LET'S GO

■ THE RESOURCE FOR THE INDEPENDENT TRAVELER

"Paints a portrait of the nation in all its grandeur and its quirkiness...Enlivened by short features on roadside attractions, local culture and legends, and the writers' memorable experiences and encounters."

—*San Francisco Chronicle*

"The guides are aimed not only at young budget travelers but at the independent traveler; a sort of streetwise cookbook for traveling alone."

—*The New York Times*

"Unbeatable; good sight-seeing advice; up-to-date info on restaurants, hotels, and inns; a commitment to money-saving travel; and a wry style that brightens nearly every page."

—*The Washington Post*

"Lighthearted and sophisticated, informative and fun to read. [Let's Go] helps the novice traveler navigate like a knowledgeable old hand."

—*Atlanta Journal-Constitution*

"A world-wise traveling companion—always ready with friendly advice and helpful hints, all sprinkled with a bit of wit."

—*The Philadelphia Inquirer*

■ THE BEST TRAVEL BARGAINS IN YOUR PRICE RANGE

"All the dirt, dirt cheap."

—*People*

"Let's Go follows the creed that you don't have to toss your life's savings to the wind to travel—unless you want to."

—*The Salt Lake Tribune*

■ REAL ADVICE FOR REAL EXPERIENCES

"The writers seem to have experienced every rooster-packed bus and lunar-surfaced mattress about which they write."

—*The New York Times*

"Value-packed, unbeatable, accurate, and comprehensive."

—*The Los Angeles Times*

"[Let's Go's] devoted updaters really walk the walk (and thumb the ride, and trek the trail). Learn how to fish, haggle, find work—anywhere."

—*Food & Wine*

LET'S GO PUBLICATIONS

TRAVEL GUIDES

Australia 9th edition
Austria & Switzerland 12th edition
Brazil 1st edition
Britain 2007
California 10th edition
Central America 9th edition
Chile 2nd edition
China 5th edition
Costa Rica 3rd edition
Eastern Europe 12th edition
Ecuador 1st edition
Egypt 2nd edition
Europe 2007
France 2007
Germany 13th edition
Greece 8th edition
Hawaii 4th edition
India & Nepal 8th edition
Ireland 12th edition
Israel 4th edition
Italy 2007
Japan 1st edition
Mexico 21st edition
Middle East 4th edition
New Zealand 7th edition
Peru 1st edition
Puerto Rico 2nd edition
South Africa 5th edition
Southeast Asia 9th edition
Spain & Portugal 2007
Thailand 3rd edition
Turkey 5th edition
USA 23rd edition
Vietnam 2nd edition
Western Europe 2007

ROADTRIP GUIDE

Roadtripping USA 2nd edition

ADVENTURE GUIDES

Alaska 1st edition
Pacific Northwest 1st edition
Southwest USA 3rd edition

CITY GUIDES

Amsterdam 4th edition
Barcelona 3rd edition
Boston 4th edition
London 15th edition
New York City 16th edition
Paris 14th edition
Rome 12th edition
San Francisco 4th edition
Washington, D.C. 13th edition

POCKET CITY GUIDES

Amsterdam
Berlin
Boston
Chicago
London
New York City
Paris
San Francisco
Venice
Washington, D.C.

LET'S GO

ROADTRIPPING
USA

THE COMPLETE COAST-TO-COAST GUIDE TO AMERICA

CAITLIN CLAIRE VINCENT EDITOR
RICHARD SHARPLESS BECK ASSOCIATE EDITOR
ADRIENNE TAYLOR GERKEN ASSOCIATE EDITOR
MICHAEL E. STEINHAUS ASSOCIATE EDITOR

RESEARCHER-WRITERS

ASHLEY RAY BUSBY
MADELEINE BÄVERSTAM
BEN COLLINS
MEGHAN DAY
WILLIAM JUSINO

HILLARY KAELL
ANNIE LEVENSON
LEE MURRAY
LAUREN SANCKEN

THOMAS BARRON MAP EDITOR
AUGUST DIETRICH MANAGING EDITOR

ST. MARTIN'S PRESS ✿ NEW YORK

HELPING LET'S GO. If you want to share your discoveries, suggestions, or corrections, please drop us a line. We read every piece of correspondence, whether a postcard, a 10-page email, or a coconut. **Address mail to:**

Roadtripping USA
67 Mount Auburn Street
Cambridge, MA 02138
USA

Visit Let's Go at **http://www.letsgo.com,** or send email to:

feedback@letsgo.com
Subject: "Let's Go: Roadtripping USA"

In addition to the invaluable travel advice our readers share with us, many are kind enough to offer their services as researchers or editors. Unfortunately, our charter enables us to employ only currently enrolled Harvard students.

CONTENTS

HOW TO USE THIS BOOK

ORGANIZATION. The book is organized into eight unique routes that will take you from ocean to ocean and to every scenic drive, classic diner, and roadside dinosaur in between. Follow just one route, or choose your own adventure by combining two or more; the **Crossroads** section at the beginning of each chapter lets you know where our routes cross paths. Each chapter begins with a **Top 5** box to help you pinpoint the best a route has to offer. To find the right route in a hurry, use the black tabs on the side of the book to guide you.

MAPS. In addition to city maps, *Let's Go Roadtripping USA* includes vertical route maps to help you navigate the road. Each map plots approximately 200 mi. of the route. The maps are oriented along your path; we've angled the text for easy reading if you rotate the book to north.

SPECIAL FEATURES. *Let's Go Roadtripping USA* includes special features to highlight the road's sights and stories in a way standard coverage can't. **Photo Op** points out quirky sights, while **Did You Know?** provides myriad fun facts and trivia along the way. The **Big Detours** are optional jaunts off the main route that guide you to wacky places and must-see sights. **From the Road** includes our researchers' memorable tales, and **In the Passenger Seat** introduces you to characters they met along the way. **Local Story** and **Local Legend** gives a closer look at culture and undiscovered gems; **No Work, All Play** is your ticket to the best festivals and celebrations. Whet your appetite for regional cuisine with **On the Menu.** We know you're traveling on a budget, so we've incorporated **The Big Splurge** to tell you when an extravagance is worth the sticker shock and the **The Hidden Deal** to help your pennies go further.

RANKINGS. *Let's Go* lists establishments in order of value, starting with the best. Our absolute favorites are denoted by the ⚑**Let's Go thumbs-up.**

PHONE CODES AND TELEPHONE NUMBERS. Phone numbers in this guide are marked with the ☎ icon. All include the area code and local number. In many cities, all 10 digits are required even for local calls; often in more remote areas only the final seven are needed for local calls.

WHEN TO USE IT

ONE YEAR BEFORE. Some national parks' summer accommodations and campgrounds fill up many months in advance. Use our coverage to make your plans and secure your spot.

ONE MONTH BEFORE. Take care of insurance, and write down a list of emergency numbers and hotlines. Make a list of packing essentials (see **Packing**). Make sure you understand the logistics of your itinerary (ferries, distance between gas and rest stops, etc.). Make any reservations if necessary.

2 WEEKS BEFORE. Leave an itinerary and a photocopy of important documents with someone at home. Check all of the fluids in the vehicle you are planning on taking, and make sure the tires are in good shape. It's a good idea to have a tune-up, just in case.

ON THE ROAD. The **Appendix** contains metric conversion tables and a basic introduction to French and Spanish terms, which may come in handy during the portions of the roadtrips that occur in Eastern Canada and Mexico. Arm yourself with a journal, some sunglasses, and plenty of gas, and hit the road!

A NOTE TO OUR READERS. The information for this book was gathered by *Let's Go* researchers from May through August 2006. Each listing is based on one researcher's opinion, formed during his or her visit at a particular time. Those traveling at other times may have different experiences since prices, dates, hours, and conditions are always subject to change. You are urged to check the facts presented in this book beforehand to avoid inconvenience and surprises.

RESEARCHER-WRITERS

Ashley Ray Busby   *The Pacific Coast*

This native Californian (NorCal, mind you) went back to her roots—hard. With coverage as sunny as the climate and a full lexicon of California slang at her disposal, Ashley had her editors back East buying Joni Mitchell records and gobbling down avocado sandwiches. Ashley's research was a happy mix of tireless effort and serendipity—no other researcher stumbled onto quite as many festivals, and no one covered them so brilliantly.

Madeleine Bäverstam   *The Oregon Trail*

Dedicated, thorough, and endlessly enthusiastic, Madeleine joined the team at the last minute to research Kansas, Nebraska, and Wyoming. Drawing on her backpacking experience from *Let's Go: Britain 2005*, this history and literature enthusiast and musician zoomed along rural mountain roads, tamed the wild jackalope, charmed her editors with vivid, masterful text, and did her fellow pioneers proud.

Ben Collins   *The Deep South*

As a veteran of *Let's Go: USA 2006*, we knew Ben would be up to the task of blazing a new trail, and with his perpetual smile, laid-back vibe, and penchant for tangy barbecue, we knew he'd be perfect for the South. When he wasn't busy learning to love Civil War battlefields, falling hard for Southern towns, and developing the slightest hint of a twang, Ben sent back polished copy and entertaining features—everything we needed for a brand-new route.

Meghan Day   *Route 66*

Fresh from her tiny hometown in Maine, Meghan drove into town ready for serious adventure. Tackling the Mother Road is serious business, but Meghan was prepared. Wowing us with her melodious prose and tireless dedication, Meghan breathed fresh life into every dusty mile and roadside diner of Route 66. She endured stifling desert heat and a missing phone charger, all while writing precise copy and thrilling marginalia—not to mention napkin poetry.

William Jusino   *The National Road*

Determined and meticulous, this fearless researcher tackled the daunting 3000-mile journey across the middle of America with ease. Ever the tireless bargain-hunter, Bill made use of his refined taste buds to track down the country's best deals at even the most luxurious establishments. When he wasn't keeping his editors entertained with stories from the road, Bill sent in thoroughly researched and well-written copy.

Hillary Kaell
The Southern Border

It takes a real sense of adventure to drive through Florida swamps, Louisiana bayous, and Arizona deserts during the dog days of summer, but we're delighted that Hillary was up to the task. From watermelon thumps, to recyclable roadrunners, to public art masquerading as a Prada boutique, Hillary covered everything under the blazing sun and then some. Even when the going got tough, Hillary's dedication to the book and to our readers never faltered.

Annie Levenson
The East Coast

This Jacksonville native may have started out close to home, but she ranged far and wide in her pursuit of the East Coast's hidden gems. Hunting down new establishments and rewriting swaths of coverage with panache and aplomb, Annie astonished her editors and left them clamoring for each week's fresh batch of features. Dogged by interminable rainstorms and a broken arm, Annie nevertheless drove and wrote with tenacious good cheer.

Lee Murray
The Great North

A native of upstate New York, Lee made it his mission to discover the best of the Great North, and discover it, he did. Armed with the rugged outdoorsmanship of Meriwether Lewis, the technical skills of a budding engineer, and the audacious good-nature of his ginger-colored hair, he traipsed through his route with a constant grin. Lee tackled a long route with the self-assurance of one who knows what lies ahead: gorgeous national parks and the great blue Pacific.

Lauren Sancken
The Oregon Trail

Last seen trekking through the furnace-like Southwest for *Let's Go: USA 2006*, Lauren researched the western Oregon Trail with boundless energy and earnest resolve from her home base in Seattle. She tackled Oregon, British Columbia, and the rigorous Big Detour, downing coffee like nobody's business. Her colorful descriptions, sense of adventure, and good humor made our jobs delightfully easy.

REGIONAL EDITORS AND RESEARCHER-WRITERS

Amber Johnson — *Researcher-Writer*, Let's Go: New York City

Kate Penner — *Researcher-Writer*, Let's Go: New York City

Carl Hughes — *Editor*, Let's Go: New York City

CONTRIBUTING WRITERS

Mike Marriner crossed the country in a neon-green RV, interviewing self-made men and women for his book, *Roadtrip Nation: A Guide to Discovering Your Path In Life.*

Professor Burt Vaux has a Ph.D. in Linguistics and currently teaches at the University of Wisconsin-Milwaukee. He has published extensively and taught at Harvard University.

ACKNOWLEDGMENTS

TEAM ROADTRIP THANKS: Our fantastic ▓researchers, without whom this book would be nothing more than a bunch of blank pages. Prod, who spent weeks and weeks tweaking old designs and creating new ones. August, our proofers, wheelchair calls ("Well, baby, I'm wheelchair accessible, but the bar is not"), and quotes of the day.

CAITLIN THANKS: Adrienne, Rich, and Michael, for hard work and constant hilarity; Ben, for making the Deep South route a reality; wheelchair accessible phone calls, for adding some sweet irony to the summer; olive bread, Picard, and pillus; and Mom, Dad, Jordan, and Paul.

ADRIENNE THANKS: Team ROAD, for everything; histamine, for nothing; my amazing mother, Marilyn, for friendship; Danielle, for smiles and 'mingos; Brian, for surviving another year of this; Rachel, Silvia, and Katherine, for editing parties; TeamEllery, for always deserving a thumbpick; Tom, Richard, and Chase, for making a good book great.

RICH THANKS: Michael, Caitlin, Adrienne, August, and Tom, for dedication and humor. Annie and Ashley, for working harder than me. Richard, Matthew, and Geoffrey, for Muppets, domesticity, and kindness. My family, for talking. Zach, for correspondence and being my friend.

MICHAEL THANKS: Caitlin, for leadership and keeping us on track; Rich, for humor and his surprising history; Adrienne, for saving us; August, the most balla ME ever, for his life lessons; Tom, for his BA, with all that knowledge; and Bill, for his dedication. Love to Dan, Joel, Anne, and Witchy for helping me live the dream; to G&P and B&B; and to Betsy. Finally, to M and D, to whom I am forever indebted.

TOM THANKS: Michael, Rich, Adrienne, Caitlin, and August for all their hard work, 6 Exeter for keeping me company, and last, but not least, Mapland.

Editor
Caitlin Claire Vincent
Associate Editors
Richard Sharpless Beck, Adrienne Taylor Gerken,
Michael E. Steinhaus
Managing Editor
August Dietrich
Map Editor
Thomas M. Barron
Typesetters
Victoria Esquivel-Korsiak
Chase Mohney

LET'S GO

Publishing Director
Alexandra C. Stanek
Editor-in-Chief
Laura E. Martin
Production Manager
Richard Chohaney Lonsdorf
Cartography Manager
Clifford S. Emmanuel
Editorial Managers
August Dietrich, Samantha Gelfand,
Silvia Gonzalez Killingsworth
Financial Manager
Jenny Qiu Wong
Publicity Manager
Anna A. Mattson-DiCecca
Personnel Manager
Sergio Ibarra
Production Associate
Chase Mohney
IT Director
Patrick Carroll
Director of E-Commerce
Jana Lepon
Office Coordinators
Adrienne Taylor Gerken, Sarah Goodin

Director of Advertising Sales
Mohammed J. Herzallah
Senior Advertising Associates
Kedamai Fisseha, Roumiana Ivanova

President
Brian Feinstein
General Manager
Robert B. Rombauer

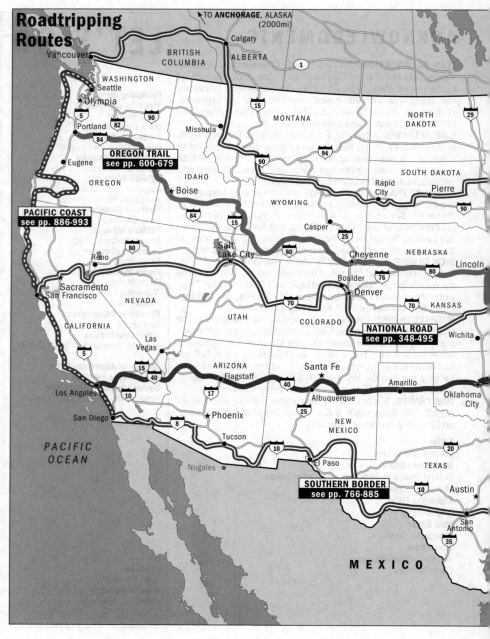

Roadtripping Routes

TO **ANCHORAGE**, ALASKA (2000mi)

Calgary

BRITISH COLUMBIA

ALBERTA

1

Vancouver

WASHINGTON

Seattle

Olympia

5　82　90

MONTANA

NORTH DAKOTA

29

Portland

84

Missoula

94

OREGON TRAIL
see pp. 600-679

Eugene

OREGON

IDAHO

90

SOUTH DAKOTA

Boise

Rapid City

Pierre

PACIFIC COAST
see pp. 886-993

84

WYOMING

15

Casper

90

25

Reno

80

Salt Lake City

80

Cheyenne

NEBRASKA

Lincoln

Sacramento

San Francisco

NEVADA

Boulder

76

80

70

Denver

70

KANSAS

CALIFORNIA

UTAH

COLORADO

Wichita

Las Vegas

NATIONAL ROAD
see pp. 348-495

5

15

ARIZONA

40

Santa Fe

Flagstaff

40

Amarillo

Oklahoma City

Los Angeles

10

17

Albuquerque

San Diego

8

Phoenix

25

NEW MEXICO

20

Tucson

10

PACIFIC OCEAN

Nogales

El Paso

TEXAS

10

Austin

SOUTHERN BORDER
see pp. 766-885

San Antonio

35

M E X I C O

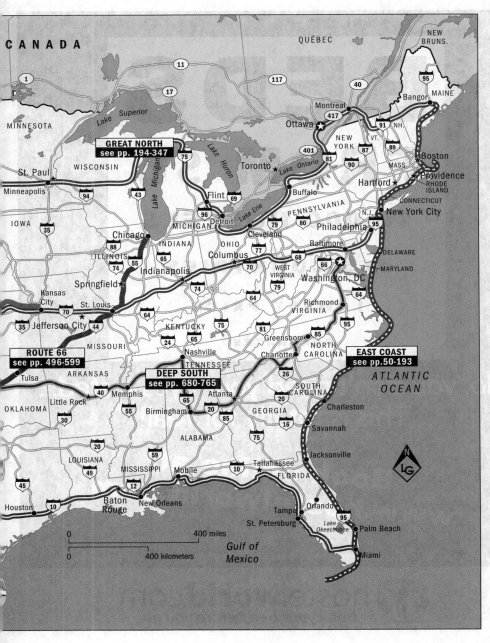

CANADA

QUÉBEC

NEW BRUNS.

MINNESOTA

Lake Superior

GREAT NORTH
see pp. 194-347

WISCONSIN

St. Paul

Minneapolis

IOWA

MICHIGAN

Lake Huron

Lake Michigan

Toronto

Lake Ontario

Montreal

Ottawa

NEW YORK

Bangor MAINE

NH.

VT.

Boston

MASS

Providence

RHODE ISLAND

Hartford

CONNECTICUT

New York City

Buffalo

PENNSYLVANIA

N.J.

Flint

Detroit

Lake Erie

Cleveland

Philadelphia

DELAWARE

Chicago

INDIANA

OHIO

Columbus

Baltimore

MARYLAND

ILLINOIS

Indianapolis

WEST VIRGINIA

Washington, DC

Springfield

Kansas City

St. Louis

Richmond

VIRGINIA

Jefferson City

MISSOURI

KENTUCKY

ROUTE 66
see pp. 496-599

Greensboro

NORTH CAROLINA

EAST COAST
see pp.50-193

Nashville

Tulsa

ARKANSAS

TENNESSEE

Charlotte

ATLANTIC OCEAN

OKLAHOMA

Little Rock

Memphis

DEEP SOUTH
see pp. 680-765

SOUTH CAROLINA

Birmingham

Atlanta

Charleston

GEORGIA

ALABAMA

Savannah

LOUISIANA

MISSISSIPPI

Mobile

Jacksonville

Tallahassee

FLORIDA

Houston

Baton Rouge

New Orleans

Tampa

Orlando

St. Petersburg

Lake Okeechobee

Palm Beach

Miami

Gulf of Mexico

N

LG

0   400 miles

0   400 kilometers

XI

the road

HISTORY

THE FIRST ROADTRIP

For a $50 bet, Horatio Nelson Jackson set out from San Francisco in 1903 to cross the country by car in 90 days, challenging the belief that the newfangled "horseless carriages" were an impractical and unreliable means of travel. Though he did not own a car and had practically no driving experience, Jackson enthusiastically struck out for New York with his mechanic and a two-cylinder, 20-horsepower Winton Touring Car named the *Vermont*. A blowout 15 mi. into their journey was the first of many mechanical setbacks encountered along their often-unpaved route, but Jackson persevered, winning the hearts of the public and acquiring a goggle-sporting bulldog named Bud along the way. Sixty-three days, 12 hours, and 30 minutes after they began, the triumphant trio crossed the Harlem River into Manhattan. The media raved about the trip's success, and Americans began to reconsider the possibilities of the automobile. Thus, the great American roadtrip was born.

HISTORY OF THE ROAD

THE EARLY ROADS. Although John Calhoun had proposed a cross-country network of roads to Congress almost a century before Jackson's trip, in 1903 this system was still far from complete. There were roads in most parts of the country, but they were almost universally "unimproved"—that is, made of packed dirt or gravel, wide enough for only a single carriage to pass, and unfit for long trips. The state of roads a traveler could expect to encounter varied widely by region. In the East, rural roads were often indirect, ill-placed, and haphazardly maintained. In the South, where 96% of public roadways were classified as "unimproved" as of 1904, the norm

was an unmapped dirt road that became muddy quagmire during the soggy Southern rains. Farther west, roads were constructed along the edges of rectangular townships and plots of public land. Although the resulting grid system was well-organized, the roads themselves were little more than wagon ruts.

THE FIRST HIGHWAYS. By the early 20th century, America's national roads were changing. With the growing popularity of the automobile, more and more attention was turned toward the quality of the nation's highways. The members of the new **American Automobile Association** (**AAA,** founded in 1903) began to clamor for improvements as they tried to drive their new vehicles over narrow, bumpy, unpaved roads. In 1908, the association held its first annual National Good Roads Convention to inaugurate the **Good Roads Movement,** which pushed for raised, graded, and ditched highways that wouldn't flood or wash out with every rain. The country's first "good road" appeared in 1909 as a mile of concrete highway outside Detroit, Michigan (not coincidentally the birthplace of the Model T).

In 1913, industrialists Carl Fischer, Frank Seiberling, and Henry Joy envisioned a paved road from coast to coast, and by 1915 their dream had been realized. The **Lincoln Highway,** as it was known, became the first transcontinental American road, stretching almost 3400 mi. from New York to California. The **Federal-Aid Road Act** of 1916 created a system of federal funding for the local construction, while the **Federal Highway Act** of 1921 established the Bureau of Public Roads to oversee the laying down of a numbered system of paved, two-lane highways throughout the states. Eventually, the Lincoln Highway became integrated into this growing highway network, and the first era of standardized road-building began nationwide.

Throughout the 40s and 50s, highway construction continued steadily as more Americans discovered the joys of the road. Hordes of motorists travelled along cross-continental highways like Route 66 and Route 40, developing the lore and romance of the national roadtrip. Though vastly improved from the dirt roads that preceded them, these highways were still only two-lane roads and would soon be overshadowed by the advance of multi-lane, high-speed interstates.

HIGH-SPEED INTERSTATES. The Federal-Aid Act of 1944, later cemented in the **Federal-Aid Highway Act** of 1956, created the National System of Interstate Highways, an interregional network of high-speed routes. The Interstate program was touted as the greatest public works program in history and promised to connect all of the principle cities and metropolitan areas in the country. Designed to reach a length of 42,500 mi. when finished, the highway system would be 30 times as long as the Great Wall of China and would pave a surface area the size of West Virginia. It was a fitting project for transitional post-war America and, in conjunction with the older Federal-Aid and state-run highway projects, would be the capstone of the national effort to make the continent accessible by car.

Construction of the Interstate system continued throughout the 60s, as environmental concerns became influential and Cold War tension made national security a high priority. In 1966, the **Department of Transportation** was formed to develop and organize an efficient national transportation system that would consider both the environment and national defense. The Bureau of Public Roads was absorbed into this new department as the **Federal Highway Administration (FHWA).** During the 70s and 80s, interstate construction reached a state of virtual completion.

THE ROAD TODAY. President Dwight D. Eisenhower's dream of a well-organized interstate highway system has today been realized—a comprehensive, well-maintained, and efficient network connects the cities and states of the US. The original plan was for the interstates and the old highways to co-exist, but as the interstates became the dominant arteries for transportation, classic two-lane highways drifted into obscurity. On the old highway maps, the interstates were mapped out in red ink and the two-lane highways were colored in blue ink, hence these classic roads became known as **Blue Highways.**

The Blue Highways of America now represent an alternative to the commerce, congestion, anonymity, and pollution of the interstate system. They embody all that is central to the experience of the American roadtrip: the myth of the road, road culture, vintage diners, and 50s motels with large neon signs.

Several of the Blue Highways have found their way into legend. **US Route 66,** which runs from Chicago to Los Angeles, has become synonymous with American road culture. Created by a congressional act in 1925 and completely paved by 1938, Route 66 saw the westward migration of thousands of families from the Dust Bowl of the midwest to the greener fields and vineyards of California during the Depression, the subject of John Steinbeck's *The Grapes of Wrath* (1939). Later, Route 66 would facilitate the movement of thousands more westward-bound, adventure-seeking travelers, as well as the development of the modern service station and motel. Route 66 was officially decommissioned by 1985, but the "Main Street of America" remains a standard road-trip route as well as a pop culture legend.

Another classic highway is **US Route 40,** the "National Road," which spans the 3200 miles from Atlantic City to San Francisco. Sometimes called the "Golden Highway," Route 40 roughly parallels the old Lincoln Highway, and, in its heyday in the 1950s, was the transcontinental route of choice for many travelers. Like Route 66, Route 40 has been largely replaced by the modern Interstate system, but it still remains a road-culture standard in all its neon-light and roadside-diner glory.

Recently, the US Department of Transportation has begun to recognize roads with special historic, scenic, or cultural significance through its **Scenic Byways Program.** Since 1992, the program has funded almost 1500 roadways in 48 states, designating routes as National Scenic Byways or as All-American Roads. Famous and well-loved byways include the Blue Ridge Parkway through the southern Appalachian mountains, the San Juan Skyway in Southern Colorado, and the Pacific Coast Highway, as well as parts of Routes 40 and 66.

HISTORY OF THE CAR

Far from a new innovation, the automobile that made Horatio Jackson's journey a reality was the product of a gradual process of development. The first **self-propelled vehicle** was a steam-powered military tractor invented in 1769 by French engineer Nicolas Joseph

Cugnot. (Two years later, Cugnot also became the first person to experience a motor vehicle accident, when he drove one of his contraptions into a stone wall.) Some early vehicles also used electrical power. In the mid- 1830s, Scottish inventor Robert Anderson constructed the first **electric carriage.** These battery-powered vehicles, clunky and expensive as they were, were the dominant form of automobile in the US until about 1900.

Around the turn of the century, **gasoline-powered cars** began to outsell other types of vehicles. Largely results of the late 19th-century innovations of German engineers Karl Benz (as in Mercedes-Benz) and Gottlieb Daimler (as in Daimler-Chrysler), these gas-fueled automobiles featured a more powerful internal combustion engine, the grand-daddy of engines used in cars today.

Although Americans like to think of their country as the birthplace of the automobile, the world's first actual **car manufacturers** were Frenchmen: René Panhard and Emile Levassor in 1889, and Armand Peugot in 1891. The first "modern" automobile was also a European creation. In 1901 William Bayback designed a 35-horsepower Mercedes model with a maximum speed of 53 mph. Gasoline-powered automobiles were not manufactured in the US until 1893, when bicycle mechanic brothers Charles and Frank Duryea of Springfield, MA, started constructing a small number of expensive limousines. The first car to be mass-produced in the US was the **Curved Dash Oldsmobile**—425 of these vehicles were processed in Detroit in 1901. When **Henry Ford** started manufacturing small, black, lightweight cars for only $850 in Detroit in 1908, he cemented the city's identity as the Motor City and ignited what would become a nationwide fascination with cars. For the first time, automobiles were cheap and available to a wide cross-section of American society.

THE EARLY YEARS. The Ford Model T was only the first car to capture the attention of the American public. Its debut marked the beginning of America's love affair with the automobile, and the simple, no-frills design of the Model T was rapidly replaced with bigger, fancier, and faster models. By the late 1920s, auto manufacturers were producing ever grander and more stylish cars. Throughout the 50s car size increased, and designs became increasingly impractical. Hall-

marks of the 1950-era automobile include the outlandish **space fins,** while the late 60s saw the advent of the **muscle car.**

These increasingly ostentatious car designs reflected more than just changing styles; they were indications of the changing mentality surrounding the car in American culture. The early Fords were primarily farmers' cars, designed to be efficient and practical. Later, however, the car became a status symbol and means of self-expression. Ownership was widespread during America's post-war boom. Teenagers, in particular, began to own and preen over their automobiles, and the acquisition of a driver's license became a rite of passage into adulthood and a sign of independence. It wasn't until the oil embargo and new government safety restrictions of the 1970s that manufacturers and consumers began to rein in their enthusiasm for gas-guzzling automobiles.

Increased car ownership combined with an extensive road network prompted the growth of the residential **suburb,** transforming the American city from a residential center into a place of industry. America's car obsessions have also given rise to various roadside industries. The **fast-food joint,** today an American icon, evolved to its present form in the 1950s (the ubiquitous McDonald's was founded by Ray Kroc in 1954), when long road-trips made eating on the go a necessity. The **drive-in movie theater,** a favorite spot for many a hot-rodding suburbanite, peaked during the 1950s.

TODAY. Today, driving and car culture have evolved into a massive industry. The road continues to shape the American imagination, influencing art, film, literature, and personal identity. More than half of US citizens drive automobiles, and there are many more cars than licensed drivers. In 2001, there were 191 million drivers out of 281 million American citizens, who owned 226 million motor vehicles. Americans now drive over two trillion miles a year, and even though the days of the hot rod and the muscle car are over, individuals continue to spend vast amounts of time and money on their automobiles. Meanwhile, the US government continues to pump money into the road infrastructure, spending over $75 billion each year on the highway system.

Indeed, it is fair to say that cars, like baseball games, are an American obsession. AAA is currently second only to the Catholic church in terms of membership in the US, with more than

45 million members and around 1000 offices. Magazines devoted to automobiles, like the popular *Car and Driver*, abound, and radio stations feature car-themed shows (such as National Public Radio's *Car Talk*). Clubs like the **Antique Automobile Club of America** (which has over 400 chapters and 60,000 members nationwide), host conferences, shows, festivals, and "meets," at which old-car enthusiasts congregate by the thousands. Established in 1977, the **Society for Commercial Archaeology (SCA)** devotes itself to preserving the sights and symbols of 20th-century roadside culture, publishing a journal and hosting annual conferences and tours.

The automobile in America isn't just a mode of transportation; it is a way of life. Almost any American will reminisce fondly about his or her first automobile, and the Sunday after-dinner drive is as American as apple pie. None of these are quite as iconic, however, as the American roadtrip.

LIFE ON THE ROAD

ROADTRIP ATTITUDE

What is it that makes a roadtrip different from an average, ordinary vacation? Like the car and the open road, the roadtrip has acquired a specific meaning. The type of roadtrip ingrained in American tradition revolves around the journey and the experience of travel itself.

At one extreme, a roadtrip can be a marathon, a test of endurance, a major undertaking. Visiting one category of sight is a popular way of planning out a trip—taking a tour of America's mystery spots, hitting up all of the missions in California, or visiting all of the lobster shacks on the East Coast, for example. Event-based trips are also popular—baseball roadtrips from one stadium to the next are an American tradition. Pilgrimages to rock concerts (ask your parents about Woodstock), Shakespeare festivals, and historical tours, like the Lewis and Clark Trail, are all fair game.

At the other end of the spectrum, a roadtrip can also evolve with only a vague direction and a desire for knowledge and experience. Exploring a specific region or driving a historic two-lane highway are both good ways to start out, as is following one of the cardinal directions. This kind of trip revolves around discovering the lives and culture of the people who live along the way—seeing every historical site, stopping at every diner, mingling at every bar. It is all about the digression, all about the culture, and all about the detour.

ROADTRIP TRADITIONS

FRIENDS. From Bonnie and Clyde to Thelma and Louise, roadtrippers traditionally travel in pairs; roadtrip culture is oriented around the experience of a shared journey. Picking the right friend or friends to bring along requires care, but a trusty companion in the front seat makes the miles go by faster. Bringing a friend also means you have an extra navigator—unless your travel companion of choice, like John Steinbeck's, happens to be a dog.

WHO TO TAKE ALONG:

The Adventurer: Adventurers are outgoing and unafraid to deviate from pre-arranged plans to see a sight recommended by a complete stranger. They revel in long conversations with people they've never met before and happily find the best local places. The adventurer's motto is: "Sure, sounds like a hoot!"

The Navigator: These godsends couldn't get lost if you blindfolded them and left them in the middle of the forest. They have lodestones in their foreheads, know how to read maps, and yet always know the right moment to ask for directions. The navigator's motto is: "See? Here we are!"

The Optimist: These positive individuals somehow know how to make changing a tire in the snow on the New Jersey turnpike feel like a rousing good time. They take adversity with a grain of salt and keep the big picture in mind. The optimist's motto is: "Good thing the radiator overheated, otherwise we would never have seen this sunrise."

CAR GAMES. Miles of uninterrupted cornfields have inspired an extensive collection of **road games** to alleviate the interstate boredom blues. Some old favorites are "I Spy" and "Twenty Questions," but there are many others which serve the same purpose.

Sweet and Sour. Whenever a car goes by the window, each player waves and smiles. If a person waves and smiles back (sweet), you get a point. If the person frowns or ignores you (sour), no points.

Howdy Doody. One player says a name, and the next player uses either the first or the last name to create another name. Example: Will Smith to Will Rogers to Mister Rogers.

Ghost. You spell out words: the first person says a letter, the next person has to add a letter, and you continue adding letters in order. If you add a letter that cannot form a word, you lose. If you add a letter that completes a word, you also lose.

Counting Cows. Teams count cows throughout the day on their side of the car (while trying to distract the other team). If you pass a cemetery on your side of the car, you lose all your cow points.

The Quiet Game. Shut up kids. Mom and Dad are having a conversation.

WHO NOT TO TAKE ALONG:

The Whiner: For the whiner, the grass is always greener in the other lane. Any bump in the road or fly on the windshield will set them off, and there is nothing worse than a whiner's tirade, especially when you're changing a tire in the snow on the New Jersey turnpike. The whiner's motto is: "Are we there yet?"

The Backseat Driver: With their constant driving critiques, multiple maps, and exclamations at every less-than perfect turn, backseat drivers can quickly ruin any roadtrip, or at least, drive you a little bit crazy. The Backseat Driver's motto is: "You were supposed to take a left back there."

The Parent: Though they mean well, parents have an uncanny knack for taking the fun out of roadtripping. They will turn down the volume of your music, throw off your game with potential hook-ups, and reminisce about their own roadtrip at age 22 (without their parents). Of course, they might also pay for gas. The parent's motto: "You're going on a roadtrip? Do you have a job?"

CAR RITUALS. There is also a repertoire of **roadtrip superstitions.** Details vary by region, but standards include holding your breath while driving past graveyards, across state lines, or through tunnels, making wishes when you see a hay wagon or at the end of a tunnel, raising your feet while crossing bridges or railroad tracks, and touching the ceiling of your car when you drive through a yellow traffic light. Another common ritual is the **"punchbuggy"** game, in which the first person to see a Volkswagon Beetle shouts "punchbuggy!" and punches the ceiling or (in a more risky version) the arm of the person next to him or her. Variations of this classic, taken very seriously by the finest of roadtrippers, include shouting "p-diddle" or extending the ritual to include pink cars, limousines, or cars with one headlight. These rituals may seem silly, but what if they aren't? Just something to keep in mind.

ROAD ETIQUETTE

A growing concentration of rushed drivers on America's highways means road etiquette is increasingly important. Unfortunately, road rage incidents are no myth. Tailgating, gratuitous horn-honking, driving with high beams on when approaching or following other cars, eye contact with aggressive drivers, and obscene language and gestures are all road taboos. On highways with two or more lanes, the left-hand lane (the "fast lane") is for passing, and on any road, it is standard politeness to let faster cars pass. One of the most offensive gestures in the US is extending the middle finger of either hand. Also known as "giving someone the finger," this gesture is considered not only rude, but obscene.

Also, roadtrips mean long times in small spaces, and things can get a little "Lord of the Flies" if you're not careful. Play nice, share the candy, and don't talk without the conch shell.

FOOD ON THE ROAD

Today, most interstates and many highways are lined with fast-food joints, but the real richness and variety of American road food is best found at local, non-chain ice-cream parlors, hot-dog stands, barbecue pits, delis, and diners.

Diners have historically been places where entire communities congregate to enjoy a home-style meal in a comfortable atmosphere. The first roadside diner was little more than a horse-drawn wagon in 1872. Later diners included the Art Deco eateries of the 30s and the stainless steel restaurants in the 50s. The classic diner, a modular, factory-made structure, still appears along many roadsides, and usually promises warm (if greasy) food, considerate service, and a piping hot cup of coffee.

REGIONAL TREATS

With a little extra attention and a discerning eye, a roadtripper can experience a variety of flavor, ranging from the spicy chiles of New Mexico to the sweet maple syrup of Vermont. Enjoying such regional delights is a highlight of any roadtrip.

NORTHEAST. America's English settlers first landed in the Northeast, combining their staples of meats and vegetables with uniquely American foodstuffs such as turkey, maple syrup, clams, lobster, cranberries, and corn. The results yielded such treasures as Boston brown bread, **Indian pudding,** New England **clam chowder,** and **Maine boiled lobster.** The shellfish are second to none.

SOUTHEAST. Be prepared for some good ol' down-home cookin'. Fried chicken, biscuits, grits, collard greens, okra, and sweet potato pie are some of the highlights of Southeastern cuisine. **Virginia ham** is widely renowned, and ham biscuits provide a savory supplement to lunch and dinner dishes. In addition to the famed collection of animal by-products that make up **"soul food"**—pig's knuckles and ears, hog maws, and chitterlings (boiled or fried pig intestines) among others—Southern cuisine has a strong African and West Indian influence in its sauces and spices.

LOUISIANA. Chefs in New Orleans are among the country's best, and **Creole** or **Cajun** cooking tantalizes the taste buds. Smothered crawfish, fried catfish, **jambalaya** (rice cooked with ham, sausage, shrimp, and herbs), and **gumbo** (a thick stew with okra, meat, and vegetables) are delicacies. The faint of taste buds beware: spicy Cajun and creole cooking can fry the mouth.

TEXAS. From juicy tenderloins to luscious baby back ribs to whole pig roasts, Texans like to slow cook their meats over an open fire, flavoring the meat with the smoke from burning mesquite or hickory. Eat at any of the state's many **barbecue** joints, though, and they'll tell you that the real secret is in the tangy sauce. For those in the mood for something ethnic, enchiladas, burritos, and fajitas are scrumptious **Tex-Mex** options.

MIDWEST. Drawing on the Scandinavian and German roots of area settlers, Midwest cuisine is hearty, simple, and plentiful. The Scandinavian influence brings **lefse** (potato bread) and the indomitable **lutefisk** (fish jellied through a process of soaking in lye). The comfort food of the Midwest could only be the **Bratwurst,** a type of German sausage, usually made from pork, that is seen in every ballpark and church picnic in the region. Breads include German Stollen and Swedish Limpa Rye, complementing an assortment of meats, cheeses, soups, and relishes.

CALIFORNIA. Fresh fruits and vegetables are grown throughout California and the Central Valley; avocado and citrus fruits are trademark favorites. Southern California has more Mexican influences, while the long coastline allows for excellent seafood throughout the state. California is also home to the spiritual mother of all road stops, **In-N-Out Burger,** where you can get a simple and cheap 50s-style burger that has been nowhere near a microwave, heat lamp, or freezer. Do you want a malt with that double-double?

SOUTHWEST. The Mexican staples of corn, flour, and chiles are the basic components of Southwestern grub. Salsa made from tomatoes, chilies, and **tomatillos** adds a spicy note to nearly all dishes, especially cheese- and chicken-filled quesadillas and ground beef tacos. In most Southwest road food stops, you can get **green chile,** a spicy extra, on pretty much anything you want.

PACIFIC NORTHWEST. In close proximity to the arctic water frequented by **halibut** and **salmon,** many cities in the Pacific Northwest have superior seafood, which can be found in everything from chowder to tacos. Washington is also known for its juicy **apples** and **mountain huckleberries,** while Oregon boasts the microbrewery capital of North America and has the beer to prove it. British Columbia is known for **bannock,** a biscuit-like cake made from flour, lard, and honey. Some varieties incorporate local delicacies such as salmon.

CANADA. Canadian specialties vary by region. Newfoundland boasts the food with rather unusual names, including **bangbelly** (salt pork in a spiced bun,) **toutons** (salt pork with white raisin bread), **figgy duff** (a raisin pudding), and **Jigg's Dinner** (a large meal prepared in a pot containing salt beef, cabbage, turnips, carrots and potatoes).

Smoked salmon is a favorite in British Columbia, and Quebec is well-known for its **maple syrup** (served on everything from pancakes to omelettes to meats) and varieties of **poutine,** a tasty combination of french fries, cheese curds, and a thick, dark gravy sauce.

ROADTRIP CULTURE

LITERATURE

"Afoot and light-hearted, I take to the
open road ... From this hour, freedom!"
—Walt Whitman, 1856

The roadtrip that you are about to embark on is the stuff of poetry. The journey along the open road in search of a new life, some new experiences, and a new understanding of America has fueled the creativity of authors long before the first Model T rolled off the assembly line. Generations of writers have used life on the road to inspire both critiques and celebrations of American culture.

FICTION

Around the World in Eighty Days (1872) by Jules Verne. Phileas Fogg's madcap quest to circumnavigate the world and win a £20,000 bet.

Roughing It (1872) by Mark Twain. Semi-autobiographical journal of Twain's journeys through the "Wild West" and disillusionment with the American Dream.

Adventures of Huckleberry Finn (1884) by Mark Twain. A boy's misadventures along the Mississippi River typify the American roadtrip spirit.

Grapes of Wrath (1939) by John Steinbeck. A Depression-era journey westward and one of American literature's angriest works.

The Adventures of Augie March (1953) by Saul Bellow. An expansive, over-abundant chronicle of a Chicago youth's quest for fulfillment.

Lolita (1955) by Vladimir Nabokov. Famous and controversial. Humbert Humbert is a classic anti-hero.

On the Road (1957) and just about everything else written by Jack Kerouac. A Beatnik's odyssey and the seminal text of road literature.

The Getaway (1958) by Jim Thompson. Two bank robbers flee across the country and cut a violent swath across America.

Rabbit Run (1960) by John Updike. The story of Harry "Rabbit" Angstrom's flight from his former life and search for new meaning.

Travels with Charley: In Search of America (1962) by John Steinbeck. A veteran writer takes to the road with his dog (Charley) to rediscover his homeland.

In Cold Blood (1966) by Truman Capote. An analysis of a crime and the mystery as to why two men would drive over 400 miles to kill four people whom they did not know.

Another Roadside Attraction (1971) by Tom Robbins. The story of comedic genius and 1960s counterculture recounting how a troupe of carnies come into the possession of the embalmed body of Jesus Christ. Also check out the classic story of the hitchhiking small-town girl in *Even Cowgirls Get the Blues.*

Zen and the Art of Motorcycle Maintenance (1974) by Robert Pirsig. A cross-country roadtrip both physical and philosophical.

Blue Highways: A Journey into America (1983) by William Least Heat-Moon. A trip through the backroads of small-town America.

Christine (1983) by Stephen King. Christine is a red and white 1958 Plymouth Fury with a thirst for blood.

Road Fever (1991) by Tim Cahill. The documentation of an attempt to travel from Tierra del Fuego to the tip of Alaska in 25½ days.

Interstate (1995) by Steven Dixon. The telling and retelling of a father's search for the perpetrators of a seemingly random act of road violence.

Amnesia Moon (1995) by Jonathan Lethem. The post-apocalyptic journey of a boy named Chaos.

NON-FICTION & POETRY

A Hoosier Holiday (1916) by Theodore Dreiser. A precursor to the "road novel," this work documents a roadtrip Dreiser took with fellow artist Franklin Booth.

The Air-Conditioned Nightmare (1945) by Henry Miller. An account of Henry Miller's 1940-1941 journey through America and his criticism of American culture.

The Electric Kool-Aid Acid Test (1968) by Tom Wolfe. Documents Ken Kesey and the band of Merry Pranksters' drug-fueled journey through America.

Out West (1987) by Dayton Duncan. The narrative of a man and his Volkswagon trip westward, following the trail of Lewis and Clark.

The Lost Continent: Travels in Small Town America (1990) by Bill Bryson. A search across 38 states for the essence of small-town life.

American Nomad (1997) by Steve Erickson. The non-fiction account of Erickson's road journey after covering the 1996 presidential election for *Rolling Stone*.

Songs for the Open Road: Poems of Travel and Adventure (1999) by The American Poetry & Literacy Project. Collection of 80 poems by 50 British and American poets, about travel and journeys.

Driving Visions (2002) by David Laderman. Discusses the cultural roots of the Road Movie and analyzes its role in literary tradition.

Ridge Route: The Road That United California (2002) by Harrison Irving Scott. An in-depth look at highway construction over the grapevine.

RV Traveling Tales: Women's Journeys on the Open Road (2003) edited by Jaimie Hall & Alice Zyetz. An anthology of women writers and their experiences living on the road.

FILM

Counterculture, existential, visionary, or just slapstick, road movies tell the story of rebels, outlaws, and nomads. If you want to learn just about everything there is to know about the genre, pick up a copy of David Laderman's in-depth study, *Driving Visions*.

MOVIES

The Wild One (1953): Marlon Brando and his motorcycle gang, rebelling against whatever you've got, terrorize a town and disrupt a motorcycle race.

North-By-Northwest (1959): Cary Grant crosses the country to try to reclaim his identity in one of the Hitchcock's best. Look for the famed crop-dusting scene.

It's a Mad, Mad, Mad, Mad World (1963): A dying thief's last words spark a cross-country dash to find buried treasure in 182 mad, mad, mad, mad minutes.

Bonnie and Clyde (1967): The world's most notorious and romanticized bank robbers, played by Warren Beatty and Faye Dunaway, drive across the Midwest robbing banks during the Great Depression.

Easy Rider (1969): Peter Fonda and Dennis Hopper play two non-conforming bikers searching for America on a motorcycle trek from L.A. to New Orleans.

Two-Lane Blacktop (1971): James Taylor and Dennis Wilson, as "The Driver" and "The Mechanic," drag race their way across the US.

The Blues Brothers (1980): On a mission from God, Jake and Elwood Blues find themselves amongst hundreds of wrecked cars, 106 miles from Chicago, with a

full tank of gas, half a pack of cigarettes, and in the dark wearing sunglasses.

National Lampoon's Vacation (1983): The now-classic Griswold family summer vacation journey to Wally-World.

Sesame Street Presents: Follow That Bird (1985): Big Bird, forlorn and feeling like he does not belong, searches for himself out on the road.

Pee-Wee's Big Adventure (1985): Pee-Wee, a loner and a rebel, goes on a cross-country quest to find his stolen bicycle in the basement of the Alamo.

Rainman (1988): Selfish yuppie Charlie Babbitt travels cross-country with his autistic brother Raymond.

The Land Before Time (1988): Littlefoot and Co.'s pre-roads roadtrip to find the idyllic Great Valley. Watch out for sharp-teeth and revel in being seven again.

My Own Private Idaho (1991): Gus Van Sant directs this gay interpretation of Henry IV, in which River Phoenix and Keanu Reeves search across the country and across the Atlantic for maternal support.

Thelma and Louise (1991): A housewife and a waitress shoot a rapist and make their getaway in a 1966 Thunderbird.

Highway to Hell (1992): In a retelling of the Orpheus myth, Las Vegas newlyweds have to go to hell and bargain with Satan.

Bottle Rocket (1996): Luke and Owen Wilson look to become thieves and go on the lam in a movie Martin Scorsese called one of the ten best films of the 90s.

The Straight Story (1999): An elderly man hits the road in a tractor in David Lynch's heartfelt tale of fraternal reconciliation.

Road Trip (2000): Four college students hop in a car and travel cross-country to retrieve a mistakenly mailed incriminating video tape.

Y tu Mamá También (2001): Two amorous teenage boys, ditched by their girlfriends, travel by car through Mexico with an older woman in search of a hidden beach.

About Schmidt (2002): After retirement and his wife's death, Jack Nicholson sets out in a Winnebago to crash his daughter's wedding.

Horatio's Drive: America's First Road Trip (2003): Directed by Ken Burns, the story of the Horatio Jackson, America's first roadtripper.

The Motorcycle Diaries (2004): A dramatization of the motorcycle roadtrip Che Guevara took during his youth that inspired his life's work.

Transamerica (2005): A pre-operative, male-to-female transsexual embarks on unexpected journey after discovering she has fathered a son.

Cars (2006): The animated saga of Lightning McQueen, a hot-shot car who gets stranded in Radiator Springs.

MUSIC

Traveling music has been around since bards have been writing ballads, and oral travel poetry dates back before Homer. In America, there is a strong folk tradition of travel songs, with artists such as Woodie Guthrie singing Kerouacian tunes about rambling through the dust bowl and living the itinerant life. Distinct from the folk ballad is the "hot-rod song" of the early 60s, primarily about fast cars and flashy lifestyles.

ALBUMS

THE EAST COAST

Bruce Springsteen: The Wild, the Innocent, and the E Street Shuffle (1973). The Boss didn't really write about anything other than the road. "Rosalita" will have you wishing you could disobey your parents all over again.

THE DEEP SOUTH

Robert Johnson: King of the Delta Blues Singers (1961). More myth than man, Johnson supposedly sold his soul to the devil in Clarksdale, MS in exchange for his guitar skills. This will have you travelin' down dirt roads looking for your lost woman in no time.

THE GREAT NORTH

Wilco: Yankee Hotel Foxtrot (2002). We're not entirely sure why this works, but something about this record suggests snow-covered plains. "Heavy Metal Drummer" is particularly irresistible.

THE NATIONAL ROAD

Bob Dylan: Highway 61 Revisited (1965). Any Dylan will do, but this is as good as it gets. Crank up the volume and play "Like a Rolling Stone" as you set out. There's just no other way.

ROUTE 66

AC/DC: Highway to Hell (1979). Ignore the fact that the lead singer drank himself to death six months after the album's release, and revel in the chunky, hard-stompin' riffs of these all-time rock anthems.

THE OREGON TRAIL

Woody Guthrie: Woody Guthrie Sings Folk Songs (1962). This collection from the God of Folk even has a song called "Oregon Trail" on it. The perfect soundtrack when fording the river and dying of dysentery.

THE SOUTHERN BORDER

Johnny Cash: Complete Live at San Quentin (2000). Recorded in California in 1969, this album is Cash at his Texas outlaw best, singing about a Mississippi jail, among other things. Country never sounded this crazy.

THE PACIFIC COAST

Joni Mitchell: Blue (1971). For the contemplative hippie in all of us. Sounds even better if waves can be heard in the distance, and "California" is everybody's favorite.

SONGS

Aerosmith, "On the Road Again"

The Allman Brothers, "Ramblin' Man"

Audioslave, "I am the Highway"

B-52s, "Love Shack"

The Beatles, "Why Don't We Do It In the Road?"

The Beach Boys, "Fun Fun Fun"

Black Sabbath, "Hard Road"

Michelle Branch, "Breathe"

Garth Brooks, "Callin' Baton Rouge"

Cake, "Stick Shifts and Safety Belts"

Johnny Cash, "City of New Orleans"

Kelly Clarkson, "Since U Been Gone"

The Clash, "Train In Vain (Stand By Me)"

Tom Cochrane, "Life is a Highway"

Sheryl Crow, "Every Day is a Winding Road"

Deep Purple, "Highway Star"

John Denver, "Take Me Home, Country Roads"

The Doobie Brothers, "Rockin' Down the Highway"

Bob Dylan, "Highway 51 Blues"

Eve 6, "Open Road Song"

Fastball, "The Way"

Golden Earring, "Radar Love"

Woody Guthrie, "Hard Travelin'"
Sammy Hagar, I Can't Drive 55"
Jimi Hendrix, "Crosstown Traffic"
Elton John, "Blues for My Baby and Me"
Mike Jones, "Still Tippin'"
John Mayer, "Why Georgia"
Don McLean, "American Pie"
The Mekons, "Lost Highway"
Willie Nelson, "On the Road Again"
Elvis Presley, "Long Lonely Highway"
Prince, "Little Red Corvette"
John Prine, "Paradise"
Queen, "Bohemian Rhapsody"
R.E.M., "It's the End of the World as We Know It"
Simon & Garfunkel, "America"
Lynyrd Skynyrd, "Sweet Home Alabama"
Bruce Springsteen, "Born to Run"
Steppenwolf, "Born to be Wild"
James Taylor, "Carolina in my Mind"
Livingston Taylor, "Truck Driving Man"
Bobby Troup, "Route 66"
U2, "Where the Streets Have No Name"
Kanye West f. Paul Wall, "Drive Slow"

ON THE WEB

These roadside culture websites list all the funky stuff we know you really want to see along the way or anything you'd want to know before leaving. After all, no roadtrip is truly complete without a visit to the two-headed calf of Ft. Cody, NE.

www.driveinmovie.com. The drive-in is not quite a thing of the past; this site lists places where you can still enjoy the big screen from the comfort of your car.

www.roadfood.com. Lists and reviews a variety of roadside eateries, all presumably serving homestyle, greasy, classic American roadtrip food.

www.chowhound.com. A food-obsessed forum that will direct you to whatever food you desire anywhere in the country.

www.roadsideamerica.com. A guide to "offbeat tourist attractions," classic American kitsch, and just plain weirdness.

HOLIDAYS

2007 HOLIDAYS	
January 1	New Year's Day (US)
January 15	Martin Luther King, Jr. Day (US)
February 19	Presidents Day (US)
April 6-9	Easter Weekend (CAN)
May 21	Victoria Day (CAN)
May 28	Memorial Day (US)
July 1	Canada Day (CAN)
July 4	Independence Day
September 1	Labor Day (US)
October 8	Columbus Day (US)
October 8	Canadian Thanksgiving (CAN)
November 11	Veterans Day (US); Remembrance Day (CAN)
November 22	Thanksgiving (US)
December 25	Christmas Day
December 26	Boxing Day (CAN)

FESTIVALS

FESTIVAL	LOCATION
Tournament of Roses *December 29 to January 1*	Pasadena, CA *Pacific Coast*
Denver March Pow Wow *January*	Denver, CO *Oregon Trail*
Mardi Gras *January to February*	New Orleans, LA *Southern Border*
Daytona 500 *February*	Daytona Beach, FL *East Coast*
Houston Livestock Show & Rodeo *February to mid-March*	Houston, TX *Southern Border*
South by Southwest *March*	Austin, TX *Southern Border*
St. Patrick's Day Celebration *March 17*	Savannah, GA *East Coast*
Cinco de Mayo *May 5*	Los Angeles, CA *Pacific Coast*
Memphis in May *May*	Memphis, TN *Deep South*
Gullah Festival *Memorial Day Weekend*	Beaufort, SC *East Coast*
San Francisco Pride *June*	San Francisco, CA *Pacific Coast*
Rose Festival *June*	Portland, OR *Oregon Trail*
Int'l Country Music Fan Fair *mid-June*	Nashville, TN *Deep South*

FESTIVAL	LOCATION
Colorado Shakespeare Festival *late June to mid-August*	Boulder, CO *National Road*
Freedom Fest *2 weeks leading up to July 4*	Philadelphia, PA *National Road*
Cheyenne Frontier Days *July*	Cheyenne, WY *Oregon Trail*
Kansas City Blues & Jazz Festival *July*	Kansas City, MO *Oregon Trail and National Road*
Wild Pony Roundup *last consecutive W and Th in July*	Assateague Island, VA *East Coast*
Ohio State Fair *early August*	Columbus, OH *National Road*
Newport Jazz Festival *August*	Newport, RI *East Coast*

FESTIVAL	LOCATION
Bumbershoot *Labor Day Weekend*	Seattle, WA *Pacific Coast*
Monterey Jazz Festival *September*	Monterey, CA *Pacific Coast*
Head of the Charles Regatta *September*	Boston, MA *East Coast*
Austin City Limits *September*	Austin, TX *Southern Border*
Great American Beer Festival *end of September and beginning of October*	Denver, CO *National Road*
International Balloon Fiesta *early October*	Albuquerque, NM *Route 66*
Helldorado Days *third week of October*	Tombstone, NM *Southern Border*

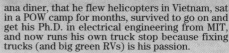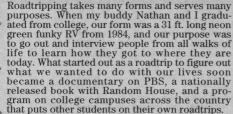

Roadtripping takes many forms and serves many purposes. When my buddy Nathan and I graduated from college, our form was a 31 ft. long neon green funky RV from 1984, and our purpose was to go out and interview people from all walks of life to learn how they got to where they are today. What started out as a roadtrip to figure out what we wanted to do with our lives soon became a documentary on PBS, a nationally released book with Random House, and a program on college campuses across the country that puts other students on their own roadtrips.

While creating *Roadtrip Nation* in the last few years, we've logged more than 14 months on the road, traveled at least 45,000 mi., been to every contiguous state, and met more amazing, eccentric, and brilliant people than we could have ever met inside our comfort zones. And we discovered that when you boil everything down—the photo ops, the scenic drives, the endless cheeseburgers—you discover the real beauty of roadtripping comes from the people you meet along the way.

Without those people, a roadtrip becomes, well, a mere trip. People give your expedition texture. They push you to a deeper level—a level that makes your roadtrip not just a fun vacation, but a change-your-life-forever-experience.

Here's the difference. Imagine a roadtrip in Maine. Some drivers will just coast through, only stopping to eat lobster at some cheeseball restaurant with a big neon sign. Those people miss the chance to meet Manny the lobsterman on the docks. Through him, we were able to spend a day out on his boat, the Jarvis Bay. On that boat, we weren't just in Maine, we were living Maine. We helped bring in the day's catch, downed a few shipyard brews as we watched the sun slip into the Atlantic, and retired to Manny's pad to cook up a few lobster tails. The meal was the best we've ever had, but what we remember the most is Manny.

It might seem tough to find interesting characters on the road, but opportunities pop up with every twist and turn of the journey. Say you get a flat tire on the Texas/Louisiana state line. You pull into the most classic truck stop you've ever seen, and out comes a tattooed 60-year-old man with a cigarette plastered to his mouth, Vietnam vet medals pinned to the mesh on his trucker's hat, and a rough beard grown to cover the scars on his face. Do you sit in the waiting room reading a 3-year-old issue of *Entertainment Weekly* until your tire is neatly primped, or do you hang with "Doc" as he puts the tire back on, learning a bit about him and going out to coffee with him afterwards? If you choose the latter option, you will learn, over a 3hr. cup of coffee at a typical Louisi-

ana diner, that he flew helicopters in Vietnam, sat in a POW camp for months, survived to go on and get his Ph.D. in electrical engineering from MIT, and now runs his own truck stop because fixing trucks (and big green RVs) is his passion.

Yep, meeting people on the road is where it's at, but HOW do you meet them?

The first rule is Carpe Diem. Seize the Day. It's not just a rule, but also a roadtrip philosophy, a perspective thwack on how you live your life, and an elevation of intensity that milks the experience out of every day. To live the rest of your life at this high pace would be not only tiring, it would be impossible. But while you're on the road for that finite amount of time, you really have nothing to lose. If Manny offers you a day on his boat, you put off your plans to go to Boston. If the founder of Starbucks, who also owns the Seattle Supersonics, offers you tickets to the basketball game that night, you have a quiet, relaxing evening some other time. If the guy who decoded the human genome wants to have coffee with you the next morning, and you're an 8hr. roadtrip away, fire up the engine and drive all night. You can sleep when you get home. Carpe Diem, roadtrip-style.

Secondly, leave your prejudices at home. On the road, nothing is as it seems. The moment you start judging people is the moment you close yourself off from an authentic connection. If we would have seen Doc as some low-level mechanic not worth our time, we would have missed out on one of the best cups of coffee of our lives.

Third, make a project out of it. Wrapping your roadtrip in some creative framework gives you the excuse to get in doors you wouldn't normally be able to open, and meet people you wouldn't normally be able to meet. Our excuse was to film an independent documentary about learning how people got to where they are today. So we interviewed the Lobsterman on his boat, we captured the story of the founder of Starbucks, and we learned where the guy who decoded the human genome was when he was our age. Your project could be doing a coffee table book on the best bakeries in the Pacific Northwest, taking photos of the best breakfast burritos in every state, surfing the northernmost point break in Maine, or finding the best concert venues down the eastern seaboard. Get creative. Open your mind. Put a little twist on things to wrap a mission around your expedition.

The degree of commitment to achieving "the mission" ranges from slacker to obsessive, but by thinking differently about your journey you'll meet people you would have never imagined. And who knows where it could go? I thought I would be in medical school right now.

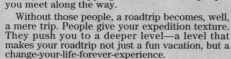

Mike Marriner crossed the country in a neon green RV, interviewing self-made men and women from the CEO of National Geographic *to the head sylist for Madonna. He is a founder of roadtripnation.com and an author of* Roadtrip Nation: A Guide to Discovering Your Path In Life. *See www.roadtripnation.com/campus/bring for information on hitting the road with RTN on one of their future roadtrips.*

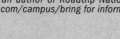

essentials

BEFORE YOU GO

ENTRANCE REQUIREMENTS

Passport. Required of all visitors who are not citizens of the US, Canada, or Mexico (required of Canadians and Mexicans as of Jan. 1, 2008).

Visa. Generally required of all visitors who are not citizens of the US or Canada, but requirement can be waived for residents of certain countries (including Australia, New Zealand, Ireland, and the UK) if staying fewer than 90 days.

Driving Permit. Required for those planning to drive. Foreign licenses are accepted, although an **International Driving Permit** (p. 14) may be preferable.

VITAL DOCUMENTS

PASSPORTS

REQUIREMENTS

As of January 1, 2008, citizens of all countries other than the US will need valid passports to enter the US. Returning home with an expired passport is usually illegal and may result in a fine, or it may not be possible at all. Passports must be valid for at least six months (for visitors to the US) or one day (for visitors to Canada) beyond the intended stay. Your passport is the most convenient method of identification.

NEW PASSPORTS

Citizens of the US, Canada, Australia, Ireland, New Zealand, and the UK can apply for a passport at a passport office or court of law. Many post offices also accept passport applications. Any new passport or renewal applications must be filed well in advance of the departure date, though most passport offices offer rush services for a very steep fee, typically US$60-200.

PASSPORT MAINTENANCE

Photocopy the page of your passport with your photo. Carry one copy in a safe place, apart from the original, and leave a copy at home. Consulates recommend that you carry an expired passport or an official copy of your birth certificate in a part of your baggage separate from other documents.

If you lose your passport, immediately notify the local police and the nearest embassy or consulate of your home government. To expedite its replacement, you will need to know all information previously recorded and show an ID and proof of citizenship, as well as pay a fee and include a police report. Replacements take approximately 10 days to process, but some consulates offer three-day rush service for an additional fee. A replacement may be valid only a limited time. Any visas stamped in your old passport will be irretrievably lost. In an emergency, some consulates immediately provide temporary traveling papers that will permit you to re-enter your home country.

VISAS

Citizens of some non-English speaking countries need a visa—a stamp, sticker, or insert in your passport specifying the purpose of your travel and the permitted duration of your stay—in addition to a valid passport to enter the US. Canadian citizens do not need to obtain a visa for admission; citizens of Australia, New Zealand, and most European countries (including the UK and Ireland) can waive US visas through the **Visa Waiver Program (VWP).** Visitors qualify if they are traveling only for business or pleasure (not work or study), are staying for fewer than 90 days, have proof of intent to leave (e.g., a return plane ticket), possess an I-94W form (arrival and departure certificate issued upon arrival), are traveling on particular air or sea carriers (most major carriers qualify—contact the carrier for details), and have no visa ineligiblities.

As of October 2004, visitors in the VWP must possess a **machine-readable passport** to be admitted to the US without a visa, although most countries in the VWP have been issuing such passports for some time and many travelers will not need new passports. **Children** from these countries who normally travel on a parent's passport will also need to obtain their own machine-readable passports. Additionally, as of June 2005, the following requirements are in place for the use of **biometric** identifiers as visa waivers: Passports issued before October 26, 2005 do not require biometric identifiers; passports issued between October 26, 2005 and October 25, 2006 require either a digital photograph or an integrated data chip; passports issued after October 26, 2006 require an integrated data chip. See http://travel.state.gov/visa or contact your consulate for a list of countries participating in the VWP as well as the latest info on biometric deadlines.

For stays of longer than 90 days in the US, all foreign travelers (except Canadians) must obtain a visa. Travelers eligible to waive their visas who wish to stay for more than 90 days must receive a visa before entering the US. In Canada, citizens of some non-English speaking countries also need a visitor's visa if they're not traveling with a valid green card. Citizens of the US, Australia, Ireland, New Zealand, the UK, as well as many other countries do not need a visa. See www.cic.gc.ca/english/visit/visas.html for a list of countries whose citizens are required to hold visas, or call your local Canadian consulate. Visitor's visas cost CDN$75 and can be purchased from the **Canadian Embassy** (☎ 202-682-1740) in Washington, D.C. US citizens can take advantage of the **Center for International Business and Travel** (☎ 800-929-2428; www.cibt.com), which secures visas to almost all countries for a varying service charge.

IDENTIFICATION

When you travel, always carry at least two forms of identification on your person, including at least one photo ID; a passport and a driver's license or birth certificate is usually adequate. Never carry all of your IDs together; split them up in case of theft or loss, and keep photocopies of all of them in your luggage and at home.

The **International Student Exchange Card (ISE)** is an identification card available to students, faculty, and ages 12-26. The card provides discounts,

medical benefits, access to a 24hr. emergency crisis line, and the ability to purchase student airfares. The card costs $25; call ☎ 800-255-8000 for more info, or visit www.isecard.com.

The **International Student Identity Card (ISIC),** the most widely accepted form of student ID, provides discounts on some sights, accommodations, food, and transport; access to a 24hr. emergency line; and insurance benefits for US cardholders. Applicants must be full-time secondary or post-secondary school students at least 12 years old. The **International Teacher Identity Card (ITIC)** offers teachers the same insurance coverage as the ISIC and similar, but limited, discounts. For travelers who are 25 years old or younger but are not students, the **International Youth Travel Card (IYTC)** provides many of the same benefits. Each of these identity cards costs $22 or equivalent. ISICs, ITICs, and IYTCs are valid one year from the date of issue. To learn more about ISICs, ITICs, and IYTCs try www.myisic.com. Many student travel agencies issue the cards; for a list of issuing agencies or more info, check with the **International Student Travel Confederation** (**ISTC;** www.istc.org).

CUSTOMS

Upon entering the US or Canada, you must declare certain items from abroad and pay a duty on the value of those articles if they exceed the allowance established by the local customs service. Note that goods and gifts purchased at **duty-free** shops abroad are not exempt from duty or sales tax; "duty-free" means that you need not pay a tax in the country of purchase. Upon returning home, you must declare all articles acquired abroad and pay a duty on the value of articles in excess of your home country's allowance. To expedite your return, make a list of any valuables brought from home and register them with customs before traveling abroad; be sure to keep receipts for all goods acquired abroad.

PERMITS AND INSURANCE

INTERNATIONAL DRIVING PERMIT

If you do not have a license issued by a US state or Canadian province or territory, you might want an **International Driving Permit (IDP).** While the US and Canada accept foreign licenses for up to a year, it may ease interaction with police if your license is written in English. You must carry your home license with your IDP at all times. IDPs are valid for a year, and must be issued in the country from which your license originates. To apply, contact the national or local branch of your automobile association.

CAR INSURANCE

While the minimum level varies by state, insurance is required in all states of the US; proof of insurance must be kept in the car at all times. Insurance costs depend on type of coverage and how big of a "risk" the driver poses. It may vary depending on age, sex, driving record, and credit history. Common types of coverage include **liability insurance,** the most standard and most often required type, which protects against the cost of damage to other people or property; **uninsured** or **under-insured motorist insurance,** which protects against damages to you caused by those driving illegally without insurance or without sufficient coverage; and **collision insurance,** which protects against the cost of damage caused to your vehicle in a collision in which you are at fault. Remember that if you are driving a conventional vehicle on an unpaved road in a rental car, you are almost never covered by insurance.

Most US insurance policies cover drivers in Canada as well; check with your provider before departure to obtain proof of coverage. For helpful info about the different types of insurance and statistics on which are required in each state, consult www.autoinsuranceindepth.com.

EMBASSIES

Contact the nearest embassy to obtain info regarding the visas and permits necessary to travel to the US and Canada. Listings of foreign embassies in the US as well as US embassies abroad can be found at www.embassyworld.com. The **US State Department's Bureau of Consular Affairs** (http://travel.state.gov) provides a list of US embassy and consulate websites. The **Canadian Ministry of Foreign Affairs** (www.dfait-maeci.gc.ca/world/embassies/menu-en.asp) lists the websites of its overseas embassies and consulates. General info for US citizens traveling to Canada can be found at www.amcits.com.

MONEY

CURRENCY AND EXCHANGE

The currency chart below is based on August 2006 exchange rates between US dollars (US$) and Australian dollars (AUS$), Canadian dollars (CDN$), European Union euros (EUR€), New Zealand dollars (NZ$), and British pounds (UK£). Check the latest exchange rates in a large newspaper, or try a currency converter on websites like www.xe.com or www.bloomberg.com.

US DOLLARS	
AUS$1 = US$0.75	US$1 = AUS$1.33
CDN$1 = US$0.91	US$1 = CDN$1.10
EUR€1 = US$1.29	US$1 = EUR€0.77
NZ$1 = US$0.63	US$1 = NZ$1.58
UK£1 = US$1.87	US$1 = UK£0.53

As a general rule, it's cheaper to convert money in the US than abroad. While currency exchange is available in most airports and border towns, it's wise to bring enough local currency to last for the first 24-72hr. of your trip. When changing money, try to go only to banks that have at most a 5% margin between their buy and sell prices. Since you lose money with every transaction, convert large sums, but no more than you'll need.

If you use traveler's checks or bills, carry some in small denominations (the equivalent of $50 or less) for times when you are forced to exchange money at disadvantageous rates, but bring a range of denominations since charges may be levied per check cashed. Store your money in a variety of forms; ideally, at any given time you will be carrying some cash, some traveler's checks, and an ATM and/or credit card.

TRAVELER'S CHECKS

Traveler's checks are one of the safest and least troublesome means of carrying funds. Check issuers provide refunds if the checks are lost or stolen, and many provide additional services, such as toll-free refund lines abroad, emergency message services, and stolen credit card assistance. American Express and Visa are the most recognized brands. Many banks and agencies sell them for a small commission. They are readily accepted in the US and Canada. Ask about refund hotlines and the location of refund centers when purchasing checks, and always carry some cash.

American Express: Checks available with commission at select banks, at all AmEx offices, and online (www.americanexpress.com; US residents only). American Express cardholders can also purchase checks by phone (☎800-721-9768).

Visa: Checks available at banks worldwide. AAA (p. 29) offers commission-free checks to its members. For the nearest office, call Visa (☎800-227-6811).

Travelex: Issues Visa traveler's checks. Members of AAA and affiliated automobile associations receive a 25% commission discount on purchases. US and Canada ☎800-287-7362; UK ☎0800 62 21 01.

CREDIT, DEBIT, AND ATM CARDS

Where they are accepted, credit cards are a convenient way to pay your expenses. Credit cards may also offer services such as insurance or emergency help, and are sometimes required to reserve hotel rooms or rental cars. **MasterCard** and **Visa** are the most welcomed; **American Express** cards work at some ATMs and at AmEx offices.

ATMs are widespread in the US and Canada. Depending on the system your home bank uses, you can likely access your personal bank account from the road. ATMs get the same exchange rate as credit cards, but there is often a limit on the amount of money you can withdraw per day (usually around $500). Credit cards don't usually come with PINs; if you intend to use credit cards at ATMs to get cash advances, request a PIN from your credit card company before leaving. The two major international ATM networks are **Cirrus** (☎800-424-7787; www.mastercard.com) and **Visa/PLUS** (☎800-843-7587; www.visa.com). Most ATMs charge a transaction fee that is paid to the bank that owns the ATM.

Debit cards are as convenient as credit cards but have a more immediate impact on your funds. A debit card can be used wherever its associated credit card company (usually MasterCard or Visa) is accepted, yet the money is withdrawn directly from the holder's checking account. Debit cards often

also function as ATM cards and can be used to withdraw cash from associated banks and ATMs throughout the US and Canada. Ask your local bank about obtaining one.

GETTING MONEY

WIRING MONEY

It is possible to arrange a **bank money transfer,** which means asking a bank back home to wire money to a bank in the US. This is the cheapest way to transfer cash, but it's also the slowest, usually taking several days or more. Money transfer services like **Western Union** are faster and more convenient than bank transfers—but also much pricier. Western Union has many locations worldwide. To find one, visit www.westernunion.com, or call in the US or Canada ☎800-325-6000, in Australia 1800 173 833, and in the UK 0800 833 833. To wire money using a credit card (Discover, MasterCard, Visa), call in the US and Canada 800-225-5227, in the UK ☎0800 833 833. Money transfer services are also available to **American Express** cardholders and at selected **Thomas Cook** offices.

US STATE DEPARTMENT (US CITIZENS ONLY)

In serious emergencies only, the US State Department will forward money within hours to the nearest consular office, which will then disburse it according to instructions for a $30 fee. If you wish to use this service, you must contact the Overseas Citizens Service division of the US State Department (☎202-647-5225 or 888-877-8339).

COSTS

The cost of your roadtrip will vary considerably, depending on where you go, how you drive, and where you stay. Significant expenses will include food, lodging, car maintenance, and gasoline. Before you go, spend some time calculating a reasonable daily **budget.** Don't forget to factor in emergency reserve funds (at least $200) when planning how much money you'll need.

TIPS FOR SAVING MONEY

Some simpler ways to stay within your budget include searching out opportunities for free entertainment, splitting accommodation and food costs with trustworthy fellow travelers, and buying food in supermarkets rather than eating out. Camping (see p. 35) is often a good way to save money, as is doing your laundry in the sink (unless this is explicitly prohibited). That said, don't go overboard. Though preserving your budget is important, don't scrimp at the expense of your health or a great travel experience.

FOOD AND LODGING

To give you a general idea, bare-bones lodging on the road (camping or sleeping in hostels) starts at about $12 per night, and a basic sit-down meal costs about $5-10. A slightly more comfortable day (sleeping in hostels/guesthouses and the occasional budget hotel, eating one meal per day at a restaurant, going out at night) would cost about $60-75, and for a luxurious day, the sky's the limit. In general, prices vary depending on the region and are usually higher along both coasts and around major cities or tourist attractions than in some parts of the South, West, and Midwest.

GASOLINE

Gas prices in the US have risen steeply over the past few years. A gallon of gas now costs about $2.90 ($0.70 per L), but prices vary widely according to state gasoline taxes. In Canada, gas costs as much as CDN$1 per L (CDN$3.80 per gallon). It is more than worth your while to shop around for the best price. Gas prices fluctuate quickly, but there are a number of websites entirely devoted to helping you find good gas prices. For average gas prices by state, check out **www.fuelgaugereport.com.** There's also a gas cost calculator: enter the start and end points of your trip, and the make, model, and year of your car to get approximate fuel costs for your roadtrip. Two websites, **www.fuelmeup.com** and **www.gasbuddy.com,** let travelers enter a zip code and then provide high, low, and average gas prices for that zip code, as well as the gas stations at which those prices can be found. However, because both rely on info submitted by other consumers, coverage can be spotty, especially in rural areas.

In general, it is a good idea to fill up your car before entering urban areas. Gas tends to be more expensive in cities, and you never know when you will get stuck in a traffic jam with the fuel needle flirting with empty. Similarly, fill up before entering a large rural stretch of road where there may not be a gas station when you need it.

In some cities, and at night, gas stations require you to **pay before you pump.** At most gas stations in the US, you'll be able to pay with a credit card, either inside the station or at the pump; however, at some rural stations you may only be able to pay by cash or check, so carry enough cash to fill up, just in case.

Most gas stations offer gas in three or four **octane levels;** usually, higher octane ratings have a higher price. Octane is the measurement of the "antiknock" quality of the gasoline, or its ability to resist undesired spontaneous combustion due to increased temperature and pressure. Higher octane gas experiences fewer spontaneous explosions, making it easier on your engine. Most cars come with a recommendation for which grade to use. If the recommended grade is not posted on the sticker on the back of the fuel filler door, consult your owner's manual.

TIPPING

In the US, it is customary to tip wait staff and cab drivers 15-20% (at your discretion). Tips are usually not included in restaurant bills unless you are in a party of six or more. In hotels, porters expect at least a $1 per bag tip to carry your bags. Tipping is less compulsory in Canada; a good tip signifies remarkable service. In general, anyone who offers a service and then waits around afterward is expecting a tip. In restaurants, waiters are tipped based on the quality of service; good service deserves at least 15%.

TAXES

In the US, sales tax is usually 4-10%, depending on the item and the place. Usually taxes are not included in the prices of items. In many states, groceries are not taxed. In Canada, you'll quickly notice the 6% goods and services tax (GST) and an additional sales tax in some provinces. Visitors can claim a rebate of the GST they pay on accommodations during stays of less than one month and on most goods they buy and take home, so save your receipts and pick up a GST rebate form while in Canada. To qualify for a rebate, total purchases must reach CDN$200, and the rebate application must be made within 11 months of the date of the purchase. A brochure detailing restrictions is available from local tourist offices.

ESSENTIALS

PACKING

When packing for your roadtrip, consider what you'll be doing along the way; pack comfortable clothes and shoes for driving, and if you plan to do a lot of hiking or camping, also consult our **Outdoors** section (see p. 35). You might want to bring a small cooler for bottled water and road-friendly snacks. Depending on your car and the number of people you are taking with you on your trip, space considerations may vary.

Luggage: In addition to your main pieces of luggage, a **daypack** (a small backpack or courier bag) is useful for storing essentials like your water bottle and copy of *Let's Go* for on-foot exploration.

Clothing: Whether your route takes you east-west or north-south, count on climates varying by region and elevation. Regardless of the season, those headed into the great outdoors should bring a waterproof **rain jacket,** sturdy shoes or **hiking boots,** and **thick socks.** Cotton socks are not recommended, as they tend to soak up and retain moisture. Keep the intense sunlight out of your eyes with a wide-brimmed **hat** or **sunglasses.** Those headed to the highlands or to mountainous national parks should pack a wool sweater or medium-weight fleece for the chilly nights. You may also want outfits for going out, and maybe a nice pair of shoes.

Converters and Adapters: In the US and Canada, electricity is 120 volts AC. Appliances from anywhere outside of North America will need an adapter (which changes the shape of the plug; $5) and a converter (which changes the voltage; $20-30). Don't make the mistake of using only an adapter (unless appliance instructions state otherwise).

Cellular Phones: A cell phone (see p. 32) can be a lifesaver on the road; it is highly recommended that travelers carry one, especially when traveling alone.

Toiletries: Most common toiletries are readily available throughout the US and Canada. Contact lenses are likely to be expensive and difficult to find on the road, so bring extra pairs and enough solution for your entire trip. Carry a copy of your prescription in case you need emergency replacements.

First-Aid Kit: For a basic first-aid kit, pack bandages, pain relievers, antibiotic cream, a thermometer, a Swiss Army knife, tweezers, moleskin, decongestant, motion-sickness remedy, diarrhea or upset-stomach medication (Pepto Bismol or Imodium), an antihistamine, sunscreen, insect repellent, and burn ointment.

Film: Film and developing in the US are affordable (around $10 per roll of 24 color exposures) and commonly available, so it is relatively easy to develop film while traveling. Less serious photographers may want to buy a disposable camera.

Other Useful Items: For safety purposes, you might consider bringing a **money belt** and **padlock.** Basic **outdoors equipment** (plastic water bottle, compass, waterproof matches, pocketknife, sunglasses, sunscreen, hat) may also prove useful. Quick repairs of torn garments can be done on the road with a needle and thread; also consider bringing electrical tape for patching tears. Other things you're liable to forget are an umbrella, sealable **plastic bags** (for damp clothes, soap, food, and other spillables), an **alarm clock,** safety pins, rubber bands, earplugs, garbage bags, and a small calculator.

Important Documents: Don't forget your driver's license and car insurance forms, passport, traveler's checks, ATM and/or credit cards, adequate forms of identification, and photocopies of the aforementioned in case these documents are lost or stolen.

For Your Car: When traveling in the summer or in the desert, bring substantial amounts of **water** (a suggested 5L per person per day) for drinking and for the radiator (p. 26). It is also a good idea to carry extra **food.** Make sure you take **good maps** and **sunglasses.** A **compass** and a **car manual** can also be useful. You should always carry a **spare tire** and **jack, jumper cables, extra oil, flares,** a **flashlight,** and **heavy blankets** (in case your car breaks down at night or in the winter). An empty **gas container** in your trunk can come in handy if you need to carry fuel to your car from a distant gas station. For more car-related essentials, see **Car Care on the Road,** p. 25.

SAFETY AND HEALTH

GENERAL ADVICE

In any type of crisis situation, the most important thing to do is **stay calm.** The emergency numbers in the box above are some of your best resources when things go wrong.

EMERGENCY 911. For emergencies in the US and Canada, dial ☎**911.** This number is toll-free from all phones, including coin phones and cell phones. In a very few remote communities, 911 may not work. If it does not, dial 0 for the operator. In national parks, it is usually best to call the **park warden** in case of emergency.

DRUGS AND ALCOHOL

In the US, the drinking age is 21; in Canada it is 19, except in Alberta, Manitoba, and Québec, where it is 18. Most localities restrict where and when alcohol can be sold. Sales usually stop at a certain time at night and are often prohibited entirely on Sundays. Drinking restrictions are particularly strict in the US. The youthful should expect to be asked to show government-issued identification when purchasing any alcoholic beverage.

Driving under the influence is a serious crime in the US and Canada. **Don't do it.** All 50 states, the District of Columbia, and all Canadian provinces have laws which make it a crime to drive with a blood alcohol concentration (BAC) above a certain level, in most cases, 0.08%, which can be achieved with as few as two drinks in one hour. A DUI conviction usually results in license suspension or revocation, and in 30 states, repeat offenders may have their cars taken away. Most states have zero-tolerance laws for those under 21, with severe consequences for those found to have consumed *any* amount of alcohol. In many states, **open containers** of alcoholic beverages in the passenger compartment of a car will result in heavy fines; a failed breathalyzer test will mean fines, a suspended license, imprisonment, or all three. Drivers under 21 should be aware that they may be convicted of underage possession if any alcohol is present in their vehicle.

Narcotics, such as heroin and cocaine, are highly illegal in the US and Canada. Though it may be partially decriminalized in some areas of Canada, marijuana is still illegal in most provinces and throughout the US. If you carry prescription drugs while you travel, keep a copy of the prescription with you, especially at border crossings. A letter from your doctor is advisable if you carry large amounts of prescription drugs.

SPECIFIC CONCERNS

NATURAL DISASTERS

EARTHQUAKES. Earthquakes occur frequently in certain parts of the US, particularly California, but most are too small to be felt. If a strong earthquake does occur, it will last at most 1-2 minutes. Open a door to provide an escape route and protect yourself by moving underneath a sturdy doorway or table. If you are outside, move to an open area free from buildings, trees, and power lines.

TORNADOES AND HURRICANES. Tornadoes have been reported in every US state, though they are most common in the Great Plains during the spring and summer. If you are inside during a tornado, move to a basement or interior location away from windows. If you are outside, lie flat on the ground in a low place away from power lines. Hurricanes are most common on the Atlantic and Gulf of Mexico coasts. Often, these areas are evacuated in anticipation of particularly severe hurricanes. If you are not advised to evacuate, stay inside, away from windows.

LANDSLIDES AND MUDSLIDES. Heavy rain, flooding, or snow runoff combined with hilly terrain can lead to landslides or mudslides, particularly on slopes where vegetation has been removed. This will most likely not be a concern in cities; however, if you are hiking after a heavy rainfall, be aware of the possibility of a slide. If you are caught in a mudslide or landslide, try to get out of its path and run to high ground or shelter. If escape is not possible, curl into a ball and protect your head.

FOREST FIRES. Dry spells are common in the western US, and 2005 marked the sixth consecutive year of drought for much of this area. In 2003, forest fires ravaged much of the eastern Cascades, as well as parts of California and Oregon. If you are hiking or camping and smell smoke, see flames, or hear fire, leave the area immediately. To prevent forest fires, always make sure campfires are completely extinguished; during high levels of fire danger, campfires will most likely be prohibited. Before you go hiking or camping, be sure to check with local authorities for the level of fire danger in the area.

TERRORISM

In light of the September 11, 2001 terrorist attacks, there is an elevated threat of further terrorist activities in the US. Terrorists often target landmarks popular with tourists; however, the threat of an attack is generally not specific or great enough to warrant avoiding certain places or modes of transportation. Keep aware of developments in the news and watch for alerts from federal, state, and local law enforcement officials. Also, due to heightened security, allow for extra time at border crossings, and be sure you have the appropriate documents. For more info on security threats to the US, visit the US Department of Homeland Security's website at www.dhs.gov.

PERSONAL SAFETY

EXPLORING

To avoid unwanted attention, try to blend in as much as possible. Familiarize yourself with your surroundings before setting out, and carry yourself with confidence. Check maps in shops and restaurants rather than on the street. If you are traveling alone, be sure someone at home knows your itinerary, and never tell anyone you meet that you're by yourself. When walking at night, stick to busy, well-lit streets and avoid dark alleyways. If you ever feel uncomfortable, leave the area as quickly and directly as you can.

Let's Go warns of neighborhoods that should be avoided when traveling alone or at night. There is no sure-fire way to avoid all the threatening situations you might encounter while traveling, but a good **self-defense course** will give you concrete ways to react to unwanted advances. **Impact, Prepare,** and **Model Mugging** can refer you to local self-defense courses in Australia, Canada, Switzerland and the US. Visit the website at www.modelmugging.org for a list of chapters. Workshops (2-4hr.) start at $50; full courses (20hr.) run $350-500.

PROTECTING VALUABLES

Never leave your belongings unattended; crime occurs in even the most demure-looking hostel or hotel. Bring your own padlock for hostel lockers, and don't ever store valuables in a locker. There are a few steps you can take to minimize the finan-cial risk associated with traveling. First, **bring as little with you as possible.** If it's not replaceable, don't bring it on the road. Second, buy a few combination **padlocks** to secure your belongings in your pack or in a hostel locker. Third, be sure to lock your car whenever you park it, even for a few minutes. Keep all bags and especially valuables out of sight, in the trunk, or under your seat. Fourth, **carry as little cash as possible.** Especially in big cities, roadtrippers might want to keep traveler's checks and debit or credit cards in a **money belt**—not a "fanny pack"—along with their passport or ID cards. Fifth, keep a small cash reserve separate from your main stash.

In large cities **con artists** often work in groups. Beware of certain classics: stories that require money, rolls of bills "found" on the street, mustard spilled (or saliva spit) onto your shoulder to distract you while they snatch your bag. **Never let your passport or bags out of your sight.** Beware of **pickpockets** in crowds. Also, be alert in public telephone booths: if you must say your calling card number, do so quietly; if you punch it in, make sure no one can look over your shoulder.

If you will be taking electronic devices, such as a laptop computer or PDA, check whether your homeowner's insurance covers loss, theft, or damage when you travel. If not, you might consider purchasing a low-cost separate insurance policy. **Safeware** (☎ 800-800-1492; www.safeware.com) specializes in covering computers and charges $90 for 90-day comprehensive international travel coverage up to $4000.

PRE-ROADTRIP HEALTH

In your **passport,** write the names of any people you wish to be contacted in case of a medical emergency, and list any allergies or medical conditions you may have. While traveling, be sure to keep all medication with you in your carry-on luggage. For tips on packing a **first-aid kit** and other health essentials, see p. 18.

IMMUNIZATIONS

The following vaccines should be kept up to date for travelers over two years old: MMR (measles, mumps, and rubella); DTaP or Td (for diphtheria, tetanus, and pertussis); IPV (for polio); Hib (for *haemophilus* influenza B); and HepB (for Hepatitis B). For recommendations on immunizations and prophylaxis, consult the Centers for Disease Control and Prevention, and check with a doctor for guidance.

INOCULATION REQUIREMENTS.
The US and Canada do not require visitors to carry vaccination certificates, nor do they require specific vaccinations for entry. Consult your doctor four to six weeks before departure. In addition to **booster shots for measles and tetanus,** consider the following vaccines and prescriptions:
Hepatitis A: Vaccine or immune globulin.
Hepatitis B: Recommended for those who might be exposed to blood or bodily fluids.

INSURANCE

Travel insurance covers four basic areas: medical/health problems, property loss, trip cancellation/interruption, and emergency evacuation. Though regular insurance policies may well extend to travel-related accidents, you may consider purchasing separate travel insurance if the cost of potential trip interruption or emergency medical evacuation is greater than you can absorb. Prices for travel insurance generally run about $50 per week for full coverage, while trip cancellation/interruption may be purchased separately at a rate of $3-5 per day depending on length of stay.

Medical insurance (especially university policies) often covers costs incurred abroad; check with your provider. **US Medicare** does not cover foreign travel, though in rare circumstances it pays for care in Canada and Mexico. **Canadian** provincial health insurance plans increasingly do not cover foreign travel; check with the provincial Ministry of Health or Health Plan Headquarters. **Homeowners' insurance** (or your family's coverage) often covers theft during travel and loss of documents up to $500.

ISIC and **ITIC** (see p. 14) provide basic insurance benefits to US cardholders, including $165 per day of in-hospital sickness for up to 60 days and $25000 of accident-related medical reimbursement. Cardholders have access to a 24hr. helpline for medical, legal, and financial emergencies overseas. **American Express** (☎800-528-

4800) grants most cardholders collision, rental theft, and up to $100,000 accident coverage on flight purchases made with the card.

INSURANCE PROVIDERS
STA offers a range of insurance plans that can supplement your basic coverage. Other private insurance providers in the US and Canada include: **Access America** (☎800-284-8300; www.accessamerica.com); **Berkely Group** (☎800-797-4514; www.berkely.com); **Travel Assistance International** (☎800-821-2828; www.europ-assistance.com); and **Travel Guard** (☎800-826-4919; www.travelguard.com).

USEFUL ORGANIZATIONS

The US **Centers for Disease Control and Prevention** (CDC; ☎877-FYI-TRIP; www.cdc.gov/travel) maintains an international travelers' hotline and an informative website. Their comprehensive booklet *Health Information for International Travel* (a.k.a. The Yellow Book), an annual rundown of disease, immunization, and health advice, is available free online. For detailed info on travel health, including a country-by-country overview of diseases (and a list of travel clinics in the US), try the *International Travel Health Guide*, by Stuart Rose, MD ($35; www.travmed.com). For info on medical evacuation services and travel insurance firms, check http://travel.state.gov/medical.html, and for general health info, contact the **American Red Cross** (☎800-564-1234; www.redcross.org).

STAYING HEALTHY

Common sense is the simplest prescription for good health on your roadtrip. Drink lots of fluids to prevent dehydration and constipation, and wear sturdy, broken-in shoes and clean socks.

ON THE ROAD

ENVIRONMENTAL HAZARDS

Heat exhaustion and dehydration: Heat exhaustion, characterized by dehydration and salt deficiency, can lead to fatigue, headaches, and wooziness. Avoid it by drinking plenty of fluids, eating salty foods (e.g., crackers), and abstaining from dehydrating beverages (e.g., alcohol, coffee, tea, and caffeinated soda). Continuous heat stress can eventually lead to heatstroke, characterized by a rising temperature, severe headache, and cessation of sweating. Victims should be cooled off with wet towels and taken to a doctor. The risk of heat exhaustion is greatest while traveling through desert areas, where the combination of heat and dryness can result in rapid water loss.

Hypothermia and frostbite: A rapid drop in body temperature is the clearest sign of overexposure to cold. Victims may shiver, feel exhausted, have poor coordination or slurred speech, hallucinate, or suffer amnesia. *Do not let hypothermia victims fall asleep.* To avoid hypothermia, keep dry, wear layers, and stay out of the wind. When the temperature is below freezing, watch out for frostbite. If skin turns white, waxy, and cold, do not rub the area. Drink warm beverages, get dry, and slowly warm the area with dry fabric or steady body contact.

Sunburn: Always wear sunscreen (at least SPF 30) when outdoors. If you are planning on spending time near water, in the desert, or in the snow, you are at a higher risk of getting burned, even on a cloudy day. If you get sunburned, drink more fluids than usual and apply an aloe-based lotion. Severe sunburns can lead to sun poisoning, a condition that affects the entire body, causing fever, chills, nausea, and vomiting. Sun poisoning should be treated by a doctor.

Air Pollution: While traveling through urban areas, especially greater Los Angeles and Denver, air pollution can be a serious problem. Fortunately, many of the possible effects—wheezing, tightness in the chest, bronchitis—tend to reverse themselves once exposure stops. Long-term exposure can result in serious problems such as lung cancer and heart disease. To protect yourself, heed daily pollution warnings. Pollution is often worst during the winter and in early morning.

Altitude Sickness: Many mountainous areas are high enough for altitude sickness to be a concern. Symptoms may include headaches, dizziness, and sleep disruption. To minimize effects, avoid rapid increases in elevation, and allow your body a couple of days to adjust to a new elevation before exerting yourself and take special care when driving. Note that alcohol is more potent and UV rays stronger at high elevations.

INSECT-BORNE DISEASES

Many diseases are transmitted by insects—mainly mosquitoes, fleas, ticks, and lice. Be aware of insects in wet or forested areas, and while hiking

or camping. Use an insect repellent that has a 30-35% concentration of DEET. Wear long pants and long sleeves (fabric need not be thick or warm; tropic-weight cottons can keep you comfortable in the heat) and consider buying a **mosquito net** for travel in coastal or humid regions. Natural repellents can be useful supplements: taking vitamin B-12 pills regularly can eventually make you smelly to insects, as can garlic pills. Calamine lotion or topical cortisones (like Cortaid) may stop insect bites from itching, as can a bath with a half cup of baking soda or oatmeal. **Ticks**—responsible for Lyme and other diseases—can be particularly common in rural and forested regions of the Northeast and the Pacific Northwest.

Lyme disease: A bacterial infection carried by ticks and marked by a circular bulls-eye rash of 2 in. or more. Later symptoms include fever, headache, fatigue, and aches and pains. Antibiotics are effective if administered early. Left untreated, Lyme can cause problems in joints, the heart, and the nervous system. If you find a tick attached to your skin, grasp the head with tweezers as close to your skin as possible and apply slow, steady traction. Removing a tick within 24hr. greatly reduces the risk of infection. Do not try to remove ticks with petroleum jelly, nail polish remover, or a hot match. Tick bites usually occur in moist, shaded environments and heavily wooded areas. If you are going to be hiking in these areas, wear long pants and sleeves and an insect repellent with DEET.

West Nile Virus: The West Nile Virus has been detected in all 48 continental states and is transmitted through the bite of an infected mosquito. Most victims do not have any symptoms, but some develop mild flu-like symptoms; less than 1% develop more severe symptoms including meningitis or encephalitis. Those at highest risk are the elderly and those with lowered immune systems, but people of all ages can develop a serious illness. To minimize the risk of infection, limit outdoor activity in dawn, dusk, and early evening, wear long clothes, and use DEET.

FOOD- AND WATER-BORNE DISEASES

Prevention is the best cure; be sure that your food is properly cooked and the water you drink is clean. The tap water in the US and Canada is treated to be safe for drinking. Culprits include raw shellfish, unpasteurized milk and dairy products, and sauces containing raw eggs. Peel fruits and vegetables before eating them.

Beware of food from markets or street vendors that may have been "washed" in dirty water or fried in rancid oil. Juices, peeled fruits, and exposed coconut slices are all risky.

Giardiasis: A parasite that is acquired by drinking untreated water from streams or lakes. Symptoms include swollen glands or lymph nodes, fever, rashes or itchiness, and digestive problems. Boil water, wear shoes, and eat only cooked food.

Gastroenteritis/Stomach Flu: Caused by a class of viruses called Noroviruses and spreads via contact with the bodily fluids of infected people, including exposure to contaminated food, touching contaminated objects and then placing the hands in or near the mouth, and direct contact with infected persons. Symptoms appear within 48hr. of infection and include vomiting, nausea, chills, diarrhea, and abdominal cramping. Though the symptoms usually pass within a few days, the disease can be contagious for several weeks and a doctor should be consulted if any of these symptoms develop.

OTHER INFECTIOUS DISEASES

Rabies: Transmitted through the saliva of infected animals; fatal if untreated. By the time symptoms (thirst and muscle spasms) appear, the disease is in its terminal stage. If you are bitten, wash the wound thoroughly, seek immediate medical care, and try to have the animal located. A rabies vaccine, which consists of 3 shots given over a 21-day period, is available and recommended for developing-world travel, but is only semi-effective. Rabies is found all over the world, and is often transmitted by dog bite.

Hepatitis B: A viral infection of the liver transmitted via blood or other bodily fluids. Symptoms, which may not surface until years after infection, include jaundice, loss of appetite, fever, and joint pain. It is transmitted through activities like unprotected sex, injections of illegal drugs, and unprotected health work. A 3-shot vaccination sequence is recommended for health-care workers, sexually active travelers, and anyone planning to seek medical treatment abroad; it must begin 6 months before traveling.

Hepatitis C: Like Hepatitis B, but the mode of transmission differs. IV-drug users, those with occupational exposure to blood, hemodialysis patients, and recipients of blood transfusions are at the highest risk, but the disease can also be spread through sexual contact or sharing items like razors and toothbrushes that may have traces of blood on them. No symptoms are usually exhibited, but they can include loss of appetite, abdominal pain, fatigue, nausea, and jaundice. If untreated, Hepatitis C can lead to liver failure.

AIDS and HIV: For detailed info on Acquired Immune Deficiency Syndrome (AIDS) in North America, call the US Centers for Disease Control's 24hr. hotline at ☎800-342-2437, or contact the Joint United Nations Programme on HIV/AIDS (UNAIDS), 20, ave. Appia, CH-1211 Geneva 27, Switzerland (☎41 22 791 3666; fax 22 791 4187).

Sexually Transmitted Infections (STIs): Gonorrhea, chlamydia, genital warts, syphilis, herpes, and other STIs are more common than HIV and can cause serious complications. There is no cure for herpes or the virus that causes genital warts. Both Hepatitis C and syphilis can be fatal if untreated. Though **condoms** may protect you from some STIs, they are far from completely effective. Oral or even tactile contact can lead to transmission. If you think you may have contracted an STI, see a doctor immediately.

OTHER HEALTH CONCERNS

MEDICAL CARE ON THE ROAD

Medical care in the US and Canada is among the best in the world. In case of medical emergency, call ☎911 from any phone and an operator will dispatch paramedics, a fire brigade, or the police as needed. Emergency care is also readily available at any emergency room on a walk-in basis. If you do not have insurance, you will have to pay for medical care. Appointments are required for non-emergency medical services.

If you are concerned about obtaining medical assistance while traveling, you may wish to employ special services. The *MedPass* from **GlobalCare, Inc.,** 2001 Westside Pkwy., Alpharetta, GA 30004, US (☎800-860-1111; www.globalcare.net), provides 24hr. international medical assistance and medical evacuation resources. The **International Association for Medical Assistance to Travelers** (**IAMAT;** ☎716-754-4883, in Canada 519-836-0102; www.iamat.org) has free membership and info on immunization requirements and sanitation.

Those with medical conditions (such as diabetes, allergies to antibiotics, epilepsy, heart conditions) may want to obtain a **Medic Alert** membership (first year $35, annually thereafter $20), which includes a stainless steel ID tag and a 24hr. collect-call number. Contact the Medic Alert

Foundation, 2323 Colorado Ave., Turlock, CA 95382, US (☎ 888-633-4298; www.medicalert.org).

WOMEN'S HEALTH

Unsanitary conditions and even stretching the distance between pit stops can contribute to **urinary tract (including bladder and kidney) infections.** Over-the-counter medicines can sometimes alleviate symptoms, but if they persist, see a doctor. **Vaginal yeast infections** may flare up in hot and humid climates. Wearing loose-fitting trousers or a skirt and cotton underwear will help, as will over-the-counter remedies like Monistat or Gyne-Lotrimin, which should only be used if you have been previously diagnosed with a yeast infection and have exactly the same symptoms. **Tampons, sanitary pads,** and **contraceptive devices** are widely available in the US and Canada. **Abortion** is legal in both the US and Canada.

CAR SAFETY

ROAD RULES

While driving, be sure to buckle up. ▨**Seatbelts** are required by law in many regions of the US and Canada. Children under 40 lb. should only ride in a specially designed car seat, available for a small fee from most car rental agencies, and children under 12 should ride in the backseat. Sleeping in your car is one of the most dangerous (and often illegal) ways to get your rest. Let's Go does not recommend hitchhiking under any circumstances; it is particularly dangerous for women and solo travelers. It is *never* a good idea to pick up hitchhikers.

The **speed limit** in the US varies considerably from region to region. Most urban highways have a limit of 55 mph (89 kph), while rural routes range from 65 mph (104 kph) to 75 mph (120kph). Heed the speed limit; not only does it save gas, but most local police forces and state troopers make use of radar to catch speed demons. The speed limit in Canada is 50 kph (31mph) in cities and 80 kph (49 mph) on highways. On rural highways the speed limit may be 100 kph (62 mph).

Don't tailgate. Most rear-end collisions are a result of following too closely, so use the **two-second rule** to determine a safe following distance— choose a fixed object ahead of you on the road and start counting slowly when the vehicle in front of you passes it. If you reach the object before two seconds, you're following too closely.

Driving at night requires extra caution. Switch from your brights to normal lights so as not to blind any oncoming drivers, and stay alert. Be aware of **weather conditions,** and drive appropriately. Try to avoid **driving in fog,** but if you have to, go slowly and keep your headlights on dim or use foglights. In the **rain,** roads get slippery, so it is a good idea to slow down and allow extra time for breaking, especially right after it has started raining and roads are slick with dust and oil. Usually you are required to keep your headlights on while it's raining, even during the day.

Finally, **winter driving** can be especially hazardous; be aware of the temperature and of road conditions. It can be hard to tell if roads are icy (bridges and overpasses can be icy even when the rest of the road is clear), and braking can take extra time.

> **NAPTIME.** Even if you don't fall asleep at the wheel, just being sleepy can endanger you by slowing your reaction time and handicapping your driving skills. Crash rates rise at night and in the mid-afternoon, as drowsiness reduces responsiveness, contributes to tunnel vision, and impairs decision-making and concentration. The only antidote for drowsiness is sleep. Slapping yourself, turning the radio up, or sticking your head out the window may entertain you and fellow drivers, but is no substitute for rest. Walking around every couple of hours will make you a more alert driver, but is also not a reliable solution. You'll be most alert at the wheel if you sleep on a regular schedule in a cool, dark, quiet place. Avoid caffeine and alcohol before bedtime, and try to get some kind of exercise during the day.

BEFORE YOU LEAVE

It is a good idea to have your car checked over by a mechanic a few weeks before you depart to allow time to fix any problems. Things like worn brakes or strained shock absorbers, while not always in need of immediate replacement, may fail on you after you've put them through a rigorous, long-distance roadtrip.

ESSENTIALS

Fuel-injected vehicles may benefit from a few doses of **fuel system cleaner** both before you go and on the road—though it might cost you $10-15 per bottle (typically, one bottle is dumped into one tank of gas), it is cheaper than having the fuel system overhauled. At the same time, don't consider cleaner a substitute for necessary repairs uncovered during a pre-departure inspection.

In order to make minor repairs on your car, or to keep it moving after a problem, you will need to carry several tools, including a **wrench** (an adjustable wrench can handle many sizes of bolts but may be too large for small spaces), a **flashlight** or two (a larger flashlight for illuminating things at night, and a smaller **pen light** for slim crevasses), a few good **screwdrivers** with both **Phillips** and **flat-head** ends (these should range in size from small to large, and should be long enough to reach down into concealed engine spaces—if your vehicle has star, square, or other special types of screw, make sure that you have the correct screwdriver on hand), and a couple of different kinds of **pliers** (one for gripping larger items and a narrower needle-nosed pair for reaching into tight spaces).

Other vital items include extra oil, extra coolant, a jack, a tire iron, a full-sized spare tire, extra gasoline, extra clean water, a tire pressure gauge, road flares, hose sealant, a first-aid kit (see p. 18), jumper cables, fan belts, extra windshield washer fluid, plastic sheeting, string or rope, a larger tow rope, duct tape, an ice scraper, rags, a funnel, a spray bottle filled with glass cleaner, a compass, matches, blankets, and food. Even if you don't have a tow hitch or are traveling alone, carry along a tow rope. Having one on hand will make it easier for others to help get you out of your jam.

CAR CARE ON THE ROAD

TIRE CARE
Check your **tire pressure** periodically throughout your trip. Most tires are stamped with the appropriate pressure to which they ought to be inflated. If not, look at the inside of your driver's side door or in your vehicle's owner's manual. The pressure is represented in **PSI** (pounds per square inch). You can use a **tire pressure gauge** to determine the PSI of your tires—this small tool is often shaped like a pen with a metal bulb at one end, and will cost $10-40, depending on the model (digital models are typically priced higher). **Overinflation** and **underinflation** are both dangerous and can contribute to skidding, flats, and blowouts, as well as reducing your gas mileage.

Be aware that climate shifts can have a large impact on tire PSI—make sure to check it after periods of changing temperature. Since hot temperatures will give you inaccurate readings, check the PSI after your tires have cooled down from driving. Regular tire maintenance should also include **tire rotations** every 6000 mi. (9700km). If your tires are worn or bald, consider having them replaced entirely before taking a roadtrip. Tires that are dangerously worn can cause the car to start vibrating violently and make lots of noise.

FLUID, HOSE, AND FILTER CARE
Long days of driving mean that you will need to change your **oil** and your **oil filter** more frequently than you normally would. Three thousand miles (4800km) should be the absolute maximum distance you drive before you change your oil and oil filter. If conditions are extremely dusty, it may be necessary to change your oil even more frequently. You should check your oil level every few days by taking your vehicle's **dipstick** and sliding it into the engine's oil level test tube. The dipstick will often be resting in this tube, but to get an accurate measurement, wipe it off first and then plunge it in and out of the tube, checking the actual oil level against the level recommended on the dipstick or in your vehicle's owner's manual. Test the level after your vehicle has been at rest for at least several minutes. If your level is low, add more oil.

Dust will also collect in your **air filter** and clog it. Though air filter replacements are normally recommended every 20,000 mi. (32,300km), you will want to have yours inspected during each oil change. Replacement air filters may cost $15-40, but if your filter is dirty, the money will be well spent—your air filter doesn't just sieve the junk out of your air, it also protects your fuel system.

Other essentials you should have inspected before your journey and after hard driving include your **brake fluid, transmission fluid, fuel filter, PCV breather filter** (which filters gases from engine combustion and protects your oil system, and which should be replaced every 30,000 mi. or 48,300km), **automatic transmission filter, spark plugs,** and your **distributor cap** and **rotor.** It is cheaper to replace all of these than it is to fix a single catastrophe caused by ignoring one of them.

Hoses and **belts** are extremely important to monitor for wear and damage—even very small problems with vacuum hoses, for instance, will prevent your vehicle from starting. **Fan belts** are notorious for snapping in the most remote places. It is worthwhile to carry along a few extra fan belts, but it is better to get failing belts replaced. Replace any fan belt if it looks loose, cracked, or if it is glazed or shiny. In an emergency, **panty hose** can serve as a very temporary substitute.

CHANGING A FLAT TIRE

To change a tire, you will need, at the very least, a **jack,** a sturdy **tire iron** capable of withstanding a couple hundred pounds of pressure, and a **full-sized spare tire.** Park your vehicle securely on level ground with the emergency brake applied. Turn on your **emergency flashers** to alert other vehicles that you are stalled on the side of the road. At night, it may be helpful to light a couple **road flares,** especially if your vehicle is not entirely off of the road. Place the jack on smooth ground (you may need to lay down a flat board for the jack), and locate the place underneath the vehicle where the jack will do its lifting. There are usually flat panels close to each wheel, perhaps behind it or to its sides. Locate this area, and align it with the jack. Do not pump the jack yet—you will need to loosen the tire's **lugnuts.** If you have a **hubcap,** remove it and set it aside.

Practice changing your tire before you leave—if the lugnuts are fastened too tightly, they may be difficult or impossible for you to loosen on your own. Choose a lugnut to loosen, place the tire iron against it, and loosen it until it spins freely. After loosening the first lugnut, loosen the opposite lugnut. The third lugnut you loosen should be next to the first. The fourth will be opposite the third. Repeat this pattern until every lugnut is loose.

Before jacking up the car, make sure your spare tire is on the ground outside of the car. Raise the jack slowly and carefully, making sure that your vehicle is stable. Never place anything else underneath the vehicle, or reach under the vehicle while it is propped up by a jack. Use the jack to raise your vehicle far enough for your tire to rotate freely. Once the vehicle is raised, remove the loosened lugnuts and place them in your hubcap or another secure area. Carefully remove the tire.

Take the spare tire and align its holes with the tire studs on the wheel hub. If you can't see the tire's air valve facing you, the tire is probably on backwards. Once the spare tire is resting against the wheel hub, replace the lugnuts in the same order you removed them, and tighten them down with your fingers. Do not use the tire iron yet. Slowly lower your vehicle, remove the jack, and use the tire iron to tighten the lugnuts. As with loosening, tighten the lugnuts in opposite pairs. Drive slowly for a few hundred feet to make sure that the tire is on correctly. Gradually increase your speed, and make your way down to the next service station to buy yourself another spare.

OVERHEATING

In the US and some parts of Canada, summer days can reach shocking levels of heat. Take **several gallons of clean water** with you—this can be used for drinking or for pouring into your radiator if you experience overheating or loss of coolant. Dedicate about 1½ gallons (5.6L) of water per person per day solely for drinking, and carry an additional few gallons for your radiator. The water should be clean to prevent damage to your radiator; however it is possible to use impure stream or lake water to top off your radiator. Just be sure to have the radiator flushed afterwards. Also carry a gallon of **coolant** along with you. Coolant needs to be mixed with water after being poured into the radiator, so don't substitute water with more coolant.

On a hot day, you can help prevent overheating by turning off your **air conditioning** system. This would seem to be exactly the time when you need A/C the most, but the it takes a toll on your vehicle's cooling mechanisms. If your car has a temperature gauge, check it frequently. If not, stop periodically and check for signs of overheating—any sort of boiling noise coming from under your hood is a strong indicator that you need to let the vehicle cool down for a while—and check your hoses for leaks. Turning the **heater** on full blast will also help cool the engine. If your car overheats, pull off the road and turn the heater on full force to let the engine blow off its steam. If radiator fluid is steaming or bubbling, turn off the car for 30min. or more. If not, run the car in neutral at about 1500 rpm for a few minutes, allowing the coolant to circulate. Never pour water over the engine, and never try to lift a searingly hot hood. Be warned that if you turn on the heater, the heat may actually be enough to melt the plastic fins which cover your car's vents—put them in an open and loose position in case they become trapped later on.

If you open your radiator cap, always wait 45min. or more until the coolant inside of the radiator loses its heat—otherwise, you may be spattered with boiling coolant. Even after waiting, you may still be spattered with warm coolant, so stand to the side whenever opening the cap. Remember that 'topping off' your radiator does not mean filling it completely. Instead, there is probably a tank or reservoir with a filling indicator somewhere near the radiator. Pour a small amount of water and coolant into the radiator (in a 50/50 mixture) and wait for it to work its way into the system and raise the reservoir. Some vehicles need the engine running in order to draw the coolant in.

Coolant leaks are sometimes just the product of overheating pressure, which forces coolant out of the gaps between the hoses and their connections to the radiator. If not, or if there are other holes in the hose, it helps to have **hose sealant** on hand with you. Many hose sealants also double as temporary gas tank sealants and cost between $7-15. If you apply sealant, treat it as a very short-term solution, and get the vehicle to a service station as soon as possible. Drive slowly and keep your heater on to avoid stressing the seal. Always put the radiator cap back on—coolant will erupt from your vehicle if you don't.

BATTERY FAILURES AND FLUBS

If you turn the key in the ignition and nothing happens, or if the engine refuses to start, you may have a dead battery. Recharging the battery at a service station may be your only option if your battery is too drawn down. It helps to have the tools on hand to remove your battery (and often the accompanying battery cover) from your vehicle. A **screwdriver** and **wrench** are usually required for this task. However, your first option should be to try and **jump start** your car. This may require waiting for a while on the side of the road with your hood raised, and is one of the reasons why you should always have jumper cables on hand. Since many batteries are run down through simple carelessness (forgetting to turn off headlights, etc.), it's a good idea to devise a simple system to help you remember to turn off all your lights when leaving the vehicle. Also, many vehicles have lights in places that are not obvious, such as below the rearview mirror. Check these periodically to make sure that they are not on.

To safely jump start your vehicle, position the two cars close to one another while making sure that there is no contact between them. Set the emergency brakes, turn off both engines, and take out the keys before you open the hoods. If the battery looks damaged or cracked, do not attempt to jump start; you'll need to call for a tow. Identify the positive posts on both batteries, and attach the red cable to the positive post of the dead battery, then the positive post of the working battery. Do not let the red clips contact the clips on the black cable. Attach one clip on the black cable to the negative post on the working battery, and then attach the other clip to bare metal on the disabled vehicle's engine frame (or another part of the disabled car with exposed, unpainted metal), as far as possible from the battery—otherwise, the battery's hydrogen gas could ignite. Start the working vehicle, and rev it for a few moments before starting the disabled vehicle. Once both vehicles are running, disconnect the cables in reverse order, starting with the black cable attached to the bare metal. Do not kill the engines or allow the cables to contact one another until they are completely disconnected. Afterwards, drive around for 30min. or more to allow the alternator to recharge the battery.

LEAVING YOUR KEYS IN THE CAR

Lockouts can be particularly troublesome in remote areas, since locksmiths are uncommon and often expensive. Prevent lockouts by keeping a **spare copy** of your vehicle's door key somewhere on your person at all times, perhaps in a money belt. If you do happen to find yourself locked out, it may be possible to get assistance from local police services. Though they may be reluctant to provide assistance if there are other options in the area, in some towns the police are the only agency with locksmithing equipment. Be prepared to prove your ownership of the vehicle afterwards.

As a very last resort, if you simply cannot wait for the police, many vehicles have **small triangular windows** next to the main roll-down windows, especially in the rear. If you can reach the lock from this window, use a stone or other blunt object to break the glass. Take care not to cut yourself—wrap a cloth around your hand and arm before reaching for the lock. You can temporarily patch the damage with a **plastic sheet** or **tarp,** folded over several times until it is quite thick, and sealed to the car with **duct tape** on every edge. Keep it taut to resist the wind.

ROAD HAZARDS

SKIDDING

Avoid skids by reducing your speed whenever driving in wet or icy conditions. If you find yourself in a skid, **do not apply the brakes.** This will only make things worse, and may cause your vehicle to roll over. Instead, at the beginning of a skid, ease off of both the brake and gas. The most important thing to do is to control the steering wheel. Grip the wheel firmly with both hands. **Steer into the skid.** If you are skidding to the right, then take the wheel and firmly turn it to the right. Once you feel the vehicle straightening out, carefully tug the wheel back toward a straight position. At this point, you may need to press down on the gas pedal a bit to push the vehicle onto its new course.

Afterwards, slow down—you were probably skidding because you were traveling faster than you could safely handle. You may want to pull over and inspect your vehicle for damage. Prioritize a **brake inspection.** Your skid probably sapped a few months off of the life of your brake pads.

BLOWOUTS

You should become familiar with the feel of your car under normal driving conditions—the first sign of a tire rupture will probably involve a change in the way the vehicle feels while you are driving. A deflating tire may not be obvious at first, especially if you have the windows rolled up or are playing loud music. You might notice that the car doesn't turn as easily, or it might feel a bit more wobbly than usual. Pull over to a safe place at the first sign of trouble—make sure that you stop somewhere off the road, away from blind corners, and on level ground. You will feel a tire blowout (or tread separation) right away—the car will suddenly become much more difficult to steer, especially on turns, and you may be tugged in a particular direction.

To handle a tire blowout, absolutely **do not slam on the brakes,** even though this may be your first instinct. A blown tire (especially a blown front tire) will reduce your braking capability, and slamming on the brakes will just send you in an uncontrolled skid—at worst, the car may even roll over. The same advice applies to steering—even though your vehicle may be pulled out of its original direction, don't compensate by wrenching the wheel forcefully the other way around. Instead, grip the wheel firmly while you take your foot off of the gas, steering only enough to keep the vehicle in a straight line or away from obstructions. Let the vehicle come to a complete stop—don't worry about damaging the wheel of the blown tire, since a blowout is an emergency situation, and your safety is more important.

CRITTERS

One of the dangers of driving in rural areas is that the long distances tend to lull you. You might not check the **speedometer** as often as you should, or you might be tempted to gaze at the scenery instead of the road. This may seem safe for stretches at a time, but don't do it—some areas of the US are rife with wildlife such as **deer, moose,** or **bears.** If you aren't paying attention, you could find yourself poised to collide with any one of these creatures.

TRUCKS AND GRAVEL

Roads are repaired in sections, so you may find yourself cruising along comfortably on a smooth road when the pavement suddenly ends and your excessive speed sends you slamming into deep potholes and roadside brush. One useful indicator of potential road trouble is the presence of **black tire marks**—these are created by the tag axles of large trucks as they hit dips in the road. If you see these markings, reduce your speed dramatically.

The large number of RVs and trucks on major roads means that there is a chance you could suffer a chipped or cracked windshield from flying debris—if you see a large vehicle trundling toward you on the road, pull as far away from the center as possible and slow down. Hopefully, stones flung in your direction will just bounce off your windshield if you keep it slow. You can take other measures to reduce the risk of rock damage. Consider having **protective covers** placed on your headlights. Though not required, it is good to have a **gas tank cover** placed over your gas tank.

STEEP GRADES

Some parts of the road take you up **steep grades.** Make sure your **brake system** is in good order before you set out, and that your **brake pads** aren't worn. Don't attempt to run up steep hills too quickly—it might cause you to overheat or blow your transmission. On downhill grades, go slower than you typically would, since controlling a skid on a downhill slope is one of the hardest things you should never have to do. Travel slowly in case you meet an oncoming truck—flung gravel will punish reckless speeders. Finally, if you blow a tire on a slope (much more likely if you speed), you will need to keep going until you find a flat and level place to stop, meaning that you might have to absorb damage to your wheels.

INCIDENTS AND ACCIDENTS

If you see flashing lights in your rearview mirror, you're being **pulled over.** Slow down and move onto the shoulder as soon as you can. Turn off the engine, keep your hands on the wheel, and wait for an officer to come to your window. Don't fumble for your license and registration until you're asked for it. Excuses usually won't get you out of a ticket, but respect and courtesy go a long way.

If you're involved in an **accident,** even a minor fender-bender, stay calm and call the police. Never move an injured person unless he or she is in danger, but move your car out of traffic if

you can. Exchange info with the other driver involved; get the driver's license number, insurance company info, address, phone number, and license plate number, as well as the names and contact information of any witnesses. You may need to file an accident report and contact your insurance company.

CAR ASSISTANCE

In addition to **911** service in the US and Canada and, most **automobile clubs** offer free towing, emergency roadside assistance, travel-related discounts, and random goodies in exchange for a modest membership fee. Travelers should strongly consider membership in one if planning an extended roadtrip.

American Automobile Association (AAA; ☎800-222-4357; www.aaa.com). Emergency assistance, free trip-planning services, maps, guidebooks, and 24hr. emergency road service anywhere in the US. Free towing and commission-free American Express traveler's cheques from over 1000 offices across the country. Discounts on Hertz car rental (5-20%) and various motel chains and theme parks. Basic membership $48, each extra person $24. To sign up, call ☎800-564-6222.

Canadian Automobile Association (CAA), 1145 Hunt Club Rd., #200, Ottawa, ON K1V 0Y3 (☎800-222-4357; www.caa.ca). Affiliated with AAA (see above), the CAA provides the same membership benefits, including 24hr. emergency roadside assistance, free maps and tourbooks, route planning, and various discounts. Basic membership CDN$70-90. Call ☎800-564-6222 for membership services.

 ROAD INFORMATION. Dialing ☎511 in many states across the nation will get you helpful info, including details on area traffic, construction projects, road closures, detours, and weather conditions.

GETTING AROUND

NAVIGATING

On most road signs and maps, "I" refers to interstate highways (as in "I-90"), "U.S." (as in "U.S. 1") to US highways, and "Rte." (as in "Rte. 7") to state and local highways. For Canadian highways,

"TCH" refers to the **Trans-Canada Hwy.**, while "Hwy." or "autoroute" refers to standard routes.

Most US roads are named with an intuitive **numbering system.** Even-numbered interstates run east-west and odd ones run north-south, decreasing in number toward the south and the west. Except for a few cases, primary (two-digit) interstates have unique numbers nationwide. North-south routes begin on the West Coast with I-5 and end on the East Coast with I-95. The southernmost east-west route is I-4 in Florida. The northernmost east-west route is I-94, stretching from Montana to Wisconsin. Three-digit numbers signify branches of other interstates that often skirt large cities, and generally are numbered by adding a multiple of 100 to the number of its parent interstate (as in I-285, a branch of I-85). Traditionally, if an interstate has three digits that start with an even number, then it is bounded on both ends by other interstates, and if it begins with an odd digit, it meets another interstate at only one end.

A good **map** is a roadtripper's best friend; make sure you have one before starting your journey. *Rand McNally's Road Atlas*, covering all of the US and Canada, is one of the best commercial guides (available at bookstores, gas stations, and online at www.randmcnally.com; $9). Free maps of the interstate and national highway systems can be found online from the US Department of Transportation at www.fhwa.dot.gov/hep10/nhs/.

YOUR WHEELS

For a life-changing, classic American road-trip, any car will do. If you already own one, drive it. Some people think that off-road vehicles like pickup trucks and SUVs are necessary, while others prefer flashy red sportcars. In truth, most of America's roads are paved and navigable by any car.

CAR RENTAL

National car rental agencies usually allow you to pick up a car in one city and drop it off in another for a hefty charge, sometimes in excess of $1000. The drawbacks of car rentals include high prices (a compact car rents for $25-45 per day) and high minimum ages (usually 25). Some branches rent to drivers ages 21-24 for an additional (often steep) charge, but policies vary from agency to agency. **Alamo** (☎800-462-5266; www.alamo.com), **Dollar** (☎800-800-3665; www.dollar.com), **Enterprise** (☎800-736-8222; www.enterprise.com), and **Thrifty** (☎800-367-2277; www.thrifty.com) all rent to ages 21-24 for varying surcharges. **Rent-A-Wreck** (☎800-944-7501; www.rent-a-wreck.com) specializes in supplying vehicles that are past their prime for lower-than-average prices; a bare-bones compact less than eight years old rents for around $20-25. There may be an additional charge for a **collision and damage waiver (CDW),** which usually comes to about $12-15 per day. Major credit cards (including MasterCard and American Express) will sometimes cover the CDW if you use their card to rent a car; call your credit card company for specifics.

Because it is mandatory for all drivers in the US, check that you are covered by **insurance.** Be sure to ask whether the price includes insurance against theft and collision. Some credit cards cover standard insurance. If you rent, lease, or borrow a car, and you are not from the US or Canada, you will need a **green card** or **International Insurance Certificate** to certify that you have liability insurance that applies abroad. Green cards can be obtained at car rental agencies, car dealerships, and some travel agents and border crossings. Driving a conventional rental on an **unpaved road** is almost never covered by insurance.

Instead of a traditional rental, **Adventures on Wheels,** 42 Hwy. 36, Middletown, NJ 07748 (☎800-943-3579 or 732-495-0959; www.wheels9.com), will sell you a motor home, minivan, station wagon, or compact car, organize its registration and insurance, and guarantee that they will buy it back after your travels. Cars with a buy-back guarantee start at $2500. Buy a camper van for $6500, use it for six months, and sell it back for $3000-4000. The main office is in New Jersey; there are others in L.A., San Francisco, Las Vegas, Denver, Montreal, and Miami. Vehicles can be picked up at one office and dropped off at another.

CAR TRANSPORT SERVICES

Car transport services match drivers with car owners who need cars moved from one city to another. Would-be travelers give the company their desired destination and the company finds a car that needs to go there. Expenses include gas, tolls, and your own living expenses. Some companies insure their cars; with others, your security deposit covers any breakdowns or damage. You must be over 21, have a valid license, and agree to drive about 400 mi. per day on a fairly direct route. More info on auto transport options (including overseas and listings by state) can be found at www.movecars.com. **Auto Driveaway Co.,** 310 S. Michigan Ave., Chicago, IL 60604 (☎800-346-2277; www.autodrive-away.com), and **Across America Driveaway,** 9839 Indianapolis Blvd., Highland, IN 46322 (☎800-677-6686; www.schultz-international.com), are two transport companies.

CAMPERS AND RVS

Much to the chagrin of more purist outdoorsmen, the US and Canada are havens for the home-and-stove on wheels known as the recreational vehicle (RV). Most national parks and small towns cater to RV travelers, providing campgrounds with large parking areas and electrical outlets ("full hook-up"). The costs of RVing compare favorably with the price of staying in hotels and renting a car, and the convenience of bringing along your own bedroom, bathroom, and kitchen makes it an attractive option. **Renting** an RV is also a possibility. **Cruise America,** 11 W. Hampton Ave., Mesa, AZ 85210 (☎800-671-8042 or 480-464-7300; www.cruiseamerica.com) rents and sells RVs in the US and Canada. Rates vary widely by region, season (July and August are most expensive), and type of RV, but prices for a standard RV are around $800 per week.

MOTORCYCLES

The revving engine, worn leather, and wind-in-your-face thrill of motorcycling have built up a cult following, but motorcycling is one of the most dangerous ways to experience the open road. Helmets are required in many states and always recommended; wear the best one you can find. Those considering long trips should contact the **American Motorcyclist Association,** 13515 Yarmouth Dr., Pickerington, OH 43147 (☎800-262-5646; www.ama-cycle.org), the linchpin of US biker culture. And of course, take a copy of Robert Pirsig's *Zen and the Art of Motorcycle Maintenance.*

KEEPING IN TOUCH BY MAIL

SENDING MAIL

First-class letters sent and received within the US take one to three days to reach their destination and cost $0.39; postcards are $0.24. Priority Mail packages up to 1 lb. generally take two to three days and cost $4.05. All days specified denote business days. For more details, see www.usps.com. For Canadian mailing information, visit Canada Post at www.canadapost.ca.

RECEIVING MAIL

Mail can be sent to the US or Canada through **Poste Restante or General Delivery** to almost any city or town with a post office. Address letters to:

Elvis PRESLEY
General Delivery
Post Office Street Address
Memphis, TN 38101 or Kelowna, BC V1Z 2H6
USA or CANADA

The mail will go to a special desk in the central post office, unless you specify a post office by street address or postal code. As a rule, it is best to use the largest post office in the area; mail may be sent there regardless of what is written on the envelope. It is usually safer and quicker to send mail express or registered. When picking up mail, bring a form of photo ID, preferably a passport.

SENDING MAIL OVERSEAS

For mailing letters abroad, the marking "par avion" is universally understood. The **standard letter** rate for international postage is $0.84 to most countries ($0.63 to Canada or Mexico). A standard postcard costs $0.75 ($0.55 to Canada or Mexico). For packages up to 4 lb., use **Global Priority Mail** for delivery to major locations in three to five business days for a flat rate (small envelope $5.25, large envelope $9.50). If regular airmail is too slow, **Federal Express** (☎800-247-4747) can get a letter from New York to Sydney in two business days for a whopping $41. By **US Express Mail,** a letter would arrive within four business days and cost about $20. **Surface mail** is by far the cheapest and slowest way to send mail. It takes one to three months to cross the Atlantic and two to four to cross the Pacific—appropriate for sending large quantities of items you won't need to see for a while.

BY TELEPHONE

DOMESTIC CALLS

The simplest way to call within the US and Canada is to use a coin-operated **pay phone,** which charges $0.35 for local calls. You can also buy **prepaid phone cards** that carry prepaid phone time. Phone rates tend to be highest in the morning, and lowest Sunday and at night.

US and Canadian phone numbers consist of a three-digit area code and a seven-digit local number. Let's Go lists all 10 digits, although often only the final seven are needed for in-city dialing. Before purchasing any calling card, compare rates with other cards, and make sure that it serves your needs (a local phonecard is generally better for local calls, for instance).

MOBILE PHONES

While pay phones can be found in almost every city and town, you can avoid much of the hassle of scrounging up change or a card by using a cell phone. Cell phone reception is clear and reliable in cities and along major highways throughout most of the US, though in remote areas reception can be spotty. Your provider may also slap on hefty additional fee (up to $1.25 per min.) for roaming or extended areas. Call your service provider to check their coverage policies in the area of your destination.

The international standard for cell phones is **GSM,** a system that began in Europe and has spread to much of the rest of the world. Some cell phone companies in the US and Canada use GSM in certain regions (e.g., T-Mobile and AT&T), but most employ other services such as **TDMA, CDMA, I-den,** and **AMPS.** You can make and receive calls in the US and Canada with a GSM or GSM-compati-ble phone, but you will only get coverage in relatively populated areas, and your phone will only work if it is from North America or if it is a **tri-band** phone. American GSM networks use different frequencies than those used in Europe; a tri-band phone allows you to use the European 900MHz and 1800MHz frequencies as well as the North American 1900MHz frequency.

If you are using a GSM phone in the US or Canada, you will need a **SIM (subscriber identity module) card,** a country-specific, thumbnail-sized chip that gives you a local phone number and plugs you into the local network. You may need to **unlock** your phone in order to insert a SIM card. Many companies will offer to unlock your phone for fees (from $5-50), but call your provider; some will unlock your phone for free upon request. If your provider won't unlock your phone, your best bet is to look online for an unlocking service, but bear in mind that getting your phone unlocked may violate your service agreement. Many SIM cards are prepaid, meaning that they come with calling time included and you don't need to sign up for a monthly service plan. Incoming calls are frequently free. When you use up the prepaid time, you can buy additional cards or vouchers. For more info on GSM phones, check out www.telestial.com, www.orange.co.uk, www.roadpost.com, or www.t-mobile.com.

Renting a cell phone is possible but usually more expensive than a short-term prepaid contract. A good option, especially if you want to make occasional calls over a short period, is to buy a cell phone with a **prepaid contract,** which allows a customer to buy a certain amount of minutes each month. Phones such as those provided by **Ecallplus** (www.ecallplus.com), **AT&T** (www.att.com), or **Verizon** (www.verizon.com) provide this type of service. Before you buy a used cell phone, make sure it is compatible with the service you want.

INTERNATIONAL CALLS

To make international calls from the US or Canada, a **calling card** is probably your cheapest bet. You can often make **direct international calls** from pay phones, but if you aren't using a calling card, you may need to drop your coins as quickly as your words. Where available, prepaid phone cards (see below) and major credit cards can be used for direct international calls, but they are pricey.

PLACING INTERNATIONAL CALLS. To call North America from abroad or to call abroad from North America dial:

1. The **international dialing prefix.** To make a call out of Australia, dial 0011; the Republic of Ireland, Mexico, New Zealand, or the UK, 00; Canada or the US, 011.
2. The **country code.** To call Australia, dial 61; the Republic of Ireland, 353; Mexico, 52; New Zealand, 64; the UK, 44; Canada or the US, 1.
3. The **city/area code.**
4. The **local number.**

TIME DIFFERENCES

Because the US is divided into three different time zones, regions can vary between five and eight hours behind **Greenwich Mean Time (GMT).** New York, NY, is five hours behind GMT, while Los Angeles, CA, is eight hours behind. Most areas observe Daylight Savings Time, so clocks are set forward 1hr. in the spring and backward 1hr. in the fall. Clocks change at 2am, local time.

8AM	9AM	10AM	11AM	NOON
Alaska	Seattle L.A. Las Vegas	Denver Missoula Boise	Chicago St. Louis Houston	Toronto Boston Miami

BY EMAIL AND INTERNET

If your email provider won't let you check your e-mail from the web, your best bet for reading email from the road is to use a free **web-based email account** (www.gmail.com and www.yahoo.com are two options). Most public libraries in the US and Canada offer free Internet access, and Internet cafes abound. Check the "Vital Stats" boxes of major cities for establishments with Internet access. For lists of additional cybercafes in the US and Canada, check out www.cypercaptive.com or www.cybercafe.com.

Increasingly, travelers find that taking their **laptop computers** on the road can be a convenient option for staying connected. Laptop users can call an Internet service provider via a modem using long-distance phone cards specifically intended for such calls. They may also find Internet cafes that allow them to connect laptops to the Internet. Travelers with wireless-enabled computers may be able to take advantage of Internet "hotspots" where they can get online for free or for a small fee. Newer computers can detect hotspots automatically; otherwise, websites like www.jiwire.com, www.wi-fihotspotlist.com, and www.nodedb.net can help you find them. For info on insuring your laptop, see p. 20.

ACCOMMODATIONS

HOTELS AND MOTELS

HOTELS

Commonly found in the downtowns of cities, hotels were born in the age before cars, when traveling from city to city was difficult and often expensive and lodging was a grand affair suited to the occasion. The hotels came to symbolize the height of sophistication and luxury—to stay in a hotel was emblematic of wealth and class. Though hotels still dominate the downtowns of most major American cities, today many of them are franchises, and brand names like Radisson, Hilton, Ritz-Carlton, Marriott, Hyatt, Sheraton, and the ever-present Holiday Inn appear on street corners from New York to New Orleans. These franchises strive to maintain the old style of city lodging, but some of the unique extravagance of the 19th century has been lost. Most cities still boast at least one lavish independent hotel, usually a relic from this golden age, which is usually the absolute cream of the hotel crop. None of these hotels, of course, is cheap.

Hotel rooms in the US vary widely in cost depending on the region in which the hotel is located. The cheapest hotel single in the Northeast would run about $60 per night, while it is possible to stay for $30 per night in a comparable hotel in the South, West, or Midwest. You'll typically have a private bath and shower, although some places may offer shared bathrooms.

MOTELS

With car culture in the US came a new kind of lodging. As motorists began driving long distances, they began to need places to sleep along the way, and the motor hotel, now universally known as the motel, was born. In the 1910s, organized tent camps and motor cabins appeared along roads to popular destinations. Throughout WWI and the Great Depression, "cottage courts" and "motor courts" replaced tourist camps as the lodging norm on the road. These courts offered stand-alone cabins or "bungalows" for touring visitors, and often featured amenities like gas and food. With the appearance of the interstate, motor courts began to unite their rooms under one roof and package them as "motels."

Just as the grand city hotel had its golden age in the mid-19th century, the motel flourished in the 1950s; colorful names, distinct architecture, idiosyncratic themes, and garish signs lined America's highways, each competing for the attention of the rising tide of roadtrippers. Today's motels are still car-oriented; the horizontal layout of some motels allows guests direct access to cars parked right outside their doors. Interstates are lined with familiar brand names such as Motel 6, Super 8, Comfort Inn, Red Roof Inn, Howard Johnson, Travelodge, Econolodge, Best Western, and Hampton Inn. Most rooms cost between $35 and $60 per night; again, expect to pay more near cities and in the Northeast than in rural areas or the West.

HOSTELS

Hostels are generally dorm-style accommodations, often in large single-sex rooms with bunk beds, though some hostels do offer private rooms for families and couples. They sometimes have kitchens and utensils, bike or moped rentals, storage areas, and laundry facilities. There can be drawbacks: some hostels close during certain daytime "lockout" hours, have a curfew, don't accept reservations, impose a maximum stay, or, less frequently, require that you do chores.

HOSTELLING INTERNATIONAL

Joining the youth hostel association in your own country automatically grants you membership privileges in **Hostelling International (HI),** a federation of national hosteling associations. HI hostels are scattered throughout the US and Canada and may accept reservations via the **International Booking Network** on HI's web page (www.hihostels.com), which also lists the web addresses and phone numbers of all national associations. Other hosteling websites include www.hostels.com and www.hostelplanet.com.

Most HI hostels also honor **guest memberships**—you'll get a blank card with space for six validation stamps. Each night you'll pay a nonmember supplement (one-sixth the membership fee) and earn one guest stamp; get six stamps, and you're a member. Most student travel agencies sell HI cards, as does **Hostelling International-Canada (HI-C),** 205 Catherine St. #400, Ottawa, ON K2P 1C3 (☎613-237-7884; www.hihostels.ca).

 BOOKING HOSTELS ONLINE. One of the easiest ways to ensure that you've got a bed for the night is by reserving online. Click to the **Hostelworld** booking engine through **www.letsgo.com,** and you'll have access to bargain accommodations with no added commission.

OTHER TYPES OF ACCOMMODATIONS

YMCAS

Young Men's Christian Association (YMCA) lodgings are usually cheaper than a hotel but more expensive than a hostel. Not all YMCA locations offer lodging; those that do are often located in urban downtowns. Many YMCAs accept women and families; most will not lodge those under 18 without parental permission.

YMCA of the USA, 101 N. Wacker Dr., Chicago, IL 60606 (☎800-872-9622; www.ymca.net). Provides a listing of the nearly 1000 YMCAs across the US and Canada, with prices, services, and contact info.

YMCA Canada, 42 Charles St. E. 6th fl., Toronto, ON M4Y 1T4 (☎416-967-9622; www.ymca.ca). Info on YMCAs in Canada.

YWCA of the USA, 1015 18th St. NW, Ste. 1100, Washington, DC 20036 (☎202-467-0801; www.ywca.org). Publishes a directory ($8) on YWCAs across the USA.

BED AND BREAKFASTS

For a cozy alternative to hotel rooms, bed & breakfasts (B&Bs; private homes with rooms available to travelers) range from the acceptable to the sublime. Rooms generally cost $50-70 for a single and $70-90 for a double in the US and Canada, but on holidays or in expensive locations, prices can soar. For more info, check out **Bed & Breakfast Inns Online** (☎800-215-7365; www.bbonline.com), **InnFinder** (www.inncrawler.com), or **Innsite** (www.innsite.com).

UNIVERSITY DORMS

Many colleges and universities open their residence halls to travelers when school is not in session (May-Sept.)—some do so even during term-time. Getting a room may take a couple of phone calls and require advance planning, but rates tend to be low, and many offer free local calls and Internet access. Some universities that host travelers include the University of Texas in Austin, TX (☎512-476-5678), Ohio State University in Columbus, OH (☎614-292-8266), and McGill University in Montréal, QC (☎514-398-6367).

THE OUTDOORS

Camping is probably the most rewarding way to slash travel costs. Considering the number of public lands available for camping in both the US and Canada, it may also be the most convenient. Well-equipped campsites (usually including prepared tent sites, toilets, and water) go for $5-25 per night in the US and CDN$10-30 in Canada. **Backcountry camping,** which lacks all of the above amenities, is often free but can cost up to $20 at some national parks. Most campsites are first come, first served. The **Great Outdoor Recreation Pages** (www.gorp.com) provides excel-
lent general info for travelers planning on spending time outdoors.

USEFUL RESOURCES

A variety of publishing companies offer hiking guidebooks to meet the educational needs of novice or expert. For info about camping, hiking, and biking, write or call the publishers listed below to receive a free catalog.

Family Campers and RVers/National Campers and Hikers Association, Inc., 4804 Transit Rd., Bldg. #2, Depew, NY 14043 (☎800-245-9755; www.fcrv.org). Membership fee ($25 per family) includes their publication *Camping Today.*

The Mountaineers Books, 1001 SW Klickitat Way, Ste. 201, Seattle, WA 98134 (☎206-223-6303; www.mountaineersbooks.org). Over 600 titles on hiking, biking, natural history, and conservation.

Sierra Club Books, 85 2nd St., 2nd fl., San Francisco, CA 94105 (☎415-977-5500; www.sierraclub.org). Publishes general resource books on camping and women traveling in the outdoors, as well as books on hiking in Arizona, Florida, Arkansas, the Rockies, the California Desert, and Northern California.

Wilderness Press, 1200 5th St., Berkeley, CA 94710 (☎800-443-7227 or 510-558-1666; www.wildernesspress.com). Carries over 100 hiking guides and maps, mostly for the western US.

Woodall Publications Corporation, 2575 Vista Del Mar Dr., Ventura, CA 93001 (☎877-680-6155; www.woodalls.com). Annual campground directories.

NATURE PRESERVES

US NATIONAL PARKS

National Parks protect some of the most spectacular scenery in North America. Though their primary purpose is preservation, the parks also host recreational activities such as ranger talks, guided hikes, marked trails, skiing, and snowshoe expeditions. For more info, contact the **National Park Service,** 1849 C St. NW, Washington, D.C. 20240 (☎202-208-6843; www.nps.gov).

The larger and more popular parks charge a $4-20 entry fee for cars. The **National Parks Pass** ($50), available at park entrances, allows the passport-holder's party entry into all national parks for one year. National Parks Passes can also be bought through the National Park Foun-

ESSENTIALS

dation, P.O. Box 34108, Washington, D.C. 20043 (☎202-619-7289; www.nationalparks.org). For an additional $15, the Parks Service will affix a **Golden Eagle Passport** hologram to your card, which will allow you access to sites managed by the US Fish and Wildlife Service, the US Forest Service, and the Bureau of Land Management. Senior citizens qualify for the lifetime **Golden Age Passport** ($10), which entitles the holder's party to free park entry, a 50% discount on camping, and reductions on various recreational fees. Persons eligible for federal disability benefits can enjoy the same privileges with the free **Golden Access Passport.**

Most national parks have both backcountry and developed **camping.** Some welcome RVs, and a few offer grand lodges. At the more popular parks in the US, reservations are essential and available through the National Park Service Reservation Center (☎800-365-2267 or 301-722-1257; http://reservations.nps.gov) no more than five months in advance. Indoor accommodations should be reserved months in advance. Smaller campgrounds often observe policies of first come, first served, and many fill up by late morning.

US NATIONAL FORESTS

Often less accessible and less crowded, **US National Forests** (www.fs.fed.us) are a purist's alternative to parks. While some have recreation facilities, most are equipped only for primitive camping—pit toilets and no water are the norm. When charged, entrance fees are $10-20, but camping is generally $3-4 or free. Necessary wilderness permits for backpackers can be obtained at the US Forest Service field office in the area. *The Guide to Your National Forests* is available at all Forest Service branches and the main office (USDA Forest Service, 1400 Independence Ave. SW, Washington, DC 20250; ☎202-205-1760). This booklet includes a list of all national forest addresses; request maps and other info directly from the forests you plan to visit. Reservations are available for most forests with a $9 service fee, but are usually only needed during high season at the more popular sites. Call the National Recreation Reservation Center (☎877-444-6777, outside US 518-885-3639; www.reserveusa.com) up to one year in advance.

CANADA'S NATIONAL PARKS

Less touristed than their southern counterparts, these parks boast plenty of natural splendor. Park entrance fees are CDN$3-7 per person, with family and multi-day passes available. Reservations are offered for a limited number of campgrounds for CDN$7. For these reservations or info on the over 40 parks and historical sites in the network, call **Parks Canada** (☎888-773-8888) or consult their web page (www.pc.gc.ca). Annual passes are available (CDN$63 per adult, CDN$125 for families or groups of 7 or fewer).

WILDERNESS SAFETY

Stay warm, stay dry, and stay hydrated. The vast majority of life-threatening wilderness situations can be avoided by following this simple advice. Prepare yourself for an emergency by always packing rain gear, a hat and mittens, a first-aid kit, a reflector, a whistle, high-energy food, and extra water for any hike. Dress in warm layers of wool or synthetic materials designed for the outdoors; never rely on cotton for warmth, as it is useless when wet. For info about outdoor ailments and medical concerns, see **Safety and Health,** p. 18.

WILDLIFE

If you are hiking in an area that might be frequented by **bears,** sing or make noise as you walk to warn them of your approach. If you see a bear, keep your distance. No matter how cute they appear, don't be fooled—bears are powerful and dangerous animals. If you see a bear at a distance, calmly walk (don't run) in the other direction. If the bear pursues you, back away slowly while speaking in low, firm tones. If you are attacked by a bear, get in a fetal position to protect yourself, put your arms over your neck, and play dead. Remain calm and don't make any loud noises or sudden movements. Don't leave food or other scented items (e.g., trash, toiletries, the clothes that you cooked in) near your car or tent. Putting these objects into canisters is now mandatory in some national parks. **Bear-bagging**—hanging edibles and other good-smelling objects far from camp in a tree out of reach of hungry paws—is the best way to keep your toothpaste from becoming a condiment. Bears are also attracted to any **perfume,** as are bugs; cologne, scented soap, deodorant, and hairspray should stay at home.

LEAVE NO TRACE. The idea behind environmentally responsible tourism is to leave no trace of human presence behind. A camp stove is a safer and more efficient way to cook than using vegetation, but if you must make a fire, keep it small and use only dead branches or brush rather than cutting vegetation. Make sure your campsite is at least 150 ft. (50m) from water supplies or bodies of water. If there are no toilet facilities, bury human waste (but not paper) at least 4 in. (10cm) deep and above the high-water line, and 150 ft. or more from any water supplies and campsites. Always pack your trash in a plastic bag and carry it with you until you reach the next trash receptacle. For more info on these issues, contact one of the organizations listed below.

Earthwatch, 3 Clock Tower Pl., Ste. 100, Box 75, Maynard, MA 01754 (☎800-776-0188 or 978-461-0081; www.earthwatch.org).

International Ecotourism Society, 1333 H St. NW, Ste. 300, East Tower, Washington, D.C. 20005 (☎202-347-9203; www.ecotourism.org).

National Audubon Society, 700 Broadway, New York, NY 10003 (☎212-979-3000; www.audubon.org).

Poisonous **snakes** are hazards in many wilderness areas of North America and should be avoided. The two most dangerous are coral snakes and rattlesnakes. Coral snakes reside in the southwestern US and Mexico and can be identified by black, yellow, and red bands. Rattlesnakes live in desert and marsh areas and will shake the rattle at the end of their tail when threatened. Don't attempt to handle or kill a snake; if you see one, back away. If you are bitten, wash the wound with soap and water, apply a dry dressing (but not a tourniquet), immobilize the limb, and keep it below the level of the heart. Do not apply ice, as this may worsen the bite. Seek immediate medical attention for any snakebite that breaks the skin.

In the desert areas of the Southwestern US and Mexico, travelers should also be on the lookout for poisonous **lizards.** The two dangerous types of lizards are Gila monsters and Mexican beaded lizards. Gila monsters are large lizards (around 12-18 in.) with dark, highly textured skin marked by pinkish mottling, and thick, stumpy tails. The Mexican beaded lizard resembles the Gila monster, but with uniform spots rather than bands of color. Both are poisonous, though they are docile in nature and unlikely to bite unless antagonized.

Though often mistakenly thought to be exclusively desert dwellers, **scorpions** can also be found throughout the grassland, savannah, jungle, and forest regions of North America. The coloration of these arachnids (eight legs, not six) varies greatly, though they are generally brown or black. Scorpions range from the typical 1 in. to the more impressive (and scary) 8 in., and are active mostly at night. Scorpions usually sting in self-defense, and stings are usually excruciatingly painful but not life-threatening. Nevertheless, if stung, you should seek immediate medical attention.

Mountain regions are the stomping grounds for **moose.** These big, antlered animals have been known to charge humans, so never feed, walk toward, or throw anything at a moose. If a moose charges, get behind a tree. If it attacks, get on the ground in a fetal position and stay still.

Mosquitoes will be your main source of agony during the summer. The volume of mosquitoes after spring thaw can be unbearable without some sort of protection. Though these creatures start cropping up in spring, peak season runs from June through August before tapering off at the approach of fall. Mosquitoes can bite through thin fabric, so cover up with thicker materials. Products with **DEET** are useful, but the mosquitoes can be so ravenous that nothing short of a **mosquito hood** and netting will stop every jab. (see p. 22)

OUTDOORS EQUIPMENT

WHAT TO BUY
Good camping equipment is both sturdy and light.

Sleeping Bags: Most sleeping bags are rated by season. "Summer" bags are effective for temperatures down to 30-40°F (around 0°C) at night; "4-season" or "winter" bags are for temperatures 0°F (-17°C). Bags are made of **down** (warm and light, but expensive; miserable when wet) or of **synthetic** material (heavy, durable; warm when wet). Prices range $50-250 for a summer synthetic to $200-300 for a down winter bag. **Sleeping bag pads** include foam pads ($10-30), air mattresses ($15-50), and self-inflating mats ($30-120). Bring a **stuff sack** to store your bag and keep it dry.

Tents: The best tents are free-standing (with their own frames and suspension systems), set up quickly, and only require staking in high winds. Low-profile dome tents are the best all-around. Worthy 2-person tents start at $100, 4-person at $160. Make sure your tent has a rain fly and waterproofed seams. Other useful accessories include a **battery-operated lantern,** a plastic **groundcloth,** and a nylon **tarp.**

Backpacks: Internal-frame packs mold well to your back, keep a lower center of gravity, and flex adequately to allow you to hike difficult trails, while **external-frame packs** are more comfortable for long hikes over even terrain, as they carry weight higher and distribute it more evenly. Make sure your pack has a strong, padded hipbelt to transfer weight to your legs. Sturdy backpacks cost from $125-420—your pack is an area where it doesn't pay to economize.

Boots: Be sure to wear hiking boots with good **ankle support.** They should fit snugly and comfortably over 1-2 pairs of **wool socks** and a pair of thin **liner socks.** Break in boots over several weeks before you go to spare yourself blisters.

Other Necessities: Synthetic layers, like those made of polypropylene or polyester, and a pile jacket will keep you warm even when wet. A **space blanket** ($5-15) helps retain body heat and doubles as a groundcloth. Plastic **water bottles** are vital; look for shatter- and leak-resistant models. Carry **water-purification tablets** for when you can't boil water. Although most campgrounds provide campfire sites, you may want to bring a small **metal grate** or **grill.** For places that forbid fires, you'll need a **camp stove** (the classic Coleman starts at $50) and a propane-filled **fuel bottle.** Also bring a **first-aid kit, flashlight, pocketknife, insect repellent,** and **waterproof matches** or a **lighter.**

WHERE TO BUY IT

The mail-order and online companies below offer lower prices than many retail stores. A visit to a local camping or outdoors store will give you a sense of the look and weight of certain items.

Campmor, 400 Corporate Dr., Mahwah, NJ 07430 US (☎800-525-4784; www.campmor.com).

Discount Camping, 880 Main North Rd., Pooraka, South Australia 5095, Australia (☎08 8262 3399; www.discountcamping.com.au).

Eastern Mountain Sports (EMS), 1 Vose Farm Rd., Peterborough, NH 03458, US (☎888-463-6367; www.ems.com).

L.L. Bean, Freeport, ME, US 04033 (☎800-441-5713; www.llbean.com).

Mountain Designs, 433a Nudgee Rd. Hendra 4011, P.O. Box 824, Nundah, Queensland 4012, Australia (☎07 3114 4300; www.mountaindesigns.com).

Recreational Equipment, Inc. (REI), Sumner, WA 98352, US (US and Canada ☎800-426-4840, elsewhere 253-891-2500; www.rei.com).

OTHER CONCERNS

SUSTAINABLE TRAVEL

As the number of travelers on the road continues to rise, the detrimental effect that they can have on natural environments becomes an increasing concern. With this in mind, Let's Go promotes the philosophy of sustainable travel. Through a sensitivity to issues of ecology and sustainability, today's travelers can be a powerful force in preserving and restoring the places they visit.

Americans are notorious for the pollution generated by their dependence on cars and gas-guzzling SUVs. However, recent EPA reports indicate that air pollution is declining and air quality is improving nationwide. This is due, in part, to improvements in car and fuel technology such as **catalytic converters, cruise control, fuel injection, overdrive transmission,** and **radial tires.** While roadtripping will probably never be the most eco-friendly mode of travel, there are things you can do to maximize the benefits of this technology and reduce pollution from your roadtrip.

Choosing a more **fuel efficient car** can help preserve the environment and your budget. Consider driving a vehicle that makes use of an alternative fuel source or a **hybrid vehicle** that combines the use of an internal combustion engine with an electric motor. Both of these types of vehicles emit dramatically lower levels of pollution and greenhouse gases. For more info on fuel economy, alternate fuel sources, and finding and comparing the gas mileages of different cars, consult www.fueleconomy.gov.

Leaving your car running for a long time means more pollution, so **avoid idling** if you can. Consider parking and going in instead of driving through at fast-food restaurants. Also, newer cars don't need to be warmed up in cold weather by idling. Besides reducing your chances of being stranded on some lonesome highway, **regular tune-ups** diminish pollution from your car and increase fuel efficiency. Maintaining recommended **tire pressure** also improves gas mileage, and be sure to replace your air filter as needed—consult your owner's manual. Another way to maximize fuel efficiency is **to accelerate smoothly and maintain a steady speed.** Here's where cruise control comes in handy. There may be an appeal in the classic tire-squealing, gravel-throwing start, but it's hard on your tires and a waste of fuel. **Be savvy with your air conditioner.** Limiting air-conditioner use can increase fuel efficiency. Additionally, repair air conditioner leaks immediately, as some air conditioners contain ozone-depleting chlorofluorocarbons. **Don't speed.** Not only is speeding illegal and dangerous, but it also wastes fuel. Finally, **bring your friends.** Carpooling means fewer cars on the road and reduces traffic and pollution.

SOLO ROADTRIPPERS

While roadtrips are a great opportunity to spend quality time with your friends, there is a certain romance to flipping the top back and finding your own way across the country. However, any solo traveler is a more vulnerable target of harassment and street theft. As a lone roadtripper, try not to stand out as a tourist, look confident, and be especially careful in deserted or very crowded areas. If questioned, never admit that you are traveling alone. Maintain regular contact with someone at home who knows your itinerary.

MORE INFORMATION

Connecting: Solo Traveler Network, 689 Park Rd., Unit 6, Gibsons, BC V0N 1V7, CAN (☎604-886-9099; www.cstn.org). Bimonthly newsletter features going solo tips, single-friendly tips, and travel companion ads. Membership US$30/CDN$35.

Travel Companion Exchange (TCE), P.O. Box 833, Amityville, NY 11701, US (☎800-392-1256 or 631-454-0880; www.whytravelalone.com). Subscription $48.

Traveling Solo, Eleanor Berman. Globe Pequot ($18).

WOMEN ROADTRIPPERS

Women taking roadtrips on their own inevitably face some additional safety concerns, but it's easy to be adventurous without taking undue risks. If you are concerned, consider staying in hostels that offer single rooms that lock from the inside or in religious organizations with rooms for women only. **Picking up hitchhikers is never safe,** especially for women traveling alone.

Dress conservatively, especially in rural areas. Wearing a conspicuous **wedding band** sometimes helps to prevent unwanted overtures. The best answer to verbal harassment is no answer at all; feigning deafness, sitting motionless, and staring straight ahead will usually be effective. Don't hesitate to seek out a police officer or a passerby if you are being harassed. Memorize the emergency numbers in places you visit, and consider carrying a whistle on your keychain. A self-defense course (see p. 20) will both prepare you for a potential attack and raise your level of awareness of your surroundings. Also be sure you are aware of the health concerns that women face when traveling (see p. 24). **RAINN** (☎800-656-4673; www.rainn.org) can refer travelers to rape crisis centers and counseling services.

FURTHER READING

Active Women Vacation Guide, Evelyn Kaye. Blue Panda Publications ($18).

The Bad Girl's Guide to the Open Road, Cameron Tuttle. Chronicle Books ($15).

A Journey of One's Own: Uncommon Advice for the Independent Woman Traveler, Thalia Zepatos. Eighth Mountain Press ($15).

GLBT ROADTRIPPERS

Large US and Canadian cities are generally accepting of all sexualities and gender identities, and thriving gay, lesbian, bisexual, and transgendered (GLBT) communities can be found in most cosmopolitan areas. Most college towns are also GLBT-friendly. Still, in rural areas homophobia and transphobia can be rampant, and GLBT travelers should take extra caution. As evidenced by anti-same-sex marriage initiatives recently passed in many states and occasional violent attacks against GLBT people, homophobia and transphobia are still too common. You must always be aware of your surroundings. It is safer to avoid public displays of affection until you know you are in a safe environment. **Out and About** (www.planetout.com) offers a bi-weekly newsletter and a comprehensive site addressing GLBT travel concerns. The online newspaper **365gay.com** (www.365gay.com/travel/travelchannel.htm) also has a travel section.

To avoid hassles at border crossings, transgendered travelers should make sure that all of their travel documents consistently report the same gender. It may also be helpful to dress in a gender-neutral manner during travel or to present the gender listed on your documents until you've crossed the border. Many countries (including the US and Canada) will amend the passports of post-operative transsexuals to reflect their true gender, though governments are generally less willing to amend documents for pre-operative transsexuals and other transgendered individuals.

INFORMATION SERVICES

Gay's the Word, 66 Marchmont St., London WC1N 1AB, UK (☎44 20 7278 7654; www.gaystheword.co.uk). The largest gay and lesbian bookshop in the UK, with fiction and non-fiction titles.

Giovanni's Room, 345 S. 12th St., Philadelphia, PA 19107, USA (☎215-923-2960; www.queerbooks.com). An international lesbian and gay bookstore with mail-order service (carries many of the publications listed below).

International Gay and Lesbian Travel Association, 4331 N. Federal Hwy. 304, Fort Lauderdale, FL 33308, USA (☎800-448-8550; www.iglta.org). An organization of over 1200 companies serving gay and lesbian travelers worldwide.

International Lesbian and Gay Association (ILGA), Avenue des Villas 34, B-1060 Brussels, Belgium (☎32 2 502 2471; www.ilga.org). Provides political info.

FURTHER READING

Damron Men's Travel Guide, Damron Road Atlas, Damron Accommodations Guide, Damron City Guide, and *Damron Women's Traveller.* Damron Travel Guides ($11-19). For info, call ☎800-462-6654 or 415-255-0404 or visit www.damron.com.

The Gay Vacation Guide: The Best Trips and How to Plan Them, Mark Chesnut. Kensington Books ($15).

Gayellow Pages USA/Canada, Frances Green. Gayellow Pages ($23, CD version $10). Also publishes smaller regional editions. Visit Gayellow pages at www.gayellowpages.com.

Spartacus International Gay Guide. Bruno Gmunder Verlag ($33).

ROADTRIPPERS WITH DISABILITIES

Federal law dictates that all public buildings in the US should be wheelchair accessible, and laws governing building codes make disabled access more the norm than the exception. However, traveling with a disability still requires planning. Those with disabilities should inform airlines and hotels of their disabilities when making reservations; some time may be needed to prepare accommodations, even if they consider themselves wheelchair accessible. Certified guide dogs entering the US must have originated from or lived for six months in an area that is free from rabies (including Australia, Canada, Ireland, New Zealand, and the UK), or they must have unexpired vaccination certificates. For a list of rabies-free areas, see www.cdc.gov/travel/diseases/rabies.htm. In all areas of the US, guide dogs are legally allowed, free of charge, on public transit and in all "public establishments," including hotels, restaurants, and stores.

If you are planning to visit a national park or attraction in the US run by the National Park Service, obtain a free Golden Access Passport, which is available at all park entrances and from federal offices relating to land, forests, or wildlife. The passport entitles disabled travelers and their families to free park admission and provides a lifetime 50% discount on all campsite and parking fees.

USEFUL ORGANIZATIONS

Accessible Journeys, 35 W. Sellers Ave., Ridley Park, PA 19078, USA (☎800-846-4537; www.disabilitytravel.com). Designs tours for wheelchair users and slow walkers. The site has tips and forums for all travelers.

Mobility International USA (MIUSA), 132 E. Broadway, Ste. 343, Eugene, OR 97440 (☎541-343-1284; www.miusa.org). Provides a variety of books and other publications containing information for travelers with disabilities.

Society for Accessible Travel and Hospitality (SATH), 347 Fifth Ave., Ste. 610, New York, NY 10016 (☎212-447-7284; www.sath.org). An advocacy group that provides free online travel information. Annual membership $45, students and seniors $20.

MINORITY ROADTRIPPERS

While attitudes in the US and Canada differ drastically from region to region, racial and ethnic minorities sometimes face blatant and, more often, subtle discrimination or harassment. Verbal harassment is now less common than unfair pricing, false info on accommodations, or unfriendly service at restaurants. Remain calm and report discriminating individuals to a supervisor and establishments to the **Better Business Bureau** (www.bbb.org); contact the police in extreme cases. Let's Go always welcomes reader input regarding discriminating establishments. Be aware that racial tensions do exist, even in large, ostensibly progressive areas, and try to avoid confrontations.

In towns along the US-Mexico border, the **Border Patrol** for the US Immigration and Naturalization Service (INS) remains on a constant lookout for Mexican nationals who have crossed the border illegally. In border towns, they may pull over anyone who looks suspicious, search their vehicles for smuggled goods or people, and ask for identification.

FURTHER RESOURCES

United States Department of Justice (www.usdoj.gov).

Go Girl! The Black Woman's Book of Travel and Adventure, Elaine Lee. Eighth Mountain Press ($18).

The African-American Travel Guide, Wayne C. Robinson. Hunter Publishing ($16).

DIETARY CONCERNS

Most major US and Canadian cities are vegetarian-friendly, especially those on the West Coast. While **vegetarians** should have no problem finding suitable cuisine as they travel, **vegans** may still meet with some blank stares, especially along routes through small-town America. Let's Go often indicates vegetarian options in restaurant listings; other places to look for vegetarian and vegan cuisine are local health food stores or large natural food chains such as ▨**Trader Joe's** and **Wild Oats.** Vegan options are more difficult to find in smaller towns and inland; be prepared to make your own meals. The travel section of the The Vegetarian Resource Group's website (www.vrg.org/travel) has a comprehensive list of organizations and websites geared toward helping vegetarians and vegans on the road. For more info, consult the *Vegetarian Journal's Guide to Natural Foods Restaurants in the US and Canada,* published by the Vegetarian Resource Group ($18). Vegetarians will also find numerous resources on the web; try www.vegdining.com, www.happycow.net, and www.vegetariansabroad.com, for starters.

Travelers who keep **kosher** should contact synagogues in larger cities for info on kosher restaurants; your own synagogue should have lists of Jewish institutions across the nation. You may also consult the restaurant database at www.shamash.org/kosher. The *Jewish Travel Guide* ($19) lists synagogues, kosher restaurants, and Jewish institutions in the US and Canada.

INFORMATION SERVICES

North American Vegetarian Society, P.O. Box 72, Dolgeville, NY 13329, US (☎518-568-7970; www.navsonline.org). Publishes the *Healthy Dining Guide* ($15).

Vegetarian Resource Group, P.O. Box 1463, Dept. IN, Baltimore, MD 21203, US (☎410-366-8343;

www.vrg.org). Website has a travel section with general info and listings of vegetarian businesses, as well as dining guides for American cities and a formidable collection of links to vegetarian resources on the web.

OTHER RESOURCES

WORLD WIDE WEB

Almost every aspect of budget travel is accessible via the web. Listed here are some sites to start off your surfing; other relevant web sites are listed throughout the book.

ROADTRIP WEBSITES

America's Byways: www.byways.org. Lists Scenic Byways and All-American Roads as well as suggested itineraries through scenic areas.

Information Roadtrip: www.informationroadtrip.com. A nifty tool for your roadtrip research, including links, attractions, planning tips, and suggestions galore.

Roadtrip America: www.roadtripamerica.com. Almost everything you'd want to know before taking a roadtrip, from info on maps and planning to pop-culture landmarks to a forum for answers to your roadtrip queries.

Roadtrip Planning: www.roadtripplanning.com. Helpful tips, driving directions, and links to attractions and tourist destinations.

INFORMATION ON THE US AND CANADA

CIA World Factbook: www.odci.gov/cia/publications/factbook/index.html. Vital statistics on geography, government, and people.

Tourism Offices Worldwide Directory: www.towd.com. Lists tourism offices for all 50 states and Canada, as well as consulate and embassy addresses.

US Department of State Guide to Travel and Living Abroad: www.state.gov/travel. Lists travel warnings and has info about laws and considerations regarding passports, visas, and citizens living abroad.

WWW.LETSGO.COM. Let's Go's website features valuable advice at your fingertips. Our resources section is full of info you'll need before you hit the road, and our forums are buzzing with advice from other travelers. Visit **www.letsgo.com** to read blog entries posted by our researchers Ashley (Pacific Coast) and Meghan (Route 66) in the summer of 2006.

Many people believe that regional variation in the US is disappearing, thanks to the insidious and pervasive influence of television and mainstream American culture. There is hope for those of us who relish linguistic and cultural diversity, though: recent research by William Labov at the University of Pennsylvania and by Scott Golder and myself at Harvard University has found that regional variation is alive and well, and along some dimensions is even increasing between the major urban centers.

Consider, for instance, the preferred cover term for sweetened carbonated beverages. As can be seen in the map below, Southerners generally refer to them as coke, regardless of whether the beverages in question are actually made by the Coca-Cola Company; West and East coasters (including coastal Florida, which consists largely of transplanted New Yorkers) and individuals in Hawaii and the St. Louis, Milwaukee, and Green Bay spheres of influence predominantly employ soda. The remainder of the country prefers pop.

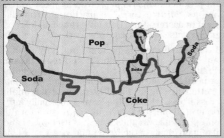

National television advertisements and shows generally employ soda, presumably due to the concentration of media outlets in soda areas New York City and California, but this has had no effect on the robust regional patterns. (The three primary terms do appear, however, to be undermining traditional local expressions such as tonic in Boston and cocola in the South.)

Another deeply entrenched, regionally conditioned food product is the long sandwich made with cold cuts. Its unmarked form in the US is submarine sandwich or just sub. Pennsylvanians (and New Jerseyites in the Philadelphia sphere of influence) call it a hoagie, New Yorkers call it a

hero, western New Englanders call it a grinder, Mainers call it an Italian sandwich, and people in the New Orleans area call it a po' boy.

Confrontation between traditional regional terms and newer interlopers has created subtle variations in meaning in some areas. In the Boston sphere of influence, for instance, grinder is commonly relegated to hot subs, whereas sub is used for cold ones. Similarly, in stores in northern Vermont grinder refers to large (12 in.) subs, whereas hoagie is used for their small (6 in.) counterpart. Many in the Philadelphia area divide up the sub domain in the same manner as Boston, but hoagie is used for the cold version and steak sandwich for the hot one.

In other cases, the dialectical picture is so evenly distributed that there is no clear national standard, as with the terms for the machine out of which one drinks water in schools and other public spaces.

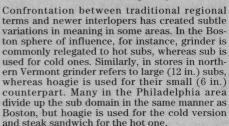

The preferred term in the southeastern half of the US is water fountain, whereas in the northwestern half it's drinking fountain. If you're in eastern Wisconsin or the Boston area, be sure to elicit bubbler from the locals.

These examples should suffice to show that regional variation is alive and well in the US. But where did these differences come from, and how have they resisted the influence of the American media juggernaut? The second question has a relatively straightforward answer: humans are generally unaware of the properties of their language, and normally assume that the way they behave and speak is the way everyone else does and should behave and speak. You, for example, were probably unaware before reading this that a large swathe of the US doesn't share your term for

The maps employed in this chapter were designed by Prof. Vaux on the basis of previously published materials (primarily William Labov's forthcoming *Atlas of North American English* and Frederick Cassidy's *Dictionary of American Regional English*) and his online survey of English dialects. Specific references are available on request by emailing the author at vaux@post.harvard.edu. Please note that all generalizations made here reflect statistical predominance, not absolute invariance. One can find individuals who say *soda* in the South, for example, but these are in the minority.

The examples adduced in this chapter are primarily lexical, due to the difficulty of conveying subtleties of pronunciation in a publication intended for non-linguists.

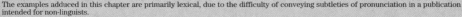

water fountains. Since humans are generally unaware of the idiosyncrasies of their own speech, it is to be expected that they would typically fail to notice that what is said on TV differs from their own forms.

SETTLEMENT PATTERNS AND THE ORIGINS OF THE AMERICAN DIALECTS

The other question, involving the origins of linguistic variation, can be answered in part by considering the history of US settlement by speakers of English.

The continental US was settled by three main waves of English speakers: Walter Raleigh brought settlers primarily from the southwest of England to form the Chesapeake Bay Colony in 1607; Puritans from East Anglia came to the Massachusetts Bay Colony in 1620; and Scots-Irish, Northern English, and Germans came to America through Philadelphia in large numbers beginning in the 18th century. Settlers then moved horizontally westward across the country from these three hearths, giving rise to the three main dialect areas in the US: the South, the North, and the Midlands. The fourth area on the map, the West, contains a mixture of features imported from the other three.

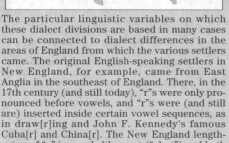

The particular linguistic variables on which these dialect divisions are based in many cases can be connected to dialect differences in the areas of England from which the various settlers came. The original English-speaking settlers in New England, for example, came from East Anglia in the southeast of England. There, in the 17th century (and still today), "r"s were only pronounced before vowels, and "r"s were (and still are) inserted inside certain vowel sequences, as in draw[r]ing and John F. Kennedy's famous Cuba[r] and China[r]. The New England lengthening of "a" in words like aunt ("ahnt") and bath ("bahth") was also imported from the British dialect of East Anglia.

Other features cannot be connected to British antecedents so transparently, but nicely demonstrate the North/South/Midlands boundary. One of my favorite examples is the large wasplike critter that is usually seen when it stops by puddles to collect mud, which it then rolls into a ball and carries off to construct a nest. Northerners call this a mud wasp, midlanders and westerners call it a mud dauber, and southerners call it a dirt dauber. Another such example is the small freshwater lobster-like critter, which is a crayfish in the North, a crawdad in the Midlands, and a crawfish or mudbug in the South.

The North breaks into two main areas, the Northeast and the Inland North. The Northeast and its crony, southeast coastal Florida, are roughly the home of sneakers; the rest of the country uses tennis shoes or gym shoes as the generic term for athletic shoes. The Inland North is most famous for pop and for the so-called "Rust Belt Vowel Shift." This is a change in the pronunciation of most of the American vowels that produces what is perceived by most Americans as "Midwestern," even though it is also found in eastern Rust Belt cities such as Rochester, Syracuse, and Utica, New York.

The Midlands region is home not only to mud dauber, but also to the oft-noted regionalisms warsh and the needs X-ed construction, as in the car needs warshed. The Midlands and the South together are home to catty-corner (diagonally across from), which in the North is normally kitty-corner. (My personal favorite expression for this concept is kitty wampus, which is used by a handful of individuals in the Upper Midwest.)

The South is home to the "pin-pen merger" ("i" and "e" are pronounced identically before "m," "n," and "ng"), preservation of the contrast in pronunciation between "w" and "wh" (as in witch and which respectively), use of y'all to address a group of individuals, multiple modal constructions (as in I might could do that), nekkid for "naked," and commode for "toilet."

The inland part of the South features gems such as rolling for the act of covering a house and/or its front yard in toilet paper. In the rest of country, this is generally called tp'ing or toilet papering. (It's wrapping in the Houston area.)

AMERICAN DIALECTS YOU HAVE TO HEAR

Since, as we have just seen, regional variation is alive and well in the US, where should one go to hear the most satisfying range of dialects? Here are some of my favorites, which also provide a representative sample of the main dialect groups in the country. (If you get to one of these locales and have trouble finding a really juicy local accent, try a police station, working-class bar, or farm.)

THE NORTHEAST

No linguistic tour of the Northeast would be complete without visiting the two main linguistic spheres of influence in the area, Boston and New York City. Though locals would probably die rather than admitting it, the two actually share a large number of linguistic features, such as pronouncing can (is able) differently than can (con-

tainer), wearing sneakers and drinking soda, having no word for the roly poly/potato bug/sow bug/doodlebug (though the critter itself is just as rampant in the Northeast as anywhere else in the country), and pronouncing route to rhyme with moot and never with out.

Perhaps the most striking feature shared by these two areas is the behavior of "r": it disappears when not followed by a vowel (drawer is pronounced draw), and conversely gets inserted when between certain vowels (drawing comes out as drawring). Because these dialects don't allow "r" to follow a vowel within a syllable, they end up preserving vowel contrasts that were neutralized before "r" in other dialects. This is heard in the "3 Maries": Mary, marry, and merry are each pronounced differently, whereas in most of the country all three are homophonous. Similarly mirror and nearer have the same first vowel in most of the US, but not in Boston and New York City. Bostonians and New Yorkers pronounce words like hurry, Murray, furrow, and thorough with the vowel of hut, whereas most other Americans use the vowel in bird. And of course there's the first vowel in words like orange and horrible, which in most of the US is the same as in pore, but in Boston and New York City is closer to the vowel in dog.

New York City

Though New York City shares many important features with Boston and other parts of the Northeast, it is also in many ways a linguistic island, undergoing little influence from the rest of the country and—despite the ubiquity of New York accents on TV and in movies—propagating almost none of its peculiarities to the outside world. Its lack of linguistic influence can be connected to its stigmatization: two surveys in 1950 and the 1990s found that Americans considered New York City to have the worst speech in the country.

When you visit the New York City area (including neighboring parts of New Jersey and Long Island), be sure to listen for classic New Yorkisms. This includes the deletion of "h" before "u" (e.g. huge is pronounced yuge, and Houston becomes Youston), and the rounding of "a" to an "o"-like vowel before "l" in words like ball and call (the same vowel also shows up in words like water, talk, and dog). New Yorkers who don't have a thick local accent may not have these particular features, but they are sure to have other shibboleths like stoop (small front porch or steps in front of a house), on line instead of in line (e.g. We stood on line outside the movie theater for three hours), hero for sub, pie for pizza, and egg cream for a special soft drink made with seltzer water, chocolate syrup, and milk. You can also tell New Yorkers by their pronunciation of Manhattan and forward: they reduce the first vowel in the former (it comes out as Mn-hattan), and delete the first "r" in the latter (so it sounds like foe-ward). Believe it or not, it is also common in the New York City area to pronounce donkey to rhyme with monkey (which makes sense if you consider the spelling), even though they typically aren't aware that they are doing so.

New England

Moving up the coast to New England, we find that most people don't actually sound like John F. Kennedy, but they do all use cellar for basement (at least if it's unfinished), bulkhead for the external doors leading out of the cellar, and rotary for what others call a roundabout or traffic circle. New England itself is divided by the Connecticut River into two linguistically distinct areas, Eastern and Western.

Eastern New England: Boston

You can hear great Eastern New England speech almost anywhere in Maine, New Hampshire, Rhode Island, or Massachusetts, especially if you stay away from more affluent areas in the bigger cities, but I'll focus here on the Boston area. (Revere, South Boston, Somerville, and Dorchester are traditionally considered to harbor especially thick local accents.) Thanks to park your car in Harvard Yard and Nomar Garciaparra many Americans are familiar with the Boston pronunciation of -ar-, which generally comes out as something very similar to the Southern pronunciation of -ay- (Boston park sounds like Southern pike). The sequence -or- also has an interesting outcome in many words, being pronounced like the vowel in off. For instance, the Boston pop group LFO, in their 1999 song "Summer Girls," rhymed hornet with sonnet.

In the domain of vocabulary, be sure to get a frappe (or if you're in Rhode Island, a cabinet), a grinder, harlequin ice cream with jimmies or shots on it, and of course a tonic. (Frappes are milkshakes, harlequin is Neapolitan ice cream, and jimmies and

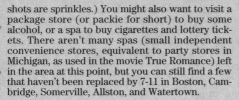
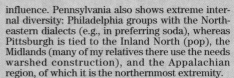
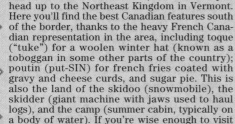
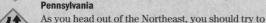
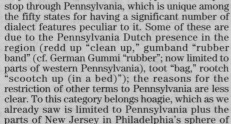

shots are sprinkles.) You might also want to visit a package store (or packie for short) to buy some alcohol, or a spa to buy cigarettes and lottery tickets. There aren't many spas (small independent convenience stores, equivalent to party stores in Michigan, as used in the movie True Romance) left in the area at this point, but you can still find a few that haven't been replaced by 7-11 in Boston, Cambridge, Somerville, Allston, and Watertown.

The towns where you'll hear the best Boston accents (and classic local terms like wicked and pissa) also feature many triple deckers, three-family houses with three front porches stacked on top of one another. These seem to be less common in Connecticut, but if you happen to pass through that area, be sure to look out for tag sales (yard sales). Connecticut is also home to the term sleepy seed for the gunk that collects in the corner of your eye after you've been sleeping; not all Connecticutians have this expression, but your trip will have been worthwhile if you find someone who does.

Western New England: Vermont

West of the Connecticut River, I recommend you head up to the Northeast Kingdom in Vermont. Here you'll find the best Canadian features south of the border, thanks to the heavy French Canadian representation in the area, including toque ("tuke") for a woolen winter hat (known as a toboggan in some other parts of the country); poutin (put-SIN) for french fries coated with gravy and cheese curds, and sugar pie. This is also the land of the skidoo (snowmobile), the skidder (giant machine with jaws used to haul logs), and the camp (summer cabin, typically on a body of water). If you're wise enough to visit the Northeast Kingdom, be sure to check out how they pronounce the "a" and the "t" in the name of the local town Barton.

THE MIDLANDS

Pennsylvania

As you head out of the Northeast, you should try to stop through Pennsylvania, which is unique among the fifty states for having a significant number of dialect features peculiar to it. Some of these are due to the Pennsylvania Dutch presence in the region (redd up "clean up," gumband "rubber band" (cf. German Gummi "rubber"; now limited to parts of western Pennsylvania), toot "bag," rootch "scootch up (in a bed)"); the reasons for the restriction of other terms to Pennsylvania are less clear. To this category belongs hoagie, which as we already saw is limited to Pennsylvania plus the parts of New Jersey in Philadelphia's sphere of influence. Pennsylvania also shows extreme internal diversity: Philadelphia groups with the Northeastern dialects (e.g., in preferring soda), whereas Pittsburgh is tied to the Inland North (pop), the Midlands (many of my relatives there use the needs warshed construction), and the Appalachian region, of which it is the northernmost extremity.

Philadelphia and its satellites in southern New Jersey are perhaps best known for their pronunciation of water, which comes out as something like wooder. This conveniently shows up in the local term water ice, which refers to something between Italian ice and a snow cone. Residents of the Philly sphere of influence are also more likely than other Americans to bag school rather than skip school or play hooky. When you make your trip to Philly to hear these choice linguistic tidbits and you run short of money, be sure to ask where the MAC machine is, not the ATM or cash machine.

You should also make a special effort to visit the opposite end of the state, anchored by the beautiful city of Pittsburgh, which (unknown to most Americans) has its own distinctive dialect. Here the "aw" sound is replaced by something approaching "ah," as in dahntahn for downtown; "ay" similarly loses its "y" in certain situations, as in Pahrts for Pirates and Ahrn City for Iron City. The "o" in this region is very rounded in words like shot, and comes out sounding a lot like the New York vowel in ball. It is also popular to delete the "th-" at the beginning of unstressed words in certain collocations, such as up 'ere (for up there), like 'at, and 'n 'at (for and that, which western Pennsylvanians are fond of ending sentences with).

In terms of vocabulary, Pittsburgh and environs have some real whoppers, such as yins or you 'uns, used to address a group of two or more people; jagoff meaning "a jerk or loser" (shared with Chicagoland); jumbo "bologna sandwich"; and slippy "slippery."

These days many Pittsburgh residents don't have the traditional dialect, but you're sure to come across at least a few of the items just discussed. You'll have even better luck if you visit some of the unknown small towns in western Pennsylvania such as Franklin, Emlenton, and Oil City, which have satisfying variants of the Pittsburgh speech patterns and also happen to be unusually scenic.

Cincinnati

From Pittsburgh you're in striking distance of Cincinnati, one of the better representatives of the Midlands dialect region. Here, instead of inserting "r," as we saw in Boston and New York

City, they insert "l": saw comes out as sawl, drawing as drawling, and so on. In the Cincinnati area one can also find drive-through liquor stores (and for some people, regular liquor stores) referred to as pony kegs. (Elsewhere in the US, on the other hand, pony keg usually refers to a small keg.)

THE RUST BELT

Milwaukee

Moving westward, the next interesting dialect zone is the Inland North or Rust Belt, within which I recommend Milwaukee, WI (not to be confused with Zilwaukee, MI.) Here, in the land so eloquently etymologized by Alice Cooper in *Wayne's World*, you will find—especially if you visit an area where there hasn't been much immigration, such as West Allis—not only the classic speech features identified with the Midwest (as canonized for example in the Da Bears skit on "Saturday Night Live"), but also features characteristic of areas other than the Midwest (freeway, otherwise associated with the West Coast; bubbler, most familiar from the Boston area; soda, otherwise characteristic of the West and East coasts). Milwaukeeans share some features with the rest of Wisconsin: they pronounce Milwaukee as Mwaukee and Wisconsin as W-scon-sin rather than Wis-con-sin; they refer to annoying Illinoisans as FIB's or fibbers (the full form of which is too saucy to explain here), and they eat frozen custard and butter burgers. They also share some features with the Upper Midwest, notably pronouncing bag as baig and using ramp or parking ramp for "parking garage" (the same forms surface in Minnesota and Buffalo). Milwaukee is also known for the cannibal sandwich, raw ground sirloin served on dark rye bread and covered with thin-sliced raw onions.

Milwaukee is only an hour and a half drive north of Chicago, yet it lacks many of the classic Chicagoisms, such as jagoff, gaper's block (a traffic jam caused by drivers slowing down to look at an accident or other diversion on the side of the road), black cow (root beer with vanilla ice cream, known elsewhere as a root beer float), expressway, and pop. It also differs from the more northern reaches of Wisconsin with respect to many of the classic Upper Midwestern features so cleverly reproduced in the movie Fargo, such as the monophthongal "e" and "o" in words like Minnesota and hey there. You can find the occasional inhabitant of Wisconsin's northern border with Minnesota who has Upper Midwest terms like pasties, whipping shitties (driving a car in tight circles, known elsewhere as doing donuts), hotdish (elsewhere called a casserole), and farmer matches (long wooden matches that light on any surface), but for the most part these are less commonly used

than in Minnesota and the Dakotas (and the Upper Peninsula of Michigan in the case of pasties).

THE WEST

The San Fernando Valley

Moving ever westward, we come next to the West Coast. Here it is more difficult to find hardcore traditional dialects, largely because the West was settled relatively recently, and by individuals from a wide variety of different locales; one is hard-pressed to find any Californian (or other Westerner) whose family has been there for more than two generations. Perhaps the best place to start is the San Fernando Valley of California, home of the Valley Girl. Many of the Valley Girl quirks immortalized in Frank Zappa's 1982 song "Valley Girl" and the 1995 film Clueless are now profoundly out of favor, such as gnarly, barf out, grodie (to the max), gag me with a spoon, rad, for sure, as if, and bitchin'. Others are now ubiquitous throughout the US, such as totally, whatever, sooo X (as in, That's so like 5 years ago), and the use of like to report indirect speech or state of mind (as in, I was like, "No way!"). Others are still used in the area but have yet to infiltrate the rest of the country, such as flip a bitch or bust a bitch (make a U-turn) and bag on (make fun of, diss).

And if you're interested in figuring out whether someone's from northern or southern California, I recommend seeing if they use hella or hecka to mean "very" (e.g. that party was hella cool; characteristic of northern California), and if they refer to freeway numbers with or without "the" before them (Southern Californians refer to "the 5", "the 405", and so on, whereas northern Californians just use "5" and "405").

THE SOUTH

Looping back around the country we come to the South, which is perhaps the most linguistically distinct and coherent area in the US. This is not only home to obvious cases like y'all, initial stress on Thanksgiving, insurance, police, and cement, and the other features mentioned above, but also showcases feeder road (small road that runs parallel to a highway), wrapping (tp'ing), doodlebug (the crustacean that rolls into a ball when you touch it) in the Houston area, and party barns (drive-through liquor stores) in Texas (bootlegger, brew thru, and beer barn are also common terms for this in the South). The South as a whole differs from the rest of the country in pronouncing lawyer as law-yer, using tea to refer to cold sweet tea, and saying the devil's beating his wife when it rains while the sun is shining (elsewhere referred to as a sunshower, or by no name at all). The South is so different from the rest of the country that almost anywhere you go you will hear a range of great accents, but I especially recommend the Deep South (start with Mississippi or Alabama) and New Orleans.

New Orleans

Louisiana is famous for the Cajuns, a local group descended from the Acadians, French people who were exiled from Nova Scotia and settled in southern Louisiana in the 1760s. Some Cajuns still speak their own special creole, Cajun French, and this in turn has influenced the English dialect of the region. This can be seen in local expressions such as: by my house for "in/at my place" (e.g., he slept by my house last night), which is claimed to be based on the French expression chez moi; make dodo meaning "to sleep," based on Cajun French fais do do; make groceries meaning "do grocery shopping," cf. French faire le marché; and lagniappe, French for "a little something extra," e.g., when your butcher gives you a pound and two ounces of hot sausage but only charges you for a pound.

Some of the creole elements that have made their way into the local English dialect may be of African rather than French origin, such as where ya stay (at)? meaning "where do you live?", and gumbo, referring to a traditional southern soup-like dish, made with a rich roux (flour and butter) and usually including either sea food or sausage. The word gumbo is used in Gullah (an English-based creole spoken on the Sea Islands off the Carolina coast) to mean okra, and appears to have descended from a West African word meaning okra.

The New Orleans dialect of English also includes words drawn from other sources, such as yat (a typical neighborhood New Orleanian), neutral ground (the grassy or cement strip in the middle of the road), po' boy (basically a sub sandwich, though it can include fried oysters and other seafood and may be dressed, i.e., include lettuce, tomatoes, pickles, and mayonnaise), hickey (a knot or bump you get on your head when you bump or injure it), and alligator pear (an avocado).

HAWAII

Last but not least we come to Hawaii, which in many ways is the most interesting of the fifty states linguistically. Many Americans are aware of Hawaiian, the Austronesian language spoken by the indigenous residents of the Hawaiian Islands before the arrival of colonizers from Europe and

Japan. Fewer, however, know of the English-based creole that has arisen since that time, known as Hawaiian Pidgin English, Hawaiian Creole English, or just Pidgin. This variety of English is spoken by a fairly large percentage of Hawaiians today, though they tend not to use it around haole (Caucasian) tourists.

Pidgin combines elements of all of the languages originally spoken by settlers, including Portuguese (cf. where you stay go? meaning "where are you going?", or I called you up and you weren't there already meaning "I called you up and you weren't there yet"), Hawaiian (haole, makapeapea "sleepy seed," lanai "porch," pau "finished"), Japanese (shoyu "soy sauce"), and even Californian/surfer (dude, sweet, awesome, freeway). They also have some English expressions all their own, such as shave ice (snow-cone) and cockaroach (cockroach).

The syntax (word order) of Pidgin differs significantly from that of mainland English varieties, but resembles the English creoles of the Caribbean in important ways. This includes deletion of the verb be in certain contexts (e.g., if you one girl, no read dis meaning "if you're a girl, don't read this"), lack of inversion of the subject and finite verb in questions and subordinate clauses (e.g. doctah , you can pound my baby? Meaning "doctor, can you weigh my baby?", or how dey came up wid dat? meaning "how did they come up with that?"), null subjects (e.g. cannot! meaning "I can't!", or get shtrawberry? meaning "do you have strawberry [flavor]?"), and the use of "get" to express existential conditions ("there is," "there are"), as in get sharks? meaning "are there sharks [in there]?".

IN CONCLUSION

This tour only begins to scratch the surface of the range of English varieties to be found in the US, but it should provide enough fodder to keep you busy for a while on your travels, and with any luck will enable you to provide some entertainment for your hosts as well. And if the info I've provided here isn't enough to sate your thirst for American dialects, I urge you to visit the Sea Islands, where Gullah is still spoken, Tangier Island in Chesapeake Bay, and Ocracoke Island, off the coast of North Carolina. Each of these islands features a variety of English that will shock and titillate you; I'll leave the details for you to discover.

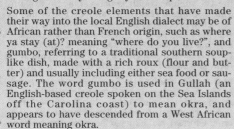

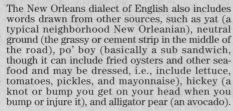

Bert Vaux *is Ph.D. in Linguistics and currently teaches at the University of Wisconsin-Milwaukee. He has written extensively and taught popular classes on linguistics and dialects at Harvard University.*

WWW.LETSGO.COM
HERE TODAY, WHEREVER YOU'RE HEADED TOMORROW.

Whether you're planning your next adventure or are already far afield, letsgo.com will play companion to your wanderlust.

Peruse our articles and descriptions as you select the spots you're off to next. If we're making your decision harder, consult fellow travelers on our written and photo forums or search for anecdotal advice in our researchers' blogs.

If you're itching to leave, there's no need to shake that pesky travel bug. From embassy locations to passport laws, we keep track of all the essentials, so find out what you need to know fast, book that high-season hostel bed, and hit the road.

READY. SET. LET'S GO

the east coast

TOP 5

1. Discover the party that just won't quit at Miami's **South Beach.**
2. Whip up a mint julep, find yourself a porch, and soak up **Savannah's** quiet charm.
3. Make haste to New York City, where **Shakespeare in the Park** is free all summer long.
4. Find authentic Southern barbecue on the back of a truck at **Curtis' Barbeque,** in Putney, VT.
5. Blaze your way up the spectacular Precipice Trail in **Acadia National Park.**

The East Coast route is a testament to the radical regional diversity of the US. This is where the country began, and American history, whether in Boston's cobbled streets or Savannah's easy grandeur, is happily unavoidable. There's a reason people who live on the coast are so proud of it; many of the country's literary, political, scientific, and philosophical luminaries lived and worked near the Atlantic. From Key West, former playground of Ernest Hemingway's six-toed cat to Bar Harbor, former playground of New England's old money, the Eastern Seaboard is yours for the taking.

You'll set off in idyllic **Key West,** (p. 52), home to some of the best nightlife in the country and hordes of Ernest Hemingway look-alikes. The road will pass through **Key Largo** (p. 55) before plunging into the **Everglades** (p. 57). Alligators and mosquitoes give way to all-night bacchanalia in **South Beach, Miami** (p. 57). The rest of Florida hosts a bevy of landmark sights, from the **Kennedy Space Center** in **Cape Canaveral** (p. 69) to the **International Speedway** at **Daytona Beach** (p. 71) to the **Fountain of Youth** in **St. Augustine** (p. 73). After the **Cumberland Island National Seashore** (p. 79), you'll reach **Savannah** (p. 81), one of the route's true highlights. The historic homes and plantations keep coming in **Charleston** (p. 85).

Past **Myrtle Beach** and the **Grand Strand** (p. 91), you'll steel your nerves and brave **Cape Fear** (p. 93). The road will coast through North Carolina's **Outer Banks** (p. 99) on its way to **Kitty Hawk** (p. 100), where the Wright Brothers are inescapable—on signs, storefronts, even license plates. **Virginia Beach** (p. 102) will be your last stop in the present before the road visits the smithies and taverns of **Colonial Williamsburg** (p. 106). **Chincoteague Wildlife Refuge** (p. 107) will ease you back into the present, and **Assateague Island National Seashore** (p. 107) features free-ranging wild

horses. The road then leaves Maryland for Delaware, where the Lewes-Cape May Ferry heads into New Jersey. **Lucy the Elephant** (p. 118), in Margate, is the finest example of zoomorphic architecture in New Jersey, and its surreal quality is a good prelude to **Atlantic City** (p. 350), where the streets of the Monopoly Board lead to gaudy casinos and wide beaches. Up the Garden State Expressway, the road will artfully dodge **New York City** (p. 119). Make sure you don't do the same. The best pizza on the coast is tucked away in **New Haven, CT** (p. 142), and sprawling **Indian Casinos** (p. 145) also line the Connecticut coast.

Providence, RI (p. 147), home of Brown University, the Rhode Island School of Design, and a spectacular public art installation, is a roadtripper's paradise. **Newport** (p. 151) follows, and its mansions, embodying giddy absurdity, are jaw-dropping sights. Then it's off to **Cape Cod** (p. 154), where the lighthouses nearly outnumber the Nantucket Reds. At **Plimoth Plantation,** you'll find that **Plymouth Rock** (p. 160) is smaller than you thought. Then it's off to the East Coast's apotheosis of Colonial history: **Boston** (p. 161).

Heading into northern Massachusetts, the road enters **Salem** (p. 173), either the scariest place on the coast or the most hilarious, depending on your disposition. If the salty sea

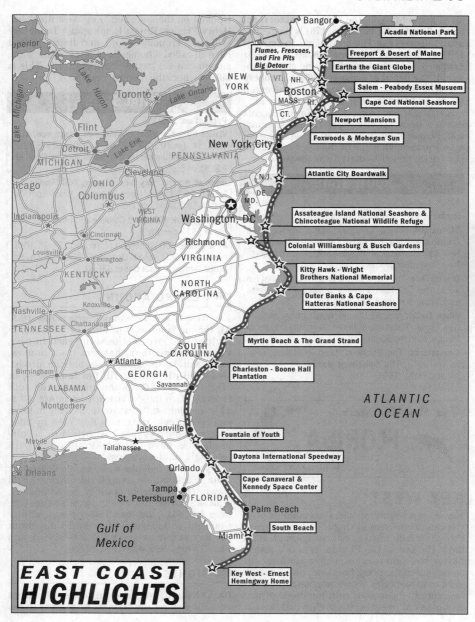

EAST COAST

Bangor

Acadia National Park

Flumes, Frescoes,
and Fire Pits
Big Detour

Freeport & Desert of Maine

Eartha the Giant Globe

NEW
YORK

VT. NH.

Boston

MASS.

R.I.

CT.

Salem - Peabody Essex Musuem

Cape Cod National Seashore

Newport Mansions

New York City

Foxwoods & Mohegan Sun

PENNSYLVANIA

N.J.

Atlantic City Boardwalk

DE.

MD.

Washington, DC

Assateague Island National Seashore &
Chincoteague National Wildlife Refuge

Richmond

Colonial Williamsburg & Busch Gardens

VIRGINIA

Kitty Hawk - Wright
Brothers National Memorial

NORTH
CAROLINA

Outer Banks & Cape
Hatteras National Seashore

SOUTH
CAROLINA

Myrtle Beach & The Grand Strand

Atlanta

GEORGIA

Charleston - Boone Hall
Plantation

Savannah

ATLANTIC
OCEAN

Jacksonville

Fountain of Youth

Tallahassee

Daytona International Speedway

Orlando

Cape Canaveral &
Kennedy Space Center

Tampa

St. Petersburg   FLORIDA

Palm Beach

Gulf of
Mexico

Miami

South Beach

EAST COAST
HIGHLIGHTS

Key West - Ernest
Hemingway Home

air is getting to you, the **Flumes, Frescoes, and Family Camping Big Detour** (p. 176) is the perfect inland distraction. The fried clams in **Essex** (p. 178) are delicious, and **Yarmouth, ME** is home to **Eartha** (p. 185), the largest rotating globe in the world. The **Desert of Maine** (p. 185) is a stupefying sight, and soon afterwards the route enters **Mt. Desert Island** (p. 188), the end of the road.

So whether you prefer sucking down piña coladas in a straw hat or swirling the finest brandy with Boston brahmins, the East Coast Route will take you through some of the most fascinating parts of the country—don't forget the sunscreen!

ROUTE STATS

Miles: c. 2000

Route: Key West, FL to Bar Harbor, ME.

States: 14; Florida, Georgia, South Carolina, North Carolina, Virginia, Maryland, Delaware, New Jersey, New York, Connecticut, Rhode Island, Massachusetts, New Hampshire, Maine.

Driving Time: You could drive it in 4 days, but what fun would that be? Take 3 weeks to sample the diverse environments of the Atlantic coast.

When To Go: Anytime, though winter brings snow to New England and late summer brings the danger of hurricanes to the South.

Crossroads: The National Road in Atlantic City, NJ (p. 350); **The Southern Border** in the Everglades, FL (p. 769).

The Sunshine State

FLORIDA

Welcomes You!

KEY WEST

Key West's economy once depended on shipwrecks; locals would ring a bell to proclaim their good luck when a boat ran aground. These days, the last of the Florida Keys is a tourist haven, welcoming cruise ships, families with small children, spring breakers, and a sizable gay population. Key West's popularity makes it an expensive stay, but with hundreds of bars and tropical breezes, it's well worth a visit.

Hooked on the so-called "Key West lifestyle," Henry Flagler, Ernest Hemingway, Tennessee Williams, Truman Capote, and Jimmy Buffett have all called it home. Key West is as far south as you can get in the continental US. This is mile 0, where the roadtrip begins.

VITAL STATS

Population: 25,811

Visitor Info: Key West Chamber of Commerce, 402 Wall St. (☎305-294-2587 or 800-527-8539; www.keywestchamber.org), in old Mallory Sq. Open M-F 8:30am-6:30pm, Sa-Su 9am-6pm.

Internet Access: Key West Library, 700 Fleming St. (☎305-292-3595). Open M and W 10am-8pm, Tu and Th-Sa 10am-6pm. Free.

Parking: Park 'N Ride, at Caroline and Grinnell St. ($2 per hr., $13 per day.)

Post Office: 400 Whitehead St. (☎305-294-9539), 1 block west of Duval St. Open M-F 8:30am-5pm, Sa 9:30am-noon. **Postal Code:** 33040

GETTING AROUND

Key West lies at the end of **Overseas Hwy. (U.S. 1),** 155 mi. southwest of Miami. The island is divided into two sections; the eastern part, known as **New Town,** harbors tract houses, chain motels, shopping malls, and the airport. Beautiful old houses fill **Old Town,** west of White St. **Duval St.** is the main north-south thoroughfare in Old Town; **Truman Ave. (U.S. 1)** is a major east-west route. Driving in town can be difficult; traversing Key West by bike, foot, or moped is your best bet. Most accommodations have free parking. Do not park overnight on the bridges.

If you don't feel like walking, the **Conch Tour Train** is a 90min. narrated ride through Old Town. (Leaves from Mallory Sq. at 3840 N. ☎305-294-5161. Runs daily 9am-4:30pm. $25, ages 4-12 $12.) **Old Town Trolley** runs a similar tour, but you can get on and off throughout the day at ten stops. (☎305-296-6688. Tours 9am-5:30pm. $25, ages 4-12 $12.)

SIGHTS

ON LAND. No one should leave Key West without visiting the ■**Ernest Hemingway Home,**

a Caribbean-style mansion where "Papa" wrote *For Whom the Bell Tolls* and had some nasty fights with the second of his four wives. Take a tour with hilarious guides who relate strange-but-true Hemingway history, then enjoy the garden with 46 descendants of Hemingway's cat, half of which have six toes. *(907 Whitehead St. ☎ 305-294-1136; www.hemingway-home.com. Open daily 9am-5pm. $11, ages 6-12 $6.)* Even in Key West, the best things in life are free. At the ▧Chicken Store, you can adopt your very own chick—assuming you meet a few qualifications. You'll crow with joy when you see these gypsy chickens. *(1229 Duval St. ☎ 305-294-0070; www.thechickenstore.com. Open daily 10am-5pm.)* Originally built in 1890 as naval quarters, the **Harry S. Truman Little White House Museum** provides a fascinating look at both President Truman and his getaway in Key West, used at points by John Kennedy, Dwight Eisenhower, and Bill Clinton. *(111 Front St. ☎ 305-294-9911; www.trumanlittlewhitehouse.com. Open daily 9am-5pm. $11, children $5. Grounds open 8am-6pm. Free.)* The **Audubon House** shelters antiques and engravings by naturalist and painter John James Audubon, but the highlight is the tropical garden and reflecting pool. *(205 Whitehead St. ☎ 305-294-2116; www.audubon-house.org. Open daily 9:30am-5pm; last entry 4:30pm. $10, students $6.50, ages 6-12 $5.)*

ON WATER. The **Mel Fisher Maritime Heritage Society Museum** showcases the discovery and salvaging of the Spanish galleon *Atocha*, which sank off the Keys in 1622 and was uncovered after a 16-year search. The museum also has an entire floor dedicated to the study of the 17th- and 18th-century slave trade. *(200 Greene St. ☎ 305-294-2633; www.melfisher.org. Open daily 9:30am-5pm. $11, students $9.50, ages 6-12 $6.)* The **Key West Shipwreck Historeum Museum** exhibits the remains of the *Isaac Allerton*, the 594-ton ship that sank in 1856. Cheesy shows every 20min. emphasize that the museum is kid-oriented. The museum's **Lookout Tower,** which stands 65 ft. tall, offers one of the best views of the island. *(1 Whitehead St., in Mallory Sq. ☎ 305-292-8990; www.shipwreckhistoreum.com. Open daily 9:40am-5pm. $10, ages 4-12 $5, under 4 free.)* At the **Mallory Sq. Dock,** street entertainers and kitsch-hawkers work the crowd, while boats parade in revue during the **Sunset Celebration** each evening. *(☎ 305-292-7700. 2hr. before sunset.)* At the opposite end of Duval St., you'll come to the southernmost point in the continental US at the fittingly named **Southernmost Beach.** A large, red-and-black conical monument marks the spot: "90 miles to Cuba." The **glass bottom boat** *Discovery* cruises to the reefs and back. *(251 Margaret St. ☎ 305-293-0099. 2-2½hr. cruises daily 11:30am, 3:30, 6pm. $35, ages 5-12 $16.)*

🍴 FOOD

Expensive trendy restaurants line **Duval St.,** while side streets offer lower prices and fewer crowds.

Camille's Restaurant, 1202 Simonton St. (☎ 305-296-4811). It's always time for breakfast at

ALL CONCHS ARE CREATED EQUAL

In 1860, South Carolina seceded from the United States, precipitating the Civil War. Today, Key West, the self-dubbed Conch Republic, carries on that legacy. On April 23, 1982, Key West citizens raised their flag to protest the establishment of a border patrol blockade on U.S. 1, just north of the Keys. Key West residents feared that the time-intensive search of visitors' cars would cause impatient tourists to travel elsewhere. To show the world their displeasure, they staged a tongue-in-cheek secession, publishing a Proclamation of Secession and declaring war on the United States by hitting a federal agent over the head with a loaf of Cuban bread. They quickly surrendered and asked for foreign aid. The Conch Republic website (www.conchrepublic.com) reports that the "nation" is "still waiting" for the aid. While the fledgling nation never earned the recognition of the US government, the protest was successful—the border patrol blockade was lifted soon after the secession. Though the Conch Republic's original demands have been met, it remains "independent" and has staged several additional battles against the US. The Republic has even been involved in international incidents. Each year, the Conch Republic has a week-long independence celebration at the end of April to reaffirm the nation's right to life, liberty, and the pursuit of tourism.

Camille's, where you can get Belgian waffles ($3) or buttermilk pancakes ($5) all day long. The bustling establishment also serves chicken salad sandwiches ($7) with a pickle on the side. Open daily 8am-3pm and 6-10pm. AmEx/D/MC/V. ❷

Blue Heaven, 729 Thomas St. (☎305-296-8666). Feast on healthy breakfasts with fresh banana bread ($2.25) or Caribbean lunches like the Jamaican jerk chicken sandwich ($8). Open in summer M-Tu and Th-Sa 8am-3pm and 6-10:30pm, Su 8am-2pm and 6-10:30pm; in winter M-Sa 8am-3pm and 6-10:30pm, Su 8am-2pm. AmEx/D/MC/V. ❷

Flora & Flipp on Flkeming, 811 Fleming St. (☎305-296-1050). It doesn't look like much from the outside, but this hole-in-the-wall is a real Mom-and-Pop sandwich place. Try the Very Veggie ($4.75) or a robust smoked turkey and avocado sandwich ($5.50). The shop also sells groceries, wine, and beer. Open M-Sa 9:30am-7pm, Su 11am-4pm. Cash only. ❶

El Siboney, 900 Catherine St. (☎305-296-4184). This authentic establishment gives you a real taste of Havana. Entrees, like half a roasted chicken ($9), come with rice, black beans, and plantains. Save room for sangria ($2.25) and flan ($3). Open daily 11am-9:30pm. Cash only. ❷

Karr Breizh Crêperie, 512½ Duval St. (☎305-296-1071). Watch the owner create an array of French crepes, from classic banana, strawberry, and Nutella ($8) to the savory mozzarella and pesto Italian *galette* ($9.50). Open M-Th and Su 9am-6pm, F-Sa 9am-10pm. Cash only. ❸

ACCOMMODATIONS

Key West is packed from January through March, so reserve rooms far in advance. During the summer, prices drop and many places have vacancies. **Pride Week** (www.pridefestkeywest.com) in June and **Fantasy Fest** (www.fantastyfest.net) on Halloween are particularly busy. In Old Town, B&Bs dominate, and "reasonably priced" still means over $50. Rates decrease as you move further south and away from Duval St. Some of the guesthouses in Old Town are exclusively for gay men.

Angelina Guesthouse, 302 Angela St. (☎305-294-4480), 2 blocks from Duval St. This 1920s bordello is now a haven for budget-conscious travelers. A/C, communal fridge, pool, and swing. No TVs or phones. Breakfast included. No spring breakers. Shared bathroom. Rooms May-Dec. $69; Dec.-Apr. $99. D/MC/V. ❸

Key West Youth Hostel and Seashell Motel, 718 South St. (☎305-296-5719). While the hostel's cleanliness leaves something to be desired, it's the cheapest game in town. Common bathroom and kitchen. Linen included. Key deposit $5. Dorms $31; private rooms in summer $75-85, in winter $95-105. MC/V. ❶

Eden House, 1015 Fleming St. (☎305-296-6868), 5 blocks from downtown. A brightly painted hotel with a hostel-like atmosphere. Clean, simple rooms with bath. Pool, jacuzzi, hammock area, and kitchens. Bikes $10 per day. Rooms with

CONCH 101

You've heard Key West residents refer to themselves as conchs. You've tasted the conch fritters and conch chowder. You've even blown a conch shell. Now it's time to leave Key West, and you're wondering how you're ever going to live without that special mollusk. Well, never fear-anyone can buy and prepare conch in their own homes. Because conch are usually still within their shells in the grocery store, it can be difficult to tell whether a conch is fresh. A fresh conch's shell is shiny, and the meat, if exposed, should be firm. Never buy conch that smells overly fishy. Once you've got your conch, you have to remove it from its shell. Make a hole at the top of the shell with a hammer and screwdriver. Alternatively, you can put the shell in boiling water for a few minutes and then pull out the conch. Then you should be able to cut the muscle and remove the conch meat. Remove the eyes, the foot, and the tough protective nail with a sharp knife. Cut away the dark-colored skin and then you've got your prize: the white stuff. Pound it with a mallet until flat, and you're ready to get cooking. Conch can be used in salads, fritters, and chowders, all with tasty results. Of course, if all this talk of protective nails, hammers, and sharp knives sounds a little extreme, you can always start planning your next trip to Key West-they'll do the cooking for you.

shared bath in summer $90, in winter $135. AmEx/D/MC/V. ❹

Casablanca Hotel, 900 Duval St. (☎305-296-0815), in the center of town. This charming B&B once hosted Humphrey Bogart and James Joyce. Pool, beautiful courtyards, cable TV, and large bathrooms. Breakfast included. Rooms June-Nov.. $125-155; Dec.-May $225-255. AmEx/D/MC/V. ❺

Wicker Guesthouse, 913 Duval St. (☎305-296-4275). Pastel decor, private baths, A/C, and cable TV. Most rooms have kitchenettes. No phones. Kitchen, pool access, and free parking. Breakfast included. Reservations recommended. Rooms May-Dec. $110-250; late Dec.-Apr. $165-350. AmEx/D/MC/V. ❺

Boyd's Campground, 6401 Maloney Ave. (☎305-294-1465; www.boydscampground.com). Take a left off U.S. 1 onto Macdonald Ave., which becomes Maloney. This campground sprawls over 12 oceanside acres and has full facilities. Sites in summer $50, with water and electricity $60, with full hookup $75; in winter $60/$70/$60-85. MC/V. ❸

🍸 NIGHTLIFE

Nightlife in Key West revs up at 11pm and winds down in the wee hours of the morning. The action centers around upper **Duval St.** Key West nightlife reaches its peak in the 3rd week of October's **Fantasy Fest** (☎305-296-1817; www.fantasyfest.net), when decadent floats filled with drag queens, pirates, and wild locals take over Duval St.

▨ The Green Parrot, 601 Whitehead St. (☎305-294-6133). Though off the beaten path of Duval St., this bar warranted a nod from *Playboy* as Key West's best bar. A real area hangout; stop by and meet a crowd of local characters. Open daily 10am-4am. Cash only.

Capt. Tony's Saloon, 428 Greene St. (☎305-294-1838). The oldest bar in Key West and reputedly one of Tennessee Williams's preferred watering holes. Bras and business cards festoon the ceiling, and the city's old hanging tree still grows right through the bar. Nightly live music. Open daily 10am-2am. D/MC/V.

Sloppy Joe's, 201 Duval St. (☎305-294-5717). For the best party you'll most likely forget, stop by

Hemingway's favorite hangout. Prepare to be blown away by the house specialty, the Sloppy Rita ($7.25). Mostly blues in the afternoon and rock at night. 21+. Open M-Sa 9am-4am, Su noon-4am. AmEx/D/MC/V.

Rick's, 202 Duval St. (☎305-296-5513). This trendy entertainment complex boasts a bar with live music downstairs, a dance floor upstairs, and a strip club around back. Tu $2 longneck Buds. Open M-Sa 11am-4am, Su noon-4am. AmEx/D/MC/V.

GLBT NIGHTLIFE

Known for its wild, outspoken gay community, Key West hosts more than a dozen fabulous drag lounges, night clubs, and private bars that cater to a gay clientele. Most clubs welcome straight couples and lesbians, but check with the bouncer. Gay clubs line **Duval St.** south of Fleming Ave.

Aqua, 711 Duval St. (☎305-294-0555; www.aquakeywest.com). The hottest drag club in Key West. Nightly cabaret shows (9:30pm) play to a crowd of female tourists. Dancing after the show. Cover after 8:30pm $10. Happy hour daily 3-8pm. Open daily 3pm-last customer. MC/V.

KWEST MEN, 705 Duval St. (☎305-292-8500). By day, it's a mild-mannered bar. By night, it's a raunchy, male strip club. Happy hour 3-8pm. Strip show 10pm. Open daily 3pm-4am. AmEx/D/MC/V.

The Bourbon Street Pub, 724 Duval St. (☎305-294-9354; www.bourbonstreetpub.com). Boys in very tiny undies dance to the nightly line-up of music videos. Open M-Sa 11am-4am, Su noon-4am. Sister club **801 Bourbon,** 801 Duval St. (☎305-296-1992) hosts a nightly drag show. Open M-Sa 11am-4am, Su noon-4am. Cover $5.

🚗 APPROACHING KEY LARGO: 99 MILES

From Key West, follow **U.S. 1 N** into town.

KEY LARGO

Over half a century ago, Hollywood stars Humphrey Bogart and Lauren Bacall immortalized the name "Key Largo" in their hit movie. Quick-thinking locals of Rock Harbor, where some scenes were shot, changed the name of their town to Key Largo to attract tourists. The plan worked. While some visitors still come to see the relics of the moviemaking past, more are drawn to Key Largo's greatest natural assets: miles of coral reefs and incredible fishing.

VITAL STATS

Population: 12,886

Visitor Info: Key Largo Chamber of Commerce/Florida Keys Visitors Center, 106000 U.S. 1 (☎305-451-1414 or 800-822-1088; www.keylargo.org), at Mi. 106. Open daily 9am-6pm.

Internet Access: Key Largo Library Branch, 101485 Overseas Hwy. (☎305-451-2396), in the Tradewinds Shopping Center. Open M and W 10am-8pm, Tu and Th-Sa 10am-6pm. Free.

Post Office: 101000 U.S. 1 (☎305-451-3155), at Mi. 100. Open M-F 8am-4:30pm, Sa 10am-1pm.

Postal Code: 33037.

▤ GETTING AROUND. The **Overseas Hwy. (U.S. 1)** bridges the Keys and the southern tip of Florida, stitching the islands together. Mile markers section the highway and replace street addresses beginning with Mi. 0 in Key West. In Key Largo, U.S. 1 is a divided highway, and establishments are considered oceanside, east of U.S. 1, or bayside, to the west.

◉▨ SIGHTS AND OUTDOORS. Key Largo is the self-proclaimed "Dive Capital of the World," and diving instructors advertise on highway billboards. The best place to dive is the nation's first underwater sanctuary, the **▨John Pennekamp Coral Reef State Park,** Mi. 102.5 oceanside. The park extends 3 mi. into the Atlantic Ocean, safeguarding a part of the reef that runs the length of the Keys. While Pennekamp's reefs are its main attraction, the park also has miles of mangroves reaching finger-like into the salt water. (☎305-451-1202; www.pennekamppark.com. $3.50-6 per vehicle.) Stop by the park's **visitors center** for maps, boat and snorkeling tour info, an aquarium, and films about the park's habitat. To see the reefs, visitors must take their own boats or rent. (☎305-451-9570, for reservations ☎305-451-6325. 18 ft. motor boat $135 per 4hr., $210 per day. Canoes and kayaks $12 per hr. Deposit required. Open daily 8am-5pm.) **Scuba trips** depart from the visitors center. (☎305-451-6322. Trips 9:30am and 1:30pm. 2-tank dive $45. Equipment rental surcharge. Deposit required. Certification required. Classes available.) A **snorkeling tour**

allows visitors to experience the reefs. (☎305-451-6300. Tours 9am, noon, 3pm. Equipment $6. Deposit required. $29, under 18 $24.) The park also rents snorkeling equipment ($10) for use in the beach area. **Glass Bottom Boat Tours** provides a crystal-clear view of the reefs without wetting your feet. (☎305-451-1621. Tours 9:15am, 12:15, 3pm. $22, under 12 $15.) Head to any local marina to charter a spot on a fishing boat. At Mi. 100 oceanside, the **Holiday Inn Hotel** also offers scuba, snorkel, and boat trips. The best known is the **Key Largo Princess,** which offers 2hr. glass-bottom boat tours. (☎305-451-4655; www.keylargoprincess.com. Tours 10am, 1, 4pm. $25, children $15.) Aside from its busy dock, the Holiday Inn Hotel has become a tourist destination in its own right; it houses the *African Queen*, the boat from the 1952 film starring Humphrey Bogart and Katharine Hepburn.

▧ FOOD. Seafood restaurants of varying price, specialty, and view litter the **Overseas Hwy.** With bright pink walls and trophies over the mantle, **The Hideout Restaurant ❶,** Mi. 103.5 oceanside, at the end of Transylvania Ave., could be your 1970s living room. Their blueberry hotcakes ($4.25) will keep you truckin' all day. (☎305-451-0128. Open M-Th and Sa-Su 11:30am-2pm, F 11:30am-2pm and 5-9pm. Cash only.) At **Hobo's ❷,** Mi. 101.5 oceanside, loyal barflies swap stories over $0.35 shrimp, $0.45 wings, and $1 drafts during happy hour (M-F 3-6pm). For something a little more substantial, try the Hobo's Fish Sandwich ($8) followed by $4 key lime pie. (☎305-451-5888. Open daily 11am-10pm. MC/V.) **Mary Mac's Kitchen ❶,** Mi. 99 bayside, cooks up bowls of chili ($4) and overwhelming hamburgers ($4.50) for its heavily local crowd. The windows feature neon beer signs, and the walls are adorned with license plates. (☎305-451-3722. Open M-Sa 7am-9:30pm. AmEx/D/MC/V.) Try **The Fish House ❺,** Mi. 102.5 oceanside, which serves fish caught daily by local fishermen. Enjoy the Catch of the Day ($21) after a long day in the sun. (☎305-451-4665. Open daily 11:30am-9:30pm. AmEx/D/MC/V.)

▥ ACCOMMODATIONS. Ed and Ellen's Lodgings ❸, Mi. 103.5 oceanside, on Snapper Ave., has large, clean rooms with cable TV, A/C, mini-fridges, and microwaves. Ed and Ellen, the cheerful owners, live out back and are eager to help. (☎305-451-9949 or 888-333-5536. Doubles in summer $49-59; in winter $59-79. MC/V.) Closer to downtown Key Largo is **Hungry Pelican ❸**, Mi. 99.5 bayside, which features tropical flowers and cozy rooms with double beds, fridges, and cable TV. Guests can use the paddle boats, canoes, sailboat, and hammocks. (☎305-451-3576. Continental breakfast included. Rooms from $60. AmEx/D/MC/V.) Next door, the **Bay Cove Motel ❹**, Mi. 99 bayside, offers free use of hammocks, barbecue grills, and swings overlooking the water. (☎305-451-1686. Rooms $75-95. MC/V.) Reservations are recommended for the popular **John Pennekamp State Park Campground ❶** (see p. 56). The 47 sites are clean, convenient, and worth the effort required to obtain them. Ninety percent are available through advance registration, and fill a year in advance for the winter; during the summer call a few months in advance for weekends. The other 10% are first come, first served. Beware the pesky insects that descend at nightfall. (☎305-451-1202; www.pennkamppark.com. Showers. Laundry. Open 8am-sunset. Sites $24, with electricity $26. AmEx/D/MC/V.)

❖ NIGHTLIFE. Key Largo, unlike its sister to the south, isn't known for its nightlife. Locals relax at the sports bar **Sharkey's**, at Mi. 100 oceanside; take a left at Caribbean Dr. and follow the bend. The pool tables, darts, and $1.50 drafts keep the local crowd happy. (☎305-453-0999. Open noon-2am. MC/V.) If you can't get enough of the great outdoors, try **Coconuts**, in the Holiday Inn at Mi. 100 oceanside. There's a tiki bar outside—inside, bands play Friday and Saturday nights. (☎305-453-9794. W ladies night. Su karaoke. Open 11am-2am. AmEx/D/MC/V.)

⚲ APPROACHING THE EVERGLADES: 29 MILES
Drive north on **U.S. 1** until **Florida City**. Turn right onto **Palm Dr.**, and follow the signs into the park.

THE EVERGLADES

The Everglades National Park makes a spectacular detour on your trip. Encompassing the entire tip of Florida and spearing into Florida Bay, the Everglades spans 1.6 million acres of one of the world's most fragile ecosystems. Species found nowhere else in the world inhabit these lands and waters: American alligators, dolphins, sea turtles, and various birds and fish, as well as the endangered Florida panther, Florida manatee, and American crocodile.

 PAGE TURN. See p. 57 in the **Southern Border** for complete coverage of the Everglades.

⚲ APPROACHING MIAMI: 43 MILES
Follow signs to **S.R.-821 N.** Get on **S.R.-824 N**, and head into downtown Miami.

MIAMI

No longer purely a vacation spot for "snowbirds" (wealthy East Coasters escaping harsh winters), Miami's heart pulses to a beat all its own, fueled by the largest Cuban population this side of Havana. Appearance rules in this city, and nowhere is this more clear than on the shores of South Beach, where visual delights include Art Deco hotels and tanned beach bodies. South Beach (SoBe) is also host to a nightclub scene that attracts some of the world's most beautiful people. But it's not all bikinis and glitz—Miami is the entry point for one of America's great natural habitats, the Everglades, as well as the gateway to the Florida Keys and the Caribbean.

VITAL STATS

Population: 360,000

Visitor Info: Miami Beach Visitors Center, 1920 Meridian Ave. (☎305-674-1300). Open M-F 9am-6pm, Sa-Su 10am-4pm. **Coconut Grove Chamber of Commerce,** 2820 McFarlane Rd. (☎305-444-7270). Open M-F 9am-5pm.

Internet Access: Miami Public Library, 101 W. Flagler St. (☎305-375-2665). Open M and W-Th 9am-8pm, Tu and F-Sa 9am-5pm, Su 1-5pm. Free.

Parking: Miami Heat Parking, Biscayne Blvd., opposite American Airlines Arena., charges $4 per day.

Post Office: 500 NW 2nd Ave. (☎305-639-4284), downtown. Open M-F 8am-5pm, Sa 9am-1:30pm. **Postal Code:** 33101.

EAST COAST

Miami

⚑ FOOD
Versailles, 2

◾ NIGHTLIFE
Tobacco Road, 3

Miami

GETTING AROUND

Three highways crisscross the Miami area. **I-95,** which runs along the east side of the city and is the most direct north-south route, merges into **U.S. 1 (Dixie Hwy.)** just south of downtown. **Rte. 836 (Dolphin Expwy.),** the major east-west artery through town, connects I-95 to **Florida's Turnpike,** which circles the outer edges of the city in the west. Downtown Miami has a systematic street layout: streets run east-west, avenues run north-south, and both are numbered. Miami is divided into NE, NW, SE, and SW quadrants by **Flagler St.** and **Miami Ave.**

The heart of **Little Havana** lies on **Calle Ocho (SW 8th St.)** between SW 12th and SW 27th Ave. **Coconut Grove,** south of Little Havana, centers around the shopping and entertainment district on **Grand Ave.,** and **Virginia St. Coral Gables,** an upscale residential area, is around the intersection of **Coral Way** and **Le Jeune Rd. (SW 42nd Ave.).** Although public transportation is safe and reliable, it's difficult to get around without a car in downtown Miami. Blocks are long, and pedestrians (the few and the proud) often have to cross many-laned roads with no crosswalks.

Several causeways connect Miami to **Miami Beach.** The most useful is **MacArthur Causeway,** which becomes **5th St.** Numbered streets run east-west across the island, increasing as you go north. In South Beach, **Collins Ave. (Rte. A1A)** is the main north-south drag and runs parallel to club-filled **Washington Ave.** and beachfront **Ocean Dr.** The commercial district sits between 6th and 23rd St. One-way streets, traffic jams, and limited parking make driving around **South Beach (SoBe)** frustrating. Tie on your most stylish sneakers, park the car, and enjoy the small island at your leisure.

 When visiting Miami, it's best to avoid Liberty City, which is considered an unsafe area and has little to offer tourists.

SIGHTS

SOUTH BEACH. The hot bodies, Art Deco design, and sparkling sand of South Beach

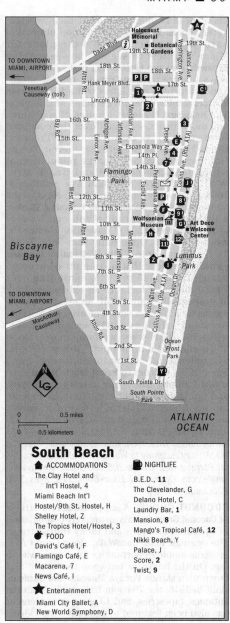

EAST COAST

South Beach

🏠 ACCOMMODATIONS
The Clay Hotel and
   Int'l Hostel, 4
Miami Beach Int'l
   Hostel/9th St. Hostel, H
Shelley Hotel, Z
The Tropics Hotel/Hostel, 3

🍴 FOOD
David's Café I, F
Flamingo Café, E
Macarena, 7
News Café, I

⭐ Entertainment
Miami City Ballet, A
New World Symphony, D

🌙 NIGHTLIFE

B.E.D., 11
The Clevelander, G
Delano Hotel, C
Laundry Bar, 1
Mansion, 8
Mango's Tropical Café, 12
Nikki Beach, Y
Palace, J
Score, 2
Twist, 9

make these 17 blocks seem like their own universe. **Ocean Drive** is part fashion show and part raging party, and it's the place for Miami's hottest to see and be seen. Along **Espanola Way** and **Lincoln Rd.**, pedestrian walkways feature outdoor dining, tourist shops, and overpriced boutiques while **Miami Beach Visitors Center** offers free maps and advice. The **Holocaust Memorial,** a series of sculptures and monuments, was built over the course of four years by sculptor Kenneth Treister. Guided tours are sometimes offered free by Holocaust survivors, a large population of which immigrated to Miami Beach after WWII. (1933-1945 Meridian Ave. ☎305-538-1663. Open daily 9am-9pm. Free.) Next to the Memorial is the **Miami Beach Botanical Garden,** a little tropical paradise you can wander around for free. (2000 Convention Center Dr. ☎305-673-7256. Open daily 9am-5pm. Tours Tu-Su 11am. Free.) The **Wolfsonian Museum** examines the cultural impact of art and design from 1885 to 1945, exhibiting over 70,000 pieces. It includes an exhaustive look at propaganda from WWII, an array of political cartoons, and a series of original Norman Rockwell paintings. (1001 Washington Ave. ☎305-531-1001; www.wolfsonian.org. Open M-Tu and Sa-Su noon-6pm, Th-F noon-9pm. $7, students and seniors $5. F after 6pm free.) Since 1936, visitors to **Parrot Jungle Island** have walked among free-flying parrots, flamingos, and orangutans. Other attractions include an albino alligator, parrot and reptile shows throughout the day, and—a treat for Napoleon Dynamite fans—a real, live liger. (1111 Parrot Jungle Trail. From downtown Miami, take the MacArthur Causeway to Watson Island. Look for signs for Parrot Jungle Trail ☎305-258-6453; www.parrotjungle.com. Open daily 10am-6pm. $25, ages 3-10 $20, under 3 free.)

COCONUT GROVE. A stroll through the streets of **Coconut Grove** reveals an unlikely combination of upscale boutiques and tacky tourist traps. The open-air mall, **CocoWalk,** along Grand Ave. presents ample opportunities for people-watching. On the bayfront between the Grove and downtown stands **Vizcaya Museum and Gardens.** Built in 1916, the 70-room Italian villa features antiques, tapestries, and 10 acres of gardens. It has also been featured in numerous rap videos.

(3251 S. Miami Ave. ☎305-250-9133; www.vizcayamuseum.com. Open daily 9:30am-5pm; last entry 4:30pm. $12, ages 6-12 $5. Gardens free.)

BAYSIDE MARKETPLACE. Miami's outdoor, ocean-front shopping center caters to cruiseship guests and tourists with money to burn. Stores and restaurants are mainly chains or tourist boutiques. One redeeming feature is the free concerts held most nights and some afternoons. (On the waterfront, off Biscayne Blvd., between NE 4th St. and NE 6th St. Open M-Th 10am-10pm, F-Sa 10am-11pm, Su 11am-9pm.) From Bayside you can take a boat tour with **Island Queen Cruises** to see "Millionaires' Row," mansions built on exclusive islands that can only be seen from the water. Ogle Enrique Iglesias's palatial mansion and Al Capone's former abode from afar. (☎305-379-5119; www.islandqueencruises.com. Departures daily every hr. 11am-4, 5:30, 7:30pm. $16)

NORTH MIAMI. The **Museum of Contemporary Art (MOCA),** is known for its often eccentric exhibits and displays. Having played host to Versace dresses and steel drummers alike, MOCA supports uncommon means of artistic expression. (770 NE 125th St. ☎305-893-6211; www.mocanomi.org. Open Tu-Sa 11am-5pm, Su noon-5pm. $5, students and seniors $3, under 12 free.)

CORAL GABLES. Dade County Commissioner George Merrick began building his "perfectly designed" city in 1921 to counter the sprawl of an emerging Miami. Merrick's city—now called Coral Gables neighborhood—is replete with fountains, tree-lined esplanades, and Mediterranean-style houses. A drive down Granada Blvd. gives a taste of true Miami glamor. At the roundabout, stop to check out the imposing **Biltmore Hotel,** where Esther Williams once made aquatic movie masterpieces. Those who can afford the hefty price tag for a room may enjoy a complimentary carriage ride through Coral Gables. (1200 Anastasia Ave. ☎305-445-1926; www.biltmorehotel.com.) For a more wallet-friendly but equally grandiose activity, check out the **Venetian Pool,** a beautiful Spanish-inspired swimming pool built in 1924. Even if you're not into swimming, the 820,000 gal. oasis deserves a quick look, if only for its role in the first Hollywood Tarzan movie. (2701 De

Soto Blvd. ☎305-460-5306; www.venetianpool.com. Open June-July M-F 11am-7:30pm, Sa-Su 10am-4:30pm; Aug. M-F 11am-5:30pm, Sa-Su 10am-4:30pm; Sept.-Oct. Tu-F 11am-5:30pm, Sa-Su 10am-4:30pm; Nov.- Mar. Tu-Su 11am-4:30pm; Apr.-May Tu-F 11am-5:30pm, Sa-Su 10am-4:30pm. Nov.-Mar. $6.25/$3.25; Apr.-Oct. $9.50, ages 3-12 $5.25.)

FOOD

Miami has a wide variety of restaurants, and most don't come cheap. For less expensive fare, check out **Little Havana** and **Little Haiti** or head to the open-air snack counters in South Beach and along **Calle Ocho**. In South Beach, restaurants can be found up and down **Ocean Dr.** and along **Lincoln Rd.**, west of Washington St. and Espanola Way. Go at least one block inland from the beach to find cheaper prices.

David's Cafe, 1058 Collins Ave. (☎305-672-8707). In the 1940s, David opened an American-style diner. When it was bought by Cuban owners in the early 1960s, they changed the food but kept the name and the decor. An institution in SoBe, David's Cafe has open-air counters where you can get churros ($3), Cuban espresso ($0.75), or batidos (fruit shakes; $3) on the go. Lunch specials $5. Open daily 24hr. AmEx/MC/V. ❶

News Cafe, 800 Ocean Dr. (☎305-538-6397). Though the food is outstanding, you're really paying for one of the best people-watching locations on Ocean Dr. Go in the evening for dessert (chocolate fondue for 2; $13) and gaze at the stylish hardbodies strolling by. Open daily 24hr. AmEx/DC/MC/V. ❷

Macarena, 1334 Washington Ave. (☎305-531-3440). This festive eatery serves up Spanish delights alongside wine from its own vineyards. Live Flamenco dancing F night. Open M-Tu 7pm-midnight, W-Su 7pm-4am. Cover after 10pm $10-20. AmEx/DC/MC/V. ❸

Flamingo Cafe, 1454 Washington Ave. (☎305-673-4302). Overwhelming amounts of delicious food for staggeringly low prices. Breakfast plate with eggs, toast, and meat $3. Beef tacos $4. Frijoles con queso $2.75. Open M-Sa 7am-9:30pm. Cash only. ❶

Versailles, 3555 SW 8th St. (☎305-444-0240), in Little Havana. Miami-Cuban to the core. Sit in the company of power-brokers as you enjoy classic Cuban dishes like ropa vieja with sweet plantains ($10.50). Entrees $8-24. AmEx/MC/V. ❸

ACCOMMODATIONS

Nothing comes cheap in South Beach and rooms are no exception. Even so, choosing a place to stay is all about attitude. If young bohemian isn't your thing, cruise down Collins Ave. to hot-pink Art Deco hotels. In general, high season for Miami Beach runs from late December through mid-March; during the low season, hotel clerks are often quick to bargain. **The Miami Beach Visitors Center** (p. 57) can help you find a place. Camping is not allowed on Miami Beach.

The Tropics Hotel/Hostel, 1550 Collins Ave. (☎305-531-0361), across the street from the beach. This quiet refuge from the intense SoBe scene offers large, comfortable rooms and access to a lovely patio, pool, and outdoor kitchen. Linen included. Laundry $1. Internet access $1 per 10min. Key deposit $10. Reservations required Feb.-Apr. Dorms $26; private doubles $102. MC/V. ❷

The Clay Hotel and International Hostel (HI-AYH), 1438 Washington Ave. (☎305-534-2988). This historic Mediterranean-style building was once the center of Al Capone's Miami gambling syndicate and now hosts an international crowd. Kitchen and A/C. Lockers $1 per day. Laundry $1. Internet $4 per hr. Key deposit $10. Reservations required. Dorms in summer $24, members $23; in winter $27/$25. Private rooms $48-78/$60-160. MC/V. ❷

Miami Beach International Travelers Hostel/9th St. Hostel (HI-AYH), 236 9th St. (☎305-534-0268), right in the heart of SoBe's club scene. Common room with TV and fridge. Storage room and safety deposit boxes are strongly recommended. Laundry $1. Internet access $5 per hr. Dorms $21, members $19; singles $67-111. MC/V. ❷

Hotel Shelley, 844 Collins Ave. (☎305-531-3341). With marble bathrooms and bright, white bedspreads, the Shelley offers luxury without sucking your wallet dry. Complimentary cocktails, and VIP passes to nearby clubs. Continental breakfast included. Rooms M-F from $65, Sa-Su from $95. AmEx/DC/MC/V. ❸

ENTERTAINMENT

For the latest on Miami entertainment, check out the "Living Today," "Lively Arts," and Fri-

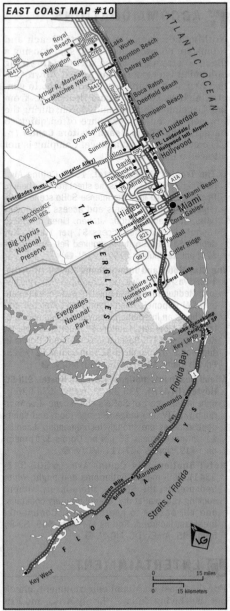

EAST COAST MAP #10

day's "Weekend" section of the *Miami Herald*. Weekly *Oceandrive*, *New Times*, *Street*, and *Sun Post* also list local happenings. *TWN* and *Miamigo*, the major gay papers, are available free in paper boxes along Ocean Dr. Events occur regularly at the **Orange Bowl** (☎305-643-7100) and the **American Airlines Arena** (☎786-777-1000); the latter is home to the Miami Heat NBA team. Look for concerts at the **New World Symphony Orchestral Academy,** 541 Lincoln Rd. (☎305-673-3331; www.nws.edu. Tickets from $36.) The **Miami City Ballet,** 2200 Liberty Rd., and its performance school, known for cutting-edge ballet, also has performances throughout the year. (☎305-929-7000; www.miamicityballet.org. Tickets from $20.) **Carnaval Miami,** the nation's largest Hispanic festival, fills 23 blocks of Calle Ocho in early March with salsa dancing and the world's longest conga line.

🞐 NIGHTLIFE

Nightlife in the Art Deco district of South Miami Beach starts late and continues until well after sunrise. Clubs are centered on **Ocean Dr., Collins Ave.,** and **Washington Ave.,** between 7th and 18th St. The scene is transient; what's there one week may not be there the next; call in advance before heading out. Many clubs don't demand cover until after midnight, and the $20 (and up) door charge can include an open bar. However, willingness to pay a steep cover is no guarantee of admission. Difficult doormen can prove impossible after 1am, so show up early. Many clubs have dress codes, and everyone always dresses to the nines, even on so-called "casual" nights.

🞐 **Delano Hotel,** 1685 Collins Ave. (☎305-672-2000). What happens when a $3500 per night hotel sets up a lounge in its lobby and courtyard? Jaw-dropping decor and the poshest atmosphere in SoBe—and maybe the continent. Splurge for a $1300 bottle of champagne, or, more realistically, dress in your finest and head over for a cocktail ($15). No cover. Open daily 5pm-1 or 2am. AmEx/D/DC/MC/V.

🞐 **Mansion,** 1235 Washington Ave. (☎305-532-1525; www.mansionmiami.com). An assault on all the senses, the lavish Mansion hosts concerts, boxing matches, even political debates. Mostly known as a bumping club with lines around the corner. The VIP section is littered with celebrities sipping Cristal. Cover $20. Open daily 10pm-5am. AmEx/D/DC/MC/V.

Mango's Tropical Cafe, 900 Ocean Dr. (☎305-673-4422). All that noise you hear while walking up Ocean Dr. is coming from here. Mango's is the main Latin-inspired venue in SoBe and is always filled with tourists. Order a stiff and delicious CoCo-Loco ($8) and stay for a set of live music, ending with a bar-top dance extraordinaire by alluring waitresses and buffed-up waiters. Not for the faint of heart. Cover $5-20. Open daily 11am-5am. AmEx/D/MC/V.

B.E.D., 929 Washington Ave. (☎305-532-9070). The acronym stands for Beverage, Entertainment, and Dining, which pretty much sums up the attraction of this venue. Patrons lounge on sexy beds as they enjoy dinner, drinks, and the atmosphere of silky seduction that oozes from every corner of this SoBe favorite. No cover. Open W-Sa and Su 8pm-5am. AmEx/D/MC/V.

The Clevelander, 1020 Ocean Dr., (☎786-276-1414; www.clevelander.com). A casual atmosphere that attracts all ages for dancing by the outdoor pool and bar. Bikini contests in the afternoon give way to dancing to Top 40 and 80s hits at night. No cover. Open daily 11am-3am. AmEx/MC/V.

Nikki Beach, 1 Ocean Dr. (☎305-538-1111). Trendy beach club packed with hot, young people listening to house music spun by local DJs. Beach area is filled with a weird mix of beds, teepees, and lawn chairs. You can walk around back to the beach area for free. Cocktails $10. Cover after 7pm $20. Open M-Th 11am-6pm, F-Su 11am-5am.

Tobacco Road, 626 S. Miami Ave. (☎305-374-1198), at SW 7th St. Fun, laid-back, and the oldest bar in Miami. Munch on killer burgers ($6-7) to the rhythm of local bands belting out the blues and old-fashioned rock 'n' roll. Shows ($5) often held on the top floor. Open daily 11:30am-5am. AmEx/D/MC/V.

GLBT NIGHTLIFE

South Beach's gay scene may be somewhat diminished since its heyday, but the gay and mixed clubs are still dance-club staples, attracting partiers of every inclination.

❦ Palace, 1200 Ocean Dr. (☎305-531-9077) Offers a glimpse of what Ocean Dr. was like in the 80s. A laid-back bar with wild dancing and impromptu drag shows. Music is a mix of Top 40, 70s, and 80s. Passersby are often pulled off the street to join the party. No cover. Open daily 10am-11pm. AmEx/MC/V.

Twist, 1057 Washington Ave. (☎305-538-9478). A popular 2-story club with an outdoor lounge, a rockin' dance floor, and 6 bars. Straight couples welcome. No cover. Open daily 1pm-5am. AmEx/D/MC/V.

Laundry Bar, 721 Lincoln Ln. N (☎305-531-7700). Men and women alike flock to Laundry Bar, where the chic clientele sips cocktails to DJ-spun beats and the hum of laundry machines. A great place to do laundry and get a drink before dinner. 21+ from 10pm. No cover. Open daily 7am-5am. AmEx/D/MC/V.

Score, 727 Lincoln Rd. Mall (☎305-535-1111; www.scorebar.net). Plenty of style and plenty of attitude. Mostly men frequent this multi-bar hot spot, where a packed dance floor grooves all night, especially on Tu Latin Night. Cover $5-10. Open M-Sa 3pm-5am, Su 3pm-2am.

⚐ APPROACHING FORT LAUDERDALE: 53 MILES

From Florida City, follow **U.S. 1 N** until it becomes **I-95 N.** Follow signs to Ft. Lauderdale.

FORT LAUDERDALE

Over the past two decades, Fort Lauderdale has transformed from a city known as a beer-stained spring break mecca to the largest yachting center in North America. City streets and highways may be fine for the commoner's transportation needs, but Fort Lauderdale adds another option: canals. Intricate waterways connect ritzy homes with the intracoastal river and even mere mortals can cruise the canals via the Water Taxi, an on-the-water bus system. "The Venice of America" also has 23 mi. of beaches where spring break mayhem still reigns supreme, making Fort "Liquordale" fun even for those who can't afford a yacht.

VITAL STATS

Population: 167,000

Visitor Info: Greater Fort Lauderdale Convention and Visitors Bureau, 100 E. Broward Blvd., Ste. 200. (☎954-765-4466 or 800-227-8669; www.sunny.org). Open M-F 8:30am-5pm.

Internet Access: Public Library, 100 S. Andrews Ave. (☎954-357-7444). Open M-Th 9am-9pm, F-Sa 9am-5pm, Su noon-5:30pm. Free.

Post Office: 1900 W. Oakland Park Blvd. (☎954-765-5720). Open M-F 7:30am-7pm, Sa 8:30am-2pm. **Postal Code:** 33310.

EAST COAST

GETTING AROUND

Fort Lauderdale is bigger than it looks. The city extends westward from its 23 mi. stretch of beach to encompass nearly 450 sq. mi. Streets and boulevards run east-west and avenues run north-south. All are labeled NW, NE, SW, or SE according to quadrant. The two major roads in Fort Lauderdale are **Broward Blvd.** and **Andrews Ave.** The brick-and-mortar downtown centers around **U.S. 1 (Federal Hwy.)** and **Las Olas Blvd.**, about 2 mi. west of the oceanfront. Yachts fill the inlets of the **Intracoastal Waterway** between downtown and the waterfront. **The Strip** (a.k.a. Rte. A1A, Fort Lauderdale Beach Blvd., 17th St. Causeway, Ocean Blvd., or Seabreeze Blvd.) runs 4 mi. along the beach between **Oakland Park Blvd.** to the north and **Las Olas Blvd.** to the south. North-south **I-95** connects West Palm Beach, Fort Lauderdale, and Miami. **Rte. 84/I-75 (Alligator Alley)** runs 100 mi. west from Fort Lauderdale across the Everglades to small cities on Florida's Gulf Coast. Florida's **Turnpike** runs parallel to I-95.

SIGHTS

THE WATERFRONT. Fort Lauderdale Beach doesn't have a dull spot on it, but most of the action is between Las Olas Blvd. and Sunrise Blvd. Alongside the canal system is the **Las Olas Waterfront,** where people stroll and enjoy the clubs, restaurants, shopping, and bars. *(E. Las Olas Blvd. to SW 2nd St.)* The **Water Taxi** offers a relaxing way to beat rush-hour traffic and maneuver through town. The friendly captains will steer right up to any Las Olas restaurant or drop you off anywhere along the Intracoastal Waterway or New River. Alternatively, ride the entire route for an intimate view of the colossal houses along the canal. *(651 Seabreeze Blvd., on Rte. A1A. ☎954-467-6677; www.watertaxi.com. Call 30min. before pickup. Runs daily 9am-midnight. $5, seniors and under 12 $2.50; 1-day pass $7; 3-day pass $12.)* If traveling with a family or young children, take a tour aboard the tourist-targeted **Jungle Queen.** The captain explains the changing scenery as the 550-passenger riverboat cruises up the New River. *(801 Seabreeze Blvd., at the Bahia Mar Yacht Center, on Rte. A1A, 3 blocks south of Las Olas Blvd. ☎954-462-5596; www.jungle-queen.com. 3½hr. tours daily 10am, 2, 7pm. $14.50, under 12 $10.25; 7pm tour $33/$18 with barbecue dinner. Cash only.)* **Aloha Watersports** is the best beach spot for watersport equipment rentals and trips. Charter a sailboat or enjoy the serene blue water from above on a parasailing trip. Speed boats and wave runners are also available. *(301 Seabreeze Blvd. (Rte. A1A). ☎954-462-7245. Parasailing $75 per hr. Single kayak $20 per hr. Waverunner $65 per 15min. Open daily 9am-5pm.)*

DRY LAND. In the midst of Ft. Lauderdale's urban sprawl is the **Hugh Taylor Birch State Park,** an enclave of subtropical trees and animals. Bike, jog, or drive through the 2 mi. stretch of mangroves and royal palms, or canoe through the fresh lagoon filled with herons, gophers, tortoises, and marsh rabbits. There are also areas for picnicking, fishing, birding, and swimming. *(3109 E. Sunrise Blvd., west off Rte. A1A. ☎954-564-4521. Open daily 8am-sunset. Gate on Rte. A1A open 9am-5pm. $4 per vehicle, $1 per pedestrian. Canoes $5.30 per hr. Cabins and primitive sites available by reservation; call ahead.)* It's a bird! It's a plane! No, it's Jai Alai. This fast paced game—with players hurling balls up to 180 mph—is relatively unknown to most Americans; think of it as racquetball on steroids. Place your bets on a match at **Dania Jai-Alai,** which sports one of the largest *frontons* (courts) in the state. *(301 E. Dania Beach Blvd., off U.S. 1, 10min. south of Fort Lauderdale. ☎954-927-2841. Games Tu and Sa noon and 7pm, W-F 7pm, Su 1pm. Tickets from $2.)*

MUSEUMS. Cast your line at the International Game Fishing Association's **Fishing Hall of Fame and Museum,** where life-size mounts of record fish finally settle the long-standing question, "How big was it?" Interactive fishing simulations allow visitors to feel the bite, while exhibits describe the technology and history of fishing. The 18min. film, *Journeys,* in the big-screen theater, shows record-holders reminiscing about the lure of the sport. *(300 Gulf Stream Way, off I-95 at Griffin Rd., Exit 23. ☎954-922-4212; www.igfa.org. Open daily 10am-6pm. $6, seniors and children $5.)* For a different kind of high-seas adventure, doggy-paddle over to the **International Swimming Hall of Fame and Museum,** where exhibits on the sport, its greatest athletes, and sequined bathing costumes await. *(1 Hall of Fame

Dr., off Rte. A1A. ☎954-462-6536; www.ishof.org. Open daily 9am-7pm. $8, seniors $6, students $4, under 12 free.) Fort Lauderdale's **Museum of Art** is home to an extensive collection of American impressionist painter William Glacken's work. There are also remarkable temporary exhibits which showcase everything from laser shows to photojournalism. *(1 E. Las Olas Blvd. ☎954-525-5500; www.moafl.org. Open M, W and F-Su 11am-7pm, Th 11am-9pm. Tours Sa-Su 1:30pm. $6, students and seniors $5, ages 12-18 $3.)*

▚ FOOD

Locals and tourists alike flock to **Las Olas Blvd.** for a mixture of casual and upscale restaurants and the best people-watching in the city.

▨ The Floridian, 1410 E. Las Olas Blvd. (☎954-463-4041). A low-key local favorite whose walls are covered with photos of the celebrities who have visited. Try the burger platter, served with a heaping mound of fries ($7.25), with one of the excellent milkshakes ($4), and you might never want to leave. Free Wi-Fi. Open 24hr. AmEx only. ❷

Noodles Panini, 821 E. Las Olas Blvd. (☎954-462-1514). Named for a pasta-lover called Noodles Panini, the restaurant serves . . . wait for it . . .noodles and panini. French jazz plays as customers scarf down bombolotti ($13) and grilled portobello panini ($10). Open Tu-Th 11:30am-10pm, F-Sa 11:30am-11pm, Su 10:30am-10pm. AmEx/D/MC/V. ❸

Big City Tavern, 609 E. Las Olas Blvd. (☎954-727-0307). An elegant eatery in the heart of the Las Olas strip serving patrons beneath art and a finely paneled ceiling. Enjoy chicken rigatoni ($17) or almond crusted trout ($21) in the brick-lined interior or on the bustling patio. Open daily 10:30am-11pm. AmEx/D/MC/V. ❺

Squiggy's N.Y. Style Pizza, 207 SW 2nd St. (☎954-522-6655), in Old Town. Whether you're between bars or looking for a treat before heading home, Squiggy's is the place for those late-night munchies. This no-nonsense pizza shop serves gooey slices of Sicilian pie ($2.25, after 8pm $3) and $3 domestic beers late into the night. Open M 11am-11:30pm, Tu-W 11am-3am, Th-Su 11am-4am. AmEx/D/MC/V. ❶

▟ ACCOMMODATIONS

Thank decades of spring breakers for the abundant hotels lining the beachfront. Motels just north of the strip and a block west of Rte. A1A are the cheapest. Generally, it's easy to find a room at any time of the year. High season runs from mid-February to early April, and many hotels offer low-season deals. The *Fort Lauderdale News* and the *Miami Herald* occasionally publish listings from local residents who rent rooms to tourists in spring. Sleeping on the well-patrolled beaches is illegal.

▨ Fort Lauderdale Beach Hostel, 2115 N. Ocean Blvd. (☎954-567-7275; www.fortlauderdalehostel.com), off NE 21st St. After a long day at the beach, backpackers mingle in the tropical courtyard. A/C, a pool table, 2 lounges, and free Internet access. Breakfast included. Free lockers. Linen deposit $10. Free parking. Reception 8am-noon. Reservations recommended Dec.-June. Dorms $22; private rooms $45-55. $5 off 1st night with *Let's Go* in hand. MC/V. ❶

The Bridge II, 506 SE 16th St. (☎954-522-6350). Sunburned travelers take a break from the beach by jumping in this hostel's pool. A/C, free Internet access, laundry facilities, and kitchens. Reception 8:30am-11:30am and 4:30-9pm. Linen deposit $10. 4-bed dorms for ages 18-35 $25. MC/V. ❶

Floyd's Hostel/Crew House, 445 SE 16th St. (☎954-462-0631; www.floydshostel.com). A homey hostel catering to international travelers and boat crews. Free food, lockers, laundry, and Internet access. Passport or American driver's license required. No Florida residents. Linen deposit $10. 4-bed dorms $23. Private rooms $50. AmEx/D/MC/V. ❶

Tropic-Cay Beach Hotel, 529 N. Ft. Lauderdale Beach Blvd. (☎954-564-5900 or 800-463-2333), off Belmar St. One of the best deals on the beach. The spacious rooms and outdoor patio bar make it a spring breaker's paradise. A/C, pool, kitchens available. 21+ during spring break. Key deposit $10. Doubles in summer $59-79; in winter $109-129. AmEx/D/MC/V. ❸

Tropi-Rock Resort, 2900 Belmar St. (☎954-564-0523 or 800-987-9385), 2 blocks west of Rte. A1A at Birch Rd. This yellow-and-orange hotel provides a resort atmosphere at affordable prices. Lush hibiscus garden with caged birds and tiki bar. Gym, Internet access, tennis courts, free local calls, and refrigerators. Rooms Apr. to mid-Dec. from $75; mid-Dec. to Apr. from $100. AmEx/D/MC/V. ❹

EAST COAST

NIGHTLIFE

As any local will tell you, the *real* Fort Lauderdale nightlife action is in **Old Town.** Two blocks northwest of Las Olas Blvd. on 2nd St. near the **Riverwalk** district, the 100 yd. stretch of Old Town is packed with raucous bars, steamy clubs, cheap eats, and a stylish crowd. Considerably more expensive, and geared specifically toward tourists, the **Strip,** along A1A and across from the beach, is home to several popular nightspots.

Tarpon Bend, 200 SW 2nd St. (☎954-523-3233). Always the busiest place on the block, it feels like an upscale version of a raucous beach party. Live, loud rock music most nights. Happy hour daily 4-7pm with 2-for-1 drinks. Open M-Sa 11:30am-4am, Su noon-4am. AmEx/D/MC/V.

Elbo Room, 241 S. Ft. Lauderdale Beach Blvd., (☎954-463-4615), at the corner of Rte. A1A and Las Olas Blvd. This booming sidewalk bar is one of the most packed scenes on the Strip. Casual, fun, and perfect for wandering in off the beach. Nightly live rock. Domestic beers $3. Imported beers $4. Open M-F 11am-2am, Sa 11am-3am, Su noon-2am. Cash only.

Capone's, 310 SW 2nd St. (☎954-524-1969). A small club where you can get down to hip-hop and house among other stylish folk. No cover. Happy hour F 5-10pm with 3-for-1 drinks. Open W-Th and Sa 9pm-4am, F 5pm-4am. AmEx/MC/V.

The Voodoo Lounge, 111 SW 2nd St. (☎954-522-0733). With 18,000 sq. ft. of dance floors, plush, roped-off VIP tables, and its own clothing line, the Voodoo Lounge is Ft. Lauderdale's answer to South Beach. The party doesn't get going until midnight or later; come too early and you'll be grinding under the blacklights all alone. Su drag shows midnight and 2am. Cover for men $10; for women Sa $5. Open W-Su 10pm-4am. AmEx/D/MC/V.

APPROACHING PALM BEACH AND WEST PALM BEACH: 45 MILES

From Ft. Lauderdale, follow **U.S. 1 N** into town.

PALM BEACH AND WEST PALM BEACH

Nowhere else in Florida is the line between the "haves" and the "have-nots" as visible as the intracoastal waterway dividing the aristocratic vacationers of Palm Beach Island from the blue-collar residents of West Palm Beach. Five-star resorts and mansions reign over the "Gold Coast" island, while auto repair shops and fast-food restaurants characterize the mainland. Budget travel may be difficult here, but the region still offers some unique museums and stunning houses.

GETTING AROUND

I-95 runs north-south through the center of West Palm Beach, then continues north to Daytona and Jacksonville. The more scenic coastal highway **Rte. A1A** also travels north-south, crossing over Lake Worth at the **Flagler Memorial Bridge** to run along the beach in Palm Beach. Large highways cut through urban areas and residential neighborhoods; finding your way around can be a bit confusing. Stick to the major roads like north-south **U.S. 1** (which turns into **S. Dixie Hwy.**), Rte. A1A, east-west **Palm Beach Lakes Blvd.,** and **Belvedere Rd.** The heart of downtown West Palm Beach is **Clematis St.,** across from the Flagler Memorial Bridge, and the nearby outdoor mall **CityPlace,** 700 Rosemary Ave.; both contain affordable restaurants and wild nightclubs.

SIGHTS

The prize of blue-collar West Palm Beach is **Ragtops,** 2119 S. Dixie Hwy., as fine a collection of Americana as you'll find anywhere. It just so happens that all the items have four wheels and some serious muscle under the hood. Once a Cadillac dealership, the five show floors are now home to over 70 beautiful classic cars, and should you fall in love with one, you need not leave brokenhearted—most of the cars are for sale. (☎561-655-2836; www.ragtopsmotorcars.com. Open M-Sa 10am-6pm. $8, seniors and under 12 $6.) The **Norton Museum of Art,** 1451 S. Olive Ave., is well known for its collection of European, American, contemporary, and Chinese art. The museum displays works by Cézanne, Matisse, O'Keeffe, and Pollock. Stop by the central garden, which features its own fountain of youth. (☎561-832-5196; www.norton.org. Open M-Sa 10am-5pm, Su 1-5pm; May-Oct. Tu-Sa 10am-5pm, Su 1-5pm. Tours F-Su 2pm. $8, ages 13-21 $3. Special exhibits $10/$4, under 13 free.) If you're visiting in early spring, catch the training seasons of the **St. Louis Cardinals** and **Florida Marlins,** who hold training camp at **Roger Dean Stadium** in Jupiter, 15 mi. to the north. During the rest of the season, single-A Minor league baseball teams play nightly. (4751 Main St., Jupiter. Take I-95 N to Exit 73. ☎561-966-3309; www.rogerdeanstadium.com. Spring training $8-22; Minor league $7.) For a glimpse of lions and tigers and bears, check out the **Palm Beach Zoo,** 1301 Summit Blvd., where kids play in the interactive fountain. (☎561-547-9453. Open daily 9am-5pm. $13, seniors $10, ages 3-12 $9.)

To the east, in Palm Beach, just walking around is one of the most enjoyable (and affordable) activities. Known as the "Rodeo Drive of the South," **Worth Ave.,** between S. Ocean Blvd. and Cocoanut Row, outfits Palm Beach's rich and famous in the threads of fashion heavyweights. Walk or drive along **Ocean Blvd.** to gawk at spectacular mansions owned by celebrities and millionaires. One particularly remarkable complex is **The Breakers,** 1 S. County Rd., a sprawling Italian Renaissance-style resort with a regal driveway flanked by tall palms. If you can't afford the bare-minimum $259 price tag for a night of luxury, live vicariously though a guided tour. (☎561-655-6611 or 888-273-2537. Tours W 2pm. $15.)

A trip to Palm Beach County is incomplete if you don't take the time to relax on one of its picturesque beaches. Although most of the beachfront property in Palm Beach is private, more public beaches can be found in **West Palm Beach.** Good options on Palm Beach include the popular **Mid-town Beach,** 400 S. Ocean Blvd., and **Phipps Ocean Park,** 2185 S. Ocean Blvd., which has tennis courts for public use. (☎561-585-9203. Open 8am-8pm. Tennis courts open M-F 8am-12:30pm and 2-7:30pm, Sa-Su 8am-12:30pm.)

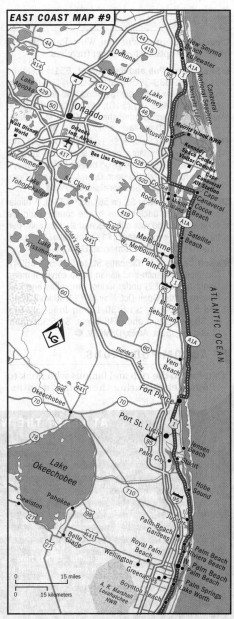

EAST COAST

FOOD

Clematis St., in downtown West Palm Beach, offers lively options for budget travelers.

O'Shea's Irish Pub and Restaurant, 531½ Clematis St. (☎561-833-3865), at Rosemary St. The perfect place for that neighborhood pub feel. After a bit of shepherds pie ($10), stick around for Guinness and sports around the bar. Open M-F 10am-3am, Sa-Su 10am-4am. AmEx/MC/V. ❸

Pizza Girls, 114 Clematis St. (☎561-833-4004). The slices here put ordinary pizza to shame. Try an enormous slab ($2.50) with garlic bread ($3), and they'll have to roll you out the door. Open M-W 11am-10pm, Th-Sa 11am-11pm, Su noon-9pm. MC/V. ❶

Sloan's, 112 Clematis St. (☎561-833-3335). A miniature ice-cream truck cruises by the counter, and the walls are painted with sundaes and shakes. Silly, perhaps, but the ice cream ($4) is no joke. Open M-F 11am-11pm, Sa-Su 11am-noon. D/MC/V. ❶

Maison Carlos, 207 Clematis St. (☎561-659-6524). This elegant French and Italian bistro serves a mean sirloin burger ($9) under indoor umbrellas and low-hanging lights. Open Oct.-May M-F 11:30am-2:30pm and 5:30-10pm, Sa 5:30-10pm; June-July Tu-F 11:30am-2:30pm and 5:30-10pm, Sa 5:30-10pm. Closed Aug.-Sept. AmEx/D/MC/V. ❹

▲ ACCOMMODATIONS

Catering to the rich and famous who flock to Palm Beach during the winter months, extravagant resorts and hotels are arguably the most notable attraction lining the Gold Coast. Many reasonably priced B&Bs are booked far in advance; reserve a room before you arrive. West Palm Beach is the best bet for an affordable room near the action, but the absolute cheapest options are the chain hotels near the highway.

◆ Hibiscus House Downtown Bed & Breakfast, 213 S. Rosemary Ave. (☎561-833-8171 or 866-833-8171; www.hibiscushousedowntown.com), just down the block from CityPlace. Large, airy rooms right by the action. After a late night at the house bar, wake up to a gourmet breakfast. Rooms in summer from $110; in winter from $130. AmEx/D/MC/V. ❺

◆ Hibiscus House Bed & Breakfast, 501 30th St. (☎561-863-5633 or 800-203-4927), at the corner of Spruce St. Flanked by historic houses, Hibiscus Downtown's sister establishment is a quiet, antique-filled home with a heated pool out back. Call ahead for reservations in winter. Rooms Dec.-Mar. from $150; Apr.-Nov. from $100. AmEx/D/MC/V. ❺

Hotel Biba, 320 Belvedere Rd. (☎561-832-0094; www.hotelbiba.com), in West Palm Beach. Fun, funky, and eclectic. Don't be fooled by its lackluster turquoise exterior; Hotel Biba, with quirky furniture and an elegant courtyard, has become a haven for travelers with a sense of style. Beautiful bodies lounge on the pool deck and gather in the garden bar for drinks in the evening. Break-

AT LEAST THE WORST IS OVER?

Charley, Ivan, Jeanne, and Katrina are persona non grata in the southeastern US. Over the last few years, these hurricanes tore through the East Coast, displacing thousands of people and causing an estimated $1 trillion in damages. The East Coast's tempestuous relationship with hurricanes is getting messier—the number of storms hurtling towards the coast is increasing. According to the National Oceanic and Atmospheric Administration (NOAA), the Southeast is likely to see more hurricanes in the years to come. Hurricane seasons come in cycles of high and low activity depending on atmospheric and oceanic conditions. From 1971 to 1994 hurricane activity was relatively low, but in 1995 the new active cycle began, bringing an increase in the frequency and power of storms. The 2005 season broke records in several categories, including total number of hurricanes and number of category five hurricanes. Some scientists have suggested that global warming may be a contributing factor. Others have argued that the current active cycle may seem unusually powerful only because of improvements in record keeping and satellite imagery since the last cycle. Whatever the cause, NOAA warns that the current cycle could last for 10-40 years. It may be time for southeast

fast included. Rooms Apr.-Nov. from $109; Dec.-Mar. from $180. AmEx/D/MC/V. ❺

Heart of Palm Beach Hotel, 160 Royal Palm Way (☎561-655-5600). This hotel is reasonably inexpensive way to stay in Palm Beach; it's just down the street from the beach and ritzy Worth Ave. Internet access, refrigerators, TV, balconies, heated pool. Reservations recommended. Rooms mid-Apr. to mid-Dec. from $129; mid-Dec. to mid-Apr. from $350; under 18 free with parents. AmEx/MC/V. ❺

🎭 NIGHTLIFE

West Palm Beach's nightlife centers on Clematis St. and nearby CityPlace. Shuttles run between the two locations. Clematis St. in downtown West Palm Beach offers a lively option for travelers on the cheap, with a Wednesday to Saturday nightlife scene that rivals any college town. For 23 years, **Ray's Downtown Blues,** 519 Clematis St., has featured local bands as well as national acts. The early show (6:30-10:30pm) draws mainly indie rock and emo bands; from 10:30pm to 2am it's all blues, baby. (☎561-835-1577. Open daily 6:30pm-2am. AmEx/D/MC/V.) Down the street at the **Monkey Club,** 219 Clematis St., a crowd of hip yuppies frolics in a building reminiscent of a Caribbean Colonial mansion. (☎561-833-6500. Open Th 9pm-3am, F-Sa 9pm-4am. AmEx/MC/V.)

🚩 APPROACHING COCOA BEACH AND CAPE CANAVERAL: 140 MILES

From West Palm Beach, take **U.S. 1 N** to Ft. Pierce, and take **Route A1A N** into Cocoa Beach.

COCOA BEACH AND CAPE CANAVERAL

Cape Canaveral and the surrounding "Space Coast" were hot spots during the Cold War. Once the great Space Race began, the area took off—it became the base of operations for every major space exploration, from the Apollo moon landings to the current International Space Station effort. During summer launch dates, tourists pack the area and hotel prices follow NASA into the stratosphere. The town of Cocoa Beach is full of beach bums and surfers; make sure to catch a wave while in the area.

🚗 GETTING AROUND

The Space Coast, 50 mi. east of Orlando, consists of mainland Cocoa and Rockledge, oceanfront Cocoa Beach and Cape Canaveral, and Merritt Island. Both **I-95** and **U.S. 1** run north-south on the mainland, while **Rte. A1A (N. Atlantic Ave.)** is the beach's main drag. East-west **Rte. 520** connects Cocoa Beach with the mainland, while **Rte. 528** connects Cape Canaveral to Merritt Island.

👁 SIGHTS

SPACE SIGHTS. All of **NASA's** shuttle flights take off from the **Kennedy Space Center,** 18 mi. north of Cocoa Beach on Rte. 3. The **Kennedy Space Center Visitors Complex (KSC)** provides a huge welcome center, complete with two 3D IMAX theaters, a Rocket Garden, and exhibits on the latest in-space exploration. KSC offers two tours of their 220 sq. mi. grounds. The **Kennedy Space Center Tour** features the three main attractions: the LC 39 Observation Gantry, where visitors can see the launchpads and assembly buildings; the Apollo/Saturn V Center, which houses a 363 ft. rocket; and the International Space Station Center. Meet a real space pioneer face-to-face at the daily **Astronaut Encounter,** in which astronauts of the past and present discuss their other-

EAST COAST

worldly experiences. The **NASA Up Close Tour** provides access to facilities that are restricted on the standard tour. Guides take you to the shuttle launch pad, the gigantic VAB building (where the shuttle is put together), and the Crawler Transporter. Check NASA's **launch schedule**—you may have a chance to watch Endeavor, Atlantis, or Discovery thunder off into the blue yonder above the Cape. A combo package will get you admission to the visitors complex and transportation to a viewing area to watch the fiery ascension. The **Cape Canaveral: Then and Now Tour** goes to the first launch site, the Air Force Space and Missile Museum, and the Cape Canaveral Lighthouse. *(Follow Rte. A1A N as it joins Rte. 528 W onto Merritt Island, then to Rte. 3 N. ☎321-452-2121 or 321-449-4444; www.kennedyspacecenter.com. Open daily 9am-6pm. Tours 9am-2:45pm. Standard KSC grounds tour $31, ages 3-11 $21. "Maximum Access" tour $38/$28, including admission to the Astronaut Hall of Fame and space simulators. Up Close and Cape Canaveral tour $22/$16. Astronaut Encounter $23/$16. Launch viewing $18/$14.)*

OUTDOORS. Surrounding the NASA complex, the 140,000-acre **Merritt Island National Wildlife Refuge** teems with sea turtles, manatees, 21 endangered species, and over 300 species of birds. Spot wildlife from your car on the 7 mi. **Black Point Wildlife Drive**, or hike the 5 mi. **Cruickshank Trail** for a closer look at the marshes. *(Take Rte. A1A/528 off Cape Canaveral, over Merritt Island, onto the mainland, and take U.S. 1 N through Titusville. Turn east onto Rte. 406, cross the bridge, and bear right on S.R. 402. ☎321-861-0667; www.merrittislandwildlife.org. Open daily sunrise-sunset. Visitors center open M-F 8am-4:30pm, Sa-Su 9am-5pm. Free.)* **Canaveral National Seashore,** on the northeastern shore of the refuge, covers 67,000 acres of undeveloped beach and dunes. Launch boats at nearby Playalinda Beach, or swim under lifeguards' supervision from June to Sept. *(Take Rte. 406 E off U.S. 1, in Titusville. ☎321-867-0677. Open daily Apr.-Oct. 6am-8pm; Nov.-Mar. 6am-6pm. Closed 3 days before and 1 day after NASA launches. $3 per person.)*

BEACHES. They don't call it Cocoa Beach for nothing—by the Atlantic you'll find windswept surfers and sunbathers galore. For volleyball, fishing, and a boardwalk that extends over the Atlantic, there's the **Cocoa Beach Pier.** *(401 Meade Ave., off Rte. A1A. ☎321-783-7549. Free.)* Those low on essentials like surf wax and sunscreen will find them at **Ron Jon Surf Shop.** Boards cover the walls of the two-story building, which has, oddly enough, attracted a large tourist following. *(4275 N. Atlantic Ave. ☎321-799-8840. Open 24hr.)*

☙ FOOD

Prime beachside real estate and live music make the pastel-colored **Coconuts on the Beach ❷**, 2 Minutemen Causeway, at Rte. A1A, a popular hangout for folks of all ages. Try the classic crab cake ($7) for lunch or the coconut-crusted mahi-mahi ($15) for dinner while chilling on the deck and watching surfers. (☎321-784-1422. Open daily 11am-10pm. AmEx/D/MC/V.) The **Sunrise Diner ❶**, 365 W. Cocoa Beach Causeway, at Rte. 520, serves Greek food alongside typical diner fare. Gyro ($5) or corned beef ($5.50), it's all delicious; be sure to save room for pie ($2), baked fresh daily. (☎321-783-5647. Open daily 6am-9pm. AmEx/D/MC/V.) Chandeliers hang over a collection of teapots at **The Tea Room ❶**, 6006 N. Atlantic Ave. (Rte. A1A), which combines home cookin' and a little TLC. Locals regularly take advantage of the dirt-cheap prices and relaxed, friendly atmosphere, chowing down Belgian waffles ($3) and $6 chicken salad sandwiches. (☎321-783-5527. Open Tu-F 7:30am-2pm, Sa-Su 8am-2pm. Cash only.) For an authentic Cuban meal, try **Roberto's Little Havana ❷**, 26 N. Orlando Ave., where *tostones* ($2.25) and Cuban sandwiches ($6.25) are served up in a casual dining room. (☎321-784-1868. Open Tu-Th and Su 6am-3pm and 5-9pm, F-Sa 6am-3pm and 5-10pm. AmEx/D/MC/V.)

⚷ ACCOMMODATIONS

Wary of wild teenagers, some hotels in Cocoa Beach rent rooms only to guests who are 21+. Across from the beach, **Motel 6 ❸**, 3701 N. Atlantic Ave. (Rte. A1A), offers clean, comfortable rooms at cheaper rates than most accommodations in the area. (☎321-783-3103; www.motel6.com. A/C, TV, heated pool, laundry, and shuffleboard. Rooms $60-70. AmEx/D/MC/V.) The hot-pink and wondrously tacky **Fawlty Towers Resort ❸**, 100 E. Cocoa Beach

Causeway, off Rte. A1A, includes a heated pool and a tiki bar, and the entire video collection of Fawlty Towers. (☎321-784-3870 or 800-887-3870. Rooms in summer $60-70; in winter $130-140. AmEx/MC/V.) Partying teens and vacationing families alike flock to the **Cocoa Beach Comfort Inn ❹**, 3901 N. Atlantic Ave., which offers visitors enormous rooms with all the perks, including pool, A/C, cable TV, coffeemakers, and an outdoor bar. (☎321-783-2221. 18+. Rooms May-Oct. $70-80; Nov.-Apr. $100-130. AmEx/D/MC/V.) Eight miles down the road in Cocoa proper, the **Dixie Motel ❸**, 301 Forrest Ave., is a family-owned establishment with clean rooms, floor-to-ceiling windows, A/C, cable TV, and a swimming pool. (☎321-632-1600. From A1A, take Rte. 528 W. Laundry available. 21+. Rooms $55. AmEx/MC/V.) Pitch your tent at scenic **Jetty Park Campgrounds ❷**, 400 E. Jetty Rd., at the northern tip of Cape Canaveral. There are hundreds of sites, which include sewer hookup, showers, laundry, a playground, a swimming beach, a volleyball court, and a dump site. (Follow Rte. A1A N. ☎321-783-7111. Reserve 3 months ahead. 3-week maximum stay. Sites May-Dec. $20, with water and electricity $25, with full hookup $30; Jan.-Apr. $30/$35/$40. MC/V.)

◗ NIGHTLIFE

Bars line Rte. A1A by the ocean, all with outdoor patios to catch the cool night breezes. One of the best is **Coconuts on the Beach**, 2 Minutemen Causeway (see p. 70), which has live rock music every Tu-Su 8:30-11pm. (☎321-784-1422. Open daily 11am-10pm. AmEx/D/MC/V.) Take Rte. A1A N to Port Canaveral at Exit B to find a row of brightly lit bars. At the end of the row, **Grills**, 505 Glen Cheek Dr., has live rock and reggae every W-Su on a patio. (321-868-2226. Open M-Th 11am-10pm, F-Su 11am-midnight or later. AmEx/D/MC/V.)

◖ DETOUR
DISNEY WORLD
Take I-4 W to Exit 64 for the Magic Kingdom and MGM Studios. Take Exit 65 for the Animal Kingdom and Exit 67 for EPCOT Center.

Disney World is the Rome of central Florida: all roads lead to it. Within this Never-Never-land, theme parks, resorts, theaters, restaurants, and nightclubs all work together to form the "happiest place on earth." The four main parks are the Magic Kingdom, EPCOT, MGM Studios, and Animal Kingdom, but Disney offers innumerable other attractions with different themes and—of course—separate admissions. (☎407-939-6244; www.disneyworld.com. 1 park $67, ages 3-9 $55; 4-day Park Hopper Pass $248/$211.)

🎫 **APPROACHING DAYTONA BEACH: 79 MILES**
From Cocoa Beach, take **Rte. A1A/528 N** past Cape Canaveral. Take **U.S. 1 N** until you hit Daytona Beach.

DAYTONA BEACH

When locals first started auto-racing on the hard-packed shores of Daytona Beach more than 60 years ago, they combined two aspects of life that would come to define the city's entire mentality: speed and sand. Daytona played an essential role in the founding of the **National Association of Stock Car Auto Racing (NASCAR)** in 1947, and the Daytona International Speedway still hosts several big races each year. Though races no longer occur on the sand, 23 mi. of Atlantic beaches still pump the lifeblood of the community.

VITAL STATS

Population: 64,422

Visitor Info: Daytona Beach Area Convention and Visitors Bureau, 126 E. Orange Ave. (☎800-854-1234 or 386-255-0415; www.daytonabeachcvb.org), on City Island. Open M-F 9am-5pm.

Internet Access: Volusia County Library Center, 105 E. Magnolia Ave. (☎386-257-6036). Open M-Th 9am-7pm, F 9am-5pm, Sa 9am-3pm, Su 1–5pm. Free.

Post Office: 220 N. Beach St. (☎386-226-2618). Open M-F 8:30am-5pm, Sa 10am-noon. **Postal Code:** 32115.

◗ GETTING AROUND

U.S. 1 parallels the coast and the barrier island. **Atlantic Ave. (Rte. A1A)** is the main drag along the shore. **International Speedway Blvd. (U.S. 92)** runs east-west from the ocean through the downtown area to the racetrack. Daytona Beach is a collection of smaller towns; many street numbers are not consecutive and navigation can be difficult, so stick to the main roads. To avoid the gridlock on the beach, arrive early (8am) and leave early (around 3pm). Visitors must pay $5 to drive onto the beach, and police enforce the 10 mph speed limit. Free parking is plentiful during most of the year but sparse during spring break (usually mid-Feb. to Apr.), **Speedweek, Bike Week, Biketoberfest,** and the **Pepsi 400.**

🐚 SIGHTS

The ■**Museum of Arts and Sciences**, 352 S. Nova Rd., combines traditional and decorative art, natural history, and science in its displays. The museum complex includes several miniature museums, two trains, and nature trails. Check out the **Cuban Museum**, donated by President Batista just two years before his overthrow, for a look into the country's artistic and historical past. Visit the enormous giant sloth, or see the **Root Family Museum,** which has classic cars, Coke paraphernalia, and hundreds of teddy bears on display. (☎386-255-0285; www.moas.org. Open M-Sa 9am-5pm, Su 11am-5pm. $13, students and seniors $11, ages 6-17 $7, under 6 free.)

The center of the racing world, the **Daytona International Speedway** hosts the Daytona 500 every February. **Speedweek** precedes the legendary race, while the Pepsi 400 heats up the track in early July. Next door, **Daytona USA,** 1801 W. International Speedway Blvd., includes a simulation ride, an IMAX film, and a program on NASCAR commentating. Included with admission is a walk through a hall of winning cars, an exhibit on the history of car racing, and the NASCAR IMAX movie. The **Speedway Tour** is a chance to see the garages, grandstands, and 31° banked turns up close; you can even take a photo on Victory Lane. The **Richard Petty Driving Experience** puts fans in a stock car for a 150 mph ride-along. (☎386-947-6800, NASCAR tickets 385-253-7223. Open daily 9am-7pm. Tours every 30min. daily 9:30am-5pm. $21.50, seniors $18.50, ages 6-12 $15.50. Tours $8.50. Richard Petty ☎800-237-3889. 14+. $134. Speedway $8.50. NASCAR simulator $5.)

To learn about the origins of the race, go to the **Halifax Historical Museum,** 252 S. Beach St., which also displays Spanish artifacts, old cameras, and a

victrola. Upstairs, play with a spinning wheel and antique toys to your inner child's content. (☎386-255-6976; www.halifaxhistorical.org. Open Tu-Sa 10am-4pm. $4, ages 3-12 $1.) Daytona Beach was the only place to allow young Jackie Robinson to suit up for his AAA spring training in 1946. During the summer, check out the single-A Daytona Cubs on the diamond where he played at **Jackie Robinson Ballpark,** 105 E. Orange Ave. (☎386-257-3172. Games Apr.-Aug. Tickets $6.)

🍴 FOOD

Glass bottles and signs line the walls of ■**The Dancing Avocado Kitchen ❷,** 110 S. Beach St., welcoming vegans and carnivores alike. Enjoy the "dancer" sandwich (avocado, cheese, sprouts, and tomato; $6.25) or the portobello veggie panini ($6.25) while people-watching from the patio. (☎386-947-2022. Open M-Sa 8am-4pm. AmEx/D/MC/V.) One of the most famous (and popular) seafood restaurants in the area is **Aunt Catfish's ❺,** 4009 Halifax Dr., at Dunlawton Ave., next to the Port Orange Bridge. Order anything that resides under the sea and you're in for a treat, though the lobster tails ($16) and catfish ($10) receive the most praise. The relaxed atmosphere means diners don't need to dress up, but with nightly crowds, you might want to call ahead for reservations. (Take Rte. A1A S. to Dunlawton Ave., turn right, and follow the road over the bridge; Halifax Dr. is on the right. ☎386-767-4768; www.auntcatfish.com. Open M-Sa 11:30am-10pm, Su 9am-10pm. D/MC/V.) Arabic music plays in **Pasha's Middle East Cafe ❶,** 919 W. International Speedway Blvd., where you'll find fresh falafel ($4.25) and baklava ($1.25). After you eat, stock up on dates and pistachios in the attached grocery. (☎386-257-7753. Open M-Sa 10am-7pm, Su noon-6pm. MC/V.)

🏠 ACCOMMODATIONS

Almost all of Daytona's accommodations cluster on **Atlantic Ave. (Rte. A1A),** either on the beach or across the street; those off the beach offer the best deals. Spring break and race events drive prices to absurdly high levels, but low-season rates are more reasonable. Almost all the motels facing the beach cost $59 for a low-season single; on the other side of the street it's $39. The **Camellia Motel ❷**, 1055 N. Atlantic Ave. (Rte. A1A), across the street from the beach, is an especially welcoming retreat with cozy, bright rooms, free local calls, cable TV, and A/C. (☎386-252-9963. Reservations recommended. Rooms $45-69. MC/V.) Near the boardwalk, you'll find the **Daytona Shore Inn ❷**, 805 N. Atlantic Ave., a clean motel with cable TV, fridges, and microwaves. (☎386-253-1441. Singles $39. AmEx/D/MC/V.) For a truly unique sleeping experience, try the **Travelers Inn ❷**, 735 N. Atlantic Ave. Each of the 22 rooms has a different theme: find the force with Yoda in the *Star Wars* room or dream of checkered flags in the NASCAR room. (☎386-253-3501 or 800-417-6466. Key deposit $10. Singles $35-45; doubles $55-65. AmEx/D/MC/V.) **Tomoka State Park ❶**, 2099 N. Beach St., 8 mi. north of Daytona in Ormond Beach, has 100 sites under a tropical canopy. Enjoy saltwater fishing, nature trails, and a sculpture museum. Unfortunately, no swimming is allowed. (☎386-676-4050, reservations 800-326-3521. From A1A N, take Granada Blvd. west to N. Beach St. Open daily 8am-sunset. $4 per vehicle. Sites $22.50. AmEx/D/MC/V.)

📷 NIGHTLIFE

When spring break hits, concerts, hotel-sponsored parties, and other events answer the call of students. News travels fastest by word of mouth, but the *Calendar of Events* and *SEE Daytona*

Beach make good starting points. On mellow nights, head to the boardwalk to play volleyball or shake your groove-thang to rock or jazz at the **Oceanfront Bandshell,** an open-air amphitheater. Dance clubs thump along Seabreeze Blvd., just west of N. Atlantic Ave. **Ocean Deck,** 127 S. Ocean Ave., behind the Wendy's, stands out among the clubs because of its live music on the beach and laid-back atmosphere. Sip the house specialty Red Tide ($5) while grooving to reggae, jazz, and calypso. (☎386-253-5224. Nightly live music 9:30pm-last customer. 21+ after 9pm. Open daily 11am-3am. Kitchen closes 2am. AmEx/D/MC/V.) **Razzle's,** 611 Seabreeze Blvd., has been a fixture in Daytona for 20 years. Its high-energy dance floors, flashy light shows, and popular ladies' night each W keep locals and tourists happy. (☎386-257-6236. 18+. Cover $5-10. Open M 8pm-midnight, Tu-Sa 8pm-3am. AmEx/D/MC/V.)

⚑ APPROACHING ST. AUGUSTINE: 43 MILES

Continue following **Rte. A1A** to St. Augustine.

ST. AUGUSTINE

In 1513, Spaniard Ponce de León came to these shores in search of the legendary Fountain of Youth. Fifty-two years later, Pedro Menéndez de Aviles founded St. Augustine in 1565, making it the first European colony in North America and the oldest continuous settlement in the US. Though Wal-Marts and drive-thrus have sprung up alongside

GREASED LIGHTING

The National Association of Stock Car Racing, or NASCAR, has the most live spectators of any sport in America. NASCAR claims 40 million so-called "hardcore fans," who spend 9 hours per week on NASCAR-related media and spend $900 a year on NASCAR products. And it's not just Southerners, either; the proportion of fans in each region closely matches the proportion of Americans as a whole. Though NASCAR hasn't been around very long, its fans may not be aware of its unconventional origins. NASCAR was born during Prohibition, when bootleggers ran alcohol from their workshops to their thirsty clients. "Coppers" were, of course, in hot pursuit, so bootleggers had to be fast, and they worked hard to make their vehicles faster and faster. The bootleggers tested their new designs by driving around long ovals—the precursors of the NASCAR tracks we see today. It was only a matter of time before they started competing with one another and, when people began attending the races, promoters realized they had a viable spectator sport on their hands. The races moved from empty fields to the beaches of Daytona, and NASCAR was officially formed in 1947. The first race was held in Charlotte, North Carolina, in 1949. Even without the cops in the rear view mirror, they

buildings made of coquina shell, St. Augustine's historic district and Spanish flavor remain intact. This city's pride lies in its provincial cobblestone streets, coquina-rock walls, and antique shops, rather than in its token beaches. Most consider the Fountain of Youth a legend, but don't be too sure—St. Augustine looks awfully good for its age.

VITAL STATS

Population: 12,157

Visitor Info: St. Augustine Visitors Center, 10 Castillo Dr. (☎904-825-1000; www.oldcity.com), at San Marco Ave. Open daily 8:30am-5:30pm.

Internet Access: St. Johns County Public Library, 1960 N. Ponce de Leon Blvd. (☎904-827-6940). Open M-W 9:30am-9pm, Th-F 9:30am-6pm, Sa 9:30am-5pm, Su 1-5pm. Free.

Post Office: 99 King St. (☎904-825-0628). Open M-F 8:30am-5pm, Sa 9am-1pm. **Postal Code:** 32084.

⌐ GETTING AROUND

Most of St. Augustine's sights lie within a 10-15min. walk from the Pirate Haus Inn and Hostel and motels. Narrow streets and frequent one-ways can make driving in St. Augustine unpleasant. Free parking is scarce—park at your accommodations or be prepared to pay a fee. The city's major east-west routes, **King St.** and **Cathedral Pl.,** run through downtown and become the Bridge of Lions that leads to the beaches. **San Marco Ave.,** or **Avenida Menendez,** runs north-south. **Castillo Dr.** diverges from San Marco Ave. near the center of town. **Saint George St.,** a north-south pedestrian route, contains most of the shops and many of the sights in town. While St. Augustine can certainly be navigated by foot, **Sightseeing Trains,** 170 San Marco Ave., shuttle travelers on a trolley that hits all the major attractions on its 20 stops. (☎904-829-6545 or 800-226-6545. Runs every 15-20min. 8:30am-5pm. 3-day pass $18, ages 6-12 $6. MC/V.)

⊙ SIGHTS

FOUNTAIN OF YOUTH. No trip to St. Augustine would be complete without a trek down beautiful Magnolia Ave. to the **Fountain of Youth,** the legend that sparked Ponce de León's voyage to the New World. Forget L.A.'s pricey plastic surgeons—eternal youth comes cheap around these parts—about $5.75, to be exact, in the form of admission to the famed Fountain of Youth. With animatronic Spanish figures and brightly painted dioramas, it's the ultimate in tacky fun. To capture the historical significance of the place, take a swig of the sulfurous libation, and try to ignore the fact that the water now runs through a pipe. (*11 Magnolia Ave. Take a right right on Williams St. from San Marco Ave., and continue until it dead-ends into Magnolia Ave. ☎904-829-3168 or 800-356-8222. Open daily 9am-5pm. $6.50, seniors $5.50, ages 6-12 $3.50.*)

SPANISH HERITAGE. The oldest masonry fortress in the continental US, **Castillo de San Marcos National Monument** has 14 ft. thick walls built of coquina, a material chosen because the shell rock does not shatter under cannon fire. The fort, a four-pointed star complete with drawbridge and moat, contains a museum, a large courtyard, garrison quarters, a jail, a chapel, and the original cannon brought overseas by the Spanish. (*1 Castillo Dr., off San Marco Ave. ☎904-829-6506. Monument open daily 8:45am-5:15pm; last entry 4:45pm. Grounds open 5:30am-midnight. Ranger-led tours every hr. starting 10am. $6, under 16 free.*) One of the most significant religious sights in the US is the **Shrine of our Lady de la Leche and Mission of Nombre de Dios,** where the first Mass in the US was held over 400 years ago. A 208 ft. cross commemorates the city's founding, and the shaded lawns and view of Matanzas Bay make for a lovely stroll. Casual visitors should be respectful of those there for religious purposes. (*27 Ocean St., off San Marco Ave. ☎904-824-2809. Open M-F 8am-5pm, Sa 9am-5pm, Su 9:30am-5pm. Mass M-F 8am, Sa 5pm, Su 7, 9, 11am, 6pm. Donation suggested.*)

HISTORIC BUILDINGS. Visitors can take a spirited student-led tour through ▨**Flagler College,** a small liberal arts institution housed in the restored Spanish Renaissance-style **Ponce de León Hotel.** Constructed by railroad and Standard Oil tycoon Henry Flagler in 1888, the hotel served as a luxury playground for America's social elite. Celebrity heavyweights such as John Rockefeller and Will Rogers once strolled through the gorgeous interior, much of which was designed by Louis Comfort Tiffany. (☎904-819-6383; www.flagler.edu. Tours every hr. daily mid-May to mid-Aug. 10am-3pm. $6, under 12 $1.) In 1947, Chicago publisher and art lover Otto Lightner converted the Alcazar Hotel into the **Lightner Museum** to hold a collection of cut, blown, and burnished glass, as well as old clothing and oddities. Today, the museum houses everything from antique musical instruments to a Russian bath steam room. (75 King St. ☎904-824-2874; www.lightnermuseum.org. Open daily 9am-5pm; last entry 4:30pm. 18th-century musical instruments play daily 11am and 2pm. $8, military $6, students and ages 12-18 $2.) For the best view of the nation's oldest city and its surrounding waters, climb the 219 stairs of the **St. Augustine Lighthouse and Museum,** Florida's oldest lighthouse. Tour the 19th-century tower and keeper's house to learn about marine archaeological studies in the area waters. (81 Lighthouse Ave., off Rte. A1A. ☎904-829-0745; www.staugustinelighthouse.com. Open daily 9am-6pm. Tower, house, and grounds $8, seniors $7, ages 6-11 $5; house and grounds $5/$4/$3.)

HISTORICAL SIGHTS. Not surprisingly, the oldest continuous settlement in the US holds some of the nation's oldest artifacts. The **Gonzalez-Alvarez House** is not technically the oldest in the nation, but forgive the hyperbole—it's 300 years young. Constructed in the early 18th century, the house now serves as a tourist attraction, containing exhibits on the Spanish, British, and American heritage of the area; a museum; and ornamental gardens. (14 Saint Francis St. ☎904-824-2872; www.oldesthouse.org. Open daily 9am-5pm; tours every 30min. Last tour 4:30pm. $8, seniors $7, students $4.)

GATORS AND GILLS. The **St. Augustine Alligator Farm** allows visitors to get up close and personal with some of nature's finest reptiles, including 15 ft. long Maximo. The park, which has been delighting visitors since 1893, is the only place in the world where all 23 known crocodilian species live. Check out the white alligator from the Louisiana bayou, who, according to legend, bestows good luck on viewers. (On Rte. A1A S. ☎904-824-3337. Open daily 9am-6pm. Presentations every hr. Feeding daily noon and 3pm. $18, ages 5-11 $10.) The world's original oceanarium, **Marineland** was once the premier attraction in Florida, drawing thousands for its dolphin show. Several bankruptcies and a hurricane later, Marineland is rebuilding with an emphasis on small animal interactions. While the extravagant dolphin shows are no more, visitors can now play with the dolphins (10min.; $65), swim with them (1hr.; $150), and participate in research projects. And of course, adults and kids can still watch Flipper cruise through the 1.3 million-gallon tank. (9600 Oceanshore Blvd., off Rte. A1A, 14 mi. south of St. Augustine. ☎888-279-9194. Open daily 8:30am-4:30pm. $5, under 12 $2.50.)

▓ FOOD

The bustle of daytime tourists and the abundance of budget eateries make lunch in St. Augustine's historic district a delight, especially among the cafes and bars of **Saint George St.**

▨ **Bunnery Bakery and Cafe,** 121 Saint George St. (☎0904-829-6166). A casual cafe that offers hearty, Southern-style breakfasts. Try the eggs, biscuits, gravy, and grits ($6) or a hulking stack of pancakes ($4), and you'll be drawling in no time. In the afternoon, the Bunnery offers veggie paninis and salads. Open daily 8am-3pm. Cash only. ❶

Cafe del Hidalgo, 35 Hypolita St. (☎904-823-1196). St. Augustine may have been founded by Spaniards, but this restaurant honors Italy. Patrons line up for gelato ($4), then relax at the huge wooden tables. Free Internet access. Open M-Th and Sa-Su 9:30am-9pm, F-Sa 9:30am-10pm. AmEx/D/MC/V. ❶

Scarlett O'Hara's, 70 Hypolita St. (☎904-824-6535), at Cordova St. Monster "Big Rhett" burgers ($6) and full slabs of ribs ($15.50) are consumed by patrons who will never go hungry again. Live music, usually classic or Southern rock, entertains nightly out on the porch. Happy hour M-F 4-7pm with 2-for-1 drinks. Open daily 11am-12:30am. AmEx/D/MC/V. ❸

Pizzalley's, 117 St. George St. (☎904-825-2627). Scarf down a slice of pizza ($2.35) or a tremendous meatball sub ($6.50) in this inviting eatery. Open M-Th and Su 11am-8:30pm, F-Sa 11am-9pm. MC/V. ❶

▛ ACCOMMODATIONS

▨ **Pirate Haus Inn and Hostel,** 32 Treasury St. (☎904-808-1999; www.piratehaus.com), just off

St. George St. From Rte. A1A N, take Cordoba to Charlotte St. Hands-down the best place to stay in town, with spotless dorms, beautiful private rooms, and a great location. Weary travelers are pampered by a common room, full kitchen, Internet access, parking, and a pancake breakfast. Key and linen deposit $5. Dorms $16.50; private rooms $50-75. MC/V. ❶

Sunrise Inn, 512 Anastasia Blvd. (☎904-829-3888). The best option among the motels along Rte. A1A. Spacious rooms with kitchens. Access to a Holy Bible free of charge. A/C, cable TV, and pool. Singles M-Th and Su $34, F-Sa $44; doubles $39/$49. MC/V. ❷

Seabreeze Motel, 208 Anastasia Blvd. (☎904-829-8122). Clean rooms with fridge and pool access. A/C, cable TV, and free local calls. Rooms with kitchenettes available for weekly rentals. Singles M-Th and Su $49, F-Sa $59; doubles $59/$69. D/MC/V. ❸

Anastasia State Park, 1340a Rte. A1A (☎904-461-2033; www.floridastateparks.org/anastasia), 4 mi. south of the historic district. Nearby Salt Run and the Atlantic provide great windsurfing, swimming, and hiking. Within the park are the coquina quarries used to build the Castillo de San Marco. Reception 8am-sunset. Reservations recommended. Sites with water and electricity $23. Day-use $5 per vehicle, $1 per pedestrian. AmEx/D/MC/V. ❶

■ NIGHTLIFE

St. Augustine supports a variety of bars, many on Rte. A1A and Saint George St. *Folio Weekly* contains event listings. Local string musicians play on the two stages in the **Milltop,** 19½ Saint George St., a tiny yet illustrious bar above an old mill in the restored district. Sip a tall draft for $2.50 on Tuesday or Wednesday and enjoy the acoustic crooners. (☎904-829-2329. Daily music 1pm-midnight. Cover F-Sa $2. Open daily 11:30am-midnight. D/MC/V.) Sample your choice of 24 drafts at the **Oasis Deck and Restaurant,** 4000 Rte. A1A S, at Ocean Trace Rd. Up a flight of rickety stairs, there's live rock and reggae daily 8pm-12:30am and F 4-7pm. (☎904-471-3424. Gator tail $6. Open daily 6am-1am. Happy hour daily 4-7pm with $1.50 drafts. AmEx/D/MC/V.)

■ APPROACHING JACKSONVILLE: 40 MILES
From St. Augustine, take **U.S. 1 N** into town.

JACKSONVILLE

At almost 850 sq. mi., Jacksonville is geographically the largest city in the continental US. Because Jacksonville lacks top-draw tourist attractions, it's often overshadowed by cities to the south. However, Jacksonville's beautiful beaches, big-city museums, and revitalized downtown make it an undiscovered treat. While Jacksonville rolls up its carpets at 10pm, during the day visitors will find much to enjoy.

VITAL STATS

Population: 777,000

Visitor Info: Jacksonville and the Beaches Convention and Visitors Bureau, 550 Water St., Ste. 1000 (☎904-798-9111 or 800-733-2668; www.visitjacksonville.com). Open M-F 8am-5pm.

Internet Access: Jacksonville Main Public Library, 303 N. Laura St. (☎904-630-2665). Open M-Th 9am-8pm, F-Sa 9am-6pm, Su 1-6pm. Free.

Post Office: 311 W. Monroe St. (☎904-353-3445). Open M-F 8:30am-5pm, Sa 9am-1pm. **Postal Code:** 32202.

■ GETTING AROUND

Three highways intersect in Jacksonville, forming a cross with a C around it. Because Jacksonville is so large, it can take over an hour to get from one end to the other; be sure to leave a half-hour for transportation between most points. **I-95** runs north-south, while **I-10** starts downtown and heads west. **I-295** forms the giant "C" on the western half of the city, and **Arlington Expwy.** becomes **Atlantic Blvd. (Rte. 10)** heading to the beach. The St. Johns River snakes throughout the city.

■ SIGHTS

One of the nicest things to do in Jacksonville—weather permitting, of course—is to walk. San Marco, across the bridge from downtown, offers restaurants, shops, and

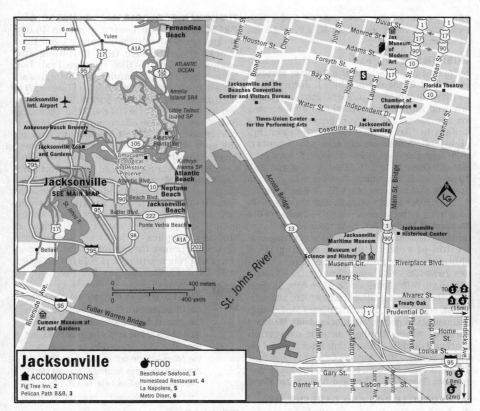

Jacksonville

🏠 **ACCOMODATIONS**
Fig Tree Inn, **2**
Pelican Path B&B, **3**

🍴**FOOD**
Beachside Seafood, **1**
Homestead Restaurant, **4**
La Napolera, **5**
Metro Diner, **6**

people-watching. Five Points, near the Cummer Museum, has an edgier mix of tattoo parlors and coffee shops. The newly completed Northbank Riverwalk allows joggers and strollers alike to enjoy the river for 2½ miles.

BEACHES. Miles of uncrowded white sands can be found at **Jacksonville Beach.** Fishermen stake out spots on the **Jacksonville Beach Pier** while golfers take advantage of the more than 20 area golf courses. Free parking lots run all along the beach, but they fill up quickly and there are no bathrooms. The **Boardwalk** is abuzz with activity, from musical festivals to sandcastle-building contests. Surfing and volleyball tournaments take place in May. (☎904-241-1515. $4 to fish, $1 per pedestrian. Open 6am-

10pm.) Those looking for a less crowded stretch of sand should try **Atlantic Beach** to the north. Staple Florida attractions are nearby, including a dog track, mini golf, go-karts, and a water park. (To reach the Atlantic Ocean take Rte. 90/Beach Blvd. or Rte. 10/Atlantic Blvd. heading east from downtown for about 30min.)

ANHEUSER-BUSCH BREWERY. Visitors from all over the globe unite under the banner of brewsky at the Anheuser-Busch Brewery Tour. Most are awed by their sneak peak at the factory where beer is born, though all are blown away by the "hospitality room," in which beer-lovers sample any two of Busch's 12 beers; designated drivers enjoy free soda and pretzels. (111 Busch Dr., Exit 360 off I-95,

10min. north of downtown. ☎ 904-696-8373; www.budweisertours.com. Tours M-Sa every 15min. 9am-4pm. Free.)

MUSEUMS. The beautiful gardens and reflecting pools behind the **Cummer Museum of Art and Gardens** line the St. Johns River south of downtown. Indoors, Baroque, Modern, and American Colonial exhibits impress art connoisseurs, while children and adults delight in "Art Connections," the exciting, high-tech, hands-on art education center. *(829 Riverside Ave. ☎ 904-356-6857; www.cummer.org. Open Tu and Th 10am-9pm, W and F-Sa 10am-5pm, Su noon-5pm. Free tours Tu 7pm, Su 3pm. $8, students and seniors $5. Tu 4-9pm free. Tu-F 1:30-4:30pm college students with ID free.)* Jacksonville's newest museum, the **Jacksonville Museum of Modern Art,** next door to the fountains of Hemming Plaza, offers a rotating collection of eclectic pieces, ranging from photography to interactive mechanical statues. *(☎ 904-366-6911; www.jmoma.org. Open Tu and F 11am-5pm, W-Th 11am-9pm, Sa 11am-4pm, Su noon-4pm. Tours $4; reservations required. $6; students, seniors, and under 12 $4. W 5-9pm free.)* Model-ship enthusiasts may enjoy the **Jacksonville Maritime Museum,** which displays antique navigation tools and models of ships that once docked on the St. Johns. *(1015 Museum Cir. Unit 2, Southbank Riverwalk Main St. ☎ 904-398-9011; www.jaxmarmus.com. Open M-F 10:30am-3pm, Sa-Su 1-5pm. Free.)*

JACKSONVILLE ZOO AND GARDENS. The Zoo has been largely redone in the last few years and now features lovely gardens and world-class exhibits. The AZA-honored "Range of the Jaguar" features big cats, while another area allows visitors to pet giraffes. *(Take I-95, Exit 358A to Heckscher Dr. E. ☎ 904-757-4463; www.jaxzoo.org. Open daily 9am-5pm. $11, seniors $9.50, ages 3-12 $6.50.)*

JESSE BALL DUPONT PARK. For a cool escape from the asphalt downtown, climb into the Treaty Oak, 200-year-old tree more than 70 ft. tall. Conservationists falsely said that the oak was the site of a settler-Indian treaty in order to save it from the axe. *(Corner of Prudential and Main St., on the south bank of the river. Open daily sunrise-sunset. Free.)*

TIMUCUAN ECOLOGICAL AND HISTORIC PRESERVE. This preserve contains 46,000 serene acres of saltwater marshes and tidal creeks teeming with fish, dolphins, and eagles. The 2 mi. Willie Browne Trail is a biker's paradise, meandering through salt marsh and maritime hammocks. *(Take I-95 N to Rte. 105 E, off Exit 124A. Signs point to the major sights and the visitors center. ☎ 904-641-7155. Open daily 8am-sunset. Free.)* One of the park's two historical sights is the **Ribault Monument,** marking the spot where, in 1562, French Huguenot Jean Ribault claimed the land for King Charles IX. Near the visitors center, **Fort Caroline National Memorial** was the site of a 1565 battle between Spanish and French Huguenot forces—the first armed conflict between European powers over a New World settlement. Today, visitors can try their hand at storming a replica of the fort, while the less aggressive peruse the museum's Native American and French artifacts. *(12713 Ft. Caroline Rd. ☎ 904-641-7155. Open daily 9am-5pm. Free.)*

PHOTO OP. In May of 1901, the entire city of Jacksonville burned to the ground in the greatest fire in Southern history. A grand total of 2300 buildings were destroyed, but they were soon replaced by the buildings of the future—made out of concrete. Look for the small plaque in Heming Plaza that states "Here started the Great Fire of 1901."

⚞ FOOD

Even a city as large as Jacksonville has a small-town diner, ⬛**The Metro Diner** ❷, 3302 Hendricks Ave., where locals gather for brunch. Enjoy the friendly banter over French toast ($6) or one of the daily blackboard specials. *(☎ 904-398-3701; www.metrodinerjax.com. Open daily 7am-2:30pm. AmEx/D/MC/V.)* You'll feel right at home at **The Homestead** ❹, 1712 Beach Blvd., where Southern favorites are served up for loyal locals. If you're brave, try the fried chicken gizzards ($5); the less adventurous can stick to the fried chicken for $13. *(☎ 904-249-9660. Open M-W and Su 11am-9:30pm, Th-Sa 11am-*

1979: Muppet Fozzy Bear utters the immortal line: "A bear in his natural habitat—a Studebaker."

EAST COAST

10pm. AmEx/D/MC/V.) Beach bums take a break from the rays at the **Beachside Seafood Market and Restaurant ❷,** 120 N. 3rd St. (Rte. A1A), by 2nd Ave., where the cooks fry up fish baskets ($7) and perch sandwiches ($5) with their own fresh catches. (☎904-241-4880. Open Tu-Sa 11am-9pm, Su 5-9pm. MC/V.) Spray-painted murals welcome hungry patrons to **La Nopalera ❷,** 1629 Hendricks Blvd., where you can get huge platters of tacos and enchiladas for $7-8. (☎904-399-1768. Open M-Th 11am-10pm, F-Sa 11am-10:30pm, Su noon-9pm. AmEx/MC/V.)

ACCOMMODATIONS

Inexpensive hotels abound along I-95 and on the Arlington Expwy. heading to the ocean. The cheapest options are the chains north of the city off I-95. Just steps from the sands of Jacksonville Beach, **Fig Tree Inn Bed and Breakfast ❹,** 185 4th Ave. S, offers six differently themed rooms, all including TV, VCR, and private baths. Enjoy your breakfast or afternoon tea on the front porch of this beach-style shingle cottage. (☎904-246-8855 or 877-217-9830. Singles M-F $75-85, Sa-Su $75-95. AmEx/D/MC/V.) Farther north, the **Pelican Path Bed and Breakfast ❺,** 11 N. 19th Ave., overlooks the ocean. Rooms include DVD player, fridge, and a full breakfast. (☎904-249-1177 or 888-749-1177. Rooms $125-175. AmEx/D/MC/V.) **Kathryn Abbey Hanna Park ❶,** 500 Wonderwood Dr., in Mayport, has 293 wooded sites near the beach, all with full hookup, and four cabins with A/C. Twenty miles of bike paths and a water playground are also on site. (☎904-249-4700. Cabin stay 2-night min. Reception 8am-9pm. Reservations recommended several months in advance for cabins. Apr.-Oct. Tent sites Apr.-Oct. $21, Nov.-Mar. $15; RV sites $34/$26; cabins $34/$26. MC/V.)

ENTERTAINMENT

Acts ranging from Ringo Starr to the Dixie Chicks to Gilbert and Sullivan theater companies have performed at the historic **Florida Theatre,** 128 E. Forsyth St. (☎904-355-2787), built in 1927. The theater hosts more than 300 performances per year; check out www.floridatheatre.com for upcoming shows and pric-

ing. **The Times-Union Center for Performing Arts,** 300 W. Water St. (☎904-633-6110), offers traveling Broadway shows, the Jacksonville Symphony, and local college productions. A different kind of popular culture thrives at the **Alltel Stadium** (☎904-633-2000), at E. Duval and Haines St., home to the NFL's Jaguars. The **Jacksonville Baseball Grounds,** 301 A. Philip Randolph Blvd., offers AA minor-league baseball from April through August for mere peanuts (☎904-358-2846. Tickets $5.50-19.50.) Much of Jacksonville's nightlife centers on **Jacksonville Landing,** at Main St. and Independent Dr., a riverfront area packed with restaurants, shops, and live entertainment. (☎904-353-1188. Open M-Th 10am-8pm, F-Sa 10am-9pm, Su noon-5:30pm.)

⚲ APPROACHING CUMBERLAND ISLAND: 65 MILES

From Jacksonville, take **Rte. A1A N** to the Cumberland Island Ferry. Take the ferry (every 30min. 6am-10pm; $3.25) and continue on A1A N. Just over the ferry is the **Kingsley Plantation.** When her husband died, former slave Anna Kingsley took over control of the plantation, including the slaves that worked it. Today, visitors can see the remains of the slave quarters, house, and barn. (☎904-251-3537. Open daily 9am-5pm. Free.) In Fernandina Beach, take **A1A/200 W** to **I-95 N.** Get off at **Exit 29** and take **Rte. 40 E** to the town of St. Mary's.

The Peach State

GEORGIA

Welcomes You!

CUMBERLAND ISLAND

Off the coast of southeastern Georgia, near the tiny town of St. Mary's, **Cumberland Island National Seashore** remains an astoundingly untouched piece of nature, with herds of wild horses roaming the 36,500 acres of the park. Up to 500 visitors per day can wander on near-deserted beaches, but be sure to pack a lunch, as only limited water is available on the island. (Day-use $4.) The park is only accessible by a ferry that leaves twice a day, so plan your visit ahead of time. Ferries leave from St.

EAST COAST

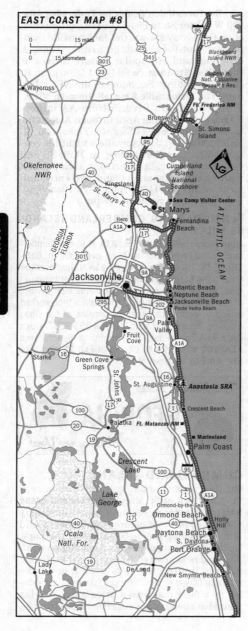

EAST COAST MAP #8

Mary's to two docks on the island. Tickets are sold at the visitors center on the mainland daily 8am-6pm. (☎912-882-4335 or 877-860-6787. Ferries depart from St. Mary's Mar.-Nov. daily 9, 11:45am; Dec.-Feb. M and Th-Su 9, 11:45am. Return from Cumberland Island Mar.-Sept. 10:15am, 2:45, 4:45pm; Oct.-Feb. 10:15am, 4:45pm. $15, seniors $12, under 13 $10.) On the southern end of the island, **Dungeness,** the ruins of the former home of Carnegie sibling Thomas and his wife Lucy, now lies covered in palm trees and ivy. A tour leaves from the Sea Camp dock 15min. after the ferry arrives. The **Ice House Museum,** located in the Carnegie's old ice house, documents the history of the island beginning with Native American settlers. (Open daily 8am-4pm. Free.) In St. Mary's, the **Cumberland Island Mainland Museum,** 169 Osborne St., provides info on the history of Cumberland. (☎912-882-4335. Open daily 1-4pm. Free.) If you wish to spend the night on the island, come prepared—aside from water, all provisions must be carried in and out. The only developed campground, **Sea Camp ❶,** is a 15min. walk from the Sea Camp dock and has cold water showers and bathrooms. (Sites $4.)

◪ **APPROACHING ST. SIMONS ISLAND: 26 MILES** Take **Rte. 40 W** back to **I-95 N.** Exit at **Rte. 17/25** and follow signs to St. Simon's Island.

ST. SIMONS ISLAND

St. Simons Island has long been a popular resort and vacation destination, with plenty of sun and fun for all. The beach is always busy by the pier and lighthouse; visitors can rent kayaks and sailboats. The Village, along Mallery St., is a fun, funky strip of restaurants and shops. **Neptune Park** is home to the **St. Simons Island Lighthouse.** The second lighthouse built on the island (the first was destroyed during the Civil War), it dates from 1872 and rises 104 ft. Climb 129 steps to the top for a breathtaking view of the area. (☎912-638-4666. Open M-Sa 10am-5pm, Su 1:30-5pm. $6, ages 6-12 $3.) Heading north on Frederica Rd. leads to **Fort Frederica,** a fort established by Georgia founder James Oglethorpe. A movie explains the fort's history and a walking tour leads visitors through the meager remains of the town to the fort itself. (☎912-638-3639; www.nps.gov/fofr. Open daily 8am-5pm. 7-day access $3.) Just before the Fort on Frederica Rd. lies **Christ Episcopal Church,** the 2nd-oldest Episcopal parish in the state. Built by shipbuilders, the ceiling looks like the hull of a ship. Across the street, the **Wesley Memorial Monument** celebrates Reverend Charles Wesley, who conducted the parish's first services in 1736. (☎912-638-8683. Open daily 2-5pm. Free.) Off Demere Rd. lies the frighteningly named **Bloody Marsh,** where Oglethorpe's men ambushed Spanish troops fighting to retake the island in 1742. The Marsh didn't really run red with blood—there were only 12 deaths—but the Spanish returned to St. Augustine and never again tried to take Georgia. (Open daily 8:30am-4pm. Free.)

The local favorite, **Dressner's Village Cafe ❶,** 223 Mallery St., serves basic Southern fare, three-egg veggie omelettes (with grits and biscuits, of course; $5) and delectable French toast ($4) with pecans and raisins. (☎912-634-1217. Open M-W 7:30am-2:30pm, Th-F 7:30am-2:30pm and 5:30-8pm, Sa-Su 8am-2:30pm and 5:30-8pm. MC/V.) **Zuzu's ❷,** 119 Mallery St., is an old-fashioned ice-cream shop with veggie meal options. Relax with a portobello mushroom sandwich ($6.50) and a milkshake ($3.50) after a day at the beach. (☎912-638-8655. Open 11am-9pm. MC/V.) For cheap accommodations in the heart of town, try 🢔**Queen's Court ❸,** 437 Kings Way, a clean, pretty motel located only a couple of blocks from the Village and the beach. (☎912-638-8459. Singles from $70; doubles from $76. MC/V.) The least expensive accommodations on the island are available at **Epworth by the Sea ❸,** 100 Arthur J. Moore Dr., a Methodist center that mostly hosts large groups for retreats and other events. (☎912-638-8688; www.epworthbythesea.org. Reservations required. Rooms $61-110. MC/V.)

🢔 APPROACHING SAVANNAH: 65 MILES
From St. Simon's Island, take **U.S. 17 N** to Savannah.

SAVANNAH

General James Oglethorpe and his band of 120 vagabonds founded Savannah in 1733, designing the city around over 20 beautiful green squares. Oglethorpe's design escaped Sherman's march through the South as it did modern-day expan-

sion. It now remains Georgia's greatest treasure. This is a walking city, with tree-lined roads and park benches so that tired travelers can "set for a spell." Be sure to strike out on foot and enjoy the streets that Sherman found too pretty to burn.

VITAL STATS
Population: 130,000
Visitor Info: Savannah Visitors Center, 301 Martin Luther King Jr. Blvd. (☎912-944-0455; www.savannahgeorgia.com), at Liberty St. Open M-F 8:30am-5pm, Sa-Su 9am-5pm.
Internet Access: Gallery Espresso, 234 Bull St. (☎912-233-5348). Free Wi-Fi.
Parking: A parking pass ($8), obtained at the public parking desk across from the visitors center, allows 2-day unlimited use of all metered parking, city lots, and garages.
Post Office: 2 N. Fahm St. (☎912-235-4619), at Bay St. Open M-F 7am-6pm, Sa 9am-3pm.
Postal Code: 31402.

EAST COAST

📭 GETTING AROUND

Savannah rests on the coast of Georgia at the mouth of the **Savannah River,** which runs north of the city along the border with South Carolina. The city stretches south from bluffs overlooking the river. The restored 2½ sq. mi. **downtown historic district,** bordered by **E. Broad St., Martin Luther King Jr. Blvd., Gwinnett St.,** and the river, is best explored on foot. Do not stray outside these borders; the historic district quickly deteriorates into an unsafe area. On the banks of the Savannah River, **River St.** is lined with shops, restaurants, and nightlife. The nearby **City Market,** by Franklin Sq., is another pleasant area to stroll and shop.

 PHOTO OP. At the eastern edge of the strip, there's a statue of **Savannah's Waving Girl.** Florence Martus waved at ships entering the harbor every day for over 30 years.

👁 SIGHTS

Most of Savannah's 21 squares contain some distinctive centerpiece, such as monuments or fountains. Elegant antebellum houses and drooping, vine-entangled trees often cluster around the squares, adding to the classic Southern aura. Simply visiting Savannah's squares is an excellent way to appreciate the beauty of the city. Bus and horse carriage tours leave from the visitors center, but walking can be more rewarding. The **Old Town Trolley Tours** allow on-and-off privileges at their 16 historic stops. (☎912-233-0083. Trains every 20min. 9am-4:30pm. $23, ages 4-12 $10.) Savannah's **free bus** system, Catham Area Transit (CAT) stops at 28 locations in the historic district. (Buses every 20min. M-Sa 7am-7pm, Su 9:40am-5pm. Free.)

HISTORIC HOUSES. Savannah is known for its beautiful, early 19th-century homes, which have been preserved thanks to a vocal preservation movement. Though all the historic homes are lovely, unless you have a particular interest in architecture, pick one tour as a representative of the genre. Built in 1820, the **Davenport House Museum** was the first home to be saved from the wrecking ball by the seven women of the Savannah Historical Foundation. Energetic docents show visitors the cantilevered staircase, beautiful marble fireplaces, and truly hideous 1820s wallpaper. (☎912-236-8097; www.davenporthousemuseum.org. 324 E. State St., on Columbia Sq. Open M-Sa 10am-4pm, Su 1-4pm. Tours every 30min.; last tour 4pm. $8, ages 7-18 $5. Seniors, military, AAA 10% discounts.) An example of English Regency architecture, the **Owens-Thomas House** includes three false doors, a bridge connecting two areas of the house, and an emphasis on symmetry. The Marquis de Lafayette stayed here in 1825. (124 Abercom St., on Oglethorpe Sq. ☎912-790-2003. Open M noon-5pm, Tu-Sa 10am-5pm, Su 1-5pm. Tours every 30min.; last tour 4:30pm. $9; seniors, military, AAA $8; students $6; ages 6-12 $4.) The **Green Meldrim House** is a Gothic Revival mansion that served as General Sherman's Savannah headquarters following his famed "march to the sea." It was from this house that Sherman wrote the famous telegram to President Lincoln, giving him the city as a gift. (14 W. Macon St., on Madison Sq. ☎912-232-1251. Open Tu and Th-F 10am-4pm, Sa 10am-1pm. Tours every 30min. $7, students $2.) The **Mercer-Williams House Museum,** built in 1868 and restored in 1969, is one of the town's most famous literary sites. Though the docents won't tell you, here lived Jim Williams, accused and acquitted four times of shooting hustler Danny Hansford in the case that inspired *Midnight in the Garden of Good and Evil.* (429 Bull St. ☎912-236-6352 or 877-430-6352. Open M-Sa 10:30am-4pm, Su 12:30-4pm. Tours every 40min. $12.50, students and ages 6-12 $8.)

FORT PULASKI NATIONAL MONUMENT. Savannah's four forts once protected the city's port from Spanish, British, and other invaders. The most intriguing, Fort Pulaski National Monument marks the Civil War battle where Union forces first used rifled cannons to decimate the Confederate opposition. (15 mi. east of Savannah on U.S. 80 E and Rte. 26. ☎912-786-5787. Open daily in summer 8:30am-6:45pm; in winter 9am-5pm. $3, under 16 free.)

JULIETTE GORDON LOW BIRTHPLACE. Girl Scout or not, you might want to check out this Victorian-era home. Guides tell stories of four generations of the Gordon family, with an emphasis on the near-deaf, quirky Juliette, who founded the Girl Scouts in 1912. (10 E. Oglethorpe Ave. ☎912-233-4501. Open M-Sa 4pm, Su 1-4pm. Tours every 15-25min. $8; adult Girl Scouts, students, ages 6-18 $7; current Girl Scouts $6.)

SAVANNAH HISTORY MUSEUM. Conveniently located in the same building as the visitors center, the Savannah History Museum has displays on Savannah history, a cotton gin, a steam locomotive, and memorabilia such as Forest Gump's bench. (303 Martin Luther King Jr. Blvd. ☎912-238-1779. Open M-F 8:30am-5pm, Sa-Su 9am-5pm. $4.25; seniors, students, active military, ages 6-11 $3.75.)

TELFAIR MUSEUM OF ART. The oldest art museum in the South, the Telfair Museum of Art was once a Regency-style mansion. Now it houses major works of the Ashcan School and the statue *Bird Girl*, depicted on the cover of *Midnight in the Garden of Good and Evil.* (121 Barnard St. ☎912-232-1177. Open M noon-5pm, Tu-Sa 10am-5pm, Su 1-5pm. $9; seniors, military, AAA $8; college students $6; ages 6-12 $4.) The ◙**Jepson Center for the Arts** is the new Contemporary wing of the Telfair and houses photographic, abstract, and modern pieces. The most stunning artistic feat is the building itself—with grand staircases, airy exhibit halls, and an outdoors sculpture garden,

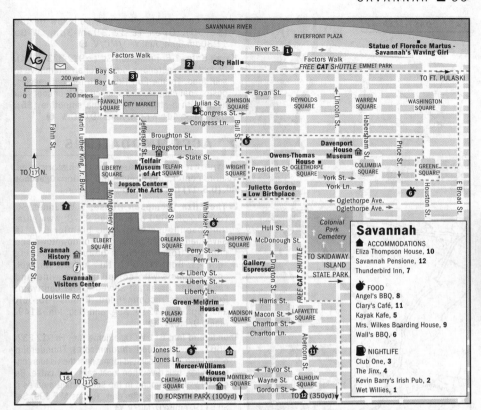

Savannah

🏠 ACCOMMODATIONS
Eliza Thompson House, **10**
Savannah Pensione, **12**
Thunderbird Inn, **7**

🍎 FOOD
Angel's BBQ, **8**
Clary's Café, **11**
Kayak Kafe, **5**
Mrs. Wilkes Boarding House, **9**
Wall's BBQ, **6**

🍸 NIGHTLIFE
Club One, **3**
The Jinx, **4**
Kevin Barry's Irish Pub, **2**
Wet Willies, **1**

it's an architectural triumph well worth visiting. *(207 W. York, on Telfair Sq. ☎912-790-8800. Open M noon-5pm, Tu-Sa 10am-5pm, Su 1-5pm. $9, seniors and military, college students $6, ages 6-12 $4.)*

🍴 FOOD

Mrs. Wilkes' Boarding House, 107 W. Jones St. (☎912-232-5997). A Southern institution where friendly folks gather around large tables for soul food served homestyle. The dining room fills up quickly with strangers uniting over fried chicken, okra, greens, cornbread, and more. All-you-can-eat $15. Open M-F 11am-2pm. Cash only. ❹

Clary's Café, 404 Abercorn St. (☎912-233-0402). Clary's has been serving up some of Savannah's best breakfasts since 1903. With blueberry pancakes ($5), sourdough French toast ($5), and free Wi-Fi, you might never want to leave. Open M-Th 7am-4pm, F 7am-5pm, Sa 8am-5pm, Su 8am-4pm. AmEx/D/MC/V. ❶

Wall's BBQ, 515 E. York Ln. (☎912-232-9754), in an alley between York St. and Oglethorpe Ave. This hole-in-the-wall serves up mouth-watering barbecue. Don't devour your delicious barbecue sandwich ($5.30) or ribs ($12.75) inside; most locals know to order and then savor their meal in one of the neighboring squares. Open Th-Sa 11am-9pm. Cash only. ❷

Angel's BBQ, 21 W. Oglethorpe Ln. (☎912-495-0902), hidden in an alley off Whitaker and Hull. It doesn't look like much inside, but you won't mind when you taste the grub. Try one of the

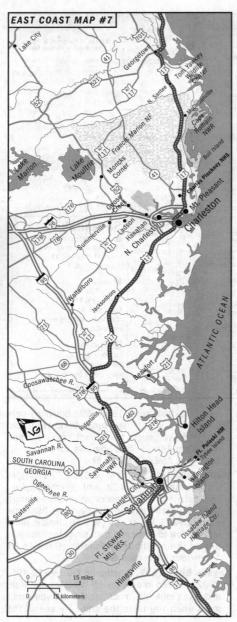

huge pork sandwiches with coleslaw on top ($5.50). Open Tu 11:30am-3pm, W-Sa 11:30am-6pm. AmEx/D/MC/V. ❷

Kayak Kafe, 1 E. Broughton St. (☎912-233-6044). Perfect for vegetarians looking for an alternative to soul food. Try the Ebb Tide, with roasted veggies, pesto, goat cheese, and spinach ($7), or cool your heels with a strawberry-banana smoothie ($5). Open M-Sa 11am-6pm. AmEx/D/MC/V. ❷

ACCOMMODATIONS

Downtown motels cluster near the historic area, visitors center, and Greyhound station. **Ogeechee Rd. (U.S. 17)** has several budget options.

The Eliza Thompson House, 5 W. Jones St. (☎912-236-3620 or 800-348-9378; www.eliza-thompsonhouse.com). The premier B&B in Savannah, located in the heart of downtown and minutes from the city's beautiful, bustling squares. Built in 1847, this historic inn welcomes guests with complimentary wine and cheese and breakfast served in the courtyard. Reservations recommended. Rooms Feb.-July and Sept.-Nov. $210; Aug. and Dec.-Jan. $149. AmEx/D/MC/V. ❺

Thunderbird Inn, 611 W. Oglethorpe Ave. (☎912-232-2661; www.thethunderbirdinn.com). Thunderbird offers large, well-decorated rooms near the visitors center. Fridge, hair dryer, free local calls, and cable. Be careful walking around in the surrounding area as it may become unsafe after dark. Rooms M-F $99, Sa-Su $119. AmEx/D/MC/V. ❹

Savannah Pensione, 304 E. Hall St. (☎912-236-7744). A former hostel, Savannah Pensione is a bit run-down, offering little more than a bed and a roof, but is located only minutes from some of Savannah's greatest sights. The surrounding area may be unsafe at night. Bike rental $10. Reception 7-10am and 5-11pm; call ahead for late-night check-in. Rooms with shared bath $40-55. Cash only. ❷

Skidaway Island State Park (☎912-598-2300 or 800-864-7275), 6 mi. southeast of downtown off Diamond Causeway; follow Liberty St. east from downtown until it becomes Wheaton St.; turn right on Waters Ave., and follow it to Diamond Causeway. The park has 88 sites with bathrooms, hot-water showers, electricity, and water, as well as miles of hiking trails. Open daily 7am-10pm. Reservations recommended. Sites $22, with hookup $24. ❶

ENTERTAINMENT

Green is the theme of the **St. Patrick's Day Celebration on the River** (☎912-234-0295), a five-day, beer- and fun-filled party that packs the streets and warms celebrants up for the annual **St. Patrick's Day Parade** (☎912-233-4804), the second-largest in the US. During the annual **NOGS Tour of the Hidden Gardens of Historic Savannah** (☎912-961-4805), in late April, private-walled gardens are opened to the public, who can join in a special Southern tea. **First Friday for the Arts** (☎912-232-4903) occurs on the first Friday of each month in City Market, when art galleries open their doors to visitors. **First Saturday on the River** (☎912-234-0295) brings arts, crafts, entertainment, and food to historic River St. each month. The free *Connect Savannah*, found in restaurants and stores, has the latest in news and entertainment.

NIGHTLIFE

The waterfront area on **River St.** is one of the five places in the nation where you can walk with an open container of alcohol. Not surprisingly, it brims with endless dining opportunities, street performers, and a friendly pub ambience.

Wet Willies, 101 E. River St. (☎912-233-5650). If sugary drinks are your pleasure, this is the place for you. Try the Call a Cab, the strongest drink in the house ($5-7). Tequila wings $8. M-Tu Karaoke. F-Sa DJ. Open M-Th and Su 11:15am-1am, F-Sa 11:15am-2am. Cash only.

Kevin Barry's Irish Pub, 117 W. River St. (☎912-233-9626). Hosts a laid-back crowd relaxing over Guinness and Irish folk music. Nightly music after 8:30pm. 21+ after 7pm. Open M-Sa noon-3am, Su 12:30pm-2am. AmEx/D/MC/V.

The Jinx, 127 W. Congress St. (☎912-236-2281), located downtown off Barnard St. This hot spot was recently voted the best place in Savannah to hear live music. They sell earplugs ($1) for those who can't handle the pounding hip hop, metal, and indie rock. Open M-Sa 4pm-3am. AmEx/D/MC/V.

Club One, 1 Jefferson St. (☎912-232-0200), near Bay St. Features a great alternative scene and a GBLT-friendly atmosphere. Come to see the Lady Chablis, a drag queen and transsexual featured in *Midnight in the Garden of Good and Evil*. Cover Th-Sa $5-16. Shows Th-Sa 10:30pm, 12:30am. Open M-Sa 5pm-3am, Su 5pm-2am. AmEx/D/MC/V.

APPROACHING CHARLESTON: 108 MILES

From Savannah, take **U.S. 17 N.** Carefully observe all posted speed limits—the smaller towns between the 2 cities are notorious speed traps. Once in Charleston, get off at **Calhoun St.** and follow signs to parking, major attractions, and the visitors center.

The *Palmetto State*
SOUTH CAROLINA
Welcomes You!

CHARLESTON

During the early 1800s, Charleston was the richest city in the nation, topping even Boston and New York. The vast riches generated by rice and cotton plantations were used to build stately town-houses and intricate furniture, many of which remain on display in the city. Charleston today is a funky mix of old and new, plantations and college culture. So sit back with a mint julep and experience the capital of the old South.

VITAL STATS

Population: 115,540

Visitor Info: Charleston Visitors Center, 375 Meeting St. (☎843-853-8000 or 800-868-8118; www.charlestoncvb.com), across from Charleston Museum. Open daily 8:30am-5pm.

Internet Access: Charleston Public Library, 68 Calhoun St. (☎843-805-6801). Open M-Th 9am-9pm, F-Sa 9am-6pm, Su 2-5pm.

Post Office: 83 Broad St. (☎843-577-0690). Open M-F 9am-5pm. **Postal Code:** 29402.

GETTING AROUND

Old Charleston lies at the southernmost point of the 1 mi.-wide peninsula below **Calhoun St.** The major north-south routes through the city are **Meeting St., King St.,** and **E. Bay St.** The area north of the visitors center is run-down and uninviting. **Savannah Hwy. (U.S. 17)** cuts across the peninsula heading south to Savannah and north across two towering bridges to Mt. Pleasant and Myrtle Beach. Charleston is a great walking city, but when the heat is oppressive, visitors may want to make use of alternate transportation. The **Downtown Area Shuttle (DASH)** is made up of trolley routes that circle downtown. (Operates daily 8am-11pm; schedule and hour vary by route. $1.25, seniors $0.60; 1-day pass $4; 3-day $9.) **The Bicycle Shoppe,** 280 Meeting St., between George and Society St., offers bike rentals. (☎843-722-8168. $5 per hr., $20 per day. Deposit required. Open M-F 9am-7pm, Sa 9am-6pm, Su 1-5pm.)

◉ SIGHTS

Charleston's historic homes, monuments, churches, galleries, and gardens can be seen by foot, car, bus, boat, trolley, horse-drawn carriage, or on one of the several ghost tours that leave from City Market. **City Market,** downtown at Meeting St., stays abuzz in a restored 19th-century building. (Open daily from about 6am-11:30pm.)

PLANTATIONS AND GARDENS. The 738-acre, still-working ▧**Boone Hall Plantation** in Mt. Pleasant features a plantation house, slave cabins, and the gorgeous Avenue of Oaks, a much-photographed half-mile drive of oaks thickly draped in Spanish moss. A fun, interactive Gullah presentation teaches visitors about slave culture through storytelling and dance. *(1235 Long Point Rd., off U.S. 17. ☎843-884-4371; www.boonehallplantation.com. Open Apr.-Aug. M-Sa 8:30am-6:30pm, Su 1-5pm. Sept.-Mar. M-Sa 9am-5:30pm, Su 1-4pm. $14.50, ages 6-12 $7.)* The 300-year-old **Magnolia Plantation and Gardens** is the most majestic of Charleston's plantations, with fabulous gardens and miles of walking paths along the marsh. Guided tours lead groups through the plantation home, rice fields, and surrounding flora, but visitors will enjoy just stopping to smell the flowers. *(On Rte. 61, 10 mi. northwest of town off U.S. 17. ☎843-571-1266 or 800-367-3517. Open Mar.-Oct. daily 8am-*

5:30pm; in winter call for hours. Gardens $14, seniors $13, ages 6-12 $8; with house $21/$20/$15; with nature trail $21/$20/$13; with swamp garden $21/$20/$14.) A bit farther down the road, **Middleton Place** is a manicured plantation with working stables, gardens, a house, a restaurant, and an inn, as well as demonstrations of 18th- and 19th-century crafts. *(4300 Ashley River Rd. on Rte. 61, 14 mi. northwest of downtown. ☎843-556-6020 or 800-782-3608; www.middletonplace.org. Open daily 9am-5pm. Gardens $25, under 16 $15. House tour $10.)* The long trek out to **Cypress Gardens** may be worth it to visitors who wish to paddle boats out onto eerie, gator-filled swamps. *(3030 Cypress Gardens Rd., off Rte. 52. ☎843-553-0515; www.cypressgardens.info. Open daily 9am-5pm. $10, seniors $9, ages 6-12 $5.)*

CHARLESTON MUSEUM. Across the street from the visitors center stands the Charleston Museum, the country's oldest museum, founded in 1773. The museum contains outstanding exhibits on the Revolutionary War and the Civil War, as well as an exhaustive look into the cultural history of the Low Country. *(360 Meeting St. ☎843-722-2996; www.charlestonmuseum.org. Open M-Sa 9am-5pm, Su 1-5pm. $10, ages 3-12 $4.)*

HISTORIC HOMES. Charleston has a number of beautiful late 18th- and early 19th-century homes, so unless you particularly adore cabinets and cantilevered staircases, choose just one of the tours. The **Nathaniel Russell House** features a free-flying staircase, masterful iron balconies, and exceptional guides. *(51 Meeting St. ☎843-724-8481. Open M-Sa 10am-5pm, Su 2-5pm. $10, under 6 free.)* The view of the Charleston harbor from the **Edmonston-Alston House** is gorgeous; if it doesn't take your breath away, the springy joggling board will. *(21 E. Battery St. ☎843-722-7171. Open M and Su 1:30-4:30pm, Tu-Sa 10am-4:30pm. $10, students $8.)* George Washington rented the **Heyward-Washington House** during his trip through the South in 1791. Home to Thomas Heyward, Jr., a signer of the Declaration of Independence, the house features timeless American furniture and a lush garden. *(87 Church St. ☎843-722-2996. Open M-Sa 10am-5pm, Su 1-5pm. $9, ages 3-12 $4.)* Built in 1803, The **Joseph Manigault House** is a stunning example of Neoclassical architecture. Be sure to check out the Gate Temple, a gorgeous outdoor vestibule that stays cool in the muggy summer months. *(350 Meeting St. ☎843-722-2996. Open M-Sa 10am-5pm, Su 1-5pm. $9, ages 3-12 $4.)*

PATRIOTS POINT, FORT SUMTER, AND FORT MOULTRIE. Climb aboard four naval ships, including a submarine and the aircraft carrier *Yorktown*, in **Patriots Point Naval and Maritime Museum**, the world's largest naval museum. Exhibits include a Congressional Medal of Honor display, several aircraft, and a flight simulator. *(40 Patriots Point Rd., across the Cooper River in Mt. Pleasant. ☎843-884-2727; www.patriotspoint.org. Open daily 9am-5pm. $14, seniors and military $12, ages 6-11 $7. Flight simulator $4.50.)* **Fort Sumter Tours** has boat excursions to the National Historic Site where the Civil War began in April 1861. Tours leave from Patriot's Point in Mt. Pleasant and Liberty Square in Charleston. *(Fort Sumter: ☎843-883-3123, Tours: ☎843-881-7337; www.nps.gov/fosu. $14, ages 6-11 $8.)* Confederate troops attacked Fort Sumter from **Fort Moultrie** to begin the Civil War. The fort now sports anti-aircraft guns alongside 1860s cannons. *(1214 Middle St. Follow Coleman Blvd. off U.S. 17 as it becomes Rte. 703, and take a right onto Middle St. ☎843-883-3123. Open daily 9am-5pm. $3, seniors $1, under 16 free. After 4pm free.)*

CHARLES PINCKNEY NATIONAL HISTORIC SITE. The site lies on what was once the property of Charles Pinckney, a South Carolina delegate to the 1787 Constitutional Convention and former state governor. The grounds cover 28 acres and feature a half-mile long history and nature trail, an 1828 Low Country cottage, and a museum with exhibits on rice agriculture, plantation life, the Gullah, and the American Revolution. *(1254 Long Point Rd., 6 mi. north of Charleston, off U.S. 17, in Mt. Pleasant. ☎843-881-5516; www.nps.gov/chpi. Open daily 9am-5pm. Free.)*

BEACHES. Folly Beach is popular with students from the Citadel, College of Charleston, and University of South Carolina. *(Over the James Bridge and U.S. 171, about 20 mi. southeast of Charleston. ☎843-588-2426. Open 9am-6pm.)* The more exposed **Isle of Palms** extends for miles down toward the less-crowded **Sullivan's Island.** *(Across the Cooper Bridge, drive 10 mi. down U.S. 17 N, and turn right onto the Isle of Palms Connector. ☎843-886-3863. Open 9am-7pm.)*

Charleston

■■ ACCOMMODATIONS
Bed, No Breakfast, 9
Campground at James Island County Park, 2
Charleston's NotSo Hostel, 3
Motel 6, 1

● FOOD
Andolini's Pizza, 13
Gaulart & Maliclet, 15
Hominy Grill, 4
Hyman's Seafood Company, 14
Jestine's Kitchen, 12
Papa Zuzu's, 10

■ NIGHTLIFE
A.C.'s Bar and Grill, 7
Music Farm, 6
Raval, 8
The Terrace on Marion Sqare, 11
Tonik, 5

SOUTH CAROLINA AQUARIUM. With waterfalls and towering tanks, the aquarium has become Charleston's greatest attraction. Exhibits showcase aquatic life from the region's swamps and oceans. Stare down the fishies at the 330,000-gal. Great Ocean Tank, which rises two full stories. *(At the end of Calhoun St., on the Cooper River, overlooking the harbor. ☎843-720-1990; www.scaquarium.org. Open Apr. to mid-Aug. M-Sa 9am-6pm, Su noon-6pm; mid-Aug. to Apr. M-Sa 9am-5pm, Su noon-5pm. $15, seniors $13, ages 3-11 $8.)*

BULL ISLAND. To get away from human civilization, take a 30min. ferry to Bull Island, a 6 mi. long island off the coast of Charleston. The island is home to several endangered species, including the loggerhead turtle and red wolf. On the island there are 16 mi. of hiking trails popular with bird-

EAST COAST

ers. *(Ferries depart from Garris Landing, off Seewee Rd., 16 mi. north of Charleston off U.S. 17. ☎843-884-7684. Departs Mar.-Nov. Tu and Th-Sa 9am and 12:30pm; returns noon and 4pm; Dec.-Feb. Sa 10am; returns 3pm. Round-trip $30, under 12 $15.)*

GIBBES MUSEUM OF ART. With one of the best collections of art in the Southeast, the museum features portraits and miniatures, as well as an extensive collection of Japanese block prints. Rotating exhibits highlight local and regional artists. *(135 Meeting St. ☎843-722-2706; www.gibbesmuseum.org. Open Tu-Sa 10am-5pm, Su 1-5pm. Tours Tu and Sa 2:30pm. $9; seniors, students, military $7; ages 6-12 $5.)*

🍴 FOOD

Charleston has some of the best food in the country. While restaurants in high-traffic areas cater to big-spending tourists, there are plenty of budget options. Step off the main drag to find the Southern cooking, barbecue, and fresh seafood that have made the Low Country famous.

🍴 **Gaulart & Maliclet (Fast and French),** 98 Broad St. (☎843-577-9797). Strangers bond over shared countertops and steaming veggie croque baguettes ($3.85). From the portraits on the wall to the chocolate croissants ($2.60), it's all French, and all *magnifique.* Open M 8am-4pm, Tu-Th 8am-10pm, F-Sa 8am-10:30pm. AmEx/D/MC/V. ❶

🍴 **Papa Zuzu's,** 340 King St. (☎843-534-1666). The screen door sticks, and there's limited seating, but Papa Zuzu's serves up some of the best gyros and pitas you'll find anywhere. Grab the Greek veggie pita ($5.25) or the hummus pita ($5.25) and chow down in a nearby park. Open M-Th and Su 11am-9pm, F-Sa 11am-10pm. Cash only. ❶

Jestine's Kitchen, 251 Meeting St. (☎843-722-7224). Serving up some of the best Southern food in Charleston, Jestine's has become a local favorite for its fried green tomatoes ($5), chicken livers, and okra and greens ($2). There must be something in the food—Jestine herself lived to be 117. Open Tu-Th 11am-9:30pm, F-Sa 11am-10pm, Su 11am-9pm. MC/V. ❷

Hyman's Seafood Company, 215 Meeting St. (☎843-723-6000). This restaurant has offered 15-25 kinds of fresh fish daily ($7-15) served in 8 styles since 1890. Try the Charleston crab cakes ($17). Voted the #1 seafood restaurant in South Carolina 6 years running. No reservations; expect long waits. Open daily 11am-11pm. AmEx/D/MC/V. ❹

Hominy Grill, 207 Rutledge Ave. (☎843-937-0930). With low lights and white tablecloths, this is down-home cooking gone slightly upscale. Stop by for 2 eggs and hominy grits ($4.50) in the morning, or fried chicken with peace sauce ($14) in the evening. Open M-Th 7:30am-2:30pm and 5:30-9:30pm, F-Sa 5:30-10pm, Sa-Su 9am-2:30pm. AmEx/MC/V. ❸

Andolini's Pizza, 82 Wentworth St. (☎843-722-7437), just west of King St. Perfectly hidden from the uber-trendy King St. shoppers, Andolini's is fabulously funky, with statues, lightbulb signs, and a loft. Amazing pizza at unbeatable prices. A large slice with any topping, a salad, and a drink runs $6. Cheese pizza $13. Calzones from $5.50. Open M-Th 10:30am-10pm, F-Su 10:30am-11pm. AmEx/D/MC/V. ❶

 DID YOU KNOW? South Carolina is known for 4 different variations of barbecue sauce. In northwest South Carolina, the sauce is tomato-based with a hint of sweet relish; in northeast South Carolina, the sauce is vinegar-based with no tomato; in central South Carolina, the sauce is mustard-flavored; in southern South Carolina, the sauce is vinegar-based with a hint of mustard.

🏨 ACCOMMODATIONS

Motel rooms in historic downtown Charleston are expensive. Cheap motels are a few miles out of the city, around Exits 209-211 on I-26 W. in North Charleston, or across the Ashley River, on U.S. 17 in Mt. Pleasant.

🏨 **Charleston's NotSo Hostel,** 156 Spring St. (☎843-722-8383). A scrupulously clean hostel near the bright lights of downtown Charleston. 2 fully-equipped kitchens, a wrap-around porch with hammocks, laundry, parking, and free Wi-Fi. Be careful walking around at night, as the hostel borders an unsafe neighborhood. Reception daily 10am-1pm and 5-10pm. Dorms $19; private rooms $30-60. AmEx/D/MC/V. ❶

Bed, No Breakfast, 16 Halsey St. (☎843-577-2821). The only budget option within walking distance of downtown, this charming 2-bedroom inn offers guests an affordable way to stay in the historic heart of the city. Shared bathroom. Reservations recommended. Rooms $85-125. Cash only. ❹

Motel 6, 2058 Savannah Hwy. (☎843-556-5144), 5 mi. south of town. Be sure to call ahead to reserve one of these clean rooms; the immensely popular motel is often booked solid for days. Singles M-Th and Su $50, F-Sa $60; doubles $56/$66. AmEx/D/MC/V. ❸

Campground at James Island County Park, 871 Riverland Dr. (☎843-795-4386 or 800-743-7275). Take U.S. 17 S to Rte. 171, and turn left onto Riverland Dr. Spacious, open sites. The spectacular park features 16 acres of lakes, bicycle and walking trails, a climbing wall, and a small water park. Bike and boat rental. Primitive sites $17; tent sites $27; with hookup $29. Day use $1. AmEx/D/MC/V. ❶

🎸 NIGHTLIFE

With nearby colleges and a constant tourist presence, Charleston's nightlife thrives. Free copies of *City Paper*, available in stores and restaurants, list events.

🎸 A.C.'s Bar and Grill, 467 King St. (☎843-577-6742). Hipsters and the Man mingle at this loud, friendly neighborhood dive. Locals come for the cheap beer ($2-3.25), pool tables, and Frogger. Su brunch 11am-4pm with $1 mimosas. Open daily 11am-2am. AmEx/D/MC/V.

Music Farm, 32 Ann St. (☎843-722-8904; www.etix.com). From hippie jam bands to bluegrass, Music Farm is the place for live music in Charleston. Housed in what was once a train station, Music Farm seats 1000 for the big-name acts that come through town. Tickets $5-20. Open daily 9pm-2am. Box office open M-F noon-4pm. AmEx/MC/V.

Raval, 453 King St. (☎843-853-8466). This is one funky Tapas bar. It may seem like a typical wine bar, but in the back, a DJ spins house and hip-hop on F-Sa. Tapas $4-12. Open M-Sa 5pm-2am, Su 6:30pm-2am. AmEx/D/MC/V.

The Terrace on Marion Square, 145 Calhoun St. (☎843-937-0314). 3 fl. above the bustle of King St., a crowd catches the breezes in this rooftop bar. Try the specialty, a 1 gal. fishbowl of booze ($12-15). Open Tu-F 4-11pm, Sa 11am-11pm, Su brunch 11am. AmEx/MC/V.

Tonik, 479 King St. (☎843-709-5050). This bar and lounge has big black couches and art on the walls. F live music, generally 80s cover bands. Sa dancing. Jager bombs $3. Cover Th-F men $5. Open Th-Sa 10pm-2am. AmEx/D/MC/V.

◤ APPROACHING GEORGETOWN: 60 MILES
Follow **U.S. 17 N**; it becomes **Church St.** in Georgetown.

GEORGETOWN

Don't plan on hurrying through Georgetown. In this decidedly Southern town, everyone takes their time. Stroll through the downtown area or along the waterfront, and take a moment to enjoy the peace and quiet. It might not be the most happening place along the route, but it gives visitors a chance to while away an afternoon.

VITAL STATS

Population: 9000

Visitor Info: Georgetown County Chamber of Commerce, 531 Front St. (☎843-546-8436; www.georgetownchamber.com). Open M-Sa 9am-5pm.

Internet Access: Georgetown County Library, 405 Cleland St. (☎843-545-3300). Open June-Aug. M-Th 9am-8pm, F-Sa 9am-5pm; Sept.-May M-Th 9am-8pm, F-Sa 9am-5pm, Su 2-5pm. Free

Post Office: 1101 Charlotte St. (☎843-546-5515). Open M-F 8:30am-5pm, Sa 9am-noon. **Postal Code:** 29440.

▤ GETTING AROUND. From **U.S. 17,** turn right onto **Front St.** to reach downtown Georgetown. **U.S. 17 (Church St.)** bends to run parallel to the waterfront and Front St.

◉ SIGHTS. Located right next to the chamber of commerce, **Kaminski House Museum,** 1003 Front St., is a 1769 house decorated with period English and American furnishings, including examples of Charleston's finest cabinet-making. Friendly tour guides lead visitors through the home, explaining its particular history and satirizing its inhabitants. (☎843-546-7706 or 888-233-0383. Tours every hr. M-Sa 10am-4pm, Su 1-4pm. $7, ages 6-12 $3, under 6 free.) The **Rice Museum,** 633 Front St., presents the history of rice culture in the county and illustrates how dependence on a single agricultural product shaped the era's history. The

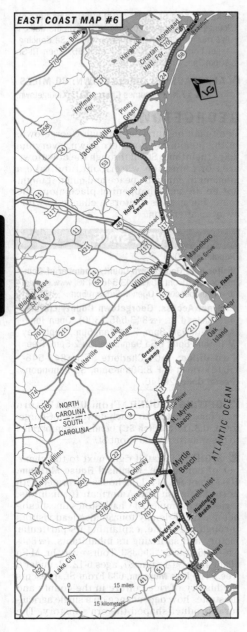

EAST COAST MAP #6

museum also contains the hull of the oldest boat manufactured in the colonies. (☎843-546-7423; www.ricemuseum.org. Open M-Sa 10am-4:30pm. $7, seniors $5, ages 6-21 $3.) **Swamp Fox Tours** gives narrated tram rides through the historical district, highlighting major points of interest and local stories. (Tours leave from 624 Front St. ☎843-527-1112; www.swampfoxtours.com. Tours every hr. M-Sa 10am-4pm. $7.50, ages 6-12 $4.) The visitors center also has brochures for a self-guided walking tour to major historic sights. The **Hampton Plantation State Historic Site,** 1950 Rutledge Rd. in McClellanville, off U.S. 17 south of Georgetown, focuses on Low Country rice culture. The tour of the white, stately plantation house uses cutaway sections of wall and ceiling to show its evolution from farmhouse to grand manor. (☎843-546-9361. Park grounds open daily 9am-6pm. Mansion tours daily every hr. Memorial Day to Labor Day 11am-4pm; Labor Day to Memorial Day M and Th-Su 1-4pm. Last tour 3pm. Tours $4, ages 6-16 $3.)

FOOD AND ACCOMMODATIONS. The owners of **Front Street Deli ❶,** 809 Front St., left corporate America to open a small-town sandwich shop with large, tasty sandwiches like roast beef ($5) or chicken parmigiana ($5). If you was us, their investment paid off. (☎843-546-2008. Open M-Sa 10am-4pm. Cash only.) The **Thomas Cafe ❷,** 703 Front St., is a no-frills restaurant that focuses on what matters—the food. They serve up Low Country favorites, like jambalaya and shrimp and grits, each for $8. (☎843-546-7776. Open M-Sa 7am-2pm, Su 11am-3pm. AmEx/D/MC/V.) The cool, dark **Dogwood Cafe ❶,** 713 Front St., features classic Southern fare like fried pickles ($3.75) and BLT sandwiches ($5.25) made with fried green tomatoes. (☎843-545-7777. Open M-Sa 11am-10pm. AmEx/D/MC/V.)

Downtown Georgetown is peppered with B&Bs, but for budget options, visitors will have to resort to more generic hotels and motels. The **Budget Inn ❷,** 412 James St., just off U.S. 17, offers cable, fridge, microwave, and phone for less than motels bordering U.S. 17. (☎843-546-4117. Rooms $40. AmEx/D/MC/V.) The **Harbor Inn ❸,** 600 Church St., has clean, spacious rooms with cable TV and fridge, as well as a large outdoor pool. (☎843-546-5111.

Continental breakfast included. Singles $60; doubles $66. AmEx/D/MC/V.) The **Carolinian Inn ❹**, 706 Church St., has standard amenities and a beautiful view of a nearby marsh. Don't be frightened by the deer head in the lobby. (☎800-722-4667; www.carolinianinn.com. Free Wi-Fi. Rooms from $75. AmEx/D/MC/V.)

⚐ **APPROACHING MURRELLS INLET: 20 MILES**
Take **U.S. 17 N** to **Bus. U.S. 17,** and follow it until hitting Murrells Inlet.

MURRELLS INLET

Ten miles south of Myrtle Beach lies tiny Murrells Inlet, which stretches along Bus. U.S. 17. The town is famous as a fishing village, and provides day access to its multiple marinas for a reasonable fee. The Huntingtons built the sprawling ▩**Brookgreen Gardens,** U.S. 17, opposite Huntington Beach State Park south of Murrells Inlet, to showcase wife Anna Hyatt Huntington's sculpture. Over 1200 sculptures now preside over the beautiful gardens and reflecting pools. Tours of the gardens and wildlife trail are available in addition to summer drama, music, and food programs. (☎843-235-6000; www.brookgreen.org. Open daily 9:30am-5pm. 7-day pass $12, seniors and ages 13-18 $10, ages 6-12 $5.)

With picnic tables overlooking the inlet, busy **Creek Ratz ❸**, off Bus. U.S. 17, offers a great view for cheap. Try the yellowfin tuna philly ($9) or the flounder po' boy ($8.25), two of the house specialties. (☎843-357-2891. Open daily 11am-11pm. AmEx/D/MC/V.) For 50 years, **Lee's Inlet Kitchen ❺**, 4460 Bus. Hwy. 17, has served fresh, local seafood, like crab-stuffed flounder ($23). It's expensive, but it's definitely worth the splurge. Be sure to get here early—the place fills up fast. (☎843-651-2881; www.leesinletkitchen.com. Open M-Sa 5-10pm. AmEx/MC/V.) Decorated with Mardi Gras beads and memorabilia, **Flo's Place ❸**, 3797 Bus. Hwy. 17, serves up authentic Cajun cuisine. Make sure to sample the alligator stew ($7.25) for a real taste of the swamp. (☎843-651-7222; www.flosplace.com. Open daily 11:30am-10pm. AmEx/MC/V.) The family-owned **Brookwood Inn ❸**, off Bus. U.S. 17, offers travelers a quiet, shady place to hang their hats. There are hammocks and a pool under elegant oak trees, along with the standard fridge and TV set. (☎843-651-2550. Rooms in summer $65-75; in winter $45-65. AmEx/D/MC/V.) **Huntington Beach State Park Campground ❶**, 16148

Ocean Hwy., 3 mi. south of Murrells Inlet on U.S. 17, is located in a diverse environment including lagoons, salt marshes, and a beach. Take advantage of the boating access and nature trails. Be careful: gators come within yards of the sites. (☎843-237-4440. Open daily Apr.-Oct. 6am-10pm; Nov.-Mar. 6am-6pm. Sites Apr.-Oct. $17, with water and electricity $23, with full hookup $25; Nov. and Mar. $15/$21/$23; Dec.-Feb. $14/$20/$21. Day-use $5, children $3. AmEx/D/MC/V.)

⚐ **APPROACHING MYRTLE BEACH: 10 MILES**
Follow **U.S 17 N** to **Bus. U.S. 17,** which becomes **Kings Hwy.**

MYRTLE BEACH AND THE GRAND STRAND

A long time ago, one restaurant must have put up the gaudy sign that ignited an advertising arms race. Driving through Myrtle Beach, neon and pastel assault the senses, and you're never far from an elaborately decorated mini-golf course. While lovers of the absurd will adore Myrtle Beach, those seeking to escape its incessant tackiness will find lovely beaches and excellent state parks further along the Grand Strand.

EAST COAST

VITAL STATS

Population: 23,000

Visitor Info: Myrtle Beach Chamber of Commerce, 1200 N. Oak St. (☎843-626-7444 or 800-356-3016; www.mbchamber.com), at 12th Ave. N. Open M-F 8:30am-5pm, Sa 9am-5pm, Su 10am-2pm.

Internet Access: Chapin Memorial Library, 400 14th Ave. N (☎843-918-1275). Open June-Aug. M and W 9am-6pm, Tu and Th 9am-8pm, F 9am-5pm, Sa 9am-1pm; Sept.-May M and W 9am-6pm, Tu and Th 9am-8pm, F-Sa 9am-5pm. Free.

Mini Golf: Absolutely everywhere.

Post Office: 505 N. Kings Hwy. (☎843-626-9533), at 5th Ave. N. Open M-F 8:30am-5pm, Sa 9am-1pm. **Postal Code:** 29577.

▐ **GETTING AROUND**

U.S. 17 splits into a business route and a bypass 4 mi. south of Myrtle Beach, then rejoins before the town of North Myrtle Beach (not to be confused with north Myrtle Beach). Most attractions are on **Kings Hwy.**, or **Bus. U.S. 17**. Parallel to Kings Hwy. is **Ocean Blvd.**, which follows the shoreline, flanked on either side by cheap pastel motels. Cross streets are numbered, but be aware that the town is split into a southern half and a northern half. **Rte. 501** runs west toward Conway and **I-95**.

👁 SIGHTS

The boulevard and the beach are both "the strand," and while you're on it, the rule is see and be seen. Fashionable teens strut their stuff, low riders cruise the streets, and older beachgoers showcase their sunburns. Coupons are everywhere—never pay full price for any attraction. Pick up a copy of the *Monster Coupon Book*, *Sunny Day Guide*, *Myrtle Beach Guide*, or *Strand Magazine* at any visitors center or hotel.

The colossal **Broadway at the Beach**, at U.S. 17 Bypass and 21st Ave. N, is a sprawling complex designed to stimulate and entertain with theaters, a water park, mini golf, 20 restaurants, nightclubs, 100 shops, and other attractions. Of course, it's all ridiculously decorated, with buildings shaped like pyramids or topped with enormous frogs. The info centers and booths sell tickets for major attractions at a discount. (☎ 843-444-3200 or 800-386-4662. Open in summer daily 10am-11pm.) Several amusement parks line the beach, with unapologetically tacky decor and carnival games. One such park is **Family Kingdom**, 300 4th Ave. S, which includes a wooden roller coaster, a merry-go-round, and pastels galore. (☎843-946-9821. Open M-F and Su 4pm-midnight, Sa 1pm-midnight. Single rides $1.50-3.75, unlimited rides $19.50.) South Carolina's most visited attraction is Broadway's **Ripley's Aquarium**, 1110 Celebrity Cir., where guests roam through a 330 ft. underwater tunnel and gaze at the sharks swimming above. With piped mood music, it's quite gaudy, but it does have an excellent collection of animals. (☎843-916-0888 or 800-734-8888; www.ripleysaquarium.com. Open daily 9am-11pm. $17, ages 5-11 $10, ages 2-4 $4.) The reptile capital of the world is **Alligator Adventure**, on U.S. 17 in North Myrtle Beach at Barefoot Landing, where visitors are mesmerized by snakes, lizards, and frogs. Don't miss the odd-hour gator feedings and the park's enormous resident, Utan—the largest crocodile ever exhibited in the US. (☎843-361-0789; www.alligatoradventure.com. Open daily 9am-9pm. $15, seniors $13, ages 4-12 $10.)

Most visitors to Myrtle Beach putter over to one of the many elaborately themed **mini golf** courses on Kings Hwy. Get behind the wheel (again) at the **NASCAR Speedpark**, across from Broadway at the Beach on the U.S. 17 Bypass. The park provides seven different tracks, catering to those who have the need for speed with go-karts and Thunder Road, in which visitors drive around steep curves. (☎843-918-8725. Open daily 10am-11pm. $1 per ride; unlimited rides $25, 55+ and under 13 $16.)

DID YOU KNOW? The South and North Carolina state dance is 🕺 **the shag.** The shag is a form of swing dancing that originated on the strands between Myrtle Beach, South Carolina, and Wilmington, North Carolina, in the 1940s.

🍴 FOOD

The Grand Strand tempts hungry motorists with over 1800 restaurants serving every type of food in every imaginable setting. Massive all-you-can-eat joints beckon from beneath the glow of every traffic light. **U.S. 17** offers countless steakhouses, seafood buffets, and fast-food restaurants. With license plates covering the walls and ceiling and discarded peanut shells crunching underfoot, the **River City Cafe ❶**, 404 21st Ave. N, celebrates a brand of American informality bordering on delinquency. Peruse the enthusiastic signatures of patrons on tables and walls as you polish off a burger with Cajun seasoning ($3.65) and fries ($1.85) while sitting at one of the picnic tables on the front porch. (☎843-448-1990. Open daily 11am-10pm. D/MC/V.) Be sure to bring an appetite to **Manny's ❶**, 1701 S. Kings Hwy., where deli sandwiches come stuffed with meat and cheese. Try the pastrami sandwich ($4.35) or a Manny's sub ($5.25), brimming with turkey, ham, and bologna. (Off 17th Ave. S. ☎843-946-6817. Open M-Sa 11am-9pm, Su 11am-4pm. Cash only.) Take a break from the soft hues of Ocean Dr. at **Dagwood's Deli ❷**, 400 11th. Ave. N, where beach bums and businessmen come together to enjoy the Dagwood Dipper (turkey and swiss with dipping mayo; $6.25). The triple-decker Bumstead's Club ($6.55) is also quite tasty. (☎843-448-0100. Open M-Sa 11am-6pm. MC/V.) **Goodberry's ❶**, 1205 Celebrity

Dr., offers a refreshing taste of authenticity in the form of frozen custard. Hungry pedestrians polish off old favorites and unique concoctions. (☎843-448-8000. Open daily 10am-11pm. AmEx/D/MC/V.)

ACCOMMODATIONS

There are hundreds of motels lining **Ocean Blvd.**, with those on the ocean fetching higher prices. Cheap motels also dot **U.S. 17.** From October to March, prices plummet as low as $25-35 per night for one of the luxurious hotels right on the beach. The **Hurl Rock Motel ❸**, 2010 S. Ocean Blvd., has big, clean rooms with microwave, fridge, and TV. The motel also has a pool and hot tub and is right across the street from the beach. (☎843-626-3531 or 888-487-5762. 21+. Rooms in summer $60, in winter $35. AmEx/D/MC/V.) Closer to the action of the boardwalk, **Coral Sands Motel ❸**, 301 N. Ocean Blvd., offers standard rooms and laundry facilities. (☎843-448-3584 or 800-248-9779. Singles in summer $60, in winter $25; doubles $70/$35. AmEx/D/MC/V.) Across the street from the ocean, the family-owned **Sea Banks Motor Inn ❸**, 2200 S. Ocean Blvd., has large, clean rooms with mini-fridges, cable TV, and laundry, as well as pool and beach access. (☎843-448-2434 or 800-523-0603. Singles in summer $68, in winter $25; doubles $82/$30. AmEx/D/MC/V.) Just a few miles south of Myrtle Beach, **Myrtle Beach State Park ❶**, 4401 S. Kings Hwy., offers over 300 sites bordering on a gorgeous beach. The park also includes picnic areas, laundry facilities, a general store, and miles of bike trails. (☎843-238-5325 or 866-345-7275. Sites with water and electricity Apr.-Oct. M-Th and Su $26, F-Sa $29; full hookup $29/$32. Rates vary in winter. Day use $4, ages 6-15 $1.50. AmEx/D/MC/V.)

NIGHTLIFE

The New Orleans-style nightclub district of **Celebrity Sq.**, at Broadway, at the Beach, facilitates stepping out with 10 clubs, ranging in theme from classic rock to Latin. With karaoke every night at 9:30pm, **Broadway Louie's** allows your inner diva to take the stage. (☎843-445-6885. 21+ after 7pm. Happy hour 4-7pm. Open daily Mar.-Nov. noon-2am; Dec.-Feb. 4pm-2am. AmEx/D/MC/V.) One cover ($5-10) gains you access to three neighboring clubs. **Club Boca** is a dance club playing Latin and house. (☎843-444-3500. Open daily 10pm-

3am. AmEx/D/MC/V.) Listeners sip fishbowl drinks ($8-10) at **Froggy Bottomz** while listening to live music, usually Top 40. (☎643-444-3500. Open daily 9:45pm-2:30am. AmEx/D/MC/V.) **Malibu's** is a surf bar where locals ride the waves. (☎843-444-3500. Open daily 9pm-2 or 4am. AmEx/D/MC/V.)

◤ APPROACHING CAPE FEAR: 67 MILES

From Myrtle Beach, take **U.S. 17 N.** To bypass North Myrtle Beach traffic, take **S.C. 31** to **Rte. 9** and then rejoin U.S. 17.

The Tar Heel State
NORTH CAROLINA
Welcomes You!

WILMINGTON AND CAPE FEAR

Situated on the Carolina coast at the mouth of the Cape Fear River and only a few miles from the beaches of the Atlantic, Wilmington has long been an important center for shipping and trade. Home to the largest film production facility east of L.A., the city is sometimes referred to as "Wilmywood" and "Hollywood East." Over 400 feature films and TV projects have been shot along the picturesque Cape Fear coast since 1983, including the hit TV series *Dawson's Creek.* Even if you don't glimpse a celebrity, the historic downtown has plenty to offer, from memorials and excellent restaurants to picturesque views of the waterfront.

VITAL STATS
Population: 76,000
Visitor Info: Cape Fear Coast Convention and Visitors Bureau, 24 N. 3rd St. (☎910-341-4030 or 800-222-4757), in the 1892 courthouse. Open M-F 8:30am-5pm, Sa 9am-4pm, Su 1-4pm.
Internet Access: New Hanover County Public Library, 201 Chestnut St. (☎910-798-6302). Open M-W 9am-8pm, Th-Sa 9am-5pm, Su 1-5pm. $2 per day.
Parking: There are 3 parking decks—2 on 2nd St., 1 on Water St. M-F $1 per hour, $5 per day; Sa-Su free.
Post Office: 152 Front St. (☎910-313-3293). Open M-F 9am-5pm, Sa 9am-noon. **Postal Code:** 28401.

EAST COAST

▣ GETTING AROUND

Wilmington proper is north of Cape Fear. In town, **Bus. U.S. 17** is called **Market St.** and runs midway through downtown. Downtown is bounded by **Red Cross St.** to the west, **Castle St.** to the east, and **Front St.** along the water. The streets running parallel to Front St. are all numbered and form a grid. **U.S. 421** runs the length of Cape Fear. A free trolley, the blue and brown **Wave** (☎910-343-0106), runs downtown every 20min.

◉ SIGHTS

CAPE FEAR MUSEUM. The museum documents and celebrates all aspects of Cape Fear life—political, cultural, and scientific. The interactive habitat exhibits and the lighted diorama of the battle of Fort Fisher are particularly interesting. For basketball fans, there's also an exhibit on hometown hero Michael Jordan. *(814 Market St. ☎ 910-341-4350; www.capefearmuseum.com. Open M-Sa 9am-5pm, Su 1-5pm; Labor Day to Memorial day Tu-Sa 9am-5pm, Su 1-5pm. $5; students, military, and seniors $4; ages 3-17 $1.)*

BELLAMY MANSION MUSEUM. Once the residence of planter John D. Bellamy, this mansion is a terrific example of antebellum architecture. The 22 rooms have been restored, and two gallery spaces have displays focusing on the arts, historic preservation, and architecture. *(503 Market St. ☎910-251-3700; www.bellamymansion.org. Open Tu-Sa 10am-5pm, Su 1-5pm. $8, ages 5-12 $4.)*

BURGWIN-WRIGHT MUSEUM HOUSE AND GARDENS. Built on top of an abandoned jail, the house is an example of Georgian architecture. Check out the kitchen for demonstrations of open-hearth cooking. *(224 Market St. ☎910-762-0570. Open Tu-Sa 10am-4pm; last tour 3:30pm. $8, ages 5-12 $4.)*

CAPE FEAR SERPENTARIUM. With red lighting and in-depth descriptions of death by snake bite, the Serpentarium doesn't shy away from shocking its visitors. Snakes and crocodiles are rated on a scale of deadliness, from 1 to 5 skull-and-crossbones. If you aren't frightened yet, just listen to the eerie background music. *(20 Orange St. ☎910-762-1669; www.capefearserpentarium.com. Open M-F 11am-5pm Sa-Su 11am-6pm. $8, under 2 free.)*

LOUISE WELLS CAMERON ART MUSEUM. Dedicated to North Carolina's artistic heritage, the Louise Wells Cameron Art Museum displays the work of artists such as Mary Cassatt. Traditional media are supplemented by exhibits on commercial design and computer-generated art. *(3201 S. 17th St. ☎910-395-5999; www.cameronartmuseum.com. Open W-Th and Sa-Su 11am-5pm, F 11am-9pm. $7, ages 6-18 $2.)*

BATTLESHIP NORTH CAROLINA. With its crew of 2300, the *North Carolina* served in every major battle of WWII. Visitors can climb inside the bowels of this floating city, which includes a barber and ice cream shops. The museum provides insight into the lives of WWII sailors and the ship's battles. *(Off U.S. 17, south of Wilmington. ☎910-350-1817; www.battleshipnc.com. Open daily 8am-8pm; last entry 7pm. $9, seniors and military $8, ages 6-11 $4.50, under 6 free.)*

WILMINGTON RAILROAD MUSEUM. For over 150 years, Wilmington was home to the Atlantic Coast Line Railroad, and the old transportation headquarters now houses the Wilmington Railroad Museum. In addition to pictures and models, it also contains a caboose, a steam engine, and a box car. *(501 Nutt St. ☎910-763-2634. Open mid-Mar. to mid-Oct. M-Sa 10am-5pm, Su 1-5pm; mid-Oct. to mid-Mar. M-Sa 10am-4pm. $5, seniors and military $4.50, children $3.)*

FORT FISHER. Fort Fisher was the Confederacy's last major stronghold. The fort was able to withstand the shock of torpedo shells and other blasts because it consisted almost entirely of sand and dirt, but it was finally captured in January 1865. The visitors center has exhibits on the Civil War, including cannons and rifles while the recreation site has a crowded beach and a number of nature-oriented programs. *(On U.S. 421, 20 mi. south of Wilmington. ☎910-458-5538. Historic site open M-Sa 9am-5pm, Su 1-5pm. Recreation area open daily in summer 6am-9pm. Free.)* The **North Carolina Aquarium**, also at Fort Fisher, allows visitors to view and interact with the state's aquatic life. Visitors can touch the animals in the Touch Tanks and see the staff feed the fishies. *(☎910-458-8257. Open daily 9am-5pm. $8, seniors $7, ages 6-17 $6.)*

THE LATIMER HOUSE. Built in the popular "Italianate" style, this 1952 home contains period furnishings and artwork, including portraits of the wealthy Latimer family. Be sure to check out the period clothing and hair wreath. *(126 S. 3rd St. ☎910-762-0492; www.latimerhouse.org. Open M-F 10am-3:30pm, Sa noon-5pm. Walking tours W and Sa 10am. $8, students $4.)*

▓ FOOD

Wilmington's downtown is flush with trendy cafes, many of which have outdoor seating. **Caffé Phoenix ❸,** 9 S. Front St., has a chic, European feel with abundant greenery and colorful art on the walls. Try the pear and fennel salad ($5.50) or the *spinaci con prosciutto* ($12)— all served with freshly baked bread. (☎910-343-1395. Open M-Sa 11:30am-10pm, Su 11am-4pm. AmEx/D/MC/V.) Though housed in a building constructed in 1881, the **Roudabush Cafe ❷,** 33 S. Front St., caters to a modern palate. Patrons enjoy portobello mushroom, red pepper, and goat cheese sandwiches ($7) or grilled chicken and gouda ($7) in a restored wood interior. (☎910-763-3176. Open M-F 11am-4pm, Sa-Su 9am-4pm. AmEx/D/MC/V.) With funky chairs, a shelf of poetry, and free Wi-Fi, **Bella's ❶,** 19 Market St., draws college students like moths to a porch light. The Mediterranean Harvest sandwich (hummus and veggies; $6) and smoothies ($4) will appeal to anyone. (☎910-762-2777. Open daily 8am-midnight. AmEx/D/MC/V.) The **Caprice Bistro ❺,** 10 Market St., serves upscale French cuisine at intimate tables. After dinner, head upstairs to the sofa bar to relax with cocktails. (☎910-815-0810; www.capricebistro.com. Open M-Th and Su 5-10:30pm, F-Sa 5pm-midnight. Sofa bar open until 2am. AmEx/MC/V.)

▐ ACCOMMODATIONS

Wilmington's best lodging comes in the form of B&Bs; you'll find most of them in the historic downtown area. Though rooms usually cost $100-200 per night, the personalized experience, breakfasts, unique rooms, and riverfront views make them worth the extra cash. Those seeking less expensive lodging will find nearly every budget chain on **Market St.,** between College Rd. and 23rd St. Rates generally run $50 during the summer, $35 in winter, with weekend rates $5-10 higher than weekday prices. **The River Inn ❺,** 314 S. Front St., offers large, lavishly decorated rooms overlooking the river, as well as a home-cooked breakfast. (☎910-763-4891; www.theriverinnwilmington.com. Rooms $140-150. D/MC/V.) The **Super 8 ❷,** 3604 Market St., has large, clean rooms. (☎910-343-9778 or 800-800-8000. Free Wi-Fi. Rooms in summer $50, in winter $45. AmEx/D/MC/V.) **Travel Inn ❷,** 4401 Market St., provides basic rooms with tiny showers. (☎910-763-8217. Pool and cable TV. Rooms in summer M-F $50, Sa-Su $55; in winter from $35. AmEx/D/MC/V.) The **Carolina Beach State Park ❶,** about 18 mi. south of the city on U.S. 421, offers campsites as well as hiking, picnic areas, and a marina. You'll find hungry Venus flytraps growing in the park, so guard your victuals well. (☎910-458-8206. Restrooms, hot showers, laundry facilities, water, and grills. No RV hookups. No reservations. Sites $15. Day-use free. AmEx/D/MC/V.)

◤ APPROACHING BEAUFORT: 98 MILES

From Wilmington, take **U.S. 17 N** to Jacksonville, then take **Rte. 24 E.** Rte. 24 will become **Rte. 70 E.**

BEAUFORT

A tiny town near Morehead City on Cedar Island, Beaufort is home to a beautiful, quaint downtown with a celebrated history. It may be small, but Beaufort offers a relaxed weekend of window-shopping and strolling by the river.

VITAL STATS

Population: 4000

Visitor Info: Beaufort Historic Site (☎252-728-5225; www.beauforthistoricsite.org), at Turner St. Open M-Sa 9:30am-5pm, Su noon-4pm.

Internet Access: Carteret County Public Library, 210 Turner St. (☎252-728-2050). Open M-Th 8:30am-9pm, F 8:30am-6pm, Sa 8:30am-5pm. Free.

Post Office: 701 Front St. (☎252-728-4821). Open M-F 9am-12:50pm and 2-4pm, Sa 10am-noon. **Postal Code:** 28516.

▐ GETTING AROUND. Turner St. leads south from **U.S. 70** to the main part of Beaufort, including the historic downtown. **Front St.** runs along the water downtown and is home to most of the shops and restaurants.

◘ SIGHTS. The **Beaufort Historic Site,** at 100 Turner St., is composed of six historic buildings owned by the Beaufort Historic Society. The **Mattie King Davis Art Gallery** features rotating paintings and sculptures by local artists as well as several restored buildings. Be sure to visit the **Apothecary Shop** and **Doctor's Office,** built in 1859, for a glimpse of dusty bottles and grisly medical instruments. Visitors can also tour the **Carteret County Courthouse,** the oldest wood-framed courthouse in the state, the **Josiah Bell House,** and the **Old Jail,** among other historic buildings. (☎252-728-5225; www.beauforthistoricsite.org. Art Gallery open M-Sa 10am-4pm. Tours M-Sa 10, 11:30am, 1, 3pm. Tours $8, ages 6-12 $4.) The **Beaufort Historical Association** gives double-decker bus tours to the nearly 100 historical buildings throughout town. (☎252-728-5225. Tours M, W, F 11am and 1:30pm; Sa 11am. $8, ages 6-12 $4.) A block or so away lies the **Old Burying Ground,** a cemetery deeded to the town in 1731. The site has a pamphlet for a self-guided walking tour with stories about the interred. Most of the graves face east because those buried wanted the sun on their faces on the morning of Judgment Day. (☎252-728-5225. Open daily 8am-5pm. Tours June-Sept. Tu-Th 2:30pm. $6, children $3.) Those looking for a more fantastical historical experience can follow the **Ghost Walk,** which leads ghost hunters to the **Hammock House**—purportedly once owned by Blackbeard—and ends at the Old Burying Ground. (Tours depart from Front St. across the street from the Inlet Inn; look for a flag marked with a red cross. ☎252-342-0715. Call ahead for hours. $10, under 12 $8.)

The **North Carolina Maritime Museum,** 315 Front St., features exhibits on Blackbeard, who met his end just miles from Beaufort, along with model ships and an underwater observation chamber that you can climb inside. Those who haven't yet satisfied their nautical cravings can head across the street to the **Harvey W. Smith Watercraft Center,** an extension of the museum, and see small watercraft being handbuilt by experts, as well as displays of tools and the "half-models" used to design ships. (☎252-728-7317; www.ah.dcr.state.nc.us/sections/maritime. Open M-F 9am-5pm, Sa 10am-5pm, Su 1-5pm. Free.) **Fort Macon State Park** lies a few miles south of Beaufort at Atlantic City Beach. Constructed between 1826 and 1834, the fort is a pentagonal structure that was used in both the Civil War and the Spanish-American War. Check out the soldiers' quarters, the commissary, and the "hot shot furnace," which heated nonexplosive cannonballs in order to destroy wooden marine vessels. (Take Rte. 70 S, then head east over the Highrise Bridge and take a left on E. Ft. Macon Rd., which heads right to the fort. ☎252-726-3775. Swimming area open daily 10am-5:45pm. Fort open daily 9am-5:30pm. Tours daily every hr. 10am-3pm. Free.)

◘ FOOD. Downtown Beaufort has a generous array of tasty, elegant restaurants. The **Beaufort Grocery Co. ❸,** 117 Queen St., serves delicious sandwiches, like the "fuhgeddabou-

WEH 'E DEH AT?

In the small towns between Cape Fear and the St. Johns River, you might hear the musical lilt of Gullah, a dialect that combines elements of West African languages and 17th- and 18th-century English. Gullah arose as a pidgin dialect that allowed slaves from different communities in Africa to communicate with each other and their owners. The language, along with traditional art forms like quilting and basket weaving, has survived for hundreds of years in insular Gullah communities along the East coast. Recently, however, tourist resorts have sprung up in Gullah areas, and rising property taxes are forcing the Gullah to leave the area. Without a close community, the long-term survival of the language is seriously threatened, and the area has been designated one of the 11 most endangered places in America by the National Trust for Historic Preservation. The Gullah and outsiders are working to preserve this unique culture by digitally recording the language and introducing a bill that would establish a "Heritage Corridor" to protect Gullah land. Though Gullah culture is endangered, the community is working to ensure that the answer to "weh 'e deh at?"—where is it?—remains the same as it has for 300 years.

dit" (turkey, red pepper, greens, bacon; $9) and the "sonnamabeach" (ham, capocolla, salami, and cheeses; $10) in a casual cafe setting. (☎252-728-3899. Open Memorial Day to Labor Day daily 11:30am-3:30pm and 5:30-9:30pm; Labor Day to Memorial Day M and W-Su 11:30am-3:30pm and 5:30-9:30pm. D/MC/V.) The **Spouter Inn ❷**, 218 Front St., makes superb sandwiches, like the Islander (veggies in pita with balsamic vinaigrette; $6) and the One Eye Terrible (ham, salami, and swiss; $7.50). The restaurant overlooks the calm waters of Taylor's Creek. (☎252-728-5190. Open 11:30am-2:30pm and 5-9pm. AmEx/MC/V.) Part pool hall, part casual restaurant, the **Royal James Cafe ❶**, 117 Turner St., offers a refreshing break from the expensive eateries downtown and serves burgers ($1.75) and draft beers ($2) to a young local crowd. (☎252-728-4573. Open 9am-2am. Cash only.) A few streets away from the waterfront, **Roland's BBQ ❷**, 815 Cedar St., cooks up real Carolina barbecue plates ($5) and half racks of ribs ($8). It's take-out only, so take your Q and head for the riverbanks. (☎252-728-1953. Open Tu-Th 10:30am-7:30pm, F-Sa 10:30am-8pm. D/MC/V.)

ACCOMMODATIONS. Beaufort is happily devoid of chain accommodations. Unfortunately, it isn't easy on the pocketbook. For cheaper accommodations, travelers can stay in neighboring Morehead City, a few miles south, where cheap motels line Rte. 70. One of only two hotels in town, the **Inlet Inn ❺**, 601 Front St., has 35 enormous rooms with porches on the first two floors, fridges, fireplaces, and continental breakfast. (☎252-728-3600; www.intlet-inn.com. Waterfront rooms in summer $135-155; non-waterfront $115-135. Rooms in other seasons $75-115. AmEx/D/MC/V.) The **Pecan Tree Inn ❺**, 116 Queen St., has seven lovely rooms, porches with rocking chairs, and a 5000 sq. ft. garden. Use of bicycles, Wi-Fi, and continental breakfast with fresh baked bread is included. (☎252-728-6733; www.pecantree.com. Rooms Apr.-Oct. $130-175, Nov.-Mar. $100-140. AmEx/D/MC/V.)

NIGHTLIFE. The Dock House, 500 Front St., is the place to go in town for a beer and live music, usually classic rock or beach. Sit outside and enjoy the breeze coming off the

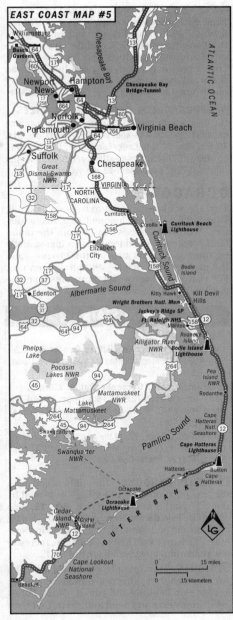

EAST COAST MAP #5

water. (☎252-728-4506. Open daily 11:30am-2am. Kitchen closes 10pm. MC/V.) Hidden behind the shops and restaurants of Front St., the **Backstreet Pub,** 124 Middle Ln., is decorated with tattered flags and life preservers. Locals chat over beers ($3) and live blues on the weekends. (☎252-728-7108. Open daily noon-2am. Cash only.)

◪ APPROACHING OCRACOKE: 61 MILES
The only way to reach Ocracoke is by ferry, which departs from **Cedar Island.** From Beaufort, take **Rte. 70 E** to **Rte. 12 N** to Cedar Island. (☎252-225-3551 or 800-856-0343. Reservations required. $15 per vehicle, $1 per pedestrian, $3 per cyclist.)

OCRACOKE

Tiny Ocracoke was once extremely isolated, allowing for the development of a unique dialect. With ferry access daily from the mainland, Ocracoke's economy relies increasingly on tourism, and as a result the brogue—and the natives' way of life—is fading from use. For visitors, the town still represents a unique escape from the hustle of mainland life.

VITAL STATS

Population: 770

Visitor Info: Ocracoke Visitors Center (☎252-928-4531), located off Rte. 12 by the ferry. Open daily 9am-6pm.

Internet Access: Ocracoke Public Library, on Back Rd. (☎252-928-4436.) Open M and Th noon-4pm and 7-9pm, Tu-W and F noon-4pm, Sa 9am-1pm. Free.

Post Office: Off Rte. 12, at the northern end of town (☎252-928-4771). Open M-F 9am-2pm and 3-5pm, Sa 10am-1pm. **Postal Code:** 27960.

⬛ GETTING AROUND. The entire island, with the exception of Ocracoke village, is owned by the U.S. National Park Service. **Rte. 12,** also called the **Irvin Garrish Hwy.,** stretches the length of the island and forms the major road in Ocracoke. It's hard to get lost in Ocracoke; there are few roads, and most lead back to Rte. 12.

◪ SIGHTS. Most people come to Ocracoke for the beaches; there are several public access points along the island. Those interested in watersports need look no farther than

the booths lining Rte. 12 in town, and many visitors also rent bikes to pedal through the island. The **Ocracoke Lighthouse,** on Lighthouse Rd., was built in 1823 and stands 75 ft. tall. A boardwalk leads to the lighthouse, but alas, no one can go inside. The **Ocracoke Preservation Society Museum,** near the ferry terminal, displays artifacts from life on Ocracoke Island, including a parlor with a cast-iron stove and a kitchen with a hand-pump, highlighting the recent installation of running water in 1970. The museum also has a room devoted to the Ocracoke brogue, including a video illustrating the pronunciation, grammar, and vocabulary—"dingbatters" are non-natives of the island. (☎252-928-7375. Open M-F 10am-5pm, Sa 11am-4pm. Free.) The **Pony Pasture,** on Rte. 12, acts as the stomping grounds for a herd of semi-wild horses, said to be descendants of horses left here by shipwrecked explorers in the 16th or 17th century.

◪◪ FOOD AND ACCOMMODATIONS.
Unlike most Ocracoke establishments, **Howard's Pub ❷,** 1175 Irvin Garrish Hwy., is open 365 days a year. During the day, enjoy hush puppies ($4.50) or a cheeseburger ($7); when night falls, drink up to the strains of live acoustic guitar. (☎252-928-4441; www.howardspub.com. Music begins 9 or 10pm. Open M-Th and Su 11am-10pm, F-Sa 11am-midnight. D/MC/V.) The **Flying Melon Cafe ❷,** on Rte. 12 and Ocean View, is decorated with brightly colored roosters. While you wait for your eggs, biscuit, and grits ($3.50) or fish-of-the-day sandwich ($6.50), pass the time coloring on the tablecloth. (☎252-928-2533. Open Tu-Sa 9am-2pm and 5-9pm, Su 9am-2pm. MC/V.) Shed the beach gear before heading to the elegant **Back Porch Restaurant ❺,** at Rte. 12 and Back Rd., to enjoy the Back Porch salad (apples, stilton, and walnuts; $9), or the salmon and ginger for $19. (☎252-928-6401. Open daily 5-9:30pm. MC/V.)

For bright rooms at low prices, visit the **Sand Dollar Motel ❹,** 70 Sand Dollar Rd. Rates include refrigerators, microwaves, A/C, cable TV, pool, and breakfast. (☎252-928-5571 or 866-928-5571. Open Apr. to late Nov. Rooms May-Aug. from $80; Sept.-Nov. and Apr. from $45. AmEx/D/MC/V.) **Blackbeard's Lodge ❺,** 111 Back Rd., offers ship-shape wood-paneled rooms. The swing and rocking chairs on the porch provide a spot to relax, and the large game room downstairs feels like a ship's cabin. (☎252-928-3421, reservations 800-892-5314; www.blackbeardslodge.com. A/C, cable TV, and pool. Rooms in summer $125; in winter $53-62. AmEx/D/MC/V.) Because Ocracoke is part of the **Cape Hatteras National Seashore ❶**, there are plenty of places to camp just steps from the beach. The campground has water and restrooms, but those in search of electricity and heated showers will be disappointed. The 136 sites may be reserved from March to October; the rest of the year they're first come, first served. (☎800-365-2267. Sites $20. MC/V.)

⚐ APPROACHING CAPE HATTERAS: 60 MILES
Free ferries run between **Ocracoke** and **Cape Hatteras** (40min.; daily 5am-midnight). The ferry is subject to rush hour traffic; arrive early to avoid a wait.

CAPE HATTERAS
Hatteras Island, covered almost entirely by the **Cape Hatteras National Seashore**, stretches 70 mi. and includes several small towns. Gorgeous, duned public access beaches line Rte. 12, many of which are deserted save for a lonely swimmer or fisherman. While heading up the coast, drivers can look out to the ocean to marvel at the feared "Graveyard of the Atlantic," the cause of more than 600 shipwrecks. Storms still uncover the remains of unlucky vessels. A few miles north of the ferry, the **Frisco Native American Museum and Natural History Center** is an interactive museum about the history of the island's first inhabitants. The museum consists mostly of local artifacts, such as baskets, bead-work, and a Hopi *kiva* drum. (☎252-995-4400. Open M by appointment, Tu-Su 11am-5pm. $5, seniors $3.) At the southern end of Hatteras Island on Rte. 12 lies the **Cape Hatteras Lighthouse.** As the rangers proudly proclaim, the 210 ft. structure is the tallest brick lighthouse in the world. While you wait for your chance to climb the 248 steps to the top, visit the old keeper's quarters, now a museum with displays on the lighthouse. (☎252-995-4474. Open daily Memorial Day to Labor Day 9am-6pm; Labor Day to Memorial Day 9am-5pm. Museum free. Lighthouse $6, seniors and children $3.) The top half of the island consists of the **Pea Island National Wildlife Refuge,** established in 1938 to preserve the island's unique barrier island habitat. The **visitors center** has info about local wildlife and marks the beginning of the **North Pond Wildlife Trail,** which stretches a half mile to the sound. More intrepid explorers can bike or walk the 4 mi. of service road that encircle the pond and connect back to Rte. 12. (☎252-987-2394. Open in summer daily 9am-4pm; hours vary in winter.)

⚐ APPROACHING ROANOKE ISLAND: 17 MILES
From Cape Hatteras, take **Rte. 12 N** to **U.S. 64 W.**

ROANOKE ISLAND
Roanoke Island was the location of the first (failed) English settlement in the New World. A second settlement on the island was established in 1587 and mysteriously disappeared sometime during the next three years. Though it is most

SPEAKING LIKE AN O'COCKER

Ocracoke was founded in the 1700s and until recently has been fairly isolated from the rest of North Carolina. The island developed its own dialect that sounds completely different from that of the mainland. Speakers pronounce the long i sound (as, for example, in the word high) as "oy." On the mainland, the sound has changed to an "ah" sound (as in "ah'm tahrd" for "I'm tired"). Similarly, Ocracoke residents pronounce ending r sounds, as in the words "car" or "near," while mainland North Carolineans often use a soft r, pronouncing those words as "cah" or "neuh." In addition to the different pronunciation, speakers of the Ocracoke brogue have a specialized vocabulary, some of which was originally used in 18th century England.

So you think you can talk like a native? Try some of these phrases on for size: **Haint** - a ghost. **Mommick** - to bother. **Quamish** - sick to the stomach. **Pizer** - porch. **O'cocker** - a native of Ocracoke.

Now, put it all together: The haint on the pizer mommicked the O'cocker until he was quamish. And if you think that's real brogue, you must be a dingbatter.

[the local story]

famous for its role in early English settlement of the continent, the island also features parks, gardens, and inexpensive food.

VITAL STATS

Population: 6000

Visitor Info: Outer Banks Visitors Bureau, 1 Visitors Center Circle (☎252-473-2138). Open daily 9am-6pm.

Internet Access: Manteo Public Library, on the corner of Burnside Rd. and Hwy. 64 (☎252-473-2372), in Manteo. Open M and Th 10am-7pm, Tu-W and F 9am-5:30pm, Sa 10am-4pm. Free.

Post Office: 212 Hwy. 64 Ste. B (☎252-473-2534). Open M-F 9am-4:30pm, Sa 10am-noon. **Postal Code:** 27954.

GETTING AROUND. U.S. 64 is the largest road on Roanoke Island. It serves as the main thoroughfare of Manteo at the northern end of the island.

SIGHTS. The **Fort Raleigh Visitors Center** has information about the famed lost colony and daily programs explaining and re-enacting pieces of its history. (☎252-473-2111. Visitors center open daily June-Aug. 9am-6pm; Sept.-Mar. 9am-5pm.) This vanished colony is the inspiration for *The Lost Colony*, a musical theatrical extravaganza performed every night in the summer. (☎252-473-3414; www.thelostcolony.org. Shows June-Aug. M-Sa 8:30pm. $16, seniors $15, under 11 $8.) The theater is located on the **Fort Raleigh National Historic Site,** 1409 National Park Rd., which has a restored fort marking the location of the first attempted settlement.

Flowers perfume the air of the romantic **Elizabethan Gardens,** 1411 National Park Dr., where visitors can wander among fountains, finely tended gardens, and a statue of Virginia Dare, the first English child born in the New World. (☎252-473-3234; www.elizabethangardens.org. Open June-Aug. M-Sa 9am-8pm, Su 9am-7pm; Aug.-June hours vary. $8, seniors $7, ages 6-18 $5, under 5 free.) Down the road, the **North Carolina Aquarium** has gators, otters, a touch tank, and an exhibit on hurricanes. (☎866-332-3475. Open daily 9am-5pm. $8, seniors $7, ages 6-17 $6.) Facing the Manteo Waterfront, **Roanoke Island Festival Park,** staffed largely by

accented actors in 16th-century garb, features *Elizabeth II*, a replica of a 16th-century English merchant ship. It also includes a settlement site with craft demonstrations, an art gallery, an interactive museum, and a film depicting native reaction to the European arrival. (Follow signs from the highway. ☎252-475-1500; www.roanokeisland.com. Open in summer daily 9am-6pm. Last entry 5:30pm. $8, students $5, under 6 free.) During the summer, students from the **North Carolina School of the Arts** perform theatre and ballet at the park's outdoor pavilion. (☎252-475-1506. Call ahead for schedule. Free.)

FOOD AND ACCOMMODATIONS. Manteo, where food and accommodations are located, is the largest town on Roanoke Island. Grab a folding chair for some down-home cooking at **T.L.'s Family Restaurant ❷,** in Manteo. Have a short stack of pancakes ($3) at any time of day, or brave the grilled beef liver with gravy and onions for $8. (☎252-473-3489. Open M-Sa 6am-8:30pm, Su 6am-2pm. D/MC/V.) On the waterfront near Festival Park, you'll find **Poor Richard's Sandwich Shop & Pub ❷** serving up reuben sandwiches and burgers ($6). There's live folk and 60s rock on the weekends. (☎252-473-3333. Sandwich shop open M-Sa 8am-3pm. Bar open M-Sa 5pm-midnight, Su noon-midnight. MC/V.) The **Duke of Dare Motor Lodge ❸,** offers a no-nonsense place to rest your head. Large, clean rooms include cable and pool access for some of Manteo's cheapest rates. (☎252-473-2175. Rooms in summer $68, in winter $54. MC/V.) With flowerbeds, a basketball hoop, and wood-paneled rooms, the **Dare Haven Motel ❹,** Rte. 64/264, shows that cheap can be pretty. (☎252-473-2322. Singles $74, doubles $80. AmEx/D/MC/V.)

APPROACHING BODIE AND KITTY HAWK: 18 MILES
From Roanoke Island, take **U.S. 64 E** to **U.S. 158.**

BODIE AND KITTY HAWK

Bodie Island is composed of four towns, with Nags Head at the southern end and Kitty Hawk to the north. The island is the most trafficked of the Outer Banks, due to easy access from the mainland and the Wright Brothers' historic flight in

1903. Despite crowds in the summertime, there are more than enough beaches, restaurants, and kites to go around.

VITAL STATS

Population: 3000

Visitor Info: Aycock Brown Welcome Center, Mi. 1.5 on U.S. 158 (☎252-261-4644), in Kitty Hawk. Open daily 9am-6pm.

Internet Access: Dare County Library, 400 Mustian St. (☎252-441-4331), Mi. 8.5 in Kill Devil Hills, 1 block west of U.S. 158. Open M and Th-F 9am-5:30pm, Tu-W 10am-7pm, Sa 10am-4pm. Free.

Post Office: 3841 N. Croatan Hwy. (☎252-261-2211), in Kitty Hawk. Open M-F 9am-4:30pm, Sa 10am-noon. **Postal Code:** 27949.

GETTING AROUND. Bodie is the northernmost of the Outer Banks islands. It is joined to the mainland by **U.S. 158** and serves as a major point of entry to the Outer Banks for travelers coming south over the **Wright Memorial Bridge.** For much of Bodie Island, **Rte. 12 (Virginia Dare Tr.)** parallels U.S. 158 (called the **Bypass**), with Rte. 12 east of the Bypass along the beach. Directions on Bodie Island are usually given in terms of distances in miles from the bridge. Traffic calls for extra caution and travel time, especially on Saturdays and Sundays.

SIGHTS. The **Wright Brothers National Memorial,** Mi. 8 on U.S. 158, marks the spot where bicycle mechanics Orville and Wilbur Wright took to the skies. Exhibits in the visitors center document the brothers' triumph over gravity. Outside, stone markers show the distance of the four flights taken the morning of December 17, 1903. The **Centennial Pavilion** contains a replica of the plane the brothers used and a timeline of subsequent developments in aviation. (☎252-441-7430. Open daily June-Aug. 9am-6pm; Sept.-May 9am-5pm. $4, under 16 free.) Nearby **Jockey's Ridge State Park,** Mi. 12 on U.S. 158, includes the east coast's largest naturally occurring sand dune, around 100 ft. high and containing some 30 million tons of sand. The museum at the visitors center explains the origins of the big pile of sand. (☎252-441-7132. Open daily June-Aug. 8am-9pm.; Nov.-Feb. 8am-6pm;

Mar., Oct. 8am-7pm; Apr.-May and Sept. 8am-8pm. Free.) The 158 ft. **Currituck Beach Lighthouse,** on the northern tip of the island, 20 mi. north of Kitty Hawk on Rte. 12, was completed in 1875 to fill the final "dark spot" on the state's coast. Visitors can climb the 214 steps to the top of the unpainted brick structure. (☎252-453-4939. Open for climbing daily 10am-6pm. $6, under 8 free.) At the southernmost tip of the island, off the Bypass, is the **Bodie Island Lighthouse,** first lit in 1872. Standing 150 ft. high, the lighthouse is painted with a distinctive white and black striped pattern, each stripe 22 ft. thick. Climbing the lighthouse is not permitted because it is still in use, but the old keeper's house serves as a museum. (☎252-441-5711. Open daily 9am-6pm.) **Public beaches** line the beach road. The beaches are free, but parking is limited—walking is your best bet.

 DID YOU KNOW? Pirates in the Outer Banks used to tied lanterns around their horses' heads to simulate boats bobbing at anchor to lure passing ships onto the offshore sandbars. This practice resulted in the name **Nags Head.**

FOOD. The popular and sometimes crowded, **Tortuga's Lie ❷,** Mi. 11 on Beach Rd. in Nags Head, serves Caribbean-influenced fare, like jerk chicken ($8) and Creole crawdad fett ($8.50) in a low-key, beachy setting. Sandwiches, burgers, and vegetarian options are also available. (☎252-441-7299; www.tortugaslie.com. W sushi night. Open daily 11:30am-10:30pm. AmEx/D/MC/V.) The fun and lively **Chilli Peppers ❷,** Mi. 5.5 on U.S. 158, specializes in top-notch Tex-Mex, like shrimp quesadillas ($7) and veggie burritos ($6.50) in a sun-dried tomato wrap. Happy hour daily 3-5pm. (☎252-441-8081; www.chillipeppers.com. Open daily 11am-10pm. Bar open 11am-2am. AmEx/D/MC/V.) At the **Rundown Cafe ❸,** at Mi. 1 on Rte. 12, food and atmosphere are anything but. The Asian and Caribbean-influenced menu includes coconut fried chicken salad ($10.50) and Jamaican fish soup ($4). At the rooftop Tsunami Bar, patrons enjoy the ocean breeze over a drink. (☎252-255-0026. Open daily 11:30am-10pm.

AmEx/D/MC/V.) The walls at **Stack 'em High ❶**, at Mi. 9 on the Bypass, are covered with riffs on popular sayings, but the food is by-the-book southern. Have a short stack of pancakes ($4) or eggs, grits, and toast ($4.50) in the casual dining room. (☎252-261-8221. Open daily 6:30am-1pm. MC/V.)

⚑ ACCOMMODATIONS. Most visitors stay in houses rented by the week (weekend rentals are sometimes available in the low-season), which range from one-bedroom cottages to oceanfront mansions. The **Outer Banks Motor Lodge ❸**, 1509 S. Virginia Dare Tr., at Mi. 9.5, has large, inexpensive rooms by the ocean. (☎252-441-77404 or 877-625-6343. Cable, fridge, microwave, and pool. Laundry. Rooms in summer from $59; in winter from $39. D/MC/V.) At Mi. 8.5, **The Cavalier Motel ❹**, 601 S. Virginia Dare Tr., has a play area with pool, volleyball net, and shuffleboard. (☎252-441-5585; www.thecavaliermotel.com. Rooms in summer from $88; in winter from $34. D/MC/V.) **Outer Banks Adventure Bound ❶**, 1004 W. Kitty Hawk Rd., offers tent camping, 1½ mi. inland. The campground, which is little more than an open field, has hot showers, volleyball, and shuffleboard courts. (☎252-255-1130. Sites $20. Cash only.)

▧ NIGHTLIFE. During the summer, tourists flood Bodie Island, and bars respond with nightly music and dancing. At Mi. 10.5 on the Bypass, Kelly's Restaurant and Tavern has two bars, a large dance floor, and pool tables. Bands play dance music nightly for a friendly, casual crowd. (☎252-441-4116. Music in summer Tu-Su 10pm-2am; hours vary in winter. M wet T-shirt contest. Cover $2-5. Open daily in summer 4:30pm-2am, in winter 4:30pm-1am. AmEx/D/MC/V.) Winner of the bronze medal at the World Beer Competition, the Outer Banks Brewing Station, Bypass Mi. 8.5, has 6 of its own beers on tap (16 oz. $4). On weekends, regional acts play everything from rock to hip hop. (☎252-449-2739; www.obbrewing.com. Music 10:30pm-2am. W ladies night. Su open mic. Cover $5. Open 11:30am-2am. AmEx/D/MC/V.)

⚐ APPROACHING VIRGINIA BEACH: 88 MILES
From Bodie and Kitty Hawk, take **U.S. 158 W** to **U.S. 168 N**. There is a $2 toll after you enter Virginia. After

60 mi., take **I-64 W** to **I-264 E**, which splits into **21st** and **22nd St.** in downtown Virigina Beach.

VIRGINIA BEACH

This boardwalk-centered town overflows with the all-you-can-eat buffets, age-old motels, and cheap discount stores that are the hallmarks of seemingly every beach town in America. So load up on saltwater taffy, homemade fudge, and tacky t-shirts, because the best part of a Virginia Beach vacation is not getting wrapped up in the stuffiness that plague more pretentious resort towns.

⬛ GETTING AROUND

In Virginia Beach, east-west streets are numbered while north-south avenues, running parallel to the beach, have ocean names. The main east-west thoroughfares are **Virginia Beach Blvd.**, **I-264**, and **Laskin Rd.** Prepare to feel like a thimble on a Monopoly board: **Atlantic** and **Pacific Ave.** comprise the main drag. **Arctic**, **Baltic**, and **Mediterranean Ave.** are farther inland.

VITAL STATS

Population: 430,000

Visitor Info: Virginia Beach Visitors Center, 2100 Parks Ave. (☎757-437-4919 or 800-822-3224; www.vbfun.com), at 22nd St. Open daily June-Aug. 9am-8pm; Sept.-May 9am-5pm.

Internet Access: Virginia Beach Public Library, 4100 Virginia Beach Blvd. (☎757-219-2640). Open June-Sept. M-Th 10am-9pm, F-Sa 10am-5pm; Oct.-May M-Th 10am-9pm, F-Sa 10am-5pm, Su 1-5pm. Free.

Post Office: 201 Virginia Beach Blvd. (☎757-463-5925). Open M-F 7:30am-7pm, Sa 10am-3pm. **Postal Code:** 23452.

SIGHTS

CONTEMPORARY ART CENTER OF VIRGINIA. The constantly changing galleries showcase photography, installations, and video. Would-be collectors are in luck—many of the works featured are for sale. *(2200 Parks Ave. ☎ 757-425-0000; www.cacv.org. Open Tu-F 10am-5pm, Sa 10am-4pm, Su noon-4pm. In summer $7; seniors, students, and military $5; in winter $5/$3.)*

VIRGINIA BEACH. Toned and tanned bods drag surfboards through the thick, heavy sand of Virginia Beach. The boardwalk, with lanes for walking and biking, runs 3 mi. past a pier and amusement park. Live music plays at bandshells at 24th St. and 31st St. *(☎ 757-491-7866.)*

BACK BAY NATIONAL WILDLIFE REFUGE. Composed of islands, dunes, forests, marshes, ponds, and beaches, this remote national refuge is a sanctuary for an array of endangered species and other wildlife, not to mention tourists tired of Virginia Beach's joyful tackiness. With nesting bald eagles and peregrine falcons, the natural wonderland is open to the public for camping, hiking, fishing, and photography—but only on foot. Driving is prohibited beyond the Visitor Contact Station. The Back Bay Tram is also available to transport visitors around the refuge. *(Take General Booth Blvd. to Princess Anne Dr.; turn left, then take Sandbridge Rd., and continue approximately 6 mi. Turn right on Sandpiper Rd., which leads to the visitors center. ☎ 757-721-2412; www.backbay.fws.gov. Open daily sunrise-sunset. $5 per vehicle May-Oct. Tram ☎ 757-721-7666 or 757-426-3643; www.bbrf.org. Departs daily 9am, returns 12:45pm. $8, seniors and under 12 $6.)* Also in the refuge, False Cape State Park got its name because ships used to touch shore here in the 17th century, mistakenly thinking that they had landed at the nearby Cape Henry (where America's first English settlers landed in 1607). False Cape State Park is located 4 mi. within the refuge, and can only be reached by foot, bicycle, or the tram. *(4001 Sandpiper Rd. ☎ 757-426-7128 or 800-933-7275, tours 888-669-8368 or 757-480-1999; www.dcr.state.va.us/parks. No hookups.)*

VIRGINIA AQUARIUM AND MARINE SCIENCE CENTER. Virginia's largest aquarium is home to hundreds of species of fish, including crowd-pleasing sharks and sea turtles. A wooden boardwalk connects the main building with the Marsh Pavilion. The museum also houses a six-story IMAX theater and offers excursions for dolphin observation in summer and whale watching in winter. *(717 General Booth Blvd., 1 mi. drive or 30min. walk south down Pacific Ave., which becomes General Booth Blvd. ☎ 757-425-3474, excursions 757-437-2628; www.vmsm.com. Open daily in summer 9am-7pm; in winter 9am-5pm. $12, seniors $11, ages 3-11 $8.)*

FOOD

Cuisine and Co., 3004 Pacific Ave. (☎ 757-428-6700; www.cuisineandcompany.com). This sophisticated eatery serves gourmet lunches and rich desserts in a sleek, clean environment. Take your vegetarian (avocado, mushrooms, sprouts, swiss; $4.25) to a cafe armchair, and be sure to save room for a slab of killer chocolate cake ($4.25). Open Labor Day to Memorial Day M-Sa 9am-7pm, Su 9am-6pm. AmEx/D/MC/V. ❶

The Jewish Mother, Pacific Ave. (☎ 757-422-5430; www.jewishmother.com). Heal what ails you with some matzoh ball soup ($3.25) or a hot pastrami on rye ($8.50). The restaurant also offers some decidedly unkosher options, like a bacon cheeseburger ($9)—oy, gevalt! Open daily 8am-2am. AmEx/D/MC/V. ❷

Chicho's, 2112 Atlantic Ave. (☎ 757-422-6011; www.chichoshr.com), at 29th St. One of the most popular spots on the strip with pizza ($3 per slice) and hot 'n' spicy wings ($6). Live reggae some weekends, starting at 10pm. Open M-Th and Su 11:30am-midnight, F-Sa 11:30am-2am. AmEx/D/MC/V. ❶

ACCOMMODATIONS

Angie's Guest Cottage, Bed and Breakfast, and HI-AYH Hostel, 302 24th St. (☎ 757-428-4690; www.angiescottage.com). Barbara "Angie" Yates and staff welcome guests to an old house with a fantastic location. Kitchen, barbecue grill, ping-pong, and boogie boards. No A/C. Linen $2. Street parking first come, first served with a $20 deposit. Reception 9am-9pm. Check-out 10am. 2-night min. stay for nonmembers. Reservations recommended. Apr.-Oct. 4- to 9-bed dorms $21, members $17; Oct.-Apr. $17/$14. Private singles $38. Cash or check only. ❶

First Landings, 2500 Shore Dr. (☎757-412-2300 or 800-933-7275; www.dcr.state.va.us), about 8 mi. north of town on Rte. 60. Picnic areas, swimming on a sprawling beach, a bathhouse, and boat launching areas. Cabins include full kitchen, furnishings, fireplace, and A/C. Call several months ahead for reservations. Sites $24, with hookup $30; cabins May-Sept. $126; Sept.-Nov. and Apr.-May $90; Dec.-Mar. $68. AmEx/D/MC/V. ❺

The Castle Motel, 2700 Pacific Ave. (☎757-425-9330). Quite possibly the best bang for your buck as motels go. Spacious, clean rooms come with cable TV, refrigerator, and outdoor pool. The beach is just 2 blocks away. Rooms in summer M-F from $90, Sa-Su from $130; call for winter rates. AmEx/D/MC/V. ❺ *GROSS*

◧ NIGHTLIFE

Peabody's, 209 21st St., at Pacific Ave. (☎757-422-6212; www.peabodysvirginiabeach.com). This venerable club offers something for everyone—pounding dance music, pool tables, and occasional live music. ▨**Fierce dodgeball matches** on the dance floor every F before the music starts. Th ladies night. F college night. F-Sa 21+. Cover $5. Open Th-Sa 7pm-2am. AmEx/D/MC/V.

Mahi Mah's, 615 Atlantic Ave. (☎757-437-8030; www.mahimahs.com), at 7th St., inside the Ramada Hotel. During the summer, a band plays every night from 7-11pm, with music ranging from bluegrass to 70s R&B. Seafood, sushi, and an extensive wine list. W karaoke. Happy hour daily 3-7pm. Open daily 7am-2am. AmEx/D/MC/V.

Harpoon Larry's, 216 24th St. (☎757-422-6000; www.harpoonlarrys.com), at Pacific Ave., serves tasty fish in an everyone-knows-your-name atmosphere. The amicable staff welcomes twenty- and thirtysomethings to the loud, friendly bar. Specials include oysters (M; $0.35) and rum runners (Tu and Th 7-9pm; $2.50). W $0.25 jalapeño poppers. Open May-Sept. daily noon-2am; hours vary in winter. AmEx/MC/V.

Lunasea, 206 22nd St. (☎757-437-4400). With a sand pit in the back and a patio out front, this restaurant and bar offers locals a place to relax. If the volleyball gives you an appetite, there are chimichangas ($10) and crabcakes ($9). Tu and Th live music, usually acoustic. Sa local DJ. W $2 Pabst. Open M-Th 6pm-2am, F-Su 11:30am-2am. AmEx/D/MC/V.

◰ **APPROACHING HAMPTON: 30 MILES**
From Virginia Beach, take **I-264 W** to **I-64 W**. Take **Exit 267** to Hampton.

HAMPTON

With a small, active downtown with museums, restaurants, and shops, Hampton has a big city feel on a tiny scale. The town's relaxed, uncommercialized approach to tourism makes it a refreshing break from East Coast beach resorts.

VITAL STATS

Population: 150,000

Visitor Info: Hampton Visitors Center, 120 Hampton Ln. (☎757-727-1102 or 800-800-2202; www.hamptoncvb.com). Open daily 9am-5pm.

Internet Access: Hampton Public Library, 4207 Victoria Blvd. (☎757-727-1312; www.hamptonpubliclibrary.org). Open M-Th 9am-9pm, F-Sa 9am-5pm, Su 1-5pm. Free.

Post Office: 809 Aberdeen Rd. (☎757-826-0299). Open M-F 8am-7pm, Sa 9am-3pm. **Postal Code:** 23670.

◧ GETTING AROUND

Off the highway, take a left onto **Settlers Landing Rd.,** the main drag through downtown. The **Hampton River** runs between downtown and the Hampton University campus.

◉ SIGHTS

▨**VIRGINIA AIR AND SPACE CENTER.** With simulators, build-your-own paper airplanes, and a B-24, the museum will have even the stodgiest visitor shouting, "I want to be a fighter pilot!" The flight simulators let visitors step into the cockpit of a number of different jets with slightly less risk than the real thing. The enormous IMAX theater plays films on everything from volcanos to space travel. (*600 Settlers Landing Rd.* ☎757-727-0900 *or 800-296-0800; www.vasc.org. Open M-W 10am-5pm, Th-Su 10am-7pm. $9, seniors and military $8, children $7. IMAX $8/$7/$6.75.*)

HAMPTON UNIVERSITY MUSEUM. The Emancipation Proclamation was first read at

Hampton University in 1863; the University's museum is dedicated to African-American history, containing over 9000 artifacts and works of art. *(In the Huntington Bldg., on the Hampton University campus. Follow Settlers Landing Rd. over the Hampton River, and take a right into the Hampton University campus. ☎ 757-727-5308. Open M-F 8am-5pm, Sa noon-4pm. Free.)*

HAMPTON HISTORY MUSEUM. The museum gives an interactive view of the oldest permanent English-speaking settlement in America. Starting with the Kecoughtan tribes, exhibits continue through the Civil War to the present day. *(120 Old Hampton Ln. ☎ 757-727-1610 or 800-800-2202. Open M-Sa 10am-5pm, Su 1-5pm. $5; ages 4-12, seniors, and military $4.)*

SANDY BOTTOM NATURE PARK. Visitors can rent boats and canoes to explore the lake, learn about the local animals and habitats at the **Nature Center,** or go birding at the observation tower. Ten trails run through the park, all marked and most fairly level. *(1255 Big Bethel Rd. From I-64, take Exit 261A. ☎ 757-825-4657; www.hampton.gov/ sandybottom. Canoes $4 per hr., $15 per day. Park open daily sunrise-sunset. Nature Center open M-Th 9am-6pm, F-Su 9am-7:30pm. Free.)*

HAMPTON CAROUSEL. This antique carousel, located at the Buckroe Beach Amusement Park from 1921 until the city bought it in 1985, is one of only 70 such carousels still functioning in the US. In addition to being a great ride for kids, it's also an unexpected example of American folk art; the horses and oil paintings are all originals. *(On Settlers Landing Rd., by the Virginia Air and Space Center. ☎ 757-727-0900. Open M-W noon-5pm, Th-Su noon-7pm. $1.50, 5 rides $5.)*

THE COUSTEAU SOCIETY. The U.S. headquarters for the Cousteau Society, the building hosts a small museum about the life and work of underwater explorer Jacques-Yves Cousteau. Although best appreciated by those already somewhat familiar with Cousteau's work, it has several nifty pieces, including the remains of a mechanical, remote-controlled shark named Allison, and one of the claustrophobia-inducing mini-subs Cousteau used to explore the depths from the deck of the *Calypso*. *(710 Settlers Landing Rd. ☎ 757-722-9300 or 800-441-4395. Open in summer daily 9:30am-4pm; in winter W-Su 9:30am-4pm. Free.)*

FOOD

Most of Hampton's restaurants are downtown, and nice options are on **Queens Way. La Bodega Hampton ❶,** 22 Wine St., serves inexpensive sandwiches on freshly baked bread like the Navigator (turkey, sun-dried tomatoes, and gouda; $6). La Bodega also sells gourmet food and a variety of wines, specializing in local vineyards. (☎ 757-722-8466; www.labodegahampton.com. Open M-F 7:30am-6pm, Sa 10am-3pm. AmEx/D/MC/V.) For some southern comfort, try the **Grey Goose Tearoom ❷,** 101 W. Queens Way, where you'll find Virginia ham croissants ($6.50) and steaming Brunswick stew for only $4. (☎ 757-723-7978. Open M-Sa 11am-3pm. AmEx/D/MC/V.) **Marker'20 ❷,** 21 E. Queens Way, serves microbrews and fresh seafood in a pub atmosphere. Try their signature crab dip ($7.50) or a thick 10 oz. burger for $5.50. (☎ 757-726-9410; www.marker20.com. Open daily 11am-2am. AmEx/MC/V.)

ACCOMMODATIONS

Most accommodations in Hampton are generic hotel chains of varying rates and qualities. The **Little England Inn ❺,** 4400 Victoria Blvd., provides three rooms in a sprawling house in a residential neighborhood only a few blocks from Settlers Landing Rd. Enjoy the roof garden with hot tub and lounge chairs. (☎ 757-722-0985 or 800-606-0985; www.littleenglandinn.com. Breakfast included. Rooms $145. AmEx/D/MC/V.) A few miles from downtown, the **Hampton Manor Motel ❷,** 1515 W. Pembroke Ave., offers clean, inoffensive rooms with cable, fridge, freezer, and microwave. (☎ 757-723-0727. Laundry. Rooms $40. AmEx/D/MC/V.) The **Sandy Bottom Nature Park ❶,** bounded by I-64, Big Bethel Rd., and Hampton Road Center Pkwy., has nine sites with picnic tables and barbecue, but no electricity or water. (☎ 757-825-4657; www.hampton.gov/sandybottom. Quiet hours 10pm-7am. No reservations. Sites $10; cabins $40. $60 deposit required for cabins. AmEx/D/MC/V.)

DETOUR
BUSCH GARDENS
Located 30 mi. west of Hampton, off I-64.

Busch Gardens puts its own spin on Williamsburg's colonial theme. The park is divided into themed sections such as "Italy," "Germany," and "New France," with appropriate restaurants and rides. A train runs around the park's perimeter from the entrance to New France on the other side, and a skyride provides a view of the park and quicker journey from England to France. The park features four roller coasters: the hurtling **Apollo's Chariot**, the tamer **Big Bad Wolf**, the **Loch Ness Monster**, and the hilariously named **Alpengeist**. There are tons of snack stands, but those in search of a heartier meal can try the **Trapper Smokehouse** ❸, which smokes meat on a huge grill and serves up half-racks of ribs ($11) and baby back ribs ($15). The **Ristorante della Piazza** ❷ offers basic Italian pasta dishes like chicken parmesan ($7.50) with breadsticks. (☎800-343-7946; www.buschgardens.com. Open M-Th and Su 10am-9pm, F-Sa 10am-10pm. $52, ages 3-6 $45. Restaurants open 11:30am-8:30 or 9:30pm.)

⚑ APPROACHING WILLIAMSBURG: 2 MILES
From Busch Gardens, take **I-64 W** to Williamsburg.

WILLIAMSBURG

Colonial Williamsburg manages to recreate the world of colonial America faithfully, appealing to tourists but not pandering to them. The result is a town where men in wigs and tights hardly draw a glance. A few blocks away from the historical madness, the College of William and Mary provides great cafes, bookstores, and nightlife. Travelers who visit in late fall or early spring avoid the crowds but miss the special summer programs.

VITAL STATS

Population: 12,000

Visitor Info: Colonial Williamsburg Visitors Center, 100 Visitors Center Dr. (☎757-229-1000 or 800-447-8679; www.colonialwilliamsburg.com). Open daily 8:45am-9pm.

Internet Access: Williamsburg Library, 7770 Croaker Rd. (☎757-259-4040). Open M-Th 10am-9pm, F 10am-6pm, Sa 10am-5pm, Su 1-5pm. Free.

Post Office: 425 N. Boundary St. (☎757-229-0838). Open M-F 8am-5pm, Sa 9am-2pm. **Postal Code:** 23185.

▣ GETTING AROUND

The **Colonial Pkwy.** enters Williamsburg from the east, curving south to intersect with **Rte. 5** and **Francis St. Duke of Gloucester St.**, the focal point of Colonial Williamsburg's sights, runs parallel to Francis St., one block north. Cars are not permitted within the historic area. A shuttle runs from the visitors center to the colonial area, though a short walking path is also available. The **Orientation Walking Tour,** included with admission, begins at the shuttle stop and introduces visitors to the main sights of the town.

▣ SIGHTS

At **Colonial Williamsburg,** the world's largest living history museum, you'll see drummer boys and bayonet-wielding soldiers walking alongside visitors on cell phones. Many of the costumed interpreters have spent years learning their craft, and one of the most interesting ways to experience Williamsburg is to see a wigmaker, brickmaker, or silversmith at work. Visitors who want to dress the part can rent costumes inside the visitors center. There are over 80 original 18th-century buildings in the historic area, and 500 more have been reconstructed. The **Public Gaol** (pronounced "jail") on Market Sq. shows what happened to those colonists who stole a horse or failed to honor the sabbath. The **Governor's Palace,** at the head of the village green, housed seven colonial governors (as well as Patrick Henry and Thomas Jefferson). Five hundred swords and guns festoon the walls of the building, which has been restored to its appearance in the days of Governor Dunmore, the last of the British colonial governors. At the **Raleigh Tavern,** on Duke of Gloucester St., tours explain the significance of the tavern in town life. Tours of the **Capitol** focus on the events and philosophies that led up to the American Revolution. Performances occur throughout the day at the reconstructed **Play Booth Theater.** The original was an indoor theater, but this incarnation was built to resemble open-air English theaters of the colonial era. Those interested in the painstaking process that transformed a sleepy 1920s town into colonial Williamsburg will enjoy touring **Bassett Hall.**

EAST COAST

Multimillionaire John D. Rockefeller financed the initial venture, and his home is preserved as it looked when he lived there in the 1930s. (☎757-229-1000 or 800-447-8679. Most exhibits open daily 9am-5pm. Capital City pass $34, ages 6-17 $15; includes access to over 40 sites and orientation walk, but not the Governor's Palace or Bassett Hall. Governor's Key to the City pass $48/$24; includes Governor's Palace, Bassett Hall, and 2nd day.)

🍴 FOOD

The Cheese Shop ❶, in Merchant's Sq., is a popular stop for a quick, tasty meal. Doubling as a gourmet food store, the restaurant sells fresh sandwiches like veggie focaccia ($5) and prosciutto ($5.75), perfect for eating on the patio out front. Go early or late to avoid the lunchtime rush. (☎757-220-0298. Open M-Sa 10am-8pm, Su 11am-6pm. AmEx/D/MC/V.) With art on the walls and a jug of espresso beans on the counter, **Aromas ❷**, 431 Prince George St., caters to the college crowd up the road. While you enjoy the Prince George portobello wrap ($6.25) or cheese fondue ($9), read one of the "recycled" newspapers left by earlier customers. (☎757-221-6676; www.aromasworld.com. Free Wi-Fi. Open M-Th 7am-10pm, F-Sa 7am-11pm, Su 8am-8pm. MC/V.) Walk a few minutes down Prince George St. to **The College Delly ❷**, 336 Richmond Rd., a student favorite that serves all the classic late night foods. (☎757-229-6627. Burgers $3.75. Medium pizza $11.25. Subs $6.25. Open daily 10:30am-2am. MC/V.) **The Old Chickahominy House ❷**, 1211 Jamestown Rd., 1½ mi. from the historic district, serves plantation breakfasts with ham, bacon, sausage, eggs, grits, and biscuits ($8.50) in a down-home setting. (☎757-229-4689. Open daily 8:30-10:15am and 11:30am-2:15pm. MC/V.)

🔑 ACCOMMODATIONS

There are many chain hotels and motels along Rte. 60. Make reservations in advance in the summer, but during quieter times, you can often get major discounts as a walk-up at the Lodging and Dining desk in the visitors center. Three blocks from the historic area, the

Bassett Motel ❸, →Nice 800 York St., has large, standard rooms. (☎757-229-5175. Rooms in summer $59; call for winter rates. MC/V.) Just up the road, the **Quarterpath Inn ❹**, 620 York St., has clean, basic rooms with pool access. (☎757-220-0960 or 800-446-9222. Rooms in summer M-Th and Su $75, F-Sa $90; in winter $45/$49. AmEx/D/MC/V.) For those who can afford it, the **Liberty Rose ❺**, 1022 Jamestown Rd., is a romantic Victorian B&B with lavishly decorated rooms. (☎757-253-1260 or 800-545-1825; www.libertyrose.com. Rooms from $185. AmEx/D/MC/V.)

🎵 NIGHTLIFE

Though Williamsburg rolls up the welcome mat early in the evening, the nearby College of William and Mary provides plenty of great options. Don't be fooled by the name—**Paul's Deli**, 761 Scotland St., has a young, laid-back bar scene. Have a pitcher of Budweiser ($6.50) and listen to the guitarist who plays on Wednesdays. (☎757-229-8976. M open mic. Open daily 10:30am-2am. MC/V.) Next door, the **Green Leafe**, 765 Scotland St., appeals to college kids and townies alike with 30 beers on tap and over 100 bottled brews. (☎757-220-3405; www.greenleafe.com. Th any Virginia draft $1.50. Su mug night. Open 10:30am-2am. AmEx/D/MC/V.)

🚗 APPROACHING ASSATEAGUE AND CHINCOTEAGUE: 145 MILES

From Williamsburg, take **I-64 E** to **U.S. 13 N.** Just after switching to U.S. 13, pay a $12 toll and continue to **Rte. 175 E**, which takes you to Chincoteague.

ASSATEAGUE AND CHINCOTEAGUE

Crashing waves, windswept dunes, wild ponies galloping free—if it sounds like the stuff of a childhood fantasy, that's because it is. Local legend has it that ponies first came to Assateague Island by swimming ashore from a sinking Spanish galleon. A less romantic and more likely theory is that miserly colonial farmers put their horses out to graze on Assateague to avoid mainland taxes. Whatever their origins,

1976: Julius "Dr. J" Irving dunks from the free-throw line, predating the Air Jordan logo by 2 decades.

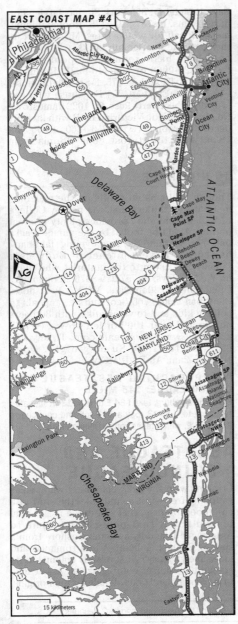

EAST COAST MAP #4

EAST COAST

the famous ponies now roam free across unspoiled beaches and picturesque forests.

VITAL STATS

Population: 4300

Visitor Info: Barrier Island Visitors Center, 7206 National Seashore Ln./Rte. 611 (☎410-641-1441), in Berline, MD. Open daily 9am-5pm. **Chincoteague Chamber of Commerce,** 6733 Maddox Blvd. (☎757-336-6161; www.chincoteague.com), in Chincoteague. Open M-Sa 9am-4:30pm.

Internet Access: Island Library, 4077 Main St. (☎757-336-3460), in Chincoteague. Open M-Tu 10am-5pm, W and F-Sa 1-5pm, Th 4-8pm. Free.

Post Office: 4144 Main St. (☎757-665-7412). Open M-F 8am-4:30pm, Sa 8:30am-noon. **Postal Code:** 23336.

GETTING AROUND

Assateague Island is the longer barrier island facing the ocean, while **Chincoteague Island** is nestled between Assateague and the mainland eastern shore. Chincoteague is developed, but Assateague is entirely parkland. Maryland and Virginia share Assateague Island, which is divided into three parts: the **Assateague State Park** (in Maryland), the **Assateague Island National Seashore** (Maryland), and the **Chincoteague Wildlife Refuge** (Virginia), which is actually on Assateague. Driving the length of Assateague Island is neither permitted nor possible—there aren't any roads.

SIGHTS

ASSATEAGUE. The ⌘**Chincoteague National Wildlife Refuge** stretches across the Virginia side of the island. Avid birdwatchers flock here to see rare species such as peregrine falcons, snowy egrets, and black-crowned night herons. During the **Pony Penning,** held the last consecutive Wednesday and Thursday in July, local firemen herd the ponies together for a swim from Assateague to Chincoteague Island, where they are auctioned off. Head to the visitors center, located just inside the refuge, to learn about biking, hiking, walking, and bird and nature tours. Guided wildlife bus tours are also available. (*Tours Memorial Day to Labor Day* daily 10am, 1, 4pm. $12, seniors $10, children $5.) Trails include the 3 mi. pony-populated **Wildlife Loop** (open 3pm-sunset for vehicles; 24hr. for pedestrians and bicyclists), the 1½ mi. **Woodland Trail,** and the quarter-mile **Lighthouse Trail.** The last leads to the **Assateague Lighthouse,** which is closed to visitors for repairs. Park rangers request that visitors resist the urge to feed the ponies, who, if overfed by guests, could starve in the winter months when visitors have left the islands. Gawk from a safe distance—the ponies may appear to be harmless, but they can be temperamental. *(8231 Beach Rd., off Maddox Blvd. ☎ 757-336-6122; http://chinco.fws.gov. No pets permitted. Park open daily May-Sept. 5am-10pm; Oct. and Apr. 6am-8pm; Nov.-Mar. 6am-6pm. Visitors center open daily Memorial Day to Labor Day 9am-5pm; Labor Day to Memorial Day 8am-4:30pm. 7-day pass $10 per vehicle.)*

CHINCOTEAGUE. The **Oyster & Maritime Museum** is the only nonprofit museum in Chincoteague. Originally focused on the seafood industry, it has turned its attention to local history. Don't miss the 1865 Barbier & Frenestre first-order Fresnel lens from the old Assateague Lighthouse, one of only 21 in the US. Its light could be seen from 23 mi. away. *(7125 Maddox Blvd. ☎ 757-336-6117. Open May-Sept. M-Sa 10am-5pm, Su noon-5pm. Free.)* The **Chincoteague Pony Centre,** capitalizing on a children's book set in Chincoteague, has a museum dedicated to all things "Misty"—including a few of her descendants. The center also offers pony rides and showcases veterans of the pony swim in shows every night at 8pm. *(6417 Carriage Dr. Heading north on Main St., turn right on Church St., left on Chicken City Rd., and right on Carriage Dr. ☎ 757-336-2776. Open in summer M-Sa 9am-10pm. Rides M-Sa 9am-1pm and 3:30-6pm. $6. Museum $5. Shows $8, children $5.)*

🍴 FOOD

Visitors eat and sleep on Chincoteague. The **Sea Star ❶,** 4121 Main St., serves "gourmet carry-out" from a brightly painted booth. Specialties include the Harv ($5.50), with roast beef and havarti cheese on sourdough, and the Super Veggie ($5.25), with avocado, veggies, and swiss. (☎ 757-336-5442. Open M-Sa 11am-6pm, Su 11am-4pm. Cash only.) **AJ's on the**

Creek ❸, 6585 Maddox Blvd., has treats like artichoke hearts stuffed with crab ($12) and salty oyster sandwiches ($7). The restaurant has a casual atmosphere and a great view of the water. (☎ 757-336-5888. Open M-Sa 11:30am-9pm. AmEx/D/MC/V.) For coffee and scones, stop by **Main Street Shop & Coffee House ❶,** 4288 Main St. The shop also sells quirky clothes, jewelry, and housewares in rainbow colors. (☎ 757-336-6782. Open M-F 8:30am-5pm, Sa-Su 8:30am-4pm. AmEx/D/MC/V.)

🏨 ACCOMMODATIONS

The **Sea Hawk Motel ❹,** 6520 Maddox Blvd., across the street from the Chincoteague Bay, has large rooms with free Wi-Fi and pool access. (☎ 757-336-6527; www.seahawkchincoteague.com. Rooms late May to Sept. $75-80, Oct. to early May $45. AmEx/D/MC/V.) Located closer to the shops of Main St., the **Lighthouse Inn ❹,** 4218 Main St., has soft beds, pool access, and free Wi-Fi. (☎ 757-336-3383 or 888-336-6777; www.mylighthouseinn.com. Rooms in summer M-F $90, Sa-Su $100; in winter $50/$60. AmEx/D/MC/V.) Camping is not permitted on the Virginia side of Assateague; those wishing to camp may use **Assateague State Park** in Maryland (see Ocean City). **Maddox Family Campground ❷,** across from the visitors center, is a sprawling, 500-site complex with a grocery store, arcade, pool, and bath house. (☎ 757-336-3111. Open Mar.-Nov. Tent sites $33; RV sites $36, with full hookup $39. AmEx/D/MC/V.)

🚗 APPROACHING OCEAN CITY: 51 MILES

The road from Chincoteague to Ocean City is slightly confusing; look for signs along the way. From Chincoteague, take **Rte. 175 W** to **U.S. 13 N.** Take U.S. 113 N, then **Rte. 376 E** to **Rte. 661 S** for Assateague State Park; take **Rte. 50** from U.S. 113 for Ocean City.

OCEAN CITY

Ocean City is like an all-you-can-eat buffet—at first, you're overwhelmed by all the choices, but then you look closer and realize there's nothing there worth eating. The city features a strip of Atlantic beach crowded with tourists looking for fun in the form of garish amusement parks, mini-golf, and crowded boardwalks. From June to August, the city is packed and hotel rates skyrocket; the low season allows travelers to enjoy the beaches for reasonable prices.

VITAL STATS

Population: 7200

Visitor Info: Ocean City Visitors Center, 4001 Coastal Hwy. (☎800-626-2326; www.ococean.com), at 40th St., in the Convention Center. Open M-F 8:30am-5pm, Sa-Su 9am-5pm.

Internet Access: Ocean City Public Library (☎410-289-7297), on Coastal Hwy., between 14th and 15th St. Open M, W, F 10am-6pm, Tu and Th 10am-8pm, Sa 10am-2pm.

Parking: Available at the visitors center at 40th St. for free. Also at the Hugh T. Cropper Inlet Lot, at the southern end of the island. 1st 30min. free, $1.50 per hr., $0.25 per additional 10min.; weekends $2 per hr., $0.50 per additional 10min.

Post Office: 7101 Coastal Hwy. (☎410-524-7611). Open M-F 9am-5pm, Sa 9am-noon.
Postal Code: 21842.

GETTING AROUND

Within Ocean City, numbered streets run east-west across the narrow strip of land linking the ocean to the bay. Numbers increase from south to north. Avenues run north-south through town, as does the **Coastal Hwy.** The **Boardwalk** parallels the ocean, running from the southern tip to 27th St. Most hotels are in the lower numbered streets near the ocean, while most clubs and bars are uptown toward the bay. Parking downtown can be extremely difficult during the summer; the city offers a $1 Park-and-ride service off Rte. 50 just west of town.

SIGHTS

Ocean City's star attraction is its beautiful **beach.** The wide stretch of surf and sand runs the entire 10 mi. of town and can be accessed by turning east onto any side street off Philadel-

phia and Baltimore Ave. At the inlet, **Trimper's Amusements** has a Ferris wheel, a century-old Hershell carousel, and a tilt-a-whirl (☎410-289-8617. Open M-F 1pm-midnight or later, Sa-Su noon to midnight or later. Unlimited rides 1-6pm $20.) For a larger park, try the **Jolly Roger Amusement Park,** 2901 Coastal Hwy., which includes multiple go-kart tracks, mini-golf, rides, and the huge Splash Mountain water park. (☎410-289-4902; www.jollyroger-park.com. Rides open Memorial Day to Labor Day daily 2pm-midnight. Splash Mountain open Memorial Day to Labor Day daily 10am-8pm. Unlimited rides $15. Splash Mountain day pass $33, under 42 in. $11.) The **Ocean City Life-Saving Station Museum,** at the southern tip of the Boardwalk, contains artifacts from the history of the United States Life-Saving Service, as well as over a hundred different "sands of the world," antique swimsuits, and an all-things-mermaid collection. (☎410-289-4991. Open June-Sept. daily 10am-10pm; May and Oct. daily 10am-4pm; Nov.-Dec. and Apr. Sa-Su 10am-4pm; Jan.-Mar. call for hours. Free programs in summer 10:30am. $3, 6-12 $1.)

FOOD

Ocean City's cuisine is plentiful and cheap, but don't expect gourmet quality. Just outside Ocean City on Rte. 50 is **TC Diner ❷,** 12744 Ocean Gateway, which serves breakfast all day long in a relaxed environment. Have a short stack of pancakes ($4) or a spicy Spanish omelette ($7), served with homefries. (☎410-213-4700. Open daily 6am-3pm. MC/V.) **Brass Balls Saloon & Bad Ass Cafe ❷,** on the Boardwalk between 11th and 12th St., is known for its drinks and beachy-slow service, but their Oreo waffles ($5.25) and cheeseburgers with waffle fries ($8) are worth the wait. (☎410-289-0069; www.brassballssaloon.com. Open Mar.-Sept. daily 8:30am-1:30am. D/MC/V.) The **Kitchen Restaurant ❷,** 106 Wicomico St., stands out from the cluttered offerings of the Boardwalk with its down-home atmosphere. Try their specialty, French toast ($5), or experiment with the creamed chipped beef ($7.75) served on a biscuit. (☎410-289-2244. Open daily 7am-2pm. MC/V.) **Biggies ❷,** at 18th St. and Coastal Hwy., serves gyros (chicken; $7) and subs (tuna salad;

$5.75) to hungry beachgoers. (☎410-289-3222. Open daily 11am-3am.AmEx/D/MC/V.)

ACCOMMODATIONS

In July and August, it's almost impossible to find a room in town for under $100. After the crowds subside in September, prices are much more reasonable. Though it's not as close to the neon lights of downtown as some might like, the **Maridel Motel ❹**, 101 42nd St., has clean rooms with all the standard amenities and pool access. (☎410-289-7665 or 800-333-1734; www.marideloc.com. Key deposit $5. Rooms July-Aug. M-Th and Su $95, F-Sa $125; Sept.-Oct. and Mar.-June $40/$70. Closed Nov.-Feb. MC/V.) The **Atlantic House Bed & Breakfast ❺**, 501 N. Baltimore Ave., at 5th St., offers a full breakfast buffet, a great location, and a wholesome change of pace. The 1920s house has a hot tub, a front porch, off-street parking, and even complimentary beach chairs, umbrellas, and towels. (☎410-289-2333; www.atlantichouse.com. Closed Nov.-Apr. Rooms with shared bath $160. D/MC/V.) The **Cabana Motel ❺**, 1900 Philadelphia Ave., at 19th St., offers rooms with little more than a bed, but they're close to the action. (☎410-922-4419. Rooms July-Sept. $115-125, May-June $45-55. D/MC/V.) A few miles south of town, ponies roam the uncrowded beaches at **Assateague State Park ❶**, 7307 Stephen Decatur Hwy., off Rte 611. Sharing a campsite with wild horses can be a great experience, but watch out for "presents" they may leave behind. (☎410-641-2918, reservations 888-432-2267. Sites $30, with water and electricity $40. AmEx/D/MC/V.)

NIGHTLIFE

Like everything else in Ocean City, clubs are sprawling spectacles with tourist-targeted themes. The veteran of the bayside clubs, **Fager's Island,** at 60th St. in the bay, has hordes walking the plank to its island location. During the summer, modern rock bands play nightly, while a DJ spins nearby. No one seems to know the source of the tradition, but the *1812 Overture* booms at every sunset, rain or shine. (☎410-524-5500. Cover Th-Sa $5-10. Open daily 11am-2am. AmEx/D/MC/V.) Professional party-goers will no doubt be impressed by **Seacrets,** on 49th St., an entertainment complex that works a tiki-bar-gone-wild-motif. This oasis features 17 bars, and patrons can be served on rafts in the bay. Barefoot partygoers wander from bar to bar, sipping the Pain in the Ass—a frozen rum runner mixed with piña colada ($5.75)—to the strains of live bands. (☎410-524-4900; www.seacrets.com. Cover $5-10. Open daily 11am-2am. AmEx/D/MC/V.) Another mega-club, the **Party Block,** at 17th St. and Coastal Hwy., offers patrons one cover to flirt between three clubs. **Paddock** has live modern rock, **Rush** spins hip-hop and house, and the **Big Kahuna** features Top-40 beats. (☎410-289-6331. W bikini contest. Budweiser bottles $1.75. Cover after 10pm $7-10. Open Apr.-Sept. daily 8:30pm-2am. AmEx/D/MC/V.)

⚐ APPROACHING REHOBOTH BEACH: 27 MILES

Take **Coastal Hwy. N,** which becomes **U.S. 1.**

The First State DELAWARE Welcomes You!

REHOBOTH BEACH

Rehoboth Beach strikes a balance between neon insanity and inactivity. The small downtown area has great shops and restaurants, and when the sun sets there are plenty of low-key places. Along with families and young professionals, Rehoboth Beach hosts a sizable gay population.

VITAL STATS
Population: 1500
Visitor Info: Rehoboth Beach Chamber of Commerce, 501 Rehoboth Ave. (☎302-227-2233 or 800-441-1329; www.beach-fun.com). Open M-F 9am-5pm, Sa-Su 9am-1pm.
Internet Access: Rehoboth Beach Public Library, 226 Rehoboth Ave. (☎302-227-8044). Open M and F 10am-5pm, Tu and Th noon-8pm, W 10am-8pm, Sa 10am-3pm. Free Wi-Fi.
Post Office: 179 Rehoboth Ave. (☎302-227-8406), at 2nd St. Open M-F 9am-5pm, Sa 8:30am-12:30pm.
Postal Code: 19971.

EAST COAST

⌐ GETTING AROUND

The town's main drag is **Rehoboth Ave.**, which heads straight for the water. The downtown area is small and packed with shops and restaurants. The **Boardwalk** runs for 17 blocks along the water. **Atlantic Cycles,** 18 Wilmington Ave., offers bike rentals, complete with helmet, lock, and maps. (☎302-226-2543. Open daily May-Sept. 7am-7pm; Apr. and Oct. 9am-5pm. $5 per hr., $20 per day.)

⑥ SIGHTS

Coming from Ocean City, you'll first encounter **Bethany Beach,** which is popular with families. Navigate through ongoing construction to find the **Delaware Seashore State Park,** with opportunities for camping, swimming in the ocean or bay, and crabbing and clamming. There is also a marina packed with fishing boats and concession stands. (☎302-227-2800; www.destateparks.com. Open Apr.-Nov. daily 8am-4:30pm; Dec.-Mar. M-F 8am-4pm. $8.) Slightly north of the park is the **Indian River Life-Saving Station Museum and Historic Site,** 130 Coastal Hwy., in one of six life-saving stations built along Delaware's coast to rescue shipwreck victims. 30min. tours describe the methods used to save sailors from the sea and the rescuers from boredom. (☎302-227-6991. Open Apr.-Oct. daily 8:30am-4pm; hours vary in winter. $3.50, ages 6-12 $1.) Just south of Rehoboth lies **Dewey Beach,** a favorite with the younger crowd and home to plenty of hotels, motels, and food markets.

🍴 FOOD

Rehoboth is known for high-quality beach cuisine at bargain prices. ◀**Cafe Papillon ❶,** 42 Rehoboth Ave., in the Penny Lane Mall, offers light, authentic French fare. Chefs serve fresh Nutella crepes ($4.50) and croissants ($5.50) on a small outdoor patio. (☎302-227-7568. Open May-Sept. daily 8am-11:30pm. Cash only.) **Royal Treat ❶,** 4 Wilmington Ave., serves up stacks of pancakes ($4) and oxymoronic Italian French toast ($4.25). Ice cream is sold in the afternoon. (☎302-227-6277. Open June-Aug. daily 8-11:30am and 1-11:30pm. Cash only.) **Taste ❹,** 122 Rehoboth Ave., combines Asian, Mediterranean, and French cuisine, serving everything from bruschetta ($10) to pad thai ($16). All meals are served in a brightly colored, casual setting. (☎302-226-4250. Open daily 5-10pm. AmEx/D/MC/V.) Just a block from the water, **Sammy's Kitchen ❷,** 32A Wilmington Ave., displays prize catches on the walls and serves delicious seafood, pancakes, and burgers. (☎302-227-1168. Tuna melt $7. Burgers $6.50. Open 24hr. AmEx/D/MC/V.) **S.O.B's Deli ❷,** 56 Baltimore Ave., assembles classic sandwiches and creatively named "specialty hoagies" like the Soprano Combo with ham, salami, and provolone for $7. (☎302-226-2226. Open May-Sept. M-Th and Su 11am-9pm, F-Sa 11am-10pm. AmEx/D/MC/V with $10 min.)

⌐ ACCOMMODATIONS

Like other resort towns on the coast, rates skyrocket during the summer months and then drop off sharply as the weather cools. The **High Seas Motel ❹,** 12 Christian St., is just a block south of the main drag and serves free doughnuts in the morning. (☎302-227-2022; www.highseasde.com. Rooms June M-F $65, Sa-Su $100; July-Sept. $95/$130; Apr. and Oct. $45/$60. Closed Nov.-Mar. AmEx/D/MC/V.) The **Summer Place Hotel and Condominiums ❹,** 30 Olive Ave., offers 23 rooms in a building with a guesthouse feel. (☎302-226-0766 or 800-815-3925; www.rehobothsummerplace.com. Closed Sept.-Apr. Rooms May to mid-June M-F $80-95, Sa-Su $85-105; mid-June to Aug. $80-95/$120-155. AmEx/D/MC/V.) **Big Oaks Family Campground ❷,** a few miles north of town, off U.S. 1 on Rd. 270, offers a cheaper alternative to town lodging. There's a swimming pool and game room on the grounds, as well as shuttle service to the beach. (☎302-645-6838. Tent sites $36; RV sites $41, with full hookup $45. Cash only.) Camping is also available 5 mi. south on U.S. 1, at the **Delaware Seashore State Park ❶.** Sites are sandy and crowded, but near a swimming area. (☎302-539-7202, reservations 877-987-2757. Sites $27, with full hookup $35. AmEx/D/MC/V.)

🎵 NIGHTLIFE

Rehoboth partygoers head out early to maximize their time before 1am last calls. Try the

Shelter Pale Ale ($4) at the ▨**Dogfish Head Brewings & Eats,** 320 Rehoboth Ave., which brews its own beer on-site and in a larger brewery nearby. On the weekends, artists perform original live music beneath hanging canoes. (☎302-226-2739; www.dogfish.com. F-Sa live music 10pm-1am. No cover. Open M-Th and Su noon-midnight, F-Sa noon-1am. AmEx/MC/V.) **Sydney's Blues and Jazz Restaurant,** 236 Rehoboth Ave., features live weekend acts in a sophisticated setting. (☎302-227-1339; www.sydneybluesandjazz.com. Music F-Sa 9pm, Su 5-8pm. Cover varies. Happy hour daily 5-7pm with $5 martini of the day. Open M-W and Su 5-11pm, Th-Sa 5pm-1am. AmEx/D/MC/V.) The supercasual **Summer House Saloon,** 228 Rehoboth Ave., is ideal for meeting friends for a beer ($3) and a relaxed night out. (☎302-227-3895; www.summerhousesaloon.com. Open M-F 5pm-1am, Sa-Su 4pm-1am. AmEx/D/MC/V.)

▨ **APPROACHING LEWES: 8 MILES**
From Rehoboth Beach, take **U.S. 1 N** to **U.S. 9,** which becomes **Kings Hwy.**

LEWES

Explored by Henry Hudson and founded in 1613 by the Dutch, Lewes (LEW-iss) was the first town in the first state in America. Today, year-rounders populate the town's Victorian homes, and savvy tourists come for the beach in the summer months. While it isn't exactly happening, it's a beautiful area in which to spend a calm weekend.

VITAL STATS

Population: 2900

Visitor Info: Fisher-Martin House Info Center, 120 Kings Hwy. (☎302-645-8073 or 877-465-3937; www.leweschamber.com), off Savannah Rd. Open M-F 10am-4pm, Sa 9am-3pm, Su 10am-2pm.

Internet Access: Lewes Public Library, 111 Adams Ave. (☎302-645-2733), at Kings Hwy. Open M-Th 10am-8pm, F 10am-5pm, Sa 10am-2pm. Internet guest pass allows use 3 times per year.

Post Office: 116 Front St. (☎302-645-0235). Open M-F 8:30am-5pm, Sa 8am-12:30pm. **Postal Code:** 19958.

▐ **GETTING AROUND. Cape Henlopen Dr. (Rte. 19)** runs along the coast into Cape Henlopen State

Park. **Kings Hwy. (U.S. 9)** runs out from the city and intersects with **U.S. 1.**

◔ **SIGHTS.** Comprising sand dunes and scrub pines 1 mi. east of Lewes on the Atlantic Ocean is the 4000-acre ▨**Cape Henlopen State Park,** where children frolic in the waves under the watchful eyes of lifeguards. In addition to its expansive beach, the park is home to a ¼ mi. fishing pier, sparkling white "walking dunes," and a 2 mi. paved trail ideal for biking or in-line skating. (From the south, follow Rte. 9 E toward the ferry. ☎302-645-8983. Park open daily 8am-sunset. Day-use $8 per car.) Bike rentals are free at the **Seaside Nature Center,** the park's museum on beach and ocean wildlife, which also hosts weekly lectures and leads hikes. (☎302-645-6852. Bike rental 9am-3pm; 2hr. limit. Open daily July-Aug. 9am-5pm; Sept.-June 9am-4pm.) **The Zwaanendael Museum,** 102 Kings Hwy., is a bright two-story space filled with relics of maritime history and exhibits on the settlement of Delaware, lighthouses, and shipwrecks. The building itself is a replica of the old town hall in Hoorn, Holland. (☎302-645-1148. Open Tu-Sa 10am-4:30pm, Su 1:30-4:30pm. Free.) Historic buildings cluster around the **Lewes Historical Society,** 110 Shipcarpenter St., near 2nd St. A tour of the complex takes you through a doctor's office, country store, and old schoolhouse, all of which were moved here from other parts of Delaware. The society also runs trolley tours of historic Lewes that leave from Ryves Holt House, at the corner of 2nd and Mulberry St. (☎302-645-7670; www.historiclewes.org. Museums open May to mid-June Sa 11am-4pm; Mid-June to Oct. M-Sa 11am-4pm, Su 1-4pm. Trolley tours late June to Sept. Tu-Th 11:30am, $5. Buildings $5, under 12 free. Self-guided audio tour $5.)

⬛ **FOOD.** Clustered primarily on **2nd St.,** downtown Lewes has a number of tasty cafes. ▨**Cafe Azafran ❷,** 109 Market St., serves gourmet Mediterranean dishes such as "Ricardo's Panini" ($6.25) with pesto, artichokes, cheese, roasted peppers, and spinach on Italian bread. The cafe's walls are decorated with art for sale, and on sunny days patrons enjoy the outdoor patio. (☎302-644-4446. Free Wi-Fi. Open daily

6:30am-3:30pm and 6-10pm. MC/V.) The **Second Street Grille ❸**, 115 W. 2nd St., has a chic, European feel. They offer sandwiches and salads for lunch, as well as fried calamari for $11. (☎302-644-4121. M live piano 5-7pm. Open M, W-Th, Su 11am-9pm, F-Sa 11am-10pm. MC/V.) **Books by the Bay Cafe ❶**, 111 Bank St., serves coffee and cake ($4) in the morning before switching over to creatively named sandwiches, like the Pilgrim's Feast panini (turkey, stuffing, cranberries; $5.50). While you wait for your sandwich, browse through the small bookshop. (☎302-644-6571. Open daily 7am-5pm. MC/V.) Consistently voted "Best Ice Cream" by *Delaware Today*, **Kings Homemade Ice Cream Shop ❶**, 201 2nd. St., is always full of lactose lovers. Try a scoop of Oh! Cookie for $2.75. (☎302-645-9425. Open May-Oct. daily 11am-11pm. Cash only.) Once a sea captain's house, **The Buttery ❹**, at 2nd and Savannah St., is the best spot for fine dining and people-watching in Lewes. The menu changes seasonally; try the smoked salmon BLT ($12) in the summer. (☎302-645-7755. Reservations recommended. Open M-Th and Su 11am-2:30pm and 5-9pm, F-Sa 11am-2:30pm and 5-10pm. Su brunch 10:30am-2:30pm. D/MC/V.)

⚑ ACCOMMODATIONS. The least expensive accommodations downtown are the well-furnished rooms at the **Vesuvio Motel ❹**, 105 Savannah Rd., right by the shops of Front St. and 2nd St. (☎302-645-2224. Rooms Apr.-Sept. $75-95; Oct.-Mar. $50-65. AmEx/MC/V.) You can't get any closer to downtown than the **Zwaanendael Inn ❹**, 142 2nd St., which sits between shops and restaurants on the main thoroughfare. The cheapest rooms include continental breakfast, but no TV. (☎302-645-6466; www.zwaanendaelinn.com. Rooms in summer $75-95; in winter $45-55. AmEx/D/MC/V.) The campsites at **Cape Henlopen State Park ❶** are just a short hike from the beach and have an amazing view of the dunes. There are 150 wooded sites with water, but no electricity. (☎302-645-8983, reservations 877-987-2757. Campground open Apr.-Nov. Sites $27, with water $29. AmEx/D/MC/V.)

⚐ APPROACHING CAPE MAY: 5 MILES
A ferry runs between Lewes, DE, and Cape May, NJ, cutting 2-3hr. off the drive. From Lewes, take **Rte. 9 E** and follow the signs. The ferry often sells out during the summer, so call ahead for reservations. (☎800-643-3779; www.capemaylewesferry.com. Call ahead for schedule. One-way Apr.-Oct. $29 for car and driver; $9.50 per additional passenger, under 6 free. Nov.-Mar. $23/$7.) From the ferry terminal, take **U.S. 9 (Ferry Rd.)** to **Rte. 626 (Seashore Rd.)**, which turns into **Broadway Rd.** and leads to **Beach Ave.** and the ocean.

CAPE MAY

At the southern end of New Jersey's coast, Cape May is the oldest seashore resort in the US, and the money here is no younger. Once the summer playground of Upper East Side New Yorkers, the town still shows signs of affluence in the elegant restaurants of Beach Ave. However, Cape May is a steal for budget travelers, with sparkling beaches, cheap accommodations, and a boardwalk and downtown that invite strolling.

⬛ GETTING AROUND

The **Garden State Pkwy.** leads into Cape May from the north, culminating at Cape May Harbor. Parallel to the parkway are **U.S. 9** and **Rte. 626**. As Rte. 626 heads south toward the tip of the cape, it becomes **Seashore Rd.** and then **South Broadway**, running parallel to **Lafayette St. (Rte. 633)**.

VITAL STATS
Population: 4000
Visitor Info: Welcome Center, 609 Lafayette St. (☎609-884-9562). Open daily 9am-4:30pm.
Internet Access: Cape May County Library, 30 Mechanic St. (☎609-463-6350). Open in summer M-Th 8:30am-9pm, F 8:30am-4:30pm, Sa 9am-4:30pm; in winter M-F 8:30am-9pm, Sa 9am-4:30pm, Su 1-5pm.
Post Office: 700 Washington St. (☎609-884-3578). Open M-F 9am-5pm, Sa 8:30am-12:30pm. **Postal Code:** 08204.

SIGHTS

THE BEACH. Cape May's sands, which are studded with famous "Cape May diamonds" (quartz pebbles), actually do sparkle. Beach tags, available from roaming vendors, are required for beachgoers over 11. You can also purchase tags at the **Beach Tag Office.** *(At Grant and Beach Dr. ☎ 609-884-9522. Open daily 6am-10pm; for swimming 10:30am-5pm. Tags required Memorial Day to Labor Day. $4 per day, $13 per week.)* The **South End Surf Shop** rents beach necessities. *(311 Beach Ave. ☎ 609-898-0988. Foam surfboards $20 per day, $75 per week. Driver's license required. Open Apr.-Sept. daily 9am-10pm.)* Bike the beach with the help of **Shields' Bike Rentals.** *(11 Gurney St. ☎ 609-884-2453. $5 per hr., $10 per day; tandems $10 per hr. Open daily 7am-7pm.)* Beach Dr., which runs parallel to the ocean, makes for a beautiful walk. In the summer, artists sell their work on the street. Crawling with pedestrians hunting for heavenly fudge and saltwater taffy, Washington St. supports several popular food stores and eateries.

CAPE MAY POINT STATE PARK. Those in search of exercise and a view of the seashore can ascend the 199 steps of the 1859 **Cape May Lighthouse** in Cape May Point State Park, west of town at the end of the point. The 157 ft. lighthouse was built on the site in 1859, and the 1893 oil house now serves as a combined gift shop and visitors center. Three clearly marked trails feature excellent birdwatching in the marsh and oceanside dunes. The behemoth bunker next to the lighthouse is a WWII gun emplacement, used to scan the shore for German U-boats. There's a sandy beach, too, but swimming is not allowed. *(Lighthouse and museum ☎ 609-884-5404; www.njparksandforests.org. Visitors center ☎ 609-884-2159. Park open daily sunrise-sunset. Lighthouse open in summer daily 9am-8pm; hours vary in winter. Visitors center and museum open July-Aug. M-Tu and Su 8:30am-5pm, W-F 8:30am-4pm, Sa 8:30am-6pm; Sept.-June daily 8:30am-3:30pm. Lighthouse $5, ages 3-12 $1.)*

WILDLIFE. Due to the close proximity of fresh and saltwater, migratory birds flock to Cape May for a break from the long southbound flight. Sneak a peek at over 300 types of feathered vacationers at the **Cape May Bird Observa-tory,** a birdwatcher's paradise. Bird maps, field trips, and workshops are available, along with advice about where to go for the best bird-watching. *(701 E. Lake Dr., on Cape May Point. ☎ 609-884-2736; www.njaudubon.org. Open M-Tu and Th-Su 9am-4:30pm.)* For a look at some larger creatures, hop on the **Cape May Whale Watcher.** *(☎ 800-786-5445; www.capemaywhalewatcher.com. 3hr. tours Mar.-Dec. 1pm. $35, ages 7-12 $20.)*

MID-ATLANTIC CENTER FOR THE ARTS (MAC). The MAC runs walking and 30min. trolley tours of the city's major historical sites, including the **Emlen Physick Estate,** a Victorian mansion that showcases the luxury of the upper classes and the living conditions of their servants. Trolley tours run throughout the city and along the beachfront. MAC also runs unique cultural events such as **Sherlock Holmes Weekends** (early Mar. and Nov.) and **Victorian Week** in early Oct. *(1048 Washington St. ☎ 609-688-5404 or 800-275-4278; www.capemaymac.org. Physick Estate $10, ages 3-12 $5. Trolley tour $9/$4.50.)*

CAPE MAY AIRPORT AVIATION MUSEUM. This museum displays vintage aircraft in a WWII-era hangar. Visitors are allowed to jump in the cockpit of most of the planes, so bring your aviator goggles. *(500 Forrestal Rd., at Cape May Airport. Take Exit 4A off the Garden State Pkwy. and follow the signs. ☎ 609-886-8787; www.usnasw.org. Open late Mar. to early Jan. daily 9am-5pm; late Jan. to early Mar. M-F 8am-5pm. $5, ages 3-12 $3.)*

FOOD

Cape May's cheapest food is found in generic pizza and ice-cream shops along **Beach Ave.** Tastier (but more expensive) options can be found on side streets.

Marybeth's Beachfront Cafe, 314 Beach Dr. (☎ 609-898-6050). This casual beachfront diner serves Big Breakfasts (eggs, hotcakes, bacon, sausage, homefries; $8) and light, fresh wraps, like the Thai chicken ($7). Open Apr.-Oct. daily 9am-3pm and 4:30-10pm. MC/V. ❷

George's Place, 301 Beach Ave. (☎ 609-884-6088), at Beach Dr. and Perry St. This diner blends all-American favorites with Greek cuisine, serving pancakes ($4) alongside *spanakopita* (filo dough with spinach and feta; $8). Feta omelette ($6.50). Open daily 7am-3pm and 5-9pm. Cash only. ❷

Freda's Gourmet Shop, 210 Ocean St. (☎609-884-0707), by Washington St. Mall. The crowded shop lacks atmosphere, so get your specialty wrap to go. If "Jen's Wrap" (spinach, sun-dried tomatoes, portobello mushroom, couscous, brie; $7.50) doesn't tickle your fancy, standard favorites like pastrami ($5.75) are also available. Open in summer daily 11:15am-5pm; in winter M and F-Su 11:15am-5pm. MC/V. ❷

The Mad Batter, 19 Jackson St. (☎609-884-5970; www.madbatter.com). Start the morning right with orange-and-almond French toast ($6.75) or a 3-egg omelette ($7.25). For lunch, try a Waldorf chicken croissant ($9.25) on the beautiful porch. Open daily 8am-3pm and 5-10pm. AmEx/D/MC/V. ❸

ACCOMMODATIONS

Cape May's streets are lined with pricey, beautiful Victorian B&Bs, but budget accommodations are available too. Prices drop farther from the shore. Campgrounds line U.S. 9, just north of Cape May.

Hotel Clinton, 202 Perry St. (☎609-884-3993), at S. Lafayette St. Breezy, homey rooms, 2 porches overlooking a busy street, and charismatic Italian proprietors. Reservations recommended. Open mid-June to Sept. Singles with shared bath M-F $35, Sa-Su $40; doubles $45/$50. Cash only. ❷

Parris Inn, 204 Perry St. (☎609-884-8015). A variety of spacious, comfortable rooms and apartments less than 3 blocks from the beach, most with A/C and TV. Reservations recommended. Rooms with shared bath Apr.-Sept. $35-45. AmEx/D/MC/V. ❷

Poor Richard's Inn, 17 Jackson St. (☎609-884-3536; www.poorrichardsinn.com). The large rooms at this elegant inn are furnished with antiques and similarly aged TVs. Breakfast included. Rooms July-Aug. $120-165, Sept.-June $110-150. AmEx/D/MC/V. ❺

Seashore Campsites, 720 Seashore Rd./Rte. 626. (☎609-884-4010 or 800-313-2267; www.seashore-campsite.com). Connected to Cape May by the Seashore Line. Wooded campground features mini-golf, pool, lake, playground, store, and laundry facilities. June-Sept. tent sites $37; RV sites $40, with full hookup $44. AmEx/D/MC/V. ❷

NIGHTLIFE

A young crowd congregates at **Cabana's,** 429 Beach Ave. Alternative and blues bands play Tu-Sa, with original acts on Thursdays. (☎609-884-4800; www.cabanasonthe-beach.com. Cover F-Sa $5. Happy hour 4-7pm. Open daily 11:30am-2am. AmEx/D/MC/V.) **Martini Beach,** 429 Beach Ave., serves martinis in an intimate, unpretentious environment. Sit back with a Red Door martini ($12) and enjoy the live jazz. (☎609-884-1925; www.martinibeachcapemay.com. M karaoke. Sa DJ. No cover. Open daily 3pm-2am. AmEx/D/MC/V.) **Carney's,** 411 Beach Ave., offers nightly cover bands playing everything from Top 40 to modern rock. The "other room" caters to an older crowd, with Irish singalongs F-Su. (☎609-884-4424. Cover F-Sa $5. Happy hour 3-6pm with half-price drinks and

JOISEY AND BAGELS

Step off the Lewes-Cape May ferry, and you'll notice an immediate change. It's not just the accents-suddenly, everywhere you look, there are bagels. These doughnut-shaped bundles of joy are ubiquitous once you cross the border. Such a popular food begs the question: where in the world did these things come from? Supposedly, the first bagel was made in 1683 as a tribute to King Jan Sobieski of Poland, who had just saved the Austrians from almost-certain defeat at the hands of the Turks. A Viennese baker was so overcome by gratitude that he wanted to present the king with a token of his appreciation. The clever baker shaped the dough in a ring, like a stirrup, to honor the king's skill as a horseman. An earlier legend has it that bagels were invented in the early 1600s and used during childbirth. Instead of "biting the bullet," a laboring woman would "bite the bagel." The newborn child would then use a bagel as a teething device. Bagels made their way to America in the 1880s with the immigration of Eastern European Jews, and it's the historically high population of Jews in New Jersey that makes these ringed delicacies so prevalent in the area. So have a bagel with a "shmear" of cream cheese and some lox, and say your thanks to that anonymous Viennese baker.

free hot dogs. Open daily 11:30am-2am. AmEx/D/MC/V.) Entertainment ranges from DJs to solo artists at **Ugly Mug**, 426 Washington St. Mall. After a few Hammer Shots (rums and pineapple juice; $5), you won't care. (☎609-884-3459. Music 10pm-2am. No cover. Open daily 10:30am-2am. AmEx/D/MC/V.)

☊ APPROACHING OCEAN CITY: 32 MILES From Cape May, take the **Garden State Pkwy. N** to **Exit 25.** There is a $0.70 toll.

OCEAN CITY

Billing itself as "America's favorite family resort," Ocean City features a busy boardwalk and beachside mini-golf. A few blocks from the shore, the beach attractions give way to a calmer downtown area with cafes and stores. The family-oriented atmosphere means that there's not much to do after dark, so it's best to take full advantage of the daytime activities.

VITAL STATS

Population: 15,500

Visitor Info: Ocean City Regional Chamber of Commerce (☎609-399-2629 or 800-232-2465), on the Howard Stainton Memorial Causeway. Open M-Sa 9am-5pm, Su 10am-3pm. Information booth on the boardwalk at 8th Ave.

Internet Access: Ocean City Free Public Library, 1735 Simpson Ave. (☎609-399-2434 or 609-399-2143), off 17th St. Open M-F 9am-9pm, Sa 9am-5pm, Su 1-5pm.

Parking: Lots available near the beach for $10-15 per day. Metered parking ($0.25 per hr.) along Asbury Ave. for up to 4hr.

Post Office: 859 Ocean Ave. (☎609-399-0475). Open M-F 8:30am-5pm, Sa 9am-1pm. **Postal Code:** 08226.

▣ GETTING AROUND. The boardwalk stretches 2½ mi. along the beach toward the north end of the island. **Bay St.** runs parallel to the ocean on the west. Most hotels lie between the beach and **Ocean Ave.** between 1st and 9th St. Downtown centers on **Asbury Ave.** between 6th and 14th St. Free parking can be found in some residential areas, but all parking fills up quickly in summer.

◕ SIGHTS. In the summer, Ocean City's **beaches** are its best attraction. Those over 11 must wear **beach tags,** available on the boardwalk at the end of 8th Ave. (☎800-232-2465. Open June to Labor Day daily 6am-10pm; swimming 9:30am-5:30pm. Beach tag $5 per day, $8 per week.) **Surf Buggy Centers,** at 8th Ave. and Broadway, rents bikes and surreys for seashore exploration. (☎609-399-2468; www.surfbuggycenters.com. Bikes $5 per hr., $15 per day; surreys $15 per hr. Open daily 6am-noon.) The **7th Street Surf Shop,** 654 Boardwalk, rents surfboards and offers lessons in surfing and gnarly lingo. (☎609-391-1700. Surfboards $10 per hr., $30 per day. $50 deposit. Credit card or driver's license required. Open daily 7:30am-11:30pm.) Those looking for a wilder ride than the ocean can offer can ride the chutes at **Gilligan's Island,** at Plymouth Place on the Boardwalk. (☎609-399-0483. Open 9:30am-6:30pm. Day pass $23, under 48" $20.) The **Bayside Center,** 520 Bay Ave., has an environmental center with exhibits on local animals, a lifeguard museum, and models of local buildings. During the summer, the center also offers guided beach walks, starting at 59th and Central Ave. (☎609-525-9244. Open daily 10am-6pm. Free. Beach walks July-Aug. Tu 9am, W 6:30pm. $1, children $0.50.) Once a month, the **Second Friday Art Walk** showcases local artists on the sidewalk of Asbury Ave. (☎609-814-0308). The **Ocean City Art Center,** 1735 Simpson Ave., offers classes in everything from dance to basket weaving and organizes art shows. (☎609-399-7628; www.oceancityarts-center.org. Open M-Th 9am-9pm, F-Sa 9am-4pm.) In the same building, the **Ocean City Historical Museum** displays remnants of the *Sindia*, a large bark that ran aground in Ocean City in 1901, an old-fashioned telephone switchboard, and a taffy machine. (☎609-399-1801; www.ocnjmuseum.org. Open in summer M-F 10am-4pm, Sa 11am-2pm; in winter M-F 1-4pm, Sa 11am-2pm. Free.) The **Boardwalk Concert Series** at the **Music Pier** runs M nights July-Aug. with family-friendly musical acts. (☎609-525-9248. Tickets available at the Music Pier Box Office in the Ocean City Chamber of Commerce. $25.)

▤▮ FOOD AND ACCOMMODATIONS. Ocean City's boardwalk is lined with storefronts that provide the cheapest, if not the most well-rounded, meals in town, selling pizza and South Jersey favorites like Italian ice (also, redundantly, called "water ice"), funnel cakes, and custard. Downtown, streets are lined with a number of casual, inexpensive eateries. **Kibbitz Down the Shore ❸**, 846 Central Ave., is a New York-style deli dishing out massive portions—the reubens (half $8, whole $11.30) have a full pound of corned beef. For something a bit lighter, feed your soul with some matzoh ball soup for $4.25. (☎609-398-0880. Open daily 11am-8pm. AmEx/D/MC/V.) **The Chatterbox ❷**, at 9th St. and Central Ave., has been serving buttermilk pancakes ($4) and "chatter burgers" ($7) for 70 years. During peak times, there's a line out the door. (☎609-399-0113. Open daily 7am-11pm. AmEx/D/MC/V.) The **Panini Grill ❷**, 953 Asbury Ave., serves the Capri (tomato, mozzarella, balsamic vinaigrette; $6) and 10 other types of panini. If you're all sandwiched out, there's also pizza ($12) and a variety of breakfast options. (☎609-391-1111. Open M-Th and Su 8am-8:30pm, F-Sa 8am-9pm. AmEx/MC/V.) While it has little ambience, **Nags Head Fine Foods ❷**, 801 Asbury Ave., serves delicious sandwiches, like the $7 roast turkey with apples and cheddar. (☎609-391-9080. Open M-Sa 11:30am-2pm and 5-8pm. Cash or check only.)

Ocean City has plenty of quaint but pricey B&Bs. For cheaper (if less luxurious) accommodations, there's the family-run **Glen Nor Inn ❹**, 1015 Central Ave. Rooms are small, but they include all the standard amenities plus doughnuts in the morning. (☎609-399-4138 or 800-320-4138; www.glennorinn.com. Most rooms 2-night min. stay. Open Memorial Day to Labor Day. Rooms $80-90. MC/V.) The **Homestead Hotel ❺**, 805 E. 8th St., offers more distinctive accommodations in a European-style building with views of the city and the ocean. Rooms include stovetop, fridge, microwave, and flat-screen TV. (☎609-391-0200; www.homesteadhotel.info. Rooms in summer $130-150; in winter $80-100. AmEx/D/MC/V.) The **Tradewinds Motel ❺**, at 9th and Wesley Ave., has a pool and standard rooms with TV and fridge. (☎609-399-2789. 21+. Open May-Oct. Rooms July-Aug. $145. AmEx/D/MC/V.)

◪ DETOUR
LUCY THE ELEPHANT
9200 Atlantic Ave. In Margate City, off the Garden State Pkwy. at Exit 36. Follow signs to Margate and Lucy.

Originally built in 1881 by land developer James Lafferty as a marketing gimmick, Lucy has always been a sight for the public. It's no wonder; at 65 ft. and 90 tons, she's hardly the average pachyderm. After she fell into disrepair in the 1960s, the Save Lucy Committee convinced the city to donate land for a site and raised $62,000 to move her down the beach to her present location. (☎609-823-6473; www.lucytheelephant.org. Open mid-June to Labor Day M-Sa 10am-8pm, Su 10am-5pm; Labor Day to Oct. M-F 11am-4pm, Sa-Su 10am-5pm; Nov.-Dec. W-F 11am-4pm, Sa-Su 10am-5pm; May to mid-June M-F 11am-4pm, Sa-Su 10am-5pm. Closed Jan.-Mar. Tours every 30min. $5, children $3.)

◤ APPROACHING ATLANTIC CITY: 5 MILES
From Margate, take **Atlantic Ave.** west into town.

ATLANTIC CITY

Atlantic City was once a premier getaway, but lately, even Miss America has taken flight. It's easy to see why. During a 1970s refurbishment effort, giant casino-resorts were built over the rubble of the old boardwalk, sacrificing the city's old-time charm in hopes of attracting tourist dollars with glitz and glamor. Today, the Boardwalk is the safest and most interesting part of the city, but poverty and crime lurk around the fringes of downtown. Still, tourists stream into the city hoping to win big, and visitors can enjoy themselves if they avoid leaving the labyrinthine casinos.

PAGE TURN. See p. 350 in **National Road** for complete coverage of Atlantic City.

◤ APPROACHING ASBURY PARK: 78 MILES
From the **Atlantic City Expwy. W**, take **Exit 7N** to the **Garden State Pkwy. N**. After 60 mi., take **Exit 98** and merge onto **NJ-138 E**. Follow **NJ-18N**, and then take **Exit 10A**, heading for Asbury Park.

ASBURY PARK. Built from the ground up by developer James Bradley, Asbury Park is now best known as the hometown of rocker Bruce Springsteen. Having suffered under economic changes that hurt many Jersey Shore resort towns, Asbury Park has attempted an economic, commercial, and cultural renewal, but the city has few attractions to offer outside its role in rock 'n' roll history. With over 2000 pieces, the **Asbury Park Library**, 500 1st. Ave., has the world's largest collection of published material relating to Bruce Springsteen and the E-Street Band. (☎ 732-774-4221. Open M-W 11am-8pm, Th 9am-5pm, F-Sa noon-5pm.) The **Stone Pony**, 913 Ocean Ave., is a landmark rock venue that originally opened in 1974 and reopened in 2000. It may not be worth the pilgrimage for a casual fan. (☎ 732-502-0600. Open M and W-F 11am-4:30pm, Sa noon-5pm.) The **Stephen Crane House**, 508 4th. Ave. (☎ 732-775-5682) has nothing to do with rock, but was the teenage home of the author of the *Red Badge of Courage*. The house is not open for tours but hosts occasional lectures.

◪ APPROACHING NEW YORK CITY: 53 MILES
Follow **I-95** to the **Lincoln Tunnel** ($6), which leads you to Midtown. To bypass the city, skip ahead to p. 142; otherwise, sit back and enjoy the ride.

The *Empire State*
NEW YORK
Welcomes You!

NEW YORK CITY

The self-proclaimed "Capital of the World" puts its money where its mouth is. Eight million New Yorkers pack themselves into the city limits, and each one can tell you exactly why theirs is the greatest city on earth. This is where the legendary Yankees hold court, the lights of Broadway never dim, and every street corner promises a hot dog and a pretzel. Towering skyscrapers form the hub of American business by day, and the pounding beats of legendary clubs thump forth from neon-tinged shadows by night. When an act of terrorism destroyed the twin towers of the World Trade Center on September 11, 2001, New Yorkers were awakened to both horror and heroism. The city has moved

on, but it hasn't forgotten. For more info, check out ◪*Let's Go: New York City.*

VITAL STATS

Population: 8.1 million

Visitor Info: NYC & Company, 810 7th Ave. (☎ 212-484-1222; www.nycvisit.com). Open M-F 8:30am-6pm, Sa-Su 9am-5pm. Also in Grand Central and Penn Station.

Internet Access: Alt.Coffee, 139 Ave. A (☎ 212-529-2233), between 8th and 9th St. Open M-F 7:30am-1:30am, Sa-Su 10am-2am. $10 per hr.

Post Office: 421 8th Ave. (☎ 212-330-2902), at W. 32nd St. Open 24hr. **Postal Code:** 10001.

▶ GETTING AROUND

NYC is comprised of five boroughs: the Bronx, Brooklyn, Manhattan, Queens, and Staten Island. Flanked on the east by the East River (actually a strait) and on the west by the Hudson River, **Manhattan** is an island, measuring 13 mi. long and 2½ mi. wide. **Queens** and **Brooklyn** are on the other side of the East River. **Staten Island,** southwest of Manhattan, is the most residential borough. North of Manhattan sits the **Bronx,** the only borough connected by land to the rest of the US. The **Metropolitan Transit Authority (MTA)** runs the city's subways, buses, and trains. The **subway** system is open 24hr.; once inside, a passenger may transfer onto any other train without restrictions. The subway is much more useful for traveling north-south than east-west, but crosstown shuttle buses run on several streets, including 14th, 23rd, 34th, 42nd, 57th, 79th, and 86th St. Maps are available in any station. **Buses,** often slower than subways, stop roughly every two blocks and run throughout the city. Blue signposts announce bus numbers; glass-walled shelters display schedules and route maps. Be sure to grab a borough bus map. **MetroCards** for subways and buses have a pre-set value (12 rides for the price of 10) and allow free bus and subway transfers within 2hr. The 1-day ($7), 7-day ($24), and 30-day ($76) "Unlimited Rides" MetroCards (as opposed to $2 "Pay-Per-Ride" cards) are good for tourists staying for a while.

BOROUGHS

MANHATTAN

Above 14th St., Manhattan is an organized grid of avenues running north-south and streets running east-west. Street numbers increase as you travel north. Avenues are slightly less predictable: some are numbered, while others are named. The numbers of the avenues increase as you go west. **Broadway** defies the pattern, cutting diagonally across the island at 23rd St. **Central Park** and **5th Ave.** (south of 59th St., north of 110th St.) separate the city into the East Side and West Side. **Washington Heights** is located north of 155th St.; **Morningside Heights** (above 110th St. and below 125th St.) is sandwiched between **Harlem** (110th St. to the 150s) and the **Upper West Side** (59th to 110th St., west of Central Park). The museum-heavy **Upper East Side** is across Central Park, above 59th St. on 5th Ave. **Midtown** (42nd to 59th St.) includes Times Square and the Theater District. **Lower Midtown** (14th to 41st St.) includes **Herald Square**, **Chelsea**, and **Union Square**. Below 14th St., the city dissolves into a confusing tangle of old, narrow streets that aren't numbered south of Houston St. The bohemian **East Village** and **Alphabet City** are grid-like, with alphabetized avenues from Ave. A to Ave. D, east of 1st Ave. Intellectual **Greenwich Village**, to the west, is especially complicated west of 6th Ave. Moving south, trendy **SoHo** (South of Houston St.) and **TriBeCa** (Triangle Below Canal St.) are just west of historically ethnic enclaves **Little Italy**, **Chinatown**, and the **Lower East Side**. The **Financial District/Wall Street** area, at the tip of Manhattan, was set over the original Dutch layout and is full of narrow, winding, one-way streets.

BROOKLYN

The **Brooklyn-Queens Expwy. (BQE)** links to the **Belt Pkwy.** and circumscribes Brooklyn. Ocean Pkwy., Ocean Ave., Coney Island Ave., and diagonal Flatbush Ave. run from the beaches of southern Brooklyn (**Coney Island** and **Brighton Beach**) to the heart of the borough in **Prospect Park**. The streets of western Brooklyn, including **Park Slope**, are aligned with the western shore and intersect central Brooklyn's main arteries at a 45-degree angle. In northern Brooklyn (including **Williamsburg,**

Greenpoint, **Brooklyn Heights**, and **Downtown Brooklyn**), several avenues—Atlantic Ave., Eastern Pkwy., and Flushing Ave.—travel east into Queens.

QUEENS

The streets of Queens resemble neither the orderly grid of Upper Manhattan nor the haphazard angles of Greenwich Village. Streets generally run north-south and are numbered from west to east, from 1st St. in **Astoria** to 271st St. in **Glen Oaks**. Avenues run perpendicular to streets and are numbered from north to south, from 2nd to 165th Ave. Pick up the useful Queens Bus Map, free and available on most Queens buses.

THE BRONX

Major highways divide the Bronx. The **Major Deegan Expwy. (I-87)** runs up the western border, next to the Harlem River. The **Cross-Bronx Expwy. (I-95)** runs across the borough, turning north on its easternmost edge. Up the center of the borough runs the **Bronx River Pkwy.** Many avenues run north-south, including **Jerome Ave.** on the western side and **White Plains Rd.** and **Boston Rd.** to the east. East-west streets include **Tremont Ave., Fordham Rd.,** and the **Pelham Pkwy.**

STATEN ISLAND

Sometimes referred to as New York's "forgotten borough," quiet Staten Island is very spread out. It has a limited tourist infrastructure, making a vehicle necessary. Pick up bus route maps at the Chamber of Commerce, 130 Bay St. (☎718-727-1900), left from the ferry station.

> **AREA CODES:** 212, 347, or 646 (Manhattan); 718 (other 4 boroughs); 917 (cell phones). All calls made within and between these 5 area codes must be dialed using 10-digit dialing.

 ## SIGHTS

THE STATUE OF LIBERTY AND ELLIS ISLAND

STATUE OF LIBERTY. The Statue of Liberty, long a symbol of hope for immigrants, stands at the entrance to New York Harbor. In 1886, the French government presented Frederic-Auguste Bartholdi's sculpture to the US as a sign of goodwill. The statue's crown and torch were closed in September 2001; views are limited to the 150 ft. concrete pedestal. *(Subway: 4, 5 to Bowling Green; R, W to Whitehall St.; 1, 9 to South Ferry. ☎ 212-363-3200; www.statueofliberty.org. Liberty Island open daily 9am-5pm. Ferries leave for Liberty Island from the piers at Battery Park every 30min. M-F 9:15am-3:30pm, Sa-Su 9am-4pm. Ferry reservations ☎ 212-269-5755; www.statuereservations.com. Tickets for ferry with access to Liberty Island and Ellis Island $11.50, seniors $9.50, ages 4-12 $4.50, under 4 free.)*

ELLIS ISLAND. Accessible via the same ferry as the Statue of Liberty, Ellis Island was the processing point for millions of immigrants from 1897 to 1938. Each day, as many as 5000 immigrants would wait in the main building's vaulted Registry Room until they were called forward to be questioned by inspectors. Despite the long wait and the often harrowing medical exams that they were forced to undergo, only 1-2% of immigrants failed to pass inspection. Of those that were granted entry to the US, one-third settled in New York City. *(☎ 212-363-3200; www.ellisisland.org. Audio tour $5; seniors, students, and under 17 $4. 45min. guided tours throughout the day. Free.)*

FINANCIAL DISTRICT AND CIVIC CENTER

FINANCIAL DISTRICT. Once the northern border of the New Amsterdam settlement, Wall St. is named for the wall built in 1653 to shield the Dutch colony from British invasion. By the early 19th century, the area was the financial capital of the US. On the southwest corner of Wall and Broad St. stands the **New York Stock Exchange.** This 1903 temple to capitalism sees billions of dollars change hands daily. The exchange, founded in 1792 at 68 Wall St., is now off-limits to tourists. Around the corner, at the end of Wall St., stands the seemingly ancient **Trinity Church,** with its delicately crafted steeple. *(74 Trinity Place. ☎ 212-602-0800; www.trinitywallstreet.org. Open M-F 7am-6pm, Sa 8am-4pm, Su 7am-4pm.)* With a fence erected in 1771, **Bowling Green** is Manhattan's oldest park. It was restored in the 1970s following decades of neglect. *(Intersection of Battery Pl., Broadway, and Whitehall St.)* The **Custom House** was completed

in 1907, when the city still derived most of its revenue from customs. The magnificent Beaux Arts building, designed by Cass Gilbert, is fronted by sculptures of four women representing America, Europe, Africa, and Asia. *(1 Bowling Green St.)*

WORLD TRADE CENTER SITE (GROUND ZERO). The site where the World Trade Center once stood is sobering. The poignancy of the vastly empty landscape can only really be understood in person. However, it won't be empty for long. Construction for the memorial, Reflecting Absence, began in the summer of 2006 and is scheduled for completion by the eighth anniversary of the attacks, September 11, 2009. *(On the corner of Liberty and West St. The Tribute Center, 120 Liberty St. between Church and Greenwich St., is scheduled to open in September 2006 and will feature exhibits and an education center. ☎ 212-422-3520; www.tributenyc.org. Open M and W-Sa 10am-6pm; Tu and Su noon-6pm. 1hr. walking tours of the site, led by those affected by the attacks, M-F 1 and 3pm; Sa-Su noon, 1pm, 2pm, and 3pm. $10, under 12 free; reserve at www.telecharge.com.)*

CIVIC CENTER. The city's center of government is located north of its financial district. The New York City mayor's office is in **City Hall;** around it are courthouses, civic buildings, and federal buildings. The building's interior is closed indefinitely to the public. *(Broadway at Murray St., off Park Row.)* The **Woolworth Building,** a 1913 neo-Gothic skyscraper built for $15.5 million to house the offices of F.W. Woolworth's five-and-dime store empire, looms south of City Hall. *(233 Broadway, between Barclay St. and Park Pl. Closed to the public.)* A block and a half south on Broadway lies ◙**St. Paul's Chapel.** Inspired by the design of London's St. Martin-in-the-Fields, this modest chapel was built between 1764 and 1766 and is Manhattan's oldest church—George Washington prayed here regularly. *(Between Vesey and Fulton St. ☎ 212-233-4164; www.stpaulschapel.org. Chapel open M-F 9am-3pm, Su 7am-3pm. Free.)*

SOUTH STREET SEAPORT. The shipping industry thrived here for most of the 19th century, when New York City was the most important port city in the US. In the 20th century, shipping was replaced by bars, brothels, and crime. Now a 12-block "museum without walls," the seaport displays old schooners, sailboats, and houses. Sadly, it is also a monument to unimaginative consumerism: **Pier 17** houses a three-story mall full of chain stores. A gigantic Pizzeria Uno is the most visible dining option in the area. Still, kids and nautical history buffs may enjoy a visit. *(Bounded by FDR Dr., Water St., Beekman St., and John St. Subway: 2, 3, 4, 5, A, C, J, M, Z to Fulton St./Broadway/Nassau St. Visitors center: 12 Fulton St. ☎ 212-748-8600; www.southstseaport.org. Open daily 10am-5pm. Admission to ships, shops, and tours $8, students and seniors $6, under 12 free. Walking around the museum is free.)* Built in 1911 by a Hamburg-based company, the *Peking* is the second-largest sailing ship ever launched. An intensive 12-year restoration has returned this four-masted barque to her former glory. For information on the ship's rich history, catch the 15min. 1929 film of the ship's passage around Cape Horn, shown daily 10am-6pm. *(On the East River, off Fulton St., next to Pier 16. Open daily 10am-5pm. Free with Seaport Museum admission from visitors center.)* In addition to the *Peking*, there are seven ships open to the public. Some are stationary, like the 325 ft. iron-hulled, full-rigged *Wavertree* (1885; currently undergoing restoration) and the *Ambrose*, a floating lighthouse built in 1908 to mark the entrance to New York Harbor. Others take to the open seas: the *Pioneer* (1885) offers 2- and 3hr. tours.

GREENWICH VILLAGE

WASHINGTON SQUARE. Washington Square Park is at the center of Village life. On the north side of the park is **The Row,** a stretch of 1830s brick residences that were once populated by writers, dandies, and professionals. Use caution here late at night. During the day, you'll find a motley mix of musicians, misunderstood teenagers, homeless people, and romping children in the park. At the north end of the park stands the **Washington Memorial Arch,** built in 1889 to commemorate the centennial of George Washington's inauguration. Until 1964, 5th Ave. actually ran through the arch. Residents complained about the noisy traffic, so the city cut the avenue short.

NEW YORK UNIVERSITY. With 48,000 students in 14 schools, NYU is the country's largest private university. On the southeast side of the park looms the rust-colored **Elmer Holmes Bobst Library,** NYU's central library and one of the largest in the country. On the same block stands NYU's Reuben Nakian-designed **Loeb Student Center,** which is garnished with pieces of scrap metal, supposedly meant to represent birds in flight. An enormous concrete monolith, known simply as the **Picasso,** sits in a green square at the center of NYU's three 30-story Silver Towers. Proclaimed by *The New York Times* to be the city's ugliest piece of public art, the 36 ft., 60-ton structure made of black stone and concrete is Norwegian artist Carl Nesjar's adaptation of Picasso's 24 in. *Bust of Sylvette.* **Gould Plaza,** which houses an aluminum sculpture by Dadaist Jean Arp, sits a few steps east on W. 4th St., in front of NYU's Stern School of Business and the Courant Institute of Mathematical Sciences.

CHRISTOPHER PARK AND ENVIRONS. The intersection of Seventh Ave., Christopher St. and W 4th St. forms a green triangle, home to one statue, two sculptures, and a few benches, known (mistakenly) as Sheridan Square and (correctly) as **Christopher Park.** The park owes its common misidentification to the statue of General Sheridan that stands at the triangle's eastern tip. The 1969 Stonewall Riots, arguably the beginning of the modern gay rights movement, took place here. Off 10th St. and 6th Ave., you'll see an iron gate and street sign marking **Patchin Place.** Theodore Dreiser, e. e. cummings, and Djuna Barnes lived in the 145-year-old buildings that line this path. The Village's narrowest building, **75½ Bedford Street,** only 9½ ft. in width, housed writer Edna St. Vincent Millay in the 1920s. Anthropologist Margaret Mead and actors Lionel Barrymore and Cary Grant each lived at 75½ Bedford after Millay's departure. *(Near the corner of Commerce St.)*

LOWER MIDTOWN

UNION SQUARE. At the intersection of 4th Ave. and Broadway, Union Square and the surrounding area sizzled with high society before the Civil War. At the nexus of a number of neighborhoods, Union Sq. has become the crossroads of downtown. In the square itself, the scent of herbs and fresh bread wafts through the air, courtesy of the ◪**Union Square Greenmarket.** Farmers, fishermen, and bakers from all over the region come to sell fresh produce, jellies, and baked goods. In late November, the south end of Union Square is transformed into the Union Square Holiday Market. *(Between Broadway and Park Ave. S, between 14th and 17th St. Greenmarket open M, W, F-Sa 8am-6pm.)* New York's first skyscraper over 20 stories high, the **Flatiron Building** was also as one of the first buildings in which exterior walls were hung on a steel frame. This photogenic building (originally the Fuller Building) was named for its resemblance to the clothes-pressing device. Constructed in 1902, its triangular shape produced wind currents that made women's skirts billow; police coined the term "23 skiddoo" to shoo gapers from the area. The building is now all commercial space. Among its tenants is **St. Martin's Press,** the company that publishes this book. *(175 5th Ave., off the southwest corner of Madison Sq. Park.)*

HOTEL CHELSEA AND PRIESTS. Hotel Chelsea is hallowed literary ground. Some 150 books have been penned here, including works by Arthur Miller, Mark Twain, Vladimir Nabokov, Thomas World, and O. Henry. *(222 W. 23rd St., between 7th and 8th Ave. ☎ 212-243-3700; www.hotelchelsea.com.)* Founded in 1817, **General Theological Seminary** is the oldest Episcopal seminary in America. Hidden behind a rather unfortunate 1960s exterior is a compound of ivy-covered, Gothic Revival brick buildings, home to about 100 seminarians. The grounds are open to the public year-round and, if you're lucky, you may catch some aspiring priests playing tennis. *(175 9th Ave., between 20th and 21st St. ☎ 212-243-5150; www.gts.edu. Gardens open daily 11am-3pm.)*

HERALD SQUARE. Herald Square is located between 34th and 35th St., between Broadway and 6th Ave., is a mecca for shopping. Ever since King Kong first climbed the **Empire State Building** in 1933, the skyscraper has attracted scores of tourists. The limestone-and-granite structure stretches 1454 ft. into the sky and its 73 elevators run through 2 mi. of shafts. *(350 5th Ave., at 34th St. ☎ 212-736-3100. Open daily 8am-midnight; last elevator up at 11:15pm. $18, seniors $16, under 12 $12.)* East on 34th St. stands department store Goliath **Macy's,** which sprawls over 10 floors and houses two million square feet of merchan-

dise ranging from designer clothes to housewares. The store sponsors the **Macy's Thanksgiving Day Parade,** a NYC tradition buoyed by 10-story Snoopys, marching bands, and floats. *(151 W. 34th St., between Broadway and 7th Ave. ☎ 212-695-4400. Open M-F 10am-9pm, Sa 10am-10pm, Su 11am-8pm.)*

MIDTOWN

FIFTH AVENUE. A monumental research library in the style of a classical temple, the main branch of the ◪**New York Public Library,** between 40th and 42nd St., contains the world's seventh-largest research library and an immense reading room. Featured in the film *Ghostbusters,* two marble lions representing Patience and Fortitude guard the library against illiteracy—and ghosts. *(42nd St. and 5th Ave. ☎ 212-869-8089; www.nypl.org. Open Tu-W 11am-7:30pm, Th-Sa 10am-6pm. Free.)* Behind the library, **Bryant Park** features free summertime cultural events, like classic film screenings and live comedy. *(☎ 212-768-4242; www.bryantpark.org. Open daily 7am-9pm.)* Designed by James Renwick, the twin spires of **St. Patrick's Cathedral** stretch 330 ft. into the air, making it the largest Catholic cathedral in the US. *(51st St. ☎ 212-753-2261. Open daily 7am-10pm.)* The **Plaza Hotel,** on 59th St., at the southeast corner of Central Park, was constructed in 1907 at an astronomical cost. Its 18-story, 800-room French Renaissance interior flaunts five marble staircases, ludicrously named suites, and a Grand Ballroom.

ROCKEFELLER CENTER. Rockefeller Center got its start in the Roaring 20s, when tycoon John D. Rockefeller, Jr. wanted to move the Metropolitan Opera to Midtown. The plans fell through when the Great Depression struck in 1929, so Rockefeller made the center a media hub instead. The main entrance is on 5th Ave. between 49th and 50th St. **The Channel Gardens,** so named because they sit between the **Maison Française** on the left and the **British Empire Building** on the right, usher pedestrians toward **Tower Plaza.** This sunken space, topped by the gold-leafed statue of Prometheus, is surrounded by the flags of over 100 countries. During spring and summer, an **ice-skating rink** lies dormant beneath an overpriced cafe. The rink, which is better for people-watching than for skating, reopens in winter in time for the annual **Christmas tree lighting,** one of New York City's greatest traditions. Behind Tower Plaza is the **General Electric Building,** a 70-story skyscraper. **NBC,** which makes its home here, offers an hour-long tour that traces the history of the network, from its first radio broadcast in 1926, through the heyday of TV programming in the 1950s and 60s, to today's sitcoms. The tour visits six studios, including the infamous 8H studio, home of *Saturday Night Live,* and 6A studio, home of *Late Night with Conan O'Brien.* (☎ 212-664-3700. *Departs from the NBC Experience Store in the GE Building M-Th every 30min., F-Su every 15min. M-Sa 8:30am-5:30pm, Su 9:30am-4:30pm. No children under 6. $18.50, seniors and ages 6-16 $15.50.)*

RADIO CITY MUSIC HALL. After narrowly escaping demolition in 1979, this Art Deco landmark received a complete interior restoration. Radio City's main attraction is the Rockettes, a high-stepping, long-legged dance troupe whose annual Christmas and Easter extravaganzas are legendary. The Stage Door Tour takes you through the Great Stage and various rehearsal halls. *(50th St. at 6th Ave. ☎ 212-247-4777; www.radiocity.com. Departs every 30min. daily 11am-3pm. $17, seniors $14, under 12 $10.)*

PARK AVENUE. A luxurious boulevard with greenery running down its center, **Park Avenue,** between 45th and 59th St., is lined with office buildings and hotels. Completed in 1913, the **Grand Central Terminal** is a train station of monumental proportions. On the classical facade on 42nd St., you'll find a beautiful sculpture of Mercury, the Roman god of transportation. An information booth sits in the middle of the commuter-filled concourse. For a dizzying array of chocolates, cheeses, breads, meats, and pastries, swing by the **Grand Central Market,** located on the main level. *(Between 42nd and 45th St.)* Several blocks uptown is the *crème de la crème* of Park Avenue hotels, the **Waldorf-Astoria.** Cole Porter's piano sits in the front lounge, and every US President since Hoover has spent a night or two here. *(301 Park Ave., between 49th and 50th St.)* The dark and gracious **Seagram Building,** the only building in the city designed by Ludwig Mies Van der Rohe, stands a few blocks uptown. *(375 Park Ave., between 52nd and 53rd St.)*

UNITED NATIONS AND THE CHRYSLER BUILDING. Founded just after WWII to serve as a "center for harmonizing the actions of nations," the **United Nations** is located in international territory along what would be 1st Ave. The UN complex consists of the Secretariat Building (the skyscraper), the General Assembly Building, the Hammarskjöld Library, and the Conference Building. The only way into the General Assembly Building is by guided tour. *(1st Ave., between 42nd and 48th St. ☎ 212-963-4475, tours 212-963-3242; www.un.org. 1hr. tours depart from the UN visitors' entrance at 1st Ave. and 46th St. every 15min. M-F 9:15am-4:45pm, Sa-Su 9:30am-4:45pm. $12, 62+ $8.50, students $8, ages 5-14 $7.)* One of New York's most iconic buildings, the **Chrysler Building** is a monument to the car. The building's spire is meant to evoke a 1930 Chrysler's radiator grill. Other motoring mementos include gargoyles styled after hood ornaments and hubcaps. *(On 42nd St. and Lexington Ave.)*

TIMES SQUARE. At the intersection of 42nd St., 7th Ave., and Broadway, Times Sq. is a non-stop, neon-lit, overcrowded, overstimulating feast of excess. The square was once the epicenter of New York seediness, filled with peep shows, prostitutes, and drug dens. Today the smut has been replaced by 30 ft. tall video screens, Disney musicals, and nearly 40 million tourists per year. This is techno-commercial postmodernity at its most apocalyptic. Stop by the **Times Square Information Center,** in the restored Embassy Movie Theatre on 7th Ave., between 46th and 47th St., for free bathrooms, free Internet access, and a theater ticketing service. *(☎ 212-869-1890; www.timessquarenyc.org. Open daily 8am-8pm.)*

THEATER DISTRICT. New York's theater district, centered on Broadway just north of Times Square, is home to approximately 40 theaters, of which 22 have been declared historical landmarks. **Shubert Alley,** half a block west of Broadway, between 44th and 45th St., was originally built as a fire exit between the Booth and Shubert Theaters, and is now a pedestrian zone where theater groupies cluster after shows to get their playbills signed by their favorite actors. *(From 41st to 54th St., between 6th and 8th Ave.)*

CARNEGIE HALL. Amid 57th St.'s galleries and stores, New York City's musical center is Carnegie Hall. Since hosting Tchaikovsky's American debut in 1891, Carnegie Hall has featured such classical icons as Caruso, Toscanini, and Bernstein; jazz greats like Dizzy Gillespie, Ella Fitzgerald, and Thelonious Monk; and even rock 'n' rollers such as The Beatles and The Rolling Stones. *(881 7th Ave., at W. 57th St. ☎ 212-247-7800, tours 212-903-9765; www.carnegiehall.org. 1hr. tours M-F 11:30am, 2, 3pm. $9, students and seniors $6, under 12 $3.)*

CENTRAL PARK. Central Park was founded in the mid-19th century when wealthy New Yorkers advocated the creation of a park in the style of the public grounds of Europe. Frederick Law Olmsted and Calvert Vaux designed the park in 1858; their Greensward plan took 15 years and 20,000 workers to implement. With 58 mi. of pedestrian paths lined by 26,000 trees, it's a great place to escape Manhattan's traffic, pollution, and noise. Expansive fields like the **Sheep Meadow,** from 66th to 69th St., and the **Great Lawn,** from 80th to 85th St., complement developed spaces such as the **Mall,** between 66th and 71st St., the **Shakespeare Garden,** at 80th St., and the **Imagine Mosaic,** commemorating the music of John Lennon, on the western side of the park at 72nd St. Don't miss free summer shows at **Central Park Summerstage** and **Shakespeare in Central Park.** *(☎ 212-310-6600; www.centralparknyc.org.)*

 Central Park is fairly safe during the day, but less so at night. Don't be afraid to go to events in the park at night, but take large paths and go with someone. Do not wander the darker paths at night.

UPPER EAST SIDE

TEMPLE EMANU-EL. The largest synagogue in the world, Temple Emanu-El was completed in 1929 for its German-American congregation. Its 65th St. entrance features an intimidating Romanesque limestone facade trimmed with archways representing the twelve tribes of Israel. Tours are available after morning services and on Saturdays at noon. *(1 E. 65th St., at 5th Ave. ☎ 212-744-1400; www.emanuelnyc.org. Open daily 10am-5pm. Services M-Th and Su 5:30pm, call for F and Sa service schedule.)*

CARL SCHURZ PARK AND GRACIE MANSION. The 15-acre park, built in 1896, overlooks the turbulent waters of the East River. **Gracie Mansion,** at the northern end of the park, has been the official "home" of the mayor of New York City since 1942. Almost all of the objects in the recently restored Gracie Mansion were made in New York, and many of the paintings and prints depict scenes of the city. The privately funded Gracie Mansion Conservancy was established in 1981 to preserve, maintain, and enhance the mansion and its surroundings. *(Between 84th and 90th St. Park open sunrise-1am. ☎ 212-570-4751. 50min. tours Mar. to mid-Nov. W 10, 11am, 1, 2pm by reservation only. $7, seniors $4, students free.)*

UPPER WEST SIDE

LINCOLN CENTER. Inspired by John D. Rockefeller's belief that "the arts are not for the privileged few, but for the many," this 15-acre center for the performing arts is home to 12 facilities that can accommodate nearly 18,000 spectators in all. A reinterpretation of the public plazas in Rome and Venice, Lincoln Center was initially dismissed by *The New York Times* as "a hulking disgrace." Since then, its spare and spacious architecture and the performances it hosts have made Lincoln Center one of New York's beloved public spaces. *(Between 62nd and 66th St.)*

APARTMENTS. Perhaps Manhattan's most famous apartment building, the **Dakota Apartments** counts Lauren Bacall, Leonard Bernstein, Roberta Flack, and Boris Karloff as former residents. The Dakota provided the eerie setting for Roman Polanski's New York horror classic, *Rosemary's Baby,* and the sidewalk outside was the site of resident John Lennon's tragic assassination on December 8, 1980. The interior is closed to the public. *(1 W 72nd St., at the corner of Central Park W.)* The upscale **Ansonia Apartments** complex, completed in 1904, was once the grande dame of Beaux Arts apartments. While the inside is closed to the public, the building's exterior—complete with weathered stone ornaments and rounded corner towers—is still worth a look. Soundproof walls and thick floors once enticed musically-inclined tenants like Enrico Caruso, Arturo Toscanini, and Igor Stravinsky. *(2109 Broadway, between 73rd and 74th St.)*

EAST COAST

COLUMBIA UNIVERSITY. This world-famous university was chartered in 1754 as King's College, but it lost its original name in the American Revolution. The campus, designed by prominent New York architects, is urban—don't come looking for leafy quads. Its centerpiece, the majestic Roman-Classical **Low Library,** looms over **College Walk,** the school's central promenade, which bustles with academics, students, and quacks. Just to the east of Low Library stands **St. Paul's Chapel,** a small but beautiful space with magnificent acoustics, which holds free choral and chamber concerts on Tuesdays and Saturdays (www.columbia.edu/cu/earl/stpauls.html). **Morningside Park,** where Meg Ryan discussed her sexual fantasies in *When Harry Met Sally,* is just east of the campus along Morningside Dr. *(Morningside Dr. and Broadway, from 114th to 120th St. ☎ 212-854-1754; www.columbia.edu. Group tours late fall through spring; no regularly scheduled public tours.)*

CHURCHES. The still-unfinished **Cathedral of St. John the Divine,** under construction since 1892, is the largest in the world. It features altars and bays dedicated both to the sufferings of Christ and to the experiences of immigrants, victims of genocide, and AIDS patients. *(Amsterdam Ave., between 110th and 113th St. Subway: 1 to Cathedral Pkwy./110th St./Broadway. ☎ 212-316-7540, tours 932-7347; www.stjohndivine.org. Open M-Sa 7am-6pm, Su 1pm. Tours Tu-Sa 11am, Su 1pm. $5, students and seniors $4. Parish box office ☎ 212-662-2133.)* Inspired by the Chartres Cathedral, **Riverside Church** has an observation deck in its tower and an amazing view, as well as the world's largest carillon (74 bells), a gift of John D. Rockefeller, Jr. *(490 Riverside Dr., at 120th St. Subway: 1 to 116th St./Columbia University. ☎ 212-870-6792; www.theriversidechurch.org. Open daily 7am-10pm. Tours Su 12:30pm, after services, and upon request. Free.)*

LOWER EAST SIDE

TEMPLES AND SYNAGOGUES. The **Sung Tak Buddhist Association** occupies a former synagogue. Look for the two imposing stone staircases on either side of a Chinese emporium, with a giant, white Buddha at the top. The interior reflects the building's multicultural past in its juxtaposition of Middle Eastern and Asian architectural styles. Services are held daily. *(15 Pike St., between E. Broadway and Henry St. ☎ 212-587-5936. Open daily 9am-6pm. Free.)* The Moorish-style **Eldridge St. Synagogue** was built in 1886 as the first synagogue for New York's Eastern European Jews. It now presides over a crowded, noisy block of Chinatown. The synagogue hosts community events almost every Sunday, including lectures, concerts, and festivals. *(12 Eldridge St., south of Canal St. ☎ 212-219-0888; www.eldridgestreet.org. Tours Tu-Th and Su 11am-4pm. Tours $5, students and seniors $3.)*

HARLEM

SUGAR HILL. African-Americans with "sugar" (that is, money) moved here in the 1920s and 30s. Musical legends Duke Elling-

AMATEUR NIGHT AT THE APOLLO

The Apollo Theater, 253 W. 125th St. is world-famous as the club where legends like James Brown, Ella Fitgerald, and Aretha Franklin all got their start. Shows here can be pricey, but you can save money—and see the promising talent of tomorrow—by going to Amateur Night, an Apollo tradition since 1934. This contest for up-and-coming artists packs the theater every Wednesday night. Audiences vote by applause for their favorite singing, dancing, comedy, and hip-hop acts. Winners are invited back for monthly "show off" nights every two months. The stakes are high—a big-time victory at the Apollo can be a ticket to national recognition. Not all acts make it big, though. Booing is permitted, even encouraged, during performances that don't immediately grab the raucous crowd's attention. If the boos last more than a few seconds, the "Executioner" appears, sending the dejected artist off-stage. But don't worry, "getting executed" is a right of passage that many big names have endured. Luther Vandross performed here six times before completing a song.

☎ 212-531-5301; www.apollotheater.com. First-time contestant shows $15.24; show off nights $15.34.

ton and W.C. Handy lived in the neighborhood, while leaders W.E.B. DuBois and Thurgood Marshall inhabited apartments at 409 Edgecombe Ave. Some of the city's most notable gangsters also operated here. The area was the birthplace of Sugarhill Records, the rap label that created the Sugarhill Gang. Their 1979 single Rapper's Delight became the first hip-hop song to enter the Top 40. Today, skyrocketing real estate prices in Manhattan have made Sugar Hill's beautiful brownstones prized possessions once more. *(143rd to 155th St., between St. Nicholas and Edgecombe Ave. Subway: A, B, C, D to 145th St./St. Nicholas Ave.)*

THE SCHOMBURG CENTER FOR RESEARCH IN BLACK CULTURE. This research branch of the **New York Public Library** houses the city's vast archives, manuscripts, and rare books on black history and culture. Scholar Arturo Schomburg collected some five million photographs, oral histories, and pieces of art. The center also houses the American Negro Theater, famous during the 1940s, and the Langston Hughes Auditorium. *(515 Malcolm X Blvd./Lenox Ave., at 135th St. Subway: 2 or 3 to 135th St. ☎ 212-491-2200; www.schomburgcenter.org. Research and reference open Tu-W noon-8pm, Th-F noon-6pm, Sa 10am-6pm. Exhibition house open Tu-Sa 10am-6pm.)*

CITY COLLEGE. City College was the nation's first public college and the alma mater of Woody Allen, Colin Powell, Edward Koch, and Walter Mosley. Architect George Brown Post employed the Gothic style associated with Oxford and Cambridge, but, seeking to identify the college as a "workingman's school," he insisted on rust-streaked and iron-spotted schist instead of marble or ivory. *(Admissions office at 138th St. and Convent Ave., campus from 130th to 140th St. Enter at 138th St. ☎ 212-650-7000, tours ☎ 212-650-6977; www.ccny.cuny.edu.)*

WASHINGTON HEIGHTS

FORT TRYON PARK. Fort Tryon Park has one of the most majestic landscapes in the city. Inside are the crumbling remains of Fort Tryon, a Revolutionary War bulwark captured by the British in 1776, and the well-tended Heather Garden. *(Subway: C to 155th St./St. Nicholas Ave., 163rd St.; 1, A, C to 168th St./Broadway; A to 175th St., 181st St., 190th St.; 1, 9 to 181st St./St. Nicholas Ave., 191st St.)* The ▧**Cloisters,** the

Met's palatial sanctuary of medieval art, overlooks the park from its perch. Fragments of 12th- and 13th-century French monasteries are incorporated into the building's own medievalist architecture; the building is as much of an attraction as the artwork it houses. *(☎ 212-923-3700; www.metmuseum.org. Open Mar.-Oct. Tu-Su 9:30am-5:15pm; Nov.-Feb. Tu-Su 9:30am-4:45pm. Tours Mar.-Oct. Tu-F 3pm, Su noon. $20, students and seniors $10, children under 12 free.)*

MORRIS-JUMEL MANSION. The Morris-Jumel Mansion is Manhattan's oldest free-standing house, built in 1765, and has famous bedchambers, Napoleonic ornaments, and regal furniture. The gardens afford a great view of the Harlem River. Ring the doorbell for admission, even if the museum looks closed. *(65 Jumel Terr., between 160th and 162nd St. ☎ 212-923-8008; www.morrisjumel.org. Open W-Su 10am-4pm. $3, students and seniors $2, under 12 free. 1hr. tour of building $3.50, under 12 $2.50; 1½hr. tour of building, grounds, and neighborhood $7.)*

BROOKLYN

FULTON LANDING. Fulton Landing is reminiscent of the days when the ferry—not the subway or the car—was the primary means of transportation between Brooklyn and Manhattan. Completed in 1883, the nearby ▧**Brooklyn Bridge**—spanning the gap between lower Manhattan and Brooklyn—is the product of elegant calculation, careful design, and human exertion. A walk across the bridge at sunrise or sunset is one of the most beautiful strolls New York City has to offer. *(From Brooklyn: entrance at the end of Adams St., at Tillary St. Subway: A, C to High St./Cadman Plaza E. From Manhattan: entrance at Park Row. Subway: 4, 5, 6, J, M, Z to Brooklyn Bridge/City Hall.)*

PROSPECT PARK. Central Park designers Frederick Law Olmsted and Calvert Vaux also designed Brooklyn's Prospect Park. While Manhattan's park incorporated existing swamps and bluffs, Prospect Park's "nature" was constructed entirely from scratch. Supposedly, the two designers liked Prospect Park better. The 80 ft. tall **Soldiers and Sailors Arch,** in the middle of **Grand Army Plaza,** was built in the 1890s to commemorate the Union's Civil War victory. The park also contains a children's museum, tennis courts, a carousel, and a zoo. *(Bounded by Prospect Park W,*

Flatbush Ave., Ocean Ave., Parkside Ave., and Prospect Park SW. Subway: 2, 3 to Grand Army Plaza; F to 15th St./Prospect Park; B, Q, S to Prospect Park. ☎ 718-965-8951; www.prospectpark.org.)

BROOKLYN BOTANIC GARDEN. This 52-acre oasis was founded in 1910 by the Brooklyn Institute of Arts and Sciences on a reclaimed waste dump. The artificial scenery is so convincing that water birds flock to the site. Favorite spots include the Discovery Garden; the discovery center in the Steinhardt Conservatory; the Fragrant Garden with mint, lemon, violet, and other aromatic flora; and the Japanese Hill-and-Pond Garden. (1000 Washington Ave.; other entrances on Eastern Pkwy. and Flatbush Ave. Subway: S to Botanic Garden; B, Q, S to Prospect Park; 2, 3 to Eastern Pkwy./Brooklyn Museum. ☎ 718-623-7000, events hotline 718-623-7333; www.bbg.org. Open Apr.-Sept. Tu-F 8am-6pm, Sa-Su 10am-6pm; Oct.-Mar. Tu-F 8am-4:30pm, Sa-Su 10am-4:30pm. $5, students and seniors $3, under 16 free. Tu and Sa 10am-noon free.)

BROOKLYN PUBLIC LIBRARY. The striking Art Deco main branch of the Brooklyn Public Library stands majestically on Grand Army Pl. Its front doors are flanked by two large pillars with gold engravings and the words, "Here are enshrined the longings of great hearts." The library has spawned 53 branches and contains 1.6 million volumes. Temporary exhibitions are on the 2nd floor. (Corner of Eastern Pkwy. and Flatbush Ave. Subway: 2, 3 to Grand Army Plaza. ☎ 718-230-2100; www.brooklynpubliclibrary.org. Open M and F 9am-6pm, Tu-Th 9am-9pm, Sa 10am-6pm.)

CONEY ISLAND. An elite resort until the subway made it accessible to the masses, **Coney Island** is now a rickety slice of Americana. The legendary **Cyclone,** built in 1927, was once the most terrifying roller coaster in the world. The National Register has designated it a historic place, and couples have even been married on it. (At Astroland, 1000 Surf Ave. Open M-Th 10am-10pm, F noon-6pm, Sa-Su noon-4pm. Individual rides $2.50-6; M-F 6hr. unlimited-ride pass $23.) Meet sharks and other beasties at the **New York Aquarium.** (At Surf and W. 8th St. Subway: F, Q to W. 8th St./NY Aquarium. ☎ 718-265-3474; www.nyaquarium.com. Open May-Oct. M-F 10am-6pm, Sa-Su 10am-7pm; Nov.-Apr. daily 10am-4:30pm. $12, seniors and ages 2-12 $8.)

QUEENS

SOCRATES SCULPTURE PARK. Led by sculptor Mark di Suvero, artists transformed this former landfill into an artistic exhibition space with 35 stunning day-glo and rusted-metal abstractions. On Wednesday evenings in August, stop by the **Summer Solstice Celebration,** which screens a variety of independent and foreign films beginning at sunset. (At the end of Broadway, across the Vernon Blvd. intersection. Subway: N, W to Broadway. ☎ 718-956-1819; www.socratessculpturepark.org. Open daily 10am-sunset. Free.)

THE STEINWAY PIANO FACTORY. The Steinway company has manufactured world-famous pianos here ever since it moved from its original location in the Village during the 1860s. The 12,000 parts of a typical Steinway piano, which weighs anywhere from 750-1365 lb., include a 340 lb. plate of cast iron and tiny bits of Brazilian deer skin. If you're interested in visiting, make plans in advance to take the tour, which takes you through the process of construction. (1 Steinway Pl., at 19th Rd. and 77th St. ☎ 718-721-2600; www.steinway.com/factory. Free tours every other Th; call ahead for info.)

FLUSHING AND FLUSHING MEADOWS PARK. Formerly a 1255-acre swamp, nestled between Corona and Flushing, **Flushing Meadows-Corona Park** was a huge rubbish dump until city planners decided to turn the area into fairgrounds for the 1939 and 1964 World's Fairs. The park now holds **Shea Stadium** (home of the Mets), the **USTA National Tennis Center** (where the US Open is played), and the simple but interesting **New York Hall of Science.** (4701 111th St., at 48th Ave. Subway: 7 to 111th St. ☎ 718-699-0005; www.nyhallsci.org. Open July-Aug. Tu-Su 9:30am-5pm; Sept.-June Tu-W 9:30am-2pm, Th-Su 9:30am-5pm. $9; seniors, students, and ages 5-17 $6; ages 2-4 $2.50; under 2 free. Sept.-June and F 2-5pm free.) The **Unisphere,** a 380-ton steel globe in front of the New York City Building, is the retro-futuristic structure featured in the 1997 movie *Men In Black.* (Subway: 7 to Flushing/Main St; 7 to 111th St. or Willets Point.)

THE BRONX

YANKEE STADIUM. The "House That Ruth Built" opened in 1923, and it remains one of the Bronx's main attractions. Inside the 11½-

acre park (the field itself measures only 3½ acres), monuments honor Yankee greats like Lou Gehrig, Joe DiMaggio, and the Bambino himself. A new Yankee Stadium is currently under construction on the nearby site previously occupied by Macombs Dam Park, so catch a game in this historic shrine while you can. Stick close to the stadium area; the neighborhood gets really bad, really fast. *(E. 161st St., at River Ave. Subway: 4, B, D to 161st St./ Yankee Stadium. ☎718-579-4531; www.yankees.com. 1hr. tours daily at noon, except on game days. $14, students and seniors $7.)*

THE BRONX ZOO. The Bronx Zoo/Wildlife Conservation Park is the largest urban zoo in the US. It houses over 4000 animals in a 265-acre expanse of recreated natural habitats. Grab a free map at the entrance. The **World of Reptiles** is home to a poison dart frog, a timber rattlesnake, and Samantha the python, the largest snake in the US. More benign beasts wander free in the Park's "protected sanctuary," allowing for interactions between inhabitants and visitors. If you get tired of all the kids, work out your aggression at the crocodile feedings Mondays and Thursdays at 2pm. *(Subway: 2, 5 to West Farms Sq./E. Tremont Ave. Follow Boston Rd. for 3 blocks to the Bronx Park S gate. Bus: Bx9, Bx12, Bx19, Bx22, and Q44 pass various entrances to the zoo. ☎718-367-1010; www.bronxzoo.com. Open daily M-F 10am-5pm, Sa-Su 10am-5:30pm. Parts of the zoo closed Nov.-Apr. $12, seniors and ages 2-12 $9. W free.)*

NEW YORK BOTANICAL GARDEN. Across from the zoo, the 250-acre New York Botanical Garden, created in 1891, serves as a research laboratory and plant museum, with rare specimens, like the Japanese pagoda tree, the Kobus magnolia, and the Daybreak Yoshino cherry. The 50-acre native forest is the last of the woodlands that once covered the city. Although it costs a few extra dollars to enter, the gorgeous domed **Conservatory** are worth a visit. *(Bronx River Pkwy. Exit 7W and Fordham Rd. Subway: 4 to Bedford Park Blvd./Lehman College; B, D to Bedford Park Blvd. Walk 8 blocks east or take the Bx26 bus. Train: Metro-North Harlem line from Grand Central Terminal to Botanical Garden. ☎718-817-8700; www.nybg.org. Open Apr.-Oct. Tu-Su 10am-6pm; Nov.-Mar. Tu-Su 10am-5pm. $13, students and seniors $11, children 2-12 $5. Call for tour info.)*

BELMONT. Arthur Ave. is the center of this uptown **Little Italy,** where you'll find wonderful homestyle southern Italian cooking. *(Centering on Arthur Ave. and E. 187th St., near the Southern Blvd. entrance to the Bronx Zoo. Subway: B, D to Fordham Rd./Grand Concourse. Walk 11 blocks east or take Bx12 to Arthur Ave. and head south.)* To get a concentrated sense of the area, stop into **Arthur Avenue Retail Market,** an indoor market with a cafe, butcher, grocer, cheese shop, and deli. *(2334 Arthur Ave., between 186th and Crescent St. ☎718-295-5033. Open M-Sa 6am-6pm.)*

EDGAR ALLEN POE COTTAGE. Poe lived in this cottage from 1846 to 1849 with his tubercular cousin and wife, Virginia. The writer married her when he was 26 and she 13. It was in this cottage that Poe wrote "Annabel Lee," "Eureka," and "The Bells," which refers to the bells of nearby Fordham University. The museum, a small clapboard structure, displays a slew of Poe's manuscripts and macabre effects, including the bed in which his young bride died. *(E. Kingsbridge Rd. and Grand Concourse, 5 blocks west of Fordham University. Subway: 4 to Kingsbridge Rd./Jerome Ave. or B, D to Kingsbridge Rd./Grand Concourse. ☎718-881-8900. Open Sa 10am-4pm, Su 1-5pm. $3, students and seniors $2.)*

STATEN ISLAND

Staten Island has a limited tourist infrastructure and is quite difficult to traverse without a car. The **Staten Island Ferry** is itself a sight not to be missed; it offers the best and cheapest (free) tour of NY's harbor. *(Departs from South Ferry. Subway: N, R to Whitehall St.; 1, 9 to South Ferry.)*

■SNUG HARBOR CULTURAL CENTER. Founded in 1801, Sailors' Snug Harbor served as a home for retired sailors for 175 years. The iron fence kept old mariners from quenching their thirst at nearby bars. Purchased by the city and opened in 1976 as a cultural center, this national landmark now includes 28 historic buildings scattered over 83 acres of parkland. In the restored Main Hall, one of the Center's most breathtaking buildings, the **Newhouse Center for Contemporary Art** shows temporary exhibits. *(1000 Richmond Terr. Bus S40. ☎718-448-2500; www.snug-harbor.org. Free tours of the grounds Apr.-Nov. Sa-Su 2pm, starting at the visitors center. Newhouse Center: ☎718-448-2500, ext. 508. Open Tu-Su; hours vary. $3, seniors and under 12 $2.)*

MUSEUMS

Whether you're looking to examine medieval armor, dinosaur fossils, or abstract paintings, New York City has a museum for you. For listings of current and upcoming exhibits, consult *The New Yorker*, *New York* magazine, or Friday's *New York Times* "Weekend" section. Beware: most museums are closed on Mondays and packed elbow-tight on weekends. Many request a "donation" in place of an admission fee—don't be embarrassed to give as little as a dollar.

UPPER WEST SIDE

AMERICAN MUSEUM OF NATURAL HISTORY. For generations of New York's schoolchildren, future paleontologists, and pretty much anyone with a pulse, the Natural History Museum has been a can't-miss opportunity to marvel at dinosaur skeletons, stargaze at the Hayden Planetarium, or buy mineral slabs and rubber snakes at the gift shop. The undisputed champion of the museum's exhibits is the fourth-floor **dinosaur hall**, which displays real fossils in most exhibits. *(Central Park W, between 77th and 81st St. ☎ 212-769-5100; www.amnh.org. Open daily 10am-5:45pm. Suggested donation $14, students and seniors $10.50, ages 2-12 $8.)*

NEW YORK HISTORICAL SOCIETY. Founded in 1804, this block-long Neoclassical building houses a library and New York's oldest continuously operating museum. The Society's extensive, six-million-object collection, displayed in the **Henry Luce III Center** on the fourth floor, includes 132 Tiffany lamps, an array of children's toys, George Washington's bed, Napoleon's chair, 435 Audubon watercolors, and a display about September 11, 2001. *(2 W. 77th St., at Central Park W. ☎ 212-873-3400; www.nyhistory.org. Open Tu-Su 10am-6pm. $10, students and seniors $5, children free.)*

NEW YORK TRANSIT MUSEUM. Embrace your inner subway nerd. This museum, housed in the now-defunct Court St. subway station (yes, the entrance is, in fact, a subway stop), details the birth and evolution of New York's mass transit system. Exhibits include old subway maps, turnstiles, and restored trains, as well as an in-depth look at how the subway was constructed. The museum is also home to one of the best tourist shops in New York—souvenirs include subway-emblem-emblazoned socks ($6.50), t-shirts ($20), and Metro-Card playing cards ($4.50) for all those poker cravings along the road. *(Corner of Schermerhorn St. and Boerum Pl. ☎ 718-694-1600; www.mta.info/museum. Open Tu-F 10am-4pm, Sa-Su noon-5pm. $5, seniors and children $3. W seniors free.)*

UPPER EAST SIDE

METROPOLITAN MUSEUM OF ART. Founded in 1870 by a group of distinguished philanthropists and artists, the Met has more than two million works of art spanning over 5000 years. You could camp out here for a month and still not see everything the museum has to offer. Highlights are the fully intact Temple of Dendur, given to the US by Egypt in 1965, and the European paintings collection. The Costume Institute houses over 75,000 costumes and accessories from the 17th century to the present. *(1000 5th Ave., at 82nd St. Subway: 4, 5, 6 to 86th St./Lexington Ave. ☎ 212-879-5500; www.metmuseum.org. Open Tu-Th and Su 9:30am-5:30pm, F-Sa 9:30am-9pm. Suggested donation $15, students and seniors $10, under 12 free.)*

GUGGENHEIM MUSEUM. The Guggenheim's most famous exhibit is the building itself. Frank Lloyd Wright's inverted white, ridged shell was hailed as a modern masterpiece. Though critics feared that the design would overshadow the art housed within, the collection of modern and postmodern paintings has put those concerns to rest. *(1071 5th Ave., at 89th St. Subway: 4, 5, 6 to 86th St./Lexington Ave. ☎ 212-423-3500; www.guggenheim.org. Open M-W and Sa-Su 10am-5:45pm, F 10am-8pm. $18, students and seniors $15, under 12 free. F 6-8:30pm "pay what you wish.")*

FRICK COLLECTION. Built in the style of an 18th-century mansion, the magnificent former residence of industrialist Henry Clay Frick was transformed into an art connoisseur's museum in 1935. The collection, two-thirds of which belonged to Frick himself, includes impressive Western masterpieces from the early Renaissance through the late 19th century. Frick's favorite organ music sometimes plays in the relaxing Garden Court. *(1 E. 70th St., at Fifth Ave. Subway: 4, 5, 6 to 68th St./Hunter College. ☎ 212-288-0700;*

www.frick.org. Open Tu-Sa 10am-6pm, Su 11am-5pm. $15, seniors $10, students $5. No children under 10 admitted, under 16 must be accompanied by an adult.)

MUSEUM OF THE CITY OF NEW YORK. This fascinating museum recounts the history of the Big Apple through a vast, 1.5 million-object collection. Highlights include an extensive photography exhibit documenting New York's evolution during the first half of the 20th century, a toy gallery, a fascinating theater exhibit, and a collection of 19th-century vehicles used by the police and fire departments. Cultural history of all varieties is on parade—don't miss the model ships, hot pants, and the Yankees' World Series trophies—if you can stomach the sight of them. *(1220 5th Ave., at 103rd St. Subway: 4, 5, 6 to 103rd St. ☎212-534-1672; www.mcny.org. Open Tu-Su 10am-5pm. Suggested donation $9; students, seniors, and children $5; under 12 free.)*

THE JEWISH MUSEUM. The museum's permanent exhibits span two floors and 4000 years of Jewish art, beginning with ancient Biblical artifacts and ceremonial objects and moving to contemporary masterpieces by Marc Chagall, Frank Stella, and George Segal. Culminating in postmodernity, the museum includes a deconstructivist *mezuzah* and an interactive Talmud exhibit. *(1109 5th Ave., at 92nd St. Subway: 4, 5, 6 to 96th St. ☎212-423-3200; www.jewishmuseum.org. Open M-W and Su 11am-5:45pm, Th 11am-9pm, F 11am-5pm. $10, students and seniors $7.50, children under 12 free. Th 5-9pm "pay what you wish.")*

WHITNEY MUSEUM OF AMERICAN ART. In 1929, the Metropolitan Museum declined a donation of over 500 works from the Greenwich Village sculptor and collector Gertrude Vanderbilt Whitney, so she founded her own museum instead. This museum, unique in its aim to champion the work of living American artists, has assembled a 12,000-object collection of 20th- and 21st-century American art, the largest in the world. *(945 Madison Ave., at 75th St. Subway: 4, 5, 6 to 77th St. ☎212-570-3676; www.whitney.org. Open W-Th and Sa-Su 11am-6pm, F 1-9pm. $15, students and seniors $10, under 12 free. F 6-9pm "pay what you wish.")*

LOWER EAST SIDE

LOWER EAST SIDE TENEMENT MUSEUM. This museum, dedicated to the experience of New York's immigrants in the early 20th cen-

tury, offers one of the most personal and fascinating approaches to New York City history around. The museum can only be seen by guided tour, so it's best to reserve ahead. One tour focuses on the lives of two Depression-era families, one German-Jewish, another Sicilian-Catholic. A second tour focuses on the hardships of turn-of-the-century garment workers. A third, focusing on the life of a Sephardic Jewish family, is led by a costumed guide. *(108 Orchard St., between Broome St. and Delancey St. ☎212-431-0233, tickets 866-811-4111; www.tenement.org. Tours limited to 15. Buy tickets online at least 24hr. in advance. $15, students and seniors $11.)*

MIDTOWN

⊠ MUSEUM OF MODERN ART (MOMA). In the 1920s, when the conservative Met Museum refused to display modernist work, scholar Alfred Barr responded by holding the first exhibit of what would become the MoMA. As the ground-breaking works of the 20th century have gone from shockers to masterpieces, the contemporary MoMA has shifted from revolution to institution. Still, it's one of the best museums of its kind in the world, with over 100,000 paintings, 2000 videos, and 25,000 photographs. *(11 W. 53rd St., between 5th and 6th Ave. ☎212-708-9400. Open M, W-Th, Sa-Su 10:30am-5:30pm, F 10:30am-8pm. $20, seniors $16, students $12, under 17 free.)*

MUSEUM OF TELEVISION AND RADIO. More an archive than a museum, this shrine to modern media contains over 200,000 TV and radio programs donated by the major networks. You can watch *I Love Lucy* episodes, listen to the original announcement of the Pearl Harbor attacks, or wonder at the popularity of the *Newlywed Game*. Most shows arrive with their original commercials intact. *(25 W. 52nd St., between 5th and 6th Ave. ☎212-621-6800; www.mtr.org. Open Tu-W and F-Su noon-6pm, Th noon-8pm. $10, students and seniors $8, under 14 $5.)*

BROOKLYN

⊠ BROOKLYN MUSEUM OF ART (BMA). If it weren't for the Met, the BMA would be NYC's most magnificent museum. Oceanic and New World art collections reside on the 1st floor; ancient Greek, Roman, Middle Eastern, and Egyptian galleries are on the 3rd floor.

Free tours of the museum are offered most weekends around 1:30pm, but call or check the website for times. *(200 Eastern Pkwy., at Washington Ave. Subway: 2 or 3 to Eastern Pkwy./Brooklyn Museum. ☎ 718-638-5000; www.brooklynmuseum.org. Open W-F 10am-5pm, Sa-Su 11am-6pm; 1st Sa of each month 11am-11pm. $8, students and seniors $4, under 12 free. Audio tours $3. 1st Sa of each month free.)*

QUEENS

AMERICAN MUSEUM OF THE MOVING IMAGE.
This museum, dedicated to the art of film and television production, features fascinating exhibits explaining television and film production, along with cool movie memorabilia. Check out the Yoda puppet from *The Empire Strikes Back*, the chariot from *Ben Hur*, and the jowl-enhancing mouthpiece worn by Marlon Brando in *The Godfather*. *(35th Ave., at 36th St. Walk 1 block down Steinway St., turn right onto 35th Ave. Subway: R, G, V to Steinway. ☎ 718-784-0077; www.movingimage.us. Open W-Th 11am-5pm, F noon-8pm, Sa-Su 11am-6:30pm. $10, students and seniors $7.50, ages 5-18 $5, under 4 free. F 4-8pm free.)*

ISAMU NOGUCHI GARDEN MUSEUM.
The stunning, recently restored home of the Noguchi Museum showcases over 240 works by the celebrated sculptor Isamu Noguchi, whose works probe the relationship between the natural and the manmade. The building, a converted factory, encircles a climate-controlled garden. *(32-37 Vernon Blvd., at 10th St. and 33rd Rd., in Long Island City, Queens. ☎ 718-204-7088; www.noguchi.org. Open W-F 10am-5pm, Sa-Su 11am-6pm. $10, students and seniors $5.)*

GALLERIES

New York City's galleries provide a riveting—and free—introduction to the contemporary art world. To get started, pick up a free copy of *The Gallery Guide* at any major museum or gallery. Most galleries are open Tuesday to Saturday, from 10 or 11am to 5 or 6pm. In the summer galleries are usually only open on weekend afternoons, and many are closed from late July to early September.

Artists Space, 38 Greene St., 3rd fl. (☎ 212-226-3970; www.artistsspace.org), at Grand St. Subway: 1, 9 to Canal St./Varick St.; A, C, E to Canal St./Ave. of the Americas (6th Ave.). Nonprofit gallery founded in 1972. Champions work by emerging and unaffiliated artists as well as work in digital media. The gallery presents works in all media, but the focus is on works in architecture and design. The Irving Sandler Artists File, containing slides and digitized images of works by more than 3000 artists, is open F-Sa to critics, curators, and the public by appointment. Open Tu-Sa 11am-6pm. Closed Aug.

The Drawing Center, 35 Wooster St. (☎ 212-219-2166; www.drawingcenter.org), between Grand and Broome St. Subway: 1, 9 to Canal St./Varick St.; A, C, E to Canal St./Ave. of the Americas (6th Ave.). Specializing in original works on paper, this nonprofit space sets up high-quality, rotating exhibits. Open Tu-F 10am-6pm, Sa 11am-6pm. Closed Aug. Suggested donation $3. More space at the **Drawing Room,** 40 Wooster St.

525 W. 22nd St., between 10th and 11th Ave. Houses a handful of excellent, petite galleries of contemporary art in 1 space, including the **303 Gallery** (☎ 212-255-1121; www.303gallery.com). Many galleries cater to art-students. Call for hours.

529 W. 20th St., between 10th and 11th Ave. This 11-floor colossus houses over 20 contemporary art galleries, including the **ACA Galleries** (☎ 212-206-8080; www.acagalleries.com) and the **Dorfman Projects** (☎ 212-352-2272; www.dorfman-projects.com). Call for hours.

Leo Castelli, 59 E. 79th St., Apartment 3A (☎ 212-249-4470; www.castelligallery.com), between Park and Madison Ave. Subway: 6 to 77th St. Founded in 1957 by Leo Castelli, a highly influential art dealer known for showcasing the early efforts of Frank Stella and Andy Warhol. A selection of both established and up-and-coming artists. Open mid-Aug. to late June Tu-Sa 10am-6pm.

FOOD

New York is a diner's paradise. Whether expense-accounting your way through a seven-course tasting menu in Midtown or scouring Queens for the best kebab vendor, you won't have trouble finding the perfect meal. If you are one of those lucky few with a rumbly in your tumbly and a charge card in your wallet, the city can be your "hunny pot" of culinary delight.

CHINATOWN

■ **Doyers Vietnamese Restaurant,** 11 Doyers St. (☎212-693-0725), between Bowery and Pell St. Follow the steps downstairs on one of those staircases-beneath-the-sidewalk so characteristic of Chinatown. You won't come here for the decor, which includes palm trees, year-round Christmas decorations, and prominently displayed posters illustrating the Heimlich Maneuver. Appetizers are delicious and often unusual—try the shrimp paste grilled on sugar cane ($6.25). Open M-Th and Su 11am-9:30pm. AmEx only. ❷

■ **Joe's Shanghai,** 9 Pell St. (☎212-233-8888; www.joeshanghairestaurant.com), between Bowery and Mott St. From fried turnip cakes ($3.25) to crispy whole yellowfish ($14), the Shanghai specialties served here draw huge crowds. Joe's is so well known for its delicious *xiao long bao* (crab meat and pork dumplings in savory soup) that the waiter will probably ask if you want them immediately after you sit down. Be prepared for communal tables, long lines on weekends, and prices higher than those of a typical Chinatown restaurant. Open daily 11am-11:15pm. Cash only. ❸

LITTLE ITALY AND NOLITA

■ **Lombardi's Coal Oven Pizza,** 32 Spring St. (☎212-941-7994), between Mott and Mulberry St. Recognized as the nation's oldest pizzeria (1905), Lombardi's claims to have created the New York-style coal-oven pizza, and it has the checkered-tablecloth-and-exposed-brick atmosphere to match. A large pie ($15.50) feeds 3. The line is invariably out the door. Open M-Th 11:30am-11pm, F-Sa 11:30am-midnight, Su 11:30am-10pm. Cash only. ❸

Rice, 227 Mott St. (☎212-226-5775; www.riceny.com), between Prince and Spring St. Rice offers every permutation of its namesake you can imagine, and others that you probably haven't. The basics—basmati, brown, sticky, Japanese, and Thai black—are all here, as are more exotic varieties. Rice entrees $4-9.50. Open daily noon-midnight. Cash only. ❷

Cafe Colonial Restaurant, 276 Elizabeth St. (☎212-274-0044; www.cafecolonialny.com), at Houston St. This colorful, laid-back Brazilian cafe serves great sandwiches and salads ($8.50-11) and larger entrees at dinner (grilled salmon $17; Brazilian-style pork ribs $18). For dessert, the Brazilian flan pudding ($6.75) is scrumptious. Open daily 8am-11pm. AmEx/MC/V. ❸

GREENWICH VILLAGE

■ **Chez Brigitte,** 77 Greenwich Ave. (☎212-929-6736), between 7th Ave. and Bank St. This hole-in-the-wall French bistro has no pretensions and a selection friendly to even the most strapped budget. As its menu boasts, it "serves 250 people, 11 people at a time" from its counter daily. Meat and fish sandwiches on French bread $5-7. Entrees $8-9.50. Open daily 11am-10pm. Cash only. ❷

Sacred Chow, 227 Sullivan St. (☎212-337-0863; www.sacredchow.com), between W. 3rd St. and Bleeker. This delightful vegan restaurant, with a logo depicting a meditating cow, serves creative and delicious cuisine without any animal products, refined sugar, or white flour. Mix and match from the tapas selection (3 for $12), or go for one of the heaping heros ($8.50). Open M-Th 11am-10pm, F-Sa 11am-11pm. AmEx/D/MC/V. ❷

MEATPACKING DISTRICT

■ **Restaurant Florent,** 69 Gansevoort St. (☎212-989-5779; www.restaurantflorent.com), between Greenwich and Washington Ave. The board above the counter at this funky diner reads, "Go Out—Your Nightlife Needs U," and the French bistro fare is sure to keep the hipsters energized. *Salade niçoise* $15. Open 24hr. Cash only. ❹

Spice Market, 403 W. 13th St. (☎212-675-2322), at 9th Ave. A worthwhile splurge, Spice Market is the latest effort of celebrity chef Jean-Georges Vongerichten, who, despite his French roots, pays homage to Asian street food. Vongerichten's updates on Asian appetizers, like mushroom-stuffed egg rolls and chicken samosas in a cilantro-yogurt sauce, may be the best part of the meal ($8-12). Entrees $15-29. Open M-F noon-3pm and 5:30pm-midnight, Sa-Su noon-4pm and 5:30pm-midnight. AmEx/D/MC/V. ❹

CHELSEA

■ **Chef & Co.,** 8 W. 18th St. (☎646-336-1980; www.chefandco.com), between 5th and 6th St. Chef & Co. is a world-famous catering company, serving 30-40 events around New York daily. Leftovers go to this Chelsea store, where you'll find a wide array of gourmet treats—all for $10.50 per lb. The ideal place to stock your picnic basket. Everything half-price daily 3-4pm. Open M-F 11am-4pm. AmEx/D/MC/V. ❷

Rosa Mexicano, 9 E. 18th St. (☎212-533-3350; www.rosamexicano.com), at 5th Ave. Extraordinary Mexican cuisine in a colorful setting. *Flautas de pollo* (rolled crispy chicken tacos) $7.50. Open M-Tu 11:30am-10:30pm, W-Sa 11:30am-11:30pm, Su 11am-10pm. AmEx/D/MC/V. ❸

THEATER DISTRICT

⊠**Empanada Mama,** 763 9th Ave. (☎212-698-9008), between 51st and 52nd St. Empanadas are an artery-clogging Latin American specialty—a combination of meat, cheese, and vegetables wrapped in dough and fried. Empanada Mama, a narrow, always-jammed Hell's Kitchen find, offers over 40 variations, from the pizza (mozzarella and cheese; $2), to the Viagra (crab meat, scallops, and shrimp; $3). Don't miss the dessert empanadas ($2). Open daily 10am-midnight. AmEx/D/MC/V. ❶

Say Cheese!, 649 9th Ave. (☎212-265-8840), between 45th and 46th St. This cute Hell's Kitchen soup-and-sandwich joint looks like a funky kindergarten cafeteria and smells like home. It specializes in all permutations of grilled-cheese sandwiches ($4.25-7.50). If you're feeling low, try Mama's Special, a bowl of rich tomato soup with grilled cheese on sourdough ($6.50). Open M-F noon-9pm, Sa-Su 10am-9pm. AmEx/D/MC/V. ❶

UPPER EAST SIDE

Barking Dog Luncheonette, 1678 3rd Ave. (☎212-831-1800), at 94th St. A haven for Upper East Siders and their 4-legged friends (who are permitted to eat on the patio). Known for tasty American comfort food served in a homey, canine-themed atmosphere. Try the buttermilk-battered half chicken ($13), which comes with gravy, mashed potatoes, and homemade biscuits (for humans). Daily sunset specials (M-F 5-7pm, $13-17) include soup or salad and dessert. Sandwiches $6-8. Open daily 8am-11pm. Cash only. ❷

Mon Petit Café, 801 Lexington Ave. (☎212-355-2233), at 62nd St. This welcoming and unpretentious Parisian-style bistro is the perfect place to relax after a day of sightseeing. While dinner entrees ($16.50-20) aren't cheap, breakfast and lunch are good budget options. Omelettes $7.25-11. *Croque monsieur* $10.75. Some nights feature live music. Open M-Sa 8am-11pm, Su 11am-6pm. AmEx/MC/V. ❸

UPPER WEST SIDE

⊠**Big Nick's Burger and Pizza Joint,** 2175 Broadway (☎212-362-9238, 212-724-2010), at 77th St. Big Nick's has satisfied West Siders for over 40 years. Its sizable reputation rivals its telephone book-like menu (a hefty 27 pages). Burgers and pizza rule the menu, but you can also get all-day breakfast, vegan, and vegetarian options. Wrestle with a plate-sized burger ($5-7.50). Open 24hr. Cash only. ❷

Good Enough to Eat, 483 Amsterdam Ave. (☎212-496-0163; www.goodenoughtoeat.com), between 83rd and 84th St. The Vermont cabin-style decor, complete with miniature white picket fences, quilts, and mismatched cow-motif dishware, is the perfect match for the homey American cuisine at this Upper West Side gem. Try the macaroni and cheese ($11). Open M-Th 8am-4pm and 5:30-10:30pm, F 8am-4pm and 5:30-11pm, Sa 9am-4pm and 5:30-11pm, Su 9am-4pm and 5:30-10:30pm. AmEx/MC/V. ❷

LOWER EAST SIDE

Freeman's (☎212-420-0012; www.freemansrestaurant.com), at the end of Freeman Alley, off Rivington between the Bowery and Chrystie St. Finding this restaurant, tucked away at the end of a tiny alley, is nearly as fun as eating here. Nosh on traditional American cuisine in a "hunting lodge" complete with antlers and stuffed geese. Macaroni and cheese $12. Open M-F 6:30-11:30pm, Sa-Su 11am-4pm and 6:30-11:30pm. AmEx/MC/V. ❸

Clinton St. Baking Company, 4 Clinton St. (☎646-602-6263; www.clintonstreetbaking.com), between E. Houston St. and Stanton St. 6 years ago, this was just a small muffin shop with a loyal following. Today, it's a full-service American restaurant with some of the best baked goods in the city. Lines form early on weekends for their blueberry pancakes ($10) and biscuit sandwiches ($8). Open M-F 8am-4pm and 6-11pm; Sa 10am-4pm and 6-11pm, Su 10am-4pm. Breakfast and lunch cash only; dinner AmEx/MC/V. ❷

HARLEM AND MORNINGSIDE HEIGHTS

⊠**Amir's Falafel,** 2911A Broadway (☎212-749-7500), between 113th and 114th St. Small, clean, and simple (read: counter service and easy takeout), with Middle Eastern staples like

Shawarma and baba ghanoush. Numerous vegetarian selections (platters from $5.50). Open daily 11am-11pm. Cash only. ❶

Miss Maude's Spoonbread Too, 547 Lenox (6th) Ave. (☎212-690-3100; www.spoonbread-inc.com), between 137th and 138th St. Heaping portions of delicious, down-home soul food. The restaurant is famous for spoonbread and sweet potato pie ($3.50), and the macaroni and cheese ($3.50) is phenomenal. Entrees include Louisiana catfish ($13) and Southern fried chicken ($11). Open M-Th noon-9:30pm, F-Sa noon-10:30pm, Su 11am-9:30pm. AmEx/MC/V. ❷

BROOKLYN

Chip Shop, 381 5th Ave. (☎718-832-7701), at 6th St. Downstairs, this restaurant is as properly British as can be, with yellow walls, royal paraphernalia, and excellent fish and chips ($10.50-11.50). Upstairs is Bali-inspired, with succulent chicken *korma* ($9). Open M-Th noon-10pm, F noon-11pm, Sa 11am-10pm, Su 11am-11pm. Cash only. ❷

Sea, 114 N. 6th St. (☎718-384-8850; www.sea-estaurant.com), between Berry St. and Wythe Ave. Sleek and chic, with fluorescent lighting and thumping music, this Thai restaurant feels as much like a dance club as it does a place to eat, but the food won't disappoint. The lunch special ($6.50-7.50) is an unbeatable value; entrees come with an appetizer and a mountain of rice. Pad thai $7. Duck with curry sauce $13. Th-Su DJ. Open M-Th and Su 11:30am-11:30pm, F-Sa 11:30am-2am. MC/V. ❷

QUEENS

Elias Corner, 24-02 31st St. (☎718-932-1510). A fantastic seafood restaurant with a distinctly Greek character, Elias Corner has no fixed menu, just an ever-changing selection of fish caught the morning of your meal. Reservations aren't accepted; arrive early to guarantee you'll snag a table. Prices depend on the catch of the day, but the average meal starts around $10. Open daily 4-11pm or midnight. Cash only. ❷

Telly's Taverna, 28-13 23rd Ave. (☎718-728-9056). A really big, really popular, and really Greek fish and steak house. Try the octopus ($10) and *Saganaki* ($9). Open M-Th 3pm-midnight, F-Sa 3pm-1am, Su noon-midnight. D/MC/V. ❷

ACCOMMODATIONS

Accommodations in New York City are Very expensive, with a capital "V." You can expect a dorm room in a hostel to cost around $35, with private rooms closer to $50. Hotel singles start around $60, with the upper limit around the highest number you can think of, plus three.

HOSTELS

Central Park Hostel, 19 W. 103rd St. (☎212-678-0491; www.centralparkhostel.com), between Manhattan Ave. and Central Park W. This 5-story brownstone boasts hand-painted murals in the lobby, a funky tiled floor, spotless rooms with A/C, and a nice downstairs TV lounge. Internet access $2 per 20min. Shared bathrooms. Lockers available. Linen and towels provided. Key deposit $2. Reservations recommended. Dorms $26-35; private doubles $85-95. Cash only. ❶

New York International HI-AYH Hostel, 891 Amsterdam Ave. (☎212-932-2300; www.hinewyork.org), at 103rd St. Large youth hostel with 96 dorm-style rooms and 624 beds. Soft carpets, tight security, spotless bathrooms, and A/C. Kitchens, dining rooms, communal TV lounges, and large outdoor garden. Linen and towels included. Internet access $2 per 20min. Check-in after 4pm. Check-out 11am. 10- to 12-bed dorms $33; 6- to 8-bed dorms $35-38; 4-bed dorms $38, members $30/$32-35/$35. AmEx/MC/V. ❶

Jazz on Harlem, 104 W. 128th St. (☎212-222-5773; www.jazzonthepark.com), near Lenox (6th) Ave. This new hostel from the owners of the Jazz on the Park hostel was recently converted from a brownstone apartment complex and offers clean, secure lodging in the heart of Harlem. Sparkling hardwood floors, new furniture, and A/C make for a comfortable stay. TV lounge, lockers, and luggage storage. Reception 24hr. 10- to 14-bed dorms $24; 4- to 6-bed dorms $28; private rooms from $85. MC/V. ❶

Big Apple Hostel, 119 W. 45th St. (☎212-302-2603; www.bigapplehostel.com), between 6th and 7th Ave. This hostel provides a clean and safe place to sleep in a great location. Kitchen with refrigerator, luggage room, big deck with grill, common rooms, and laundry facilities. Internet access

1971: TAKI 183, a kid from Washington Heights, is the first graffiti writer to garner national attention

$1 per 8min. Check-in and check-out 11am. Aug.-Sept. reservations accepted on website only. 4-bed dorms $28; private rooms $77. MC/V. ❷

Chelsea International Hostel, 251 W. 20th St. (☎212-647-0010; www.chelseahostel.com), between 7th and 8th Ave. Full of funky (mostly European) travelers, this hostel has small rooms at unbeatable prices. The neighborhood is safe (there's a police station right across the street). Free pizza W night. Kitchens, laundry room, and TV rooms. Internet access $1 per 8min. Key deposit $10. Passport required. Reception 24hr. Reservations recommended. Rooms $28, with private bath $32. AmEx/D/MC/V. ❶

Jazz on the Park, 36 W. 106th St./Duke Ellington Blvd. (☎212-932-1600; www.jazzonthepark.com), between Manhattan Ave. and Central Park W. A brightly colored hostel with fun decor, 255 beds, and live jazz on weekends. Internet access $1 per 9min. Linen, towels, and breakfast included. Laundry. Check-in 11am. Check-out 1pm. Reservations required June-Oct. 10- to 12-bed dorms $27; 6- to 8-bed dorms $29; 4-bed dorms $32; private rooms from $75. MC/V. ❷

HOTELS AND GUEST HOUSES

🏨 **Carlton Arms Hotel,** 160 E. 25th St. (☎212-679-0680; www.carltonarms.com), between 3rd and Lexington Ave. This brutally hip hotel couldn't be more proud, sporting the Latin phrase for "There's no mint on your pillow." What it lacks in mints, TV, and phones, it makes up for in cool decor. Each room is decorated by a different artist. 11C is the "good daughter/bad daughter" room—half the room is festooned in teeny-bopper posters; the other in horror-movie pics. All rooms have A/C and sink; some have private baths. Check-in noon. Reservations recommended. Singles $70, with private bath $87. MC/V. ❹

🏨 **Gershwin Hotel,** 7 E. 27th St. (☎212-545-8000; www.gershwinhotel.com), between Madison and 5th Ave. This boutique hotel's red facade is ornamented with stunning glass, and its modern lobby has a Warhol vibe. Private rooms with bathrooms, cable TV, A/C, and phones. Wi-Fi $10 per day. Reception 24hr. Check-in 3pm. Check-out 11am. 6- to 10-bed dorms $33-45; private rooms from $109. AmEx/MC/V. ❸

Hotel Belleclaire, 250 W. 77th St. (☎212-362-7700 or 877-468-3522; www.hotelbelle-claire.com), at Broadway. In a landmark building with marble staircases and an attractive modern lobby, this Scandinavian-chic boutique hotel offers fluffy comforters on sleek white beds. Full gym. Check-in 3pm. Check-out noon. Rooms with shared bath $109-119, with private bath $199-219. AmEx/D/MC/V. ❺

Larchmont Hotel, 27 W. 11th St. (☎212-989-9333; www.larchmonthotel.com), between 5th and 6th Ave. Clean, European-style rooms in a whitewashed brownstone on a quiet block. A/C, closets, desks, phones, TVs, and wash basins in all rooms. Wear your cotton robe and slippers to the shared bath. Continental breakfast included. Check-in 3pm. Check-out noon. Reservations recommended. Singles $80-115; doubles $109-135; queens $129-145. AmEx/MC/V. ❹

Hotel Newton, 2528 Broadway (☎212-678-6500 or 888-468-3558; www.newyorkhotel.com), between 94th and 95th St. Likely one of the best values in Manhattan, this classy, recently renovated hotel boasts clean and spacious rooms with A/C, TVs, and private baths. Internet access $1 per 9min. Check-in 2pm. Check-out noon. Singles and doubles from $99. AmEx/D/DC/MC/V. ❹

Crystal's Castle Bed & Breakfast, 119 W. 119th St. (☎212-722-3637; www.crystal-scastle-bandb.com), between Lenox (6th) Ave. and Adam Clayton Powell Blvd. This 100-year-old brownstone is family owned. All rooms have private baths and TVs. Continental breakfast included. Check-in 10pm. Check-out 1pm. Call at least 1 month in advance for reservations. Singles $76; doubles $97. Call for discounts May-Sept. and Dec.-Jan. 15. MC/V. ❹

Chelsea Star Hotel, 300 W. 30th St. (☎212-244-7827 or 212-877-6969; www.starhotelny.com), at 8th Ave. Madonna reportedly stayed here once as a struggling artist. Stay in one of the 16 themed rooms, or choose a regular "luxe" room. Clean and coveted. All rooms with shared bathrooms. Safe deposit box $5. Reception 24hr. Check-in 1pm. Check-out 11am. Reservations recommended. Dorms $35; singles $79-89; doubles $95-105. AmEx/D/MC/V. ❷

🎵 ENTERTAINMENT

Publications with noteworthy entertainment and nightlife sections are the Village Voice,

New York magazine, and the Sunday edition of The New York Times. The New Yorker has the most comprehensive theater survey.

THEATER

Broadway tickets are pricey, starting at around $45. TKTS, Duffy Square, at 47th St. and Broadway, sells tickets for many Broadway and some larger Off-Broadway shows at a 25-50% discount on the day of the performance. The lines begin to form an hour or so before the booths open, but they move fairly quickly. (☎212-768-1818. Tickets sold M-Sa 3-8pm for 8pm performances, W and Sa 10am-2pm for matinees, Su 11am-7pm for matinees and evening performances.) **Shakespeare in the Park** (☎212-539-8750; www.publictheater.org) is a New York City summer tradition. From June through August, two plays are presented at the outside Delacorte Theater in Central Park, near the 81st St. entrance on the Upper West Side, just north of the main road. Tickets are free, but lines form extremely early.

OPERA

The **Metropolitan Opera Company's** premier outfit performs on a Lincoln Center stage as big as a football field. You can stand in the orchestra for $16 or all the way back in the Family Circle for $12. (☎212-362-6000; www.metopera.org. Season Sept.-May M-Sa. Box office open M-Sa 10am-8pm, Su noon-6pm. Upper balcony around $65. Student rush tickets M-Th $25, F-Sa $35.) It may not be the juggernaut that the Met is, but this smaller **New York City Opera** has gained a reputation for inventive programming and reasonable prices. (☎212-870-5630; www.nycopera.com. Box office open M 10am-7:30pm, Tu-Sa 10am-8:30pm, Su 11:30am-7:30pm. Tickets $12-105. Student rush tickets $10 day of performance.) **Dicapo Opera Theatre,** 184 E. 76th St., between 3rd and Lexington Ave., is a small company that garners standing ovations after almost every performance. (☎212-288-9438; www.dicapo.com. Shows Th-Sa 8pm and Su 4pm. Tickets around $40.)

DANCE

The **New York State Theater** in Lincoln Center is home to the late George Balanchine's ☒**New York City Ballet.** Tickets for the *Nutcracker* in December sell out almost immediately. (☎212-870-5570; www.nycballet.com. Season Nov.-Mar. Tickets from $30. Student rush tickets $12; call ☎212-870-7766.) The **American Ballet Theatre** troupe dances at the Metropolitan Opera House. (☎212-477-3030, box office 212-362-6000; www.abt.org. Tickets from $25.) **City Center,** 131 W. 55th St. (☎212-581-1212; www.citycenter.org), has the city's best dance, from modern to ballet, including the ☒**Alvin Ailey American Dance Theater** (☎212-767-0590; www.alvinailey.org). **De La Guarda** (think disco in a rainforest) performs at 20 Union Sq. E. (☎212-239-6200. Standing-room only. $65; rush tickets $20 2hr. before show. Box office open Tu-Th 1-8:15pm, F 1-10:30pm, Sa 1-10pm, Su 1-7:15pm.) Other dance venues include **Dance Theater Workshop,** 219 W. 19th St. (☎212-924-0077; www.dtw.org), between 7th and 8th Ave.; **Joyce Theater,** 175 8th Ave. (☎212-242-0800; www.joyce.org), between 18th and 19th St.; and **Thalia Spanish Theater,** 41-17 Greenpoint Ave. (☎718-729-3880), in Queens.

MUSIC

JAZZ

The **JVC Jazz Festival** comes into the city from June to July. All-star performances from past series have included Elvin Jones, Ray Charles, Tito Puente, and Mel Torme. Tickets go on sale in early May, but many events take place outdoors in the parks and are free. Check the newspaper for listings. An old-school jazz club, the **Village Vanguard,** 178 7th Ave., serves its music straight-up—no food, and no talking during sets. The club is in a windowless, wedge-shaped basement 70 years thick with the memories of John Coltrane, Lenny Bruce, Leadbelly, Miles Davis, and Sonny Rollins. (☎212-255-4037; www.villagevanguard.net. All ages welcome. Cover M-Th and Su $20, F-Sa $25. $10 drink min. Reservations recommended. Sets M-Th and Su 9 and 11pm; F-Sa 9, 11pm, and sometimes 12:30am. $10 discount with student ID for M-Th and Su 11pm set.) The **Cotton Club,** 656 W. 125th St., on the corner of Riverside Dr., has been around since 1923 and has seen jazz greats like Lena Horne, Ethel Waters, and Cab Calloway. (Subway: 1 to 125th St./Broadway. ☎212-663-7980 or 800-640-7980; www.cottonclubnewyork.com. M evening swing/big band. Buffet dinner and jazz show Th-Sa evening. M and Th-Sa evening 21+; call for age restrictions at other events. Su brunch and gospel show $30; dinner jazz show $38. Call 2 weeks in advance for reservations.) **Smoke,** 2751 Broadway, between 105th and 106th St., may no longer be a den of fumes, but the music keeps it smokin'. Surprise guests have included legends like Dr. Lonnie Smith, George Benson, and Ronnie Cuber; the regular lineup includes Cedar Walton, Larry Willis, and George Coleman. (☎212-864-6662; www.smokejazz.com. Cover F-Sa $25 with $10 drink min. per set. No cover M-Th and Su, with $15 drink min. per set. Sets usually M-Th and Su 6:30, 7:45, 9, 11pm, 12:30am; F-Sa 8, 10, 11:30pm, 1am. Tu and Th jam sessions 6-8:30pm. Open daily 5pm-4am.)

ROCK, POP, PUNK, AND FUNK

New York City has a long history of producing bands on the forefront of popular music and performance. **Music festivals** provide the opportunity to see tons of bands at a (relatively) low price. The **CMJ Music Marathon** (☎917-606-1908; www.cmj.com) runs for four nights in the fall and includes over 400 bands and workshops on the alternative music scene. The **Macintosh New York Music Festival** presents over 350 bands over a week-long period in July.

■**SOBs (Sounds of Brazil),** 204 Varick St., at W. Houston St., is a dinner-dance club that has some of NYC's best live music and hip-hop's best talents, including Talib Kweli and the Black Eyed Peas. Monday nights begin with a 1hr. Latin dance class at 7pm ($5); Latin bands play at 9pm. (☎212-243-4940; www.sobs.com. Sa samba 6:30pm-4am $20. Box office at 200 Varick St. open M-F 11am-6pm, Sa noon-6pm. Usually 21+, occasionally 18+. Opens M-Sa at 6:30pm.) The ■**Knitting Factory,** 74 Leonard St., between Broadway and Church St., is a multi-level performance space featuring several shows each night. There are two shows nightly—one at the bar, one on the main stage—ranging from avant-garde and indie rock to jazz and hip-hop. (☎212-219-3006; www.knittingfactory.com. Cover $5-25. Tickets from $8. Box office open M-Sa 10am-2am, Su 2pm-2am. Bar open 6pm-4am.)

CLASSICAL

Lincoln Center has the greatest selection in its halls. The **Great Performers Series** packs the Avery Fisher and Alice Tully Halls and the Walter Reade Theater from October until May with quality classical music, films, and world premieres. (☎212-875-5456; www.lincolncenter.org. Tickets $20-60.) Avery Fisher Hall presents the annual **Mostly Mozart Festival,** which features Mozart along with some Schubert, Beethoven, and Haydn. Show up early; there are usually recitals 1hr. before the main concert that are free to ticket holders. (☎212-875-5456; www.lincolncenter.org. July-Aug. Tickets $25-70.) The **New York Philharmonic** begins its regular season in mid-September. Students and seniors can sometimes get $10 tickets on the day of performances; call ahead. (☎212-875-5656; www.newyorkphilharmonic.org. Tickets $20-80.) For a few weeks in late June, the Philharmonic holds **free concerts** (☎212-875-5709) on the Great Lawn in Central Park, at Prospect Park in Brooklyn, at Van Cortlandt Park in the Bronx, and elsewhere.

Music schools promise low-cost, high-quality music—a gift for a weary budget traveler. Except for opera and ballet productions ($5-12), concerts at the following schools are free and frequent, especially during the school year (Sept.-May). The best options are the **Juilliard School of Music,** Lincoln Center (☎212-769-7406; www.juilliard.edu), the **Mannes College of Music,** 150 W. 85th St. (☎212-580-0210; www.mannes.edu), and the **Manhattan School of Music,** 120 Claremont Ave. (☎212-749-2802; www.msmnyc.edu).

SPORTS

Most cities are content to have one major team in each big-time sport. New York City has two baseball teams, two hockey teams, NBA and WNBA basketball teams, two football teams . . . and one lonely soccer squad. The beloved **New York Mets** bat at **Shea Stadium** in Queens. (☎718-507-6387. Tickets $5-70.) The **Yankees** play ball at **Yankee Stadium** in the Bronx. (☎718-293-4300. Tickets $12-115.) Both the **Giants** and the **Jets** play football across the river at **Giants Stadium** in East Rutherford, NJ. The **New York/New Jersey Metrostars** play soccer in the same venue. (☎201-935-3900. Tickets from $25.) The NBA's **Knickerbockers** (that's the **Knicks** to you), the WNBA's **Liberty,** and the NHL **Rangers** play at **Madison Square Garden,** the

"World's Most Famous Arena." (☎212-465-5800; from $22, $8, and $25, respectively).

🔊 NIGHTLIFE

Whether you prefer a Chelsea nightclub or a Harlem jazz club, a smoky Brooklyn bar or a Lower East Side be-seen-ery, New York has it all. Try the *Village Voice*, *New York* magazine, *The New York Press*, and *The New York Times* (particularly the Sunday edition) for daily, weekly, and monthly nightlife calendars.

BARS

LOWER EAST SIDE

☒ **The Back Room,** 102 Norfolk St. (☎212-228-5098), between Rivington and Delancey St. This faithful rendition of a Prohibition-era speakeasy is appropriately difficult to find. Go through the iron gate by the "Lower East Side Toy Company" sign. Head to the back of the courtyard, and go up the stairs to your right. You'll find yourself in a classy parlor-like space, where twentysomethings drink liquor out of teacups and bottles of beer wrapped in paper bags. A sliding bookcase gives way to a "secret" 2nd bar. Open Tu-Sa 7:30pm-2am.

Happy Ending, 302 Broome St. (☎212-334-9676; www.happyendinglounge.com), between Eldridge and Forsyth St. This bar and lounge was converted from a massage parlor (yes, *that* kind). Mirrors etched with naked women remain, and the saunas have become semi-private booths, their waist-high shower heads left intact. The canopy outside still reads "Xie He Health Club"; you're in the right place. Th 10pm "Something Tight" gay dance party. Mixed drinks $6-10. Open Tu-Sa 10pm-4am, Su 7pm-4am.

SOHO AND TRIBECA

☒ **Circa Tabac,** 32 Watts St. (☎212-941-1781), between 6th Ave. and Thompson St. Despite Bloomberg's ban, this lounge is a specially licensed smoker's haven. Decor recalls a Prohibition-era speakeasy: jazz soundtrack, protective curtains, suede seats, and Art Deco pieces. State-of-the-art air purifiers and odor killers keep the air clear. 180 kinds of cigarettes ($9-25) available, plus beer ($5-6) and cocktails ($8-12). Open daily 4pm-4am. AmEx/MC/V.

Milady's, 160 Prince St. (☎212-226-9069), at Thompson St. Down-to-earth decor, friendly staff, low prices, and Manhattanites drunk enough to leave their scowls at home make Milady's a welcome break from the SoHo scene. Beer $3.50-5. Mixed drinks under $7. Open daily 11am-4am. AmEx/D/DC/MC/V.

GREENWICH VILLAGE

☒ **Employees Only,** 510 Hudson St. (☎212-242-3021), between W. 10th St. and Christopher St. In this bar with a 20s feel, skilled bartenders in white chef uniforms—all with handlebar moustaches—mix some of the best vintage cocktails in the city. There's no sign other than the neon "Psychic" in the window; one is often on hand. Open daily 6pm-4am. AmEx/D/MC/V.

The White Horse Tavern, 567 Hudson St. (☎212-243-9260), at W. 11th St. Students playing drinking games and locals reminiscing about the tavern's $0.20 beers. Poet Dylan Thomas drank himself to death here. Jack Kerouac was a regular, too. Beer $4-5. Open M-Th and Su 11am-2am, F-Sa 11am-4am. Cash only.

MEATPACKING DISTRICT

☒ **Flatiron Lounge,** 37 W. 19th St. (☎212-727-7741; www.flatironlounge.com), between 5th Ave. and Avenue of the Americas (6th Ave.). Candlelight and tinkling jazz provide respite from the neighborhood's frenetic nightlife. The 30 ft. mahogany bar was salvaged from The Ballroom, which hosted the likes of Frank Sinatra. Today, it provides the setting for a 30s-inflected menu of classic cocktails. Try the NY Sour (rye whiskey, fresh lemon juice, a dash of orange, and a float of dry red wine; $12). Open M-W and Su 5pm-2am, Th-Sa 5pm-4am. AmEx/MC/V.

Cielo, 18 Little W. 12th St. (☎212-645-5700), between Washington and Greenwich St. A proudly exclusive and surprisingly intimate dance club centered on a sunken dance floor. High-caliber DJs spin electronica, nu-jazz, future soul, and deep house every night. The clientele is stylish and the door is tightly guarded; plan your outfit well. Cover $10-20. Extremely expensive bottle service only at tables. Open W-Sa 10pm-4am. MC/V.

EAST VILLAGE

☒ **d.b.a.,** 41 1st Ave. (☎212-475-5097; www.drinkgoodstuff.com), between E. 2nd and 3rd St. For your inner alcohol connoisseur. With 19 premium beers on tap ($5-6), well over 100 bottled imports and microbrews, 50 bourbons, 130 single-malt whiskeys ($5-8), and 45 different tequilas, this friendly space lives up to its motto: "drink good stuff." Outdoor beer garden open until 10pm; space heaters keep it toasty on cold winter nights. Happy hour daily 5-7pm; $4 drinks. Open daily 1pm-4am. AmEx/D/DC/MC/V.

Joe's Pub, 425 Lafayette St. (☎212-539-8777; www.joespub.com), between Astor Pl. and E. 4th St., at the Joseph Papp Public Theater. Everything from Norwegian acid-folk to chamber music and dance contests is featured at this popular, intimate venue for big names and up-and-coming musical acts. Late night DJs spin hip-hop, rock, and 80s hits for a packed, dancing crowd. Open daily 6pm-4am. AmEx/D/MC/V.

CHELSEA

Barracuda, 275 W. 22nd St. (☎212-645-8613), between 7th and 8th Ave. Classic movies play on TVs above the bar and dramatic red lighting directs patrons to a plush back lounge of armchairs, booths and sofas at this gay-friendly hangout that draws a mixed crowd. Frequent live music. Drinks from $6. Happy hour M-F 4-9pm; 2-for-1 drinks. Open daily 4pm-4am. Cash only.

The Roxy, 515 W. 18th St. (☎212-645-5156; www.roxynyc.com), at 10th Ave. Catering to both gay and straight crowds, The Roxy boasts a series of gigantic and luxurious spaces for drinking and dancing. Downstairs, you'll find high ceilings, a beautiful dance floor, and pounding techno and house. Upstairs is a more intimate setting, where the DJ focuses on pop and hip-hop. Madonna used to party here. Beer $5. W indoor Roller Disco (cover $25); free roller skating classes W 6:30-7:45pm. Sa gay night. Open W 8pm-2am, F 11pm-4am, Sa 11pm-6am. MC/V.

UPPER EAST SIDE

Metropolitan Museum Roof Garden, 1000 5th Ave. (☎212-535-7710). On the 5th fl. of the Met, this lovely patio bar (open only in summer) affords spectacular views of Central Park and the Manhattan skyline. It's an ideal place to start the evening with a glass of wine ($9), a beer ($7), or a martini ($10). Enter at the main entrance and take the elevator from the 1st fl. Open (weather permitting) May-Oct. Tu-Th 10am-4:30pm, F-Sa 10am-8:15pm, Su 10am-4:30pm. AmEx/D/MC/V.

The Big Easy, 1768 2nd Ave. (☎212-348-0879; www.bigeasynyc.com), at 92nd St. A post-grad hang-

out for those who miss their college years, with 4 beer pong tables in the back and a Skee-Ball machine up front. W karaoke. Happy hour daily 5-8pm. Open M-F 5pm-4am, Sa-Su noon-4am. MC/V.

UPPER WEST SIDE

Dive 75, 101 W. 75th St. (☎212-3627518), between Columbus and Amsterdam St. All the joys of your favorite dive without the unusable bathrooms. Locals lounge on comfy couches—watching the TV, enjoying pop-rock jukebox tunes, and pondering the eerily glowing fish tank. A stack of board games sits in the corner. Happy hour 5-7pm with $2.50 Budweiser and $4 mixed drinks. Open M-Th 5pm-4am, F 2:30pm-4am, Sa-Su noon-4am. AmEx/D/DC/MC/V.

The Dead Poet, 450 Amsterdam Ave. (☎212-595-5670), at 81st St. Photos, quotes, and books from some of history's most well-known wordsmiths line the walls of this cozy, dimly lit tavern. Thankfully, the place doesn't take itself too seriously, and the diversions aren't all highbrow: pool, darts, and sports on TV keep the laid-back crowd entertained. Drink 500 pints of Guinness and you'll get your own plaque on the wall. Happy hour M-F 4-8pm with $3 pints. Open M-Sa 8am-4am, Su noon-4am. AmEx/D/DC/MC/V.

BROOKLYN

▨ Galapagos, 70 N. 6th St. (☎718-384-4586; www.galapagosartspace.com), between Kent and Wythe St., in Williamsburg. Once a mayonnaise factory, this space is now one of the coolest nightspots in the city. The industrial decor centers on a giant reflecting pool—formerly the mayonnaise tank. M "Smut" 8pm. Tu-W live rock bands ($6-7). Sa after 10pm DJs (no cover). Happy hour M-Sa 6-8pm. Open M-Th and Su 6:30pm-2am, F-Sa 6pm-4:30am. AmEx/MC/V.

Gowanus Yacht Club, 323 Smith St. (☎718-246-1321), at President St. A friendly outdoor patio with the feel of a rowdy neighborhood barbecue. The proprietor describes the decor as "garage-sale chic meets Gilligan's Island," with a "Captain Ahab mounts Ginger" vibe. 10 kinds of hotdogs (including a vegan "Not Dog"). Open daily 4pm-2am. Cash only.

GLBT NIGHTLIFE

Gay nightlife in New York City is centered in **Chelsea,** especially along 8th Ave. in the 20s, and in **Greenwich Village,** on Christopher St.

g, 223 W. 19th St. (☎212-929-1085; www.glounge.com), between 7th and 8th Ave. A brightly colored, oval-shaped bar popular with pumped-up and pretty Chelsea men cruising to the sounds of DJs spinning house. Shirtless bartenders serve famous frozen cosmos ($7). Happy hour M-F 4-9pm. Open daily 4pm-4am. Cash only.

Stonewall Bar, 53 Christopher St. (☎212-463-0950), at 7th Ave. S. Entrance at 113th 7th Ave. S. The site of the legendary 1969 Stonewall Riots, the Stonewall is still a lively gay bar, though it encounters far less resistance from law enforcement today than it did in 1969. M hip-hop. W and Sa Latin. Th pop. Enter the Su night male amateur strip contest (appropriately named "Meatpacking") for a chance to win $200. Happy hour M-F 3-9pm with 2-for-1 drinks. Cover M, W, Sa-Su $6. Open daily 3pm-4am. Cash only.

SBNY, 50 W. 17th St. (☎212-691-0073; www.splashbar.com), between 5th and 6th Ave. One of the most popular gay mega-bars, the newly renamed and renovated Splash Bar New York (formerly known simply as Splash) is an enormous 2-fl. complex. Industrial decor provides a sleek backdrop for a crowded scene. Themed parties nightly. Happy hour M-Sa 4-9pm; 2-for-1 beers and mixed drinks. Cover after 11pm M-W $5, Th $10, F $20. Open M-Th and Su 4pm-4am, F-Sa 4pm-5am, Su 3pm-4am. AmEx/D/MC/V.

Henrietta Hudson, 438 Hudson St. (☎212-924-3347; www.henriettahudsons.com), between Morton and Barrow St. A young, clean-cut lesbian crowd, along with an assortment of gay and straight males, frequents this friendly Greenwich Village institution. Different music every night: M old school, Tu requests, W karaoke, Th world, F house, Sa pop, Su Latin. Cover Sa-Su $7-10. Happy hour M-F 5-7pm with $3 beers. Open M-F 4pm-4am, Sa 1pm-4am, Su 3pm-4am. AmEx/MC/V.

Chi Chiz, 135 Christopher St. (☎212-462-0027), at Hudson St. A hot spot for attractive, well-groomed African-American and Latino gay men, along with a growing lesbian contingent on the weekends. Pool table in back. Happy hour daily 5-9pm with 2-for-1 drinks. Open daily 4pm-4am. Cash only.

The Cubbyhole, 281 W. 12th St. (☎212-243-9041), at W. 4th St. Hanging fish, seaweed, and kites put this bar somewhere between a magical underwater garden and a kindergarten classroom. Though predominantly lesbian, the crowd is truly mixed, with straight and gay men warmly welcomed. Happy hour M-F 4-7pm, Sa 2-7pm, Su 2-10pm. Open M-F 4pm-3am, Sa-Su 2pm-3am. Cash only.

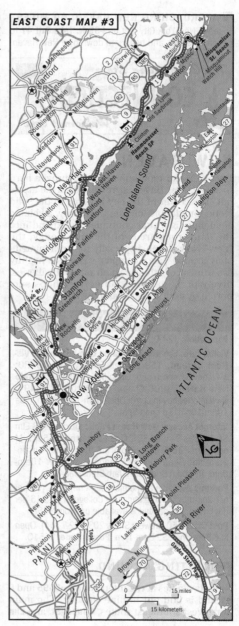

EAST COAST MAP #3

EAST COAST

▲ APPROACHING NEW HAVEN: 80 MILES

To leave New York City, get on **I-95 N.** Take **Exit 47** to get on **CT-34 W,** and head into downtown New Haven.

The Constitution State
CONNECTICUT
Welcomes You!

NEW HAVEN

Despite a bad reputation that has proven hard to shake, New Haven is growing from the inside out. The center of the city is home to the solid stone foundations of Yale University, a shining academic light that continues to expand into the dangerous areas of the city. Today, the "new" New Haven, especially the area immediately around Yale's campus, sustains a healthy assortment of ethnic restaurants, art galleries, dive-y pizza parlors, and coffee shops supported by both students and townies.

VITAL STATS

Population: 124,000

Visitor Info: Greater New Haven Convention and Visitors Bureau, 169 Orange St. (203-777-8580; www.newhavencvb.org). Open M-F 8:30am-5pm. **Info New Haven,** 1000 Chapel St. (☎203-773-9494; www.infonewhaven.com). Open M-Th 10am-9pm, F-Sa 10am-10pm, Su noon-5pm.

Internet Access: New Haven Public Library, 133 Elm St. (☎203-946-8130). Open June to mid-Sept. M noon-8pm, Tu-W 10am-6pm, Th 10am-8pm, F noon-5pm; mid-Sept. to May M noon-8pm, Tu-W 10am-6pm, Th 10am-8pm, Sa 10am-5pm. Free.

Parking: Available at meters along Chapel St. ($1 per hr.; 2hr. max.) or in garages on College St. ($8-15 per day). Free 2hr. parking is available on Wooster St.

Post Office: 50 Brewery St. (☎203-782-7104). Open M-F 8am-6pm, Sa 8am-1pm. **Postal Code:** 06510.

▐ GETTING AROUND

New Haven lies at the intersection of **I-95** and **I-91** and is laid out in nine squares. The main northwest-southeast routes, **Chapel St.** and **Elm St.**, run one-way in opposite directions along the Yale campus and border **New Haven Green.** Cross streets **College** and **Temple St.** frame the green's other edges and are bordered by restaurants and bars. At night, don't wander too far from the immediate downtown and campus areas; surrounding neighborhoods, especially south of the green, can be unsafe.

◉ SIGHTS

The majority of the sights and museums in New Haven are located on or near the Yale University campus. Most of the campus buildings were designed in the English Gothic or Georgian Colonial styles, many of them with intricate moldings and a few with gargoyles. Bordered by Chapel, College, Grove, and High St., the charming **Old Campus** contains Connecticut Hall, which is the university's oldest remaining building. The **Yale Visitors Center** faces the New Haven Green and is the starting point for **campus tours.** *(149 Elm St. ☎203-432-2300; www.yale.edu. Open M-F 9am-4:30pm, Sa-Su 11am-4pm. 1¼hr. tours M-F 10:30am and 2pm, Sa-Su 1:30pm. Free.)*

YALE UNIVERSITY ART GALLERY. The Yale gallery holds over 100,000 pieces from around the world, including works by Monet, Van Gogh, Matisse, and Picasso. The museum also includes a display of fine furniture—unexpectedly culminating in stacking plastic chairs. *(1111 Chapel St., at York St. ☎203-432-0600. Open Tu-W and F-Sa 10am-5pm, Th 10am-8pm, Su 1-6pm. Free.)*

PEABODY MUSEUM OF NATURAL HISTORY. The Peabody Museum houses Rudolph F. Zallinger's Pulitzer Prize-winning mural depicting the "Age of Reptiles" in a room containing dinosaur skeletons. Be sure to check out the prehistoric skulls and Egyptian mummy. *(170 Whitney Ave., at Exit 3 off I-91. ☎203-432-5050. Open M-Sa 10am-5pm, Su noon-5pm. $7, seniors $6, college students and ages 3-18 $5.)*

YALE CENTER FOR BRITISH ART. The Center for British Art is housed in the last building designed by architect Louis I Kahn. The museum contains 2000 paintings, the most complete collection of British art outside the UK. *(1080 Chapel St. ☎203-432-2800; www.yale.edu/ycba. Open Tu-Sa 10am-5pm, Su noon-5pm. Free.)*

STERLING MEMORIAL LIBRARY. Sterling Memorial Library is designed to resemble a monastery—even the telephone booths are shaped like confessionals. The design is not without a sense of humor, though—the Cloister Hall has carved stone corbels portraying students sleeping, lounging, and smoking. *(120 High St., 1 block north of the Yale Visitors Center. ☎ 203-432-1818. Open June-Sept. M-Th 8:30am-9:45pm, F 8:30am-4:45pm, Sa 10am-4:45pm; Sept.-June M-Th 8:30am-1:45am, F 8:30am-9:45pm, Sa 10am-6:45pm, Su noon-1:45am.)*

BEINECKE RARE BOOK AND MANUSCRIPT LIBRARY. Paneled with 900 lb. sheets of Vermont marble cut thin enough to be translucent, Beinecke Rare Book and Manuscript Library is a massive modern structure containing 600,000 rare books and manuscripts. The building protects one of the five Gutenberg Bibles in the US as well as an extensive collection of John James Audubon's prints. *(121 Wall St. ☎ 203-436-1254. Open M-Th 8:30am-8pm, F 8:30am-5pm, Sa 10am-5pm. Free.)*

OTHER SIGHTS. East Rock Park provides an excellent sunset view of New Haven and Long Island Sound from an overlook 325 ft. above sea level. *(Outside the campus, accessible from East Rock Rd. northeast of the city. ☎ 203-946-6086. Free.)* Those interested in New Haven's history should visit the Amistad Memorial, a 14 ft., three-sided, bronze sculpture cast in bronze, across the Green from where the Amistad revolt occurred. *(In front of New Haven City Hall, on Elm St.)*

▄ FOOD

New Haven supports an enviable variety of cheap, high-quality cafes, including several all-vegetarian eateries. For authentic Italian cuisine, work your way along Wooster St. in **Little Italy**, 10min. east of downtown off Chapel St. Indian restaurants dominate the neighborhood southwest of downtown, near **Howe St.**

Pepe's, 157 Wooster St. (☎203-865-5762). Claims to be the inventor of the American pizza, originally known as "tomato pie" ($13). Try a red or white sauce "New Haven" pie ($21.50). Be prepared to wait for a table. Open M-Th 4-10pm, F-Sa 11:30am-10:30pm, Su 2-10pm. AmEx/D/MC/V. ❸

Libby's, 139 Wooster St. (☎203-772-0380), next door to Pepe's. Serves 10 types of cannoli and

delicious gelato ($2). Open M and Su 11:30am-9pm, W-Th 11:30am-10pm, F-Sa 11:30am-11pm. Cash only. ❶

Louis' Lunch, 263 Crown St. (☎203-562-5507). One of several establishments claiming to be the birthplace of the burger. Cooked in vertical cast-iron grills, these burgers ($4.50)—and burgers are all they make—are too fine for ketchup. Open Tu-W 11am-4pm, Th-Sa noon-2am. Cash only. ❶

Tandoor, 1226 Chapel St. (☎203-776-6620). Decorated with holiday lights year-round. Try the *alu mattar* ($5) or another cheap, delicious lunch special (11:30am-3pm). Those unfamiliar with Indian cuisine or just really hungry may prefer to try the enormous Tandoori Dinner, which includes soup, appetizer, dessert, and three mini-entrees for $18. Open daily 11:30am-10:30pm. AmEx/D/MC/V. ❶

▐ ACCOMMODATIONS

Inexpensive lodgings are sparse in New Haven, especially around Yale Parents' Weekend (mid-Oct.) and Commencement (early June). For a variety of budget-friendly options, head 10 mi. south on I-95 to Milford.

Hotel Duncan, 1151 Chapel St. (☎203-787-1273), in the heart of the Yale campus, has the most affordable rates in the downtown area. Guests enjoy spacious rooms and ride in the oldest manually operated elevator in the state. Reservations recommended. Singles $44-50; doubles $70. AmEx/D/MC/V. ❷

The Colony, 1157 Chapel St. (☎203-776-1234 or 800-458-8810; www.colonyatyale.com). Because of its location just steps from downtown, this hotel is able to charge a premium for basic rooms with free Wi-Fi. Singles $110; doubles $120. AmEx/MC/V. ❺

Mayflower Motel, 219 Woodmont Rd. (☎203-878-6854 or 888-800-6854; www.milford-motel.com), just off the highway at Exit 40. Offers very large rooms with free Wi-Fi, HBO, and access to a laundromat. Key deposit $4. Singles $57; doubles $67. AmEx/D/MC/V. ❸

◗ NIGHTLIFE

The **Yale Repertory Theatre,** 1120 Chapel St., hosts productions with professionals and students at the Yale School of Drama. (☎203-432-1234; www.yalerep.org.) The **New Haven Symphony Orchestra,** 247 College St., performs at the Shubert Theater year-round. (☎203-562-5666; www.shubert.com. Box office open M-F 9:30am-5:30pm, Sa 10am-2pm. Tickets $25-50.)

■ **Toad's Place,** 300 York St. (☎203-562-5589; www.toadsplace.com), has hosted the likes of Bob Dylan, the Rolling Stones, and George Clinton. Toad's also features dance parties Sa nights during the school year. Cover $5-35 for shows, $10 for dance nights. Dance party 21+. Open on show nights 7pm-2am. AmEx/D/MC/V.

Bar, 254 Crown St. (☎203-495-1111), is a hip hangout with a pool table, lounge room, dance floor/theater, five homemade beers ($4) at the bar, and brick-oven pizza. Party every Tu night attracts a large gay crowd. Th college night with $1 drafts. Su live indie rock. Cover Tu $5, F-Sa $6. Open M-Tu and Su 4pm-1am, W-Th 11:30am-2:30am, F 11:30am-2am, Sa 4pm-2am. AmEx/D/MC/V.

Alchemy, 223 College St. (☎203-777-9400). 3 levels of dancing. W live music downstairs. Th-Sa 9-11:30pm penny wells. Cover W $12 for open bar upstairs; Th-Sa 21+ $7, 18-21 $10. Open M-Th 9pm-1am, F-Sa 9pm-2am. AmEx/D/MC/V.

Playwright, 144 Temple St. (☎203-752-0450; www.playwrightirishpub.com). Looks more Sunday morning than Sa night—the facade and interior were cobbled together from parts of abandoned Irish and British churches, and it caters to an older crowd. F live music 5-7pm. F-Sa DJ. Open M-Th and Su noon-1am, F-Sa noon-2am. AmEx/D/MC/V.

■ **DETOUR**

HAMMONASSET BEACH STATE PARK

1288 Boston Post Rd. (U.S. 1). Take I-95 N to Exit 62. Turn right off the exit ramp; proceed 1 mi. to the park entrance.

Covering nearly 1000 acres, Hammonasset Beach State Park has a long stretch of beach, two interpretive nature walks, an educational Nature Center, and a launch for smaller watercraft. The park is favored by families and features 550 campsites. (☎203-245-2785, reservations 877-668-2267; www.dep.state.ct.us. Open daily 8am-sunset. $10 per vehicle. Campground open May-Oct. Sites $15. AmEx/D/MC/V.)

■ **APPROACHING CLINTON: 23 MILES**
From New Haven, take **U.S. 1 N** into town.

CLINTON

Founded in 1663, Clinton was the original home of the school that would become Yale University. Still a relatively rural community, much of the town's life centers on outdoor pursuits. The **Clinton Town Beach,** at the end of Waterside Ln., is small and uncrowded, offering a volleyball court, basketball net, and playground. (☎860-669-6901. Open daily 6am-10pm. $25; free before 9am and after 3pm.) The **Clinton Chamber of Commerce,** 50 East Main St., provides free maps of the town and a guide to stores and activities. (☎860-669-3889; www.clintonct.com. Open M-F 9am-3pm.) Visitors can also pick up a walking guide of the town that highlights colonial buildings.

The **M. Sarba Fine Art Cafe ❶,** 95 E. Main St., is located in the former home of Civil War General Horatio Wright and serves a variety of gourmet coffees and lighter fare, such as delicious spinach au gratin and strawberry toast, both $5.25. (☎860-669-5062; www.sarba.com. Open Tu-F 9am-4:30pm, Sa 8am-6pm, Su 9am-4pm. MC/V.) **Saldamarco's ❶,** 86 E. Main St., offers heavy subs stuffed with meatballs and mozzarella ($5.50). The shop also sells pizza ($8.50) and has a mini-grocery with roadtripping necessities like chocolate-chip cookies. (☎860-669-3469. Open M-Tu 9am-6pm, W-Sa 9am-9pm, Su 10am-2pm. AmEx/D/MC/V.) The town has a few quaint inns, but those looking to splurge should head to the **Clinton Motel ❹,** 163 E. Main St. Rooms include fridge, microwave, bathtub, and pool access. (☎860-669-8850. Rooms M-Th and Su $72, F-Sa $92. AmEx/D/MC/V.) The rooms are basic at the **Holiday Motel ❷,** 345 E. Main St., but the motel has a pool, and the rates are the cheapest in town. (☎860-664-3971. Rooms $48. AmEx/D/MC/V.)

■ **APPROACHING OLD SAYBROOK: 10 MILES**
Continue on **U.S. 1 N.**

OLD SAYBROOK

The small town of Old Saybrook has an amazing array of historical homes. The quaint downtown doesn't cater to tourists, but there

1901: The first posted speed limits go up in Connecticut; 12 mph on open roads, 8 mph in cities.

are a variety of excellent places to eat, and the local attractions make it a pleasant stroll.

VITAL STATS

Population: 10,000

Visitor Info: Chamber of Commerce, call for location. (☎860-388-3266; www.oldsaybrookct.com). Open M-F 9am-4pm.

Internet Access: Acton Public Library, 66 Old Boston Post Rd. (☎401-395-3184). Open in summer M-Th 10am-8:30pm, F-Sa 9am-5pm; in winter M-Th 10am-8:30pm, F-Sa 9am-5pm, Su 1-5pm. Free.

Post Office: 36 Main St. (☎860-388-4479). Open M-F 8:30am-5pm, Sa 8:30am-1pm. **Postal Code:** 06475.

GETTING AROUND. Boston Post Rd. (U.S. 1) runs approximately parallel to I-95 in town. Rte. 154 crosses both U.S. 1 and I-95 and becomes **Main St.** in town. Main St. has mostly restaurants and shops, while the hotels lie along **Boston Post Rd.**

SIGHTS. Most attractions in Old Saybrook celebrate the town's rich history. Stop by the Chamber of Commerce for a **walking tour** of the city, which traces the architectural history from the 18th-century Colonial buildings to the 19th-century Federal style. **Fort Saybrook Monument Park** (☎860-395-3152) lies at the end of Main St. Standing on land once owned by local tribes, the fort was built in 1636 as the first fortification in southern New England. The land was later acquired by the Connecticut Valley Railroad, and the remains of the roundhouse and turning station are still there. The park consists of 18 acres, more than half of which are marshland. The **Old Saybrook Historical Society** occupies the **General William Hart House,** 350 Main St., which was built in 1767 by a general in the Revolutionary War. (☎860-388-2622. Open F-Su 1-4pm. $2, under 12 free.)

Don't miss the **Florence Griswold Museum,** 96 Lyme St., in nearby Old Lyme. In the late 19th century, Florence Griswold opened her home to boarders, including artist Harry Ward Ranger, who founded an art colony there. Over 200 artists, mostly Impressionists, eventually came and painted at the estate, inspired to paint by their surroundings.

Today, visitors can see both the grounds and much of the art that was created on-site, including several paintings on the home's doors. (☎860-434-5542; www.flogris.org. Open Tu-Sa 10am-5pm, Su 1-5pm. $8, students and seniors $7, ages 6-12 $4.)

FOOD AND ACCOMMODATIONS. In downtown Old Saybrook, **Caffe Toscana ❷,** 25 Main St., serves fantastic mozzarella sandwiches ($6) on the sunny outside porch. Patrons can also take advantage of the pile of newspapers. (☎860-388-1270. Open M-F 7am-4pm, Sa 8am-4pm, Su 8am-noon. Cash only.) **Savory ❷,** 254 Main St., serves a rotating selection of gourmet choices, like the onion and chevre tart ($4), in a crisp, modern storefront. Side dishes and entrees are sold by weight, while sandwiches, like the Thai shrimp wrap, are all $7. (☎860-395-0755. Open M-Sa 11am-7pm, Su 11am-5pm. AmEx/D/MC/V.) The **Monkey Farm Cafe ❷,** 571 Boston Post Rd., at the junction of Main St. and U.S. 1, is a great local dive with darts and PacMan. Have a burger ($6) or Philly steak grinder ($7), or come back later for a cold one with the regulars. (☎860-388-4866. Open 9am-1am. Cash only.) **Pat's Kountry Kitchen ❸,** 70 Mill Rock Rd,. off U.S. 1 north of town, serves hearty meals in a dining room forever decorated for Christmas. For breakfast, try the clam hash and toast ($7), and be sure to thank Santa for it. (☎860-388-4784. Open M-Tu and Th-Sa 7am-9pm, Su 7am-12:30pm and 2-9pm. AmEx/D/MC/V.)

The well-kept **Sandpiper Inn ❹,** 1750 Boston Post Rd., has rooms with access to a heated outdoor pool, continental breakfast, and free Wi-Fi. (☎860-399-7973; www.sandpiperinnct.com. Rooms M-Th and Su $89, F-Sa $110. AmEx/D/MC/V.) The **Saybrook Motor Inn ❹,** 1575 Boston Post Rd., offers spacious rooms with TV. (☎860-399-5926. Rooms M-Th and Su $65, F-Sa $95. AmEx/D/MC/V.) The **Heritage Motor Inn ❹,** 1500 Boston Post Rd., is a family-owned motel with basic rooms and a pool. (☎860-388-3743. Rooms M-Th and Su $85, F-Sa $125. AmEx/D/MC/V.)

DETOUR
CONNECTICUT CASINOS

Follow U.S. 1 to I-395 and take Exit 79A to Rte. 2A E. Mohegan Sun is 1 mi. away, on Mohegan Sun Blvd. Follow 2A to Rte. 2 to reach Foxwoods, 9 mi. farther.

Foxwoods and Mohegan Sun, two tribally owned casinos in southeastern Connecticut, bring sin to the suburbs. The 4.7 million sq. ft. **Foxwoods** (☎800-FOXWOODS; www.fox-woods.com) complex contains a casino complete with 6400 slot machines, as well as a nonsmoking section. Nearby **Mohegan Sun** (☎888-226-7711; www.mohegansun.com) offers a flashier environment, with the Casino of the Earth making use of Native American motifs.

APPROACHING MYSTIC: 27 MILES
From Old Saybrook, take **U.S. 1 N** into town, where it becomes **Main St.**

MYSTIC
When Herman Melville's white whale, Moby Dick, became a legend, Connecticut's coastal towns were busy seaports full of dark, musty inns and tattooed sailors. Today, there's nothing mystical about this bright, beautiful town overlooking the water. With history, a cute downtown, and natural beauty, Mystic has something for everyone—even Julia Roberts fans.

VITAL STATS

Population: 4000

Visitor Info: Mystic Tourist and Information Center (☎860-536-1641; www.visitmystic.com), Building 1D in Old Mystick Village, off Rte. 27. Open mid-June to Sept. M-Sa 9:30am-5:30pm, Su 10am-5pm; Oct. to early June M-Sa 9:30am-5pm, Su 10am-4pm.

Internet Access: Mystic & Noank Library, 40 Library St. (☎860-536-7721). Open late Sept. to early June M-W 10am-9pm, Th-F 10am-5pm, Sa 9am-1pm; mid-June to early Sept. M-W 10am-9pm, Th-F 10am-5pm, Sa 10am-5pm. $0.25 per 15min.

Post Office: 23 E. Main St. (☎860-536-8143). Open M-F 8:30am-5pm, Sa 8:30am-12:30pm. **Postal Code:** 06355.

GETTING AROUND. Downtown Mystic lies along **U.S. 1,** which becomes **Main St.** between **Greenmanville Ave. (Rte. 27)** to the east and the Mystic River to the west. **Rte. 184** runs north-south to Groton. Most attractions lie along Rte. 27 south of I-95, which roughly parallels U.S. 1.

SIGHTS. Located along the Mystic River, **Mystic Seaport,** off Rte. 27, offers a depiction of 19th-century whaling. In 17 acres of recreated village, actors in period dress entertain visitors with interactive skits, a functioning wood-only shipyard, and three splendid ships. (☎860-973-2767; www.mysticseaport.org. Open daily Apr.-Oct. 9am-5pm; Nov.-Mar. 10am-4pm. $17.50, students and seniors $15.50, ages 6-12 $12.) A few dollars more entitles visitors to a **Sabino Charters** cruise along the Mystic River on an authentic 1908 coal-fired steamboat. (☎860-572-5351. 30min. cruises mid-May to early Oct. daily every 30min. 11:30am-3:30pm. $5.50, ages 6-17 $4.50. 1½hr. cruise 4:30pm. $12/$10.) The **Mystic Aquarium and Institute for Exploration,** 55 Coogan Blvd., takes visitors underwater through video feeds from marine sanctuaries around the US and features an impressive collection of seals, penguins, sharks, and beluga whales. (North of Rte. 27 off U.S. 1. ☎860-572-5955; www.mysticaquarium.org. Open daily 9am-6pm. $19.75, seniors $18.75, ages 3-17 $14.25.) Only 1½ mi. east of downtown, the **Denison Pequotsepos Nature Center,** 109 Pequotsepos Rd., offers excellent birdwatching and indoor exhibits about local wildlife. (☎860-536-1216; www.dpnc.org. Visitors center open M-Sa 9am-5pm, Su 10am-4pm. Park open daily sunrise-sunset. $6, seniors and ages 6-12 $4.)

FOOD AND NIGHTLIFE. On U.S. 1 just north of Main St., **Rice Spice Noodles ❷,** 4 Roosevelt Ave., serves Thai favorites like *tom yum* soup ($5) and pad thai ($9), as well as other specialties. (☎860-572-8488. Open M-F 11:30am-2:30pm and 5-9:30pm, Sa-Su 11:30am-9:30pm. AmEx/D/MC/V.) **Bartleby's ❷,** 46 W. Main St., serves delicious sandwiches along with your caffeinated drink of choice. When you're done, the tables double as chessboards. (☎860-245-0017. Open M-Sa 7am-8:30, Su 8am-8pm. MC/V.) Locals recommend **Cove Fish Market ❸,** in a shack on Old Stonington Rd., 1 mi. east of downtown, for its excellent seafood. Order at the shack, then take your crab cakes ($9.50) or fried oyster roll ($8) to the nearby picnic tables. (☎860-536-0061; www.cove-fish.com. Open M-Th and Su 11am-8pm, F-Sa 11am-9pm. Fish market open daily 10am-7pm. MC/V.) The popular **Mystic Pizza ❸,** 56 W. Main St., has been serving its "secret recipe" pizzas for 30 years. The pizzeria's renown stems largely from the 1988 Julia Roberts movie *Mystic Pizza,* which was filmed here. (☎860-536-3737. Pies $11. Open daily 11am-

11pm. AmEx/D/MC/V.) When locals need to kick back a cold one in Mystic, the younger crowd heads to **Margarita's,** 12 Water St., downtown, a loud, casual bar that mostly serves chips and salsa. (☎860-536-4589. M-Th and Su 9pm-midnight $4 margaritas and $2 Coronas. Open M-Th 4pm-1am, F-Sa 4pm-2am, Su noon-1am. Kitchen closes 10pm. AmEx/D/MC/V.)

ACCOMMODATIONS. It's almost impossible to find budget-friendly lodgings in Mystic; make reservations well in advance. At the intersection of Rte. 27 and I-95, the **Econolodge ❹,** 251 Greenman Ave., has standard motel rooms with TV, mini-fridge, microwave, pool access, and free continental breakfast. (☎860-536-9666. Rooms M-Th and Su $79-89, F-Sa $109. AmEx/D/MC/V.) For reasonably priced rooms, head 6 mi. out of town to Groton. The **Windsor Motel ❸,** 345 Gold Star Hwy. (Rte. 184), in Groton, offers large rooms with standard amenities. (☎860-445-7474. Singles M-Th and Su $45, F-Sa $60-65; doubles $50/$70. AmEx/D/MC/V.) The **Seaport Campground ❷,** on Rte. 184, has a pool, a mini-golf course, a fishing pond, and a laundromat. (Take Rte. 27 west 3 mi. to Rte. 184. ☎860-536-4044; www.seaportcampground.com. Open mid-Apr. to mid-Nov. Sites with water and electricity mid-May to mid-Sept. $36; mid-Apr. to mid-May and mid-Sept. to mid-Nov. $28; with full hookup $42/$34. D/MC/V.)

APPROACHING MISQUAMICUT AND WATCH HILL: 17 MILES
From Mystic, take **U.S. 1 N** to Misquamicut.

The Ocean State
🔱 RHODE ISLAND
Welcomes You!

MISQUAMICUT AND WATCH HILL

The town of Westerly is split into several fire districts, two of which are Misquamicut and Watch Hill. The towns are connected to U.S. 1 by U.S. 1A, which loops towards them. While Misquamicut is a fun, crowded beach town, Watch Hill caters to more affluent tourists. Far west on the Rhode Island coast lies **Misquamicut State Beach,** a half-mile stretch of crowded sand. (☎401-596-9097. Lifeguards on duty 9am-6pm. Park open 9am-sunset.) Farther down the coast, **Watch Hill Beach** is a favorite with locals. (Open M-F 10am-7pm, Sa-Su 9am-6pm. $6, ages 13-17 $4, under 13 $1. Parking $10.) Watch Hill is also home to many beautiful old houses and the **Flying Horse Carousel,** the country's oldest merry-go-round. (Open M-F 11am-9pm, Sa-Su 10am-9pm. Ages 2-12 only. Outside horse $1, inside horse $0.50.)

Hungry beachgoers get off the sand to get down at **Paddy's ❸,** 159 Atlantic Ave. Sandy patrons chow on Kahuna burgers ($11) during the day, then dance to live bands every weekend evening. (☎401-596-2610; www.paddysbeach.com. Open daily 11am-1am. Cover F-Sa $5-10. MC/V.) The **Bay Street Deli ❷,** 112 Bay St., has creatively christened sandwiches like the Carousel (turkey, cheese, sprouts; $7). Just don't eat it right before riding its namesake. (☎401-596-6606. Open daily 8am-8pm. MC/V.) Accommodations are cheaper in Misquamicut than in Watch Hill, and cheaper still as you move away from the beach. Just down the road from Misquamicut Beach, the **Tradewinds Motel ❹,** 4 Rabbit Run, has rooms with A/C and fridge. (☎401-596-5557; www.tradewindsmotel.com. Rooms late June-Sept. M-Th and Su $80, F-Sa $95; Sept. to late June $60/$70. AmEx/D/MC/V.) Take U.S. 1 a few miles north to Charlestown, home to **Burlingame State Camp Ground ❶,** 1 Burlingame Park Rd. The park has 750 sites, as well as bathroom facilities, a playground, swimming in Watchaug Pond, and hiking trails. (☎401-322-7994 or 401-322-7337. Open mid-Apr. to Oct. Sites $20; cabins $35. No hookups. Cash only.)

APPROACHING PROVIDENCE: 47 MILES
From Watch Hill, take **U.S. 1 N** to **Rte. 108 S** to visit the **Point Judith Lighthouse.** Visitors can explore the small park surrounding the lighthouse, but the building itself belongs to the Coast Guard and is off-limits. (On Point Judith Rd. ☎401-789-0444. Free.) Take U.S. 1 N until it becomes **Broad St.** in Providence.

PROVIDENCE

Providence manages to blend its colorful history as the birthplace of the American Industrial Revolution with its current status as home to two world-class universities. The cobblestone streets are crowded with cheap, funky places to eat, and the young, artsy inhabitants support a multitude of performance spaces. When the bonfires of WaterFire are aflame, it feels like the best place on earth—or at least the East Coast—to hang your hat.

VITAL STATS

Population: 174,000

Visitor Info: Providence/Warwick Convention and Visitors Bureau, 1 Sabin St. (☎800-233-1636). Open M-Sa 9am-5pm. **Roger Williams National Memorial Information Center,** 282 N. Main St. (☎401-521-7266). Open daily 9am-4:30pm.

Internet Access: Providence Public Library, 225 Washington St. (☎401-455-8000). Open M and Th noon-8pm, Tu-W 10am-6pm, F-Sa 9am-5:30pm. Free.

Parking: The **Providence Place Mall,** located by the visitors bureau on Francis St., has all-day parking ($1 per 3 hr.)

Post Office: 2 Exchange Terr. (☎401-421-5214). Open M-F 8am-5pm, Sa 8am-2pm. **Postal Code:** 02903.

▐ GETTING AROUND

I-95 and the **Providence River** run north-south and split Providence into three sections. West of I-95 is **Federal Hill;** between I-95 and the Providence River is **Down City;** and east of Providence is **College Hill,** home to Brown University and Rhode Island School of Design (RISD). **I-195** cuts across Providence, running east-west, and connects it to Seekonk, MA. A jaunt down **Benefit St.** in College Hill reveals notable historic sights and art galleries. **Providence Link,** run by the **Rhode Island Public Transit Authority (RIPTA),** has trolleys ($1.50; $6 per day) that run through the city with stops at major sights. Walking is really the best ways to see the city during daylight hours.

◉ SIGHTS

RISD MUSEUM OF ART. The world-renowned Rhode Island School of Design (RISD) occasionally shows the work of its students and professors at the **RISD Museum of Art.** The museum's three-floor maze of galleries also exhibits Egyptian, Indian, Impressionist, medieval, and Roman artwork, as well as a gigantic 12th-century Japanese Buddha. (224 Benefit St. ☎401-454-6500; www.risd.edu/museum.cfm. Open Tu-Su 10am-5pm. $8, seniors $5, students and ages 5-18 $3. Su 10am-1pm and last Sa of each month free. Guided tours Sa-Su 2pm.)

BROWN UNIVERSITY. Established in 1764, Brown boasts several 18th-century buildings, including the **Carliss-Brackett House,** now the Office of Admission. (45 Prospect St. ☎401-863-2378; www.brown.edu/admission. Open M-F 8am-4pm. 1hr. walking tours M-F 9am-4pm. Free.)

RHODE ISLAND STATE CAPITOL. The stunning marble dome of the Rhode Island State Capitol is visible from nearly every vantage point in the city. Visitors can take free 50min. tours; book at least two weeks in advance. (☎401-222-3983; www.state.ri.us. Open M-F 8:30am-4:30pm. Tours every hr. M-F 9am-1pm. Free.)

HISTORICAL SIGHTS. The factory that started the American Industrial Revolution is preserved in Pawtucket at the **Slater Mill Historic Site.** Situated by the rushing Blackstone River, the site has a large waterwheel and working water-powered machinery from the early 19th century. (67 Roosevelt Ave., in Pawtucket, north of the city on I-95. ☎401-725-8638; www.slatermill.org. Open daily May-June 11am-3pm; July-Sept. 10am-5pm; hours vary in winter. 1½hr. tours. $9, seniors $8, ages 6-12 $7.) In addition to founding Rhode Island, in 1638 Roger Williams founded the first **First Baptist Church of America.** Visitors should register with the church office. (75 N. Main St. ☎401-454-3418. Open M-F 9am-3:30pm. Free.) The **John Brown House Museum** is a prime example of Georgian style, with symmetry and squirrel-printed French wallpaper. The 1hr. tour includes a brief video introducing the house and the Brown family, who endowed Brown University. Those less enamored of furniture may prefer the walking tours of Benefit St. (52 Power St. ☎401-331-8575. Open Tu-Sa 10am-4pm. $8, students and seniors $6, ages 7-17 $4. Tours $12, seniors $10, under 12 $6.)

CHILDREN'S MUSEUM. Children go into a frenzy when they see the water activities and giant

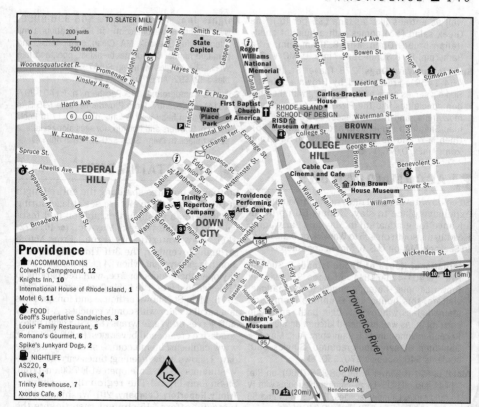

Providence

🏠 ACCOMMODATIONS
Colwell's Campground, 12
Knights Inn, 10
International House of Rhode Island, 1
Motel 6, 11

🍴 FOOD
Geoff's Superlative Sandwiches, 3
Louis' Family Restaurant, 5
Romano's Gourmet, 6
Spike's Junkyard Dogs, 2

🍸 NIGHTLIFE
AS220, 9
Olives, 4
Trinity Brewhouse, 7
Xxodus Cafe, 8

teeth in this small but packed museum. Best enjoyed by the very young or exceedingly young at heart. *(100 South St. ☎401-273-5437. Open Sept.-Mar. Tu-Su 9am-6pm, Apr.-Aug. daily 9am-6pm. $6.50. First Su of month 5-8pm and June to Labor Day F free.)*

🍴 FOOD

Providence has a wide variety of delicious, inexpensive culinary options for the budget traveler. **Atwells Ave.,** on Federal Hill just west of downtown, has a distinctly Italian flavor. **Thayer St.,** on College Hill to the east, is home to offbeat student hangouts and ethnic restaurants. **Wickenden St.,** in the southeast corner of town, also has a diverse selection of inexpensive eateries.

🦪 **Louis' Family Restaurant,** 286 Brook St. (☎401-861-5225). Serves eclectic breakfast and lunch fare to scores of college students. Try the pumpkin pancakes ($3.25) or vegan chili ($2.25). Homemade collages cover the walls, generating a friendly atmosphere. Open daily 5am-3pm. AmEx/D/MC/V. ❶

Geoff's Superlative Sandwiches, 163 Benefit St. (☎401-751-2248), in College Hill. Attracts a mixed crowd with about 85 creatively named sandwiches, like the Dead Head (provolone and veggies; $5.50) and the Kevorkian (pastrami, bacon, cheddar, hot sauce; $7). Grab a green treat (or 2) from the huge pickle barrel to complement your meal. Open M-F 8am-9pm, Sa-Su 9:30am-9pm. AmEx/D/MC/V. ❶

Roma Gourmet, 310 Atwells Ave. (401-331-8620). This gourmet grocery serves huge, delicious grinders (prosciutto and mozzarella; $7) as well as entrees like lasagna ($5 per lb.). The Greek salad ($5) comes with a hunk of crusty Italian bread. Open M-Th 8:30am-6pm, F-Sa 8am-7pm, Su 8:30am-5pm. AmEx/D/MC/V. ❷

Spike's Junkyard Dogs, 273 Thayer St. (☎401-454-1459). Frequented by Brown students, Spike's serves pizza and subs along with their hot dog specialties like the Pizza Dog (pizza sauce, mozzarella, and Italian spices; $3) and the German Shepherd (sauerkraut and mustard; $2.75). Open M-W and Su 11am-midnight, Th-Sa 11am-2am. AmEx/D/MC/V. ❶

🏠 ACCOMMODATIONS

Steep downtown motel rates make Providence an expensive place to stay. Rooms fill up far in advance for graduation in May and early June. Head 10 mi. south on I-95 to **Warwick** or **Cranston** or to **Seekonk, MA,** on U.S. 6, for cheaper motels.

International House of Rhode Island, 8 Stimson Ave. (☎401-421-7181), off Hope St. near the Brown campus. Catering largely to international visitors, this house has 6 unique rooms and stained-glass windows. Fridge, bath, and TV in each room, as well as shared kitchen and laundry. Reception June-July M-F 9am-4pm; Aug.-May M-F 9am-5pm. Reservations required. Singles $60, students $40; doubles $70/$50. ❸

Motel 6, 821 Fall River Ave. (508-336-7800), on Rte. 144A, just off I-95. Large, comfortable rooms with TV and table. Laundry facilities. Rooms M-Th and Su $60, F-Sa $70. AmEx/D/MC/V. ❸

Knights Inn, 48 Mink St. (☎508-336-8050; www.knightsinnseekonk.com), on U.S. 6 about 1 mi. after entering Seekonk, MA. Clean, comfortable, and standard rooms. Continental breakfast, pool, and free Wi-Fi. 21+. Singles M-Th and Su $75, F-Sa $79; doubles $82/$92. AmEx/D/MC/V. ❹

Colwell's Campground, 119 Peckham Ln. (☎401-397-4614), in Coventry. From Providence, take I-95 S to Exit 10, then head west 8½ mi. on Rte. 117 to Peckham Ln. Showers and hookups for sites along a lake, a perfect place to swim. Sites $20-22. Cash only. ❶

🎵 ENTERTAINMENT

Stationary bonfires spanning the entire length of the downtown rivers are set ablaze during ▧**Water Fire,** a public art exhibition and festival held every few weeks May-Oct. (☎401-272-3111; www.waterfire.org. Free.) From March through November, the 3rd Thursday of each month is **gallery night,** when 24 galleries across the city open their doors for free, with free parking in 11 designated lots. The **Cable Car Cinema and Cafe,** 204 S. Main St., shows arthouse and foreign films in a small theater with comfy couches. A friendly staff serves up veggie wraps ($4.35), vegan baked goods, ice cream, and beverages. (☎401-272-3970; www.cablecarcinema.com. 3 shows during the day, 2 shows in the evening; times vary. $8.50; M-W students $6.50. Cafe open M-F 7:30am-11pm, Sa-Su 9am-11pm.) The regionally acclaimed **Trinity Repertory Company,** 201 Washington St., typically offers $15 student rush tickets the

ELEMENTAL

Crowds line the banks of the river and pour over the bridges. People press against the railings, anxiously waiting for sunset. Those who have seen this before sip drinks calmly, while the uninitiated stare intently at the river, afraid they'll miss the moment when the cords of wood are set aflame. This is WaterFire, Providence's public, on-going art installation. As the sun sets, 100 braziers floating on the river are set aflame, releasing aromatic smoke and sparks that rise into the night. Nearby, live musicians play everything from jazz to waltzes, and vendors sell food to the crowds. The fires burn until 1am, as workers continually refuel the flames. When artist Barnaby Evans created the project in 1994, he intended it to be a one-time installation, but WaterFire was so popular that supporters were able to establish it as a nonprofit arts organization. The Providence River is set aflame roughly every 2 weeks from May to October, allowing residents to experience WaterFire as the seasons change. Figures suddenly rush towards the bridge, and a collective quiver goes through the masses of people. The first fire has been lit. WaterFire has begun.

For more information on WaterFire, call ☎401-272-3111 or see www.waterfire.org

day of performances. (☎401-351-4242; www.trinityrep.com. Box office open M-F noon-5pm. Tickets $40-50.) The **Providence Performing Arts Center,** 220 Weybosset St., hosts high-end productions like Broadway musicals. (☎401-421-2787; www.ppacri.org. Box office open M-F 10am-6pm, Sa noon-5pm. Tickets $33-66. Box office M-Th 10am-3pm.)

🔊 NIGHTLIFE

Brownies, townies, and RISDs rock the night away at several hot spots throughout town. For film, theater, and nightlife listings, read the "Weekend" section of the *Providence Journal* or pick up a free *Providence Phoenix.*

Xxodus Cafe, 276 Westminster St. (☎401-351-0353; www.blackrep.org). Serves up cocktails ($6) in a sleek lounge and hosts regular poetry readings, musical performances, and battling MCs. The cafe is also home to the Providence Black Repertory Company, which puts up more formal theatrical performances celebrating black creativity. Xxodus open M-Th 9pm-1am, F-Sa 9pm-2am. Theater tickets $18, student matinees $10. AmEx/D/MC/V.

AS220, 115 Empire St. (☎401-831-9327), between Washington and Westminster St. Ataqueria, bar, gallery, and performance space wrapped into one. It's nonprofit and totally uncensored. The chalkboard outside lists the acts and times for upcoming performances. Cover under $10. Open M 6pm-1am, Tu-F 5pm-1am, Sa noon-1am, Su 6pm-1am.

Trinity Brewhouse, 183 Fountain St., (☎401-854-0368; www.trinitybrewhouse.com), behind Trinity Repertory Theatre. The Trinity brews award-winning beer ($3.50) and features a live jazz band W and Su nights. No cover. Open M-Th and Su 9am-1am, F-Sa 9am-2am. AmEx/D/MC/V.

Olives, 108 N. Main St., (☎401-751-1200). Martinis are their game; throw one back for $7-9. W-Sa night live rock music. Cover F-Sa $5. Open Tu-Th and Su 5pm-1am, F-Sa 5pm-2am. AmEx/D/MC/V.

🚩 APPROACHING NEWPORT: 34 MILES
From Providence, take **I-195 E** to **Rte. 24 S,** which becomes **Rte. 114 S.**

NEWPORT

Money has always found its way into Newport. Once a center of transatlantic shipping, the coastal town later became the summer escape for the elite of America's elite. Today, the awe-inspiring mansions of big-business tycoons still remain, but they are only a part of this high-priced tourist town—world-famous music festivals and the beautiful landscape are now the big draws.

VITAL STATS

Population: 26,000

Visitor Info: Newport County Convention and Visitors Bureau, 23 America's Cup Ave. (☎401-845-9123 or 800-976-5122; www.gonewport.com), 2 blocks from Thames St., in the Newport Gateway Center. Open Labor Day to Memorial Day daily 9am-5pm; Memorial Day to Labor Day F-Sa 9am-6pm.

Internet Access: Public Library, 300 Spring St. (☎401-847-8720). Open in summer M 11am-8pm, Tu-Th 9am-8pm, F-Sa 9am-6pm; in winter M 12:30-9pm, Tu-Th 9:30am-9pm, F-Sa 9:30am-6pm. Free.

Parking: Parking at the visitors center is $2 per day with use of the Rhode Island Public Transit Authority ($1.50 per ride, $6 per day). Free parking is available on Broadway, Spring St., and Bellevue Ave., but the 2hr. limit is strictly enforced.

Post Office: 320 Thames St. (☎401-847-0700). Open M-F 8:30am-6pm, Sa 9am-1pm. **Postal Code:** 02840.

🚩 GETTING AROUND

Running parallel to the shore, **Thames St.** is home to the tourist strip and the wharves, while **Bellevue Ave.** is lined with many of Newport's mansions. Walking is the best way to navigate the downtown area. The mansions are a mile or two away from downtown, so you may wish to drive or take RIPTA buses.

🔆 SIGHTS

OCEAN DRIVE. In the Fort Adams area, Ocean Drive winds along the coast with startling views of the rocky beach, tide pools, and luxurious inns and mansions lining Newport's shoreline. There are plenty of places to pull over to walk along the coast or take a dip, but watch out—private owners do not appreciate trespassing. Stop at **Brenton Point State Park** to take in the view, play on the fields, or visit the **Portuguese Navigators Monument,** which celebrates the Portuguese sailors who revolutionized modern exploration. The point was chosen because of its resemblance to Sagres, a promontory in Portugal where Prince Henry founded a school of navigation in 1419. (☎401-847-2400. Open sunrise-sunset. Free.)

MANSIONS. George Noble Jones built the first "summer cottage" in Newport in 1839, thereby kicking off the creation of an extravagant string of palatial summer estates. Most of the mansions lie south of downtown on Bellevue Ave. Self-guided tours and tours led by the **Preservation Society of Newport** provide a chance to ogle the decadence. (424 Bellevue Ave. ☎401-847-1000; www.newportmansions.org. Open daily in summer 10am-5pm; in winter 10am-4pm.) The five largest mansions are **The Elms,** 367 Bellevue Ave., **Chateau-sur-Mer,** 474 Bellevue Ave., **Rosecliff,** 548 Bellevue Ave., the **Marble House,** 596 Bellevue Ave., and **The Breakers,** 44 Ochre Point Ave. Of these, The Breakers, once owned by the Vanderbilts, is the largest and most popular, with 70 rooms of unchecked opulence. Also well worth checking out is the Marble House, which features over 500,000 cubic ft. of marble, silk walls, and more gold-leaf than you can shake a monocle at. (☎401-847-1000. Open daily 10am-5pm. $10-15 per house, ages 6-17 $4. Combination tickets for 2 houses $22/$6.)

BEACHES. Newport's gorgeous beaches are frequently as crowded as its streets. The most popular sandy spot is **Easton's Beach,** also known as First Beach. (On Memorial Blvd. ☎401-845-5810.) Starting at Easton's Beach or Bellevue Ave., the **Cliff Walk** traverses Newport's eastern shore as a 3½ mi. walking trail. The Cliff Walk can be accessed along a number of roads that intersect with Bellevue Ave. Wildflowers and a rocky shoreline mark one side, while mansions border the other. (www.cliffwalk.com. Open 24hr.)

FORT ADAMS STATE PARK. Fort Adams State Park has a 19th-century fort, a small (but free) beach, and picnicking areas galore. (South of town on Ocean Dr., 2½ mi. from the visitors center. ☎401-841-0707; www.fortadams.org. Park open daily sunrise-sunset. Free. Tours daily every hr. 10am-4pm. $8, students and seniors $7, ages 5-17

$5.) The park also features the **Museum of Yachting,** but your time is better spent watching the boats circling on Narragansett Bay. (☎401-847-1018. Open mid-May to Oct. daily 10am-5pm. $5, seniors and under 12 $4.)

OTHER SIGHTS. The oldest synagogue in the US, the restored **Touro Synagogue,** dates back to 1763. George Washington sent a letter to the synagogue in 1790, pledging his support for religious freedom. (85 Touro St. ☎401-847-4794; www.tourosynagogue.org. Tours every 30min. July-Aug. M-F and Su 10am-5pm; Sept.-June call for times. $5.) The **Tennis Hall of Fame** celebrates the history of the sport with displays on champions like Arthur Ashe, Althea Gibson, and Billie Jean King. A colorful exhibit on tennis-ball canisters through history rounds out the collection. (194 Bellevue Ave. ☎401-849-3990 or 800-457-1144; www.tennisfame.com. Open daily 9:30am-5pm. $9, students and seniors $7, under 16 $5.) The **Newport Historical Society** celebrates Newport's Colonial history and its emergence as a resort town with the **Museum of Newport History.** They also own the **Great Friends Meeting House,** the state's oldest place of worship, and two Colonial-era buildings. Tours of **Colony House** depart every 30min. from 11:30am to 2pm, while tours of the meeting house and **Wanton-Lyman-Hazard House** depart M, W, F-Sa 3pm and 4pm respectively. All of their properties are open for 30min. tours from late June to August. (Newport Historical Society: 82 Touro St. ☎401-846-0813. Open Tu-F 9:30am-4:30pm, Sa 9:30am-noon. Museum of Newport History: 127 Thames St. ☎401-841-8770. Open June-Sept. daily 10am-4pm; Sept.-Dec. Th-Sa 10am-4pm, Su 1-4pm. $4. Great Friends Meeting House: At Farewell and Marlborough St. Tours $2-5.)

▶ FOOD

While many Newport restaurants are pricey, cheap food can be found with a little extra effort. Your best bet is on **Thames St.,** where inexpensive eateries and ice-cream parlors line the street.

Panini Grill, 186 Thames St. (☎401-847-7784), offers creative twists on old favorites, like the Greek panini (red peppers, cucumbers, feta, hot peppers, olives; $5) and turkey portobello melt ($6). This funky shop attracts a young crowd in search of free Wi-Fi and late night eats. Open M-Th and Su 11am-10pm, F-Sa 11am-2am. MC/V. ❶

Gary's Handy Lunch, 462 Thames St. (☎401-847-9480). Decorated like a 50s diner with food that's stood the test of time. Start your day right with eggs ($2.75), and return later for burgers ($2.55). Open M-Th and Sa 5am-3pm, F 5am-7:30pm, Su 5am-1pm. Cash only. ❷

Franklin Spa, 229 Spring St. (☎401-847-3540). Good, hearty breakfasts ($7-8) like the "Portuguese Sailor" (chorizo sausage and eggs) are prepared right before your eyes. Open M-W 6am-2pm, Th-Sa 6am-3pm, Su 7am-1:30pm. Cash only. ❷

Roll Your Own, 408 Thames St. Though the walls are plain and the dining room is just a bunch of chairs, Roll Your Own has no trouble luring in burrito fans. Though you can't actually make your own—a blatant case of false advertising—you can dictate just what goes on your chicken ($8) or veggie ($7) burrito. Open daily 11am-2am. AmEx/D/MC/V. ❷

ACCOMMODATIONS

With over 250 guesthouses and inns scattered throughout the city, small, private lodgings abound in Newport. During the summer, it's hard to find anything for under $100, and weekends are even pricier. Many hotels and guesthouses book solid two months in advance for summer weekends, especially during festivals. For less expensive lodging, it's best to head out of town. **Rte. 114 (W. Main Rd.)** hosts a variety of chain motels about four miles from Newport.

Twin Lanterns, 1172 W. Main Rd. (☎401-682-1304 or 866-682-1304), 7 mi. north of Newport. A relatively inexpensive, family-owned motel with eight clean, one-room cabins with full-size bed, A/C, TV, fridge, and private bathroom. Reservations recommended. Cabins $54. Cash only. ❸

Newport Gateway Hotel, 31 W. Main Rd. (☎401-847-2735 or 800-427-9444), in Middletown, has very large rooms with pull-out bed, A/C, and cable TV. Free continental breakfast and shuttle to downtown Newport. Open Mar.-Nov. Rooms M-Th and Su $89, F-Sa $179. AmEx/D/MC/V. ❹

Melville Ponds Campground, 161 Bradford Ave. (☎401-682-2424), off Rte. 114. Though it's only 5 mi. north of Newport, this campground feels

EAST COAST MAP #2

EAST COAST

like another universe. When the sun goes down, you can't see your hand in front of your face—but you can see the stars and hear the water rushing by. Fishing, hiking, volleyball courts. Open Apr.-Nov. Tent sites $22; RV sites $30, with full hookup $35. Cash only. ❶

Travelodge, 1185 W. Main Rd. (☎401-849-4700 or 800-862-2006). Offers standard rooms with cable, but it's no bargain, especially since it's 3 mi. north of Newport. Free Wi-Fi and a heated pool. Continental breakfast included. Rooms M-Th and Su $85-99, F-Sa $169-179. AmEx/D/MC/V. ❹

🎵 ENTERTAINMENT

Newport gives lovers of classical, folk, jazz, and film each a festival to call their own from June to August. Festival tickets, as well as accommodations, fill up months ahead of time, so start looking early. The **Newport Music Festival** brings in classical musicians from around the world for over 60 concerts during two weeks in July. (☎401-846-1133, box office 401-849-0700; www.newportmusic.org. Box office open M-F 10am-6pm, Sa 10am-1pm. Tickets $25-45.) Bring a picnic to Fort Adams State Park and partake of the festivities of one of the oldest and best-known jazz festivals in the world, the **Newport Jazz Festival.** In early August, guitars replace saxophones at the **Newport Folk Festival.** Former acts include Bob Dylan, Joan Baez, and the Indigo Girls. (☎401-847-3700; www.festivalproductions.net. Jazz festival $65 per day, under 12 $5; folk festival $55/$5.) Over the course of six days in June, the **Newport International Film Festival** screens over 70 feature, documentary, and short films in the **Jane Pickens Theater** and the **Opera House Cinema,** both on Truro St. (☎401-846-9100; www.newportfilmfestival.com. Tickets $10.)

🎷 NIGHTLIFE

Pubs and clubs line Thames St., Newport's liveliest nighttime drag. Be sure to bring proper ID, as area clubs are very strict. Across the hall from one another are two crowded spots, the **Rhino Bar and Grille** and the **Mambo Room,** 337 Thames St. While the Rhino Bar has everything from karaoke on Tuesdays to reggae on Thursdays,

the Mambo Room always has a DJ spinning hip-hop and Top 40. If you're feeling brave, try the Rough Rider, a 72 oz. fishbowl ($22) designed for four. (☎401-846-0707. F ladies night. Cover F-Sa $5, good for both establishments. Rhino open M-F 4pm-1am, Sa-Su noon-1am. Mambo open Th-Sa 9pm-1am. AmEx/D/MC/V.) **One Pelham East,** 270 Thames St., doesn't bother with the slick look of many Newport clubs. The live rock, cover, and acoustic sets are enough to draw a crowd of faithful regulars. (☎401-847-9460. Drinks $4.50-5.50. Nightly live music. Cover M-Sa $3-15. Open daily 3pm-1am. Cash only.) Don't be fooled by the name of **The Newport Blues Cafe,** 286 Thames St.; it hosts a variety of live music ranging from blues to rock to jazz. Previous acts include the Allman Bros. and Sugar Daddy. (☎401-841-5510. Drinks $4-6.50. Nightly live music from 9:30pm. Cover varies, usually F-Sa $5-10. Open daily 6pm-1am. Kitchen closes 10pm. AmEx/D/MC/V.)

TIP **Cape Cod** is one of New England's premier vacation destinations, attracting tourists with small towns, sandy beaches, sun-drenched landscapes, and 🍂**cranberry bogs.** It resembles a bent arm, with **Hyannis** at the biceps, **Chatham** at the elbow, **Cape Cod National Seashore** tattooed onto the forearm, and **Provincetown** at the clenched fist. **Rte. 6** is your best bet if you're in a hurry, but those with time should take **U.S. 6A** and **Rte. 28** along the cape's inner and outer coasts, respectively.

📍 **APPROACHING PROVINCETOWN: 120 MILES**
Take **Rte. 114 N** to **Rte. 24 N.** Take **I-195 E** to **Rte. 25 N,** then switch to **Rte. 6 E** on the Cape.

The Bay State
MASSACHUSETTS
Welcomes You!

PROVINCETOWN

Provincetown has changed quite a bit since the Pilgrims landed here briefly in 1620. In the early 20th century, the town's popularity soared with resident artists and writers like Norman Mailer, Tennessee Williams, and Edward Hopper. Provincetown's tradition of open-mindedness has attracted a large gay community, making it a premier destination for gay vacationers, who fill the town to capacity in summer. Although far from cheap, P-town has better options for outdoor activities, dining, and nightlife than the rest of Cape Cod.

VITAL STATS

Population: 3400

Visitor Info: Provincetown Chamber of Commerce, 307 Commercial St. (☎508-487-3424; www.ptownchamber.com), on MacMillian Wharf. Open June-Sept. M-Sa 9am-5pm, Su 10am-4pm; hours vary in winter.

Internet Access: Provincetown Public Library, 356 Commercial St. (☎508-487-7094; www.ptownlib.com). Open M and F 10am-5pm, Tu and Th noon-8pm, W 10am-8pm, Sa 10am-2pm, Su 1-5pm. Free.

Post Office: 219 Commercial St. (☎508-487-0368). Open M-F 8:30am-5pm, Sa 9am-noon. **Postal Code:** 02657.

GETTING AROUND

P-town's main drag, **Commercial St.,** runs along the harbor, centered on **MacMillian Wharf. Standish St.** divides the town into the East and West Ends. The East End is crowded with galleries. It's easy to navigate Provincetown by foot, but it's a bit of a trek out to the beaches. **Arnold's,** 329 Commercial St., rents bikes. (☎508-487-0844. Bikes $4 per hr., $21 per day.)

SIGHTS

The **Provincetown Art Association and Museum,** 460 Commercial St., has an eclectic collection of art, tied together only by the fact that it all relates somehow to Provincetown. The museum showcases mainly 20th-century art, though exhibits are ever-rotating. (☎508-487-1750; www.paam.org. Open M-Th 11am-8pm, F 11am-10pm, Sa-Su 11am-5pm. $5, under 12

free. F after 5pm free.) The **Pilgrim Monument,** the tallest all-granite structure in the US at 253 ft., and the **Provincetown Museum,** on High Pole Hill just north of the center of town, commemorate the Pilgrims' first landing. Hike up to the top of the tower for stunning views of the Cape and the Atlantic; unfortunately, you have to gaze through wire fencing. (☎508-487-1310. Open daily July-Aug. 9am-7pm; Apr.-June and Sept.-Oct. 9am-5pm. Last entry 45min. before close. $7, students and seniors $5, ages 4-14 $3.50. Su 9am-noon free.) A large bas-relief **monument,** in the small park at Bradford and Ryder St., depicts the signing of the Mayflower Compact on Nov. 11, 1620, in Provincetown Harbor.

OUTDOORS

P-town's miles of shoreline provide spectacular scenery and more than enough space to catch some sun. At the west end of Commercial St., the 1¼ mi. **Breakwater Jetty** stretches into the bay, providing fantastic views of marsh, sand, and Provincetown. Follow it all the way to the end to find a secluded peninsula with empty beaches, two working lighthouses, and the remains of a Civil War fort (free). At **Race Point Beach,** waves roll in from the Atlantic, while **Herring Cove Beach,** at the west end of town, offers calm, protected waters. Directly across from Snail Rd., on U.S. 6, an unlikely path leads to a world of rolling **sand dunes;** look for shacks where writers such as Tennessee Williams, Norman Mailer, and John Dos Passos spent their days.

Those not content just looking at the Cape Cod Bay can rent a kayak from **Venture Athletics,** 237 Commercial St. The shop also offers 2-3hr. guided tours of the harbor. (☎508-487-2395. Single kayaks $25 per 4hr.; double kayaks $45. Guided tours $45-65. Open daily 9am-6pm.) Today, Provincetown seafarers have traded harpoons for cameras, but they still pursue the same beast—**whale-watching cruises** rank among P-town's most popular attractions. Most companies guarantee sightings. (3hr. tour $27-30. Coupons at the Chamber of Commerce.) **Dolphin Fleet** (☎508-240-3636 or 800-826-9300) and **Portuguese Princess** (☎508-487-2651 or 800-422-3188) both leave from MacMillian Wharf.

1872: The first roadside diner, a horse-drawn wagon, opens for business in Providence, Rhode Island.

▄ FOOD

Sit-down meals in Provincetown tend to be expensive. Fast-food joints line the Commercial St. extension (next to MacMillian Wharf) and the Aquarium Mall, farther west on Commercial St.

▓Tofu A Go-Go, 338 Commercial St. (☎508-487-6237). An off-beat restaurant with deliciously fresh vegetarian and vegan options in hearty portions. Try the tofu tahini salad ($8.50), or if you're feeling particularly herbivorous, the Spriulicious soup ($6), made with green algae. Open June-Aug. M-Th 11:30am-4pm, F-Su 11:30am-9pm; Aug.-June hours vary. Cash only. ❸

Karoo Kafe, 338 Commercial St. (☎508-487-6630). A campy, self-titled "fast-food safari," which serves up falafel ($6.75) and chicken *sosatie* ($7.25), a South African dish. Open daily June-Aug. 11am-9pm; Mar.-May and Sept.-Nov. hours vary. AmEx/D/MC/V. ❷

Cafe Edwidge, 333 Commercial St. (☎508-487-4020). Though the cafe is open for dinner, it's Edwidge's breakfast dishes, like the fruit-topped French toast ($9), that draw crowds. Open in summer 8:30am-1pm and 6-11pm; hours vary in winter. AmEx/D/MC/V. ❸

Angel Foods, 467 Commercial St. (☎508-487-6666), offers grilled veggie sandwiches ($7) in a grocery store lined with dried fruit and organic juice. Entrees are sold by the pound: the Mediterranean chicken pasta ($8 per lb.) and curried chicken salad ($10 per lb.) are two of the best. Open M-Th and Su 7am-8pm, F-Sa 7am-9pm. AmEx/D/MC/V. ❷

▄ ACCOMMODATIONS

Provincetown teems with expensive places to rest your head, mainly located on Bradford St.

▓ Somerset House, 378 Commercial St. (☎508-487-0383 or 800-575-1850; www.somerset-houseinn.com). A 14-room guesthouse with sleek, stylish rooms and art on the walls. All rooms include fridge, DVD, and A/C, and hosts Bob and Dan serve cocktails every afternoon. 4-night min. stay in high season. Sa barbecue in summer. Doubles late June-Aug. $150-285; May-June and Sept.-Oct. $110-195; Nov.-Apr. $75-160. AmEx/MC/V. ❺

Outermost Hostel, 28 Winslow St. (☎508-487-4378), just steps from the heart of town. A hostel with 5 cottages and kind management. Key deposit $10. Reception 5:30-9:30pm. Open May to mid-Oct. Dorms $25. Cash only. ❶

Sunset Inn, 142 Bradford St. (☎508-487-9810 or 800-965-1801; www.sunsetinnptown.com). This was the inspiration for Edward Hopper's painting *Rooms for Tourists*. The Inn has lost some of the painting's romance, but it has simple, well-kept rooms with shared bath and continental breakfast. Open Apr.-Dec. Rooms mid-June to Sept. $95-100; Apr. to mid-June and Sept.-Dec. $50-70. D/MC/V. ❹

Cape Codder Guests, 570 Commercial St. (☎508-487-0131). It may be a 15min. walk to downtown, but the Cape Codder is easy on the wallet. Rooms with shared bath are small but bright, and there's a peaceful garden in the front. Free parking. Continental breakfast included. Rooms June-Sept. $35-72; Sept.-June $30-60. AmEx/D/MC/V. ❸

Dunes' Edge Campground, 386 Rte. 6 (☎508-487-9815; www.dunes-edge.com), just outside downtown Provincetown. 100 wooded sites that border the Cape Cod National Seashore. Open May-Sept. Tent sites $30-35, with electricity and water $38-43. MC/V. ❷

▄ ENTERTAINMENT

P-town's gay community comes out in droves for **Carnival,** a "Gay Paree!" held every August. Be sure to book rooms well in advance, as visitors flood into town for the week-long celebration and colorful parade (☎800-761-0182; www.ptown.org). On the first weekend in November, gay singles gather for **Meet Your Man in Provincetown,** a whirlwind weekend of speed-dating and clubbing (☎800-637-8696; www.ptown.org). The **Art House,** 214 Commercial St., has everything from drag shows to Shakespeare. Before the show, have a crepe ($5.50) on the comfy couches of the attached cafe. (☎508-487-9222. Cafe open 7am-10 or 11pm. Tickets $20, students and seniors $17.)

▄ NIGHTLIFE

Nightlife in P-town is almost totally GLBT-oriented.

Crown & Anchor, 247 Commercial St. (☎508-487-1430). A massive complex with a restaurant, 2 cabarets, the chill Wave video bar, and the Paramount dance club. Try a Crown lemonade ($8) by the pool out back. Beer $4-4.75. Mixed drinks $4-8. Cabaret shows $20-25. Cover $10; no cover for Wave. Open daily in summer 5pm-1am. Paramount open F-Sa 9pm-1am. AmEx/D/MC/V.

Atlantic House, 6 Masonic Pl. (☎508-487-3821), just off Commercial St., Founded in 1798 by gay whalers, the Atlantic House still attracts its fair share of seamen. Choose from 3 different scenes: the low-key "little bar" with sing-along jukebox; the Leather & Levis "macho bar"; and the "big room," where you too can be a dancing queen. Beer $3. Mixed drinks $4. Cover for big room $5-10. Little bar open daily noon-1am. Macho bar and big room 10pm-1am. Cash only.

Vixen, 336 Commercial St. (☎508-487-6424). The only major club for women, with a casual bar and Ms. PacMan out front and a steamy dance floor in back. On Th sip a Vixen-original Putka ($8), and enjoy the live rock 'n' roll. No cover. Open daily noon-1am. Cash only.

Governor Bradford, 312 Commercial St. (☎508-487-2781). Don't be fooled by the traditional decor; the Governor hosts drag karaoke nightly at 9:30pm. Ladies as well as gents sing along as a wigged beauty cavorts behind them. Drinks around $5. No cover. Open M-Sa 11am-1am, Su noon-1am.

◤ APPROACHING CAPE COD NATIONAL SEASHORE: 20 MILES
From Provincetown, take **U.S. 6 W.** Cape Cod National Seashore runs nearly the entire length of the Cape's "inner forearm."

CAPE COD NATIONAL SEASHORE

As early as 1825, the Cape had suffered so much erosion that the town of Truro required locals to plant beach grass and keep their cows off the dunes. These conservation efforts culminated in 1961, when President Kennedy and the National Park Service created the Cape Cod National Seashore. Park rangers at the **Salt Pond Visitors Center,** at Salt Pond, off U.S. 6 in Eastham, provide maps, schedules for guided tours, and additional information about the park. (☎508-255-3421. Open daily June-Sept. 9am-5pm; Oct.-May 9am-4:30pm.) At the northern end of the Cape, the **Province Lands**

Visitors Center, off U.S. 6 in Provincetown, provides similar assistance. (☎508-487-1256. Open May-Oct. daily 9am-5pm.) The seashore spans the Lower and Outer Cape from Provincetown to Chatham, comprising six beaches. Of the six, **Marconi,** in Wellfleet, is a favorite of surfers, while **Race Point,** in Provincetown, ½ mi. from the parking lot, offers more secluded waters. Parking at the beaches is expensive (up to $10 per day). Among the best of the seashore's 11 self-guided nature trails is the **Great Island Trail,** in Wellfleet. It traces an 8 mi. loop through pine forests and grassy marshes and has views of the bay and Provincetown.

Camping in the National Seashore is illegal, but there are commercial campgrounds just off park land. ◤**Truro Hostel ❶,** 111 N. Pamet Rd., in Truro, sits high atop a bluff overlooking the ocean and offers a large kitchen, a porch, and access to Ballston Beach. The hostel is in a turn-of-the-century Coast Guard station, located on the National Seashore, so walking and biking trails abound. (From U.S. 6, take the Pamet Rd. exit, which becomes N. Pamet Rd. ☎508-349-3889 or 888-901-2086. Key deposit $10. Open June-Sept. 6- to 8-bed dorms $28, members $25. MC/V.) Eastham's **Mid-Cape Hostel (HI-AYH) ❶,** 75 Goody Hallet Dr., features communal bungalow living in a woodsy location. You don't have to go far to do some birdwatching—the spacious kitchen has a great view of birds perching in the front yard. (From Provincetown, follow U.S. 6, take the Rock Harbor exit at the Orleans Center rotary. Turn left onto Bridge Rd., then left again onto Goody Hallet Dr. ☎508-255-2785 or 888-901-2085. All-you-can-eat pancake and waffle breakfast $4. Open May-Sept. Dorms $25, members $22. MC/V.)

◤ APPROACHING CHATHAM: 35 MILES
From Provincetown, take **U.S. 6 W** to **Rte. 137 S,** which dead-ends into **Rte. 28.** Take Rte. 28 E into town, where it becomes **Main St.**

CHATHAM

Chatham's an expensive stay, popular with an affluent family crowd. Though budget travelers may not want to spend the money to spend the night in Chatham, it's a pleasant stop for an afternoon, with a quaint downtown and historically relevant museums.

GETTING AROUND. Main St. is home to most of the town's shopping and restaurants. Heading north on **Shore Rd.** leads to the ocean.

SIGHTS. One of the best (and cheapest) things to do in Chatham is walk along **Main St.,** which is home to shops, restaurants, and galleries. Stop by the visitors center for a **walking guide,** illustrated in painstaking detail. Run by the Chatham Historical Society, the 250-year-old **Old Atwood House Museum,** 347 Stage Harbor Rd., houses artifacts and pieces of art documenting over two centuries of life in Chatham. Be sure to check out Chatham resident Alice Stahlknecht's haunting Depression-era paintings of townspeople, including one with untied shoelaces. (☎508-945-2493. Open June and Sept.-Oct. Tu-Sa 1-4pm; July-Aug. Tu-Sa 10am-4pm. $5, students $3, under 12 free.) The **Chatham Fish Pier,** on Shore Rd. north of the intersection with Main St., attracts many summer tourists. In the afternoon (2-4pm), visitors can watch the fishing fleet bring in haddock, cod, lobster, and halibut that they can purchase in local fish markets later that same day. They can also see the **Fisherman's Monument,** built to honor the town's fishing industry. The monument, called the Provider, is a little unusual: an abstraction of an upturned hand is supported by a structure of poles over a base of fish and shellfish in relief. Built from 1818 to 1820

by the town postmaster for his bride-to-be, the **Josiah Mayo House,** 540 Main St., is maintained as an accurate representation of a home from that era. Guides conduct tours, highlighting period architecture and furniture. (☎508-945-4084. Open July-Sept. Tu-Th 11am-4pm. Free.) The **Old Grist Mill** is a small windmill built in the late 18th century to grind corn. The mill itself is locked, but it is surrounded by a small park. (From the rotary, take Main St. toward the water, take a right on Cross St., then a left on Shattuck.)

FOOD AND ACCOMMODATIONS. Chatham's **Main St.** has tasty, inexpensive options for hungry diners. **Sandi's Diner ❶,** 639 Main St., serves breakfast classics like pancakes ($4) and eggs benedict ($6) on mismatched plates. Sandi herself buzzes around refilling coffee cups and wiping down tables. (☎508-945-0631. Open M and W-F 6am-2pm, Sa 6am-1pm, Su 7-11:30am. Cash only.) **Chatham Cookware Cafe ❷,** 524 Main St., might sound like Martha Stewart's favorite store, but it's actually a cafe with a bakery in the front and a soup-and-sandwich counter in the back. The sandwiches are creative reincarnations of old favorites like the "hungry pilgrim" (smoked turkey, cranberries, and stuffing; $7) and the BLAT ($6), a BLT with avocado. (☎508-945-1250. Open daily 6:30am-4pm. MC/V.) The **Anytime Cafe ❸,** 512 Main St., serves sophisticated pizzas like the Blanco (olive oil, garlic, chevre, and sun-dried tomatoes; $17) alongside deep-fried cheese sticks ($7). They also serve a variety of wraps and paninis, with plenty of veggie options. (☎508-945-4080. Open M-W and Su 11am-10pm, Th-Sa 11am-11pm. AmEx/D/MC/V.)

Chatham is by no means budget friendly. In the summer, there's almost nowhere to stay for under $100. Your best bet is to stay in the **Mid-Cape Hostel ❶** (see p. 157) or head farther west to nearby towns **Harwich** or **Dennis,** where you'll find options for $50 or less.

APPROACHING HARWICH PORT: 7 MILES
From Chatham, take **Rte. 28 W.** The road provides a glimpse of the quintessential Mid-Cape, crossing shallow tidal rivers and wide salt marshes while passing countless cottages, ice-cream shops, clam shacks, and mini-golf courses.

HARWICH PORT. As it enters Harwich Port, Rte. 28 passes Cape favorite **Bonatt's Bakery**

❶, 537 Rte. 28. Stop in for coffee and one of their famous "meltaway" pastries for under $3. (☎508-432-7199. Open daily 7am-1:30pm. AmEx/D/MC/V.) A little farther down, the **Trampoline Center,** 296 Rte. 28, returns the bounce to travelers' steps by allowing them to jump on one of the outdoor trampolines set into the ground. (☎508-432-8717. Open June to Labor Day daily 9am-11pm. $5 per 10min.) If you haven't done enough driving yet, take the wheel at **Bud's Go Karts,** 9 Sisson Rd. (☎508-432-4964. Open in summer M-Sa 9am-11pm, Su 10am-11pm. $6.)

◪ APPROACHING HYANNIS: 11 MILES
Continue on **Rte. 28 W** to head into Hyannis.

HYANNIS

Mostly a transportation hub (ferries to Nantucket and Martha's Vineyard depart from here) and industrial city, Hyannis offers less charm than the villages farther down the Cape. However, the town does boast a long Main St. lined with trendy stores, brewpubs, and motels. Hyannis' fame comes from its proximity to JFK's famous summer home in Hyannisport and its excellent beaches.

VITAL STATS
Population: 16,000
Visitor Info: Hyannis Area Chamber of Commerce, 1481 Rte. 132 (☎508-362-5230 or 877-492-6647). Open M-Tu 10am-4pm, Th-Sa 9am-5pm, Su 10am-2pm.
Internet Access: Hyannis Public Library, 401 Main St. (☎508-775-2280). Open M and Th-F 11am-5pm, Tu-W 11am-8pm. Free.
Post Office: 385 Main St. (☎508-775-2603). Open M-F 8:30am-6pm, Sa 9am-1pm. **Postal Code:** 02601.

▛ GETTING AROUND. Rte. 28 runs through Hyannis as **Main St. Barnstable Rd.** and **High-school Rd.** both intersect with Main St. running north to south.

◖ SIGHTS. Veterans Park, on Ocean St., includes the **Korean War Veterans Memorial** and the **John Fitzgerald Kennedy Memorial.** (Park open daily 9am-9pm.) Nearby are family-friendly **Veterans' Beach** and **Kalmus Beach.**

The **John F. Kennedy Museum,** 397 Main St., has a small collection of memorabilia and pictures from the former president's life, from his childhood in Massachusetts to his presidency. (☎508-775-7778. Open Memorial Day to Columbus Day M-Sa 9am-5pm, Su noon-5pm; hours vary Columbus Day to Memorial Day. $5, ages 10-17 $2.50.) At Hyannis Harbor, visitors can ride the seven seas on the *Sea Gypsy* through **Pirate Adventures.** The trips on a pirate boat (of dubious historical accuracy, mind you) require 16 passengers and provide a fun, if somewhat bizarre, experience. Face-painting is included. (☎508-430-0202; www.pirateadventures.com. Reservations required. $20.) **Hy-Line Cruises** offers ferries to Nantucket and Martha's Vineyard. (☎508-778-2600 or 800-492-8082; www.hylinecruises.com. $33, ages 5-12 $16.50.)

▟ FOOD AND ACCOMMODATIONS. Hyannis has a lot of pricey restaurant options along Main St., but budget options are available as well. **Thai House ❷,** 304-306 Main St., has inexpensive Thai food in a storefront decorated with strings of lights. The combination plate ($8) lets you choose from 9 entrees, like pad thai or red curry chicken, and comes with two appetizers. (☎508-862-1616. Open M-Sa 11am-10pm, Su 4-9:30pm. AmEx/MC/V.) The **Egg and I ❸,** 523 Main St., serves everything from fried chicken fingers ($6.50) to portobello mushroom salads ($10). Whatever the logic behind the menu, it seems to be working—they've been around for 35 years. (☎508-771-1596. Open daily 6am-1am. AmEx/D/MC/V.) The **Box Lunch ❶,** 357 Main St., offers creative sandwiches and "rollwiches" like the Humpty Dumpty (deviled-egg salad and bacon; $5) and Hum Vee (hummus, avocado, sprouts; $5.75). The shop is just a counter, so make your way to the nearby park to eat. (☎508-790-5855. Open in summer M-W and Sa 9am-6pm, Th-F 9am-8pm, Su 9am-5pm; hours vary in winter. MC/V.)

Hyannis has plenty of accommodations, but during the summer the prices downtown are around $100. Cheaper options line Rte. 28, south of town. Just a mile south of Hyannis, the **Windrift Motel ❸,** 115 Rte. 28, has comfortable, standard rooms. Guests can make use of the outdoor pool and gobble down free doughnuts and coffee in the morning. (In West Yarmouth. ☎508-775-4697 or 800-354-4179. Rooms M-Th and Su $58, F-Sa $72. D/MC/V.) Closer to downtown, the **Cascade Motor Lodge ❹**, 201 Main St., offers free bike rentals and rooms with fridge and TV. (☎508-775-9717; www.cascademotorlodge.com. Outdoor pool. Rooms June-Sept. M-Th and Su $78-82, F-Sa $93-97; Sept.-June $54-58/$64-68. AmEx/D/MC/V.) The **Hyannis Travel Inn ❹**, 18 North St., is within walking distance of all of Hyannis's sights and has two pools (one indoor, one outdoor). Each room comes with a fridge, a balcony, and free Wi-Fi. (☎508-775-8200 or 800-352-7190. Continental breakfast included. Rooms M-Th and Su $90-109, F-Sa $129. AmEx/D/MC/V.)

⚐ APPROACHING PLYMOUTH: 33 MILES
From Hyannis, follow **Rte. 132 N** to **U.S. 6 W** to **Rte. 3 N**. Take **Exit 6** for downtown Plymouth.

PLYMOUTH

Your textbook may say otherwise, but the Pilgrims' first step onto the New World was *not* at Plymouth. They stopped first at Provincetown (see p. 154), then promptly left because the soil was inadequate.

VITAL STATS

Population: 52,000

Visitor Info: Waterfront Tourist Information Center (☎508-747-7525 or 800-872-1620), on Water St. Open June to Labor Day daily 8am-8pm; Apr.-May and Labor Day to Nov. 9am-5pm.

Internet Access: Plymouth Public Library, 132 South St. (☎508-830-4250; www.plymouthpublicli-brary.org). Open M-W 10am-9pm, Th 10am-6pm, F-Sa 10am-5:30pm. Free.

Post Office: 6 Main St. (☎508-746-8175). Open M-F 9am-1:30pm and 2:30-5pm, Sa 9am-noon. **Postal Code:** 02360.

◢ SIGHTS. Plymouth is extremely proud of its place in American history. **Plymouth Rock** is a small stone that has been dubiously identified as the rock on which the Pilgrims disembarked the second time. A symbol of liberty during the American Revolution, it has since moved three times before ending up beneath a portico on Water St., at the

foot of North St. After several vandalizations and one dropping (in transit), it's cracked and under "tight" security. A few miles south of town on Rte. 3, the historical theme park **Plimoth Plantation** recreates the Pilgrims' early settlement. In the **Pilgrim Village,** costumed actors play the roles of villagers carrying out their daily tasks, while **Hobbamock's Homesite** represents a Native American village of the same period. (☎508-746-1622; www.plimoth.org. Open Apr.-Nov. daily 9am-5pm. $21, ages 6-12 $12.) Docked off Water St. in Plymouth, the **Mayflower II** is a 1950s scale replica of the Pilgrims' vessel, staffed by actors who recapture the atmosphere of the original ship. (Open Apr.-Nov. daily 9am-5pm. $8, ages 6-12 $6. Combined admission with Plimoth Plantation $24/$14.) The **Pilgrim Hall Museum,** 75 Court St., contains objects owned by the Pilgrims, including a hat stained with Pilgrim sweat. (☎508-746-1620; www.pilgrimhall.org. Open Feb.-Dec. daily 9:30am-4:30pm. $6, seniors $5, ages 5-17 $3.) Atop a hill on Allerton St., the **National Monument to the Forefathers,** erected in 1889 to pay homage to the Pilgrims, is the largest solid granite statue in the nation. (Take Samoset St. west to Allerton St.) The **1749 Court House,** in Town Sq., has a museum on the first floor and a real courtroom on the second. The courthouse was the Plymouth court for over 70 years, hosting young attorneys like John Adams and James Otis. (☎508-830-4075. Open late June to Columbus Day M-Sa 10:30am-4:30pm, Su noon-4:30pm. Free.) At the courthouse, visitors can pick up brochures for a "Walk Through History," a walking tour around historic Town Sq.

◤ FOOD AND ACCOMMODATIONS. Plymouth has plenty of restaurants for a Pilgrim-worthy feast, mostly clustered on Main St. The **Water Street Cafe ❷**, 25 Water St., serves a hearty breakfast of two eggs, meat, pancakes or French toast, homefries, and coffee ($6) to a laid-back, local crowd. For lighter fare, try the Water St. salad ($6.25), with roasted red peppers, feta, potatoes, artichokes, and chicken. (☎508-746-2050. Open daily 5:30am-3pm. MC/V.) **Namaste ❶**, 56 Main St., offers Indian favorites like chana masala ($5.50) and chicken vindaloo ($6) in a quiet, elegant environment. All dishes can be made extra hot for patrons with asbestos tongues and cast-iron stomachs. (☎508-747-2353. Open Tu-Su 11:30am-10pm. AmEx/D/MC/V.) **Jubilee ❷**, 22 Court St., caters on the weekends; during the week it serves gourmet sandwiches like the veggie hummus roll-up for $6.75 and ham and brie for $6.25. (☎508-747-3700. Open M-F 10am-3pm. AmEx/MC/V.)

Within easy walking distance of downtown, the **Blue Anchor Motel and Guest Rooms ❹**, 7 Lincoln St., has roomy, well-decorated digs and a comfortable front porch. (☎508-746-9551. Open May-Oct. Rooms with shared bathroom May-Sept. $75-85; Apr. and Oct. $65. AmEx/D/MC/V.) A few miles south of Plymouth on Rte. 3A, the **Whispering Oaks Motel ❸**, 517 State Rd. 3A, has large standard rooms. (☎508-224-2500. 21+. Rooms M-Th and Su $68, F-Sa $79. AmEx/D/MC/V.) The **Myles Standish State Forest ❶**, on Cranberry Rd., has 400 sites in forested areas alongside 16 ponds. The park also has miles of hiking and biking trails. (Take Rte. 3 N to Exit 3 and make a left, then a right onto Long Pond Rd. ☎508-866-2526, reservations 877-422-6762. Open Memorial Day to Labor Day. Reservations recommended. Sites $14. MC/V.)

◪ APPROACHING BOSTON: 40 MILES
Take **Rte. 44 W** out of town to **Rte. 3 N.**

BOSTON

For a long time, Boston *was* the United States. During America's fledging and formative years in the 17th and 18th centuries, the city played a starring role in the country's fight for independence. In the 19th century, some of America's most influential doers and thinkers called Bos-

ton home, unabashedly dubbing it the "Hub of the Universe." In the 20th century, the Boston experienced the same growing pains sweeping the rest of the nation, including immigration booms, civil-rights battles, and problems with urban expansion and renewal. Today, Boston is a restless stew of distinct communities, cultural attractions, and urban parks. While the Freedom Trail is a nice place to start, wandering around Boston's many districts, jumble of streets, and rarely square squares will give you a better glimpse of this evolving metropolis. For more comprehensive coverage of the Boston area, see ◪*Let's Go: Boston.*

VITAL STATS

Population: 600,000

Visitor Info: Greater Boston Convention and Visitors Bureau, 2 Copley Pl., Ste. 2 (☎888-SEE-BOSTON; www.bostonusa.com;), has a booth at Boston Common, at Ⓣ Park St. Open M-F 8:30am-5pm. Downtown's **National Historic Park Visitor Center,** 15 State St. (☎617-242-5642; www.nps.gov/bost), has Freedom Trail info and tours. Ⓣ State. Open daily 9am-5pm.

Internet Access: Boston Public Library, 700 Boylston St. (☎617-536-5400; www.bpl.org), at Ⓣ Copley. Open M-Th 9am-9pm, F-Sa 9am-5pm. Free.

Post Office: 25 Dorchester Ave. (☎617-654-5302), behind South Station at Ⓣ South Station. Open 24hr.
Postal Code: 02205.

ROCKS FOR JOCKS

When is a rock not just a rock? When it's Plymouth Rock. Every history textbook has it that the Pilgrims disembarked from the Mayflower on Plymouth Rock. But what's often glossed over is that the historical evidence for that claim is fairly meager. In William Bradford's journal describing the Pilgrims landing in 1620, rocks are conspicuously absent. The first reference to a rock isn't made until nearly a hundred years later, when it was mentioned in regard to the town boundaries. So where did all this rock business come from? The rock was first identified in 1741 by a 95-year-old man who claimed that his father, who had arrived in the New World in 1623, had pointed out the rock to him. It wasn't until 1774 that Ephraim Spooner declared the rock's identity to the citizens of Plymouth, and maps began to plot the its location for the first time. The newly christened Plymouth Rock was broken that same year when citizens attempted to move it. Despite the damage done to the rock, its symbolic significance is still very much intact. The rock's fame has grown over the years, even as its size has decreased due to the work of souvenir hunters. The Pilgrims (who, incidentally, weren't called Pilgrims until 1793) may or may not have landed at Plymouth Rock, but it's the

GETTING AROUND

Boston is situated on a peninsula jutting into Massachusetts Bay. **I-93/U.S. 1/Rte. 3** runs north-south along the city's eastern edge. The Charles River divides Boston and its neighbor to the north, Cambridge; **Storrow Dr.** and **Memorial Dr.** run along its southern and northern banks.

Boston's heart is the grassy **Boston Common,** sandwiched between **Beacon Hill** to the north, downtown to the south and east, and **Back Bay** to the west. Back Bay is Boston's most navigable area. Major avenues **Beacon St., Commonwealth Ave., Newbury St.,** and **Boylston Ave.** run parallel to Storrow Dr.; alternating one-way cross streets are named alphabetically from Arlington to Hereford as you head west. Elsewhere, driving is more complicated. **The Big Dig** still wreaks havoc on the roads of the waterfront, and the labyrinthine cobblestone paths of Boston's colonial downtown are almost impossible to negotiate.

Luckily for out-of-towners, Boston's metro system is clean, efficient, and cheap. Known as the Ⓣ, the subway has 5 colored lines—Red, Blue, Orange, Green (which breaks into lines B-E), and Silver—that radiate from Downtown. "Inbound" trains head toward Ⓣ Park St. or Ⓣ Downtown Crossing; "outbound" trains head away from those stops. All Ⓣ stops have maps and schedules. (☎617-222-5000; www.mbta.com. Lines run daily 5:30am-12:30am; "Night Owl" buses run F-Sa until 2:30am. Fares $1.25, ages 5-11 $0.60, seniors $0.35.) Holes in the Ⓣ's coverage are somewhat filled by an extensive (though sometimes sluggish) bus system, which links to the subway lines. Many buses use Harvard Sq. as their home base, leaving from the underground hub in the Harvard T station or from Johnston Gate. Buses cost $0.90 (monthly pass; $31), but you must have exact change (or a token), and there is no free transfer between buses and the subway. Most buses run from M-Sa about 5am-1am, Su 6am-1am.

For sightseeing in Boston's compact center, it makes sense to park and walk. Parking garages are pricey (up to $20 per day), but they are often the only option; metered parking is limited, and ticketing is relentless. Resident parking permits are required for street parking in many residential neighborhoods.

👁 SIGHTS

REVOLUTIONARY SIGHTS

Passing the landmarks that put Boston on the map, the 2½ mi. **Freedom Trail** is a great introduction to the city's history. Following the Freedom Trail on your own is fairly simple (just follow the faded red line painted on or paved into the sidewalk), but the National Park Service does offer free 1½hr. tours from April to November, departing from their **visitors center.** Bring a bit of cash ($9) if you want to visit the historical sites, since some have entrance fees. (Visitors center at 15 State St., opposite Old State House. T: State. ☎617-242-5642; www.nps.gov/bost. Tours in summer M-F 10, 11am, noon, 2pm; in winter noon and 2pm. Arrive 30min. before tour to get a ticket.)

BEACON HILL. The Trail first runs uphill to the **Robert Gould Shaw Memorial,** honoring the first black regiment of the Union Army in the American Civil War and their Bostonian leader. On July 19, 1863, Shaw led the Massachusetts 54th in an assault on Fort Wagner, South Carolina, where he and 62 members of his regiment were killed. The larger-than-life, high-relief bronze sculpture (by Augustus St.-Gaudens, a popular Boston-area sculptor) was dedicated on May 31, 1897, in a ceremony attended by surviving soldiers of the 54th as well as prominent activists and thinkers of the era. Opposite the memorial is the gold-domed **Massachusetts State House.** (Tours ☎617-727-3676. Open M-F 10am-4pm. 40min. tours depart every 20min.; tour pamphlet available at tourist desk. Free.)

DOWNTOWN. Passing the **Park Street Church,** the Trail reaches the **Granary Burial Ground,** where John Hancock, Samuel Adams, Elizabeth Goose ("Mother Goose"), and Paul Revere rest. **Kings Chapel & Burying Ground** is America's oldest Anglican church; the latest inhabitants are Unitarian. The city's first cemetery, next door, is the final resting place of that other midnight rider, William Dawes. (58 Tremont St. Chapel ☎617-227-2155. Chapel open Memorial Day to Labor Day M 9:30am-4pm, Tu-W 10-11:30am and 1:30-4pm, Th-Sa 10am-4pm, Su 2-4pm;

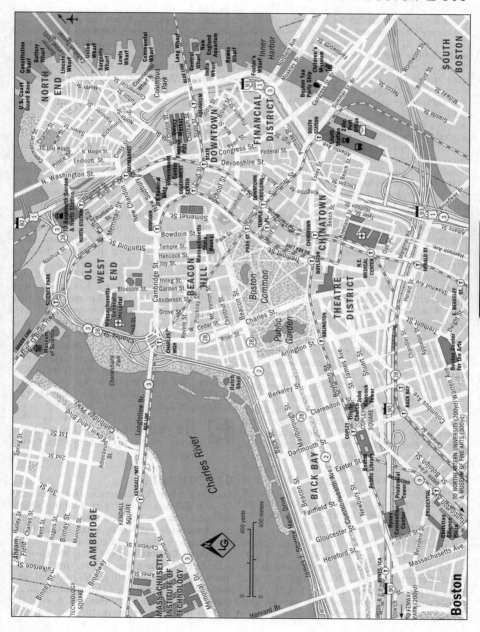

EAST COAST

Labor Day to Memorial Day Sa 10am-4pm. Burying Ground open daily June-Oct. 8am-3pm; Nov.-May 9am-3pm. Chapel $1-3. Burying Ground free.) Within the walls of the **Old South Meeting House,** Ben Franklin was baptized and Samuel Adams gave the speech that led to the Boston Tea Party. *(310 Washington St. ☎617-482-6439; www.oldsouthmeetinghouse.org. Open daily Apr.-Oct. 9:30am-5pm; Nov.-Mar. 10am-4pm. $5, students and seniors $4, ages 6-18 $1.)* Formerly the seat of British government, the ◪**Old State House** is the oldest public building in Boston. Preserved and run by the Bostonian Society as a museum of the history of Boston, the Old State House is perhaps the most interesting and well-organized of the stops along the Freedom Trail. *(206 Washington St. ☎617-720-1713. Open daily 9am-5pm. $5, students and seniors $4, ages 6-18 $1.)* Stand under the Old State House balcony and look right for the ring of cobblestones; this marks the site of the Boston Massacre. The **Faneuil Hall** and **Quincy Market** complex, a former meeting hall and current mega-mall, houses a food court and carts selling kitschy items. *(Faneuil Hall ☎617-523-1300. Open M-Sa 10am-9pm, Su noon-6pm.)*

NORTH END. Heading into the heavily Italian-American North End, the Trail crawls through Big Dig rubble to the **Paul Revere House,** where a self-guided tour helps visitors navigate meticulously recreated 18th-century rooms. *(19 North Sq. ☎617-523-2338; www.paulreverehouse.org. Open mid-Apr. to Oct. daily 9:30am-5:15pm; Nov.-Dec. and early Apr. daily 9:30am-4:15pm; Jan.-Mar. Tu-Su 9:30am-4:15pm. $3, students and seniors $2.50, ages 5-17 $1.)* The **Old North Church** is where Robert Newman was instructed by Revere to hang lanterns— "one if by land, two if by sea"—warning patriots in Charlestown that the British were coming. The church still houses such Revolutionary relics as George Washington's wig and tea from the Boston Tea Party. *(193 Salem St. ☎617-523-6676. Open daily 9am-5pm. Suggested donation $3.)*

CHARLESTOWN. The Battle of Bunker Hill is the focus of much of the rest of the Trail, which heads across the Charles River to the **U.S.S. Constitution** (a.k.a. "Old Ironsides") and its companion museum. *(☎617-426-1812; www.ussconstitutionmuseum.org. Ship open Apr.-Oct. Tu-Su 10am-6pm; Nov. Mar. Th-Su 10am-4pm. Museum*

open daily May-Oct. 9am-6pm; Nov.-Apr. 10am-5pm. Free.) The Trail winds through residential Charlestown toward the **Bunker Hill Monument,** which is actually on Breed's Hill—fitting given that the entire Battle of Bunker Hill was fought there. A grand view awaits at the top of the obelisk's 294 steps. *(Monument Sq. Visitors lodge open daily 9am-5pm. Monument open daily 9am-4:30pm. Free.)*

DOWNTOWN

In 1634, colonists designated **Boston Common** a grazing ground for their cattle. Today, street vendors, runners, and tourists roam the green and congregate near the **Frog Pond,** a wading pool in summer and a skating rink in winter. *(Ⓣ Park St.)* Across Charles St. from the Common is the lavish **Public Garden,** the nation's first botanical garden. Bronze versions of the title characters from the children's book *Make Way for Ducklings* point the way to the **Swan Boats,** graceful paddleboats that float around a quiet willow-lined pond. *(☎617-522-1966. Park open daily sunrise-sunset. Boats open Apr.-June daily 10am-4pm; June 20 to Labor Day daily 10am-5pm; Sept. M-F noon-4pm, Sa-Su 10am-4pm. 15min. ride $2.75, seniors $2, ages 2-15 $1.25.)* Steps from the Common is the pedestrian mall at **Downtown Crossing.** The city's biggest budget shopping district revolves around legendary **Filene's Basement,** a chaotic feeding frenzy for bargain-hunters. *(426 Washington St. Ⓣ Downtown Crossing. ☎617-542-2011; www.filenesbasement.com. Open M-F 9:30am-8pm, Sa 9am-8pm, Su 11am-7pm.)*

 DID YOU KNOW? The first football game in America was played in Boston Common in 1862.

BEACON HILL

Looming over the Common is aristocratic Beacon Hill, an exclusive residential neighborhood that was the first spot on the Shawmut Peninsula settled by Puritans. Antique shops, pricey cafes, and ritzy boutiques line charming **Charles St.,** the neighborhood's main artery. For generations, the Hill was home to Boston's intellectual, political, and social elite, christened the "Boston Brahmins." For a taste of Brahmin life, visit the **Nichols House Museum,** restored to its 19th-century state. *(55 Mt. Vernon St., off Charles St. T: Charles/MGH. ☎617-227-6993. Open May-Oct. Tu-Sa noon-5pm; Nov.-Apr. Th-Sa noon-5pm. $5, under 12 free. Entrance by tour only.)* Boston was the first city in the US to outlaw slavery, and many African-Americans moved to the Beacon Hill area after the Civil War. The **Black Heritage Trail** is a free 2hr. 1½ mi. walk through important Beacon Hill sights of Boston's abolitionist era. The tour begins at the foot of Beacon Hill, near the Shaw Memorial, and ends at the **Museum of Afro-American History.** *(46 Joy St. ☎617-725-0022; www.afroammuseum.org. Museum open M-Sa 10am-4pm. Suggestion donation $5. Heritage Trail: ☎617-742-5415. Tours daily Memorial Day to Labor Day 10am, noon, 2pm; Labor Day to Memorial Day by appointment. Free.)* Also at the foot of the hill is the **Bull & Finch Pub,** 84 Beacon St., the inspiration for the bar in *Cheers*.

WATERFRONT

The Waterfront district refers to the wharves along Boston Harbor from South Station to the North End. The excellent ◪**New England Aquarium** features cavorting penguins, an animal infirmary, and briny beasts in a four-story tank. *(On Central Wharf at ⓣ Aquarium. ☎617-973-5200; www.neaq.org. Open Sept.-June M-F 9am-5pm, Sa-Su 9am-6pm; July-Aug. M-Th 9am-6pm, F-Su 9am-7pm. $18, students and seniors $14, ages 3-11 $10.)* The Long Wharf, north of Central Wharf, is **Boston Harbor Cruises'** departure point for sightseeing cruises and whale-watching. *(☎617-227-4321; www.bostonharborcruises.com. Open Apr.-Oct. 45min. cruises depart on the half-hour 10:30am-4:30pm. $14, students and seniors $12, under 12 $10. 3hr. whale-watches $35/$32/$29. Reservations recommended.)*

BACK BAY

Back Bay was initially an uninhabitable tidal flat tucked into the "back" corner of the bay until it was filled in at the end of the late 19th century. Today elegant Back Bay's stately brownstones and shady promenades are laid out in an easily navigable grid. Running through Back Bay, fashionable **Newbury St.,** accessible from ⓣ Hynes/ICA, is where Boston's trendiest strut their stuff and empty their wallets.

COPLEY SQUARE. Named for painter John Singleton Copley, Copley Sq. is popular with both lunching businessmen and Newbury St.

tourists. The square is dominated by H.H. Richardson's Romanesque **Trinity Church,** reflected in the 14 acres of glass used in I.M. Pei's stunning John Hancock Tower, now closed to the public. *(206 Clarendon St. ⓣ Copley. Church ☎617-536-0944. Open daily 9am-6pm. $4.)* Facing the church, the dramatic ◪**Boston Public Library** is an art museum in disguise; don't miss John Singer Sargent's *Triumph of Religion* murals or the hidden courtyard. *(☎617-536-5400; www.bpl.org. Open M-Th 9am-9pm, F-Sa 9am-5pm.)* The 50th floor of the **Prudential Center** next door to Copley Sq. is home to the **Prudential Skywalk,** which offers a 360° view of Boston from a height of 700 ft. *(ⓣ Prudential. ☎617-859-0648. Open Mar.-Oct. daily 10am-9:30pm, Nov.-Feb. 10am-8pm. $10.50, seniors $8.50, under 12 $7.)*

CHRISTIAN SCIENCE PLAZA. Down Massachusetts Ave. from Newbury St., the 14-acre Christian Science Plaza is Boston's most unappreciated public space. This epic expanse of concrete, centered on a smooth reflecting pool, is home to the Byzantine-revival "Mother Church," a.k.a. **First Church of Christ, Scientist,** a Christian denomination of faith-based healing founded in Boston by Mary Baker Eddy. *(175 Huntington Ave. ⓣ Symphony. ☎617-450-2000. 30min. tours Th-Sa noon-4pm, Su 11:15am. Free.)* The adjacent **Mary Baker Eddy Library,** another of Boston's library/museum hybrids, has exhibits on Mrs. Eddy's life and a surreal "Hall of Ideas," where holographic words bubble out of a fountain. Step inside the **Mapparium,** a three-story stained glass globe that depicts the world as it was in 1934 and details the changes that have occurred since then. The globe's perfect acoustics let you whisper in the ear of Pakistan and hear it in Suriname. *(200 Massachusetts Ave. ☎617-222-3711. Open Tu-Su 10am-4pm. $6, students and 62+ $4.)*

JAMAICA PLAIN

Jamaica Plain offers everything quintessentially un-Bostonian: ample parking and Mother Nature. Although it's one of Boston's largest green spaces (over 265 acres), many Boston residents never make it to the lush **Arnold Arboretum,** which has flora and fauna from all around the world. *(ⓣ Forest Hills. ☎617-524-1718. Visitors center open M-F 9am-4pm, Sa 10am-4pm, Su noon-4pm. Arboretum open daily sun-*

rise-sunset. *Free.)* Nearby, **Jamaica Pond** is a popular skinny-dipping spot and a great place for a quiet sail. To conclude your JP junket, salute beer-guzzling patriots at the **Sam Adams Brewery.** At the end of the tour, experts teach you how to "taste" beer. *(30 Germania St. Ⓣ Stony Brook.* ☎ *617-368-5080. Tours W-Th 2pm; F 2 and 5:30pm; Sa every 30min. 11am-2pm. Tastings 21+. Suggested donation $2.)*

🏛 MUSEUMS

If you're planning a museum binge, consider a **CityPass** (www.citypass.com), which covers the JFK Library, MFA, the Museum of Science, Harvard's Museum of Natural History, the Aquarium (see p. 165), and the Prudential Center Skywalk (see p. 165). Passes, available at museums or online, are valid for nine days. ($39, ages 3-17 $22.)

◪ **Museum of Fine Arts,** 465 Huntington Ave. (☎617-267-9300; www.mfa.org), in Fenway. Ⓣ Museum. One of the world's finest collections of Asian art with exceptional exhibits of Classical, Egyptian, European, and American works. Enter at the Huntington Ave. entrance to experience the museum's more traditional grandeur, or arrive through the soaring granite-and-glass West Wing. Open M-Tu 10am-4:45pm, W 10am-9:45pm, Th-F 10am-4:45pm (West Wing open until 9:45pm), Sa-Su 10am-5:45pm. $15, students and seniors $13, ages 7-17 M-F $6.50. M-Tu after 3pm, W after 4pm, Sa-Su free.

◪ **Isabella Stewart Gardner Museum,** 280 The Fenway (☎617-566-1401; www.gardnermuseum.org). Ⓣ Museum. This astounding private collection remains exactly as eccentric Mrs. Gardner arranged it in her Venetian palazzo over a century ago. In 1990, 13 major works were stolen in the largest art robbery in US history. The as-yet unclaimed $5 million reward might be incentive enough to test out your sleuthing skills. The mansion still houses some remarkable works of art and is built around a lush, 4-story glass-roofed garden courtyard. Open Tu-Su 11am-5pm. M-F $10, Sa-Su $11; seniors $7; students $5; under 18 and those named "Isabella" free with ID.

Museum of Science, Science Park (☎617-723-2500; www.mos.org). Ⓣ Science Park. Make your way through a sea of wide-eyed, field-trip-

ping 4th-graders to get a look at the Museum's over 400 exhibits, 5-story dome Omnimax Theater, and planetarium. Open M-Th and Sa-Su 9am-5pm, F 9am-9pm. $15, seniors $13, ages 3-11 $12. IMAX $9, ages 3-11 $7.

The Museum of Bad Art (MOBA), 580 High St. (☎781-444-6757; www.museumofbadart.org). Ⓣ Forest Hills. Located in the basement of the Dedham Community Theater, the collection rotates through gallery exhibits of 20-25 of the worst paintings of all time. The museum's curators discover their disaster pieces at garage sales, in garbage piles, or through word of mouth, then usually title the finds themselves (for example, "In the Cat's Mouth"). Open M-F 6-10pm, Sa-Su 1-10pm. Free.

JFK Library and Museum, Columbia Pt. (☎617-514-1600; www.jfklibrary.org). Ⓣ JFK/UMass. Dedicated to "all those who through the art of politics seek a new and better world" and designed by I.M. Pei, this enormous, white, oceanside edifice contains 21 exhibits chronicling the life of President John F. Kennedy and First Lady Jacqueline Onassis. Worth a visit just for the building's dramatic views of the Harbor surrounding Columbia Pt. Open daily 9am-5pm. $10, students and seniors $8, ages 13-17 $7.

🍴 FOOD

Once known as barren gastronomical wasteland whose only claim to fame was baked beans, Boston still may not be a culinary paradise, but its cuisine has certainly become much more palatable. Trendy bistros, fusion restaurants, and a globetrotting array of ethnic eateries have taken their place alongside the long-standing "chowda" shacks, greasyspoons, and soul-food joints.

DOWNTOWN

Downtown is the most heavily toured part of Boston, so expect mediocre food, big crowds, and high prices. The best and most affordable options downtown are the sandwich shops on almost every corner and the diverse food court inside Quincy Market (see p. 162). Fresh seafood shops line Boston's Waterfront district.

No Name, 15½ Fish Pier (☎617-338-7539). T: South Station. Famous for its delicious seafood chowder, No Name has been serving Boston reasonably priced seafood since 1917. No awards here for snazzy presentation, but the seafood can't be beat. Entrees $5-23. Open M-Sa 11am-10pm, Su 11am-9pm. D/MC/V. ❷

Zuma's Tex-Mex Grill, 7 N. Market St. (☎617-367-9114). Ⓣ Government Ctr. Zuma's is reasonably priced, colorful, and rowdy—everything you could want from a Tex-Mex restaurant. Entrees $8-13. Open M-Th 11:30am-11pm, F-Sa 11:30am-1pm, Su noon-10pm. AmEx/D/DC/MV/V. ❸

Durgin Park, 340 Fanueil Hall Marketplace (☎617-227-2038). Ⓣ Government Ctr. This legendary tourist hot spot doubles as a belly-busting New England family-style restaurant and a good watering hole for the after-work crowd. Established in 1826, Durgin Park has been serving up local favorites for longer than you, your parents, and even your grandparents have been around. Entrees $7-30. Open M-Sa 11:30am-10pm, Su 11:30am-9pm. AmEx/DC/MC/V. ❹

NORTH END

Boston's Italian-American enclave is the place to go for authentic Italian fare, with over 100 restaurants packed into one square mile. Most establishments line **Hanover St.,** accessible from Ⓣ Haymarket. After dinner, try the *cannoli* ($2-4) and other Italian sweets at **Mike's Pastry,** 300 Hanover St., or **Modern Pastry,** 257 Hanover St.

 DID YOU KNOW? In 1919, a massive tidal wave of molasses flooded Boston's North End, killing 21 people. It was known as the Great Molasses Flood.

Trattoria Il Panino, 11 Parmenter St. (☎617-720-1336), at Hanover St. Ⓣ Haymarket. Unquestionably one of the finest North End restaurants for food service and value, Trattoria Il Panino serves up Italian delicacies to the crowds that gather anxiously in front of the door every night. *Gnocchi alla sorrentina* (potato dumplings with tomato, basil, and mozzarella; $14). Open daily 11am-11pm. AmEx/D/DC/MC/V. ❸

L'Osteria, 104 Salem St. (☎617-723-7847). Ⓣ Haymarket. A lively, family-owned restaurant, L'Osteria has been serving a variety of Italian favorites for over 20 years. Juicy veal *Piemontese,* stuffed with prosciutto and mozzarella $20. Entrees $12-23. Open M-Th and Su noon-10pm, F-Sa noon-11pm. AmEx/MC/V. ❸

Dolce Vita, 221 Hanover St. (☎617-720-0422). Ⓣ Haymarket. From the moment you enter the radi-

ant dining room of this restaurant, owner Franco Graceffa will make certain you have a good time. Servers recommend traditional Sicilian dishes (the kitchen's forte) or adapt dishes to individual tastes. Open daily 11am-11pm. AmEx/MC/V. ❸

CHINATOWN

Chinatown is *the* place for cheap, filling Asian food anytime. Stuck between the skyscrapers of the Financial District and the chaos of the Big Dig, the neighborhood is slightly grimy and run-down, but the prices are unbeatable and most places stay open until late (3-4am). Ⓣ Chinatown.

Ocean Wealth, 8 Tyler St. (☎617-423-1338). Ⓣ Chinatown. Ocean Wealth claims the loyalty of Greater Boston's Chinese residents with its unbeatable lobster special: $11 for 2 lobsters lightly fried in your choice of seasoning. Delicious crustaceans aside, Ocean Wealth serves up Chinatown's best Cantonese cuisine. If seafood is what you crave, your server will bring the live fish out in a bucket to prove that it's still hopping. Open daily 11am-4am. MC/V. ❸

East Ocean City, 25-29 Beach St. (☎617-542-2504). Ⓣ Chinatown or Downtown Crossing. Live lobsters and crabs stare out at you from their tanks at the door of this popular Chinatown restaurant. Although the vegetarian selection is strong, this spot specializes in seafood, featuring unusual dishes like fried bean cake with minced shrimp ($9.50). Open M-Th 11:30am-10pm, F 11:30am-11pm, Sa noon-11pm, Su noon-10pm. AmEx/MC/V. ❷

Ginza, 16 Hudson St. (☎617-338-2261). Ⓣ Chinatown. Ginza's mouthwatering sushi doesn't come cheap, but the sake bombs will ease the pain your bill inflicts. Entrees $17-46. Open M-Th 11:30am-2:30pm and 5-11pm, F 11:30am-2:30pm and 5pm-3:30am, Sa noon-3:30am, Su noon-11pm. AmEx/DC/MC/V. ❹

BACK BAY

The diverse eateries of the Back Bay line elegant **Newbury St.,** accessible from Ⓣ Hynes/ICA or Ⓣ Back Bay. Though Newbury is known as Boston's expensive shopping district, affordable restaurants do exist.

Parish Café, 361 Boylston St. (☎617-247-4777). Ⓣ Arlington. Locals crowd tables and bar stools to order sandwiches ($9-20) designed by the city's hottest chefs, who do marvelous things with chicken, portobello, lobster, brioche, and focaccia. Open M-Sa 11:30am-2am, Su noon-2am. Kitchen closes 1am. AmEx/DC/MC/V. ❸

Kashmir, 279 Newbury St. (☎617-536-1695), at Gloucester St. ⓣ Hynes/ICA. Marble floors, traditional carpets, and plush red seats create a setting as light and exotic as the subtle Indian curries and vegetarian dishes. Your cheapest bet is the all-you-can-eat buffet M-F 11:30am-3pm ($9), Sa-Su noon-3pm ($12). Open daily 11:30am-11pm. AmEx/D/MC/V. ❷

Island Hopper, 91 Massachusetts Ave. (☎617-266-1618). ⓣ Hynes/ICA. Trendy yet casual, Island Hopper serves huge portions flavored with authentic Southeast Asian spices. Try the delicious curry chicken ($13) and finish with fried ice cream ($6). Lunch combos $7. Open M-Th 11:30am-11pm, F-Sa 11:30-midnight, Su noon-11pm. AmEx/MC/V. ❸

SOUTH END

The long waits and hefty bills here are worth it: the Sound End's upscale restaurants meld flavors and techniques from around the world with amazing results. Most eateries line **Tremont St.,** accessible from ⓣ Back Bay.

🅖 Addis Red Sea, 544 Tremont St. (☎617-426-8727), near ⓣ Back Bay. Spicy, curry- and veggie-heavy Ethiopian cuisine in an intimate setting. Entrees are served utensil-free with spongy *injera* bread on traditional *mesob* tables. Entrees $7-15. Open M-F 5-11pm, Sa-Su noon-11pm. AmEx/D/DC/MC/V. ❸

Flour, 1595 Washington St. (☎617-267-4300; www.flourbakery.com). ⓣ Prudential, Mass. Ave., or Back Bay. Harvard graduate Joanne Chang left the lucrative world of consulting for the even more lucrative world of desserts and opened this wildly popular cafe in 2004. Baked goods $1-4. Open M-F 7am-9pm, Sa 8am-6pm, Su 9am-3pm. D/DC/MC/V. ❶

Franklin Cafe, 278 Shawmut Ave. (☎617-350-0010; www.franklincafe.com). ⓣ Back Bay. Hidden away in a residential area of the South End, this trendy dinner-and-drinks spot is clearly the place to be for locals in the know. The food justifies the long wait on weekend nights. Salads $5-9. Entrees $14-20. Open daily 5pm-2am. AmEx/D/DC/MC/V. ❸

🄰 ACCOMMODATIONS

Finding cheap accommodations in Boston is hard. Rates and bookings are highest in summer and during college-rush times in September, late May, and early June. Reservation services promise to find discounted rooms. Try **Boston Reservations** (☎617-332-4199) or **Central Reservation Service** (☎800-332-3026). Listed prices do not include Boston's **12.45%** room tax.

🅖 Fenway Summer Hostel (HI), 575 Commonwealth Ave. (☎617-267-8599), in Fenway. ⓣ Kenmore. The best hostel in Boston with a penthouse common room with a 360° view of Boston. Breakfast included. Linens included. Open June-Aug. Dorms $38, members $35; private rooms $92/$89. MC/V. ❷

🅖 Oasis Guest House, 22 Edgerly Rd. (☎617-267-2262; www.oasisgh.com), at Stoneholm St. ⓣ Hynes/ICA. Though its name and the camel on its logo might hint at an exotic lodging experience, Oasis is still closer to Symphony Hall than the Sahara. Its 16 rooms, all outfitted with TVs, are clean and homey, if small. Reservations recommended. Rooms May to mid-Nov. $69-99; mid-Nov. to Apr. $90-150. AmEx/MC/V. ❸

🅖 Newbury Guest House, 261 Newbury St. (☎617-437-7666; www.newburyguesthouse.com), between Gloucester and Fairfield St. ⓣ Copley or Hynes/ICA. Combining the colonial and the cosmopolitan, the Newbury Guest House is a charming B&B in a 19th-century brownstone. Victorian architecture and 21st-century amenities (cable TV, private bath, Wi-Fi). Reception 24hr. Check-in 3pm. Check-out noon. Rooms $150-250. AmEx/D/DC/MC/V. ❺

American Youth Hostels, 12 Hemenway St. (☎617-536-1027; www.hiayh.org), in Back Bay. From ⓣ Hynes/ICA, walk down Massachusetts Ave., turn right on Boylston St., then left onto Hemenway St. AYH in Boston is the US headquarters of Hostelling International (HI), the world-wide hosteling syndicate with 4500 hostels in 71 countries. Reception 24hr. Check-in noon. Check-out 11am. Dorms $35-38, members $32-35. AmEx/MC/V. ❷

Copley House, 239 W. Newton St. (☎617-236-8300; www.copleyhouse.com). ⓣ Prudential. A small studio and 1-bedroom apartment complex in Back Bay, Copley House offers fully equipped studios for short-term residents. Each of the 55 rooms includes a kitchenette, private bath, cable TV, and local phone access. Limited parking $10 per night. Rooms in summer $95-105; in winter $85-135. AmEx/D/DC/MC/V. ❹

Greater Boston YMCA, 316 Huntington Ave. (☎617-927-8040). ⓣ Symphony. Access to world-class athletic facilities and location near Boston's cultural attractions make the surprisingly hefty price tag more palatable. 18+. Breakfast included. Key deposit $5. Reception 24hr. Check-out 11am. Men only Sept.-May. Singles $46, with bath $66; doubles $66; triples $81; quads $96. MC/V. ❸

♫ ENTERTAINMENT

The best publications for entertainment listings are the weekly *Boston Phoenix* and *Dig* (both free from streetside boxes), and the *Boston Globe's* Thursday *Calendar* section. In addition to selling tickets to most major theater shows, **Bostix** sells half-price, day-of-show tickets from booths at Faneuil Hall and Copley Sq. (☎617-723-5181; www.bostix.com. Open M-Sa 10am-6pm, Su 11am-4pm. Tickets daily 11am. Cash only.) The **Charles Playhouse,** 74 Warrenton St., hosts the infamous Blue Man Group. (Ⓣ Boylston. ☎617-426-6912; www.broadwayinboston.com. Box office open M-Tu 10am-6pm, W-Th 10am-7pm, F-Sa 10am-9pm, Su noon-6pm. Tickets from $46.) The **Boston Lyric Opera** performs at the Shubert Theater, 265 Tremont St. (☎617-542-4912. Tickets $34-159.) At storied **Fenway Park,** diehard fans cheer on their 2004 World Series Champion Red Sox. The nation's oldest, smallest, and most expensive baseball park, Fenway is home to the Green Monster, the towering left-field wall. (Ticket Office, 4 Yawkey Way. Ⓣ Kenmore. ☎617-482-4769. $12-70.) If you're a basketball or hockey fan, head to the **TD Banknorth Garden,** 50 Causeway St., Ⓣ North Station, which hosts basketball's **Celtics** and hockey's **Bruins.** (Celtics ☎617-854-8000. $10-140. Bruins ☎617-624-2327. $19-99.)

◗ NIGHTLIFE

Before you set out to paint the town red, there are a few things to keep in mind. Boston bars and clubs are notoriously strict about age requirements (usually 21+), so bring backup ID. Puritanical zoning laws require that all nightlife shuts down by 2am. The T stops running at 12:30am, so bring extra cash for a taxi ride home.

DANCE CLUBS

Boston is a town for pubbers, not clubbers. The city's few clubs are on or near Kenmore Sq.'s **Lansdowne St.,** near Ⓣ Kenmore.

Avalon, 15 Lansdowne St. (☎617-262-2424). Ⓣ Kenmore. Purported to be Boston's hippest full-on dance club, Avalon features a huge sunken dance floor, obscene sound system, and masses of college students working up an adrenaline high. The longest running gay night in the country Su. F-Sa 19+, Su 21+. Cover $10-15. Open F-Su 10pm-2am. AmEx/MC/V.

Pravda 116, 116 Boylston St. (☎617-482-7799). Ⓣ Boylston. The mood-enhancing caviar, red decor, and 116 brands of vodka may recall Mother Russia, but capitalism reigns supreme at Pravda, the favored haunt of Boston's yuppified twentysomethings. Cover W $15, F-Sa $10. Bar open W-Sa 5pm-2am. Club open W and F-Sa 10pm-2am. AmEx/D/MC/V.

Europa/Buzz, 51-67 Stuart St. (☎617-267-8969). Ⓣ Boylston. Which face and name you get depends on the night, but this club is usually filled with good-looking types. On Sa the club is called Buzz and hosts Best of Boston's 2004 Best Gay Dance Party. Cover $10-15. Th-F 19+, Sa 21+. Open Th-Sa 10pm-2am.

Axis, 13 Lansdowne St. (☎617-262-2437). Ⓣ Kenmore. The little sister of nearby Avalon, Axis provides a smaller, less-crowded clubbing experience with more of a punk feel. Drag shows M night. The biggest draws are the weekly concerts, when college kids from all over come in to hear everything from alt-rock to rap. Strict dress code. F-Sa 19+, Su 21+. Cover $7-20. Open M and F-Su 10pm-2am. AmEx/D/MC/V.

BARS AND PUBS

Boston's large student population means the city is filled with countless great bars and pubs. Most tourists stick to the various faux Irish pubs around **downtown,** while the **Theater District** is the premier after-dark destination of the city's international elite. The shamelessly yuppie meat markets on Back Bay's **Boylston St.** are also popular.

The Littlest Bar, 47 Province St. (☎617-523-9766). No shamrock-flaunting imitation, the Littlest Bar is a true Irish pub, sandwiched into a room the size of your closet. The convivial space packs in about 38 drinkers—a mix of tourists, locals, and visiting Irish students. Nightly $4 pints. No cover. Open daily 8:30am-2:30am. Cash only.

Vox Populi, 755 Boylston St. (☎617-424-8300). Serving 20 of the most creative martinis in Boston in a hip but unpretentious milieu, this swanky bar is Boylston St.'s "It" spot. A mostly twenty- and thirtysomething crowd on the prowl (voted Boston's "best place to find

EAST COAST

a relationship of limited duration") downs $10 drinks. Open daily 11:30am-1am. Kitchen closes M-W 11pm, Th-Sa 11:30pm, Su 10pm. AmEx/D/MC/V.

Daisy Buchanan's, 240 Newbury St. (☎617-247-8516). ⓣ Hynes/ICA. Newbury St. may have plenty in common with East Egg, but somehow Daisy Buchanan's has skipped the ostentation and become a gem of a bar. It's home to cheap beer ($3-6), shots ($6), and cocktails ($6), as well as a notably un-Newbury crowd. Open daily 11am-2am. Kitchen closes M-Sa 10pm, Su 7pm. Cash only.

Purple Shamrock, 1 Union St. (☎617-227-2060). ⓣ Government Ctr. Just across the way from Quincy Market, the Purple Shamrock attracts an older crowd of regulars relaxing after work, while a younger crowd drops by this combination restaurant, nightclub, and Irish pub on weekends. A selection of draft beers and specialty drinks (chocolate cake martini; $8) are available after 9:30pm. 21+ after 9pm. Cover Th-Sa $5. Open daily 11:30am-2am. AmEx/D/MC/V.

GLBT NIGHTLIFE

For listings of GLBT nightlife, pick up a free copy of *Bay Windows*, a gay weekly available everywhere, or check the free *Boston Phoenix* and *Improper Bostonian*. The **South End's** bars and late-night restaurants, accessible from ⓣ Back Bay, are all gay-friendly (sorry ladies, these are mostly for the boys). Lesbians flock to **Jamaica Plain's** bookstores and cafes, many of which are queer-owned.

Ramrod and Machine, 1254-1256 Boylston St. (☎617-266-2986; www.ramrodboston.com). ⓣ Hynes/ICA. A gay institution for 22 years, Ramrod and Machine offer the full range of nightlife experience, from friendly drinking to kinky fetishism. Ramrod is a traditional bar: video machines, pool tables, and Th karaoke. Machine's club nights (cover $5-8) offer blisteringly loud house and scantily-clad male models gyrating on platforms. M 19+. Open daily noon-2am. Cash only.

Chaps/Vapor, 100 Warrenton St. (☎617-422-0862). ⓣ N.E. Medical. A young, attractive male crowd moves in time with urban beats at Chaps/Vapor, one of Boston's most popular gay bars and dance clubs. Their renowned theme nights (W Latino night, Th "Music Factory," and Sa "Evolution") attract throngs of partygoers, especially W and Sa when a younger crowd turns out in droves. W and Su 19+. Cover usually $4-10. Open M-Sa 3pm-2am, Su noon-2am. AmEx/D/MC/V.

Club Cafe, 209 Columbus Ave. (☎617-536-0966; www.clubcafe.com). ⓣ Arlington. Atop a glass-roofed fitness club, this restaurant-cafe and 2 bars cater to the South End's "guppie" (gay-yuppie) crowd. Regulars know that the "club" moniker is deceiving: Club Cafe is more restaurant than bar, and certainly not so much club, making it a good place to actually have conversations. Bar open daily 11:30am-2am. Club open M-W 11:30am-2:30pm and 5:30-10pm, Th-F 11:30am-2:30pm and 5:30-11pm, Sa 5:30-11pm, Su 11am-3pm and 5:30-10pm. AmEx/D/DC/MC/V.

⛴ APPROACHING CAMBRIDGE: 3 MILES

Head northwest on **Congress St.,** and bear left onto **Merrimac St.** Bear left onto **New Chardon St.,** and take a right onto **Cambridge St.** Continue onto **Rte. 3 N,** turning right on the ramp to stay on Rte. 3. Get onto **Memorial Dr.,** and turn right onto **Massachusetts Ave.** to head into Cambridge. To save yourself the high parking fee in Cambridge, park the car in Boston and take the Red Line to ⓣ Harvard.

CAMBRIDGE

Separated from Boston only by a small river, Cambridge is often called Boston's "Left Bank" for its liberal politics and bohemian flair. The city has thrived as an intellectual hotbed since the colonial era, when it first became the home of prestigious Harvard University, the nation's first college. The Massachusetts Institute of Technology (MIT), the country's foremost school for science and technology, moved here in the early 20th century. Cambridge's counterculture has died down since its 1960s heyday, but the city remains vibrant, with tons of bookstores and coffee shops, a large student population, and great food and nightlife.

VITAL STATS

Population: 101,000

Visitor Info: Cambridge Office for Tourism, (☎617-441-2884; www.cambridge-usa.org), in Harvard Sq. The office runs a booth outside ⓣ Harvard with plenty of maps and info. Call for hours.

Internet Access: Adrenaline Zone, 40 Brattle St. (☎617-876-1314), in Harvard Sq. Open M-Th and Su 11am-11pm, F-Sa 11am-midnight. $2 per 24min.; $5 per hr.

Post Office: 770 Mass. Ave. (☎617-275-8777), in Central Sq. Open M-F 7am-7pm, Sa 7:30am-2pm. **Postal Code:** 02138.

⊡ GETTING AROUND

Cambridge is easily reached by public transit—it's just a 10min. Ⓣ ride from downtown Boston. Cambridge's main artery, **Massachusetts Ave. ("Mass Ave.").** The **Kendall/MIT** stop is just across the river from Boston, near MIT's campus. The Red Line continues to Ⓣ **Central Sq.,** a bar-hopper's paradise; **Harvard Sq.,** the city's heart; and largely residential **Porter Sq.** Harvard Sq. sits at the intersection of Mass. Ave., Brattle St., JFK St., and Dunster St.

◉ SIGHTS

HARVARD YARD. Just off Mass Ave., Harvard Yard is the center of undergraduate life at **Harvard University.** The student-led tours offered by **Harvard Events and Information,** Holyoke Ctr. Arcade (across Dunster St. from the Ⓣ), are the best way to tour the university's dignified red-brick-and-ivy campus and learn about its history. (☎ 617-495-1573; www.harvard.edu. Open M-Sa 9am-5pm. Tours Sept. to mid-May M-F 10am and 2pm, Sa 2pm, June to mid-Aug. M-Sa 10, 11:15am, 2, 3:15pm.) The massive **Harry Elkins Widener Memorial Library** houses nearly 5 million of Harvard's 13.3 million books, making it the world's largest university library. Unfortunately, even the most persistent tourists are not allowed entry. The college's oldest standing building (built in 1720), **Massachusetts Hall,** once housed Revolutionary-era troops and is now home to the President's offices. The building was occupied in 2001 for three weeks by student protesters. The east side of Mass. Hall faces the Charles Bulfinch-designed **University Hall,** also the site of a student occupation (in 1969) and fronted by the famous **John Harvard statue.** The most photographed monument here is known as "The Statue of the Three Lies" because: 1) the statue does not depict John Harvard, but actually a college student; 2) Harvard did not found the college, but only donated his library to it; and 3) the college was not founded in 1638 as the statue indicates, but in 1636.

 DID YOU KNOW? The first book published in the US, the *Bay Psalm Book,* was printed in Cambridge in 1640.

HARVARD MUSEUMS. The ▧**Fogg Art Museum** is home to one of America's preeminent collections of Impressionist and post-Impressionist works, watercolors by William Blake, an extensive Picasso collection, and the finest collection of Ingres outside of France. True to its focus on European painting and sculpture, the Fogg arrays its works around a central courtyard modeled after a 16th-century Italian palazzo. Inside the Fogg, the **Busch-Reisinger Museum** is dedicated to modern German work. *(32 Quincy St. ☎ 617-495-9400; www.artmuseums.harvard.edu/fogg. Tours M-F 11am. Open M-Sa 10am-5pm, Su 1-5pm. $7.50, students and seniors $6, under 18 free.)* One admission ticket covers the connected maze of the **Harvard Museum of Natural History,** the **Botanical Museum,** and the **Peabody Museum of Archeology and Ethnology.** The museum's most famous display is its spectacular glass flowers—over 3000 incredibly life-like, life-sized, and magnified glass models of plants. Basic museum exhibits are mixed in with George Washington's pheasants, a narwhal skeleton, and a popular 42 ft. ▧**chronosaurus.** *(26 Oxford St. ☎ 617-495-3045; www.peabody.harvard.edu. Open daily 9am-5pm. $7.50; students, seniors, and children $6. Sept.-May W 3-5pm and Su 9am-noon free.)* The **Sackler Museum** has one of the best collections of Asian and near-Eastern art in the world. Wonderful Chinese jades and bronzes reside on the fourth floor, and be sure to check out the beautiful illustrations from Muslim manuscripts on the second floor. *(485 Broadway. ☎ 617-495-9400. Tours W 5pm. Open M-Sa 10am-5pm, Su 1-5pm. $6.50, students and seniors $5, under 18 free.)* Founded in 1889, the **Harvard Semitic Museum** was moved to its present location in 1903 and has since become the Harvard Department of Near-Eastern Languages and Civilizations. Exhibits at the museum's galleries focus on both the artifacts' significance and their aesthetic appeal and include a re-creation of a house from ancient Israel. *(6 Divinity Ave. ☎ 617-495-4631. Open M-F 10am-4pm, Su 1-4pm. Free.)*

MIT SIGHTS. Kendall Sq. (Ⓣ Kendall/MIT) is home to the **Massachusetts Institute of Technology (MIT),** the world's leading institution in the study of science. Free campus tours begin at the **MIT Info Center** and includes visits to the Chapel and Kresge Auditorium, which touches the ground in only three places. *(In Lobby 7/Small Dome building. 77 Mass Ave. ☎ 617-*

EAST COAST

253-1000; www.mit.edu. Tours M-F 10:45am and 2:45pm.) The ◪**MIT Museum** features technological wonders in dazzling multimedia exhibitions. Highlights include a gallery of "hacks" (elaborate, if nerdy, pranks) and the world's largest hologram collection. *(265 Mass Ave. ☎617-253-4444. Open Tu-F 10am-5pm, Sa-Su noon-5pm. $5; college students with ID, seniors, and ages 5-18 $2.)*

OTHER SIGHTS. The small ◪**Harvard Book & Binding Service** is easy to miss but claims a devoted following. Robert Marshall, the friendly Renaissance man who runs the shop, will proudly take customers on a tour of his collection, which includes an original copy of Paradise Lost and an impressive collection of Greek and Roman coins ($10-750). Aside from the rare and ancient books that rival the cost of a college education, most used books go for $2. *(5 JFK St., 3rd fl. ☎617-233-6756. Open daily 9am-5pm.)* The elegant lemon-yellow **Longfellow House**, was the home of famous 19th-century American poet Henry Wadsworth Longfellow, who lived here for over 40 years until his death in 1882. *(105 Brattle St. ☎617-876-4491; www.nps.gov/long. Accessible by guided tour only. House open in summer W-Su 10am-4:30pm. Grounds open daily sunrise-sunset. $3.)* Until the Revolutionary War began, tree-lined Brattle St. was referred to as **Tory Row** because the stately mansions along the street were home to British sympathizers, known as Loyalists or Tories. Nearly 300 years later, the homes still house Cambridge's most blue-blooded families.

◪ FOOD

Situated comfortably between the din of Harvard Sq. and the suburban stuffiness of residential Cambridge, ◪**Darwin's Ltd. ❷**, 148 Mt. Auburn St., is the perfect spot for a quick lunch or a leisurely latte. The staff at the deli counter creates the best sandwiches ($5.75-7.25), all named after local streets. *(☎617-354-5233. Open M-Sa 6:30am-9pm, Su 7am-9pm. Cash only.)* One of the Square's most popular establishments, ◪**Pinocchio's,** 74 Winthrop St., has survived rampant commercialization and doesn't seem to be going anywhere fast. Students flock to "Noch's" every night for the famous crispy-gooey Sicilian pizza ($2.25 per slice, 2 for $4), like tomato basil. *(☎617-876-4897. Open M-W 11am-1am, Th-Sa 11am-2am, Su 1pm-midnight. MC/V with $10 min.)* **Punjabi Dhaba ❷**,

225 Hampshire St., is a self-proclaimed "Indian Highwayside Cafe" with an odd fusion of a no-frills, fast-food atmosphere with delicious Indian favorites. (In Inman Sq. Ⓣ #69 Bus. Entrees $5-9. Open daily noon-midnight. MC/V.) A hotspot for cash-strapped students, **Felipe's Mexican Taqueria ❶**, 83 Mt. Auburn St., satisfies any craving for delightfully greasy south-of-the-border fare for less than $5. Felipe's may have only six main offerings (burritos, super burritos, quesadillas, tacos, tostadas, and platos), but when the post-clubbing munchies hit, those six are all you need. (☎617-354-9944. Open M-W and Su 10am-midnight, Th-Sa 11am-2am. Cash only.) **Atasca ❸**, 50 Hampshire St., is the perennial winner of *Boston Magazine*'s "Best Portuguese Restaurant" award and offers delectable Iberian cuisine in a romantic setting. (Ⓣ Kendall. ☎617-734-7028. Open M-Th and Su 11am-10pm, F-Sa 11am-11pm. AmEx/D/DC/MC/V.)

◪ ACCOMMODATIONS

The **Cambridge Bed & Muffin ❹**, 267 Putnam Ave., offers five clean, private bedrooms, one muffin-room (kitchen), and two shared bathrooms. The owner cheerfully provides extra quilts and daily continental breakfast. (☎617-576-3166; www.bedandmuffin.com. Ⓣ Harvard. Rooms $80, with 2-night stay $65. Cash only.) The highway interchanges of north Cambridge aren't exactly great scenery, but the **Cambridge Gateway Inn ❹**, 211 Concord Turnpike, is one of the best deals around for the budget traveler. (☎617-661-7800; www.cambridgegateway-inn.com. Ⓣ Alewife. Free Wi-Fi and HBO. Singles from $90. AmEx/D/MC/V.) The **Irving House ❺**, 24 Irving St., has 44 simple rooms less than a 10min. walk from Harvard Sq. Complimentary drinks, teacakes, and brownies are provided until 10pm. (☎617-547-4600. Ⓣ Harvard. Free Internet access. Singles $75-185, with private bath $90-265. AmEx/D/MC/V.)

◪ NIGHTLIFE

On weekend nights, Harvard Sq. is equal parts gathering place, music hall, and three-ring circus, with tourists, locals, students, and pierced suburban punks enjoying the varied street performers. Bars abound in Harvard Sq., but Cambridge's best nightlife options are in Central Sq. a bar-hopper's heaven. ◪**The People's Republik,** 878 Mass Ave., keeps the proletariat happy with cheap beer and cheeky chalkboards with adages like "Drink beer—it's cheaper than gasoline." (Ⓣ Central. ☎617-491-6969. No cover. Open M-W and Su noon-1am, Th-Sa noon-2am. Cash only.) **The Cantab Lounge,** 738 Mass Ave., has arcade games, heaping nachos ($4-6), and a diverse clientele, but it makes a name for itself with its live entertainment and music. Little Joe Cook and the Trillers play every F and Sa starting at 9pm. The Underground downstairs hosts open mic (M-Tu 8pm), an acclaimed poetry slam (W 8pm), and local DJs every F-Sa. (Ⓣ Central. ☎617-354-2685. Cover F-Sa $8. Open M-W 8am-1am, Th-Sa 8am-2am, Su noon-1am. Cash only.) The **Enormous Room,** 567 Mass Ave., is so exclusive that is doesn't even have a sign on the door. Look for the door with an elephant on it and head up the stairs to an avant-garde haven. (Ⓣ Central. ☎617-491-5550. F-Sa cover after 9:30pm $3. Open M-F and Su 5:30pm-1am, Th-Sa 7pm-2am. AmEx/MC/V.)

⚑ APPROACHING SALEM: 16 MILES
From Boston, take **I-93 N** to **I-95 N,** which splits into I-95 and Rte. 128. Take **Rte. 128 N** to **Rte. 114 E,** which leads into town.

SALEM

Salem can't seem to get over 1692, the year in which witch hysteria gripped the town. Although Salem has more to offer than witch kitsch, its infamous past has spawned a Halloween-based tourist trade that culminates in the month-long Haunted Happenings festival in October. The town also has a fantastic art museum and a legacy as the birthplace of author Nathaniel Hawthorne.

VITAL STATS

Population: 40,400

Visitor Info: Salem Visitors Center, 2 New Liberty St. (☎978-740-1650). Open daily 9am-5pm.

Internet Access: Salem Public Library, 370 Essex St. (☎978-744-0860). Open M-Th 9am-9pm, F-Sa 9am-5pm, Su 1-5pm. Free.

Parking: 2hr. metered parking is readily available along Derby St. and in a lot at the Museum Place Mall for $0.25 per hr.

Post Office: 2 Margin St. (☎978-744-4671). Open M-F 8am-5pm, Sa 8am-1pm. **Postal Code:** 01970.

⬛ GETTING AROUND

Most of Salem's attractions center on **Essex St.** and **Derby St.,** which run east-west parallel to **Rte. 107** (leading to Beverly). **Washington St.** runs north-south, becoming **Rte. 114** (leading to Danvers) south of Derby St. **U.S. 1A** runs parallel to Washington St. Taking Derby St. north will lead you to the waterfront.

⬢ SIGHTS

◪**PEABODY ESSEX MUSEUM.** The Peabody houses an enormous collection of attractively displayed Asian Art from China, Japan, and India. The museum also has collections of maritime and contemporary art; a highlight is the Yin Yu Tang house, which was dismantled, shipped from China, and reassembled for display. *(East India Sq.* ☎*978-745-9500 or 866-745-1876; www.pem.org. Open daily 10am-5pm. $13, seniors $11, students and under 16 $9. Yin Yu Tang additional $4.)*

HOUSE OF THE SEVEN GABLES. The so-called "second most famous house in America," the Turner-Ingersoll Mansion became famous as Nathaniel Hawthorne's "House of the Seven Gables." Many changes were made to the home in 1910 to make it more closely resemble the house in the book, including the addition of a secret passageway to nowhere. *(54 Turner St.* ☎*978-744-0991; www.7gables.org. Open daily July-Oct. 10am-7pm; Nov.-June 10am-5pm. $12, seniors $11, ages 5-12 $7.25.)*

SALEM MARITIME NATIONAL HISTORICAL SITE. Down the waterfront from the witch-oriented section of town, the site is dedicated to Salem's colonial and maritime history. The **Orientation Center** shows a film entitled *To the Farthest Part of the Rich East* every 30min. throughout the day. Guides lead tours of the **1817 Custom House,** where Hawthorne worked, and tours of the **1762 Derby House** and **1672 Narbonne House,** owned by wealthy Salem residents. Visitors can also tour the *Friendship,* a three-masted ship constructed in the late 18th century. *(193 Derby St. Orientation Center open daily 9am-5pm. Tour times vary; call ahead. $5, ages 6-15 and seniors $3.)*

WITCH HYSTERIA. Salem certainly doesn't try to minimize the most infamous event in its history. Most of the museums that have opened to capitalize on the witch craze are over-wrought, tacky, and not worth the price of admission. The **Witch House**, once home to witch-trial judge Jonathan Corwin, is the only home with legitimate historical ties to the trials. The museum focuses on everyday life in the 17th century, turning only briefly to its role in the trials. *(310½ Essex St. ☎978-744-8815; www.salemweb.com/witchhouse. Open May-Nov. daily 10am-5pm. Guided tours every hr. $8, seniors $6, ages 6-14 $4.)* The **Salem Witch Trials Memorial** consists of stones with the names and dates of the 20 individuals killed during the hysteria. *(Free.)* The **Salem Witch Museum** uses testimony from contemporary documents in a live-action exhibit called "Witches: Evolving Perceptions." *(Washington Sq. ☎978-744-1692; www.salemwitchmuseum.com. Open daily July-Aug. 10am-7pm; Sept.-June 10am-5pm. $7.50, seniors $6.50, ages 6-14 $4.50.)* The **Salem Wax Museum of Witches and Seafarers** displays life-sized statues of major figures from the trials, including Colonel Lieutenant John Hathorne, ancestor of author Nathaniel Hawthorne and supposedly the only person never to regret his involvement. A series of full-scale dioramas documents Salem history. *(288 Derby St. ☎800-298-2929; www.salemwaxmuseum.com. Open daily 10am-8pm. $6, ages 6-14 $4.)* The "Hysteria Pass" is available for $10 and grants access to the wax museum and to the **Salem Witch Village,** actually a series of indoor dioramas meant to illustrate views of witches through history. Practicing witches give tours meant to explain witchcraft as a legitimate way of life. *(282 Derby St. ☎978-740-9229; www.salemwitch-village.net. Open daily 10am-8pm. Tours on the half-hr.)*

WALKING TOURS. Like everything else in Salem, walking tours of the city focus on witchcraft and hangings. Expect tours to be over the top. If you're into the witch mania, you may as well go all-out. The **Spellbound Tour,** led by a licensed ghost hunter, takes visitors on a quest for Salem's spectral un-dead. *(190 Essex St. ☎978-745-0138. Tours Mar.-Oct. 8pm; Nov. 5:30pm. $13, students and seniors $10, under 13 $7.)* **Salem Trolley Tours** provides a more historical way to see the city. The tour takes visitors through the city to several non-witch-related sites. *(☎978-744-5469. Tours Apr.-Oct. daily 10am-5pm. $12, seniors $10, ages 5-14 $3.)*

FOOD

Voted "Best Breakfast" for 20 years running, **Red's Sandwich Shop ❶,** 15 Central St., probably hasn't changed its decor in as many years. No matter—stop by for a stack of chocolate-chip pancakes ($5.25) and a hearty serving of local gossip. Red's also has diner-style sandwiches, salads, and "American chop suey" ($5.75) for lunch. (☎978-745-3527. Open M-Sa 5am-3pm, Su 6am-1pm. Cash only.) Only a few doors down from the visitors center, **Fuel ❶,** 196 Essex St., serves creative fare such as the apple-and-strawberry salad ($5.25) and the Green Monster wrap (lettuce, broccoli, snow peas, sprouts, pine nuts, cheese; $5.50). You can also design your own wrap or salad from a list of ingredients: choose wisely, for with great power comes great responsibility. (☎978-741-0850. Free Wi-Fi. Open M-F 11am-5pm, Sa-Su 8am-5pm. Cash only.) The **Derby Deli Cafe ❶,** 245 Derby St., offers deli options like the smoked turkey ($4.50), as well as paninis and salads. (☎978-741-2442. Open M-Sa 8am-5pm, Su 8am-4pm. MC/V.)

ACCOMMODATIONS

Salem has a large number of B&Bs and quaint inns in historic houses, most outside the price range of the budget traveler. The most reasonable option is the **Clipper Ship Inn ❹,** 40 Bridge St., off U.S. 1A, the "only motel in downtown Salem." The 60 larger-than-average rooms have A/C and cable TV, but guests have to drive into the downtown area—or take a long walk—to reach the most famous attractions. (☎978-745-8022. Rooms M-Th and Su $75-105, F-Sa $85-115. AmEx/D/MC/V.) Take Rte. 114 W to Danvers to find cheaper options. The **Days Inn ❹,** 152 Endicott St., has large, standard motel rooms with fridge, microwave, iron, and Wi-Fi. (Take Rte. 114 W to Rte. 128 N Exit 24. Laundry, outdoor pool. Continental breakfast included. Rooms M-Th and Su $70, F-Sa $80. AmEx/D/MC/V.) Just north of its intersection with Rte. 114 is **Motel 6 ❸,** 65 Newbury St. Rooms include a bed and little else. (☎978-774-8045. 21+. Singles M-Th and Su $60, F-Sa $66; doubles $66/$72. AmEx/D/MC/V.)

BIG DETOUR. Explore the kooky side of New Hampshire on the **Flumes, Frescoes, and Fire Pits Big Detour,** p. 176.

⚑ APPROACHING ROCKPORT: 22 MILES
Take **Rte. 128 N** to **Rte. 127,** which leads into town.

ROCKPORT

Cape Ann, on which Rockport is located, claims to be the "home of the perfect vacation." While that's up for discussion, Rockport is well worth a visit. With historic and offbeat sights and a beautiful waterfront, it's got something for everyone. The area can be an expensive stay, but luckily budget travelers will be content just walking the streets of Bearskin Neck.

VITAL STATS

Population: 7300

Visitor Info: Rockport Chamber of Commerce, 3 Whistlestop Mall, off Rte. 127 N (☎978-546-6575). Open M-F 9am-5pm.

Internet Access: Rockport Public Library, 17 School St. (☎978-546-6934). Open M and W-Th 1-8pm, Tu 1-5pm, Sa 10am-5pm, Su 1-6pm. Free.

Parking: Free parking is available in a lot ½ mi. from downtown; a shuttle runs 11am-7pm for $1.

Post Office: 39 Broadway (☎978-546-2667). Open M-F 9am-5pm, Sa 8:30am-noon. **Postal Code:** 03870.

▐▄ GETTING AROUND

Rte. 127 leads into **Main St.** and **Broadway,** two of the town's central streets. Main St. turns to run along the water and leads into **Mt. Pleasant St.** to the southeast and **Beach St.** to the northwest. This stretch along the beach is the main commercial and tourist section of town, with numerous restaurants, shops, and accommodations. The intersection of Main St., Mt. Pleasant St., and Bearskin Neck forms **Dock Sq.,** the center of the downtown.

👁 SIGHTS

BEARSKIN NECK. One of the country's oldest artist colonies, Bearskin Neck is now also one of Rockport's most tourist-oriented areas, featuring gift shops, ice-cream stores, and, of course, galleries aplenty. Most of the galleries highlight painting, but a few display sculpture and jewelry. Though the area is certainly geared towards tourists, it avoids kitsch, making it a enjoyable area for walking and window-shopping. *(At the center of town, off Dock Sq. From Broadway, take a left onto Mt. Pleasant St., then a right onto Bearskin Neck. There is not a lot of space to drive, so parking and walking is easiest.)*

MOTIF NO. 1. A sort of "little fish shack that could," Motif No. 1 is still just a fish shack, but perhaps the most famous fish shack in the world. At the end of Bradley Wharf in Bearskin Neck, the red fish shack is the most often-painted building in America. Legend has it that the building received its name when artist Lester Hornby saw yet another student's drawing featuring this popular subject—or motif—and christened it "motif no. 1." Visitors can try their hand at painting, but the building itself is locked.

THE PAPER HOUSE. In 1922, Elis F. Stenman, a mechanical engineer from Cambridge, was experimenting with newspapers as an insulation material for his summer cottage. After the walls survived a harsh New England winter with minimal damage, Stenman decided to leave them exposed, and the paper house was born. While it has a wood frame and a normal roof, the walls and the furniture that Stenman continued to add until his death in 1942 are made entirely of newspapers. About 100,000 newspapers were used to construct the home, a grandfather clock, a radio cabinet, and a writing desk. *(52 Pigeon Hill. Follow Rte. 127 north to Pigeon Cove, take a left onto Curtis St., then make a left onto Pigeon Hill. The house is on the right; there are signs marking the way. ☎978-546-2629. Open Apr.-Oct. daily 10am-5pm. $1.50.)*

HALIBUT POINT STATE PARK. Occupying the land around the Babson Farm Quarry off Rte. 127, Halibut Point State Park features a ½ mi., self-guided walking tour around the 60 ft. deep quarry. Brochures detailing the tour and its sights are available at the visitors center, which highlights the history and natural habitat of the park and the artifacts left over from the quarry. Visitors can also follow a path down to a beach of huge rocks, but wear shoes suitable for climbing over stones and exploring tidepools. *(On Gott Ave. Take Rte. 127 N out of downtown Rockport, and turn right on Gott Ave. ☎978-546-2997. Open Memorial Day to Columbus Day daily 8am-9pm. Free.)*

FLUMES, FRESCOES & FIRE PITS

WE TOOK THAT FACE FOR GRANITE

Length: 384 miles
Days: 3 days
Starting point: Salem
Highlight: Franconia Notch State Park

From Salem, take Rte. 128 S to I-93 N. Cross the border into New Hampshire, and take Rte. 111 E for 4½ mi., past the North Salem Village Shops. Make a right at the traffic light, and follow the road 1 mi.

1 AMERICA'S STONEHENGE. Step within an ordinary New Hampshire forest to find a maze of stone structures, supposedly constructed 4000 years ago. It's unclear who built the structures—Native Americans, seafaring Europeans, or rascally kids—and there are a number of chambers and the frighteningly named "sacrificial table." If you can't decide whether it's all true or an elaborate hoax, ask the alpaca out back. They know everything, but unfortunately, they aren't talking. (☎603-893-8300; www.stonehengeusa.com. $9, seniors $8, ages 6-12 $6. Open Jan. to early June and Labor Day to Oct. 9am-5pm; late June to Labor Day 9am-6pm; Nov.-Dec. 9am-4:30pm.)

From America's Stonehenge, take I-93 N to Exit 9. Take Rte. 3 to Rte. 28 N, which leads to Bear Brook State Park. The museum is inside the park, about ½ mi. down on the right.

2 MUSEUM OF FAMILY CAMPING. Trek to the museum to learn the history of S'mores and Coleman Stoves. There's even a Hall of Fame dedicated to those who made breakthroughs in the wide world of camping. When you've had your fill of canteens and cooking pots, head over to the Snowmobile Museum across the lawn. Inside you'll find 50 years of technological improvements, from an old black buggy with three skis to a tricked-out low rider. A few even sport leopard-print seats. (☎603-485-3782; www.ucampnh.com/museum. Open Memorial Day to Columbus Day daily 10am-4pm. Free.)

Hop back onto I-93 N, and stay the course until Exit 34A towards the Gilman Visitors Center.

3 FRANCONIA NOTCH STATE PARK. In the heart of the White Mountains, Franconia Notch State Park offers rushing waterfalls, fantastic views of miles upon miles of trees, and a glacially formed lake. The rangers at the **Gilman Visitors Center**, at Exit 34A off I-93, suggest trails and provide maps of the area. (☎603-745-8391. Open daily 9am-5pm.) The entire park is gorgeous, but **The Flume Gorge** is a must-see. A walking loop (2 mi.) takes visitors up a series of wooden stairs to the top of the 800 ft. gorge, surrounded by lichen-covered walls of Conway granite. (☎603-271-3556. Open daily May-June and Sept.-Oct. 9am-5pm; July-Aug. 9am-5:30pm. $10, ages 6-12 $7.) Formed by glacial melting 25,000 years ago, **Glacier Basin** is a 20 ft. deep pothole fed by the Pemigewasset River. The waterfall emits a cool spray, shrouding the basin in a fine mist. The **Old Man of the Mountain**, a rock formation that looked like a face, once looked out over Profile Lake. The Old Man's visage collapsed in 2003, but a **Historical Site and Museum** remain to pay homage to New Hampshire's trademark. **Echo Lake Beach** offers over-heated hikers a place to cool off. Visitors can also rent canoes and kayaks for $10 per hr. (☎603-745-8391. Lifeguards mid-June to Aug. daily 10am-5pm. $3, ages 6-11 $1.) Campers can pitch their tents at **Lafayette Campground ❶**, centrally located within the park. The sites are heavily wooded, and are located at the heads of several trails. The campground is very busy on the weekends—make reservations a few weeks in advance. (Take Rte. 93 to Exit 34B, and head south to the pull-off. ☎603-823-9513, reservations 603-271-3628. Open mid-May to mid-Oct.; no water Jan.-May. Coin operated showers. Sites $19, premium sites mid-June to Sept. $24. D/MC/V.)

From Franconia Notch State Park, take I-93 N to Rte. 117 W. Then follow Rte. 10 S to I-91 S.

4 DARTMOUTH COLLEGE. Located in the heart of New Hampshire, Hanover is almost entirely subsumed by Dartmouth College. Wheelock St. and Main St., home to restaurants and shops, are the main thoroughfares of the town. The lower level of the **Baker-Berry Library** houses the Orozco Frescoes, 24 panels tracing American civilization. Beware: Orozco's vision of American history is not a sunny one. (☎603-646-2560; www.dartmouth.edu/~library/Orozco. Call ahead for hours. Free.) Visitors can tour Dartmouth's campus on student-led tours, which leave from the **Office of Admissions**, 6016 McNutt Hall. (☎603-646-2875. Tours M-F 10am, 12:30, 3pm, Sa noon. Free.) The **Dirt Cowboy Cafe ❶**, 7 S. Main St., serves baguette sandwiches to hungry students. The busy shop also makes pineapple-banana-mango smoothies for $4. (☎802-643-1323; www.dirtcowboycafe.com. Gruyere swiss sandwich $4. Free Wi-Fi. Open daily 7am-6pm. MC/V.)

From Hanover, NH, take I-89 N to Rte. 14 at Exit 2. Follow Rte. 14 about 5 mi. towards S. Royalton, then make a right on Dairy Hill Rd. There's a sign for the monument on your right.

5 JOSEPH SMITH BIRTHPLACE MONUMENT. Mormons believe that there are two holy sites in the world: Bethlehem and Sharon, VT, birthplace of the religion's founder, Joseph Smith. Step out of your car to hear otherworldly music mysteriously emanating from the hills. Gushing missionary tour guides lead you through a museum detailing the Prophet's life, including a 9min. video complete with strategically placed tissue boxes. The monument itself is a 38½ ft. granite shaft that guides insist was erected thanks to a miracle. (☎802-763-7742; www.lds.org/placestovisit. Open May-Oct. M-Sa 9am-7pm, Su 1:30-6pm; Nov.-Apr. M-Sa 9am-5pm, Su 1:30-5pm. Free.)

From the Joseph Smith Birthplace Monument, take I-89 S to I-91 S. Take Exit 4, and make a left onto Rte. 5 headed towards Putney. The smoke will be visible to your right just after exiting the highway.

6 CURTIS' BARBEQUE. Hard to believe, but it's true—**Curtis' Barbeque ❸** has been cooking up ribs in New England for 35 years. Curtis Tuff started selling his slabs on the side of the road, but has since made his permanent residence in a couple of bright blue schoolbuses in Putney. Tuff cooks the ribs ($25 per slab) and chicken ($7 per ½ chicken) on a wood-fired open pit. If you're lucky, you may even catch a glimpse of pet pig CJ running around. Here's hoping he never strays too close to the flames. (☎802-387-5474; www.curtisbbqvt.com. Open Apr.-Oct. 9am-"you have to put on your headlights." Cash only.)

BACK TO THE ROUTE. From Putney, head south on I-91, then east on Rte. 9. Near the town of Keene, get onto Rte. 101. Stay on Rte. 101A past Milford, then get on U.S. 3 S. Switch to I-95 N at Woburn, then take 128 N. To finish the drive in style, take 127A into Rockport.

OUTDOORS. The **North Shore Kayak Outdoor Center** allows adventurous types to paddle through the Rockport harbor and to neighboring islands, Straitsmouth and Thatcher Island. Guides lead inexperienced kayakers on tours, while experts are welcome to take a boat out themselves. (☎978-546-5050. *Tours $35-45, under 13 $20-30. Kayak rentals $30 per half-day, $45 per full day. Tandem kayaks $40/$60. Open daily 9am-8pm.*)

■ FOOD

Rockport is a dry town, so no restaurants or stores sell alcohol. Some, however, do allow visitors to bring their own. At **Roy Moore Lobster Company ❷**, in Bearskin Neck, the morning's catch is boiled and buttered for lunch. Take your lobster (price varies, usually $8-9 per lb.), clam chowder ($3), or baked stuffed clams ($1 each) to the back deck, which overlooks the water. (☎978-546-6696. Open daily 8am-6pm. MC/V.) **Top Dog ❶**, in Bearskin Neck, serves a wide array of dogs—hot dogs, that is—such as the "Chihuahua" (jalapeño peppers, salsa, and cheese; $3.50) and the "Golden Retriever" (macaroni and cheese; $3.50). Diners get a free meal if they are ordering when the Red Sox hit a home run. (☎978-546-0006; www.topdogrockport.com. Open daily 11am-9pm. Cash only.) **The Greenery ❷**, 15 Dock Sq., offers light fare in a casual cafe atmosphere. Diners can opt for self-service or the whole shebang; either way, the blueberry pancakes ($6.25) and the avocado special (avocado, cheese, veggies, and garlic on pita; $7) are delicious. (☎978-546-9593. Open daily 7am-10pm. AmEx/D/MC/V.)

■ ACCOMMODATIONS

Like many towns along the New England coast, Rockport has a plethora of accommodations, most of which are hard on the pocketbook. During the summer, there's nothing in the area for under $100. On Bearskin Neck, the **Bearskin Neck Motor Lodge ❺**, 64 Bearskin Neck, has porches with fantastic views of the harbor and ocean and eight rooms just steps from the area attractions. (☎978-546-6677. Reservations recommended. Rooms June-Sept. $149-159; Apr.-May and Oct. $99. AmEx/D/MC/V.) The **Peg Leg Inn ❺**, 18 Beach St., across the street from Front Beach, offers 14 colonial-style rooms with beautiful views of the water. Rooms are spacious and have TV, refrigera-

tor, and microwave. (☎978-546-2352 or 800-346-2352; www.pegleginn.com. Continental breakfast included. Open Apr.-Dec. Rooms $145-180. AmEx/MC/V.) The **Turks Head Inn ❺**, 151 South St., lies farther out of town in a residential neighborhood and has fairly typical rooms with access to a beach and an indoor swimming pool. (Take Broadway until it hits Mt. Pleasant St. Turn right onto Mt. Pleasant St., which becomes South St. ☎978-546-3436; www.turksheadinn.com. Open late spring to late fall. Rooms from $119. AmEx/D/MC/V.) The **Sandy Bay Motor Inn ❺**, 183 Main St., is conveniently located across the street from the "park-and-ride" lot, with easy access to the shuttle into town. The establishment has rooms with TV, as well as a heated pool, hot tub, and laundry facilities. (☎978-546-7155 or 800-437-7155. Rooms from $120. AmEx/D/MC/V.)

◪ APPROACHING ESSEX: 11 MILES
From Rockport, take **Rte. 127 S** to Gloucester, then switch to **Rte. 133 W,** which leads into Essex.

ESSEX

Tiny Essex—without even a traffic light to its name—is known for two distinctive features: its many antiques shops and flea markets, and Lawrence "Chubby" Woodman, who, in 1916, dipped the clam in vegetable oil and cornmeal and invented the fried clam. **The White Elephant,** 32 Main St., and **RC Schonick Antiques,** 67 Main St., are among the town's endless stores devoted to serious antiquing. On the weekends, deal-hunters flock to **Todd Farm,** a few miles north on 1-A in Rowley, for anything that can be sold. (☎978-948-3300. Open Th-Su 10am-4pm.) **Essex Shipbuilding Museum and Store,** at 66 Main St., has exhibits on schooners, dories, Chebaco boats, and privateers. (☎978-768-7541; www.essexshipbuildingmuseum.org. Open W-Su 10am-5pm. $7, students and seniors $6, ages 6-12 $5.)

To experience Essex's clamming history, head to **Woodman's ❺**, 121 Main St., for fried clams ($18) served the way Chubby liked 'em. Proud of its history, Woodman's has a black-and-white picture of the shop dating from 1919. (☎978-768-7541; www.woodmans.com. Open daily 11am-10pm. Cash only.) Across the street is **Tom Shea's ❸**, 122 Main St., which offers a formal dining experience, serving seafood delicacies like clam chowder ($5), coconut beer battered shrimp ($11) and scallops wrapped in bacon ($9). Enjoy the view of the Essex River. (☎978-768-6931; www.tomsheas.com. Open daily 11:30-9pm. AmEx/D/MC/V.) Visitors can stay at the town's only hotel, the **Essex River House Motel ❺**, 132 Main St., where each room has a name, like the Puritan or the Tattler. The rooms are smallish, but nicely decorated. (☎978-768-6800. Rooms $108-130. D/MC/V.)

⚲ APPROACHING RYE AND HAMPTON BEACH: 31 MILES

From Essex, take **Rte. 133 N.** Switch to **U.S. 1-A N** in Rowley, then change to **U.S. 1 N** in Newburyport. As you approach Hampton, switch back to **U.S. 1-A,** which runs along the coast as **Ocean Blvd.**

The Granite State
NEW HAMPSHIRE
Welcomes You!

RYE AND HAMPTON BEACH

New Hampshire may not have much shoreline, but it certainly tries to make the most of it. Unfortunately, that means crowded beaches, gaudy boardwalks, and motels everywhere. Hampton Beach is packed with tourists during the summer; drive farther north and you'll find more peaceful shores.

VITAL STATS

Population: 5,200/15,000

Visitor Info: Hampton Beach Chamber of Commerce (☎603-926-8717; www.hampton-beach.org), on Ocean Blvd. Open 9:30am-9pm.

Internet Access: Rye Public Library, 581 Washington Rd., (☎603-964-8401), off U.S. 1A near Wallis Sands State Beach, in Rye. Open M, W, F 9am-5pm; Tu and Th 9am-8pm; Sa 9am-3pm. Free.

Post Office: 25 Stickney Terr. (☎603-926-6413), in Hampton Beach. Open M-F 8:30am-5pm, Sa 8:30am-noon. **Postal Code:** 03870.

⬛ GETTING AROUND. U.S. 1A runs along the shore in both towns. In Hampton Beach it becomes one-way heading north, so southbound drivers must take **Ashworth Ave.** and double back. Parking is tight in Hampton. Beach meters charge $1 per 40min. and lots are $5-7 for all-day parking.

⬛ SIGHTS. Entering town, you'll first come upon the crowded sands and arcades of **Hampton**

Beach. The downtown area is saturated with motels and storefronts. **North Hampton State Beach** is a thin strip of sandy beach far less crowded than Hampton Beach itself. (Head north on Rte. 1A. ☎603-436-1552. Open 24hr.) Between Odiorne State Park and Rye Beach lies **Wallis Sands State Beach,** the prettiest of the beaches between Hampton and Rye. (☎603-436-9404. Open mid-June to Labor Day daily 8am-8pm.) For the fisherman, the marina in **Rye Harbor** offers the perfect opportunity to catch the big one. (☎603-964-9008.) Stands sell whale-watching tours and trips around the **Isles of Shoals,** nine islands off the coast that were once popular resort communities. Try **Granite State Whale Watch** (☎603-964-5545 or 800-962-5364. Whale-watching daily 8:30am and 1:30pm. $27, ages 4-17 $18.). **Atlantic Queen II** also organizes half-day fishing tours as well as whale-watching tours. (☎800-942-5364 or 603-964-5220. Fishing tour 8am. Whale-watching 1pm. Fishing $31, ages 4-16 $22. Whale-watching $32/$22.). North of Rye along U.S. 1A, **Odiorne State Park** consists of open fields and a rocky beach more suitable for looking at than for swimming. It features the **Seacoast Science Center,** with exhibits on aquaculture, radar, and a ship-wreck off the coast. Visitors can play a 3-D underwater video game and pick up a free 1hr. audio tour of the seven distinct natural habitats featured in the park. (☎603-436-8042; www.seacentr.org. Open daily 10am-5pm. $3, ages 3-12 $1, under 3 free.) Along with meandering trails, the park also includes the remains of **WWII's Fort Dearborn,** built in response to Pearl Harbor. (☎603-436-7406. Open sunrise-sunset. $3, under 12 free.)

⬛⚲ FOOD AND ACCOMMODATIONS.

Along with the henna tattoo stands and arcades, **Ocean Blvd.** is crowded with fast-food joints, burger stands, and pizza parlors. For a sit-down meal, try the **Purple Urchin ❷,** 167 Ocean Blvd., right across from the visitors center. The menu mainly features seafood, like the fried-haddock sandwich ($9), but also includes a good selection of salads, including a tomato-and-mozzarella plate for $8. (☎603-929-0800. Open daily noon-10pm. AmEx/D/MC/V.) Just past Rye Harbor State Park, **Ray's Seafood ❸,** 1677 Ocean Blvd., serves only lobster they catch themselves. Try the lobster quesadilla ($8) or baked mushrooms ($7), stuffed with lobster. (☎603-436-2280. Open M and W-Su 11:30am-10pm. AmEx/D/MC/V.)

Hampton Beach is filled to the brim with hotels and motels that are close to the beach. The farther you go from the ocean, the less you'll pay. The **Regal Inn ❺**, 162 Ashworth Ave., offers large, clean rooms within walking distance of Hampton Beach. (☎603-926-7758 or 800-445-6782. Rooms M-Th and Su $99, F-Sa $109-119. AmEx/D/MC/V.) The **Jammer Motel ❹**, 52 Ashworth Ave., has some of the best prices around. Some rooms don't have A/C, but all are clean and have a TV and access to a pool. (☎603-926-3925. Rooms without A/C $90, with A/C $135. Cash only.) The strip along Rye Beach has a number of quaint inns, but few budget options. **Rye Beach Motel and Cottages ❺**, on Old Beach Rd., has motel rooms with refrigerators and microwaves as well as cottages that can be rented by the week. The quiet residential location is perfect for those who want to escape the chaos of the Hampton Beach, but the lack of A/C can make the rooms a little stuffy on hot summer days. (☎603-964-5511. Rooms M-Th and Su $99, F-Sa $119. D/MC/V.)

◪ APPROACHING PORTSMOUTH: 11 MILES
From Rye, take **1A N** into town.

PORTSMOUTH

Portsmouth was once a center of New England, home to signers of the Declaration of Independence. The town has undergone a rebirth, focusing on tourism, but it has avoided the temptation towards tackiness and maintains a vibrant, funky downtown.

VITAL STATS

Population: 21,000

Visitor Info: Greater Portsmouth Chamber of Commerce, 500 Market St. (☎603-436-5526; www.portcity.org). Open daily 9am-5pm. **Info kiosk** in Market Sq. Open May to mid-Oct. daily 10am-5pm.

Internet Access: Portsmouth Public Library, 8 Islington St. (☎603-427-1540), at the corner of Middle and State St. Open M-Th 9am-9pm, F 9am-5:30pm, Sa 9am-5pm. Free.

Parking: The garage at the corner of Hanover and Market St. is your best bet ($0.75 per hr.).

Post Office: 80 Daniel St. (☎603-431-1301). Open M-F 7:30am-5:30pm, Sa 8am-12:30pm. **Postal Code:** 03801.

▤ GETTING AROUND

State St. (U.S. 1) and **Congress St.** are the two major roads that run northeast-southwest through town. The central intersecting road is **Market St.**, which runs southeast-northwest. The town is best navigated by foot; drivers will miss the cafes and shops that line the streets. **Seacoast Trolley** has 11 stops around Portsmouth and surrounding areas. (☎603-431-6975. Runs in M-Th and Su every hr. 11am-3pm. Partial loop $3.50, full loop with reboarding privileges $7.)

◉ SIGHTS

STRAWBERY BANKE MUSEUM. Modern Portsmouth sells itself with its past, and the Strawbery Banke Museum is a prime example of this. Each building has been restored to illustrate life in the region in various time periods, from a Revolutionary War-era tavern to an early 20th-century Russian immigrant's home. A different group of buildings is open each day. Most are self-guided, but guided tours begin in the visitors center on the hour. *(At the corner of Marcy and Hancock St. From there, follow the signs that lead toward the harbor. ☎603-433-1100; www.strawberybanke.org. Open May-Oct. daily 10am-5pm; Nov.-Apr. Sa-Su 10am-2pm. $15, seniors $14, ages 5-17 $10.)*

PRESCOTT PARK. Across the street from the Strawbery Banke Museum, Prescott Park runs along the bank of the Piscataqua River. The small, well-tended gardens and lawns offer a pleasant respite with an amazing view. *(Open 24hr.)*

THE USS ALBACORE. The *USS Albacore* was a research submarine used to test brakes, sonar equipment, and escape mechanisms. Visitors can explore a small museum before navigating the cramped sub. You don't have to be a Navy buff to find looking through the spy-glass exciting. *(600 Market St. ☎603-436-3680. Open May-Oct. daily 9:30am-5pm; Nov.-Apr. hours vary. $5, seniors and military with ID $4, ages 7-17 $3.)*

JOHN PAUL JONES HOUSE. The famous captain stayed here for a few months in 1781; in 1905, his mummified body was found under the streets of Paris and reburied in the US. The museum serves as a historical catch-all, with furniture, tar-dipped firebuckets, and china galore. (At the corner of Middle and State St. ☎ 603-436-8420; www.portsmouthhistory.org. Open late May to mid-Oct. daily 11am-5pm. $8, seniors $7, children free with adult.)

MUSIC HALL. The Music Hall, a 125-year-old theater, shows mainstream, independent, and foreign films during the summer, and hosts live musical and dance performances during the winter. Visitors can tour the horseshoe balcony, which has overlooked performances by Suzanne Vega, Buffalo Bill, and Patti Lapone. Schedules of movies and events are available outside the theater. (28 Chestnut St. ☎ 603-436-2400; www.themusichall.org. Box office open M-Sa noon-6pm or until 30min. after shows. Live acts $20-35. Movies $8, students and seniors $6. Tours June-Sept. F 2pm. $6.)

NEWCASTLE SCENIC DRIVE. Drive, bike, or jog this scenic loop onto the nearby island of Newcastle. From Portsmouth, take Rte. 1B and follow the 5 mi. loop over bridges, past beautiful homes, and through the trees. Return to Portsmouth by taking Rte. 1A heading east into town.

NORTH CEMETERY. One of Portsmouth's oldest graveyards, the North Cemetery is the resting place for some of the city's most prominent citizens, including William Whipple, a signer of the Declaration of Independence, and John Langdon, who signed the US Constitution. (On Maplewood Ave., near Deer St. Free.)

PORTSMOUTH BLACK HERITAGE TRAIL. The Portsmouth Black Heritage Trail offers a different means to experience the city's celebrated history. Plaques throughout the city mark sites important in African-American history, like the Wharf and the People's Baptist Church. Brochures are available at the Strawbery Banke Museum Visitors Center, the museum shop, or the Chamber of Commerce. (☎ 603-431-2768; www.seacoastNH.com/blackhistory.)

SANDY POINT DISCOVERY CENTER. Popular with birdwatchers, Sandy Point is one of only three points where the public can explore the Great Bay Estuary and has a ½ mi. boardwalk. The Discovery Center houses exhibits about the estuary's wildlife and runs programs and kayak trips for all ages. (89 Depot Rd. Take I-95 S to Exit 3 for Rte. 33. ☎ 603-778-0015; www.greatbay.org. Discovery Center open W-Su 10am-4pm. Grounds open daily sunrise-sunset. Free.)

🍴 FOOD

Portsmouth supports a number of offbeat cafes, with an emphasis on fresh, local, and vegetarian fare. A local landmark, **The Friendly Toast ❷**, 121 Congress St., is cluttered with ghastly artifacts of the 1950s: mannequin limbs, pulp novels, Formica, and bad art. The French toast ($5.60), made with thick, homemade bread, is heavenly, while massive items like the "mission burrito" ($8) are a tasty struggle to finish. (☎ 603-430-2154. Breakfast

OLD MAN DEAD AT 12,000

Lincoln, NH – A medical examiner announced today that the Old Man of the Mountain, a Lincoln native, passed away during the night. Said one crying child, "I'm so sad. He rocked." The 12,000-year-old had been a fixture in the community. A neighbor first realized something was amiss when he did not see Mr. Mountain on his morning stroll. "I always wave good morning to the Old Man," reported the 65-year-old, "but today I was just waving at air." Further investigation revealed that the Old Man had fallen to his death during the night. The autopsy concluded that the proximal cause of Mr. Mountain's fall was water damage, which caused his center of gravity to shift. Residents of Lincoln expressed grief at Mr. Mountain's untimely end. Said neighbor Bald Mountain, "I'll truly miss seeing the Old Man's face every day—that regal nose, that jutting chin." The Old Man's friend Eagle Cliff added, "Though his profile is gone, I know that he's still looking down on us somehow." The Old Man of the Mountain is survived by his father, the Man in the Moon, as well as his four siblings, who reside on Mount Rushmore. Unfortunately, they were unable to attend his funeral. Those wishing to pay their respects may purchase a New Hampshire state quarter for $0.25. Proceeds go to the Old Man in the Mountain Foundation, which helps young granite slabs achieve the goal of becoming

served all day. Open M-Th 7am-10pm, F-Sa 24hr., Su 7am-9pm. AmEx/D/MC/V.) Semi-inebriated folk trail out the door of nearby pubs and into **Gilley's Lunchcart ❶**, 175 Fleet St., for heavenly burgers ($2.75) and cheese fries ($2.75). The place is tiny—it was once hauled into town each day as a lunchcart—but the food makes up for the squeeze. (☎603-431-6343. Open daily 11:30am-2am. Cash only.) Check out **The Juicery ❷**, 51 Hanover St., which serves an entirely organic, vegetarian menu. Grab your juice or Peaches & Cream smoothie ($4.75) and head to the streets; the restaurant doesn't have much seating. (☎603-431-0693. Open M-Th 9am-5pm, F-Sa 9am-6pm, Su 10am-4pm. AmEx/D/MC/V.) The **Ceres Bakery ❶**, 51 Penhallow St., off Congress St., serves creative sandwiches, like the Asian marinated tofu ($5) on freshly baked bread. Soup offerings ($3.50) change daily. (☎603-436-6518. Open M-F 7am-5pm, Sa 7am-4pm. Cash only.)

☗ ACCOMMODATIONS

Portsmouth isn't budget-friendly when it comes to finding a place to hang your hat. Cheaper options can be found at the rotary where U.S. 1, I-95, and Rte. 4 meet. **Motel 6 ❸**, located an easy 5min. drive from Portsmouth, offers clean rooms and an outdoor pool. (Take Maplewood Ave. north to the rotary, and make a right onto Rte. 4. Get off at Exit 1; the motel is on your right. ☎603-334-6606. Singles M-Th and Su $66, F-Sa $86. AmEx/D/MC/V.) Take the rotary to U.S. 1 Bypass S and you'll find the **Meadowbrook Inn ❹**. The rooms are extremely large, with a couch and coffee table, as well as microwave, fridge, and TV. (☎603-436-2700 or 800-370-2727. Continental breakfast included. Rooms M-Th and Su $89, F-Sa $109. AmEx/D/MC/V.) An alternative for campers is **Camp Eaton ❶**, in York Harbor, about 10 mi. north of Portsmouth off U.S. 1. The wooded sites are a bit expensive for a campground but have immaculate bathrooms and well-kept grounds. (☎207-363-3424. Take U.S. 1 N into York village. Make a right onto York St., and follow it to the beach. Open May-Oct. Tent sites $41; RV sites $56. MC/V.)

☖ APPROACHING PORTLAND: 51 MILES
From Portsmouth, follow **I-95 N** to Portland. There is a $1.75 toll just after you enter Maine. **Exit 7** takes you into downtown Portland.

The Pine Tree State
MAINE
Welcomes You!

PORTLAND

Tucked between forested land and a wild sea, Portland is the largest port town in Maine. The city thrives as an urban center in an otherwise rural area, with a mixture of industry, arts, and well-preserved relics of colonial times. In summer, the streets fill with the exuberant sounds of parades and festivals. Meanwhile, laughter can be heard long into the night in the old port district, where pubs beckon the city's spirited youth to set even the coldest night aflame.

VITAL STATS

Population: 64,000

Visitor Info: Visitor Information Center, 245 Commercial St. (☎207-772-5800), between Union and Cross St. Open M-F 8am-5pm, Sa 10am-5pm.

Internet Access: Portland Public Library, 5 Monument Sq. (☎207-871-1700). Open M, W, F 9am-6pm; Tu and Th noon-9pm; Sa 9am-5pm. Free.

Parking: There's a garage by the public library (1st 30min. free, each additional 30min. $0.50 with library validation). Another garage is on Pearl St., between Fore and Milk St. (1st hr. $2, each additional hr. $1.25).

Post Office: 400 Congress St. (☎207-871-8464). Open M-F 8am-7pm, Sa 9am-1pm. **Postal Code:** 04101.

☗ GETTING AROUND

Downtown Portland rests in the middle of a peninsula jutting into the Casco Bay, along **Congress St.**, between **State St.** and **Pearl St.** A few blocks south of Congress St. along the waterfront lies the **Old Port,** between Commercial and Middle St. These two districts contain most of the city's sights and attractions. **I-295** (off I-95) forms the northwestern boundary of city. It's best to park your car and navigate the downtown area on foot.

👁 SIGHTS

PORTLAND MUSEUM OF ART. Along with several galleries of temporary exhibits, the museum has an excellent collection of Impressionist and post-Impressionist art, including works by Degas, Monet, and Picasso. *(7 Congress Sq. ☎207-775-6148; www.portlandmuseum.org. Open Memorial Day to Columbus Day M-Th and Sa-Su 10am-5pm, F 10am-9pm; Columbus Day to Memorial Day Tu-Su 10am-5pm. Tours daily 2pm, F also 6:30pm. $10, students and seniors $8, ages 6-17 $4. F 5-9pm free.)*

VICTORIA MANSION. Built in 1860 by a luxury hotelier, this mansion has a free-flying staircase, chairs with cloven hooves, and a portrait of cupid that looks suspiciously like the owner. Guides lead 45min. tours through the home, which still has 90% of its original furnishings. *(109 Danforth St., off High St. ☎207-772-4841; www.victoriamansion.org. $10, ages 6-17 $3. Open May-Oct. M-Sa 10am-4pm, Su 1-5pm. Tours every 30min.)*

PARKS. It's worth your time to take the scenic detour to the functioning **Portland Head Light** in **Fort Williams Park.** Families play on the large green spaces of the park, which offers numerous views of the rocky shoreline and nearby islands, including a lighthouse off the coast. Inside is the **Port Head Light Museum,** with a timeline that documents the history of the lighthouse. Unfortunately, there is no access to the tower. *(From State or York St., go south along Rte. 77 to Cape Elizabeth, turn left at the flashing signal onto Shore Rd., and proceed to the park. Open sunrise-sunset. Museum open June-Oct. daily 10am-4pm; Nov.-Dec. and Apr.-May Sa-Su 10am-4pm. $2, ages 6-18 $1.)* Across the Casco Bay Bridge, **Two Lights State Park** park is a great place to picnic or walk along the shimmering ocean. *(From State or York St., go south along Rte. 77 to Cape Elizabeth. ☎207-799-5871; www.state.me.us/doc/parks. $3, children $1.)*

PORTLAND OBSERVATORY. Not only is it the last maritime signal tower in the US, at 86 ft. it's also the best view in town. Tours provide a detailed history and an enthusiastic explanation of signaling in general. *(138 Congress St. ☎207-774-5561; www.portlandlandmarks.org. Open daily 10am-5pm; last tour 4:40pm. $5, ages 6-16 $3, under 6 free.)*

SHIPYARD BREWING CO. While it takes about eight days to brew a batch of beer at the Shipyard Brewing Co., it will only take 30min. to tour the brewery and try the free sample. *(86 Newbury St. ☎207-761-0807. Open in summer M-F 3-5pm, Sa-Su noon-5pm; in winter M-F 3-5pm, Sa noon-5pm. Tours every 30min. Free.)*

MUSEUM OF AFRICAN CULTURE. Those interested in African art will enjoy the museum's headdresses and spirit masks, some of which are hundreds of years old. The two-room museum also showcases modern-day black-and-white photographs and film screenings. *(122 Spring St. ☎207-871-7188; www.tribalartmuseum.com. Film screenings F 5pm. Open Tu-F 10:30am-4pm, Sa 12:30-4pm. Suggested donation $5.)*

OFFSHORE ISLANDS. These rocky islands are ideal for an afternoon of hiking or biking. **Casco Bay Lines,** on State Pier near the corner of Commercial and Franklin St., runs ferries daily to **Long Island,** where waves crash on an unpopulated beach, and **Peaks Island,** home to tidepools and wooded areas. The **Sunset Cruise** takes travelers past several islands as night falls. *(☎207-774-7871; www.cascobaylines.com. Long Island M-F 5am-9:30pm, Sa 6:30am-9:30pm, Su 7:45am-9:30pm. Round-trip $8.25, seniors and ages 5-9 $4.10. Peaks Island daily 5:45am-11:30pm. $6.25/$3.25. Sunset Cruise $13/$6.50.)* On Peaks Island, **Brad's Recycled Bike Shop** rents bikes. *(115 Island Ave. ☎207-766-5631. $5 per hr., $14 per day. Open daily 10am-6pm.)*

🍴 FOOD

Portland's harbor overflows with the fruits of the ocean, but non-aquatic and vegetarian fare isn't hard to find.

Gilbert's Chowder House, 92 Commercial St. (☎207-871-5636). This restaurant may have swordfish on the walls, but it's another aquatic animal that gets the praise. Make sure to try the clam chowder (small $4.50; bread bowl $7.75), and if you're still hungry, there are clam cakes ($2.50), clam strips ($7), and, well, clam everything. Open daily 11am-11pm. AmEx/D/MC/V. ❷

Federal Spice, 225 Federal St. (☎207-774-6404), just off Congress St. Serves up vegetarian wraps and soft tacos, like the Mediterranean veggie ($4.75) and Thai red curry tofu ($5.25). The small

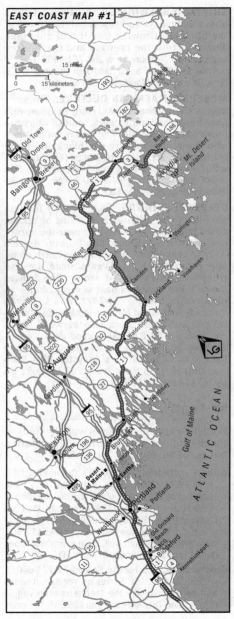

EAST COAST MAP #1

EAST COAST

shop also features local artists and local brewskies. Open M-F 11am-9pm, Sa 11am-6pm. Cash only. ❶

Flatbread Company, 72 Commercial St. (☎207-772-8777). Organic pizza is the specialty and the view is a combination of ocean and parking garage. The sun-dried tomato flatbread (half $8.25, whole $15), baked in a wood-fired clay oven, is ample distraction. Open M-Th and Su 11:30am-10pm, F-Sa 11:30am-10:30pm. AmEx/MC/V. ❸

Becky's Diner, 390 Commercial St. (☎207-773-7070). Serves diner-style breakfasts, like bacon, eggs, and toast ($4.75), 362½ days a year until 4pm. Becky's also serves burgers and sandwiches, but be sure to save room for a slice of pie ($3.75) on the swivel chairs. Open daily 4am-9pm. AmEx/D/MC/V. ❶

⚑ ACCOMMODATIONS

Portland has some inexpensive accommodations during the winter, but prices jump steeply during the summer, especially on weekends. Standard chain motels can be found off Rte. 25 about 10min. west of town.

The Inn at St. John, (☎207-773-6481 or 800-636-9127), 939 Congress St., is surrounded by fast-food joints and gas stations, but its old-fashioned upscale decor makes it an elegant choice. The spacious Victorian rooms include fridge, continental breakfast, and Wi-Fi. Rooms in summer M-Th and Su $85-115, F-Sa $115-175; in winter $55-65/$80-125. AmEx/D/MC/V. ❺

Motel 6, (☎207-775-0111), 1 Riverside St., is among the cheapest of the chains. The basic rooms are clean and near downtown. Singles M-Th and Su $64, F-Sa $80; doubles $70/$86. AmEx/D/MC/V. ❸

Wassamki Springs, (☎207-839-4276; www.wassamkisprings.com), 56 Saco St., in Scarborough. Take I-95 to Exit 7A, then take Rte. 22 W to Saco St. This is the closest campground to Portland. There are over 100 sites clustered around a lake encircled by sandy beaches. Laundry, volleyball and basketball courts, and free weekend activities are all included. Reservations recommended July-Aug. Open May to mid-Oct. Sites mid-June to Sept. $39, with hookup $41; May to mid-June and Sept.-Oct. $22/$24. MC/V. ❷

♪ ENTERTAINMENT

Signs for theatrical productions are ubiquitous, and schedules are available at the visitors center. Info on Portland's jazz, blues, and club scene packs the *Casco Bay Weekly* (www.cascobayweekly.com) and *FACE*, both of which are free. Traditionally held the first Sunday in June, the **Old Port Festival** (☎207-772-6868) fills the blocks from Federal to Commercial St. with as many as 50,000 people enjoying free public entertainment, including a battle of the bands and parade. Every Thursday afternoon in summer, the **Alive at Five** music series in Monument Sq. offers working people a reason to make it through the day. (☎207-772-6828. July-Aug. Th 5-7:30pm.) On Friday afternoons in summer, the **Weekday Music Series** (☎207-772-6828; July-Aug. F noon) has a more low-key selection of bands that play at noon in Post Office Sq. between Middle and Exchange St.

☒ NIGHTLIFE

The Old Port area, known as "the strip"—especially **Fore St.** between Union and Exchange St.—livens up after dark. **Brian Boru,** 57 Center St., provides a mellow Irish pub scene with live music, mainly covers of 90s and reggae, on the weekends. (☎207-780-1506. Su $2.50 pints. Open daily 11am-1am. AmEx/D/MC/V.) **Gritty MacDuff's,** 396 Fore St., brews its own beer (pints $4) and entertains a largely local crowd with live jazz, blues, and rock. (☎207-772-2739. Th pitchers $9. Tu and Su live music. Open daily 11:30am-1am. AmEx/D/MC/V.) **Una Wine Bar & Lounge,** 505 Fore St., mixes speciality martinis ($7-9) for the older, sophisticated crowd. The bar also serves tapas in a low-key environment. (☎207-828-0300. Open M-Sa 4:30pm-1am, Su 6pm-1am. AmEx/MC/V.)

☒ APPROACHING CAMDEN: 80 MILES

Take **I-295 N** to **U.S. 1** to **Exit 28.** Head left on the **Blue Star Memorial Hwy.** After 30 mi., get onto **U.S. 1,** which becomes **Atlantic Hwy.** Make a left onto **Camden Rd.,** and head into town.

☒ DETOUR
EARTHA
2 Delorme Dr., in Yarmouth, off I-295.

The **world's largest rotating globe** and the largest printed representation of the earth, Eartha was finished in July of 1998, stealing the title of world's largest from a globe in Wellesley, MA. Forty-two feet in diameter and weighing 5600

lb., the globe has a circumference of 130 ft. and rotates on an axis at 23.5°, just like the real thing. (Open M-Th 9:30am-6pm, F-Sa 9:30am-7pm, Su 9:30am-6pm. Free.)

☒ DETOUR
THE DESERT OF MAINE
95 Desert Rd. In Freeport, 2 mi. off I-295, at Exit 20.

Nestled between Maine's lush forests and its famous coast is . . . a desert? Maine's only desert is actually the result of the Tuttle family's mishandling of their family farm through overgrazing, overforesting, and neglecting to rotate crops. These poor techniques caused massive soil erosion that exposed a hidden glacial sand deposit that spread to become the Desert of Maine—complete with (plastic) camels. A narrated trolley tour takes visitors out on the dunes, while the **Barn Museum** has sand art and samples from around the globe. Visitors can also **camp ❶** on the forested part of the property. (☎207-865-6962; www.desertofmaine.com. Open daily 8:30am-5:30pm. Tours 9am-4:30pm. $8.75, ages 13-16 $6.25, ages 5-12 $4.25. Sites $21, full hookup $36. A/C units $2. AmEx/D/MC/V.)

CAMDEN

Camden is chock-full of Teva-clad hikers, bikers, and kayakers taking advantage of the nearby outdoor attractions. The town's outdoor activities are its largest draw, but the downtown area, full of restaurants, shops, and t-shirt vendors, makes for an enjoyable afternoon.

VITAL STATS

Population: 5200

Visitor Info: Camden-Rockport-Lincolnville Chamber of Commerce (☎207-236-4404; www.camdenme.org), at the public landing. Open mid-May to mid-Oct. M-F 9am-5pm, Sa 10am-5pm, Su 10am-4pm; mid-Oct. to mid-May M-F 9am-5pm.

Internet Access: Camden Public Library, 55 Main St. (☎207-236-3440; www.camden.lib.me.us). Open M, W and F-Sa 9:30am-5pm, Tu and Th 9:30am-8pm, Su 1-5pm. Free.

Parking: Free 2hr. parking is available on Main St.

Post Office: 28 Chestnut St. (☎207-236-3570). Open M-F 8:30am-5pm, Sa 9am-noon. **Postal Code:** 04843.

⌕ GETTING AROUND. U.S. 1 heads right into town, becoming **Main St.** Most restaurants and shops lie around Main St. and **Elm St.**, near the large public green.

◙ SIGHTS. Camden Hills State Park is home to Mt. Battie, an 800 ft. hill popular with hikers for its gorgeous view. The park includes 25 mi. of trails, as well as a scenic road up Mt. Battie. (☎207-236-3109. Open sunrise-sunset. $3, ages 5-11 $1.) Intrepid paddlers can also sea kayak in the harbor or take a tour, offered by **Maine Sports.** The company rents boats out of its store off U.S. 1, south of town in Rockport, while tours leave from Camden Harbor. (☎207-236-7120 or 800-722-0826. Open daily 9am-8pm. Single kayaks $25-40 per day; tandems $30-50. Canoes $30 per day. 2hr. tour $35, ages 10-15 $30, 4hr. tour $75/$60.) **Day tours** are available on a variety of boats at the public dock and range from $20-30 in price. Times are on display at the Chamber of Commerce, but most boat owners sit at the public landing displaying their signs. (*Schooner Olad* ☎207-236-2323. *Betselma* ☎207-236-4446. *Surprise* ☎207-236-4687.) The **Maine State Ferry Service,** 5 mi. north of Camden in Lincolnville, runs to quaint and residential **Islesboro Island.** (☎207-789-5611. 30min. 5-9 per day; last return trip 4:30pm. Round-trip $6, with bike $11.75. Car and driver $17.50.) The ferry also has an agency at 517A Main St., on U.S. 1 in Rockland, which runs to Vinalhaven and North Haven. (☎207-596-2202. Round-trip $12, with bike $23.50; car and driver $34.50.)

◪⌂ FOOD AND ACCOMMODATIONS. At the ▨**Camden Deli ❷**, 37 Main St., patrons enjoy gourmet sandwiches like the meaty Islander (roast beef, turkey, cheddar, horseradish; $7.25) and the artichoke-and-spinach wrap ($6.25). Two seating areas offer gorgeous ocean views. (☎207-236-8343. Open daily 7am-10pm. AmEx/D/MC/V.) Moose heads and swordfish cover the walls at **Cappy's Chowder House ❸**, 1 Main St., where the clam chowder is served in a mug for $7. (☎207-236-2254. Open daily 11am-11pm. MC/V.)

The downtown area is full of expensive B&Bs, but less expensive options are available on U.S. 1, just outside of town. Less than a mile north of Camden, **Beloin's on the Maine Coast ❸**, 254 Belfast Rd., offers travelers spacious rooms with a view, as well as beach access. (☎207-236-3262; www.beloins.com. Open mid-May to mid-Oct. Rooms mid-May to June $56; July-Sept. $80; Sept. to mid-Oct. $64. AmEx/D/MC/V.) **Camden Hills State Park ❶**, 1¼ mi. north of town on U.S. 1, is almost always full in summer. Be sure to make a reservation for one of the 107 wooded sites. (☎207-236-3109, reservations 207-287-3824. Reception 7am-10pm. Open mid-May to mid-Oct. Sites $20. AmEx/D/MC/V.)

⌖ APPROACHING BELFAST: 20 MILES
From Camden, take **U.S. 1 N** into Belfast.

BELFAST

This small town has a funky feel, with a co-op, countless cafes, and a gallery-filled downtown area. Like Camden, it pushes its outdoor opportunities, but it also celebrates its history as a shipbuilding center. Belfast is the kind of town that will win you over without even trying that hard.

VITAL STATS
Population: 6400
Visitor Info: Belfast Information Center, 15 Main St. (☎207-338-5900). Open July-Aug. M-Th 10am-6pm, F-Su 10am-8pm; Sept.-June daily 10am-6pm.
Internet Access: Belfast Public Library, 106 High St. (☎207-338-3884; www.belfast.lib.me.us). Open M 9:30am-8pm, Tu and Th-F 9:30am-6pm, W noon-8pm, Sa 10am-2pm. Free.
Parking: Free parking behind the visitors center.
Post Office: 1 Franklin St. (☎207-338-1820). Open M-F 8am-5pm, Sa 8am-noon. **Postal Code:** 04915.

⌕ GETTING AROUND. Belfast sits at the mouth of the **Passagasswakeag River,** on Penobscot Bay. **Main St.** and **High St.** are the main commercial and shopping streets in downtown Belfast; their intersection forms the center of town.

◙ SIGHTS. A visitor could spend an entire afternoon at the **Penobscot Marine Museum,** at U.S. 1 and Church St. in Searsport. The museum has 13 buildings, including four historic homes, several boats, and a large collection of nautical paintings. Be sure to check out "lobstah," an exhibit dedicated to Maine's favorite crustacean. (☎207-548-2529; www.penobscotmarinemuseum.org. Open Memorial Day to late Oct. M-Sa 10am-5pm, Su noon-5pm; last entry 4pm. $8, seniors $6, ages 7-15 $3.) North of Belfast on U.S. 1, **Moose Point State Park,** 310 W. Main St., has 2 mi. of hiking trails overlooking the Penobscot Bay. (☎207-548-2882. Open May-Oct. sunrise-sunset. Entrance fee $2, 5-11 $1.) Constructed in the mid-1800s using granite from nearby Mt. Waldo, **Fort Knox** was part of a plan to protect the Penobscot River against British invasion. Info panels guide visitors through the **Fort Knox State Historic Site,** from the storage vaults to the powder magazine. (Take U.S. 1 N to Rte. 178; the fort is the 1st right. ☎207-469-6553. Open May-Oct. 9am-sunset. $3, ages 5-12 $1.)

▧ FOOD AND ACCOMMODATIONS. The **▧Belfast Co-op ❷,** 123 High St., has delicious organic fare like the Greek salad ($7) and grilled-chicken pesto sandwich ($7). The store attracts an outdoorsy, relaxed crowd of locals who mingle in the cafe. (☎207-338-2532. Open daily 8am-7pm. AmEx/D/MC/V.) The **Lookout Bar and Grill ❷,** 37B Front St., sports a marine theme and a casual bar atmosphere. Try the onion teriyaki burger ($8), or shoot some pool with locals. (☎207-388-8900; www.thelookoutpub.com. Open daily 11:30am-1am. Kitchen closes 10pm. MC/V.)

Belfast's historic B&Bs occupy the gorgeous houses downtown, but rates are over $100 during the summer. An accommodations pamphlet is available at the visitors center downtown. The **Seascape Motel and Cottages ❹,** 2202 Searsport Ave. off Rte. 1, provides one of the best deals in the area. The well-furnished rooms include continental breakfast and use of the heated pool. (☎207-338-2130 or 800-477-0786; www.seascapemotel.com. Rooms M-Th and Su $89, F-Sa $99. MC/V.) A few miles north of town, the **Yankee Clipper Motel ❹** has spacious rooms complete with an easy-chair, A/C, and cable TV. (☎207-338-2220 or 877-338-2220. Rooms M-Th and Su $70, F-Sa $80-90. AmEx/D/MC/V.) **Searsport Shores Camping Resort ❷,** 209 W. Main St., in Searsport, has ¼ mi. of gorgeous beach, as well as laundry facilities and a video arcade. (☎207-548-6059. Tent sites $25-42; RV sites $42-52; cabins $80. MC/V.)

▨ APPROACHING ELLSWORTH: 27 MILES From Belfast, take **U.S. 1 N** to Ellsworth.

ELLSWORTH

Fuel and stock up here—this town, the largest between Bar Harbor and Bangor, is more of a pit stop than an attraction. The **Stanwood Wildlife Sanctuary,** 289 High St., was built in 1958 as a memorial for Cordelia J. Stanwood, a leading ornithologist and wildlife photographer. The homestead on the property was placed on the National Registry of Historic Places in 1973, ensuring that no urban expansion would ever invade in the area. The 165 acres of woodland are home to wild birds. (☎207-667-8460. Open May-Oct. daily 10am-4pm. Open year-round. Donations accepted.)

On your right as you drive uphill out of town, **China Hill ❷,** 301 High St., has everything from lo mein ($7) to cheeseburgers served with fried rice ($5.25). The lunch specials include an entree, egg roll, and fried rice for $4-6. (☎207-667-5308. All-you-can-eat buffet $11. Open M-Th and Su 11am-9pm, F-Sa 11am-10pm. AmEx/D/MC/V.) Those in need of a good night's sleep should consider the **Ellsworth Motel ❸,** 24 High St., an affordable place to stay on the main road. The cheerful yellow building has a pool and comfortable rooms with TV. (☎207-667-4424. Rooms $54-64. MC/V.)

◪ DETOUR
STANWOOD WILDLIFE SANCTUARY
289 High St. In Ellsworth, on U.S. 1

The **Stanwood Wildlife Sanctuary** was built in 1958 as a memorial for Cordelia J. Stanwood, who spent her life establishing herself as a leading ornithologist and wildlife photographer. The homestead on the property was placed on the National Registry of Historic Places in 1973, ensuring no urban expansion would ever invade in the area. The 165 acres of woodland are home to owls and other wildfowl. (☎207-667-8460. Sanctuary open May-Oct. daily 10am-4pm. Trails and grounds open year-round.)

◪ DETOUR
GREAT MAINE LUMBERJACK SHOW
In Trenton, off Rte. 3

In the 1870s, Maine was one of America's important logging centers. Lumberjacks used to challenge each other to the "Olympics of the Forest," an event the Great Maine Lumberjack Show reenacts nightly during the summer. As seen on ESPN, the 14 events include axe throwing, log rolling, and cross-cut sawing. The show also offers hands-on activities for kids to try. Don't miss the **Lumber-**

Jills, a group of women who keep up with (and sometimes outlast) their male counterparts. (☎207-667-0067; "log" onto www.mainelumberjack.com. Shows mid-June to Labor Day daily 7pm. $8.25, ages 4-11 $6.25, seniors $7.75. Box office opens 6pm.)

APPROACHING MT. DESERT ISLAND: 20 MILES
From Ellsworth, head south on **High St.** for nearly 3 mi. This will turn into **Bar Harbor Rd.,** which you can follow to the island.

MT. DESERT ISLAND

There's no better place to end your roadtrip than Mt. Desert Island, where gorgeous sights meet a hopping small town. Acadia National Park is easily the most beautiful place on the East Coast, and allows roadtrippers to stretch their legs on trails overlooking lakes and mountains.

GETTING AROUND

Mt. Desert Island is shaped roughly like a lobster claw, 16 mi. long and 13 mi. wide. The claw reaches from the north to the south and is dotted with small towns. The island's only links to the mainland are **Rte. 3,** which runs down the arm of the claw from the north, and the vehicle **ferry** to Yarmouth, Nova Scotia, which leaves from Bar Harbor. (☎888-249-7245; www.catferry.com. $63 one-way.) The island's main roads are Rte. 3, and **Rte. 102,** which traces the western drive. To the east, on Rte. 3, lies **Bar Harbor,** the island's largest town. **Seal Harbor,** also on Rte. 3, sits on the southeast corner of the island. South on Rte. 198, near the cleft of the claw, is **Northeast Harbor.** Across Somes Sound on Rte. 102 is ruggedly scenic **Southwest Harbor.** At the southern tip of the island, on the west half of the claw, sits the town of **Bass Harbor,** and up the western coast on Rte. 102 lie the hamlets of **Seal Cove, Pretty Marsh,** and **Somesville.**

ACADIA NATIONAL PARK

Roughly half of Mt. Desert Island plus several other small islands constitute Acadia, New England's only national park. The park has activities that appeal to a wide range of visitors. Park Loop Rd. allows you to see the vistas without leaving your car, while challenging trails allow intrepid hikers to climb the cliffs. Whether you're a hiker, biker, runner, or watcher, Acadia is a sublimely beautiful place to visit.

VITAL STATS
Area: 48,000 acres
Visitor Info: Hulls Cove Visitors Center (☎207-288-3338), off Rte. 3. Open mid-June to late Aug. daily 8am-6pm; mid-May to mid-June and mid-Sept. to Oct. daily 9am-5pm. **Park Headquarters** (☎207-288-3338), on Rte. 233., 3 mi. west of Bar Harbor, near Eagle Lake. Provides visitor info during the low season. Open M-F 8am-4:30pm.
Gateway Town: Bar Harbor (p. 191)
Fees: 7-day pass $20 per vehicle, $5 per motorcycle.

GETTING AROUND

Though visitors are welcome to drive into Acadia, most of the beauty of the place is off-limits to cars, thanks to John D. Rockefeller. Fearing the island would one day be overrun by automobiles, millionaire Rockefeller funded the creation of 51 mi. of carriage roads, which are now accessible only to hikers and mountain bikes. The one-way **Park Loop Rd.** is the only car access to the eastern area of the park. The **Island Explorer** is a free shuttle system consisting of eight different routes that runs from late June to October and allows you to dump the car and explore the island.

SIGHTS

A good way to see Acadia is to drive the Park Loop Rd. About 4 mi. south of Bar Harbor on Rte. 3, Park Loop Rd. runs along the shore of the island, where waves crash against vertical cliffs. The road eventually makes a 27 mi. circuit of the eastern section of the island and passes by several premier hiking trails. Begin your drive on Park Loop Rd. at the Hulls Cove Visitors Center by turning left onto the one-way road to Sand Beach. The first stop is **Sieur de Monts Spring,** where over 300 floral species thrive in the Wild Gardens of Acadia. The original **Abbe Museum,** built in honor of the native Wabanaki people, is also here, though it pales in comparison to the newer branch in Bar Harbor. (☎207-288-3519. Open late May to mid-Oct. 9am-4pm. $2, children $1.) The next stop is **Sand Beach,** the only sandy beach in the otherwise rocky park. The water may look enticing, but the

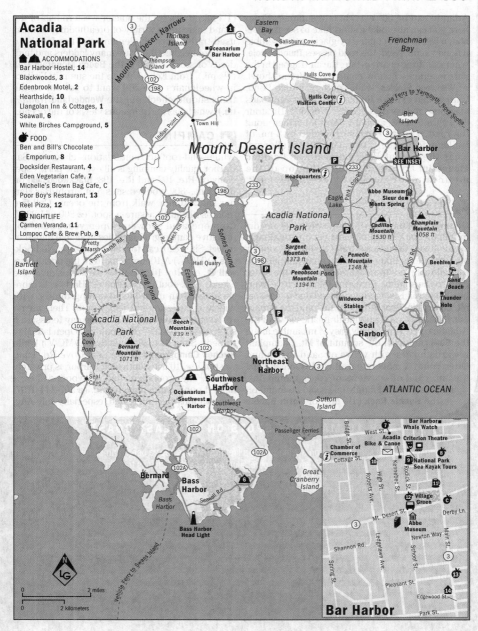

Acadia National Park

ACCOMMODATIONS
Bar Harbor Hostel, **14**
Blackwoods, **3**
Edenbrook Motel, **2**
Hearthside, **10**
Llangolan Inn & Cottages, **1**
Seawall, **6**
White Birches Campground, **5**

FOOD
Ben and Bill's Chocolate Emporium, **8**
Docksider Restaurant, **4**
Eden Vegetarian Cafe, **7**
Michelle's Brown Bag Cafe, **C**
Poor Boy's Restaurant, **13**
Reel Pizza, **12**

NIGHTLIFE
Carmen Veranda, **11**
Lompoc Cafe & Brew Pub, **9**

Atlantic can be 50° even in late summer. From here you can also take a short hike to see the **Beehive,** a 520 ft. hill sculpted by glaciers to resemble a honeycomb. Next, the road passes **Thunder Hole,** where, at three-quarters tide, the air trapped in the narrow granite hollow emits a thunderous howl. At **Wildwood Stables,** ½ mi. south of Jordan Pond, tourists can explore Rockefeller's carriage roads via horse and carriage. (☎207-276-3622. 1hr. tour $16, ages 6-12 $8, ages 2-5 $4.50.). Farther along the road is **Jordan Pond,** surrounded by 3 mi. of trails; unfortunately, no swimming is allowed. Near the end of Park Loop Rd. is **Cadillac Mountain;** try the detour to the top of the mountain for the best view in the park.

⚑ HIKING

Getting out of the car is the only way to see Acadia in full; the park is full of short yet breathtakingly scenic hikes. ⚑**Precipice Trail** (1½ mi.), a popular and strenuous hike, has iron rungs and ladders that allow hikers to make their way up the sheer cliffs to the summit. Peregrine falcons circle overhead; the trail is sometimes closed due to nesting. **Mt. Champlain/Bear Brook** (2¼ mi.) and the strenuous **Beehive** (¾ mi.), provide dramatic views of the Atlantic coast. A relatively easy ½ mi. amble along the **Bowl** trail from the summit of Mt. Champlain rewards hikers with views of Sand Beach and Otter Point. A moderate trail circles **Jordan Pond** (3¼ mi.) and offers views of lakes, mountains, and forests. Good family hikes can be found on the **Bubble Rock** (1¼ mi.) or **North Bubble**

(1¼ mi.) trails. On the quieter western half of the island there are a variety of breathtaking and less used trails. More challenging and not for those afraid of heights (there are many ladders and hundreds of stone steps) is the **Beech Mountain Trail** (1½ mi.), from Echo Lake to the summit. Visitors in wheelchairs who still want to get out on the trails should check out the **Wonderland Trail** (½ mi.), which has and gorgeous views of the ocean.

⚑ CAMPING

While solid-roof accommodations cluster in Bar Harbor, quality camping is all over the park, especially on Rte. 102 and Rte. 198. **Blackwoods ❶,** on Rte. 3, has 300 wooded sites 5 mi. from Bar Harbor and a 10min. walk from the ocean. Call five months ahead to assure a spot. (☎800-365-2267. Coin-operated showers. Open year-round for primitive camping; all facilities available mid-Mar. to Oct. Sites $20; call for rates Nov.-Apr. No hookups. D/MC/V.) A 10min. walk from the ocean, **Seawall ❶,** off Rte. 102A on the western side of the island, 4 mi. south of Southwest Harbor, is more secluded than most island campgrounds, with widely spaced sites and deep woods. There are no reservations, so come early in the day to assure a spot. (☎800-365-2267. No hookups. Open late May to Sept. Sites $14; RV sites $20. D/MC/V.) **White Birches Campground ❶,** on Seal Cove Rd. 1 mi. west of Rte. 102, in Southwest Harbor, is privately owned. The grounds include 40 wooded sites, a heated pool, and a playground. (☎207-244-3797. Reservations recommended, especially July-Aug.

TOP 10 MAKEOUT SPOTS ON THE EAST COAST

You and that special someone are on the roadtrip of a lifetime. Maybe you've been married for years; maybe you met on the side of the road and gave each other a jump. Regardless, lovers traveling the East Coast will find miles of romantic beaches and stirring sunsets. Here, distilled for your convenience, are the ten best places to lock lips on the Eastern seaboard.

10. Sunset Celebration, Key West, Florida. There's nothing more romantic than snuggling with your honey as an Elvis impersonator shakes his butt.

9. WaterFire, Providence, Rhode Island. You think candlelight is romantic? Try 100 bonfires.

8. Rockport, Massachusetts. As you're looking out at Motif No. 1, shack up and form a popular motif of your own. Ever done it at a place called Bearskin Neck? Neither had we.

7. Breakwater Jetty, Provincetown, Massachusetts. The wind blows through your hair, salty water laps at the jetty, and there's a gorgeous view of the Cape. And hey, you might even catch a glimpse of a speedo-clad

[the local story]

Open mid-May to mid-Oct. June-Sept. sites $27, with water and electricity $30; mid-May to mid-June and Sept.-Oct. $24/$27. MC/V.)

◪ APPROACHING BAR HARBOR: 0 MILES
Exit at the park's western entrance on **Rte. 233.** You are in Bar Harbor.

BAR HARBOR

Bar Harbor serves as a gateway town for visitors to Acadia, but it has plenty to offer itself. During the summer, the downtown area is crowded with visitors licking ice-cream cones and checking out the terrific galleries. Though Bar Harbor is full of B&Bs, a hostel makes the town accessible to the budget traveler as well. It's a small town, to be sure, but Bar Harbor has plenty of museums, shops, and bars to keep visitors happy—especially those at the end of the road.

VITAL STATS

Population: 4800

Visitor Info: Chamber of Commerce, 93 Cottage St. (☎207-288-5103). Open June-Oct. M-F 8am-6pm, Sa-Su 10am-6pm; Nov.-May daily 8am-5pm.

Internet Access: Jesup Memorial Library, 34 Mt. Desert St. (☎207-288-4245). Open Tu and Th-Sa 10am-5pm, W 10am-7pm. Free.

Post Office: 55 Cottage St. (☎207-288-3122). Open M-F 8am-4:30pm, Sa 9am-noon. **Postal Code:** 04609.

◪ GETTING AROUND

Bar Harbor's streets are all state highways, most of which are known by other names within the town itself. **Rte. 3** runs through Bar Harbor, becoming **Mt. Desert St.** and then runs along the water as **Main St.** On the waterfront, **Cottage St.** and **West St.** run parallel to Mt. Desert St. Both Mt. Desert St. and Cottage St. are home to shops, restaurants, and bars.

◉ SIGHTS

If you're interested in the Wabanaki, Maine's first Native American inhabitants, the **Abbe Museum,** 26 Mt. Desert St., is the place to go. The museum showcases all types of creative expression, from paintings and beaded purses to arrowheads. (☎207-288-3519; www.abbemuseum.org. Open May-Oct. daily 9am-5pm. $6; ages 6-15 $2.) In summer, the historic **Criterion Theatre,** 35 Cottage St., hosts mainstream movies, puppet shows, and the occasional concert. The theater, constructed in 1937, has a floating balcony complete with bar. (☎207-288-3441. 2 movie showings nightly. Box office opens 30min. before show. $7.50, seniors $6.50, under 12 $5.50; balcony seats $8.50. Live shows $12-25. Puppet shows $4.) The local piers, at the junction of Main and West St., are starting points for a variety of excursions into Frenchman Bay. The **Margaret Todd** is a four-masted schooner that runs three daily tours of the bay. (☎207-288-4585; www.downeastwind-

---

6. John Pennekamp State Park, Key Largo, Florida. Coral reefs, mangroves, and brilliant blue skies make this a gorgeous spot. Though dusk is popular with lovers, it's also when the noseeums come out for love bites.

5. Savannah, Georgia. Savannah's 21 squares provide green, secluded spots for a midday tête-a-tête. Beware the camera-laden trolley tours.

4. Mystic, Connecticut. Julia Roberts did it. So it must be good.

3. Assateague Island, Virginia. Wild horses roam free along the coast, and chicks totally dig that, you stud. Watch out, they bite.

2. Kitty Hawk, North Carolina. Feel like you're walking on the clouds at the spot where the Wright brothers took to the sky.

1. Lucy the Elephant, Margate, New Jersey. Duh—it's a giant elephant.

Honorable Mention: Atlantic City, New Jersey. Because this gambling town is hooker-free

jammer.com. $32, seniors $30, under 12 $22.) **Bar Harbor Whale Watch,** 1 West St., sets sail several times a day for 3-4hr. tours and offers a refund if no whales are sighted. (☎207-288-2386; www.whalesrus.com. $49, ages 6-14 $26, 5 and under $8.) **Beal & Bunker** runs ferries from the Northeast Harbor town dock to Great Cranberry Island. (☎207-244-3575. Open late June to early Sept. daily 7:30am-6pm; hours vary in winter. 15min.; 6 per day. $16, ages 3-12 $10.)

The largest of two **Mount Desert Oceanarium** locations lies in South Harbor, off Main St. at the end of Clark Point Rd. The hands-on displays feature sea stars, urchins, sea cucumbers, anemones, and other creatures. The second oceanarium is **Hull's Cove Oceanarium,** 1351 Rte. 3, just north of town, and has a lobster hatchery and museum exhibits dedicated to the crustacean. Guess the weight of their "big lobster" and win that many pounds of lobster meat. (☎207-244-7330; Hull's Cove ☎207-288-5005. Open M-Sa mid-May to mid-Oct. 9am-5pm. Oceanarium $8, ages 4-12 $6; Hull's Cove $12/$7; combination ticket $15/$10.)

OUTDOORS

Along the **Shore Path** are some of the area's largest waterfront "cottages," most dating from the late 1800s or early 1900s. These homes recall the gilded age of Bar Harbor, when only the most rich and famous inhabited the island. Those on foot can head to **Bar Island** at low tide, when a gravel path with tidepools, accessible via Bridge St., is exposed for 2-3hr. (Take Bridge St. from West St.) For those who want to bike in the park or navigate the harbor, **Acadia Bike & Canoe,** 48 Cottage St., has the goods. The company also leads day and overnight sea kayaking tours. (☎207-288-9605 or 800-526-8615. Open May-Oct. daily 8am-6pm. Mountain bikes $18 per day; road bikes $24 per day. Single kayaks $45 per day, tandems $55.) **National Park Sea Kayak Tours,** 39 Cottage St., specializes in ecological tours, pointing out local birds and marine life. (☎207-288-0342 or 800-347-0940. 4hr. tours $43-46. Open daily 8am-9pm.)

FOOD

You'll have to hike a lot to work off all the delicious food you'll find in Bar Harbor. Only vegetarians have a good excuse to leave without eating lobster.

■ **Reel Pizza,** 33 Kennebec Pl. (☎207-288-3828; www.reelpizza.com), at the end of Rodick Pl. off Main St. Combination movie theater and pizzeria shows 2 films each evening for $6 and serves up creative pies, such as the "Hawaii 5-O" with ham, pineapple, green pepper, and macadamia nuts (large $16.50). The 1st 3 rows of the "theater" are comfy couches and chairs. Open daily 4:30pm-last screening. MC/V. ❸

Ben and Bill's Chocolate Emporium, 66 Main St. (☎207-288-3281), near Cottage St. Scoops out 48 flavors of homemade ice cream, including—no kidding—lobster. Come hungry; the small is 2 gigantic scoops. Small $4. Open mid-Feb. to Jan. daily 8:30am-11pm. MC/V. ❶

Eden Vegetarian Cafe, 78 West St. (☎207-288-4422; www.barharborvegetarian.com). This stylish cafe is pricey, but worth every penny. Everything on the menu is organic and vegetarian, from portobello mushroom steak ($16) to pesto pasta ($14.50). Reservations recommended. Open daily 5-9pm. D/MC/V. ❹

Michelle's Brown Bag Cafe, 164 Main St. (☎207-288-5858). The eatery serves up light, fresh sandwiches, like the Village Green (greens, cucumbers, tomatoes, sprouts, hummus; $6.50). Half of a sandwich and small salad for $7. Open M-F 10am-8pm, Sa-Su 10am-3pm. AmEx/D/MC/V. ❷

Poor Boy's Restaurant, 300 Main St. (☎207-288-4148). Local favorite for good food at great prices. The extensive menu features lobster in no fewer than 10 incarnations. Catch the early-bird special before 7pm, with 9 entrees and all-you-can-eat pasta for $9. Lobster meal includes bisque, lobster, baked potato, and dessert for $19. Reservations recommended. Open daily 4:30-10pm. AmEx/D/MC/V. ❸

Docksider Restaurant, 14 Sea St. (☎207-276-3965), outside of Bar Harbor in Northeast Harbor. It's located right on the harbor, so the lobster doesn't have to travel far to reach your plate. Try their specialty, the lobster roll ($18), and relax in the casual dining room. Open daily 11am-9pm. MC/V. ❺

ACCOMMODATIONS

Lodging is easy to find in Bar Harbor—it seems that every other building is an inn or a B&B. Affordable accommodations, on the other hand, are another story; grand hotels and even grander prices recall the island's exclusive resort days. Cheaper establishments assemble on Rte. 3 north of Bar Harbor. Hotel and B&B prices can more than double over the course of a week (especially July-Aug.), depending on how busy it is. Book as early as possible to get the best deal.

Bar Harbor Hostel, 321 Main St. (☎207-288-5587; www.barharborhostel.com). This spotlessly clean old house is right in the heart of downtown Bar Harbor, 2 mi. from Acadia. The friendly owner acts as a 2nd mother, doling out advice and Band-Aids. Movie nights, free Wi-Fi and breakfast. Check-in 5-10pm. Lockout 10am-5pm. Curfew midnight. Reservations only with deposit. Open May-Nov. Dorms in summer $25, in winter $20; private rooms $80/$50. MC/V. ❶

Llangolan Inn & Cottages, 865 Rte. 3 (☎207-288-3016; www.acadia.net/llangolan). Lovely B&B 5 mi. north of the park. Clean rooms are tastefully decorated. Inn with 5 rooms (shared bath for 2 rooms) open year-round; 8 cottages with stove, pots, and pans open May to mid-Oct. Home-cooked continental breakfast for those staying in the Inn. Rooms $70-80; cottages $85. AmEx/D/MC/V. ❹

Edenbrook Motel, 96 Eden St. (☎207-288-4975 or 800-323-7819). Located between Bar Harbor and Acadia's main entrance, this motel has decent rooms with a great view. Open mid-May to mid-Oct. Rooms in summer $76; in winter $50. AmEx/D/MC/V. ❹

Hearthside, 7 High St. (☎207-288-4533). A comfortable B&B on a back street a short walk from downtown. A/C and private bath; some rooms have fireplaces. Free afternoon tea. Rooms in summer $110-150; in winter $75-120. AmEx/D/MC/V. ❺

NIGHTLIFE

Although the surrounding scenery is the town's best offering, roadtrippers looking for nightlife won't be disappointed in Bar Harbor. For live music in a relaxed setting, head to the **Lompoc Cafe & Brew Pub,** 36 Rodick St., off Cottage St. Locals adore this evening haunt, where you can sip a pint of Dark and Stormy ($6) while playing bocce on the porch. Live music—mainly rock, acoustic, and indie on Friday and Saturday nights. (☎207-288-9392. Th open mic. No cover. Open May-Oct. daily 11:30am-1am. MC/V.) With pool tables and old movie posters on the walls, **Carmen Verandah,** 119 Main St., has a cool, relaxed atmosphere. That all changes at 9:30pm, when DJs spin Tuesday through Friday and it turns into a wild dance party. (☎207-288-2766. Mojitos $6.50. Sa live music. M open mic. Cover $2-5. AmEx/D/MC/V.)

THE END OF THE ROAD

Acadia National Park's beauty is unmatched on the Eastern Seaboard. Set up camp, take a relaxing trek through the wilderness, and taste the fruits of the ocean with a tall blueberry ale. Congratulations on a journey well done. But don't head back home yet—the rugged Great North is just around the corner. Who knows what adventures await off U.S. 1?

SPEED LIMIT 65

EXIT TO

Bangor, ME   46mi.
on the great north route, p. 196

Atlantic City, NJ   616 mi.
on the national road route, p. 350

the great north

TOP 5

1. Lose yourself in the **Great Corn Maize** in North Danville, Vermont.
2. Sip *café au lait* or catch the **Festivale Internationale de Jazz** in Montreal, Québec.
3. See a housing-project-turned-installation-art at the **Heidelberg Project** in Detroit, Michigan.
4. Get caught in a **bison jam** in one of the world's largest calderas, Yellowstone National Park.
5. Relax at the **Vandusen Botanical Garden** after an authentic meal in Vancouver's Chinatown.

The Great North Route is a many-splendored thing: the first half of the trip is marked by some of the most vibrant cities in the US and Canada, while the second half travels through many of the largest and most beautiful national parks in North America. The Great North offers the best of both worlds, whether you enjoy sipping steaming espresso in the coffee shops of Montréal and Minneapolis-St. Paul or backcountry camping in the serene wilderness of Yellowstone, Grand Teton, and Banff National Parks. So don your raccoon skin cap and grab your rifle—the rugged North awaits.

GREAT NORTH

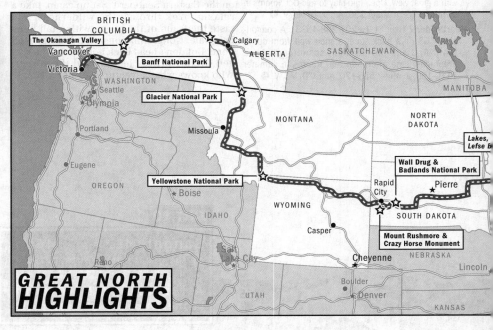

GREAT NORTH
HIGHLIGHTS

The road begins on the rocky coast of Maine, where you'll find the first and largest statue of Paul Bunyan in **Bangor** (p. 196). After traveling through central Maine and the ski country of northern New Hampshire and Vermont, the road takes a sweet turn toward **Waterbury,** where you'll find the **Ben & Jerry's Factory** (p. 208) and its ice-cream graveyard of lost and forgotten flavors. The route then heads north across the border into Canada, to the francophone city of **Montréal** (p. 213), home to McGill University and the "Underground City," which makes pedestrian travel in the winter much more pleasant.

The road continues through Ontario, where you'll see Parliament Hill in **Ottawa** (p. 224) before passing into New York, home of the **Thousand Island Seaway** (p. 231) and the **Jell-O Museum** of LeRoy (p. 234). Continue on to **Niagara Falls** (p. 235), where, in a bizarre reversal, the American side of the falls has serene parks and wilderness while the Canadian side features bright lights and rampant consumerism. Next, the route travels south around the shore

of Lake Erie, offering the opportunity to sample the original buffalo wings at the Anchor Bar in Buffalo (p. 238). The road along the lake hits small towns and big cities, visiting the **Rock and Roll Hall of Fame** in **Cleveland** (p. 245) and the **Motown Historical Museum** in **Detroit** (p. 252) before crossing over to Michigan's Upper Peninsula over the **Mighty Mac** bridge (p. 257).

From there, the road travels past the cheese factories of **Wisconsin** (p. 262) on its way to the Twin Cities, **Minneapolis** and **St. Paul,** home of the **Mall of America** (p. 271) and its indoor roller coaster. Leaving the Twin Cities, the road shifts from the big cities and Great Lakes to the oddities of the Midwest, but not before embarking on the **Lakes, Lewis, and Lefse Big Detour** (p. 276) through the heart of Minnesota. Beginning with the **Jeffers Petroglyphs** (p. 278) in western Minnesota, the road finds a hotbed of roadside sights in western South Dakota, from the bizarre landscape of the **Badlands** (p. 281), to the kitschy animatronic dinosaurs of **Wall Drug** (p. 283), to the manmade wonders of **Mt. Rushmore** (p. 286). From there, the road strikes out of the natural wonders of **Wind Cave** (p.

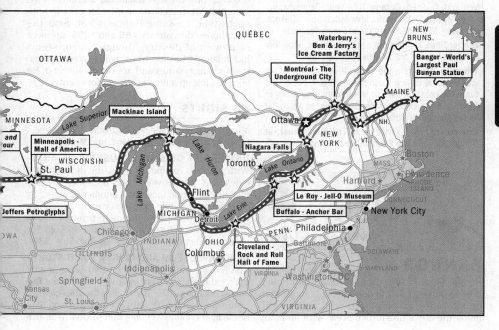

287) and **Jewel Cave** (p. 287), then north to the gigantic **Crazy Horse Memorial** (p. 287) and the shootouts and casinos of **Deadwood** (p. 288)— what more could a roadtripper ask for?

After leaving South Dakota, the road continues toward the vast expanses of some of North America's most majestic lands. The road travels by the geysers and mudpots of **Yellowstone National Park** (p. 293), the pristine trout streams of **Livingston** (p. 301), the alpine lakes of the **Waterton-Glacier Peace Park** (p. 309), the mineral springs and backcountry beauty of **Banff National Park** (p. 320), and the Great Divide of **Yoho National Park** (p. 325) before rediscovering civilization in **Vancouver** (p. 337). Finally, feed your inner scone fiend in self-consciously British **Victoria** (p. 344) as you gaze out over the harbor and ponder that eternal question: "Exactly how far away *am* I from Wall Drug?"

ROUTE STATS

Miles: c. 3800

Route: Bangor, ME to Victoria, BC.

States and Provinces: 16; Maine, New Hampshire, Vermont, Québec, Ontario, New York, Pennsylvania, Ohio, Michigan, Wisconsin, Minnesota, South Dakota, Wyoming, Montana, Alberta, and British Columbia.

Driving Time: Two to three weeks minimum; allow four to appreciate the natural beauty of the north.

When To Go: While the snow of winter may make camping and driving much more difficult, those who brave the cold can take on some of the best skiing in North America. Depart in mid-September to watch the leaves change all along the route.

Crossroads: Near-misses with **The East Coast**, at Bangor, ME, and **The Pacific Coast**, at Vancouver, BC.

The Pine Tree State

MAINE

Welcomes You!

BANGOR

Bangor is more of a transportation hub than a destination—its sights don't provide more than an afternoon's distraction. Still, visitors will enjoy the city's downtown area, with its many cafes, including a bakery run by monks. Though there's a giant statue of Paul Bunyan, Bangor's forests are gone—those in search of trees should pack up and hit the road for Acadia.

VITAL STATS

Population: 31,500

Visitor Info: Bangor Region Chamber of Commerce, 519 Main St. (☎207-947-0307; www.bangorregion.com). Open M-F 8am-5pm.

Internet Access: Bangor Public Library, 145 Harlow St. (☎207-947-8336). Open June 19-Sept. 7 M-Th 9am-7pm, F 9am-5pm; Sept. 5-June 10 M-Th 9am-8pm, F 9am-5pm. Free.

Post Office: 202 Harlow St. (☎207-941-2016). Open M-F 7:30am-6pm, Sa 8am-1pm. **Postal Code:** 04401.

GETTING AROUND

Rte. 2 runs east-west through the heart of Bangor as **State St.** on the west side of Kenduskeag Stream, and **Hammond St.** on the east side. **Main St.** runs north-south along the Penobscot River, crossing Hammond St. near the courthouse downtown. **I-95** and **I-395** intersect southwest of the city. Though Bangor seems like it should be easy to navigate, streets downtown change names and are poorly marked. Be sure to pick up a map at the visitors center.

SIGHTS

Most sights in Bangor center around the intersection formed by **State, Hammond,** and **Main St.**

UNIVERSITY OF MAINE MUSEUM OF ART. With just two exhibition halls, the museum is a quick visit, but it's well worth the time. The permanent collection includes a number of works by Maine artists, while temporary exhibits feature everything from photographs to prints. (*Norumbega Hall, 40 Harlow St. ☎207-561-3350; www.umma.umaine.edu. Open M-Sa 9am-5pm. $3.*)

BANGOR MUSEUM AND CENTER FOR HISTORY. The Bangor Museum is currently revamping its main exhibition hall, but operates tours of the **Thomas A. Hill House.** The 1hr. tour of the 19th-century home focuses on Bangor's early history. The home also contains a collection of Civil War arti-

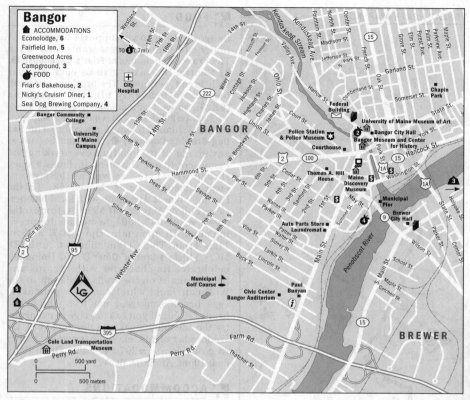

Bangor

🏠 ACCOMMODATIONS
Econolodge, 6
Fairfield Inn, 5
Greenwood Acres
Campground, 3
🍴 FOOD
Friar's Bakehouse, 2
Nicky's Cruisin' Diner, 1
Sea Dog Brewing Company, 4

facts, including an apothecary kit complete with opium and whiskey. *(From the direction of City Hall, walk southwest down Main St., and take a right on Union St. ☎ 207-942-1900. Open Tu-Sa 10am-4pm. Tours 10am-3pm. $5, seniors $4.)*

COLE LAND TRANSPORTATION MUSEUM. The museum, covering more than an acre, houses over 200 vehicles built or used in Maine, as well as Bangor's WWII Memorial and Vietnam Veterans Memorial. *(405 Perry Rd. Take Odlin Rd. south from Hammond St. to Perry Rd., and turn left. ☎ 207-990-3600. Open daily May to mid-Nov. 9am-5pm. $6, seniors $4, under 19 free.)*

LEONARD'S MILLS. A historic reconstruction of a 1790s logging and milling community, Leonard's Mills contains the **Maine Forest and Logging Museum.** "Living history days" are scheduled several times each summer, highlighting blacksmiths and woodsmen and featuring events such as axe-throwing. The site also features a picnic ground, an amphitheater, and a system of trails. *(Located off Rte. 178 in the Pembascot Experimental Forest. Take Rte. 9 E, and turn left onto Rte. 178. ☎ 207-581-2871; www.leonardsmills.com. Open 24hr. Free. Living history days $7, children $2.)*

OTHER SIGHTS. The **Maine Discovery Museum** has water games, supersized body parts, and a recording studio for kids to enjoy. *(74 Main St. ☎ 207-262-7200. Open Tu-Sa 9:30am-5pm, Su noon-5pm. $6.)* The **Police Museum,** located inside the police station, has enough displays of brass knuckles and guns to unnerve even the most upstanding citizen. *(35 Court St. ☎ 207-947-7382. Open M-F 9am-5pm. Free.)*

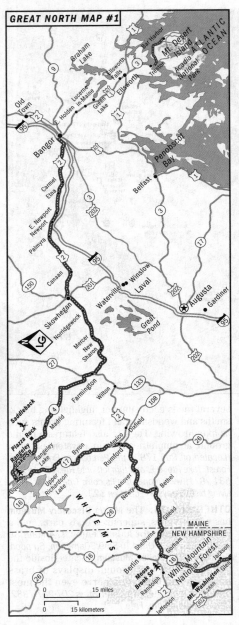

GREAT NORTH MAP #1

🍴 FOOD

Bangor's downtown supports a variety of funky cafes, Indian restaurants, and delis. The Franciscan monks at **Friar's Bakehouse ❶**, 21 Central St., take "give us each day our daily bread" seriously. The brothers sell fresh bread and heavenly blueberry muffins ($1.25), as well as a small selection of sandwiches. (☎207-947-3770. Open Tu-F approximately 7:13am-2:52pm. Cash only.) The **Sea Dog Brewing Company ❸**, 26 Front St., takes advantage of its location overlooking the Penobscot River. The menu includes a spicy shrimp wrap ($10), as well as the mysteriously named vegetarian chicken ($8). Try the Bluepaw Wheat Ale, made with local blueberries. (Follow May St. off Main St. toward the river. ☎ 207-947-8004; www.seadogbrewing.com. Th open mic. Open M-W and Su 11am-11pm, Th-Sa 11am-midnight. AmEx/D/MC/V.) **Nicky's Cruisin' Diner ❷**, 957 Union St., celebrates its character with records and license plates on the walls. Wake up to the Wolfman Jack, which includes pancakes, eggs, bacon, sausage, home fries, and baked beans ($6.50). If you can manage to eat again, try the salisbury steak and potatoes ($8). On Wednesday nights, classic car owners gather to go cruisin'. (☎207-942-2430. Open daily 6am-10pm. AmEx/D/MC/V.)

🏠 ACCOMMODATIONS

Bangor has a fair share of hotel and motel chains, with most accommodations on **Odlin Rd.**, west of downtown near the airport. One of the better deals is the **Econolodge ❹**, 327 Odlin Rd., where rooms have a refrigerator, a microwave, and a coffeemaker. There's also a pool and laundry facilities. (☎207-945-0111. Continental breakfast included. Rooms M-Th and Su $70, F-Sa $75. AmEx/D/MC/V.) The **Fairfield Inn ❺**, 300 Odlin Rd., has a gym, sauna, hot tub, and indoor pool available 24hr. Rooms have cushy beds as well as fridge and microwave. Continental breakfast included. (☎207-990-0001. Rooms $129. AmEx/D/MC/V.) A few miles outside of town, **Greenwood Acres Campground ❶**, on Rte. 178, has everything from a paintball range to a slushie machine. The 54 sites and cabin are wooded, though the cabins don't have water or electricity. (Take Rte. 9 E until it splits, then take Rte. 178 N 1 mi. ☎207-989-8898 or 888-989-8898. Open Apr.-Oct. Sites $17, with full hookup $27; cabins $25-40. D/MC/V.)

APPROACHING NEWPORT: 27 MILES

Leaving Bangor, stay on **State St.** heading west. It becomes **U.S. 2** outside of town.

NEWPORT. Newport refers to itself as the "Hub of Maine" because it sits at the intersection of U.S. 2 and the I-95 freeway. Stop here to enjoy beautiful Sebasticook Lake. **Lakeside Christie's Campground ❶**, 83 Christie's Camp Rd., accommodates tents and RVs and has six comfortable cabins equipped with kitchen, picnic table, porch, and toilet. Christie's also has access to fishing, boating, swimming, and basketball, and rents bicycles, paddle boats, canoes, and kayaks. (3 mi. east of town center, off U.S. 2. ☎207-368-4645 or 800-688-5141. Open May-Nov. Rentals $10-15 per day. Lakefront sites $21; RV hookups $23; cabins $350-400 per week. Day-use $2 per person. Reservations recommended. D/MC/V.)

> **? DID YOU KNOW?** Maine has more moose per sq. mi. than any other state.

APPROACHING CANAAN: 16 MILES

Continue along **U.S. 2** for about 16 mi. until you reach Canaan.

CANAAN. The most unique attraction in this small town is **The Charles Lindbergh Crate Museum**, 241 Easy St. This eccentric museum is a collection of Lindberghabilia displayed inside a giant packing crate—the one in which Charles Lindbergh's famous *Spirit of St. Louis* airplane was shipped back to America after he completed the first solo transatlantic flight in 1927. The crate was originally given to a retired Naval officer who converted it into a vacation home in New Hampshire, but it is now located in the backyard of collector Larry Ross. (From U.S. 2, make a right onto Easy St., across from the Canaan Post Office. Follow the street about 1½ mi. uphill. Look for a small sign on a mailbox. ☎207-474-9841. Tours by appointment, or just stop by to take a look on your own. Free.) Enjoy the view by the side of

the Kennebec River at the Kennebec Banks Rest Stop, 2 mi. east of Skowhegan on U.S. 2, and take advantage of the picnic tables. Also nearby is the **Lake George Regional Park,** a great place for swimming, boating, picnicking, and relaxing on a sandy beach. (Day-use $3.)

APPROACHING SKOWHEGAN: 9 MILES

From Canaan, continue on **U.S. 2 W.**

SKOWHEGAN

Skowhegan is the largest city between Bangor and St. Johnsbury, VT, but its biggest claim to fame is the **World's Tallest Indian Statue.** From the Chamber of Commerce, 23 Commercial St. (U.S. 2), it's easy to see the 62 ft. statue tucked among the trees. It was erected by Bernard Langlais in 1969 in honor of Maine's Abnaki Indians and in observance of Maine's 150th year as a state. Sadly, the statue fell into disrepair, but the town rallied around their tallest citizen and raised $20,000 to "Save the Indian." Also worth a stop is the **Skowhegan History House,** 66 Elm St., an 1839 Greek Revival homestead turned into a museum of Skowhegan antiques and Civil War artifacts. (From Chamber of Commerce, drive straight onto Elm St. where U.S. 2 merges with Rte. 201. At the intersection with Pleasant St., nestled back on the left. ☎207-474-6632. Open June-Sept. Tu-Sa 1-5pm. $2, children and seniors $1.) The **Margaret Chase Smith Library,** 56 Norridgewock Ave., is a congressional research library honoring the first female senator. Lining the ceiling is an impressive display of the 95 robes worn by Ms. Smith as she received various honorary degrees. (Drive west from the History House; Elm St. will become Norridgewock Ave. ☎207-474-7133; ww.mcslibrary.org. Open M-F 10am-4pm.) If you're driving by in the winter, hit the slopes at **Eaton Mountain Ski Resort,** 89 Lambert Rd. Lights cover the mountain for night skiing, and the base lodge has equipment rentals as well as a restaurant, lounge, and game room. If traveling in summer, you can pitch a tent for outdoor snoozing. (☎207-474-2666; www.eatonmountain.com. Lift tickets $23, ½-day $19. Sites $12, with hookup $15-18. AmEx/D/MC/V.)

APPROACHING FARMINGTON: 28 MILES

From Skowhegan, it's a winding drive down **U.S. 2** along the Kennebec and Sandy Rivers to Farmington. U.S. 2 bypasses downtown, so turn right onto **Rte. 4** to get onto **Main St.**

FARMINGTON

Farmington is home to the **University of Maine at Farmington.** The presence of the college has turned Farmington into the cultural center of the region, but a quiet rural lifestyle still lingers. Farmington is the starting point for thousands who come to see the fall foliage, enjoy the area's many outdoor activities, or head to **Sugarloaf Ski Resort,** a 40min. drive north. There are several upscale restaurants in downtown Farmington. **The Granary Brew Pub & Restaurant ❹,** 147 Pleasant St., serves diners on an inviting deck that looks out onto the forested valley. The restaurant no longer brews its own beers on location, but nearby Oak Pond Brewing Company prepares their own handcrafted beers for the customers. (From Main St., take a left on Broadway. ☎207-779-0710; www.thegranarybrewpub.com. Lunch $7-14. Dinner $14-20. Open M-Sa 11am-10pm, Su for brunch. AmEx/D/MC/V.) **Gifford's Ice Cream ❶,** 293 Main St. (Rte. 4), is Maine right down to its icy sweet core, with flavors like Maine Deer Tracks (vanilla, fudge, and peanut butter cup) and Maine Blueberry. A "small" cone is a heaping two scoops. (☎207-778-3617; www.giffordsicecream.com. Cones $2-3. Cash only.) **Quad M's Cabin Restaurant ❸,** 476 Fairbanks Rd. (Rte. 4), is a country-style surf-and-turf restaurant in a charming log cabin. Try your hand at the "Big Quad"—a 64 oz. cut of Black Angus sirloin ($60). If you do manage to finish this hunk of meat, you get the next one for free. (☎207-778-2776. Entrees $10-14. Open M, W-Th and Su 6am-8pm, F-Sa 6am-9pm. MC/V.) Motels are primarily located on Rte. 2, near the west side of town. The **Colonial Valley Motel ❷,** 593 Wilton Rd. (Rte. 2), offers clean rooms with simple early-American decor. (☎800-684-2800. Singles $44; doubles $52. AmEx/D/MC/V.)

◪ APPROACHING RANGELEY: 40 MILES
Leaving Farmington, drive north on **Rte. 4.** Be sure to fill up in Farmington since service stations are few and far between. 3 mi. outside the town of Madrid is a turnout where you can park at the base of charming Smalls Falls. 6 mi. from Madrid, roadtrippers can stretch cramped legs by hiking a flat section of the **Appalachian Trail** to **Piazza Rock;** it's an easy 1½ mi.

trek through woodland to an enormous overhanging boulder that seems to be suspended in mid-air.

RANGELEY

The Rangeley Lakes region is home to 110 lakes and ponds, 150 mi. of snowmobile trails, and an assortment of eccentric artists and inquisitive moose. Rangeley is the largest hamlet on the lakes, and its one major street is the main drag of this pastoral corner of Maine. A 691-acre recreation area located on Rangeley Lake, **Rangeley Lake State Park ❶** features picnicking, swimming, a boat launch, a playground, hiking trails, restrooms, showers, and forested campsites. (37 mi. from Farmington on Rte. 4; take a left on South Shore Dr. The park turn-off is 5 mi. on the right. ☎207-864-3858, reservations ☎207-287-3824; www.campwithme.com. Check-in after 1pm. Check-out before 11am. Curfew 11pm. Open May-Sept. Reservations by phone M-F 9am-4pm. MC/V.) For wintertime roadtrippers, **Saddleback Mountain's** location deep in Maine's snow belt means exceptional snow conditions. Skiers enjoy uncrowded, well-groomed trails, glade skiing, untracked powder, and natural snow trails, along with plenty of beginner routes. The 1830 ft. drop makes this mountain one of Maine's largest. (☎207-864-5671; www.saddlebackmaine.com.)

There are several dining options in Rangeley, but locals adore the **Red Onion ❸,** 2511 Main St., for its Italian fare. Best known for its homemade pizza dough, the Red Onion also serves sandwiches ($5-6), seafood ($8-11), and pasta dishes ($9-10). Everything is available to go. (☎207-864-5022. Open daily 11am-10pm. AmEx/D/MC/V.)

◪ APPROACHING OQUOSSOC: 7 MILES
Take **Pleasant St.** out of town; it turns into **Rte. 4/16.** Oquossoc is located at the narrow strip of land between Rangeley and Mooselookmeguntic Lakes.

OQUOSSOC. Oquossoc is little more than a few stores at a crossroads; however, as lodging in the area can cost an arm and a leg, Oquossoc's Own B&B ❸, 32 Rangeley Ave., is definitely worth a stop. The best deal around, this B&B has been open year-round since 1980. Repeat customers enjoy its cozy atmosphere and excellent food. Volleyball and croquet are available, as well as a grill for guest use and a living room that serves as a lounge. (Follow signs from Rte. 4 in Oquossoc.

☎207-864-5584. Singles $40; doubles $70. AmEx/D/ MC/V.) The Bald Mountain Trail is on Bald Mt. Rd., ¾ mi. south of Oquossoc, off Rte. 4. Along this 1¾ mi. trail are picnic tables and a 30 ft. lookout tower that gives a 360-degree view of the surrounding mountains.

⚑ APPROACHING RUMFORD: 36 MILES

From Oquossoc, head south on **Rte 17.** 17 mi. later, you'll reach **Angel Falls,** a scenic hanging falls. Its 90 ft. plummet onto the rocks below is one of the longest drops in the state. Finding the trailhead is tricky–ask at the **Coos Canyon Rest Area and Campground** (22 mi. south of Oquossoc) for detailed directions. Make a right at the intersection with **U.S. 2** to proceed west into Rumford.

RUMFORD

Rumford is a typical, run-of-the-mill New England post-industrial town. Though its glory days are long gone, it boasts many architectural treasures from an earlier time. If you can stand the smell of the Mead paper mill, New England's largest, it's worth seeing the shiny giant **Paul Bunyan Statue.** He stands in front of the **River Valley Chamber of Commerce,** at the intersection of U.S. 2 and Rte. 108. (☎207-364-3241. Free Wi-Fi. Open M-F 8am-4pm.) The city was built around **Penacook Falls,** which, at 180 ft., are the tallest east of Niagara. The falls are best appreciated by walking around town and viewing them from the three bridges that span the river. **Mexico Chicken Coop ❸,** 32 Bridge St. (U.S. 2), in the nearby town of Mexico, has a shabby exterior that hides the good food inside. A family restaurant where chicken is king, the Coop is also known for its fresh seafood. (☎207-364-2710. Lunch $3-6. Dinner $10-19. Open M-Th and Su 11am-8pm, F-Sa 11am-9pm. AmEx/D/MC/V.) About 4 mi. west of Rumford on Rte. 2 is **Madison Resort Inn and Camping ❹,** an inn, restaurant, and campground. It includes 60 units of motel rooms as well as a pool, health club, sauna, waterfront nature trail, canoes, and riverside wooded campsites ❶. (☎207-364-7973 or 800-258-6234; www.madisoninn.com. Live entertainment some evenings. RV hookups but no sewer. Sites $25; singles $80; doubles from $90. AmEx/D/MC/V.)

⚑ APPROACHING BETHEL: 23 MILES

Follow **U.S. 2 W** out of Rumford. At Newry, 17 mi. from Rumford, follow U.S. 2 as it curves and goes south.

BETHEL. Bethel is one of Maine's most beautiful mountain villages. Nearby, along U.S. 2, is the **Sunday River Ski Resort.** Skiers enjoy 126 trails, which are available for hiking and biking in the summer. (☎207-824-3000; www.sundayriver.com.) Near the turn-off to Sunday River, turn right and follow the signs for 3 mi. to the **Artist's Covered Bridge,** so named because of its picturesque appearance. Also at this turn-off is the **Sunday River Brewing Company ❸,** 1 Sunday River Rd. This restaurant makes several of its brews and its own unique barbecue. (☎207-824-3541. Barbecue from $12. Entrees $8-16. AmEx/D/MC/V.) For a cheaper option, the **Crossroads Diner and Deli ❷,** on U.S. 2 at Parkway just before the turn-off to downtown, is a great kickback to an earlier era. (☎207-824-3673. Breakfast $3-5. Sandwiches and soups $5-8. Blue-plate dinner specials $7-11. Open M-Th and Su 5:30am-8pm, F-Sa 5:30am-9pm. MC/V.) The **Inn at Rostay ❸,** 186 Mayville Rd. (U.S. 2), has rooms with hand-sewn quilts. The main house serves a country breakfast ($6) and a three-course dinner for $12. (On U.S. 2, 1 mi. east of town. ☎207-824-3111 or 888-754-0072; www.rostay.com. Rooms M-F from $55, Sa-Su from $60. AmEx/D/MC/V.)

⚑ APPROACHING SHELBURNE: 16 MILES

After Bethel, **U.S. 2** continues west, entering New Hampshire near Shelburne.

SHELBURNE. Shelburne is best known for the **Shelburne Birches,** part of the White Mountain National Forest. The **White Birches Camping Park ❶,** 218 U.S. 2, is the best place to camp in the area, offering tent sites and a pool. (☎603-466-2022. Sites $16; full hookup $27. D/MC/V.)

⚑ APPROACHING GORHAM: 6 MILES

6 mi. from Shelburne, **U.S. 2** passes through Gorham as **Main St.**

GORHAM

Gorham is the gateway to the **White Mountains National Forest,** set at the crossroads of U.S. 2 and Rte. 16. The railroad capital of the White Mountains, Gorham celebrates its past in the **Train Within a Train** exhibit, 25 Railroad St., behind the info office and playground. Inside an actual granary boxcar, a computerized, miniature Androscoggin Valley train system is fully operational. A variety of railroad paraphernalia can be found in another boxcar as well as in the nearby depot, which also serves as the town's **historical museum.** (Open daily May-Nov. 1-5pm. Donations requested.) Also near Gorham, 44 clean campsites sit off the highway at **Moose Brook State Park ❶,** 30 Jimtown Rd. The park's great location positions campers between the park and nearby cities. Moose Brook and Perkins Brook run through the campground with walking trails leading along the banks and a swimming and picnic area close by. (1 mi. west of Gorham off U.S. 2. Turn north onto Jimtown Rd.; the office is on the right. ☎603-271-3628. Check-in 1-8pm. Check-out noon. Open May to mid-Oct. Sites $18. No hookups. MC/V.)

An influx of national chains into Gorham has coincided with the closure of many of the town's locally-owned restaurants. However, one restaurant that has weathered Gorham's changing times since 1947 is **Mary's Pizza ❷,** 9 Cascade Flats. The first restaurant in Gorham's former Italian District on the west side of town, this award-winning establishment is still run by the original family and makes all their own pasta and sauces on the premises. (Take U.S. 2/Rte. 16 W, and follow Rte. 16 N until they diverge; 4 mi. later, turn right onto Cascade Flats Rd. ☎603-752-6150. Pizza $6-17. Pasta $7-10. AmEx/D/MC/V.) With clean, simple rooms, the **Gorham Motor Inn ❸,** 324 Main St. (U.S. 2), west of town, is the cheapest accommodation in town. (☎603-466-3381. Rooms July-Oct. M-F $69-99; Nov.-June $38-68. AmEx/D/MC/V.)

⚐ APPROACHING PINKHAM NOTCH: 13 MILES
Take **Main St.** to **Rte. 16 S,** which will take you into the **White Mountain National Forest.** Occupying 780,000 acres of national forest maintained by the US Forest Service, the White Mountains provide an immense playground for outdoor enthusiasts. The forest contains one of the oldest mountain ranges in North America and many moose and black bears.

PINKHAM NOTCH

Pinkham Notch, New Hampshire's easternmost pass, lies in the shadow of the tallest mountain in the Northeast—the 6288 ft. **Mt. Washington.** Pinkham's proximity to the peak makes it more

crowded and less peaceful than some neighboring towns, but secluded areas can still be found not too far off the beaten path. The **AMC's Pinkham Notch Visitors Center** lies between Gorham and Jackson, on Rte. 16. (☎603-466-2727; www.outdoors.org. Open daily 6:30am-10pm.) Stretching from just behind the Pinkham Notch Visitors Center all the way up to the summit of Mt. Washington, **Tuckerman's Ravine Trail** demands 4-5hr. of steep hiking each way. Mt. Washington is one of the most dangerous small mountains in the world due to highly unpredictable weather, including high winds that frequently reach hurricane force. Exercise caution when climbing. A temperature warmer than 72°F has never been recorded atop Mt. Washington, and the average temperature on the peak is a chilly 26.9°F. The summit also boasts the highest wind speed ever recorded (a whopping 231 mph). With proper measures, however, the trek up the mountain is stellar. Those lucky enough to hike on a clear day are rewarded with a view of five states and Canada. A less daunting option is the **Lion's Head Trail,** which diverges from the Tuckerman's Ravine Trail by about 2 mi. A popular option is to go up Tuckerman's Ravine and return via Lion's Head. For the less adventurous, the **Glen Ellis Falls** trail just south of Pinkham is a lovely 0.3 mi. jaunt to an impressive waterfall.

Adventurous roadtrippers can take the **Mt. Washington Auto Road,** a paved and dirt road that winds 8 mi. to the summit. The road begins 3 mi. north of the visitors center on Rte. 16. Owners of vehicles sturdy enough to reach the top receive a free "This Car Climbed Mt. Washington" bumper sticker. (☎603-466-3988. Road open daily June-Aug. 7:30am-6pm; May-June and Sept.-Oct. 8am-5pm. Call ahead to check weather conditions. $20 per car; free audio tour included. $7 per additional passenger, ages 5-12 $5.) If you are afraid (or certain) that your car might not make it, tours are available through **Great Glen Stage Tours,** across from the Auto Road. (☎603-466-2333. Tours daily 8:30am-5pm. $26, seniors $23, ages 5-12 $11.)

Many of the region's lodging options are on or near Mt. Washington. Accessible by car, the **Joe Dodge Lodge ❸,** immediately behind the Pinkham Notch Visitors Center, offers over 100 comfortable bunks, including seven family rooms, as well as a library and living room. (☎603-466-2727. Breakfast and dinner included. Common bathroom. Reservations recommended. Rooms in summer $62, under 15 $39; in winter $56/$37. AmEx/D/MC/V.)

▼ APPROACHING NORTH CONWAY: 15 MILES
Continue on **Rte. 16** to North Conway.

NORTH CONWAY

With its proximity to ski resorts in winter, foliage in the fall, and hiking and shopping year-round, North Conway is one of New Hampshire's most popular vacation destinations. As the gateway to the White Mountains from the eastern seaboard, it caters to the yuppie crowd and is more expensive than other towns in the region. Rte. 16, the congested main road, is home to outlet stores as well as a variety of smaller local shops. The town of Conway, a little farther south, has fewer touristy shops but excellent food and lodging options.

VITAL STATS

Population: 2100

Visitor Info: Mt. Washington Valley Chamber of Commerce and Visitors Bureau, P.O. Box 2300 (☎800-367-3364; www.mtwashingtonvalley.org).

Internet Access: North Conway Public Library, 2719 White Mtn. Hwy. (☎603-356-2861). Open M-Tu 12-5pm, W-Th 12-6pm, F noon-5pm.

Post Office: 78 Grove St. (☎603-356-2293). Open M-F 9am-5pm, Sa 9am-noon. **Postal Code:** 03860.

� GETTING AROUND. North Conway is about 28 mi. south of Gorham and 5 mi. north of Con-

way, along **Rte. 16** and **U.S. 302.** In North Conway, Rte. 16 and U.S. 302 merge, running through town as the main drag. Conway sits near the junction of U.S. 302, Rte. 16, **Rte. 112,** and **Rte. 153.**

◢ OUTDOORS. Numerous stores in the North Conway area rent outdoor equipment. For ski goods in winter or biking gear during the warmer months, **Joe Jones,** 2709 White Mtn. Hwy., in North Conway, has it all. (☎603-356-9411. Open July-Aug. daily 9am-8pm; Sept.-June M-Th and Su 8:30am-6pm, F-Sa 8:30am-8pm. Alpine skis, boots, and poles $20 per day; cross-country equipment $15/$29; snowboards $25/$49. Bikes $30 per day. MC/V.) A second branch, **Joe Jones North** (☎603-356-6848), lies a few miles north of town on Rte. 302. **Eastern Mountain Sports (EMS),** just north on White Mtn. Hwy. in the lobby of the Eastern Slope Inn, sells camping equipment and rents tents (2-3 person $25 for the first day, $12 each additional day; 4-6 person $30/$15), sleeping bags ($20/$10), snowshoes ($20/$10), packs ($15/$7), and skis ($30/$15). The knowledgeable staff provides firsthand info on climbing and hiking and offers a summer climbing school. A one-day beginner lesson costs $220 for one person, $175 each for two people, or $160 each for three. (☎603-356-5433. Open in summer M-Sa 8:30am-9pm; in winter M-Th and Su 8:30am-6pm, F-Sa 8:30am-9pm. MC/V.)

▼ FOOD. For sports fans who will appreciate autographed Red Sox bats and other New

MOOSE STOPPINGS

As you're driving through New Hampshire's White Mountains, it's wise to keep an eye out for errant moose. These large and awkward creatures don't exactly have the wits to stay out of the road, and a collision can have deadly consequences. Yet to the surprise of unassuming, prudent drivers, there is another side to the moose story—the hundreds of tourists just waiting for the chance to see one. Moose mania is everywhere. Tour guides rattle off places where the antlered animals congregate. Local shops stock clothing and souvenirs branded with every imaginable pun on the creature ("nice rack" gets pretty old). If you really must see a moose, there are steps you can take to improve your chances. Moose tend to emerge around sunrise and twilight, often near still bodies of water. The Kancamungus Scenic Highway and other isolated throughways provide the best odds for spotting a moose from the road. If your tracking skills aren't up to par, **Gorham Moose Tours** boasts a 93% success rate.

Gorham Moose Tours, at Rte. 16 in Gorham (☎877-986-6673). Tour departs daily June to mid-Aug. 6:30pm; mid-Aug. to mid-Sept. 6pm; mid-Sept. to mid-Oct. 5:30pm. $20, ages 5-12 $15, under 4 $5.

[the local story]▶

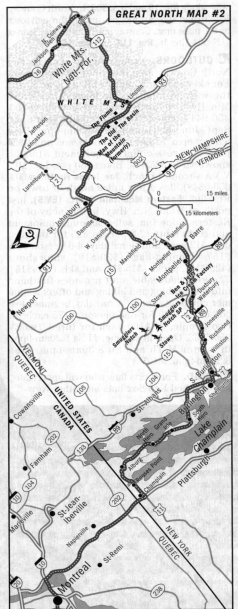

GREAT NORTH MAP #2

GREAT NORTH

England sports paraphernalia, **Delaney's ❸**, north of town along Rte. 16, is the place to stop. The restaurant offers an unorthodox juxtaposition of American bar fare ($7-11) and beautifully prepared sushi rolls. (☎603-356-7776; www.delaneys.com. Open daily 11:30am-11pm. AmEx/D/MC/V.) A bagful of penny candy from **Zeb's General Store ❶**, 2675 Main St. (Rte. 16), will energize you while you explore the shop, which sells only New England-made products, from maple syrup to moose memorabilia. Thirsty tourists can indulge in the $1 homemade soda. (☎603-356-9294. Open mid-June to Dec. M-Su and Th 9am-6pm, F-Sa 9am-8pm; low-season hours vary. AmEx/MC/V.) Several miles south in Conway, pink, green, and purple paint decorates the walls and ceilings of **Cafe Noche ❷**, 147 Main St., while colorful paper cutouts flutter through the air. Locals recommend the Montezuma Pie (Mexican lasagna; $8.75) or the garden burger ($4.25) among the multitude of authentic Mexican options. (☎603-447-5050. Lunch $5-8, dinner $7-11. Open daily 11:30am-9pm. AmEx/D/MC/V.)

🛏 ACCOMMODATIONS. Located in the heart of Conway and maintained by incredibly friendly folks, the **⊠White Mountains Hostel (HI-AYH) ❶**, 36 Washington St., off Rte. 16 at the intersection of Rte. 153, is meticulously clean and environmentally friendly. The hostel has 43 comfy bunks, a kitchen, and a common room. Each bed comes with clean linen and a pillow. (☎603-447-1001. Laundry $3. Reception 7:30-10am and 5-10pm. Check-out 10am. Reservations recommended. Dorms $22, non-members $25; private rooms $48. MC/V.) The hostel at the beautiful **Cranmore Mt. Lodge ❶**, 859 Kearsarge Rd., in North Conway, has 22 bunks. The lodge is about 2 mi. from downtown, but the living room, pool, jacuzzi, cable TV, refrigerator, and duck pond that are at guests' disposal justify the trip. (☎603-356-2044 or 800-356-3596. Linens and towel $3. Check-in 3-11pm. Check-out 11am. Dorms $20. AmEx/D/MC/V.)

 If you camp, be aware that **bears** are a threat. Keep food hung and well away from sleeping areas, and do not keep anything that smells of food in or near your tent. **Moose** can be a danger for drivers as well, so keep a watchful eye.

APPROACHING FRANCONIA NOTCH: 52 MILES
From North Conway, take **Rte. 16** 5 mi. south to Conway. In Conway, take a right to head west on **Rte. 112**, also known as the ▧**Kancamagus Scenic Hwy.** Fill up your tank at Conway, as no gas is available for the entire 35 mi., then head west on the clearly marked byway to enjoy scenic splendor all the way to Lincoln. This stretch of Rte. 112 requires at least 1hr. to drive, though the vistas typically lure drivers to one of many scenic outlooks. In Lincoln, Rte. 112 is known as **Main St.** From Main St. merge onto **I-93 N** to pass through the Franconia Notch area of the White Mountains on the way to Franconia Notch State Park.

FRANCONIA NOTCH STATE PARK

Imposing granite cliffs, formed by glacial movements that began during an ice age 400 million years ago, tower on either side of the **Franconia Notch Pkwy. (I-93)** and create one of the more scenic spots in the White Mountains. Traveling north from Lincoln on I-93, ▧**The Flume,** Exit 34A on I-93, is a 2 mi. walk cutting through a spectacular granite gorge. Although only 12-20 ft. apart, the moss-covered canyon walls are 70-90 ft. high. Take a leisurely stroll over century-old covered bridges and past the 345 ft. **Avalanche Falls.** Tickets can be purchased from the **The Flume Visitors Center.** (☎603-745-8391; www.flumegorge.com. Open May-Oct. daily 9am-5pm. $10, ages 6-12 $7. AmEx/D/MC/V.) Between Exits 34A and 34B on I-93, visitors can find a well-marked turn-off for **The Basin,** a 5-10min. walk that takes you to a 20 ft. whirlpool carved out of a massive base of granite by a 15 ft. waterfall. (Free.)

Franconia Notch State Park was once home to the famous **Old Man of the Mountain,** but in May 2003, the rock formation partially collapsed and sent New Hampshire into mourning. The viewing areas at between Exit 34A and 34B on I-93 are still open and explain the Old Man's demise.

Ten miles north of the town of Lincoln (take Exit 34B off I-93), the 80-passenger **Cannon Mountain Aerial Tramway** climbs over 2000 ft. in 7min. and carries visitors to the summit of the **Cannon Cliff,** a 1000 ft. sheer drop into the cleft between Mt. Lafayette and Cannon Mountain. The tram offers unparalleled vistas of Franconia Notch along its ascent. Once at the top, a short walk will bring you to an **observation tower** (over 4200 ft.) overlooking the Notch. (☎603-823-8800. Open daily mid-May to mid-Oct. and mid-Dec. to mid-Apr. 9am-5pm. Trains run every 15min. Round-trip

$10, ages 6-12 $6. One-way $8. AmEx/D/MC/V.) In winter, the tram takes skiers up the mountain, which has 58 trails. (Ski passes M-F 9am-4pm $42, Sa-Su 8:30am-4pm $54. AmEx/D/MC/V.) Right next to the tramway station sits the one-room **New England Ski Museum,** which features a new exhibit each year alongside permanent memorabilia such as a timeline of skis from 1905 to the present. (☎603-823-7177. Open daily mid-May to mid-Oct. and mid-Dec. to mid-Apr. noon-5pm. Free.)

APPROACHING ST. JOHNSBURY: 34 MILES
Head north through Littleton on **I-93.** Soon you'll cross the Connecticut River to Vermont. Take **Exit 1** onto **Rte. 18** and bear right, then take a left onto **U.S. 2 (Portland Rd.).**

The Green Mountain State **VERMONT** *Welcomes You!*

ST. JOHNSBURY

At the first town meeting in 1790, Colonel Ethan Allen suggested that St. Johnsbury be named in honor of Hector St. Jean de Crevecoeur, French Consul to the United States. However, de Crevecoeur himself thought that St. John was too cliché and suggested the name St. Johnsbury to make it unique in the world—a distinction that remains today. Over time, a booming economy based on maple products and platform scales developed in St. Johnsbury. Those days are long gone, but St. Johnsbury has assimilated well into the quickly growing Vermont tourist industry, no doubt aided by its placement at the junctions of U.S. 2 and U.S. 5, interstates 91 and 93, and the Maine Central and Canadian Pacific railroads.

VITAL STATS
Population: 7600
Visitor Info: Northeast Kingdom Chamber of Commerce, 51 Depot Sq., Ste. 3 (☎802-748-3678 or 800-639-6379; www.nekchamber.com). Free Wi-Fi.
Internet Access: St. Johnsbury Athenaeum, 1171 Main St. (☎802-748-8291). Open M and W 10am-8pm, Tu and Th-F 10am-5:30pm, Sa 9:30am-4pm.
Post Office: 1153 Main St. (☎802-748-3301). Open M-F 8am-5pm, Sa 9am-noon. **Postal Code:** 05819.

GREAT NORTH

GETTING AROUND. U.S. 2 comes into town from the east over a bridge and heads uphill to **Main St.,** which is lined with Victorian mansions. Spanning the bottom of the hill is **Railroad St.,** while Main St. covers the top of the hill. Parking is just $0.05 per 30min. at any of the meters that line the streets.

SIGHTS. The **Fairbanks Museum,** 1302 Main St., has one of the best collections of impressive odds and ends in New England—from North American wildlife to a portrait of Abe Lincoln made from thousands of shimmering bugs—hence its affectionate nickname, the "Cabinet of Curiosities." The museum was given as a gift to the town of St. Johnsbury from Franklin Fairbanks, the inventor of Fairbanks platform scales. The museum now sits in a Victorian mansion, the cornerstone of the **Main St. Historic District.** (☎802-748-2372; www.fairbanksmuseum.org. Open May-Oct. M-Sa 9am-5pm, Su 1-5pm; Nov.-Apr. Tu-Sa 9am-5pm, Su 1-5pm. Planetary shows July-Aug. Sa-Su 1:30pm. $5, seniors $4. D/MC/V.) A short distance from the intersection of U.S. 2 and Main St. is the **St. Johnsbury Athenaeum, Art Gallery, and Public Library,** 30 Main St. Named for Athena, the goddess of wisdom, this beautifully constructed building contains an impressive art gallery for a small town. (☎802-748-8291. Open M and W 10am-8pm, Tu and Th-F 10am-5:30pm, Sa 9:30am-4pm. Free.) Also in downtown St. Johnsbury is the **Octagon** building and annex. The structure now houses offices for the US Air Force, Army, and Marines—there isn't much to tour, but the 1854 building is worth a look just for its odd shape. If you're visiting in March or April, you may be lucky enough to see maple syrup being tapped. An alternative to the real thing is to visit the **Maple Grove Farms,** 1052 Portland St., the largest packager of maple syrup in the US. Here, visitors can tour a museum, tasting room, and candy factory and see the **world's largest can of maple syrup** at 10 ft. tall. (1 mi. east of town on U.S. 2. ☎802-748-5141; www.maplegrove.com. Open M-F 10am-2pm. In fall 1hr. tours every 15min. $1, under 13 free. Cash only for tour; gift shop accepts AmEx/MC/V.)

 DID YOU KNOW? Vermont contains over a hundred covered bridges, including the 450 ft. **Cornish Bridge,** the nation's longest covered bridge, in Windsor, Vermont.

FOOD AND ACCOMMODATIONS. A typical diner, **Anthony's Diner ❷,** 321 Railroad St., serves sandwiches ($4-7) and dinners ($10-15). Try the "Exploring Salad" ($8.25) with sweet and sour salad dressing. (☎802-748-3613. Open M-Th 6:30am-8pm, F-Sa 6:30am-8:30pm. MC/V.) Lodging rates throughout Vermont have been on the rise in recent years, but are exorbitant around St. Johnsbury. The **Yankee Traveler Motel ❺,** 342 Portland St. (U.S. 2), is unremarkable but conveniently located. (☎802-748-3156. Heated outdoor pool and A/C. Continental breakfast included. Free Wi-Fi. Rooms from $109. AmEx/D/MC/V.)

APPROACHING DANVILLE: 7 MILES
Head west along **Main St.** toward St. John's Academy, then turn right at the signs for **U.S. 2.** After 7 mi. you will reach Danville.

DANVILLE. Danville is home to the national headquarters of the **American Society of Dowsers,** 184 Brainerd St. Here you can observe the art of dowsing, which uses forked sticks or pendulums to find water under the ground. Walking around the backyard labyrinth clears the mind for the necessary "sensitivity and awareness" for proper dowsing. (Make a left onto Brainerd St. from Rte. 2 in the town center; it'll be on your right. ☎802-684-3417. Open M-F 9am-5pm. Free.)

APPROACHING NORTH DANVILLE: 5 MILES
From Danville town center, at blinking yellow light, follow **Hill St. (Badger Hwy.)** north for 5 mi. At the North Danville town center (a church and library), make a left onto the dirt **McReynolds Rd.** After 100 ft., make a right onto **Old North Church Rd.,** follow it for 3 mi., then make another right onto **Wheelock Rd.** for 1 mi.

NORTH DANVILLE. A short but worthwhile detour is to the village of **North Danville** to visit the **Great Vermont Corn Maze,** 1404 Wheelock Rd., two miles of pathways and five acres of an a"maize"ingly perplexing cornfield. On the first two weekends of October, the Haunted Maze opens in the spirit of Halloween. Victims take a hayride to the site, where they walk half a mile through haunted forest and cornfield. A "Starlight Maze" is available for an added challenge. (☎802-748-1399. Open July daily 10am-5pm, Aug.-Sept. daily 10am-

5pm and 7-10:30pm, early Oct. 10am-4pm. Last entry 1hr. before closing. $9, ages 4-14 and 62 and over $7.) Nineteen miles from Danville, in **Plainfield,** on U.S. 2 is a rest stop at the **Maple Valley Country Store and Cafe ❶.** At this hippie-esque local hangout, roadtrippers cruising through early should try the breakfast sandwich (tofu, sprouts and tomato; $3.50). The veggie burgers ($6.25) are excellent, as are the smoothies made with Ben & Jerry's ice cream ($4-6). The store is also home to a gift shop and serves pizza. (☎802-454-8626. Breakfast $2-4. Lunch and dinner $3-9. Open daily 6am-8pm. AmEx/MC/V.)

⚑ APPROACHING MONTPELIER: 36 MILES
U.S. 2 approaches Montpelier about 10 mi. from Danville. Exit U.S. 2 at **Main St.**

MONTPELIER

Chartered in 1781, Montpelier became the capital of Vermont in 1805. For decades, the community has made efforts to restore historical buildings and locally owned businesses. Now, a beautiful capitol dome shines over the city, and the downtown bursts with cafes, markets, and bookstores. Although it's the least populous of the state capitals, Montpelier's small-town charm makes it one of the loveliest.

VITAL STATS
Population: 8000
Visitor Info: Central Vermont Chamber of Commerce, 134 State St. (☎802-828-5981; www.central-vt.com). Open M-F 6:30am-5pm; Sa-Su 9am-5pm.
Internet Access: Kellogg-Hubbard Library, 135 Main St. (☎802-223-3338). Open M-Th 10am-8pm, F 10am-5:30pm, Sa 10am-1pm. Free.
Post Office: 87 State St. (☎802-229-1718). Open M-F 8am-5:30pm, Sa 9am-12:30pm. **Postal Code:** 05602.

🄴 GETTING AROUND. U.S. 2 skirts the city's southern edge, tracing the north bank of the Winooski River. From the east, a right on **Main St.** leads to downtown. U.S. 2 briefly turns into Main St., and then continues west as **State St.** Continuing straight after the intersection of U.S. 2 and Main St. puts you on **Memorial Dr.,** which roughly parallels U.S. 2 on the other side of the river.

🄶 SIGHTS. The best views of the Montpelier countryside come from the 54 ft. observation tower in **Hubbard Park,** on Hubbard Park Dr., the highest point in the city. Don't expect a view of Montpelier—it's blocked by the trees—but you'll get a great look at Camel's Hump, Vermont's second-tallest mountain, in all of its dromedarian splendor to the west. The park has nearly 180 wooded acres for hiking and cross-country skiing. (From the rotary at Main St., follow Rte. 12 north. Make a left shortly thereafter onto Winter St. and follow into the park.) **Morse Farm Maple Sugarworks,** 1168 County Rd., is home to the oldest maple-harvesting family in Vermont. See the trees and take the tour to learn how many gallons of sap it takes to make syrup. A "creatures exhibit" stars Yxon the Alpaca and Sombrero the Goat. (Take Main St. 2½ mi. north of town and turn right on County Rd. ☎800-242-2740; www.morsefarm.com. Open daily in summer 9am-8:30pm; in winter 9am-5pm. Free tours and tastings M-F 8am-2pm.)

🄵🄵 FOOD AND ACCOMMODATIONS. The **New England Culinary Institute's** three restaurants in Montpelier are also classrooms; students-in-training spend weeks and months cooking and training in each location. The **Main St. Grill ❹,** 118 Main St., serves American fare at reasonable prices, with entrees ranging $11-15. (☎802-223-3188. Open Tu-F 11:30am-2pm and 5:30-9pm, Sa 9am-2pm and 5:30-9pm, Su 10am-2pm and 5:30-9pm. AmEx/D/MC/V.) **La Brioche ❷,** 89 Main St., lets students experiment with bakery food; they prepare eye-pleasing cakes, pastries, and sandwiches. Lunches with a sandwich, soup, and a cookie ($6-7) are available to go. (☎802-229-0443. Open M-F 6:30am-6pm, Sa 7am-5pm. AmEx/D/MC/V.) **Sarducci's ❸,** 3 Main St., dishes out Italian cuisine from a wood-burning oven. The dining room overlooks the Winooski River. (☎802-223-0229. Lunch $6-8. Dinner $9-17. Open M-Th and Su 4:30-9pm, F-Sa 4:30-9:30pm. AmEx/D/MC/V.)

Betsy's B&B ❹, 74 E. State St., is a Victorian home downtown with rates better than local motels. Offering bay windows, wood floors, antique furnishings, and oriental rugs, Betsy's has been recognized for its exemplary environmental management by the state of Vermont. Betsy's serves breakfasts of blueberry pancakes with maple syrup or omelettes filled with Cabot cheese. (E. State St., off Main St. ☎802-229-0466; www.betsysbnb.com. All rooms with private baths. Singles $60-90; doubles $80-100. Rates lowest in winter, highest in Oct. AmEx/D/MC/V.)

⚑ APPROACHING WATERBURY: 12 MILES
Between Montpelier and Waterbury, **U.S. 2** is a windy drive paralleling **I-89.**

WATERBURY

Waterbury sits on the banks of the Winooski River, where mountain peaks rise on the horizon. Every trip warrants a stop at the ▨**Ben & Jerry's Factory,** on Rte. 100 N, off Exit 10 from I-89, where Ben & Jerry's premium ice cream began with two schoolboys running at the back of the pack in gym class. In 1978, armed with diplomas from a $5 ice cream-making correspondence course at Penn State, they converted an abandoned gas station into their first ice cream parlor, launching a double-scoop success story. Whether you're into "Karamel Sutra" or just "Makin' Whoopie Pie," the 30min. tours give you a taste of the founders' passion, ending with free samples. Behind the factory sits the ice cream graveyard, a collection of tombstones for discontinued flavors such as "Peanuts! Popcorn! Mix 'em in a pot. Plop 'em in your ice cream! Well, maybe not. 2000-2000." (Go north for 1 mi. on Rte. 100, and look for it on your left. ☎802-846-1500. Tours daily Nov.-May 10am-5pm, June 9am-5pm, July-Aug. 9am-8pm, Aug.-Oct. 9am-6pm. $3, seniors $2, under 13 free.) The **Ziemke Glass Blowing Studio,** 3033 Stowe Rd. (Rte. 100), is also worth a stop. (☎802-244-6126. Demonstrations of glass blowing M-Tu and Th-Su 10am-5pm. Open daily 10am-6pm.)

For dinner, head over to **The Alchemist ❷,** 23 S. Main St. (Rte. 2). You'll want to arrive early, even on weeknights, to avoid the 2hr. waits at this popular local hangout. Try a panini ($6) with a pint of their famous Mortal Sin IPA ($3.50) or one of the six other brews made under your feet in the basement. (☎802-244-4120; www.alchemistbeer.com. Open M-Th 4pm-midnight, F-Sa 3pm-1am, Su 3pm-midnight. Kitchen closes 10pm. AmEx/D/MC/V.) Unfortunately, Waterbury's only motel recently burned down, which makes affordable lodging problematic. There is one $70 room (shared bath, $80 during foliage season) at the beautiful **Old Stagecoach Inn ❹,** 18 North Main St. (☎802-

244-5056; www.oldstagecoach.com. Full breakfast included. AmEx/D/MC/V.) More extensive lodging options are available in Stowe. For more information, the **Waterbury Tourism Council** runs an info booth on the side of Rte. 100, about ¼ mi. north of the intersection with I-89.

⚑ APPROACHING STOWE: 10 MILES
From Waterbury, head north on **Rte. 100** to Stowe.

STOWE

Stowe curves gracefully up the side of Mt. Mansfield, Vermont's highest peak (4393 ft.). A mecca for outdoor enthusiasts in all seasons, but especially during the winter, the village tries to live up to its aspirations as a ritzy European skiing hotspot. Yet despite Stowe's reputation as a mountain resort, the prices are generally more reasonable than throughout the rest of Vermont.

VITAL STATS

Population: 4300

Visitor Info: Stowe Area Association, 51 Main St. (☎802-253-7321 or 800-247-8693; www.gostowe.com). Open June to mid-Oct. and mid-Dec. to Mar. M-Sa 9am-8pm, Su 9am-5pm; mid-Oct. to mid-Dec. and Apr.-May M-F 9am-5pm.

Internet Access: Stowe Free Library, 90 Pond St. (☎802-253-6145). Open M, W, F 9:30am-5:30pm; Tu and Th 2-7pm; Sa 10am-3pm.

Post Office: 105 Depot St. (☎802-253-7521). Open M-F 8am-5pm, Sa 9am-noon. **Postal Code:** 05672.

▛ GETTING AROUND. Stowe is located 10 mi. north of I-89 Exit 10, 27 mi. southwest of Burlington. The ski slopes lie along **Mountain Rd. (Rte. 108),** northwest of Stowe.

▟ OUTDOORS. In summer, Stowe's frenetic pace drops off somewhat, but it still burns with the energy of outdoor enthusiasts. Stowe's 5½ mi. asphalt **recreation path** runs parallel to Mountain Rd.'s ascent and begins behind the church on Main St. Perfect for biking, skating, and strolling in summer, the path also accommodates cross-country skiing and snowshoeing in winter. A few miles past Smuggler's Notch on Mountain Rd. (Rte. 108), the road shrinks to one lane and winds past huge boulders and 1000 ft. high cliffs.

Fly fishermen should head to the **Fly Rod Shop**, 2703 Waterbury Rd. (Rte. 100), 2½ mi. south of Stowe, to pick up the necessary fishing licenses, rent fly rods and reels, and enroll in the free fly-fishing classes in the shop's pond. (☎802-253-7346 or 800-535-9763. Open Apr.-Oct. M-Sa 9am-6pm, Su 9am-5pm; Nov.-Mar. daily 9am-5pm. Classes in summer W 4-6pm and Sa 9-11am. Rods and reels $15 per day. Non-Vermont resident licenses $15 per day.) **Umiak**, 849 S. Main St. (Rte. 100)., three-quarters of a mile south of Stowe Center, rents kayaks and canoes in the summer. During the snowy season, Umiak runs moonlight snowshoeing tours with wine and cheese. (☎802-253-2317. Open in summer daily 9am-6pm; hours vary in winter. Snowshoe tours $39. River trips $42. Kayaks $38 per day, $28 per half-day.) **AJ's Ski and Sports** (see **Skiing**, below) also rents out summer equipment at good rates. (Mountain bikes $27 per day; canoes $42; kayaks $40.)

SKIING. Every winter, skiers pour onto some of the Northeast's finest slopes. **Stowe Mountain Resort** (☎802-253-3000 or 800-253-4754; www.stowe.com) offers two-day lift tickets for $74-102 (depending on season), 48 trails (16% beginner, 59% intermediate, 25% expert), and impressive summer facilities: a golf course and country club, alpine slides, a gondola, a scenic toll road ($16 per car), and a skate park. If Stowe is packed, try **Smuggler's Notch Resort** on the other side of the notch. The hills are alive with cross-country skiing on 50km of groomed trails and 45km of backcountry skiing at the **Von Trapp Family Lodge**, 2 mi. off Mountain Rd. from Luce Hill Rd. Budget travelers beware: lodging prices soar in high season. However, there's no charge to visit, and rentals and lessons are inexpensive. (☎802-253-5719 or 800-826-7000. Trail fee $16. Ski rentals $20 per day. Lessons $15-50 per hr. Ski school package includes all 3 for $40.) **AJ's Ski and Sports**, 350 Mountain Rd., rents equipment at better rates than the resorts. (☎802-253-4593 or 800-226-6257; www.smuggs.com. Skis, boots, and poles: downhill $26 per day, cross-country $16 per day. Snowboard and boots $26 per day. Open in winter M-Th and Su 8am-8pm, F-Sa 8am-9pm; in summer daily 9am-6pm. AmEx/D/MC/V.)

For complete info on skiing statewide, contact **Ski Vermont**, 26 State St., P.O. Box 368, Montpelier 05601. (☎802-223-2439; www.skivermont.com. Open M-F 7:45am-4:45pm.) Cheaper lift tickets can be found during low season—before mid-December and after mid-March.

FOOD AND NIGHTLIFE. The **Depot Street Malt Shoppe ❶**, 57 Depot St., is reminiscent of decades past. Sports pennants and vinyl records line the walls, while rock favorites liven up the outdoor patio seating. The cost of a 1950s-style flavored Coke has been adjusted for inflation, but prices remain reasonable, with nothing above $7 on the menu. (☎802-253-4269. Meals $3-6. Open daily 11:30am-9pm. AmEx/D/MC/V.) Fans of little green men and all things not of this planet will enjoy **Pie in the Sky ❸**, 492 Mountain Rd. "Out of This World" pizzas include the "Blond Vermonter" with olive oil, Vermont cheddar, apples, and ham. Stuff yourself for $7 with "all-you-can-eat-pizza" M-F 11:30am-2pm. (☎802-253-5100. Pizza $8-17. Open daily 11:30am-10pm. MC/V.)

The **Sunset Grille and Tap Room ❸**, 140 Cottage Club Rd., off Mountain Rd., allows its guests to face off at air hockey and pool tables while following sporting events on over 15 TVs. The adjacent restaurant offers award-winning barbecue. (☎802-253-9281. Lunch $5-10. Dinner $6-20. Kitchen open daily 11:30am-midnight. Bar open until 2am. D/MC/V.) The weekday specials and six homemade microbrews served up in **The Shed ❹**, 1859 Mountain Rd., make this brewery stand out. (☎802-253-4364. Tu night $3 pint night. Open daily 11:30am-midnight. AmEx/D/MC/V.)

ACCOMMODATIONS. A converted 19th-century farmhouse and adjacent motel, the **Riverside Inn ❸**, 1965 Mountain Rd., 2 mi. from town, offers a number of great perks and some of the best rates around. The friendly owners loan out their mountain bikes. (☎802-253-4217 or 800-966-4217; www.rivinn.com. Rooms $49-89. AmEx/MC/V.) **Smuggler's Notch State Park ❶**, 6443 Mountain Rd., 8 mi. west of Stowe, keeps it simple with hot showers, tent sites, and lean-tos. The natural beauty and seclusion of the park's sites make up for its lack of amenities. (☎802-253-4014. Reservations recommended; $6 fee. Open late May to mid-Oct. 4-person sites $14-16; lean-tos $21-23. MC/V.)

GREAT NORTH

1863: Pierre Lallement invents the velocipede, a predecessor to the bicycle.

⚐ APPROACHING BURLINGTON: 36 MILES
From Stowe, turn around and take **Rte. 100** back to **Waterbury,** then continue west on **I-89** to Burlington. Be sure to notice the set of **granite whale tails** protruding from the hillside on the north side of the road between Exits 12 and 13. The $100,000 sculpture nearly found a home with the Hartford Whalers hockey team, but instead found its way to I-89. I-89 enters Burlington from the east and takes a right turn north of town along Lake Champlain. Take **Exit 14W** from I-89 into south Burlington and onto **Rte. 2 (Main St.),** which will take you into downtown Burlington.

BURLINGTON

Tucked between Lake Champlain and the Green Mountains, the largest city in Vermont offers spectacular views of New York's Adirondack Mountains across the sailboat-studded waters of Champlain. Several colleges, including the University of Vermont (UVM), give the area a youthful, progressive flair. On a warm day, the city resembles a mountain beach town; if you're lucky enough to catch some rays, visit the boardwalk or the brand new ECHO aquarium and science center. On a rainy day, walk along Church St., where numerous cafes offer a taste of the hip and laid-back Vermont atmosphere.

VITAL STATS

Population: 39,000

Visitor Info: Lake Champlain Regional Chamber of Commerce, 60 Main St. (☎802-863-3403; www.vermont.org). Open M-F 8am-5pm; May to mid-Oct. also Sa-Su 10am-5pm.

Internet Access: Fletcher Free Library, 235 College St. (☎802-864-7146). Open M-Tu and Th-F 8:30am-6pm, W 8:30am-9pm, Sa 9am-5pm, Su noon-6pm. Free.

Parking: Outdoor parking is available at the corners of Pearl and N. Champlain St.; College and Lake St.; and St. Paul and Maple St. Indoor parking is available at Cherry St. between N. Winooski Ave. and Church St.; College St. between Pine and Battery St. (free shuttle); and Main St. at S. Winooski Ave.

Post Office: 11 Elmwood Ave. (☎802-863-6033), at Pearl St. Open M-F 8am-5pm, Sa 9am-1pm. **Postal Code:** 05401.

⌐ GETTING AROUND

In Burlington, **U.S. 2** is known as **Main St.** The major north-south streets downtown are **St. Paul St., Pine St.,** which is one block to the west of St. Paul, and **Battery St.,** which runs next to the lake. **Church St.** also runs north-south but is mainly a pedestrian stretch full of restaurants and shops. Major east-west streets are (from south to north) **Main St., College St., Cherry St.,** and **Pearl St.** Driving around Burlington can be a nightmare, with stoplights or signs at every intersection snarling traffic into gridlock as seen in much bigger cities. Park as soon as possible—nothing is outside of walking distance. Drivers get 2hr. of free parking in all city-owned garages every day, and garages and meters are free after 6pm and on weekends.

 DID YOU KNOW? In 1981, Burlington elected (and subsequently reelected 3 times) a socialist mayor, Bernie Sanders.

◐ SIGHTS

Architecture buffs can delight in **S. Willard St.,** where **Champlain College** occupies many of the Victorian houses that line the street. The pastoral **City Hall Park,** in the heart of downtown, and **Battery St. Park,** on Lake Champlain near the edge of downtown, provide an escape into the cool shade on hot summer days. With an amazing view across Lake Champlain, the **Burlington Community Boathouse,** at the base of College St., operates a small snack bar and offers platforms and seating for those who just want to enjoy the stunning sunsets over Lake Champlain. (☎802-865-3377. Open mid-May to mid-Oct.) The **Spirit of Ethan Allen III** runs a narrated, 500-passenger scenic cruise that departs from the boathouse at the bottom of College St. (☎802-862-8300; www.soea.com. Cruises daily late May to mid-Oct. 10am, noon, 2, 4pm. $13, children $6. Nightly sunset cruise $18/$13.) Visitors have the opportunity to discover ecology, culture, and history at **ECHO,** 1 College St., a science center and lake aquarium built in a renovated former naval station. Though most of the exhibits are designed for younger crowds, they

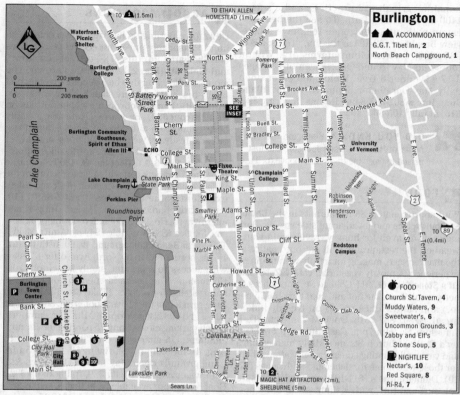

Burlington

ACCOMMODATIONS
G.G.T. Tibet Inn, **2**
North Beach Campground, **1**

FOOD
Church St. Tavern, **4**
Muddy Waters, **9**
Sweetwater's, **6**
Uncommon Grounds, **3**
Zabby and Elf's
Stone Soup, **5**

NIGHTLIFE
Nectar's, **10**
Red Square, **8**
Rí-Rá, **7**

are interesting for anyone curious about the inhabitants of the largest US freshwater lake outside of the Great Lakes—including "Champ," Lake Champlain's own Loch Ness Monster, first sighted in 1609 by Samuel de Champlain himself. (☎802-864-1848; www.echovermont.org. Open daily 10am-5pm. $9, students and seniors $8, ages 3-17 $7.)

The **Ethan Allen Homestead** rests northeast of Burlington on Rte. 127 in the Winooski Valley Park. In the 1780s, Allen and his Green Mountain Boys forced the surrender of Fort Ticonderoga in New York, and later were instrumental in establishing Vermont statehood. Today, 1hr. tours tell the story of Vermont's most unique and legendary character. (☎802-865-4556; www.ethanallenhomestead.org.) **Magic Hat Artifactory,** 5 Bartlett Bay Rd., 3 mi. south of Burlington off Rte. 7, offers free brewery tours and tastings. (☎802-658-2739; www.magichat.net. Tours W-F 3, 4, 5pm; Sa noon, 1, 2, 3pm.) Just 7 mi. south of Burlington on Rte. 7 is the ■**Shelburne Museum,** which houses an impressive collection of Americana, including the enormous paddleboat *Ticonderoga,* alongside paintings by Degas, Cassatt, Manet, Monet, Rembrandt, and Whistler. (☎802-985-3346; www.shelburnemuseum.org. Open daily May-Oct. 10am-5pm. Tickets valid for 2 days. $18, ages 6-18 $9; after 3pm $10/$5. Half-price for Vermont residents.) Just north of the museum is **Shelburne Farms,** 1611 Harbor Rd., which was built in 1886 and encompasses a castle-like farm and the majestic **Inn on Lake Champlain ⑤.** Today, the complex is a nonprofit environmental education center for sustainable agricultural practices and a scenic 1400-acre working farm. To see the beautiful estate without an entrance fee, have a lakeview breakfast ($3-12) at the inn. (Tours: ☎802-985-8686; www.shelburnefarms.org. Wagon tours mid-May to mid-Oct. $6, seniors $5, ages 3-17 $4, under 3 free. Welcome center open daily May-Oct. 9am-5:30pm; Nov.-Apr. 10am-5pm. Inn: ☎802-985-8498. Rooms in spring $95-315, in fall $105-365. MC/V.)

 DID YOU KNOW? Burlington was the home of Horatio Nelson Jackson, the first person to cross the US by automobile (p. 1).

▤ FOOD

With approximately 85 restaurants in the **Church St. Marketplace** and its adjacent side streets, Burlington is a haven for hungry travelers. In warm weather, the restaurants spill out onto patios in the marketplace, making for a truly vibrant dining experience. A mostly vegetarian cafe, **▤Zabby and Elf's Stone Soup ❷**, 211 College St., specializes in hefty meals from the hot and cold bars ($6.75 per lb.) and sandwiches ($7-8) on freshly baked bread. (☎802-862-7616. Open M 7am-7pm, Tu-F 7am-9pm, Sa 9am-7pm. Cash only.) At **Sweetwater's ❸**, 120 Church St., incredibly high ceilings and vast wall paintings create an airy atmosphere for those who come for delicious sandwiches ($7-10). Dinner entrees ($11-16) are standard American surf and turf, with a slight Asian influence. (☎802-864-9800. Open M-Sa 11:30am-11pm, Su 11:30am-midnight. Full bar open until midnight. AmEx/D/MC/V.) Everything on the menu is under $9 at the **Church St. Tavern ❷**, 103 Church St., including many vegetarian options. (☎802-658-1309. Open M-Sa 11:30am to close, Su noon-last customer. Kitchen closes 10pm. AmEx/MC/V.) Local students get their caffeine buzz at **Uncommon Grounds ❶**, 42 Church St., which roasts and grinds its coffee on the premises. (☎802-865-6227. Open M-Th 7am-10pm, F 7am-11pm, Sa 8am-11pm, Su 9am-9pm. Coffee and refill $1.50. Teapot $1.80. Cash only.) An equally appealing option is **Muddy Waters ❶**, 184 Main St., where the outdoors meets the indoors in its rustic decor. (☎802-658-0466. All coffee drinks $3, smoothies $4.25. Open M 7:30am-6pm, Tu-F 7:30am-midnight, Sa 8:30am-midnight, Su 8:30am-10pm. Cash only.)

▣ ACCOMMODATIONS

Downtown Burlington has very few accommodations. Reasonably priced hotels and guesthouses line **Shelburne Rd. (Rte. 7)**, south of downtown, and **Main St. (Rte. 2)**, east of downtown. The motels on Rte. 7 tend to be a generation older and family-run, and hence are slightly cheaper (singles from $40) than the corporate chain options on Rte. 2 (from $80). Be warned: rates vary wildly here—almost on a day-to-day basis—depending on local festivals, weather conditions, and day of the week. Call ahead to guarantee the most affordable visit. The **G.G.T. Tibet Inn ❷**, 1860 Shelburne Rd. (Rte. 7), greets you with a large picture of the Dalai Lama behind the reception desk and offers excellent value and rates. (☎802-863-7110; www.ggtibetinn.com. Pool, TV, A/C, fridges, and microwaves. Breakfast included during peak season. Singles $33-79; doubles $49-89. AmEx/MC/V.) The **North Beach Campground ❶**, 60 Institute Rd., 1½ mi. north of town by North Ave., offer 137 sites with access to a pristine sandy beach on Lake Champlain. The beach is open to non-campers and is stellar for picnics. (Take Rte. 127 to North Ave.; turn left at the high school. ☎802-862-0942 or 800-571-1198. Beach open 24hr. for campers; beach parking closes 9pm. $5 parking fee for non-campers. Lifeguards on duty daily mid-June to Aug. 10am-5:30pm. Showers $0.25 per 5min. Campgrounds open May to mid-Oct. Sites $23, with water and electricity $29, full hookup $32.) Boat rentals are available from **Umiak.** (☎802-253-2317. Canoes $15 per hr., kayaks $10-15 per hr. Open daily 10am-5pm.)

▣ NIGHTLIFE

With several colleges in the area, Burlington's nightlife scene is always alive and kicking. **Nectar's,** 188 Main St., rocks with inexpensive food, including the locally acclaimed gravy fries ($3.50), and nightly live tunes of all genres—check the monthly schedule. Saturday 80s nights are a favorite. (☎802-658-4771. Open daily 10am-2am. AmEx/MC/V.) One of Burlington's most popular night spots, the **Red Square,** 136 Church St., hosts live music nightly. Bands play in the alley if the crowd gets large. (☎802-859-8909. Open M-Sa 4pm-2am, Su 8pm-2am. No kitchen. AmEx/MC/V.) For a laid-back pint, try **Rí-Rá,** 123 Church St., a traditional

Irish pub. Wednesday nights feature live Celtic music starting at 7pm. (☎802-860-9401; www.rira.com. Beer $2-4.50. Open M-W 11:30am-1am, Th-Sa 11:30am-2am, Su 11:30am-midnight. AmEx/D/MC/V.)

⚐ APPROACHING THE CHAMPLAIN ISLANDS: 20 MILES
From **Main St.** in Burlington, turn left on **U.S.2/U.S. 7 (Ethan Allen Hwy.).** Merge with **I-89 N** for about 6 mi. Take **Exit 17** for **U.S. 2 W.**

THE CHAMPLAIN ISLANDS

U.S. 2 heads north through the rural Champlain Islands. Nestled between the Adirondacks and Green Mountains, these mostly flat islands of "New England's West Coast" have avoided exploitation despite the allure of their natural beauty and their prime location between Montréal and Burlington, and still devote their land to farms, orchards, vineyards, and sandy beaches. North of Winooski, the Sandbar Causeway connects to the south end of the Champlain Islands. The northern end of the islands is connected to New York by Rouses Point Bridge, west of Alburg.

SOUTH HERO. This town is known as the "Garden Spot of Vermont" due to an especially long agricultural season. **Grand Isle State Park ❶**, 36 E. Shore Rd. S, offers near-perfect camping, with the waves of Lake Champlain lapping against the shore. Because South Hero is less marshy, there are fewer bugs in this campground than on North Hero. (2 mi. north of town on the east side of the road. ☎802-372-4300; www.vtstateparks.com. 36 lean-tos and 117 sites. Showers, RV sites, swimming, fishing, boat ramp, volleyball courts, and playground. Dump station; no hookups. Rowboat and kayak rentals $7.50 per hr., $20 per half-day, $35 per day. Reception 2-9pm. Quiet hours 10pm-7am. Sites $16-18; lean-tos $23-25. Day-use $2.50 per adult, $2 per child. MC/V.)

NORTH HERO. For a short time during the summer, the island hosts the famous **Royal Lipizzaner Stallions** at **Knight Point State Park.** Originally bred for the exclusive use of the Hapsburg royal family of Austria, the magnificent horses return each summer to North Hero and give spectacular performances under the direction of Colonel Ottomar Herrmann. (☎802-372-6400. Shows mid-July to Aug. Th-F 6pm, Sa-Su 2:30pm; free open barn

other times. $17, seniors $14, ages 6-12 $10, under 6 free. Reservations recommended.)

Called the "Finest General Store on the Planet" in Yankee Magazine, **Hero's Welcome ❶**, 3537 U.S. 2, stocks anything you could ever (or never) need, from slinkies to DVDs, fish bait to film. They also house a deli with excellent sandwiches ($4-6) named after local famous islanders, such as the "Hero" (roast beef and horseradish), after Ethan Allen, who, according to local legend, died while walking back from the island in a winter storm. (☎802-372-4121. Open in summer daily 6:30am-8pm; in winter generally M-Sa 6:30am-6pm, Su 8am-6pm. D/MC/V.) North Hero offers a few other restaurants, but they tend to be expensive during the summer months. The **Lake Champlain Islands Chamber of Commerce**, near Hero's Welcome, offers more information. (☎802-372-8400 or 800-262-5226; www.champlainislands.com. Open M-F 8am-5pm, Sa-Su 10am-2pm.)

⚐ APPROACHING MONTRÉAL: 47 MILES
From the islands, it's a quick 8 mi. drive through New York to the US-Canada border. Get on **I-87 (Adirondack Northway)** heading north, which will almost immediately bring you to customs and turn into **Autoroute (Hwy.) 15.** Just east of Montréal, Autoroute 15 merges with **Autoroutes 10 and 20** to cross the St. Lawrence River via the **Pont Champlain (Champlain Bridge).** Right after you cross the massive river, take the exit for Centre-Ville (Downtown) along the **Autoroute Bonaventure (Hwy. 10).** Follow the expressway to the end, where it becomes **rue Université.**

⚐ LEAVING THE US
See Vital Documents (p. 13) for info on passport, visa, and identification requirements. Until returning to the US, all prices listed are in Canadian dollars.

Bienvenue à **QUÉBEC** *La Belle Province*

MONTRÉAL

This island city has been coveted territory for over 300 years. War and sieges dominated Montréal's early history as British forces strove to wrest it from French control. Today's invaders are not French, British, or American generals, but rather, visitors eager to experience a diverse, cosmopolitan city. Only an hour from the US border, Montréal is the second-largest French-speaking city in the world. Fashion that rivals Paris, a nightlife comparable to London, and international cuisine all attest to the city's prominent European legacy. With its global flavor and large student population, it is hard not to be swept up by the energy coursing through the *centre-ville*.

VITAL STATS

Population: 1.6 million

Visitor Info: Infotouriste, 1001 rue de Square-Dorchester (☎877-266-5687; www.tourisme-montreal.org), on N. Ste-Catherine between rue Peel and rue Metcalfe. Open daily July-Aug. 8:30am-8pm; Sept.-June 9am-6pm.

Currency Exchange: Custom House, 905 blvd. Maisonneuve (☎514-844-1414). Open M-F 8:30am-6pm, Sa 9am-4pm. **Calforex,** 1250 rue Peel (☎514-392-9100). Flat CDN$2.75 fee. Open M-W 8:30am-7pm, Th-Sa 8:30am-9pm, Su 10am-6pm; low season Sa 10am-7pm.

Internet Access: Bibliothèque Nationale du Québec, 1700 rue St-Denis (☎514-873-1100). Open daily 10am-midnight for limited access.

Post Office: 1250 rue Université (☎800-267-1177). Open M-F 8am-5:45pm. **Postal Code:** H3B 3B0.

▐ GETTING AROUND

Two major streets divide the city, making navigation simple. The one-way **Blvd. St-Laurent** (also called **"le Main,"** or **"The Main"**) runs north through the city, splitting Montréal and its streets east-west. The Main also serves as the unofficial French/English divider; English **McGill University** lies to the west, while **St-Denis,** a street running parallel to St-Laurent, lies to the east and defines the French student quarter (also called the *Quartier Latin*). **Rue Sherbrooke,** which is paralleled by **de Maisonneuve** and **Ste-Catherine** downtown, runs east-west almost the entire length of Montréal. The **Underground City,** a network of shops and restaurants, runs north-south, stretching from **rue Sherbrooke** to **rue de la**

Gauchetière and **rue St-Antoine.** Pick up a free map from the tourist office.

Parking is expensive and often difficult to find along the streets. Try lots on the city's outskirts for reasonable prices, and consider using the convenient **STM Métro and Bus** (☎514-288-6287; www.stm.info). The four Métro lines and most buses run daily 5:30am-12:30am (CDN$2.50; 6 tickets $11.50; 1-day pass CDN$9; 3-day CDN$17). Reasonable parking is available at the McGill Residences ($14 per day, CDN$30 per week) or the Université de Montréal (CDN$10 per day) for those who stay in their accommodations.

NEIGHBORHOODS

When first founded, Montréal was limited to the riverside area of present-day **Vieux Montréal.** It has since evolved from a settlement of French colonists into a cosmopolitan metropolis. A stroll along **rue Ste-Catherine,** the flashy commercial avenue, is a must. European fashion is all the rage, conversations mix English and French, and upscale retail shops intermingle with tacky souvenir stores and debaucherous clubs. Its assortment of peep shows and sex shops has earned it the nickname "Saint-Vitrine" (holy windows).

A small **Chinatown** lines rue de la Gauchetière. At the northern edge of the city's center, **Little Italy** occupies the area north of rue Beaubien between rue St-Hubert and Louis-Hémon. Rue St-Denis, home to the city's elite at the turn of the century, still serves as the **Quartier Latin's** main street. Restaurants of all flavors are clustered along **rue Prince Arthur.** Nearby, **Sq. St-Louis** hosts a beautiful fountain and sculptures. **Blvd. St-Laurent,** north of Sherbrooke, is perfect for walking or biking. Many attractions between **Mont-Royal** and the **Fleuve St-Laurent** (St. Lawrence River) are free. **Le Village,** the gay village, is located along rue Ste-Catherine Est between rue St-Hubert and Papineau.

◉ SIGHTS

MONT-ROYAL, LE PLATEAU, AND THE EAST

Package tickets *(forfaits)* for the Biodôme, Funiculaire, and Gardens/Insectarium are a

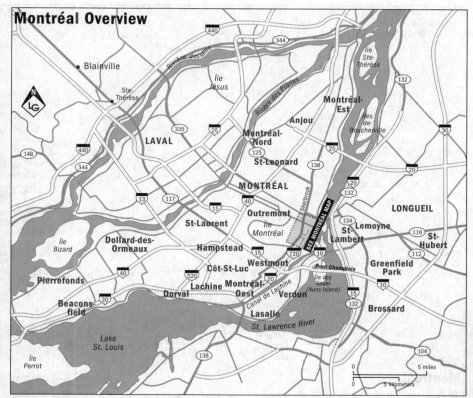

Montréal Overview

decent deal. Tickets are good for 30 days. (Any 2 sights CDN$21.50, students and seniors CDN$16.25, children 5-17 CDN$9.25. All 3 sights CDN$31.50/$23.75/$15.75.)

■**BIODÔME.** The fascinating Biodôme is the most recent addition to Olympic Park. Housed in the former Olympic Vélodrome, the Biodôme is a "living museum" of four complete ecosystems: a Tropical Forest, a Laurentian Forest, a St-Laurent marine ecosystem, and a Polar World. (*4777 av. Pierre-de-Coubertin. M: Viau. ☎514-868-3000; www.biodome.qc.ca. Open daily in summer 9am-6pm; low season 9am-5pm. CDN$12.75, students and seniors CDN$9.50, ages 5-17 CDN$6.50.*)

■**ST. JOSEPH'S.** The dome of **St. Joseph's Oratory** is the second-highest dome in the world after St. Peter's Basilica in Rome. An acclaimed

religious site that attracts pilgrims from all over the globe, St. Joseph's is credited with a long list of miracles and unexplained healings. The **Votive Chapel,** where the crutches and canes of thousands of healed devotees hang for all to see, stays warm with the heat of 10,000 candles. (*3800 ch. Queen Mary. M: Côte-des-Neiges. ☎514-733-8211; www.saint-joseph.org. Open daily 9am-8pm; museum open 10am-5pm.*)

OLYMPIC PARK. The world's tallest inclined tower (*le Tour Olympique*) is the glory of Olympic Park, built for the 1976 summer games. Take the **Funiculaire** to the top of the tower for a breathtaking view. (*3200 rue Viau. M: Viau, Pie-IX. ☎514-252-4737; www.rio.gouv.qc.ca. Guided tours every hour, alternating every 30min. French and English. Tours CDN$8, with tower admission CDN$17. Funiculaire open*

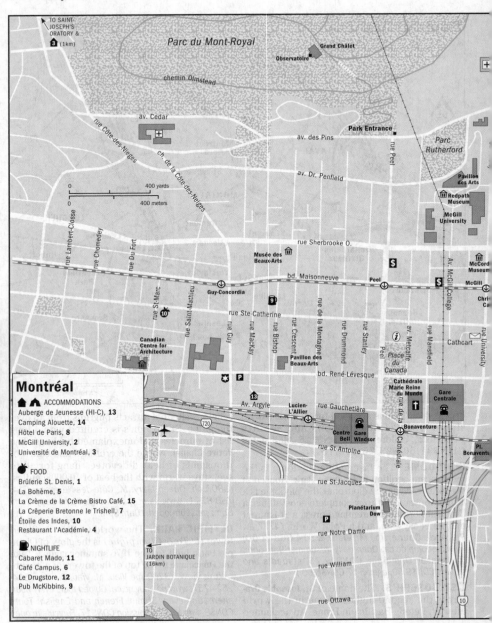

TO SAINT-
JOSEPH'S
ORATORY &
3 (1km)

Parc du Mont-Royal

Grand Châlet

Observatoire

chemin Olmstead

av. Cedar

Park Entrance

Parc Rutherford

av. des Pins

rue Peel

Pavillon des Arts

av. Dr. Penfield

Redpath Museum

McGill University

0   400 yards
0   400 meters

rue Sherbrooke O.

Musée des Beaux-Arts

McCord Museum

bd. Maisonneuve

Peel

McGill

Guy-Concordia

Chri Ca

9

rue Ste-Catherine

10

Canadian Centre for Architecture

Pavillon des Beaux-Arts

bd. René-Lévesque

Place du Canada

Cathédrale Marie Reine du Monde

Gare Centrale

13

Av. Argyle

Lucien-L'Allier

rue Gauchetière

720

TO ✈

Centre Bell

Gare Windsor

Bonaventure

Pl. Bonaventu

rue St-Antoine

rue St-Jacques

Planétarium Dow

P

rue Notre Dame

TO JARDIN BOTANIQUE (16km)

rue William

rue Ottawa

Montréal

🏠🏕 ACCOMMODATIONS
Auberge de Jeunesse (HI-C), **13**
Camping Alouette, **14**
Hôtel de Paris, **8**
McGill University, **2**
Université de Montréal, **3**

🍎 FOOD
Brûlerie St. Denis, **1**
La Bohème, **5**
La Crème de la Crème Bistro Café, **15**
La Crêperie Bretonne le Trishell, **7**
Étoile des Indes, **10**
Restaurant l'Académie, **4**

📖 NIGHTLIFE
Cabaret Mado, **11**
Café Campus, **6**
Le Drugstore, **12**
Pub McKibbins, **9**

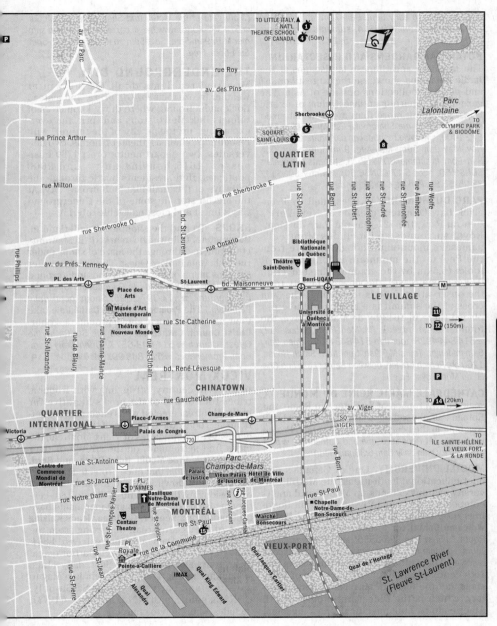

P

av. du Parc

TO LITTLE ITALY,
NAT'L
THEATRE SCHOOL
OF CANADA, ❹ (50m)

❶

rue Roy

av. des Pins

Sherbrooke ⓜ

❺

Parc
Lafontaine

TO
OLYMPIC PARK
& BIODÔME

rue Prince Arthur

❻

SQUARE
SAINT-LOUIS ❼

❽

QUARTIER
LATIN

rue Milton

rue Sherbrooke E.

rue St-Denis

rue Berri

rue St-Hubert

rue St-Christophe

rue St-André

rue St-Timothée

rue Wolfe

rue Amherst

rue Sherbrooke O.

rue Phillips

bd. St-Laurent

rue Ontario

av. du Prés. Kennedy

Bibliothèque
Nationale
de Québec

Théâtre
Saint-Denis

Pl. des Arts

St-Laurent

bd. Maisonneuve

Berri-UQAM

LE VILLAGE

ⓜ

Place des
Arts

Musée d'Art
Contemporain

Théâtre du
Nouveau Monde

rue Ste-Catherine

Université de
Québec
à Montréal

❶❶

TO ❶❷ (150m)

rue St-Alexandre

rue de Bleury

rue Jeanne-Mance

rue St-Urbain

bd. René-Lévesque

P

CHINATOWN

rue Gauchetière

av. Viger

TO ❶❹ (20km)

QUARTIER
INTERNATIONAL

Place-d'Armes

Champ-de-Mars

SQ.
VIGER

Victoria

Palais de Congrès

720

rue Berri

TO
ÎLE SAINTE-HÉLÈNE,
LE VIEUX FORT,
& LA RONDE

Centre de
Commerce
Mondial de
Montréal

rue St-Antoine

Parc
Champs-de-Mars

rue St-Jacques

Palais
de Justice

Vieux Palais
de Justice

Hôtel de Ville
de Montréal

PL.
D'ARMES

Basilique
Notre-Dame
de Montréal

rue Notre Dame

rue de la Commune

Centaur
Theatre

rue St-François-Xavier

rue St-Sulpice

rue St-Vincent

rue Jacques-Cartier

VIEUX
MONTRÉAL

Chapelle
Notre-Dame-de-
Bon-Secours

rue St-Paul

Marché
Bonsecours

❶❺

Pl.
Royale

Pointe-à-Callière

rue St-Jean

rue St-Pierre

IMAX

Quai
Alexandra

Quai King Edward

Quai Jacques-Cartier

VIEUX-PORT

Quai de l'Horloge

St. Lawrence River
(Fleuve St-Laurent)

daily mid-June to early Sept. 9am-7pm; early Sept. to mid-June 9am-5pm. CDN$14, students and seniors CDN$10.50, ages 5-17 CDN$7.)

BOTANICAL GARDENS AND INSECTARIUM. The Japanese and Chinese landscapes at the **Jardin Botanique** showcase the largest *bonsai* and *penjing* collections outside of Asia. The gardens also harbor an **insectarium** of exotic bugs, including more than a dozen fist-sized spiders. (*4101 rue Sherbrooke Est. M: Pie-IX.* ☎514-872-1400; www.ville.montreal.qc.ca/jardin. Open daily Nov.-May 9am-5pm; May-Aug. 9am-6pm; Sept.-Oct. 9am-9pm. In summer CDN$12.75, students and seniors CDN$9.50, ages 5-17 CDN$6.50; in winter CDN$11/ $8.25/$5.50. Parking CDN$8 per day.)

PARC DU MONT-ROYAL. Designed by Frederick Law Olmsted, creator of New York's Central Park, the 127-year-old Parc du Mont-Royal surrounds and includes Montréal's namesake mountain. Though the hike from rue Peel up the mountain is longer than it looks (5.5km by the gradual Olmsted Trail, 0.6km by staircase), the view of the city from the observation deck is rewarding. The 30m cross at the summit is a replica of the cross placed there in 1643 by de Maisonneuve, the founder of Montréal. (*M: Mont-Royal or bus #11.* ☎514-844-4928, tour info 514-843-8240. Open daily 6am-midnight. Tours M-F 9am-5pm from Smith House, 1260 ch. Remembrance, between Beaver Lake and Chalet du Mont-Royal. Free.)

CATHÉDRALE MARIE REINE DU MONDE. A scaled-down replica of St. Peter's in Rome, this Roman Catholic cathedral stirred tensions when it was built in the heart of Montréal's Anglo-Protestant area. (*At René-Lévesque and Cathédrale.* ☎514-866-1661. Open daily 6am-6:30pm. Free.)

MCGILL UNIVERSITY. One of Canada's premier educational institutions, the McGill University campus extends up Mont-Royal and is composed predominantly of Victorian buildings on pleasant greens. Stop by the **McGill Welcome Center** for a tour. (*Burnside Hall Bldg., Room 115.* ☎514-398-6555; welcome@mcgill.ca. Tours available M-F. Call or email 48hr. in advance to reserve.) The campus includes the site of the 16th-century Native American village of **Hochelaga** and the **Redpath Museum of Natural History,** which is the oldest building in North America to be built specifically as a museum.

(Main gate at rue McGill and Sherbrooke. M: McGill. ☎514-398-4086; www.mcgill.ca/redpath. Open in summer M-Th 9am-5pm, Su 1-5pm; in winter M-F 9am-5pm, Su 1-5pm. Free.)

THE UNDERGROUND CITY

Montréal residents don't let the winter weather freeze their *joie de vivre*, and instead flock underground, where thirty kilometers of tunnels link Métro stops and form the ever-expanding "prototype city of the future," with restaurants, cinemas, theaters, hotels, two universities, two department stores, 1700 businesses, 1615 housing units, and 2000 boutiques. Here, residents bustle through the hallways of this mall-like "sub-urban" city. At the McGill stop lie some of the Underground City's finest and most navigable offerings.

SHOPS. To find the shopping wonderland **Pl. Bonaventure,** follow signs marked "Restaurants et Commerce" through the maze of shops under rue de la Gauchetière Ouest. The visitors center supplies maps of the tunnels and underground attractions. (*900 rue de la Gauchetière Ouest. M: Bonaventure.* ☎514-397-2325. Shops open daily 9am-9pm.) The **Promenades de la Cathédrale** take their name from their above-ground neighbor, **Christ Church Cathedral.** (*635 rue Ste-Catherine Ouest. Church* ☎514-843-6577. Open daily 8am-6pm. Promenades ☎514-849-9925.)

VIEUX MONTRÉAL

In the 17th century, struggling with Iroquois tribes for control of the area's lucrative fur trade, Montréal erected walls encircling the settlement. Today, the remnants of those ramparts delineate the boundaries of Vieux Montréal, the city's first settlement, on the stretch of river bank between **rue McGill, Notre-Dame,** and **Berri.** The fortified walls that once protected the quarter were torn down long ago in the interest of expansion, but the beautiful 17th- and 18th-century mansions of politicos and merchants have retained their splendor. **Guidatour** leads **walking tours** of Vieux Montréal, departing from the Basilique Notre-Dame-de-Montréal. (☎514-844-4021 or 800-363-4021; www.guidatour.qc.ca. 1½hr. tours mid-June to late Sept. daily 11am, 1:30pm in English, 11am in French; late May to mid-June and early Oct. tours Sa-Su only. CDN$15, students CDN$13, ages 6-12 CDN$7, includes admission to church.)

■BASILIQUE NOTRE-DAME DE MONTRÉAL.
Towering above the Place d'Armes and its memorial to Maisonneuve is the most beautiful church in Montréal. One of North America's largest churches and a historic center for the city's Catholic population, the neo-Gothic Basilique Notre-Dame de Montréal has hosted everyone from Québec separatists to the Pope. Don't miss the Sacred Heart Chapel's bronze altarpiece and the sound-and-light spectacular *Et la lumière fut*—"And then there was light." *(110 rue Notre-Dame Ouest. M: Place-D'Armes.* ☎ *514-842-2925; www.basiliquenddm.org. Open M-F 8am-4:30pm, Sa 8am-4:15pm, Su 12:30-4:15pm. CDN$4. Light show Tu-Th 6:30pm, F 6:30 and 8:30pm, Sa 7 and 8:30pm. CDN$10, seniors CDN$9, under 18 CDN$5.)*

 MUSEUMS

McCord Museum, 690 rue Sherbrooke Ouest (☎514-398-7100; www.mccord-museum.qc.ca). M: McGill or bus #24. The McCord's exhibits range from toys to wedding gowns, lawn ornaments to photographs. Displays chronicle Montréal's development and quirks. Open Tu-F 10am-6pm, Sa-Su 10am-5pm. CDN$10, seniors CDN$7.50, students CDN$5.50, ages 6-12 CDN$3.

Musée des Beaux-Arts, 1380 and 1379 rue Sherbrooke Ouest (☎514-285-2000; www.mmfa.qc.ca), 5 blocks west of the McGill entrance. The museum's small permanent collection features art ranging from ancient cultures to 20th-century works. Don't miss the collection of creative decorative arts, which includes an 18th-century French sleigh and a cactus hat stand. Open Tu 11am-5pm, W-F 11am-9pm, Sa-Su 10am-5pm. Tours W and Su 1:30 (French) and 2:30pm (English). CDN$15, students and seniors CDN$7.50, children under 13 free.

Pointe-à-Callière: Montréal Museum of Archaeology and History, 350 Place Royale (☎514-872-9150; www.pacmusee.qc.ca), off rue de la Commune near Vieux-Port. M: Place d'Armes. This museum and historic site uses the products of 10 years of archaeological digs in an underground tour of the city's past. Free guided tours with admission 1:30pm (French) and 2:30pm (English). Open in summer M-F 10am-6pm, Sa-Su 11am-6pm; in winter Tu-F 10am-5pm, Sa-Su 11am-5pm. CDN$12, seniors CDN$8, students CDN$6.50, ages 6-12 CDN$4.50, under 5 free.

Musée d'Art Contemporain, 185 rue Ste-Catherine Ouest (☎514-847-6226; www.macm.org), at Jeanne-Mance. M: Place-des-Arts. Canada's premier modern art museum concentrates on the work of Canadians. Open in summer M-Tu and Th-Su 11am-6pm, W 11am-9pm; in winter Tu-Su 11am-6pm, W 11am-9pm. CDN$8, seniors CDN$6, students CDN$4, under 12 free. W free after 6pm.

Canadian Centre for Architecture, 1920 av. Baile (☎514-939-7026; www.cca.qc.ca). M: Guy-Concordia or Atwater. Houses one of the world's most important collections of architectural prints, drawings, photographs, and books. Tours in summer Sa-Su 10:30am and 1:30pm (English); in winter Sa-Su 1:30pm. Open Tu-W and F-Su 11am-6pm, Th 11am-9pm. CDN$10, seniors CDN$7, students CDN$5, under 12 CDN$3. Th free after 5:30pm.

 FOOD

In Montréal, chic restaurants rub shoulders with funky cafes, and everyone can find something to fit their taste. Stop by **Chinatown** or **Little Italy** for outstanding examples of their culinary heritages. The western half of **Ste-Catherine** and the area around **Blvd. St-Laurent** north of Sherbrooke offer a large range of choices. By far the best and affordable restaurants cluster on **rue St-Denis.** Many restaurants, even upscale ones, have no liquor license; head to the nearest *dépanneur* or **SAQ** (Societé des alcools du Québec) to buy wine. For further guidance, consult the free *Restaurant Guide*, published by the **Greater Montréal Convention and Tourism Bureau** (☎514-844-5400), which lists over 130 restaurants by type of cuisine.

■ **Restaurant l'Académie,** 4051 rue St-Denis (☎514-849-2249), at the corner of av. Duluth. M: Sherbrooke. An elegant culinary experience where lunchtime indulgence is reasonably priced and the atmosphere is refined without being stuffy. Recognized for their *moules frites* (steamed mussels; CDN$10). Open daily noon-10pm. AmEx/DC/MC/V. ❹

■ **La Crème de la Crème Bistro Café,** 21 rue de la Commune Est (☎514-874-0723), in Vieux Montréal. A brick cafe on the waterfront that combines Greek cuisine and Provençal decor, La Crème serves tasty baguette sandwiches (with salad; CDN$7-11) and slices of cake (CDN$4). Open daily 11am-midnight, closed Jan. depending on weather. MC/V. ❷

Brûlerie St. Denis, 3967 rue St-Denis (☎514-286-9158). M: Sherbrooke. A fun student cafe where the food and coffee are excellent, the waiters are friendly, and the patrons seem to know each other already. *Café du jour* CDN$1.50. Bagel "Belle Hélène" CDN$4.50. Open daily 8am-11pm. AmEx/MC/V. ❷

Étoile des Indes, 1806 Ste-Catherine Ouest (☎514-932-8330), near St-Mathieu. A local favorite for Indian food. Spicy Bangalore *phal* dishes are only for the brave, but the homemade cheese *paneer* plates are for everyone. The butter chicken (CDN$10) is phenomenal. Lunch specials including soup CDN$6-9. Dinners CDN$5-15. Open M-Sa 11:30am-2:30pm and 5-11pm, Su 5-11pm. MC/V. ❸

La Bohème, 3625 rue St-Denis (☎514-286-6659). M: Sherbrooke, overlooking the Square Saint-Louis. The high quality and beautiful presentation of the classic French cuisine far surpasses the price. Lunch CDN$12-17. Dinner CDN$9-27. All meals include soup or salad, dessert, and coffee or tea. MC/V. ❸

La Crêperie Bretonne le Trishell, 3470 rue St-Denis (☎514-281-1012). M: Sherbrooke. Montréalers have been known to line up for a taste of le Trishell's melt-in-your-mouth crepes and fondues. Strawberry crepe CDN$6.75. Open M-F 11:30am-10:30pm, Sa-Su noon-10:30pm. AmEx/MC/V. ❸

🏠 ACCOMMODATIONS

The **Infotouriste** (☎877-266-5687) is the best resource for info about hostels, hotels, and *chambres touristiques* (rooms in private homes or small guesthouses). Inquire about B&Bs at the **Downtown Bed and Breakfast Network,** 3458 ave. Laval, near Sherbrooke; the managers run their own modest hideaway and maintain a list of 80 other homes downtown. (☎800-267-5180; www.bbmontreal.qc.ca. Open daily 9am-9pm. Singles CDN$55-85; doubles CDN$65-95. AmEx/MC/V.) The least expensive *maisons touristiques* and hotels cluster around **rue St-Denis,** which abuts Vieux Montréal. Canada Day and the Grand Prix in July make accommodations scarce.

🏠 **Auberge de Jeunesse, Montréal Youth Hostel (HI-C),** 1030 rue MacKay (☎514-843-3317; www.hostellingmontreal.com). M: Lucien-L'Allier;

from the station exit, cross the street and head right. The hostel is on the 1st real street on the left, across from the parking lot. Bath in every room, kitchen, laundry, pool tables, Internet, and a cafe. Linen CDN$2.30; no sleeping bags. 1-week max. stay. Reception 24hr. Check-in 1pm. Check-out 11am. The 240 beds fill quickly in summer; reservations strongly recommended. Dorms CDN$30, members CDN$26; private doubles CDN$75/$65. MC/V. ❷

McGill University, Bishop Mountain Hall, 3935 rue de l'Université (☎514-398-6367; www.mcgill.ca/residences/summer). M: McGill. Follow Université along the edge of campus; when the road seems to end in a parking lot at the top of the steep hill, bear right—it is the circular grey stone building with lots of windows. Kitchenettes on each floor. 1000 beds. Free Internet access in lobby, common room with TV. Towels and linens provided. Laundry facilities. Continental breakfast included M-Th 7:30-9:30am. Reception 7am-10pm; there is a guard for late check-in. Check-in 3pm. Check-out noon. Open mid-May to mid-Aug. Singles CDN$45, students and seniors CDN$40. MC/V. ❷

Université de Montréal, Residences, 2450 rue Edouard-Montpetit (☎514-343-8006; www.studiohotel.ca). Metro: Edouard-Montpetit. Follow the signs up the steep hill. Located in a tranquil, remote neighborhood on the edge of a beautiful campus, the East Tower affords a great view. Free local calls. Laundry facilities. TV lounge. Internet CDN$5 per day. Continental breakfast CDN$5 per person. Cafe open M-F 7:30am-2:30pm. Parking CDN$10. Reception 24hr. Check-in 3pm. Check-out noon. Open mid-May to early Aug. Singles CDN$40; doubles CDN$50. 10% student discount. MC/V. ❷

Hôtel de Paris, 901 rue Sherbrooke Est (☎514-522-6861 or 800-567-7217; www.hotel-montreal.com). M: Sherbrooke. This European-style 19th-century apartment houses pleasant hotel rooms with private bath, TV, telephone, and A/C. Some rooms contain kitchenettes. The hotel's 100 hostel beds are not as good a deal as Montréal's other hostels. Linen CDN$3. Single-sex dorms CDN$20; rooms CDN$80-155. AmEx/MC/V. ❶

Camping Alouette, 3449 rue de l'Industrie (☎450-464-1661 or 888-464-7829; www.campingalouette.com), 30km from the city. Follow Autoroute 20 south, take Exit 105, and follow the signs. A nice alternative to the lack of privacy at Montréal's bustling hostels is this secluded campground. Nature trail, pool, laundry facilities, a small store, volleyball courts, a dance hall, and a daily shuttle to and from Montréal (30min., CDN$12 round-trip). Sites for up to 2 campers CDN$28, with hookup CDN$36. MC/V. ❶

🎵 ENTERTAINMENT

Like much of the city, Vieux Montréal is best seen at night. Street performers, artists, and *chansonniers* in various *brasseries* set the tone for lively summer evenings of clapping, stomping, and singing along. Real fun goes down on **St-Paul,** near the corner of St-Vincent. For a sweet Sunday afternoon in summer, **Parc Jeanne-Mance** reels with bongos, dancing, and handicrafts.

FESTIVALS

On any given day, you're likely to find a festival somewhere in Montréal. To keep track of the offerings, pick up a copy of *Mirror* (English) or *Voir* (French) in any theater and in many bars and cafes. In summer, keep your eyes peeled for *ventes-trottoirs,* "sidewalk sales" that shut down major streets. In mid-June, Montréal reels from its always-entertaining **Fringe Festival** (☎514-849-3378; www.montrealfringe.ca), which offers theater, dance, and music events at various spots throughout the Plateau Mont-Royal. It wouldn't be Montréal without high-spirited **Fête Nationale** (☎514-849-2560; www.cfn.org), on St-Jean-Baptiste Day, June 24, a celebration of Québecois pride through local music performances and cultural events. Two of Montréal's signature summer festivals draw crowds from all over the world. In early June, the **Mondial de la Bière** offers tastings of over 300 brands of beer, port, scotch, and whiskey. (☎514-722-9640; www.festivalmondialbiere.qc.ca. Free. Tasting coupons CDN$1.) In the first week of July, jazz fiends take over the city for the **Montréal International Jazz Festival** (☎514-871-1881; www.montrealjazzfest.com). The show brings together over 300 performers. A month later, **Divers/Cité** (☎514-285-4011; www.diverscite.org), a gay pride week, rocks the city in and around Emilie-Gamelin Park.

SPORTS

Montréal also has its share of sporting events. Between October and April, hockey's **Canadiens** (aka Les Habitants—"the locals"—or Les Habs) play at the **Centre Bell,** 1250 rue de la Gauchetière Ouest. (☎514-989-2841, tickets 514-790-1245. M: Bonaventure. CDN$23-150.) Spin to victory during the one-day **Tour de l'Île,** an amateur cycling event with over 45,000 participants. (☎514-521-8356.)

THEATER

Montréal lives up to its cultured reputation with a vast selection of theater in French and English. The **Théâtre du Nouveau Monde,** 84 rue Ste-Catherine Ouest, stages French productions. (☎514-878-7878, tickets 514-866-8668; www.tnm.qc.ca. M: Place-des-Arts. Tickets from CDN$18.) In mid-July, the theater is turned over to the bilingual **Festival Juste pour Rire/Just for Laughs** (☎514-790-4242; www.hahaha.com). The renowned **National Theatre School of Canada,** 5030 rue St-Denis, stages excellent "school plays." (☎514-842-7954; www.ent-nts.qc.ca. Most shows free.) The city's exciting **Place des Arts,** 260 Blvd. de Maisonneuve Ouest (☎514-842-2112; www.pda.qc.ca;), at rue Ste.-Catherine Ouest and Jeanne Mance, houses the **Opéra de Montréal** (☎514-985-2258; www.operademontreal), the **Montréal Symphony Orchestra** (☎514-842-9951; www.osm.ca), and **Les Grands Ballets Canadiens** (☎514-849-0269; www.grandsballets.qc.ca). **Théâtre Saint-Denis,** 1594 rue St-Denis (☎514-849-4211; http://theatrestdenis.com;), hosts Broadway-style productions. Peruse the *Calendar of Events,* available at tourist offices and newspaper stands, or call **Tel-Spec** for ticket info. (☎514-790-2222; ww.tel-spec.com. Open M-Sa 9am-9pm, Su noon-6pm.) **Admission Ticket Network** has tickets throughout Québec. (☎514-790-1245 or 800-678-5440; www.admission.com. Open daily 8am-midnight.)

💺 NIGHTLIFE

Combine a loosely enforced drinking age of 18 with thousands of taps flowing unchecked 'til 3am and the result is the unofficially titled "nightlife capital of North America." Most pubs and bars offer a happy hour (usually 5-8pm) when bottled drinks may be two-for-one and mixed drinks may be double their usual potency. In summer, restaurants often spill onto outdoor patios. Avoid crowds of drunken American college students by ducking into one of the laid-back local pubs along **rue St-Denis** north of Ste-Catherine. Alternatively, join in the fun on **rue Ste-Catherine,** especially around **rue Crescent.** Tamer fun can be found in the pedestrian-only section of **rue Prince Arthur** at **rue St-Laurent.**

Café Campus, 57 rue Prince Arthur (☎514-844-1010; www.cafecampus.com). Unlike the more touristy meat-market discothèques, this hip club gathers a friendly student and twentysomething crowd. Fun and happy Tu retro, Th "Hit-Moi" (Top Ten), Su French music. Drinks CDN$3.50-5.50. Cover CDN$3-6. Open Tu and Th-Su 8:30pm-3am. Cash only.

Pub McKibbins, 1426 rue Bishop (☎514-288-1580). Fine drinks are served in this warmly lit Irish pub. Trophies and tokens ornament the walls and dartboards entertain the crowds, while a fieldstone fireplace warms the room in winter. Live music nightly around 9 or 10pm, including live Irish bands. Open daily 11:30am-3am. Kitchen closes 10pm. AmEx/MC/V.

GLBT NIGHTLIFE

In recent years, Montréal has reached out to the GLBT community, making it one of the most popular gay travel destinations in the world. The ideological capital of the first province in North America to allow gay marriage, the city was also the recent host of the world's first Outgames in 2006. Most of Montréal's gay and lesbian hot spots can be found in the **gay village,** one of the world's largest and safest, along rue Ste-Catherine between St-Hubert and Papineau. While most of the village's establishments cater to men, there are a few lesbian-friendly locales.

Le Drugstore, 1366 rue Ste-Catherine Est (☎514-524-1960). M: Beaudry. A 3-story megaplex bar basking in the glow of colored lights. The crowd is usually mixed sex, though the crowd is mostly female on F. Open daily 8am-3am. Cash only.

Cabaret Mado, 1115 Ste-Catherine Est (☎514-525-7566). M: Beaudry. This cabaret is the home of the wildest drag shows in town. Come Tu for "le Mardi à Mado." Straight-friendly, especially weekends. Drinks CDN$4-5. Cover CDN$5-10. Open daily 11am-3am. AmEx/MC/V.

⚑ APPROACHING SAINT-EUSTACHE: 21 MILES
Getting out of Montréal to the west can be a harrowing experience. The easiest way to reach Saint-Eustache is to take **rue St-Antoine,** which merges onto **Hwy. 720.** Take Hwy. 720 2.5km south to **Hwy. 15,** then take Hwy. 15 22km to the northwest until it connects with **Hwy. 344** at **Exit 19.** Continue west *(ouest)* on Hwy. 344 for about 6 mi. to St.-Eustache.

SAINT-EUSTACHE. The area of Saint-Eustache near the highway brims with chain restaurants and shops. **Old Saint-Eustache,** the heart of the town established in the 18th century, is worth seeing. If you're hungry, try **La Chitarra ❹,** 168 rue St-

---

PARLEZ-VOUS HIGHWAY SIGNS?

Though you can get around Québec quite easily without any knowledge of French, driving in the province and the metro region can be a bit harrowing without a rudimentary knowledge of common highway signage vocabulary. It only takes a few wrong turns to find yourself in Saskatchewan.

Nord - north
Sud - south
Est - east
Ouest - west
Prochaine sortie - next exit
Chemin (Ch.) - route

Le Boulevard (Boul.) - boulevard
Une Autoroute (Auto.) - highway
La rue - street
Le pont - bridge
Attention - caution
Travaux - work

Passing on the right is illegal in Quebec, and speed limit signs are in kilometers per hour. If you blow by a cop at 100 mph and get pulled over, don't say we didn't warn you.

Louis, which lists an extensive selection of *cuisine Italienne*, including pasta, steak, and seafood. Try *ombria* (lamb with goat cheese; CDN$16), a regional specialty. (☎450-974-2727. Entrees CDN$9-19. Open M-Tu and Sa-Su 4:30-10pm, W-F 11am-10pm. AmEx/MC/V.) The only hotel in Saint-Eustache, **L'Auberge Saint-Eustache ❹**, 40 Dubois St., offers 39 rooms that are spacious but sparsely decorated. (From Hwy. 148 west, turn right on Grignon St., and immediately make another right on Dubois St. ☎514-473-6825. Rooms CDN$79-85. MC/V.)

⚐ APPROACHING OKA: 10 MILES
Follow **Hwy. 344** to Oka.

OKA. A small town on the banks of the Ottawa River, Oka is home to small diners and ice-cream shops as well as a couple of B&Bs. Take a break from the road here at the popular sand beach at **Parc National d'Oka ❶**, 2020 Chemin d'Oka, or spend the night; showers, swimming, boating, and picnicking all await. (☎450-479-8365; www.parcsquebec.com. Parking CDN$6.25 per day. Open daily May to mid-Oct. 8am-10pm. Tent sites CDN$21; RV sites CDN$31. Day-use CDN$3.50, ages 6-17 CDN$1.50, under 6 free. AmEx/MC/V.)

⚐ APPROACHING MONTEBELLO: 47 MILES
Continue along **Hwy. 344** heading west. Between Grenville and St-Andre-Est, Hwy. 344 merges with 148, continuing west as **Hwy. 148.**

MONTEBELLO

In the town of Montebello, be sure to check out **Fairmont le Château Montebello**, 392 Notre Dame St. (Hwy. 148). Château Montebello may just be the world's largest log building; trying to squeeze the whole star-shaped marvel into one photograph is challenging. You can wander around the 260 sq. km of waterfront property or call to reserve a tour. To stay at the Château is incredibly pricey, however, starting at CDN$149 per person per night and fluctuating wildly. If you don't want to pay CDN$5 per hour to park, leave your car at the Infotouriste and take a pleasant 15min. trail through the historic Manoir Papineau to get to the château. (☎819-423-6341 or 800-441-1414; www.fairmont.com.) Be sure not to wash your car before a visit to **Parc Omega**, Hwy. 323 N, since deer slobber will inevitably ruin the effort. Majestic elk, buffalo, ducks, and boars roam

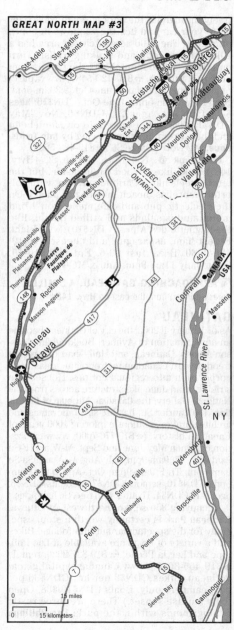

GREAT NORTH MAP #3

freely throughout the park and will walk right up to your car and lick the windows in hopes of a treat. The 1500-acre enclosed area has a 10km driving loop and walking trails. (Turn onto Hwy. 323 in Montebello; the park is 4km north on the left. ☎819-423-5487; www.parc-omega.com. Open daily June-Oct. 9:30am-6pm; Nov.-May 10am-5pm. June-Oct. CDN$16, ages 6-15 CDN$11, ages 2-5 CDN$6; Nov.-May CDN$13/$9/$5.) For more info on Montebello and the surrounding area, swing by **Info Touristique,** 502 Notre Dame St. (☎819-423-5602).

⬛Le Zouk ❸, 530 Notre Dame St. (Hwy. 148), looks like a wood cabin inside, but the terrace feels like a Caribbean resort, with colorful umbrellas, beach music, and plants. On their eclectic pub and cafe menu, you'll find mountainous salads and grilled panini, like the baguette des Alpes (CDN$10), with Black Forest ham, asparagus, and cheese. (☎819-423-2080. Breakfast $3-6. Entrees $10-19. Open daily 11am-9pm. AmEx/MC/V.)

◪ APPROACHING GATINEAU: 41 MILES
Enter Gatineau from the east on **Hwy. 148.**

GATINEAU

As of January 1, 2002, the city of Gatineau became an amalgamation of Aylmer, Buckingham, Masson-Angers, Gatineau, and Hull—part of a recent trend toward Canadian metropolitan areas' reincorporation into regional entities. Housed in a striking, sand-dune-like structure across from the National Gallery, the **Canadian Museum of Civilization,** 100 Laurier St., has life-sized dioramas and architectural re-creations exploring 1000 years of Canadian history. (☎819-776-7000; www.civilization.ca. Open May-June and Sept. M-W and F-Su 9am-6pm, Th 9am-9pm; July-Aug. M-W and Sa-Su 9am-6pm, Th-F 9am-9pm; Oct.-Apr. daily 9am-6pm. CDN$10, seniors CDN$7, students CDN$6, ages 2-12 CDN$4. Th after 4pm free. Su half-price.)

Occupying 356 sq. km northwest of Ottawa, **Gatineau Park** is certainly worth a stop, especially for the spectacular autumn foliage. Bikes and a variety of boats are available at Lac Philippe and Lac la Pêche. (☎819-827-2020, rentals ☎819-456-3016; www.canadascapital.gc.ca/gatineau. Bikes CDN$8 per hr., CDN$36 per day; campers only. Boats CDN$10/$38. Open daily sunrise-sunset.) There are three rustic campgrounds within the park: **Lac Philippe**

Campground ❶, which offers 248 sites with facilities for family camping, trailers, and campers; **Lac Taylor Campground ❶,** which has 33 semi-rustic sites; and **Lac la Pêche Campground ❶,** with 36 sites accessible only by canoe. (Take Hwy. 5 N, and exit at Old Chelsea. ☎819-456-3016; www.gatineau-park-camping.ca. Permit CDN$26. Check-in 1:30pm. Sites CDN$5. MC/V.)

◪ APPROACHING OTTAWA: 1 MILE
Cross the **Alexandra Bridge,** which will take you into the Parliament Hill area of the city.

OTTAWA

Legend has it that in the mid-19th century, Queen Victoria chose Ottawa as Canada's capital by closing her eyes and pointing a finger at a map. In reality, perhaps political savvy, rather than blind chance, guided her to this once-backwater logging town known for its saloons and bar fights. Held by neither the French nor the English, Ottawa was the perfect compromise. Forced to attempt to forge national unity while preserving local identities, Ottawa continues to play cultural diplomat to the rest of Canada.

VITAL STATS

Population: 800,000

Visitor Info: National Capital Commission Information Center, 90 Wellington St. (☎613-239-5000; www.canadascapital.gc.ca), opposite the Parliament Building. Open daily early May to early Sept. 8:30am-9pm; early Sept. to early May 9am-5pm.

Currency Exchange: Accu-Rate Foreign Exchange, 111 Albert St. (☎613-596-0612; www.accu-rate.com).

Internet Access: Ottawa Public Library, 120 Metcalf St. (☎613-580-2945). Open M-Th 10am-9pm, F 10am-6pm, Sa 10am-5pm, Su 1-5pm. Free.

Parking: Park for free Sa-Su in the **World Exchange Plaza,** on Queen St. between O'Connor and Metcalfe.

Post Office: 59 Sparks St. (☎613-844-1545). Open M-F 8am-6pm. **Postal Code:** K1P 5A0.

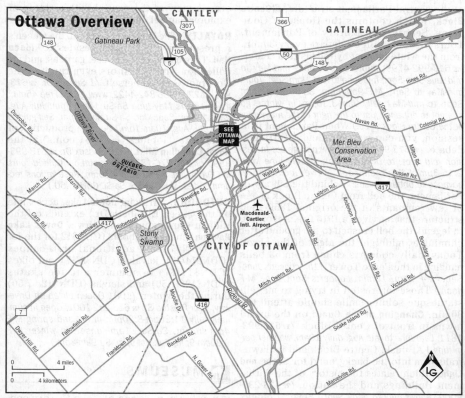

Ottawa Overview

GETTING AROUND

The **Rideau Canal** divides Ottawa into the eastern lower town and the western upper town and is lined with bike paths and walkways. The canal is a major access route and the world's longest skating rink during the winter. West of the canal, Parliament buildings and government offices line **Wellington St.**, a major east-west artery, which runs directly into the heart of downtown. **Laurier Ave.** is the only other east-west street permitting traffic from one side of the canal to the other. East of the canal, Wellington St. becomes **Rideau St.**, surrounded by a fashionable shopping district. North of Rideau St., the Byward Market hosts a summertime open-air market and most of Ottawa's nightlife. **Elgin St.** runs north-south from Hwy. 417 (the Queensway) to the War Memorial just south of Wellington near Parliament Hill. **Bank St.**, which runs parallel to Elgin St. three blocks to the west, leads to the town's older shopping area. Parking downtown is hard to find, and Ottawa is notorious for prompt ticketing of vehicles.

SIGHTS

THE HUB. Parliament Hill, on Wellington at Metcalfe St., towers over downtown with its distinguished neo-Gothic architecture. The **Centennial Flame** at the south gate was lit in 1967 to mark the 100th anniversary of Confederation. The Prime Minister can be spotted at the central Parliament structure, ☒**Centre Block,** which contains the House of Commons, Senate, and Library of Parliament. Tours of Centre Block depart every 30min. from the white **Infotent** by the visitors center. *(☎613-992-4793. Infotent open daily mid-May to mid-June 9am-5pm; mid-June to Aug. 9am-8pm. Tours mid-May to Sept. M-F 9am-8pm, Sa-Su 9am-5pm; Sept. to mid-May daily 9am-3:30pm. In winter, go straight to entrance just to the right of the main door of the Centre Block. Free.)* When Parliament is in session, you can watch Canada's officials debate. *(☎613-992-4793; www.parl.gc.ca. In session mid-Sept. to Dec. and Feb. to mid-June M-Th 2:15-3pm, F 11:15am-noon. Arrive about 2hr. in advance to obtain passes.)* Behind the Library of Parliament, the bell from Centre Block is one of few remnants of the original 1859-1866 structure that survived a 1916 fire. According to legend, the bell crashed to the ground after chiming at midnight the night of the blaze. Today, daily concerts chime from 53 bells hanging in the Peace Tower. *(1hr. concerts June-Sept. M-F 2pm. 15min. concerts Sept.-June M-F noon.)* Those interested in trying to make a statuesque soldier smile should attend the 30min. **Changing of the Guard** on the broad lawns in front of Centre Block. *(☎613-993-1811. Late June to late Aug. daily 10am, weather permitting.)* At dusk, Centre Block and its lawns transform into the background for **Sound and Light,** which relates the history of the Parliament Buildings and the nation. *(☎613-239-5000. Shows July to early Sept.)* Several blocks west along Wellington St. stand the **Supreme Court of Canada** and the **Federal Court.** *(☎613-995-5361; www.ssc-csc.gc.ca. Open daily June-Aug. 9am-5pm; Sept.-May hours vary. Free tours every 30min. except Sa-Su noon-1pm. Tours alternate between French and English.)*

CONFEDERATION SQUARE. East of the Parliament Buildings at the junction of Sparks, Wellington, and Elgin St. stands **Confederation Square** and the enormous **National War Memorial,** dedicated by King George VI in 1939. The structure, a life-size representation of Canadian troops marching under the eye of the angels of liberty, symbolizes the triumph of peace over war. At **Nepean Point,** several blocks northwest of Rideau Centre and the Byward Market, visitors can share a pan-

oramic view of the capital with a statue of explorer Samuel de Champlain.

ROYALTY. The Governor General, the Queen's representative in Canada, resides at **Rideau Hall.** Take a tour of the house, gardens, and art collection—many visitors even run into the Governor General herself. *(1 Sussex Dr. ☎613-991-4422 or 866-842-4422; www.gg.ca. Free 45min. guided tours May-June Sa-Su 10am-4pm; July-Aug. daily 1-5pm; Sept.-Oct. Sa-Su noon-4pm. Self-guided tours July-Aug. 10am-1pm.)* See the production of collectors' "loonies" (CDN$1 coins) at the **Royal Canadian Mint.** *(320 Sussex Dr. ☎613-993-8990 or 800-276-1871; www.mint.ca. Guided tours M-F 9am-7pm, Sa-Su 9am-4:30pm. Reservations recommended. M-F CDN$5, Sa-Su CDN$3.50.)*

OUTDOORS. Artificial **Dow's Lake,** accessible by the Queen Elizabeth Dr., extends off the Rideau Canal south of Ottawa. **Dow's Lake Pavilion** rents pedal boats (CDN$12 for the 1st hr., CDN$7 each additional hr.), canoes (CDN$14/$7), kayaks (CDN$9/$7) and bikes (CDN$11/$7) in summer and ice skates (CDN$12/$7.50) and sleighs (CDN$12/$7.50) during the winter. *(1001 Queen Elizabeth Driveway, near Preston St. ☎613-232-1001. Open in summer daily 11:30am-8:30pm; in fall and spring M-F 4pm-sunset, Sa-Su 11am-sunset; in winter M-F 9:30am-9pm, Sa 9am-9pm, Su 9am-8pm.)*

🏛 MUSEUMS

☒ **National Gallery,** 380 Sussex Dr. (☎613-990-1985, tickets 888-541-8888; www.gallery.ca). A glass-towered building adjacent to Nepean Pt. holds the world's most comprehensive collection of Canadian art. The facade is a reinterpretation of the nearby neo-Gothic Library of Parliament. Don't miss Rideau Chapel, a church reconstructed inside the Gallery. Open May-Sept. M-W and F-Su 10am-5pm, Th 10am-8pm; Oct.-Apr. W and F-Su 10am-5pm, Th 10am-8pm. CDN$6, students and seniors CDN$5, ages 12-19 CDN$3. Th after 5pm free.

Canadian Museum of Contemporary Photography, 1 Rideau Canal (☎613-990-8257; http://cmcp.gallery.ca), between the Château Laurier and the Ottawa Locks. Showcases an impressive rotation of temporary exhibits. Open May-Sept. M-W and F-Su 10am-5pm, Th 10am-8pm; Oct.-Apr. W and F-Su 10am-5pm, Th

TO RIDEAU HALL, ACCU-RATE FOREIGN EXCHANGE (700m)

HULL

Alexandra Bridge

Nepean Point

Royal Canadian Mint

Canadian War Museum

Riverside Path

Ottawa River

National Gallery

Peacekeeping Monument

Rue Bruyere

St. Andrew St.

Gulguee Ave.

St. Patrick St.

Rue Murray

Parent Ave.

Dalhousie St.

Majors Hill Park

Mackenzie Ave.

U.S. Embassy

Clarence St.

Rue York

BYWARD MARKET

Byward Market

Rue George

Rue Rideau

Supreme Court

Riverside Path

Infotent

Centre Block

PARLIAMENT BUILDINGS

Château Laurier

Sussex Dr.

Centennial Flame

Canadian Museum of Contemporary Photography

National War Memorial

Rue Wellington

CONFEDERATION SQ.

Sparks St. Mall

Rideau Centre

Congress Centre

Nicholas St.

Waller St.

Kent St.

Rue Bank

O'Connor St.

Metcalfe St.

Rue Queen

National Arts Centre

Rue Albert

Rue Slater

Elgin St.

MacKenzie King Bridge

Colonel Dr.

Ottawa Public Library

Laurier Ave.

Laurier Bridge

TO LAURIER HOUSE (500m)

Rue Gloucester

Ontario Courthouse

Nepean St.

City Hall

Queen Elizabeth Dr.

Rideau Canal

UNIVERSITY OF OTTAWA

Université St.

Ottawa

🛏 ACCOMMODATIONS
Ottawa International Hostel (HI-C), **8**
University of Ottawa Residences, **9**

🍎 FOOD
Byward Café, **5**
D'Arcy McGee's Irish Pub, **7**
Mamma Grazzi's Kitchen, **4**
Medithéo, **1**

🛏 NIGHTLIFE
The Honest Lawyer, **6**
The Lookout, **3**
Zaphod, **2**

Rue Lisgar

Rue Cooper

TO 🏛 CANADIAN MUSEUM OF NATURE (400m)

Somerset St.

TO 🚉 (1km), DOW'S LAKE (4mi)

Rue MacLaren

GREAT NORTH

10am-8pm. CDN$4, students and seniors CDN$3, ages 12-19 CDN$2. Th after 5pm free.

Canadian War Museum, 1 Vimy Pl. (☎819-776-8600; www.warmuseum.ca), next to the National Gallery. Documents the history of the Canadian armed forces, from colonial skirmishes to UN Peacekeeping missions. See Hitler's armored car, and walk through a mock WWI trench. Open May-June and Sept.-Oct. M-W and F-Su 9am-6pm, Th 9am-9pm; July-Aug. M-W and Sa-Su 9am-6pm, Th-F 9am-9pm; Oct.-Apr. Tu-W and F-Su 9am-5pm, Th 9am-9pm. CDN$10, seniors CDN$7, students CDN$6, ages 3-12 CDN$4. Th after 4pm free. Su half-price.

Canadian Museum of Nature, 240 McLeod St. (☎613-566-4700; www.nature.ca), at Metcalfe St. A multimedia exploration of the natural world. Open May to early Sept. M-W and F-Su 9:30am-5pm, Th 9:30am-8pm; Oct.-Apr. Tu-W and F-Su 9am-5pm, Th 9am-8pm. Donations requested.

⌕ FOOD

Ottawa's **Byward Market,** on Byward St. between York and George St., is full of tables displaying produce, plants, and sweet maple syrup. (☎613-562-3325; www.byward-market.com. Open in warmer weather daily 8am-5pm.) **York, George,** and **Clarence St.** are packed with cafes, great restaurants, and bars.

☒ Mamma Grazzi's Kitchen, 25 George St. (☎613-241-8656; www.mammagrazzis.com). This Italian hideaway in one of the oldest parts of Ottawa is tucked away in a grand building. Thin-crust pizza (CDN$10-16) is worth the wait. Open M-Th and Su 10:30am-10pm, F-Sa 10:30am-11pm. AmEx/MC/V. ❸

Meditheo, 77 Clarence St. (☎613-562-2500; www.meditheo.com). Whether it's the alluring atmosphere, the exotic Mediterranean and Spanish cuisine, or that 3rd glass of sangria (CDN$6), the world looks different from inside this unique eatery. Entrees CDN$22-34. Open M-F 11am-11pm, Sa-Su 11am-2am. AmEx/MC/V. ❺

Byward Café, 55 Byward Market (☎613-241-2555), at George St. Fun pop music and a huge array of baked goods and savory deli dishes bring both young and old to eat, drink, and relax on the covered patio. Panini

CDN$4.50. Open daily in summer 8am-11pm; in winter 8am-6pm. AmEx/MC/V. ❷

D'Arcy McGee's Irish Pub, 44 Sparks St. (☎613-230-4433; www.darcymcgees.ca). Whether lured in by the traditional Celtic music or chased in by the traditional Canadian weather, visitors to D'Arcy's are never sorry they came. Hearty pub food and Irish dishes CDN$6-19. W live music. Open M-Tu and Su 11am-1am, W-Sa 11am-2am. AmEx/MC/V. ❸

⌕ ACCOMMODATIONS

In downtown Ottawa, the only way to stick to your budget is to avoid hotels. Reservations are recommended, especially if you're staying through Canada Day (July 1). **Ottawa Bed and Breakfast** represents 10 B&Bs in the Ottawa area. (☎613-563-0161. Singles CDN$70-100; doubles CDN$90-110.)

☒ Ottawa International Hostel (HI-C), 75 Nicholas St. (☎613-235-2595; www.hihostels.ca), in downtown Ottawa. The site of Canada's last public hanging, the former Carleton County Jail now "incarcerates" travelers in tiny cells. Jail tours (7pm nightly; CDN$12, guests CDN$7.50). Kitchen, Internet access, laundry, and a friendly atmosphere. Linen CDN$2.50. Parking CDN$5 per day. Reception in summer 24hr.; in winter 7am-2am. Check-in 1pm. Check-out 11am. Dorms CDN$25, members CDN$23; private rooms CDN$55/$59. AmEx/MC/V. ❷

University of Ottawa Residences, 90 University St. (☎613-564-5400 or 877-225-8664), in the center of campus, an easy walk from downtown. Clean dorms in a concrete landscape. Free Internet access. Parking CDN$10 per day. Check-in 4:30pm. Check-out 10:30am. Open early May to late Aug. Singles CDN$40, students CDN$30; doubles CDN$60/$45. MC/V. ❷

⌕ ENTERTAINMENT

Ottawans celebrate everything, even the bitter Canadian cold. The city explodes for the all-important **Canada Day,** July 1, which involves fireworks, partying in Major's Hill Park, and concert. During the first three weekends of February, **Winterlude** (☎800-465-

1922: The American Association of Highway Officials standardizes the octagonal stop sign.

1867; www.canadascapital.gc.ca/winterlude) lines the Rideau Canal. Ice sculptures and a working ice cafe illustrate how it feels to be an Ottawan in the winter—frozen. In early May, the **Tulip Festival** (☎613-567-4447 or 800-668-8547; www.tulipfestival.ca) showcases more than a million buds around Dow's Lake, while pop concerts and other events center on Major's Hill Park. Music fills the air during the **Dance Festival** (☎613-947-7000; www.canadadance.ca) in late June and the **Jazz Festival** (☎613-241-2633; www.ottawajazzfestival.com) in late July.

⬛ NIGHTLIFE

Many of Ottawa's nightclubs have been purchased by the same owner, so prices among establishments are fairly uniform.

The Honest Lawyer, 141 George St. (☎613-562-2262), near Dalhousie St. If you were to mix an arcade, a college library, and a law office, this cavernous bar is what you'd get. A bowling alley, pool table, and foosball tables round out this sports bar that attracts a more mature crowd. The 130 oz. "Beerzooka" is, well, a lot of beer (CDN$35). Specials every night, including M all-you-can-eat wings (CDN$13). F-Sa 21+. Cover CDN$3 after 11pm. Open M-Tu 3pm-2am, W-F 11:30am-2am, Sa 3pm-2am, Su 6pm-2am. AmEx/MC/V.

Zaphod, 27 York St. (☎613-562-1010; www.zaphodbeeblebrox.com), in Byward Market. Named for a character in the classic sci-fi spoof *The Hitchhiker's Guide to the Galaxy,* this popular alternative rock club showcases local musicians. Pangalactic Gargle Blasters CDN$6.50. W-Sa live bands. Cover CDN$5-20. Open daily 4pm-2am. AmEx/MC/V.

The Lookout, 41 York St. (☎613-789-1624; www.thelookoutbar.com), next to Zaphod on the 2nd floor. A gay club with intense dancing. The Th evening crowd is mostly male, but women flock here on F. Sa night drag shows. No cover. Open daily noon-2am. Cash only.

⬛ APPROACHING SMITH FALLS: 48 MILES

From Ottawa, take **Hwy. 417 (Queensway)** west to **Hwy. 7,** which will meet **Hwy. 15** 17 mi. before Smiths Falls. Hwy. 15 enters Smiths Falls as **Union St.** from the north at a T-junction with **Cornelia St.** Turn right on Cornelia St., then take a left onto **Elmsley St.**

SMITHS FALLS

Smiths Falls was named after Thomas Smyth, an American who received the land after the Revolutionary War for remaining loyal to the British crown. With the advent of the Rideau Canal and later the junction of several major railroads, Smiths Falls became a manufacturing hub. Though past its prime, the town now retains a small-town charm. The **Rideau Canal Museum,** 34 Beckwith St., houses five floors of high tech displays, images, and artifacts. Exhibits cover everything from the construction of the canal to modern influences on the local lifestyle. (☎613-284-0505; www.rideauinfo.com/museum. Open mid-May to mid-Oct. daily 10am-4:30pm. $4, seniors CDN$3.50, ages 6-18 CDN$2.50.) The air surrounding **Hershey's Factory,** 1 Hershey Dr., is heavy with the sweet smell of chocolate, tempting those with a sweet tooth well before the self-guided tour of the production line ends at the endless (and unavoidable) gift shop. The best part of the tour? A free full-size chocolate bar at the end. (Follow Elmsley St. ½ mi. south until it turns into Queen St.; the factory is on the left. ☎613-283-3300; www.hersheys.com/discover/smithsfalls.asp. Open M-F 9am-6pm, Sa 9am-5pm, Su 10am-5pm. Free.)

Star Pizza ❷, 6 Russell St. E., is a classic diner that has changed very little since it first opened in the 1960s. Red bar stools line the counter where customers eat standard diner fare. (☎613-283-8459. Open M-W noon-10pm, Th-Sa noon-1am, Su noon-9pm. AmEx/MC/V.) **Montgomery's on Main ❹,** 117 Main St., offers rooms that shine with class. Breakfasts are served on the sun deck. (☎613-284-0947. Rooms CDN$65-80. Cash only.)

⬛ APPROACHING KINGSTON: 60 MILES

Take **Rte. 15 S** until it ends and meets with **Rte. 2.** Make a right onto Rte. 2, which becomes **Ontario St.,** and proceed over the LaSalle Causeway into downtown Kingston.

KINGSTON

The "Limestone City" was chosen for its strategic location as the western gateway to the Thousand Islands, the southern end of the Rideau Canal, and the source of the St-Lawrence River. Kingston was built by the

British following the War of 1812 for refugee Loyalists from New York.

VITAL STATS

Population: 110,000

Visitor Info: Information Office, 209 Ontario St. (☎888-855-4555; www.cityofkingston.ca). Open daily in summer 9am-9pm; in winter 9am-6pm.

Internet Access: Kingston-Frontenac Public Library, 130 Johnston St. (☎613-549-8888). Open May-Sept. M-Th 9am-9pm, F-Sa 9am-5pm; Oct.-Apr. M-Th 9am-9pm, F-Sa 9am-5pm, Su 1-5pm. Free.

Post Office: 120 Clarence St. (☎613-530-2260). Open M-F 9am-5:30pm. **Postal Code:** K7L 1X7.

▐ GETTING AROUND. Rte. 15 enters Kingston from the north and meets with **Rte. 2** across the river from downtown. Running east-west, **Ontario St.** serves as Kingston's main drag along the waterfront downtown, while **Princess St.** (Rte. 2 west of the causeway) cuts diagonally from the waterfront through the heart of the city. Parking is free M-F after 5:30pm.

◪ SIGHTS. Kingston offers several free museums, including the **Correctional Service of Canada Penitentiary Museum,** 555 King St. W. The museum follows the history of Canada's federal penitentiary system, detailing the early history of Canadian penitentiaries and showing contraband weapons, escape devices, and punishment equipment. (From Ontario St., turn onto West St. for 1 block, then left onto King St. for 1 mi. ☎613-530-3122; www.penitentiarymuseum.ca. Open May-Sept. M-F 9am-4pm, Sa-Su 10am-4pm; Oct.-Apr. M-F by appointment only. Donations requested.) The more lighthearted **Original Hockey Hall of Fame,** at York and Alfred St., is hockey's "first hall of fame" and the oldest hall of fame in Canada. Memorabilia from hockey greats, including Wayne Gretzky's Edmonton Oiler rookie sweater, and the oldest hockey sweater, all await. (From Ontario St., turn onto Princess St. After ¾ mi., make a right onto Alfred St. ☎613-544-2355; www.ihhof.com. Open June 15 to Labor Day daily 10am-3pm; Labor Day to June 15 by appointment. CDN$5, seniors CDN$4, students CDN$3, under 13 CDN$2.)

Scare yourself silly on one of the **Haunted Walks of Kingston,** which depart from the **Fort Henry National Historic Site,** 200 Ontario St. Just after sunset, these lantern-lit tours wind through Kingston's spooky streets and historic 19th-century fortress, exploring burial grounds ravaged by grave-robbers and the places of public execution. Watch out for the ghost of a murdered young mother-to-be and the ghosts of the two young lovers killed in Deadman's Bay. (☎613-549-6366; www.hauntedwalk.com. Tours May daily 8pm; June daily 8, 9pm; July-Sept. daily 7, 8, 9pm. Reservations strongly recommended.) Kingston boasts lively festivals, such as the **Busker's Rendezvous** (www.kingstonbuskers.com) in mid-July when over 100 street performers from all over the world perform downtown. Another major festival is the **Limestone City Blues Festival** (www.kingstonblues.com) at the Grand Theatre stage in Confederation Park during the third week in August, a favorite of local Blues Brother Dan Aykroyd.

▐▐ FOOD AND ACCOMMODATIONS. Housed in an 1870s building, the **Kingston Brewing Company ❸,** 34 Clarence St., off Ontario St., was the first public house in Ontario to receive a license to brew its own beer and wine on the premises. Try the "Dragon's Breath Ale" or "Regal Lager" (CDN$5 per pint) to wash down the pub grub and barbecue offerings. Outside, streetside and courtyard patios are fringed with hanging white lights. (☎613-542-4978; www.kingstonbrewing.com. Entrees CDN$8-20. Tours available. Open daily 11am-2am. AmEx/MC/V.) **Darbar ❸,** 479 Princess St., off Ontario St., is one of a host of affordable Indian restaurants and a student favorite. Darbar offers delicious Indian fare such as tandoor (CDN$8-11), curries (CDN$11-13), and vegetable dishes. (☎613-548-7053. Open M-Th and Su 11:30am-2pm and 5-9:30pm, F-Sa 11:30am-2pm and 5-10pm. AmEx/MC/V.)

During its career days, the 210 ft. *Alexander Henry* was a Canadian Coast Guard ship used primarily as a navigation aid and ice breaker. Today, *Alexander Henry* is busier than most retirees, serving as the **Alexander Henry Ship B&B ❸,** 55 Ontario St., and accommodating over 50,000 guests since 1986. If seasickness isn't a worry, you'll find the place comfortable and hotel-like, though the rooms with single beds are a bit cramped. (☎613-542-2261; www.marmuseum.ca. Continental breakfast included. Parking available at the museum. Check-in 4:30pm at the Marine Museum. Check-out 10am. Open May-Oct. Singles CDN$35-65; doubles CDN$65-95. AmEx/MC/V.)

◪ APPROACHING CAPE VINCENT: 13 MILES

The route returns to the US over water, crossing the St. Lawrence River and Lake Ontario to **Wolfe Island,** then to Cape Vincent by **ferry.** From Kingston, ferries depart nearly every hr. for Wolf Island. (☎613-548-7227. 25min. ride. May-Oct. 19 trips per day 6:15am-2am. Free.) On Wolfe Island, follow the well-marked signs leading to the next dock. Ferries depart Wolfe Island for Cape Vincent nearly every hr. (☎315-783-0638 or 613-385-2402. 10min ride. Runs daily 8am-7pm, with additional rides as needed. Car and driver CDN$12; passengers CDN$2.) Be prepared to show identification and proof of citizenship upon boarding the ferry and landing in Cape Vincent. See **Vital Documents** (p. 13) for information on passport and visa requirements. For those who want to avoid the ferry, it's a 67 mi. detour. Take **Rte. 15 N** to **Hwy. 401 E** and exit for the **Thousand Islands Bridge,** a toll bridge that brings you to the US and **I-81.** Take **Exit 50S** and follow **Rte. 12** to **Rte. 12E** at Clayton, which leads into Cape Vincent.

The Empire State
NEW YORK
Welcomes You!

CAPE VINCENT

Cape Vincent is nestled at the head of the scenic **Thousand Island Seaway,** which spans 100 mi. from the mouth of Lake Ontario to the first of the many locks on the St. Lawrence River. Surveys conducted by the US and Canadian governments determined that there are 1864 "islands" in the seaway, where an island is defined as having at least 1 sq. ft. of land above water year-round and two trees growing on it. The region is also a fisherman's paradise, with some of the world's best bass and muskie catches.

Aubrey's Inn ❶, 126 S. James St., serves up some of the best deals in the seaway next to an indoor mural of the Tibbetts Point Lighthouse. (☎315-654-3754. Giant breakfasts $2-6. Lunch $3-6. Open M-Sa 7am-9pm, Su 7am-8pm. AmEx/D/MC/V.) The **Tibbetts Point Lighthouse Hostel (HI-AYH) ❶,** 33439 County Rte. 6, provides maritime-themed accommodations in an old keeper's quarters. (Go west

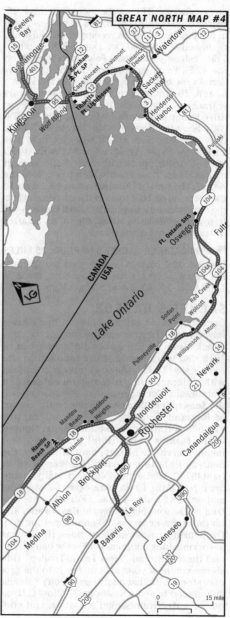

on Broadway and follow the shore for 3 mi. ☎315-654-3450. 36 beds; family rooms available. Check-in 5-10pm. Reservations recommended July-Aug. Open mid-May to mid-Oct. Dorms $18, members $15. Cash only.) **Burnham Point State Park ❶,** on Rte. 12 E., 4½ mi. east of Cape Vincent, has a wonderful view of the water and 51 sites but lacks a beach. However, the admission fee grants entrance to any park in the system, so you can drive to any of the nearby beaches. (☎315-654-2324. Showers. Reception late May to early Sept. daily 7am-9pm. Sites $13-19, with electricity $19-23. Day-use $6 per car, after 4pm $4. AmEx/D/MC/V.) For roadtrippers with time, Cape Vincent makes a nice base from which to explore the region. The town of **Alexandria Bay, NY,** 26 mi. to the north, offers boat tours of the islands and tells the romantic story surrounding **Boldt Castle.** A 400 ft. tower on **Wellesley Island, ON,** offers amazing 360-degree views of the islands.

⚐ APPROACHING SACKET'S HARBOR: 25 MILES
Take **Rte. 12 E** south to Limerick, then turn right onto **Rte. 180 W.** South of Dexter, turn right onto **Rte. 3 W.** Turn right at **C.R. 62** to enter Sacket's Harbor.

SACKET'S HARBOR

Once a busy port on the shores of Black River Bay, Sacket's Harbor was the site of two naval attacks from British forces during the War of 1812 that were successfully repelled by the Americans. Today, the town revels in its past with a vibrant string of waterfront shops and restaurants. For a preview of the road ahead, the **Seaway Trail Discovery Center,** at the corner of Ray and W. Main St., offers interactive exhibits pertinent to the entire route. Housed in the former Union Hotel (c. 1817), these include maritime history, natural history, the Seaway lighthouses, and the War of 1812. (☎800-732-9298. Open May-Oct. daily 10am-5pm; Nov.-Apr. Tu-Sa 10am-5pm. $4, students and seniors $3, ages 4-17 $2.) For a more terrestrial attraction, **Old McDonald Has A Farm,** and on that farm he has a 200-animal petting zoo, Oz-themed hayride, and pony rides. He also has a working, fully automated 400-cow dairy farm, and the additional "Moo Town Trolley" ride shows you how your milk makes it to the grocery store. With that many cows, you're almost guaranteed to see a newborn. (Follow C.R. 62 out of waterfront Sacket's Harbor, and con-

tinue for 2 mi. after the intersection with Rte. 3. ☎315-583-5737; www.oldmcdonaldhasa-farm.com. Open May-Oct. 10am-5pm. $6. Milking tours $2. Pony rides $2.) Housed in a former waterfront train station, **Sacket's Harbor Brewing Co. ❹,** 212 W. Main St., offers eight beers ($4-5 per pint), including the award-winning 1812 Ale. (☎315-646-2752; www.1812ale.com. Entrees $11-29. Th half-priced pints. Open M-Th 5-9:30pm, F 5-10pm, Sa 11:30am-10pm, Su 11:30am-9:30pm. AmEx/D/MC/V.)

◢ DETOUR
SANDY ISLAND BEACH
24 mi. from Sacket's Harbor on C.R. 15, in Pulaski.

Sandy Island Beach is New York's smallest state park, but it is the area's best beach. Unlike the other rocky beaches, Sandy Island is a natural sand beach in the Eastern Lake Ontario Dune system. If it gets too crowded, two other beaches are a few miles away and your admission is good for all three. (☎315-387-2657. Open daily sunrise-sunset. $6 per car.)

⚐ APPROACHING OSWEGO: 50 MILES
Follow **Rte. 3 W** for 35 mi., then merge right onto **Rte. 104B.** After 6 mi., veer onto **Rte. 104 W,** which enters Oswego as **Bridge St.**

OSWEGO

This small city offers a wealth of historical attractions. Established in a strategic location at one of the few natural water routes to the Great Lakes from the Atlantic, Oswego was in high demand for centuries. Rebuilt time and time again by Britain and the US after attacks, the **Fort Ontario State Historic Site,** 1 E. 4th St., was established as a historic site in 1949. Today, it has been restored to its 1867-1872 appearance, and costumed interpreters host demonstrations. (☎315-343-4711. Open May-Oct. Tu-Su 10am-5pm. $4, students and seniors $3, under 12 free.) In 1944, 982 refugees fled the Nazi regime from 18 war-torn countries; Oswego became their home for the next 18 months. **Oswego Safe Haven,** 2 E. 7th St., is a museum that documents the lives of the Holocaust refugees who found sanctuary at the Fort Ontario Emergency Refugee Shelter. (☎315-342-3003; www.oswegohaven.org. Open Tu-Su in summer 11am-5pm; in fall and winter 11am-4pm.)

Enjoy your food on a patio with river views at **Bridie Manor ❷,** 1830 Bridie Sq., housed in a former flour mill (c. 1833). The restaurant serves tavern fare ($2-8) alongside Italian dishes ($9-14) and seafood ($13-15). Drafts are always $1.50. (☎315-342-1830. Lunch $2-7. Open M-Th 11am-9pm, F-Sa 11am-9pm, Su noon-9pm. Bar closes 2am. AmEx/D/MC/V.) Local art is displayed throughout the **Oswego Inn ❸**, 180 E. 10th St. (☎800-721-7341. Continental breakfast included. Singles $55-105; doubles $65-115. AmEx/D/MC/V.)

🏁 APPROACHING ROCHESTER: 74 MILES
Take **Rte. 104** to **I-590** to **I-490**, which leads into downtown Rochester. For a longer but more scenic route along the lake, follow the Seaway signs along Rte. 104 until it meets I-590.

ROCHESTER

Rochester is New York's third-largest urban area and has an inventive metropolitan feel that enhances its historic past. Few American cities have had such a lasting social and political impact; both Susan B. Anthony and Frederick Douglass spent their most active years in Rochester and are buried in Rochester's Mount Hope Cemetery. The presence of two top universities, the University of Rochester and Rochester Institute of Technology, as well as the headquarters of Bausch and Lomb, Eastman Kodak, and Xerox, have shaped Rochester's modern identity.

VITAL STATS

Population: 220,000

Visitor Info: Greater Rochester Visitors Association, 45 East Ave., Ste. 400 (☎800-677-7282; www.visitrochester.com). Open Memorial Day to Labor Day M-F 8:30am-5pm, Sa 9am-5pm, Su 10am-3pm; Labor Day to Memorial Day M-F 8:30am-5pm.

Internet Access: Central Library of Rochester and Monroe County, 115 South Ave. (☎585-428-7300). Open July-Aug. M and Th 9am-9pm, Tu-W and F 9am-6pm; June M and Th 9am-9pm, Tu-W and F 9am-6pm, Sa 9am-5pm; Sept.-May M and Th 9am-9pm, Tu-W and F 9am-6pm, Sa 9am-5pm, Su 1-5pm. Free.

Parking: Rochester has the highest per-capita auto-theft rate in New York. Metered street parking is available, but the city has numerous affordable garages downtown with security guards (around $4 per day).

Post Office: 216 Cumberland St. (☎585-546-6425). Open M-F 8:30am-5pm, Sa 9am-noon. **Postal Code:** 14603.

🚻 GETTING AROUND. I-490 forms part of the **Inner Loop** that encircles the downtown core. The **Genesee River** runs north and south through the middle of town, paralleled on the west by **State St.** and on the east by **South Ave.** and **Clinton Ave.** Cutting through the inner-loop east-west is **Main St.**

🎯 SIGHTS. Once the home of women's rights pioneer Susan B. Anthony, the **Susan B. Anthony House,** 17 Madison St., is now a museum. It was in this red-brick house that she was arrested for voting in 1872. (From Main St., head west ½ mi., and turn right onto Madison St. ☎585-235-6124; www.susanbanthonyhouse.org. Open Labor Day to Memorial Day W-Su 11am-4pm; Memorial Day to Labor Day Tu-Su 11am-5pm. Last tour 1hr. before close. $6, seniors $5, students and children $3.) The reproduction of Sesame Street at the **Strong Museum National Museum of Play,** 1 Manhattan Sq., has helped make the museum the nation's leading hands-on history center for the young and young-at-heart. The building contains the largest collection of toys and dolls in the world in addition to an assortment of Americana. (From Main St., turn south onto S. Clinton Ave. Turn left onto Woodbury Ave. At the next light, cross Chestnut St. into the parking lot. ☎585-263-2700; www.strongmuseum.org. Open M-Th and Sa 10am-6pm, F 10am-8pm, Su noon-6pm. $9, seniors $8, ages 2-17 $7, under 2 free. Parking free.)

In 1888, George Eastman produced a flexible film camera that launched an amateur photography company later known as Eastman Kodak. The **George Eastman House,** 900 East Ave., holds works by over 10,000 photographers and the **world's largest collection of American cameras,** including the first Kodak Brownie and a camera that belonged to Ansel Adams. (☎585-271-3361; www.eastman.org. Open Tu-Sa 10am-5pm, Th 10am-8pm, Su 1-5pm. Tours M-Sa 10:30am, 2pm; Su 10:30am. $8, seniors $6, students $5, ages 5-12 $3, under 5 free.) At the thriving **High Falls Entertainment District,** 60 Brown's Race (☎585-325-2030), check out the dazzling laser light show projected on the walls of the river gorge, nightclubs, restaurants and shops. High Falls is also a National Register Historic District with old mills and factories from Rochester's glory days. The 850 ft. Pont-de-Rennes pedestrian bridge sits across the High Falls waterfall. (☎585-325-2030. Laser shows in summer most Th-Sa 9:30pm.)

🍴🍺 FOOD AND ACCOMMODATIONS.

Rochester is famous for its local take on hot dogs, or "white hots," which are unsmoked to maintain a white color. You can try them in the equally famous "garbage plates" ($5.50-6.50), a customizable mountain of sides, sauces, condiments, and meat, at **Nick Tahou Hots ❶**, 320 Main St. W. (☎585-436-0184. Open daily 8am-8pm. Cash only.) A second location, **Nick Tahou Hots II ❶**, 2260 Lyell Ave., is open 24hr. (☎585-429-6388. Cash only.) One of the most popular joints in Rochester is **Dinosaur Bar-B-Que ❷**, 99 Court St., which offers a dazzling array of barbecued meat options. (☎585-325-7090; www.dinosaurbarbque.com. Sandwiches $4-7. Platters $6-10. Ribs $11-20. Open M-Th 11am-midnight, F-Sa 11am-1am, Su noon-10pm. AmEx/D/MC/V.) Locals congregate at **Jines Restaurant ❷**, 658 Park Ave., which has Greek, Italian, and American dishes amid Art Deco furnishings. Breakfast specials include banana-bread French toast ($5.25); for lunch, try the lamb and feta burger for $7. (☎585-461-1280. Open M-Sa 7am-10pm, Su 7am-8pm. AmEx/D/MC/V.) The inside of **Charlie's Frog Pond ❷**, 652 Park Ave., has funky, colorful straw-like sculptures and paintings by a local painter, Ramon Santiago. An eclectic selection of daily dinner specials includes duck with Kahlua cream sauce and the "Horny Toad" ($6.50), which consists of ground beef, an English muffin, chili, and cheese. (☎585-271-1970. Breakfast $4-8. Sandwiches $3-8. Open in summer M-Sa 7:30am-10pm, Su 8am-3pm; in winter M-Th 7:30am-9pm, F-Sa 7:30am-10pm, Su 8am-3pm.

AmEx/MC/V.) Affordable lodging near Rochester can be found at chain motels in Henrietta.

🔄 DETOUR
JELL-O MUSEUM

23 E. Main St. Take I-490 W from Rochester, merge onto I-90 W (NY State Thruway), and exit onto Rte. 19 southbound. LeRoy is 4 mi. south of the interstate. The gallery is behind the Historic LeRoy House.

The Jell-O factory offers self-guided tours with a guided introduction. Get your fill of Jell-O memorabilia, souvenirs, and trivia—did you know that the citizens of Salt Lake City consume more lime Jell-O per year than any other city?—and receive a free package of the world's wiggliest dessert. (☎585-768-7433; www.jellomuseum.com. Open May-Oct. M-Sa 10am-4pm, Su 1-4pm; Nov.-Mar. M-F 10am-4pm. $3, ages 6-11 $1.50, under 6 free.)

🚗 APPROACHING YOUNGSTOWN: 88 MILES

At the end of **I-390 N**, veer left onto the **Lake Ontario State Pkwy.**, which becomes **Rte. 18 (Lake Rd.).** 40 mi. after the parkway ends, turn right onto **Rte. 18F** to enter Youngstown. Look across the lake for the impressive skyline of **Toronto** and the **CN Tower,** once the world's tallest freestanding structure. There are no services on this stretch, but they can be found throughout the Erie Canal corridor roughly 10 mi. south.

YOUNGSTOWN

The sleepiness of the village of Youngstown you see today belies its bloody, martial past. Strategically located where the Niagara flows into Lake Ontario, its position was of great mil-

TALL TALES

The vast wilderness of the Great North motivated early settlers to create equally grand tall tales. The story of Paul Bunyan seems to be an amalgamation of early Québécois legends of a fur-trading *voyageur* and American north woods stories of a massive lumberjack. According to the tale, Paul outgrew his father's clothes when he was just a week old, and he soon grew so large that his parents decided he would have to live outside. Stories of Paul Bunyan revolve around a legendary logging camp of gargantuan men led by Paul, who frequently performed physical feats of Herculean proportions. So large were Paul and his men that the pan used to fry their flapjacks was the size of a lake and had to be greased by skaters with slabs of bacon on their feet. Paul is often credited with creating some of the area's most beautiful topography; it is said that when his trusty sidekick, Babe the Blue Ox, became thirsty, Paul dug out the Great Lakes as a watering trough, and the leftover soil formed the Thousand Islands. The Mississippi River was born when the camp's water wagon sprung a leak, the Dakota plains were clear-cut by Paul and his men, and Babe's burial mound formed the Black Hills. Today Paul is immortalized in countless statues scattered across the North, often with

itary importance—whichever nation controlled the mouth of the Niagara controlled commerce on the upper Great Lakes. In 1678, René-Robert Cavelier, Sieur de La Salle, built the first fortifications at ☒**Old Fort Niagara.** For the next 150 years, four nations fought desperately for it. It remained an active military post until 1963, when it was converted into a museum. Especially impressive is the "French Castle," a stone fortress built to look like a chateau to catch the Iroquois off-guard. July brings re-enactments with over 1000 living-history demonstrators. (☎716-745-7611; www.old-fortniagara.org. Open June M-F 9am-6:30pm, Sa-Su 9am-7:30pm; July-Aug. daily 9am-7:30pm; May and Sept.-Oct. M-F 9am-5:30pm, Sa-Su 9am-6:30pm; Apr. daily 9am-5:30pm; Nov.-Mar. daily 9am-4:30pm. $10, seniors $9, ages 6-12 $6.) **Whirlpool Jet Boat Tours,** S. Water St., in nearby Lewiston, sends visitors racing through the perilous Devil's Hole rapids of the Niagara Gorge to the massive whirlpool in the Lower Niagara River. (☎888-438-4444. Trips Apr.-Oct. $47, ages 6-13 $39.)

Campers can stay among great blue herons at **Four Mile Creek State Park ❶**, 1 Four Mile Creek Dr., which has 275 campsites, including 21 on a bluff overlooking Lake Ontario. (4 mi. east of Youngstown via Route 18F or the Robert Moses Pkwy. ☎716-745-3802, reservations 800-456-2267. Showers, store, hiking trails. Check-in 3pm. Check-out 11am. Open mid-Apr. to mid-Oct. Tent sites $13-16, with electricity $19-22; waterfront sites $19-22/$25-28. AmEx/D/MC/V.)

▣ APPROACHING NIAGARA FALLS: 13 MILES
Continue south along **Rte. 18F (Lower River Rd.).** In Lewiston, 18F becomes **Center St.** Turn right onto the **Robert Moses Pkwy.** heading toward Niagara Falls. Keep an eye out; along the way you'll drive over the famous **Niagara Power Project.**

NIAGARA FALLS

Niagara Falls, one of the seven natural wonders of the world, is flat-out spectacular. The Ontario side of Niagara is full of flashy Vegas-style attractions—a trend that has horrified residents over the past few decades—while the New York side is mainly a park area and is something of a ghost town. The giant falls are

best viewed from the Canadian side of the Niagara River, but prices tend to be more reasonable on the American side.

VITAL STATS

Population: NY 56,000, ON 79,000

Visitor Info: US: Orin Lehman Visitors Center (☎716-278-1796), on Prospect St., in front of the Falls Observation Deck. Open M-F 8am-7pm, Sa-Su 10am-6pm. **CAN: Niagara Falls Tourism,** 5515 Stanley Ave. (☎905-356-6061 or 800-563-2557; www.discoverniagara.com). Open daily 8am-8pm.

Internet Access: Niagara Falls Public Library, 1425 Main St. (☎716-286-4894; www.niagara-fallspubliclib.org). Open M-W 9am-9pm, Th-F 9am-5pm; Sept.-May M-W 9am-9pm, Th-F 9am-5pm, Sa 9am-5pm. Free.

Parking: Parking on the US side is cheaper and more plentiful than on the Canadian side. There is free parking at the **Seneca Niagara Casino,** Niagara St., a 5min. walk from the falls.

Post Office: 615 Main St. (☎716-285-7561). Open M-F 8:30am-5pm, Sa 8:30am-2pm. **Postal Code:** 14302.

▣ GETTING AROUND

Niagara Falls spans the US-Canadian border. The **Robert Moses Pkwy.** runs along the river to the sights on the US side of the falls. On the US side, **Niagara St.** is the main street, ending in the west at the **Rainbow Bridge** to Canada (pedestrians $0.50, cars $2.50; fees include return). In Canada, **Roberts St. (Rte. 420)** is the main east-west street and **Stanley Ave.** is the main north-south street, but **Clifton Hill** is where the attractions are. Slightly downriver, the **Whirlpool Bridge** also adjoins the two countries. **People Movers** buses tourists through the 30km area on the Canadian side of the falls, stopping at attractions along the way. (☎877-642-7275. Runs mid-June to early Sept. daily 9am-11pm; Sept. to mid-June hours vary. Day pass CDN$7.50, children CDN$4.50.)

◉ SIGHTS

AMERICAN SIDE. Most local attractions are centered in or around **Niagara Falls State Park,**

which was designed by Frederick Law Olmsted and is the oldest state park in America. Especially serene are the **Three Sisters Islands** off **Goat Island** in the Upper Rapids. For over 150 years, the ■Maid of the Mist boat tour has entertained kings and commoners alike with awe-inspiring (and wet) views from the foot of the falls. (☎716-284-8897. Open daily 9:45am-5:45pm, extended hours in summer. Tours depart in summer every 15min. from base of observation deck. $11.50, ages 6-12 $6.75. Observation deck $1.) The **Cave of the Winds Tour** hands out souvenir (read: ineffective) yellow rain-coats and sandals for a drenching hike to the base of the Bridal Veil Falls, including an optional walk to the Hurricane Deck, where strong waves slam down from above. (☎716-278-1730. Open May to mid-Oct. 9am-7:30pm, hours vary depending on season and weather conditions. Trips depart every 15min from Goat Island. Must be at least 42 in. tall. $8, ages 6-12 $7.) The **Niagara Gorge Discovery Center,** in Pros-pect Park, has gorge trail hikes and a simulated elevator ride through the geological history of the falls. (☎716-278-1780. Open daily 9am-6:30pm. $5, children $3.) The **Aquarium of Niagara** houses the endangered Peruvian Penguin alongside 1500 aquatic animals. (701 Whirlpool St., across from the Discovery Center. ☎716-285-3575; www.aquariu-mofniagara.org. Open daily 9am-5pm. $8, seniors $6.50, children $5.50.) The **Niagara Scenic Trolley,** provides tours of the park and is the easiest form of transportation between the sights on the Amer-ican side. (☎716-278-1730. Runs May-Aug. daily 9am-10pm every 10-20min. $2, children $1.) The **Master Pass,** available at the visitors center, covers admission to the Maid of the Mist, the Cave of the Winds Tour, the Discovery Center, the aquarium, and the trolley ($24.50, ages 6-12 $17.50).

Just north of Niagara Falls is the **Niagara Power Authority Visitor Center,** 5777 Lewiston Rd., in Lewiston, which offers spectacular views of the famous power project and Niagara Gorge, and interactive exhibits about electricity, hydropower, and the plant that generates a quarter of New York's power supply. (Take the Robert Moses Pkwy. north 4 mi. to the Power Vista exit. Turn left onto Rte. 104 for 1 mi.; the entrance is on the right. ☎716-285-3211. Open daily 9am-5pm. Free.)

 DID YOU KNOW? In 1859, Jean François Gravelet became the 1st person to cross Niagara Falls on a tightrope.

CANADIAN SIDE. On the Canadian side of Niagara Falls, **Queen Victoria Park** provides the best view of **Horseshoe Falls.** Starting 1hr. after sunset every night, the falls are illuminated for 3hr. At 10pm on Fridays and Sundays in sum-mer (and also on Canadian and American holi-days), a free fireworks display lights up the sky. Bikers, in-line skaters, and walkers enjoy the 32km **Niagara River Recreation Trail,** which runs from Fort Erie to Fort George and passes many historical sights dating back to the War of 1812. Far above the crowds and excitement, **Skylon Tower** has the highest view of the falls at 520 ft. above ground and 775 ft. above the base of the falls. The tower's **Observation Deck** offers a calm-ing, unobstructed vista. (5200 Robinson St. ☎716-356-2651. Open daily 8am-midnight. CDN$11, children CDN$6.50.) The **Adventure Pass** includes entrance to the Maid of the Mist boat tour; Journey Behind the Falls, White Water Walk, and the Butterfly Conservatory. It also offers CDN$2 discounts for the **Spanish Aero Car,** an aerial cable ride over the rapids' whirlpool waters, and all-day transportation on the People Mover. (www.niagaraparks.com. Adventure Pass CDN$38, children CDN$24. Aero Car: ☎905-354-5711. Open in summer daily 9am-6:45pm. CDN$11, children CDN$6.50.) The adventurous will enjoy **Journey Behind the Falls,** a tour that takes visitors behind Horseshoe Falls. (☎905-354-1551. Open daily 9am-5:30pm; extended hours in summer. CDN$11, children CDN$6.50.) **White Water Walk** is a long boardwalk next to the Niagara River Rapids. (☎905-374-1221. Open in summer daily 9am-8pm. Tours available. CDN$8, children CDN$5.) The **But-terfly Conservatory** is located on the grounds of the world-famous Niagara Parks Botanical Gar-dens. (☎905-358-0025. Open in summer daily 9am-9pm. CDN$11, children CDN$6.50.)

For those who wish to escape the glitz and glam, a 10 mi. drive north along the **Niagara Pkwy.,** which Winston Churchill called the "pret-tiest Sunday afternoon drive in the world," will lead you through the heart of the Niagara wine region to the town of **Niagara-on-the-Lake.** Across the river from Youngstown, Niagara-on-the-Lake is full of gorgeous Victorian homes and inns. Every summer the town hosts the Shaw Festival, which features performances of the works of George Bernard Shaw and his contem-poraries. (☎905-468-2172; www.shawfest.com. Mar.-Nov. Tickets CDN$25-86.)

CASINOS. For those who wish to try their luck, Niagara Falls has seen the influx of three very popular full-service casinos in the last decade. Note that you must be 19 to gamble in Ontario and 21 in New York. **Casino Niagara** opened in 1996 and quickly became Canada's most profitable business. It recently underwent a complete renovation. *(5705 Falls Ave., in Ontario. ☎905-374-3598; http://casinoniagara.com. Open 24hr.)* Also on the Ontario side, the **Niagara Fallsview Casino Resort** revels in gorgeous Belle Époque decor. There is a free shuttle between Fallsview and Casino Niagara. *(6380 Fallsview Blvd. ☎888-FALLSVUE; http://fallsviewcasinoresort.com. Open 24hr.)* After intense debate in the US, land was transferred from the city of Niagara Falls to the Seneca Nation of Indians, who built the **Seneca Niagara Casino & Hotel**, which has a modern woodlands theme and cheap eating options. *(310 4th St. ☎716-299-1100; http://senecaniagaracasino.com. Open 24hr.)*

▓ FOOD

Restaurants and nightclubs line the **Clifton Hill** entertainment district, and more affordable places can be found west of **Victoria Ave.** In a sea of expensive dining on the Canadian side, the oldest restaurant in town, **Simon's Restaurant ❶**, 4116 Bridge St., in Ontario, one block from the HI hostel, is still a local favorite, thanks to its huge breakfasts (CDN$6), giant homemade muffins (CDN$1), and homestyle dinners for CDN$6-10. *(☎905-356-5310. Open M-Sa 5:30am-7pm, Su 5:30am-2pm. Cash only.)* For a lovely dining experience overlooking the Upper Rapids, the Tudor-style **Red Coach Inn ❹**, 2 Buffalo Ave., in New York, offers lunches for $9-13 and steak and seafood dinners for $22-34. (Across from the Goat Island car bridge. ☎716-282-1459; www.redcoach.com. Lunch $9-13. Dinner $22-34. Open daily 11:30am-10pm. AmEx/D/MC/V.)

▓ ACCOMMODATIONS

Niagara is a popular honeymoon destination. In Canada, cheap motels (from CDN$35) advertising free wedding certificates line **Lundy's Ln.**, while moderately priced B&Bs overlook the gorge on **River Rd.** between the Rainbow Bridge and the Whirlpool Bridge. In New York, cheap motels line **Niagara Falls Blvd. (Rte. 62)** from I-190 eastward. Excellent camping is also available 14 mi. away at **Four Mile Creek State Park** (p. 235).

▓ Hostelling International Niagara Falls (HI-AYH), 4549 Cataract Ave. *(☎905-357-0770 or 888-749-0058; www.hihostels.ca)*, in Ontario. Just off Bridge St. A remarkable, well-equipped hostel with a laid-back atmosphere and convivial, rainbow-colored interior. Organic vegetable garden and fair trade organic coffee. Activities include Su vegan potluck (6-9pm) and a drum circle. Continental breakfast CDN$2.75. Lockers CDN$2. Linen included. Internet CDN$3 per hr. Reception in summer 24hr.; in winter 8am-midnight. Check-out 11am. Quiet hours 11pm-7am. Reservations recommended May-Nov. Dorms CDN$25, members CDN$21; singles CDN$52/$48. AmEx/D/MC/V. ❶

Backpacker's International Hostel, 4219 Huron St. *(☎905-357-4266 or 800-891-7022; www.backpackers.ca)*, at Zimmerman Ave., in Ontario. A well-maintained hostel in a historic home with clean dorm rooms. Family-run and owned. Bike rentals CDN$15 per day. Breakfast, linens, and parking included. Free Internet access. Reception 24hr. with reservation. Dorms CDN$20; doubles CDN$50-60. Cash only. ❶

Hostelling International Niagara Falls (HI-AYH), 1101 Ferry Ave. *(☎716-282-3700)*, off Memorial Pkwy., in New York. 38 beds in a former private schoolhouse. Bicycles available. Kitchen, TV lounge, and free parking. Family rooms available. Linens $1.75. Check-in 7:30-9:30am and 4-11pm. Open mid-Jan. to mid-Dec. Dorms $17. MC/V. ❶

▓ APPROACHING NORTH TONAWANDA: 12 MILES

Continue on the **Robert Moses Pkwy.** Exit as if for I-190 N, but instead continue on **Rte. 384 (Buffalo Ave.)** toward Buffalo. Rte. 384 will become **River Rd.** as it heads into North Tonawanda.

NORTH TONAWANDA. Downtown North Tonawanda has a lovely path along the **Erie Canal** where you can stretch your legs. Also in North Tonawanda is the **Herschell Carrousel Factory Museum**, 180 Thompson St., home of the merry-go-round. Learn the history of the wooden carousel, see horse-carving, restoration demonstrations, and organ roll production, and finish your trip with a ride on one of two antique carousels. (☎716-693-1885. From Rte. 384, make a left onto Thompson St. just after the fork in the road. Open June-Aug. M-Sa 10am-4pm, Su noon-4pm; Apr.-May and Sept.-Dec. W-Su noon-4pm. $5, seniors $4, ages 2-12 $2.50. Guided tours $4, children $2.)

⚑ APPROACHING BUFFALO: 14 MILES

Continue south on **Rte. 384,** which will become **Delaware Ave.** and lead you downtown in **Niagara Sq.**

BUFFALO

At the turn of the 19th century, Buffalo—the "Queen City of the Lake" —was the playground of Gilded Age grandeur, home to more millionaires than any other American city. When the steel industry collapsed and the Erie Canal became obsolete, those glory days became a thing of the past. Still, don't underestimate a city that easily shrugs off seven feet of snow in one storm. Buffalo's past has given it a cultural and architectural legacy that is equal to much larger and pricier cities. From the downtown skyline to funky Elmwood Village, Buffalo balances small-town warmth with big-city culture.

VITAL STATS
Population: 280,000
Visitor Info: Visitors Center, 617 Main St. (☎716-852-2356 or 800-283-3256; www.visitbuffalonia-gara.com), in the Theater District. Open daily in summer 10am-4pm; in winter 10am-2pm.
Internet Access: Buffalo and Erie County Public Library, 1 Lafayette Sq. (☎716-858-8900), at Washington St. Open in summer M-W and F-Sa 8:30am-6pm, Th 8:30am-8pm; in winter also Su 1-5pm. $1.
Post Office: 701 Washington St. (☎716-856-4603). Open M-F 8:30am-5:30pm, Sa 8:30am-1pm. **Postal Code:** 14203.

⮐ GETTING AROUND

Buffalo is one of the few American cities with a radial layout like Washington, D.C.; **Niagara Square** forms its center. The principal spokes, in a clockwise direction, are **Niagara St. (Rte. 266), Delaware Ave. (Rte. 384), Main St. (Rte. 5), Broadway, Clinton St.,** and **Seneca St. (Rte. 16).** Buffalo's expressways are rarely called by their

posted names, so if asking for directions from locals, I-290 is the "Youngmann," Rte. 198 is the "Scajaquada," and Rte. 33 is the "Kensington."

⦿ SIGHTS

BUFFALO ZOO. At the Buffalo Zoo, over 23 acres shelter 1500 exotic and domestic animals in the country's third-oldest zoo. Hands-on summer activities include feeding giraffes and washing elephants, but by far the best attraction is Surapa, the amazing painting elephant. (300 Parkside Ave. ☎716-837-3900; www.buffalozoo.org. Open daily July to Labor Day 10am-5pm; Labor Day to June 10am-4pm. $8.50, seniors $5, ages 2-14 $5, under 2 free.)

ALBRIGHT-KNOX ART GALLERY. The Albright-Knox Art Gallery houses an internationally recognized collection of over 6000 modern pieces, including works by Picasso and Rothko. (1285 Elmwood Ave. ☎716-882-8700; www.albrightknox.org. Open W-Th and Sa-Su 10am-5pm, F 10am-10pm. $10, students and seniors $8, under 13 free. F 3-10pm free.)

ARCHITECTURE. Architecture buffs can take a 2hr. self-guided walking tour of historic downtown Buffalo. Pick up the free guide, Walk Buffalo, at the visitors center. Buffalo has stunning examples of 20th-century architecture. Don't miss **City Hall,** in Niagara Sq., Buffalo's Art Deco masterpiece. Other highlights are the **Guaranty Building** (28 Church St.), the piece-de-resistance of American skyscraper pioneer Louis Sullivan; the creepy gothic towers of the **Richardson Complex,** at Buffalo State College; the former **Buffalo Psychiatric Center,** 400 Forest Ave., designed by H.H. Richardson; and the Gilded Age mansions of **Millionaires Row,** along Delaware Ave., between Summer and Bryant St. The area also showcases the largest number of "Prairie School" works by Frank Lloyd Wright outside of Chicago, including the **Darwin D. Martin House Complex,** an estate of five buildings by the architectural master. (125 Jewett Pkwy. ☎716-856-3858; www.darwinmartinhouse.org. Call for tour schedules and reservations. $12, students $8.) Buffalo is also home to Frederick Law Olmsted's first public park system, an interconnected series of green gems linked by tree-lined parkways, the centerpiece being **Delaware Park.**

FESTIVALS. During the year, Buffalo is home to a host of festivals. What began as a happy hour in 1987 has morphed into today's **Thursday at the Square,** drawing over 10,000 people weekly into Lafayette Square during the summer months for free concerts by regional and national acts. (☎716-837-3900.) America's second largest food festival, the **Taste of Buffalo,** features inventive traditional and ethnic foods from over 50 local restaurants. The festival takes place alongside three stages of live entertainment for a weekend in July in Niagara Square. (☎716-856-3150; www.tasteofbuffalo.com. $1-3.50.) The historic Allentown neighborhood plays host to the **Allentown Art Festival** each summer, one of the largest and oldest outdoor art festivals in the country. (☎716-881-4269; www.allentownartfestival.com.) And what would Buffalo be without the **National Buffalo Wing Festival?** Over Labor Day weekend in Dunn Tire Park, the festival features chicken wings from across the country, wing-eating contests, and the crowning of Miss Buffalo Wing. (☎716-565-4141; www.buffalowing.com. $5, children under 8 free.)

⚡ FOOD

Elmwood Village, up Elmwood Ave. between Virginia and Forest Ave., and **Allentown,** which runs the length of Allen St., are full of funky coffee shops and ethnic restaurants.

🦞 **Anchor Bar,** 1047 Main St. (☎716-886-8920). On a busy night in 1964, Teressa Bellissimo cooked up an unusual midnight snack of chicken wings and Buffalo wings were born. Try 10 wings for $8 or a bucket of 50 for $25. F-Sa live jazz 9pm-midnight. Open M-Th 11am-11pm, F 11am-1am, Sa noon-1am, Su noon-11pm. AmEx/D/MC/V. ❷

Broadway Market, 999 Broadway St. (☎716-893-0705). Over 40 vendors have served German, Polish, and Eastern European foods here for more than a century. Homemade kielbasa...yum! Open M-F 8am-5pm. AmEx/MC/V. ❸

Gabriel's Gate, 145 Allen St. (☎716-886-0602). A friendly saloon-like restaurant with rustic furniture, mounted animal heads, and a big chandelier. Enjoy the famous "Richmond Ave." burger ($6) or the vegetarian portobello sandwich ($6) on the comfy shaded patio. Open M-W and Su 11:30am-midnight, Th 11:30am-1am, F-Sa 11:30am-2am. AmEx/MC/V. ❷

Charlie the Butcher's Kitchen, 1065 Wehrle Dr. (☎716-633-8330), in Williamsville. From downtown, follow Main St. (Rte. 5) east, and make a right on Union Rd. (Rte. 266) and a left on Wehrle Dr. Most locals head here for a taste of Buffalo's famous Beef on Weck, thinly sliced roast beef au jus on a Kummelwick roll. For the true Buffalo experience, pile on the horseradish. Open M-Sa 10am-10pm, Su 11am-9pm. AmEx/MC/V. ❸

🏠 ACCOMMODATIONS

Budget lodgings are a rarity in downtown Buffalo, but chain motels can be found near the airport and off I-90. Family-run independent motels

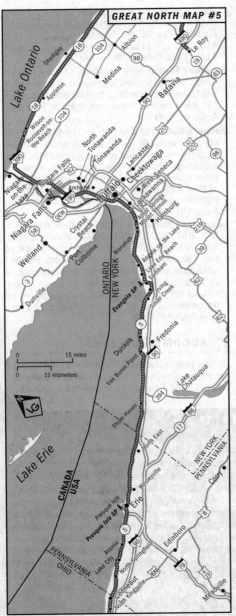

GREAT NORTH MAP #5

for under $50 per night are along **"the Boulevard" (Rte. 62),** about 15min. from downtown.

Hostel Buffalo (HI-AYH), 667 Main St. (☎716-852-5222; www.hostelbuffalo.com.) A bright, clean 50-bed facility in a centrally located neighborhood. The friendly staff makes travelers feel at home and offers free nightly movies. Common rooms, a kitchen, a pool table, Internet access ($1 per 15min.), free linen, and laundry facilities. Reception 8-10am and 5-10pm. Check-out 10am. Reservations recommended. Dorms $23, members $20; private rooms $50-75. AmEx/MC/V. ❶

Lenox Hotel & Suites, 140 North St. (☎716-884-1700; www.lenoxhotelandsuites.com.), at Delaware Ave. The large and luxurious rooms at this historic hotel are only 5min. from Elmwood Village nightlife. Singles $69-79; studio suites $89-99. AmEx/D/MC/V. ❸

🎵 ENTERTAINMENT

Buffalo has a thriving Theatre District, with seven different venues in the heart of downtown and several more sprinkled throughout the city. The heart of the scene is **Shea's Performing Arts Center,** 646 Main St., a beautifully restored 1920 vaudeville theater that features Broadway musicals, concerts, and a free film series. (☎716-847-0850, box office 716-852-5000; www.sheas.org. Box office open M-F 10am-5pm. Tours Tu and Th 10am and 1pm. $8, seniors $4.) The **Studio Arena,** 710 Main St., is a resident theater that has hosted the likes of Glenn Close and Jon Voight. (☎716-856-5650; www.studioarena.org. Box office open M-F 10am-5pm.) **Kleinhans Music Hall,** 71 Symphony Circle, is home to the Buffalo Philharmonic Orchestra and was recognized as a national historic landmark before it was even 50 years old. (☎716-885-5000; www.bpo.org. Box office open M-F 9am-6pm. Tickets $18-60.)

The success of the local sports franchises is testament to the fervor of the fans. Tailgating is an art form before **Bills** football games at **Ralph Wilson Stadium,** 1 Bills Dr., just south of town in Orchard Park. (☎716-648-1800.) **HSBC Arena,** 1 Seymour H. Knox, III Plaza (☎716-855-4100), downtown, is home to hockey's **Sabres** and Buffalo's professional lacrosse team, the **Bandits.**

☕ NIGHTLIFE

Downtown bars and clubs are concentrated on **Chippewa St.** and **Franklin St.**, but live music can be found at numerous establishments throughout the city. From Thursday to Saturday the bars are open until 4am, and thousands of Western New Yorkers stay out all night. Pick up a copy of *Artvoice* for event listings.

Nietzsche's, 248 Allen St. (☎716-886-8539; www.nietzsches.com). Music is burned into the walls at this legendary club where Ani DiFranco and the 10,000 Maniacs got their big breaks. Beer from $2.50. Live bands every night. Open daily noon-4am. Cash only.

D'Arcy McGee's Irish Pub and Sky Bar, 257 Franklin St. (☎716-853-3600). An authentic Irish pub on the 1st fl., a nightclub on the 2nd, and Buffalo's only open-air rooftop lounge on top. Patrons can ride a glass elevator up to the sky bar to relax above the bustling scene below. Cover for sky bar after 10pm $2-3. Open M-W 11am-midnight, Th-Su 11am-4am. AmEx/D/MC/V.

Club Marcella, 622 Main St. (☎716-847-6850; www.clubmarcella.com). An energetic gay nightclub where clubbers of all persuasions party on 2 dance floors. W and F-Su drag shows. 18+. Cover usually $3. Open W-Su 9pm-4am. MC/V.

☛ APPROACHING LACKAWANNA: 6 MILES
Take **Rte. 5 W** and exit onto **Ridge Rd.**

LACKAWANNA

In Lackawanna, the triple dome of the **Buffalo and Erie County Botanical Gardens,** 2655 South Park Ave., rises like a crown above the green cushion of the surrounding park. Frederick Law Olmsted, the father of modern landscape architecture, designed the surrounding South Park in 1888. Events at the gardens include orchid shows, rare plant sales, Buffalo Philharmonic Orchestra concerts, and the annual Hot Luck ethnic food festival during the third week of July. (☎716-827-1584; www.buffalogardens.com. Open M-W and F-Su 10am-5pm, Th 10am-6pm. $5, students and seniors $4.) **The Our Lady of Victory Basilica and National Shrine,** at S. Park Ave. and Ridge Rd., was built in 15th- and 16th-century Renaissance style, with copper-topped towers and a huge copper dome. (☎716-828-9433; www.ourlady-ofvictory.org. Open daily 7am-7pm. Tours Su 1pm. Free.) The **Grand View Drive-In Movie Theater,** Rte. 5 and Lake St., near Angola, shows new releases. (☎716-549-2450. Shows in summer 9:30 and 11:30pm; call ahead for times in winter. $6, ages 6-11 $3.) **Graycliff Manor,** 6472 Old Lake Shore Rd., is another example of Frank Lloyd Wright's Prairie Houses in the region. (☎716-947-9217. Tours Tu-F 11am, 2pm; Sa every hr. 11am-3pm; Su every hr. noon-4pm.) The maritime-themed **Hoak's Restaurant ❷,** 4100 Lake Shore Rd., has a patio right on Lake Erie. Entrees include shrimp skewers ($12) and perch ($12), as well as sandwiches and steak. (☎716-627-7988. Open M-Th 11am-11:30pm. AmEx/D/MC/V.)

☛ APPROACHING DUNKIRK: 37 MILES
Continue along on **Rte. 5** westbound.

DUNKIRK

The **Dunkirk Historical Lighthouse and Veterans Park Museum** is located at the end of Point Dr. The keeper's quarters house a museum of war memorabilia as well as various lighthouse paraphernalia. (☎716-366-5050; www.dunkirklighthouse.com. Open M-Tu and Th-Sa May-June 10am-2pm; July-Aug. 10am-4pm. $1. Tours $5, ages 4-12 $2.) If you haven't gotten your daily dose of **giant carvings of Native American heads**, drive along Lakeshore Dr., on the west side of town, to see a gnarly 15 ft. giant (Ong-Gwe-Ohn-Weh) carved into an existing tree trunk. In the 1970s, Peter Wolf Toth traveled the country carving these wooden heads as part of his "Trail of Whispering Giants" project, which now reaches across the country. If you happen to be in town on February 2nd, don't miss **Dunkirk Dave,** the town groundhog, who comes out on his special day to forecast the coming of spring.

Lodging on beautiful Lake Erie is desirable, but expensive. The **Pines Motel ❸,** 10684 W. Lake Rd., south of town, in Ripley, has a half-mile of private lake access. The rooms are

---

1903: Orville and Wilbur Wright make the roadtrip obselete.

decorated to enhance the knotty pine walls. (☎716-736-7463 or 800-736-8850; www.thepineslakeerie.com. Rooms mid-May to mid-Sept. $50-70; mid-Apr. to mid-May and mid-Sept. to mid-Nov. $45-50. AmEx/D/MC/V.)

🛣 APPROACHING ERIE: 48 MILES

The **Seaway Trail** continues on to Erie as **NY 5** becomes **PA 5.**

The Keystone State

PENNSYLVANIA

Welcomes You!

ERIE

The city of Erie and the Great Lake are named after the Erie tribe of Native Americans, who inhabited the region until a fierce battle with the Iroquois in the 1600s. This little corner of land (called the "Erie Triangle") was originally chartered to four states—due to less-than-precise territorial descriptions. The dispute was finally settled in 1792, when all four states gave up their claims and Pennsylvania purchased its only seashore from the federal government. After many years of population decline, Erie is experiencing a renaissance of sorts following the revitalization of its downtown area.

VITAL STATS

Population: 104,000

Visitor Info: Erie Area Convention and Visitors Bureau, 208 E. Bayfront Pkwy. (☎814-454-7191; www.visiteriepa.com), next to the Maritime Museum. Open M-F 8:30am-5pm.

Internet Access: Erie County Public Library, 160 E. Front St. (☎814-451-6900). Open M-Th 9am-8:30pm, F-Sa 9am-5pm, Su 1-5pm. $1 per hr.

Post Office: 2108 E. 38th St. (☎814-898-7303). Open M-F 8am-5pm, Sa 8am-12:30pm. **Postal Code:** 16515.

📇 GETTING AROUND. Rte. 5 becomes **6th St.** in the downtown area, where it is divided into E. 6th St. and W. 6th St. by **Perry Sq.** at **State St.** Leaving town to the east, Rte. 5 becomes **E. Lake Rd.** Numbered streets start on the Erie shore and increase as they go inland (southeast).

◆ SIGHTS. The biologically diverse **Presque Isle State Park,** on Peninsula Dr., juts out 7 mi. into Lake Erie, covering 3200 acres. Enjoy nature as you swim, hike, bike, fish, windsurf, cross-country ski, or ice skate. Be sure to take a free pontoon boat ride through the lagoons at Misery Bay. (☎814-871-4251. Open daily in summer 5am-11pm; in winter 5am-9pm. Beaches open Memorial Day to mid-Sept. Pontoon rides 11am, 1, 2pm. Free.) The constantly evolving **Erie Maritime Museum,** 150 E. Front St., chronicles local history like the Battle of Lake Erie during the War of 1812. A video of museum staff shooting actual cannons at the sides of a ship is particularly interesting, and the results are on display with the shells still embedded. The brig *Niagara* docks at the museum from September to May. (☎814-452-2744; www.brignigara.org. Open Apr.-Dec. M-Sa 9am-5pm, Su noon-5pm; Jan.-Mar. Th-Sa 9am-5pm, Su noon-5pm. $6, seniors $5, ages 6-17 $3.)

 DID YOU KNOW? Over time, Presque Isle has shifted 3 mi. to the east, heading toward New York. To keep the island from drifting away, Erie has employed shoreline management since the 1800s, creating breakwaters to hold the island in place.

🍴 FOOD AND ACCOMMODATIONS. The **Quaker Steak & Lube Restaurant ❸,** 7851 E. Peach St., revolves around road culture. Full-size cars are displayed on the roof and the walkway, and there's even a motorcycle behind the bar and a "convertible room" with a retractable roof. The restaurant serves creatively named dishes like the "LubeBurger" ($8) and "O-Rings Ontenna" ($6-10), a stack of onion rings on an onion antenna with a baby moon hubcap. (☎814-864-9464; www.quakersteakandlube.com. Lunch buffet $8. Open M-Th and Su 11am-11pm, F-Sa 11am-1am. MC/V.) **El Canelo ❷,** 2709 W. 12th St., serves delicious Mexican fare in a festive atmosphere with plenty of red brick, sombreros, and Mexican flags. (☎814-835-2290. Combination dinners $6-7. Fajitas $10. M-Tu 6-8pm $1 drafts. Open M-Th 11am-10pm, F-Sa 11am-11pm, Su 11am-9pm. AmEx/D/MC/V.)

The Lighthouse Inn ❸, 3704 E. Lake Rd. (Rte. 5), is a friendly, family-run motel with spacious rooms. The inn's restaurant serves breakfast and lunch. (3 mi. east of downtown. ☎814-899-9300; www.erielighthouseinn.com. Rooms in June $45-75; July-Aug. $49-77; Sept.-May $40-50. AmEx/D/MC/V.) The **El Patio Motel ❹**, 2950 W. 8th St., at Peninsula Dr., has white balconies and a pool. The funky rooms are close to beautiful Presque Isle have access to a pool, volleyball, basketball, and shuffleboard. (Just outside the entrance to Presque Isle. ☎814-838-9772; www.elpatioerie.com. Singles M-Th and Su $59, F-Sa $89; doubles $69/$104. AmEx/D/MC/V.) Visitors crowd to the beach tent sites at **Sara's Beachcomber Campground ❶**, 50 Peninsula Dr. Since there's no overnight camping in Presque Isle State Park, the location can't be beat. (☎814-833-4560; www.sarasbeachcomber.com. Check-in 9am. Check-out 1pm. Open Apr.-Oct. Tent sites $20; RV sites with full hookup $24-28. Cash only.)

◙ DETOUR
ASHTABULA COVERED BRIDGE FESTIVAL

From Rte. 531 in Ashtabula, take Rte. 11 south to the junction with Rte. 46. Follow Rte. 46 southbound into Jefferson, where it intersects with W. Jefferson St.

Ashtabula County is known for its 16 historical covered bridges. The Covered Bridge Festival is held on the second weekend in October, during the foliage season, and features parades, arts and crafts, antique cars, farmers markets, and tours. Self-guided tour maps of the bridges are available year-round. (☎440-576-3769; www.covered.bridgefestival.org. $4, under 12 free.)

◤ APPROACHING GENEVA-ON-THE-LAKE: 54 MILES

Take **Rte. 5 W** out of Erie. In Conneaut, take **U.S. 20** to **Rte. 7 N.** From Rte. 7, turn onto **Rte. 531 W** along Lake Rd. Rte. 531 leads through tiny Ashtabula and into Geneva-on-the-Lake.

The Buckeye State
OHIO
Welcomes You!

GENEVA-ON-THE-LAKE
By the end of WWII, Geneva-on-the-Lake was widely known as the playground of Lake Erie.

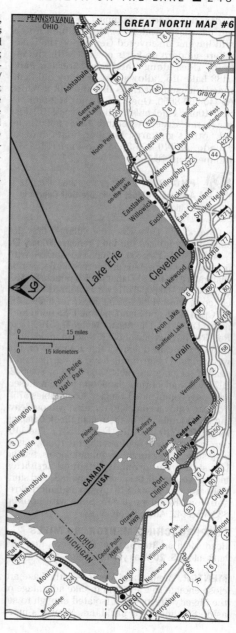

GREAT NORTH MAP #6

Today, the resort maintains a 1950s ambience but caters to modern visitors. Chain hotels still haven't discovered Geneva-on-the-Lake, where modern go-karts coexist with vintage kiddy rides along "the Strip." **Erieview Park,** 5483 Lake Rd., allows you to enjoy old-fashioned amusement rides like the Tilt-a-Whirl. (☎440-466-8650. Open M-Th and Su 2-9pm, F-Sa 2-10pm. 1 ticket $2; full-day pass $15.) Just down the street, **Adventure Zone,** 5600 Lake Rd., offers go-karts, bumper boats, and an arcade. (☎440-466-3555. Go-kart rides $5. Bumper boat $3.75.)

PHOTO OP. Geneva-on-the-Lake has **America's Oldest Miniature Golf Course** in continuous play.

Overlooking Lake Erie, the village's first fire station now houses the **Old Firehouse Winery ❸,** 5499 Lake Rd. (Rte. 531), which is decorated with fire engine memorabilia and serves barbecue ribs (half rack $13, full $17) that pack a punch. (☎440-466-9300 or 800-862-6751; www.oldfirehousewinery.com. Sandwiches $6.50. Mexican dishes $8-13. Open M-Th and Su noon-9pm, F-Sa noon-midnight. D/MC/V.) The **Anchor Motel ❹,** 5196 Lake Rd. (Rte. 531), is one of the few accommodations in the area that doesn't raise its rates on the weekends. The grounds have gas grills and a shaded picnic area. (☎440-466-0726 or 800-642-2978; www.anchormotelandcottages.com. Reservations recommended. Singles $65; doubles $75.) You can enjoy a complete vacation without leaving the boundaries of the **Indian Creek Camping Resort ❷,** 4710 Lake Rd. E (Rte. 531). The 110-acre campground features a game room, a grocery store, a restaurant, swimming pools, fishing lakes, and laundromats. Planned activities include volleyball, basketball, hayrides, and shuffleboard. (☎440-466-8191; www.indiancreekresort.com. Key deposit $15. Sites with hookup $32; RVs $42. AmEx/D/MC/V.)

⚑ APPROACHING MENTOR: 30 MILES
Head south on **Rte. 531** out of Geneva. Rte. 531 turns into **U.S. 20 W** as you head into Mentor.

MENTOR. Mentor and Mentor-On-the-Lake are close enough to Cleveland to take advantage of the big-city lifestyle, yet isolated enough to set aside 800 acres for parkland. Mentor's most impressive sight is the **James A. Garfield National Historic Site,** 8095 Mentor Ave. (U.S. 20). President Garfield purchased this farm in 1876, when he was still a congressman, and it was here that he launched his presidential campaign. The home was nicknamed "Lawnfield" by reporters due to the expansive lawn used for press appearances. (☎440-255-8722; www.wrhs.org. Open May-Oct. M-Sa 10am-5pm, Su noon-5pm; Nov.-Apr. Sa-Su noon-5pm. $7, seniors $6, ages 6-12 $5, under 6 free.) **Headlands Beach State Park** is a great destination for sunbathers and sunset-watchers. (From U.S. 20, head north on Heisley Rd., which ends at the beach. Free.)

⚑ APPROACHING CLEVELAND: 24 MILES
From Mentor, take **U.S. 20 W** to **Rte. 306 N.** Get onto **Rte. 2 W,** and follow it along the coast of Lake Erie into downtown Cleveland. Exit and make a left onto **E. 9th St.,** then make a right onto **Euclid Ave. (Rte. 6)** to go into **Public Sq.**

CLEVELAND

Ridiculed for having a river so polluted it caught fire (twice) and branded the "Mistake on the Lake," Cleveland has gone to great lengths over the past decade to correct its beleaguered image. The industrial ooze that once lapped up on the shores of Cleveland is now gone, and Cleveland has made valiant efforts to spruce up its civic center. Yet the city is still struggling to reinvent itself. Hip coffee shops and music venues abound on the eastern and western edges of Cleveland, and residents are hopeful that these enclaves will become increasingly integrated with the museums and playhouses downtown.

VITAL STATS

Population: 480,000

Visitor Info: Cleveland Convention and Visitors Bureau, 50 Public Sq. (☎216-621-7981; www.travelcleveland.com), in the rotunda of the Terminal Tower. Open daily 9am-9pm.

Internet Access: Cleveland Public Library, 325 Superior Ave. (☎216-623-2800; http://cpl.org). Open in summer M-Sa 9am-6pm; in winter M-Sa 9am-6pm, Su 1-5pm. Free.

Post Office: 2400 Orange Ave. (☎216-443-4494). Open M-F 7am-8:30pm, Sa 8:30am-3:30pm. **Postal Code:** 44101.

▣ GETTING AROUND

Terminal Tower, in **Public Sq.,** at the intersection of Detroit Ave. and Ontario St., forms the center of downtown and splits the city east and west. Street numbers correspond to the distance of the street from Terminal Tower. To reach Public Sq. from **I-90** or **I-71,** take the Ontario St./Broadway exit. While the downtown area and **University Circle** are relatively safe, the area between the two around 55th St. can be rough and should be avoided at night. **The Flats,** along both banks of the Cuyahoga River, and **Coventry Rd.,** in Cleveland Heights, are the best spots for food and nightlife.

◉ SIGHTS

DOWNTOWN. The aspirations of a new Cleveland are revealed in the new downtown—a self-declared "Remake on the Lake." The centerpiece is I.M. Pei's glass pyramid which houses the ▧**Rock and Roll Hall of Fame.** Blaring music invites visitors into a dizzying retrospective of rock music. Take a tour through rock history on the "Mystery Train," listen to the "500 Songs that Shaped Rock and Roll," and ogle memorabilia from Elvis's jumpsuits to Jimi Hendrix's guitar. *(751 Erieside Ave.* ☎ *216-781-7625; www.rock-hall.com. Open in summer M-F and Su 10am-5:30pm, Sa 10am-9pm; in winter daily 10am-5:30pm. $20, seniors $16, ages 9-12 $11, under 9 free.)* Next door, the **Great Lakes Science Center** trots out high-tech toys like infrared cameras and a solar car to create interactive exhibits that are fun for all ages. Click your heels together, hang on to Toto, and stick your hand into a mini-tornado. *(601 Erieside Ave.* ☎ *216-694-2000; www.glsc.org. Open daily 9:30am-5:30pm. Science center or OMNIMAX $9, seniors $8, ages 3-17 $7. Both $13/$11/$9.)*

THE WILD SIDE. Nearly 20,000 acres of undeveloped land comprise the **Cleveland Metroparks,** perfect for biking, horseback riding, and hiking; the trail along the northern edge of Big Creek Reservation's Lake Isaac is a great place to listen for songbirds. The **Cleveland Lakefront State Park,** near downtown, is 14 mi. of beaches, bike trails, and great picnic areas. The soft sand at Edgewater Beach beckons sunbathers and swimmers. *(8701 Lakeshore Blvd. NE.* ☎ *216-881-8141. Open daily 6am-11pm. Free.)* The **Cleveland Metroparks Zoo,** 5

mi. south of Cleveland on I-71 at the Fulton Rd. exit, offers a more manicured look at Mother Nature, from North America's largest primate collection to the Australian Adventure walk. Along the African Savannah and the Northern Trek, you can catch glimpses of Siberian tigers, red pandas, and hissing cockroaches. *(3900 Wildlife Way.* ☎ *216-661-6500; www.clemetzoo.com. Open Memorial Day to Labor Day M-F 10am-5pm, Sa-Su 10am-7pm; Labor Day to Memorial Day daily 10am-5pm. Apr.-Oct. $9, ages 2-11 $4, under 2 free; Nov.-Mar. $6/$4.)*

UNIVERSITY CIRCLE. While much has been made of Cleveland's revitalized downtown, the city's cultural nucleus still lies in **University Circle,** a part of Case Western University's campus, 4 mi. east of the city. The **Cleveland Museum of Art** closed its doors in January 2006 as it embarks on the first stage of a renovation project. Call ahead for opening dates. *(11150 East Blvd.* ☎ *614-421-7340; www.clevelandart.org.)* Nearby, the **Cleveland Museum of Natural History** showcases a menagerie of animals preserved by taxidermists, while live river otters and great horned owls populate the Wildlife Center outside. *(1 Wade Oval Dr.* ☎ *216-231-4600; www.cmnh.org. Open M-Tu and Th-Sa 10am-5pm, W 10am-10pm, Su noon-5pm. $7.50; students, seniors, and ages 7-18 $5.50; ages 3-6 $4.50.)* The **Cleveland Botanical Garden** provides a peaceful respite from urban life with traditional Victorian and Japanese gardens both indoors and out. The Eleanor Armstrong Smith Glasshouse recreates a Costa Rican cloud forest and the spiny desert of Madagascar. *(11030 East Blvd.* ☎ *216-721-1600; www.cbgarden.org. Open Apr.-Oct. M-Sa 10am-5pm, Su noon-5pm; Nov.-Mar. open Tu-Sa 10am-5pm, Su noon-5pm. $7.50, children 3-12 $3.)*

CUYAHOGA VALLEY NATIONAL PARK. Just 10 mi. south of Cleveland lies the northern edge of the scenic Cuyahoga Valley National Park. The park's lifeline is the **Cuyahoga River,** which winds 30 mi. through dense forests and open farmland, passing stables, aqueducts, and mills along the way. The best way to see the park is to hike or bike its long trails. The **Ohio & Erie Canal Towpath Trail** runs through shaded forests and past the numerous locks used during the canal's heyday, when it served as a vital link between Cleveland and the Ohio River. The park's **visitors center** has maps and information on the canal. *(To reach the park take I-77 S to Rockside Rd. Take a left after the exit, continue to Canal Rd., and make a right into the park.*

☎800-445-9667; www.nps.gov/cuva. Open daily 10am-4pm. Park open daily sunrise-sunset.)

OBERLIN. Two young missionaries from the East Coast founded the Oberlin Collegiate Institute in 1833. Their commitment to coeducation and racial integration left its imprint on the small town of Oberlin; three years before the Civil War broke out, local abolitionists swarmed the nearby village of Wellington to rescue a fugitive slave who was being returned to captivity. Progressive politics are still alive and well in Oberlin, as Birkenstocked students from **Oberlin College** pad around S. Main St. and dream of a free Tibet. The college's **Conservatory of Music** is one of the best in the nation, and free recitals are open to the public year-round. (☎440-775-8044; www.oberlin.edu/con.) The **Allen Memorial Art Museum** features a strong collection of 17th-century Dutch and Flemish canvases, although its modern holdings are also vast. (87 N. Main St. ☎440-775-8665; www.oberlin.edu/allenart. Open Tu-Sa 10am-5pm, Su 1-5pm. Free.) Town-gown relations are at their rosiest during the **Big Parade,** held on the first Saturday in May, while mid-June's **Juneteenth** celebration commemorates the signing of the Emancipation Proclamation in 1865. (To reach Oberlin, take I-90 W to Exit 140; then follow Rte. 53 for 6 mi. into Oberlin's downtown area.)

⃕ FOOD

Colorful cafes grace **Coventry Rd.,** in **Cleveland Heights,** between Mayfield Rd. and Euclid Heights Blvd. The sounds of Italian crooners fill the sidewalks of **Little Italy,** around **Mayfield Rd.** Over 100 vendors hawk fresh produce, meat, and cheese at the old-world-style **West Side Market,** 1979 W. 25th St., at Lorain Ave. (☎216-664-3387; www.westsidemarket.com. Open M and W 7am-4pm, F-Sa 7am-6pm.)

Tommy's, 1824 Coventry Rd. (☎216-321-7757; www.tommyscoventry.com), in Cleveland Heights. This bright, spacious cafe stays busy throughout the day serving vegetarian fare like falafel ($5), although meat-eaters get in on the action with juicy burgers ($6). Open M-Th 7:30am-10pm, F-Sa 7:30am-11pm, Su 9am-10pm. MC/V. ❷

Lelolai Bakery and Cafe, 1889 W. 25th St. (☎216-771-9956), in Ohio City. Revered for its velvety flan ($2) and sandwiches slathered with garlic mayonnaise ($4-6), this Hispanic bakery also offers buttery breakfast pastries ($1.50) that are perfect with a steaming cup of café con leche. Open M-W 8am-5pm, Th-Sa 8am-6pm. MC/V. ❶

Mama Santa's, 12305 Mayfield Rd. (☎216-231-9567), in Little Italy, just east of University Circle. Mama Santa's has kept hordes of college students and courting couples happy for over 40 years with its sumptuous Sicilian pizzas and welcoming atmosphere. Cheese pizzas $5.50-6.50. Open M-Th 11am-10pm, F-Sa 11am-11:30pm. MC/V. ❷

China Sea Express, 1507 Euclid Ave. (☎216-861-0188), downtown. A delicious all-you-can-eat lunch buffet ($5.75) includes wonton soup, lo mein, General Tso's chicken, crab rangoon, and all of the other expected Chinese staples. Entrees $4-8. Open M-Th and Su 11am-9pm, F-Sa 11am-11pm. Buffet served M-F 11am-3pm. AmEx/D/MC/V. ❶

⃔ ACCOMMODATIONS

With hotel taxes (not included in the prices listed below) as high as 14.5%, cheap lodging is hard to find in Cleveland. Prices tend to be lower in the suburbs or near the airport. Most accommodations will not rent to those under 21.

▨ Cuyahoga Valley Stanford Hostel (HI-AYH), 6093 Stanford Rd. (☎330-467-8711; www.stanfordhostel.com), in Peninsula, 22 mi. south of Cleveland in the Cuyahoga Valley National Park. Housed in a 19th-century farm house, this idyllic hostel offers cozy dorms and nightly cricket serenades. Kitchen, living room, and access to trails along the old Erie & Ohio Canal towpath. Linen $3. Reception 7-9am and 5-10pm. $16.50, under 18 $8.25. Cash only. ❶

Danes Guest House, 2189 West Blvd. (☎216-961-9444). Follow I-90 west of downtown to the West Blvd. exit. 2 rooms in a 1920s colonial revival house are a particularly good deal for travelers in groups. Homemade breakfast included. Singles $55-70; doubles $65-80. Cash only. ❸

Motel 6, 7219 Engle Rd. (☎440-234-0990), off I-71 at Exit 235, 15 mi. southwest of the city. Comfy rooms with cable TV and A/C close to restaurants, stores, and a park-and-ride lot. Singles M-Th and Su $46, F-Sa $56; doubles $52/$62. AmEx/D/MC/V. ❸

♫ ENTERTAINMENT

The **Cleveland Orchestra** performs at **Severance Hall,** 11001 Euclid Ave. (☎216-231-7300 or 800-

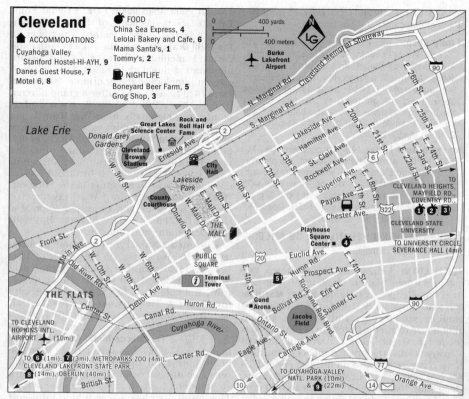

Cleveland

ACCOMMODATIONS
Cuyahoga Valley
   Stanford Hostel-HI-AYH, **9**
Danes Guest House, **7**
Motel 6, **8**

🍎 FOOD
China Sea Express, **4**
Lelolai Bakery and Cafe, **6**
Mama Santa's, **1**
Tommy's, **2**

🍺 NIGHTLIFE
Boneyard Beer Farm, **5**
Grog Shop, **3**

686-1141; www.clevelandorch.com. Box office open M-F 9am-5pm. Tickets from $25.) **Playhouse Square Center,** 1519 Euclid Ave., a 10min. walk east of Terminal Tower, is the second-largest performing arts center in the US. (☎614-771-4444; www.playhouse-square.org. Box office open daily 11am-6pm.) Inside, the **State Theater** hosts the **Cleveland Opera** (☎614-575-0900; www.clevelandopera.org) and the **Cleveland Ballet** (☎614-426-2500; www.clevelandballet.com). Football reigns supreme in Cleveland, where the **Browns** grind it out at **Cleveland Browns Stadium.** (☎216-241-5555. Tickets from $25.) Baseball's **Indians** hammer the hardball at **Jacobs Field,** 2401 Ontario St. (☎216-420-4200. Tickets from $5.) If you can't catch a game, the best way to see the field is on a 1hr. sta-

dium tour. (☎216-420-4385. Tours Apr.-June and Sept. M-F 1 and 2pm, Sa when the Indians are away every hr. 10am-2pm; mid-June to Aug. M-Sa every hr. 10am-2pm. $6.50, seniors and under 15 $4.50.) The **Cavaliers** play basketball at the **Gund Arena,** 1 Center Ct. (☎216-420-2000). In summer, the WNBA's **Rockers** (☎216-263-7625) play in the same building.

🎵 NIGHTLIFE

A few pubs and music venues stay open at major hotels downtown. The **Warehouse District** features upscale clubs, while edgier crowds favor nightspots along **Coventry Rd.** in Cleveland Heights or along **W. 25th St.** in Ohio City. For more info on clubs and concerts, pick up a free copy of *Scene* or the *Free Times.* The *Gay*

People's Chronicle and *OUTlines* are available at gay clubs, cafes, and bookstores.

■ **Grog Shop,** 2785 Euclid Heights Blvd. (☎216-321-5588), at Coventry Rd. in Cleveland Heights. A mainstay of Cleveland's alternative music scene. A move to a larger, less dingy location in the summer of 2003 had purists waxing nostalgic about a lost era, but the Grog continues to host the best in underground rock and hip-hop. Cover varies. Open M-F 7pm-2:30am, Sa-Su 1pm-2:30am. AmEx/D/MC/V.

Boneyard Beer Farm, 748 Prospect Ave. (☎216-575-0226), in the Gateway District. Serves over 120 beers from around the world for brew lovers. Skull and crossbones decor, faux cow-skin chairs, and barrels of peanuts make this a great place to enjoy a brew. Beer $3-6.50. Open M-F 4pm-2:30am, Sa 7pm-2:30am.

⌐ APPROACHING VERMILION: 38 MILES
Take **U.S. 6 W** to Vermilion.

VERMILION. A classic shipbuilding town, Vermilion is a great place to brush up on your nautical knowledge. At the **Inland Seas Maritime Museum,** 480 Main St. (off U.S. 6), interactive exhibits, model ships, and a 1910 steamship pilot house relate the history of the Inland Seas (code for "Great Lakes"). Harrowing tales of shipwrecks and the original timber of the *U.S. Brig Niagara* are also on display. (☎440-967-3467 or 800-893-1485; www.inlandseas.org. Open daily 10am-5pm. $6, seniors and children $5.) If you're passing through in mid-August, check out the annual **Duck Derby,** in which thousands of sponsored ducks race down the Vermilion River (☎440-967-4477). The ■**Main Street Soda Grill ❶,** 5502 Liberty Ave., is a blast from the past. Grab a phosphate (soda water and flavored syrup; $1.50), a Coney burger ($3.50), or an egg creme (milk, soda water, and chocolate syrup; $1.75), and then marvel at the 1930s paraphernalia. (☎440-967-4002. Open M-Th and Su 11am-9pm, F-Sa 11am-10pm. MC/V.)

⌐ APPROACHING SANDUSKY: 20 MILES
U.S. 6 enters downtown Sandusky from the east along **Cleveland Rd.,** and then turns into **Washington St.**

SANDUSKY

Consistently ranked the "best amusement park in the world" by *Amusement Today,*

■**Cedar Point Amusement Park,** 1 Cedar Point Dr., off U.S. 6, has many of the world's highest and fastest roller coasters. The towering **Top Thrill Dragster** takes the cake in both categories, launching thrill-seekers 420 ft. before plummeting down at 120 mph. Fifteen other coasters, including the enormous **Millennium Force** (310 ft., 93 mph), offer a grand adrenaline rush. (☎800-237-8386; www.cedarpoint.com. Open daily June-Aug. 10am-11pm; Sept. to early Oct. hours vary. $40, military $30, seniors and under 4 ft. tall $10.) Though most visit Sandusky for Cedar Point, the waterfront business district, established in 1818, has one of the most beautiful collections of historic architecture in the Midwest. **Washington Park,** along Washington St., between Wayne St. and Jackson St., contains a lovely floral park and the historic "Boy with the Boot" statue and fountain.

A devoted staff serves customers at **Markley's ❶,** 160 Wayne St., on the corner of Market St., downtown. For lunch, try the Little Sister sandwich platter (bacon cheeseburger, fries, and cole slaw; $5), the house specialty for 45 years. They also serve breakfast all day, fresh doughnuts, and pies. (☎419-627-9441. Open M-Th and Su 6am-2pm, F-Sa 6am-7pm. MC/V.) The **Mecca Motel ❸,** 2227 Cleveland Rd. (U.S. 6), has lower rates than the chain hotels surrounding Cedar Point and runs a shuttle service to the amusement park so you don't have to miss out on the action. The motel also has a free 9-hole mini-golf course and a swimming pool. (☎800-986-3222; www.mhdcorp.com. Rooms $50-73. D/MC/V.)

⌐ APPROACHING PORT CLINTON: 14 MILES
Head west on **U.S. 6,** which follows **Washington St.** to **Tiffin Ave.** and **Venice Rd.** From Venice Rd., take **U.S. 2** to Port Clinton.

PORT CLINTON

The **African Safari Wildlife Park** is Port Clinton's biggest attraction, and the rare white zebras, buffalo, and giraffes are as curious about you as you are about them. Activities at the park include rides on camels or ponies and the Pork Chop Downs pig races. (☎419-732-3606; www.africansafariwildlifepark.com. Open daily June-Aug. 9am-7pm; mid-Mar. to May and Sept.-Oct. 9am-5pm. Last entry 1hr. before close. $16, ages 3-16 $10, under 3 free.) After meeting the animals, treat yourself to ice cream ($1.50), sundaes ($2.50), or deep-fried delectables ($1.50-5) at **Brown's Dairy Plaza** ❶, 425 Fremont Rd. (☎419-734-4995. Open daily 11am-10pm. Cash only.)

🚗 APPROACHING TOLEDO: 39 MILES
Take **U.S. 2** through Oregon to reach Toledo.

TOLEDO

The 🏛**Toledo Zoo** is home to over 4700 animals and 700 species, including polar bears, seals, primates, and elephants. Visit the **Hippoquarium** with underwater viewing of Nile River hippos, or go nose to nose with wolves in the Arctic Encounter Wolf Exhibit. (From downtown, take N. Michigan St. south past I-75 until it becomes Anthony Wayne Trail. The zoo is 2 mi. ahead. ☎419-385-5721; www.toledozoo.org. Open daily May to Labor Day 10am-5pm; Labor Day to Apr. 10am-4pm. $8.50, seniors and ages 2-11 $5.50, under 2 free.) The Grecian-style **Toledo Museum of Art**, 2445 Monroe St., has exhibits spanning the centuries from ancient Egypt to the present. (☎800-644-6862; www.toledomuseum.org. Open Tu-Th and Sa 10am-4pm, F 10am-10pm, Su 11am-5pm. Free.)

🍴**Tony Packo's Cafe** ❷, 1902 Front St., was made famous by M*A*S*H star Jamie Farr, whose character Klinger frequently craved a Packo's dog. The wieners are even part of the decor; celebrity-autographed buns line the walls. Try the M*O*A*D ($7.50), also known as the "mother of all dogs." (☎419-691-6054; www.tonypackos.com. Open M-Th 11am-10pm, F-Sa 11am-11pm, Su noon-9pm. AmEx/D/MC/V.) The **Maumee Bay Brewing Company** ❸, 27 Broadway St., runs a restaurant and the **Toledo Brewing Hall of Fame.** Try Walter's burger ($7.50), or the pizzas ($8) with your brew. (☎419-243-1302. Open M-F 11am-10pm, Sa 1:30-11pm. AmEx/D/MC/V.) There are few affordable motels in downtown Toledo, but chain motels starting at $40 are clustered to the south near I-475 and I-80/90. The **Classic Inn** ❷, 1821 E. Manhattan Blvd., near the junction of I-75 and I-280, has standard motel rooms with access to an outdoor swimming pool and a free deluxe breakfast. (☎419-729-1945. Singles $40-52; doubles $50-57. MC/V.)

🚗 APPROACHING DETROIT: 58 MILES
There really isn't anything to see between Toledo and Detroit, so don't feel guilty about taking the interstate.

GREAT NORTH MAP #7

GREAT NORTH

From downtown, take **Summit St. (Rte. 65 E)** to **I-280**, which connects to **I-75** north of town. Take I-75 to **Grand River Ave.**, which leads into downtown.

The *Great Lakes State*
MICHIGAN
Welcomes You!

DETROIT

Heavyweight champ Joe Louis is one of Detroit's best-known native sons and a fitting icon for the city; Detroit resembles an aging slugger, caught up on the ropes in the seventh round but determined to stay standing until the final bell. Violent race riots in the 1960s spurred a massive exodus to the suburbs, while the decline of the auto industry in the late 1970s chiseled away the city's industrial base and left behind a weary, crumbling shell of Motown's glory days. Detroit continues to shrink with each succeeding census, and yet the stalwarts who have stayed behind love their city with an almost cultish ferocity. With a generation of young DJs reinventing the Detroit sound, this plucky boomtown won't go down without a fight.

VITAL STATS

Population: 870,000

Visitor Info: Convention and Visitors Bureau, 211 W. Fort St., 10th fl. (☎313-202-1800 or 800-338-7648; www.visitdetroit.com). Open M-F 9am-5pm.

Internet Access: Detroit Public Library, 5201 Woodward Ave. (☎313-833-1000). Open Tu-W noon-8pm, Th-Sa 10am-6pm.

Post Office: 1401 W. Fort St. (☎313-226-8075). Open 24hr. **Postal Code:** 48233.

GETTING AROUND

Detroit lies on the Detroit River, which connects Lake Erie and Lake St. Clair. Across the river to the south, the town of Windsor, Ontario, can be reached by a tunnel just west of the Renaissance Center (toll $3.50), or by the **Ambassador Bridge** ($2.75). Those planning to make the crossing should expect delays because of the heightened security. Detroit can be a dangerous town, but it is generally safe during the day; expect to be approached by panhandlers, and avoid walking alone at night. Office buildings and sports venues dominate the downtown, while up-and-coming neighborhoods like **Corktown** open out to the west. Driving is the best way to get around town.

Detroit's streets form a grid, though streets tend to end suddenly and reappear several blocks later. The numbered Mile roads run east-west and measure the distance away from downtown. **Eight Mile Rd.** is the city's northern boundary. **Woodward Ave. (Rte. 1)** is the city's main north-south artery and divides both city and suburbs into "east side" and "west side." **Gratiot Ave.** flares out northeast from downtown, while **Grand River Ave.** shoots west. **I-94** and **I-75** also pass through downtown. Streets tend to end suddenly and reappear several blocks later; for a particularly helpful map, check *Visit Detroit*, available at the Detroit Visitors Bureau.

SIGHTS

DETROIT ZOO. Exotic animals like tigers and red pandas roam the suburban grounds of the Detroit Zoological Park. The National Amphibian Conservation Center allows visitors to get up close and personal with enormous salamanders, while the Arctic Ring of Life exhibit showcases polar bears and offers a trek through the Tundra. (*8450 W. Ten Mile Rd., just off the Woodward Exit of Rte. 696 in Royal Oak. ☎248-398-0900; www.detroitzoo.org. Open M-Tu and Th-Su 10am-5pm, W 10am-8pm. $11, seniors $9, ages 2-12 $7.*)

CAMPUS MARTIUS PARK. The same firm that gave the Bellagio casino in Las Vegas its famous fountains designed the centerpiece of Detroit's newest public space. The park borrows its name from an 18th-century military drill ground and has already emerged as a center for activity with its shaded gardens and a skating rink during the winter months. (*800 Woodward Ave., between Fort and Michigan Ave. ☎313-962-0101. Open M-Th 7am-10pm, F 7am-midnight, Sa 9am-midnight, Su 9am-8pm.*)

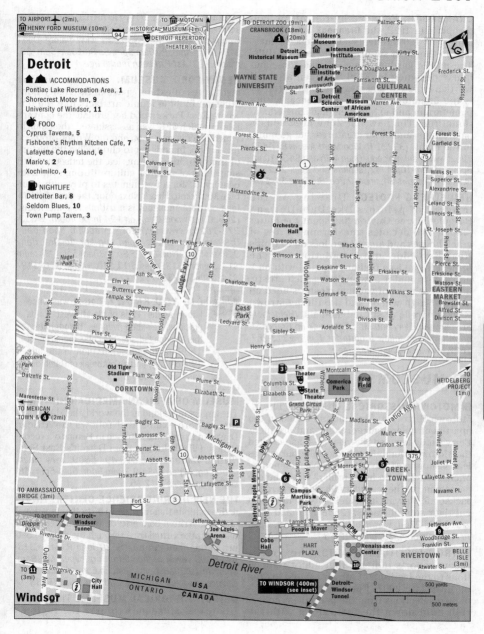

Detroit

ACCOMMODATIONS
Pontiac Lake Recreation Area, **1**
Shorecrest Motor Inn, **9**
University of Windsor, **11**

FOOD
Cyprus Taverna, **5**
Fishbone's Rhythm Kitchen Cafe, **7**
Lafayette Coney Island, **6**
Mario's, **2**
Xochimilco, **4**

NIGHTLIFE
Detroiter Bar, **8**
Seldom Blues, **10**
Town Pump Tavern, **3**

GREAT NORTH

CRANBROOK. Founded by Detroit philanthropists in 1922, the **Cranbook Schools** give more than 1600 students a world-class education in the posh suburb of Bloomfield Hills. The public gardens, several museums, and house designed by Eliel Saarinen are well worth a look. Far and away the best of the lot is the **Cranbrook Institute of Science**, with a planetarium and exhibits emphasizing educational fun. The new Bat Zone area houses bats, sloths, and other creatures that go bump in the night. *(39221 N. Woodward Ave. ☎877-462-7262; www.cranbrook.edu. Open M-Th and Sa-Su 10am-5pm, F 10am-10pm. $7, seniors and ages 2-12 $5. Planetarium shows $4, under 2 free. Bat Zone $4/$1.)*

HEIDELBERG PROJECT. Drawing on the imagery of painters like Dubuffet and Basquiat, Tyree Guyton has spent the better part of two decades transforming a row of crack houses and abandoned lots on Detroit's Near East Side into installation art. The project began as a building painted with pink polka dots, and it now includes such artistic oddities as rows of vacuum cleaners lined up in waist-high weeds and a building strewn with hundreds of stuffed animals. *(Heidelberg St., between Ellery and Mt. Elliott; pick up Gratiot St. downtown, and follow it north for 1 mi. ☎313-267-1622; www.heidelberg.org. Free.)*

🏛 MUSEUMS

🎵 MOTOWN HISTORICAL MUSEUM. The Motown Historical Museum is housed in the apartment where entrepreneur and producer Berry Gordy founded Hitsville, USA, and created the Motown sound. Knowledgeable tour guides lead visitors past the hat and gloves donned by Michael Jackson in his "Thriller" video, before descending to the legendary **Studio A,** where the Jackson 5, Marvin Gaye, and Smokey Robinson cut their soulful tracks. *(2648 W. Grand Blvd. ☎313-875-2264; www.motownmuseum.com. Open Tu-Sa 10am-6pm. $8, under 12 $5.)*

DETROIT INSTITUTE OF ARTS. The most recent reports indicate that major renovations to the Institute of Arts are slated to drag on until late 2007. For the moment, handpicked selections from the permanent collection hold down the fort, along with the signature Diego Rivera mural depicting scenes from Detroit's industrial history. *(5200 Woodward Ave. ☎313-833-7900; www.dia.org. Open W-Th 10am-4pm, F 10am-9pm, Sa-Su 10am-5pm. $6, children $3. 1st F of each month free.)*

HENRY FORD MUSEUM. The astonishing eight acres of exhibit space in the Henry Ford Museum include iconic artifacts like the bus where Rosa Parks stood her ground, the convertible in which JFK was assassinated, the chair in which Lincoln was shot, and the Wright Brothers' flight shop. In addition to chronicling the history of transportation in America, the museum takes snapshots of popular culture through the 20th century; sit for a few minutes to play with a vintage Mr. Potato Head. Next door, the **Greenfield Village** outdoor museum is a tribute to Americana. *(20900 Oakwood Blvd., off I-94 in Dearborn. ☎313-271-1620; www.hfmgv.org. Museum open daily 9:30am-5pm. Village open mid-Apr. to Oct. daily 9:30am-5pm, Nov.-Dec. F-Su 9:30am-5pm. Museum $14, seniors $13, ages 5-12 $10. Village $20/$19/$14; both $26/$24/$20.)*

 DID YOU KNOW? Detroit was once known as the "Paris of the Midwest" for its gracious, tree-lined avenues. Unfortunately, this all changed after the catastrophic fire of 1805, rapid industrialization in the late 19th century, and an outbreak of Dutch disease around 1950.

MUSEUM OF AFRICAN AMERICAN HISTORY. The largest of its kind in the world, the MAAH features a core exhibit that follows the African Diaspora from a marketplace in Benin to a reconstructed 1960s lounge from Detroit's East Side. *(315 E. Warren Rd. ☎313-494-5800; www.maah-detroit.org. Open W-Sa 9:30am-5pm, Su 1-5pm. $8, seniors and ages 3-12 $5.*

THE NEW DETROIT SCIENCE CENTER. Interactive exhibits that manage to be both educational and fun. Write a concerto on the stringless laser harp, or take virtual trips through the rings of Saturn in the planetarium. *(5020 John R. St. ☎313-577-8400; www.sciencedetroit.org. Open M-F 9am-5pm, Sa 10:30am-6pm, Su noon-6pm. Museum $12, seniors and ages 2-12 $11; with IMAX $15/$13.)*

DETROIT HISTORICAL MUSEUM. The Detroit Historical Museum explores the region's transformation from "frontiers to factories"—visitors can tour a streetscape of old-town Detroit and gawk at a working piece of the Cadillac assembly line. *(5401 Woodward Ave. ☎313-833-1805; www.detroithistorical.org. Open W-F 9:30am-5pm, Sa 10am-5pm, Su 11am-5pm. $5, college students $3.50, seniors and ages 5-18 $3.)*

⚑ FOOD

Gourmet restaurants may have cast their lots with the northern suburbs, but city dwellers continue to dine in the city's ethnic neighborhoods. At **Greektown,** Greek restaurants and bakeries line one block of Monroe St., east of Beaubien St. To snag a pierogi, cruise Joseph Campau Ave. in **Hamtramck** (Ham-TRAM-eck), a Polish neighborhood northeast of Detroit. **Mexican Town,** just west of downtown, is packed with restaurants, markets, and nightspots. No one should miss the **Eastern Market,** at Gratiot Ave. and Russell St., an 11-acre produce-and-goodies festival. (☎313-833-1560. Open M-Sa 7am-5pm.)

Cyprus Taverna, 579 Monroe St. (☎313-961-1550). Serves *moussaka* (eggplant casserole; $9), and other Greek specialties in the heart of Greektown. Lunch specials from $6.25. Entrees $10-13. Open M-Th and Su 11am-1:30am, F-Sa 11am-4am. AmEx/D/MC/V. ❸

Lafayette Coney Island, 118 W. Lafayette Blvd. (☎313-964-8198). Perhaps Detroit's most famous culinary establishment, Lafayette doles out coney dogs ($2.50) and chili-cheese fries ($3.25) to loyal customers. Open M-Th 7:30am-4am, F-Sa 7:30am-5am, Su 9:30am-4am. Cash only. ❶

Xochimilco, 3409 Bagley St. (☎313-843-0129). Draws the biggest crowds in Mexican Town with delicious enchiladas and burrito platters ($5-8). Murals, great service, and warm chips are just a few of the details that separate Xochimilco (so-she-MIL-co) from its competition. Open daily 11am-2am. AmEx/MC/V. ❷

Fishbone's Rhythm Kitchen Cafe, 400 Monroe St. (☎313-965-4600), in Greektown. Fishbone's brings Mardi Gras to the Motor City with zydeco music and Cajun dishes like deep-fried alligator ($11) and seafood gumbo ($6). Nightly live jazz. Open M-Th and Su 11am-midnight, F-Sa 11am-2am. AmEx/D/MC/V. ❹

Mario's, 4222 2nd St. (☎313-832-6464), downtown. An elegant, old-fashioned Italian eatery. All meals include antipasto platters, salad, and soup. Live bands and ballroom dancing take over on the weekends. Entrees from $18. Open M-Th 11:30am-11pm, F 11:30am-midnight, Sa 4pm-midnight, Su 2-10pm. AmEx/D/MC/V. ❺

⌂ ACCOMMODATIONS

Staying in downtown Detroit often leaves travelers with the choice of high-end hotels or questionable dives. There are a few options along **E. Jefferson Ave.,** near downtown, but it may be easier to find chain motels in the northern suburbs or across the border in **Windsore.** For a mix of convenience and affordability, look along **Telegraph Rd.** off I-94, west of the city.

Shorecrest Motor Inn, 1316 E. Jefferson Ave. (☎313-568-3000 or 800-992-9616), located 3 blocks east of the Renaissance Center. Rooms include A/C, fridges, free Wi-Fi, and data ports. Key deposit $20 when paying with cash. Free parking. Reservations recommended. 21+. Singles $69; doubles $89. AmEx/D/MC/V. ❸

University of Windsor, 401 Sunset Ave. (☎519-253-3000, ext. 7041), in Windsor, Ontario. Rents functional rooms with refrigerators, A/C, and shared bathrooms. Free Internet access and use of university facilities. Open early May to late Aug. Dorms CDN$29; private rooms CDN$79. AmEx/MC/V. ❶

Pontiac Lake Recreation Area, 7800 Gale Rd. (☎248-666-1020), in Waterford, 45min. northwest of downtown. Take I-75 to Rte. 59 W, turn right on Will Lake northbound, and left onto Gale Rd. Follow the signs. 176 wooded sites with electricity and showers. Vehicle permit $8. Sites $16. AmEx/D/MC/V. ❶

♫ ENTERTAINMENT

THEATER

Though the era of Motown has come and gone, a vibrant music scene lives on in the Motor City. The **Detroit Symphony Orchestra** performs at **Orchestra Hall,** 3711 Woodward Ave., at Parsons St. (☎313-576-5111; www.detroitsymphony.com. Open M-F 10am-6pm. Tickets $20-105. Half-price student and senior rush tickets 1½hr. prior to show.) Dramatic works are performed in the restored **Theater District,** around Woodward Ave. and

Columbia St. The **Fox Theatre,** 2211 Woodward Ave., near Grand Circus Park, features dramas, comedies, and musicals in a 5000-seat theater. (☎313-983-3200. Box office open M-F 10am-6pm. Tickets $25-100.) The **State Theatre,** 2115 Woodward Ave. (☎313-961-5450, tickets 248-645-6666), hosts concerts, while the acclaimed **Detroit Repertory Theatre,** 13103 Woodrow Wilson Ave., shakes things up with a commitment to race-transcendent casting. (☎313-868-1347; www.detroitreptheatre.com. Shows Th-F 8:30pm, Sa 3 and 8:30pm, Su 2 and 7:30pm. Tickets from $17.)

SPORTS

Baseball's **Tigers** round the bases at new **Comerica Park,** 2100 Woodward Ave. (☎313-471-2255. Tickets $5-60.) Football's **Lions** hit the gridiron at **Ford Field,** 2000 Brush St. (☎800-616-7627. Tickets $40.) Inside the **Joe Louis Arena,** 600 Civic Center Dr., the **Red Wings** play hockey, and zealous fans chuck octopi onto the ice. (☎313-645-6666. Tickets $20-40.) Basketball's **Pistons** hoop it up at **The Palace at Auburn Hills,** 2 Championship Dr., in Auburn hills. (☎248-377-0100. Tickets $10-80.)

FESTIVALS

Detroit's festivals draw millions of visitors. Most outdoor events take place at **Hart Plaza,** a downtown oasis that hugs the Detroit River. A recent and successful downtown tradition, the ▧**Detroit Electronic Music Festival** (☎313-393-9200; www.demf.org) lures over a million ravers to Hart Plaza on Memorial Day weekend. Jazz fans jet to the riverbank during Labor Day weekend for the **Ford Detroit International Jazz Festival** (☎313-963-7622; www.detroit-jazzfest.com), which features more than 70 acts on three stages. The international **Freedom Festival** (☎313-923-7400), a week-long extravaganza in late June, celebrates the friendship between the US and Canada. The continent's largest fireworks display ignites the festivities on both sides of the border. **Detroit's African World Festival** (☎313-494-5853) fills Hart Plaza on the third weekend in August for free reggae, jazz, and gospel concerts. The nation's oldest state fair, the **Michigan State Fair** (☎313-369-8250), at Eight Mile Rd. and Woodward Ave., beckons with art and livestock two weeks before Labor Day.

 NIGHTLIFE

For info on the trendiest hot spots, pick up a free copy of *Orbit* in record stores and restaurants. The *Metro Times* also has complete entertainment listings. *Between the Lines,* also free, has GLBT entertainment info. Bars abound in the area around the stadiums, though their popularity fluctuates with game nights. More bars are sprinkled throughout **Greektown** and **Bricktown,** the most pedestrian-friendly section of town. Avoid walking alone downtown at night.

Town Pump Tavern, 100 Montcalm St. (☎313-961-1929; www.thetownpumptavern.com), behind the Fox Theatre. Good pints and atypical bar fare like roasted turkey-and-gouda sandwiches ($7) and pizzas ($7). Free Wi-Fi. Pints $3.75-5. Open M-Sa 11am-2am, Su noon-2am. Kitchen closes 10pm. AmEx/D/MC/V.

Detroiter Bar, 655 Beaubien St. (☎313-963-3355), in Bricktown. Catch the Lions or Tigers game alongside locals in this old-fashioned American pub. Burgers $4.75-6.75. Sandwiches $3.50-6. Open daily 10am-2am. AmEx/D/MC/V.

Seldom Blues, 400 Renaissance Ctr. (☎313-567-7301). The food is pricey ($13-35), but this joint is well known among Detroiters for the nightly jazz performances and the view over the Detroit River. Open M-Th 11:30am-10pm, F 11:30am-midnight, Sa 5pm-midnight, Su 11:30am-4pm. AmEx/D/MC/V.

⏴ APPROACHING FLINT: 68 MILES

Take **I-75 N.** Merge off I-75 onto **I-475,** and exit at **Saginawa St.,** which will take you to downtown Flint.

FLINT

Most recently known as the hometown of independent filmmaker Michael Moore and the subject of the movie *Roger and Me,* Flint has seen the industries of lumbering, carriage-manufacturing, and automobile-building all come and go. It still clings stubbornly to life despite its economic slumps. One of Flint's major attractions is **Crossroads Village & Huckleberry Railroad,** 6140 Bray Rd., where visitors can wander among 1860s villagers in period dress and partake in old-fashioned fun. (☎810-736-7100 or 800-648-7275. Open June-Aug. Tu and Th-Su 10am-5pm, W 10am-8pm. $9, seniors $8, ages 3-12 $7; with train and boat $13/$12/$10.50.) Over 90,000 visitors annually enjoy the collection at the **Flint Institute of Arts,** 1120 E. Kearsley St., which encompasses more than 6,000 works including paintings by John Singer Sargent and a *Prancing Horse* sculpture from the Han Dynasty. (☎810-234-1695; www.flintarts.org. Open Tu-Sa 10am-5pm, Su 1-5pm. Free.) The **Robert T. Longway Planetarium,** Michigan's largest planetarium, has Sky Theater planetarium shows and laser shows. (☎810-237-3400; www.longway.org. Open M-F 8:30am-4:30pm, Sa-Su noon-4:30pm. Laser shows M-F 2pm, Sa-Su 1:30 and 2:30pm. $5, under 12 $4.) Try your luck at **Gillie's Coney Island Restaurant ❶,** 6524 N. Dort Hwy., in Mt. Morris, which has cheap eats and slot machines. (From downtown Flint, take Rte. 54 N; the restaurant will be on your right. ☎810-686-1200; www.gilliesconeyisland.com. Sandwiches $1.50-5.75. Dinner $7-9. Open 24hr. AmEx/D/MC/V.)

☈ APPROACHING FRANKENMUTH: 21 MILES

Head north on the **Dort Hwy. (Rte. 54).** Near Clio, Rte. 54 turns into **Rte. 83,** which takes you toward Frankenmuth.

FRANKENMUTH

Frankenmuth was founded in 1845 by a band of Bavarian missionaries who came to Michigan to convert the Chippewa Indians to Christianity. "Michigan's Little Bavaria" maintains much of its original identity nowadays with some of the most authentic Bavarian architecture found anywhere in the US. (Note: the "Bavarian" McDonald's is excluded from this statement.)

VITAL STATS

Population: 4800

Visitor Info: Frankenmuth Visitors Center, 635 S. Main St. (☎989-652-6106 or 800-386-8696; www.frankenmuth.org). Open June-Aug. M-W 8am-5pm, Th-F 8am-8pm, Su noon-5pm; Sept.-May. M-F 8am-5pm, Sa 10am-5pm, Su noon-5pm.

Internet Access: Wickson James E Memorial Library, 359 S. Franklin St. (☎989-652-8323). Open June-Aug. M-Th 9am-9pm, F 9am-5pm, Sa 10am-5pm; Sept.-May M-Th 9am-9pm, F 9am-5pm, Sa 10am-5pm, Su 1-4pm. Free.

Post Office: 119 N. Main St. (☎989-652-6751). Open M-F 8:30am-5pm, Sa 9am-noon. **Postal Code:** 48734.

❏ GETTING AROUND. Rte. 83 enters Frankenmuth from the south and becomes **Main St.** in town. The main intersections with Main St. are at **Curtis Rd.** and **Genesee St.**

☉ SIGHTS. The holiday season never ends at **Bronner's Christmas Wonderland,** 25 Christmas Ln., the world's largest Christmas store. The European-style marketplace is the size of 1½ football fields, and the landscaped grounds cover 27 acres. You can see 400 nativity scenes from around the world, 200 types of nutcracker, a replica of the Silent Night Memorial Chapel in Oberndorf, Austria, and over 10,000 twinkling lights on Christmas Ln. at night. (☎989-652-9931; www.bronners.com. Open Jan.-May M-Th and Sa 9am-5:30pm, F 9am-9pm, Su noon-5:30pm; June-Dec. M-Sa 9am-9pm, Su noon-7pm.) The **Frankenmuth River Place** shopping area, 925 S. Main St., is set up as a miniature European village and features a nightly "Lights Fantastic" laser show. (☎800-600-0105; www.frankenmuth-riverplace.com.)

☎⊓ FOOD AND ACCOMMODATIONS. The streets of Frankenmuth are lined with multitudes of candy, fudge, and taffy shops. If you're famished, try the all-you-can-eat dinner ($18) at the **Bavarian Inn ❹,** 713 S. Main St., a Frankenmuth tradition that includes platters of Frankenmuth Chicken, baked dressing, mashed potatoes, *gemuese* (hot vegetable), chicken *nudelsuppe,* *stollen* (fruit and nut bread), *krautsalat* (cole slaw), and homemade ice cream. If you haven't had enough, additional German *wiener schnitzel, kasseler rippchen, sauerbraten,* and *bratwurst* are available. (☎989-652-9941; www.bavarianinn.com. Open M-Th and Su 11am-9:30pm, F-Sa 11am-9pm. AmEx/D/MC/V.) **Zehnders ❹,** 730 S. Main St., has a similar all-you-can-eat deal with chicken, dressing, noodle soup, cabbage salad, chicken liver pâté, cheese spread with garlic toast, freshly baked bread, mashed potatoes, egg noodles, and ice cream for $17.50. (☎800-863-7999; www.zehnders.com. Open Apr.-Dec. daily 11am-9:30pm; Jan.-Mar. M-Th and Su 11am-8pm, F-Sa 11am-9:30pm. D/MC/V.)

If you'd like to stay in Frankenmuth without paying resort prices, the **Frankenmuth Motel ❸,** 1218 Weiss St., is an affordable option. (☎800-821-5362. Rooms $49-89. AmEx/D/MC/V.) If you want the real German experience, stay at the **Bavarian Inn Lodge ❺,** 1 Covered Bridge Ln. The seven-acre building

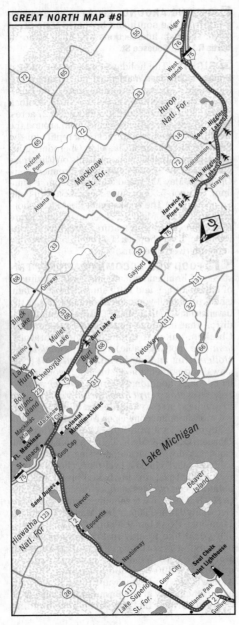

GREAT NORTH MAP #8

features five pools, indoor mini-golf, four tennis courts, two lounges, and nightly entertainment. (Across the covered bridge on Cass River. ☎888-775-6343; www.bavarianinn.com. Rooms from $109. AmEx/D/MC/V.)

◪ APPROACHING BAY CITY: 22 MILES
Continue on **Rte. 83** heading north. Rte. 83 becomes **Rte. 15** as it reaches Bay City.

BAY CITY. Lush pine forests once fueled Bay City's prosperous lumber industry. Though the city's former prosperity is not as evident these days, it still boasts several waterfront parks and historic districts. The Friendship Shell amphitheater in **Wenonah Park** hosts fireworks shows and concerts during the summer. (☎989-893-0343; www.bayartscouncil.org.) **Midland Street Historic District** is known as the entertainment capital of mid-Michigan and backs up that reputation with a high density of bars, many of which host live jazz and rock music. Head to the **Midland Street Pub ❶**, 610 E. Midland St., for a pint ($1-3.25) and some cheap pub fare ($3-5) in front of a beautiful 1920s wooden bar. (☎989-895-0556. Open M-Sa 11am-2am, Su noon-midnight. AmEx/D/MC/V.)

◪ APPROACHING ROSCOMMON: 83 MILES
In Bay City, take **Center Ave. (Rte. 15/25)** across the bridge onto **Jenny St.** From Jenny St., turn north onto **Euclid Ave. (Rte. 13),** which becomes **Huron Rd.** Huron Rd. becomes Main St. as it enters the town of Standish to the north. From Take **Old Rte. 76 NW** toward the town of Sterling. Taking Rte. 76 instead of the freeway between Standish and West Branch is worth it. Giant pine trees line the stick-straight road, allowing you to see for miles through tunnel-like greenery. Hop on **I-75** and exit at Roscommon.

ROSCOMMON. Roscommon is a small village on the banks of the Ausable River's South Branch, known for its clear blue waters. Born a typical lumber town when the railroad made its way through town, Roscommon's main business is now tourism. The **Firemen's Memorial,** 1 mi. south of Roscommon, ½ mi. east of Rte. 18 on County Rd. 103, stands 12 ft. tall. The third weekend in September is the **Michigan Firemen's Memorial Festival** (☎989-275-5880; www.firemensmemorial.org), when thousands of visitors from all over the US come to honor the valiant fire fighters who lost their lives protecting their communities. **North Higgins Lake State Park,** 11747 N. Higgins Lake Dr., and **South Higgins Lake State Park,** 106 State Park Dr., both have campgrounds and nice, sandy beaches. North Higgins also contains the **Civilian Conservation Corps (CCC) Museum,** which describes the successful New Deal program that reforested much of Michigan. (☎800-447-2757. Open daily 8am-10pm. $4 per vehicle.)

◙ DETOUR

HARTWICK PINES STATE PARK
4216 Granger Rd. Located on Rte. 93 in Grayling, at Exit 259 off I-75.

The 9762 acres of **Hartwick Pines ❶** are home to 49 acres of one of Michigan's last and largest stands of old-growth pine forests. The 1¼ mi. Old Growth Forest Foot Trail leads to the **Logging Museum,** a recreated logging camp. (☎989-348-7068. Grounds open daily 8am-10pm. Museum open daily June-Aug. 9am-6pm; Sept.-Oct. and May 9am-4pm. Sites $15-19, with electricity $23; cabins $40. Day-use $4. Tours 11am, 1, 3pm. Free.)

◙ APPROACHING GAYLORD: 28 MILES
Continue north on **I-75,** and take **Exit 282** toward Gaylord/Alpena. Turn right onto **W. Main St.**

GAYLORD

In the 1960s, Gaylord recreated itself as an Alpine village to attract tourists. These days the town's main attractions are its Swiss architecture and its status as the Ski Capital of Michigan. In 1965, Gaylord chose Pontresina, Switzerland, as its sister city, and Pontresina sent a boulder from the Swiss Alps as a gift to the town. You can see the **Pontresina Stone** on the corner of the courtyard lawn at S. Otsego Ave. and W. Main St. ◙**The Cross in the Woods,** 7078 Rte. 68, is one of Michigan's best-known monuments. The cross was inspired by Kateri Tekakwitha, a Native American woman who erected crosses in the woods around the area. This particular cross was crafted from a redwood tree, and its crucified Jesus was created by renowned Michigan sculptor Marshall M. Fredericks. The cross—55 ft. high and 22 ft. wide—is truly monumental. The **Museum of the Cross in the Woods** keeps the largest collection of nun dolls in the US, but (amazingly) fails to include any of those punching-nun puppets. (Take Exit 310 from I-75 north of town, and follow Rte. 68 W. ☎231-238-8973; www.cross-inthewoods.com. Cross open 24hr. Free.)

La Senorita ❸, 737 W. Main St., serves sizzling pans of fajitas ($11-13). Daily lunch specials are $5.50. (☎989-732-1771. Open M-Th 11am-10pm, F-Sa 11am-11pm, Su noon-10pm. Bar closes midnight. AmEx/D/MC/V.) **The Timberly Motel ❷,** 881 S. Otsego Ave., is less Alpine and less pricey than the rest of Gaylord with plain but large rooms. (☎989-732-5166. Singles in summer $48, in winter $38; doubles $58/$42. AmEx/D/MC/V.)

◙ APPROACHING MACKINAW CITY: 58 MILES
Continue north on **I-75.** Take **Exit 337 (Old U.S. 31/ M-108/Nicolet)** into downtown Mackinaw City.

MACKINAW CITY

First things first, Mackinac is pronounced "MACK-i-naw," so curb the urge to rhyme your syllables by saying "MACK-i-nack." The Mackinac Bridge ("Mighty Mac") soars over the intersection of Lake Michigan and Lake Huron, connecting Mackinaw City to St. Ignace in the Upper Peninsula. Measuring 950 ft. longer than the Golden Gate Bridge, the 5 mi. span is the third-longest suspension bridge in the world.

VITAL STATS
Population: 860
Visitor Info: Michigan Dept. of Transportation Welcome and Travel Information Center (☎231-436-5566), on Nicolet St., off I-75 at Exit 338. Open daily mid-June to Aug. 8am-6pm; Sept. to mid-June 9am-5pm.
Internet Access: Mackinaw Area Public Library, 528 W. Central Ave. (☎231-436-5451). Open M-Tu and Th-F 11am-5pm, W 1-9pm. Free.
Post Office: 306 E. Central Ave. (☎231-436-5526). **Postal Code:** 49701.

▉ GETTING AROUND. I-75 runs through town and across the Mackinac Bridge (toll $2.50). **U.S. 23** enters Mackinaw City from Cheboygan to the east. **Nicolet St.** and **Huron St.** are the main north-south thoroughfares. **Central Ave.,** the main east-west street, leads west to **Wilderness State Park.**

◙ SIGHTS. A local tradition that is not to be missed is the annual **Labor Day Bridge Walk,**

where Michigan's governor leads thousands north across the bridge to St. Ignace. Chain motels and tacky gift shops dominate the town, although the **Mackinac State Historic Parks** are well worth a look. Colonial enthusiasts should buy a combination ticket, good for seven days from date of purchase, for unlimited admission to all three. ($20, ages 6-17 $12.50. Available at all 4 sights.) Just west of the Mackinac Bridge's southern landfall, **Colonial Michilimackinac Fort** guards the straits between Lake Michigan and Lake Huron. The site reconstructs a fort built in 1715 by French fur traders that was recently unearthed by a tireless team of archaeologists. (☎231-436-4100. Open daily early May-early June and late Aug. to mid-Oct. 9am-4pm; mid-June to late Aug. 9am-6pm. $9.50, ages 6-17 $6.) A 5min. walk away, the **Old Mackinac Point Lighthouse** opened in 2005 as a restoration project in progress. Warped wood and cracked plaster walls give visitors a sense of the work that remains to be done, although the four-story climb to the tower already offers a sweeping view of the surrounding straits. (Open daily mid-May to early June and mid-Aug. to mid-Oct. 9am-4pm; mid-June to mid-Aug. 9am-5pm. $6, ages 6-17 $3.50, under 6 free.) **Fort Mackinac** (on Mackinac Island; see below) and **Old Mill Creek Historic State Park,** a complex with a working sawmill and nature trails located 3½ mi. south of Mackinaw City on U.S. 23, round out the list of Mackinac State Historic Parks. (☎231-436-4100. Open daily early May to mid-Oct. 9am-4pm; mid-July to late Aug. 9am-5pm. $7.50, ages 6-17 $4.50.)

FOOD AND ACCOMMODATIONS. Family-oriented restaurants cluster around Central St., near Shepler's Dock in Mackinaw City. **Cunningham's ❸,** 312 E. Central St., serves homemade pasties ($6.50), pies, and fresh fish. (☎231-436-8821. Dinner specials $8.50. Open daily in spring 8am-8pm; in summer 8am-10pm; in fall 8am-9pm. AmEx/D/MC/V.) At the laid-back **Audie's ❸,** 314 N. Nicolet St., huge sandwiches ($6.50-11) keep diners happy. Try the "Perchwich Deluxe" ($8.75), made with local fish. (☎231-436-5744; www.audies.com. Lunch specials $5.75. Dinner specials $9.25. Open daily 7:30am-10pm. MC/V.) For the best pasties in town, head to the ▓**Mackinaw Pastie & Cookie Co. ❶,** 117 W. Jamet St., which serves

variations of the U.P.'s favorite meat pie for $5.50. (☎231-436-8202. Open daily 9am-10pm. MC/V.)

Lakeshore accommodation options abound on U.S. 23, south of the city. The best deals in the area lie across the Mackinac Bridge on **Bus. I-75** in St. Ignace (p. 259). For an outdoor escape, try one of the 600 sites at **Mackinac Mill Creek Campground ❶,** 3 mi. south of town on U.S. 23. The grounds provide beach access, fishing, and trails. (☎231-436-5584. Internet access, public showers, pool. Sites $18-35; cabins $40. AmEx/D/MC/V.)

⚓ APPROACHING MACKINAC ISLAND: 7 MILES
Ferry lines leave Mackinaw City (in summer every 30min. 7:30am-9pm). **Shepler's** offers the fastest service. (☎800-828-6157; www.sheplersferry.com. Round-trip $19, ages 5-12 $9.50. Bikes $7.50.) Catamarans operated by **Arnold Transit Co.** are another fun way to get to the island. (☎800-542-8528. Round-trip $20, ages 5-12 $10. Bikes $7.50.)

MACKINAC ISLAND

Mackinac Island, a 16min. ferry ride from the mainland, has been a destination for summer vacationers since the 1870s. Railroad barons lined the south-facing bluffs with elegant Victorian homes and, by banning automobiles from the island in 1896, tried to guarantee that Mackinac would retain its genteel, unhurried atmosphere for years to come. The slew of shops pressing Mackinac fudge on daytrippers proves that the early inhabitants weren't entirely successful, although there are still quiet corners of the island to explore. Walk off the ferry landing, cross the garish strip that is Main St., and never look back.

VITAL STATS

Population: 500

Visitor Info: Mackinac Island Chamber of Commerce and Visitors Center (☎906-847-3783; www.mackinacisland.org.), on Main St. Open daily June-Sept. 8am-6pm; Oct.-May 9am-5pm.

Internet Access: see Mackinaw City (p. 257)

Post Office: 35 Market St. (☎906-847-3821). Open M-F 9am-4pm, Sa 9-11am. **Postal Code:** 49757.

⬛ GETTING AROUND. Travel on the island is limited to foot, bicycle, and horse-drawn carriage.

Michigan State Hwy. M-185, one of the few US highways without motorized vehicles, encircles the island as **Lake Shore Dr.** and **Huron St.**

 DID YOU KNOW? The name of Mackinac island was shortened from "Michilimackinac," which means "large turtle" in the Chippewa and Ottawa languages.

◙ SIGHTS. Escape the touristy Main St. for a quiet look at what made the island popular in the first place—its beautiful fauna and rolling hills. Commanding a lofty view of the island's southern harbor **Fort Mackinac** was a hotly contested piece of military architecture during the War of 1812. Today cannon firings, carefully restored buildings, and the sounds of fife and drum lure a steady stream of tourists up to the bluffs. Tickets to the fort also allow access to four museums on island history that are housed in refurbished period buildings. (☎231-436-4100. Open daily early May to mid-June. and late Aug. to mid-Oct. 9:30am-4:30pm; mid-July to late Aug. 9:30am-8pm. $9.50, ages 6-17 $6, under 6 free.) Travelers willing to don a three-cornered hat should inquire into week-long volunteer opportunities at the fort, which include free housing on the island. Call for details. **Mackinac Island Carriage Tours,** Main St., sends horse-drawn buggies on a 2hr. trot around the southern half of the island, veering as far east as the Arch Rock formation before circling back to showcase the sumptuous grounds of the Grand Hotel. Keep an eye out for weepy devotees of the 1980 Christopher Reeve film *Somewhere in Time,* which was set at the hotel. (☎906-847-3307; www.mict.com. Tours daily early May to mid-Oct. 9am-3pm; July-Aug. 9am-5pm. $19, ages 5-12 $8.) For those who would like to take the reins themselves, **Jack's Livery Stable,** 331 Mahoney Ave., off Cadotte Ave., rents saddle horses and buggies. (☎906-847-3391. Saddle horses $30 per hr. 2-person horse and buggy $48 per hr.; 4-person $60 per hr. Open daily in summer 8am-6pm; in winter 9am-5pm.) Encompassing 80% of the island, **Mackinac Island State Park** features a circular 8¼ mi. shoreline road that takes about an hour by bike.

▐▜ FOOD AND ACCOMMODATIONS. Take your cue from the locals and "shop across" in Mackinaw City for food; everything is more expensive on the island, whether you buy it in a restaurant or a convenience store. **Mighty Mac ❶,** on Main St., keeps it cheap, serving quarter-pound burgers for under $4. (☎906-847-8039. Open daily 8am-8pm.) The **Pink Pony ❸,** 100 Main St., serves handmade pastas, fresh salads, and fish under the watchful eyes of the pink horses on the wall. (☎906-847-3341. Entrees from $10. Open daily 8am-10pm.) Hotel rates on the island generally reach into the stratosphere, but **McNally Cottage ❹,** offers a haven for thrifty travelers. Situated at the heart of downtown, this B&B has been owned and operated by the same family every summer since its construction in the 1880s. (☎906-847-3565; www.mcnallycottage.net. Reservations recommended. Open May-Sept. Rooms $55-175. Cash or check only.)

▐▜ APPROACHING ST. IGNACE: 6 MILES
From the mainland, hop onto **I-75** and cross the **Mackinac Bridge** ($2.50). Take the 1st exit onto **U.S. 2 E** to enter St. Ignace.

ST. IGNACE. Founded in 1671 by Father Marquette and named for St. Ignatius of Loyola, St. Ignace is Mackinaw City's sister city in the Upper Peninsula. Be sure to take a stroll along the **Huron Boardwalk** on the waterfront downtown, where open-air exhibits relate the history of St. Ignace. **Castle Rock** began as the lookout of the Ojibway Indians. The lookout tower rises 200 ft. above St. Ignace with spectacular views of Mackinac Island and Lake Huron. You can also find yet another **Paul Bunyan statue** at Castle Rock, 4 mi. north of the Mackinac Bridge. (Exit 348 off I-75. ☎906-643-8268. $0.50 to climb.) A beloved local diner, **Bentleys B-n-L Cafe ❷,** 62 N. State St., has colorful 50s decor and memorabilia. Get a shake ($3) with your fried whitefish dinner ($7). Lunch specials are a steal for $4.25. (☎906-643-7910. Open mid-May to Nov. daily 7am-11pm, Feb. to mid-May 7am-8pm. Cash only.) Affordable motels are along N. State St. (Bus. I-75) away from the town center. For luxurious accommodations in the heart of town, try the **Colonial House Inn ❸,** 90 N. State St., a beautiful B&B and motel complex. (☎906-643-6900. Motel singles M-Th and Su $59, F-Sa $69; doubles $69/$79. B&B rooms from $79. D/MC/V.)

▐▜ APPROACHING GULLIVER: 75 MILES
Head out on **U.S. 2 W.** Just after St. Ignace, encounter the unusual at **Michigan's Mystery Spot,** 150 Martin

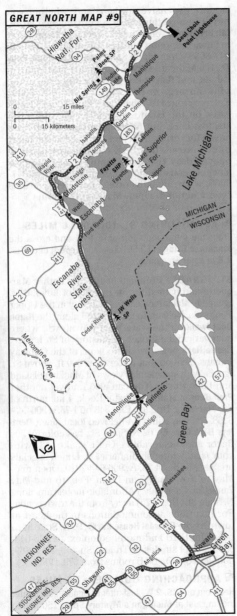

GREAT NORTH MAP #9

0   15 miles

0   15 kilometers

GREAT NORTH

Lake Rd., where "the laws of physics and gravity do not apply." For fun with optical illusions, this classic tourist trap has tours, but don't fret if you miss it—there's an identical attraction in Montana, a thousand miles down the road. (5 mi. west of St. Ignace off U.S. 2. ☎906-643-8322. Open daily mid-May to mid-June 9am-8pm; mid-June to Labor Day 8am-9pm; Labor Day to late Oct. 9am-7pm.)

GULLIVER. Take a quick break at **Seul Choix Point Lighthouse,** 672 NW Gulliver Lake Rd. French fur traders caught in a storm took refuge here and named the bay Seul Choix, meaning "only choice." In 1892, the Seul Choix Point Lighthouse was completed. Today, you can climb to the top of the 79ft. tower for an impressive view from the only operable lighthouse on the north shore. (From Gulliver, turn south onto County Rd. 432, then right onto County Rd. 431. ☎906-283-3183. Open June to mid-Oct. daily 10am-6pm. Museum $5. $2 donation to climb tower.)

APPROACHING MANISTIQUE: 13 MILES
Return to **U.S. 2 W,** which becomes **Lakeshore Dr.** in Manistique.

MANISTIQUE. The restored iron-smelting village of Manistique is now a popular tourist destination on Lake Michigan. The city's central location makes a great base for the many outdoor activities in the Upper Peninsula. The wood and cement **Manistique Boardwalk** lines 2 mi. of Lake Michigan shoreline. In front of the Chamber of Commerce, on the north side of Rte. 2, is yet another **Paul Bunyan statue.** Are you getting tired of these yet? It's usually crowded inside **Marley's Bar & Grill ❶,** 127 Walnut St., which has served basic bar fare under the same pressed-tin ceiling for over 100 years. Try the chicken cordon bleu sandwich on homemade bread for $5.75. (☎906-341-8297. Open M-Th 11am-12:30am, F-Sa 11am-2:30am, Su noon-midnight. AmEx/D/MC/V.)

DETOUR
PICTURED ROCKS NATIONAL SEASHORE
From Manistique, head west on Rte. 94. In Shingleton, continue straight onto C.R. H-15. Make a left onto C.R. H-58 and a right onto Miners Castle Rd. a few miles later.

With the largest surface area of any freshwater lake in the world and an average depth of 500 ft., Lake Superior contains enough water to fill the other four Great Lakes. The **Pictured**

Rocks National Seashore hugs Lake Superior's wild shoreline for 40 mi., offering spectacular views of the colorfully striated sandstone cliffs, along with sand dunes, waterfalls, forests, lakes, and a lighthouse. From **Miners Castle,** a rock formation mentioned in Henry Wadsworth Longfellow's *The Song of Hiawatha*, you can see grand views of the cliffs in either direction. A pleasant 1 mi. hike along the **North Country National Scenic Trail** leads down the cliffs through wild blueberry patches to **Miners Beach,** a beautiful sand beach on frigid waters. (☎906-387-3700; www.nps.gov/piro. Free.)

APPROACHING ESCANABA: 55 MILES
If you skip the Pictured Rocks National Seashore, it's a straight 55 mi. shot down **U.S. 2 W/Rte. 35** to Escanaba. From Pictured Rocks, take **Miners Castle Rd.,** and make a right onto **C.R. H-58** toward Munising. In Munising, make a left onto **Rte. 28,** then follow **Rte. 94 W** to **Rte. 67 S.** Turn onto **U.S. 41 S** in Trenary, which will merge with U.S. 2 W/Rte. 35 to bring you to Escanaba.

ESCANABA

A pleasant town on the southern side of the Upper Peninsula, Escanaba has a few noteworthy sights. The **Sand Point Lighthouse** was built in 1867 and operated until 1939, when it was closed because the changing contour of Escanaba Harbor no longer necessitated its use. After that, the lens and lantern were removed and the tower shortened. You can visit the lighthouse and the **Delta County Historical Museum** next door, which houses 50 years of memorabilia ranging from vintage costumes to a blacksmith shop. (From U.S. 2, turn east onto Ludington St., then left onto Jenkins Dr. ☎906-789-6790. Open daily June-Aug. 9am-5pm; Sept. 1-4pm.) The arrival of the first cold front in early September marks the departure of thousands of **monarch butterflies** from their summer home near Escanaba. Each year, the butterflies fly over 1900 mi. from Michigan to their winter home near Zitácuaro, Mexico. The dates of migration are unpredictable, but good viewing locations are Point Peninsula and Stonington Peninsula.

The **Swedish Pantry ❷,** 819 Ludington St., is consistently packed with locals enjoying Swedish specialties. The *kroppkakor* (ham

dumplings; $8-10) and the *kottbullar* (swedish meatballs with lingonberries; $8-10) are definitely worth a taste. (☎906-786-9606. Open in summer M-F 8am-8pm, Sa 8am-4pm; in winter M-F and Su 8am-7pm, Sa 8am-3pm. AmEx/D/MC/V.) The **Hiawatha Motel ❷,** 2400 Ludington St., has comfy beds, movie rentals, and some rooms with kitchenettes. (At U.S. 2 and Rte. 41. ☎800-249-2216. Continental breakfast included. Singles from $40. AmEx/D/MC/V.)

APPROACHING CEDAR RIVER: 54 MILES
Continue on **Rte. 35 (Lakeshore Dr.).**

> Before Cedar River, Rte. 35 enters the Central Time Zone, where it is 1hr. earlier.

CEDAR RIVER. Cedar River is the only town between Escanaba and Menominee, so if you're hungry, stop for a bite to eat at the **Lighthouse Inn ❸,** N. 8241 Rte. 35. Pictures of Cedar River back in its logging days line the walls of this small restaurant, which kind of feels like being inside a Lake Michigan tugboat. Try the "broasted" half chicken ($9), made using a process patented in Beloit, WI, in 1954. (☎906-863-2922. Open M-Th and Su 11am-10pm, F-Sa 11am-midnight. MC/V.) The 678 acres of **J.W. Wells State Park ❶,** N. 7670 Rte. 35, are covered in thick forests that almost look like a Michigan rainforest. The park offers 7 mi. of trails and 3 mi. of sandy beach with swimming and picnic areas. (☎906-863-9747. Day-use $4. Sites with electricity $17. AmEx/D/MC/V.)

APPROACHING MENOMINEE: 25 MILES
Continue southwest on **Rte. 35** to Menominee.

MENOMINEE. The first inhabitants of Menominee were an Algonquin-speaking Native American tribe; the name Menominee translates to "wild rice," which once grew abundantly here. Menominee is known for its historical waterfront district, which was once the world's greatest lumber shipping port. Take some time to travel down **First St.** between 10th and 4th Ave. to see an eclectic assortment of building styles, from Tudor to French château. According to Menominee legend, the **Spirit Stone** brought luck to whomever made an offering to the stone. The stone now sits in front of the **Menom-**

inee Welcome Center, 1343 10th Ave. (☎906-863-6496. Open daily 8am-6pm.)

◤ APPROACHING MARINETTE: 1 MILE
Continue along **Rte. 35** to the junction with **U.S. 41**, and cross the **Interstate Bridge.** In Marinette, U.S. 41 is known as **Marinette Ave.**

MARINETTE
Named in honor of a 19th-century Native American trading post owner known as Queen Marinette, Marinette County is the waterfall capital of Wisconsin, with over 14 waterfalls located within a one-day drive. Most are located within the county park system. (☎ 715-732-7530; www.marinettecounty.com. Day-use $3.) Between Menominee and Marinette, the Menominee River flows into Green Bay. The surrounding bodies of water provide Menominee and Marinette with boating, fishing, swimming, and even ice boating in the winter. Exhibits at the **Marinette County Historical Society Logging Museum** include a logging camp in miniature and the Evancheck log cabin. Special exhibits honor Queen Marinette and the Menominee Indians. (On Stephenson Island, between Menominee and Marinette. ☎ 715-732-0831. Open Memorial Day to Labor Day Tu-Sa 10am-4:30pm, Su noon-4pm.) For information on Marinette and the surrounding area, visit the **Wisconsin Travel Information Center,** 1680 Bridge St. (☎ 715-732-4333; http://travelwisconsin.com. Open M-Sa 8am-4pm.)

The **Brothers Three ❸,** 1302 Marinette Ave., is famous for its thin-crust pizza made with Wisconsin cheese. (☎ 715-735-9054. Large $15. Open M-W 11am-10pm, Th-Sa 11am-11pm. D/MC/V.) To satisfy your dairy cravings, **Seguins House of Cheese,** W. 1968 U.S. 41, offers a variety of Wisconsin cheeses, **▉cheese curds,** spreads, and sausages. (☎ 800-338-7919; www.seguinscheese.com. Open daily 8am-8pm. MC/V.)

◤ APPROACHING PESHTIGO: 7 MILES
Take **U.S. 41 S.**

PESHTIGO. Peshtigo was the site of the deadliest forest fire in U.S. history. At least 1,200 people perished in Northern Wisconsin on Oct. 8, 1871—coincidentally, the same day as the Great Chicago Fire—when a nearby prairie fire fueled by strong winds suddenly swept through the town. The **Peshtigo Fire Museum,** 400 Oconto Ave., showcases period life and the few items that survived the inferno, including the Catholic church's tabernacle, saved by a priest who flung it into the river in desperation. (☎ 715-582-3244. Open daily 10am-4:30pm. Donation suggested.)

HOOK, LINE, AND SINKER

When you're out on the open road, it can be tempting to ignore your bank account's activity. After all, who wants to pore over online bank reports when there's a great big world out there? The problem is, you're most vulnerable to identity theft when you're traveling and using your card frequently. There are plenty of opportunities for ill-intentioned people to overhear your card number and try to use it themselves. Would-be thieves will initially make a small charge to your account. They're fishing for a person who isn't paying attention, and if they see that you don't close out the card, they'll quickly reel you in—by cleaning out your account. These charges generally stand out, even though they are so tiny, because they tend to come from overseas. If you notice unauthorized activity on your account, close out the card as soon as possible by calling your bank's security number. Closing the card presents a problem for the roadtripper, because the bank will mail a new card to your permanent address, which is probably miles away. However, you don't need to end the roadtrip early. Many banks will issue temporary ATM cards so that you can still access your account. Just go to a local branch of your bank and ask for a temporary ATM card to use until you return home.

-Annie Levenson

◙ APPROACHING SUAMICO: 38 MILES
Continue on **U.S. 41 S.**

SUAMICO. Located within the Brown County Reforestation Camp, the **Northeastern Wisconsin Zoo**, 4418 Reforestation Rd., is home to lions, moose, penguins, and their friends. Together, the zoo and Reforestation Camp make up a 1560-acre recreation area with trails, picnic areas, and trout ponds. (Exit at C.R. B/Sunset Beach Rd./School Lane Rd. Follow C.R. B W for 2 mi. to City Rd. IR/Reforestation Rd. Turn right and travel 1 mi. to the zoo. ☎920-434-7841; www.newzoo.org. Open daily Apr.-Oct. 9am-6pm; Nov.-Mar. 9am-4pm. $4, seniors and ages 3-15 $2.)

◙ APPROACHING GREEN BAY: 10 MILES
U.S. 41 enters Green Bay from the north and borders the city along the west side. To enter downtown, head from the highway onto **Dousman St.** or **Shawano St.** and head east.

GREEN BAY

Green Bay is the oldest settlement in the Midwest, established in 1634 when French fur trappers explored the area. Today, the city is well known for its rowdy, cheese-headed football fans. In the fall, the city is crowded with Packers football fans trying to get a seat in the revered Lambeau Field. Winter brings hockey season as the Green Bay Gamblers play at the Resch Center.

VITAL STATS

Population: 101,000

Visitor Info: Packer Country Regional Tourism Office, 1901 S. Oneida St. (☎920-494-9507 or 888-867-3342; www.packercountry.com). Open M-F 8am-4:30pm.

Internet Access: Brown County Library, 515 Pine St. (☎920-448-4400). Open Memorial Day to Labor Day M-Th 9am-8pm, F 9am-5pm, Sa 9am-1pm; Labor Day to Memorial Day M-Th 9am-9pm, F-Sa 9am-5pm, Su noon-4pm. Free.

Post Office: 300 Packerland Dr. (☎920-498-3849). Open M-F 7:30am-6:30pm, Sa 8am-3pm. **Postal Code:** 54303.

▐ GETTING AROUND. Downtown Green Bay is surrounded by a rectangular loop of freeways.

U.S. 41 runs north-south along the western edge of Green Bay, while **I-43** borders the city to the north and east. **Rte. 172** flanks Green Bay to the south.

◙ SIGHTS. At the ▧**National Railroad Museum,** 2285 S. Broadway, there are more than 70 trains on display, including one that will take you on a ride around the block. Take a break and sit in the cab of the world's largest steam locomotive, "Big Boy." (☎920-437-7623; www.nationalrrmuseum.org. Open M-Sa 9am-5pm, Su 11am-5pm. Rides May-Oct. daily 10, 11:30am, 1, 2:30, 4pm. May-Sept. $9, seniors $8, ages 4-12 $6.50; Oct.-Apr. $8/$6/$5.) **Heritage Hill State Park,** 2640 S. Webster Ave., has managed to fit four periods of Wisconsin history into 48 acres. Barter with a fur trader (1672-1825), march alongside soldiers at Fort Howard (1836), get your horse shod at a blacksmith shop (1871), or churn butter with the farmers at the Belgian Farm (1905) in one of the 25 historical buildings. (2640 S. Webster Ave., off Rte. 172. ☎800-721-5150; www.heritagehillgb.org. Open Apr.-Oct. Tu-Sa 10am-4:30pm, Su noon-4:30pm. Tours Sept.-Oct. M-F 1:30pm, Sa 11am and 1:30pm. Tu-Th $8, seniors $7, ages 5-17 $6; F-Su $10/$7/$6.) **Bay Beach Amusement Park,** 1313 Bay Beach Rd., is your ticket to the days before Six Flags and $60 admission fees. Free admission to the park includes 16 old-fashioned rides, as well as concessions, volleyball and softball facilities, and games. (Off I-43 on Webster Ave., on the Green Bay waterfront. ☎920-391-3671. Open late May to mid-Aug. daily 10am-9pm; mid-Aug. to late Aug. daily 10am-6pm; early May and Sept. Sa-Su 10am-6pm. Tickets $0.25.)

Bicycling is huge in Wisconsin; the state leads the nation with nearly 1000 mi. of trails. The historical **Fox River Trail,** in downtown Green Bay, is a great place to start. Once a footpath for Native Americans traveling between villages, the trail begins on the east side of the Fox River between E. Mason and Walnut St. and ends in Greenleaf, WI. (☎920-448-4466; www.foxrivertrail.org. Open daily 5am-9pm. $3.)

▧▐ FOOD AND ACCOMMODATIONS. Located in the old Dousman Street Station, the **Titletown Brewing Company ❹,** 200 Dousman St., has walls lined with old photographs of historical Green Bay. Specialty brews on tap include Johnny "Blood" McNally Red Ale and Grandma's root beer. (☎920-437-2337; www.titletownbrew-

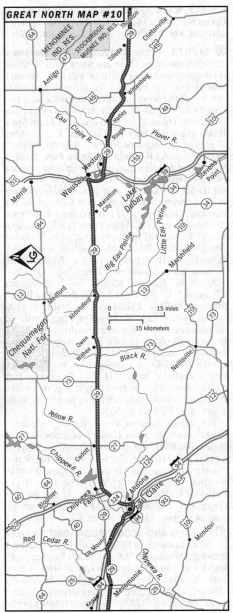

GREAT NORTH MAP #10

ing.com. Open M-F 11am-10pm, Sa-Su 11am-11pm. Bar closes 2am.) In the shadow of Lambeau Field, **Kroll's ❶**, 1990 S. Ridge Rd., has been a long-time local burger favorite. (☎920-468-4422. Open 10:30am-11pm. D/MC/V.)

Motels are expensive and scarce on the east side of the city. **Days Inn ❹**, 406 N. Washington St., is the most affordable. (☎920-435-4484. Rooms $59-110. AmEx/D/MC/V.) Cheaper accommodations can be found on the west side closer to the stadiums. **Motel 6 ❷**, 1614 Shawano Ave., is a decent option. (☎920-494-6730. Singles $36-42; doubles $42-48. AmEx/D/MC/V.) The **Bay Motel ❷**, 1301 S. Military Ave., has clean rooms close to Lambeau Field. The rooms are (predictably) more expensive on game weekends. (☎920-494-3441. Singles $42-52; doubles $49-59. AmEx/D/MC/V.)

APPROACHING WAUSAU-MOSINEE: 93 MILES
Leaving Green Bay, head west through residential areas on **Shawano St.,** which becomes **Rte. 29 W** outside of town. Continue on Rte. 29 for 86 mi. To get to the visitors center, take Exit 171 to the **Bus. Rte. 51 S;** to go downtown, take Exit 171 to **Bus. Rte. 51 N** through Schofield for 3 mi. into Wausau.

WAUSAU-MOSINEE

Wausau was founded in 1845 as "Big Bull Falls." At the request of the postmaster, the name was changed to something more appropriate for ladies to write on envelopes, and Wausau and Mosinee were chosen. Today, Marathon County is the world leader in the production of the medicinal root ginseng. Whitewater canoeing and kayaking on the Wisconsin River are also big attractions.

VITAL STATS

Population: 38,000

Visitor Info: Wausau/Central Wisconsin Convention & Visitors Bureau, 10204 Park Plaza, Ste. B (☎715-355-8788 or 888-948-4748; www.wausaucvb.com), off Exit 185 on I-39/51 in Mosinee. Open daily 9am-5pm.

Internet Access: Marathon County Public Library, 300 N. 1st St. (☎715-261-7200). Open M-Th 9am-8:30pm, F 9am-5pm, Sa 9am-1pm. Free.

Post Office: 235 Forest St. (☎715-261-4200). Open M-F 8am-6pm, Sa 8am-2pm. **Postal Code:** 54403.

GETTING AROUND. Rte. 29 enters Wausau from the south, between **Schofield** and **Rothschild.** Southwest of Wausau, Rte. 29 connects with **Rte. 51.** At the north side of town, Rte. 29 continues to the west and Rte. 51 continues north.

SIGHTS. Changing exhibits at the **Leigh Yawkey Woodson Art Museum,** 700 N. 12th St., at Franklin St., display artwork from around the world. The museum is home to permanent painting and decorative arts collections as well as "Birds in Art," a world-class collection of avian art. (☎715-845-7010; www.lywam.org. Open Tu-F 9am-4pm, Sa-Su noon-5pm. Free.) **Hsu Ginseng Enterprises,** T6819 County Rd. W, specializes in all things ginseng. It seems that Wisconsin's cool summers and virgin soil are perfect for producing the roots for food and medicinal products. (☎800-388-3818; www.hsuginseng.com.) **Artsblock,** 401 N. Fourth St., was built around the historical Grand Theater, adding 75,000 sq. ft. of performance space. The three buildings connected by the new space—the Grand Theater, the Center for the Visual Arts, and the Great Hall—host events ranging from Broadway productions to staged spectaculars. (Bordered by Scott, 4th, Jefferson, and 5th St. ☎715-842-0988; www.onartsblock.org. Box office open M-F 8:30am-5pm. Tickets $19-97.)

The peak at **Rib Mountain State Park,** 4200 Park Rd., is one of the oldest geologic formations on earth. An observation tower provides views of the entire Wisconsin River Valley. (☎715-842-2522. Park access $10.) **Granite Peak,** 3605 N. Mountain Rd., is one of America's oldest ski resorts and one of the Midwest's biggest. (☎715-845-2846; www.skigranitepeak.com. Open mid-Nov. to Mar. daily 9am-9pm. Lift tickets mid-Dec. to mid-Mar. $48, seniors and ages 6-12 $36; mid-Nov. to mid-Dec. $38/$26.)

FOOD AND ACCOMMODATIONS. Walk through the doors (or, rather, the mine shaft) of the ⬛Wausau Mine Company ❸, 3904 W. Stewart Ave., and discover that the **Mother Lode Eatery** restaurant and **Rusty Nail Saloon** have been carved to resemble the caverns within the mine, along with original mining artifacts. Try the Virgil Cristo burger ($6), named after the miner dummy who keeps watch over the bar. (Turn north on Rte. 51/39 junction, and exit at Sherman St. Turn left on Sherman St., then right on 28th St., and continue 1 mi. ☎715-845-7304. Open M-F 11am-10pm, Sa-Su 11am-11pm. AmEx/D/MC/V.) Rock

music greets patrons of **Hudson's Classic Grill ❸,** 2200 W. Stewart Ave., a 50s bar and grill where the walls are lined with Burma Shave signs. Choose between booths and the outdoor patio and beer garden. Try the "spark plugs" (jalapeno poppers; $6) for a warm up. (☎715-849-8586. Open M-Th and Su 11am-11pm, F-Sa 11am-midnight. AmEx/D/MC/V.) Rooms at the **Nite Inn ❷,** 425 Grand Ave., in Schofield, are available with kitchenettes. (☎715-355-1641; www.theniteinn.com. Singles $32; doubles $59. AmEx/D/MC/V.)

APPROACHING CHIPPEWA FALLS: 90 MILES
Head west on **Stewart Ave.** from downtown and merge onto **Rte. 29,** which takes you through the heart of dairy country. Merge onto **Rte. 124 N,** and cross the bridge over the Chippewa River.

CHIPPEWA FALLS

Chippewa Falls was named one of the top 10 small towns in the U.S. in 1997 by *Time Magazine*, and it's easy to see why: museums, gardens, and the Chippewa River make this picturesque city worth visiting. The industrial area is full of historical buildings, including the Chippewa Shoe Factory, which started out making shoes for lumberjacks and rivermen.

VITAL STATS

Population: 13,000

Visitor Info: Chippewa Falls Area Visitors Center, 10 S. Bridge St. (☎715-723-0331 or 888-723-0024; www.chippewachamber.org). Open in summer M-F 8am-5pm, Sa 10am-3pm; in winter M-F 8am-5pm.

Internet Access: Chippewa Falls Public Library, 105 W. Central St. (☎715-723-1146). Open M and Th 10am-8pm, Tu-W and F 10am-5:30pm, Sa 10am-12:30pm. Free.

Post Office: 315 N Bridge St. (☎715-723-5805). **Postal Code:** 54729.

GETTING AROUND. Rte. 29 borders Chippewa Falls to the south. **Rte. 124** becomes **Bridge St.** as it comes from the south and crosses the river. It curves north on the other shore, intersecting with Rte. 29 and **Rte. 178,** eventually becoming **N. High St.** and **Jefferson St.**

SIGHTS. The **Old Abe State Trail,** 711 N. Bridge St., connects Chippewa Falls to Cornell and is open year-round for biking, horseback riding, and cross-country skiing. (☎800-866-6264; www.wiparks.net. Day-use $4.) **Leinenkugel's Brewery,** 1 Jefferson Ave., is Chippewa Falls's oldest business and has been brewing German-style beer in the North Woods of Wisconsin since 1867. A tour shows the original spring that was the brewery's water source and the caves where the beer was kept before the advent of refrigeration. After the tour, hang out in the recently opened Leinie Lodge, where you can sip two free beer samples. (☎715-723-5557 or 888-534-6437; www.leinie.com. 45min. tours every 30min.; last tour 60-90min. before close. Open M-Th and Sa 9am-5pm, F 9am-8pm, Su 11am-4pm. Reservations recommended. Free.)

The history of manufacturing and processing in Chippewa Falls dates back to the 1840s. In the 1950s, the town was the site of Seymour Cray's invention of the supercomputer, which set the benchmark for speed. The **Chippewa Falls Museum of Industry and Technology,** 21 E. Grand Ave., has interactive exhibits on regional industries, photos, and documents from Cray's collection. (☎715-720-9206; www.cfmit.com. Open Tu-F 1-5pm, Sa 10am-3pm. $3, children $1.) The **XMI Neckwear Factory Outlet,** 8336 Rte. 178, sells a huge selection of ties at reduced prices. The company was founded in New York City and expanded production to Chippewa Falls in 1987. Their neckties are frequently worn by Bryant Gumbel, Tom Brokaw, and David Letterman. If you aren't that into ties yourself, you can always buy one for your dad. (☎715-723-1999. Open M-F 8am-4pm.)

🍴🏨 FOOD AND ACCOMMODATIONS. Since 1944, **Olson's Ice Cream Parlor & Deli ❶,** 611 N. Bridge St., has been serving over 20 different "Homaid" ice creams made daily in flavors ranging from chocolate-chip cookie dough to peach pie. Sandwiches ($4-5), soups ($2-4), and salads ($3-6) are served in the deli. (☎715-723-4331. Open daily 10am-9pm. Cash only.) The **Indianhead Motel ❷,** 501 Summit Ave., has simple rooms with desks, clean beds, and little decoration. (Off Rte. 29 S, east of town. ☎715-723-9171 or 800-306-3049; www.indianheadmotelchippewa.com. Singles $49; doubles $59. AmEx/D/MC/V.)

◪ APPROACHING EAU CLAIRE: 12 MILES
Take **Rte. 124 S.** Merge with **U.S. 53 S** to get to **Birch St.,** which will take you downtown.

EAU CLAIRE

Eau Claire (French for "clear water") was one of Wisconsin's busiest lumber towns in the 1800s, thanks to its location at the junction of the Eau Claire and Chippewa Rivers. Today, Eau Claire might have been named "Routes Encombrées" for its perpetual, ever-changing road construction, which confuses tourists and locals alike. The **Paul Bunyan Logging Camp,** 1110 Carson Park Dr., welcomes visitors with the Henry O. Strand Interpretive Center, a hands-on introduction to Wisconsin's logging industry with—of course—another giant Paul Bunyan statue. The camp's log cabins duplicate the rugged conditions faced by early settlers. (Follow Main St. until it ends at Graham Ave. Turn left on Graham, go 2 blocks, and turn right on Lake St. ☎715-835-6200. Open Apr.-Sept. daily 10am-4pm. $4, children $1.50. Beneath the towering pines of Carson Park next door, the exhibits at the **Chippewa Valley Museum** begin with the arrival of the Ojibwe Indians and continue through the days of European settlers and the changing social roles of farm life. (☎715-834-7871; www.cvmuseum.com. Open daily M and W-Sa 10am-5pm, Tu 10am-8pm, Su 1-5pm. $4, children $1.50. Combination ticket with camp $7/$2.50.)

"Let no one hunger for lack of a better sandwich" is the motto at the **Acoustic Cafe ❶,** 505 S. Barstow St. The food is excellent, and the hip atmosphere makes up for the limited choices. (☎715-832-9090. Soup and sandwich $5. Nightly live music. Free Wi-Fi. Open M-Th 8am-10pm, F-Sa 8am-midnight, Su 11am-9pm. MC/V.) **Erbert & Gerbert's ❶,** at 405 Water St. and 3003 London Rd., is a popular regional sandwiches chain, serving unique subs and clubs. (☎715-835-9995. Open M-Sa 10:30am-11pm, Su 10:30am-10pm.) **▨Maple Manor Motel ❷,** 2507 S. Hastings Way, is an ordinary motel on the outside, but inside it's a quaint B&B. Each room has its own unique flavor; the Wisteria is a vision in purple. (☎715-834-2618 or 800-624-3763; www.themaplemanor.com. Singles $30-40; doubles $40-60. AmEx/D/MC/V.) The **Highlander Inn ❷,** 1135 W. MacArthur Ave, has large rooms. (☎715-835-2261 or 877-568-0773. Rooms $38-50. AmEx/D/MC/V.)

⚑ APPROACHING MENOMONIE: 23 MILES
Follow **U.S. 12** to downtown Menomonie.

MENOMONIE

The land around beautiful Menomonie, on man-made Lake Menomonie and the Red Cedar River, was first inhabited by Native Americans. The **Mabel Tainter Theater,** 205 Main St., was built in 1890 in Richardson Romanesque style. The beautiful Victorian theater has been restored to its original splendor and is considered to be one of the most architecturally significant theaters in the US. (☎715-235-0001; www.mabeltainter.com. Self-guided tours M-F 10am-5pm. Suggested donation $1.) For nearly 70 years, thousands of children have enjoyed reading the adventures of Caddie Woodlawn, a young pioneer tomboy who fought for peaceful relations between the pioneers and her Native American friends. The **Caddie Woodlawn Historic Park,** 12 mi. south of Menomonie on Rte. 25, contains the original Woodlawn home, made famous in Caddie's granddaughter's books. Many of the buildings and sites mentioned in the book can be seen along Rte. 25 or the Red Cedar Bike Trail. (Open spring-fall daily sunrise-sunset. Free.) No trip to Wisconsin is complete without stopping at a cheese factory, and **Eau Galle Cheese Factory,** N6765 Rte. 25, 20min. south of Menomenie in Durand, is as good as any. Sample cheesy morsels while observing the cheese-making process. (☎715-283-4211; www.eaugallecheese.com. Open M-Sa 9am-5:30pm; Su 11am-4:30pm.)

If you're in need of a little pick-me-up, **Legacy Chocolates ❶**, 544 S. Broadway, is revered for its high quality truffles, chocolates, and gourmet beverages. The spiel about chocolate being one of nature's most nutritious and easily digested foods makes it especially hard to resist. (☎715-231-2580; www.legacychocolates.com. Free Wi-Fi. Open M-Sa 6:30am-6pm, Su 8:30am-4pm.) Stop by **Bullfrog "Eat My Fish" Farm ❶**, N1321 Bullfrog Rd./566th St., to enjoy a day of fishing at a tranquil stocked trout farm, then grill up your catch and have a picnic next to the pond. Presentations and tours of the fish hatchery and workshops are also offered. (From Rte 25., follow C.R. Y to 566th St. and follow the yellow fish pointers. ☎715-664-8775; www.eatmyfish.com. Pole rental $2.50. Cleaned fish from $6 per lb. Open "casually" daily noon-6pm. MC/V.)

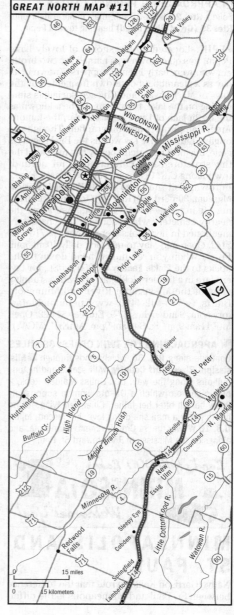

GREAT NORTH MAP #11

⚲ APPROACHING PEPIN: 41 MILES
Follow **Rte. 25 S** for 35 mi., then make a right onto **Rte. 35 (Great River Road)** heading toward Pepin.

PEPIN. Located on the shores of lovely Lake Pepin, this quiet town was named for two brothers who were early French trappers. Known in its day as a steamboat boomtown frequented by the likes of Mark Twain and Chicago socialites summering on the lake, today Pepin is best known as the birthplace of **Laura Ingalls Wilder**, the famous American pioneer autobiographer. Though the original Little House (as well as the Big Woods) is gone, the local historical society has recreated the tiny structure Laura chronicled. (7 mi. north of town along C.R. CC. Open sunrise-sunset. Free.) In town, visit the **Laura Ingalls Wilder Historical Museum**, 306 3rd St. (Rte. 35), for artifacts from her life in pioneer-era Wisconsin. Ask about the nearby cemetery where some of the characters mentioned in her books were buried. (☎715-442-2142. Open mid-May to mid-Oct. daily 10am-5pm. Free.) When you're hungry, head down to the docks to the **Pickle Factory ❹**, 250 1st St., for tavern fare in a former pickle factory with a stunning view of the Mississippi River and Minnesota Bluffs. (☎715-442-4400; www.pepinpicklefactory.com. Sandwiches $7-9. Entrees $11-22. Open M-F 11am-9pm, Sa-Su 7am-9pm. AmEx/D/MC/V.)

⚲ APPROACHING THE TWIN CITIES: 66 MILES
Continue along **Rte. 35,** which winds through ■ **Mississippi River Bluff Country,** with scenic and historic pull-offs along the way. Don't miss Maiden Rock, a precipice from which a Dakota woman supposedly threw herself after her father, Chief Red Wing, forced her to marry a man she didn't love. In Prescott, follow **U.S. 10 W** over the St. Croix River into Minnesota, and alongside the Mississippi River toward St. Paul.

Land of 10,000 Lakes
MINNESOTA
Welcomes You!

MINNEAPOLIS AND ST. PAUL

Native Garrison Keillor wrote that the "difference between St. Paul and Minneapolis is the differ-

ence between pumpernickel and Wonder bread." For years, St. Paul, viewed as a conservative, Irish-Catholic town, contrasted sharply with its young, metropolitan neighbor. Remnants of this distinction are evident in Minneapolis's big venues and bigger skyscrapers and St. Paul's traditional capitol and cathedrals, but it is impossible to typecast the cities' diverse residents.

VITAL STATS

Population: 380,000/290,000

Visitor Info: Minneapolis Convention and Visitors Association, 250 Marquette Ave. S. (☎612-335-6000; www.minneapolis.org), in a kiosk at the Convention Center. Open M-Sa 8am-4:30pm, Su noon-5pm. **St. Paul Convention and Visitors Bureau,** 175 W. Kellogg Blvd., ste. 502 (☎651-265-4900; www.visitstpaul.com), in the River Centre. Open M-F 8am-4:30pm.

Internet Access: Minneapolis Public Library, 300 Nicollet Mall (☎612-630-6000; www.mplib.org). Open M and Th 10am-8pm, Tu-W 10am-6pm, F-Sa 10am-5pm. Free.

Parking: Lots near the Warehouse District are often the cheapest. Meter time limits are strictly enforced.

Post Office: 100 S. 1st St. (☎612-349-4713), at Marquette Ave. on the river. Open M-F 7am-8pm, Sa 9am-1pm. **Postal Codes** 55401.

▶ GETTING AROUND

Downtown Minneapolis lies about 10 mi. west of downtown St. Paul via **I-94. I-35** splits in the Twin Cities, with **I-35 W** serving Minneapolis and **I-35 E** serving St. Paul. **I-494** runs to the airport and the Mall of America, while **I-394** heads to downtown Minneapolis from the western suburbs. **Hennepin Ave.** and the pedestrian **Nicollet Mall** are the two main roads in Minneapolis; **Kellogg Blvd.** and **7th St.** are the primary thoroughfares in St. Paul. Driving in the Twin Cities can be challenging, though a commuter rail system is in the planning stages.

◉ SIGHTS

MINNEAPOLIS

LAKES AND RIVERS. In the land of 10,000 lakes, Minneapolis boasts many of its own:

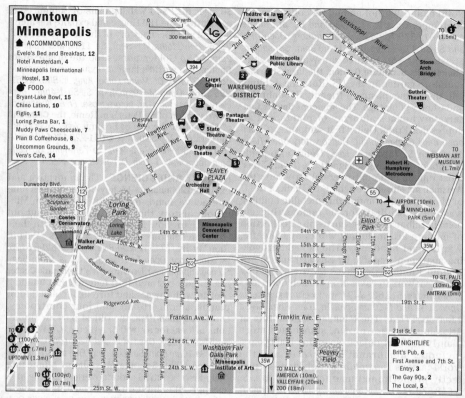

Downtown Minneapolis

▲ **ACCOMMODATIONS**
Evelo's Bed and Breakfast, **12**
Hotel Amsterdam, **4**
Minneapolis International
    Hostel, **13**
🍴 **FOOD**
Bryant-Lake Bowl, **15**
Chino Latino, **10**
Figlio, **11**
Loring Pasta Bar, **1**
Muddy Paws Cheesecake, **7**
Plan B Coffeehouse, **8**
Uncommon Grounds, **9**
Vera's Cafe, **14**

🎭 **NIGHTLIFE**
Brit's Pub, **6**
First Avenue and 7th St.
    Entry, **3**
The Gay 90s, **2**
The Local, **1**

GREAT NORTH

the city contains 22 lakes, alongside 150 parks and 100 golf courses. **Lake Calhoun,** on the west end of Lake St., is the largest of the bunch and a recreational paradise. Scores of in-line skaters, bicyclists, and runners loop the lake on all but the coldest days. Encircled by stately mansions, the serene **Lake of the Isles** has lovely views but no public access to the water. Just southeast of Lake Calhoun on Sheridan St., **Lake Harriet** lures the locals with tiny paddleboats and a band shell with free concerts on summer nights. The city maintains 28 mi. of lakeside trails around the three lakes for strolling and biking. **Calhoun Rentals**, three blocks east of Lake Calhoun, rents out bikes for exploring the paths. (*1622 W. Lake St.* ☎*612-827-8231. Open daily 10am–6pm, extended hours in summer. $25-40 per day. Credit card and*

driver's license required.) At the northeast corner of Lake Calhoun, **The Tin Fish** offers canoe, kayak, and paddleboat rentals on the side of the restaurant pavilion. (*3000 Calhoun Pkwy. E.* ☎*612-555-1234; www.thetinfish.com. Open M-Sa 11am-9pm, Su 11am-7pm. All boats $10 per hr. $20 deposit and driver's license or credit card required.*) **Minnehaha Park** offers striking views of the impressive **Minnehaha Falls,** immortalized in Longfellow's *Song of Hiawatha*. (*Falls are off Minnehaha Ave. at Minnehaha Pkwy.*)

MUSEUMS. Lakes are only the beginning of Minneapolis's appeal—locals and visitors have plenty to do during the (at least) six months of frigid winter. A few blocks southwest of downtown, the world-renowned ■**Walker Art Center** counts daring exhibits by Lichtenstein,

Rothko, and Warhol among its collections of contemporary art. (*725 Vineland Pl., at Lyndale Ave. ☎612-375-7622; www.walkerart.org. Open Tu-W and Sa-Su 11am-5pm, Th-F 11am-9pm. $8, seniors $6, students $5.*) Next to the Walker lies the **Minneapolis Sculpture Garden,** the largest urban sculpture garden in the US. Rotating exhibits join the iconic, postcard-friendly Spoonbridge and Cherry sculpture. The adjacent **Cowles Conservatory** houses an array of plants and an impressive Frank Gehry fish sculpture. (*Garden open daily 6am-midnight. Conservatory open Tu-Sa 10am-8pm, Su 10am-5pm. Free.*) Gehry also holds the honor of having designed the Twin Cities' most unique and controversial structure: the **Weisman Art Museum,** on the East Bank of the U of M campus. The undulating metallic building was the rough draft for his famous Guggenheim in Bilbao and hosts an inspired collection of modern art, including works by O'Keeffe, Warhol, and Kandinsky. The thought-provoking apartment replica, by Edward and Nancy Reddin Kienholz, engages all the senses by asking viewers to eavesdrop at each door. (*333 E. River Rd. ☎612-625-9494; www.weisman.umn.edu. Open Tu-W and F 10am-5pm, Th 10am-8pm, Sa-Su 11am-5pm. Free.*) The **Minneapolis Institute of Arts,** south of downtown, showcases more than 100,000 art objects spanning 5000 years, including Rembrandt's *Lucretia* and the world-famous *Doryphoros,* Polykleitos's perfectly proportioned man. (*2400 3rd Ave. S. ☎612-870-3131; www.artsmia.org. Open Tu-W and F-Sa 10am-5pm, Th 10am-9pm, Su 11am-5pm. Free.*)

ST. PAUL

ARCHITECTURE. History and architecture define stately St. Paul. Nowhere is this more evident than along ◼**Summit Ave.,** the nation's longest continuous stretch of Victorian houses, including the childhood home of novelist **F. Scott Fitzgerald** and the Minnesota **Governor's Mansion.** (*Fitzgerald: 599 Summit Ave. Currently a private residence. Governor's Mansion: 1006 Summit Ave. ☎651-297-8177. Tours May-Oct. F 1-3pm. Reservations required. Free.*) Also on Summit Ave., the magnificent home of railroad magnate **James J. Hill**—the largest and most expensive home in the state when it was completed in 1891—offers 1¼hr. tours. (*240 Summit Ave. ☎651-297-2555. Open W-Sa 10am-3:30pm, Su 1-3:30pm. Reservations recommended. $8, seniors*

$6, ages 6-12 $4.) **Walking tours** of Summit Ave. depart from the Hill House and explore the architectural and social history of the area. (*☎651-297-2555. 1½hr. tours May-Sept. Sa 11am and 2pm, Su 2pm. $4-8.*) Golden horses top the ornate **State Capitol,** the world's largest unsupported marble dome. (*75 Rev. Dr. Martin Luther King, Jr. Blvd. ☎651-296-3962. Open M-F 9am-4pm, Sa-Su 1-4pm. Tours every hr.; last tour 1hr. before close. Free.*) A scaled-down version of St. Peter's in Rome, the **Cathedral of St. Paul,** at the end of Summit Ave., overlooks the capitol. (*239 Selby Ave. ☎651-228-1766. Open M-Th 7am-5:30pm, F 7am-4pm, Sa 7am-7pm, Su 7am-5pm. Tours M, W, F 1pm. Donations accepted.*)

HISTORY AND SCIENCE. The innovative and exciting ◼**Minnesota History Center** houses nine interactive, hands-on exhibit galleries on Minnesota history that entertain young and old alike. Learn how Minnesotans cope with their extreme seasons or admire Prince's "Purple Rain" attire. (*345 Kellogg Blvd. W. ☎651-296-6126; www.mnhs.org. Open Tu 10am-8pm, W-Sa 10am–5pm, Su noon-5pm. Free.*) Downtown's **Landmark Center** is a grandly restored 1894 federal court building replete with towers and turrets, a collection of pianos, a concert hall, and four courtrooms. Out front, **Rice Park,** the oldest park in Minnesota, is ideal for a stroll or a picnic. (*75 W. 5th St. ☎651-292-3230. Open M-W and F 8am-5pm, Th 8am-8pm, Sa 10am-5pm, Su noon-5pm. Free tours Th 11am, Su noon.*) The **Science Museum of Minnesota** includes a beautiful atrium overlooking the Mississippi, an exhibit on the human body, and a paleontology hall. (*120 W. Kellogg Blvd. ☎651-221-9444; www.smm.org. Open mid-June to early Sept. M-Sa 8:30am-11pm; early Sept. to mid-June M-W 9:30am-5pm, Th-Sa 9:30am-9pm, Su noon-7pm. $22, students and seniors $16, ages 4-12 $12.50; with Omnitheater and 3D cinema $29/$22.50/$18.50.*)

AMUSEMENTS. Located on 500 wooded acres in suburban Apple Valley, the **Minnesota Zoo** houses local and exotic animals in their natural habitats, including 22 endangered and threatened species, a Tiger Lair exhibit, and native beavers, lynx, and wolverines. (*13000 Zoo Blvd. Take Rte. 77 S to the Zoo exit, and follow signs. ☎952-431-9500 or 800-366-7811; www.mnzoo.org. Open June-Aug. daily 9am-6pm; Sept. and May M-F 9am-4pm, Sa-Su 9am-6pm; Oct.-Apr. daily 9am-4pm. $12, seniors $8.25, ages 3-12 $7.*) From St. Paul, escape to **Como Park,** off Lexington Pkwy., where you can visit the small zoo and impressive conservatory with an award-winning collection of Bonsai trees and orchids. *(1225 Estabrook Dr. ☎651-487-8200; www.comozoo-conservatory.org. Open daily 10am-6pm. Suggested donation $2.)* In Shakopee, even the most daring thrill-seekers can get their jollies at **Valleyfair,** a quality amusement park with six roller coasters, a water park, and the heart-stopping Power Tower, which drops over 10 stories. *(1 Valleyfair Dr. Take I-35W south to Rte. 13 W. ☎800-386-7433; www.valleyfair.com. Open June-Aug. daily; May and Sept. hours vary. Call for hours, usually 10am-10pm; water park closes earlier. $34, over 60 and under 48 in. $10, under 3 free. After 5pm, $17/$10.)*

MALL OF AMERICA. Welcome to the largest mall in America. With more than 520 specialty stores and 60 restaurants and nightclubs extending for over 2 mi., the "MoA" is the consummation of an American love affair with all that is obscenely gargantuan. Don't settle for just shopping and eating; the complex also boasts a movie megaplex, an aquarium, and the largest indoor amusement park in the world. *(60 E. Broadway, in Bloomington. From St. Paul, take I-35E S to I-494 W and exit at 24th Ave. ☎952-883-8800; www.mallofamerica.com. Open M-Sa 10am-9:30pm, Su 11am-7pm.)*

 PHOTO OP. Check out the statue of **Mary Tyler Moore,** famous for turning the world on with her smile, at Nicollet and 7th St.

 FOOD

In the Twin Cities, many forgo restaurants for area cafes (see p. 272). For cook-it-yourself-ers, pick up fresh produce at the **Minneapolis Farmers Market,** off 94W at E. Lyndale Ave. and 3rd Ave. N. The market offers over 450 booths of fruits, vegetables, flowers, and crafts that claim to constitute the "largest open-air market in the upper Midwest." (☎612-333-1737. Open late Apr. to late Dec. daily 6am-1pm.)

MINNEAPOLIS

Uptown Minneapolis, near Lake St. and Hennepin Ave., has funky restaurants where the Twin Cities' young socialites meet after work. In downtown Minneapolis, the **Warehouse District,** on 1st Ave. N between 8th St. and Washington Ave., and **Nicollet Mall,** a 12-block pedestrian stretch of Nicollet Ave., has eateries ranging from burgers to Tex-Mex. South of downtown, Nicollet turns into **Eat Street,** a 17-block stretch of international cuisine.

■ **Chino Latino,** 2916 Hennepin Ave. (☎612-824-7878), at Lake St., Uptown. Drinks like the signature watermelon mojito ($8.50) characterize this Latin-Asian fusion restaurant. With a chic *satay* bar ($7-9) and unusual dishes that often require instruction from the waitstaff, Chino Latino is for the hip. Entrees $13-40. Open M-Th and Su 4:30pm-1am, F-Sa 4:30pm-2am. Reservations recommended. AmEx/MC/V. ❹

Bryant-Lake Bowl, 810 W. Lake St. (☎612-825-3737; www.bryantlakebowl.com), at Bryant St., near

A REALLY COOL CELEBRATION

In January 1885, a visiting reporter from New York City described Minnesota's capital city as "another Siberia, unfit for human habitation." The local Chamber of Commerce decided to show East Coasters how wonderful their icy city was by throwing a giant outdoor festival in the middle of winter, thus initiating the annual St. Paul Winter Carnival. The festival revolves around a concocted feud between King Boreas, ruler of the winds and lover of all things cold, and his arch nemesis, Vulcanus Rex, the God of Fire. Each year, the members of the king's court reside within a massive ice castle constructed from 27,000 bathtub-sized bricks of ice carved from Lake Phalen. In Mardi Gras fashion, elaborate floats are outfitted for the festival's opening and closing parades. The celebration includes activities like ice-carving contests, snow sculpting, curling, ice skating, and car races on ice. For the past half century, one of the festival's highlights has been a treasure hunt organized by the local *St. Paul Pioneer Press,* which publishes cryptic daily clues to the location of a medallion hidden in an unnamed public park. The medallion's finder wins up to $10,000. Previous hiding places have included a White Castle box, a baby diaper, an Oreo cookie, and—of course—a block of ice.

Uptown. Built in the 1930s, this funky bowling alley, bar, and cabaret serves quality food at friendly prices. The breakfast "BLB Scramble" (eggs and vegetables; $6.25), ravioli, soups, and sandwiches ($5-9) ensure that the stylish patrons throw strikes on full stomachs. Bowling $3.75 per game. Happy hour 3-6pm. Entrees $9-12. Open daily 8am-1am. AmEx/D/MC/V. ❸

Figlio, 3001 Hennepin Ave. S (☎612-822-1688), at W. Lake St. in the Calhoun Sq. complex, Uptown. Italian fare with flair. Twin City residents have awarded Figlio the title of "Best Late Night Dining" for many years. Scrumptious sandwiches from $9. Pizzas from $11. Open M-Th and Su 11:30am-1am, F-Sa 11:30am-2am. AmEx/D/MC/V. ❹

ST. PAUL

In St. Paul, the upscale **Grand Ave.,** between Lexington and Dale, is lined with laid-back restaurants and bars, while **Lowertown,** along Sibley St. near 6th St. downtown, is a popular nighttime hangout. Near the University of Minnesota (U of M) campus between the downtowns, **Dinkytown,** on the East Bank of the river, and the **Seven Corners** area of the West Bank, on Cedar Ave., cater to student appetites—including late-night cravings.

🖾 **Mickey's Diner,** 36 W. 7th St. (☎651-222-5633), at St. Peter St. A diner on the National Register of Historic Places, Mickey's offers food that outshines its chrome-and-vinyl decor. Take a spin at a counter stool, or groove to some oldies on the jukebox at each booth. Open 24hr. AmEx/D/MC/V. ❶

Cossetta, 211 W. 7th St. (☎651-222-3476). What began as an Italian market in 1911 now serves eat-in specialities. Try the veal parmigiana ($7) or the famous pizza ($12-22). Open M-Th and Su 11am-9pm, F-Sa 11am-10pm. MC/V. ❸

Loring Pasta Bar, 327 14th Ave. SE (☎612-378-4849; www.loringcafe.com), in Dinkytown, near the U of M campus. A whimsical restaurant with dishes ranging from tasty potstickers ($8) to pasta ($7-16). Nightly live music. Su night tango DJ. Open M-F 11:30am-10pm, Sa noon-11pm, Su 11am-2pm and 4:30-10pm. MC/V. ❸

Day By Day Cafe, 477 W. 7th St. (☎651-227-0654; www.daybyday.com). Started in 1975 by an alcoholism treatment center, Day By Day now serves the community all day breakfast ($4.50-8), and lunch and dinner specials ($7.50-9) in its library-like dining room. F live music 7-10pm. Open M-F 6am-8pm, Sa 6am-3pm, Su 7am-3pm. Cash only. ❷

Cafe Latte, 850 Grand Ave. (☎651-224-5687), at Victoria St. More substantial than a cafe, and more gourmet than its prices and cafeteria-style setup would suggest. This cafe, bakery, pizzeria, and wine bar combo is also famous for its desserts. Chicken-salsa chili $5. Turtle cake $4. Open M-Tu and Su 9am-10pm, W-Th 9am-11pm, F-Sa 9am-noon. AmEx/D/MC/V. ❶

🍴 CAFES

Cafes are an integral part of the Twin Cities' nightlife. Particularly in Uptown Minneapolis, quirky coffeehouses caffeinate the masses and draw crowds as large as those at any bar. Most of these creatively decorated coffeehouses complement their java with some of the cheapest food in town.

🖾 **Uncommon Grounds,** 2809 Hennepin Ave. S (☎612-872-4811), at 28th St., Uptown. The self-described "BMW of coffee shops" uses secret ingredients to make the tastiest coffees ($2-5) and teas around. With velour booths and relaxing music in a Victorian house, this coffeehouse lives up to its name. Free Wi-Fi. Open M-F 5pm-1am, Sa-Su 10am-1am. Cash only. ❶

Vera's Cafe, 2901 Lyndale Ave. (☎612-822-3871; www.verascafe.com), between 29th and Lake St., Uptown. The "vintage cafe for the hip and saucy," Vera's serves a mixed gay and straight crowd its signature "White Zombie" ($4.60) and all-day breakfast ($5-6). Occasional events on the patio. Free Wi-Fi. Open daily 7am-midnight. MC/V. ❶

Plan B Coffeehouse, 2717 Hennepin Ave. (☎612-872-1419), between 27th and 28th St., Uptown. Animated conversation and mismatched furniture in a laid-back earth-tone atmosphere. Try the "tripper's revenge" ($3.75). Free Wi-Fi. Open M-Th and Su 9am-midnight, F-Sa 9am-1am. D/MC/V. ❶

Muddy Paws Cheesecake, 2528 Hennepin Ave. (☎612-377-4441; www.muddypawscheesecake.com), at 25th St., Uptown. This modern cafe offers a host of sandwiches, wraps, and salads ($6.25) and plenty of reading material on comfy sofas. For dessert–or, dare we say, as an entree–try one of over 100 cheesecake flavors ($3.25 per slice). Free Wi-Fi. Open M-Th 10am-10pm, F-Sa 10am-11pm, Su 10am-8pm. MC/V. ❶

🏠 ACCOMMODATIONS

The Twin Cities are filled with unpretentious, inexpensive accommodations. Minneapolis caters to a younger crowd and consequently has cheaper hotels; St. Paul offers finer establishments for those with thicker wallets. Visitors centers have lists of **B&Bs**, while the **University of Minnesota Housing Office** (☎612-624-2994; www.umn.edu/housing/offcampus.htm) keeps a list of local rooms ($15-60) that can be rented on a daily or weekly basis. The section of I-494 at Rte. 77, near the Mall of America, is lined with budget chain motels from $40. The nearest private campgrounds are about 15 mi. outside the city; the closest state park camping is in the **Hennepin Park** system, 25 mi. away. Call **Minnesota State Parks** (☎651-296-6157 or 888-646-6367).

Minneapolis International Hostel, 2400 Stevens Ave. S (☎612-522-5000; www.minneapolishostel.com), south of downtown, near the Institute of Arts. Clean hostel with a strong community atmosphere. Internet access, living room, porch, and patio. Check-in 1pm. Check-out 11am. Reception 8am-midnight. Reservations recommended. Dorms $25; singles $35. AmEx/MC/V. ❶

Evelo's Bed and Breakfast, 2301 Bryant Ave. S. (☎612-374-9656), in south Minneapolis, just off Hennepin Ave. Owners rent out 3 lovingly tended rooms in this 1897 Victorian home. Flowers in each room, continental breakfast, and shared bath. Reservations and deposit required. Rooms $65-85. AmEx/D/MC/V. ❸

Hotel Amsterdam, 828 Hennepin Ave. (☎612-288-0459; www.gaympls.com), in downtown Minneapolis, between 8th and 9th St. Located above the Saloon nightclub, this hotel offers food, lodging, and entertainment geared toward the GLBT community. "The inn that's out" has a colorful lounge with TV and free Internet access. Reception 24hr. Reservations recommended. Singles $49; doubles $55-70. MC/V. ❷

Exel Inn, 1739 Old Hudson Rd. (☎651-771-5566; www.exelinns.com), in St. Paul. Take Exit 245 off I-94 E. Clean rooms with cable TV and easy access to St. Paul and the Mall of America. Free Wi-Fi. Reservations recommended. Singles $56-66; doubles $63-73. AmEx/D/MC/V. ❸

♫ ENTERTAINMENT

THEATER
Rumored to be second only to New York City in number of theaters per capita, the Twin Cities are alive with drama and music. The renowned **▧Guthrie Theater,** 818 S 2nd St.,

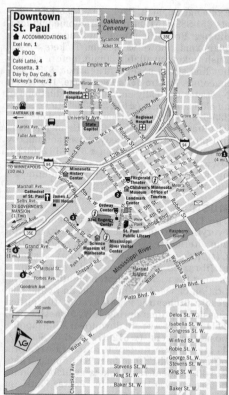

located in their recently completed Minneapolis venue, draws praise for its mix of daring and classical productions. (☎612-377-2224; www.guthrietheater.org. Shows Aug.-June. Box office open daily 10am-8pm. Tickets $16-60. Rush tickets 10min. before show $15; line starts 1-1½hr. before show.) The historic **State Theatre,** 805 Hennepin Ave., the **Orpheum Theatre,** 910 Hennepin Ave. N, and the **Pantages Theatre,** 710 Hennepin Ave., comprise the **Hennepin Theater District** in downtown Minneapolis, with Broadway shows and musical events. (☎612-339-7007; www.hennepintheaterdistrict.com. Box office open M-F 10am-6pm, Sa noon-3pm. Broadway shows $30-80; concerts $25-50.) The tongue-in-cheek public-radio variety show **▧A Prairie Home Companion** is broadcast live from the **Fitzgerald Theater,** 10 E.

GREAT NORTH

Exchange St., in St. Paul. (☎651-290-1200, tickets 651-989-5151; http://prairiehome.publicradio.org. Box office open Tu-F noon-6pm, Sa 10am-2pm. Shows Sa 4:45pm. Tickets $32-42. Rush tickets available 30min. before shows, but line starts several hr. earlier; $15.) The ingenious **Théâtre de la Jeune Lune,** 105 1st St. N, stages critically acclaimed productions in an old warehouse. (☎612-332-3968, tickets 612-333-6200. Open M-F 10am-6pm. Tickets $36-64.) **Brave New Workshop,** 2605 Hennepin Ave., in Uptown, stages comedy shows and improv in an intimate club. (☎612-332-6620; www.bravenewworkshop.com. Box office open M-Th 9:30am-5pm, F 9:30am-8pm, Sa 10am-11pm. Tickets $14-27.)

MUSIC

The Twin Cities' vibrant music scene offers everything from opera and polka to hip-hop and alternative. For more info, read the free *City Pages* (www.citypages.com), available at libraries, most cafes, and newsstands around town. **Sommerfest,** a month-long celebration of Viennese music put on by the **Minnesota Orchestra,** is the best of the cities' classical options during July. **Orchestra Hall,** 1111 Nicollet Ave., in downtown Minneapolis, hosts the event. (☎612-371-5656 or 800-292-4141; www.minnesotaorchestra.org. Box office open M-F 10am-5pm, Sa 1-5pm. Tickets $15-43. Student rush tickets available 30min. before show; $10.) Nearby, **Peavey Plaza,** on Nicollet Mall, holds free nightly concerts and occasional film screenings. The **Saint Paul Chamber Orchestra,** the **Schubert Club,** and the **Minnesota Opera Company** all perform at St. Paul's glass-and-brick **Ordway Center For The Performing Arts,** 345 Washington St., which also hosts touring productions. (☎651-224-4222; www.ordway.org. Box office open M-F 10am-6pm, Sa-Su 11am-3pm. Tickets $30-60.)

SPORTS

The puffy **Hubert H. Humphrey Metrodome,** 900 S. 5th St., in downtown Minneapolis, hosts baseball's **Minnesota Twins** (☎612-375-7454; www.twinsbaseball.com) and football's **Minnesota Vikings** (☎612-338-4537; www.vikings.com). The NBA's **Timberwolves** (☎612-337-3865; www.timberwolves.com) and WNBA's **Lynx** (☎612-673-8400; www.wnba.com/lynx) play at the **Target Center,** 601 1st Ave., between 6th and 7th St., in downtown Minneapolis. The cities' NHL team, the **Wild,** takes to the ice at St. Paul's **Xcel Energy Center.** (☎651-222-9453; www.wild.com.) The soccer craze hits the Midwest with the minor-league **Thunder,** at the **National Sports Center** (☎763-785-5600), in suburban Blaine.

FESTIVALS

In late January and early February, the **St. Paul Winter Carnival,** near the state capitol, cures cabin fever with ice sculptures, ice fishing, skating contests, and a giant ice palace. On the 4th of July, St. Paul celebrates the **Taste of Minnesota** with fireworks, concerts, and regional and ethnic cuisine from local vendors. The **Minneapolis Riverfront Fourth of July Celebration and Fireworks** is a day for the family with trolley rides, concerts, food, and fireworks. (☎612-378-1226; www.minneaplis-riverfront.com.) On its coattails rides the 10-day **Minneapolis Aquatennial,** which has concerts and art exhibits glorifying the lakes. (☎612-518-3486; www.aquatennial.org.) In the two weeks prior to Labor Day, everyone heads to the nation's largest state fair, the **Minnesota State Fair,** at Snelling and Como St., in St. Paul. (☎651-288-4427; www.mnstatefair.org. $9, seniors and ages 5-12 $8, under 5 free.)

◧ NIGHTLIFE

Minneapolis's vibrant youth culture feeds the Twin Cities' nightlife. Anchored by strong post-punk influences, the area's thriving music scene has spawned, among others, Soul Asylum, Hüsker Dü, and The Replacements. A cross-section of the diverse nightlife options can be found in the downtown **Warehouse District** on Hennepin Ave.; in **Dinkytown,** by U of M; and across the river on the **West Bank** (bounded on the west by I-35 W and to the south by I-94), especially on **Cedar Ave.** Even the top floor of the **Mall of America** invites bar-hopping until the wee hours. The Twin Cities card hard, however, even for cigarettes.

Brit's Pub, 1110 Nicollet Mall (☎612-332-3908; www.britspub.com), between 11th and 12th St. Patrons can play a game of lawn bowling on the rooftop garden ($5 per hr.). 18 different beers, a Stilton burger ($9), and fish and chips ($7-13) add to the English flavor. Open daily 11am-2am. AmEx/D/MC/V.

The Local, 931 Nicollet Mall (☎612-904-1000; www.the-local.com), at 10th St., in Mineapolis. Irish pub that doubles as a restaurant and bar. Outdoor patio and dark interior make for a mellow and intimate night out. Open M-Th 11am-11pm, F 11am-midnight, Sa 9am-midnight, Su 9am-11pm. AmEx/D/MC/V.

First Ave. and the 7th St. Entry, 701 1st Ave. N (☎612-338-8388; www.first-avenue.com), in downtown Minneapolis. Rocks with the area's best live music several nights a week, including concerts with the hottest rock bands in the nation. Music from grunge to world beat. Cover $6-10, for concerts $6-30. Open daily 5pm-3am. AmEx/MC/V.

The Gay 90s, 408 Hennepin Ave. (☎612-333-7755; www.gay90s.com), at 4th St. This gigantic complex hosts gay and lesbian partiers in its 8 bars, though the straight crowd is also sizable. M 9pm-1am 2-for-1 drinks. W-Su drag shows 9:15pm. M-Tu and F-Sa 21+, W-Th and Su 18+. Cover $3-5 after 9pm. Open M-Sa 8am-2am, Su 10am-1am. Cash only.

 BIG DETOUR. Explore the Scandinavian heritage of Minnesota on the **Lakes, Lewis, and Lefse Big Detour,** p. 276.

⚑ APPROACHING LE SUEUR: 57 MILES
From downtown Minneapolis, take **I-35W S** to **I-494 W**. Continue along **U.S. 169 S** to Le Sueur.

LE SUEUR. Entering Le Sueur along U.S. 169, drivers are greeted by a monstrous billboard cutout of the **Jolly Green Giant** and Sprout (his diminutive peapod pal) standing guard over the valley, much like in the commercials. The valley is just as you'd expect, with rolling green hills covered in bushy trees and farmland. The **Le Sueur Museum,** 709 N. 2nd St., documents the history of the Green Giant. Exhibits, videos, and jolly green statues tell the history of the canning company, from its start in 1903 under C.N. Cosgrove to its purchase in 1979 by the Pillsbury Company. (☎507-665-2050. Open Memorial Day to Labor Day Tu-F 10am-4:30pm, Sa 1-4:30pm. Free.) The **W.W. Mayo House,** 118 N. Main St., is where Dr. William Worrall Mayo set up his medical practice in 1859. Tours of the house by costumed interpreters relate the lives of the two famous families who called it home.

(☎507-665-3250; www.mayohouse.org. Open June-Aug. Tu-Sa 10am-4:30pm; late May and Sept.-Nov. Sa 1-4:30pm. $3, seniors $2, children $1, under 6 free.)

⚑ APPROACHING ST. PETER: 11 MILES
Continue along **U.S. 169,** which enters St. Peter from the north as **N. Minnesota Ave.**

ST. PETER

St. Peter lures visitors with the beauty and refuge of the Minnesota River Valley and surrounding bluffs. One of Minnesota's oldest cities, St. Peter is built on the rich black soil that makes the surrounding area some of the most fertile farmland in the country. **Gustavus Adolphus College** was founded here in 1876, and the 2500-student college is one of the best private liberal arts colleges in the Midwest. It hosts the annual **Nobel Conference** on the first Tuesday and Wednesday of October, the first ongoing educational conference in the US to earn official authorization from the Nobel Foundation. The **Treaty Site History Center,** 1851 N. Minnesota Ave., has exhibits on the ramifications of the treaty in which the Sioux transferred much of the Dakota Territory to the United States. (1 mi. north of St. Peter at the intersection of U.S. 169 and Rte. 22 W. ☎507-934-2160. Open Tu-Sa 10am-4pm, Su 1-4pm. $3, ages 13-18 $0.50, under 13 free.) The adjacent **Traverse des Sioux State Historic Site** is a short trail with interpretive signs down to the site of the signing, an ancient Minnesota River crossing. At **Whiskey River ❸,** on Rte. 99, just east of town over the bridge, you can stick to the classic Whiskey River burger ($9) or expand your horizons with the beer-cheese soup ($4), made from Wisconsin cheese. (☎507-934-5600; www.riversp.com. F live music. Open M-Th 11am-9:30pm, F 11am-10:30pm, Sa 7am-10:30pm, Su 9am-9:30pm. AmEx/D/MC/V.)

 PHOTO OP. Before you head out of St. Peter, get your picture taken at the **Pearly Gates,** located next to the Chamber of Commerce, 101 S. Front St., at Rte. 99.

⚑ APPROACHING NEW ULM: 28 MILES
Take **U.S. 169** out of St. Peter. Turn onto **Rte. 99 W** headed toward Nicollet. In Nicollet, Rte. 99 meets **U.S. 14** and continues west to New Ulm. Follow **C.R.**

LAKES, LEWIS & LEFSE

YOU'RE TWINE TOO HARD

Length: 312 miles
Days: 2 days
Starting point: Minneapolis-St. Paul
Highlight: the World's Largest Ball of Twine

From downtown Minneapolis, take I-94 W to Exit 127 at Sauk Centre. Turn right onto Main St. (Rte. 28), then make a left onto Sinclair Lewis Ave.

■ SINCLAIR LEWIS' BOYHOOD HOME. Though born across the street, Sinclair Lewis was brought up in this little house, at 810 Sinclair Lewis Ave. The tiny town became the thinly-veiled subject of his hit novel, *Main Street*, much to the chagrin of his gossipy neighbors. Lewis went on to be the first American to win the Nobel Prize in Literature and turn down a Pulitzer. He also wrote for the likes of the *Saturday Evening Post* and *Cosmopolitan*—before the days of "55 new ways to please your man." (☎320-352-5201. Open Memorial Day to Labor Day Tu-Sa 1-5pm. $5, students $3.50, ages 6-12 $2.)

Backtrack to I-94 W, and take Exit 103/Alexandria. Follow Rte. 29 N until it becomes Broadway. The museum is on your left, just before the park.

■THE RUNESTONE MUSEUM. In 1898, Swedish-American farmer Olof Öhman discovered a strange stone on his farm in nearby Kensington. The stone had unusual markings that were later discovered to be Nordic runes. Since then, the Kensington Runestone has sparked sharp debate as to its authenticity (it is dated 1362) and the likelihood of whether or not Vikings ventured into North America's interior in the 14th century. Head to the **Runestone Museum,** 206 Broadway, to watch the 22min. intro video, view the exhibits, and decide for yourself as you gaze at the stone. (☎320-763-3160. Open in summer M-F 9am-5pm, Sa 9am-4pm, Su 11am-4pm; in winter M-F 10am-5pm, Sa 10am-4pm. $6, seniors $5, students $3, under 7 free.)

Walk for a block until you see a really big statue.

■ BIG OLE. Standing proudly at the end of Broadway, Big Ole is a 28 ft. tall, four-ton Viking statue that was built for the Minnesota Pavilion at the 1965 World's Fair in New York City. Since his move to Alexandria after the fair, Big Ole has suffered vandals lighting his Christmas cape on fire, a broken sword, and structural failure due to heavy snowfall.

Continue back along Broadway, but ignore the interstate and follow Rte. 28 south to Starbuck. In Starbuck, turn left onto Main St. (Rte. 29). The World's Largest Lefse is on the left.

4 THE WORLD'S LARGEST LEFSE. In 1983, this predominantly Norwegian-American community decided that for their Centennial Celebration, they would make the world's largest lefse—a Scandinavian flatbread made of potato, milk, and flour, cooked on a griddle, and rolled up with butter and sugar. The finished product, made from 30 lb. of potatoes, 35 lb. of flour, 1 lb. of sugar, and 4 lb. of shortening, measured at 9 ft., 8 in. across. Today you can see a picture and life-sized plaque memorializing the dish at Main St. and E. 5th St. After paying homage to the plaque, head over to the nearby (and pragmatically named) **Bakery ❶**, to try a normal-sized lefse of your own. (☎320-239-2123. Lefse $4. Open M and W-Sa 6am-2pm. Cash or check only.)

Continue south along Rte. 29. At the fork in the road, turn left onto C.R. 41 to enter the park.

5 GLACIAL LAKES STATE PARK. This small state park offers a relaxing environment among native prairies and several kettle lakes. The day-use picnic area is a great place for a lunch break, and the park offers swimming, fishing, boating (canoe rentals available), hiking and horseback trails, and 38 tree-lined **campsites ❶**. (☎320-239-2860. Open daily sunrise-sunset. Water, showers, and flush toilets available in summer. Sites $11, with electricity $15. Day-use $7 per vehicle. Cash only.)

Continue south along C.R. 41, and make the 1st right onto T-50 to return to Rte. 29 S. In Benson, turn onto U.S. 12 E to Wilmar. In Wilmar, turn onto Bus U.S. 71 S (1st St.), and drive south for about a mile until you see the museum on your right next to the Menards.

6 THE SCHWANKE MUSEUM. The Schwanke Museum, 3310 S. Hwy. 71, is a privately owned collection of 89 cars, 130 tractors, 15 trucks, 70 gas engines, 18 gas pumps, and many more related artifacts. Those interested in historical farming equipment and the Green Revolution in the US will find themselves in heaven. (☎320-235-7045. Open May-Nov. M-Sa 1-4pm; Nov.-Dec. F-Sa 1-4pm. $5, under 12 $2.)

Head back north along Bus U.S. 71, and get back onto U.S. 12 E. Once in Darwin, make a right onto C.R. 14. The ball is a few blocks down, on the left.

7 WORLD'S LARGEST BALL OF TWINE. Housed in a plexiglass gazebo to guard against weather and rodentia alike, the "world's largest ball of twine rolled by one man" was Francis A. Johnson's life project. For 39 years, starting in 1950, he spent 4 hours a day wrapping the ball until his death. Finished, it weighs 17,400 lb. and is 12 ft. in diameter. The adjacent museum offers the story in more detail. (☎320-235-7045. Museum open Memorial Day to Labor Day; hours vary.)

Continue east on U.S. 12 to Dassel. The museum will be on your left.

8 THE OLD DEPOT MUSEUM. Housed in a former railroad depot, the Old Depot Museum, 651 W. Hwy. 12, houses original equipment from the old days of the railroad. Artifacts include baggage carts, track inspectors' bicycles, flashing signals, and one of the nation's largest collections of antique lanterns. (☎320-275-3876. Open Memorial Day to Labor Day 10am-4:30pm. $2.50, under 12 $1.)

BACK TO THE ROUTE. Get back on U.S. 12 E. The highway will merge with I-394 and lead you back into downtown Minneapolis.

37 into the southeastern section of New Ulm, and make a right onto **Broadway,** the main drag in town.

NEW ULM

German heritage is still evident in this small city full of manicured yards and well-kept homes. New Ulm's **August Schells Brewery,** 1860 Schells Rd., founded in 1860, is the second-oldest family-owned brewery in the US. Today, the fifth generation of Schells crafts the acclaimed beer in the original brewery. (Head south on Broadway and turn west on 18th St. ☎507-354-5528 or 800-770-5020; www.schellsbrewery.com. Open in summer daily 11am-5pm; in winter Sa-Su noon-3pm. Tours in summer M-F 2:30 and 4pm, Sa-Su 1, 2, 3, 4pm; in winter Sa 1 and 2:30pm, Su 1 and 2:30pm. $2.) The New Ulm **Glockenspiel,** at 4th North and Minnesota St., guards the city center. Three times each day (noon, 3, and 5pm) the stage door slides up and entertains viewers with wood-chip carvings moving mechanically to the chiming bells. The 45 ft. tall clock is one of the world's only free-standing carillon clock towers. The **Hermann Monument,** at Center St. and Monument St., honors the hero Hermann, who liberated Germany from the Romans. (☎507-359-8344. Open Memorial Day to Labor Day daily 10am-7pm. $1.) The **Heritage Tree,** at 1st S and Minnesota St., was erected recently to celebrate New Ulm's 150th anniversary. These are common decorations in German villages that tell local history in a whimsical and public manner.

Veigel's Kaiserhoff ❸, 221 N. Minnesota St., has been a New Ulm institution and "home to those famous barbecue ribs" for over 65 years. Their first order of barbecue ribs sold for $0.45, but today you'll have to fork over $13-17. Jukeboxes sit by each table, so you can impose your musical taste on everyone in the dining room for just a quarter. (☎507-359-2071. Open daily 11am-9pm. D/MC/V.) The small **Colonial Inn ❸,** 1315 N. Broadway, has 24 basic units with A/C and refrigerators. (☎507-354-3128. Rooms $45-55. AmEx/D/MC/V.)

⚐ APPROACHING SLEEPY EYE: 14 MILES
From Broadway, take **U.S. 14 W.** Just after leaving New Ulm, you will see your 1st **Wall Drug** sign, one of many on the trip toward Wall, South Dakota. The landscape also loses its rolling green hills and settles into flatness as you prepare to cross the Great Plains. The importance of corn is only made more apparent by the trucks you'll see in small towns near Sleepy Eye, selling ears of corn

for as little as $3 per 15 ears. U.S. 14 passes through the heart of Sleepy Eye as **Main St.**

SLEEPY EYE. Sleepy Eye is named after a Dakota chief with droopy eyelids, Ish Tak Ha Ba. The **Sleepy Eye Depot Museum,** 100 Oak St. NW, displays artifacts from the Sleepy Eye area, including a permanent display about the state-champion drum-and-bugle corps. Next to the Depot Museum is a granite obelisk erected in honor of Chief Sleepy Eye. (Turn right 1 block before the main intersection downtown. ☎507-794-5053. Open May-Dec. Tu-Sa 10am-4pm. Free.) **Sleepy Eye Lake** features swimming beaches, parks, picnic areas, and boat landings. As you're driving out of town, don't miss the **Linus Statue** in front of the Dyckman Library on U.S. 14. Linus Mauer, a Sleepy Eye native and friend of Charles Schulz, the creator of the Peanuts comic, was the inspiration for Charlie Brown's highly intelligent and blanket-loving best friend. Info is available at the **Sleepy Eye Convention and Visitors Bureau,** 232 E. Main St. (☎507-794-4731 or 800-290-0588. Open M-F 9am-4pm.)

⬛ DETOUR
JEFFERS PETROGLYPHS
27160 County Rd. 2. From Sleepy Eye, take U.S. 14 W to U.S. 71 S. Go 3 mi. east on Cottonwood C.R. 10, and travel 1 mi. south on C.R. 2.

The Jeffers petroglyphs are one of Minnesota's most intriguing artifacts. American Indians carved records into these islands of exposed rock nearly 5000 years ago. The rock outcroppings feature bison, turtles, thunderbirds, human figures, and other images frozen in time. (☎507-628-5591. Open Memorial Day to Labor Day M-F 10am-5pm, Sa 10am-8pm, Su noon-8pm; Sept. and May F-Sa 10am-5pm, Su noon-5pm; Oct.-Apr. by appointment. $5, seniors $4, children 6-12 $3.)

⚐ APPROACHING WALNUT GROVE: 39 MILES
Continue west along **U.S. 14** to Walnut Grove.

WALNUT GROVE. Most famous as the setting for Laura Ingalls Wilder's third book, *On the Banks of Plum Creek,* and the location for the enormously popular TV series *Little House on the Prairie,* Walnut Grove bears little resemblance to the land Wilder described. Nevertheless, the town pays homage to its most famous daughter with the **Laura Ingalls Wilder Museum,** 330

Eighth St. (C.R. 5), off U.S. 14. The Ingalls family arrived in Walnut Grove in 1874, when Laura was only seven. The museum complex houses an early settler's home, a chapel, and a depot building that contains original items belonging to the Ingalls family. (☎507-859-2358 or 888-528-7298; www.walnutgrove.org. Open June-Aug. daily 10am-6pm; May and Sept. M-Sa 10am-5pm, Su noon-5pm; Apr. and Oct. M-Sa 10am-4pm, Su noon-4pm; Mar. and Nov.-Dec. M-Sa 10am-4pm; Jan.-Feb. M-F 10am-4pm. $4, ages 6-12 $2, under 6 free.) The only remaining building from the 1870s is the hotel directly across the street from the museum, today a private residence. To stand on the banks of Plum Creek and see the depression that is all that remains of the Ingalls' first home in Walnut Grove, head to the **Ingalls Dugout Site,** located on a private farm 1½ mi. north of town off C.R. 5, on the right. (Open May-Oct. sunrise-sunset. $3 per car.)

⛿ APPROACHING PIPESTONE: 52 MILES
Continue west on **U.S. 14** until it intersects with **Rte. 23** 7 mi. past Balaton. Take Rte. 23 S to Pipestone.

PIPESTONE. The historic downtown of Pipestone has a decidedly different flavor than any other Midwestern town; many of the buildings were crafted from the Sioux Quartzite mined in the town quarries. The **Pipestone National Monument,** 36 Reservation Ave., provides relief from the surrounding plains. The monument is a Native American quarry, where visitors can watch pipes and carvings being crafted. The **Circle Tour** (¾ mi.) leads past Winnewissa Falls, Leaping Rock, and a marker from the Nicollet Expedition. (☎507-825-5464; www.nps.gov/pipe. Open daily in summer 8am-6pm; in winter 8am-5pm. $3, under 16 free.) Constructed in 1888, the **Calumet Inn ❹,** 104 West Main St., is a historical landmark. (☎507-825-5871 or 800-535-7610; www.calumetinn.com. Modern and antique rooms available. Rooms in summer $72-103; in winter $82-133. AmEx/D/MC/V.)

⛿ APPROACHING MADISON: 43 MILES
Follow **Rte. 30** to **Rte. 34.**

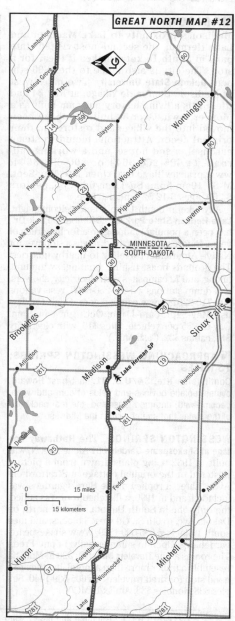

GREAT NORTH

The Mt. Rushmore State
SOUTH DAKOTA
Welcomes You!

MADISON

Madison's proximity to Lake Madison and Lake Herman, the second-most-visited state park in South Dakota, makes it ideal for a stop. The city is also home to the 1800-student **Dakota State University.** Two miles west of Madison, the **Prairie Village,** at Rte. 34 and Rte. 81, is a living history museum built as a pioneer town. Over 50 buildings have been moved into the village and restored in their original decor. Attractions include a steam carousel, a sod house, and a working railroad. (☎605-256-3644 or 800-693-3644; www.prairievillage.org. Open late May-Sept. M-Sa 10am-5pm, Su 11am-6pm. $5, seniors $4.50, ages 6-12 $2, under 5 free.)

Any lake in South Dakota is a welcome sight. **Lake Herman State Park ❶,** 23409 State Park Dr., has been a popular camping area for hundreds of years. Before settlers arrived, it was a stopover for Native Americans traveling to nearby quarries. The grounds boast fishing, boating, swimming, hiking, and 72 campsites with electricity, showers, and dump stations. (☎605-256-5003, reservations 800-710-2267; www.campsd.com. Open for day-use May-Sept. 6am-11pm; Oct.-Apr. 6am-9pm. Day-use $5 per vehicle. Sites $10, with electricity $14; cabins $32. Cash only.)

⚐ APPROACHING WESSINGTON SPRINGS: 75 MILES
Continue on **Rte. 34/U.S. 81.** Just past Howard, ovines replace bovines and fields of corn and wheat become wild, untamed grassland—the real backbone of the plains that stretch across the Midwest.

WESSINGTON SPRINGS. The **Hathaway Cottage at Shakespeare Garden,** 501 Alene Ave. N, was built in 1932 using plans drawn from a picture postcard of the original cottage at Stratford-on-Avon. Later, a replica of the Bard's gardens was included, and in 1995, a thatched roof was added, the only one in South Dakota. (Travel north on Dakota Ave. to 6th St. Go west 3 blocks, and then south 1 block. ☎605-539-1529; www.shakespeare-garden.org. Open in summer daily 1-5pm. Free.) The rooms at the **Travelers Motel ❶,** 320 E. Main St. resemble a trailer more than a motel, but they're a good stop for tired travelers. (☎605-539-1440. Singles $28; doubles $33. AmEx/D/MC/V.)

⚐ APPROACHING CHAMBERLAIN: 67 MILES
From Wessington Springs, drive west on **Rte. 34** until you hit **Rte. 45.** Turn left to go south on Rte. 45 until you reach **I-90,** and head west.

CHAMBERLAIN

Nearly 200 years ago, the Lewis and Clark expedition spent three days at Camp Pleasant watching thousands of bison graze on the nearby bluffs. The **Lewis and Clark Information Center,** off I-90 at Mi. 264, is accessible from both the east and west. It offers information on these early River Trippers and offers panoramic views of the Missouri River valley. (☎605-895-2188. Open May-Oct. daily 8am-6pm. Free.) One of Chamberlain's main sights is the **Akta Lakota Museum,** 1301 N. Main St., at St. Joseph's Indian School. Akta Lakota means "to honor the people," and the museum honors the Lakota people, offering a living lesson on how their culture has changed over the past few centuries. (☎605-734-3452 or 800-798-3452; www.aktalakota.org. Open Memorial Day to Labor Day M-Sa 8am-6pm, Su 9am-5pm; Labor Day to Memorial Day M-F 8am-5pm. Donations accepted.)

The **Derby Cafe ❶,** 138 S. Main St., is a relatively new addition to Chamberlain. On Friday and Saturday evenings the cafe has steak dinners; the rest of the week, it serves up breakfast, sandwiches ($5), soups, and the best espresso within 100 mi. (☎605-234-1380. Open M-Th 7am-6pm, F-Sa 7am-9pm. D/MC/V.)

⚐ APPROACHING MURDO: 73 MILES
Continue west on **I-90** to **Exit 192.**

MURDO. At the **Pioneer Auto Museum,** Exit 192 off I-90, in Murdo, there are over 275 old cars and other vehicles among an eclectic mix of Americana, including the only surviving "General Lee" from *The Dukes of Hazzard.* The museum's pride and joy is Elvis's '76 Harley. (☎605-669-2691; www.pioneerautoshow.com. Open Memorial Day to Labor Day 8am-9pm; hours vary in winter. $8.50, ages 6-13 $4.25, under 6 free.)

🕐 Just after Murdo, I-90 enters the Mountain Time Zone, where it is 1hr. earlier.

⚐ APPROACHING MIDLAND: 12 MILES
Continue west on **I-90** to **Exit 170.**

 218-219 B.C.E.: Hannibal and his 37 war elephants roadtrip over the Alps in mid-winter.

MIDLAND. As you pass into the Mountain time zone and set your watch back, you may think you've gone a little too far when you see the statue of Lulu, the *T. Rex* guarding Exit 170 near the **1880 Town and Longhorn Ranch,** in Midland. The town showcases a collection of transplanted buildings from an early South Dakotan town. The buildings range from Indian relics to a 14-sided barn built in 1919. A museum houses more valuable collections, including Buffalo Bill memorabilia, a tribute to Casey Tibbs, the 19-time World Champion Rodeo Cowboy, and movie props from *Dances with Wolves.* (☎605-344-259 or 605-669-2387. Open daily June-Sept. 6am-sunset; May and Oct. 8am-sunset. $8, seniors $7, ages 13-18 $5, 6-12 $4, under 5 free.)

⚑ APPROACHING KADOKA: 33 MILES
Keep driving west on **I-90** until an alien landscape emerges from the plains. Don't worry—there aren't any aliens. Turn off at **Exit 52** for Kadoka.

KADOKA. Located on the outskirts of the Badlands, Kadoka is home to the **Badlands Petrified Garden.** This museum features a fluorescent mineral exhibit and some impressive prehistoric Badlands fossils. The outdoor park includes the largest petrified trees and logs found in the Badlands Area. (☎605-837-2448. Open mid-Apr. to Oct. daily 7am-7pm. $5, ages 6-16 $2.50, under 6 free.)

⚑ APPROACHING THE BADLANDS: 136 MILES
Continue west on **I-90** until you reach **Exit 131,** then follow **Rte. 240 W** toward Badlands National Park.

THE BADLANDS

When they first saw these mountainous rock formations rising out of the prairie, early explorers were less than enthusiastic. General Alfred Sully called these arid and treacherous formations "Hell with the fires out," and the French translated the Sioux name for the area, *mako sica,* as *les mauvaises terres,* meaning "bad lands." Late spring and fall in the Badlands offer pleasant weather that can be a relief from the extreme temperatures of mid-summer and winter; however, even at their worst, the Badlands are worth a visit. Deposits of iron oxide lend layers of marvelous red and brown hues to the land, and the moods of the Badlands change with the time, season, and weather. According to geologists, they erode about 2 in.

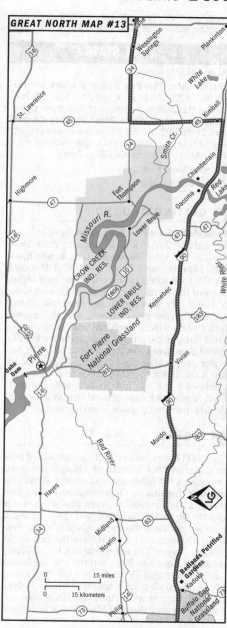

GREAT NORTH MAP #13

GREAT NORTH

every year. At that rate they will disappear in 500,000 years—hurry and visit before it's too late.

VITAL STATS

Area: 244,000 acres

Visitor Info: The Ben Reifel Visitors Center (☎605-433-5361; www.nps.gov/badl), 5 mi. inside the park's northeastern entrance. Open daily 9am-4pm. **White River Visitors Center** (☎605-455-2878), 55 mi. to the southwest, off Rte. 27, in the park's less-visited southern section. Open in summer daily 8am-7pm.

Gateway Town: Wall (p. 283).

Fees: $15 per vehicle.

▣ GETTING AROUND

Badlands National Park lies just south of I-90. The highlight of the park is the amazing drive along the 31½ mi. long ▨**Badlands Loop Scenic Byway (Rte. 240)**, between Exit 131 and Exit 110, off I-90. The road winds in and out of the rock formations of the North Unit, offering stunning vistas of the White River drainage area. Go during evening for your best chance to beat the summer heat and crowds, see wildlife, and catch the colorful hues of the sunset against the rocks. The gravel **Sage Creek Rim Rd.**, west of Rte. 240, has fewer people and more animals. Highlights are the Roberts Prairie Dog Town and the park's herds of bison and antelope; across the river from Sage Creek campground lies another prairie dog town and popular bison territory.

◉ SIGHTS

The 244,000-acre park protects large tracts of prairie and stark rock formations. **Hiking** is permitted throughout the entire park, although officials discourage climbing on the formations and request that you stick to high-use trails. The south unit is mostly uncharted territory, and the occasional path is most likely the tracks of wildlife. Five hiking trails begin off Loop Rd. near the Ben Reifel Visitors Center. The **Notch Trail** (1½ mi., 1½-2hr.) demands surefootedness and the will to climb a shaky ladder at a 45° angle. Not for the faint of heart, the trail blazes around narrow ledges before making its way to the grand finale: an unbelievable view of the Cliff Shelf and White River

Valley. The moderate **Cliff Shelf Nature Trail** (½ mi., 30min.) consists of stairs, a boardwalk, and unpaved paths. It is your best bet for coming face-to-face with wildlife. **Door Trail** (¾ mi., 20min.) cuts through buttes and crevices for spectacular views of the countryside. **Window Trail** (¼ mi., 10min.), more of a scenic overlook than an actual hike, consists of a wheelchair-accessible ramp that looks over a splendid view.

Those interested in exploring the area on horseback can check out **Badlands Trail Rides,** 1½ mi. south of the Ben Reifel Visitors Center, on Rte. 377. While the trails do not lead into the park, they do cover territory on the park's immediate outskirts. (☎605-309-2028. Open in summer daily 8am-7pm. 30min. rides $20; 1hr. rides $25.)

PHOTO OP. The Ranch Store, off Exit 131 on the eastern entrance to the Badlands Loop, has the **World's Largest Prairie Dog.** And no, it won't dig tunnels in your backyard or eat your flowers—it's a 6-ton statue. Out back behind the gift shop, they have the real thing; a maze of prairie-dog tunnels populated by hungry dogs. For $0.50 you can buy a bag of peanuts to keep 'em satisfied. (☎605-433-5477. Open June-Sept. daily 7:30am-8pm.)

▤ FOOD

A true South Dakota experience, the **Cuny Table Cafe,** 8 mi. west of the White River Visitors Center, on Rte. 2, is truly a restaurant in the middle of nowhere. The restaurant is packed at lunchtime; try the Indian Tacos (home-cooked fry bread piled with veggies, beans, and beef) for $5. (☎605-455-2957. Open daily 5:30am-5:30pm. Cash only.) About 60 mi. north, by the main visitors center, the **Cedar Pass Lodge Restaurant ❷** has buffalo burgers ($6.25), fry bread ($2.50), and fantastic views to the north of the Badlands. (☎605-433-5460. Open daily in summer 7am-8:30pm; in fall 8am-4:30pm. AmEx/D/MC/V.)

▥ ACCOMMODATIONS

In addition to standard lodging and camping, **backcountry camping** allows an intimate introduction to this austere landscape, but be sure to bring water. Campers are strongly urged to contact one of the rangers at the visitors center before heading out and to be extra careful of bison, which can be extremely dangerous. When it comes to indoor accommodations, the two best options are essentially identical. Within the park, the **Cedar Pass Lodge ❸**, 1 Cedar St., next to the Ben Reifel Visitors Center, rents cabins with A/C and showers. (☎605-433-5460; www.cedarpasslodge.com. Reservations recommended. Open mid-Apr. to mid-Oct. Cabins with private bath in summer $55, in spring and fall $65. 2-bedroom with shared bath $70/$80. Cottage $85/$90. AmEx/D/MC/V.) The **Badlands Inn ❸**, on Rte. 44, in Interior, sits outside the park, but all rooms have a wide view of the Badlands and access to an outdoor pool. (☎605-433-5401 or 800-341-8000; www.badlandsinn.com. Open mid-May to mid-Sept. Rooms in summer $70; in spring and fall $55. AmEx/D/MC/V.) If you'd rather sleep under the stars, the **Sage Creek Campground ❶**, 13 mi. from the Pinnacles entrance south of Wall, is on a flat open field in the prairie with pit toilets and no water. (Take Sage Creek Rim Rd. off Rte. 240. No reservations. Free.) You pay for the view at the **Cedar Pass Campground ❶**, south of the Ben Reifel Visitors Center, which has organized sites with water and flush toilets, but no showers. It's best to get there before 6pm in summer, since sites fill before evening, and no reservations are accepted. (Sites $10. AmEx/D/MC/V.)

◥ APPROACHING WALL: 39 MILES
Head out of the park on **Rte. 240 W** to Wall.

WALL

Wall is world famous for the presence of ◢**Wall Drug,** 510 Main St. You absolutely can't miss it, because the highway is lined for hundreds of Wall Drug billboards and Wall Drug signs, most of them erected by enterprising individuals. Signs have been seen on the Paris Metro, the buses of London, and rail lines in Kenya, at the Taj Majal, the Great Wall of China, and both poles. At the actual store, you can purchase nearly anything, especially if it's useless and has your name on it. Opened in 1931, the drug store has turned into a sprawling complex that includes innumerable novelty shops, an arcade, an 80 ft. dinosaur, and a guitar and banjo played by a machine. (☎605-279-2175; www.walldrug.com. Open daily 6:30am-

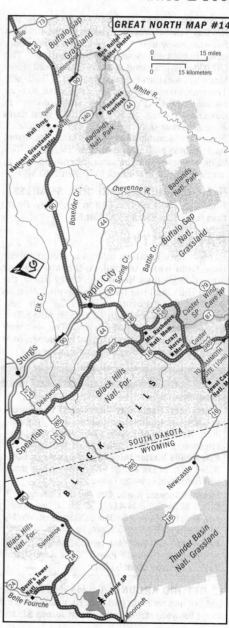

GREAT NORTH MAP #14

10pm.) Two blocks south of Wall Drug is the **Buffalo Gap National Grassland Visitors Center,** 708 Main St., whose slogan is, "Anyone can love the mountains, but it takes soul to love the prairie." The 591,000-acre grassland is one of 20 national grasslands and includes intermingled bits of Badlands. There are no established hiking trails, but you can mountain bike, ATV, hunt, fish, and birdwatch in designated areas. (☎605-279-2125. Open daily June-Aug. 8am-6pm; Sept.-May M-F 8am-4:30pm. Free.) The **Sunshine Inn ❸,** 608 Main St., offers basic rooms with A/C and cable TV. (☎605-279-2178; www.sunshineinnatwallsd.com. Rooms in summer $55-65; in winter $45-55. AmEx/D/MC/V.)

⧉ APPROACHING RAPID CITY: 56 MILES
From Wall, travel west on **I-90** to Rapid City. Downtown Rapid City is located off **Exit 57.**

RAPID CITY

Rapid City's location makes it a convenient base from which to explore the surrounding attractions; Mount Rushmore, Crazy Horse, the Black Hills, and the Badlands are all within an hour's drive of downtown Rapid City. The second-largest city in South Dakota, it also offers the most amenities in the region. The area welcomes three million tourists each summer, over 50 times the city's permanent population.

VITAL STATS

Population: 60,000

Visitor Info: Rapid City Chamber of Commerce and Visitors Information Center, 444 Mt. Rushmore Rd. N (☎605-343-1744; www.rapidcity-cvb.com), in the Civic Center. Open M-F 8am-5pm. **Black Hills Visitor Information Center** (☎605-355-3700), at Exit 61, off I-90. Open daily in summer 8am-8pm; in winter 8am-5pm.

Internet Access: Rapid City Public Library, 610 Quincy St. (☎605-394-4171), at 6th St. Open June-Aug. M-Th 9am-9pm, F-Sa 9am-5:30pm; Sept.-May M-Th 9am-9pm, F-Sa 9am-5:30pm, Su 1-5pm.

Post Office: 500 East Blvd. (☎605-394-8600), east of downtown. Open M-F 8am-5:30pm, Sa 8:30am-12:30pm. **Postal Code:** 57701.

⧉ GETTING AROUND. Rapid City's roads are laid out in a sensible grid pattern, making driving along its wide streets easy. **Saint Joseph St.** and **Main St.** are the main east-west thoroughfares and **Omaha St.** is two-way. **Mount Rushmore Rd. (U.S. 16)** is the main north-south route. Many north-south roads are numbered, and numbers increase from east to west, beginning at **East Blvd.**

◪ SIGHTS. Rapid City's Civic Center supplies a glossy brochure and map of the **Rapid City Star Tour,** which leads to 12 free attractions, including a jaunt up Skyline Dr. for a bird's-eye view of the city and the seven concrete dinosaurs of **Dinosaur Park,** as well as a magical trip to **Storybook Island,** an amusement park. In Memorial Park, check out America's largest **Berlin Wall Exhibit,** featuring two pieces of the wall. The **Journey Museum,** 222 New York St., traces the history of the Black Hills, detailing the geology, archaeology, and people of the region, with skull castings of a *Tyrannosaurus rex,* a holographic story tent, and a mercantile trading post. (☎605-394-6923; www.journeymuseum.org. Open M and W-Su 8am-5pm, Tu 8am-8pm. $6, seniors $5, students $4.) And just in case the other 41 feel slighted by their lack of immortalization on nearby Mt. Rushmore, the **City of Presidents** is an ongoing project to create life-size bronze statues of every president at intersections in Rapid City. Tip your hat at James Monroe in front of the **Presidents Information Center,** 631 Main St., as you pick up your free map. (☎605-484-2162. Open June-Sept. daily 10am-9pm. Free.) The 8 mi. **Rapid City Recreational Path** runs along Rapid Creek.

◪◪ FOOD AND NIGHTLIFE. The **Millstone Family Restaurant ❷,** 2010 W. Main St., at Mountain View Rd., cooks up large portions of chicken ($6-8), spaghetti and meatballs ($8), and pork ribs for $9. (☎605-343-5824. Open daily 6am-11pm. AmEx/D/MC/V.) **Pauly's Sub Co. ❶,** 2060 W. Main St., west of downtown, shares space with **Java Junkie,** creating a one-stop spot for cheap coffee ($1.50) and subs ($3-7) of all varieties. (☎605-348-2669. Pauly's open M-Sa 10am-9pm, Su 11am-8pm. Java Junkie open M-F 6:30am-7pm, Sa 8am-6pm, Su 8am-4pm. MC/V.) Nightlife options line Main St., between 6th St. and Mt. Rushmore Rd. For a beer as black as the Hills, throw back a Smokejumper Stout ($3.75) at the **Firehouse Brewing Company,** 610 Main St. The company brews several beers and serves sandwiches, burgers, and salads ($6-10) in a restored 1915 firehouse. (☎605-348-1915; www.firehousebrewing.com. Sa-Su live music. Open M-Th 11am-11pm, F-Sa 11am-midnight, Su 11am-10pm. AmEx/D/MC/V.)

 ACCOMMODATIONS. Rapid City accommodations are expensive in summer, and motels often fill weeks in advance, especially during the **Sturgis Motorcycle Rally** in mid-August. Budget motels surround the junction of I-90 and Rte. 59 by the Rushmore Mall. Large billboards guide the way to **Big Sky Lodge ❹**, 4080 Tower Rd., 5min. south of town on a service road, off Mt. Rushmore Rd. The rooms are very clean and the doubles have great views of Rapid City and the surrounding valley. (☎605-348-3200 or 800-318-3208. Free Wi-Fi. Open May-Oct. Mid-June to mid-Aug. singles $69, doubles $79. Call ahead for prices in winter. D/MC/V.) **Camping** is available at **Badlands National Park** (p. 281), **Black Hills National Forest** (p. 285), and **Custer State Park** (p. 286).

> **TIP**
> **HOG HEAVEN.** Unless you've got a Harley underneath you, the Black Hills are best avoided during the first two weeks in August, when the **Sturgis Rally** takes over the area. Nearly 500,000 motorcyclists roar through the hills, filling up campsites and motels and bringing traffic to a standstill.

◪ DETOUR
REPTILE GARDENS
5 mi. south of Rapid City on U.S. 16.

Reptile Gardens was opened in the winter of 1937 (four years before Mt. Rushmore was completed) by Earl Brockelsby, who noted that the biggest draw at other attractions was the thrill of seeing a rattlesnake close-up. Reptile Gardens is more fun than your average zoo, with a giant Australian croc, tortoises, komodo dragons, and exhibits like "death row," which is filled with the world's most poisonous snakes. (☎605-342-5873 or 800-335-0275; www.reptilegardens.com. Open Apr.-Dec. daily 8am-7pm; hours vary in spring and fall. $12.50, seniors $11, ages 5-12 $7.50, under 5 free.)

◪ DETOUR
BLACK HILLS NATIONAL FOREST
U.S. 16 snakes toward Custer through the Black Hills.

The Lakota called this region "Paha Sapa," meaning Black Hills, for the hue that the Pon-derosa pines take on from a distance. The region was considered to be so sacred that they would visit, but never settle. The Treaty of 1868 gave the Black Hills and the rest of South Dakota west of the Missouri River to the tribe, but when gold was discovered here in the 1870s, the US government snatched back 6000 sq. mi. Today, the area attracts millions of visitors with a trove of natural treasures and is protected by an assortment of state and national parks, monuments, and forests. Mining, logging, ranching, and recreation all take place in close proximity. The forest itself provides opportunities for backcountry hiking, swimming, biking, and camping, as do park-run campgrounds and tent sites. **Forest Service Visitor Centers** are available on U.S. 385 at Pactola Lake (☎605-343-8755; open late May to early Sept. daily 8:30am-6pm) and in Rapid City (p. 284). **Backcountry camping** in the national forest is free and allowed 1 mi. away from any campground or visitors center and at least 200 ft. from the side of the road. Leave your car in a parking lot or just pull off. Open fires are prohibited, but fires in provided grates are allowed. **Campgrounds ❶** include: **Pactola,** on the Pactola Reservoir just south of the junction of Rte. 44 and U.S. 385; **Sheridan Lake,** 5 mi. northeast of Hill City on U.S. 385; and **Roubaix Lake,** 14 mi. south of Lead on U.S. 385. All three have some sites in winter. All national forest campgrounds are quiet and wooded, offering fishing, swimming, and pit toilets. (☎877-444-6777; www.reserveusa.com. No hookups. Sites $17-20. Cash only.) The Wyoming side of the forest permits some campfires and horses, and draws fewer visitors.

◪ DETOUR
RUSHMORE BORGLUM STORY
U.S. 16A in Keystone.

If you'd like to know more about the man behind the mountain, visit the Rushmore Borglum Museum. A 22min. movie documents the progress of the mountain and tells the story of Gutzon Borglum. Borglum, who encountered opposition from those who felt the work of God could not be improved, defended the project, insisting that "there is not a monument in this country as big as a snuff box."

(☎605-666-4448; www.rushmoreborglum.com. Open June-Aug. M-Sa 8am-7pm; Su 9am-7pm; May, Sept., and early Oct. 9am-3pm. $7, seniors $6.50, ages 7-17 $3.25, under 7 free.)

▶ APPROACHING MT. RUSHMORE: 23 MILES
Traveling from Rapid City through the Black Hills along **U.S. 16,** you'll pass the town of Keystone. Just after Keystone, turn west (right) onto **Rte. 244,** which will lead to Mt. Rushmore after 2 mi.

MOUNT RUSHMORE
🏛**Mount Rushmore National Memorial** boasts the faces that launched a thousand minivans. Historian Doane Robinson originally conceived of this "shrine of democracy" in 1923 as a memorial for frontier heroes; sculptor Gutzon Borglum chose four presidents instead. In 1941, the 60 ft. heads of Washington, Jefferson, Roosevelt, and Lincoln were "finished" due to Borglum's death. The **Info Center** details the monument's history and has ranger tours every hour on the half-hour. A state-of-the-art **visitors center** chronicles the monument's history and the lives of the featured presidents. (Info center ☎605-574-3198, visitors center 605-574-3165. Both open daily in summer 8am-10pm; in winter 8am-5pm.) From the visitors center, it's half a mile along the planked wooden **Presidential Trail** to **Borglum's Studio.** (Open in summer daily 9am-6pm. Ranger talks every hr.) In summer, the **Mount Rushmore Memorial Amphitheater** hosts a patriotic speech and film nightly at 9pm, and lights flood the monument from 9:30 to 10:30pm. (☎605-574-2523; www.nps.gov/moru. Trail lights extinguished at 11pm.)

Horsethief Campground ❶ lies 2 mi. west of Mt. Rushmore on Rte. 244 in the Black Hills National Forest. President George H. W. Bush fished here in 1993; rumor has it that the lake was overstocked with fish to guarantee presidential success. (☎605-574-2668, reservations 800-657-5802; www.horsethief.com. Water and flush toilets. Reservations recommended on weekends. Sites late May to early Sept. $18, with electricity $21.50, with full hookup $32-35.50; early May and mid-Sept. to Oct. $13.50/$16/$24-26.50. Cash only.) The commercial **Mt. Rushmore KOA/Palmer Gulch Lodge** ❷, 7 mi. west of Mt. Rushmore, on Rte. 244, has campsites, cabins, two pools, a spa, laundry, nightly movies, a small strip mall, free Wi-Fi, and $3 shuttles

to Mt. Rushmore. (☎605-574-2525 or 800-562-8503; www.palmergulch.com. Reservations recommended. Open May-Sept. Tent sites $33-61; RV sites $33-61. AmEx/D/MC/V.)

▶ APPROACHING CUSTER STATE PARK: 20 MILES
From Mt. Rushmore, backtrack on **Rte. 244** to **U.S. 16A/Iron Mountain Rd.,** and head south to **Custer State Park.** Large RVs (greater than 13 ft. 5 in. wide or 12 ft. 4 in. tall) will need to continue west on Rte. 244 to follow U.S. 16 into the town of Custer, then head east on U.S. 16A to enter the park.

CUSTER STATE PARK
Peter Norbeck, governor of South Dakota in the late 1910s, loved to hike among the thin, towering rock formations that haunt the area south of Sylvan Lake and Mt. Rushmore. In order to preserve the land, he created Custer State Park. The spectacular **Needles Hwy. (Rte. 87)** follows his favorite hiking route—Norbeck designed this road to be especially narrow and winding so that newcomers could experience the pleasures of discovery. For those who love roller-coaster freeways, 🏛**Iron Mountain Rd. (U.S. 16A)** from Mt. Rushmore to near the Norbeck Visitors Center (see below) takes drivers through a series of one-lane tunnels, "pigtail" curves, and alpine meadows. The park's **Wildlife Loop Road** twists past prairie dog towns, bison wallows and corrals, and wilderness areas near prime hiking and camping territory. Pronghorns, elk, deer, and burros loiter by the side of the road, and traffic will often stop for some of Custer's 1500 bison to cross the road. Do not get out—bison are dangerous. At 7242 ft., **Harney Peak** is the highest point east of the Rockies and west of the Pyrenees. The hike is a strenuous 6 mi. round-trip. The 3 mi. **Sunday Gulch Trail** offers the most amazing scenery of all the park's trails. The park also provides 30 lower-altitude trails. At **Sylvan Lake,** on Needles Hwy., you can hike, fish, boat, or canoe. (☎605-575-2561. Paddleboats $5 per 30min.) Fishing is allowed anywhere in the park, but a South Dakota fishing license is required. ($16 per day, $34 per 3 days.)

The **Peter Norbeck Visitors Center,** on U.S. 16A, ½ mi. west of the State Game Lodge (where Eisenhower and Coolidge stayed), serves as the park's info center. (☎605-255-4464; www.custerstatepark.info. Open daily

Apr.-May and Oct.-Nov. 9am-5pm; June-Aug. 8am-8pm; Sept. 8am-6pm. Weekly entrance pass May-Oct. $5 per person or $12 per vehicle; Nov.-Apr. $2.50/$6.) The visitors center offers info about walk-in **primitive camping**, which is available for $2 per night in the **French Creek Natural Area ❶**. Eight **additional campgrounds ❶** have sites with showers and restrooms. No hookups are provided. (☎800-710-2267; www.campsd.com. Open daily 7am-9pm. Over 200 of the 400+ sites can be reserved; the entire park fills in summer by 3pm. Sites $13-18.) The **Legion Lake Resort,** on U.S. 16A, 6 mi. west of the visitors center, rents mountain bikes. (☎605-255-4521. $10 per hr., $25 per half-day, $40 per day.) The strong granite of the Needles makes for great rock climbing. For more info contact **Sylvan Rocks,** in Hill City, 20 mi. north of Custer City. (☎605-484-7585; www.sylvanrocks.com. Open in summer M-Tu and Th-Su 8am-10am.)

◣ DETOUR
MAMMOTH SITE
1800 U.S. 18 Bypass. From Custer, take U.S. 89 S to U.S. 18 W.

The Mammoth Site is the only in situ (bones left as found) mammoth fossil display in America. Remains of more than 50 mammoths have been found among other prehistoric animals that were trapped in a spring-fed sinkhole. The first remains were discovered in 1974 when excavation began for a housing project. (☎605-745-6017; www.mammothsite.com. Open mid-May to mid-Aug. daily 8am-8pm; mid-Aug. to early Sept. daily 8am-6pm; mid- to late Sept. daily 8am-5pm; Oct. daily 9am-5pm; Nov.-Feb. M-Sa 9am-3:30pm, Su 11am-3:30pm; Mar. to mid-May daily 8am-5pm. $7, seniors $6.50, ages 5-12 $5.)

◣ DETOUR
WIND CAVE NATIONAL PARK
From Custer, take Rte. 89 S to U.S. 385 S. The park is about 18 mi. from Custer.

In the cavern-riddled Black Hills, the subterranean scenery often rivals the above-ground sites. After the Black Hills formed from shifting plates of granite, warm water filled the cracked layers of limestone, eroding it to form the fourth-largest cave in the world. Bring a sweater on all tours—Wind Cave remains a constant 53°F, while Jewel Cave is 49°F. Discovered in 1821, scientists estimate that only 5% of the cave's volume has been explored. Wind Cave houses over 95% of the world's "boxwork"—a honeycomb-like lattice of calcite crystals. (☎605-745-4600. Tours June-Aug. daily 8:40am-6pm; in winter call ahead. Tours $7-23.) The **Wind Cave National Park Visitors Center,** in Hot Springs, can provide more info. (☎605-745-4600; www.nps.gov/wica. Open mid-June to mid-Aug. daily 8am-7pm; mid-Aug. to late Sept. daily 8am-6pm; late Sept. to mid-Oct. daily 8am-5pm; mid-Oct. to mid-June hours vary.)

◣ DETOUR
JEWEL CAVE NATIONAL MONUMENT
From Custer, take U.S. 16 west for 13 mi.

Distinguishing itself from nearby Wind Cave's boxwork, the walls of Jewel Cave are covered with a layer of calcite crystal. Enticed by the cave's twinkling walls, the cave's discoverers filed a mining claim for "jewels," only to realize that giving tours would be more profitable. The popular **Jewel Cave Discovery** tour gives you a quick peek at the main room of the caverns. ($4, free with National Parks Pass.) The **Scenic Tour** (½ mi., 1¼hr.; 723 stairs) highlights chambers with the most interesting formations. (In summer every 20min. 8:20am-6pm; in winter call ahead. $8, ages 6-16 $4, under 6 free.) The **Lantern Tour** is an illuminating journey that lasts 1¾hr. (In summer every hr. 9am-5pm; in winter call ahead. $8, ages 6-16 $4.) The **Visitors Center,** next to the parking lot, has more information. (☎605-673-2288. Open daily June to mid-Aug. 8am-7:30pm; Oct. to mid-May 8am-4:30pm.) The **Roof Trail** behind the visitors center provides a memorable introduction to the Black Hills through a trek across the "roof" of Jewel Cave.

◣ DETOUR
CRAZY HORSE MEMORIAL
Take a left off Rte. 385/U.S. 16, 17 mi. southwest of Mt. Rushmore.

In 1947, Lakota Chief Henry Standing Bear commissioned sculptor Korczak Ziolkowski to sculpt a memorial to Crazy Horse. A famed warrior who garnered respect by refusing to sign treaties or live on a government reservation, Crazy Horse was stabbed in the back by a white soldier in 1877. The Crazy Horse Memo-

GREAT NORTH

rial, which at its completion will be the **world's largest sculpture,** is being carved into the Black Hills the Lakota hold sacred as a spectacular tribute to the revered Native American leader and warrior. The first blast rocked the hills on June 3, 1948, taking off 10 tons of rock. On the memorial's 50th anniversary, the completed face (all four of the Rushmore heads could fit inside it) was unveiled. With admissions funding 85% of the cost, Ziolkowski's wife Ruth and seven of their 10 children carry on his work, currently concentrating on the horse's head, which will be 219 ft. high. Part of Crazy Horse's arm is also visible, and eventually, his entire torso and head, as well as part of his horse, will be carved into the mountain. The memorial includes the **Indian Museum of North America,** the **Sculptor's Studio-Home,** and the **Native American Educational and Cultural Center,** where artisans' works are displayed and sold. The orientation center shows a moving 17min. video entitled "Dynamite and Dreams." (☎605-673-4681; www.crazyhorse.org. Open daily in summer 7am-dark; in winter 8am-4:30pm. Nightly laser show on the memorial after sunset; ask for ticket to return. $10, under 6 free; $25 per vehicle.)

⌐ APPROACHING CUSTER: 14 MILES
Custer is located along **U.S. 16,** west of Custer State Park.

CUSTER. Custer has plenty of places to refuel after a day of exploration. **The Wrangler ❷,** 302 Mt. Rushmore Rd., is a local family restaurant, serving up breakfasts ($4-6), deluxe bison burgers ($6), and dinners ($8-10) that are dependably good. (☎605-673-4271. Open M-Sa 5am-8pm, Su 6am-8pm.) **Sage Creek Grille ❸,** 607 Mt. Rushmore Rd., downtown, serves upscale food at reasonable prices. Try the delicious salads ($4-8), sandwiches ($7-9), and buffalo and elk burgers for $9. (☎605-673-2424. Open Tu-F 11am-2pm, Th-Sa 5-8pm.) An anomaly among campgrounds, **Fort Welikit ❶,** 24992 Sylvan Lake Rd., has private bathrooms on large sites. (☎605-673-3600 or 888-946-2267; www.blackhillsrv.com. Tent sites $9 per person; RV sites $24, with hookup $28. D/MC/V.) The **Shady Rest Motel ❷,** 238 Gordon Rd., sits on the hill overlooking Custer and has homey cabins. (☎605-673-4478 or 800-567-8259. Open Mar.-Oct. Singles $60; doubles $65. MC/V.) The **Rocket Motel**

❸, 211 Mt. Rushmore Rd., in west Custer, has very clean, tastefully furnished rooms with free Wi-Fi and cable TV. (☎605-673-4401. Open Apr.-Oct. Singles from $50; doubles $65. AmEx/D/MC/V.) If your interest in Custer goes beyond food and sleep, visit the **Custer Visitors Center,** 615 Washington St., for information. (☎605-673-2244 or 800-992-9818; www.custersd.com. Open mid-May to Aug. M-F 8am-5pm, Sa 9am-5pm, Su 10am-4pm; Sept. to mid-May M-F 8am-5pm.)

⌐ APPROACHING DEADWOOD: 52 MILES
Continue up **U.S. 385 N/16 E** toward Hill City. Go north on U.S. 385 until you reach Deadwood, making a right onto **U.S. 85 N** to enter downtown.

DEADWOOD

Gunslingers Wild Bill Hickok and Calamity Jane sauntered into Deadwood during the height of the Gold Rush in the summer of 1876. Bill stayed just long enough—three weeks—to spend eternity here. At her insistence, Jane and Bill now lie side-by-side in the Mount Moriah Cemetery, just south of downtown, off Cemetery St. ($1, ages 5-12 $0.50.) Gambling takes center stage in this authentic western town—casinos line **Main St.,** and many innocent-looking establishments have slot machines and poker tables waiting in the wings. There's live music outside the **Stockade** at the **Buffalo-Bodega Complex,** 658 Main St. (☎605-578-1300), which is packed with throngs of 24hr. gambling spots. **Saloon #10,** 657 Main St., was forever immortalized by Wild Bill's murder. Hickok was shot holding black aces and eights, thereafter known as the "dead man's hand." The chair in which he died is on display, and every summer the shooting is reenacted on location. (☎605-578-3346 or 800-952-9398; www.saloon10.com. Open daily 8am-2am. Reenactments in summer daily 1, 3, 5, 7pm.) Onlookers follow the scene outdoors as **shootouts** happen daily along Main St. (2, 4, 6, 7:30pm)—listen for gunshots and the sound of Calamity Jane's whip. The **Deadwood History and Information Center,** 3 Siever St., behind Main Street's Silverado, can help with any questions. (☎605-578-2507 or 800-999-1876; www.deadwood.org. Open daily in summer 8am-7pm; in winter 9am-5pm.) Right outside Deadwood is Kevin Costner's new museum **Tatanka: Story of the Bison,** 1 mi. north on Rte. 85, an educational center with a spectacular outdoor sculpture of riders pursuing bison over a cliff. The cafe serves dishes with bison meat for $4-8. (☎605-584-5678; www.storyofthebison.com. Open May 15-Oct. 15 daily 9am-5pm. $6.50, seniors $5.50, children $4.50.)

The chain motels in town are all much more expensive than the **Thunder Cove Inn ❸**, 311 Cliff Ave., off U.S. 85 south of town, which has 30 large rooms with free Wi-Fi and reclining chairs. The inn is located at a Deadwood trolley stop. (☎605-578-3045 or 800-209-7361. Rooms $65-130. D/MC/V.) The **Whistlers Gulch Campground ❷**, off U.S. 85, has a pool, laundry facilities, and showers. (☎605-578-2092 or 800-704-7139; www.whistlergulch.com. Open May-Sept. Sites $22, with full hookup $36. D/MC/V.)

◤ **APPROACHING SUNDANCE: 47 MILES**
Take **U.S. 85 N** to **I-90 W.**

The Equality State
WYOMING
Welcomes You!

SUNDANCE. You won't find a film festival here, but if you know of Butch Cassidy, then surely you've heard of the Sundance Kid. Sundance sits at the southern foot of the Wyoming Black Hills in the shadow of a mountain named **Wi Wacippi Paha** (Temple of the Sioux). The **Crook County Museum and Art Gallery,** 309 Cleveland St., tells the story of several famous people from Crook County. The museum has displays of some items related to these famous men as well as cowboy guns, saddles, branding irons, and the Sundance Kid's court records. (☎307-283-3666. Open M-F 8am-5pm, Sa 8am-noon. Free.) The **Budget Host Arrowhead Motel ❸**, 214 Cleveland St., is the cheapest lodging in town. (☎307-283-3307 or 800-283-4678. Singles $59; doubles $69. AmEx/D/MC/V.) The Black Hills National Forest extends throughout the area, and the **Bearlodge Ranger Station,** 121 S. 21st St., directs visitors to the west. (☎307-283-1361. Open M-F 7:30am-4:30pm.)

◤ **APPROACHING DEVILS TOWER: 30 MILES**
Devils Tower is a short 21 mi. drive from Sundance along **U.S. 14 W.** Turn north onto **Rte. 24,** and follow it 9 mi. to the visitors center.

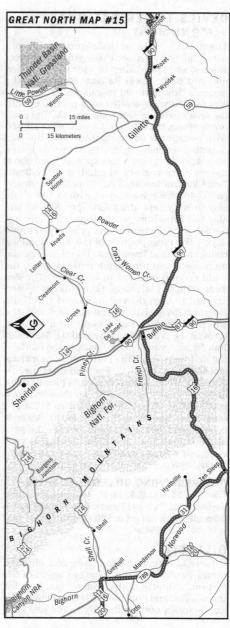

GREAT NORTH MAP #15

0   15 miles

0   15 kilometers

GREAT NORTH

DEVILS TOWER NATIONAL MONUMENT

The massive column that figures so prominently in Native American myths, geological studies, and space alien movies is the centerpiece of **Devils Tower National Monument,** the nation's first national monument. The tower was formed when molten rock pushed up into the area's existing sedimentary rock. The cooling igneous rock formed a tall mass ribbed with hexagonal columns, and when the surrounding sedimentary rock was eroded by the elements, the tower was exposed. Read about the rock and register to climb it at the **Devils Tower Visitors Center,** 3 mi. from the entrance. (☎307-467-5283; www.nps.gov/deto. Open late May to early Sept. daily 8am-7pm; Mar. to late May and Sept.-Nov. usually 9am-5pm. Entrance fee $10 per vehicle or $5 per person, good for 7 days.) The most popular of the several hiking trails, the paved **Tower Trail** (1¼ mi.), loops the monument and provides terrific views of the multi-faceted columns of the tower. The **Red Beds Trail,** a 3 mi. loop, takes hikers up and around the bright red banks of the Belle Fourche River. Hikers can connect with the shorter **Valley View Trail** (½ mi.) for a flat walk through the prairie dog town and the **South Side Trail** (½ mi.), which climbs back to the bluffs of the Red Beds Trail. The park maintains a **campground ❶** near the Belle Fourche River. (☎307-467-5283. Water, bathrooms, grills, picnic tables, and lots of noisy prairie dogs; no showers. Open roughly Apr.-Oct.; call ahead. Sites $12. Cash only.) For hookups, the **Fort Devils Tower ❶** campground, 601 Rte. 24, just outside the park at the intersection of Rte. 24 and 112, is your cheapest option. (☎307-467-5655. Sites with electricity $21, with full hookup $26. MC/V.)

⚑ APPROACHING GILLETTE: 61 MILES
Take **Rte. 24 S** to **U.S. 14 W.** Drive past the scenic Keyhole State Park and Reservoir on your way to the interstate; when you get to **I-90** in Moorcroft, go west until you reach Gillette.

GILLETTE

Gillette is Wyoming's fourth-largest city and proudly calls itself the "Energy Capital of the Nation." Gillette is the commercial hub for the oil, gas, and coal industries, as evinced by the factories outside the city to the east. If it were a country of its own, Campbell County would be the sixth-largest coal-producing nation in the world. ◪**Coal mine tours** are provided by RAG Coal West, Inc., at Eagle Butte Coal Mine. They depart from the Chamber of Commerce, just south of I-90 on S. Douglas Hwy./Rte. 59. (☎307-686-0040 or 800-544-6136. Tours June-Aug. M-F 9, 11am, 1:15pm. Reservations recommended. Free.) The free **Rockpile Museum,** 900 W. 2nd St., rises above the landscape as a symbol of Gillette's history. One hundred years ago it marked the end of the cattle drive for weary cowboys, and today it has exhibits on ranching life. The saddles, rifles, and pioneer items are impressive, as is the video presentation of explosive surface coal mining. (☎307-682-5723. Open June-Aug. M-Sa 9am-7pm, Su 1-5pm; Sept.-Mar. M-Sa 9am-5pm. Free.)

Lula Bell's Cafe ❶, 101 N. Gillette Ave., offers no-frills eatin' alongside customers in cowboy hats. Breakfast doesn't get more basic than "Meat and Eggs" ($6). Later, try the burgers for $5-7 or the chicken-fried steak for $8-10. (☎307-682-9798. Open M-Sa 5am-9pm, Su 5am-5pm. MC/V.)

⚑ APPROACHING BUFFALO: 70 MILES
Between Gillette and Buffalo, jump on **I-90 W.**

BUFFALO. Buffalo has a historic main street dating back to 1804, complete with bronze sculptures, murals, and an old-fashioned soda fountain. The city is home to one of the west's premier frontier-history museums. The **Jim Gatchell Museum,** 100 Fort St., overflows with 15,000 artifacts from Indians, soldiers, and settlers, and features carefully crafted dioramas of local battles. (☎307-684-9331; www.jimgatchell.com. Open mid-Apr. to Dec. daily 9am-6pm. $4, seniors $3, ages 6-17 $2, under 6 free.) Before leaving Buffalo, swing by the **Bighorn National Forest Ranger Office,** 1415 Fort St., where you can obtain maps and information before continuing through the forest to Ten Sleep. (☎307-684-7806. Open M-F 8am-4:30pm.) From the outside, **Grandma's ❷,** 845 Fort St., looks like a motel, but inside is a rustic restaurant that serves comfort food ($8-9), sandwiches ($6-7), and large breakfasts for $5-7. (☎307-684-0713. Open daily 6am-3pm. MC/V.)

⚑ APPROACHING TEN SLEEP: 64 MILES
Take **U.S. 16 W,** otherwise known as the **Cloud Peak Skyway.** Make sure your brakes are in good shape

before attempting the descent into the stunning **Ten Sleep Canyon,** wherein rests the hamlet of Ten Sleep.

TEN SLEEP

Don't rush to get to Ten Sleep; the town is nothing more than a bit of civilization on the far edge of the **Bighorn National Forest** and the **Bighorn Mountains.** Ten Sleep earned its name because it took the Sioux "ten sleeps" to travel from there to their main winter camps. The Bighorns erupt from the hilly pasture land of northern Wyoming, providing a dramatic backdrop for grazing cattle, sprawling ranch houses, and valleys full of wildflowers. Visitors can hike through the woods or follow **U.S. 16** in the south to waterfalls, layers of prehistoric rock, and views above the clouds. Within the forest is the **Cloud Peak Wilderness,** which offers utter solitude. Registration at major trailheads is required to enter the Cloud Peak area. The most convenient access to the wilderness area is from the trailheads off U.S. 16, around 20 mi. west of Buffalo. To get to the top of 13,175 ft. Cloud Peak, most hikers enter at **West Ten Sleep Trailhead,** accessible from Ten Sleep. Thirty-five **campgrounds** (☎877-444-6777; www.reserveusa.com) fill the forest. There is no fee to camp at the uncrowded **Elgin Park Trailhead,** 16 mi. west of Buffalo off U.S. 16, which promises good fishing along with parking and toilets. **Doyle Campground ❶,** near a fish-filled creek, has 19 sites with toilets and water. Drive 26 mi. west of Buffalo on U.S. 16, then south 6 mi. on Hazelton Rd./County Rd. 3—it's a rough ride. (☎307-684-7981. Sites $10. Cash only.) Many other campgrounds line U.S. 16. Campgrounds rarely fill up in the Bighorns, but if they do, free **backcountry camping** is permitted at least 100 yd. from the road. Contact the Bighorn National Forest's Tongue District for more information (☎307-674-2600).

⏷ APPROACHING CODY: 111 MILES

From Ten Sleep, continue on **U.S. 16** for 25 mi. to Worland. Turn right on **N. 10th St.,** which is actually U.S. 16 in disguise. Continue heading northwest for 30 mi. through Manderson to the town of Basin. In Basin, turn left onto **C St.,** which becomes **S.R. 30** as you head west out of town. Follow S.R. 30 for 26 mi.; it will bend sharply to the north (right) at the intersection with C.R. 8 and 40, but stay on S.R. 30 as it passes through Burlington. When the road

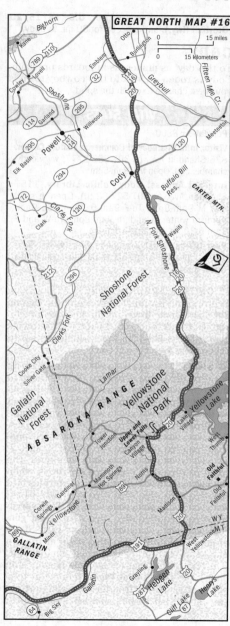

GREAT NORTH MAP #16

GREAT NORTH

dead-ends, turn west (left) on **U.S. 14/16/20 (Greybull Hwy.),** and proceed for 30 mi. to Cody.

CODY

To this day, as numerous billboards proclaim, Cody *is* rodeo—a visit to this cowboy town is your best chance to catch the sport.

VITAL STATS

Population: 8800

Visitor Info: Chamber of Commerce Visitors Center, 836 Sheridan Ave. (☎307-587-2777; www.cody-chamber.org). Open M-F 8am-5pm.

Internet Access: Cody Public Library, 1157 Sheridan Ave. (☎307-527-8820). Open in summer M 9am-8pm, Tu-F 9am-5:30pm, Sa 9am-4pm; in winter M and Th 9am-8pm, Tu-W and F 9am-5:30pm, Sa 9am-4pm. Free.

Post Office: 1301 Stampede Ave. (☎307-527-7161). Open M-F 8am-5:30pm, Sa 9am-noon. **Postal Code:** 82414.

GETTING AROUND. Cody is 54 mi. from Yellowstone National Park along the **Buffalo Bill Cody Scenic Byway,** at the junction of Rte. 120, U.S. 14A, and U.S. 14/16/20. The town's main drag is **Sheridan Ave.,** which turns into **Yellowstone Ave.** west of town.

SIGHTS. Praised for its breathtaking scenery and Western charm, Cody is home to the longest-running rodeo in the US. For 63 straight years, the **Cody Nite Rodeo** has thrilled audiences every night in summer with bucking broncos, fearless bull riders, steer wrestlers, and more. (☎307-527-9453. Shows June-Aug. 8pm, grounds open at 7pm. $16, ages 7-12 $8.) Over the 4th of July weekend, the town attracts the country's cowboys when the **Buffalo Bill Cody Stampede** rough-rides into town. (☎307-587-5155 or 800-207-0744; www.codystampederodeo.com. $18. Reservations recommended.) There are **street gunfights** every afternoon, when 12th St. is blocked off and actors in period attire fire blanks at each other in a noisy, smoky skit. (On 12th St. in front of the Irma Hotel. Daily 6pm.) The **Cody Trolley Tour** offers a 1hr. tour of the city, visiting frontier sites and portraying the Old West. (☎307-527-7043; www.codytrolleytours.com. Tours depart from the Irma Hotel June-Sept. M-Sa 11am, 3, 6pm, Su 11am and 3pm. $18, seniors $16, ages 5-17 $8, under 5 free.) The highlight of town is the ■**Buffalo Bill Historical Center,** 720 Sheridan Ave., a complex of five museums with innovative exhibits and displays. The Buffalo Bill Museum showcases local history, while the Whitney Gallery of Western Art includes pieces by Paxson, Bierstadt, Moran, and Sitting Bull. The complex also includes the Plains Indian Museum, the Draper Museum of Natural History, and the Cody Firearm Museum, which houses over 2700 guns. (☎307-587-4771; www.bbhc.org. Open May to mid-Sept. daily 8am-8pm; Apr. and mid-Sept. to Oct. daily 10am-5pm; Nov.-Mar. Tu-Su 10am-3pm. $15, seniors $13, students $10, ages 5-12 $6.) Six miles west of Cody on U.S. 14/16/20, the **Buffalo Bill Dam** celebrates man's ability to control the flow of water to fit human needs. Built between 1904 and 1910, it measures 350 ft. in height. (☎307-527-6076. Visitors center open daily June-Aug. M-F 8am-8pm, Sa-Su 8am-6pm. Free.) West of the dam, strange rock formations, created millions of years ago by volcanic eruptions in the Absarokas, dot the dusty hillsides.

Rafting trips on the Shoshone provide livelier diversions. To make arrangements, call **Wyoming River Trips,** 233 Yellowstone Hwy./Rte. 14. (☎307-587-6661 or 800-586-6661; www.wyomingrivertrips.com. Open May-Sept. 2hr. trip $26-36; half-day trip $65.) For equine adventures, try **Cedar Mountain Trail Rides,** 1 mi. west of the rodeo grounds on the left. (☎307-527-4966. $25 per hr., $125 per day.)

FOOD AND ACCOMMODATIONS. Wyoming license plates and chile peppers line the walls in the **Noon Break ❶,** 927 12th St., a little chile cafe that's "taming the wild Western pepper." Green or red chile dishes are the best ($3.50-5), but you can also get breakfast, sandwiches ($5.50), or Mexican food. (☎307-587-9720. Open M-Sa 7am-2pm. Cash only.) **Peter's Cafe and Bakery ❶,** at 12th St. and Sheridan Ave., offers cheap breakfasts (3 buttermilk pancakes $4.50) and thick subs from $3.75. (☎307-527-5040. Open M-F 6:45am-8pm, Su 6:45am-4:15pm. MC/V.)

Room rates go up in the summer; the most reasonably priced motels (from around $70 in summer) line **W. Yellowstone Ave.** The **Rainbow Park Motel ❸**, 1136 17th St., has wood-paneled rooms. (☎307-587-6251; www.rainbowpark-motel.com. Open Mar.-Nov. Singles in summer $60-75, in late fall $38-45; doubles $75-90/ $45-60. AmEx/D/MC/V.) On the Western side of town, the **Gateway Motel and Campground ❹**, 203 Yellowstone Ave., has four one-bed cabins with bath, A/C, cable, and free Wi-Fi, and a slightly more expensive motel. (☎307-587-2561; www.gatewaycamp.com. Cabins from $69.) **Buffalo Bill State Park** offers two campgrounds on the Buffalo Bill Reservoir. The **North Shore Bay Campground ❶** is located 9 mi. west of town on U.S. 14/16/20. (☎307-527-6274. Sites $12. Day-use $4. Cash only.)

⚲ APPROACHING YELLOWSTONE NATIONAL PARK: 52 MILES

Follow the **Buffalo Bill Cody Scenic Byway (U.S. 14/ 16/20)** westbound to the **East Entrance** of Yellowstone. Along the way, you'll pass Shoshone Canyon and drive through the Shoshone National Forest.

YELLOWSTONE NATIONAL PARK

Established in 1872, Yellowstone National Park has the distinction of being the first national park in the world. Yellowstone also happens to be the largest active volcano in the world, with over 300 geysers and more than 10,000 geothermal features spewing steam and boiling water—as well as less-than-savory sulfur gases—from beneath the earth's crust. The park's hot springs are popular among local wildlife; bison and elk gather around the thermal basins for warmth and easier grazing during the winter months. Today, Yellowstone is still recovering from extensive wildfires that burned over a third of the park in 1988. The effects are especially evident in the western half of the park, where young saplings rise through a graveyard of charred tree stumps. Despite the fires, Yellowstone retains its rugged beauty. With the reintroduction of wolves in 1995, all of the animals that lived in the Yellowstone area before the arrival of Europeans still roam the landscape, with the exception of the black-footed ferret.

VITAL STATS

Area: 2.2 million acres

Visitor Info: Most regions of the park have their own central visitors centers. All centers offer general info and backcountry permits, but each has distinct hiking and camping regulations and features special regional exhibits. The main visitors center, **Albright** (☎307-344-2263; www.nps.gov/yell), at Mammoth Hot Springs, features exhibits on the history of Yellowstone and the origins of America's National Parks, along with stuffed examples of wildlife. Open daily late May to early Sept. 8am-7pm; early Sept. to May 9am-5pm. The closest visitors center to the East Entrance is **Fishing Bridge** (☎307-242-2450). Open daily late May to Aug. 8am-7pm; Sept. 9am-6pm.

General Park Information: ☎307-344-7381. **Weather:** ☎307-344-2113. **Road Report:** ☎307-344-2117. **Radio Info:** 1610AM.

Gateway Towns: Pahaska (WY) to the east, West Yellowstone (MT) to the west (p. 299), Gardiner (MT) to the north, and Cooke City (MT) to the northeast.

Fees: $25 per vehicle.

▄ GETTING AROUND

Yellowstone is huge; either Rhode Island or Delaware could fit within its boundaries. Yellowstone's roads form a figure-eight, with side roads leading to park entrances and some of the lesser-known attractions. The natural wonders that make the park famous are scattered along the **Upper** and **Lower Loops**. Construction and renovation of roads is ongoing; call ahead (☎307-344-7381) or consult the extremely helpful *Yellowstone Today*, available at the entrances and visitors centers, to find out which sections will be closed during your visit. Travel through the park can be slow regardless of construction. The speed limit is at most 45 mph and is closely radar-patrolled; steep grades, tight curves, and frequent animal crossings can also cause delays.

The bulk of Yellowstone National Park lies in the northwest corner of Wyoming, with slivers in Montana and Idaho. There are five entrances to the park; West Yellowstone, MT, and Gardiner, MT are the most developed entrance points, as they are closest to interstates 15 and 90. The East Entrance to the park is 53 mi. west of Cody along **U.S. 14/16/20.** The southern entrance to the park is bordered by **Grand Teton National Park.** The only road within the park that is open year-round is the northern strip between the North Entrance and Cooke City. All other roads are only open from May through October.

🌀 SIGHTS

Xanterra (☎307-344-7311) organizes tours ($26, under 17 $13), horseback rides (1hr. $33, 2hr. $52), and chuck wagon dinners ($51, ages 5-11 $41). These outdoor activities are expensive, however, and Yellowstone is best explored on foot. Visitors centers give out self-guided-tour pamphlets with maps for each of the park's main attractions ($0.50). Trails to these sights are accessible from the road via walkways, usually extending ¼-1½ mi. from the road.

Yellowstone is set apart from other national parks and forests in the Rockies by its geothermal features—the park protects the largest geothermic area in the world. The bulk of these wonders can be found on the western side of the park between Mammoth Hot Springs in the north and Old Faithful in the south. The most dramatic thermal fissures are the **geysers.** Hot liquid magma close to the surface of the earth superheats water from snow and rain until it boils and bubbles, eventually building up enough pressure to burst violently through the cracks.

While bison-jams and bear-gridlock may make wildlife seem more of a nuisance than an attraction, they afford a unique opportunity to see a number of native species in their natural environment. The best times for viewing are early morning and just before dark, as most animals nap during the hot midday. The road between Tower-Roosevelt and the northeast entrance, in the untamed **Lamar River Valley,** often called the "Serengeti of Yellowstone," is where most of Yellowstone's wolf packs roam. Bison are best spotted between Fishing Bridge and Canyon, and elk between Norris and Canyon. Many visitors

park along the sections of road with sweeping vistas of the floodplains around dusk with binoculars, so get there early if you want a spot. Some species take to the higher elevations in the heat of summer, so travel earlier or later in the season (or hike to higher regions) to find the best viewing .

Yellowstone can be dangerous. While roadside wildlife may look tame, these large beasts are unpredictable and easily startled. Stay at least 75 ft. from any animal, and keep at least 300 ft. between yourself and bears. Both black bears and grizzly bears inhabit Yellowstone; consult a ranger about proper precautions before entering the backcountry. If you should encounter a bear, inform a ranger. Bison, sometimes naively regarded as overgrown cows, can run up to 30 mph; visitors are gored every year. Finally, "widow makers"—dead trees that can fall over at any time, especially during high winds—are always a threat in forests, but are especially common in burn areas.

OLD FAITHFUL AREA. Yellowstone's trademark attraction, 📷**Old Faithful,** is no longer the most predictable or largest of the large geysers, but its high frequency has consistently pleased audiences since its discovery in 1870. Eruptions usually shoot 100-190 ft. in the air, occurring every 45min. to 2hr. (average 90min.) and lasting about 1½-5min. Predictions for the next eruption, usually accurate to within 10min., are posted at the Old Faithful Visitors Center. (Open late Apr. to late May daily 9am-5pm; late May to early Nov. 8am-7pm.) Old Faithful lies in the **Upper Geyser Basin,** 16 mi. south of the Madison area and 20 mi. west of Grant Village. This area has the largest concentration of geysers in the world, and boardwalks connect them all. The spectacular rainbow spectrum of **Morning Glory Pool** is an easy 1½ mi. hike from Old Faithful, and provides up-close-and-personal views of hundreds of hydrothermal features along the way, including the tallest predictable geyser in the world, **Grand Geyser,** and the graceful **Riverside Geyser,** which spews at a 60° angle across the Firehole River. Between Old Faithful and Madison, along the

Firehole River, lie the **Midway Geyser Basin** and the **Lower Geyser Basin.** The **Excelsior Geyser Crater,** a large, steaming lake created by a powerful geyser blast, and the **Grand Prismatic Spring,** the largest hot spring in the park, are both located in the Midway Geyser Basin. The basin is about 5 mi. north of Old Faithful and worth the trip. Two miles north is the less developed but still thrilling **Firehole Lake Drive,** a 2 mi. side loop through hot lakes, springs, and dome geysers. Eight miles north of Old Faithful gurgles the **Fountain Paint Pot,** a bubbling pool of hot, milky white, brown, and grey mud. Four types of geothermal activity present in Yellowstone (geysers, mudpots, hot springs, and fumaroles) are found along the trails of the Firehole River. There's a temptation to wash off the grime of camping in the hot water, but swimming in the hot springs is prohibited. You can swim in the **Firehole River,** near Firehole Canyon Dr., south of Madison Junction. Prepare for chilly water; the name of the river is deceptive.

NORRIS GEYSER BASIN. Fourteen miles north of Madison and 21 mi. south of Mammoth, the colorful Norris Geyser Basin is both the oldest and the hottest active thermal zone in the park. The geyser has been spewing water and steam at temperatures up to 459°F for over 115,000 years. The area has a ½ mi. northern **Porcelain Basin** loop and a 1½ mi. southern **Back Basin** loop. **Echinus,** in the Back Basin, is the largest known acidic geyser, with a pH similar to vinegar; it erupts 40-60 ft. every 1-4hr. Its neighbor, **Steamboat,** is the tallest active geyser in the world, erupting over 300 ft. for anywhere from 3-40min. Steamboat's eruptions, however, are entirely unpredictable; the last eruption occurred in 2002, after two years of inactivity.

 Beware: the crust around many of Yellowstone's thermal basins, geysers, and hot springs is thin, and boiling, acidic water lies just beneath the surface. Stay on the marked paths and boardwalks at all times. In the backcountry, keep a good distance from hot springs and fumaroles.

MAMMOTH HOT SPRINGS. The hot spring terraces resemble huge wedding cakes at Mammoth Hot Springs, 21 mi. to the north of the Norris Basin and 19 mi. west of Tower in the northwest corner of the upper loop. Shifting water sources, malleable travertine limestone deposits, and temperature-sensitive, multi-colored bacterial growth create the most rapidly changing natural structure in the park. The **Upper Terrace Drive,** 2 mi. south of Mammoth Visitors Center, winds 1½ mi. through colorful springs and rugged travertine limestone ridges and terraces. When visiting, ask a ranger where to find the most active springs, as they vary in intensity from year to year. Some go dormant for decades, their structures gradually crumbling, only to revive unexpectedly to build new domes and cascades. In recent years, **Canary Spring,** on the south side of the main terrace, has been expanding into virgin forest, killing trees and bushes in its path. Inquire at ranger stations about area trails that provide wildlife viewing. **Swimming** is permitted in the **Boiling River,** 2½ mi. north, where a hot spring flows into the Gardner River.

GRAND CANYON. The east side's featured attraction, the ▓**Grand Canyon of the Yellowstone,** wears rusty red and orange hues created by hot water running over the rock. The canyon is 800-1200 ft. deep and 1500-4000 ft. wide. For a close-up view of the mighty **Lower Falls** (308 ft.), hike down the short, steep **Uncle Tom's Trail** (over 300 steps). **Artist Point,** on the southern rim, and **Lookout Point,** on the northern rim, offer broader canyon vistas and are accessible from the road between Canyon and Fishing Bridge. Keep an eye out for bighorn sheep along the canyon's rim. **Stagecoach rides** along the canyon are available at Roosevelt Lodge. (☎ 307-344-7311. June-Sept. $9.25, ages 2-11 $7.50.)

YELLOWSTONE LAKE AREA. Situated in the southeast corner of the park, **Yellowstone Lake** is the largest high-altitude lake in North America and a protective sanctuary for cutthroat trout. While the surface of the lake may appear calm, geologists have found geothermal features at the bottom. Geysers and hot springs in **West Thumb** dump 3100 gal. of water into the lake per day. Notwithstanding this thermal boost, the temperature of the lake remains quite cold, averaging 45°F during the summer. Visitors to the park once cooked trout on fishing lines in the boiling water of the **Fishing Cone** in the West Thumb central basin, but this is no longer permitted. Along the same loop on the west side of the lake, check out the **Thumb Paint Pots,** a field of puffing miniature mud volcanoes and chimneys. On the northern edge of the lake is the rustic **Fishing Bridge,** where fishing has been prohibited in an effort to help the endangered native trout. The sulphurous odors of **Mud Volcano,** 6 mi. north of Fishing Bridge, can be distinguished from miles away, but the turbulent mudpots, caused by the creation of hydrogen sulfide gas by bacteria working on the naturally-occurring sulfur in the spring water, are worth the assault on your nose. The unusual geothermal mudpots, with their rhythmic belching, acidic waters, and cavernous openings, have appropriately medieval names, such as **Dragon's Mouth, Sour Lake,** and **Black Dragon's Cauldron.**

◪ OUTDOORS

Most visitors to Yellowstone never get out of their cars and therefore miss out on over 1200 mi. of trails in the park. Options for exploring Yellowstone's more pristine areas range from short day hikes to long backcountry trips. When planning a hike, pick up a **topographical trail map** ($9-10 at any visitors center or general store) and ask a ranger to describe the network of trails. Visitors centers also have day-hike pamphlets for each major park area. Some trails are poorly marked, so be sure of your skill with a map and compass before setting off on more obscure paths. The 1988 fires scarred over a third of the park; hikers should consult rangers and maps about which areas were damaged. Burned areas have less shade, so pack hats, extra water, and sunscreen.

In addition to the self-guided trails at major attractions, many worthwhile sights are only a few miles off the main road. The **Fairy Falls Trail** (5¼ mi., 2½hr. round-trip), 3 mi. north of Old Faithful, provides a unique perspective on the Midway Geyser Basin and up-close views of 200 ft. high Fairy Falls. This easy round-trip trail begins in the parking lot marked Fairy Falls just south of Midway Geyser Basin. A more strenuous option is to follow the trail beyond the falls up **Twin Buttes,** a 650 ft. elevation gain, which turns this trail into a moderate, 4hr. round-trip

hike. The **Natural Bridge** (1 mi., easy) trailhead is located just south of the Bridge Bay Campground. The trail to the top of **Mount Washburn** (5½ mi., 4hr. round-trip; 1380 ft. elevation gain) is enhanced by an enclosed observation area with sweeping views of the park's central environs, including the patchwork of old and new forests and herds of bighorn sheep. This trail begins at Chittenden Rd. parking area, 10 mi. north of Canyon Village, or Dunraven Pass, 6 mi. north of Canyon Village. A more challenging climb to the top of **Avalanche Peak** (4 mi., 4hr.; final elevation 10,568 ft.) starts 8 mi. west of the East Entrance on East Entrance Rd. A steep ascent up several switchbacks opens to stunning panoramas out over Yellowstone Lake and the southern regions of the park, west to the Continental Divide and east to Shoshone National Forest. Wildlife-viewing opportunities in this area are superb. There are dozens of extended backcountry trips in the park, including treks to the Black Canyon of the Yellowstone, in the north-central region, and to isolated Heart Lake in the south.

Fishing and **boating** are both allowed within the park. Permits are required for fishing which is catch-and-release only. (Fishing permits $15 per 3 days, $20 per week; ages 12-15 free.) In addition to Yellowstone Lake, popular fishing spots include the Madison and Firehole Rivers; the Firehole is available for fly-fishing only. To go boating or even floating on the lake, you'll need a **boating permit,** available at backcountry offices (check *Yellowstone Today*), Bridge Bay marina, and the South, West, and Northeast entrances to the park. (Motorized vessel permit $10 per week; nonmotorized boats $5.) **Xanterra** rents row boats, outboards, and dockslips at Bridge Bay Marina. (☎307-344-7311. Mid-June to early Sept. Rowboats $9.50 per hr., $43 per 8hr.; outboards $45 per hr.; dockslips $15-20 per night.)

▨ FOOD

Buying food in the park can be expensive; stick to **general stores** at each lodging location. The stores at Fishing Bridge, Lake Village, Grant Village, and Canyon Village sell lunch counter-style food. (Open daily 7:30am-9pm, but times may vary.) For other restaurants, see West Yellowstone (p. 299).

Grizzly Pad Grill and Cabins, 315 Main St. (☎406-838-2161), on Rte. 212 on the eastern side of Cooke City. Try the Grizzly Pad Special—a milkshake, fries, and large cheeseburger ($8). Alternatively, pick up a sack lunch ($8). Open late May to mid-Oct. daily 7am-9pm; Jan. to mid-Apr. hours vary. MC/V. ❷

Ka-Bar Restaurant (☎406-848-9995), on U.S. 89 just as it enters Gardiner. Wash down meat-laden pizzas (8 in. $6.25) with cheap pints ($2-3). Don't let the rustic exterior fool you; this is one of the tastiest and most filling places to enjoy dinner after a romp in the park. Open daily 11am-10pm. MC/V. ❶

Helen's Corral Drive-In (☎406-848-7627), a few blocks north on U.S. 89, in Gardiner. Rounds up super ½ lb. buffalo burgers and pork chop sandwiches ($5-8) in a lively atmosphere. Open in summer daily 11am-10pm. Cash only. ❶

The Miner's Saloon, 108 Main St. (☎406-838-2214), on Rte. 212 in downtown Cooke City. The best place to go for a frosty Moose Drool beer ($3). Tasty burgers and fish tacos $6-7. Sa-Su live music. Open daily noon-2am. Kitchen closes 10pm. Cash only. ❷

ACCOMMODATIONS

The park's high season extends from mid-June to mid-September. Lodging within the park can be hard to come by on short notice, but is sometimes a better deal than the motels along the outskirts of the park. During peak months, the cost of a motel room can skyrocket to $100, while in-park lodging remains relatively inexpensive. **Xanterra** controls all accommodations within the park, employing a code to distinguish between cabins: "Roughrider" means no bath, no facilities; "Budget" offers a sink; "Pioneer" has a shower, toilet, and sink; "Frontier" is bigger and more plush; and "Western" is the biggest and most comfortable. Public facilities are available near cabins that lack private baths. (☎307-344-7311; www.travelyellowstone.com. Reservations strongly recommended. AmEx/D/MC/V.)

Old Faithful Inn, 30 mi. southeast of the West Yellowstone entrance, between Madison and Grant on the lower loop. In the heart of key attractions and a masterpiece unto itself. Admire the 6-story central lobby and stone fireplace from numerous balconies and stairways, all built of solid tree trunks. Constructed in 1904 by architect Robert Reamer as an embodiment of the natural surroundings, it is the quintessential example of "parkitecture." Open mid-May to mid-Sept. Budget cabins $62; Frontier cabins $96; hotel rooms from $85, with bath from $109. ❸

Roosevelt Lodge, in the northeast portion of the upper loop, 19 mi. north of Canyon Village. A favorite of Teddy Roosevelt, who seems to have frequented every motel and saloon west of the Mississippi. The lodge provides scenic accommodations and is located in a relatively isolated section of the park. Open June to early Sept. Roughrider cabins with wood-burning stoves $59; Frontier cabins with bath $96. ❸

Canyon Lodge and Cabins, in Canyon Village, overlooking the Grand Canyon of Yellowstone. Less authentic than Roosevelt's cabins, but centrally located and more popular with tourists. Open early June to mid-Sept. Pioneer cabins $61; Frontier cabins $85; Western cabins $123-132. ❸

Mammoth Hot Springs, on the northwest part of the upper loop near the north entrance. A good base for early-morning wildlife-viewing excursions in the Lamar Valley to the east. Open early May to mid-Oct. Budget cabins $68; Frontier cabins (some with porches) from $96; hotel rooms $76, with bath $102. ❸

Lake Lodge Cabins, 4 mi. south of Fishing Bridge, southeast corner of the lower loop. A cluster of cabins from the 1920s and 50s, all close to Yellowstone Lake. Open mid-June to late Sept. Pioneer cabins $61; Western cabins $123. Next door, **Lake Yellowstone Hotel and Cabins** has yellow Frontier cabins with bath but no lake view for $103. ❸

CAMPING

Campsites fill quickly during the summer months. Call Park Headquarters (☎307-344-7381) for info on campsite vacancies. Permits for backcountry camping must be obtained in person no more than 48hr. in advance from a ranger station. You can reserve a permit beginning in April of the year in question by filling out a "trip planning worksheet" and mailing it, along with a $20 fee, to the **Central Backcountry Office,** in Mammoth next to the visitors center, P.O. Box 168, Yellowstone National

Park 82190. (☎307-344-2160. Open daily 8am-5pm.) The seven **National Park Service campgrounds** ❶ do not accept advance reservations. During the summer, these smaller campgrounds generally fill by 10am, and finding a site can be frustrating. Their popularity arises from their stunning locations; most are well worth the effort to secure a spot. Two of the most beautiful campgrounds are **Slough Creek Campground,** 10 mi. northeast of Tower Junction (29 sites; vault toilets; open June-Oct.; $12; cash only) and **Pebble Creek Campground** (32 sites; vault toilets; no RVs; open early June to late Sept.; $12; cash only). Both are located in the northeast corner of the park, between Tower Falls and the Northeast Entrance, and offer relatively isolated sites and good fishing. Travelers in the southern end of the park might try **Lewis Lake,** halfway between West Thumb and the South Entrance, a rugged campground with several walk-in tent sites that tend to fill up late in the day, if at all. (85 sites. Vault toilets. Open mid-June to early Nov. Sites $12. Cash only.) **Tower Falls,** between the Northeast Entrance and Mammoth Hot Springs, has sites situated atop a hills, with fine views over mountain meadows. (32 sites. Vault toilets. Open mid-May to late Sept. Sites $12. Cash only.) **Norris** (116 sites; water and flush toilets; open late May to late Sept.; $12); **Indian Creek,** between the Norris Geyser Basin and Mammoth Hot Springs (75 sites; vault toilets; open mid-June to mid-Sept.; $12; cash only); and **Mammoth** (85 sites; water and flush toilets; $14; cash only) are less scenic but still great places to camp. The lodges at Mammoth and Old Faithful have showers, but no laundry facilities.

Xanterra ❶ runs five of the 12 developed campgrounds within the park (all sites $17, except Fishing Bridge RV, $34; AmEx/D/MC/V). **Canyon,** with 272 spacious sites on forested hillsides, is the most pleasant, while **Madison,** with 277 sites on the banks of the Firehole River, has the advantage of being in the heart of the park's western attractions. **Grant Village** (425 sites) and **Bridge Bay** (432 sites), both near the shores of Yellowstone Lake, are relatively open with little vegetation to provide privacy except at the small tent sites. Finally, **Fishing Bridge RV** (RVs only) provides closely packed parking spots for the larger motor homes and those desiring full hookups. Canyon, Grant Village, and Fishing Bridge RV have showers ($3; towel rental $0.75) and coin laundry facilities (open daily 7am-9pm). All five sites have flush toilets, water, and dump stations. (Advance reservations ☎307-344-7311, same-day 307-344-7901. Campgrounds usually open mid-May to early Oct., though Canyon has the shortest season, mid-June to mid-Sept. The two largest Xanterra campgrounds, Grant Village and Bridge Bay, are the best bet for last-minute reservations.)

⊠ DETOUR
GRAND TETON NATIONAL PARK
Head out of Yellowstone's South Entrance via the John D. Rockefeller Jr. Memorial Parkway (U.S. 89), which runs for 7½ mi. to the adjacent park.

The Teton Range is the youngest in the entire Rocky Mountain system. Glaciers more than 2000 ft. thick sculpted the jagged peaks, carved U-shaped valleys, and gouged out Jenny, Leigh, and Phelps lakes. Though the Shoshone Indians called them the "hoary-headed fathers," French trappers dubbed the three most prominent peaks—South Teton, Grand Teton, and Middle Teton—"les trois tetons," meaning "the three breasts." Admission to Grand Teton is included with the Yellowstone entrance fee, and the park is usually less crowded than its more-famous northern neighbor. Traveling south from Yellowstone along the eastern shore of **Jackson Lake,** the **Colter Bay Visitor Center and Indian Arts Museum,** is on the right about 10 mi. past the park entrance. In addition to providing maps and information, the center displays an array of Native American objects. (☎307-739-3594; www.nps.gov/grte. Open daily late May to early Sept. 8am-7pm; early May to late May and early Sept.-Oct. 8am-5pm.) One of the most famous views of the mountains is across **Jenny Lake,** off Teton Park Rd. in the middle of the park. Jenny Lake Overlook offers classic Teton views, including Mount Teewinot, and many of the park's best hiking trails depart from the vicinity of the **Jenny Lake Visitor Center,** next to the Jenny Lake Campground at the southeastern corner of Jenny Lake. (☎307-739-3343. Open mid-May to early Sept. daily 8am-7pm; early to late Sept. daily 8am-5pm.) The popular **Jenny Lake Loop** (6¾ mi. round-trip, 4hr.) is an easy trail that connects to more difficult trails, including the moderate **Inspiration Point** (5¾ mi. round-trip, 4hr., moderate) and the strenuous **Cascade Canyon** trail to **Lake Solitude** (18½ mi. round-trip, 10 hr., 2252 ft. elevation change). For those with limited time or limited desire to hike, **Signal Mountain Road** (accessible from Teton Park Rd.

just south of the Signal Mountain Lodge) offers stunning vistas of the park.

Cheap eats can be found at the **John Colter Cafe Court** ❸, in Colter Bay. (☎307-543-2811. Breakfast $3-6. Lunch $6-10. Dinner $8-18. Open daily 6:30am-10pm. D/MC/V.) The park's accommodations are managed by the **Grand Teton Lodge Company** (☎800-628-9988; http://gtlcreservations.com). An affordable option is **Colter Bay Village,** which has 66 tent cabins and 166 log cabins near Jackson Lake. (☎800-628-9988. Open late May to early Oct. Tent cabins $39; log cabins from $77. MC/V.) Five of the park's seven **campgrounds** are filled on a first come, first served basis (☎307-739-3603). **Signal Mountain** ❶, off Teton Park Rd. on the shores of Jackson Lake, has wooded sites with lake access and mountain views. (☎307-543-2831. 81 sites. Marina and camp store. Fills by 10am. Open mid-May to mid-Oct. Sites $15. AmEx/D/MC/V.) Latecomers can almost always find a site at **Gros Ventre** ❶, in the southeast corner of the park. (☎800-628-9988. 360 sites. Dump station. Sites $15. MC/V.)

PHOTO OP. Replicate photographer Ansel Adams's classic view of the Snake River and Tetons at the ◪**Snake River Overlook,** on U.S. 91.

🔢 APPROACHING WEST YELLOWSTONE
When you're ready to leave the park, continue north along **Rte. 89,** or head west to the Tower Roosevelt area, then south to **Canyon Village,** the Grand Canyon of Yellowstone. Continue west from Canyon Village along **U.S. 287/20** to exit the park through the **West Yellowstone** exit.

WEST YELLOWSTONE

Much of West Yellowstone is, unsurprisingly, park-oriented. The **Yellowstone Historic Center,** 104 Yellowstone Ave., on the corner of Can-

yon St., has extensive exhibits on park flora and fauna, earthquakes, fires, and historical development. See old "Snaggletooth," a favorite former Grizzly resident, and watch a riveting video on the 1988 fires. (☎406-646-1100. Open mid-May to mid-Oct. daily 9am-9pm. $6, seniors $5, students and children $4.) In the likely event that you didn't see them in the park, the **Grizzly and Wolf Discover Center,** 201 S. Canyon St., gives visitors an opportunity view the legendary grizzly bear and gray wolf. The center is home to bears and wolves that are unable to survive on their own in the wild. The animals are most active early and late in the day, so plan your visit accordingly. (☎800-257-2570; www.grizzlydiscoverctr.org. Open June-Aug. daily 8am-8:30pm; Sept. reduced hours. $8, ages 6-12 $4, under 6 free.)

Stockpile provisions at the **Food Round-Up Grocery Store,** 107 Dunraven St. (☎406-646-7501. Open daily in summer 7am-10pm; in winter 7am-9pm. MC/V.) The **Timberline Cafe** ❸, 135 Yellowstone Ave., prepares travelers for a day tromping through the park with large soup-and-salad ($5.75) and potato ($7.50) bars, as well as homemade pies ($4 per slice). For a high-energy meal with all the fixin's, chow down on the homestyle chicken-fried steak with soup and salad for $14. (☎406-646-9349. Breakfast $5-10. Lunch $6-9. Dinner $12-24. Open daily 6:30am-10pm. AmEx/D/MC/V.) At the **Gusher Pizza & Sandwich Shoppe** ❷, at the corner of Madison and Dunraven, food is only half of the fun—partake of the full video game room, pool tables, and casino. (☎406-646-9050. Open daily 11:30am-10:30pm. D/MC/V.)

The **West Yellowstone International Hostel** ❶, 139 Yellowstone Ave., at the **Madison Hotel,** provides some of the best indoor budget accommodations around the park. The friendly staff and welcoming lobby make travelers feel right at home. (☎800-838-7745. Internet $5 per hr. Open late May to mid-Oct. Dorms $23, nonmembers $25; singles and doubles $33-42. Motel rooms from $65. AmEx/D/MC/V.) The **Lazy G Motel** ❸, 123 Hayden St., has 15 spacious 1970s-style rooms with queen-size beds, refrigerators, Wi-Fi, and cable TV. (☎406-646-7586. Reservations recommended. Open May-Mar. Singles $56; doubles $69. D/MC/V.)

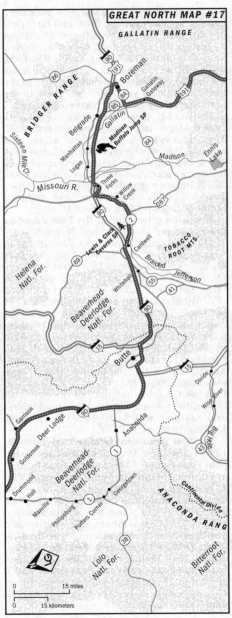

⬐ DETOUR
BIG SKY
1 Lone Mountain Trail. Off U.S. 191 45 mi. south of Bozeman.

The world-class ski area **Big Sky** has over 150 trails and short lift lines. The Lone Peak trams reach an altitude of 11,166 ft. for extreme skiing options. (☎ 800-548-4486; www.bigskyresort.com. Open mid-Nov. to mid-Apr. daily 9am-4pm. Lift tickets $69, ages 14-21 $48, seniors $30, ages 11-13 $25. Rentals $28, under 21 $20. Snowboards $35.) In summer, scenic **lift rides** soar up Big Sky. (Open mid-June to early Oct. daily 9:45am-4:30pm. $16, seniors $10, ages 11-17 $9, under 10 free.) Full suspension mountain bike rentals are also available, and include lift ($37 per hr., $75 for 8hr.).

▶ APPROACHING BOZEMAN: 89 MILES
From West Yellowstone, take **U.S. 191/287 N** to Bozeman through Yellowstone's northwestern corner and the Gallatin National Forest.

BOZEMAN
Surrounded by world-class hiking, skiing, and fishing, Having recently become a magnet for outdoor enthusiasts, Bozeman gives off a hip and youthful Western vibe.

VITAL STATS

Population: 27,500

Visitor Info: Bozeman Chamber of Commerce (☎406-586-5421; www.bozemanchamber.com), 1003 N. 7th Ave. Open M-F 8am-5pm.

Internet Access: Bozeman Public Library, 220 E. Lamme St. (☎406-582-2400). Open M-Th 10am-8pm, F-Sa 10am-5pm. Free.

Post Office: 32 E. Babcock St. (☎406-586-2373). Open M-F 9am-5pm. **Postal Code:** 59715.

⬐ GETTING AROUND. I-90/U.S. 191 enters Bozeman from the southeast, and U.S. 191 splits off to become **Main St.** in town. Main St. runs east-west, and has major intersections with **Rte. 86, 7th Ave.,** and **19th Ave. (Rte. 412).**

◐ ⚠ SIGHTS AND OUTDOORS. Get friendly with dinosaurs and other artifacts of Rocky Mountain history at the **Museum of the Rockies,** 600 West Kagy Blvd., near the university. Dr. Jack Horner (the model for *Jurassic Park*'s Alan Grant) and other paleontologists make this their base for excavating prehistoric remains throughout the West. See the world's largest *T. rex* skull and a Rube Goldberg-like machine that demonstrates Earth's energy cycles. (☎406-994-3466; www.montana.edu/wwwmor. Open in summer daily 8am-8pm; in winter M-Sa 9am-5pm, Su 12:30-5pm. $9.50, ages 5-18 $6.50.) Standing on the site of the old county jail, **The Pioneer Museum,** 317 W. Main St., offers a look at the gallows and jail cells, along with an account of early Bozeman history. (☎406-522-8122; www.pioneermuseum.org. Open mid-May to mid-Sept. M-Sa 10am-5pm; mid-Sept. to mid-May Tu-Sa 11am-4pm. $3, under 12 free.)

The warm, shallow **Madison River** makes tubing a popular, relaxing, and cheap way to pass long summer days. Rent tubes ($4-15) at **Big Boys Toys,** 28670 Norris Rd. (☎406-587-4747; www.bigboystoysrentals.com. Canoes $30 per day. Open daily 8am-6pm.) **Montana Whitewater** shoots the rapids of the Gallatin River, 7 mi. north of the Big Sky area on U.S. 191. Trips meet at the office, between mileposts 55 and 56 on U.S. 191. (☎800-348-4376; www.montanawhitewater.com. Half-day $45, children $35; full day $77/$62.)

◤ FOOD. Affordable eateries aimed at the college crowd line **W. College St.** near the university. Now a popular chain throughout Montana, the original **Pickle Barrel ❶** resides at 809 W. College St. Enormous sandwiches with fresh ingredients and free pickles have drawn MSU students for years. (☎406-587-2411. Hefty 9 in. sandwiches $5.25-6. Open daily in summer 10:30am-10pm; in winter 11am-10:30pm. Cash only.) The quirky **Cateye Cafe ❸**, 23 N. Tracy Ave., is popular among locals and the college crowd, serving an eclectic melange of sandwiches and entrees ($7-16). Try the Melazane Sammy, with eggplant and mozzarella, for $7.75. (☎406-587-8655. Open M and W 7am-2:30pm, Th-F 7am-2:30pm and 5-9pm, Sa 7am-2pm and 5-9pm, Su 7am-2pm. MC/V.) **La Parrilla ❷**, 1533 W. Babcock St., wraps up just about everything in their giant 1 ft. tortillas ($5-9), including homemade barbecue, fiery jambalaya, and fresh seafood. (☎406-582-9511. Open daily 11am-9pm. AmEx/D/MC/V.)

◤ ACCOMMODATIONS. Budget motels line **Main St.** and **7th Ave.** north of Main. **Bozeman**

Backpacker's Hostel ❶, 405 W. Olive St., has a kitchen, three dogs, and the cheapest beds in town. (☎406-586-4659. Laundry facilities. Dorms $18; private rooms with shared bath $38.) In the heart of downtown, the **Imperial Inn ❷** offers rooms with A/C, cable TV, free Wi-Fi, and a computer in the lobby. (☎406-586-3354; www.innbozeman.com. Singles in summer $49, in winter $39; doubles $59/49. AmEx/D/MC/V.) The **Bear Canyon Campground ❶**, 4 mi. east of Bozeman at Exit 313 off I-90, has great views of the surrounding mountain ranges. (☎800-438-1575. Laundry, showers, and pool. Open May to mid-Oct. Sites $15, with water and electricity $13, with full hookup $28. D/MC/V.)

◤ NIGHTLIFE. Get the lowdown on music and nightlife from the weekly *Tributary* or *The BoZone*. Locals and travelers thirsty for good beer and great live music head over to the **◤Zebra Cocktail Lounge,** 320 E. Main St., in the basement at Rouse Ave. The large selection of beers and the hipster atmosphere always draw a young, cool crowd. (☎406-585-8851. W-Sa DJ or bands. Open daily 8pm-2am. AmEx/D/MC/V with $10 min.) The **Rocking R Bar,** 211 E. Main St., offers hot drink specials every night. (☎406-587-9355. Happy hour Tu-Th 5-9pm. Open daily 11am-1:30am. D/MC/V.) Often voted the best bar in Bozeman, **Montana Ale Works,** 601 E. Main St., offers over 30 microbrews. (☎406-587-7700. Open daily 4pm-midnight. Kitchen closes 11pm. AmEx/D/MC/V.)

◤ DETOUR
LIVINGSTON
26 mi. east of Bozeman off I-90.

Surrounded by three renowned trout fishing rivers—Yellowstone, Madison, and Gardiner—the small town of Livingston is an angler's heaven; the film *A River Runs Through It* was shot here and in Bozeman. Livingston's Main St. features a strip of early 20th-century buildings, including bars (with gambling), restaurants, and fishing outfitters. If fishing's your thing, **Dan Bailey's,** 209 W. Park St. in Livingston, sells licenses and rents gear. (☎406-222-1673 or 800-356-4052. Open in summer M-Sa 7am-7pm, Su 7am-noon; in winter M-Sa 8am-6pm. 2-day fishing license $25. Rod and reel $20; waders and boots $15.)

⊠ DETOUR
LEWIS AND CLARK CAVERNS
20 mi. from Three Forks on Rte. 2.

At **Lewis and Clark Caverns ❶**, visitors can take a tour of the extensive limestone and calcite caves. The 2 mi. tour has steep grades, and stooping and bending are required to descend the 600 steps into the caverns. Be sure to dress warmly; temperatures in the caverns hover around 50°F year-round. Aboveground camping is also available. (☎ 406-287-3541. Tours May-Sept. daily 9:15am-6:30pm. $10, ages 6-11 $5. MC/V.)

⋒ APPROACHING BUTTE: 91 MILES
Take **I-90 W** about 30 mi. to the **Three Forks** exit, and continue west along **Rte. 2.**

BUTTE
"A mile high, a mile deep, and a mile wide" is a popular expression about Butte; the city perches 1 mi. high in the Rocky Mountains. One nearby mine reaches 1 mi. deep, and another, the Berkeley Pit, is 1 mi. wide. The ⊠**World Museum of Mining,** 155 Museum Way, presents a realistic look at a mining camp in the 1880s. Located on the site of the silver and zinc **Orphan Girl Mine,** the 22-acre museum presents the history of mining in exhibits on rock mining and includes Hell Roarin' Gulch, a town lined with over 50 reconstructed mining camp businesses. Daily tours circle the museum on the Orphan Girl Express mini train, pulled by a 1911 tram engine. Also available is a 1hr. underground tour into the mine itself with a professional miner who demonstrates mining techniques. (☎ 406-723-7211; www.miningmuseum.org. Open in summer M-W and Su 9am-5:30pm, Th-Sa 9am-9pm; in winter daily 9am-5:30pm. $7, seniors $6, ages 13-18 $5, ages 5-12 $2. Mine tour $10, students and seniors $8.) The **Mineral Museum,** 1300 W. Park St., located on the Montana Tech Campus, displays classic mineral specimens from Butte's underground mines, as well as a 27½ troy-ounce gold nugget and a 400 lb. smoky quartz crystal called "Big Daddy." (☎ 406-496-4414. Open Memorial Day to Labor Day 9am-6pm; May and Sept.-Oct. M-F 9am-4pm, Sa-Su 1-5pm; Nov.-Apr. M-F 9am-4pm. Free.) The **Mai Wah Museum,** 17

W. Mercury St., was built in honor of the Chinese miners who came to Butte to work the mines. (☎ 406-723-6731; www.maiwah.org. Open Memorial Day to Labor Day Tu-Sa 11am-5pm.) Visible as a tiny dot to the east of Butte, **Our Lady of the Rockies,** seated on the Continental Divide, is the tallest Madonna statue in America at 90 ft.; her "gaze" overlooks peaks and valleys for nearly 100 mi. Bus tours to her base leave daily from the Butte Plaza Mall at 3100 Harrison Ave. (☎ 800-800-5239; www.ourladyoftherockies.org. 2½hr. tours June-Sept.; 2-3 per day. Call for times. $12, seniors $10, ages 13-17 $9, under 13 $5.)

What mining town would be complete without pasties? Get yours at **Park Street Pasties ❶**, 800 W. Park St., for $3.50. (☎ 406-782-6400. Open M-F 8am-6pm. AmEx/D/MC/V.) Located in the historic Uptown district of Butte, the **Finlen Hotel and Motor Inn ❸**, 100 E. Broadway, was opened in 1924 and has been in constant operation ever since. These hotel rooms once housed Copper Kings; they now provide lodging for nostalgic visitors. (☎ 800-729-5461; www.finlen.com. Singles $48-52; doubles $58-68. AmEx/D/MC/V.)

⋒ APPROACHING DEER LODGE: 37 MILES
Hop on **I-90 W** to Deer Lodge.

DEER LODGE
Nestled within a sheltered valley, Deer Lodge has always offered gold seekers, ranchers, and settlers the opportunity for a good life. The trout-filled waters of the Clark Fork, Little Blackfoot, Nevada Creek Reservoir, and Blackfoot Rivers all flow through the area. Today, the town is home to the **Old Prison Museums** complex, a collection of four museums plus other free exhibits. The **Frontier Museum,** 1153 Main St., has the largest display of cowboy collectibles between Cody and Calgary and the largest collection of (empty) whiskey bottles this side of Kentucky. While still a territory, Montana chose Deer Lodge to hold its prison, and very slowly constructed it by inmate labor. Today, you can incarcerate yourself in the ⊠ **Old Montana Prison,** 1160 Main St. The fortress held at least one member of Butch Cassidy's Wild Bunch, and is the final resting place of the "galloping gallows,"

Montana's official mobile gallows until they outlawed hanging in the late 1990s. The **Montana Auto Museum,** 1160 Main St., showcases over 120 classic cars. The collection is sure to make a motorhead drool; offerings include Model Ts, Model As, V-8 Fords, a DeSoto Air-Flow, a 1929 Hudson, and a 1903 Ford. Across the street from the Prison, the **Yesterday's Playthings Museum** is Montana's foremost doll and toy museum. (☎406-846-3111; www.pcmaf.org. Prison and Auto museums open daily in summer 8am-8pm; in winter 8:30am-5pm. Frontier and Playthings museums open daily in summer 8am-6pm; in winter 8:30am-5pm. 1½hr. tours daily in summer 10am and 2pm. Each museum $6, ages 10-15 $5; all museums $9/$5.)

◪ DETOUR
GARNET GHOST TOWN
Take Bear Gulch Rd. north from I-90/U.S.12, and follow the signs.

Montana's history claims more than 600 mining camps and towns, many of which vanished almost as quickly as they had appeared when inhabitants fled, following rumors of other strikes. Visit Garnet to see Montana's best-preserved ghost town, once a mining camp. (☎406-522-3856; www.montana.com/ghosttown. $3, under 16 free.)

 DID YOU KNOW? The tiny town of Ismay (pop. 26) temporarily changed its name to **Joe, Montana** in 1993 to honor the professional football player.

◪ APPROACHING MISSOULA: 81 MILES
Take **I-90/U.S 12 W** toward Missoula.

MISSOULA

A liberal haven in a largely conservative state, Montana's second-largest city attracts new residents every day with its revitalized downtown and bountiful outdoor opportunities. Home to the University of Montana, downtown Missoula is lined with bars and coffeehouses that cater to the large student population. Four different mountain ranges and five major rivers surround Missoula, supporting skiing during the winter and fly fishing, hiking, and biking during the summer.

VITAL STATS

Population: 57,000

Visitor Info: Missoula Chamber of Commerce, 825 E. Front St. (☎406-543-6623; www.missoulachamber.com.), at Van Buren. Open M-F 8am-5pm.

Internet Access: Missoula Public Library, 301 E. Main St. (☎406-721-2665). Open M-Th 10am-9pm, F-Sa 10am-6pm, Su 1-5pm. Free.

Post Office: 200 E. Broadway St. (☎406-329-2222). Open M-F 8am-5:30pm. **Postal Code:** 59801.

▣ GETTING AROUND

The Clark Fork River divides Missoula into northern and southern halves. From west to east, the city's principal routes are **Reserve St.** (portions of which are **U.S. 93**), **Orange St.,** and **Higgins Ave.** The principal east-west route is **Broadway St. (Bus I-90/Rte. 200).** Downtown lies north of the river, around the intersection of N. Higgins Ave. and Broadway St. The University of Montana lies southeast of downtown, accessible by heading south on **Madison St.** from Broadway. Businesses outside of downtown have parking lots, and meters ($0.05 per 6min.) are readily available in the downtown area during business hours.

◉ SIGHTS

Missoula's hottest sight is the **Smokejumper Center,** 5765 Rte. 10, the nation's largest training base for aerial firefighters who parachute into flaming forests. (Just past the airport, 7 mi. northwest of town on Broadway. ☎406-329-4934. Open Memorial Day to Labor Day daily 8:30am-5pm; Labor Day to Memorial Day by appointment. 4-5 tours per day; call for times. Free.) The **Carousel,** in Caras Riverfront Park, is a hand-carved merry-go-round. (☎406-549-8382. Open daily June-Aug. 11am-7pm; Sept.-May 11am-5:30pm. $1.50, seniors and under 19 $0.50.) **Out to Lunch,** also in Caras Riverfront Park, offers free musical performances in summer; call the Missoula Downtown Association for info. (☎406-543-

4238; www.missouladowntown.com. June-Aug. W 11am-1:30pm. Free.)

Pick up the *Missoula Gallery Guide* brochure at the tourist office for a self-guided tour of Missoula's art galleries. See regional art at the **Dana Gallery**, 246 N. Higgins Ave. (☎406-721-3154; www.danagallery.com. Open M-F 10am-6pm, Sa 10am-4pm; 1st F of each month until 8pm. Free.) The **Gallery Saintonge**, 216 N. Higgins Ave., displays photographs. (☎406-543-0171. Open Tu-F 10am-5:30pm, Sa 10am-4pm. Free.) The **Montana Museum of Art & Culture,** on the UM campus is also particularly noteworthy. (☎406-243-2019. Open July-Aug. W-Sa 11am-3pm; Sept.-June Tu-Th 11am-3pm, F-Sa 4-8:30pm. Free.) The **Historical Museum at Fort Missoula,** in Building 322 at Fort Missoula, on South Ave. one block west of Reserve St., displays 22,000 artifacts of Missoulan history. (☎406-728-3476; www.fortmissoulamuseum.org. Open Memorial Day to Labor Day M-Sa 10am-5pm, Su noon-5pm; Labor Day to Memorial Day Tu-Su noon-5pm. $3, seniors $2, students $1.)

The **Western Montana Fair and Rodeo,** held at the beginning of August, has live music, a carnival, fireworks, and concession booths. (☎406-721-3247; www.westernmontanafair.com. Open daily 10am-midnight. $6.) Soak your weary feet at the **Lolo Hot Springs,** 35 mi. southwest of Missoula on Rte. 12 in the Lolo National Forest. The 103°-105°F springs were a meeting place for local Native Americans and were frequented by Lewis and Clark in 1806. Today ,you can swim in a pool fed by the springs. (☎406-273-2290 or 800-273-2290; www.lolohotsprings.com. Changing rooms available. Open daily 10am-10pm. $7, under 13 $5.)

◤ OUTDOORS

Nearby parks, recreation areas, and surrounding wilderness areas make Missoula an outdoor enthusiast's dream.

BIKING AND HIKING

Bicycle-friendly Missoula is located along both the Trans-America and the Great Parks bicycle routes, and all major streets have designated bike lanes. **Open Road Bicycles and Nordic Equipment,** 517 S. Orange St., has bike rentals. (☎406-549-2453. $3.50 per hr., $17.50 per day. Open M-F 9am-6pm, Sa 10am-5pm,

Su 11am-3pm.) The national **Adventure Cycling Association,** 150 E. Pine St., is the place to go for info about local trails, including the Trans-America and Great Parks routes. (☎406-721-1776 or 800-755-2453; www.adventurecycling.org. Open spring to fall M-F 8am-5pm.) The **Rattlesnake Wilderness National Recreation Area,** 11 mi. northeast of town off the Van Buren St. exit on I-90, and the **Pattee Canyon Recreation Area,** 3½ mi. east of Higgins on Pattee Canyon Dr., are highly recommended for their biking trails.

The **Rattlesnake Wilderness National Recreation Area,** named for the river's shape (there are no rattlers for miles), is 11 mi. northeast of town, off the Van Buren St. exit from I-90, and makes for a great day of hiking. Other popular areas include **Pattee Canyon** and **Blue Mountain,** south of town. Maps ($7) and info on longer hikes in the Bitterroot and Bob Marshall areas are at the **US Forest Service Information Office,** 200 E. Broadway; the entrance is at 200 Pine St. (☎406-329-3511. Open M-F 8am-4pm.) For rentals, stop by **Trailhead,** 221 E. Front St. (☎406-543-6966; www.trailheadmontana.com. Tents $10-14; sleeping bags $7. Open M-F 9:30am-8pm, Sa 9am-6pm, Su 11am-6pm.)

SKIING

Alpine and Nordic **skiing** keep Missoulians busy during winter. With a 1500 ft. vertical drop, three lifts and 23 runs, **Marshall Mountain** is a great place to learn how to ski, and has night skiing. (☎406-258-6000. Lift tickets $24, children $19.) Experienced skiers should check out the extreme **Montana Snowbowl,** 12 mi. northwest of Missoula, with a vertical drop of 2600 ft., an average annual snowfall of 300 in., and over 35 trails. (☎406-549-9777 or 800-728-2695; www.montanasnowbowl.com. Open Nov.-Apr. daily 9:30am-4pm. Lift tickets $34, children $14. Rentals $13.)

WATER ACTIVITIES

The Blackfoot River, along Rte. 200 east of Bonner, is an excellent place to tube or raft on a hot day. Call the **Montana State Regional Parks and Wildlife Office,** 3201 Spurgin Rd., for info about rafting locations. (☎406-542-5500. Open M-F 8am-5pm.) Rent tubes or rafts from the **Army and Navy Economy Store,** 322 N. Higgins. (☎406-721-1315; www.armynavyeconomy.com. Tubes $4 per day. Rafts $50 per day, credit card required. Open M-F 9am-7:30pm, Sa 9am-5:30pm, Su 10am-5:30pm. AmEx/D/MC/V.) **Hiking** opportunities also abound in the Missoula area. The relatively easy 30min. hike to the "M" (for the U of M, not Missoula) on Mount Sentinel, has a tremendous view of Missoula and the surrounding mountains.

Western Montana is **fly-fishing** country, and Missoula is at the heart of it all. Fishing licenses are required and can be purchased from the **Department of Fish, Wildlife, and Parks**, 3201 Spurgin Rd. (☎406-542-5500), or from sporting goods stores. **Kingfisher**, 926 E. Broadway, offers licenses ($25-70) and fishing trips. (☎406-721-6141; www.kingfisherflyshop.com. Trips from $260. Open daily in summer 7am-7pm; hours vary in winter.)

🥢 FOOD

Missoula, the culinary capital of Montana, has a number of innovative, delicious, and inexpensive eating establishments. Head downtown, north of the Clark Fork River along **Higgins Ave.**, and check out the array of restaurants and coffeehouses that line the road. Walk through the gift shop pharmacy to reach ⬛**Butterfly Herbs ❶**, 232 N. Higgins Ave., where the hummus sandwich ($4), chai milkshake ($3), and organic green salad ($2.50) are exciting alternatives to diner fare. (☎406-728-8780; www.butterflyherbs.com. Open M-F 7am-7pm, Sa-Su 9am-5:30pm. MC/V.) **Worden's ❶**, 451 N. Higgins Ave., is a popular deli, serving a wide variety of world-class sandwiches in three sizes: 4 in. ($4.25), 7 in. ($5.75), and 14 in. ($10.75). You can also pick up groceries while munching. (☎406-549-1293; www.wordens.com. Open M-Th 8am-11pm, F-Sa 8am-midnight, Su 9am-10pm. AmEx/D/MC/V.) **Tipu's Tiger ❸**, 115½ S. 4th St. W., is one of the only all-veggie establishments and was the first Indian restaurant in Montana. (☎406-542-0622. All-you-can-eat lunch buffet $7 until 4:30pm. Open daily 11:30am-9:30pm. AmEx/D/MC/V.) At **Taco del Sol ❶**, 422 N. Higgins Ave., get a Mission Burrito and other Mexican favorites for under $4. (☎406-327-8929; www.tacodelsol.com. Open M-Sa 11am-10pm, Su noon-9pm. MC/V.)

🛏 ACCOMMODATIONS

There are no hostels in Missoula, but there are plenty of inexpensive alternatives on Broad-

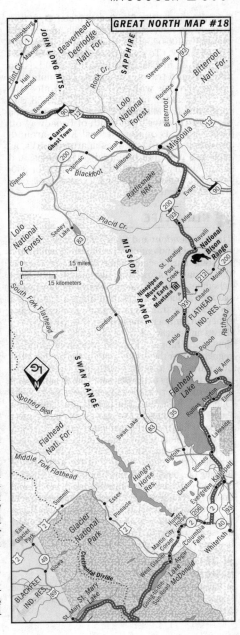

way. Rooms at the **City Center Motel ❸,** 338 E. Broadway, have cable TV, fridges, and microwaves. (☎406-543-3193. Singles $48-54; doubles $59-64. MC/V.) To reach the **Aspen Motel ❷,** 3720 Rte. 200 E., in East Missoula, take I-90 East to Exit 107 and travel ½ mi. east. The motel has spacious rooms with A/C, cable TV, coffee, Wi-Fi, and breakfast included. (☎406-721-9758. Singles $40.) The **Missoula/El-Mar KOA Kampground ❶,** 3450 Tina Ave., just south of Broadway off Reserve St., is one of the best KOAs around, providing shaded tent sites apart from RVs, as well as a pool, hot tub, mini-golf courses, and 24hr. laundry facilities. (☎406-549-0881 or 800-562-5366. Tent sites $25-30; RV sites $30-60; cabins $42-48. AmEx/D/MC/V.)

◈ NIGHTLIFE

The *Independent* and *Lively Times,* available at newsstands and cafes, offer the lowdown on the Missoula music scene, while the *Entertainer,* in the Friday *Missoulian,* has movie and event schedules. College students swarm the downtown bar area around Front St. and Higgins Ave. during the school year. Bars have a more relaxed atmosphere in summer. **Charlie B's,** 420 N. Higgins Ave., draws an eclectic clientele of bikers, farmers, students, and hippies. Framed photos of longtime regulars cover the walls—park at the bar for 10 or 20 years and join them. Hungry boozers can weave their way to the **Dinosaur Cafe ❶** at the back of the room for Creole delights. (☎406-549-3589. Open daily 8am-2am.) The popular **Iron Horse Brew Pub ❷,** 501 N. Higgins Ave., always packs a crowd; the patio fills up during summer. (☎406-728-8866; www.ironhorsebrewpub.com. Pints $2.50-4. Open daily 11am-2am. AmEx/D/MC/V.) Follow the advice of the "beer coaches" at **The Kettle House Brewing Co.,** 602 Myrtle, one block west of Higgins between 4th and 5th, and "support your local brewery." The Kettle House serves an assortment of beers, including their hemp beer, "Fresh Bongwater Pale Ale." (☎406-728-1660; www.kettlehouse.com. Pints $2.75-4. Open M-F noon-9pm; no beer served after 8pm. D/MC/V.)

◪ DETOUR
NATIONAL BISON RANGE

In Ravalli, take Rte. 200 W. Following the signs, and take a right onto Rte. 212 after 5 mi.; the entrance to the park is 5 mi. north, on your right.

The National Bison Range was established in 1908 to save bison from extinction. At one time 30-70 million bison roamed the plains, but after years of hunting the population dropped to less than 1000. The range is home to 350-500 bison as well as deer, pronghorn, elk, bighorn sheep, and mountain goats. The Red Sleep Mountain self-guided tour offers a view of the Flathead Valley and the best chance for wildlife observation, but shorter free routes exist. Sunrise and sunset are the best wildlife viewing times. The Wild West comes alive the first Monday and Tuesday of October during the **Roundup,** in which wranglers gather the bison together to do checkups and herd-size management. (☎406-644-2211. Visitors center open mid-May to Oct. daily 8am-6pm; Nov. to mid-May M-F 8am-4:30pm. Red Sleep Mountain Dr. open mid-May to mid-Oct. daily 7am-sunset. Red Sleep Mountain Dr. $4 per vehicle.)

◪ APPROACHING ST. IGNATIUS: 41 MILES
Take **Broadway** north to its intersection with **U.S. 93 N,** and head out of town and into the quiet mountain country of Western Montana.

ST. IGNATIUS. Named for the Jesuit Mission for which it is best known, St. Ignatius sits just east of U.S. 93 at the foot of the Mission Mountains on the Flathead Indian Reservation. While there's not much to see in town, **St. Ignatius Catholic Mission,** the brick building just off the highway, is worth a look. Built in 1891 at the request of the local Salish and Kootenai tribes, the mission features 58 frescoes and murals painted by the mission cook, Brother Carignano. (☎406-745-2768. Open daily 9am-8pm. Donations accepted.) Across the highway from town, Col. Doug Allard's mini-empire constitutes most of the services offered in St. Iggy's, starting with **Col. Doug Allard's Indian Museum and Trading Post,** which houses traditional native clothing and artifacts, as well as a small display of stuffed (dead) animals. Perhaps most impressive, however, is the World Champion Stick Game Tournament Trophy, replete with actual sticks, that Col. Allard himself has awarded to various stick game all-stars. (☎406-745-2951. Open daily 9am-5pm. Free.) Head to **The Malt Shop ❶,** 101 1st. St., for burgers, hot dogs, and tasty sandwiches ($1-5). The huckleberry milkshake ($3.25) is delightful. (☎406-

745-3501. Open M-Sa 10:30am-10pm, Su 11:30am-9pm. MC/V.)

◥ DETOUR
NINEPIPES MUSEUM OF EARLY MONTANA
40962 U.S. 93. In Charlo, on U.S. 93. Look for the large log cabin-style buildings on the right, just after the Ninepipes Reservoir.

Chronicling the histories and traditions of the nearby Ninepipes Refuge and the surrounding area, the museum displays photographs and artifacts of Native Americans, trappers, miners, loggers, and frontiersfolk. Fine Native American beadwork and dioramas depicting life in the Old West make this roadside attraction worth investigating. (☎406-644-3435. Open W-Su 11am-5pm. $4. Free guided tours possible; call ahead. AmEx/D/MC/V.) The adjacent **Ninepipes Lodge and Restaurant ❹**, 69286 U.S. 93, offers lodging and dining for the road-weary. Try the seafood quiche ($9) while gazing out over the Mission Range reflected in the Ninepipes Reservoir. (☎406-644-2588. Singles $73; doubles $78-83. Restaurant open daily 11am-2am. AmEx/D/MC/V.)

⬚ APPROACHING POLSON: 28 MILES
Follow **U.S. 93 (Main St.)** through town, around the courthouse rotary, and on out to the west shore of beautiful Flathead Lake, which the highway follows straight to Polson, on its southwestern corner.

POLSON AND FLATHEAD LAKE
On the southern side of Flathead Lake, Polson has a small town's share of outdoor activities and art, but the real reason to stop here is the ◪**Miracle of America Museum**, 36094 Memory Ln. With displays of old posters, uniforms, motorcycles, and weapons, the museum is the life's work of proprietor Gil Mangels. A re-created general store, saddlery, barber shop, soda fountain, and gas station sit among such oddities as an 1898 sheep-powered treadmill. The museum celebrates Live History Day the 3rd weekend in July. (Off U.S. 93 just before town. ☎406-883-6804. Open June-Sept. daily 8am-8pm; Oct.-May M-Sa 8am-5pm, Su 1:30-5pm. $4, ages 3-12 $1.) Fresh fruit stands line **Flathead Lake**, the largest natural lake west of the Mississippi. Renowned for its fish and adjacent cherry trees, the lake is skirted by U.S. 93 between

Polson and Kalispell. The largest island you'll see as you drive along the shore is the 2000-acre **Wild Horse Island State Park,** accessible only by boat, where the Salish-Kootenai Indians used to pasture their horses to prevent theft by neighboring tribes. Today, Montana allows a few neutered and vaccinated "wild" horses to roam free. The waters near Polson have some of best Class II and Class III rafting around, and the **Flathead Raft Co.,** 1501 U.S. 93, prepares visitors for the experience. The famous Buffalo Rapids of the Lower Flathead River are especially good at folding your raft in half and tossing your shipmates overboard. (☎406-883-5838 or 800-654-4359; www.flatheadraftco.com. Open M-F 9am-7pm, Sa-Su 9am-6pm. $42, seniors $36, ages 8-12 $34.) A local secret, **Blacktail Mountain Ski Resort,** in Lakeside, is one of the newest ski areas in the country. The lone ski lodge is a welcome break from the crowded ski resorts scattered throughout the Rocky Mountains—you won't find any lift lines here. (☎406-844-0999; www.blacktailmountain.com. Lift tickets $34, ages 13-17 $24, ages 8-12 $15.)

M&S Meats ❶, 86755 U.S. 93, just after Dayton, is worth a stop for some of the best jerky you'll ever taste ($18 per lb.). Jerky and sausage are made with either beef or bison meat. (☎406-844-3414 or 800-454-3414; www.msmeats.com. Open M-F 7:30am-6pm, Sa-Su 9am-6pm. D/MC/V.) Most lodging on the lake is expensive, but there are some affordable options. **Edgewater Motel ❹**, 7140 U.S. 93, in Lakeside, has rooms with kitchenettes, some facing the lake. (☎406-844-3644 or 800-424-3798. Open in summer. Singles from $70; cabins $115. AmEx/D/MC/V.) The **Cherry Hill Motel ❸**, 1810 U.S. 93, in Polson, offers clean and comfortable rooms just north of the museum. (☎406-883-2737. Singles $59; doubles $67. MC/V.)

⬚ APPROACHING KALISPELL: 51 MILES
Drive 51 mi. along the western shore of the lake via **U.S. 93** north to reach Kalispell.

KALISPELL
Nestled between the ski-haven Big Mountain and gorgeous Flathead Lake, Kalispell mixes rampant outdoorsmanship with the art and culture of the largest urban center of north-

western Montana. While it may not take long to get a feel for the town proper, Kalispell is a gateway to the wild Montana countryside.

VITAL STATS

Population: 15,000

Visitor Info: Chamber of Commerce, 15 Depot Park (☎406-758-2800), in Depot Park, on Main St. at Center St. Open M-F 8am-5pm.

Internet Access: Flathead County Library, 247 1st Ave. E. (☎406-758-5819), 1 block off Main St. (U.S. 93). Open M-Th 10am-8pm, F 10am-5pm, Sa 11am-5pm. Free.

Post Office: 350 N. Meridian Rd., (☎406-755-6450), right off U.S. 2 west of Main St., at 3rd St. Open M-F 8:30am-5:30pm, Sa 10am-2pm. **Postal Code:** 59904.

⊏ GETTING AROUND. Kalispell is laid out in a grid centered on the intersection of **Main St. (U.S. 93)** and **Idaho St. (Rte. 2),** the older highway around which the town's businesses first developed. Numbered avenues flank Main St., increasing in number as they move out in both directions, with East and West designating their orientation. Numbered streets count southward from **Center St.,** while streets north of Center bear state names.

◪ SIGHTS. Museums, small stores, and galleries give the downtown area around Main St. more character than most towns of this size. **The Hockaday Museum of Art,** 302 2nd Ave. E., houses a collection of art inspired by Glacier National Park, along with rotating exhibits of nationally renowned and emerging artists. (☎406-755-5268. Open Tu-F 10am-6pm, Sa 10am-5pm, Su noon-4pm. $5, seniors $4, students $2, ages 6-18 $1.) The **Conrad Mansion National Historic Site Museum,** 6 blocks east of Main St. on 4th St. E, shows 26 beautifully furnished rooms in their original 1895 condition, along with pleasant gardens and a Victorian gift shop. (☎406-755-2166; www.conradmansion.com. Open daily 10am-5pm. Tours every hr. until 4pm. $8, under 12 $3.) **The M,** 124 2nd Ave. E, has displays on the history and culture of Northwestern Montana, including a cross-section of a tree that is older than the United States. (☎406-756-8381; www.yourmuseum.org. Open Tu-Sa 10am-5pm. $6.)

⊠⊏ FOOD AND ACCOMMODATIONS. A variety of chain restaurants line U.S. 93 and U.S. 2, but a few local eateries can be found. **Bojangles Diner ❸,** 1319 U.S. 2 W, is a 50s-style throwback replete with a jukebox and trains. (☎406-755-3222. Breakfasts $2-11. Burgers and sandwiches $6-8, dinners $8-11. Open daily 6am-8pm. AmEx/D/MC/V.) **D.G. Barley's Brewhouse & Grill ❸,** 285 North Main St., at the junction of U.S. 93 and U.S. 2, serves up Southwestern fare worthy of any cowgirl in a kitschy, glam-ranch atmosphere. (☎406-756-2222. Steaks $14-23. Salads $7-13. Burgers $6-8. Open M-Th and Su 11am-10pm, F-Sa 11am-11pm. AmEx/D/MC/V.) **Avalanche Creek Restaurant & Coffeehouse ❶,** 38 1st Ave. E., serves some of the valley's finest soups ($3-4), salads ($3-7), and sandwiches ($4-7) among the works of local artists. (☎406-257-0785. Open M-F 7am-5pm, Sa 9am-3pm. AmEx/D/MC/V.)

A few chain motels dot the sides of Main St. (U.S. 93) on the south side of town, just past the courthouse. Older, privately-run endeavors crop up along **Idaho St.** (U.S. 2), heading east. The **◪Kalispell Grand Hotel ❹,** 100 Main St., has provided the finest that "frontier hotels" have to offer since 1912, with vintage architecture blending seamlessly with high-speed Internet access and jetted bathtubs. (At 1st St. ☎800-858-7422; www.kalispellgrand.com. Singles $84-97; doubles $91-104. AmEx/D/MC/V.) **Blue & White Motel ❸,** 640 E. Idaho St. (Rte. 2), 6 blocks east of Main St., spruces up the motel experience with an indoor swimming pool, a sauna, and a jacuzzi. (☎800-382-3577. Singles $59; doubles $75. D/MC/V.)

⊠ DETOUR
BIG SKY WATER PARK
Just before the intersection of U.S. 2 and Rte. 206.

As Montana's biggest water park, Big Sky is the place to cool down. Some of the water park's 10 waterslides make 360-degree turns while others steeply drop 50 ft. The park also has a mini-golf course. (☎406-892-5025; www.bigskywaterslide.com. Open Memorial Day to Labor Day daily 10am-8pm. $20, ages 3-10 $15. After 4pm $20/$15.)

⊓ APPROACHING HUNGRY HORSE: 27 MILES
Head east on **E. Idaho St. (U.S. 2).**

HUNGRY HORSE. Named after two starving horses, Tex and Jerry, who survived the bitter winter of 1900, Hungry Horse advertises itself as the "friendliest dam town in the West." The impressive **Hungry Horse Dam** controls the flow of the Flathead River. Stop by **The Huckleberry Patch ❶**, 8868 U.S. 2, which specializes in Montana's local berry, a tart, blueberry-like fruit. For a treat, try the huckleberry milkshakes ($3). The restaurant serves pancake breakfasts ($4-8) made with, of course, huckleberries. (☎406-387-5000 or 800-527-7340; www.huckleberrypatch.com. Open in summer daily 7am-11am. AmEx/D/MC/V.)

APPROACHING GLACIER NATIONAL PARK: 11 MILES

Continue on **U.S. 2 E** for a few more miles to bring you to West Glacier. Turn left onto **Going-to-the-Sun Rd.**, which brings you into the park.

GLACIER NATIONAL PARK

Glacier National Park makes up most of the Waterton-Glacier Peace Park; although technically one park, Waterton-Glacier is actually two distinct areas: the small Waterton Lakes National Park in Alberta, and the enormous Glacier National Park in Montana. Waterton-Glacier transcends international boundaries to encompass one of the most strikingly beautiful portions of the Rockies. The massive Rocky Mountain peaks span both parks, providing sanctuary for endangered bears, bighorn sheep, moose, mountain goats, mountain lions, and gray wolves—it's the only area in the lower 48 states with its historical predators intact. Perched high in the Northern Rockies, Glacier is sometimes called the "Crown of the Continent," and the alpine lakes and glaciers shine like jewels.

GETTING AROUND

Linking West Glacier and St. Mary, **Going-to-the-Sun Rd.**, the only road through the park, is a spectacular 52 mi. scenic drive climbing 3000 ft. through cedar forests, mountain passes, and arctic tundra. (Allow 2-3hr. or more. Closed in winter.) **U.S. 2** skirts the southern border of the park. At "Goat Lick," about halfway between East and West Glacier, mountain goats traverse steep cliffs to lick up natural salt deposits. **U.S. 89** heads north along the east edge of the park through St. Mary.

HIKING

Most of Glacier's scenery lies off the main roads and is accessible only by foot. An extensive trail system has something for everyone, from short, easy day hikes to rigorous backcountry expeditions. Stop by one of the visitors centers for free day hike guides. Beware of bears and mountain lions. Familiarize yourself with the precautions necessary to avoid an encounter, and ask rangers about wildlife activity.

Avalanche Lake (4 mi. round-trip, 3hr.) is a breathtaking trail and by far the most popular day hike in the park. Starting north of Lake McDonald on the Going-to-the-Sun Rd., this moderate hike climbs 500 ft. to picture-perfect panoramas.

Iceberg Lake (7 mi., 5 hr.), begins at the trailhead at the Swiftcurrent Motor Inn in Many Glacier. The trail climbs steeply for the 1st ½ mi., then inclines more gradually. The lake rivals the beauty of any in the world, circled by mountains with turquoise blue water and icebergs that float in the lake year-round.

Trail of the Cedars (¾ mi. loop, 20min.) begins at the same trailhead as Avalanche Lake and is an easy walk that also has a shorter hike.

Grinnell Glacier Trail (11 mi. round-trip, 7hr.) passes near several glaciers and follows along Grinnell Point and Mt. Grinnell, steadily gaining 1600 ft. Trailhead at the Many Glacier Picnic Area.

Hidden Lake Nature Trail (3 mi. round-trip, 2hr.), beginning at the Logan Pass Visitors Center, is a short and modest 460 ft. climb through alpine meadows and over the Continental Divide to a beautiful view of Hidden Lake. A favorite place for mountain goats and Columbian ground squirrels.

St. Mary Falls (1¾ mi. round-trip, 1hr.). Beginning off Going-to-the-Sun Rd. between Logan Pass and St. Mary, this trail descends 260 ft. to bring you to an small but impressive cataract in the St. Mary River.

OUTDOORS

Opportunities for bicycling are limited and confined to roadways and designated bike paths; cycling on trails is strictly prohibited. Although the Going-to-the-Sun Rd. is a popular route,

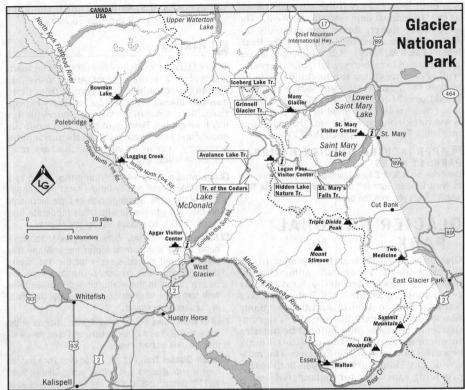

Glacier
National
Park

only experienced cyclists with appropriate gear and legs of titanium should attempt this grueling ride; the sometimes nonexistent road shoulder can create hazardous situations. The **Inside North Fork Rd.**, which runs from Kintla Lake to Fish Creek on the west side of the park, is good for **mountain biking**, as are the old logging roads in the Flathead National Forest. Equestrian explorers should check that trails are open; there are steep fines for using closed trails. Two-hour **trail rides** from Mule Shoe Outfitters are available at Many Glacier and Lake McDonald. (Many Glacier ☎ 406-732-4203; Lake McDonald ☎406-888-5121. May to early Sept. daily 8:30, 10:45am, 1:15, 3:30pm. $50.)

The **Glacier Park Boat Co.** (☎406-257-2426) runs boat tours ($12-16) that explore Glacier's lakes. **Glacier Raft Co.,** in West Glacier, leads trips down

the middle fork of the Flathead River. (☎800-235-6781. Half-day $43, under 13 $33; full day with lunch $74/$51.) You can rent **rowboats** ($12 per hr.) at Lake McDonald, Many Glacier, Two Medicine, and Apgar; **canoes** ($12 per hr.) at Many Glacier, Two Medicine, and Apgar; **kayaks** ($12 per hr.) at Apgar and Many Glacier; and **outboards** ($20 per hr.) at Lake McDonald and Two Medicine. No permit is needed to fish in the park, and some limits are high in the main lakes. Some areas, however, are severely restricted, and certain species may be catch-and-release. Pick up *Fishing Regulations*, available at visitors centers, for info.

🍴 FOOD

Moderately priced restaurants exist in major villages within the park, but more affordable options are found outside the park. **Polebridge Mercantile Store ❶,** on Polebridge Loop Rd., ¼ mi. east of N. Fork Rd., has homemade pastries ($1-3) as splendid as the surrounding peaks. Gas, gifts, groceries, and pay phones are also available. (☎406-888-5105. Open daily June-Sept. 8am-9pm; Oct.-May 8am-6pm. MC/V.) Sample Montanan delicacies at the **Whistle Stop Restaurant ❷,** in East Glacier, best known for its omelettes and huckleberry French toast. (☎406-226-9292. Open mid-May to mid-Sept. daily 7am-9pm. AmEx/D/MC/V.)

ACCOMMODATIONS

Staying indoors within Glacier is expensive, but several affordable options lie just outside the park boundaries. On the west side of the park, the small, electricity-less town of **Polebridge** provides access to Glacier's remote and pristine northwest corner. From Apgar, take Camas Rd. north, and take a right onto the poorly marked gravel Outside North Fork Rd., just past a bridge over the North Fork of the Flathead River. (Avoid Inside North Fork Rd.—your shocks will thank you.) From Columbia Falls, take Rte. 486 northbound. To the east, inexpensive lodging is just across the park border in **East Glacier.** The distant offices of **Glacier Park, Inc.** (☎406-756-2444; www.glacierparkinc.com) handle reservations for all in-park lodging.

Brownies Grocery (HI-AYH), 1020 Rte. 49 (☎406-226-4426), in East Glacier Park. Check in at the grocery counter and head up to the spacious hostel. Kitchen, showers, linens, laundry, and a view of the Rockies. Internet $1.75 per 15min. Key deposit $5. Check-in by 9pm. Reservations recommended; credit card required. Open mid-May to Sept., weather permitting. Dorms $16, members $13; private singles $21/$18; doubles $29/$26; family rooms $41/$38; tent sites $10. MC/V. ❶

North Fork Hostel, 80 Beaver Dr. (☎406-888-5241), in Polebridge. The wooden walls and kerosene lamps are reminiscent of a hunting lodge. Showers and a beautiful, fully equipped kitchen, but no flush toilets. During the winter, old-fashioned wood stoves warm frozen fingers. Open Apr.-Oct. Canoe rentals $20 per day; mountain bikes free. Linen $3. Check-out noon. Call ahead. Dorms $15; teepees $30 per person; cabins $35; log homes $70. AmEx/D/MC/V. ❶

Backpacker's Inn Hostel, 29 Dawson Ave. (☎406-226-9392), in East Glacier, at the Mexican restaurant. 14 clean beds in coed rooms. Hot showers. Sleeping bags $1. Open May-Sept. Dorms $12; singles $25; doubles $35. AmEx/D/MC/V. ❶

Swiftcurrent Motor Inn (☎406-732-5531), in Many Glacier Valley. One of the few budget motels in the area. Most cabins have shared bath. Open early June to early Sept. 1-bedroom cabins $45; 2-bedroom $55; cottage with private bath $75. AmEx/D/MC/V. ❷

CAMPING

Visitors planning overnight backpacking trips must obtain the necessary **backcountry permits.** With the exception of the **Nyack/Coal Creek** camping zone, all backcountry camping must be at designated campsites equipped with pit toilets, tent sites, food preparation areas, and food hanging devices. (June-Sept. $4 per person, ages 9-16 $2; Oct.-May free. For an additional $20, reservations are accepted beginning in mid-Apr. for trips between June 15 and Oct. 31. AmEx/D/MC/V.) Pick up a free and indispensable *Backcountry Camping Guide* from a visitors center or the **Backcountry Permit Center,** next to the visitors center in Apgar, which also has valuable info for those seeking to explore Glacier's less-traveled areas. (Open July to mid-Sept. daily 7am-4pm; May-June and mid-Sept. to Oct. daily 8am-4pm.) The park also maintains 13 campgrounds (8 with flush toilets), ranging from $6-17 per night. The largest and closest to the West Glacier Entrance is **Apgar Campground ❶,** with 192 wooded sites just off Lake McDonald (Open May to mid-Oct. Sites $15. AmEx/D/MC/V.)

DETOUR
CATTLE BARON SUPPER CLUB
At the intersection of U.S. 89 and the road to Many Glacier, in Babb.

The **Cattle Baron Supper Club ❺** might just be the nicest surprise you'll ever find in the middle of nowhere; inside the beautiful dining room, complete with murals and an enormous pine tree that grows right through the middle of the building, waiters in tuxedos serve amazing steaks ($23-26). The food may be expensive, but the Cattle Baron has been

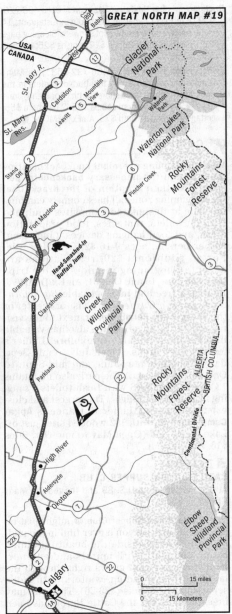

GREAT NORTH MAP #19

known to convert vegetarians. (☎406-732-4033. Open daily 5-10pm. Bar open until midnight. D/MC/V.)

◪ APPROACHING CARDSTON: 35 MILES

From St. Mary, take **U.S. 89 N** to the **Piegan/Carway Border Crossing** (open daily 7am-11pm). In Canada, U.S. 89 becomes **Hwy. 2,** heading north to Cardston.

◪ LEAVING THE US

See **Vital Documents** (p. 13) for info on passport and visa requirements.

The Sunshine Province
ALBERTA
Welcomes You!

CARDSTON

Cardston, located in the Lee Creek Valley where the foothills of the Rockies meet the Great Plains, became the center of the Canadian Mormon Church after some of Brigham Young's descendents migrated there. There are several worthwhile attractions in town, including the **Fay Wray Fountain,** just over the bridge past the visitors center, which honors the hometown girl who was hoisted to fame by King Kong. The ◪**Remington Carriage Museum,** 623 Main St., houses over 250 horse-drawn vehicles, the largest collection in the New World. Watch master craftsmen at work in the restoration shop or take a carriage ride. (☎403-653-5139; www.remingtoncentre.com. Open daily mid-May to mid-Sept. 9am-6pm, mid-Sept. to mid-May 10am-5pm. CDN$9, seniors CDN$8, ages 7-17 CDN$5, under 7 free.)

Cardston's hotels are pricey; a cheaper and friendlier option is to stay at one of the town's many B&Bs. **Temple Sunset View ❷,** 221 3rd St. E, welcomes guests with beautiful gardens and a patio with a fabulous view. Giant Canadian breakfasts of pancakes, eggs, bacon, and toast with homemade jelly will get you going in the morning. (☎403-653-3539. Singles CDN$35; doubles CDN$45. Cash only.)

◪ APPROACHING FORT MACLEOD: 39 MILES

From Cardston, **Hwy. 2** is a straight shot all the way to Calgary. The road north from Cardston might just be flatter than South Dakota. Keep on the lookout for locusts dive-bombing your car and delicate little white butterflies reenacting the Boston massacre on your bumper. Just before you arrive, you'll pass Canada's largest wind farm.

FORT MACLEOD. In Alberta's early lawless days, a trading post for Canada's illegal whiskey trade was established in nearby Lethbridge, affectionately nicknamed Fort Whoop-Up. After news trickled back to Ottawa, the federal government marched a force of Mounties out in 1874 to establish Fort Macleod and keep order. More recently, Fort Macleod gained fame as the town where the Academy Award-winning film *Brokeback Mountain* was filmed—many of the buildings featured in the film are located in town and sport large movie posters. Fort Macleod preserves Canada's past in its many wood frame buildings from the 1890s and its brick and sandstone structures from the 1900s. At the ⬛**Fort Museum of the North-West Mounted Police,** 219 25th St., Mounties circle the fort on horseback on their "Musical Ride." (☎403-553-4703; www.nwmpmuseum.com. Open mid-May to June daily 9am-5pm; July-Aug. daily 9am-6pm, early May and early Sept. W-Su 10am-4pm. CDN$7.50, seniors CDN$7, ages 12-17 CDN$5.50, ages 6-11 CDN$4.50. Musical Ride July-Aug. W-Su 10, 11:30am, 2, 3pm.) When you're hungry, head over to the homey log-cabin atmosphere of **Aunty Lynda's Cafe & Grill ❸**, 2323 7th Ave., for cheap breakfasts (CDN$2-8), burgers, sandwiches, pastas, salads (CDN$6-9), and delicious desserts. (☎403-553-2655. Entrees CDN$15-22. Open daily 7am-9pm. AmEx/MC/V.) The **Red Coat Inn Motel ❸**, 359 Main St., was home to Ang Lee and the actors while filming, with comfortable accommodations, high-speed Internet access, microwaves, indoor pool, and real mugs for your coffeemaker. (☎403-553-4434; www.redcoatinn.com. Singles CDN$60-120; doubles CDN$80. MC/V.)

◤ **DETOUR**
HEAD-SMASHED-IN BUFFALO JUMP
Located 18km from Fort MacLeod on Rte. 785.

For over 10,000 years, Native Americans stampeded buffalo off strategically placed sandstone cliffs. Legend has it that this particular buffalo jump got its name from a young brave who wanted to witness the falling buffalo. Standing in the shelter of an overhanging ledge, he was trapped by the mounting bodies. When his people came to collect the buffalo, they found him with his skull crushed and named the place "Head-Smashed-In." Today you can visit the jump that was used for at least 5700 years along with its excellent interpretive center. (☎403-553-2731; www.head-smashed-in.com. Open daily mid-May to mid-Sept. 9am-6pm; mid-Sept. to mid-May 10am-5pm. CDN$9, seniors CDN$8, ages 7-17 CDN$5, under 7 free.)

 DID YOU KNOW? The United Nations named Head-Smashed-In a UNESCO World Heritage Site; ten-meter-deep beds of bone and tools make this one of the best-preserved buffalo jumps in North America.

◤ **APPROACHING HIGH RIVER: 68 MILES**
Continue north on **Rte. 2** toward High River.

HIGH RIVER. The best way to see High River is to follow the 14km **Happy Trails** pathway system, which winds by a number of murals that transform the concrete walls of downtown shops into historical works of art. Exhibits rotate at the **Museum of the Highwood,** 406 1st St. SW, but some of the quirky themes include "Hair's to You," a century of women's hairstyles, or "Sitting Pretty: Chairs and More." Local history and reference material is also archived here. (☎403-652-7156. Open mid-May to Sept. M-Sa 10am-5pm, Su 12:30-5pm; Oct. to mid-May Tu-Sa noon-4pm, Su 12:30-5pm. CDN$2.50, students and seniors CDN$2, under 13 free.) The food is as unique as the atmosphere at the **Whistle Stop Cafe ❶**, 406 1st St. SW, adjacent to the Museum of Highwood, in the dining car of an old train. Try the brie and cucumber sandwich or a chicken mango quesadilla, both CDN$7. (☎403-652-7156. Open M-Sa 10am-4pm, Su 10am-3pm. MC/V.)

◤ **APPROACHING CALGARY: 41 MILES**
Continue north on **Rte. 2** toward Calgary.

CALGARY

Mounties founded Calgary in the 1870s to control Canada's flow of illegal whiskey, but oil made the city what it is today. Petroleum fuels Calgary's economy and explains why the city hosts the largest number of corporate headquarters in Canada outside of Toronto. As the host of the 1988 Winter Olympics, Calgary's dot on the map grew larger; already Alberta's largest city, this thriving young metropolis is the fastest-growing in all of Canada.

VITAL STATS

Population: 990,000

Visitor Info: Calgary Chamber of Commerce, 100 6th Avenue SW (☎403-750-0400). Open M-F 8am-4:30pm.

Internet Access: Calgary Public Library, 616 Macleod Trail SE (☎403-260-2600). Open June-Aug. M-Th 10am-9pm, F-Sa 10am-5pm; Sept.-May M-Th 10am-9pm, F-Sa 10am-5pm, Su noon-5pm. CDN$2 per hr.

Post Office: 207 9th Ave. SW (☎403-974-2078). Open M-F 8am-5:45pm. **Postal Code:** T2P 2G8.

GETTING AROUND

Calgary is 126km east of Banff along the **Trans-Canada Hwy. (Hwy. 1),** which becomes **16th Ave.** in town. The city is divided into quadrants: **Centre St.** is the east-west divider, while the **Bow River** splits the north and south. Avenues run east-west; streets north-south. Derive cross streets from the first digit of the street address: 206 7th Ave. SW, for example, would be found on 7th Ave. at 2nd St.

◉ SIGHTS

CALGARY TOWER. To get your bearings quickly, take a trip up the Calgary Tower. The 191m tower, built in 1967, was the first of its kind. Now the tower has a grill, observation deck, and revolving dining room. (*101 9th Ave. SW. ☎403-266-7171; www.calgarytower.com. Open in summer daily 7am-10:30pm; in winter daily 9am-9pm. CDN$13, seniors CDN$11, ages 2-17 CDN$10.*)

OLYMPIC SIGHTS. For two glorious weeks in 1988, the world's eyes were on Calgary for the Winter Olympics. Almost 20 years later, the world has moved on, but the city still clings relentlessly to its Olympic stardom. Visit the **Canada Olympic Park** and its looming ski jumps and twisted bobsled and luge

tracks. The **Olympic Hall of Fame** honors Olympic achievements with displays, films, and a hockey simulator. (*10min. northwest of downtown on Hwy. 1. ☎403-247-5452. Open July-Aug. daily 9am-5pm; Apr.-May. and Sept.-early Oct. daily 10am-4pm. CDN$6. Tours CDN$15; includes chair-lift and entrance to ski-jump buildings, Hall of Fame, and ice-house.*) In summer, the park opens its hills and a lift to **mountain bikers.** (*Open mid-May to June M-F noon-9pm, Sa-Su 9am-6pm; July-early Sept. M-F 9am-9pm, Sa-Su 9am-6pm; Sept. to mid-Oct. M-F noon-sunset, Sa-Su 9am-6pm. Hill access CDN$19, ages 13-24 CDN$15, seniors and ages 5-12 CDN$12. Front-suspension bike rental CDN$20 per 2hr., CDN$35 per day.*) Keep an eye out for ski-jumpers, who practice at the facility year-round. The miniature mountain (113m) also opens for recreational **downhill skiing** in winter. The **Olympic Oval,** an enormous indoor speed-skating track on the University of Calgary campus, remains a major international training facility. Speedskaters work out in the early morning and late afternoon; sit in the bleachers to observe the action for free. (*☎403-220-7890; www.oval.ucalgary.ca. Public skating hours vary. CDN$4.75, children and seniors CDN$2.75. Skate rental CDN$3.75.*)

PARKS AND MUSEUMS. Devonian Gardens is one of the world's largest indoor parks, spanning three levels of the Toronto Dominion Square and housing 20,000 plants. A visit to the peaceful gardens will reveal waterfalls and fountains in the Sun Garden, flower-banked pathways in the Quiet Garden, or fish and turtles to feed. (*317 7th Ave. SW. ☎403-268-5207. Open daily 9am-9pm. Free.*) Footbridges stretch from either side of the Bow River to **Prince's Island Park,** a natural refuge only blocks from the city center. In July and August, Mount Royal College performs **Shakespeare in the Park.** (*☎403-240-6908. Call for shows and times. "Pay what you will."*) Calgary's other island park, **St. George's Island,** is accessible by the river walkway to the east or by driving. It houses the **Calgary Zoo,** including a botanical garden and children's zoo. For those who missed the Cretaceous Period, life-sized plastic dinosaurs are also on exhibit. (*Parking off Memorial Dr. on the north side of the river. 1300 Zoo Rd. NE. ☎403-232-9300; www.calgaryzoo.org. Open daily 9am-5pm. CDN$16, seniors CDN$14, ages 13-17 CDN$10, ages 3-12 CDN$8.*)

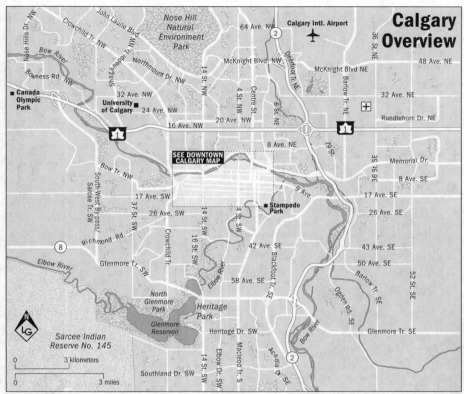

Calgary Overview

SEE DOWNTOWN CALGARY MAP

■ Stampede Park

Nose Hill Natural Environment Park

Canada Olympic Park

University of Calgary

North Glenmore Park

Heritage Park

Glenmore Reservoir

Sarcee Indian Reserve No. 145

Calgary Intl. Airport

0 3 kilometers
0 3 miles

STAMPEDE. The more cosmopolitan Calgary becomes, the more tenaciously it holds on to its frontier roots. The Stampede draws one million cowboys and tourists each July for world-class steer wrestling, bareback and bull-riding, and pig races. The festival spills into the streets from early in the morning (free pancakes for all) through the night. *(Stampede Park is just southeast of downtown, bordering the east side of Macleod Trail between 14th Ave. SE and the Elbow River.* ☎ *800-661-1767; www.calgarystampede.com. CDN$12, seniors and ages 7-12 CDN$6, under 7 free.)*

⚡ FOOD

The small ⬛**Thi-Thi Submarine ❶,** 209 1st St. SE, manages to pack in two plastic seats, a bank of toaster ovens, and the finest Vietnamese submarines in Calgary. Most meaty subs cost under CDN$6; the veggie sub is an unreal CDN$3.25. (☎403-265-5452. Open M-F 11am-7pm, Sa 11:30am-7pm. Cash only.) A generational anomaly and worthy destination, ⬛**Peter's Drive In ❶,** 219 16th Ave. NE, is one of the city's last remaining drive-ins. Hordes of chummy patrons attest to the swell quality. Drive in or walk to the service window. Famous milkshakes cost CDN$3.25, and burgers are under CDN$5. (☎403-277-2747. Open daily 9am-midnight. Cash only.) **Take 10 Cafe ❷,** 304 10th St. NW, became a local favorite by offering dirt-cheap, high-quality food. (☎403-270-7010. Omelettes and wok dishes CDN$8. Open M-F 9am-4pm, Sa-Su 8:30am-3pm. AmEx/MC/V.) **Wicked Wedge ❶,** 618 17th Ave. SW,

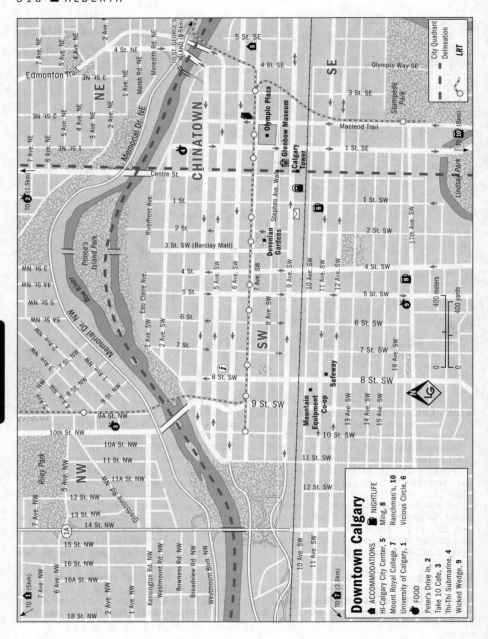

7 Ave. NE
5 Ave. NE
4 Ave. NE
2 Ave. NE

Edmonton Trail

4 St. NE
Marsh Rd. NE
Meredith Rd. NE

TO ST. GEORGE'S ISLAND (0.5km)

5 St. SE
5

4 St. SE

Olympic Way SE

SE

3 St. SE

Stampede Park

Olympic Way SE

NE

3 St. NE
1 Ave. NE

7 Ave. NE
6 Ave. NE
5 Ave. NE
4 Ave. NE
3 Ave. NE
2 Ave. NE

2 St. NE
1 St. NE

Memorial Dr. NE

CHINATOWN

Olympic Plaza
Glenbow Museum

Macleod Trail

TO 10 (8km)

7 Ave. NE

Centre St.

TO 2 (1.5km)

Calgary Tower

1 St. SE

Lindsay Park

Stephen Ave. Walk

1 St.

1 St. SW

Riverfront Ave.

6

2 St.

2 St. SW

17th Ave. SW

3 St. SW (Barclay Mall)

Devonian Gardens

Bow River

Prince's Island Park

4 St.

4 St. SW

Eau Claire Ave.

5 St.

5 St. SW

6 St.

6 St. SW

3 St. NW
4A St. NW
5 St. NW
5A St. NW

Memorial Dr. NW

5 Ave. SW
6 Ave. SW
7 Ave. SW
9 Ave. SW
10 Ave. SW
11 Ave. SW
12 Ave. SW

16 Ave. SW

8 Ave. SW

SW

7 St. SW

8 St. SW

8 St. SW

8

9

9 St. SW

400 meters
400 yards

2 Ave. NW
3 Ave. NW
4 Ave. NW
5 Ave. NW
6 Ave. NW
7 Ave. NW
8 Ave. NW

1 Ave. SW
2 Ave. SW
7 St.

Safeway

9 St. SW

Mountain Equipment Co-op

13 Ave. SW
14 Ave. SW
15 Ave. SW

10 St. SW

9A St. NW

3

N

10th St. NW

11 St. NW
11A St. NW
12 St. NW
13 St. NW
14 St. NW

10A St. NW

11 St. SW

Riley Park

NW

Kensington Rd. NW
Westmount Rd. NW
Bowness Rd. NW
Broadview Rd. NW
Westmount Blvd. NW

Gladstone Rd. NW

1A

12 St. SW

5 Ave. NW

15 St. NW
16 St. NW
16A St. NW

7 Ave. NW
6 Ave. NW

TO 1 (5km)

2 Ave. NW
1 Ave. NW

18 St. NW

TO 4 (2.5km)

10 Ave. SW
11 Ave. SW

Downtown Calgary

City Quadrant Delineation
LRT

serves large, topping-heavy pizza (CDN$3.75 per slice) to Calgary's post-party scene. (☎403-228-1024. Open M-W 11am-last customer, Th-Sa 11am-3am, Su noon-10pm. MC/V.)

ACCOMMODATIONS

Busy and sometimes impersonal, the **HI-Calgary City Centre ❶**, 520 7th Ave. SE, near downtown, has some nice accessories; the clean kitchen, lounge areas, laundry, and backyard with barbecue are pluses, as are free parking and Wi-Fi in the rooms. (☎403-269-8239. 120 beds. Dorms CDN$27, members CDN$23; private rooms CDN$68/$60. MC/V.) The **University of Calgary ❶**, in the ex-Olympic Village in the NW quadrant, is popular with conventioneers and is often booked solid. (Coordinated through **Cascade Hall,** 3456 24th Ave. NW. Take 16th Ave. NW/Trans-Canada west to University Dr. N, then make a left onto 24th Ave. ☎403-220-3203; www.ucalgary.ca/residence. Internet access CDN$15. Parking CDN$4. Rooms available May-Aug. Dorms CDN$23, youth CDN$17; singles CDN$33/$27. MC/V.) In the SW quadrant, **Mount Royal College ❷** offers visitors modern apartment complexes with linens, free parking, and Internet access. (From 16th Ave. NW, take Crowchild Trail S to Mount Royal Gate W. Make a left at the end of Mt. Royal Gate; they're on your left. ☎403-440-6275; www.mtroyal.ab.ca/residence. Mid-May to mid-Aug. bedrooms in 4-bedroom apartment with 2 baths, kitchen, and living room CDN$45.50. MC/V.)

NIGHTLIFE

A very relaxing bar, **Vicious Circle,** 1011 1st St. SW, offers a solid menu, colored mood lights, and a disco ball, plus pool tables, couches, eclectic art, and a TV. Kick back on the summer patio seating and sample one of the 141 different martinis for CDN$8.50. (☎403-269-3951; www.viciouscircle.ca. W live music. Happy hour M-Sa 4-7pm and all day Su. Open M-Th 11:30am-1am, F 11:30am-2am, Sa-Su 1pm-2am. AmEx/MC/V.) For an ultra-hip lounge, stop by **Ming,** 520 17th Ave. SW,

which, though a little smoky, offers modern decor and original martinis like the "Jane Goodall" or "Mother Teresa" along with an equally creative menu. (☎403-229-1986. Open daily 4pm-2am. AmEx/MC/V.) If line-dancing is more your thing, **Ranchman's,** 9615 Macleod Trail, will let you do-si-do to your heart's content. (☎403-253-1100. Cover CDN$6. Open M-Sa 10:30am-2am. MC/V.)

APPROACHING CANMORE: 62 MILES

From Calgary, take **Rte. 1 W** (marked by the Maple Leaf sign) all the way to Lake Louise.

CANMORE. Canmore got its start over 100 years ago, when miners were lured to the valley by rich coal deposits. Worldwide attention turned to the sleepy town in 1988, when the Nordic skiing events of the Winter Olympic Games were held here. Effort has been put into creating the charming downtown area, which today offers a walk past family shops and homey restaurants. The **Canmore Museums,** 907 7th Ave., include a Geoscience Center with ancient stones and bones, the historic North West Mounted Police Barracks, and artifacts from local mines. (☎403-678-2462; www.cmags.org. Open M-F noon-5pm, Sa-Su noon-4pm. CDN$3, students and seniors CDN$2.) The **HI Canmore ❶,** on Indian Flats Rd., offers plush accommodations, but the beds are closely packed. (☎403-678-3200. Internet, laundry, linens. Reservations required. 4- to 6-bed coed dorms CDN$27, members CDN$20; private rooms CDN$81/$60. MC/V.)

APPROACHING BANFF TOWNSITE: 15 MILES

Continue west on **Hwy. 1** to Banff National Park. All traffic will be forced to stop to pay the entrance fee to the park. Your pass will get you into any of the other national parks in the area (Jasper, Yoho, Kootenay, Glacier, and Mt. Revelstoke), so purchase as many days as you want to explore them.

BANFF TOWNSITE

Less townsite than chic resort, Banff provides the weary traveler with fine dining and luxury lodgings just below majestic, snow-capped peaks. A stroll downtown reveals decadent candy shops and jewelry boutiques alongside sports outfitters and equipment rental. The

GREAT NORTH

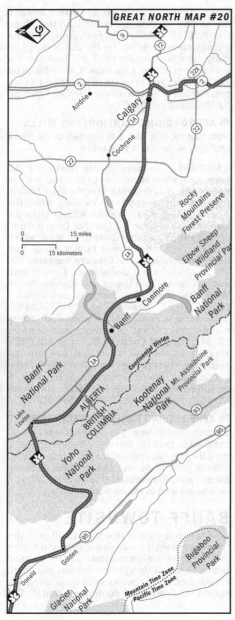

GREAT NORTH MAP #20

GREAT NORTH

chilly weather hasn't affected the people—Banff residents are warm and welcoming.

VITAL STATS

Population: 8000

Visitor Info: Banff Visitor Centre, 224 Banff Ave., includes **Banff/Lake Louise Tourism Bureau** (☎403-762-8421; www.banfflakelouise.com) and **Parks Canada** (☎403-762-1550). Open daily July-Aug. 8am-8pm; mid-May to June and early to mid-Sept. 8am-6pm; late Sept. to mid-May 9am-5pm.

Internet Access: Banff Library, 101 Bear St. (☎403-762-2611). Sign up in advance. Open June-Aug. M-Th 10am-8pm, F-Sa 10am-6pm; Sept.-May daily 10am-8pm. Free.

Post Office: 204 Buffalo St. (☎403-762-2586). Open M-W 8:30am-5:30pm, Th-F 8:30am-7pm, Sa 9am-5pm. **Postal Code:** T0L 0C0.

GETTING AROUND

The Banff townsite is located off the **Trans-Canada Highway (Hwy. 1). Banff Ave.** leads to downtown, where restaurants, shops, and bars reside. Parallel to and west of Banff Ave. is **Bear St.,** where the movie theater and the Whyte Museum are located. Accommodations scatter the downtown area, with pricier options clustered closer to town. Parking is ample in and around the downtown area.

SIGHTS

There are numerous outdoor activities in Banff National Park (see p. 320), but a quiet day in the townsite can prove rewarding as well. The **Whyte Museum of the Canadian Rockies,** 111 Bear St., explores the history and culture of the Canadian Rockies over the last two centuries in the **Heritage Gallery,** while temporary exhibits focus on the natural history of the region. Displays include works by Canadian painters. (☎403-762-2291; www.whyte.org. Open daily 10am-5pm. CDN$6, students and seniors CDN$3.50.)

OUTDOORS

There are countless outdoor opportunities in Banff National Park (p. 320). Before you head out, however, you'll need to rent equipment in town. Here are several options:

Mountain Magic Equipment, 224 Bear St. (☎403-762-2591). One of the few places in Banff to rent mountaineering packages (CDN$40 per day). They also offer the usual bike (CDN$9 per hr., CDN$28 per day), ski (from CDN$30 per day), and cross-country (from CDN$15 per day) rentals. Open daily 9am-9pm.

Bactrax Rentals, 225 Bear St. (☎403-762-8177). Rents mountain bikes (CDN$8-12 per hr., CDN$30-42 per day). Bike tours CDN$20-60 per hr. including all equipment. Ski packages from CDN$20 per day; snowboard packages CDN$28. Also offers camping equipment rentals (CDN$3-20 per day). Open daily Apr.-Oct. 8am-8pm; Nov.-Mar. 7am-9pm.

Wilson Mountain Sports (☎403-522-3636), in the Lake Louise Samson Mall. Rents bikes (CDN$15 per hr., CDN$39 per day) and camping and fishing gear. Mountaineering (CDN$39 per day) and rock climbing packages (CDN$19 per day). Open daily mid-June to Sept. 9am-9pm; Oct. to Apr. 8am-8pm; May to mid-June 9am-8pm.

▓ FOOD

Like everything else in town, Banff restaurants tend toward the expensive. The Banff and Lake Louise hostels serve affordable meals in their cafes (CDN$5-9). **Nourish ❸,** 215 Banff Ave., is a relaxed vegetarian cafe hidden upstairs in a touristy mall—try the *spanakopita* for CDN$12. (☎403-760-3933. Entrees CDN$8-15. Open daily 11:30am-9pm. MC/V.) **Aardvark's ❶,** 304A Caribou St., does big business selling pizza after the bars close. It's often standing-room-only as hungry revelers jostle for a spot. (☎403-762-5500. Breakfast CDN$2-5. Slices of pizza CDN$3. Small pie CDN$8-10; large CDN$16-22. Subs CDN$5-8. Open daily 9am-4am. MC/V.) **Chaya ❷,** 118 Banff Ave., serves a terrific assortment of pan-Asian food in a tiny space. (☎403-760-0882. Dishes CDN$8-9. Open daily 11:30am-8:30pm. Cash only.)

▓ ACCOMMODATIONS

Finding a cheap place to stay in Banff has become exceedingly difficult; the number of visitors soars into the millions every year. Residents offer rooms in their homes, occasionally at reasonable rates (CDN$75-140; in

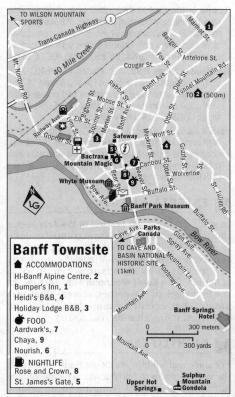

Banff Townsite

⌂ ACCOMMODATIONS
HI-Banff Alpine Centre, **2**
Bumper's Inn, **1**
Heidi's B&B, **4**
Holiday Lodge B&B, **3**

◆ FOOD
Aardvark's, **7**
Chaya, **9**
Nourish, **6**

▣ NIGHTLIFE
Rose and Crown, **8**
St. James's Gate, **5**

winter CDN$60-100). Check the list at the back of the *Banff and Lake Louise Official Visitor Guide*, available free at the visitors centers. The hostel does provide an alternative to camping, and several inns in town run on the not-so-expensive-compared-to-everything-else side. For more options, stop by the Banff tourist office, which supplies free accommodations guides, replete with general price rankings. For more options inside the park, see p. 320.

HI-Banff Alpine Centre (☎403-762-4122), 3km uphill from Banff Townsite on Tunnel Mountain Rd. This monster hostel sleeps 215 and has 3 lounges and kitchens. Laundry and hot showers. Free Wi-Fi. Check-in 3pm. Check-out 11am. Dorms CDN$30-32, members CDN$26-28. MC/V. ❶

Bumper's Inn (☎403-762-3386 or 800-661-3518; www.bumpersinn.com), at the corner of Banff Ave. and Marmot St. This cozy, quiet inn is 1½km from downtown and offers comfortable suites with an outdoor courtyard. Rooms CDN$101-150. AmEx/MC/V. ❺

The Holiday Lodge B&B, 311 Marten St. (☎403-762-3648), on Marten St., between Elk and Moose St. This quaint inn has heritage home decor and private baths with showers. Doubles in summer CDN$65-130; in winter CDN$45-115. MC/V. ❹

Heidi's B&B, 214 Otter St. (☎403-726-3806), between Wolf and Caribou St., 3 blocks away from downtown. Comfortable rooms have private baths and tubs with jets. Rooms in summer CDN$70-85; in winter CDN$50. Cash only. ❹

🎵 ENTERTAINMENT

In summer, the **Banff Festival of the Arts** keeps tourists occupied. A wide spectrum of events, from First Nations dance to opera, are performed from May to mid-August. Some shows are free; stop by the visitors center for a schedule. The **Banff Mountain Film Festival,** in the first week of November, screens films and videos that celebrate mountaineers. (For times and info, call ☎403-762-6301.)

🍷 NIGHTLIFE

For some real wildlife, check out Banff's bars. Ask the visitors center to find out which nightspots are having "locals' night," featuring cheap drinks. **Banff Ave.** hosts a ton of bars, restaurants, kitschy gift shops, and banks.

❤ Rose and Crown, 202 Banff Ave. (☎403-762-2121), upstairs at the corner of Caribou St. Ample room for dancing and billiards (CDN$1.25), even on busy nights. Living room for watching sports and live music every night at 10pm, and a rooftop patio with unparalleled views. Pints CDN$5-7. Cover Sa CDN$2-3. Su Jam Night with happy hour 9pm-last customer. Open daily 11am-2am. AmEx/MC/V.

St. James's Gate, 205 Wolf St. (☎403-762-9355). A laid-back Irish pub. Ask the bartenders to recommend one of 32 international beers on tap. F-Sa live jigs. Open daily 11am-2am. AmEx/MC/V.

🚶 APPROACHING BANFF NATIONAL PARK: 0 MILES

Don't move. You are already in the park.

BANFF NATIONAL PARK

Banff is Canada's best-loved and best-known natural park, with 6641 sq. km of peaks, forests, glaciers, and alpine valleys. It also became Canada's first national park only days after the Canadian Pacific Railway's completion in 1885. The park's name comes from Banffshire, Scotland, the birthplace of two Canadian Pacific Railway financiers who convinced Canada's first Prime Minister that a "large pecuniary advantage" might be gained from the region, telling him that "since we can't export the scenery, we shall have to import the tourists." Banff's natural beauty, along with the laid-back attitude it affords, has attracted hordes of young people to Banff Townsite (p. 317).

VITAL STATS
Area: 1.6 million acres
Visitor Info: Banff Visitor Centre, 224 Banff Ave. (p. 318).
Gateway Towns: Banff, Lake Louise
Fees: CDN$9, seniors CDN$7.75, ages 6-16 CDN$4.50.

🧭 GETTING AROUND

Banff National Park hugs the Alberta side of the Alberta/British Columbia border, 128km west of Calgary. The **Trans-Canada Hwy. (Hwy. 1)** runs east-west through the park, connecting it to Yoho National Park (p. 325) in the west. The **Icefields Pkwy. (Hwy. 93)** connects Banff with Jasper National Park to the north and Kootenay National Park to the southwest. Civilization in the park centers on the towns of **Banff** and **Lake Louise,** 58km apart on Hwy. 1. The more serene **Bow Valley Pkwy. (Hwy. 1A)** parallels Hwy. 1 from Lake Louise to 8km west of Banff, offering excellent camping, hostelling, sights, and wildlife. The southern portion of Hwy. 1A is restricted at night in late spring and early summer to accommodate wildlife. Parking in Banff National Park is plentiful.

👁 SIGHTS

The **Banff Park Museum National Historic Site,** 92 Banff Ave., is western Canada's oldest natural history museum, with rooms of stuffed specimens dating to the 1860s. (☎403-762-1558. Open daily mid-May to Sept. 10am-6pm; Oct. 1 to mid-May 1-5pm. Tours daily in summer 3pm; in winter Sa-Su only. CDN\$4, seniors CDN\$3.50, children CDN\$2.) Banff National Park would not exist if not for the **Cave and Basin Mineral Springs,** once rumored to have miraculous healing properties. The **Cave and Basin National Historic Site,** a refurbished bath house built circa 1914, is now a small museum detailing the history and science of the site. Access to the low-ceilinged cave containing the original spring is inside the building. Five of the pools are the only home of the park's most endangered species: the small Banff Springs snail, *Physella johnsoni.* (☎403-762-1566. Open in summer daily 9am-6pm; in winter M-F 11am-4pm, Sa-Su 9:30am-5pm. Tours daily 11am. CDN\$4, seniors CDN\$3.50, children CDN\$2.) The **springs** are southwest of the city on Cave Ave. For a dip in the hot water, follow the smell to the Upper Hot Springs pool, a 40°C (104°F) sulfurous cauldron on Mountain Ave. (☎403-762-1515; www.hotsprings.ca. Open daily mid-May to early Sept. 9am-11pm; early Sept. to mid-May M-Th, Su 10am-10pm, F-Sa 10am-11pm. Swimsuits CDN\$2, towels CDN\$2, lockers CDN\$1. CDN\$7.50, seniors and children 3-17 CDN\$6.50.)

◤ OUTDOORS

A visitor sticking to paved byways will see a tiny fraction of the park and the majority of the park's visitors. Those interested in the endless outdoor options can hike or bike on more than 1600km of trails. Grab a free copy of the *Mountain Biking and Cycling Guide* or *Dayhikes in Banff* and peruse trail descriptions at information centers. For still more solitude, pick up *The Banff Backcountry Experience* and an overnight **camping permit** at a visitors center and head out to the backcountry. (CDN\$9 per person per day. CDN\$12 surcharge for advance reservations. AmEx/MC/V.) Be sure to check with the rangers at the information center for current weather, trail, and wildlife updates.

HIKING

Two easy trails are within walking distance of Banff Townsite, but longer, more rigorous

trails abound farther away. The best escapes are found in the backcountry. Restaurants are few and far between so, unless you plan to throttle elk with your bare hands, bring your own food on hikes. Let's Go does not recommend throttling elk.

Fenland (2km, 1hr.). Follow Mt. Norquay Rd. to the outskirts, look for signs across the tracks on road's left side. This flat, easy trail crosses area is inhabited by beaver, muskrat, and waterfowl, but it is closed for elk calving in late spring.

Tunnel Mountain (2.25km, 2hr.). Follow Wolf St. east from Banff Ave., and turn right on St. Julien Rd. to reach the head of the steep, moderately difficult trail. After a rise of 260m, there is a dramatic view of the **Bow Valley** and **Mt. Rundle.** Tunnel Mountain has the distinction of being the Rockies' smallest mountain.

Aylmer Pass (26.5km round-trip, 8hr.). This strenuous trail leaves from the shore of Lake Minnewanka on Lake Minnewanka Rd. (the extension of Banff Ave. across the Trans-Canada from town). Parking just above tour boat area. A steep climb to the summit yields a panoramic view of the lake and surrounding scenery. The trail can be abridged by hiking only 11.6km to the lookout, cutting the final 250m ascent.

Johnston Canyon (5½km, 2hr.). West of the Norquay Interchange on Hwy. 1, then 18km along the Bow Valley Pkwy. (Hwy. 1A). A popular moderate-to-strenuous ½-day hike. A catwalk along the edge of the deep limestone canyon runs 1km over the thundering river to the canyon's lower falls, then another 1.5km to the upper falls. The trail continues for a rugged 3.25km to 7 blue-green cold-water springs, known as the **Inkpots,** in a valley above the canyon. More than 42km of trails beyond the Inkpots are blissfully untraveled and punctuated with campgrounds roughly every 10km.

Sulphur Mountain (5.5km, 2hr.). Winds along a well-trodden trail to the peak, where a spectacular view awaits; the **Sulphur Mountain Gondola** charges half-price for the 8min. downhill trip if you buy your ticket at the top. (☎403-762-2523. Round-trip CDN\$23.50, ages 6-15 CDN\$11.75, under 6 free.) The **Panorama Restaurant ❹** (☎403-762-7486), perched atop the mountain, serves breakfast (CDN\$9) and lunch buffets (CDN\$17) from mid-May to mid-August. AmEx/MC/V.

BACKCOUNTRY

Backcountry trekking is the way to see Banff. Banff's wild backcountry, replete with mind-boggling scenery, belies the civilized tourist trap that the townsite has become. Amateurs and experts alike should beware of dangerous and changing conditions on strenuous trails that do not receive as much maintenance as more accessible routes; consult park rangers for information. Trails to ask about include **Egypt Lake** (12.4km one-way, 2 days), **Twin Lakes** (8.7km one-way, 2 days), **Mystic Pass** (37km, 3 days), **Skoki Loop** (34km, 3 days), **Assiniboine Loop** (55km, 4 days), **Sawback Trail** (74km, 5 days), and **Mystic Pass-Flint's Park-Badger Pass Trail** (76km, 5 days).

BIKING

Biking is permitted on public roads, highways, and certain trails in the park. Spectacular scenery and a number of hostels and campgrounds make the **Bow Valley Pkwy. (Hwy. 1A)** and the **Icefields Pkwy. (Hwy. 93)** perfect for extended cycling trips. Every store downtown seems to rent bikes; head to **Bactrax** (see p. 319) for HI discounts. Parks Canada publishes a free *Mountain Biking and Cycling Guide* that describes trails and roadways where bikes are permitted; pick up a copy at bike rental shops or visitors centers.

WATERSPORTS

Fishing is legal in most of the park during specific seasons, but natural bait and lead weights are not. Get a **permit** and check out regulations at the info center. (Permits CDN$9 per day; season pass CDN$30.) **Bourgeau Lake,** a 7km hike in, is home to a particularly feisty breed of brook trout. Closer to the road, try **Herbert Lake,** off the Icefields Pkwy., or **Lake Minnewanka,** on Lake Minnewanka Rd. northeast of Banff. Lake Minnewanka Rd. passes **Johnson Lake,** where shallow warm water makes for a perfect swimming hole.

Hydra River Guides runs rafting trips along the Kicking Horse River. (☎ 403-762-4554 or 800-644-8888; www.raftbanff.com. Up to Class V rapids. CDN$95; includes lunch, transportation, and gear. HI members discount 10%.) **Blast Adventures** leads half-day inflatable kayak trips on the rowdy Kananaskis River. (☎ 403-609-2009 or 888-802-5278; www.blastadventures.com. CDN$72; includes transportation, gear, and snacks.)

▲ ACCOMMODATIONS

Enormous, modern hostels in Banff and Lake Louise anchor a chain of cozier hostels from Calgary to Jasper. Rustic hostels provide more of a wilderness experience (read: no electricity or flush toilets), and often have some of the park's best hiking and cross-country skiing right in their backyards. Wait-list beds become available at 6pm, and the larger hostels try to save a few stand-by beds for shuttle arrivals. Beds go quickly, especially during the summer, so make reservations as early as possible. Reservations can be made through the southern **Alberta HI administration.** (☎ 866-762-4122; www.hihostels.ca). Free reservations are held until 6pm, but can be guaranteed until later with a credit card.

Rampart Creek Wilderness Hostel (HI), 34km south of the Icefield Centre. Close to several world-famous ice climbs (including Weeping Wall, 17km north), this hostel is a favorite for winter mountaineers and anyone who likes a rustic sauna after a hard day's hike. Wood-burning sauna, full-service kitchen. Reservations recommended. Closed mid-Apr. to mid-May and mid-Oct. to mid-Nov. 12-bed coed cabins CDN$27, members CDN$23. MC/V. ❶

Castle Mountain Wilderness Hostel (HI), in Castle Junction, 1.5km east of the junction of Hwy. 1 and Hwy. 93 south, between Banff and Lake Louise. One of the hardest hostels to find, Castle Mountain offers a quieter alternative to the hubbub of its big brothers. Comfortable common area with huge bay windows. Friendly staff, hot showers, kitchen, laundry, electricity, and volleyball. Check-in 5-10pm. Check-out 10am. Dorms June-Oct. CDN$23-27, Sept. CDN$27; members CDN$19-23/$23. MC/V. ❶

Mosquito Creek Wilderness Hostel (HI), 103km south of the Icefield Centre and 26km north of Lake Louise. Across the creek from the Mosquito Creek campground. Close to the Wapta Icefield. Enormous living room with wood stove, wood-burning sauna, kitchen, and pump water. Check-in 5-10pm. Check-out 11am. 16-bed coed cabins CDN$27, members CDN$23; private rooms CDN$66/$58. MC/V. ❶

▲ CAMPING

A chain of campgrounds stretches between Banff and Jasper. Extra-large, fully hooked-up grounds lie closer to the townsites; for more trees and fewer vehicles, try more remote sites farther from Banff and Lake Louise. At park campgrounds that allow fires, a **campfire permit** (including firewood) costs CDN$7. Sites are first come, first served; arrive early. The sites below are listed from south to north and have no toilets or showers unless otherwise noted.

Tunnel Mountain Village, 4km from Banff Townsite on Tunnel Mountain Rd. With nearly 1200 sites, this is a camping metropolis. Trailer/RV area has 321 full RV sites, Village 2 has 188 sites, and Village 1 houses a whopping 618. Fires allowed in Village 1 only; all villages have showers. Village 2 is open year-round; 1 and 3 closed Oct. early May. Sites CDN$24, with electricity CDN$28; RV sites with full hookup CDN$33. AmEx/MC/V. ❶

Two Jack, 13km northeast of Banff, across Hwy.1. 381 main sites (CDN$19) with no showers. 80 lakeside sites (CDN$24) with showers. Open mid-May to Aug. AmEx/MC/V. ❶

Johnston Canyon, 26km northwest of Banff on Bow Valley Pkwy. 140 sites. Access to Johnston Canyon Trail. Showers. Open early June to mid-Sept. Sites CDN$24. AmEx/MC/V. ❶

Protection Mountain, 15km east of Lake Louise and 11km west of Castle Junction on the Bow Valley Pkwy. (Hwy. 1A). 89 spacious sites (14 RV sites) in a basic campground. Open late June to early Sept. Sites CDN$19. AmEx/MC/V. ❶

Lake Louise, 1.5km southeast of the visitors center on Fairview Rd. On Bow River, not the lake. Plenty of hiking and fishing awaits. Showers. 189 trailer sites with electricity, open year-round. 220 tent sites, open mid-May to Sept. Tent sites CDN$24; RV sites CDN$28. AmEx/MC/V. ❶

Mosquito Creek, 103km south of the Icefield Centre and 26km north of Lake Louise. 32 sites with hiking access. Pit toilets. Open year-round. Sites CDN$14. AmEx/MC/V. ❶

Rampart Creek, 147km north of Banff, 34km south of the Icefield Centre, across from Rampart Creek hostel and amazing ice climbing. Pit toilets. Open late June to early Sept. Sites CDN$14. AmEx/MC/V. ❶

🛌 APPROACHING LAKE LOUISE: 35 MILES
Continue on **Hwy. 1 W** to Lake Louise.

LAKE LOUISE TOWNSITE

The highest community in Canada (1530m), Lake Louise and the surrounding glaciers have often passed for Swiss scenery in mov-

ies and are the emerald in the Rockies' tiara of tourism. The lake was named in 1884 in honor of Queen Victoria's daughter, and its beauty is nothing short of royal.

VITAL STATS
Population: 1200
Visitor Info: Lake Louise Visitor Centre (☎403-522-3833), at Samson Mall on Village Rd. Open daily in summer 9am-7pm; in spring and fall 9am-5pm; in winter 9am-4pm.
Internet Access: The Depot (☎403-522-3870), in the Samson Mall. Open M-F 7am-6pm, Sa-Su 7am-5pm. Free.
Post Office: Mail services at The Depot (see above). **Postal Code:** TOL 1E0.

▐ GETTING AROUND

The townsite's center, to the right off Hwy. 1/Hwy. 93, is literally that—a small shopping center with a few restaurants and a market. Parking is ample in the city center and at motels and campsites around the lake.

⚠ OUTDOORS

The **Lake Louise Sightseeing Lift,** up Whitehorn Rd. and across the Trans-Canada Hwy. from Lake Louise, cruises up **Mt. Whitehorn.** (☎403-522-3555; www.skilouise.com. Open May daily 9am-4pm; June to Sept. daily 8:30am-6pm. Last ascent 30min. before close. CDN$23, ages 6-15 CDN$11.50, under 6 free. To enjoy breakfast at the top, add CDN$2; for lunch, add CDN$6.)

HIKING

You can view the water and its surrounding splendor from several hiking trails that begin in the neighborhood and climb along the surrounding ridgelines. But be warned, with beauty comes crowds; expect masses of tourists (and bears).

Lake Agnes Trail (3½km round-trip, 2½hr.), and the **Plain of Six Glaciers Trail** (5.3km round-trip, 4hr.) both end at teahouses and make for a lovely, if sometimes crowded, day hike with views down to the Lake. Open in summer daily 9am-6pm.

Moraine Lake, 15km from the village, at the end of Moraine Lake Rd. and off Lake Louise Dr. (no trailers or long RVs). Moraine lies in the awesome **Valley of the Ten Peaks,** opposite glacier-encrusted **Mt. Temple.** Join the multitudes on the **Rockpile Trail** for an eye-popping view of the lake and a lesson in ancient ocean bottoms (10min. walk to the top). To escape the camera-wielding hordes, try one of the lake's more challenging trails, either **Sentinel Pass** via Larch Valley (6km one-way, 5-6hr.), with stunning views from flower-studded meadows, or **Wenkchemna Pass** via Eiffel Lake (9.7km one-way, full day), which carries hikers the length of the Valley of the Ten Peaks with incredible views in both directions. Be sure to arrive before 10am or after 4pm to see the view instead of the crowds.

Paradise Valley, depending on how you hike it, can be an intense day hike or a relaxing overnight trip. From the **Paradise Creek Trailhead,** 2.5km up Moraine Lake Rd., the loop through the valley runs 18km through subalpine and alpine forests and along rivers (7½hr.; elevation gain 880m). One classic backpacking route runs from Moraine Lake up and over **Sentinel Pass,** joining the top of the Paradise Valley loop after 8km. A **backcountry campground** marks the midpoint from either trailhead. Grizzly activity often forces the park wardens to close the area in summer; check with the wardens before hiking in this area.

WINTER SPORTS

Winter activities in the park range from world-class ice climbing to ice fishing. Those 1600km of hiking trails make for exceptional **cross-country skiing (Moraine Lake Rd.** is closed to vehicle traffic in the winter, and is used for cross-country skiing, as are the backcountry trails), and three allied resorts offer a range of **skiing and snowboarding** opportunities from early November to mid-May. All have terrain parks for snowboarders. Shuttles to all the following three resorts leave from most big hotels in the townsites, and Banff and Lake Louise hostels typically have ticket and transportation **discounts** available for guests. Multi-day passes good for all three resorts are available at the **Ski Banff/Lake Louise** office, 225 Banff Ave. (☎403-762-4561), in Banff, at all resorts, and online (www.skibig3.com). Passes include free shuttle service and an extra night of skiing at **Mount Norquay** (3-day passes CDN$198-225).

Sunshine Mountain (☎403-762-6500, snow report 403-760-7669; www.skibanff.com). 3168 acres on 3 mountains, with the most snowfall (10m) in the area, this mountain attracts loyal followers. Lift tickets CDN$65; seniors CDN$53, ages 13-17 CDN$50; ages 6-12 CDN$24.

Lake Louise (☎403-522-3555, snow report 403-762-4766; www.skilouise.com). The second-largest ski area in Canada (4200 ski-able acres), with amazing views, over 1000m of vertical drop, and the best selection of expert terrain. Some simpler slopes cover plenty of the mountain. Lift tickets CDN$85; students under 25 and seniors CDN$72; ages 6-12 CDN$55.

Mt. Norquay (☎403-762-4421; www.banffnorquay.com). A locals' mountain: small and close to town. The Canadian Rockies' only night-skiing on Friday. Lift tickets CDN$52; students, ages 13-17, and 55+ CDN$40; ages 6-12 CDN$17. Night-skiing CDN$24/$22/$12.

FLOUR POWER

Passing by the many lakes and streams in the Rockies, you may notice that they have an unusual color. When looking at the swimming-pool turquoise or glowing blue of the water, you might wonder if this is some kind of gimmick perpetuated by the park wardens to bring in the tourists. Many years ago, a visitor to Lake Louise claimed that he had solved the mystery of the beautiful water: it had obviously been distilled from peacock tails. Turns out he was a bit off the mark. The actual cause of the color is "rock flour." This fine dust is created by the pressure exerted by the glacier upon rocks trapped in the ice; the resulting ground rock is washed into streams and lakes in the glacial meltwater. Suspended particles trap all colors of the spectrum except for the blues and greens, which are reflected back for your visual pleasure. The glacially-fed lakes are too cold to grow murky algae, and the water is free from the dirt sediment that would interfere with their color. This means, however, that the water is usually free of large populations of fish as well—it's pleasing to the eye, but not so nice to the touch. The floury water is just as safe as any other water in the mountains as long as you filter it first, but only try it as a last resort: you'll have to go through plenty of clogged filters before the water becomes potable.

FOOD

There are more food options in Banff than Lake Louise, so if you plan to dine out, it's best to stay in the city. The town's main shopping center, however, has a grocery and a few restaurant options. The **Village Market**, in the Samson Mall, has fresh produce and the basics. (☎403-522-3894. MC/V.) **Laggan's Deli ❶**, in Samson Mall, is always crowded. Thick sandwiches (CDN$6) or fresh-baked loaves (CDN$3) are perennial favorites. (☎403-522-2017. Open daily June-Sept. 6am-8pm; Oct.-May 6am-7pm. Cash or traveler's checks only.) The **Lake Louise Village Grill & Bar Family Restaurant & Lounge ❶**, also in the Samson Mall, is as versatile as its name suggests, with steaks (CDN$12-24), breakfast options, sandwiches, and Chinese food. (☎403-522-3879. Salads CDN$5-12. Sandwiches and burgers CDN$8-12. Chinese entrees CDN$13-18. Open daily 11am-10:30pm. Bar open until 2am. MC/V.)

ACCOMMODATIONS

There are several campsites near Lake Louise (p. 324), and one hostel in town. **Lake Louise International Hostel (HI) ❶**, 500m west of the visitors center in Lake Louise Townsite, on Village Rd. toward the Park Warden's office, is more like a resort than a hostel—it boasts a reference library, a stone fireplace, two full kitchens, a sauna, and a nice cafe with free Wi-Fi. (☎403-522-2200. Hub for mountaineering tours. Internet access CDN$2 per 15min. Check-in 3pm. Check-out 11am. Reservations recommended. Dorms CDN$27-38, members CDN$23-34. Private rooms CDN$85-106/$78-99. MC/V.) There are also a handful of inns in Lake Louise, but they tend to be pricey. The posh **Lake Louise Inn ❺**, 210 Village Rd., has a swimming pool, suites with kitchens and fireplaces, and several restaurants. (☎403-522-3791 or 800-661-9237; www.lakelouise.com. Rooms in summer CDN$201-250, in winter CDN$101-150. AmEx/MC/V.)

APPROACHING YOHO NATIONAL PARK: 16 MILES

From Lake Louise, continue west on **Hwy 1**. When you cross the Continental Divide, you enter British Columbia and Yoho National Park. Descend the Kicking Horse Canyon toward Field, the gateway to Yoho National Park.

The Pacific Province

BRITISH COLUMBIA

Welcomes You!

YOHO NATIONAL PARK

A Cree expression for awe and wonder, Yoho is the perfect name for this park. It sports some of the most engaging names in the Rockies, such as Kicking Horse Pass, named after Captain John Hector, who was kicked in the chest by his horse. Driving down Yoho's narrow pass on Hwy. 1, visitors can see geological forces at work: massive bent and tilted sedimentary rock layers exposed in sharply eroded cliff faces, and rock bridges formed by water that has carved away the stone. Beneath these rock walls, Yoho overflows with other natural attractions, including the largest waterfall in the Rockies—Takakkaw Falls—and 500 million-year-old fossils.

VITAL STATS

Area: 325,000 acres

Visitors Info: Yoho National Park Visitor Centre (☎250-343-6783), in Field on Hwy. 1. Open daily in summer 9am-7pm; in spring and fall 9am-5pm; in winter 9am-4pm.

Gateway town: Field.

Fees: CDN$9, seniors CDN$7.75, children CDN$4.50.

GETTING AROUND

The park lies on the **Trans-Canada Hwy. (Hwy. 1)**, next to Banff National Park. Within Yoho is the town of **Field**, 27km west of Lake Louise on Hwy. 1. Parking is available at campsites and most lookout points and trailheads.

SIGHTS

The **Great Divide** is both the boundary between Alberta and BC as well as the Atlantic and Pacific watersheds. Here a stream forks, with one arm flowing 1500km to the Pacific Ocean and the other flowing 2500km to the Atlantic via the Hudson Bay. It is also the site of **Burgess Shale,** a layer of sedimentary rock containing imprints of the insect-like, soft-bodied organisms that inhabited the world's oceans prior to the Cambrian Explosion. Discovered in 1909, the unexpected complexity of these 505 million-year-old specimens changed the way paleontologists thought about evolution. Larger, clumsier animals known as humans have since lobbied to protect the shale from excessive tourism: educational hikes led by the **Yoho-Burgess Shale Foundation** are the only way to see it. (☎ 800-343-3006. July to mid-Sept. only. Call ahead. Full day 20km hike CDN$65, under 12 CDN$25.) A steep 6km loop to the equally old and trilobite-packed **Mt. Stephen Fossil Beds** is CDN$45. For easier sightseeing, follow the 14km of the Yoho Valley Rd. to views of the **Takakkaw Falls,** Yoho's most splendid waterfall, and the highest-altitude major falls in the Canadian Rockies.

🥾 HIKING

The park's six **backcountry campgrounds** and 400km of trail make for an intense wilderness experience, with countless quickly accessed trails exhibiting scenery equal to that of the larger parks. Before setting out, pick up **camping permits** (CDN$9 per person per day), maps, and the free *Backcountry Guide to Yoho National Park* at the visitors center. Whiskey Jack Hostel (see p. 326) is also well stocked with trail info. The park's finest terrain is in the Yoho Valley, accessible only after the snow melts in mid- to late summer.

Iceline Trail (via Little Yoho 21km, via Celeste Lake 17.5km; 695m elevation change). Starts at the hostel. Takes hikers through forests of alder, spruce, and fir before leading them above the treeline, over glacial moraines, and past the striated rock and pools of Emerald Glacier. Moderate.

Emerald Triangle (19¾km round-trip; 880m elevation change). The route travels through the Yoho Pass to the Wapta Highline trail, Burgess Pass, and back to the start. Most of the journey is

above treeline with breathtaking views over diverse landscape. Moderate.

Mt. Hunter Lookout to Upper Lookout (12¾km one-way; 440m elevation change). Cuts through lower altitudes, with a nice view of Kicking Horse and Beaverfoot valleys, leading to 2 former fire towers. Moderate.

Wapta Falls (4.6km round-trip; 30m elevation change). The trailhead is not marked on Hwy. 1 for westbound traffic as there is no left-turn lane. Continue 3km to the west entrance of the park, turn around, and come back east. Highlights include the Kicking Horse River's 30m drop. The least ambitious of the hikes, and thus, the least spectacular. Easy.

🍴 FOOD

The most convenient food stop in Yoho is the ⬛**Truffle Pigs Cafe and General Store ❷,** on Stephen Ave. in Field, which sells basic foodstuffs, excellent coffee, microbrews, wine, and camping supplies. Local crafts line the walls, and the owners peddle sandwiches (CDN$6-9), breakfast (CDN$2-7), and delicious dinners (CDN$12). You may end up staying all day. The restaurant also has the only **ATM** in the area. (☎ 250-343-6462. Open in summer daily 8am-10pm; in winter M-Sa 10am-7pm. AmEx/MC/V.)

🏠 ACCOMMODATIONS

With one of the best locations of the Rocky Mountain hostels, the ⬛**Whiskey Jack Hostel (HI) ❶,** 13km off Hwy. 1 on the Yoho Valley Rd., blurs the line between civilization and nature. It offers a kitchen, plumbing, propane light, access to Yoho's best high-country trails, and the splendor of the Takakkaw Falls from the porch. Reserve through the Banff Hostel. (☎ 403-762-4122. Open late June-Sept., depending on snow. Dorms CDN$27, members CDN$23. MC/V.)

The three official **frontcountry campgrounds** offer a total of 200 sites, all accessible from the highway. All sites are first come, first served, but only Monarch and Kicking Horse fill up regularly in summer. ⬛**Takakkaw Falls Campground ❶** is situated beneath mountains, glaciers, and the magnificent falls 14km up curvy Yoho Valley Rd. It offers only pump water and pit toilets, and campers must park in the Falls lot and haul their gear 650m to the peaceful sites. (35 sites. Open late June until snow. Sites CDN$16. AmEx/MC/V.) **Monarch Campground ❶** sits at the junction of Yoho Valley Rd. and Hwy. 1. (46 sites and 10 walk-ins. No campfires. Open early May and June-early Sept. Sites CDN$16. AmEx/MC/V.) **Kicking Horse ❶**, another kilometer up Yoho Valley Rd., has toilets. (86 sites. Hot showers. Open mid-May to mid-Oct. CDN$24. AmEx/MC/V.) A fourth campground, **Hoodoo,** is presently closed for regrowth after a prescribed fire. Reserve one of two backcountry alpine huts through the Alpine Club of Canada. (☎403-678-3200. CDN$22.)

⚐ APPROACHING GOLDEN: 35 MILES

From Yoho, haul keel west on **Hwy. 1.** Golden is a bit south of the intersection with **Hwy. 95.** The drive through the Kicking Horse Canyon is stunning but dangerous—watch out for impatient drivers attempting ridiculous passing feats on this 2-lane road. This stretch is BC's top priority for expansion, so construction will also be ongoing for the next few years.

GOLDEN. Surrounded by six national parks (Glacier, Yoho, Banff, Jasper, Kootenay, and Mount Revelstoke), Golden is a convenient base for regional exploration and outdoor activities. At the foot of Kicking Horse Ski Mountain, the **Kicking Horse Hostel ❶**, 518 Station Ave., matches its location with ski-lodge decor, complete with skis and snowshoes hanging from the walls. (Exit for the city center off Hwy. 1, then make an immediate left onto Station Ave. ☎250-344-5071. Kitchen, free linens. Coed dorms CDN$25. Cash only.)

⚐ APPROACHING GLACIER NATIONAL PARK: 52 MILES

Take **Hwy. 95 N** to **Hwy. 1 W.**

GLACIER NATIONAL PARK

This aptly named national park (not to be confused with the Glacier National Park in Montana) is home to over 400 monolithic ice floes that cover one-tenth of its 1350 sq. km area. The jagged peaks and steep, narrow valleys of the Columbia Range not only make for breathtaking scenery but also prevent development in the park. In late summer, brilliant

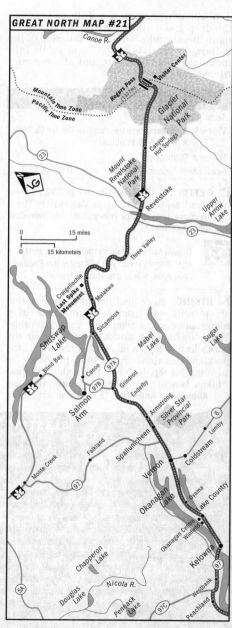

GREAT NORTH MAP #21

explosions of mountain wildflowers offset the deep green of the forests. In the winter, more literal explosions shake the calm of the valleys—scientists fire 105mm shells into mountain sides to create and observe controlled avalanches.

VITAL STATS

Area: 333,000 acres

Visitor Info: Rogers Pass Information Centre (☎250-837-7500), on Hwy. 1 in Glacier.

Gateway Town: Roger

Fees: CDN$7, seniors CDN$6, under 16 CDN$3.50.

GETTING AROUND. Glacier is 350km west of Calgary and 723km east of Vancouver. There are no roads in the park other than the **Trans-Canada Highway (Hwy. 1).**

 Glacier National Park straddles 2 time zones. After Rogers Pass, you will enter the Pacific Time Zone, where it is 1hr. earlier.

HIKING. More than 140km of rough, often steep trails lead from the highway, inviting mountaineers to attempt the unconquerable. While the highway works its way through the park's lush valleys, a majority of the area in the parkland lies above the treeline, providing for incredibly steep, high altitude, highly beautiful hikes. Leaving from the info center, the easy **Abandoned Rails Trail** (1.2km one-way, 1hr.) follows the 1885 Canadian Pacific Railway bed over the top of historic Rogers Pass. Free guided tours are available during July and August from the visitors center. From the Beaver River Trailhead, **Copperstain Trail** (16km one-way, 6hr., 449m elevation change) leads uphill through alpine meadows. This trail is often combined with the longer Beaver Valley Trail to create a four-day backpacking loop. The challenging **Balu Pass Trail** (10km round-trip, 4hr., 788m elevation change) begins at the west edge of Rogers Centre parking lot, near Rogers Pass Information Centre, and rises to the Ursus Major and Ursus Minor peaks. As their names might suggest, they provide an excellent opportunity to see bears. This trail is prime bear habitat; check with park wardens before embarking. **Hermit Trail** (2.8km one-way, 2hr.) climbs nearly 800m into the Hermit Glacier, hanging high over Rogers Pass.

CAMPING. Glacier has two recently rebuilt campgrounds: **Illecillewaet ❶** (ill-uh-SILL-uh-way-et), 3.5km west of Roger's Pass (60 sites; open late June to early Oct.; CDN$19; MC/V), and smaller **Loop Brook ❶,** another 3km west on Hwy. 1 (20 sites; open July to early Sept.; CDN$19; MC/V). Both offer flush toilets, kitchen shelters with cook stoves, and firewood. The park has no vehicle-accessible sites until late June; **Canyon Hot Springs** (see below) is the closest alternative for drivers. Backcountry campers must purchase a **backcountry pass** from the Parks Canada office in Revelstoke (☎205-837-7500; CDN$9 per day; MC/V) or from the Rogers Pass Information Centre.

BLASTING THE PASS

When the Canadian Pacific Railway was plotting routes for its trans-Canada line in the 1880s, it was faced with the decision of heading north, through the Yellowhead Pass, or south, over a steeper pass in the Rockies and an as-yet-undiscovered pass through the Selkirk range, where Glacier National Park sits today. The railroad decided (against the advice of its engineers) to take the southern route, in order to prevent US railroads from making a land grab in southern BC. To find a pass through Selkirk, Canadian Pacific hired A.B. Rogers, an American engineer, offering him a $5000 bonus if he actually found a pass. Rogers was known for three things: an immense mustache, superhuman endurance, and an uncontrollable temper resulting in a constant stream of profanity. The men who had ventured into the unknown wilderness with him were kept in constant fear of their boss's unpredictable anger. Rogers did find his pass, a narrow slot that today bears his name. The Canadian Pacific was completed in 1882 and Rogers received his $5000. He was more interested in glory than money, however, and had the check framed. His check lasted longer than his pass—avalanches closed the route so frequently in win-

◪ DETOUR
CANYON HOT SPRINGS
On Hwy. 1.

At Canyon Hot Springs, two spring water swimming pools simmer at 26°C and 40°C (86°F and 106°F) to ease aching muscles. (☎250-837-2420; www.canyonhotsprings.com. Firewood included. Showers CDN$1. Swim pass CDN$7.50, seniors and ages 4-14 CDN$6.50, under 4 free. Open daily July-Aug. 9am-10pm; May-June and Sept. 9am-9pm. Sites CDN$28, with water and electricity CDN$36. Day-use CDN$10.50, seniors and ages 4-14 CDN$9.50.)

⚐ APPROACHING REVELSTOKE: 39 MILES
Follow **Hwy. 1 W** to Revelstoke.

REVELSTOKE

Located on both the Columbia River and the Canadian Pacific Railway, Revelstoke was born as a transfer station for boats and trains. Although still largely a stopover for travelers to the Rockies, Revelstoke is finally coming into its own. Revelstoke's laid-back social life complements the physical rigors of the area activities. Excellent hostels, surprisingly lively outdoor entertainment in the town center, and extensive outdoor pursuits make Revelstoke a welcoming destination.

VITAL STATS

Population: 7500

Visitor Info: Visitors Centre (☎205-837-3522; www.revelstokecc.bc.ca), at the junction of Mackenzie and Victoria Rd. Open daily July-Aug. 8:30am-9:30pm; May-June 9am-5pm. **Parks Canada** (☎205-837-7500), at Boyle Ave. and 3rd St. Open M-F 8:30am-noon and 1-4:30pm.

Internet Access: Revelstoke Public Library, 600 Campbell Ave. (☎205-837-5095). Open Tu noon-8pm, W noon-7pm, Th 10am-4pm, F-Sa 10am-5pm. Free.

Post Office: 307 W. 3rd St. (☎205-837-3228). Open M-F 8:30am-5pm. **Postal Code:** V0E 2S0.

▣ GETTING AROUND

Revelstoke is on the **Trans-Canada Hwy. (Hwy. 1),** 285km west of Banff. The town is easily navi-gated on foot or by bike, hence the lack of traffic and abundance of parking spaces downtown. **Mt. Revelstoke National Park** lies just east of town on Hwy. 1. Most of the town is on the east bank of the river, and **Victoria Rd.** is the main street that curves parallel to the highway.

◉ SIGHTS

By now, you've undoubtedly seen several Canadian-Pacific trains, whose route was later shared by the Trans Canada Highway. The **Revelstoke Railway Museum,** 719 W. Track St., off Victoria Rd., tells of the construction of the Trans-Canada line, which was completed a few miles from Revelstoke in 1885. Other exhibits include a steam engine and a passenger car. (☎877-837-6060; www.railwaymuseum.com. Open daily July-Aug. 9am-8pm; May-June and Sept. 9am-5pm; Mar.-Apr. and Oct.-Nov. M-Tu and Th-Su 9am-5pm; Dec.-Feb. M-Tu and F-Su 11am-4pm. CDN$6, seniors CDN$5, ages 7-16 CDN$3, under 7 free.) The mechanical marvels of the **Revelstoke Dam** is one of North America's largest hydroelectric developments. (☎205-814-6697. Open mid-Apr. to mid-Oct. daily 9am-5pm. CDN$5, seniors CDN$4, ages 7-17 CDN$3.) The town also hosts a **blues festival** during the 3rd weekend in June, a **lumberjack competition** in early July, and a **railroad festival** in August (www.revelstokecc.bc.ca/events).

⚠ OUTDOORS

SUMMER ACTIVITIES

A relaxing aquatic experience can be found with **Natural Escapes Kayaking,** 1115 Pineridge Crest. (☎205-837-2679; www.naturalescapes.ca. Kayaks CDN$25 per 2hr. Lessons from CDN$45.) The 140 bolted routes on Begbie Bluffs offer exceptional **sport climbing** (from the small parking area almost 9km down 23 S from Hwy. 1, the bluffs are a 10min. walk; take the left fork). Rogers Pass and the surrounding peaks offer limitless of year-round opportunities to hone one's mountaineering skills. **Glacier House Resort** has a large range of equipment rentals and trips year-round. (☎205-837-9594; www.glacierhouse.com. Canoe rentals CDN$35 per half-day; kayak rentals CDN$30 per half-day. 90min. lessons CDN$30. Guided canoe

GREAT NORTH

tours CDN$49-119. Mt. Revelstoke guided day hikes CDN$89 per day.)

WINTER ACTIVITIES

Winter in Revelstoke brings 60-80 ft. of powder, and excellent downhill skiing. **Powder Springs Resort,** 5km outside town, maintains one chairlift and 21 trails with a 1000 ft. vertical drop on the bottom third of Mt. MacKenzie. (☎800-991-4455; www.catpowder.com. Lift tickets CDN$28-32.) The **Powder Springs Inn,** 200 3rd St. W. (☎205-837-5151; www.catpowder.com), offers reasonable hotel and skiing packages and rents skis. The **SameSun Backpacker Lodge** (p. 330) also offers liftticket packages from CDN$29. **Parks Canada** offers excellent advice and brochures on area nordic trails and world-class backcountry skiing. They also provide info on area snowmobiling, as does **Great Canadian Snowmobile Tours,** by Frisby Ridge, 6km north of town on West Side Rd. (☎205-837-5030 or 877-837-9594; www.snowmobilerevelstoke.com. Snowmobiles CDN$190-295 per day. CDN$2500 credit card deposit required. 22+. Reservations recommended.)

MT. REVELSTOKE NATIONAL PARK

Adjacent to town, Mt. Revelstoke National Park has astounding scenery and furnishes convenient access to nature. It is a favorite of mountain bikers and hikers. The park requires a **National Parks Permit** (CDN$7, seniors CDN$6, under 16 CDN$3.50) that can be purchased at the **Parks Canada Office** in Revelstoke or at the gate. The park is too tiny to offer extensive backcountry opportunities, but it does boast two backcountry campgrounds, **Eva Lake,** a 6km hike, and **Jade Lake,** a 9km hike. (Each has 4 sites. No pumped water. Jade Lake is equipped with a bear pole. Open July-Sept. Contact park office for fee information.) Two boardwalks off Hwy. 1, on the east side of the park, provide access to the trails. **Skunk Cabbage Trail** (1.3km, 30min.) leads through acres of stinking perfection: skunk cabbage plants tower at heights of over 1.5m. **Giant Cedars Trail** (500m, 15min.) has majestic, over-600-year-old trees growing around babbling brooks. **Meadows in the Sky Parkway** (Summit Rd.) branches off Hwy. 1 between the town's two exits, leading 26km up 16 switchbacks. From there, you can take a 1km hike up Mt. Revelstoke to subalpine meadows.

◢ FOOD

The town's market is **Cooper's Supermarket,** 555 Victoria St. (☎205-837-4372. Open daily 8am-9pm.) Revelstoke's streets, especially **Mackenzie Ave.,** are lined with wonderful cafes, restaurants and bars, including a collection of Chinese-Western hybrids.

Chalet Deli and Bakery, 555 Victoria St. (☎205-837-5552), across the parking lot from Cooper's. This bakery is also a lunch spot with a hot deli, pizza by the slice (CDN$2.50), fresh baked bread (loaves CDN$3), and sandwiches (CDN$5.50). Open M-Sa 6am-6pm. MC/V. ❶

Main Street Cafe, 317 Mackenzie Ave. (☎205-837-6888), at 3rd St. Serves breakfast (CDN$5-8) and sandwiches (CDN$5-6) on a lovely patio. Open M-F 8am-5pm, Sa 8am-4pm, Su 8am-3pm. MC/V. ❶

Hong Kong Restaurant, 113 Mackenzie Ave. (☎205-837-2360). It may not be the fanciest of Chinese restaurants, but the filling combination platters are a great deal at CDN$8.50. Entrees CDN$7.50-15. MC/V. ❷

⌂ ACCOMMODATIONS

▨ **SameSun Backpacker Lodge ❶,** 400 2nd St. W (☎877-562-2783; www.samesun.com). The friendly staff hosts a lively youth hostel scene and a more sedate older crowd in the private rooms. Several kitchens, full bathrooms, living room with TV, and a constant mellow soundtrack. Pool table and backyard barbecue. Internet CDN$3 per 30min. Reception 24hr. Dorms CDN$23; singles CDN$49. MC/V.

Martha Creek Provincial Park, 1224 Stanley St. (☎250-825-4212), in Nelson, 22km north of Revelstoke on Hwy 23. Beach and a boat launch. The campground tends to be full of RVs, so get there early if you want a good spot. Open May-Sept. Sites CDN$14. Cash only. ❶

Williamson's Lake Campground, 1818 Williamson Lake Rd. (☎888-676-2267; www.williamsonlakecampground.com), 5km southeast of town on Airport Way. Farther from the highway than competitors, next to a peaceful swimming hole. Laundry. Free showers. Reception 8am-9:30pm. Open mid-Apr. to Oct. Tent sites CDN$16; RV sites CDN$21.50. MC/V. ❶

DETOUR

ENCHANTED FOREST

Between Revelstoke and Sicamous on Hwy. 1.

What started as a couple's hobby turned into a major tourist stop with the completion of the Trans-Canada Hwy. Looking slightly out of place among pines and ferns, over 350 colorful, slightly kitschy, concrete figurines of fairy-tale creatures inhabit a lush, old-growth forest. Also on-site is British Columbia's tallest tree house. Nearby fish ponds and beaver dams are accessible via row boat. (☎ 866-944-9744; www.enchantedforestbc.com. Open daily mid-May to mid-Oct. 8am-8pm or 30min. before sunset. CDN$6.50, ages 3-15 CDN$5, under 3 free.)

 PHOTO OP. On Hwy. 1 at Craigellachie, the **Last Spike Monument** stands in honor of the completion of the transcontinental Canadian Pacific Railway; the last spike was pounded in here on November 7th, 1885.

APPROACHING SICAMOUS: 48 MILES

Follow **Hwy. 1 W** for 74km to Sicamous.

SICAMOUS. The houseboat capital of Canada and gateway to the nearby Shuswap Lakes, Sicamous is also home to the **D Dutchman Dairy ❶**, 1321 Maeir Rd. Savor 40 flavors of ice cream (2 scoops CDN$3.25) and wander around the petting zoo to see llamas, cows, donkeys, and a camel. (Follow the signs to the left of Hwy. 1 after entering town. ☎ 250-836-4304; www.dutchmendairy.ca. Open daily 8am-9pm. Cash only.)

APPROACHING KELOWNA: 77 MILES

Continue south on **Rte. 97A** through the Okanagan Valley. Just before Vernon, merge onto **Rte. 97 S**, and continue through the Okanagan Valley to **Kelowna.**

KELOWNA

In the heart of the Okanagan Valley, Kelowna (kuh-LOW-nuh) is one of Canada's richest agricultural regions and a popular tourist destination. The town's fruit stands, wineries, and independent shops draw thousands every summer. In winter, those not skiing in Whis-tler find the slopes of Big White Ski Resort equally rewarding.

VITAL STATS

Population: 105,000

Visitor Info: Tourism Kelowna, 544 Harvey Ave. (☎250-861-1515; www.tourismkelowna.org). Open May-Sept. M-F 8am-7pm, Sa-Su 9am-7pm; Oct.-Apr. M-F 8am-5pm, Sa-Su 10am-3pm.

Internet Access: Okanagan Regional Library Kelowna Branch, 1380 Ellis St. (☎250-762-2800). Open Apr.-Sept. M and F-Sa 10am-5:30pm, Tu-Th 10am-9pm. Oct.-Mar. M and F-Sa 10am-5:30pm, Tu-Th 10am-9pm, Su 1-5pm. Free.

Post Office: 101-591 Bernard Ave. (☎250-868-8480). Open M-F 8:30am-5:30pm, Sa 9am-5pm. **Postal Code:** V1Y 7G0.

GETTING AROUND

At the eastern shore of Okanagan Lake, Kelowna lies on **Hwy. 97 (Harvey Ave.),** which runs east-west across the lake and bisects the town. In the east, Hwy. 97 becomes the **Okanagan Hwy.** and curves north, intersecting **Hwy. 33** by the golf course. The floating bridge across the lake is unique in Canada. Traffic is notoriously terrible in Kelowna, as the bridge creates a massive bottleneck.

SIGHTS

PARKS AND BEACHES. The sun is Kelowna's main attraction, warming Okanagan parks and beaches for an average of 2000hr. per year. **City Park** and **Waterfront Park,** on the west end of downtown, are popular hangouts. **Boyce Gyro Park,** on Lakeshore Rd. south of the Okanagan Bridge, features beach volleyball. **Kelowna Parasail Adventures** transforms patrons into living kites, floating them high above the lake. *(1310 Water St., at the docks of Grand Okanagan Resort north of City Park. ☎250-868-4838; www.parasailcanada.com. Open May-Sept. daily 9am-sunset. CDN$55.)* Take a sail around the lake with **Go With the Wind Cruises.** *(On Waterfront Walkway. ☎250-763-5204; www.gowiththewind.com. CDN$25 per hr., 2hr. min. Reservations recommended. Open May-Oct. daily 9am-6pm.)*

GREAT NORTH

1908: Henry Ford's $850 Model T zooms onto the market.

KELOWNA MUSEUM. The museum houses regional artifacts, including those of the Okanagan and other First Nations, as well as rotating temporary exhibits. *(470 Queensway Ave. ☎ 250-763-2417; www.kelownamuseum.ca. Open M-Sa 10am-5pm. CDN$2, children CDN$1.)*

WINE AND FRUIT. Over the past few years, the Okanagan Valley has become the center of the Canadian wine industry. Kelowna and the surrounding area are home to 12 of the valley's wineries, all of which offer tastings. Contact the Visitors Center or call **Okanfana Wine Country Tours** at ☎ 866-689-9463 for a complete list of the pricey tours. Wine and cheese parties are common during the **Okanagan Wine Festival,** held over 10 days in early October, for four days during another wine festival in late April, and for three days at the **Icewine Festival** in late January. Events range from free tastings to expensive ticketed events, though many of the events cost less than CDN$50. *(☎ 250-861-6654; www.owfs.com. Tickets CDN$8-195.)* **Mission Hill,** overlooking the west bank of Okanagan Lake, is one of Kelowna's most respected wineries, offering tours of an underground wine cavern, bell tower, and outdoor amphitheater, with tastings of four wines. *(1730 Mission Hill Rd. Cross the bridge west of town, turn left on Boucherie Rd., and follow the signs. ☎ 250-768-6448; www.missionhillwinery.com. Open daily July-Sept. 10am-7pm; Oct.-June 10am-5pm. Tours daily July-Aug. every 30min. 10am-5pm; May-June and Sept. every hr. 11am-4pm; Oct.-Apr. 11am, 1, 3pm. CDN$5.)* **Kelowna Land and Orchard,** the town's oldest family-owned farm, offers a 45min. hayride that explains farming techniques. The tour finishes at the orchard's farm stand. *(3002 Dunster Rd. Take KLO Rd. to E. Kelowna Rd., then make a left onto Dunster Rd. ☎ 250-763-1091; www.k-l-o.com. Open daily Apr.-Oct. 9am-4pm; call for winter hours. Tours Apr.-Oct. 1pm. CDN$6.50, students CDN$3, under 12 free.)*

⚠ OUTDOORS

Equipment rental is available at **Sports Rent,** 3000 Pandosy St. *(☎ 250-861-5699; www.sportsrentkelowna.com. Bikes from CDN$25 per day; in-line skates CDN$11; kayaks CDN$30; canoes CDN$35. Ski packages from CDN$24 per day. Open daily May-Sept. 9am-6pm; Oct.-Apr. 9am-8pm.)*

HIKING AND BIKING. While Kelowna's main attraction is Okanagan Lake, surrounding areas offer excellent opportunities for off-road fun. Ponderosa pines dominate this hot, dry landscape. **Knox Mountain,** just north of the city, features many hiking trails as well as a paved road to the summit. Hike, bike, or drive to the top for a spectacular view of Kelowna and Okanagan. While you're there, don't pass up a chance to check out one of the city's natural secrets, ⚠**Paul's Tomb.** A secluded gravel beach named for the grave of one of Kelowna's early settlers, it's only a 2km walk or bike from either the trailhead at the base of the mountain or the one at the lookout halfway up. **Bear Creek Regional Park's** 20km of trails include a challenging hike that ascends to the canyon rim to view the city and lake. Much of the large and popular **Okanagan Mountain Provincial Park** was ravaged by a wildfire in 2003, leaving portions of the park scarred. Though the park has since reopened, ask at the visitors center for updates on trail conditions.

The **Kettle Valley Railbed (KVR),** another biking trail, passes through scenic **Myra-Bellevue Provincial Park** and the stunning **Myra Canyon** and then through the only desert in western Canada. The railbed through Myra Canyon stretches 12km, but the bike trail continues all the way to Penticton.

In addition, there are 18 regional parks within a 40km radius of Kelowna, providing everything from picnic areas to swim spots, and in some cases nature and hiking trails. Highlights include the **Mission Creek Regional Park,** with over 12km of hiking trails and a connection to the **Mission Creek Greenway,** with 7km of trails leading to the waterfront; and **Glen Canyon Regional Park,** offering hikes along the old concrete flume and the cliff edges.

WINTER SPORTS. In the winter, downhill skiing is the most popular outdoor activity in the Okanagan Valley. **Big White Ski Resort** offers 15 lifts serving over 100 trails throughout 7355 acres of terrain. The resort completed a CDN$130 million expansion at the beginning of the 2004 season, adding two new chairlifts and a state-of-the-art terrain park. (On a clearly marked access road off Hwy. 33, east of town. ☎ 250-765-3101; www.bigwhite.com. Open mid-Nov. to late Apr. Lift tickets CDN$65, ages 13-18 CDN$56. Night skiing CDN$25. Ski or snowboard rental CDN$36.) Those preferring a smaller, less crowded mountain should head to **Crystal Mountain**, with 22 trails and an 800 ft. drop located at the top of Glenrosa Rd., 10min. from the Westbank overpass of Hwy. 97. (☎250-768-5189; www.crystalresort.com. Open mid-Nov. to mid-Dec. Sa-Su 9am-3:30pm; mid-Dec. to mid-Jan. daily 9am-3:30pm; mid-Jan. to Mar. Th-Su 9am-3:30pm. Lift tickets CDN$39, ages 13-17 CDN$34. Ski rental CDN$26; snowboards CDN$27.)

CLIMBING. The area around Kelowna boasts numerous spots for climbers. Along the Kettle Valley Railbed, in the Myra-Bellevue Provincial Park are the **Boulderfields,** with six main areas and 25 independent walls, almost all of advanced difficulty. **Idabel Lake,** lying near Okanagan Falls on Rte. 33 off Hwy. 97, boasts the best bouldering routes in the area. The most popular climbing in the area at **Kelowna Crags,** by Chute Lake Mountain Park. The area offers climbs of a range of difficulties, as well as a trail to the top for spectators to see the lake vista and relax in well-worn chairs constructed from stones. (Follow Lakeshore Ave. to Chute Lake Rd. Follow the road for 2 mi. after it becomes a dirt road, 1 mi. after the sign marking the edge of Kelowna.)

🍴 FOOD

Kelowna overflows with fresh produce. Find juicy delights at the stands outside town along **Benvoulin Rd.** and **KLO Rd.,** or head south on **Lakeshore Dr.** to the pick-your-own cherry orchards. **Bernard Ave.** is lined with restaurants and cafes.

The Bohemian Bagel Cafe, 363 Bernard Ave. (☎250-862-3517; www.vtours.com/boh). Rich breakfast and lunch offerings in a colorful atmosphere on the main drag. The soup-salad-sandwich special is a steal at CDN$8. Open Tu-F 7:30am-2:30pm, Sa 8:30am-2:30pm, Su 9am-1pm. AmEx/MC/V. ❶

The Pier Marina Pub & Grill, 2035 Campbell Rd. (☎250-769-4777), just across the floating bridge outside Kelowna. This unassuming joint serves up hot lunches in huge portions, like calamari (CDN$7), burger and sandwich "two-fisted feasts" (CDN$10-13),

and dinners (CDN$12-21). Meals are served on a great dock patio. Open daily 11am-midnight. MC/V. ❸

Le Triskell Creperie, 467 Bernard Ave. (☎250-763-5151). This long, narrow restaurant with Parisian artwork manages to find the essence of a sidewalk bistro. Crepes CDN$5-13. Open M-W 9am-2pm, Th-Sa 9am-2pm and 5-9pm. MC/V. ❷

Tripke Bakery Konditorei & Cafe, 567 Bernard Ave. (☎250-763-7666). Use the breakfasts (CDN$3-11) or sandwiches (CDN$7-9) as your excuse for leaving with a hoard of their delectable pastries (under CDN$5). Open M-Sa 8am-5:30pm. MC/V. ❶

🛏 ACCOMMODATIONS

Warm, dry summer days attract thousands, so make reservations, even at campgrounds. If everything is full, there are inns and chain hotels along **Lakeshore Dr.** and **Hwy. 97** in either direction. Kelowna has a plethora of B&Bs—stop by the visitors center for a list.

Kelowna International Hostel, 2343 Pandosy St. (☎250-763-6024; www.kelowna-hostel.bc.ca). 1 block from the beach in a colorful home. This laid-back hostel is a budget paradise, with super-friendly hosts, a comfortable lounge, and daily activities. Pancake breakfast included. Internet CDN$1 per 30min. Reception 7am-11pm. Dorms CDN$20; private doubles CDN$40. MC/V. ❶

SameSun Backpacker's Lodge, 245 Harvey Ave. (877-562-2783; www.samesun.com), just across the floating bridge. This lively hostel features keg parties and barbecues almost every night in summer. Key deposit CDN$5. Dorms CDN$25; private rooms CDN$69-80. Credit card and ID required. MC/V. ❶

Bear Creek Provincial Park, (☎800-689-9025 or 494-6500), 9km north of Hwy. 97 on Westside Rd. Day use area and camping. Shaded lakeside sites, 400m of Okanagan lake shore, boat launch, and a walking trail along the waterfront. Sites CDN$22. Cash only. ❶

⛰ APPROACHING PENTICTON: 40 MILES
Continue south on scenic **Hwy. 97** to Penticton.

PENTICTON

Indigenous peoples named the region between Okanagan and Skaha Lakes Pen-tak-tin, "a place to stay forever." Today, Penticton is known more commonly as the "Peach City," complete with a giant peach on the

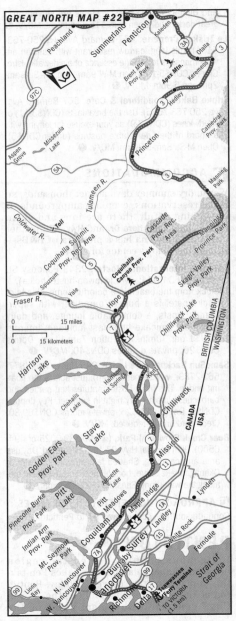

GREAT NORTH MAP #22

GREAT NORTH

waterfront that would make Roald Dahl proud. Penticton is more than an agricultural mecca, however; the city bustles with tourists during the summer.

VITAL STATS

Population: 31,000

Visitor Info: Penticton Wine and Information Center, 533 Railway St. (☎800-663-5052; www.penticton.org), at Power and Eckhardt St. Free Internet access and Wi-Fi. Open July-Sept. daily 8am-8pm; Oct.-June M-F 9am-6pm, Sa-Su 10am-5pm.

Internet Access: Penticton Public Library, 785 Main St. (☎250-492-0024). Open in summer M, W, F-Sa 10am-5:30pm, Tu and Th 10am-9pm; in winter M, W, F-Sa 10am-5:30pm, Tu and Th 10am-9pm, Su 1-5pm.

Post Office: 56 W. Industrial Ave. (☎250-492-5769). Open M-F 8:30am-5pm. **Postal Code:** V2A 6J8.

▶ GETTING AROUND

Penticton lies at the junction of **Hwy. 3** and **Hwy. 97,** at the southern extreme of the Okanagan Valley. **Okanagan Lake** borders the north end of town, while smaller **Skaha Lake** lies to the south. **Main St.** bisects the city from north to south, turning into **Skaha Lake Rd.** as it approaches the lake.

👁 SIGHTS

S.S. SICAMOUS AND S.S. NARAMATA. While lounging on the beachfront, meander over to the *S.S. Sicamous* and *S.S. Naramata,* restored steel-hulled ships from 1914 that transported goods and passengers to the communities along the Okanagan. Tours offer a window into the leisure and luxury of the early Okanagan Valley; for those who are truly intrigued, the *Sicamous* also hosts a musical about life on the ship. Just adjacent is the small but fragrant and calming **Rose Garden** in which to sit or stroll. (*1099 Lakeshore Dr.* ☎*250-492-0403; www.sssicamous.com. Open daily June-Sept. 9am-9pm; Apr.-May and Oct. to mid-Dec. 9am-6pm; mid-Jan. to Mar. 9am-5pm. CDN$5, students and seniors CDN$4, ages 5-12 CDN$1.*)

SUMMERLAND. Just 12 mi. north of Penticton on Hwy. 20, the town of Summerland is home to ornamental gardens and the preserved portion of the 1910 **Kettle Valley Steam Railway** today operating as a tourist attraction. The 1½hr. tour provides views of vineyards and the highest bridge on the original railway. *(Take Hwy. 97 to Summerland exit. Follow Prairie Valley Rd. then turn right on Doherty Ave. ☎877-494-8424; www.kettlevalleyrail.org. Tours July-Sept. M and Th-Su 10:30am and 1:30pm; late May-June and Oct. M and Sa-Su 10:30am and 1:30pm. CDN$18, seniors CDN$17, ages 13-17 CDN$15, ages 3-12 CDN$11.)*

PENTICTON MUSEUM. The museum chronicles the history of Penticton's gold trails and the Kettle Valley Railway, as well as First Nations history, preserved in over 8000 artifacts. *(785 Main St., in the same building as the library. ☎250-490-2451. Open July-Aug. M-Sa 10am-5pm; Apr.-June and Sept.-Oct. Tu-Sa 10am-5pm; Nov.-Mar. Tu-Sa 10am-4pm. Suggested donation CDN$2, children CDN$1.)*

◤ OUTDOORS

LAKEFRONT

In the summer, the Penticton tourist trade revolves around **Lake Okanagan** and **Lake Skaha.** Youths head toward Skaha Lake Park to the south for tubing down the Okanagan River. **Coyote Cruises,** 215 Riverside, rents tubes for CDN$11 and provides a free shuttle for the return. *(☎250-492-2115. Open daily late June to Sept. 10am-6pm.)* **Pier Water Sports,** 45 N. Martin St., just beyond the Peach on the beach pier, rents water vessels for those with an active spirit and a few extra bucks. *(☎250-493-8864. Open daily 9am-8pm. Jet skis CDN$85 per hr.; kayaks and pedal boats CDN$16 per hr. Banana boat rides CDN$11.)*

HIKING AND BIKING

Although the lakes are the star attractions, those looking for land-based adventures will not be disappointed. Visit Munson Mountain, an extinct volcano with "PENTICTON" spelled out in letters 50 ft. high and 30 ft. wide, for a bird's eye view of the valley. (Take Vancouver Ave. north of town and turn right on Tupper Ave., then left on Middle Bench Rd., to Munson Mt. Rd. The road ends just below the summit.) Bikers, walkers, and runners will enjoy dozens of pathways and trails in the

city and surrounding hills, many of which offer panoramic views of the lakes. The abandoned tracks of the Kettle Valley Railway run through Penticton and along both sides of Okanagan Lake and are the site of the Trans-Canada Trail in this area. Traveling north, you'll pass through orchards, vineyards, and wineries, all with a fantastic view of the lake. Those looking for a daytrip from Penticton can travel 21km at a gradual ascent to Glenfir, or 41km to Chute Lake. For a short, moderate hike, follow the trail down the western side of the river channel to Sage Mesa for stunning views. (Take Vancouver Ave. north to the intersection with Vancouver Pl. ☎250-496-5220; www.kettlevalleytrail.com.)

CLIMBING

The **Skaha Bluffs,** southeast of town on Valley View Rd., feature some of Canada's best rock climbing. For hikers and spectators, there are trails throughout the park. Check out *Skaha Rock Climbs*, by Howie Richardson, for detailed info on climbs. **Skaha Rock Adventures,** 437 Martin St., offers guide and instructional services. (☎250-493-1765; www.skaharockclimbing.com. Open M-F 9am-5pm. Guided climbing and lessons from CDN$110.)

SKIING

Apex Mountain Resort, off Green Mountain Rd., west of Penticton on Hwy. 3, offers the best downhill skiing in the area. Apex has downhill, cross-country, and night skiing on over 60 runs with a 2000 ft. vertical drop. They also boast a halfpipe and terrain park for boarders and an extensive glade area for the adventurous. In the summer, ski slopes become a dream come true for mountain bikers. (☎877-777-2739; www.apexresort.com. Night skiing F-Sa 4:30-9:30pm. Lift tickets CDN$53, ages 13-18 CDN$43, ages 8-12 CDN$32. Ski rentals CDN$35/$35/$22. Night skiing CDN$12.)

◤ FOOD

The **Penticton Farmers Market ❶,** 100 Block Main St., in Gyro Park, sells local produce and baked goods. (☎250-770-3276. Open June-Oct. Sa 8:30am-noon.) You can't miss fruits and vegetables at family stands (look for signs on the side of the road) both north and south of town on Hwy.

97 and 3A. Locals line up at **Il Vecchio Delicatessen ❶**, 317 Robinson St., for delicious sandwiches at incredible prices. (☎250-492-7610. Open M-Sa 8:30am-6pm. Cash only. **The Dream Cafe ❷**, 67 Front St., is an organic oasis with light sandwiches and dinners; try the spring rolls (CDN$8) or the mango roasted chicken sandwich for CDN$9.50. (☎250-490-9012. Open Apr.-Oct. daily 9am-11pm; Nov.-Mar. Tu-Su 9am-11pm. AmEx/MC/V.) **Isshin Japanese Deli ❷**, 101-449 Main St. is a local favorite, serving affordable, fresh sushi (CDN$2-4 per piece, CDN$8-25 per roll) and heaping noodle dishes for CDN$6-13. (☎250-770-1141. Open M-F 11:30am-2:30pm and 5-9pm, Sa noon-2:30pm and 5-9pm. AmEx/MC/V.)

ACCOMMODATIONS

Penticton is a resort city year-round; cheap beds are few and far between. It's essential to make reservations in summer. If possible, avoid the hotels that lurk along Skaha Lake Rd. and take advantage of the beautiful hostel. Campgrounds along Skaha Lake are costly and often tightly packed. The **Penticton Hostel (HI) ❶**, 464 Ellis St., is a large, well-maintained hostel only 10min. from the beach. Relax in the comfy lounge or enjoy the hot water, powered by rooftop solar panels. (☎250-492-3992. Laundry CDN$2. Reception 8am-noon and 5-10pm. Dorms CDN$22-24, members CDN$18-20; private rooms CDN$48-60/$40-46. MC/V.) North of town on Hwy. 97, **Okanagan Lake Provincial Park ❶**, has 168 sites on two campgrounds (North and South, with a connected walking trail). The North park is more spacious, with a good swimming beach. (☎250-494-6500 or 800-689-9025. Free firewood and showers. Reservations recommended. Sites CDN$22. Cash only.)

APPROACHING HOPE: 144 MILES

In Kaleden, turn west onto **Hwy. 3A**. In Keremeos, turn west onto the **Crowsnest Hwy. (Hwy. 3)**. Check your tank before you leave—few services exist as you breach the Cascade Mountains.

HOPE

Despite its fame as the Chainsaw Carving Capital of Canada, visitors will find quiet Hope, halfway between Penticton and Vancouver, a tranquil stay. Hope's location at the intersection of several highways ensures easy arrival and departure. Seven hikes of varying lengths and difficulties begin in or near town. The lush **Rotary Trail** (20min.), on Wardle St., is a casual walk with views of the Fraser and Cocquihalla Rivers. **Mt. Hope Lookout** (45min.) offers an impressive view of the town and surrounding area. This trail continues past the lookout to become the **Mt. Hope Loop** (4hr. round-trip). The hike begins at intersection of Hwy. 1 and **Old Hope Princeton Way,** off the dirt road behind the picnic tables. Pause for a pleasant diversion at **Kawkawa (a.k.a. Suckers) Creek,** off Union Bar Rd., enhanced in 1984 to aid the late summer and midfall salmon spawning. The boardwalk along the creek leads to a swimming hole. For biking, hiking, fishing, and hunting needs, stop by **Cheyenne Sporting Goods,** 267 Wallace St. (☎604-869-5062. Open M-Th and Sa 8:30am-5:30pm, F 8:30am-8pm.) The **Visitors Centre,** 919 Water St., provides the riveting, self-guided **Rambo Walking Tour** (*First Blood* was filmed here) in addition to sharing info on Fraser River Canyon and Manning Park. (☎604-869-2021. Open July-Aug. daily 8am-8pm; May-June and Sept. to mid-Oct. daily 8am-6pm; mid-Oct. to Apr. M-Sa 10am-4pm.)

Locals feast on generous portions of homemade cherry pie (CDN$4 per slice) at the **Home Restaurant ❷**, 665 Old Hope Princeton Hwy. (☎604-869-5558. Open daily 6am-11pm. MC/V.) **The Blue Moose Cafe ❶**, 322 Wallace St., offers Internet (CDN$0.10 per min.) and a variety of coffees (CDN$2-4), smoothies (CDN$4), and beer (CDN$5) along with sandwich options. (☎604-869-0729; www.bluemoosecafe.com. Open M-Sa 7:30am-10pm, Su 8:30am-10pm. AmEx/MC/V.) **Holiday Motel ❸**, 63950 Old Yale Rd., features an outdoor swimming pool, playground, volleyball court, and fire pit. (Follow signs from Exit 168 off Hwy. 1. ☎604-869-5352. Rooms with cable TV CDN$50-120; tent sites CDN$20-30. AmEx/MC/V.) Campers can head for the big trees at the spacious and secure **Coquihalla Campsite ❶**, 800 Kawkawa Lake Rd., off 6th Ave. on the banks of the Coquihalla River. (☎888-869-7118. Open Apr.-Oct. Sites CDN$20-28. MC/V.)

DETOUR
OTHELLO-QUINTETTE TUNNELS

A 10min. drive east of Hope along Kawkawa Lake Rd. Follow the signs, turning right on Othello Rd., off Kawkawa Lake Rd., and right again on Tunnel Rd.

In the **Coquihalla Canyon Recreation Area,** the Othello-Quintette Tunnels, which were blasted through solid granite, provide evidence of the daring engineering that led to the opening of the Kettle Valley Railway in 1916. The railway has since been turned into an easy footpath, allowing hikers to walk through the dark tunnels leading to narrow bridges over rapids that shoot through the gorge. These tunnels have served as the backdrop to many Hollywood adventure films.

Ⅷ APPROACHING VANCOUVER: 92 MILES
Head west toward Vancouver along **Hwy. 7.**

VANCOUVER

Even more so than most cities in North America, Vancouver boasts a thriving multicultural populace; the Chinese influence is so strong that it is commonly joked that Cantonese will soon become Canada's third national language. You'll find Asian flavor in everything from the peaceful manicured gardens to the raucous annual festivals in one of the largest Chinatowns in North America. Surrounded on three sides by water and closely hemmed in by the Coast Mountain Range, Vancouver can never stray far from its humble logging-town roots. From the hip neighborhood of Gastown to the therapeutic walks of Stanley Park, Vancouver's diversity, location, and worldly atmosphere keep its residents friendly and the tourist influx constant.

VITAL STATS

Population: 2 million

Visitor Info: 200 Burrard St. (☎604-683-2000; www.tourismvancouver.com), on the plaza level near Canada Place. Open daily 8:30am-6pm.

Internet Access: Vancouver Public Library, 350 W. Georgia St. (☎604-331-3600). Open M-Th 10am-9pm, F-Sa 10am-6pm, Su 1-5pm. Free.

Parking: EasyPark, 150 W. Pender St. (☎604-682-6744). CDN$2 per hr., CDN$7 per day.

Post Office: 349 W. Georgia St. (☎604-662-5725). Open M-F 8am-5:30pm. **Postal Code:** V6B 3P7.

▐ GETTING AROUND

Vancouver lies in the southwestern corner of mainland British Columbia. It is divided into distinct regions, mostly by waterways. South of the city flows the Fraser River, and to the west lies the Georgia Strait, which separates the mainland from Vancouver Island. **Downtown** juts north into the Burrard Inlet, and **Stanley Park** goes even farther north. The **Lions Gate** suspension bridge over Burrard Inlet links Stanley Park with North and West Vancouver (West Van), known collectively as the **North Shore;** the bridges over **False Creek** south of downtown link downtown with **Kitsilano** ("Kits") and the rest of the city. West of Burrard St. is the **West End. Gastown** and **Chinatown** are just east of downtown. The **University of British Columbia (UBC)** lies to the west of Kitsilano on Point Grey. **Hwy. 99** runs north-south from the US-Canada border through the city along **Oak St.,** through downtown, then over the Lions Gate bridge. It temporarily joins with the **Trans-Canada Hwy. (Hwy. 1)** before splitting off again and continuing north to Whistler. Roadtrippers may want to consider using the **Park 'n' Ride** system (☎604-953-3333; www.translink.bc.ca), or making the use of free parking lots at major transit hubs.

 The area east of Gastown, especially around **Hastings** and **Main St.,** can often be dangerous. Go with a group during the day, and stay away entirely after dark.

👁 SIGHTS

▧ VANCOUVER ART GALLERY. This gallery hosts fantastic temporary exhibitions and houses a permanent collection of contemporary art and design from the West Coast. *(750 Hornby St., in Robson Sq. ☎604-662-4700; www.vanartgallery.bc.ca. Open in summer M, W and F-Su 10am-5:30pm, Tu and Th 10am-9pm; hours vary in winter. CDN$15, seniors CDN$11, students CDN$10, under 12 free. Tu 5-9pm donations accepted.)*

▧ VANDUSEN BOTANICAL GARDEN. Fifty-five tranquil acres purchased from the Canadian Pacific Railway in 1966 are the site of the stunning Vandusen Botanical Garden, which showcases 7500 species from six continents. A nice place for a picnic or an evening stroll, the grounds also feature an international sculpture collection, while more than 60 species of

Vancouver Overview

★ ACCOMMODATIONS
Vancouver Hostel Jericho Beach (HI), **1**
UBC Lodgings, **9**

🍴 FOOD
Benny's Bagels, **10**
Mongolian Teriyaki, **7**
Montri's Thai Restaurant, **4**
The Naam, **5**
Sophie's Cosmic Cafe, **6**
WaaZuBee Cafe, **3**

🍸 NIGHTLIFE
The King's Head, **2**
Koerner's Pub, **8**

birds can be seen in areas such as the Fragrance Garden, Children's Garden, Bonsai House, Chinese Medicinal Garden, and the Elizabethan Maze, which is planted with 3000 pyramidal cedars. Daily tours are given at 2pm. If you'd rather stroll the garden on your own, follow a self-guided tour tailored to show the best of the season. (*5251 Oak St., at W. 37th Ave. ☎ 604-257-8665; www.vandusengarden.org. Open daily June to mid-Aug. 10am-9pm; mid-Aug. to Sept. and May 10am-8pm; Oct. and Mar. 10am-5pm; Apr. 10am-6pm; Nov.-Feb. 10am-4pm. Apr.-Sept. CDN$8, seniors CDN$6, ages 13-18 CDN$5.60, ages 6-12 CDN$4.50, under 6 free; Oct.-Mar. CDN$6/$4.25/$4/$2.75.*)

■**VANCOUVER AQUARIUM.** If you've never seen a white whale, head here for the must-see version of Melville's muse. A visit to the aquar-

ium, on Stanley Park's eastern side not far from the entrance, is like spending time at the British Columbia coastline with playful otters, white beluga whales (a huge tank allows for outdoor and underwater viewing), dolphins, and interactions with smaller, more delicate species. (*☎ 604-659-3474; www.vanaqua.org. Open daily July-Aug. 9:30am-7pm; Sept.-June 10am-5:30pm. Shows every 2hr. 10am-5:30pm. CDN$18.50, students and seniors CDN$14, ages 4-12 CDN$11, under 4 free.*)

CHINATOWN. Southeast of Gastown, the neighborhood bustles with restaurants, shops, bakeries, and **the world's narrowest building,** 8 W. Pender St. In 1912, the city expropriated all but a 1.8m (6 ft.) strip of Chang Toy's property in order to expand the street; he built on the land anyhow, and today the building is a symbol of Chinatown's perseverance. The serene **Dr. Sun Yat-Sen Classical Chinese Garden** maintains imported plants, carvings, and rock formations in the first full-size garden of its kind outside China. The neighboring park is free but lacks the ornate beauty of the actual gardens. *(578 Carrall St. ☎ 604-662-3207; www.vancouverchinesegarden.com. Open daily mid-June to Aug. 9:30am-7pm; May to mid-June and Sept. 10am-6pm; Oct.-Apr. 10am-4:30pm. Tours every hr. 10am-6pm. CDN$8.75, students and seniors CDN$7, under 5 free.)* Don't miss the sights, sounds, smells, and tastes at the **night market,** when vendors set up stands selling nearly anything every weekend along Keefer St. east of Main. *(F-Su 6:30-11pm.)* Chinatown is relatively safe, but surrounding areas are some of Vancouver's less savory sections and should be avoided.

BLOEDEL FLORAL CONSERVATORY. Go from the tropics to the desert in 100 paces inside this 43m diameter triodetic dome, constructed of Plexiglas bubbles and aluminum tubing. The conservatory, which is maintained at a constant 18°C (65°F), is home to 500 varieties of exotic plants and 150 birds. The conservatory is located inside beautiful Queen Elizabeth Park, whose elevation also affords views of downtown Vancouver. *(1 block east of Cambie and 37th Ave. ☎ 604-257-8584. Open Apr.-Sept. M-F 9am-8pm, Sa-Su 10am-9pm; Oct. and Feb.-Mar. daily 10am-5:30pm; Nov.-Jan. daily 10am-5pm. CDN$4.30, seniors CDN$3, ages 13-18 CDN$3.20, ages 6-12 CDN$2.15.)*

UNIVERSITY OF BRITISH COLUMBIA (UBC). The high point of a visit to UBC is the breathtaking ▨**Museum of Anthropology.** The high-ceilinged glass-and-concrete building houses totems and carvings, highlighted by Bill Reid's depiction of Raven discovering the first human beings in a giant clam shell. *(6393 NW Marine Dr. ☎ 604-822-5087; www.moa.ubc.ca. Open May-Sept. M and W-Su 10am-5pm, Tu 10am-9pm; Sept.-May Tu 10am-9pm, W-Su 10am-5pm. CDN$9, students and seniors CDN$7, under 6 free. Tu after 5pm free.)* Across the street, caretakers tend to the **Nitobe Memorial Garden,** rated as one of the finest classical Shinto gardens outside of Japan. *(☎ 604-822-9666; www.nitobe.org. Open mid-May to Aug. daily 10am-6pm; mid-Mar. to mid-May and Sept.-Oct. daily 10am-5pm. CDN$4, seniors CDN$3, stu-*

dents CDN$2.50, under 6 free.) The **Botanical Gardens** are a collegiate Eden, encompassing eight gardens in the central campus. The garden includes the largest collection of rhododendrons in North America. *(6804 SW Marine Dr. ☎ 604-822-9666; www.ubcbotanicalgarden.org. Open daily mid-May to Aug. 10am-6pm; mid-Mar. to mid-May and Sept.-Oct. 10am-5pm. CDN$6, seniors CDN$4, students CDN$3, under 6 free.)*

STANLEY PARK. Established in 1888 at the tip of the downtown peninsula, the 1000-acre Stanley Park is a testament to the foresight of Vancouver's urban planners. The thickly wooded park is laced with cycling and hiking trails and surrounded by a 10km seawall promenade popular with cyclists, runners, and in-line skaters. *(☎ 778-257-8400. A free shuttle runs between major destinations throughout the park late June to Sept. every 30min. 10am-6:30pm.)* On the south side of the park, the **Lost Lagoon** brims with fish, birds, and the odd trumpeter swan on the south side of the park and provides a utopian escape from the skyscrapers. Nature walks start from the Nature House, underneath the Lost Lagoon bus loop at the west side of Alberni St. *(☎ 604-257-8544. Walks Su 1-3pm. CDN$8, under 12 free. Nature House open June-Aug. F-Su 11am-7pm.)* The park's edges feature restaurants, tennis courts, a running track, swimming beaches staffed by lifeguards, and an outdoor theater, the **Malkin Bowl.** *(☎ 604-687-0174.)* For warm, chlorinated water, take a dip in the **Second Beach Pool.** *(Next to Georgia St. park entrance. ☎ 604-257-8371. CDN$4.50, ages 13-18 CDN$3.50, seniors CDN$3.25, ages 6-12 CDN$2.25.)*

DID YOU KNOW? Think that the totem poles in Stanley Park are fake? Think again. They are actually authentic and among the most valuable totems in the world.

H.R. MACMILLAN SPACE CENTRE. The space center runs a motion-simulator ride, a planetarium, a solar observatory, an exhibit gallery, and laser-light rock shows. *(1100 Chestnut St. ☎ 604-738-7827; www.hrmacmillanspacecentre.com. Laser shows Th-Sa 9:30, 10:45pm. Open July-Aug. daily 10am-6pm; Sept.-June Tu-Su 10am-5pm. CDN$14, students and seniors CDN$10.75, ages 5-10 CDN$10.50, under 5 free. Laser-light show CDN$10.50.)*

GRANVILLE ISLAND. This hidden gem, underneath the Granville Street bridge, has shops ranging from umbrella designers to silversmiths, a public market with fresh produce and seafood, and a waterfront location with frequent musical performances. *(1689 Johnston St. ☎ 604-666-5784; www.granvilleisland.bc.ca. Open daily 9am-7pm.)*

▲ OUTDOORS

BEACHES. Follow the western side of the Stanley Park seawall south to **Sunset Beach Park,** a strip of grass and beach extending all the way along **English Bay** to the Burrard Bridge. **Kitsilano Beach,** across Arbutus St. from Vanier Park, is a favorite for tanning and beach volleyball (the water is a bit cool for swimming). For smaller crowds, more kids, and free showers, visit **Jericho Beach** (head west along 4th Ave., and follow signs). A cycling path at the side of the road leads uphill to the westernmost end of the UBC campus. West of Jericho Beach is the quieter **Spanish Banks;** at low tide the ocean retreats almost 1km, allowing long walks on the flats. Most of Vancouver's 31km of beaches are patrolled by lifeguards from late May to Labor Day between 11:30am and 9pm. *(For information on beaches, call the Parks and Recreation department mid-May to mid-Sept. ☎604-738-8535; mid-Sept. to mid-May ☎604-665-3424; www.city.vancouver.bc.ca/parks/rec/beaches/)*

GROUSE MOUNTAIN. The ski hill closest to downtown Vancouver has the crowds to prove it. The very steep and well-traveled 2.9km **Grouse Grind Trail,** also known as "Mother Nature's Stairmaster," is a popular hiking trail among Vancouverites in the summer. It charges straight up 853m to the top of the mountain but rewards hikers with a beautiful view of downtown. *(☎604-984-0661; www.grousemountain.com. Slopes lit for skiing mid-Nov. to mid-Apr. daily sunrise-10:30pm. Lift tickets CDN$42, seniors and ages 13-18 CDN$30, ages 5-12 CDN$18. Tramway CDN$27, seniors CDN$24, ages 13-18 CDN$15, ages 5-12 CDN$10. Skyride CDN$5.)*

CYPRESS BOWL. Cypress Bowl in West Vancouver provides a less-crowded skiing alternative to Grouse Mountain. It boasts the most advanced terrain of the local mountains on its 23 runs at prices comparable to Grouse Mtn. The 16km of groomed trails at Hollyburn cross-country ski area are open to the public. In summer, the cross-country trails have hiking and berry-picking. *(Go west on Hwy. 1, and take Exit 8/Cypress Bowl Rd. ☎604-922-0825; www.cypressmountain.com. Open daily Dec. 9am-4pm; Dec.-Mar. 9am-10pm. Lift tickets CDN$44, ages 13-18 CDN$32; half-day CDN$32/$30.)*

MOUNT SEYMOUR. At Mount Seymour Provincial Park, trails leave from Mt. Seymour Rd. and a paved road winds 11km to the top. The Mt. Seymour ski area has the cheapest skiing around. Its marked terrain is also the least challenging, although the spectacular backcountry is preferred by many pro snowboarders. *(☎604-986-2261; www.mountseymour.com. Call ahead for seasonal hours. Lift tickets CDN$34, ages 13-18 CDN$28, seniors CDN$24, ages 6-13 CDN$18, under 6 free.)*

▨ FOOD

From Vietnamese noodle shops to Italian cafes, Vancouver has your corner of the globe covered. Vancouver's **Chinatown** and the **Punjabi Village** along Main and Fraser, around 49th St., both serve cheap, authentic food. Restaurants in **downtown** compete for the highest prices in the city. The **West End** caters to diners seeking a variety of ethnic cuisines (check out the globe-spanning lineup on Denman St.), while **Gastown** has funky coffee shops. Many cheap establishments along Davie and Denman St. stay open around the clock. Dollar-a-slice, all-night **pizza joints** pepper downtown.

WEST END, DOWNTOWN, AND GASTOWN

☙ **Subeez Cafe,** 891 Homer St. (☎604-687-6107), downtown. Serves a hipster crowd with delicious upscale dishes like baked brie with peach chutney (CDN$9), organic beef burgers (CDN$10), and the mushroom-and-herb frittata (CDN$9). Lengthy wine list, large bar, and home-spun beats (DJs W and F-Sa 9pm-midnight). Open M-F 11:30am-1am, Sa 11am-1am, Su 11am-midnight. MC/V. ❸

La Luna Cafe, 117 Water St. (☎604-687-5862), in Gastown. Loyal patrons swear by the coffee, roasted on site. Satisfying sandwiches (CDN$4-6) and homemade soups (CDN$4). Internet CDN$1 per 15min. Open M-F 7:30am-5pm, Sa 10am-5pm. MC/V. ❶

The Dish, 1068 Davie St. (☎604-689-0208). This long-time Vancouver staple prides itself on large portions and creative, healthy dishes. Vegetarian sandwiches and entrees are available, including the roasted veggie wrap (CDN$5) and the lentil stew on rice (CDN$6.50). Carnivores will not be disappointed by the deli-style sandwiches (CDN$5-6) and entrees like curry chicken on rice (CDN$6.50). Open M-Sa 7am-10pm, Su 9am-9pm. MC/V. ❷

Samurai Sushi House, 1108 Davie St. (☎604-609-0078). A range of cheap, not-so-dainty sushi options makes this Japanese restaurant a backpackers' favorite. Lunch specials include salad, soup, and sushi for CDN$7. Open M-Th and Su 11am-midnight, F-Sa 11am-1am. MC/V. ❷

COMMERCIAL DRIVE

Mongolian Teriyaki, 1918 Commercial Dr. (☎604-253-5607). Diners fill a bowl with 4 types of meat, veggies, 16 sauces, and noodles, and the chefs cook and serve it with miso soup, rice, and salad for CDN$4 (large bowl CDN$6). Open daily 11am-9:30pm. MC/V. ❶

WaaZuBee Cafe, 1622 Commercial Dr. (☎604-253-5299), at E. 1st St. Sleek, metallic decoration, ambient music, huge murals, and an enormous wine list. Entrees such as spinach-and-ricotta lagnoilotti pasta or Thai prawns run CDN$11-16. Chicken, lamb, beef, tuna, and veggie burgers CDN$9-11. Open M-F 11:30am-1am, Sa 11am-1am, Su 11am-midnight. AmEx/D/MC/V. ❹

KITSILANO

☒ **Sophie's Cosmic Cafe,** 2095 W. 4th Ave. (☎604-732-6810). Colorful walls decorated with lunch boxes and antique hats make Sophie's a homey place to enjoy a big breakfast or a diner-style lunch. Omelettes, waffles, Middle Eastern hot cereal, sandwiches, and hearty entrees are done with flair and old-fashioned charm. Entrees CDN$5-10. Open daily 8am-9:45pm. AmEx/D/MC/V. ❷

The Naam, 2724 W. 4th Ave. (☎604-738-7151; www.thenaam.com), at MacDonald St. One of the most diverse vegetarian menus around, with great prices to boot. Beautifully presented entrees such as Crying Tiger Thai stir-fry (CDN$9) and several

kinds of veggie burgers for under CDN$7. Tofulati dairy-free ice cream CDN$3.50. Daily live music 7-10pm. Open 24hr. MC/V. ❷

Montri's Thai Restaurant, 3629 W. Broadway (☎604-738-9888). Voted the best Thai restaurant 6 years running by *Vancouver* magazine. It's worth sampling the *Thai Gai-Yang* (chicken in coconut milk; CDN$12) along with the traditional but perfectly done pad thai (CDN$10). Open Tu-Su 5-10pm. AmEx/MC/V. ❸

Benny's Bagels, 2505 W. Broadway (☎604-731-9730). Benny's can start, end, or continue your day with bagels (CDN$1.35), sandwiches (CDN$5.50-7.50), and beer (CDN$3). Open M-Th and Su 7am-1am, F-Sa 24hr. MC/V. ❶

CHINATOWN

☒ **Hon's Wun-Tun House,** 268 Keefer St. (☎604-688-0871). This award-winning Cantonese noodle house is the place to go. Pick from over 300 options—reading the menu might take as long as eating what you finally order. Noodle bowls CDN$4-8. Open M-Th and Su 8:30am-9pm, F-Sa 8:30am-10pm. Cash only. ❷

Superior Tofu, Ltd., 163 Keefer St. (☎604-682-8867; www.superiortofu.com). If you're down with the soybean, you'll be in heaven. This deli-style vegetarian restaurant's menu incorporates tofu or soy milk into all of its veggie dishes. Open daily 5:30am-6pm. MC/V. ❷

⚑ ACCOMMODATIONS

Vancouver B&Bs are a good deal for couples or small groups, with singles generally from CDN$45 and doubles from CDN$55. Check out www.bedsandbreakfasts.ca/vancouver_area.htm for more information. **HI hostels** are good for clean and quiet rooms; some non-HI options can be seedy.

HOSTELS

☒ **Vancouver Hostel Downtown (HI),** 1114 Burnaby St. (☎604-684-4565 or 888-203-4302), in the West End. Sleek, clean 225-bed facility in a quiet neighborhood surrounded by downtown, the beach, and Stanley Park. Library, kitchen, Internet access (CDN$4 per hr.), lockers, laundry (CDN$3), and rooftop patio. Free pub crawls M and W; frequent tours of Granville Island. Reception 24hr. Reservations recommended June-Sept.

Dorms CDN$28-31, members CDN$24-27; doubles CDN$66-74/$59-66. MC/V. ●

☑ SameSun Hostel, 1018 Granville St. (☎604-682-8226; www.samesun.com), at the corner of Nelson, next to the Ramada Inn. Funky, laid-back, colorful hangout in an area with great nightlife. Internet, pool table, lockers (bring your own lock). Laundry (CDN$2). Dorms CDN$27, members CDN$23; doubles CDN$60/$53, with bath CDN$65/$60. MC/V. ●

C&N Backpackers Hostel, 927 and 1038 Main St. (☎604-682-2441 or 888-434-6060; www.cnn-backpackers.com). At the 1038 location, cheap meal deals with the **Ivanhoe Pub** (CDN$2.50 breakfast all day) make living above the bar a bargain, but across the street is a quieter location. Laundry CDN$2. Bikes CDN$10 per day. Reception 8am-10:30pm. Dorms CDN$18; doubles CDN$45. AmEx/MC/V. ●

Seymour Cambie Hostel, 515 Seymour St. (☎604-684-7757 or 877-395-5535; www.cambiehostels.com), in Gastown. The quieter of 2 downtown Cambie hostels. Movie nights (M and Su), soccer games (July-Sept.), free tours of Granville Island Brewery (Tu noon, 2, 4pm). Breakfast CDN$2.50. Free lockers (bring your own lock). Laundry CDN$2. Internet CDN$4 per hr. Dorms CDN$20-23; private rooms CDN$45. MC/V. ●

Cambie International Hostel, 300 Cambie St. (☎877-395-5335; www.cambiehostels.com), in Gastown. The Cambie offers easy access to the busy sights and sounds of Gastown (including those of the bar downstairs) in one of the neighborhood's older buildings. Though it can be noisy at night, mornings have free breakfast at the bakery next door. Common room, Internet access (CDN$4 per hr.), and laundry (CDN$2). Reception 24hr. Dorms CDN$22; singles CDN$43. MC/V. ●

Vancouver Hostel Jericho Beach (HI), 1515 Discovery St. (☎888-203-4303), in Jericho Beach Park. Follow 4th Ave. west past Alma, and bear right at the fork. Practically on the beach, with a great view across English Bay, this is a homey hostel with 280 beds in 14-person dorm rooms. 10 4-bed family rooms. Cafe (breakfast CDN$6; dinner CDN$7-8), kitchen, TV room, free linen. Laundry CDN$2.50. Parking CDN$3 per day. Open May-Sept. Dorms CDN$24, members CDN$20; family rooms CDN$50-60. ●

Pacific Spirit Hostel at UBC Lodgings, Place Vanier Residence, 1935 Lower Mall (☎604-822-1000; www.ubcconferences.com). Private rooms with access to TV lounges, microwave and fridge, and campus pubs. Internet CDN$10 per day. Linen included. Laundry CDN$2.50. Open May-Aug. Singles CDN$25. ●

CAMPING

Capilano RV Park, 295 Tomahawk Ave. (☎604-987-4722; www.capilanorvpark.com), at the foot of Lions Gate Bridge in North Van. By far the most convenient camping location, with pool, jacuzzi, and laundry facilities. Reception 8am-9pm. Tent sites CDN$28-30; RV sites with full hook-up from CDN$46. ●

ParkCanada, 4799 Hwy. 17 (☎604-943-5811), in Delta, near the Tsawwassen ferry terminal. Take Hwy. 99 S to Hwy. 17, then go east for 2.5km. The campground is next to a water park and has a pool. Tent sites CDN$19; RV sites from CDN$21. ●

🎵 ENTERTAINMENT

MUSIC AND THEATER

The renowned **Vancouver Symphony Orchestra** (☎604-876-3434; www.vancouversymphony.ca; tickets CDN$25-78) plays from September to May in the refurbished **Orpheum Theatre** (☎604-665-3050), at the corner of Smithe and Seymour. The VSO often joins forces with other groups such as the **Vancouver Bach Choir.** (☎604-921-8012; www.vancouverbachchoir.com. Tickets CDN$35-90.) The **Vancouver Playhouse Theatre Co.** (☎604-873-3311), at Dunsmuir and Georgia St., and the **Arts Club Theatre** (☎604-687-1644; www.artsclub.com), on Granville Island, stage low-key shows, often including local work. **Theatre Under the Stars** puts on outdoor musicals in the summer in Stanley Park's Malkin Bowl. (☎604-687-0174; www.tuts.bc.ca. Tickets CDN$20-30.) The world-famous improvisational theater company **Theatresports League** performs competitive improv, comedies, and improv jam sessions at the Arts Club New Revue Stage on Granville Island. (☎604-687-1644; www.vtsl.com. Tickets CDN$10-18.) The **Ridge Theatre,** 3131 Arbutus, shows arthouse, indie, European, and vintage film double features. (☎604-738-6311; www.ridgetheatre.com. CDN$5, seniors and children CDN$4.) The **Hol-**

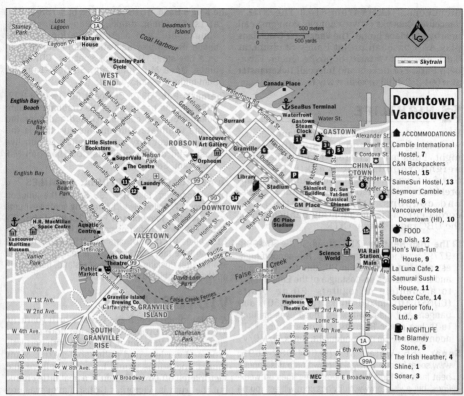

Downtown Vancouver

▲ ACCOMMODATIONS
Cambie International Hostel, **7**
C&N Backpackers Hostel, **15**
SameSun Hostel, **13**
Seymour Cambie Hostel, **6**
Vancouver Hostel Downtown (HI), **10**

🍴 FOOD
The Dish, **12**
Hon's Wun-Tun House, **9**
La Luna Cafe, **2**
Samurai Sushi House, **11**
Subeez Cafe, **14**
Superior Tofu, Ltd., **8**

🍸 NIGHTLIFE
The Blarney Stone, **5**
The Irish Heather, **4**
Shine, **1**
Sonar, **3**

lywood Theatre, 3123 W. Broadway, shows indie films, documentaries, and second-run, mainstream double features for less than other theaters downtown. (☎ 604-515-5864; www.hollywoodtheatre.ca. Films CDN$6, seniors and under 14 CDN$3.50.)

FESTIVALS

Vancouver's diverse cultural makeup brings festivals of all shapes and sizes to the city. As with almost everything else, buying tickets in advance for these festivals often results in reduced prices. The **Chinese New Year** celebration involves fireworks, music, and dragons in the streets of Chinatown and beyond. The **Vancouver International Jazz Festival** attracts over 500 performers and bands for 10 days of jazz, from acid to swing. (☎ 604-872-5200 or 888-438-5200; www.jazzvancouver.com. Late June to early July. Events $10-60.) The **Vancouver Folk Music Festival** hosts folk performers from all around the world on the third weekend of July. (☎ 604-602-9798 or 800-985-8363; www.thefestival.bc.ca. Tickets $40-55 per day, weekend $130.) The **Vancouver International Film Festival** showcases movies from over 50 countries with over 500 screenings. The emphasis is on Canadian films, East Asian films, and documentaries. (☎ 604-683-3456; www.viff.org. Late Sept. to early Oct. Tickets $6-8.)

SPORTS

One block south of Chinatown on Main St. is **BC Place Stadium,** 777 S. Pacific Blvd., home to the CFL's **BC Lions** and the world's largest air-supported dome. (☎ 604-669-2300; www.bcplacestadium.com. Tickets from $15.) The NHL's **Vancouver Canucks** (www.canucks.com/gm) call nearby **GM Place** home. The **Vancouver Canadians** play AAA baseball in Nat Bailey Stadium, at 33rd. Ave. and Ontario, opposite Queen Elizabeth Park. For tickets and info call **Ticketmaster** at ☎604-280-4400 or visit www.ticketmaster.ca.

◧ NIGHTLIFE

Vancouver's nightlife centers on dance clubs, with lively beats and DJs spinning every night. Pubs are scattered through the city's neighborhoods. The weekly *Georgia Straight* (www.straight.com) publishes comprehensive event listings, restaurant reviews, and coupons. *Discorder* (http://discorder.citr.ca) is the monthly publication of the UBC radio station CITR.

◪ **The Irish Heather,** 217 Carrall St. (☎604-688-9779; www.irishheather.com). The second-highest seller of Guinness in BC, this true Irish pub and bistro serves up nostalgia of the Emerald Isle to a clientele of regulars. 20 oz. drafts (CDN$6.10), mixed drinks (CDN$6.50), and bangers and mash will keep those eyes smiling. Tu-Th live music 8pm-last customer. Open M-Th noon-11pm, F-Sa noon-midnight. AmEx/D/MC/V.

Sonar, 66 Water St. (☎604-683-6695; www.sonar.bc.ca). Partygoers crowd onto this popular beat factory's large dance floor. Long lines on weekends, but a visit to www.clubvibes.com will get you on the guest list. International DJs spin house (W), techno (F), and hip-hop (Sa). Open W 9pm-2am, F-Sa 9pm-3am. AmEx/D/MC/V.

Shine, 364 Water St. (☎604-408-4321; www.shinenightclub.com), in the basement. Named the "sexiest club in Canada" in 2001 by *Flare Magazine*, this ultra-hip club draws in crowds with its sleek decor and nightly specials. M favorite sets, Tu DJ party, W reggae, Th 90s, F-Sa hip-hop and pop, Su techno and house. Beer CDN$6-8. Cover M-Th and Su CDN$3, F-Sa CDN$10. Open M-Tu 10pm-2am, W-Th 9pm-2am, F-Sa 9pm-3am, Su 9pm-2am. AmEx/MC/V.

The Blarney Stone, 216 Carrall St. (☎604-687-4322). For a more raucous Irish experience, join the university crowd for music 4 nights a week by Killarney, a Celtic-rock band that has played here for 20 years. Cover F-Sa CDN$7. Open W-Sa 7pm-2am. MC/V.

The King's Head, 1618 Yew St. (☎604-738-6966), at 1st St. Cheap drinks, cheap food, relaxing atmosphere, and a great location near the beach. Bands play acoustic sets nightly at 9pm on a tiny stage. Daily drink specials. CDN$3.50 pints. Open M-F 9am-1am, Sa 8am-1am, Su 8am-midnight. AmEx/MC/V.

Koerner's Pub, 6371 Crescent Rd. (☎604-822-0983), in the basement of the Graduate Student Building on UBC campus. Owned and operated by the Graduate Student Society, this is the place to meet sexy brains. Mellow M with live music and open jam. Pints CDN$5. Open M-F noon-1am, Sa 4pm-1am.

◪ **APPROACHING VICTORIA: 68 MILES**
From Vancouver, take **Hwy. 99 S** until the junction with **Hwy. 17.** Follow Hwy. 17 heading southwest until you reach the **Tsawwassen Ferry Terminal.** (☎888-223-3779; www.bcferries.com. 8-16 per day. CDN $11; bikes CDN$2.50; cars CDN36-38.) You will need to take the 1½hr. ferry trip across to Vancouver Island. After docking on Vancouver Island, head south on Hwy. 17 until you get to Victoria.

VICTORIA

A fitting place to end the Great North roadtrip, Victoria is the proper British side note to more cosmopolitan Vancouver, complete with perfectly groomed gardens and polite society tea. Many tourist operations would have you believe that Victoria fell off Great Britain in a neat little chunk, but the truth is, Victoria's British flavor was created in the 1950s to attract tourists. Today, double-decker buses motor past art galleries, countless "English" pubs, and waterfront cafes. Victoria lies within easy distance of Vancouver Island's outdoor paradise, making it a destination for both leisure and adventure.

VITAL STATS

Population: 330,200

Visitor Info: Tourism Victoria, 812 Wharf St., (☎250-953-2033), at Government St. Open daily July-Aug. 8:30am-6:30pm; Sept.-June 9am-5pm.

Internet Access: Central Library, 735 Broughton St. (☎250-382-7241). Open M and F-Sa 9am-6pm, Tu-Th 9am-9pm, Su 1-5pm. Free.

Post Office: 706 Yates St. (☎250-267-1177). Open M-F 8am-5pm. **Postal Code:** V8W 2L9.

GETTING AROUND

Victoria surrounds the **Inner Harbour,** a boulevard meant for pedestrians. The main north-south streets are **Government St.** and **Douglas St.** To the north, Douglas St. becomes **Hwy. 1,** which runs to Nanaimo. **Blanshard St.,** one block to the east, becomes **Hwy. 17.** BC Ferries depart Swartz Bay to Vancouver's Tsawwassen terminal. (☎888-223-3779; www.bcferries.com. 8-16 per day; CDN$11; bikes CDN$2.50, cars CDN$36-38.)

SIGHTS

If you don't mind becoming one with the flocks of tourists heading to the shores of Victoria, wander along the **Inner Harbour.** You'll see boats come in and admire street performers on the Causeway as the sun sets behind neighboring islands.

BUTCHART GARDENS. The elaborate and world-famous Butchart Gardens sprawl across 55 acres, 13 mi. north of Victoria, off Hwy. 17. Immaculate landscaping includes the magnificent **Sunken Garden** (a former limestone quarry), the Rose Garden, Japanese and Italian gardens, and fountains. The gardens sparkle with live entertainment and lights at night, while Saturday evening fireworks shows in July and August draw out the locals. (*Bus #75 "Central Saanich" from downtown.* ☎250-652-4422; www.butchartgardens.com. *Open daily mid-June to Aug. 9am-11:30pm; call ahead for win-*ter hours. CDN$23, ages 13-17 CDN$11.50, ages 5-12 CDN$2.50, under 5 free.)

ROYAL BRITISH COLUMBIA MUSEUM. This thorough museum houses exhibits on the biological, geological, and cultural history of the province. Step into a coastal ecosystem, temperate forests, and an ice age, complete with woolly mammoth. (*675 Belleville St.* ☎250-356-7226; www.royalbcmuseum.bc.ca. *Open daily 9am-5pm. CDN$12.50, seniors and ages 6-18 CDN$8.70, under 6 free. IMAX and Museum CDN$21, students CDN$18.20, seniors and ages 6-18 CDN$17, under 6 CDN$5.)*

VANCOUVER ISLAND BREWERY. After a few days of hiking, biking, and museum-going, unwind with a tour of the Vancouver Island Brewery. The 1hr. tour has 20min. of touring and 40min. of drinking. (☎250-361-0007; www.vanislandbrewery.com. *Tours M and Th 1pm, F 1 and 3pm, Sa 3pm. CDN$6. 19+ to taste.)*

DOWNTOWN SIGHTS. The **Parliament Buildings** light up Victoria's skyline in the evenings and majestically preside over the Inner Bay during the day. Stroll through the buildings and admire the 19th-century architecture of Francis Rattenburg. (*501 Belleville St.* ☎250-387-3046; www.legis.gov.bc.ca. *Tours in summer daily 9am-5pm; hours vary in winter, call ahead. Free.)* The **Fairmont Empress Hotel** is one of Victoria's most popular icons, with ivy-covered brick and regal flair. Staying the night is pricey, but a free visit to the tea room and grounds is well-worth the stop. (*721 Government St.* ☎250-384-8111.)

A SPOT OF TEA

For nearly a century, the grand Fairmont-Empress Hotel has hosted formal afternoon tea, one of England's oldest and most famous traditions. While tea, including many afternoon tea services, can be found throughout Victoria, none have the history nor the majesty of high tea at the Empress. The menu includes fresh fruit topped with Chantilly cream, small tea sandwiches in flavors like carrot and ginger, traditional English scones, a wide selection of freshly prepared pastries, and their "Tea at The Empress" blend, whose ingredients are known only to a group of select insiders. The menu is, however, only part of the experience. The gorgeous tea lobby is a sight in itself, and the dress code—smart casual; shorts, ripped or torn jeans, tank tops, sleeveless shirts, short shorts or cut-offs, and running shoes are all forbidden—lends a regal air to the services. The hotel has played host to the rich and famous throughout the centuries, including Edward Prince of Wales, Katherine Hepburn, and Barbra Streisand. The afternoon tea service allows you to join their ranks, even if for just an hour.

The Empress Hotel. 721 Government St. (☎250-389-2727). Tea service $45.50.

OUTDOORS. The flowering oasis of **Beacon Hill Park,** off Douglas St., south of the Inner Harbour, pleases walkers, bikers, and picnickers; it borders the gorgeous Dallas Rd. scenic drive. Mountain bikers can tackle the **Galloping Goose,** a 100km trail beginning downtown and continuing to the west coast of the island through rainforests and canyons. **Ocean River Sports,** 1824 Store St., offers kayak rentals, tours, and lessons. (☎381-4233 or 800-909-4233; www.oceanriver.com. Open M-Th 9:30am-6pm, F 9:30am-8pm, Sa 9:30am-5:30pm, Su 11am-5pm. Single kayak CDN$40 per day; double CDN$60.)

▓ FOOD

A diverse array of food awaits in Victoria, if you know where to go. Many **Government St.** and **Wharf St.** restaurants raise their prices for summer tourists. **Chinatown** extends from Fisgard and Government St. to the northwest. **Cook St. Village,** between McKenzie and Park St., has an eclectic mix of creative restaurants.

Rebar, 50 Bastion Sq. (☎250-361-9223). Perhaps the healthiest, best-tasting cuisine in Canada. Mosaic walls, an eclectic menu of organic breakfast treats, salads, and pastas will make even the pickiest of diners happy. Dishes $5-12. Open M-W 8:30am-9pm, Th-Sa 8:30am-10pm, Su 7:30am-3:30pm. ❸

John's Place, 723 Pandora St. (☎250-389-0711; www.johnsplace.ca). Dishes up Canadian fare with a spicy Mediterranean and Asian twist. Fluffy Greek omelettes ($8), sweet chile prawns ($14), and banana chocolate cheesecake ($2) are just some of the delights that await. Open M-Th 7am-9pm, F 7am-10pm, Sa 8am-4pm and 5-10pm, Su 8am-4pm and 5-9pm. AmEx/MC/V. ❸

James Bay Tea Room and Restaurant, 332 Menzies St. (☎250-382-8282), at Superior St., behind the Parliament Buildings. A trip to Victoria is not complete without a spot of tea. The Sa and Su High Tea (CDN$12) is delightful and significantly less expensive than the famous High Tea at the Empress Hotel. Open M-Sa 7am-5pm, Su 8am-5pm. AmEx/MC/V. ❷

Ali Baba Pizza, 1101 Blanshard St. (☎250-385-6666; www.alibabapizza.com). Ali Baba Pizza is continually voted the best pizza on the island for good reason. One slice will fill up any of the 40 thieves. If you want something gourmet, choose from 6 sauces, 3 types of crust, and fancy Italian toppings. Open M-Th 10am-midnight, F-Sa 10am-2am, Su 11am-11pm. AmEx/MC/V. ❷

▛ ACCOMMODATIONS

Victoria has a plethora of budget accommodations. A number of flavorful hostels and B&B-hostel hybrids make a night in Victoria an altogether pleasant experience. More than a dozen campgrounds lie in the greater Victoria area.

Ocean Island Backpackers Inn, 791 Pandora St. (☎250-385-1788 or 888-888-4180; www.oceanisland.com), downtown. This hostel boasts a better lounge than most clubs, tastier food than most restaurants, and accommodations comparable to many hotels. Linen and locker included. Internet access CDN$1 per 15min. Parking CDN$5. Reception 24hr. Dorms CDN$19-24, members CDN$18-22; private rooms CDN$25-59. MC/V. ❶

Victoria International Hostel (HI), 516 Yates St. (☎250-385-4511). Colorful barracks-style dorms and private rooms in downtown. Laundry CDN$3.50. Dorms CDN$21-24, members CDN$17-20; private rooms CDN$52/$60. MC/V. ❶

Paul's Motor Inn, 1900 Douglas St. (☎866-333-7285; www.paulsmotorinn.com), just past Chinatown. Offers cozy hotel rooms with TV, fridge, and queen beds. Rooms CDN$72-170. ❹

Goldstream Provincial Park, 2930 Trans-Canada Hwy. (☎250-391-2300 or 800-689-9025), 10 mi. northwest of Victoria, offers tent sites in a forested riverside area with great hiking trails and swimming in the Goldstream River. Toilets and showers. Sites CDN$22. ❶

▊ NIGHTLIFE

English pubs, watering holes, and clubs abound throughout town. Live music is available practically every night, and the free weekly *Monday Magazine* (www.mondaymag.com) will keep you updated on who's playing when and where.

Irish Times Pub, 1200 Government St. (☎250-383-7775). For a cheap and swanky time, head here. Happy hour daily 3-6pm with CDN$0.69 oysters. W pizza and pints CDN$10. Live Irish music daily. Open daily 11am-1am. AmEx/D/MC/V.

Upstairs Cabaret, 15 Bastian Sq. (☎250-385-5483). The college venue for live music and dancing. F-Sa nights DJs bring a crowd. Cover CDN$7. Doors open 9pm. AmEx/D/MC/V.

Darcy's Pub, 1127 Wharf St. (☎250-380-1322; www.darcyspub.ca), just below Upstairs. Caters to a drinking, people-watching, lively-without-dancing crowd. Outdoor seating right on the Square makes it a prime spot in summer. M and W chicken wings $5. Tu bottomless pasta CDN$5. Open M-Th and Su 11am-midnight, F-Sa 11am-1am. AmEx/MC/V.

Steamers Public House, 570 Yates St. (☎250-381-4342; www.steamerspub.ca). Attracts a college-age dancing crowd and serves everything from burgers (CDN$9-10) to flatbread (CDN$9-

10). It's the best Su entertainment in town. M open mic. Tu jazz night. Open daily 11:30am-2am. AmEx/MC/V.

THE END OF THE ROAD

You've braved wild animals, giant cities, forbidding mountain passes, and that dreaded Canadian "eh" for nearly 4000 miles across North America. Take a moment to revel in your success—clamber onto a double-decker bus, indulge in some crumpets and Earl Grey tea, and explore British Columbia's outdoor paradise. You've conquered the Great North, and nothing can stop you now. Head south for the Pacific Coast or the Oregon Trail to continue the adventure.

EXIT TO

Seattle, WA   108 mi.
on the pacific coast route, p. 982

Portland, OR   254 mi.
on the oregon trail route, p. 673

SPEED LIMIT 65

the national road

TOP 5

1. Traverse the **Continental Divide** in **Rocky Mountain National Park** (p. 428).
2. Relive the major events of "Give 'Em Hell" Harry's presidency at the **Truman Library** (p. 408).
3. Celebrate the fact that you're halfway there at the **Middle of the US** (p. 412).
4. Visit the quintessential roadside attraction at the site of the **world's largest hairball** (p. 413).
5. Plan an escape at former maximum security prison **Alcatraz** (p. 482).

For roadtrippers who don't want to mess around, the 3000+ mile National Road puts all others to shame. This route cuts across the middle of the country, from sea to shining sea. For the first stretch, you'll follow the Old National Road, much of which is today's U.S. 40. Construction on this road began in 1811, and the road reached its original terminus, Wheeling, West Virginia in 1818. By 1833, it had been extended to Vandalia, Illinois; from the start of the route to Vandalia, Old National Road Markers, as well as Madonna of the Trail statues, are still visible on the roadside.

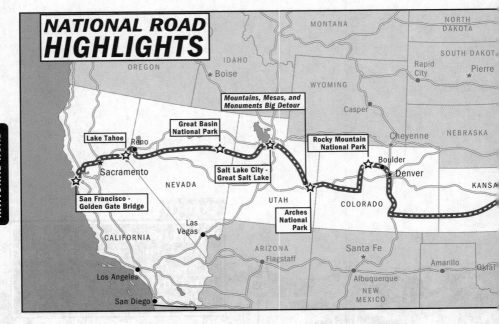

Start your trip in **Atlantic City, NJ**—check out **Lucy the Elephant** (p. 354), but don't spend all your quarters at the slots here; save some for **Reno, NV** (p. 461), still 2700 mi. down the road. From here, continue on to **Philadelphia** (p. 355), revered by some as the birthplace of the nation and revered by more as the birthplace of the cheesesteak sandwich, before passing through **Baltimore** (p. 365). Soon enough you'll enter the foothills of the **Blue Ridge Mountains.** Stop at scenic **Harpers Ferry National Historic Park** (p. 371) before rolling through Ohio and into Indiana, home of the world-famous **Indianapolis Motor Speedway** (p. 390). Pass into the West under the arch at **St. Louis** (p. 397) and then through Missouri, home state of ragtime legend **Scott Joplin** (in Sedalia, p. 406). Next is Kansas, home of the **world's largest hairball** (p. 413). By now, you'll be on **U.S. 50,** another famous continent-crosser, paralleling the historic **Lincoln Highway.** It's a long, straight shot to Colorado, and then to **Denver** (p. 420) up into the mountains, winding through the **Rocky Mountains National Park** (p. 428), and passing by some of the nation's best skiing at **Vail** (p. 433). This area also hosts unparalleled opportunities for summertime activities, including rafting and mountain biking.

The stunning scenery continues into Utah; our route takes you through **Moab** (p. 441), gateway to the spectacular **Mountains, Monuments, and Mesas Big Detour** (p. 442), and then north to **Salt Lake City** (p. 450) and its namesake Great Salt Lake. From there, it's on to northern Nevada, where U.S. 50 is known as **"The Loneliest Road,"** tracing the route of the short-lived **Pony Express** (p. 460). The road here is a black ribbon winding across the desert, broken by the occasional cow, cactus, or mining town. You'll pass **Great Basin National Park** (p. 454) and then Reno—"the biggest little city in the world"—before the welcome blue oasis of **Lake Tahoe** (p. 464), which somehow offers pristine wilderness and casino-sponsored debauchery side-by-side. Continuing west, you'll come down from the **Sierra Nevada** through California's Central

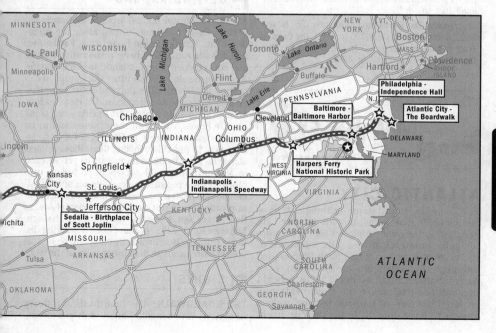

NATIONAL ROAD

Valley. **Berkeley** (p. 474) is a bibliophile's dream and home to **Chez Panisse** (p. 477), the birthplace of California cuisine. Go west, young roadtripper, until you can go west no more, ending your journey in **San Francisco** (p. 479). Watch the sun set over the **Golden Gate Bridge** (p. 486), a grand end to a grand transcontinental roadtrip.

ROUTE STATS

Miles: c. 3000

Route: Atlantic City, NJ to San Francisco, CA.

States: 14; New Jersey, Pennsylvania, Delaware, Maryland, West Virginia, Ohio, Indiana, Illinois, Missouri, Kansas, Colorado, Utah, Nevada, and California.

Driving Time: Give yourself at least 3-4 weeks to experience what the road has to offer.

When To Go: Almost any time you feel like taking off for California. Go in winter and ski in Colorado (but keep in mind that driving conditions can be treacherous) or go in summer and explore the wilderness along the way (but keep in mind that prices and temperatures are higher). The bottom line? Just go.

Crossroads: The East Coast in Atlantic City, NJ (p. 350); **Route 66** in St. Louis, MO (p. 397); **The Oregon Trail** in Independence, MO (p. 408); **The Pacific Coast** in San Francisco, CA (p. 479).

The Garden State

NEW JERSEY

Welcomes You!

ATLANTIC CITY

For 70 years, board game enthusiasts have been wheeling and dealing with Atlantic City geography, famously depicted on the Monopoly game board. Meanwhile, the opulence of the original Boardwalk and Park Place faded into neglect and then into casino-driven tackiness. Gambling, legalized in the 1970s, brought mega-dollar casinos to the Boardwalk and restored the flow of tourists, but the casinos appear to have done little for the city itself.

Highlights center on the Boardwalk, where blaring announcements invite pedestrians to step into the casinos and try their luck.

VITAL STATS

Population: 41,000

Visitor Info: Atlantic City Visitors Welcome Center (☎609-449-7100), on the Atlantic Expwy., 1 mi. after the Pleasantville Toll Plaza. Open daily 9am-5pm. **Atlantic City Convention Center and Visitors Bureau Info Center** (☎888-228-4748; www.atlanticcitynj.com), on the Boardwalk at Mississippi Ave. Open daily Labor Day to Memorial Day 9:30am-5:30pm; Memorial Day to Labor Day M-W 9:30am-5:30pm, Th-Su 9:30am-8pm. Free.

Internet Access: Atlantic City Library, 1 N. Tennessee Ave. (☎609-345-2269). Open M-W 10am-8pm, Th-Sa 9am-5pm.

Post Office: 1701 Pacific Ave. (☎609-345-5583), at Illinois Ave. Open M-F 8:30am-5:30pm, Sa 8:30am-12:30pm. **Postal Code:** 08401.

GETTING AROUND

Attractions cluster on and around the **Boardwalk,** which runs northeast-southwest along the Atlantic Ocean. Parallel to the Boardwalk, **Pacific Ave.** and **Atlantic Ave.** offer cheap restaurants, hotels, and convenience stores. Atlantic Ave. and Pacific Ave. can be dangerous after dark, and areas beyond the Boardwalk's flurry of activity are desolate and unsafe. Getting around is easy on foot on the Boardwalk. **Jitneys,** 201 Pacific Ave., small shuttle buses, run to all the casinos and most major points of interest. (☎609-344-8642; www.jitneys.net. $2 per ride). **Rolling Chair Rides** appear along the Boardwalk as frequently as yellow cabs in Manhattan. (☎609-347-7500. $5 for up to 5 blocks.) Free parking is available on some residential streets, but you're only likely to find spots in unsafe areas. You can also try **Oriental Ave.** at **New Jersey Ave.** near the Garden Pier Historic Museum for free 3hr. parking at easy walking distance from the Boardwalk. Be careful at night: this area is more desolate than other parts of the city.

SIGHTS

THE BOARDWALK. The Boardwalk is a flurry of activity and seagulls, lined with gift shops,

Atlantic City

▲ ACCOMMODATIONS
Comfort Inn, **5**
Inn of the Irish Pub, **7**
Red Carpet Motel, **2**
Rodeway Inn, **8**
Shady Pines Campground, **1**

● FOOD
Bill's Gyro and Souvlaki, **9**
Inn of the Irish Pub, **6**
Tony's Baltimore Grille, **4**
White House Sub Shop, **3**

food stalls selling pizza, funnel cakes, stromboli, and ice cream, and, of course, the casinos (see p. 352). There's often live music playing, usually paid for by casinos trying to attract gamblers. Visitors can walk, ride bikes between 6 and 10am, or take advantage of the ubiquitous rolling chairs. Most of the action along this 8 mi. stretch takes place south of the Showboat. Those under 21 play for prizes at the many arcades that line the Boardwalk, including **Central Pier Arcade & Speedway.** It feels like real gambling, but the teddy bear in the window is easier to win than the convertible on display at Caesar's. The pier also has go-karts and paintball. *(At the Boardwalk and Tennessee Ave. ☎609-345-5219. Open M-Th and Su 10am-midnight, F-Sa 10am-2am. Single go-kart $7; double $12. Must be 12 and 54 in. tall to ride alone. Paintball $5 per 30 shots.)* The historic **Steel Pier** juts into the coastal waters with a ferris wheel that spins riders over the Atlantic. It also offers the rest of the usual amusement park attractions: a roller coaster, a carousel, and games of "skill" aplenty. *(On the Boardwalk at Virginia Ave. ☎609-345-4893 or 866-386-6659; www.steelpier.com. Open M-F 3pm-midnight, Sa-Su noon-1am. Tickets $0.75, 35 for $25.)* When you tire of spending money, check out the historic **Atlantic City Beach,** pretty much the only free activity in town. Just west of Atlantic City, **Ventnor City Beach** offers more tranquil shores.

MUSEUMS. For a quieter way to spend the afternoon, explore the **Atlantic City Art Cen-**ter, which displays the work of local and regional artists. *(On Garden Pier at New Jersey Ave. and the Boardwalk. ☎609-347-5837; www.acartcenter.org. Open daily 10am-4pm. Free.)* On the same pier, the **Atlantic City Historical Museum** contains memorabilia from the history of the "Queen of Resorts," including displays on the Miss America Pageant, Monopoly, and sand art. *(☎609-347-5839; www.acmuseum.org. Open daily 10am-4pm. Free.)*

OTHER SIGHTS. The tallest lighthouse in New Jersey and the third tallest in the nation, **Absecon Lighthouse** has been painted with several different color schemes since it was built in 1868. Now yellow and black, it contains a small museum and a stunning view of the city and ocean. *(31 S. Rhode Island Ave. Drive northeast on Pacific Ave. from midtown. ☎609-449-1360; www.abseconlighthouse.org. Open July-Aug. daily 10am-5pm; Sept.-Dec. and Mar.-June M and Th-Su 11am-4pm; hours vary in winter. $5, seniors $4, ages 4-12 $3.)*

🏛 CASINOS

All casinos on the Boardwalk fall within a dice toss of one another. The farthest south is the elegant **Hilton,** between Providence and Boston Ave. (☎609-347-7111 or 800-257-8677; www.hiltonac.com), and the farthest north is the gaudy **Showboat,** at Delaware Ave. and Boardwalk (☎609-343-4000 or 800-621-0200; www.harrahs.com). Donald Trump's glittering **Trump Taj Mahal Hotel and Casino,** 1000 Board-

A MONOPOLY ON MONOPOLY

If you've ever played the classic board game Monopoly, you will probably recognize many of the street names in Atlantic City. Charles Darrow, who invented the game in 1935, named Monopoly's properties after streets and neighborhoods in and around Atlantic City. Millions of copies of the game have been printed, making it the most popular commercial board game in history. But even with the game's continued success, Parker Brothers has decided it is time for a change—Atlantic City is being taken off the board. Many versions featuring other cities have been sold over the years, but the official version has always featured Atlantic City. Starting in 2006, the new version of monopoly will hit stores, without any A.C. locales. To make their decision, Parker Brothers created an online poll to allow visitors to vote on which legendary US properties will replace the existing ones. Atlantic City has not dealt with the change well; after years of publicity from the game, the city's citizens are outraged by the decision. Monopoly purists are none too pleased either, having grown attached to Water Works, B&O Railroad, and Boardwalk. Other changes will include greater denominations of money, modern scenarios on Chance and Community Chest cards, and higher property values, but the location is the sticker. Alas, it seems Atlantic City didn't have a monopoly on the game after all.

walk, (☎609-449-1000; www.trumptaj.com), at Virginia Ave., is an Atlantic City landmark and too ostentatious to be missed. In true Monopoly form, Trump owns another hotel casino on Boardwalk: the **Trump Plaza**, at Mississippi and the Boardwalk (☎609-441-6000 or 800-677-7378; www.trumpplaza.com). Many a die is cast at **Caesar's Boardwalk Resort and Casino,** 2100 Pacific Ave., at Arkansas Ave. (☎800-443-0104; www.caesarsatlanticcity.com). At Indiana Ave., **The Sands** (☎609-441-4000; www.acsands.com) stands tall and flashy with its seashell motif. All casinos are open 24hr. and are dominated by slot machines.

■ FOOD

Although not recommended by nutritionists, $0.75 hot dogs and $2 pizza slices are readily available on the Boardwalk, and there is no shortage of ice-cream parlors. Some of the best deals in town await at the casinos, where all-you-can-eat lunch ($7) and dinner ($11) buffets abound. Tastier, less tacky fare can be found farther from the seashore.

White House Sub Shop, 2301 Arctic Ave. (☎609-345-8599), at Mississippi Ave. According to rumor, Sinatra had these immense subs (half $6, whole $12) flown to him while on tour. Pictures of sub-lovers Joe DiMaggio, Wayne Newton, and Mr. T overlook the team making each sandwich to order. Open M-Th 10am-9:30pm, F-Sa 10am-10pm. Cash only. ❷

Inn of the Irish Pub, 164 St. James Pl. (☎609-344-9063; www.theirishpub.com). Locals lounge downstairs and foreign students and hostelers stay upstairs at this hostel-and-bar combo. Serving hearty pub-style food all night, it's packed with carousers at all hours. Wash down a liverwurst and onion sandwich ($2.40) with a domestic pint ($2). Dinner specials $6. Domestic drafts $1. Open 24hr. Cash only. ❶

Tony's Baltimore Grille, 2800 Atlantic Ave. (☎609-345-5766), at Iowa Ave. It's hard to resist this old-time Italian atmosphere with personal jukeboxes and cheap prices. Pizza $8. Seafood platter with shrimp, crab cakes, and scallops $12. Open daily 11am-3am. Bar open 24hr. Cash only. ❹

Bill's Gyro and Souvlaki, 1607 Boardwalk (☎609-347-2466), near Kentucky Ave. Thousands of customer-signed dollar bills adorn the walls, stools, cash registers, and counter at this bright establishment. The menu offers 24hr. breakfast (omelette $3) and gyros ($5.75). Open 24hr. AmEx/D/MC/V. ❶

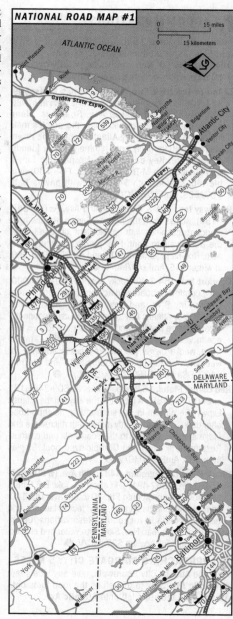

NATIONAL ROAD MAP #1

▲ ACCOMMODATIONS

Motels are located 2-6 mi. out of town on U.S. 40 and U.S. 30, as well as in Absecon, 8 mi. west of town on U.S. 30. Rates may vary wildly between weekdays and weekends, so call ahead.

Inn of the Irish Pub, 164 St. James Pl. (☎609-344-9063; www.theirishpub.com), between New York Ave. and Tennessee Ave. Spacious, clean rooms near the Boardwalk. Enjoy the porch's rocking chairs and refreshing Atlantic breeze. The downstairs bar offers lively entertainment and a friendly atmosphere. Key deposit $5. No parking. Single with shared bath M-Th and Su $25, F-Sa $30; double with shared bath $40/$45; with private bath $60/$65. AmEx/D/MC/V. ❷

Rodeway Inn, 124 S. North Carolina Ave. (☎609-345-0155), across from the Resorts Casino. Rooms have standard amenities with an excellent location just off the Boardwalk to boot. Free parking. Laundry available. Rooms in summer M-Th and Su $75, F-Sa $90; in winter $45. AmEx/D/MC/V. ❹

Comfort Inn, 154 S. Kentucky Ave. (☎609-348-4000; www.comfortinnboardwalkac.com), between Martin Luther King Blvd. and New York Ave. Basic rooms with—true to Atlantic City swank—a jacuzzi. Continental breakfast, free parking, and a heated pool. Rooms with ocean views are extra, but come with fridge, microwave, and a bigger jacuzzi. Reserve in advance for weekends and holidays. Rooms M-Th and Su from $100, F-Sa from $180. AmEx/D/MC/V. ❺

Red Carpet Motel, 1630 Albany Ave. (☎609-348-3171 or 866-749-6985). A bit out of the way, off the Atlantic Expwy. Be careful in the surrounding neighborhood after dark. Standard, comfy rooms with microwave and fridge and free shuttles to the Boardwalk and casinos. Restaurant in lobby and Olympic-sized pool. Singles from $50. AmEx/D/MC/V. ❸

Shady Pines Campground, 443 S. 6th Ave. (☎609-652-1516 or 800-352-4917), in Absecon. Take Exit 5 from the Expwy., then left onto Rte. 30 to 6th Ave. This 140-site campground has a pool, playground, laundry, and new showers and restrooms. Reservations recommended. Open Mar.-Nov. Sites with water and electricity $37, with full hookup $39. MC/V. ❷

▲ APPROACHING MARGATE CITY: 5 MILES
From the Atlantic City Boardwalk, take any side street to **Pacific Ave.** Stay to the left as the road turns onto **Albany Ave.,** then turn left onto **Atlantic Ave.**

MARGATE CITY. Trim beachfront houses and condos replace the glitz and grit of the Atlantic City boardwalk. If you didn't get your fill of over-the-top fun, check out **Lucy the Elephant** at 9200 Atlantic Ave. Originally built in 1881 as a marketing gimmick, Lucy has always been in the public eye. It's no wonder—at 60 ft. and 90 tons, she's hardly the average pachyderm. (☎609-823-6473; www.lucytheelephant.org. Open Apr. W-F 11am-4pm, Sa-Su 10am-5pm; May to mid-June M-F 11am-4pm, Sa-Su 10am-5pm; mid-June to Labor Day M-Sa 10am-8pm, Su 10am-5pm. Tours every 30min. $5, children $3.) If you've grown too attached to Lucy to leave for a meal, head to **I Love Lucy's Beach Grille ❶,** the food stand right in front of her trunk. (☎609-822-7268. Burgers $4.50. Open Memorial Day to Labor Day M-F 10am-5pm. Cash only.) **Ventura's Greenhouse Grill ❸,** 106 S. Benson Ave., serves seafood lunch and dinner in a tiki bar setting. (☎609-822-0140. Lobster bisque $10. Clams casino $12. Open 11am-2am. Kitchen closes 10pm. AmEx/MC/V.)

▲ APPROACHING MAYS LANDING: 18 MILES
Leaving Margate City, take **Ventnor Ave.** back towards Atlantic City and make a left onto **Albany Ave. (U.S. 40).** Stay left to stay on **U.S. 40** when it splits from **U.S. 322** to become the **Harding Highway.** Continue on it for 5 mi.

MAYS LANDING. When you enter well-maintained Mays Landing, be sure to note the **American Hotel** on your left and the courthouse on your right, both built in the late 1830s. The American Hotel has replaced its beds with bookshelves and now forms part of the **Atlantic County Library,** 40 Farragut Ave. (☎609-625-2776. Free Internet access. Open M-Th 9am-9pm, F-Sa 9am-5pm.) More homey than your typical diner, **Chef John's Main St. Cafe ❷,** 6033 W. Main St., has $5 lunch specials with savory french fries. (☎609-625-5500. Breakfast $1.50-8. Sandwiches $5-9. Breakfast served M-F until 11:30am, Sa-Su all day. Open M-Th 9am-3pm, F 9am-8:30pm, Sa 7am-8:30pm, Su 7am-3pm. AmEx/D/MC/V.)

▲ APPROACHING WOODSTOWN: 35 MILES
Turn onto **Cape May Ave./Harding Hwy.** and proceed for 20 mi. Bear right, and after 10 mi., take

the second exit at the traffic circle. Take **U.S. 40** until you hit Woodstown.

WOODSTOWN. Locals congregate under pictures of chefs at the **Woodstown Diner ❷**, 16 E. Ave., on U.S. 40. (☎856-769-1140. Breakfast $2-7.50. Lunch $3.50-7. Dinner $5-16. Open daily 6am-10pm. AmEx/D/DC/MC/V.) Victorian homes line Woodstown's leafy main streets, but you won't have much luck finding a room for a night.

APPROACHING CAMDEN: 30 MILES
From Woodstown, turn right at **N. Main St. (Rte. 45)** which becomes **Woodstown Rd.** after 7 mi. Turn left on **Commissoners Rd. (Rte. 45/77).** Bear right to take the ramp to Bellmawr, and drive for 10 mi. Get on the ramp for **Route 42 N,** and follow it for 4 mi. as it becomes **I-76 W.** Take **Exit 2** on **I-676 N** to **Camden/Ben Franklin Bridge,** then take **Exit 3** to **Morgan Blvd.** Turn left onto Morgan Blvd., and follow signs to the waterfront.

CAMDEN

For years Camden languished along with its smaller counterparts farther down the shore; however, a revitalization program introduced a little over a decade ago has since yielded noticeable results. Although much of Camden is not safe for tourists, the waterfront area is a pleasant exception, offering attractions that, while a bit expensive, are worth a stop. Camden fought a long battle to host the Navy's most decorated battleship, the **USS New Jersey,** which was in service until the early 1990s and has been moored here since 2001. Visitors can take a tour (1½hr.) of the prize, docked next to the Tweeter Center just south of the aquarium, at the **USS New Jersey Naval Museum and Veterans Memorial.** Tours offer a look at life on a modern battleship, complete with weapons, radio rooms, officers's quarters, and a mess area. (☎866-877-6262; www.battleshipnewjersey.org. Open daily 9am-5pm. Self-guided tours $13.50; ages 6-11, seniors, and veterans $9; under 6 free. Guided tours $15; ages 6-11, seniors, and veterans $10; under 6 free. Tour of weapons systems $17; ages 6-11, seniors, and veterans $11; under 6 free. Active military in uniform free.) Also in the waterfront area is the **Adventure Aquarium,** 1-3 Riverside Dr. The aquarium features live seal exhibits, penguin

feedings, and a chance to ⊠**swim with sharks** for $115. (☎856-365-3300; www.adventureaquarium.com. Open daily 9:30am-5pm. $17, seniors and children $14, under 2 free.) The destinations are all within walking distance of each other, and a free shuttle bus runs regularly.

APPROACHING PHILADELPHIA: 1 MILE
To get on **Federal St.,** follow signs for **U.S. 30.** After crossing **Broadway,** turn left onto the **Ben Franklin Bridge.** Take the exit for **Independence Hall** to access the central attractions.

The Keystone State
PENNSYLVANIA
Welcomes You!

PHILADELPHIA

With his band of Quakers, William Penn founded the City of Brotherly Love in 1682. But it was Ben, not Penn, who planted the seeds of the metropolis it is today. Benjamin Franklin, the ingenious American ambassador, inventor, and womanizer, almost single-handedly built Philadelphia into an American colonial capital. Today, sightseers will eat up Philly's historic attractions, world-class museums, and architectural accomplishments—not to mention the city's native cheesesteaks and endless culinary offerings.

VITAL STATS

Population: 1.5 million

Visitor Info: Independence Visitors Center and National Park Service Visitors Center, (☎215-965-7676), on Market St., between 5th and 6th St. inside the welcome center. Open daily in summer 8:30am-7pm; in winter 8:30am-5pm.

Internet Access: Free Library of Philadelphia, 1091 Vine St. (☎215-686-5322). Open M-W 9am-9pm, Th-Sa 9am-5pm. Free.

Post Office: 2970 Market St. (☎215-895-8980), at 30th St., across from the Amtrak station. Open daily 6am-midnight. **Postal Code:** 19104.

GETTING AROUND

The construction of **I-676** and **I-95** through Philadelphia's center has made navigating the already-challenging grid of one-way streets and alleys even more difficult. I-676 runs east-west through the **Center City** area, which is bordered by I-95 on the east and I-76 just across the Schuylkill River. Within the city, numbered north-south streets ascend in value from the **Delaware River** on the east past the **Schuylkill River** on the west, and serve as good reference points. The first street is **Front St.**; the others follow consecutively from 2nd to 69th.

Seeing attractions in the historic district is best done on foot. There is no shortage of expensive parking lots (about $11 per day) in Center City. Outside of the area around the convention center and Independence Hall, lot prices get somewhat cheaper, and virtually all lots offer day-long specials if you are in by 9 or 10am and out by 6pm. There is a somewhat cheaper lot ($5-11) on Race St. between 10th and 9th St. Metered spots ($1 per hr.) also exist throughout the city except in the immediate area of **Independence Mall**. Also, while most Center City meters give you 2hr., the spots at the Delaware River end of Chestnut and Market St. up above **Penn's Landing** offer 4hr. time slots. Meters in **University City** offer 3hr. slots.

SIGHTS

INDEPENDENCE MALL

Often referred to as the birthplace of the nation, this historic area of downtown Philadelphia is home to the city's most time-honored attractions, all must-sees for any visit.

INDEPENDENCE NATIONAL HISTORICAL PARK.
A small green framed by Market, Walnut, 2nd, and 7th St., the park is home to several historical buildings. At night, the **Lights of Liberty Show** relates the story of the American Revolution. An elaborate audio program narrates a 1hr., half-mile tour through the part while a $12 million laser light show illuminates five key sites in the downtown area. (☎ 215-542-3789 or 877-462-1776; www.lightsofliberty.org. Open daily June-Aug. 9am-6pm; Sept.-May 9am-5pm. Light show starts at the PECO Energy Liberty Center at 6th and Chestnut St. Tu-Sa sunset. Reservations required. $19.50, students and seniors $16.50, ages 6-12 $13.)

INDEPENDENCE HALL AND VISITORS CENTER.
Instead of wandering blindly through the park, begin your trip down American history memory lane at the impressive Independence Visitors Center. They dispense detailed maps and brochures, offer a small exhibit detailing each historical site, and provide electronic trip-planners that cater to the desires of each individual visitor. Revolutionary history abounds at **Independence Hall**, one of the most popular of Philadelphia's historic landmarks. Delegates signed the Declaration of Independence here in 1776 and reconvened in 1787 to endorse the US Constitution. Today, knowledgeable park rangers lead visitors on a brief but informative tour through the nation's first capitol building. (On Chestnut St. ☎ 215-925-6101. Open daily 9am-5pm. Free tours every 15min. Tickets distributed at the visitors center.)

CONGRESSIONAL SIGHTS.
Capital of the fledgeling nation, Philadelphia's **Congress Hall** was host to the first assembly of Congress from 1790-1800. While soaking up years of history, visitors can rest in plush Senate chairs. (At Chestnut and 6th St. Open daily 9am-5pm. Free.) The First Continental Congress united against the British in **Carpenters' Hall**, now a small museum heralding such architectural achievements as Old City Hall and the Pennsylvania State House. (320 Chestnut St. ☎ 215-925-0167. Open Mar.-Dec. Tu-Sa 10am-4pm; Jan.-Feb. W-Sa and Su 10am-4pm. Free.)

LIBERTY BELL AND CONSTITUTION CENTER.
While freedom still rings at the **Liberty Bell Center**, the **Liberty Bell** does not (inauspiciously, it cracked the first time it was rung). The petite bell is also visible through a glass wall from Chestnut St. (On Market St., between 5th and 6th St. ☎ 215-965-2305. Open daily 9am-5pm. Free.) The stunning **National Constitution Center** invites visitors to become "delegates" as they learn about the history of the Constitution and the ideas for which it stands. A 17min. presentation on the history of the Constitution wows visitors—touchscreens and monitors replace dusty artifacts here. The museum can seem imposing, but it is well organized and free of any overdone flag-waving. (525 Arch St., in Independence National Historical Park. ☎ 215-409-6600;

NATIONAL ROAD

NATIONAL ROAD

Philadelphia

◆ ACCOMMODATIONS
Alexander Inn, 14
Bank St. Hostel (HI), 8
Chamounix Mansion
International Youth
Hostel (HI), 1
La Reserve (Bed and Breakfast
Center City), 15

● FOOD
Abner's Cheesesteaks, 12
Bassett's Ice Cream, 6
Famous 4th St. Deli, 24
Geno's Steaks, 22
Jamaican Jerk Hut, 17
Jim's Steaks, 18
Pat's King of Steaks, 21
Pico de Gallo, 16
Pink Rose Pastry Shop, 23

Rangoon, 5
Ray's Cafe and Tea House, 4
Sang Kee Peking Duck House, 2
Singapore, 3
Smokey Joe's, 11
Tandoor India Restaurant, 10

■ NIGHTLIFE
Copabanana, 19
The Five Spot, 7
The Khyber, 9
Moriarty's, 13
Monk's Belgian
Cafe, 22

Delaware River

Christopher Columbus Blvd.

Benjamin Franklin Bridge

Penn's Landing

Delaware Ave.

Front St.

U.S. OLD CITY

Independence
National
Historical
Park

CHINATOWN

CENTER CITY

PARKWAY/MUSEUM
DISTRICT

RITTENHOUSE
SQUARE
DISTRICT

HISTORIC
DISTRICT

SOCIETY
HILL

WASHINGTON
SQUARE
DISTRICT

AVENUE OF THE ARTS

DREXEL
UNIVERSITY

Schuylkill River

Fairmount Park

PHILADELPHIA

CAMDEN

www.constitutioncenter.org. Open M-F and Su 9:30am-5pm, Sa 9:30am-6pm. Last presentation 4:10pm. $9, seniors and under 12 $7.)

OTHER SIGHTS. The rest of the park preserves residential and commercial buildings of the Revolutionary era. On the northern edge of the Mall, a white building replicates the size and location of Ben Franklin's home in **Franklin Court.** His original abode was unsentimentally razed by the statesman's heirs in 1812 in order to erect an apartment complex. The home features an underground museum, a 20min. movie, a replica of Franklin's printing office, and a working post office—the first post office in the nation and the only one not to fly the American flag, as there wasn't one in 1775. *(318 Market St., between 3rd and 4th St. ☎ 215-965-2305. Open summer daily 9am-5pm. Free.)* On a more somber note, a statue of the first American president and army general presides over the **Tomb of the Unknown Soldier,** in Washington Sq., where an eternal flame commemorates the fallen heroes of the Revolutionary War.

SOCIETY HILL

Society Hill proper begins on Walnut St., between Front and 7th St., east of Independence Mall. The neighborhood is rich with history, boasting century-old townhouses and cobblestone paths under electric "gaslights." America's oldest firehouse, historic **Head House Square,** at 2nd and Pine St., now houses restaurants and boutiques. Bargain hunters can test their skills at the outdoor crafts fair. *(☎ 215-790-0782. Open June-Aug. Sa noon-11pm, Su noon-6pm. Workshops Su 1-3pm. Free.)* Each January sequin- and feather-clad-participants join in a rowdy New Year's Day Mummer's parade, which began in celebration of the masked festival actors known as "mummers." South of Head House Sq., the **Mummer's Museum** swells with glamorous old costumes. *(1100 S. 2nd St., at Washington Ave. ☎ 215-336-3050; www.riverfrontmummers.com/museum.html. Open May-Sept. Tu 9:30am-9:30pm, W-Sa 9:30am-4:30pm, Su noon-4:30pm; Oct.-Apr. Tu-Sa 9:30am-4:30pm, Su noon-4:30pm. Free concerts Tu 8pm. $3.50; students, seniors, and under 12 $2.50.)*

CENTER CITY

As the financial hub of Philadelphia, Center City barely has enough room to accommodate the professionals who cram into the area bounded by 12th, 23rd, Vine, and Pine St.

Though rife with activity during the day, the region retires early at night.

ART AND ARCHITECTURE. The country's first art museum and school, the **Pennsylvania Academy of Fine Art** has displays of artwork by Winslow Homer and Mary Cassatt, while current students and accomplished alumni get their own exhibits each May. *(118-128 N. Broad St., at Cherry St. ☎ 215-972-7600; www.pafa.org. Open Tu-Sa 10am-5pm, Su 11am-5pm. 45min.-1hr. tours Tu-F 11:30am and 12:30pm, Sa-Su noon-1pm. $7, students and seniors $6, ages 5-18 $5.)* Presiding over Center City, the granite and marble **City Hall** took 30 years to build and is currently undergoing a $125 million cleaning project. At 548 ft., it remains the nation's largest working municipal building and, until 1908, it reigned as the tallest building in the US, aided by the 37 ft. statue of William Penn at its peak. A "gentlemen's agreement" prohibited building anything higher than Penn's hat until entrepreneurs overturned it in 1987. A commanding view of the city still awaits visitors in the tower. *(At Broad and Market St. ☎ 215-686-2840. Open M-F 9:30am-4:30pm. City Hall tour daily 12:30pm; ends at the tower 2pm. Tower Tour daily every 15min. 9:15am-4:15pm. Reservations recommended. $1.)* They may or may not rule the world, but the Freemasons of Philadelphia have a stunning **Masonic Temple** just north of City Hall. *(1 N. Broad St. ☎ 215-988-1917. Tours Tu-F 11am, 2, 3pm; Sa 10 and 11am. $8, students $6, under 12 and 65+ $5.)*

RITTENHOUSE SQUARE

Masons of a different ilk left their mark in the brick-laden **Rittenhouse Square District,** a ritzy neighborhood southeast of Center City. This part of town cradles the musical and dramatic pulse of the city, housing several performing arts centers. The square itself provides the best free entertainment in the city in terms of people-watching.

RITTENHOUSE MUSEUMS. For the best results, digest lunch completely before viewing the bizarre and often gory medical abnormalities displayed at the highly intriguing **Mütter Museum.** Among the potentially unsettling fascinations are a wall of human skulls and a collection of preserved body parts of famous people, including John Marshall's bladder stones and a cancerous section of John Wilkes Booth's neck. The museum also contains a Level 4 biohazard suit., a medicinal herb garden, and a bizarre gift shop. *(19 S. 22nd St. ☎ 215-563-3737, ext. 211; www.collphyphil.org. Open daily 10am-5pm. $12; students, seniors, and ages 6-18 $8.)* Just south, the nondescript exterior of the **Rosenbach Museum and Library** hides an enormous, must-see collection of rare books and manuscripts, from the original manuscript of James Joyce's *Ulysses* to Lewis Carroll's copy of *Alice in Wonderland. (2010 Delancey St. ☎ 215-732-1600; www.rosenbach.org. Open Tu and Th-Su 10am-5pm, W 10am-8pm. 1hr. tours Tu-Su 11am-4pm; $8, students and seniors $5. Tu free.)*

PARKWAY AND MUSEUM DISTRICT

BENJAMIN FRANKLIN PARKWAY. Once nicknamed "America's Champs-Elysées," the Benjamin Franklin Parkway has one of the best art museums in the country but has seen better days. Of the city's five original town squares, **Logan Circle** was the sight of public executions until 1823. It now delights hundreds of children who frolic in its **Swann Memorial Fountain.** Designed by Alexander Calder, the fountain represents the Wissahickon Creek and the Schuylkill and Delaware Rivers—the three bodies of water that surround the city.

SCIENCE MUSEUMS. A modern assemblage of everything scientific, the interactive **Franklin Institute** would make the old inventor proud. A skybike allows visitors to pedal across a tightrope suspended nearly four stories high. *(222 N. 20th St., at Race St. ☎ 215-448-1200; www.fi.edu. Open daily 9:30am-5pm. $13.75, seniors and ages 4-11 $11. IMAX $9. Museum and IMAX $18.75, seniors and ages 4-11 $16.)* Part of the Institute, the newly renovated **Fels Planetarium** flashes laser shows on Saturday nights. *(222 N. 20th St. ☎ 215-448-1388. $8.)* Opposite Fels, the **Academy of Natural Sciences** allows budding archaeologists to try digging up fossils. The animal center is home to over 100 beasties awaiting your visit. *(1900 Ben Franklin Pkwy., at 19th St. ☎ 215-299-1000; www.acnatsci.org. Open M-F 10am-4:30pm, Sa-Su 10am-5pm. $9, seniors and military $8.25, ages 3-12 $8.)*

ART MUSEUMS. Sylvester Stallone may have etched the sight of the **Philadelphia Museum of Art** into the minds of movie buffs everywhere when he bolted up its stately front steps in *Rocky*, but it is the artwork within that has earned the museum its fine reputation. The collections of Impression-

ist and northern Renaissance works are particularly strong. *(At Benjamin Franklin Pkwy. and 26th St. ☎ 215-763-8100; www.philamuseum.org. Open Tu-Th and Sa-Su 10am-5pm, F 10am-8:45pm. Tours 10am-3pm. $12, seniors $9, students and ages 13-18 $8. Su "pay what you wish.")* A cast of *The Gates of Hell* outside the **Rodin Museum** guards the portal of human passion, anguish, and anger in the most extensive collection of the sculptor's works this side of the Seine. One of the original casts of *The Thinker* (1880) marks the museum entrance. *(At Benjamin Franklin Pkwy. and 22nd St. ☎ 215-568-6026; www.rodinmuseum.org. Open Tu-Su 10am-5pm. Suggested donation $3.)*

FAIRMOUNT PARK. Philly's finest outdoor opportunities can be found in the resplendent Fairmount Park. The faux-Grecian ruins by the waterfall behind the Museum of Art are the abandoned **Waterworks,** built between 1819 and 1822. Free tours of the Waterworks' romantic architecture, technology, and social history meet on Aquarium Dr., behind the art museum. *(☎ 215-685-4935; www.fairmountwaterworks.org. Open Tu-Sa 10am-5pm, Su 1-5pm.)* Farther down the river, the line of crew clubs forming historic **Boathouse Row** make Philadelphia's place in the rowing world clear. The Museum of Art hosts tours of Boathouse Row on Wednesday and Sunday, as well as trolley tours to mansions in Fairmount Park. The area near Boathouse Row is also the city's most popular in-line-skating spot. In the northern arm of Fairmount Park, trails follow the secluded Wissahickon Creek for 5 mi. The **Japanese House and Garden** is designed in the style of a 17th-century *shoin;* the authentic space offers the utmost tranquility. *(Off Montgomery Dr., near Belmont Ave. ☎ 215-878-5097; www.shofuso.com. Open May-Oct. Tu-F 10am-4pm, Sa-Su 11am-5pm; hours vary in winter. 30-45min. tour included with ticket. $4, students and seniors $3.)* Some neighborhoods surrounding the park are not safe, and the park is not safe at night.

▚ FOOD

Street vendors are at the heart of Philadelphia culinary tradition, hawking cheesesteaks, hoagies, cashews, and soft pretzels. Ethnic eateries cluster in several specific areas: hip **South St.,** between Front and 7th St.; **18th St.** around Sansom St.; and **2nd St.,** between Chestnut and

Market St. The nation's third-largest Chinatown is bounded by 11th, 8th, Arch, and Vine St. Philadelphia's original farmers market (since 1893), the ⊠**Reading Terminal Market,** at 12th and Arch St., across from the Pennsylvania Convention Center, is the largest indoor market in the US. A food court on steroids, the market has everything from traditional Amish meat mongers to trendy Asian-fusion stalls. (☎215-922-2317; www.readingterminalmarket.org. Open M-Sa 8am-6pm. Amish merchants open W-Th 8am-3pm, F-Sa 8am-5pm.)

HISTORIC DISTRICT

⊠ **Famous 4th St. Delicatessen,** 700 S. 4th St. (☎215-922-3274), at Bainbridge St. This deli rivals New York's finest. A landmark since 1923, it has acquired a cult following for its hot corned-beef sandwiches ($10.75). The best cookies in the city. Open daily 8am-9pm. AmEx/MC/V. ❸

Pink Rose Pastry Shop, 630 S. 4th St. (☎215-592-0565; www.pinkrosepastry.com). Serves up homemade delicacies at tables graced with fresh flowers and grandmotherly decorations. Breakfast and lunch $2.50-8.25. Open M-Th 8am-10:30pm, F 8am-11pm, Sa 9am-11pm, Su 9am-10:30pm. AmEx/D/MC/V. ❷

Jim's Steaks, 400 South St. (☎215-928-1911; www.jimsteaks.com), at 4th St. Customers arrive in droves, clamoring for the authentic hoagies ($3.50-5) and fries ($1.25). Pass the time in line by inspecting the wall of fame, which includes Pat Sajak and Kobe Bryant. Open M-Th 10am-1am, F-Sa 10am-3am, Su 11am-10pm. Cash only. ❶

CHINATOWN

Singapore, 1006 Race St. (☎215-922-3288), between 10th and 11th St. The health-conscious flock here for the kosher-vegetarian roast "pork" with black-bean sauce ($7). Open daily 11am-11pm. AmEx/MC/V. ❷

Rangoon, 112 9th St. (☎215-829-8939), between Cherry and Arch St. Simple pink and plastic decor complements the spicy scents of Burmese cuisine. Crisp lentil fritters $9. Open M-Th and Su 11:30am-9:30pm, F-Sa 11:30am-10pm. MC/V. ❷

Sang Kee Peking Duck House, 238 9th St. (☎215-925-7532), near Arch St. Locals pack in for the extensive menu. Duck requires lengthy preparation, but they serve so much of it you are always just minutes away from the delectable fowl (half $16.50, whole $24.50).

Entrees $6-10. Open M-Th and Su 10am-10:45pm, F-Sa 10am-11:45pm. Cash only. ❷

Ray's Cafe and Tea House, 141 N. 9th St. (☎215-922-5122). Ideal for a quick snack on the run or a lingering meal over a book. Delicious dishes like rice noodle soup ($7). Hot mint-chocolate latte $2.50. Open M-Th 9am-9pm, F 9am-10pm, Sa 11:30am-10pm, Su 11:30am-10pm. AmEx/MC/V. ❷

CENTER CITY

⊠ **Jamaican Jerk Hut,** 1436 South St. (☎215-545-8644). While chefs jerk Negril garlic shrimp ($15) to perfection, Bob Marley tunes blast in the veranda. F-Sa live music 7pm. Cover $2. Open M-Th 11am-10pm, F-Sa 11am-11pm, Su 5-10pm. Cash only. ❸

Pico de Gallo, 1501 South St., (☎215-772-3003), on the corner of South and 15th St. This fun Mexican place makes no attempt at authenticity, but every meal is a fiesta. The plantain, roasted pork, and organic black bean burrito ($8) will challenge even the hungriest roadtripper. Fresh squeezed juices $3.25. Open daily noon-10pm. Cash only. ❷

Bassett's Ice Cream (☎215-925-4315), in Reading Terminal Market at 12th and Arch St. Established in 1861, Bassett's is the oldest ice creamery in the state, and some say the best in the nation. Originals like pumpkin ice cream may be throwbacks to the olden days, but modern concoctions—moose tracks, mocha chip, and rum raisin—also await. 2 scoops $2.75. Open M-Sa 8am-6pm. Cash only. ❶

UNIVERSITY CITY

⊠ **Tandoor India Restaurant,** 106 S. 40th St. (☎215-222-7122). Cheap Indian restaurants are a dime a dozen at college campuses, but this is a highlight. Lunch buffet daily 11:30am-3:30pm; $6. Dinner buffet daily 4-10pm; $9. Student discount 20%. Open daily 11:30am-10pm. AmEx/D/MC/V. ❷

Smokey Joe's, 210 S. 40th St. (☎215-222-0770), between Locust and Walnut St. Hearty meals at student-friendly prices make this a popular UPenn bar and restaurant. Sandwiches $4.75-6. Pints $2. Open M-Sa 11am-2am, Su 4pm-2am. AmEx/D/MC/V. ❶

Abner's Cheesesteaks, 3813 Chestnut St. (☎215-662-0100; www.abnerscheesesteaks.com), at 38th St. This bright, spacious, and sparkling-clean joint is a local favorite with the professional set and UPenn students. Cheesesteak, large soda, and fries $6.20. Open M-Th 11am-midnight, F-Sa 11am-3am, Su 11am-11pm. AmEx/D/DC/MC/V. ❶

ACCOMMODATIONS

Aside from the two hostels, inexpensive lodging in Philadelphia is uncommon. If reserved a few days in advance, comfortable rooms close to Center City can be found for around $60. The motels near the airport at Exit 9A on I-95 sacrifice location for affordable rates. **Bed and Breakfast Connections/Bed and Breakfast of Philadelphia,** in Devon, PA, books rooms in Philadelphia and southeastern Pennsylvania. (☎215-610-687-3565; www.bnbphiladelphia.com. Open M-F 9am-5pm. Reserve at least 1 week in advance; registration fee $10. Singles $60-90; doubles $75-250.) Most hotels and hostels listed are not parking-friendly; park in a lot or plan to pay meters.

Chamounix Mansion International Youth Hostel (HI-AYH), 3250 Chamounix Dr. (☎215-878-3676; www.philahostel.org), in West Fairmount Park. Take I-76 W to Exit 339, take a left on Belmont, a left on Ford Rd., and a left on Chamounix Rd. An energetic staff maintains this lavish hostel. Kitchen, piano, TV/VCR, and bikes. Linen $3. Laundry $2. Internet access $1 per 5min. Free parking. Check-in 8-11am and 4:30pm-midnight. Lockout 11am-4:30pm. Curfew midnight. Dorms $21, members $18. MC/V. ●

Bank Street Hostel (HI-AYH), 32 S. Bank St. (☎215-922-0222; www.bankstreethostel.com), between Chestnut and Market St. Social hostel in an alleyway in the historic district. Kitchen, A/C, TV, pool table. Linen $3. Laundry $3. Internet access $1 per 4min. Lockout 10am-4:30pm. Curfew M-Th and Su 12:30am, F-Sa 1am. Dorms $23, members $20. MC/V. ●

Alexander Inn, 12th and Spruce St. (☎215-923-3535; www.alexanderinn.com). 48 spacious rooms with Wi-Fi, cable TV, A/C, breakfast buffet, access to a fitness room, and just about everything else you could imagine. Check-in 3pm. Check-out noon. Singles $99; doubles from $109. AmEx/D/DC/MC/V. ●

La Reserve (Bed and Breakfast Center City), 1804 Pine St. (☎215-735-1137; www.lareserve-bandb.com). Take I-676, to the 23rd St. exit and bear right. 10 blocks down, turn left on Pine St. A stately house with a Steinway in the entryway and 8 guest rooms with 19th-century decor. Full breakfast and A/C. Rooms $89-159. AmEx/D/DC/MC/V. ●

Timberlane Campground, 117 Timberlane Rd. (☎856-423-6677; www.timberlanecampground.com), in Clarksboro, NJ. Take U.S. 295 S to the first turnoff for Exit 18A, follow the campground signs for ½ mi., and turn right on Friendship Rd. Timberlane is 1 block down on the right. Hot showers, toilets, fishing pond, pool, and batting cages. Reservations recommended. Sites $28, with hookup $32. MC/V. ●

ENTERTAINMENT

Old City, the area framed by Chestnut, Vine, Front and 4th St., comes alive for the **First Friday** celebration, when art galleries, museums, and restaurants open their doors to entice visitors with free food. (☎800-440-7000; www.oldcity.org.) The **Academy of Music,** at Broad and Locust St., was modeled after Milan's La Scala and hosts the **Pennsyl-**

A BEEFY RIVALRY

In a town known for its cheesesteaks and, not surprisingly, for its staggering obesity rate, every Philadelphian has a favorite corner shop to loudly champion whenever the subject of cheesesteaks arises. Even after Mayor Street created a city-wide "Health and Fitness Czar" (shortly after Philly surpassed Houston in 2000 as "fattest city" in a *Men's Health* survey), cheesesteak consumption remained astronomical. Philadelphia is bursting with shops serving up the caloric concoctions, but none are more famous than **Pat's King of Steaks** (☎215-468-1546; www.patskingofsteaks.com) and his cross-street rival, the larger, more neon **Geno's Steaks** (☎215-389-0659; www.genosteaks.com). Pat Olivieri founded his cheesesteak shop on a corner in 1930, amidst rumors that he invented the famous sandwich. Some 36 years later, Joe Vento was inspired by some alleyway graffiti to name his shop, and later his son, Geno. The flashier Geno's boasts visits from Justin Timberlake and Jessica Simpson, while the more sedate Pat's has hosted Steve Case and Larry King. Tourists can sample either side of the controversy (or both) for $6.25 per steak daily at 9th St. and Passyunk Ave. Just be prepared to order quickly,

vania Ballet. (☎215-551-7000; www.paballet.org. Tickets $20-85.) The **Philadelphia Orchestra** performs from September to May at the **Kimmel Center,** 260 S. Broad St. (☎215-790-5800 or 215-893-1999; www.kimmelcenter.org. Box office open daily 10am-6pm. Tickets $5, student rush tickets Tu and Th 30min. before show $8.)

With 5000 seats under cover and 10,000 on outdoor benches and lawns, the **Mann Music Center,** on George's Hill near 52nd and Parkside Ave. in Fairmount Park, hosts big-name entertainers like Tony Bennett and Willie Nelson, as well as jazz and rock concerts. (☎215-546-7900, tickets 215-893-1999; www.manncenter.org. Pavilion seats $10-32. Lawn tickets for June-Aug. free on day of performance.) **The Trocadero,** 1003 Arch St., is the oldest operating Victorian theater in the US and hosts local as well as big-name bands. (☎215-922-5483; www.thetroc.com. Advance tickets through Ticketmaster. Box office open M-F noon-6pm, Sa noon-5pm. Tickets $6-16.) The **Robin Hood Dell East,** on Ridge Ave., near 33rd St. in Fairmount Park, brings in top names in pop, jazz, and gospel in July and August. During the school year, the students of the **Curtis Institute of Music,** 1726 Locust St. (☎215-893-5252; www.curtis.edu.), give free concerts.

Baseball's **Phillies** (☎215-463-1000; www.phillies.com) play at the new **Citizens Bank Park,** on Pattison Ave. between 11th and Darien St. Football's ▓**Eagles** (☎215-463-5500; www.philadelphiaeagles.com) play at **Lincoln Financial Field,** at Broad St. and Pattison Ave. Across the street, fans fill the **First Union Center** to watch the NBA's **76ers** (☎215-339-7676; www.sixers.com) and the NHL's **Flyers** (☎215-755-9700; www.philadelphiaflyers.com).

◕ NIGHTLIFE

Check the Friday *Philadelphia Inquirer* for entertainment listings. The free Thursday *City Paper* and the Wednesday *Philadelphia Weekly* have weekly listings. A diverse club crowd jams to live music on weekends along **South St.** Many upscale pubs line **2nd St.** near Chestnut St. and Market St., close to the Bank St. hostel. Continuing south to Society Hill, especially near **Head House Sq.,** an older crowd fills dozens of streetside bars and cafes. **Delaware Ave.,** or **Columbus Blvd.,** running along Penn's Landing, has become a hot spot

full of nightclubs and restaurants that attracts droves of yuppies and students. Gay and lesbian weeklies *Au Courant* (free) and *PGN* (free) list events. Most bars and clubs that cater to a gay clientele are along **Camac, S. 12th,** and **S. 13th St.**

The Five Spot, 5 S. Bank St. (☎215-574-0070), off Market St. between 2nd and 3rd St. The classic lounge is perfect for hearty drinking, while the cramped dance floor hosts swingers of all abilities. 1st Sa of the month "Peek-a-Boo Review"; $15. Su gay night. Dress to impress. Drinks $5-12. Cover $5. Open daily 9pm-2am. AmEx/D/MC/V.

Moriarty's, 1116 Walnut St. (☎215-627-7676; www.moriartysrestaurant.com), near 11th St. and the Forest Theater. This Irish pub draws a sizeable crowd late into the night with a quiet, comfortable bar scene. Over 30 beers on tap and private booths galore. Open M-Sa 11am-2am, Su noon-2am. Kitchen closes 1am. AmEx/D/MC/V.

Monk's Belgian Cafe, 626 S. 16th St. (☎215-545-7005; www.monkscafe.com), in Rittenhouse Sq. Don't let the simple exterior fool you—Monk's carries 200-225 beers at any given time, and their expert staff promises to find the right brew for you. Domestic beers $4.50. Belgian drafts $6-7. Open daily 11:30am-2am. Kitchen closes 1am. AmEx/D/MC/V.

The Copabanana, 344 South St. (☎215-923-6108), at South and 4th St. The hottest club north of Havana and a great place to start off your night. Tangy margaritas and lighter fare than the nearby cheesesteak joints. Happy hour M-F 5-7pm with $2 off cocktails. Open daily noon-2am. AmEx/D/MC/V.

The Khyber, 56 S. 2nd St. (☎215-238-5888; www.thekhyber.com). A speakeasy during Prohibition days, the Khyber now gathers a young crowd to listen to a range of punk and heavy metal at volumes that will make your socks hurt. The ornate wooden bar was shipped over from England in 1876. Nightly live music 10pm. Cover $10-18. Open daily 11am-2am. Cash only.

◈ APPROACHING MEDIA: 13 MILES

Take **I-76 W** to **Exit 339** for **City Ave./U.S. 1 S.** Continue down U.S. 1 across **I-476** toward Media. Exit for **Rte. 252.** After 11 mi., turn left onto **Providence Rd.** Proceed 1½ mi., and take a right on **State St.**

MEDIA. Architecturally eclectic restaurants and shops, many of which date from the 19th century, line State St., Media's main drag. As you enter town, notice the **armory** on State St. just after Monroe St., still in use by the Army National Guard. A large stone bank marks the center of town at **Veterans Sq.** Two blocks to the north stands Media's **courthouse,** its most significant architectural attraction, built in four stages from 1851-1929. Restaurants in Media are not overly expensive, but don't come expecting cheap eats. For a light bite, head to the **Coffee Club ❶,** 214 W. State St., near Orange St., which offers coffee, pastries, smoothies, wraps, sandwiches, and several vegetarian selections. (☎610-891-6600. Sandwiches $3-6. Open M-Th 7am-7pm, F-Sa 7am-10pm, Su 7am-3pm. AmEx/D/MC/V.) The glass and wood of **Iron Hill Brewery and Restaurant ❸,** 30 E. State St., stand out among the old buildings of Media. Sample the selection of homemade brews. (☎610-627-9000. Lunch $8-12. Pizza $10-13. Happy hour M-Th 5-7pm. Open M-Sa 11:30am-9 or 11pm, Su 11am-9 or 11pm. AmEx/D/DC/MC/V.)

⚑ APPROACHING BRANDYWINE: 12 MILES
Take **Baltimore Ave.** It becomes the **Baltimore Pike** and merges onto **U.S. 1** 1½ mi. from town.

BRANDYWINE BATTLEFIELD PARK. The **Brandywine Battlefield Park** is on a small section of the 10 sq. mi. area where a critical Revolutionary War battle took place. A ticket grants access to the two houses on the site, inhabited by "living historians" on special occasions throughout the year—men costumed as the Marquis de Lafayette and George Washington, who adopt accents and tell their life stories. (☎610-459-3342; www.ushistory.org/brandywine. Open Tu-Sa 9am-5pm, Su noon-5pm. $5, seniors and ages 6-17 $3.50.)

⚑ APPROACHING WILMINGTON: 10 MILES
Continue on **U.S. 202 (Concord Pike)** 1½ mi. past I-95, and turn right onto **N. Market St.**

WILMINGTON

In 1683, a Swedish Ship, the *Kalmar Nyckel*, sailed from Europe to the banks of what was then called the "South River," leaving its passengers to establish the colony of New Sweden. These days,

the city of Wilmington might as well be named DuPontville, because, from the grand Hotel DuPont downtown to the DuPont mills along the Brandywine River, there's no escaping the name.

VITAL STATS

Population: 73,000

Visitor Info: Greater Wilmington Convention and Visitors Bureau, 100 W. 10th St. (☎302-652-4088; www.visitwilmingtonde.com), at Market and Orange St. Open M-F 9am-5pm.

Internet Access: Wilmington Library (☎302-571-7400), at 10th and Market St., downtown. Open M-Th 9am-8pm, F 9am-5pm, Sa 11am-3pm. Free.

Post Office: 1101 N. King St. (☎302-656-0228), at 11th St. downtown. Open M-F 5am-6:30pm, Sa 5am-3pm. **Postal Code:** 19801.

▣ GETTING AROUND. In the city's center, numbered streets run east-west, starting at the southern end with **Front St.** and running from 2nd to 15th St., then continuing with 16th St. on the other side of the Brandywine River. Major north-south roads in the downtown area include **Walnut St., King St.,** and **Market St.** To the west, restaurants crowd on north-south **Union St.** and **Lincoln St.** Take **Pennsylvania Ave.** from the city center for easy access to these streets.

◈ SIGHTS. The DuPont estates are among the most popular tourist attractions in the area. Closest to downtown Wilmington, the **Hagley Museum and Library** emphasizes the home and work life of the DuPonts, with tours of the original family mansion and black powder works. Mechanical minds will love the enormous stone mills, water turbines, steam engines, and powder testers. Brace yourself when the guide demonstrates the power of blasting powder. (Take Rte. 202 N for 1¼ mi., turn onto Rte. 141 S for 2 mi., turn right onto the bridge, and look for the main entrance on the right. ☎302-658-2400; www.hagley.lib.de.us. Tours Mar.-Dec. daily 9:30am-4:30pm; Jan.-Mar. M-F 1:30pm, Sa-Su 9:30am-4:30pm. $11, students and seniors $9, ages 6-14 $4.) The ritzy **Nemours Mansion and Gardens,** 1600 Rockland Rd., shows a more glamorous side of DuPont but is closed for heavy renovations until March 2007. (☎302-651-6912. Tours May-Dec. Tu-Sa 9, 11am, 1, 3pm; Su 11am,

1, 3pm. $10.) The Brandywine River Museum, Rte. 1, in Chadds Ford, PA, displays an extensive collection of works by N.C., Andrew, and Jaime Wyeth in a restored mill house. (From Wilmington, take Rte. 52 N to Rte. 1 and follow it east. ☎610-388-2700; www.brandywinemuseum.org. Open daily 9:30am-4:30pm. $8; seniors, students, and ages 6-12 $5.)

▐▌▐ FOOD AND ACCOMMODATIONS. Restaurants can be found in two areas: **Union** and **Lincoln St.**, and the **Trolley Square District**, up Delaware Ave. **Mrs. Robino's ❷**, 520 N. Union St., is a great family-run restaurant in Wilmington's Little Italy which serves delicious homemade pasta and sauces. (☎302-652-9223; www.mrsrobinos.com. Pasta $6-11. Platters $7-12. Open M-Th 11am-9pm, F-Sa 11am-10pm, Su noon-9pm. D/MC/V.) For Irish pub fare, try **Kelly's Logan House ❸**, 1701 Delaware Ave., in Trolley Square, which dates back to the Civil War. Appetizers ($6-9) include the "Not-So-Healthy" fries with cheese, bacon, jalapeños, and ranch dressing. (☎302-652-9493; www.loganhouse.com. Burgers $7-9. Pasta $10. Happy hour daily 4-7pm. Open M 11am-midnight, Tu-Sa 11am-1am, Su noon-10pm. AmEx/D/MC/V.)

Chain hotels and motels dominate the northern portion of the city; some cheaper motels lie south of the city on **Dupont Hwy.** (Rte. 13) in **Newcastle**, but you get what you pay for. A slight cut above the rest in this area are the large rooms at the **Delaware Motel and Trailer Park ❷**, 235 S. DuPont Hwy., south of the city, near the junction of Rte. 13 and U.S. 40. (☎302-328-3114. Singles $50; doubles $60. AmEx/D/DC/MC/V.)

▞ APPROACHING HAVRE DE GRACE: 41 MILES
Proceed down **King St.** After crossing **E. 2nd St.**, bear right, then take a left onto **Bus. Rte. 13 S.** Follow signs for **U.S. 13**, which joins **U.S. 40 W.** Turn left on **Otsego Rd.** at the sign for Havre de Grace.

HAVRE DE GRACE. Located where the Susquehanna River meets the Chesapeake Bay,

Havre de Grace is home to residents who once made their living by fishing and building boats. Both industries remain, though more for the benefit of tourists than for commercial purposes. At the corner of Lafayette and Concord St. in the southeast corner of town is the **Concord Point Lighthouse.** Short and stubby, this lighthouse, while officially decommissioned in 1975, still illuminates the port. You can brave the granite spiral stairs and metal ladder for a nice free view of the bay. Next door, an active wooden boat-building shop is located at the back of the small **Havre de Grace Maritime Museum.** (☎410-939-4800. Open June-Aug. daily 11am-5pm; Sept.-May M and F-Su 11am-5pm. Boat building Tu 6-9:30pm. $2, students and seniors $1.) A local favorite, **La Cucina ❷**, 103 N. Washington St., is a combination pizza parlor and gourmet Italian restaurant. Identity crisis aside, it's a good place for either a quick bite or a relatively inexpensive meal. (☎410-939-1401. Pizzas $8-15. Pastas $8.50-11. Open M-Th 10:30am-10pm, F-Sa 10:30am-11pm, Su noon-9pm. AmEx/D/MC/V.)

▞ APPROACHING ABERDEEN: 4 MILES
Continue down **U.S. 40** for 4 mi. to reach Aberdeen.

ABERDEEN

Just 2½ mi. past Havre de Grace lies the town of Aberdeen, which Baltimore Orioles fans know as the hometown of their beloved **Cal Ripken, Jr.,** who broke Lou Gehrig's record for most consecutive baseball games ever played. "Real" is the best word to describe the ▞US Army Ordnance Museum, on the Aberdeen Proving Ground; there are few photos or replicas, just real guns, real mortars, and real tanks. The M65 cannon by the parking lot is as tall as the trees around it. (Take Rte. 715 N, and follow the signs. After passing the checkpoint, take a left at the 4th light, and a right into the parking lot in front of the tanks. ☎410-278-3602. Open daily 9am-4:45pm. Free.)

Two quirky roadside diners occupy the Aberdeen Area. The **New Ideal Diner ❸** on U.S. 40 just past Bel Air Ave., is a prettied-up railway car. The diner specializes in seafood; the prices are on the high side, but items like burgers ($5-6) are yummy and affordable. (☎410-272-1880. Seafood up to $21. Open daily 6am-8pm. Cash only.) The 14-page menu at the chrome-and-neon **White Marsh Double T Diner ❸**, 10741 Pulaski Hwy. (U.S. 40), is sure to have something you want. This is one of the better diners on this stretch of U.S. 40. (In White Marsh, at the corner of Ebenezer Rd. ☎410-344-1020. Burgers $5-8. Open 24hr. AmEx/D/MC/V.)

⚐ APPROACHING ROSEDALE: 20 MILES
Cross the **Baltimore Beltway,** and follow **U.S. 40.**

ROSEDALE. Diners and motels abound on this stretch of the road, but tiny Rosedale is home to a pleasing pair. The chrome **Happy Day Diner ❷,** 8302 Pulaski Hwy., has a limited selection, but the food is delicious and cheap. A plate of French toast, two eggs, bacon, and sausage is $5. (☎410-687-2129; www.happydaydiner.com. Open M-F 6am-10pm, Sa-Su 24hr. AmEx/D/MC/V.) **Duke's Motel ❸,** 7905 Pulaski Hwy., has some of the cheapest accommodations around. (☎410-686-0400. Key deposit $5. Singles $54; doubles $59. D/MC/V.)

⚐ APPROACHING BALTIMORE: 6 MILES
Stay on **U.S. 40** as it crosses **I-895/I-95.** About 1½ mi. past the beltway, veer right, following signs for **U.S. 40/Orleans St.**

BALTIMORE

Nicknamed "Charm City" for its mix of small-town hospitality and big-city flair, Baltimore impresses visitors with its lively restaurant and bar scene, first-class museum, and devotion to history. The pulse of the city lies beyond its star attraction, the glimmering Inner Harbor, in Baltimore's over-stuffed markets, coffee shops, and diverse citizenry. The city's Southern heritage is evident in Roland Park, where friendly neighbors greet you from front porches in a "Bawlmer" accent.

VITAL STATS

Population: 650,000

Visitor Info: Baltimore Area Visitors Center, 100 Light St. (☎877-225-8466 or 410-837-7024; www.baltimore.org). Open daily 9am-6pm.

Internet Access: Enoch Pratt Free Library, 400 Cathedral St. (☎410-396-5430). Open June-Aug. M-W 10am-8pm, Th 10am-5:30pm, F-Sa 10am-5pm; Sept.-May M-W 10am-8pm, Th 10am-5:30pm, F-Sa 10am-5pm, Su 1-5pm. Free.

Post Office: 900 E. Fayette St. (☎410-347-4202). Open M-F 7:30am-10pm, Sa 8:30am-5pm. **Postal Code:** 21233.

▣ GETTING AROUND

Baltimore lies 35 mi. north of Washington D.C. and about 150 mi. west of the Atlantic Ocean. **Baltimore Street** (east-west) and **Charles Street** (north-south) divide the city. **U.S. 40** runs east-west through the northern end of downtown, while the **Jones Falls Expressway (I-83)** cuts into Baltimore from the north. The **Baltimore Beltway (I-695)** and a series of other ring roads circle the city, which lies just off north-south **I-95.** The main arteries serving the Inner Harbor and downtown Baltimore are mostly one-way and include Charles St. and **St. Paul St./Light St.,** which runs south (both intersect U.S. 40). **Pratt St.** runs east, **Lombard St.** runs west, and both end at **Frederick Rd. (Rte. 144).** Some neighborhoods in Baltimore, including around Orleans St. and west of Martin Luther King, Jr. Blvd., are not safe at night

The best bet for parking is to bring a roll of quarters, as meters are plentiful but hungry (generally $1 per hr.), with many enforced 24hr. Garages are easy to find throughout downtown and are most expensive near the Inner Harbor (up to $12 daily). A long stretch of 4hr. parking meters lies along Key Hwy. just south of the Inner Harbor; take St. Paul St. south past the Inner Harbor and turn left on Key Hwy. In **Little Italy,** there are many options on Albemarle St., just north of Eastern St. ($7 flat rate). Baltimore sights cluster together, so your best bet is to park and walk.

◉ SIGHTS

Commercial shopping and restaurants frequented by non-locals crowd the **Inner Harbor,** home to the National Aquarium. An excursion to the Johns Hopkins University campus and nearby Druid Hill Park escapes the glitz (and grime) of the city.

THE NATIONAL AQUARIUM. The National Aquarium is perhaps the one thing (besides Baltimore's murder rate) that sets the city apart from all other major American cities. Though a visit outdoors to watch slap-happy seals play is free, it's worth the time and money to venture inside. The eerie **Wings in the Water** exhibit showcases 50 species of stingrays in an immense pool. In the **Tropical Rainforest,** parrots and a pair of two-toed sloths peer through the dense foliage in a 157 ft. glass pyramid. At the **Marine Mammal Pavilion,** dolphins perform every hour on the half-hour. *(Pier 3, 501 E. Pratt St. ☎410-576-3800; www.aqua.org. Open M-Th 9am-5pm, F-Sa 9am-8pm, Su 9am-7pm. $22, seniors $21, ages 3-11 $13.)*

BALTIMORE MARITIME MUSEUM. Several ships, most of which belong to the Baltimore Maritime Museum, grace the harbor by the aquarium. Visitors clamber through the interior of the **USS Torsk,** the intricately painted submarine that sank the last WWII Japanese combat ship. You can also board one of the survivors of the Pearl Harbor attack, the Coast Guard cutter Roger B. Taney, and ascend the octagonal lighthouse on Pier 5. For these historic sites and more, purchase the Seaport Day Pass, which grants access to the Maritime Museum, the Museum of Industry, Baltimore's World Trade Center, and the USS Constellation—the last all-sail warship built by the US Navy. Water taxi service is included. *(Piers 3 and 5. ☎410-396-3453; www.baltomaritimemuseum.org. Open in summer M-Th and Su 10am-5:30pm, F-Sa 10am-6pm; in winter F-Su 10:30am-5pm. $8, seniors $6, ages 4-14 $4.)*

WALTERS ART MUSEUM. With over 50 centuries of art in three buildings, the Walters Art Museum houses one of the largest private art collections in the world. The ancient art collections include sculpture, jewelry, and metalwork from Egypt, Greece, and Rome, and are the museum's pride and joy. Byzantine, Romanesque, and Gothic art are also on display. The **Hackerman House** displays art from China, Korea, Japan, and India among dark wooden furniture, patterned rugs, and plush velvet curtains. *(600 N. Charles St. ☎410-547-9000; www.thewalters.org. Open W-Su 10am-5pm. Tours W noon and Su 1:30pm. $8, seniors $6, students $5, under 19 free. Sa 10am-noon and 1st Th of each month free.)*

EDGAR ALLAN POE HOUSE. Gothic author Edgar Allan Poe lived in this now-preserved historical landmark from 1833-1835. In between doses of opium, Poe penned famous stories such as *The Tell-Tale Heart* and *The Pit and the Pendulum,* as well as macabre poems like *The Raven* and *Annabel Lee.* The house contains period furniture and exhibits relating to Poe, all maintained by a staff eager to regale visitors with Poe stories. Steer clear of the neighborhood at night. *(203 N. Amity St., near Saratoga St. ☎410-396-7932; www.eapoe.org. Open Apr.-July and Oct.-Dec. W-Sa noon-3:30pm; Aug.-Sept. Sa noon-3:45pm. $4, under 13 free.)*

JOHNS HOPKINS UNIVERSITY. Approximately 3 mi. north of the harbor, prestigious Johns Hopkins University (JHU) radiates out from 33rd St. JHU was the first research university in the country and is currently a world leader in medicine, public health, and engineering. The campus was originally the Homewood estate of Charles Carroll, Jr., the son of the longest-lived signer of the Declaration of Independence. One-hour campus tours begin at the **Office of Admissions** in Garland Hall. *(3400 N. Charles St. ☎410-516-8171; www.jhu.edu. Tours Sept.-May M-F 10am, noon, 3pm. Call ahead for summer hours, ☎410-516-5589.)* One mile north of the main campus, the **Evergreen House** is an exercise in excess—even the bathroom of this elegant mansion is plated in 23-carat gold. Purchased in 1878 by railroad tycoon John W. Garret, the house, along with its collections of fine porcelain, impressive artwork, Tiffany silver, and rare books, was bequeathed to JHU in 1942. *(4545 N. Charles St. ☎410-516-0341. Open M-F 10am-4pm, Sa-Su 1-4pm. Tours every hr. 10am-3pm. $6, seniors $5, students $3.)*

🍴 FOOD

If you're blowing through Baltimore with some cash to burn, forget the overpriced eateries that crowd the Inner Harbor and head to some of Baltimore's more-upscale choices, scattered throughout the city. You'll find cheaper options if you search hard enough. Be sure not to leave without a taste of the region's famous 🦀**crab cakes.**

🦀 **Corks,** 1026 S. Charles St. (☎410-752-3810). A hidden retreat specializing in fine contemporary American cuisine infused with classic French techniques and Asian influences. Semi-formal attire. Appetizers $10-15. Entrees $24-30. Reservations recommended. Open M-Th 5-10pm, F-Sa 5-11pm, Su 5-9:30pm. AmEx/D/DC/MC/V. ❺

The Helmand, 806 N. Charles St. (☎410-752-0311; www.helmand.com). The best Afghan restaurant in town, with dishes like *kaddo borani* (pan-fried and baked pumpkin in a yogurt-garlic sauce; $3). Plenty of vegetarian options and enough dessert to satisfy any sweet tooth. Open M-Th and Su 5-10pm, F-Sa 5-11pm. AmEx/D/MC/V. ❸

NATIONAL ROAD

Baltimore

▲ ACCOMMODATIONS
The Admiral Fell Inn, 12
Aunt Rebecca's B & B, 5
Capital KOA Campground, 13
Radisson Plaza Lord
  Baltimore, 6
White Elk Motel, 3

● FOOD
Alonso's, 4
Attman's Deli, 7
Babalu Grill, 8
Corks, 14
The Helmand, 1
Iggy's, 10

■ NIGHTLIFE
Fletcher's, 11
Grand Central, 2
Howl at the Moon, 9

Broadway
Bethel St.
Gough St.
Bank St.
Bond St.
Dallas St.
Spring St.

FELLS POINT

Thames St.
Wills St.
Dock St.

Caroline St.

Central Ave.

Aisquith St.

Madison St.

Monument St.

Constitution St.

Calvert St.

St. Paul St.

Charles St.

Cathedral St.

Centre St.

Hamilton St.

Park Ave.

Howard St.

Pratt St.
Eden St.
Lombard St.
Baltimore St.

LITTLE ITALY

Eastern Ave.
Fleet St.
Aliceanna St.
Lancaster St.
Fawn St.
Stiles St.
High St.
President St.

Lloyd St.
Watson St.
Exeter St.
E. Lombard St.
Albemarle St.

Baltimore Public
Works Museum
and Streetscape

Pier 6
Concert
Pavilion

Market Pl.

Holocaust
Memorial

Baltimore
Maritime Museum

National Aquarium

Inner Harbor

Rash Field

Federal
Hill Park

FEDERAL HILL

Key Hwy.

Warren Ave.

Hughes St.
Churchill St.
Hamburg St.

Lee St.

Hanover St.

Conway St.

Light St.

Redwood St.

Lexington St.

City Hall

Commerce St.

Guilford St.

Gay St.

Front St.

Low St.

Orleans St.

High St.

Exeter St.

Hillen St.

Forrest St.

Front St.

McElderry St.

Colvin St.

Fayette St.

Watson St.

TO JOHNS HOPKINS, BALTIMORE MUSEUM OF ART,
THEATER PROJECT, (500yd)
ROLAND PARK (2mi),
(3mi), EVERGREEN HOUSE (4mi),
(6mi)

Water St.

Harborplace

Maryland
Science
Center

Light St.

TO (15mi)

Conway St.

Charles St.

Liberty St.

The Walters
Art Museum

Sharp St.

Hamilton St.

Centre St.

Park Ave.

Howard St.

TO ARENA
PLAYERS (200ft)

Franklin St.
Orchard St.

Paca St.

Greene St.

Pearl St.

Mulberry St.

Saratoga St.

Lexington St.

Fayette St.

Martin Luther King Jr. Blvd.

TO EDGAR ALLEN
POE HOUSE (300yd)

Edgar Allen
Poe's Grave

Eutaw St.

Redwood St.

Lombard St.

Pratt St.

Camden St.

Camden
Station

Oriole Park
at Camden Yards

Russell St.

Penn St.

Portland St.

Washington St.

Sterrett St.

Hamburg St.

M&T Bank
Stadium

Warren Ave.

Hamburg St.

0   400 meters
0   400 yards

Attman's Deli, 1019 E. Lombard St. (☎410-563-2666), on Baltimore's "Corned beef row." Made a name for itself serving hot pastrami ($6) and corned beef sandwiches ($6) just like you'd find in New York City. The reuben ($7.50) was voted Baltimore's best. Open M-Sa 8am-6:30pm, Su 8am-5pm. AmEx/D/MC/V. ❷

Babalu Grill, 32 Market Pl. (☎410-234-9898), in Power Plant Live. Popular appetizers include Cuban-style turnovers with seasoned beef and avocado salsa ($6). Babalu turns into a hot salsa club at night. Cover 10-11pm $5, after 11pm $10. Open M 5-10pm, Tu-Th 11:30am-2:30pm and 5-10pm, F 11:30am-2:30pm and 5-11pm, Sa 5-11pm, Su 4-9pm. Club open Th-Sa 10pm-2am. AmEx/D/DC/MC/V. ❹

Iggy's, 410 S. High St. (☎410-685-6727), near Little Italy. From U.S. 40, head south on Broadway to Eastern and turn right. Local favorite serves sandwiches ($3-5) and soups ($3). Open M-Sa 7am-2:30pm. Cash only. ❶

Alonso's, 415 W. Cold Spring Ln. (☎410-235-3433), in the Roland Park neighborhood. Take Exit 9A from I-83 N. Famous for 1 lb. burgers ($12). The vegetable panini ($8) and crab-cake sandwich ($14) are more manageable. Open M-Th and Su 11am-11pm, F-Sa 11am-midnight. AmEx/D/MC/V. ❸

🏠 ACCOMMODATIONS

Hotels dominate the Inner Harbor, and budget lodgings elsewhere are hard to find. There are motels on **Washington Blvd.,** 4-10 mi. south of the downtown area. Take Light St. west to Conway St. Turn left to get on I-395 S, following it to I-95 S. Take Exit 50A onto Caton Ave., and turn right on Washington Blvd.

▨ Aunt Rebecca's B&B, 106 E. Preston St. (☎410-625-1007; www.auntrebeccasbnb.com), in the Mount Vernon district. Full of gilded mirrors and chandeliers. Only 3 bedrooms, but if you book one you'll save big over the downtown hotels. Free parking. Breakfast included. Queen bedroom $110. AmEx/D/MC/V. ❺

White Elk Motel, 6195 Washington Blvd. (☎410-796-5151), in Elkridge, 10 mi. south of downtown. While a bit out of the way, a landscaped entrance and cottage-inn-style rooms with bathtubs make this a comfy place. Singles $55; doubles $60. AmEx/D/MC/V. ❸

Radisson Plaza Lord Baltimore, 20 W. Baltimore St. (☎410-539-8400 or 800-333-3333), between Liberty and Charles St. A national historic landmark built in 1928, this is the oldest hotel in Baltimore. The location—6 blocks from the Inner Harbor—and historic flavor are unbeatable. Parking $25 per night. Reservations recommended. Rooms from $189. AmEx/D/DC/MC/V. ❺

The Admiral Fell Inn, 888 S. Broadway (☎410-522-7377 or 866-583-4162; www.harbormagic.com), at Thames St. Blast to the past with themed rooms that include canopied beds and armoires. Internet access $4 per day. Parking $15 per night. Rooms $219 and up. AmEx/D/DC/MC/V. ❺

Capitol KOA, 768 Cecil Ave. N. (☎410-923-2771 or 800-562-0248), in Millersville, between D.C. and Baltimore. Take U.S. 50 E to Rte. 3 N. Bear right after 8 mi. onto Veterans Hwy., turn left under the highway onto Hog Farm Rd., and follow the signs. Pool, volleyball courts, and bath-shower facilities. Free Wi-Fi. Open Apr.-Oct. Sites $33, with hookup $44; cabins $58-67. D/MC/V. ❷

🎵 ENTERTAINMENT

At **Harborplace,** street performers are constantly amusing tourists with magic acts and juggling during the day. On weekend nights, dance, dip, and dream to the sounds of anything from country to calypso. The **Baltimore Museum of Art,** 10 Art Museum Dr., offers summer jazz concerts with award-winning musicians in its sculpture garden. (☎443-573-1701. Open May-Sept. Sa 7pm. $20.) More jazz can be found from May to October at the canvas-topped **Pier 6 Concert Pavilion,** 731 Eastern Ave. (☎410-625-3100. Tickets $15-30.)

The **Theater Project,** 45 W. Preston St., near Maryland St., experiments with theater, poetry, music, and dance. (☎410-752-8558. Box office open 1hr. before shows. Shows Th-Sa 8pm, Su 3pm. $15, seniors $10.) The **Arena Players,** the first black theater group in the country, performs comedy, drama, and dance at 801 McCullough St., at Martin Luther King, Jr. Blvd. (☎410-728-6500. Box office open M-F 10am-2pm. Tickets from $15.) The **Showcase of Nations Ethnic Festivals** celebrate Baltimore's ethnic neighborhoods during the summer, featuring a different culture each week. (☎877-225-8466.) The beloved **Baltimore Orioles** play ball at **Camden Yards,** at the corner of Russell and Camden St. (☎410-685-9800; www.orioles.mlb.com. Tickets $7-50.) The Baltimore **Ravens** play in **Ravens Stadium** (☎410-481-7328; www.ravenszone.net).

◉ NIGHTLIFE

Neighborhood bars in **Mount Vernon** know their middle-aged patrons by name, while the loud and sweaty dance floors of **Fells Point** and **Power Plant Live** cater to a college and twentysomething crowd. Be prepared for the 1:30am last call. If you make it through the dozens of bars in Fell Point, head to **Canton** for a similar scene.

Howl At The Moon, 22 Market Pl., (☎410-783-5111; www.howlatthemoon.com), in Power Plant Live. A dueling-piano bar where the crowd runs the show, with frequent sing- (or "howl-") alongs. Crowd ranges from just-barely-adults to could-be-your-parents. Happy hour F 5-8pm with free buffet. Cover $3-8. Open W-Th 7pm-2am, F 5pm-2am, Sa 7pm-2am. AmEx/D/DC/MC/V.

Grand Central, 1001-1003 N. Charles St. (☎410-752-7133; www.centralstationpub.com), at Eager St. Chill under chandeliers from the set of *A Few Good Men* and *Batman* or play some pool with a mixed gay and straight crowd. Happy hour daily 4-8pm; $1 off beer. $2 Skyy vodka drinks Su. The disco club next door is the spot for bumping and grinding W-Su 9pm-2am. Cover for dance club $6. Dance club 18+. Open daily 4pm-2am. AmEx/D/MC/V.

Fletcher's, 701 S. Bond St. (☎410-558-1889; www.fletchersbar.com), offers live bands F-Su. Most often features rock, rap, and blues acts. Happy hour M-Th 4:30-6:30pm and all day Su. Cover $7-13. Surcharge for under 21 at some shows $3. Doors open at 7, 8, or 9pm. AmEx/D/MC/V.

◪ APPROACHING ELLICOTT CITY: 10 MILES

The route out of Baltimore follows the old **National Road,** or **Rte. 144,** which is not U.S. 40. From downtown, get on **Lombard St.** heading west and take a soft left to proceed on Rte. 144 W. 10 mi. from Baltimore, **Frederick Rd.** (Rte. 144) becomes **Main St.** as it crawls into Ellicott City, an old Quaker mill town nestled into an idyllic hillside.

ELLICOTT CITY. The most memorable experience of your stop here may be just marveling at the city's physical location on the descending Patapsco River. Today, antique shops in equally antique buildings line the brick sidewalks along Main St. Housed in the oldest railroad terminal in America, the **B&O Railroad Station Museum,** 2711 Maryland Ave., at Main St., relates the his-

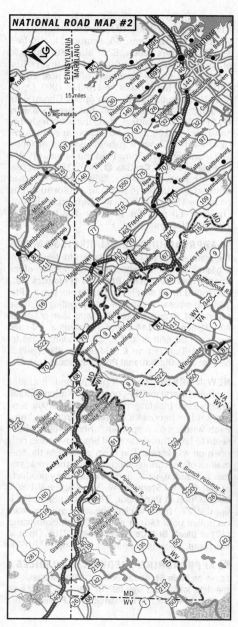

NATIONAL ROAD MAP #2

tory of the area's railroad and its role in the Civil War. (☎410-461-1945; www.ecborail.org. Open W-Su 11am-4pm. $5, seniors $4, children $3.) The **visitors center**, 8267 Main St., has info on self-guided walking tours of the town's historical sites. (In the basement of the post office; enter from Hamilton St. ☎410-313-1900. Open M-F 10am-5pm, Sa-Su noon-5pm.) Cheap eats are hard to find on Main St., but **Fisher's Bakery ❶**, 8143 Main St., offers everything from simple sandwiches ($3.25-6) to extra-large eclairs. (☎410-461-9275; www.fishersbakery.com. Open M-Th and Su 8am-5pm, F-Sa 8am-6pm. MC/V.) **La Palapa Grill & Cantina ❸**, 8307 Main St., featuring burritos ($10-12), fajitas ($13-15), and seafood specialties ($15-17) in a colorful dining room. (☎410-465-0070; www.lapalapagrill.com. Open M-Th and Su 11:30am-9:30pm, F-Sa 11:30am-10:30pm. MC/V.)

⚑ APPROACHING NEW MARKET: 30 MILES
The road becomes 2-lane and rural, with few lights or services. The gradual hills signal the approach of the Appalachian Mountains. **Rte. 144 (Frederick Rd.)** flirts with **U.S. 40** after leaving Baltimore; stay on Rte. 144 and proceed around the rotary, getting off at the second exit, to pass through the small town of Lisbon. After Lisbon, **Rte. 144** curves and stops at a T-intersection. Turn right onto **Rte. 27**, following signs for **Mt. Airy**. Turn left on **E. Ridgeville Blvd.**, which becomes the **Old National Pike** after about 1½ mi.

NEW MARKET. The self-proclaimed "antiques capital of Maryland" lies on the old National Road. With several buildings dating from the 1700s, New Market has become a center for antique shops, each with its own specialty. Shopkeepers here seem to have found the good life; most stores only open on weekends. The town guide lists the specialties of the various shops. During the week, you can find fudge, jams, and other touristy products at the **General Store**, 26 W. Main St. (☎301-865-2350. Open M 9am-5pm, Tu-Sa 9am-8pm, Su 1-6pm. MC/V.) In the back of the store, you can feast on pulled pork ($6) or a pound of chicken wings ($7) at **Blue's BBQ Co ❷**. (☎301-685-2100. Open M 9am-5pm, Tu-Sa 9am-8pm, Su 11am-6pm. MC/V.)

⚑ APPROACHING FREDERICK: 10 MILES
Leave on **Main St**. About 3 mi. past New Market, take the right fork at the sign for "To West 40." Stay west on **Rte. 144**, which is **E. Patrick St**. in Frederick.

FREDERICK

Frederick lies at the southeastern corner of a region littered with Civil War sites. Like neighboring Harper's Ferry (p. 371), the city was at the center of the battle lines, alternately occupied by Union and Confederate forces. Modern-day Frederick has a pleasant, well-kept downtown with an assortment of boutiques and pricey restaurants.

VITAL STATS

Population: 53,000

Visitor Info: Frederick Visitors Center, 19 E. Church St. (☎301-228-2888 or 800-999-3613; www.cityof-frederick.com). Open daily 9am-5pm.

Internet Access: C. Burr Artz Library, 110 E. Patrick St. (☎301-694-1630), downtown. Open M-Th 10am-9pm, F-Sa 10am-5pm, Su 1-5pm. Free.

Post Office: 201 E. Patrick St. (☎301-662-2131), between East and Caroll St. Open M-F 8am-6pm, Sa 8am-2pm. **Postal Code:** 21701.

▐ GETTING AROUND. Rte. 144, the old National Road, runs one-way west through Frederick, where it is known as **Patrick St.** At the center of town it intersects the main north-south thoroughfare, one-way **Market St.** Shops and restaurants congregate on these streets and surrounding blocks. To head east, use **South St.,** just south of Patrick St., or **Church St.,** one block to the north. Most streets have 2hr. parking meters, but **parking** can be tight. There are several garages in town, including one off E. Patrick St. by the library (M-F $1 per hr., $5 max.) and another off Church St. by the visitors center (M-F $1 per hr., $5 max. per day).

◪ SIGHTS. Civil War history is well preserved in Frederick. The **National Museum of Civil War Medicine,** 48 E. Patrick St., focuses on "immersion exhibits," including seven life-sized dioramas with accompanying audio that depict battlefield medical scenes—somewhat grisly, but worth the trip. (☎301-695-1864; www.civilwarmed.org. Open M-Sa 10am-5pm, Su 11am-5pm. $6.50; seniors, military, and students $6; ages 10-16 $4.50; under 9 free.) Recreated after floods, the house and gardens of the **Barbara Fritchie House & Museum,** 154 W. Patrick St., hearken back to the days when Fritchie cheered Union soldiers even as the Rebs approached. According to legend, as General Stonewall Jackson marched into town, Fritchie, then 95 years old, proudly waved her Union flag. Civil War buffs will appreciate original furnishings, documents, and quilts. (☎301-698-0630. Open Apr.-Sept. M and Th-Sa 10am-4pm, Su 1-4pm.) The **Mt. Olivet Cemetery,** 515 S. Market St., has graves from the Civil War era, including those of Francis Scott Key, the author of the national anthem, and Thomas Johnson, the first governor of Maryland. (Head south from Patrick St. on Carroll St., turn right onto South St., then left onto Market St. ☎301-662-1164. Open daily sunrise-sunset.) For those less into Civil War lore, **Wonder Book and Video,** 1306 W. Patrick St., is a worthwhile stop, with 30 aisles of books packed floor to ceiling. Comics and videos are also available. (2½ mi. west of town, in the Golden Mile Marketplace. ☎301-694-5955. Open daily 10am-10pm.)

▧▐ FOOD AND ACCOMMODATIONS. Frederick offers simple yet enjoyable dining options. A local favorite, family-owned **Nido's ❸,** 111 E. Patrick St., serves Italian fare like cheese tortellini ($9) with homemade sauces. (☎301-624-1052. Pastas $7-11. Entrees $8-21. Reservations recommended. M-Th 11:30am-2:30pm and 4:30-9:30pm, F-Sa 11:30am-10pm, Su 3-9pm. AmEx/MC/V.) At the **Mountain View Diner ❸,** 1300 W. Patrick St., customers can see the Blue Ridge Mountains off to the west as they enjoy a California chicken salad ($9) or burger. (☎301-696-1300. Entrees $9-19. Open M-Th 7:30am-11pm, F-Sa 7:30am-midnight, Su 7:30am-10pm. AmEx/D/DC/MC/V.) The best bet for budget lodging in Frederick is **Masser's Motel ❷,** 1505 W. Patrick St., 3¼ mi. west of the town center, which offers simple rooms, some with microwaves and fridges. (☎301-663-3698. Singles $42; doubles $48. MC/V.)

▐ APPROACHING KNOXVILLE: 18 MILES
Head west on **W. Patrick St. (Rte. 144)**. Proceed ½ mi. to the intersection with **Jefferson St.,** and make a soft left at the sign for **U.S. 340 W.** Continuing west on U.S. 340, and turn left on **Keep Tryst Rd.** Take the first right on **Sandy Hook Rd.** for Knoxville.

KNOXVILLE. Backpackers, travelers, and scouting troops all find respite at the homey ▨**Harpers Ferry Lodge ❶,** 19123 Sandy Hook Rd. Housed in a single-level building, it has a fully equipped kitchen, showers, laundry, and lounge. For $5, indulge in the all-you-can-eat pancake breakfast.

(☎301-834-7652; www.harpersferryhostel.org. Reception Mar. 14-Nov. 14 7-9am and 6-10pm. Lockout 9am-6pm. Reservations recommended. Tent sites $10; dorms $23, members $20. D/MC/V.)

▐ APPROACHING HARPERS FERRY: 5 MILES
Continue on **U.S. 340.** At the sign for Harpers Ferry, turn left to enter the **Harpers Ferry National Historic Park** or right to enter the town of Harpers Ferry on **Washington St.**

The Mountain State
WEST VIRGINIA
Welcomes You!

HARPERS FERRY

A pastoral hillside town overlooking the Shenandoah and Potomac rivers, Harpers Ferry earned its fame when a band of abolitionists, led by John Brown, raided the US Armory in 1859. Although Brown was captured and executed, the raid brought the issue of slavery into the national spotlight. Brown's adamant belief that violence was the only means to overcome the problem of slavery soon gained credence, and the town became a major theater of conflict, changing hands eight times during the Civil War. Today, Harpers Ferry attracts more mild-mannered guests, ranging from outdoors enthusiasts to field trippers looking for a taste of American history, who come to enjoy the surrounding wilderness.

VITAL STATS

Population: 300

Visitor Info: Jefferson County Convention and Visitors Bureau (☎304-535-2627; www.jefferson-countycvb.com), on Washington St., just off U.S. 340. Open daily in summer 9am-6pm; in winter 9am-5pm. **Cavalier Heights Visitors Center** (☎304-535-6298; www.harpersferryhistory.org), off U.S. 340, inside Harpers Ferry National Historic Park. Open daily 8am-5pm.

Internet Access: Harpers Ferry-Bolivar Library (☎304-535-2301), 151 Polk St. Open M-Tu, F-Sa 10am-5:30pm, W-Th 10am-8pm. Free.

Post Office: 1010 Washington St. (☎304-535-2479). Open M-F 8am-4pm, Sa 9am-noon. **Postal Code:** 25425.

GETTING AROUND

Harpers Ferry lies just south of the Potomac River and is surrounded on three sides by Harpers Ferry National Historic Park. **U.S. 340** runs just south of town; most attractions are located on **Washington St.,** which runs east-west through town. Parking is generally free at Washington St. establishments but is not permitted on the streets of the **Lower Town** area of the National Historic Park; visitors must park at the Cavalier Heights Visitors Center unless they are staying at accommodations with parking within walking distance of town. Shuttles leave the lot for town every 10min.; the last pickup is at 6:45pm.

SIGHTS

The **Harpers Ferry National Historic Park,** comprising most of historic Harper's Ferry, consists of several museums, all of which are included with admission to the park. The park also offers occasional reenactments of Harpers Ferry's history. The shuttle from the parking lot stops at **Shenandoah St.,** where a phalanx of replicated 19th-century shops greets visitors. The **Dry Goods Store** displays clothes, hardware, liquor, and groceries, complete with an 1850s price list. The **Harpers Ferry Industrial Museum,** on Shenandoah St., describes the methods used to harness the powers of the Shenandoah and Potomac Rivers and details the town's status as the terminus of the nation's first successful rail line. At the **Black Voices from Harpers Ferry,** at the corner of High and Shenandoah St., visitors can listen to audio clips of the memoirs of fettered and freed slaves expressing their opinions of John Brown and his raid. Next door on High St., the plight of Harpers Ferry's slaves is further illustrated in the **Civil War Museum.** Informative displays detail the importance of Harpers Ferry's strategic location. (☎304-535-6298. Open daily in summer 8am-6pm; in winter 8am-5pm. $6 per vehicle; $4 per pedestrian, bike, or motorcycle.)

The **John Brown Museum,** on Shenandoah St., just beyond High St., is the town's most captivating historical site. A 30min. video chronicles Brown's raid of the armory with a special focus on the moral and political implications of his actions. A daunting, steep staircase hewn into the hillside off High St. follows the **Appalachian Trail** to **Upper Harpers Ferry,** which has fewer sights but is laced with interesting historical tales. Allow 45min. to ascend past **Harper's House,** the restored home of town founder Robert Harper, and **St. Peter's Church,** where a pastor flew the Union Jack during the Civil War to protect the church. Just a few steps uphill from St. Peter's lie the ruins of **St. John's Episcopal Church,** which was built in 1852 and used as a hospital and barracks during the Civil War before being abandoned in 1895.

OUTDOORS

Pick up trail maps at the park's visitors center before setting off into the wilderness. The moderately difficult **Maryland Heights Trail,** located across the railroad bridge in the Lower Town of Harpers Ferry, winds 4 mi. through the steep Blue Ridge Mountains that include precipitous cliffs and crumbling Civil War-era forts. The demanding 7½ mi. **Loudon Heights Trail** starts in Lower Town off the Appalachian Trail and leads to Civil War infantry trenches and scenic overlooks. For less strenuous hiking, the 2½ mi. **Camp Hill Trail** passes by the Harper Cemetery and ends at the former Stoner College. History dominates the **Bolivar Heights Trail,** starting at the northern end of Whitman Ave. The **Chesapeake & Ohio Canal** towpath, at the end of Shenandoah St. and over the railroad bridge, serves as a reminder of the town's industrial roots and is the departure point for a day's bike ride to Washington, D.C.

River & Trail Outfitters, 604 Valley Rd., 2 mi. out of Harpers Ferry, off U.S. 340, in Knoxville, MD, rents canoes, kayaks, inner tubes, and rafts. They also organize everything from scenic daytrips to placid rides down the Shenandoah River ($21) to wild overnights. (☎301-695-5177; www.rivertrail.com. Canoes $55 per day. Raft trips $50-60, under 17 $40. Tubing $32 per day.) At **Butt's Tubes, Inc.,** on Rte. 671, off U.S. 340, adventurers can buy a tube for the day and sell it back later. (☎800-836-9911; www.buttstubes.com. Open M-F 10am-3pm, last pickup 5pm; Sa-Su 10am-4pm, last pickup 6pm. $12-20.) At the **Appalachian Trail Regional Headquarters and Information Center,** 799 Washington St., a 10 ft. relief map shows the whole trail, and more sedentary visitors can learn about the trail on a computer monitor. (☎304-535-6331; www.appalachiantrail.org. Open mid-May to Oct. M-F 9am-5pm, Sa-Su 9am-4pm; Nov. to mid-May M-F 9am-5pm.)

FOOD

Harpers Ferry has sparse offerings for hungry hikers on a budget. U.S. 340 welcomes fast-food fanatics with various chain restaurants. The historic area, especially around High and Potomac St., caters to the lunch crowd with burgers, salads, and steaks but vacates at dinnertime. Across the street from the Hillside Motel, the **Cindy Dee Restaurant ❷**, 19112 Keep Tryst Rd., at U.S. 340, fries enough chicken ($6) to clog all of your arteries. The apple dumplings ($3.50) are delectable. (☎301-695-8181. Open M-Th and Su 6am-10pm, F-Sa 6am-11pm. D/MC/V.) **The Anvil ❸**, 1270 Washington St., serves delightfully non-greasy pub food for lunch, and fresh fish and beef for dinner. Don't miss the slot machines in the "gaming room" behind the door opposite the bar. (☎304-535-2582. Open W-Su 11am-9pm. AmEx/D/MC/V.)

ACCOMMODATIONS

There are B&Bs in town as well as in nearby Charles Town (west of Harpers Ferry, on U.S. 340). The **Hillside Motel ❷**, 19105 Keep Tryst Rd., 3 mi. from town in Brunswick, has 19 clean rooms inside a beautiful stone motel. (☎301-834-8144. Singles $45; doubles $55. Cash only.) Fishing fanatics might try **Anglers Inn ❹**, 867 Washington St., with fly-fishing packages available. All rooms come with a private bath. (☎304-535-1239; www.theanglersinn.com. Rooms $85-165. AmEx/D/MC/V.) **Greenbrier State Park ❶**, on U.S. 40 E off Rte. 66, has 165 campsites and an outdoor recreation area near a lake. (☎301-791-4767 or 888-432-2267; http://reservations.dnr.state.md.us. Reservations required. Open May-Sept. Sites $20, with hookup $25. MC/V.)

⚐ APPROACHING SHARPSBURG: 17 MILES

Head east on **U.S. 340** for about 4½ mi., passing into Virginia and then Maryland. Cross Harpers Ferry Rd., and turn right on **Keep Tryst Rd.** Take the first right onto **Sandy Hook Rd.**, which becomes **Harpers Ferry Rd.** This section of road is quite narrow, and there are a number of unsigned sharp curves. Exercise caution and avoid driving this stretch at night or in snowy conditions. Continue on Harpers Ferry Rd. until it becomes **Mechanic St.** in Sharpsburg.

The Old Line State

MARYLAND

Welcomes You!

SHARPSBURG. This historic Civil War town hasn't changed much since the 19th century—the town's residents have fought hard to keep it the way it is. One of the few places to eat is **American Deli Coffee ❶**, 100 E. Main St., on the corner of Mechanic and Main St. The small deli serves up fresh sandwiches ($5-6) and wraps ($4.50-5.50). "The Boss" (roast beef, swiss, horseradish, barbecue sauce, and onions; $5.75) is scrumptious. (☎301-432-7686. Open M-Sa in summer 11am-5pm; in winter 11am-3pm. Cash only.)

⚐ APPROACHING ANTIETAM NATIONAL BATTLEFIELD: 1 MILE

Take **Mechanic St.** to **Main St.**, and turn right. After 1 mi., take a left onto **S. Church St. (Rte. 65)**.

ANTIETAM NATIONAL BATTLEFIELD. Sep-

tember 17, 1862, the day of the Battle of Antietam in the Civil War is said to have been the single bloodiest day in US history. Nearly 25,000 soldiers died at Antietam, more than in the American Revolution, War of 1812, and Mexican-American War combined. Though neither side won decisively, the Union Army did manage to stop General Lee's advance towards Harrisburg. Inside the park, a stone observation tower offers a view of the expansive fields and nearby farmhouses. There are several fairly flat hiking trails through the area. Be sure to stick to them to avoid nettles, snakes, and ticks. A driving tour leads past the major sites of the battle. The **Antietam National Battlefield Visitors Center** distributes a driving guide, and a short film plays every 30min. Ranger tours of the battlefield (around 2hr.) run daily at 1:30pm from the visitors center and are preceded by a 1hr. documentary narrated by James Earl Jones. (☎301-432-5124. Open daily in summer 8am-7pm; in winter 8:30am-5pm. $4.)

⚐ APPROACHING HAGERSTOWN: 17 MILES

Take **E. Main St.** out of Sharpsburg, where it becomes **Rte. 34.** Turn left onto **Alt. U.S. 40** which becomes **Frederick St.** As you come into Hagerstown, make a soft left onto **Baltimore St.** and a right onto **Locust St.**, which is 1 block east of the center of town.

HAGERSTOWN

Once a principal town on the C&O Railway, Hagerstown remains the capital of this region of Maryland. It is home to the **Maryland Symphony Orchestra,** which performs at an inconspicuous theater at 13 S. Potomac St. (☎301-797-4000; www.marylandsymphony.org. Tickets $11-79.) The **Washington County Museum of Fine Art,** located in the beautiful Hagerstown City Park, occasionally features the work of local artists and students. (☎301-739-5727, www.washcomuseum.org. Open Tu-F 9am-5pm, Sa 9am-4pm. Free.)

For sheer quantity of food, **Ryan's ❸,** in the strip mall on U.S. 40 just west of town, takes the cake and barely dents the wallet, offering an all-you-can eat buffet that includes steak cooked to order. (☎301-766-4440. Dinner after 4pm $9. Weekday lunch 10:45am-4pm; $6.50. Breakfast buffet Sa-Su 7:30-10:30am; $7. Open M-Th and Su 10:45am-9:30pm, F-Sa 10:45am-10pm. AmEx/D/MC/V.) A pleasant family eatery, **Richardson's Restaurant ❸,** 710 Dual Hwy. (U.S. 40), serves sirloin steak ($14) and other classy cuisine. (☎301-733-3660. Dinner buffet $10. Open M-Th 7am-9pm, F-Sa 7am-10pm. D/MC/V.) Chain hotels and motels abound just outside the city, but you can't beat the **Holiday Motel ❸,** 12 N. Prospect St., for its prime location downtown. The rooms are worn but come with refrigerators and TV. (☎301-790-0844. Key deposit $5. Rooms $52. AmEx/D/DC/MC/V.)

⧉ DETOUR
GETTYSBURG NATIONAL MILITARY PARK

From Hagerstown, head east on Jefferson Blvd. (Rte. 64/804) to Smithsburg. Turn right on Foxville Rd., which becomes Rte. 77. After passing through Catoctin Mountain Park, get on U.S. 15 N toward Gettysburg, watching for signs that direct you to the visitors center (between S.R. 134 and Taneytown Rd.).

In the sweltering heat of July 1-3, 1863, Union and Confederate forces clashed spectacularly at Gettysburg. Though the Union ultimately prevailed, their victory came at the cost of more than 50,000 casualties. Four and a half months later, President Lincoln arrived in Gettysburg to dedicate the Gettysburg National Cemetery, where he delivered the Gettysburg Address on November 19, 1863. Today, the **Soldiers' National Monument** stands on the spot where Lincoln delivered his speech. A good place to start is the **Gettysburg National Military Park Visitors Center,** 97 Taneytown Rd., which distributes free driving tour maps and houses the Gettysburg Museum of the Civil War. (☎717-334-1124; www.nps.gov/gett. Open daily June-Aug. 8am-6pm; Sept.-May 8am-5pm. Free.) The information desk at the visitors center can set you up with a **licensed battlefield guide** on a first come, first served basis (arrive early), or you can make reservations at least seven days in advance. (☎717-334-4474 or 877-438-8929. $45 for 1-6 people per vehicle, with reservation $60.)

⧉ APPROACHING CUMBERLAND: 58 MILES

Turn left on **Franklin St.** and head out of town. Merge onto **I-70.** About 60 mi. from Hagerstown off **Exit 50,** idyllic **Rocky Gap State Park** offers fishing, boating, and swimming in beautiful blue Lake Habeeb. (☎888-432-2267; http://reservations.dnr.state.md.us. Call ahead. Sites $25, with electricity $30; cabins $50. MC/V.) 19 mi. from Hagerstown, **U.S. 40** and I-70 become one. To get to Cumberland, take the exit for **I-68 W** and get off at **Exit 43C.**

CUMBERLAND. The site of the C&O Canal and several railroads, Cumberland once served as the gateway to the west. The **C&O Canal National Historic Park Visitors Center,** 13 Canal St., explains the significance of the waterway. (☎301-722-8226. Open daily 9am-5pm. Free.) The same building that houses the visitors center is also home to the restored **Western Maryland Scenic Railroad,** which attracts train lovers to its old diesel and steam locomotives and runs daily excursions to Frostburg and back. Views from the train beat most of what you would see from behind the wheel. (☎301-759-4400 or 800-872-4650; www.wmsr.com. Trains depart May-Sept. Th-Sa and Su 11:30am; Oct. daily 11:30am; Nov.-Dec. Sa-Su. 11:30am. $23, seniors $21, children $18.) Conveniently close is **Kramers Deli ❷,** 13 Canal St., on the 2nd fl., which sells wraps and sandwiches. (☎301-722-8004. Sandwiches $5-7. Open M-F 10am-8pm, Sa 10am-7pm, Su 10am-7pm. AmEx/D/DC/MC/V.)

⧉ APPROACHING LAVALE: 6 MILES

In Cumberland, **Greene St.** ends at a marker indicating the start of the National Road. Turn left, then take your first right to cross the river. Take a left on **Mechanic St.,** which curves right onto **Frederick St.** Cross Liberty St. and take a left on **Centre St.,** which becomes **Alt. U.S. 40 W;** follow this out of town toward Lavale.

LAVALE. Lavale is a small town with little to do, but you can catch a few winks at the clean **Slumberland Motel,** 1262 National Hwy. (☎301-729-2880. Singles $55; doubles $57. AmEx/D/MC/V.) The first visible **tollhouse** on this road, Maryland's only surviving tollhouse, is perched high above the ground. (Open Sa-Su 1:30-4:30pm. Free.)

APPROACHING FROSTBURG: 8 MILES
Continue on **Alt. U.S. 40 W/National Hwy.** out of town and into Frostburg.

FROSTBURG. While parts of Main St. are empty, Frostburg has a few worthwhile attractions. The nearby campus of **Frostburg State University** supplies the town with cultural events and a lively student population. At the **Thrasher Carriage Museum,** 19 Depot St., a collection of horse-drawn carriages reminds visitors that, in the days before the automobile, those heading west along this route settled for much slower transportation. The variety of carriages represents the diversity of their owners, from the milkman to the president. (From U.S. 40, take a right onto Depot St. ☎301-689-3380; www.thrashercarriage.com. Open W-Su 10am-4pm. $4, ages 6-18 $2, under 6 free.) Standing amid the empty storefronts of Main St., the **Princess Restaurant ❶,** 12 W. Main St. (Alt. U.S. 40), at Broadway St., feels like a blast from the past. A turkey and cheese sub is just over $4, and some full meal platters (including meatloaf) come with two sides and a roll for under $6. (☎301-689-1680. Open M-Sa 6am-8pm. D/V.) **Failingers Hotel Gunter ❸,** 11 W. Main St., has 14 polished rooms in a hotel built in 1896. (☎301-689-6511. Singles $72; doubles $78. MC/V.)

APPROACHING GRANTSVILLE: 15 MILES
Continue on **Alt. U.S. 40 W (National Rd.)** toward Grantsville.

GRANTSVILLE. Pretty much the only attraction in Grantsville is the **Penn Alps,** 125 Casselman Rd., a village that offers a selection of local arts and showcases local history. In the village, **Stanton's Mill** looks rickety for a reason; it has stood here since 1797 and still mills flour today. The nearby **Casselman River Bridge** also dates back to the beginning of the 19th century. This beautiful stone arch was in use from 1813 to 1932. Adjacent to the

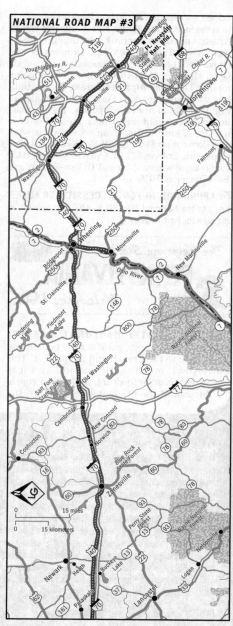

NATIONAL ROAD MAP #3

bridge, a collection of old buildings houses artists in residence at the **Spruce Forest Artisanal Village.** Artists undergo a rigorous selection process to win a coveted spot in the village. Drop-ins are welcome. (☎301-895-3332. Mill open daily 10am-6pm. Open May-Oct. M-Sa 10am-5pm and by appointment.) The **Penn Alps Restaurant ❸** was built largely by volunteers as Penn Alps expanded to bring visitors in from the highway. The German-inspired restaurant serves hearty and affordable meals. A smoked sausage sandwich with sauerkraut runs $4.50. (☎301-895-5985; www.pennalps.com. Entrees $11-21. Open in summer daily 7am-8pm; in winter M-Tu and Th 7am-7pm, W and F-Su 7am-8pm. MC/V.)

APPROACHING FORT NECESSITY: 26 MILES
Keep to the **National Pike (U.S. 40),** and turn left at the sign for **Fort Necessity.**

The Keystone State
PENNSYLVANIA
Welcomes You!

FORT NECESSITY NATIONAL BATTLEFIELD. Leave those Civil War sites behind and jump back to the French and Indian War. This battlefield, much more tranquil and less crowded than Gettysburg, includes a reproduction of the original stockade fort, the Mt. Washington Tavern, and Gen. Edward Braddock's Grave. While the notion of entering the West in Pennsylvania seems a bit far-fetched, the stockade bears witness to the fact that this wooded area was once the frontier. The tavern has an exhibit on the National Road along with period furnishings. (☎724-329-5512. Visitors center open daily 9am-5pm. Grounds open sunrise-sunset. $5.)

DETOUR
KENTUCK KNOB AND FALLINGWATER
Turn right at the sign for Kentuck Knob onto Chalk Hill-Ohiopyle Rd. The house is 5¾ mi. down the road.

Contemporary architect Frank Lloyd Wright chose a beautiful site at **Kentuck Knob** to construct a house three years before his death. Part of an 80-acre estate, the home is post-modern architecture writ large. Steeply priced tours explore the house and sculpture garden (☎724-329-1901. Open Tu-Sa and Su Mar.-Dec. 9am-4pm; Jan.-Feb. 11am-3pm. 1½hr. tours Tu-F $10, ages 6-18 $8; Sa-Su $15/$12.) Down the way, the world-renowned **Fallingwater,** "the most famous private residence ever built" exemplifies Wright's organic architecture, striking a balance with the landscape. (☎724-329-8501; www.wpconline.org/fallingwater/visit.htm. Open Mar.-Nov. Tu-Sa and Su 10am-4pm.)

APPROACHING UNIONTOWN: 10 MILES
Follow **U.S. 40** around Uniontown; take the exit for **U.S. 40 W/Bus. U.S. 40/Main St. Uniontown.** At the bottom of the ramp, turn right to proceed for 1 mi. to downtown Uniontown on **Main St. (Bus. U.S. 40).**

HOW'S MY (KID) DRIVING?

During a roadtrip, "How's My Driving?" bumper stickers are a common sight. Plastered to the back of tractor-trailer trucks, these stickers boast a threatening toll-free number for tattling on abrupt lane changes or wide turns. As you drive through New Jersey, Delaware, and Pennsylvania, you might see these stickers somewhere unexpected: on teenagers' cars. Inspired by truck stickers, Delaware residents James Pugh and Kevin Brown started a teen monitoring service from their homes, charging $25 per year. In return, parents receive a simple black-and-white bumper sticker bearing the company name, HowsMyKidDrivingToday.com, a toll-free number, an identification code, and the truth of how their teen is really driving. An answering service logs the feedback into a computer, and Pugh and Brown relay the information to the parents. A similar service, Tell-My-Mom.com, was started in Wisconsin in 2001, and several others have formed over the last few years. These services may be exploiting parental paranoia, but the fears may be warranted. 16-year-old drivers are involved in fatal one-car collisions almost five times more often than drivers over ages 20. Reactions to these services have been mixed, but the services will likely continue to expand as more teenagers get

UNIONTOWN. Little has changed since Uniontown served as a provisioning stop on the National Road. Today, the town remains primarily service-oriented. Grab a bite at **Meloni's ❷**, 105 W. Main St. (Bus. U.S. 40), where hearty entrees come at moderate prices. (☎724-437-0820. Pasta $5-8. Open M-Th 11am-10pm, F-Sa 11am-11pm, Su noon-9pm. AmEx/D/V.) Two miles west of Uniontown, the **MG Motel ❷**, 7909 National Pike (U.S. 40), offers small, neat rooms, some with TVs. (☎724-437-0506. Singles $49; doubles $55. AmEx/D/MC/V.) Cheery folks from the Fayette County Historical Society manage the **Searight Toll House,** 5 mi. west of Uniontown, one of only two left in Pennsylvania. See where the travelers of yore had to pay for their passage. (☎412-439-4422. Open mid-May to mid-Oct. Tu-Sa and Su 10am-4pm. $1.)

ⓝ APPROACHING BROWNSVILLE: 12 MILES
Proceed west on **Main St.** until **Bus. U.S. 40** turns into **U.S. 40 W.** Follow the signs indicating the original **National Road** into Brownsville.

BROWNSVILLE. Brownsville once served as a junction between the National Road and the Monongahela River heading to Pittsburgh; in the 1940s more freight went down this river than any other river in the world. Though considerably less busy today than in its days of glory, Brownsville is home to the interesting **Flatiron Building and Frank L. Melaga Art Museum,** 69 Market St. A two-room museum with artifacts from the coal mining and coca-cola industries, on which Brownsville thrived for years, the museum also features paintings by Frank Melaga, a Brownsville native who painted signs for local businesses as well as emotional portraits of area workers and coal miners. (From U.S. 40, turn left at the light for Market St.; the building is down the hill, on the right. ☎724-785-9331. Open M-Sa 11am-5pm, Su noon-6pm. Museum open by appointment only.) Built in three stages, **Nemacolin Castle,** 100 Front St., displays an unassuming exterior that hides a collection of 22 rooms, each furnished with different architectural styles from 150 years of American history. (☎724-785-6882. Open June-Aug. Tu-Su 11am-5pm; Mar.-Oct. Sa-Su 11am-5pm. $7, under 13 $3.)

ⓝ APPROACHING SCENERY HILL: 11 MILES
Continue following the **National Road** markers across the Monongahela River, and rejoin **U.S. 40** after about 3 mi. 8 mi. from Brownsville, check out the **Madonna of the Trail,** U.S. 40. This 16 ft. statue is one of 12 (the 1st of 5 along the National Road) erected in 1928 by the Daughters of the American Revolution in honor of "pioneer mothers of the covered wagon days."

SCENERY HILL. Scenery Hill has little to offer besides the **Hill's Tavern at Century Inn ❹**, 2175 E. National Pike (U.S. 40). Once host to Andrew Jackson, this tavern, built in 1794, remains active as an elegant B&B and restaurant. If you head inside the actual **Tavern ❸**, check out the flag from the Whiskey Rebellion to the right of the entrance. Lunch items include peanut soup made from Thomas Jefferson's recipe ($5), Welsh rarebit ($8), and rainbow trout ($12). Dinner takes a heftier bite out of the wallet. (☎724-945-6600; www.centuryinn.com. Rooms $80-150. MC/V.)

ⓝ APPROACHING WASHINGTON: 9 MILES
Continue on **U.S. 40** to Washington.

WASHINGTON

When entering Washington, be sure to check out the majestic US capitol-style **County Courthouse** at the corner of Main and Beau St. At the **Pennsylvania Trolley Museum,** 1 Museum Rd., an earlier era lives on. Visitors can ride restored vintage streetcars down a 3 mi. track. (Take I-79 north and Exit 49 for "Meadow Lands," then follow the blue signs for the museum. ☎724-228-9256; www.patrolley.org. Open Memorial Day to Labor Day M-F 11am-4pm, Sa-Su 11am-5pm; Apr.-Dec. Sa-Su 11am-5pm. $6, seniors $5, ages 2-15 $3.50.) Visitors to the **LeMoyne House,** 49 E. Maiden St. (U.S. 40), can see where runaway slaves hid and learn about Dr. LeMoyne, the staunch abolitionist who ran this stop on the Underground Railroad. (☎724-225-6740; www.wchspa.org. Open Tu-F 11am-4pm. $4, students $2.) Visitor info is available at the **Washington County Tourism Promotion Agency,** 273 S. Main St., north of the railroad tracks. (☎866-927-4969; www.washpatourism.org. Open M-F 9am-4:30pm.) The **New Tower Restaurant and Lounge ❷**, 680 W. Chestnut St. (U.S. 40), caters to locals and travelers looking for a quick no-fuss bite to eat. (☎724-222-5952. Breakfast $3-6. Dinner with 2 sides and salad $8-10. Open Tu-Th 7am-10pm, F-Sa 7am-11pm, Su 7am-8pm. D/MC/V.) Washington has very few motels, but the chains that cluster on **W. Chestnut St. (U.S. 40)** at the exits for I-70, 2 mi. west of town, offer rooms for as low as $46 per night. Just outside the city, the **Washington KOA**, 7 KOA

Rd., has campsites with access to laundry, a game room, and a pool. (Off Vance Station Rd. Follow signs from U.S. 40/U.S. 19. ☎ 724-225-7590 or 800-562-0254. Free Wi-Fi. Sites $22, with hookup $28; cabins $38. D/MC/V.)

⛏ APPROACHING WHEELING: 26 MILES

Take **Main St.** north and turn left on **Chestnut St.**, which becomes **U.S. 40.** 7 mi. from Washington, the **S-Bridge** is visible on the north side of U.S. 40. The bridge was built in an S-shape because the river was at an angle to the road, and it was easier to construct straight arches over the river. 17 mi. from Washington, the road leaves Pennsylvania and enters West Virginia; 9 mi. later, U.S. 40 turns right to head into Wheeling. On your way into town, notice the next **Madonna of the Trail** monument on the right. From here, U.S. 40 takes a long, scenic route around the hills to downtown Wheeling. The fastest way to get into Wheeling, however, is on **I-70 W.**

The Mountain State

WEST VIRGINIA

Welcomes You!

WHEELING

Once the thriving economic and political center of West Virginia, Wheeling today has a warm, small-town feel. The **Kruger Street Toy and Train Museum,** 144 Kruger St., displays 20,000 toys in a gorgeous restored Victorian-era schoolhouse. (☎ 304-242-8133, www.toyandtrain.com. Open June-Oct. M and W-Su 10am-6pm; Nov.-Dec. daily 10am-6pm; Jan.-May F-Su 10am-6pm. $8.50, seniors $7.50, students $5.) The answer to that eternal question, "Why does West Virginia exist?" can be found at the **West Virginia Independence Hall,** 1528 Market St., which narrates the history of the division between the regions of Richmond and Wheeling. The building marks the site where West Virginia became a state. (Proceed south on Main St. to 16th St., and turn left. ☎ 304-238-1300. Open Mar.-Dec. M-Sa 10am-4pm.) $3, students $2.) From Main St., at 10th St., you can view the **Wheeling Suspension Bridge,** just south of the current I-70/U.S. 40 bridge. Built in 1849 to carry the National Road across the Ohio River, this 1010 ft. suspension bridge opened 34 years before the Brooklyn Bridge.

The 🍴**Coleman's Fish Market ❶,** 22nd and Market St., serves up fried and steamed delicacies from the sea. Most items, including the shrimp and the fish sandwich, are under $5. (Behind Centre Market. ☎ 304-232-8510. Open M-Tu 10am-5:30pm, W-Th and Sa 8:30am-5:30pm, F 8:30am-7pm. Cash only.) **Michael's Beef House ❶,** 2200 Market St., has hot roast beef sandwiches ($3.25-4.25), chicken salad ($3.50), and other affordable sandwiches. Vegetarians beware: you will find little to munch on here. (☎ 304-232-2231. M-Th and Sa 10am-5:30pm, F 10am-6pm. Cash only.)

THE TOY BOY

Let's Go had the opportunity to speak with Allan Miller, the founder and curator of The Kruger Street Toy and Train Museum. He has collected toys since the age of 9, starting with his father's model train sets.

LG: What sorts of people visit the museum?

AM: We see people from all sorts of walks of life. They all find things they like, but they are not the same things. We try not only to keep different types of toys, but toys from a variety of eras, too. You're going to see trains from the turn of the last century and trains that are only a few years old. We want everyone who comes to the museum not only to enjoy their visit but to find something that they connect with. We get to see a lot of people as five-year-olds again.

LG: What are some of the fun things you get to do on the job?

AM: As the curator, I put together the various exhibits. What I find fun about that is to play off our visitors in a way—a lot of our exhibits were born out of suggestions from our visitors. We are supposed to understand what the customers want, what the people want to see. They are coming to experience things from their past

⬛ DETOUR

FORMER WEST VIRGINIA PENITENTIARY

818 Jefferson Ave. From downtown Wheeling, take Rte. 2 S (Main St./Chapline St. in Wheeling) for 12 mi. to Moundsville, then turn left on 8th St. The penitentiary is 2 blocks ahead.

If you can't wait until Alcatraz (2586 mi. down the road), tour this Civil-War-era structure where West Virginia still conducts its Mock Prison Riot training. You can even spend the night with reservations; just watch out for the ghosts. (☎304-845-6200; www.wvpentours.com. Open Apr.-Nov. Tu-Su 10am-4pm. $8, seniors $7, ages 6-12 $5.)

▶ APPROACHING BRIDGEPORT: 4 MILES

Continue on **Main St.,** which enters Ohio 1 mi. from Wheeling and becomes **U.S. 40.** Continue straight ahead even though there is not a "U.S. 40" sign for nearly 2 mi.

The Buckeye State
OHIO
Welcomes You!

BRIDGEPORT. Bridgeport doesn't have much going on, but the homey and scenic **Hillside Motel ❷,** 54481 National Road (U.S. 40), is an excellent place to spend the night. (☎740-645-9111. Singles $43; doubles $52. D/MC/V.)

▶ APPROACHING CAMBRIDGE: 46 MILES

U.S. 40 merges with **I-70** 22 mi. from Wheeling. Take it, and get off at **OH Exit 178.** Make a right at **Southate Pkwy.,** and take it into Cambridge.

CAMBRIDGE

Cambridge was and still is at the heart of a glass-producing region. **Mosser Glass Inc.,** 9279 Cadiz Rd. (U.S. 22 E), is the largest operational glass factory in Cambridge. (☎740-439-1827. Open M-F 8am-4pm. Tours 8am-10am and 11:15am-2:30pm.) Inside **Boyd's Crystal Art Glass,** 1203 Morton Ave., on the corner of Woodlawn Ave., workers are busy producing specialty glass. (From U.S. 40, turn left onto 11th St., which becomes Morton Ave. ☎740-439-2077. Open June-Aug. M-F 7am-3:30pm. Showroom open M-F 8am-4pm.) The **Degenhart Paperweight and Glass Museum,** 65323 Highland Hills Rd., at Cadiz Rd. (U.S. 22) and I-77, has glass samples from different companies and eras, each with informative explanations. (From town, take U.S. 22 E; the museum is on the left just before the I-77 exit. ☎740-432-2626. Open Apr.-Dec. M-Sa 9am-5pm, Su 1-5pm; Jan.-Mar. M-F 10am-5pm. $1.50, seniors $1, under 18 free.)

The **National Road Heritage Market ❶,** 738 Wheeling Ave., sells an assortment of "made in Ohio" products, with everything from crafts to farm-fresh butter. The market sells ice cream ($1.50-2.50) in a variety of flavors, and the owner possesses a wealth of knowledge about the Cambridge area. (☎740-432-8789 or 866-334-6446. Open M-Sa 10am-7pm, Su noon-5pm. D/MC/V.) ⬛**Theo's Restaurant ❷,** 632 Wheeling

that bring back positive memories.

LG: Do you still get to play with the toys?

AM: Of course, of course. I pride myself on the fact that everything on the shelves actually works. I've been known to take the toys out of the cases and wind them up and play with them. One of the things that we've tried to do is not display the toy as an artifact but as how you'd remember it from childhood.

LG: Anything else to add?

AM: You have to forget that we have the word "museum" in our name. Our museum is different because everyone in the family is going to enjoy it; everyone is going to find something they like. There are not a whole lot of these types of things in life. They don't usually hit across generations, across sexes, across ethnic groups. There's a universal language of play. To me, it's magical.

The Kruger St. Toy and Train Museum, 144 Kruger St. (☎304-242-8133; www.toyandtrain.com.) Open June-Oct. M and W-Su 10am-6pm; Nov.-Dec. daily 10am-6pm; Jan.-May F-Su 10am-6pm. $8.50, students $5.

Ave. (U.S. 40), serves delightfully cheap and non-greasy food. Their specialty is the Coney Island Hot Dog ($1.25), which is perfectly accompanied by a wedge of freshly baked pie for $1.50. (☎740-432-3878. Barbecue $6-7. Steak $9. Open M-Sa 10am-9pm. D/MC/V.) The cozy, family-run **Budget Inn ❷**, 6405 Glenn Hwy. (U.S. 40), 2 mi. west of town, has sweet and comfy rooms. (☎740-432-2304. Singles $32; doubles $40. D/MC/V.)

⛽ APPROACHING NEW CONCORD: 8 MILES
Follow **U.S. 40 W** to New Concord.

NEW CONCORD. New Concord's most noteworthy attraction is the **John and Annie Glenn Historic Site,** 6872 W. Main St. At this small museum, the town of New Concord memorializes its hero, John Glenn. Learn the story of this small-town Ohioan, US senator, and astronaut while exploring different facets of American history. (☎740-826-3305; www.johnglennhome.org. Open Apr. to Labor Day W-Sa 10am-4pm, Su 1-4pm; Labor Day to mid-Nov. W-Sa 10am-4pm, Su 1-4pm. $6, seniors $5, students $3.) Right next door is the **Jitterbug Coffee House ❶**, 68 ½ W. Main St., the perfect spot for all of your java jitters. The warm staff serves a variety of hot and iced coffees, including the coconut-flavored "Gilligan" ($2.80) and the "Curious George" (coffee with banana and chocolate milk, $2.90.) (☎740-826-2233. Free Wi-Fi. Open M-Th 6:30am-8pm, F 6:30am-10pm, Sa 8am-10pm. MC/V.)

⛽ APPROACHING NORWICH: 4 MILES
Continue on **U.S. 40** out of town toward Norwich.

NORWICH. Norwich is a small town whose only claim to fame is the fantastic ▨**National Road/Zane Grey Museum,** 8850 E. Pike (U.S. 40). All the bits and pieces of National Road history come together at this museum along with exhibits of highlighted sights you've already passed and some still yet to come. Check out the world's largest vase. (From U.S. 40, look for the large sign for "Baker's Motel" and turn left into the museum. ☎740-872-3143. Open May-Sept. M-Sa 9:30am-5pm, Su noon-5pm. $7, students $3, children 5 and under free.) **Baker's Motel ❷**, 8855 E. Pike, has

a convenient location and comfortable rooms. (☎740-872-3232. Singles $36; doubles $55. AmEx/D/MC/V.)

⛽ APPROACHING ZANESVILLE: 13 MILES
Follow **U.S. 40** to Zanesville.

ZANESVILLE

Amelia Earhart described Zanesville as the "most recognizable city in the country" due to its Y-shaped bridge. The current Y-bridge is the fifth of its kind since 1814. On the opposite side of town, your best bet for a glimpse of the bridge is on your way out. (As you leave town on U.S. 40, just after the Y-bridge, take the first left on Pine St. and then turn left on Grandview Ave., following signs for **"Y-Bridge Overlook."**) From **Zane's Landing Park,** roadtrippers can ride the **Lorena Sternwheeler** down the Muskingum River, accompanied by "riverboat music" and dinner at night. (Take Market St. west until it ends at the park. ☎740-455-8883 or 800-246-6303. Call for cruise schedule. $6, seniors $5, ages 2-12 $3. Dinner cruises $30.)

The original incarnation of a roadside favorite, ▨**Classic Denny's ❷**, 4990 E. Pike, has a regular Denny's menu, but with red and white leather seats with chrome finishing that look like they came right out of your grandfather's Chevy. If you love classic cars, try to drop in on a Friday during June or July; Denny's hosts classic car shows that pack the parking lot with the area's best cars and their proud owners. (☎740-450-8387. Open 24hr. AmEx/D/DC/MC/V.) At **Nicol's Restaurant ❶**, 730 Putnam Ave., home-style entrees with two sides are less than $7, while lunch specials with soup or salad run $4. Don't forget Nicol's homemade ice cream ($2) or pie ($2-2.25) for dessert. (From Main St. or Market St., turn left onto 4th St. or 5th St., turn left at Canal St., and take the first right onto Putnam Ave. ☎740-452-2577. Open M-W and Su 7am-8pm, Th-Sa 7am-9pm. Cash only.) Hotels in Zanesville are surprisingly expensive and cluster around the U.S. 40 junction with I-70, though there are a number of other chains downtown. Your best bet is to head back to Cambridge to spend the night (p. 379).

1903: Horatio Nelson Jackson completes the first transcontinental roadtrip at a blistering 20 mph.

APPROACHING NEWARK: 30 MILES

Take **Main St. (U.S. 40)** out of town, bearing left on the Y-bridge to stay on U.S. 40. Take a right on **OH 13/Jacksontown Rd. SE** toward Newark.

NEWARK. A visit to Newark requires a brief detour from U.S. 40, but it's worth the brief digression. At the **Dawes Arboretum**, 7770 Jacksontown Rd., visitors can walk through beautifully landscaped grounds, including an "all-season garden," which features different plants depending on the month. (Turn right onto Rte. 13, and head north; the arboretum is on the left. ☎ 740-323-2355 or 800-443-2937; www.dawesarb.org. Open daily sunrise-sunset. Free.)

APPROACHING BUCKEYE LAKE: 15 MILES

Return on **OH 13** back to **U.S. 40 W;** get off at **OH 79 S/Hebron Rd.** Make a left onto **Union Ave.** toward Buckeye Lake.

BUCKEYE LAKE. If you're hungry, don't miss the pizza at **Catfish Charley's ❷**, 11048 Hebron Rd. (Rte. 79), in Buckeye Lake Village. (☎ 740-928-7174. All-you-can-eat spaghetti W; $7. 8 in. pizza $7. Calzones $6. Open M-Th and Su 11am-10pm, F-Sa 11am-11pm. AmEx/D/DC/MC/V.) **KG's Grub Shack ❶**, 10960 Hebron Rd., doesn't have a lot of seating but serves tasty chicken. A three-piece "snack" with a biscuit costs $4. (☎ 740-928-4782. Open M-Th and Su 11am-9pm, F-Sa 11am-10pm. AmEx/D/MC/V.) The well-maintained **Buckeye Lake/Columbus East KOA ❸**, 4460 Walnut Rd., offers shaded tent sites, a pool, laundry, and a miniature golf course. (☎ 740-928-0706. Open Apr.-Oct. Sites $31, with full hookup $38-40; cabins $48-59. AmEx/D/DC/MC/V.)

APPROACHING COLUMBUS: 30 MILES

Return to **U.S. 40** via **OH 79 N.** In Bexley, U.S. 40 strays from Main St. The sign for U.S. 40 is small and hard to see; if you miss the turn, **Main St.** will also take you into downtown, albeit on a less scenic path.

COLUMBUS

Less a single, coherent metropolis than a collection of freeway exits, Columbus crept past Cleveland in 1990 as Ohio's most populous city. White-collar workers hit the freeways at 5pm and make for the inner-ring suburbs, while immigrants and young artists keep parts of downtown aglow after dark. The capital's museums and galleries are well worth a day or two of exploration.

VITAL STATS

Population: 711,000

Visitor Info: Visitor Center in Easton Town Center, 160 Easton Town Ctr. (☎ 614-416-7000; www.experiencecolumbus.com), on the 1st fl. of the Easton Town Center Mall. From Broad St. (U.S. 40), take the exit for I-270 and get off at the Easton Way exit. Open M-Sa 10am-9pm, Su noon-6pm.

Internet Access: Columbus Metropolitan Library, 96 S. Grant Ave. (☎ 614-645-2275). Open M-Th 9am-9pm, F-Sa 9am-6pm, Su 1-5pm. Free.

Post Office: 850 Twin Rivers. (☎ 614-469-4267). Open M-F 8am-7pm, Sa 8am-2pm. **Postal Code:** 43215.

GETTING AROUND

The city is laid out in a simple grid, but it can be frustrating to get around since left turns are rarely permitted. **High St.,** running north-south, and **Broad St. (U.S. 40),** running east-west, are the main thoroughfares. High St. heads north from the towering office complexes downtown to the lively galleries and restaurants in the **Short North,** continuing on to Ohio State University (OSU). South of downtown lies historic German Village. There is little free parking available in Columbus except on evenings and weekends at certain meters. There is free parking available in German Village. Lots downtown tend to be expensive ($12 per day). Meters proliferate on almost every street but time limits and prices vary widely.

SIGHTS

OSU AND VICINITY. Ohio State University (OSU) lies 2 mi. north of downtown. **The Wexner Center for the Arts** was the first public building designed by controversial Modernist Peter Eisenman. The center now sports a five-story "permanent scaffold," an aesthetic of unfinished construction that matches its commitment to avant-garde visual art and performance. *(1871 N. High St. ☎ 614-292-3535; www.wexarts.org. Open Feb.-June Tu-W and Su 11am-6pm, Th-Sa 11am-8pm. Free. Films $5, students and seniors $4, under 12 $2.)*

MUSEUMS. The **Columbus Museum of Art** has an unusually strong permanent collection of early modern canvases, from European luminaries like Matisse and Klee to lesser-known Americans like George Bellows. Other highlights include a collection of local folk art and a great children's exhibit that allows kids to walk into a Dutch studio. Don't miss the giant "ART" sign towering right behind the museum. (*480 E. Broad St.* ☎ *614-221-6801; www.columbusmuseum.org. Open Tu-W and F-Su 10am-5:30pm, Th 10am-8:30pm. $6; students, seniors, and ages 6-18 $4. Su free.*) The submarine-shaped **Center of Science and Industry (COSI)** allows visitors to explore space from the safety of an armchair, create their own short stop-animation films, and enjoy arcade games like Pong, Centipede, and Space Invaders. A seven-story Extreme Screen shows action-packed films. (*333 W. Broad St. Take Broad St./U.S. 40 W past High St.; the museum is on the left just after crossing the river.* ☎ *614-228-2674; www.cosi.org. Open M-Sa 10am-5pm, Su noon-6pm. $12.50, seniors $10.50, ages 2-12 $7.50. Extreme Screen $6. Combination ticket $17.50, seniors $15.50, ages 2-12 $12.50.*) James Thurber's childhood home, the **Thurber House,** showcases major events of the famous *New Yorker* writer's life. It also serves as a literary center, hosting seminars with authors like John Updike. (*77 Jefferson Ave., off E. Broad St. From Broad St., turn right on Jefferson Ave., just past I-71.* ☎ *614-464-1032. Open daily noon-4pm. Free. Tours Su $2.50, students and seniors $2.*)

ARTS DISTRICT. The **Short North Arts District** is rife with galleries to browse. On the first Saturday of each month from 6 to 10pm, the district fills with an eclectic crowd for the free **Gallery Hop Night,** in which artists, purveyors, and appreciators come together for street performances, hors d'oeuvres, and champagne. The eccentric **Gallery V** exhibits and sells contemporary paintings and sculptures along with handcrafted jewelry. (*694 N. High St.* ☎ *614-228-8955. Open Tu-Sa 11am-5pm. Free.*) The **Kathryn Gallery** features contemporary American and European artists, and has a back room for private viewing of individual works. (*642 N. High St.* ☎ *614-222-6801. Open Tu-Th 11am-6pm, F-Sa 11am-8pm, Su 11am-5pm. Free.*)

GERMAN VILLAGE. For some good Germanica, march down to the **German Village,** south of Capitol Sq. This area, first settled in 1843, is now the largest privately funded historical restoration in the US, and is full of stately homes and beer halls. The **German Village Society Meeting Haus** provides info on local happenings, including summertime performances of Shakespeare in Schiller Park. (*588 S. 3rd St.* ☎ *614-221-8888. Open M-F 9am-4pm, Sa 10am-2pm; hours vary in winter.*) **Schmidt's Fudge Haus** concocts tasty chocolate delicacies named for local celebrities. (*220 E. Kossuth St.* ☎ *614-444-2222. Truffles and other candies $12-17 per lb. Open M-Th noon-4pm, F-Sa noon-7pm, Su noon-3pm.*)

OTHER SIGHTS. The **Franklin Park Conservatory and Botanical Garden** cultivates lush greenery from various parts of the world and is a good break from the variable Ohio weather. (*1777 E. Broad St.* ☎ *614-645-8733; www.fpconservatory.org. Open Tu and Th-Su 10am-5pm, W 10am-8pm. $6.50, students and seniors $5, ages 2-12 $3.50.*) About 10 mi. north of downtown, the surreal **Field of Corn** contains 109 7 ft. concrete ears of corn that pay homage to the town's agrarian roots. (*4995 Rings Rd., in Dublin. From Columbus, take I-70 W to I-270 N; take Exit 15 and turn right on Tuttle Crossing Blvd. Turn left onto Frantz Rd. The field is visible at the intersection of Frantz Rd. and Rings Rd. Open 24hr. Free.*)

ᗧ FOOD

By far the best place for budget eats in Columbus is the **North Market**, 59 Spruce St., in the Short North Arts District. From every corner of this restored marketplace, vendors offer a variety of wines, meats, cheeses, fruits, and prepared ethnic foods from sushi to barbecue to fresh produce. (Take High St. north to Spruce St., and turn left. ☎ 614-463-9664; www.northmarket.com. Open Tu-F 9am-7pm, Sa 8am-5pm, Su noon-5pm. Some merchants open M 9am-5pm.) **High St.** is lined with a variety of cafes and coffee shops, all tasty and reasonably priced.

▩ **Katzinger's Delicatessen,** 475 S. 3rd St. (☎614-228-3354). Katzhinger's charges a whopping $11.25 for its incredible half-pound Reuben. But with Black Angus corned beef shipped down from Detroit and Bill Clinton's personal approval, Katzinger's can't be beat for sandwiches ($9-12) or Sunday morning bagels and lox. Open M-F 8:30am-8:30pm, Sa-Su 9am-8:30pm. AmEx/MC/V. ❸

Schmidt's Sausage Haus, 240 E. Kossuth St. (☎614-444-6808; www.schmidthaus.com), serves Bavarian

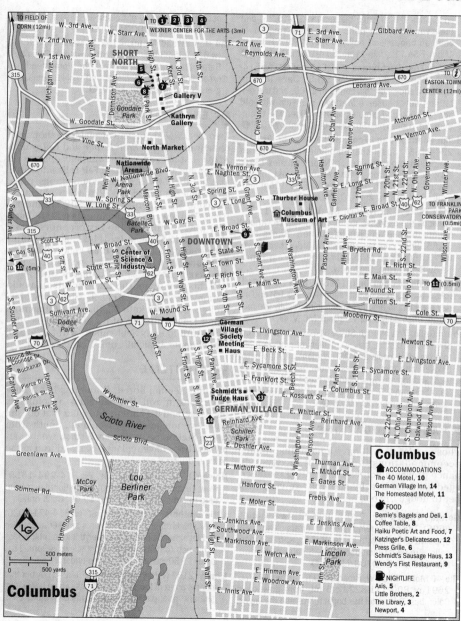

Columbus

🏠 ACCOMMODATIONS
The 40 Motel, **10**
German Village Inn, **14**
The Homestead Motel, **11**

🍴 FOOD
Bernie's Bagels and Deli, **1**
Coffee Table, **8**
Haiku Poetic Art and Food, **7**
Katzinger's Delicatessen, **12**
Press Grille, **6**
Schmidt's Sausage Haus, **13**
Wendy's First Restaurant, **9**

🍸 NIGHTLIFE
Axis, **5**
Little Brothers, **2**
The Library, **3**
Newport, **4**

specialties like sausage platters ($9.25-10.25) and their vanilla cream puffs ($4), while traditional oompah bands lead polkas. Open M-Th 11:30am-10pm, F-Sa 11:30am-11pm, Su 4-10pm. D/MC/V. ❸

Wendy's First Restaurant, 257 E. Broad St. (☎614-464-4656), at the corner of 5th St. Dave Thomas started Wendy's on this corner in 1969, and the restaurant now houses a Wendy's museum with old ads, articles, and pictures of Dave. Open M-F 10am-8pm, Sa 10am-7pm, Su 11am-6pm. AmEx/MC/V. ❶

Haiku Poetic Art and Food, 800 N. High St. (☎614-294-8168). Sushi chefs produce their edible art amid chic Japanese decor. Noodle dishes ($10-13), such as *udon tempura,* might just inspire poetry. Open M-Th 11am-11pm, F-Sa 11am-midnight, Su 4-10pm. AmEx/D/MC/V. ❸

Coffee Table, 731 N. High St. (☎614-297-1177). Provides the espresso fix for an eclectic crowd and seems to have an Elvis infatuation. Drinks from $1.55. Huge cookies and "sinful fudge bar brownies" $1.50. Open M-Th 7am-10pm, F 7am-11pm, Sa-Su 8am-11pm. Cash only. ❶

Bernie's Bagels and Deli, 1896 N. High St. (☎614-291-3448). Serves healthy sandwiches ($3-5) and all-day breakfast in a subterranean joint. Nightly live rock music. Open daily 11am-2:30am. MC/V. ❶

Press Grille, 741 N. High St. (☎614-298-1014), in the Short North District, serves a variety of modern foods to a crowd of locals and OSU students. Try the pesto chicken with fontina cheese, portobello, bacon, lettuce, and tomato on sourdough bread ($7). Open M-Sa 11:30am-2:30am, Su 1pm-2:30am. Kitchen closes 1am. AmEx/DC/MC/V. ❷

■ ACCOMMODATIONS

Those under 21 will have a hard time finding accommodations in Columbus; a city ordinance prevents hotels from renting to underaged visitors. Nearby suburbs are your best bet to dodge the ban.

German Village Inn, 920 S. High St. (☎614-443-6506). The newly remodeled inn offers clean, well-appointed rooms with cable TV, A/C, and free local calls. Breakfast included. 21+. Singles $54; doubles $59. AmEx/D/DC/MC/V. ❸

The 40 Motel, 3705 W. Broad St./U.S. 40 (☎614-276-2691 or 800-331-8223), 5 mi. from downtown Columbus. This motel has bright rooms and the largest

neon sign in the city of Columbus. Singles $42; doubles $44. AmEx/D/DC/MC/V. ❷

The Homestead Motel, 4182 E. Main St./U.S. 40 (☎614-235-2348), 7 mi. from downtown Columbus. Better than most area motels, the Homestead has exceedingly spacious, clean, and well-lit rooms. Singles $35; doubles $40. MC/V. ❷

■ ENTERTAINMENT

Two free, weekly papers available in shops and restaurants, *The Other Paper* and *Columbus Alive,* list arts and entertainment options. In early August, the **Ohio State Fair** rolls into town, as it has for 150 years, with competitions, rides, and concerts. (☎888-646-3976; www.ohiostatefair.com. $8, seniors and ages 5-12 $7, under 5 free.) The always formidable **Ohio State Buckeyes** play football in the historic horseshoe-shaped **Ohio Stadium** (☎614-292-2624). Major league soccer's **Columbus Crew** kicks off at **Crew Stadium.** (☎614-447-2739; www.crewstadium.com. Tickets $35.) Columbus' brand-new NHL hockey team, the **Blue Jackets,** plays in Nationwide Arena. (☎614-246-3350; www.bluejackets.com. Tickets $6-10.) The **Clippers,** a Minor league affiliate of the NY Yankees, play from April to early September. (☎614-462-5250; http://clippersbaseball.com. Tickets $6-10.)

■ NIGHTLIFE

If you're feeling bored, Columbus has a sure cure: rock 'n' roll. Bar bands are a Columbus mainstay, and it's hard to find a bar that doesn't have live music on the weekend. South from Union Station is the **Brewery District,** where barley and hops have replaced coal and iron in the once industrial area.

Newport, 1722 N. High St. (☎614-294-1659; www.newportmusichall.com). Big national acts stop here to strut their stuff. Cover $5-40. Cash only.

Little Brothers, 1100 N. High St. (☎614-421-2025; www.littlebrothers.com). Features smaller alternative and local bands performing everything from bluegrass to hip-hop to heavy metal. Most shows 8-9pm. 18+. Cover $5-30; surcharge for those under 21.

Library, 2169 N. High St. (☎614-299-3245). A bar that attracts a mix of locals and students, where beer chugging and pool playing replace traditional study techniques. Beer $2-3. Happy hour daily 3-9pm. Open M-Sa 3pm-2:30am, Su 7pm-2:30am. MC/V.

Axis, 775 N. High St. (☎614-291-4008). Attracts gay and lesbian partygoers. T3rd F of each month "steam" party with showers from the ceiling. 18+. Cover $3-6. Open F-Sa 10pm-2:15am.

⚑ APPROACHING SPRINGFIELD: 32 MILES

From **Broad St.,** proceed west out of the downtown area on **U.S. 40.** U.S. 40 mostly bypasses the tiny towns; you can take "Old U.S. 40" for brief stretches to pass through Summerford and South Vienna, ending up back on U.S. 40.

SPRINGFIELD

A town proud of its manufacturing heritage, Springfield flourishes as the site of Wittenberg University, the Clark County Seat, and the gateway to Buck Creek State Park.

VITAL STATS

Population: 64,000

Visitor Info: Springfield Area Convention and Visitors Bureau, 333 N. Limestone St., #201 (☎937-325-7621 or 800-803-1553; www.springfield-clark-countyohio.info). Open M-F 8am-5pm.

Internet Access: Clark County Public Library, 201 S. Fountain Ave. (☎937-328-6903). Open M-F 9am-9pm, Sa 9am-6pm, Su 1-5pm. Free.

Post Office: 150 N. Limestone St. (☎937-323-6498). Open M-F 8am-6pm, Sa 8am-1pm. **Postal Code:** 45501.

⌷ GETTING AROUND. In Springfield, **U.S. 40 W** becomes **North St.** and runs one-way through town. One block south, U.S. 40 E runs the other way as **Columbia St.** The two are intersected by **Limestone St.,** which runs one-way north, and **Fountain Ave.,** which runs one-way south.

◪ SIGHTS. The **Heritage Center of Clark County,** 117 S. Fountain Ave., exhibits cars, surgical instruments, steamrollers, fire trucks—all made right in Springfield—in a built-on addition to a restored marketplace. The center also houses a large National Road history museum, complete with a refurbished Conestoga wagon and an original stone mile marker. (☎937-324-0657. Open Tu-Sa 9am-5pm. Free.) A collection of paintings by mostly American artists adorns the pastel-

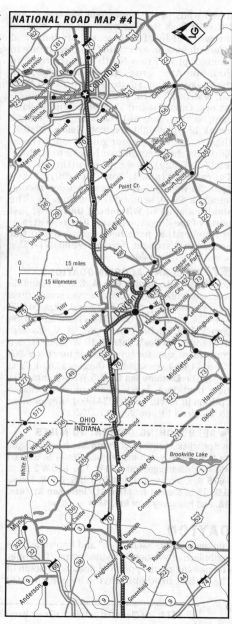

NATIONAL ROAD MAP #4

toned walls of the **Springfield Museum of Art,** 107 Cliff Park Rd. The museum also exhibits the work of local high school students and offers classes on everything from sculpture to photography. (From North St., turn right on Fountain Ave., cross the small bridge, and then take an immediate left onto Cliff Park Rd. ☎937-325-4673; www.spfld-museum-of-art.org. Open Tu and Th-F 9am-5pm, W 9am-9pm, Sa 9am-3pm. $3.) The large, prairie-style Frank Lloyd Wright **Westcott House,** 1340 E. High St., is now open for guided tours. (From North St., head south two blocks to High St. ☎937-327-9291; www.westcotthouse.org. Tours W-F 11am, 1, 3pm, Sa hourly 11am-4pm, Su hourly 1-4pm. Reservations recommended. $8.50, seniors $7, students $6.) The small campus of **Wittenberg University,** just north of the downtown area, lies in an area of old homes that have been converted to frat houses and student dorms. (☎800-677-7558; www.wittenberg.edu.)

🍴🛏 FOOD AND ACCOMMODATIONS.
Locals flock to **Station One ❶,** 325 N. Fountain Ave., a neighborhood bar that serves scrumptious sandwiches ($3-5), subs ($4-7), and pizza. (☎937-324-3354. Pizza $4-12. Open M-Sa 11am-2:15am, Su 3pm-2:15am. Kitchen closes 9pm. MC/V.) If you're downtown, **Wa Bee's Cafe ❶,** 10 W. Main St., is a convenient spot for breakfast or lunch. (☎937-327-9143. Chicken salad $3. Burgers $2.50-4. Cash only.) The **Executive Inn ❷,** 325 W. Columbia St., right next door, is one of the most affordable options in town. (☎513-324-5601. Key deposit $5. Singles $40; doubles $45. D/MC/V.)

🚗 APPROACHING DAYTON: 30 MILES
In Springfield, continue on **North St.,** following signs for **U.S. 40 W,** which merges with **Rte. 4 S.** Stay on Rte. 4, which merges with **I-70 W.** Take I-70 W 2 mi. to **I-675 S.** Continue to **Exit 13** for **U.S. 35 W.** Follow U.S. 35 to the exit for **Main St./Jefferson St./Rte. 48,** and follow signs for **Rte. 48 N** into town.

DAYTON
Nicknamed the "Gem City," and known as "the birthplace of aviation," Dayton has much to offer the passing roadtripper. Originally the home of the Wright brothers, Dayton's economy still revolves around the sprawling Wright-Patterson Air Force Base, but has attempted to take advantage of the recent centennial of the first human flight to reinvent itself as a tourist destination.

VITAL STATS

Population: 166,000

Visitor Info: Dayton/Montgomery County Convention and Visitors Bureau, 1 Chamber Plaza, Ste. A (☎937-226-8211), at 5th and Main St. Open M-F 8am-5:30pm.

Internet Access: Dayton Metro Library, 215 E. 3rd St. (☎937-227-9500), at the corner of St. Clair. Open June-Aug. M-Th 9am-9pm, F-Sa 9am-5:30pm; Sept.-May M-Th 9am-9pm, F-Sa 9am-5:30pm, Su 1-5pm. Free.

Post Office: 1111 E. 5th St. (☎937-227-1122). Open M-F 7am-6pm, Sa 8am-2pm. **Postal Code:** 45401.

🚗 GETTING AROUND. I-75 runs north-south through the city just west of the downtown area. **U.S. 35,** a controlled-access highway for much of its length, runs east-west near downtown. **Rte. 48** runs primarily on **Main St.** north-south through the center of downtown. Numbered streets run east-west perpendicular to Main St., and **Monument Ave.** is one block north of **1st St.**

🏛 SIGHTS. At the 🗽**United States Air Force Museum,** 1100 Spaatz St., at the Wright-Patterson Air Force Base, visitors pour through the museum for the 300-odd aircraft dating from the beginning of human flight. Also onsite is the **National Aviation Hall of Fame.** View recent enshrinees or sign up to see the Presidential Aircraft and Development/Test Flight Hangars. (Follow I-70 E to I-675, take Exit 15 for the Col. Glenn Hwy., and follow the signs. ☎937-255-3286; www.wpafb.af.mil/museum. Open daily 9am-5pm. Free.) More aviation fun is on display at the **Wright Brothers Aviation Center,** in Carillon Historical Park, where the intricate history of the Wright brothers is told in intricate detail. Displays include actual items belonging to the Wright Brothers, including their 1903 plane. (☎937-293-2841. Open Tu-Sa 9:30am-5pm, Su noon-5pm. $8, seniors $7, ages 3-17 $5.)

Those tired of aviation paraphernalia will appreciate the **Dayton Art Institute,** 456 Bel-

1974: The Cleveland Indians' "10-cent Beer Night" game devolves into an ugly riot.

monte Park N. In addition to some contemporary pieces, the institute displays Peter Rothermel's magnificent *King Lear*, created in 1858. Some smaller collections of Asian, African, European, and Native American art are also on display. (From Jefferson St., take a left on Monument Ave. Cross the bridge and turn right onto Riverview Ave., then head left on Belmont Park N. ☎937-223-5277; www.daytonartinstitute.org. Open M-W and Sa-Su 10am-4pm, Th-F 10am-8pm. Free.) At **Sunwatch Prehistoric Indian Village,** 2301 W. River Rd., archaeologists have reconstructed an Indian village that dates back about 500 years. (From Edwin C. Moses Blvd. downtown, turn left and proceed southwest past the I-75 exits, and take a left onto W. River Rd. ☎937-268-8199; www.sunwatch.org. Open Tu-Sa 9am-5pm, Su noon-5pm. $5, seniors and ages 6-17 $3.)

🍴🛏 FOOD AND ACCOMMODATIONS. For standard Irish fare, try **Flanagan's Pub ❶,** 101 E. Stewart St., near Broad St., where a lunch crowd gathers to enjoyburgers and beer. (☎937-228-5776. Burgers $3-5. Drafts $1.50. Open M-Sa 11am-2:30am. AmEx/D/MC/V.) **Smokin Bar-B-Que ❶,** 200 E. 5th St., makes the entire intersection smell like hickory smoke—your mouth will water from blocks away. (☎937-586-9790. Burgers $4. Open M-Th 10:30am-9pm, F-Sa 10:30am-4am. AmEx/D/DC/MC/V.) Some of the cheapest rooms in town are at the **Econolodge ❸,** 2140 Edwin C. Moses Blvd., just west of Exit 51, on I-75. (☎937-222-9929. Continental breakfast included. Rooms from $50-60. MC/V.)

◄ DETOUR
ENGLEWOOD METROPARK
Instead of continuing straight on Rte. 48/U.S. 40, head east on U.S. 40. The "East Park" entrance is on your left.

Englewood provides a shade relief off the road before the route heads into the fairly natureless Indiana stretch. The park has three small waterfalls and several miles of flat hiking trails, as well as fishing and canoeing. Maps are available inside the park. (☎937-278-2623; www.metroparks.org. Open daily 8am-sunset.)

🏁 APPROACHING RICHMOND: 44 MILES
Head north on **Rte. 48,** which joins **U.S. 40 W** for a brief stretch, and then take a left at the **National**

Road/U.S. 40 sign. Fill up your tank at the Indiana border; there are few gas stations for the next 28 mi.

The Hoosier State
INDIANA
Welcomes You!

RICHMOND

Ohio may have been the beginning of the Midwest, but you'll know you've reached America's heartland when you come to Richmond. Flat and full of chain establishments and wide open road, the "gateway to eastern Indiana" feels like America in all its small-town glory. Check out the next **Madonna of the Trail,** 22nd St. and U.S. 40, at the entrance to Glen Miller Park. A stop at the **Indiana Football Hall of Fame,** 815 N. A St., might evoke fond (or perhaps not-so-fond) memories of high-school gym class. Eight high-school football coaches mortgaged their homes in the 1970s to buy this building, which honors the best players and coaches from Indiana high schools. The walls of the aging museum's rooms are filled with photographs of high-school teams, hall of fame members, and winners of the college scholarships that the center awards each year. (☎765-966-2235. Open M-F 10am-4pm. $1, ages 14-16 $0.50.)

Richmond residents lament the loss of most local eateries, but it's still possible to catch a bite of local flavor. Low-key and mellow **Little Sheba's ❶,** 175 Fort Wayne Ave., is known for sandwiches with quirky names. Try the "Stupid Idiot" or the "Dr. Jetmore's Flamethrower." (☎765-962-2999. Spaghetti and other pastas with salad and garlic bread F-Sa $7-9. Open M-Th 11am-9pm, F-Sa 11am-10pm. AmEx/D/MC/V.) Expect little decor and a simple menu at the unpretentious **Main Street Diner ❶,** 1600 E. Main St. (U.S. 40), where a chef salad bowl is $6 and omelettes are $3-6. The Main St. Dagwood ($4) is sure to fill you up. (☎765-962-7041. Open M-Sa 6:30am-1:30pm, Su 8am-1:30pm. Cash only.) The **Holiday Motel ❷,** 3004 E. Main St., offers comfortable rooms at the right price. (☎765-962-3561. 21+. Singles $27; doubles $47. AmEx/D/MC/V.)

🏁 APPROACHING CENTERVILLE: 5 MILES
Continue on **U.S. 40** for another 5 mi. toward Centerville. The stretch of U.S. 40 from Richmond to Knight-

NATIONAL ROAD

stown, including Centerville and Cambridge City, forms part of Indiana's **"Antique Alley."**

CENTERVILLE. As you enter Centerville, venture to **Webb's Antique Mall,** 200 W. Union St., which hosts an 85,000 sq. ft. collection of antique merchants with multiple booths filled with signs, plates, books, clothing, records, furniture, and everything else that you didn't know you needed. (At the traffic light, turn right on Morton St., then take a left on Union St. ☎ 765-855-5551; www.webbsantiquemalls.com. Open daily Mar.-Nov. 8am-6pm; Dec.-Feb. 9am-5pm.) The antique mall is also home to the **Station Stop Restaurant ❶,** a good place for a quick lunch in a cozy setting that fits right in with all the other knickknacks around. (☎ 765-855-5551. Sandwiches $4-6. Pie $3. Cash only.) **The Shake Shoppe ❶,** 215 E. Main St. (U.S. 40) is a also good stop for lunch, a scoop of ice cream ($1-2) or $3 candy. (☎ 765-855-1514. M-F 10am-9pm, Sa 11am-9pm, Su 2-8pm. Cash only.) Rooms are small but clean at the **Richmond Motel ❷,** U.S. 40 E, 5 mi. from Richmond. (☎ 765-855-5616. Breakfast included. Singles $34; doubles $45. MC/V.) The **City View Motel ❷,** 5149 U.S. 40, 4 mi. from Richmond, also has small and affordable rooms. (☎ 765-962-2943. Singles $30; doubles $38. AmEx/D/MC/V.)

⚐ APPROACHING CAMBRIDGE CITY: 10 MILES
Continue west on **U.S. 40** toward Cambridge City, where U.S. 40 becomes **E. Main St.**

CAMBRIDGE CITY. Six native sisters of Cambridge City helped turn pottery into an American art form. A small collection of their vaunted work is on display at the **Museum of Overbeck Art Pottery,** 33 W. Main St. (U.S. 40), in the Cambridge City Public Library. (☎ 765-478-3335. Open M-Sa 10am-noon and 2-5pm, or by appointment. Free.)

⚐ APPROACHING NEW CASTLE: 22 MILES
Take **U.S. 40** to **Rte. 3 N,** and follow it for about 8 mi.

NEW CASTLE. New Castle is home to the **Indiana Basketball Hall of Fame,** 1 Trojan Ln., which glorifies hoops and the best Hoosiers to play the game, including Larry Bird, George McGinnis, and Kent Benson. (Turn right at the Shell Station; the museum is on the left. ☎ 765-529-1891. Open Tu-Sa 10am-5pm and Su 1-5pm. $4, seniors $3, children $2.) The **New Castle Inn ❷,** 2005 S. Memorial Dr., has big rooms and a great location. (☎ 765-

529-1670. Singles $31; doubles $36. AmEx/D/DC/MC/V.) The **Steve Alford All-American Inn ❸,** 21 E. Executive Dr., off Memorial Dr. (Rte. 3), offers cozier rooms than many neighboring chains. (☎ 765-593-1212. Singles $55. MC/V.)

⚐ APPROACHING INDIANAPOLIS: 48 MILES
Take **Rte. 3 S** to **U.S. 40 W.** When you reach the beltway, head north on **I-465** to the exit for **I-70.** Follow I-70 W to **Exit 88A/Ohio St.**

INDIANAPOLIS

Surrounded by flat farmland, Indianapolis feels like a model Midwestern city. Locals shop and work all day among downtown's skyscrapers before returning to sprawling suburbia. Life ambles here—until May, that is, when 250,000 spectators invade the city and the road warriors of the Indianapolis 500 claim the spotlight. Though Indianapolis has been known in the past as "Napville," and "India No Place," Indiana's sprawling state capital resolved to build a cultural infrastructure that would outlast the seasonal boom of the Indianapolis 500.

VITAL STATS

Population: 860,000

Visitor Info: Indianapolis Convention and Visitors Association, 1 RCA Dome, Ste. 100. (☎317-639-4282; www.indy.org). Open M-F 8:30am-5pm.

Internet Access: Indianapolis/Marion County Interim Public Library, 202 N. Alabama St. (☎317-269-1700). Open June-Aug. M-Tu 9am-9pm, W-F 9am-6pm, Sa 9am-5pm; Sept.-May M-Tu 9am-9pm, W-F 9am-6pm, Sa 9am-5pm, Su 1-5pm. Free.

Post Office: 125 W. South St. (☎317-464-6804). Open M 7:30am-5pm, Tu-F 8am-5pm, Sa 8am-noon. **Postal Code:** 46204.

▤ GETTING AROUND

While most attractions are within several miles of the city center, you should be prepared to drive. Indianapolis does not lend itself well to walking. The downtown, called **Center City,** is marked by a dense cluster of skyscrapers. **Washington St.** divides the city north-south; **Meridian St.** divides it east-west. The two meet just south of Monument Circle

TO SPEEDWAY  (4mi)
TO INDIANAPOLIS MUSEUM OF ART (2.5mi)
16th St.
TO  (.5mi)
TO INDIANAPOLIS CHILDREN'S MUSEUM (1.5mi)
TO (4mi),
BROAD RIPPLE (6mi)

15th St.
14th St.
Ransom St.
13th St.
Drake St.
12th St.
Cora St.
Smith St.
15th St.
14th St.
13th St.
12th St.

Crispus Attucks Museum
11th St.
10th St.
9th St.
St. Clair
Walnut St.

St. Joseph St.
Sahm St.

MASSACHUSETTS AVENUE ARTS DISTRICT
St. Clair

Walker Theater
North St.
CANAL WALK DISTRICT

North St.

Indiana University Purdue University Indianapolis
Michigan St.
Allegheny St.
Vermon St.
Tippecanoe St.
New York St.

Military Park

University Park

Michigan St.

New York St.
Miami St.

Ohio St.

Market St.
Monument Circle
State House
Court St.
Hilbert Circle Theater
City Market
Market St.
Washington St.

NCAA Hall of Champions
Eiteljorg Museum
Washington St.
Indiana State Museum
Maryland St.

WHITE RIVER STATE PARK
Washington Ave.

TO INDIANAPOLIS ZOO (3.4mi)

Circle Center Mall

WHOLESALE DISTRICT

Pearl St.

Chesapeake St.
Georgia St.
RCA Dome
Jackson Pl.
Conseco Fieldhouse

Union Station

South St.
Henry St.
Merrill St.

South St.
Empire St.
Henry St.

Louisiana St.
Lord St.

Stevens St.

McCarty St.
Wyoming St.
Ray St.

McCarty St.
Buchanan St.

N

0 200 yards
0 200 meters

Prospect St.

Morris St.
Kansas St.
Sanders St.

Morris St.

Indianapolis

▲ ACCOMMODATIONS
All Nations Bed and Breakfast, **1**
Indiana State Fair Campgrounds, **8**
Motel 6, **2**
Methodist Tower Inn, **4**

🍎 FOOD
Bazbeaux Pizza, **10**
Don Victor's, **13**
Shapiro's, **12**
Union Jack Pub, **3** & **7**

🎭 NIGHTLIFE
The Jazz Cooker, **9**
Patio, **6**
The Slippery Noodle, **11**
Vogue, **5**

NATIONAL ROAD

downtown. **I-465** circles the city, while **I-70** cuts through the city east-west. Outside the beltway (I-465) both east and west of the city, **Washington St.** is **U.S. 40.** Metered parking is abundant almost everywhere along Indianapolis's wide, straight streets, including downtown and near Circle Centre Mall.

SIGHTS

EITELJORG MUSEUM OF AMERICAN INDIANS AND WESTERN ART. Near the entrance to the White River State Park, this museum features an impressive collection of art depicting the Old West, including works by Georgia O'Keeffe and Frederick Remington. The museum also highlights a collection of Native American artifacts. (*500 W. Washington St. ☎317-636-9378; www.eiteljorg.org. Open May-Sept. M 10am-5pm, Tu-Sa 10am-5pm, Su noon-5pm.; Oct.-Apr. Tu-Sa 10am-5pm, Su noon-5pm. Tours daily 1pm. $7; seniors $6, students, and ages 5-17 $4.*)

INDIANA STATE MUSEUM. This huge museum lets visitors follow the "Hoosier Heritage Trail" through a series of in-depth exhibits on Indiana history—so in-depth, in fact, that it starts off with the birth of the earth, and wraps up by exploring what the future might hold for the Hoosier State. (*650 W. Washington St. ☎317-232-1637; www.indianamuseum.org. Open M-Sa 9am-5pm, Su 11am-5pm. $7, seniors $6.50, children $4. IMAX $8.50/$7/$6.*)

INDIANAPOLIS MUSEUM OF ART. It may be far from downtown, but the Indianapolis Museum of Art showcases American, African, and Neo-Impressionist works along with nature trails, a historic home, botanical gardens, a greenhouse, and a theater. (*4000 Michigan Rd. ☎317-923-1331; www.ima-art.org. Open Tu-W and F-Su 10am-5pm, Th 10am-9pm. $7, seniors $5, college students and children free. Th free.*)

CRISPUS ATTUCKS MUSEUM. Chronicling the history of the Crispus Attucks High School, formed in 1927 to educate African-Americans in Indianapolis, the understated Crispus Attucks Museum is worth a visit. (*1140 Dr. Martin Luther King, Jr. St., on the Crispus Attucks Middle School campus. Look for the visitor entrance; enter the office and ask to be let in. ☎317-226-2432. Open M-F 10am-2pm. Free.*)

RACING ATTRACTIONS. The country's passion for fast cars peaks during the **500 Festival,** an entire month of parades and hoopla leading up to race day at the **Indianapolis Motor Speedway.** The festivities begin with time trials in mid-May and culminate with "Gentlemen, start your engines" of the **Indianapolis 500** the Sunday before Memorial Day. Tickets for the race go on sale the day after the previous year's race and usually sell out within a week. In quieter times, buses full of tourists drive around the 2½ mi. track at tamer speeds. (*4790 W. 16th St., off I-465 at the Speedway Exit. ☎317-481-8500; www.indy500.com. Track tours daily 9am-4:40pm. $3, ages 6-15 $1.*) The **Speedway Museum,** at the south end of the infield, includes **Indy's Hall of Fame** and a collection of cars that have tested their mettle on the track over the years. (*☎317-484-6747. Open daily 9am-5pm. $3, ages 6-15 $1.*)

OTHER SIGHTS. A majestic stained-glass dome graces the marble interior of the **State House.** (*200 W. Washington St., between Capitol and Senate St. ☎317-233-5293. Open M-F 8am-4pm. 1hr. tours 1hr. by appointment only. Free.*) No sports fan should miss the **NCAA Hall of Champions,** which covers all 28 college sports. Relive the passion of the Final Four in the March Madness Theater and try your hand at hitting a buzzer beater in the 1930s-style gymnasium. (*700 W. Washington St. ☎317-916-4255; www.ncaa.org/hall_of_champions/global/home.htm. Open June-Aug. M-Sa 10am-5pm, Su noon-5pm; Sept.-May Tu-Sa 10am-5pm, Su noon-5pm. $3, students $2, under 5 free.*) Animal lovers should check out the seemingly cageless **Indianapolis Zoo,** which holds a large dolphin pavilion with a new underwater observation dome. A unique enclosed desert exhibit allows desert animals like meerkats to be available for viewing year round. (*1200 W. Washington St. ☎317-630-2001; www.indyzoo.com. Open June-Aug. M-Th 9am-5pm, F-Su 9am-6pm; Sept.-Oct. M-Th 9am-4pm, F-Su 9am-5pm; Nov. daily 9am-4pm; Dec. daily noon-9pm. $13.50, seniors and ages 2-12 $8.50.*)

FOOD

Ethnic food stands, produce markets, and knick-knack vendors fill the spacious **City Market,** 222 E. Market St., a renovated 19th-century building. (☎317-634-9266; www.indianapoliscitymarket.com. Open M-F 6am-4pm, Sa 11am-3pm.) Moderately priced restaurants cluster in Indianapolis's newly constructed **Circle Centre,** 49 W. Maryland St. (☎317-681-8000). **Massachusetts Ave.** is home to some of the liveliest restaurants and bars in town; in the summer, outdoor patios fill with diners every night.

Bazbeaux Pizza, 334 Massachusetts Ave. (☎317-255-5711), and 832 E. Westfields Blvd. Indianapolis' favorite pizza. Construct your own masterpiece ($6) from 53 toppings. Pizza from $11. Open M-Th and Su 11am-10pm, F-Sa 11am-11pm. MC/V. ❷

Don Victor's, 1032 S. East St. (☎317-637-4397). The best Mexican food in town. Burrito and enchilada platters ($6), as well as more authentic dishes such as *menudo* and *pozole*. The 2-person Fiesta Platter ($21) is a good way to sample various dishes. Open M-Th and Su 11am-9pm, F-Sa 11am-10pm. ❷

Shapiro's, 808 S. Meridian St. (☎317-631-4041; www.shapiros.com). Head south on Meridian St. past South St. When it diverts onto Madison St., take a quick right on Henry St., and then a quick left to get back on Meridian St. Over 100 years of practice have given this kosher-style deli ample time to turn food production into a science. Huge deli sandwiches $7-10. Open daily 6:30am-8pm. AmEx/D/DC/MC/V. ❷

Union Jack Pub, 6225 W. 25th St. (☎317-243-3300), and 924 Broad Ripple Ave. (☎317-257-4343). From I-465, take Exit 16A and head east on Crawfordsville Rd. Turn left onto High School Rd., then right onto 25th St. This cozy spot showcases loads of race memorabilia, rows of drivers' helmets, and an Indy racecar. Chicago-style pizzas $16-20. Open M-W 11am-11pm, Th-Sa 11am-midnight, Su noon-11pm. MC/V. ❸

🏠 ACCOMMODATIONS

Budget motels line the I-465 beltway, 5 mi. from downtown. Make reservations a year in advance for the Indy 500.

Motel 6, 6330 Debonair Ln. (☎317-293-3220), at Exit 16A off I-465. Clean, pleasant rooms with A/C and cable TV. Singles $35; doubles $40. ❷

All Nations Bed and Breakfast, 2164 N. Capitol Ave. (☎317-923-2622), ½ mi. north of downtown. Large, tasteful rooms with themes stemming from various countries offer luxurious accommodations at a reason-

able price. Each room has a private bath and some have sofabeds. Rooms $75-100. ❹

Methodist Tower Inn, 1633 N. Capitol Ave. (☎317-925-9831). A short walk from Monument Circle. Large rooms with TV and A/C and is the cheapest option near downtown. Singles $81; doubles $86. AmEx/D/MC/V. ❹

Indiana State Fair Campgrounds, 1202 E. 38th St. (☎317-927-7520). 170 sod-and-gravel sites, mostly packed with RVs. To get close to nature, go elsewhere. Especially busy during the state fair. Primitive sites $16, with full hookup $25. D/MC/V. ❶

🎵 ENTERTAINMENT

The **Walker Theatre,** 617 Indiana Ave., used to house the headquarters of African-American entrepreneur Madame C.J. Walker's beauty enterprise. Today, the landmark hosts arts programs, including the monthly **Jazz on the Avenue.** (☎317-236-2099. Tours M-F 9am-5pm. Jazz every 4th F 6-10pm. $10.) The **Indianapolis Symphony Orchestra** performs from late June to August in the **Hilbert Circle Theater** on Monument Circle. (☎317-639-4300; www.indyorch.org. Box office open M-F 9am-5pm, Sa 10am-2pm.) Basketball lovers watch the **Pacers** hoop it up at the **Conseco Fieldhouse,** 125 S. Pennsylvania St. (☎317-917-2500. Tickets from $10.) The WNBA's **Indiana Fever** take over in the summer. (☎317-239-5151. Tickets $8-90.) Football's **Colts** hit the gridiron at the **RCA Dome,** 100 S. Capital Ave. (☎317-239-5151).

🍸 NIGHTLIFE

Somewhat bland by day, the **Broad Ripple** area, 6 mi. north of downtown at College Ave. and 62nd St., transforms into a center for nightlife after dark. Partiers fill the clubs and bars and spill out onto the sidewalks until about 1am on weekdays and 3am on weekends.

The Jazz Cooker, 925 E. Westfield Blvd. (☎317-253-2883; www.thejazzcooker.com). Heats up when the Steve Ball Trio begins jamming. The attached **Monkey's Tale** is a nice, relaxed bar. F-Sa live music 7-10pm. Bar open M-Sa until 3am, Su until 12:30am. AmEx/D/DC/MC/V.

Vogue, 6259 N. College Ave. (☎317-255-2828). By far the hottest club in town. Hosts national acts like Pink and Jurassic 5. Shows 8pm; call for schedule. Cover

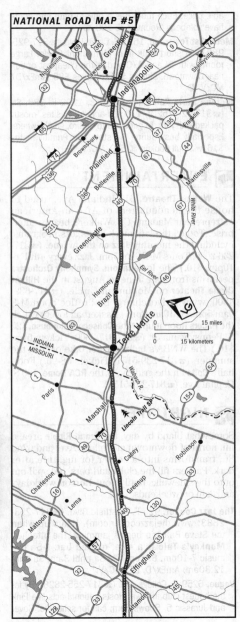

NATIONAL ROAD MAP #5

$3-5; F ladies free. Open W 9pm-3am, F-Sa 10pm-3am. MC/V.

The Slippery Noodle, 372 S. Meridian St. (☎317-631-6974), downtown. The oldest bar in Indiana and one of the country's best venues for nightly live blues. 21+. Cover Th-Sa $5. Open M-F 11am-3am, Sa 12:30pm-3am, Su 4pm-12:30am. AmEx/D/DC/MC/V.

◪ APPROACHING TERRE HAUTE: 66 MILES

Head west on **Washington St.;** it becomes **U.S. 40** after crossing the beltway (I-465). U.S. 40 becomes **Wabash Ave.** toward Terre Haute.

TERRE HAUTE

Terre Haute was once called the "crossroads of America" by virtue of its existence at the junction of U.S. 40 and U.S. 41. Deceptively large, the city today retains only a shadow of its former importance. Industries power the area close to downtown, but outlying areas have become a little more run-down.

VITAL STATS

Population: 60,600

Visitor Info: Terre Haute Chamber of Commerce, 630 Wabash Ave., Ste. 105 (☎812-232-2391). Open M-F 8am-4pm.

Internet Access: Vigo County Public Library, One Library Sq. (☎812-232-1113). Open M-Th 9am-9pm, F 9am-6pm, Sa 9am-5pm, Su 1-5pm. Free.

Post Office: 70 Rose Ave. (☎812-232-9133). Open M-F 7:30am-4:30pm, Sa 8:30am-noon. **Postal Code:** 47803.

▤ GETTING AROUND. U.S. 40 and **U.S. 41** (locally **3rd St.**) intersect in downtown Terre Haute. U.S. 40 heads east-west, while U.S. 41 heads north-south. The **Wabash River** forms the western border of town.

◪ SIGHTS. During the school year, the **Children's Science and Technology Museum,** 523 Wabash Ave., takes its weather-related exhibits on the road to give children hands-on science education. During the summer, those exhibits, along with the museum's permanent collection of interactive teaching tools, are on display. (☎812-235-5548. Open Tu-Sa 9am-4pm. $3, children $2.50.) Quite a bit of self-glorification goes on at the **Clabber Girl Museum,**

900 Wabash Ave., at 9th St., which waxes poetic about Hulman & Co.'s wonderful and benevolent deeds for the American home-maker. Demonstrations show the baking powder manufacturing process, while an eclectic collection of old telephones and telegraphs, an early 20th-century kitchen, World War II-era posters, and goods at the "country store" also await the baking powder connoisseur. (☎812-478-7223; www.clabbergirl.com. Open M-F 10am-6pm, Sa 9am-3pm. Free.) **St. Mary-of-the-Woods College's Providence Center,** 1¾ mi. from Terre Haute, is a beautiful wooded site for spiritual retreats. A simple **labyrinth** provides a tranquil setting for prayer, reflection, and walking meditation. (From Rte. 150, turn left at the sign for St. Mary-of-the-Woods College. The main entrance is on the right. ☎812-535-4531. Open daily sunrise-sunset. Free.)

 FOOD AND ACCOMMODATIONS. For a refreshing change from chain restaurants, try **Gerhardt's Bierstube ❸,** 1724 Lafayette Ave., where German music and beer complement menu items like *Wiener Schnitzel* ($13) and *kassler rip-pchen* (pork chop steamed in beer) for $10. (From downtown, head north on 7th St. to Lafayette Ave. and turn right. ☎812-466-9249. Open Tu-Th 11am-2pm and 4-9pm, F 11am-2pm and 4-10pm, Sa-Su 4-10pm. MC/V.) The **Coffee Cup Family Restaurant ❶,** 1512 Lafayette Ave. and 2919 S. 3rd St., serves typical American fare, but at better prices than the rest of town. (☎812-466-7200. Sandwiches $3-5. Open daily 6am-9pm. MC/V.) At **Coffee Break ❶,** 663 Wabash Ave., perk up with a selection of coffee and espresso drinks ($1-3.50), or enjoy a sandwich ($6) in a cushy chair. (☎812-478-3975; www.coffeebreakevents.com. Open M-F 7am-5:30pm. MC/V.) Clean and cheap, the ▣**Midtown Motel ❷,** 400 S. 3rd St., is comfortable, spacious, and close to both U.S. 40 and the center of town. (☎812-232-0383. Singles $44; doubles $50. AmEx/D/MC/V.) The **Woodbridge Motel ❷,** 4425 Wabash Ave., is a great alternative to the chain motels a few miles away. (☎812-877-1571. Rooms $35. D/MC/V.)

◪ **APPROACHING MARSHALL: 15 MILES**
Hop on **U.S. 40 W.** 1¼ mi. past **3rd St.,** there is an unla-beled curve—follow it around to the left and merge with **I-70.** Rejoin U.S. 40 in about 2½ mi. 14½ mi. from Terre Haute, turn left at the sign for **Marshall/Historic National Road.**

Set your clocks back 1hr. once you cross the border into Illinois—you are in the Central Time Zone.

MARSHALL
The small town of Marshall is home to the **Lincoln Trail State Park,** perfect for a bit of relaxation on a sunny day. This 1000-acre rustic, wooded park offers flat hiking through American beech woods, fishing, picnicking, and inexpensive camping around a 146-acre lake. (From the center of town, head south on Rte. 1 for 3 mi. ☎217-826-2222. No swimming.)

The **Lincoln Trail Restaurant ❷,** 16895 E. 1350th Rd., is a convenient spot for a hot meal while you're exploring the park or camping. Their omelettes ($5) are exceptional, and homemade pastries ($2) are perfect snacks for the road. (Follow the signs from inside the park. ☎217-826-8831. Open daily 6am-8pm. AmEx/D/MC/V.) An alternative to the busy chain eateries by the interstate, **Bishop's Cafe ❶,** 710 Archer Ave., caters to a crowd that prefers home cooking. Locals come for the baskets ($6), which include a sandwich with fries and slaw. Drivers can grab an early breakfast here (served until 10:30am) before pushing westward. (☎217-826-9933. Breakfast $3-5. Open M-Sa 5am-1:30pm, Su 6am-2pm. Cash only.) For a good night's rest, interesting **Archer House ❹,** 717 Archer Ave., at Rte. 1, is the oldest hotel in Illinois. Built in 1841, this B&B was originally a stage-coach stop on the National Road and has beautifully-furnished suites with private baths. (☎217-826-8023. Rooms $75. Cash only.) An affordable option with clean, simple rooms is the **Lincoln Motel ❷,** 1002 N. 2nd St. (☎217-826-3040. Singles $30; doubles $39. MC/V.)

◪ **APPROACHING LERNA: 37 MILES**
Head out of town on **Archer Ave.;** it rejoins **U.S. 40.** On your way, notice the stone arch bridge (c. 1828) about ½ mi. west of town, remarkably still in use. Con-

tinuing west, follow the sign for the **National Road (Rte. 121)** heading into Greenup. Take **Rte. 130 N** to Lerna.

LERNA. Lerna's only worthy attraction is the **Lincoln Log Cabin State Historic Site,** 400 S. Lincoln Hwy. Rd. At this "living history" museum and working 1840s farm, actors play members of the Lincoln family and their wealthy neighbors, the Sargeants. They maintain the farm using techniques from the period, and answer questions in character. (☎217-345-6489; www.lincolnlogcabin.org. Open Apr.-Oct. W-Sa and Su 9am-5pm; Nov.-Mar. until 4pm. Free.)

▼ **APPROACHING EFFINGHAM: 22 MILES**
Following **Rte. 121,** you'll pass over a covered wooden bridge spanning the Embarras (say "umbraw") River. It was built in the late 1990s to the specifications of one originally built by Abe and Thomas Lincoln. After the bridge, make a left at the dead end, which dumps you back on **U.S. 40** and becomes **W. Fayette St.** in Effingham.

EFFINGHAM

Effingham moves at an easy, slow pace, though it is surprisingly cosmopolitan for its rural location. Locals reside in the proud shadow of a 198 ft. tall steel cross erected on the outskirts of town.

VITAL STATS

Population: 12,400

Visitor Info: Convention and Visitors Bureau, 210 E. Jefferson St. (☎217-342-5310 or 800-772-0750), inside City Hall, at the corner of 3rd St. Open M-F 8am-noon and 1-5pm.

Internet Access: Helen Matthes Library, 100 E. Market Ave. (☎217-342-2464). Take N. 3rd St. from Fayette Ave. and turn left at the sign. Open M-Th 10am-7pm, F 10am-5pm, Sa 10am-1pm. Free.

Post Office: 210 N. 3rd St. (☎217-342-6016), 3 blocks north of Fayette St. Open M-F 7:30am-5:30pm, Sa 8:30am-12:30pm. **Postal Code:** 62401.

▣ **GETTING AROUND.** Main east-west streets in Effingham include **Fayette Ave. (U.S. 40), Jefferson Ave.,** and **Washington Ave.,** each of which is lined with shops and restaurants. Jefferson Ave. runs one-way east between Banker St. and 3rd St., while Washington Ave. runs one-way west. The main north-south thoroughfare through the center of town is **3rd St. (Rte.**

45). At the western edge of downtown is **Keller Dr.** (Henrietta St. on the other side of Fayette Ave.), another main drag. There is free 2hr. street parking in the downtown area; most other establishments have parking lots.

◪ **SIGHTS.** Effingham has its share of quirky roadtrip attractions. The 20-odd pristine Corvettes at the ◪**Mike Yager Mid-America Designs Corvette Museum,** 1 Mid America Pl., off Rte. 45, is enough to make any car buff drool. The walls are almost as fun as the cars; the airplane hangar-sized garage is set up with 1950s- and 60s-style wall decorations and storefronts. Ask about **Funfest,** at which thousands of cars descend on the town for some serious partying. The **Volkswagon Funfest** takes place the first weekend of June, and the much larger **Corvette Funfest** takes place around the third weekend of September. (Take N. 3rd St.; the museum is on the right. ☎217-347-5591; www.mamotorworks.com. Open M-Sa 8am-5pm; occasionally closed to rotate cars. Free.) It's visible from U.S. 40 on the way out of town, but for the full experience, you have to drive up close to the ◪**Cross at the Crossroads,** off Pike Ave. On the outskirts of Effingham, this gargantuan 181-ton steel cross stands a whopping 198 ft. tall and 113 ft. across, surrounded by black stone monuments representing each of the ten commandments. Quite simply, this "world's biggest" has to be seen to be believed. (Take W. Fayette St. out of downtown, turn left on Raney St., then right on Pike Ave. ☎217-347-2846; www.crossusa.org. Visitors center open daily 9:30am-8pm.) If you need a break from motel television channels, the old Art Deco **Heart Theatre,** at the corner of 3rd and Jefferson St., shows movies in the center of town. (☎217-342-5555; www.effinghamheart.com. Movies generally M-Th 7pm, F-Sa 4:15 and 7pm. $6, students, seniors, and before 6pm $5.)

▚▐ **FOOD AND ACCOMMODATIONS.** Some of the best grub in town is served at **El Rancherito ❷,** 1313 Keller Dr. Huge portions of sizzling hot, authentic, and non-greasy Mexican food is guaranteed to stuff and satisfy even the hungriest roadtripper. Try a skillet of mouth-watering fajitas ($9.25-10) or one of the combination dinners ($7)—*relleno,* burrito, or enchilada. (Take W. Fayette Ave. heading west out of downtown, and turn right on Keller Dr. ☎217-342-4753. Lunch $3.50-6. Open M-Th and Su 11am-10pm, F-Sa 11am-11pm. D/MC/V.) For a plethora of steak varieties ($8-14) in an unpretentious setting, stop by **Niemerg's Steak House ❸**, 1410 W. Fayette Ave. A smattering of other options include fish dinner specials ($7-9), eggs ($2), and the special "country-fried chicken dinner" ($6). Try to save room for a slice of homemade pie ($2) for dessert. (☎217-342-3921. Open daily 6am-2am. AmEx/D/MC/V.)

Roadtrippers looking for a night's lodgings in Effingham should try the **Paradise Inn ❷**, 1000 W. Fayette Ave. (U.S. 40), which offers standard, well-maintained rooms in a convenient location. (☎217-342-2165. Singles $36; doubles $46. D/MC/V.) The cheapest rates in town are at the **Abe Lincoln Motel ❷**, 1108 W. Edgar Ave. (☎217-342-4717. Singles $34; doubles $39.)

■ APPROACHING VANDALIA: 33 MILES
Follow **U.S. 40** out of Effingham. The giant Effing ■ **cross** is to the left after you turn right off Henrietta St. and onto the **Old National Road.** U.S. 40 turns right in Vandalia; proceed straight at the "National Road" sign for 1 block on **Gallatin Ave.** until you reach the **Madonna of the Trails Statue.** This statue marks the original end of the 591 mi. National Road from Cumberland, MD, to Vandalia, IL.

VANDALIA
It's hard to believe that tiny Vandalia was once the capital of Illinois. Relics of this golden age exist, however, in the form of the majestic state house. The **Vandalia Statehouse State Historic Site,** 315 W. Gallatin St., at the corner of 3rd St., is where Abraham Lincoln first served as a state representative; this imposing white-painted brick building was the Illinois State House from 1836-1839. The simply furnished interior is open for tours. Across the street is tiny **Lincoln Park,** complete with a statue of a young Abraham Lincoln sitting on a bench. (☎618-283-1161. Open Mar.-Oct. W-Su 9am-5pm; Nov.-Feb. W-Su until 4pm. Suggested donation $2, under 17 $1.) Two blocks from the State House, the **Evans Public Library,** 215 S. 5th St., houses the life mask of Abraham Lincoln made by Leonard Volk. While a reproduction of Volk's mask is on display at the State House, the real

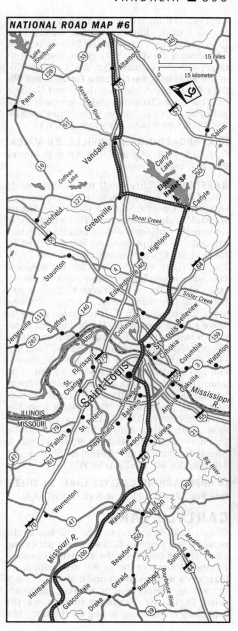

NATIONAL ROAD MAP #6

(and eerie) thing sits in the "Lincoln Room" at the back of the library. (☎618-283-2824. Free Internet access. Open M-Th 9am-7pm, F-Sa 9am-5pm.) Nearby, you can quench your thirst with an originally-flavored Coke ($1.75) at the **Something Special Soda Fountain and 50s Cafe ❶**, on the corner of 4th St. and Gallatin St. You'll need to suck hard to get their thick milkshakes ($3.75) through the straw. (☎618-283-1810. Open M-Sa 9am-5pm. MC/V.)

◪ APPROACHING GREENVILLE: 20 MILES
Follow **U.S. 40 W** out of town. Turn right to go north on **Rte. 127,** toward Greenville.

GREENVILLE. This small town, the county seat of Bond County, is home to the picturesque Greenville College. Worth a visit is the **Richard W. Bock Sculpture Museum.** This museum, in Greenville College's oldest building, houses around 300 sculptures and 500 sketches by Richard Bock, who worked closely with Frank Lloyd Wright. (☎618-664-6724; www.greenville.edu/campus/bock. Follow signs for Greenville College. The museum is on College St. just before the intersection with Spruce St. Open by appointment only. Free.) The sizable menus at **Annie's Home Cookin' ❶**, 110 N. 2nd St., come with a warning that everything is homemade. Their half-pound hamburgers ($2.75-5) will satisfy any burger lover, and the Southwest chicken sandwiches ($3.50) are a good, light alternative. It's not the fastest kitchen in town, but the food is worth the wait. (Near the corner of 2nd St. and College St., 1 block from the Bock Museum. ☎618-664-0128. Open daily 6am-9pm. Cash only.) Affordable rooms can be found at the **Budget Host Inn ❷**, 1525 S. State Rte. 127, near U.S. 40. (☎618-664-1950. Singles $43; doubles $48. AmEx/D/MC/V.)

◪ APPROACHING CARLYLE LAKE: 21 MILES
Take **Rte. 127 S** for 21 mi. until you reach Carlyle.

CARLYLE LAKE

Carlyle Lake is second only to Chicago as the most-visited place in Illinois. State parks and campsites operated by the US Army Corps of Engineers encircle the 26,000-acre man-made lake, each with its own combination of camping, sailing, fishing, hunting, boating, and swimming facilities. Strong winds make for especially challenging sailing on the lake. The small county seat of Carlyle, at the southwest corner of the lake, serves park users.

VITAL STATS

Population: 3400

Visitor Info: Carlyle Lake Visitors Center, 801 Lake Rd. (☎618-594-5253), east off Rte. 127. Open in summer daily 10am-6pm; hours vary in winter.

Internet Access: Case-Halstead Library, 571 Franklin St. (☎618-594-5210), at 6th St. Open M-Th noon-8pm, F-Sa 9am-2pm. Free.

Post Office: 1080 Fairfax St. (☎618-594-3322), at 11th St. Open M-F 8:30am-5pm, Sa 9am-11pm.
Postal Code: 62231.

☍ GETTING AROUND. Carlyle Lake occupies three counties; primary access points include those near the towns of **Carlyle, Keyesport,** and **Boulder.** Eldon Hazlet State Park is 4 mi. north of Carlyle off **Rte. 127.** The **Dam West, Dam East,** and **McNair** areas lie just north of the town of Carlyle, while the **Coles Creek** facility and **South Shore State Park** both lie on the southeastern shore of the lake between Carlyle and Boulder.

In the town of Carlyle, Rte. 127 runs north-south through downtown as **12th St.;** getting to most places requires turning off Rte. 127 before this point, so check out directions in advance to avoid having to backtrack. All north-south streets in town are numbered, from 1st St. in the east to 24th St. in the west. **U.S. 50** joins with Rte. 127 and runs north-south above **Franklin St.,** joining it on the way out of town. Most restaurants and services are concentrated along Franklin St. or **Fairfax St.,** one block north.

⚠ OUTDOORS. Eldon Hazlet State Park attracts families for summer lakeside getaways. Park day-use is free, and the lake is stocked with farm-reared fish. Hunting is permitted in winter. (From Rte. 127, head east on Hazlet Park Rd. ☎618-594-3015. Visitors center open M-F 8am-noon and 12:30-4pm. Swimming pool $3.)

▓▐ FOOD AND ACCOMMODATIONS. Windows at the **Dockside Diner ❷,** 5 Resort Dr., offer a good view of the boats moored in the nearby lake. With a log-cabin exterior, the diner was built to accommodate the growing tourist crowd. The varied dinner menu includes a reuben or "dockside dog" ($6), entrees like homemade lasagna ($10), and the "Jack Daniels Steak," which tops the menu at $16. (☎618-594-4657. Open M-Th and Su 6am-9pm, F-Sa 6am-10pm. AmEx/D/MC/V.) For a nice dinner that won't empty your wallet, try **Patrick's ❸**, 870 Franklin St., at 9th St., an Irish pub slightly more elegant than most. Dishes like pork chops ($11), prime rib ($13-22), and baked roughy ($12.50) fill the menu. (☎618-594-8115. Open M-W and Su 4-9pm, Th 11am-2pm and 4-9pm, F 11am-2pm and 4-10pm, Sa 4-10pm. AmEx/D/MC/V.)

Campsites ❶ are mostly scattered near the lake, with a few abutting the lakefront directly; these offer shady trees and gorgeous views across the water. Only 65 sites allow reservations; the rest are first come, first served. Sites are often booked on summer weekends in June and July. (☎618-594-3015. Sites $7, with hookup $11; cabins $35. Cash only.) Two campgrounds here are run by the US Army Corps of Engineers. **Coles Creek ❶** has 148 campsites, a beach, showers, and laundry. (Sites $12-24. Cash only.) **McNair ❶**, has 32 sites and a beach. (Sites $12. Cash only.) For indoor accommodations, green is in at the **Motel Carlyle ❷**, 570 12th St., from the light green doors to the dark green carpet. (☎618-594-8100. Singles $48; doubles $52. MC/V.)

◤ APPROACHING ST. LOUIS: 50 MILES
Take **I-64/U.S. 50 W**; at the large highway split, stay left for **I-55/I-70/I-64/St. Louis.** Take the exit for the **Martin Luther King, Jr. Memorial Bridge** toward downtown St. Louis.

 In Missouri, minor state routes have letters, not numbers. From your cell phone, you can contact the State Highway Patrol at ☎ 55.

ST. LOUIS

Lying directly south of the junction of the Mississippi, Missouri, and Illinois rivers, St. Louis gained prominence in the 18th and 19th centuries as the US expanded west. The Gateway Arch rises above the sprawling city, framing it against the river that nurtured its growth. Combining Southern hospitality, Midwestern pragmatism, and Western optimism, St. Louis offers a mix of fast-paced urban life and relaxation.

VITAL STATS

Population: 348,000

Visitor Info: Visitors Center, 308 Washington Ave. (☎314-241-1764; www.explorestlouis.com), at Memorial Blvd. Open daily 9:30am-4:30pm. Branch inside **America's Convention Center** (☎314-342-5160), at the corner of 7th St. and Washington Ave. Open M-F 8:30am-4pm, Sa 9am-2pm.

Internet Access: St. Louis Central Library, 1301 Olive St. (☎314-241-2288). Open M 10am-9pm, Tu-F 10am-6pm, Sa 9am-5pm. Free.

Post Office: 1720 Market St. (☎314-436-4114). Open M-F 8am-8pm, Sa 8am-1pm. **Postal Code:** 63101.

▐ GETTING AROUND

U.S. 40/I-64 runs east-west through the center of the entire metropolitan area, while **I-70, I-44 (U.S. 50),** and **I-55** all head downtown from other outlying areas. Downtown is defined as the area east of **Tucker Blvd.** between **Martin Luther King** and **Market St.,** which divides the city north-south. Numbered streets parallel the Mississippi River, with addresses increasing to the west. St. Louis' neighborhoods are well defined, with attractions and restaurants concentrated in several distinct areas. The historic **Soulard** district borders the river south of downtown. **Forest Park** and **University City,** home to **Washington University** and old, stately homes, lie west of downtown. **The Hill,** an Italian neighborhood, lies south of these. St. Louis is very much a driving town; parking comes easily along the wide streets, and traffic moves quickly along interstates.

◉ SIGHTS

JEFFERSON EXPANSION MEMORIAL. The ▨**Gateway Arch**—the nation's tallest monument at 630 ft.—towers gracefully over all of St.

NATIONAL ROAD

Louis and southern Illinois, serving as a testament to the city's historical role as the "Gateway to the West." The ground-level view is impressive, and the arch frames downtown beautifully from the Illinois side, but the 4min. tram ride to the top in quasi-futuristic elevator modules is more fun. Waits are shorter in mornings and evenings, but are uniformly long on Saturday. Beneath the arch, the underground **Museum of Westward Expansion** adds to the appeal of the grassy park complex known as the **Jefferson Expansion Memorial.** The museum radiates in a semi-circle from a statue of a surveying Jefferson, celebrating the Louisiana Purchase and Westward expansion. *(☎ 314-982-1410; www.gatewayarch.com. Open daily in summer 8am-10pm; in winter 9am-6pm. Free. Tram $10, ages 13-16 $7, ages 3-12 $3.)*

DOWNTOWN. It's a strike either way at the **International Bowling Museum and Hall of Fame** and the **St. Louis Cardinals Hall of Fame Museum,** which share a home across from Busch Stadium. The mildly amusing bowling museum traces the largely speculative history of the sport and allows visitors to roll four free frames, while the baseball museum exhibits memorabilia of St. Louis hardball. *(111 Stadium Plaza. ☎ 314-231-6340. Open Apr.-Sept. daily 9am-5pm, game days until 6:30pm; Oct.-Mar. Tu-Sa and Su 11am-4pm. $7.50, ages 5-12 $4; both $8.50/$7.50.)* Historic **Union Station,** 1 mi. west of downtown, houses a shopping mall, food court, and entertainment center in a magnificent building that was once the nation's busiest railroad terminal. *(At 18th and Market St. ☎ 314-421-6655; www.stlouisunionstation.com. Open M-Sa 10am-9pm, Su 10am-6pm.)* "The Entertainer" lives on at the **Scott Joplin House,** just west of downtown near Jefferson Ave., where the ragtime legend tickled the ivories and penned classics from 1900 to 1903. The 45min. tour delves into Joplin's long-lasting influence on American music. *(2658 Delmar Blvd. ☎ 314-340-5790. Tours Apr.-Oct. M-F every 30min. 10am-4pm, Su noon-5pm; Nov.-Mar. M-F every 30min. 10am-4pm, Sa 10am-4pm, Su noon-5pm. $2.50, ages 6-12 $1.50.)*

 DID YOU KNOW? St. Louis was the site of the "demonic possession" that inspired William Peter Blatty to write *The Exorcist* in 1971.

SOULARD. In the early 1970s, the city proclaimed this area, bounded by I-55 and 7th St., a historic district due to its former populations of German and Eastern European immigrants, many of whom worked in the breweries. Today, it is an attractive, tree-lined neighborhood packed with 19th-century brick townhouses. The district surrounds the bustling **Soulard Farmers Market,** known for its fresh, inexpensive produce. *(730 Carroll St. ☎ 314-622-4180. Open W-Sa 7am-7pm; hours vary among merchants.)* At the end of 12th St., the **Anheuser-Busch Brewery,** the largest brewery in the world, produces the "King of Beers." The 1½hr. tour includes a glimpse of the famous Clydesdales, two beer samples, and dozens of fun factoids for both beer- and history-lovers. *(1127 Pestalozzi St., at 12th and Lynch St. Take bus #40 "Broadway" south from downtown. ☎ 314-577-2626; www.budweisertours.com. Tours June-Aug. M-Sa 9am-5pm, Su 11:30am-5pm; Sept.-May M-Sa 9am-4pm, Su 11:30am-4pm. Free.)* Open since 1959, the internationally acclaimed 79-acre **Missouri Botanical Garden** thrives north of Tower Grove Park on grounds which once belonged to entrepreneur Henry Shaw. The Japanese Garden and numerous fountain plazas are guaranteed to soothe the weary traveler. *(4344 Shaw Blvd. From downtown, take I-44 W. ☎ 800-642-8842; www.mobot.org. Open June-Aug. M 9am-8pm, Tu-Su 9am-5pm; Sept.-May daily 9am-5pm. Free tours daily 1pm. $8, under 12 free.)*

FOREST PARK. Forest Park contains three museums, a zoo, a 12,000-seat amphitheater, a grand canal, and countless picnic areas, pathways, and flying golf balls. Marlin Perkins, the late host of TV's *Wild Kingdom,* turned the **St. Louis Zoo** into a world-class institution, with black rhinos, Asian elephants, and a top-notch penguin and puffin habitat. *(☎ 314-781-0900; www.stlzoo.com. Open daily June-Aug. 8am-7pm; Sept.-May 9am-5pm. Free. Children's Zoo $4, under 2 free.)* Atop **Art Hill,** a statue of King Louis IX, the city's namesake, raises his sword in front of the **St. Louis Art Museum,** which contains works by Rothko, Pollock, and a number of other great modern artists. *(☎ 314-721-0072; www.slam.org. Open Tu-Th and Sa-Su 10am-5pm, F 10am-9pm. Tours W-Sa and Su 1:30pm. Free. Special exhibits usually $10, students and seniors $8, ages 6-12 $6. F free.)* The **Missouri History**

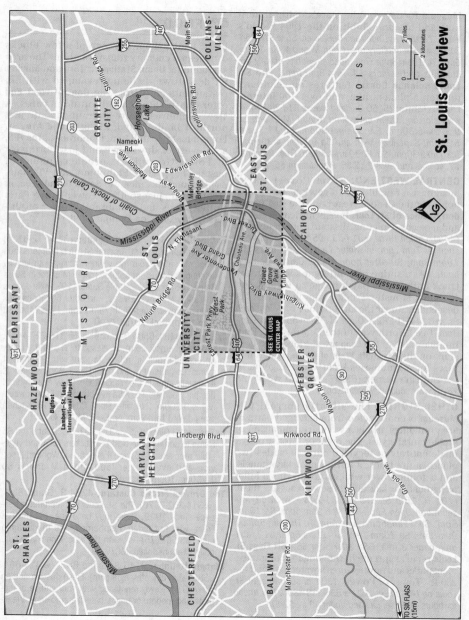

St. Louis Overview

Museum focuses on the state's cultural heritage and has an exhibit on the 1904 World's Fair. *(Located at Lindell and DeBaliviere St. ☎314-454-3124; www.mohistory.org. Open M and W-Su 10am-6pm, Tu 10am-8pm. Free. Special exhibits usually $5, students and seniors $4. Tu 4-8pm free.)* The **St. Louis Science Center** features an Omnimax theater, a planetarium, and over 700 interactive exhibits. *(5050 Oakland Ave. ☎314-289-4444; www.slcs.org. Open early June to Aug. M-Th and Sa 9:30am-5:30pm, F 9:30am-9:30pm, Su 11:30am-5:30pm; Sept.-May M-Th and Sa 9:30am-4:30pm, F 9:30am-9:30pm, Su 11:30am-4:30pm. Free. Omnimax $7, seniors and ages 2-12 $6. Planetarium $6/$5.)*

CENTRAL WEST END. From Forest Park, head east a few blocks to gawk at the Tudor homes of the Central West End. The vast **Cathedral Basilica of St. Louis** boasts intricate ceilings and mosaics depicting Missouri church history. *(4431 Lindell Blvd. ☎314-533-0544. Open daily in summer 7am-7pm; in winter 7am-sunset. Tours M-F 10am-3pm, Su after noon Mass. Call to confirm hours.)* At a shrine of a different sort, monster truck enthusiasts pay homage to **Bigfoot**, the "Original Monster Truck," who lives with his descendants near the airport. *(6311 N. Lindbergh St. ☎314-731-2822. Open M-F 9am-6pm, Sa 9am-3pm. Free.)* Northwest of the Central West End, the sidewalks of the **Loop** are studded with gold stars on the **St. Louis Walk of Fame**, which features local luminaries from Maya Angelou to Ike and Tina Turner. *(6504 Delmar Blvd. ☎314-727-7827; www.stlouiswalkoffame.org.)*

OTHER SIGHTS. The slightly surreal **City Museum** is constructed from salvaged parts of area buildings and is a wonderful amalgam of architectural styles. The outdoor "Monstrocity," made entirely of recycled parts, includes two planes, a fire truck, a ferris wheel, sky tunnels, and a gothic tower with gargoyles. It's a killer playground for kids and those who act like them. *(701 N. 15th St. ☎314-231-2489; www.citymuseum.org. Open Sept.-May W-F 9am-5pm, Sa 10am-5pm, Su 11am-5pm; June-Aug. Tu-Th 9am-5pm, F 9am-1am, Sa 10am-1am, Su 11am-5pm. $12, children under 3 free. F-Sa after 5pm $8.)* **Six Flags St. Louis** reigns supreme in the kingdom of amusement parks and now features a water park and the 230 ft. "Tower of Power." *(30min. southwest of St. Louis on I-44 at Exit 261. ☎636-938-4800. Call ahead for hours. $39, seniors and under 48 in. $24.)*

FOOD

In St. Louis, the difference of a few blocks can mean a culinary transformation. The area surrounding **Union Station,** at 18th and Market St. downtown, is being revamped with hip restaurants and bars. The **Central West End** offers coffeehouses and outdoor cafes. A slew of impressive restaurants awaits just north of Lindell Blvd. along **Euclid Ave.** St. Louis's historic Italian neighborhood, **The Hill,** southwest of downtown and just northwest of Tower Grove Park, produces plenty of pasta. Cheap Thai, Philippine, and Vietnamese restaurants spice the **South Grand** area, at Grand Blvd., just south of Tower Grove Park. Coffee shops and restaurants cluster on **University City Loop,** on Delmar Blvd.

☒ **City Diner,** 3139 South Grand. (☎314-772-6100; www.citydiner.us), at Arsenal St. This fabulous 50s diner will satisfy your every diner craving with kitschy ketchup and mustard bottles. Try the Mushroom Swiss Burger ($6) or the Vegetable Burrito ($9), while dozens of Marilyn Monroes, Elvises, and other 50s icons look on in approval. Open M-Th 7am-11pm, F-Sa 24hr., Su 7am-10pm. AmEx/D/MC/V. ❸

☒ **Blueberry Hill,** 6504 Delmar Blvd. (☎314-727-4444; www.blueberryhill.com), at Westgate St., on the Loop. An eclectic rock 'n' roll restaurant with 9 different rooms. Call ahead to find out if Chuck Berry is playing; he usually jams in the "Duck Room" 1 W each month. Big, juicy burgers $5. F-Sa live bands and some weeknights 9:30pm. 21+ after 9pm. Cover $4-15. Kitchen open daily 11am-9pm. AmEx/D/MC/V. ❸

In Soo, 8423 Olive Blvd. (☎314-997-7473), at 82nd St. Home to some of the best pot stickers ($5) and vegetable moo-shu ($16) you'll ever taste. Wonderful service and even better food. Open M and W-Su 11:30am-10pm. Cash only. ❸

Ted Drewes Frozen Custard, 4224 S. Grand Blvd. (☎314-352-7376). The St. Louis summertime experience since 1929. There may be a line, but the Fox Treat—with hot fudge, raspberries, and macadamia nuts ($3.50-5.75)—is worth the wait. Open May-Aug. daily 11am-midnight. MC/V. ❶

Mangia Italiano, 3145 S. Grand Blvd. (☎314-664-8585; www.dineatmangia.com). Fresh pasta made on site ($5-9). Newly renovated with your choice of intimate and modern or bright, cafe-like ambience. Week-

St. Louis Center

▲ ACCOMMODATIONS
Babler State Park, **17**
Congress Airport Inn, **1**
Huckleberry Finn Youth Hostel
(HI-AYH), **15**
The Mayflair, **10**
The Royal Budget Inn, **8**

● FOOD
Amighetti's, **14**
Arcelia, **13**
Blueberry Hill, **5**
City Diner, **18**
Imo's, **3**
In Soo, **2**
Kaldi's Coffeehouse and
Roasting Company, **6**
Mangia Italiano, **19**
Ted Drewes Frozen
Custard, **20**

■ NIGHTLIFE
AMP, **12**
The Big Bang, **9**
Clementine's, **16**
Mississippi Nights, **7**
Novak's, **11**
The Pageant, **4**

VENICE

Mississippi River

Mississippi River

Broadway

North Florissant St.

Cass Ave.

Natural Bridge Ave.

Spring Ave.

Grand Blvd.

70

Page Blvd.

Goodfellow Blvd.

Page Blvd.

THE LOOP

Big Bend Blvd.

Dr. Martin Luther King Dr.

Delmar Blvd.

Washington Pl.

DeBaliviere Ave.

Union Blvd.

Kingshighway Blvd.

Skinker Blvd.

Forest Park Pkwy.

Lindell Blvd.

Forest Park

St. Louis
Art Museum

Missouri
History
Museum

Walk of Fame

St. Louis
Zoo

St. Louis
Science Center

Municipal
Opera

CENTRAL
WEST END

Oakland Ave.

McCausland Ave.

Clayton Ave.

Manchester Ave.

Mackland Ave.

Hampton Ave.

THE HILL

Southwest Ave.

Wilson Ave.

Bischoff Ave.

Marconi Ave.

Shaw Blvd.

Missouri
Botanical
Garden

Tower Grove Park

Magnolia Ave.

Kingshighway

Vandeventer Ave.

Chouteau Ave.

Forest Park Ave.

Cathedral
Basilica
of St. Louis

Powell Hall

St. Louis
Black
Repertory

Fox Theatre

Scott Joplin
House Museum

Washington Ave.

Olive St.

Pine St.

Market St.

DOWNTOWN

Union Station

Savvis Center

Busch
Stadium

Cardinals
Hall of Fame

Bowling
Museum

Gateway Arch

Museum
of Western
Expansion

Casino
Queen

President
Casino

Edward
Jones
Dome

LACLEDE'S
LANDING

Sullivan Blvd.

Lafayette
Park

Compton Hill
Reservoir Park

Russell Blvd.

Park Ave.

Lafayette Ave.

Gravois Ave.

Jefferson Ave.

Grand Blvd.

Shenandoah Ave.

Arsenal St.

SOULARD

Soulard Farmers Market

Anheuser-
Busch
Brewery

Lynch St.

Broadway

7th St.

Cherokee St.

Chippewa St.

Mississippi River

Arsenal St.

Chippewa St.

Watson Rd.

Hampton Ave.

Jamieson Ave.

Lansdowne Ave.

Landstowne Ave.

Wabash Ave.

Big Bend Blvd.

WEBSTER
GROVES

Repertory
Theatre of
St. Louis

Laclede Station Rd.

Murdoch Ave.

Mackenzie Rd.

Chippewa St.

Gravois Ave.

Morganford Rd.

TO GRANT'S
FARM (2mi)

TO SIX
FLAGS
(25mi)

TO ▲ (15mi)

TO + ST. LOUIS INTL. AIRPORT,
BIGFOOT ♣ (10mi)

1 mile

1 kilometer

NATIONAL ROAD

end nights jazz.. Open M-F 10:30am-10pm and Sa-Su 12:30-10:30pm. AmEx/D/MC/V. ❷

Amighetti's, 5141 Wilson Ave. (☎314-776-2855; www.amighettis.com), at Marconi St. Probably the city's most famous sandwich joint, serving the "special sandwich" (small $3.40, large $5.50) for 3 generations. Open M 8am-3pm, Tu-F 7:30am-6pm, Sa 7:30am-6pm; in summer Tu-F until 7pm. MC/V. ❷

Arcelia, 2001 Park Ave. (☎314-231-9200; www.arcelias.com). Big combination platters ($5.50-10.25) feature usual suspects like burritos and enchiladas, but this bustling Mexican eatery also offers more authentic dishes such as *mole de pollo* and *menudo* ($8). Open Tu-Th 11am-2pm and 5-10pm, F-Sa 11am-10pm, Su noon-9pm. AmEx/D/DC/MC/V. ❸

Imo's, 8437 Olive Blvd. (☎314-997-1444), and other numerous locations. Imo's makes the city's favorite St. Louis-style thin crust pizza (from $7) and receives shout-outs from rap superstar Nelly. Lasagna $5.50. Open M-Th 10am-midnight, F-Sa 11am-1:30am, Su 10am-midnight. AmEx/DC/MC/V. ❷

Kaldi's Coffeehouse and Roasting Company, 700 De Mun Ave. (☎314-727-9955), in Clayton. From downtown, take I-64 W to Exit 34B: Clayton Rd./Skinker Blvd. Proceed straight to Clayton Rd., and take a right onto De Mun Ave. An eclectic crowd sips espresso drinks and munches on fresh baked goods and veggie delights. Hummus plate $4.50. Open daily 7am-11pm. AmEx/D/MC/V. ❶

ACCOMMODATIONS

Most budget lodging is far from downtown. For chain motels, try **Lindbergh Blvd. (U.S. 67)** near the airport, or the area north of the I-70 junction with I-270 in Bridgeton, 5 mi. beyond the airport. **Watson Rd.** near Chippewa is littered with cheap motels. Take I-64 or I-44 W to Hampton Blvd. S, turn right on Chippewa St., and cross the River des Peres to Watson Rd. (Rte. 366).

Huckleberry Finn Youth Hostel (HI-AYH), 1908 S. 12th St. (☎314-241-0076), at Tucker Blvd. Take Broadway/7th St. S toward Soulard, turn right just past Geyer Ave. onto Allen Ave., and then take a right on 12th St.; it's on the right. A full kitchen, free parking, and proximity to Soulard bars make this hostel a great option. Dorms $20. Cash only. ❶

Congress Airport Inn, 3433 N. Lindbergh Blvd. (☎314-739-5100), 1 mi. south of I-70. This clean, no-frills

hotel puts you close to the Loop. Singles $50; doubles $55. AmEx/D/DC/MC/V. ❸

Royal Budget Inn, 6061 Collinsville Rd. (☎618-874-4451), in Fairmont City, Illinois, 20min. east of the city, off I-55/I-70 at Exit 6. Clean rooms with a Taj Mahal flavor make for a fun budget option. Key deposit $2. Rooms $40. Cash only. ❷

The Mayfair, 806 St. Charles St. (☎314-421-2500). Constructed at the height of the Jazz Age, the Mayfair has hosted famous musicians and politicians from Irving Berlin to Harry Truman. Standard rooms are spacious, with marble-topped sinks and soft beds. Rooms from $109; suites from $119. AmEx/D/DC/MC/V. ❺

Dr. Edmund A. Babler Memorial State Park (☎636-458-3813 or 877-422-6766), 20 mi. west of downtown, just north of Hwy. 100. Tent and RV sites and a shower house. Tent sites $8; RV sites with electrical hookup $14. Cash only. ❶

ENTERTAINMENT

Founded in 1880, the **St. Louis Symphony Orchestra** is one of the country's finest. **Powell Hall,** 718 N. Grand Blvd., holds concerts for the orchestra. (☎314-534-1700. Performances late Sept. to early May Th-Sa 8pm, Su 3pm. Box office open late May to mid-Aug. M-F 9am-5pm; mid-Aug. to late May M-Sa 9am-5pm and before performances. Tickets $10-95, students half-price.)

St. Louis offers theatergoers many options. The outdoor **Municipal Opera,** also known as the "Muny," presents hit musicals on summer nights in Forest Park. (☎314-361-1900. Box office open June to mid-Aug. daily 9am-9pm. Tickets $8-54.) Productions are also regularly staged by the **St. Louis Black Repertory,** 634 N. Grand Blvd. (☎314-534-3807), and by the **Repertory Theatre of St. Louis,** 130 Edgar Rd. (☎314-968-4925). The **Fox Theatre,** 537 N. Grand Blvd., was originally a 1930s movie palace, but it now hosts Broadway shows, classic films, and country and rock music stars. (☎314-534-1111. Open M-Sa 10am-6pm, Su noon-4pm. Tours Tu, Th, Sa 10:30am. Tu $5, Th and Sa $8; under 12 $3. Call for reservations.) **Metrotix** (☎314-534-1111) has tickets to most area events.

Gambling is permitted on the river for those over 21. The **President Casino on the Admiral** floats below the Arch on the Missouri side. (☎314-622-1111 or 800-772-3647; www.presidentscasino.com. Open M-Th 8am-4am, F-Su 24hr. Entry $2.) On the Illinois side, the **Casino**

Queen lays claim to "the loosest slots in town." (☎618-874-5000 or 800-777-0777; www.casino-queen.com. Open daily 9am-7am.) The **St. Louis Cardinals** swing away at **Busch Stadium.** (☎314-421-3060. Tickets $9-55.) The **Rams** toss the pigskin at the **Edward Jones Dome.** (☎314-425-8830. Tickets $40-49.) The **Blues** hockey team plays at the **Savvis Center** at 14th St. and Clark Ave. (☎314-843-1700. Tickets from $15.)

🎤 NIGHTLIFE

The music scene rules the night in St. Louis. The *Riverfront Times* (free at many bars and clubs) and the *Get Out* section of the *Post-Dispatch* list weekly entertainment. For a summary of the gay night scene find a copy of *EXP*, available in many shops and clubs. The *St. Louis Magazine*, published annually, lists seasonal events. St. Louis offers **Laclede's Landing,** a collection of restaurants, bars, and dance clubs housed in 19th-century industrial buildings north of the Arch on the riverfront. In the summer, bars take turns sponsoring "block parties," with food, drink, music, and dancing in the streets. (☎314-241-5875. Generally open 9pm-3am, with some places open for lunch and dinner.) Other nightlife hot spots include the bohemian **Loop** along Delmar Blvd., **Union Station,** the strip of gay bars and clubs along **Manchester St.** and **Vandeventer St.,** and the gay-friendly **Soulard** district.

Novak's, 4121 Manchester St. (☎314-531-3699; www.novaksbar.com). This favorite of the St. Louis GLBT community attracts gay and straight alike with mega-amplified karaoke (W, F, Su), extensive patio seating, and plenty of games. Whether you're dancing or just chilling, Nancy Novak might take your picture. Open M, W, and F-Sa 4pm-3am, Tu 4pm-midnight, Th 4pm-2am, Su noon-3am. AmEx/D/MC/V.

Amp, 4199 Manchester Ave. (☎314-652-5267), at Boyle St. Leather couches, local art, and psychedelic music screens make this a terrific place to chill in the wee hours. Proprietors Rusty and Niel welcome all. Ask for the house cosmopolitan. Open M-F 6pm-3am, Sa 8pm-3am. AmEx/D/MC/V.

The Big Bang, 807 N. 2nd St. (☎314-241-2264), at Laclede's Landing. Dueling pianists in a massive brick room lead the enthusiastic crowd in a rock 'n' roll sing-along. Cover F-Sa $6. Open M-Th and Su 7pm-3am, F-Sa 5pm-3am. AmEx/D/DC/MC/V.

The Pageant, 6161 Delmar Blvd. (☎314-726-6161). Line up early for a spot in the fantastic 33,000 sq. ft. nightclub and major concert venue, which hosts national acts from The Roots to AFI. Call for ticket and cover prices. 18+. Doors usually open 7pm. The classy **Halo Bar** is open daily 7pm-3am. AmEx/MC/V.

Mississippi Nights, 914 N. 1st St. (☎314-421-3853), at Laclede's Landing. St. Louis's favorite place for music since 1979 has a history of bringing in the best national acts of all genres. Cover from $6. Doors usually open 7 or 8pm. AmEx/D/MC/V.

Clementine's, 2001 Menard St. (☎314-664-7869), in Soulard. St. Louis's oldest gay bar (established in 1978) also houses the crowded **Oh My Darlin' Cafe.** Open M-F 10am-1:30am, Sa 8am-1:30am, Su 11am-midnight. AmEx/D/MC/V.

🚗 APPROACHING WASHINGTON: 66 MILES

Head west out of St. Louis on **I-44/U.S. 50.** I-44 entrance ramps can be accessed from **Tucker Blvd.** or **S. Jefferson Ave.** south of downtown. From I-44, take **Exit 251** for **Rte. 100 W.** Curve to the right and continue straight at the light onto Rte. 100 toward Washington. After about 8 mi., turn right at the light onto **S. Point Rd.,** which becomes **5th St.;** cross Rte. 47 and head into the center of town on **3rd St.**

WASHINGTON

Washington and its neighbor Hermann were both settled in the early- to mid-19th century by Catholic German families; the area's greenery and rolling hills reminded them of Germany's Rhine Valley. Today, some industry in Washington continues, including the manufacture of corncob pipes at the Missouri Meerschaum Company. Washington is also home to the **Washington Historical Society Museum,** at the corner of 4th and Market St. Aside from various exhibits and archives on the area, the museum houses the Four Rivers Genealogical Society. (☎636-239-0280; www.washmohistorical.org. Open Mar.-Dec. Tu-Sa 10am-4pm. Free.)

The best place in town to eat is **Cowan's ❷,** 114 Elm St., which feels like a very large living room. The spaghetti and meatball dinner ($8) comes bottomless with salad and toast. Finish up with a wedge of homemade pie for $3. (Take Market St. to 2nd St., and turn left. ☎636-239-3213. Sandwiches $5.50-7. Open M and W-Sa 6am-8pm, Su 6am-7pm.) **La Dolce Vita Restaurant ❷,** 4 Lafayette St., offers a selection of light sandwiches and salads ($7.50), as well as glasses of wine ($4).

Outdoor seating is plentiful. (At the corner of Front St. and Lafayette St., by the riverfront. ☎636-390-8180; www.ladolcewinery.com. Open M-Th 11am-6pm, F-Su 11am-8pm.) In the same building, you'll find two lovely rooms at **La Dolce Vita ❺**, a beautiful B&B overlooking the Missouri River. (☎636-390-8180. Rooms $110.)

◥ APPROACHING HERMANN: 27 MILES
Take **Jefferson St.** to **Rte. 100 W.** Rte. 100 becomes **1st St.** before joining with **Rte. 19** and turning south onto **Market St.**

HERMANN

Surrounded by Missouri wineries, Hermann depends heavily on tourism for revenue; tourist-oriented development of this picturesque valley (centered on the area's German heritage) has made it the "B&B capital of Missouri." The artifacts on display at the **Historic Hermann Museum,** 312 Schiller St., chronicle the history of early German immigrants in this area, and the **Deutsch Market** inside sells works by local artisans. (Take Market St. to 4th St., and turn left; it's on the corner of 4th in the old German School. ☎573-486-2017; www.historichermann.com. Open Apr.-Oct. Tu-Su 10am-4pm. $12.) On the way out of Hermann is the **Stone Hill Winery,** the oldest and most lauded winery in Missouri. Stone Hill lets visitors tour the grounds and caves where the wine ages, and tours relate the history of the winery and the story of Hermann. Visitors can taste samples of wine and grape juice at the end of the tour. (☎573-486-2221 or 800-909-9463; www.stonehillwinery.com. Open M-Th 8:30am-7pm, F-Sa 8:30am-8pm, Su 10am-6pm. $1.50.)

On Rte. 100, the **Rivertown Restaurant ❷,** 222 E. 1st St., offers ravenous roadtrippers old-fashioned cooking amidst kitschy trinkets, antique kitchenware, and assorted old trophies. Daily lunch specials are under $6, and dinner plates, like roast beef, go for about $7. (☎573-486-3298. Sandwiches $1.60-5. Steaks $8-12. Open M 7am-2pm, Tu-Sa 7am-8pm, Su 7am-1pm. MC/V.) To find a B&B, call or stop by the Hermann **visitors center,** 312 Market St. (☎573-486-2744 or 800-932-868; www.hermannmo.com. Open Apr.-Oct. M-Sa 9am-5pm, Su 11am-4pm; Nov.-Mar. M-Sa 9:30am-4pm, Su 11am-4pm.) The **Hermann Motel ❸,** 112 E. 10th St., provides pleasant rooms with TVs. (☎573-486-3131. Continental breakfast included. Rooms $42-70. AmEx/D/MC/V.)

◥ APPROACHING JEFFERSON CITY: 43 MILES
From Hermann, **Rte. 100** meanders along the scenic Missouri River, passing numerous wineries. It does test driving skills a bit, running up and down roller-coaster hills; exercise caution. 42 mi. from Hermann, the road rejoins **U.S. 50** near the town of Linn; turn right here to head west on U.S. 50. U.S. 50 becomes the **Whitton Expwy.** in downtown Jefferson City.

JEFFERSON CITY

As one might expect from the capital of Missouri, Jefferson City is refreshingly relaxed and low-key. Because there's virtually no industry, government is the main business in town, and it operates at a slow pace—the Missouri legislature has been known to spend seven years on the passage of a bill. Situated above the Missouri River, the tall capitol building is the focal point of downtown.

VITAL STATS

Population: 40,000

Visitor Info: Jefferson County Convention and Visitors Bureau, 213 Adams St. (☎573-632-2820 or 800-769-4183; www.visitjeffersoncity.com), just north of High St. Open M-F 8am-5pm.

Internet Access: Missouri River Regional Library, 214 Adams St. (☎573-634-2464), off High St. Open M-Th 9am-9pm, F-Sa 9am-6pm, Su 1-5pm.

Post Office: 131 W. High St. (☎573-636-4186), across from the capitol building. Open M-F 8am-4:30pm, Sa 9am-noon. **Postal Code:** 65101.

▛ GETTING AROUND. Jefferson City is surprisingly easy to navigate. **Whitton Expwy. (U.S. 50)** runs east-west just south of the downtown area. **McCarty St., High St.,** and **Main St./Capitol Dr.** are north of U.S. 50 and run parallel to it. North-south streets through downtown are named for the first six U.S. Presidents, though unfortunately not in order. **Missouri Blvd.** (Bus. U.S. 50), a major thoroughfare, runs parallel to U.S. 50 west of downtown and then north-south within the downtown area itself. **U.S. 54** runs north-south through the entire area. Street parking is available and sometimes metered.

◙ SIGHTS. The ▣**Missouri State Capitol Building** overlooks the Missouri River from High St. Informative tours explain Missouri's government and showcase the plush legislative floor when the legislature is not in session. The highlight of the tour is a visit to the Thomas Hart Benton mural on the 3rd fl., which sheds considerable light on Missouri's history. (☎573-751-4127. Open daily 8am-5pm. Tours every hr. M-F 8am-11am and 1-4pm. Free.) Near the capitol, the **Missouri Governor's Mansion,** 100 Madison St., allows visitors to tour the 1st fl. of the first family's home, a stately brick mansion on a bluff overlooking the Missouri River. (☎573-751-7929; www.missourimansion.org. Tours by appointment only. Reserve 24hr. in advance. Free.) Five centuries worth of veterinary medicine are on display at the **Veterinary Museum,** 2500 Country Club Dr. Visitors can learn about instruments, animal specimens, diseases, and surgery. (Take U.S. 50 W to the exit for Rte. 179; turn right at the bottom of the ramp, and take the next right onto Country Club Dr. ☎573-636-8737. Open M-F 9am-4pm, Sa by appointment. Free.)

FOOD AND ACCOMMODATIONS. The usual assortment of chain restaurants is laid out along Missouri Blvd. If you do nothing else while passing through town, indulge in a few scoops of freshly made ice cream at ■**Central Dairy** ❶, 610 Madison St., a long-standing Jefferson City landmark. It may take you a few minutes to decide on one of their 40 flavors, but the waffle cones ($2) are kind to the wallet. (☎573-635-6148. Open M-Sa 8am-6pm, Su 10am-6pm. Cash only.) The great Greek options at **Johnny's Pizza and Steak House** ❷, 2102 Missouri Blvd., are a fine alternative to most of the boulevard's other offerings. A filling *souvlaki* wrap with pork or chicken is $7. (☎573-635-3737. Open M-Th 11am-10pm, F-Sa 11am-11pm AmEx/D/DC/MC/V.) **Bone's Lounge** ❸, 210 Commercial Ave., is really two restaurants in one; the carpeted ground floor serves hearty meals, while a bar dominates upstairs with neon decorations, plastic furnishings, and a young clientele. (☎573-636-8955. Sandwiches $4-7. Open daily 11am-1am. AmEx/MC/V.)

Most accommodations, including an assortment of chain motels, lie on U.S. 54 just south of downtown. Unusually comfortable beds, clean rooms, and powerful showers at the ■**Budget Inn** ❷, 1309 Jefferson St., make for a pleasant stay in "Jeff City." (☎573-636-6167. Singles $34; doubles $39. AmEx/D/MC/V.) A more-upscale hotel in this area is the **Hotel DeVille** ❸, 319 W. Miller St., which

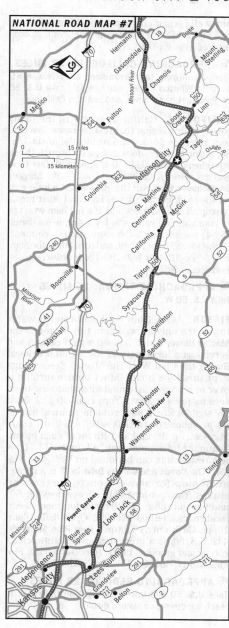

NATIONAL ROAD MAP #7

NATIONAL ROAD

has well-furnished rooms in a range of sizes. (☎573-636-5231; www.devillehotel.com. Rooms from $65. AmEx/D/MC/V.)

◤ APPROACHING CALIFORNIA: 23 MILES
From downtown, take **Broadway** or **Jefferson St.** south to **Whitton Expwy.** and turn left; take **U.S. 50 W.** Push that pedal down, and head for California.

CALIFORNIA. California is one of the many towns in this region that feature attractive centers, river overlooks, and residential areas. U.S. 50, unfortunately, does not pass through those stretches of town. U.S. 50 is lined with fast food and gas stations, but the good stuff—like **Burger's Smokehouse ❶**, 32819 Rte. 87—is just a little way off the road. Burger's cures ham and other meats to ship all around the world. If a full ham won't fit in your car, you can settle for a simple sandwich ($3-4) packed with the same signature meat. (Take Rte. 87 S for 2¾ mi. and turn left at the sign. ☎573-796-3134 or 800-203-4244; www.smokehouse.com. MC/V.)

◤ APPROACHING TIPTON: 15 MILES
Take **U.S. 50 W.**

TIPTON. Aside from the 8-ball-topped water tower, the only attraction in tiny Tipton is the **Maclay Home,** which housed a girls' school and served as a headquarters for a Union general during the Civil War. The Maclay descendants kept this 1858 home intact before turning it over to a nonprofit foundation that now oversees its preservation. (Turn right off U.S. 50 at the sign for Rte. B and cross the railroad tracks; it's just ahead on the left. ☎660-433-2101. Tours May-Oct. on the 2nd and 4th Su of each month 2-4pm, or by appointment. $3, under 13 $1.) A few restaurants can be found on U.S. 50 in Tipton. The **Cones and Coneys Drive-in ❶** is a convenient stop for above-average burgers and shakes. The foot-long chili cheese dogs ($2.50) and banana splits ($3.50) make for good, cheap road snacks. (☎660-433-9922. Open daily 10am-10pm. Cash only.) Tipton's **Twin Pine Motel ❷**, 442 U.S. 50, is a great deal, with large, clean rooms and gracious hosts. (☎660-433-5525. Singles $38-47; doubles $55. AmEx/MC/V.)

◤ APPROACHING SEDALIA: 25 MILES
Take **U.S. 50** into town. Turn right on **Ohio Ave.** to reach the downtown historic district.

SEDALIA
Sedalia is a quiet, well-to-do city with a graceful and relaxed air. Home of the Missouri State Fair for 11 days every August, Sedalia livens up, welcoming city and country dwellers numbering over 345,000, who fill the town's hotels, bars, and restaurants.

VITAL STATS

Population: 20,000

Visitor Info: The Chamber of Commerce, 600 E. 3rd St. (☎660-826-2222; www.visitsedaliamo.com.), inside the reconstructed Katy Depot. Open June-Aug. M-F 9am-5pm, Sa 10am-3pm; Sept.-May in summer M-F 9am-5pm. **Visitor Info Caboose,** on the west side of U.S. 65, just south of U.S. 50. Open M-F 10am-3pm.

Internet Access: Sedalia Public Library, 219 W. 3rd St. (☎660-827-7323), at Kentucky St. Open M and W-F 9am-6pm, Tu 9am-7pm, Sa 9am-5pm. $1 per hr.

Post Office: 405 E. 5th St. (☎660-826-8887), at Washington Ave. Open M-F 8am-5:30pm, Sa 8am-noon. **Postal Code:** 65301.

◱ GETTING AROUND. U.S. 50 is known as **Broadway Blvd.** and runs east-west through the entire area (where 8th St. would be). North of Broadway on **Ohio Ave.** and the surrounding streets lies the downtown historic district. The Missouri State Fairgrounds and State Fair Community College lie along **16th St.** (south of Broadway) to the west. **Limit Ave.** (U.S. 65) runs north-south through the area and is home to many motels, chain hotels, and chain restaurants.

◪ SIGHTS. Ragtime was born and bred in Sedalia thanks to native son Scott Joplin. People relive his memory each year at the **Scott Joplin Ragtime Festival,** a series of concerts held each June. The rest of the time, pick up ragtime music and memorabilia at the **Scott Joplin Ragtime Store,** 321 S. Ohio St. (☎660-826-2271 or 866-218-6258; www.scottjoplin.org. M-Sa 9am-4pm. Call ahead.) Worth a brief stop, the **Daum Museum of Contemporary Art,** 3201 W. 16th St., has an excellent permanent collection of modern paintings and sculptures. (From U.S. 50, go south on U.S. 65 to 16th St., then head west. ☎660-530-5888. Open Tu-F 11am-5pm, Sa-Su 1-5pm. Free.) Visit the **Bothwell Lodge State Historic Site,** 19349 Bothwell State

Park Rd., where John Homer Bothwell, an influential (and eccentric) Sedalia resident, originally built this 12,000 sq. ft. castle as his vacation residence. Tours run through the house, disclosing Bothwell's secret hiding places and his system of cooling the house, which involved air from underground caves. (From U.S. 50, head north on U.S. 65 for 6¼ mi. until you reach the right turn for Bothwell Lodge. ☎660-827-0510. Open daily in summer 9am-4pm; hours vary in winter. Tours $2.50, ages 6-12 $1.50.) The **Katy Depot Railroad Heritage Site**, 600 E. 3rd St., highlights its role as a railroad junction, home to the shops and stockyards of the MKT (Missouri-Kansas-Texas) and Missouri Pacific Railroads (☎660-826-2222. Open M-F 9am-5pm, Sa 10am-3pm. Free.)

⬛🍴 FOOD AND ACCOMMODATIONS.

Town favorite **McGrath's ❸**, 2901 W. Broadway (U.S. 50), dishes out meat-oriented pub fare amidst items hand-picked by the owner at estate sales and flea markets. There is a regular menu but there are no set recipes—each dish is cooked to customer specifications. (☎660-826-9902. Steak, chicken, and fish $7.50-24.50. Open M-Sa 5-10pm. AmEx/MC/V.) The elegant dining room in Hotel Bosworth's **Ivory Grille ❸**, 103 E. 4th St., is a relaxed setting for an excellent meal. Dinner entrees are not the cheapest bet in town ($13-30), but the all-you-can-eat express lunch buffet ($8) is a fantastic option. (☎660-829-0060. Open Tu-F 11am-2pm and 5-10pm, Sa 5-10pm. MC/V.) The squat structure of **Eddie's Drive-In ❶**, 115 W. Broadway (U.S. 50), is a holdover from the glory days of automobile travel. Don't be fooled by the name—you don't actually eat out of your car. (☎660-826-0015. Steakburgers $1.70-5. Open M-Sa 7:30am-8pm. MC/V.)

Sedalia offers a range of accommodations, but some aren't very well maintained. Rates approximately double during fairtime and the Scott Joplin Ragtime Festival. The rooms at the **Sunset Motel ❷**, 3615 S. Limit Ave. (U.S. 65), are as basic as can be, but they are some of the most affordable in town. (☎660-826-1446. Singles $38; doubles $45.) The **Sho-Me-Kort Motel ❸**, 1217 S. Limit Ave., has done some repair and painting work on its rooms recently, and a new guest laundry room is available. (On U.S. 65, just south of the intersection with U.S. 50. ☎660-826-2488. Singles $50; doubles $55. AmEx/D/MC/V.) At the landmark **Hotel Bothwell ❹**, 103 E. 4th St., at Ohio St.,

rooms come in all shapes, sizes, and prices, but all are ornately furnished. (☎660-826-5588. Singles $49; suites $94. MC/V.)

⚑ APPROACHING KNOB NOSTER: 18 MILES
Take **Broadway Blvd. (U.S. 50 W)** out of town.

KNOB NOSTER. While in Knob Noster, venture to **Knob Noster State Park,** a 3,567-acre park that caters to naturalists and equestrians alike with its mixture of prairie and second-growth forest. Camping is available; reserve sites at the Missouri Centralized Reservation System, online at www.mostateparks.com. (From U.S. 50, take the exit for Rte. 23. At the top of the ramp, turn left and proceed straight for 1¼ mi. to the park entrance. ☎877-422-6766. Visitors center open M-F 8am-4:30pm, Sa-Su 9am-4:30pm. Sites $8, with electricity $14, with full hookup $17.) Knob Noster's **Hometown Cafe ❶**, 111 N. State St., is a patriotic local diner that celebrates the B-2 Spirit stealth bombers stationed nearby with a colorful mural. The friendly staff serves basic sandwiches ($3-5) and breakfast items, including breakfast sandwiches ($2.25) on toast or a biscuit. (From U.S. 50, turn onto McPherson St., and turn left onto N. State St. ☎660-563-7482. Open M 6am-2pm, Tu-F 6am-8pm, Sa 7am-8pm, Su 7am-2pm. MC/V.)

⚑ APPROACHING WARRENSBURG: 9 MILES
Take **U.S. 50 W** and take the exit for **Rte. 13.** Turn left at the top of the ramp, then turn right at **Young St. (Bus. U.S. 50).** To reach the town center, proceed 2 blocks to the light at **Holden St.** and turn left.

WARRENSBURG. A speech given at the **Old Warrensburg Courthouse,** 302 N. Main St., as part of the 1870 Old Drum Trial gave rise to the phrase "Man's best friend is his dog." The pathos-filled speech has been faithfully inscribed for all to read on a monument on the lawn of the historic courthouse; the monument is topped by a statue of the famous dog, "Old Drum" himself. The tavern directly to the left of the courthouse, **Old Barney's Tavern on the Square ❶**, 112 Hout St., serves pork tenderloin sandwiches and "Macho Taco" quesadillas ($6 each) to hungry locals. (☎660-747-9038. Open M-Sa 6:30am-1:30am. MC/V.) **Java Junction ❶**, 112 N. Holden St., has plenty of seating, exposed interior bricks, and all the caffeine that a downtown worker could crave. (☎660-747-0725.

NATIONAL ROAD

Coffee $1.25. Muffins and pastries $1.40. Open M-F 7am-6pm, Sa 8am-midnight. D/MC/V.)

▣ DETOUR
POWELL GARDENS
1609 NW U.S. 50. On the north side of U.S. 50. Follow the signs.

Colorful, carefully sculpted flowerbeds surround bridges and mini-waterfalls at Powell Gardens. Concentrated into three small sites, the grounds take visitors from the heat of the prairie to the comfort of the shaded rock-and-waterfall garden. Mazes can make for fun diversions or peaceful meditation breaks. Driving is not permitted in the gardens. (☎816-697-2600; www.powellgardens.org. Open daily Apr.-Oct. 9am-6pm; Nov.-Mar. 9am-5pm. $8, seniors $7, ages 5-12 $3.)

▥ APPROACHING INDEPENDENCE: 50 MILES
Take **U.S. 50** and get off at the **Colburn Rd.** exit. Stay left to remain on **Rte. 291.** At the **23rd St.** light, turn left. Drive 2 mi. and turn right onto **S. Main St.**

INDEPENDENCE
Now in the shadow of larger Kansas City, Independence is the hometown of President Harry S. Truman. During the era of westward expansion, this city stood on the edge of a vast wilderness; Independence was the last waystation for pioneers seeking a new life. Today, modernized antebellum estates and thriving century-old businesses let this suburb maintain its legacy.

PAGE TURN. See p. 602 in **Oregon Trail** for complete coverage of Independence, Kansas City, Lawrence, Topeka, and Manhattan.

▥ APPROACHING JUNCTION CITY: 20 MILES
Take **Rte. 18 W** out of Manhattan. 8¼ mi. from town, Rte. 18 exits to the right. Take that exit and fork right to rejoin **I-70** heading west, and then take **Exit 300** for Junction City attractions.

JUNCTION CITY. The ▨**Geary County Historical Society Museum,** 530 N. Adams St., has the usual slew of historical exhibits, but its live demonstration of historic undergarments, "Undercover Story," makes it a must-visit. Middle-aged and elderly women parade in period undergarments dating from the 1880s through the 1920s as the museum director narrates. (☎785-238-1666.

Open Tu-Su 1-4pm. Call Museum Director Gaylynn Childs in advance of your visit to arrange for "Undercover Story." Free.) Be sure to check out **Freedom Park** and the **Atomic Cannon,** just south of I-70 at Exit 301. A climb up a shadeless switchback trail leads to the cannon, one of 20 designed during the Cold War to launch nuclear shells. Seven survived and one is on public display today. Across the Kansas River in Fort Riley, visitors can learn about the cavalry's role in war and in the expansion of the American frontier at the aging **US Cavalry Museum.** You can also take a 28-stop, 10 mi. driving tour around the rest of the 19th-century buildings of the fort. Pick up the driving tour guide at the Cavalry Museum, where the tour starts. Entrance to the museum requires passing through a military police checkpoint—bring photo ID, proof of car registration, and insurance. (☎785-239-2737. Open M-Sa 9am-4:30pm, Su noon-4:30pm. Free.)

▥ APPROACHING ABILENE: 44 MILES
From **I-70,** take **Exit 275,** and turn left onto **Rte. 15,** which becomes **Buckeye** in Abilene.

The Sunflower State KANSAS *Welcomes You!*

ABILENE
The famous birthplace of President Dwight D. Eisenhower began as a cowtown but remains prosperous today thanks to industry on its outskirts. With a small but entertaining collection of sights and museums, as well as excellent food and motels, Abilene is a good place for a stopover.

VITAL STATS

Population: 6500

Visitor Info: Abilene Convention and Visitors Bureau, 201 NW 2nd St. (☎785-263-2231; www.abilenekansas.org). Open M-Sa 8am-6pm, Su 10am-4pm.

Internet Access: Abilene Public Library, at NW 4th St. and Broadway. Open M-W 9am-6pm, Th noon-7pm, F 9am-5pm, Sa 9am-noon. Free.

Post Office: 217 N. Buckeye (☎785-263-2691), at 3rd St. Open M-F 8am-4:30pm, Sa 9am-11:30pm. **Postal Code:** 67410.

NATIONAL ROAD

GETTING AROUND. Buckeye (Rte. 15) is the major north-south axis stretching from I-70 into town. Numbered streets run east-west and count up in both directions from **1st St.** For example, an address on NW 2nd St. is west of Buckeye and one block north of 1st St., while one on SE 4th St. is east of Buckeye and three blocks south of 1st St.

SIGHTS. The museum at the **Eisenhower Center,** 200 SE 4th St., at Buckeye, focuses on Eisenhower's military and presidential careers as well as the work of his wife, Mamie. Newly revised and updated, the museum still glorifies Ike's presidency, but some newer exhibits question some elements of Ike's legacy. Other attractions include the family's 19th-century home and a visitors center that shows a film every hour. (☎877-746-4453; www.eisenhower.archives.gov. Museum and visitors center open daily in summer 8am-5:45pm; in winter 9am-4:45pm. $8, seniors and military $6, under 16 $1, under 8 free.) Housed inside the County History Museum, the **Museum of Independent Telephony,** 412 S. Campbell St., displays examples of telephone technology dating from the 1880s, including switchboards, switching stations, and some foreign equipment. (From Buckeye turn left on SE 3rd St., and proceed past the Eisenhower Center. Follow Campbell St. around to the right. ☎785-263-2681. Open in summer M-F 9am-5pm, Sa 10am-8pm, Su 1-5pm; in winter M-Sa 10am-5pm, Su 1-5pm. $4, seniors $3, under 15 $2.) Just south of the Eisenhower Center, **Old Abilene Town,** on SE 6th St., recreates the Abilene of cowtown days with replicas of 19th-century buildings and gunfight reenactments. (☎785-263-1868. Buildings open M-F 9am-4pm, Sa 9am-5pm, Su 12:30-5pm. Stagecoach rides Sa 10am-5pm, Su 12:30-5pm. Reenactments Sa-Su 11:30am, 1:30, 3:30pm. $3.) Live specimens greet visitors at the **Greyhound Hall of Fame,** 407 S. Buckeye, where you can learn about greyhounds (the dog, not the bus) and racing. (☎800-932-7881; www.greyhoundhalloffame.com. Open daily 9am-5pm. Free.)

FOOD AND ACCOMMODATIONS. You'll probably hear about the ◪**Brookville Hotel** ❸, 105 E. Lafayette Dr., even before you arrive in Abilene. There is only one item on the menu at this Midwestern institution: "One-half Skillet Fried Chicken," served family style with cottage cheese, sweet-and-sour cole slaw, mashed potatoes, creamed corn, biscuits, and ice cream. (Take Buckeye 1 block north of I-70 to Lafay-

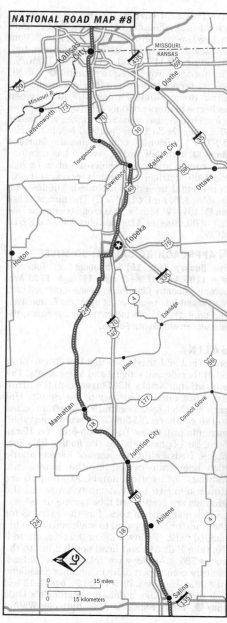

NATIONAL ROAD MAP #8

ette Dr., and turn right. ☎ 785-263-2244; www.brookvillehotel.com. Open Tu-F 5-8pm, Sa 11:30am-2pm and 4:30-8pm, Su 11am-2:30pm and 5-7:30pm. Reservations recommended. $12.50, ages 3-11 $7, under 3 $3 AmEx/D/MC/V.) The historic Kirby House Restaurant ❹, 205 NE 3rd St., serves Midwestern fare in a former Victorian home. Come for casual Fridays, when barbecue platters are only $10. (☎ 785-263-7336; www.kirby-house.com. Sandwiches and salads $7-8. Open M-Sa 11am-2pm and 5-8pm. AmEx/ D/MC/V.) A friendly couple runs the **Diamond Motel** ❷, 1407 NW 3rd St., which has comfortable rooms in a quiet residential area. (☎ 785-263-2360. Refrigerators, microwaves, and A/C. Continental breakfast included. Singles $33; doubles $36. AmEx/D/MC/V.) The **Budget Lodge Inn** ❷, 101 NW 14th St., has clean rooms. (☎ 785-263-3600. Singles $25; doubles $35. AmEx/D/ MC/V.)

ᴍ APPROACHING SALINA: 30 MILES
Take **Buckeye (Rte. 15) S** for about 5 mi. Turn right onto **1700 Ave.**, at the "Salina 19" sign. **1700 Ave.** becomes **Country Club Rd.** in Salina. Curve left onto **Marymount Rd.**, take your 1st right onto **E. Iron Ave.**, and drive 1¾ mi. into the center of downtown, the intersection with **Santa Fe Ave.**

SALINA

Salina is a mid-sized town that has little to offer other than decent lodging and a few sights. The educational **Smoky Hill Museum**, 211 W. Iron Ave., presents the history of the Smoky Hill region, which spans central Kansas from Salina to the south. (☎ 785-309-5776; www.smokyhill-museum.org. Open Tu-F noon-5pm, Sa 10am-5pm, Su 1-5pm. Free.) At the **Rolling Hills Zoo**, 625 N. Hedville Rd., 65 acres of Kansas prairie have been transformed into the "naturalistic habitats" of exotic animals. Although there don't seem to be that many animals, the grounds are pretty, and this "prairie oasis" surpasses many urban zoos. Pay the extra $3 for the tram, or be prepared to walk across the unshaded park. (Follow I-135 or 9th St. north to I-70, take Exit 244 and head south 2 mi. to the zoo. ☎ 785-827-9488; www.rollinghillswildlifeadventure.com. Open daily in summer 8am-5pm; in winter 9am-5pm. $9, seniors $8, ages 2-12 $5.)

It may look like a deli, but **Martinelli's Little Italy** ❸, 158 S. Santa Fe Ave., between Walnut St. and E. Iron Ave., is actually a great little Italian restaurant. (☎ 785-826-9190. Open M-Sa 11am-10pm, Su 11am-9pm. MC/V.) **Capers** ❷, 109 N. Santa Fe Ave., is a trendy cafe. The funky, colorful furnishings invite lingering, while the country music reminds you that you're not in Starbucks anymore, Toto. (☎ 785-823-7177. Sandwiches $6-7. Open M-Sa 7am-6pm. AmEx/D/MC/V.) For accommodations, the **Travelers Lodge** ❷, 245 S. Broadway, offers clean, comfortable rooms. (☎ 785-827-9351. Outdoor pool. Free Wi-Fi. Singles $30; doubles $33-40.) Nearby, the **Village Inn** ❷, 453 S. Broadway, has basic rooms. (☎ 785-827-4040. Outdoor pool. Singles $33; doubles $40.)

◪ DETOUR
▨ MUSHROOM ROCK STATE PARK
From Salina, take Rte. 140 W for 19 mi., then turn onto Rte. 141 S for about 4 mi. Turn west onto the dirt road, and follow it for about 3 mi.

The huge, creviced, mushroom-shaped rocks at Mushroom Rock State Park are truly unique; the natural sculptures resemble petrified UFOs on top of stone landing posts. (200 Horsethief Rd. ☎ 785-546-2565. Open 24hr. Free.)

ᴍ APPROACHING ELLSWORTH: 38 MILES
Head west on **Iron Ave.**, turn right on **College St.**, then left on **State St.** 7 mi. past Broadway, turn left to continue on State St., which becomes **Rte. 140.** From Rte. 140, take **Rte. 156** into town and bear right to get onto **Douglas Ave.**

ELLSWORTH. Texas Longhorn cattle were once herded through the lawless streets of Ellsworth, and the town's main street, **Douglas Ave.**, has purposefully preserved itself as it was in the 1870s. To equip yourself with contemporary cowboy gear, start at **Drovers Mercantile**, 119 N. Douglas Ave., which sells hats, boots, and spurs. (☎ 785-472-4703; www.droversmercantile.com. Open M-Sa 10am-5pm.) At the **Hodgden House Museum Complex**, 104 W. Main St., off Douglas Ave., a set of preserved buildings recall Ellsworth's dusty, up-roarin' history. (☎ 785-472-3059. Open Tu-Sa 9am-5pm, Su 1-5pm.)

ᴍ APPROACHING GREAT BEND: 40 MILES
Leave Ellsworth on **Rte. 156.** Outside of Great Bend, fork right to get on **U.S. 56 W.** U.S. 56 runs straight through the area; head north on **Main St.** to reach down-

town shops and businesses, or continue west on U.S. 56 to reach chain motels.

GREAT BEND. Great Bend serves mainly as a support city for the region's dominant industry, agribusiness. The **Kansas Quilt Walk,** 1400 Main St., in Courthouse Sq., surrounds the courthouse on the sidewalk, and showcases Kansan quilt patterns from the late 19th and early 20th centuries. The **visitors center,** 3111 10th St., west of downtown, is around the rear side of the Convention Center, through an unmarked doorway. (☎620-792-2750; www.visitgreatbend.com. Open M-F 8:30am-noon and 1-5pm.) **Delgado's Restaurant ❷,** 2210 10th St., is a good bet for Mexican fare. (☎620-793-3786. Open M-F 11am-2pm and 5-8:30pm.) Across from Courthouse Sq., the **Home Field Bar and Grille ❶,** 2017 Forest Ave., lays claim to the best burgers ($3.50-7) in Great Bend. (☎620-793-6420. Open M-Th 11am-2pm and 4:30-10pm, F 11am-2pm and 4:30pm-midnight, Sa 11am-10pm. Cash only.)

◪ **APPROACHING FORT LARNED: 23 MILES**
Follow **U.S. 56 W** from Great Bend to Kinsley. U.S. 56 aligns with the **Santa Fe Trail.** Stay straight to remain on **Rte. 156.**

◪ **DETOUR**
PAWNEE ROCK STATE PARK
In Pawnee Rock, turn right onto Centre St.

Pawnee Rock was once a major landmark on the Santa Fe Trail, rising high above this flat area. It served as both a lookout point and a signpost. Erosion and development have shortened what once was the only interruption in a vast, uncultivated landscape. An observation deck set as high as the original height of the rock allows visitors to view the area from the same perspective as travellers did ages ago. (☎785-272-8681. Open daily 8am-sunset. Free.)

FORT LARNED. This fort once defended the Santa Fe Trail against "hostile Indians." The **Fort Larned National Historic Site** consists of nine 1860s-era stone buildings. The officers' quarters have been recreated, but otherwise there isn't much to see here. (☎620-285-6911. Open daily 8:30am-5pm. $3, under 16 free.) At the **Santa Fe Trail Center,** on Rte. 156, exhibits explore this ancient transportation route. (☎620-285-2054. $4, students $2.50, children $1.50.)

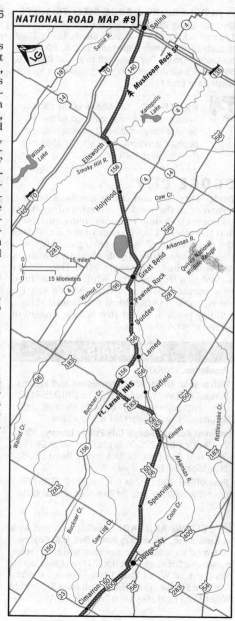

NATIONAL ROAD MAP #9

◪ APPROACHING DODGE CITY: 70 MILES
Continue along **Rte. 156** until the junction with **Rte. 183**; take Rte. 183 S to **U.S. 56.** Follow U.S. 56 through Kinsley, where it merges with **U.S. 50.** On the outskirts of Dodge City, head left to get on **Bus. U.S. 50 W,** the main drag of Dodge City (known in town as **Wyatt Earp Blvd.**)

PHOTO OP. The **Middle of the US** is in Kinsley, where a large road sign by the U.S. 50 interchange features 2 arrows pointing in opposite directions; New York City 1561 mi., San Francisco 1561 mi.

DODGE CITY

Dodge City was and still is the most famous cowtown of the west. Silhouettes of cowboys on horses welcome visitors driving into town, and the smell of beef hangs in the air. This is the dusty heart of meat-packing country, and the factories still provide the town with its economic base 125 years after Dodge City served as a frontier post. While it can be hard to separate what's real from what's just for show, you'll find that local residents display a genuine pride in Dodge that is independent of all the cowboy hoopla.

VITAL STATS

Population: 25,000

Visitor Info: Dodge City Convention and Visitors Bureau, 400 W. Wyatt Earp Blvd. (☎620-225-8186; www.visitdodgecity.org). Open in summer daily 8:30am-6:30pm; in winter M-F 8:30am-5pm.

Internet Access: Dodge City Public Library, 1001 2nd Ave. (☎620-225-0248), up the hill at Elm St. Open M-W 9am-6pm, Th 9am-8pm, F 9am-6pm, Sa 10am-5pm, Su 1-5pm. Free.

Post Office: 700 Central Ave. (☎800-275-08777). Open M-F 8:30am-5pm, Sa 9am-noon. **Postal Code:** 67801.

▐ GETTING AROUND. Dividing east and west at **Central Ave., Wyatt Earp Blvd. (Bus. U.S. 50),** runs east-west through the entire area and is the reference point for most directions. Downtown Dodge lies north of Wyatt Earp Blvd. between Central Ave. and **5th Ave.**; Boot Hill lies on **Front St.,** next to Wyatt Earp Blvd., between 3rd and 5th Ave.

◎ SIGHTS. The **Boot Hill Museum,** on Front St., between 3rd and 5th Ave., is a 1950s-era re-creation of Dodge City's legendary frontier. While some locals lament that the museum has gone downhill, it is still Dodge's main attraction. (☎620-227-8188; www.boothill.org. Open in summer daily 8am-8pm; in winter M-F 9am-5pm, Su 1-5pm. $8, students and seniors $7.50.) Located 4 mi. east of town on U.S. 400, the wooden **Coronado Cross** marks the spot where the Spanish explorer Coronado supposedly crossed the Arkansas River in 1541 in search of the mythical "Cities of Gold." On your way back, check out **Fort Dodge,** which once guarded the Santa Fe Trail.

▐◪ FOOD AND ACCOMMODATIONS.
Dodge City is dominated by chain restaurants, but the steak houses here in cow country are worth a look. **Casey's Cowtown ❸,** 503 E. Trail St., serves steak ($10-20) in all shapes and sizes. Place settings here automatically include a steak knife, but Casey's also offers chicken, seafood, and salads. (Take 1st. south across the railroad tracks, and turn left on Trail St. ☎620-227-5225. Sandwiches and salads $6-8. Open M-Sa 11am-10pm. MC/V.) Authentic Mexican food brings south-of-the-border flavor to the Sunflower State at **Casa Alvarez ❸,** 1701 W. Wyatt Earp Blvd. (☎620-225-7164. Fajitas $11. Combo plates $6-8.50. Open M-Th 10:30am-2pm and 5-9pm, F-Sa 11am-9:30pm, Su 10am-8pm. Cash only.) The **Thunderbird Motel ❷,** 2300 W. Wyatt Earp Blvd., offers free Wi-Fi and clean rooms. (☎620-225-4143. Singles $35; doubles $40. AmEx/D/MC/V.) The **Bel Air Motel ❷,** 2000 E. Wyatt Earp Blvd., is a clean single-level motel with basic rooms. (☎620-227-7155. Singles $24; doubles $30-32. MC/V.)

◪ APPROACHING GARDEN CITY: 50 MILES
Wyatt Earp Blvd. (Bus. U.S. 50) rejoins **U.S. 50/U.S. 400 W** outside of town. Take U.S. 50 toward Garden City. During the 50yr. period when this area was part of the **Santa Fe Trail,** continuous use by wagons scarred the land with deep ruts. Check them out off the side of U.S. 50/400 on your way out of Dodge City. 28 mi. west of the city, pull off at the marked overlook for a good view of cattle, farms, and lots of grass. U.S. 50 turns north just outside of Garden City; head straight into town on **Fulton St.,** it rejoins U.S. 50 after Holcomb.

GARDEN CITY

Though it has a large population, Garden City doesn't cater much to tourists. The **Finney County Historical Museum**, 403 S. 4th St., is the home to the **world's largest hairball** as well as displays of historical significance to the county, including an excellent exhibit on the Santa Fe Trail. (☎316-272-3664. Open in summer M-Sa 10am-5pm, Su 1-5pm; in winter daily 1-5pm. Free.) At the **Sandsage Bison Range and Wildlife Area**, on Rte. 83, is where the buffalo roam; call ahead for a driving tour to see the beasts in their natural home. The refuge also protects other native animals, including quail, ground squirrels, jackrabbits, and deer. (☎620-276-9400; www.gardencity.net/fofgr.)

 PHOTO OP. The **world's largest hairball** weighs 20 lb. (it weighed 55 lb. when it was first removed in 1993) and is nearly 36 in. in circumference. Ripley's Believe It or Not reportedly offered the museum $1,000 for the hairball, but the Finney County Historical Museum rejected the bid and keeps the ball on a stand by the information desk.

Hanna's Corner Restaurant ❶, 2605 N. Taylor, is a neighborhood hangout in the shadow of a beef packing plant. Besides a large breakfast selection and cheap sandwiches ($3-6), Hanna's also offers meaty dinners for $6-12. (☎620-276-8044. Open Tu-Th 5:30am-8pm, F-Sa 5:30am-9pm, Su 6am-1:30pm.) The **Continental Inn ❷**, 1408 Jones Ave., has recently renovated rooms and an outdoor pool. (☎620-276-7691. Singles from $40; doubles from $48. AmEx/D/MC/V.) The **Garden City Inn ❸**, 1202 W. Kansas Ave, at the corner of Taylor Ave. and Kansas Ave., has an indoor pool, a hot tub, and free Wi-Fi. (☎620-276-7608; www.gardencityinnkansas.com. Continental breakfast included. Singles from $50; doubles from $60. AmEx/D/MC/V.)

⚑ APPROACHING HOLCOMB: 5 MILES
Take **Fulton St.**, and turn right on **Main St.** Follow **Bus. U.S. 50** as it turns left on **Kansas St.** and then right onto **Taylor St.** Turn left on **Mary St.** Turn right on **Jones Ave.** to head into Holcomb.

HOLCOMB. This town became infamous as the site of grisly murders depicted in Truman Capote's *In Cold Blood*. The house where the murders took place is on the outskirts of town;

you may be able to find it, but people live there, and they don't want to be disturbed. Pay attention to the "NO TRESSPASSING" signs. Holcomb is also home to the **world's largest beef-packing plant**, a Tyson plant formerly known as IBP. (3105 N. IBP Rd.; turn left from Jones Rd. at the sign. ☎620-277-2614. Some tours available. Call ahead.)

⚑ APPROACHING SYRACUSE: 45 MILES
Follow **Jones Ave.** and turn left on **U.S. 50.** After about 44 mi., U.S. 50 becomes **E. Ave. A** in Syracuse.

 After Holcomb, U.S. 50 passes from the Central Time Zone to the Mountain Time Zone, where it is 1hr. earlier.

SYRACUSE. Sixteen miles from the border of Colorado, Syracuse is the last cowtown in Kansas, and it is convenient for a fresh tank of gas before heading into Colorado. While in Syracuse, check out the **Hamilton County Museum**, at Gates St. and E. Ave. From the unassuming exterior, this museum doesn't look like much, but the spacious interior is impressive, showcasing old collections of everything from pens to stuffed birds to typewriters that once belonged to townspeople. Don't miss the giant mammoth tusk, discovered just outside of town. (☎620-384-7496. Open in summer M-F 1-5pm; in winter M-W 10am-4pm. Free.) The owners of **Cynthia's Syracuse Pizzaria ❶**, 208 N. Main St., take great pride in both their pizza and their dining room. Several signs politely remind guests to keep the staff aware of any spills or dropped food, but you won't want to drop any of the freshly baked pizza. (☎620-384-5928. Pizza $8-15. Open M-Th 11am-1:30pm and 4-8:30pm, F-Sa 11am-1:30pm and 4-9:30pm. MC/V.)

⚑ APPROACHING LAMAR: 50 MILES
Continue west on **U.S. 50/U.S. 400**; it becomes a major thoroughfare in Lamar.

The Centennial State
COLORADO
Welcomes You!

LAMAR

Thirty-two miles inside the state border, Lamar may be in Colorado, but it doesn't

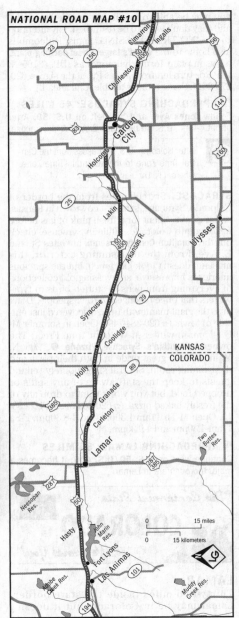

NATIONAL ROAD MAP #10

NATIONAL ROAD

resemble the mountainous terrain depicted on postcards and license plates. As the buzzing flies constantly remind you, Lamar, like much of west Kansas, is a land of cows. This region is known as "Big Timbers" after the giant cottonwood trees that once stood on the banks of the Arkansas River. The **Big Timbers Museum,** 7517 U.S. 50, focuses on settlement in the area. (☎719-336-2472. Open daily in summer 10am-5pm; in winter 1:30-4:30pm. Free.) At the northwest corner of Main and Beech St. by the **Welcome Depot,** the familiar **Madonna of the Trail** (see p. 377) returns for a final visit. (☎719-336-3483. Visitors center open daily 8am-6pm.)

Fresh and healthy (not to mention fabulous) sandwiches and wraps can be found at **Elm St. Perk ❶,** 117 W. Elm St. Their extensive menu of wraps and panini ($3.75-5) rotates daily, and their great coffee and espresso drinks are $1.50-4.75. Their squishy furniture might keep you sedentary. (Heading north, turn left onto Elm St. from Main St. ☎719-336-7109. Open M-F 6am-5pm, Sa 7am-2pm. MC/V.) For a heartier meal, you may consider **Hickory House ❸,** 1115 N Main St. Enjoy stick-to-your-ribs classics like a chicken-fried steak dinner ($9) under paintings of mountain scenes while you remember that the real Rockies aren't far off. (☎719-336-5018. Open M-Sa 5:30am-10pm. AmEx/D/MCV.) The spacious rooms at **El Mar Budget Host Motel ❷,** 1210 S. Main St., have comfortable furnishings with access to a pool. (☎719-336-4331; www.elmarmotel.com. Free Wi-Fi. Continental breakfast included. Singles $40; doubles $50. AmEx/D/MC/V.) Rooms at the **Passport Inn ❷,** 113 N. Main St., are a solid bet. (☎719-336-7746. Free Wi-Fi. Continental breakfast included. Singles $32-35; doubles $40-45. AmEx/D/MC/V.)

⚑ APPROACHING HASTY: 21 MILES
Follow **U.S. 50 W** out of Lamar.

HASTY. Hasty is not much more than a dusty collection of homes and small farms near the John Martin Reservoir. Head to **Valley Grocery ❶,** 100 S. Main St., to refill a water jug, pick up some basic sandwiches ($3-4), or stock up on basic fishing gear. (☎719-829-4810. Open daily 7am-7pm. MC/V.) The **John Martin Reservoir State Park ❶** is worth a look and offers two campsites: the slightly shaded **Hasty Campground ❶** (full hookup $18), with flush toilets, showers, and proximity to Lake Hasty, and the totally shadeless **Point Campground ❶** (sites $14), which offers better views of the reservoir. You can swim in the lake, water-ski, or jet-ski in the reservoir, and you'll have a good chance of glimpsing a prairie dog. (Follow the signs to the park. ☎719-829-1801. Visitors center open daily 8am-4pm. Park entrance fee $5. MC/V.)

◢ APPROACHING LA JUNTA: 33 MILES
Continue past the fort on **Rte. 194 S.** Follow signs to get on **U.S. 50 W** after about 2 mi. Turn left off U.S. 50 onto **Colorado Ave.**

LA JUNTA. The ▧**Koshare Indian Museum,** 115 W. 18th St., is the reason to stop in La Junta. Along the entire route there are countless museums about the "settlement" of the west, but this museum is devoted to the people who were already here. At the back of the building is the original *Kiva*, a log-roofed theater built in 1949 in which today's Koshare Indian Dancers perform on weekends in June and July. (☎719-384-4411; www.koshare.org. Open daily in summer 10am-5pm; in winter Tu-Su 12:30-4:30pm. $4, students and seniors $3. Shows $5/$3.) The crowded and kitschy **Copper Kitchen ❶,** 116 Colorado Ave., offers a large variety of breakfast and lunch options. Brave souls can try a meal of Rocky Mountain oysters ($6.50), and the very ravenous should try a chili burger ($4.50), with two burger patties and red or green chili. (☎719-384-7216. Breakfast $1-5. Lunch $3-6. Open M-Sa 6am-2pm, Su 6am-12:30pm. MC/V.) The **Bamboo Panda ❶,** 313 Colorado Ave., is clean and bright, with generous portions of great Chinese food. Lunch specials with rice and egg roll are only $5.25. (☎719-384-9880. Open M-Sa 11am-9pm, Su 11am-8pm. MC/V.) The **Travel Inn ❷,** 110 E. First St., has clean and moderately-priced rooms. (☎719-384-2504. Singles $36; doubles $38.50. AmEx/D/MC/V.)

◢ APPROACHING PUEBLO: 61 MILES
About 58 mi. from La Junta, **U.S. 50** and **Rte. 96** join. When they split 3 mi. later, take the exit for Rte. 96 (4th St.) into the center of Pueblo.

PUEBLO

A longtime steel town and once Colorado's second largest city, Pueblo is often shunned by residents of more mountainous regions for its flatness and supposed lack of sophistication. Today much of the steel business is gone, but Pueblo, like dad in a mid-life crisis, is trying to rediscover its hip side. New restaurants have opened, artists have moved into old ware-house spaces, and preservation efforts have created some interesting attractions. The **Rosemount Museum,** 419 W. 14th St., is one of Pueblo's most worthwhile sights. More a castle than a home, this 37-room Victorian mansion is decked out with an elegant original interior. Hour-long tours detail the architecture and furnishings of the house, from the English tile fireplaces to the gold foil trim on some walls and ceilings. (4 blocks west of Santa Fe Ave. at Greenwood St. ☎719-545-5290; www.rosemount.org. Open Feb.-Dec. Tu-Sa 10am-4pm. $6, under 20 $4.) The **El Pueblo History Museum,** 301 N. Union Ave., includes many exhibits on the settlement of the area from the 1780s to the 1860s, including Native American displays. (☎719-583-0483; www.coloradohistory.org. Open Tu-Sa 10am-4pm. $4; seniors, children, and students $3.)

Don't let the name fool you at the ▧**Steel City Diner and Bakeshop ❹,** 121 W. B St. Run by a couple who met while training at the Culinary Institute of America, this place has an innovative menu with items like butternut squash ravioli with goat cheese ($8.50) and Colorado lamb sirloin ($21). It may be expensive, but a meal here has quality that far exceeds the cost. Lunch items (under $10) provide a more affordable way to taste what they have to offer. (Take Union Ave. south to B St. and turn right. ☎719-295-1100. Entrees $13-22. Open Tu 11am-2pm, W-Sa 11am-2pm and 5-9pm. MC/V.) The **Bramble Tree Inn ❷,** 115 E. 8th St., has small rooms in good condition, with standard amenities. (☎719-542-1061. Rooms $36. MC/V.) The **Traveler's Motel ❷,** 1012 N. Santa Fe Ave., is a bare-bones motel with gaudy concrete interiors. (☎719-543-5451. Singles $26; doubles $31-35. AmEx/D/MC/V.)

◢ APPROACHING CAÑON CITY: 36 MILES
Take **I-25 N** from downtown Pueblo to **Exit 101** for **U.S. 50 W.** Proceed 35 mi. to Cañon City, where U.S. 50 becomes **Royal Gorge Ave.** Note the junction with **Rte. 115 N;** you will be returning here later.

CAÑON CITY

For Coloradans, the mountain town of Cañon City will always be associated with prisons; Colorado's first territorial prison was here, and there are still several correctional facilities in the area. Going back several hundred million years, dinosaurs were also plentiful in these parts, and many sets of fossilized remains have been discovered, especially in the area of Florissant National Monument. Today, as other mountain regions have become more touristed, Cañon City has flourished and is a great base for exploring the surrounding area.

VITAL STATS

Population: 16,000

Visitor Info: Cañon City Chamber of Commerce, 403 Royal Gorge Blvd. (☎719-275-2331; www.canyoncity-colorado.com), at 4th St. Open M-F 8am-5pm.

Internet Access: Cañon City Public Library, 516 Macon Ave. (☎719-269-9020). Open M-Th 9:30am-7pm, F 9:30am-5pm, Sa 9:30am-2pm. Free.

Post Office: 1501 Main St. (☎719-275-6877). Open M-F 8:30am-5:30pm, Sa 9am-noon. **Postal Code:** 81212.

GETTING AROUND. U.S. 50 runs east-west through the entire area and is known as **Royal Gorge Ave.** The town itself mostly lies north of U.S. 50 in an easily navigable downtown area; numbered streets head north from U.S. 50. **Royal Gorge** is about 10 mi. west of Cañon City on U.S. 50.

SIGHTS. At the western edge of downtown, the **Museum of Colorado Prisons,** 201 N. 1st St., presents a series of cell displays highlighting disciplinary methods, famous riots, prison breaks, and individual prisoners. An actual gas chamber is located in the front yard. Ghost walks in Cañon City (90min.) meet at the museum. (☎719-269-3015; www.prisonmuseum.org. Open in summer daily 8:30am-6pm; in winter F-Su 10am-5pm and by appointment. $7, seniors $6, children $5. Ghost walks M and F-Su 6:15pm. $8, children $5.) The **Royal Gorge Route Train Ride,** 401 Water St., provides a 2hr., 24 mi. train ride through the Royal Gorge. It may not be cheap, but the luxury train is a good way to kick back and enjoy the canyon. (Take 3rd St. south to Santa Fe Depot at Water St., behind the Dinosaur Depot. ☎303-569-1000 or 888-724-5748; www.royalgorgeroute.com. Runs mid-June to mid-Aug. daily 9:30am, 12:30, 3:30, and 7pm; dinner train Sa 7pm. Reservations recommended. Coach $30, children $20; first class $40/$30. Dinner train $80. Locomotive ride $99.)

OUTDOORS. Years ago it was free to walk over the Royal Gorge Bridge, the world's highest suspension bridge, but today they charge an exorbitant price at the **Royal Gorge Park.** Admission for the amusement-park-style area includes a trip on the world's steepest incline railway or the world's longest single-span aerial tram above it. The scenery from the air is spectacular, but to see the bridge for free, park in the parking lot and take the trail down to an overlook. (Take U.S. 50 W 10 mi. from Cañon City. ☎719-275-7507 or 888-333-5597; www.royalgorge-bridge.com. Bridge open in summer 7am-sunset; rest of year daily 10am-6:30pm. $21, ages 4-11 $17.) **Tunnel Drive,** a 2 mi. trail through three tunnels, offers views of the Arkansas River. It's best explored in early morning when the reflections off the river are brilliant. (Head west on U.S. 50 past the prison; it's on the left.) The Arkansas River reaches a hilly point around Cañon City where it produces some fantastic rapids. Four companies based in and around the city offer rafting excursions: **Adventure Quest Expeditions** (☎719-269-9807 or 888-448-7238; www.aqerafting.com); **Raft Masters,** 2315 E. Main St. (☎800-568-7238; www.raftmasters.com.); **Whitewater Adventure Outfitters,** 50905 U.S. 50 W (☎719-275-5344 or 800-530-8212; www.waorafting.com); and **Echo Canyon River Expeditions,** 45000 U.S. 50 W (☎800-595-3246; www.raftecho.com). All trips are around $55-105 per person, depending on duration of trip.

FOOD AND ACCOMMODATIONS. The **Good Thyme Cafe ❶,** 412 Main St., has a basic menu of fresh sandwiches and salads ($5-6), but try to save room for a slice of one of their homemade cakes and pies. (☎719-275-0222. Breakfast $3-7. Open M-F 7am-3pm, Sa 7am-2pm. D/MC/V.) Motels line U.S. 50 near downtown as well as E. Main St., south of U.S. 50. It's good to reserve ahead, especially on weekends. **The Knotty Pine Motel ❷,** 2990 E. Main St., 2 mi. east of downtown, has clean rooms in a red wooden structure that matches its surroundings. (☎719-275-0461. Wi-Fi. 21+. Singles in summer $49; in winter $34. Doubles $55-60/$39-46. MC/V.) The **Skyline Motel ❷,** 219 Main St., only has six basic rooms, but if you find a room available, you'll pay less than you'll pay anywhere else in town. The rooms come with kitchens, but not cable TV. (☎719-275-5814. Rooms $25. Cash or check only.)

APPROACHING COLORADO SPRINGS: 45 MILES
A bit of backtracking is required here—from Cañon City, follow **Royal Gorge Blvd. (U.S. 50)** back east out

of town to the junction with **Rte. 115 N,** which becomes **Nevada Ave.** in town.

COLORADO SPRINGS

Once a resort town frequented only by America's elite, Colorado Springs is now the second most-visited city in Colorado. When early gold seekers discovered bizarre red rock formations here, they named the region Garden of the Gods, in part due to a Ute legend that the rocks were petrified bodies of enemies hurled down from the sky. Today, the US Olympic Team trains here, while jets from the US Air Force Academy roar overhead.

VITAL STATS

Population: 370,000

Visitor Info: Colorado Springs Chamber of Commerce, 515 S. Cascade Ave. (☎719-635-7506). Open in summer M-F 8am-6pm; in winter 8:30am-5pm.

Internet Access: Penrose Public Library, 20 N. Cascade Ave. (☎719-531-6333). Open M-Th 10am-9pm, F-Sa 10am-6pm, Su 1-5pm. Free.

Post Office: 201 E. Pikes Peak Ave. (☎719-570-5336), at Nevada Ave. Open M-F 7:30am-5:30pm, Sa 8am-1pm. **Postal Code:** 80903.

▐ GETTING AROUND

Colorado Springs is laid out in a grid of broad thoroughfares. **Nevada Ave.** is the main north-south strip from which numbered streets ascend moving westward. **I-25** from Denver cuts through downtown, dividing **Old Colorado City** from the eastern sector of the town, which remains largely residential. **Colorado Ave.** and **Pikes Peak Ave.** run east-west across the city. Just west of Old Colorado City lies **Manitou Springs** and the **Pikes Peak Area.** Colorado Ave., the main street through town, becomes **Manitou Ave.** as it extends into Manitou Springs.

◉ SIGHTS

Olympic hopefuls train at the **US Olympic Complex,** 1750 E. Boulder St., at the corner of Union St. The best times to get a glimpse of athletes in training are 10-11am and 3-4pm. (☎719-866-4618 or 888-659-8687. Tours M-Sa 9am-4pm. Free.) The **Pioneer's Museum,** 215 S. Tejon Ave., recounts the settling of the city. (☎719-385-5990;

www.cspm.org. Open in summer Tu-Sa 10am-5pm, Su 1-5pm; in winter Tu-Sa 10am-5pm. . Free.) Just north of Lake St., the **World Figure Skating Museum and Hall of Fame,** 20 1st St., traces the history, art, and science of skating through film and photos. It boasts an extensive collection of medals and skating outfits. (☎719-635-5200. Open M-Sa 10am-4pm. $3, seniors and ages 6-12 $2.) Potters at **Van Briggle Pottery,** on 21st St. (Rte. 24), demonstrate their skill during free tours through the studio and showroom. Witness the spinning, casting, and etching process that has produced pieces displayed in museums throughout the world. (☎800-847-6341. Open M-Sa 8:30am-5pm. Tours M-Sa 9am-4pm. Free.) If you want to do serious hiking anywhere in the Colorado Springs/Pikes Peak Region, buy the *Pikes Peak Discovery Atlas,* which contains detailed topographical maps of the whole region. **Pikes Peak Tours,** 132 E. Las Animas, offers whitewater rafting trips on the Arkansas River, as well as a combo tour of the US Air Force Academy and the Garden of the Gods. They also offer tours of Pikes Peak and the Royal Gorge. (☎719-633-1181 or 800-345-8197. Open daily 8am-5pm. Tours $30-85.)

PHOTO OP. Sam's, a bar at **Rum Bay Bourbon Street** in Colorado Springs, is officially the **world's smallest bar,** according to the *Guinness Book of World Records.* You will barely have room to turn around with your drink; Sam's has a diminutive 109.57 sq. ft. of space and a maximum occupancy of 5 people–a bartender and 1 person at each of the bar's 4 seats.

▤ FOOD

Students fill the outdoor tables in front of the cafes and restaurants lining **Tejon Ave.**

■ **Poor Richard's Restaurant,** 324½ N. Tejon St. (☎719-632-7721). A popular local hangout with great New York-style pizza (slices from $3.50; pizzas from $13), healthy sandwiches ($7), and salads ($4-7) as well as a good selection of microbrews from in and around Colorado ($3-3.50). Tu live folk music. W bluegrass. Th Celtic. Open M-Tu and Su 11am-9pm, W-Sa 11am-10pm. AmEx/D/MC/V. ❶

■ **Savelli's,** 301 Manitou Ave. (☎719-685-3755). Cheery waitresses bring out Italian food at this friendly restaurant. The pasta ($5-9) is tasty, but the specialty

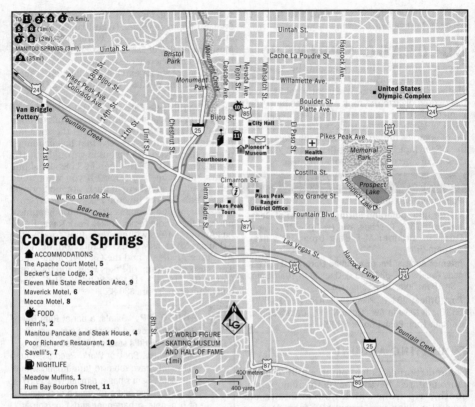

Colorado Springs

🏠 ACCOMMODATIONS
The Apache Court Motel, **5**
Becker's Lane Lodge, **3**
Eleven Mile State Recreation Area, **9**
Maverick Motel, **6**
Mecca Motel, **8**

🍴 FOOD
Henri's, **2**
Manitou Pancake and Steak House, **4**
Poor Richard's Restaurant, **10**
Savelli's, **7**

🎵 NIGHTLIFE
Meadow Muffins, **1**
Rum Bay Bourbon Street, **11**

here is the pizza ($5-18), which comes in baked-in, deep-dish gourmet, and stone-baked thin crust varieties. Open M-Sa 11am-9pm, Su noon-9pm. ❷

Henri's, 2427 W. Colorado Ave. (☎719-634-9031). Henri's has served chimichangas ($8) and a wide variety of *cervezas* for over 50 years. The house special, Tacos *al carbone* ($9.25), are a popular favorite. Drop in for a margarita during happy hour (M-F 4-6pm) or check out the strolling mariachi singers at night F-Sa. Open M-Th and Su 10:30am-8pm, F-Sa 10:30am-9pm. AmEx/D/MC/V. ❷

Manitou Pancake and Steak House, 26 Manitou Ave. (☎719-685-9225), feels like a pleasant country home. Enjoy a filling country-style breakfast or lunch in the breezy dining room under the open rafters. An all-you-can-eat breakfast buffet is only $8.50; most lunch items $5-9. Open daily 6am-2pm. D/MC/V. ❷

🏠 ACCOMMODATIONS

Motels line **Nevada Ave.** near downtown, but the best options can be found farther west in Manitou Springs. Campgrounds clutter Rte. 67, 5-10 mi. north of **Woodland Park,** which lies 18 mi. northwest of the Springs on U.S. 24. Try **Colorado, Painted Rocks,** or **South Meadows,** near Manitou Park. (Generally open May-Sept. Sites $13-15. MC/V.) Unless otherwise posted, you can camp on national or forest property for free if you are at least 500 ft. from a road or stream. The **Pikes Peak Ranger District Office,** 601 S. Weber St., has maps. (☎719-636-1602. Open M-F 8am-4:30pm.)

Mecca Motel, 3518 W. Colorado Ave. (☎719-475-9415). Well-kept rooms with microwaves, refrigerators, a pool with a slide, and a public hot tub. Rooms $50. MC/V. ❷

Beckers Lane Lodge, 115 Beckers Ln. (☎719-685-1866), at the south entrance of the Garden of the Gods. Clean rooms with microwaves and fridges. Heated outdoor pool and barbecue area. Rooms $50. AmEx/D/MC/V. ❷

The Apache Court Motel, 3401 W. Pikes Peak Ave. (☎719-471-9791). The Apache Court Motel features pink adobe rooms with microwaves, fridges, and a common hot tub. Rooms $22. MC/V. ❶

Maverick Motel, 3620 W. Colorado Ave. (☎719-634-2852 or 800-214-0264). Expect an explosion of pastels the moment you walk in. Rooms come with fridge and microwave. Rooms $40-55. MC/V. ❷

Eleven Mile State Recreation Area, (☎719-748-3401 or 800-678-2267), from U.S. 24, take County Rd. 90, then turn onto County Rd. 92. Farther afield, visitors can camp on Lake George reservoir; hiking and fishing are popular activities. Showers and laundry (wash $1.50; dry $1). Reception M-F 7am-8pm, 7am-9pm Sa-Su. Vehicle passes $5 per day. Sites $12, with electricity $16. MC/V. ❶

▧ NIGHTLIFE

Bars in Colorado Springs fill with students until late into the night.

Rum Bay Bourbon Street, 20 N. Tejon St. (☎719-634-3522). A multi-level bar and club complex with 8 clubs included under 1 cover charge ($5, $10 after 11pm). The main Rum Bay Club features Top 40. Masquerade is a disco club, Copy Cats is a karaoke bar, and Fat City is a lounge with live blues. Drinks $6-7. Th ladies night. Rum Bay open Tu-Sa 11am-2am; other clubs 4pm-2am. MC/V.

Meadow Muffins, 2432 W. Colorado Ave. (☎719-633-0583). Wagons hanging from the ceiling were used in *Gone With The Wind*, and the windmill-style fan was in *Casablanca*. Tu-Sa live music. W karaoke. Sa ladies night. Open daily 11am-2am. MC/V.

◪ APPROACHING DENVER: 70 MILES

Take **Cimarron (U.S. 24) W** from downtown or east from Old Colorado City to **I-25 N.** For the first part of the drive, an unbroken chain of Rocky Mountains greets drivers on the left, while plains can be seen on the right. Proceed about 68 mi. north to Denver. For downtown and sights, take **Exit 210A** for **U.S. 40/ Colfax Ave.**

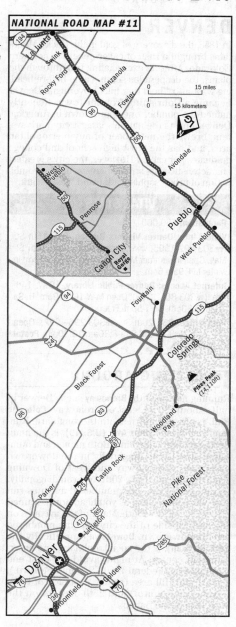

NATIONAL ROAD MAP #11

DENVER

In 1858, the discovery of gold in the Rocky Mountains brought a rush of eager miners to northern Colorado. After an excruciating trek through the plains, the desperados set up camp before heading west into "them thar hills." Overnight, Denver became a flourishing frontier town. Recently named the number one sports town in America, Denver boasts the nation's largest city park system, brews the most beer of any metropolitan area, and has the most high-school and college graduates per capita. However, the city's greatest characteristic is its atmosphere—a unique combination of urban sophistication and Western grit.

VITAL STATS

Population: 560,000

Visitor Info: Denver Visitors Bureau, 918 16th St. (☎303-892-1505; www.denver.org), at the 16th St. Mall. Open in summer M-F 9am-5pm, Sa 9am-1pm; in winter M-F 9am-5pm.

Internet Access: Denver Public Library, 10 W. 14th Ave. (☎303-865-1363). Open M-W 10am-9pm, Th-Sa 10am-5:30pm, Su 1-5pm. Free.

Post Office: 951 20th St. (☎303-296-4692). Open M-F 7am-10:30pm, Sa-Su 8:30am-10:30pm. **Postal Code:** 80202.

⌐ GETTING AROUND

Running north-south, **Broadway** slices Denver in half. About 2½ mi. east of Broadway, **Colorado Blvd.** is another north-south thoroughfare. Running east-west, **Colfax Ave. (U.S. 40),** is the main north-south dividing line. Both named and numbered streets run diagonally in the downtown area; east of Broadway and west of Downing Ave., only those above 20th Ave. run diagonally. In the rest of the city, numbered avenues run east-west, increasing as you head north. Named streets run north-south. Many of the avenues on the eastern side of the city become numbered streets downtown. **Downtown** (specifically the **16th St. Mall**), is the social, culinary, and entertainment center. At night, avoid the west end (Colfax Ave., Federal Blvd., S. Santa Fe Blvd.), the Capitol Hill area (on the east side of town beyond the Capitol) and 25th-34th St. on the west side of the Barrio.

◉ SIGHTS

Many of the best sights in Denver center on downtown, which makes touring on foot easy.

COLORADO STATE CAPITOL. The beautiful **Capitol Building** is a sensible place to start a visit to the Mile High City. Marked by a small engraving, one step leading to the building's entrance sits one mile above sea level. Free tours show visitors the governor's office and the House and Senate chambers. *(200 E. Colfax Ave. ☎303-866-2604. Open M-F 7am-5:30pm. 30min. tours M-F 9am-3:30pm. Free.)*

DENVER ART MUSEUM. Near the Capitol stands the Denver Art Museum (DAM). Recently overhauled, the museum includes the original seven-story building and a new, uniquely shaped annex next door. The DAM houses a world-class collection of Native American art and pre-Colombian artifacts. *(100 W. 14th Ave. Pkwy. ☎720-865-5000; www.denverartmuseum.org. Tours daily of special exhibits; call for times. Open Tu and Th-Sa 10am-5pm, W 10am-9pm, Su noon-5pm. $13, students and seniors $10, ages 6-18 $5.)*

SIX FLAGS. Make a splash at the Island Kingdom water park at Six Flags Elitch Gardens, across the freeway from Mile High Stadium. The Boomerang, Mind Eraser, and the Flying Coaster keep thrill-seekers screaming. *(2000 Elitch Cir., at Speer Blvd. ☎303-595-4386. Open in summer daily 10am-10pm; in spring and early fall Sa-Su, hours vary. $45, under 4 ft. $21.)*

OCEAN JOURNEY. Denver's brand new aquarium guides visitors through two spectacular underwater exhibits: the **Colorado River Journey,** descending from the Continental Divide to the Sea of Cortez in Mexico, and the **Indonesian River Journey,** emptying from the volcanic Barisan Mountains in Sumatra into the South China Sea. The aquarium houses over 15,000 exotic marine creatures, including several species of sharks, sea otters, and the magnificent Napoleon wrasse. *(700 Water St. ☎303-561-4450 or 888-561-4450; www.oceanjourney.org. Open M-Th and Su 10am-10pm, F-Sa 10am-11pm. $13.25, seniors $10, ages 4-12 $8.)*

DENVER MUSEUM OF NATURE AND SCIENCE. This gigantic museum hosts a variety of fun exhibits, including the Hall of Life and the Prehistoric Journey room. Ride the skies in the museum's **Gates Planetarium,** with a variety of

NATIONAL ROAD

Denver

⌂ ACCOMMODATIONS
Broadway Plaza Motel, **10**
Budget Host Inn, **1**
Cherry Creek State Park, **13**
Hostel of the Rocky Mtns., **7**

🍴 FOOD
Benny's Restaurante y Cantina, **12**
The Buckhorn Exchange, **9**
Domo, **8**
Mercury Cafe, **5**
Wazee Lounge & Supper Club, **6**

🍸 NIGHTLIFE
The Church, **11**
El Chapultepec, **4**
Foxhole Lounge, **3**
Wynkoop Brewery, **2**

300 yards
300 meters

TO CHEESMAN PARK (500yd)
BLUEBIRD THEATER (1mi),
MUSEUM OF NATURE AND
SCIENCE (2.2mi)

TO 13 (10mi)

TO 70

TO BLACK AMERICAN
WEST MUSEUM (900yd)

TO 12 (0.45mi)

State Capitol
Colorado History Museum

Museum of Western Art
Brown Palace Hotel

Greek Amphitheater
Denver Art Museum

Civic Center Park

Coors Field

18th St. Mall

Writer Square
Larimer Square

Denver Performing Arts Complex

Colorado Convention Center

Union Station

Metropolitan State College
Community College of Denver

UNIVERSITY OF COLORADO - DENVER

St. Elizabeth's

Pepsi Center

CONFLUENCE PARK

TO 1 (0.75mi)
GERMINAL STAGE THEATER (1.25mi)

TO SIX FLAGS & OCEAN JOURNEY (300yd)

TO 10 (300yd),
11 (150yd), &
ELLSWORTH AVE. (1.1mi)

TO MUSEO DE LAS AMERICAS (900yd),
ROXBOROUGH STATE PARK (30mi)

TO 3 (300yd)

TO COORS BREWERY (6mi)
TO 9 (500yd)

TO 8

Benedict Fountain Park

Skyline Park

Marion St.
Downing St.
Clarkson St.
Ogden St.
Emerson St.
Washington St.
Corona St.
E. 13th Ave.
E. 16th Ave.
E. 17th Ave.
E. 18th Ave.
E. 19th St.
E. 20th Ave.
E. 22nd Ave.
E. 2nd Ave.

Pearl St.
Pennsylvania St.
Logan St.
Grant St.
Sherman St.
Lincoln St.
Broadway
Bannock St.
Cheyenne Pl.
Cleveland Pl.
Court Pl.
Glenarm Pl.
Tremont Pl.
Welton St.
California St.
Stout St.
Champa St.
Curtis St.
Arapahoe St.
Lawrence St.
Larimer St.
Market St.
Blake St.
Wazee St.
Wynkoop St.
Wewatta St.
Delgany St.

Colfax Ave.
W. 14th Ave.
E. 13th Ave.
W. 14th Ave.
W. Colfax Ave.

Speer Blvd.
Cherry Creek
Auraria Pkwy.
Klamath St.
Osage St.
Mariposa St.
Delaware St.

13th St.
14th St.
15th St.
16th St.
17th St.
18th St.
19th St.
20th St.
21st St.
22nd St.
23rd St./Park Ave.
24th St.
Court Pl.
Glenarm Pl.

shows on infinity and beyond. *(2001 Colorado Blvd., at Montview St. ☎ 800-925-2250; www.dmns.org. Open daily 9am-5pm. $10, children and seniors $6. IMAX or planetarium and museum $15/$10.)*

BLACK AMERICAN WEST MUSEUM. Denver resident Paul W. Stewart had a lifelong desire to tell the public about a fact that was "not recorded in history books"—that one out of every three cowboys was black. The small museum, mostly a collection of photos with brief explanations, details the role black Americans played in settling the west. There are also exhibits about Justina Ford, an early 20th-century physician to Denver's poor and minority residents. *(3091 California St. ☎ 303-292-2566, www.blackamericanwestmuseum.com. Open June-July Tu-Sa 10am-5pm; Sept.-May W-F 10am-2pm, Sa-Su 10am-5pm. $6, seniors $5.50, ages 5-12 $4.)*

OTHER SIGHTS. Located in nearby Golden, the **Coors Brewery** is the world's largest one-site brewery. Free tours take visitors through the brewing process and provide free samples. *(Take I-70 W to Exit 264, head west on 32nd Ave. for 4½ mi., then turn left on East St. and follow the signs. ☎ 303-277-2337. 1½hr. tours every 30min. M-Sa 10am-4pm.)* At the **Colorado History Museum,** interesting exhibits document Colorado's multi-faceted history, including a series of intricate historical dioramas made by the WPA in the 1930s. *(1300 Broadway, at 13th St. ☎ 303-866-3682. Open M-Sa 10am-5pm, Su noon-5pm. $7, students and seniors $6, children $5.)* The **Museo de Las Americas** exhibits work by Latin American artists, including photographers, painters, and fabric makers. *(861 Santa Fe Dr., between 8th and 9th Ave., south of downtown. ☎ 303-571-4401; www.museo.org. Open Tu-Sa 10am-5pm. $4, students and seniors $3.)*

PARKS. Denver has more public parks per square mile than any other city, providing prime space for bicycling, walking, or lolling. **Cheesman Park,** at 8th Ave. and Humboldt St., offers picnic areas, manicured flower gardens, and a view of snow-capped peaks. **Confluence Park,** at Cherry Creek and the South Platte River, lures bikers and hikers with paved riverside paths. Free live music is the name of the game at **Confluence Concerts,** along the banks of the South Platte. *(☎ 303-455-7192. July-early Aug. Th 6:30-8pm.)* One of the best parks for sporting events, **Washington Park,** at Louisiana Ave. and Downing St., hosts impromptu vol-

leyball and soccer games on summer weekends. Wide paths for biking, jogging, and in-line skating encircle the park, and the two lakes in the middle are popular fishing spots. At **Roxborough State Park,** visitors can hike and ski among rock formations in the **Dakota Hogback** ridge. *(Take U.S. 85 S, turn right on Titan Rd., and follow it 3½ mi. ☎ 303-973-3959. Open sunrise-sunset.)*

 PHOTO OP. 40 mi. west of Denver, the road to the top of **Mount Evans** (14,264 ft.) is the **highest paved road** in North America. (Take I-70 W to Rte. 103 in Idaho Springs. ☎ 303-567-2901. Open late May to early Sept. $10.)

 FOOD

Denver offers a full range of cuisines, from traditional Southwestern to Russian. Al fresco dining and people-watching are available along the **16th Street Mall.** Gourmet eateries are located southwest of the Mall on **Larimer St.** Sports bars and trendy restaurants occupy **LoDo.** Outside of downtown, **Colorado Blvd.** and **6th Ave.** also have their share of posh restaurants. **E. Colfax Ave.** offers a number of reasonably priced ethnic restaurants.

▧ **Mercury Cafe,** 2199 California St. (☎ 303-294-9281), at 22nd St. Decorated with a new-age flair and political posters, the Merc specializes in home-baked bread, vegan desserts, and veggie specials. Live local bands play in the dining room, while the upstairs dance area hosts swing and tango lessons Th and Su. Salads $6-9. Enchiladas $6-8. Open Tu-F 5:30-11pm, Sa-Su 9am-3pm and 5:30-11pm. Dancing Tu-Th and Su until 1am, F-Sa until 2am. Cash only. ❸

▧ **Domo,** 1365 Osage St. (☎ 303-595-3666; www.domorestaurant.com). Take Colfax Ave. to Osage St. (east of I-25) and head south 1 block. One of the top Japanese restaurants in the nation. Filling traditional dishes ($14-23) are served in the outdoor Japanese garden or airy interior. Open Th-Sa 11am-2pm and 5-10pm. MC/V. ❺

Benny's Restaurante y Tequila Bar, 301 E. 7th Ave. (☎ 303-894-0788; www.bennysrestaurant.com). A local favorite for cheap, tasty Mexican food, including huevos rancheros ($6.75) and fish tacos ($8). Open M-F 11am-11pm, Sa 9am-11pm, Su 9am-10pm. AmEx/D/MC/V. ❷

Wazee Lounge & Supper Club, 1600 15th St. (☎303-623-9518), in LoDo. The black-and-white tile floor, stained glass, Depression-era wood paneling, and bleached mahogany create a unique bohemian ambience. Wazee's award winning pizza $6-8. Strombolis $8. Happy hour M-F 4-6pm. Open M-Sa 11am-2am, Su noon-midnight. AmEx/D/DC/MC/V. ❷

The Buckhorn Exchange, 1000 Osage St. (☎303-534-9505; www.buckhorn.com). Take Colfax Ave. to Osage St., and head south 3 blocks. Denver's oldest restaurant, famous for its hunting-themed walls. Carnivores will delight in mammoth steaks. Dinner $18-40. Open M-Th 11am-2pm and 5:30-9pm, F 11am-2pm and 5-10pm, Sa 5-10pm, Su 5-9pm. AmEx/D/DC/MC/V. ❹

ACCOMMODATIONS

Inexpensive hotels line **E. Colfax Ave.,** as well as Broadway and Colorado Blvd.

Hostel of the Rocky Mountains, 1717 Race St. (☎303-861-7777), off E. Colfax Ave. Take E. Colfax Ave. east of the Capitol, and turn left on Race St. The best value in Denver. Free Internet access. Linen $2. Laundry. Key deposit $5. Reception 7am-11:30pm. No curfew. Dorms $20; private rooms $45. MC/V. ❶

Broadway Plaza Motel, 1111 Broadway (☎303-893-0303), south of the Capitol. Clean rooms near downtown. Singles $45-55; doubles $65. V. ❷

Budget Host Inn, 2747 Wyandot St. (☎303-458-5454), on the corner of 27th St. and Wyandot St. Comfortable rooms conveniently located near Six Flags Elitch Gardens. $15 off Six Flags tickets. Singles from $45; doubles from $55. AmEx/D/MC/V. ❷

Cherry Creek State Park, 4201 S. Parker Rd. (☎303-699-3860), in Aurora, an urban area situated around Cherry Creek Lake. Take I-25 to Exit 200, then head north for about 3 mi. on I-225, and take the Parker Rd. Exit. Pine trees provide limited shade. Boating, fishing, swimming, and horseback riding available. Arrive early. Open May-Dec. Sites $14, with electricity $18. Cash or check only. ❶

ENTERTAINMENT

THEATER

The **Denver Performing Arts Complex (DPAC),** at Speer Blvd. and Arapahoe St., is the largest arts complex in the nation. DPAC is home to the Denver Center for the Performing Arts, Colorado Symphony, Colorado Ballet, and Opera Colorado. (Tickets M-Sa 10am-6pm. ☎303-893-4100 or 800-641-1222.) The **Denver Center Theater Company** (☎303-893-4000) offers one free Saturday matinee per play. In the intimate **Geminal Stage Denver,** 2450 W. 44th Ave., every seat is a good one. (☎303-455-7108. Shows F-Su. $14-18.) **The Bluebird Theater,** 3317 E. Colfax Ave. (☎303-322-2308), is an old theater-turned-music venue.

FESTIVALS

Every January, Denver hosts the nation's largest livestock show and one of its biggest rodeos, the **National Western Stock Show & Rodeo,** 4655 Humboldt St. Cowboys compete for prize money while over 10,000 head of cattle, horses, sheep, and rabbits compete for "Best of Breed." Between big events, all sorts of oddball fun take place, including western battle re-creations, monkey sheep herders, and rodeo clowns. (☎303-295-1660; www.nationalwestern.com. Tickets $10-20.) The whole area vibrates during the **Denver March Pow-Wow,** at the Denver Coliseum, when over 1000 Native Americans from all over North America dance in full costume to the beat of the drums. (☎303-934-8045; www.denvermarchpowwow.org. $6.) During the first full week of June, the **Capitol Hill People's Fair** is one of the largest arts and crafts festivals in Colorado. (☎303-830-1651; www.peoplesfair.com.) Originally named to celebrate Denver's dual personalities as the Queen City of the Plains and the Monarch Metropolis of the Mountains, **The Festival of Mountain and Plain: A Taste of Colorado** (☎303-295-6330; www.atasteofcolorado.com) packs Civic Center Park on Labor Day weekend.

SPORTS

Denver's baseball team, the **Colorado Rockies,** plays at **Coors Field,** at 20th and Blake St. (☎303-762-5437 or 800-388-7625.) Football's **Denver Broncos** play at the **Mile High Stadium,** 2755 W. 17th Ave. (☎720-258-3333), which is used by soccer's **Colorado Rapids** (☎303-299-1599) during the spring and summer. The NBA's **Denver Nuggets** and the NHL's **Colorado Avalanche** share the state-of-the-art **Pepsi Center,** 1000 Chopper Cir. (☎303-405-1100).

NIGHTLIFE

Downtown Denver, in and around the 16th St. Mall, is an attraction in itself. A copy of the weekly *Westword* gives the lowdown on LoDo, where much of the action begins after dark.

El Chapultepec, 1962 Market St. (☎303-295-9126), at 20th St. A be-boppin' jazz holdover from the Beat era of the 50s with a menu of cheap Mexican food ($3-9). The regulars are a mix of older and younger locals who come for the nightly live music from 9pm. No cover; 1 drink minimum per set. Open daily 8am-2am. Cash only.

The Church, 1160 Lincoln St. (☎303-832-3528). In a remodeled chapel complete with stained-glass windows and an elevated altar area, the Church offers 4 full bars, a cigar lounge, and a sushi bar Sa-Su. Th 18+, F-Su 21+. Cover $5-15 after 10pm. Open Th-Su 9pm-2am. AmEx/D/MC/V.

Wynkoop Brewery, 1634 18th St. (☎303-297-2700; www.wynkoop.com), in LoDo. Colorado's first brewpub serves fresh beer ($3.75-4.50) and homemade root beer, along with full lunch and dinner dishes. An independent improv troupe, Impulse, performs downstairs Th-Sa (☎303-297-2111). Happy hour M-Th 3-6pm and 10pm-midnight, F-Sa 3-6pm, Su 3-6pm and 9pm-midnight. Free brewery tour Sa 1-5pm. Kitchen open M-Sa 11am-2am, Su 10am-midnight. AmEx/D/MC/V.

Foxhole Lounge, 2936 Fox St. (☎303-369-4653; www.foxholesundays.com). A popular, GLBT-friendly neighborhood bar that caters to a younger set. Foxhole has the largest outdoor patio in Denver. Happy hour 6-8pm with $3 Long Island iced teas. No cover. Su gay night. Open M-Sa 6pm-2am; Su 3pm-2am. MC/V.

APPROACHING BOULDER: 30 MILES
Take **I-25 N** to **Exit 217** for **U.S. 36 W**, the **Denver-Boulder Turnpike.**

BOULDER

The 1960s have been slow to fade in Boulder. A liberal haven in an otherwise conservative region, the city brims with fashionable coffee shops, teahouses, and juice bars. Boulder is home to both the central branch of the University of Colorado (CU) and Naropa University, the only accredited Buddhist university in the US. Seek spiritual enlightenment through meditation workshops at Naropa, or pursue a physical awakening through

Boulder's incredible outdoor activities, including biking, hiking, and rafting along Boulder Creek.

VITAL STATS

Population: 95,000

Visitor Info: Boulder Chamber of Commerce and Visitors Service, 2440 Pearl St. (☎303-442-1044; www.boulderchamber.com.), at Folsom. Open M-Th 8:30am-5pm, F 8:30am-4pm.

Internet Access: University of Colorado Information (☎303-492-6161), in the University Memorial Center (UMC). Open in summer M-F 7am-10pm, Sa 9am-11pm, Su noon-10pm; in winter M-F 7am-11pm, Sa 9am-midnight, Su noon-11pm. Free.

Post Office: 1905 15th St., at Walnut St. (☎303-938-3704). Open M-F 7:30am-5:30pm, Sa 10am-2pm. **Postal Code:** 80302.

GETTING AROUND

Boulder is a small, manageable city. The most developed area lies between **Broadway (Rte. 7/Rte. 93)** and **28th St. (Rte. 36),** two busy north-south streets. Broadway, 28th St., Arapahoe Ave. and Baseline Rd. border the **University of Colorado (CU)** campus. The area around the school is known as **the Hill.** The pedestrian-only **Pearl Street Mall,** between 9th and 15th St., is lined with cafes, restaurants, and posh shops. Be alert for bicyclists and careless pedestrians. Avoid meandering around the Hill alone after dark.

SIGHTS

The intimate **Leanin' Tree Museum of Western Art,** 6055 Longbow Dr., presents an acclaimed collection of over 200 paintings and 80 bronze sculptures, depicting people and scenes from the old West. (☎303-530-1442, ext. 299; www.leanintree-museum.com. Open M-F 8am-5pm, Sa-Su 10am-5pm. Free.) **The Celestial Seasonings Tea Company,** 4600 Sleepytime Dr., lures visitors with tea samples and tours of the factory, including the Peppermint Room. (☎303-581-1202. Open M-Sa 10am-3pm, Su 11am-3pm. Tours every hr. Free.)

Boulder supports many outdoor activities in the nearby mountains. Starting at **Scott Carpenter Park,** hiking and biking trails follow Boulder Creek to the foot of the mountains. **Chautauqua Park,** south of the Hill, has many trails varying in length and difficulty that climb up and around the Flatirons. From the auditorium, the **Enchanted Mesa/McClintock Trail** (2 mi.) is an easy loop through meadows and ponderosa pine forests. A more challenging hike, **Greg Canyon Trail** starts at the Baird Park parking lot and rises through the pines above Saddle Rock, winding back down the mountain past Amphitheater Rocks. Before heading into the wilderness, grab a map at the entrance to Chautauqua Park. Beware of mountain lions, and dispose of garbage in the designated receptacles to avoid attracting bears.

🍴 FOOD

The streets on **the Hill,** which surround CU, as well as those along the Pearl St. Mall, burst with eateries, natural food markets, and colorful bars. Twice a week from April through October, Boulder shuts down 13th St. between Canyon and Arapahoe for a lively **Farmers Market.** Most produce and other foods for sale are organic, and samples are widely available. (Open Apr.-Oct. W 4-8pm, Sa 8am-2pm.)

■ **Dushanbe Teahouse,** 1770 13th St. (☎303-442-4993). Built by artists in Tajikistan, and then piece-mailed from Boulder's sister city of Dushanbe. Lays out a scrumptious spread from cultures spanning the globe, focusing on East and Southeast Asia. Breakfast $5-8. Lunch $7-9. Dinner $9-12. Brunch Sa-Su 8am-3pm. Open M-Th 8am-9pm, F 8am-10pm, Sa 3-10pm, Su 5-9pm. AmEx/D/MC/V. ❸

■ **Half Fast Subs,** 1215 13th St. (☎303-449-0404). A standout among sandwich shops. Makes over 90 oven-baked subs. Cheesesteak, stuffed, and vegetarian subs galore go for ridiculously inexpensive prices ($3.50-5). Happy hour (M-F 5-7pm) with 7 in. subs for $3.75. Open M-W and Su 11am-10pm, Th-Sa 11am-1:30am. AmEx/D/MC/V. ❶

Rio Grande, 1101 Walnut St. (☎303-444-3690). Fresh Mexican fare and live local groups which are excellent. Express lunch items are filling ($5.75-6.50). Great collection of premium tequilas. Th live music 9-11pm. Open M-W 11am-2pm and 5-10pm, Th 11am-2pm and 5-10:30pm, F-Sa 11am-10:30pm, Su 11am-10pm. AmEx/MC/V. ❷

Moongate Asian Bistro, 1628 Pearl St. (☎303-565-9787), boasts tasty noodle bowls, salads, and spring rolls each for $4-7. Open M-Th and Su 11am-10pm, F-Sa 11am-11pm. AmEx/D/MC/V. ❶

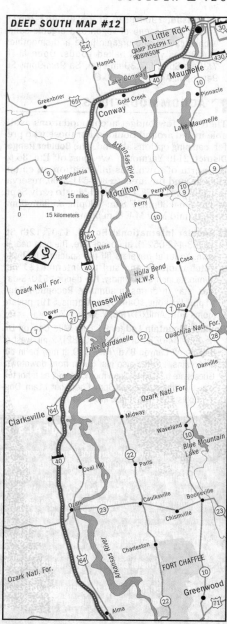

DEEP SOUTH MAP #12

Cafe Prasad, 1904 Pearl St. (☎303-447-2667). Serves a full menu of vegan and organic sandwiches ($6-7) and organic juice and smoothies ($4-6), as well as baked goods. Open M-Th 7:30am-8pm, F 7:30am-9pm, Sa 9am-9pm, Su 9am-8pm. AmEx/D/MC/V. ❷

⚐ ACCOMMODATIONS

There are few budget accommodations available in and around Boulder. For those who prefer, **camping** options abound. The **Boulder Ranger District,** 2140 Yarmouth Ave., just off Rte. 36 to the north of town, has information on campsites around the area. (☎303-541-2500, reservations 877-444-6777. Open mid-May to early Sept. M-Th 8am-4:30pm, F 8am-5:30pm, Sa 9am-3pm; Sept. to mid-May M-F 8am-5pm.)

⚐ Boulder International Hostel, 1107 12th St. (☎303-442-0522), at College Ave. The best deal in town. Youthful travelers fill the spacious lobby to watch cable TV and surf the Internet ($1 per 20min.). Linen $5. Laundry. Key deposit $10. 3-day max. stay in dorms in summer. Reception 8am-11pm. Lockout 10am-5pm. Dorms $19; private rooms $49. AmEx/D/MC/V. ❶

Boulder Mountain Lodge, 91 Four Mile Canyon Dr. (☎435-444-0882 or 800-458-0882), 2 mi. west of Boulder off Canyon Blvd./Hwy. 119. It may be in the mountains, but it's also just 5min. from downtown. Guests are treated to clean rooms as well as a hot tub by the stream. Check-in 3pm. Check-out 11am. Doubles $59-189. AmEx/MC/V. ❸

Chautauqua Association (☎303-442-3282, ext. 11), off Baseline Rd., at the foot of the Flatirons; turn at the Chautauqua Park sign and take Kinnikinic to Morning Glory Dr. Chautauqua has lodge rooms as well as private cottages. Reception June-Aug. M-F 8:30am-7pm, Sa-Su 9am-5pm; Sept.-May M-F 8:30am-5pm, Sa-Su 9am-3pm. Reservations recommended. Rooms from $89. AmEx/D/MC/V.) ❺

Arapahoe/Roosevelt National Forest (☎303-541-2500, reservations 877-444-6777). Information available at Boulder Ranger District (see above). Most sites have water; none have electric hookups. Open mid-May to Oct. Sites $8-17. Cash only. ❶

Kelly Dahl (☎303-541-2500, reservations 877-444-6777), 17 mi. west on Hwy. 119. The closest campground to Boulder. 46 sites lie among pine trees and picnic tables with open views of the Continental Divide. Sites $14. Cash only. ❶

Rainbow Lakes (☎303-541-2500, reservations 877-444-6777), 6½ mi. north of Nederland off Hwy. 72; turn at the Mountain Research Station (CR 116) and follow the dirt road for 5 mi. A primitive, quiet camping experience. No water. Sites $8. Cash only. ❶

♫ ENTERTAINMENT

An exciting street scene bumps through both the Mall and the Hill; the university's kiosks have the lowdown on happenings. From June to August, find live music and street performances on Pearl St. Mall. (Tu and Th-F noon-

MEALS ON WHEELS

Roadtrips and good food are not generally synonymous terms, at least in the history of the American roadtrip. Roadtrippers spend the majority of their money on gas, cheap motels, and kitschy roadside attractions, leaving pittance for food. In an effort to save money, roadtrippers limit meal options to the three sandwiches (or rather two slices of bread plus condiment) on the menu for under $5. Or worse, they skip the restaurant altogether and simply munch on honey-roasted peanuts and $1 gas station burritos in between highway exits. But just because you're driving from coast-to-coast doesn't mean that your meals should be anything less than square. All you need for a dinner that will make your grandmother proud is...your car engine. For every wad of cash you pour into your gas tank, a huge amount of heat is produced under the hood. In order to harness this engine cooking power, you need heavy duty aluminum foil and some space next to the manifold (hint: it's metal and hot). Then head to a local grocery store and pick up your meal of choice; if you're still tied to your microwave oven, start off with a pre-prepared frozen meal. Otherwise, pick up some fish or chicken (other meats tend to get tough) and a few vegetables. Wrap these morsels tight in the foil and secure them on a hot (i.e. metal) part of the engine with wire. By the time you reach your destination of

1:30pm.) From late June to early Aug., the **Colorado Shakespeare Festival** draws over 50,000 people, making it the third-largest festival of its kind. (☎303-492-0554; www.coloradoshakes.org. Tickets from $10.) The **Colorado Music Festival** performs at Chautauqua Park July through August. (☎303-449-1397; www.coloradomusicfest.org. Tickets from $10.) The local indie music scene is on display at the popular **Fox Theater and Cafe,** 1135 13th St. (☎303-447-0095; www.foxtheater.com Shows usually around 8pm. Call ahead for schedule and prices.)

🎵 NIGHTLIFE

The city overflows with nightlife hot spots, each catering to a young crowd with its own unique spin.

🍺🍺 Mountain Sun Pub and Brewery, 1535 Pearl St. (☎303-546-0886). The place to go for bluegrass, funk, and the best brews in town. Try the "kind crippler." Acoustic performances Su 10pm-1am. $2 pints daily 4-6pm and 10pm-1am. Open M-Sa 11:30am-1am, Su noon-midnight. Cash only.

The Sink, 1165 13th St. (☎303-444-7465; www.the-sink.com). A Boulder classic, the Sink still awaits the return of its one-time janitor, Robert Redford, who quit his job and headed to California in the late 1950s. Students fill the place for late-night drinking and great pizzas ($5-18) amid wild graffiti and low ceilings. Open M-Sa 11am-2am, Su noon-2am. Kitchen closes 10pm. D/MC/V.

The West End Tavern, 926 Pearl St. (☎303-444-3535), has a rooftop bar with a view of downtown and a moderately priced menu. Draft beers $4-5. Open M-Sa 11am-11:30pm, Su 11:30am-11:30pm. Bar open until 1:30am. MC/V.

⛰ APPROACHING ESTES PARK: 38 MILES

Head north on **28th St.** to **U.S. 36 W.** Allow 1hr. from Boulder to **Estes Park,** and another 30min. to get into **Rocky Mountain National Park** itself. About halfway to Estes Park, U.S. 36 W becomes **Main St.** in the city of Lyons; consider stopping at **Lyons Soda Fountain ❶,** 400 Main St., on the corner of Main St. and 4th St., for one of their famous malts or milkshakes ($5). Their "Hungry Lyon" sandwiches ($2.50) are also quite tasty. (☎303-823-5393; www.lyonsicecream.com. Open Tu-W and Su 10am-8pm, M 11am-8pm, F-Sa 9am-8pm. MC/V.) Gas gets even more expensive beyond the park—the next gas spot with decent prices is Kremmling., so fill up in Boulder.

> ⚠ The route through Rocky Mountain National Park from Estes Park to Grand Lake is closed from mid-Oct. to June. If you are traveling during this time, you will need to head back out to Estes Park and take Rte. 7 to Rte. 72 to Rte. 119 down to I-70.

ESTES PARK

As the gateway town to Rocky Mountain National Park, Estes Park sits in the valley below the Front Range, the first of the Rockies. Though a prime location for tourists, quaint Estes Park has

choice, the meal will be steamed through, perfect for your dining delight. Cooking by engine is not an exact science and can be dangerous to both you and your car if done incorrectly. Odds are, your first meal will not meet with Martha Stewart's approval, but don't worry—you have 3,000 mi. to perfect it.

Salmon with Lemon and Soy Sauce
Ingredients:
- ¼ lb. salmon filet
- 1 lemon, sliced
- 2 teaspoons olive oil
- 2 soy sauce packets

Cut the salmon filet in half. Tear two squares of tin foil and spread the dull side evenly with olive oil. Place a salmon portion on each square and place lemon slices on it. Pour contents of one soy sauce packet over each portion and wrap up into a tight packet. Tuck each packet next to the manifold. Drive 40 mi. at 65 mph. If the salmon does not flake easily, replace and drive another 5 mi. Delish!

resisted the commercialization and glitz of other mountain towns.

■ GETTING AROUND. Trail Ridge Rd. runs from Estes Park through the Rocky Mountain National Park. **I-34,** known as **Fall River Rd.,** and **I-36,** known as **N. St. Vrain Ave.,** also run through Estes Park.

◙ SIGHTS. The **Stanley Hotel ❺,** 333 Wonderview Ave., found itself in the spotlight as the "Overlook Hotel" in the film adaptation of Stephen King's novel *The Shining,* and in several other movies, including "Dumb and Dumber." Tours of the hotel show its connections to Stephen King and its other appearances in pop culture; ghost-story-telling sessions take place on weekends. A glass of milk and cookies are provided. (☎970-586-3371 or 800-976-1377; www.stanleyhotel.com. 8 tours daily 10am-5pm; ghost stories F-Sa 9pm. Tours and ghost stories $10. Rooms $179-1200. AmEx/D/MC/V.) The **Estes Park Area Historical Museum,** 200 4th St., offers an account of the town's history, including info on local wildlife, the area's Native American tribes, and the history of the fur trapping and gold mining industry. (☎970-586-6256. Open May-Oct. M-Sa 10am-5pm, Su 1-5pm; Nov.-Apr. F-Sa 10am-5pm, Su 1-5pm. Free.)

▓▐ FOOD AND ACCOMMODATIONS. Locals flock to **The Notchtop Bakery & Cafe ❷,** 459 E. Wonderview, for freshly baked breads, pastries, and pies. (In the upper Stanley Village Shopping Plaza, east of downtown off Rte. 34. ☎970-586-0272. Sandwiches and wraps $6-7. Open M-Sa 7am-8pm, Su 7am-

Prospect Dr., keeps eight of its signature beers on tap and also maintains a seasonal rotation of brews. (☎970-586-5421. Open daily 11am-11pm. AmEx/D/DC/MC/V.) In the heart of downtown, **Local's Grill ❷,** 153 E. Elkhorn Ave., is a self-proclaimed "world-famous gathering place." Customers crowd the front patio for gourmet sandwiches ($5-8) and pizza. (☎970-586-6900. Open M-Th 11am-9pm, F-Su 11am-10pm. AmEx/D/MC/V.) The intimate seating area at **Sweet Basilico Cafe ❷,** 401 E. Elkhorn Ave., overflows with patrons seeking focaccia bread sandwiches ($6.50-7.25) and freshly made pastas ($8-11). Be prepared to wait, even during the week. (☎970-586-3899. Open June-Sept. M-F 11am-10pm, Sa-Su 11:30am-10pm; Oct.-May Tu-Su 11am-2:30pm and 4:30-9pm. AmEx/D/MC/V.)

The tidy, dorm-style rooms at **The Colorado Mountain School ❷,** 341 Moraine Ave., are open to travelers unless booked by mountain-climbing students. (☎970-586-5758. Reception June-Sept. daily 8am-5pm; hours vary in winter. Dorms $35. AmEx/D/MC/V.) **Saddle & Surrey Motel ❹,** 1341 S. Saint Vrain (Rte. 7), offers clean and comfy rooms with access to a heated outdoor pool and spa. (☎800-204-6226. Singles $85; doubles $95. D/MC/V.) Rooms at the beautiful **Baldpate Inn ❺,** 4900 S. Saint Vrain (Rte. 7) don't come cheap, but is located at the doorstep of Rocky Mountain National Park,. (☎970-586-6151, www.baldpateinn.com. Reservations recommended. 2-night min. stay. Rooms from $100; cabins from $180. MC/V.)

▓ APPROACHING ROCKY MOUNTAIN NATIONAL PARK: 3 MILES
From Estes Park, take **U.S. 34 W** into the park.

ROCKY MOUNTAIN NATIONAL PARK

Of all the US national parks, Rocky Mountain National Park is closest to heaven, with over 60 peaks exceeding 12,000 ft. A third of the park lies above the treeline, and Longs Peak tops off at 14,256 ft. Here among the clouds, the alpine tundra ecosystem supports bighorn sheep, dwarf wildflowers, and arctic shrubs interspersed among granite boulders and crystal lakes. Crea-

mots also call the park home. Mountain lions are very rare but occasionally seen.

VITAL STATS

Area: 266,000 acres

Visitor Info: Park Headquarters and Visitors Center (☎970-586-1206), 2½ mi. west of Estes Park on Rte. 36, at the Beaver Meadows entrance to the park. Open mid-June to late Aug. M-W 8am-8pm, Th-Su 8am-9pm; Sept. to mid-June daily 8am-5pm.

Fees: 7-day pass $20 per vehicle, $10 per motorcycle. Backcountry camping permit $20.

▣ GETTING AROUND. U.S. 36 and **U.S. 34** both lead into Rocky Mountain National Park. **U.S. 36** is the main route into the park; it's about 2 mi. shorter than U.S. 34 and passes the **Beaver Meadows Visitors Center,** the campgrounds at Moraine Park and Glacier Basin, and the trailheads at Sprague Lake and Bear Lake. **U.S. 34,** less crowded, passes the Aspenglen campground, provides access to Old Fall River Rd., and goes by the smaller **Fall River Visitors Center.**

▣ SIGHTS. Moraine Park Museum, off Bear Lake Rd., 1½ mi. from the Beaver Meadows entrance, has exhibits on the park's geology and ecosystem, as well as comfortable rocking chairs with a view of the mountains. Many exhibits explain how tectonic action and glaciers shaped the park. (☎970-586-8842. Open June-Aug. daily 9am-5pm. Free.) The park's most popular trails are all accessible from the Bear Lake Trailhead at the south end of Bear Lake Rd. Parking is available halfway down the road, and a shuttle bus leads from this parking area to the scenic (and very busy) trailhead.

▣ OUTDOORS. The star of the park is **Trail Ridge Rd. (U.S. 34),** a 48 mi. stretch across the park that rises 12,183 ft. above sea level into frigid tundra. The drive takes roughly 3hr. by car with traffic and a few stops, though it is possible to get to the other side of the park in 90min. Beware of slow-moving tour buses and people stopping to ogle wildlife. The road usually closes for the year in mid-October and reopens Memorial Day weekend, but it is also sometimes closed or inaccessible due to icy conditions, even in June. Heading west, steal a view of the park from the boardwalk along the highway at **Many Parks Curve. Rainbow Curve** and the **Forest Canyon Overlook** offer impressive views of the tree-carpeted landscape. The **Tundra Communities Trail** provides a look at the fragile alpine tundra. Signposts along the paved trail explain local geology and wildlife. The **Lava Cliffs** attract crowds, but it's worth the hassle. After peaking at **Gore Range,** a mighty 12,183 ft. above sea level, Trail Ridge Rd. runs north to the **Alpine Visitors Center.**

A wilder alternative to Trail Ridge Rd. is **Old Fall River Rd.,** a one-way dirt road that leads uphill through part of the park and passes **Chasm Falls.** The road rejoins Trail Ridge Rd. behind the Alpine Visitors Center. RVs and trailers should not take Old Fall River Rd. because of steep hills. This road is closed in winter and does not usually open until the 4th of July. **Bear Lake Rd.,** south of Trail Ridge Rd., leads to campgrounds and the most popular hiking trails within the park. **Flattop Mountain** (4½ mi., 3hr.), the most challenging and picturesque of the Bear Lake hikes, climbs 2800 ft. to a vantage point along the Continental Divide. **Nymph** (½ mi., 15min.), **Dream** (1 mi., 30min.), and **Emerald Lakes** (1¾ mi., 1hr.) are a series of three glacial pools offering inspiring glimpses of the surrounding peaks. Forking left from the trail, **Lake Haiyaha** (2¼ mi., 1¼hr.) includes switchbacks through dense sub-alpine forests and superb views of the mountains. A scramble over the rocks at the end grants a view of Lake Haiyaha. Numerous trailheads lie in the western half of the park, including the **Continental Divide** and its accompanying hiking trail.

▣ CAMPING. Visitors can camp a total of seven days anywhere within the park. In the backcountry, the maximum stay increases to 14 days during the winter. Water spigots are available but are turned off during the winter. Reservations are taken at Glacier Basin and Moraine Park up to five months in advance, but the other sites are first come, first served, and fill up quickly. Backcountry permits are available from the **Backcountry Permits and Trip Planning Building,** directly adjacent to the park headquarters at Beaver Meadows. (☎970-586-1242. Open daily mid-May to late Oct. 7am-7pm; Nov. to mid-May 8am-5pm. $20.) The only national park campground on the western side of the park is **Timber Creek ❶**, 10 mi. north of Grand Lake. (☎800-365-2267. Sites in summer $20; in winter $14. AmEx/D/MC/V.) Campsites can also be found in the surrounding **Arapaho National Forest ❶**. (☎970-887-4100. Sites in summer $20; in winter $14. AmEx/D/ MC/V.) **Stillwater Campground ❶**, west of Grand Lake on the shores of Lake Granby, has 127 tranquil sites. (Open year-round. Sites $16, with water $19, with full hookup $21. AmEx/D/MC/V.) **Green Ridge Campground ❶**, on the south end of Shadow Mountain Lake, is also a good bet with 78 sites. (☎877-444-6777; www.reserveusa.com. Open mid-May to mid-Nov. Sites $13. AmEx/D/MC/V.)

⚐ APPROACHING GRAND LAKE: 4 MILES
Turn off **U.S. 34** at the sign for Grand Lake, and stay right at the fork in the road.

GRAND LAKE

Grand Lake, the "snowmobile capital of Colorado," offers spectacular cross-country routes and is the jumping-off point for several hiking trails.

VITAL STATS

Population: 450

Visitor Info: Grand Lake Chamber of Commerce, (☎970-627-3402; www.grandlakechamber.com). Call ahead for hours and location.

Internet Access: Juniper Library, 316 Garfield St. (☎970-627-8353). Open M and F 10am-6pm, W-Th 10am-8pm, Sa noon-4pm. Free.

Post Office: 520 Center Dr. (☎970-627-3340). Open M-F 8:30am-5pm. **Postal Code:** 80442.

⬛ GETTING AROUND. Trail Ridge Rd. runs through Grand Lake. **Shadow Mountain Lake** and **Grand Lake** both border town.

⬛ OUTDOORS. Lake Verna (7 mi., 3½hr. round-trip), starts at the East Inlet Trailhead at the east end of Grand Lake. This moderate hike gains a total of 1800 ft. in elevation as it passes **Adams Falls** and **Lone Pine Lake** and rewards hikers with open views of **Mt. Craig** before re-entering the forest. (Turn off U.S. 34 at the sign for Grand Lake, and stay left at the fork for W. Portal Rd. The North Inlet Trailhead is off a dirt road to the left. The East Inlet Trailhead lies at the end of the

road; proceed straight onto CR 339, and the trailhead is to the left.) **Deer Mountain** (6 mi., 3hr. round-trip), leaving from Deer Mountain Trailhead, is a moderate hike with a 1000 ft. rise. The light foliage affords views of the Rockies all the way up. For fun in the snow, **Lone Eagle Lodge**, 720 Grand Ave., offers unguided snow mobile rentals that include suits, helmets, boots, fuel, oil, and a map. (☎970-627-3310 or 800-282-3311; www.loneeaglelodge.com. Reservations recommended. 1hr. deposit required. 4hr. single rental $105; double $125; 8hr. rental $165/$185.)

⬛⬛ FOOD AND ACCOMMODATIONS. At the far end of town, **Pancho and Lefty's ❸**, 1120 Grand Ave., has an outdoor patio overlooking Grand Lake and a bar large enough to fit most of its residents. Try the *rellenos fritos* ($12-13), and wash it all down with a margarita for $4.50. (☎970-627-8773. Live music on some weekends. Open June-Sept. daily 11am-9pm; Sept.-June M-Th 11am-8pm, F-Su 11am-9pm. D/MC/V.) The **Bear's Den ❸**, 612 Grand Ave., serves hearty meals, like chicken-fried steak ($14.50), and box lunches ($7.75-8.75-) with chips, a pickle, and dessert—perfect for taking on the road or trail. (☎970-627-3385. Open M-F 5-10pm, Sa-Su 11:30am-2:30pm and 5-10pm. D/MC/V.)

Perched on a cliff overlooking the Rockies, the hand-built **⬛Shadowcliff Hostel (HI-AYH) ❶**, 405 Summerland Park Rd., is sure to delight. The friendly staff almost equal the magnificent view. (☎970-627-9220. Kitchen, showers, wood-burning stove. Internet access $3 per day. Linens included. 7-night min. stay for cabins. Reservations recommended. Open June-Sept. Dorms $23, members $20; private rooms with shared bath $45; 6- to 8-bed cabins $100. AmEx/D/MC/V.) Cozy rooms and the only heated, indoor pool in Grand Lake await at **Sunset Motel ❹**, 505 Grand Ave., which boasts a yellow front and baby-blue trim. (☎970-627-3318. Singles in summer from $95; in winter from $45. MC/V.) **Bluebird Motel ❹**, 30 River Dr., 2 mi. west of town on Rte. 34, overlooks Shadow Mountain Lake and the Continental Divide and has affordable rooms with microwaves and fridges. (☎970-627-9314. Singles in summer $85; in winter $45. MC/V.)

⚐ APPROACHING HOT SULPHUR SPRINGS: 25 MILES
Continue west on **U.S. 34** to **U.S. 40 W.**

NATIONAL ROAD

HOT SULPHUR SPRINGS. As the name suggest, Hot Sulphur Springs is known for its naturally luxurious hot springs. Many people in the area treat themselves to a soak at the **Hot Sulphur Springs Resort and Spa ❸**, 5609 C.R. 20. This tranquil spot, where signs exhort you to keep quiet, is fed by natural mineral hot springs, ranging from 96-110° F. While a snack bar is available, food facilities are limited, so pack a lunch. If you can't drag yourself away, the motel-style rooms are small, but clean, and have log-style wooden furniture. (☎970-725-3306. Open daily 8am-10pm. Hot springs $16.50. Private bath $12 per hr. Rooms $98-108. D/MC/V.)

APPROACHING KREMMLING: 17 MILES
Continue on **U.S. 40 W** for 17 mi.; it becomes **W. Park Ave.** in Kremmling.

KREMMLING

Forty-two miles from Grand Lake, Kremmling offers few cultural attractions or restaurants; the area serves primarily as a regional base for outdoor sports. **Mad Adventures**, on U.S. 40, east of town, will outfit you for class I-III rafting on the Colorado River. (☎970-726-5290; www.madadventures.com. Half-day trips $44, ages 4-11 $37; full day $64/$54.) Before leaving Kremmling, consider taking a ride down **Trough Rd.**, 2 mi. south of town. It ascends gradually for 8½ mi. to a turn-off at **Inspiration Point**, providing a stupendous view of the impossibly steep Gore Canyon and the headwaters of the Colorado River, which slices through the canyon far below.

The **Moose Cafe ❶**, 115 W. Park Ave., serves all-day breakfast and lunch. Try the "Moose omelette," which is filled with a little bit of everything, but no moose ($9.25). The "moose latte" ($5) is an espresso milkshake with chocolate and caramel sauce. (☎970-724-9987. Breakfast $3.50-9.25. Hot sandwiches $6-7.50. Open daily 6am-2pm. MC/V.) **Big Shooters Coffee ❶**, 204 W. Park Ave., has a selection of coffee drinks ($1.25-5), ice cream ($1.50-5.50), and pastries ($2) baked fresh daily. (☎970-724-3735. Open M-F 6am-7pm, Sa-Su 7am-6pm. MC/V.) The prices at **Hotel Eastin ❷**, 105 S. 2nd St., off W. Park Ave., are just about the lowest in town. Some rooms still have original antique furnishings from when the hotel first opened in 1906. (☎970-724-3261; www.hoteleastin.com. Free Wi-Fi. Rooms $29-46. AmEx/MC/V.) **Bob's Western Motel ❸**, 110 W. Park Ave., has a variety of basic rooms. (☎970-724-3266. Singles $50; doubles $60. AmEx/D/MC/V.)

DETOUR
LOWER CATARACT LAKE TRAIL AND WHITE RIVER NATIONAL FOREST
Take Rte. 9 S for 12½ mi., and turn right onto Heeney Rd. 30. After 5 mi., turn right on Cataract Creek Rd. The campground is 2 mi. along the road, and the trailhead is ¾ mi. farther. This route is not recommended in wintertime.

The lake is magnificent, surrounded by sloping hills on all sides and the higher rocky peaks off in the distance to the south. The highlight of the area is the wonderful **Lower Cataract Loop Trail** and neighboring **Cataract Creek Campsite** (entrance fee $5). There are seven mostly sunny open-area lakeside **campgrounds ❶**, operated by the National Forest Service (sites $9-13), and several are accessible from Rte. 9 and Heeney Rd. 30. There are also four primitive drive-in camping sites ($10), perfect for sleeping under the stars.

APPROACHING FRISCO: 50 MILES
Take **Rte. 9 S** until it joins with **I-70 W.** Follow I-70 for 3 mi. to **Exit 203** for **Rte. 9 S/Frisco.**

FRISCO

The mountains stare down from all sides at the droves of tourists who come to Frisco to bike the mountain trails or ski in the area. Downtown, expensive restaurants and sport shops cater to seasonal visitors.

VITAL STATS

Population: 2400

Visitor Info: Summit County Visitors Center, 300 Main St. (☎800-424-1554; www.townoffrisco.com), on the corner of 3rd St. Open daily 8am-6pm.

Internet Access: Frisco-Summit County Library, 37 County Rd. 1005 (☎970-668-5547). Take Summit Blvd. south of Main St. Open M-Th 9am-9pm, F-Sa 9am-5pm, Su 1-5pm. Free.

Post Office: 35 W. Main St. (☎970-668-0610), at Madison. Open M-F 8:30am-5pm, Sa 9am-12:30pm. **Postal Code:** 80443.

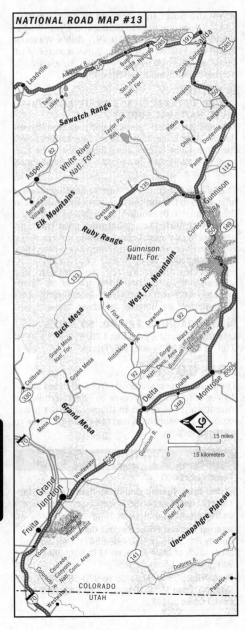

NATIONAL ROAD MAP #13

⌐ GETTING AROUND. Frisco is extremely easy to navigate. **I-70** borders the town to the northwest. **Summit Blvd. (Rte. 9),** home to motels, Wal-Mart, Safeway, and other large stores, runs north-south along the eastern edge of town from I-70 to Main St. before heading southeast. **Main St.,** the town's principle commercial street, runs east-west from I-70 on the west to Summit Blvd. on the east and is home to restaurants, lodging establishments, and local stores.

⚞ OUTDOORS. In the summer, Frisco, Breckenridge, and surrounding Summit County are a biking haven, with some 70 mi. of paved trails and many more mountain paths. A popular moderate route circles **Dillon Reservoir** (18 mi., 2hr.). Biking the easier route to Breckenridge along the **Blue River Pathway** (9½ mi., 1½hr.) is also popular. Each of these trails can be accessed near the parking lot by the Frisco Bay marina, at the end of Main St. Bike rentals are available at **Wilderness Sports,** 400 Main St. (☎970-668-8804. Bikes $18-38 per day. Open in summer daily 8:30am-6pm.) Miles of hiking trails crisscross the area and go up into the mountains. The fun, moderate climb up to 1350 ft. **Mt. Royal** (4½ mi., 2-3hr. round-trip) offers great views of Lake Dillon and Frisco. (To get to the trailhead, take Main St. heading west. Just before the entrance to I-70, turn left into the parking lot for the Tenmile Canyon Trailhead. Park and follow the bike path a half-mile southeast along the mountain's base.) **Ten-Mile Meadows** (10 mi., 5-6hr. round-trip), off W. Main St., after the entrance to I-70, is considered one of the most difficult and rewarding trails in the area, passing a series of meadows and a view of the Swan River Valley.

Summit County offers some of Colorado's best skiing. **Breckenridge** (☎970-453-5000 or 800-789-7669; www.breckenridge.com) is 9 mi. south of Frisco on Rte. 9. One of the most popular ski resorts in the country, Breckenridge has a 3400 ft. vertical drop, 146 trails, one of the best halfpipes in North America, and 2043 acres of skiable terrain accessible by 28 lifts. In the summer, most mountains offer hiking, biking, and various other outdoor activities; consult the **Breckenridge Activities Center,** 137 S. Main St., at Washington St., for details. (☎970-453-5579 or 877-864-0868. Open daily 9am-5pm.)

FOOD AND ACCOMMODATIONS. The **Pika Bagel Bakery and Cafe ❶**, 401 Main St., proudly bakes its pastries at an elevation of 9100 ft. The "Cool One" sandwich ($3) features cucumbers and herb cream cheese. (☎970-668-0902. Sandwiches $3.50-6.50. Open daily 7:21am-3:08pm. D/MC/V.) The **Backcountry Brewpub and Pizzeria ❸**, 720 Main St., offers light items like the smoked-turkey-club wrap with chipotle ranch dressing ($8), but pizza (from $8.25) is their specialty. (☎970-668-2337; www.backcountrybrewery.com. Pints $4. Open daily 10am-11pm. MC/V.) The **Boatyard Pizzeria and Grill ❸**, 304 Main St., serves gourmet pizzas starting at $11. (☎970-668-4728. Open M-Sa 11am-10pm, Su 4-10pm. MC/V.)

South of Frisco, in Breckenridge, you can find reasonably priced, smoke-free accommodations at the **⚑Fireside Inn (HI-AYH) ❷**, 114 N. French St., two blocks east of Main St., at the corner of Wellington Rd. Set in a mining cottage that dates back to 1870, the beautiful inn is well-maintained and has an indoor hot tub great for après-ski. (☎970-453-6456; www.firesideinn.com. Breakfast $3-6. Reception daily 8am-9:30pm. Dorms in summer $25; in winter $38. Private rooms $65/$180. MC/V.) **New Summit Inn ❹**, 1205 N. Summit Blvd., off Dillon Dam Rd., has rooms with refrigerators and mountain views. (Take Summit Blvd. one block south from I-70. ☎970-668-3220. Free Wi-Fi. Continental breakfast included. Rooms in summer $50-84; in winter $99-220. MC/V.) The **Snowshoe Motel ❹**, 521 Main St., has modern rooms in downtown Frisco. (☎970-668-3444. Hot tub, sauna, and free Wi-Fi. Rooms in summer $55-75; in winter $75-125. AmEx/D/MC/V.) **Heaton Bay Campground ❶**, on Dillon Dam Rd., has 72 shady spots northwest of the reservoir with water and outhouse style toilets. "D" loop is the quietest, but "C" loop has hookups. (☎877-444-6777; www.reserveusa.com. 2-night min. stay on weekends. 10-day max. stay. Reservations required. Sites $14. AmEx/D/MC/V.)

APPROACHING VAIL: 36 MILES
Follow **Main St.** to **I-70 W.** Take **Exit 176** for Vail.

VAIL

The largest, one-mountain ski resort in all of North America, Vail has its fair share of ritzy hotels and boutiques, but it's the mountain that wows skiers with its prime powder and famed back bowls. With skiers and employees from around the world, the resort has an international feel unlike other Colorado ski towns. Discovered by Lord Gore in 1854, the Vail area was swarmed by prospectors during the 1870s gold rush. According to legend, the Ute tribe adored the area's rich supply of game but became so upset with the white settlers that they set fire to the forest, creating the open terrain beloved by so many visitors today.

VITAL STATS

Population: 4500

Visitor Info: Vail Visitors Center, S. Frontage Rd. (☎800-525-3875), in Vail Village. Open daily in summer 8am-7pm; in winter 8am-6pm.

Internet Access: Vail Public Library, 292 W. Meadow Dr. (☎970-479-2184). Open M-Th 10am-8pm, F 11am-6pm, Sa-Su 11am-6pm. Free.

Post Office: 1300 N. Frontage Rd. W. (☎970-476-5217). Open M-F 8:30am-5pm, Sa 8:30am-noon.

Postal Code: 81657.

GETTING AROUND. Vail consists of **East Vail, Vail Village, Lionshead Village, Cascade Village,** and **West Vail.** Vail Village and Lionshead Village, which are the main centers of action, are pedestrian-only.

SIGHTS. The **Ski Hall of Fame** is housed in the **Colorado Ski Museum,** on the third level of the Vail Transportation Center. A fascinating exhibit focuses on the 10th Mountain Division and its training in the Rockies for the rigors of fighting in the mountains of Italy during WWII. (☎970-476-1876. Open June-Sept. and Nov.-Apr. Tu-Su 10am-5pm. Free.) In the summer, the **Gerald R. Ford Amphitheater,** at the east edge of Vail Village, presents a number of outdoor concerts, dance festivals, and theater productions. (☎970-476-2918. Box office open June-Sept. daily 11am-5pm. Lawn seats $19-23.) Next door in the lovely **Betty Ford Alpine Gardens,** stroll through the peaceful meditation and rock gardens. (☎970-476-0103. Open May-Sept. sunrise-sunset. Tours M, Th, Sa 10:30am. Free.) The **Vilar Center for the Arts,** in Beaver Creek, hosts performances of everything from Shakespeare to Broadway. (☎970-845-8497 or 888-920-2787; www.vilarcenter.org. Box office open M-Sa 11am-5pm.)

⚒ OUTDOORS. The mountain's 193 trails, 34 lifts, 5289 skiable acres, and seven legendary back bowls are certainly worth the expense. (☎800-892-8062; www.vail.com.) Before slaloming, visit **Ski Base**, 610 W. Lionshead Cir., for equipment. In the summer, the store becomes **Wheel Base Bike Shop.** (☎970-476-5799. Skis, poles, and boots from $23 per day. Snowboard and boots from $22 per day. Bikes $44 per day. Open daily in summer 9am-6pm.; in winter 8am-7pm.) The **Eagle Bahn Gondola** in Lionshead and the **Vista Bahn Chairlift,** part of Vail Resort, whisk hikers and bikers to the top of the mountains. Tickets and passes can be purchased at the LionsHead Summer Pass Office, located below Garfinkel's Restaurant (see below) near the base of the Gondola, or at the Vail Village Pass Office. (☎970-476-9090. Eagle Bahn open in summer daily 10am-4pm; in winter F-Su 10am-4pm. Day pass $18, ages 65-69 and 5-12 $11. Bike haul $30. Vista Bahn open mid-July to early Sept. F-Su 10am-4pm.)

🍴🍸 FOOD AND NIGHTLIFE. You'll never need to cook breakfast in Vail as long as the griddle is hot at **DJ McCadams Classic Diner ❷**, 616 W. LionsHead Plaza, on the west end of Lionshead Village. During the winter, locals ski in around the clock to warm up with DJ's crepes ($5.50-7), omelettes ($4-6.50), and pasta frittatas from $7.50. (☎970-476-2336. Open in summer daily 7am-1pm, F 10pm-3am; in winter M 7am-1pm, Tu 7am-midnight, W-Sa 24hr., Su midnight-1pm. Cash only.) With Alabama-style barbecue, **Moe's Original BBQ ❷**, 675 W. Lionshead Cir., describes itself as "A Southern Soulfood Revival." Their box lunches ($8-12) might be the best deal in town. (☎970-479-7888. Open M-Sa 11am-9pm. MC/V.) Right in the heart of Vail Village, **The Red Lion ❹**, Hanson Ranch Rd. and Bridge St., was built by its owners as a hotel, but they had so many children there were no rooms left for guests. (☎970-476-7676. Barbecue brisket $13. Open daily 10am-midnight or 2am. Kitchen closes 10pm. AmEx/D/DC/MC/V.)

With two bars and seven decks, **The Tap Room ❷**, 333 Bridge St., in Vail Village, caters to those looking for good, rowdy fun. Wash down one of their famous burgers ($6-12) with your drink of choice, and soak up the mountain air at one of Vail's coolest after-the-slopes

bars. (☎970-479-0500. Open daily 11:30am-2am. Kitchen closes 10pm. AmEx/D/MC/V.) **Garfinkel's ❸**, 536 E. Lionshead Cir., draws a young crowd to a large beer selection and generous portions. (☎970-476-3789. Meals $8-11. Open June-Sept. and Nov.-Apr. daily 11am-2am. Kitchen closes 10pm. AmEx/MC/V.)

🏨 ACCOMMODATIONS. Cheap lodging is not part of Vail's mentality. Rooms rarely dip below $175 per night in winter, and summer lodging is often equally pricey. The **Roost Lodge ❸**, 1783 N. Frontage Rd., in West Vail, provides relatively affordable lodging. The rooms are impressively clean and include breakfast, cable TV, fridge, microwave, and access to a jacuzzi, sauna, and heated, indoor pool. (☎970-476-5451 or 800-873-3065. Continental breakfast in winter. Singles in summer $59-69; in winter $99-129. AmEx/D/MC/V.) **Lionshead Inn ❺**, 705 W. Lionshead Cir., has good deals on luxury accommodations in the summer. In addition to an exercise room, game room, hot tub, fireplace lounge, and free Internet access, the Inn offers plush robes, down comforters, and balconies in every room. (☎970-476-2050 or 800-283-8245; www.lionsheadinn.com. Continental breakfast included. Singles in summer from $89; in winter from $199. AmEx/D/MC/V.) The **Holy Cross Ranger District ❶**, 24747 U.S. 24, in Minturn, provides info on summer campgrounds near Vail. Most sites are primitive with picnic tables and fire grates. (☎970-827-5715. Ranger District open M-F 8am-5pm. Sites $10-15. MC/V.)

🚗 APPROACHING LEADVILLE: 24 MILES Take **I-70 W** to **Exit 171** for **U.S. 24 S**, which becomes **Poplar St.** in Leadville.

LEADVILLE

Leadville has a rich history as a mining town. Fortunes were made and lost overnight as 13 major minerals including gold, silver, lead, zinc, and molybdenum were mined here. The mining history is documented in the town's six museums; Leadville has the most museums per capita of any city in Colorado. With an elevation of 10,152 ft., it is the highest incorporated city in the US and also marks the beginning of a cluster of **"fourteeners"** (mountain peaks over 14,000 ft.), which attract hikers and thrill-seekers from far and wide.

VITAL STATS

Population: 2800

Visitor Info: Leadville Chamber of Commerce, 809 Harrison Ave. (☎719-486-3900). Open daily 9am-5pm.

Internet Access: Lake County Public Library, 1115 Harrison Ave. (☎719-486-0569). Open M and W 10am-8pm, Tu and Th 10am-5pm, F-Su 1-5pm. Free.

Post Office: 130 W. 5th St. (☎719-486-9397). Open M-F 8am-5pm, Sa 9am-noon. **Postal Code:** 80461.

☗ **GETTING AROUND. Front St., Poplar St., Harrison Ave., Mountain View Dr., Mt. Massive Dr.,** and **McWethy Dr.** form a loop around the downtown area. **6th St.** is the main thoroughfare within this loop.

◪ **SIGHTS.** The **National Mining Hall of Fame and Museum,** 120 W. 9th St., showcases the mining that resulted when the '49ers headed to Colorado in search of gold. The best part of the museum is the second floor, which features three recreated mines and a set of dioramas. The crystal room is also worth a look. (☎719-486-1229; www.mininghalloffame.org. Open May-Oct. daily 9am-5pm; Nov.-Apr. M-Sa 10am-4pm. $6, ages 6-11 $3.) The **Healy House and Dexter Cabin Museum,** 912 Harrison Ave., both date from the first decades of the town's founding. Dexter Cabin was the lavish mountain hideaway of Colorado's first millionaire, James Dexter, while Healy House is a Greek Revival home with a opulent interior. (☎719-486-0487. Open May-Oct. daily 10am-4:30pm. $5, seniors $4.50, ages 6-16 $3.50.) The **Mineral Belt Trail,** a 12½ mi., all-season, paved loop, circles the town, following old railroad rights-of-way and paths through California and Slaughterhouse Gulches. Along the way it passes the remnants of several old mines, tunnels, and shafts. The trail is closed to motor vehicles but is popular for biking.

▦▟ **FOOD AND ACCOMMODATIONS.** Locals enjoy the relaxed atmosphere at the **Golden Burro ❷,** 710 Harrison Ave. Try their signature breakfast item, the "Golden Breakfast Burrito" ($8.75) with green chili. (☎719-486-1239. Open daily in summer 6:30am-9pm; hours vary in winter. AmEx/D/DC/MC/V.) **Rosie's Brewpub ❸,** 1115 E. 7th St., brews their beer at a higher elevation than any other brewery in North America, and serves flavorful pub food like an inside-out buffalo burger, stuffed with spinach and blue cheese ($9), and homemade potato skins for $7. (☎719-486-2349. Pints $3.50. Open M-Sa 11am-11pm, Su 11am-10pm. AmEx/D/MC/V.) The **Columbine Inn and Suites ❹,** 2019 N. Poplar St., has an indoor spa and well-maintained rooms. (☎719-486-5650. Laundry and free Wi-Fi. Continental breakfast included. Singles in summer $75-115; in winter $65-95. AmEx/D/MC/V.)

Right in downtown Leadville, the **Delaware Hotel ❹,** 700 Harrison Ave., has well-decorated Victorian rooms with period furnishings. (☎719-486-1418 or 800-748-2004; www.delawarehotel.com. Free continental breakfast. Rooms June-Sept. and Dec.-Mar. $79-99; Apr.-May and Oct.-Nov. $85. AmEx/D/MC/V.)

◪ **APPROACHING BUENA VISTA: 34 MILES**
Follow **U.S. 24 E,** heading south.

BUENA VISTA. Buena Vista may lack the cultural opportunities of the larger Salida down the road, but it offers easy access to the fourteeners, hot springs, and rafting in the summer, and snowmobiling and cross-country skiing in the winter. One of the nicest resorts in Colorado, the **Cottonwood Hot Springs Inn and Spa,** 18999 C.R. 306, steams the stress away with four soaking pools of varied sizes, shapes, and temperatures, a 112° hot tub, and cold pools. (From U.S. 24, turn right onto C.R. 306. ☎719-395-6434. Open daily 8am-midnight. No children after dark. $10, F-Su $15.)

◪ **APPROACHING SALIDA: 30 MILES**
About 2 mi. south of Buena Vista, get on **U.S. 285 S,** and turn left onto **Rte. 291.**

SALIDA

Residents are proud of what they consider to be Colorado's last unspoiled mountain town. Though tourists have yet to discover Salida, the artists have; excellent galleries congregate on several streets. Salida's downtown district is composed of galleries, restaurants, and outlets catering to outdoor enthusiasts.

VITAL STATS

Population: 5600

Visitor Info: Salida Chamber of Commerce, 406 U.S. 50 (☎719-539-2068). Open M-Sa 9am-5pm.

Internet Access: Salida Regional Library, 405 E St. (☎719-539-4826). Open M-F 9am-8:30pm, Sa 9am-5:30pm, Su 1-5pm. Free.

Post Office: Salida Main Post Office, 310 D St. (☎719-539-2548), at 3rd St. Open M-F 7:30am-5pm, Sa 8:30am-noon. **Postal Code:** 81201.

GETTING AROUND. Rte. 291 runs along the northeastern edge of town, along the Arkansas River. It is called **Grand Ave.** as it approaches town, **1st St.** in downtown, and **Oak St.** as it heads south to **Rainbow Blvd. (U.S. 50),** which runs east-west at the southern edge of town. Lettered streets run northeast-southwest between U.S. 50 and the Arkansas River, while numbered streets parallel the river, starting with 1st St., running northwest-southeast.

SIGHTS. In the last decade Salida has seen a new gallery or two open each year, leading some locals to wonder if it might be on its way to becoming the best little art town in America. Salida's 15 or so **downtown galleries** concentrate on 1st St. between E and G St. Salida is a stopping point on the **Monarch Crest Trail** (28 mi., 4½hr.), a grueling mountain bike trail from Salida to Monarch Pass that includes 14 mi. along the Continental Divide and a spectacular view of the Rockies. The **Midland Trail** (8 mi., 1hr.) is a more intermediate ride, with minimal climbing and great views of the Sawatch Range. Bike rentals and more information on bike trails are available at **Otero Cyclery,** 104 F St. (☎719-539-6704. Open daily 9am-6pm. Full-suspension bikes $45 for the 1st day, $35 per additional day.) While there are rafting companies located all along the Arkansas River, Salida is conveniently next to **Brown's Canyon,** a relaxing section of the Arkansas River. Thrill-seekers also use Salida as a jumping-off point for the challenging **Royal Gorge** (p. 416). **Canyon Marine Whitewater,** 10015 U.S. 50, leads trips several times per day. (5 mi. west of Salida on U.S.

50. ☎800-539-4447; www.canyonmarine.com. Open daily 7am-10:30pm. Brown's Canyon half-day trip $43, under 12 $37; full day $75/$65. Royal Gorge half-day trip $58, full day $85.) A number of **hiking** trails run through the Salida area, and it's a good base for hiking the fourteeners. Check www.salida.com/html/hiking.htm for good hiking tips and directions to several of the trailheads.

FOOD AND ACCOMMODATIONS. At **Laughing Ladies ❺,** 128 W. 1st St., Napa Valley-trained chefs serve California-inspired cuisine at a high-end, downtown fixture. Dinner entrees ($18-22) like molasses barbecued duck and crispy chicken with red-eye gravy are delicious. (☎719-539-6209. Open M and Th 5-8pm, F 5-8:30pm, Sa 5-9pm, Su 9am-2pm and 5-8pm. D/MC/V.) The owners of Laughing Ladies also opened a place down the street for lunch, the **Downtown Bakery and Deli ❷,** 124 F St. Fresh sandwiches ($6.25-8) are made to order, and specials like focaccia pizza ($5.25) are also available. (☎719-539-4248. Open W-Sa 6am-8pm, Su 8am-2pm. D/MC/V.) At **Fiesta Mexicana ❸,** 1220 E. U.S. 50, heaping portions of fresh, authentic Mexican fare will leave you stuffed. Try the *enchiladas a la Fiesta,* with steak and chicken, for $11.25. (☎719-539-5203. Entrees $11-13. Combo plates $8-9.50. Open M-Th and Su 11am-10pm, F-Sa 11am-11pm. AmEx/D/MC/V.) For old-fashioned country cooking, try **Country Bounty ❸,** 413 U.S. 50 W, where even oatmeal ($2) is made fresh to order. The "Country Bounty Meatloaf" ($12.50) is made with ground elk and bison. (☎719-539-3546. Breakfast $3-7. Sandwiches $5-10. Entrees $9-15. Open daily 6am-9pm. AmEx/D/MC/V.) The rooms at the **Budget Lodge ❷,** 1146 U.S. 50 E, are small, but the owner is friendly and the price is right. (☎719-539-6695 or 877-909-6695. Singles in summer $38, in winter $32-35; doubles $45/$35-38. D/MC/V.)

APPROACHING GUNNISON: 57 MILES
From downtown, head to **U.S. 50** and turn right. About 5 mi. west of town, fork right, and then turn left to stay on **U.S. 50 W.** There are lots of bikers here; pay careful attention. 23 mi. from Salida, U.S. 50 crosses the Continental Divide at **Monarch Pass** (11,312 ft.) and becomes **Tomichi Ave.** in Gunnison.

GUNNISON. Gunnison is ideal for an afternoon rest stop. The **Pioneer Museum,** 801 E.

Tomichi Ave. (U.S. 50), has a large collection of western hats and about 50 antique cars. (☎970-641-4530. Open mid-May to Sept. M-Sa 9am-5pm, Su 1-5pm. $7, ages 6-12 $1.) The **Gunnison National Forest Office,** 216 N. Colorado Ave., has info on area forest service lands. (☎970-641-0471. Open M-F 7:30am-4:30pm.) As U.S. 50 curves left at the western edge of town, look left for the **giant white "W"** carved into W Mountain—the "W" is for Western State College, located in Gunnison. ■**Farrells' Restaurant ❷,** 310 N. Main St., serves sandwiches ($6-7) and fresh breads to patrons on a shady back patio. (☎970-641-2655. Open M-F 7am-3pm. MC/V.) Accommodations in Gunnison are easy to find but somewhat expensive during the summer. The **Gunnison Inn ❸,** 412 E. Tomichi Ave., has good-sized rooms. (☎970-641-0700 or 866-641-0700. Laundry and free Wi-Fi. Singles in summer from $65; in winter from $55. AmEx/D/MC/V.)

◥ DETOUR
CRESTED BUTTE
Take Rte. 135 27 mi. north of Gunnison.

Crested Butte was settled by miners in the 1870s. The coal was exhausted in the 1950s, but a few years later the steep powder fields began attracting skiers. Thanks to strict zoning rules, the historical downtown is a throwback to early mining days. Three miles north of town, **Crested Butte Mountain Resort,** 12 Snowmass Rd., offers over 800 acres of bowl skiing. (☎800-544-8448; www.skicb.com. Open mid-Dec. to mid-Apr. Lift tickets $74, early season discounts available.) In summer, Crested Butte becomes the mountain biking capital of Colorado. In 1976, a group of cyclists rode from Crested Butte to Aspen, starting what is now the oldest mountain biking event in the world. Every September, experienced bikers repeat the trek over the 12,705 ft. pass to Aspen and back during the **Pearl Pass Tour,** organized by the **Mountain Biking Hall of Fame,** 331 Elk Ave., which relates the short history of the sport. (☎970-349-1880. Museum open daily in summer noon-8pm; hours vary in winter. $3.) During the last week of June, the town hosts the **Fat Tire Bike Festival** (www.ftbw.com), four days of biking, racing, and fraternizing. The friendly folks at the **Sunshine Deli ❷,** 214 Elk Ave., will be happy to grill you some banana-battered French toast ($4.50)

for "brekkie," or one of their signature sandwiches for lunch ($7). The "Joker" sandwich, with turkey, muenster cheese, red peppers, and curry mayonnaise, will wake up your taste buds. (☎970-349-6866. Open daily 8am-4pm. MC/V.)

◥ APPROACHING CURECANTI NATIONAL RECREATION AREA: 74 MILES
The **Curecanti National Recreation Area** begins along **U.S. 50,** 6 mi. from Gunnison.

CURECANTI NATIONAL RECREATION AREA
You wouldn't know it by looking, but the large bodies of water in this area are man-made, created by dams on the Gunnison River. Curecanti is primarily used for fishing, boating, sailing, and horseback riding. The moderately strenuous **Dillon Pinnacles Trail** (4 mi.) ascends 600 ft. through sagebrush and conifers to an up-close view of the large set of spires. (Trailhead off U.S. 50, 6 mi. west of the Elk Creek Visitors Center.) If you have time, the strenuous **Curecanti Creek Trail** (4 mi., 2-3hr. round-trip) goes down into the upper Black Canyon and then along the tumbling Curecanti Creek. At the end, look across the Morrow Point Reservoir to view the 700 ft. Curecanti Needle, a granite spire. (11 mi. west of Elk Creek Visitors Center, turn right onto Rte. 92, and continue 5¾ mi. to the Pioneer Point Trailhead.) **Morrow Point Boat Tours** leave from Pine Creek Boat Dock, 12 mi. west of Elk Creek Visitors Center, and rushes through the upper Black Canyon. For 1½hr., park rangers discuss the area's geology, wildlife, history, and the dams and reservoirs. (☎970-641-2337. Tours in summer M and W-Su 10am and 12:30pm. Reservations required. $15, under 13 $7.50.) **Elk Creek Marina** has boat rentals and guided fishing trips. (☎970-641-0707. Boat rentals $30 per hr., $95 per half-day, $135 per day. Guided fishing trips $300.)

Due to its low elevation, **camping ❶** in Curecanti is not as picturesque as that in the National Parks or at the Forest Service sites near Heeney and Twin Lakes. On the other hand, campsites are generally convenient to the road and easily obtained. Curecanti's four major campsites, primarily sheets of asphalt, turn into a city of RVs in the summer, and offer water, toilets, grills, and picnic tables. **Elk Creek** and **Lake Fork** are the most developed and have showers. (☎970-641-2337. Sites $10-15, with electricity $16-21.)

NATIONAL ROAD

⚠ APPROACHING BLACK CANYON: 48 MILES
Turn right at the sign for **Rte. 347/Black Canyon** and go 6 mi. to **Black Canyon National Park.**

BLACK CANYON NATIONAL PARK

Native American parents used to tell their children that the light-colored strands of rock streaking through the walls of the 53 mi. Black Canyon were hairs of a blond woman—if they got too close to the edge they would get tangled and fall. Visitors today should remember this lesson—the beautiful canyon can be very dangerous to unwary and unprepared visitors.

VITAL STATS

Area: 30,000 acres

Visitor Info: South Rim Visitors Center (☎970-249-1914, ext. 423; www.nps.gov/blca), on South Rim Dr. Open daily in summer 8am-6pm; in winter 8:30am-4pm.

Gateway Town: Montrose (p. 439).

Fees: $8 per vehicle. Free wilderness permits required for inner canyon use.

📭 GETTING AROUND. The **South Rim** is easily accessible by a 6 mi. drive off U.S. 50 at the end of Rte. 347; the wilder **North Rim** can only be reached by an 80 mi. detour around the canyon followed by a gravel road from Crawford off Rte. 92. This road is closed in winter. The **East Portal Rd.,** accessed from South Rim Rd. near the park entrance, takes you down to the East Portal, inside the canyon at the side of the river. East Portal Rd. is closed in winter, and vehicles over 22 ft. long are prohibited. Stay in first gear as you proceed down the road. Be advised that both North and South Rim Roads are dead-ends, and driving around the canyon takes 2-3hr.

🏔 OUTDOORS. The spectacular 6 mi. 📷**South Rim Road** traces the edge of the canyon, and boasts a jaw-dropping vista of Chasm View, where you can peer down a 1850 ft. drop to the streaked Painted Wall. For an even better view of the Painted Wall—arguably the most impressive in the park—head to the **Painted Wall View** overlook. Hiking routes into the canyon follow unmarked drainage gullies. The Park Service discourages inexperienced hikers from taking these steep and

strenuous routes; consult a park ranger at the visitors center before attempting. A drainage is by nature wide at the top and narrow at the bottom, so it can be very difficult to find your way back. Setting up cairns (piles of rocks) is permitted but discouraged, so knock down your cairns on your return. Park rangers recommend taking mental notes of the terrain. Leave early in the morning to avoid the afternoon heat. A couple of hiking routes skirt the edge of the canyon and provide a more in-depth experience than the short overlooks. The moderate **Oak Flat Loop Trail** (2 mi.) begins near the visitors center and gives a good sense of the terrain below the rim. From the South Rim, you can scramble down the popular **Gunnison Route,** which drops 1800 ft. over 1 mi. Allow 1½-2hr. for the descent, and even longer for the climb out. If you're feeling courageous, tackle the more difficult **Tomichi** or **Warner Routes,** which are both good as overnight trips. A free wilderness permit (from the South Rim Visitors Center) is required for inner-canyon routes, and you are required to check-out on your return. Bring at least one gallon of water per person per day.

The sheer walls of the Black Canyon make for a **rock climbing** paradise. This rock is not for beginners or the faint of heart; some of the best climbers in the world travel here to tackle the difficult rock walls. All climbers must carry a full rack of gear and register at the visitors center. Anglers from all over Colorado trek to the Black Canyon for **fly fishing.** Gunnison River Expeditions runs fly-fishing float trips in Black Canyon and walk-wade trips on the Gunnison. (☎970-872-3078. Float-trip $400 per person. Walk-wades $100.) **Gunnison Gorge National Conservation Area** is a particularly popular stretch of the river. Non-motorized boaters have access to the area via the Chukar Boater Put-In and the Gunnison Forks Boater Take-Out. The only land access is by hiking one of four trails from the rim of the gorge. Access roads are rough, requiring 4WD and high-clearance, and some are impassable when wet.

🏕 CAMPING. The **South Rim Campground ❶** has 102 sites with pit toilets, charcoal grills, and water. (Turn right from the entrance to South Rim Park; head down E. Portal Rd. to the base of the canyon beside the river. ☎970-641-2337. Water, pit toilets, grills. Sites $12, with electricity $16. Cash only.) Eleven primitive hike-in only campsites are available in the **Gunnison Gorge National Conservation**

Area ❶, northwest of Montrose. Sites are first come, first served; pay at the trailhead. (☎970-240-5300. Pit toilets. 2-night max. stay. Day-use $5. Sites $10. Cash only.)

APPROACHING MONTROSE: 15 MILES
Take **Rte. 347 S** to **U.S. 50 W,** following the signs for Montrose.

MONTROSE

The quiet community of Montrose serves as both the center of a farming region and a gateway to the spectacular beauty of southwest Colorado. Amidst the sounds of "nature music" at the **Ute Indian Museum,** 17253 Chipeta Dr., you can learn the history of the Ute people. Though they once inhabited much of present-day Colorado and Utah, the Utes now have only a small reservation at the southern end of the state. (Take U.S. 550 S; the museum is on your right. ☎970-249-3098. Open mid-May to Oct. M-Sa 9am-4:30pm, Su 11am-4pm; Nov. to mid-May Tu-Sa 9am-4:30pm. $3.50, seniors $3, students $1.50.)

For tasty sandwiches ($5-6) and delightful omelettes ($7), head to the **Daily Bread Bakery and Cafe ❶,** 346 Main St. Vegetarians will love the Garden Delight, with avocado, mushrooms, sprouts, tomatoes, and cheese. (☎970-249-8444. Open daily 6am-4pm. Cash only.) **La Cabana at Sicily's ❸,** 1135 E. Main St. (U.S. 50), offers solid Italian and Mexican food in a garden-like atmosphere. (☎970-240-9199. Pasta $8-11. Entrees $14-19. Open M-W 11am-9pm, Th-Su 11am-10pm. D/MC/V.) **Camp Robber Cafe ❹,** 228 Main St., caters to locals with its Southwestern flavors. (☎970-240-1590. Open M-Sa 11am-3pm and 5-9pm, Su 9am-2pm. AmEx/MC/V.) The family-owned **Canyon Trails Inn ❸,** 1225 E. Main St., has small and clean single rooms with access to an outdoor hot tub. (☎970-249-3426 or 800-858-5911; www.canyon-trailsinn.com. Rooms from $50. MC/V.) The **Western Motel ❸,** 1200 E. Main St., offers tidy rooms, a pool, hot tub, and continental breakfast. (☎800-445-7301. Reception 24hr. Checkout 10am. Singles in summer $50-55, in winter $45; doubles $65/$48. AmEx/D/MC/V.)

APPROACHING GRAND JUNCTION: 69 MILES
U.S. 50 becomes **5th St.** entering Grand Junction.

GRAND JUNCTION

Grand Junction takes its name from its position at the junction of the Colorado and Gunnison Rivers. The name aptly describes the town's role as a transportation hub for the masses heading to southern Utah and the Colorado Rockies. If you need big-city services, Grand Junction is the best place to stop; the next stop with a population over 10,000 is Salt Lake City.

VITAL STATS

Population: 48,000

Visitor Info: Grand Junction Visitors Bureau, 740 Horizon Dr. (☎970-256-4060; www.grandjunction.net). Head east to 7th St., turn left, and then turn right on Horizon Dr. Open M-Sa May-Sept. 8:30am-8pm; Oct.-Apr. 8:30am-5pm.

Internet Access: Mesa County Library, 530 Grand Ave. (☎970-243-4442). Open June-Aug. M-Th 9am-9pm, F-Sa 9am-5pm; Sept.-May M-Th 9am-9pm, F-Sa 9am-5pm, Su 1-5pm. Free.

Post Office: 241 N. 4th St. (☎970-244-3400). Open M-F 7:45am-5:15pm, Sa 10am-1:30pm. **Postal Code:** 81501.

GETTING AROUND. Grand Junction lies on the **Colorado River** near **I-70.** In town, streets run north-south, increasing in number from west to east, and avenues run east-west. **Grand Ave.** runs one block north of **Main St.,** and contains many hotels and restaurants. **North Ave. (U.S. 6)** runs one block north of Grand Ave.

SIGHTS. There are lots of **sidewalk sculptures** in downtown Grand Junction; don't miss the dinosaur riding a bicycle at 3rd and Main St. The **Museum of Western Colorado,** at 5th St. and Ute Ave., has several excellent exhibits, including one on the infamous Alfred Packer, tried and convicted of cannibalism. See Bill Cody's gun from 1881, and head up the Educational Tower for a 360-degree view of the surrounding area. (☎970-242-0971. Open May-Sept. M-Sa 9am-5pm, Su noon-4pm; Oct.-Apr. Tu-Sa 10am-3pm. $5.50, seniors $4.50, ages 3-12 $3.)

OUTDOORS. The Grand Junction area has a smorgasbord of outdoor activities nearby. The best hiking around Grand Junction

NATIONAL ROAD

1912: Salt Lake City policeman Lester Wire sets up the first red-green electric traffic lights.

awaits in the **Colorado Canyons National Conservation Area** just west of the Colorado National Monument. **Pollock, Rattlesnake,** and **Knowles Canyons** all feature beautiful hikes. (Take I-70 to Exit 19, and head south 1¼ mi. to Kings View Estates subdivision. Follow the Kings View Rd. westbound, and look for signs to the trailhead.) The **Mt. Garfield Trail** (1½mi., 2hr. round-trip) is a great option for a short hike to amazing views of this otherworldly rockscape. Wild horses are sometimes visible from the top during winter and early spring. (Take Exit 42 from I-70, and travel south on 37 Three-tenths Rd. to G Seven-tenths Rd. Take a right and go west to 35 Five-tenths Rd. Turn right and cross I-70 to the trailhead.) The Kokopelli area, the 18-Mile Rd. area, and the Tabeguache area each attract many mountain bikers in search of adventure. A bevy of mountain bike shops offer advice and rent bikes. **Ruby Canyon Cycles,** 301 Main St., is a bike shop with full-day rentals. (☎970-241-0141. Open M-F 9am-6pm, Sa 9am-5pm. Mountain bikes $50 per day. Enduros $60 per day. Street bikes $20 per day.) Near the visitors center on North Ave., **Board and Buckle Ski and Cyclery,** 2822 North Ave., rents bikes and skis. (☎970-242-9285. Open in summer M-F 9am-6pm, Sa 9am-5pm; in winter daily 7am-7pm. Bikes $35 per day. Skis $13.50 per day.)

⛺🍴 FOOD AND NIGHTLIFE. Thursday nights in summer, downtown transforms into the **Farmers Market Festival,** with local produce, live music, and extended Main St. restaurant hours. (☎970-245-9697. June-Aug. Th 4:30-8pm.) Massive, mouth-watering breakfasts ($5.50-7.25) are the specialty at **Crystal Cafe ❷,** 314 Main St., but hot lunches and decadent baked goods don't fall short. Sandwiches ($7.50) include the massive quarter-pound tuna-steak sandwich with onion relish. (☎970-242-8843. Open M-F 7am-2pm, Sa 8am-noon. D/MC/V.) The **Rockslide Restaurant and Brew Pub ❹,** 401 S. Main St., has a fun, modern brewhouse atmosphere. The Big Bear Stout comes in a half-gallon growler for $8.50. (☎970-245-2111. M-F 4-6pm and 10pm-midnight half-price appetizers. Open M-Th 11am-midnight, F-Sa 11am-2am, Su 8am-midnight. MC/V.)

Weaver's Tavern, 103 N. 1st St., is a hip sports bar with tons of drink specials. (☎970-241-4010.

F 4-8pm $1.25 well wine, Su 8pm-midnight $2 you-call-its. Open daily 11am-2am. AmEx/D/MC/V.) The **Mesa Theater,** 538 Main St., features live music on summer weekends. (☎970-241-1717; www.mesatheater.com. Th under 21. Hours and cover vary. MC/V.)

🛏 ACCOMMODATIONS. Between 3rd and 4th St., **Hotel Melrose ❷,** 337 Colorado Ave., offers well-kept dorms and private rooms in the heart of the city. The historical building has a kitchen available for guests. (☎970-242-9636. Laundry $6. Check-out 11am. Dorms $22; private rooms from $45. AmEx/D/MC/V.) Camping is available at **Fruita State Park ❶,** 10 mi. west of town, off Exit 19 from I-70. (☎800-678-2267 or 970-858-9188. 80 sites with showers and hookups. $5 per vehicle. Sites $12-20. MC/V.)

🚶 APPROACHING COLORADO NATIONAL MONUMENT: 4 MILES
Proceed north on **5th St.** 3 blocks past Main St. to **Grand Ave.,** and turn left. At the intersection with 1st St. head straight onto **Broadway/Rte. 340.** After about 1 mi., turn left onto **Monument Rd.** at the sign for the monument.

COLORADO NATIONAL MONUMENT

On the outskirts of Grand Junction, Colorado National Monument is a 32 sq. mi. sculpture of steep cliff faces, canyon walls, and obelisk-like spires wrought by the forces of gravity, wind, and water. The monument was established in 1911, largely due to the efforts of John Otto, who blazed many of the trails used today and badgered the government to protect this dreamworld of rock.

VITAL STATS

Area: 20,500 acres

Visitor Info: Colorado National Monument Visitors Center (☎970-858-3617; www.nps.gov/colm), 4 mi. east of the western entrance. Open daily in summer 8am-6pm; in winter 9am-5pm.

Gateway Towns: Fruita, Grand Junction (p. 439).

Fees: $7 per vehicle.

🚗 GETTING AROUND. For those without time to explore on foot, the 23 mi. **Rim Rock Dr.**

runs along the edge of red canyons across the mesa top from Grand Junction to Fruita between the two entrances.

⚑ OUTDOORS. Rim Rock Dr. provides views of awe-inspiring rock monoliths, the Book Cliffs, Grand Mesa, and the city of Grand Junction. Grand View offers a panoramic look back into the multiple layers of the canyon. At the next overlook, Independence Monument, visitors can glimpse the park's highest free-standing rock formation. While driving affords great views, the hiking trails that crisscross the monument are the only way to fully appreciate the scope and scale of this canyon country. There are a number of short walks that whisk hikers away from the road and immerse them in the terrain. The **Window Rock Trail** (½ mi. round-trip) leaves from a trailhead on the Saddlehorn campground road and offers expansive vistas through piñon-juniper woodland over the Grand Valley, as well as views of Monument Canyon, Wedding Canyon, and many of the monument's major rock formations. **Otto's Trail** (1 mi. round-trip), east on Rim Rock Dr. to Pipe Organ, is gentle and offers good views of monoliths. The **Coke Ovens Trail** (1 mi. round-trip), a few miles down Rim Rock Dr. from the visitors center to Coke Ovens, ambles to an overlook of the Coke Ovens. The **Devil's Kitchen Trail** (1½ mi.) begins off the park drive just past the east entrance, and drops into Devils Kitchen, a natural grotto surrounded by enormous upright boulders.

There are a number of primitive trails, good for long or overnight hikes. The moderately strenuous **Monument Canyon Trail** (6 mi.) allows hikers to view eerie, skeletal rock formations up close. The trail descends 600 ft. from the mesa top to the canyon floor and then wanders amid giant rocks, including Independence Monument, Kissing Couple, and the Coke Ovens, before emerging on Rte. 340 (Broadway/Redlands Rd.). The **Ute Canyon Trail** and **Liberty Cap Trail** (14 mi., 8hr. round-trip each) are also scenic backcountry hikes ideal for overnight trips.

⚑ CAMPING. Backcountry camping is allowed anywhere ¼ mi. from the roads and 100 yd. from the trails. A free required permit is available at the visitors center. **Saddlehorn Campground ❶**, a quarter-mile north of the visitors center, offers 80 beautiful, secluded sites on the mesa's edge. Sites are first come, first served. (☎970-858-3617. Water and bathrooms. No showers. Sites $10. Cash only.)

⚑ APPROACHING MOAB: 102 MILES
Leave the monument from the west entrance and turn left at the T onto **Rte. 340.** Go 2½ mi. to **I-70 W.** Take **Exit 202** for **Rte. 128 S.** After rounding a corner about 4 mi. past the bridge, you will see the 1st of the area's hallmark red spires. Rte. 128 dead-ends at **U.S. 191;** from here, turn left toward Moab.

The Beehive State
UTAH
Welcomes You!

MOAB

Moab, about 70 mi. from the Colorado/Utah border, first flourished in the 1950s, when uranium miners rushed to the area and transformed the town into a gritty desert outpost. Today, the mountain bike has replaced the Geiger counter, as outdoors enthusiasts rush into town eager to bike the slickrock, raft whitewater rapids, and explore Arches and Canyonlands National Parks.

VITAL STATS

Population: 4800

Visitor Info: Moab Information Center, 3 Center St. (☎435-259-8825 or 800-635-6622), at corner of Main St. Open daily in summer 8am-9pm; in winter 8am-6pm.

Internet Access: Grand County Library, 257 E. Center St. (☎435-259-1111). Open M-W 9am-8pm, Th-F 9am-7pm, Sa 9am-5pm. Free.

Post Office: 50 E. 100 N (☎435-259-7427). Open M-F 8:30am-5:30pm, Sa 9am-1pm. **Postal Code:** 84532.

⚑ GETTING AROUND. Moab sits 30 mi. south of I-70 on **U.S. 191,** just south of the junction with **Rte. 128.** The town center is 5 mi. south of the entrance to Arches National Park and 38 mi. north of the turn-off to the Needles section of Canyonlands National Park. U.S. 191 becomes **Main St.** for 5 mi. through downtown.

MOUNTAINS, MESAS & MONUMENTS

EMBARK ON A PARK LARK

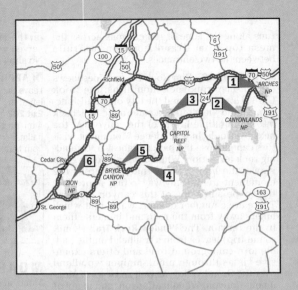

Length: 688 miles
Days: 5 days
Starting point: Moab
Highlight: Bryce Canyon National Park

Head north on U.S. 191, passing the junction with Rte. 128. The entrance is 5 mi. north of Moab.

■ ARCHES NATIONAL PARK. Here, thousands of sandstone arches, spires, pinnacles, and fins tower above the desert floor in overwhelming grandeur. Some arches are so perfect in form that early explorers believed they were constructed by a lost civilization. Deep red sandstone, green piñon pines, juniper bushes, and a strikingly blue sky combine in an unforgettable palette of colors. While most visitors come in the summer, 100°F temperatures make hiking difficult; bring at least one gallon of water per person per day. The weather is best in the spring and fall, when temperate days and nights provide a more comfortable stay. In the winter, white snow creates a brilliant contrast to the red arches. While the striking red slickrock around Arches may seem worthy enough, the park's real points of interest lie off the paved road. Load up on water and sunscreen and seek out the park's thousands of natural arches, each one pinpointed on the free pamphlet distributed at the entrance. The most popular hike in the park leads to the oft-photographed **Delicate Arch.** The trail (3 mi., 2½hr.) leaves from the Wolfe Ranch parking area and climbs 480 ft. To view the spectacular Delicate Arch without the 3 mi. hike, take the **Delicate Arch Viewpoint Trail** (300 ft., 15min.), which begins in the Viewpoint parking area, 14 mi. from the entrance. **Tower Arch** (3½ mi., 2-3hr.) can be accessed from the trailhead at the Klondike Bluffs parking area via Salt Valley Rd. This moderate hike explores one of the remote regions of the park and is a good way to escape the crowds. Salt Valley Rd. is often washed out—check at the visitors center before departing.

The park's only campground, **Devil's Garden ❶,** 18 mi. from the visitors center, has 52 excellent campsites nestled amid piñons and giant, red sandstone formations. The campsite is within walking distance of the Devil's Garden and Broken Arch trailheads. (☎435-719-2299. Bathrooms and water. 1-week max. stay. Sites $10. Cash only.) If the heat becomes unbearable at Arches, the aspen forests of the **Manti-La Sal National Forest** offer a respite. Take Rte. 128 along the Colorado River, and turn right at Castle Valley, or go south from Moab on U.S. 191, and turn left at the Shell Station. There are a number of campgrounds in the forest including **Warner Lake ❶,** where beautiful sites sit 4000 ft. above the national park and are invariably several degrees cooler. (☎435-259-7155; www.reserveusa.com. Sites $10. MC/V.)

Take U.S. 191 N to Hwy. 313 S.

2 CANYONLANDS NATIONAL PARK. Canyonlands is a vast, rugged park of red sandstone sculpted by the Green and Colorado Rivers. Its stone canyons, mesas, arches, and spires are divided into four districts: **Island in the Sky,** the **Needles,** the **Maze,** and the **Rivers.** It is nearly impossible to see more than one or two of them in a single trip; they are not directly connected, and it takes roughly 2-3 hr. to travel between them. Island in the Sky is the most popular and accessible district, drawing a majority of the park's visitors, while the Needles, Maze, and Rivers entice those more interested in backcountry trips. Canyonlands is very hot and dry in summer; bring at least one gallon of water per person per day and a good supply of sunblock. The **visitors center,** near the Island in the Sky entrance, is the only place in the park where water is available. (☎ 435-719-2313. Open daily 8am-6pm.)

Trails in Canyonlands are marked with cairns (small rock piles); do not disturb them or build new ones. The **Mesa Arch** is a popular destination in Island in the Sky, lying ¼ mi. uphill from its trailhead, 6 mi. from the visitors center. The rocky, but easy trail is a loop, passing many outcroppings of slickrock. The arch itself lies on a cliff edge 2200 ft. above the Colorado River; the sweeping view from the arch is unforgettable. Wake up early and watch the sunrise from the arch, but take caution along the cliff edge. **Grand View Point** (2 mi., 1½hr. round-trip), 13 mi. from the visitors center, provides a gorgeous panoramic view of the mighty rivers that carved the canyons. The rocky, moderate **Upheaval Dome trail** (¾-1¾ mi., 1-1½hr. round-trip) leads to the mysterious Upheaval Dome, a circular rock deformation nearly 3 mi. across. Geologists are still not sure how this odd structure formed. Two popular theories are explained on signs in front of the dome: one states that an ancient "salt bubble" rose through the layers of denser rock above it, shaping the rock into a circular form, while the other states that the area is a crater left by a meteorite 500-1000 ft. in diameter. In either case, the enormous phenomenon is unlike anything else in the park and has fantastic viewpoints. **Backcountry hiking** is permitted in the park; a permit ($5) is required and is available at the visitors center—consult with a ranger before heading out. **Rock climbing** is popular in Island in the Sky; the other park districts lack hard stone and established routes. Permits are not required unless trips will include overnight stays in the backcountry. As with most parks, changing the rock face or using white chalk is prohibited; consult a park ranger for more information on climbing routes and regulations.

Camping ❶ is allowed in the park; there are some developed campgrounds with vault toilets, picnic tables, and fire grates, and several primitive sites. All sites are first come, first served with self-registration. (No water or hookups. Sites $10. Cash or check only.)

Take Rte. 313 N to U.S. 191 N. At the interchange, get on I-70 W to Exit 149 to get on Rte. 24.

3 CAPITOL REEF NATIONAL PARK. Capitol Reef is an oasis in the desert. With about 2700 fruit trees bearing antique and heirloom varieties of cherries, peaches, apricots, apples, and pears, Capitol Reef has the largest orchard system of any national park. The **◢Fruita orchards** lie off the roads near the visitors center; visitors are welcome to eat as much ripe fruit as they like while in the orchards, but there is a nominal fee for taking fruit out of the orchards. The flooding of the Fremont River helps to irrigate the orchards that Mormon settlers started planting around 1880. A one-room Mormon schoolhouse still stands near the park entrance. Mormons were not the only ones that favored this area— Native Americans who settled in the area long ago left ancient petroglyphs on rock walls near the park entrance. From May to September, the park offers many free ranger-guided programs, providing lessons about the Fruita Schoolhouse, historic Gifford farm, the park's geology, and more at the campground amphitheater. More information can be found at the **visitors center,** 9 mi. west of the park entrance. (☎ 435-425-3791, ext. 111. Open daily 8am-6pm.)

You can see the Reef's towering and colorful landforms from your car on the 25 mi. **scenic drive,** 1hr. round-trip, that wiggles around the cliffs, washes, and canyon floors on paved and improved dirt roads. The easy **Capitol Gorge Trail** (1 mi.) runs off the scenic drive. Another easy trail, the **Grand Wash** (2¼ mi.), on Rte. 24, 4 mi. east of the visitors center, leads visitors along sheer canyon walls. These and other canyon trails can become inundated with water during flash floods, common in late summer and early fall; check at the visitors center for weather and flood information. The park's premier hike is a backcountry route, the **Halls Creek Narrows** (22 mi. round-trip). Marked with cairns but not otherwise maintained, the steep trail leads down to the Halls Creek drainage and then south to the Narrows themselves. It begins near the Halls Creek overlook. Some hiking experience and a topography map (available at the visitors center) are required.

The park's main campground, **Fruita ❶**, off Rte. 24, 1¼ mi. south of the visitors center, has first come, first served sites with water, restrooms, picnic tables, and an RV dump station. (Sites $10. Cash or check only.)

Continue on Rte. 24 for 6¼ mi. to Rte. 12, which leads through the monument and towards Escalante and Cannonville.

4 GRAND STAIRCASE-ESCALANTE NATIONAL MONUMENT. Big, wild, and best suited to backcountry adventures, Grand Staircase is unlike the other national parks and monuments you've seen so far. No main roads run through the monument, and the high, rugged, remote region was the last place in the continental U.S. to be mapped. **Rte. 12** provides a dizzying view of the monument's cliffs and plateaus as you approach Escalante, but be sure to keep your eyes on the road. The staircase itself is comprised of exposed rock layers rising in a series of cliffs from Lake Powell to Bryce Canyon. Information can be found at the **Escalante Interagency Visitor Center,** 755 W. Main St., in Escalante. (☎ 435-826-5499. Open daily in summer 7:30am-5:30pm; in winter 8am-5pm.)

Some relatively easy routes along the canyon floors exist, but much of the monument is extremely dangerous for the careless and unprepared. **Hiking** most routes without a guide is not advised unless you have a firm grasp of the landscape and geographical organization. Two beautiful, narrow slot canyons, **Spooky** and **Peek-A-Boo** (3-4 mi., 3-5hr.), are suitable for hikers with some experience, and require no climbing gear. To get to the trailheads, head 26 mi. down **Hole-In-The-Rock Rd.,** 5 mi. east of Escalante, and turn left at **Dry Fork.** The moderate **Calf Creek Falls Trail** (6 mi., 3-5hr. round-trip) is the only developed trail in the monument, and leads to a beautiful 126 ft. waterfall and crystal clear swimming hole. It is accessible from the **Calf Creek Recreation Area,** 15 mi. east on Rte. 12 (day-use $2). **Excursions of Escalante,** 125 E. Main St., in Escalante, offers guided trips through the most pristine, unvisited canyons in the monument; guides say that they have never seen anyone else on their trips. The owner, Rick Green, has been exploring the area for 20 years, and only shares his knowledge of the unnamed, unpublished canyons he has found with his staff and his customers. (☎ 800-839-7567. Open M and W-Su 11am-5pm. Hikes leave at 9am and generally return at 5 or 6pm. $100-145; includes full gear, lunch, and transportation.)

Guides for Excursions of Escalante also grill up some amazing burgers at the **Trailhead Cafe and Grill ❷,** 125 E. Main St. The hand-packed burgers ($8-9) and grilled chicken ($8) are flavored with fresh herbs and garlic from their own garden. The fruit smoothies ($4) are a tasty way to beat the canyon heat. (☎ 435-826-4714. Open M and W-Su 11am-5pm. Cash only.) Several motels line Rte. 12 between Escalante and U.S. 89; most have basic rooms starting at $50-60 per night. The **Padre Motel ❸,** 20 E. Main St., across the street from the Trailhead Cafe and Grill, offers remodeled rooms with free Internet access and satellite TV. (☎ 435-826-4276; www.padremotel.com. Open Mar.-Sept. Singles from $50; doubles from $65. AmEx/MC/V.)

Take Rte. 12 W through the town of Tropic to Bryce Canyon.

5 BRYCE CANYON NATIONAL PARK. One of the West's most vivid landscapes, Bryce Canyon brims with haunting, slender rock pinnacles known as hoodoos. What it lacks in Grand Canyon-esque magnitude, Bryce makes up for in intricate beauty, especially early in the morning or late in the evening when the sun's rays bring the hoodoos to life. As Ebenezer Bryce, a Mormon carpenter with a gift for understatement, once said, the canyon is "one hell of a place to lose a cow." To limit park traffic, the Park Service has a free shuttle service that takes visitors to the visitors center, lodge, and scenic overlooks in air-conditioned comfort. (Shuttle runs daily every 12min. 9am-6pm. Free.) Private vehicles can travel park roads, but the Park Service urges visitors to leave their cars outside the park. The **visitors center** is just inside the park. (☎ 435-834-5322; www.nps.gov/brca. Open daily May-Sept. 8am-8pm; Oct.-Nov. and Apr. 8am-6pm; Nov.-Mar. 8am-4:30pm. Entrance fee $20 per vehicle; $10 per pedestrian.)

Bryce's 18 mi. main road winds past spectacular lookouts, with **Bryce and Inspiration Points** providing quintessential postcard-worthy views of the canyon. One oft-missed viewpoint is **Fairyland Point,** at the north end of the park, 1 mi. off the main road, which has the best sights in the park. A range of hiking trails lures visitors from their cars. The **Rim Trail** can be accessed anywhere along the rim and has very little elevation change (11 mi., 4-6hr.). The moderate **Navajo/Queen's Garden Loop** (3 mi., 2-3hr.) is an excellent way to experience the canyon and see some of the park's most famous vistas. A less-traveled trail with great views of hoodoos and wildflowers in the summer is the **Tower Bridge Trail** (3½ mi., 3-4hr.). A more challenging option is the **Peek-A-Boo Loop** (3½ mi., 3-4hr.), which winds in and out of hoodoos. A word to the wise: the air is thin—if you start to feel short of breath, take a rest. Very sturdy shoes or hiking boots are a must for hiking into the canyon. Campgrounds are available in the park; ask at the visitors center.

Take Rte. 12 W to its terminus at the U.S. 89 interchange; get on U.S. 89 S. Take Exit 149 for Rte. 9, which leads into the park.

⑥ ZION NATIONAL PARK. Zion is Utah's most developed and popular national park, with over 2.5 million visitors exploring its wonders annually. Its sandstone cliffs are among the world's highest, and it features the stunning Virgin River. The park stands as a refuge for at least five rare or endangered species, including the peregrine falcon, mexican spotted owl, and Zion snail, found only at the park. The park's expansive **visitors center,** near the south entrance, 14 mi. from the east entrance, offers park information and backcountry permits. (☎435-772-3256, backcountry information 435-772-0170. Open daily 8am-5pm.) The long, dark **Zion-Mt. Carmel Tunnel** connects the park's east entrance to Zion Canyon. Built in the 1920s, it was never intended for very large vehicles—any vehicle 7 ft. 10 in. or more in width or 11 ft. 4 in. or more in height will require traffic control to get through the tunnel and must pay a fee of $15 per vehicle.

Most of the park's attractions are found in and around Zion Canyon; Rte. 9 intersects with the **Zion Canyon Scenic Drive** 4¾ mi. from the east entrance. The scenic drive is closed to private vehicles and only accessible by a **shuttle bus,** which stops at all of Zion Canyon's trailheads and points of interest. (Runs daily in summer 5:45am-11pm; in winter 6:45am-10pm. Frequency varies, but can run as often as every 6min. Free.) Park at the visitors center if you can find a spot., or try parking in Springdale and riding the free town shuttle to the park. The easy **Riverside Walk** (2 mi., 1½hr. round-trip), a paved walk following the Virgin River into a narrow canyon, is the park's most popular trail. Here, you can see a unique "desert swamp" environment, a wet home to plant life. The trailhead is at the **Temple of Sinawava** shuttle stop. If you are feeling intrepid, get your feet wet, and continue beyond the end of the path through the **Zion Narrows** (1-5hr. round-trip). Wear sturdy shoes or boots with ankle support, and carry a light jacket. The trails leading to the algae-rich **Emerald Pools** are also popular. You can usually see a small waterfall here. The easy **Lower Emerald Pool Trail** (1¼ mi., 1hr. round-trip) and moderate **Middle Emerald Pools Trail** (2 mi., 2hr. round-trip) connect with each other; the trailhead is at the **Zion Lodge** stop. The **Watchman Campground ❶,** south of the visitors center, has electrical hookups and sites by the river. (☎800-365-2267; www.reserveusa.com. Nov.-Mar. first come, first served; Apr.-Oct. by reservation only. Sites $16, with electricity $18, river sites $20. Cash only.) The **South Campground ❶,** 1½ mi. north of the park's south entrance, has first come, first served sites with no hookups. Drinking water, restrooms, picnic tables, dump stations, and fire grates are available, but gathering firewood is prohibited, so bring your own. (Open Mar.-Oct. Sites $16. Cash only.)

Take Rte. 9 to Rte. 17 N, then take I-15 N for a little over 100 mi. until you reach I-70 E. Follow I-70 another 150 mi. to get to Green River. Gas is scarce, so budget it well.

☷ SIGHTS. The **Dan O'Laurie Canyon Country Museum,** 118 E. Center St., highlights the Native Americans who once lived here, the 1950s mining boom, and the geology of the area. (☎435-259-7985. Open in summer M-F 10am-6pm, Sa-Su noon-6pm; in winter M-F 10am-3pm, Sa-Su noon-5pm. $3.) About 15 mi. south of downtown Moab, **Hole 'N the Rock,** 11037 S. U.S. 191, is not exactly what the name purports. Early in the century, a couple blasted a set of cozy, cavernous rooms for themselves out of entrada sandstone, and you can tour the unique, naturally climate-controlled home. (Take U.S. 191 S 16 mi. from Moab. ☎435-686-2250. Open daily in summer 8:30am-5pm; in winter 9am-5pm. 10min. tours every 12-15min. $5, ages 6-12 $3.50.)

☊ OUTDOORS. Mountain biking and **rafting** are the big draws in Moab. The popular **Slickrock Trail** (10 mi.) rolls up and down the slickrock (which is actually sandstone) outside of Moab. The trail doesn't have a big vertical gain, but the level of technical skill required makes it an expert level trail, and temperatures often reach 100°F. **The Porcupine Rim Trail** (21 mi. one-way), a local favorite of moderate difficulty, offers great views of Castle Valley and starts near two metal stack tanks on the north side of Sand Flats Rd., 11 mi. from Moab. **Poison Spider** (12 mi., moderate), with an 860 ft. elevation change, is another popular route, though only skilled bikers should take the Portal Trail portion of the route, as it has exposure to dangerous cliffs. The trailhead is on Potash Rd. (Rte. 279), at the Dinosaur Tracks sign. **Rim Cyclery,** 94 W. 100 N, rents bikes and has trail info. (☎435-259-5333. Open M-Th and Su 9am-6pm, F-Sa 8am-6pm. Bikes $34-50 per day; includes helmet, pump, and water bottle.) Countless rafting companies are based in Moab. The **Moab Adventure Center,** 225 S. Main St., offers good deals on rafting trips as well as arranges horseback, motorboat, canoe, jeep, and helicopter expeditions. (☎435-259-7019 or 800-453-7450. Half-day $39-45, children $35; full day $55/$43.)

☷⋔ FOOD AND ACCOMMODATIONS. Retro booths at the **☷Moab Diner and Ice Cream Shoppe ➋,** 189 S. Main St., takes you back to the 1950s. The Sweetwater Skillet ($5.75) includes fried potatoes, bacon, green

onions, bell peppers, two eggs, and cheese. (☎435-259-4006. Open M-Th and Su 6am-10pm, F-Sa 6am-10:30pm. D/MC/V.) **☷Eclectica Coffee ➋,** 352 N. Main St., offers coffee, breakfast, lunch specialties ($6), and delicious pastries. (☎435-259-6896. Open M-Sa 7:30am-2:30pm, Su 7:30am-1pm. MC/V.) The **Peace Tree Juice Cafe ➋,** 20 S. Main St., will cool you off with smoothies ($2.50-5) and juice. (☎435-259-6333. Open daily 8am-6:30pm. AmEx/MC/V.) **Marianne's Bakery ➊,** 92 E. Center St., is a little bake shop with sandwiches like the "Zip-A-Dee-Do-Da" (tuna with mustard, onions, and hot sauce; $6.50). Day-old pastries are $0.75. (☎435-259-8268. Free Wi-Fi. Open M-F 7am-5pm, Sa 7am-3pm. D/MC/V.)

Chain motels clutter Main St., but rooms in Moab are not cheap and fill up fast from April to October. **Lazy Lizard International Hostel ➊,** 1213 S. U.S. 191, is 1 mi. south of Moab. The kitchen, VCR, laundry, and hot tub draw a mix of college students and backpackers, and the owners will give you the lowdown on the area. (☎435-259-6057. Reception 8am-11pm. Check-out 11am. Reservations recommended. Tent sites $6; dorms $9; private rooms from $22; cabins $27-47. AmEx/D/MC/V.) The Moab area features 1000 campsites, so finding a place to sleep shouldn't be a problem. **Goose Island, Hal Canyon, Oak Grove, Negro Bill,** and **Big Bend Campgrounds ➊,** all on Rte. 128, sit on the banks of the Colorado River, 3-9 mi. northeast of downtown Moab. (☎435-259-2100. Fire pits but no hookups or showers. Sites $5-10.)

BIG DETOUR. To explore the stunning scenery in Utah, take the **Mountains, Mesa, and Monuments Big Detour,** p. 442.

⛰ APPROACHING GREEN RIVER: 53 MILES
Take **U.S. 191 N** until it merges with **I-70 W;** get off at **Exit 164 (Rte. 19)** toward Green River.

GREEN RIVER

The town of Green River straddles the calm section of the waterway famous for its raging rapids to the north and south. An oasis in the vast desert traversed by the interstate, Green River once acted as a remote desert hideout for the Wild Bunch and other outlaws. Robber rumors aside, today Green River is known as a base for rafting the Green and Colorado Rivers and for its flourishing melon industry. If you're in town for the August harvest or the September festival, the watermelon and cantaloupe can't be missed.

VITAL STATS

Population: 900

Visitor Info: Green River Visitors Center, 885 E. Main St. (☎435-564-3526), in the John Wesley Powell Museum. Open daily June-Aug. 8am-8pm; Sept.-May 8am-5pm.

Internet Access: Green River City Library, 85 S. Long St. (☎435-564-3349). Open M-F 10am-6pm. Free.

Post Office: 20 E. Main St. (☎435-564-3329). Open M-F 8:30am-noon and 1-4:30pm, Sa 8:30-11:30am.
Postal Code: 84525.

GETTING AROUND. Green River lies along **I-70** just east of its intersection with **U.S. 191,** 185 mi. southeast of Salt Lake City. **Main St.,** the only road in town, runs between two exits off I-70.

SIGHTS. Outdoor activities steal the show in Green River, but the **John Wesley Powell Museum,** 885 E. Main St., captivates history buffs with Colorado River lore and a slideshow with narrated excerpts from Powell's journals. Artifacts from his expedition, including a replica of his boat, the *Emma Dean,* are on display. (☎435-564-3427. Open daily June-Aug. 8am-8pm; Sept.-May 8am-5pm. $3, ages 3-12 $1.)

OUTDOORS. The town's grandest offering is the river itself, and rafting trips depart frequently from late spring through early fall. Two reputable local outfitters are **Moki Mac River Expeditions,** 100 S. Sillman Ln. (☎435-564-3361 or 800-284-7280; www.moki-mac.com), and **Holiday Expeditions,** 1055 E. Main St. (☎435-564-3273; www.bikeraft.com). Both offer daytrips on the Green River for about $55-60 as well as multi-day trips on the Green, the Colorado, and other area rivers. To see the terrain from the banks, try the **Green River Scenic Drive** along Hastings Rd., off Main St. This drive traces the river through Gray Canyon for almost 20 mi., offering access to biking, hiking, and swimming. The drive starts from Hastings Rd., off Main St., east of downtown and the Powell

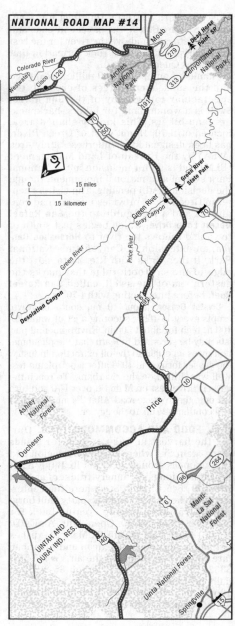

Museum. Turn north on Hastings Rd. 8 mi. out at Swasey Beach; the pavement ends and the road stays just above the river for the rest of the drive, ending at a rock formation that resembles Queen Nefertiti.

Thanks to an uplift 40-60 million years ago and the subsequent forces of erosion, the spectacular topography of the **San Rafael Swell** is a wonderland for hikers, backpackers, and bikers. This kidney-shaped area, located off I-70, 19 mi. west of Green River, has been designated a Wilderness Study Area (WSA) by the Bureau of Land Management (BLM) and is up for inclusion in the National Park system as a national monument, though the decision is still pending. The visitors center in Green River provides info on road conditions and a free guide to the **San Rafael Desert Loop Drive,** which begins just south of town and follows the river to **Horseshoe Canyon,** an extension of Canyonlands National Park. It then links with Rte. 24 to skirt the edge of the sawtooth ridge that marks the eastern rim of the swell, called **San Rafael Reef,** before intersecting with I-70.

Crystal Geyser, about 10 mi. south of town, erupts every 14-16hr., shooting a jet of water 80-100 ft. high for about 30min. Environmental purists may be surprised to learn that the phenomenon owes its origin to the oil extraction industry; the geyser formed in 1936 after a petroleum test well was drilled on the riverbank. To reach the geyser, drive east on Main St. over I-70 and turn left onto the frontage road. After 2¾ mi., turn right and continue 4½ mi. to the geyser.

▓▐ FOOD AND ACCOMMODATIONS. During the harvest in August, look for **stands** along Main St., where fresh watermelon and cantaloupe is around $0.17 per lb. Enjoy a hot breakfast alongside hungry truckers at **West Winds ❷,** 545 E. Main St., where the center-cut pork chops ($11) and two-patty chili burgers ($7.75) keep people coming back for more. (☎435-564-8240. Open 24hr. AmEx/D/MC/V.) **Ben's Cafe ❷,** 115 W. Main St., dishes out ample portions of Mexican and American fare as jukebox tunes fill the air. (☎435-564-3352. Breakfast $3.75-7. Lunch $5-8. Open daily in summer 6:30am-11pm; in winter 7am-10pm. AmEx/D/DC/MC/V.) Right next door, **Ray's Tavern ❷,** 26 S. Broadway, has rafting t-shirts on the walls, and diners helping themselves to ½ lb. burgers, chicken teriyaki, and pizzas ($9-14) at tree-trunk tables. (☎435-564-3511. Open daily 11am-10pm. AmEx/D/MC/V.)

One of the cheapest motels in town is **Budget Inn ❷,** 60 E. Main St., across the street from the Green River Community Park. The inn offers large rooms with comfy queen-size beds, cable TV, and A/C. (☎435-564-3441. Reception 24hr. Singles $35; doubles $40. AmEx/D/MC/V.) **Robbers Roost Motel ❷,** 225 W. Main St., offers tidy, basic rooms. (☎435-564-3452; www.robbersroost-motel.com. Reception 7am-2am. Check-out 10:30am. Singles $31; doubles $41. MC/V.) **Green River State Park,** 145 S. Green River Blvd., has 40 grassy sites and showers. (☎435-564-3633; www.reserveamerica.com. No hookups. Check-in 3pm. Check-out 2pm. Sites $15. MC/V.) **Backcountry camping** is usually allowed (check with the BLM in advance), and developed sites are available at **Goblin Valley State Park,** south of the swell near Temple Mountain and Crack Canyon just off Rte. 24.

◪ APPROACHING PRICE: 63 MILES
Take **I-70 W** to **U.S. 191 N/U.S. 6 W.** At Wellington, take **Exit U.S. 191/6** to take the 78 mi. Scenic Backcountry Byway through **Nine-Mile Canyon.** The marked turn-off for **Silver Creek Rd.** toward Nine-Mile Canyon is 51 mi. from I-70. If you're not up for the strenuous drive, take U.S. 191 N to **Exit 243** for **Bus. U.S. 6** through Price.

PRICE

Price's attractions include prehistoric displays and proximity to outdoor sights. The **College of Eastern Utah's Prehistoric Museum,** 155 E. Main St., displays fossils and skeletons from the Cleveland-Lloyd Quarry and has exhibits on Nine-Mile Canyon and prehistoric life in Utah. The enormous Huntington mammoth skeleton is the most complete of its kind in the world. Extensive exhibits explain what we can learn from teeth, claws, eggs, footprints, and even fossilized dino droppings. (☎435-637-5060. Open Apr.-Sept. daily 9am-6pm; Oct.-May M-Sa 9am-5pm. $4, ages 2-12 $2.) Next door, in the lobby of **Price City Hall,** 185 E. Main St., you can see a **WPA mural,** by artist Lynn Fausett, depicting the history of the area. (☎435-636-3185. Open M-F 8am-5pm.)

The **Log Palace Restaurant ❶**, 150 N. Hospital Dr., serves American fare in a log cabin built from trees that died of natural causes (i.e. not from an axe). French toast stuffed with strawberry cream cheese ($6) will satisfy any morning sweet tooth. (From the center of town, head north one block, and turn left on Rte. 100 N. ☎435-636-0779. Breakfast $3-8. Sandwiches $5-9. Open M-Sa 6am-8pm, Su 7am-9pm. AmEx/D/MC/V.) The **Greek Streak ❷**, 84 S. Carbon Ave., is a good stop for filling plates of *souvlaki* ($4-10), greek salad ($5-6.50), and visions of Crete in the midst of Utah. (☎435-637-1930. Open M-F 9am-9pm, Sa 11am-9pm. MC/V.) Price's **Budget Host Inn Motel and RV Park ❸**, 145 N. Carbonville Rd., has large, clean rooms. (☎435-637-2424. Tent sites $28; singles $50; doubles $55. AmEx/D/MC/V.)

◪ **APPROACHING HEBER CITY: 125 MILES**
Head west on **Rte. 100**. After crossing over the viaduct, take **U.S. 6 W/U.S. 191 N** through Helper and follow **U.S. 191 N** as it forks off to the right. A designated scenic byway, this section runs through the **Ashley National Forest** and **Uintah and Ouray Indian Reservations**. At Duchesne, take a right off U.S. 191, and follow **U.S. 40 W** to Heber City.

HEBER CITY

This small farming community lies in the shadow of its wealthier neighbor, Park City, but it still charms those passing through. Heber City is home to the **Heber Valley Historic Railroad,** 450 S. 600 W. This scenic railroad goes into Provo Canyon (3hr. round-trip), though the shorter trip to Soldier Hollow (1½hr.) and one-way trips are also available. (☎435-654-5601. Provo Canyon $28, seniors $23, children $18. Soldier Hollow $22/$18/$14.)

The upscale ◪**Snake Creek Grill ❺**, 650 W. 100 S, seems somewhat out of place in Heber City. Eclectic main dishes ($13-22) include the chef's specialties: 10-spice salmon with red curry, Japanese-noodle stir-fry, and blue cornmeal-crusted red trout. (☎435-654-2133; www.snakecreekgrill.com. Open W-Sa 5:30-9:30pm, Su 5:30-8:30pm. AmEx/D/MC/V.) The **Hub Cafe ❷**, 1165 S. Main St., has standard fare like ham steak ($9) and club sandwiches ($6.75). The delicious biscuits and gravy ($5) are served until noon. (☎435-654-5463. Open daily 6am-10pm. MC/V.) **Mac's Motel ❸**, 670 S. Main St., has clean rooms with microwaves and free Wi-Fi. (☎435-654-0612; www.macsmotel.net. Singles $54. AmEx/D/MC/V.) Rooms at the **Alpine**

Lodge ❷, 90 N. Main St., are clean and pleasant. (☎435-657-0224. Singles $45; doubles $55. MC/V.) The **High Country Inn Motel ❸**, 1000 S. Main St., has a spa for guests in winter. (☎435-654-0201. Singles $61; doubles $72. AmEx/D/MC/V.)

◪☷**DETOUR**
BIG COTTONWOOD CANYON SCENIC BYWAY
Head west out of Heber City on Rte. 100 N (Rte. 113), and turn right at the sign for Rte. 224. After the road becomes dirt, travel 7½ mi. to Guardsman Pass (closed in winter), forking left at the sign for Brighton. Continue west on Rte. 152 to the canyon.

Spanning over 22,000 acres, the stunning Big Cottonwood Canyon includes parts of the Wasatch Mountains. While the area is perhaps best known for its skiing, summertime travelers will find an array of forested camping areas and recreational opportunities. Spectacular hiking lies just over Guardsman Pass. The **Mill B South Fork** trail leads to Lake Blanche, with lovely views of the forest along the way. The trailhead is 9½ mi. from the stop sign at the bottom of the road to Guardsman Pass, on the left. The **Lillian** trail is strenuous but not technically challenging and offers great canyon and lake views. An easy hike (½ mi.) to the second bridge leads to a shaded bench by the water with a view of the canyon. The **Wetland Loop** (¾ mi.), an easy interpretive trail, takes you around wetlands at the edge of Brighton and explains the local ecosystem. The **Pine Creek Nature Trail** (1¼ mi.) is a relaxing path that leads through a zone inhabited by songbirds, chipmunks, rabbits, as well as other predatory species like coyotes, mountain lions, and golden eagles. Tread softly, watch for tracks, and you may spot some of these creatures yourself. (Emergency☎435-654-1791. $5 per vehicle.) The **Little Deer Creek Campground ❶**, which has 17 shady tent sites with water and flush toilets, but no electricity or showers (☎800-322-3770. Sites $11. AmEx/MC/V.) **Pine Creek Campground ❶**, in Oak Hollow Loop, has 122 secluded tent sites surrounded by trees. (☎800-322-3770. Water, showers, picnic tables, and grills. Gates open 8am-10pm. Reservations recommended; $7 fee. Sites $17. AmEx/MC/V.)

◪ **APPROACHING SALT LAKE CITY: 15 MILES**
After leaving the canyon, turn right onto **Rte. 190**. Go 1½ mi., and take **I-215 W** to **I-15 N**. Take **Exit 310**, following the signs to downtown **Salt Lake City.** If con-

ditions are iffy, skip the detour and follow **U.S. 40** to **I-80 W** directly to Salt Lake City.

SALT LAKE CITY

Tired from five months of travel across the plains, Brigham Young looked out across the Great Salt Lake and said: "This is the place." He believed that in this desolate valley his band of Mormon pioneers had finally found a haven where they could practice their religion freely. Though Mormons make up less than half of Salt Lake City's population today, Temple Square is still the focal point of downtown and the Church of Jesus Christ of Latter-Day Saints (LDS) continues to hold tremendous sway over the city. The cultural mix has created a city vibrant enough to have hosted the 2002 Winter Olympics. As the only American city with world-class skiing within 30min. of downtown, Salt Lake City also serves as home base for visitors to the seven surrounding ski meccas.

VITAL STATS

Population: 180,000

Visitor Info: Salt Palace Convention Center and Salt Lake City Visitors Bureau, 90 S. West Temple (☎801-534-4902; www.visitsaltlake.com), in Salt Palace Convention Center. Open M-F 8:30am-6pm, Sa-Su 9am-5pm.

Internet Access: Salt Lake Public Library, 209 E. 500 South (☎801-524-8200). Open M-Th 9am-9pm, F-Sa 9am-6pm, Su 1-5pm. Free.

Parking: Metered parking ($0.25 per 20min.) is available. Garages frequently offer 2hr. free parking.

Post Office: 230 W. 200 South (☎801-532-2906). Open M-F 8am-5pm, Sa 9am-2pm. **Postal Code:** 84101.

GETTING AROUND

Like most in cities in Utah, Salt Lake City's streets follow a grid system. Brigham Young designated **Temple Square** as the heart of downtown. Street names increase in increments of 100 and indicate how many blocks east, west, north, or south they lie from Temple Sq.; the "0" points are **Main St.** (north-south) and **South Temple** (east-west). State St., West Temple, and North Temple are 100-level streets. Occasionally, streets are referred to as 13th South or 17th North, which are the same as 1300 South or 1700 North. Local address listings often include two cross streets. For example, a building on 13th South (1300 South) might be listed as 825 E. 1300 South, meaning the cross street is 800 East (8th East). The streets are wide but can become congested during rush hour.

SIGHTS

LATTER-DAY SIGHTS. The center of the Mormon religion, **Temple Square** encloses the seat of the highest Mormon authority and the central temple. The square has two **visitors centers.** (North: 50 E. North Temple St. ☎801-240-4872. Open daily 9am-9pm. South: 50 W. South Temple St. ☎801-240-2534. Open daily 9am-9pm.) Visitors can wander around the 10-acre square, but the temple is not open to the public. Tours leave from the north and south gates every 15min. *Joseph Smith,* a film about the life of the Church's founding prophet, are screened at the **Joseph Smith Memorial Building.** (15 E. South Temple St. ☎800-537-9703; www.lds.org/events. Open M-Sa 9am-9pm. Tours every 15min. Reservations required. Free.) Temple Sq. is also home to the **Mormon Tabernacle** and its famed choir. Weekly rehearsals and performances are free. In the summer, there are frequent free concerts at **Assembly Hall,** next door. (Assembly Hall ☎800-537-9703 or 801-240-3323. Organ recitals M-Sa noon-12:30pm, Su 2-2:30pm; in summer M-Sa noon-12:30pm and 2-2:30pm, Su 2-2:30pm. Choir rehearsals most Th 7:30-9:30pm. Choir broadcasts Su 9:30am. Arrive at least 15min. early.) The **Church of Jesus Christ of Latter Day Saints Office Building** is the tallest skyscraper in town. Take the elevator to the 26th floor for a view of the Great Salt Lake to the west. (40 E. North Temple St. ☎801-240-3789. Observation deck open M-F 9am-4:30pm. Free.) The church's genealogical materials are accessible at the **Family Search Center,** 15 E. South Temple, in the **Joseph Smith Memorial Building.** The collection is housed in the **Family History Library,** which is free for visitors to browse. (35 N. West Temple. ☎801-240-2331. Search Center open M-Sa 9am-9pm. Library open M 7:30am-5pm, Tu-Sa 7:30am-10pm.)

 DID YOU KNOW? The site for the Salt Lake City Temple was selected in just four days, but it took 40 years to build.

NATIONAL ROAD

CAPITOL HILL. At the northern end of State St. stands Utah's beautiful **State Capitol.** Unfortunately, due to renovations, visitors haven't been able to tour the building for several years. Call ahead for availability. (☎801-538-3000.) Down State St., **Hansen Planetarium** has exhibits on black holes and the international space station, as well as laser and IMAX shows. (*15 S. State St. ☎801-531-4925. Open M-Th 10:30am-9pm, F-Sa 10:30am-11pm, Su 10:30am-8pm. Free. Shows and IMAX $8, ages 12 and under $5. All shows before 5pm $5.*)

PIONEER MEMORIAL MUSEUM. In Salt Lake City, "pioneer" refers to those who came to Utah with Joseph Smith and in the 22 years thereafter (1847-1869) to help found the Mormon Church. This huge museum has hundreds of photographs and hand-crafted personal items, but the highlights are several sets of "character dolls" and a 1902 horse-drawn steam fire engine. (*300 N. Main St., across from the State Capitol. ☎801-538-1050. Open June-Aug. M-Sa 9am-5pm, Su 1-5pm; Sept.-May M-Sa 9am-5pm. Free.*)

MUSEUMS. Early Mormon history is recounted at the **Museum of Church History and Art.** The museum contains an original 1830 Book of Mormon and Brigham Young's famous prayer bell. (*45 N. West Temple St. ☎801-240-3310. Open M-F 9am-9pm, Sa-Su 10am-7pm. Free.*) Exhibits wow art enthusiasts at the expanded **Utah Museum of Fine Arts,** on the University of Utah campus. The museum includes pieces from around the world, with a notable Japanese collection. (*☎801-581-7332. Open M-F 10am-5pm, Sa-Su noon-5pm. $5; students, seniors, and children $3.*) Also on campus, the **Museum of Natural History** has displays on the history of the Wasatch Front, with an emphasis on anthropology, biology, and paleontology. (*☎801-581-6927. Open M-Sa 9:30am-5:30pm, Su noon-5pm. $4, ages 3-12 $2.50, under 3 free.*) The **Salt Lake Art Center** shows an impressive array of contemporary art from around the country and rotates exhibits every 2-3 months. (*20 S. West Temple St. ☎801-328-4201. Open Tu-Th and Sa 11am-6pm, F 11am-9pm. Donation suggested.*)

RED BUTTE GARDEN AND ARBORETUM. In the hills above the city, the Arboretum offers 4 mi. of hiking and paved trails with almost guaranteed wildlife encounters. The Arbore-tum also features the Red Butte Canyon, herb gardens, and wildflowers. The Garden has an outdoor summer concert series with blues, folk, jazz, and R&B, entertaining attendees with musicians like Herbie Hancock and the Indigo Girls. (*300 Wakara Way, at the University of Utah. ☎801-581-4747; www.redbuttegarden.org. Open May-Aug. M-Sa 9am-9pm, Su 9am-5pm; Apr. and Sept. M-Sa 9am-7:30pm, Su 9am-5pm; Oct.-Mar. daily 10am-5pm. $6; students, seniors, and children $4.*)

CITY CREEK CANYON. City Creek Canyon offers scenic picnicking and recreation close to the city. The one-way, 5¾ mi. drive climbs 1300 ft. Picnicking pavilions must be reserved in advance. Wildlife is abundant in the area. (*Take B St. north. ☎801-596-5065. Open daily to pedestrians 8:30am-10pm, last entry 8pm; Memorial Day to Sept. to vehicles on even-numbered days; bicycles on odd-numbered days. $3. Picnic pavilions $3-25.*)

▄ FOOD

Good, cheap restaurants are sprinkled around the city and its suburbs. For a quick bite, **ZCMI Mall** and **Crossroads Mall,** both across from Temple Sq., have standard food courts.

▨ **Sage's Cafe,** 473 E. 300 South (☎801-322-3790). Calling themselves "culinary astronauts," the talented chefs at this classy eatery produce delectable dishes. Try the basil-and-walnut pesto pasta ($14.50) or the "Rabbit's Pick" sandwich (carrot butter, avocado, and veggies; $7). Open M-Th 11:30am-2:30pm and 5-10pm, F 11:30am-2:30pm and 5-11pm, Su 9am-10pm. AmEx/D/MC/V. ❹

▨ **Ruth's Diner,** 2100 Emigration Canyon Rd. (☎801-582-5807; www.ruthsdiner.com). The best breakfasts in town and a bar with live music nightly. Originally run out of a trolley car, Ruth's is the second-oldest restaurant in Utah and has been a Salt Lake landmark for 70 years. Huge omelettes like the "Rutherino" ($6-7) and brownie sundaes ($6). Open daily 8am-10pm. AmEx/D/MC/V. ❷

Red Iguana, 736 W. North Temple (☎801-322-4834; www.rediguana.com), in the bright-orange building. Famous for its *mole,* this popular eatery serves authentic Mexican food in a festive atmosphere. Burritos, enchiladas, and tacos $5-8. Combo plates $10-12. Open M-Th 11am-10pm, F 11am-11pm, Sa 10am-11pm, Su noon-9pm. AmEx/D/MC/V. ❷

Salt Lake City

⌂ **ACCOMMODATIONS**
The Avenues Hostel
   (HI-AYH), **3**
City Creek Inn, **2**
Ute Hostel
   (AAIH/Rucksackers), **9**

🍎 **FOOD**
Orbit, **4**
Red Iguana, **1**
Ruth's Diner, **8**
Sage's Cafe, **5**

🎵 **NIGHTLIFE**
Avalon, **10**
Circle Lounge, **6**
Totem's, **7**

Orbit, 540 W. 200 South (☎801-322-3808; www.orbitslc.com), close to the dance clubs in the old industrial district. With a sports bar and patio seating, Orbit boasts sleek decor and a diverse clientele. Sandwiches $7-10. Pizzas $8-10. Entrees $10-16. Open M and W-Th 11am-2:30pm, F 11am-9pm, Sa 9am-9pm, Su 9am-3pm. AmEx/D/MC/V. ❸

🏠 ACCOMMODATIONS

Affordable chain motels cluster at the southern end of downtown, around 200 West and 600 South, and on North Temple.

City Creek Inn, 230 W. North Temple (☎801-533-9100; www.citycreekinn.com), a stone's throw from Temple Sq. This solid family-owned and operated motel has 33 immaculate, ranch-style rooms

for cheap. Free coffee. Singles $54; doubles $64. AmEx/D/MC/V. ❸

The Avenues Hostel (HI-AYH), 107 F St. (☎801-359-3855), a 15min. walk from Temple Sq., in a nice residential area. Keep an eye out—there is no sign marking the hostel. A new entertainment system, 2 kitchens, laundry, and free Wi-Fi make the hostel one of the best budget options around. Key deposit $5. Free parking. Reception 7:30am-10:30pm. Reservations recommended July-Aug. and Jan.-Mar. Dorms $15; private rooms $25-35. MC/V. ❶

Ute Hostel (AAIH/Rucksackers), 21 E. Kelsey Ave. (☎801-595-1645 or 888-255-1192), near the intersection of 1300 South and Main St. Young domestic and international travelers crash at this cozy, friendly hostel. Free tea, coffee, and Wi-Fi. Linen included. Res-

NATIONAL ROAD

ervations recommended July-Sept. and Jan.-Mar. Dorms $20; private rooms $30-35. Cash only. ❶

ENTERTAINMENT

Salt Lake City's sweltering summer months are jammed with evening concerts. The **Temple Square Concert Series** presents free outdoor concerts in Brigham Young Historic Park, with music ranging from string quartets to acoustic guitar. (☎801-240-2534. Concerts Tu and F 7:30pm. Free.) The **Utah Symphony Orchestra** performs in Abravanel Hall, 123 W. South Temple. (☎801-533-6683; www.utah-symphony.org. Office open M-F 10am-6pm, Sa 10am-2pm. Tickets $15-40.)

NIGHTLIFE

The free *City Weekly* lists events and is available at bars, clubs, and restaurants. Famous for teetotaling, the early Mormon theocrats made it illegal to serve alcohol in public places. Hence, all liquor-serving institutions are "private clubs," serving only members and "sponsored" guests. To get around this law, most bars and clubs charge a "temporary membership fee"—essentially a cover charge. Nonetheless, Salt Lake City has an active nightlife, centering on S. West Temple and the run-down blocks near the railroad tracks.

Avalon, 3605 S. State St. (☎801-266-0258; www.theavalontheater.com). Avalon has live rock and Top 40 for all ages. Most shows 7pm; call or check website for exact times. MC/V.

Circle Lounge, 328 S State St. (☎801-531-5400). An upscale jazz-martini-sushi bar with live music. Cover $12. Open M-Sa 6pm-2am. AmEx/MC/V.

Totem's, 538 S. Redwood Rd. (☎801-975-0401). Perfect for dinner and dancing, with live music on some nights. Open M-Th 7am-midnight, F 7am-1am, Sa 10am-midnight, Su 10am-10pm. AmEx/D/MC/V.

DETOUR
GREAT SALT LAKE

From downtown, follow 600 N west to I-15 S, and take the 1st exit for I-80 W. Take Exit 104 for access to the south shore; there is also a scenic overlook from the highway about 3½ mi. past the exit, near mi. 101. To get to the island, take Exit 335 from I-15, and follow signs to the causeway.

The Great Salt Lake is so salty that only blue-green algae and brine shrimp can survive in it. The salt content varies from 5-27%, providing the unusual buoyancy credited with keeping the lake free of drownings. Decaying organic material on the shore gives the lake its pungent odor, which locals prefer not to discuss. **Antelope Island State Park,** in the middle of the lake, is a favorite of visitors. There, you have a fair chance of spotting the island's namesake species, as well as deer, bobcats, and coyotes. The size of Manhattan, the island is home only to animals, a sole park ranger, and his family. (☎801-625-1630. Open daily in summer 7am-10pm; in winter 7am-6pm. $9 per vehicle, $4 per bicycle and pedestrian.) On the south shore, **Saltair,** just across from Exit 104, has a souvenir shop, free restrooms, and showers. The beach itself is nearly nonexistent, but many tourists use this spot to access the water. (☎801-250-4388. Open May-Sept. daily 9am-9pm.) About 1½ mi. west of Saltair is the **Great Salt Lake State Marina,** the starting point for a variety of cruises on the lake. Some offer talks on the history and geology of the lake, while others offer dinner at sunset. (☎801-252-9336; www.gslcruises.com. Cruises $12-18. Dinner cruises $39-52.)

APPROACHING DELTA: 21 MILES
Follow **I-80 W** to **Rte. 36** toward Tooele. Rte. 36 runs across a sparsely populated area of the state, ending about 88 mi. from Salt Lake City. Follow signs for **U.S. 6 W** to Delta. If you need to fill up before cutting to the western part of the state, gasoline is available in the tiny town of Lynndyl. The dunes are open for enjoyment at the **Little Sahara Recreation Area,** just over 100 mi. from Salt Lake City. Primitive camping with drinking water is available. (Turn off U.S. 6, head about 6 mi. on a dirt road to the visitors center, and turn right at the sign. ☎435-433-5960. Visitors center open M and W-Su 10am-7pm.) Entering Delta, **U.S. 6** and **U.S. 50 W** merge to become **Main St.**

DELTA

Delta is the largest in a cluster of desert towns near a wide section of the Sevier River, and the largest outpost until Ely, Nevada, 170 mi. west. Rockhunting—prowling the desert for minerals—is a popular activity here. The **Great Basin Museum,** 328 W. 100 North, has a collection of local memorabilia as well as exhibits on beryllium mining and geology. Ask a volunteer to operate the black light in the mineral fluorescence display. Outside is an exhibit on the Topaz Internment Camp, where Japanese-Americans were held during WWII. Don't miss the 3D map, which shows the roadtrip route from Green River to the Nevada border. (☎435-864-5013. Open M-Sa 10am-4pm. Free.)

Locals drink from their own mugs at **Top's City Cafe ❸**, 313 W. Main St. The "Big Daddy" burger ($8), with swiss cheese and mushrooms, is a house specialty. (☎435-864-2148. Entrees $8-17. Open daily 6am-10pm. MC/V.) **The Pizza House ❷**, 69 S. 300 East, serves filling Italian and American food and claims to have the "best pizza in the West." (☎435-864-2207. Open M-Th 11am-9:30pm, F-Sa 11am-10pm. AmEx/D/MC/V.) The **Diamond D Motor Lodge ❷**, 234 W. Main St., is one of the best values in town. (☎435-864-2041. Laundry. Free Wi-Fi. Singles $33; doubles $37-41. AmEx/D/MC/V.) The **Budget Motel ❷**, 75 S. 350 East, offers pleasant rooms. (☎435-864-4533. Singles $37; doubles $39. MC/V.) Small but homey, the **Deltan Inn Motel ❷**, 347 E. Main St., has well-maintained rooms with standard amenities. (☎435-864-5318. Singles $35; doubles $39-42. AmEx/D/MC/V.)

 Don't forget to fill up on gas before leaving Delta—there are many miles between here and the next pump!

◼ APPROACHING GREAT BASIN: 93 MILES
Head west on **Main St. (U.S. 6/50)**, following the signs for Ely. The last gas station is 6 mi. west of Delta, in Hinckley. Just after the cattle guard, exactly 3 mi. from the state border, turn left at the sign for Great Basin National Park. Turn left at the stop sign onto **Rte. 487**, and right at the junction with **Rte. 488** in the town of Baker. The park lies 5 mi. down the road.

The Silver State
NEVADA
WELCOME TO FABULOUS LAS VEGAS NEVADA
Welcomes You!

 At the border, U.S. 6/50 enters the Pacific Time Zone, where it is 1hr. earlier.

GREAT BASIN NATIONAL PARK

Established in 1986, Great Basin National Park preserves ancient glaciers, prehistoric pine trees, diverse fauna, and miles of unmaintained trails. The basin area extends through much of Nevada, and is so named because no precipitation falling in the region reaches the ocean. Eastern Nevada's Snake Range forms the spine of the park, with various creeks, lakes, and forest spreading out from its peaks. Despite the desolation of the area's vast desert, high alpine areas created by the towering ranges support ecological diversity, including the ancient bristlecone pine and the mountain lion.

VITAL STATS

Area: 77,100 acres

Visitor Info: Lehman Caves Visitors Center (☎775-234-7331; www.nps.gov/grba), at the end of Rte. 488. Open daily May-Oct. 7:30am-5:30pm; Nov.-Apr. 8am-4:30pm. **Great Basin Visitors Center** (☎775-234-7331), on Rte. 487, just north of Baker. Open daily 8am-5:30pm.

Gateway towns: Baker, Ely (p. 457).

Fees: None.

▤ GETTING AROUND

Rte. 488 is the only paved road that enters the park, running west to the **visitors center** and providing access to all four of the park's developed campgrounds. Improved gravel roads grant access to the park's northern reaches and central drainage, while a high-clearance dirt road ventures into the park's southern mountains. The town of Ely bills itself as a gateway to the park and offers most comforts, but Baker (5 mi. from the visitors center) also provide basic services.

◢ OUTDOORS

SCENIC DRIVE
Just down the hill from the visitors center, the paved **Wheeler Peak Scenic Drive** (1½hr. round-trip) winds 12 mi. up to an elevation of 10,000 ft. Full of sharp curves and switchbacks, the road demands caution. As the road climbs, it passes first through greasebrush and sagebrush, then piñon pines and

junipers, then ponderosa pines, white fir, and mountain mahogany, and finally through spruce, limber pine, and high alpine aspen groves. As late as June, snowbanks line the summit area and make the warm desert weather at the base a pleasant memory. **Mather Overlook** features an awe-inspiring view of jagged **Wheeler Peak** and **Wheeler Glacier;** in the other direction, the road stretches across the flat basin you crossed on your way west to the park. For a closer view of the peak, stop at **Wheeler Peak Overlook.**

HIKING AND BIKING

Because much of the park remains undeveloped, exploring its far reaches requires good hiking boots, plenty of water, several days' worth of food, and strong legs. Luckily, for those not enthusiastic about hauling a heavy pack through the backcountry, the park's other notable features, **Bristlecone Groves, Lexington Arch,** and **Lehman Cave,** are accessible via shorter excursions, though the route to Lexington Arch requires high-clearance 4WD. Several trails along the Wheeler Peak Scenic Drive grant ample opportunities to stretch weary legs. For a less crowded jaunt, try the longer trails departing from the Baker Creek Trailhead. The **Mountain View Nature Trail** (30min., easy) begins at the Rhodes Cabin next to the visitors center and provides a brief glimpse of park ecology and geology for those pressed for time. Stop by the visitors center for a trail guide and watch for the signs along the way. The only day hike flagged for winter use, the **Lehman Creek Trail** (7 mi., 4-6hr. round-trip) passes through a range of habitats over its 2000 ft. elevation change. It departs from the end of Wheeler Peak Scenic Drive or the Lehman Creek campgrounds.

Although bicycling in the park is limited to roads, mountain bikers will relish excellent riding at the **Sacramento Pass Recreation Site,** east of the park along U.S. 6/50. Some of the best trails in the area explore **Black Horse Canyon,** accessible off U.S. 6/50 via the marked forest road, ¾ mi. south of Sacramento Pass.

LEHMAN CAVES. Absalom Lehman came across these splendid caves in 1885, and soon he was charging visitors for the pleasure of exploring them by candlelight. The caves continue to delight travelers with their fantastic formations. The Park Service prohibits self-guided tours, offering three options for guided tours: entrance

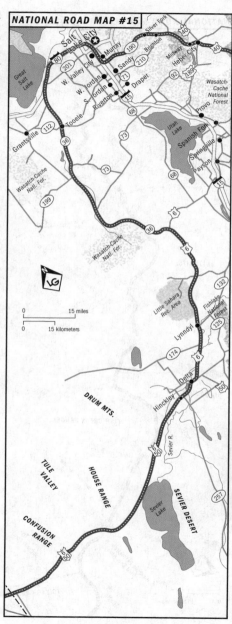

NATIONAL ROAD MAP #16

UTAH
NEVADA

SNAKE RANGE

SCHELL CR. RANGE

Humboldt-Toiyabe National Forest

Baker

Great Basin National Park

Humboldt-Toiyabe National Forest

Majors Place

Ely

EGAN RANGE

BUTTE MTS.

Humboldt-Toiyabe National Forest

White R.

Newark Lake

DIAMOND MTS.

Eureka

FISH CREEK RANGE

Fish Cr.

Antelope Wash

Humboldt-Toiyabe National Forest

Coils Cr.

Hickson Petroglyph BLM Rec. Area

Willow Cr.

Humboldt-Toiyabe National Forest

Austin

TOIYABE RANGE

0   15 miles
0   15 kilometers

into the first room only, the Gothic Palace; a 1hr. tour of the Gothic Palace, Lodge Room, and Inscription Room; and a 1½hr. tour of the entire cave including the spectacular **Grand Palace Room.** The cave remains at 50°F all year, a refreshing break from the sun in the summer months; just be sure to bring an extra layer. (☎ 775-234-7331, ext. 242. Free. Tours mid-June to mid-Aug. every 30min. 8am-4:30pm; Sept.-May every 2hr. 9am-3pm. Reservations recommended. 1hr. tour $8, ages 5-15 $4. 1½hr. tour $12. No children under 5 permitted on the 1½ mi. tour.)

LEXINGTON ARCH. A mammoth, six-story limestone sculpture in the wild southeast section of the park, Lexington Arch demonstrates nature's powerful craftsmanship. The moderate 3½ mi. hike switches back and forth up several hundred feet before paralleling a drainage ditch back to the base of the arch. The majority of the trail, which gains a total of 820 ft. in elevation, sits on Forest Service land. (Drive south 12 mi. from the intersection of Rte. 487 and 488 through Garrison, UT. At the sign for Lexington Arch, follow the rough, high-clearance dirt road 12 mi. to the trailhead.)

BRISTLECONE TRAIL. The Great Basin bristle-cones, gnarled but beautiful trees, are the world's oldest living organisms. Bristlecones survive on high mountain slopes by deadening themselves until more hospitable times allow them to flourish again. The oldest trees are found in some of the most inhospitable locations and can be over 3,000 years old. Although there are several bristlecone groves throughout the park, the grove below Wheeler Peak offers the easiest access. Follow the Wheeler Peak Scenic Drive to the end and take the trail (2¾ mi., moderate) from **Bristlecone Trailhead** to the trees. Tours of the grove depart from the trailhead at 10am daily during the summer. The **Alpine Lakes Loop Trail** (2¾ mi., 1-3hr. round-trip) is a highly-trafficked trail that allows quick access to two scenic lakes, **Lake Stella** and **Lake Teresa,** as well as views of Wheeler Peak, which looms overhead. The trailhead is at the end of Wheeler Peak Scenic Drive.

◢ FOOD

Catering to those unwilling to trek to Baker or pack their own grub, the visitors center's **Lehman Caves Cafe ❶,** at the end of Rte. 488, serves break-fast ($5), sandwiches ($5), and ice cream ($1.50-

3), and peddles park memorabilia. (☎775-234-7221. Open June-Aug. daily 8am-5pm; Apr.-May and Sept.-Oct. daily 8am-4pm. D/MC/V.) For a more substantial menu, check out **T&D's ❷**, a restaurant, bar, and convenience store in downtown Baker. The store stocks grocery and camping essentials, and the restaurant serves breakfasts ($3-4), sandwiches and burgers ($4-7), and Mexican food. (☎775-234-7264. Restaurant open M and Su 7am-8pm, Tu-Th 11am-8pm, F-Sa 7am-8:30pm. Store open daily 8am-7pm. D/MC/V.)

ACCOMMODATIONS

Four developed campsites, several primitive sites along Snake and Strawberry Creeks, and nearly unlimited backcountry camping accommodate Great Basin visitors. All four developed campgrounds are first come, first served and reservations are not allowed. Both Upper Lehman and Wheeler Peak Campgrounds host evening ranger talks during summer months. Scenic **primitive camping**, which offers pre-dug fire pits, rewards those willing to travel gravel roads. **Snake Creek Rd.,** 5 mi. south of Baker along Rte. 487, follows the fertile watershed Snake Creek area and allows easy access to six primitive sites. **Strawberry Creek Rd.,** 3 mi. from the U.S. 6/50 and Rte. 487 junction, leads to four primitive sites along Strawberry Creek. (☎775-234-7331. Both campgrounds have tables and pit toilets, but no water. Sites $10.) For those not into camping, there are a few budget accommodations in the area.

Border Inn (☎775-234-7300). Straddling the Utah/Nevada border along U.S. 6/50, the Border Inn boasts sizable rooms with small TVs and VCRs. Singles $35-42. MC/V. ❷

Silver Jack Motel, 14 Main St. (☎775-234-7323), in Baker. Simple rooms close to the mountains. Sites with full hookup $22; private rooms $55-66. AmEx/MC/V. ❸

Wheeler Peak Campground (9890 ft.) offers scenic sites nestled among aspen groves and alpine meadows in the shadow of Wheeler Peak. Access to the sites is at the end of the serpentine Wheeler Peak Scenic Dr., a road which is not recommended for vehicles over 24 ft. in length. 37 sites. Pit toilets and potable water. Open June-Sept. Sites $12. Cash only. ❶

Baker Creek Campground (7530 ft.), south down the graded gravel road from Rte. 488. A serene spot on the banks of Baker Creek. 32 sites. Pit toilets and potable water. Open May-Oct. Sites $12. Cash only. ❶

Upper and **Lower Lehman Creek Campgrounds,** close to the visitors center and Lehman Caves, guard the banks of Lehman Creek along the 1st 3 mi. of the Wheeler Mountain Scenic Dr. Both campgrounds crowd quickly, so arrive early. Sites 17-24 at Upper are more removed and spacious. Both campgrounds have pit toilets and potable water. Open May-Oct. Sites $12. Cash only. ❶

⚐ APPROACHING LAS VEGAS: 255 MILES
In Majors Place, take a left from **U.S. 6/50** for the 255 mi. trek south on **U.S. 93.** It's not a daytrip by any stretch, but Las Vegas offers a glittery change of scenery from the Nevada desert.

LAS VEGAS

Rising out of the Nevada desert, Las Vegas is a shimmering tribute to excess. Those who embrace it find a mirage made real, an oasis of vice and greed, and one hell of a good time. The modern incarnation of the city was founded on gambling, whoring, and mob muscle. And while the mob has more or less slunk away, the others remain indivisible features of this playground town. Nowhere else in America do so many shed their inhibitions and indulge with such abandon. A word of caution: know thy tax bracket. Walk into the city with a good idea of what you want to spend and get the hell out when you've spent it. In Las Vegas, there's a busted wallet and a broken heart for every garish neon light.

PAGE TURN. See p. p. 582 in **Route 66** for complete coverage of Las Vegas.

⚐ APPROACHING ELY: 305 MILES
Get on **I-515 N,** and take **Exit 76B** to **I-93 N.** Continue on I-93, and turn left onto **NV 318** (also known as the Extraterrestrial Highway). Stay on NV 318/NV 38, and turn right onto **U.S. 6/U.S. 50.** Entering Ely, U.S. 6 heads left; stay on **U.S. 50.**

ELY

This mining town hardly fits the profile of a typical "gateway" city. Yet its barren surroundings and the convergence of several highways make Ely (rhymes with "really") a hub for much trans-Nevadan traffic. In the early 20th century, development of the area's copper resources brought an influx of residents and a railroad system, but today's Ely is a shadow of its former self. Remnants of past glory remain—like the stately Nevada Hotel and Casino, once the state's tallest building.

VITAL STATS

Population: 4000

Visitor Info: White Pine County Chamber of Commerce, 636 Aultman St. (☎775-289-8877). Open M-F 9am-5pm.

Internet Access: White Pine County Library, 900 Campton St. (☎775-289-3737), 1 block south of Aultman St. Open M-Th 9am-6pm, F 9am-5pm; 1st and 3rd Sa of each month 10am-2pm. Free.

Post Office: 2600 Bristlecone Ave. (☎775-289-9276). Open M-F 8:30am-5pm, Sa 10am-2pm.
Postal Code: 89301.

⌘ GETTING AROUND. U.S. 6, 50, and **93** meet in Ely and radiate toward Reno, Las Vegas, Utah, Idaho, and California. Approaching the town from the southeast, U.S. 50 runs along **Great Basin Blvd.** before turning west onto **Aultman St.,** Ely's main drag. Great Basin Blvd. serves as the division between numbered north-south streets. Lettered streets run east-west, east of Great Basin Blvd.

◆ SIGHTS. In 1983, the railroad through East Ely shut down, leaving behind an office and depot full of old equipment and records. Relics from the depot are on display at the **Nevada Northern Railway Museum,** 1100 Ave. A, in East Ely. A tour goes through the restored office building and well-informed guides share their knowledge of the railroad, town, and surrounding region. There's also a train ride on the old line, pulled by a 94-year-old coal-fired locomotive. Or you can drive a locomotive 14 mi. yourself—$590 for the steam locomotive, $390 for the diesel. (Where U.S. 50 turns left on Aultman St., turn right and then left onto 11th St. E. ☎775-289-2085 or 866-407-8326; www.nevadanorthernrailway.net. Open M-F 8am-5pm; Sa-Su hours vary. Tours $4. Train rides M and W-F 1 per day, Sa-Su 2 per day. $15-60, ages 4-12 $12-45.) The **White Pine Public Museum,** 2000 Aultman St., displays a hodgepodge of artifacts ranging from stuffed birds to telegraph equipment. (☎775-289-4710. Hours vary; call ahead. Free.)

▚▐ FOOD AND ACCOMMODATIONS. Aultman St. has several steak-and-potatoes chop houses, including restaurants in the downtown casinos. **La Fiesta ❷,** on McGill Hwy., prepares *Taquitos La Fiesta* ($10) and lunch specials. (☎775-289-4112. Open daily 11am-10pm. MC/V.) For a change of pace, **Twin Wok ❷,** 700 Great Basin Blvd., offers Chinese and Japanese cuisine. Try Mandarin entrees ($8-10) or pricier hibachi selections ($13) with soup or salad, vegetables, and rice. (☎775-289-3699. Open daily 11am-10pm. AmEx/MC/V.)

Many of Ely's hotels and motels are located on Aultman St. The best option is the grand **Hotel Nevada ❷,** 501 Aultman St., a relic from another era. Many rooms are shrines to celebrities who have stayed here, like Mickey Rooney and Wayne Newton. (☎775-289-6665 or 888-406-3055. Singles from $40. AmEx/D/MC/V.) **The White Pine Motel ❷,** 1301 Aultman St., has basic rooms. (☎775-289-4600. Rooms $45. AmEx/D/MC/V.)

◥ DETOUR
GARNET FIELDS ROCKHOUND AREA
5¼ mi. west of Ely on U.S. 50. Turn right at the sign.

"Pockets" in volcanic rock were created by quickly-cooling lava; carefully break these rocks open and with luck, red garnet will shine inside. The top of Garnet Hill affords a view of the goldish-colored pit mine and waste dumps in Ruth, a by-product of the region's mining. (Open 24hr.)

◤ APPROACHING EUREKA: 77 MILES
Follow **Aultman St. (U.S. 50 W)** out of town. Don't forget to fill up before leaving Ely—the next chance is 77 mi. down the road.

EUREKA

Eureka boomed in population and wealth after the discovery of silver in the area. The mine quickly busted, however, leaving behind a smattering of late-1870s buildings and little else. A bit of mining remains, but Eureka has never regained its 19th-century prosperity. U.S. 50, known as Main St., runs straight through the center of town. The **Eureka County Sentinel Museum,** 10 N. Monroe St., contains the printing press that produced the local *Eureka Sentinel,* a daily from 1871 to 1960. The original wall, papered with decaying posters from the Opera House and old news stories, is fascinating. (☎775-237-5010. Open May-Oct. daily 10am-6pm; Nov.-Apr. Tu-Sa 10am-6pm. Free.) The

Eureka Courthouse, 10 S. Main St., is restored and elegant. Ask someone to show you the old jail back. (☎ 775-237-5263. Open M-F 8am-noon and 1-5pm. Free.) Nevadan artists display their work at the **Opera House,** 31 S. Main St. (☎ 775-237-6006. Open M-F 8am-noon and 1-5pm. Free.)

D.J.'s Drive-In and Diner ❷, 509 S. Main St., is a burger-and-sandwich joint that serves sandwiches ($3-6) and rib, seafood, and chicken dinners ($7-8), as well as a pizza and ice cream. (☎ 775-237-5356. Open daily 10am-10pm. Cash only.) The **Sundown Lodge,** 60 N. Main St., offers clean rooms. Prices fluctuate, so call ahead. (☎ 775-237-5334. Singles $38; doubles $45. AmEx/D/MC/V.)

◪ DETOUR
HICKISON PETROGLYPH RECREATION AREA
Off U.S. 50 W, 45 mi. from Eureka. Turn right on a dirt road to reach the site.

A free interpretive guide discusses a short loop trail, which leads to prehistoric designs carved into rock faces. The designs, somewhat harder to see than those at Grimes Point, consist mostly of curved lines. (☎ 775-635-4000. Free.)

◪ DETOUR
SPENCER HOT SPRINGS
Off Rte. 376, just east of U.S. 50 W, 58 mi. from Eureka. Watch for the turnoff near mi. 99, take the dirt road 10 mi.; the springs are on the left.

Surrounded by mountains and isolated from civilization, Spencer Hot Springs is worth a stop. While the springs are well known to locals and legal to use, there aren't any signs pointing to these rock-lined pools, nor any gatekeepers asking for money. (Open 24hr. Free.)

◪ DETOUR
TOQUIMA CAVE
From U.S. 50 W, turn left on Rte. 376. Proceed ¼ mi., and turn left onto the dirt road. Turn left on another dirt road after 5½ mi., and continue 1½ mi. Continue straight for 11 mi., and turn left at the sign.

A bit of a drive down a dirt road, Toquima Cave, carved into volcanic rock, is filled with prehistoric art, including painted pictographs and carved petroglyphs. (Open 24hr. Free.)

◪ APPROACHING AUSTIN: 70 MILES
Continue on **U.S. 50 W** toward Austin.

AUSTIN

The only sign of civilization for miles around, Austin has dwindled significantly since its days as a major mining camp. It is a good 2hr. drive from Austin to Fallon, however, so Austin makes a good place for a stop. A developed network of mountain biking trails goes through the nearby **Toiyabe National Forest,** just south of town. Trails range in difficulty and length; pick up a trail guide and Forest Service map at the **Austin Ranger District Office,** just west of town (☎ 775-964-2671; open M-F 8am-4:30pm), or at the **Chamber of Commerce,** on the second floor of the Austin Courthouse (☎ 775-964-2200; open M-F 9am-5pm). Based on a Roman design, the three-story **Stokes Castle** was built as a luxury summer home for Ansen Stokes, a mine developer and railroad magnate.

CONQUER THE CANYONS

A canyoneering adventure through slot canyons and narrows might be paralled only by sky-diving for its sheer excitement value. Slipping sideways, nose against the rocks, sun and shadows gleaming through red canyons as you maneuver your body into acrobatic poses, canyoneering is the pinnacle of athletic and aesthetic prowess rolled into one. Canyoneering, broadly defined as the act of traveling through a canyon, is a sport native to the Southwest and perfectly suited to Grand Staircase-Escalante's hidden canyons. You get a view into the Earth's layers that you can't see from the road and won't find hiking. Consider the hefty $100 per day cost as tuition for the most amazing geology lesson you'll ever take. The best part, though, is the 100 ft. rappel at the end of certain canyons, a once-in-a-lifetime opportunity to become a human spider. Your heart may race, and you may get claustrophobic at times, but at the end of the tunnel, you'll definitely want to go back for more.

Excursions of Escalante, 125 E. Main St. (☎ 800-839-7567; www.excursions-escalante.com), in Escalante, leads guided canyoneering tours. Open M and W-Su 11am-5pm. Full-day canyoneering tour $100-145; meals,

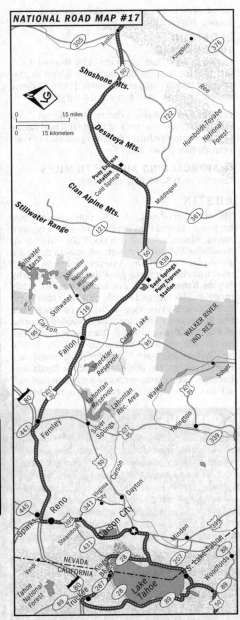

NATIONAL ROAD MAP #17

NATIONAL ROAD

Today, it lies in ruin. (Just west of the Chevron Station and left on Castle Rd. Free.)

Austin offers few dining options. For a decent meal, the **International Cafe and Bar ❶**, 59 N. Main St., is the place to go. (☎ 775-964-1225. Breakfast $3-6. Sandwiches and burgers $5-6. Dinner entrees $7.50-19. Open daily 6am-9:30pm. Cash only.) The **Toiyaba Cafe ❷**, 150 Main St., serves basic sandwiches ($5-9) and other diner fare. (☎ 775-964-2220. Open daily 6am-9pm. AmEx/D/MC/V.) Austin's motels line U.S. 50. **Lincoln Motel ❷**, 60 N. Main St., provides minimalist rooms with thin walls. (☎ 775-964-2698. Singles $30; doubles $37. MC/V.) The **Pony Canyon Motel ❷**, 30 Main St., has nicer rooms, but no A/C. (☎ 775-964-2605. Singles $38; doubles $48. AmEx/MC/V.)

APPROACHING COLD SPRINGS: 49 MILES
Follow **U.S. 50 W** out of town.

COLD SPRINGS. Cold Springs is a small outpost on the way to Fallon; blink, and you'll miss it. The **Cold Springs Pony Express Station** delights history buffs as one of the few Pony Express stations in good condition. After a 1½ mi. hike, visitors can walk around the inside, now overgrown with bushes, and read about the site on small plaques. Refill your tank and your stomach at the **Cold Springs Station ❶**, near mi. 83, an affordable and cozy restaurant. Eggs, bacon, hash browns, and toast ($6) and chili-cheese dogs ($5) grace the menu and there is even room to camp. (☎ 775-423-1233; www.coldspringsstationnv.com. Restaurant open M-Sa 8am-8pm, Su 8am-6pm. Sites $10, with hookup $20. MC/V.)

 PHOTO OP. In the 25 mi. between Sand Springs and Fallon, watch (or listen) for Navy jets overhead; Fallon is the home of the **Naval Fighters Weapons School**, a.k.a. "Top Gun."

APPROACHING FALLON: 61 MILES
Continue on **U.S. 50** into downtown Fallon.

FALLON. The self-proclaimed "Oasis of Nevada," Fallon is at the center of a fertile farming region, created when the Newlands Project built two dams and a canal, bringing water to the desert. While artifacts are few at the **Churchill County**

Museum, 1050 S. Maine St., this local history museum has extensive displays on the natural history of northwestern Nevada. Highlights include a display on the Hidden Cave as well as a large mineral and rock collection. (☎775-423-3677. Open Apr.-Oct. M-Sa 10am-5pm, Su noon-5pm; Nov.-Mar. M-Sa 10am-4pm, Su noon-4pm. Donations accepted.) At **La Fiesta ❸,** 60 W. Center St., friendly waiters in tuxedo shirts and bow ties serve delicious Mexican food in spotlessly clean restaurant. (From U.S. 50, head south 1 block on Maine St., and turn right. ☎775-423-1605. Open daily 11am-10pm. D/MC/V.) The **Value Inn ❷,** 180 W. Williams Ave., has clean rooms. (☎775-423-5151. Singles $39; doubles $49. AmEx/D/MC/V.)

✈ APPROACHING RENO: 63 MILES
Head west out of Fallon on **U.S. 50.** 9½ mi. west of town, the road divides; take **Alt. U.S. 50** to **I-80** and Reno. Take **Exit 13** off I-80, and turn left onto **Virginia St.** to reach the casino towers.

RENO

With decadent casinos only a throw of the dice away from snow-capped mountains, Reno embodies both the opportunist frenzy and the natural splendor of the West. Catering to those interested in making a fast buck or saying a quick vow, the self-proclaimed "biggest little city in the world" has earned a reputation for gritty glamor, crazed gamblers, and delirious lovers.

VITAL STATS

Population: 207,000

Visitor Info: Reno-Sparks Convention and Visitors Authority, 1 E. 1st St. (☎800-367-7366; www.renolaketahoe.com), on the 2nd fl. of the Cal-Neva Bldg. Open M-F 8am-5pm.

Internet Access: Washoe County Library-Downtown Reno Branch, 301 S. Center St. (☎775-327-8300). Open M 10am-8pm, Tu-Th 10am-6pm, F and Su 10am-5pm. Free.

Post Office: 50 S. Virginia St. (☎775-786-5936). Open M-F 8:30am-5pm. **Postal code:** 89501.

▟ GETTING AROUND

Most major casinos are downtown between **West** and **Center St.** and **2nd** and **6th St.** The neon-lit streets are heavily patrolled, but don't stray far east of the city center at night. **Virginia St.** is Reno's main drag; south of the **Truckee River** there are cheaper accommodations, outlying casinos, and strip mall after strip mall. The town of **Sparks,** a few miles northeast along I-80, has several casinos frequented by locals. The *Reno/Tahoe Visitor Planner,* available at info kiosks throughout the city, has a local map and is a helpful city guide.

◉ SIGHTS

There's far more to Reno culture than nightlife. Roadtrippers won't want to miss the **◪National Automobile Museum,** 10 Lake St. S. By far the best car collection along this roadtrip route, the museum boasts rare cars, early model years, and one-of-a-kind prototypes from the private collection of the late gambling magnate Bill Harrah. (☎775-333-9300. Open M-Sa 9:30am-5:30pm, Su 10am-4pm. 1½hr. tours M-Sa 10:30am and 1:30pm, Su 12:30pm; free. $9, seniors $7, children $3.) The **Nevada Museum of Art,** 160 W. Liberty St., is in a striking structure inspired by the Black Rock Desert. Rotating exhibits feature artists like Diego Rivera, Edward Hopper, and Dennis Oppenheim. (☎775-329-3333. Open Tu-W, F, Su 11am-6pm; Th 11am-8pm. $10, students and seniors $8, ages 6-12 $1, under 6 free.) After hearing that a diseased cottonwood tree needed to be cut down, a local family commissioned woodcarvers to transform the trunk's four branches into fish shapes. The result was the **Truckee River Trout Tree,** a unique and intricate piece of public art. (From downtown, take either 4th or 2nd St. west about ½ mi., turn left on Keystone Ave., and keep right.)

▤ FOOD

The cost of eating out in Reno is low, but the food quality doesn't have to be. Casinos offer all-you-can-eat buffets, but you can escape the clutches of these giants via inexpensive eateries outside of the mainstream.

Blue Moon Gourmet Pizza, 190 California St. (☎775-324-2828). Pizzas with a range of gourmet toppings, including goat cheese, sun-dried tomatoes, and roasted garlic ($17). A good selection of local and imported beers and wines rounds out the menu at this cool local hangout. Open M-F 11am-9pm, Sa 1-9pm, Su 1-8pm. MC/V. ❹

Bangkok Cuisine, 55 Mt. Rose St. (☎775-322-0299), near S. Virginia St. Delicious Thai food

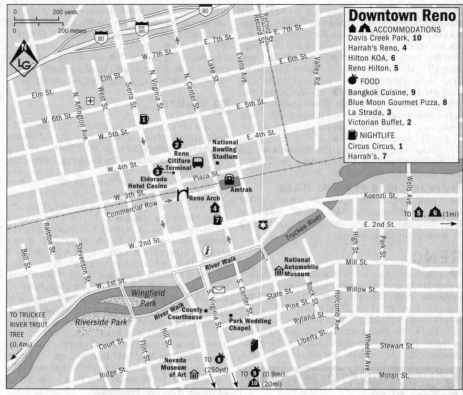

Downtown Reno

▲▲ ACCOMMODATIONS
Davis Creek Park, **10**
Harrah's Reno, **4**
Hilton KOA, **6**
Reno Hilton, **5**

🍅 FOOD
Bangkok Cuisine, **9**
Blue Moon Gourmet Pizza, **8**
La Strada, **3**
Victorian Buffet, **2**

🎭 NIGHTLIFE
Circus Circus, **1**
Harrah's, **7**

served in an elegant setting, a welcome respite from Reno's steaks and burritos. Huge menu with soups ($4-7), noodles ($8-12), fried rice ($8-12), and curries ($8-10). Open M-Sa 11am-10pm, Su 4-10pm. AmEx/D/MC/V. ❸

Victorian Buffet, 407 N. Virginia St. (☎775-329-4777), inside the Silver Legacy. The huge domed ceiling with replica mining tower makes this casino feel more like Las Vegas than anywhere else in Reno. Carving station, seafood, pizza, desserts, and tons of fresh fruit. Breakfast $12. Dinner $18. Open M-Th and Su 7:30am-2pm and 4:30-9pm, F-Sa 7:30am-2pm and 4:30-10pm. AmEx/D/MC/V. ❺

La Strada, 345 N. Virginia St. (☎775-348-9297), in the Eldorado Hotel. Award-winning northern Italian cuisine in the heart of the Eldorado. Pastas made fresh daily ($10-20), in addition to beef and fish entrees ($13-30). Open M-Tu and F-Su 5-10pm. AmEx/D/MC/V. ❹

🏨 ACCOMMODATIONS

While weekend prices at casinos are usually high, weekday rates and off-season discounts mean great deals. Rates can vary widely, however, so call ahead. **Eldorado,** 345 N. Virginia (☎800-648-5966 or 775-786-5700) and **Silver Legacy,** 407 N. Virginia St. (☎800-687-7733 or 775-325-7401), offer good deals along with their central locations and massive facilities. Rates generally hover around $60 for a single.

Harrah's Reno, 219 N. Center St. (☎800-427-7247 or 775-786-5700), between E. 2nd St. and Commercial Row. 2 towers of luxurious rooms, 7 restaurants, a pool, and a health club leave little to be desired. The 65,000 sq. ft. casino draws crowds with Reno's highest table limits. Sammy's Showroom and the

Plaza host top performers. Free valet parking. Rooms $49-89. AmEx/D/MC/V. ❸

Reno Hilton, 2500 E. 2nd St. (☎800-648-5080 or 775-789-2000), off Hwy. 395, at the Glendale exit. More than 2000 elegant rooms, a 9000-seat outdoor amphitheater, a driving range, a 50-lane bowling center, a health club and spa, and a shopping mall make the Hilton Reno's biggest. Try your luck in the casino, or check out the Ultimate Rush reverse bungee for something even more stomach-churning. Rooms $35-149. AmEx/D/MC/V. ❷

Davis Creek Park (☎775-849-0684), 18 mi. south on U.S. 395 to Rte. 429. Follow the signs ½ mi. west. Volleyball courts and trout-packed Ophir Creek Lake. First come, first served. Showers and toilets on site. Sites $14. Cash only. ❶

Hilton KOA, 2500 E. 2nd St. (☎888-562-5698 or 775-789-2147), next to the Hilton. There's no grass, but campers have access to the Hilton's pool, tennis courts, and fitness center. Sites $40-50. MC/V. ❷

🎵 ENTERTAINMENT

The renowned annual **Reno Rodeo** gallops into town for eight days in late June. (☎775-329-3877; www.renorodeo.com. $10-25.) Reno heats up with the popular **Artown** festival every July. The event features dance, jazz, painting, and theater. (☎775-322-1538; www.renoisartown.com.) August roars in with the chrome-covered, hot-rod splendor of **Hot August Nights,** a celebration of classic cars and rock 'n' roll. (☎775-356-1956; www.hotaugust-nights.com.) The weekend after Labor Day, witness the **Great Reno Balloon Race** (☎775-826-1181; www.renoballoon.com), in Rancho San Rafael Park. In mid-September, the **National Championship Air Races** (☎775-972-6663; www.airrace.org), at Reno/Stead Airport, draws international contestants who take to the sky as spectators look on. Nearby Virginia City hosts **Camel Races** (☎775-847-0311) the weekend after Labor Day, in which both camels and ostriches scoot about town.

Almost all casinos offer live nighttime entertainment, but few shows are worth the steep admission prices. **Harrah's,** 219 N. Center St., is an exception, with several nightly shows in Sammy's Showroom. (☎775-786-3232. Tickets from $30.) At **Circus Circus,** 500 N. Sierra, a small circus on the midway above the casino floor performs "big top" circus shows. (☎775-329-0711. Every 30min. M-Th 11:30am-11:30pm, F-Su 11:15am-11:45pm. Free.)

🏔 APPROACHING CARSON CITY: 33 MILES
Head east from **Virginia St.** to **U.S. 395 S.** Bear right on **N. Carson St.** in Carson City.

CARSON CITY

At the crossroads of traffic bound for Lake Tahoe and home to three large casinos, this former mint town lacks the quaint, homey feel of other capital cities. Thirty miles from Reno and only 10 mi. from Lake Tahoe, Carson City is a good overnight stop before a day of outdoor exploration.

VITAL STATS

Population: 53,000

Visitor Info: Carson City Convention and Visitors Bureau, 1900 S. Carson St. (☎775-687-7410; www.carson-city.org). Open M-F 8am-5pm.

Internet Access: Carson City Library, 900 N. Roop St. (☎775-887-2244; www.carson-city.nv.us/library/index.htm). Open M and F-Sa 10am-6pm, Tu-Th 10am-9pm. Free.

Post Office: 1111 S. Roop St. (☎775-884-2300). Open M-F 8:30am-5pm, Sa 9am-2pm. **Postal Code:** 89701.

🅴 GETTING AROUND. Rte. 50/Hwy. 530 runs east-west in the eastern half of Carson City. When it runs into **U.S. 395,** Rte. 50 turns 90 degrees and follows U.S. 395 north-south through the center of the city. A few blocks east, **N. Roop St. runs** parallel to U.S. 395.

🎰 SIGHTS. Occupying part of the building that once contained a US Mint, the **Nevada State Museum,** 600 N. Carson St., highlights aspects of Nevada's past and present with displays on silver mining, ghost towns, animal and plant life of the desert, and the Native Americans that inhabited the area. There is also an emphasis on prehistory, with a good exhibit on the history of Earth. (☎775-687-4810. Open daily 8:30am-4:30pm. $5, seniors $3, under 18 free.) Railroad buffs won't want to miss the **Nevada State Railroad Museum,** 2180 S. Carson St., which showcases a collection of cars and engines from the historic Virginia & Truckee Railroad. The museum also hosts an annual railroad symposium. (☎775-687-6953. Open daily 8:30am-4:30pm. $4, seniors $3, under 18 free.)

🍴 FOOD AND ACCOMMODATIONS. At **Red's Old 395 Grill ❹,** 1055 S. Carson St., covered wagons, horses, and sleighs hang suspended from the ceiling. Patrons devour delicious, home-smoked barbecue or sip one of the 101 beers next to an old Carson City DPW steam roller. (☎775-887-0395. Lunch $5-8. Wood-fired pizzas $7-8. Dinner entrees $12-18. Happy hour daily 4-6pm with $2 drafts and well drinks. Open M-Th and Su 11am-10pm, F-Sa 11am-11pm. AmEx/D/MC/V.) **B'Sghetti's ❸**, 318 N. Carson St., attracts locals with its upbeat service, easygoing atmosphere, and savory pasta dishes. The gnocchi ($10.50), with your choice of sauce, is tasty. (☎775-887-8879. Soups, salads, and sandwiches $7-10. Pasta $8-12. Open M-Sa 11am-9pm, Su 4-9pm. AmEx/D/MC/V.)

Carson City has the usual set of casino hotels and motels, but rooms fill fast on weekends, especially during events. Motels line Carson St. throughout town. Call ahead to check rates, which change frequently. **The Best Value Inn ❸**, 2731 S. Carson St., offers rooms with refrigerators, coffeemakers, free Wi-Fi, and comfy chairs. (☎775-882-2007; www.bestvaluecarsoncity.com. Singles $42-79. AmEx/D/MC/V.) Rooms at the **Desert Hills Motel ❸**, 1010 S. Carson St., are decorated with different themes and have access to an outdoor hot tub. (☎775-882-1932 or 800-652-7785. Singles from $55. AmEx/D/MC/V.)

🚗 APPROACHING LAKE TAHOE: 10 MILES
U.S. 50 merges with **Rte. 28** on the eastern edge of the lake before heading into South Lake Tahoe.

LAKE TAHOE

Coming over the Sierra Nevada Mountains from Carson City, the green-blue of Lake Tahoe is a welcome sight indeed. The vast lake stretches for miles, surrounded by rugged peaks. In a town without a low season, visitors can try everything from keno to kayaking. No matter the reason for visiting, the centerpiece of every experience is the lake itself, the highest alpine lake in North America and one of the cleanest lakes in the world.

VITAL STATS

Population: 34,000

Visitor Info: Lake Tahoe Basin's Taylor Creek Visitors Center (☎530-543-2674), 3 mi. north of South Lake Tahoe on Rte. 89. Open mid-June to late Sept. daily 8am-5:30pm; late May to mid-June and Oct. Sa-Su 8am-4:30pm.

Internet Access: South Lake Tahoe Branch Library, 1000 Rufus Allen Blvd. (☎530-573-3185). Open Tu-W 10am-8pm, Th-Sa 10am-5pm. Free.

Post Office: 1046 Al Tahoe Blvd. (☎530-544-8133). Open M-F 8:30am-5pm, Sa noon-2pm. **Postal Code:** 96151.

🧭 GETTING AROUND

Lake Tahoe is divided into two main regions, **North Shore** and **South Shore.** The North Shore includes **Tahoe City,** CA, and **Incline Village,** NV, while **South Lake Tahoe,** CA, and **Stateline,** NV, make up the South Shore. **Lake Tahoe Blvd. (U.S. 50)** is the main drag in South Lake Tahoe and Stateline. **Rte. 89** traces the lake's western shore. Major streets in South Lake Tahoe include **Ski Run Blvd., Wildwood Ave.,** and **Park Ave.** If you want to ⬛loop the lake (2½-4hr.), you can circumnavigate all but about 16 mi. of the shore by heading north on **Rte. 28** to **Rte. 89 S** and back to **U.S. 50** in South Lake Tahoe. This route, once named "The Most Beautiful Drive in America," provides spectacular views and bypasses the busiest section of the lake.

🥾 HIKING

Hiking is a great way to explore the Tahoe Basin. Always bring a jacket and drinking water. Ask where the snow has (or has not) melted—it's usually not all gone until July. After decades of work, the 165 mi. **Tahoe Rim Trail** has finally been completed. The trail, which circles the lake along the ridge tops of Lake Tahoe Basin, welcomes hikers, equestrians, and, in most areas, mountain bikers. Camping is allowed on most of the trail, though permits for camping and hiking are required in the Desolation Wilderness ($10 per person). On the

NATIONAL ROAD

1868: The US grants its first patent for a mechanical lawn mower. Lawn races follow soon after.

western shore, the route comprises part of the Pacific Crest Trail. Popular trailheads include **Spooner Summit**, at the U.S. 28/50 junction, and **Tahoe City**, off Rte. 89 on Fairway Dr.

SOUTH SHORE

The southern region of the basin offers moderate to strenuous hiking trails; stop by the Taylor Creek Visitors Center for maps and info. For many visitors, picturesque **Emerald Bay** is an essential stop. This crystal-clear pocket of the lake is home to Tahoe's only island and most photographed sight—tiny, rocky Fannette, accessible by boat. ◪**Emerald Bay State Park**, from which you can drive ¾ mi. to access the **Bayview Trail** into Desolation Wilderness, offers hiking and biking trails of varying difficulty, along with camping and rock climbing. (☎530-541-3030. Entrance fee $3.) Possibly the most popular South Shore trail, the **Eagle Falls Trail** (1 mi.) offers a moderate hike into Desolation Wilderness to **Eagle Lake**. A strenuous trail continues past Eagle Lake several miles to the **Velma Lakes**, a series of lakes surrounded by the nearby mountains. Accessible from **D.L. Bliss State Park** (p. 465) and ending at Vikingsholm is one of the best hikes in Tahoe, the **Rubicon Point Trail** (5½ mi.), which wraps around Emerald Bay. If you make it the full distance, you can take a shuttle back to D.L. Bliss ($1.75-5); inquire at the park visitors center for details. Those looking for a more leisurely excursion can enjoy the nature trails around the Taylor Creek Visitors Center. (3 mi. north of South Lake Tahoe on Rte. 89.) The **Lake of the Sky Trail** (½ mi.) is dotted with informative signs about the lake's origins, its early inhabitants, and current wildlife.

NORTH SHORE

At 10,778 ft., **Mount Rose** is one of the tallest mountains in the region as well as one of the best climbs. The panoramic view from the summit offers views of the lake, Reno, and the Sierra Nevadas. The 12 mi. round-trip trek starts out as an easy dirt road but ascends switchbacks for the last couple of miles. (Take Rte. 431 N from Incline Village to reach the trailhead.) The **Granite Chief Wilderness**, west of Squaw Valley, is a spectacular outdoor destination; its hiking trails and mountain streams wind through secluded forests in 5000 ft. valleys to the summits of 9000 ft. peaks. The **Alpine Meadows Trailhead**, at the end of Alpine Meadows Rd. off Rte. 89 between Truckee and Tahoe City,

and the **Pacific Crest Trailhead**, at the end of Barker Pass Rd. (Blackwood Canyon Rd.), grant access to the wilderness.

▲ OUTDOORS

BIKING

Miles of excellent trails and killer views make Tahoe a hot spot for mountain biking. The lake's premier ride is the **Flume Trail**, in Nevada State Park, which begins near the picnic area at Spooner Lake. This 23 mi. single-track loop has magnificent views of the lake from 1500 ft. off the deck. (Entrance fee $5.) **Flume Trail Mountain Biking**, at Spooner Lake, rents bikes and runs shuttles to popular trails. (☎775-749-5349. Bikes $39-45 per day. Shuttles $10-15. Open May-June daily 9am-6pm; July-Aug. daily 9am-7pm; Sept.-Oct. daily 9am-5pm.) Other tire trails include **Mr. Toad's Wild Ride**, a 3 mi., 2200 ft. descent south of South Lake Tahoe off Rte. 89, and **McKinney/Rubicon Rd.**, a loop ride to difficult peaks from Rte. 89, north of Tahoma. For rentals in South Lake Tahoe, check out **South Shore Bike & Skate**, 1056 Ski Run Blvd. (☎775-541-1549. Bikes $25-45 per day.) Cyclists can cover parts of the Lake Tahoe loop; the **Pope-Baldwin Bike Path** on the South Shore runs parallel to Rte. 89 for over 3 mi. past evergreen forests until it joins the **South Lake Tahoe Bike Path** (via bike lanes on U.S. 50), which goes through South Lake Tahoe and into Nevada.

ROCK CLIMBING

There are many climbs in Lake Tahoe, but proper safety precautions and equipment are a must. Inexperienced climbers can try bouldering in **D.L. Bliss State Park**. A host of popular climbing spots are scattered along the South Shore; the super-popular, beginner-friendly **Ninety-Foot Wall** at Emerald Bay, **Twin Crags** at Tahoe City, and **Big Chief**, near Squaw Valley are some of the more famous area climbs. **Lover's Leap**, in South Lake Tahoe, is an incredible (and crowded) route spanning two giant cliffs. East of South Lake Tahoe, off U.S. 50, the **Phantom Spires** have amazing ridge views, while **Pie Shop** offers serious exposure.

SKIING

With its world-class alpine slopes, knee-deep powder, and notorious California sun, Tahoe is a skier's mecca. There are 15 ski resorts in the Tahoe area. Visitors centers provide info, coupons, maps, and free publications like *Ski Tahoe* and *Sunny Day*. All the major resorts offer lessons and rent equipment. For the best slopes, try **Squaw Valley,** site of the 1960 Olympic Winter Games. (☎775-583-6985 or 888-766-9321; www.squaw.com. Lift tickets from $60.) **Heavenly** also offers great powder. (☎775-586-7000; www.skiheavenly.com. Lift tickets from $49.) One of the best ways to enjoy Tahoe's pristine snow-covered forests is to cross-country ski. **Spooner Lake,** at the junction of U.S. 50 and Rte. 28, offers 57 mi. of machine-groomed trails and incredible views. (☎775-749-5349. Lift tickets $19, children $3.) **Tahoe X-C,** off Rte. 28, on Dollar Hill, maintains 40 mi. of trails for all abilities that wind through North Shore forests. (☎775-583-5475. Lift tickets $18, children $6.) Snowshoeing is easier to pick up than cross-country skiing, and equipment is available at many sporting goods stores for about $15 per day. Check local ranger stations for ranger-guided winter snowshoe hikes.

BEACHES

Many beaches dot Lake Tahoe. On the North Shore, **Sand Harbor Beach,** U.S. 28, 2 mi. south of Incline Village, has gorgeous granite boulders and clear waters that attract swimmers, sunners, snorklers, and boaters to its marina. **Tahoe City Commons Beach,** just off North Lake Blvd., in the heart of the city, contains a playground for kids, a sandy beach for sunbathing, and pristine lake waters for swimming. Boats, jet skis, wakeboards, and waterskis can be rented at **Tahoe Water Adventures,** 120 Grove St. (☎530-583-3225.) The West Shore offers family-oriented **Meeks Bay,** equipped with picnic tables, volleyball courts, barbecue pits, campsites, and a store. (10 mi. south of Tahoe City.) **D.L. Bliss State Park,** on Rte. 89, 17 mi. south of Tahoe City, is home to **Lester Beach** and **Calawee Cove Beach,** on striking Rubicon Bay. It's also the trailhead for the Rubicon Trail. **Baldwin Beach** and neighboring **Pope Beach,** near the southernmost point of the lake off Rte. 89, are shaded expanses of shoreline popular with South Lake Tahoe crowds. For kayak tours, lessons, and rentals check out **Kayak Tahoe,** 3411 Lake Tahoe Blvd., near Johnson Blvd. (☎530-544-2011. Single kayaks $60 per day; tandems $80. Tours $30-80. Lessons $32-180.) **Nevada Beach,** off U.S. 50, 3 mi. north of South Lake Tahoe, is close to the casinos and offers a sandy sanctuary with a view of sun-kissed mountains. **Zephyr Cove Beach,** U.S. 50, 8 mi. south

of the intersection with Rte. 28, hosts a young crowd keen on beer and bikinis. This beach offers boat rentals, jet skis, parasailing, and towel-side cocktail service.

LAKES

Many lakes are accessible from hiking routes and may offer a bit more privacy than Tahoe. **Angora Lakes,** a pair of mountain lakes accessible by car except for a final half-mile walk, are popular with families. (Take Rte. 89 N. from South Lake Tahoe for 3 mi. Turn left onto Fallen Leaf Rd., and left again onto Tahoe Mountain Rd. Continue ½ mi. and turn right onto Forest Service Rd. #1214. Open daily 6am-10pm. Free.)

▓ FOOD

Sprouts Natural Foods Cafe, 3123 Harrison Ave. (☎530-541-6969), at Alameda Ave. Natural foods in large portions, and everything is done just right. Try the breakfast burrito with avocados ($6), one of the smoothies and fresh juices ($3.50-4), or a shot of wheat grass ($1.50-2). Open daily 8am-9pm. Cash only. ❶

The Red Hut Cafe, 2723 Lake Tahoe Blvd. (☎530-541-9024). A friendly staff has been dishing out homestyle cooking since 1959 at this Tahoe original. Waffles piled with fruit and whipped cream $6.25. Avocado burgers $7.50. Open daily 6am-2pm. Cash only. ❷

Lakeside Beach Grill, 4081 Lakeshore Blvd. (☎530-544-4050), on the beach between Park and Stateline Ave. The real draw is the spectacular view as you enjoy your meal outside overlooking the lake. Try one of the inventive lunch entrees ($8-15), like the calamari sandwich ($12). Garlic lovers will love the garlic fries ($5). Open June-Sept. daily 11am-3pm and 5-8pm. AmEx/D/MC/V. ❹

Orchid Thai, 2180 Lake Tahoe Blvd. (☎530-544-5541). Terrific fare, including vegetarian options like the Pad Basil Garden ($8) or crispy tofu ($5). Carnivores will be sated with Pottery Shrimp ($12) and a wide range of curries ($7-14). Open M-Sa 11am-10pm, Su 3-10pm. AmEx/D/MC/V. ❸

▌ ACCOMMODATIONS

On the South Shore, the blocks bordering U.S. 50 on the California side of the border support the bulk of the area's motels. Glitzy and cheap, motels in South Lake Tahoe cost next to nothing midweek. Accommodations are more expensive along the North Shore.

Tahoe Valley Lodge, 2214 Lake Tahoe Blvd. (☎800-669-7544 or 530-541-0353; www.tahoevalley-lodge.com). Immaculate rooms take the mountain motif to an extreme, with alpine-themed bedspreads and wallpaper. DVD players and free Wi-Fi. Reception 24hr. Rooms from $125. AmEx/D/MC/V. ❺

Tahoe Retreat, 2446 Lake Tahoe Blvd. (☎530-544-6776). The basic rooms vary in size, but are clean and very convenient to local attractions. Some rooms have kitchenettes. Rooms $55-70. AmEx/D/MC/V. ❸

Doug's Mellow Mountain Retreat, 3787 Forest Ave. (☎530-544-8065). Coming from the north, turn left onto Wildwood Rd., west of downtown Stateline, and take a left on Forest Ave. It's the 6th house on the left. Mellow Doug supplies a modern kitchen, barbecue, and fireplace in this woodsy house in a residential neighborhood. Linen included. Dorms $15; private rooms $25. Cash only. ❷

Best Tahoe West Inn, 4107 Pine Blvd. (☎800-700-8246 or 530-544-6455), off Park Ave. Within walking distance of the casinos but also close to the beach. Modern rooms are chock full of amenities, and some have kitchenettes. Pool, jacuzzi, and sauna. Reception 7am-11pm. Rooms $34-170. AmEx/D/MC/V. ❸

◪ CAMPING

The Taylor Creek Visitors Center provides up-to-date info on camping. **Rte. 89** is rife with campgrounds between Tahoe City and South Lake Tahoe. Sites can be booked on weekends in July and August, so it pays to reserve in advance; call the **California State Parks Reservation Center** (☎800-444-7275) or the **National Recreation Reservation System** (☎877-444-6777; www.reserve-usa.com). Backcountry camping is allowed in designated wilderness areas with a permit from the Forest Service.

Nevada Beach (☎775-588-5562), off U.S. 50, 10½ mi. south of the junction with Rte. 28. 54 sites near a peaceful, family-oriented beach. Water, but no showers. Sites $22-24. MC/V. ❶

Fallen Leaf Lake (☎530-544-0426). Take Rte. 89 to U.S. 50, and head 3 mi. north; turn left on Fallen Leaf Rd. 206 sites by Fallen Leaf Lake. Reservations recommended. Sites $20. MC/V. ❶

D.L. Bliss State Park (☎530-525-7277), off Rte. 89, 10½ mi. north of U.S. 50. Access to Lester Beach and

trailheads for the Rubicon and Lighthouse Trails. Grills, water, flush toilets, and showers. Open late May to Sept. Sites $25-35. MC/V. ❶

◪ NIGHTLIFE

Nightlife in South Lake Tahoe centers around casinos, which are busy at all hours.

Club Nero, 55 U.S. 50 (☎775-586-2000), in Caesar's Place, a large casino with restaurants and clubs. A hotspot for dancing and drinking. M $1 drinks. Tu Latino night. W wet T-shirt contests and free for ladies. Th-Sa ladies night. Su $1 drafts. Cover $5-25. Open daily 9pm-last customer. AmEx/D/MC/V.

Altitude Nightclub (☎775-586-6705), off U.S. 50, in Harrah's (☎800-427-7247 or 775-588-6611), the slot machine heaven replete with restaurants, bars, and cocktail lounges. Hosts its fair share of foam parties. Cover $10-20. Open M-Tu and Th-Sa 10pm-last customer. AmEx/D/MC/V.

The Brewery, 3542 Lake Tahoe Blvd. (☎530-544-2739). Stop in and try one of the 7 microbrews on tap, including favorites like the Bad Ass Ale and Alpine Amber (pints $4, pitchers $12). Pizzas (from $12) come full of toppings. A laid-back atmosphere makes this spot a local favorite. Open M-Th and Su 11am-10pm, F-Sa 11am-2am. AmEx/D/MC/V.

◪ APPROACHING PLACERVILLE: 66 MILES
Follow **U.S. 50 W** through the granite cliffs and tall conifers of El Dorado National Forest. Continue west; the road enters Gold Country around Placerville.

◪ DETOUR
SLY PARK
4771 Sly Park Rd. From U.S. 50, take the exit for Sly Park Rd. Turn left, and proceed 4¼ mi.

A heavily wooded pine forest shades dark sandy beaches around a pristine lake. Mountain bikers enjoy the 8½ mi. loop trail around the water, while the lake offers a lovely place to swim or take out a small boat. Though the views are less spectacular than Tahoe's, Sly Park's natural pine beds provide a very comfortable place for **camping ❶**. (☎530-644-254. Reserve ahead for weekend camping; $8 fee. Open daily 6am-10pm. Sites $20-25. Day-use $8. AmEx/D/MC/V.)

PLACERVILLE
After gold was found in California in 1849, "gold fever" brought a stampede of more than half a

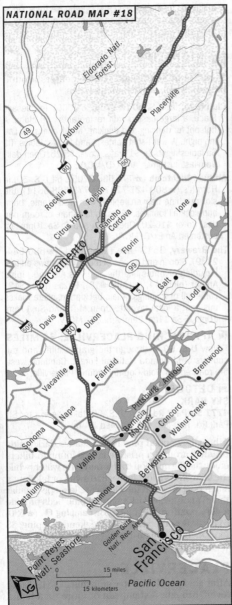

NATIONAL ROAD MAP #18

million prospectors over the next decade. Five years after the big discovery, the panning gold was gone, and miners dug deeper and deeper into the rock. All but a few mines were abandoned by the 1870s. Today, restaurants and shops fill its restored historic downtown. Beyond downtown, however, chain stores dominate and Placerville's Gold Rush charm is nowhere to be found.

VITAL STATS

Population: 10,000

Visitor Info: Placerville Chamber of Commerce, 542 Main St. (☎530-621-5885). Open M-F 9am-5pm.

Internet Access: El Dorado County Library, 345 Fair Ln. (☎530-621-5540). Open M-W 10am-8pm, Th-Sa 10am-5pm. Free.

Post Office: 3045 Sacramento St. (☎530-642-5280). Open M-F 8:30am-5pm, Sa 8:30am-noon. **Postal Code:** 95667.

GETTING AROUND. Between Sacramento and Lake Tahoe on **U.S. 50,** Placerville is positioned to snare campers, boaters, and skiers. Most streets, like **Main St.,** run parallel to U.S. 50 to the north. **Rte. 49** bisects the town, running north to Auburn (10 mi.), and south to Calaveras County.

SIGHTS. Placerville was once known as "Hangtown, USA," for doling out speedy justice at the end of a rope. Nowadays, tourists are drawn to Placerville's orchard-covered hills. Drivers can tour the apple orchards and wineries off U.S. 50 in the area known as **Apple Hill;** the fall is particularly busy with events, concerts, and apple-picking. A complete listing and map of orchards is available from the visitors center and at many orchards. **Larsen Apple Barn,** 2461 Larsen Dr. (☎530-644-1415), in Camino, has 12 varieties of apples and a large picnic area. Most orchards are only open September through December, but **Boa Vista Orchards,** 2952 Carson Rd. (☎530-622-5522), stays open year-round, selling fresh pears and cherries, along with many other seasonal fruits, from a huge open barn. For free wine tasting, try **Lava Cap Winery,** 2221 Fruitridge Rd. (☎530-621-0175; www.lavacap.com; open daily 11am-5pm), **Madroña Vineyards,** 2560 High Hill Rd., in Camino (☎530-644-5948; www.madronavineyards.com; open daily 11am-5pm), or the sophisticated **Boeger Winery,** 1709 Carson Rd. (☎530-622-8094; open daily 10am-5pm). Visitors in late June should not miss **Brewfest** (☎530-672-3436), when hordes of locals pony up $25 for a small tasting glass and wander to over 30 downtown businesses for beer.

⛏️ FOOD AND ACCOMMODATIONS. Those seeking a Dukes of Hazzard experience should saunter into **⛏️Poor Red's ❸**, 6221 Pleasant Valley Rd., off Main St., in El Dorado, 5 mi. south of Placerville on Rte. 49. The bar and dining room of this barbecue joint are always packed. Their famous two-glass "Golden Cadillac" ($7) is responsible for 3% of American consumption of Galliano. (☎530-622-2901. Sandwiches $6. Entrees $9-17. Open M-Sa 5-11pm, Su 2-11pm. AmEx/MC/V.) The historic **Cozmic Cafe and Bar ❷**, 594 Main St., is in an old soda works building that dates from 1859. There is a pub upstairs and a walk-in mine shaft with seating in the back. (☎530-642-8481. Sandwiches $6-7. Smoothies $3.50-5. Th open mic. Sa live band. Open M-Sa 7am-8pm, Su 8am-6pm. Upstairs pub open Th-Sa 7-11pm. D/DC/MC/V.) **Sweetie Pies ❷**, 577 Main St., is known for its huge cinnamon buns ($3), sandwiches ($7), and breakfast menu ($5-11). The homemade pies (slice $3.25) are particularly tempting. (☎530-642-0128; www.sweetiepies.biz. Open M-F 6:30am-3pm, Sa 7am-3pm, Su 7am-1pm. MC/V.)

The **Motherlode Motel ❸**, 1940 Broadway, is a great deal, offering good-sized rooms and a pool. (☎530-622-0895. Singles $52-56; doubles $68. AmEx/D/MC/V.) The **National 9 Inn ❸**, 1500 Broadway, has spotless rooms, cable TV, A/C, free Wi-Fi, and comfortable king beds. (☎530-622-3884. Singles $60-70; doubles $75. AmEx/D/MC/V.) Camping is plentiful in the Eldorado National Forest, east of town. **Sand Flat ❶**, U.S. 50, 28 mi. east of town, has 29 sites at 3800 ft. (Vault toilets and water. No reservations. Sites $12. Cash only.) **Dispersed camping** is free and does not require a permit, although campfire permits (free) are required for fires and stoves.

⛏️ APPROACHING SACRAMENTO: 45 MILES Follow **U.S. 50,** which merges with **Bus. I-80** to become a freeway. Take the **10th St. exit** to downtown Sacramento.

SACRAMENTO

Sacramento is the indistinct capital of a highly distinctive state. In 1848, Swiss emigré John Sutter, fleeing debtor's prison back home, purchased 48,000 dusty acres from the Miwok tribe for a few trinkets. His trading fort became the central pavilion for the influx of gold miners to the valley in the 1850s. Over the next century, mansions and suburban bungalows gradually changed the landscape, paving the way for future residents Ronald Reagan and the Brady Bunch. Sacramento balances the nonstop bustle of San Francisco to the west with the tranquility of the mountains to the east, remaining as slow-paced as any small town (especially in the summer, when temperatures can soar to 115°F). But don't let the city's daytime friendliness fool you; some areas can be dangerous at night.

VITAL STATS

Population: 460,000

Visitor Info: Old Sacramento Visitors Center, 1002 2nd St. (☎916-442-7644). Open M-Th and Su 10am-5pm, F-Sa 9am-6pm.

Internet Access: Sacramento Public Library, 828 I St. (☎916-264-2700), between 8th and 9th St. Open Tu-Th 10am-8pm, F 10am-6pm, Sa 10am-5pm, Su noon-5pm. Free.

Post Office: 801 I St. (☎916-556-3415). Open M-F 8am-5pm. **Postal Code:** 95814.

📍 GETTING AROUND

Sacramento is at the center of the **Sacramento Valley.** Five major highways converge on the capital: **I-5** and **Rte. 99** run north-south, with I-5 to the west, **I-80** runs east-west between San Francisco and Reno, and **U.S. 50** and **Rte. 16** bring traffic westward from Gold Country. Downtown, numbered streets run north-south and lettered streets run east-west in a grid. The street number on a lettered street corresponds to the number of the cross street (2000 K St. is near the corner of 20th St.). The capitol building, parks, and endless cafes and restaurants occupy the area around **10th St.** and **Capitol Ave.** Old Sacramento is located just west of downtown, on the Sacramento River.

◉ SIGHTS

GOVERNMENT BUILDINGS. Debates about the budget and water shortages occur daily in the elegant **State Capitol.** (At 10th St. and Capitol Ave. ☎916-324-0333. 1hr. tours every hr. daily 9am-

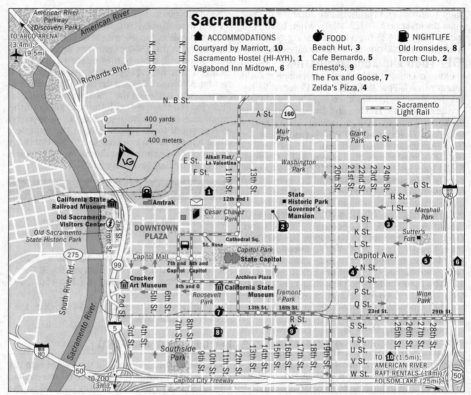

Sacramento

🏠 ACCOMMODATIONS
Courtyard by Marriott, **10**
Sacramento Hostel (HI-AYH), **1**
Vagabond Inn Midtown, **6**

🍎 FOOD
Beach Hut, **3**
Cafe Bernardo, **5**
Ernesto's, **9**
The Fox and Goose, **7**
Zelda's Pizza, **4**

🖥 NIGHTLIFE
Old Ironsides, **8**
Torch Club, **2**

Sacramento
Light Rail

4pm. Free.) Colonnades of palm trees and grassy lawns transform **Capitol Park** into a shaded oasis in the middle of downtown's busy bureaucracy. The **State Historic Park Governor's Mansion** was built in 1877, and its faded, weathered exterior makes it look not a year younger. The mansion served as the residence of California's governor and his family until then-governor Ronald Reagan opted to rent his own pad. *(At 16th and H St. ☎916-324-0539. Open daily 10am-4pm. Tours every hr. $4, ages 6-16 $2, under 6 free.)*

OLD SACRAMENTO. This 28-acre town of early 19th-century buildings attracts nearly five million visitors annually. Tourists tread wooden-planked sidewalks, browsing gift shops or eating at restaurants. Attractions include a restored riverboat, California's first

theater, and a military museum. The 100,000 sq. ft. 🚂**California State Railroad Museum** exhibits 23 historic locomotives, half of which you can walk through, and is regarded by many as the finest railroad museum in North America. *(125 I St. ☎916-445-6645; www.csrmf.org. Open daily 10am-5pm. $8, ages 6-17 $4, under 6 free. 40min. train rides from the Train Depot in Old Sacramento Apr.-Sept. Sa-Su. $8, ages 6-17 $3, under 6 free.)*

CALIFORNIA HISTORY. Sutter's Fort was the only remaining property of John Sutter after the rest were overrun by gold-seekers. These days, busloads of tourists and local school children come to see the restored fort and its educational exhibits. *(2701 L St., between 26th and 28th St. ☎916-445-4422. Open daily 10am-5pm. $4, ages 6-12 $2, under 6 free.)*

CALIFORNIA STATE MUSEUM FOR HISTORY, WOMEN, AND THE ARTS.

At this museum dedicated to the history of women in California, multimedia exhibits include a virtual trip on a 1936 bus and a video of immigrant stories. *(1020 O St. ☎916-653-0563; www.californiamuseum.org. Open Tu-Sa 10am-5pm, Su noon-5pm. $7.50, ages 6-13 $5, seniors $6, under 6 free.)*

CROCKER ART MUSEUM.

This small museum packs in excellent art with permanent works by Brueghel, Rembrandt, and David, as well as rotating exhibits. What makes the Crocker stand out, however, is its contemporary Californian art, including pieces by local artist Robert Arneson. *(216 O St. ☎916-264-5423; www.crockerartmuseum.org. Open Tu-W and F-Su 10am-5pm, Th 10am-9pm. $6, seniors $4, students $3, under 7 free. Su 10am-1pm free.)*

SACRAMENTO ZOO.

Chimps, giraffes, lions, white tigers, and an albino alligator are among the nearly 400 critters at the Sacramento Zoo. The zoo sits in a eucalyptus-filled park and emphasizes protection of endangered species and the restoration of natural habitats. *(On William Land Park Dr., off I-5 at the Sutterville exit. ☎916-264-5885; www.saczoo.com. Open daily 10am-4pm. $7.50, ages 3-12 $5.50, under 3 free.)*

🏔 OUTDOORS

The **American River** winds through Sacramento, and its rushing waters make **river rafting** an opportunity for those seeking adventure. Rent rafts at **American River Raft Rentals,** 11257 S. Bridge St., in Rancho Cordova, 14 mi. east of downtown on U.S. 50. (Exit on Sunrise Blvd., and take it north 1½ mi. to the American River. ☎916-635-6400. Open daily 9am-6pm; rentals available until 1:30pm. 4-person rafts $44; kayaks $30-50. Launch fee $2. Return shuttle $4 per person.) The **American River Recreation Trail and Parkway,** spanning 23 mi. from Discovery Park to Folsom Lake, is a nature preserve with a view of the downtown skyline. Hundreds of people cycle, jog, swim, fish, hike, and ride horses along the paths every day. You can enter the trail in Old Sacramento or at designated points along the river. **Folsom Lake State Recreation Area,** 25 mi. east on I-80, hosts a giant 18,000-acre reservoir perfect for swimming, boating, fishing, and wakeboarding. Over 100 mi. of trails wind through the surrounding hills. (☎916-988-0205. Open daily 6am-10pm. $3-8 per vehicle.)

🍴 FOOD

Food in Sacramento is plentiful and good, thanks to a hip midtown, immigrant populations, and Californian culinary inventiveness. Many eateries are concentrated on **J St.** or **Capitol Ave.,** between 19th and 29th St. The stretch of **Fair Oaks Blvd.** between Howe and Fulton St. is home to restaurants of all price ranges. Old Sacramento is filled with more expensive and gimmicky restaurants.

🍴 Zelda's Pizza, 1415 21st St. (☎916-447-1400), at N St. Posters of Italy and Christmas lights enliven this windowless joint. The Chicago-style pizzas are loaded with everything from standard pepperoni and mushrooms to feta and spinach. Open M-Th 11:30am-2pm and 5-10pm, F 11:30am-2pm and 5-11:30pm, Sa 5-11:30pm, Su 5-9pm. Cash only. ❷

Ernesto's, 1901 16th St. (☎916-441-5850; www.ernestosmexicanfood.com), at the corner of S St. Dishes out upscale Mexican food at reasonable prices. Huge burritos ($7.50-10), quesadillas ($7), and salads ($6.50-11). Open M-W 11am-10pm, Th 11am-11pm, F-Sa 9am-midnight, Su 9am-10pm. AmEx/D/MC/V. ❸

Cafe Bernardo, 2726 Capitol Ave. (☎916-443-1189; www.cafebernardo.com), at 28th St. Decorated in earth tones and stainless steel, Cafe Bernardo serves excellent sandwiches ($7-8.50), soups ($2-4), and salads ($3-7) with freshly baked bread. Open M-Th and Su 7am-10pm, F-Sa 7am-11pm. MC/V. ❷

The Fox and Goose, 1001 R St. (☎916-443-8825; www.foxandgoose.com), at 10th St. Situated in a huge brick factory, the Fox and Goose blends English public house with American alternative culture. Primarily a brunch spot with standard sandwiches, fish and chips ($7.50), and Cornish pasties ($6.25). M open mic nights. W-Sa live music. Open M-F 7am-midnight, Sa-Su 8am-2am. AmEx/MC/V. ❷

Beach Hut, 2406 J St. (☎916-442-1400). A fun beach-themed spot. The "Surfin' Cow" sandwich ($6.50) has roast beef, avocado, bacon, and cream cheese. Domestic drafts $2.75-4.50. Open M-Sa 10am-8pm, Su 11am-5pm. AmEx/MC/V. ❷

ACCOMMODATIONS

Sacramento has many hotels, motels, and B&Bs, but advance reservations are always a good idea. **W. Capitol Ave.** has many cheap hotels. Within Sacramento proper, **16th St.** has hotels and motels. Rates fluctuate, but standard chain hotel and motel rooms usually go for $50-150 per night.

Sacramento Hostel (HI-AYH), 900 H St. (☎916-443-1691; reservations 800-909-4776, ext. 40), at 10th St. Built in 1885, this pastel Victorian mansion looks more like a B&B than a hostel. Huge modern kitchen, 3 lounges, library, laundry, TV/VCR, and a selection of video rentals ($1). Parking $5 per night. Check-in 7:30am-10pm. Check-out 9:30am. Dorms $25, members $20. AmEx/D/MC/V. ❷

Vagabond Inn Midtown, 1319 30th St. (☎916-454-4400; www.vagabondinn.com), at N St. Moderately sized, well-kept rooms, and extra perks. Rooms have cable TV, phone, Internet access, and free newspapers. Continental breakfast included. Pool and spa available. Rooms from $70. AmEx/D/MC/V. ❸

Courtyard by Marriott, 4422 Y St. (☎916-455-6800), at the UC Davis Medical Center. Rooms have cable TV and free Wi-Fi. Rooms $94-150. AmEx/D/MC/V. ❹

ENTERTAINMENT

In summer, Sacramento bustles with free afternoon concerts and cheap food. The Friday *Sacramento Bee* contains a supplement called *Ticket*, which gives a rundown of events. For music and activities, check free weeklies such as *Sacramento News and Review* and *Inside the City. Alive and Kicking* has music and arts schedules.

If you're visiting Sacramento in the spring, scream alongside **Sacramento Kings** fans, reputed to be the loudest in the NBA, at the **Arco Arena,** 1 Sports Pkwy. (☎916-649-8497, 530-528-8497, or 209-485-8497.) Minor league

baseball fans can catch the **Sacramento Rivercats** at **Raley Field,** 400 Ballpark Dr., in West Sacramento. (☎800-225-2277. Season runs early Apr.-Sept.) On the second Saturday of each month, art galleries stay open late for the **Second Saturday Art Walk.** Art lovers wander and check out the scene. (www.sacramento-second-saturday.org. Open 6-10pm. Free.) The **Friday Night Concert Series,** in César Chávez Park, at 10th St. and I St., has live bands (rock, blues, jazz, folk, and pop), food stands, and beer gardens. Local bars often offer post-concert specials. (☎916-442-2500; www.downtownsac.org. Open June-Oct. F 5-9pm. Free.) Over 100 bands attract thousands every Memorial Day weekend at the **Dixieland Jazz Jubilee,** in Old Sac. (☎916-372-5277; www.sacjazz.com. Tickets $18-40.) **Shakespeare Lite,** in St. Rose of Lima Park, at 7th and K St., boasts comedic versions of the Bard's work. (☎916-442-8575. Runs June to mid-July Th noon-1pm. Free.) The **California State Fair** doesn't skimp on spinning rides, fairway food, or pig races. (☎916-263-3000; www.bigfun.org. Runs mid-Aug. to early Sept. Tickets $8, seniors $6, children $5.)

NIGHTLIFE

Capital-dwellers hang in brass- and mahogany-lined bars and coffeehouses. Sacramento's midtown venues, on the other hand, entertain a clientele with few more body piercings than their representatives in the government. Nightclubs are scattered around Sacramento's periphery.

Old Ironsides, 1901 10th St. (☎916-443-9751; www.theoldironsides.com), at S St. The 1st bar to get its liquor license after Prohibition, Old Ironsides has 2 rooms, one for grooving and one for boozing. Drafts $2-4. Tu Lipstick DJ spins indie and Britpop. W open mic. Th-Sa live music. Cover Tu after 9:30pm and Th-Sa $3-10. Open M-F 11am-1:30am, Sa-Su 6pm-1:30am. MC/V.

Torch Club, 904 15th St. (☎916-443-2797; www.torchclub.net), at I St. The ultimate blues venue in town, voted "Best Place To Hear Blues" by Sacramento News and Review Readers Choice Awards. Cover varies. Open daily noon-2am. Cash only.

⚲ APPROACHING DAVIS: 14 MILES

Take **Bus. I-80/U.S. 50 W** until it merges with **I-80.** Exit at **Richards Blvd. N,** following signs for downtown Davis.

DAVIS

Davis prides itself on higher education, agriculture, and two-wheeled transportation. Residents fancy themselves to be living in the model eco-conscious town—and their self-image is certainly substantiated. Not only is Davis a leader in recycling, its streets sport energy-saving traffic signals and as many bikes as residents (more per capita than any other US city). The character of the city is shaped largely by the diverse students of the University of California at Davis (UCD), and activity centers on the campus and downtown.

VITAL STATS

Population: 64,000

Visitor Info: Davis Visitors Bureau, 105 E St., Ste. 300 (☎ 530-297-1900; www.davisvisitor.com). Open M-F 8:30am-4:30pm. **UC Davis Information Center** (☎ 530-752-2222), at Memorial Union. Open in summer M-F 9am-4pm; in spring and fall M-Th 8am-7pm, F 8am-5pm; in winter M-F 8am-5pm.

Internet Access: Yolo County Library, 315 14th St. (☎ 530-757-5591). Open M 1-9pm, Tu-Th 10am-9pm, F-Sa 10am-5:30pm, Su 1-5pm. Free.

Post Office: 2020 5th St. (☎ 530-756-1081). Open M-F 7am-5:30pm, Sa 9am-4pm. **Postal Code:** 95616.

⬛ GETTING AROUND. UC-Davis lies in the southwest corner of the city, bound by **I-80** and **Rte. 113. Vic Fazio Hwy. (Rte. 113), Anderson Rd., F St.,** and **Pole Line Rd.** are all major north-south thoroughfares. **W. Covell Blvd.** runs east-west until F St., where it changes to **E. Covell Blvd.** Similarly, **Russell Blvd.** runs east-west until **A St.,** where it becomes **5th St.**

⬛ SIGHTS. Of the UC schools, the **University of California at Davis** tops the list in agriculture. It is also one of only a handful of schools in the country with a department specializing in viticulture (vine cultivation) and enology (wine making). Step into nature at the **UCD Arboretum,** which features trees and plants from Mediterranean climates around the

world. (Take Russell Blvd. to LaRue Rd. Follow it to the parking lot. ☎ 530-752-4880. Open 24hr. Free.) Davis is marked by more than 40 mi. of **bike trails.** For trail maps and ratings, stop by the visitors bureau or a bike shop in town. **Ken's Bike and Ski,** 650 G St., rents bikes and gives advice about biking around the city. (☎ 530-758-3223; www.kensbikeski.com. Open M-F 9am-8pm, Sa 9am-7pm, Su noon-5pm. Street bikes $8 per half-day, $12 per day; mountain bikes $16/$29.) For some practice before hitting the rocks outside, check out the **Rocknasium,** 720 Olive Dr., Ste. Z, in a warehouse just past Redrum Burger, which offers climbing for all levels. (☎ 530-757-2902; www.rocknasium.com. Open M-F 11am-11pm, Sa 10am-9pm, Su 10am-6pm. $12, students $10. Equipment rental $8/$6.) For cultural entertainment, check out the recently opened **Mondavi Center for the Arts,** on Mrak Hall Dr. at Old Davis Rd. Built for UCD by wine tycoon Robert Mondavi, this striking sandstone performance center draws heavyweights such as Joshua Redman, Ladysmith Black Mambazo, and Salman Rushdie. (1 Shields Ave. ☎ 530-754-2787; www.mondavi-arts.org. Box office open M-F 10am-6pm, Sa noon-6pm, and 1hr. before performances. Tickets $20-50.)

⬛⬛ FOOD AND ACCOMMODATIONS. Wednesday nights in summer bring locals to Central Park (at 4th and C St.) for the renowned **Davis Farmers Market.** (☎ 530-756-1695; www.davisfarmersmarket.org. Open Apr.-Sept. W 4:30-8:30pm, Sa 8am-1pm; Oct.-Mar. W 2-6pm, Sa 8am-1pm.) The **⬛Davis Food Co-op,** 620 G St., has organic produce, fresh deli foods, and international wines. They also offer 15min. of free Internet access. (☎ 530-758-2667; www.daviscoop.com. Open daily 8am-10pm. AmEx/D/MC/V.) **Redrum Burger ❶,** 978 Olive Dr., delights true carnivores with full 1 lb. burgers ($10). Less ambitious eaters can settle for the sandwiches ($5-7), but super-thick milkshakes ($3.75) complement patties of any kind. (☎ 530-756-2142. Open daily 10am-10pm. AmEx/D/MC/V.) The outdoor seating at **Thai Bistro ❷,** 234 E St., is a great place to enjoy some of the best Thai food in town. (☎ 530-747-0123; www.thaibistrodavis.com. Satays $6-9. Open M-Th 11am-

3pm and 5-9:30pm, F-Sa 11am-3pm and 5-10pm, Su 5-9:30pm. MC/V.)

Motels in Davis don't come cheap, and rooms are scarce during university events. **University Park Inn & Suites ❹**, 1111 Richards Blvd., off I-80 at the Richards Blvd. exit, is just six blocks from campus. It has 45 spotless rooms with cable TV, refrigerators, A/C, and a pool. (☎530-756-0910; www.universityparkinn.com. Continental breakfast included. Singles $80-85; doubles $95-105. AmEx/D/MC/V.) The **Aggie Inn ❹**, 245 1st St., is also convenient to the UCD campus. It offers pleasant rooms with free Wi-Fi, refrigerators, and microwaves. Guests also have access to a fitness room and computer station. (☎530-756-0352; www.aggieinn.com. Continental breakfast included. Singles $99-105; doubles $109-115. AmEx/D/MC/V.)

■ NIGHTLIFE. At night, students party at **The Graduate**, 805 Russell Blvd., in the University Mall. Friday evenings attract swarms of students with drink specials. The walls usually reverberate with mainstream pop and hip-hop, but The Graduate occasionally hosts country dance nights. Check the website's calendar for events and specials. (☎530-758-4723; www.davisgrad.com. Happy hour 2:30-6pm and 9-10pm with $1 beers and $3 drink specials. Open daily 11am-2am. AmEx/D/MC/V.) An older, sophisticated crowd gathers at **Sophia's Thai Bar**, 129 E St., a tiny bar with tropical decor, aquariums, outdoor seating, and occasional live music. (☎530-758-4333. Tu trivia night. Happy hour M-F 5-7pm. Open M-Sa 5pm-2am, Su 5-10pm. AmEx/MC/V.)

◪ APPROACHING FAIRFIELD: 27 MILES
Take **I-80** and exit at **N. Texas St.**; follow it south until it turns west onto **Texas St.**

FAIRFIELD. Fairfield's most roadtrip-worthy attraction is the **Jelly Belly Factory**, 1 Jelly Belly Ln. While waits can be unbearably long in summer, the 40min. tour, an artful mix of observation of the factory floor and video presentations, leaves you sugar-high and jelly bean enlightened. They even sweeten the deal with a small bag of free jelly beans. Don't miss the opportunity to buy "Belly Flops"—irregularly sized jelly beans—which are sold cheaply at the factory store. (From downtown, take Pennsylvania Ave. south to Rio Vista Rd., turn right, and exit at Chadbourne Rd. Turn left on Courage Dr. and then left onto N. Watney Way. ☎800-953-5592. Open daily 9am-4pm. Free.) **Joe's Buffet ❶**, 834 Texas St., near Jackson St., offers food that's a little less sugary. When you order a sandwich at this old-style delicatessen, they slice the fresh meat right onto it; the messy result is fantastic. (☎707-425-2317. Sandwiches $5. Open M-Sa 10am-4pm. Cash only.) The **Travis Lodge ❸**, 1349 Texas St., has clean rooms near the highway. (☎707-425-6465. Singles $55; doubles $65. AmEx/D/MC/V.)

◪ APPROACHING BERKELEY: 35 MILES
Continue straight onto **W. Texas St.** to get back onto **I-80** toward Berkeley. About 15 mi. past the Carquinez Bridge, take the **University Ave.** exit to downtown Berkeley and the UC Berkeley (Cal) campus.

BERKELEY

Famous as an intellectual center and a haven for iconoclasts, Berkeley lives up to its reputation. Although the peak of its political activism occurred in the 1960s and 70s—when students attended more protests than classes—UC Berkeley continues to foster an alternative atmosphere. The vitality of the population infuses the streets, which overflow with hip cafes and top-notch bookstores. Telegraph Ave., with its street-corner soothsayers, hirsute hippies, and itinerant musicians, remains one of the town's main draws.

 DID YOU KNOW? Berkeley native Roy Jacuzzi invented the whirlpool bath in 1968. The jacuzzi was first showcased at California's Orange County Fair.

▐ GETTING AROUND

To prevent people from using residential streets as cut-offs to bypass traffic-filled main streets, Berkeley installed rows of planters to interrupt many streets. Use main streets to navigate as close to your destination as possible before cutting in. The heart of town, **Telegraph Ave.**, runs south from the UC Berkeley Student Union, while the **Gourmet Ghetto** north of campus hosts California's finest dining. Beware of bicycles and unwary pedestrians.

VITAL STATS

Population: 105,000

Visitor Info: Berkeley Convention and Visitor Bureau, 2015 Center St. (☎510-549-7040; www.visitberkeley.com), at Milvia St. Open M-F 9am-1pm and 2-5pm. **UC Berkeley Visitors Center,** 101 University Hall (☎510-642-5215; www.berkeley.edu), at the corner of University Ave. and Oxford St. Open M-F 8:30am-4:30pm.

Internet Access: Berkeley Public Library, 2090 Kittredge St. (☎510-981-6100). Open M-Tu noon-8pm, W-Sa 10am-6pm, Su 1-5pm. Free.

Post Office: 2000 Allston Way (☎510-649-3155), at Milvia St. Open M-F 9am-5pm, Sa 10am-2pm. **Postal Code:** 94704.

SIGHTS

TELEGRAPH AVENUE. You haven't really visited Berkeley until you've strolled the first five or so blocks of Telegraph Ave. The action is close to the university, where Telegraph Ave. is lined with a motley assortment of cafes, bookstores, and secondhand clothing and record stores. Businesses come and go at the whim of the marketplace, but the scene—a rowdy jumble of 60s and 90s counterculture—persists. Vendors push tie-dye, Tarot readings, and jewelry; the disenfranchised hustle for change; and characters looking like Old Testament prophets carry on hyper-dimensional conversations, transmitting knowledge accrued through years of Berkeley experience. (Runs south from Sproul Plaza to Oakland.)

UC BERKELEY. In 1868, the private College of California and the public Agricultural, Mining, and Mechanical Arts College united as the **University of California.** The 178-acre university in Berkeley was the first of nine U of C campuses, so by seniority it has sole right to the nickname "Cal." The campus is bounded on the south by Bancroft Way, on the west by Oxford St., on the north by Hearst Ave., and on the east by Tilden Park. Enter through **Sather Gate** into **Sproul Plaza,** both sites of celebrated sit-ins and bloody confrontations with police. Tours leave from **Sather Tower,** the tallest building on campus; its observation level offers a great view. (Tours M-Sa 10am, Su 1pm. $2.) ⚑**Berkeley Art Museum (BAM),** 2626 Bancroft Way, is most respected for its 20th-century American and Asian art. BAM is also associated with the **Pacific Film Archive,** which screens selections from its Asian, European, and American holdings. (☎510-642-0808; www.bampfa.berkeley.edu. Open W and F-Su 11am-5pm, Th 11am-7pm. $8; students, seniors, and ages

THE PANACHE OF PANISSE

As greasy diner food becomes less appealing, take the opportunity to visit a culinary icon in Berkeley, CA. Save your pocket change, make reservations a month ahead of time, and indulge in dinner at **Chez Panisse,** the birthplace of California cuisine. After a trip to France, Alice Waters, the owner and executive chef of Chez Panisse, began preparing food for her friends in the traditional French style but used fresh local produce instead of traditional ingredients. The results were so good that Waters opened her own restaurant, and Chez Panisse and California cuisine were born. Because of Waters' culinary innovations, her restaurant has been rated one of the best in the world. Most top restaurants today follow Chez Panisse's model, and aspiring chefs study the restaurant in culinary school. Dishes like tea-smoked quail with asparagus, mustard greens, and sesame oil or lavender honey ice cream are phenomenal. If the hefty price tag of the *prix-fixe* menu is still too much for you, you can splurge more reasonably at the cheaper cafe upstairs.

Chez Panisse, 1517 Shattuck Ave. (☎510-548-5525; www.chezpanisse.com), between Cedar and Vine St. Reservations recommended. Prix-fixe menu M $50, Tu-Th $65, F-Sa $85.

[the big splurge]

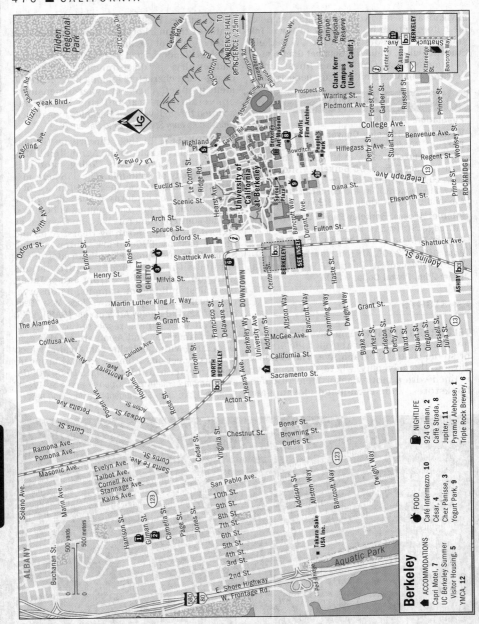

Berkeley

ACCOMMODATIONS
Capri Motel, **7**
UC Berkeley Summer
Visitor Housing, **5**
YMCA, **12**

FOOD
Café Intermezzo, **10**
César, **4**
Chez Panisse, **3**
Yogurt Park, **9**

NIGHTLIFE
924 Gilman, **2**
Café Strada, **8**
Jupiter, **11**
Pyramid Alehouse, **1**
Triple Rock Brewery, **6**

12-17 $5. 1st Th of each month free.) UC Berkeley is also host to one of the finest science museums and most stunning views in the Bay Area, the **Lawrence Hall of Science.** Ever-changing exhibits stress hands-on science activities catering to children but fun for all ages. Visit the renowned Planetarium and check out the outdoor "Forces that Shape the Bay" display. *(On Centennial Dr. ☎510-642-5132; www.lawrencehallofscience.org. Open daily 10am-5pm. $9.50, seniors and ages 5-18 $7.50, ages 3-4 $5.50. Planetarium shows $3, 18 and under $2.50.)*

OTHER SIGHTS. For off-campus fun, check out ▨**Takahara Sake USA, INC.,** where visitors can learn the history and science of sake-making and sample 15 different types of Japan's fire-water and plum wine. *(☎510-540-8250; www.takarasake.com. Open daily noon-6pm. Free.)* When you're ready to get out of town, Berkeley is happy to oblige. In the pine and eucalyptus forests east of the city lies the beautiful anchor of the East Bay park system, **Tilden Regional Park.** Hiking, biking, running, and riding trails crisscross the park and provide impressive views of the Bay Area. *(Take Spruce St. to Grizzly Peak Blvd. to Canon Ave. ☎510-635-0135; www.ebparks.org. Open daily sunrise-sunset.)* Also inside the park, the small, sandy beach at **Lake Anza** is a popular swimming spot during the hot summer days. *(☎510-843-2137. Open in summer daily 11am-6pm. $3.50, seniors and children $2.50.)*

➔ FOOD

Berkeley's **Gourmet Ghetto,** at Shattuck Ave. and Cedar St., is the birthplace of California Cuisine. The north end of **Telegraph Ave.** caters to student appetites and wallets, with late-night offerings along **Durant Ave.** A growing number of international establishments are helping to diversify the area. **Solano Ave.** is great for Asian cuisine, while **4th St.** is home to some more upscale eats.

▨ **Chez Panisse,** 1517 Shattuck Ave. (☎510-548-5525, cafe 510-548-5049; www.chezpanisse.com). See **The Panache of Panisse,** p. 475. ❺

▨ **Café Intermezzo,** 2442 Telegraph Ave. (☎510-849-4592), is a veggie-lover's paradise, serving salads ($4-7), sandwiches on freshly baked bread

($5), and tasty soups ($3), all at deliciously low prices. Open daily 10am-10pm. Cash only. ❶

César, 1515 Shattuck Ave. (☎510-883-0222), north of Cedar St., in the Gourmet Ghetto, is a great place for drinks and a light meal, with savory tapas ($4-10), *bocadillos* (small sandwiches on french bread; $8), desserts ($6-7), and a long list of spirits. Open M-Th and Su noon-11pm, F-Sa noon-11:30pm. ❸

Yogurt Park, 2433 Durant Ave. (☎510-549-2198), just west of Telegraph Ave., is an icon of Berkeley gastronomic life, serving huge portions of frozen yogurt ($2-2.50) made fresh daily. Open daily 11am-midnight. Cash only. ❶

⌂ ACCOMMODATIONS

There are few cheap accommodations in Berkeley. The **Berkeley-Oakland Bed and Breakfast Network** (☎510-547-6380; www.bbonline.com/ca/berkeley-oakland) coordinates great East Bay B&Bs with a range of rates. No-frills motels line **University Ave.** between Shattuck and Sacramento St.; ritzier joints are downtown, especially on **Durant Ave. UC Berkeley Summer Visitor Housing,** at Stern Hall, has simple dorms, shared baths, and free Internet access. (☎510-642-5796 or 510-642-5925. Parking $6 per day. Rooms $55. Open June to mid-Aug. D/MC/V.)

YMCA, 2001 Allston Way (☎510-848-6800; www.baymca.org), has a communal kitchen, shared bath, computer room, free Wi-Fi, TV lounge, pool, and fitness center. 18+. 10-night max. stay. Reception daily 8am-9:30pm. Singles $39-46; doubles $50-60. AmEx/D/MC/V. ❷

Capri Motel, 1512 University Ave. (☎510-845-7090), at Sacramento St. Tasteful rooms with cable TV, A/C, and fridge. 18+. Rooms from $65. AmEx/D/MC/V. ❸

☾ NIGHTLIFE

▨ **Jupiter,** 2181 Shattuck Ave. (☎510-843-8277), features a beer garden, live blues and jazz, and pizza ($7.50-13). Open M-Th 11:30am-1am, F 11:30am-2am, Sa noon-2am, Su noon-midnight. MC/V.

Caffè Strada, 2300 College Ave. (☎510-843-5282), at Bancroft Way, is a glittering jewel of the caffeine-

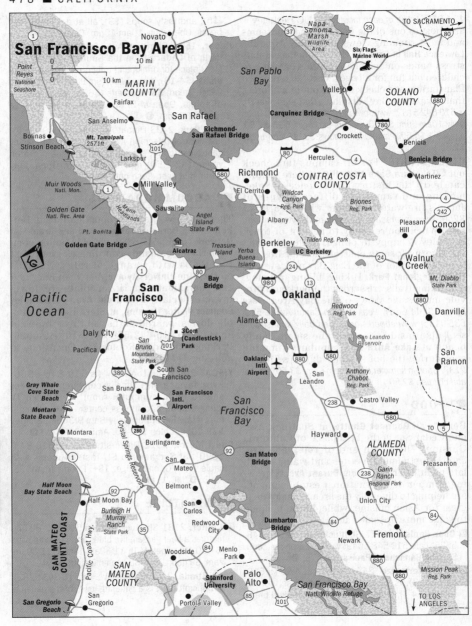

San Francisco Bay Area

0 _____ 10 mi
0 _____ 10 km

TO SACRAMENTO

Napa-Sonoma Marsh Wildlife Area

Six Flags Marine World

Point Reyes National Seashore

Novato

MARIN COUNTY

Fairfax

San Anselmo

San Rafael

Bolinas

Stinson Beach

Mt. Tamalpais 2571ft

Larkspur

San Pablo Bay

Vallejo

SOLANO COUNTY

Carquinez Bridge

Crockett

Benicia

Benicia Bridge

Richmond-San Rafael Bridge

Hercules

Martinez

Muir Woods Natl. Mon.

Golden Gate Natl. Rec. Area

Marin Headlands

Pt. Bonita

Mill Valley

Sausalito

Richmond

El Cerrito

Wildcat Canyon Reg. Park

Albany

CONTRA COSTA COUNTY

Briones Reg. Park

Pleasant Hill

Concord

Golden Gate Bridge

Alcatraz

Angel Island State Park

Treasure Island

Yerba Buena Island

Berkeley

UC Berkeley

Tilden Reg. Park

Walnut Creek

Mt. Diablo State Park

Pacific Ocean

San Francisco

Bay Bridge

Oakland

Danville

San Ramon

Daly City

280

3Com (Candlestick) Park

San Bruno Mountain State Park

Redwood Reg. Park

San Leandro Reservoir

Pacifica

Gray Whale Cove State Beach

Montara State Beach

South San Francisco

San Bruno

Oakland Intl. Airport

San Leandro

Anthony Chabot Reg. Park

Montara

Millbrae

San Francisco Intl. Airport

San Francisco Bay

Castro Valley

Burlingame

Crystal Springs Reservoir

Hayward

ALAMEDA COUNTY

San Mateo Bridge

Half Moon Bay State Beach

San Mateo

Belmont

Garin Ranch Regional Park

Pleasanton

Half Moon Bay

Burleigh H Murray Ranch State Park

San Carlos

Union City

SAN MATEO COUNTY COAST

Redwood City

Dumbarton Bridge

Newark

Fremont

Woodside

Menlo Park

Pacific Coast Hwy.

SAN MATEO COUNTY

Stanford University

Palo Alto

San Francisco Bay Natl. Wildlife Refuge

Mission Peak Reg. Park

San Gregorio Beach

San Gregorio

Portolá Valley

TO LOS ANGELES

TO 5

fueled intellectual scene. Open daily in summer 6am-11pm; in winter 6am-midnight. Cash only.

Pyramid Alehouse, 901 Gilman St. (☎510-528-9880), has meals designed to complement their gold medal-winning ales and lagers. Open M-Th and Su 11:30am-10pm, F-Sa 11:30am-11pm. Brewery tours M-F 5:30pm, Sa-Su 2 and 4pm. AmEx/D/MC/V.

924 Gilman, 924 Gilman St. (☎510-524-8180; www.924gilman.org), is a legendary all-ages club and a staple of California punk. Maintained by volunteers, the venue is nonprofit and dedicated to non-corporate music and community service and is alcohol- and drug-free. Cover $5-9. Shows F-Sa. Cash only.

Triple Rock Brewery, 1920 Shattuck Ave. (☎510-843-2739; www.triplerock.com), north of Berkeley Way, is boisterous and friendly and was the 1st (and to many the best) of Berkeley's many brew-pubs. Take a seat at the antique wood bar and try the award-winning Red Rock Ale. Pints $4-4.25. Open M-W and Su 11:30am-midnight, Th-Sa 11:30am-1am. Rooftop garden closes 9pm. MC/V.

⚲ APPROACHING SAN FRANCISCO: 14 MILES Head south on **Shattuck Ave.,** past downtown Berkeley. Just after crossing Derby St., Shattuck forks right onto **Adeline St.;** follow that fork, and turn right ¼ mi. later at the light onto **Ashby St.** Proceed down Ashby St. 2 mi. to **I-80 W.**

SAN FRANCISCO

If California is a state of mind, then San Francisco is euphoria. Welcome to the city that will take you to new highs, leaving your mind spinning, your taste buds tingling, and your calves aching. The dazzling views, daunting hills, one-of-a-kind neighborhoods, and laid-back, friendly people fascinate visitors. Though smaller than most "big" cities, the city manages to pack an incredible amount of vitality into its 47 sq. mi., from its thriving art communities and bustling shops to the pulsing beats in some of the country's hippest nightclubs and bars. For more coverage of the City by the Bay, see *Let's Go: San Francisco.*

▮ GETTING AROUND

San Francisco sits at the junction of several major highways, including **I-280, U.S. 101, Hwy. 1,** and **I-80.** From the east, **I-80** runs across the Bay Bridge (westbound-only toll $3) into the **South of Market Area (SoMa)** and then connects with U.S. 101 just before it runs into **Van Ness Ave. Market St.,** one of the city's main thoroughfares, runs on a diagonal from the Ferry Building near the bay through downtown and to the Castro in the southwest.

VITAL STATS

Population: 736,426

Visitor Info: California Welcome Center (☎415-956-3493; www.sfvisitor.org), on Pier 39 at the Great San Francisco Adventure. Open M-Th and Su 9am-9pm, F-Sa 9am-10pm.

Internet Access: At the California Welcome Center (see above). Free. For complete listings of Internet cafes in SF, check www.surfandsip.com.

Parking: Look for spots in residential Richmond and the Sunset District, or park in a garage for the day ($9-26). Options otherwise are very limited.

Post Office: 170 O'Farrell St. (☎415-956-0131), at Stockton St., in the basement of Macy's. Open M-Sa 10am-5:30pm, Su 11am-5pm. **Postal Code:** 94108.

Neighborhood boundaries get a bit confusing; a good map is a must. Touristy **Fisherman's Wharf** sits at the northeast edge of the city. Just south of the wharf is **North Beach,** a historically Italian area, and south of North Beach lies **Chinatown.** Wealthy **Nob Hill** and **Russian Hill** round out the northeast of the city. Municipal buildings cluster in the **Civic Center,** which lines Market St. and is bounded on the west by Van Ness Ave. On the other side of Van Ness Ave. is hip **Hayes Valley.** Retail-heavy **Union Square** is north of Market St. and gives way in the west to the rougher **Tenderloin,** which, incidentally, is not the meat-packing district.

The **Golden Gate Bridge** stretches over the Bay from the **Presidio** in the city's northwest corner. Just south of the Presidio, **Lincoln Park** reaches westward to the ocean, while vast **Golden Gate Park** dominates the western half of the peninsula. Near Golden Gate Park sits the former hippie haven of **Haight-Ashbury.** The trendy **Mission** takes over south of 14th St. The diners and cafes of the "gay mecca" of the **Castro** dazzle on Castro and Market St.,

San Francisco

🏠 ACCOMODATIONS
Red Victorian Bed Breakfast & Art, **7**
International Guesthouse, **18**

⭐ ENTERTAINMENT
Bottom of the Hill, **12**
Cafe du Nord, **8**
Castro Theatre, **11**
Fillmore, **1**
The Independent, **2**
Oberlin Dance Company, **13**

🍎 FOOD
Herbivore, **17**
Kan Zaman, **3**
Kate's Kitchen, **4**
Mitchell's Ice Cream, **20**
Nirvana, **15**
Pork Store, **6**
Taqueria Cancún, **14**

🍺 NIGHTLIFE
The Bar-on Castro, **10**
El Rio, **19**
Noc Noc, **5**
Pink, **9**
SF Badlands, **16**
Wild Side West, **21**

Golden Gate Bridge
Golden Gate National Recreation Area
Crissy Field
Lincoln Blvd.
Doyle Dr.
Lincoln B7/
Presidio
Baker Beach
W. Pacific Ave
Park Presidio Blvd.
Californi
Arguello Blvd
Gear
6th Ave.
8th Ave.
10th Ave.
Lake St.
California St.
Clement St.
Geary Blvd.
Anza St. INNER RICHMOND
Balboa St.
Univers
San Fran
Cabrillo St.
Fulton St.

Land's End
China Beach
SEA CLIFF
California Palace of the Legion of Honor
Lincoln Park
Point Lobos
El Camino del Mar
OUTER RICHMOND
34th Ave.
22nd Ave.
19th Ave.
25th Ave.
28th Ave.
30th Ave.

Sutro Baths
Cliff House
Seal Rocks
Pt. Lobos Ave.
46th Ave.
43rd Ave.

Beach Chalet
Golden Gate Park
Kennedy Dr.
Middle Dr.
Stow Lake
Japanese Tea Garden
Lincoln Way

Ocean Beach
Great Hwy.
Lincoln Wy.
Irving St.
Judah St.
Kirkham St.
Lawton St.
Moraga St.
Noriega St.
Ortega St.
Pacheco St.
Quintara St.
Rivera St.
Santiago St.
Taraval St.
Ulloa St.
Vicente St.
Wawona St.

Sunset Blvd.
34th Ave.
31th Ave.
28th Ave.
25th Ave.
22th Ave.
16th Ave.
10th Ave.
7th Ave.
Funston Ave.

Parnassus Ave.
U HA Frede
University of Calif at San Francisc Medical Cente
INNER SUNSET
10th Ave.

OUTER SUNSET
18th Ave.
19th Ave.
14th Ave.
FOREST HILL
Laguna Honda Blvd.
Dewey Blvd.
Clarendon Ave
Laguna He Hospita

McCoppin Sq.
PARKSIDE

PACIFIC OCEAN
San Francisco Zoo
Skyline Blvd.
Sunset Blvd.
Stern Grove
Sloat Blvd. 35
WEST PORTAL
Vicente St.
West Portal Ave.
Portola Dr.
Yerba Buena Ave.
ST. FRANCIS WOOD
Montere
City Colle
San Fran
De

0 ──── 1 mile
0 ──── 1 kilometer

Golden Gate National Recreation Area
STONESTOWN
San Francisco State University
Ocean Ave.
Miramar Ave.

Harding Park
Lake Merced
Font Blvd.
Lake Merced Blvd.
Junipero Serra Blvd.
Garfield St.
Holloway Ave.
INGLESIDE

Fort Funston
PARK MERCED

N LG

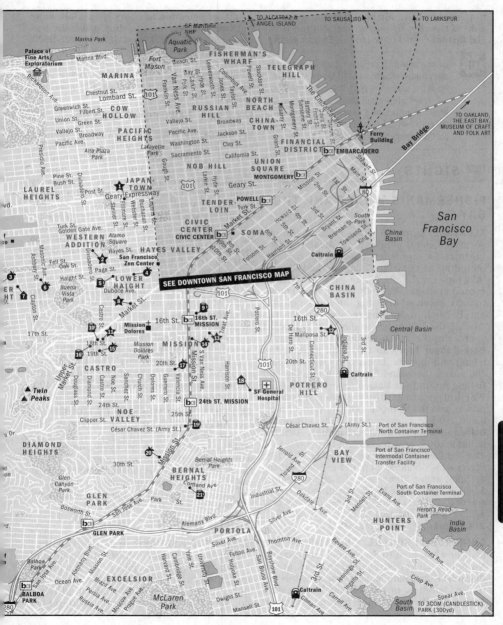

TO ALCATRAZ &
ANGEL ISLAND

TO SAUSALITO

TO LARKSPUR

SF Maritime
NHP

Aquatic
Park

Marina Park

Palace of
Fine Arts/
Exploratorium

Marina Blvd.

Fort
Mason

Beach St.

FISHERMAN'S
WHARF

Richardson Ave.

MARINA

Chestnut St.

Lombard St.

TELEGRAPH
HILL

The Embarcadero

TO OAKLAND,
THE EAST BAY,
MUSEUM OF CRAFT
AND FOLK ART

Greenwich St.

COW
HOLLOW

Union St.

Vallejo St.

Broadway

PACIFIC
HEIGHTS

Pacific Ave.

Filbert St.

Green St.

RUSSIAN
HILL

NORTH
BEACH

CHINA-
TOWN

Ferry
Building

Presidio Ave.

Alta Plaza
Park

Pacific Ave.

Jackson St.

Clay St.

FINANCIAL
DISTRICT

Bay Bridge

EMBARCADERO

San
Francisco
Bay

LAUREL
HEIGHTS

Pine St.
Bush St.

Divisadero St.

Post St.

JAPAN-
TOWN

Geary Expressway

NOB HILL

Larkin St.

Hyde St.

Leavenworth St.

UNION
SQUARE

MONTGOMERY

WESTERN
ADDITION

Turk St.
Golden Gate Ave.

Fillmore St.

Webster St.

Buchanan St.

Steiner St.

Geary St.

TENDER
LOIN

POWELL

Mission St.

2nd St.

China
Basin

Masonic Ave.

Fell St.
Oak St.

Alamo
Square

Hayes St.

CIVIC
CENTER

CIVIC CENTER

SOMA

Folsom St.

Harrison St.

Caltrain

Ashbury Ave.

2

HAYES VALLEY

San Francisco
Zen Center

4

CHINA
BASIN

Clayton St.

3

6

LOWER
HAIGHT

5

Haight St.

Page St.

Buena
Vista
Park

Duboce Ave.

7

SEE DOWNTOWN SAN FRANCISCO MAP

16th St.

9

16th St.
MISSION

16th St.

12

Central Basin

17th St.

10

11

Mission
Dolores

Mission
Dolores
Park

MISSION

14

De Haro St.

Mariposa St.

Indiana St.

3rd St.

Upper
Market St.

CASTRO

16

18th St.

19th St.

15

Sanchez St.

Church St.

Dolores St.

20th St.

17

S. Van Ness Ave.

Valencia St.

Guerrero St.

Harrison St.

20th St.

Connecticut St.

Caltrain

Twin
Peaks

Douglass St.

Diamond St.

Castro St.

Noe St.

24th St.

18

SF General
Hospital

POTRERO
HILL

DIAMOND
HEIGHTS

NOE
VALLEY

Clipper St.

24th St. MISSION

25th St.

César Chavez St. (Army St.)

César Chavez St.

(Army St.)

Port of San Francisco
North Container Terminal

19

Glen
Canyon
Park

30th St.

20

Mission St.

Bernal Heights
Park

BERNAL
HEIGHTS

Jerrold Ave.

Toland St.

BAY
VIEW

Port of San Francisco
Intermodal Container
Transfer Facility

GLEN
PARK

Bosworth St.

San Jose Ave.

Park
St.

Cortland Ave.

21

Industrial St.

Oakdale Ave.

Silver Ave.

Port of San Francisco
South Container Terminal

Heron's Head
Park

India
Basin

GLEN PARK

Alemany Blvd.

PORTOLA

Silver Ave.

Thornton Ave.

HUNTERS
POINT

Balboa
Park

EXCELSIOR

Ocean Ave.

Alemany Blvd.

Mission St.

Harvard St.

Cambridge St.

Yale St.

University St.

Felton Ave.

Holyoke St.

San Bruno Ave.

Bayshore Blvd.

Revere Ave.

3rd St.

Mendell St.

Evans Ave.

Jennings St.

Ingalls St.

Crisp Ave.

Innes Ave.

Spear Ave.

BALBOA
PARK

San Jose Ave.

Brazil Ave.

Persia Ave.

Russia Ave.

Moscow St.

Prague St.

McLaren
Park

Dwight St.

Mansell St.

Gilman Ave.

Caltrain

Carroll Ave.

South
Basin

TO 3COM (CANDLESTICK)
PARK (300yd)

San
Francisco
Bay

NATIONAL ROAD

northwest of the Mission. On the opposite side of the city, the skyscrapers of the **Financial District** crowd down to the **Embarcadero.**

When parking facing uphill, turn front wheels away from the curb, and, if driving a standard, leave the car in first gear. If your car starts to roll, it will stop when the tires hit the curb. When facing downhill, turn the wheels toward the curb and leave the car in reverse. Always set the emergency brake.

👁 SIGHTS

FISHERMAN'S WHARF AND THE BAY

ALCATRAZ. In its 29 years as a maximum-security federal penitentiary, **Alcatraz Prison** harbored a menacing cast of characters, including Al "Scarface" Capone and George "Machine Gun" Kelly. There were 14 separate escape attempts, but only one man is known to have survived crossing the Bay—unfortunately for him, he was recaptured. On the "rock," the cell-house audio tour immerses visitors in the infamous days of Alcatraz. A **Park Ranger Tour** can take you around the island and discuss its history. Over the past 200 years, the island has been a hunting and fishing ground for Native Americans, a Civil War outpost, a Military prison, a federal prison, and the birthplace of the Native American Civil Rights movement. Now part of the **Golden Gate National Recreation Area,** Alcatraz is home to diverse plants and birds. *(Take the Blue and Gold Fleet from Pier 41. ☎415-773-1188, tickets 415-705-5555. 14 ferries per day 9:30am-4:15pm; arrive 20min. early. $16.50, seniors $14.75, ages 5-11 $10.75. Reservations recommended. Park Ranger tours free. Evening tour $23.50, seniors and ages 12-17 $20.75, ages 5-11 $14.25; call for times and availability.)*

GHIRARDELLI SQUARE. Ghirardelli Sq. is a mall in what used to be a chocolate factory. No golden ticket is required to gawk at the **Ghirardelli Chocolate Manufactory's** vast selection of goodies, or the **Ghirardelli Chocolate Shop and Caffe,** with drinks, frozen yogurt, and a smaller selection of chocolates. Both hand out **free samples,** but the shop is usually less crowded. *(Mall 900 N. Point St. ☎415-775-5500. Stores open M-Sa 10am-9pm, Su 10am-6pm. Manufactory ☎415-771-4903. Open M-Th and Su 9am-11pm, F-Sa 9am-midnight. Shop ☎415-474-1414. Open M-Th 8:30am-9pm, F 8:30am-10pm, Sa 9am-10pm, Su 9am-9pm.)*

MARINA AND FORT MASON

🖼 **PALACE OF FINE ARTS.** With its open-air domed structure and curving colonnades, the Palace of Fine Arts was originally built to commemorate the opening of the Panama Canal, testifying to San Francisco's recovery from the 1906 earthquake. It serves today as a monument to all artistic endeavors. The **Palace of Fine Arts Theater,** located directly behind the rotunda, hosts dance and theater performances and film festivals. *(On Baker St., between Jefferson and Bay St., next to the Exploratorium. ☎415-563-6504; www.palaceoffinearts.com. Open daily 6am-9pm. Free.)*

FORT MASON. Fort Mason Center is home to some of the most innovative and impressive resources in San Francisco. The array of outstanding attractions seem to remain unknown to both tourists and locals, making it a quiet waterfront counterpart to the tourist blitz of nearby Fisherman's Wharf. The grounds are also the headquarters of the **Golden Gate National Recreation Area.** *(☎415-441-3400; www.fortmason.org.)*

SAN FRANCISCO MUSEUM OF MODERN ART ARTISTS GALLERY. Over 1200 Bay Area artists show, rent, and sell work here. Monthly curated exhibits are downstairs, while most other pieces are sold upstairs. Every May, the gallery hosts a benefit sale at which all works are half-price. *(In Bldg. A., on the 1st fl. ☎415-441-4777. Open Tu-Sa 11:30am-5:30pm. Free.)*

NORTH BEACH

WASHINGTON SQUARE. Washington Sq., bordered by Union, Filbert, Stockton, and Powell St., is North Beach's *piazza*, a pretty, not-quite-square, tree-lined lawn. The wedding site of Marilyn Monroe and Joe DiMaggio, the park fills every morning with tai chi enthusiasts. By noon, sunbathers, picnickers, and Bocce Ball players take over. **St. Peter and St. Paul Catholic Church** beckons sightseers to its dark nave. Ten stained glass windows on the upper walls depict the Ten Commandments, though the real highlight is the rose window. *(666 Filbert St. ☎ 415-421-0809.)* Turn-of-the-century San Francisco philanthropist and party-girl Lillie Hitchcock Coit donated the **Volunteer Firemen Memorial** in the middle of the square.

COIT TOWER. At the top of Telegraph Hill (also built by Lillie Hitchcock Coit), the Coit Tower stands 210 ft. high and commands a spectacular view of the city and the bay. During the Depression, the government's Works Progress Administration employed artists to paint the colorful and subversive murals in the lobby. *(☎ 415-362-0808. Open daily 10am-7pm. Elevator $3.75, seniors $2.50, ages 6-12 $1.50, under 6 free.)*

CITY LIGHTS BOOKSTORE. Beat writers came to national attention when Lawrence Ferlinghetti's City Lights Bookstore published Allen Ginsberg's *Howl*, which was banned in 1956 and then subjected to an extended trial. The judge found the poem "not obscene," and City Lights has been a landmark ever since. It has expanded since its Beat days and now stocks a wide selection of fiction and poetry, but it remains committed to publishing young poets and writers under its own label. *(2261 Columbus Ave. ☎ 415-362-8193. Open daily 10am-midnight.)*

CHINATOWN

WAVERLY PLACE. Find this little alley and you'll want to spend all day gazing at the incredible architecture. The fire escapes are painted in pinks and greens and held together by railings cast in intricate Chinese patterns. *(Between Sacramento and Washington St. and between Stockton St. and Grant Ave.)* **Tien Hou Temple** is the oldest Chinese temple in the city. *(125 Waverly Pl. Open daily 10am-4pm.)*

ROSS ALLEY. Once lined with brothels and opium dens, today's **Ross Alley** has the look of old Chinatown. The narrow street has stood in for the Orient in such films as *Big Trouble in Little China, Karate Kid II,* and *Indiana Jones and the Temple of Doom.* Squeeze into the doorway to see fortune cookies being shaped at the ◪**Golden Gate Cookie Company.** *(56 Ross Alley. ☎ 415-781-3956. Bag of cookies $3, with "funny," "sexy," or "lucky" fortunes $5. Open daily 10am-8pm.)*

NOB HILL AND RUSSIAN HILL

THE CROOKEDEST STREET IN THE WORLD. The famous curves of **Lombard St.**—installed in the 1920s so that horse-drawn carriages could negotiate the extremely steep hill—serve as an icon of SF. From the top, pedestrians and passengers enjoy the view of city and harbor. The view north along Hyde St. isn't too shabby either. *(Between Hyde and Leavenworth St. at the top of Russian Hill.)*

GRACE CATHEDRAL AND HUNTINGTON PARK. The largest Gothic edifice west of the Mississippi, **Grace Cathedral** is Nob Hill's stained-glass crown. Inside, modern murals mix San Franciscan and national historical events with saintly scenes. The cathedral is particularly famous for the Ghiberti doors that replicate the Doors of Paradise. The altar of the AIDS Interfaith Memorial Chapel celebrates the church's "inclusive community of love." *(1100 California St., between Jones and Taylor St. ☎ 415-749-6300; www.gracecathedral.org. Open M-F and Su 7am-6pm, Sa 8am-6pm. Tours M-F 1-3pm, Sa 11:30am-1:30pm, Su 1:30-2pm. Suggested donation $5.)*

UNION SQUARE AND THE TENDERLOIN

MAIDEN LANE. When the Barbary Coast (now the Financial District) was down and dirty, Union Sq.'s **Morton Alley** was dirtier. Around 1900, murders on the Alley averaged one per week and prostitutes waved to customers from second-story windows. After the 1906 earthquake and fires destroyed most of the brothels, merchants moved in and renamed the area **Maiden Lane** in hopes of changing the street's image. It worked. Today, the pedestrian-only street is as virtuous as they come and makes a pleasant place to stroll or sip espresso while sporting your new Gucci shades.

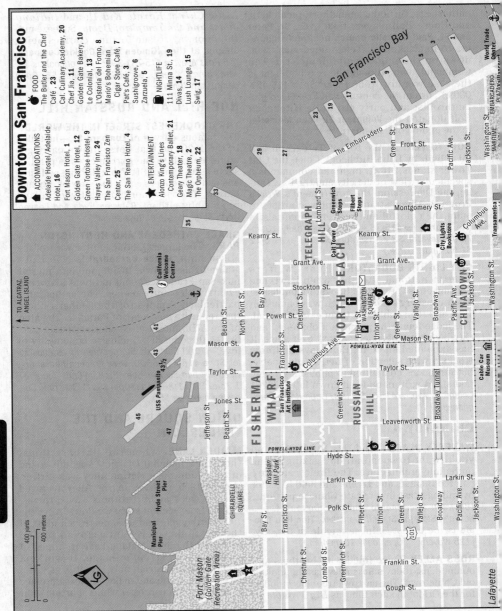

Downtown San Francisco

♦ FOOD
The Butler and the Chef
   Café, **23**
Cal. Culinary Academy, **20**
Chef Jia, **11**
Golden Gate Bakery, **10**
Le Colonial, **13**
L'Osteria del Forno, **8**
Mario's Bohemian
   Cigar Store Café, **7**
Pat's Café, **3**
Sushigroove, **6**
Zarzuela, **5**

▲ ACCOMMODATIONS
Adelaide Hostel/Adelaide
   Hotel, **16**
Fort Mason Hotel, **1**
Golden Gate Hotel, **12**
Green Tortoise Hostel, **9**
Hayes Valley Inn, **24**
The San Francisco Zen
   Center, **25**
The San Remo Hotel, **4**

★ ENTERTAINMENT
Alonzo King's Lines
Contemporary Ballet, **21**
Geary Theatre, **18**
Magic Theatre, **2**
The Orpheum, **22**

NIGHTLIFE
111 Minna St., **19**
Divas, **14**
Lush Lounge, **15**
Swig, **17**

San Francisco Bay

NATIONAL ROAD

Ferry Building

The Embarcadero

JUSTIN HERMAN PLAZA

Steuart St.
Spear St.
Main St.
Beale St.
Howard St.
Folsom St.
Fremont St.

Drumm St.

Embarcadero Center

EMBARCADERO

FINANCIAL DISTRICT

California St.

Battery St.

Beale St.

1st St.

Mission St.

2nd St.

1st St.

Pine St.

Sansome St.

Montgomery St.

Kearny St.

Grant Ave.

Pine St.

Bush St.

Stockton St.

Maiden Ln.

Geary St.

Market St.

MONTGOMERY

BART/MUNI

CALIFORNIA STREET LINE

POWELL

POWELL-HYDE LINE

UNION SQUARE

UNION SQUARE

Powell St.

POWELL-HYDE LINE

Sacramento St.

Hang Gallery

Martin Lawrence Gallery

Mason St.

Post St.

Sutter St.

Kabuki Hot Springs

O'Farrell St.

Ellis St.

Taylor St.

Turk St.

Jones St.

Eddy St.

Leavenworth St.

Golden Gate Ave.

Hyde St.

TENDERLOIN

Larkin St.

Surrey Bikes and Blades

Polk St.

Van Ness Ave.

Clay St.

Sacramento St.

Pine St.

Bush St.

Sutter St.

Post St.

Geary St.

Van Ness Ave.

Grace Cathedral

CALIFORNIA STREET LINE

St. Mary's Cathedral

Gough St.

Ellis St.

Eddy St.

JEFFERSON SQUARE

Turk St.

McAllister St.

Fulton St.

Franklin St.

War Memorial Opera House

CIVIC CENTER

City Hall

Louise M. Davies Symphony Hall

Grove St.

Hayes St.

Gough St.

HAYES VALLEY

Fell St.

Oak St.

Page St.

Haight St.

California St.

San Francisco Museum of Modern Art

Yerba Buena Gardens

Sony Metreon

San Francisco Shopping Center

Yerba Buena Center for the Arts

Moscone Center

California Academy of Sciences

Folsom St.

Howard St.

Mission St.

4th St.

3rd St.

5th St.

6th St.

7th St.

SOUTH OF MARKET

509 Cultural Center

CIVIC CENTER

Market St.

BART/MUNI

8th St.

9th St.

10th St.

11th St.

12th St.

Van Ness Ave.

US 101

Mission St.

Otis St.

Harrison St.

Bryant St.

Brannan St.

Townsend St.

King St.

Berry St.

SBC Park

Caltrain Depot

South Park

San Francisco-Oakland Bay Bridge

Bryant St.

Harrison St.

Folsom St.

Howard St.

6th St.

7th St.

8th St.

9th St.

280

280

80

80

2nd St.

3rd St.

4th St.

5th St.

Transbay Terminal

Essex St.

THE PRESIDIO

When Spanish settlers forged their way up the San Francisco peninsula from Baja California in 1769, they established *presidios*, or military outposts, as they went. San Francisco's **Presidio,** the northernmost point of Spanish territory in North America, was dedicated in 1776. Today the Presidio is home to many nonprofit organizations as well as residential housing. Baker Beach offers sunbathing and views of the Golden Gate and lies at the northwest end of the Presidio. Crissy Field is another popular recreation area, where people head for a picnic or a game of frisbee.

LINCOLN PARK

COASTAL TRAIL. The Coastal Trail loops around the interior of Lincoln Park for a scenic and sometimes hardcore coastal hike. The entrance to the trail is not well marked, so be careful not to mistakenly tackle a much more difficult cliffside jaunt. The path leads first into **Fort Miley,** a former army post. Near the picnic tables rests the **USS San Francisco Memorial.** The *USS San Francisco* sustained 15 major hits in the battle of Guadalcanal in November 1942. Nearly 200 men died in the clash, but the ship survived and went on to fight in further battles. The Coastal Trail continues for a 3 mi. hike into **Land's End,** famous for its views of both the Golden Gate Bridge and the "sunken ships" that signal treacherous waters below. Biking is permitted on the trail, although parts contain stairs and bumpy terrain better suited for mountain bikes. From Land's End, onlookers can hike an extra 6 mi. into the Presidio and on to the arches of the Golden Gate Bridge. *(Begins at Pt. Lobos and 48th Ave.)* For hikers and bikers who aren't so inclined, the walk along **El Camino Del Mar** originates close to the Coastal Trail but runs farther in from the shore. Enjoy the forested views of the **Palace of the Legion of Honor** before finishing "The Path of the Sea" at **China Beach.** *(Begins at Pt. Lobos and Sea Rock Dr.)*

BEACHES. Swimming is permitted but dangerous at scenic **China Beach,** at the end of Seacliff Ave. on the eastern edge of Lincoln Park. Once the camping grounds of Chinese fisherman, this beach is somewhat hidden down a long flight of stairs. Adolph Sutro's 1896 **bathhouse** lies in ruins on the cliffs. Cooled by ocean water, the baths were capable of packing in 25,000 occupants at a time. **Ocean Beach,** the largest and most popular of San Francisco's beaches, begins south of Pt. Lobos and extends down the northwestern edge of the city's coastline. The undertow along the point is dangerous, but die-hard surfers brave the treacherous currents and the ice-cold water anyway. **Bakers Beach,** a local favorite, is located in the Presidio west of the Golden Gate Bridge. Its proximity to the Golden Gate make it a popular sunbathing spot on summer days.

GOLDEN GATE SIGHTS

GOLDEN GATE BRIDGE. When Captain John Fremont coined the term "Golden Gate" in 1848, he meant to name the harbor entrance to the San Francisco Bay after the mythical Golden Horn port of Constantinople. In 1937, however, the colorful name became permanently associated with Joseph Strauss's copper-hued engineering masterpiece—the Golden Gate Bridge. Built for $35 million, the bridge stretches across 1¼ mi. of ocean, its towers looming 966 ft. above the bay. On sunny days, hundreds of people take the 30min. walk across. Only the adventurous would attempt the trek on windy days, when the bridge can sway up to 27 ft. in each direction. The views from the bridge are amazing, as they are from the Vista Point in Marin County just after the bridge. To see the bridge itself, it's best to get a bit farther away; Fort Point and Fort Baker in the Presidio, Land's End in Lincoln Park, and Mt. Livermore on Angel Island all offer spectacular views on clear days.

GOLDEN GATE PARK. Take your time to enjoy this park. Museums (p. 488) and cultural events pick up where the lush flora and fauna leave off, and athletic opportunities abound. The park has a municipal golf course, equestrian center, sports fields, tennis courts, and stadium. On Sundays, park roads close to traffic, and bicycles and in-line skates come out in full force. The Golden Gate Park Visitors Center is in the Beach Chalet on the western edge of the park. (☎ 415-751-2766. *Open daily 9am-5pm.*) Surrey Bikes and

Blades, 50 Stow Lake Dr., in Golden Gate Park, rents equipment. (☎ *415-668-6699. Bikes from $6 per hr., $20 per day; in-line skates $6/$20. Open daily 10am-sunset.)*

GARDENS. The **Garden of Fragrance** is designed especially for the visually impaired; all labels are in Braille and the plants are chosen specifically for their textures and scents. Near the Music Concourse off South Dr., the **Shakespeare Garden** contains almost every flower and plant ever mentioned by the Bard. *(Open in summer daily sunrise-sunset; in winter Tu-Su sunrise-sunset. Free.)* The **Japanese Cherry Orchard,** at Lincoln Way and South Dr., blooms intoxicatingly the first week in April. Created for the 1894 Mid-Winter Exposition, the elegant **Japanese Tea Garden** is a serene collection of wooden buildings, small pools, graceful footbridges, carefully pruned trees, and lush plants. Don't leave without trying the tea. (☎ *415-752-4227. Open daily in summer 8:30am-6pm; in winter 8:30am-5pm. $3.50, seniors and ages 6-12 $1.25. Free in summer 8:30-9:30am and 5-6pm; in winter 8:30-9:30am and 4-5pm.)*

FINANCIAL DISTRICT

TRANSAMERICA PYRAMID. Certain areas of the Financial District's architectural landscape rescue it from the otherwise banal functionality of the business area. The leading lady of the city's skyline, the **Transamerica Pyramid,** is, by all descriptions, impressive. Though its shape may be architecturally awkward, its individuality makes it stand out. Planned as an architect's joke and co-opted by one of the leading architectural firms in the country, the building has earned disdain from purists and reverence from city planners. *(600 Montgomery St., between Clay and Washington St.)*

JUSTIN HERMAN PLAZA. When not overrun with skateboarders, the Plaza is often home to bands and rallyists who provide lunch-hour entertainment. U2 rock star Bono was arrested here in 1987 for spray painting "Stop the Traffic—Rock and Roll" on the fountain. Recently, the plaza has been the starting point for **Critical Mass,** a pro-bicyclist ride that takes place after 5pm on the last Friday of every month. If you happen to be around

on a rare hot day, walk through the inviting mist of the **Vaillancourt Fountain** to cool off.

JAPANTOWN AND PACIFIC HEIGHTS

SAINT DOMINIC'S ROMAN CATHOLIC CHURCH. Churchgoers and architecture buffs appreciate Saint Dominic's towering altar, carved in the shape of Jesus and the 12 apostles. With its imposing stone and Gothic architecture, St. Dominic's is a must see, especially its renowned ▓shrine of Saint Jude. *(2390 Bush St. ☎ 415-567-7824. Open M-Sa 6:30am-5:30pm, Su 7:30am-9pm. Mass M-F 6:30, 8am, 5:30pm; Sa 8am and 5:30pm; Su 7:30, 9:30, 11:30am, 1:30, 5:30, 9pm.)*

FUJI SHIATSU AND KABUKI SPRINGS. After a rigorous day hiking the hills, reward your weary muscles with an authentic massage at **Fuji Shiatsu.** *(1721 Buchanan Mall, between Post and Sutter St. ☎ 415-346-4484. Massage $41-44. Open M-F 9am-8:30pm, Sa 9am-6:30pm, Su 10am-6:30pm.)* Alternatively, head to the bathhouse at **Kabuki Hot Springs** to relax in the sauna and steam-room, or enjoy the *Reiki* (light touching) treatment to heal, rejuvenate and restore energy balance. *(1750 Geary Blvd. ☎ 415-922-6000; www.kabukisprings.com. Open daily 10am-10pm. M-F $20, Sa-Su $25. Men only M, Th, and Sa; women only Su, W, and F; coed Tu.)*

CIVIC CENTER

ARCHITECTURE. Referred to as "The Crown Jewel" of American Classical architecture and with a dome to rival St. Paul's cathedral and an area of over 500,000 sq. ft., **City Hall** reigns supreme over the Civic Center. *(1 Dr. Carlton B. Goodlett Pl., at Van Ness Ave. ☎ 415-554-4000. Open M-F 8am-8pm. Free.)* The seating in the $33 million glass-and-brass **Louise M. Davies Symphony Hall** was designed to give audience members a close-up view of performers. Its **San Francisco Symphony** is highly esteemed. Rush tickets available at the box office (during business hours) the day of performances. *(201 Van Ness Ave. ☎ 415-552-8000. Open M-F 10am-6pm, Sa noon-6pm. Rush tickets $20.)* The recently renovated **War Memorial Opera House** hosts the **San Francisco Opera Company** and the **San Francisco Ballet.** *(301 Van Ness Ave., between Grove and McAl-*

lister St. Box office at 199 Grove St. ☎415-864-3330. Open M-F 10am-6pm and 2hr. before each show.)

MISSION

MISSION DOLORES. Founded in 1776, the **Mission Dolores** is thought to be the city's oldest building. Bougainvillea, poppies, and birds-of-paradise bloom in its cemetery, which was featured in Hitchcock's *Vertigo.* (3321 16th St., at Dolores St. ☎415-621-8203. Open daily May-Oct. 9am-4:30pm; Nov.-Apr. 9am-4pm. $5, ages 5-12 $3.)

MISSION MURALS. A walk east or west along 24th St. takes you past magnificent murals. Continuing the Mexican mural tradition made famous by Diego Rivera and Jose Orozco, the murals have been a source of pride for Chicano artists and community members since the 1980s. Standouts include the political murals of **Balmy Alley**, off 24th St., between Harrison and Folsom St., a three-building tribute to guitar god **Carlos Santana** at 22nd St. and Van Ness Ave., the face of **St. Peter's Church** at 24th and Florida St., and the murals that cover the **urban life skills center** on 19th St., between Valencia and Guerrero St.

CASTRO

THE CASTRO. Stores throughout the area cater to gay-mecca pilgrims, with everything from rainbow flags and pride-wear to the latest in GLBT books, dance music, and trinkets of the unmentionable variety. Many local shops, especially on colorful **Castro St.**, also double as novelty galleries. Discover just how anatomically correct Gay Billy is at **Does Your Father Know?**, a one-stop kitsch-and-camp overdose. To read up on gay history and culture, try at **A Different Light Bookstore.** (489 Castro St. ☎415-431-0891.)

WALKING TOURS. For a tour of the Castro that includes sights other than biceps and abs, check out **Cruisin' the Castro.** Once run by resident Trevor Hailey, the tour has recently taken on a new leader whose 3hr. walking tours cover Castro life and history from the Gold Rush to today. (☎415-550-8110; www.cruisinthecastro.com. Tours Tu-Sa 10am. $45; lunch included. Reservations required.)

HAIGHT-ASHBURY

FORMER CRIBS. The former homes of counterculture legends still attract visitors. From the corner of Haight and Ashbury St., walk just south of Waller St. to check out the house occupied by the **Grateful Dead** when they were still the Warlocks. (710 Ashbury St.) Look across the street for the **Hell's Angels** house. If you walk back to Haight St., go right three blocks, and make a left on Lyon St., you can check out **Janis Joplin's** abode. (122 Lyon St., between Page and Oak St.) Cross the Panhandle, continue three blocks to Fulton St., turn right, and wander seven blocks toward the park to see where the Manson "family" planned murder and mayhem at the **Charles Manson** mansion. (2400 Fulton St., at Willard St.)

SAN FRANCISCO ZEN CENTER. Appropriately removed from the havoc of the Haight, the **San Francisco Zen Center** offers a peaceful retreat. The temple is called Beginner's Mind Temple, so don't worry if you don't know where to begin looking for your chi. The best option for most is the Saturday morning program, which includes a meditation lecture at 8:45am followed by activities and lunch. (300 Page St., at Laguna St. ☎415-863-3136. Open M-F 9:30am-12:30pm and 1:30-5pm, Sa 8:30am-noon. Call ahead for schedule. Sa morning program $6.)

🏛 MUSEUMS

▧SAN FRANCISCO MUSEUM OF MODERN ART (SFMOMA). This black-and-white cylindrical museum houses 5 spacious floors of photography, painting, media, and sculpture, with an emphasis on architecture and design. It houses the largest selection of 20th-century American and European art this side of New York. (151 3rd St., between Mission and Howard St. ☎415-357-4000; www.sfmoma.org. Open June-Aug. M-Tu and F-Su 10am-5:45pm, Th 10am-8:45pm; Sept.-May M-Tu and F-Su 11am-5:45pm, Th 11am-8:45pm. 4 free gallery tours per day. $12.50, seniors $8, students $7, under 13 free. 1st Tu of each month free.)

▧EXPLORATORIUM. Over 4000 people can visit the Exploratorium at one time, and when admission is free it usually fills up. Over 650 displays—including miniature tornadoes, computer planet-managing, and giant bubble-makers—explain the wonders of the world. Heighten your sense of touch in the Tactile Dome, a dark maze of tunnels, slides, and crevices. *(3601 Lyon St. ☎415-563-7337 or 415-561-0360; www.exploratorium.edu. Open Tu-Sa 10am-5pm. $13; students, seniors, ages 9-17 $10; ages 4-12 $8. 1st W of each month free. Tactile Dome $3/$6/$8.)*

CALIFORNIA PALACE OF THE LEGION OF HONOR. Outside the museum, a copy of Rodin's *Thinker* beckons visitors into the courtyard, where a glass pyramid recalls the Louvre. A thorough catalogue of great masters, from the medieval to the modern, hangs inside, and extensive statuary and decorative art collections are spread throughout. Just outside the Palace, a Holocaust memorial depicts a single, hopeful survivor looking out through a barbed-wire fence to the beauty of the Pacific. *(In the middle of Lincoln Park. ☎415-863-3330; www.legionofhonor.org. Open Tu-Sa and Su 9:30am-5pm. $10, seniors $7, ages 13-17 $6, under 12 free. 1st Tu of each month free.)*

CALIFORNIA ACADEMY OF SCIENCES. The California Academy of Sciences houses multiple museums specializing in different fields of science. The **Steinhart Aquarium,** home to over 600 aquatic species, is livelier than the natural history exhibits. Watch the food chain do its thing at animal feedings throughout the week. At the **Natural History Museum,** the Hotspot exhibit features live animals and endangered species. *(875 Howard St. ☎415-750-7145; www.calacademy.org. Snake feeding F 1pm; fish feeding M and W 2pm; penguin feeding daily 11am and 3:30pm. Open daily June-Aug. 9am-6pm; Sept.-May 10am-5pm. Combined admission $7; seniors, students, and ages 12-17 $4.50; ages 4-11 $2. 1st W each month free.)*

YERBA BUENA CENTER FOR THE ARTS. The center includes an excellent theater and gallery space, with programs emphasizing performance, film, viewer involvement, and local multi-cultural work. It is surrounded by the **Yerba Buena Rooftop Gardens,** a vast expanse of concrete, fountains, and foliage. Also on the grounds is a restored 1906 carousel. *(701 Mission St. ☎415-978-2787; www.yerbabuenaarts.org. Open Tu-W and F-Su noon-5pm, Th noon-8pm. $6, students and seniors $4.)*

MUSEUM OF CRAFT AND FOLK ART (MOCFA). The art doesn't just hang on walls at the MOCFA. The museum brings together a fascinating collection of crafts and functional art (clothing, furniture, jewelry) from past to present, near and far. Highlights included everything from 19th-century Chinese children's hats to unorthodox war-time commentary. *(51 Yerba Buena Ln. ☎415-227-4888; www.mocfa.org. Open Tu-F 11am-6pm, Sa-Su 11am-5pm. $5, seniors $4, under 18 free. 1st Tu of each month free.)*

CABLE CAR POWERHOUSE AND MUSEUM. After the steep journey up Nob Hill, you'll understand the importance of the vehicles celebrated at the Cable Car Powerhouse and Museum. The modest building is the working center of San Fran's extensive cable car system. Look down on 57,300 ft. of cable whizzing by, or learn about the cars, some of which date back to 1873. *(1201 Mason St. ☎415-474-1887. Open daily Apr.-Oct. 10am-6pm; Nov.-Mar. 10am-5pm. Free.)*

 GALLERIES

509 CULTURAL CENTER AND LUGGAGE STORE. The Luggage Store and its annex, the 509, present exhibitions, performances, and education initiatives, though the often-graphic art exhibits probably won't be Grandma's favorites. Regular events include comedy Open mic, improv music concerts, and a theater festival each June. *(1007 Market St. ☎415-865-0198. Open mic Tu 9pm. Concerts Th 8pm. Suggested donation $6-10.)* Next door to 509, the **Cohen Alley** houses a 3rd venue for the area's creative talent; the alley is leased to the Luggage Store, which has made it an artistic showcase.

SAN FRANCISCO ART INSTITUTE. Before he set off across the country to create some of America's most iconic images, Ansel Adams got his start at the **San Francisco Art Institute.** The oldest art school west of the Mississippi, the Institute is lodged in a converted mission and has produced a number of American greats including Mark Rothko, Imogen Cunningham, Dorothea Lange, and James

Weeks. To the left as you enter is the **Diego Rivera Gallery,** one wall of which is covered by a huge 1931 Rivera mural. *(800 Chestnut St. ☎ 415-771-7020 or 800-345-7324; www.sfai.edu. Open daily 9am-9pm. Free.)*

MARTIN LAWRENCE GALLERY. The gallery displays works by pop artists like Warhol and Haring, who once distributed his work for free to New York commuters in the form of subway station graffiti; his playful works now command upwards of $13,000 in print form. The gallery also houses studies by Picasso and America's largest collection of work by Marc Chagall. *(366 Geary St. ☎ 415-956-0345. Open M and Su 10am-6pm, Tu-W 9am-8pm, Th-Sa 9am-9pm. Free.)*

HANG. Artistic works hang from the exposed ceiling beams of this chrome warehouse. An annex recently opened directly across the street. *(556 Sutter St. ☎ 415-434-4264; www.hangart.com. Open M-Sa 10am-6pm, Su noon-5pm. Free.)*

 FOOD

For the most up-to-date listings of restaurants in town, try the *Examiner*, the *S.F. Bay Guardian*, and the *Bay Area Vegetarian*. **Chinatown** is filled with cheap restaurants the sheer number of which can baffle even the savviest of travelers. Some locals claim that Chinese restaurants in **Richmond** are better than those in Chinatown. In **North Beach's** tourist-friendly restaurants, California cuisine merges with the bold palate of Italy. In the **Financial District,** corner cafes vend Mediterranean grub at rock-bottom prices. The dominance of Mexican specialties and gigantic burritos is undeniable in the **Mission.**

FISHERMAN'S WHARF

Pat's Café, 2330 Taylor St. (☎ 415-776-8735), between Chestnut and Francisco St. With playful yellow swirls on the building's facade, Pat's bright decor welcomes diners to a hearty home-cooked meal like mom would make. Burgers, sandwiches, and big breakfasts $5-10. Open M and Th-Su 5:30-9pm, Tu-W 7:30am-3pm. D/MC/V. ❷

CHINATOWN

☒ **Chef Jia,** 925 Kearny St. (☎ 415-398-1626), at Pacific St. Insanely cheap and delicious food. A local crowd comes for lunch and dinner specials ($4.80) or the celebrated signature dishes like prawns rolled in lettuce and pine nuts ($11). Open M-F 11:30am-10pm, Sa-Su 5-10pm. Cash only. ❷

Golden Gate Bakery, 1029 Grant Ave. (☎ 415-781-2627), in Chinatown. This tiny bakery's moon cakes, noodle puffs, and vanilla cream buns (all $0.75-1.50) bring all the boys to the yard. Open daily 8am-8pm. Cash only. ❶

NORTH BEACH

☒ **L'Osteria del Forno,** 519 Columbus Ave. (☎ 415-982-1124), between Green and Union St. Acclaimed Italian roasted and cold foods, plus homemade breads. Terrific thin-crust pizza (slices $3-4) and focaccia sandwiches ($5-7). Open M, W-Th, and Su 11:30am-10pm, F-Sa 11:30am-10:30pm. Cash only. ❷

Mario's Bohemian Cigar Store Café, 566 Columbus Ave. (☎ 415-362-0536), at the corner of Washington Sq. The Beats frequented this laid-back cafe, which still serves first-rate chow. Panini $5-7.50. Open daily 10am-11pm. MC/V. ❷

NOB HILL AND RUSSIAN HILL

Zarzuela, 2000 Hyde St. (☎ 415-346-0800), at Union St. Spanish homestyle cooking and a festive upscale setting make *chorizo al vino* (sausage in wine sauce; $6.75) the highlight of the evening. Entrees $9-20. Open Tu-Th 5:30-10pm, F-Sa 5:30-10:30pm. D/MC/V. ❸

Sushigroove, 1916 Hyde St. (☎ 415-440-1905), between Union and Green St. This chic sushi-sake joint (sushi and maki $3-7) serves up a lot of rolls but nothing that has seen the inside of an oven. Open M-Th and Su 5:30-10pm, F-Sa 5:30-10:30pm. AmEx/MC/V. ❷

UNION SQUARE AND THE TENDERLOIN

☒ **Le Colonial,** 20 Cosmo Pl. (☎ 415-931-3600; www.lecolonialsf.com), off Post St., between Taylor and Jones St. Exquisite French-Vietnamese cuisine in a stunning French-inspired building. The veranda, with its high, white adobe walls, ivy-clad lattice, and overhead heating lamps, offers the best opportunity to revel in the architecture and sip a signature mojito ($8). Entrees $20-35. Call for dress code. Open M-W and Su 5:30-10pm, Th-Sa 5:30-11pm. AmEx/D/MC/V. ❺

The California Culinary Academy, 625 Polk St. (☎415-292-8229), between Turk and Eddy St. Academy students cook behind a window visible from the high-ceilinged Carême dining room. The Tu-W prix-fixe 3-course lunch ($14) and dinner ($24) indulges patrons with ambitious culinary combinations. Wine with each course is a steal at $5. The Th-F grand buffet lunch ($22) and dinner ($38) draws large crowds; reserve 1 week ahead. Open Tu-F 11:30am-1pm and 6-8pm. AmEx/D/MC/V. ❹

SOUTH OF MARKET AREA (SOMA)

▣ **The Butler and the Chef Cafe,** 155A S. Park Ave. (☎415-896-2075; www.thebutlerandthechef.com). Advertising itself as San Francisco's only authentic French bistro, this stellar reproduction of a Parisian street cafe serves breakfast crepes ($4-10) and baguette sandwiches ($7). Open M-Sa 8am-4pm, Su 10am-5pm. AmEx/D/DC/MC/V. ❷

HAIGHT-ASHBURY

▣ **Pork Store Cafe,** 1451 Haight St. (☎415-864-6981), between Masonic Ave. and Ashbury St. A breakfast joint that strives to help your inner fat kid blossom—they proudly stock only whole milk. The 2 delicious healthy options ("Tim's Healthy Thursdays" $7.50 and "Mike's Low Carb Special" $7.25) pack enough spinach, avocado, and salsa to hold their own against the Piggy Special (two eggs with your choice of two pancakes or French toast; $6.25). Open M-F 7am-3:30pm, Sa-Su 8am-4pm. AmEx/D/MC/V. ❷

Kan Zaman, 1793 Haight St. (☎415-751-9656), at Schrader St. Delicious Middle Eastern fare like falafel sandwiches ($5). Top it off with a hookah session ($9-14) and some arabic tea. W and Su belly dancing 9pm, F-Sa 9 and 10:30pm. Open M-Th 5pm-midnight, F 5pm-2am, Sa noon-2am, Su noon-midnight. MC/V. ❷

Kate's Kitchen, 471 Haight St. (☎415-626-3984), near Fillmore St. Start your day off right with one of the best breakfasts in the neighborhood (served all day), like the "Farmer's Breakfast" ($4.25) or the "French Toast Orgy" (with fruit, yogurt, granola, and honey; $8). It's often packed, so sign up on the waiting list outside. Open M 9am-2:45pm, Tu-F 8am-2:45pm, Sa-Su 8:30am-3:45pm. Cash only. ❷

MISSION AND THE CASTRO

▣ **Taquería Cancún,** 2288 Mission St. (☎415-252-9560), at 19th St. Delicious burritos (grilled chicken; $4) and scrumptious egg dishes served with chips and salsa, small tortillas, and choice of sausage, ham, or salsa ($5). Open M-Th and Su 9am-1:45am, F-Sa 9am-3am. Cash only. ❶

▣ **Mitchell's Ice Cream,** 688 San Jose Ave. (☎415-648-2300), at 29th St. This takeout parlor gets so busy that you have to take a number at the door. Mitchell's boasts a list of awards almost as long as the list of flavors (from caramel praline to Thai iced tea), and will chocolate dip any scoop. Cone $2.10. Pint $5.10. Open daily 11am-11pm. Cash only. ❶

Herbivore, 983 Valencia St. (☎415-826-5657). If you are unfamiliar with vegan cuisine, the sandwiches are a safe and tasty bet ($7.75) and come with potatoes and salad). Pastas and wraps vary from Thai to Shawarma. Open M-Th and Su 9am-10pm, F-Sa 9am-11pm. MC/V. ❸

Nirvana, 544 Castro St. (☎415-861-2226), between 18th and 19th St. Playfully concocted cocktails such as "nirvana colada" and "phat margarita" ($8-9) complement Burmese cuisine (from $8) with a twist. Mango-glazed chicken $14.50. Open M-Th 4:30-9:30pm, F-Sa noon-10:30pm, Su noon-9:30pm. MC/V. ❸

▛ ACCOMMODATIONS

For those who don't mind sharing a room with strangers, many San Francisco hostels are homier and cheaper than budget hotels. Book in advance if at all possible, but since many don't take reservations for summer, you might have to just show up or call early on your day of arrival. B&Bs are often the most comfortable and friendly, albeit expensive, option. Beware that some of the cheapest budget hotels may be located in areas requiring extra caution at night.

HOSTELS

◙ **San Francisco International Guesthouse,** 2976 23rd St. (☎415-641-6173), in the Mission. Look for the blue Victorian with yellow trim near the corner of Harrison St. With hardwood floors, tapestries festooning the walls, and comfortable common areas, this hostel feels like the well-designed room of your tree-hugger college roommate. Free Internet access. Passport with international stamps "required." 5-night min. stay. No reservations, but chronically filled to capacity. All you can do is try calling a few days ahead of time. Dorms $22. Cash only. ❶

◙ **Green Tortoise Hostel,** 494 Broadway (☎415-834-1000; www.greentortoise.com), off Columbus Ave., in North Beach. A ballroom preceded this super-mellow, friendly pad, allowing today's fun-seeking young travelers to hang out amid abandoned finery in the spacious common room. There's even a sauna. Breakfast (daily) and dinner (M, W, F) included. Tu free beer. Key deposit $10. Females ask for the window bed. Reception 24hr. Check-out 11am. Reservations recommended. Dorms $25; private rooms $32-65. MC/V. ❶

Adelaide Hostel and Hotel, 5 Isadora Duncan Ln., (☎877-359-1915; www.adelaidehostel.com), at the end of a little alley off Taylor St., between Geary and Post St. in Union Square. The bottom 2 floors, recently renovated with fresh paint and new furniture, entice a congenial international crowd. Check-out 11am. Reservations recommended. Dorms $26; private rooms from $70. AmEx/D/DC/MC/V. ❶

Fort Mason Hostel (HI-AYH), Bldg. #240 (☎415-771-7277), at the corner of Funston and Pope St., in Fort Mason. Beautiful surrounding forest and wooden bunks provide a campground feel. Not a place for partiers—strictly enforced quiet hours (11pm) and no smoking or alcohol. Movies, walking tours, dining room, and parking. Laundry (wash $1, dry $1). Check-in 2:30pm. Reservations recommended. Dorms $28, under 13 $17. AmEx/D/MC/V. ❶

HOTELS AND GUESTHOUSES

◙ **The San Remo Hotel,** 2237 Mason St. (☎415-776-8688; www.sanremohotel.com), between Chestnut and Francisco St., in Russian Hill. Built in 1906, this pension-style hotel features small but elegantly furnished rooms with antique arm-

oires, bedposts, lamps, and complimentary back-scratchers. Shared bathrooms. Check-out 11am. Reservations recommended. Rooms $55-75. AmEx/DC/MC/V. ❸

◙ **Hayes Valley Inn,** 417 Gough St. (☎415-431-9131, reservations 800-930-7999; www.hayes-valleyinn.com), in Hayes Valley. European-style B&B with small, clean rooms, shared bath, and lace curtains. Bedrooms range from charming singles with daybeds to extravagant turret rooms with wraparound windows and queen-size beds. All rooms have cable TV, phone, and sink. Breakfast included. Check-in 3pm. Check-out 11am. Singles $73-84; doubles $84-95; turret rooms $94-105. AmEx/D/DC/MC/V. ❹

The Red Victorian Bed, Breakfast, and Art, 1665 Haight St. (☎415-864-1978; www.redvic.com), west of Belvedere St., in the Upper Haight. Inspired by the 1967 "Summer of Love," proprietress Sami Sunchild nurtures guests. Continental breakfast included. Reception 9am-9pm. Check-in 3-6pm or by appointment. Check-out 11am. Reservations recommended. Rooms $89-22. MC/V. ❹

San Francisco Zen Center, 300 Page St. (☎415-863-3136; www.sfzc.org), near Laguna St. in the Lower Haight. Even if rigorous soul-searching is not for you, the Zen Center offers breezy, unadorned rooms whose courtyard views instill a meditative peace of mind. Breakfast included. All meals included in the discounted weekly (10% off) or monthly (25% off) rates. Rooms $66-108. MC/V. ❸

Golden Gate Hotel, 775 Bush St. (☎415-392-3702 or 800-835-1118; www.goldengatehotel.com), between Mason and Powell St., in Union Sq. A positively charming B&B, with a staff as kind and solicitous as the rooms are plush and inviting. Continental breakfast and afternoon tea (4-7pm) included. Reservations recommended. Doubles $85, with bath $130. AmEx/DC/MC/V. ❹

🎵 ENTERTAINMENT

MUSIC

The distinction between bars, clubs, and live music venues is hazy in San Francisco. Almost all bars will occasionally have bands, and small venues have rock and hip-hop shows. Look for the latest live music listings in *S.F. Weekly* and *The Guardian*. Hardcore audiophiles might snag a copy of *Bay Area Music (BAM)*. ◼**Café du Nord,** 2170 Market St., is one of San Francisco's best music venues. Live music—from pop and groove to garage rock—plays every night, and the Monday Night Hoot showcases local singing and songwriting. (Between Church and Sanchez St., in the Castro. ☎415-861-5016. 21+. Cover $5-10 after 8:30pm. Open 1hr. before showtime. Call ahead for schedule.) Both local acts and bands with their sights set on the national stage perform at **The Independent,** 628 Divisadero St., where live performances nearly every night feature genres as diverse as reggae, indie rock, and hip-hop. (At Hayes St., in the Lower Haight. ☎415-771-1422; www.independentsf.com. Free movie screenings M 8pm; 2 drink min. Open daily; hours vary.) An intimate rock club with a tiny stage, **Bottom of the Hill,** 1233 17th St., is the best place to see up-and-coming artists before they move to bigger venues. Most Sunday afternoons feature local bands and ◼**all-you-can-eat barbecue.** (Between Missouri and Texas St., in Potrero Hill. ☎415-626-4455; www.bottomofthehill.com. 21+; some shows open to all ages. Cover $7-12. Open M-Tu and Sa 8:30pm-2am, W-F 4pm-2am, Su hours vary.) Bands that pack stadiums may play the legendary **Fillmore,** 1805 Geary Blvd., for its history, but the venue's bread and butter is still mid-size groups like Jurassic 5 and The Black Keys. The Fillmore was the foundation of San Francisco's 1960s music scene, and performers like Janis Joplin, The Grateful Dead, and Jefferson Airplane all performed here. (At Fillmore St., in Japantown. ☎415-346-6000; www.thefillmore.com. Box office open Su 10am-4pm. Tickets $15-40.)

THEATER, FILM, AND DANCE

Downtown, **Mason St.** and **Geary St.** constitute **"Theater Row,"** the city's center for theatrical entertainment. **TIX Bay Area,** located in a kiosk in Union Sq., at the corner of Geary and Powell St., is a Ticketmaster outlet and sells half-price tickets the day of performances. (☎415-433-7827; www.theaterbayarea.org. Open Tu-Th 11am-6pm, F-Sa 11am-7pm, Su 10am-3pm.) **Magic Theatre,** in Fort Mason Center, stages international and American premieres. (☎415-441-8822; www.magictheatre.org.) A famous landmark, **The Orpheum,** 1192 Market St., at Hyde St., near the Civic Center, hosts big Broadway shows. (☎415-512-7770.) **Geary Theater,** 415 Geary St., is home to the renowned **American Conservatory Theater,** one of the best theater companies in the country. (At Mason St. in Union Sq. ☎415-749-2228; www.act-sfbay.org.) The ◼**Castro Theatre,** 429 Castro St., near Market St., shows eclectic films, festivals, and double features, some featuring live organ music. (☎415-621-6350; www.thecastrotheatre.com.) The ◼**Oberlin Dance Company,** 3153 17th St., mainly stages dance performances, but it also has theatrical productions and art exhibitions. (Between S. Van Ness Ave. and Folsom St., in the Mission. ☎415-478-2787; www.odctheater.org. Box office open W-Sa 2-5pm.) At **Alonzo King's Lines Contemporary Ballet,** 26 7th St., dancers combine elegant classical moves with athletic flair to the music of great living jazz and world-music composers. (In Hayes Valley. ☎415-863-3040; www.linesballet.org. Tickets $20-70.)

FESTIVALS

If you can't find a festival going on in San Francisco, well, you just aren't trying hard enough. Cultural, ethnic, and queer special events take place year-round. For two consecutive weekends in April, the Japanese **Cherry Blossom Festival** lights up the streets of Japantown with hundreds of performers. (☎415-563-2313.) For a bit of high culture, consider the free **San Francisco Shakespeare Festival,** every Saturday and Sunday in September in the Presidio. (☎415-558-0888. Shows Sa 7:30pm, Su 2:30pm.) The **San Francisco Blues Festival,** held the 3rd weekend in September, is the oldest blues festival in America and attracts some of the biggest names in the business. (In Fort Mason. ☎415-979-5588.) The oldest film festival in North America, the **San Francisco International Film Festival** shows more than 100 international films of all genres over two weeks. Films are shown at 12 venues throughout the city, but the **Kabuki Theatre,** 1881 Post St., and the **Castro Theatre,** 429 Castro St., are two main venues. (☎415-561-5000; www.sffs.org. $11, students $10; matinees $7.50.) If films are your thing, you may also want to check out the **San Francisco International Gay and Lesbian Film Festival,** California's second-largest film festival and the world's largest gay and lesbian media event. It takes place during the 11 days leading up to Pride Day. (☎415-703-8650.) The High Holy Day of the queer calendar, **Pride Day** celebrates with a parade and events downtown starting on Market St. at Davis St. at 10:30am. (☎415-864-3733; www.sfpride.org.) Finally, the leather-and-chains gang lets it all hang out at the **Folsom Street Fair,** Pride Day's raunchier, rowdier little brother. (On Folsom St., between 7th and 12th St. ☎415-861-3247; www.folsomstreetfair.com.)

SPORTS

Baseball's **Giants** play at the **Pacific Bell Park,** 24 Willie Mays Plaza, in SoMa (☎415-972-2000 or 888-464-2468; www.sfgiants.com. Tickets $13-68.) **Candlestick Park** is now home to the five-time Super Bowl champion **49ers.** (☎415-464-9377, tickets 415-656-4900; www.sf49ers.com. Tickets $49-94.)

🏮 NIGHTLIFE

Nightlife in San Francisco is as varied as the city's personal ads. Everyone from the "shy first-timer" to the "bearded strap daddy" can find places to go at night. The spots listed below are divided into bars and clubs, but the lines get blurred in SF after dark, and even cafes hop at night. Check out the nightlife listings in the *S.F. Weekly, S.F. Bay Guardian,* and *Metropolitan.* San Francisco is not particularly friendly to those under 21.

BARS

🏮 **Noc Noc,** 5574 Haight St. (☎415-861-5811), near Fillmore St., in the Lower Haight. This lounge, creatively outfitted as a modern cavern, seems like the only happening place before 10pm—neo-hippies mingle at bar stools, or relax on the padded floor cushions. Open daily 5pm-2am. MC/V.

🏮 **111 Minna St.** (☎415-974-1719), at 2nd St., in SoMa. Funky gallery by day, hipster groove-spot by night. The bar turns club W 5-10pm for a crowded night of progressive house music. Cover $5-15. Gallery open Tu-F noon-5pm. Bar open Tu 5-9pm, W 5-11pm, Th-F 5pm-2am, Sa 10pm-2am. AmEx/D/MC/V.

Lush Lounge, 1092 Post St. (☎415-771-2022), at Polk St., in Nob Hill. Oh-so-lush, with ample vegetation and sassy classic Hollywood throwback decor. Kick back as the best of the 80s, from ABBA to Madonna, streams through the speakers. Raspberry cosmos $5. Watermelon martinis $3. Open daily 4pm-2am. Cash only.

Swig, 561 Geary St. (☎415-931-7292; www.swig-bar.com), between Taylor and Jones St., in Union Square. With an artful, intimate back room and an upstairs VIP lounge, this recently opened bar has already entertained Eminem, D12, and The Wallflowers. Open daily noon-2am. No cover. AmEx/MC/V.

CLUBS

🏮 **El Rio,** 3158 Mission St. (☎415-282-3325), between César Chavez and Valencia St., in the Mission. Each area in this sprawling club has its own bar, but the patio is center stage for the young urbanites who play cards and smoke cigars. Diverse queer and straight crowd. Tu-W and Sa-Su live Bay area bands. Su live salsa (mainly GLBT) 3-8pm; salsa lessons 3-4pm. Pool table and jukebox in the bar area. Cover M $3, Th free or $2, Su $7. Open M 5pm-1am, Tu-Sa 5pm-2am, Su 3pm-midnight. Cash only.

Pink, 2925 16th St. (☎415-431-8889), at S. Van Ness Ave., in the Mission. Filled with the scent of gardenias, this venue plays it *très chic.* Pink satin and gossamer draperies lend a lounge feel on weekdays, but expect a throng of clubbers F-Sa. DJs spin a mix of world music, soulful house, Cuban jazz, and Afro beats. Cover $5, F-Sa $10. Open Tu-Th and Su 9pm-2am, F-Sa 9pm-3am. MC/V.

GLBT NIGHTLIFE

Politics aside, nightlife alone is enough to earn San Francisco the title of "gay mecca." Generally, the boys hang in the Castro neighborhood, while the girls gravitate to the Mission, around Valencia St. All frolic along Polk St. (several blocks north of Geary Blvd.), and in SoMa. Polk St. can seem seedy and SoMa barren, so keep a watchful eye.

■ **Divas,** 1081 Post St. (☎415-474-3482; www.divassf.com), at Polk St., in the Tenderloin. With a starlet at the door and a savvy pinstriped madame working the bar, this transgender nightclub is simply fabulous. Tu talent night. F-Sa drag show. Cover $7-10. Open daily 6am-2am. Cash only.

■ **The Bar on Castro,** 456 Castro St. (☎415-626-7220), between Market and 18th St. An urbane Castro staple with padded walls and dark plush couches perfect for eyeing the stylish young crowd or scoping the techno-raging dance floor. Happy hour M-F 4-8pm with $2 pints and well drinks. Open M-F 5pm-2am, Sa-Su 1pm-2am. Cash only.

SF Badlands, 4121 18th St. (☎415-626-0138), near Castro St. Strutting past the sea of boys at the bar, cruise a circular dance floor where the latest Top 40 divas shake their thangs. Cover F-Sa $2. Drinks $4-5. Open daily 2pm-2am. Cash only.

Wild Side West, 424 Cortland Ave. (☎415-647-3099), at Wool St., in Bernal Heights. The oldest lesbian bar in SF is a favorite for women and men. The backyard jungle has benches, fountains, and statues. Open daily 1pm-2am. Cash only.

THE END OF THE ROAD

Navigate the crookedest street in the world, plan your escape from Alcatraz, walk across the Golden Gate Bridge, then head to the beach to contemplate the Pacific. You've finished a colossal coast-to-coast trek, the National Road. But don't rest on your laurels—the road awaits. Route 66 and the Pacific Coast are only a few highway exits away.

EXIT TO

Palo Alto, CA   33 mi.
on the pacific coast route, p. 944

Los Angeles, CA 381 mi.
on route 66, p. 596

SPEED LIMIT 65

route 66

TOP 5

1. Get a rabbit autograph from Montana at **Henry's Rte. 66 Emporium and Rabbit Ranch** (p. 518)
2. Rummage through atomic junk at the **Black Hole Surplus Store and Museum** (p. 553)
3. Pretend you're Don Henley and stand on a corner in **Winslow, AZ.**
4. Slither around Santa Fe's **Rattlesnake Museum** while practicing your parseltongue.
5. Bypass all other Rte. 66 museums until the **Oklahoma Rte. 66 Museum** in Clinton, Oklahoma.

Route 66 is *the* roadtrip. Born of America's love affair with the automobile, Route 66 is the final resting place of classic car culture, known variously as the "Main Street of America," the "Mother Road," and the "Will Rogers Highway." Route 66 appeared in Steinbeck's *The Grapes of Wrath* (the term "Mother Road" comes from here), has been memorialized in song by Bobby Troup, and—most importantly—has been driven by millions. Whether you're searching for yourself or just a good burger and a cheap motel room, Route 66, in all its neon-lit glory, delivers.

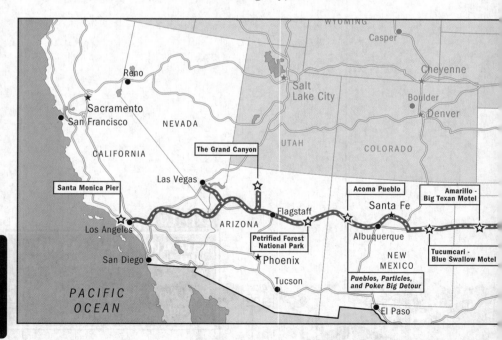

Continuously paved by 1938, Rte. 66 saw the westward migration of thousands of families heading to California, looking to escape the dust and poverty of the Great Depression. It also spawned the motel, the drive-through, and, of course, the assortment of mom-and-pop businesses that sprang up along the way.

While Route 66 was eventually eclipsed by the many-laned sterility of the Interstate Highway and officially decommissioned in 1985, the road is experiencing a revival in the form of thousands of modern-day migrants, who seek to re-create the classic journey of generations past. From its lakeside beginnings in **Chicago, IL** (p. 498), which offers world-class architecture (not to mention deep-dish pizza), our route follows the original as closely as possible, through the rolling countryside of Illinois and Missouri, home to **Henry's Rte. 66 Emporium and Rabbit Ranch** (p. 518) and one hell of a milkshake at **Ted Drewes Frozen Custard** (p. 400) in **St. Louis.** From there, the next stop is **Meramec Caverns** (p. 520)—if the caverns' reputation as Missouri's biggest tourist attraction doesn't

reach you, the sheer number of signs surely will. After passing the oddly Gothic **Jasper County Courthouse** (p. 524), it's on to the lonely, dusty plains of Oklahoma, where traffic is sparse, cows are many, and almost every town has a street (or at least a park) named after **Will Rogers.** Rte. 66 passes through El Reno, OK, where **Johnnie's Grill** (p. 534) proudly cooks up the **world's largest hamburger** each May, before traversing **Texas** and entering **New Mexico,** where you, too, can stay in "Tucumcari tonight" at the **Blue Swallow Motel** (p. 543).

Rte. 66 then cuts a magnificent swath across **New Mexico, Arizona,** and **Nevada** through miles and miles of scrubby desert, where skies are blue and sweeping, and colorful little trading posts line the road, peddling Navajo crafts, road snacks, and, of course, Rte. 66 souvenirs. The road passes through **Santa Fe** (p. 546), where Spanish colonial architecture, Native American influence, and green chiles come together in one spicy, delicious mix, and then explores New Mexico on the **Pueblos, Particles, and Poker Big Detour** (p. 552). The route continues on

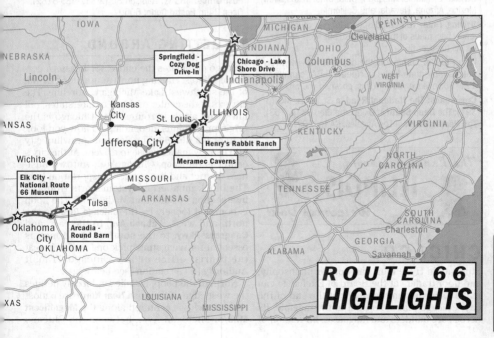

ROUTE 66 HIGHLIGHTS

ROUTE 66

through charming **Albuquerque** (p. 551), the stunning and scenic pueblo country of Arizona, and the one and only **Petrified Forest National Park** (p. 562). Take it easy in **Winslow, AZ** (p. 564) before reaching **Flagstaff,** where you can take a brief jaunt off 66 to visit the **Grand Canyon** (p. 570). Ponder the mind-boggling engineering of the 726 ft. **Hoover Dam** (p. 580), and play the tables in **Las Vegas** (p. 582) if you're feeling lucky. Or—if you really want to gamble—get hitched at the **Little White Wedding Chapel** (p. 582). Continue across the punishing Mojave Desert toward **Los Angeles** (p. 902), the sprawling city of the stars. Finally, the near-perfect roadtrip reaches its near-perfect end at **Santa Monica** (p. 598). There's never been a better time to get your kicks, so pack your sunglasses and bring a camera—the journey has begun.

ROUTE STATS

Miles: c. 2400

Route: Chicago, IL to Santa Monica, CA.

States: 8; Illinois, Missouri, Oklahoma, Texas, New Mexico, Arizona, Nevada, and California.

Driving Time: You could spend forever cruising the lonely backroads of the Southwest, but allow at least 3 weeks to savor 66.

When To Go: Summer in the desert is hot—very, very hot. Summertime highs in Needles, CA, can reach 120°F. We leave you with this; go when you wish.

Crossroads: The National Road in St. Louis, MO (p. 397); **The Deep South** in Oklahoma City, OK (p. 763), **The Pacific Coast** in Los Angeles, CA (p. 902).

The Land of Lincoln
ILLINOIS
Welcomes You!

CHICAGO

Students in Hyde Park can ponder philosophy, and floor traders at the Board of Exchange can make electronic millions, but at the end of the day, Chicago places its trust in the tangible. Its heroes are builders and magnates; its version of the American Dream raises a glass to anyone who can get ahead in this clamorous boom-town. Long a city of immigrants and underdogs, Chicago knows how to rub elbows with sophistication and then hop on the wheezing, clanking El for the long ride home.

VITAL STATS

Population: 2.9 million

Visitor Info: Visitor Information Center, 77 E. Randolph St. (☎312-744-2400), in the Chicago Cultural Center. Open M-Th 8am-7pm, F 8am-6pm, Sa 9am-6pm, Su 10am-6pm. **Water Works Visitor Center,** 163 E. Pearson St. (☎312-742-8811), at Michigan Ave. in the Water Tower Pumping Station. Open daily 7:30am-7pm.

Internet Access: Chicago Public Library, Harold Washington Library Center, 400 S. State St. (☎312-747-4999), at Congress. Open M-Th 9am-7pm, F-Sa 9am-5pm, Su 1-5pm. Free.

Parking: 524 S. Wabash Ave. (☎312-648-9770). Open 24hr. $12 per 12hr.; $18 per day.

Post Office: 433 W. Harrison St. (☎312-983-8182). Open 24hr. **Postal Code:** 60607.

GETTING AROUND

Chicago dominates the entire northeastern corner of Illinois, running north-south along 29 mi. of the southwest Lake Michigan shoreline. The city sits at the center of a web of interstates, rail lines, and airplane routes. And Chicago is the origin or terminus, depending on how you look at it, of **Old Rte. 66.** The flat and sprawling city grid usually makes sense to drivers. At the city's center is the **Loop,** Chicago's downtown business district and the public transportation hub. The block numbering system starts from the intersection of State and Madison St. The Loop is bounded loosely by the **Chicago River** to the north and west, **Wabash Ave.** to the east, and **Congress Pkwy.** to the south. A good map is essential for navigating; pick one up for free at the tourist office or any Chicago Transit Authority (CTA) station (see below).

North of the Loop, LaSalle Dr. loosely defines the west edge of the posh **Near North** area; most of its activity is centered along the **Magnificent Mile** of Michigan Ave., between the Chicago

Otel.com

Are you aiming for a budget vacation**?**

DO NOT DISTURB

Chicago Overview

Mount Prospect

Evanston
Northwestern University

Skokie

Rosemont

Chicago O'Hare International Airport

Norridge

Schiller Park

Franklin Park

Oak Park

Lincoln Park

Elmhurst

Hillside

CHICAGO

SEE DOWNTOWN CHICAGO MAP

Grant Park

Cicero

Burnham Park

University of Chicago

Lake Michigan

Jackson Park

Chicago Midway Airport

Marquette Park

Rainbow Park

Bridge-view

Bedford Park

Burbank

Oak Lawn

Calumet Park

Calumet Park

Wolf Lake

Lake George

Orland Park

Alsip

Calumet Park

Calumet City

Hammond

ROUTE 66

River and Oak St. A trendy restaurant and night-life district, **River North** lines N. Clark St., just north of the Loop and west of Michigan Ave. The **Bucktown/Wicker Park** area, at the intersection of North, Damen, and Milwaukee Ave., is the place to be for artsy, cafes and cutting-edge nightlife. **Lincoln Park** revolves around the junction of N. Clark St., Lincoln Ave., and Halsted St. To the north, near the 3000 block of N. Clark St. and N. Halsted St., sits **Lakeview,** a gay-friendly area teeming with food and nightlife that becomes Wrigleyville in the 4000 block. **Andersonville,** 5 mi. farther up N. Clark St. north of Foster Ave., is the center of the Swedish-American community, though immigrants from Asia and the Middle East have recently settled here. It is a good idea to stay within the boundaries made apparent by tourist maps, as much of Chicago is unsafe at night; especially avoid the South Side neighborhood.

Competition for parking in downtown Chicago is ferocious, and parking lot prices are extreme. To avoid driving and parking in the city, daytrippers can leave their cars in one of the suburban park-and-ride lots ($1.75-10.75 per day depending on station). In the city, the **Chicago Transit Authority (CTA),** 350 N. Wells, 7th fl. (☎312-836-7000 or 888-968-7282; www.transitchicago.com), runs efficient subways and buses. The **elevated rapid transit train system,** called the **El,** encircles the Loop. (Runs 24hr. $2; day pass $5.) Late-night service is infrequent and unsafe in many areas. Helpful CTA maps are available at many stations and at the visitors center.

Parking lots west of the South Loop and across the canal from the **Sears Tower** generally have the best rates, but avoid parking in the Loop if possible. Also, beware the 45 mph speed limit on **Lake Shore Drive,** a scenic freeway that hugs Lake Michigan and offers express north-south connections.

👁 SIGHTS

Tourist brochures, bus tours, and strolls through the downtown area reveal only a fraction of Chicago's eclectic attractions. Chicago's sights range from well-publicized museums to undiscovered back streets, from beaches and parks to towering skyscrapers, and seeing it all requires some off-the-beaten-path exploration. Fortunately, Chicago is one of a growing number of cities worldwide to have a **Greeter** program (☎312-744-8000; www.chicagogreeter.com), whose volunteer staff of knowledgeable Chicagoans will show you around.

THE LOOP

When the Great Fire of 1871 razed Chicago's downtown, the burgeoning metropolis had an opportunity to start anew. Bounded by the river on one side and Lake Michigan on the other, the city was forced to build up rather than out. Drawing on new technologies, including steel-frame construction and the elevator brake, the Windy City assembled a daring skyline regarded today as one of America's most elegant.

TOURS. Visitors can take a crash course on columns and cornices through **walking tours** organized by the **Chicago Architecture Foundation.** Two-hour tours of skyscrapers start at the foundation's gift shop. Highlights include the stained-glass windows of the Marquette Building, the Art Deco flourishes of the Board of Trade, and the revolutionary aesthetics of Mies van der Rohe. (224 S. Michigan Ave. ☎ 312-922-3432, ext. 240; www.architecture.org. Historic Skyscrapers tours May-Sept. daily 10am, 3pm; Oct. M-Tu and Th-Su 10am, 3pm, W 5:30pm; Nov.-Apr. daily 10am. Modern Skyscrapers tours daily 1pm. $14, students and seniors $11.)

SEARS TOWER. A few blocks west on Jackson, the 1454 ft. tall **Sears Tower** is undoubtedly Chicago's most recognizable landmark. Early in 1997, the Petronas Towers in Malaysia edged out the Sears Tower as the tallest building in the world; however, the tower can still claim the highest occupied floor. The ear-popping elevator ride to the 103rd-floor skydeck earns visitors a view of four states on a clear day. (233 S. Wacker Dr.; enter on Jackson St. ☎312-875-9696; www.theskydeck.com. Open daily May-Sept. 10am-10pm; Oct.-Apr. 10am-8pm. Lines usually at least 1hr. $12, seniors $10, children 3-11 $8.60.)

THE PLAZA. The **Bank One Building and Plaza** is one of the world's largest bank buildings, luring gazes skyward with its diamond-shaped, diagonal slope. Back on the ground, Marc Chagall's vivid mural *The Four Seasons* lines the block and defines a public space used for concerts and lunchtime entertainment. One block north, the Methodist **Chicago Temple,** the world's tallest church, sends its delicate steeple heavenward. (77 W. Washington St., at the cor-

Downtown Chicago

■ ACCOMMODATIONS
Arlington House, **1**
Hostelling International
   Chicago (HY-AYH), **15**
Hotel Wacker, **5**
International House, **16**
Ohio House Motel, **10**

■ NIGHTLIFE
Berlin, **3**
The Green Mill, **2**
Sweet Home Blue
   Chicago, **4**

♥ FOOD
Al's #1 Italian Beef, **7**
Ed Debevic's, **8**
Gino's East of Chicago, **9**
Heaven on Seven, **13**
Lou Malnati's, **12**
Lou Mitchell's, **14**
Pizzeria Uno, **11**
Portillos Hotdogs, **6**

TO WRIGLEY
FIELD (3mi)
North Ave
TO STEPPENWOLF
THEATER (500yd),
OAK PARK (7mi)

Second
City
TO (1mi),
(3mi)

Chicago
Historical
Society
TO LINCOLN
PARK (1mi)
International
Museum of
Surgical Science

W. Schiller St.
Goethe St.
Division St.
Elm St.
Cedar St.
Bellevue Pl.
Walton St.
Oak St.

La Salle St.
Rush St.
Oak St.
Beach

Locust St.
Hudson Ave.
Sedgwick St.
Orleans St.
Franklin St.
Wells St.
La Salle St.
Clark St.
Dearborn St.
State St.
Larabee St.

Delaware Pl.
John Hancock
Center
E. Chestnut
Chicago Water
Tower
Water Tower Place
Pearson St.
Chicago Ave.
Superior St.
Museum of
Contemporary Art

NEAR
NORTH

Huron St.
Erie St.
Ontario St.
Ohio St.
Grand Ave.
Illinois St.
W. Hubbard St.

RIVER
NORTH

Merchandise
Mart
Kinzie St.
Wrigley
Building
Tribune
Tower
E. North Water St.

N. Kingsbury St.
Chicago River
Canal St.
Clinton St.

Wacker Dr.
S. Water St.
E. Lake St.
Lake St.

State of
Illinois Building
Wacker Dr.

TO MUSEUM
OF HOLOGRAPHY
(1.1mi)
Washington St.

Northwestern
Station

Franklin St.

Goodman
Theatre
City Hall
Daley
Plaza
Civic Opera House
Chicago Temple
Randolph St.
E. Randolph Dr.
Chicago
Cultural
Center
Millenium Park

Madison St.
Bank One Plaza
Monroe St.
E. Monroe Dr.

THE LOOP

Union
Station
Sears Tower
and Observ.
Adams St.
Symphony
Center
Art Institute
of Chicago
Petrillo
Music Shell
Jackson Blvd.
E. Jackson Dr.
Monadnock Building
Chicago
Architecture
Foundation
Grant Park

Van Buren St.
Congress Pkwy.
Congress Dr.
Harold
Washington
Library Center
Auditorium Theater
Harrison St.
Columbia
College
E. Balbo Dr.

S. Wells St.
W. Polk St.
E. 8th St.
9th St.
E. 11th St.
Roosevelt Rd.
Canal St.
Clinton St.
Chicago River
South Branch

W. 14th St.
E. 13th St.
Michigan Ave.
Indiana Ave.
Clark St.
State St.
Wabash Ave.
Columbus Dr.
S. Lake Shore Dr.
Lake Shore Dr.

Field Museum
Of Natural
History
John G. Shedd
Aquarium
Solidarity Dr.
Adler
Planetarium

TO COMISKEY PARK,
MUSEUM OF SCIENCE
& INDUSTRY, HYDE PARK,
U. OF CHICAGO
Soldier
Field
Burnham
Park
Harbor

Outer
Harbor

Olive
Park

Navy Pier

Lake
Michigan

Monroe
Harbor

Chicago
Harbor

McClurg St.
Michigan Ave.
Ohio St.

0   300 yards
0   300 meters

ner of Clark and Washington St. ☎ 312-236-4548; www.chicagotemple.org. Free.)

STATE STREET. State and Madison St., the most famous intersection of "State Street, that great street," is the focal point of the Chicago street grid as well as another architectural mecca. Louis Sullivan's signature **Carson Pirie Scott** store is adorned with ornate ironwork and wide Chicago windows. Sullivan's other masterpiece, the **Auditorium Building,** now a part of Roosevelt University, sits several blocks south at the corner of Congress St. and Michigan Ave. Once Chicago's tallest building, it typifies Sullivan's obsession with form and function, housing a hotel and an opera house with some of the world's finest acoustics.

OTHER ARCHITECTURAL WONDERS. Burnham and Root's **Monadnock Building** deserves a glance for its alternating bays of purple and brown rock. (53 W. Jackson Blvd.) The $144 million **Harold Washington Library Center** is a researcher's dream come true, as well as a postmodern architectural delight. (400 S. State St. ☎ 312-747-4300. Open M-Th 9am-7pm, F-Sa 9am-4:30pm, Su 1-4:30pm.) On the north side of the Loop, the glass **State of Illinois Building** offers an elevator ride to the top that gives a thrilling view of a sloping atrium, circular floors, and hundreds of employees.

NEAR NORTH

MAGNIFICENT MILE. Chicago counts Paris as one of its sister cities, and the Magnificent Mile must be the Windy City's answer to the Champs-Elysées. Expensive shopping on the order of Tiffany and Cartier lines the stretch of N. Michigan Ave. between the Chicago River and Oak St. Several of these retail stores were designed by the country's foremost architects and merit a look. At Pearson Ave., the squat **Chicago Water Tower** and **Pumping Station** stand out among the orgy of consumption. Built in 1869, these buildings were the only ones in the area to survive the Great Chicago Fire. One block north, the **John Hancock Center** has an exoskeleton of steel girders and glass that casts a stunning figure on the skyline. (875 N. Michigan Ave. ☎ 312-751-3681. Observation deck open daily 9am-11pm. Adults $10, seniors $7.50, ages 5-12 $6.)

TRIBUNE TOWER. Critics of the Tribune Tower, a skyscraper built in 1925, dubbed it the

"Cathedral of Commerce" for its marriage of Gothic religious architecture and American money-grubbing. *The Chicago Tribune* still publishes the largest newspaper in town from the upper floors of this building. (435 N. Michigan Ave.)

NAVY PIER. With a concert pavilion, dining options, nightspots, sightseeing boats ($12), a spectacular Ferris wheel ($5), a crystal garden with palm trees, and an IMAX theater, the mile-long pier is like Las Vegas, Mardi Gras, a Shakespeare festival, and a state fair all rolled into one. Explorers can rent bicycles to navigate the Windy City or hop on a free trolley to State St.; consider taking advantage of reasonable parking rates on the Pier and ride in to get a close-up of downtown. (600 E. Grand Ave. ☎ 312-595-7437 or 800-595-7437; www.navypier.com. Bike rental open daily June-Sept. 8am-11pm; May 8am-8pm; April and Oct. 10am-7pm. $9 per hr., $36 per day.)

OAK PARK

Gunning for the title of the most fantastic suburb in the US, Oak Park is the Chicago sight for any architecture aficionado. The **Oak Park Visitors Center,** 158 N. Forest Ave., offers both metered parking and garage parking for $0.20 per hr. (10 mi. west of downtown, take I-290 W. to Harlem St. ☎ 708-848-1500 or 888-625-7275; www.visitoakpark.com. Open daily in summer 10am-5pm; in winter 10am-4pm.)

UNITY TEMPLE. When Frank Lloyd Wright designed this cubical church, his "jewel box," he declared it the beginning of modern architecture. It was a personal project for Wright, who was a member of the congregation that moved into the completed building. (1 mi. north on Harlem Ave. From I-290, turn east on Lake for ½ mi. to Kenilworth Ave. 875 Lake St. ☎ 708-383-8873; www.unitytemple-utrf.org. Open M-F 10:30am-4:30pm, Sa-Su 1-4pm. Tours M-F by appointment; Sa-Su 1, 2, 3pm. $8, students and seniors $6, under 5 free.)

FRANK LLOYD WRIGHT HOME AND STUDIO. Frank Lloyd Wright's house showcases the evolution of his creative ideas, from conception to reality. Visitors can see not only the studio where he planned his work, but also his house, which was the constantly evolving subject of his architectural experimentation. (From Rte. 66, go north to Chicago Ave. and head east for 3 blocks. 951 Chicago Ave. ☎ 708-848-1976;

www.wrightplus.org. Open daily 10am-5pm. 45min. tours M-F 11am, 1, 3pm; Sa-Su every 20min. 11am-3:30pm. $12, seniors and ages 7-18 $10.)

ERNEST HEMINGWAY BIRTHPLACE AND MUSEUM. Throughout the year, fans flock to the Ernest Hemingway Birthplace and Museum to take part in the many events honoring the architect of the modern American novel. The museum features rare photos of Hemingway, his letters, and other memorabilia. *(Birthplace: 339 N. Oak Park Ave. Museum: 200 N. Oak Park Ave. ☎708-848-2222; www.ehfop.org. Open M-F and Su 1-5pm, Sa 10am-5pm. $7, students and seniors $5.50.)*

THE LAKE. ◪**Lincoln Park** extends across five miles of lakefront on the north side, with winding paths and natural groves of trees. The **Lincoln Park Zoo** is usually filled with herds of children fascinated by the gorillas and lions. *(☎312-742-2000; www.lpzoo.com. Open daily 10am-5pm; in summer Sa-Su until 7pm. Free.)* Next door, the **Lincoln Park Conservatory** is a veritable glass palace of plants from various ecosystems. *(☎312-742-7736. Open daily 9am-5pm. Free.)* **Grant Park,** covering 14 lakefront blocks east of Michigan Ave., follows the 19th-century French park style: symmetrical and ordered, with corners, a fountain, and wide promenades. The Grant Park Concert Society hosts free summer concerts in the **Petrillo Music Shell.** *(520 S. Michigan Ave. ☎312-742-4763.)* Colored lights illuminate **Buckingham Fountain** from 9 to 11pm. Just to the south, the new **Millennium Park** also hosts free concerts and performances, as well as exercise and dance classes. *(☎312-742-1168; www.millenniumpark.org.)* On the north side, Lake Michigan lures swimmers and sunbathers to **Lincoln Park Beach** and **Oak St. Beach.** Beware, though: the rock ledges are restricted areas, and swimming from them is illegal. Although the beaches are patrolled 9am-9:30pm, they can be unsafe after dark. The **Chicago Parks District** has further info. *(☎312-742-7529.)*

MUSEUMS

Chicago's museums range from some of the largest collections in the world to one-room galleries. The first five listings (known as the Big Five) provide a diverse array of exhibits,

while a handful of smaller collections target specific interests. Lake Shore Dr. has been diverted around Grant Park, linking the Field Museum, Adler, and Shedd. This compound, known as Museum Campus, offers a free shuttle between museums. Visitors who plan on seeing the Big Five plus the Hancock Observatory can save money by purchasing a CityPass that grants admission to the sights for nine days, as well as discount coupons for some restaurants and shops. *(☎707-256-0490; www.citypass.com. $50, ages 3-11 $39.)*

◪**ART INSTITUTE OF CHICAGO.** It's easy to feel overwhelmed in this expansive museum, with a collection spanning four millennia of art from Asia, Africa, Europe, and beyond. Make sure to see Chagall's stunning America Windows—the artist's stained-glass tribute to the country's bicentennial—as well as Grant Wood's *American Gothic,* Edward Hopper's *Nighthawks,* and Monet's *Wheatstacks. (111 S. Michigan Ave., at Adams St., in Grant Park. ☎312-443-3600; www.artic.edu/aic. Open M-W 10:30am-5pm, Th-F 10:30am-9pm, Sa-Su 10am-5pm. $12, students and seniors $7, under 12 free. Th and F 5pm-9pm free.)*

SHEDD AQUARIUM. The Shedd, the world's largest indoor aquarium, has over 6600 species of fish and marine life in 206 tanks. The Oceanarium features beluga whales, dolphins, seals, and penguins in a giant pool that appears to flow into Lake Michigan. See piranhas and tropical fish of the rainforest in the "Amazon Rising" exhibit or wave to sharks in the "Caribbean Reef" exhibit. *(1200 S. Lake Shore Dr., in Grant Park. ☎312-939-2438; www.sheddaquarium.org. Open May-Sept. daily 9am-6pm; Sept.-May M-F 9am-5pm, Sa-Su 9am-6pm. Feedings M-F 11am, 2, 3pm. $8, seniors and ages 3-11 $6. Combined admission $23/$16.)*

FIELD MUSEUM OF NATURAL HISTORY. Sue, the Field Museum's mascot and the largest *T. rex* skeleton ever unearthed, towers over excellent geology, anthropology, botany, and zoology exhibits. Other highlights include Egyptian mummies and an exhibit on the evolution of Earth and its creatures. *(1400 S. Lake Shore Dr., at Roosevelt Rd. in Grant Park. ☎312-922-9410; www.fieldmuseum.org. Open daily 9am-5pm, last tickets sold 4pm. $12; students, seniors, and ages 3-11 $6.)*

ROUTE 66

1871: Cyrus Avery, the "Father of Route 66," is born in Pennsylvania.

ROUTE 66 MAP #1

MUSEUM OF SCIENCE AND INDUSTRY.
This museum features the Apollo 8 command module, a full-sized replica of a coal mine, and a host of interactive exhibits on topics from DNA to the Internet. Stop by the Yesterday's Main Street exhibit for a scoop at the 1920s-style ice-cream parlor. *(5700 S. Lake Shore Dr., at 57th St., in Hyde Park. ☎ 773-684-1414; www.msichicago.org Open daily June-Aug. 9:30am-5:30pm; Sept.-May 9:30am-4:30pm. $11, seniors $9.50, ages 3-11 $7; with Omnimax $17/$14.50/$12.)*

ADLER PLANETARIUM. Traditional and digital sky shows bring you face to face with the awesome glory of the cosmos at America's first planetarium, now over 75 years old. Aspiring astronauts can learn their weight on Mars, read the news from space, and explore a medieval observatory. *(1300 S. Lake Shore Dr., on Museum Campus, in Grant Park. ☎ 312-922-7827. Open daily 9:30am-4:30pm. Sky show daily every hr. $16, seniors $15, ages 4-17 $14. Special exhibits $4. Sept.-Dec. M-Tu free.)*

MUSEUM OF CONTEMPORARY ART. The white-and-chrome immensity of this cutting-edge museum provides an ideal backdrop for the ambitious rotating exhibitions within. The beautiful view of Lake Michigan is the only unchanging feature in the MCA's ultra-modern exhibition space. See Warhol's iconic Marilyn or a selection of Calder's mobiles. Call to see what is on display—their collection also includes works by Bruce Nauman, Francis Bacon, and Joseph Beuys. *(220 E. Chicago Ave., 1 block east of 3 Michigan Ave. ☎ 312-280-2660; www.mcachicago.org. Open Tu 10am-8pm, W-Su 10am-5pm. $10, students and seniors $6, under 12 free. Tu free.)*

MUSEUM OF HOLOGRAPHY. This unconventional museum explores the wild world of holograms, including fantastic hologram pictures of famous people. *(1134 W. Washington Blvd., just west of the Loop. ☎ 312-226-1007. Open W-Su 12:30-5pm. $4, under 12 $3.)*

INTERNATIONAL MUSEUM OF SURGICAL SCIENCE. This quirkily specific museum details the history of healthcare around the world, from a room filled by the original apparatus for X-rays to a fully tricked-out apothecary. If you've never seen a human skull, this is your chance. *(1524 N. Lake Shore Dr., at North Ave. ☎ 312-642-6502; www.imss.org. Open May-*

Sept. daily 9am-4pm; Oct.-Apr. M-Sa 10am-4pm. $6, students and seniors $3. Tu free.)

FOOD

Chicago's many culinary delights, from pizza to po' boy sandwiches, are among its main attractions. One of the best guides to city dining is the monthly *Chicago* magazine, which includes an extensive restaurant section, indexed by price, cuisine, and quality. It can be found at tourist offices and newsstands throughout the city.

PIZZA

Lou Malnati's, 439 N. Wells St. (☎312-828-9800; www.loumalnatis.com), downtown. A Chicago mainstay for over 30 years. Lou used to be in business with the founders of Pizzeria Uno's, but in the mid-70s, irreconcilably divided over recipes, they went their separate ways. Today rivalry remains fierce over whose pies are Chicago's finest. Pizzas $4.50-20. Open M-Th 11am-11pm, F 11am-11:30pm, Sa 11am-midnight, Su noon-10pm. AmEx/D/MC/V. ❸

Pizzeria Uno's, 29 E. Ohio St. (☎312-321-1000), at the corner of Wabash and Ohio St. It may look like any other Uno's, but this is where the legacy of deep-dish began in 1943. Pizza (large $20) takes 45min. to prepare, but the world-famous pies have a taste worth the wait. Individual-sized pies ($5) only take 25min. Open M-F 11:30am-1am, Sa 11:30am-2am, Su 11:30am-11:30pm. AmEx/D/DC/MC/V. ❸

Gino's East of Chicago, 633 N. Wells St. (☎312-988-4200; www.ginoseast.com), at Ontario, 7 blocks west of Michigan Ave. The writing on the wall proclaims this the best pizza around. Signs invite you to make your own mark on the already heavily decorated surfaces of the restaurant. Appetizers ($3-8), deep-dish or thin-crust pizza ($11-22), and pasta ($10). Lunch combos $6.25. Open M-Th 11am-9pm, F-Sa 11am-11pm, Su noon-9pm. MC/V. ❸

THE LOOP

Lou Mitchell's, W. Jackson St. (☎312-939-3111), at the corner of Jefferson St., 2 mi. west of the start of Rte. 66. Recently inducted into the Restaurant Hall of Fame, this retro diner has been stuffing faithful customers for 80 years. Start the day with "the world's finest cup of coffee" ($1.75) or end with a piece of homemade pie. Lines are long but move fast. Female customers get free Milk Duds and

doughnut holes while they wait. Open M-Sa 5:30am-3pm, Su 7am-3pm. Cash only. ❷

Heaven on Seven, 111 Wabash Ave. (☎312-263-6443; www.heavenonseven.com), in the Garland building. Mardi Gras beads festoon shelves and shelves of hot sauce at this folksy Louisiana-style eatery. Heat lovers can try the Angry Burger ($8), topped with the hottest sauce they make. Open M-F 8:30am-5pm, Sa 10am-3pm. Cash only. ❸

RIVER NORTH

Ed Debevic's, 640 N. Wells St. (☎312-644-1707; www.eddebevics.com), at Ontario, across from Gino's East Pizza. Valet parking ($7) or on-street metered parking. Half 1950s diner, half sassy spectacle, with the slogan "eat and get out." Ed Debevic's features uniformly irreverent, poodle-skirted waitresses who dance on countertops. Appetizers from $3. Burgers $8. Shakes $4. Open M-Th and Su 11am-9pm, F-Sa 11am-11pm. AmEx/D/DC/MC/V. ❸

Portillo's Hotdogs, 100 W. Ontario St. (☎312-587-8910; www.portillos.com), at Clark St. Portillo's won so many "Silver Platter" awards for its tasty hot dogs that it retired for 5 years to give the competition a chance. Try the famous all-beef hot dog on a poppy-seed bun ($2), best with a schooner of beer (from $3). Open M-F and Su 10am-midnight, drive-in until 1am; Sa 10am-1am, drive-in until 2am. MC/V. ❶

Al's #1 Italian Beef, 169 W. Ontario St. (☎312-943-3222; www.alsbeef.com), at N. Wells St. You can get some of America's best sandwiches at this no-frills, fast-beef eatery. Sandwiches $6. Burgers $4. Open M-Th 10am-midnight, F-Sa 10am-3am, Su 11am-10pm. AmEx/D/DC/MC/V. ❶

SOUTH SIDE

Dixie Kitchen and Bait Shop, 5225A S. Harper St. (☎773-363-4943), in Hyde Park. Metered lot across the street. Tucked in a parking lot on 52nd St., Dixie's looks like a garage sale exploded. You might want to eat with your eyes first—coffee cans, bottles, signs, and even a gas pump decorate the walls. Fried catfish $10.50. Open M-Th and Su 11am-10pm, F-Sa 11am-11pm. AmEx/D/MC/V. ❷

Manny's Coffee Shop & Deli, 1141 S. Jefferson St. (☎312-939-2855; www.mannysdeli.com), 1 block east of Rte. 90, off the Madison St. exit. Serving up "Chicago's best corned beef since 1942," this enormous and locally worshipped kosher coffee shop serves up huge and affordably priced servings cafeteria-style. 2 eggs and corned beef hash $5.25. Open M-Sa 5am-4pm. ❶

LINCOLN PARK

Penny's Noodle Shop, 950 W. Diversey Ave. (☎ 773-281-8448), at Sheffield Ave. One of the best budget options in town, Penny's presents generous portions of Asian noodles (all under $7) in a bright, inviting setting. Open M-Th and Su 11am-10pm, F-Sa 11am-10:30pm. MC/V. ❷

Cafe Ba-Ba-Reeba!, 2024 N. Halsted St. (☎ 773-935-5000; www.cafebabareeba.com), just north of Armitage. With a rich and dark wood interior and artistic signs announcing upcoming wine tastings and cooking classes, Ba-Ba-Reeba has unbeatable tapas ($4-8) and frequent flamenco performances. Reservations recommended. Open M-Th and Su 5-10pm, F-Sa noon-midnight. AmEx/D/DC/MC/V. ❸

BUCKTOWN/WICKER PARK

The Smoke Daddy, 1804 W. Division St. (☎ 773-772-6656; www.thesmokedaddy.com), in Wicker Park. Pulled pork ($8.50) and finger-lickin' rib platters ($9.50-20) definitely justify the neon "WOW" sign dangling out front. Live blues and jazz daily 9:30pm. Open M-W and Su 11:30am-11pm, Th-Sa 11:30am-1am. AmEx/MC/V. ❷

Alliance Bakery & Cafe, 1736 W. Division St. (☎ 773-278-0366). When the owners of an 80-year-old Polish bakery scrape together the cash to buy an adjacent storefront next to their bakery, you might expect them to use it for storing flour. In Wicker Park, however, they have converted the space into a luminous coffeehouse where twentysomethings type away at their laptops. Open M-Sa 6am-9pm, Su 7am-9pm. AmEx/MC/V. ❶

Handlebar, 2311 W. North Ave. (☎ 773-384-9546). Launched in 2003 by a local brewer who loved bicycling, Handlebar features bar stools made out of the rims of bicycle wheels. Dive into a dish of West African groundnut stew ($7.75), or swing by for brunch Sa-Su. Open M-W 4pm-midnight, Th-F 4pm-2am, Sa 10pm-2am, Su 10am-midnight. AmEx/D/DC/MC/V. ❷

▌ ACCOMMODATIONS

It's easy to find a cheap, convenient place to rest your head at one of Chicago's many hostels. The motels on **Lincoln Ave.** in Lincoln Park

are moderately priced. Motel chains off the interstates, about 1hr. from downtown, are out of the way and more expensive (from $35), but are an option for late arrivals. **At Home Inn Chicago** (☎ 800-375-7084) offers a reservation and referral service for many downtown B&Bs. Most have a two-night minimum stay, and rooms average around $120. Chicago has a **15% tax** on most accommodation rates.

■ **Hostelling International Chicago (HI-AYH),** 24 E. Congress Pkwy. (☎ 312-360-0300; www.hichicago.org), off Wabash St. in the Loop. The location offers easy access to the major museums during the day, but be careful on the deserted streets of the Loop at night. Foosball, pool tables, and fun organized outings give the hostel a lively social atmosphere to match the bright decor. Laundry. Internet $1 per 10min. Reception 24hr. Check-out 11am. Reservations recommended. Dorms $39, members $36. MC/V. ❷

Arlington House, 616 W. Arlington Pl. (☎ 773-929-5380; www.arlingtonhouse.com), in Lincoln Park. A giant renovated nursing home, this massive hostel is so full in the summer that it's a scramble to get one of their 140+ dorm beds. Private and double rooms are also available, but they get pricey fast. Laundry $1.75. Internet $1 per 4min. Key deposit $10. Reception 24hr. Reservations recommended. International guests have priority for dorms. Dorms $28; private rooms with shared bath from $63. MC/V. ❶

International House, 1414 E. 59th St. (☎ 773-753-2270), at the corner of 59th and Blackstone on the University of Chicago campus. The marble floors and ornate trim make the International House seem more like a snazzy hotel than a student residential hall. Guests must be affiliated with some institution of learning (being a "student of life" does not count). Laundry, coffee shop, tennis courts, game room, and weight room access. Reservations recommended. Dorms $52; singles $62; doubles $67. MC/V. ❸

The Write Inn, 211 N. Oak Park Ave. (☎ 708-383-4800; www.writeinn.com), in Oak Park. This historic building transports guests into the 1920s with select antique furnishings and quilt-laden box-frame beds. Free Wi-Fi. Reception 24hr. Reservations recommended. Rooms from $79. AmEx/MC/V. ❹

Hotel Wacker, 111 W. Huron St. (☎ 312-787-1386), at the corner of N. Clark St. A giant, green, formerly neon sign on the corner makes this place easy to find. It unsuccessfully mimics classier hotels, but you won't get a room for this price and location anywhere else. Key and linen deposit $5. Reception 24hr. Singles $60; doubles $65. Cash only. ❸

Ohio House Motel, 600 N. LaSalle St. (☎312-943-6000), at Ohio St. This 2-story inn looks out of place among its skyscraping neighbors, but it puts guests within easy walking distance of Near North and Loop attractions. TV and private baths. Free parking. Reservations recommended. Queen or 2 twin beds $90; 2 double beds $120. AmEx/MC/V. ❹

♫ ENTERTAINMENT

The free weeklies *Chicago Reader* and *New City*, available in many bars, record stores, and restaurants, list the latest events. The *Reader* comes out each Thursday and reviews all major shows with times and ticket prices. *Chicago* magazine includes theater reviews alongside exhaustive club, music, dance, and opera listings. *The Chicago Tribune* includes an entertainment section every Friday. *Gay Chicago* provides info on social activities as well as other news for the area's gay community.

THEATER AND COMEDY

One of the foremost theater centers of North America, Chicago's more than 150 theaters feature everything from blockbuster musicals to off-color parodies. Downtown, the recently formed **Theater District** centers on State St. and Randolph and includes the larger venues in the city. Smaller theaters are scattered throughout Chicago. Most tickets are expensive. Half-price tickets are sold on the day of performance at **Hot Tix booths**, at 108 N. State St., and on the 6th fl. of 700 N. Michigan Ave. Purchases must be made in person. (☎312-977-1755. Open M-F 10am-7pm, Sa 10am-6pm, Su noon-5pm.) **Ticketmaster** (☎312-559-1212; www.broadwayinchicago.com) supplies tickets for many theaters; ask about discounts at all Chicago shows. The "Off-Loop" theaters on the North Side put on original productions, with tickets usually under $18. Both Gary Sinise and John Malkovich got their start at the ◪**Steppenwolf Theater**, 1650 N. Halsted St. (☎312-335-1888; www.steppenwolf.org). **Bailiwick Repertory**, 1225 W. Belmont Ave. (☎773-

883-1090; www.bailiwick.org), is a mainstage and experimental studio space.

The most famous comedy club in town, ◪**Second City**, 1616 N. Wells St. (☎312-642-8189; www.secondcity.com), at North Ave., spoofs Chicago life and politics. Alums include Bill Murray, John Candy, and John Belushi. Most nights a free improv session follows the show. Watch improv actors compete to bust your gut at **Comedy Sportz**, 2851 N. Halsted, where two teams of comedians create sketches based on audience suggestions. (☎773-549-8080. Tickets $17. Shows Th 8pm, F-Sa 8 and 10:30pm.)

DANCE, MUSIC, AND OPERA

Ballet, comedy, live theater, and musicals are performed at **Auditorium Theatre**, 50 E. Congress Pkwy. (☎312-922-2110; www.auditoriumtheatre.org. Box office open M-F 10am-6pm.) From October through May, the sounds of the **Chicago Symphony Orchestra** resonate throughout **Symphony Center**, 220 S. Michigan Ave. (☎312-294-3000; www.cso.org). **Ballet Chicago** performs throughout theaters in Chicago. (☎312-251-8838; www.balletchicago.org. Tickets $12-45.) The acclaimed **Lyric Opera of Chicago** performs from September through March at the **Civic Opera House**, 20 N. Wacker Dr. (☎312-332-2244; www.lyricopera.org). While other places may demand more of your wallet than your wallet is prepared to give, the **Grant Park Music Festival** affords a taste of classical music for free. From mid-June through late August, the acclaimed **Grant Park Symphony Orchestra** plays a few free evening concerts per week at the Grant Park **Petrillo Music Shell**. (☎312-742-4763; www.grantparkmusicfestival.com. Usually W-Su; schedule varies.)

FESTIVALS

The city celebrates summer on a grand scale. During the first week in June, the **Blues Festival** celebrates the city's soulful music. The **Chicago Gospel Festival** takes place in mid-June, and Nashville moves north for the **Country Music Festival** at the end of June. In early July, the **Taste of Chicago** festival cooks for eight days. Seventy-plus restaurants set up booths with endless samples in Grant Park, while crowds chow down to the blast of big-name bands. The Taste's fireworks are the city's biggest. The **¡Viva Chicago!** Latin music festival steams up in late August, while the **Chicago Jazz Festival** scats over Labor Day weekend. All festivals center on the Grant Park Petrillo Music Shell. The Mayor's Office's **Special Events Hotline** (☎312-744-3370; www.cityofchicago.com/specialevents.com.) Pick up an official visitor's guide at the visitors center for a list of upcoming events.

The regionally famous **Ravinia Festival** (☎312-847-266-5100; www.ravinia.org), in the northern suburb of Highland Park, runs from late June to early September. During the festival's 14-week season, the Chicago Symphony orchestra, ballet troups, folk and jazz musicians, and comedians perform. On certain nights, the Orchestra allows free lawn admission with student ID. (Shows 8pm, occasionally 4:30 and 7pm; call ahead. Lawn seats $10-15, other seats $20-75.)

SPORTS

The National League's **Cubs** step up to bat at **Wrigley Field**, 1060 W. Addison St., at N. Clark St. (☎773-404-2827; www.cubs.com. Tickets $17-60.) The **White Sox**, Chicago's American League team, swing on the South Side at **Comiskey Park**, 333 W. 35th St. (☎312-674-1000. Tickets $14-55) The **Bears** of the NFL play at the renovated **Soldier Field**, 425 E. McFetridge Dr. (☎888-792-3277. Tickets $45-65.) Basketball's **Bulls** have won three NBA championships at the **United Center**, 1901 W. Madison, just west of the Loop. (☎312-943-5800. Tickets $30-450.) Hockey's **Blackhawks** skate onto United Center ice when the Bulls aren't playing. (☎312-455-4500. Tickets $25-100.) **Sports Information** (☎312-976-4242) has additional info.

▨ NIGHTLIFE

Chicago is proud of the innumerable blues performers who have played here. Jazz, folk, reggae, and punk clubs groove, step, jam, and pogo all over the **N. Side**. The **Bucktown/Wicker Park** area stays open late with bars and clubs. Some of the best dancing in town is at **Rush St.** and **Division St.** Full of bars, cafes, and bistros, **Lincoln Park** is frequented by singles and young couples, both gay and straight. The center of gay culture is between 3000 and 4500 **N. Halsted St.** For more upscale raving and discoing, there are plenty of clubs near **River North**, in **Riverwest**, and on **Fullerton St.**

BARS AND BLUES JOINTS

▨ **The Green Mill,** 4802 N. Broadway Ave. (☎773-878-5552). Once a Prohibition-era speakeasy favored by Al Capone, the Green Mill has phased out gangsters and gun-runners in favor of elegant live jazz. Things get lively again late in the evening. The jam sessions on weekends after main acts finish (no cover) are reason enough to chill until the wee hours. Cover $5-15. Open M-Sa noon-5am, Su noon-4am. AmEx only.

Kingston Mines, 2548 N. Halsted St. (☎773-477-4647). Mick Jagger and Bob Dylan have been known to frequent this venerable club, which has dueling blues acts alternating on 2 stages. Live blues daily from 9:30pm. Appetizers $6. Cover $8-15. Open M-F and Su 8pm-4am, Sa 8pm-5am. AmEx/D/MC/V.

The Hideout, 1354 W. Wabansia Ave. (☎773-227-4433). Tucked away in a municipal truck parking lot, this bar and performance space lures hipsters with indie rock shows and families with a late-Sept. block party. Cover Tu-F $5-10. Open M 8pm-2am, Tu-F 4pm-2am, Sa 7pm-3am. Cash only.

B.L.U.E.S., 2519 N. Halsted St. (☎773-528-1012; www.chicagobluesbar.com). Chicago's oldest blues bar focuses on local blues acts and packs in patrons elbow-to-elbow on weekends. Albert King, Bo Diddley, Wolfman Washington, and Dr. John have played here. Live blues every night 9:30pm-2am. Cover M-Th $6-8, F-Sa $8-10. Open M-F and Su 8pm-2am, Sa 8pm-3am. AmEx/D/DC/MC/V.

Sweet Home Blue Chicago, 736 N. Clark St. (☎312-642-6261; www.bluechicago.com), at Grand St. This live music joint is one of the newest hot spots for classic Chicago blues. A sister location is just down the street at 536 N. Clark St. Cover $8. Open M-F 8pm-2am; Sa 8pm-3am. AmEx/D/MC/V.

DANCE CLUBS

Berlin, 954 W. Belmont Ave. (☎773-348-4975; www.berlinchicago.com), just off Halsted St. Anything goes at Berlin, a black-and-neon, gay-friendly mainstay of Chicago's nightlife. Crowds pulsate to house dance music amid drag contests and disco nights. W ladies night. Cover F-Sa $3. Open M-F 4pm-4am, Sa 2pm-5am, Su 4pm-2am. Cash only.

Funky Buddha Lounge, 728 W. Grand Ave. (☎312-666-1695; www.funkybuddha.com). Trendy, eclectic dance club where hip-hop and funk blend with leopard and velvet decor. W soul and R&B night. Cover after 10pm $10 for women, $20 for men. Open M-W 10pm-2am, Th-F 9pm-2am, Sa 9pm-3am, Su 6pm-2am. AmEx/MC/V.

The Apartment, 2251 N. Lincoln Ave. (☎773-348-5100). On a street packed with generic pubs, this heavily themed club stands out. Sit on sofas in front of the fireplace and play Playstation 2, lounge in the master bedroom, or chat in the faux kitchen. A duckie-curtained bathtub of beer satisfies most requests, but if you have more mixed cravings, just head downstairs to the **Lion's Head Pub.** No cover. Open W-Th 9pm-2am, F-Sa 9pm-3am. AmEx/D/MC/V.

Hydrate, 3458 N. Halsted St.(☎773-975-9244; www.hydratechicago.com). The red-lit club is a favorite of the gay-oriented stretch of Halsted St. Smiling, heavily muscled male bartenders bring in, unsurprisingly, a smiling, heavily male crowd. W drag show 9:30pm. Go-go dancers nightly. No cover.

Spin, 3200 Halsted St. (☎773-327-7711; www.spinnightclub.com), at Belmont St. Themed nights and a fabulous disco ball make Spin a popular new club on the gay scene in the Lincoln Park area. M free pool, W hip-hop, Th retro video night, F shower contest. Lots of boys and girls. M-Tu and Th-F 4pm-2am, W 8pm-2am, Sa 2pm-3am, Su 2pm-2am. Cash only.

⚐ APPROACHING RIVERSIDE: 14 MILES
Just west of the Art Institute of Chicago on Adams St., an unimposing road sign marks the beginning of "The Mother Road," **Rte. 66.** To begin at the very beginning, follow **Lake Shore Dr.** to **Jackson St.,** then turn west on **Adams St.** Follow Adams St. 2½ mi. west

until you hit **Ogden St.** then angle left on Ogden St., and continue 10 mi. to **Harlem Ave. (I-43).** Turn right on Harlem Ave. to reach Riverside.

RIVERSIDE. Run by the Stanga family for over 20 years, the **Riverside Family Restaurant ❷,** 3422 S. Harlem Ave., serves giant portions of Czech food for cheap, cheap, cheap. Enormous plates of *wiener schnitzel,* duck, or pork come with delicious, warm rye bread and your choice of sauerkraut, applesauce, cabbage, or beets, plus dessert and a bottomless cup of coffee—all for an astounding $6-8. Be sure to try the apricot *kolashky* ($1) for dessert. (☎708-442-6055. Open Tu-Sa 11am-8pm, Su 11am-7pm. Cash only.)

⚐ APPROACHING BERWYN: 3 MILES
From Riverside, continue north on **Harlem Ave.**

 DID YOU KNOW? Illinois produces more swiss cheese than any other state in the US.

BERWYN. Nothing starts a road trip quite like a jolt of wry sobriety in the form of a 50 ft. tower of impaled cars in the middle of a parking lot. The **"Spindle,"** as the structure is named, is just one of several artistic statements scattered throughout the Cermak Plaza in the town of Berwyn. Don't miss the flattened VW as you enter from Harlem Ave. (1¾ mi. north of Ogden St. intersection, on Harlem Ave. Turn right after 26th St.)

BELLOW'S CHICAGO

The late Saul Bellow set a number of his brainy, bombastic novels in his adopted hometown of Chicago. Indeed, some of the most memorable passages in his fiction hinge upon the geography of the city he loved.

1. In *The Adventures of Augie March,* Bellow's breakout novel of 1953, the title character steals books from Carson Pirie Scott, 1 S. State St. Instead of fencing the books for profit, however, Augie ends up reading most of them and re-examining his priorities in life.

2. Charlie Citrine of *Humboldt's Gift* pays off mobster Rinaldo Cantabile at the tumbledown Russian Baths, 1916 W. Division St.

3. The title character of Bellow's *Herzog* graduated from McKinley High School, 2040 W. Adams, and pronounced to the Class of 1934 that "the main enterprise of the world...is the upbuilding of a man." Today the school has been razed to make room for a multiplex cinema.

4. With graves dating back to the 1860s, the Jewish Waldheim Cemetary, 1800 S. Harlem Ave., is the largest Jewish burial site in Chicago. This made it an unlikely, but somehow perfect place for the marriage proposal at the very end of Bellow's 1997 novella *The Actual.*

ⓝ APPROACHING LEMONT: 20 MILES

Turn left on **Harlem Ave.** and drive 10½ mi. south. Then turn right onto **Joliet Rd.** Rte. 66 is well-marked through these parts—look for the brown-and-white signs by the roadside leading you down "Historic Route 66." To follow the original Rte. 66 alignment, follow Joliet Rd. for 7 mi. until it merges with **I-55** where Rte. 66 has been paved over. Continue on I-55 S/Rte. 66. Take **Exit 271A** for **Lemont Rd.**, and drive south for 3 mi. Head west after crossing the bridge, where Lemont Rd. becomes **State St.** and turn left onto **Main St.**

LEMONT

This town, 6 mi. south of where Joliet Rd. joins I-55, offers a surprisingly interesting historic district. Almost out of place in its grandeur atop the hill overlooking Lemont, the lavishly carved **Hindu Temple of Greater Chicago**, 10915 Lemont Rd., is a religious and community center for the Hindus of Chicago. (1¼ mi. north of downtown Lemont. ☎630-972-0300. Open daily 9am-9pm; in winter open until 8pm.) Thousands of cookie jars of all shapes and sizes are on display in the **Cookie Jar Museum**, 111 Stephen St. Tragically, none of them contain cookies. Call Lucille, founder and proprietor, in the early evening for appointments to visit the museum. (☎630-257-5012.)

At the same location for 75 years, in the various guises of pharmacy, garage sale, and convenience store, **Budnik's**, 400 Main St. (☎630-257-6224), sells everything from cigars to china. **Lemont Lanes Bowling Alley**, 1015 State St., may look like your typical ball-hurling venue, but it also dishes out a dirt-cheap breakfast of champions. (☎630-257-1994. Omelettes $5. Pancakes $3.50. Open Tu-Sa 7am-9pm. Cash only.) In the same building as the bowling alley, **Vito and Nick's Pizza ❸**, 1015 State St., serves delectable slices. (☎630-257-9536; www.vitoandnick.com. Pizzas $10-13. Sandwiches $6. Cash only.) **Nick's Tavern ❷**, 221 Main St., is the home of the Nickburger ($5), and features colored hanging lights, holographic wallpaper, and figurines from JFK to giant hamburgers. (☎630-257-6564. Open M-Sa 10am-midnight. Grill open until 10:30pm. Cash only.)

ⓝ APPROACHING JOLIET: 14 MILES

Leave Lemont the only way you can: south on **I-55**. To continue following Rte. 66, exit I-55 8 mi. south of Lemont, at **Exit 269**. Head south on **Joliet Rd.** Joliet Rd. is marked as **Rte. 53**, but every mile or so, you should see the easily distinguishable Historic Rte. 66 markers. Call it wild speculation, but 9 mi. south from picking up Joliet Rd. you'll find the **Ilinois State Police.** Hit the gas too hard here, and you might find yourself a quarter-mile down the road quicker than you expected, at one of Joliet's most well-known landmarks, the **Department of Corrections.**

JOLIET

For lunch or a tour of the Rte. 66 welcome center, stick to the north side of Joliet, though supermarkets, gas stations, and banks abound farther south. Folks at the **Joliet Historical Museum and Welcome Center,** 214 N. Ottawa St., are only too happy to share the stories of the blue Cadillacs in the lobby. The Rte. 66 memorabilia collection is showcased as part of the official Joliet Route 66 Welcome Center. Entrance to the welcome center (and Rte. 66 gift shop) is free. (☎815-722-7225. Open Tu-Sa 10am-5pm, Su noon-5pm. Tours Tu-Sa 11am and 3pm. Joliet Historical Museum $5, students and seniors $4, children $3.) A restored vaudeville theater guarded by massive two-story columns, the **Rialto Square Theatre,** 102 N. Chicago St., was designed to resemble the Hall of Mirrors at Versailles and is supposedly haunted. (☎815-726-6600. Box office open M-F 9am-5pm, Sa 9am-noon.) Three miles south of Joliet, racecar enthusiasts can watch the pros get their kicks at the **Chicagoland Speedway,** which sits on 930 acres and seats over 75,000. **Rte. 66 Raceway,** Chicagoland's sister track, is nearby. (☎815-727-7223; www.chicagolandspeedway.com.)

Follow the lunch crowd to the **Sandwich Shoppe ❶**, 79 N. Chicago St., for $5 subs or $4 salads. (☎815-723-8071. Open M-F 8am-3pm. Cash only.) The **Chicago Street Pub ❷**, 75 N. Chicago St., has classy beer ads and mirrors along with its reasonably priced fare. Try their flagship meal, the Guinness-braised beef stew ($7.50), while indulging in a draught of ale. (☎815-727-7171; www.chicagost.com. Sandwiches $6.50. Live music M, W, Sa 9pm. Cover W and Sa $3. Open M-F 11am-10pm, Sa 5-10pm, Su 1-8pm. MC/V.) Low-cost lunches, prepared by students of culinary art at Joliet Junior College, are available across the lobby from the Historical Society at the **Renaissance Room ❸**,

214 N. Ottawa St. Wednesdays and Fridays feature an all-you-can-eat lunch buffet for $7. (☎815-280-1443. Open M-F 11am-1:30pm, Sa by reservation only, Su 10am-2pm. D/MC/V.) For a cheap night of sleep, the **Hotel Plaza ❷**, 26 Clinton St., has standard rooms with minimal amenities. (☎815-726-6195. Key deposit $5. Singles $28; doubles $34. Cash only.)

APPROACHING WILMINGTON: 16 MILES
Take **Ottawa St.** left, following signs for **Rte. 6 W, Rte. 53 S**, and **Rte. 66**. Expect to see cornfield after cornfield; they're "knee-high by the fourth of July"

WILMINGTON. Nothing says Rte. 66 like the 28 ft. tall Gemini Giant, the first of three giants you'll encounter along the way and the mascot of the **Launching Pad Drive-In ❶**, at the corner of Daniels St. and Rte. 66. Rte. 66 wallpaper and map-covered tabletops let you trace your path while enjoying tasty eats. (☎815-476-6535; www.launchingpadrt66.com. Hamburgers $1.10. Shakes $2. Open daily 9am-10pm. Cash only.) From May to September, Mr. Van Duyne of the **Van Duyne Motel ❷**, 107 Bridge St., offers canoe trips ($35) up the river and opens his Rte. 66 memorabilia-lined balcony for cookouts and socializing. The spotless rooms in the motel each come with mini-fridge, microwave, cable TV, and a private bathroom. (1 mi. south of central Wilmington. ☎815-476-2801. Singles $45-60. D/MC/V.)

APPROACHING BRAIDWOOD: 2 MILES
Continue south on **Rte. 66**. Keep your eyes peeled for the fireflies that cavort through the fields at dusk.

BRAIDWOOD. Elvis, Marilyn, James Dean, and Betty Boop welcome you to the parking lot of the **Polka Dot Drive-In ❶**, 222 N. Front St. Even without the celebrities, you could hardly miss the spinning, neon-pink sign of this chrome-and-checkered 50s diner, which was originally located in a white bus decorated with rainbow polka dots. Stop by the first Saturday in August for the annual Rte. 66 roadster cruise. (☎815-458-3377. Burgers $1.50. Chicken $7.25. Open daily in summer 11am-9pm; in winter 11am-8pm. MC/V.) Right across the tracks is the clean and comfortable **Braidwood Motel ❷**, 120 N. Washington St. Rooms have fridges and cable TV. (☎815-458-2321. Reception 24hr. Check-out 11am. Singles $30; doubles $38. AmEx/D/MC/V.)

APPROACHING GARDNER: 9 MILES
Continue south on **Rte. 66** for 6 mi. If your hunger pangs are too intense to wait, stop by the ◙ **Riviera Restaurant ❷**, 5650 Rte. 53. "Al Capone passed gas here in 1932," proclaims the sign by the toilet in the bathroom, and Gene Kelly danced through the parking lot on his way to Hollywood. Watch out for resident ghost Charley. (☎815-237-2344. Open Tu-Th 5-9pm, F-Sa 5-10pm, Su 4-9pm. Cash only.) Turn right on **E. Washington St.** to head into downtown Gardner.

GARDNER. From E. Washington St., follow the brown, historical directional signs to the **two-cell jail**, a local landmark. Built in 1906 and used up until the 60s, this tiny building holds an old cast-iron-stove and just two small jail cells. Also on-site are papers detailing the feats of the legendary Rev. Christiansen. (Open daily. Free.) Find a haven of wall-scribbling at **Curley's**, 114 Depot St., an ancient beer-meets-arts-and-crafts establishment. (☎815-237-8060. Beer $2. Open M 3pm-1:30am, Tu-Su 11am-1:30am. Cash only.)

APPROACHING DWIGHT: 10 MILES
Heading south on **Rte. 66,** watch for turns in the road; they are all marked by familiar brown signs. 3 mi. south of Gardner, take a right onto **Rte. 53** and go over the railroad tracks, then follow the signs directing you left on **Rte. 66** 10 mi. later.

DWIGHT. Another railroad town over the tracks, Dwight prides itself on its refurbished windmill. As you pass through the south end of town, the **Becker Marathon Gas Station** on the left dates back to 1932. To see downtown Dwight, head east toward the railroad tracks and turn right onto E. Main St. The garish "Mother Road" decorations on the outside match the part-"God Bless America," part-"God Bless Route 66" interior of the **Old 66 Family Restaurant ❷**, 105 S. Old 66, 2 mi. south of town. This restaurant does a brisk business, and for good reason. (☎815-584-2920. Burgers $3. Chicken bucket $8. Open M-Th and Su 5am-9pm, F-Sa 5am-10pm. D/MC/V.)

APPROACHING PONTIAC: 17 MILES
Continue south, following the brown **"Historic Rte. 66"** signs. Even where Rte. 66 has been paved over or routed under I-55, divergent rows of telephone poles peeling off into the distance reveal the old path of the Mother Road. Nine miles south of **Dwight,** you'll diverge from I-55 to follow the **railroad.** One mile into

ROUTE 66

Odell, you'll see the **Standard Oil Company Gas Station** (with sign proudly proclaiming "87 mi. from Chicago, 2361 from L.A."). This restored station was the recent winner of the "Best Preservation Project on all of Rte. 66" award. Don't roll in on an empty tank—you can fill up on 66 memorabilia, but not on gas.

PONTIAC. Famed for its ornate courthouse and extensive veterans memorials, Pontiac has several elegant swinging bridges abutting the Chatauqua recreation area; the popular saying is: "Pontiac has three swinging bridges, and we're a swinging town!" The **Pontiac Route 66 Museum,** 110 W. Howard St., has a wealth of memorabilia, including a map stamped at every post office on Rte. 66 and original diner booths. (☎815-844-4566. Open M-F 11am-3pm, Sa 10am-4pm. Free.) When Rte. 66 was rerouted away from the railroad tracks, the whole **Old Log Cabin Food and Spirits** building, just off the northbound side of Rte. 66, was jacked up and turned around to keep it facing the road. Decorated with discarded telephone poles by the founding Selotis brothers in the early 1920s, today the log cabin is one of the dining highlights of the road, putting kitsch to shame with its genuine laid-back reverence for the old road and extremely friendly and road-knowledgeable staff. (☎815-842-2908. Shockingly bright bottles of Rte. 66 pop $1.50. Open M-Tu 5am-4pm, W-Sa 5am-8pm.)

◢ APPROACHING BLOOMINGTON AND NORMAL: 32 MILES
Continue south on **Rte. 66** with railroad tracks and stocky telephone poles to your left. After 7¾ mi. look to the right to see signs detailing a historical stretch of original 66 known as **Dead Man's Curve,** which was an accident-heavy right-angle turn until it was altered after WWII. Shortly afterwards, check out the 6 bright orange original Burma Shave ads from 1927, spaced 100 paces apart and reading, "The wolf—is shaved—so nice and trim—red riding hood—is chasing him—Burma Shave." 29 mi. south of **Pontiac,** Rte. 66 is not a straight shot, so pay close attention to signs.

BLOOMINGTON AND NORMAL

The "twin cities" of Bloomington and Normal, about 127 mi. from Chicago, are home to an array of food and lodging establishments, as well as a significant student population, thanks to the presence of **Illinois State University** in Normal and **Illinois Wesleyan University** in Bloomington. If driving is already getting you down, take advantage of the **Constitution Trail,** a joint Bloomington/Normal recreational venture, including over 20 mi. of trails throughout the two cities. Built for Supreme Court Justice and longtime Lincoln associate David Davis, the **David Davis Mansion** displays the elegant home and lifestyle of one of Illinois's most celebrated politicians. (☎309-828-1084. Tours W-Sa 9am-4pm. Suggested donation $2, children $1.) The majestic **Ewing Manor,** 48 Sunset Rd., at the corner of Towanda Ave. and Emerson St., looms like a castle above the surrounding wooded area. Although visitors can tour the manor only by appointment, in the summer locals gather for a **Shakespeare festival** put on in the theater out back. The manor has two lovely gardens, one Japanese and the other Elizabethan. (☎309-829-6333; www.ewingmanor.ilstu.edu. Shakespeare Festival: ☎309-438-8110; www.thefestival.org. Seats from $20; students from $16.)

Playboy ranked **Pub II ❶,** 102 N. Linden St., among its top 100 campus bars. With sports posters galore and video games, Pub II doesn't disappoint its fun-loving patrons. (☎309-452-0699. Burgers $2.50. Open in summer M-Sa 11am-1am, Su 4pm-1am; in winter M-Sa 11am-1am, Su noon-1am. MC/V.) Standard chain motels are found around Normal and Bloomington, particularly to the north near Normal. For a break from roadside digs, visit stately, antique-laden **Davis Inn Bed & Breakfast ❹,** 1001 E. Jefferson St., across from the David Davis Mansion in Bloomington. (☎309-829-6854; www.davisinnbb.com. Rooms F-Su from $99, M-Th from $59.)

◢ APPROACHING SHIRLEY: 9 MILES
From Bloomington, head south on **Center St.** through town, following the signs toward I-55. 4 mi. south of where Bloomington and Normal meet, things get tricky. Rte. 66 effectively doubles back on itself, finally heading south again on **Beich Rd.,** parallel to I-55. Just hold on tight and follow the signs.

SHIRLEY

Signs advertise no services in Shirley, but keep going to the 18-acre **Funks Grove Nature Preserve.** Funks Grove produces some of the finest maple sirop in the Midwest. And yes, they do mean "sirop"—according to the FDA, "sirop" with an "i" means it's 100% natural. To buy the sweet stuff, continue a half-mile south of Funk's Grove to the small store. (☎309-874-3360. Maple candy $1. Open by chance or appointment.) Follow the signs down Funks Grove Rd. to the **Funks Grove Church and Cemetery**, 1 mi. off Rte. 66. Behind the 1864 church is a modest monument to the more than 50 Irish immigrants who came to Illinois in the 1850s to help construct the Chicago and Alton Railroad. Across the road, in the **Church of the Templed Trees**, felled trunks form the pews and stumps the altar of an outdoor sanctuary. The friendly folks at the **Sugar Grove Nature Center** will show you everything you ever wanted to know about sugar. The center is closed in winter, but butterfly tours, firefly campfires and other activities are free and open to the public May-Sept. (Head right at the "Sirop" arrow 4 mi. south of Shirley, on Funk's Grove Rd., and take a right at the sign for Funks Grove Church. ☎309-874-2174; www.funksgrove.com.) At the junction of I-55 and U.S. 36, 4 mi. further down Rte. 66, the epic truck stop, **Dixie Trucker's Home ❷** keeps its parking lot rumbling with rigs, gargantuan portions, and all-day breakfast. Also on-site is the Rte. 66 Hall of Fame with polaroid pictures of the hundreds of truckers who have passed through. (☎309-874-2323. Burgers $5. Country meatloaf $8. Open 24hr.)

◪ APPROACHING LINCOLN: 26 MILES
Continue south on **Rte. 66** through the small town of **Atlanta**, pausing to see the **Hot Dog Giant**, the second of 3 iconic fiberglass **Muffler Men** on Rte. 66. A few yards away, Atlanta's 3-in-one **1908 Clocktower, Library, and Museum** is definitely worth a glimpse. 23 mi. south of Bloomington, you'll pass **Lawndale** and enter Lincoln.

LINCOLN. The only town to be named for Abraham Lincoln during his lifetime, the town of **Lincoln** is home to a white, gilt courthouse and refurbished movie theater. Campsites at **Camp-a-While ❶**, 1779 1250 Ave., 1¼ mi. north of Lincoln and 2 mi. west of Rte. 66, have a great deal of privacy in the midst of cornfields. Sites include hookups, hot showers, laundry, and laptop Internet hookup. (☎217-732-8840. Sites $10; RVs $20. Cash only.) History buffs can visit the **Postville Courthouse**, a careful reproduction of the original courthouse Lincoln visited twice a year as a lawyer in 1840. (☎217-732-8930. Open

Tu-Sa Mar.-Oct. noon-5pm; Nov.-Feb. noon-4pm. Suggested donation $2, children $1.)

◪ APPROACHING SPRINGFIELD: 29 MILES
Continue south on **Rte. 66.** As you pass through **Broadwell**, stop by the **Pig Hip Restaurant Museum.** Now retired after serving thousands of Pig Hip sandwiches from 1937 to 1991, Ernie, "the Old Coot on 66," still loves talking to travelers. 9 mi. past Broadwell, turn right on **Elm St.** About 1 mi. later, turn right, then turn right again. Follow **I-55** to **Exit 105,** passing through **Sherman,** then **Springfield.**

SPRINGFIELD

Home of Abe Lincoln and the corn dog, Springfield could not be any more American. Inexorable Lincoln-mania is clearly the tourist focus of the town, but amidst the dated storefronts of 5th St. and under the domes of the stately legislative buildings, business—primarily the running of the state—gets done. Springfield also honors its portion of Rte. 66; the city is home to the "International Route 66 Mother Road Festival," several classic diners, and the historic Rte. 66 signs on portions of 2nd and 5th St.

VITAL STATS

Population: 111,000

Visitor Info: Springfield Convention and Visitors Bureau, 109 N. 7th St. (☎217-789-2360). Open M-F 8am-5pm.

Internet Access: Lincoln Public Library, 326 S. 7th St. (☎217-753-4900). Open June-Aug. M-Th 9am-9pm, F 9am-6pm, Sa 9am-5pm; Sept.-May M-Th 9am-9pm, F 9am-6pm, Su noon-5pm. Free.

Post Office: 411 E. Monroe St. (☎217-753-3432), at Wheeler St. Open M-F 7:45am-5pm. **Postal Code:** 62701.

▤ GETTING AROUND

Getting around in Springfield is fairly simple. **N. Grand Ave.** is one of the city's main thoroughfares, running east-west through town. Streets run north-south and are numbered; main arteries include **5th St.,** which borders the Lincoln Neighborhood and Oak Park Cemetery, and **7th St. N. Grand Ave.** is known as **N. Grand Ave. W,** west of the intersection with **5th St.,** and **N. Grand Ave. E,** east of the intersection. The only

ROUTE 66

real difficulty is the prevalence of one-way streets, but excellent downtown maps detailing the location of historic sights are available throughout the city. To enter downtown, take 6th St.; to leave downtown, take 5th St. Both connect with I-55 south of the downtown area.

⑤ SIGHTS

The sleepy state capital plays curator to the 16th president's legacy; many of Springfield's sights revolve around Lincoln's life and family. For variety, there are also Rte. 66-related attractions and oddball distractions.

SHEA'S GAS STATION MUSEUM. Looking as though Rte. 66 exploded into one happy jumble of signs, car parts, and Mother Road memorabilia, this eclectic museum is a priority for any roadtripper along Rte. 66. Owner Bill Shea will be more than happy to explain how it all began with an adding machine in 1955. (2075 Peoria Rd. ☎217-522-0475. Open Tu-F 7am-4pm, Sa 7am-noon. Suggested donation $2.)

LINCOLN SIGHTS. Abraham Lincoln's old haunts have been turned into a pedestrian-only pilgrimage site called the **Lincoln Neighborhood.** Abe-o-philes can take 25min. tours of the fully restored **Lincoln Home,** which features his original writing desk in the parlor where he was offered the presidential nomination. Several other houses in the area have also been renovated and serve as miniature museums dedicated to the original neighborhood. (☎217-492-4241, ext. 244; www.nps.gov/liho. Open daily 8:30am-5pm; extended hours in summer. Tickets available at the visitors center. Free.) The final resting place of Honest Abe, Mary Todd Lincoln, and three of the Lincoln children is in the **Lincoln Tomb,** under an obelisk in the Oak Ridge Cemetery. (1500 Monument Ave. ☎217-782-2717. Open daily Mar.-Oct. 9am-5pm; Nov.-Feb. 9am-4pm. Free.)

THE DANA-THOMAS HOME. Built in 1902, the stunning home was one of Frank Lloyd Wright's early experiments in Prairie Style and features the largest collection of original furniture and art glass of any Wright structure. Tours describe the house and the eccentric millionaire who lived there. (301 E. Lawrence Ave. ☎217-782-6776. Open Tu-Sa and Su 9am-4pm. Tours approximately every 20min. Suggested donation $3, under 17 $1.)

OTHER SIGHTS. The **Museum of Funeral Customs** features a history of American embalming and funeral customs, including exhibits on Lincoln's funeral affairs and mourning jewelry, as well as the history of formaldehyde. Check out the massive Cadillac hearse and harmonica-sized chocolate coffins. (1440 Monument Ave. ☎217-544-3480. Open Tu-Sa 10am-4pm, Su 1-4pm. $4, children $1.50.) The **Illinois State Museum** has everything you ever wanted to know about Illinois, though you'll need a hearty helping of Illinois pride or general patriotism to really appreciate it. The highlight is the replica of an Alaskan Tlingit totem pole, complete with its own Lincoln tribute, outside the building. (502 S. Spring St. ☎217-782-7386; www.museum.state.il.us. Open M-Sa 8:30am-5pm, Su noon-5pm. Donations accepted.) In 1858, Lincoln delivered his famous "House Divided" speech at the **Old State Capitol;** the building is open for guided tours today. (☎217-785-7961. Open Mar.-Oct. daily 9am-5pm; Nov.-Feb. Tu-Sa 9am-4pm.)

⫶ FOOD

Springfield offers an array of dining options, ranging from classic American to Italian to Southern home cooking. Springfield is also home to several classic Rte. 66 diners and fast-food joints; even if you're just passing through, these are ones you shouldn't miss.

Krekel's Custard, 2121 N. Grand Ave. (☎217-525-4952). Eat-in, eat-out, or drive-thru since 1949, the shakes and burgers here are legendary. The "concretes" ($2.50) are not for the faint of heart. Milkshakes from vanilla and chocolate to lemon and pineapple $2.25. Cheeseburgers $2. Open M-Sa 10:30am-9pm. Cash only. ❶

Cozy Dog Drive-In, 2935 5th St. (☎217-525-1992; www.cozydogdrivein.com). Run by the Waldmire family since 1949, Cozy Dog is the birthplace of the corn dog and one of the all-time greats of the road. You might be surprised to learn that the 'cozy-dog' was almost called a 'crusty cur.' Pick up postcards ($0.25), maps, a Cozy Dog ($1.75), a Rte. 66 Root Beer, bottled in Wilmington ($1.75), or other quick road food. Open M-Sa 8am-8pm. Cash only. ❶

Trout Lily Cafe, 218 S. 6th St. (☎217-391-0101; www.troutlilycafe.com). A little girl's dream room meets a French cafe in this friendly establishment decorated with local art and colorful murals. An excellent selection of specialty and drip coffees

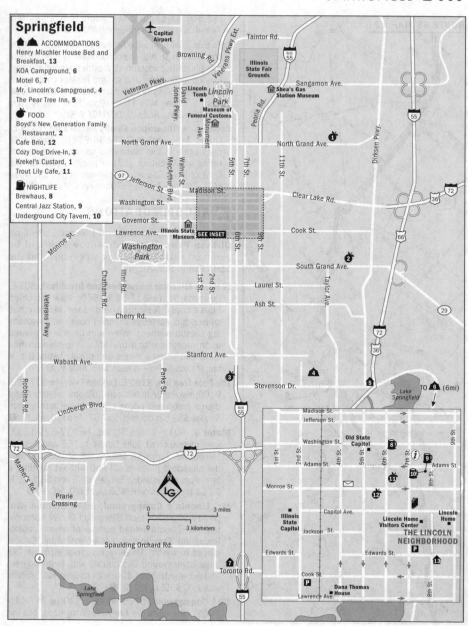

Springfield

■ ▲ ACCOMMODATIONS
Henry Mischler House Bed and
Breakfast, **13**
KOA Campground, **6**
Motel 6, **7**
Mr. Lincoln's Campground, **4**
The Pear Tree Inn, **5**

🍎 FOOD
Boyd's New Generation Family
   Restaurant, **2**
Cafe Brio, **12**
Cozy Dog Drive-In, **3**
Krekel's Custard, **1**
Trout Lily Cafe, **11**

▮ NIGHTLIFE
Brewhaus, **8**
Central Jazz Station, **9**
Underground City Tavern, **10**

Capital
Airport

Taintor Rd.

Browning Rd.

Veterans Pkwy. Ext

Illinois
State Fair
Grounds

BUS
55

Veterans Pkwy.

Lincoln
Tomb

David
Jones Pkwy.

Lincoln
Park

Museum of
Funeral Customs

Sangamon Ave.

Shea's Gas
Station Museum

Peoria Rd.

Dirksen Pkwy.

55

North Grand Ave.

North Grand Ave.

MacArthur Blvd.

Walnut St.

Lincoln
Monument
Ave.

5th St.

7th St.

11th St.

🍅
1

97

Jefferson St.

Madison St.

36

72

Washington St.

Clear Lake Rd.

Governor St.

6th St.

9th St.

Cook St.

66

Lawrence Ave.

Illinois State
Museum

SEE INSET

Washington
Park

South Grand Ave.

2

Monroe St.

Chatham Rd.

Illini Rd.

1st St.

2nd St.

Laurel St.

Taylor Ave.

Ash St.

29

Veterans Pkwy

Cherry Rd.

Parks St.

Stanford Ave.

72

36

Wabash Ave.

3

4

Stevenson Dr.

5

Lake
Springfield

TO
6 (6mi)

Robbins Rd.

Lindbergh Blvd.

BUS
55

72

72

Mather's Rd.

Prarie
Crossing

N
LG

0   3 miles
0   3 kilometers

Spaulding Orchard Rd.

4

Lake
Springfield

Toronto Rd.

7

55

Madison St.
Jefferson St.

Washington St.

Old State
Capitol

8

9th St.

1st St.

2nd St.

4th St.

5th St.

6th St.

7th St.

i

9

Adams St.

Adams St.

8th St.

Monroe St.

11

10

12

Illinois
State
Capitol

Capitol Ave.

Lincoln Home
Visitors Center

Lincoln
Home

Jackson St.

THE LINCOLN
NEIGHBORHOOD

P

Edwards St.

Edwards St.

13

Cook St.

P

8th St.

Dana Thomas
House

Lawrence Ave.

ROUTE 66

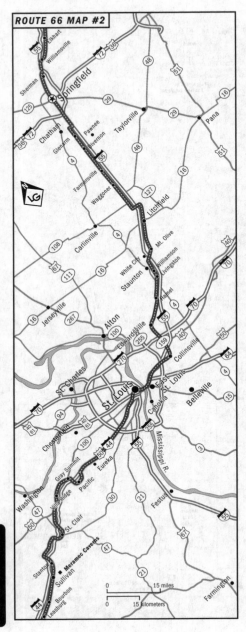

ROUTE 66 MAP #2

15 miles

15 kilometers

($2.50). Live music M-F noon-1pm. Open M-F 7am-4:30pm, Sa 9am-3pm. MC/V. ❶

Cafe Brio, 524 E. Monroe St. (☎217-544-0574), at the corner of 6th St. With chairs nonchalantly mismatched, this plant-filled restaurant provides a sophisticated take on rustic decor and stylized Tex-Mex cuisine. Salads $6-9. Shrimp BLT $9. Marinated Portobello mushroom $7. Open M-Th 11am-10pm, F-Sa 11am-11pm, Su 11am-3pm. AmEx/D/DC/MC/ V. ❸

Boyd's New Generation Family Restaurant, 1831 S. Grand Ave. East (☎217-544-9866). The South rises again in this homestyle southern eatery, featuring whole catfish ($8) or nuggets ($6) for the faint of heart. Su all-you-can-eat buffet $9. Open M-Th 7:30am-3pm, F 7:30am-7pm. V only. ❷

ACCOMMODATIONS

There are cheap lodgings off I-55 and U.S. 36 on **Dirksen Pkwy.** Rooms downtown should be reserved early for holiday weekends and the **State Fair** in mid-August.

Henry Mischler House Bed and Breakfast, 802 E. Edwards St. (☎217-525-2660; www.mischlerhouse.com). New proprietor Jane Murphy has infused this gorgeous Victorian house with welcoming sumptuousness. Wine and cheese is offered upon reception, and breakfast is served on fine china and silver. 8 rooms with private baths. Breakfast included. Rooms from $85. MC/ V. ❹

The Pear Tree Inn, 3190 S. Dirksen Pkwy. (☎217-529-9100; www.druryhotels.com). Rooms slightly larger than a motel and prices slightly lower than an inn. Singles $52-62; doubles $57-67. AmEx/D/MC/V. ❸

Motel 6, 6011 S. 6th St. Rd. (☎217-529-1633; www.motel6.com). Take 5th St. to I-55 and Exit 90, Toronto Rd. Turn right onto S. 6th St. This is about the cheapest place you'll find without needing a tent. Pool and laundry. Singles M-Th and Su $40, F-Sa $44; doubles $46/$50. AmEx/D/MC/V. ❷

Mr. Lincoln's Campground, 3045 Stanton Ave. (☎217-529-8206), off Stevenson Dr. RV hookups, tent sites, and a limited number of private cabins. Reception 8am-8pm; in winter until 6pm. Cabins closed in winter. Make reservations early as this large campground fills quickly with festival-goers and snowbirds. Sites $20, with hookup $22; cabins with A/C $35. D/MC/V. ❶

KOA Campground, 5775 W. Farm 140 (☎217-498-7002). The sites are fairly close together, but the campground is removed from the road in the sweeping countryside south of Springfield. Reception 24hr. Open Apr.-Nov. Sites $16; RVs $23; cabins $28. MC/V. ❶

📷 NIGHTLIFE

Locals crowd around the bar and lounge in wooden booths in the **Brewhaus,** 617 E. Washington St., one of the most popular nightspots around. Chat with the friendly bartenders or have proprietor Patty give you a primer on Scotch. (☎217-525-6399. Beer $1-3. Mixed drinks $5. Open M-F 7am-1am, Sa 8am-1am, Su 5pm-1am. AmEx/D/DC/MC/V.) The **Underground City Tavern,** 700 E. Adams St., is a more sophisticated option, with live music Sa-Su featuring a mix of local acoustic acts and more famous groups. Local artists and musicians gather here throughout the week and a guitar is generally within reach. (☎217-789-1530. Mixed drinks $3.50-6. Sandwiches $3. Cover varies. Open M-F 2pm-3am, Sa noon-3am, Su noon-midnight. MC/V.) Way upstairs, on the 30th floor of the Hilton, **Central Jazz Station** caters to the out-of-town crowd and has a stunning view of Springfield that cannot be topped. (☎217-789-1530. Live music F-Sa. Open M-Th 5pm-11pm, F-Sa 5pm-3am, Su 7pm-3am. MC/V.)

📷 APPROACHING FARMERSVILLE: 29 MILES

Take **5th St.** south to **I-55.** At **Exit 88,** you'll see signs for Historic 66. From Springfield, the bevy of towns on the way south to St. Louis pride themselves on their Rte. 66 status, and many host restaurants that hearken back to the days of Mother Road glory. Directly south of Springfield, **Glenarm, Pawnee,** and **Divernon** are all home to necessities like gas, mom-and-pop diners, and motels. Head left at the T and then back onto I-55. Take **Exit 80** past the giant Lincoln to reach Farmersville.

PHOTO OP. On your way to Farmersville, keep an eye out for a **giant tribute to Abraham Lincoln**—he's perched in a wagon, absorbed in a law book.

FARMERSVILLE. As Rte. 66 climbs over I-55 at **Farmersville,** keep an eye out for an old 66 standby: **Art's Restaurant and Motel ❷,** at Exit 72 off I-55. Current owner Gloria prides herself on her supersized portions, so get ready for the hearty meal that awaits. Afterwards, sleep it off at the newly renovated rooms next door.

(☎217-227-3777. Entrees $8. Gigantic truckers' breakfast $6. Open M and Su 7am-3pm, Tu-Sa 7am-8pm. For motel: ☎217-227-3266. Singles $30-35; doubles $40-45. D/MC/V.) Along Rte. 66, look for **Frances Marten's Our Lady of the Highways Shrine.** Erected in 1956, the statue of the Virgin Mary prays for the road safety of those who pass under her gaze. A series of Burma Shave style signs leading southward spells out the Hail Mary.

📷 APPROACHING LITCHFIELD

7 mi. south of the Shrine, Rte. 66 heads up over **I-55,** so that I-55 is now to the west (right) of the road. At **Litchfield,** drivers have the choice of heading straight through town on the 1940-1977 alignment of Rte. 66 or diverging to the left on the older alignment, dating from 1930-1940. The newer alignment leads to chain motels and fast food, while the older alignment passes the **Skyview Drive-In** and the **Ariston Cafe.**

LITCHFIELD

Litchfield is a town proud to be on Rte. 66. The **Sky View Drive-In,** on the Rte. 66 1930-1940 alignment, just north of Union St., still shows movies for $2 in the summer months, just like the in the old days. (☎217-324-4451. Films F-Su. Call for showtimes.) Numerous annual celebrations in Litchfield include an April reenactment of 1800s life and a July International Chili Society district cook-off. Nearby **Lake Lou Yaeger** offers beachfront, watersports availability, campgrounds, and playgrounds. (Take Union Ave. heading east, then turn left on Yaeger Lake Trail. ☎217-324-4771.) The **Ariston Cafe ❹,** at the corner of Rte. 66 and Union St., on the 1930-1940 alignment, has been serving roadies since the 1920s. (☎217-324-2023; www.ariston-cafe.com. Appetizers $6. Entrees $7-15. Steak $22. Open M-F 11am-10pm, Sa 4-10pm, Su 11am-9pm. AmEx/D/MC/V.)

📷 APPROACHING STAUNTON: 13 MILES

Take **I-16** back to the 1940-1977 alignment of **Rte. 66.** After 7 mi., you'll pass through **Mt. Olive,** the final resting place of Mary "Mother" Jones, and "General" Alexander Bradley, both instrumental in the fight for the rights of mine workers, in the **Union Miners Cemetery.** 1 mi. past the cemetery, look to the right to see the restored 1926 **Russel Soulsby Shell Gas Station.** Approximately 10½ mi. south of central Litchfield, Rte. 66 reaches a T intersection; take a left to rejoin the old route, and continue on over **I-55.** The road forks in a number of places but is clearly marked and leads directly into Staunton.

STAUNTON. "Hare it is!" proclaim the signs for **Henry's Rte. 66 Emporium and Rabbit Ranch,** 1107 Historic Rte. 66 Rd., as if you could miss the two giant tractor trailers out front with "Humpin' to Please" painted on them. Henry's Emporium embodies the joy of Rte. 66 culture—38 rabbits in the "Rabbit Ranch," 15 Volkswagen rabbits, and one Rte. 66 enthusiast extraordinaire hop among an ever-expanding collection of memorabilia. Rich Henry has worked and lived on Rte. 66 all his life, and he can talk a blue streak. Ask to pet Montana, the most famous of his rabbits, and she might even autograph a brochure for you. (☎618-635-5655; www.henrysroute66.com. Open daily 9am-4pm or whenever Rich Henry is around.)

☒ APPROACHING EDWARDSVILLE: 19 MILES
Continue on **Rte. 66** from Henry's Emporium for 10 mi. to hit the town of Hamel. Just north of Hamel, on the eastern side of I-55, is a repainted sign for the famous **Meramec Caverns** of Staunton, MO. Across Rte. 66 from the Meramec Barn is **St. Paul's Church,** where the neon-blue cross at the top has been lighting roadtrippers' ways for years. 7 mi. later, you'll reach the town of Edwardsville. The next manifestation of Rte. 66 is **E. Vandalia St.,** which becomes **W. Vandalia** after intersecting with Main St.

EDWARDSVILLE. Edwardsville is home to the **Southern University of Illinois.** Gas and amenities are available, including a new library and some excellent eating and lounging options. **Sacred Grounds Cafe ❷,** 233 N. Main St., off E. Vandalia, is a student-friendly coffee shop offering ample space to relax with a book, spread out over a board game, or just gobble down some health food. (☎618-692-4150. Wraps, salads, quiche, or panini $4. Open daily 7am-11pm. MC/V.) Chalkboards at the **Stagger Inn Again ❷,** 104 E. Vandalia St., are festooned with specials and quips, and the wooden bar, checkered floors, and spacious dining area draw potential diners through the saloon doors for a night out or a lunch on the go. Try the Nightmare (a chili burger with jalapenos) for $6.50. (☎618-656-4221. Sandwiches $5. Open M-W 11am-1am, Th 11am-2am, F-Sa 11am-2:30am, Su 3pm-1am. MC/V.) For a relaxing jaunt through nature, head to the **Watershed Nature Center,** 1591

Tower Avenue, a 40-acre nature preserve with wetlands, forests, hiking trails, and a 3000 ft. walkway. (From Main St., take Lincoln St. to Eberhart St., and then to Tower Ave. ☎618-692-7578. Open sunrise-sunset. Free.)

☒ APPROACHING MITCHELL: 10 MILES
5 mi. past **Main St.,** W. Vandalia becomes **Chain of Rocks Rd.,** which takes you to Mitchell.

MITCHELL. Now a quiet town of metal yards and auto shops laced with old railroad tracks, Mitchell used to be the last big stop before St. Louis on Rte. 66. You can still knock back brews with the local crowd at the **Luna Cafe ❶,** 201 E. Chain of Rocks Rd. Rumor has it that Al Capone used to come to this legendary old Rte. 66 bar, tucked under a blinking vintage neon sign, when he feared foul play in St. Louis. (☎618-931-3152. Hamburgers $3. Drinks $2-3. Open M-F and Su 7am-2am, Sa 7am-3am. Cash only.)

☒ APPROACHING COLLINSVILLE: 13 MILES
Take I-55 S to Rte. 159 S to get to downtown Collinsville. Head south on **Morrison St.** as your hamburger dreams materialize over the horizon.

 PHOTO OP. Collinsville is home to the **World's Largest Catsup Bottle,** a giant painted water tower dating from 1949.

COLLINSVILLE. Pick up your catsup postcards and catsup paraphernalia at **Ashmann's Drugs,** 209 E. Main St. (Open daily 9am-9:30pm.) As you head down Main St., keep an eye to the left for an ancient Bull Durham Tobacco sign painted on a brick wall. For cheap eats, stop into **Bert's Chuckwagon BBQ ❷,** 207 E. Clay St. On the outside of the A-frame building is a giant mural of Biblical scenes (check out Mary's mirrored eyes) painted by the owner's sons. Inside is tasty barbecue and Tex-Mex. (☎618-344-7993. Rib tips $3. Full side $10. AmEx/D/MC/V.) Outside of Collinsville, the **Cahokia Mounds** are the remnants of the prehistoric Native American city of Cahokia. Archaeologists are fairly certain that some were burial mounds. **"Monks Mound,"** the largest Indian mound north of Mexico, is named for Trappist Monks who set up camp on top of the mound in the 1800s. (Take I-55 S to I-255 S. Take Exit 24, and turn left onto

Collinsville Rd. ☎618-346-5160. Museum open Apr.-Sept. daily 9am-5pm, Oct.-Mar. W-Sa and Su 9am-5pm. Park open daily sunrise-sunset. Suggested donation $2, children $1.)

🖩 APPROACHING ST. LOUIS: 15 MILES

Take **Main St.** in Collinsville west to **St. Louis Rd.,** which turns into **Collinsville Rd.** Turn left to take **I-255 N** to **I-55 S/I-70 W,** which will take you toward St. Louis. There will be a number of exit options for St. Louis, each for a major street or intersection. It is best to decide which part of the city you want to see, and look at a map beforehand to determine where it is most efficient to exit.

The Show - Me State
MISSOURI
Welcomes You!

ST. LOUIS

Directly south of the junction of three rivers— the Mississippi, Missouri, and Illinois—St. Louis marks the transition between the Midwest and the West. Known as the "Gateway to the West," a theme expressed by the soaring Gateway Arch, the sprawling city is also at the cross- roads of Route 66 and the National Road. Stay on Rte. 66 to continue your classic roadtrip journey, or take the other fork in the road, fol- lowing I-40 straight to San Francisco.

PAGE TURN. See p. 397 in the **National Road** for complete coverage of St. Louis.

🖩 APPROACHING PACIFIC: 32 MILES

From downtown St. Louis, hop on **I-44 W.** On either side of the route, cliffs fall away sharply—be careful, as the route is narrow and frequently traveled by giant tractor trailers. Continue on **I-44** to **Exit 261,** at Eureka, and follow **Old Rte. 66** to Pacific.

PACIFIC. Pacific is home to the **Old Rte. 66 Flea Market,** where everything you'll ever need (and a lot you won't) awaits. (☎636-257-

8333. Open Sa-Su 8am-5pm.) Roadtrippers in Pacific can stop for munchies at **Smitchell's Dairy and Diner ❶,** 724 W. Osage St., a diner with sparkly red and silver booths, Rte. 66 napkin dispensers, and creative "concrete" shakes. (☎636-257-6609. Concretes from $3. Hamburgers $2.75. Open M-Th and Su 11am-10pm, F-Sa 11am-11pm. MC/V.)

🖩 APPROACHING GRAY SUMMIT: 5 MILES

Head west along **W. Osage St. (Bus. I-44).** Join **I-44** briefly, crossing over I-50 and onto **Rte. 100.**

GRAY SUMMIT. In Gray Summit, I-44 and the old alignment of Rte. 66 rejoin. The **Diamonds Restaurant and Inn,** constructed in 1928 on this spot and once known as America's largest roadside restaurant, has now been turned into **Diamonds Tri-County Truck Stop ❷,** just past the junction of Rte. 66 and Rte. 100 in Villa Ridge. The new owner is involved in an evolving quest to recapture the former glory of this Rte. 66 favorite. (☎636-742-2508. Buttermilk hot- cakes $3.75. Sandwiches $3-5.50. Open M-Th and Su 5am-9pm, F-Sa 24hr. MC/V.) An exten- sion of the Missouri Botanical Garden (see p. 398), the **Shaw Nature Reserve,** across from the Diamonds Restaurant signs, provides hiking trails, wildflower gardens, and horticultural exhibits in the former home of Confederate Colonel Thomas William Bouldin Crews. (☎636-451-3512. Grounds open daily 7am-sunset. Visi- tors center open M-F 8am-4:30pm, Sa 9am-5pm. $3, seniors $2, under 12 free.)

🖩 APPROACHING STANTON: 22 MILES

Continue along **Rte. 66,** crossing over the highway 6¾ mi. from Gray Summit and continuing parallel to the railroad tracks. 11 mi. south of Grey Summit on Rte. 66, the **Indian Harvest** store, in the 2 giant blue-and-white teepees, has bison sausage and jewelry made by the Navajo and the Zuni tribes in New Mexico. (Entrance fee is a promise to make a purchase of at least $2.) Continue southwest into St. Clair. Just past the intersection with **Rte. 30,** head north over I-44, then head left on the outer road and follow the signs for the Meramec Caverns into Stanton

STANTON

Stanton may be all about the Meramec Cav- erns, but before heading to the caves, be sure

ROUTE 66

to check out the **Jesse James Wax Museum,** at Exit 230 off I-44, just after the turnoff for the caverns. In this memorial to the legendary bandit, rooms are devoted to wax reenactments of key moments in James' life, including the first bank robbery on record in the US. (☎573-927-5233. Open June-Aug. daily 9am-6pm; Sept.-Oct. and Apr.-May Sa-Su 9am-5pm. $6, ages 5-11 $2.50, under 5 free.) The **Meramec Caverns** cannot be missed after the miles of advertisements on barns and billboards. Reputedly where Jesse James and his gang once hid their loot, the 26 mi. of caverns are now one of Missouri's biggest tourist draws. Other cave-side attractions include riverboat and mining tours. (☎573-468-3166. Caverns open daily Mar. 9am-5pm; Apr. and Sept. 9am-6pm; May-June 9am-7pm; July-Aug. 8:30am-7:30pm; Nov.-Dec. 9am-4pm. Tours every 30min. $14, ages 5-11 $7, under 5 free.) The **Meramec Caverns Motel ❷,** in La Jolla Natural Park, provides riverfront lodging adjacent to the caves. (☎537-468-4215. Open Apr.-Oct. Singles $50; doubles $55. AmEx/D/MC/V.) Meramec Caverns' **La Jolla Natural Park ❶** has comfortable, shaded campsites along the river, at the mouth of the caverns. Amenities include bathrooms, showers, a supply store, a concession stand, and canoe and raft rentals. (☎573-468-3166. Open Apr.-Oct. Sites $15, with hookup $19. Cash only.) On your way back to Rte. 66, stop by the **Riverside Reptile Ranch,** the best thing that's ever happened to a petting zoo. Here you can stroke a snake, test the jaw strength of baby alligators with your finger, get wrapped up in a Burmese python, or watch the scaly creatures from behind glass—just keep an eye out for Zeus, the giant American alligator who paddles freely through the grounds. (☎573-927-6253. Open daily 10am-7pm. $6, ages 5-12 $5, under 5 free.)

> **?** **DID YOU KNOW?** Meramec Caverns is known as the birthplace of the bumper sticker.

⚐ APPROACHING LEASBURG: 16 MILES
From Stanton, follow **Rte. 66** into Sullivan. Motels and gas stations are located along the west side, while fast-food restaurants assemble to the east. To continue on Rte. 66, follow **Elmont St.** right, then turn left at the stop sign as you enter town. Follow the **outer road** south from Sullivan, and about 10 mi. later you'll hit Leasburg.

LEASBURG. Located in **Onondaga Caves State Park,** just south of Leasburg, the **Onondaga Caves** feature an active river and spring. (Head left from Rte. 66 through Leasburg, following signs for the caves. ☎573-245-6576. Visitors center open daily 10am-4pm. Cave tours Mar.-Oct. daily 9am-5pm. $9, ages 13-19 $7, ages 6-12 $5, under 6 free.) Camping is permitted in the park at the **Onondaga Caves Campgrounds ❶,** which offer showers, bathrooms, laundry, and a general store. (☎573-345-6576. Call for availability and opening dates. Sites $7, with hookup $12. Cash only.) On busy nights, it seems like every car in town pulls up in front of **Ike's Chat 'n' Chew ❷,** 2344 Rte. H. (☎573-245-6268. Steak, potatoes, and salad $8. Open daily 8am-6pm. Cash only.)

⚐ APPROACHING CUBA: 6 MILES
Continue on **Rte. 66** to Cuba.

CUBA. 🔪**Missouri Hick Barbecue ❸,** 913 E. Washington St., at the entrance to Cuba, is decorated with saddles and farm equipment and provides a welcome break from diner fare. (☎573-885-6791. Beef brisket $6. Pulled chicken $5.50. Open in summer M-Th and Su 11am-9pm, F-Sa 11am-10pm; in winter M-Th and Su 11am-8pm, F-Sa 11am-9pm. AmEx/D/MC/V.) The **Wagon Wheel Motel ❶,** 901 E. Washington St., offers prices that are almost as low as they were when the motel first opened in 1934. (☎573-885-3411. Reservations recommended. Singles $13-16; doubles $18. Cash only.)

⚐ APPROACHING ST. JAMES: 14 MILES
Roughly 14 mi. south of Cuba on Rte. 66, turn right on **Jefferson St. (Rte. 68)** and then right onto **Sidney St.** at the first light.

ST. JAMES. The area south of Cuba is grape country, and St. James is no exception. The **St. James Winery,** 540 Sidney St., has 15min. tours, daily wine samplings, and excellent grape juice for drivers. (☎800-280-9463; www.stjameswinery.com. Open daily 11am-4pm. Tasting room open M-Sa 8am-7pm, Su 11am-7pm. Free.)

DID YOU KNOW? Bobby Troup wrote "Get Your Kicks on Route 66" while driving to Los Angeles in 1946.

APPROACHING ROLLA: 11 MILES

In St. James, head right at **Jefferson St. (Rte. 68)**, crossing I-44. Go west on the **outer road** and turn left 8½ mi. later on **Bishop Ave. (U.S. 63)** into Rolla.

ROLLA

Touted as Missouri's "center of everything," Rolla is home to classic diners, quirky motels, and a state university, as well as a convenient gateway to outdoor attractions. Rolla's stretch of Rte. 66 is truly unique; few other places can transition from Stonehenge at one end of town to the Totem Pole Trading Post at the other.

VITAL STATS

Population: 16,000

Visitor Info: Rolla Chamber of Commerce and Visitors Center, 1301 Kingshighway St. (☎573-364-3577; www.rollachamber.org). Open Nov.-Apr. M-F 8am-5pm, Sa 9am-3pm; May-Oct. M-F 8am-5pm, Sa 9am-3pm, Su 1-5pm.

Internet Access: Rolla Public Library, 900 Pine St. (☎573-364-2604). Open M-Th 9am-9pm, F-Sa 9am-5pm, Su 1:30-5pm. Free.

Post Office: 501 W. 8th St. (☎573-364-1775). Open M-F 7:45am-5:15pm, Sa 8:30am-12:30pm. **Postal Code:** 65401.

GETTING AROUND. Rte. 66 cuts through town on **U.S. 63,** which is known in town as **Bishop Ave.** and runs north-south. Numbered streets run east-west through downtown. To reach downtown, head east on **10th St.** or south on **Pine St.,** which runs parallel to Bishop Ave. a few blocks to the east. **Kingshighway St.** heads west from U.S. 63, becoming **Martin Springs Dr.** in the west and running parallel to **I-44.**

SIGHTS. Compare your wheels to 66 roadsters of the past at **Memoryville USA,** 2220 Bishop Ave., an antique automobile restoration shop and museum. Memoryville has a reputation for giving new life to outdated cars; an array of shiny, polished classics, enough to delight any true auto fan, is on display in the museum. (☎573-364-1810. Museum open M-F 9am-6pm, Sa-Su 9am-5:30pm. Shop open daily 9am-4:30pm. $4.75, seniors $3.50, ages 6-12 $2.) In case you still have holes in your 66 memorabilia collection, head to the **Route 66 Nostalgia Gift Shop,** 12601 Bishop Ave. The adjoining **Route 66 Motors** showcases old cars, and most are available for purchase. (☎573-265-5200. Open M-Sa 9am-5pm.) For a break from the automobile, head over to the **Stonehenge Replica,** at 14th St. and Bishop Ave., on the campus of the University of Missouri at Rolla. Approximately 160 tons of granite compose the giant rock structure. Though it's smaller than the original, the replica includes features the original lacked, such as an opening through which the North Star can be seen. (☎573-341-4111. Open daily sunrise-sunset. Free.) Don't miss the historic **Totem Pole Trading Post,** 1413 Martin Springs Dr. A well-known Rte. 66 landmark, the Trading Post has been offering gas and souvenirs since 1933. (☎573-364-3519. Open daily 7:30am-9pm.)

FOOD AND ACCOMMODATIONS. At **Granny's Saw Mill ❷,** at the corner of 9th and Pine St., let Granny fill you up with giant pancakes ($1.50) or a burger ($3.50) made with ½ lb. of juicy ground beef. (☎573-364-8383. Open M-F 5am-2pm, Sa 5am-1:30pm. AmEx/MC/V.) A movie theater-turned-restaurant, the **All Star Sports Bar and Grill ❷,** 1100 N. Pine St., serves satisfying portions of appetizers, pastas, and steaks during the day and occasionally hosts live musical acts at night. (In the historical Uptown Theater. ☎573-368-3000. Cover up to $5. Open M-Sa 11am-1am, Su noon-midnight. AmEx/MC/V.) For a night of quirky elegance, **Zeno's Motel and Steakhouse ❸,** 1621 Martin Springs Dr., offers a motel-meets-antique-shop atmosphere and an adjoining steakhouse. The Scheffer family has been running this establishment since the 1950s. Nearly all the antiques decorating the rooms and lobby are for sale. (☎573-364-1301. Entrees $10-20. Singles from $50; doubles from $62. AmEx/D/DC/MC/V.) Motels cluster along **Martin Springs Dr.** on the western edge of Rolla. The rock-bottom rates, however, are on the south side of the city at **Budget Deluxe Motel ❷,** 1908 N. Bishop Ave., which offers

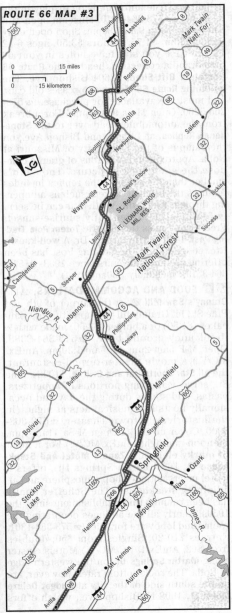

ROUTE 66 MAP #3

0   15 miles

0   15 kilometers

adequate rooms. (☎573-364-4486. Singles from $28.50; doubles from $35. MC/V.) Eight miles south of Rolla on Rte. 66, **Vernelle's Motel ●** offers wood-paneled rooms straight out of the glory days of Rte. 66. (Take Sugartree Rd., and then turn onto Arlington Rd. ☎573-762-2798. Singles from $27; doubles from $30. Cash only.) Another option is the family-owned **Rustic Motel ❷,** 812 S. Bishop Ave., which offers clean rooms with just a hint of rustic charm. (☎573-364-6943. Singles M-Th $43, F-Su $50. AmEx/D/MC/V.)

◪ APPROACHING ST. ROBERT: 21 MILES

Veer southwest (left) off **Kingshighway St.** onto **Martin Spring Dr.,** which runs parallel to I-44. Although the road becomes narrow and is relatively unmarked, follow its curves across the 1-lane bridge and through the backwoods of ramshackle log cabins. Just before the bridge over the Big Piney River, about 20 mi. southwest of Rolla, head left across the highway, and detour over the creek and steel-trussed bridge. Just over 2 mi. after detouring through the Ozark hamlet of **Devil's Elbow,** rejoin the highway, heading left, and follow it into St. Robert.

ST. ROBERT. Small St. Robert is home to several roadside classics. **Jack's Route 66 Diner ●,** 126 St. Robert Blvd., serves up sandwiches ($3-5), dinner plates ($3), and shakes ($3) in a blinding chrome and red-pleather interior. (☎573-336-8989. Open daily 6am-midnight. AmEx/D/DC/MC/V.) The **Sweetwater BBQ ❸,** 14076 Rte. Z, makes mouth-watering barbecue in a small cabin on a hill at the northeastern entrance to St. Robert. (Take Exit 163 from I-44, and head east on S. Outer Rd. ☎573-336-8830. Special pork and rib plates $7.50-8.75. Open daily 11am-8pm. AmEx/MC/V.) The **Deville Motor Inn ❸,** 461 Old Rte. 66, is another Rte. 66 standard with a restaurant and clean cinderblock rooms. (☎573-336-3113. Singles from $44; doubles from $50. AmEx/MC/V.)

◪ APPROACHING LEBANON: 31 MILES

Stay on **Rte. 66,** continuing through to Waynesville, passing over I-44, and veering left at the fork on the west edge of town. Follow **S. Outer Rd.** from **Exit 153,** steering right on **Rte. 17** to the intersection with **Rte. P** and **Rte. NN.** 2 mi. later, head right to Laquey on P, then left at the fork in town onto **Rte. AA.** Head right at **Rte. AB;** Hazelgreen is 9 mi. down the road. At the junction with **Rte. F** 13 mi. later, turn north, crossing I-44, and head into Lebanon.

LEBANON. Head to the **Peggy Palmer Summers Memorial Library,** 915 S. Jefferson Ave., to see the Rte. 66 museum with replicas of a diner and a 30s cabin-style motel room recreated with authentic furniture. (☎417-532-2148. Free Internet access. Open M-Sa 9am-5pm.) Next to the museum within the library is **Maria's Route 66 Cafe ❶,** where chrome and a piano key floor meet burritos and smoked brisket. (☎417-588-7922. Burritos $2.40. Open M-Sa 9am-5pm. Cash only.) One of the best lodging options on this stretch of road is the **◆Munger Moss Motel ❷,** a holdout from the glory days of the old road. Pass through at night, and the glowing red, blue, yellow, and green blinking sign beckons like a siren. Each pleasantly furnished room has hand-quilted bedspreads, and many are decorated in Rte. 66 memorabilia, all for the cost of your standard roadside motel. The gift shop has a great selection of Rte. 66 memorabilia. (☎417-532-3111. Reservations recommended. Singles from $40; doubles from $47. AmEx/MC/V.)

⚐ APPROACHING SPRINGFIELD: 47 MILES
Leaving Lebanon, turn right at the junction with **Rte. W,** then left onto the **Outer Rd.** 9 mi. later, in Phillipsburg, cross to the south side of the interstate, following **Rte. CC.** Watch closely for signs in this area as they are sometimes small green Rte. 66 signs rather than the historic brown ones you're accustomed to. Veer right in Marshfield, 12 mi. later, then head left onto **Rte. OO.** Continue across the junction with Rte. B on the way to Springfield.

SPRINGFIELD

The largest city in southern Missouri and hometown of hunky Brad Pitt, Springfield seems to grow out of the surrounding cattle fields. As Rte. 66 enters town from the northeast, the stretch of fast-food restaurants, cheap motels, and gas stations are in stark contrast to the old-time heart of downtown, where the ghost of Wild Bill Hickock seems as lively as the multitude of coffee shops, swanky bars, and hip restaurants.

VITAL STATS

Population: 150,000

Visitor Info: Springfield Convention and Visitors Bureau, 815 St. Louis St. (☎800-678-8767; www.springfieldmo.org). Open M-F 8am-5pm.

Internet Access: Springfield-Greene County Library Center, 4653 S. Campbell St. (☎417-874-8110). Open M-Sa 8am-9pm, Su 1-5pm. Free.

Post Office: 500 W. Chestnut Expwy. (☎417-864-0199). Open M-F 7:30am-5:30pm. **Postal Code:** 65801.

▛ GETTING AROUND

Downtown Springfield is just south of I-44. **U.S. 160** is known as **S. Campbell Ave.** in the city; running north-south, this is one of Springfield's main thoroughfares. Other major streets include **Sunshine St.,** which is labeled E. Sunshine St. or W. Sunshine St. relative to Campbell Ave., and the **Chestnut Expwy.,** which runs east-west north of Sunshine St.

◉ SIGHTS

More than just a retail store, **Bass Pro Shops,** 1935 S. Campbell Ave., is an outdoorsman's indoor amusement park. The store includes acres of merchandise plus a restaurant with a 20,000-gallon aquarium, a firing range, a four-story waterfall, a taxidermy museum, and the Archery Hall of Fame. (☎417-887-7334. Open M-Sa 7am-10pm, Su 9am-6pm.) Although the owners of Bass Pro Shops donated the land, **Wonders of Wildlife, The American National Fish and Wildlife Museum,** 500 W. Sunshine St., is not affiliated with the store. The museum features live animals swimming below and flying overhead. (☎888-521-9497; www.wondersofwildlife.org. Open daily 9am-6pm. $11, children $6.50.) For a relaxing walk, visit Springfield's "oasis of serenity," the **Mizumoto Japanese Stroll Garden,** 2400 S. Scenic Ave., in Nathanael Greene Park. (☎417-864-1049. Open Mar.-Oct. M and Th-Su 9am-7:30pm. $3, under 12 free.) Just north of Springfield, **Fantastic Caverns,** 4872 N. Farm Rd. 125, offers tours via Jeep-drawn tram. (☎417-833-2010; www.fantasticcaverns.com. Open daily 8am-sunset. $17, ages 6-12 $9.50, under 6 free.) Trade in your road-worn paperbacks at the **Well-**

Fed Head, 331 S. Campbell Ave., which buys, sells, and trades books. (☎417-832-9333. Open M 11am-6pm, Tu-Sa 11am-9pm.)

▧ FOOD

Springfield's streets are studded with quirky coffeehouses, hearty cafes, and a few laid-back bars.

Casper's, 600 W. Walnut St. (☎417-866-9750). Don't be fooled by the bland exterior—inside, Casper's chile haven is decorated with a riot of blue, orange, and most colors in between. Open Sept.-May M-F 10:30am-4pm. Cash only. ❷

Rasta Grill, 319 W. Walnut St. (☎417-831-7221; www.rastagrill.com), at S. Campbell St. Blue walls and fish create an underwater atmosphere for unique Caribbean cuisine. Thai chicken burrito $7. "Rasta pasta" with jerk chicken and spicy sauce $9. Open M-Th 11am-10pm, F-Sa 11am-1am. AmEx/MC/V. ❸

Mudhouse Downtown Coffeehouse, 323B S. Ave. (☎417-832-1720). Mudhouse roasts its own beans (espresso $1.50), throws its own ceramics, and whips up smoothies ($3) and sandwiches ($5). Live music F. Open M-Sa 7am-midnight, Su 8:30am-11pm. AmEx/D/MC/V. ❶

Nonna's Italian American Cafe, 306 South Ave. (☎417-831-1222), at McDaniel St. Cheery, yellow, art-bedecked walls complement the family atmosphere of this bistro. Sandwiches $5-6. Entrees $5-7. Open daily 11am-4:30pm. AmEx/MC/V. ❷

▐ ACCOMMODATIONS

Walnut St. Inn, 900 E. Walnut St. (☎417-864-6346; www.walnutstinn.com), in the historic district. The bedside chocolate-chip cookies sum up the decadence of this Victorian hotel. Reservations recommended. Rooms $89-169. AmEx/D/DC/MC/V. ❹

Rail Haven Best Western, 203 S. Glenstone Ave. (☎417-866-1963). Just pretend not to see the blue hallmark of America's biggest lodgings chain; this well-kept motel has ties to the motor courts of Old 66. Free Wi-Fi. Singles from $45; doubles from $49. AmEx/D/MC/V. ❷

Merigold Inn, 2006 S. Glenstone Ave. (☎866-881-2833). Quirky statues and a popcorn machine in the lobby and wood furnishings in each room. Singles from $20; doubles from $35. AmEx/D/DC/MC/V. ❶

Springfield KOA Campground, 5775 W. Farm Rd. 140 (☎800-562-1228 or 417-831-3645). Take Chestnut St. westbound, and turn left on Hazeltine to reach Farm Rd. 140. Over 60 pleasant sites, some with hookup. Sites from $22, with hookup from $28; cabins $40-50. AmEx/D/MC/V. ❶

▨ NIGHTLIFE

The intersection of Walnut St. and South Ave. has some of the best nightlife options in the area.

South Avenue Pizza and The Bar Next Door, 305-307 South Ave. (☎417-831-5551). Long bar and restaurant on downtown's main strip, featuring pizza ($10-20) and abundant veggie options. Live music Tu-Sa. Restaurant open M-Th 11am-10pm, F 11am-11pm, Sa noon-11pm. Bar open M until 10pm, Tu-Sa until 1:30am. AmEx/D/MC/V.

Ernie Biggs Dueling Piano Bar, 312 South Ave. (☎417-865-4782; www.erniebiggs.com). Get in early to find a table at this popular downtown joint with nightly acts. Th $3 drinks. Cover $5. No reservations. Open W 8pm-1:30am, Th-Sa 7pm-1:30am. Piano shows 8pm. AmEx/D/MC/V.

Joe's Repair Shop and Saloon, 2251 E. Kearney St. (☎417-862-7100). An old-style saloon updated with a "shoe-tree" (leave a pair if you're feeling generous), free pool, karaoke, and the famous "walleye Wednesday" for fish fans. Domestic drafts $1.50. Open M-Sa 11am-1:30am, Su 11am-midnight. AmEx/MC/V.

▨ APPROACHING CARTHAGE: 56 MILES

Leave Springfield on **W. Chestnut Expwy.** This road becomes **Rte. 266;** follow it westward. The road from Springfield south to Carthage is one of the most untouched stretches of Missouri's Rte. 66; decrepit stone buildings with Rte. 66 signs stand amid functioning cattle ranches. Follow Rte. 66 straight where Rte. 96 diverges. 2 mi. later, cross Rte. 96 and head right over the creek and bridge, turning left when the back road crosses Rte. 96. Follow **Rte. 66/96** until it becomes **Central Ave.** Turn left on **Main St.** and continue to **Courthouse Sq.** in Carthage.

CARTHAGE

Miles of cattle and little else give way to the chateau-like turrets of the Jasper County Courthouse in elegant but diminutive Carthage. Carthaginians proudly trace their history parallel to the rise and fall, and rise again, of ancient Carthage, and pride themselves on being emblematic of Missouri's contentious position in the Civil War—Carthage was the site of two major battles.

VITAL STATS

Population: 13,000

Visitor Info: Chamber of Commerce, 107 E. 3rd St. (☎417-358-2373; www.visit-carthage.com). Open M-F 8:30am-5pm.

Internet Access: Carthage Public Library, 612 S. Garrison Ave. (☎417-237-7040), at the corner of 7th St. Open M-W 9am-8pm, Th-F 9am-6pm, Sa 9am-4pm. Free.

Post Office: 226 W. 3rd St. (☎417-358-2307). Open M-F 8am-4:40pm, Sa 8:30am-noon. **Postal Code:** 64836.

GETTING AROUND. Rte. 66/96 enters Carthage from the east and runs just north of downtown as **Central Ave.** Numbered streets, starting with **2nd St.** one block south of Central Ave., run east-west through town. In the eastern section, east-west streets take the names of trees; **Oak St.** is two blocks south of Central Ave. **Rte. 571,** known as **Garrison Ave.,** is a main north-south drag.

SIGHTS. Downtown Carthage centers on the spired, castle-like **Jasper County Courthouse,** where the historic cannons and exhibits on the county's past are on display. (☎417-358-0421. Open M-F 8:30am-4:30pm. Free.) Down the street at the **Carthage Civil War Museum,** 205 Grant St., army figurines and mannequins portray the town's role in Missouri politics and the Civil War. (☎417-237-7060. Open M-Sa 8:30am-5pm, Su 1-5pm. Free.) More local history is illustrated at **Kendrick Place,** at Garrison Ave. and Rte. V, north of town, where period-garbed guides take visitors through a pioneer home dating from the 1850s, outlining Carthage history, the role of the town in the Civil War, and life during the late 1800s. (☎417-358-0636. Open Mar.-Dec. Tu-Sa 10am-5pm; Jan.-Feb. 10am-4pm. Free.) For another step back in time, take a **Victorian Homes Driving Tour** (☎417-359-8181) through downtown Carthage. Audio commentary is available at the visitors bureau. As you leave town, don't miss the **Route 66 Drive-In,** 17231 Old 66 Blvd. Built in

1949, it is the last of the six original drive-in theaters named after the Mother Road. (☎417-357-5959. $5, under 12 $2.)

FOOD AND ACCOMMODATIONS. A 50s-style diner with pink-Cadillac booths, the **Carthage Deli ❶,** 301 S. Main St., features diner favorites as well as Italian sodas and espresso drinks. (☎417-358-8820. Sandwiches $3-4. Open M-F 7am-5pm, Sa 8am-4pm. MC/V.) To satisfy late-night cravings, **CD's Pancake Hut ❶,** 301 S. Garrison St., serves dishes like steak with two eggs, toast, hashbrowns, and coffee for $6. (☎417-359-9807. Open 24hr. AmEx/D/DC/MC/V.) The relaxed **Stone's Throw Dinner Theater,** 796 S. Stone Ln. (Rte. 66), presents comedies, mysteries, and dramas. (☎417-358-9665. Call ahead for hours. $20, seniors $18, students and children $16.) At the **Grand Avenue B&B ❹,** 1615 Grand Ave., each room is adorned in the style of a different 19th-century author; you'll hardly be roughing it in the Mark Twain room. (☎888-380-6786. Breakfast included. Rooms $74-109.) The **Best Budget Inn ❸,** 13011 Rte. 96, offers comfy rooms overlooking a pond on the east side of Carthage. (☎417-358-6911. Rooms from $45. D/MC/V.)

APPROACHING JOPLIN: 12¾ MILES
From **Central Ave.,** turn left on **Garrison Ave.,** then right on **Oak St.** Bear left at the fork on the western edge of town and left again at the T in front of the Carthage cemetery.

JOPLIN. Joplin is noted for its **Thomas Hart Benton mural** in the Municipal Building at 3rd St. and Broadway. The **Joplin Museum Complex,** in Schifferdecker Park, at the corner of Old Rte. 66 and Schifferdecker Ave., contains a glorified rock display, a cookie cutter collection, and a salute to the area's mining past. (☎417-623-1180. Open Tu 10am-7pm, W-Sa 10am-5pm, Su 2-5pm. $2, under 5 free.) The **Red Onion Cafe ❸,** at the corner of 4th and Virginia St., is an island of gourmet sandwiches ($6-8) in the sea of fast food. The Kentucky bourbon pecan pie ($4) is finger-lickin' good. (☎417-623-1004. Salads $5-7. Open M-Th 11am-8pm, F-Sa 11am-9pm. AmEx/MC/V.) **Wok & Roll ❶,** 231 7th St., in an old Rte. 66 gas station, has been converted into the classiest

ROUTE 66 MAP #4

of Chinese buffets. (☎417-782-6400. Buffet $6-8. Open daily 11am-9pm. AmEx/D/DC/MC/V.)

The stretch from Joplin to Afton will take you over 3 states in record time. Consequently, many area businesses have toll-free numbers to keep their customers from paying out-of-state long-distance charges.

⚲ APPROACHING RIVERTON: 11 MILES

Follow **7th St.** out of Joplin and turn right at the "Rte. 66 Next Right" sign onto an ancient alignment featuring white Rte. 66 shields on the narrow stretches of concrete. Be careful on the rises over railroad tracks, where oncoming traffic is difficult to see. Where bustling I-44 heads straight from Missouri to Oklahoma, **Rte. 66** pays a 13 mi. tribute to southeastern Kansas. After passing by Galena, follow **7th St.** for 3 mi.

The Sunflower State

KANSAS
Welcomes You!

RIVERTON. For any souvenir needs, be sure to stop at **Eisler Bros. Old Riverton Store.** Located in a neat, cheery, red-and-white roadside shack right along Historic Rte. 66, Eisler Bros. is part deli, part grocery store, and part Rte. 66 souvenir shop and has been offering a little bit of everything since 1925. (☎620-848-3330. Open M-Th 7:30am-8pm, F-Sa 7:30am-9pm, Su 12:30-7pm. AmEx/MC/V.)

⚲ APPROACHING BAXTER SPRINGS: 5 MILES

Cross over at the junction with **Rte. 400,** heading straight and then left, passing an old, white, trussed bridge along the way. Entering town, turn left, then right on **Aron Ln.,** which turns into **Military Ave.**

BAXTER SPRINGS. Located in the Baxter National Bank, the **Cafe on the Route ❸,** 1101 Military Ave., is a long-standing Rte. 66 eatery, with upscale dining and downscale prices. The menu features delicious salads ($6), pasta ($6-8), and meat entrees ($8-14). (☎620-856-5646. Open M-Th 11am-2:30pm and 4-8pm, F-Sa 11am-2:30pm and 4-8:30pm, Su 11am-2pm.

AmEx/D/MC/V.) Upstairs, **The Little Brick Inn ❷** offers spacious rooms, each with private bath and TV. (☎ 620-856-5646. Rooms $45-65. Breakfast included. AmEx/D/MC/V.)

📷 APPROACHING MIAMI: 16 MILES
Leaving town, head left on **Roberts St.**, swinging right to detour behind the businesses and then merging left again onto **U.S. 69** as you head into Oklahoma. Go through Quapaw, 4 mi. over the border, then pass into Commerce, Mickey Mantle's hometown. Locals will be happy to point out the little house where Mickey, the Commerce Comet, grew up.

MIAMI. Don't blow your cover by mispronouncing Miami—properly said, it's "My-AM-uh." Check out **Waylan's Ku-Ku Hamburgers ❶**, 915 N. Main St., a 1960s chain whose yellow-and-green cuckoos are the last of their breed. The restaurant serves up burgers ($2-4), shakes, malts, and sundaes. (☎918-542-1696. Open M-Th 10am-11pm, F-Sa 10am-midnight. MC/V.)

📷 APPROACHING AFTON: 14 MILES
At the west end of Miami, turn south on **U.S. 69**, continuing straight through Narcissa, 7 mi. later. Keep going until you hit Afton.

AFTON. There is little reason to stop in Afton, although a decent night's sleep can be had at the **Route 66 Motel ❷**, 21751 S. U.S. 69 (Rte. 66), which has standard amenities (☎918-257-8313. Singles $44; doubles $47. AmEx/D/MC/V.)

📷 APPROACHING VINITA: 11 MILES
Continue on **U.S. 69** into Vinita.

VINITA. Entering Vinita from the north, the first major attraction is the **Will Rogers Rodeo Grounds** to the left. The **Will Rogers Memorial Rodeo,** which attracts some of the best cowboys in the country, takes place here over four days every August. (Info ☎918-256-7133.) Instead of following Rte. 66 all the way through town, stop by the **World's Largest**

McDonald's. Spanning the Will Rogers Expwy., the giant glass paean to fast food includes McMeeting rooms, McGiftshops, and McBathrooms, in addition to all your McFood needs. (Turn left at the Rodeo, and follow the road for about ½ mi. Turn right just before the overpass. ☎918-256-5571. Open daily 5:30am-midnight.) The **Clanton Cafe ❷**, 319 E. Illinois St., has offered unique meal options since 1927, including Vinita's famed "Calf Fries" (cow testicles; $5), as well as tamer cow-part options. (☎918-256-9053. Burgers $2-4. Open M-F 5:30am-8pm, Su 11am-2pm. D/MC/V.) Each room in **The Relax Inn ❷**, 110 W. Dwain Willia, has dark wood paneling and cable TV. (☎918-256-6492. Singles from $34; doubles from $39. AmEx/D/MC/V.)

📷 APPROACHING FOYIL: 27 MILES
In the heart of downtown Vinita, head left on **Wilson St.** Leave town on **Rte. 66,** following it southwest through the mini-towns of White Oak and Chelsea until reaching Foyil.

FOYIL. One of the stranger attractions along the Oklahoma stretch of Rte. 66 is **Totem Pole Park.** Artist Ed Galloway's masterpiece is a meadow of brightly colored totem poles, including the **world's largest totem pole** (90 ft.), birdbaths, and an 11-sided **"Fiddle House"** that once held over 300 fiddles. The building now serves as the museum and visitors center. (Turn east at the northern end of town on Rte. 28A, following the road for about 4 mi. to get to the park. ☎918-342-9149. Open daily 11am-3pm. Suggested donation.)

📷 APPROACHING CLAREMORE: 10 MILES
Returning to **Rte. 66,** continue west for 8 mi. to reach Claremore.

CLAREMORE
What Abe Lincoln is to Illinois, cowboy/entertainer Will Rogers is to Oklahoma, and Claremore is the center of Rogers mania. The Will Rogers Memorial Museum sits on Will Rogers Blvd., next to Rogers State University, while Will Rogers sculptures and memorials line the streets. A veritable oasis of antique stores line Will Rogers Blvd., all the while maintaining its early Sooner look.

VITAL STATS

Population: 16,000

Visitor Info: Claremore Convention and Visitors Bureau, 419 W. Will Rogers Blvd. (☎918-341-8688; www.claremore.org). Open M-F 8:30am-5pm.

Internet Access: Will Rogers Library, 1515 N. Florence St. (☎918-341-1564). Open M-Tu 9:30am-8pm, W-Th 9:30am-6pm, F-Sa 9:30am-5pm. Free.

Post Office: 400 W. 9th St. (☎918-343-8917). Open M-F 8am-5pm, Sa 9am-noon. **Postal Code:** 74017.

Ｆ GETTING AROUND. Rte. 65 runs northeast-southwest through Claremore as **Lynn Riggs Blvd.,** and streets are arranged in an easily navigable grid system south of Rte. 65. Numbered streets run roughly east-west through the city, while avenues run north-south. **Will Rogers Blvd.,** the city's major streets, is one block southwest of 4th St.

Ｇ SIGHTS. Will Rogers fanfare is everywhere in Claremore—if he was merely a name when you entered town, he'll seem like an old friend when you leave. At the **Will Rogers Memorial Museum,** 1720 W. Will Rogers Blvd., the Will Rogers statue out front watches over Claremore from high on a hill to the northeast of town. Inside, video reels and a barrage of paintings, clippings, and photographs pay homage to the life of Oklahoma's favorite son. (☎800-324-9455. Open daily 8am-5pm. Tours by appointment. Suggested donation $4, seniors and children $3.) At the **Will Rogers Birthplace Ranch,** 2 mi. east of Oologah, the white log cabin where Will Rogers grew up has largely been preserved. The view from atop the hill remains quietly breathtaking, interrupted only by the horses, goats, and a peacock that wander the grounds. (Head northwest on Will Rogers Blvd. and take Rte. 88 for 12 mi. north toward Oologah. ☎918-275-4201. Open daily sunrise-sunset. Tours by appointment. Suggested donation $3-4.) If you haven't found yourself spelling out Oklahoma in song yet, a visit to the **Lynn Riggs Memorial,** 121 N. Weenonah St., will give you a kick-start. Riggs wrote **Green Grow the Lilacs,** upon which Rogers and Hammerstein based their smash hit *Oklahoma!* (☎918-627-2716. Open M-F 9am-noon and 1-4pm. Suggested donation $3.)

The **J.M. Davis Arms and Historical Museum,** 333 N. Lynn Riggs Blvd., features the over 20,000-piece collection of J.M. Davis, making it the world's largest privately owned gun collection. The collection includes 1,200 beer steins, Native American artifacts, and a 500-year-old Chinese hand cannon. (☎918-341-5707. Open M-Sa 8:30am-5pm, Su 1-5pm.)

ＦＦ FOOD AND ACCOMMODATIONS. Unusual variety characterizes the cooking at the **Hammett House,** 1616 W. Will Rogers Blvd. Pies ($3) come in flavors like lemon pecan and sour cream raisin, and their lamb and turkey fries (cousins to calf fries; p. 534) have a thankful resemblance to chicken. (☎918-341-7333. Sandwiches and salads $6. Entrees $10-20. Open Tu-Sa 11am-9pm. AmEx/D/DC/MC/V.) Get a home-style meal at Claremore's oldest restaurant, **Dot's Cafe ❷,** 301 W. Will Rogers Blvd. Their specialty is homemade chili ($4), but the burgers ($2.50) are also delicious. (☎918-341-9718. Open M-W and F-Su 7am-2pm, Th 7am-8pm. Cash only.) The **Claremore Motor Inn ❷,** 1709 N. Lynn Riggs Blvd., has well-kept rooms. (☎918-342-4545; www.cmi66.com. Singles from $44; doubles from $49. AmEx/D/MC/V.) On the way to the Will Rogers Birthplace Ranch, **Hawthorn Bluff Campground ❶,** 9¾ mi. north of Claremore, has swimming and basic sites. (☎918-443-2319. Sites $14, with electricity $18. AmEx/D/MC/V.)

PHOTO OP. In Catoosa, about 11 mi. beyond Claremore, the main attraction is a **giant blue whale,** once a waterslide and now merely a picnic area and roadside gawking point.

ＦＦ APPROACHING TULSA: 15 MILES
Follow **Will Rogers Blvd.** westbound to **Rte. 66,** turn left, and continue west on Rte. 66. Just past Catoosa, head right on **Ford Ave.,** 1 mi. past **Spunky Creek,** then left on **Cherokee St.** at the T-intersection 2 mi. later. Head left under the interstate, continuing about 1 mi. to **11th St.** Turn right on 11th St. to head into Tulsa.

TULSA

Though Tulsa is not Oklahoma's political capital, it is in many ways the state's center of commerce and culture. First settled by Creek Native Americans arriving on the Trail of

Tears and named for the old Alabama settlement "Tulsey-town," Tulsa's location on the banks of the Arkansas River made it an optimal trading outpost. It was once known as The Oil Capital of the World, but for roadtrippers it is most notable as the home of Cyrus Avery, the "Father of Rte. 66."

VITAL STATS

Population: 390,000

Visitor Info: Tulsa Convention and Visitors Bureau, 2 W. 2nd St., #150 (☎918-585-1201 or 800-558-3311; www.visittulsa.com). Open M-F 8am-5pm.

Internet Access: Tulsa Public Library, 400 Civic Center (☎918-596-7977), at 4th St. and Denver Ave. Open May.-Aug. M-Th 9am-9pm, F-Sa 9am-5pm; Sept.-Apr. M-Th 9am-9pm, F-Sa 9am-5pm; Su 1-5pm. Free.

Parking: American Parking, at 4th St. and Cincinnati Ave. (☎918-587-4141). 12hr. or less $1.50.

Post Office: 333 W. 4th St. (☎918-732-6651). Open M-F 7:30am-5pm. **Postal Code:** 74103.

⬛ GETTING AROUND

Tulsa is divided into quadrants. Downtown surrounds **Main St.** (north-south) and **Admiral Blvd.** Numbered east-west streets ascend to the north and south of Admiral Blvd. Named avenues run north-south in alphabetical order; those named after western cities are west of **Main St.**, while eastern cities lie to the east.

👁 SIGHTS

The ⬛**Philbrook Museum,** 2727 S. Rockford Rd., presents tasteful exhibits of Native American and European art in a renovated 1920s Italian villa that is an attraction in its own right. In the summer the museum hosts films, lectures, and art classes. (Follow the signs from Utica Ave. ☎800-324-7941; www.philbrook.org. Open Tu-W and F-Su 10am-5pm, Th 10am-8pm. $7.50, students and seniors $5.50.) Perched amid the Osage Hills, 2 mi. from downtown, the **Thomas Gilcrease Museum,** 1400 Gilcrease Museum Rd., houses the world's largest collection of Western American art as well as 250,000 Native American artifacts. See feather bonnets, cowboy

sculptures, and wonderful themed gardens. (Take the Gilcrease Rd. exit off I-244. ☎918-596-2700; www.gilcrease.org. Open Tu-Su 10am-4pm. Free. Special exhibits $7, seniors $6, ages 13-18 $5, under 13 free.) In 1964, Oral Roberts had a dream in which God commanded him, "Build Me a University!" Roberts took these orders seriously, and the ultra-modern spectacle of **Oral Roberts University,** 7777 S. Lewis Ave., was born. At the visitors center, tourists can see a multimedia presentation on Roberts' life. (6 mi. south of downtown. ☎800-678-8876; www.oru.edu. Open June-Aug. M-Sa 9am-5pm, Su 1-5pm; Sept.-May M-Sa 10am-4:30pm, Su 1-4:30pm.)

 PHOTO OP. At the Canning Entrance to Oral Roberts University, visitors are greeted by an 80 ft. tall sculpture of praying hands.

Tulsa thrives during the **International Mayfest** (☎918-582-6435) in mid-May. August brings both **Jazz on Greenwood,** which includes concerts at Greenwood Park, 300 N. Greenwood Dr., as well as the **Intertribal Powwow,** at the Tulsa Fairgrounds Pavilion. The Powwow attracts Native Americans and thousands of onlookers for a three-day festival of food, crafts, and nightly dance contests. (☎918-744-1113. $5.)

🍽 FOOD

Tulsa has the usual fast-food chains lining I-44, but if it's real food you're after, skip these, and head for the more original establishments scattered around town—don't miss **Weber's Root Beer,** a local favorite, in the orange shack on Peoria Ave. Upscale food is available downtown, but many restaurants cater to business-people and close at 2pm on weekdays and altogether on weekends.

Mama Lou's, 5688 W. Skelly Dr. (☎918-445-1700), take the W. 49th St. exit off I-44. The famous 2x2 includes 2 hot cakes, 2 eggs, 2 strips of bacon, and 2 sausage links for less than $5. Tuna melt $5. Open 24hr. AmEx/D/MC/V. ❷

Desi Wok, 3966 S. Hudson Ave. (☎918-621-6565; www.desiwok.net), at 41st St. This casual restaurant is one of only 2 Indian restaurants in Tulsa. The chicken *tikka masala* is excellent ($7), and vegetarians will salivate over the *saag*

Tulsa

🏠 ACCOMMODATIONS
Desert Hills Motel, **4**
Gateway Motor Hotel, **9**
Towers Hotel & Suites, **14**
Western Capri Motel, **10**

🍎 FOOD
Brook Restaurant & Bar, **12**
Coney Island, **2**

Desi Wok, **15**
In the Raw Sushi Bar, **7**
Mama Lou's, **8**
Metro Diner, **3**
Queenie's Cafe, **6**
Weber's Root Beer, **13**

📻 NIGHTLIFE
Boston's, **5**
Club Majestic, **1**
Suede Lounge, **11**

paneer (spinach and cheese curd; $7). Open M-Th and Su 11am-10pm, F-Sa 11am-11pm. AmEx/D/DC/MC/V. ❸

Brook Restaurant & Bar, 3401 S. Peoria Ave. (☎918-748-9977), in an old movie theater. Classic Art Deco appeal with a menu of chicken, burgers, wraps, and salads ($7-8). Open M-Sa 11am-1am, Su 11am-11pm. AmEx/D/MC/V. ❸

Metro Diner, 3001 E. 11th St. (☎918-592-2616), on Rte. 66, on the way into town. In an old Rte. 66 filling station, the Metro has chrome and 50s kitsch diner appeal, with an *I Love Lucy* theme. Salads, sandwiches, and dinner entrees $4-10. Homemade pies $2. Open M-Th and Su 6am-10pm, F-Sa 6am-midnight. AmEx/D/MC/V. ❷

In the Raw Sushi Bar, 3321 S. Peoria Ave. (☎918-744-1300). Serves fresh sushi with quirky nick-

names to match. Try the "volcano roll" with shrimp and jalapeno ($11) or "deep-fried goodness" with soft-shell crab and yellowtail ($7). Sushi rolls $5-24. Open Tu-Th 11:30am-2pm and 5-10pm, F 11:30am-2pm and 5-11pm. AmEx/D/MC/V. ❹

Queenie's Cafe, 1834 Utica Sq. (☎918-749-3481). Excellent sandwiches ($6-7) and baked goods like the Mt. St. Helen's Fudge Torte ($3.50 per slice) and signature Linzer cookies. Open M-F 7am-7pm, Sa 8am-6pm, Su 9am-2pm. MC/V. ❷

Coney Island, 123 W. 4th St. (☎918-587-2821). A chain that started on the East Coast and migrated westward to become a Tulsa tradition. The original in Tulsa is on 4th and Cherokee, where they have been serving little all-beef wieners since 1926. 3 Coneys plus drink $4. Open M-Sa 10am-8pm. MC/V. ❶

ACCOMMODATIONS

Decent budget accommodations are scarce downtown, but they are plentiful off I-44 on the east and west sides of Tulsa.

Towers Hotel & Suites, 3355 E. Skelly Dr. (☎918-744-4263). Take Exit W. 49th St. off I-44. Designed like a medieval fortress, with stone-walled rooms, bathroom chandeliers, and whirlpools. The ultimate in budget castle luxury. (☎918-744-4263. Singles from $41; doubles from $51. AmEx/D/MC/V. ❷

Desert Hills Motel, 5220 E. 11th St. (☎918-834-3311). Look for the neon cactus sign. This motel offers clean, if dimly lit rooms, although non-smoking options are limited. Key deposit $5. Rooms from $32. AmEx/D/MC/V. ❷

Western Capri Motel, 5320 W. Skelly Dr. (☎918-446-2644). The vintage sign on this recently renovated motel proves that it's the cheapest option on the strip. There are few decorations in the rooms but in a good "thank God they didn't bother" kind of way. Rooms $30. MC/V. ❶

Gateway Motor Hotel, 5600 W. Skelly Dr. (☎918-446-6611). Rooms with cable TV and DVD/VCR players. Key deposit $2. Singles $34-39; doubles $40-43. AmEx/D/MC/V. ❷

NIGHTLIFE

Check out the free *Urban Tulsa,* at local restaurants, and *The Spot* in the Friday *Tulsa World* for up-to-date specs on arts and entertainment. Bars line **Brookside,** an area along S. Peoria Ave., and 15th St. east of Peoria. At the **Suede Lounge,** 3340 S. Peoria Ave., a martini lounge/champagne bar, imbibe your lip-smacking libation while dancing to a combination of live music and canned tunes. (☎918-743-0600. Cover up to $10. Open Tu-Sa 7pm-2am.) A true sports bar and grill, **Boston's,** 1738 Boston Ave., serves up everything from chips and salsa ($3) to chicken-fried steak ($8). On Tuesdays enjoy "Red Dirt" music, a distinctive Oklahoman sound. (☎918-583-9520. Cover Th-Sa $5. Happy hour daily 3-7pm with $1.50 domestic beers. Open M-F 11am-2am. AmEx/D/MC/V.) If you are in the mood to dance on the weekend, check out **Club Majestic,** 124 N. Boston Ave. (☎918-584-9494. Cover varies. Open Th-Sa 9pm-2am. AmEx/D/MC/V.)

APPROACHING SAPULPA: 11 MILES

Head southwest on **11th St.** Curve left passing **Denver Ave.** as 11th St. turns into **12th St.** ¼ mi. later, turn left and cross the river. Continue on **Southwest Blvd.** toward Sapulpa. Follow Southwest Blvd. until it becomes **Frankoma Rd.** Rte. 66 heading into Sapulpa is also known as **Mission St.;** turn right on Mission St., following the railroad tracks.

SAPULPA. Named for Chief Sapulpa, the Lower Creek Native American who established a trading post here in 1850, Sapulpa was once an oil and gas town. It is now known for **Frankoma Pottery,** 9549 Frankoma Rd., which has produced pieces made from Oklahoma clay since 1938. (☎918-224-5511; www.frankoma.com. Open M-Sa 9am-5pm. Free.) The blue bubbliness of **Happy Burger ❶,** 215 N. Mission St., has been leaving customers giddy with grease since the early 1950s. (☎918-224-7750. Burgers $2. Slushies $1.25. Open M-F 10:30am-9pm. Cash only.)

APPROACHING BRISTOW: 21 MILES

1 mi. after turning onto **Mission St.** at the northeastern edge of Sapulpa, turn right onto **Dewey St.** There is no historic 66 sign at this turn, but you will see the signs for Rte. 66 and 33. Follow Rte. 66 through Kelleyville, site of Oklahoma's worst train disaster in 1917, and on to Bristow.

BRISTOW. Bristow began in 1897 as a trading post for the Cherokee Nation, and as you drive through it's hard to miss the historical brick streets and vintage brick buildings. Rte. 66 is the main street of Bristow, where people seem relatively unconcerned with the Mother Road. **Russ's Ribs ❷,** 223 S. Main St., however, displays its Rte. 66 pride with hand-stenciled 66 shields and vintage signs as well as messages tacked on the walls from everyone who passes through. Sample some of the excellent barbecue like the rib sandwich ($4), or try the frog legs basket for $6.50. (☎918-367-5656. F 6pm all-you-can-eat $9.50. Open Tu-Th 10:30am-7pm, F-Sa 10:30am-8pm. MC/V.)

APPROACHING STROUD: 16 MILES

Take a right on **4th St.** (Watch out—the sign is hard to see). Turn left onto **Poland St.** ½ mi. later, then head straight toward Stroud.

STROUD. Home to the Sac and Fox Nation, one of Oklahoma's 39 Native American tribes,

ROUTE 66 MAP #6

Stroud sports many buildings built prior to statehood. As you leave, stop by the **Stable Ridge Vineyard**, 2016 Hwy 66 W. The tasting room is located in Stroud's historic Catholic Church, and the wine is delicious. (☎800-359-3990; www.stableridgevineyards.com. Open M-F 11am-6pm, Sa 10am-7pm, Su 1-5pm.) A Rte. 66 classic, the ◪**Rock Cafe** ❷, 114 W. Main St., was a favorite eatery of Pixar's *Cars* film crew and features multi-ethnic cuisine in a stone cabin. Alligator burgers ($4.15), crepes ($4.50), and *jagerschnitzel* and *spaetzle* ($6.50) are just a few of the tantalizing options. (☎918-968-3990. Open daily 6am-9pm. D/MC/V.) Rooms at the **Skyliner Motel** ❷, 717 W. Main St., beneath the dazzling sign, are clean and cheap. (Just before Jct. 99, on Rte. 66. ☎918-968-9556. Singles M-Th $42, F-Su $48; doubles $50/$65. AmEx/D/MC/V.) Equally nice accommodations can be found across the street at the **Sooner Motel** ❷, 412 N. 8th St. (☎918-968-2595. Singles from $35. AmEx/D/MC/V.)

⌖ APPROACHING DAVENPORT: 8 MILES
Continue along **Rte. 66,** and don't miss the Burma-Shave signs welcoming you to Davenport.

DAVENPORT. Davenport is home to the first spherical oil tank, erected in 1925 to the northeast of town. **Garwooly's Game Room** ❷, 1023 Broadway, at the eastern side of town, covers the nightlife bases with a dim dining area, squeaky clean chrome and tile ice-cream parlor, and adjoining checkered dance floor. (☎918-377-2230. Indian Taco made with fry bread $4. Chicken-fried steak $7. Open M-Sa 10am-9pm. D/MC/V.)

⌖ APPROACHING CHANDLER: 4 MILES
Continue following **Rte. 66.**

CHANDLER. In Chandler, you can see buildings that survived the 1897 tornado and some authentic ghost signs on the sides of old buildings. The town is also home to the **Lincoln County Historical Society Museum**, 719 Manvel St., at 8th St., which displays a complete Oklahoma pioneer history with period clothing, a 19th-century buggy, a buffalo skull, and a flush-toilet outhouse from 1902. (☎405-258-2425. Open M-F 9:30am-4pm, Sa by appointment. Suggested donation $2.) The **Lincoln Inn Motel** ❸, 740 E. 1st St., offers snug wooden duplexes that have faced Rte. 66 for the last 62 years. (☎405-258-0200. Singles $40; doubles $45. AmEx/MC/V.)

🏨 APPROACHING LUTHER: 18 MILES

Follow **Manvel St.** as it curves left, heading west toward Luther.

LUTHER. South of the pecan grove at the west end of Luther, the **Tres Suenos Vineyards,** 19691 E. Charter Oak Rd., offers free tours and tastings, if you don't mind the 10min. drive on unpaved, dusty road. Twelve wines are bottled here; you can taste any of them, but be sure to try the Chenin, made from an American grape. (☎405-277-7089; www.tressuenos.com. Open Th-Sa noon-6pm or by appointment.)

🏨 APPROACHING ARCADIA: 8 MILES

Continue west on **Rte. 66.** As you enter Arcadia, look to the right to see remnants of the **Rock of Ages gas station.**

ARCADIA. Arcadia's main attraction is the **Round Barn.** Originally built in 1898 and restored in 1992, the structure is now a historic landmark. The bottom level is a museum of all the round barns around the world, while upstairs features dances and events. Speak on the center platform for an especially thrilling acoustical phenomenon. (☎405-396-2761; www.arcadiaroundbarn.org. Open Tu-Sa and Su 10am-5pm. Free.) The rustic charm of the Old West lives in the grey wooden exterior of 🏨**Hillbillee's Cafe and Bed & Breakfast ❸,** 208 E. Rte. 66. The cafe features license plate siding and serves three square meals a day, while the B&B has six themed rooms including Doc Holliday's, Shady Lady's, and Miss Kitty's, each decorated with Western memorabilia. Although the Old West never had luxury like this, some similarities ring true—while there are private baths with huge tubs, none of the rooms have telephones. Pool and hot tub are available for guest use in the spring and summer. (☎405-396-2982; www.hillbillees.com. Omelettes $5. Fried chicken dinner for 4 $15. Live music F-Sa. Cafe open M-Th 11am-9pm, F 11am-10pm, Sa 8am-10pm, Su 8am-3pm. Rooms from $65. AmEx/D/MC/V.)

🏨 APPROACHING EDMOND: 15 MILES

Continue on **Rte. 66** to reach Edmond.

EDMOND. The site of both the first church and the first school in Oklahoma Territory, Edmond is now largely overrun with popular commercial establishments and looks it was erected within the last 15 years. Hidden amongst the plentiful food chains is **El Parian ❸,** 315 S. Broadway Ave., a restaurant serving an extensive menu of authentic Mexican food. The El Parian special (one asada taco, one fajita quesadilla, and one fajita enchilada; $10) is delicious. (☎405-359-1068. Open M-Th and Su 10:30am-9pm, F-Sa 10:30am-9:30pm. D/MC/V.) Lodging is plentiful in Edmond, and it is cheaper than the chain motel alternatives in Oklahoma City. **Stafford Inn ❸,** 1809 E. 2nd St., rents elegant brick-walled rooms with jacuzzis and king-size beds. (☎405-340-8197. Continental breakfast included. Singles $55; doubles $59. AmEx/D/MC/V.) **Broadway Suites ❷,** 1305 S. Broadway, provides excellent value with suites or kitchenette units, as well as VCRs for $10 per night and laundry. (☎800-200-3486. Kitchenette units $37; suites $75. AmEx/D/MC/V.)

🏨 APPROACHING OKLAHOMA CITY: 18 MILES

From Edmond on **Rte. 66,** turn left at Broadway, following the **Memorial Rd.** exit. Go left at the yield sign.

OKLAHOMA CITY

In the late 1800s, Oklahoma's capital was a major transit point on cattle drives from Texas to the north, and today its stockyards are a fascinating window into a world not often seen by outsiders. Lying along the Santa Fe Railroad, the city was swarmed by over 100,000 homesteaders when Oklahoma was opened to settlement in 1889, and it continues to celebrate American westward expansion at one of the nation's largest museums devoted to the West.

PAGE TURN. See p. 763 in the **Deep South** for complete coverage of Oklahoma City.

🏨 APPROACHING YUKON: 15 MILES

Take **I-44 W** through Bethany. On the west end of town, watch for an old steel trussed bridge. Head left across the highway here, and immediately swing right onto the frontage road to cross the bridge and continue on **Rte. 66** to Yukon.

YUKON. You'll know when you've hit Yukon when the giant "Yukon's Best Flour" sign towers above you. **Garth Brooks Blvd.** may also tip you off that you've stumbled into the hometown of the King of Country himself. Park your pickup truck and rest your broken heart at the **Green Carpet Inn ❷,** 10 E. Main St., where the floral floor coverings compete with riotous striped curtains and tropical bedspreads. (☎405-350-9900 or 800-583-0290. Singles $40; doubles $46. AmEx/D/MC/V.)

☑ APPROACHING EL RENO: 14 MILES

Continue west on **Rte. 66.** As you enter El Reno, 66 becomes **Rock Island Ave.** Look to the right when you first enter to see the historic **Oasis Drive-In** sign, which promises 5 burgers for $1.

EL RENO

Located at the intersection of Rte. 66 and the old Chisholm Trail, El Reno has a rich history and the buildings to back it up. The city was the site of three land runs, events where tens of thousands of settlers made a mad dash over newly opened territory to stake the largest claim they could. Thousands of dead German and Italian POWs from WWII also lie beneath Reno's red dirt. More recently, the 1988 film *Rain Man* was shot here, and Dustin Hoffman fever still runs high.

VITAL STATS

Population: 16,000

Visitor Info: EL RENO Convention and Visitors Bureau, 206 N. Bickford St. (☎888-535-7757; www.elreno.org). Open M-F 9am-5pm.

Internet Access: El Reno Carnegie Library, 215 E. Wade St. (☎405-262-2409). Open M-Th 9am-7pm, F 9am-5pm, Sa 9am-1pm. Free.

Post Office: 203 N. Evans Ave. (☎405-262-5095). Open M-F 8:30am-5pm, Sa 9-11am. **Postal Code:** 73036.

☞ GETTING AROUND.

El Reno is laid out in a simple grid; most streets run east-west, while most avenues run north-south. **U.S. 40** runs just south of town, while **Bus. U.S. 40** splits off to become **Sunset Dr.,** a major road, in town. **U.S. 81** enters El Reno from the north, turning into **Choctaw Ave.** on its way through town; downtown is centered at the intersection of Choctaw Ave. and Sunset Dr. Parking is generally plentiful.

☒ SIGHTS.

In town, you can take the **Heritage Express Trolley**—the only rail-based trolley in Oklahoma—which runs from Heritage Park into El Reno's historic downtown. (☎405-262-5121. Boards at 300 S. Grand St. Call for schedule.) **Heroes Plaza,** 206 N. Bickford Ave., pays tribute to the 206 Canadian men and women killed in 20th-century wars. (☎405-262-1188; www.heroesplaza.org. Free.) The **Canadian County Historical Museum,** 300 S. Grand St., features an 1892 hotel, a jail, and a caboose. (☎405-262-5121. Open W-Sa 10am-5pm, Su 1-5pm. Free.) Four miles west of El Reno, **Fort Reno,** 7107 W. Cheyenne St., was established in 1885 as an Indian military camp to monitor the local Cheyenne and Arapaho populations. Troops from the fort, including two companies of Buffalo Soldiers, oversaw the first great Land Run, making sure no Sooners crossed the line too, well, soon. The fort was the birthplace of Black Jack, the riderless black horse in JFK's funeral, and also served as a German POW camp in WWII. The restored 1936 Officer's Quarters serves as the visitors center and provides info on the buildings. (Take the Fort Reno exit off Bus. 1-40 and turn right. ☎405-262-3987; www.fortreno.org. Open M-F 10am-5pm, Sa-Su 10am-4pm.) Outside of town, **Lake El Reno** has four miles of shoreline and is perfect for recreational activities like water skiing, swimming, boating, and fishing. The lake is also home to a herd of buffalo.

 PHOTO OP. The truly lucky will pass through El Reno on the 1st Saturday in May, for **Onion Fried Burger Day,** when Johnnie's cranks out the **World's Largest Hamburger,** an 800 lb. onion fried burger bonanza.

▓☞ FOOD AND ACCOMMODATIONS.

Check out the countertop at **Sid's Diner ❶,** 300 S. Choctaw Ave., one block south of U.S. 81, for photos of Dustin Hoffman and hundreds of other historic shots. While you're there, enjoy the steak and shake special for $5. (☎405-262-7757. Open daily 7am-8:30pm. Cash or check only.) El Reno is also famous as home of the scrumptious "Onion Fried Burger" at **Johnnie's Grill ❶,** 301 S. Rock Island St. Grilled onions are pressed into the burger patty and cooked together. (☎405-262-4721. Onion fried burger $2.50. Open M-Sa 6am-9pm, Su 11am-8pm. Cash or check only.) Crazy chicken hats cover racks outside the door of the **Squawk-N-Skoot ❷**, 200 S. Choctaw, where the most popular menu items are frog legs ($1.50) and calf fries ($4), a.k.a. bull testicles. (☎405-422-3622. Open M-Th 11am-9pm, F-Sa 11am-10pm. D/MC/V.) **The Budget Inn ❷**, 1221 W. Sunset Dr., has lacy decor, laundry, and cable TV. (☎405-262-0251. Singles $35; doubles $45. AmEx/D/MC/V.) Turn left onto U.S. 81 S. as you enter town to reach the **Economy Express ❷**, 2851 S. U.S. 81, which has clean and basic rooms. (☎405-262-1022. Singles from $39; doubles from $42. AmEx/D/MC/V.)

⚐ APPROACHING HINTON: 29 MILES
Leave El Reno on **Sunset Dr.** which becomes **Bus. I-40 W.** Take the Fort Reno turnoff onto **Rte. 66.** 11 mi. later turn right onto **U.S. 281.** Spur for about 2 mi., then take a left at the top of the hill onto the old 2-lane road (watch carefully because it's easy to miss). Turn left at the bottom of the hill to rejoin U.S. 281. Continue on the frontage road through Bridgeport. From **I-40** take **Exit 101** to reach Hinton.

HINTON. Just off Rte. 66 along U.S. 281, the **Hinton Country Inn ❷** follows true Rte. 66 style, combining a gas station, convenience store, and motel. The decorative woodwork around the mirrors was done by the current owner. (☎405-542-3198. Singles from $36. AmEx/D/MC/V.) For a brief and pleasant rest stop, take a departure from Rte. 66, following U.S. 281 5 mi. south of I-40 through Hinton to the **Red Rock Canyon State Park ❶**, where basic campsites await in the heart of the canyon. (☎405-542-6344; www.oklahomaparks.com. Open M-F 8am-5pm. Tent sites from $8; RV sites from $15. AmEx/D/MC/V.)

⚐ APPROACHING WEATHERFORD: 24 MILES
As you drive past Hydro on Rte. 66, check out the structure sporting historic gas pumps on the right. It used to be **Lucille's,** a landmark filling station and market that was sold on e-Bay following Lucille's death in 2000. New owner Rich Koch is currently restoring the station as well as building **Lucille's Roadhouse** in Weatherford in its honor.

WEATHERFORD. Weatherford is extremely proud of native son Thomas P. Stafford—the 18th man in space. The **Stafford Air and Space Museum,** Exit 84 from I-40, includes replicas and artifacts of air and space travel from the Wright brothers' plane to the actual desk that responded to Apollo 13's infamous report, "Houston, we have a problem here." (☎580-772-6143; www.staffordairandspacemuseum.com. Open M-Sa 9am-5pm, Su 1-5pm. $5, under 18 free.)

⚐ APPROACHING CLINTON: 15 MILES
From the north **I-40** service road in Weatherford, continue to the T intersection. Turn left to cross I-40 and right to follow the **south service road.** Skip one crossover and take the next (no choice as the south side dead ends) to cross I-40 and head into Clinton. Turn right at the intersection with **Bus. I-40/Gary Blvd./Rte. 66.**

CLINTON

Clinton's provenance reflects relations between settlers and Native Americans in the Great Plains. Deeded the land by the federal government, the Native Americans that had been condensed into the area were prohibited from selling more than half of their 160-acre allotments. Determined to found a town in the rich valley, J.L. Avant and E.E. Blake secretly bought half allotments from four different men, and in 1902 the amalgamated town was dubbed Clinton for Judge Clinton Irwin. As the headquarters of the National Highway 66 Association for almost three decades, Clinton has an abundance of Rte. 66 pride and the first state-sponsored Rte. 66 museum.

VITAL STATS

Population: 9000
Visitor Info: Clinton Chamber of Commerce, 101 S. 4th St. (☎580-323-2222; www.clintonok.org). Open M-F 9am-5pm.
Internet Access: Clinton Public Library, 751 Frisco Ave. (☎580-323-2165). Open M and W 9am-6pm, Tu and Th 9am-6pm, F 9am-5pm, Sa 9am-1pm.
Post Office: 212 S. 11th St. (☎508-323-0712.) Open M-F 8am-4:30pm, Sa 9-11am. **Postal Code:** 74103.

⬚ GETTING AROUND. Clinton is centered on the intersection of **Bus. I-40** and **U.S. 183.** I-40 runs just south of downtown. In town, U.S. 183 is known as **Cox St.,** and Bus. I-40 is called **Gary Blvd.,** one of the city's main drags. Numbered streets run north-south, starting with **1st St.** in the east.

⊙ SIGHTS. On the way into Clinton, the much-advertised **Cherokee Trading Post,** 6101 NE Service Rd., sells crafts of every variety, including beautiful jewelry, moccasins, cacti, and postcards. (Take Exit 71 from I-40. ☎580-323-5524. Open M-Th and Su 7am-10pm, F-Sa 8am-11pm.) **McLain Rogers Park,** at the corner of 10th and Bess Rogers St., has a pool with a three-story waterslide and plenty of snacks (☎580-323-7870. $2.50 to swim.) The **Cheyenne Cultural Center,** 2250 NE Rte. 66, displays work by Cheyenne craftspeople and artists and exhibits on Cheyenne regional history and culture. (☎580-323-6224. Open Tu-Sa 10am-5pm. Free.) Finally, don't miss the **⊠Oklahoma Rte. 66 Museum,** 2229. W. Gary Blvd. The state's tribute to Rte. 66 traces the road decade by decade. Be sure to take advantage of the inspiring (and free) audio tour by notable Rte. 66 author Michael Wallis. Also at the museum is the **"World's Largest Curio Cabinet,"** filled with Rte. 66 souvenirs. (☎580-323-7866. Open Memorial Day to Labor Day M-Sa 9am-7pm, Su 1-6pm; Labor Day to Memorial Day M-Sa 9am-5pm, Su 1-5pm. $3, seniors $2.50, ages 6-18 $1, under 6 free.)

🍴🛏 FOOD AND ACCOMMODATIONS. At the **Cherokee Trading Post Cafe ❷,** 6101 NE Service Rd., a juicy buffalo burger runs only $6. (Take Exit 71 from I-40. ☎580-323-5524. Sandwiches $4-7. Open M-Th and Su 7am-10pm, F-Sa 8am-11pm. AmEx/D/MC/V.) Check in for a little heartbreak and hang up your blue suede shoes at the **Best Western Trade Winds Courtyard Inn ❷,** 2128 Gary Blvd., where the King himself rocked around the clock each time he came through Clinton. Now a Best Western franchise, Elvis's favorite Clinton motel is still under the same management as it was during his reign, and lodgers can rent his room, with original furnishings. (☎800-321-2209 or 580-323-2610. Singles from $29; doubles $45; Elvis Suite $70. AmEx/D/MC/V.) At the **Glancy Motel ❶,** 217 Gary Blvd., the giant red vintage sign and the 70s-style wrought iron indicate the age of the motel, but rooms are comfortable enough. (☎580-323-0112. No non-smoking singles. Singles $25; doubles $30. Cash only.) Rooms at the **Relax Inn ❶,** 1116 S. 10th St., aren't ritzy, but they're clean and cheap. (☎580-323-1888. Rooms from $28. AmEx/D/MC/V.)

🚩 APPROACHING CANUTE: 20 MILES
Follow old **Rte. 66,** paralleling I-40 W. On the way, you'll pass through Foss, little more than a dusty ghost town. 5 mi. north of town, an incongruous man-made reservoir provides opportunities for lakeside camping, swimming, water sports, and boat rentals. Later on you'll hit Canute.

CANUTE. Canute has few diversions to slow your cross-country progress, but Elvis fans can stop at **Kupka's Station,** a gas station where the king was known to stop and fuel up. A convenient spot for camping, the local **KOA Campground ❶,** Exit 50 off I-40, offers a general store, pool, and laundry facilities. (☎580-592-4409. Store open daily in summer 8am-9pm; in winter 8am-7pm. Sites $20; RVs $30-33; cabins $40. D/MC/V.)

🚩 APPROACHING ELK CITY: 9 MILES
Turn right at the 4-way stop in Canute and another right 1 mi. west to pass under the interstate. Turn left to take the **service road** into Elk City, following **Bus. 40** as you enter town.

ELK CITY

Although Elk City's biggest—in all senses—attraction is heralded by a giant neon Rte. 66 sign at the west end of town, the small historic downtown is relatively unconcerned with the tourist traffic just to the north and offers an assortment of homey dining and loitering options, in no-frills settings with no-frills prices. Meanwhile, the standard bevy of fast-food regulars lines Rte. 66.

VITAL STATS

Population: 10,500

Visitor Info: Elk City Chamber of Commerce, 1016 Airport Industrial Rd. (☎800-280-0207; www.elkcity-chamber.com). Open M-F 9am-5pm.

Internet Access: Elk City Carnegie Library, 221 W. Broadway (☎580-225-0136). Open M, W and F 10am-6pm; Tu and Th 10am-9pm; Sa 10am-2pm. Free.

Post Office: 101 S. Adams Ave. (☎508-225-0294), at Broadway Ave. Open M-F 8:30am-4:30pm, Sa 9am-11am. **Postal Code:** 73644.

🚗 GETTING AROUND. Streets in Elk City form a grid; avenues run north-south, while streets are numbered and run east-west. An exception to this is **Broadway Ave. (Bus. I-40)**, which runs east-west one block south of **3rd. St.**, both major Elk City thoroughfares. Parking in the area is pretty much everywhere.

◙ SIGHTS. The **National Rte. 66 Museum**, right along Rte. 66, is Elk City's pride and joy. Part of a complex of four museums, it features a map of the road made out of t-shirts, plus state-by-state displays of the history of Rte. 66. Two giant Kachina dolls guard the grounds, and the exterior of the museum recreates an Old West Rte. 66 townscape. Next door, the **Old Town Museum** features regional history, including a display on Elk City's own Miss America 1981, Susan Powell, and a rotating display of local collections. Also in the complex, the **Farm and Ranch Museum** has vintage machiner, and the **Transportation Museum** allows you to ring the bell on a 1917 fire truck. (All museums ☎580-225-6266. Open Memorial Day to Labor Day M-Sa 9am-7pm, Su 1-5pm; Labor Day to Memorial Day M-Sa 9am-5pm, Su 2-5pm. Any one museum $3. Combination ticket $5; students, seniors, ages 6-16 $4; under 6 free.)

◭⋔ FOOD AND ACCOMMODATIONS. The French Silk Pie at the ⊠**Country Dove Tea Room ❶**, 610 W. 3rd St., is glorious. If you feel the need to justify it with a meal, the soups and sandwiches are also local legends. (☎580-225-7028. Open M-Sa 11am-2pm, pie and drinks until 5pm. MC/V.) The wooden trellises of **Lupe's Cocina y Cantina ❸**, 905 N. Main St., seclude diners enjoying chicken chalupas ($6), and fajitas ($8). The fried ice cream is particularly delectable. (☎580-225-7109. Open M-F 11am-10pm, Sa 4-10pm. AmEx/D/MC/V.) Satiate sweet teeth at **The Sugar Shack ❶**, 521 S. Main St. Although their main gig is decorating cakes, the peanut butter fudge ($1) and enormous cinnamon rolls ($1.50) are also delightful. (☎580-243-1670. Open Tu-F 8:30am-5:30pm, Sa 9am-noon. AmEx/D/MC/V.) Rooms at the **Flamingo Inn ❷**, 2000 W. 3rd St., all come with pink and black tiling around the sink area. A limited number of rooms with microwaves and refrigerators are available at no extra charge. (☎580-225-1811. Singles from $35; doubles from $40. AmEx/D/MC/V.)

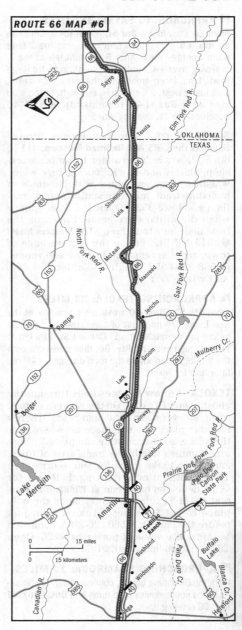

ROUTE 66 MAP #6

ROUTE 66

◥ APPROACHING SAYRE: 16 MILES

From Elk City, follow **3rd St.** out of town. Continue on **Rte. 66** 4 mi., then turn right onto the 2-lane north frontage road. After 6 mi. turn left at the T, crossing over I-40 onto the south side frontage road. 1 mi. later, cross onto the north side again, continuing west. 2½ mi. later, turn right at the stop sign onto **Bus. I-40** (unmarked). Bus. 1-40 becomes **4th St.** heading into Sayre.

SAYRE. Worth a stop as you pass through Sayre is the ◪**RS & K Railroad Museum,** 411 N. 6th St. Like a railroad annex to Santa's workshop, Shirley and Ray Killian's garage whirs, whistles, toots, and chugs with hundreds of miniature trains and train station paraphernalia. (☎580-928-3525. Open M-F 9am-9pm or when the Killians are home. Knock on the front door for a tour. Free.) The **Western Motel ❷,** 315 NE Rte. 66, on the eastern edge of town, rents unremarkable but clean rooms. (☎508-928-3353. Singles $33; doubles $56. AmEx/D/MC/V.)

◥ APPROACHING TEXOLA: 23 MILES

From **4th St./Bus. 40** cross the north fork of the Red River. 1½ mi. west of town, take a right just before the overpass onto **El Camino St.** Turn left at the stop sign onto **Old Rte. 66,** then bear right onto the frontage road where the road diverges. 14¾ mi. later, exit for Texola.

TEXOLA. Follow tumbleweeds through the ghost town of Texola. On the western edge of town, an ever-so-truthful sign reads "There's no other place like this place anywhere near this place, so this must be the place." About nine families live in the main area of town, and it won't take much for you to drive past Texola without even noticing. Pull over for some delicious barbecue at **Windmill Restaurant ❸,** 21 Texola #A, pretty much the only place to eat for miles. (Take a right just before the church. ☎580-526-3965. Sandwich $5. Mesquite smoked pork ribs $8.25. Open Tu-Sa 6:30am-9pm. AmEx/D/MC/V.)

◥ APPROACHING SHAMROCK: 13 MILES

From the Oklahoma border, continue 13 mi. to Shamrock. The south service road turns into **Bus. I-40/Old Rte. 66** entering town.

The Lone Star State **TEXAS** *Welcomes You!*

SHAMROCK

The historic **U-Drop Inn Cafe,** at the corner of Rte. 66 and U.S. 83, was built in 1936 as the Conoco Tower Service Station. At the time, the cafe was said to be the "swankiest of swank eating places" and the "most up-to-date edifice of its kind between Oklahoma City and Amarillo." These days, the green and peach Art Deco construction has been renovated into a museum and tourist information center (☎806-256-2501; www.shamrocktx.net. Open M-F 9am-noon and 1-5pm, Sa 10am-4pm. Free.) One of the oldest buildings in town, the **Pioneer West Museum,** 204 N. Madden St., used to be a boarding house for construction workers. Now the small museum hosts history exhibits. (☎806-256-3941. Open M-F 1-4pm.) The **Texan Movie Theater,** 205 N. Main St., shows feature films Friday and Saturday nights if there are at least five people in the audience. (☎806-256-1212. $4, children $2.50.)

The chicken-fried steaks ($7) at **Mitchell's Family Restaurant ❷,** I-40 and Hwy. 83 E, are legendary. (Across I-40 on U.S. 83. Take the 1st right after the overpass. ☎806-256-2141. Open daily 6am-9:30pm. D/MC/V.) Sleep at the reasonably priced and "cowboy owned" **Route 66 Inn ❷,** 800 E. Hwy. 66. (☎806-256-3225. Singles $30; doubles $38. AmEx/D/MC/V.) Rub the Blarney Stone outside the **Irish Inn ❸,** 301 I-40 East. The inn offers Internet access in the lobby, a 24hr. pool, golf, free breakfast buffet, and guest laundry. (☎806-256-2106. Singles $49; doubles $63. AmEx/D/MC/V.)

◥ APPROACHING MCLEAN: 21 MILES

Jog left over the **I-40** access, following **Rte. 66** as you leave town on the south frontage road. Just over 14 mi. down the road, cross the interstate at **Exit 146** and 2 mi. later turn left on the north frontage road. At the stop sign at **Exit 143,** take a right onto **First St.** in McLean.

MCLEAN

Credit for the development of the West is often given to the rifle and the six-gun, but Rte. 66 reminds us to see the significance of tools at all levels of function, from the windmill to barbed wire. The **Devil's Rope Museum**, dedicated jointly to barbed wire and Rte. 66, features over 2550 different types of barbed wire and displays on everything associated or done with the material. There's also a history of cattle brands. The **Texas Old Rte. 66 Association and Museum** is in the same building. (Entering town on Rte. 66, turn left on Kingsley St. ☎ 806-779-2225; www.barbwiremuseum.com. Open Feb.-Dec. 15 Tu-Sa 10am-4pm. Donations suggested.) Farther down Rte. 66 in the heart of McLean, the **McLean-Alanreed Area Museum** has an area ranching exhibit, a memorial to local veterans, and history of McLean and Alanreed. (☎ 806-779-2731. Open W-Sa 10am-4pm. Free.) Leaving town, glance to the south to see a bright orange **1920s Phillip's 66 service station,** the first Phillip's 66 station in Texas.

The **Red River Steakhouse ❸,** 101 Rte. 66 West, is a blend of barn and saloon, with bandana napkins, mounted deer heads, doodles by patrons, and license plates along the walls. (☎ 806-779-8940. Jalapeno cheeseburger $6. Catfish $10. Open Tu-Sa 11am-9pm. AmEx/D/DC/MC/V.) Virtually next door on Rte. 66, the **Cactus Inn Motel ❷,** 101 Pine St., offers singles and suites including kitchenettes, couches, and TVs. Cacti-spotted landscapes complement the antlers and boots mounted on the walls. (☎ 806-779-2346. Singles $43; suites $48. AmEx/D/MC/V.)

⚐ APPROACHING AMARILLO: 73 MILES
1 mi. west of McLean, take a left before the overpass. 10 mi. later, cross under to the far side of I-40, then take a left on **Johnson Ranch Rd.** at **Exit 132.** Continue on the south frontage road through Alanreed. Follow the interstate westbound to **Exit 124** and cross to the south service road. 3 mi. later turn left to stay on the frontage road passing through Jericho, Groom, Lark and Conway, an uneventful stretch of road save for the enormous cross you'll see to the right in Groom. 7 mi. beyond Conway, cross to the north side of the road, and turn left on the north frontage road. As this turns into **Farm Market Rd. 2575,** go straight until **FM**

PHOTO OP. 19 stories high and weighing in at 1250 tons, the **second-largest cross** in the Western Hemisphere is on the roadside in Groom.

1912, and turn right. When FM 1912 intersects **U.S. 60 (Amarillo Blvd.)** and **Bus I-40,** go left.

AMARILLO

Named for the yellow clay of nearby Lake Meredith, Amarillo began as a railroad construction camp in 1887 and evolved into a Texas-size truck stop. Big steaks and bigger canyons are available, and horns are affixed to just about everything possible. After years of cattle and oil, Amarillo is now the prime overnight stop for motorists en route from Dallas, Houston, or Oklahoma City to Denver and other Western destinations.

VITAL STATS

Population: 170,000

Visitor Info: Amarillo Convention and Visitors Bureau, 401 S. Buchanan St. (☎ 806-374-8474; www.amarillo-cvb.org). Open M-F 8am-5pm. **Texas Travel Info Center,** 9700 I-40 East (☎ 806-335-1441), at Exit 76. Open daily 8am-6pm.

Internet Access: Amarillo Public Library, 413 E. 4th Ave. (☎ 806-378-3054). Open M-Th 9am-9pm, Sa 9am-6pm, Su 2-6pm. Internet card $5.

Post Office: 505 E. 9th Ave. (☎ 806-468-2148). Open M-F 7:30am-5pm. Postal Code: 79105.

▣ GETTING AROUND. Amarillo sprawls at the intersection of **I-27, I-40,** and **U.S. 87/287. Rte. 335 (the Loop)** encircles the city. **Rte. 66** runs east-west through town as **Amarillo Blvd.** parallel to I-40. Very much a driver's city, Amarillo is fairly easy to navigate, and parking is abundant.

◩ SIGHTS. The recently reopened **Amarillo Botanical Gardens,** 1400 Streit Dr., now include a large entry court in addition to the tropical conservatory, fragrance gardens, and butterfly gardens. (In Medical Center Park, north of I-40. ☎ 806-352-6513; www.amarillobotanicalgardens.org. Open Tu-F 9am-5pm, Sa-Su 1-5pm.

$4, 60+ $3, ages 4-12 $2.) At **Cadillac Ranch,** Stanley Marsh III planted 10 Cadillacs—ranging from model years 1948 to 1963—at the same angle as the Great Pyramids in a wheat field west of Amarillo, and, as one local notes, "they didn't take root, neither." (Get off I-40 at the Hope Rd. Exit (62A), 9 mi. west of Amarillo, cross to the south side of I-40, turn right at the end of the bridge, and drive half a mile down the highway access road. Free.)

⁂♖ FOOD AND ACCOMMODATIONS. At **Dyer's BBQ ❸,** on I-40 at Georgia, expect heaping portions and a friendly vibe. The rib plate includes ribs, potato salad, cole slaw, baked beans, apricots, and onion rings for $8.75—sharing is advised. (☎806-358-7104. Quesadillas $4.70. Open M-Sa 11am-10pm, Su 11am-9pm. AmEx/D/MC/V.) For a taste of West Texas Mexican fare, **Tacos Garcia ❸,** 1100 S. Ross, at 11th St. Try the *carne guisada* (stewed beef simmered with fresh vegetables served with beans, rice, guacamole, and tortillas; $9), and satisfy your sweet tooth with flaky, fresh *sopaipillas*—a pastry covered in sugar and honey—three for $2.75. (☎806-371-0411; www.tacosgarcia.com. Open M 10:30am-9:30pm, Tu-Sa 10:30am-10pm, Su 10:30am-3:30pm. AmEx/D/MC/V.) The world-famous **Big Texan Steak Ranch ❺,** 7701 I-40 E, promises a free 72 oz. steak dinner if you can eat it in under an hour. (1 in 7 men and 1 in 2 women do!) Call for a free limo pick-up from any I-40 hotel, motel or RV park. (☎806-372-6000; www.bigtexan.com. 10 oz. sirloin $18. AmEx/D/MC/V.)

Amarillo provides over 4000 beds for travelers to leave their boots under. Budget motels proliferate along the entire stretch of I-40, I-27, and U.S. 87/287 near town. Prices rise near downtown but grab a book of coupons at the visitors center to save a few dollars. One popular option is the **Big Texan Motel ❸,** 7701 I-40 E, where the western pioneer facade sets the mood for the saloon doors to the bathroom. (☎806-372-6000 or 800-657-7177; www.bigtexan.com. Singles $55; doubles $60. AmEx/D/MC/V.) One of the cheaper I-40 options is **La Kiva Hotel and Conference Center ❸,** 2501 I-40 E. A free hot breakfast is served in the atrium. (Take Exit 72A. ☎806-379-6555. Singles $55; doubles $60. AmEx/D/MC/V.) **KOA Kampground ❶,** 1100 Folsom Rd., has a pool in summer.

(Take I-40 to Exit 75, head north to Rte. 60, then go east 1 mi. ☎806-335-1792. Laundry, propane, free Wi-Fi, cable TV, cafe, and swimming pool. Reception daily June-Aug. 8am-10pm; Sept.-May 8am-8pm. Sites $22, with water and electricity $30, with full hookup $31.)

PHOTO OP. Thomas Cree's Little Tree, or the Bois d'Arc tree, was the 1st tree planted in Texas. The original tree, planted by settler Thomas Cree in 1888, was accidentally poisoned by pesticides in 1969, but its descendant sits on U.S. 60, 11 mi. northeast of Amarillo.

◥ DETOUR
PALO DURO CANYON
23 mi. south of Amarillo; take I-27 to Exit 106 and head east on Rte. 217.

Palo Duro Canyon, known as the "Grand Canyon of Texas," spans 20,000 acres of breathtaking beauty. The 16 mi. scenic drive through the park begins at the headquarters. Rangers allow backcountry hiking, but the majority of visitors stick to interconnected marked trails. Temperatures in the canyon frequently climb to 100°F; bring at least two quarts of water. The park headquarters, just inside the park, has trail maps and info on park activities. (☎806-488-2227. Open daily in summer 7am-10pm; in winter 8am-5pm. $3, under 12 free.) The official play of Texas, the musical ■**Texas Legacies,** 1514 5th Ave., performs in the largest outdoor amphitheater in the world. With the canyon as its backdrop, the epic drama includes a tree-splitting lightning bolt and fireworks. (☎806-655-2181; www.epictexas.com. Barbecue dinner $8.50. Backstage tours $2. Shows June-Aug. Tu-Sa 8:30pm. Tickets $11-27, under 12 $7-23.) **Old West Stables,** a quarter-mile farther along, rents horses and saddles. (☎806-488-2180. Rides Apr.-Oct. 10am, noon, 2, 4pm; June-Aug. 10am, noon, 2, 4, 6pm. Reservations recommended. 1hr. guided tour $35.) The largest history museum in the state of Texas, the **Panhandle-Plains Historical Museum,** 2503 4th Ave., in nearby Canyon, displays an impressive collection of "cowboy" art as well as the popular Pioneer Town, a full-sized replica of a Panhandle settlement, and working oil derrick. (12 mi. west of Palo Duro

Canyon State Park. ☎ 806-651-2244; www.panhandleplains.org. Open June-Aug. M-Sa 9am-6pm, Su 1-6pm; Sept.-May M-Sa 9am-5pm, Su 1-6pm. $7, 65+ $6, ages 4-12 $3.)

▶ APPROACHING WILDORADO: 22 MILES
Follow **Amarillo Blvd.** through town. For the original old Rte. 66, head right onto **Indian Hill Rd.** just before the I-40 overpass into a residential neighborhood. Continue 4½ mi. to the T, then head right, following the north frontage road toward Wildorado.

WILDORADO. If hunger or a snooze should take you, Wildorado is a surprising oasis. The decrepit, almost unreadable sign for "Jessie's Cafe" hides what is today **Randy's of Wildorado ❹**, 708 W. I-40, an elegant lunchtime eatery and genuine upscale dining establishment featuring fresh seafood. (☎ 806-426-3287. Appetizers $5-12. Pan-fried red snapper $20. Open Tu-Th 11am-2pm and 5-9pm, F-Sa 11am-2pm and 5-10pm. AmEx/D/MC/V.) Next door, the brightly painted **Royal Inn ❷** has bright rooms with floral wallpaper. (☎ 806-426-3315. Singles $38; doubles $42. AmEx/D/MC/V.)

▶ APPROACHING VEGA: 14 MILES
In Wildorado, cross to the north service road to stay on **Rte. 66.** 12 mi. past Wildorado on Rte. 66, head left on **Bus I-40** after crossing over the road to enter Vega on **Vega Blvd.**

VEGA. The folks in Vega take great pride in being on an original alignment of Rte. 66. Dot Leavitt, proprietress of **Dot's Mini Museum,** 105 N. 12th St., has seen—and collected—it all. The outbuildings next to her house contain a voluminous and eclectic collection of memorabilia amassed since 1944, including a room full of cowboy hats and a boot tree. Self-professed to be "Rte. 66-obsessed" she'll gladly chat with passersby. (Turn right off Vega Blvd. ☎ 806-267-2367. Call ahead for hours. Free.) Have a meal at the informal **Hickory Inn Cafe ❷**, 1004 Vega Blvd., almost the only place to eat in Vega. (☎ 806-267-2569. Biscuits and gravy $3. Big boy burger $6.50. Open M-Sa 6am-2pm. D/MC/V.)

▶ APPROACHING ADRIAN: 15 MILES
Continue west on **Vega Blvd.**

ADRIAN. As they say in Adrian, "When you're here, you're halfway there!" From the sign across from the **Midpoint Cafe ❷,** on Rte. 66, it's 1139 mi. to either end of the Mother Road. The decor is one part antique kitchen, two parts "We love Rte. 66." (Take Exit 23A off I-40. ☎ 941-729-0429; www.midpointroute66cafe.com. Sandwiches $6. Dessert $4. Open M-F 8am-4pm, Sa 8am-3pm, Su 8am-2pm. MC/V.) Entering town from the east, an old pickup truck with a star-spangled "66" greets visitors next to the **Antique Ranch ❷**, 106 E. Rte. 66. Antique cabinets and kitchenware decorate this restaurant that serves the best barbecue around. (☎ 806-538-9944. Barbecue sandwich $3.50-3.75. Open M-F 10am-7pm. AmEx/D/MC/V.)

▶ APPROACHING TUCUMCARI: 64 MILES
Take **I-40** from **Exit 18 (Gruhlkey Rd.)** and take the interstate 20 mi. to the New Mexico border, passing the ghost town of Glenrio, where an abandoned gas station is the only building for miles. Entering from the interstate, the **New Mexico Visitors Center,** on the north side, has every map you could ever need. If you use the metal toilets, you can press a button on your way out approving or condemning the facilities. Continue on I-40 to **Exit 369,** heading right at the stop on the exit, then immediately left on the frontage road. Continue on the I-40 to **Exit 369,** heading right at the stop on the exit, then immediately left on the frontage road. Take **Exit 356** to cross the interstate in San Jon, then turn right and continue west through town. Continue on the north frontage road from San Jon. 21 mi. down the road, head right under the interstate and then join I-40 W. Get off at **Exit 335** and enter Tucumcari on **Tucumcari Blvd.**

Land of Enchantment
NEW MEXICO
Welcomes You!

 At the border you cross into the Mountain Time Zone, where it is 1hr. earlier.

TUCUMCARI

The road between Amarillo and Albuquerque is a long one, and in the heyday of Rte. 66, Tucumcari made its name as the town with 2000 rooms for weary travelers. "Tucumcari

ROUTE 66

ROUTE 66 MAP #7

Tonight" became a popular slogan for travelers, and the wall-to-wall motels lining Tucumcari Blvd. do not disappoint. The strip of neon signs lights up the night—recent renovation and Rte. 66 preservation efforts have brought attention to signs like the Blue Swallow, the bluebird of happiness to drivers for decades.

VITAL STATS

Population: 6000

Visitor Info: Tucumcari/Quay County Chamber of Commerce, 404 W. Tucumcari Blvd. (☎505-461-1694; www.tucumcarinm.com). Open M-F 8am-noon and 1-5pm.

Internet Access: Tucumcari Public Library, 602 S. 2nd St. (☎505-461-0295). Open M 9:30am-7pm, Tu-F 9:30am-5:30pm, Sa 9am-1pm. Free.

Post Office: 222 S. 1st St. (☎505-461-0370). **Postal Code:** 88401.

GETTING AROUND. Tucumcari sits just north of **I-40; U.S. 54** runs into town from the north. **Bus. U.S. 54** is known as **Tucumcari Blvd.** in town and is home to the city's famous motel strip. Getting around is fairly simple; streets run north-south and are numbered, while avenues run east-west. Most establishments have parking lots; parking is plentiful almost everywhere.

SIGHTS. The **Tee Pee Trading Post,** 924 E. Tucumcari Blvd., has been peddling "damn fine stuff" to Rte. 66 travelers from inside a concrete tee pee since the 1940s. (☎505-461-3773. Open M-Sa 8:30am-6pm, Su 8:30am-7pm.) Dinosaur enthusiasts should swing by the **Mesalands Dinosaur Museum,** at 1st and Laughlin St. As one of the world's foremost paleontological sites, Tucumcari's main attraction is a dinosaur museum featuring touchable bronze castings of beasts and bones as well as coprolites, also known as fossilized dino droppings. (☎505-461-3466; www.mesalands.edu. Open Mar. to Labor Day Tu-Sa 10am-6pm; Labor Day to Mar. Tu-Sa noon-5pm. $5.50, seniors $4.50, students $3.50, ages 4-12 $3.) The **Tucumcari Historical Museum,** 416 S. Adams Ave., is a 1903 schoolhouse overflowing with historical artifacts from the region. (☎505-461-4201. Open in summer M-Sa 9am-6pm; in winter Tu-Sa 8am-5pm. $2.50.) The lovely **Odeon Theater,** 123 S.

2nd St., was built in the 1930s and still shows movies. (☎ 505-461-0100. $5, under 12 and 60+ $4.) **Ute Lake State Park,** in Logan, just north of Tucumcari on U.S. 54, is a narrow glistening strip of natural beauty. (☎ 505-487-2284; www.nmparks.com. Open 24hr. Free.)

⛨ ☖ FOOD AND ACCOMMODATIONS.
Tucumcari's motel magnificence comes with unvarnished but satisfying meal options that have been around as long as the route itself. **Del's Restaurant ❹,** 1202 E. Tucumcari Blvd., is hard to miss considering the huge cow perching atop its sign. Del's features a great selection of American and Mexican foods as well as a fortune-telling machine. (☎ 505-461-1740; www.delsrestaurant.com. Appetizers $3-8. Red chile pork enchiladas $8.50. Open M-Sa 7am-9pm. AmEx/D/MC/V.) The best breakfast option in town is **La Cocina de Raul ❶,** 321 E. Tucumcari Blvd., dubbed the "no-name restaurant" by locals since the sign reads simply "restaurant." You can enjoy a classic breakfast of 2 eggs, 2 strips of bacon, 2 pancakes and hashbrowns for $3. (☎ 505-461-8406. Open M-Sa 6:30am-2pm, Su 7am-2pm. Cash only.) Vintage burger posters line the walls of **Rubee's Diner ❷,** 605 W. Tucumcari Blvd. (☎ 505-461-1463. Burritos $3.50-4.50. Open M-F 7am-7pm, Sa 7am-4pm. Cash only.)

Tucumcari is known for its legendary "2000 Rooms," and the motels that sprawl along Rte. 66 backs up the hype. The **Blue Swallow Motel ❷,** 815 E. Rte. 66 Blvd., is perhaps Rte. 66's most celebrated motel. The pink motel with bright blue carports has well-decorated rooms, and, according to the sign under the neon swallow, "100% refrigerated air." (☎ 505-461-9849; www.blueswallowmotel.com. Singles $41; doubles $52. AmEx/D/MC/V.) Another option, the **Best Western Pow Wow Inn ❷,** 801 W. Tucumcari Blvd., is one of the original Rte. 66 tourist courts, though it has been refashioned and redecorated into a modern version of its former self. Rooms have uniformly carved furniture, highly coordinated color schemes, and access to an inviting pool. (☎ 505-461-0500. Rooms $47-53. AmEx/D/MC/V.) The bright orange **Buckaroo Motel,** 1315 W. Tucumcari Blvd./Rte. 66, has served Rte. 66 travelers for decades with 70s decor and low prices. (☎ 505-461-1650. Singles $22.50-28; doubles $30. AmEx/D/MC/V.)

◪ APPROACHING SANTA ROSA: 52 MILES
Head west on **Tucumcari Blvd.** as it joins **I-40** at **Exit 329.** Take I-40 to **Exit 321,** crossing to the south side of I-40 and taking the frontage road through the tunnel 11 mi. later to Montoya. Cross to the south side of the interstate at **Exit 311** and continue through Newkirk and Cuervo, where you will rejoin I-40. Take the interstate to **Exit 277** for Santa Rosa. Turn right after exiting onto **Bus I-40/Historic 66.**

SANTA ROSA

Halfway between Albuquerque and Amarillo, Santa Rosa is an oasis amidst the arid surrounds. Santa Rosa got its start as a ranching

---

HEAT: IT'S WHAT'S FOR DINNER

Whether cooked in fiery dishes or offered as a novelty hot sauce in tourist shops, the chile pepper is the icon of New Mexican cuisine. Its spicy flavor comes from the chemical *capsaicin,* which resides not in the seeds, as many believe, but in the pod's membranes and the soft tissue that supports the seeds. The chemical is thought to be an evolutionary adaptation to prevent mammals from eating the pods. Unable to taste *capsaicin,* birds eat but can't digest the seeds, thus helping with their dispersal; mammals, who can digest the seeds, taste the heat and avoid chiles entirely. In the summer, farmers' markets brim with chiles of all kinds. All told, New Mexico produces about 100,000 tons of chiles each year, the most in the US. Most common is the New Mexico green chile, with a 6 in. pod and a firm, crisp texture, but chiles range from fat, orange *habañeros* to skinny, red *de arboles* to the stubby, green *jalapeño.* The *habañero* is the undisputed king of heat, its orange variety topping out at eight times the heat of a regular *jalapeño.* Its juice can actually blister bare skin. When the fire hits, the best remedy is milk or yogurt; the chemical *casein* in dairy products helps prevent the tongue's nerves from sensing *capsaicin.* Resist the urge to reach for water—it will only help the fire spread.

ROUTE 66 MAP #8

[map of Route 66 showing Santa Fe, Albuquerque, Rio Rancho, Grants, Acoma Pueblo, El Malpais Nat. Mon. and Cons. Area, and surrounding roads and towns including Pecos, Glorieta, La Cienega, Algodones, Bernalillo, Isleta, Mesita, Laguna, Cubero, McCartys, San Fidel, Milan, Bluewater, Prewitt, Thoreau, with a 15 miles / 15 kilometers scale]

TIP There's gas in Cuervo, but it's best to fill up before leaving Tucumcari to avoid making inconvenient detours before Santa Rosa, 52 mi. from Tucumcari. Passersby are few along some of the road, and the vultures would be only too happy for the company.

community, and grew under the propriety of Don Celso Baca, an officer in Kit Carson's brigade. Less gaudy than neighboring Tucumcari, the city has equal claim to Old 66, with a main drag lined with ancient motels, landmark "billboards," and friendly diners. The train scene in the film *Grapes of Wrath* features the Pecos River railroad bridge on the western side of town, though Santa Rosa's principal draw is its lakes; the Blue Hole and Perch Lake both host some of the state's best scuba diving.

VITAL STATS

Population: 2800

Visitor Info: Santa Rosa Visitors Center, 486 Parker Ave. (☎505-472-3763). Open M-F 9am-5pm.

Internet Access: Moise Memorial Public Library, 208 5th St. (☎505-472-3101). Open M-F 10am-6pm, Sa 9am-noon. Free.

Post Office: 120 S. 5th St. (☎505-472-3734), at Rte. 66. Open M-F 8:30am-5pm, Sa 9:45-11:45am.

Postal Code: 88435.

☞ GETTING AROUND. Unlike many other cities along the route, Santa Rosa is not laid out in a grid. **Rte. 66,** also known as **Will Rogers Dr.,** runs east-west through the city and is the principal road. Streets are numbered starting in the west, and run roughly northwest-southeast through town. Parking is readily available. Continue on Rte. 66 over the crest of the hill to get the full effect of Santa Rosa's magnificent perch.

◙ SIGHTS. Fins, street rods, trucks, and vintage chrome shine at the awesome Santa Rosa **Route 66 Auto Museum,** 2766 Will Rogers Dr. Inside-are a collection of lovingly restored roadsters and exhibits paying homage to a past of drive-thrus, cruisin', and backseats. (☎505-472-1966. Open M-Sa 7:30am-6pm, Su

10am-5pm. $5, under 12 free.) In the middle of an arid desert, Santa Rosa is blessed with 13 lakes and watering holes. The most famous is the **Blue Hole**, which draws scuba fanatics and casual swimmers alike with its 80 ft. depth, clarity, and constant 64°F temperature. (To reach the Blue Hole from Rte. 66, turn left on 4th St. and left again onto Lake Dr. Follow the signs and turn left onto Blue Hole Rd. Permits required for diving, call ☎505-472-3763.) Along the same route, **Park Lake** features a two-story water slide. Northeast of town on Rte. 91, **Santa Rosa Lake** was built to ease the flooding of the Pecos River so cowboys could ford their cattle. The lake offers fishing and watersports.

Santa Rosa also hosts a number of festivals. **Santa Rosa Days,** during Memorial Day weekend, draws over 40 softball teams for a tournament, in addition to hosting an arts and crafts fair, pony rides, amusement rides, and goat roping. (☎505-472-3763.) The **Guadalupe County Fair,** during the first weekend in August, features a pet parade, flower show, barbecue, rodeo, chili cook-off, and horseshoe contest (☎505-472-3652.) **Santa Rosa de Lima Fiestas,** the third weekend in September, includes mariachis and a fiesta dance (☎505-472-3652). Also in September, the **Route 66 Festival** includes a street dance, hot rod contest, and a motorcycle rally. (☎505-472-3763.)

⛟ FOOD AND ACCOMMODATIONS. On the eastern edge of Rte. 66's jaunt though town, the **Route 66 Restaurant ❷,** 1819 Rte. 66, at the top of the hill, has been feeding roadies since the 1950s. The interior is a testimony to the town's road-fever. (☎505-472-9925. Entrees $3-7. Open M-Sa 6am-9pm. MC/V.) **Joseph's Cafe ❸,** 865 Rte. 66, with landmark **Fat Man** billboards (symbols of American prosperity during WWII and the Vietnam War) is a Rte. 66 legend. Hungry folk look forward to it for miles, and weary travelers can relax with a margarita within easy walking distance of a bevy of motels. The *carne adovada* (pork marinated in spicy chili sauce; $8.50) is a favorite. (☎505-472-3361. Entrees $6-13. Open daily 6am-10pm. AmEx/D/DC/MC/V.) Just as you enter town off Exit 277 you'll see the sign for the **Silver Moon Cafe ❷,** 3701 Rte. 66, which has been serving Mother Road burgers (2 patties with all the trimmings; $7.50) since 1959.

(☎505-472-3162; Open M-F 6:30am-9:30pm, Sa-Su 6:30am-10pm. MC/V.) The informal family eatery **Mateo's Restaurant ❷,** 500 Rte. 66, is known for its fresh doughnuts ($4 per half dozen)—but call to order ahead or they might be gone. (☎505-472-5720. Sandwiches $4-7. Dinner plates $6-8. Open M-F 6am-7:30pm, Sa-Su 7am-8pm. AmEx/D/MC/V.)

Like Tucumcari's, Santa Rosa's stretch of Rte. 66 is lined with vintage motels offering decent rooms at very reasonable rates. The giant sunny beacon of the **Sun N' Sand Motel ❷,** 1120 Rte. 66, leads to comfortable rooms with fridge, TV, and the ever essential A/C. (☎505-472-5268. Singles $33; doubles $39. AmEx/D/MC/V.) Rooms at the **Sunset Motel ❶,** 929 Rte. 66, are recently renovated with hand decorated walls. (☎505-472-2607. Singles $25-30; doubles $35-40. AmEx/D/MC/V.)

◪ APPROACHING LAS VEGAS: 58 MILES Follow **Rte. 66** out of Santa Rosa as it curves to the right, and join **I-40** heading west. During the mapping of the road, an outgoing governor with rivals in the town of Moriarty decided to thwart the town by bypassing it completely with the extravagant loop through Santa Fe. Only later did alignments head in a gas-efficient, but far less interesting, straight line. Get off at **Exit 256,** and take **U.S. 84 N** through Dilia and Romeroville until you hit the junction with **I-25** just over 55 miles from Santa Rosa. Although it isn't on Rte. 66, heading 3 mi. east from Romeroville on **I-25** will bring you to the other Las Vegas—Las Vegas, New Mexico.

LAS VEGAS

Unlike its northern namesake, this Las Vegas supplies in history what it lacks in razzle and dazzle. In 1899, Las Vegas was the biggest city in the New Mexico territory, and it flourished when the railroad was routed through town at the turn of the century. What remains today is a town frozen in time, with nine historic districts and 900 buildings on the National Register of Historic Places. The **City of Las Vegas Museum and Rough Riders Memorial Collection,** 727 Grand Ave., chronicles the history of Roosevelt's "Rough Riders," the US Cavalry regiment involved in the Spanish-American war. In addition to Rough Riders artifacts and local history paraphernalia, the museum also includes an annotated photo display of the hanging of the notorious Black Jack, reported

ROUTE 66

to have said to the priest ministering to him: "Padre, make it snappy. I haven't much time. I have to be in hell and eat dinner with the Devil at noon." Due to a mistake with the rope tension, his head was "cut plumb off." (☎505-454-1401. Open May-Sept. Tu-Su 10am-4pm; Oct.-Apr. Tu-Sa 10am-4pm. Free.)

Estella's Cafe ❷, 148 Bridge St., offers the best Northern New Mexican food in town. (☎505-454-0048. Entrees $4-7. Open M-W 11am-3pm, Th-Sa 11am-8pm. Cash only.) **The Plaza Drug Store ❶**, 178 Bridge St., serves ice cream cones ($1.50) from an old-fashioned soda fountain in a standard drug store. (☎505-425-5221. Open M-Sa 8am-6pm. MC/V.) In addition to being a fully stocked liquor store, bar, and dance club, **Dick's Deli ❷**, 705 Douglas Ave., makes sandwiches to be reckoned with. Order a gourmet option ($6-8) or build your own. (☎505-425-8261. Deli open M-F 10am-10pm, Sa 10am-11:30pm. Club open until 2am. AmEx/MC/V.) **Charlie's Spic and Span Bakery and Cafe ❸**, 715 Douglas Ave., has a full espresso bar and fresh baked goods daily. Breakfast is served all day. (☎505-426-1921. Open M-Sa 6:30am-5:30pm, Su 7am-3pm. AmEx/MC/V.) Budget motels can be found all along Grand Ave., between I-25 Exits 343 and 347. The **Town House Motel ❷**, 1215 Grand Ave., has clean rooms with massive TVs and charming features. (☎505-425-6717. Singles from $40; doubles from $49. AmEx/D/MC/V.) Next door, the **Sunshine Motel ❷**, 1201 Grand Ave., has pleasant rooms. (☎505-425-3506. Singles $35-40; doubles $44-49. AmEx/D/MC/V.)

◤ **APPROACHING PECOS: 44 MILES**
Take **I-25** back to where you left **Rte. 66,** then follow Rte. 66 (I-25 south frontage road) into Pecos, crossing the interstate at Sands and again at Rowe (Exit 307). Turning left onto **Rte. 50** in "downtown" Pecos.

PECOS. The main attraction in Pecos is the **Pecos Wilderness Area and Historical Park.** The **Pecos Wilderness** protects 233,667 acres of high country in the heart of the Sangre de Cristo Mountains, punctuated by the second-highest peak in New Mexico, 13,103 ft. **Trunchas Peak.** Winters are long and snowy, but from late spring to early autumn this is an ideal spot for backcountry hiking. The upper Pecos River is the premier trout-fishing site in the Southwest,

so don't be surprised to find campgrounds crowded with Texan fishermen. Once you get a few miles into the backcountry, you'll find yourself alone amid beautiful mountains, forests, and rivers. In 1625, Spanish colonists established an elaborate adobe mission on the wealthy **Pecos Pueblo.** In 1680, the inhabitants of the pueblo joined a united Indian force against the Spanish and, having killed the priest and destroyed the church, built a ceremonial kiva in the convent of the mission. The power of Pecos Pueblo gradually declined through disease, conflict and migration, but the ruins of the mission, later rebuilt, and the pueblo are still accessible in the form of a 1¼ mi. self-guided tour. Stop in at the **visitors center** on Rte. 66 just a few miles before the town of Pecos for more information. (☎505-757-6414. Open M-F 8am-5pm. Free.)

◤ **APPROACHING SANTA FE: 20 MILES**
From **Rte. 50,** rejoin **I-25** at Glorieta, continuing to **Exit 294,** 10¼ mi. down the road. Take the north frontage road 10 mi. to Santa Fe. Just as you enter Santa Fe, be sure to check out ◪**Bobcat Bite ❸**, which could easily be missed, but shouldn't be. Every car in town is generally parked outside this pink adobe roadhouse, constructed in 1954, and if you've got a hankering for a hunk of meat or just a taste of New Mexico's finest green chiles, you're in the right place. (☎505-983-5319. Green chile cheeseburger $6.70. Open W-Sa 11am-7:50pm. Cash or check only.)

SANTA FE

Everyone who isn't selling something seems to be a tourist in this city where the winding streets, beautiful adobe buildings, exquisite museums, and smell of incense in the streets bring to life a time long forgotten in much of the rest of the region. Founded by the Spanish in 1608, Santa Fe's prime location at the convergence of the Santa Fe Trail, an old trading route running from Missouri, and the Camino Real ("Royal Road"), has always brought commerce and bustle. In recent years, Santa Fe has skyrocketed in popularity, becoming one of the leading vacation destinations in the US and leading to an influx of gated communities and California millionaires. In many spots, prices have risen accordingly, but Santa Fe's architecture, museums, and scenery make the bargain hunt well worth the time.

Santa Fe

▲▲ ACCOMMODATIONS
Hyde State Park, **1**
Kings Rest Court Motel, **13**
Santa Fe Intl. Hostel
  and Pension, **14**
Silver Saddle Motel, **15**
Thunderbird Inn, **12**

ⓘ FOOD
Cafe Paris, **5**
Maria's, **17**
The Shed, **6**
Tia Sophia's, **8**
Upper Crust Pizza, **11**

NIGHTLIFE
Cowgirl Hall of Fame, **10**
Second St. Brewery, **16**
Swig, **7**

🏛 MUSEUMS
Georgia O'Keeffe
  Museum, **2**
Institute of American
  Indian Arts, **9**
Museum of Fine Arts and
  St. Francis Auditorium, **3**
Museum of Indian Arts &
  Culture Laboratory of
  Anthropology, **19**
Museum of International
  Folk Art, **18**
Palace of the Governors, **4**

VITAL STATS

Population: 62,000

Visitor Info: Visitor Info Center, 491 Old Santa Fe Trail (☎505-875-7400 or 800-545-2040; www.santafe.com). Open daily 8am-6:30pm; off season until 5pm. **Santa Fe Convention and Visitors Bureau,** 201 W. Marcy St. (☎800-777-2489). Open M-F 8am-5pm.

Internet Access: Santa Fe Public Library, 145 Washington Ave. (☎505-955-6781). Open M-Th 10am-6pm, F-Sa 10am-6pm, Su 1-5pm. Free.

Parking: Public lots throughout town run $9-10 per day. The visitors center has free parking (M-F 2hr. free, Sa-Su free all day).

Post Office: 120 S. Federal Pl. (☎505-988-6351), next to the courthouse. Open M-F 7:30am-5:45pm, Sa 9am-1pm. **Postal Code:** 87501.

🔲 GETTING AROUND

The streets of downtown Santa Fe seem to wind and wander without rhyme or reason. It is helpful to think of Santa Fe as a wagon wheel, with the **Plaza** in the center and roads leading outwards like spokes. **Paseo de Peralta** forms a loop around the downtown area, and the main roads leading out toward I-25 are **Cerrillos Rd., St. Francis Dr.,** and **Old Santa Fe Trail.** Narrow streets make driving troublesome; park your car and pound the pavement. The downtown area is compact and lined with interesting shops, restaurants, and sights, and the Plaza area is restricted to pedestrians. Parking lots are abundant, and closely-monitored metered spaces line the streets near Plaza and **Canyon Rd.**

ROUTE 66

Hand-held cell-phones are illegal to use while driving in Santa Fe. Hands-free devices, however, are permitted.

👁 SIGHTS

The grassy **Plaza de Santa Fe** is a good starting point for exploring the museums, sanctuaries, and galleries of the city. Since 1609, the plaza has been the site of religious ceremonies, military gatherings, markets, cockfights, and public punishments—now, it shelters ritzy shops and dozens of artisans selling their crafts. **Historic walking tours** leave from the blue doors of the Palace of the Governors on Lincoln St. (May-Oct. M-Sa 9:30am and 1:30pm. $10.)

MNM MUSEUMS. Sante Fe is home to six imaginative, world-class museums. Four are run by **The Museum of New Mexico.** A worthwhile four-day pass includes admission to all four museums and can be purchased at any of them. (☎505-827-6463; www.museumofnewmexico.org. Open Sept.-May Tu-Su 10am-5pm; May-Sept. daily 10am-5pm. $8, under 12 free. 4-day pass $18. Museum of Fine Arts and Palace of the Governors are both free F 5-8pm.) Inhabiting a large adobe building on the northwest corner of the plaza, the **Museum of Fine Arts** dazzles visitors with the works of major Southwestern artists, as well as contemporary exhibits of controversial American art. (107 W. Palace Ave. ☎505-476-

5072. Open Sept.-May Tu-Sa 10am-5pm; May-Sept. daily 10am-5pm. $8, under 12 free.) The **Palace of the Governors** is the oldest public building in the US and was the seat of seven successive governments after its construction in 1610. The *hacienda*-style palace is now a museum with exhibits on Native American, Southwestern, and New Mexican history and the artwork of the mysterious Sesseger hides. (On the north side of the plaza. ☎505-476-5100; www.palaceofthegovernors.org. Open Sept.-May Tu-Sa 10am-5pm; May-Sept. daily 10am-5pm. $8, under 12 free.) The fascinating **Museum of International Folk Art** houses the largest collection of folk art in the world, including over 10,000 handmade dolls, doll houses, and other toys. Other galleries display ethnographic exhibits. (706 Camino Lejo. ☎505-476-1200; www.moifa.org. Open Sept.-May Tu-Sa 10am-5pm; May-Sept. daily 10am-5pm. $8, under 12 free.) Next door, the **Museum of Indian Arts and Culture Laboratory of Anthropology** displays Native American photos and over 10 million artifacts from New Mexico archaeological sites. (710 Camino Lejo. ☎505-476-1250; www.indianartsandculture.org. Open Sept.-May Tu-Sa 10am-5pm; May-Sept. daily 10am-5pm. $8, under 12 free.)

OTHER PLAZA MUSEUMS. The popular **Georgia O'Keeffe Museum** attracts the masses with the artist's famous flower paintings, as well as some of her more abstract works. The collection, complemented by a brief biographical documentary, spans her entire life and is the first museum dedicated to an internationally

STAIRWAY TO HEAVEN

The Loretto Chapel is one of the biggest tourist attractions in Santa Fe, primarily for its "miraculous staircase," a 33-step spiral staircase that stands without any visible support. Architects are at a loss to explain the architectural phenomenon, though the people of Santa Fe have their own explanations. The Sisters of Loretto first came to Santa Fe in 1852 and immediately began construction on a chapel. The chapel was nearing completion when constructors realized that there was no way to get from the chapel to the choir loft, since it was too high for ordinary stairs. Carpenter after carpenter measured the space and announced that building a staircase was impossible. The sisters prayed for aid, and one day a man entered the chapel with only a hammer, a saw, and a T square. The stranger offered to build a stairway and finished his work in just a few months, leaving before the nuns could pay him. The resulting staircase is a structure which the laws of Physics say should have crumpled the moment someone stepped on it. Yet, the staircase has remained intact for over 100 years. Extensive tests have been made on the wood itself, only to find that it cannot be matched to any existing species. Many sisters believe that the mysterious carpenter was St. Joseph, the patron saint of craftsmen, though to this day, the staircase and its strange creator remain a mystery.

acclaimed female artist. *(217 Johnson St. ☎505-946-1017; www.okeeffemuseum.org. Open daily 10am-5pm; Nov.-May M-Tu and Th-Su 10am-5pm. $8, seniors $7, under 17 and students with ID free. F 5-8pm free. Audio tour $5.)* Downtown's **Institute of American Indian Arts Museum** houses an extensive collection of contemporary Indian art with an intense political edge and many inviting interactive exhibits. *(108 Cathedral Pl. ☎505-983-8900. Open M-Sa 9am-5pm, Su noon-5pm. $4, students and seniors $2, under 16 free.)* The **New Mexico State Capitol** was built in 1966 in the form of the Zia sun symbol. The House and Senate galleries are open to the public, and the building contains an impressive art collection. *(5 blocks south of the Plaza on Old Santa Fe Trail. ☎505-986-4589. Open June-Aug. M-F 6am-7pm; Sept.-Apr. M-F 6am-6pm, Sa 8am-5pm. Free tours June-Aug. M-F 10am and 2pm.)*

CHURCHES. Santa Fe's Catholic roots are evident in the Romanesque **St. Francis Cathedral,** built from 1869 to 1886 under the direction of Archbishop Lamy to help convert Westerners to Catholicism. The basilica features wide doors and a tintinnabulum, in case the Pope needs to enter on horseback. *(213 Cathedral Pl., 1 block east of the Plaza on San Francisco St. ☎505-982-5619. Open daily 7:30am-5:30pm. Free.)* The **Loretto Chapel** was the first Gothic building west of the Mississippi River and dates to the 1870s. The church is famous for its "miraculous" spiral staircase—architects still cannot figure out how it was accomplished. *(207 Old Santa Fe Trail., 2 blocks south of the cathedral. ☎505-982-0092. Open M-Sa 9am-5pm, Su 10:30am-5pm. $2.50, seniors and children $2.)* About five blocks southeast of the plaza lies the **San Miguel Mission,** at the corner of DeVargas St. and the Old Santa Fe Trail. Built in 1610 by the Tlaxcalan Indians, the mission is the oldest functioning church in the US. Also in the church is the San Jose Bell, the oldest bell in the US, made in Spain in 1356. *(☎505-988-9504. Open M-Sa 9am-5pm, Su 9am-4pm, mass at 5pm; may close earlier in winter. $1.)*

GALLERIES. Santa Fe's most successful artists live and sell their work along **Canyon Rd.** Pick up a map and guide to the businesses featured here at the visitors center or at any one of the galleries. To reach the galleries, depart the Plaza on San Francisco Dr., take a left on Alameda St., a right on Paseo de Peralta, and a left on Canyon Rd. Most galleries are open 10am-

5pm and contain interesting and often fantastically expensive collections. The **Michael Smith Gallery** is full of beautiful, intricately woven baskets. *(526 Canyon Rd. ☎505-995-1013. Open daily 10am-5pm.)* The **Hahn Ross Gallery** has hip, enjoyable, and pricey works. *(409 Canyon Rd. ☎505-984-8434. Open daily 10am-5pm.)*

OUTDOORS. The nearby **Sangre de Cristo Mountains** reach heights of over 12,000 ft. and offer countless opportunities for hikers, bikers, skiers, and snowboarders. The **Pecos** and **Río Grande Rivers** are playgrounds for kayakers, rafters, and canoers. Before heading into the wilderness, stop by the **Public Lands Information Center,** 1474 Rodeo Rd., near the intersection of St. Francis Rd. and I-25, to pick up maps, guides, and friendly advice. *(☎505-438-7542 or 877-276-9404; www.publiclands.org. Open M-F in summer 8am-5pm; in winter 8am-4:30pm.)* The Sierra Club Guide to *Day Hikes in the Santa Fe Area* and the Falcon Guide to *Best Easy Day Hikes in Santa Fe* are good purchases for those planning to spend a few days hiking. The closest **hiking** trails to downtown Santa Fe are along Rte. 475 on the way to the Santa Fe Ski Area. On this road, 10 mi. northeast of town, the **Tesuque Creek Trail** (4 mi., 2hr.) leads through the forest to a flowing stream. The best **skiing** is 16 mi. northeast of downtown, at **Ski Santa Fe.** In the towering Sangre De Cristo Mountains on Rte. 475, the ski area operates six lifts, servicing 43 trails on 600 acres of terrain with a 1650 ft. vertical drop. *(☎505-982-4429. Open late Nov. to early Apr. daily 9am-4pm. Lift tickets $51, ages 13-20 $41, under 13 and 61+ $37. Rental packages from $18. Lessons from $65.)*

▨ FOOD

Even fly-bys through Santa Fe should take a time-out to sample some of the best food the Southwest has to offer. Green chili is New Mexico's specialty, and most dishes come with the offer to have them smothered in the zesty sauce. Take them up on it, but the spiciness can vary, so keep your personal temperature gauge in mind. The **Santa Fe Farmers Market,** near the intersection of Guadalupe St. and Paseo de Peralta, has fresh fruits and vegetables. *(☎505-983-4098. Open late Apr. to early*

Nov. Tu and Sa 7am-noon. Call for indoor winter location and hours.)

■ **Maria's,** 555 W. Cordova Rd. (☎505-983-7929; www.marias-santafe.com). This restaurant is known for serving the best margarita in Santa Fe among 100 other delicious concoctions ($5-45). House margarita $5.50. Appetizers $2-9. Maria's combination plate $15. AmEx/MC/V. ❺

■ **Tia Sophia's,** 210 W. San Francisco St. (☎505-983-9880). It looks unassuming with a few decorative baskets and narrow walk space, but as the long waits will testify, the food is exceptional. The most popular item is the Atrisco plate ($6)—chile stew, cheese enchilada, beans, *posole*, and a *sopapilla*. Open M-Sa 7am-2pm. MC/V. ❸

Cafe Paris, 31 Burro Alley (☎505-986-9162). The black forest cake is dreamy, and the lemon tart ($6) inspires joy, but you won't notice from behind your enormous cappuccino ($4). Seafood crepe $10.75. Open Tu-Su 8am-5pm. AmEx/D/DC/MC/V. ❹

The Shed, 113½ E. Palace Ave. (☎505-982-9030), up the street from the Plaza. The beautiful vine-lined patio feels like a garden so you won't notice the 15min. wait. Lots of vegetarian dishes, like quesadillas ($6) and excellent blue corn burritos ($8.75). Meat-eaters will enjoy the red chile enchiladas ($8.75). Open M-Sa 11am-2:30pm and 5:30-9pm. AmEx/D/MC/V. ❸

Upper Crust Pizza, 329 Old Santa Fe Trail (☎505-982-0000). This pizza place has won awards for the best pizza in Santa Fe nearly every year for the last decade. Small pizza $8. Open in summer 11am-11pm; in winter 11am-10pm. D/MC/V. ❸

ACCOMMODATIONS

Hotels in Santa Fe tend toward the expensive side. As early as May they become swamped with requests for rooms during **Indian Market** and **Fiesta de Santa Fe.** Make reservations early. In general, the motels along **Cerrillos Rd.** have the best prices, but even these places run $40-60 per night. Downtown, B&Bs and spa inns dot most corners, but unless your budget is liberal, steer clear. Nearby camping is pleasant during the summer and easier on the wallet. Two sites for free primitive camping are **Big Tesuque** and **Ski Basin Campgrounds.** These campgrounds are both off Rte. 475 toward the Ski Basin and have pit toilets.

Santa Fe International Hostel and Pension, 1412 Cerrillos Rd. (☎505-988-1153). This miscellaneously furnished hostel is a great place to meet other travelers. Easily accessible, with a fully stocked kitchen, Internet ($2 per day) laundry, and a sitting room. Guests perform one 10min. task each morning though you can get out of it for $35. Dorms $14, nonmembers $15; private rooms $25. Cash only. ❶

Thunderbird Inn, 1821 Cerrillos Rd. (☎505-983-4397). Slightly closer to town than most and an excellent value considering the alternatives. Large rooms with A/C and cable TV, some with fridges and microwaves. Reception 24hr. Singles $50-60; doubles $65-70. AmEx/D/MC/V. ❸

Silver Saddle Motel, 2810 Cerrillos Rd. (☎505-471-7663). Beautiful adobe rooms with cowboy paraphernalia have A/C and cable TV. Reception 7am-11:30pm. Singles from $59; doubles from $65. AmEx/D/MC/V. ❸

Kings Rest Court Motel, 1452 Cerrillos Rd. (☎505-983-8879). Pleasant rooms in this old tourist court come with their own carport. Singles $65; doubles $70. AmEx/D/DC/MC/V. ❸

Hyde State Park Campground (☎505-983-7175), 8 mi. from Santa Fe on Rte. 475. This campground offers over 50 sites with water, pit toilets, and shelters. Sites $10, with hookup $14. ❶

ENTERTAINMENT

Iambic pentameter and distinguished acting invade the city each summer when **Shakespeare in Santa Fe** raises its curtain. The festival shows plays in an open-air theater on the St. John's College campus from late June to late August. (Tickets available at show or call ☎505-982-2910. Shows F-Su 7:30pm. Reserved seating tickets $15-32; lawn seating is free, but a $5 donation is requested.) The **Santa Fe Opera,** on Opera Dr., 7 mi. north of Santa Fe on Rte. 84/285, performs outdoors against a mountain backdrop. Nights are cool; bring a blanket. (☎800-280-4654 or 877-999-7499; www.santafeopera.org. Shows July W and F-Sa; Aug. M-Sa. Performances begin 8-9pm. Tickets $25-170; rush standing-room tickets $8-15.) The **Santa Fe Chamber Music Festival** celebrates the works of Baroque, Classical, Romantic, and 20th-century composers in the **St. Francis Auditorium of the Museum of Fine Arts** and the **Lensic Theater.** (☎505-983-2075, tickets 505-982-1890; www.sfcmf.org. Mid-July to mid-Aug. Tickets $16-40, students $10.)

In the third week of August, the country's largest and most impressive **Indian Market** floods the plaza. The **Southwestern Association for Indian Arts** (☎505-983-5220) has more info. Don Diego de Vargas's peaceful reconquest of New Mexico in 1692 marked the end of the 12-year Pueblo Rebellion, now celebrated in the three-day **Fiesta de Santa Fe** (☎505-988-7575). Held in mid-September, festivities begin with the burning of the **Zozobra** (a 50 ft. marionette) and include street dancing, processions, and political satires. The *New Mexican* publishes a guide and a schedule of events.

🐟 NIGHTLIFE

Santa Fe nightlife tends to be more mellow than in nearby Albuquerque. The **Cowgirl Hall of Fame,** 319 S. Guadalupe St., has live hoe-downs that range from bluegrass to country. (☎505-982-2565. Sa-Su ranch breakfast. Happy hour 3-6pm and midnight-1am. 21+ after midnight. Cover $3-5. Open M-F 11am-2am, Sa 8:30am-2am, Su 8:30am-midnight. AmEx/D/MC/V.) The **Second Street Brewery,** 1814 Second St. at the railroad tracks, caters to an artsy crowd with live music. (☎505-982-3030. Live music daily 9pm. Open M-Sa 11am-2am, Su noon-midnight. AmEx/D/MC/V.) For an upscale option try a swig at **Swig,** 135 West Palace Ave., where the tapas are great and you can find something to complement them at one of four bars. The soundtrack is hip-hop and house. (☎505-955-0400. Cover F-Sa $7. Open Tu 5pm-midnight, W-Sa 5pm-2am. AmEx/D/MC/V.)

 BIG DETOUR. Explore the quirky side of New Mexico on the **Pueblos, Particles, and Poker Big Detour,** p. 552.

⊠ DETOUR
COCHITI PUEBLO
At Exit 264 off the interstate, go west, turning right onto Rte. 16. Go 8 mi. and then right onto Rte. 22. Take a left into the Cochiti Pueblo Reservation, and then a right onto Forest Rte. 266. The parking area is 5 mi. from the turnoff.

An excellent spot for picnicking, The **Kasha-Katuwe Tent Rocks Natural Monument** has two easy trails through magnificent slot canyons and towering tent rock formations; one (20min. round-

trip) leads up to a small cave, the other (40min. round-trip), has a steep climb up a well-marked path at the end, but leads hikers to a spectacular view. (505-761-8700. Monument open daily in summer 7am-8pm; in winter 8am-5pm. $5 per vehicle.) Nearby, the **Cochiti Lake Campground ●** is high on the pueblo, with toilets, showers, cooking pits, and lake access. (☎505-465-0307; www.reserve-USA.com. Sites $5, with hookup $12. MC/V.)

⚑ APPROACHING BERNALILLO: 47 MILES
Follow **Cerillos Rd.** out of Santa Fe, passing under I-25 and turning right at **NM 599.** Turn left onto the frontage road and continue to Waldo. Join **I-25** and take the interstate to Algodones at **Exit 248.** Take a right from the off-ramp and a left at the stop sign, taking **NM 313 S** to Bernalillo.

BERNALILLO. The **Coronado State Monument,** 485 Kuaua Rd., has recreated Indian ruins and a reconstructed *kiva.* The small museum has original murals from the *kiva* and town walls. (☎505-867-5351. Open daily 8:30am-5pm. $3, under 17 free.) The **Range Cafe ④,** 925 Camino del Pueblo, is a exhibition space for local artists that offers a mix of Mexican and American dishes. (☎505-867-1700. Sandwiches $6-9. Entrees $8-15. Open M-Th and Su 7:30am-9pm, F-Sa 7:30am-9:30pm. AmEx/D/MC/V.) **The Coronado Campground ●,** just north of Rte. 66 entering town, is a good place to sleep. (☎505-980-8756. Sites $10, with water and electricity $22. Cash only.)

⚑ APPROACHING ALBUQUERQUE: 18 MILES
In Bernalillo, turn right onto **Camino del Pueblo** to find **I-25.** Continue through Alameda to Albuquerque.

ALBUQUERQUE

At the crossroads of the Southwest, Albuquerque buzzes with history and culture, nurturing ethnic restaurants, offbeat galleries, quirky cafes, and raging nightclubs. Rte. 66 may no longer appear on maps, but it's alive and kicking here. The mythic highway radiates a palpable energy that gives shops, restaurants, and bars a distinctive spirit found nowhere else in the state. Downtown Albuquerque may lack East Coast elegance, but it has a cosmopolitan feel of its own, fed by a unique combination of students, cowboys, bankers, and government employees.

PUEBLOS, PARTICLES & POKER

GONE FISSION IN NEW MEXICO

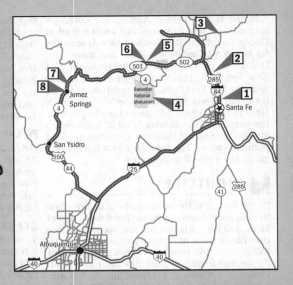

Length: 160 miles
Time: 2 days
Starting point: Santa Fe
Highlight: Black Hole Surplus Store

From Santa Fe, take St. Francis Dr./NM 84/285 N to Tesque. Take Exit 172, and follow the signs to Tesque Village to reach the Foundry.

1 SHIDONI FOUNDRY. The Shidoni Foundry is an 8-acre complex of beautiful sculpture gardens, galleries, and a bronze foundry. Stop by on a Saturday to see a bronze pour, or just stick to a free self-guided tour. (☎505-988-8001; www.shidoni.com. Open M-F 10:30-10:45am, noon-1pm, and 3-3:15pm; Sa 9am-5pm. Free.)

Retrace your steps back to NM 84/285 N, and take it to Exit 175.

2 CAMEL ROCK CASINO. Casinos are advertised at regular intervals along the highways in New Mexico, though the Camel Rock Casino is the best bet for your gambling needs. With rows of shimmering slot machines, towering columns, and the occasional Elvis impersonator, Camel Rock has all the obligatory extravagance necessary for a classic gambling experience. (☎800-462-2635; www.camelrockcasino.com.)

Return to NM 84/285 N to Espanola. Take Hwy. 76 7 mi. east to Chimayo.

3 EL SANCTUARIO DE CHIMAYO. Built between 1814 and 1816, **El Sanctuario de Chimayo** is known by locals as 'little Lourdes' and considered holy by many. Over 30,000 worshippers make the pilgrimage to this tiny chapel every Good Friday to celebrate Easter. The chapel seems even smaller in comparison to the massive 6 ft. crucifix. (☎505-351-4889. Open daily June-Sept. 9am-5pm; Oct.-Apr. 9am-4pm. Mass Su noon. Free.)

From Chimayo, return to NM 84/285, and head south, branching off to NM 502 W as you follow signs to Los Alamos. Turn left onto NM 4, and head south 12 mi. to Bandelier National Park.

4 BANDELIER NATIONAL MONUMENT. Bandelier National Monument features the remnants of over 2400 cliff dwellings and pueblos amid 50 sq. mi. of mesas and rugged canyons. The park centers around **Frijoles Canyon,** the site of many natural caves and settlements along the canyon floor that were occupied for roughly 500 years. The **Main Loop Trail** (1½ mi.) begins at the back porch of the visitors center and passes the ruins of **Tyuonyi Pueblo** and the **Long House,** an 800 ft. section of adjoining multi-storied stone homes. Those with more time should go a half-mile farther to **Alcove House,** a *kiva* carved high above the canyon floor. (☎505-672-3861; www.nps.gov/band. Open daily in summer 9am-5:30pm; in winter 8am-4:30pm. Entrance fee $12 per vehicle.)

Continue on NM 4 as it curves to the west. Turn right onto NM 501/W. Jemez Rd. 6 mi. later to enter Los Alamos. Turn left onto Diamond Dr. and right onto Canyon Rd., which becomes Central Ave.

5 **BRADBURY SCIENCE MUSEUM.** The **Bradbury Science Museum,** at 15th and Central Ave., explains the history of the mysterious P.O. Box 1663 during the heydey of the Manhattan Project and the Los Alamos National Laboratory. You may be expecting just another science museum swarming with third-graders, but this one has bombs. Big ones. (☎505-667-4444; http://bsm.lanl.gov. Open M and Su 1-5pm, Tu-Sa 10am-5pm. Free.)

From Central Ave., turn right on NM 502, turn right on Diamond Dr., and then take a left onto Arkansas Ave.

6 **BLACK HOLE SURPLUS STORE AND MUSEUM.** The **Black Hole Surplus Store and Museum,** 4015 Arkansas Ave., a quirky gem of an atomic junkyard that sells all the junk the laboratory doesn't want anymore, including 50-year-old calculators, fiber-optic cables, flow gauges, time-mark generators, optical comparators, and other technological flotsam. Former lab scientist and owner Ed Grothus is happy to give visitors the politically-edged "nickel tour," detailing some of the most remarkable features of his "nuclear waste" from the Los Alamos National Laboratory. Leave with your very own $2 atomic-bomb detonator cable or a $0.25 WWII army fork. (☎505-662-5053. Open M-Sa 10am-5pm.)

Backtrack on Arkansas Ave., and turn right on Diamond Dr. Turn right onto NM 4. (Trinity Dr.). Follow the extremely curvy road for 33 mi. to Jemez Springs. You will pass through a number of natural preserves and have several chances to stop for a magnificent view of the Valle Grande. The State Monument will come into view a few miles into Jemez Springs.

7 **JEMEZ STATE MONUMENT AND SODA DAM.** Over 600 years ago, the Jemez people built villages in the mountain valley and on top of mesas. In the 17th century, Spanish colonists built a Catholic Mission directly in the middle of the valley, and the Jemez villages were soon abandoned. The ruins of the **Church of San Jose de los Jemez** are some of the most spectacular ruins in the Southwest. (☎505-829-3530. Open M and W-Su 8:30am-4:30pm. $3, under 17 free.) One of the many natural hot springs in the region, **Soda Dam** doesn't have a visitors center, but you can swim in the pool. It may smell like sulfur, but you won't mind when you're basking in the warm water amid thousands of years of minerals. If you're feeling adventurous, try out the natural waterslide.

Follow NM 4 for a short way to reach downtown Jemez Springs.

8 **LOS OJOS RESTAURANT AND SALOON.** A true Old West watering hole, Los Ojos Restaurant and Saloon ❹, 17596 NM 4, is a true Old West watering hole with antlers and guns mounted on the wall. Not only is it the best restaurant in town, but it has an eclectic mix of New Mexican cuisine. Try the Jemez burger with swiss cheese and black olives for $8. (☎505-829-3547. Open M-Th and Su 11am-8:30pm, F-Sa 11am-9:30pm. MC/V.)

BACK TO THE ROUTE. 15 mi. past Jemez, turn onto NM 550 S to Bernalillo. Take I-25 N to Exit 282. Then take U.S. 84 N back to Santa Fe.

VITAL STATS

Population: 450,000

Visitor Info: Albuquerque Visitors Center, 401 2nd St. NW (☎505-842-9918; www.abqcvb.org), 3 blocks north of Central Ave., in the Convention Center. Open M-F 9am-5pm. **Old Town Visitors Center,** 303 Romano St. NW (☎505-243-3215; www.itsatrip.org), in the shopping plaza west of the church. Open daily Apr.-Oct. 9am-5pm; Nov.-Mar. 9:30am-4:30pm.

Internet Access: Albuquerque Public Library, 501 Copper NW (☎505-768-5141). Open M and W-Sa 10am-6pm, Tu 11am-7pm. $3.

Parking: 2025 Central Ave. NW (☎505-924-3950). $1 per 30min., $8 per day max.

Post Office: 1135 Broadway NE (☎505-346-8044), at Mountain St. Open M-F 7:30am-6pm. **Postal Code:** 87101.

GETTING AROUND

Rte. 66 is known in Albuquerque as **Central Ave.,** and it is the main thoroughfare of the city, running through all of its major neighborhoods. Central Ave. runs east-west, while **I-25** runs north-south; the two divide Albuquerque into quadrants. All downtown addresses come with a quadrant designation: NE, NW, SE, or SW. The campus of the **University of New Mexico (UNM)** spreads along Central Ave. from University Ave. to Carlisle St. **Nob Hill,** the area of Central Ave. around **Carlisle St.,** features coffee shops, bookstores, and galleries. **Downtown** lies on Central Ave., between **10th St.** and **Broadway. Old Town Plaza** sits between **San Felipe, North Plaza, South Plaza,** and **Romero.**

SIGHTS

OLD TOWN. When the railroad cut through Albuquerque in the 19th century, it missed Old Town by almost 2 mi. As downtown grew around the railroad, Old Town remained untouched until the 1950s, when the city realized that it had a tourist magnet right under its nose. Just north of Central Ave. and east of Río Grande Blvd., the adobe plaza looks today much like it did over 100 years ago, save for the ubiquitous restaurants, gift shops, and jewelry vendors. Sure it's a tourist trap, but Old Town is an architectural marvel, and a stroll through is worthwhile. On the north side of the plaza, the quaint **San Felipe de Neri Church** has stood the test of time, dating back to 1706. (*Open daily 9am-5pm. Accompanying museum open M-Sa 10am-4pm. Free.*) **Walking tours** of Old Town meet at the Albuquerque Museum. (*1hr. tours Tu-Su 11am. Free with admission.*)

OLD TOWN MUSEUMS. To learn about the beautiful stone that is the lifeblood of so many New Mexican artisans, stop by the ▣**Turquoise Museum.** The museum has been in a family of Turquoise experts for generations and lapidary demonstrations take place daily at 10am. The collection room features gorgeous stones from over 60 mines. (*2107 Central Ave. NW. ☎505-247-8650. Open M-Sa 10am-4pm. $4, seniors and children $3.*) Nearby, the **National Atomic Museum** has enthralling exhibits on nuclear physics, the social history of the Cold War, and the Manhattan Project. The museum is moving to a new location at the end of 2007, so call ahead. (*1905 Mountain Rd. NW. ☎505-245-2137. Open daily 9am-5pm. $5.60, 60+ and ages 6-17 $4, under 6 free.*) To the northeast, the **Albuquerque Museum** showcases New Mexican art and history. The comprehensive exhibit on the Conquistadors and Spanish colonial rule is especially impressive with full suits of armor and weaponry as well as replicated New Mexican homes from the 18th century. Even if you choose not to go in, be sure to see the beautiful sculpture gardens outside. (*2000 Mountain Rd. NW. ☎505-243-7255; www.cabq.gov/museum. Open Tu-Su 9am-5pm. Tours of the sculpture garden Tu-F 10am. $4, seniors $2, ages 4-12 $1. 1st W of each month free.*) No visit to Old Town would be complete without seeing the **Rattlesnake Museum,** which lies just south of the plaza. With over 30 species ranging from the deadly Mojave to the tiny Pygmy, this is the largest collection of live rattlesnakes in the world. Have myths debunked, and get your picture taken with a snake. (*202 San Felipe NW. ☎505-242-6569. Open M-Sa 10am-6pm, Su noon-6pm. $3.50; seniors, students, military $2.50; under 18 $1.50.*) Just outside the main Old Town area, Spike and Alberta, two statuesque dinosaurs, greet tourists outside the **New Mexico Museum of Natural History and Science.** The museum features a five-story "dynatheater," a planetarium, and a Seismosaurus, the longest dinosaur ever unearthed. (*1801*

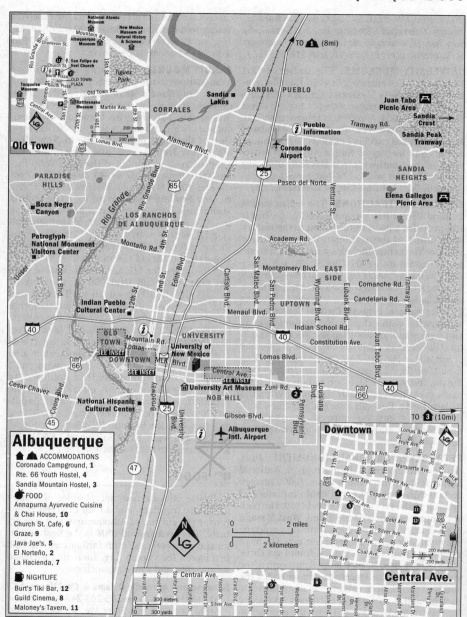

Old Town

National Atomic Museum
New Mexico Museum of Natural History & Science
Mountain Rd.
Albuquerque Museum
Charlevoix St.
Rio Grande Blvd.
Church St.
San Felipe de Neri Church
North Plaza
OLD TOWN PLAZA
South Plaza
Turquoise Museum
Romero
San Felipe St.
Old Town Rd.
Rattlesnake Museum
Central Ave.
20th St.
19th St.
18th St.
Marble Ave.
Lomas Blvd.
Tiguex Park
0 200 meters
0 200 yards

TO **1** (8mi)

SANDIA PUEBLO
Sandia Lakes
CORRALES
Alameda Blvd.
Pueblo Information
Coronado Airport
Juan Tabo Picnic Area
Tramway Rd.
Sandia Crest
Sandia Peak Tramway

PARADISE HILLS
Boca Negra Canyon
Rio Grande
Rio Grande Blvd.
85
Paseo del Norte
Ventura St.
SANDIA HEIGHTS
Elena Gallegos Picnic Area

Petroglyph National Monument Visitors Center
LOS RANCHOS DE ALBUQUERQUE
Montaño Rd.
4th St.
Academy Rd.

Unser
Coors Blvd.
12th St.
Indian Pueblo Cultural Center
2nd St.
Edith Blvd.
Carlisle Blvd.
San Mateo Blvd.
San Pedro Blvd.
Montgomery Blvd.
EAST SIDE
Comanche Rd.
Candelaria Rd.
Tramway Rd.

40
OLD TOWN
SEE INSET
DOWNTOWN
SEE INSET
Mountain Rd.
Lomas
MLK Blvd.
66
UNIVERSITY
University of New Mexico
Central Ave.
SEE INSET
University Art Museum
Zuni Rd.
NOB HILL
Menaul Blvd.
UPTOWN
Wyoming Blvd.
Eubank Blvd.
Indian School Rd.
Constitution Ave.
40
Lomas Blvd.
Louisiana Blvd.
Pennsylvania Blvd.
Juan Tabo Blvd.
66
TO **3** (10mi)

Cesar Chavez
Coors Blvd.
National Hispanic Cultural Center
Broadway
25
University Blvd.
Gibson Blvd.
Albuquerque Intl. Airport
2

45
47

N
LG
0 2 miles
0 2 kilometers

Albuquerque

⌂ ⌂ ACCOMMODATIONS
Coronado Campground, **1**
Rte. 66 Youth Hostel, **4**
Sandía Mountain Hostel, **3**

🍴 FOOD
Annapurna Ayurvedic Cuisine & Chai House, **10**
Church St. Cafe, **6**
Graze, **9**
Java Joe's, **5**
El Norteño, **2**
La Hacienda, **7**

🍸 NIGHTLIFE
Burt's Tiki Bar, **12**
Guild Cinema, **8**
Maloney's Tavern, **11**

Downtown

Lomas Blvd.
Fruit Ave.
Roma Ave.
11th St.
10th St.
9th St.
8th St.
Marquette Ave.
4th St.
3rd St.
2nd St.
MLK Blvd.
LG
Kent Ave.
Tijeras Ave.
66
Park Ave.
Central Ave.
Copper
11th St.
Gold Ave.
Silver Ave.
10th St.
8th St.
Lead Ave.
5th St.
4th St.
1st St.
66
Coal Ave.
Iron Ave.
5
11
12
0 200 meters
0 200 yards

Central Ave.

Central Ave.
Harvard Dr.
Cornell Dr.
Stanford Dr.
Columbia Dr.
Princeton Dr.
Vassar Dr.
Silver Ave.
Girard Blvd.
Richmond Dr.
Dartmouth Dr.
Bryn Mawr Dr.
Wellesley Dr.
Tulane Dr.
Carlisle Blvd.
Amherst Dr.
Hermosa Dr.
Solano Dr.
Aliso Dr.
Morningside Dr.
Montclaire Dr.
Sierra Dr.
Graceland
9
8
0 300 meters
0 300 yards

Mountain Rd. NW. ☎505-841-2800; www.nmnaturalhistory.org. Open daily 9am-5pm; Jan. and Sept. Tu-Su 9am-5pm. $6, seniors $5, children $3; with Dynatheater or Planetarium ticket $11/$9/$5; both $16/$13/$7.)

UNIVERSITY MUSEUMS. The **University Art Museum** features changing exhibits that focus on 20th-century New Mexican paintings and photography. (Near the corner of Central Ave. and Cornel St. ☎505-277-4001; http://unmartmuseum.unm.edu. Open Tu-F 9am-4pm. Free.) The **Maxwell Museum of Anthropology** has excellent exhibits on the culture and ancient history of Native American settlement in the Southwest. (On University Blvd., just north of MLK Blvd. ☎505-277-4405; www.unm.edu/~maxwell. Open Tu-F 9am-4pm, Sa 10am-4pm. Free.)

CULTURAL ATTRACTIONS. The **Indian Pueblo Cultural Center** has a commercial edge, but it still provides a good introduction to the history and culture of the 19 Indian Pueblos of New Mexico. The center includes a museum, a store, and a restaurant. (2401 12th St. NW. ☎505-843-7270; www.indianpueblo.org. Museum open daily 9am-4:30pm. Art demonstrations Sa-Su 11am-2pm. Indian dances Sa-Su 11am and 2pm. $4, seniors $3, students $1.) The **National Hispanic Cultural Center** has an art museum with exhibits that explore folk art and representations of Hispanic social and cultural life in America. (1701 4th St. SW, at the corner of Bridge St. ☎505-246-2261; www.nhccnm.org. Open Tu-Su 10am-5pm. $3, seniors $2, under 16 free.) During the 2nd week of October, hundreds of aeronauts take flight in hot-air balloons during the **Balloon Fiesta.** Beneath a surreal sky filled with the colorful giants, the entire city enjoys a week of barbecues and musical events (☎888-422-7277; www.balloonfiesta.com.)

PETROGLYPH NATIONAL MONUMENT. Just outside Albuquerque, the Petroglyph National Monument features more than 20,000 images etched into lava rocks by Pueblo Indians and Spanish settlers between 1300 and 1680. The park encompasses much of the 17 mi. **West Mesa,** a ridge of black basalt boulders formed by volcanic activity that occurred 130,000 years ago. The most accessible petroglyphs can be found via three short trails at **Boca Negra Canyon,** 2 mi. north of the visitors center. The **Rinconada Canyon Trail,** 1 mi. south of the visitors center, has more intricate rock art and is an easy 2½ mi. desert hike along the base of the West Mesa. To see the nearby vol-

canos, take Exit 149 off I-40, and follow Paseo del Volcán to a dirt road. (Take I-40 to Unser Blvd./Exit 154, and follow the park signs. ☎505-899-0205. Park open daily 8am-5pm. $1 per vehicle.)

SANDÍA MOUNTAINS. Rising a mile above Albuquerque to the northeast, the sunset-pink crest of the **Sandía Mountains** gives the mountains their name, which means "watermelon" in Spanish. The crest beckons to New Mexicans, drawing thousands to hike and explore. One of the most popular trails in New Mexico, **La Luz Trail** (7½ mi. one-way) climbs the Sandía Crest, beginning at the Juan Tabo Picnic Area. (From Exit 167 on I-40, drive north on Tramway Blvd. 10 mi. to Forest Rd. 333. Follow Trail 137 for 7 mi., and then take Trail 84 to the top.) The Sandía Mountains have excellent mountain biking trails. Warm up on the moderate **Foothills Trail** (7 mi.), which starts at the Elena Gallegos Picnic Area, off Tramway Blvd., and skirts along the bottom of the mountains. The most popular place for biking is at the **Sandía Peak Ski Area,** 6 mi. up Rte. 536 on the way to Sandía Crest. Bikers of all skill levels can take their bikes up the chairlift and then ride down on 15 mi. of mountain trails and rollers. (☎505-242-9052; www.sandiapeak.com. Bikes $40 per day. Helmets required. Chairlifts run June-Aug. F-Su 10am-4pm. Full-day lift ticket $16.) The peak is also a serviceable ski area for those who can't escape north to Taos or south to Ruidoso. Six lifts service 25 short trails on 200 acres. The summit has a vertical drop of 1700 ft. (☎505-242-9052; www.sandiapeak.com. Open Dec. 17-Jan. 2 daily 9am-4pm; Jan. 5-Mar. 13 W-Su 9am-4pm. Full-day lift ticket $41, ages 13-20 $33, under 13 $31, 62+ $30. Rentals from $18; lessons from $50.)

ᴎ FOOD

A diverse ethnic community, hordes of hungry interstate travelers, and a load of green chiles render the cuisine of Albuquerque surprisingly tasty. The area around **UNM** is the best bet for inexpensive eateries. A bit farther east, **Nob Hill** is a haven for yuppie fare, including avocado sandwiches and iced cappuccinos.

■ **Annapurna Ayurvedic Cuisine & Chai House**, 513 San Mateo Blvd. NE (☎505-262-2424), on the corner of Yale Blvd. and Silver Ave. Wonderful Indian vegetarian options are designed to promote healing and balance. Determine which body type you are to maximize effects. Try the house chai ($2.50) or the Malaysian stir-fry ($7). Open M-W 7am-8pm, Th-Sa 7am-9pm, Su 10am-2pm. MC/V. ❷

Java Joe's, 906 Park Ave. SW (☎505-765-1514), 1 block south of Central Ave. This lively, casual restaurant has hearty wraps ($6) and great breakfast burritos ($3.25). Lots of vegetarian dishes and occasional live music. Open daily 6:30am-3:30pm. MC/V. ❶

El Norteño, 6416 Zuni St. (☎505-256-1431), at California. A family-run establishment renowned as the most authentic and varied Mexican joint in town. The walls feature murals of Mexico, and the vast repertoire runs from chicken *mole* ($8) to *caldo de res* (beef stew) to beef tongue ($7-9). Lunch buffet M-F 11am-2pm ($6). Open daily 8:30am-9pm. AmEx/D/MC/V. ❷

Graze, 3128 Central Ave. SE (☎505-268-4729). Patrons are encouraged to eat what they like from the eclectic menu without the limits of conventional courses. Chickpea fries $10. Parmesan crusted veal scaloppini $13. Open M-Th 11am-10pm, F-Sa 11am-11pm, Su noon-9pm. The associated bar **Gulp** is next door and features free live music Th and Sa. Open M-Th noon-1am, F-Sa noon-2am, Su noon-midnight. No cover. AmEx/D/MC/V. ❹

Church St. Cafe, 2111 Church St. NW (☎505-247-8522; www.churchstreetcafe.com), in Old Town. This New Mexican eatery is in the Casa de Ruiz, which dates back to 1706, making it one of the oldest buildings in the state. Glass-topped wagon-wheel

tables and great lunch options. Salads $6-7. Open M-Sa 8am-9pm, Su 8am-4pm. AmEx/D/MC/V. ❸

La Hacienda, 302 San Felipe NW (☎505-243-3131), in Old Town. With huge wooden beams, elaborate chairs, and stained glass lamps, this restaurant appeals to aesthetic sensibilities as well as tastebuds. Entrees $9-15. Open daily 11am-9pm. AmEx/D/DC/MC/V. ❹

◣ ACCOMMODATIONS

Cheap motels line **Central Ave.**, even near downtown. Though many of them are worth their price, be sure to evaluate the quality before paying. During the October **Balloon Festival**, rooms are scarce, so call ahead for reservations.

Route 66 Youth Hostel, 1012 Central Ave. SW (☎505-247-1813), at 10th St. Friendly hostel located between downtown and Old Town. Dorm and private rooms are simple but clean. Proprietor prepares dinner 6pm. Key deposit $5. Reception 7:30-10:30am and 4-11pm. Check-out 10:30am. Each guest responsible for 1 of 10 easy chores. Dorms $17; private rooms $22.50-25, with bath $33. Cash or check only. ❶

Sandía Mountain Hostel, 12234 Rte. 14 N (☎505-281-4117), in nearby Cedar Crest, 10 mi. from the Sandía Ski Area. Take I-40 E to Exit 175 and go 4 mi. north on Rte. 14. This wooden building offers a living room with fireplace and kitchen, plus a family of donkeys out back. Hiking and biking trails are across the street. Linen $1. Coin-op laundry. Tent sites $8; dorms $14; private cabins $32. MC/V. ❶

OH, BILLY!

Lawrence Murphy owned the only general store in Lincoln in the 1870s. When John Tunstall and Alexander McSween opened a rival store in 1878, Murphy saw red, and his assistant James Dolan had Tunstall killed. One of Tunstall's men, William H. Bonney vowed to get revenge. Bonney, a.k.a. **Billy the Kid,** rounded up a posse called the Regulators who wreaked havoc in Lincoln, killing Tunstall's assassins along with the sheriff. Dolan's men fought back, burning McSween's house with his family inside. McSween himself was shot unarmed on the doorstep as he came out to propose a truce. Billy the Kid, then only a peach-fuzzed teenager, escaped and spent the next two years on the run. The new Lincoln sheriff, Pat Garrett, finally caught up with Billy in nearby Fort Sumner. Billy was subsequently put on trial for killing the sheriff. Sentence to hang, Billy was in jail awaiting execution in Lincoln on April 28, 1881 when he made his famous escape. While in the outhouse, he grabbed a pistol hidden by an accomplice, burst out, and killed one of his two guards. Billy then killed the other guard with the man's own shotgun and fled on a horse. Less than 3 months later, Garret caught up with Billy again, and this time, he did not give the slippery Kid a chance to escape. Garret shot

Coronado Campground (☎505-980-8256), about 15 mi. north of Albuquerque. Take I-25 to Exit 242, and follow the signs. A pleasant campground on the banks of the Río Grande. Adobe shelters offer a respite from the heat. Toilets, showers, and water. Open M and W-Su 8:30am-5pm; self-service pay station after hours. Tent sites $10, with shelters and picnic tables $18; full hookup $22. Cash only. ❶

☕ NIGHTLIFE

Albuquerque is an oasis of interesting bars, jamming nightclubs, art-film houses, and university culture. Check flyers posted around the university area or pick up a copy of *Alibi*, the free local weekly, for info on live music. Most nightlife huddles on and near **Central Ave.**, downtown, and near the university; **Nob Hill** establishments tend to be the most gay-friendly. **Maloney's Tavern**, 325 Central Ave. NW, is covered in black and white shots of classic moments of the silver screen. Classy bar food like burgers and sandwiches ($8-9.50) is available until 10pm. (☎505-242-7422; www.maloneystavern.com. No cover. Open M-Sa 11am-2am, Su 11-midnight. AmEx/D/MC/V.) **Burt's Tiki Bar**, 313 Gold St. SW, is 1 block south of the Central Ave. strip of clubs, and the difference shows in its friendly, laid-back atmosphere. Surf and tiki paraphernalia line the walls and ceiling, while anything from funk to punk to hip-hop takes the stage. (☎505-247-2878. Live music Tu-Sa. No cover. Open Tu-Sa 9pm-2am. AmEx/D/MC/V.) The offbeat **Guild Cinema**, 3405 Central Ave. NE, runs indie and foreign films. (☎505-255-1848. Films M-Th 4:30, 7pm; F-Su 2, 4:30, 9:15pm. $7; students, seniors, and all shows before 5pm $5. Cash only.)

◪ APPROACHING ACOMA PUEBLO AND SKY CITY: 64 MILES

Here the old route joins the interstate; follow **Rte. 66 W** out of Albuquerque on **I-40.** Bypass the Santa Fe route (since you've already been to Santa Fe) and take I-40 all the way to **Exit 117.** In Mesita turn right onto the north service road, and follow it 5 mi. to the junction with **NM 124.** Turn right onto NM 124, and pass through the tiny towns of Paraje, Budville, Cubera, Villa de Cubero, and San Fidel. Cross to the I-40 south service road 17 mi. later in McCartys **(Exit 96).** 1 mi. past the exit you will see signs to the Acoma Pueblo and Sky City.

DID YOU KNOW? Villa de Cubero was where Ernest Hemingway holed up to write *The Old Man and the Sea,* although little is left to suggest its role as literary foil to Hemingway's ocean.

ACOMA PUEBLO AND SKY CITY. Arguably the oldest continuously inhabited area in North America, **Sky City,** on the **Acoma Pueblo,** peers over the edge of the high mesa. Accessible only by a narrow staircase, Sky City avoided Spanish rule until 1599, when its residents were brutally enslaved by Don Juan de Onate. Between seven and 13 families live on the mesa, which lacks electricity and running water. Perched high above the rocky world below, the **San Esteban Rey Mission** on the pueblo is a gravity-defying architectural feat and a stunning example of Southwestern pueblo architecture. Visitors must buy a bus pass at the visitors center to ride up to the pueblo with a guide. Photographs are prohibited unless you buy a photography pass ($10), and video cameras are forbidden. Bring cash if you plan on ascending the pueblo, as resident native artists often lay out their renowned hand-painted pottery. All are welcome September for the **Harvest Dance and Annual Feast of San Estevan** at Old Acoma. (☎505-552-7860; www.skycity.com. Open daily. Tours daily Apr.-Oct. 8am-6pm; Nov.-Mar. 8am-5pm. Last tour 1hr. before closing. $10, seniors $9, children $7.)

◪ APPROACHING GRANTS: 37 MILES

From the service road leading from McCartys, pass under **I-40** after 5½ mi. RVs should backtrack to I-40 and take it to **Exit 89** due to the low, narrow tunnel. Cross onto the north side 7 mi. later at the Sky City turnoff, and continue on **NM 117.** Enter Grants on Santa Fe Ave./NM 122.

GRANTS

Grants first appeared on the map when the three Grant brothers were given a contract to build the Santa Fe railroad through the area. After the railroad boom, Grants became a shoot-'em-up Old West town, and the population scraped as low as 350. Grants got its big chance in 1950 when a Navajo named Paddy Martinez overheard some prospectors in a cafe discussing a valuable yellow mineral they called carnotite, and found the rock near his sheep pastures outside of town. Grants became a mining town, and the uranium wealth made the town glow until the last of the mines was tapped out in the 1980s.

VITAL STATS

Population: 8800

Visitor Info: Grants Chamber of Commerce, 100 N. Iron Ave. (☎505-287-4802; www.grants.org), in the New Mexico Mining Museum. Open M-Sa 9am-4pm. **El Malpais Info Center,** (☎505-783-4774) 23 mi. south of I-40 on Rte. 53. Open daily 8:30am-4:30pm.

Internet Access: Mother Whiteside Memorial Library, 525 High St. (☎505-287-7927). Open M-F 9am-5pm, Sa 9am-3:30pm. Free.

Post Office: 816 W. Santa Fe Ave. (☎505-287-3143). Open M-F 8:50am-5pm, Sa 8:30am-noon. **Postal Code:** 87020.

GETTING AROUND. Although streets in Grants are laid out erratically, getting around is fairly simple. **Rte. 66** runs through the center of town as **Santa Fe Ave.;** most attractions, restaurants, and accommodations can be found along this strip. **I-40** runs just south of town, parallel to Santa Fe Ave.

SIGHTS. Grant's mining history is panned out in the **New Mexico Mining Museum,** 100 N. Iron Ave., where you can almost feel yourself glow as you descend into a restored mine shaft under the museum. Walk through the mine to learn about every aspect of mining uranium. (☎505-287-4802. Open M-Sa 9am-4pm. $3, students and seniors $2, under 6 free.) The volcanic past of the Grants area has created an abundance of interesting natural phenomena. **Malpais National Monument,** south of town on Rte. 53 (☎505-285-4641), is home to 17 mi. of lava tube caves, ice caves, spatter cones, and rugged terrain. Miles of hiking trails lead to sandstone bluffs, natural arches, ancient Native American trade routes, and over 30 volcanic craters. Despite its spectacular landscape, the monument does not receive the traffic of some of its neighbors, making it a perfect spot to escape the crowds and head into some true wilderness. Continuing on Rte. 53, the **Ice Caves,** 12000 Ice Caves Rd., are a collapsed lava tube forming a cave that remains 31°F year-round. Admission to the ice caves also includes admission to the **Bandera Vol-**

cano, a gaping maw of fire 10,000 years ago, and now just a hole. Tickets to the attractions can be purchased at the converted logging saloon and dance hall, now the **Old Time Trading Post.** (☎888-423-2283; www.icecaves.com. Open daily 8am-1hr. before sunset. $9, ages 5-12 $4.)

FOOD AND ACCOMMODATIONS. Everything's bigger in Texas, but that doesn't include the **Uranium Cafe ❷,** 519 W. Santa Fe Ave. Their inch-thick yellow cakes ($3) are larger than the plate; eat two and they're free. The smaller Silver Yellow Cakes ($1.75) are still generously dinner-plate-sized, an inch thick, and enough for a boy scout troop. Burgers are also "Uranium size." (☎505-287-7540. Open M-F 7am-2pm, Sa 8am-2pm. AmEx/D/MC/V.) **El Cafecito ❶,** 820 E. Santa Fe Ave., is hands-down the best Mexican food in town. The prices don't hurt either. (☎505-285-6229. Entrees $1.50-6. Open M-F 7am-9pm, Sa 7am-8pm. D/MC/V.) **La Ventana Steakhouse ❹,** 1101 Guise St., at First St., is the local pick for an upscale meal. (☎505-287-9393. Appetizers $4.25-7.25. Steaks $10-20. Open daily 11am-11pm. AmEx/D/MC/V.) The **Canton Cafe ❷,** 1212 W. Santa Fe Ave., serves above-average, all-you-can-eat-buffet Chinese food. (☎505-287-8314. Dinner buffet $7. Open daily 11am-9pm. D/MC/V.) Entering town on Santa Fe Ave., look to the left for chain accommodations, which cluster with the fast-food joints at the east end of town. Continuing west on Santa Fe Ave., Grants has a neon strip to rival Santa Rosa and Tucumcari. Several of the original Rte. 66 motels are still great budget options. The **Sands Motel ❷,** 112 McArthur St., lauded through billboards west of town, has its own mini-strip coming from the east. Rooms come with microwaves, refrigerators, and sparkling bathrooms. (☎505-287-2996; www.sandsmotelonroute66.com. Singles from $31; doubles from $38. AmEx/D/MC/V.) The **Southwest Motel ❶,** 1000 E. Santa Fe Ave., rents simple but nice rooms. (☎505-287-2935. Singles $23; doubles $35. MC/V.) Across the street, rooms at the **Desert Sun Motel ❶,** 1121 E. Santa Fe Ave., are clean and pleasant with a fridge and free coffee available. (☎505-287-7925. Singles $20; doubles $25. AmEx/D/MC/V.)

APPROACHING THOREAU: 22 MILES
Leaving Grants, follow **Rte. 122** through the suburb of Milan. Continue south 9½ mi. through Prewitt until you reach Thoreau.

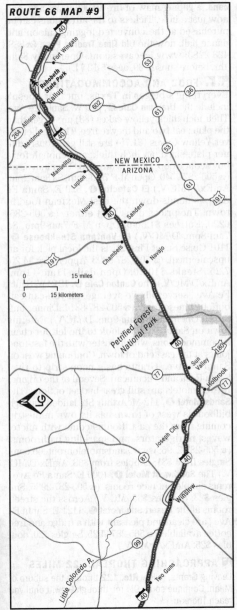

ROUTE 66 MAP #9

ROUTE 66

THOREAU. Although signs as far east as Albuquerque advertise a multitude of jewelry and souvenir stops, one of the best places to splurge is in the tiny town of Thoreau (pronounced "THREW"). Less blazingly publicized than the stores clustering around the Continental Divide, the **Navajo Cooperative Store,** 23 1st St., has jewelry, clothing, and other souvenirs. Profits from the store support The Gathering Place, a community-based organization run by the Navajo people to provide community services. (☎ 505-862-8075. Open M 8:30am-5pm, Tu-F 8:30am-6:30pm, Sa 9am-5pm.) Five miles west of town is the **Continental Divide;** rain falling east of the line makes its way to the Atlantic, while rain falling on the west ends up in the Pacific.

◪ APPROACHING GALLUP: 25 MILES
Enter **I-40** at **Exit 47,** and take it to **Exit 36,** 11 mi. later. Take the north service road 14 mi. to Gallup.

GALLUP

At the intersection of Rte. 66 and U.S. 666, Gallup is the gateway to some of the more beautiful stretches of New Mexico. Native American vendors fill parking lots, and "trading posts" crammed with silver and local turquoise line the downtown streets. If you can overlook the gaudy signs and ubiquitous turquoise vendors, the landscape and proximity to the Petrified Forest National Park, Chaco Culture National Historic Park, Navajo Reservation, and El Morro National Monument make Gallup a worthwhile stop.

VITAL STATS

Population: 20,000

Visitor Info: Gallup Visitors Center, 701 Montoya Blvd. (☎505-863-4909 or 800-242-4282; www.gallupnm.org), just off Rte. 66. Open daily Sept.-May 8am-5pm; June-Aug. 8am-6pm. **Gallup Chamber of Commerce,** 103 Rte. 66 (☎505-722-2228). Open M-F 8:30am-5pm.

Internet Access: Octavia Fellin Library, 115 W. Hill St. (☎505-836-1291). Open M-Th 9am-8pm, F-Sa 10am-6pm. Free.

Post Office: 500 S. 2nd St. (☎505-863-3491). Open M-F 8:30am-5pm, Sa 10am-1:30pm. **Postal Code:** 87301.

🄴 GETTING AROUND. Almost all you need to know about getting around in Gallup is that **Rte. 66,** the city's main drag, runs parallel to and south of **I-40.** Numbered streets run roughly north-south; **2nd St.** is also a main artery, known as N. 2nd St.

◪ SIGHTS. For a small town, Gallup has its share of local attractions. In addition to supplying all the info on Gallup you could ever want, the **Gallup Chamber of Commerce** also houses the town's **Navajo Code Talker Museum,** 103 Rte. 66, paying tribute to the over 400 Navajo whose "code" was never broken by enemy forces during WWII. The museum details the use of the Navajo language as a military code, the Navajo involvement in WWII, and Ronald Reagan's declaration of August 14 as "National Navajo Code Talkers Day." (☎505-722-2228. Open M-F 8am-5pm. Free.) The **Gallup Cultural Center,** 201 Rte. 66, houses the Storyteller Museum, Kiva Cinema, Angela's Cafe con Leche, the Ceremonial Gallery, the Wisdom Keeper Book Store/Gift Shop, and seasonal artist presentations. (☎505-863-4131. Open M-Sa 8am-8pm. Free.) **Gilbert Ortega's,** 3306 Rte. 66, does a bustling trade. Get used to it; the Ortega empire covers everything from jewelry to tacos and extends far down the road toward Arizona. (☎505-722-6666. Open daily 8am-8pm.) For an amazing selection of turquoise jewelry and other locally produced goods, **Richardson's Trading Company and Cash Pawn, Inc.,** 222 Rte. 66, deals in goods purchased from, and pawned by, local artists and citizens (☎505-722-4762. Open M-Sa 9am-6pm.) The nearby **Red Rock State Park** provides ample camping and hiking opportunities. The park museum features kachina dolls, pottery, blankets, jewelry, and regional art. During the warmer months, Red Rock is the site of concerts, rodeos, and motorcycle races; call ahead to make sure the park is open for camping. (On the east side of Gallup. Take Ford Canyon Rd. 5 mi. north, crossing over I-40 at Exit 22 to reach the park. ☎505-863-1337, camping ☎505-863-1329; www.redrockgallup.com. Museum open Sept.-May M-Sa 8am-4:30pm; June-Aug. daily 8am-4:30pm. Trading post with camping registration open daily 8:30am-4:30pm. Sites $10; RV $18.)

◪◪ FOOD AND ACCOMMODATIONS. For westbound travelers, **Earl's Restaurant ❸,** 1400 Rte. 66, at the east end of town, has been a first stop for roadtrippers since the 1940s. (☎505-863-4201 or 505-863-3285. Hand-pressed hamburgers $7-9. Open M-Th 6am-9pm, F-Sa 6am-9:30pm, Su 7am-9pm. AmEx/MC/V.) **The Ranch Kitchen,** 3001 Rte. 66, 2 mi. west of town on Rte. 66, dishes up hearty portions of inventive Mexican and American cuisine, like the popular turkey sandwich with guacamole and green chile ($7), or traditional Native American lamb stew ($7) with fry bread. (☎505-722-2537. Open daily Mar.-Oct. 7am-10pm; Oct.-Mar. 7am-9pm. AmEx/D/MC/V.) **Angela's Cafe con Leche ❷,** in the Greyhound station on Rte. 66 downtown, has a variety of gourmet coffee drinks, as well as fresh salads ($7.25), soup ($3-4), sandwiches ($7.25), and quiche ($7.25) in an exclusively French-style restaurant. (☎505-722-7526. Open M-F 8am-4pm. MC/V.) Located on a section of the old Rte. 66 alignment, **Virgie's ❸,** 2720 Rte. 66, is topped with a blinking beacon of Rte. 66 splendor and has tasty Mexican dishes. (☎505-863-5152. Fajitas $8.25. Open M-Sa 7am-10pm. AmEx/D/DC/MC/V.)

At the east end of town, Rte. 66 is lined with dirt-cheap motels (in some cases, the emphasis is on the dirt). Without a doubt, though, the best lodging in Gallup is the sprawling **El Rancho Hotel and Motel ❸,** 1000 Rte. 66. The hotel was built by the brother of film pioneer D.W. Griffith, though conflicting stories claim that Griffith actually had no brother and the man claiming to be R.E. Griffith was little more than a trickster. The motel does have cinematic claim to fame, though; it has been the longtime lodging choice of celebrities passing through, and most have had a room or a dish in the restaurant named after them. (☎505-863-9311. Singles from $52; doubles from $61. AmEx/D/MC/V.) A good bet for those watching their bottom line is the **Capitan Motel ❷,** 1300 Rte. 66, which has clean, well-maintained rooms with fridges, cable TV, and spacious bathrooms. (☎505-863-6828. Singles from $38; doubles from $42. AmEx/D/MC/V.) An even cheaper option is the **Desert Skies Motel ❶,** 1703 W. Rte 66, which has all the basics. (☎505-863-4485. Singles $30; doubles $36. MC/V.) The historical **Roadrunner Motel ❷,** 3012 Rte. 66, offers clean rooms on the eastern edge of town. (☎505-863-3804. Singles from $30; doubles from $38. AmEx/D/MC/V.)

⌖ APPROACHING HOUCK: 34 MILES

Approximately 9 mi. west of town on **Rte. 66**, 3½ mi. past the I-40 overpass, head left on **Rte. 118**. Follow the south frontage road 4 mi., under I-40, and then curve right over the railroad tracks. The tiny, old town of Manuelito is 15 mi. out of Gallup. The view leaving town is stunning and expansive; a riverbed cuts away on one side, and snow-capped mountains rise on the far side of the tracks. Attractions and gas are few and far between, although curio shops virtually wallpaper the strip. Just past the Arizona border, the **Painted Cliffs Welcome Center** will outfit roadtrippers with maps and info. (☎928-688-2448. Open M-F 8am-5pm.) Just east of the welcome center, cross under I-40 to the south frontage road. Continue 5½ mi. to join **I-40**. Take the interstate to **Exit 351** to reach Houck.

The Grand Canyon State

ARIZONA

Welcomes You!

 If you're traveling between April and October, you'll enter the Pacific Time Zone as you cross into Arizona, where it is 1hr. earlier. From November-March there is no change.

HOUCK. Houck is yet another town brimming with Ortega family stores. In addition to Ortega jewelry, you'll find **Indian City** and **Chee's Indian Store.** (On Allentown Rd. ☎928-688-2691. Open daily 7am-7pm.) The adjacent food stand is little more than a shack, but it has phenomenal Indian tacos ($5) and fry bread ($2) with honey, sugar, or cheese. (Next to Indian City. Cash only.) Three and a half miles farther down the road is the **Ft. Courage Trading Post,** in case you need to stock up on whatever it is they sell at trading posts. The exit also includes a post office and a gas station. (☎928-688-2723. Post office open M-F 8:30am-12:30pm and 1-5pm, Sa 9am-noon.)

⌖ APPROACHING SANDERS: 10 MILES

From Houck, follow the interstate 1½ mi. to **Exit 346/Pine Springs Rd.** For the next 7 mi., original **Rte. 66** is a nasty piece of narrow dirt road, so you might want to stay on the interstate to **Exit 339.** Those who take the dirt road can find age-old **Querino Trading Post,** which stocks everything from shampoo to ice cream.

(☎928-688-3047. Cash only.) Follow the dirt road 6¼ mi., or stay on **I-40** to **Exit 340.** At Exit 340, follow the north frontage road 2 mi. to Sanders.

SANDERS. Sanders is home to the pink, white, and chrome **Route 66 Diner and Pizza Shack ❷,** on the south side of the interstate. This roadside classic serves shakes ($1.75) and cobblers ($2), large breakfasts, sandwiches, and dinner plates, not to mention pizza. (☎928-688-2537. Open M-F 8am-8pm, Sa 10am-8pm. MC/V.)

⌖ APPROACHING CHAMBERS: 6 MILES

Continue on **I-40.** Chambers is at the junction of I-40 and **Rte. 191.**

CHAMBERS. Chambers has offered respite to many a traveler at the **Best Western Chieftain Motel ❹,** the only motel for miles. The adjacent restaurant provides non-fast-food meals. (☎800-657-7632. All you can eat breakfast buffet included. Singles $87; doubles $93. Restaurant open daily 6am-8pm. AmEx/D/MC/V.)

⌖ APPROACHING PETRIFIED FOREST NATIONAL PARK: 28 MILES

Continue through Navajo, where gas is available at the 24hr. Texaco station. Take **Exit 311** from **I-40.**

PETRIFIED FOREST NATIONAL PARK

Spreading over 60,000 acres, the Petrified Forest National Park looks like an overturned, psychedelic crayon box. Some 225 million years ago, when Arizona's desert was swampland, volcanic ash covered the logs, slowing their decay. Silica-infused water seeped through the wood, and the silica crystallized into quartz, combining with iron-rich minerals to produce rainbow hues. Colorful sediment was laid down in this floodplain, creating the stunning colors that stripe the park's badlands.

VITAL STATS

Area: 93,500 acres

Visitor Info: Painted Desert Visitors Center (☎928-524-6228), off I-40 at the north entrance to the park. Open daily June-Aug. 7am-7pm; Sept.-May 8am-5pm.

Gateway towns: Gallup (p. 560), Sun Valley (p. 563), Holbrook (p. 563).

Fees: 7-day pass $10 per vehicle. $5 per bike.

⊑ GETTING AROUND. Roughly speaking, the park can be divided into two parts: the northern Painted Desert and the southern Petrified Forest. A 28 mi. road connects the two sections. With lookout points and trails at intervals along the road, driving from one end of the park to the other is a good way to take in the full spectrum of landscapes. An entrance station and visitors center welcomes visitors to both ends of the park, and a restaurant is located at the northern end.

◙ SIGHTS. Most travelers opt to drive the 28 mi. park road from north to south, which takes at least 45min. From the north, the first stop is **Tiponi Point.** From the next stop at **Tawa Point,** the **Painted Desert Rim Trail** (1 mi. one-way) skirts the mesa edge above the Lithodendron Wash and the Black Forest before ending at **Kachina Point.** The panoramas from Kachina Point are among the best in the park, and the point provides access to the **Painted Desert Wilderness,** the park's designated region for backcountry hiking and camping. As the road crosses I-40, it enters the Petrified Forest portion of the park. The next stop is the 100-room **Puerco Pueblo.** A short paved trail through the pueblo offers viewpoints of nearby petroglyphs. Hundreds of petroglyphs can be seen from a distance at **Newspaper Rock.** The road then wanders through the eerie moonscape of **The Tepees** before arriving at the 3 mi. **Blue Mesa** vehicle loop. The **Long Logs** and **Giant Logs Trails,** near the southern visitors center, are littered with fragments of petrified wood. Both trails are less than 1 mi. and fairly flat, but they travel through the densest concentration of petrified wood in the world. Don't pick up the petrified wood; taking fragments is illegal and unlucky. One wall of the visitors center is covered with notes from people who took petrified wood and sent it back to the park with good riddance. At the southern end of the park, near U.S. 180, the **Rainbow Forest Museum** provides a look at petrified logs up close and serves as a visitors center. (☎928-524-6822. Open daily June-Aug. 7am-7pm. Free.)

⚐ CAMPING. There are no campgrounds in the park, but **backcountry camping** is allowed in the Painted Desert Wilderness with a free permit, available at the Painted Desert Visitors

Center and Rainbow Forest Museum. Water is available at the visitors centers. In case of emergency, call the ranger dispatch (☎928-524-9726). No fires are allowed. Motels and diners line Rte. 66, but there are none right around the park. Gallup and Holbrook offer more lodging and eating options.

◪ DETOUR
STEWART'S PETRIFIED WOOD
Take Exit 303 from I-40.

A number of curio shops west of the park hawk bits of the petrified wood. Some even offer "petrified rocks straight from the factory." By far the most entertaining of these shops is Stewart's Petrified Wood; keep an eye out for the giant dinosaurs munching on mannequins. If you get to the school bus perched on a cliff, mannequin poised to sail off the edge, you've gone just a bit too far. Charles and Gazell Stewart have used every kooky advertising ploy in the book to lure visitors into their rock shop—from the papier-mâché dinos to the ostrich pen next door. The store itself has fossils and rocks. (☎800-414-8533; www.petrifiedwood.com. Open daily 9am-sunset.)

◪ APPROACHING SUN VALLEY: 24 MILES
Get back on **I-40** and take **Exit 294** for Sun Valley.

SUN VALLEY. Between Stewart's rock haven and Holbrook is Sun Valley. Barring extreme need for pause, it's best to press on to Holbrook for food and service. The **Sun Valley RV Park ❶** sells petrified wood and has RV sites, as well as shelters for tenters. (☎928-524-2972. Tent sites $10; RV sites $30. Cash or check only.)

◪ APPROACHIING HOLBROOK: 9 MILES
Continue on **I-40 W** and take **Exit 286** for Holbrook.

HOLBROOK

All of the Rte. 66 attractions of the surrounding miles converge on tiny Holbrook. Every curio shop hawks petrified wood and Rte. 66 schlock, and the town may have more giant plastic dinosaurs and Rte. 66 murals per capita than anywhere else on the planet. Founded in 1882, Holbrook has always been a tourist mecca, first as home to one of the first Fred Harvey railroad restaurants, and later as a Rte. 66 stopping point, where tourists could hunker down in concrete teepees.

ROUTE 66

VITAL STATS

Population: 5,000

Visitor Info: Holbrook Chamber of Commerce, 100 E. Arizona Ave. (☎800-524-2459). Open daily 8am-5pm.

Internet Access: Holbrook Public Library, 451 N. 1st Ave. (☎928-524-3732). Open M 10am-5pm, Tu-Th 10am-7pm, F 1-5pm, Sa 10am-2pm. Free.

Post Office: 100 W. Erie. St. (☎928-524-3311). Open M-F 9am-5pm, Sa 10am-noon. **Postal Code:** 86025.

▐▆ GETTING AROUND. Navajo Blvd. is Holbrook's main north-south thoroughfare. At the west end of town, **N. 8th Ave.** also runs north-south. **W. Florida St.** and **W. Hopi Dr.** are the two main roads running east to west.

◙ SIGHTS. On the eastern approach into Holbrook along Rte. 66, the first of the giant plastic dinosaurs since Stewart's Petrified Wood Store line the highway, beckoning curious visitors into the **International Petrified Forest, Dinosaur Park, and Museum of the Americas,** 1001 Forest Dr. (at Exit 292). Guests can visit the extensive pottery collection and small dinosaur bone collection of the Museum of the Americas, and a short, looping drive among the scattered stone dinos is also available. (☎928-524-9178 or 928-524-9315. Open daily 8am-6pm. $10 per vehicle.) **Julien's Roadrunner Shop,** 109 W. Hopi Dr., has Rte. 66 trinkets galore, as well as a great collection of signs and t-shirts amassed over the past 33 years. (☎928-524-2388. Open M-F 8am-5pm, Sa 8am-4:30pm.) For a sense of local history, the **Navajo County Courthouse and Museum,** on Rte. 66 at the corner of E. Arizona St. and Navajo Blvd., has a small museum including a claustrophobic jail cell embellished with murals. In summer the small performance space outside the courthouse features Navajo dancing with professional dancers and children in traditional garb. (☎928-524-6558. Open daily 8am-5pm. Navajo dance June-July M-F 6:30-8:30pm. Free.) A few miles west of Holbrook, the historic **Geronimo Trading Post,** with geode pillars and a stand of teepees, has been luring travelers with postcards, jewelry, and petrified wood for years. (At Exit 290, off I-40. ☎928-288-3241. Open daily in summer 7am-7pm; in winter 8am-5pm.)

▆▐ FOOD AND ACCOMMODATIONS. When *Glamour* wanted a picturesque small-town diner for a photo shoot, **Joe and Aggie's Cafe ❸,** 120 W. Hopi Dr., fit the bill. You'd have to ask owners Stanley and Alice Gallegos if the models indulged in the hearty Mexican cuisine. (☎928-524-6540. Cheese enchilada plates $6.75. Open M-Sa 6am-8pm. AmEx/D/MC/V.) Across the street, **Romo's Cafe ❷,** 121 W. Hopi Dr., may not have made the pages of a fashion mag, but its Mexican specialties are very popular. (☎928-524-2153. Meals $3-9. Open M-F 9am-8pm, Sa 10am-8pm. AmEx/D/MC/V.) The concrete teepees of the **Wigwam Motel ❸,** 811 W. Hopi Dr., are surprisingly comfortable, each with private bath, TV, and A/C. (☎928-524-3048. Singles from $46. MC/V.) If the wigwams won't fit your budget, the **Holbrook Inn ❶,** 235 W. Hopi Dr., has standard rooms within teepee eyeshot. (☎928-524-3809. Free Wi-Fi. Singles $25; doubles $30. AmEx/D/MC/V.)

▐ APPROACHING JOSEPH CITY: 11 MILES
Continue on I-40 W. At **Exit 277,** take the north frontage road to Joseph City.

JOSEPH CITY. The giant "Here it Is" sign of the **Jackrabbit Trading Post,** 5½ mi. down the road at Exit 269, should be familiar—remember Henry's Rte. 66 Emporium and Rabbit Ranch's "Hare it is" sign (p. 518) back in Staunton, IL? The photo-op with the giant plastic rabbit is too good to miss. The store sells the usual Rte. 66 paraphernalia and great trinkets. (☎928-288-3230. Open M-Sa 8am-6:30pm, Su noon-6:30pm.)

▐ APPROACHING WINSLOW: 22 MILES
To continue into Winslow, follow the south frontage road, and head north on **Bus. I-40** into town; follow **3rd St.** through town.

WINSLOW

If you don't already know that Winslow was inspiration for the Eagles song "Take it Easy," the folks in Winslow won't let you forget it. "Standing on a corner in Winslow, AZ; such a fine sight to see" has been taken to the extreme, with an entire intersection and three out of the four corners dedicated to that happy moment. If you can possibly get away from the Eagles-mania, Winslow is a small, leisurely paced town, with one amazing hotel and a few small restaurants.

VITAL STATS

Population: 9,550

Visitor Info: Winslow Chamber of Commerce and Visitors Center, 101 E. Second St. (☎928-289-2434). Open daily 8am-5pm.

Internet Access: Winslow Public Library, 136 Halifax St. (☎207-872-1978). Open M-Tu 9am-8pm, W-F 1-8pm, Sa 9am-4pm. Free.

Post Office: 223 N. Williamson Ave. (☎928-289-2131). Open M-F 9am-5pm, Sa 10am-1pm. **Postal Code:** 86041.

GETTING AROUND. N. Williamson Ave. and **N. Berry Ave.** are two main arteries in Winslow. **Rte. 66** heads one-way west, and **W. 2nd St.** runs one-way east.

SIGHTS. What's that voice in the air? Is it God? No, it's Don Henley. **Roadworks Gifts and Souvenirs,** 101 W. 2nd St., pumps Eagles music onto the infamous corner, and sells a full variety of "Standin' on the corner" memorabilia. (☎928-289-5423. Open daily 8am-6:30pm.) The **Old Trails Museum,** 212 N. Kinsley Ave., or "Winslow's Attic," is the repository for every sort of historical Winslow knickknack, including Anasazi artifacts, souvenirs from the La Posada Hotel, and Santa Fe Railroad memorabilia. Run by the historical society, the museum is staffed by society members happy to talk about their town. (☎928-289-5861. Open Apr.-Oct. Tu-Sa 1-5pm; Nov.-Mar. Tu, Th, Sa 1-5pm. Free.) The ancient but newly renovated **Winslow Theater,** 115 Kinsley Ave. (☎928-289-4100), shows feature flicks nightly at 7pm, with Saturday and Sunday matinees at 3pm. Two miles east of Winslow at Exit 257, off I-40, the **Homolovi Ruins State Park** offers easy walks among pueblo ruins, as well as a beautiful **campground ❶.** (☎928-289-4106. Open daily 8am-5pm. Day-use $5 per vehicle. Water hookups Mid-Apr. to mid-Oct. only. Sites $10, with hookup $15. MC/V.)

FOOD AND ACCOMMODATIONS. **Bojo's Grill and Sports Club ❸,** 117 W. 2nd St., has great sandwiches ($5.25-7.25) and Mexican options. (☎928-289-0616. Open daily 11am-9pm. AmEx/D/MC/V.) A Rte. 66 historic family restaurant since 1955, **Falcon Family Restaurant ❷,** 113 E. 3rd St., serves reasonably priced American and Mexican dishes. (☎928-289-2628. Green chile burger $6.50. Entrees $6-9. Open daily 5:30am-9pm. AmEx/D/MC/V.) Nearby, the **La Posada Hotel ❹,** 303 E. 2nd St., is a sprawling *hacienda* of tiled elegance. At roughly the same price as some higher-end motels, a stay here includes plush rooms, some with their own balconies, landscaped outdoor patios, decadent downstairs lounges, a game room, and a library. (☎928-289-4366; www.laposada.org. Check-out noon. Rooms from $89. AmEx/D/MC/V.) The **Motel 10 ❷,** 725 W. 3rd St., at the west end of town, has well-maintained rooms. (☎928-289-3211. Singles from $33; doubles from $36. AmEx/D/MC/V.)

DETOUR
METEOR CRATER

18 mi. west of Winslow. Turn right on I-40 W at the edge of town, and follow it until you hit Meteor Crater.

At Meteor Crater, visitors drive up the side of the first proven meteor impact site and hike the ridge of the crater, 2½ mi. in diameter. A museum on the rim details the story of the crater, including how its moon-like terrain has made it a training ground for Apollo astronauts. (☎928-289-2362. Open daily mid-May to mid-Sept. 6am-6pm; mid-Sept. to mid-May 8am-5pm. Tours 9:15am and 2:15pm. Closed-toed shoes required. $12, seniors $11.) There is also an **RV park ❶** near the park entrance. (☎928-289-4002. Sites with water and electricity $22, with sewer $24. AmEx/D/MC/V.)

APPROACHING FLAGSTAFF: 22 MILES

Continue on **I-40** heading west. At **Exit 211,** go north on the frontage road, **Townsend-Winona Rd.,** and follow it through Winona to the northeast end of Flagstaff. Turn left on **U.S. 89,** 10 mi. after the turn-off, and follow it south into downtown Flagstaff.

FLAGSTAFF

Born on the 4th of July, Flagstaff began as a rest stop along the transcontinental railroad, its mountain springs providing precious refreshment on the long haul across the continent to the Pacific Ocean. These days, Flag-

ROUTE 66 MAP #10

Wupatki National Monument

Winona

Mormon Lake

Flagstaff

Sedona

Kaibab National Forest

Bellemont

Parks

Partridge Cr.

TO THE GRAND CANYON (55mi)

Williams

Pine Springs

Cataract Cr.

Ash Fork

0   15 miles
0   15 kilometers

Big Chino Wash

Seligman

Prescott National Forest

JUNIPER MTS.

TO HAVASUPAI RESERVATION

Yampai

Trout Cr.

Nelson

AQUARIUS MTS.

Peach Springs

Truxton

Valentine

Big Sandy

Hackberry

Truxton Wash

Red Lake

Kingman

HUALAPAI MTS.

TO HOOVER DAM (60mi), LAS MEAD (80mi), LAS VEGAS (100mi)

Sacramento Wash

staff is still a major stopover on the way to the Southwest's must-sees. Trains plow through town 72 times a day, while travelers pass through on their way to the Grand Canyon, Sedona, and the Petrified Forest, all within a day's drive. The outdoorsman will never be bored here, but Flagstaff caters to the fashionistas as well, with outlet malls and great downtown boutiques. The city's citizens welcome all to their unusual rock formations during the day and their hopping breweries at night; many of them wandered into town with a camera in hand and ended up staying.

VITAL STATS

Population: 53,000

Visitor Info: Flagstaff Visitors Center, 1 E. Rte. 66 (☎928-774-9541; www.flagstaff.com), in the Amtrak station. Open daily Memorial Day to Labor Day 7am-7pm; Labor Day to Memorial Day 8am-5pm.

Internet Access: Cline Library (☎928-523-2171), on the NAU campus. Take Riordan Rd. east from Rte. 66. Open M-Th 7:30am-10pm, F 7:30am-6pm, Sa 10:30am-5pm, Su noon-10pm. Free.

Post Office: 104 N. Agassiz St. (☎928-779-3559). Open M-F 9am-5pm, Sa 9am-1pm. **Postal Code:** 86001.

GETTING AROUND

Downtown lies between **Leroux St.** and **Aspen St.,** 1 block north of **Rte. 66;** the visitors center, hostels, and inexpensive restaurants and bars are all within a half-mile of this spot. **S. San Francisco St.,** a block east of Leroux St., hosts many outdoors shops. Split by Rte. 66, the touristy northern area of Flagstaff is the center of downtown. The area south of the tracks is less developed but has hostels and vegetarian eateries.

SIGHTS

LOWELL OBSERVATORY. In 1894, Percival Lowell chose Flagstaff as the site for an astronomical observatory. He spent the rest of his life here, devoted to the study of heavenly bodies and culling data to support his theory that life existed on Mars. The Lowell Observatory, where Lowell discovered Pluto, is both a tribute to his genius and a high-powered research center sporting five mammoth telescopes. During the day, admission includes tours of the telescopes, as well entrance to a museum with hands-on astronomy exhibits. If you have stars in your eyes, come back at night for an excellent program about the night sky and constellations. *(1400 W. Mars Hill Rd., 1 mi. west of downtown off Rte. 66. ☎928-233-3211; www.lowell.edu. Open daily Nov.-Mar. noon-5pm; Apr.-Oct. 9am-5pm. Free guided tours every hr. 10am-4pm. Evening programs June-Aug. M-Sa 8pm; Apr.-May and Sept.-Oct. W and F-Sa 7:30pm; Nov.-Mar. F-Sa 7:30pm. $5, students and seniors $4, ages 5-17 $2.)*

MUSEUM OF NORTHERN ARIZONA. The
Museum of Northern Arizona details anything and everything about the land and peoples of the Colorado Plateau. The museum has a wonderful geology gallery, but most of its space is dedicated to the area's diverse cultures, traditions, and artistic works. It also hosts the annual Hopi (4th of July weekend), Navajo (first weekend in Aug.), and Hispanic (last weekend in Oct.) heritage marketplaces, celebrating each group's art and culture. *(3 mi. north of downtown Flagstaff on U.S. 180. ☎928-774-5213; www.musnaz.org. Open daily 9am-5pm. $5, seniors $4, students $3, ages 7-17 $2.)*

WALNUT CANYON NATIONAL MONUMENT.
Dotted with the ruins of 13th-century Sinaguan dwellings, Walnut Canyon National Monument is as interesting geologically as it is culturally. The shadier north side of the Canyon is home to Ponderosa Pines and Douglas Firs, while the southern side, fully exposed to sun, is filled with desert juniper and yucca. The steep **Island Trail** (1 mi. loop) snakes down into the canyon past 25 cliff dwellings. The **Rim Trail** (¾ mi.) offers views of the canyon and passes rim-top sights. A glassed-in observation deck in the visitors center overlooks the canyon. *(☎928-526-3367. Entrance fee $5. Open daily 8am-6pm.)*

SUNSET CRATER VOLCANO NATIONAL MONUMENT.
The 1000 ft. cinder cone of Sunset Crater Volcano National Monument is the result of nearly 200 years of periodic volcanic eruptions beginning in AD 1065. It may not be Pompeii, but it's still pretty cool. The easy **Lava Flow Nature Trail**, 1½ mi. east of the visitors center, wanders 1 mi. through the rocky black terrain—tinged with yellow and red—that gave the formation its name. Hiking up Sunset Crater itself is not allowed, but the **Lenox Crater Trail** is a tough scramble up the loose cinders of a neighboring cone, followed by a quick slide down. The **visitors center** has more information. *(12 mi. north of Flagstaff on U.S. 89. ☎928-526-0502. Open daily in summer 8am-6pm; in winter 8am-5pm. $5, under 16 free.)*

WUPATKI NATIONAL MONUMENT. Wupatki
has gorgeous views of the Painted Desert and fascinating Puebloan sights. The Sinagua people moved here in the 11th century after a Sunset Crater eruption forced them to evacuate the land to the south, but archaeologists speculate that in less than 200 years, drought, disease, and over-farming led them to abandon these stone houses. The remnants of five pueblos form a loop off U.S. 89. The largest and most accessible, **Wupatki**, on a ½ mi. loop trail from the visitors center, is three stories high. The spectacular **Doney Mountain Trail** rises ½ mi. from the picnic area to the summit. Get info and trail guide brochures at the visitors center. Backcountry hiking is not permitted. *(30 mi. northeast of Flagstaff, off U.S. 89. Visitors center ☎928-526-0502. Open daily in summer 8am-6pm; in winter 9am-5pm. Monument open daily 8am-5pm.)*

OTHER SIGHTS. North of town near the
museum, the **Coconino Center for the Arts** hosts exhibits, festivals, performers, and even a children's museum. *(2300 N. Fort Valley Rd. ☎928-779-2300; www.culturalpartners.org. Open usually Tu-Sa 11am-5pm, and sometimes also Su 11am-5pm. See online calendar for exact hours. Free.)* At the **Arizona Historical Society Pioneer Museum**, history buffs can peruse displays covering the social and cultural history of Northern Arizona in the former Coconino Country Hospital for the Indigent. One excellent exhibit, "Playthings of the Past," covers antique toys. *(2340 N. Fort Valley Rd. ☎928-774-6272. Open M-Sa 9am-5pm. $3, seniors $2, under 14 free. 1st Sa of month free.)* Buy or trade new or used books for the road at **Starlight Books**. *(15 N. Leroux St. ☎928-774-6813. Open M 10am-5pm, Tu-Th 10am-6pm, F-Sa 10am-8pm, Su noon-3pm.)*

◪ OUTDOORS

With the northern **San Francisco Peaks** and the surrounding **Coconino National Forest**, Flag-

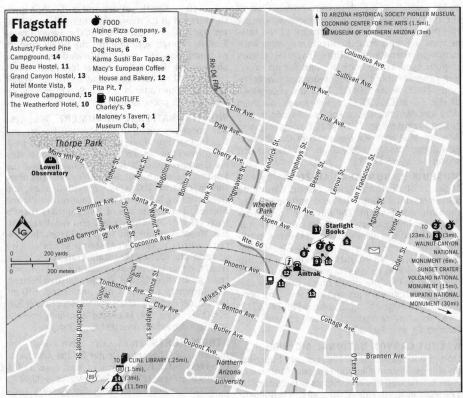

Flagstaff

ACCOMMODATIONS
Ashurst/Forked Pine
Campground, **14**
Du Beau Hostel, **11**
Grand Canyon Hostel, **13**
Hotel Monte Vista, **5**
Pinegrove Campground, **15**
The Weatherford Hotel, **10**

FOOD
Alpine Pizza Company, **8**
The Black Bean, **3**
Dog Haus, **6**
Karma Sushi Bar Tapas, **2**
Macy's European Coffee
  House and Bakery, **12**
Pita Pit, **7**

NIGHTLIFE
Charley's, **9**
Maloney's Tavern, **1**
Museum Club, **4**

TO ARIZONA HISTORICAL SOCIETY PIONEER MUSEUM,
COCONINO CENTER FOR THE ARTS (1.5mi),
MUSEUM OF NORTHERN ARIZONA (3mi)

Thorpe Park
Mars Hill Rd
Lowell
Observatory

Columbus Ave.
Sullivan Ave.
Hunt Ave.
Elm Ave.
Dale Ave.
Fine Ave.
Cherry Ave.
Kendrick St.
Humphreys St.
Beaver St.
Leroux St.
San Francisco St.
Agassiz St.
Verde St.
Sitgreaves St.
Park St.
Bonito St.
Mogollon St.
Artec St.
Toltec St.
Wheeler Park
Birch Ave.
Aspen Ave.
Starlight Books
Santa Fe Ave.
Walnut St.
Sycamore St.
Summitt Ave.
Spring St.
Grand Canyon Ave.
Coconino Ave.
Rte. 66
Elden St.

TO (23mi.), (3mi)
WALNUT CANYON
NATIONAL
MONUMENT (6mi),
SUNSET CRATER
VOLCANO NATIONAL
MONUMENT (15mi),
WUPATKI NATIONAL
MONUMENT (30mi)

Phoenix Ave.
Amtrak
Kingman St.
Tombstone Ave.
Florence St.
Globe St.
Clay Ave.
Malpais Ln.
Mikes Pike
Benton Ave.
Cottage Ave.
Butler Ave.
Dupont Ave.
Blackbird Roost St.

0   200 yards
0   200 meters

TO CLINE LIBRARY (.25mi),
(1.5mi),
89 (3mi),
(11.5mi)

Northern
Arizona
University

Brannen Ave.
O'Leary St.

Rio De Flag

---

staff offers numerous options for the outdoorsman. Due to the 7000 ft. altitude, bring plenty of water, regardless of the season. In late spring and summer, rangers may close trails if the risk of fire gets too high. The mountains occupy national forest land, so **backcountry camping** is free.

SKIING. The **Arizona Snowbowl** operates four chairlifts and a tow rope and maintains 32 trails. Majestic **Humphrey's Peak** (12,633 ft.) is the backdrop for the Snowbowl, though the skiing takes place at 11,500 ft. on **Agassiz Peak.** With an average snowfall of 260 in. and a vertical drop of 2300 ft., the Snowbowl rivals the big-time resorts of the Rockies and easily outclasses its Arizona competition. (*Take U.S. 180 about 7 mi. north to the Fairfield Snowbowl turn-off.* ☎928-779-

1951; www.arizonasnowbowl.com. Open daily 9am-4pm. Lift tickets $44, seniors and ages 8-12 $25.) **Equipment rental** is available on the mountain. (Ski package $22 per day; snowboards $29 per day.)

HIKING. In the summer, these peaks attract hikers and bikers aplenty. The Coconino National Forest has trails for hikers of all abilities. Consult the **Peaks Ranger Station,** 5075 N. U.S. 89A (☎928-526-0866), for trail descriptions and possible closures. For the more energetic hiker, the **Elden Lookout Trail** is ideal for jaw-dropping, mountain-top views. The trail climbs 2400 ft. in only 3 mi.; it is demanding, but the view makes up for it. The trail begins at the Peaks Ranger station. The most popular trail in the area is the hike to **Humphrey's Peak,** Arizona's highest mountain. This

9 mi. round-trip hike begins in the first parking lot at the Snow Bowl ski area. For a longer hike, the moderate to strenuous 17½ mi. round-trip **Weatherford Trail** offers excellent opportunities for bird- and animal-spotting. The trailhead can be found next to Schultz Tank, about 7 mi. from Flagstaff.

MOUNTAIN BIKING. Flagstaff promises excellent mountain biking. The **Schultz Creek Trail** leads bikers into an extensive network of trails in the San Francisco Mountains. Take U.S. 180 N to Schultz Pass Rd. (Forest Service Rd. 420) and park in the dirt lot just as the road becomes unpaved. The trail climbs north along the bottom of a ravine and after almost 4 mi. splits into **Sunset Trail** heading south and **Little Elden Trail** heading east. Sunset Trail climbs through the woods before cresting and descending along **Brookbank Trail** down glorious single-track dropoffs and switchbacks. This 4 mi. stretch spits out riders bearing big grins of satisfaction onto Forest Service Rd. 557. This road can either be used to ride 4 mi. back to the trailhead or to access the renowned and technically challenging **Rocky Ridge Trail,** which leads to the same trailhead.

■ FOOD

Flagstaff will make epicurean roadtrippers happy with its diverse selection of eateries. Vegetarian, organic, and just-plain-good food abound here.

Macy's European Coffee House and Bakery, 14 S. Beaver St. (☎928-774-2243), behind Du Beau Hostel. A cheery, earthy hangout serving only vegetarian food and excellent vegan selections. Specials ($4-7) change daily. Get there early, and start the day with a bowl of granola ($4) and a cup of fresh-roasted coffee ($1.50-4). Open M-Th and Su 6am-8pm, F-Sa 6am-10pm. Kitchen closes M-Th and Su 7pm, F-Sa 9pm. MC/V. ●

The Black Bean, 12 E. Rte. 66 (☎928-779-9905). Enormous, creatively stuffed wraps like veggie parmesan, Thai peanut chicken or tofu, or La Baja, featuring chicken, guacamole, and mango-pineapple salsa ($5.50-6.25). Build your own burrito ($4-7). Open May-Sept. M-Th and Su 11am-9pm, F-Sa 11am-11pm; Oct.-Apr. daily 11am-9pm. AmEx/D/MC/V. ●

Dog Haus, 1302 Rte. 66 (☎928-774-3211). The ultimate in drive-thru hotdogs ($2-3) and hamburgers ($2-4). Try the guacamole burger ($4) with bacon

and tomato. Open M-Th 7am-10pm, F-Sa 7am-11pm, Su 8am-10pm. AmEx/D/MC/V. ●

Karma Sushi Bar Tapas, 6 E. Rte. 66 (☎928-774-6100), downtown. This trendy sushi bar has dozens of creative rolls ($5-12), as well as noodles ($6-8) and standard Japanese appetizers ($3-8). Try the sunset roll (tuna, salmon, carrot, and caviar; $6.50). Reservations recommended. Open M-F 11am-2pm and 5-10pm, Sa-Su 5-10pm. D/MC/V. ●

Alpine Pizza Company, 7 Leroux St. (☎928-779-4109). Comfortably worn-in wood paneling sets the mountain-town tone of this eatery. Pool tables, foosball, and neon beer ads. Small pizza $8. Happy hour Tu-Th 4-8pm. Open daily 11am-10pm. MC/V. ●

▐ ACCOMMODATIONS

Cheap motels line Rte. 66 entering town, but there are great inexpensive lodging deals for almost as cheap in the heart of downtown. Free backcountry camping is available around Flagstaff in designated areas. Pick up a map from the **Peaks Ranger Station,** 5075 N. U.S. 89A (☎928-526-0866). All backcountry campsites must be located at least 200 ft. away from trails, waterways, wet meadows, and lakes. For more info, call the **Coconino National Forest Line.** (☎928-527-3600. Open M-F 7:30am-4:30pm.)

Du Beau Hostel, 19 W. Phoenix Ave. (☎800-398-7112; www.dubeauhostel.com). The hotel of hostels, 1 block from Rte. 66 and downtown Flagstaff. The funky lounge space with leather futons, foosball, pool, and an electric jukebox sees a regular flow of international travelers. Breakfast included 7-10am. Internet access $2 per 30min. 24hr. reception. Key deposit $5. Dorms $16-18; private rooms $34-41. MC/V. ●

Grand Canyon Hostel, 19 S. San Francisco St., (☎928-779-9421 or 888-442-2696; www.grandcanyonhostel.com). Du Beau's sister hostel with the same great value, friendly atmosphere, and free breakfast. Dorms $15-18; private rooms $30-37. MC/V. ●

Hotel Monte Vista, 100 N. San Francisco St. (☎928-779-6971 or 800-545-3068; www.hotelmonte-vista.com), downtown. A classy hotel with quirky, antique decor and a faux peeling-brick lounge used in the film *Casablanca*. Private rooms named for the movie stars who once slept there. Rooms M-Th and Su $85-95, F-Sa $105-115. AmEx/D/MC/V. ●

The Weatherford Hotel, 23 N. Leroux St. (☎928-779-1919). The oldest hotel in Flagstaff, dating from 1898, the Weatherford has 8 large rooms with balconies, antique furniture, and bay windows. No TVs or in-room phones. Reservations recommended. Rooms $65-105. AmEx/D/MC/V. ❸

Pinegrove Campground (☎877-444-6777; www.reserveamerica.com), 5 mi. south of Lakeview at the other end of Upper Lake Mary. Set in a charming locale, with drinking water and flush toilets. $12 per vehicle. ❶

Ashurst/Forked Pine Campground, on both sides of Ashurst lake (a smaller, secluded lake on Forest Rd. 82E). Turn left off Lake Mary Rd., across from Pine Grove Campground. Water and flush toilets on-site, and the fishing is stupendous. 64 sites are available first come, first served. $10 per vehicle. ❶

🎵 ENTERTAINMENT

In the second weekend of June, the annual **Flagstaff Rodeo** comes to town with competitions, barn dances, a carnival, and a cocktail waitress race. Competitions and events go on from Friday to Sunday at the Coconino County FairGrounds. (On Rte. 89A, just south of town; ask at the Flagstaff Visitors Center for details.) On the 4th of July, the town celebrates its birthday with street fairs, live music, barbecues, a parade, and, of course, fireworks. On Labor Day, the **Coconino County Fair** arrives with rides, animal competitions, and carnival games. **Theatrikos,** a local theater group, stages plays year-round. (11 W. Cherry Ave. ☎928-774-1662; www.theatrikos.com. Box office open Tu-F 11am-5pm. Tickets $5-14.)

🍸 NIGHTLIFE

Charley's, 23 N. Leroux St., plays live jazz and blues in the Weatherford Hotel, one of the classiest buildings in town. (☎928-779-1919. Happy hour 5-7pm. Open daily 11am-10pm. Bar open until 1am.) If country is your thing, check out the **Museum Club,** 3404 E. Rte. 66, the premier spot for honky-tonk action. Five trees support the building, constructed in 1918. (☎928-526-9434. Th ladies night with 2-for-1 drinks. F-Sa live country music. Happy hour daily 11am-7pm. Cover F-Sa $5. Open daily 11am-3am. MC/V.) For lively drinks surrounded by the young

and stylishly attired, head to **Maloney's Tavern,** 101 N. Leroux St. (☎928-214-9519; www.maloneystavern.com. Happy hour 4-7pm. Open daily 11am-1am. AmEx/D/MC/V.)

🚗 APPROACHING PARKS: 17 MILES

From Flagstaff, curve left on **Rte. 66** under the rail tracks, and right ½ mi. later. After 4 mi., join **I-40 W.** Follow I-40 for 5½ mi., take **Exit 185** for Bellemont, and head north on the frontage road. After 2 mi., the road enters the **Kaibab National Forest,** and 1¾ mi. beyond that turns to dirt; the pavement resumes 3 mi. later. Parks is 1 mi. beyond the paved road.

PARKS. Just to the south of Rte. 66, the **Parks General Store,** 101 Parks Rd., is also the local gas station, antique shop, post office, hair-dresser, massage parlor, gunsmith, chain-saw sharpening stop, real estate office, and video rental store. (☎928-635-1310. Open daily in summer 6:30am-6:30pm; in winter 7am-6pm.) Next door is the **Ponderosa Forest RV Park ❶,** which offers woodland sites for tents and campers, with showers, laundry, and propane. (☎928-635-0456. Sites $21, with water and electricity $25, with full hookup $28. AmEx/D/MC/V.)

🚗 DETOUR
DEER FARM PETTING ZOO
6752 Deer Farm Rd. At Exit 171, 6 mi. down the road from Parks, take a left on Deer Farm Rd.

The Deer Farm Petting Zoo gives friendly deer, donkeys, wallabies, llamas, and reindeer the opportunity to maul your pockets as you circulate among the animals and the small children feeding them. If you buy food in a cup instead of at the quarter machines, you get more food and a souvenir cup. (☎928-635-4073 or 800-926-3337. Open daily 9am-6pm. $7.50, 62+ $6.50, ages 3-13 $4.50.)

🚗 APPROACHING WILLIAMS: 16 MILES
Backtrack to **I-40 W** from **Deer Farm Rd.,** and take it to **Exit 165.** Turn left from the off-ramp into Williams, entering town on **Bus. I-40/Railroad Ave.**

WILLIAMS

The closest town to the South Rim of the Grand Canyon, Williams bills itself as the "Gateway to the Grand Canyon." This fortunate geography ensures a steady flow of tourists, and Williams offers small-town America

KAIBAB PLATEAU

TO NORTH ENTRANCE STATION, **2** (7mi), KAIBAB PLATEAU VISITORS CENTER (32mi), **5** (5mi),

3 **4**

Ken Patrick Tr.

67

Uncle Jim Tr.

NORTH RIM

WALHALLA PLATEAU

Widforss Forest Tr.

VG

6
7

North Rim Visitors Center

Komo Point Tr.

N. Kaibab Tr.

8
9

Bright Angel Point

0   1 mile
0   1 kilometer

GRAND CANYON

N. Kaibab Tr.

Bright Angel Creek

BRIGHT ANGEL CANYON

■ Isis Temple

Shiva Temple ■   ■ Cheops Pyramid

10

River Tr.

Osiris Temple ■

Tonto Tr.

↑ Shelter

Tonto Tr.

Plateau Point

S. Kaibab Tr.

Cedar Ridge

Yavapai Observation Station 🏛

Mather Point

■ Yaki Point

Bright Angel Tr.

Indian Gardens

Canyon View Information Plaza

Desert View Dr.

Powell Point

Hopi Point

Maricopa Point

Mohave Point

Trailview Overlook

13

14 Market Plaza ✉

11
12

GRAND CANYON VILLAGE

15

16

The Abyss

17

Pima Point

Rim Tr.

✚

Hermit Tr.

Hermit Rd.

Backcountry Park Entrance Rd. Office

SOUTH RIM

TO DESERT VIEW (25mi), CAMERON, EAST ENTRANCE GRANDVIEW TRAIL (10mi), **18** (25mi)

Hermits Rest ■

TO SOUTH KAIBAB NATIONAL FOREST, SOUTH ENTRANCE STATION (1mi), TUSAYAN AND **19** (1.2mi) (10mi), **20** (23mi)

180

64

S. Entrance Rd.

Grand Canyon: North and South Rims

🏠 🏕 **ACCOMMODATIONS**

Bright Angel Lodge, **11**
Cottonwood Campground, **2**
Desert View Campground, **18**
Grand Canyon Inn, **20**
Grand Canyon Lodge, **9**
Jacob Lake Inn, **3**
Kaibab National Forest, **5**
Maswik Lodge, **16**
Mather Campground, **15**
North Rim Campground, **7**
Phantom Ranch, **10**
Ten-X Campground, **19**

🍎 **FOOD**

Bright Angel Dining Room and Soda Fountain, **12**
Canyon Village Marketplace, **14**
Deli in the Pines, **6**
El Tovar Dining Room, **13**
Grand Dining Room at the North Rim, **8**
Jacob Lake Dining Room, **4**
Maswik Cafeteria, **17**

Colorado River

ROUTE 66

with trees (instead of cacti) and the leisurely pace of country living.

⚑ GETTING AROUND. Getting around in Williams is relatively easy, as **Rte. 66** runs through downtown. One block south of Rte. 66 is **Railroad Ave.,** another main drag. Streets in Williams are numbered and run north-south, while most avenues run east-west. Most of Williams's downtown is centered between Railroad Ave. and Rte. 66 between **1st** and **4th St.**

◪ SIGHTS. The **Grand Canyon Railroad** departs from the Williams railroad depot for the Grand Canyon at 10am daily, arriving 3hr. later, and returning later that day. (☎800-863-0546 or 800-635-4061. Tickets $60-155.) Grand Canyon National Park entrance tickets can be purchased here. For more info on the Grand Canyon, see p. 573. **Pete's Rte. 66 Gas Station Museum,** 101 E. Rte. 66, has every kind of Rte. 66 car memorabilia crammed into a corner garage gas station. (☎928-635-2675. Open daily 9am-10pm.) For more small-town America, check out the **Cowpuncher's Reunion Rodeo** during the first weekend in August or the **Cool Country Cruise-In & Rte. 66 Festival** during the third weekend in August.

▨◪ FOOD AND NIGHTLIFE. ▨**Twister's 50's Soda Fountain ❶,** 417 E. Rte. 66, is a glittering chrome soda fountain and Rte. 66 gift shop with sparkling vintage cars out front. (☎928-635-0266. Ice cream $1.85-5. Burgers $5. Open in summer M-Sa 8am-9pm, Su 8am-5pm; in winter daily 8am-8pm. MC/V.) Once a gas station, **Cruisers ❸,** 233 W. Rte. 66, has the vintage signs to verify it as one of the great Rte. 66 diners. (☎928-635-2445. Open daily

11am-10pm. AmEx/D/MC/V.) At the east end of town, **Pancho McGillicuddy's Mexican Cantina and Espresso Bar ❸,** 141 Railroad Ave., is your "standard" Mexican-Irish blend, although the food seems to favor the south-of-the-border side of the family. The daily lunch specials ($5-6) are great deals. (☎928-635-4150. Entrees $7.50-13. Open daily 11am-10pm. AmEx/D/DC/MC/V.) **Rod's Steakhouse ❹,** 301 Rte. 66, is a tribute to steak, from the steer-shaped menus, the beef-themed walls, and beef-inspired art. (☎928-635-2671. Lunch $6-7. Dinner entrees $11-15. Steaks $13-24. Open M-Sa 11:30am-9:30pm. AmEx/D/MC/V.) The **Sultana,** 301 W. Rte. 66, used to have the town's speak-easy in the basement; today it is a pleasantly cavernous pub with $4 drafts. (☎928-635-2021. Open daily 10am-1am. MC/V.)

⚑ ACCOMMODATIONS. The **Red Lake Hostel ❶,** 8 mi. north of Williams on Rte. 64, has simple rooms in a converted motel. The common room has a microwave and a refrigerator, and outdoor barbecue facilities are available. (☎928-635-4753. Reception M-Th and Su 6am-8pm, F-Sa 6am-9pm. Sites $10; RV sites $14; dorms $15; private rooms $33.) The **Red Garter Bed and Bakery ❹,** 137 W. Railroad Ave., has a mannequin hanging out the front suite, beckoning guests to stay in rooms once occupied by the town madams. New ownership has transformed the Red Garter from brothel to classy B&B, though it is still "slightly haunted." (☎928-635-1484; www.redgarter.com. Rooms $95-120. AmEx/D/MC/V.) The **Rte. 66 Inn ❷,** 128 E. Rte. 66, may not look like the most historic motel around, but it has been accommodating guests in cute pastel rooms since the 1930s. Rooms have TV, microwave, fridge, and elegant white wood furnishings. (☎928-635-4791. Singles M-Th and Su $45; F-Sa $49. Doubles $49/$55. AmEx/D/MC/V.) The **Williams Circle Pines KOA ❶,** 5333 Rte. 64, has camping options with access to mini-golf, bicycle rentals, game room, heated indoor pool and two spas, nightly family movies, an outdoor cafe, and seasonal activities like horseback riding, Sunday evening hayrides, and Grand Canyon tours. (☎928-635-2626 or 800-562-9379. Open Mar.-Oct. Sites from $21; RVs from $25; cabins $48-58. AmEx/D/MC/V.)

⛰ APPROACHING THE GRAND CANYON: 90 MILES

From Williams, take **I-40 E** to the junction with **I-64 N.** Turn left onto I-64 N, and follow it for 88 mi. to the Grand Canyon National Park. To bypass the Grand Canyon, skip ahead to p. 577.

GRAND CANYON

Each year, millions of people from across the globe are drawn to the magnificent Grand Canyon. Skeptics often wonder if it deserves its grandiose reputation, but seeing one sunrise or sunset in the canyon is enough to make a believer out of even the most reluctant visitor. First, there's the space: 277 mi. long and over 1 mi. deep, the enormous crevice overwhelms the human capacity for perception. Then there's the color: the shifts in hue translate to millions of years of geologic history and make the panoramic view even more awe-inspiring. Grand Canyon National Park is divided into three sections: the popular South Rim, the more serene North Rim, and the canyon gorge itself, which begins at Lake Powell, AZ, and feeds into Lake Mead, NV. Between the National Park area and Lake Mead are the Hualapai and Havasupai Reservations, which offer separate entrances into the canyon. Traveling between rims takes approximately 5½hr. via the long drive to the Lee's Ferry bridge or even longer via a grueling 13 mi. hike.

VITAL STATS

Acres: 1.2 million acres

South Rim Visitor Info: Canyon View Information Plaza (☎800-858-2808; www.grandcanyon.com or www.nps.gov/grca), across from Mather Point by the park entrance. To get there, park at Mather Pt., then walk ½ mi. to the info plaza.

North Rim Visitor Info: North Rim Visitors Center (☎928-638-2611), on Rte. 67 just before the Lodge. Open May-Oct. daily 8am-5pm. **Kaibab Plateau Visitors Center** (☎928-643-7298), at Jacob Lake, next to the Inn. Issues backcountry permits and has displays on the canyon and its ecosystem. Open daily 8am-5pm, but hours may vary.

Gateway Towns: Williams (p. 570), Flagstaff (p. 565), Kanab, UT

Fees: 7-day pass $25 per car, $12 for travelers using other modes of transportation.

SOUTH RIM

In the summer, everything on two legs or four wheels comes to this side of the Grand Canyon, primarily for the fantastic and easily accessible views from the rim. If you plan to visit at this time, be sure to make reservations for everything far in advance and prepare to battle crowds. A friendly Park Service staff, well-run facilities, and beautiful scenery generally make for enjoyable visits despite the high volume of people. Fewer tourists brave the canyon in the winter, so most hotels and facilities close during the low season.

▣ GETTING AROUND

Posted maps and signs in the park make navigation easy. Lodges and services concentrate in **Grand Canyon Village,** at the west end of **Park Entrance Rd.** To the east lie the visitors center, campground, and general store, while most of the lodges and the **Bright Angel Trail** are in the west section. The **South Kaibab Trail** is off **Desert View Dr.** east of the village. Free shuttle buses to eight rim overlooks run along **Hermit Rd.** (closed to private vehicles February through December) in the west. Avoid walking on the drive; the rim trails are safer and more scenic.

⛰ OUTDOORS

There are several ways to explore the Canyon. **Mule trips** from the South Rim are an option, but they're expensive and are often booked up to one year in advance. (☎303-297-2757. Day trip to Plateau Point 6 mi. down the Bright Angel Trail $143, lunch included; overnight including lodging at Phantom Ranch and all meals $375.) The view of the Grand Canyon from a **whitewater raft** is another popular option but usually costs $1500-3500, depending on trip length. Trips into the Grand Canyon vary from 7 to 18 days and generally require one-year advanced booking. The *Trip Planner* (available by request at the info center or online) lists several guides licensed to offer trips in the canyon. Most guides run out of Flagstaff or Page, AZ. Calmer **rafting** trips are also available for those not quite ready for a wet and wild time in the heart of the canyon. Drifting from Glen Canyon Dam to Lee's Ferry generally takes half a day.

Aramark-Wilderness River Adventures arranges such trips. (☎928-645-3296 or 800-922-8022. $62, children $52.) If the views from the rim fail to dazzle or astound you, try the higher vantages provided by one of the park's many **flightseeing** companies, located at the Grand Canyon Airport. **Grand Canyon Airlines** flies 45min. tours hourly in the summer. (☎866-235-9422; www.grandcanyonairlines.com. Reservations recommended. $119, under 11 $89.)

HIKING

Hikes in and around the Grand Canyon can be broken down into day-hikes and overnight hikes. Confusing an overnight hike for a day-hike can be a dangerous mistake, so heed the warnings of rangers and don't attempt to get to the Colorado River and back in one day. All overnight trips require permits obtained from the **Backcountry Office**, located on the west side of Parking Lot E near Maswik Lodge (permit $10; camping fee $5). Permits often take up to four months to obtain, so request one as early as possible via the Internet (www.nps.gov/grca), mail (P.O. Box 129, Grand Canyon, AZ 86023), or walk-up. For day-hikes into the canyon, be prepared to retrace every footstep uphill on the way back. An enjoyable hike usually means beginning before 7am or after 4pm; it's best to consult a ranger at the Canyon View Information Plaza before leaving. Park Service rangers also lead a variety of guided hikes; times and details are listed in *The Guide*.

The Rim, Bright Angel, South Kaibab, and River Trails are the only South Rim trails regularly maintained and patrolled by the Park Service. While other trails do exist, they are only for experienced hikers and may contain steep chutes and technically challenging terrain. Consult a ranger and *The Guide* before heading out.

Rim Trail (9½ mi. one-way, 4-6hr.). With only a slight elevation change (about 200 ft.) and the security of the nearby shuttle, the Rim Trail is an excellent way to see the canyon from several angles. The trail is wheelchair accessible to Maricopa Point in the west and has 8 viewpoints along Hermit Rd. and 3 east of it. Convenient access to viewpoints makes this trail the most crowded, but toward the eastern and western ends, hikers have a bit more room. Hopi Point's panoramic

> Seeing the canyon from the inside is harder than it looks. Even the young of body and heart should recall that there are no easy trails, and what starts as a downhill stroll can become a nightmarish 50° incline on the way back. Also, note that the lower you go, the hotter it gets; when it's 85°F on the rim, it's around 100°F at Indian Gardens and around 110°F at Phantom Ranch. Heat stroke, the greatest threat to a hiker, is marked by a monstrous headache and dry, red skin. **For a day-hike, take at least a gallon of water per person; drink at least a quart per hour hiking uphill under the hot sun.** Footwear with excellent tread is also necessary; the trails are steep, and every year careless hikers take what locals morbidly call "the 12-second tour." Parents should think twice about bringing children more than 1 mi. down any trail.

canyon views make it a great place to watch the sunset; *The Guide* lists sunrise and sunset times.

Bright Angel Trail (18 mi. round-trip, 1-2 days). Bright Angel's many switchbacks and water stations make it the best choice of moderate hikers. Depending on distance, the trail can be either a day or overnight hike. Departing from the Rim Trail near the western edge of the Grand Canyon Village, the first 1-2 mi. attract droves of day-hikers looking for a taste of canyon descent. Rest houses are strategically stationed 1½ and 3 mi. from the rim, each with water May-Sept. **Indian Gardens**, 4½ mi. down, offers restrooms, picnic tables, 15 backcountry campsites open year-round, and blessed shade. From rim to river, the trail drops 4460 ft. The round-trip is too strenuous for a day-hike—do not attempt to make it one. With a permit, overnighters can camp at Indian Gardens or on the canyon floor at Bright Angel Campground. Day-hikers are advised to go no farther than Indian Gardens (9¼ mi. round-trip) or Plateau Point (12¼ mi. round-trip). The **River Trail** (1¾ mi.) links the Bright Angel with South Kaibab at the base of the canyon.

South Kaibab Trail (7 mi. one-way to Phantom Ranch, 4-5hr.) is for those seeking a more challenging descent. Beginning at Yaki Point (7260 ft.), Kaibab is steep and tricky and lacks shade or water, but it rewards intrepid hikers with a better view of the canyon. The South Kaibab avoids the safety and obstructed views of a side-canyon route as it winds directly down the ridge, offering panoramic views across the canyon. Day-hikes to Cedar Ridge (3 mi. round-trip) and Skeleton Point (6 mi. round-trip) are reasonable only for experienced hikers due to the trail's steep grade. Kaibab meets up with Bright Angel at the Colorado River. Fewer switchbacks and a rapid descent make the South Kaibab Trail 1¾ mi. shorter than the Bright Angel to this point—guests staying at the Phantom Ranch or Bright Angel Campground can access them via either trail.

FOOD

Fast food has yet to develop in the South Rim (the closest McDonald's is 7 mi. south in Tusayan), but, fortunately, you can find better-quality meals at fast-food prices.

Canyon Village Marketplace (☎928-638-2262), at Market Plaza, 1 mi. west of Mather Point on the main road, has a deli counter with the cheapest eats in the park, groceries, camping supplies, and enough Grand Canyon apparel to clothe your extended family. Sandwiches $6. Open daily 7am-8pm. AmEx/D/MC/V. ❶

Maswik Cafeteria (☎928-638-2631), in Maswik Lodge. Serves soups, salads, country favorites, and Mexican dishes. Sandwiches $3-5. Hot entrees $6-7. Open daily 6am-10pm. AmEx/D/DC/MC/V. ❶

Bright Angel Dining Room (☎928-638-2631), in Bright Angel Lodge, is popular with families and serves breakfast, sandwiches, and Southwestern-style entrees. Breakfast $5-11. Hot sandwiches $7-10. Dinner $10-15. Open daily 6:30am-10pm. AmEx/D/DC/MC/V. ❸

Soda Fountain (☎928-635-0266), just outside the dining room of the Bright Angel Lodge. The Soda Fountain has the basics, including 13 flavors of ice cream, snack-bar sandwiches, soda, and candy. Sandwiches $5. Ice cream $2. Open M-Sa 8am-9pm, Su 8am-5pm. Hours vary; call ahead. AmEx/D/DC/MC/V. ❷

El Tovar Dining Room (☎928-638-2631, ext. 6432), in the El Tovar Hotel in the Grand Canyon Village. The classiest dining in the park. The grandly appointed dining room has a great view of the canyon and food that lives up to its surroundings. Splurge on the grilled lamb chops with cucumber mint yogurt ($30). Reservations recommended. Open daily 6:30-11am, 11:30am-2pm, and 5-10pm. AmEx/D/DC/MC/V. ❺

ACCOMMODATIONS

Indoor lodging within the park requires months of advance planning, but a few options exist just outside the park and even more within an hour's drive in neighboring Williams and Flagstaff. Summer rooms in the park should be reserved 11 months in advance (☎888-297-2757, or write Xanterra, 14001 E. Iliff, Ste. 600, Aurora, CO 80014). That said, there are frequent cancellations; if you arrive unprepared, check for vacancies or call the hotel switchboard (☎928-638-2631) and ask to be connected with the proper lodge.

Bright Angel Lodge (☎928-638-2631), in Grand Canyon Village, sits in a historic building right on the rim. Close to Bright Angel Trail and shuttle buses. Singles and doubles with shared bath $56, with private bath $68; 1- to 2-person cabins $89. AmEx/D/DC/MC/V. ❸

Maswik Lodge (☎928-638-2631), at the west end of Grand Canyon Village. Small, clean cabins with showers. Rooms with 2 queen-size beds and ceiling fans also available. Singles $76; doubles $120. AmEx/D/DC/MC/V. ❹

Phantom Ranch (☎928-638-2631), on the canyon floor, a day's hike down the South Kaibab Trail or Bright Angel Trail. Reservations are necessary and can be made up to 13 months in advance. If you're dying to sleep on the canyon floor but have no reservation, go to the Bright Angel transportation desk at 6am on the day prior to your planned stay and try the waiting list. Breakfast $18; lunch $11; stew dinner $22-32, vegetarian option $22. Single-sex dorms $31; 1- or 2-person cabins $83. AmEx/D/DC/MC/V. ❷

Grand Canyon Inn (☎928-635-9203 or 800-635-9203; www.grand-canyon-inn.com), in Valle, at Hwy. 180, 25min. from the park entrance. Clean, spacious rooms and a pool. Reservations recommended in summer. Singles $49; doubles $69. AmEx/D/MC/V. ❸

1956: The federal government begins construction on the US Interstate Highway system.

ROUTE 66

▨ CAMPING

Lodgings in the park are usually filled before you've even decided to visit the Grand Canyon, so camping is a good second option. Some reservations can be made through **SPHERICS** (☎ 800-365-2267). If you do run out of options, you can camp for free in the **Kaibab National Forest,** along the south border of the park, though no camping is allowed within a quarter-mile of U.S. 64. Dispersed camping sits conveniently along the oft-traveled N. Long Jim Loop Rd.— turn right about a mile south of the south entrance station. For quieter, more remote sites, follow signs for the Arizona Trail into the national forest between miles 252 and 253 on U.S. 64. Fires are heavily restricted or even banned in some areas; make sure you know the rules. For more info, contact the **Tusayan Ranger Station** (☎ 028-638-2443), Kaibab National Forest, P.O. Box 3088, Tusayan 86023.

Ten-X Campground (☎ 928-638-2443), in Kaibab National Forest, 10 mi. south of Grand Canyon Village, off Rte. 64. Away from the highway, Ten-X offers quality sites surrounded by pine trees. Toilets and water. First come, first served. Open May-Sept. Sites $10. ❶

Mather Campground (☎ 800-365-2267; http://reservations.nps.gov), in Grand Canyon Village, 1 mi. south of the Canyon Village Marketplace; follow signs from Yavapai Lodge. 327 shady, relatively isolated sites. Those on foot or bike can snag a spot in a communal hiker/biker site; they are usually available on a walk-up basis. 7-night max. stay. For Apr.-Dec. reserve up to 5 months in advance; Jan.-Mar. first come, first served. Sites $18. ❶

Desert View Campground (☎ 928-638-7888), 25 mi. east of Grand Canyon Village. Far from the South Rim, but perfect for avoiding crowds. Sites with toilets. No hookups, campfires, or reservations. Open mid-May to Oct. Sites $10. ❶

NORTH RIM

If you're looking to avoid the South Rim's crowds, the park's North Rim is rugged and serene, with a view almost as spectacular as that from the South Rim. Unfortunately, it's hard to reach by public transit and is a long drive by car. From October 15 to November 30,

the North Rim is open for day use only, and from December 1 to May 15, it closes entirely. In summer, sunsets from the Grand Canyon Lodge are spectacular and worth the long trip.

▣ GETTING AROUND

To reach the North Rim from the South Rim, take **Rte. 64 E** to **U.S. 89 N,** which runs into **Alt. 89;** from Alt. 89, follow **Rte. 67 S** to the edge—but don't go over it. The drive is over 220 mi. Snow closes Rte. 67 from early December to mid-May, and park facilities (including the lodge) close from mid-October to mid-May. The visitor parking lot, 12 mi. south of the park entrance, is near the end of Rte. 67, close to both the visitors center and North Rim Lodge. Parking is also available at the North Kaibab and Widforss trails and at scenic points along the road to Cape Royal.

▨ OUTDOORS

Hiking in the leafy North Rim seems like a trip to the mountains—the mountain just happens to be upsidedown. While the temptation to plunge down into the canyon is strong, it would be an extraordinarily bad idea. The North Rim is at a surprisingly high elevation, so the air is very thin, and there are no easy trails down into the canyon. You should never attempt to hike to the river and back in a single day. Info on trails can be found in the North Rim's version of *The Guide.* Day-hikes of various lengths beckon the active North Rim visitor. The **Bright Angel Point Trail** (½ mi. round-trip, 30min.) departs from the lodge area, and the **Cape Royal Trail** (¾ mi. round-trip, 30min.) departs from the Cape Royal parking area. Both offer impressive views of the canyon for little effort. The **Widforss Trail** (10 mi. round-trip, 6hr.) is a more challenging day-hike but offers views of both canyon and forest and can be tailored into a shorter hike. The **North Kaibab Trail** (28 mi. round-trip) is the only maintained trail into the canyon on the North Rim and is for only the most experienced hikers. Consult rangers before beginning this hike. Pick up the invaluable *Official Guide to Hiking the Grand Canyon* ($12), available at any of the visitors centers and gift shops. Overnight hikers must get permits from the **Backcountry Office** in the ranger station, just north of the campground entrance, 11½ mi. from the park entrance. ($10 permit plus $5 per person per night. Open daily 8am-noon and 1-5pm.) Park rangers run nature walks, lectures, and evening programs at the North Rim Campground and Lodge. The info desk or campground bulletin boards have schedules. **Mule trips** through **Canyon Trail Rides** circle the rim or descend into the canyon. (In the lodge lobby. ☎435-679-8665. 1hr. $30, half-day $55, full-day $105. Reservations recommended. Open May-Oct. daily 7:30am-5pm.)

FOOD

Grand Dining Room at the North Rim (☎928-638-2612, ext. 160). On the edge of the canyon, the North Rim Lodge's dining room treats guests to sweeping views. The breakfast buffet ($8) and lunch options (salads and burgers $6-10) are generic but affordable. Dinners (from $13) do justice to the grand atmosphere. Open daily 6:30-10am, 11:30am-2:30pm, 5-9:30pm. Reservations required for dinner. AmEx/D/MC/V. ❸

Deli in the Pines, at the North Rim Lodge. Specializes in no-frills dining on the go. Salads, sandwiches, and burgers $3-7. Pizza by the slice $2.50-4. Open daily 7am-9pm. ❶

Jacob Lake Dining Room (☎928-643-7232; www.jacoblake.com), 30 mi. north of the park entrance, is a good alternative to North Rim establishments. The old-fashioned diner counter, full restaurant, and tempting bakery offer a variety of options. Pick up a gravity-defying milkshake ($4) to make the remaining drive more enjoyable. Breakfast $4.50-7. Dinner $12-17. AmEx/D/MC/V. ❸

ACCOMMODATIONS

Staying inside on the North Rim is pricey and requires advance planning, but there are still many lodging options. If you can't find lodging within the park, many less-expensive accommodations can be found 80 mi. north in Kanab, UT.

Grand Canyon Lodge (☎928-638-2611, reservations 888-297-2757), on the edge of the rim. This swank but rustic lodge is the only indoor lodging in the park. The overlook near the reception area is open to all and is a great place to relax in the comfort of leather sofas. Reception

24hr. Reserve as early as 6 months in advance, or 2 years in advance for the 4 rim-view cabins. Open mid-May to Oct. Motel rooms $96; cabins $97-128. AmEx/D/DC/MC/V. ❺

North Rim Campground (☎800-365-2267), on Rte. 67 near the rim, is the only park campground on this side of the chasm, with spacious sites among the ponderosas. Reservations recommended in summer. Groceries, showers ($1.25 per 5min.), and laundry ($2). No hookups. Open mid-May to mid-Oct. Sites $15-20. ❶

Jacob Lake Inn (☎643-7232; www.jacoblake.com), 44 mi. north of the North Rim entrance at Jacob Lake. Lodge, gift shop, and cafe (see p. 577). Reception daily May-Oct. 7am-9pm; Nov.-Apr. 8am-8pm. Cabins $72-96; motel units $94-123. AmEx/D/DC/MC/V. ❸

Kaibab National Forest (☎928-635-5607). Runs from north of Jacob Lake to the park entrance. You can camp for free, as long as you're ¼ mi. from the road, water, or official campgrounds, and 1 mi. from any commercial facility. A strict fire ban is in effect. ❶

Cottonwood Campground, 7 mi. down the North Kaibab Trailhead. A good resting place for those doing an overnight hike into the canyon. Drinking water available May-Oct. Requires $5 camping permit from the Backcountry Office (p. 576). ❶

APPROACHING ASH FORK: 76 MILES
Take **I-40 W** to **Exit 146,** then make a right for Ash Fork.

ASH FORK. Those in need of beautification need look no farther than the 1960 DeSoto parked on the roof of the **DeSoto Salon**, 314 W. Lewis Ave. Joe DeSoto and family will make you as glamorous as their giant rooftop hood-ornament. (☎928-637-9886. Open W-Sa 9am-5pm.)

APPROACHING SELIGMAN: 17 MILES
From Ash Fork, rejoin **I-40 W** for 4¾ mi. to **Exit 139.** Don't turn left onto the road marked "Old Rte. 66." Take a right on **Crookton Rd.** Continue for about 17 mi. to the Rte. 66 celebration that is Seligman, and turn left at the T-intersection.

SELIGMAN
The Rte. 66 enthusiasm in Seligman is hard to miss. The town was founded at the junction of the main line of the Santa Fe Railroad, and when Rte. 66 was routed along the main street of the town, tourist accommodations flourished. When I-40 cut the town off the

ROUTE 66

main thoroughfare, local residents were quick to react; Seligman was where the **Arizona Route 66 Association**—the nation's first—was founded to bring fame back to the road as a destination rather than a thoroughfare. Rte. 66 through Seligman is crowded with outrageous Rte. 66 kitsch, including Marilyn Monroe and James Dean cutouts leaning on antique cars lining the street. A semi-functioning barber shop, **Delgadillo's Rte. 66 Gift Shop, Museum and Visitors Center,** 217 E. Rte. 66, is also lined with memorabilia from appreciative travelers world-wide; add your business card to the wall. You even can get a trim ($15) from the iconic Angel Delgadillo if he has time. (☎928-422-3352. Open daily 8am-6pm.) **The Rusty Bolt Gift Shop,** 115 E. Rte. 66, is hard to miss, with dressed-up mannequins perched on the 2nd fl. balcony and Eagles cover tunes perpetually blasting in the otherwise quiet street. (☎928-422-0106. Open daily in summer 8am-8pm; in winter 8am-6pm.)

Juan Delgadillo's (brother to Angel) **Snow Cap Ice Cream Shop ❶,** 301 E. Chino Ave., is decorated year-round in holiday decorations and prides itself on serving "Dead Chicken" and great shakes ($3). Juan's sons Bob and John are a couple of world-class pranksters who are sure to entertain while they take your order. (Open daily 9:30am-6pm. Cash only.) The cuisine at the **Road Kill Cafe ❹,** 592 W. Rte. 66, may not be exactly true to the name, but the decor certainly seems to be. Enjoy a foot-high pile of onion rings ($6) or the meat of your choice ($7-15) in the company of an entire herd of dead animals. Try the "chicken that almost crossed the road" for $11. (☎928-422-3554. Open daily 7am-10pm. AmEx/D/MC/V.) The **Deluxe Inn ❷,** 203 E. Chino, a 1932 motel, has spacious rooms with wood furnishings, large welcome mats, and nature photography lining the walls. (☎928-422-3244. Singles from $42; doubles from $45. AmEx/MC/V.) At the **Rte. 66 Inn ❷,** 500 W. Rte. 66, rooms are pleasantly decorated with TVs and doilies. (☎928-422-3204. Singles $47; doubles $52. AmEx/D/DC/MC/V.)

◤ APPROACHING GRAND CANYON CAVERNS: 24 MILES

Head west on **Rte. 66** out of Seligman to reach the Grand Canyon Caverns.

GRAND CANYON CAVERNS

A giant green plastic dinosaur guards the entrance to **Grand Canyon Caverns,** the largest registered dry cavern in the US. Tours of the enormous rooms, 210 ft. underground, are led by guides eager to point out the unique features of this one-time fallout shelter, including a mummified bobcat and enough toilet paper for three weeks of nuclear fallout. (☎928-422-3223 or 928-713-2671; www.gccaverns.com. 45min. tours daily every 30min. $13; seniors, military, and ages 5-12 $12. 25min. tours $10/$8. Explorer's tour $45; reservations and deposit required.) **The Grand Canyon Cavern Restaurant ❶,** conveniently located at the entrance to the caverns, serves diner cuisine cafeteria-style. (Entrees $2-7. Open M-Th and Su 6am-7pm, F-Sa 6am-10pm. AmEx/D/MC/V.) The pink, 70s-inspired rooms at **Grand Canyon Caverns Inn ❹,** also at the caverns' entrance, are the only option for miles in either direction. (☎928-422-3223. Mar.-Oct. rooms from $72; Nov.-Feb. from $62. AmEx/D/MC/V.) The motel also has bike rentals and a convenience store. (Bikes $4 per hr., $25 per day.)

◤ DETOUR
HAVASUPAI RESERVATION

3 mi. from the Caverns. Follow signs for Supai and the Havasupai Reservation, 60 mi. north on Rte. 18. Follow the road north approximately 60 mi., ending in a series of narrow hairpin turns down to the canyon rim and the trailhead down to the village of Supai and the Supai waterfalls.

Meaning "people of the blue-green water," the Havasupai live in a protected enclave at the base of the canyon, bordered by the Grand Canyon National Park. Ringed by dramatic sandstone faces, their village, Supai, rests on the shores of the Havasu River and is only accessible from a 10 mi. trail starting at the Hualapai Hilltop. Two miles down the path from the village is an astounding sight—three waterfalls of crystal-clear water. The village has a post office, general store, and cafe (☎928-448-2591). Prices are high because everything must be brought in by mule or helicopter; bringing your own food is advised. Reservations for the campground, lodge, and mules can be made by calling the **Havasupai Tourist Enterprise.** (☎929-448-2237. Mules leave from the Hualapai Hilltop daily 10am. One-way $75.)

Camping permits are required for overnight hiking, so reservations should be made far in advance. The Havasupai tribe operates the **Havasupai Campground ❶** and the Havasupai Lodge, both on the canyon floor. The campground, 2 mi. past Supai, lies between Havasu and Mooney Falls, bordering the Havasu River's blue-green water and swimmer-friendly lagoons. There are no showers or flush toilets. (☎928-448-2121; www.kaibab.org/supai. Register in the Supai tourist office. Entrance fee $30. Sites $10.) The trail from Supai to the campground extends to **Mooney Falls** (1 mi. from campground), **Beaver Falls** (3 mi.), and the **Colorado River** (8 mi.). The hike down to Mooney Falls is steep; exercise caution—shoes with good tread are a must. Swimming and frolicking are both permitted and encouraged in the lagoons at the bottom of the falls.

◄ APPROACHING PEACH SPRINGS: 6 MILES
From the Grand Canyon Caverns, continue west along **Rte. 66** to reach Peach Springs.

PEACH SPRINGS. The headquarters of the Hualapai Tribe and once the western terminus of the Santa Fe Railroad, Peach Springs is where you will find the **River Runners**, a rafting outfitter offering day trips on the Colorado River. (☎888-255-2219 or 888-216-0076; www.grandcanyonresort.com. Trips Mar.-Oct. $310 per person; includes round-trip transport, food, helicopter uplift, life jackets, and a souvenir mug.) Peach Springs also prides itself on having the only access road directly into the bottom of the Grand Canyon. The **Diamond Creek Restaurant ❸**, 900 Rte. 66, serves Hualapai favorites like catfish baskets ($11) and Hualapai stew ($9), beef tips, and vegetables served with fry bread. (☎928-769-2800. Entrees $5-12. Open daily 6am-9pm. AmEx/D/MC/V.) The new and adjoining **Hualapai Lodge ❹**, 900 Rte. 66, has comfortable, upscale rooms. (☎888-255-9550. Rooms $89-99. AmEx/D/MC/V.)

◄ APPROACHING HACKBERRY: 23 MILES
Along **Rte. 66** from Peach Springs, the road is expansive and empty, save for would-be towns along the main road. Truxton, 9½ mi. beyond Peach Springs, and Valentine, 9 mi. farther on, are quickly passed. Stop in Hackberry, 5 mi. past Valentine.

HACKBERRY. The **Hackberry Visitor Center & General Store** is a must see Rte. 66 roadside store. Once you get past the vintage cars outside, you'll find a recreated 50s diner, 1955 Marilyn Monroe calendars ($25), glass-bottled cokes ($1.25), and other Rte. 66 memorabilia and souvenirs. (☎928-769-2605. Open daily in summer 7am-7pm; in winter 10am-5pm.)

◄ APPROACHING KINGMAN: 23 MILES
From Hackberry, continue on **Rte. 66**, and enter Kingman on **Andy Devine Ave.**

KINGMAN

Kingman has always prided itself on being a transportation town; the railroad and Rte. 66 running straight through Kingman brought in voyagers aplenty, including Clark Gable and Carole Lombard, who were married in the Old Courthouse. The town is as Rte. 66 crazy as any, hosting the Rte. 66 Fun Run the first weekend in May.

VITAL STATS

Population: 20,000

Visitor Info: Powerhouse Visitors Center, 120 W. Rte. 66 (☎866-427-7866; www.kingman-chamber.org). Open daily Mar.-Nov. 9am-6pm; Dec.-Feb. 9am-5pm.

Internet Access: Kingman Public Library, 3269 N. Burbank St. (☎928-629-2665). Open M 10am-6pm, Tu 9am-8pm, W-F 9am-6pm, Sa 9am-5pm. Free.

Post Office: 1901 Johnson Ave. (☎928-753-2480). Open M-F 8:30am-5:30pm, Sa 9am-noon. **Postal Code:** 86401.

▮ GETTING AROUND. Most avenues in Kingman run east-west, while streets are numbered and run north-south (though just north of the downtown area some streets also run east-west). Rte. 66 enters Kingman from the northeast and is known in town as **Andy Devine Ave.;** many of the city's sights and establishments lie along this road. Downtown centers on the area near **4th St., Beale St.,** and Andy Devine Ave.

◙ SIGHTS. A converted 1907 power station that hosts a decent Rte. 66 gift shop, the **Powerhouse Visitors Center,** 120 W. Rte. 66, now serves as Kingman's visitors center. The top floor houses an extensive, lovingly curated Rte. 66 transportation museum featuring exhibits on Burma Shave, *The Grapes of Wrath*, and Seligman's role in the development of Historic Rte. 66. Road buffs can while away the hours in the Rte. 66 of Arizona Reading Room upstairs. (☎928-753-9889. Open daily Mar.-Nov. 9am-6pm; Dec.-Feb. 9am-5pm. Museum $4.) At the **Mohave Museum of History and Arts,** 400 W. Beale St., exhibits focus on the area, arts and Indian culture, and the life and career of actor Andy Devine, a native of Kingman. An outdoor display highlights a 19th-century Santa Fe Caboose, as well as wagons, mining equipment, and farm machinery. (☎928-753-3195; www.mohavemuseum.org. Open M-F 9am-5pm, Sa-Su 1-5pm. $4, under 13 free.)

▟▛ FOOD AND ACCOMMODATIONS. The easily spotted **Mr. D'z Route 66 Diner ❷,** 105 E. Andy Devine Ave., at 1st St., is a pink, blue, and chrome tribute to the kitschy Rte. 66 diner, serving breakfast, lunch, and dinner with the hoot of a train whistle. Try their sweet potato fries for $4.25. (☎928-718-0066. Breakfast from $3.50. Sandwiches from $2.50. Open daily 7am-9pm. AmEx/MC/V.) **El Palacio ❷,** 401 Andy Devine Ave., is the local Mexican cantina of choice, with a comprehensive and exclusively Mexican menu. (☎928-718-0019. Salads $5.50-8. Entrees $7-9. Open daily 11am-9pm. AmEx/D/MC/V.) For any sandwich you can dream up and coffee to match, head to **Kingman Deli ❶,** 419 E. Beale. Take 4th St. (☎928-753-4151. Sandwiches $4-6. Open M-F 9am-3pm, Sa 10am-2pm. AmEx/MC/V.)

The historic **Hotel Brunswick ❷,** 315 E. Andy Devine Ave., offers a variety of rooms, ranging from austere "cowboy rooms" with shared bathrooms to expansive suites. (☎928-718-1800. Breakfast included. Singles $35-66; suites $115. AmEx/D/MC/V.) Guests at the **Hilltop Motel ❷,** 1901 E. Andy Devine Ave., will find basic, clean rooms. (☎928-753-2198; www.hilltopmotelaz.com. Reservations recommended. Singles $36-55; doubles $85. AmEx/D/MC/V.)

▟ APPROACHING LAKE MEAD: 56 MILES
Take **Andy Devine Ave.** through town until it becomes **Beale Ave.,** which becomes **Rte. 93 N** at the edge of town. To bypass Lake Mead, Hoover Dam, and the glamorous glitz of Las Vegas, skip ahead to p. 588.

The Silver State **NEVADA** *Welcomes You!*

LAKE MEAD. The largest reservoir in the US, Lake Mead was created when Hoover Dam was constructed across the Colorado River in the 1930s. First-time visitors will benefit from a trip to the **Alan Bible Visitors Center,** 4 mi. east of Boulder City on Rte. 93, where the helpful staff has brochures and maps. (☎702-293-8990; www.nps.gov/lame. Open daily 8:30am-4:30pm. Entrance fee $3 per pedestrian, $5 per vehicle.) Falling water levels have left Lake Mead roughly half its usual depth, forcing boat ramps to close and exposing previously submerged hazards. Despite these conditions, Lake Mead is still a haven of water recreation. Park service-approved outfitters rent boats and more on the shores; www.funonthelake.com has more info. Popular **Boulder Beach,** the departure point for many water-based activities, is accessible from Lakeshore Dr., at the south end of the lake.

▟ APPROACHING HOOVER DAM: 16 MILES
Continue on **Rte. 93 N** to reach Hoover Dam.

HOOVER DAM. Built to subdue the flood-prone Colorado River and give vital water and energy to the Southwest, this ivory monolith took 5000 men five years to construct. By the time the dam was finished in 1935, 96 men had died. Their labor rendered a 726 ft. colossus that pumps more than four billion kilowatt-hours of power to Las Vegas and L.A. A lasting tribute to America's "think big" era, the dam is a spectacular feat of engineering, weighing 6.6 million tons and measuring 660 ft. thick at its base and 1244 ft. across the canyon at its crest. Tours and an interpretive center explore the dam's history and future. (☎866-291-8687. Open daily 9am-5pm. Self-guided tours $11, seniors and military $9, ages 7-16 $6.)

▟ APPROACHING LAS VEGAS: 30 MILES
Head north on **Rte. 93.** Take **Exit 61** to **I-215 W.**

Las Vegas

0   1000 yards
0   1 kilometer

N
LG

Harris Ave.
Bonanza Rd.
Mesquite St.
Cedar St.

Main St. Station
The Fremont St. Experience
Golden Gate
The Plaza
Golden Nugget

Valley Medical Center
University Medical Center

Fremont St.
Carson Ave.
Bridger Ave.
Clark Ave.
Bonneville Ave.
Gass Ave.
Hoover St.
Coolidge St.

Charleston Blvd.

Colorado Ave.
Utah St.
Franklin Ave.
Sweeney Ave.
Little White Wedding Chapel

Hassett St.
Oakey Blvd.

New York St.
Philadelphia St.
Stratosphere
Canosa Ave.
St. Louis Ave.

Oakey Blvd.

Jaycee Park

Sahara Ave.

Guinness World Records Museum
Sahara
Wet 'n' Wild

Karen Ave.

Circus Circus
Riviera Blvd.
Riviera

Las Vegas Country Club

Stardust
Channel 8 Dr.
Las Vegas Hilton
Convention Center Dr.
Las Vegas Convention Center
Debbie Reynolds Dr.
Desert Inn Rd.
Pinehurst Dr.

Golden Arrow St.

Sunrise Hospital & Medical Ctr.

Fashion Show Mall
Sierra Vista St.
Dumont St.
Commanche St.
Cherokee Ln.
Ottawa St.

Spring Mountain Rd.
Wynn
Treasure Island
Mirage
Venetian
Elm Dr.
Twain Ave.
Katie St.

Harrah's
Imperial Palace
Flamingo Las Vegas
Caesar's Palace
Northrup St.
Palo Verdes St.
Flamingo Rd.

Rio Suite Hotel and Casino
The Palms
Bellagio
Jockey Club
Aladdin
Paris
Bally's
Hard Rock Hotel

University of Nevada Las Vegas

Rochelle Ave.

Monte Carlo
New York, New York
MGM Grand
Thomas & Mack Center

E. Harmon Ave.

Tropicana
Luxor
Hacienda Ave.
Mandalay Bay
The Four Seasons
Diablo Dr.
Dewey Dr.

Las Vegas International Golf Center
Tropicana Ave.
Reno Ave.
Gus Giuffre Ave.
Hacienda Ave.
Richard St.

Liberace Museum

Russell Rd.
TO GOLD N'STRIKE (24mi)
TO 26 (4mi)

McCarran International Airport

Las Vegas

▲ ACCOMMODATIONS
Aruba Hotel and Spa, **4**
Barbary Coast, **13**
Excalibur, **25**
Silverton, **26**
Sin City Hostel, **3**
USAHostels Las Vegas, **1**

🍴 FOOD
Battista's Hole in the Wall, **15**
Carnival World Buffet, **9**
Dishes, **14**
El Sombrero Cafe, **2**
Le Village Buffet, **17**
Nine Fine Irishmen, **23**
Paymon's Mediterranean Cafe, **22**
Peppermill, **5**
Trattoria del Lupo, **16**
Victorian Room, **7**

🍸 NIGHTLIFE
The Beach, **6**
Body English, **19**
Club Paradise, **20**
Fontana Bar, **12**
Ghost Bar, **10**
Gipsy, **24**
Hookah Lounge, **21**
Rain, **11**
Red Square, **18**
V Bar, **8**

ROUTE 66

LAS VEGAS

Rising out of the Nevada desert, Las Vegas is a shimmering tribute to excess. Gambling, whoring, and mob-muscle built this city and continue to add to its mystique. Those who embrace it find a mirage made real, an oasis of vice and greed, and one hell of a good time. Those not immediately enthralled by its frenetic pace may still find sleeping (and decision-making) nearly impossible, with sparkling casinos, cheap gourmet food, free drinks, and spectacular attractions at every turn. Nowhere else do so many shed inhibitions and indulge with such abandon. A word of caution: know thy tax bracket; walk in knowing what you want to spend and get the hell out when you've spent it. In Las Vegas, there's a busted wallet and a broken heart for every garish neon light.

VITAL STATS

Population: 1.3 million

Visitor Info: Las Vegas Convention and Visitors Authority, 3150 Paradise Rd. (☎702-892-0711 or 877-847-4858), at the corner of Paradise and Convention Center Dr., 4 blocks from the Strip in the big pink convention center by the Hilton. Open M-F 8am-5pm.

Internet Access: Clark County Library, 1401 E. Flamingo Rd. (☎702-507-3400). Open M-Th 9am-9pm, F-Su 10am-6pm. Free.

Post Office: 4975 Swenson St. (☎702-736-7649), near the Strip. Open M-F 8:30am-5pm. **Postal Code:** 89119.

⊑ GETTING AROUND

Las Vegas has two major casino areas. The **downtown** area, around **2nd** and **Fremont St.,** has been converted into a pedestrian promenade. Casinos cluster together beneath a shimmering space-frame structure covering over five city blocks. The other main area is the **Strip,** a collection of mammoth hotel-casinos along **Las Vegas Blvd.** Parallel to the east side of the Strip and in its shadow is **Paradise Rd.,** also lined with casinos. Some areas of Las Vegas are unsafe, so remain on well-lit pathways, and don't wander too far from major casinos and hotels. Valet parking your car at a major

casino and sticking to Fremont St. are safe bets. The neighborhoods just north of Stewart St. and west of Main St. in the downtown vicinity are especially dangerous.

Despite, or perhaps as a result of, its reputation for debauchery, Las Vegas has a **curfew.** Those under 18 are not allowed in most public places at night (M-Th and Su 10pm-5am, F-Sa midnight-5am), unless accompanied by an adult. Laws are even harsher on the Strip, where no one under 18 is allowed unaccompanied 9pm-5am—ever. **The drinking and gambling age is a strictly enforced 21**.

◉ SIGHTS

Before casinos suck you dry of greenbacks, explore some of the simpler oddities of the city. Fans of classical music and kitsch will be delighted by the **Liberace Museum,** 1775 E. Tropicana Ave., which displays the showman's velvet, rhinestone, fur, and suede stage costumes. (☎702-798-5595. Open Tu-Sa 10am-5pm, Su noon-4pm. $12.50, students and seniors $8.50, under 11 free.) The **Auto Collections** on the 5th fl. of the Imperial Palace Casino, 3535 Las Vegas Blvd. S, is a worthwhile destination. Visitors can feast their eyes on 300 classic cars and dream of how they're going to spend their jackpot. (☎702-794-3174; www.autocollections.com. Enter through the casino to get admission coupons. Open daily 9:30am-9:30pm. $7, seniors and under 12 $3.)

From 3min. drive-through whirlwinds to elaborate fantasy-themed extravaganzas, the **Little White Wedding Chapel,** 1301 Las Vegas Blvd., is a mainstay of the city's matrimonial traditions. Vegas luminaries like Frank Sinatra and Liberace as well as celebrities Michael Jordan and Britney Spears have been hitched here. The drive-through wedding tunnel begins at a romantic $40 (plus a donation to the minister) and possibilities only end with the imagination. (☎702-382-5943 or 800-545-8111. No reservations required for drive-through services. Have your marriage license ready. Open 24hr.) Way out in Primm Valley at **Buffalo Bill's Casino,** along I-15, the **Desperado Roller Coaster** is the tallest and fastest bad-boy in the Vegas area; it's also one of the best coasters in the West. (☎702-386-7867.

Open M-Th 11am-9pm, F 11am-midnight, Sa 10am-midnight, Su 10am-10pm. $7.)

🏛 CAINO

Casinos spend millions attracting big spenders to Las Vegas. Efforts to bring families to Sin City are evident everywhere, with arcades and thrill rides at every turn. Still, Vegas is no Disneyland. With steamy nightclubs, topless revues, and scantily-clad waitresses serving free liquor, it's clear that casinos' priorities center on the mature, moneyed crowd. Casinos, bars, and some wedding chapels are open 24hr., so whatever your itch, Vegas can usually scratch it. Look for casino "funbooks" that feature deals on chips and entertainment. Cash goes in a blink when you're gambling, so it pays to have a budget. There are far more casinos harboring far more attractions than can be listed here; use the following as a compendium of the best, but explore Vegas for yourself—there are ways to fulfill fantasies where you'd least expect it.

THE STRIP

The undisputed locus of Vegas's surging regeneration, the Strip is a fantasyland of neon, teeming with people, casinos, and restaurants. The nation's 10 largest hotels line the legendary 3.5 mi. stretch of Las Vegas Blvd., named an "All-American Road" and a "National Scenic Byway." Despite the sparkling facade, the Strip's seedy underbelly still shows; porn is peddled behind family fun centers, and denizens of the night sporting open alcohol containers wander in search of elusive jackpots.

Mandalay Bay, 3950 S. Las Vegas Blvd. (☎702-632-7777; www.mandalaybay.com). Undoubtedly Vegas's hippest casino, Mandalay Bay tries to convince New York and L.A. fashionistas they haven't left home. With swank restaurants and chi-chi clubs, gambling seems an afterthought. Shark Reef has aquatic beasts from all over the globe, including 15 species of shark. ($16, ages 5-12 $12, under 5 free.) Afterwards you may or may not want to check out the surf and sand beach, complete with 6 ft. waves.

Bellagio, 3600 S. Las Vegas Blvd. (☎693-7444; www.bellagio.com). The world's largest five-star hotel, made famous in the remake of *Ocean's Eleven.* Houses a gallery of fine art, the world's tallest chocolate fountain, and a floral conservatory that changes with the seasons. Check out the carefully choreographed dancing fountains in front of the casino and see the water leap several stories high to well-known classical pieces. Shows M-F 3-8pm every 30min. and 8pm-midnight every 15min., Sa-Su noon-8pm every 30min. and 8pm-midnight every 15min. Free.

Venetian, 3355 S. Las Vegas Blvd. (☎702-414-1000; www.venetian.com). Singing gondoliers serenade passengers on the chlorinated "canal" that runs through this palatial casino. Elaborate ceilings, the Guggenheim Hermitage Museum,

FACING A LIQUID ASSETS SHORTAGE

Asked to support faux Venetian canals, ubiquitous gushing fountains, elaborate water ballets, and more than 1.5 million residents, all amid the southern Nevada desert, Las Vegas' water supply is, not surprisingly, perpetually in short supply. Despite its underground springs, Las Vegas (Spanish for "the meadows") has not seen heavy natural irrigation since prehistoric times. Explosive urban sprawl, coupled with irresponsible use of water at big-name casinos, is rapidly outstripping the supply of water allotted to Nevada by the states sharing rights to Colorado River. Las Vegas's share, which is the lowest of the cities sharing the river, is a meager 300,000 acre-feet of water. With more than 5000 people moving to the area each month, the only conceivable solution may be to cut the ceaseless influx of residents. Southern Nevada is rapidly exhausting its stores of conserved water, forcing it to dip into reserves that neighboring Arizona does not yet need to rely on. The expansion of Arizona's urban areas make this solution less viable with each passing year. Experts are fearful that water restrictions may not solve the growing problem, and it is far from clear that a population accustomed to gluttonous water use is willing to change its ways.

and Madam Tussaud's wax museum evoke a little bit of old Europe, while Blue Man Group adds some edge.

Caesar's Palace, 3570 S. Las Vegas Blvd. (☎877-427-7243; www.caesarspalace.com). At Caesar's, busts abound: some are plaster, and others are barely concealed by cocktail waitress' low-cut get-ups. The 160 boutiques in the Forum Shops provide numerous opportunities to leave your winnings in Vegas.

Wynn, 3131 S. Las Vegas Blvd. (☎702-770-7000; www.wynnlasvegas.com). This latest addition to the Strip more than competes with the Bellagio for classiest casino. The gambling floor is tastefully decorated, with flashing slot machine lights noticeably absent. Even if table limits are high, the dealers are friendly and the grounds are beautiful.

Luxor, 3900 S. Las Vegas Blvd. (☎702-262-4444; www.luxor.com). This architectural marvel recreates the majestic pyramids of ancient Egypt in opaque glass and steel. Popular with young adults but still family-friendly, Luxor has an IMAX theater, a full-scale replica of King Tut's Tomb, and numerous clubs.

Paris, 3655 S. Las Vegas Blvd. (☎702-946-7000; www.parislasvegas.com). From restaurants that resemble French cafes to replicas of the Arc de Triomphe, the French Opera House, and the Eiffel Tower, this resort adds a Parisian *je ne sais quoi* to Las Vegas.

The Mirage, 3400 S. Las Vegas Blvd. (☎702-791-7111; www.mirage.com). This tropical oasis is home to a 20,000 gal. aquarium, a lush indoor rainforest, and several rare white tigers and lions. A volcano that puts science fair projects to shame erupts every 15min.

MGM Grand, 3799 S. Las Vegas Blvd. (☎702-891-7777; www.mgmgrand.com). A huge bronze lion guards Las Vegas's largest hotel (5000 rooms) as it glows like the Emerald City from *The Wizard of Oz.* Watch the big cats frolic in the tunnel overhead in the Lion Habitat. The MGM often hosts world-class sporting events and concerts.

New York, New York, 3790 S. Las Vegas Blvd. (☎702-740-6969; www.nynyhotelcasino). An eye-catching, fun-filled casino brings a slice of the Big Apple to Sin City. Towers mimic the Manhattan skyline, the streets of a miniature Greenwich Village lead to an **ESPNZone,** and a walk

under the Brooklyn Bridge brings you to the Manhattan Express, the wildest ride on the Strip.

Treasure Island (TI), 3300 S. Las Vegas Blvd. (☎702-894-7111; www.treasureisland.com). Catering to a younger crowd with raucous party clubs and chic loungers, the pirate's cove is the place to go for a big night out. See the *Sirens of TI* for a sea battle in one of Vegas' most scantily-clad shows. Shows daily 7, 8:30, 10, 11:30pm.

Circus Circus, 2880 S. Las Vegas Blvd. (☎877-434-9175; www.circuscircus.com). Though less glamorous than its younger neighbors, the free circus acts are reminiscent of the Strip's early, outlandish days. While parents run to card tables and slot machines, children flock to one of the world's largest indoor theme parks.

Aladdin, 3667 S. Las Vegas Blvd. (☎702-785-5555; www.aladdincasino.com). As much a sight as a casino. The Desert Passage retail area is a replica of a North African town, complete with "weather patterns," ambient noise, and 140 shops.

 CASINO TIPPING. While gambling, players are served free cocktails, and $1 is the standard tip for servers. Leave at least $1 per person for the drink server and bussers at a buffet. Many players reward a good table-game dealer with a $1 tip next to their main bet.

DOWNTOWN AND OFF-STRIP

The tourist frenzy that grips the Strip is less noticeable in "old" Downtown Vegas. **Glitter Gulch** has smaller hotels, cheaper alcohol and food, and table limits as low as $1. Years of decline were reversed with Las Vegas's citywide rebound and the 1995 opening of the Fremont Street Experience. Now, a protective canopy of neon and construction of a pedestrian promenade have aided the area's renaissance, making it almost as entertaining as the Strip and much more welcoming to the budget traveler.

Golden Gate, 1 Fremont St. (☎702-385-1906; www.goldengatecasino.com). Opened in 1906, Las Vegas' oldest hotel and casino now anchors the Fremont Street Experience and offers a thoroughly modern good time. Grab a famous 99-

cent shrimp cocktail and sharpen your gambling skills in the relaxed atmosphere.

Golden Nugget, 129 E. Fremont St. (☎702-385-7111; www.goldennugget.com). An outpost of Strip-like class downtown, this four-star hotel charms gamblers with marble floors, chandeliers, and high-end gambling.

Palms, 4321 W. Flamingo Rd. (☎702-942-7777; www.palms.com). The ultimate venue to spot celebrities and party with the young and beautiful. The Skin Pool Lounge has swings and cabanas to enjoy before you hit the bars and clubs on the property.

Hard Rock Hotel, 4455 Paradise Rd. (☎702-693-5000; www.hardrockhotel.com). The largest night scene in Vegas, the Hard Rock is furbished with all sorts of music memorabilia and often the stars to go along with it. Feels more like a giant lounge than a casino, especially thanks to The Joint, a tiny venue that attracts rockers for intimate concerts.

Las Vegas Hilton, 3000 Paradise Rd. (☎702-732-5111; www.lvhilton.com). Look for the enormous "Las Vegas Hilton" sign. Its $70 million Star Trek: The Experience immerses you in the Trekkie universe with slot machines on "the bridge." Entrance includes admission to the Star Trek Museum, which presents the cultural phenomenon with astonishing intricacy. (☎888-GO-BOLDLY/462-6535. Open daily 11am-11pm. $37; seniors and under 12 $34.)

🍴 FOOD

From swanky eateries run by celebrity chefs to gourmet buffets, culinary surprises are everywhere in Las Vegas, and usually at a great price. Everyone comes to gorge at Vegas' gigantic buffets. The trick to buffet bliss is to find places that are more than glorified cafeterias, which can be difficult. Beyond buffets, Vegas has some of the world's best restaurants, though few have prices palatable to the budget traveler.

🍴 **Battista's Hole in the Wall,** 4041 Audrie St. (☎702-732-1424), behind the Flamingo. 3 decades worth of celebrity photos, an accordion player, mini liquor bottles and the head of "Moosolini" (the Fascist moose) adorn the walls. Dinner ($19-35) includes all-you-can-drink wine.

Reservations recommended. Open daily 5-10:30pm. AmEx/D/DC/MC/V. ❹

🍴 **Le Village Buffet,** 3655 Las Vegas Blvd. (☎702-946-7000), in the Paris. French cuisine at 5 stations, each representing a different region. Begin with heaps of fresh shellfish and cheeses, and then order fresh fruit crepes. Beef and veal sit at carving stations, while a pastry chef prepares more than 40 *gateaux*. Lunch $18. Dinner $25. Open daily 7am-10pm. AmEx/D/DC/MC/V. ❹

Dishes, 3300 S. Las Vegas Blvd. (☎702-894-7111), in Treasure Island. A classy buffet ranging from sushi to made-to-order salads and pastas. The carving stations and scrumptious desserts are hard to beat. Breakfast $12-18. Lunch $15. Dinner $20-26. Open daily 7am-10:30pm. AmEx/D/DC/MC/V. ❸

Peppermill, 2985 S. Las Vegas Blvd. (☎702-735-4177). A Vegas favorite straight from the 70s, this Day-Glo purple restaurant serves up heaping plates of comfort food ($8-20). Open 24hr. AmEx/MC/V. ❷

Paymon's Mediterranean Cafe, 4147 S. Maryland Pkwy. (☎702-731-6030). Some of the best Mediterranean food in the city. Try the delicious combo plate with hummus, tabouli, falafel, bourrani, and stuffed grape leaves ($15), or a big falafel and hummus pita sandwich ($7-8). Attached to the **Hookah Lounge** (p. 588). Open M-Th 11am-1am, F-Sa 11am-3am, Su 11am-5pm. AmEx/MC/V. ❹

El Sombrero Cafe, 807 S. Main St. (☎702-382-9234). Where locals go for authentic Mexican food. Small room, huge portions, efficient service. Huge combination plates ($11-12) offer a lot of food for a little money. Lunch $6.50-7.50. Open M-Sa 11am-9:30pm. AmEx/D/MC/V. ❸

Trattoria del Lupo, 3590 S. Las Vegas Blvd. (☎702-632-7777), in Mandalay Bay. Celebrity chef Wolfgang Puck's first Italian restaurant. Gourmet appetizers $7.50-18. Pizza del Lupo, with shrimp, braised pancetta, and leeks $14. Open M-Th and Su 11:30am-11pm, F-Sa 11:30am-midnight. AmEx/D/MC/V. ❹

Nine Fine Irishmen (☎702-740-6463), in New York, New York. A bit too trendy to be a proper pub, but the Irish favorites are beautifully garnished. Steak and stout $10. Bangers and mash $17. Cover F-Sa $5 men only. Open daily 11am-3am. AmEx/D/MC/V. ❹

Carnival World Buffet, 3700 W. Flamingo Rd. (☎ 702-752-9720), in the Rio. One of the most upscale international cafeterias you will see. The line can be long, but the 12 themed food stations, from sushi to Mexican, are sure to delight those who wait. Breakfast $14. Lunch $17. Dinner $24. Open daily 7am-11pm. AmEx/D/MC/V. ❺

Victorian Room, 3595 S. Las Vegas Blvd. (☎ 702-737-7111), in Barbary Coast. Home to the best night-owl breakfast special (11pm-7am; breakfast $3-8) and excellent Chinese food. Also serves pasta, steak, and seafood. Fast, friendly service around the clock. Entrees $7-30. Open 24hr. AmEx/D/MC/V. ❹

▟ ACCOMMODATIONS

Room rates in Las Vegas fluctuate greatly, and a room that normally costs $30 can cost hundreds during a convention weekend. **Vegas.com** (www.vegas.com) and **casino websites** often list some of the best rates. Free publications like *What's On In Las Vegas, Today in Las Vegas, 24/7,* and *Vegas Visitor* list discounts, coupons, general info, and schedules of events. Booking through a travel company online can also yield slightly cheaper quotes, and you should book two to three months in advance if a casino hotel is your plan. Hotels along the Strip are the center of the action and within walking distance of each other, but they sell out quickly and

are much more expensive than comparable, off-Strip hotels. A number of motels concentrate around **Sahara Rd.** and **South Las Vegas Blvd.** If you stay downtown, it's best to stay at one of the casinos near the **Fremont Street Experience** (p. 584). Budget motels also stretch along the southern end of the **Strip,** across from Mandalay Bay. The **9% hotel tax** (11% for downtown Fremont St.) are not included in the prices listed below.

▨ **Barbary Coast,** 3595 S. Las Vegas Blvd. (☎ 702-737-7111 or 888-227-2279; www.barbarycoast-casino.com), at Flamingo Rd. The best location on the Strip, mere minutes from Bally's. Low table limits make this popular with a young crowd. Restaurants, bars, and casino floor always buzzing. Rooms M-Th and Su from $49, F-Sa from $90. AmEx/D/MC/V. ❹

▨ **Excalibur,** 3850 S. Las Vegas Blvd. (☎ 702-597-7777; www.excalibur.com), at Tropicana Ave. The best value of all of the major resort casinos. This King Arthur-themed castle features a moat and drawbridge, 2 pools, a modern spa and fitness center, a large casino and poker room, and a monorail station to Luxor and Mandalay Bay. Many of the 4000 rooms have been recently renovated. Rooms M-Th and Su $51-80, F-Sa $79-129. AmEx/D/DC/MC/V. ❸

USAHostels Las Vegas, 1322 Fremont St. (☎ 702-385-1150 or 800-550-8958; www.usahostels.com). Though it's far from the Strip's action, this hostel's staff keeps guests entertained.

BURMA-SHAVE

In 1927, a study emerged showing that the average person spent less than 18 seconds reading a billboard or magazine advertisement. Burma-Shave decided to use this to their advantage and created a fantastic new advertising gimmick. Six red Burma-Shave signs were spaced 300 ft. apart along a highway such that a car traveling 35mph would take 3 seconds to travel between each post. Given this 3 second approach, each advertisement experience would last 18 seconds. The number of Burma-Shave ads multiplied steadily; at the height of their popularity, there were over 7000 Burma Shave ads across America. The last Burma-Shave ads were placed in 1963, but many still flavor the roads today. Here are some classics:

- To kiss / a mug / that's like a cactus / takes more nerve / than it does practice. / Burma-Shave
- If you think / she likes your bristles / walk barefooted / through some thistles. / Burma-Shave
- Nobody likes / to dance or dine / accompanied by / a porcupine. / Burma-Shave
- The wolf is shaved / so neat and trim / Red Riding Hood / is chasing him. / Burma-Shave.
- To steal / a kiss / he had the knack / but lacked the cheek / to get one back. / Burma-Shave.

Nightly organized events like champagne limo tours of the Strip ($20). Laundry. Breakfast included. Free Wi-Fi. Passport, proof of international travel or out-of-state college ID required. Key deposit $10. Dorms M-Th and Su $15-21, F-Sa $17-24; suites $40-45/$47-53. MC/V. ❷

Sin City Hostel, 1208 S. Las Vegas Blvd. (☎702-868-0222; www.sincityhostel.com). North of the heart of the Strip but south of Fremont St., this new hostel balances the excitement of the city with a restful atmosphere, allowing the young crowd to sleep it off in peace after partaking of wild clubbing tours. International passport or student ID required. Breakfast included. Dorms $19-21; private rooms with shared bath $39-41. AmEx/D/MC/V. ❷

Aruba Hotel and Spa, 1215 Las Vegas Blvd. (☎702-383-3100; www.arubalasvegas.com). Conveniently located at the north end of the Strip, this hotel has an outdoor pool, exercise room, and popular theme nights at the affiliated bar. Rooms $50-100. AmEx/MC/V. ❸

Silverton, 3333 Blue Diamond Rd. (☎702-263-7777 or 866-946-4373; www.silvertoncasino.com). This Old West mining-town-themed gambling den has recently-renovated rooms. Free Las Vegas Blvd. shuttle until 10pm. Rooms from $70. AmEx/D/MC/V. ❹

Goldstrike, 1 Main St. (☎800-634-1359) in Jean, NV, 20min. from the Strip off I-15 at Exit 12. A genuine Vegas experience at cut-rate prices. Inexpensive restaurants, loose slots, and low-limit tables. Making a reservation may net cheaper prices. Rooms M-Th and Su $35, F-Sa $70-90. AmEx/D/DC/MC/V. ❸

🎵 ENTERTAINMENT

Vegas entertainment revolves around the casinos. Big bucks will buy you a seat at a made-in-the-USA phenomenon: the **Vegas spectacular.** These stunning, casino-sponsored productions feature waterfalls, explosions, fireworks, and casts of hundreds. You can also see Broadway plays and musicals, ice revues, and individual entertainers in concert. All hotels have city-wide ticket booths in their lobbies. Check out some of the free show guides—*Showbiz, Today in Las Vegas, What's On*—for listings.

For a more opinionated perspective, check out one of the independents—*Las Vegas Mercury, City Life, Las Vegas Weekly*—or the *Las Vegas Review-Journal's* weekly entertainment supplement, *Neon*. Some "production shows" are topless; many are tasteless, but there are a few exceptions: the ▓**Cirque de Soleil's** creative shows—*O, Mystere*, and the racy *Zumanity*—are bank-busting (from $88) yet awe-inspiring displays of human agility and physical strength channeled as artistic expression at the Bellagio, Treasure Island, and New York, New York. "Limited view" tickets are discounted, and the view isn't that limited. **Blue Man Group** at the Venetian, a production that pushes the limits of stage entertainment with percussion sets and audience participation. (☎800-258-3626. Tickets from $70.)

For a show by one of the musical stars who haunt the city, e.g. **Celine Dion** (Caesar's Palace), **Gladys Knight** (Flamingo), or **Wayne Newton** (Stardust), you'll have to fork over a minimum of $55. Incredible impersonator/singer/dancer **Danny Gans** entertains at the Mirage (about $100). The tricks of **Lance Burton's** (a mainstay at the Monte Carlo) are good, old magic ($66-75), while **Penn and Teller** at the Río are far darker (from $75). With a bit of everything, former street performer **The Amazing Jonathan** stages one of Vegas's edgiest productions ($55-65). Chicago's classic comedic institution **The Second City** also graces the stage at the Flamingo for a reasonable $40.

💀 NIGHTLIFE

Nightlife in Vegas gets rolling around midnight and runs until everyone drops—or runs out of money. Dress codes at dance clubs are strictly enforced, so call ahead before heading out. In a city that never sleeps, inebriated club-hoppers bounce from one happening joint to the next to the next to the next...

CLUBS

Ghost Bar and **Rain,** 4231 W. Flamingo Rd. (☎702-938-2666 and 702-940-7246), at the Palms. Indisputably the hottest nightspots, drawing partiers in droves. You may wait in line for hours, but once you're in, groove with Vegas' hottest bodies while

DJs throw down on the 1s and 2s. Ghost Bar is on the 55th fl., with a deck and 360-degree view of Vegas. Open M-Sa 8pm-5am. Cover M-Th and Su $10, F-Sa $25. Rain has over 25,000 sq. ft. of dance floor and intense displays of fire, fog, and, of course, rain. Cover Th $10, F-Sa $25. Open Th 11pm-5am, F-Sa 10pm-5am. AmEx/D/MC/V.

Body English, 4455 Paradise Rd. (☎702-693-4000), inside of the Hard Rock Hotel. Imagine a European rock star's mansion, add lots of black leather, and you have it. World-class DJs spin mostly rock and hip-hop. Cover for men $30, for women $20. Open F-Su 10:30pm-4am. AmEx/D/MC/V.

Gipsy, 4605 Paradise Rd. (☎702-731-1919). This enormous GLBT club heats up every night of the week with Latin (M), drag queens (Th), go-go dancers (F), cabaret shows (Su), and wild dance parties to create one of the town's most swinging scenes. Happy hour daily 9pm-midnight. Cover varies. Open daily 9pm-last customer. Cash only.

The Beach, 365 Convention Center Dr. (☎702-731-1925; www.beachlv.com). At this tropical-themed club, DJs spin Top 40 and hip-hop on 2 levels, creating as close to a frat party scene as you can get in Las Vegas. Cover men M-Th and Su after midnight $5, F-Sa after midnight $10; women Tu $10. Open M-Th and Su 10pm-4am, F-Sa 10pm-6am. AmEx/D/MC/V.

Club Paradise, 4416 Paradise Rd. (☎702-734-7990), opposite Hard Rock Casino. Repeatedly voted best gentlemen's cabaret (read: strip joint) in the US. Safe, and the g-strings stay on. As sophisticated as a topless bar gets. Cover before 9pm $10, after 9pm $20. Open M-F 5pm-8am, Sa-Su 6pm-8am. AmEx/D/MC/V.

BARS

Red Square, 3950 Las Vegas Blvd. (☎702-632-7407), in Mandalay Bay. Probably the sweetest bar on the Strip, this Miami Beach import pulls off post-Communist chic with ease. Serves amazing martinis, frozen vodkas, and caviar, Red Square is the hippest way to enjoy the fall of the Soviet Union. Open M-Th and Su 5pm-2am, F-Sa 5pm-4am. AmEx/MC/V.

V Bar, 3355 Las Vegas Blvd. (☎702-414-3200). This elegant bar in the Venetian deftly recreates the New York lounge scene. A minimalist design and mellow beats make V Bar equally suitable for hanging low or dancing. Open daily 5pm-4am. AmEx/D/MC/V.

Hookah Lounge, 4147 S. Maryland Pkwy. (☎702-731-6030). Features 20 flavored tobaccos and a funky, intimate vibe that attracts pre-club crowds. Full bar and flavored teas. Happy hour daily 5-7pm with half-price cocktails. Open M-Th 5pm-1am, F-Sa 5pm-3am. AmEx/D/MC/V.

Fontana Bar, 3600 S. Las Vegas Blvd. (☎702-693-7111). The talented crooners who perform nightly at this flawless bar in the Bellagio conjure up images of the Las Vegas of yore. Sit back and enjoy the lakefront view. Open M-Th and Su 5pm-1am, F-Sa 5pm-2am. AmEx/D/MC/V.

⌖ APPROACHING OATMAN: 132 MILES

Take **I-93 S.** Bear left, and continue on **Beale Ave.** and **Historic Rte. 66** to get back to Kingman. From Kingman, take Take **I-40 W** 4 mi. to **Exit 44.** Turn right from the off-ramp and left ½ mi. later onto **Oatman Hwy.** The last stretch between Kingman and Oatman is an intense series of hair-raising switchbacks along cliffsides in an otherworldly landscape of craggy peaks and undulating valleys. Check your gauges and make sure the sun won't be in your eyes; after dark, the unlit roads are downright treacherous.

The Grand Canyon State
ARIZONA
Welcomes You!

OATMAN

Harleys and burros vie rather bizarrely for the right of way in Oatman, and leather-clad bikers stage mock-gunfights in the heart of town during the week. (Sa-Su 1:30 and 3:30pm in the center of town.) The town was originally founded to support the nearby mining interests of the present-day ghost town, Gold Road, and it became the traditional last stop before venturing across the Mojave, but the road leading to the town was later bypassed in favor of a looping but flatter by-way. Oatman displays its own Wild West version of hospitality at the **Oatman Visitors Center,** an old, open-air outhouse. The display in the gold mine next door answers more questions about the town. Across the street, the **Oatman Jail** displays various instruments of imprisonment as well as photos and clippings about the town. Stop at the **Oatman Post Office,** 251 Main St., to have your mail marked with the special Oatman cancellation stamp, one of the few small-town cancellation stamps left in America. (☎928-768-3990. Open M-F 9am-4pm.)

 PHOTO OP. Oatman is famous for its (state-protected) wild burros that migrate daily from the hills to Main St. Signs warning visitors not to feed the burros junk food are as plentiful as the burros themselves. You can't name one (that's reserved for townspeople), but you can definitely get a photo.

The **Oatman Hotel,** 181 Main St., is famous as the location of Clark Gable and Carole Lombard's 1939 honeymoon. The hotel is also an informal museum where you can read about the history of the town and see the original 1920s rooms. Downstairs, the colorful bar is wallpapered in over 25,000 signed dollar bills. You can leave one behind, like Ronald Reagan did, if you can find a spot! (☎928-768-4408. Open M-Th and Su 10:30am-6pm, F-Sa 8am-6pm. Suggested donation $1.) Three miles outside of Oatman proper, 49er wannabes can tour **Gold Road Mine's** now-defunct mine shafts that run directly under Rte. 66. 45min. tours are conducted throughout the day and take visitors deep into the old mine. When you're done, the gift shop stocks t-shirts proudly proclaiming, "Rte. 66—Been on it, Been under it!" (☎928-768-1600; www.goldroad-mine.com. Open daily 10am-5pm. Tours $12.50, under 12 $6.) Oatman was named in honor of the Oatmans, a family of pioneers who were ambushed by Native Americans on their way west. Two of the Oatman daughters, Olive and Mary, were taken captive, and their brother was left for dead. Mary died in captivity, but Olive was rescued by the US Army at age 14. The namesake **Olive Oatman Restaurant and Saloon ❷,** 171 Main St., has heaping Navajo tacos, fry bread, and live music on the weekends. (☎928-768-1891; www.oatmangold.com/olive. Entrees $5-8. Open daily 8:30am-4:30pm. AmEx/D/MC/V.)

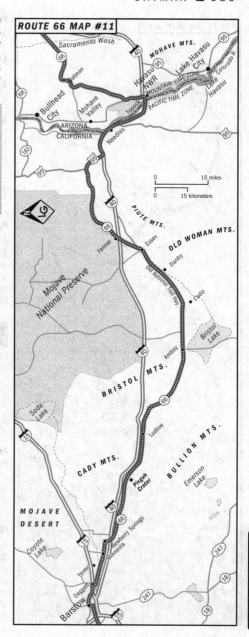

ROUTE 66 MAP #11

ROUTE 66

ROUTE 66 MAP #12

⚑ APPROACHING GOLDEN SHORES: 18 MILES

2 mi. beyond Oatman, bear left at the fork, following signs for Golden Shores, and continue on **Rte. 66.**

GOLDEN SHORES. The town of Golden Shores has the basics for the traveler in need, but the hint of palm trees and the scent of impending California along the banks of the Colorado River impel most roadsters onward. Enjoy diner deals and a life-size Marilyn Monroe cut-out at **Linda's Cafe ❷,** 12826 S. Hwy 66. Every night after 4pm, get two all-you-can-eat shrimp or chicken dinners for $10. (☎928-768-8011. Open Tu-Sa 8am-8pm, Su 8am-2pm. Cash only.)

⚑ APPROACHING MOABI REGIONAL PARK: 7 MILES

5 mi. beyond Golden Shores at Topock (the Mojave word for "bridge"), take **Exit 1** to join **I-40** heading west into California, the promised land of Rte. 66 travelers. About 2 mi. from the border, you will reach Moabi Regional Park.

PHOTO OP. About 30 mi. southeast of Topock, near Lake Havasu City, is **London Bridge,** which was dismantled in the 1960s, because it was unable to support London traffic. It was later moved and reassembled in Arizona. Take I-40 E from Topock and head south on Rte. 95 to see for yourself.

MOABI REGIONAL PARK. The Moabi Regional Park ❶, Moabi Park Rd., offers a chance to cool off in the Colorado River and provides an alternative to the nondescript motels of nearby Needles. (☎760-326-3831. Entrance fee $10. Sites $15-22, with hookup $25-35. D/MC/V.)

⚑ APPROACHING NEEDLES: 11 MILES

Approaching Needles on **I-40,** take the **95 S/E Broadway exit** approximately 10½ mi. from the border into town, making a right onto **Broadway** and following as it swings into town. The original alignment of **Rte. 66** actually cuts away to the left of the interstate, then veers right again to enter town on Broadway.

The Golden State

CALIFORNIA

Welcomes You!

DID YOU KNOW? Needles was the home of Charlie Brown cartoonist Charles Schulz. The town is featured in the comic strip as the desert home of Spike.

If you're traveling between November and March, you'll enter the Pacific Time Zone as you cross into California, where it is 1hr. earlier. From April to October there is no change.

NEEDLES

Needles, famed for its unrelenting summer heat, has wide streets lined with dingy motels and truck stops. Needles was the birthplace of comic-strip artist Charles Schulz and the home of his character "Spike." The iconic **Rte. 66 Motel**, 91 Desnok St., might look familiar as the backdrop for several scenes from the film adaptation of *The Grapes of Wrath*. (☎760-326-3611.)

At **Route 66 Burger ❶**, 701 Broadway, you can pick up Mexican-American fast food at great prices. (☎760-326-2342. Roast-beef sandwich $5.50. Shakes $2.50. *Churros* $1. Open M-F and Su 8am-9pm. Cash only.) The **Wagon Wheel ❸**, 2420 Needles Hwy., is the ultimate truck stop, with meals ranging from an all-you-can-eat salad bar for $4 to a truck-size half-pound burger for $7. (☎760-326-4361. Open daily 5am-10pm. MC/V.) At **Lucy's Mexican Restaurant ❷**, 811 Front St., just off Rte. 66, Lucy herself serves up popular Mexican fare. Try the chile *relleno* dinner, with 2 *rellenos*, rice, beans, and a tortilla for $7.50. (☎760-326-4461. Entrees $4-8. Open Th-Su 11am-8pm. Cash only.) The **Hungry Bear ❹**, 1906 Needles Hwy., is a classic, family-style diner with booths upholstered in Rte. 66-themed fabric. Entrees, like pork chops and club sandwiches, run $6-12. (☎760-326-2988. Open M-Th and Su 5:30am-9pm, F-Sa 5:30am-9:30pm. AmEx/D/MC/V.) Clean rooms with orange-sherbet-colored walls can be found at the **Needles Inn ❶**, 2306 W. Broadway. (☎760-326-0300; www.needlesinn.com. Singles $30; doubles $36. AmEx/D/MC/V.)

APPROACHING AMBOY: 60 MILES
It's a lonely road across the desert; fill up on gas before leaving Needles. From Broadway, head left onto **Needles Hwy.** after crossing the tracks. Continue until **Park Rd.**, then turn left and join **I-40** ½ mi. later. 6 mi. down I-40, take the **U.S. 95/Searchlight/Vegas exit,** and make a right on **Rte. 66.** 6½ mi. later, turn left onto **Goffs Rd.,** following signs for Goffs. Pass through Goffs 14 mi. later. The town of Fenner, another 9½ mi. down the road, is even smaller than Goffs but has the only gas station for miles. 5 mi. past Fenner, head right at the T intersection. Another 2 mi. will bring you through Essex, which has little besides a small auto-repair shop. 25 mi. past Essex is Amboy.

AMBOY. Roy's Cafe and Motel is somewhere between comic and picturesque, with a bright 1950s-era sign vying for customer attention with what must be imaginary competition. The motel is now only a historical sight, but you can stop for soda or water in the former cafe. (Open daily 8am-3pm. Cash only.) Heading west from Amboy, the rising mountains on the north side of the road are countered by an equally surprising geological feature to the south—a volcanic crater set back from the road across a volcanic field. A modest hike up the walls of **Amboy Crater** affords a view not only of a depression of caked mud inside the crater, but also the surrounding plains and mountains.

APPROACHING LUDLOW: 15 MILES
Continue on **Rte. 66** for a rather bumpy 15 mi. past Amboy Crater to the town of Ludlow.

LUDLOW. Until 1988, Ludlow residents had to dial an operator to place a call, and incoming calls were placed through an operator to numbers Ludlow 1, 2, 3, etc. Different extensions had distinctive rings, and it was up to residents to decipher their ring and determine when to pick up. A veritable metropolis in the desert hinterlands, Ludlow now offers a 24hr. gas station and mini-mart as well as the **Ludlow Cafe ❷**, which caters to folks on

ROUTE 66

the go with telephones in most booths. (☎760-733-4501. Entrees $4-8. Open daily 6am-9pm. MC/V.) Rooms are available at the **Ludlow Motel ❷**, 68315 Ludlow Rd. (☎760-733-4338. Singles $50; doubles $52. AmEx/MC/V.)

⚐ APPROACHING NEWBERRY SPRINGS: 27 MILES

Take a right on **Crucero Rd.** to head under I-40, then take a left to Newberry Springs.

NEWBERRY SPRINGS. Newberry Springs is home to the now semi-famous **Bagdad Cafe ❷**, 46548 National Trail Hwy., which inspired for the movie of the same title. (☎760-257-3101. Entrees $4-9. Open daily 7am-7pm. AmEx/MC/V.) Lodging in town is scarce, but for the way-farer who happens to end up in Newberry Springs at nightfall, **The Barn,** 44560 National Trails Hwy., has dancing "every so often." Drinks are cheap (beer $2), as are cups of locally grown pistachios ($1), with flavors like garlic. (☎760-257-4110. Open daily 10am-10pm. MC/V.) The motel part of the **Newberry Mountain R.V. and Motel Park ❶**, 47800 National Trails Hwy., has yet to be resurrected, but the RV park is up and running, with a manmade lake and a paddle boat. (☎760-257-0066. Showers, laundry. Reception 8am-10pm. Tent sites $13; RV sites $22.   AmEx/D/MC/V.)

⚐ APPROACHING DAGGETT: 11 MILES

Continue on **Rte. 66/National Trails Hwy.** to Daggett.

DAGGETT. What used to be the mining and railroad town of Daggett is now pretty much dried up, but the **Daggett Museum,** 33703 2nd St., offers a look at the town's rustic past. Displays cover everything from barbed wire to beaded purses and the folks who used to own them. (☎760-254-2629. Open Sa-Su 1-4pm. Free.)

⚐ APPROACHING BARSTOW: 9 MILES

About 2 mi. down **Rte. 66** from Daggett, curve left onto the **Nebo Access Rd.,** then right onto the high-way. At the **Marine Corps exit,** 4½ mi. down the road, turn left under **I-40,** right on **E. Main St.,** and right on **Montara Rd.** into Barstow.

BARSTOW

Barstow, a classic rest-stop town of inexpensive motels and fast-food chains, may be what the Joad family was hoping for as they crossed into California. Downtown streets are lined with small shops, and the Italian Renaissance-style railroad depot adds Old World grandeur to this gateway to the California desert.

VITAL STATS

Population: 23,000

Visitor Info: Barstow Chamber of Commerce, 409 E. Fredericks St. (☎760-256-8617), off Barstow Rd. Open M-F 10am-4pm.

Internet Access: Barstow Public Library, 304 Buena Vista St. (☎760-256-4850). Open M and W noon-8pm, Tu and Th-F 10am-6pm, Sa 9am-5pm. Free.

Post Office: 425 S. 2nd Ave. (☎760-256-9304). Open M-F 9am-5pm, Sa 9am-noon. **Postal Code:** 92311.

🄴 **GETTING AROUND.** Barstow sits at the junction of **I-15** and **I-40** and at the convergence of a number of California state routes. Most avenues run north-south; streets run east-west. Downtown centers on the intersection of **1st Ave.** and **Main St. (Rte. 66).** Main St. is known as W. Main St. or E. Main St. on the respective sides of 1st Ave. **Barstow Rd.** parallels 1st Ave. a few blocks east.

🄶 **SIGHTS.** In the Casa del Desierto Train Station, a piece of pseudo-Italian Renaissance architecture, the **Route 66 Mother Road Museum,** 681 N. 1st Ave., focuses on Rte. 66's development from a collection of old trails to the epic "Mother Road." (☎760-255-1890. Open F-Su 11am-4pm. Free.) The **Mojave River Valley Museum,** 207 E. Virginia Way, traces the history of the area. (☎760-256-5452. Open daily 11am-4pm. Free.) Eight miles north of Barstow lies the arid beauty of the **Rainbow Basin Natural Area.** Hikers investigate the colorful canyon by day and gaze at a sky unpolluted by city lights at night. Nearby **Owl Canyon Campground ❶** offers primitive camping. (Head north on N. 1st St., take a left onto Fort Irwin Rd., continue for 7 mi., then turn left onto Fossil Bed Rd. Follow the signs down this dirt-and-gravel road for 3 mi. ☎760-

256-8313; www.ca.blm.gov/barstow. Sites $6.) For more info on Rainbow Basin Natural Area, contact the **California Desert Information Center,** 831 Barstow Rd. (☎760-255-8760; www.caohwy.com/c/caldesic. Open daily 9am-5pm.) The ghost town of **Calico** is a collection of touristy craft stores and mini-attractions like "Calico Woodworking" and the "Mystery Shack." (On Ghost Town Rd., off I-15, 10min. north of Barstow. ☎800-862-2542; www.calicotown.com. Open 9am-5pm. $6, ages 6-15 $3.)

■ ☰ FOOD AND ACCOMMODATIONS.

Every restaurant chain imaginable has a branch on Main St., but Barstow's local cuisine may be more promising. The aroma of savory dishes fills the festive dining room of **Rosita's Mexican American Food ❸,** 540 W. Main St. (☎760-256-9218. Mexican combination plates $9-13. Lunch specials Tu-F under $5. Open Tu-Sa 11am-9pm, Su 11am-8pm. AmEx/D/MC/V.) For some hearty Italian food, head to **DiNapoli's Firehouse Italian Eatery ❹,** 1358 E. Main St. Traditional pizzeria fare is served in a refurbished firehouse, complete with the front of a fire engine and a fire pole. (☎760-256-1094. Dinner entrees $8-15. Open M-Sa 11am-9pm. AmEx/D/DC/MC/V.) The world-class doughnuts ($5.50 per dozen) at the **Starlight Donut Shop ❶,** 101 W. Main St., are just the tip of the iceberg. Their list of offerings includes ice cream, egg rolls, tamales, hot dogs, burgers, and croissants. (☎760-256-5974. Open 24hr. Cash only.)

E. Main St. offers an endless line of motels. Prices fluctuate depending on the season, day, and whether Vegas accommodations are full. The **Route 66 Motel ❷,** 195 W. Main St., constructed in 1922, features amazingly comfortable round beds inside stucco, cottage-like units, with vintage cars and signs decorating the outside. (☎760-256-7866. Rooms from $35. AmEx/D/MC/V.) The **Desert Inn ❷,** 1100 E. Main St., is a newly renovated motel with HBO and A/C. (☎760-256-2146. Singles $32; doubles $40. AmEx/D/DC/MC/V.) The massive sign for **El Rancho Motel ❷,** 112 E. Main St., advertises the clean rooms of the white-and-green cottage motel. (☎760-256-2401. Rooms from $37. AmEx/D/MC/V.)

⛰ APPROACHING VICTORVILLE: 30 MILES

Leaving Barstow, follow **Rte. 66** through Hodge, Helendale, Oro Grande, and on to Victorville.

VICTORVILLE. Victorville offers little long-term diversion, but it is home to a few excellent eateries as well as the **California Rte. 66 Museum,** 16849 Rte. 66. Worth a stop, the museum holds an impressive collection of Rte. 66 memorabilia coupled with a refreshing array of modern artistic takes on the Old Road. (☎760-951-0436. Open M and Th-Sa 10am-4pm, Su 11am-3pm. Free.) The new Southern roadhouse in town, **Johnny Reb's ❷,** 15051 7th St., offers an entertaining break from diner fare. As the building instructs, "put some South in your mouth." (☎760-955-3700. Cajun sausage $3.50. Grits $2. Open M-Th 7am-9pm, F-Sa 7am-10pm. AmEx/D/MC/V.) Inexpensive lodging options are scarce in Victorville, though chain motels are abundant at the west end of town and along I-15. The **New Corral Motel ❸,** 14643 7th St., has clean rooms. (☎760-245-9378. Singles $48; doubles $53. AmEx/D/DC/MC/V.)

⛰ APPROACHING SAN BERNARDINO: 37 MILES

Take **7th St.** out of town, then pick up **I-15 S.** Follow I-15 over the mountainous **Cajon Pass** 6¾ mi. Head right at the **Cleghorn Rd. exit,** then curve left 6½ mi. farther on, heading left to join the interstate. Almost 2 mi. beyond that, bear right onto the ramp southbound. Immediately shift into the left lane for **Exit 215** to San Bernardino. As soon as the highway splits, exit for Devore, and turn left at the stop sign onto **Cajun Blvd.** Take a right onto **Kendall Rd.,** and just a few miles beyond, head under the railroad trestle. Continue on **Rte. 66** into San Bernardino, 7 mi. farther.

SAN BERNARDINO

San Bernardino, the seat of America's largest county, is a generic Southern California smog-bowl. It may call itself the hub of the Inland Empire, but the only real empires in this sulfurous city are the rampant corporate franchises—the side benefit of which is cheap food and lodging for those en route to a more palatable destination.

VITAL STATS

Population: 182,000

Visitor Info: San Bernardino Convention and Visitors Bureau, 201 N. E St., Ste. 103. (☎909-889-3980). Open M-Th 7:30am-5:30pm, F 7:30am-4:30pm.

Internet Access: Norman F. Feldheym Library, 555 W. 6th St. (☎909-381-8201). Open M-W 10am-8pm, Th-Sa 10am-6pm. Free.

Post Office: 2160 N. Arrowhead Ave. (☎909-881-2523). Open M-F 9am-5pm, Sa 10am-3pm. **Postal Code:** 92405.

GETTING AROUND. Although traffic in San Bernardino may be a little overwhelming for roadtrippers used to open stretches of Arizona desert, getting around in San Bernardino is relatively simple; the city is laid out in a grid, with numbered streets running north-south and lettered streets east-west. **Rte. 66** enters the city from the north on **I-15,** becoming **Mt. Vernon Ave.** in town. The area along Mt. Vernon Ave. (Old Rte. 66) can be unsafe, especially at night, so stick to the north end of town or **Hospitality Ln.,** which crosses Waterman Ave. just north of I-10.

SIGHTS. Will Rogers performed his last show at the historic **California Theater,** 562 W. 4th St. (☎909-386-7361), and entertainers like Buster Crabbe and Rita Hayworth also performed here. Today, the theater is home to the California Theater of Performing Arts, which hosts popular musicals and shows like *Cats* and *Phantom of the Opera.* Don't miss the giant Will Rogers mural outside. San Bernardino also hosts the **Rte. 66 Rendezvous Weekend** (www.route-66.org.), a Rte. 66 weekend open to all vehicles made between 1900 and 1973, and any model Viper, Corvette, or Prowler. The **original McDonald's,** 1398 N. E St., was established by Richard and Maurice "Mac" McDonald in 1948, but don't expect $0.15 burgers anymore. The only thing offered at this half-hearted historic site is a growing display of Golden Arches memorabilia and Happy Meal toys. (☎909-885-6324. Open daily 10am-5pm.)

FOOD AND ACCOMMODATIONS. Lined with tributes to James Dean and Elvis, **Molly's ❷,** 350 N. D St., at Court St., has healthy

options with just enough creativity to draw in the out-of-towners. (☎909-888-1778. Sandwiches $6.25. Omelettes $6-6.50. Open M-F 6am-3pm, Sa 7am-2pm, Su 7:30am-2pm. AmEx/D/MC/V.) Family-owned since 1937, **Mitla's ❷,** 602 Mt. Vernon Ave., has enormous Mexican specialties, many of them for rock-bottom prices. (☎909-888-0460. Taco, enchilada, and tamale plate $6.25. Open Tu-W 9am-2pm and 4:30-8pm, Th-F 9am-9pm, Sa 9am-8pm, Su 9am-8pm. AmEx/D/MC/V.) At the **Guesthouse Inn ❸,** 1280 S. E St., the rooms have fridges, microwaves, and free continental breakfast. (☎909-888-0271. Singles M-Th and Su $54; F-Sa $64; doubles $64/$74. AmEx/MC/V.)

APPROACHING RIALTO: 5 MILES
From San Bernardino, head out of town on **5th St.,** which turns into **Foothill Blvd.** toward Rialto, 2 mi. west of **Mt. Vernon Rd.**

RIALTO. The historic stop in Rialto is the **Wigwam Motel ❸,** 2728 W. Foothill Blvd. As with the Holbrook wigwams, these concrete structures are a blend of modern convenience and antique quirkiness, featuring TV, A/C, and wagon-wheel headboards. (☎909-875-3005. Singles M-Th and Su $65; F-Sa $75; doubles $76/$85. AmEx/D/DC/MC/V.)

APPROACHING PASADENA: 35 MILES
In summer, juice-mongers operate from inside the giant orange on the south side of the road in **Rancho Cucamonga.** Just a few miles ago, towns were as hard to come by as water in the stretch of punishing Mojave Desert across eastern California. From San Bernardino to L.A., however, the urban sprawl of countless strip-mall towns blends together in one commercialized, brand-happy stretch of suburbia that might send east-west roadies into population-density shock. Those with an itch for the ocean might consider hitting I-10 directly onto the beach, bypassing the urban sprawl leading into Los Angeles. Upland, 16 mi. from San Bernardino, is home to the **Madonna of the Trail statue,** a statue that marks the end of the National Road and the Californian cousin to Illinois's Madonna of the Highway. From Upland, continue through Claremont, Laverne, San Dimas, and Glendora. Continue on **Foothill Blvd.** through Azusa, Duarte, Monrovia, and Arcadia. 1 mi. after entering Arcadia, take a right onto **Colorado Blvd.,** and follow it into Pasadena.

PASADENA

Nationally, Pasadena is known as the home of the Rose Bowl; for Californians, it's a serene, ritzy suburb. Old Town combines historic sights with a lively entertainment scene, and wide boulevards lined with trendy eating and shopping options, side streets with world-class museums, and graceful architecture make Pasadena quite distinct from its noisy downtown neighbor.

VITAL STATS

Population: 134,000

Visitor Info: Convention and Visitors Bureau, 171 S. Los Robles Ave. (☎626-795-9311; www.pasadena-cal.com). Open M-F 8am-5pm, Sa 10am-4pm.

Internet Access: Pasadena Central Library, 285 E. Walnut St. (☎626-744-4066). Open M-Th 9am-9pm, F-Sa 9am-6pm, Su 1-5pm. Free.

Post Office: 967 E. Colorado Blvd. (☎626-432-4835). Open M-F 8:30am-5pm. **Postal Code:** 91106.

GETTING AROUND

Pasadena sits on the northeast edge of the sprawling metropolis that is L.A. **Rte. 66** approaches Pasadena from the west and runs through the city as **Colorado Blvd. I-210** parallels Colorado Blvd. to the north; downtown Pasadena and many attractions, including **Old Town Pasadena,** lie between I-210 and Colorado Blvd. Avenues in Pasadena run north-south; streets and boulevards run east-west. On the west edge of the city, the **Arroyo Pkwy. (I-110)** runs north-south. It turns into the **Pasadena Fwy.** as it heads southwest toward L.A., serving as the major route between the cities.

SIGHTS

Besides sports, Pasadena's main draw is **Old Town Pasadena,** a series of trendy shops and restaurants bordered by Walnut St. and Del Mar Ave., between Pasadena Ave. and Arroyo Pkwy.

NORTON SIMON MUSEUM OF ART. This world-class private collection chronicles Western art from Italian Gothic to 20th-century abstract. The museum features paintings by Raphael, Van Gogh, Monet, and Picasso, as well as rare etchings by Rembrandt and Goya. The Impressionist and post-Impressionist hall, the Southeast Asian sculptures, and the 79,000 sq. ft. sculpture garden by California landscape artist Nancy Goslee Power are particularly impressive. *(411 W. Colorado Blvd., at Orange Grove Blvd. ☎626-449-6840; www.nortonsimon.org. Open M, W-Th, Sa-Su noon-6pm, F noon-9pm. $8, seniors $4, students with ID and under 18 free. 1st F of each month 6-8pm free.)*

ROSE BOWL. In the gorge that forms the city's western boundary stands Pasadena's most famous landmark. The sand-colored, 90,000-seat stadium is home to "the granddaddy of them all," the annual college football clash on Jan. 1 between the champions of the Big Ten and Pac 10 conferences. The Bowl Championship Series comes every four years, and the UCLA Bruins play regular-season home games here as well. *(1001 Rose Bowl Dr. ☎626-577-3100; www.rosebowlstadium.com.)* The Bowl also hosts an enormous monthly **flea market** that attracts upwards of 2000 vendors selling nearly one million items. *(☎626-577-3100. Held the 2nd Su of each month 9am-3pm. $7, 12 and under free.)*

ARTS. The **Pasadena Playhouse** fostered the careers of William Holden, Dustin Hoffman, and Gene Hackman. Founded in 1917 and restored in 1986, it offers some of L.A.'s finest theater. *(39 S. El Molino Ave., between Colorado Blvd. and Green St. ☎626-356-7529; www.pasadenaplayhouse.org.)* Housed in the concrete labyrinth of the **Pasadena Civic Auditorium** is the centerpiece of the city's Spanish-influenced architecture. The auditorium hosted television's **Emmy Awards** each year until 1998, when the ceremonies moved to Los Angeles. Since it is a rented venue, events are constantly changing, but the auditorium usually hosts the Pasadena Symphony and the Distinguished Speaker Series, which hosts guests from Shimon Peres to Bob Woodward to Rudy Giuliani. *(300 E. Green St., at Marengo St. ☎626-449-7360. Box office open M-Sa noon-6pm.)* The **Pasadena Museum of California Art** displays feature Californian art, architecture, and design from 1850 to the present. *(490 E. Union St. ☎626-568-3665. Open W-Su noon-5pm. $6, students and seniors $4.)*

ROUTE 66

SCIENCES. Some of the world's greatest scientific minds do their work at the **California Institute of Technology (Caltech).** Founded in 1891, Caltech has amassed a faculty that includes several Nobel laureates and a student body that prides itself on both its staggering intellect and its loony practical jokes. *(1201 E. California Blvd., about 2½ mi. southeast of Old Town. ☎626-395-6327. Tours M-F 2pm. Free.)* The **NASA Jet Propulsion Laboratory,** about 5 mi. north of Old Town, executed the journey of the Mars Pathfinder. *(4800 Oak Grove Dr. ☎818-354-9314. Free tours by appointment.)*

FOOD

Eateries line **Colorado Blvd.** from Los Robles Ave. to Orange Grove Blvd. in Old Town. The restaurants and sights around the boulevard make it pleasant and walkable.

Fair Oaks Pharmacy and Soda Fountain, 1516 Mission St. (☎626-799-1414), at Fair Oaks Ave. in South Pasadena. From Colorado Blvd., go south 1 mi. on Fair Oaks Ave. to Mission St. This old-fashioned drugstore has been serving travelers since 1915. Hand-dipped shakes and malts $5. Sandwiches $5.50. Soda fountain open M-Th 9am-9pm, F-Sa 9am-10pm, Su 9am-8pm. Lunch counter open M-Th and Su 11am-6pm, F-Sa 11am-8pm. AmEx/D/MC/V. ❶

Pita! Pita!, 927 E. Colorado Blvd. (☎626-356-0106; www.citycent.com/pitapita), 1 block east of Lake Ave. Never has a flatbread deserved so many exclamation points. Free appetizers of green olives, yellow peppers, and toasted pita. Great salad options $5.25-7.25. Spicy chicken pita $6. Lamb kebab with salad, rice, and beans $8.45. Open M-Th and Su 8am-9pm, F-Sa 8am-10pm. AmEx/D/MC/V. ❷

Pie 'n' Burger, 913 E. California Blvd. (☎626-795-1123; www.pienburger.com), just east of S. Lake Ave.. A classic 1963 diner, complete with Formica counters and plaid wallpaper. Burgers ($6) and pies (19 varieties; $3.50-4) are your best bets. Open M-F 6am-10pm, Sa 7am-10pm, Su 7am-9pm. Cash only. ❸

ACCOMMODATIONS

Pasadena Motor Inn, 2097 E. Colorado Blvd. (☎626-796-3122). The narrow hallways may feel a bit like your college dorm, but the rooms are large and comfortable, with fridges and balconies. Singles $55, doubles $60. Cash deposit $20. AmEx/D/MC/V. ❷

Saga Motor Hotel, 1633 E. Colorado Blvd. (☎626-795-0431; www.thesagamotorhotel.com). This apartment-like hotel offers pleasant peach-colored rooms. Singles from $85; doubles from $91. AmEx/D/DC/MC/V. ❹

Astro Motel, 2818 E. Colorado Blvd. (☎626-449-3370). Zany 70s bedspreads, floral wallpaper, carved bedsteads, and antique glass lamps lend chaotic comfort to this colorful budget option. Singles $48; doubles $60. MC/V. ❷

APPROACHING LOS ANGELES: 10 MILES
From **Colorado Blvd.,** turn left onto **Arroyo Pkwy.,** which immediately feeds into **CA-110.** Take CA-110 18 mi. southwest into the heart of Los Angeles.

LOS ANGELES

There's a reason why 17 million people choose to live in the sprawling collection of neighborhoods and freeways known as the City of Angels. Yes, the traffic is terrible, the smog is worse, the socioeconomic divisions are tense, and the plastic surgery rate is high. However, many find L.A.'s ever-changing scene enthralling and battle to seek out the trendiest beaches, freshest clubs, hottest artists, and best ethnic food as the sun shines through their car windows. In this movie-obsessed town, everyone either works in the industry, wants to work in the industry, or is related to someone who does. Cruise through the city and watch the sun set over the Pacific in Santa Monica, or stay to see the sights and the stars; either way, it's one hell of a show.

PAGE TURN. See p. 902 in the **Pacific Coast** for complete coverage of Los Angeles.

APPROACHING SANTA MONICA: 16 MILES
Get on **CA-110 W.** Exit at **Sunset Blvd.,** and turn left from the off-ramp, crossing the freeway. Bear right on **Figueroa St.** (following signs to Sunset Blvd.), and turn right. 3 mi. later, turn left onto **Manzanita St.,** which immediately turns into **Santa**

TO PACIFIC
PALISADES (2mi),
MALIBU (8mi)

Montana Ave.
Idaho Ave.
Washington Ave.
California Ave.

3rd St.
Lincoln Park
Wilshire Blvd.

Douglas Park

Wilshire Blvd.

Arizona Ave.
Santa Monica Blvd.

Broadway

Colorado Ave.

Memorial Park

Bergamot Station Arts Center

Olympic Blvd.

SANTA MONICA

Santa Monica Fwy.

Michigan Ave.

Delaware Ave.

Pico Blvd.

Virginia Ave.

Kansas Ave.

Santa Monica College

Bay St.
Grant St.
Pacific St.
Pearl St.

California Heritage Museum

OCEAN PARK

Ocean Park Blvd.
Oak St.
Hill St.
Ashland Ave.

Dewey St.
Marine St.

Rose Ave.

Penmar Golf Course

Museum of Flying

Santa Monica Airport

Dewey Ave.
Warren Ave.

Flower Ave.

Sunset Ave.
Vernon Ave.
Indiana Ave.
Brooks Ave.
Broadway Ave.
Westminster Ave.

VENICE

Brooks Ave.

Lake St.

California Ave.

Palms Blvd.
Vienna Wy.
Carlton Wy.

Victoria Ave.

Lucille Ave.

Venice Blvd.

Venice Canals

Venice Fishing Pier

Washington Blvd.

Venice Beach

Washington Blvd.

MARINA DEL REY

Maxella Ave.

Santa Monica Bay

Santa Monica State Beach

Santa Monica Pier Aquarium

Santa Monica Pier & Pacific Park

Santa Monica Place

Int'l. Chess Park

Perry's Beach Rentals
Bicknell Ave.

Pacific St.
Strand St.

Ocean Front Walk

Boardwalk

Santa Monica

🔺 **ACCOMMODATIONS**
Los Angeles / Santa Monica Hostel, **2**
Ocean Lodge Hotel, **6**
Pacific Sands Motel, **3**

🍎 **FOOD**
Big Dean's "Muscle-In" Cafe, **5**
Bread & Porridge, **1**
Fritto Misto, **4**
Omelette Parlor, **7**

Monica Blvd. Follow Santa Monica Blvd. through West Hollywood, Beverly Hills, and West Los Angeles to reach Santa Monica. At the junction with I-10, turn left at **Lincoln St.**, and follow it to **Olympic St.** The intersection of Lincoln and Olympic is the official end of Route 66, but to reach the famously eclectic **Santa Monica Pier,** continue west on Santa Monica Blvd.

SANTA MONICA

Finally—the Pacific! After mile upon mile of open road, from the shores of Lake Michigan across flat Oklahoma plains and through the Arizona desert, Santa Monica awaits on the edge of the dazzling blue expanse. But Santa Monica is known as much for its shore scene as its shore; the promenade and the pier are popular destinations.

■ **GETTING AROUND. Rte. 66** enters Santa Monica from the east on **Santa Monica Blvd.** Just north of the boulevard, the **Santa Monica Fwy. (I-10)** runs west from L.A. to the **Pacific Coast Hwy.** Pedestrian **Third St. Promenade** heads north from **Broadway** to **Wilshire Blvd.** Much of Santa Monica is best seen by foot or bike.

VITAL STATS

Population: 87,000

Visitor Info: Santa Monica Visitors Center, 1920 Main St., Ste. B (☎310-393-7593), 2nd fl. Open daily 9am-6pm.

Internet Access: Santa Monica Public Library, 601 Santa Monica Blvd. (☎310-434-2608). Open M-Th 10am-9pm, F-Sa 10am-5:30pm, Su 11am-5pm. Free.

Parking: Lots near Third St. Promenade; 1st 2hr. free 6am-5:59pm, then $3 per hr. Santa Monica Place Mall, 2nd and Broadway, has free parking for up to 3hr. Meters $1 per hr. All-day beach parking $6-10.

Post Office: 1248 5th St. (☎310-576-6786), at Arizona Blvd. Open M-F 9am-6pm, Sa 9am-3pm. **Postal Code:** 90401.

■ **SIGHTS.** Filled with gawkers and hawkers, the area on and around the carnival pier is the hub of tourist activity. Farther inland, along Main St. and beyond, are galleries, design shops, and museums. Cars are prohibited on the ultra-popular **Third Street Promenade,** a three-block stretch of mosaic art tiles, fashionable stores, movie theaters, and lively restaurants. The Promenade truly heats up when the sun sets, the ocean breeze kicks in, and the ivy-lined mesh dinosaur sculptures spurt water into fountains. On Wednesday and Saturday mornings, the area becomes a **farmers market** selling flowers and produce, with Saturdays featuring exclusively organic products. (Between Broadway and Wilshire in downtown Santa Monica. Exit off 4th St. from I-10.) The famed **Santa Monica Pier** is the heart of Santa Monica Beach and home to the carnival-esque **Pacific Park.** Adrenaline addicts over 4 ft. tall can twist and turn on the five-story West Coaster or soar 100 ft. above the ocean in the first solar-powered Ferris wheel. (☎310-458-8900; http://santamonicapier.org. Pier open 24hr. Park open in summer M-Th and Su 11am-11pm, F-Sa 11am-12:30am; hours vary in winter. Tickets $2.25.)

■ **FOOD AND ACCOMMODATIONS.** Giant, colorful table umbrellas sprout from sidewalk patios along the Third St. Promenade and Ocean Ave., punctuating Santa Monica's upscale eating scene. Menus nod to deep-pocketed health buffs, offering organic and vegetarian choices. The cheery waitstaff at ■**Fritto Misto** ❸, 601 Colorado Ave., at 6th St., urge you to create your own pasta (from $7) and bring your own bottle. (☎310-458-2829. Vegetarian entrees $7-12. Open M-Th 11:30am-10pm, F-Sa 11:30am-10:30pm, Su 11:30am-9:30pm. D/MC/V.) You don't need to venture far from the beach for the "burger that made Santa Monica famous" at **Big Dean's "Muscle-In" Cafe** ❷, 1615 Ocean Front Walk. (☎310-393-2666. Veggie burgers $5. Happy hour M-F 4-8pm. Open M-F 11am-sunset, Sa-Su 11:30am-sunset. MC/V.) You can't beat the half-price omelettes offered up at the **Omelette Parlor** ❸, 2732 Main St., from 6-7am. For lunch try the Garden of Eatin' salad ($8.50), but make no mistake, this place is a breakfast destination. (☎310-399-7892. Open M-F 6am-2:30pm; Sa-Su 6am-4pm. MC/V.) **Bread & Porridge** ❸, 2315 Wilshire Blvd., prides itself on exceptional service and an egalitarian division of labor—dishwashers, busboys, servers, cashiers, and cooks all rotate jobs and share tips. (☎310-453-4941. Pancakes $6-8. Omelettes $10. Entrees $8-13. Open M-F 7am-2pm, Sa-Su 7am-4pm. AmEx/MC/V.)

Accommodations in Santa Monica range from cheap oceanfront hostels to expensive oceanfront hotels. The closer you stay to the beach, the more you dish out. Depending on the hostel/hotel, the tax on your room may be 8.5% or 14%. The best budget option available is the ◙Los Angeles/Santa Monica Hostel ❶, 1436 2nd St., which has prime access to the beach and Santa Monica hot spots and sponsors tours and activities. The hostel has Internet access, video games, nightly movie showings, library, self-service kitchen, laundry, and a travel store. (☎310-393-9913. Check-in 2pm-midnight. Dorms $29, members $26; private rooms from $66. MC/V.) **The Ocean Lodge Hotel ❺**, 1667 Ocean Ave., has

spacious and clean rooms close enough to smell the ocean water. (☎310-451-4146. Rooms $135-150. Parking $10. AmEx/MC/V.) At the epicenter of what's happening, **Pacific Sands Motel ❺**, 1515 Ocean Ave., has modest rooms and a heated pool. (☎310-395-6133. Rooms from $105. AmEx/D/MC/V.)

THE END OF THE ROAD

Sink your toes into the sand, ride the Ferris wheel on the pier, take a picture next to the plaque on the grass at Ocean Ave. and Santa Monica Blvd., and dip your feet in the Pacific. You've finished "the Journey," the Mother Road, the Will Rogers Highway, the Main Street of America. Now that you've mastered Route 66, why stop the adventure? Replenish your stock of chocolate-covered coffee beans, and head north for the Pacific Coast or meet up with the Southern Border in San Diego.

EXIT TO

Malibu, CA   36 mi.
on the pacific coast route, p. 917

San Diego, CA 120 mi.
on the southern border route, p. 878

SPEED LIMIT 65

the oregon trail

TOP 5

1. Conquer the mighty **Jackalope**, in Douglas, Wyoming.
2. Take one small step for roadtrippers at Idaho's **Craters of the Moon National Monument.**
3. Encounter **Carhenge,** in Alliance, Nebraska, and see your car in a whole new way.
4. Immerse yourself in the beauties of Oregon on the **Columbia River Scenic Highway.**
5. Skim through hundreds of dusty volumes at **Powell's City of Books** in Portland, Oregon.

You learned about it in history class, and maybe spent hours honing your bison-hunting, river-fording, and epitaph-writing skills on the computer game, but this is your chance to experience the real thing—and without dying of cholera or dysentery. Stretching 2000 miles from Independence, Missouri, to Oregon City, Oregon, our route traces the path of the determined pioneers across the prairies of Kansas, over the mountain passes of Wyoming, and along the Columbia River in Oregon. Gather your oxen, pack your grain, and, above all, heed your inner Lewis and Clark.

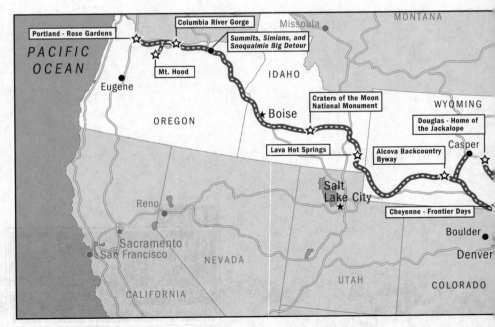

By the mid-1860s, over 300,000 pioneers had emigrated from the crowded east to the fertile valleys of the West Coast. While the original journey, a four- to six-month undertaking, offered settlers the opportunity to stake claims in new lands, it also posed great risks. One in 10 people traveling the trail died en route, many claimed by cholera. Wagons were full and space was limited; most travelers walked. Barefoot. Today's travels are less treacherous, but reminders of pioneers past still line the way, including famous **Alcove Spring** (p. 614), **Chimney Rock** (p. 623), **Scotts Bluff** (p. 623), and, of course, **Independence Rock** (p. 635)—make it here by July 4th, and you'll be in Oregon before the winter. The route also crosses the original **Pony Express** trails, pathways of daring young adventurers who embodied the roadtripping spirit.

But the modern Oregon Trail offers far more than just historical sights. From sprawling **Kansas City** (p. 605) in the East, through laid-back **Boise** (p. 652), to funky **Portland** (p. 673) in the West, the cities that line the road are varied and vibrant. Many revel in their Wild Western heritage; **Douglas, WY** (p. 627) bills itself as the **"Jackalope Capital of the World,"** while **Cheyenne, WY** (p. 628) celebrates **Frontier Days** with rodeos, parades, and square dances each July. Others take full advantage of their natural resources, offering everything from kiteboarding (**Hood River, OR**; p. 668) to mountain climbing (**Enterprise** and **Joseph, OR**; p. 660) to natural hot springs (**Lava Hot Springs, ID**; p. 643). Like the towns along the way, the Oregon Trail's landscape is just about as varied as it gets. From the sweeping prairies of Kansas and Nebraska, you'll climb into the towering Rocky Mountains of southern Wyoming (don't miss the **Scenic Alcova Backcountry Byway**; p. 632), pass through the spectacularly bizarre rock formations of **Craters of the Moon National Monument** (p. 646) in Idaho, and follow the beautiful **Columbia River Gorge** (p. 664) along the waterfalls that line the **Historic Columbia River Highway** (p. 672). Try out the **Summits, Simians, and Snoqualmie Big Detour** (p. 666) for a rugged drive through Washington State, passing through **Mt. Rainier National Park** and the **Snoqualmie Valley**.

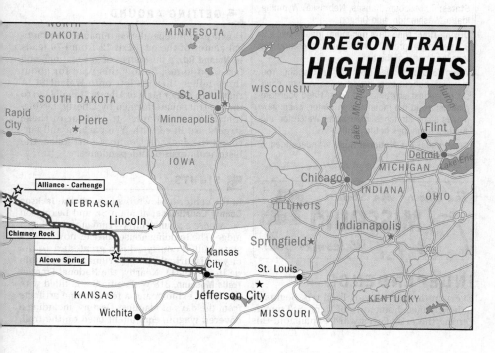

The Oregon Trail isn't a big-city route by any stretch of the imagination, so don't expect mega-malls or cosmopolitan downtowns. Instead, prepare for the tiny hamlets that line the rural highways of the Great Plains and Rocky Mountains—places where motel rooms and ice-cream cones are cheap, owners are friendly, stoplights are few, and cows are plentiful. Fortunately, even the tiniest towns aren't completely devoid of attractions, and the open road between them has an appeal of its own. And, of course, near Alliance, NE, you'll pass by what is perhaps the epitome of all roadtrip culture—delightfully wacky **Carhenge** (p. 622), modeled after England's famous Stonehenge, but constructed entirely out of old automobiles.

It's a long, arduous road, but the views along the way are unparalleled, far better than any computer game or textbook. Get going—Oregon awaits!

ROUTE STATS

Miles: c. 2000

Route: Independence, MO to Oregon City, OR.

States: 7; Missouri, Kansas, Nebraska, Wyoming, Idaho, Washington, and Oregon.

Driving Time: Nine days minimum; ideally, allow 2-3 weeks to appreciate the scenic drives and historic landmarks of the trail.

When To Go: Pioneers started in mid-spring. You, however, benefit from paved roads, so you could set off almost any time you want. Heed your forerunners; avoid the mountains in winter, when snow makes some stretches impassable. Watch for late-summer tornadoes in the plains.

Crossroads: The National Road in Independence, MO (p. 602).

The Show - Me State

MISSOURI

Welcomes You!

INDEPENDENCE

Every authentic Oregon Trail trip begins in Independence, hometown of Harry S. Truman. During the era of westward expansion, this city stood on the edge of a vast wilderness, truly the last waystation for pioneers. The romantic sense of journey lingers, between the hills of the East and the prairies of the Midwest. Modernized antebellum estates and hundred-year-old businesses allow this suburb to remain a trailhead to the West.

VITAL STATS

Population: 115,000

Visitor Info: Tourist Information Center and Truman Home Ticket Center, 223 N. Main St. (☎816-254-9929), at Main St. and Truman Rd. Open M-F 8:30am-5pm.

Internet Access: Mid-Continent Public Library, South Independence Branch, 13700 E. 35th St. (☎816-461-2050). Open M-Th 9am-9pm, F 9am-6pm, Sa 9am-5pm.

Post Office: 301 Lexington St. (☎816-521-3608). Open M-F 8am-5pm, Sa 8am-noon. **Postal Code:** 64050.

■ GETTING AROUND

Downtown Independence remains the practical center of the city. **Exit 12** from **I-70** leads to **Noland Rd.,** a busy strip of gas stations and fast-food joints. Follow this road for about three miles, then go left onto **Walnut St.** A right onto either **Main** or **Liberty St.** will lead to the central square formed by Liberty, Lexington, Main, and Maple St. All four of these streets are lined with free parking and surround the Jackson County Courthouse, the historical nexus of Independence.

◉ SIGHTS

In the center of downtown stands the **Jackson County Courthouse,** at Main St. and Lexington St., where a young Harry Truman worked as a judge. The building houses offices now, but its statue-filled courtyard is a great start to the city's historical sites. (Truman Courtroom ☎816-881-4431). Nearby, the **National Frontier Trails Museum,** 318 W. Pacific St., is filled with historical exhibits and a few genuine artifacts from the days of Manifest Destiny, including a covered wagon, equipment used on the trail,

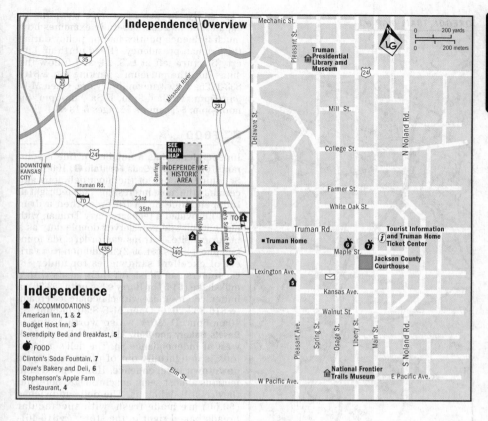

Independence Overview

Mechanic St.

Pleasant St.

Truman Presidential Library amd Museum

Mill St.

Delaware St.

College St.

N Noland Rd.

Farmer St.

White Oak St.

Truman Rd.

Truman Home

Tourist Information and Truman Home Ticket Center

Maple St.

Jackson County Courthouse

Lexington Ave.

Kansas Ave.

Walnut St.

Pleasant Ave.

Spring St.

Osage St.

Liberty St.

Main St.

S Noland Rd.

Elm St.

National Frontier Trails Museum

W Pacific Ave.

E Pacific Ave.

0   200 yards
0   200 meters

Missouri River

291

35

38

DOWNTOWN KANSAS CITY

24

Truman Rd.

Sterling

SEE MAIN MAP

INDEPENDENCE HISTORIC AREA

70

23rd

35th

Noland Rd.

Lee's Summit Rd.

TO

435

40

Independence

▲ ACCOMMODATIONS
American Inn, 1 & 2
Budget Host Inn, 3
Serendipity Bed and Breakfast, 5

🍎 FOOD
Clinton's Soda Fountain, 7
Dave's Bakery and Deli, 6
Stephenson's Apple Farm
  Restaurant, 4

and the original diaries and letters of people on their way west. Exhibits explain the significance of three major trails that began in Independence: the Santa Fe, the California, and the Oregon. (☎816-325-7575; www.frontiertrailsmuseum.org. Open M-Sa 9am-4:30pm, Su 12:30-4:30pm. $5, seniors $4, ages 6-17 $3.)

Back up Main St. at the corner of Truman Rd., the **Truman Home Ticket Center** houses the **Tourist Information Center.** Tours of Truman's home, at 219 Delaware St., depart from the center following a short introductory video. The video itself acknowledges that "few memorable events took place at 219 Delaware"; the tour should probably be reserved for real Truman enthusiasts. (☎816-254-9929.

Tours Labor Day to Memorial Day Tu-Su every 15min. 9am-4:45pm. $4.) The sidewalk outside the center is the starting point for **Pioneer Trails Adventures.** These wagon rides through town are guided by the Wrangler, an in-character driver and storyteller. (☎816-456-4991 or 816-254-2466; www.pioneertrailsadventures.com. Tours $6-20.)

The graves of President Truman and his wife, his preserved office, as well as the legendary "The Buck Stops Here" sign are all on display at the extensive ◪**Truman Presidential Library and Museum,** 500 U.S. 24. Galleries focus on the different crises of the Truman administration, presenting multi-perspective analyses of its most controversial decisions,

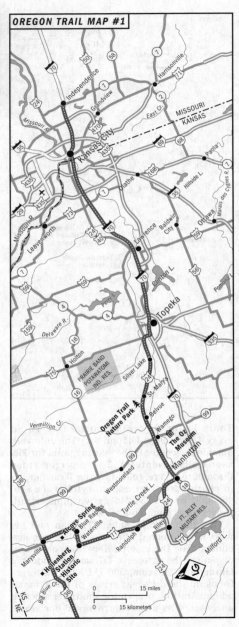

OREGON TRAIL MAP #1

especially the use of atomic weapons in Japan. The museum carefully examines how much influence politics had on policy during the Truman presidency. (Head north up Liberty St., turn left at U.S. 24, and follow the signs into the museum's parking lot. ☎816-833-1225; www.trumanlibrary.org. Open M-W 9am-5pm, Th 9am-9pm, F-Sa 9am-5pm, Su noon-5pm. $7, seniors $5, ages 6-18 $3.)

🍴 FOOD

Independence has a number of fine restaurants, but **Clinton's Soda Fountain ❶,** 100 Maple St., shines as one of the most delicious and certainly the most interesting. Located right in Independence Sq., Clinton's (then a drug store) provided a teenage Harry Truman with his first job and now serves double-duty as a historical site. Patrons can order soda fountain phosphates ($1.50-2) in addition to a variety of excellent sandwiches for under $6. Customers can finish off their meals with a milkshake ($4-5) or Harry's Favorite ($3.70), a butterscotch sundae with chocolate ice cream. (☎816-833-2046. Open M-F 8:30am-6pm, Sa 10am-6pm. D/MC/V.) Also worth a stop is **Dave's Bakery and Deli,** 214 Maple St., a block west of Independence Sq. The deli's modern look is delightfully out of place in historic downtown Independence. Home-baked confections almost seem anachronistic here, but they're still delicious. The deli sandwiches ($3.50) are made fresh, with spectacular breads baked right in the store. (☎816-461-0756. Open M-F 6am-5pm, Sa 7am-3pm. MC/V.) **Stephenson's Apple Farm Restaurant ❹,** 16401 U.S. 40, has a red barn building and low wooden rafters that are only the beginning of its rural style. Appetizers such as chicken gizzards ($5) might scare off city-slickers, but the entrees are a bit less exotic. Hickory-smoked chicken ($14) is the house specialty, with other options including hickory-smoked ham or ribs, and pork chops. (From Noland Rd., go left down U.S. 40 and take a right onto Lees Summit Rd.; Stephenson's parking lot is immediately on the left. ☎816-373-5345. Entrees $13-18. Open in summer M-Sa 11am-10pm, Su 10am-9pm; in winter M-Th 11am-9pm, F-Sa 11am-10pm, Su 10am-9pm. D/MC/V.)

ACCOMMODATIONS

Hotels are cheaper and easier to find just outside of Independence. Exit 18 off I-70 has fine budget options. Beautiful, historic, and overrun with greenery, the **Serendipity Bed and Breakfast ❷**, 116 Pleasant Ave., three blocks west of Liberty St., takes its Victorian-era decor seriously—breakfast is served by candlelight. (☎ 800-203-4299 or 816-833-4719; www.bbhost.com/serendipitybb. Check-in 4-9pm. Singles $45-70; doubles $80-85. MC/V.) Cheaper options include two **American Inn ❷** locations: Woods Chapel Rd., off Exit 18 from I-70, and 4141 S. Noland Rd. Rooms are clean and reasonably well maintained. (Woods Chapel Rd. ☎ 816-228-1080. S. Noland Rd. ☎ 816-373-8300. Singles $40-50. AmEx/D/MC/V.) The **Budget Host Inn ❷**, 15014 U.S. 40, south of I-70, is another convenient choice, with clean, if slightly worn, rooms. (☎ 816-373-7500 or 800-283-4678. Singles $35.)

 DID YOU KNOW? Most people began their journey on the Oregon Trail with over a ton of cargo, but within a day of their trip, the precious possessions would be thrown out.

■ APPROACHING KANSAS CITY: 13 MILES
From downtown Independence, return to **Noland Rd.** via **Walnut St.**, and drive 3 mi. south. Ramps onto **I-70** are very well marked. **I-70** passes through the northern part of Kansas City, close to downtown. **Exit 3A** feeds onto **The Paseo**, which is a large road parallel to, and a bit east of, **Main St.**

KANSAS CITY

With more boulevards than Paris and more fountains than Rome, Kansas City looks and acts more European than one might expect from the "Barbecue Capital of the World." When Prohibition stifled the rest of the country's fun in the 1920s, Mayor Pendergast let the good times continue to roll. The Kansas City of today maintains its blues-and-jazz reputation in a metropolis spanning two states: the highly suburbanized town in Kansas (KCKS) and the quicker-paced commercial metropolis in Missouri (KCMO).

VITAL STATS

Population: 150,000

Visitor Info: Convention and Visitors Bureau of Greater Kansas City, 1100 Main St., Ste. 2200 (☎ 816-221-5242 or 800-767-7700; www.visitkc.com), on the 22nd fl. of the City Center Sq. Bldg. Open M-F 8:30am-5pm. **Missouri Tourist Information Center,** 4010 Blue Ridge Cutoff (☎ 816-889-3330 or 800-877-1234). Follow signs from Exit 9 off I-70. Open daily 8am-5pm, except on the Chiefs' home game days.

Internet Access: Kansas City Public Library, 14 10th St. (☎ 816-701-3414). Open M-W 9am-9pm, Th 9am-6pm, F 9am-5pm, Sa 10am-5pm, Su 1-5pm. Free.

Post Office: 315 W. Pershing Rd. (☎ 816-374-9100). Open M-F 8am-8pm, Sa 8:30am-3:30pm. **Postal Code:** 64108.

GETTING AROUND

Though Kansas City is laid out in a relatively simple grid, car travel can be frustrating due to the tangle of one-way streets and turn-only lanes. East-west streets are numbered, with numbers increasing as one travels south. **Main St.**, which runs north-south and divides the city, is in fact two one-way streets located a block apart from each other. Large parking garages are available in the downtown area, but virtually every street has free or metered parking on the shoulder. This and the large dimensions of the city will likely compel travelers to drive to each site rather than to park and walk.

SIGHTS

■ STEAMBOAT ARABIA MUSEUM. In 1856, the steamboat *Arabia* struck a fallen tree and sank to the bottom of the Missouri River along with its impressive cargo of frontier artifacts. Preserved in the mud, this time capsule of 19th-century frontier life has since been excavated and restored. Delicate glassware, lovely pottery, clothing, and a vast array of other antebellum objects are now on display at the Arabia Steamboat Museum. Functioning parts of the ship chug away on a

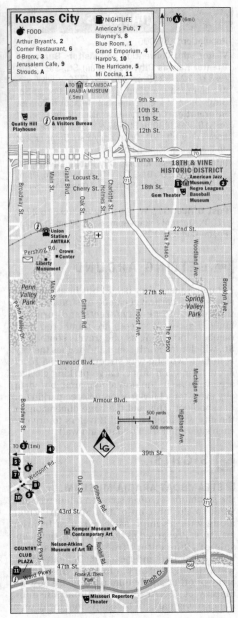

Kansas City

🍴 FOOD

Arthur Bryant's, **2**
Corner Restaurant, **6**
d-Bronx, **3**
Jerusalem Cafe, **9**
Strouds, **A**

🌃 NIGHTLIFE

America's Pub, **7**
Blayney's, **8**
Blue Room, **1**
Grand Emporium, **4**
Harpo's, **10**
The Hurricane, **5**
Mi Cocina, **11**

life-sized re-creation of the steamer's deck, complete with an enormous paddlewheel. *(400 Grand Blvd., next to the City Market. ☎816-471-4030; www.1856.com. Open M-Sa 10am-5:30pm, Su noon-5pm. $12.50, seniors $11.50, ages 4-12 $4.75.)*

COUNTRY CLUB PLAZA. The most "European-influenced" section of Kansas City is undoubtedly the Country Club Plaza, or just "the Plaza," the oldest and perhaps most picturesque shopping center in the US. Modeled after buildings in Sevilla, Spain, the Plaza boasts fountains, sculptures, hand-painted tiles, gargoyles, luxury chain stores, and latte-sipping yuppies. The Plaza is also famous for its Christmas lights, lit annually on Thanksgiving Eve. *(Along 47th St., between Main and Madison St. Free concerts May-Sept. Th 5-8pm and Sa-Su 2-5pm.)*

NELSON-ATKINS MUSEUM OF ART. This museum features one of the best East Asian art collections in the world and a sculpture park with 13 pieces by Henry Moore. The museum is under renovation until July 2007, so call ahead. Live jazz plays on Friday 5:30-8:30pm inside the Rozzelle Court Restaurant. *(4525 Oak St., 3 blocks northeast of the Country Club Plaza. ☎816-561-4000; www.nelson-atkins.org. Open Tu-Th 10am-4pm, F 10am-9pm, Sa 10am-5pm, Su noon-5pm. Free walking tours Sa 11am-2pm, Su 1:30-3pm. Free admission during renovation.)*

KEMPER MUSEUM OF CONTEMPORARY ART. Gigantic, malformed spiders adorn the lawn and outer walls of the Kemper Museum of Contemporary Art. Inside, other works—both more and less orthodox than the arachnids—are on display in cool white galleries. *(4420 Warwick Blvd., off Main St., just north of the Country Club Plaza. ☎816-753-5784; www.kemperart.org. Open Tu-Th 10am-4pm, F-Sa 10am-9pm, Su 11am-5pm. Free.)*

18TH AND VINE HISTORIC DISTRICT. The entire 18th & Vine Historic District pays tribute to great jazz musicians who lived and played there in the early 20th century. The **American Jazz Museum** brings the era back with listening stations, neon dance hall signs, and paraphernalia ranging from Ella Fitzgerald's eyeglasses to Louis Armstrong's lip salve. *(1616 E. 18th St. ☎816-474-8463; www.americanjazzmuseum.com. Open Tu-Sa 9am-6pm, Su noon-6pm. $7, under 12 $3.)* In the same building, the **Negro Leagues Baseball**

Museum documents the athletic feats of 1920s African-American ballplayers and the racism that once divided baseball and society. The museum is dominated by an indoor diamond manned by statues of a Negro League Dream Team. *(1616 E. 18th St. ☎816-474-8453; www.nlbm.com. Open Tu-Sa 9am-6pm, Su noon-6pm. $7, under 12 $3; both museums $9/$5.)*

UNION STATION AND CROWN CENTER.

The city likes to boast of its fountains and boulevards. The Bloch fountain in front of ◪**Union Station** is one of the finest. This magnificent 1914 building, renovated in 1999 and now home to restaurants, shops, and a science museum in addition to Amtrak, is the largest train station in North America outside of New York. *(30 W. Pershing Rd. Open daily 6am-midnight.)* It is linked by a skywalk to **Crown Center,** an upscale shopping center. On the 3rd floor of Crown Center is the **Hallmark Visitors Center,** where extensive family-friendly exhibits chronicle the history, design, and manufacturing process behind the famous greeting cards. *(2405 Grand Ave. ☎816-274-3613; www.hallmarkvisitorscenter.com. Open M-F 9am-5pm, Sa 9:30am-4:30pm. Free.)* It is also home to the children's **Coterie Theatre,** which features games, a maze, and theater technology demonstrations. *(☎816-474-6785. $9, under 18 $7.)* During the winter, the **Ice Terrace** is Kansas City's only public outdoor ice-skating rink. *(☎816-274-8412. Rink open Nov.-Dec. M-Th and Su 10am-9pm, F-Sa 10am-11pm; Jan.-Mar. daily 10am-9pm. Skate rental $2.50.)* The Crown Center area is dominated by the enormous WWI **Liberty Monument,** which sits on a grassy hill facing Union Station. A vast frieze is built into the hillside, depicting the horrors of war on the right and the pleasures of peace on the left.

FOOD

Kansas City's specialty is its unusually tangy barbecue. The **Westport** area, at Westport Rd. and Broadway St. just south of 40th St., has an eclectic array of cafes and coffeehouses. Ethnic eateries cluster along **39th St.,** just east of the state line. The **City Market** area has Asian grocery stores and inexpensive open-air produce markets at the intersection of 5th and Walnut St. (Open M-F and Su 9am-4pm, Sa 6am-4pm.)

◪**Arthur Bryant's,** 1727 Brooklyn Ave. (☎816-231-1123). The granddaddy of KC barbecue and a perennial candidate for best barbecue in the country. Bryant's "sandwiches" ($8) are a carnivore's delight—wimpy triangles of bread drowning in pork perfection. Open M-Th 10am-9:30pm, F-Sa 10am-10pm, Su 11am-8:30pm. AmEx/D/DC/MC/V. ❸

d-Bronx, 3904 Bell St. (☎816-531-0550), at 39th St. A New York deli in Middle America, d-Bronx has over 35 kinds of subs (half $4-6, whole $8-12), with powdered-sugar brownies ($1.50) for dessert. Open M-W 10:30am-9pm, Th 10:30am-10pm, F-Sa 10:30am-11pm. AmEx/D/MC/V. ❸

Jerusalem Cafe, 431 Westport Rd. (☎816-756-2770). Patrons enjoy vegetarian Mediterranean fare while playing backgammon. Pita sandwiches ($6-7) complement unusual appetizers (under $5). Open M-Sa 11am-10pm, Su noon-8pm. AmEx/D/DC/MC/V. ❷

Strouds, 5410 NE Oak Ridge Dr. (☎816-454-9600). Belt-bustin' steak, catfish, and fried chicken served with homemade cinnamon rolls. Open M-Th 5-9:30pm, F 11am-10:30pm, Sa 11am-9:30pm, Su 2-10:30pm. AmEx/MC/V. ❸

Corner Restaurant, 4059 Broadway St. (☎816-931-6630), in the heart of Westport. A greasy spoon famous for its all-day breakfasts, including plate-sized pancakes ($2-3). Weekday lunch specials $6. Open daily 7am-3pm. Cash only. ❷

ACCOMMODATIONS

The least expensive lodgings lie near the interstates, especially I-70, and toward Independence. Downtown hotels tend to be on the pricey side.

American Inn, 4141 S. Noland Rd. (☎816-373-8300; www.americaninn.com), off I-70 at Exit 12. Dominates the KC budget-motel market with locations throughout the city. The rooms are large and pleasant. A/C, cable TV, and outdoor pools. Singles and doubles from $42. AmEx/MC/V. ❷

Interstate Inn (☎816-229-6311), off I-70 at Exit 18. Far from downtown, but one of the cheapest, decent motels around. 21+. Singles from $29; doubles from $44. AmEx/D/MC/V. ❷

Lake Jacomo (☎816-795-8200), 22 mi. southeast of downtown. From I-70, take Rte. 291 S to Colbern Rd.; go left (east) on Colbern Rd., and head 2 mi.

down to Beach Rd. Lots of water activities, 33 forested campsites, and a marina. No swimming. Sites $12, with electricity $17, with electricity and water $18, with full hookup $24. Cash only. ❶

🎵 ENTERTAINMENT

JAZZ

In the 1920s, jazz musician Count Basie and his "Kansas City Sound" reigned at the River City bars. Twenty years later, saxophonist Charlie "Bird" Parker reasserted Kansas City's prominence in the jazz scene. The restored **Gem Theater,** 1615 E. 18th St., stages old-time blues and jazz. From October to April, the Jammin' at the Gem concert series swings in a serious way. (☎816-474-6262. Box office open M-F 10am-4pm. Tickets from $30.) Across the street, the **Blue Room,** 1600 E. 18th St., cooks four nights per week with some of the smoothest local acts in town. (☎816-474-2929. Cover F-Sa $5. Open M and Th 5-11pm, F 5pm-1am, Sa 7pm-1am.) The **Grand Emporium,** 3832 Main St., twice voted the best blues club in the US, has live music five nights a week. (☎816-531-1504. M and W-Sa live music. Cover $15, depending on act. Open M and Sa noon-2am, Tu-F 11am-2am.)

THEATER

From September to May, the **Missouri Repertory Theatre,** on the campus of the University of Missouri at Kansas City, at 50th and Oak St., stages American classics. (☎816-235-2700; www.missourirep.org. Tickets $7-48.) **Quality Hill Playhouse,** 303 W. 10th St., produces Off-Broadway plays and revues from September to June. The box office is located at 912 Baltimore Ave., Ste. 200. (☎816-421-1700. Box office open M-F 9am-5pm. Tickets $20-22.) From late June to mid-July, the **Heart of America Shakespeare Festival** (☎816-531-7728; www.kcshakes.org), in Southmoreland Park, at 47th and Oak St., puts on free shows.

SPORTS

Sports fans stampede into Arrowhead Stadium, at I-70 and Blue Ridge Cutoff, home to football's 🏈**Chiefs** (☎816-920-9400 or 800-676-5488; tickets $51-70) and soccer's **Wizards** (☎816-920-9300;

tickets $12-17). Next door, Kauffman Stadium houses the **Royals,** Kansas City's baseball team. (☎816-921-8000 or 800-676-9257. Tickets $5-22.)

🎵 NIGHTLIFE

For something besides jazz, bars and nightclubs cluster in **Westport.**

Blayney's, 415 Westport Rd. (☎816-561-3747). R&B on the dance floor, live music on the outdoor deck. Cover $2-6. Open Tu-Th 8pm-3am, F 6pm-3am, Sa 5pm-3am. AmEx/MC/V.

America's Pub, 510 Westport Rd. (☎816-531-1313). Kansas City's bachelorette party headquarters. The dance floor is usually packed, but the elevated bar stools provide a chance to relax. Th $1 drinks. Cover $6. Open W-Sa 8pm-3am. AmEx/DC/MC/V.

The Hurricane, 4048 Broadway St. (☎816-753-0884). This eclectic club hosts everything from open mic (M) to hip-hop (Th). Cover $5-15. Open M-F 3pm-3am, Sa-Su 5pm-3am. AmEx/MC/V.

Harpo's, 4109 Pennsylvania Ave. (☎816-753-3434). The keystone of Westport nightlife. The live music and $0.25 beer on Tu attract college students ready to party. Cover Tu and Sa $2-3. Open daily 11am-3am. AmEx/D/MC/V.

Mi Cocina, 620 W. 48th St. (☎816-960-6426). The place to see and be seen in Kansas City. Trendy Latin music accompanies couture-clad fashionistas. The Mexican food is generally overlooked in favor of the bar. Open M-Th 11am-10pm, F-Sa 11am-3am, Su noon-10pm. AmEx/D/DC/MC/V.

⛏ DETOUR

HARLEY-DAVIDSON VEHICLE AND POWERTRAIN OPERATIONS

11401 N. Congress Ave. 20 mi. north of downtown Kansas City. Head north on the Paseo to I-29 N/I-35 N/U.S. 71 N. When they split, continue on I-29 N toward the airport. Take Exit 12 for NW 112th St.; at the bottom of the ramp turn right. Turn left on Congress Ave., and the factory will be on the right.

It's a bit of a drive, but any true Harley fan will enjoy a stop here. After a video, a guide ushers tour groups around the assembly plant to glimpse various individual pieces being made. At the end, the assembly line for the bikes themselves reveals how everything fits together. (☎414-343-7850 or

877-883-1450. Visitors center and store open M-F 8am-3pm. 45min. tours every hr. M-F 8am-1pm. Reservations recommended. Free.)

⚑ APPROACHING LAWRENCE: 40 MILES

The easiest way to leave Kansas City is to take **Broadway St.** north. Right before reaching the Missouri River, take the ramp to **I-70 W.** The road on the way to Lawrence is an uninspiring stretch of I-70 about 25 mi. long. Tollbooths are in effect in this area, so keep quarters ready. Lawrence can be reached by either **Exit 202** or **204** off I-70. Exit 202 provides the more direct approach. Follow the exit through the tolls and straight through the intersection with **2nd St.,** as the exit ramp becomes **McDonald Rd.** Continue south until it intersects with **6th St.** Turn left, and drive east to **Massachusetts St.**

The Sunflower State
KANSAS
Welcomes You!

LAWRENCE

Forty miles from Kansas City, Lawrence was founded in 1854 by anti-slavery advocates to ensure that Kansas became a free state. Now home to the flagship University of Kansas (KU), Lawrence is a good-times college town, fully equipped with excellent restaurants and a happening music scene.

VITAL STATS

Population: 80,000

Visitor Info: Lawrence Visitors Center, 402 N. 2nd St. (☎785-865-4499 or 888-529-5267; www.visit-lawrence.com), at Locust St. Open M-Sa 8:30am-5:30pm, Su 1pm-5pm. Free Wi-Fi.

Internet Access: Lawrence Public Library, 707 Vermont St. (☎785-843-3833; www.lawrencepubliclibrary.org). Open M-F 9am-9pm, Sa 9am-6pm, Su 2-6pm. Free.

Parking: Vermont and New Hampshire St. are full of free 2hr. parking lots.

Post Office: 645 Vermont St. (☎785-843-1681). Open M-F 8am-5:30pm, Sa 9am-noon. **Postal Code:** 66045.

⬛ GETTING AROUND

Almost everything of interest is found along **Massachusetts St.** or on parallel **Vermont** and **New Hampshire St.** Numbered streets run east-west.

◉ SIGHTS

The Wild West was in full swing in Lawrence during the "Bleeding Kansas" days, giving the city quite a bit of fascinating history. The **University of Kansas Watkins Community Museum of History,** 1047 Massachusetts St., features several floors of Lawrence lore, including an exhibit on the abolitionist activist John Brown and a display on the inventor of basketball, James Naismith, who died in Lawrence. (☎785-841-4109; www.watkinsmuseum.org. Open Tu-W 10am-6pm, Th 10am-9pm, F 10am-5pm, Sa 10am-4pm. Suggested donation $3.) The main attractions, however, are two tours through downtown Lawrence. A 1½hr. driving tour, **Quantrill's Raid: The Lawrence Massacre,** beginning at 1111 E. 19th St., traces the events leading up to the slaughter of over 200 men by pro-slavery vigilantes on August 21, 1863. The 2nd tour, **House Styles of Old West Lawrence,** provides a look at 19th-century homes. There are walking (45min.) and driving (25min.) variations; pick up a map at the visitors center. The **Spencer Museum of Art,** 1301 Mississippi St., is home to an impressive collection of paintings, sculpture, and glass works from medieval and Renaissance Europe, as well as medieval Japan and dynastic China. (☎785-864-4710. Open Tu-W and F-Sa 10am-5pm, Th 10am-9pm, Su noon-5pm. Free.)

◩ FOOD

Downtown Lawrence features both traditional barbecue joints and health-conscious offerings. The **Free State Brewing Company ❷,** 636 Massachusetts St., was the first legal brewery in Kansas. This local hangout brews over 50 beers annually and always has at least five on tap, while their chef prepares sophisticated sandwiches and dinners. The turkey bacon focaccia sandwich ($6.50) goes well with a draft. (☎785-843-4555, www.freestatebrewing.com. Sandwiches $6-7. Pasta $8-10. $1.25 beer M. Open M-Sa 11am-midnight, Su noon-11pm. AmEx/D/DC/

MC/V.) **Jefferson's ❷**, 743 Massachusetts St., promotes "Peace, Love, and Hotwings" along with its entrees, all under $7. Their massive burgers, including the Jefferson Burger (bacon, cheese, and barbecue sauce; $6.50) can fill even the hungriest KU student. Unleash your artistry on a dollar bill and add it to the thousands already gracing the walls. (☎785-832-2000. Open M-W 11am-10pm, Th-Sa 11am-11pm, Su noon-10pm. AmEx/D/MC/V.) Between meals, it's possible to have any conceivable combination of fruit in a glass at the **Juice Stop ❶**, 812 Massachusetts St. Sports-named smoothies all sell for $3-6, be it the Hat Trick (papaya, peach, banana, and coconut) or the Half-pipe (guava, peach, pineapple, and banana). (☎785-331-0820. Open M-F 8am-9pm, Sa 9am-8pm, Su 10am-8pm. MC/V.) The enticing aromas wafting from **Wheatfields Bakery and Cafe ❷**, 904 Vermont St., will draw you to their large sandwiches ($5-7) on French bread, olive loaf, or focaccia. The breads, cakes, and pastries are also tempting options. (☎785-841-5553; www.wheatfieldsbakery.com. Open M-Sa 6:30am-8pm, Su 7:30am-4pm. D/MC/V.)

ACCOMMODATIONS

Inexpensive motels are hard to come by in Lawrence. The best place to look is around Iowa and 6th St., just west of the KU campus. The **Halcyon House Bed and Breakfast ❷**, 1000 Ohio St., is extremely close to local attractions and good parking. (☎785-841-0314. Rooms $49. AmEx/MC/V.) The traditional **Westminster Inn and Suites ❷**, 2525 W. 6th St., offers many amenities, including a pool. (☎785-841-8410. Breakfast included. Singles $49; doubles $54. AmEx/D/MC/V.) The **Virginia Inn ❷**, 2903 W. 6th St., right downtown, offers large rooms with microfridges. (☎785-843-6611. Singles $50. AmEx/D/MC/V.) A more luxurious but expensive stay is available at the **Eldritch Hotel ❺**, at the corner of 7th and Massachusetts St. (☎785-749-5011 or 800-527-0909. Rooms $125-155.)

NIGHTLIFE

The rowdy saloon-goers of Lawrence's past have come and gone, but late-night fun is still available; yesterday's cowboys have simply been replaced by college students. The place to be for live rock, **The Bottleneck**, 737 New Hampshire St., hosts local acts and big-name artists every night except Thursday, when Retro Dance Night takes over. (☎785-841-5483. Cover $10. Open daily 3pm-last customer.) For live music and a neighborhood bar atmosphere, head down to **Jazzhaus**, 926½ Massachusetts St. (☎913-749-3320. Cover after 9pm $2-8; Tu $1.50, but no live music. Open daily 4pm-2am. ⊛) Across the street from each other and under the same management, the **Jackpot Saloon and Music** and the **Replay Lounge**, both at 943 Massachusetts St., serve multiple facets of the clubbing community. The Replay is dark, with a bar and pinball, while the Jackpot is bright and sociable. Both put on a variety of musical acts. (Jackpot ☎785-832-1085. Shows daily. Open daily 4pm-last customer. Replay ☎785-749-7676. Shows weekly. 21+ after 10pm. Open daily from 3pm. AmEx/D/MC/V.)

◤ DETOUR
KANSAS SPEEDWAY

350 Speedway Blvd. Just after you go around the speedway on U.S. 24/U.S. 40, turn left onto Speedway Blvd. and follow it to the track.

Up to 82,000 fans pack the Kansas Speedway for NASCAR and IndyCar races. **Tours** start from the yellow security booth located at the intersection of Speedway Blvd. and Michigan Dr. and last 75-90min., leading through the stands, infield, garage, fan walk, and track. Sadly, visitors can't drive around the track. (☎913-328-3327. Tours generally Th 4pm; call ahead. $10, children $5.)

◤ APPROACHING TOPEKA: 27 MILES

Take **6th St. (U.S. 40 W)** out of town. 22½ mi. from Lawrence, exit to stay on **U.S. 40**; it joins **Rte. 4** and **I-70** toward Topeka.

TOPEKA

The capital of Kansas, Topeka is essentially a vast tract of plazas and strip malls. Though this arrangement has led to a particularly high density of fast-food joints and gas stations, intriguing restaurants and sights are still hidden throughout the city. Topeka displays its state pride at several historic sights that memorialize its role in the abolition and civil rights movements.

VITAL STATS

Population: 122,000

Visitor Info: Topeka Convention and Visitors Bureau, 1275 Topeka Blvd. (☎800-235-1030; www.topekacvb.com). Open M-F 9am-5pm.

Internet Access: Topeka and Shawnee County Public Library, 1515 10th Ave. (☎785-580-4400; www.tscpl.org), at the corner of Washburn Ave. Open M-F 9am-9pm, Sa 9am-6pm, Su noon-9pm. Free.

Post Office: 424 S. Kansas Ave. (☎785-295-9178). Open M-F 8am-5pm, Sa 9am-noon.

Postal Code: 66603.

▄ GETTING AROUND

Much of Topeka is a rough grid of four-lane roads—it's definitely a driver's city. **Topeka Blvd.** is the city's major north-south artery, featuring numerous restaurants and hotels. **Gage Blvd.,** about 2 mi. west, is a haven for gas stations and fast food. Though many east-west streets end in residential cul-de-sacs, **10th Ave.** to the north and **29th St.** to the south both span the full distance.

◉ SIGHTS

Most of Topeka's sights are not concentrated in one region, so a good bit of driving is necessary to see them all. In the center of Topeka is the **Kansas State Capitol,** at the corner of 10th Ave. and Jackson St. (☎785-296-3966). Tours M-F every hr. 8am-3pm, except noon. Free.) The new **Brown v. Board National Historic Site,** at the intersection of Monroe and 15th St., is dedicated to the groundbreaking Supreme Court decision that ruled school segregation unconstitutional. Built in a former elementary school, the museum is filled with photographs chronicling the history leading up to and resulting from the decision. In the powerful Hall of Courage exhibit, visitors pass through a narrow corridor of gigantic screens that blast footage of jeering crowds denouncing newly admitted black students. (Follow 10th Ave. to Topeka Blvd. and proceed south to 15th St. ☎785-354-4273. Open daily 9am-5pm. Free.)

The **Kansas Museum of History,** 6425 6th St., is a guide to the history of Kansas, from prehistoric native life to 20th-century developments.

Rotating special exhibits highlight particular time periods and events. (Drive north on Topeka Blvd. to 6th St.; then proceed east to the very end of the road. ☎785-272-8681; www.kshs.org. Open Tu-Sa 9am-5pm, Su 1-5pm. $5, seniors $4, students $3.) In addition to lions, giraffes, and other exotic animals, the **Topeka Zoological Park,** 635 Gage Blvd., has an indoor rainforest where visitors share the pathways with monkeys, birds, turtles, and other small jungle creatures. (☎785-368-9143. Open daily 10am-5pm. $4.50, seniors $3.50, ages 3-12 $3.) Proceeding south to Forbes Field Airport will bring you to the **Combat Air Museum,** a hangar that houses combat planes from many eras. (☎785-862-3303; www.combatairmuseum.org. Open M-Sa 9am-4:30pm, Su noon-4:30pm; last entry 3:30pm. $6, ages 6-17 $4.)

▟ FOOD

Topeka is home to several fine restaurants, though finding them can be a bit of challenge; like much in this city, they are scattered across countless strip malls. The ▨**Blind Tiger Brewery and Restaurant ❸,** 417 37th St., east of Topeka Blvd., is named for the stuffed tigers that were sometimes used to advertise Prohibition-era speakeasies. The microbrewery and restaurant are separated only by a low wall, so the buzz of the bar blends softly into the dim, trendy eating area. Finish off your meal with a Prohibition Float, made with root beer brewed right in the building. (☎785-267-2739; www.blindtiger.com. Appetizers from $6. Pasta from $11. Grill entrees from $8. Restaurant open M-Th and Su 11am-9pm, F-Sa 11am-10pm. Lounge open M-Th and Su 11am-1am, F-Sa 11am-2am. AmEx/D/MC/V.) Food preparation is a spectacle at **Kiku Japanese Steak House ❹,** 5331 22nd Pl., in the Fairlawn Plaza off Fairlawn Rd. Chefs cook food in the dynamic *hibachi* style at your table. (☎785-272-6633. Appetizers $3-10. Entrees $11-21. Reservations recommended. Open M-F 11:30am-1:30pm and 4:30-10pm, Sa-Su noon-10pm. AmEx/MC/V.) Whether you desire a hot dog ($3.75) or three-cheese quiche ($7.25), **Annie's Place ❷,** 4014 Gage Center Dr., will provide. The in-house bakery sells fabulous pies for $8-12. (☎785-273-0848, www.anniesplacetopeka.com. Open daily 11am-9pm. AmEx/D/MC/V.) **Casa Authen-**

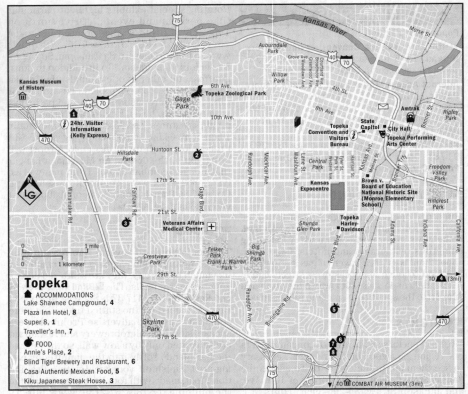

Topeka

⌂ ACCOMMODATIONS
Lake Shawnee Campground, **4**
Plaza Inn Hotel, **8**
Super 8, **1**
Traveller's Inn, **7**

🍎 FOOD
Annie's Place, **2**
Blind Tiger Brewery and Restaurant, **6**
Casa Authentic Mexican Food, **5**
Kiku Japanese Steak House, **3**

tic Mexican Food ❷, 3320 Topeka Blvd., south of 29th St., is a pleasant family restaurant with private booths and well-priced meals. The combination dinners are an excellent bargain, complete with an entree such as the house chili ($7.75) and soup or salad. (☎785-266-4503. Open M-Th 11am-10pm, F-Sa 11am-11pm, Su 11:30am-10pm. AmEx/D/MC/V.)

🏠 ACCOMMODATIONS

Hotels cluster near the highway exits, but some of the nicest and least expensive accommodations are closer to downtown. The **Plaza Inn Hotel ❸**, 3880 Topeka Blvd., is located just south of 37th St. Though it looks like every other budget hotel on the outside, the rooms are spacious and exceptionally pleasant. (☎785-

266-4591. Singles from $50. MC/V.) Nearby, the **Traveller's Inn ❷**, 3846 Topeka Blvd., offers standard rooms and an outdoor pool. (☎785-267-1222, reservations 877-524-7666. Singles $35; doubles $40. MC/V.) A safe, if predictable, bet is **Super 8**, 5968 10th Ave., right off I-70 at Exit 356. (☎785-273-5100. Singles from $50; doubles from $55. AmEx/D/MC/V.) Road-weary travelers can spend evenings fishing and swimming at **Lake Shawnee Campground ❶**, 3435 E. Edge Rd. Though there are many more RV sites than tent sites, you'll need a tent to camp right on the water's edge. (Follow 29th St. east to the edge of Topeka, then go south on Croco Rd.; E. Ridge Rd. is a short distance down to the right. ☎785-267-1156. Electrical hookups at most sites. Showers. Mid-Apr. to mid-Oct. tent sites $14; RVs $15; Mid-Oct. to mid-Apr. $11/$14.)

▶ APPROACHING ST. MARYS: 28 MILES
To leave the city, follow **Topeka Blvd.** north through downtown and over the Kansas River to **U.S. 24.** As you make your way across the Kansas prairie, be prepared for sudden speed drops; the limit swings between 70 and 20 mph. This particular strip of road follows the original Oregon Trail closely, so it is rife with **historical markers.** These big, brown signs, found in little alcoves beside the road, point out significant locations in the lives of the Oregon Trail travelers, the original roadtrippers.

ST. MARYS. The Oregon Trail Nature Park, just west of town off U.S. 24, has a series of walking trails through the prairie. The longest is a 30min. hike through the "Sea of Grass" to an outlook. The park, run by Western Resources, Inc., also has restrooms and a gigantic cylindrical mural. (From U.S. 24, follow signs right down Schoemaker Rd., just west of St. Marys. Turn left at the end onto Oregon Trail Rd. ☎785-456-2035. Open daily May-Sept. 7am-9pm; Oct.-Apr. 8am-6pm.) On the eastern outskirts of St. Marys, stop by **Froggy's ❶,** 311 W. Bertrand Ave., for delicious breakfasts and super-cheap daily grill specials. (☎785-437-6733. Open M-Sa 8am-9pm, Su noon-3pm. D/MC/V.)

▶ APPROACHING WAMEGO: 14 MILES
Continue on **U.S. 24** heading northwest to enter Wamego.

WAMEGO. Wamego plays proud host to the **Oz Museum,** 511 Lincoln Ave., a museum dedicated to Oz paraphernalia of all kinds. Enter through the lobby into the Technicolor brightness of the museum proper, where you can follow a re-creation of Dorothy's journey while marveling at first editions of Baum's novel, props from the movie, memorabilia from the stage production, and other artifacts from the Land of Oz. (Turn left on Lincoln St., shortly after crossing into Wamego; the museum is 6 blocks up on the right. ☎866-458-8686; www.ozmuseum.com. Open M-Sa 10am-5pm, Su noon-5pm. $7, ages 4-12 $4.)

▶ APPROACHING MANHATTAN:15 MILES
On the outskirts of Manhattan, **Poyntz Ave.** runs parallel to **U.S. 24.** Entering the city is easiest if you get on this road as soon as possible, thus avoiding the unpleasant snare of highway intersections at the eastern edge of the city.

MANHATTAN
Filled with Kansas State University students and a remarkable number of indoor shopping centers, Manhattan calls itself "The Little Apple." While it may be the *really* little apple compared to its big brother, Manhattan stands on its own. Its art museum, zoo, and great restaurants are all hallmarks of a lively metropolis.

VITAL STATS

Population: 48,000

Visitor Info: Manhattan Convention and Visitors Bureau, 501 Poyntz Ave. (☎785-776-8829; www.manhattancvb.org). Open M-F 8am-5pm.

Internet Access: Manhattan Public Library, 629 Poyntz Ave. (☎785-726-4741). Open M-Th 9am-8:30pm, F 9am-6pm, Sa 9am-5:30pm, Su 1-5:30pm. Free.

Post Office: 500 Leavenworth St. (☎785-776-8851). Open M-F 8:30am-4:30pm, Sa 9:30am-noon. **Postal Code:** 66502.

▣ GETTING AROUND. Businesses and official buildings are located along **Poyntz Ave.,** which degenerates into a mess of highway intersections to the east. Unfortunately, this area is the only way to reach the lodgings on **Tuttle Creek Blvd. (U.S. 24). Anderson Ave.** runs parallel to and a few blocks north of Poyntz Ave. and is home to the Kansas State University campus.

◐ SIGHTS. The prairie lives on in the city at the **Sunset Zoo,** 2333 Oak St., which features native Kansas species like prairie dogs, as well as an exotic red panda, Siberian tigers, and a snow leopard. (Follow Poyntz Ave. past Sunset Ave., and take a right on Oak St. ☎785-587-2737; www.sunsetzoo.com. Open daily Apr.-Oct. 9:30am-5pm; Nov.-Mar. noon-5pm. $4, ages 3-12 $2.) At the far end of the KSU campus, the **Beach Museum of Art,** 701 Beach Ln., exhibits contemporary sculpture and painting. (From Sunset Ave., turn right onto Anderson Ave. ☎785-532-7718; www.k-state.edu/bma. Open Tu-F 10am-5pm, Sa-Su 1-5pm. Free.)

▤◖ FOOD AND ACCOMMODATIONS.
Though a number of restaurants lie within Manhattan's shopping centers, others are scattered throughout the downtown area. The sandwiches and salads at the **4th St. Cafe ❶,**

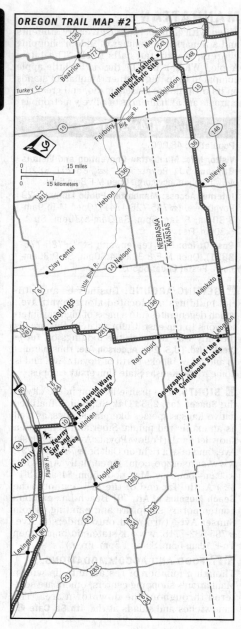

OREGON TRAIL MAP #2

15 miles

15 kilometers

Marysville

Hollenberg Station Historic Site

Beatrice

Turkey Cr.

Washington

Fairbury

Big Blue R.

Belleville

Hebron

NEBRASKA / KANSAS

Clay Center

Nelson

Little Blue R.

Mankato

Hastings

Lebanon

Red Cloud

Geographic Center of the 48 Contiguous States

The Harold Warp Pioneer Village

Minden

Ft. Kearny SHP and Rec. Area

Kearny

Platte R.

Holdrege

Lexington

---

106 S. 4th St., is a healthy and flavorful change of pace from most cafes' lunch menus. Everything on the menu is $6 or less, including the delicious pesto turkey sandwich ($5). The full coffee bar sells pastries ($1-3) and coffee beans by the pound. (Turn onto 4th St. from Poyntz Ave. ☎ 785-539-2233. Open M-F 7:30am-3pm, Sa 8am-2pm. D/MC/V.) **Harry's Uptown ❹**, 418 Poyntz Ave., serves satisfying entrees at steep prices. Unorthodox sandwiches, such as the Wild Mushroom Philly ($7), are the best deals. Best of all, Harry's offers tired roadies a chance to lounge in upholstered comfort far from the sterility of shopping malls. (☎ 785-537-1300. Entrees $12-30. Open M-Th 11am-2pm and 5-9pm, F 11am-2pm and 5-10pm, Sa 5-10pm. AmEx/MC/V.) In addition to standard burger-and-fries fare, the **Village Inn ❷**, 204 Tuttle Creek Blvd., has a special flair for crepes ($6). Stick to tradition with a fruit crepe or one of the ham, egg, and cheese crepes. (☎ 785-537-3776. Open M-Th and Su 6am-10pm, F-Sa 6am-1pm. AmEx/D/MC/V.)

Chain hotels are abundant in Manhattan, and good bargains include our old standby **Motel 6 ❸**, 510 Tuttle Creek Blvd., which has an outdoor pool. (☎ 785-537-1022. Singles M-Th and Su $50, F-Sa $56; doubles $56/$62. AmEx/D/DC/MC/V.) Those in need of a good night's sleep should consider **The Cottage at Cedar Meadows Bed and Breakfast ❹**, 15955 Cedar Meadows Rd., in Wamego. This B&B's elegance might just make the price worth it. (☎ 785-456-8654; www.thecottagebnb.com. Check in 4-8pm or by arrangement. Rooms $79-139. MC/V.)

⊼ APPROACHING ALCOVE SPRING: 43 MILES
To leave Manhattan, simply head north on **Tuttle Creek Blvd.** Outside of the city, it drops the name and becomes **U.S. 24** again. Switch to **U.S. 77 N** after driving by Tuttle Creek Lake. Just past the towns of Waterville and Blue Rapids, **Tumbleweed Rd.** appears, leading west. This dirt road is marked only by a small sign pointing the way to Alcove Spring, so it is easy to miss; the **Alcove Spring Historic Marker,** 100 yd. south of the turn, is easier to spot than the road.

ALCOVE SPRING. Carvings left in stones by emigrants still exist at Alcove Spring, which was a popular camping site for wagon trains on the Oregon Trail. Beyond this historic significance, the area is quiet and serene—a nice place to sit and watch the dragonflies. The spring itself can only be reached on foot, but the trail is well-maintained, and the walk is short. (Open daily sunrise-sunset. Free.)

⛏ APPROACHING MARYSVILLE: 18 MILES

From Alcove Spring, **Tumbleweed Rd.** arcs through the wooded hills of the countryside, where wild turkeys are more plentiful than cars. Follow Tumbleweed for 15 mi. to **Linden St.,** and take a right, which will lead you back to **U.S. 77.** Follow U.S. 77 to the intersection of **Broadway** and **Central St. (U.S. 36).**

MARYSVILLE

Pretty and quiet, Marysville is the last outpost before the long haul to Hastings, Nebraska. It was once the first major stop on the **Pony Express,** and the town proudly remembers the daring of these romantic riders. In the center of Marysville, the **Pony Express Museum,** 106 S. 8th St., contains the barn that served as the first station where courier-riders slept. The other half of the museum details the short, thrilling history of the Pony Express. The displays include a copy of the riders' oath never to drink, swear, or fight, and a bulletin seeking young men "willing to risk death daily." (☎785-562-3825. Open M-Sa 10am-5pm, Su noon-5pm. $2, ages 4-12 $0.50.) The **Marysville Chamber of Commerce,** 101 N. 10th St., has more info for visitors. (☎785-562-3101. Open M-F 9am-5pm.)

Penny's Diner ❷, 1127 Pony Express Hwy. (U.S. 36), is located in a shiny, metallic box of a building that could be straight out of a 50s sci-fi flick. Try the custom omelettes, which start at $5. (☎785-562-1234. Breakfast under $7. Lunch and dinner under $8. Open 24hr. MC/V.) The **Wagon Wheel Cafe** ❷, 703 Broadway St., is right in the heart of Marysville's brick-paved downtown. The menus are mock newspapers, so patrons can read about the history and attractions of Marysville and the surrounding region while they wait to order. In true Kansas style, the Wagon Wheel offers a full barbecue dinner ($9) with brisket, hashbrowns, beans, and cole slaw. (☎785-562-3784. Appetizers from $2.75. Sandwiches from $2. Entrees from $6.50. AmEx/D/MC/V.) To the east, accommodations can be found on the section of Center St. that has been renamed **Pony Express Hwy.** The **Oak Tree Inn** ❸, 1127 Pony Express Hwy. (U.S. 36), has excellent rooms. In addition to an exercise

center and hot tub, it shares its lot with Penny's Diner, which offers breakfast discounts to Oak Tree guests. (☎785-562-1234. Rooms from $65. Cash only.) Nearby, the **Best Western Surf Motel** ❷, 2105 Center St., offers comfortable rooms and amenities including an exercise room, whirlpool, and game room. (☎785-562-2354. Singles $52; doubles $57. AmEx/D/DC/MC.)

⛏ APPROACHING HANOVER: 17 MILES

Sticking with the Oregon Trail, head west on **Center St.** out of Marysville; it becomes **U.S. 36 W.** Head north on **Rte. 148** for about 5 mi. to reach Hanover.

HANOVER. Hollenberg Station Historic Site, 2889 23rd Rd., was a store and rest stop for Oregon Trail travelers that also served as a Pony Express relay station. The **visitors center** has a gallery on pioneer life and opens onto a short trail lined with info stations. The path sometimes has demos on the art of trail cooking—a fine skill for roadtrippers past and present. Still standing after all these years, the station at the end of the trail is open for exploration, including the attic where Pony Express riders could rest on their dash westward. (In Hanover, Rte. 243 will be on the right. ☎785-337-2635. Open Mar.-Nov. W-Sa 9am-5pm, Su 1-5pm; Dec.-Feb. by appointment only. $3, students and seniors $2.)

◤ DETOUR
THE GEOGRAPHIC CENTER OF THE US

Get back on U.S. 36 W. At the town of Lebanon, the route turns north onto U.S. 281. 1 mi. after turning onto U.S. 281 N, take a left onto Rte. 191.

In the middle of the Kansas prairie, a stone monument marks the geographic center of the United States. Established in 1898 by government surveyors, the site became the "historical" center of the contiguous states after Alaska and Hawaii joined the Union in 1959.

⛏ APPROACHING HASTINGS: 129 MILES

Get back on **U.S. 281.** From there, it is a 40 mi. journey across the Kansas-Nebraska border to the city of **Red Cloud** (birthplace of writer Willa Cather), then another 40 mi. to Hastings. The road is long, but cloud-chasing passes the time away. **U.S. 281** bends to the east after passing the Hastings city limits, then immediately takes a sharp turn to the left. At this point it changes its name to **Burlington Ave.;** this road runs through the center of Hastings.

The Cornhusker State

NEBRASKA

Welcomes You!

HASTINGS

To those who don't look too hard, Hastings is a typical residential city, but beneath its suburban skin, Hastings is a funky place fit for any roadtripper. It's the birthplace of Kool-Aid, home to a great summer festival, and a haven of cheap hotels—it doesn't get much better than that in Nebraska.

VITAL STATS

Population: 24,000

Visitor Info: Hastings Visitors Center, 100 N. Shore Dr. (☎402-461-2370; www.visithastingsnebraska.com), off Burlington Ave. near the northern edge of the city. Open M-F 10am-5pm.

Internet Access: Hastings Public Library, 517 W. 4th St. (☎402-461-2346). Open M-Th 9am-9pm, F 9am-6pm, Sa 9am-5pm. Sept.-May M-Th 9am-9pm, F 9am-6pm, Sa 9am-5pm, Su 1-5pm. Free.

Post Office: 900 E. South St. (☎402-463-3107). **Postal Code:** 68901.

GETTING AROUND. Burlington Ave. is Hastings' main drag and runs north-south through the city. Numbered streets run east-west very close together, so almost everything is found on some easy-to-locate corner.

SIGHTS. In the evening, be sure to visit **Fisher Fountain,** at the corner of Denver and 12th St. Lighting in the fountain creates amazing illuminated water displays every night between Mother's Day and Labor Day. The **Hastings Museum of Natural and Cultural History,** 1330 N. Burlington Ave, at 14th St., can provide an entire day of entertainment. The main floor is a hall of stuffed wildlife from all over the world, while the upper level extends the same treatment to birds. Best of all is the **Kool-Aid exhibit,** located on the lower level, which traces the evolution of the sugary, colorful beverage from its origins in 1927, through its development into the Kool-Aid kid (a geeky mascot with knee socks), and its final maturation into the jolly Kool-Aid man we all know and fear. (☎402-461-4629 or 800-508-4629; www.hastingsmuseum.org. Open M-W 9am-5pm, Th-Sa 9am-8pm, Su 10am-6pm. Museum and planetarium $6, ages 3-12 $4.)

FOOD AND ACCOMMODATIONS. Big Dally's Deli ❶, 801 2nd St., offers exactly 50 different sandwiches, not one of them over $6. (☎402-463-7666. Open daily 7:30am-3:30pm. AmEx/D/MC.) Tucked into a plaza at the intersection of Burlington Ave. and 4th St., **Mr. Goodcent's ❶** breaks the chain of burger and steak shops; pastas and subs dominate. The chicken parmesan pasta ($4.30) is excellent. (☎402-463-3800. Entrees $3-5.30. Open M-Th and Su 10am-9pm, F-Sa 10am-10pm. AmEx/D/MC/V.)

Three well-priced hotels are found along U.S. 281 just after entering Hastings. The **Rainbow Motel ❷,** 1000 W. J St., has amazingly comfortable and well-furnished singles. (☎402-463-2989. Singles $40. AmEx/D/MC/V.) The **X-L Motel ❷,** at the intersection of U.S. 281 and U.S. 6, has large, clean rooms, as well as a pool, sauna and laundry facilities. (☎402-463-3148. Singles $31-35; doubles $40.) The **Midlands Lodge ❷,** 910 W. J St., has a heated outdoor pool, continental breakfast, and full-sized refrigerators. (☎402-463-2428. Singles $32; doubles $38. D/MC/V.)

DETOUR
HAROLD WARP PIONEER VILLAGE

138 E. Hwy. 6. At the southern border of Hastings, U.S. 281 N takes an abrupt right turn. Turn left at this intersection to reach U.S. 6. The village is 30 mi. down U.S. 6, at the intersection with Rte. 10.

Mr. Warp's collection of antique planes, cars, newspapers, medical instruments, and handicrafts creates the king of all timelines. Twenty-six buildings, some of them hangar-sized, house relics from different aspects of life. The chronological organization is meant to provide a tour of "mankind's progress since 1830." An official **Pioneer Village Hotel** sits next door for visitors who want to see everything. (☎308-832-1181; www.pioneervillage.org. Open daily May-Aug. 8am-6pm; Sept.-Apr. 9am-4:30pm. $9.50, ages 6-12 $5.)

▣ DETOUR

FORT KEARNEY STATE HISTORICAL PARK AND RECREATION AREA

1020 V Rd. 10 mi. up Rte. 10, take Link 50A west to the fort.

The historical park is a reconstruction of Fort Kearney, which evolved from a wilderness protection post into a busy rest stop for 49ers and the Pony Express. The fort was abandoned after the Civil War, but the smithy, stockade, and powder magazine are open to visitors. The grounds take a few minutes to explore, but the recreation area to the east has over 150 acres for hiking and exploring. For a few weeks in early spring, sandhill cranes flock here on their way north. (☎ 308-865-5305. Visitors center open daily 9am-5pm. Pass $3.)

▨ APPROACHING KEARNEY: 15 MILES

Immediately west of the Harold Warp Pioneer Village, the route to Kearney turns north along **Rte. 10** toward **I-80**. From there, it's about 15 mi. to Kearney. Get off I-80 at **Exit 272**, which will lead to **2nd Ave.** in southern Kearney.

KEARNEY

Home to part of the University of Nebraska, Kearney is by no means a big city, but it can still feel like one. There are fewer people, perhaps, and the buildings are smaller, but the chic cafes, chatting shoppers, bustling bars on Central Ave., and sense of fun are very much the same.

VITAL STATS

Population: 27,000

Visitor Info: Kearney Visitors Bureau, 17 2nd Ave. (☎ 308-237-3101 or 800-652-9435; www.kearney-coc.org). Open M-F 8am-6pm, Sa 9am-5pm, Su 1-4pm.

Internet Access: Kearney Public Library, 2020 1st Ave. (☎ 308-233-3282; www.kearneylib.org). Open M-Th 8:30am-9pm, F-Sa 8:30am-6pm. Free.

Post Office: 2401 Ave. E (☎ 308-234-4814), at the corner of 23rd St. Open M-F 8am-5pm, Sa 9am-11:30am. **Postal Code:** 66847.

▣ GETTING AROUND

While Kearney has a logical layout, it can still be a little quirky. Avenues run north-south, while streets run east-west. **Central Ave.** is the axis of the city. To the east of Central Ave., avenues are numbered, while to the west they are lettered. All streets are numbered, starting with 1st St.

◉ SIGHTS

Kearney is home to one of the most spectacular historical monuments on the Oregon Trail: ▨**The Great Platte River Road Archway Monument,** 3060 1st St. The archway spans all four lanes of I-80 just east of Kearney, its towers spreading huge metallic wings. After driving under it, continue a few more miles to Exit 272 and backtrack east on 1st St. to the parking lot. Visitors don headphones and ride up to the "trail" contained by the arch. Displays chronicle the evolution of I-80 from Oregon Trail to Union Pacific Railroad to modern highway. (☎ 308-877-511-2724; www.archway.org. Open daily 9am-6pm. $10, seniors $8.50, ages 13-18 $6, ages 6-12 $3.) Back in town, the **Museum of Nebraska Art,** 2401 Central Ave., is dedicated to works and artists connected to Nebraska. Despite its limited scope, the museum contains a variety of pieces, including fiber art and wall hangings. The first floor boasts an entire gallery of paintings by the naturalist John James Audubon. (☎ 308-865-8559. Open Tu-Sa 11am-5pm, Su 1-5pm. Free.)

The **Trails and Rails Museum,** 710 W. 11th St., is just a few blocks west. Though the museum does have a gallery on railways and a train in the yard, the real attraction is a set of historic buildings transported to this site to be viewed together. The buildings are only loosely organized by era, but each is interesting in its own right. The structures include a 19th-century schoolhouse, a log cabin, and the region's first frame house. (☎ 308-234-3041; http:// bchs.kearney.net/museum.html. Open June-Aug. M-Sa 10am-6pm, Su 1-5pm; Sept.-May M-F 1-5pm. $2, under 14 free.)

▚ FOOD

Despite its location near the city limits, it's almost impossible to miss **Pane Bello ❷,** 5004 2nd Ave. The restaurant is painted in retro earth colors—burnt orange and olive green. Delicious sandwiches ($3.50-6.50) compete with flatbread pizzas ($8.50) vie for customers' affection, but the Peasant Lunch—cheese, a baguette, and fruit for less than $3—is the real winner. (☎308-233-3677. Open M-F 6:30am-9pm, Sa 7am-9pm, Su 7:30am-9pm. AmEx/D/DC/MC/V.) Watch for the sign for **The Cellar ❹**, 3901 2nd Ave., which lurks beside a cluster of businesses. Though the food is not unusual, diners recline in a peaceful, candlelit atmosphere. (☎308-236-6541. Entrees $7-16. Open M-Sa 11am-11pm. AmEx/D/MC/V.) **Tex's Cafe ❷**, 23 21st St., is homey and informal. Though the chicken-fried steak is tempting, don't forget to check out the changing nightly specials. Dinners, complete with entree and sides, run $6.25. (☎308-234-3949. Open M-F 6am-4pm, Sa 6am-1pm. Cash only.)

█ ACCOMMODATIONS

Hotels line **2nd Ave.**, which is Kearney's busiest thoroughfare. The **Midtown Western Inn ❷**, 1401 2nd Ave., is one of the friendliest hotels around, with great rooms to boot. The A/C and pool help keep summer heat at bay, but the greatest amenity of all is the recliner in each room. (☎308-237-3153; www.midtownwest-erninn.com. Singles $44; doubles $48. AmEx/MC/V.) **The AmericInn ❸**, 215 W. Talmadge St., near the south end of 2nd Ave., offers large rooms, a beautiful indoor pool, continental breakfast, and a game room. (☎308-234-7800; www.americinn.com. Singles $65; doubles $75. AmEx/D/MC/V.) At the **Budget Motel South ❷**, 411 2nd Ave., roadtrippers can find clean, functional rooms at low rates as well as an indoor pool and sauna. (☎308-237-5991. Singles $42.50; doubles $45. AmEx/D/MC/V.)

█ NIGHTLIFE

Kearney offers a small but enjoyable selection of nightlife. The microbrewery at **Thunderhead Brewing**, 18 E. 21st St., just off Central Ave., won a gold medal at the World Beer Cup in 2006. Thunderhead also hosts free local music from Thursday to Saturday. Dollar pints on Wednesdays and penny pints on Thursdays help make this a great place to have a drink, play pool, and catch a show. (☎308-237-1558; www.thunderheadbrewing.com. Open daily 10am-1am. MC/V.) In true college-town style, **The Roman**, 2004 Central

Ave., serves pizza until 12:30am and offers daily $1 drink specials. (☎308-233-5173. Open Tu-Sa 5pm-1am. AmEx/D/MC/V.)

█ **APPROACHING LEXINGTON: 30 MILES**
Follow **2nd Ave. S**, then take the ramp onto **I-80**.

LEXINGTON

Lying about 30 mi. northwest of Kearney, little Lexington is still the largest town on the road. Within its borders, the odd and entertaining **Dawson County Historical Museum**, 805 N. Taft St., houses some highly irregular objects: the remains of Big Al the mammoth, a McCabe Aeroplane with its lens-shaped wings, and a set of 3D jigsaw puzzles assembled by a resident of the area. (☎308-324-5340; www.dchs-museum.com. Open M-Sa 9am-5pm. Free.)

Enjoy seriously cheap lunch specials at the **A&D Cafe ❷**, 604 N. Washington St. (Head north up Washington St. from U.S. 30. ☎308-324-5990. Open daily 6am-3pm. MC/V.) For something quick, check out **Kirk's Nebraskaland Restaurant ❸**, off I-80 at Exit 237, south of town, on the opposite side of the highway. Kirk's serves a lot of highway traffic, so it has a little of everything. Entrees come with a salad and side for $8-10. (☎308-324-6641. Appetizers $4-7. Open M-Th and Su 6am-midnight, F-Sa 6am-1am. AmEx/D/MC/V.) The few motels in Lexington are on **Plum Creek Pkwy.**, which links I-80 to town. Approaching from U.S. 30, Plum Creek Pkwy. is the large road to the south that crosses the bridge over the Platte River. Find fine rates and pleasant rooms at the **Gable View Inn ❷**, 2701 Plum Creek Pkwy. (☎308-324-5595. Singles $36; doubles $41. AmEx/D/MC/V.) The nearby **Minute Man Motel ❷**, 801 Plum Creek Pkwy., has good rates, similar rooms, and alliteration. (☎308-324-5544. Singles $38; doubles $42. AmEx/MC/V.)

█ **APPROACHING COZAD: 18 MILES**
Continue on **I-80** and take the exit for Cozad.

COZAD. Cozad founder John Cozad was struck by the grand sound of "100th Meridian." Though he vanished after a shooting, the 100th Meridian Museum, 206 8th St., honors the meridian that gave birth to the town. It contains local artifacts, such as photos of early residents. (Head north from U.S. 30 past the 100th Meridian sign. ☎308-784-1100. Open M-F 10am-5pm. Free.)

DID YOU KNOW? As trees and fuel became scarce around 1849 (when the Oregon Trail got crowded), travelers resorted to using bison dung to get their fires going.

APPROACHING NORTH PLATTE: 64 MILES
U.S. 30 passes through tiny Gothenburg, Brady, and Maxwell before North Platte. On the eastern edge of North Platte, U.S. 30 turns north suddenly, changing its name to **Rodeo Rd.** To reach the town center, continue, trading U.S. 30 for **E. 4th St.**, the biggest of the town's east-west roads.

NORTH PLATTE

As the last stop in the Wild West and the home of Buffalo Bill Cody himself, North Platte revels in its cowboy heritage. The city names everything it can in honor of that celebrated era: Cody Park, Rodeo Rd., and the Wild West Arena, for example. Though lacking in nightlife, North Platte parties in its own way—Western-style, of course. The Nebraskaland Days festival is the greatest incarnation of this spirit, spanning 12 days in early June and stirring up an Old West fury of rodeos and parades, and crowning the whole affair with the Miss Rodeo Pageant.

VITAL STATS

Population: 24,000

Visitor Info: North Platte Convention and Visitors Bureau, 219 S. Dewey St. (☎308-532-4729 or 800-955-4528; www.visitnorthplatte.com). Open M-F 8am-5pm.

Internet Access: North Platte Public Library, 121 W. 4th St. (☎308-535-8036). Open M and Th 9am-9pm, Tu-W and F-Sa 9am-6pm. Free.

Post Office: 1302 Industrial Ave. (☎308-532-3144). Open M-F 7:30am-5:30pm, Sa 8:30am-noon. **Postal Code:** 69101.

GETTING AROUND

The major roads of North Platte intersect downtown; **4th St.** runs east-west and **Jeffers St.** runs north-south. Most accommodations are on 4th St.; most food is on Jeffers or **Dewey St.**, which runs parallel to Jeffers St. one block west. A cluster of sites lies to the northwest on **Buffalo Bill Ave.**, which joins 4th St. on the western edge of the city.

SIGHTS

North Platte manages to squeeze a huge park, the home of an American legend, and a colossal rail station into its modest borders. This impressive feat is worthy of a day's pilgrimage. **Cody Park,** 1400 N. Jeffers St., off U.S. 30, is home to everything from a merry-go-round to peacocks and is a fusion of campground, zoo, and amusement park. The Wild West monument forms the park's entrance, commemorating Buffalo Bill's first rodeo, the Old Glory Blowout. (☎800-955-4528. Open daily sunrise-sunset. $2.50 per vehicle.) Farther up Buffalo Bill Ave. is **Scout's Rest,** once Buffalo Bill's home and now the **Buffalo Bill State Historical Park,** 2921 Scout's Rest Ranch Rd. William "Buffalo Bill" Cody was a Pony Express Rider, an army scout, and a spectacular showman. It was here that he laid his head when his world-traveling Wild West Show was between tours. The ranch in back has a collection of advertisements for the shows and a small theater where you can watch surviving footage of the performances. (☎308-535-8035; www.nypc.state.ne.us/cody.html. Open Memorial Day to Labor Day daily 9am-5pm; Labor Day to Oct. 1 and late Mar. to Memorial Day M-F 10am-4pm. $3.)

The highlight of the **Lincoln County Historical Museum and Village,** 2403 N. Buffalo Bill Ave., is an exhibit on the North Platte Canteen, an organization run by local women during WWII that provided food and supplies to soldiers passing through the area. (From U.S. 30, turn right on Buffalo Bill Ave. ☎308-534-5640; www.npcanteen.net. Open May to Labor Day M-Sa 9am-5pm, Su 1-5pm; Labor Day to Oct. 1 M-Sa 9am-5pm, Su 1-5pm. $3.) Just off 4th St. sits the **North Platte Area Children's Museum,** 314 N. Jeffers Ave. Each room presents a different type of hands-on educational entertainment, allowing children to be farmers, doctors, and firefighters. (☎800-955-4528. Open W and F 10am-3pm, Th 10am-8pm, Sa 10am-5pm, Su 1-5pm. $2.50.) Older children and adults may enjoy the **Bailey Yard,** a Union Pacific train yard through which 10,000 cars can pass daily.

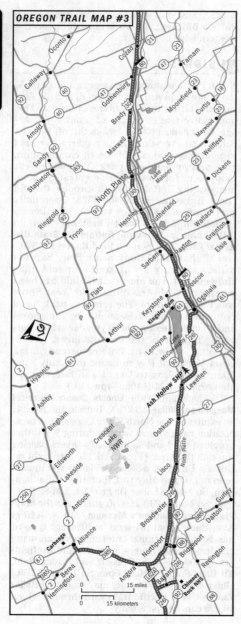

OREGON TRAIL MAP #3

FOOD

In the heart of steak country, North Platte is unabashedly a meat-eater's city. **Little Mexico Restaurant ❷**, 104 N. Jeffers St., serves 11 varieties of taco starting at just $2. (☎308-534-3052. Appetizers $6-10. Fajitas $7. Enchiladas $6. Open daily 11am-10pm. AmEx/MC/V.) The **Main Street Cafe ❷**, 517 N. Dewey St., has a small sandwich menu, but the real fun comes from joining the cafeteria-style line to see what's dished out from behind the counter. It's kind of like elementary school, but with much better food. (☎308-534-9335. Entrees $5-6. Open M-F 7am-2:30pm. MC/V.)

ACCOMMODATIONS

North Platte is graced with a cluster of budget motels. The **Rambler Motel ❷**, 1420 Rodeo Rd., on the edge of town near Scout's Rest, offers amazingly low rates for pleasant, quiet rooms, each with fridge, microwave, and pool access. (☎308-532-9290. Singles $28; doubles $35. AmEx/D/MC/V.) The **Blue Spruce Motel ❷**, 821 S. Dewey St., downtown, has rooms that are unusually large and well-furnished for the price. (☎308-534-2600. Free Wi-Fi. Singles $36; doubles $49. AmEx/D/MC/V.) A slightly upscale option, **Traveler's Inn ❷**, 602 E. 4th St., has a heated outdoor pool. (☎308-534-4020; www.bestvalueinn.com. Singles $40; doubles $55. AmEx/MC/V.) **Cody Park ❶** (p. 619) offers primitive campsites. (Sites $5.)

APPROACHING PAXTON: 34 MILES
Follow **Jeffers St.** heading south. Jeffers St. intersects **Rodeo Rd.**, which becomes **U.S. 30** outside Paxton.

PAXTON. Beef is on the menu at **◪Ole's Big Game Steakhouse ❸**, on Oak St., off U.S. 30, but every other kind of animal is on the wall. Ole's collection of hunting trophies includes the heads of a giraffe and an African elephant; however, even these are eclipsed by the full body of a gigantic polar bear that Ole took down himself. The food is just as impressive: the hamburgers (cow or buffalo; from $5) are thick and delicious, and the steaks (from $10) are no different. (☎308-239-4500; www.olesbiggame.com. Open daily 10am-midnight. AmEx/D/MC/V.)

Between Paxton and Ogallala, U.S. 30 passes into the Mountain Time Zone, where it is 1hr. earlier.

APPROACHING OGALLALA: 20 MILES
U.S. 30 becomes **1st St.**, making the approach to Ogallala a straight shot.

OGALLALA

The name is quite melodic after the first few stumbling tries—Ogallala. Like many of its neighbors, Ogallala basks in its rambunctious Old West heritage, but for visitors, Ogallala's primary attraction is the peaceful serenity of Lake McConaughy; the waters north of town are lined with beaches, fishing holes, campsites, and the first of western Nebraska's stunning hills.

VITAL STATS

Population: 5000

Visitor Info: Ogallala Visitors Center, 121 E. 2nd St. (☎308-284-4066). Open M-F 8am-5pm.

Internet Access: Goodall City Library, 203 W. A St. (☎308-284-4354). Open M-Th 9am-8pm, F-Sa 9am-5pm. Free.

Post Office: 301 N. Spruce St. (☎308-284-3251). Open M-F 8am-4:30pm, Sa 9am-11am. **Postal Code:** 69153.

GETTING AROUND. Ogallala's street layout can be a bit confusing. **1st St. (U.S. 30)** forms the central artery, running east-west through the city. Parallel streets increase sequentially as one travels north. **Spruce St.**, cutting north-south, is the other key route. Streets parallel to Spruce St. are lettered, but they come in pairs; one block east of Spruce is **E. A St.**, one block west is **W. A St.** As a result, E. E St. and W. E St. are nowhere near each other—they're 10 blocks apart.

SIGHTS. The largest attraction in Ogallala is **Lake McConaughy,** or "Big Mac," as it is affectionately known to locals. Rte. 61 runs northeast from town to the eastern end of the lake. Visitors are required to have a Nebraska State Parks sticker ($3) on their cars, available at the **visitors center,** 1475 Rte. 61, ¼ mi. before reaching the lake. Beyond the visitors center, the road leads over the magnificent

Kingsley Dam, a colossal feat of engineering. From there, five miles of shoreline present myriad possibilities: boating, fishing, swimming, **camping ❶,** or just relaxing on the beach. There is even an eagle observation post, though the birds are only present during the winter months. (☎308-284-8800. For more info on eagle viewing, call ☎308-284-2332. Primitive sites $5, with camping pad $10, with full hookup $18. MC/V.) There are also a few sights in the city itself, clustered conveniently in the **Front Street Arcade,** off 1st St. This strip of buildings is a re-created Old West main street, complete with hitching-post parking spots. The **Petrified Wood Gallery,** 525 E. 1st St., contains a large collection of wood-turned-stone, much of it brightly colored and spectacularly patterned. (☎308-284-9996 or 800-658-4390; www.petrifiedwoodgallery.com. Open Memorial Day to Labor Day M-Sa 10am-7pm; Apr. 1 to Memorial Day and Labor Day to Oct. 1 M-Sa 10am-4pm; Nov.-Dec. W-F 10am-4pm, Sa 10am-1pm.) Next door, the **Crystal Palace Revue** always seems to find itself at the center of a (staged) shootout, after which lovely young ladies put on old-style song-and-dance show that tells the story of Ogallala and the surrounding area. (☎308-284-6000. Shows daily Memorial Day to mid-Aug. 7:15pm. $4.25, ages 5-12 $2.75.)

FOOD AND ACCOMMODATIONS. Like the city itself, dining establishments in Ogallala are steeped in the character of the Old West. Part of the Crystal Palace scene, the **Front Street Steakhouse ❸,** 519 E. 1st St., is a good choice for dining in Ogallala. Local favorites include the Ogallala steak sandwich and the Crystal Palace steak sandwich for $6.50. (☎308-284-6000. Appetizers $3-7. Sandwiches $5-7. Entrees $8-12. Open daily 11am-9pm. AmEx/D/MC/V.) Lively **Hoke's Cafe ❸,** 302 E. 1st St., is a small-town diner with character. The decor is one of automobile worship—pictures and models are everywhere. (☎308-284-4654. Hot sandwiches $7-8. Country-style dinners $9. Steaks $15. Open Tu-Sa 6am-1pm and 5-8pm, Su 6am-1pm. MC/V.) **Spruce Street Sandwich Shop ❷,** 12 N. Spruce St., offers 32 different sandwiches ($4.50-7.50), as well as a guacamole burger. (☎308-284-4879. Open Tu-F 8am-7pm, Sa 8am-4pm. MC/V.)

Those who prefer not to camp at the lake will find in-town options, including the usual clump of chain motels off I-80, at the south end of Spruce St. **The Plaza Inn ❷**, 311 E. 1st St., features themed rooms, such as the Hollywood room and the Whirlpool room. (☎308-284-8416; www.staywithustheplazainn.com. Outdoor pool. Free Wi-Fi. Singles $35; whirlpool room $60. AmEx/D/DC/MC/V.) Just across the South Platte River is the **Grey Goose Lodge ❸**, 201 Chuckwagon Rd., a fine hotel with comfortable rooms and nice facilities, including an indoor pool. (☎308-284-3623 or 800-573-7148. Singles $69; doubles $74. AmEx/MC/V.)

⚑ APPROACHING WINDLASS HILL AND ASH HOLLOW: 12 MILES
Head north on **East A St.**, following signs toward Lake McConaughy until it merges into **Spruce St.** Head north for several miles to the junction with Rte. 61 and U.S. 26. Turn left, and go west on **U.S. 26.**

WINDLASS HILL AND ASH HOLLOW. Windlass Hill is named for the legend that wagons had to be lowered down its slope with a winch, though no evidence of such a device survives. The hill is quite steep, though, and visitors should be prepared for a climb. The view from the top over the lonely ravines of western Nebraska is lovely. Down the road at Ash Hollow is a small visitors center and the **Ash Hollow Cave.** Most Oregon Trail sites are only about 150 years old; this cave has been inhabited for six millennia. Displays include artifacts from the cave dating from the prehistoric era all the way to the mid-19th century when trappers and pioneers used the cave for shelter. (☎308-778-5651. Open Tu-Su 10am-4pm. $3.)

⚑ APPROACHING BRIDGEPORT: 50 MILES
Follow **U.S. 26** to where it crosses the North Platte River into Bridgeport.

BRIDGEPORT

Bridgeport's primary attractions are **Courthouse Rock** and **Jail Rock,** the first of the bizarre stone formations that mark the end of the first leg of the Oregon Trail. Less celebrated and less spectacular than Chimney Rock or Scotts Bluff, both are best viewed from Main St., 4 mi. south. A quick historical diversion is available at the **Pioneer Trails Museum,** on Main St., at the north end of town. (☎308-262-0108. Open daily 9am-6pm. Free.)

Cheap food can be found at **Karette's Drive-In ❶**, 409 Main St. (☎308-262-0790. Open daily 11am-10pm. Cash or check only.) **The Bridgeport Inn ❷**, 517 Main St., is a star among budget motels. Huge and well-furnished, the rooms look like they're from a considerably higher price bracket. (☎760-932-7380. Singles $43; doubles $50. D/MC/V.)

⚑ APPROACHING ALLIANCE: 30 MILES
Returning up **Main St.** onto **U.S. 26** and crossing the North Platte River leads to the junction with **U.S. 385.** Take U.S. 385 to **3rd St.**, the main street of Alliance.

ALLIANCE. The real reason for visiting Alliance is **◙Carhenge,** a monument exactly like England's Stonehenge—except that it was constructed entirely out of cars. Maybe profound, maybe a junkyard, it's definitely worth seeing. Surrounding the automobile monoliths is an outdoor gallery of stacked cars, automobile towers, a dinosaur car, and a vehicle-turned-salmon; it really must be seen to be believed. (Head east on 3rd St. for 3 mi., and turn north on Rte. 87. Free.) To purchase Carhenge souvenirs, visit the **Alliance Chamber of Commerce,** 124 W. 3rd St. (☎308-762-1520; www.alliancechamber.com. Open daily 8:30am-5pm.) **Ken & Dale's Restaurant ❸**, 123 E. 3rd St., is a family restaurant that serves up liver ($5), veal ($5.50), and rainbow trout ($10), among other options. (☎308-762-7252. Open M-Sa 6am-9:30pm, Su 6am-8pm. AmEx/D/MC/V.) The **West Way Motel ❷**, 1207 W. 3rd St., maintains comfortable rooms. (☎308-762-4040. Singles $34; doubles $39. D/MC/V.) The **Rainbow Motel ❶**, 614 W. 3rd St., has standard amenities as well as guest laundry facilities. (☎308-762-4980. Singles from $25; doubles from $32. AmEx/MC/V.)

⚑ APPROACHING BAYARD: 39 MILES
Head west on **3rd St.** to the junction with **Rte. 385** and return south. To take a shortcut to Chimney Rock, head west on **Link 62A,** just south of Angora. To get to Bayard, head south on **U.S. 26.**

BAYARD. Bayard serves as the jumping-off point for the **Oregon Trail Wagon Train,** 1 mi. east of Oregon Trail Rd. and 2 mi. south of Bayard. This service gives travelers with time and money a chance to experience life on the trail. Covered wagon treks wind through the Chimney Rock area, where "pioneers" cook over campfires. The four-day trek includes horse-back riding, riflery, a Pony Express delivery, and an Indian raid. For something less time-consuming, chuckwagon cookouts with a short wagon tour are also available. (☎308-586-1850; www.oregontrailwagontrain.com. Reservations required. 24hr. trek $200, children $175; 4-day trek $575/$475; cookouts $19/$9.50.) **Pizza Point ❶**, 106 E. 2nd St., is a hometown pizza joint offering personal pizzas ($3) for the solo roadtripper or large pizzas ($9.75) for entire families. (☎308-586-2255. Corndogs $1. Open M-Sa 11am-9pm, Su 4-8pm. Cash only.)

⋈ DETOUR
CHIMNEY ROCK NATIONAL HISTORIC SITE
Head south on U.S. 26, then turn west on Rte. 92. Follow the signs over dirt roads to the visitors center.

Western Nebraska was once a vast, high-elevation plain of clay and volcanic ash. As wind and water wore the surface down to present-day levels, caps of harder stone resisted erosion, protecting the ash underneath. Thus Chimney Rock, a delicate spire of vulcan material topped with stone, was formed. Visible for miles around, the Chimney was one of the best-known landmarks along the Oregon Trail, mentioned in surviving diaries more than any other landmark. Today, due to prairie conservation efforts and the threat of rattlesnakes, visitors are asked to stay at the visitors center rather than approach the rock. A closer look is achieved by driving farther down the dirt road, which terminates close to the rock near a cemetery dedicated to the pioneers. (☎308-586-2581; www.nps.gov/chro. Visitors center open Memorial Day to Labor Day daily 9am-5pm; Labor Day to Memorial Day Tu-Su 9am-5pm. $3.)

⚎ APPROACHING SCOTTSBLUFF: 24 MILES
From Chimney Rock, it's only 20 mi. west along **U.S. 26** to Scottsbluff. To go straight to the city, stay on **U.S. 26,** which runs through northwest Scottsbluff, connecting directly to **20th St.** in the eastern part of the city and **Ave. I** in the north.

SCOTTSBLUFF

Scottsbluff, Gering, and the intermediate region of Terrytown all lie in the shadow of Scotts Bluff, the towering rock formation that gives the largest of the cities its name. The cities themselves support a downtown and some worthwhile restaurants, but the bluffs dominate the skyline; manmade attractions just can't compete with nature here.

VITAL STATS

Population: 15,000

Visitor Info: Scottsbluff/Gering United Chamber of Commerce, 1517 Broadway (☎308-632-2133; ww.scottsbluffgering.net). Open M-F 8am-5pm.

Internet Access: Scottsbluff Public Library, 1809 3rd Ave. (☎308-630-6250; www.scottsbluff.org/lib). Open M-Th 9am-8pm, F-Sa 9am-6pm, Su 2-5pm. Free.

Post Office: 112 W. 20th St. (☎308-635-1121). Open M-F 8:30am-4:30pm, Sa 9:15am-11am. **Postal Code:** 69361.

▨ GETTING AROUND

Scottsbluff is the biggest city in western Nebraska but shares many of its services and much of its bustle with the smaller city of Gering to the south. The two also share the same main street, which changes its name at the border. In Gering it's called **10th St.;** in Scottsbluff, **Broadway.** This road is the largest and most direct link between the two. Unless otherwise noted, all listings are in Scottsbluff. The north-south roads in Scottsbluff are avenues. To the west of Broadway they are lettered; to the east, they are numbered. The east-west roads are streets and are numbered. **1st St.** is near the Gering border, and street numbers increase heading north. Don't confuse these with 10th St. in Gering, which runs north-south and becomes Broadway at the Scottsbluff city limits.

◎ SIGHTS

The city's name sums up its attractions well; **Scotts Bluff National Monument** is one of the largest and most accessible of the rock formations along this part of the trail. At the base of the bluff, the **Scotts Bluff Visitors Center** presents the history of the Oregon Trail. The bluff can be scaled by car, shuttle, or the **Saddle Rock Trail** (1½ mi.), which is steep and winding but worth the effort, cutting up the cliff face and straight through the rock to the other side of the bluff. For pioneers, Pony Express riders, and roadtrippers, this marks the completion of the first third of the trail. (On Rte. 92. 3 mi. west of Gering. ☎308-436-4340. Open daily 8am-7pm. $5 per vehicle. Trail maps $0.50.) For more local history, head to the **North Platte Valley Museum,** at 11th and J St., in Gering, which has objects from and dioramas of 19th-century pioneer life as well as Native American culture. Also check out the wall diagramming the evolution of the Nebraska license plate. (Head south on 10th St. in Gering; after the sign, turn right onto Overland Trails Rd. for parking. ☎308-436-5411; www.npvm.com. Open M-F 9am-4pm, Sa-Su 1-4pm. $3, ages 5-12 $1.) The **Riverside Zoo,** 1600 S. Beltline, is home to a white tiger and two African lions, as well as a moose and a red panda. (☎308-630-6236. Open Mar.-Nov. daily 9:30am-4:30pm; Dec.-Feb. Sa-Su 10am-4pm. $2.50, seniors $2, ages 5-12 $1.)

PHOTO OP. Located east of town at Lake Minatare is **Nebraska's only lighthouse.** Yup, lighthouse. Head east for 11 mi. on U.S. 26, then north for another 9 mi. on Stone Gate Rd. Once at the lake, a short jaunt down The Point Rd. leads to the structure, which, needless to say, seems a little out of place.

▓ FOOD

▓ **Scotty's,** 618 E. 27th St. (☎308-635-3314). The epitome of American dining. Burgers ($1), hot dogs ($1), and glorious french fries ($1). Open June-Aug. M-Th and Su 10am-10:30pm, F-Sa 10am-11:30pm; Sept.-May M-Th and Su 10am-10pm, F-Sa 10am-11pm. AmEx/MC/V. ❶

Wonderful House Restaurant, 829 Ferdinand Plaza (☎308-632-1668). Conventional and super yummy Chinese fare. Lunch specials (11am-3pm) include entree, egg roll, crab rangoon, rice, and fortune cookie for $5.50. Appetizers $4-7.50. Entrees $7-19. Open M-Th 11am-9:30pm, F-Sa 11am-10pm, Su 11am-9pm. AmEx/MC/V. ❸

Bush's Gaslight Restaurant & Lounge, 3315 N. 10th St. (☎308-632-7315), in Gering. Pleasant for relaxing, with a dining room fireplace and comfortable lounge. Chicken, seafood, and steak entrees at moderate to expensive prices. Entrees $9-40. Open M-Th and Su 4:30-10pm, F-Sa 4:30-11:30pm. MC/V. ❸

Prime Cut, 305 W. 27th St. (☎308-632-5353). Full steak dinners for less than $8 as well as chicken, sausage, and salad meals. Old tools and photographs lend an antique aura. Open M-Th and Su 11am-9pm, F-Sa 11am-10pm. MC/V. ❷

▓ ACCOMMODATIONS

Scottsbluff has a decent selection of hotels and motels, though they're rather scattered. Chain accommodations can be found along **E. 20th St.** and **Ave. I,** near U.S. 26.

Sands Motel, 814 W. 27th St. (☎308-632-6191). Functional rooms and some of the best rates in town. Singles from $32; doubles from $34. AmEx/D/MC/V. ❷

Lamplighter American Inn, 606 E. 27th St. (☎308-632-7108). Quite nice for its low price; spacious rooms, and an indoor pool. Singles $40; doubles $43. AmEx/MC/V. ❷

Microtel Inn, 1130 M St. (☎308-436-1951), in Gering. Unbeatable location, just minutes from the Scotts Bluff monument. Pool and fitness center. Singles $65; doubles $60. AmEx/MC/V. ❸

Capri Motel, 2424 Ave. I (☎308-635-2057). Travelers approaching Scottsbluff from U.S. 26 will find this spot easily, just down Ave. I. Pleasant and clean rooms. Singles $35; doubles $40. AmEx/MC/V. ❷

Riverside Campground, 1600 S. Beltline (☎308-632-6342), right next to the zoo. Showers and bathrooms. Gates closed 11pm-5am. Primitive sites $5, with water $10, with full hookup $15. Cash only. ❶

▓ ENTERTAINMENT

Although Scottsbluff doesn't have the bumpin' nightlife of a larger city, good fun is out there. **Theatre West Summer Repertory,** 1601 E. 27th St., at the back of the Nebraska Community College Campus, puts on a varied series of shows each summer. (☎308-632-2226. Box office open M-F 9am-4pm, Sa 1-5pm.) Fun, offbeat, and for almost everyone, **Pelini's Jazz and Comedy Club,** 15 E. 16th St., has musical nights, improv shows, stand-up comedy, and even puppetry acts. This "family nightclub" has a non-alcoholic bar in addition to the usual drinks. (☎308-632-6800. Hours vary depending on shows; call ahead.)

⚑ APPROACHING TORRINGTON: 32 MILES
Head north on **Broadway** to its end, and turn right onto **27th St.** Follow 27th until it merges with **U.S. 26**, heading toward Wyoming.

TORRINGTON. Small enough that many drivers might blast on through, Torrington has some roadtripper-friendly spots worth seeing. The **Homesteader's Museum,** 495 Main St. (U.S. 85), is a good place to stretch your legs and learn some history. The museum displays quite a collection of cowboy paraphernalia, focusing on the Homestead period after the era of overland emigration. (☎307-532-5612. Open Memorial Day to Labor Day M-W 9:30am-4pm, Th-F 9:30am-7pm, Sa noon-6pm, Su noon-4pm; Labor Day to Memorial Day M-F 9:30am-4pm. Free.) **Chicken Hut ❷,** 650 E. Valley Rd. (US. 26), gives new meaning to the phrase "tastes like chicken." Though large portions of traditionally fast, classic roadtrip fare grace the menu, the fried chicken makes contemplating a hamburger a crime. (☎307-532-4441. Open daily 10:30am-9pm. AmEx/MC/V.) **Blue Lantern Motel ❷,** on Main St. (U.S. 85), near the intersection with E. Valley Rd. (U.S. 26), offers comfortable rooms at affordable prices. (Singles $30; doubles $35. AmEx/MC/V.)

⚑ APPROACHING LINGLE: 10 MILES
Continue on **U.S. 26** to Lingle. Watch out here: U.S. 26 makes a 90 degree turn with little fanfare.

LINGLE. Right outside of town is the **Western History Center,** 2308 U.S. 26. A sort of archaeological display gallery, the Western History Center showcases mammoth remains, 10,000-year-old arrowheads, and fossils dating as far back as the Cretaceous Period. Temporary exhibits display everything from international doll collections to ornamental swords, providing an exciting alterna-

tive to traditional Oregon Trail museums. (☎307-837-3052. Open M-Sa 10am-4pm, Su 1-4pm. $1.50.)

◫ DETOUR
FORT LARAMIE NATIONAL HISTORIC SITE
965 Gray Rocks Rd. Follow the signs from the town of Ft. Laramie (pop. 256; according to the sign, "250 good people and 6 sore heads"). The fort is a few miles south of town along Gray Rocks Rd. (Rte. 160).

Fort Laramie was a critical outpost along the overland trails, serving as a central base for the US Army during its violent clashes with tribes led by Red Cloud, Crazy Horse, and Sitting Bull. The visitors center provides an informative video on Fort Laramie's role in these events and is also the starting point for self-guided tours. Audio headsets and guided tours are also available. Sights include the fully restored cavalry barracks, the captain's quarters, and "old Bedlam"—the bachelors' dormitory. The **Soldier's Bar** sells (soft) drinks for just $1, served in chilled bottles by a barkeep in 19th-century attire. (☎307-837-2221; www.nps.gov/fola. Grounds open daily sunrise-sunset. Visitors center open daily 8am-7pm. $3.)

⚑ APPROACHING GUERNSEY: 11 MILES
Follow **U.S. 26** to where it becomes **Whalen St.** in the center of Guernsey.

GUERNSEY

Guernsey divides two different landscapes; just beyond the town, the Rocky Mountains rise suddenly into view. Nineteenth-century travelers often considered Guernsey's Register Cliff to be the real marker of the Rockies' borders. Between the names carved into the cliffs long ago and the beauty of Guernsey State Park, the town maintains the adventurous feel of something new.

VITAL STATS

Population: 1150

Visitor Info: Guernsey Visitor Center, 90 S. Wyoming Rd. (☎307-836-2715). Open M-Sa 9am-7pm, Su noon-4pm.

Internet Access: North Platte County Public Library, Guernsey Branch, 108 S. Wyoming Rd. (☎307-836-2816). Open M and W noon-7pm, Tu and Th noon-5pm, F noon-4pm, Sa 9am-11am. Free.

Post Office: 401 S. Wyoming Rd. (☎307-836-2804). Open M-F 8:30am-5pm. **Postal Code:** 82214.

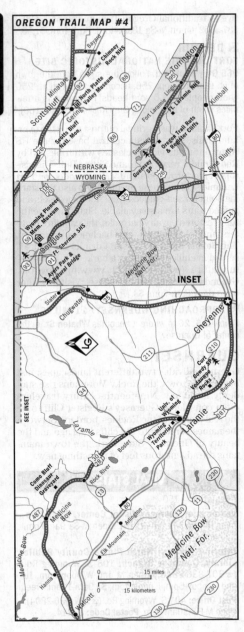

OREGON TRAIL MAP #4

INSET

SEE INSET

0   15 miles

0   15 kilometers

GETTING AROUND. U.S. 26 runs through the center of Guernsey as **Whalen St.** Most sights and establishments line the main drag of **Wyoming Ave.** south of its intersection with Whalen St.

SIGHTS. At **Oregon Trail Ruts State Historic Site,** off Wyoming Ave. about a mile down rough dirt roads, a short climb through the wooded hills reveals deep scars left in the rock by the thousands of wagons that traversed the Oregon and Mormon Trails. Two miles farther down Wyoming Ave. is **Register Cliff,** a soft, sheer face where pioneers sometimes carved their names. (☎307-836-2334. Open daily sunrise-sunset. Free.)

Just west of town on U.S. 26, Rte. 317 heads north. A few miles up Rte. 317 is **Guernsey State Park,** with 8500 acres of cliffs, forested hills, and reservoir waters. A drive through the park is rewarding, but swimming, boating, and camping are also available. The winding road leads to the visitors center, which has a few historical displays and explains of the formation of the strata in the cliffs. (☎307-836-2334. Visitors center open mid-May to Labor Day daily 10am-6pm. Park open 8am-10pm. $4 per car.)

FOOD AND ACCOMMODATIONS. **Rob's Riverview Restaurant ❷,** 501 W. Laramie St., off U.S. 26, at the west end of town, has nature-inspired decor and huge windows overlooking the North Platte. Titanic burgers (½ lb. $6) are available, as well as sandwiches like the honey mustard melt. Those on the go can grab a sandwich, chips, fruit, and two cookies for just $3. (☎307-836-2191. Entrees $5.50-7. Open daily 6am-10pm. AmEx/D/MC/V.) For a leisurely dinner, try the **Trail Inn ❷,** 27 N. Wyoming Ave., which offers Mexican, American, and Italian dishes. The Trash Can Special ($7.75), includes 10 different dishes. (☎307-836-2010. Entrees $4-9. Open Tu-Sa 11am-10pm, Su 11am-2pm. AmEx/MC/V.)

Those looking for places to stay needn't leave U.S. 26. The **Bunkhouse Motel ❷,** on U.S. 26, in town, has a fridge in every room and a barbecue pit for guest use. (☎307-836-2356. Singles $44; doubles $50. AmEx/MC/V.) The simple, clean rooms at **Sagebrush Motel ❷,** 151 W. Whalen St., come with microwaves and refrigerators. (☎307-836-2331. Singles $32; doubles $37. AmEx/MC/V.)

⚐ APPROACHING DOUGLAS: 43 MILES
Whalen St. leads west, becoming **U.S. 26** again outside of town. U.S. 26 lasts another 15 mi. before terminating at **I-25**, but the road is glorious. At the junction with I-25, turn north. **Exit 135** leads to **Bus. 1-25;** a right from here onto **S. 4th St.** leads directly to **Center St.** and downtown Douglas.

DOUGLAS

Douglas is recognized as an overland trails landmark, the setting of Owen Wister's *The Virginian*, and the descendant of Ft. Fetterman. The city puts these honors gracefully aside, however, choosing to wear a more majestic crown: home and breeding grounds of the mighty jackalope. For a supposedly reclusive creature, the deer-rabbit cross-breed shows up surprisingly often in store fronts and gift shops. One even stands sentinel on a hilltop outside the town along U.S. 30. Skeptics, beware: Douglas is proud of its chimeric mascot and does not take kindly to the suggestion that the creature is, just maybe, a myth.

VITAL STATS

Population: 5300

Visitor Info: Douglas Area Chamber of Commerce, 121 Brownfield St. (☎307-358-2950; www.jackalope.org), just off Center St., a few blocks west of downtown. Open M-F 8am-5pm.

Internet Access: Converse County Library, 300 Walnut St. (☎307-358-3644). Open M and Sa 9am-2pm, Tu and Th 9am-8pm, W and F 9am-6pm. Free.

Post Office: 129 N. 3rd St. (☎307-358-9358). Open M-F 8am-5pm, Sa 10am-12:30pm. **Postal Code:** 82633.

⚑ GETTING AROUND. Douglas is bordered by **Antelope Creek** to the west and I-25 to the south. Numbered streets run north-south through the city, with **Bus. I-25** running between 3rd and 5th St. The downtown area, home to a pleasant combination of bookshops and barbershops, is focused around the intersection of **Center St.**, a main east-west thoroughfare, and **3rd St.**

◪ SIGHTS. The first of Douglas's famed antlered rabbits was "discovered" in 1939 by a local taxidermist. Today, a giant version of the wild

creature stands, horned and alert, in **Centennial Jackalope Square,** at 3rd and Center St. Noble, fearsome, and taller than any man, he is a striking presence. The surrounding park is a pleasant picnic spot, and an info booth in the square advertises local events and relates town history. The **Pioneer Memorial Museum,** 400 W. Center St., in the state fairgrounds, is the king of local history museums, with expansive displays on cowboy, Native American, and domestic pioneer life, and a gift shop. One gallery is dedicated to area cowboys, displaying the tools and weapons of their dusty but romantic profession. Most impressive is the Native American gallery, showcasing earthenware, weavings, and, oddly enough, a teepee used in the movie *Dances With Wolves.* (☎307-358-9288. Open M-F 8am-5pm, Sa 1-5pm. Free.)

It's a bit of a drive from the city itself, but the **Ft. Fetterman Historic Site** tells an interesting chapter in the story begun at Fort Laramie. A short video, a museum, and a few surviving buildings recall this fort's central role in the "Great Sioux War" that ensued when Red Cloud, Crazy Horse, and others struck against the miners invading the Black Hills. The attacks led to the abandonment of all the forts along the Bozeman Trail except one—Fort Fetterman. Though smaller than Fort Laramie, Fetterman was closer to the action and played a more pivotal role in that legendary conflict. (☎307-358-2864 or 307-684-7629. Open daily Memorial Day to Labor Day 9am-5pm. $2.)

◪⚑ FOOD AND ACCOMMODATIONS. The dark side of Douglas is its glut of chain restaurants, but fortunately, a few independent spots still remain. The crowds that pack **The Koop ❶,** 108 N. 3rd St., testify to the fine food offered here. Don't be fooled by the generic menu; the burgers ($4-8) are truly delicious, and the curly fries are the stuff of culinary legend. Shakes, malts, and floats ($2-3) finish meals off right. (☎307-358-3509. Open M-F 6am-3pm, Sa 7am-2pm. AmEx/MC/V.) **La Costa ❸,** 1600 E. 2nd St., offers an extensive menu, with separate sections for chicken, meat, and egg dishes, along with enchiladas, burritos, and tostadas. (☎207-235-6599. Entrees $7-11. Open M-Th 11am-10pm, F-Sa 11am-10:30pm, Su 11am-9pm. AmEx/MC/V.)

One of the best is the **4 Winds Motel ❷,** 615 E. Richards St. Remodeled by new owners, this motel is sparkling clean and boasts free

Wi-Fi. Several sizes of rooms are available, allowing those with smaller (or larger) wallets to find something to their satisfaction. (☎307-358-2322. Singles from $37; doubles from $44. AmEx/MC/V.) The **Morton Mansion Bed and Breakfast** ❸ is a worthwhile stay for travelers with a little money to spare. The building, which is listed on the historic register, has a pleasantly open, airy feeling with a nicely understated decor. The seven rooms all have private baths. (☎307-358-2129. Rooms $65-125. AmEx/MC/V.) The **Plains Motel** ❷, 841 S. 6th St., has simple but cheap rooms near the fast food and gas stations of E. Richards St. (☎307-358-4484. Singles $32; doubles $34. AmEx/MC/V.)

⧉ DETOUR
AYRES NATURAL BRIDGE

From Douglas, continue heading west along I-25 N. After about 10 mi., take Exit 151 and head 5 mi. south along the road to the bridge.

La Prele Creek still flows beneath the arch it carved into a narrow band of rock that blocked its path. Far from the highway, and enclosed on either side by great red cliffs, the little park surrounding the bridge is idyllic; at the top of the narrow path that leads onto the bridge, the only sounds are birdsong and flowing water. (☎307-358-3532. Open Apr.-Oct. daily 8am-8pm. Free. Some camping permitted; consult the caretaker.)

The going gets pretty rough in the not-so-distant future, and the **Alcova Backcountry Byway** (p. 632) is nearly impossible in winter. If your car can't handle the driving, or if it's winter, head on through Douglas, continuing west on **I-25** through Casper and picking up the route at **Alcova** (p. 632).

⧉ APPROACHING CHEYENNE: 124 MILES

Turn around and head south on **I-25**, past the junction with U.S. 26. Head through the towns of Wheatland and Chugwater to Cheyenne. Stay on I-25 through the periphery of the city until it divides: I-25 will continue straight south, while U.S. 85/87 will peel off to the southeast. Stay on I-25 until the exit for **Central Ave.**, which will take you across **E. Pershing Ave.** and into the central downtown area.

CHEYENNE

"Cheyenne," the name of the Native American tribe that originally inhabited this region, was once considered a prime candidate for the name of the whole Wyoming territory. The moniker was vetoed by the notoriously priggish Senator Sherman, who pointed out that the pronunciation of Cheyenne closely resembled that of the French word *chienne*, meaning "bitch." Once one of the fastest-growing frontier towns, Cheyenne may have slowed down a bit, but its historical downtown area still exhibits traditional Western charm, complete with simulated gunfights.

⧉ GETTING AROUND

Three streets run parallel to each other through downtown—**Carey Ave., Capitol Ave.,** and **Central Ave.** Perpendicular to these streets are a series of numbered roads, increasing from south to north. Downtown is roughly between **Lincolnway** (16th St.) and **Pershing Ave.,** just north of 30th St. Free 2hr. parking is available downtown, but finding a place can be difficult. Visitors should claim a spot, then walk.

VITAL STATS

Population: 53,000

Visitor Info: Cheyenne Visitors Center, 121 W. 15th St. (☎307-778-3133 or 800-426-5009; www.cheyenne.org), on the 1st fl. of the Cheyenne Depot, at the end of Capitol Ave. Open May-Sept. M-F 8am-7pm, Sa 9am-5pm; Oct.-Apr. M-F 8am-5pm, Sa 9am-5pm, Su 11am-5pm.

Internet Access: Laramie County Public Library, 2800 Central Ave. (☎307-634-3561). Open May 16-Sept. 14 M-Th 10am-9pm, F-Sa 10am-6pm; Sept. 15-May 15 M-Th 10am-9pm, F-Sa 10am-6pm, Su 1-5pm. Free.

Post Office: 4800 Converse Ave. (☎307-772-7080). Take Lincolnway east, then head north on Converse Ave. past Dell Range Blvd. Open M-F 7:30am-5:30pm, Sa 7am-1pm. **Postal Code:** 82009.

⧉ SIGHTS

During the last full week of July, make every effort to attend the one-of-a-kind **Cheyenne Frontier Days,** a 10-day festival of nonstop

Western hoopla, appropriately dubbed the "Daddy of 'Em All." The town doubles in size as tourists arrive from all over to see the world's largest outdoor rodeo competition and partake of the free pancake breakfasts, parades, big-name country music concerts, and square dancing. The USAF Thunderbirds always stop by, too. (☎307-778-7222 or 800-227-6336; www.cfdrodeo.com. Rodeo tickets $10-22.) Even in the absence of the Frontier Days celebration, the Wild West never dies in Cheyenne, thanks to the efforts of the **Cheyenne Gunslingers.** Summer nights thunder with gunfire as these cowboys fight it out and tell corny jokes in the park at 16th St. and Carey Ave. (☎307-653-1028. Gunfights June-July M-F 6pm, Sa noon. Free.)

The **Old West Museum,** 4610 N. Carey Ave., in Frontier Park, houses an extensive collection of Western memorabilia, including the third-largest carriage collection in the world. A new exhibit considers the wild history of the Frontier Days festival, from its founding in 1897 to the tragic death of world rodeo champion Lane Frost at the horns of a bull in 1989. (☎307-778-7291; www.oldwestmuseum.org. Open in summer M-F 8:30am-5:30pm, Sa-Su 9am-5pm; in winter M-F 9am-5pm, Sa-Su 10am-5pm. $6.) The **Cheyenne Street Railway Trolley** guides visitors through historic downtown Cheyenne, with stops at museums and parks along the way. Tours depart from the Cheyenne Depot, at 15th St. and Capitol Ave. (☎307-778-3133. Tours every hr. M-F 10am-4pm; Sa 10am and 1:30pm. $8, children $4; with museum admission $14.) Whether or not you take the trolley tour, the stained-glass windows and gold-leafed rotunda of the **Wyoming State Capitol Building,** at Capitol Ave. and 24th St., are worth checking out. Self-guided tour brochures are available, but the building is sometimes closed. (☎307-777-7220. Open M-F 8:30am-4:30pm. Free.)

FOOD

While Cheyenne seems to sprout fast-food establishments from every corner, it offers few non-chain restaurants with reasonably priced cuisine.

Sanford's Grub and Pub, 115 E. 17th St. (☎307-634-3381). Sanford's swelled from humble beginnings as "a few guys drinking beer and watching reruns" to a huge restaurant with a menu so long it has a table of contents. Sandwiches and burgers ($7-8) have bizarre names like the "Pants on Fire" burger and the Hobo Sandwich. 55 beers on tap. Open daily 11am-10pm. AmEx/D/MC/V. ❷

Zen's Bistro, 2606 E. Lincolnway (☎307-635-1889; www.zensbistro.com). Vegan and vegetarian fare is complemented by an unending selection of coffees ($1.25-4), teas, and Italian sodas. The glittering front room and patio house the restaurant; the back hosts shows and readings. Open M-F 7am-10pm, Sa 9am-10pm, Su 11am-10pm. AmEx/MC/V. ❸

Driftwood Cafe, 200 E. 18th St. (☎307-634-5304), at Warren St. Mom-and-pop atmosphere to match dirt-cheap homestyle cooking. Try the Cheyenne Burger (2 cheeses, mushrooms, and bacon; $4.85). Slice of pie $2. Open M-F 7am-4pm. AmEx/MC/V. ❶

Luxury Diner, 1401A W. Lincolnway (☎307-638-8971). Easy to spot in its fire-engine-red dining car, which was in full service in the 1900s. Breakfast platters ($5-9) sport names like the Conductor, Engineer, and Caboose. Platters of chops, chicken, or fish $6-8. Open daily 6am-4pm. AmEx/MC/V. ❷

ACCOMMODATIONS

As long as your visit doesn't coincide with Frontier Days, during which rates skyrocket and vacancies disappear, it's easy to land a cheap room in Cheyenne. Seven budget motels are located on E. Lincolnway alone.

The Ranger Motel, 909 W. 16th St. (☎307-634-7995). Comfy rooms with cable TV, microwaves, and fridges. Singles from $28. AmEx/MC/V. ❶

Terry Bison Ranch, 51 I-25 Service Rd. E (☎307-634-4171). From I-25 S, take Exit 2. Go left at the bottom of the exit, then right on Terry Ranch Rd. Offers 4-person cabins with kitchenettes, 2-bed bunkhouses, RV sites, and tent sites. The ranch runs bus tours to view the local bison herds. Office open daily 8am-8pm. Tent sites $15; bunkhouses $40; cabins $80. Bison tours $10, ages 4-12 $5. D/MC/V. ❶

Pioneer Hotel, 209 W. 17th St. (☎307-634-3010). Located in a charming old building, this hotel rents rooms at fantastically low rates. Singles $20, with private bath $23; doubles $22/$25. AmEx/MC/V. ❶

◪ NIGHTLIFE

True to its Wild Western past (and present), Cheyenne is home to several rowdy nightspots. At the **Outlaw Saloon,** 3839 E. Lincolnway, at the intersection with Ridge Rd., live country music pours over the dance floor and leaks out to the patio, where there's always a good game of sand volleyball to be played. (☎307-635-7552. Free dance lessons Tu and Th 7:30-8:30pm. Happy hour M-F 5-7pm. M-Sa live music 8:30pm. Open M-F 2pm-2am, Sa noon-2am, Su noon-10pm. AmEx/MC/V.) The rowdy **Rockin' Rodeo,** 312 S. Greeley Hwy., hosts rambunctious dancing, crazed eating contests, and plenty of live music over the course of the night. (Take Central Ave. S across I-80; it's on the immediate right. ☎307-637-3800. Tu-Sa live music 9pm-1:30am. Open daily 11am-2am. AmEx/MC/V.) Drink and be merry at the **Crown Bar,** 222 W. 16th St., at the corner of Carey Ave., or drop downstairs for the games, lounge, and techno dance floor of the **Crown Underground.** (☎307-778-9202. Sa live music upstairs. Bar open M-Sa 11am-2pm, Su 11am-10pm. Underground open W and F-Sa 9pm-2am. AmEx/MC/V.)

◪ DETOUR
VEDAUWOO

28 mi. from Cheyenne on Happy Jack Rd., take a left onto Vedauwoo Rd., just past the Medicine Bow National Forest sign. Note that this dirt road is 8 mi. long and bumpy. It may be faster to continue down Happy Jack Rd. to I-80 and backtrack east to Exit 329.

Named for the towering, curved rock formations that fill it, Vedauwoo (from the Arapaho word meaning "earthborn spirits") is a spectacular sight and a prime destination for rock climbers. Families hike around the spirits' feet, while hardcore climbers scale the sheer necks and shoulders of the stone titans. (☎307-745-2300. $5 per vehicle.)

◪ DETOUR
AMES MONUMENT

Head 6 mi. east on I-80 to Exit 329, and follow the dirt roads over 2 mi. to the monument.

At the end of a dirt road through the Wyoming hills sits, oddly enough, a 60 ft. pyramid. This is the **Ames Monument,** built by the Union Pacific Railroad to honor those who contributed to the effort to build a transcontinental rail line. Its seemingly random location was once the highest point on that line at 8247 ft., before the railroad was shifted elsewhere. (Open 24hr. Free.)

◪ APPROACHING LARAMIE: 51 MILES

From **I-80, Exit 313** and **316** both lead into the city; 313 opens on **3rd St.** near town, while 316 leads to **Grand Ave.,** which runs past the University of Wyoming, then intersects **3rd St.,** downtown.

LARAMIE

Laramie is the home of the academic cowboy; the museums of the University of Wyoming mix with the Wild West heritage that the city shares with Cheyenne. The heart of Laramie, though, lies in its downtown, a pleasant jumble of antique shops, vintage clothing stores, and rare-book sellers.

VITAL STATS

Population: 27,000

Visitor Info: Laramie Chamber of Commerce, 800 3rd St. (☎800-445-5303; www.laramie-tourism.org). Open M-F 8am-5pm.

Internet Access: Albany County Library, 310 8th St. (☎307-721-2580). Open M-Th 10am-8pm, F-Sa 1-5pm. Free.

Post Office: 152 5th St. (☎307-721-8837). Open M-F 8am-5:15pm, Sa 9am-1pm. **Postal Code:** 82070.

◪ GETTING AROUND. Laramie's two critical roads are **3rd St.,** which runs north-south, and **Grand Ave.,** which runs east-west. The few blocks around their intersection comprise downtown. North of their intersection along 3rd St. are most motels, and east along Grand Ave. are municipal buildings and the University of Wyoming. There's free 2hr. parking along most streets downtown.

◪ SIGHTS. There are many museums in Laramie, thanks mainly to the University of Wyoming. Despite its name, the **Geology Museum,** at 11th and Lewis St., is a natural history museum. The centerpiece is a fossilized

Apatosaurus skeleton. In its shadow is "Big Al," one of the world's most complete *Allosaurus* skeletons. (☎307-766-4218; www.uwyo.ede/geomuseum. Open M-F 8am-5pm, Sa-Su 10am-3pm. Free.) The bizarrely pyramidal architecture of the **Centennial Complex,** 2111 Willet Dr., contains two of UW's best museums. The **American Heritage Center** is primarily a research center, but has a gallery area displaying a bit of its collection. Western pop culture fills much of the space; exhibits on Western films and TV shows surround the saddles of Hopalong Cassidy and the Cisco Kid. (Take Grand Ave. to 22nd St., and head north, then east on Willet Dr. ☎307-766-4114; www.uwyo.edu/ahc. Open June-Aug. M-F 7:30am-4:30pm, Sa 11am-5pm; Sept.-May M-F 8am-5pm, Sa 11am-5pm. Free.) Across the lobby is the **University of Wyoming Art Museum.** Exhibits are ever-changing, drawing from both traveling selections and the university's own private collection. (☎307-766-6622; www.wyo.edu/artmuseum. Open M-Sa 10am-5pm, Su 1-5pm. Free.) The **Wyoming Children's Museum and Nature Center** is a zoo/playground fusion. One room serves as a pioneer play village, while the other holds turtles, giant salamanders, and one glowering owl. (☎307-745-6332; www.wcmnc.org. Open Tu-Th 9am-noon and 3-5pm, Sa 9am-1pm. $3.50.)

The **Wyoming Territorial Park,** 975 Snowy Range Rd., hosts a pioneer village and theater, but the main attraction is the **Territorial Prison,** which once held Butch Cassidy and other famed outlaws, remembered in the restored jail's Hall of Infamy. Cassidy was pardoned after a year and a half, after promising the governor he would never rob a bank again. True to his word, he robbed trains instead. (From 3rd St., head east on Clark St. ☎307-745-6161; www.wyoprisonpark.org. Grounds open daily late June to Aug. 10am-5pm. Museum open daily June-Aug. 10am-5pm; May and Sept. 10am-3pm. Village open June-Aug. W-Su 11am-5pm. $6, ages 12-17 $3.)

🍴🏨 **FOOD AND NIGHTLIFE.** Laramie is quite hospitable to vegetarians. The menu at **Jeffrey's Bistro ❸,** 123 Ivinson St., at the corner of 2nd St., lists a number of salads ($8), or you can customize one of your own. (☎307-742-7046. Entrees $6-11. Open M-Sa 11am-9pm. AmEx/D/MC/V.) **Sweet Melissa's ❷,** 213 1st St., downtown, is a vegetarian establishment, with some

vegan items as well. Nachos ($4-8) make up much of the appetizer menu, while the entrees ($6-8) include lentil loaf and eggplant parmesan. (☎307-742-9607. Open M-Sa 11am-9pm. MC/V.) At the very core of downtown is **Grand Avenue ❷,** 301 Grand Ave., at the corner of 3rd St. This peaceful establishment serves gourmet pizzas ($12) and calzones ($5-6). The "plain" has sausage, pepperoni, and mushrooms, and it only gets more interesting from there. (☎307-721-2909. Pastas $7-10. Open Tu-Sa 11am-9pm. AmEx/MC/V.) Downtown Laramie isn't a crazed club-hopping strip, but the **Buckhorn Bar,** 114 Ivinson St., puts on a good show with two levels of games (video and otherwise), music and booze. (☎307-742-3554. F-Sa live music. 21+. No cover. Open daily 10am-2am. AmEx/D/MC/V.)

🏨 **ACCOMMODATIONS.** Unfortunately, Laramie is not a city of inexpensive motels. It does, however, have one of the more interesting motels around. An army of statues, including bears, horses, cowboys, and a few dinosaurs, monitors the parking lot of the **Gas Lite Motel ❸,** 960 3rd St. The rooms are pleasant and quite large. (☎307-742-6616. Rooms in summer $55-65; in winter $45-55. AmEx/MC/V.) **The University Inn ❸,** 1720 Grand Ave., in a residential neighborhood near the university, has clean rooms. (☎307-721-8855. Singles from $50. AmEx/MC/V.) The **Ranger Motel ❷,** 453 3rd St., boasts some of the best prices downtown. The rooms are spacious and well-equipped. (☎307-742-6677. Rooms in summer $42-46; in winter $34-38. AmEx/MC/V.)

🚗 **APPROACHING MEDICINE BOW: 57 MILES**
Head north along **3rd St.** Beyond the city limits, this road becomes **U.S. 30/287,** which arcs northwest toward Sinclair and Rawlins. 5 mi. west of Rock River, **Marshal Rd.** heads north toward the **Como Bluffs** and the legendary **Dinosaur Graveyard.** After its discovery, the area seemed to be an endless source of fossilized North American dinosaurs, yielding one of the largest skeletons ever unearthed, at nearly 70 ft. long. The graveyard seems to have run out of dinos, however, and today there isn't much to see beyond the cliffs themselves. Continue on U.S. 30 until you reach Medicine Bow.

MEDICINE BOW. Owen Wister published his novel *The Virginian* in 1902, and Medicine Bow, one of the book's settings, suddenly became famous. In 1909, the mayor had the ▨Virginian Hotel ❶, 404 Lincoln Hwy., built in Wister's honor. Each of the rooms is decorated with its own style and color scheme, and highlights include thick carpets, frilled bedspreads, and a few canopied beds or clawed bathtubs—all available at budget prices. (☎307-379-2377. Singles with shared bath $27; doubles with private bath $52. Rooms in adjacent motel $20-40. MC/V.) The **Virginian Restaurant and Saloon** ❸ serves country-style dinners ($9-10) like chicken-fried steak and calf liver. (☎307-379-2377. Restaurant open daily 6am-9pm. MC/V.) For true Wister enthusiasts, across the street from the Virginian is the **Medicine Bow Museum,** which has colorful exhibits on local history and the Old West, including a wall of cattle brands. The Owen Wister Cabin and Monument is a highlight. (☎307-379-2383. Open M-F 10am-5pm, Sa-Su 1-5pm. Donations accepted.)

◪ DETOUR
SEMINOE-ALCOVA BACKCOUNTRY BYWAY
Continue along U.S. 287/U.S. 30 W. Get on to I-80 W, get off at Exit 221. Follow the exit past the refinery, straight through the cluster of houses to 10th St., where you should turn off the main road. Watch carefully for signs to the Wyoming Backway.

The Oregon Trail did not take this path; the rather large Seminoe Mountains stood in the way. Nevertheless, the striking scenery makes it a worthy path for Oregon Trail roadtrippers. High-altitude snows can make the road impassable to cars during the winter. Though chained tires may be able to handle the passage, taking the byway is advisable only between May and November. Even during the summer months, the road is slow going and devoid of services; be prepared for a ride of several hours over gravel roads. The first miles of the route follow the North Platte River through a deepening gorge, with the Seminoe Mountains rising forbiddingly ahead. After 20 mi., you'll see a huge sand dune—just watch out for the sand that spills onto the road. About 4 mi. farther is **Seminoe State Park,** which offers good fishing, boating, and a serene **campsite** ❶. All manner of wildlife live in and around the reservoir area, even rare mountain lions and bald eagles. The park is divided into several regions, two of which—the North and South Red Hills—can be

reached directly from the Byway. (☎307-777-6323; http://wyoparks.state.wy.us/seslide.htm. Entrance fee $4 per car. Sites $12. Cash only.)

Beyond the park, the road becomes steep and winding. The next several miles are the best places to pull off; scenic vistas are everywhere, and from them you can survey the mountains and the river flowing down from them. After this, the road narrows and passes into deep forests for several miles. A 4 mi. downhill stretch past rock spires completes the mountainous leg of the journey. At the bottom of the slope is **Miracle Mile,** the five miles of stream known for their blue-ribbon trout. The fishing area is formed by **Kortes Dam,** which can be reached by following a 3 mi. detour. This side route breaks off the main road just past the bridge over Miracle Mile. There is little to do at the dam, but the sight of the giant concrete wall is very impressive. The remaining 35 mi. stretch of the byway has a harsh appeal with a rocky plain broken only by larger formations such as **Dome Rock.** At the end is the town of **Alcova,** sitting beneath the Alcova Dam.

◪ APPROACHING ALCOVA: 83 MILES
If you did not take the Seminoe-Alcova Backcountry Byway, you have some catching up to do. From Medicine Bow, head north on **WY-487** for 71 mi. Then, make a left onto **WY-220** and head into town.

ALCOVA
Alcova is the epitome of the secret, small-town America every roadtripper searches for—or at least, it comes pretty close. The town is on the northern end of the Seminoe Mountains, and the surrounding lakes and rivers are full of campgrounds and fishing spots.

Locals congregate at the **Sunset Bar & Grill** ❸, 22250 W. Rte. 220, at the bottom of the Riverview Inn's hill. It's open late, so the lonely moonlight driver can stop for a sandwich or some conversation. (☎307-472-3200. Appetizers $3-7. Sandwiches $5-7. Open M-Th 9am-midnight, F 9am-2am, Sa 8am-2am, Su 8am-midnight. AmEx/D/MC/V.) Eight cabins with full kitchens and propane grills are highlights at the ▨**Inn at Alcova** ❹, located right at the intersection of the Backcountry Byway with Rte. 220. The thematically decorated cabins can house up to five comfortably. (☎307-234-2066;

www.sloanesatalcova.com. Office in Sloanes General Store next door. Cabins $80-100. AmEx/ D/MC/V.) The **Riverview Inn ❸**, 22258 W. Rte. 220, has a magnificent view of the Gray Reef Reservoir and very comfortable rooms. (☎307-473-5829. Office in the Sunset Grill down the hill. Laundry. Singles $54; doubles $64. MC/V.)

⚐ APPROACHING CASPER: 36 MILES
Take **Rte. 220 E** all the way to Casper.

CASPER

Casper is one of the largest cities in Wyoming. But while Cheyenne distinguishes itself as a haven for gunslingers and Laramie claims the hipster throne, Casper struggles to find any sort of character. Nevertheless, pockets of good times thrive. While it's too small to be called a proper downtown, there is a stretch of E. 2nd St. that treats visitors right; it has three old movie theaters complete with flashing marquees, a set of record shops and bookstores, and the four-story western superstore, Lou Talbert Ranch Outfitters.

VITAL STATS

Population: 50,000

Visitor Info: Casper Area Chamber of Commerce, 500 N. Center St. (☎307-234-5311; www.casperwyoming.org). Open M-F 8am-6pm, Sa-Su 10am-6pm.

Internet Access: Natrona County Public Library, 307 E. 2nd St. (☎307-237-4935). Open M-Th 10am-7pm, F-Sa 10am-5pm. Free.

Post Office: 150 E. B St. (☎307-577-6480). Open M-F 8am-6pm, Sa 9am-noon. **Postal Code:** 82604.

▣ GETTING AROUND

Casper's haphazard design makes for nightmarish driving. The city is laid out around **Center St.,** which cuts north-south through the city. **1st St.** runs east-west through the downtown area, with parallel streets increasing in number as you go south. North of 1st. St., the roads are lettered. **Yellowstone Hwy.** is home to a number of establishments. Unfortunately, the street is almost impossible to follow, even with a map, since it does not stay in line with the city's rough grid, but frequently breaks off and restarts several blocks later, only to merge and vanish again.

⚆ SIGHTS

MUSEUMS. In this land of the Wild West and Oregon Trail, the **Nicolaysen Art Museum and Discovery Center** is an escape into the present. Featuring contemporary artists, rotating exhibits spotlight both locals and famed masters, like Andy Warhol. In the same building (through an Alice-in-Wonderland mini-door) is the Discovery Center, a workshop that will entertain children and their parents. (400 E. Collins Dr. ☎307-235-5247; www.thenic.com. Open Tu-Sa 10am-5pm, Su noon-4pm. Free.) The other museum of note in Casper is the **Wyoming Science Center.** (3950 S. Poplar St. ☎307-261-6130. Open M-Sa 10am-5pm. $4, children $3.)

NATIONAL HISTORIC TRAILS INTERPRETIVE CENTER. In the hills above the city, the National Historic Trails Interpretive Center lies on the northern end of the road. Despite the dull name, it is among the best of the museums along the Oregon Trail. Monuments to the California, Oregon, and Mormon trails—the major overland routes—stand in the parking lot. Painted paths lead past miniaturized landmarks such as Chimney Rock, Ft. Laramie, and the Ayres Bridge; it's a 1min. condensation of the journey thus far. Once inside, the trails vanish, but a major gallery presents the history, challenges, and people of the Oregon, California, and Mormon Trails, as well as that of the Pony Express. A full-motion river crossing simulation is available upon request, so you can feel the pain of the pioneers you heartlessly killed playing the Oregon Trail computer game back in the 90s. (1501 N. Poplar St. From Center St., head west along Collins St. to Poplar St. ☎307-261-7700. Open Apr.-Sept. daily 8am-7pm; Oct.-Mar. Tu-Sa 9am-4:30pm. $6, seniors $5, students $4, ages 6-17 $3, ages 3-5 $1.)

FORT CASPAR. Fort Caspar may have been less significant than some of its counterparts, but it still gets the last laugh. While other forts are in ruins, Caspar survives, reconstructed by the WPA in the 1930s. A museum relates the history of the fort, which was built to guard the developing railroads from attack. A reconstruction of Brigham Young's Mormon Ferry is also on the grounds. (4001 Fort Caspar Rd. ☎307-235-8462; www.fortcasparwyoming.com.

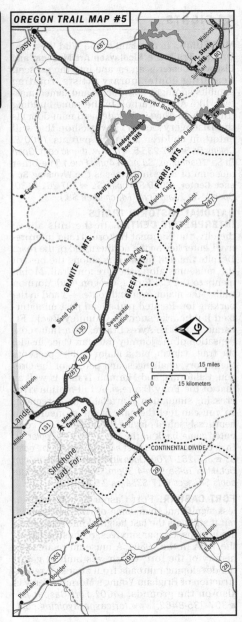

OREGON TRAIL MAP #5

Open June-Aug. M-Sa 8am-7pm; Su noon-7pm; May and Sept. M-Sa 8am-5pm, Su noon-5pm; Oct.-Apr. Tu-Sa 8am-5pm. $2, ages 6-17 $1.)

SPIRITRIDER WAGON TRAIN. Spiritrider Wagon Train gives visitors an authentic Oregon Trail experience, offering customized tours ranging from half-day wagon rides to week-long camping adventures. Though the company is very accommodating, it is best to call ahead. The week-long trip tours the Hole-in-the-Wall area, covering 55 mi. *(5897 S. Twelve Mile Rd. ☎307-472-5361; www.spiritrider-wagon-train.com. 1-week trip $1500, ages 7-17 $900. Call ahead for meeting locations.)*

◼ FOOD

The **Western Grill ❷**, 2333 E. Yellowstone Hwy., meets every requirement of a great restaurant—it's inexpensive, friendly, and has character. The menu features specialty pancakes and grill options for breakfast, as well as a variety of cheap dinners ($6-8). It also provides a great service to scurvy-suffering roadtrippers by selling individual pieces of fruit. (☎307-234-7061. Open daily 6am-9pm.) At **Eggington's ❷**, 229 E. 2nd St., the breakfast menu includes eggs benedict, while lunch features *panini* ($6.50-8) and burgers. (☎307-265-8700. Open M-Sa 6am-2:30pm, Su 7am-2:30pm.)

⬛ ACCOMMODATIONS

For the most part, Casper's accommodations fall into two classes: cheap but very basic, or pleasant but rather expensive. The biggest exception to this rule is the **Sage and Sand Motel ❸**, 901 W. Yellowstone Hwy., where the rooms are large and clean, and some have thematic decor. (☎307-237-2088. Laundry. Rooms from $53.) The **National 9 Showboat Motel ❸**, 100 W. F St., off N. Center St., has prices just beyond the budget range, but it offers cable and a continental breakfast. (☎307-235-2711. Check-out noon. Singles from $65; doubles from $76. AmEx/D/MC/V.) Those planning to stay in the area for a while will find good weekly rates at the **Yellowstone Motel ❷**, 1610 E. Yellowstone Hwy. The rooms are fairly basic, though a few large, kitchen-equipped rooms are also for rent. (☎307-234-9174. Rooms from $46; rooms with kitchenettes $59. MC/V.)

OREGON TRAIL

☒ DETOUR
INDEPENDENCE ROCK
Along Rte. 220, 24 mi. west of Alcova.

This huge and strangely smooth hill of stone was the halfway marker for pioneers heading toward Oregon. If the wagon train reached the rock by the 4th of July, then the journey was on schedule to beat the winter, thus the name "Independence Rock." You can scale the steep rock for an impressive view of the Sweetwater Valley. The rock-top is gigantic, but if you search hard enough, names can be found carved into the stone, bearing dates as early as 1850. There are few modern additions to the site—just bathrooms and informative plaques. (Open sunrise-sunset. Free.)

☒ DETOUR
DEVIL'S GATE
About 5 mi. west of Independence Rock (and visible from it), along Rte. 220.

Though the trails never passed through it, Devil's Gate was an impressive landmark associated with Independence Rock. Native legend held that a spirit had once terrorized the Sweetwater Valley in the form of a monstrous tusked beast. When daring warriors assaulted the creature, it tore the cliffs open in fury, forming the Gate. The historic site doesn't actually lead to the opening itself, but commands an excellent view of the gap. (Open sunrise-sunset. Free.)

☒ APPROACHING LANDER: 148 MILES
U.S. 287 becomes **E. Main St.** within city limits. Go straight through the intersection where **Rte. 789** breaks away to the east, and you'll find yourself on the western end of **Main St.**, which heads west.

LANDER
With the celebrated wilderness of Shoshone National Forest all around it, the city of Lander is easy to overlook. But while the tourist industry revolves around the forests and mountains, Lander's downtown is still very much alive. The town's three llama breeders are located elsewhere, but businesses of every other variety have found their way to Main St. Outdoor adventure suppliers, a military surplus store, and a smoked-meat shop lead the charge of browsable stops. A small caravan of

hot dog stands has even moved in to feed those wandering the long road.

VITAL STATS

Population: 6900

Visitor Info: Lander Chamber of Commerce, 160 N. 1st St. (☎307-332-3892 or 800-433-0662; www.landerchamber.org). Open June-Aug. M-F 9am-5pm, Sa 9am-2pm; Sept.-May M-F 9am-5pm.

Internet Access: Fremont County Public Library, 451 N. 2nd St. (☎307-332-5194). Open M-Th 10am-9pm, F-Sa 10am-4pm. Free.

Post Office: 230 Grandview Dr. (☎307-332-2126), off E. Main St. Open M-F 8am-5pm, Sa 10am-1pm. **Postal Code:** 82520.

☞ GETTING AROUND. Lander's main street is **Main St.**, appropriately enough. Main St. is short enough that it can all be seen in a single stroll. **3rd St.** is a major crossroad. Parking is available on Main St. itself, but vacant spots can be in short supply. It may be easier to just leave your car on the side streets.

☉ SIGHTS. While Main St. may be the best attraction in the city itself, the wild outskirts contain **Sinks Canyon State Park.** From Main St., head south on 5th St., which becomes Rte. 131. Seven miles down this road is the **Rise**, a calm pool into which a stream erupts to form the Popo Agie (which means "Tall Grass River" in the Crow language). Trout-food vending machines stand next to the overlook. A quarter-mile farther up the road and upstream are the **Sinks**, where the raging Popo Agie vanishes abruptly underground on its way to the Rise. The sight is truly bizarre; the river runs down into a little hollow, then simply stops (see **A Sinking Feeling**, p. 636). The **State Park Visitors Center**, 3079 Sinks Canyon Rd., is right next to the Sinks overlook, providing an overview of the area and its wildlife. (☎307-332-6333. Open daily in summer 9am-6pm, in winter 1-4pm.) Beginning 4 mi. north of the town limits but extending for millions of acres beyond is the **Wind River Indian Reservation** of the Arapaho and Shoshone Tribes. Powwows and Sundances are performed throughout the summer. Events are scheduled throughout the summer; for specific dates, contact the Lander Chamber of Commerce.

▓ FOOD AND ACCOMMODATIONS. A whole string of restaurants lines Main St. **Gannett Grill ❷**, 126 Main St., has a fascinating interior with a decor of rancher hieroglyphics. Salads ($5-6) include the "Mad Greek" and "Hail Caesar." (☎307-332-7009. Open daily 11am-10pm. AmEx/D/MC/V.) The menu of the expensive but insanely stylish **Cowfish**, 128 Main St., consists of two main sections—Cow and Fish—though there is also a Pigs & Chickens classification. The grilled sea bass ($18) is particularly good. (☎307-332-8227; www.landerbar.com. Appetizers $6-7. Entrees $10-26. Open daily 5-9:30pm. AmEx/D/MC/V.) Unusually large rooms can be found at the **Maverick Motel ❷**, 808 Main St. The free laundry room is a great service for drivers who find that their laundry bags (a.k.a. backseats), are full. (☎307-332-2300 or 877-622-2300. Singles $45; doubles $49. MC/V.) Lander also has an excellent B&B in the **Blue Spruce Inn ❹**, 677 S. 3rd St. The four rooms have private baths and are all individually decorated and named; the Brass Room is a classy alternative to Wyoming's ubiquitous cowboy decor. A large front porch makes for excellent lounging. (☎307-332-8253; www.bluespruceinn.com. Free Wi-Fi. Singles $70; doubles $90. MC/V.)

◪ DETOUR
LOOP ROAD
From Lander, head south on 5th St. This becomes Rte. 131, which feeds into Sinks Canyon. From there, the Loop Road is the only available path. It terminates on Rte. 28, 30 mi. south of Lander.

An alternative to the monotony of the interstate, the Loop Road punishes automobiles with 30 mi. of switchbacks, ledge-riders, and washed-out roads. The first few miles lead through **Sinks Canyon**, and the **Shoshone National Forest** follows. Hikers can pause at Bruce's Lot to hike the Middle Fork trail up to **Popo Agie Falls;** those who love their car's shocks can then turn around. Beyond this point, the road scissors up the cliff face in a series of dusty switchbacks. Well over 10 tiers and 6 mi. later, it climbs over the last of the rocks onto level ground. The trials are over; a minor high-altitude paradise awaits, in which miles of evergreen forests surround blue mountain lakes. By the time the road reaches 9500 ft., the snow-capped Wind River Mountains are gloriously close.

◪ DETOUR
FARSON MERCANTILE
4048 Hwy. 191. At the intersection of Rte. 28 and U.S. 191.

"Home of the Big Cone," The **Farson Mercantile ❶** is regionally famous for its ice cream and 80-year-old building. The cones have been served to locals and travelers from all over the world, even astronaut training crews. Sizes span from the not-so-small Baby Bear ($2) to the Devil's Tower ($7), one colossal cone. (☎307-273-9020. Open daily 10am-7pm. MC/V.)

◪ APPROACHING ROCK SPRINGS: 120 MILES
If you took the Loop Road, congratulations. Head south on **Rte. 28.** If you didn't, you have some catch-

A SINKING FEELING

Six miles south of Lander, the Popo Agie River tumbles down a rocky slope toward a shallow depression in a limestone cliff face and vanishes. This disappearing act is no small feat—depending on the time of year, 150 to 500 cubic feet of water from the Popo Agie (pronounced PUH-poh zyuh) flow into the cracks and fissures of "the Sinks" each second. A little over a mile later, the river reemerges at a site called "the Rise," a tranquil pool of water populated by gargantuan (but governmentally protected) rainbow trout. Though the Sinks and the Rise have been known since the Crow tribe inhabited the area, until recently no one knew whether the water that sunk at the Sinks was the same water that rose at the Rise. Because the water disappears into tiny, unexplorable passageways, it was impossible to simply drop an object into the river and see if it came out the other side. To solve the Popo Agie puzzle, scientists released dye into the Sinks and waited. And waited. More than two hours later, the dye resurfaced, having traveled a linear distance of only 1¼ mi. It seemed the puzzle hadn't been solved, after all—though the water was the same, they determined that it must flow via a slow, indirect route through the mountain. Furthermore, they found that more water wells up at the Rise than disappears at the Sinks, making Sinks Canyon a true geological mystery.

ing up to do. Head southeast on **U.S. 287 (Main St.)** for 9 mi., then get on Rte. 28 S. In Farson, take **U.S. 191 S.** It may seem broad and flat, but the **Continental Divide** lies just a few miles beyond the intersection. It is announced with little fanfare but represents an important landmark, both geologically and for the Oregon Trail, indicating the completion of the 1st ascent. **Rock Springs** is 38 mi. ahead. Entering Rock Springs, **Rte. 191** becomes **Elk St.**

ROCK SPRINGS

Though the arid beauty of the Red Desert and its wild horses surrounds the city, Rock Springs itself is not so attractive. A loop of corporate-dominated highways arcs around residential areas and a historic downtown that is now home to gambling dens and a few interesting shops. The city does come alive, however, during the last few days of July for its Red Desert Roundup rodeo. The rest of the year it serves as a convenient base of operations for trips to the Flaming Gorge.

VITAL STATS

Population: 19,000

Visitor Info: Rock Springs Chamber of Commerce, 1897 Dewar Dr. (☎307-362-3771). Open M-F 8am-5pm.

Internet Access: Rock Springs Public Library, 400 C St. (☎307-352-6667), downtown. Open M-Th 9am-8pm, F-Sa noon-5pm. Free.

Post Office: 2829 Commercial Way (☎307-362-9792). Open M-F 9am-5pm, Sa 9am-noon.

Postal Code: 82901.

◨ **GETTING AROUND.** The streets of Rock Springs are not easily navigable; you'll want to grab a street map from the info booth at the Chamber of Commerce. **Rte. 191** enters the city from the north and becomes **Elk St.,** one of the city's main thoroughfares. A little ways into the city it intersects **Center St. (Rte. 30),** which runs roughly southwest-northeast. In the western half of the city, Center St. becomes **Bridger Ave.,** and then **9th St.** The historic downtown district can be reached by taking Elk St. south past Center St. until it becomes **A St.**

◨ **SIGHTS.** A number of dinosaur museums cluster along the Oregon Trail in Nebraska and Wyoming, but none surpasses the **Western Wyo-**

ming **Community College Natural History Museum,** 2500 College Dr. The museum itself has a collection of archaeological finds from the area, but it also sponsors the set of full (cast) skeletons spread across campus. A *Triceratops,* a *Tyrannosaurus,* and the monstrous marine *Plesiosaur* are among the best of the set. Maps of skeleton locations are available in the main lobby of the campus or at the museum. (☎307-382-1666 or 307-382-1600. Open daily 9am-10pm. Free.) Sharing its building with the public library, the **Community Fine Arts Center,** 400 C St., showcases local and state artists in rotating exhibits. The permanent collection includes works by a handful of famous artists, including Norman Rockwell. (☎307-362-6212. Open M-Th 10am-6pm, F-Sa noon-5pm. Free.) The **Rock Springs Historical Museum,** 201 B. St., is located at the corner of Broadway. Over the years, it has collected thousands of personal artifacts donated by the citizens of Rock Springs, creating a collective scrapbook. (☎307-362-3138. Open M-Sa 10am-5pm. Donations accepted.)

◨◨ **FOOD AND ACCOMMODATIONS.** Rock Springs is home to every imaginable type of fast-food restaurant, most of which swarm around the I-80 restaurants. Other options are regrettably hard to find. The **Broadway Burger Station ❷,** 628 Broadway, serves hamburgers from a menu laden with Elvis references. Sit at a gleaming silver counter on sparkly red seats straight from the 50s. The final, eyebrow-raising touch comes from the animated neon sign, which endlessly raises Marilyn's skirt. (☎307-362-5858. Burgers $7. Sandwiches $4-5. Shakes and malts $2-3. Open M-Th and Sa 11am-8pm, F 11am-9pm. AmEx/D/DC/MC/V.) Hanging birds and monkeys, ceramic inlaid tables, and psychedelic murals make **Fiesta Guadalajara ❷,** 19 Elk St., a fun place to dine. The combo dishes ($6-8), which come with rice and beans, are a good deal. (☎307-382-7147. Entrees $6-9. Open M-Th 11am-9pm, F-Sa 11am-10pm, Su noon-8pm. AmEx/D/MC/V.)

There is a glut of chain hotels surrounding I-80's burn through Rock Springs on the western end of town. The **Cody Motel ❷,** 75 Center St., has clean and well-furnished rooms with fridge-and-microwave combinations. (☎307-362-6675. Rooms from $45. AmEx/D/DC/MC/V.) Back near I-80 is the pricey but pleasant **Inn**

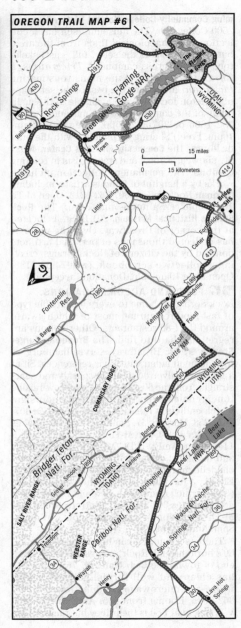

OREGON TRAIL MAP #6

at Rock Springs ❹, 2518 Foothill Blvd., which sits on Dewar Dr. west of I-80. Some of the large rooms have couches, and guests can enjoy the guest room and swimming pool. (☎ 307-362-9600. Breakfast included. Singles $85; doubles $90. AmEx/D/MC/V.)

◪ DETOUR
FLAMING GORGE NATIONAL RECREATION AREA

Take I-80 to Exit 91, and immediately get on Rte. 530 S. This will take you along the western edge of the gorge. The eastern border can be skirted via U.S. 191, off I-80 Exit 99 between Rock Springs and Green River.

Seen at sunset, the contrast between the red canyons and the aquamarine water of the Green River makes the landscape of the Flaming Gorge area appear to glow. The river was dammed in 1964, and the resulting reservoir is now the center of the Flaming Gorge National Recreation Area. The area is large enough to spill into the northern reaches of Utah, but its northern tip is just south of the town of Green River. The **scenic drive** south into the area is thus a serious undertaking, but a shorter jaunt down one edge is also possible. Elk, antelope, and bighorn sheep call the land home; these animals may not frequent the highway loop, but a turn onto one of the many side roads may lead to a sighting. Rte. 530 becomes Rte. 43 and then Rte. 44 as it meets the southern border of the area. Rte. 44 intersects with U.S. 191 in Utah near **Red Canyon.** Plenty of activities can be found along the borders of the gorge, including numerous hiking and biking trails. The Rock Springs and Green River Chambers of Commerce can provide maps of the area and phone numbers for individual campsites and marinas in the area. The Rock Springs Chamber of Commerce also sells passes required for park entrance. (Flaming Gorge Ranger District ☎ 435-784-3445; www.fs.fed.us. Day-use $2 per car.)

 DID YOU KNOW? Two hundred would-be travelers on the Oregon Trail signed up to ride in the wind-wagon, a forerunner to the airplane. Unfortunately, the contraption never got off the ground.

⚐ APPROACHING GREEN RIVER: 19 MILES

Head east on **I-80.** Much of Green River is laid out along **Flaming Gorge Way,** which is a loop between **Exits 91** and **89** off I-80. Take **Exit 91** to reach the city.

GREEN RIVER

Though not overflowing with attractions, Green River is a peaceful town and a relaxing rest stop. The tip of the long Flaming Gorge National Recreation Area is just south of town, and this scenic area defines the town and much of its economy.

VITAL STATS

Population: 11,800

Visitor Info: Green River Chamber of Commerce, 541 E. Flaming Gorge Way (☎307-875-5711). Open M-F 8:30am-5:30pm.

Internet Access: Sweetwater County Library, 300 N 1st East St. (☎307-875-3615). Open M-Th 9am-8pm, F-Sa 9am-4pm. Free.

Post Office: 350 Uinta Dr. (☎307-875-4920). Open M-F 9am-5:30pm, Sa 10:30am-noon. **Postal Code:** 82929.

☞ GETTING AROUND. Nearly all of Green river lies along **Flaming Gorge Way,** the road that forms the loop between Exits 89 and 91 off I-80. **Uinta Dr.,** which runs perpendicular to Flaming Gorge Way, is the other major road.

⊙ SIGHTS. Green River houses the **Sweetwater County Historical Museum,** 3 E. Flaming Gorge Way, an interesting mix of Oregon Trail info, dinosaur remains, and a scattershot history of immigrants in the West. (☎307-872-6435; www.sweetwatermuseum.org. Open M-Sa 10am-6pm. Free.)

🍴 FOOD. Flaming Gorge Way is home to many of Green River's restaurants. **Buckaroo's Family Restaurant ❸,** 580 E. Flaming Gorge Way, is a rope-and-boot adorned diner with some pleasantly inexpensive meals. Several choices for under $4—The Wild West, The Billy the Kid, and so forth—are supplemented by larger, more expensive dinners ($6-15) for the hungry driver. (☎307-875-2246. Open daily 6am-9pm. AmEx/D/MC/V.) All-day breakfasts and a large supply of moose paraphernalia abound at the **Krazy Moose ❷,** 211 E. Flaming Gorge Way. Omelettes ($5-6) are some of the best offerings, though the large salad list ($6-8) is also impressive. (☎307-875-5124. Breakfast $6-7. Open M-Sa 6am-9pm, Su 8am-3pm. AmEx/D/MC/V.) **Penny's Diner ❷,** 1170 W.

Flaming Gorge Way, right off the interstate, is fast, greasy, and prime roadtrip-food material. Root beer floats ($2.50) taste miraculous after a day on the dusty road. (☎307-875-3500, ext. 550. Breakfast $7. Sandwiches $6. Dinner around $8. Open 24hr. AmEx/D/DC/MC/V.)

🛏 ACCOMMODATIONS. The same stretch of road also offers a strip of good motels. The least expensive and most convenient of these is the **Mustang Motel ❷,** 550 E. Flaming Gorge Way, which has enormous rooms with refrigerators and microwaves. (☎307-875-2468. Singles $37; doubles $42. AmEx/D/MC/V.) The **Coachman Inn ❸,** 470 E. Flaming Gorge Way, right next door, is another good bet; though slightly more expensive, it also has large, comfortably furnished rooms. (☎307-875-3681. Rooms in summer $65-75; call ahead for winter rates. AmEx/D/MC/V.) The **Western Motel ❸,** 890 W. Flaming Gorge Way, has rooms equipped with A/C and TV. (☎307-875-2840. Rooms $70. AmEx/D/MC/V.)

⊠ DETOUR
FORT BRIDGER STATE HISTORIC SITE

Hop back on I-80 W, then take the Carter Mountain View exit. Make the 1st left, and go 3 mi. down the road. Make a right at the 4-way stop in town, and head another 3 mi. to Fort Bridger.

Originally a money-making supply depot established by mountain men, Jim Bridger and Louis Vasquex, Fort Bridger was obtained by Mormons in 1850, then the military in 1858. Like many of its counterparts, it served the Pony Express and later the Union Pacific Railroad. While its past may not be particularly tumultuous, the fort is remarkably well-preserved. One of the 18 standing buildings is a two-story Victorian building that was home to the commanding officer; both floors are open for viewing. At the far end of the wooded grounds is a small museum that illustrates the fort's transformation over time. Those who pass by during Labor Day weekend will be treated to the **Mountain Man Rendezvous,** a festival of 19th-century crafts and demonstrations, like a tomahawk throwing contest. (☎307-782-3842. Grounds open daily 8:30am-sunset. Museum open May-Sept. daily 8am-6pm; Oct. to mid-Nov. and mid-Mar. to Apr. Sa-Su 9am-4:30pm. $2, under 18 free.)

↖ APPROACHING KEMMERER: 70 MILES
From **Exit 39** off **I-80**, take **Rte. 412 N** to **U.S. 189**. U.S. 189 joins **U.S. 30** shortly before reaching Diamondville. The roads turn sharply left at the border; watch the signs carefully, and follow U.S. 30 into Kemmerer.

KEMMERER

Southwestern Wyoming is a pretty and peaceful place, and Kemmerer, the fossil fish capital of the world, is no exception. The town's center is a genuine village green, and its sleepy downtown charm remains largely unblemished by corporate invasion. Considering that J.C. Penney got it's start here, that is somewhat ironic.

VITAL STATS

Population: 2700

Visitor Info: Kemmerer/Diamondville Chamber of Commerce, 800 Pine Ave. (☎307-877-9761), in Herschler Triangle Park. Open M-F 9am-5pm, Sa 9am-2pm.

Internet Access: Lincoln County Library, 519 Emerald St. (☎307-877-6961), at the corner of Sage Ave. Take Emerald St. up the hill from Pine Ave. Open M-W 10am-8pm, Th-F 10am-6pm, Sa 10am-2pm. Free.

Post Office: 318 Sapphire St. (☎307-877-3432). Open M-F 8:30am-5pm, Sa 9am-noon. **Postal Code:** 83101.

▣ GETTING AROUND. Kemmerer lies along **U.S. 30,** which runs south-north, changing its name to **Central Ave.** in Diamondville. It becomes **Coral St.** at the Kemmerer line, and then **Pine Ave.** deeper in Kemmerer. Parking is generally available on the streets or in private lots.

◐ SIGHTS. Once known as The Golden Rule, the mother of all J.C. Penney stores still operates at the intersection of J.C. Penney Dr. and Pine Ave. Just a few storefronts down is the **Penney Homestead,** 107 J.C. Penney Dr., now a museum. The lower floor contains artifacts and photos from the founder's life, while the upstairs has been preserved in its original state. (☎307-877-3164. Open May-Sept. M-Sa 9am-6pm, Su 1-6pm. Free.) More local history is preserved in the **Fossil Country Frontier Museum,** 400 Pine Ave., which, in addition to the usual pioneer artifacts, gives an account of the Golden

Rule Store's transformation into the J.C. Penney franchise of today. Visitors can descend into a coal mine replica to learn about the ingenious techniques the miners used to plunder area shafts. (☎307-877-6551; www.hamsfork.net/~museum. Open June-Aug. M-Sa 9am-5pm; Sept.-May M-Sa 10am-4pm. Free.)

☎▣ FOOD AND ACCOMMODATIONS. For a little more variety, there's **Bootlegger's Steakhouse and Grill ❸,** 817 S. Main St., off Pine Ave. just south of Herschler Triangle Park. Juicy burgers ($8-9) are supplemented by baskets ($7-9), which come with shrimp, chicken fingers, or ribs. (☎307-828-3067. Open daily 5-8pm. AmEx/MC/V.)

Kemmerer's lodgings are mostly comfortable and reasonably priced budget motels. The **Antler Motel ❷,** 419 Coral St., offers a range of rooms. (☎307-877-4461. Reception 9am-9pm. Singles $32; doubles $50; triples $65. AmEx/MC/V.) Right on the Kemmerer/Diamondville line is **The Fairview Inn ❸,** 501 U.S. 30. The rooms are big and well-equipped, with large TVs, microwaves, and fridges. (☎307-877-3938. Singles from $50; doubles from $70. AmEx/D/MC/V.)

◁ DETOUR
FOSSIL BUTTE NATIONAL MONUMENT
Turn off U.S. 30 10 mi. west of Kemmerer.

Four miles from the turn-off to the monument, the **Fossil Butte National Monument Visitors Center** serves as a base-of-operations, offering info about the area before you set off on one of two hikes through fossil territory. A quick film outlines the vast array of creatures that have been preserved in the now-dry fossil lake. A mural-filled gallery comprises the rest of museum, which displays fossils and replicas of some of the finds, most dating from roughly 50 million years ago. The former location of the fossils can be reached on foot via the **Historic Quarry Trail** or the **Fossil Lake Trail.** The former is a geology hike through an abandoned quarry, showing off the rock strata. This moderately strenuous hike is about 2½ mi. and rises 600 ft. in elevation. The other hike is only about 1½ mi. long with a 300 ft. rise, winding through a nearby aspen grove. While the Fossil Lake Trail departs from the visitors center, the Historic Quarry trailhead is back down the road a short way; a small parking area marks it. (☎307-877-4455; www.nps.gov/fobu. Open daily in summer 8am-7pm; in winter 8am-4:30pm. Free.)

◖ APPROACHING MONTPELIER: 76 MILES
Follow **Pine St.** north through Kemmerer; on the outskirts of town it becomes **U.S. 30**, which takes you across the Idaho border to Montpelier. U.S. 30 becomes **4th St.;** follow it into town.

The Gem State

IDAHO

Welcomes You!

MONTPELIER

Built over the famous Oregon Trail rest stop of Clover Creek, Montpelier has long been a haven for weary travelers. The heavily commercialized intersection of U.S. 30 and U.S. 89 is balanced out by the sunny downtown blocks of Washington St., which feature an old theater, an ice-cream parlor, and sidewalk benches held up by smiling bears. The mid-20th-century aura is pleasantly tempered by some of the older buildings; one bank here was robbed of almost $17,000 by Butch Cassidy. He escaped unscathed, though a valiant deputy gave chase on a bicycle.

VITAL STATS

Population: 2800

Visitor Info: Visitor Information Center, 320 N. 4th St. (☎208-847-3800), in the National Oregon/California Trail Center. Open May-Sept. M-Th and Su 9am-5pm, F-Sa 9am-7pm.

Internet Access: Bear Lake County Library, 138 N. 6th St. (☎208-847-1664), off Washington St. Open M-Th 11am-7pm, F 9am-5pm, Sa 9am-2pm. Free.

Post Office: 804 Grant St. (☎208-847-1894). Open M-F 9am-4pm, Sa 9am-noon. **Postal Code:** 83254.

◖ GETTING AROUND. In Montpelier, **U.S. 30** is known as **4th St.** and is one of Montpelier's two main drags. The other is **Washington St. (U.S. 89)** which runs roughly north-south, perpendicular to 4th St. Parking is readily available in Montpelier, and most establishments have their own lots.

◖ SIGHTS. Montpelier's major tourist draw is the ◪**National Oregon/California Trail Center,** 320 N. 4th St. Much more than an ordinary museum, this is a westward journey led by in-character guides. After watching a film about the trails of Idaho, a guide will take you through a gun shop, wagon yard, and mercantile, listing necessary supplies and revealing tricks of the pioneering trade along the way. From there, mount the wagons, which creak through the darkness as tales of the trail are narrated. Finally, climb out at the Clover Creek camp and hear more stories about life on the trail while learning how to jack a cart out of the mud. On the way out, a huge, finely detailed woodcut of the trail through Idaho has captured the features of hundreds of people, animals, and landmarks in vivid color. (☎208-847-3800; www.oregontrailcenter.org. Open May-Sept. M-Th and Su 9am-5pm, F-Sa 9am-7pm. $8, seniors $6, ages 5-12 $5, under 5 free.)

◖◖ FOOD AND ACCOMMODATIONS. Montpelier's downtown burger and ice cream stands are supplemented by some full-fledged restaurants out on U.S. 30. It's unclear if **Butch Cassidy's Restaurant ❸,** 230 N. 4th St., is Old Western or cynically modern in style; the cowboy decor clashes amusingly with the satirical books and bottles of Grey Poupon left in each booth. (☎208-847-3501. Sandwiches $4-7. Entrees $10-18. Open daily 6am-10pm. AmEx/MC/V.)

The busy U.S. 30/89 intersection comes to the rescue for sleepy drivers, boasting a series of cheap but pleasant motels. The **Three Sisters Motel ❷,** 112 S. 6th St., at the corner of Washington St., has small rooms that include refrigerators and microwaves. (☎208-847-2324. Singles from $30. Cash only.) The **Park Motel ❷,** 745 Washington St., on the edge of downtown, is clean and well furnished. (☎208-847-1911. Singles $45; doubles $50. AmEx/D/MC/V.)

◖ APPROACHING SODA SPRINGS: 27 MILES
To the west, **4th St.** becomes **U.S. 30** again, heading on toward Soda Springs. The road is part of the **Oregon Trail/Bear Lake Scenic Byway,** and the landscape is appropriately picturesque. In Soda Springs, U.S. 30 is known as **2nd S.**

SODA SPRINGS

A hundred springs once rose from these grounds, until a city was built over them. The most spectacular of those remaining is, ironically, the man-made Soda Springs Geyser. Greenways weave through the downtown, allowing the Idaho wilderness to infiltrate the sidewalks.

VITAL STATS

Population: 3400

Visitor Info: Soda Springs Chamber of Commerce, 9 W. 2nd South (☎208-547-4964), inside City Hall. Open M-F 8am-noon.

Internet Access: Soda Springs Public Library, 149 S. Main St. (☎208-547-2606). Open M-Th 10am-8pm, F 10am-5pm. Free.

Post Office: 220 S. Main St. (☎208-547-3794). Open M-F 8:30am-5pm, Sa noon-2pm. **Postal Code:** 83276.

GETTING AROUND. Whoever chose the street names in Soda Springs was perhaps a bit misguided. **Main St.** runs north-south and forms a cross with **Hooper Ave.** All other streets are numbered: parallel to and west of Main St. is **1st West,** to the east is **1st East;** parallel to and to the south of Hooper is **1st South,** to the north is **1st North.** As if this wasn't confusing enough, these streets are divided in half at the axis streets, so there is W. 1st South as well as S. 1st West, and so on. The result is that it is shockingly easy to get lost in this very small city.

SIGHTS. Soda Springs's greatest attraction is its namesake. The springs still rise from **Geyser Park,** downtown, though the **Soda Springs Geyser** is the real thriller. The geyser was created when drillers, trying to find a source for a heated swimming pool, struck a pressurized chamber. Today, it is capped for control and allowed to erupt at the stroke of each hour. Geyser Park is also the trailhead for the **Soda Springs Pathway.** Two miles of easy-going trails cut through downtown and then into the surrounding wetlands. The trail stops at **Octagon Park,** at the corner of Hooper Ave. and Main St. The eight-sided pavilion in the center of the park makes for good picnicking. From here, the path continues north to **Hooper Springs Park** and ends in a secluded grove. Beneath a small wooden pavilion, the springs well into a low pool, easily accessible for drinking. The water is naturally carbonated and bitter, but clear and cool. Wise pioneers flavored it with sugar and syrup, but the bold still knock it back straight. (To reach Hooper Springs by car, take Hooper Ave. east to 3rd East, then north to Government Dam Rd., and head west a few hundred yards. All parks open daily sunrise-sunset. Free.) The lobby of the **Enders Building,** 76 S. Main St., is something of an attraction itself, spectacularly preserved in its original 1917 form. The second floor is a museum of local history, and barber chairs, saddles, and various antique relics are spread throughout. The collection's prize is the revolver used by the Sundance Kid; look for it at the bottom of the hallway display case. (☎208-547-4980. Open M-Sa 7am-9pm, Su 7am-8pm. Free.)

FOOD AND ACCOMMODATIONS. Soda Springs has its share of fast food along the highway, but, though hard to find, other options do exist. **Caribou Mountain Pizza and Grill ❷,** 59 W. 2nd South (U.S. 30), offers the ultimate in budget dining: all-you-can-eat. Unlimited salad and soup ($6) are available all day, while the lunch buffet (11am-1:30pm; $6) has pizza, wings, and other all-you-can-eat delights. (☎208-547-4575. Open M-Th 11am-9pm, F-Sa 11am-11pm. AmEx/MC/V.) In the Enders Building is the **Geyser View Restaurant ❸,** 76 S. Main St., particularly good if you're feeling at all carnivorous. The Geyser Burger ($7) and Geyser Chicken ($6.50) are sure bets. (☎208-547-4980. Steaks $10-17. Open M-Sa 7am-9pm, Su 7am-8pm. AmEx/D/MC/V.)

The 30 rooms of the **Enders Hotel ❸,** in the Enders Building, 76 S. Main St., feature the same antique loveliness of the building at large. The Anniversary and Honeymoon suites are perfect for the romantic pair—or the loner in need of some opulence. The Anniversary suite contains the writing desk of a Confederate general, while the Honeymoon suite has an original English bed from the 19th century. (☎208-547-4980. Rooms $65-95; Anniversary Suite $165; Honeymoon Suite $195. AmEx/D/MC/V.) For the more financially restrained, a handful of budget motels line 2nd South, including the **Caribou Lodge & Motel ❷,** 110 W. 2nd South (U.S. 30). There are a range of rooms, but even the smallest is comfortably arranged with wood paneling.

OREGON TRAIL

Free coffee is available all morning. (☎208-547-3377. Reception 7am-11pm. Singles $41; doubles $46. AmEx/D/MC/V.) The **JR Inn ❷**, 179 W. 2nd South, has big, clean rooms with standard amenities and pleasant decor. (☎208-547-3366. Singles $42; doubles $52. AmEx/D/MC/V.)

◪ **APPROACHING LAVA HOT SPRINGS: 21 MILES**
Take **2nd South (U.S. 30 W)** toward the "world-class" hot springs of Idaho, Lava Hot Springs.

LAVA HOT SPRINGS

Glittering, expensive, and fun, Lava Hot Springs embodies all the wonder and hustle of a resort city. The hot pools and the exciting river-tubing course delight the hordes of tourists who come from all over the nation to experience the naturally heated waters.

VITAL STATS

Population: 520

Visitor Info: South Bannock County Historical Center, 110 E. Main St. (☎208-776-5254). Open M-W and F-Su 10am-5:30pm, Th noon-5pm.

Internet Access: South Bannock Public Library, Lava Hot Springs Branch, 33 E. Main St. (☎208-776-5301). Open M, W, F 1-5pm; Tu and Th 1-6pm; Sa 10am-2pm. Free.

Post Office: 45 S. Center St. (☎208-776-5680). Open M-F 9am-noon and 1-4:30pm. **Postal Code:** 83246.

▤ **GETTING AROUND.** Lava Hot Springs is laid out along the **Portneuf River,** south of **U.S. 30.** Most of the town's attractions lie along **Main St.,** which runs east-west through town. In a town of Lava Hot Springs's size, parking is rarely a problem, but things can get a bit crowded when the summer tourists arrive.

◪ **SIGHTS.** The naturally heated waters (104-112°F) of the **Lava Hot Springs,** 430 E. Main St., have been in use for centuries, long before the Europeans arrived. Once hailed for their curative powers, there is no doubt that the springs have, at the very least, calming powers. The pools are set back from the road in a pleasant, tree-strewn complex. (☎208-776-5221 or 800-423-8597; www.lavahotsprings.com. Open Apr.-Sept. daily 8am-11pm; Oct.-Mar. M-Th and Su 9am-10pm, F-Sa 9am-11pm. Day pass M-Th $5, ages 3-11 and seniors $4.50; F-Su $7/$6.50.) **Tubing** is allowed on the Portneuf River. The access point is on the eastern end of town, behind the picnic pavilion. The stream runs swiftly under Main St.'s bridge and along the highway before reaching the dismount. Stands up and down Main St. compete to rent tubes and life jackets for a few dollars. Some non-water-based entertainment can be found at **Baker Ranch Wagon Rides,** 11716 S. Dempsey Creek Rd., south from 4th St. Visitors can take a mountain wagon ride powered by draft horses and then enjoy a creekside dinner with the group before the evening return trip. (☎208-776-5684. Reservations required. Operates Memorial Day-Sept. $22, ages 4-13 $17, under 4 free.)

◪◪ **FOOD AND ACCOMMODATIONS. Ye Ole Chuckwagon Restaurant ❷**, 211 E. Main St., has great hamburgers and sandwiches ($4-15) and a respectable array of vegetarian options ($3-6). The Old West motif is extensive and even includes the drinking glasses, which are transparent cowboy boots. (☎208-776-5141. Lunch $5-7. Dinner $7-14. Open daily 6:30am-10pm. MC/V.) **Johnny's ❸**, 78 E. Main St., literally rose from the ashes of the old Silver Grill Cafe that was once there to become an elegantly subdued restaurant. Tempting desserts ($1.25-5) like cheesecake and German chocolate cake round off the extensive menu. (☎208-776-5562. Open M-Th and Su 6:30am-9pm, F-Sa 6:30am-10pm. MC/V.) For ice cream, skip through the hallway to the **Riverwalk Ice Cream Shoppe ❶**, where three-scoop cones and banana splits are just $3.50. (☎208-776-5872. Open Tu-Su 1-9pm. V only.)

Most accommodations in Lava Hot Springs are on the expensive side, though a few budget rooms can be found with a bit of searching. **Aura Soma Lava ❸**, 196 E. Main St., is the best lodging in Lava Hot Springs, with motel rooms, cabins, and luxurious cottages. There are also private hot pools, fire places, and massages. (☎208-776-5800 or 800-757-1233; www.aurasomalava.com. Massages $60 per 1hr. Rooms $69, with hot tub $75; cabins $99-175; cottage $139. MC/V.) A pleasant, if slightly humbler

2005: Computer scientist Bobby Henderson founds parody religion Flying Spaghetti Monsterism.

stay is available at the **Lava Spa Motel ❸**, 359 E. Main St. This motel has a range of room sizes, and for a little extra dough, you can even get one with its own hot tub. (☎208-776-5589. Singles in summer $55; in winter $50. Doubles $75/$65. AmEx/D/DC/MC/V.) The **Home Hotel & Motel ❷**, 306 E. Main St., has budget rooms within walking distance of the hot pools and downtown Lava. (☎208-776-5507; www.home-hotel.com. Reservations recommended. Singles $35; doubles from $55. AmEx/D/MC/V.)

◪ APPROACHING POCATELLO: 38 MILES
Take **Main St.** to **Center St.**, which leads back to **U.S. 30.** 12 mi. out of Lava Hot Springs, U.S. 30 meets **I-15;** take I-15 N for another 18 mi. Take **Exit 67,** which blends conveniently into the major thoroughfare of **5th Ave.** at the southern tip of the city.

POCATELLO

A giant by mountain area standards, Pocatello draws students, thrill-seekers, and vacationers to see the Hot Springs and Yellowstone Park. This endless flux of visitors, fused with the lively population of Idaho State University, gives Pocatello a surprisingly diverse and happening feel for a small city in the heart of the potato state.

VITAL STATS

Population: 51,500

Visitor Info: Tourist Information Center, 2695 S. 5th Ave. (☎208-233-7333). Open in summer M-F 9am-6pm, Sa-Su 10am-4pm; in winter M-F 10am-4pm. **Greater Pocatello Chamber of Commerce,** 343 W. Center St. (☎208-233-1525; www.pocatelloidaho.com). Open M-F 8am-5pm.

Internet Access: Marshall Public Library, 113 S. Garfield Ave. (☎208-232-1263). Open M-Th 9am-9pm, F-Sa 9am-6pm. Free.

Post Office: 730 E. Clark St. (☎208-235-2190), off 5th Ave. Open M-F 8am-5:30pm, Sa 10:30am-2:30pm. **Postal Code:** 83201.

▐ GETTING AROUND

Pocatello is long and narrow, running from the southeast to the northwest between the **Portneuf River** and **I-15.** At the southeastern end is **Ross Park,** home to a number of Poca-tello's attractions. This part of the city is dominated by **5th Ave.**, which runs past restaurants and Idaho State University. Around the center of the city, 5th Ave. ends, running into busy **Yellowstone Ave.** The **Historic Old Town** area, Pocatello's downtown, is south of the train tracks, parallel to 5th Ave. **Benton St.** is the most direct route from 5th Ave. to downtown; **Center St.** is larger, but it runs one-way from downtown to 5th Ave. This particular area is small and easily traversed by foot. North of the Pocatello is the suburb of **Chubbuck;** the two are linked by Yellowstone Ave. Another cluster of hotels and restaurants is gathered on Chubbuck's southern border, where **I-86** divides the two cities. Most establishment have lots, so parking is easy.

◎ SIGHTS

ROSS PARK. Lovely greenery and an aquatic center make for good summer lazing at Ross Park, at the south end of 5th Ave. The park also features three major attractions. When historic Fort Hall became part of reservation territory in the 1860s, enthusiasts built a full reproduction in Pocatello, resulting in the **Fort Hall Replica,** 3002 Alvord Loop, north of S. 4th Ave. The replica buildings are furnished to recall frontier life, though two of the largest rooms house mini-museums on pioneer and Native American life in the area. (☎208-234-1795. Open Memorial Day to Labor Day daily 10am-6pm; Sept. daily 10am-2pm; mid-April to Memorial Day Tu-Sa 10am-2pm. $2.25, ages 13-17 $1.25, ages 5-11 $1.) Next door, the **Bannock County Historical Museum,** 3000 Alvord Loop, in Upper Ross Park, displays relics from Pocatello's past. The medicinal room is especially interesting, with jars of Dragon's Blood and Ethereal Oil, but unfortunately, no further explanation is offered by the yellowed labels. (☎208-233-0434. Open Memorial Day to Labor Day daily 10am-7pm; Labor Day to Memorial Day Tu-Sa 10am-2pm. $2.50, seniors and ages 12-18 $1.75, ages 6-11 $1, under 6 free.) Only North American wildlife is kept at the **Pocatello Zoo,** 3101 Ave. of the Chiefs, on the edge of Ross Park, but lack of lions isn't a serious loss: bighorn sheep, grizzly bears, coyotes, and cougars still roam the cages. One impressive enclosure contains elk, buffalo, bison, and pronghorn antelope in natural habitats. (☎208-234-6264; www.pocatellozoo.com. Open Apr. 15-Apr. 30 Sa-Su 9am-5pm; May to mid-June daily 9am-5pm; mid-June to Labor Day daily 10am-6pm; Labor Day to mid-Oct. Sa-Su 10am-4pm. $3, seniors $2.25, ages 3-11 $1.50.)

IDAHO MUSEUM OF NATURAL HISTORY.
Bigger, scarier, and more extinct fauna can be found at the impressive Idaho Museum of Natural History, on the Idaho State campus, at the intersection of 5th Ave. and Dillon St. The skeleton of a monstrous *Bison latifrons* is the museum's main prize—the 8 ft. horns are the largest horns from any bison in history. The "Dinosaur Times" exhibit has partial remains and full murals, though the most fascinating piece is the tooth whorls of an ancient shark. (☎208-282-3317; http://imnh.isu.edu. Open Tu-Sa 10am-5pm. $5, seniors $4, students $3, ages 4-11 $2.)

DOWNTOWN. The Historic Preservation Commission has a self-guided walking tour of the **Downtown Historic District,** focusing on the architecture and history behind the late 19th- and early 20th-century buildings. Pick up a pamphlet at the Chamber of Commerce. The downtown area is also a great place for exploring—herbalists, record stores, skate shops and other hole-in-the-wall establishments abound.

FOOD

Pocatello's best restaurants are scattered all over town. Vine-covered **Buddy's ❸,** 626 E. Lewis St., just north of 5th Ave., on the edge of the Idaho State campus, serves classic Italian meals to a family crowd and a few college regulars. (☎208-233-1172. Pasta $8-17. Pizza and calzones from $10-18. Open M-Sa 11am-midnight. V only.) Class practically drips from the brick walls at the **The Continental Bistro ❷,** 140 S. Main St., downtown. The menu also has an upscale slant; sandwiches ($6-9) have tasty ingredients like crab and avocado, while the pastas ($6-8.50) feature such specialties as Thai shrimp curry. (☎208-233-4433. Open M-Sa 11am-10pm. AmEx/D/DC/MC/V.) **Tastee Treat ❶,** 5231 Yellowstone Ave., in Chubbuck, offers all the delicious greasiness of classic road fare without the production-line taste of actual fast food. The proud home of the spaceburger, the sea-space burger, and the Tom burger, Tastee Treat also attracts hordes of customers with its delicious ice cream. (☎208-238-9511. Hamburgers under $3. Ice cream $1.25. Open M-Th 11am-10pm, F-Sa 11am-11pm. AmEx/D/MC/V.)

ACCOMMODATIONS

Pocatello is definitely weak in the accommodations department. There is practically nothing to choose from but chain hotels near the highway exits. The budget traveler would truly be doomed to an unhappy fate were it not for the **Thunderbird Motel ❷,** 1415 S. 5th Ave., which, luckily, consists of many buildings and many clean rooms. (☎208-232-6330; www.thunderbirdmotelid.com. Laundry. Singles $43; doubles $49. AmEx/D/MC/V.)

NIGHTLIFE

There's no cohesive feel to Pocatello nightlife, but that just means there are more ways to party. **Club Charley's,** 331 E. Center St., puts resident drag show "Charley's Angels" on the stage the first Saturday of every month, while DJs take over the rest of the time. (☎208-239-0855. M-Th karaoke. Open M-Sa 7pm-2am, Su 8pm-2am. MC/V.) **5 Mile Inn,** 4828 Yellowstone Ave., in Chubbuck, is nothing but country. Lily-livered East Coasters can experience the full power of a Western hoe-down. (☎208-237-9950. F-Sa live music 9pm-1am. Su karaoke 8pm-midnight. Open daily 10am-1:30am. AmEx/MC/V.) The **First National Bar,** 232 W. Center St., becomes a smokin' house of blues when there's someone around to play. Call ahead for the weekly schedule. (☎208-233-1516. Cover $5 or less. Open M-Sa 11am-2am, Su 11am-midnight. AmEx/D/MC/V.)

APPROACHING CRATERS OF THE MOON: 97 MILES

From the southern half of the city, the easiest escape is to head south on **5th St.** to the junction with **I-15,** and head north. Take **Exit 93** to **U.S. 26 W;** after 35 mi., it converges with **U.S. 20.** Follow the road west, crossing the Big Lost River. From the bridge, it is 16 mi. to Arco. U.S. 20/26 becomes **Front St.,** then makes a 90° turn, becoming **Grand Ave.** in Arco. Continue about 17 mi. to the entrance to the park.

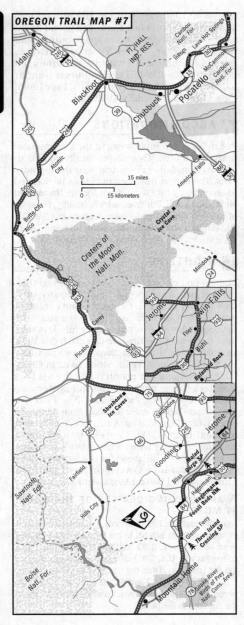

OREGON TRAIL MAP #7

CRATERS OF THE MOON

Millennia-old volcanic activity left a bizarre mark upon central Idaho. An early visitor to the other-worldly landscape of Craters of the Moon National Monument in the 1920s claimed it was "the strangest 75 sq. mi. on the North American continent." The same geological hotspot responsible for the thermal activity in Yellowstone National Park created this monument's 75,000 acres of twisted lava formations; eruptions ended only 2000 years ago and are expected to resume within the next 1000. Located 70 mi. southeast of Sun Valley at the junction of U.S. 20 and 26/93, Craters of the Moon promises visitors a fascinating mix of lava tube caves, molds of ancient trees, and long-hardened lava flows.

VITAL STATS

Area: 715,000 acres

Visitor Info: Craters of the Moon Visitors Center, (☎208-527-3257), just inside the park. Open daily Memorial Day to Labor Day 8am-6pm; Labor Day to Memorial Day 8am-4:30pm. **Arco Chamber of Commerce,** 159 N. Idaho St. (☎208-527-8977). Open M-F 8am-5pm.

Gateway Town: Arco

Fees: 7-day pass $8 per vehicle.

⊟ GETTING AROUND

Craters of the Moon is divided into three areas. The first and smallest is the **Developed Area,** where paved roads lead past several of the more impressive craters, and through some spectacularly grotesque formation clusters. The second region is the **Wilderness Area,** where only a few dirt paths disturb the natural order. The majority of the park is dominated by the **Backcountry Area.** Crisscrossed by unmaintained roads, scorched in the summer, and covered with snow in the winter, the backcountry area is not hospitable to the average driver and vehicle. The only access to the park is about 17 mi. west of Arco on **U.S. 20/26.** Immediately inside is the **visitors center,** which has videos, displays on the volcanic history of the area and the wildlife population, and printed guides. Anyone planning to camp in the Wilderness Area must obtain a free backcountry permit.

Arco, home to the nearest food and accommodations, is just 17 mi. east on U.S. 20/26. In Arco, most services are located right on the highway, which takes the names of **Grand Ave.** and **Front St.** within city limits. The highway makes a 90° turn in the middle of town, so watch the signs carefully.

 DID YOU KNOW? Arco was the 1st American city to be lit by nuclear power.

 SIGHTS

HIKING

The easiest way to visit the attractions of the developed portions of the park is to follow the 7 mi. **loop drive,** which departs from the visitors center and winds through the major sights around the monument's northern end. Several shorter trails lead to intriguing rock formations and a variety of caves. The 2 mi. **Broken Top Loop,** starting at Tree Molds parking lot, goes through Buffalo Caves and is a quick but comprehensive survey of the surrounding land; the short ■**Caves Trail,** further along the loop, leads to three large caves, each with a distinctive character. The **North Crater Flow** (½ mi.) is a lumpy field of cooled lava which has taken on fantastic shapes. The *pahoehoe* ("smooth" in Hawaiian) and *aa*

("rough" in Hawaiian) lavas produce an unlikely variety of forms. The path here is paved and mostly flat. Just a few yards down is the **North Crater Trail** (2 mi.), a steep, rocky path that leads to a volcanic vent. Next along the loop road is **Devil's Orchard** (½ mi.). The name refers to the sharp chunks of a shattered volcano that litter the area, as well as the sharp clusters of Witch's Broom which have grown upon the gnarled trees. The trail through the orchard is a half-mile loop of broad, flat sidewalk. At **Inferno Cone** (½ mi.), a tall hill of black cinder overlooks miles of volcanic terrain from the edge of the loop road. The hike up is short but extremely steep, and the path is unpaved. Between Inferno Cone and the caves is a side road breaking off the main loop, leading to the Tree Molds trailhead. From here the **Wilderness Trail** winds into the hills and craters south of the developed area. Though not very steep, this trail is long (about 5½ mi. into the wilderness before petering out), often difficult to follow through the sage brush, and brutally exposed to the sun. Don't forget sturdy shoes, water, sunscreen, and a hat, as there are no trees for miles.

CAVES

Some of the most popular attractions of the monument are the caves of the **Blue Dragon Flow,** which are actually lava tubes, or tunnels that formed when rivers of molten rock hardened on the surface. The four open caves are completely wild, with no artificial lighting,

HOWL YOU DOING?

For many years, the only wolves in Yellowstone were the pair stuffed and on display in the Albright Visitors Center. These two, along with all the other wolves in Yellowstone, were killed in 1922 when these predators were considered a menace to Yellowstone's other wildlife. When gray wolves were declared endangered in 1973, talk of bringing back the wolf population started up. After more than 20 years of public debate, 14 wolves from Canada were released into the park in 1995. Today, over 270 wolves roam the area. Although every effort has been made to reduce the concerns of opponents, the reintroduction of wolves has undoubtedly meant that some livestock and domestic animals have become prey. A wolf compensation trust, brainchild of the Bailey Wildlife Fund, has been established to pay ranchers for losses due to wolves, and this shift in the economic responsibility from ranchers to wolf supporters has created broader acceptance. Wolves seem to be a hit with the ecosystem as well as other animals and scavengers have benefited from the food remaining after wolf kills, and studies indicate that biodiversity in the ecosystem will increase now that wolves have returned.

For more on the Bailey Wildlife fund, check out www.defenders.org.

[in recent news]

pathways, or guides. **Dew Drop Cave** is actually just a deep hole scraped into the earth, and explorers are allowed to enter without a flashlight. The largest of the caves is **Indian Tunnel,** whose multiple roof openings let in a lot of light. Spelunkers will probably enjoy **Boy Scout Cave** the most of all; after you round a bend, the light disappears entirely, while the ceiling and the floor bend to meet each other. Reaching the end requires a bright light and a bent back. (Cave guides available from a box at the start of the ½ mi. caves trail.) If you plan to explore the caves, bring a flashlight since you may not be allowed to proceed in some caves without one.

FOOD

Food in the area is largely monopolized by the city of Arco. In addition to restaurants, Arco has a few grocery stores where water and other goods can be bought before any long term wilderness expeditions. With a big green rocking chair out front, **Pickle's Place ❷,** 440 S. Front St., is easy to identify. Home of the atomic burger ($6-7.25), Pickle's also dishes out classic breakfasts ($4-6.50) in plentiful portions. (☎208-527-9944. Open M-Th 6am-10pm, F-Su 6am-11pm. MC/V.) The monster sandwiches at the **Deli Sandwich Shop ❷,** 119 N. Idaho Ave., are delicious and perfect for taking into the monument. Twenty options range in size from 4 in. ($3.50) to 24 in. ($12.50). Yard long (and larger) giants can be made upon request. (☎208-527-3757. Open daily 8am-10pm. AmEx/D/MC/V.) Chicken and ribs sizzle on the backyard grill at **Grandpa's Southern Bar-B-Q ❷,** 434 W. Grand Ave. Grab a seat on the front porch for a killer pork sandwich ($7) and a dose of some small-town hospitality. (☎208-527-3362. Dinners $7-15. Open M-Sa 11am-8pm, Su noon-8pm. Cash only.)

ACCOMMODATIONS

There are 51 campsites scattered throughout the monument's single **campground ❶,** located just past the entrance station. The grounds are first come, first served, and have toilets, water, grills, and picnic tables. A tip for tent campers: site #13 is considered one of the best, as it is

private and nicely shielded from the wind. (Open year-round. No hookups. Sites in summer $10; in winter lower.) Camping at unmarked sites in the dry lava wilderness of the park is possible with a free **backcountry permit,** available at the visitors center. Campsites are completely primitive and unmarked; it is recommended that each camper bring a gallon of water for each day spent there.

Like meals, beds with roofs aren't available in the park, but in nearby Arco. Don't let the dilapidated sign fool you; the **Arco Inn Motel ❷,** 540 W. Grand Ave., is a great place to stay, with spotless rooms. (☎208-527-3100. Singles from $39; doubles from $49. AmEx/D/MC/V.) The **D-K Motel ❷,** 316 S. Front St., offers rooms ranging from family rooms to economy singles, all comfortable and equipped with microwaves, refrigerators, and coffeemakers. (☎208-527-8282. Singles $36; doubles $52. AmEx/D/MC/V.) The **Lost River Motel ❷,** 405 Hiway Dr., off Front St., near the east edge of town, has pleasant rooms with recliners and access to a hot tub. (☎208-527-3600. Reception daily 8am-11pm. Singles $41; doubles $54. AmEx/D/MC/V.)

DETOUR
SHOSHONE ICE CAVES
1561 Rte. 75. 12 mi. south of the junction of U.S. 26 S with U.S. 20.

Like Minnetonka Cave, the Ice Caves are kept naturally cool—these at a freezing 26-32°F. Unlike Minnetonka, however, the Ice Caves have fallen prey to tourist baiting; the entrance is flanked by statues of Native Americans and dinosaurs, and the grounds are dominated by a gift shop and antiques store. The cave itself is an impressive geological formation, at 1700 ft. long and 125 ft. deep. Tours depart every hour in the morning and evening, and every 30min. in the afternoon. (☎208-886-2058. Open daily May-Sept. 8am-8pm. 45min. tours daily from 9am; last tour 7pm. $6.50, seniors $5.50, ages 5-14 $3.75.)

APPROACHING TWIN FALLS: 23 MILES
From Shoshone, continue south on **U.S. 93.** Stay on U.S. 93 past the junction with I-84. The highway will cross the long **Perrine Bridge,** which spans the deep blue gash of the **Snake River Canyon.** As soon as the you cross the bridge, you'll be in Twin Falls.

TWIN FALLS

Twin Falls is like wherever you're from, only more so. Chili's is at the mall across the street from the Outback Steakhouse, a block north of Barnes & Noble, which has a Starbucks inside. Target is next to OfficeMax, behind Arby's and Applebee's. In the first mile of Twin Falls, you'll find a Sonic Burger, two McDonald's, three Subways, and a Burger King. Beyond the prepackaged glow, however, there lies a quiet, charming city that offers easy access to the outdoors; whitewater rafting trips run from Centennial Park, bike and running trails wind along the gorge, and waterfalls shine up and down the river.

VITAL STATS

Population: 39,000

Visitor Info: Twin Falls Chamber of Commerce, 858 Blue Lakes Blvd. N (☎208-733-9458), just across the bridge. Open mid-Mar. to mid-Oct. daily 8am-8pm.

Internet Access: Cyber Center, 1180 Blue Lakes Blvd. N (☎208-734-1300). Open M-F 9am-6pm, Sa 10am-4pm. $2.25 per 30min.

Post Office: 253 2nd Ave. W (☎208-733-0702), right off Shoshone St. (Rte. 74) from U.S. 93. Open M-F 8am-5:30pm. **Postal Code:** 83301.

GETTING AROUND. U.S. 93 joins up with **U.S. 30** outside Twin Falls, becoming **Addison Ave.** U.S. 30 splits off, heading southeast through downtown, and eventually becomes **Kimberly Rd.,** while U.S. 93 goes on for a few blocks and becomes **Blue Lakes Blvd. N.** Newer businesses and developments lie along Blue Lakes Blvd., while older, privately run eateries and accommodations tend to sit back on Kimberly Rd. The town's third main thoroughfare, **Shoshone St.** (Rte. 74), heads downtown diagonally from the intersection of Blue Lakes and Addison.

Downtown Twin Falls is organized in a logical numbered grid—it's just not any logic you're familiar with. **Main Ave.** and **Shoshone St.** intersect, forming an X by which all of downtown is oriented. Avenues run northwest-southeast, numbered in both directions by their distance from Main Ave.; streets run northeast-southwest, numbered relative to Shoshone St. Both avenues and streets can be marked with any of the cardinal directions. Designation changes when the street or avenue crosses either of the two main roads. Thus, 3rd St. S. does not become 3rd St. N., but 3rd St. E. as it crosses Main Ave., while four blocks northwest, 3rd St. W. becomes 3rd St. N.

SIGHTS. The **Herrett Center for Arts and Science,** at the College of Southern Idaho North Entrance, is home to the **Faulkner Planetarium,** considered to be one of the best in the world. The Herrett Center also features exhibits on stone tools, contemporary art, and the geology of North and Central America. (Just off North College Rd., from Blue Lakes Blvd. ☎208-732-6655; www.csi.edu/herrett. Open Memorial Day to Labor Day Tu-Sa 1-9pm; Labor Day to Memorial Day Tu and F 9:30am-9pm, W-Th 9:30am-4:30pm, Sa 1-9pm. Free. Planetarium shows $4, seniors $3, students $2.) **Historic Old Town** celebrated its 100th year in 2004. The downtown area sports the lovely **City Park,** which hosts free concerts Thursday nights in summer at the bandshell.

OUTDOORS. Twin Falls has a variety of attractions for outdoor enthusiasts. Closest to the city proper are the mighty **Shoshone Falls**—the "Niagara of the West"—which are actually 50 ft. longer than the real thing. The 212 ft. falls are best viewed in the spring, when snowmelt swells the Snake River and the flow has not yet been diverted to provide power to the area. (Follow Blue Lakes Blvd. to the major intersection with Falls Blvd., head east on Falls Blvd., and take a left onto 3300 East Rd. after 3 mi. ☎208-736-2265. Open daily 7am-10pm. $3 per car.) Nearby is **Twin Falls.** The title is an anachronism now, as one of the falls has vanished in the name of electric power. The other rages on, though, and in the summer it can be wider and wilder than Shoshone Falls. (From Falls Ave., head east for just under 2 mi., and turn left on 3500 East Rd. ☎208-736-2265. Open daily 8am-sunset. Free.)

Snake River Canyon, north of town, is a giant hole in the earth. The **I.B. Perrine Bridge,** a $10 million effort completed in 1976, is the longest bridge in the west, and from it, visitors can view the impressive 500 ft. drop to the golf courses in the canyon below. **Centennial Waterfront Park,** on the south rim next to the visitors center, a half-mile west of the bridge, offers impressive views and enough historical information to complement any picnic. If you'd like to experience the canyon from a slightly different angle, **Idaho Guide Service,** 563 Trotter Dr., off Elizabeth Blvd. from Blue Lakes, runs a variety of water tours, from 3hr. motor boat tours to five-day whitewater-rafting adventures. (☎208-734-4998; www.idahoguideservice.com.) If you'd rather get high than wet, **Reeder Flying Service,** 644 Airport Loop, flies helicopter tours of the canyon and the falls for as low as $25 per person. (West of U.S. 93 on the north rim of the canyon. ☎208-733-5920.)

🍴 FOOD AND ACCOMMODATIONS.

Chain restaurants with glossy menus and perky waitstaff line Blue Lakes Blvd., on the north side of town, but smaller operations can be found farther from the highway. The **Depot Grill** ❷, 545 Shoshone St. S., has drawn the local crowd since 1927 with its classic diner decor and smorgasbord lunches. Don't miss the all-you-can-eat fried chicken ($6) on Tuesdays 5-9pm. (☎208-733-0710. Sandwiches $2.50-6.50. Burgers $3-6. Seafood $8-11. Steaks $10-16. Open M 6am-midnight, Tu-Sa 24hr., Su midnight-5pm. AmEx/D/DC/MC/V.) At **Crowley's Soda Fountain** ❶, 144 Main Ave., thirsty patrons choose from malts and shakes ($3-5), smoothies ($4), Italian sodas ($3), and phosphates ($4). Sandwiches ($3-7) and wraps ($6.25) make for light meals. (☎208-733-1041. Open M-Sa 8am-5pm. MC/V.) Similarly, Blue Lakes Blvd. also has an abundance of motels. The **Old Towne Lodge** ❷, 248 2nd Ave. W, off Addison Ave., offers bright rooms at some of the best rates in town. (☎208-733-5630. Singles $43; doubles $48. MC/V.)

🚗 APPROACHING HAGERMAN: 37 MILES

Addison Ave. runs west out of town, becoming **U.S. 30.** This portion of the highway is known as the **Thousand Springs Scenic Byway.** Almost immediately after leaving Twin Falls the road sweeps past Filer, and, after 12 mi., enters the town of Buhl. From Buhl, a 17 mi. detour leads to the ridiculous geological formation of **Balanced Rock,** a 40 ft. wide stone supported on a natural pillar just 3 ft. across. In the center of Buhl, turn left onto Main St., following it for 1 mi. Take a right at the end, then an immediate left, following the signs. Continue along for 4 mi., then bear right at the fork. The road passes through farmland, plummeting suddenly into a gorge. When it re-emerges, the unlikely stone will be above the road to the right. Some 15 mi. beyond Buhl, the highway returns to Snake River and passes the **Thousand Springs.** Many white waterfalls pour from the green-bearded cliffs across the river. There are no overlooks or side roads; have cameras at the ready. The well-marked drive to the **Hagerman Fossil Beds National Monument** off U.S. 30 is less than 3 mi., ending at the Snake River Overlook. (☎208-837-4793. Open in summer 9am-6pm; in winter M and Th-Su 9am-5pm.) Continue on **U.S. 30** to Hagerman.

HAGERMAN

Hagerman's main claim to fame is the **Hagerman Fossil Beds National Monument Visitors Center,** 221 N. Front St. (U.S. 30), and the Hagerman horse skeletons. The visitors center itself has little to offer, but 20 full horse skeletons were found in the area and are believed to have been a form of North American zebra. (☎208-837-4793. Open in summer 9am-6pm; in winter M and Th-Su 9am-5pm.) If you're looking for something to eat, try the **Snake River Grill** ❸, 611 Frogs Landing. Sandwiches ($8) and entrees ($13-14) feature locally caught sturgeon and catfish, along with chicken-fried steak, ribs, and alligator. (☎208-837-6227. Open daily 7am-9pm. D/MC/V.) For some cheaper options, head to **Larry & Mary's Restaurant** ❷, 141 N. State St. The chili burger ($6.25) is a delicious house specialty, and you can amuse yourself for the rest of the trip trying to come up with other names that rhyme with Larry and Mary. (☎208-837-6475. Open daily 5am-8pm. MC/V.) One of the few lodging options in the area is the **Hagerman Valley Inn** ❸, 499 S. State St., where rooms have standard amenities. (☎208-837-6196. Rooms from $50. AmEx/D/MC/V.)

🔄 DETOUR
MALAD GORGE STATE PARK
Take Exit 147 off U.S. 30 to reach the park.

Built around the deep and narrow cleft of the Malad Gorge, the 652-acre Malad Gorge State Park is stunning—unfortunately, it runs right under the interstate. The park can be viewed by driving around its 3 mi. road. The main attraction is **Devil's Washbowl,** a green pool below the waterfall that is carving the gorge out of the rock. The view is best from a bridge that spans the canyon. From there, it is possible to hike right along the edge among the birds that flit around the gorge. (☎208-837-4505. Open daily 7am-10pm. Entrance fee $4 per vehicle. Campsites $7-12. Cash only.)

BLISS. Less than 8 mi. along U.S. 30 from Hagerman, Bliss is the last stop on the Thousand Springs Byway, the gateway back to the interstate. Those looking to sleep or eat before returning to the speedway have a final handful of options here. The **Oxbow Restaurant ❷**, Main St., is a great spot right off the highway. Breakfasts feature the pleasing oddity of the pancake sandwich ($5), while lunch includes burgers and sandwiches. (☎208-352-4250. Open daily 6am-10pm. MC/V.) The **Amber Inn Motel ❷**, off U.S. 30 at Exit 141, has simple but pretty rooms. (☎208-352-4441. Singles $37; doubles $42. AmEx/D/MC/V.)

◤ **APPROACHING GLENNS FERRY: 20 MILES** Follow **I-84** to **Exit 121**, which feeds onto **1st Ave.**, a loop which leads through Glenns Ferry and back onto the interstate.

GLENNS FERRY

Glenns Ferry is strangely quiet for an interstate city. Nestled along the Snake River, which runs slow and broad here, the town feels like a scene from *Huckleberry Finn*. The river is not as sleepy as it looks, though. Swift undercurrents made it one of the toughest river crossings pioneers once faced, and the ferry that gave the town its name wasn't built until after the golden spike was driven into the intercontinental railroad.

VITAL STATS

Population: 1600

Visitor Info: Glenns Ferry Chamber of Commerce, 108 E. 1st Ave. (☎208-366-345). Open Tu-F 11am-4pm.

Internet Access: Glenns Ferry Public Library, 298 S. Lincoln St. (☎208-366-2045), south of the train tracks. Open M-Sa 1-5pm. Free.

Post Office: 22 E. 2nd Ave. (☎208-366-7329). Open M-F 8am-4:30pm. **Postal Code:** 83623.

◪ **GETTING AROUND.** Glenns Ferry lies just south of **I-84** and just north of the **Snake River.** The city's primary street, **1st Ave.**, is a loop off the interstate, running diagonally through the center of town and then joining back up with I-84. It is known as E. 1st Ave. to the east of its intersection with **Commercial Ave.** and W. 1st Ave. to the west of the intersection.

◱ **SIGHTS.** The frustrating, occasionally deadly river crossing faced by the original Oregon Trail roadtrippers is remembered at **Three Island Crossing Park,** right on the banks of the river. The grassy riverbanks of the park look down on three islands rising from the Snake River where it widens, which helped make it possible for pioneers to ford the water. Shoshone, Bannock, and Paiute tribesmen also aided the pioneers. (Take Commercial Ave. south from 1st Ave. and across the train tracks, turning left onto Madison when Commercial Ave. ends. The park is a short distance down the road, on the left. ☎208-366-2394 or 888-634-3246. Center open W-Su 9am-4pm. Call ahead for extended summer hours. Entrance fee $4 per car.)

◾◪ **FOOD AND ACCOMMODATIONS.** Dining options are limited in the city, but what's there won't disappoint. Right on the banks of the Snake River is the **Carmela Restaurant ❹**, 1289 Madison Ave., easily recognized by the Godzilla-sized quail casting its shadow on the driveway. The restaurant serves pastas, steaks and seafood, and the vineyard outside has produced 10 wines. (☎208-366-2313. Entrees $13-21. Open in summer M-Sa 11am-9pm, Su 10am-8pm; in winter M-F 11am-8pm, Sa-Su 11am-9pm. D/MC/V.) **Hanson's Cafe ❷**, 201 E. 1st Ave., serves the enormous, 1 lb. Grande Rancher for $8. (☎208-366-9983. Sandwiches $3-6. Open in summer M-Th 7am-10pm, F-Sa 7am-11pm, Su 7am-3pm; in winter M-Th 7am-9pm, F-Sa 7am-10pm, Su 7am-3pm. MC/V.) Glenns Ferry has a handful of motels located conveniently along the 1st Ave. loop. **Hanson's Hotel ❷**, 201 E. 1st Ave., is hidden behind trees and Hanson's Cafe, but its eight garden-side rooms are worth finding. (☎208-366-9933. Singles from $35. MC/V.) The cheapest lodging in town is at the **Redford Motel ❷**, 525 E. 1st Ave., where the rooms are clean and the staff is friendly. (☎208-366-2421. Singles $33; doubles $43. MC/V.)

◤ **APPROACHING MOUNTAIN HOME: 25 MILES** From downtown Glenns Ferry, continue west along **1st Ave.** until it rejoins **I-84.** Head west for 25 mi. to

Mountain Home. Take **Exit 95** from I-84; this leads onto **American Legion Blvd.,** which passes directly into the downtown area.

MOUNTAIN HOME

Up in the high deserts, Mountain Home exists in symbiosis with the Mountain Home Air Force Base. Jets rip over the borderlands, where training exercises and battle lab tests are performed. Though this will excite aviators and conspiracy theorists, the base is largely closed for security reasons, and the main attraction around the city is the nearby state park, which offers activities ranging from sand skiing to desert stargazing.

VITAL STATS

Population: 11,150

Visitor Info: Desert Mountain Visitor Center, 2900 American Legion Blvd. (☎208-587-4464), off I-84 at Exit 95. Open in summer daily 9am-5pm; call for winter hours. **Mountain Home Chamber of Commerce,** 205 N. 3rd E (☎208-587-4334). Open M-F 9am-5pm.

Internet Access: Mountain Home Public Library, 790 N. 10th E (☎208-587-4716; www.mhlibrary.org). Open M-F 10am-7pm, Sa 9am-5pm. Free.

Post Office: 350 N. 3rd E (☎208-587-1413). Open M-F 8:30am-5pm, Sa 9:30-11:30am. **Postal Code:** 83647.

GETTING AROUND. Mountain Home's two primary roads are **American Legion Blvd.,** which runs from **I-84** westward into the center of town, and **Main St.,** which runs southeast-northwest, meeting American Legion Blvd. in the middle of town. The streets around the intersection follow a system: the first direction indicates the direction of the street, while the second number indicates which half of the street you're on.

SIGHTS. The **Bruneau Dunes State Park** is Mountain Home's center for recreation. Two large sand dunes spread over 600 acres of the park; at 470 ft., the larger of the two is the tallest in North America. You can play on the 15,000-year-old dunes and, when the fall weather cools them, even ski down them. The natural lakes at their base support bass and bluegill; fishing is allowed. Clear desert nights leave the stars intensely bright and staggeringly numerous. Head to the **Bruneau Dunes Observatory** to see them up close. (☎208-366-7919. Open daily from 9pm. $3; under 6 free.) **Camping ❶** is allowed in a range of sites across the park; contact the visitors center for more info. (Follow Main St. south from American Legion Blvd., merging into Rte. 51. After 14 mi., take a left onto Rte. 78; 2 mi. down that road is the turn-off for the park. ☎208-366-7919. Park gates open 7am-10pm. Entrance fee $4 per vehicle.)

FOOD AND ACCOMMODATIONS. Dining in Mountain Home is simple—mainly delis and cafes. Boxy and covered in red, white, and blue checks, **Grinde's Diner,** 550 Air Base Rd., is the epitome of American road culture. The two-page menu of sandwiches ($5.50-6.50) are served up swiftly, and juicy meat dinners ($6-12) are satisfying after a long day's drive. (Take Main St. to Rte. 51 to Air Base Rd. ☎208-587-5611. Open daily 7am-11pm. AmEx/D/MC/V.) The **Dilly Deli ❸,** 190 E. 2nd N, with its pickle mascot, are perfect for a quick afternoon sandwich. Try the classic three-meat, three-cheese "Triple Hitter" for $8.50. (☎208-587-0885. Open M-Sa 10:30am-4pm. AmEx/D/MC/V.) Mountain Home's budget lodgings are located around the downtown area, where American Legion Blvd. meets Main St. Clean, simple rooms are available at the **Towne Center Motel,** 410 N. 2nd East, off American Legion Blvd. (☎208-587-3373. Singles in summer $44; in winter $42. Doubles $48/$42. AmEx/D/MC/V.)

APPROACHING BOISE: 43 MILES
Follow **U.S. 30** out of Mountain Home—just take **Main St.** northwest. U.S. 30 merges with **I-84** en route to Boise. From I-84, **Exit 54** feeds directly onto **Broadway;** proceed straight through a commercial strip until you reach **Front St.** in downtown Boise.

BOISE

Built along the banks of the Boise River, Idaho's surprisingly cosmopolitan capital straddles the boundary between desert and mountains. A network of parks protects the

1971: Don Rawitsch and two friends create "The Oregon Trail" computer game at Carlton College.

natural landscape of the river banks, creating a greenbelt perfect for walking, biking, or skating. Most of the city's sights cluster in a 10-block area between the capitol and the river, making Boise extremely navigable. A revitalized downtown offers a vast array of ethnic cuisine as well as a thriving nightlife scene.

VITAL STATS

Population: 193,000

Visitor Info: Boise Convention and Visitors Bureau, 312 S. 9th St., Ste. 200 (☎208-344-7777 or 800-635-5241; www.boise.org). Open M-Th 8:30am-5pm, F 8:30am-4pm.

Internet Access: Boise Public Library, 715 S. Capitol Blvd. (☎208-384-4076; www.boisepublicli-brary.org). Open Labor Day to Memorial Day M-Th 10am-9pm, F 10am-6pm, Sa 10am-5pm, Su noon-5pm; Memorial Day to Labor Day closed. Free Wi-Fi.

Post Office: 750 W. Bannock St. (☎208-331-0037). Open M-F 8:30am-5pm. **Postal Code:** 83701.

GETTING AROUND

Boise is fairly large, but the heart of the action is the pedestrian-only **Grove,** a segment of **8th St.** between **Main St.** and **Front St.,** the two main downtown thoroughfares. There are two other important downtown streets: **Grove St.,** which runs between Main and Front St., and **Capitol Blvd.,** which runs between 8th and **6th St.** Driving in Boise is easy, thanks to wide streets and generally well-planned traffic flow, but parking is difficult; drivers in search of roadside parking spots are viciously competitive downtown, and most areas are strictly metered. Drivers will probably save themselves quarters and a good chunk of their sanity by sacrificing some money to park in one of the area garages.

SIGHTS

JULIA DAVIS PARK. The logical starting point for exploring Boise is the beautiful **Julia Davis Park.** A paddleboat pond, tennis courts, and a bandshell make this an entertaining place, while the alabaster pavilion and rose garden make it ideal for summer romance. *(Myrtle St. and Capitol Blvd. ☎208-384-4240.)* The **Boise Tour Train and River Float,** which covers about 75 city sights in 1¼hr., starts and ends in the park. At the end of the ride during the summer, visitors have the option of taking a trolley to the Boise River, where a raft will continue the tour. *(☎208-342-4796; www.boisetours.net. Tours Memorial Day to Labor Day M-Sa 10am-3pm, Su noon-3:45pm; Sept. W-Su noon-3pm; May and Oct. Sa-Su 1-2:30pm. $9, seniors $8.50, ages 3-12 $6. Train and river combo tours Memorial Day to Labor Day $34/$31.50/$21. Call ahead for times.)* To learn about Idaho and the Old West, stroll through the **Idaho Historical Museum,** which showcases replicas of a 19th-century bar, high-class Idahoan parlors, and working-class homesteads. The museum also has Native American artifacts and displays on Idaho's Basque and Chinese populations. *(610 N. Julia Davis Dr. ☎208-334-2120. Open Tu-Sa 9am-5pm, Su 1-5pm; Nov.-Apr. Tu-Sa 9am-5pm. $2, ages 6-18 $1.)* The **Boise Art Museum** displays an impressive collection of contemporary, international, and local works while offering educational programs and tours. *(670 Julia Davis Dr. ☎208-345-8330; www.boiseartmuseum.org. Open June-Aug. M-W and F-Sa 10am-5pm, Th 10am-8pm, Su noon-5pm; Sept.-May Tu-W and F-Sa 10am-5pm, Th 10am-8pm, Su noon-5pm. $5, students and seniors $3, under 6 free.)*

OLD IDAHO STATE PENITENTIARY. During its century of operation from 1870 to 1973, the Old Idaho State Penitentiary held more than 13,000 convicts. Visitors can explore the 19th-century cells, death row, gallows, and solitary confinement areas. *(2445 Old Penitentiary Rd. ☎208-334-2844. Open daily Memorial Day to Labor Day 10am-5pm; Labor Day to Memorial Day noon-5pm. $5, seniors $4, ages 6-12 $3.)*

BIRDS OF PREY CENTER. Far more impressive than the average zoo, the **World Center for Birds of Prey** is a research center and raptor breeding ground. Arrowslit windows open into the chambers, giving an up-close look at 10 species of rare and striking birds of prey, including California condors, harpy eagles, and bald eagles. *(5668 W. Flying Hawk Ln. From I-84, take Exit 50, go south on S. Cole St., and turn right. ☎208-362-8687. Open Mar.-Oct. daily 9am-5pm; Nov.-Feb. Tu-Su 10am-4pm. $5, seniors $4, ages 4-16 $3, under 4 free.)*

BASQUE MUSEUM. The last remnant of Atlantis, perhaps, is preserved at the **Basque Museum and Cultural Center,** dedicated to the

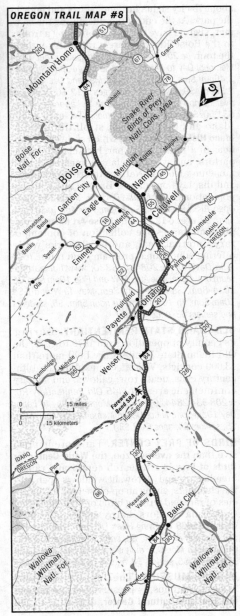

OREGON TRAIL MAP #8

culture of the Basques, an Iberian peninsula ethnic group with a language related to no other, which prompted the unlikely theory that they descended from the citizens of Atlantis. Many Basque younger sons, seeking land, immigrated to the American West to become herders. This museum recalls their heritage in Europe and their lonely lives in the Idaho pasture lands. The grounds include a gallery of Basque art and a replica of a Basque herder's house. (611 Grove St. ☎208-343-2671. Open Tu-F 10am-4pm, Sa 11am-3pm. Suggested donation.)

OTHER SIGHTS. The **Museum of Mining and Geology** has displays on mining, geology, gems, and fossils. (2455 Old Penitentiary Rd. ☎208-368-9876. Open W-Su noon-5pm. Free.) The **Capitol City Market** takes over 8th St. between Main and Bannock St. every Saturday morning in the summer. Stroll through for a look at local produce and crafts. Bikers, runners, and skaters enjoy the **Boise River Greenbelt,** 25 mi. of asphalt and grass pathways following the Boise River. If you look down on land-lubbing, throw a tube or kayak into the river; they can be rented at **Baker Park,** at the southeast end of the Greenbelt. (☎208-384-4240; www.cityofboise.org/parks. Open daily sunrise-sunset.) The 28-year-old **Boise Shakespeare Festival** hits town from June to September. (5657 Warm Springs Ave., the eastern continuation of Idaho St. ☎208-336-9221; www.idahoshakespeare.org. Tickets M-Th and Su $20-28, F-Sa $27-35.) In the **Alive After Five** series, live music fills the Grove every Wednesday from June to September at 5pm. (☎208-472-5200; www.downtownboise.org.)

🍴 FOOD

Although Idaho is world-renowned for potatoes, Boise offers hungry roadtrippers much more than spuds. The downtown area, centered around 8th and Main St., bustles with delis, coffee shops, ethnic restaurants, and several stylish bistros.

🖼 **Moon's Kitchen,** 815 W. Bannock St. (☎208-385-0472). This vintage diner and cluttered gift shop has churned out 14 magnificent flavors of shakes, malts, and floats since 1955. Shakes $4.50. Breakfast $4.50-7.50. Burgers $6-9. Open M-F 7am-7:30pm, Sa 8am-7:30pm, Su 9am-2pm. AmEx/D/MC/V. ❷

Zeppole Baking Company, 217 N. 8th St. (☎208-345-2149). Puts together gourmet sandwiches ($2-3) on famous freshly baked bread. Fresh pastries under $2. Soup and sandwich combos $4-5. Open M-F 7am-5pm, Sa 7:30am-4pm. Cash only. ❶

Gernika Basque Pub and Eatery, 202 S. Capitol Blvd. (☎208-344-2175). This is the place to experience authentic Spanish cuisine. Try the sandwiches with pork loin, lamb, or chorizo, and finish off with rice pudding. Sandwiches $6-8. Open M 11am-11pm, Tu-Th 11am-midnight, F-Sa 11am-1am. AmEx/D/MC/V. ❷

Kulture Klatsch, 409 S. 8th St. (☎208-345-0452). This hip, multicultural eatery has an extensive veggie menu, as well as a juice and smoothie bar. Breakfast $4-7. Lunch specials $5-6. Dinner $7-9. Open Tu-F 7am-3pm, Sa-Su 8am-3pm. MC/V. ❷

■ ACCOMMODATIONS

Lodgings are surprisingly hard to come by in downtown Boise. A few motels line **Fairview Ave.,** the continuation of Front and Grove St. west of town. Chain motels are concentrated around Exit 53 off I-84.

▨ Hostel Boise (HI-AYH), 17322 Can-Ada Rd. (☎208-467-6858), 15min. from downtown Boise. Take Exit 38 off I-84, and turn right onto Garrity Blvd., which turns into Can-Ada Rd. This country home has mountain views and evening campfires. Linen $1.50. Internet access $1 per 15min. Reception 7-10am and 5-10:30pm. Dorms $18, members $16; private rooms $35. MC/V. ❶

Bond Street Motel Apartments, 1680 N. Phillippi St. (☎208-322-4407), off Fairview Ave. Beautifully furnished studio and 1-bedroom apartments with kitchens. Pots, pans, dishes—even the kitchen sink. Reception M-F 8am-5pm. Reservations recommended. Studios $52; apartments $55. AmEx/D/MC/V. ❷

Budget Inn, 2600 Fairview Ave. (☎208-344-8617). One of the finer budget motels along the Oregon Trail. Bright and attractive rooms with coffeemakers and microwaves. Closer to downtown than almost any other lodging. Rooms $36-65. AmEx/D/MC/V. ❷

University Inn, 2360 University Dr. (☎208-345-7170 or 800-345-5118), next to Boise State University. Take 9th St. south, and follow signs. Rooms come with cable TV and access to a pool and 2 hot tubs.

Continental breakfast included. Check-in 3pm. Check-out noon. Rooms $60-65. AmEx/D/MC/V. ❸

■ NIGHTLIFE

The nightlife-starved roadtripper will find fulfillment in Boise; musicians perform regularly on **Main St.,** while vendors from nearby restaurants hawk food and beer.

The Balcony, 150 N. 8th St., (☎208-336-1313), on the 2nd fl. of the Capitol Terrace. DJs spin nightly, and 10 TVs surround the dance floor. All kinds of people gather at the gay-friendly bar to dance, relax on the outdoor terrace, and play pool. "Industria" brings Goth style on Su. Cover F-Sa after 9:30pm $3. Open M-F 4pm-2am, Sa-Su 2pm-2am. D/MC/V.

Bittercreek Alehouse, 246 N. 8th St. (☎208-345-1813). A casual, trendy spot in downtown Boise. Serves burgers and pitas ($6-9) as well as chowder, skewers, and other interesting choices. Wide and varied drink list. 21+ after 10pm. Open daily 11am-last customer. AmEx/D/DC/MC/V.

▨ APPROACHING PARMA: 42 MILES
Take **Front St. (U.S. 20/26)** heading west from downtown and merge left onto **I-84 W.** After 28 mi., take **Exit 26,** following **U.S. 20/26** away from the interstate. From here the drive is all sunny fields and groves, meandering 14 mi. through the tiny town of Notus and on to Parma.

PARMA. Off U.S. 20/26 in Parma is the **Old Fort Boise Replica and Museum.** The original fort was swept away when the Boise River flooded in 1853. Though the exact location of the original isn't known, it was probably somewhere northwest of where the ring of walls stands today. Enclosed within the replica is a local history museum that displays relics from an old church and pages from local high-school yearbooks. (☎208-722-6447. Open June-Aug. F-Su 1-3pm. Free.)

▨ APPROACHING ONTARIO: 19 MILES
From Parma, continue north along **U.S. 20/26.** 6 miles from town, be sure to follow the road west; going straight leads into northern Idaho, away from the trail. As soon as the road has made the turn, it crosses the Snake River into Oregon, where you'll be greeted by the city of Nyssa, Thunderegg Capitol of the World. About 8 mi. after crossing the border, U.S. 20/26 veers away. Continue straight onto **Rte. 201.** Bear

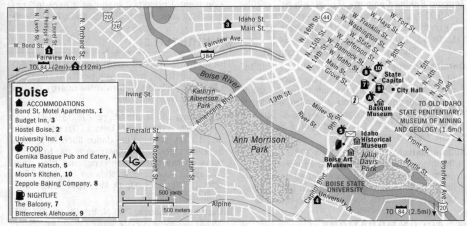

Boise

🏠 ACCOMMODATIONS
Bond St. Motel Apartments, **1**
Budget Inn, **3**
Hostel Boise, **2**
University Inn, **4**

🍴 FOOD
Gernika Basque Pub and Eatery, **A**
Kulture Klatsch, **5**
Moon's Kitchen, **10**
Zeppole Baking Company, **8**

🌙 NIGHTLIFE
The Balcony, **7**
Bittercreek Alehouse, **9**

right on **SW 4th Ave.**, leaving Rte. 201 soon after the city limits. Turn here to reach downtown Ontario.

The Beaver State
OREGON
Welcomes You!

ONTARIO

After passing over the Snake River into Oregon, a well-deserved rest is in order. Ontario, a quiet city of 11,000 people, is the ideal place to hang your hat. The city's major sight is the **Four Rivers Cultural Center,** 676 SW 5th St., which explains the historical relationships between various ethnic groups that have settled the West, including Native Americans, Europeans, Hispanics, and Japanese. The center includes a museum, a theater, and a Japanese garden. (☎541-889-8191 or 888-211-1222; www.4rcc.com. Open M-Sa 10am-5pm. $4, seniors and ages 6-14 $3, under 6 free.) Info on other attractions in Ontario is available at the **Ontario Chamber of Commerce,** 676 SW 5th Ave., in the same building as the cultural center. (☎541-889-8012 or 888-889-2012. Open M-F 8am-5pm.)

A relaxed aura emanates from **DJ's Family Restaurant ❷,** 625 E. Idaho Ave., a result of the counter seating and big, conversation-inducing tables. All sorts of pastas are available, as are hamburgers ($5-8) or sandwiches ($5-7), both generously proportioned. (☎541-889-4386. Open daily 6am-11pm. AmEx/D/MC/V.) Chain lodgings can be found up and down SW 4th Ave., with some budget establishments mixed in. The **Oregon Trail Motel ❷,** 92 E. Idaho Ave., has some of the cheapest rooms in town, which come with refrigerators and microwaves. (☎541-889-8633. Singles $35; doubles $45. AmEx/D/MC/V.) Attractive wood paneling adds some flair to the spacious rooms of the **Ontario Inn ❷,** 1144 SW 4th Ave. (☎541-823-2556; www.theontarioinn.com. Free Wi-Fi. Singles $43; doubles $49. AmEx/D/MC/V.)

◤ DETOUR
FAREWELL BEND STATE PARK

From Ontario, return west on 4th Ave. to Rte. 201, and head north along the Snake River. 25 mi. from Ontario, 3 mi. after the junction of Rte. 201 and I-84, take Exit 353.

After over 300 mi. on the Snake River, pioneers had to leave their source of fresh water behind and trek northwest to the Columbia River. Farewell Bend State Park marks one of the first truly wooded spots that the trail has seen; the shade of the pines foreshadows the evergreen slopes to the north, beyond Flagstaff Hill. The isolated **campsites ❶** of Farewell Bend make it a relaxing place to sleep, and the verdant grounds are a great place to stretch your legs escape. (☎800-551-6949. Open daily

8am-10pm. Entrance fee $3 per car. May-Sept. tent sites $15, with hookup $17; Oct.-Apr. $11/ $13. Showers $2. MC/V.)

⚑ APPROACHING BAKER CITY: 45 MILES
From Farewell Bend State Park, get back on **I-84.** Take **Exit 304,** which feeds onto the east end of **Campbell St.** in Baker City.

 Between Ontario and Baker City, Rte. 201/I-84 passes into the Pacific Time Zone, where it is 1hr. earlier.

BAKER CITY

Baker City was a gold-boom town, built by prospectors in search of the legendary Blue Bucket Mine. The lucky will arrive here in mid-July during the annual Miners' Jubilee, when covered wagons and local children parade through the streets in a patriotic procession. The town is pleasant any time of the year, however; the old-fashioned main street is lined with little businesses, and a tiny brook runs through the park by the library—it's small-town America to the core.

VITAL STATS

Population: 9900

Visitor Info: Visitor Info Center, 490 Campbell St. (☎541-523-3356 or 800-523-1235), just west of the junction with I-84. Open M-F 8am-5pm; in summer also Sa 8am-4pm.

Internet Access: Baker County Public Library, 2400 Resort St. (☎541-523-6419 or 866-297-1239; www.bakerlib.org), just south of the intersection of Campbell and Main St. Open M-Th 10am-8pm, F 10am-5pm, Sa 10am-4pm, Su noon-4pm. Free Wi-Fi.

Post Office: 1550 Dewey Ave. (☎541-523-8593). Open M-F 8:30am-5pm. **Postal Code:** 97814.

⊟ GETTING AROUND. There are only two roads of any importance to a Baker City visitor. **Campbell St.,** running west from Exit 304 on I-84, is the city's fast-food and hotel zone. Bisecting Campbell St. is north-south **Main St.,** Baker City's downtown strip. Parking is plentiful except during the Miners' Jubilee, when parking vanishes, traffic swells, roads close, and hotels fill to capacity.

⬓ SIGHTS. Baker's central attraction is the misleadingly named **Oregon Trail Regional Museum,** 2480 Grove St., off Campbell St. Those weary of pioneer memorials need not fear, as this is a museum *along* the trail, not *about* it. An interesting jumble of objects is spread throughout, from a case of Nazi relics to a scale model used in the Clint Eastwood film *Paint Your Wagon,* which was filmed nearby. The most impressive gallery is the Cavin-Warfel Collection, several rooms of gems and mineral formations which the Smithsonian once offered to buy. The crystal-in-crystal "phantoms" are mysteriously beautiful, and the giant thundereggs are impressive products of nature. (☎541-523-9308. Open daily 9am-5pm; last entry 4:15pm. $5, seniors $4.50, under 16 free with adult.) An actual Oregon Trail museum is outside of town on Flagstaff Hill, at the **National Historic Oregon Trail Interpretive Center,** 22267 Rte. 86. The museum begins on a reproduction of a stretch of the trail, complete with pioneers, oxen, wagons, and roadside graves. The rest of the museum is a stark look at the trail. (Take I-84 to Exit 302, and follow the signs. ☎541-523-1843; www.blm.gov/or/oregontrail. Open daily Apr.-Oct. 9am-6pm; Nov.-Mar. 9am-4pm. $5, seniors $3.50, under 15 free.)

The annual **Miners' Jubilee** takes its name from Baker City's mining heritage, but the huge three-day party has little to do with mining beyond a metal-detecting contest and the cartoonish miner and donkey that cavort across shop windows. A parade and carnival are the centerpieces, while bronco-riding, a bed race through downtown, and a Main St. dance add unorthodox entertainment. The schedule of events changes every year, but the festival always starts on the third Friday in July and runs through the following weekend. Ask at the visitors center about locations in Baker County where you can 🪙pan for gold.

⬓⬓ FOOD AND ACCOMMODATIONS. Food options in Baker City are generally around Campbell and Main St. An electric train chugs through **Sumpter Junction Restaurant ❷,** 2 Sunridge Ln., at Campbell St. The kitchen serves tasty burgers and sandwiches ($6-7.50), as well as a small selection of Mexican cuisine. (☎541-523-9437. Open daily 6am-10pm. AmEx/D/MC/V.) **Barley Brown's Brewpub ❸,** 2190 Main St., at the corner of Church St., has an ever-popular menu of pastas ($8-14), hearty sandwiches ($7-8), and salads ($3-10). Surely no one could resist the tempting Death Burger, named for its "killer onions." (☎541-523-4266. Open M-Sa 4-10pm. AmEx/D/MC/V.) The **Chamealeon Cafe** ❸, 1825 Main St., has simple but satisfying sandwich-and-salad lunches. Its delicious signature sandwich, Aunt Caroline's Pork Loin sandwich ($7.50), is a secret recipe. (☎541-523-7977; www.chamealeon.com. Sandwiches $4-8. Salads $6-8. Entrees $8-17. Open M-Tu 11am-3pm, W-Th 11am-8pm, F-Sa 11am-9pm. MC/V.)

Baker City sports the usual array of chain accommodations and budget motels on the outskirts of downtown, but it also has few more unusual establishments. For a great deal, try the **Bridge Street Inn** ❷, 134 Bridge St., off the south end of Main St. The rooms are spacious, clean, and come with refrigerators and microwaves. (☎541-523-6571. Continental breakfast included. Free Wi-Fi. Singles $35; doubles $48. AmEx/D/MC/V.) The **Eldorado Inn** ❸, 695 Campbell St., is not actually made of gold, but its adobe walls and red roofs exude an attractive Spanish ambience. The clean, pleasant rooms are similarly decorated, and guests have access to an indoor pool. (☎541-523-6494 or 800-537-5756; www.eldoradoinn.net. Continental breakfast included. Rooms $45-75. AmEx/D/MC/V.) The **Geiser Grand Hotel** ❹, 1996 Main St., was built in the late 19th century, when it served the rich and famous. The hotel still drips with opulence—check out the crystal chandeliers, silk damask, and gilt mirrors. (☎541-523-1889 or 888-434-7374; www.geisergrand.com. Rooms from $79. AmEx/D/MC/V.)

⚑ APPROACHING LA GRANDE: 44 MILES
Head east on **Campbell St.** to **I-84**, and take the westbound lane toward La Grande, 39 mi. to the north. The easiest way to enter La Grande from I-84 is to get off at the **Island Ave.** exit and head southwest to **Adams Ave.**

LA GRANDE

La Grande is the gateway to the evergreen wilderness of the Pacific Northwest. It lies between the two arcs of the Wallowa Whitman National Forest, with the Blue Mountains to the west and the Wallowa Mountains to the east. The Grande Ronde river, proclaimed a near-paradise by some pioneers, flows nearby. La Grande is in some ways overshadowed by its environment; it's hard to walk down Main St. without noticing the nearby hills rising into mountains.

VITAL STATS

Population: 12,500

Visitor Info: Union County Chamber of Commerce, 102 Elm St. (☎541-963-8588; www.visitlagrande.com), off Adams Ave. Open Memorial Day to Labor Day M-F 9am-5:30pm, Sa 9am-3pm; Labor Day to Memorial Day M-F 9am-5pm.

Internet Access: La Grande Public Library, 1006 Penn Ave. (☎541-962-1339). Open in summer M 10am-8pm, Tu-F 10am-6pm; in winter M 10am-8pm, Tu-F 10am-6pm, Sa 10am-2pm. Free.

Post Office: 1202 Washington Ave. (☎541-962-7539). Open M-F 8:30am-5pm. **Postal Code:** 97850.

OUT OF THE PLANE, INTO THE FIRE

While most people run from wildfires, Mark Wright is part of the elite group of aerial firefighters who jumps in.

LG: How did you start jumping?

MW: I started working for the Helena National Forest as a summer job. Among other things like cleaning picnic tables, cutting brush, and patrolling, one of the things they train you to do is put out fires. So I started out as a young firefighter putting my way through college. The "problem" is that it gets in your blood and you become addicted to it. After 4 years of firefighting through college, I got a teaching degree and ended up continuing to fight fires in my summers off. I've been doing it for the past 27 years.

LG: What does smokejumper training involve?

MW: To be a smokejumper, you need recommendations and a minimum of 2 years firefighting experience. Many people apply and only a limited number get selected to go through rookie training, which is over a month long. I would compare it to boot camp. They start their morning with calisthenics, go through daily training, and have to pass physical fitness tests. People wash out at any time, and they need to make a minimum of 15

GETTING AROUND. Getting around is a matter of knowing your bearings relative to **Adams Ave.** and **Washington Ave.** These two roads run parallel to each other one block apart, cutting the city in half from southeast to northwest. Most motels and restaurants are on or just off these streets, as is La Grande's downtown. Free parking is available on the edges of both streets.

OUTDOORS. The closest spot to experience the great outdoors is **Hilgard Junction State Park,** off I-84 Exit 252, about 8 mi. west of La Grande. The park stretches right along the interstate, but the surrounding mountains swallow it behind a convenient ridge, hiding it from view. This is an ideal **camping ❶** spot, with sites right along the banks of the Grand Ronde, a clear and gentle river ideal for summer wading. (☎800-551-6949, reservations 800-452-5687. Restrooms and potable water available. No electricity. Sites $9. MC/V.) There's more space to skip merrily among the trees a bit west of Hilgard, at **Blue Mountain Crossing Oregon Trail Interpretive Park,** which is actually much more park than interpretation; trails roll through the hills, lined with panels and signs offering information on the trials of the emigrants in these parts. Some weekends feature living history actors. (Head west on I-84 to Exit 248 and follow the signs for 3 mi. ☎541-963-7186. Open Memorial Day to Labor Day daily 8am-8pm. $5.)

FOOD AND ACCOMMODATIONS. There is a smattering of restaurants in the area around Adams and Washington Ave., downtown, and fast-food abounds at each of the town's highway exits. **Ten Depot Street ❸,** 10 Depot St., is a downtown restaurant and occasional music hall that offers emu burgers ($7.50) and emu steaks ($16)—truly an emu-vable feast. Plenty of other options are available, such as pastas ($11-14) and sandwiches ($7.50-10), including the lentil pecan burger for vegetarian diners. (☎541-963-8766. Appetizers $6-15. Entrees $11-33. Open M-Sa 5-10pm. AmEx/MC/V.) A vast and international menu is the distinguishing mark of **Foley Station ❹,** 1114 Adams Ave. Char Siu barbecue chicken and teriyaki cashew beef sit in ethnic harmony with falafel pitas and Alaskan halibut fish and chips. (☎541-963-7473. Open M-Sa 10:30am-10pm, Su 7am-10pm. MC/V.) The **Cock 'n' Bull Villa Roma ❸,** 1414 Adams Ave., in Pat's Alley, is a Christmas-light bedecked Italian restaurant. The entrees ($9-11) lean heavily toward pastas, though there is also a wide selection of sandwiches ($5.50-7.50). Menu toppers include the Cock & Bull sandwich, which is just a fancy name for turkey and roast beef. (☎541-963-0573. Open M-Th 11am-2pm, F-Sa 11am-9pm. D/MC/V.)

The numerous windows and balconies of the **Stange Manor Inn ❺,** 1612 Walnut St., let in sunlight, moonlight, and the scent of the gardens below. The elegant rooms range from singles to multi-room micro-apartments with fireplaces. (Take Penn Ave. west from Washington Ave; Walnut St. is a few blocks west of the steep hill. ☎541-963-2400; www.stange-manor.com. Breakfast included. Private bath. Rooms $98-115. MC/V.) One of La Grande's best

---

LG: What happens in a typical fire?

MW: Smokejumpers are initial attack, so we get calls right when the fire is detected and still fairly small. One of the great advantages smokejumpers have is that we are on an airplane above the fire. We take a good look at the terrain and see what the fire behavior is. People coming from the ground can only see smoke and don't know what they're getting into. Before we even jump out of the plane, we check for safety zones to see which ways we can approach the fire, pinpoint safe jump spots that are close to the fire but not endangering ourselves, and look for routes out of the fire. After we land in parachutes, the plane flies over and drops our cargo, which contains chainsaws, tools, water, freeze dried food—everything we'll need to fight the fire and camp overnight.

LG: What is one of your most memorable smokejumping experiences?

MW: This was about 21 years ago. I had just jumped a fire and we had it pretty well whipped. As I was wiping the soot off my face, the dispatcher came on the radio and asked, "Is there a smokejumper there named Mark Wright?" I knew immediately what he was going to tell me. I started hooting and hollering as he announced, "Congratulations. You have a healthy baby girl."

budget motels is the **Royal Motor Inn ❷**, 1510 Adams Ave. The rooms have very comfortable chairs and beds, as well as full desks. (☎541-963-4154 or 800-990-7575. Singles $35; doubles $40. AmEx/D/MC/V.)

 While the road into the Wallowa Mountains offers some of the most stunning scenery along the trail, it's a long 75 mi. drive. To skip this section and continue west, take **I-84** to Pendleton (p. 662).

◢ APPROACHING ENTERPRISE AND JOSEPH: 65 MILES

Take **Adams Ave.** to **Island Ave.**, and head east. Island Ave. becomes **Rte. 82 (Hell's Canyon Scenic Byway)** as it heads into the Wallowa Mountains.

ENTERPRISE AND JOSEPH

The towns of Enterprise and Joseph, situated in the Wallowa Mountains, are a powerhouse pair. The two are separated by about 6 mi. of Rte. 82, practically on the slopes of the ferociously craggy Wallowas, which bristle with evergreens and glisten with snow. The Eagle Cap Wilderness extends through the mountains south of Joseph, and much of Joseph's downtown is consumed by bike rental shops, fly-fishing stores, and hiking suppliers. Enterprise is bigger, grayer, duller, and full of motels and necessities, while Joseph is small, bright and slightly eccentric; sleep in the former, play in the latter.

VITAL STATS

Population: 1900/1100

Visitor Info: Wallowa Mountains Visitors Center, 88401 Rte. 82 (☎541-426-5546; www.josephoregon.com). Open in summer M-Sa 8am-5pm; in winter M-F 8am-5pm. Wallowa County Chamber of Commerce, 115 Tejaka Ln. (☎541-426-4622 or 800-585-4121), off Rte. 82 on the west edge of Enterprise, across the street from the visitors center. Open M-F 9am-5pm.

Internet Access: Enterprise Public Library, 101 NE 1st St. (☎541-426-3906). Open M and F noon-6pm, Tu-Th 10am-6pm, Sa 10am-2pm. Free.

Post Office: 201 W. North St. (☎541-426-5980), in Enterprise. Open M-F 9am-4:30pm. **Postal Code:** 97828.

🖃 GETTING AROUND

Maneuvering around this two-town mountain complex is quite easy, since both cities hug **Rte. 82.** This road enters Enterprise from the west, and runs east under the guise of **North St.** It then turns south as **River St.**, and continues 6 mi. to Joseph, where it becomes **Main St.** At the south end of Joseph, simply follow the signs out of town, proceeding 6 mi. to Wallowa Lake, the main gateway to the **Eagle Cap Wilderness.** Free parking is everywhere in both towns, and practically endless around the popular lake.

◪ OUTDOORS

Fun in this area revolves around its mountain wildlands. **Eagle Cap Wilderness** is gigantic at 650,000 acres, and even that is dwarfed by the encompassing **Wallowa-Whitman National Forest.** It is almost impossible to explore the area fully, but those attempting the feat can get a start at the **Wallowa Mountains Visitors Center,** which provides info on trailheads, car loops, camping areas, wildlife, and almost anything else visitors are interested in. Giant maps of the entire region are available for $6. One of the more popular, most easily accessible outdoor areas is **Wallowa Lake,** a state park nearly engulfed by the surrounding National Forest. The large lake itself is open for swimming and boating, both very popular summer activities. With no day-use fee, the mountain beach is a happening place. (Take Main St. south from Joseph for 6 mi., following the signs. ☎541-432-4185. Open for day-use 6am-9pm.)

Hikers can find a few of Eagle Cap's trailheads in Wallowa Lake's southern picnic grounds, leading up into the mountains along the Wallowa River. These are serious trails; the visitors center in Enterprise can provide maps and information on current weather and trail conditions. The peaks around Wallowa Lake aren't the exclusive playground of battle-hardened climbers. Mt. Howard (8200 ft.) is scaled by the **Wallowa Lake Tramway,** 59919 Wallowa Lake Hwy. The peak is well developed, with numerous lookouts and a system of easily accessible short trails. The view from the summit is excellent; in addition to the surrounding peaks, visitors can see four states on clear days. (☎541-432-5331; www.wallowalaketramway.com. Open daily July-Aug. 10am-5pm; May-June and Sept. 10am-4pm. $20, ages 12-17 $17, ages 3-10 $13.)

On the last full weekend of July, the **Chief Joseph Days Rodeo** tears Joseph apart; the four-day event includes dances, parades, and outdoor food. Traditional rodeo events are jazzed up with comedy rodeo acts and the new Wildest Ride contest. (☎ 541-432-1015; www.chiefjosephdays.com. $8-15, separate tickets for each day's events.)

FOOD

Dining establishments abound in Joseph; the number of restaurants crammed into the downtown area is staggering. Enterprise has a more modest selection.

Friends Restaurant, 107 N. River St. (☎ 541-426-5929), in Enterprise. This tiny diner, hiding at the corner of Main St., serves some of the best burgers for miles. Sandwiches $4-5. Entrees $7-13. Open daily 6am-9pm. Cash only. ❸

Embers Brew House, 206 N. Main St. (☎ 541-432-2739), in Joseph. A modern spot with metallic decor and plenty of vegetarian options. A healthy selection of salads ($4-8) is accompanied by all sorts of pizzas and calzones ($8-20). Appetizers $4-8. Beer $3. Open daily 11am-10pm. MC/V. ❸

Cheyenne Cafe, 209 N. Main St. (☎ 541-432-6300), in Joseph. A friendly cafe atmosphere meets friendly low prices. Big breakfasts and generously portioned lunch combos ($4-9) keep visitors going through a day of hiking. Sandwiches $4-6. Open M-Sa 6am-2pm, Su 7am-2pm. MC/V. ❷

ACCOMMODATIONS

The surest bet for available lodgings is in Enterprise, though Joseph isn't completely devoid of places to sleep. A little village clusters near Lake Wallowa, but it's fairly crowded and touristy.

Indian Lodge Motel, 201 S. Main St. (☎ 541-432-2651 or 888-286-5484; www.eoni.com/~gingerdaggett/). One of the area's best motels, right in downtown Joseph. The 16 units can fill fast in the summer, and, with their size and large TVs, it's not hard to see why. Singles in summer $47, in winter $32; doubles $46-52/$37-42. D/MC/V. ❷

Country Inn, 402 W. North St. (☎ 541-426-4986). One of the less expensive Enterprise stays. The

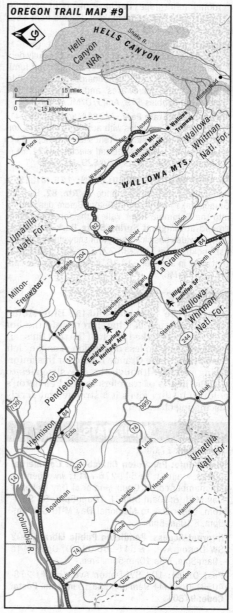

OREGON TRAIL MAP #9

rooms aren't huge, but have plenty of room for refrigerators and coffeemakers. Rooms from $58. AmEx/D/MC/V. ❸

Ponderosa Motel, 102 E. Greenwood St. (☎541-426-3186), off River St. in Enterprise. Carefully decorated rooms filled with artfully rustic, wood furniture, right down to the headboards. Rooms include coffeemakers, microwaves, and refrigerators. Singles $65; doubles $79. AmEx/D/MC/V. ❸

Wallowa Lake State Park, 72214 Marina Ln. (☎541-432-4185). Campsites with access to showers, toilets, and a dump station. Tent sites May-Sept. $17, Oct.-Apr. $13; with water and electricity $21/$17. Cabins $80/$58. Yurts $29/$29. MC/V. ❶

⚑ APPROACHING PENDLETON: 125 MILES
Retrace your route to La Grande via **Rte. 82.** From La Grande, take **I-84 W** to Pendleton. Before descending into the Columbia River Valley, the forested campground at **Emigrant Spring State Park ❶,** off Exit 234, provides basic camping with showers and electrical hookups. (☎541-983-2277 or 800-551-6949. Tent sites in summer $14-16, in winter $10-12; cabins $20-35. MC/V.)

PENDLETON

Between the Cascades and the Blue Mountains, Pendleton is a harsh return to the hot dust that has marked much of the trail thus far. Pioneers were no less disillusioned as they left the fertility of the Grande Ronde for this unforgiving valley. Although the city struggles to win the hearts of travelers today, Pendleton's colorful history gives it a strange and darkly fascinating character.

VITAL STATS

Population: 17,000

Visitor Info: Pendleton Chamber of Commerce, 501 S. Main St. (☎541-276-7411; www.pendletonchamber.com). Open Memorial Day to Labor Day M-Th 8:30am-5pm, F 10am-5pm, Sa 9am-4pm; Labor Day to Memorial Day M-Th 8:30am-5pm, F 10am-5pm.

Internet Access: Pendleton Public Library, 502 SW Dorion Ave. (☎541-966-0210). Open M-Th 10am-8pm, F-Sa 10am-5pm. Free.

Post Office: 104 SW Dorion Ave. (☎541-278-4053). Open M-F 9am-5pm, Sa 10am-1pm. **Postal Code:** 97801.

☷ GETTING AROUND. The **Umatilla River** runs east-west through Pendleton, and the majority of the city lies south of the river. The city is bisected by north-south **Main St.** All roads have a double designation giving their positions relative to these two dividers. The city is fairly narrow, and long east-west roads are all one-way, so expect to do a lot of looping. To prevent confusion, the streets names are arranged alphabetically from the river toward the south: **Byers, Court, Dorion,** and so on.

◑ SIGHTS. A system of tunnels evolved in Pendleton over the years, burrowing between the numerous brothels and saloons that sprung up here; at one point there were as many as 32 bars and 18 houses of ill repute. This whole sordid and fascinating history is told by **▨Pendleton Underground Tours,** 37 SW Emigrant Ave., which leads visitors through the completely restored and redecorated underground establishments. Tours showcase a card room, ice-cream parlor, Chinese quarters and an opium den, and the Cozy Rooms bordello. (☎800-226-6398; www.pendletonundergroundtours.org. Reservations recommended. 1½hr. tours Mar.-Oct. M-Sa 9:30am-3pm; Nov.-Feb. call for schedule. $10.) Pendleton also preserves another facet of local history at the **Tamastslikt Cultural Institute,** 72789 Hwy. 331, off Exit 216 on I-84, east of Pendleton, an interpretative center dedicated entirely to the history and future of the tribes of the Umatilla Reservation. The nautilus-shaped floor plan spirals through three sections, beginning in the coyote theatre, where a show relates the legends of the Coyote trickster, Ispilyay. From there, elaborate displays and many recordings provide a brief but detailed history of the Natitayt. (☎541-966-9748; www.tamastslikt.com. Open daily 9am-5pm. $6; students, seniors, and children $4.)

This city has been home to the rocking **Pendleton Round-Up** rodeo since 1910. If you happen to be in town in the second full week of September, don't miss the bronco-riders, clowns, and Happy Canyon Indian Pageant. The rest of the year, visit the **Round-Up Hall of Fame,** 1114 SW Court Ave. Plaques recall every champion in every event from every year, and half of the hall is filled with portraits of the annually elected Rodeo Queen and Happy Canyon Princess. Chemulwick, one of the great horses of the rodeo, has been stuffed and memorialized, honored alongside the men who rode him. (☎541-278-0815; www.pendletonroundup.com. Open May-Oct. M-Sa 10am-4pm. $3.) The **Pendleton Woolen Mills**, 1307 SE Court Pl., offers a 15min. tour that breezes through every step of the wool manufacturing process from carding and spinning to the final weaving. (☎541-276-6911 or 800-760-4844; www.pendleton-usa.com. Tours M-F 9, 11am, 1:30, 3pm. Free.)

FOOD AND ACCOMMODATIONS. Restaurants cluster around the nexus of Main St., Court Ave., and Dorion Ave. **Como's Italian Eatery ❸**, 39 SE Court Ave., is a tiny spot at the core of downtown serving standard, well-priced entrees like spaghetti and ziti. Sample Italian sweets beneath an entertaining display of postcards and pasta boxes. (☎541-278-9142. Open M-Sa 11am-9pm. MC/V.) A giant plastic Betty Boop smiles over the sidewalk of the **Main Street Diner ❷**, 349 S. Main St. The usual breakfast fare ($3-7) complements a few more adventurous lunch options. (☎541-278-1952. Sandwiches $3-7. Open M-Sa 7am-2pm, Su 8am-2pm. MC/V.) At **The Hut ❹**, 1400 SW Dorion Ave., patrons dine in the brightly lit, window-side booths or submerge themselves in the dim, deeply cushioned side room. (☎541-276-0756. Appetizers $3-6. Sandwiches $5-6.50. Entrees $7-17. Open M-Sa 11am-9pm. MC/V.)

Pendleton's accommodations are straightforward and ordinary, with one notable exception. The **Working Girls Hotel ❸**, 17 SW Emigrant Ave., is euphemistically named for the former brothel it occupies. The rooms are decorated with antiques recovered from the era; no occupants under 18 are allowed. (☎541-276-0730 or 800-226-6398. Rented through Pendleton Underground Tours. Kitchen, living area, shared bath. Rooms $65; suites $75. MC/V.) Clean and attractive rooms are available at the **Knights Inn ❸**, 105 SE Court Ave. Though the inn is right downtown, cleverly placed walls and outer walkways shield the rooms from noise and traffic. (☎541-276-3231. Singles $57; doubles $64. AmEx/MC/V.)

 BIG DETOUR. To explore Washington's rugged backcountry, take the **Summits, Simians, and Snoqualmie Big Detour** on p. 666.

APPROACHING THE DALLES: 123 MILES Continue west on **I-84**. About 45 mi. past Pendleton, you'll pass the town of **Boardman,** where the highway meets up with the **Columbia River.** Continue on I-84 to **Exit 85,** which feeds into **2nd Ave.** in The Dalles.

THE DALLES

The Dalles, a pleasant if unremarkable river city, is the central point in a broad spiral of unusual attractions spread through the area. The end of the land-bound Oregon Trail, it has long been an important nexus for Oregon Trail travelers. So close to the end, it became possible to float a wagon to Oregon City.

VITAL STATS

Population: 12,200

Visitor Info: The Dalles Area Chamber of Commerce, 404 W. 2nd St. (☎541-296-2231; www.thedalleschamber.com). Open Memorial Day to Labor Day M-F 8:30am-5pm, Sa 10am-4pm, Su 11am-3pm; Labor Day to Memorial Day M-F 8:30am-5pm.

Internet Access: The Dalles-Wasco County Library, 722 Court St. (☎541-296-2815). Open Tu-W 1-6pm, F-Sa 10am-3pm. Free.

Post Office: 101 W. 2nd St. (☎541-296-1065). Open M-F 8:30am-5pm. **Postal Code:** 97058.

GETTING AROUND. I-84 borders the edge of town along the Columbia River. **Hwy. 30** passes through down as **E. 3rd St.** and **E. 2nd St. Union St.** intersects the two near the center of town, heading down to the river.

SIGHTS. The Dalles's greatest attraction is the **Columbia Gorge Discovery Center and Wasco County Museum,** 5000 Discovery Dr., a double museum on the outskirts of town. The Wasco County Museum contains the usual displays on Native American, missionary, and military life on the Western frontier; however, unlike many similar museums, it tells the history of the area right up to the present day. The Columbia Gorge Discovery Center features an indoor gorge, teeming with (stuffed) animals and loud with (recorded) birdsong. (Head west on I-84 to Exit 82, and follow the signs. ☎541-296-8600; www.gorgediscovery.org. Open daily 9am-5pm. $8, seniors $7, ages 6-16 $4.) For some Lewis and Clark nostalgia, head to the **Rock Fort,** on the banks of the Columbia River, where Lewis and Clark camped out for three days in 1805. Clark described the campground in extreme detail in his personal diary, but these days, not much remains of the camp other than a few rocks. (At Bridgeway Rd., Bridge, and Garrison St. ☎541-296-2231. Free.) Check out **St. Peter's Landmark,** at 3rd and Lincoln St. This Gothic church from 1898 boasts a 6 ft. rooster for a spire. (☎541-296-5686.) **The Dalles Downtown Murals** include several murals, all of which detail a historical event in the city's past. The majority of the murals cluster around E. Federal St., between 2nd and 3rd St.

◼◼ FOOD AND ACCOMMODATIONS. Restaurants congregate in the downtown area and are well advertised and easy to find. You can't go wrong with ◼**Burgerville ❶,** 118 W. 3rd St., which serves the most socially and environmentally conscious fast-food you'll ever eat (Eric Schlosser, author of *Fast Food Nation,* is a fan). Electricity is generated by renewable wind energy, frying oil is reycled into biodiesel, and all of the dishes use regional ingredients like Oregon natural beef and walla walla onions. (☎541-298-5753. Burgers and shakes $3. Open daily 7am-11pm. D/MC/V.) Though it's a full restaurant, **Cafe Solara ❷,** 107C E. 2nd St., in the Columbia Court Mall, feels more like a college town coffee shop with its small tables and couches. Pita pizzas ($6) and foot-long wraps are customizable. (☎541-298-4786. Salads $3-7. Open M-F 8am-4pm. AmEx/D/MC/V.) Jump off Exit 83 to **Cousins' Restaurant ❸,** 2116 W. 6th St., which supports claims of "homestyle entrees" with a meatloaf dinner and a turkey and cranberry sauce plate. A none-too-subtle country atmosphere is created by the dancing farm animal statues outside and a door that moos, oinks, bleats, or crows when opened. (☎800-848-9378; www.cousinsthedalles.com. Breakfast $5-11. Entrees $7-13. Open daily 6am-10pm. AmEx/D/MC/V.)

Accommodations in the Dalles are fairly standard; look for the chains around Exit 83, along W. 6th St. **The Inn at The Dalles ❷,** 3550 SE Frontage Rd., sits atop a ridge. Giant windows give all its rooms glorious panoramas of the river, bridge, and dam. (Take a left immediately after getting off I-84 Exit 87. ☎541-296-1167. Singles $45; doubles $55. AmEx/D/MC/V.) The **Oregon Motor Motel ❷,** 200 W. 2nd St., is conveniently

located downtown and offers clean rooms with fridges and microwaves. (☎541-296-9111. Singles from $45; doubles from $50. AmEx/MC/V.)

 DID YOU KNOW? Thomas Jefferson originally chose war hero George Rogers Clark to explore the Louisiana Purchase with Meriwether Lewis, but Clark nominated his younger brother, William Clark, instead.

◼ APPROACHING THE COLUMBIA RIVER GORGE NATIONAL SCENIC AREA: 7 MILES Head east via **2nd St.** to the **Exit 87** on-ramps, just east of town. Follow the signs toward the interstate, but drive right past the ramps; the road will continue across the Columbia River into Washington by way of the **Dalles Bridge (U.S. 197).** After the bridge, go west on **Rte. 14,** into Washington State. Between The Dalles and Portland, you'll be driving in the heart of the Columbia River Gorge Scenic Area.

COLUMBIA RIVER GORGE NATIONAL SCENIC AREA

Stretching 80 stunning miles from The Dalles to Portland, the Columbia River Gorge carries the river to the Pacific Ocean through woodlands, waterfalls, and canyons. Heading inland along the gorge, heavily forested peaks give way to broad, bronze cliffs and golden hills covered with tall pines. Mt. Hood and Mt. Adams loom nearby, and breathtaking waterfalls plunge over steep cliffs into the river. While driving through offers spectacular vistas, roadtrippers should consider heading off-road via one of the area's many hiking or biking trails.

VITAL STATS

Area: 292,500 acres

Visitor Info: USDA Forest Service Columbia River Gorge National Scenic Area Visitors Center, 902 Wasco St., Ste. 200, (☎541-308-1700), in Hood River. Open M-F 8am-4:30pm. Columbia Gorge Interpretive Center, 9990 SW Rock Creek Dr. (☎800-991-2338; www.columbiagorge.org.), in Stevenson, WA, on Rte. 14. Open daily 10am-5pm. $6, ages 13-18 and seniors $5, ages 6-12 $4.

Gateway Towns: The Dalles (p. 663), Portland (p. 673).

GETTING AROUND

The Columbia River Gorge is traversed by several major highways: **I-84** and **U.S. 30** on the Oregon side, and **Rte. 14** in Washington. Attractions on the Washington side of the Columbia can be reached by crossing the river at the **Bridge of the Gods;** 11 mi. west of Hood River, take **Exit 44** through Cascade Locks and follow the signs ($1 toll).

SIGHTS

Two miles beyond the Bridge of the Gods turn-off near Cascades, Oregon, is the **Bonneville Dam Visitors Center.** The center has a deck for viewing the generators; though only their outer shells can be seen, their furious internal spinning can be heard and even felt through the glass. Below, windows have been built into the walls, so it is possible to see fish swimming upstream through the "fish ladders," maze-like structures built around the dam that allow the spawning creatures to continue upstream. (☎541-374-8820 or 509-427-4281. Open daily 9am-5pm. Free.) **Beacon Rock** lies 7 mi. west of the dam. Named by Louis and Clark, this titan boulder juts vertically from the water's edge. Across the street is **Beacon Rock State Park ❶,** a hillside campground and start of the Hamilton Mountain Trail. (Off Rte. 14 just west of Skamania, WA. ☎509-427-8265. Open daily 8am-sunset for day use. Sites $16. Cash or check only.)

HIKING

There is a huge array of trails in the Gorge area. For maps and information, visit the visitors center in Hood River. The forest service also has comprehensive website that contains maps, descriptions, difficulty ratings, and directions to trailheads for many area trails, at www.fs.fed.us/r6/columbia/forest/recreation/trails.

Pacific Crest Oregon (16 mi. one-way). From I-84, take Exit 44 at Cascade Locks, turn right on the Bridge of the Gods access road, and follow the signs. The trailhead is at a parking lot on the left before the bridge. This longer trail passes the canyons containing Eagle and Herman Creeks, then skirts the base of 3 small mountains. Closed in winter. Moderate.

Dog Mountain Trail (3 mi. round-trip). The trailhead is marked by a large sign, located off Rte. 14 about 14 mi. east of Stevenson, 1 mi. west of the Bridge of the Gods. This short trail is steep and rocky, but offers great vistas of Mt. Adams, Mt. Hood, and Mt. St. Helens. Closed in winter. Difficult.

Angel's Rest (4½ mi. round-trip). From I-84 W, take Exit 35 onto the Historic Columbia River Hwy., and go 7 mi. west. This trail leads through mossy, fern-filled forests, past one of the last falls in the chain, and up a ridge with excellent views. Open Mar.-Dec. Moderate.

Catherine Creek (1¼ mi. round-trip). From Rte. 14 in Washington, turn north on C.R. 1230, and proceed for 1½ mi. The paved trail passes through meadows that bloom with 90 species of wildflower Feb.-July. Easy.

BIKING

Bike trails also lace the gorge, though info on them is not quite as readily available as it is for foot trails. **Discover Bicycles,** 116 Oak St., in Hood River, sells maps in addition to renting out bikes. (☎541-386-4820; www.discoverbicycles.com. Open M-Sa 9am-6pm, Su 9am-5pm. Road bikes $6 per hr., $35 per day; mountain bikes $8/$45.) The **Post Canyon** area is home to a system of freeride trails and has become very popular with stunt and downhill riders. To reach the canyon, go west on Cascade St. in Hood River all the way to its end and turn left. Follow Country Club Rd. for 1¼ mi., then turn right onto Post Canyon Rd. For more info on freeriding in the canyon, visit www.gfra.org.

Surveyor's Ridge (23¾ mi., 3-5hr. round-trip). Take Rte. 35 S from Hood River for 31 mi., turn east onto FS 44, and follow it for 3½ mi. to the trailhead. This loop rides the edge of a ridge, offering great views. The final leg of the loop is along FS 17. Open late spring to late fall.

Three Lake Tour (18 mi., 2½-4hr. round-trip). Take 13th St. in Hood River south to Rte. 281 and continue south, turning west onto Portland Dr. The road will pass through the intersection with Country Club Rd. and become Binns Hill Rd. Follow Binns Hill Rd. for ¼ mi., then turn left onto Kinsley Rd. This leads to the trailhead beside Green Point Upper Reservoir.

SUMMITS, SIMIANS & SNOQUALMIE
SET THE PACE TO "GRUELING"

Length: 523 miles
Days: 2 days
Starting point: Pendleton
Highlight: Mt. Rainier

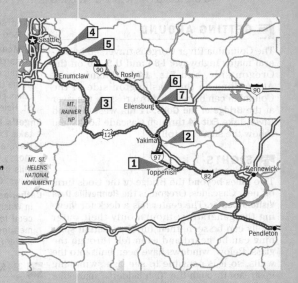

Take I-84 W from Pendleton to the junction with I-82. Follow I-82 to Exit 58, and turn left onto WA-223. Bear right onto WA-22, and continue onto U.S. 97 N. Bear left onto WA-220, and turn right on Buster Rd.

1 YAKAMA NATION CULTURAL HERITAGE CENTER. The **Yakama Nation Museum,** 100 Spilyay Loop, is the oldest Native American museum in the country and is one of the few state museums designed and managed by members of the tribe. The museum contains artifacts and exhibits detailing the history of the Yakama people. The Yakama National Cultural Heritage Center also contains a restaurant, a performing arts theater, and a library with an extensive collection of Native American literature. (☎509-865-2800; www.yakamamuseum.com. Museum open daily 8am-5pm. Free.)

Retrace your steps and get back on I-82 W. Take Exit 40 to Thorpe Rd. Bear right on Thorpe Rd., turn right onto Plath Rd., and turn left onto Gangle Rd. to reach Sagelands Vineyard.

2 SAGELANDS VINEYARD. The Yakima Valley's desert geography makes for some great wine tasting. Most wineries in the region offer tours and tastes for visitors. **Sagelands Vineyard,** 71 Gangle Rd., in Wapato, is best known for lovely berry blends and an especially fine glass of Merlot. Tours and tastings are offered throughout the day. Even if you're not in the mood for wine tasting, the vineyard has stunning views of the Yakima Valley and Mt. Adams. (☎800-967-8115; www.sagelandsvinyard.com. Open in summer daily 10am-5pm; hours vary in winter.)

Follow Hwy. 12 to Hwy. 123 into Mount Rainier National Park. Hwy. 123 is closed in winter, so call ahead and be prepared to take another, bigger detour into the park.

3 MOUNT RAINIER NATIONAL PARK. The Klickitat native people called it Tahoma, or "Mountain of God," but Rainier (ray-NEER) is simply "the Mountain" to most Washington residents. At 14,411 ft., Mt. Rainier presides regally over the Cascade Range as a giant among giants. Thousands of climbers attempt its inhospitable summit each year, and non-alpinists can explore over 305 mi. of trails that weave through old-growth forests, alpine meadows, and bubbling hot springs.

Mt. Adams and Mt. St. Helens can be seen from mountain trails like **Paradise** (1½ mi.), **Pinnacle Peak** (2½ mi.), and **Eagle Peak** (7 mi.). One of the oldest stands of trees in Washington, the **Grove of Patriarchs** grows near the Ohanapecosh Visitors Center. An easy 1½ mi. walk leads to these 500- to 1000-year-old Douglas firs, cedars, and hemlocks. The deserving favorite among the park's hikes is ◪**Camp Muir** (9 mi. round-trip), the most popular staging ground for summit attempts and a challenging day hike. The hike begins on **Skyline Trail,** a scenic 6 mi. loop reaching its peak at the 7000 ft. Panorama Point. The latter half of the hike to Muir is covered in snow throughout the year; only those skilled in snow travel with the proper equipment should attempt it. The undeniable behemoth of the park's routes is the infamous ◪**Wonderland Trail,** 94 mi. of challenging terrain that circumnavigates the whole mountain. Arguably more difficult than the mountain ascent, the route passes through every type of scenery imaginable: dark forest, bright snowfields, rushing rivers, and rocky moraines. A full hike of the route requires experience and careful planning; be sure to spend plenty of time at a ranger station before setting out. The best place to plan a backcountry trip is at the **Longmire Wilderness Information Center,** east of the Nisqually entrance. (☎360-569-4453. Open late May to early Oct. daily 7:30am-5pm.) An **entrance fee** is required ($10 per vehicle).

Take Hwy. 18 to I-90 E. Take the Snoqualmie Falls exit, and turn left onto Railroad Ave. E.

4 SNOQUALMIE FALLS. Just downstream of Snoqualmie and a few steps from the road, **Snoqualmie Falls** plummets a spectacular 270 ft. onto the rocks below. One hundred feet taller than Niagara Falls, Snoqualmie Falls is Washington's second-most popular natural attraction, following Mt. Rainier. View the falls from the vista spot above or via the steep, short hike down to the base. The view from the bottom is stunning, but be prepared for a difficult trek back. (Free.)

From Snoqualmie Falls, head back on Railroad Ave. until you reach North Bend Way. Twede's Cafe will be on the right.

5 TWEDE'S CAFE. Scenes from David Lynch's television series *Twin Peaks* were shot in **Twede's Cafe ❶,** 37 W. North Bend Way, and the sign above the restaurant won't let you forget it. Stop in for some small-town hospitality, a piece of Twin Peaks cherry pie, and a "damn fine cup of coffee." (☎425-831-5511. M-Th 6:30am-8pm, F-Sa 6:30am-9pm, Su 6:30am-7pm. MC/V.)

From Twede's, turn left on Bendigo Blvd. S, and left on the on-ramp for I-90 E. Continue on I-90 E, then take Exit 106 to U.S. 97. Stay on U.S. 97 until Exit 106. Bear right on Cascade Way, then continue onto 8th Ave. (University Way)

7 CHIMPANZEE AND HUMAN COMMUNICATION INSTITUTE. Central Washington University's Chimpanzee and Human Communication Institute (CHCI), 400 E. University Way, is home to a family of chimpanzees who have learned American Sign Language (ASL). The chimps communicate both with each other and with their human trainers using sign language and can be observed through one of the sponsored "Chimposiums." (☎509-963-2244. 1hr. chimposium Sa 9:15 and 10:45am, Su 12:30 and 2pm. $10, students $7.50.)

Head west on 8th Ave., and turn left onto Pearl St.

8 CLYMER MUSEUM OF ART. The Clymer Museum of Art, 416 N. Pearl St., contains the permanent collection of John Ford Clymer, including his covers for America's *Saturday Evening Post* and *Look* magazines, some of his early frontier work, and wildlife paintings. (☎509-962-6416. Open M-F 10am-5pm, Sa 10am-4pm, Su noon-4pm.

BACK TO THE ROUTE. Turn right onto 4th Ave. and left onto Main St. Get on I-90 heading east. Take Exit 110 to I-82 E, and exit to I-84 E. Take Exit 209 to U.S. 395. Turn right onto SW Frazer Ave., turn left on Main St., and continue back into Pendleton.

The end, along Waucoma Ridge, provides fine views. Open summer-fall. Easy to moderate.

Mosier Twin Tunnels (4½ mi., 1hr. one-way). A segment of the Historic Columbia River Hwy. too narrow for cars, between Hood River and Mosier. Offers mainly an on-road ride, with views of the river and the tunnels. Parking $3. Easy to moderate.

◪ DETOUR
MARYHILL MUSEUM AND STONEHENGE MEMORIAL

35 Maryhill Museum Dr., Goldendale, WA. After crossing the Columbia River from The Dalles, turn right to go east on Rte. 14 instead of continuing west. The museum is 15 mi. east of The Dalles, along Rte. 14, and the memorial is 3 mi. east of the museum.

A wealthy, turn-of-the-century entrepreneur named Sam Hill bought 6000 acres of riverfront property in 1907, intending to turn it into a utopian Quaker community. Originally intended to be his personal residence, the large, poured-concrete mansion overlooking the Columbia River is now the **Maryhill Museum.** Through Hill's friendship with Queen Marie of Romania, granddaughter of both Queen Victoria of England and Tsar Alexander II of Russia, the museum acquired objects from her court, including a golden gown and a reproduction of her crown. A friendship with Loie Fuller, of Folies Bergère fame, enabled Hill to acquire a number of original Rodin sculptures, including one of the smaller casts of his famous *The Thinker*. The museum's third floor displays a series of sets from the Theatre de la Mode of post-WWII France. These miniature cityscapes and dolls were meant to revitalize the fashion industry while making do with the extremely limited materials available in the wartime economy. (☎541-773-3733. Open mid-Mar. to mid-Nov. daily 9am-5pm. $7, seniors $6, ages 6-16 $2.)

Hill also built the nearby **Stonehenge WWI Memorial,** which, like the house, was constructed using only poured concrete. The memorial does not imitate the famous ruins, but the full stone structure as it was once believed to have been. The names of 13 men of Klickitat County killed in combat are inscribed on the stones. (☎541-773-3733. Grounds open daily 7am-10pm. Free.)

◪ APPROACHING HOOD RIVER: 20 MILES
On the Washington side of the Columbia River, **Rte. 14** runs about 20 mi. west from The Dalles turnoff to Bingen. Near Bingen, take the **Hood River Toll Bridge** ($0.75) across the river to Oregon. Follow the signs onto **I-84,** but don't go anywhere on it; the on-ramp flows right into the off-ramp that leads into Hood River. Turn left to enter the center of Hood River. From the Oregon side of the river, it's a straight shot on I-84.

HOOD RIVER
Built along the Oregon bank of a bend of the Columbia River, Hood River has evolved from a center for traditional sports into the windsurfing and kiteboarding capital of the Northwest.

LEWIS, CLARK...AND BIGFOOT

The Oregon Trail was plagued with river crossings, bad weather, and cholera. This wasn't quite bad enough, apparently, as pioneers managed to create a special boogie man of their own. Starr Wilkerson was a true giant, reportedly 6'8" and almost 300 lb. Unkindly nicknamed Bigfoot, Starr was something of an outcast and, hoping to escape the region (and his nickname), he hired himself out to a pioneer family. As his journey began, he fell in love with the family's daughter—however, she was smitten with another, and trouble soon set in. Tensions mounted between Starr and his rival and broke loose one night when the two were left alone. Starr was shot during the fight but still managed to kill the other man and fled camp, joining a renegade band of Indians and terrorizing the region. The rest of the ill-fated party chose to spend the winter on the trail rather than proceed to Oregon. When spring came, they were heading back to the trail when they encountered Starr once more. The object of Starr's affection angrily rejected him, and when his band slaughtered the entire party, the legend of Bigfoot was born. It is rumored that sometime later Bigfoot was slain, but legend also has it that he asked his killer not to tell anyone he was dead. With his death never certain, Bigfoot became a phantom, seen hiding behind the trees of the Oregon Trail in bloodthirsty wait.

While low-tech activities are as popular as ever, the figures cruising gloriously over the water give Hood River an extreme reputation.

VITAL STATS

Population: 6000

Visitor Info: Hood River Visitors Center, 405 Portway Ave. (☎541-386-2000 or 800-366-3530; www.hoodriver.org). Open M-F 9am-5pm, Sa-Su 10am-5pm.

Internet Access: Hood River County Library, 502 State St. (☎541-386-2535). Open M-Th 8:30am-8:30pm, F-Sa 8:30am-5pm. Free.

Post Office: 1795 12th St. (☎541-386-6280). Open M-F 9am-6pm, Sa 8am-5pm. **Postal Code:** 97031.

☞ GETTING AROUND. Hood River is an easy city to drive in, except for the occasional busy intersection regulated only by four-way stop signs. North-south streets are numbered, increasing from east to west. The most important east-west streets are **Cascade Ave.** and **Oak St.,** both close to the interstate. There is plenty of metered parking on the street sides ($0.25 per 3½hr.).

☉ SIGHTS. Hood River is the home station of the **Mount Hood Railroad,** 110 Railroad St., at the intersection of Cascade Ave. and 1st St. The excursion train, composed of early 20th-century Pullman coaches and a red caboose, winds through a valley, providing a narrated historic and scenic tour with a brief stop in the town of Parkdale. Dinner and brunch trains, in authentic restored dining cars, provide a meal to supplement the peaceful countryside ride. Specialty trips like the Train Robbery ride are occasionally offered; call ahead for dates. (☎541-386-3556 or 800-872-4661; www.mthoodrr.com. Open Apr.-Dec. Excursion train $23, seniors $21, ages 2-12 $15. Brunch train $58, dinner train $70, murder-mystery dinner train $80.) For a bit of the absurd, but nonetheless, close-up view of daintily carved animals, visit the **International Museum of Carousel Art,** 304 Oak St. (☎541-387-4622; www.carouselmuseum.com. Open M-Sa 11am-3pm, Su noon-4pm. $5, students and seniors $4, ages 5-10 $2.)

⚠ OUTDOORS. Hiking trails wrap all around Hood River in the **Columbia River Gorge National Scenic Area** (p. 664); the windsurfing and kiteboarding opportunities, however, are almost completely located in the city itself. The most important area in the windsurfing world is **Port Marina Park,** left off I-84 at Exit 64, which hosts most of the windsurfing and kiteboarding schools. North of downtown Hood River is the **Hook,** a cape which forms a windy but sheltered cove where beginners often train. Several companies rent equipment and provide instruction for the levels of windsurfers and kiteboarders. **Big Winds,** 207 Front St., at the east end of Oak St., offers 2hr. introductory windsurfing lessons to teach the basics, plus an additional 2hr. of free rentals. Kiteboarders have a 1½hr. introductory class out of the water to learn how to control a kite; most water lessons are one-on-one. (☎514-386-6086; www.bigwinds.com. Windsurfing intro lesson $65. Rentals $55 full package, $35 for only board or rig. Kiteboarding intro lesson $85. Open in summer daily 8:30am-6pm.) **Hood River Water Play,** based out of Port Marina Park, provides a 6hr. windsurfing introductory class. You can sail at the beginners' beach for free after completing the intro class. Four more levels of class are available, as well as private lessons. There are six levels of kiteboarding instruction: two basic, two intermediate, and two advanced. Each pair can be taken together. (☎541-386-9463 or 800-963-7873; www.hoodriverwaterplay.com. Windsurfing intro class $179, successive levels $85-95 for 2-3hr. classes. Kiteboarding intro class $169.)

🍴🍷 FOOD AND NIGHTLIFE. Little cafes and lunch shops cluster in Hood River, so finding somewhere to eat after a day of windsurfing is easy. In Hood River, there's no shortage of liquid refreshment. **Jean's @ 110 ❷,** 110 5th St., has serves delicious organic dishes to a young and hip crowd. (☎541-386-8755. Open M-Tu and Th-Su 8am-3pm.) For a sandwich, a salad, or a giant multi-hot-dog sandwich, try **Bette's Place ❷,** 416 Oak St. Sandwiches include standard ham and turkey, as well as the Gobbler ($7), with turkey, avocado, and cranberry sauce. The many salads ($6-7.50) include shrimp and mandarin orange, as well as cottage cheese and fruit. (☎541-386-1880. Burgers $6-7. Open daily 5:30am-3pm. MC/V.)

The ▨**Full Sail Brewing Co.,** 506 Columbia St., has 2 gold medal winners from the 2006 World Beer Championship, the Amber and IPA, along with a full pub-style menu featuring burgers and hearty appetizers. (541-386-2247. Burgers $7. Open daily noon-8pm.)

↑ ACCOMMODATIONS. Hood River accommodations can be expensive, and the smaller motels fill up quickly. The **Columbia Gorge Hostel/Bingen School Inn ❶,** one block north of the intersection of Cedar St. and Rte. 14, in Bingen, is cheap and friendly, though it's separated by a toll bridge from Hood River. The converted schoolhouse offers both huge private rooms and clean, dorm-style bunks. The old gymnasium is open for basketball and volleyball players, and the cafeteria is now a television lounge and open kitchen. (☎509-493-3363. Linen $3. Towel $1. Check-in M and Su by arrangement, Tu-Sa 8am-1pm and 6-9pm. Dorms $19; private doubles $98. MC/V.) **Praters Motel ❸,** 1306 Oak St., provides excellent gorge views from its alabaster building. The seven rooms are all decorated in the same pretty, unspoiled white as the exterior and come with refrigerators and microwaves. (☎541-386-3566. Rooms in summer $70; in winter $60. MC/V.)

↗ APPROACHING MOUNT HOOD: 43 MILES
From Hood River, take **Oak St.** eastbound until it runs into **State St.,** then drive south on **Rte. 35.** It's just over 40 mi. to the intersection with **U.S. 26,** a central point in the arc of area campsites and trailheads.

MOUNT HOOD

At 3429 meters, this majestic, snow-peaked mountain is the highest point in Oregon and one of the most climbed mountains in the world. With ski slopes at 10,000 ft. even in the middle of July, it is no wonder Mount Hood is the ideal summer training ground for the US ski team and hundreds of other aspiring olympians from around the world. The surrounding Hood River Valley and Columbia River Gorge's bountiful winds have made it the unofficial sail and kiteboard capital of the west, while the hillside fruit orchards make it one heck of a beautiful place for a basket of cherries and good picnic.

▣ GETTING AROUND

Rte. 35 connects the towns of Hood River and Government Camp northeast of Mt. Hood, and is the main road for access to many trailheads and campsites. Near the southeast edge of the mountain, Rte. 35 meets **U.S. 26,** which leads to the other major trails and camps. **Government Camp,** a ski village which lies on a single road of highway, Government Camp Loop, on U.S. 26 just east of the intersection with Rte. 35., is the closest town in proximity to the mountain and has more ski and snowboard gear than restaurants or lodgings. The town of **Hood River,** Exit 63 on I-84, offers more options for lodging, food, coffee, and pints.

◉ SIGHTS

Six miles up the steep road to Mt. Hood stands the historic **Timberline Lodge,** built in 1937 under the New Deal's Works Progress Administration. Over 2 million visitors come each year to admire this treasurehouse of woodcarvings, stone fireplaces, and artwork. (Timberline even has its own curator.) The building is so enchanting that it was the chosen setting for many Hollywood films, most famously *The Shining.* Four short **hiking trails** leave from the lodge for more views of the mountain. If the free view from the balcony of Timberline Lodge isn't enough, the **Magic Mile** express lift carries riders 1000 ft. above the clouds for spectacular views of the mountains and north ridges. (☎503-622-7979; www.timberlinelodge.com. Magic Mile open M-F 7am-1:30pm, Sa-Su 7am-3pm. $12, children $8. Rooms in summer from $95; call ahead for winter rates.) In the summer, the **Mount Hood Ski Bowl** opens its **Action Park,** which features Indy Kart racing ($3), batting cages ($1 per 10 pitches), mini-golf ($5), an alpine slide ($7), helicopter rides ($20), horseback riding ($25 per hr.), and bungee jumping ($25). Day passes are available for $16-45, covering different attractions. The Ski Bowl maintains 40 mi. of **bike trails** ($5 trail permit). **Hurricane Racing** rents mountain bikes from mid-June to October. (☎503-222-2695; www.skibowl.com. Open M-Th 11am-6pm, F 11am-7pm, Sa-Su 10am-7pm. $10 per hr., $32 per day; trail permit included.)

⬛ HIKING

Hiking trails circle Mt. Hood; simple maps are posted around **Government Camp** and at the **Mt. Hood Ranger District Station,** where you can also purchase the required Northwest Forest Pass. **Timberline Mountain Guides** (☎541-312-9242; www.timberlinemtguides.com), based out of Timberline Lodge, guides summit climbs for $375.

Mirror Lake Trail (6 mi. round-trip, 2-3hr.). Trailhead at a parking lot off U.S. 26, 1 mi. west of Government Camp. A popular day hike, this trail winds its way to the beautiful Mirror Lake. Easy to moderate.

Trillium Lake Loop (4½ mi. round-trip, 1-2hr.). Trailhead in the day-use area of the Trillium Lake Campground. A lakeside trail offering alpine wetlands. Trail can get congested on weekends. Easy to moderate.

Elk Meadows North Trail (14 mi. round-trip). Trailhead 25 mi. south of Hood River along Rte. 35, across the highway from the Polallie parking area. This trail rises sharply into the meadows around Mt. Hood, giving spectacular views of the mountain. Campsites are sheltered in the trees at the meadows' edge. Start early for a day hike or make this an overnight backpacking trip. Moderate to strenuous.

⬛ FOOD

Government Camp is small and touristy, but it is the home of **Mt. Hood Brewing Co.,** 87304 E. Government Camp Loop, where thirsty hikers and skiers can kick back with a cold one ($4 pints), traditional pub food ($8-15), and gourmet personal pizzas ($10-13). The Hogsback Oatmeal Stout and Ice Axe IPA are both award-winners. (☎503-272-3724; www.mthoodbrewing.com. Open M-Th and Su noon-9pm, F-Sa noon-10pm. MC/V.) If you're desperate for a late-night meal, the **Huckleberry Inn ❷**, 88611 Bus. U.S. 26, serves generous portions of basic fare. (☎503-272-3325. Entrees $6-9. Open 24hr.)

⬛ ACCOMMODATIONS

Most campgrounds in **Mt. Hood National Forest** cluster near the junction of U.S. 26 and Rte. 35, though they can also be found along the length of both highways on the way to Portland or Hood River. To reach **free camping** spots

THE ART OF WRITING A GOOD POSTCARD

Postcards are a roadtripper's lifeline-for $0.25, you can send a portrait of your journey to the folks back home. Some see postcards as an annoying obligation, but they can also be transcendent, offering an outsider a look into the strange yet wonderful world of roadtripping. A good postcard shows someone at home the poetry of life on the road. Unfortunately, all too many postcards are ruined by scribbled, unplanned, mental vomit. Many roadtrippers fall into the chief trap of postcard-writing, thinking that since there's so little room on the card, you shouldn't try to say anything substantial. Many postcards follow the same tired formula: "Hi, how are you? I'm in [insert town here] and it's [cute/smelly/a pit]. It's very [sunny/windy/rainy] here. I [like/love/dislike/will destroy] it. Miss you! Love, Boring McDullsville." A good postcard makes no mention of the weather (unless it leads to an account of a cave found trying to escape the rain). It may or may not mention the actual location of the roadtripper (who knows where Lander is anyway?). Instead, launch right into a short anecdote from your travels—the stranger the better. While the anecdote should always be based in fact, it's perfectly acceptable to recast events to make a better story. A good postcard should allow friends back home to see the world through your eyes, bugs on the windshield and all.

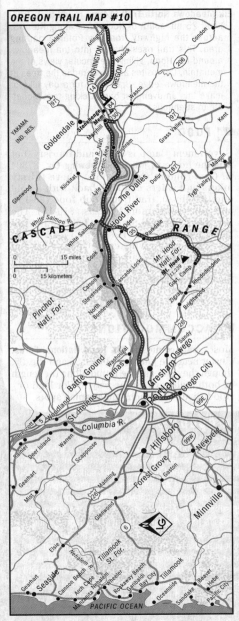

** OREGON TRAIL MAP #10**

near the mountain, take the sign toward Trillium Lake (a few miles east of Government Camp on U.S. 26), then follow a dirt road to the right ½ mi. from the entrance with sign "2650 131," and make a left toward "Old Airstrip." Campsites with fire rings line the abandoned runway. For a more expensive, less outdoorsy experience, stay in a hotel or B&B in Hood River or Government Camp, or camp on the mountain. (☎877-444-6777. Sites $9.)

Vagabond Lodge, 4070 Westcliff Dr. (☎541-386-2992), Exit 62 off I-84. 1 mi. west of Hood River. A near perfect location on 5 river-side acres, newly renovated river-view rooms, and motel prices. From the road, the modest office and street-side rooms can be deceiving; this may be one of the best-kept secrets in Hood River. Reservations recommended for the 24 riverside rooms. Singles $49-85; doubles $59-97. ❸

Lost Lake Resort (☎541-386-6366; www.lostlakeresort.org). From Rte. 35, turn east onto Woodworth Dr., right onto Dee Hwy., and then left on Lost Lake Rd. (Forest Service Rd. 13). 121 Sites with water and toilets. A 3 mi. hike around the lake provides views of Mt. Hood. Rent a canoe ($8 per hr.), or fish in the trout-stocked lake. Sites $15; RV sites without electricity $18; cabins $45-100. ❶

Trilium Lake, off U.S. 26, less than 2 mi. west of the Rte. 35/U.S. 26 intersection. The lakeside is beautiful, but the paved, popular sites are close together in some spots. Sites fill up quickly on weekends. Firewood $5. Sites $14-16. ❶

Still Creek, 1 mi. west of Trillium Lake, off US 26. Generally less crowded than Trillium Lake; even when full, the thickly-wooded grounds are quieter, as the sites are more widely spaced than those at the lake. Potable water, toilets, few RVs. Sites $14-16. ❶

⊓ APPROACHING PORTLAND: 63 MILES
Take **I-84 W** from Hood River. The biggest attraction along the highway is **seven waterfalls,** five of which are visible from the road. **Multnomah,** the most popular of the waterfalls, cascades 620 ft. from Larch Mountain and is the second-highest, year-round waterfall in the US. The road curves up to the overlook at Crown Point where **Vista House,** an octagonal stone building built in 1916, has a spectacular view of the Columbia River. The road winds down to I-84 through Corbett. 17 mi. farther west are the city limits of Portland. Take **Exit 1** off I-84 and continue through the stoplights. You'll reach

the intersection with **NE Grand Ave.** and then **NE Martin Luther King Jr. Blvd.** Turn south down MLK Jr. Blvd. to **Burnside St.**, the city's central road.

PORTLAND

Portland is a city that got it right. With a nationally renowned light-rail transit system, urban planning that has mixed parks with responsible development, and a blossoming restaurant and arts scene, Portland has hit its stride as a progressive Northwest destination. Its location on the winding Willamette River in the shadow of both Mt. Hood and Mt. Adams ensures that the city doesn't have to work hard to be beautiful, but thousands of rosebushes and landscaped riverbanks make a good thing even better. A fitting (near) end to any roadtrip, Portland embodies a fascinating integration of culture, progressivism, and the energy of a spunky teenager.

VITAL STATS

Population: 540,000

Visitor Info: Visitor Information Center, 701 SW 6th St. (☎877-678-5263; www.travelportland.com), in Pioneer Courthouse Sq. Open M-F 8:30am-5:30pm.

Internet Access: Multnomah County Library, 801 SW 10th St. (☎503-988-5234; www.multcolib.org). Open M-Th 9am-9pm, F-Sa 9am-6pm, Su 1-5pm. Free.

Parking: Parking lots line Couch St., between 4th and 6th St. ($2 per hr., $6-7per day.) Parking in central downtown is metered M-Sa 8am-6pm. Free parking can be found west of 11th or 12th St.

Post Office: 715 NW Hoyt St. (☎505-525-5398). Open M-F 7am-6:30pm, Sa 8:30am-5pm. **Postal Code:** 97205.

GETTING AROUND

Portland is divided into four manageable chunks by the **Willamette River,** which runs north-south, and **Burnside St.,** which runs east-west. The river can be crossed by a series of bridges, though the **Burnside Bridge,** located near Exit 1, is the most convenient from downtown. The city is organized as a grid, making it easy to navigate. **Old Town,** in northwest Portland, encompasses most of the city's historic sector. **China Town** is located a few blocks to the east. To the north, **Nob Hill** and the **Pearl District** are swanky, revitalized areas with upscale restaurants, tea shops, and art galleries. Central downtown, surrounding Pioneer Courthouse Sq., has a rich array of cafes, theaters, and restaurants. The **University of Portland** campus is bordered by Williams Ave. on the north. Parking in the east side of the city, around **Martin Luther King Jr. Blvd.,** is plentiful and free, while closer parking is best found in the neighboring Pearl District. The **MAX** light-rail system is free throughout much of downtown, and trips to Portland's outer neighborhoods cost less than $2 each way. (☎503-238-7433; www.trimet.org.) Bus lines run through the **Portland Transit Mall** (SW 5th and 6th Ave.)

 SIGHTS

WASHINGTON PARK

Fewer than 10 blocks west of downtown is the sprawling Washington Park, a woodland tract encompassing many of Portland's acclaimed gardens. Head west on Burnside St., past 23rd Ave., take a left on Tichner, and turn right at the first intersection onto Kingston Ave. It will eventually reach a T-junction, which is the center of the gardens area.

INTERNATIONAL ROSE TEST GARDEN. The most stunning of Washington Park's attractions, the Rose Test Garden boasts over 500 varieties of roses. The 4½ acres of crimson, pink, and yellow blooms are more than eye-candy; they're a testing ground for new breeds of roses—"Rainbow Knockout" and "Strike It Rich" are two gold-medal winners. With striking views of the city below, you'd be hard pressed to find a more peaceful setting for a picnic. (*400 SW Kingston St. ☎503-823-3636. Open daily 5am-10pm. Free.*)

JAPANESE GARDENS. Once you step into the Japanese Gardens, it's hard to believe you're still in the US. Reputed to be the most authentic this side of the Pacific, the gardens' delicate ponds, abstract sand and stone gardens, and ceremonial tea house were designed by Professor Takuma Tono. Delicate, peaceful, and truly exceptional, it's well worth a visit. (611 SW Kingston Ave., across the street from the Rose Gardens. ☎503-223-1321. Tours Apr.-Oct. daily 10:45am and 2:30pm. Open Apr.-Sept. M noon-7pm, Tu-Su 10am-7pm; Oct.-Mar. M noon-4pm, Tu-Su 10am-4pm. $8.50, seniors and college students $6.25, ages 5-18 $5.25, under 5 free.)

HOYT ARBORETUM. Forming the wooded backdrop for the rest of Washington Park's sights, the Hoyt Arboretum features 185 acres of trees, 12 mi. of trails, and flora and fauna from around the world. The visitor center has maps of popular hiking trails. (4000 Fairview Blvd. Take Kingston Ave. to Knights Ave., and turn right, then turn right on Fairview Blvd. ☎503-228-8733; www.hoytarboretum.org. Visitors center open daily 9am-4pm. Tours Apr.-Oct. Sa-Su 2pm. Grounds open daily 6am-10pm. Free.)

OREGON ZOO. This zoo boasts the most successful breeding herd of Asian elephants in the world, and many visitors flock here for a glimpse of Packy, the first elephant born in the US in the last 40 years. African savannah and rainforest enclosures contain the most exotic of the zoo's creatures, while the vast Great Northwest and Pacific Shores habitats are home to sea lions and leopards. (4001 SW Canyon Rd. ☎503-220-2493; www.oregonzoo.com. Grounds open daily Apr. 15-Sept. 15 9am-7pm; Sept. 16-Apr. 14 9am-5pm; gates close 1hr. earlier. $9.50, seniors $8, ages 3-11 $6.50.)

OTHER GARDENS AND PARKS

CLASSICAL CHINESE GARDENS. The largest Ming-style gardens outside of China, the Classical Chinese Gardens occupy a full city block and were designed by Suzhou artisans. Tranquil waterfalls, a large pond, ornate stone walkways, and an authentic tea house invite a meditative visit. (NW 3rd Ave. and Everett St. ☎503-228-8131; www.portlandchinesegarden.org. Open daily Apr.-Oct. 9am-6pm; Nov.-Mar. 10am-5pm. $7, seniors $6, students $5.50, under 5 free.)

FOREST PARK. At the northern edge of Washington park, Forest Park spans 5000 acres and is the largest urban forest reserve in the U.S. The woods, criss-crossed by 74 mi. of trails, trace Portland's far western edge. (☎503-223-5449; www.friendsofforestpark.org. Free.)

OTHER SIGHTS

◪POWELL'S CITY OF BOOKS. Downtown on the edge of the northwest district is the largest bookstore in the US. Powell's gargantuan bookstore, a cavernous 68,000 sq. ft. establishment, holds over a million new and used volumes but still retains the feel of a quirky neighborhood shop. The vaults are so large that the rooms are color coded to help browsers find their desired title. (1005 W. Burnside St. ☎503-228-4651 or 800-878-7323. Open daily 9am-11pm.)

PIONEER COURTHOUSE. Portland's most visited spot and one of the most popular outdoor venues for summer films and concerts, Pioneer Courthouse is the historic centerpiece of the **Pioneer Courthouse Sq.** Affectionately known as "Portland's Living Room," tourists and locals of every ilk hang out in the brick quadrangle. (715 SW Morrison St., at 5th Ave. and Morrison St. ☎503-223-1613; www.pioneercourthousesquare.org.)

PORTLAND ART MUSEUM. The Portland Art Museum (PAM) is the oldest art museum in the Pacific Northwest and it boasts collections from American art to Cameroonian sculpture. The new modern and contemporary center is the region's largest. (1219 SW Park St., at Jefferson St. ☎503-226-2811; www.portlandartmuseum.org. Open in summer Tu-W 10am-5pm, Th-F 10am-8pm, Su noon-5pm; in winter Tu-Sa 10am-5pm, Su noon-5pm. $10, students and seniors $9, ages 5-18 $6.)

THE GROTTO. In the far-eastern regions of Portland is the Catholic sanctuary known as the Grotto. A quiet, uncrowded forest shelters recessed statues of saints, including a shrine hewn in the cliff face overhead. Take the elevator up to the top, where a monastery sits beside a silent lake. (At NE 85th St. and Sandy Blvd. Drive east on I-84 to Exit 5. From the ramp, turn right onto Multnomah St., then right again on 82nd St. After about 1 mi., turn right onto Sandy Blvd. ☎503-254-7371; www.thegrotto.org. Grounds open daily in summer 9am-8:30pm; in winter 9am-5:30pm. Lower level free. Elevator tokens $3, ages 6-11 and seniors $2.50.)

FESTIVALS. Portland's premier summer event is the ◪**Rose Festival,** which lasts the entirety of June. The nation's second-largest floral parade is one of the highlights; finding a spot for the rose parade requires an early morning stakeout, and accommodations

OREGON TRAIL

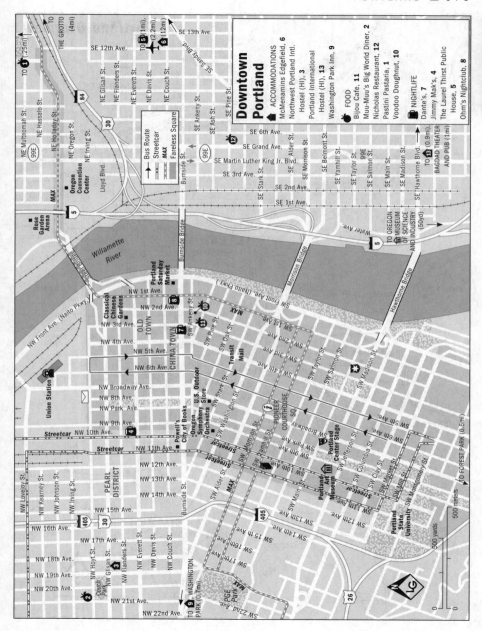

Downtown Portland

ACCOMMODATIONS
McMenamins Edgefield, **6**
Northwest Portland Intl.
 Hostel (HI), **3**
Portland International
 Hostel (HI), **13**
Washington Park Inn, **9**

FOOD
Bijou Cafe, **11**
Muu-Muu's Big World Diner, **2**
Nicholas Restaurant, **12**
Pastini Pastaria, **1**
Voodoo Doughnut, **10**

NIGHTLIFE
Dante's, **7**
Jimmy Mak's, **4**
The Laurel Thirst Public
 House, **5**
Ohm's Nightclub, **8**

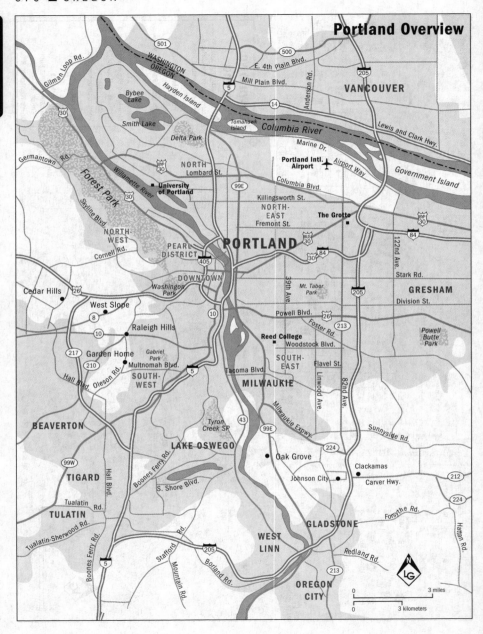

Portland Overview

should be reserved well in advance. (☎503-227-2681; www.rosefestival.org.) In early July, the three-day **Waterfront Blues Festival** draws some of the world's finest blues artists to the banks of the Willamette. (☎800-973-3378; www.waterfrontbluesfest.com. Suggested donation $8.) The **Oregon Brewers Festival**, on the last full weekend in July, is the continent's largest gathering of independent brewers, making for one incredible party at Waterfront Park. (☎503-778-5917; www.oregonbrewfest.com. Under 21 must be accompanied by parent. Mug $3; beer tokens $1 each.) The **Northwest Film Center** hosts the **Portland International Film Festival** in the last two weeks of February, with 100 films from 30 nations. (1219 SW Park Ave. ☎503-221-1156.)

FOOD

The menus in Portland are a combination of the cosmopolitan and the laid-back, with plenty of ethnic, vegetarian, and eclectic offerings. Recently, the city has become a mecca for tea connoisseurs, and the Pearl District is home to many a fine cup of oolong.

Voodoo Doughnut, 22 SW 3rd Ave. (☎503-241-4704). Possibly the only place in the world that is both a wedding chapel and a doughnut shop, Voodoo Doughnut takes fried pastry seriously. Open 22hr. per day to serve creative variations like the Butter Fingering (devil's food cake and Butterfinger), the Bacon Maple Bar, Chocolate Penetration,

and an assortment of vegan options ($1-1.50). Quirky is an understatement. Swahili lessons daily before 9am. Open M-Sa 1pm-11am. Cash only. ❶

Bijou Cafe, 132 SW 3rd Ave. (☎503-222-3187). This sunny cafe has well-deserved favorite status in Portland, and lines go out the door for weekend brunch. Gooey pecan sticky buns ($2.50), omelettes ($10), brioche french toast ($7), salads, burgers, and sandwiches ($4-9) make dining here well worth the wait. Open M-F 7am-2pm, Sa-Su 8am-2pm. MC/V. ❷

Muu-Muu's Big World Diner, 612 NW 21st Ave. (☎503-223-8169), at Hoyt St. Artful goofiness—the name of the restaurant was drawn from a hat—amidst red velvet curtains and gold upholstery. Try the Brutus salad, "the one that kills a Caesar." Appetizers $3.50-6.50. Entrees $7.50-14. Open M-F 11:30am-1am, Sa-Su 10am-1am. AmEx/D/DC/MC/V. ❷

Nicholas Restaurant, 318 SE Grand Ave. (☎503-235-5123), between Oak and Pine St. Great Lebanese and North African cuisine in a casual, authentic atmosphere. Falafel sandwiches and appetizer plates $5-6. Open M-Sa 11am-9pm, Su noon-9pm. Cash only. ❷

Pastini Pastaria, 1426 NE Broadway (☎503-288-4300). For the pasta aficionado, this place is heaven with a surprisingly cheap price tag. Fresh veggies, sundried tomatoes, authentic Italian cheeses, and ambrosial bread accompany a huge variety of pasta dishes ($7-9). A long list of gourmet salads ($5-7) is also available for those less

WHERE THE SIDEWALK ENDS

In 1948, a hole was cut through the sidewalk at the corner of SW Taylor St. and SW Naito Pkwy. (Front St.). It was expected to accommodate a mere lamp post, but greatness was thrust upon it. The street lamp was never installed, and the 24-inch circle of earth was left empty until noticed by Dick Fagan, a columnist for the Oregon Journal, who grew tired of looking at the unsightly hole from his office window. Fagan used his column, "Mill Ends," to publicize the patch of dirt, pointing out that it would make an excellent park. Fagan planted flowers in the park and regularly chronicled the comings and goings of its resident leprechaun colony, with whom he frequently conversed. According to the explanatory plaque (which is bigger than the park itself), the park has hosted weddings and is presided over by an invisible leprechaun named Patrick O'Toole. The park was added to the city's roster on St. Patrick's Day, 1976, seven years after Fagan's death. At 452.16 square inches, Mill Ends Park is officially the world's smallest. Locals have enthusiastically embraced it, planting flowers and hosting a hotly contested annual snail race on St. Patrick's Day. The park also contains a swimming pool and diving board (for butterflies) as well as a miniature Ferris wheel.

carb-inclined. Open M-Th 11:30am-9pm, F-Sa 11:30am-10pm, Su 4-9pm. AmEx/MC/V. ❷

ACCOMMODATIONS

Those looking for high-end establishments need look no farther than the blocks around Exit 1, which are rife with classy chains. The cheapest accommodations are located outside of downtown, in the suburbs; luckily, even they can be reached in just a few minutes by car. These budget spots, especially the few hostels, fill quickly. All accommodations in Portland fill up during the summer months, particularly during the Rose Festival, so make your reservations early.

Portland International Hostel, Hawthorne District (HI), 3031 SE Hawthorne Blvd. (☎503-236-3380; www.portlandhostel.org). Lively common space and a huge porch define this hostel, located in the outskirts of Portland. The outdoor stage with open mic (Th) draws a crowd. Kitchen and laundry available. Free Wi-Fi. Reception 8am-10pm. Check-out 11am. Dorms $20-23, members $17-20; private rooms $40-46. AmEx/D/MC/V. ❶

Northwest Portland International Hostel (HI), 1818 NW Glisan St. (☎503-241-2783; www.nwportlandhostel.com), at 18th Ave. This snug Victorian building has a kitchen, lockers, laundry, and a small espresso bar. Internet $1 per 16min. 34 dorm beds (coed available). Street parking permits available. Reception 8am-11pm. Dorms $20-23, members $17-20; private doubles $30-49. D/MC/V. ❶

Washington Park Inn, 840 SW King St. (☎503-226-2722). Just a few blocks from Washington Park and the Nob Hill/Pearl District. The rooms are simple but comfortable, with cable TV and free Wi-Fi. Continental breakfast included. Singles $39; doubles $49. AmEx/D/DC/MC/V. ❷

McMenamins Edgefield, 2126 SW Halsey St. (☎503-669-8610 or 800-669-8610), in Troutdale. Take I-84 to Exit 16; turn right off the ramp. This beautiful 38-acre former farm is a posh escape that keeps 2 hostel rooms. Brewery, vineyards, 18-hole golf course, movie theater, and restaurants. Live acoustic music on summer nights. No TVs or phones. Call ahead in summer; no reservations for the hostel. Dorms $30; singles $50; doubles $85-120. AmEx/D/DC/MC/V. ❷

ENTERTAINMENT

Portland's major daily newspaper, the *Oregonian*, lists upcoming events in its Friday edition, and the city's favorite free cultural reader, the *Wednesday Willamette Week*, is a reliable guide to local music, plays, and art. The **Oregon Symphony Orchestra,** 923 SW Washington St., plays from September to June. On Sundays and Mondays, students can buy $5 tickets starting one week before showtime. (☎503-228-1353 or 800-228-7343. Box office open M-F 9am-5pm; in symphony season also Sa 9am-5pm. Tickets $17-76; "Symphony Sunday" afternoon concerts $20, students $14.) The **Bagdad Theater and Pub,** 3702 SE Hawthorne Blvd., shows second-run mainstream films and has an excellent beer menu. (☎503-288-3286. Pub open M-Sa 11am-1am, Su noon-midnight. 21+ after 9pm.) **Noon Tunes,** at Pioneer Courthouse Sq., presents a plethora of rock, jazz, folk, and world music. On Thursday evenings, blues drift through the square in the **Live After 5** series. (☎503-223-1613. July-Aug. Noon Tunes Tu and Th noon; Live After 5 Th 5pm. Call ahead.) **Portland Center Stage,** in the Portland Center for Performing Arts, at SW Broadway and SW Main St., stages classics, modern adaptations, and world premieres. (☎503-274-6588. Tickets $25-55.) Basketball fans can watch the **Portland Trailblazers** at the **Rose Garden Arena,** 1 Center Ct. (☎503-321-3211; box office 503-224-4400; www.rosequarter.com.)

NIGHTLIFE

Once a rowdy frontier town, always a rowdy frontier town. Portland's nightclubs cater to everyone from the clove-smoking, college athlete to the nipple-pierced, neo-goth aesthete.

The Laurel Thirst Public House, 2958 NE Glisan St. (☎503-232-1504), at 30th Ave. Local talent makes a name for itself in 2 intimate rooms of groovin', boozin', and schmoozin'. Burgers and sandwiches $5-8. Tu free billiards. Happy hour show daily 6-8pm. Cover after 8pm $2-5. Open daily 9am-2am.

Jimmy Mak's, 300 NW 10th Ave. (☎503-295-6542), 3 blocks from Powell's Books, at Flanders St. Jam to Portland's renowned jazz artists while eating Greek and Middle Eastern dishes ($8-17). Music nightly 9:30pm. Cover $3-6. Open M 11am-3pm, Tu-W 11am-1am, Th-F 11am-2am, Sa 6pm-2am.

Dante's, 1 SW 3rd Ave. (☎503-226-6630). Rock, pop, soul, hip-hop, and DJ beats pump through this cabaret-style club on any given night. A small dance floor, open fire pit, and warm candles warm up the place, while the 2nd bar makes for more space on weekend nights. Cover $10-12. Open M-F 11am-2:30am, Sa-Su 7pm-2:30am.

Ohm Nightclub, 31 NW 1st Ave. (☎503-223-9919), at Couch St., under the Burnside Bridge. Restaurant and club dedicated to electronic music and unclassifiable beats. Weekends often bring big-name DJs. W spoken-word with live band. Th live music. Su drum 'n' bass. Music starts at 9pm. Cover $10. Open M-Th 10am-2am, F-Su 24hr. until M 2am.

⚐ APPROACHING OREGON CITY: 24 MILES
Head south on **MLK Jr. Blvd.,** which becomes **Rte. 99.**

OREGON CITY. Oregon City was once home to the only federal land office in the Oregon Territory; travelers had little choice but to end their journey here. The **End of the Oregon Trail Interpretive Center,** 1726 Washington St., is great fun for those who have just driven the route themselves. Tours lead visitors through a trio of huge wagons. (☎503-657-9336. Open Mar.-Oct. M-Sa 9:30am-5pm, Su 10:30am-5pm. Call ahead for winter hours and tour times. $7.50, ages 5-12 $5, seniors $6.50.) Finish up strong at **McMenamins Oregon City,** 102 9th St. Traditional pub grub and great ales are served at this Oregon landmark. (☎503-655-8032. Free Wi-Fi. Open M-Th 11am-midnight, F-Sa 11am-1am, Su noon-11pm.)

THE END OF THE ROAD

Lewis and Clark did it, and now you've joined the ranks of greatness. You persevered through the hardships of the trail, reaching Oregon with plenty of time to spare before winter—and you never had a problem getting your oxen to ford the river. Sample some microbreweries, head back to Portland for hopping nightlife and another stroll through the International Test Rose Garden. You've followed in the footsteps of pioneers for 2000 miles, and now it is time to blaze a new path of your own. Drive toward the ocean to join up with the Pacific Coast, or head north to the Great North.

EXIT TO

Cannon Beach, OR 79 mi.
on the pacific coast route, p. 972

Victoria, BC 254 mi.
on the great north route, p. 344

SPEED LIMIT 65

the deep south

TOP 5

1. Practice your hip swivels at **Graceland** in Memphis, Tennessee.
2. Remember the Civil Rights movement at the **Birmingham Civil Rights Institute.**
3. Discover that Honest Abe was one tall fella at the **Lincoln Memorial** in Washington, D.C.
4. Head to **Stamey's Barbecue** for the best ribs in North Carolina.
5. Peer into the massive crater at the **Petersburg National Battlefield** in Petersburg, Virginia.

Have you watched *Gone with the Wind* hundreds of times? Do you find yourself craving hushpuppies, fried okra, and country-fried steak? Do you always wish you were in the land of cotton? The South has a storied past—the effects of slavery have not yet been washed away, and the Civil Rights movement is too recent to be comfortably relegated to textbooks. But you haven't really seen America until you venture through its Southern soul. Leave your preconceptions behind and brace yourself for some serious charm—you definitely won't need Scarlett and Rhett where you're going.

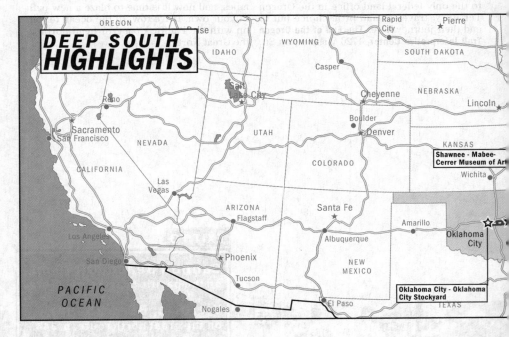

DEEP SOUTH **HIGHLIGHTS**

The route begins in **Washington, D.C.** (p. 682), the vibrant capital city and a fitting place for a roadtrip through America's past. See a show at **Ford's Theatre** (p. 688) and take advantage of the free admission to the **Smithsonian Museums** (p. 686). From there, the road swoops into Virginia heading toward **Richmond** (p. 699). The **Spotsylvania Court Battlefield** (p. 697) is the first of the multitude of Confederate sights and Civil War battlefields that you'll encounter on your trip.

Next, the road runs to North Carolina, proud to be the Tarheel State, and brimming with fields of tobacco, pastel sunsets, and rocking chairs on porches. The Triangle—**Durham** (p. 705), **Raleigh** (p. 707), and **Chapel Hill** (p. 709)—is a blend of slow-paced, small-town appeal and intellectual highbrows.

Take a moment to ponder the bizarre at the **Korner's Folly** (p. 714) before heading to **Winston-Salem** (p. 714). **Charlotte** (p. 717) is home to the **Levine Museum of the New South** (p. 717), a must-see for any roadtripper. The sharp ridges and rolling slopes of the southern Appalachian range create

some of the most spectacular scenery in the Southeast. Cruise into **Asheville** (p. 721), the prized gem of North Carolina, and fancy yourself a Southern belle at the spectacular **Biltmore Estate** (p. 721) before heading into the heart of Georgia.

Atlanta (p. 726) isn't called "Hotlanta" for nothing—trust us—they're not just talking about the weather. Sample chicken and waffles at **Gladys Knight's and Ron Winan's Chicken and Waffles** (p. 732), and wash it all down with the samples from the **World of Coca-Cola** (p. 729). You'll know when you've entered **Birmingham** (p. 737) when you see the giant statue of **Vulcan** (p. 738) and visit all the Civil Rights sights, like the **Birmingham Civil Rights Institute** (p. 738).

Don't cry when you leave Alabama—save those country woes for **Nashville** (p. 742), the center of the South's country music scene and the place for barbecue, Tennessee whiskey, and glitzy entertainment. Next, the road makes a run for **Memphis** (p. 749), home of the King and all the Elvis paraphernalia to go with it. Come in May for the **World Championship Barbecue Cook-**

DEEP SOUTH

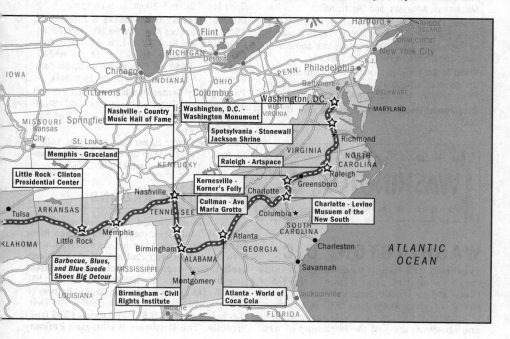

ing **Contest** (p. 752), and definitely don't leave before hitting **Graceland** (p. 749) and the **Rock 'n' Soul Museum** (p. 750). Take a fun excursion into Mississippi for the **Barbecue, Blues, and Blue Suede Shoes Big Detour** (p. 756), which runs through **Clarksdale, Oxford, Tupelo,** and **Holly Springs** and promises a rollickin' good time.

Cut across Arkansas to **Little Rock** (p. 758), home to the **Clinton Presidential Library** (p. 758). Smoke a cigar, eat some fried catfish, and look at the "little rock" itself. It's only a little ways more to **Oklahoma City** (p. 763), the end of the route and the perfect time to hook onto Route 66.

It's a long, hard road through the South, but the rewards are great. So go on; the land of cotton awaits.

ROUTE STATS

Miles: c. 2100

Route: Washington, D.C., to Oklahoma City, OK.

States: 10; Washington, D.C., Virginia, North Carolina, South Carolina, Georgia, Alabama, Tennessee, Mississippi, Arkansas, and Oklahoma.

Driving Time: You could zoom across the South in a week, but what's the point in that? Leave at least 2 or 3 weeks to hit all the sights, savor some fried okra, and develop a twang along the way.

When To Go: Yankees beware— the South sizzles in the summer. Unless your car's A/C is something fierce, beat the heat and start the trip in late spring.

Crossroads: Route 66, in Oklahoma City, OK (p. 533).

The Nation's Capital

WASHINGTON, DC

★ ★ ★ ★ ★ ★ *Welcomes You!*

WASHINGTON, D.C.

Visitors to the nation's capital often think they've seen it all after a tour of the White House and the Lincoln Memorial. But locals and savvy travelers know that D.C. is a thriving international metropolis and that monuments and museums are just the beginning of what this city has to offer. Washington, D.C.'s diamond-shaped borders encompass a bewildering array of world-class cultural and culinary delights, including the avant-garde galleries of Dupont Circle, the glittering mosaic of Adams Morgan nightlife, and the colonial chic of Georgetown. Now far more than just the world's most powerful city, D.C. has hit the big-time, with Broadway shows at the Kennedy Center, the latest bands jamming on the "New U" St. corridor, and (finally!) major-league baseball in front of positively giddy fans at RFK Stadium. For expanded coverage of the D.C. area, check out ▧*Let's Go: Washington, D.C.*

VITAL STATS

Population: 600,000 (District of Columbia); 3,500,000 (Washington metro area)

Visitor Info: D.C. Visitor Info Center, 1300 Pennsylvania Ave. NW (☎866-324-7386; www.dcvisit.com), in the Reagan International Trade Center. Ask for free maps of downtown D.C. Open M-F 8:30am-5:30pm, Sa 9am-4pm.

Internet Access: Kramerbooks & Afterwords, 1517 Connecticut Ave. NW (☎202-387-1400). Open M-Th and Su 7:30am-1am, F-Sa 24hr. Free. **The Cyberstop Cafe,** 1513 17th St. NW (☎202-234-2470). Open M-F 7am-midnight, Sa-Su 8am-midnight. $7 per 30min., $8 per hr. Free Wi-Fi.

Parking: City Center Parking, between 9th and 10th streets at I Street. Entrance at 9th and I St. M-F $8 for up to 2hr., $20 for 24hr.; Sa $15 all day; Su $10 all day.

Post Office: Martin Luther King, Jr. Station, 1400 L St. (☎202-523-2001), in the lobby. Open M-F 8am-5:30pm, Sa 8am-2pm. **Postal Code:** 20005.

▣ GETTING AROUND

D.C.'s diamond-shaped borders stretch in the four cardinal directions. The **Potomac River** forms the southwest border, its waters flowing between the District and Arlington, VA. **North Capitol, East Capitol,** and **South Capitol Street** slice the city into four quadrants: NW, NE, SE, and SW. D.C. is ringed by the **Capital Beltway** (**I-495**—except where it's part of I-95). The Beltway is bisected by **U.S. 1** and meets **I-395** from Virginia. The **Baltimore-Washington Parkway**

DEEP SOUTH

Downtown Washington, D.C.

♦ ACCOMMODATIONS

Adams Inn, 10
Hilltop Hostel, 9
Hostelling International-Washington, D.C. (HI), 31
Hotel Harrington, 22
Kalorama Guest House, 16
Washington International
Student Center, 12

● FOOD

2 Amys Neapolitan Pizzeria, 15
Burma Restaurant, 34
Cafe Luna, 21
Chinatown Express, 24
Clyde's of Georgetown, 24
The Diner, 2
Five Guys, 28
Lauriol Plaza, 8
Max's Best Ice Cream, 13
Mayur Kabab House, 29
Meskerem, 4
Moby Dick House of
Kabob, 26
New Orleans Cafe, 3
Pasta Mia, 1
Patisserie Poupon, 27
Pizza Paradiso, 17
Pot Belly Sandwich Works, 32
Yanni's, 25

♫ NIGHTLIFE

Apex, 22
The Big Hunt, 23
Brickskeller, 19
Cafe Saint-Ex, 11
Cobalt, 18
The Dubliner, 35
Eighteenth Street Lounge, 29
J.R.'s, 20
Larry's Lounge, 7
Madam's Organ, 5
Millie and Al's, 6
Pour House, 37

connects the city to Baltimore, MD. **I-595** trickles off the Capital Beltway toward Annapolis, MD, and **I-66** heads west into Virginia.

Although D.C.'s streets are spacious and relatively easy to navigate, on-street parking is scarce in the downtown area. Parking garages charge up to $25 per day in the downtown, though much cheaper parking can be found outside the city. A good idea is to park at a **Metro** station outside of the District of Columbia; once downtown, the subway and bus systems will get you where you need to go.

The Metro is operated by the **Washington Metropolitan Area Transit Authority**. The MetroRail subway system has five color-coded lines that cover the District of Columbia and extend into Maryland and Virginia, connecting to the commuter rail at several points. (☎202-637-7000; www.wmata.com. Trains run M-Th 5am-midnight, F 5am-3am, Sa 7am-3am, Su 7am-midnight. $1.35-4; 1-day pass $6.50, 7-day regional pass $22, 7-day unlimited pass $32.50. Rechargeable "farecards" available at in Metro stations.) Above ground, D.C. has an extensive **MetroBus** system. For maps and schedules, see www.wmata.com. (Some buses run 24hr.; check individual bus schedules for details. $1.25; express buses $3. Free transfers between regular buses only. Subway-to-bus transfers $0.35, express buses $2.10; purchase transfer before leaving Metro station.)

NEIGHBORHOODS

Postcard-perfect **Capitol Hill** is home to the white-marble Capitol building, the Supreme Court, and the Library of Congress, which all face one another. Extending west from the Capitol building is the grassy pedestrian **Mall,** which is punctuated by the Washington Monument and World War II Memorial before it ends at the Lincoln Memorial. The Mall is flanked by the **Smithsonian museums** and the **National Gallery of Art.** Cherry trees ring the Jefferson Memorial and the Potomac River Tidal Basin, just south and directly across the Mall from the **White House,** which is north of the Mall at 1600 Pennsylvania Ave. The State Department, the Kennedy Center, and the infamous Watergate Complex make up **Foggy Bottom,** on the west side of the city. The **Federal Triangle** area is home to a growing commercial and banking district.

Adams Morgan, in the northwest, is a hub of nightlife and good food. In **Chinatown,** authentic Chinese restaurants bump up against the vast MCI Center and its ring of sports bars. Though its cobblestone back streets are home to Washington's power elite, picturesque **Georgetown** pairs its high-end shops with enough nightlife to keep any college student entertained. **Dupont Circle,** the city's cultural nexus, has developed a powerful trinity of good food, trendy clubs, and cutting-edge art galleries. At night, travelers should avoid walking through the circle itself. Another nighttime hotspot is the **U District,** with clubs that blast trance and techno until the sun rises. Be careful in this area at night. **Upper Northwest,** a residential neighborhood, is home to American University and the National Zoo.

◉ SIGHTS

CAPITOL HILL

THE CAPITOL. The █**US Capitol** impresses visitors with a grandeur uncommon even among the city's other historical buildings and memorials. It has been the site of presidential inaugurations from Andrew Jackson's to the present day. The East Front entrance, facing the Supreme Court, brings visitors into the 180 ft. high rotunda, where soldiers slept during the Civil War. From the lower-level crypt, visitors can climb to the 2nd floor for a view of the House or Senate visitors chambers. As an alternative to waiting in line for a tour, US citizens may obtain gallery passes from the office of their representative or senator in the House or Senate office buildings near the Capitol. Gallery passes are valid M-F 9am-4pm. You can stop by the office the day of your visit, but it's recommended that you call in advance to make sure they can accommodate you. *(Metro: Capitol South or Union Station. ☎202-225-6827; www.aoc.gov. Generally open M-Sa 9am-4:30pm. Access by 30min. guided tour only. Free, but tickets are required. Same-day tickets available at the Garfield Circle kiosk on the West Front, across from the Botanic Gardens. Kiosk open from 9am until all tickets are distributed; get there about 45-60min. before opening to guarantee a ticket. Free.)* The real business of Congress, however, is conducted in **committee hearings.** Most are open to the public; check the *Washington Post*'s "Today in Congress" box for times and locations.

SUPREME COURT. In 1935, the **Supreme Court** justices decided it was time to take the nation's separation of powers literally and moved from their makeshift offices in the Capitol into a new Greek Revival courthouse across the street. Oral arguments are open to the public; show up early to get a seat. *(1 1st St. Metro: Capitol South or Union Station. ☎ 202-479-3221; www.supremecourtus.gov. In session Oct.-June M-W 10am-noon and open 1-3pm for 2 weeks every month; courtroom open when the justices are on vacation. The "3min. line" shuffles visitors through the standing gallery of the courtroom. Court open M-F 9am-4:30pm. Seating before 8:30am. Free.)*

LIBRARY OF CONGRESS. With over 126 million objects stored on 532 mi. of shelves (including a copy of *Old King Cole* written on a grain of rice and a Gutenberg Bible), the ◪**Library of Congress** is the largest library in the world. The collection was torched by the British in 1814 and then revived using Thomas Jefferson's personal collection. Visitors of college age or older can register for a library card with a valid passport or drivers's license in the James Madison Building, Room LM 140. For non-researchers, the library's beautiful fresco-lined Great Hall and rotating exhibits are open daily. Tours of the facilities are also available and take visitors to a balcony view of the spectacular main reading room. *(1st St. SE. Metro: Capitol South. ☎ 202-707-5000; www.loc.gov. Great Hall open M-Sa 10am-5:30pm. Tours M-F 10:30, 11:30am, 1:30, 2:30, 3:30pm; Sa 10:30, 11:30am, 1:30, 2:30pm. Visitors center and galleries open daily 10am-5pm. Free.)*

MONUMENTS

The monuments lining the National Mall are beautiful day or night, but you can avoid the crowds and find plenty of on-site parking if you visit at night. All of the monuments are well-lit, open for viewing until midnight, and, except for the Washington Monument, do not require tickets. The distance between monuments is deceptively long, so budget your time accordingly and consider visiting the FDR and Jefferson memorials separately from the rest to save yourself the long walk between the Mall and the tidal basin.

◪**WASHINGTON MONUMENT.** With a $9.4 million restoration project completed in 1999, this shrine to America's first president is incredible. Once nicknamed the "the Beef Depot monument" after the cattle that grazed here during the Civil War, the monument's location was supposed to form a right angle between the White House and the Capitol Building. Unfortunately, it was built too far to the east to form a perfect 90-degree angle. The beautiful Reflecting Pool mirrors Washington's obelisk. *(Metro: Smithsonian. ☎ 202-426-6841; www.nps.gov/wamo. Open daily 9am-5pm. Tours every 30min. Admission to the monument by timed ticket. Free if obtained on day of visit; arrive early. Advance ticket reservation system open 10am-10pm; ☎ 800-967-2283; www.reservations.nps.gov. Advance tickets $1.50.)*

◪**LINCOLN MEMORIAL.** The Lincoln Memorial, at the west end of the Mall, is a must-see. It was from these steps that Martin Luther King, Jr. gave his "I Have a Dream" speech during the 1963 March on Washington. Inside, a seated Lincoln presides over the admiring visitors. Though you may find Lincoln's lap inviting, climbing on the 19 ft. president is a federal offense; a camera will catch you if the rangers don't. *(Metro: Smithsonian or Foggy Bottom-GWU. ☎ 202-426-6841; www.nps.gov/linc. Open daily 8am-midnight. Free.)*

◪**VIETNAM VETERANS MEMORIAL.** Maya Lin, who designed the Vietnam Veterans Memorial, received a "B" when she submitted her memorial concept for a grade as a Yale senior. She went on to beat her professor in the public memorial design competition. In her words, the monument is "a rift in the earth—a long, polished black stone wall, emerging from and receding into the earth." The wall contains the names of the 58,235 Americans who died in Vietnam, indexed in books at both ends. *(Constitution Ave. at 22nd St. NW. Metro: Smithsonian or Foggy Bottom-GWU. ☎ 202-634-1568; www.nps.gov/vive. Open daily 8am-midnight.)*

JEFFERSON MEMORIAL. A 19 ft. hollow bronze statue of Thomas Jefferson stands in this open-air rotunda, encircled by massive Ionic columns and overlooking the Tidal Basin. Quotes from the Declaration of Independence, the Virginia Statute of Religious Freedom, and *Notes on Virginia* adorn the walls. *(A long walk from Metro: L'Enfant Plaza or Smith-*

sonian. ☎ 202-426-6841; www.nps.gov/thje. Open daily 8am-midnight. Free.)

FRANKLIN DELANO ROOSEVELT MEMORIAL. Occupying a stretch of West Potomac Park, the Franklin Delano Roosevelt Memorial deviates from the presidential tributes nearby, replacing their marble statuary with sculpted gardens, cascading fountains, and thematic alcoves. Four "rooms" each represent a phase of FDR's presidency. In April and May, the blooming cherry trees adjacent to the memorial are stunning. (A long walk from Metro: Smithsonian. ☎ 202-426-6841; www.nps.gov/fdrm. Open daily 8am-midnight. Free.)

KOREAN WAR MEMORIAL. The 19 colossal polished-steel statues of the Korean War Memorial trudge up a hill, rifles in hand, expressions of weariness and fear frozen upon their faces. The statues are accompanied by a black granite wall with over 2000 sandblasted photographic images from this war, in which 54,246 Americans lost their lives. It's worth a visit if you're already planning to see the Lincoln and/or Vietnam memorials. (At the west end of the Mall, near Lincoln. Metro: Smithsonian. ☎ 202-426-6841; www.nps.gov/kwvm. Open daily 8am-midnight. Free.)

NATIONAL WWII MEMORIAL. This arrangement of neoclassical arches and pillars is the newest addition to the National Mall. Two massive archways symbolize the major theaters of battle, and 56 granite pillars face a reflecting pool and represent the contribution of each of the US' states and territories. It's worth a visit if you're nearby. (Metro: Smithsonian or Foggy Bottom-GWU. ☎ 202-426-6841; www.nps.gov/ nwwm. Open daily 8am-midnight. Free.)

THE MALL

The Smithsonian Institution's museums on the Mall constitute the world's largest museum complex. The **Smithsonian Castle,** on the south side of the Mall, has an introduction to and info on all of the Smithsonian buildings. (Metro: Smithsonian or Federal Triangle. ☎ 202-357-2700; www.si.edu. Castle open daily 8:30am-5:30pm.)

■ **NATIONAL AIR AND SPACE MUSEUM.** This is the world's most popular museum, with 7.5 million visitors each year. Record-breaking airplanes and space vehicles hang from the ceilings. Exhibits include the Wright brothers' original biplane, which hangs in the entrance gallery, the walk-through Skylab space station, the Apollo XI command module, and a DC-7. The museum can get crowded during peak hours (11am-4pm), especially in the spring and summer. The museum also offers some costly thrills for the adrenaline or space junkie. (On the south side of the Mall. Metro: Smithsonian or Federal Triangle. ☎ 202-357-2700; www.nasm.si.edu. Free. Flight simulator $7.50. Planetarium $7.50, seniors and military $6.50, children $6.)

■ **NATIONAL GALLERY OF ART.** The National Gallery is not a part of the Smithsonian, but is considered a close cousin because of its prime Mall-front location. The West Building, the gallery's original home, contains masterpieces by Leonardo da Vinci, El Greco, Rembrandt, Vermeer, and Monet as well as a collection of 19th-century American landscapes, portraits, and sculpture. The East Building is devoted to 20th-century art, from Magritte and Matisse to Man Ray and Miró. The $5 audio tour is a good investment and guides you to the gallery's highlights. Because of its size, the gallery is rarely crowded even during peak tourist season. (Metro: Smithsonian or Federal Triangle. ☎ 202-737-4215; www.nga.gov. Open M-Sa 10am-5pm, Su 11am-6pm. Free.)

NATIONAL MUSEUM OF AMERICAN HISTORY (NMAH). The NMAH's Plexiglas-encased clutter of old goods have earned it the nickname "the nation's attic." When the Smithsonian Institution inherits quirky pop culture artifacts, like Dorothy's slippers from *The Wizard of Oz*, they end up here. The Hands On History Room contains a working telegraph and an interactive introduction to the Cherokee language. (On the north side of the Mall. Metro: Smithsonian or Federal Triangle. ☎ 202-357-2700; http://americanhistory.si.edu. Open daily 10am-5:30pm. Free.)

HIRSHHORN MUSEUM AND SCULPTURE GARDEN. The Hirshhorn is D.C.'s best collection of modern, postmodern, and post-postmodern art from around the world. The slide-carousel-shaped building has outraged traditionalists since 1966. Each floor consists of two concentric circles: an outer ring of paintings and an inner corridor of sculptures. The second floor's video art exhibits, "Video Flag" and "The Way Things Go," are both mesmerizing and unforgettable. *(On the south side of the Mall, west of Air and Space. Metro: Smithsonian.* ☎ *202-633-4674; http:// hirshhorn.si.edu. Open daily 10am-5:30pm. Free.)*

NATIONAL MUSEUM OF NATURAL HISTORY (NMNH).

The NMNH contains three floors of rocks, animals, gift shops, and displays selected from the museum's 124 million possessions. The **Hope Diamond** and dinosaur skeletons are major attractions. The Behring Hall of Mammals presents stuffed and fossilized mammals in recreations of their natural habitats. The museum is rightly proud of its new IMAX & Jazz Cafe, where you can enjoy a live performance and then take in the latest nature/action film. *(Metro: Smithsonian or Federal Triangle.* ☎ *202-633-1000; www.mnh.si.edu. Open daily 10am-5:30pm. IMAX & Jazz shows F 6-10pm $10. Free.)*

NATIONAL MUSEUM OF THE AMERICAN INDIAN.

The Smithsonian's newest addition to the Mall, the museum is lined by a cascading fountain. The exhibits present the history, culture, and beliefs of Native American peoples ranging from the Inca to the Inuit. The museum's architecture may be more engaging than some of its exhibits, but it's worth a visit nonetheless. During the morning, prisms built into the wall of the museum shine rainbows onto the atrium. *(Metro: Smithsonian or Federal Triangle.* ☎ *202-633-1000; www.nmai.si.edu. Open daily 10am-5:30pm. Free.)*

FREER GALLERY OF ART.

The Freer's collection is an intriguing jumble of American and Asian art. The permanent American collection, as dictated by Charles L. Freer himself, focuses on works by James McNeill Whistler. The rotating Asian collections have pieces from 2500 BC to the present. Bronzes, manuscripts, and jade pieces make up some of the museum's most alluring displays. *(On the south side of the Mall. Metro: Smithsonian or Federal Triangle.* ☎ *202-357-4880; www.asia.si.edu. Open daily 10am-5:30pm. Free.)*

NATIONAL MUSEUM OF AFRICAN ART AND ARTHUR M. SACKLER GALLERY.

Both museums house their exhibits in an intercon-

nected maze of galleries below the four-acre Enid A. Haupt Garden. The Museum of African Art displays artifacts from sub-Saharan Africa, such as masks, ceremonial figures, and musical instruments. *(Metro: Smithsonian or Federal Triangle.* ☎ *202-633-4600; www.nmafa.si.edu. Open daily 10am-5:30pm. Free.)* The Sackler Gallery showcases an extensive collection of manuscripts, Chinese and Japanese paintings, jade, and friezes from Egypt, Phoenicia, and Sumeria. Check ahead to see which items from the permanent collection are on display when you visit. *(Metro: Smithsonian or Federal Triangle.* ☎ *202-633-4880; www.asia.si.edu. Open daily 10am-5:30pm. Free.)*

SOUTH OF THE MALL

■ HOLOCAUST MEMORIAL MUSEUM.

Opened in 1993, the privately funded Holocaust Memorial Museum examines the atrocities of the Holocaust. Special exhibitions, which can be viewed without passes, include the **Wall of Remembrance,** a touching collection of tiles painted by American schoolchildren in memory of the 1.5 million children killed during the Holocaust, the Wexner Learning Center, and an exhibit on the current genocide taking place in Darfur, Sudan. The permanent gallery is divided into three chronologically organized floors. Arrive early to obtain tickets; during peak hours, timed-admission tickets may admit you as late as 2hr. after you pick them up. *(14th St., between C St. and Independence Ave. SW. Metro: Smithsonian.* ☎ *202-488-0400; www.ushmm.org. Open daily 10am-5:30pm, last entry 3:45pm. Free.)*

BUREAU OF ENGRAVING AND PRINTING.

The buck starts here, at the Bureau of Engraving and Printing, the largest producer of currency, stamps, and security documents in the world. Guided tours of the presses that print $696 million in money and stamps each day are available. *(At 14th and C St. SW. Metro: Smithsonian.* ☎ *202-874-2330 or 866-874-2330; www.moneyfactory.com. Ticket booth at Wallenberg Pl. on 15th St. opens Mar.-Aug. M-F at 8am to distribute free tickets for same-day tours, which run 9am-2pm. Arrive early to obtain tickets; most are gone by 9am. Tours daily Sept.-Apr. 9-10:15am, 12:30-2pm; May-Aug. 9-10:15am, 12:30-2pm, 5-7pm. Free.)*

FEDERAL TRIANGLE

■ **NATIONAL ARCHIVES.** Visitors line up at the National Archives to view the original Declaration of Independence, US Constitution, and Bill of Rights as they make their daily appearance from the recesses of a nuclear-bomb-proof vault. This building houses 16 million pictures and posters, 18 million maps, and billions of pages of text—about 2-5% of the documents the government produces each year. During peak tourist season, the line to get in can be very long, so plan accordingly. *(8th St. and Constitution Ave. NW. Metro: Archives-Navy Memorial. ☎ 202-501-5000; www.nara.gov. Open daily April to Memorial Day 10am-7pm; Memorial Day to Labor Day 10am-9pm; Labor Day to Mar. 10am-5:30pm. Free.)*

INTERNATIONAL SPY MUSEUM. Visitors navigating the movie set-like backdrops may wonder whether this is an amusement park about to blow its museum cover, but the Spy Museum has plenty of facts and artifacts from centuries of espionage. But in a city with so many free attractions, the admission price is disappointingly high unless you're a genuine espionage buff. *(800 F St. NW, at 9th St. Metro: Gallery Place-Chinatown. ☎ 202-393-7798; www.spymuseum.org. Open daily Apr.-Aug. 9am-8pm; Aug.-Oct. 10am-8pm; Oct.-Mar. 10am-6pm. Tickets with timed admission $15, seniors and military $14, children 5-11 $12, under 5 free.)*

FEDERAL BUREAU OF INVESTIGATION. The **J. Edgar Hoover Building** closed to visitors in 2002 for extensive renovations. Tours are expected to resume in spring 2007; call for details. *(935 Pennsylvania Ave. NW. ☎ 202-324-2080; www.fbi.gov.)*

FORD'S THEATRE. John Wilkes Booth shot President Abraham Lincoln during a performance at the preserved Ford's Theatre. Nonetheless, every president since 1868 has taken his chances and seen a play at here at least once a year. Of course, they sit front row center to avoid the unlucky box. Park rangers give a 15min. tour of the theater, but expect to wait up to an hour during tourist season. *(511 10th St. NW. Metro: Metro Center. ☎ 202-426-6924; www.nps.gov/foth. Open daily 9am-5pm. Free. Talks 9:15, 10:15, 11:15am, 2:15, 3:15, 4:15pm. Shows: ☎ 202-397-7328; www.fordstheatre.org. Shows Sept.-May Tu-Su 7:30pm, $25-42; Apr.-Aug. M-F noon $30-36; Sa-Su 2:30pm, $35-48.)*

OLD POST OFFICE. This classical masterpiece of arched windows, conical turrets, and a clock tower no longer houses an operational post office, although it does have a food court. If you can't make it up to the Washington Monument, the Old Post Office's soaring tower has the second-best view of the city and is rarely crowded. *(Pennsylvania Ave. and 12th St. NW. Metro: Federal Triangle. ☎ 202-289-4224; www.oldpostofficedc.com. Tower open mid-Apr. to mid-Sept. M-Sa 9am-7:45pm, Su 10am-5:45pm; mid-Sept. to mid-Apr. M-F 9am-4:45pm, Sa-Su 10am-5:45pm. Shops open M-Sa 10am-7pm, Su noon-6pm. Free.)*

NATIONAL MUSEUM OF WOMEN IN THE ARTS. In a former Masonic Temple, the National Museum of Women in the Arts showcases works by the likes of Mary Cassatt, Georgia O'Keeffe, and Frida Kahlo. This museum is the only one in the world dedicated solely to the celebration of achievements of women in the visual, performing, and literary arts, and its collection is comprised of over 3000 pieces dating from the 16th century to the present. Exhibits rotate, so check to see what's being shown before you pay. Chakika Booker's recycled tire sculptures are definitely worth a look. *(1250 New York Ave. NW. Metro: Metro Center. ☎ 202-783-5000; www.nmwa.org. Open M-Sa 10am-5pm, Su noon-5pm. $8, students and 60+ $6, under 19 free. 1st W and Su of each month free.)*

WHITE HOUSE AND FOGGY BOTTOM

■ **WHITE HOUSE.** With its simple columns and expansive lawns, the White House seems a compromise between patrician lavishness and democratic simplicity. Thomas Jefferson proposed a design for the building, but his entry lost to that of amateur architect James Hoban. Today the President's staff works in the West Wing, while the First Lady's cohorts occupy the East Wing. Staff who cannot fit in the White House work in the nearby **Old Executive Office Building.** The President's official office is the **Oval Office,** site of many televised speeches. *(1600 Pennsylvania Ave. NW. ☎ 202-456-7041; www.whitehouse.gov. Free tours of the White House can be arranged only by calling your congres-*

sional representative more than 1 month in advance. *Phone numbers for representatives available at www.whitehouse.gov.)* The **White House Visitor Center,** across 15th St. from the White House in the Commerce Department Building, has a few unimpressive exhibits on White House history if you can't get into the real thing. *(1450 Pennsylvania Ave. NW. ☎ 202-456-7041. Open daily 7:30am-4pm. Free.)*

LAFAYETTE PARK. Historic homes surround Lafayette Park north of the White House and include the Smithsonian-owned **Renwick Gallery Craft Museum,** which has some interesting works of contemporary sculpture. *(17th St. and Pennsylvania Ave. NW. Metro: Farragut North, Farragut West, or McPherson Sq. ☎ 202-633-2850; www.nmaa.si.edu. Open daily 10am-5:30pm. Free.)* The Neoclassical **Corcoran Gallery** boasts an expansive collection ranging from Colonial to contemporary American art. If a trip to the National Gallery of Art leaves you wanting more 19th- and 20th-century American art, the Corcoran's collection is excellent. *(17th St., between E St. and New York Ave. NW. ☎ 202-639-1700; www.corcoran.org. Open W and F-Su 10am-5pm, Th 10am-9pm. Free tours M-W and F noon, Th noon and 7:30pm, Sa-Su noon and 2:30pm. $8, seniors and military $6, students $4. Th 5-9pm free.)* The **Octagon House,** designed by Capitol architect William Thornton, was home to President and Mrs. Madison after the White House was burned down by British soldiers during the War of 1812. Today it is a restored example of Federalist architecture and alleg-

edly houses several ghosts. Currently undergoing renovations (and possibly ghostbusting) in 2006, the Octagon is open for prearranged group tours of 10-25 people; call in advance. *(1799 New York Ave. NW. ☎ 202-638-3221. Open Tu-Su 10am-4pm. $5, students and seniors $3.)*

KENNEDY CENTER. Completed in the late 1960s, the **John F. Kennedy Center for the Performing Arts** is a monument to the assassinated president, boasting four major stages, a film theater, three breathtaking halls replete with sumptuous red carpets, crystal chandeliers, and a roof deck with stunning views of the Potomac and the D.C. skyline. *(25th St. and New Hampshire Ave. NW. Metro: Foggy Bottom-GWU. ☎ 202-416-8341; www.kennedy-center.org. Open daily 10am-midnight. Free tours leave from the Level A gift shop M-F 10am-5pm, Sa-Su 10am-1pm; call ☎ 202-416-8340. Free.)* Across the street is the **Watergate Complex,** where President Richard "Tricky Dick" Nixon famously sent his "plumbers" on an ill-fated burglary attempt.

GEORGETOWN

🐼 **DUMBARTON OAKS ESTATE.** Home to several acres of some of the most beautiful gardens in Washington, Dumbarton Oaks was the site of the 1944 Dumbarton Oaks Conference, which helped form the United Nations charter. The estate is now a museum with an impressive collection of Byzantine and pre-

PANDAS GONE WILD

Animal sex seldom generates significant media attention, but the birth of the National Zoo's newest panda bear electrified the local and national media in 2005. In March 2005, the Zoo's animal keepers observed Mei Xiang aggressively rubbing against trees, a mating signal if there ever was one. After testing her hormone levels, they determined that she was in heat. Zookeepers attempted to mate Mei Xiang with Tian Tian, the zoo's adult male panda, the old fashioned way, but Tian Tian wasn't up to the task. After three other failed mating attempts, the zoo's staff finally opted to give nature some high-tech assistance and attempted to induce a pregnancy with Tian Tian's sperm via artificial insemination. The procedure was a success, and after a pregnancy monitored by 24hr. video surveillance, Mei Xiang gave birth to Tai Shan, a healthy male panda in June 2005. Tai Shan was instantly the toast of the Washington press and received five-star treatment by the zoo's management, who temporarily halted construction on new zoo habitats in order to give the new panda and his mother some much-needed quiet. In 2006, Tai Shan moved into the zoo's main panda habitat with his mother. Tian Tian lives in a separate habitat next door, and it is unclear whether he knows he's the father.

Columbian art, as well as a gorgeous land-scaped garden with numerous fountains and ornate terraces. Although the museum is closed for renovations through 2007, the gardens will remain open and are in bloom from mid-March through October. Unfortunately, picnicking is not allowed. *(Garden Gate entrance at 31st St. and R St. NW. Museum entrance at 1703 32nd St. NW, between R and S St. ☎202-339-6401, tour info ☎202-339-6409; www.doaks.org. Mansion open Tu-Su 2-5pm. Suggested donation $1. Gardens open daily Mar.-Oct. 2-6pm, Nov. to mid-Mar. 2-5pm. Mid-Mar. to Oct. $7; Nov. to mid-Mar. free.)*

GEORGETOWN UNIVERSITY. Archbishop John Carroll oversaw construction in 1788, and Georgetown University opened the following year, becoming the nation's first Catholic institution for higher learning. Today the original neo-Gothic spires overlook a bustling campus, with several stores, cafes, and sporting venues open to the public. *(37th and O St. on the G2 bus line from Dupont Circle. ☎202-687-3600; www.georgetown.edu. Campus tours through the admissions office; call for schedule and reservations.)*

UPPER NORTHWEST

◪ WASHINGTON NATIONAL CATHEDRAL. Since the Cathedral's construction in 1909, religious leaders from Rev. Dr. Martin Luther King, Jr. to the Dalai Lama have preached from its pulpit. The solemnity of the vast gothic nave is lightened by fanciful stained glass and sculpture. The Pilgrim Observation Gallery reveals D.C. from the city's highest vantage point. The Bishop's Garden on the Cathedral grounds is worth a detour for its blooming flowers in spring and summer. *(From downtown, follow Massachusetts Ave. NW out of town to the intersection with Wisconsin Ave. NW. From Metro: Tenleytown, take a 30-series bus toward Georgetown, or walk up Cathedral Ave. from Metro: Woodley Park-Zoo. ☎202-537-6200; www.nationalcathedral.org. Open mid-May to early Sept. M-F 10am-5:30pm, Sa 10am-4pm, Su 8am-6:30pm; early Sept. to mid-May M-F 10am-5:30pm. Su Mass 8, 9, 11am. Organ demonstration 12:45pm. Tours M-F 10am-11:30am and 12:45-4pm, Sa 10-11:30am and 12:45-3:15pm, Su 12:45-2:30pm. Guided tours $3, seniors $2, children $1. Free.)*

NATIONAL ZOO. Founded in 1889 and designed by Frederick Law Olmsted, who also designed New York City's Central Park (p. 125), the National Zoo is rarely crowded due to its size and distance from downtown. Tigers, elephants, and gorillas await. The zoo's giant pandas are perpetual Washington celebrities; their cub, Tai Shan, began receiving visitors in mid-2006. The zoo also features two endangered golden lion tamarin monkeys, who freely wander the grounds freely. *(3001 Connecticut Ave. Metro: Woodley Park-Zoo. ☎202-673-4800; www.si.edu/natzoo. Grounds open daily Apr.-Oct. 6am-8pm; Nov.-Mar. 6am-6pm. Zoo buildings open daily Apr.-Oct. 10am-6pm, Nov.-Mar. 10am-4:30pm. Free.)*

DUPONT CIRCLE

◪ PHILLIPS COLLECTION. Situated in a stately mansion, the Phillips was the nation's first museum of modern art and still turns heads with its variety of Impressionist and Post-Impressionist masters. Visitors gape at Renoir's masterpiece, *Luncheon of the Boating Party*, and works by Delacroix, Miró, and Turner. *(1600 21st St. at Q St. NW. ☎202-387-2151; www.phillipscollection.org. Open in summer Tu-W and F-Sa 10am-5pm, Th 10am-8:30pm, Su noon-5pm; in winter Tu-W and F-Sa 10am-5pm, Th 10am-8:30pm. Tu-F free; Sa-Su $12, students and seniors $10, under 19 free.)*

ART GALLERY DISTRICT. The **Art Gallery District** contains over two dozen galleries displaying everything from contemporary photographs to tribal crafts. They hold a joint open house on the first Friday of each month (6-8pm) with complimentary drinks at each venue. *(Bounded by Connecticut Ave., Florida Ave., and Q St. See www.artgalleriesdc.com for schedule.)*

EMBASSY ROW. The stretch of Massachusetts Ave. between Dupont Circle and Observatory Circle is also called **Embassy Row.** Before the 1930s, socialites lived along the avenue in extravagant townhouses; diplomats later found the mansions perfect for their purposes (and sky-high budgets). Embassy Row is too long to cover by foot, but worth a detour if you're driving through this part of the city. At the northern end of Embassy Row, flags line the entrance to the **Islamic Center.** Inside the brilliant white mosque, stunning designs stretch to the tips of spired ceilings. *(2551 Massachusetts Ave. NW. ☎202-332-8343. No shorts;*

women must cover their heads, arms, and legs. Open daily 10am-5pm; prayers 5 times daily.)

🔥 FOOD

For budget eateries, **Adams Morgan** and **Dupont Circle** are home to the *crème de la crème* of ethnic cuisine. Suburban **Bethesda, MD** (Metro: Bethesda), features over 100 restaurants within a four-block radius. For information on vegetarian-friendly restaurants in the D.C. area, look for *The Vegetarian Guide* at hotels and restaurants or visit their website at www.vegdc.com.

ADAMS MORGAN

New Orleans Cafe, 2412 18th St. NW (☎202-234-0420). With Dixieland rattling the speakers and an owner who epitomizes Southern hospitality, this popular cafe rewards its customers with great jambalaya, po' boy sandwiches ($6-9), and gumbo ($4-8). Open Tu-F 11am-9:30pm, Sa-Su 10am-10pm. AmEx/D/MC/V. ❷

The Diner, 2453 18th St. NW (☎202-232-8800). The Diner's hours and quintessential American food earn it rave reviews from local college kids and other late-night revelers. Omelettes $7-9. Pancakes $5. Burgers $6-8. Salads $5-10. Open 24hr. AmEx/D/MC/V. ❷

Meskerem Restaurant, 2434 18th St. NW (☎202-462-4100). A venerable Ethiopian restaurant, Meskerem has two levels of seating; upstairs under the skylight has a great atmosphere. The main dishes are served with *injera,* a soft flatbread for scooping up food in lieu of a fork or spoon. Entrees $7-12. Open M-Th noon-11pm, F-Sa noon-12:30am, Su Noon-11:30pm. AmEx/D/MC/V. ❷

Pasta Mia, 1790 Columbia Rd. NW (☎202-328-9114), near 18th St. Pasta Mia is an aging but perennial favorite that serves generous helpings of Italian classics ($10-13). Open M-Sa 6:30-10pm. MC/V. ❸

CHINATOWN/DOWNTOWN

🍜 **Chinatown Express Restaurant,** 744-746 6th St. NW (☎202-638-0424), between G and H St. In addition to standard Chinese fare (entrees $8-12), Chinatown Express has excellent noodle dishes made with fresh "stretched noodles" ($5.50) and steamed pork buns filled with soup ($5) that distinguish it from Chinatown's numerous other eateries. The lunch special ($5) lets you mix and match 3 dishes. Open daily 10am-11pm; lunch until 2:30pm. MC/V. ❶

Potbelly Sandwich Works, 726 7th St. NW (☎202-478-0070), between G and H St. A local chain of sandwich shops with locations throughout D.C., Potbelly serves cheap, filling sandwiches ($4) and not much else. They make up for the lack of variety with lightning-fast service and surprisingly high quality. The milkshakes ($2.70) make a great dessert. Open M-Th and Su 11am-9pm, F-Sa 11am-10pm. AmEx/D/MC/V. ❶

Burma Restaurant, upstairs at 740 6th St. NW (☎202-638-1280), between G and H St. Burmese curries, unique spices, and a plethora of

JUICY STEAKS AND ROTTEN POLITICS

Lobbyist and political power broker Jack Abramoff fell from grace in January 2006, pleading guilty to conspiracy, fraud, and tax evasion in federal court. Abramoff's crimes ranged from defrauding clients of thousands of dollars to funneling cash from political interests to pay for lavish vacations for Republican congressmen. Abramoff's influence in Congress as a lobbyist was not just built on money laundering. Abramoff opened the extravagant restaurant Signatures in 2001, guaranteeing that his congressional friends would be well-fed in addition to well-paid. With the mantra, "liberal portions in a conservative setting," Signatures billed itself as a high-end eatery for Washington's political elite, boasting walls lined with political memorabilia like a copy of Richard Nixon's pardon from Gerald Ford. Abramoff wheeled and dealed from table #40, giving away free meals to his congressional allies. During 17 months in 2002-2003, Signatures gave away $180,000 in free food and drinks. Abramoff's friends on Capitol Hill quickly distanced themselves after his indictment, leading him to remark sarcastically: "You're really no one in this town unless you haven't met me." With Abramoff headed to prison, Signatures closed in 2006, leav-

garnishes. Try the green-tea salad ($10) or the squid sautéed in garlic, ginger, and scallions ($11). Vegetarians will enjoy the papaya or tofu salads ($10). Open M-F 11am-3pm and 6-10pm, Sa-Su 6-10pm. AmEx/D/MC/V. ❷

Mayur Kabab House, 1108 K St. NW (☎202-637-9770), at the corner of 11th St. and K St., across from the Washington, D.C. Hostel. Packed with hostelers looking for cheap eats, the Kabab House serves a range of Indian and Pakistani dishes. Kababs $8. Open M-Sa 11am-10pm. MC/V. ❶

DUPONT CIRCLE

Pizza Paradiso, 2029 P St. NW (☎202-233-1245, www.eatyourpizza.com), 1 block west of Dupont Circle. This small Neapolitan pizzeria's thin-crust pizzas ($10-11) may not have descended from heaven, but they're outstanding nonetheless. Service is fast and friendly, and the delicious salads and antipasti ($5-6.50) are good alongside your pizza. Open M-Th 11:30am-11pm, F-Sa 11:30am-midnight, Su noon-10pm. MC/V. ❷

Lauriol Plaza, 1835 18th St. NW (☎202-387-0035), at T St., between Dupont Circle and Adams Morgan. Lauriol occupies half the block, with a rowdy roof deck and 3 magnificent floors of Mexican dining. Large entrees ($10-17), appetizers like fried plantains and guacamole ($4-7), and excellent margaritas ($5.50, pitchers $24). No reservations accepted, and the wait grows exponentially as the evening goes on, so arrive early. Su brunch 11:30am-3pm. Open M-Th and Su 11:30am-11pm, F-Sa 11:30am-midnight. AmEx/D/DC/MC/V. ❸

Cafe Luna, 1633 P St. NW (☎202-387-4005), near 17th St. A popular basement restaurant serving a mix of Italian, vegetarian, and low-fat fare. Huge sandwiches ($4-6) satisfy almost any appetite. Breakfast ($2-5) served all day. Pizzas $5-7. Open M-Th 8am-11:30pm, F 8am-1am, Sa 10am-1:30am, Su 10am-11:30pm. AmEx/MC/V. ❶

GEORGETOWN

▨ **Five Guys,** 1335 Wisconsin Ave. NW (☎202-337-0400), at the corner of Wisconsin Ave. and Dumbarton Ave. An oasis of cheap surrounded by Georgetown's pricey boutiques and restaurants, Five Guys's burgers are justifiably famous and surprisingly inexpensive ($4.50-5.50). You can order your fries regular or Cajun-style (medium fries $2),

but vegetarians beware: fries and grilled cheese ($2) are the only meatless items on the menu. Open M-F 11am-11pm and Sa-Su 11am-4am. AmEx/MC/V. ❶

▨ **Moby Dick House of Kabob,** 1070 31st St. NW (☎202-333-4400; www.mobysonline.com). A local favorite, the portions of Greek food at this tiny joint are enormous. Get salads ($4), gyros ($6), or kabob sandwiches ($6-9) to go, and enjoy on a quiet bench by the C&O canal. Open M-Th 10am-11pm, F-Sa 11am-4am, Su noon-10pm. MC/V. ❶

Clyde's of Georgetown, 3236 M St. NW (☎202-333-9180), between Potomac St. and Wisconsin Ave. Pop the collar on your polo shirt and you'll blend in perfectly with the preppy clientele in Clyde's leather booths. Delicious sandwiches ($8-10), salads ($13-16), seafood ($11-19), and pasta ($13-15). Open M-Th 11:30am-2am, F 11:30am-3am, Sa 10am-3am, Su 9am-2am. AmEx/D/MC/V. ❹

Patisserie Poupon, 1645 Wisconsin Ave. NW (☎202-342-3248), near Q St. Start the day with a buttery brioche, pear danish, or croissant ($1.30-2.25). Sandwiches $4-6. Salads $7-10. Open Tu-F 8am-6:30pm, Sa 8am-4pm, Su 8am-4pm. Cash only. ❶

UPPER NORTHWEST

▨ **2 Amys Neapolitan Pizzeria,** 3715 Macomb St. NW (☎202-885-5700), near Wisconsin Ave. Superb, Neapolitan-style pizzas ($9-13) in a pastel yellow and orange dining area. The "Norcia" pizza (tomato, salami, roasted peppers, mozzarella, and garlic; $13) is excellent. Many locals consider this Washington's best pizza and we wholeheartedly agree. Expect a wait. Open M 5-10pm, Tu-W 11am-10pm, Th-Sa 11am-11pm, Su noon-10pm. MC/V. ❸

Yanni's, 3500 Connecticut Ave. NW (☎202-362-8871). Find homestyle Greek cooking in this airy restaurant, adorned with classical statues and murals of Greek gods. Try charbroiled octopus, crunchy on the outside and delicately tender within, served with rice and vegetables ($13). Strong Greek coffee ($2.50) goes well with the baklava ($4.50). Entrees $6-17. Open daily 11:30am-11pm. AmEx/MC/V. ❸

Max's Best Ice Cream, 2416 Wisconsin Ave. NW (☎202-333-3111), just south of Calvert St. Known in D.C. as the premier purveyor of homemade ice cream, Max himself dishes out old favorites and exotic flavors. Discover what excellent homemade ice cream actually tastes like—this stuff is much better than anything you can buy at a supermarket. Single scoop $3. Open M-Sa noon-midnight, Su noon-10pm. Cash only. ❶

ACCOMMODATIONS

Except for a few reasonably-priced hostels, downtown D.C. accommodations are uniformly expensive. Prices are more reasonable farther from downtown and in Maryland and Virginia's suburban areas. Like other major US cities, D.C. charges a hefty **14.5% hotel tax.**

HOSTELS

Hilltop Hostel, 300 Carroll St. NW (☎202-291-9591), on the border of D.C. and Takoma Park, steps from Metro: Takoma. In the quiet suburban town of Takoma Park, 15min. from downtown D.C. The laid-back atmosphere and friendly staff attracts an international crowd of backpackers and students. Satellite TV, kitchen, game rooms, and spacious back yard. 18+. Free Internet access. Linens included. Reception 8am-midnight. Reservations recommended. Dorms $22. Cash or traveler's check only. ❶

Hostelling International-Washington D.C. (HI), 1009 11th St. NW (☎202-737-2333; www.hiwashingtondc.org), 3 blocks north of Metro: Metro Center. Use caution in this area after dark. In the heart of D.C., 5 blocks from the White House. The lack of common space and high-rise layout makes for an impersonal, hotel-like feel, but the location can't be beat. Internet access $1 per 5min. Check-in 2pm-1am; call ahead if arriving later. Check-out 11am. Reservations recommended. Dorms $32, members $29. Singles $72/$69; doubles $82/$79. MC/V. ❷

Washington International Student Center, 2451 18th St. NW (☎800-567-4150; www.washingtondchostel.com), in the middle of Adams Morgan. Temporarily closed, the hostel is expected to reopen in mid- to late 2006; call ahead for details. An incredible location, next door to some of the most fun nightlife D.C. has to offer. Towel service, kitchen, lockers, free Internet access, cable TV. No smoking. Breakfast included. Recep-

tion 8am-11pm. Coed dorms $25. Cash or traveler's check only. ❶

HOTELS AND GUEST HOUSES

Adams Inn, 1744 Lanier Pl. NW (☎202-745-3600 or 800-578-6807; www.adamsinn.com), 2 blocks north of the center of Adams Morgan. 25 rooms with A/C, tasteful furnishings, and private sinks (some with private bath). Complimentary continental breakfast and snacks. Cable TV in common area, free Internet access, and laundry facilities. Limited parking $10 per night. 2-night min. stay if staying Sa night. Reception M-Sa 8am-9pm, Su 1-9pm. Check-in 3-9pm. Check-out noon. Singles $90, with private bath $100. AmEx/D/MC/V. ❹

Hotel Harrington, 11th and E St. NW (☎202-628-8140 or 800-424-8532; www.hotel-harrington.com). Metro: Metro Center or Federal Triangle. Simply furnished rooms with cable TV and A/C in a great location. Parking $10 per day. Student discount 10%. Doubles $99-155. AmEx/D/MC/V. ❹

Kalorama Guest House, 1854 Mintwood Pl. NW (☎202-667-6369; www.kaloramaguesthouse.com). A 10min. walk from Metro: Woodley Park. Simple but elegant rooms in a quiet, well-appointed townhouse near Rock Creek Park. Breakfast included. Singles with shared bath $90, with private bath $115; doubles $100/$145. AmEx/D/MC/V. ❹

ENTERTAINMENT

MUSIC

Check the *Weekend* section in the Friday edition of the Washington Post for details on upcoming concerts, shows, and other events. Larger mainstream events take place at the sports arenas: **RFK Stadium,** 2400 E. Capitol St., in the summer (box office ☎202-608-1119; open M-F noon-5pm), and the **MCI Center,** 601 F St., year-round (box office ☎202-628-3200; open daily 10am-5:30pm). In its 73rd season, the **National Symphony Orchestra** continues to delight D.C., primarily in the Kennedy Center's concert hall (☎202-467-4600 or 800-444-1324; www.kennedy-center.org/nso). D.C. also has a diverse and thriving jazz and blues scene, with venues perfect for any budget. The **Kennedy Center** (see **Theater and Dance,** p. 694) and

Smithsonian Museums (p. 686) often sponsor free shows, especially in the summer.

THEATER AND DANCE

Arena Stage, 6th St. and Maine Ave. SW, is often called the best regional theater company in America due to its innovative takes on classics and successful productions of new works. (Metro: Waterfront. ☎202-488-3300; www.arenastage.org. Box office open M-Sa 10am-8pm, Su noon-8pm. Tickets $45-66. Discounts for students and seniors. A limited number of half-price tickets are available 1½hr. before show.) The Kennedy Center, at 25th St. and New Hampshire Ave., presents various ballet, opera, and dramatic productions. (☎202-416-8000, rush ticket info 202-467-4600; www.kennedy-center.org. Tickets $10-75.) The Shakespeare Theatre at the Lansburgh, 450 7th St. NW, at Pennsylvania Ave., puts on lively performances. Each summer the theater holds the "Free for All," a no-charge production of a Shakespearean work, usually one of the comedies. (Metro: Archives-Navy Memorial. ☎202-547-1122 or 877-487-8849; www.shakespearetheatre.org. Tickets $23-68, during preview week $13-59. Standing-room tickets available 1hr. before sold-out performances $10.) To further satisfy any Shakespearean craving, head to the famous Folger Theatre, 201 E. Capitol St. SE. The theater is a reproduction of the Bard's Globe in London, and a small museum is adjacent to the performance space. (☎202-544-7077; www.folger.edu. Box office open M-F 10am-5pm in person, M-Sa noon-4pm by phone. Student rush discount 50% 1hr. before shows.) In the 14th Street Theater District, tiny repertory companies experiment with new shows. ◪The Source Theatre, 1835 14th St. NW, between S and T St., is dedicated to the local community of artists. (Metro: U St.-Cardozo. ☎202-462-1073; www.sourcetheatre.com.) The famous ◪Woolly Mammoth Theater Company, 641 D St. NW, at 7th St. NW, offers pay-what-you-can and under-25 performances of contemporary works. (Metro: Gallery Place-Chinatown. ☎202-393-3939; www.woollymammoth.net. Tickets $28-48; under 25 $10. Rush tickets available 15min. before shows $10.)

SPORTS

The 20,000-seat MCI Center, 601 F St. NW, in Chinatown, is D.C.'s premiere sports arena. (☎202-628-3200. Metro: Gallery Pl. Chinatown. Open daily 10am-5:30pm.) Having finally earned some respect with their 2005 season, basketball's Wizards are no longer the laughingstock of the NBA. (☎202-661-5065; www.washingtonwizards.com. Regular season Oct.-Apr. Tickets $7-120.) The WNBA's Mystics play from May to September. (www.wnba.com/mystics. Tickets $8-60.) The Capitals are back with the rest of the NHL for the 2006 season, running from October to April. (☎202-661-5065; www.washingtoncaps.com. Tickets $10-100.) Washington's most successful and least-known pro sports team is soccer's D.C. United, with a strong local fan base and several MLS championship titles. (☎202-587-5000; http://dcunited.mls-net.com. Tickets $16-40.) A new stadium for D.C. United is planned, but for now they share RFK Stadium, 2400 E. Capitol St. SE, with baseball's Nationals. (☎888-632-6287; http://washington.nationals.mlb.com. Tickets $7-115.) Will Washington always remain a football town? Their beloved, if politically incorrect, Redskins still draw the faithful to FedEx Field, Raljon Dr., in Raljon, MD, from September to December. (☎301-276-6050; www.redskins.com. Tickets $40-200.)

◪ NIGHTLIFE

BARS AND CLUBS

Don't be fooled by the sea of shirt-and-tie-clad bureaucrats that flood Washington during the daytime; D.C. is a work-hard, play-hard city. With hordes of interns, campaign staffers, journalists, and other young political types, nights and weekends in the city are anything but quiet. If you ache for a pint of amber ale, swing by the Irish pub-laden Capitol Hill. Dupont Circle is home to glam GLBT nightlife, while bars in Adams Morgan and the U District stay packed well past 3am on weekend nights. For more tips, try www.dcnites.com.

DUPONT AND U DISTRICT

🍺 **Brickskeller,** 1523 22nd St. NW (☎202-293-1885). Boasts the largest selection of beer in the world, with 1072 different bottled brews from which to choose ($3.25-19). Try a "beer-tail," a mixed drink made with beer ($3.25-6.50). Monthly beer tastings Sept.-May. Open M-Th 11:30am-2am, F 11:30am-3am, Sa-Su 6pm-2am. Kitchen closes M-Th 1am, F 2am, Sa-Su 1am. MC/V.

Eighteenth Street Lounge, 1212 18th St. NW (☎202-466-3922; www.eslmusic.com/lounge). For the last decade, ESL has set the standard for the D.C. lounge scene with its top-shelf DJs, most of whom are signed to ESL's independent record label. Jazz bands often chill out the top floor while DJs work it downstairs, spinning house, hip-hop, and dance. Cover generally $10-20; no cover Tu. Open Tu-W 9:30pm-2am, Th 5:30pm-2am, F 5:30pm-3am, Sa 9:30pm-3am. MC/V.

Cafe Saint-Ex, 1847 14th St. NW (☎202-265-7839; www.saint-ex.com), at T St. This vintage aviation-themed bar, named after Antoine de Saint-Exupéry, author of *The Little Prince*, attracts a mixed crowd of alt-hippies and legal yuppies. It anchors an increasingly lively row of funky nightspots along 14th St. Upstairs bar and patio cafe. Downstairs Gate 54 lounge. Happy hour daily 5:30-7pm with $3 drinks. 21+ after 10:30pm. No cover. Open daily 11am-2am. Kitchen closes Su 10:30pm. AmEx/D/MC/V.

The Big Hunt, 1345 Connecticut Ave. NW (☎202-785-2333). The steam isn't a prop at this jungle-themed bar, where the khaki-and-flip-flops crowd hunts for potential mates. Notorious pickup joint for college kids and Hill workers pretending they're still in college. 24 brews on tap ($3.75-5). Solid pub fare, plus surprisingly delicious Guinness ice cream. Happy hour M-F 4-7:30pm. No cover. Open M-Th 4pm-2am, F 4pm-3am, Sa 5pm-3am, Su 5pm-2am. MC/V.

ADAMS MORGAN

🍺 **Madam's Organ,** 2461 18th St. NW (☎202-667-5370; www.madamsorgan.com), near Columbia Rd. A 3-fl. blues bar with an intimate rooftop patio serving soul food. Live band plays nightly on 1st fl. to an international crowd. Pool tables. Happy hour M-F 5-8pm with 2-for-1 drinks. Redheads drink Rolling Rock for half-price. Drafts $3.75-5.75. Mixed drinks $4.75-6.75. Cover M-Th and Su $2-

4, F-Sa $5-7. Open M-Th and Su 5pm-2am, F-Sa 5pm-3am. AmEx/D/MC/V.

Millie & Al's, 2440 18th St. NW (☎202-387-8131). This jukebox bar draws a party-hungry, polo-shirt-wearing crew. Think pitchers, not martinis. Cheap pizza ($1.50 per slice), subs ($3-4), and $1 Jell-O shots. Draft beer $2-3.50; bottles $3-4.25. Nightly specials 4-7pm. F-Sa DJs play rock and hip-hop. No cover. Open M-Th 4pm-2am, F-Sa 4pm-3am. MC/V.

Larry's Lounge, 1840 18th St. NW (☎202-483-1483), at the southern end of Adams Morgan. This funky bar is a long walk from the Metro, but its Singapore Slings ($6.50) are worth it. Happy hour daily 4-8pm. Open M-Th 2pm-1:30am, F-Sa 2pm-2am, Su 11:30am-1:30am. AmEx/D/MC/V.

CAPITOL HILL

The Dubliner, 520 N. Capitol St. NW (☎202-737-3773). Metro: Union Station. Pricey but classy, this Irish pub/upscale sports bar has 2 excellent house brews, Auld Dubliner Amber Ale and Auld Dubliner Irish Lager ($5 pints). A large patio morphs into a lounge as the night goes on. Live Irish music nightly around 9pm. Open M-Th and Su 7am-2am, F-Sa 7am-3am. Kitchen closes 1am. AmEx/D/MC/V.

Pour House, 319 Pennsylvania Ave. SE (☎202-546-1001; www.politiki-dc.com). Metro: Capitol South. 3 levels: German *Biergarten* atmosphere downstairs, martini bar upstairs (Tu-Sa), and a typical sports bar in between that stays packed with Hill staffers all week long. Nightly drink specials. Happy hour M-F 5:30-8pm with $2-3 beers. Open M-Th 4pm-1:30am, F 3pm-2:30am, Sa-Su 10am-2:30am. MC/V.

GLBT NIGHTLIFE

The *Washington Blade* is the best source for gay news and club listings; published every Friday, it's available in virtually every storefront in Dupont Circle. *Metro Weekly*, a gay and lesbian Washington-area magazine, is another good reference for weekend entertainment and nightlife.

🍺 **J.R.'s,** 1519 17th St. NW (☎202-328-0090), at Church St. D.C.'s busiest gay bar for good reason: hot bartenders, fun events like bachelor auctions, and great drink deals. Packed every night with hordes of "guppies" (gay urban professionals). Happy hour M-W 5-8pm with $3 mini-pitchers, $2 rail drinks and domestic beers, and $1 sodas. Open M-Th 4pm-2am, F-Sa 12:30pm-3am, Su noon-2am. MC/V.

Cobalt, 1639 R St. NW (☎202-462-6569; www.cobaltdc.com), at 17th St. No sign marks this hot spot; look for the blue light and bouncer. Shirtless bartenders serve drinks ($4.75-5.75) to a preppy gay male and straight female crowd. Tu 70s and 80s night. Cover Th $8 for open bar, F after 11pm, Sa $5. No cover M-W or Su. Open Tu-Th 10pm-2am, F-Sa 10pm-3am, Su 8:30pm-2am. Downstairs, **30°** is a relaxed lounge. Happy hour M-F 5-8pm with half-price martinis. Open M-Th and Su 5pm-2am, F-Sa 5pm-3am. MC/V.

Apex, 1415 22nd St. NW (☎202-296-0505), near P St. This 2-story dance complex is one of Dupont Circle's old standbys. DJs play a mix of house, trance, and Top 40. Sa "Liquid Ladies" night, featuring $3 Long Island iced teas, draws a crowd. Th college night with $3 mixed drinks. F drag karaoke 11pm. 18+. Cover Th $5, free with student ID; F before 10pm $8, after 10pm $10; Sa $7. Open Th-Sa 9pm-4am. MC/V.

▼ APPROACHING TRIANGLE: 30 MILES

From downtown Washington, D.C., take **I-395 S,** which becomes **I-95 S.** Follow I-95 to **Exit 150,** and take **Rte. 619 E** to the intersection with **Rte. 1** in downtown Triangle. If you hit traffic or would prefer a more leisurely drive, you can take any exit between **Exit 163** and **Exit 150** off I-95 and take **Rte. 1 S (Jefferson Davis Hwy.),** which runs parallel to the Interstate. Triangle is barely outside D.C., so there are more mini-malls than sweeping vistas, but it's a good time to fill up on supplies or gas.

The Old Dominion State

VIRGINIA

Welcomes You!

TRIANGLE

Home to Quantico Marine Base, Triangle is a busy crossroads. The **Marine Corps Heritage Center,** across from Quantico Marine Base on Rte. 1, is scheduled to open in 2007. With a design inspired by the iconic image of marines raising the US flag on Iwo Jima, the museum will have exhibits on the history of the Corps. (☎703-784-2606; www.history.usmc.mil. Call for scheduled opening date and hours.) One mile west of Rte. 1, off Rte. 619 (Joplin Rd.), **Prince William Forest Park,**

18100 Park Headquarters Rd., has 15,000 acres of preserved piedmont forest with 35 mi. of hiking trails and 20 mi. of paved roads for biking, as well as a campground and RV park. Be careful to follow speed limits within the park—deer cross the roads very frequently. (☎703-221-7181; www.nps.gov/prwi. Visitors center open daily 9am-5pm. $5 per vehicle.)

Among the numerous food options near the intersection of Rte. 1 and Rte. 619, **El Taco Rico ❷,** 18607 Rte. 1, serves tacos, burritos, quesadillas and other Mexican dishes. (☎703-221-4460. Combination meals $6-8. Lunch specials $5-6. Open M 11am-3pm, Tu-Th 11am-9pm, F 11am-10pm, Sa 11am-9:30pm, Su 11am-8:30pm. AmEx/D/MC/V.) For those looking to stay the night, **Best Value Inn ❸,** 4202 Inn St., across from Quantico Marine Base, is one of the only hotel options in town and offers free Wi-Fi and clean rooms. (☎703-221-1115. Singles $60; doubles $66. MC/V.) The **Oak Ridge Campground ❶,** inside Prince William Forest Park, has secluded campsites in a wooded setting. (☎703-221-7181; www.nps.gov/prwi. Sites $15. Cash only.)

▼ APPROACHING FREDERICKSBURG: 18 MILES

Follow **Rte. 1 S (Jefferson Davis Hwy.)** for 17 mi. After crossing the Rappahannock River, turn left onto **Rte. 17** for ½ mi. to reach downtown Fredericksburg. Signs will point you to the downtown **visitors center,** which is a good place to get oriented.

FREDERICKSBURG

Due to its strategic riverfront location halfway between the capitals of the Union and the Confederacy, Fredericksburg was the site of numerous Civil War battles. Though nearly destroyed by artillery fire during the war, Fredericksburg's downtown was rebuilt to approximate its antebellum architecture. Today, Fredericksburg attracts tourists interested in its significance as a Civil War battleground and its meticulously recreated historic attractions.

▉ GETTING AROUND.

Fredericksburg's historic downtown has two main north-south streets: **Princess Anne St.** is one-way southbound and **Caroline St.** is one-way northbound. Most historic homes and attractions are clustered around the visitor center. **Rte. 1** and **I-95** run north-south to the west of downtown, while **Lafayette Blvd.** runs southwest from downtown to Fredericksburg's Civil War battlefield. Fredericksburg has some of the **cheapest gas** between Washington, D.C. and Richmond, so fill up here rather than at pricier city gas stations.

◎ **SIGHTS.** The **Fredericksburg Area Museum,** 907 Princess Anne St., displays regional crafts and artisanal works from 1730-1860, as well as a few rotating exhibits. (☎540-371-3037; www.famcc.org. Open Mar.-Nov. M-Sa 10am-5pm, Su 1-5pm; Dec.-Feb. M-Sa 10am-4pm, Su 1-4pm. $5, ages 6-18 $1.) **Fredericksburg Battlefield Visitor Center,** 1013 Lafayette Blvd., gives a thorough summary of the region's Civil War sites, offering some small exhibits and a 22min. film. A walking tour of nearby Sunken Road battlefield is a good introduction to the numerous battles fought in the area during Grant and Lee's 1864 Overland campaign in Wilderness, Chancellorsville, Fredericksburg, and Spotsylvania. (☎540-373-6122. Open daily 9am-5pm. Free. Film $2, seniors $1, under 10 free.) The cluttered **Collector's Den,** 717 Caroline St., boasts a multitude of sports cards, coins, postcards, stamps, model trains, and other interesting collectors items ready for purchase. (☎540-373-2430. Open daily 10am-3:30pm.)

◨◪ **FOOD AND ACCOMMODATIONS.** ◪**Sammy T's ❸,** 801 Caroline St., has friendly locals, a wide variety of sandwiches, and the feel of eating in a neighbor's oversized dining room. (☎540-371-2008; www.sammyts.com. Sandwiches $6-10. Open daily 11am-10pm. AmEx/D/MC/V.) **The Soup & Taco Etc...❷,** 813 Caroline St., serves delicious soup and tacos, but, contrary to the name, little else. (☎540-899-0906. Soup of the day $5-6. Tacos $6. Combo meals $8-9. Open M 11am-5pm, Tu-Sa 11am-9pm. MC/V.) The **Heritage Inn ❷,** 5308 Jefferson Davis Hwy., has well-maintained rooms with the quality of most name-brand hotel chains. (☎540-898-1000. Free continental breakfast. Singles $39-45; doubles $50-60. AmEx/D/MC/V.) **Fredericksburg KOA Campground ❶,** 7400 Brookside Lane, 2½ mi. off Rte. 607, has excellent campsites with a fishing pond, pool, laundry, showers, and free Wi-Fi. (☎540-898-7252. Sites M-Th and Su $28, F-Sa $30; with water and electricity $32/$34; cabins $46/$48. AmEx/D/MC/V.)

◪ **APPROACHING SPOTSYLVANIA: 10 MILES** From Fredericksburg, take **Rte. 1 S (Jefferson Davis Hwy.)** for 3 mi. Turn right onto **Rte. 208 W (Courthouse Rd.),** and follow it 6½ mi. to the intersection with **Rte. 608** in downtown Spotsylvania.

SPOTSYLVANIA

The Battle of Spotsylvania Court House had some of the most cutthroat fighting of the Civil War. At the "Bloody Angle," Union and Confederate soldiers engaged in face-to-face slaughter fierce enough to fell trees with volleys of criss-crossing bullets. The ◪**Spotsylvania Court House Battlefield** does not have a visitors center, but you can explore the grounds on your own and take walking tours led by knowledgeable historians. (Follow Rte. 608 W for 5 mi., take a right onto Rte. 613 N; the battlefield will be on the right. ☎540-373-6122. Exhibit shelter open daily 10am-6pm. Bloody Angle tour in summer daily 1 and 4pm; in winter Sa-Su 1 and 4pm. Tours depart from stop 14 of driving tour. Free.) Although this battle was the greatest triumph of the legendary Confederate general Stonewall Jackson's greatest triumph, it was also his last. Accidentally shot by one of his own troops at Spotsylvania, Jackson was rushed to a small house, now the **Stonewall Jackson Shrine** in the **Spotsylvania National Military Park,** where he died on May 10, 1863. A park ranger is on duty to show visitors around. (Follow Rte. 608 E for 6 mi. to Rte 1. Take Rte. 1 S for ½ mi., then turn left onto Rte. 607; the shrine will be on the right. ☎540-373-6122. Open daily 9am-5pm. Free.)

In downtown Spotsylvania, the **Courthouse Cafe ❶,** 8955 Courthouse Rd., is a small, unpretentious diner with a wide range of American dishes. The Country Boy Special ($6.50) will keep you full all

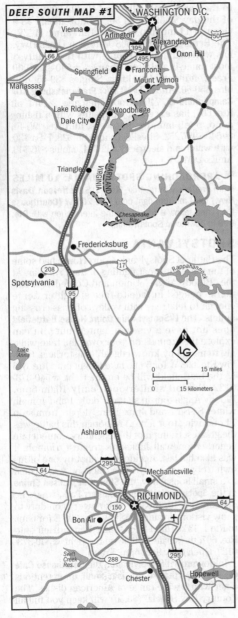

DEEP SOUTH MAP #1

day long. (☎540-582-3302. Burgers $3-5. Salads $3-6.50. Open M-Sa 7am-9pm, Su 7am-3pm. AmEx/D/MC/V.) **Captain Jack's Crab Shack ❶**, 8624 Courthouse Rd., sells crab cakes, fried shrimp, and fish for eating on the go. (☎540-582-5359; www.welovecrabs.com. Fish $4-6. MC/V.)

⛏ APPROACHING ASHLAND: 30 MILES
From Spotsylvania, follow **Rte. 608 E** for 6 mi. until hitting **Rte. 1 (Jefferson Davis Hwy.).** Turn right onto Rte. 1S and follow it for 22 mi. Turn right onto **Rte. 54** to reach downtown Ashland.

ASHLAND

An old railroad town, Ashland has a pair of good restaurants and some excellent nearby attractions. Roller-coaster addicts will not want to miss **⛺Paramount's Kings Dominion,** 1600 Theme Park Way, 6 mi. north of Ashland. King's Dominion is a 400-acre theme park with 12 roller coasters, a variety of other amusement park rides, live shows, and a water park. It's pricey, so pack a hefty lunch and plan to spend the whole day here. (☎804-876-5000; www.kingsdominion.com. From Rte. 1, follow signs to the parking lot. Open Apr.-May and Sept.-Oct. Sa-Su; Memorial Day to Labor Day daily. Call for hours. $50, seniors $39, children $34.) Ashland is also close to **Scotchtown,** 16120 Chiswell Ln., in Beaverdam. One of Virginia's first plantation houses, Scotchtown was built in 1719 and was later home to Patrick Henry, the governor of Virginia who is most famous for his 1775 "Give me liberty or give me death" speech. (☎804-227-3500; www.apva.org/scotchtown. Take Rte. 54 W 7 mi., and turn right on Rte. 671. Open Apr.-Oct. M and Th-Sa 10am-4:30pm, Su 1:30pm-4:30pm. $7, seniors $5, ages 6-18 $4.)

For a yummy lunch, try **⛺Homemades by Suzanne ❷,** 102 N. Railroad Ave., in downtown Ashland. Suzanne's brightly colored, hand-painted dining room is always packed with customers eager for fresh sandwiches and quiches ($5-7). Pies, cakes, and a variety of other outstanding desserts are $2-3 per slice. (☎804-798-8331. Open M-F 9am-2pm, Sa 9am-3pm. AmEx/D/MC/V.) The slightly more upscale **Ironhorse Restaurant ❸,** 100 S. Railroad Ave. has a sedate, earth-toned interior decorated with railroad memorabilia. The menu ranges from light sandwiches ($8) to elegant dinner options like pork tenderloin for $18. (☎804-752-6410. Open M-Th

11:30am-2:30pm and 5-9pm, F-Sa 11:30am-2:30pm and 5-10pm. AmEx/D/MC/V.) The **Twin Oaks Motel ❷**, 304 S. Washington Hwy. (Rte. 1), has clean rooms with few frills but very low prices. (☎804-798-8423. Singles $34; doubles $39. AmEx/D/MC/V.) Campers can head to the full-service **Americamps Richmond-North Campground ❶**, 11322 AirPark Road. Amenities include a pool, a laundromat, and a convenience store. (☎804-798-5298; www.americamps.com. Sites $21. AmEx/D/MC/V.)

◪ APPROACHING RICHMOND: 14 MILES
From Ashland, take **Hwy. 54 E** for ¾ mi. to **I-95 S.** Follow I-95 S to **Exit 74C** in downtown Richmond.

RICHMOND

Virginia's capital city has a survivor's history of conflicts, disasters, and triumphs. Richmond was officially chartered in 1742, but William Mayo's handiwork was burned to the ground in 1781 in a British attack led by American traitor Benedict Arnold. The city was rebuilt and went on to become the capital of the Confederate States of America during the Civil War. Richmond today is a flourishing city, home to Virginia's state government, students at Virginia Commonwealth University, and more shopping centers per capita than any other US city.

VITAL STATS

Population: 200,000

Visitor Info: Richmond Metropolitan Visitor's Bureau, 405 N. 3rd St. (☎804-783-7450; www.richmondva.org), in the Richmond Convention Center. Open daily Memorial Day to Labor Day 9am-6pm; Labor Day to Memorial Day 9am-5pm.

Internet Access: Richmond Public Library, 101 E. Franklin St. (☎646-4867; www.richmondpubliclibrary.org). Open M-W 9am-9pm, Th-F 9am-6pm, Sa 10am-5pm. Free.

Parking: The Virginia Commonwealth University Medical Center's parking lot is on Clay St. just east of the intersection with 12th St. Parking is free if validated at the Museum of the Confederacy; otherwise, $3 for 1st hr., $10 per day.

Post Office: 1801 Brook Rd. (☎775-6304). Open M-F 7am-6pm, Sa 9am-2pm. **Postal Code:** 23232.

◪ GETTING AROUND

Broad St. is the city's central artery, running east-west through downtown. Both **I-95,** going north to Washington, D.C., and **I-295** encircle the urban section of the city—the former to the east and north, the latter to the south and west. On the southeast edge of the city, **Shockoe Slip** and **Shockoe Bottom** overflow with partiers at night. Farther east, on the edge of town, the **Court End** and **Church Hill** districts comprise the city's historic center. **Jackson Ward,** to the north, recently underwent major construction to revamp its city center and revitalize the surrounding community—it is still wise to use caution in this area at night. The **Fan** is bounded by the Boulevard, I-195, the walk of statues along **Monument Avenue,** and **Virginia Commonwealth University.** The Fan has a notoriously dangerous reputation, but has become more gentrified in recent years. The pleasant bistros and boutiques of **Carytown,** west of the Fan on Cary St., and the tightly knit working community of **Oregon Hill** add texture to the cityscape. Be careful in Oregon Hill at night.

◉ SIGHTS

AROUND ST. JOHN'S CHURCH. St. John's Church is the site of Patrick Henry's famed "Give me liberty or give me death" speech. In the summer, orators re-create the 1775 speech on Sundays at 2pm. The church still serves as an active house of worship. *(2401 E. Broad St. ☎804-648-5015; www.historicstjohnschurch.org. 25min. tours M-Sa 10am-4pm, Su 1-4pm. $6, seniors $5, students $4, under 7 free. Services Su 8:30 and 11am. $5, 62+ $4, ages 7-18 $3.)* At the **Edgar Allan Poe Museum,** in Richmond's oldest standing house (c. 1737), visitors try evermore to unravel the author's mysterious death. Poe memorabilia and first editions of his works fill the museum and gardens. *(1914 E. Main St. ☎804-648-5523; www.poemuseum.org. Open Tu-Sa 10am-5pm, Su 11am-5pm. Tours every hr. $6, students and seniors $5, under 9 free.)*

CONFEDERATE SOUTH. Explore the historical legacy of the Civil War at the **Museum of the Confederacy.** With numerous battlefield artifacts and scale models of Confederate sailing ships and "ironclad" battleships, even the most hard-boiled Yankee will find something of note. Plus,

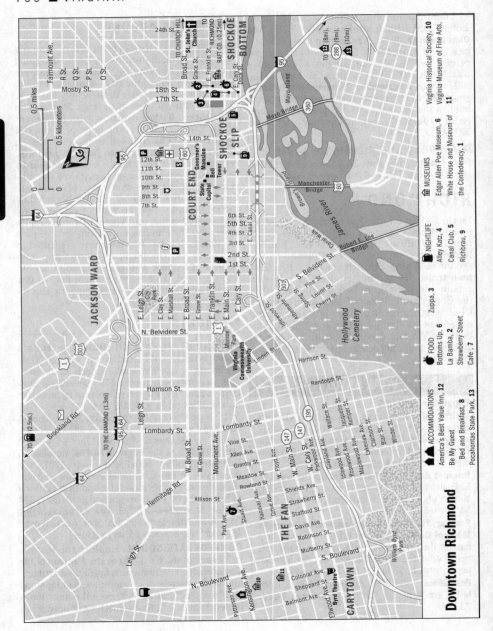

Downtown Richmond

0.5 miles
0.5 kilometers

JACKSON WARD

COURT END

SHOCKOE SLIP

SHOCKOE BOTTOM

THE FAN

CARYTOWN

Fairmount Ave.
R St.
Q St.
P St.
O St.
Mosby St.

24th St.
TO CHURCH HILL
St. John's Church
Broad St.
Grace St.
E. Franklin St.
E. Cary St.
18th St.
17th St.

TO RICHMOND RAFT CO. (0.25mi)

Dock St.

TO 12 (9mi)
288 (8mi)
13 (10m)

Mayo Island
Mayo Bridge
360

14th St.
12th St.
11th St.
10th St.
9th St.
8th St.
7th St.
60
Governor's Mansion
State Capitol
Bell Tower
6th St.
5th St.
4th St.
3rd St.
2nd St.
1st St.
E. Canal St.

Manchester Bridge
60
Belle Isle
Brown's Island

James River
Canal Walk
Robert E. Lee Bridge

E. Leigh St.
E. Clay St.
E. Marshall St.
E. Broad St.
E. Grove St.
E. Franklin St.
E. Main St.
E. Cary St.

City Park
N. Belvidere St.
S. Belvidere St.
Pine St.
Laurel St.
Cherry St.
Spring St.
301
Albemarle St.

Hollywood Cemetery

Monroe Park
Virginia Commonwealth University
Linden St.
Harrison St.
Randolph St.
Harrison St.

TO THE DIAMOND (1.3mi)
TO (2.5mi)
Brookland Rd.
64
95
301
11

Leigh St.
Lombardy St.
Lombardy St.
Vine St.
Allen Ave.
Granby St.
Meadow St.
Rowland St.
195
147
W. Floyd Ave.
W. Main St.
W. Cary St.
Grayland Ave.
Idlewood Ave.
Rosewood Ave.
Lakeview Ave.
Clairton St.
Blair St.
Winder St.
Wallace St.
Jacquelin St.
Kemper St.
Maplewood Ave.
Parkwood Ave.

Hermitaga Rd.
Allison St.

Shields Ave.
Strawberry St.
Stafford Ave.
Davis Ave.
Robinson St.
Mulberry St.
S. Boulevard
William Byrd Park

Park Ave.
Stuart Ave.
Hanover Ave.
Grove Ave.
Monument Ave.
W. Grove Ave.

N. Boulevard
Patterson Ave.
Kensington Ave.
Ellwood Ave.
Colonial Ave.
Sheppard St.
Belmont Ave.
Byrd Theatre

ACCOMMODATIONS
America's Best Value Inn, 12
Be My Guest
Bed and Breakfast, 8
Pocahontas State Park, 13

FOOD
Bottoms Up, 6
La Bamba, 2
Strawberry Street
Cafe, 7
Zuppa, 3

NIGHTLIFE
Alley Katz, 4
Canal Club, 5
Richbrau, 9

MUSEUMS
Edgar Allen Poe Museum, 6
White House and Museum of
the Confederacy, 1
Virginia Historical Society, 10
Virginia Museum of Fine Arts,
11

the exhibits on the crucial battles and campaigns of the Civil War will make your visits to actual Civil War battlefields much more interesting. Next door, friendly guides run tours through the **White House of the Confederacy,** Jefferson Davis's official residence during the Civil War. *(1201 E. Clay St. ☎804-649-1861; www.moc.org. Museum open M-Sa 10am-5pm, Su noon-5pm. White House guided tours every 30-60min. Museum $7, ages 62+ $6, ages 7-18 $3; White House $7/$6/$4; both sights $10/$9/$5.)*

FAN DISTRICT. This section of Richmond is home to the country's largest and best-preserved Victorian neighborhood. Stroll down **Monument Avenue,** a boulevard lined with graceful old houses and towering statues of Virginia heroes—Richmond's memory lane. The statue of **Robert E. Lee** faces south toward his beloved Dixie; **General Stonewall Jackson** faces north so that he can scowl at the Yankees for all eternity. The statue of African-American tennis star **Arthur Ashe** created a storm of controversy when it was added to the end of the avenue that had previously featured only Civil War generals. Though the monuments are captivating, they're also far apart, so a drive-by tour is recommended if you're in a hurry.

MUSEUM ROW. The ⧉**Virginia Historical Society** maintains an impressive collection in an even more impressive building. Marvel at the elegant classical architecture before moving on through the extensive "Story of Virginia" exhibit, which traces Virginia's past from prehistory all the way through the economic transformations and racial conflicts of the 20th century. The museum's showcase feature is a series of murals known as the "Four Seasons of the Confederacy," painted by the French artist Charles Hoffbauer between 1914 and 1921. *(428 N. Boulevard. ☎804-358-4901; www.vahistorical.org. Open M-Sa 10am-5pm, Su 1-5pm. $5, seniors $4, students $3.)* The **Virginia Museum of Fine Arts** is the largest art museum in the South, and with a new wing scheduled to open in 2007, it's getting even bigger. The museum houses a collection by some of the world's most renowned painters—Monet, Renoir, Picasso, and Warhol—as well as ancient treasures from Rome, Egypt, and Asia. *(200 N. Boulevard. ☎804-340-1400; www.vmfa.museum. Open W-Su 11am-5pm. Suggested donation $5.)*

JAMES RIVER. Flowing straight through downtown Richmond, the James River is hard to miss. The 1¼ mi. **Canal Walk** winds along the riverbank and has exhibits on Richmond's canal system and ports. *(Accessible from Tredegar St. near 5th St. Open sunrise-sunset. Free.)* For the adventurous, the **Richmond Raft Company,** 4400 E. Main St., arranges rafting trips on the James River's "urban" rapids, running right past downtown Richmond's towering office buildings. Trips last 3-6hr. and range from family-oriented excursions through gentle Class I rapids to adrenaline-charged descents through thundering whitewater. *(☎800-222-7238; www.richmondraft.com. Trips run Apr.-Oct. Sa-Su. Reservations required. Sa $60-75, Su $56-70.)*

▨ FOOD

Strawberry Street Cafe, 421 Strawberry St. (☎804-353-6860; www.strawberrystreet-cafe.com). A delicious unlimited salad bar ($8), a brunch bar ($10; Sa-Su 10am-3pm), and a variety of sandwiches ($8-10), as well as a mostly gray-haired clientele. Expect a wait. Open M-Th 11am-2:30pm and 5-10:30pm, F 11am-2:30pm and 5-11pm, Sa 10am-11pm, Su 10am-10:30pm. AmEx/MC/V. ❸

La Bamba, 19 N. 18th St. (☎804-225-8883). This Mexican restaurant covers the basics and has great variations on standard tacos, burritos, and quesadillas. The lunch menu has 40 different combos for $4-6. Dinner entrees $7-12. Open M-Th 11am-10pm, F 11am-11pm, Sa noon-10pm, Su 11am-9pm. MC/V. ❷

Bottoms Up, 1700 Dock St. (☎804-644-4400), at 17th and Cary St. Perfect for post-nightclub pizza cravings. Caters to a student and twentysomething crowd. Create your own, or try the Chesapeake (with spicy crabmeat). Slices $4.25-7. Pies $10-22. Open M-Tu and Su 11am-10pm, W-Th 11am-11pm, F-Sa 11am-2am. AmEx/D/MC/V. ❷

Zuppa, 104 N. 18th St. (☎804-249-8831), in Shockoe Bottom. This tiny cafe serves freshly baked bread, a daily selection of salads and sandwiches, as well as soups ranging from gazpacho to lobster bisque. Sandwiches $7. Soups $3-5. Open Tu-Th 11am-10pm, F 11am-2am, Sa 5pm-3am. AmEx/D/MC/V. ❶

⚑ ACCOMMODATIONS

☒ Be My Guest Bed and Breakfast, 2926 Kensington Ave. (☎804-358-9901), in the heart of Richmond. Truly a hidden deal: neither a sign nor a Yellow Pages listing marks it. Pleasing decor, breakfast, and friendly owners make this B&B a worthwhile splurge. Rooms $95-135. Cash or check only. ❹

America's Best Value Inn, 2126 Willis Rd. (☎804-271-1281 or 877-747-6884; www.bestvalueinn.com), offf I-95 at Exit 64, 10 mi. from downtown. One of the cheapest options near the city with clean, standard rooms. Rooms $44-49. AmEx/D/MC/V. ❷

Pocahontas State Park, 10301 State Park Rd. (☎804-796-4255 or 800-933-7275; www.dcr.state.va.us). Take I-95 S to Rte. 288 (Exit 67); after 5 mi., connect to Rte. 10, exit on Ironbridge Rd. heading east, and turn right on Beach Rd.; the park is 4 mi. down on the right. Showers, biking, boating, and the second-largest pool in Virginia. Rent a canoe, rowboat, kayak, or paddleboat ($6-10 per hr.). Sites with water and electricity $24. MC/V. ❶

🎵 ENTERTAINMENT

At the marvelous old **☒Byrd Theatre,** 2908 W. Cary St., movie buffs buy tickets for the latest movies from a tuxedoed agent. On Saturdays, guests are treated to midnight shows and a Wurlitzer organ concert. (☎804-353-9911; www.byrdtheatre.com. Shows $2; Sa midnight movie $3.) **Friday Cheers** presents free concerts at Brown's Island on Friday evenings during the summer. Check at the visitors center for schedules. *Style Weekly,* a free magazine available at the visitors center, and *Punchline,* found in most hangouts, list concert lineups and events. Cheer on the **Richmond Braves,** Richmond's AAA Minor League baseball team, at The Diamond, Exit 78 off I-95. (☎804-359-4444; www.rbraves.com. Tickets $3-9.)

🎭 NIGHTLIFE

Student-driven nightlife enlivens **Shockoe Slip** and the **Fan.** After dark, **Shockoe Bottom** turns into college-party central, with bars pumping bass-heavy music. Be cautious in the Bottom's alleys after dark, but do visit them.

Alley Katz, 10 Walnut Alley (☎804-643-2816). Hosts an impressive range of alternative, jazz, R&B, and other live performances throughout the week. . Open Tu-Su 9pm-2am. Cover varies. MC/V.

Richbrau, 1214 E. Cary St. (☎804-604-3018; www.richbrau.com). Part microbrewery, par pool hall, and part dance club. The downstairs restaurant has expensive food (entrees $15-25) but cheap homebrews, like the "Big Nasty Porter." A rockin' dance club and a pub with pool tables split the second floor. Happy hour M-F 4:30-6:30pm with discounted appetizers. Open daily 11:30pm-"past midnight"—usually around 2am on weekend nights. AmEx/D/MC/V.

Canal Club, 1545 E. Cary St. (☎804-643-2582; www.canalclub.com). A spacious bar that has live music most Saturdays and Sundays. Free Wi-Fi. Cover for live music $5-25. Open W-Sa 7pm-last customer, Su 9pm-last customer. MC/V.

🚗 APPROACHING PETERSBURG: 28 MILES

Get on **I-95 S** to leave the Richmond metro area. Follow I-95 for 13 mi. to **Exit 61.** Take **Hundred Rd. W** for ½ mi. to **Rte. 1 S.** Follow Rte. 1 for 10 mi. to downtown Petersburg.

PETERSBURG

One of the Confederacy's last strongholds during the waning months of the Civil War, Petersburg was under siege for over 10 months in 1864 and 1865. The city has a lot of Civil War-era history to share as well as some fascinating museums and battlefields. The **Petersburg Visitors Center,** at the end of Old Towne Rd., has a parking lot for visitors as well as information about local attractions. (☎800-368-3595; www.petersburg-va.org. Open daily 9am-7pm.) From the visitor parking lot, it's only a short walk to Petersburg's **Siege Museum,** at the corner of Bank St. and Exchange Alley. With exhibits on civilian life during the siege of Petersburg, the museum has a number of interesting artifacts, including a bullet with teeth marks from a patient undergoing emergency surgery during the siege. (☎804-733-2404. Open daily 10am-5pm. $5, seniors and children $4.) At the **Petersburg National Battlefield,** 2 mi. east of downtown off Washington St. (Rte. 36), visitors can take a driving tour and view the remains of trenches and fortifications used by both Union and Confederate armies. The final stop on the driving tour is **The Crater,** see below. (☎804-732-3531; www.nps.gov/pete. Open daily 9am-sunset. $5 per vehicle.) South of downtown Petersburg, **Pamplin Historical Park** hosts Civil War festivals with reenactments, music, and exhibits on the war. (On Rte. 1. ☎804-861-2408. Call for schedule. $13.50, ages 6-11 $7.50.)

Downtown Petersburg has a few appealing restaurants, including **Java Mio ❶,** 322 N. Sycamore St. This coffeehouse serves breakfast, sandwiches, and other light fare. (☎804-861-2700; www.javamio.com. Open M-F 7am-7pm, Sa 8am-5pm. AmEx/D/MC/V.) Petersburg's **Quality Inn ❸,** 405 E. Washington St., has a special $44 rate advertised at the Petersburg Visitor Center. The rooms are comfortable, and the hotel has a restaurant, breakfast, and pool. (☎804-861-6339. Rooms $55-70. AmEx/D/MC/V.) Outside of town, the **Picture Lake Campground ❷,** 7818 Boydton Plank Rd., has some waterfront sites, a swimming pool, and showers. (☎804-861-0174. Sites with water and electricity $30. AmEx/D/MC/V.)

▣ APPROACHING SOUTH HILL: 58 MILES
From downtown Petersburg, follow signs to **Rte. 1 S.** Follow Rte. 1 to downtown South Hill at the intersection with **Rte. 47.**

SOUTH HILL

The **South Hill Visitors Center,** 201 S. Mecklenburg Ave., is home to two small but engrossing museums, the **Model Railroad Museum** and the **Doll Museum.** The Model Railroad museum has two working, room-sized train layouts complete with detailed landscaping, as well as a collection of antique model trains. The Doll museum contains over 500 antique dolls. (☎434-447-4547 or 800-524-4347. Both museums open daily 9am-4pm. Visitors center open daily 9am-7pm. Donation suggested.) A short walk from the visitors center, the **Tobacco Farm Life Museum,** 300 W. Main St., introduces visitors to the history of tobacco production in the US and explains how tobacco is grown, harvested, processed, and sold today. The 15min. video is entertaining, if a bit dated. The two floors display artifacts and memorabilia relating to tobacco, much of which was donated by local farmers. Worth a visit, even for non-smokers. (☎434-447-2551. Open W-Sa 10am-4pm. Free.) The **Gilmore Cinema,** 835 E. Atlantic St., has two screens and bargain prices on first-run movies. (☎434-447-8551. $4, before 6pm $2; children $2.)

South of downtown, chain hotels and restaurants cluster around Exit 12, off I-85. **Brian's Steak House ❸,** 625 E. Atlantic St., serves a wide range of dishes in an informal setting. Sandwiches and other light dishes are $7-9, but steaks ($13-20) are the restaurant's specialty. (☎434-447-3169. Open daily 6am-10pm. AmEx/D/MC/V.) **Wilson Brothers Bar-B-Q ❷,** 1224 W. Danville St., specializes in pork barbecue plates and fried chicken. Fancy garnishes would only be a distraction. (☎434-447-7440. Combination plates $6-8. Open daily 5am-10pm. AmEx/D/

THE CRATER

Siege warfare is typically boring, monotonous and brutal, with each side waiting endlessly for the other to retreat. The Union Army's ten month-long siege of Petersburg during the Civil War in 1864 and 1865 was no exception, but it did have one spectacular moment. In July of 1864, when a prolonged standoff seemed inevitable, Union General Burnside (whose exaggerated facial hair gave name to what we now call "sideburns") overheard a pair of Union soldiers and former miners discussing the possibility of blowing up the Confederates from underground. Burnside was intrigued and had the solders tunnel over 500 ft. from Union trenches into no-man's-land. With the tunnel complete, the miners placed barrels of gunpowder beneath a line of Confederate artillery, lit the fuse, and hurried out of the tunnel as Union forces prepared for a surprise attack. The underground explosives exploded spectacularly and created a 30 foot-deep crater in the middle of Confederate fortifications. Unfortunately, the spectacle distracted the Union army, and by the time they reached the crater, the Confederates had regrouped and routed the Union troops who tried to scale the walls of the newly-formed crater. The remains of "The Crater" and the Union tunnel can be seen at the Petersburg

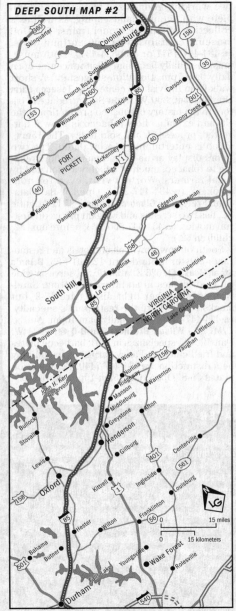

DEEP SOUTH MAP #2

DEEP SOUTH

MC/V.) Inexpensive motel rooms are available at **Budget Inn Express ❷**, 617 N. Mecklenburg Ave., near downtown. (☎434-447-8643. Rooms M-F $35, Sa-Su $40. AmEx/D/MC/V.)

◨ APPROACHING OXFORD: 45 MILES
Take **Rte. 1 S**, and get on **I-85 S**. Follow it for 9 mi. to **Exit 206 (Rte. 158)**, and take Rte. 158 W for 3 mi. to downtown Oxford. Fill up your gas tank before you arrive at Oxford; gas prices are very high in the Raleigh-Durham-Chapel Hill area.

The Tar Heel State

NORTH CAROLINA
Welcomes You!

OXFORD

Oxford is home to the Revlon cosmetics factory as well as a small museum devoted to regional history. Although the Revlon factory no longer operates tours, the **Revlon Company Store** on Rte. 158, just off Exit 206 on I-85, has a wide selection of discounted cosmetics. In the event that your shiny nose is distracting other drivers, this might be the time to "rev" yourself up. (☎919-603-3176. Open M-W 10am-5pm, Th 10am-6pm, F 7am-5pm, Sa 10am-5pm.) In downtown Oxford, the small **Granville County Museum**, 110 Court St., has a variety of exhibits on local history and a model soda fountain. The museum doubles as a visitors center with information about regional attractions and events. (☎919-693-9706. Open W-F 10am-4pm, Sa 11am-3pm. Free.)

Milano's Italian Restaurant ❷, 127 Williamsboro St., has inexpensive sandwiches and wraps ($4.50-6), along with a variety of salads ($4-8) and pasta dishes ($8-12). The dining room is always packed at lunchtime. (☎919-693-6444. AmEx/D/MC/V.) For a Southern-style breakfast, **Sunrise Biscuits ❶**, 128 Williamsboro St., serves biscuits plain ($0.80) or with egg, sausage, steak, or chicken ($1.50). If you're not a fan of biscuits, don't despair—sandwiches and other lunch items are only $2-4. (☎919-693-6178. Open M-Sa 5:30am-1:30pm, Su 6am-1pm. Cash only.)

◥ APPROACHING DURHAM: 26 MILES

From Oxford, follow **I-85 S** for 26 mi. Take **Exit 177** to downtown Durham, the first stop in the Triangle of Durham, Raleigh, and Chapel Hill.

DURHAM

Durham is the economic heart of tobacco country. Its post-Civil War economic prosperity was fueled by the success of the Duke family's tobacco empire that rose to prominence in the early 20th century. The Dukes founded Duke University, a beautiful campus centered around the elegant Duke Chapel. The University's spiritual center is Cameron Stadium, home to Duke's men's basketball team, whose fierce rivalry with the nearby UNC Tar Heels is one of the most famous in college basketball history. Durham is also home to the Research Triangle Park, responsible for inventions as inspiring as the AIDS drug AZT and as down-to-earth as Astroturf.

VITAL STATS

Population: 208,816

Visitor Info: Durham Convention and Visitors Bureau, 101 E. Morgan St. (☎919-687-0288 or 800-446-8604; www.durham-nc.com). Open M-F 8:30am-5pm, Sa 10am-2pm.

Internet Access: Durham County Public Library, 300 N. Roxboro St. (☎919-560-0100), near the visitors center. Open Aug.-May M-Th 9am-9pm, F 9am-6pm, Sa 9:30am-6pm, Su 2-6pm; June-July M-Th 9am-9pm, F 9am-6pm, Sa 9:30am-6pm. Free.

Parking: The **Nasher Museum of Art** at 2001 Campus Dr. has public parking ($2 per hr.) convenient to Duke University's central campus.

Post Office: 323 E. Chapel Hill St. (☎919-683-1976). Open M-F 8:30am-5pm. **Postal Code:** 27701.

▐ GETTING AROUND

I-85 and **I-40** run through Durham and are connected by **Rte. 147 (Durham Freeway)** which runs northeast-southwest through the center of town, separating Duke University from the downtown area. Downtown is home to shop-

ping boutiques and the Durham Bulls Athletic Park, while student-oriented restaurants and nightlife cluster around the Duke campus to the west of downtown. Durham lacks a walkable layout, and few sights or attractions except for those on the Duke campus are within walking distance of each other. Fortunately, most areas of Durham have ample on-street parking.

⬢ SIGHTS

DUKE UNIVERSITY. The Duke family's principal legacy, Duke University, is divided into East and West Campus. The majestic, neo-Gothic ▧**Duke Chapel,** completed in the early 1930s, looms above the center of West Campus. Over one million pieces of glass were used to make the 77 stained-glass windows depicting hundreds of figures from the Bible and Southern history. The chapel's carillonneur gives a free recital on the chapels' 50-bell carillon daily at 5pm. (☎919-684-2572; www.chapel.duke.edu. Open daily 8am-10pm. Free.) Nearby on Anderson St., the gorgeous **Sarah P. Duke Gardens** has over 55 acres divided into three segments: the Bloomington garden of native plants, the Culberson Asiatic arboretum, and the Terraces. (☎919-684-3698, trolley tours ☎919-668-1705. Open daily 8am-sunset. Free 1½hr. guided tours available by appointment. 45min. trolley tours M-F 8am-4pm $25.) The **Nasher Museum of Art** opened in 2005 to house rotating exhibitions from Duke University's art collections. Galleries radiate from an airy, glass-ceilinged atrium. (2001 Campus Drive. ☎919-684-5135; www.nasher.duke.edu. Open Tu-W and F-Sa 10am-5pm, Th 10am-9pm, Su noon-5pm. $5, seniors $4, students with ID $3.) Duke University's **Primate Center** is home to over 200 primates. Tours introduce visitors to the three species living in the center's indoor and outdoor habitats: lemurs from Madagascar, lorises from Asia, and galagos from Africa. (3705 Erwin Rd. at Hwy. 751. ☎919-489-3364; www.duke.edu/web/primate. Reservations required for tours. Open M-F 9am-4:30pm. $7, college students $5, seniors and children $4.)

DUKE HOMESTEAD. Visitors can explore the original farm, home, and factories where Washington Duke first planted and processed the tobacco that would become the key to the city's prosperity. The free tour includes an early factory and curing barn, as well as the restored home. The adjoining **Tobacco Museum** explains the history of the tobacco industry. The tour and museum are extensive but somewhat boring unless you have a strong interest in regional history or tobacco cultivation. *(2828 Duke Homestead Rd., off Guess Rd. ☎919-477-5498. Open Tu-Sa 10am-4pm. 45min. homestead tours depart 15min. after the hr. Free.)*

OTHER SIGHTS. The 1988 movie *Bull Durham* was filmed in Durham Athletic Park, 409 Blackwell St. The AAA farm team for the Tampa Bay Devil Rays plays here, minus Kevin Costner. *(Take Durham Bulls Stadium exit off I-40. ☎919-687-6500, tickets 956-2855; www.durhambulls.com. Games Apr.-Sept. Tickets $5-8.)* Travelers visiting the area during June and July should not miss a modern dance performance showcasing the likes of the Paul Taylor Dance Company at the American Dance Festival, hosted for six weeks at Duke. *(☎919-684-6402; www.americandancefestival.org. Tickets $12-40.)*

FOOD

Duke's campus is surrounded by affordable eateries, especially along **9th St.** A mile east of 9th St. on Main St., **Brightleaf Sq.** has renovated warehouses that hold galleries, shops, and restaurants. The American Tobacco Historic District on Jackie Robinson St. also has several good restaurants.

The Mad Hatter's Cafe and Bake Shop, 1802 W. Main St. (☎919-286-1987; www.madhattersbakeshop.com), 1 block from 9th St. A wide selection of delectable dishes made from local, organic produce including pizza, Asian noodles, and wraps. The spacious and colorful restaurant has an outdoor patio and free Wi-Fi. Pizza, soups, and wraps $7-9. Cookies $1.50-2.25. Open M-Th 7am-9pm, F-Sa 7am-11pm, Su 8am-3pm. AmEx/MC/V. ❷

Hog Heaven Bar-B-Q, 2419 Guess Rd. (☎919-286-7447). Hog Heaven specializes in North Carolina-style barbecue. Barbecue and fried chicken meals ($6-6.75) come with a choice of 2 delicious sides. Open M-Sa 11am-9pm. MC/V. ❷

Pao Lim Asian Bistro and Bar, 2505 Chapel Hill Blvd. (☎919-419-1771), just off the 15/501 Business Rte. Pao Lim pulls off Asian fusion cuisine like you've never seen it before, elegantly blending Chinese, Indian, and other flavors in reasonably priced dishes. Lunch specials $6-9. Din-

ner entrees $9-12. Open M-Th 11:30am-9:30pm, F 11:30am-10pm, Sa noon-10pm, Su noon-9:30pm. AmEx/D/MC/V. ❷

Francesca's, 706 9th St. (☎919-286-4177). Serves only beverages and desserts, but the focus pays off. Sample homemade gelato for just $2.50. Milkshakes $4. Free Wi-Fi. Open M-Th 11am-11pm, F-Sa 11am-midnight, Su 11am-10pm. MC/V. ❶

ACCOMMODATIONS

Budget lodging is scarce in Durham. Economy motels line **I-85**, especially between Exits 1-73 and 1-75 north of Duke, and **I-40** between the Research Triangle Park and Raleigh-Durham International Airport. Midweek coupon specials can reduce the price of chain hotels, but on weekends or holidays, camping may be your best option.

Best Value Carolina Duke Inn, 2517 Guess Rd. (☎919-286-0771 or 800-438-1158), off I-85 at Exit 175. Clean rooms, coin laundry facilities, and an outdoor pool. Continental breakfast included. Singles $43; doubles $50. AmEx/D/MC/V. ❷

Eno River State Park, 6101 Cole Mill Rd. (☎919-383-1686; www.ncsparks.net), off I-85 at Exit 173. 5 primitive campsites. Sites share a pit toilet and require a 1 mi. hike from the parking area. No water or electricity. Park office open daily 8am-6pm. Gate closes Nov.-Feb. 6pm; Mar. and Oct. 7pm; Apr.-Sept. 9pm. Sites $9. AmEx/D/MC/V. ❶

NIGHTLIFE

Durham's nightlife runs the gamut from classy to raunchy, with most student bars and nightclubs located near 9th St. Pick up a free copy of the weekly *Spectator* and *Independent* magazines, available at many restaurants and bookstores, for listings of Triangle events. There are numerous free concerts held in downtown Durham during the summer, such as the **Bud Light Downtown** concert series in Moore Square Park June to September (www.budlightdowntownlive.com.) The American Tobacco Historic District also has free concerts on Thursday evenings from June to August. (324 Blackwell St.; www.americantobaccohistoricdistrict.com.)

George's Garage, 737 9th St. (☎919-286-4131). George's serves great sushi and drinks into the wee hours. Sushi rolls $4.50. M jazz jam. F-Sa DJ. Every other Sa salsa lessons. Open M-Th and Su 4pm-12:30am, F-Sa 4pm-2am. AmEx/D/MC/V.

Charlie's Pub & Grill, 759 9th St. (☎919-286-4446). Since Duke bans on-campus parties, under-grads head to this no-frills bar for cheap beer. Domestic beers $2.50. Draft pitchers $8-11. Open M-Sa 11am-2am, Su noon-2am. Kitchen closes 1:30am. MC/V.

Siren's Lounge, 1803 W. Markham Ave. (☎919-416-6684; www.sirenslounge.com). This converted gas station has a 2-level lounge with trendy decorations and a college crowd. On F and Sa nights, the lounge's lower level becomes a dance floor. Th $1 drafts. Open M-Sa 7pm-2am. MC/V.

⚑ APPROACHING RALEIGH: 28 MILES
Follow **Rte. 147 S** for 7 mi. to **Exit 5A**. Take **I-40 W** for 19 mi. Take **Exit 298B** to downtown Raleigh.

RALEIGH

Home to North Carolina State University ("NC State"), Raleigh is a historic state capital with recently revamped tourist attractions. Downtown, visitors can tour the state house and numerous museums or watch artists at work in their studios at Artspace. Like Durham and Chapel Hill, Raleigh is a young city with a hot music scene, a variety of restaurants, and a college-age crowd.

VITAL STATS

Population: 276,093

Visitor Info: The Capital Area Visitor Center, 5 E. Edenton St. (☎919-715-0200 or 800-849-8499; www.visitraleigh.com), in the lobby of the North Carolina Museum of History. Open Tu-Sa 8am-5pm, Su noon-5pm.

Internet Access: North Regional Library, 200 Horizon Dr. (☎919-870-4000), in North Raleigh. Take Exit 8 from Rte. 440, head north on Six Forks Rd. for 2 mi., then turn left on Horizon Dr. Open M-F 9am-9pm, Sa 10am-5pm, Su 1-5pm. Free.

Parking: The **garage** on Blout St., between Hartett St. and Morgan St., is close to most downtown attractions ($2 1st hr., $1 per additional hr.; $9 max. per day.)

Post Office: 311 New Bern Ave. (☎919-832-1604). Open M-F 8am-5:30pm, Sa 8am-noon. **Postal Code:** 27611.

⬛ GETTING AROUND

The **I-440 "Beltline"** and portions of **I-540** loop around the city through Raleigh's northern suburbs. **I-40** runs east-west to the I-440 Beltline, connecting Raleigh to the airport and Research Triangle Park to the west of the city. **Rte. 70** runs northwest through Raleigh towards Durham. Downtown Raleigh is constructed on a grid, and most streets are one-way. Parking in downtown can be frustrating during weekdays, when on-street meters are scarce, but parking lots are scattered throughout the downtown area.

⬛ SIGHTS

⬛ARTSPACE. This collection of 46 artists' studios in three exhibition galleries features work by regional, national, and international artists. Watch them create art of all types, from watercolor and oil paintings to 3-D fabric arts. Individual studios are open to visitors while artists are at work. You can stop by, ask questions, and learn first-hand about each artist's creative process. Call ahead or check online for guided tours and special events. *(201 E. Davie St. ☎919-821-2787; www.artspacenc.org. Open Tu-Sa 10am-6pm, 1st F of each month 10am-10pm. Studio hours vary. Free.)*

MUSEUMS. Across from the capitol building in the center of downtown Raleigh are two museums worth visiting. The **Museum of Natural Sciences** has four floors of exhibits on North Carolina's natural history, geography, and wildlife. Highlights include a 15 ft. giant ground sloth unearthed near Wilmington and other specimens of record-setting, rare, or bizarre wildlife from around the state. *(11 W. Jones St. ☎919-733-7450 or 877-462-8724; www.naturalsciences.org. Open M-Sa 9am-5pm, Su noon-5pm. Free. Audio tours $2.)* Just down the block, the **North Carolina Museum of History** looks back at North Carolina history through an exhibit on the Civil War, the N.C. Sports Hall of Fame, and a collection of artifacts from North Carolina inventors, daredevils, and military aces. *(5 E. Edenton St. ☎919-715-0200; www.ncmuseumofhistory.org. Open Tu-Sa 8am-5pm, Su noon-5pm. Free.)*

STATE CAPITOL. North Carolina's capitol building was completed in 1840 and originally housed all three branches of state government. The legislature and Supreme Court have since moved out, but visitors can see the preserved house and senate chambers on the second floor. The first floor rotunda has a collection of historic flags, as well as a very unique sculpture of George Washington in the uniform of a Roman general. It's worth a quick visit, even for non-history buffs. *(1 E. Edenton St. ☎919-733-4994; www.ncstatecapitol.com. Photo ID required for entry. Open M-F 9am-5pm, Sa 10am-4pm, Su 1pm-4pm. Free.)* A few blocks from the capitol, the enormous Governor's Mansion, built in 1883, has 50 opulent rooms covering 34,000 sq. ft. Tours must be scheduled at least 10 days in advance, but are amazing. *(Blount St., between Lane St. and Jones St. ☎919-807-7948; www.ncdar.gov. Free.)*

OAKWOOD. Stretching east from the visitors center, Historic Oakwood is a Victorian neighborhood featuring some of Raleigh's most notable architecture, with attractive homes constructed in the late 19th and early 20th centuries. It's a long walk from downtown, best seen as a quick detour on your way through town. This neighborhood and the adjacent Oakwood Cemetery provide a relaxing escape from the bustle of the city center. *(Historic Oakwood is bordered by Franklin, Watauga, Linden, Jones, and Person St. Free walking tour guides available at the visitors center. Cemetery entrance at 701 Oakwood Ave. ☎919-832-6077. Open daily 8am-6pm. Free.)*

FOOD

Travelers can find good dining options in **City Market's** shops, cafes, and bars near the capitol.

The Rockford, 320½ Glenwood Ave. (☎919-821-9020), near Hillsborough St. A trendy 2nd fl. restaurant that serves delightful, inexpensive food. A popular choice is the ABC sandwich (apple, bacon, and cheddar on French toast; $7). Entrees $7.25 or less. Open M-W 11:30am-2pm and 6-10pm, Th-Sa 11:30am-2pm and 6-10:30pm, Su 6-10pm. AmEx/MC/V. ❶

Marrakesh Cafe, 2500 Hillsborough St. (☎919-341-1167). North Carolina's 1st hookah bar, offering Moroccan-influenced wraps, sandwiches ($4-5.50), and salads ($3-4). Hookah $6. Flavors include strawberry, mint, and melon. Open M-W 10am-1pm, Th-Sa 10am-3pm, Su 5pm-midnight. D/MC/V. ❶

Caffe Luna, 136 E. Hargett St. (☎919-832-6090), downtown. Decorated in gorgeous pastels, Caffe Luna serves fresh pasta that will melt in your mouth. Lunch $7.50-8.50. Dinner $12-15. Open daily 11:30am-2:30pm and 5pm-10pm. AmEx/MC/V. ❸

Roly Poly Sandwiches, 137 E. Hargett St. (☎919-834-1135; www.rolypoly.com). Serves 50 different kinds of wraps in a small downtown location. Counter service is speedy, and the selection of wraps is impressive. Wraps $3.25-7. Open M-F 10am-4pm, Sa 11am-3pm. AmEx/D/MC/V. ❶

FINDERS KEEPERS?

Nearly a century and a half after it was stolen during the Civil War, the State of North Carolina's long-lost copy of the Bill of Rights resurfaced in 2003. There's just one problem: one of the current owners of the document won't give it back. Only fourteen original copies of the Bill of Rights were written in 1789, and one of them was given to the state of North Carolina, where it was housed in the capitol building in Raleigh. In 1865, troops commanded by General William Tecumseh Sherman occupied Raleigh, and the copy of the Bill of Rights disappeared, allegedly snatched by a Union soldier. The copy was bought and sold by numerous private art collectors and dealers and finally resurfaced again in 2003. FBI agents posing as museum buyers found the copy in the possession of two men in Connecticut and seized it. One of the men relinquished his stake in the document, which he had purchased for $200,000 in 2000. The other refused, arguing that, after 140 years in private hands, the document belonged to him, not the State of North Carolina. Even though a federal appeals court ruling in 2006 stated that North Carolina was entitled to reclaim the document, the owner isn't giving up. He plans to appeal to the United States Supreme Court, that is, if they don't snag the copy for themselves.

ACCOMMODATIONS

Like Durham, Raleigh does not make it easy to find budget lodging. Shopping the chain motels with books of discount coupons from the visitors center is probably your best bet. Hotels and motels surrounds the major exits to the Rte. 440 Beltline, especially at Glenwood Ave., Forest Rd., and Capital Blvd.

Homestead Suites, 4810 Bluestone Dr. (☎919-510-8551; www.homesteadhotels.com), off Glenwood Ave. An "extended stay" hotel designed for business travelers willing to lay out extra cash but offers discounted rates with hotel coupons if there are rooms available. Spacious rooms have full kitchens, refrigerators, microwaves, coffeemakers, and free Wi-Fi. Rooms $60-79. AmEx/D/MC/V. ❷

Falls Lake State Recreation Area, 13304 Creedmoor Rd. (☎676-1027; www.ils.unc.edu/park-project/visit/fala/home.html), about 10 mi. north of Raleigh, offf Rte. 98, 1 mi. north of N.C. 50. 4 campgrounds. The main campground, **Holly Point,** is adjacent to the lake and has both open lakefront sites and secluded shady sites, showers, boat ramps, 2 swimming beaches, and a dump station. 14-day max. stay. Gates close May-Aug. 9pm; Apr. and Sept. 8pm; Mar. and Oct. 7pm; Nov.-Feb. 6pm. Reservations recommended. Sites $15, ages 62+ $10; with hook-up $20. Day-use $5 per vehicle. Cash only. ❶

NIGHTLIFE

Info on happenings in Raleigh can be found at www.raleighnow.com. Nightlife options are plentiful in Raleigh; the area around Glenwood by **Hillsborough St.** is home to a number of trendy bars.

Mitch's Tavern, 2426 Hillsborough St. (☎919-821-7771; www.mitchs.com). This 2nd fl. bar is a favorite among students and locals looking for a late-night brew. The dark, smoky charm of the tavern's interior may have been what persuaded the producers of *Bull Durham* to select this as the set for 2 scenes. Pints $2.25-3.50. Pitchers $8-13. Open M 11am-midnight, Tu-Sa 11am-2am, Su 5pm-midnight. MC/V.

The Pour House, 224 S. Blount St. (☎919-821-1120; www.the-pour-house.com.) A small downtown music venue and bar with live music ranging from rock to country. W-Sa jazz and funk. Cover $5-10 for some performances, others free. Call ahead for upcoming acts. Most shows start at 10pm. Open daily 5pm-last customer. MC/V.

Rum Runners, 208 E. Martin St. (☎919-755-6436; www.rumrunnersusa.com). A boisterous bar with a tropical flair. Rum Runners hosts interactive "dueling piano" shows where 2 pianists face off W-Sa nights. Open W 8pm-2am, Th 9pm-2am, F-Sa 7pm-2am, Su 9:30pm-2am. AmEx/D/MC/V.

Five Star, 511 W. Hargett St. (☎919-833-3311; www.heatseekershrimp.com), in downtown Raleigh. This former Chinese restaurant becomes a nightclub at around 10:30pm. Th-Sa DJs 10pm. F-Sa 21+ after 10:30pm. Cover F after 10:30pm $5-10; Sa $5. Open daily 5:30pm-2am. AmEx/MC/V.

Legends, 330 W. Hargett St. (☎919-831-8888; www.legends-club.com). A GLBT-friendly club. Tu Cabaret night. W women's night. Th "dark waves" gothic night. Su drag show 11:30pm and 12:45am. Cover $2-12. Open daily 9pm-3am. MC/V.

APPROACHING CHAPEL HILL: 24 MILES

Take **I-440 W** for ½ mi., then merge onto **I-40 W,** and take **Exit 273A** onto **Rte. 54 W.** Follow Rte. 54 W to downtown Chapel Hill.

CHAPEL HILL

Chapel Hill is the smallest of North Carolina's Triangle cities, but as the home of the University of North Carolina's main campus, it makes up for its lack of size with a vibrant college-town atmosphere. Unlike its Triangle counterparts, downtown Chapel Hill is small enough to walk and rewards pedestrians with a surprising variety of restaurants, museums, and nightlife hotspots. If you only have time to visit one city in North Carolina's Triangle area, go here.

GETTING AROUND

I-40 runs to the north and east of downtown Chapel Hill, and **Rte. 54** and **Rte. 15/501** connect the interstate to downtown. **Franklin St.** runs west of downtown and crosses into neighboring Carrboro about ½ mi. west of the downtown cross-

DEEP SOUTH

roads. Nightlife, restaurants, and attractions line Franklin St. all the way into Carrboro.

VITAL STATS

Population: 49,368

Visitor Info: Chapel Hill Orange County Visitors Bureau, 501 W. Franklin St. (☎919-9968-2060 or 888-968-2060; www.chocvb.org). Open M-F 8:30am-5pm, Sa 10am-2pm.

Internet Access: Chapel Hill Public Library, 100 Library Dr. (☎919-968-2777). From UNC, go down Franklin St. toward Durham. Turn left on Estes Dr.; it's on your right. Open M-Th 10am-9pm, F 10am-6pm, Sa 9am-6pm, Su 1-8pm. Free.

Parking: Morehead Planetarium, 250 E. Franklin St. has visitor parking ($1.25 per hr.). There is limited on-street parking along Franklin street downtown. Avoid UNC parking lots, which require permits.

Post Office: 125 S. Estes St. (☎919-929-9892). Open M-F 8:30am-5:30pm, Sa 8:30am-noon. **Postal Code:** 27514.

SIGHTS

UNIVERSITY OF NORTH CAROLINA. Chapel Hill and neighboring Carrboro are inseparable from the beautiful **University of North Carolina at Chapel Hill** campus. (☎919-962-1630; www.unc.edu. Tours M, W, F 1:30pm. Open M-F 9am-5pm. Free.) Until 1975, NASA astronauts trained at UNC's **Morehead Planetarium.** Of the 12 astronauts who have walked on the moon, 11 trained here. Today, Morehead gives live sky shows and presentations in the 68 ft. domed Star Theater and houses small exhibits on outer space. (250 E. Franklin St. ☎919-962-1236; www.moreheadplanetarium.org. Open mid-June to mid-Aug. M and Su 12:30-5pm, Tu-W 10am-5pm, Th-Sa 10am-5pm and 6:30-9pm. Call for winter hours and showtimes. Shows $5.25; students, seniors, and children $4.25. Exhibits and movies free.) UNC's **Ackland Art Museum** houses an impressive collection that focuses on post-Renaissance European painting and sculpture. (5736 S. Columbia St. ☎919-966-5736; www.ackland.org. Open W-Sa 10am-5pm, Su 1-5pm. Free.) **Blue Heaven** is a treasure trove of UNC basketball memorabilia. Operated by Carolina Pros, a nonprofit organization founded by UNC men's basketball alumni, the museum has a growing collection of signed jerseys, basketballs, and championship nets from past UNC teams. (214 W. Franklin St. ☎919-942-9993; www.carolinapros.com. Open M-F 1-5pm, Sa 1pm-4pm. $5.)

NORTH CAROLINA BOTANICAL GARDEN. These 700 acres of botanical gardens and forests operated by UNC are the largest botanical gardens in the Southeast. The gardens have walking trails through habitats that range from the seashore to the mountains. Don't miss the carnivorous plants and the giant chess set made from recycled pots and pans. (South of downtown, on Old Mason Farm Rd., off Fordham Blvd./Hwy. 15/501/54. ☎919-962-0522. Open Apr.-Oct. M-F 8am-5pm, Sa 9am-6pm, Su 1-6pm; Nov.-Mar. M-F 8am-5pm, Sa 9am-5pm, Su 1-5pm. Free.)

FOOD

Chapel Hill has numerous inexpensive restaurants along Franklin St. downtown. True to college-town form, prices are low, variety is impressive, and Wi-Fi is ubiquitous.

Mama Dip's Kitchen, 408 W. Rosemary St. (☎919-942-5837). This soul food restaurant feels like a comfy back-porch picnic, complete with rocking chairs. From the sweet potato waffles to the fried okra to the chicken and dumplings, Mama Dip's serves some of the best regional delicacies around. Entrees $8-11. Open M-Sa 8am-10pm, Su 8am-9pm. AmEx/D/MC/V. ❸

Foster's Market, 750 Martin Luther King Jr. Blvd./Airport Rd. (☎919-967-3663; www.fostersmarket.com). Turn off Franklin St. onto Columbia St., which becomes Martin Luther King Jr. Blvd./Airport Rd. This market-restaurant-coffeehouse serves pizza and sandwiches like the Jammin' Turkey Breast (with 7-pepper jelly, herb cream cheese, onions, and lettuce; $6.50). Free Wi-Fi. Open daily 7:30am-8pm. AmEx/D/MC/V. ❷

Peppers Pizza, 127 E. Franklin St. (☎919-967-7766), downtown. Whether you're eating in or taking out, Peppers has excellent pizza. The benches might be saggy, but the taste of the food makes up for it. Slices $1.75-3. Pies $11-18. Open M-W 11am-midnight, Th-Sa 11am-2:30am, Su 4-10pm. AmEx/D/MC/V. ❶

Jack Sprat Cafe, 161 E. Franklin St. (☎933-3575). A pleasant, laid-back environment frequented by students with salads and hot and cold sandwiches ($5-7), as well as coffee and desserts. Order the

"Salad Sampler" ($8), and try 3 different selections. Free Wi-Fi. Open M-Th 8am-9pm, F-Sa 8am-10pm, Su 9am-5pm. AmEx/D/MC/V. ❷

ACCOMMODATIONS

Like its companion cities, Raleigh and Durham, Chapel Hill doesn't have much in the way of discount lodging. Mid-range motels can be found at the intersection of **I-40** and **U.S. 15/501** in Chapel Hill. Hillsborough is 10 mi. west of Chapel Hill on I-40 and has cheaper lodging.

Microtel, 120 Old Dogwood St. (☎919-245-3102 or 800-771-7171), in Hillsborough. I-40 to Exit 261, then north on I-86 for 1¾ mi. New, comfortable rooms with free Wi-Fi. Continental breakfast included. Rooms $50-60. AmEx/D/MC/V. ❷

Southern Country Inn, 122 Daniel Boone St. (☎919-732-8101), in Hillsborough. Take I-40 to Exit 261, then I-86 N. Rooms are adequate and reasonably clean, but don't expect any extras. There's a campground, but campground facilities are dilapidated, so campers should look elsewhere. Key deposit $5. Singles $40; doubles $45. AmEx/D/MC/V. ❸

NIGHTLIFE

Chapel Hill has the best nightlife in the Triangle. Popular bars line Franklin St., and several live music clubs are clustered where Franklin St. becomes Main St. in Carrboro. During the summer, **Southern Village** on Market St. has a farmers' market Th 4-7pm, an outdoor movie F-Sa 7pm, and live music Su 7pm-last customer. (www.southernvillage.com.) **Cat's Cradle,** 300 E. Main St., in Carrboro, hosts local and national acts ranging from hip-hop to country. (☎919-967-9053; www.catscradle.com. 18+. Cover $5-15. Doors open 7:30-9pm; shows usually begin 8pm. MC/V.) **Local 506,** 506 W. Franklin St., has mostly indie rock. (☎919-942-5506; www.local506.com. 18+. Cover $5. Open daily 2pm-2am. Shows start around 10pm. MC/V.) The live blues and jazz at the **Blue Bayou Club,** 106 S. Churton St., in Hillsborough, is worth the drive from Chapel Hill. (☎919-732-2555. Th-Sa blues and jazz. Cover $5-15. Open M-Th 5-11pm, F-Sa 5pm-2am. D/MC/V.)

⚐ APPROACHING MEBANE: 11 MILES
Take **Rte. 86 N** to **Rte. 70 W.** Follow Rte. 70 for 10 mi. to Mebane.

MEBANE. Mebane's downtown is peppered with art galleries, thrift shops, and antique stores. Clay St. has a number of cute stores worth a look. **Sweet Tooth Heaven ❶,** 110C W. Clay St., lives up to its name, with cookies for under $1, and slices of cake or pie for around $2.50. (☎919-304-5555. Open M-Sa 8am-8pm. MC/V.) Across the street, **Strong's Neighborhood Cafe ❶,** 109 W. Clay St., serves coffee and a variety of sandwiches and salads ($6-7) as well as $5 lunch specials. (☎919-338-8050. Free Wi-Fi. Open M-F 6:30am-8pm, Sa 8am-8pm, Su 8am-6pm. MC/V.) **Nita's Cafeteria ❷,** 304 2nd St., is an eatery open for breakfast and lunch. Their specialty is the "meat and three" lunch (one meat entree with three vegetable sides) for $7. (☎919-563-0965. Open M-F 6am-2pm, Sa 6am-noon. MC/V.)

⚐ APPROACHING BURLINGTON: 10 MILES
Continue on **Rte. 70 W.**

BURLINGTON. Burlington is one of the major commercial centers of the Piedmont region of North Carolina, though it's lacking the personality you'd hope for. Its small downtown is ringed by a seemingly endless procession of strip malls and restaurants. Even if you're not aching for a cold soda or beer, it's worth stopping by **Cruze Thru,** 1305 N. Church St., just to experience a drive-through convenience store. It's not just a drive-up window, you actually pull the car through the building, and attendants get your items for you. (Open daily 7am-midnight.) For out-of-the-ordinary food options, head to **Jim's ❶,** 521 W. Elm St., in Graham, which has been serving delicious fast food for almost 50 years. (Take Rte. 70 W to Rte. 87 S, and follow Rte. 87 for 3 mi. ☎336-228-8916. Hot dogs $1. Burgers $1.25-2. Open M-Sa 11:30am-8pm. Cash only.) Next to Jim's, **El Carbonero ❷,** 517 W. Elm St., offers a mix of El Salvadoran and other Central American dishes. (☎336-228-8002. Tamales $1.50. Meat and fish dishes $10-12. Open M and W-Sa 9am-9pm, Su 9am-8pm. MC/V.)

⚐ APPROACHING SEDALIA: 12 MILES
Stay on **Rte. 70 W** toward Sedalia.

SEDALIA. Sedalia was home to the Palmer Memorial Institute, an African-American preparatory school founded in 1902 by Charlotte Hawkins Brown. Although the Institute closed in the 1970s, the ▨**Charlotte Hawkins Brown Museum,** on Rte. 70 in Sedalia, offers a fascinating glimpse into its little-known history. The museum has a 20min. video on Brown and the history of the Institute. Tours of the grounds are also available. (☎336-449-4846; www.chbrownmuseum.nchistoricsites.org. Open Apr.-Oct. M-Sa 9am-5pm; Nov.-Mar. M-F 10am-4pm. Free.)

◤**APPROACHING GREENSBORO: 10 MILES**

Follow **Rte. 70 W** to downtown Greensboro.

GREENSBORO

Along with Winston-Salem and High Point, Greensboro forms the "Piedmont Triad" of cities in central North Carolina. Greensboro was named after Nathaniel Greene, whose troops fought British forces commanded by General Earl Cornwallis at Guilford County Courthouse during the closing months of the Revolutionary War. Greensboro's colleges were centers of civil rights activism during the 1960s. The lunch counter sit-ins in downtown Greensboro helped focus national attention on the civil-rights movement.

VITAL STATS

Population: 231,543

Visitor Info: Greensboro Visitors Information Center, 317 S. Greene St., (☎336-274-2282 or 800-344-2282; www.visitgreensboronc.com). Open M-F 8:30am-5:30pm, Sa 9am-4pm, Su 1-4pm.

Internet Access: Greensboro Central Library, 219 N. Church St. (☎336-373-2471; www.greensborolibrary.org). Open M-F 9am-9pm, Sa 9am-6pm, Su 2pm-6pm. Free.

Parking: Greensboro Visitors Center, 317 S. Greene St., has free visitor parking during the day.

Post Office: 201 Edward R. Murrow Blvd. Open M-Sa 9am-5pm. 125 S. Estes St. (☎336-370-1251). Open M-F 8:30am-5:30pm, Sa 8:30am-noon. **Postal Code:** 27401.

▐ **GETTING AROUND**

Both I-85 and I-40 run south of downtown Greensboro and are connected to the downtown area by a number of wide boulevards. Most streets in the downtown area are one-way, but directions to the visitors center and other major historical attractions are clearly signposted in the downtown area. The visitors center has a helpful map of the downtown and

Greensboro metro area that indicates the location of major attractions and some hotels.

◉ **SIGHTS**

DOWNTOWN. The **Greensboro Historical Museum** has a variety of exhibits on local history, including the 1960s sit-ins and the lives of famous residents such as First Lady Dolly Madison. (130 Summit Ave. ☎336-373-2043; www.greensborohistory.com. Open Tu-Sa 10am-5pm, Su 2pm-5pm. Free.) In the Dudley Building at the North Carolina A&T campus, the **Mattye Reed African Heritage Center** is home to an impressive collection of African art ranging from ancient sculpture and textile works to contemporary African and African-American art. (1601 E. Market St. ☎336-334-3209; www.ncat.edu/~museum. Open Tu-F 10am-5pm, Sa 1-5pm. Free.) The **Weatherspoon Art Museum** contains UNC-Greensboro's extensive art collection. Exhibits rotate, but the sculpture and 20th-century art will appeal to the aesthetically-minded. (At the corner of Tate and Spring Garden St. ☎336-334-5770; www.weatherspoon.uncg.edu. Open Tu-W and F 10am-5pm, Th 10am-9pm, Sa-Su 1-5pm. Free.) Inside Greensboro's railroad station, **Carolina Model Railroaders** has two intricately detailed model railroads on display. Even for the non-hobbyist, these working mini-railroads are an impressive sight. (J. Douglas Galyon Depot. www.carolinamodelrr.homestead.com. Open Th 7-9pm, Sa 10am-5pm, Su 2-5pm. Free.) The **International Civil Rights Center and Museum** is currently under construction in the old Woolworth building where four African-American students from North Carolina A&T staged the first sit-in of the civil rights movement. Call ahead for opening information. (134 S. Elm St. ☎336-274-9199; www.sitinmovement.org.)

OUTSIDE OF DOWNTOWN. Wet 'n' Wild Emerald Pointe is an enormous water park with wave pools, tubing rivers, zip lines, and a ton of water slides. Food and drink from outside the park are not permitted inside, so be prepared to shell out extra at the concession stands. (On Holden Rd., at Exit 34, off I-85. ☎336-852-9721; www.emeraldpointe.com. Open June-Aug. Sept. daily 10am-8pm, but call ahead. Full day $28, under 48 in. $18; ½-day $19/$14.) Auto racing enthusiasts will enjoy the **Richard Petty Museum,** in Randleman, 12 mi. south of Greensboro on Rte. 220. Chronicling the epic NASCAR career of Richard Petty, a.k.a. "The King," this museum has cars, videos, and trophies galore, as well as Petty's personal collections of guns, knives, watches, and dolls. *(142 W. Academy St. ☎336-495-1143. Open M-Sa 9am-5pm. $5, students $3.)* The **Guilford Courthouse National Military Park** commemorates the Revolutionary War battle between General Nathaniel Greene's rebels and General Earl Cornwallis's British regulars in 1781. The 200-acre park has numerous monuments along walking trails, though no slides. *(2332 New Garden Rd. ☎ 336-288-1776; www.nps.gov/guco. Open daily 9:30am-5pm. Free.)*

🍴 FOOD

For a medium-sized city, Greensboro has surprisingly good dining options. **Liberty Oak ❸**, 100-D W. Washington St., serves excellent sandwiches, pasta, and salads in an airy, two-level dining room. *(☎336-273-7057. Sandwiches $8-9. Dinner entrees $11-15. Open M-F 11:30am-9:30pm, Sa noon-10pm. AmEx/D/MC/V.)* **Stamey's Barbecue ❶**, 2106 Battleground Ave., has been dishing out North Carolina-style barbecue for 75 years, and their experience shows. *(☎336-288-9275. Pork barbecue plates $4.25-5.25. Delicious peach cobbler $1.50. Open M-Sa 10am-9pm. AmEx/D/MC/V.)* **Jake's Diner ❶**, 4220 West Wendover Ave., *(☎336-297-4141)* is a gem of a diner with low prices, fast service, and tasty food. Breakfast combos ($2-5) are served all day. *(☎336-297-4141. Sandwiches $3-5. Open 24hr. AmEx/D/MC/V.)*

🏨 ACCOMMODATIONS

Greensboro has plenty of discount hotels and inexpensive campgrounds along I-40 and I-85. As with other North Carolina cities, discount hotel coupons can be helpful during weekdays and off-peak times. The **Greensboro Inn ❷**, 135 Summit Ave., has basic, clean rooms and free local calls. *(☎336-370-0135. Singles $40; doubles $45. AmEx/D/MC/V.)* **Greensboro Campground ❶**, 1896 Trox St., off I-40/I-85 at Exit 128., has a swimming pool, laundry facilities, security gate, private tent sites, and clean

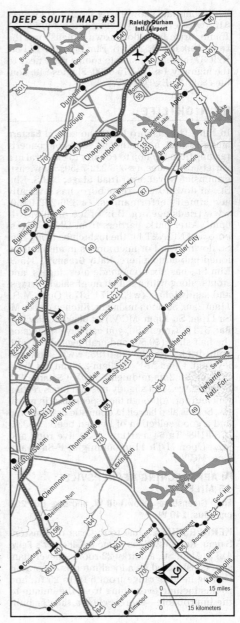

DEEP SOUTH MAP #3

DEEP SOUTH

bathrooms and showers. (☎336-274-4143. Sites $15, with electricity $20; cabins $40-50.) A 15min. drive from downtown Greensboro, the **Land Mark Inn ❷,** 2838 S. Elm St., off I-40/I-85, Exit 37, has small, simple rooms right next to the highway. (☎336-275-0800. Singles $40; doubles $50. AmEx/D/MC/V.)

☒ NIGHTLIFE

In June, Greensboro hosts the annual **Eastern Music Festival,** a month-long series of concerts ranging from hip-hop to country to classical in a variety of venues. (☎336-222-7450; www.easternmusicfestival.org.) **Triad Stage,** 232 S. Elm St., in downtown Greensboro, has critically acclaimed performances. (☎336-272-0160; www.triadstage.org. Box office open M-F 1-6pm.) After dark, partiers from UNC-Greensboro and NC A&T hit the nightclubs along Elm St. downtown. For microbrews in an old-fashioned pub atmosphere, **Natty Greene's,** 345 S. Elm St., has six homemade ales, lagers, and stouts, along with a full menu of salads, wraps, and sandwiches. (☎336-274-1373. Open M-Sa 11am-2am, Su noon-midnight. Kitchen closes M-Sa 11pm, Su 10pm. MC/V.) At **Shuka's Alley Raw Bar,** 313 S. Greene St., you can have oysters on the half shell ($0.50) and crab legs along with your drinks. (☎336-378-0198; www.shukasalley.com. Open M-F 11:30am-2:30am, Sa 4pm-2:30am, Su 2pm-midnight. MC/V.) **Solaris,** 125 Summit Ave., is a slightly upscale tapas restaurant and bar. Although they specializes in martinis, Solaris also has eight domestic drafts on tap and a good selection of bottled beers. (☎336-378-0198. Tu $4 martinis. F-Sa live rock and jazz. Open M-Th 11am-midnight, F-Sa 11am-2am. MC/V.)

🛋 APPROACHING KERNERSVILLE: 15 MILES

From Greensboro, follow **I-40 W,** and take **Exit 206** onto **Bus. 140 W.**

KERNERSVILLE. Just to the east of Winston-Salem, Kernersville is home to 🏠**Korner's Folly,** 413 S. Main St., a quirky 22-room, 7-level mansion constructed by a local interior decorator. Ceiling heights range from 6 ft. to 25 ft., and rooms include everything from the unique to the improbable—there's even a theater built

into the attic. (☎336-996-7922; www.kornersfolly.org. Open Th-Sa 10am-3pm, Su 1-5pm. $6, children $3.)

🛋 APPROACHING WINSTON-SALEM: 10 MILES

Get back on **Bus. 140,** and continue to **Exit 6** for downtown Winston-Salem.

WINSTON-SALEM

As its name suggests, Winston-Salem was originally two different towns. Salem was founded in 1766 by the Moravians, a Protestant sect from the present-day Czech Republic. One of America's most successful utopian communities, Salem was bolstered by religious fervor, dedication to education, and the production of crafts. Winston, meanwhile, rose to prominence as a center of tobacco production, home of famous tobacco mogul R.J. Reynolds. When the two towns merged in 1913, a dynamic, bustling city was born. Today, Winston-Salem has a variety of tourist-friendly services and attractions, though it's not the most thrilling town on the route.

VITAL STATS

Population: 231,543

Visitor Info: Winston-Salem Visitor Center, 200 Brookstown Ave. (☎336-728-4200 or 866-728-4200; www.visitwinstonsalem.com). Open daily 8:30am-5pm.

Internet Access: Winston-Salem Public Library, 660 W. 5th St., at Spring St. (☎336-727-2264). Open Sept.-May M-W 9am-9pm, Th-F 9am-6pm, Sa 9am-5pm, Su 1-5pm; June-Aug. M-W 9am-9pm, Th-F 9am-6pm, Sa 9am-5pm. Free.

Post Office: 1500 Patterson Ave. (☎336-721-6070). Open M-F 8:30am-5pm. **Postal Code:** 27101.

▣ GETTING AROUND

I-40 runs south of downtown, and splits into a high-speed bypass and **Bus. I-40,** which runs east-west just south of downtown. The downtown streets are numbered, and wide boulevards connect downtown to Winston-Salem's surrounding suburbs..

⊙ SIGHTS

█ REYNOLDA HOUSE AND GARDENS. Win-
ston-Salem is home to the **Reynolda House,** 2250 Reynolda Rd. One of the South's most famous houses. The Reynolda House was built by tobacco tycoon R.J. Reynolds and his visionary wife Katherine, who is credited with making the household completely self-sufficient and creating a working "village" on the grounds. Visitors can tour the house's lavish rooms and view its massive collection of American art. On Saturday nights in June and July, movies are screened on the lawn. (☎ 336-758-5150 or 888-663-1149; www.reynoldahouse.org. Open Tu-Sa 9:30am-4:30pm, Su 1:30-4:30pm; last entry 4pm. $10, seniors $9, students and children free. Movies June-July Sa 8pm. $5, students $3.) Located on the grounds of the Reynolda House, the **Reynolda Garden** is gorgeous during the spring and summer. The garden's many varieties of roses are particularly impressive, and the garden is one of the most beautiful spots in Winston-Salem. (☎ 336-758-5593. Open daily sunrise-sunset. Free.)

OLD SALEM VILLAGE. Old Salem Village takes visitors back in time to a restored Moravian village, outlining its history and traditions. The area stretches south from downtown and includes a visitors center, museums exhibiting the Moravian way of life, and a multitude of traditional Moravian homes and buildings, including cobbler and gunsmith shops. Tickets are pricey, but include admission to all of the museums and buildings, so plan on spending at least an afternoon here. (☎ 888-653-7253; www.oldsalem.org. Visitors center open M-Sa 9am-5:30pm, Su 12:30-5:30pm. Most attractions open M-Sa 9am-4:30pm, Su 1-4:30pm. $21, ages 6-16 $10.) Old Salem's **Frank L. Horton Museum Center** features a number of museums, as well as a very cool echo beneath the dome in the museum lobby. The **Toy Museum** displays toys spanning 1700 years. Don't be fooled by its name—this museum is geared toward adults and older children. All of the toys are delicate antiques housed in glass cases. (Open M-Sa 9:30am-3:30pm, Su 1:30-3:30pm. Free.) The most extensive museum in the Center is the **Museum of Early Southern Decorative Art (MESDA),** which showcases furnishings from around the Southeast, representing the period from 1690-1820. The rooms are set up entirely "ropes free" to recreate the full feel of Southern homes, and all of the furnishings are original, right down to the bricks in the fireplace. (Open M-Sa 9:30am-3:30pm, Su 1:30-3:30pm. Free 1hr. guided tours every 30min.; reservations required.)

OTHER SIGHTS. Winston-Salem is the birthplace of national doughnut company **Krispy Kreme,** and no visit to the city would be complete without stopping by the **Krispy Kreme Shop ❶,** 259 S. Stratford Rd., where you can watch the famous doughnuts being made fresh on-site. Don't expect any historical exhibits here; it's just fresh doughnuts and coffee. (☎ 336-724-2484. Doughnuts $0.69-0.89. Open M-Th and Su 6am-11pm, F-Sa 6am-midnight; drive-thru open M-Sa 6am-midnight, Su 6am-11pm. Cash only.) The **Winston Cup Museum,** 1335 Martin Luther King Jr. Dr., documents 20 years of NASCAR racing history with over 15 cars and various racing memorabilia. Race fans will enjoy it as a quick appetizer before reaching the comprehensive racing museum in Mooresville (see p. 716) later on the route. (☎ 336-724-4557. Open Tu-Sa 10am-5pm. $5, children $3.)

▧ FOOD

The **West End Cafe ❷,** 926 W. 4th St., is a laid-back local favorite that makes every kind of sandwich under the sun. Patrons line up for the curry chicken salad sandwich ($7), the Frosted Flakes-crusted brie over raspberry puree ($9), and other creative dishes. (☎ 336-723-4774. Salads $5.25-9. Burgers $5.25-6.75. Open M-F 11am-10pm, Sa noon-10pm. AmEx/D/MC/V.) The **Olive Tree ❶,** 5805 Stratford Rd., is just off I-40 and has inexpensive Greek specialties like chicken *souvlaki* and gyro wraps ($4.65). The honey-drenched baklava ($2) is delectable. (☎ 336-723-4224. Open daily 11am-9pm. Cash only.) The stylishly decorated **6th and Vine ❸,** 209 W. 6th St., offers salads ($6-8), panini ($7.50-9), and a rotating selection of entrees ($17-22). There is live music Tuesday through Thursday and sometimes Saturday. (☎ 336-725-5577; www.6thandvine.com. Open Tu-Sa 11am-last customer, Su 11am-2am. AmEx/D/MC/V.)

ACCOMMODATIONS

Winston-Salem is not hospitable to the budget traveler. The nearest campground is over 20 mi. north of the city, and there are few independently owned budget motels. There are cheap motels on the way into town at Exit 184 off I-40. On the northern side of the city, budget motels center around Rte. 52, just past Patterson Ave. The **Microtel Inn ❸**, 100 Capitol Lodging Court, between I-40 and Silas Creek Pkwy., is a great value with free local and long distance calls, clean rooms, and a pool. (☎336-659-1994 or 888-771-7171. Singles $52; doubles $55-65. AmEx/D/MC/V.) The **Innkeeper ❸**, 2113 Peters Creek Pkwy., is close to downtown and offers large rooms along with a pool, free Wi-Fi, and continental breakfast. (☎336-721-0062. Rooms from $50-60. AmEx/D/MC/V.) **Motel 6 ❷**, 3810 Patterson Ave., has some of the least expensive lodging in the city. Though a far from downtown, the clean rooms have A/C, HBO, pool access, and laundry facilities. (☎336-661-1588. Singles $50; doubles $55. AmEx/D/MC/V.)

NIGHTLIFE

Look for listings of local events in the free weekly newspaper *Go Triad* or in *Relish*, the Thursday entertainment supplement to the *Winston-Salem Journal*. On weekends from May through August, the city hosts three live music performance series of varying genres in the downtown area: **Alive After Five** every Thursday evening (Corpening Plaza, 100 W. 2nd St.), **Fourth Street Jazz and Blues** every Friday evening (W. 4th St.), and **Summer on Trade** every Saturday evening (6th and Trade St.). Check out www.winstonsalemevents.com for more info. You'll find quality live rock, roots, and reggae music at **Ziggy's**, 433 Baity St., off University Pkwy., near the Coliseum. (☎336-748-1064; www.ziggyrock.com. Beer from $2. Cover $5-25. Open Tu-Su 8pm-2am; live music starts around 9pm. MC/V.) Musicians also rock out at **The Garage**, 110 W. 7th St., at Trade St. Call ahead or check online for the acts of the night, since featured bands play New Grass, pop

punk, and everything in between. (☎336-777-1127; www.the-garage.ws. Beer from $2. Cover $5-15; under 21 $7-17. Open Th-Sa 7pm-2am, sometimes also W. Showtimes vary. MC/V.) **Speakeasy Jazz**, 410 W. 4th St. has live jazz playing most nights. (☎336-722-6555; www.speakeasyjazz.net. Cover some weekends and for big acts. Open M 11am-3pm, Tu-Th 11am-11pm, F 11am-2am, Sa 7pm-2am. MC/V.)

◪ APPROACHING STATESVILLE: 44 MILES
From Winston-Salem, take **I-40 W** to **Exit 150.** Head south on **Center St.** to downtown Statesville.

STATESVILLE. A small county seat, Statesville has a pair of nice restaurants which are good for a quick meal. **Carolina Bar-B-Q ❷**, 213 Salisbury Rd., has enormous white letters on its roof—you can't miss it. The tangy barbecue dinners ($7-8) come with hush puppies and a choice of two sides. (☎704-873-5585. Open M-Th 10:30am-8:30pm, F-Sa 10:30am-9pm. MC/V.) The **It Don't Matter Cafe ❶**, 110 Court St., is a basic diner that serves tasty breakfasts and lunches. (☎704-872-0015. Breakfast plates $2.50-4. Sandwiches $3-4. Open M-F 6:30am-3:30pm, Sa 8am-1pm. MC/V.)

◪ APPROACHING MOORESVILLE: 15 MILES
From Statesville, take **I-77 S** for 13 mi. to **Exit 36.**

MOORESVILLE
Home to numerous NASCAR race teams, NASCAR's training institute, and the Lowe's Motor Speedway, Mooresville lives up to its nickname as the "Race City USA." The **North Carolina Auto Racing Hall of Fame**, 119 Knob Hill Rd., has 35 race cars driven by NASCAR champions as well as exhibits and videos on NASCAR legends. (☎704-663-5331; www.ncarhof.com. Open M-Sa 9am-5pm, Su 12:30-4:30pm. $5, children $3.) Mooresville's **Lowe's Motor Speedway**, Exit 49 off I-85, hosts several major NASCAR events each year. (☎800-455-3267; www.gospeedway.com. NASCAR tickets $70-150; other races less expensive.) Between Mooresville and Charlotte, the **Carolina Raptor Center**, 6000 Sample Rd., is home to abandoned and injured birds of prey like falcons, owls, vultures, and bald eagles. (☎704-875-6521; www.carolinaraptorcenter.org. Bird pre-

1953: Chevrolet begins manufacturing the Corvette, an iconic American roadtrip image.

sentations Sa 11am, 1, 3pm; Su 1, 3pm. Open M-Sa 10am-5pm, Su noon-5pm. $5, seniors $4, students $3.) **Five Guys Burgers and Fries ❶**, 654 River Hwy., in Norman, has surprisingly good burgers ($4-5) and fries ($2-3)—fresh meat and healthy peanut oil ensure that you won't get a fast food hangover. (Take I-77 to Exit 36, and follow Rte. 150 W for 1 mi. ☎ 704-799-2500. Open daily 11am-10pm. AmEx/D/MC/V.)

⚑ APPROACHING CHARLOTTE: 25 MILES
Take **I-77 S** to **Exit 11.**

CHARLOTTE

Named in the mid-1700s after the wife of England's King George III, Charlotte is still referred to as the "Queen City." After a boy discovered a 17 lb. gold nugget near Charlotte in 1799, settlers flooded the region in the nation's first gold rush. Shortly thereafter, the first branch of the US Mint was established here in 1837. Now the biggest city in the Carolinas, Charlotte has expanded both outward and upward. For visitors, the city offers top-notch museums, ritzy clubs, and a wide variety of professional sports.

VITAL STATS

Population: 651,000

Visitor Info: Charlotte Visitors Center, 330 S. Tryon St. (☎800-231-4636; www.visitcharlotte.com.) Open M-F 8:30am-5pm, Sa 9am-3pm.

Internet Access: Public Library of Charlotte and Mecklenburg County, 310 N. Tryon St. (☎704-336-2572). Open M-Th 9am-9pm, F-Sa 9am-6pm, Su 1-6pm. Free.

Post Office: 201 N. McDowell St. (☎704-333-2542). Open M-F 7:30am-6pm, Sa 10am-1pm.
Postal Code: 28204.

▐ GETTING AROUND

The nucleus of Charlotte, the busy Uptown area, has numbered streets laid out perpendicular to named streets in a grid pattern. **Tryon St.**, which runs north-south, is the major crossroad. **I-77** crosses the city from north to south, providing access to Uptown, while **I-85** runs southwest-northeast, connecting Uptown to the UNC-Charlotte campus. Uptown is also accessible from **I-277**, which circles the city and is called the **John Belk Fwy.** to the south of Uptown and the **Brookshire Fwy.** to the north.

◉ SIGHTS

Charlotte has a number of museums, most of which are located in the Uptown area. The ▣**Levine Museum of the New South,** 200 E. 7th St., is a fantastic new museum that explores the history of Charlotte and the Carolina Piedmont area with outstanding interactive exhibits that will engage even the most museum-weary traveler. From a working cotton gin to a re-creation of a soda fountain that was occupied during the civil rights sit-ins, the Levine shows how the "New South" developed from the end of the Civil War to the present. (☎704-333-1887. Open Tu-Sa 10am-5pm, Su noon-5pm. $6; students, seniors, and ages 6-18 $5; under 6 free.) The **Mint Museum of Craft and Design,** 220 N. Tryon St., in Uptown, features contemporary work in glass, wood, metal, and textiles. (☎704-337-2000; www.mintmuseum.org. Open Tu-Sa 10am-5pm, Su noon-5pm. $6, college students and 62+ $5, ages 6-17 $3. Tu 10am-2pm free.) The **Mint Museum of Art,** 2730 Randolph Rd., about 2½ mi. southeast of downtown focuses on more traditional painting and ceramics. A single admission fee grants entry to both museums. (☎704-337-2000; www.mintmuseum.org. Open Tu 10am-10pm, W-Sa 10am-5pm, Su noon-5pm. $6, college students and 62+ $5, ages 6-17 $3. Tu 5-10pm. Free.) **Paramount Carowinds,** 14523 Carowinds Blvd., off I-77 is an enormous theme park with over 50 rides, roller coasters and live shows. Check the website for discounts. (☎704-588-2600 or 800-888-4386; www.carowinds.com. $50.)

🍴 FOOD

Two areas outside of Uptown offer attractive dining options at reasonable prices. **North Davidson (NoDa)**, around 36th St., houses a small artists' community in a historic neighborhood. South of the city center, the **Dilworth** neighborhood, along East and South Blvd., is lined with restaurants serving everything from authentic ethnic meals to pizza and pub fare.

☑ **Mert's Heart and Soul,** 214 N. College St. (☎704-342-4222; www.mertsuptown.com). Serves outstanding soul food, ranging from soft-shell crab to pork chops, in a dining room decorated with pictures of jazz legends. Meals come with delicious cornbread. Sandwiches $5-6. Entrees $8-12. Open M 11am-9pm, Tu-Th 11am-9:30pm, F 11am-11:30pm, Sa 9am-11:30pm, Su 9am-9:30pm. AmEx/D/MC/V. ❷

Cosmos Cafe, 300 N. College St. (☎704-372-3553; www.cosmoscafe.com), at E. 6th St. A hip spot with eccentric cuisine. The menu features everything from tapas ($6-9.50) to sushi and wood-fired pizzas ($8.75-10). The restaurant becomes a popular yuppie bar around 10:30pm. Swing by W nights for superb gourmet martinis at half price. M-Sa 2-for-1 tapas 5-7pm. Th free salsa lessons. Open M-F 11am-2am, Sa 5pm-2am. AmEx/D/MC/V. ❸

Fuel Pizza, 1501 Central Ave. (☎704-376-3835; www.therestaurantgroup.com). Excellent, New York-style pizza served in a converted gas station—thus the name. Slices $2-3. Pies $9-13. Open M-Th and Su 11am-10pm, F-Sa 11am-11pm. AmEx/MC/V. ❶

Talley's Green Grocery, 1408C E. Blvd. (☎704-334-9200; www.talleys.com), in Dilworth. This organic grocery store makes takeout sandwiches in the back. Sandwiches $8; served until 2pm. Open M-Sa 9am-9pm, Su 10am-7pm. AmEx/D/MC/V. ❷

ACCOMMODATIONS

There are several clusters of budget motels in the Charlotte area: on **Independence Blvd.** off the John Belk Freeway; off I-85 at **Sugar Creek Rd.** (Exit 41); off I-85 at **Exit 33** near the airport; and off I-77 at **Clanton St.** (Exit 7).

Best Value Inn, 3200 I-85 Service Rd. (☎704-398-3144 or 888-215-2378), off I-85 at Exit 33. A short drive from downtown, this inn has spacious, newly renovated rooms. Amenities include microfridge, outdoor pool access, free Wi-Fi, and continental breakfast. Rooms $44. AmEx/D/MC/V. ❷

The Continental Inn, 1100 W. Sugar Creek Rd. (☎704-597-8100), off I-85 at Exit 41. Free Wi-Fi, continental breakfast, and clean, basic rooms. Singles $42; doubles $55. AmEx/D/MC/V. ❷

McDowell Nature Preserve, 15222 York Rd. (☎704-583-1284; www.parkandrec.com). Go south on Tryon St. until it becomes York Rd. RV, tent, and primitive campsites in a tranquil spot. Office open Mar.-Nov. daily 7am-sunset; Dec.-Feb. F-Su 7am-sunset. Sites $9; rent-a-tent sites $38; RV sites $18. MC/V. ❶

ENTERTAINMENT

The latest expansion team to enter the NBA, the **Charlotte Bobcats,** is owned by Black Entertainment Television founder Robert Johnson. The Bobcats and Charlotte's WNBA team, the **Sting,** shoot hoops in the brand-new Charlotte Arena, 333 E. Trade St. (☎800-495-2295; www.newcharlottearena.com. Call or check website for box office hours.) Football fans can catch an NFL game when the **Carolina Panthers** play in Bank of America Stadium, 800 S. Mint St. (☎704-522-6500; www.carolinapanthers.com. Stadium tours $4, 55+ $3, ages 5-15 $2. Tickets $45-70.) Ten miles south, the Charlotte **Knights** play AAA Minor League baseball at **Knights Castle,** off I-77 S at Exit 88. (☎704-364-6637; www.charlotteknights.com. Box office open M-F 10am-5pm; game days 10am-game time. Tickets $6-10.) If sports aren't your thing, have a good laugh at **The Comedy Zone,** 516 N. College St. (☎704-348-4242; www.thecomedyzone.net. 18+. Call for prices and showtimes.)

NIGHTLIFE

To check out nightlife listings, grab a free copy of *Creative Loafing* in one of Charlotte's shops or restaurants, visit www.charlotte.creativeloafing.com, or look over the *Charlotte Observer.* Many of Charlotte's hippest clubs can be found **Uptown,** especially on **College St.**

Amos's Southend, 1423 S. Tryon St. (☎704-377-6874; www.amossouthend.com). Features live rock bands, pool, and foosball. Acts often cover rock's greats, from Led Zeppelin and Pink Floyd to Guns N' Roses and Journey. Call for showtimes, cover, and age restrictions. AmEx/D/MC/V.

The Evening Muse, 3227 N. Davidson St. (☎704-377-6874; www.theeveningmuse.com), in NoDa. A laid-back venue for a wide variety of musical acts, from acoustic and jazz to rock. Cover around $5. Open W-Th 6pm-midnight, F-Sa 6pm-2am. MC/V.

The Breakfast Club, 225 N. Caldwell St. (☎704-374-1982; www.that80sclub.com), downtown. 3 levels and an outdoor patio, all with an 80s theme. Th $2 beer and 80s music. F $1 domestics, $2 imports, and $3 mixed drinks. Open Th-Sa 8:30pm-2am. MC/V.

Thomas Street Tavern, 1218 Thomas Ave. (☎704-376-1622). Follow E. 10th St. out of Uptown; after E. 10th becomes Central Ave., turn right on Thomas Ave. A local favorite for its pool tables, extensive beer menu, and menu that ranges from pub fare to gourmet. Sandwiches $5-7. Pizzas $6-8. Open M-Sa 11am-2am, Su noon-2am. MC/V.

⚅ APPROACHING GASTONIA: 27 MILES
From Charlotte, take **I-85 S** to **Exit 10.**

GASTONIA. Gastonia is home to the **World's Largest American Flag,** 4025 W. Franklin St. (Rte. 219/74), which is flown by the United Veterans of America. Measuring 65 ft. by 114 ft., each of the flag's stripes is five feet high. The flag is sometimes on loan for special events, so call ahead for details. (☎704-868-4674; www.united-veteransofamerica.net. Free.) Transportation enthusiasts will enjoy the **C. Grier Beam Truck Museum,** 111 N. Mountain St., in Cherryville, which has an extensive display of trucks dating back to 1927. (☎704-435-3072; www.beamtruckmuseum.com. Open Th 10am-3pm, F 10am-5pm, Sa 10am-3pm. Free.)

⚅ APPROACHING GAFFNEY: 27 MILES
From Gastonia, take **I-85 S** across the South Carolina border to **Exit 96.** Take advantage of South Carolina's lower taxes on gasoline, and fill up your tank before returning to North Carolina, where taxes push prices $0.10-0.20 higher per gallon.

GAFFNEY. Gaffney celebrates South Carolina's delicious peaches with a brightly-colored town water tank called the **Peachoid.** You can see it from the off-ramp at Exit 96. Gaffney is also close to the **Cowpens National Battlefield,** off Rte. 11 (Cherokee Scenic Hwy.). The site of a decisive Revolutionary War battle between American troops commanded by General Morgan and British forces under General Cornwallis, Cowpens has a 3 mi. loop road around the battlefield, a visitors center, and a 1½ mi. walking trail that snakes through the battlefields. (☎864-461-2828, www.nps.gov/cowp. Open daily 9am-5pm. Free.)

⚅ APPROACHING SPARTANBURG: 20 MILES
From Gaffney, follow **I-85 S** and take **Exit 77** to **I-585 S.** From I-585, take **Exit 5A** to downtown Spartanburg.

SPARTANBURG

Ten miles west of downtown Spartanburg, the **BMW Zentrum** is home to the manufacturing plant that makes BMW's ultra-fast Z3 roadster. The visitors center is home to a number of famous BMW cars, including one driven by James Bond and another with a paint job by Andy Warhol. Tours of the actual plant ($5) require advance reservation. (Take Exit 60 off I-85. ☎888-868-7269; www.bmwzentrum.com. Under 12 and open-toed shoes prohibited. Open Tu-Sa 9:30am-5:30pm. Free.) The **Beacon Drive-In ❶,** 255 John B. White, Sr. Blvd. (previously Reidville Rd.) is one of the last two drive-in restaurants in the US to use curb hops. Old-fashioned fast food is delivered to your car window, though you can also eat inside alongside patrons devouring burgers and fried chicken. (☎864-585-9387. Open M-Sa 6:30am-9:30pm. Cash only.) At the **Sandwich Factory ❶,** 137 W. Main St., visitors can find lighter alternatives to fast food. Breakfast sandwiches are $2-3, while delicious wraps, sandwiches, and salads are $4-7. (☎864-585-8506. Open M-Tu 7am-4pm, W-F 7am-9pm, Sa 8am-9pm. AmEx/D/MC/V.) **Pine Ridge Campground ❶,** 199 Pineridge Campground Rd., in Roebuck, has inexpensive, wooded tent sites with hot showers, laundry facilities, Wi-Fi ($2 per day), and a swimming pool. (Take Exit 28 off I-26. ☎864-576-0302 or

The Palmetto State
SOUTH CAROLINA
Welcomes You!

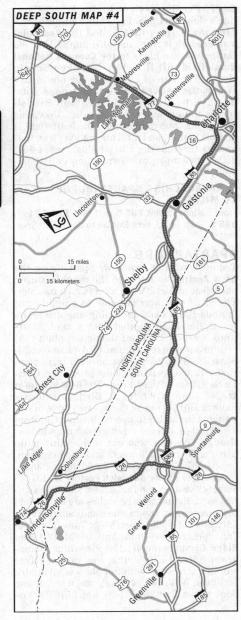

DEEP SOUTH MAP #4

866-576-0302;   www.pineridgecamp-ground.com. Sites $16, with water and electricity $19; cabins $25-35. MC/V.)

⛺ APPROACHING TRYON: 27 MILES
Take **Rte. 176 W** to Tryon. The road winds into the Blue Ridge Mountains and has some curvy stretches that are best avoided at night and in wet weather.

The Tar Heel State
NORTH CAROLINA
Welcomes You!

TRYON. Tryon's downtown is small but well-traveled by tourists who flock to the area for its picturesque views, cool temperatures, and lovely forests. Four miles past downtown, off Rte. 176, ◪**Pearson's Falls** is a nature preserve with a short trail to a stunning 60 ft. waterfall. Bring a camera for pictures, and watch the trailside for rare wildflowers. (☎828-749-3031. Open Mar.-Oct. Tu-Sa 10am-6pm, Su noon-6pm; Nov.-Feb. Tu-Sa 10am-5pm, Su noon-5pm. $3, ages 6-12 $2.)

⛺ APPROACHING SALUDA: 8 MILES
Take **Rte. 176 W** to Saluda. The road is very steep and has switchbacks and tight turns; exercise caution.

SALUDA. Once an old railway town, Saluda is now an upscale vacation destination with antique shops, boutiques, and B&Bs clustering around its downtown area. The **Purple Onion Cafe and Coffeehouse ②**, 16 Main St., has an inviting patio and a good selection of sandwiches ($6-8) and pizzas (from $7), in addition to fresh pastries. (☎828-749-1179. Th and Sa live music 7:30pm. Open daily 11am-3pm and 5-9pm. MC/V.) The **Wildflower Bakery ①**, 175 E. Main St., serves hearty breakfasts like omelettes and quiches, as well as muffins and sticky buns. (☎828-749-9224. Breakfast $3-4. Open W-Sa 8am-3pm, Su 10am-2pm. MC/V.)

⛺ APPROACHING HENDERSONVILLE: 8 MILES
Take **Rte. 176 W** to Hendersonville.

HENDERSONVILLE. A medium-sized vacation town in the Blue Ridge Mountains, Hendersonville is a blander version of Asheville that caters to families and retired couples. The **Hendersonville Visitors Center,** 201 S. Main St., has information about lodging and attractions throughout the region. (☎800-828-4224; www.historichendersonville.org. Open daily 9am-5pm.) Three miles west of downtown, **Jump Off Rock** is an ominously-named park at the end of Laurel Park Hwy. with a phenomenal view of the Blue Ridge Mountains. (Open daily sunrise-sunset. Free.) The **Western North Carolina Air Museum,** on Brooklyn Ave., off Rte. 176, has a collection of vintage airplanes on display from the "golden age of aviation" in the 1930s and 40s. (☎828-698-2482. Open Apr.-Oct. W noon-6pm, Sa 10am-6pm, Su noon-6pm; Nov.-Mar. W and Sa-Su noon-5pm. Free.)

⚑ APPROACHING ASHEVILLE: 25 MILES

Follow **I-26 W** for 19 mi., and take the **I-240 E exit** to **Asheville/US-70/UNC Asheville.** Follow I-240 E for 5 mi. to **Exit 3B** for Asheville.

VITAL STATS

Population: 70,400

Visitor Info: Chamber of Commerce and Visitor Center, 151 Haywood St., (☎828-258-6101 or 800-257-1300; www.exploreasheville.com). Take Exit 4C off I-240. Open M-F 8:30am-5:30pm, Sa-Su 9am-5pm.

Internet Access: Pack Memorial Library, 67 Haywood St. (☎828-255-5203.) Open June-Aug. M-Th 10am-8pm, F 10am-6pm, Sa 10am-5pm; Sept.-May M-Th 10am-8pm, F 10am-6pm, Sa 10am-5pm, Su 2-5pm. Free.

Parking: Wall St. Garage, off Otis St. ($0.75 per hr., $6 per day.)

Post Office: 33 Coxe Ave. (☎828-271-6429), off Patton Ave. Open M-F 7:30am-5:30pm, Sa 9am-1pm.

Postal Code: 28802.

ASHEVILLE

Hazy blue mountains, deep valleys, and spectacular waterfalls form the impressive backdrop of this small city. Once a popular retreat for the well-to-do, Asheville hosted enough Carnegies, Vanderbilts, and Mellons to fill a 1920s edition of *Who's Who on the Atlantic Seaboard.* The Great Depression devastated Asheville's high-end tourist industry, but during the past half-century, Asheville has blossomed into a bohemian haven. With funky restaurants, counter-culture bookstores, and lively nightlife, Asheville is a one-of-a-kind city that you won't want to leave.

▣ GETTING AROUND

I-40 runs east-west south of Asheville, and the **I-240** spur connects downtown Asheville to I-40 and **I-26.** Most streets in downtown Asheville are one-way. **Haywood Rd.** runs west across the French Broad River to Asheville's West End. **Biltmore Ave.** runs south from downtown to the Biltmore Estate and I-40.s

◉ SIGHTS

Unlike the sprawling mega-cities of Charlotte and Winston-Salem, Asheville's downtown is compact and fun to walk. Be sure to check out the varied skyline as you stroll; the city is a mix of bland glass-walled towers and glamorous Art Deco buildings from the 1920s. Highlights include City Hall, at the corner of Davidson and Marjorie St., and the tall, slender Jackson building, in Pack Sq. at Market St.

BILTMORE ESTATE. George Vanderbilt's palatial Biltmore Estate was constructed in the 1890s and is the largest private home in America. A self-guided tour of the house and grounds can take all day; try to arrive early. The entrance fee includes a complimentary wine tasting at the on-site winery. *(1 Approach Rd. ☎828-225-1333 or 800-543-2961; www.biltmore.com. Estate open daily Apr.-Dec. 8:30am-5pm; Jan.-Mar. 9am-4pm. Winery open daily Apr.-Dec. 11am-7pm; Jan.-Mar. noon-6pm. M-F $38-42, Sa-Su $40-46; ages 10-16 $18-20/$20-22. Audio tour $7. Rooftop tours, guided tours, and behind-the-scenes tours $15. Carriage rides $35. Trail rides $50.)*

OTHER SIGHTS. The **Asheville Art Museum,** 2 S. Pack Sq., displays rotating selections of 20th-century American artwork in an Italian Renaissance-style building. *(☎828-253-3227; www.ashevilleart.org. Open Tu-Th and Sa 10am-5pm, F 10am-8pm, Su 1-5pm. $6; students, seniors, and ages 4-15 $5.)* The **Thomas Wolfe Memorial,** 52

N. Market St., between Woodfin and Walnut St., celebrates one of the early 20th century's most influential American authors with a museum and a re-creation of his "old Kentucky home." (☎828-253-8304; www.wolfememorial.com. Open Apr.-Oct. Tu-Sa 9am-5pm, Su 1-5pm; Nov.-Mar. Tu-Sa 10am-4pm, Su 1-4pm. 30min. tours every hr. on the half-hr. $1, students $0.50.) Asheville's **Malaprops Bookstore,** 55 Haywood St., is one of the largest independent bookstores in the Southeast. With a broad selection of books, a cafe, and Internet access ($3 per 20min.), Malaprops rewards both book-lovers and casual browsers. (☎828-254-6734 or 800-441-9829; www.malaprops.com. Open M-Th 8am-9pm, F-Sa 8am-10pm, Su 8am-7pm.) Malaprops also runs a used bookstore and newsstand, **Downtown Books and News,** 67 N. Lexington Ave. (Open M-Th and Su 8am-6pm, F-Sa 8am-8pm.)

> **PHOTO OP.** Authors O. Henry (William Sidney Porter) and Thomas Wolfe are buried in the **Riverside Cemetery** on Birch St.

OUTDOORS. If the Biltmore is too much for your wallet to handle, enjoy the free **Botanical Gardens,** 151 W.T. Weaver Blvd., which contains plants native to the Carolina Mountains. The best time to visit is when the wildflowers are blooming, from April to mid-May. (☎828-252-5190; www.ashevillebotanicalgardens.org. Open daily sunrise-sunset.) Twenty-five miles southeast of Asheville on U.S. 64/74A, the scenic setting for *The Last of the Mohicans* rises up almost ½ mi. in **Chimney Rock Park.** After driving to the base of the Chimney, take the 26-story elevator to the top or walk up for a 75 mi. view. Extend your time on the mountaintop with one of five hikes that range in length from ½ to 1½ mi., some of which lead to breathtaking waterfalls. (☎828-625-9611 or 800-277-9611; www.chimneyrockpark.com. Ticket office open daily Apr.-Oct. 8:30am-5:30pm; Nov.-Mar. 8:30am-4:30pm. Park open daily Apr.-Oct. 8:30am-7pm; Nov.-Mar. 8:30am-6pm. $14, ages 6-15 $6.) Two companies arrange whitewater rafting expeditions on the French Broad River. **Blue Ridge Rafting,** in Hot Springs, and **French Broad Rafting Expeditions,** in Marshall, both offer a variety of trips at prices that depend on length and difficulty. (Blue Ridge Rafting: ☎800-303-7238; www.blueridgerafting.com.

French Broad Rafting Expeditions: ☎800-570-7238; www.frenchbroadrafting.com. Trips from $40.)

ᗌ FOOD

Laughing Seed Cafe, 40 Wall St. (☎828-252-3445). The lineup of vegetarian dishes tastes even better when served on the sunny patio; try the Curried Eggplant Napoleon. Sandwiches $7-8.50. Open M and W-Th 11:30am-9pm, F-Sa 11:30am-10pm, Su 10am-9pm. AmEx/D/MC/V. ❸

Tupelo Honey Cafe, 12 College St. (☎828-255-4404). Southern home cooking with creative twists. Sandwiches $5-8. Entrees $6-15. Open Tu-Th 9am-3pm and 5:30-10pm, F-Sa 9am-3pm and 5:30pm-midnight, Su 9am-3pm. AmEx/MC/V. ❸

Anntony's Caribbean Cafe, 1 Page Ave. Ste. 129, (☎828-255-9620), in the Historic Grove Arcade Building. Before enjoying Jamaican chicken, beef empanadas, or the roast-pork sandwich, start with plantain chips and salsa. Sandwiches $7-10. Restaurant open M-F 11:30am-9pm, Sa 11:30am-10pm, Su noon-4pm. Coffee bar open M-F 7:30am-9pm, Sa 8am-10pm, Su 8:30am-4pm. AmEx/D/MC/V. ❸

Sunny Point Cafe and Bakery, 626 Haywood Rd. (☎828-252-0055). A popular breakfast and brunch destination. Their breakfast sandwich ($7) and huevos rancheros ($7.50) are both excellent. Lunch sandwiches $7-8. Open M and Su 8:30am-2:30pm, Tu-Sa 8:30am-9:30pm. MC/V. ❷

ᐞ ACCOMMODATIONS

Bon Paul and Sharky's Hostel, 816 Haywood Rd. A real hosteler's hostel, featuring clean rooms and a friendly, relaxed atmosphere. A huge TV, extensive DVD collection, outdoor hot tub, foosball table, communal kitchen, free lockers, linens, free Wi-Fi, oparking, bicycles, and free bus station and airport pickup are just some of the perks. (☎828-350-9929; www.bonpaulandsharkys.com. Reception daily 10am-1pm and 5-10pm. Check-in 24hr. Dorms M-Th and Su $20, F-Sa $23; private rooms $50. Cash only. ❶

Arthaus Hostel, 16 Ravenscroft Rd. (☎828-225-3278; www.ashevillehostel.com). A funky, new-age hostel located downtown and offering brightly painted, spotless rooms and a communal kitchen. Laundry $5. Free Wi-Fi. Linens included. Call to arrange check-in. Restricted access noon-4pm. Dorms $20; private rooms $50-65. MC/V. ❶

Days Inn, 201 Tunnel Rd. (☎828-252-4000), in downtown Asheville. Huge rooms with A/C, cable, microwaves, refrigerators, and coffeemakers, as well as a pool, Internet access, and breakfast. Rooms M-Th and Su $60-70; F-Sa $70-80. AmEx/D/DC/MC/V. ❸

Powhatan Lake Campground ❶, 375 Wesley Branch Rd. (☎828-670-5627, reservations 877-444-6777), 12 mi. southwest of Asheville off Rte. 191. In the Pisgah National Forest, with wooded sites on a trout lake open for swimming and fishing. Sites fill quickly in summer; call for reservations. Some sites have hookups. Dump station available. Open Apr.-Oct. Gates close 10pm. Sites $17-20. Cash or check only. ❶

🎵 ENTERTAINMENT

The downtown area, especially the southeast end around the intersection of Broadway and College St., is a hot spot for music and movies. Indie flicks play at the **Fine Arts Theatre**, 36 Biltmore Ave. (☎828-232-1536; www.fineartstheatre.com. Ticket sales begin 30min. before showtimes. Box office open daily from 12:30pm. Tickets $7.50, seniors and matinees $5.50.) **Shakespeare in Montford Park,** at the Hazel Robinson Amphitheater, produces one play each summer. (☎828-254-4540; www.montfordparkplayers.org. June-Aug. F-Su 7:30pm. Free.) **Asheville Community Theatre,**

at 35 E. Walnut St., stages a variety of classic and contemporary plays and musicals throughout the year. (☎828-294-1320. Box office open M-F noon-4pm. Most shows F-Sa 8pm, Su 2:30pm. Tickets $20, students $10.) The **Asheville Tourists,** a Minor League baseball team, plays at McCormick Field from April to September. (☎828-258-0428; www.theashevilletourists.com. Tickets $7; children, seniors, and military $6.)

🍸 NIGHTLIFE

The free weekly paper *Mountain Xpress* and *Community Connections*, a free gay publication, have arts, events, and dining listings. The **Asheville Pizza and Brewing Company,** 675 Merrimon Ave., shows second-run movies for $2 and serves pizza (12 in. $10.50-11.50) and home-brewed beer. (☎828-254-1281; www.ashevillepizza.com. Th $2.50 pints. Open daily 11am-midnight. AmEx/MC/V.) **Jack of the Wood,** 95 Patton Ave., heats up at night with live celtic, bluegrass, and old-time mountain music. Fill up on corned beef and cabbage ($12) while enjoying the soundtrack. (☎828-252-5445; www.jackofthewood.com. F-Sa live music. M Trivia night 8pm. 21+ after 9pm. Cover F-Sa $5-7. Open M-F 4pm-2am, Sa noon-2am, Su 3pm-2am. AmEx/D/MC/V.) In West Asheville, the **Westville Pub,** 777 Haywood Rd., is a lively neighborhood bar with good food, locally brewed beers on tap, and live music. (☎828-225-9782. Pints $2-3.50. Nightly live music 10pm. Open

A MINOR LEAGUE TANTRUM

Asheville may have a reputation as a laid-back mountain town, but the manager of their Minor League baseball team was anything but laid-back when a call didn't go his way in June 2006. When a player on the Asheville Tourists was called out at second base, the manager of the Tourists, Joe Mikulik, launched into a bizarre tirade that caught the attention of the national media and earned him brief celebrity status. Even when Mikulik was unceremoniously tossed from the game for arguing with the second base umpire, the irate coach refused to back down. He sarcastically reenacted the previous play by sliding into second base in slow motion, and then yanked the base out of the infield and carried it back to his dugout. He then emerged from the dugout with a water bottle, and after screaming at the home plate umpire, doused home plate with water and dirt and spiked the water bottle on the soupy mess in triumph. Mikulik tossed second base back on the field and walked out of the ballpark to a chorus of boos as the stadium played "Hit the Road, Jack" over the loudspeakers. As a consequence of his shenanigans, the league suspended him for seven games and fined him $1000. Perhaps to his chagrin, the team won five out of seven games during his absence.

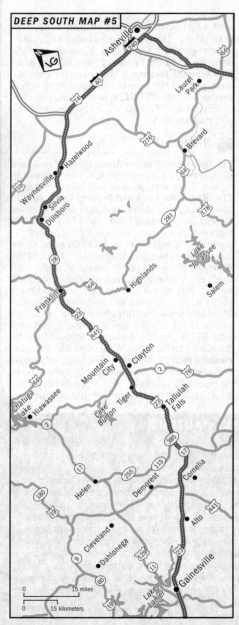

DEEP SOUTH MAP #5

DEEP SOUTH

daily noon-2am. Kitchen closes M-Th and Su 11pm, F-Sa 1am. MC/V.)

APPROACHING WAYNESVILLE: 26 MILES

From Asheville, take **Rte. 19/23 S** (which becomes **Rte. 23 S/74 W**) to **Exit 102.** Follow **Rte. 276 E** for 2 mi. to Waynesville.

WAYNESVILLE. A quiet but pretty mountain town, Waynesville has a number of charming coffee shops, boutiques, and bookstores. **Whitewater of Waynesville** runs tubing and kayaking trips on Richland Creek. (☎828-454-9565; www.whitewater-waynesville.com. Tubing trips $7-9; kayaking trips $20-45. Call for trip times and lengths.) One of the best places to eat in Waynesville is the **Whitman's Bakery and Sandwich Shop ❶,** 18 N. Main St., which has fresh pastries and sandwiches. (☎828-456-8271. Bakery open Tu-Sa 6am-5pm. Sandwich shop open Tu-Sa 11am-3pm. MC/V.)

APPROACHING FRANKLIN: 41 MILES

Take **Rte. 23/74 S** for 19 mi. Continue on **Rte. 23/441 S,** and follow signs to Franklin on Rte. 441 S.

FRANKLIN

Franklin has two worthwhile museums in its tiny, hilltop downtown. The **Scottish Tartan Museum and Heritage Center,** 86 E. Main St., has exhibits on Scottish history, tartan weaving, and the interaction between Scottish settlers and Cherokee Native Americans in colonial North Carolina. The museum's mannequins are a bit odd-looking, but the collection of over 500 family and clan tartans is impressive. (☎828-524-7472; www.scottishtartans.org. Open M-Sa 10am-5pm. $1, ages 10 and under free.) Just steps from Franklin's town center, the old county jail has been converted into the **Franklin Gem and Mineral Museum,** 25 Phillips St., which displays an extensive collection of gems, minerals, fossils, and Native American artifacts found in the region. Upstairs, you can walk inside a jail cell. (☎828-369-7831; www.fgmm.org. Open M-F noon-4pm, Sa 11am-3pm. Free.) The **Frog and Owl Mountain Bistro ❹,** 46 E. Main St., downtown, prepares critically acclaimed gourmet meals. The lunch entrees ($9-11) are delicious and significantly cheaper than dinner entrees. (☎828-349-4112.

Dinner entrees $12-25. Open daily 11am-3pm and 5:30pm-9pm. AmEx/MC/V.)

⚲ APPROACHING DILLARD: 30 MILES

From Franklin, take **Rte. 64/28 E**, and **Rte. 106 W** to **Rte. 23/441/15.** Turn left onto Rte. 23/441 S to reach Dillard, the first stop in Georgia. This route winds through a forest and has breathtaking views of a number of waterfalls. It also has steep grades and lots of tight switchback turns, so drive carefully.

The Peach State GEORGIA *Welcomes You!*

DILLARD. The **Cupboard Cafe ❸**, 7388 Hwy. 441, has a cozy dining room and a spacious covered porch with rocking chairs. The menu ranges from moderately priced comfort food to gourmet selections like roast duck. (☎706-746-5700. Open M-Th 7am-8:30pm, F-Sa 7am-9pm. MC/V.) One strip mall over from the cafe, the **Mountain Valley Inn ❸**, 13 Royalty Ln., has clean, spacious rooms and an outdoor pool. (☎706-743-5373; www.mountainvalleyinndillard.com. Rooms M-F $49, Sa-Su $65. MC/V.)

⚲ APPROACHING MOUNTAIN CITY: 4 MILES

Take **Rte. 23/441 S** to Mountain City.

MOUNTAIN CITY. The tiny town of Mountain City is home to **Foxfire**, 200 Foxfire Ln., a reconstruction of an early 1800s Appalachian mountain town. If your understanding of Appalachia is based on the movie *Deliverance*, you'll be surprised by the Foxfire Center's presentation of the richness of Appalachian culture. The gift shop has an impressive collection of books on Appalachian history and issues of *Foxfire* magazine, a student-run publication about Appalachian culture. (Turn right at Cross St., then take a left onto Foxfire Ln. ☎706-746-5828; www.foxfire.org. Self-guided tours $5, under 11 free. Call in advance for guided tours. Open M-Sa 8:30am-4:30pm.) **Black Rock Mountain State Park ❶**, Black Rock Mtn. Hwy., is Georgia's highest state park, located atop the Eastern

Continental Divide. The park has numerous scenic overlooks, 10 mi. of hiking trails, and campsites. (Follow signs from Rte. 23/411. ☎706-746-2141. Park office open daily 9am-5pm. Backcountry sites $3; tent sites $10; RV sites with water and electricity $19-21. MC/V.)

⚲ APPROACHING CLAYTON: 3 MILES

From Mountain City, take **Rte. 23/441 S** until you reach Clayton.

CLAYTON. Clayton has a number of motels and restaurants a short drive from Black Mountain and Tallulah State Parks. The **Rabun County Visitors Center**, 232 Hwy. 441 N, has maps, information on local hotels and attractions, free Internet access, and coupon books for Georgia hotels. (☎706-782-4812; www.gamountains.com. Open M-F 9am-5:30pm, Sa 10am-4pm.) Downtown Clayton has a number of touristy gift shops and antiques stores, but **Virtually Southern Books**, 108 N. Main St., is a small but very good independent bookstore. (☎706-212-3320; www.virtuallysouthern.com. Open W-Su 10am-5pm.) In addition to the chain restaurants along Rte. 441, the **Clayton Cafe ❶**, 50 N. Main St., has breakfast plates and Southern-style lunches. (☎706-782-5438. Open M-Th 6:30am-2pm and 5-8pm, F-Sa 6:30am-2pm. Cash only.)

⚲ APPROACHING TALLULAH FALLS: 12 MILES

Follow **Rte. 23/441 S** to Tallulah Falls.

TALLULAH FALLS. The primary attraction in Tallulah Falls is **Tallulah Gorge State Park**, which surrounds a massive 1000 ft. deep gorge. The park has 20 mi. of hiking trails, campsites, and a day-use area on Tallulah Falls Lake with swimming and picnic areas. Visitors can hike to overlooks, walk across a suspension bridge 80 ft. above the gorge floor, or hike down into the gorge. (☎706-754-7970. Visitors center open daily 8am-5pm. Park open daily 8am-sunset.) For a free view, continue south on Rte. 23/441, and turn left onto Old Hwy. 441. The **Tallulah Point Overlook Store**, 1 mi. down on Old Hwy. 441, has a free viewing platform and an exhibit about the Great Wallenda, the tightrope artist who crossed the gorge on a tightrope. (☎706-754-4318. Open daily 9am-5pm.)

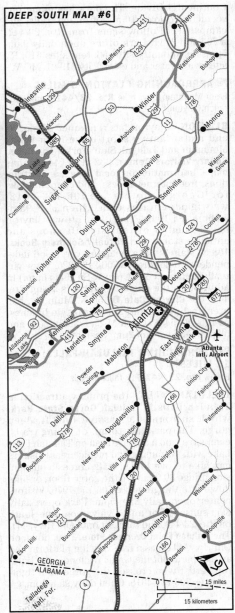

DEEP SOUTH MAP #6

DEEP SOUTH

GEORGIA
ALABAMA

Talladega
Natl. For.

0   15 miles

0   15 kilometers

APPROACHING GAINESVILLE: 43 MILES
Take **Rte. 23/441 S** for 42 mi., continuing on **Rte. 23** when 23 and 441 split. Take **Exit 24** to Gainesville.

GAINESVILLE. If you're planning to stop before you get to Atlanta, you can take advantage of Gainesville's few worthwhile restaurants and discount hotels. **2 Dog Cafe ❷**, 109 Bradford St., downtown, lives up to its claim to be a "rustic Euro soul food" restaurant. The menu includes reubens, creative pizzas, quesadillas, and vegetarian sandwiches. (☎770-287-8384. Lunch entrees $7-8. Dinner entrees $8-9. Open M-W 10:30am-2:30pm, Th-F 10:30am-2:30pm and 5pm-10pm, Sa 11am-4pm and 5-10pm. AmEx/D/MC/V.) **America's Best Value Inn ❷**, 809 Jesse Jewel Pkwy., has clean rooms and pool access. (☎770-534-0303. Breakfast included. Rooms $45-55. AmEx/D/MC/V.)

APPROACHING ATLANTA: 48 MILES
From Gainesville, take **I-985 S** (which merges with **I-85 S**) to downtown Atlanta.

ATLANTA

An increasingly popular destination for recent college grads wary of fast-paced cities, Atlanta is cosmopolitan with a smile. Northerners, Californians, the third-largest gay population in the US, and a host of ethnic groups have diversified this unofficial capital of the South, tempering its distinctly Dixie feel. An economic powerhouse, Atlanta houses 400 of the Fortune 500 companies, including the headquarters of Coca-Cola, UPS, and CNN. Nineteen colleges, including Georgia Tech, Morehouse College, Spelman College, and Emory University, also call "Hotlanta" home. The city is equally blessed with hidden gems; touring Atlanta's streets reveals an endless number of delightful restaurants and beautiful old houses.

GETTING AROUND

Atlanta sprawls across 10 counties in the northwest quadrant of the state at the junctures of **I-75, I-85** (the city "thruway"), and **I-20. I-285** (the "perimeter") circumscribes the city. Maneuvering around Atlanta's main thoroughfares, which are arranged much like the spokes of a wheel, challenges even the most experienced native. **Peachtree St.** (one of over 100 streets bearing that name in Atlanta), is a major north-south road; **Spring St.,** which runs only south, and **Piedmont Ave.,** which runs only north, are parallel to Peachtree St. On the eastern edge, **Moreland Ave.** traverses the length of the city, through Virginia Highland, Little Five Points (L5P), and East Atlanta. **Ponce de Leon Ave.** is the primary east-west road and takes travelers to most major destinations (or intersects with a street that does). To the south of "Ponce" runs **North Ave.,** another major east-west thoroughfare.

VITAL STATS

Population: 5,100,000

Visitor Info: Underground Atlanta Welcome Center, 65 Upper Alabama St. (☎404-577-2148), on the upper level of Underground Atlanta. MARTA: Five Points. Open M-Sa 10am-6pm, Su noon-6pm.

Internet Access: Central Library, 1 Margaret Mitchell Sq. (☎404-730-1700). Open M-Th 9am-9pm, F-Sa 9am-6pm, Su 2-6pm. Free.

Parking: Parking lots cluster around the **Five Points MARTA station** downtown and typically charge $10-15 per day. The parking lot at **541 Peachtree St.** charges $3 for all-day parking.

Post Office: Phoenix Station Post Office (☎524-2960), at the corner of Forsyth and Marietta St., 1 block from MARTA: Five Points. Open M-F 9am-5pm. **Postal Code:** 30303.

DID YOU KNOW? A law was recently passed which bans any further streets from being named "Peachtree" within Atlanta city limits.

Downtown is home to **Centennial Olympic Park** as well as Atlanta's major sports and concert venues. Directly southwest of downtown, the **West End** is the city's oldest historic quarter. From Five Points, head northeast to **Midtown,** from Ponce de Leon Ave. to 17th St., for museums and **Piedmont Park.** East of Five Points at Euclid and Moreland Ave., the **Little Five Points (L5P)** district is a local haven for artists and youth subculture. North of L5P, **Vir-**

ginia Highland, a trendy neighborhood east of Midtown and Piedmont Park, attracts yuppies and college kids. The **Buckhead** area, north of Midtown on Peachtree St., greets both Atlanta's professionals and rappers, housing designer shops and dance clubs.

Navigating Atlanta requires a full arsenal of transportation strategies. Midtown and downtown attractions are best explored using the **Metropolitan Atlanta Rapid Transit Authority,** or **MARTA.** (☎404-848-4711. Trains run daily 5am-1am; bus hours vary. $1.75; weekly pass $13.) The outlying areas of Buckhead, Virginia Highlands, and Little Five Points (L5P) are easiest to get to by car; once you're there, the restaurant- and bar-lined streets encourage walking.

While recent efforts to beef up police presence in high-risk areas of the city are having an effect, travelers—especially women—should exercise caution in the area south of Freedom Pkwy. and in the West End. Additionally, be aware that panhandlers throughout the city can be quite verbally aggressive.

SIGHTS

SWEET AUBURN DISTRICT

MARTIN LUTHER KING, JR. The most moving sights in the city run along Auburn Ave. in Sweet Auburn. The Reverend Martin Luther King, Jr.'s birthplace, church, and grave are all part of the 23-acre ◼**Martin Luther King, Jr. National Historic Site.** Leave your car in the parking lot at the corner of Jackson St. and John Wesley Dobbs Ave., and start your tour of the site at the visitors center, which houses poignant displays of photographs, videos, and quotations focused on King's life and the African-American struggle for civil rights. *(450 Auburn Ave. NE. MARTA: King Memorial. ☎404-331-5190; www.nps.gov/malu. Open daily June-Aug. 9am-6pm; Sept.-May 9am-5pm. Free.)* The center also gives tours of the birth home of MLK. *(501 Auburn Ave. Tours June-Aug. every 30min.; Sept.-May every hr. Arrive early. Free.)* Across the street from the visitors center stands **Ebenezer Baptist Church,** where King gave his first sermon at age

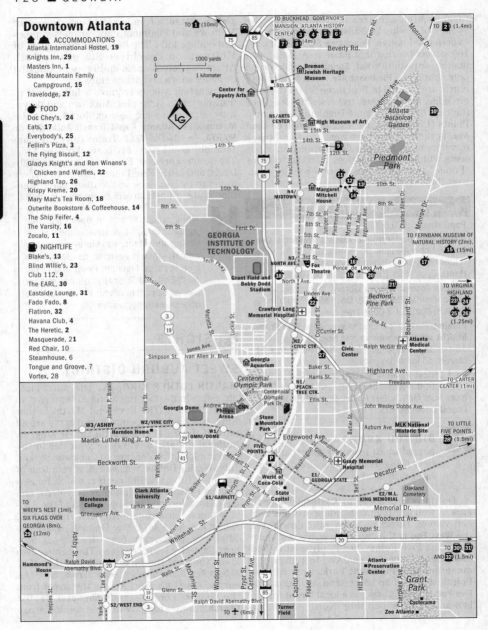

Downtown Atlanta

ACCOMMODATIONS
Atlanta International Hostel, **19**
Knights Inn, **29**
Masters Inn, **1**
Stone Mountain Family
  Campground, **15**
Travelodge, **27**

FOOD
Doc Chey's, **24**
Eats, **17**
Everybody's, **25**
Fellini's Pizza, **3**
The Flying Biscuit, **12**
Gladys Knight's and Ron Winans's
  Chicken and Waffles, **22**
Highland Tap, **26**
Krispy Kreme, **20**
Mary Mac's Tea Room, **18**
Outwrite Bookstore & Coffeehouse, **14**
The Ship Feifer, **4**
The Varsity, **16**
Zocalo, **11**

NIGHTLIFE
Blake's, **13**
Blind Willie's, **23**
Club 112, **9**
The EARL, **30**
Eastside Lounge, **31**
Fado Fado, **8**
Flatiron, **32**
Havana Club, **4**
The Heretic, **2**
Masquerade, **21**
Red Chair, **10**
Steamhouse, **6**
Tongue and Groove, **7**
Vortex, **28**

17 and co-pastored with his father from 1960 to 1968. *(407 Auburn Ave. ☎ 404-688-7263. Open June-Aug. M-Sa 9am-6pm, Su 1-6pm; Sept.-May M-Sa 9am-5pm, Su 1-5pm. Free.)* Next door, at the **Martin Luther King, Jr. Center for Nonviolent Social Change** lies a beautiful reflecting pool with an island on which King has been laid to rest in a white marble tomb. The center's Freedom Hall contains many of King's personal articles (including his Nobel Peace Prize medal), an overview of his role model, Gandhi, and exhibits on Coretta Scott King and Rosa Parks. *(449 Auburn Ave. NE. ☎ 404-526-8920. Open daily June-Aug. 9am-6pm; Sept.-May 9am-5pm. Free.)*

DOWNTOWN ATLANTA

■ **WORLD OF COCA-COLA.** Two blocks from the capitol, the World of Coca-Cola educates tourists on the rise of "the real thing" from its humble beginnings in Atlanta to its current position of world domination. Uncap the secrets of Coke as you walk through two floors of Coca-Cola history and memorabilia, complete with a "soda jerk" demonstration and TVs that loop old advertisements. The psychological barrage is so intense that even those with the strongest of willpowers will soon be craving a Coke. Luckily, visitors get to sample 46 flavors of Coke from around the world at the tour's end, from the long-lost "Tab" to Mozambique's "Krest." The World of Coca-Cola plans to move to a new location in summer 2007; call ahead for details. *(55 Martin Luther King, Jr. Dr. MARTA: Five Points. ☎ 404-676-5151; www.woccatlanta.com. Open June-Aug. M-Sa 9am-6pm, Su 11am-5pm; Sept.-May M-Sa 9am-5pm, Su noon-5pm. $9, seniors $8, ages 4-11 $5, under 4 free.)*

GEORGIA AQUARIUM. Brand-new in 2006, Atlanta's aquarium is the world's largest. Out of the aquarium's five thematic exhibits radiating from a central atrium, the deep-sea tank is the most impressive, with a moving floorway that takes visitors through a Plexiglas underwater tunnel. Keep an eye out for the ■**Wobbegong,** one of the world's ugliest creatures. The aquarium's penguins, sea lions, and coral-reef exhibit are sure to entertain. Arrive early to avoid crowds. *(225 Baker St. at Pemberton Place. MARTA: Peachtree Ctr. ☎ 404-581-4000; www.georgiaaquarium.com. Open M-F 9am-6pm, Sa-Su 8am-6pm; last entry 4:45pm. $23, seniors $19.50, ages 3-12 $17.)*

CNN. Overlooking beautiful Centennial Park is the global headquarters of the **Cable News Network (CNN).** Check out the 55min. studio tour, which reveals the reality behind the news. Sit inside a replica control room, learn the secrets of teleprompter magic, and peer into the CNN newsroom. *(At Centennial Olympic Park Dr. and Marietta St. MARTA: Omni/Dome/GWCC Station at W1. ☎ 404-827-2300; www.cnn.com/studiotour. Tours every 20min. daily 9am-5pm. $12, seniors $11, ages 4-12 $9.)*

STATE CAPITOL. On the corner of Washington and Mitchell St. is the **Georgia State Capitol Building,** a classical structure built in 1889 with Georgia's own natural resources: Cherokee marble, Georgian oak, and gold mined in Lumpkin County. Exhibits on the 4th floor detail Georgia's often tumultuous history and showcase its natural resources—don't miss the two-headed calf. *(☎ 404-463-4536; www.sos.state.ga.us. Call for tour availability. Open M-F 8am-5pm. Free.)*

OLYMPIC PARK. Amidst the commerce and concrete of bustling downtown Atlanta, you can relax at the **Centennial Olympic Park,** both a 21-acre public recreation area and a lasting monument to the 1996 Olympic Games. Eight enormous torches and an array of flags (each representing a nation that has hosted one of the modern Olympic Games) surround the park's central feature, the **Fountain of Rings,** which enthralls (and soaks) children and adults alike. Check out one of the 20min. fountain shows (daily 12:30, 3:30, 6:30, 9pm) in which the water dances to symphonic melodies and dazzling lights. *(265 Park Ave. West NW. MARTA: Peachtree Ctr. ☎ 404-222-7275; www.centennialpark.com. Visitors center open M-Tu and Th-Su 10am-6pm, W 10am-8pm. Park open daily 7am-11pm.Free.)*

CARTER PRESIDENTIAL CENTER. Just north of L5P, a charming garden and a circle of state flags surrounding the American flag welcome visitors to an engaging museum showcasing Jimmy Carter's life and presidency. Ranging from campaign memorabilia to School House Rock video clips from the energy crisis, the center's exhibits will entertain visitors of any political persuasion. *(441 Freedom Pkwy. Take bus #16 to Cleburne Ave. ☎ 404-865-7101; www.jimmycarterlibrary.org. Museum open M-Sa 9am-4:45pm, Su* *noon-4:45pm. Grounds open daily 6am-9pm. $8; students, seniors, and military $6; under 16 free.)*

GRANT PARK CYCLORAMA. The world's largest painting (42 ft. tall and 358 ft. in circumference) is in Grant Park, directly south of Oakland Cemetery and Cherokee Ave. The 117-year-old Cyclorama takes visitors back in time on a huge revolving platform in the middle of the "1864 Battle of Atlanta." *(800 Cherokee Ave. SE. Take bus #97 from Five Points. MARTA: King Memorial. ☎ 404-624-1071. Open daily 8:50am-4:30pm. $7, students and seniors $6, ages 6-12 $5.)*

ZOO ATLANTA. With over 1000 animals, including giant pandas and Sumatran tigers, this is one of the premiere zoos in the country. Though the zoo is overshadowed somewhat by Atlanta's dazzling new aquarium, animal lovers will find it a rewarding experience. *(800 Cherokee Ave. SE. Take bus #97 from Five Points. ☎ 404-624-5600; www.zooatlanta.org. Open Apr.-Oct. M-F 9:30am-4:30pm, Sa-Su 9:30am-5:30pm; Nov.-Mar. daily 9:30am-4:30pm. $18, ages 3-11 $14, seniors $13.)*

WALKING TOURS. From March to November, the **Atlanta Preservation Center** has 1-2hr. walking tours of popular areas, including Druid Hills, the setting of the film *Driving Miss Daisy.* Other tour destinations include Inman Park, Atlanta's first trolley suburb, the Fox Theatre on Peachtree St., and Historic Downtown. *(327 St. Paul Ave. NE. ☎ 404-688-3353; www.preserveatlanta.com. Office open M-F 9am-5pm. $10, ages 60+ $6, students $5.)*

WEST END

AFRICAN-AMERICAN HISTORY. Dating from 1835, the West End is Atlanta's oldest neighborhood. A tour of the historic **Wren's Nest** gives a number of twists on the typical "historic home" tour. Home to author Joel Chandler Harris, who popularized the African folktale trickster Br'er Rabbit, Wren's Nest offers a glimpse into middle-class life as it was at the beginning of the 20th century. *(1050 R.D. Abernathy Blvd. Take bus #71 from West End Station/ S2. ☎ 404-753-7735. Open Tu-Sa 10am-2:30pm. $8, ages 4-12 $5.)* The **Hammonds House,** the home-turned-gallery of Dr. Otis Hammonds, a renowned African-American physician and art lover, displays unique contemporary and older works in Georgia's only collection dedicated entirely to African-American and Haitian art. *(503 Peeples St. SW. ☎ 404-752-8730; www.hammondshouse.org. Open Tu-F 10am-6pm, Sa-Su 1-5pm. $4; students, seniors, and children $2.)* Born a slave, Alonzo F. Herndon founded Atlanta Life Insurance Co., eventually becoming Atlanta's wealthiest African-American in the early 20th Century. A Beaux-Arts Classical mansion, the **Herndon Home** was built in 1910; today it is dedicated to the legacy of Herndon's philanthropy. *(587 University Pl. NW. Take bus #3 from Five Points station to the corner of Martin Luther King, Jr. Dr. and Maple St., walk 1 block west, turn right on Walnut St., and walk 1 block. ☎ 404-581-9813; www.herndonhome.org. Tours by appointment. $5, students $3.)*

MIDTOWN

◾HIGH MUSEUM OF ART. Within the stunning Woodruff Arts Center, the recently-expanded High Museum of Art has an outstanding collection focused on American and European art, sculpture, and design. From 2006-2009, the High will host a series of visiting exhibitions from the collections of the Louvre showcasing the history of its galleries and collections from its founding to the present day. *(1280 Peachtree St. NE. MARTA: Arts Center; exit at Lombardy Way. ☎ 404-733-4400; www.high.org. Open Tu-W and F-Sa 10am-5pm, Th 10am-8pm, Su noon-5pm. $15, seniors and ages 12-17 $12, ages 6-12 $10.)*

◾ATLANTA BOTANICAL GARDEN. The **Atlanta Botanical Garden** occupies the northern end of the park and provides a peaceful refuge from everyday life. Stroll through 15 acres of gardens, a hardwood forest with trails, and an interactive children's garden. The Garden is also home to a rose garden, a formal Japanese garden, and the enormous glass-walled **Dorothy Chapman Fuqua Conservatory,** which houses an extensive orchid collection and an amazing tropical rainforest environment. *(1345 Piedmont Ave. NE. Take bus #36 or MARTA: Arts Center; on Su, bus #27 from MARTA: Five Points. ☎ 404-876-5859; www.atlantabotanicalgarden.org. Open Apr.-Sept. Tu-W and F-Su 9am-7pm, Th 9am-10pm; Oct.-Mar. Tu-W and F-Su 9am-5pm, Th 9am-10pm. $12, seniors $9, students $7; Tu $2 off.)*

BREMAN JEWISH HERITAGE MUSEUM. The Breman museum has a powerful Holocaust exhibit with a collection of interviews with

Holocaust survivors. The museum also has a gallery tracing the tumultuous history of Atlanta's Jewish community from 1845 to the present. *(1440 Spring St. NW. From MARTA: N5/Arts Center, walk 3 blocks north to 18th and Spring St. ☎ 678-222-3700; www.thebreman.org. Open M-Th 10am-5pm, F 10am-3pm, Su 1-5pm. $10, seniors $6, students $4, ages 3-6 $2.)*

MARGARET MITCHELL HOUSE. Located between the 10th St. district and Midtown is the apartment where Mitchell wrote her Pulitzer Prize-winning novel, *Gone with the Wind.* Tour the house to view her typewriter and autographed copies of the book. Included on the tour, the **Gone with the Wind Movie Museum** has memorabilia such as the portrait of Scarlett at which Clark Gable hurled a cocktail onscreen—complete with stain. The house tour will thrill *Gone with the Wind* devotees but might leave others unimpressed. *(990 Peachtree St., at 10th St., adjacent to MARTA: Midtown. ☎ 404-249-7015; www.gwtw.org. Open daily 9:30am-5pm. 1hr. tours every hr. $12, students and seniors $9, ages 6-17 $5.)*

CENTER FOR PUPPETRY ARTS. The complexity and sophistication of puppeteering will surprise and interest even those who haven't watched "The Muppet Show" in years. Exhibits show different styles of puppets and puppeteering techniques, and visitors can try their hand at controlling an animatronic puppet. *(1404 Spring St. NW, at 18th St. ☎ 404-873-3391; www.puppet.org. Open Tu-Sa 9am-5pm, Su 11am-5pm. $8, students and seniors $7, under 18 $6. Th 1-4pm free.)*

FERNBANK MUSEUM OF NATURAL HISTORY. Sporting outstanding dinosaur and sea-life exhibits and interactive discovery centers, the Fernbank is one of the best science museums in the South. *(767 Clifton Rd. NE, off Ponce de Leon Ave.; take bus #2 from North Ave. or Avondale Station. ☎ 404-929-6300; www.fernbank.edu/museum. Open M-Sa 10am-5pm, Su noon-5pm. Museum $12, students and seniors $11, ages 3-12 $10; IMAX film $10/$9/$8; both attractions $17/$15/$13.)* The adjacent **R.L. Staton Rose Garden** is small, but free. The garden blossoms from spring until December. *(At the corner of Ponce de Leon Ave. and Clifton Rd.)*

BUCKHEAD

A drive through **Buckhead,** north of Midtown and Piedmont Park, off Peachtree St. near W.

Paces Ferry Rd., reveals Atlanta's answer to Beverly Hills. The majority of these gaudy mansions were built by Coca-Cola bigwigs; the architectural style of this area has been aptly dubbed "Rococo-cola." The main drag along Peachtree Dr. is slowly turning from a hip, yuppie hangout to that of a younger, often unruly, crowd. The area, however, remains conducive to wining and dining and is strung with dance clubs and restaurants frequented by Atlanta's twentysomethings.

BUCKHEAD ATTRACTIONS. One of the most exquisite residences in the Southeast, the Greek Revival **Governor's Mansion** has elaborate gardens and one of the finest collections of furniture from the Federal Period. *(391 W. Paces Ferry Rd. ☎ 404-261-1776. Tours Tu-Th 10-11:30am. Free.)* In the same neighborhood, the **Atlanta History Center** traces Atlanta's development from a rural area to an international urban center. In celebration of the 10th anniversary of the 1996 Atlanta Olympic Games, the museum has a new gallery on the history of the Olympics and the transformation of Atlanta into an Olympic host city. Its Civil War Gallery highlights the stories of both Confederate and Union soldiers, while the Folklife Gallery details Southern culture from grits to banjos. Also on the grounds are exquisite mansions from the early 20th century, including the **Swan House,** a lavish Anglo-Palladian Revival home built in 1928, and the **Tullie Smith Farm,** an 1845 yeoman farmhouse. Abutting the homes, 33 acres of trails and gardens are perfect for an afternoon stroll. *(130 W. Paces Ferry Rd. NW. ☎ 404-814-4000; www.atlantahistorycenter.com. Open M-Sa 10am-5:30pm, Su noon-5:30pm. $15, students and seniors $12, ages 4-12 $10; house tours free with museum admission.)*

ATLANTA METRO AREA

STONE MOUNTAIN. Sixteen miles east of the city on U.S. 78, one of Georgia's top natural attractions, Stone Mountain Park, provides a respite from the city with beautiful scenery and the remarkable **Confederate Memorial.** Carved into the world's largest mass of granite, the 825 ft. "Mt. Rushmore of the South" profiles Jefferson Davis, Robert E. Lee, and Stonewall Jackson. On summer nights, be sure to check out the dazzling laser show that illu-

DEEP SOUTH

minates the side of the mountain. A cable car ($7.50) takes visitors to the top of Stone Mountain, which has a panoramic view of the Georgia landscape and a hazy view of the Atlanta skyline. *(Take bus #120 "Stone Mountain" from MARTA: Avondale. ☎770-498-5600 or 800-317-2006; www.stonemountainpark.com. Park open daily 6am-midnight. Attractions open daily in summer 10am-8pm; in winter 10am-5pm. $8 per vehicle. All day pass $22, ages 3-11 $18. Memorial and laser show free.)*

SIX FLAGS. Six Flags Over Georgia is one of the largest amusement parks in the nation. Check out the 54 mph "Georgia Scorcher" roller coaster and the "Superman" roller coaster, with a pretzel-shaped inverted loop. *(275 Riverside Pkwy., at I-20 W. Take bus #201 from MARTA Hamilton Homes. ☎770-948-9290; www.sixflags.com/georgia. Open mid-June to July M-F 10am-9pm, Sa 10am-10pm; hours vary in winter. $50, seniors and under 4 ft. $30.)*

🔪 FOOD

From Vietnamese to Italian, fried to fricasseed, Atlanta cooks options for any craving, but "soul food" nourishes the city. Head to "Chicken and Waffles" restaurants for the terrific combination. A depot for soul food's raw materials since 1923, the **Sweet Auburn Curb Market,** 209 Edgewood Ave., has an eye-popping assortment of goodies, from cow's feet to oxtails. (☎659-1665. Open M-Th 8am-6pm, F-Sa 8am-7pm.)

MIDTOWN

🔖 **Gladys Knight's and Ron Winans's Chicken and Waffles,** 529 Peachtree St. (☎404-874-9393). MARTA: North Ave. Situated on the southern border of Midtown, this upscale but reasonably priced joint screams "soul" with incredible dishes like the Midnight Train (4 fried chicken wings and a waffle; $8.75). Side dishes include collard greens, cinnamon raisin toast, and corn muffins. Open M-Th 11am-11pm, F-Sa 11am-4am, Su 11am-8pm. AmEx/D/MC/V. ❷

The Varsity, 61 North Ave. NW (☎404-881-1706), at Spring St. MARTA: North Ave. Established in 1928, The Varsity is the world's largest drive-in restaurant. Subject of a landmark Supreme Court ruling in the 1960s abolishing racial segregation in restaurants. The Varsity has since delighted patrons with cheap and delicious hamburgers ($1.15), classic Coke floats ($2.30), and famous onion rings ($1.70). Open M-Th and Su 11:30pm, F-Sa 10am-12:30am. MC/V. ❶

Eats, 600 Ponce de Leon Ave. (☎404-888-9149). Quickly whips up terrific pasta and southern meat and vegetable plates ($3.50-7). Pasta $3.75-5. Open daily 11am-10pm. Cash only. ❶

Mary Mac's Tea Room, 224 Ponce de Leon Ave. (☎404-876-1800; www.marymacs.com), at Myrtle St. MARTA: North Ave. Whether you're sipping the house specialty tea ($1.25) or enjoying the southern-style meat and vegetables, you'll appreciate the stellar service, charming tea rooms, and elegant dining hall. Entrees ($9-10) come with 2 side dishes. Open daily 11am-9pm. AmEx/MC/V. ❸

10TH STREET

The Flying Biscuit, 1001 Piedmont Ave. (☎404-874-8887; www.flyingbiscuit.com). Packed with loyal patrons, the Flying Biscuit serves breakfast feasts. Enjoy the Flying Biscuit Breakfast ($7) and the signature *Delio* (double espresso mochaccino; $3.75). Open M-Th and Su 7am-10pm, F-Sa 7am-10:30pm. AmEx/MC/V. ❷

Outwrite Bookstore and Coffeehouse, 991 Piedmont Ave. (☎404-607-0082). Rainbow beach balls grace the windows at this bookstore/cafe that specializes in gay- and lesbian-interest books. A relaxed and stylish atmosphere with remarkably friendly service. Try the espresso specialty drink "Shot in the Dark" ($2.25). Open daily 10am-11pm. AmEx/D/MC/V. ❶

Zocalo, 187 10th St. (☎404-249-7576). Woven baskets, tequila advertisements, and air-conditioned patio seating. Some of the best margaritas in Atlanta and all the Mexican favorites you'd expect. *Chiles rellenos* $10.50. *Taquitos* $8. Open M-Th and Su 11am-10pm, F-Sa 11am-11pm. AmEx/D/MC/V. ❸

VIRGINIA HIGHLAND

Doc Chey's, 1424 N. Highland Ave. (☎404-888-0777). Serves heaping mounds of noodles at super cheap prices. This pan-Asian restaurant is popular among young locals. Try the delicious lo mein ($6) or the Thai coconut red curry ($6.50-8). Open M-Th and Su 11:30am-10pm, F-Sa 11:30am-11pm. AmEx/D/MC/V. ❷

Everybody's, 1040 N. Highland Ave. (☎404-873-4545). Receives high accolades for selling Atlanta's best pizza. Creative pizza salads with greens and chicken on a bed of, well, pizza $12.50. Pizza sandwiches $8.50-9.50. Open M-Th 11:30am-11pm, F-Sa 11:30am-1am, Su noon-10:30pm. AmEx/D/DC/MC/V. ❸

Highland Tap, 1026 N. Highland Ave. (☎404-875-3673). Home of the best steaks in the Highlands and a happening bar scene. Spring for the gorgonzola crust ($2.50) with your steak. Steaks $12-28. Sandwiches $8.50-12. Open M 5pm-midnight, Tu-Th 11:30am-3pm and 5pm-midnight, F 11:30am-3pm and 5pm-1am, Sa 5pm-1am, Su 5pm-midnight. Bar open M-Sa 11:30am-3am, Su 12:30am-2am. AmEx/D/MC/V. ❹

BUCKHEAD

Fellini's Pizza, 2809 Peachtree Rd. NE (☎404-266-0082). 3 watchful gargoyles and an angel welcome customers into this pizzeria, the flagship of 5 Atlanta locations, complete with a spacious deck and mouth-watering pizza. If Hotlanta has become too warm, enjoy your slice (from $1.85) or pie ($10.50-19) inside, where classic rock is combined with a romantic atmosphere. Open M-Sa 11am-2am, Su noon-midnight. MC/V. ❶

The Shipfeifer, 1814 Peachtree Rd. (☎404-875-1106). The Shipfeifer serves up fresh Mediterranean and vegetarian food at reasonable prices. Entrees $8.25-10. Wraps $6-8. Quesadillas and burritos $5-7. Open M-Th and Su 11am-10pm, F 11am-10:30pm, Sa 11am-11pm. AmEx/D/MC/V. ❷

ACCOMMODATIONS

Hotels close to downtown Atlanta are very pricey. Stop by the Atlanta Visitors Center (p. 727) to pick up a free copy of the Georgia Travel Coupon book. Many Atlanta-area hotels have deep discounts on rooms if you use a coupon, although some do not allow coupons if you reserve a room in advance.

Atlanta International Hostel, 223 Ponce de Leon Ave. (☎875-9449 or 800-473-9449; www.hostel-atlanta.com), in Midtown. From MARTA: North Ave., and walk 3½ blocks east on Ponce de Leon to Myrtle St., or take bus #2. Look for the "Woodruff Inn: Bed and Breakfast" sign. This family-owned establishment has clean dorms in a house

with TV, pool table, and kitchen. Free coffee and doughnuts for breakfast. Internet $1 per 10min. Free Wi-Fi. Free lockers. Towels $1. Dorms $22; private rooms $50-70. AmEx/D/MC/V. ❶

Knights Inn, 1595 Blairs Bridge Rd. (☎770-944-0824), in Austell, 12 mi. west of downtown Atlanta. Take Exit 44 off I-20. Spacious, motel-style rooms come with microfridge, free Wi-Fi, and pool access. Rooms M-F $45-50, Sa-Su $50-60. AmEx/D/MC/V. ❸

Masters Inn, 2682 Windy Hill Rd. (☎770-951-2005), Exit 260 off I-75 in Marietta. Standard, clean rooms with cable TV and A/C. Singles $39-45; doubles $44-50. AmEx/D/MC/V. ❷

Travelodge, 311 Courtland St. NE (☎800-578-7878 or 404-659-4545; www.atlantatravelodge.com). The best budget option in the heart of downtown Atlanta with clean rooms and a pool. Continental breakfast included. Free parking. Reservations recommended. Rooms from $90. AmEx/D/MC/V. ❹

Stone Mountain Family Campground (☎770-498-5710), on U.S. 78. Far from the commotion of the city, this campground has stunning sites, bike rental, and a free laser show. 2-week max. stay. Sites $23-25, with water and electricity $25-29, with full hookup $32-40. Day-use $8 per vehicle. AmEx/D/MC/V. ❶

ENTERTAINMENT

For hassle-free fun, buy a MARTA pass (p. 727) and pick up the city's free publications on music and events. *Creative Loafing,* the *Hudspeth Report,* and "Leisure" in the Friday edition of the *Atlanta Journal and Constitution* contain the latest info and are available in most coffee shops and on street corners. Check for free summer concerts in Atlanta's parks.

THEATER

Every summer Turner Classic Movies and HBO present **"Screen on the Green,"** a series of free films shown once a week in the meadow behind the visitors center. The **Woodruff Arts Center** (see **Midtown,** p. 730) houses the Atlanta Symphony, the Alliance Theater Company, the Atlanta College of Art, and the High Museum of Art. Atlanta is home to a number of excellent theater groups, such as **On Stage**

Atlanta (☎404-897-1802; www.onstageat-lanta.com) and the **Stage Door Players** (☎770-396-1726; www.jackintheblackbox.org). **Atlantix,** 65 Upper Alabama St. and 3393 Peachtree Rd. NE at Lenox Sq., MARTA: Five Points, sets you up with same-day, half-price rush tickets to dance, theater, music, and other attractions throughout the city (walk-up service only). Full price advance tickets are also available online. (☎678-318-1400; www.atlantaperforms.com. Open Tu-Sa 11am-6pm, Su noon-4pm.)

SPORTS

The **Philips Arena,** 1 Philips Dr. (☎404-878-3000), hosts concerts, the **Atlanta Hawks** NBA team, and the **Atlanta Thrashers** NHL team. The National League's **Atlanta Braves,** play at **Turner Field.** (755 Hank Aaron Dr., MARTA: Georgia State, or take Braves Shuttle from Five Points. ☎404-522-7630; Ticketmaster 800-326-4000. Tickets $1-53.) 1hr. tours of Turner Field include views of the diamond from the $200,000 skyboxes. (☎404-614-2311. Open non-game days M-Sa 9am-3pm, Su 1-3pm; evening-game days M-Sa 9am-noon; no tours on afternoon or Su game days. Tickets $10, ages 13 and under $5.) See the **Atlanta Falcons** play football at the **Georgia Dome,** MARTA: OMNI/Dome/World Congress Center, the world's largest cable-supported dome. (☎404-223-8687. Open daily 10am-3pm. Tours Tu-Sa on the hr., except during events. Toclets $6, students and seniors $4.)

FESTIVALS

In the heart of Midtown, **Piedmont Park** is a hotbed of fun, free activities. Look for the **Dogwood Festival** (www.dogwood.org), an art festival in the spring, and the **Jazz Festival** (www.atlantafestivals.com) in May. In June, the park hosts the **Gay Pride Festival** (www.atlantapride.org), and on July 4th, Atlanta draws 55,000 people to the world's largest 10K race, the **Peachtree Road Race.** In July, Atlanta hosts the **National Black Arts Festival,** a two-week celebration of the art and music of the African diaspora. The festival sponsors events ranging from jazz and film to dance and spoken word at a variety of venues. (☎404-733-5000; www.nbaf.org.)

◤ NIGHTLIFE

Atlanta's rich nightlife lacks a clear focal point. Fortunately, however, it also lacks limits; young people can be found partying until the wee hours and beyond. Scores of bars and clubs along Peachtree Rd. and Buckhead Ave., in **Buckhead,** cater to a younger crowd. Pricier **Midtown** greets glamorous hipsters. Alternative **L5P** plays host to bikers and goths, while **Virginia Highland** and up-and-coming **East Atlanta** feature an eclectic mix.

BARS AND PUBS

◪ **Blind Willie's,** 828 N. Highland Ave. NE (☎404-873-2583). Blind Willie's is the quintessential blues club: the brick-lined interior is small and dark, and the bar serves mostly beer ($3-4) to its loyal patrons. Live blues, zydeco, and folk music daily around 9:30pm. Cover $3-10. Schedule varies, but usually open M-Th, F 8pm-3am, Sa 8pm-2:30am. AmEx/D/MC/V.

The Vortex, 438 Moreland Ave. (☎404-688-1828; www.thevortexbarandgrill.com), in L5P. With a front door that looks like a Halloween mask and bicycle-riding skeletons hanging from the ceiling, the Vortex will impress with its Applebee's-goes-to-hell ambience. With award-winning burgers like "Coronary Bypass" ($8) and "Italian Stallion" ($7.45), you'll need a drink to make it through the night. 18+. Open M-W and Su 11am-midnight, Th-Sa 11am-3am. AmEx/D/MC/V.

Fado Fado, 3035 Peachtree Rd. NE (☎404-841-0066). The interior of this popular bar was imported from Ireland—right down to the wood of the bar itself. The favored yuppie hang-out in Buckhead, with plenty of cozy nooks and crannies for enjoying a pint of Guinness. Free Wi-Fi. Open M-Sa 11:30am-3am, Su 11:30am-midnight. AmEx/D/MC/V.

Masquerade, 695 North Ave. NE (☎404-577-8178, concert info 404-577-2007), in Midtown. Occupying a huge turn-of-the-century mill, this bar has 3 levels: "heaven," with live music from touring bands; "purgatory," a more laid-back pub and pool house; and "hell," a dance club with everything from techno to 40s big-band jazz. Head outside for dancing or check out the 4000-seat amphitheater for your metal and punk fix. Cover from $3. MC/V.

Flatiron, 520 Flat Shoals Ave. (☎404-688-8864), in L5P. Set on the corner of Glenwood and Flat Shoals, this hot spot hosts live punk rock. On non-music nights it's a relaxed indoor-outdoor lounge with 10 beers on tap (pints $3-4) and a surprisingly large selection of tequilas ($4-10). Open M-Th 11:30am-2am, F-Sa 11:30am-3am, Su 12:30pm-2am. AmEx/D/MC/V.

Eastside Lounge, 485 Flat Shoals Ave. SE (☎404-522-7841), in L5P. This suave hideout has a well-dressed clientele and a red-tinted decor. Couches near the bar and tables in the small upstairs offer rest for the weary, but be prepared to stand with other trendsetters in the bar area. F-Sa DJ. Open M-Sa 9pm-3am. MC/V.

The EARL, 488 Flat Shoals Ave. (☎404-522-3950), in L5P. A bar and restaurant popular with hipster and goth crowds, the EARL has live music most nights ranging from hip-hop to country and serves burgers ($6-8) along with other late-night snacks. Open M 5pm-3am, Tu-Sa 11:30am-3am, Su noon-midnight. MC/V.

Steamhouse, 3041 Bolling Way (☎404-233-7980), in Buckhead. For those who like raw oysters ($8 per dozen) with their beer. A great place on hot summer evenings, the party often spills out onto the upstairs porch. Beer $3.50. Open M-Sa 11:30am-2am, Su 11:30am-midnight. MC/V.

DANCE CLUBS

■ **Tongue and Groove,** 3055 Peachtree Rd. NE (☎404-261-2325; www.tongueandgrooveon-line.com), in Buckhead. Whether you decide to kick back at one of the 2 gorgeous bars or shake it on the dance floor, this popular nightclub is a lot of fun. Cover around $10. Open W-Sa 10pm-3am. Dress code strictly enforced; no T-shirts, sneakers, or athletic apparel. MC/V.

Havana Club, 247 Buckhead Ave. (☎404-869-8484), in Buckhead. This late-night dance club plays a mix of latin and pop music. F-Sa live music. Cover $10 for men after 11pm. Open M-Sa 8pm-3am. MC/V.

Club 112, 1055 Peachtree St. NE (☎404-670-7277). A premier hip-hop club with a dark, cavernous interior. Cover $20; ladies free F before midnight, Sa before 11pm. Open Th 10pm-3am, F-Sa 9pm-3am. MC/V.

GLBT NIGHTLIFE

Atlanta is the gay capital of the south, making **Midtown** the mecca of southern gay culture. For information on gay nightlife and events, check out the free *Southern Voice,* available everywhere.

Blake's, 227 10th St. (☎404-892-5786). Midtown males flock to this friendly bar, where see-and-be-seen is a way of life. A prime location just steps from Piedmont Park, this popular bar is also a destination for the young lesbian crowd. Shows M-Th and Sa 11pm, Su 9pm. Open M-Sa 2pm-2am, Su 2pm-midnight. MC/V.

Red Chair, 550-C Amsterdam Ave. (☎404-870-0532), at the Amsterdam Walk shopping center in Midtown. A tapas-style menu and 6 huge video screens playing VH1 jams have quickly vaulted Red Chair to the top of Midtown's gay scene. 21+ after 9pm, Th 18+ until 11pm. Open W 6:30pm-3am, Th 9pm-1am, F-Sa 6:30pm-3am, Su 11:30am-3pm and 6pm-midnight. AmEx/D/MC/V.

The Heretic, 2069 Cheshire Bridge Road NE (☎404-325-3061; www.hereticatlanta.com), a little outside of the center of Midtown. Many guys head here in search of Mr. Right—or at least Mr. Right Now. If the action on the dance floor gets a little too hot for you, cool off on the outdoor patio. Cover F-Sa $4. Open M-Sa 10:30am-3am. MC/V.

◪ **APPROACHING VILLA RICA: 30 MILES**
From Atlanta, follow **Rte. 78 W.**

VILLA RICA. Villa Rica's small downtown is split by railway tracks; cross over to the other side to find the **Tin Roof Cafe ❶,** 110 Main St., next to a row of antique and thrift stores. This tiny cafe has an old-time feel, with a collection of antique bottlecaps framing the front door. The food is standard diner fare, with sandwiches like their specialty reuben ($5.50), and salads. (☎770-456-2474. Open M-Sa 7:30am-7:30pm. Cash only.)

◪ **APPROACHING TALLAPOOSA: 22 MILES**
Follow **Rte. 78 W** to Tallapoosa.

TALLAPOOSA. On your right as you drive into downtown Tallapoosa on Rte. 78, a converted gas station houses **Owen's Bar-B-Q ❶.** There's no dining room or table service, only a drive-through window, but the pork barbecue and chicken plates ($6-6.50) are tasty. Fridays and

Saturdays, Owen's has rib dinners and plates for $8. (☎770-574-9199. Open M-Sa 5:30am-2:30pm. Cash only.)

 APPROACHING ANNISTON: 32 MILES
From Tallapoosa, follow **Rte. 78 W** for 29 mi. to Oxford, AL, then turn right onto **Rte. 431/21 N** to downtown Anniston .

The Heart of Dixie
ALABAMA
Welcomes You!

Rte. 78 enters the Central Time Zone in Alabama, where it is 1hr. earlier.

ANNISTON

Primarily an iron town until the cotton industry began to flourish in 1881, Anniston was awarded the All-American City Award in 1978—and they won't let you forget it. Set in Alabama's gentle hill country to the west of the Talladega National Forest, Anniston is a good stopping point for food or a rest before finishing your trek to Birmingham.

VITAL STATS

Population: 24,000

Visitor Info: Calhoun County Chamber of Commerce, 1330 Quintard Ave. (☎256-237-3536; www.calhoun-chamber.com). Open M-F 8am-5pm.

Internet Access: Anniston Public Library, 108 E. 10th St. (☎256-237-8501). Open M-Th 9am-6:30pm, F 9am-5pm, Sa 10am-5pm, Su 1-5pm. Free Wi-Fi.

Post Office: 1101 Quintard Ave. (☎256-234-9940). Open M-F 8:30am-5pm, Sa 8am-noon. **Postal Code:** 36201.

◪ GETTING AROUND. 10th St. runs east-west through town while **Quintard Ave.** and **Rte. 431** run north-south. Parking is not difficult to find in Anniston, and the streets are easy to maneuver.

◪ SIGHTS. The **Anniston Museum of Natural History,** 1½ mi. north of downtown Anniston on McClellan Blvd. (Rte. 431), has a number of kid-oriented exhibits on Earth's geological history and Alabama's ecological habitats. The real treasure is a vast collection of stuffed and mounted birds and other animals from around the world. Thanks to a benefactor who enjoyed hunting African big game, visitors can see the rare black rhino, as well as lions, cheetahs, and giraffes up close. (☎256-237-6766; www.annistonmuseum.org. Open in summer M-Sa 10am-5pm, Su 1-5pm; in winter Tu-Sa 10am-5pm, Su 1-5pm. $4.50, seniors $4, ages 4-17 $3.50.) Across the street from the Museum of Natural History, the **Berman Museum of World History** will enthrall aspiring cowboys and Rambos with its collection of guns and weaponry. From 15th-century hand cannons to diamond-encrusted Persian scabbards, the museum showcases more ways to die than visitors could ever have previously imagined. Don't miss the flute-gun that fires when you play the right note. (☎256-237-6261; www.bermanmuseum.org. Open in summer M-Sa 10am-5pm, Su 1-5pm; in winter Tu-Sa 10am-5pm, Su 1-5pm. $3.50, seniors $3, ages 4-17 $2.50. Combination Passport to the Anniston and Berman $7, seniors $6, ages 4-17 $5.) In downtown Anniston, the Episcopal **Church of St. Michael and All Angels,** 1000 West 18th St., was built in 1887 with the patronage of John Ward Noble, one of the founders of Anniston's iron works. The majestic altar is made from Italian marble, and the stained glass windows and ark-like wooden ceiling are both gorgeous. In the entrance hall, visitors can also see an Ethiopian cross given by Emperor of Ethiopia Halie Selassie I. (☎256-237-4014. Open M-F 8am-4pm, Sa 9am-4pm. Donation suggested.)

◪▪ FOOD AND ACCOMMODATIONS. In downtown Anniston, **Lil' Cajun Cookery ❷,** 15 W. 10th St., greets customers with a big alligator head at the front door. Cajun is the specialty, with dishes like shrimp gumbo ($3.25), jambalaya ($10-11), and crawfish. (☎256-235-3888. Lunch specials $6-7. Open M-W 11am-2pm, Th 11am-2pm and 5-9pm, F-Sa 5-9pm. MC/V.) **Damn Yankees Oyster Bar ❷,** 919 Noble St., is one of the few nightlife spots in Anniston's downtown. A surf-and-turf restaurant with a lively atmosphere, Damn Yankees has fried seafood baskets ($8-10) and raw oysters. (☎256-236-7000. Oysters $5 per half-dozen. Open M 4-11pm, Tu-Th 11am-10pm, F 11am-midnight, Sa 5pm-midnight. MC/V.) Three miles south of Anniston, budget motels surround Exit 185 off I-20. The **Red Carpet Inn ❷**, 1007 Hwy. 215, may overlook a gas station and fireworks store, but it's a great deal for a budget motel. (☎256-831-6082. Free Wi-Fi. Continental breakfast included. Rooms $35-45. AmEx/D/MC/V.)

◪ APPROACHING BIRMINGHAM: 58 MILES
From Anniston, take **Rte. 431 S.** Head west on **I-20** until you hit downtown Birmingham.

BIRMINGHAM

A 180 ft. cast-iron statue of Vulcan, the Roman god of the forge, looms over the Birmingham skyline as a reminder of the city's history as an industrial powerhouse in the post-Civil War South. During the struggle for African-American civil rights, leaders like Martin Luther King, Jr. and Fred Shuttlesworth faced some of their toughest fights in what was labeled "Bombingham" after dozens of bombs rocked the city in the early 1960s. Today, industrial relics dot Birmingham's downtown, and the Civil Rights Museum and Sixteenth Street Baptist Church are reminders of the city's tumultuous past.

VITAL STATS

Population: 907,810

Visitor Info: Greater Birmingham Convention and Visitors Center, 220 9th Ave. N, 1st fl. (☎205-458-8085; www.thediversecity.org). Open M-F 8:30am-5pm.

Internet Access: Birmingham Public Library, 2100 Park Pl. (☎205-226-3600), at the corner of Richard Arrington, Jr. Blvd. Open M-Tu 9am-8pm, W-Sa 9am-6pm, Su 2-6pm. Free.

Parking: The lot on 7th Ave. N, between 22nd St. N and Richard Arrington, Jr. Blvd., charges $1 for the 1st 90min. and $4 per hr. afterwards.

Post Office: 351 24th St. N (☎202-521-7990). Open M-F 7am-8pm. **Postal Code:** 35203.

⌷ GETTING AROUND

Downtown Birmingham is organized in a grid, with numbered avenues running east-west and numbered streets running north-south. **Richard Arrington, Jr. Blvd.** is the one exception, running along what should have been called 21st St. Downtown is divided by railroad tracks run-

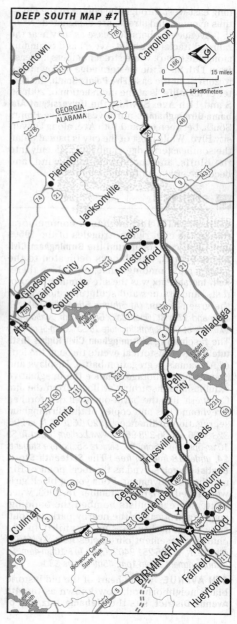

DEEP SOUTH MAP #7

GEORGIA
ALABAMA

DEEP SOUTH

ning east-west through the center of the city—thus avenues and streets are designated "N" or "S." Avenue numbers decrease as they near the railroad tracks (with 1st Ave. N and S running alongside them), while street numbers increase from 11th St. at the western edge of downtown to 26th St. at the east. **Five Points South,** the center of nightlife, is at the intersection of 20th St. S and 11th Ave. S, while the **University of Alabama-Birmingham** is northwest of Five Points South, between 6th and 10th Ave. along University Blvd. While most of the city is pancake-flat, the southeastern edge climbs up suddenly into the bluffs, and the streets curl, wind, and become very beautiful and confusing.

👁 SIGHTS

CIVIL RIGHTS. Birmingham's commemoration of the civil rights struggles of the 1950s and 1960s centers around the **Birmingham Civil Rights District,** nine blocks dedicated to the battles and bombings that took place there. **Kelly Ingram Park** was the site of numerous protests, and statues and sculptures now grace the green lawns. (*At 5th and 6th Ave. N between 16th and 17th St. Open daily 6am-10pm. Audio tours available at Civil Rights Institute Tu-Sa 10am-3pm. $5.*) The fascinating ◪**Birmingham Civil Rights Institute** looks at historical events through the lens of Alabama's segregation battle. Displays and documentary footage balance the imaginative exhibits and disturbing artifacts from the Jim Crow era, like the burnt-out shell of a torched Greyhound bus and copies of the Birmingham segregation ordinances. (*520 16th St. N. ☎205-328-9696 or 866-328-9696; www.bcri.org. Open Tu-Sa 10am-5pm, Su 1-5pm. $9, seniors $5, college students $4, under 18 free. Su free.*) The **Sixteenth Street Baptist Church** served as the focal point of Birmingham's movement. Four young black girls were killed here on September 15, 1963, when white segregationists bombed the building, spurring protests in the nearby park and outrage nationwide. A small exhibit in the church's basement chronicles its past. (*1530 6th Ave. N. ☎205-251-9402. Open Tu-F 10am-4pm, Sa by appointment 10am-1pm. 45min. tours $3.*)

4TH AVENUE. In the heart of the old historic black neighborhood, now known as the **4th Avenue District,** sits the **Alabama Jazz Hall of Fame.** Jazz greats from Erskine Hawkins to Ella Fitzgerald each gets a small display on their life work. (*1631 4th Ave. N, in the Carver Theater. ☎205-254-2731; www.jazzhall.com. Open Tu-Sa 10am-5pm, Su 1-5pm. $2. Guided tours $3.*) Two blocks away, the **Birmingham Museum of Art** is the largest municipal art museum in the South, containing over 18,000 works and a sculpture garden. The gallery also houses the Hanson Library, which features the largest collection of Wedgewood china outside the UK. (*2000 8th Ave. N. ☎205-254-2565. Open Tu-Sa 10am-5pm, Su noon-5pm. Free.*) Alabama's sports greats, from Willie "The Say Hey Kid" Mays to speedy Carl Lewis, are immortalized in the **Alabama Sports Hall of Fame.** (*2150 Civic Center Blvd., at the corner of 22nd St. N. ☎323-6665. Open M-Sa 9am-5pm. $5, seniors $4, students $3, under 6 free.*)

SMELTING. Birmingham remembers its days as the "Pittsburgh of the South" at the **Sloss Furnaces National Historic Landmark.** The blast furnaces closed 20 years ago, but they are the only preserved example of 20th-century iron smelting in the world. Visitors can walk past the massive forges and climb down into the cavernous tunnels below. Plays and concerts are held in a renovated furnace shed by the stacks. (*20 32nd St. N. ☎205-324-1911; www.slossfurnaces.com. Open Tu-Sa 10am-4pm, Su noon-4pm. Tours Sa-Su 1, 2, 3pm. Free.*) **Vulcan,** 1701 Valley View Dr., is the largest statue ever made in the US and the largest cast-iron statue in the world. The Roman god of the Forge was sculpted by Italian artist Giuseppe Moretti to represent Alabama at the 1904 St. Louis World's Fair. A 360-degree view of the region awaits at the top, but you can also get a great view of Birmingham from the base for free. If you do go up the tower, the first thing you'll see as you emerge from the elevator is Vulcan's huge iron butt. Don't worry, the view gets better. (*Go south on 20th St. S and follow the signs. ☎205-933-1409; www.vulcanpark.org. Open M-Sa 10am-10pm, Su 1-6pm. $6, seniors $5, ages 5-12 $4, under 5 $3.*)

OTHER SIGHTS. For a break from the heavy-duty ironworks, stroll the marvelously manicured grounds of the **Birmingham Botanical Gardens.** Spectacular floral displays, an elegant Japanese garden, and an enormous greenhouse occupy a 67-acre site. You can arrange a tour if you want expert commentary on the garden's flora. *(2612 Lane Park Rd., off U.S. 31.* ☎ *205-414-3900. Garden Center open daily 8am-5pm. Gardens open sunrise-sunset. Free.)* If you prefer cogs and grease to petals and pollen, the **Mercedes-Benz U.S. International Visitors Center** is a 24,000 sq. ft. museum that spares no technological expense to celebrate the history of all things Mercedes. Currently undergoing a major expansion, the center will be closed until summer 2007. *(Exit 89 off I-20/59, on Mercedes Dr., at Vance St.* ☎ *205-507-2252, or 888-286-8762.)*

🍴 FOOD

Five Points South, an old streetcar suburb at the intersection of 20th St. S and 11th Ave. S, is the best place to find great restaurants with reasonable prices.

Niki's, 1101 2nd Ave. N (☎ 205-251-1972). With 20 meats and 30 vegetable sides to choose from, this classic lunchroom keeps its faithful customers happy. There's also a tempting selection of pies ($3 per slice) and other desserts. Meat and 2 vegetable lunch $6.50-7.50. Open M-F 6am-6pm. AmEx/D/MC/V. ❷

Jim and Nick's, 1908 11th Ave. S (☎ 205-320-1060), in Five Points South. Jim and Nick's began as a roadside barbecue joint over 50 years ago and has grown into a casual restaurant. The ribs are excellent (half-rack $15, full-rack $21), as are the cheese biscuits. Open M-Th and Su 10:30am-9pm, F-Sa 10:30am-10pm. AmEx/D/MC/V. ❸

Hamburger Heaven, 1906 1st Ave. (☎ 205-951-6402), Exit 132A off I-20, in Old Irondale. Proud of its fast-food atmosphere, Hamburger Heaven was recently selected as the server of one of the Top 50 hamburgers in the world. Decide for yourself; burger combos are $5-7. Open M-Th 11am-8:30pm, F-Sa 11am-9pm. AmEx/D/MC/V. ❶

Fish Market Restaurant, 622 22nd St. S (☎ 205-322-3330; www.thefishmarket.net), at the corner of 22nd St. and 6th Ave. S. Birmingham's oldest seafood wholesaler doubles as a no-frills joint with cheap catches. Snapper and flounder are very popular, but the frog legs ($12) are especially exciting. Entrees $7.50-12. Open M-Th 10am-9pm, F-Sa 10am-10pm. AmEx/D/MC/V. ❸

Pyramids, 1207 20th St. S (☎ 205-930-0078), in Little Five Points. Inexpensive and seriously tasty

Greek and Middle Eastern food. The falafel plates ($4.25-6.75) are delicious. Open M-Th and Su 10am-3am, F-Sa 10am-5am. MC/V. ❶

🏠 ACCOMMODATIONS

Relatively cheap hotels and motels dot the greater Birmingham area along the various interstates.

Super 8, 140 Vulcan Rd. (☎ 205-945-9888), Exit 256A off I-65. In a quiet location with clean rooms, a fitness center, and free Wi-Fi. Continental breakfast included. Singles M-Th and Su $45, F-Sa $50; doubles $50/$60. AmEx/D/MC/V. ❸

Delux Inn and Suites/Motel Birmingham, 7905 Crestwood Blvd. (☎ 205-956-4440). Take Exit 132B from I-20 E. Turn right at Montevallo Rd. and left on Crestwood Blvd. Comfortable rooms with patios and pool access. Continental breakfast included. Rooms $69. AmEx/D/MC/V. ❸

Oak Mountain State Park Campground (☎ 800-252-7275), 15 mi. south of the city, in Pelham. Take Exit 246 off I-65. 10,000 acres of horseback riding, golfing, and hiking, and an 85-acre lake with a beach and fishing. Bathrooms, showers, and laundry. Park open daily 7am-8pm. 2-night min. stay required for reservations. Sites $11, with water and electricity $15, with full hookup $17. MC/V. ❶

🎵 ENTERTAINMENT

Opened in 1927, the **Historic Alabama Theater,** 1817 3rd Ave. N, is booked 300 nights of the year with films, concerts, and live performances. Their organ, the "Mighty Wurlitzer," entertains the audience before each show. (☎ 205-251-0418. Box office open M-F 9am-4pm. Order tickets at the box office 1hr. prior to show. Shows generally 7pm, Su 2pm. Organ plays 15min. before the official show time. Free.) Those visiting Birmingham in the middle of June can hear everything from country to gospel to big-name rock groups at **City Stages.** The three-day festival, held on multiple stages in the blocked-off streets of downtown, is the biggest event of the year and includes food, crafts, and children's activities. (☎ 205-251-1272 or 800-277-1700; www.citystages.org. 1-day pass $25, 3-day weekend pass $40.)

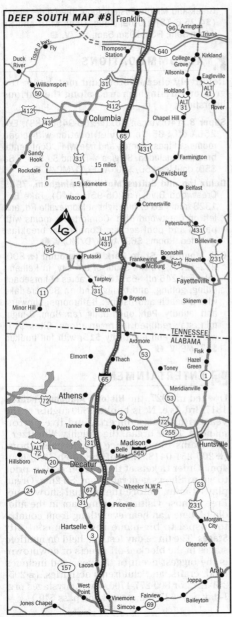

DEEP SOUTH MAP #8

DEEP SOUTH

NIGHTLIFE

Nightlife centers around **Five Points South,** at 20th St. S and 11th Ave. S. **The Garage,** 2304 10th Terrace S, is a very cool bar tucked out of sight down 23rd St. A former architecture studio turned antique store, the Garage still has all of the original materials—customers just drink among the statues and artwork. Try a Jubel German beer in the courtyard, or munch on a simple sandwich among the nymphs and Greek art. (☎205-322-3220. Open daily 11am-3am.) The hippest people jam at **The Nick,** 2514 10th Ave. S, at the corner of 26th St. It's so cool, in fact, that locals simply call it "the place." (☎205-252-3831. Nightly live rock music. Cover $5-15. Open M-F 3pm-last customer, Sa-Su 8pm-6am.) **22nd Street Jazz Cafe,** 712 22nd St. S, a small basement bar, has live jazz most Friday and Saturday nights. (☎205-252-0407. Cover F-Sa $5. Happy hour daily 4-7pm. Open M-Th and Su 4pm-midnight, F-Sa 4pm-2am. MC/V.)

APPROACHING RICKWOOD CAVERNS STATE PARK: 30 MILES

From Birmingham, take **I-65 N** for 26 mi. Take **Exit 287,** then follow signs to Rickwood Caverns State Park for 4 mi.

RICKWOOD CAVERNS STATE PARK. At Rickwood Caverns State Park, 370 Rickwood Park Rd., in Warrior, visitors can explore a mile-long underground trail through limestone caverns. The park also has an Olympic-size swimming pool fed by spring water from the caverns. (☎205-647-9692; www.ala-park.com. $1 per vehicle. 45min. tours $8, ages 6-11 $5. Swimming $3 per day. Caves open daily 10am-5pm.) The **Rickwood State Park Campground ❶** has sites with water and electric hookup. (☎205-647-9692. Bathhouse with showers in summer. Sites $14. MC/V.)

APPROACHING CULLMAN: 24 MILES

Continue on **I-65 N** for 22 mi. Take **Exit 308,** then follow **Rte. 278 E** for 2 mi. to downtown Cullman.

CULLMAN. The highlight of this little town is the **Ave Maria Grotto,** 1600 St. Bernard Dr. SE, 2 mi. east of downtown. On a wooded hillside, the Benedictine monk Joseph Zoettlis build a lifetime's worth of miniature sand and cement sculptures and replicas of famous buildings ranging from St. Peter's Basilica in Rome to the mythical Hanging Gardens of Babylon. In the heart of the grotto, a meticulously detailed cave is devoted to the Virgin Mary and sits next to replicas from the biblical city of Jerusalem. (☎256-734-4110; www.avemariagrotto.com. Open daily Apr.-Sept. 8am-6pm; Oct.-Mar. 8am-5pm. $7, seniors $5, under 12 $4.50.) **Johnny's BBQ ❷**, on Rte. 278, between downtown Cullman and I-65, has tasty and affordable barbecue in an Alabama-style tomato-based sauce. (☎256-734-8539; www.johnnysbbq.com. Pork and chicken plates $5-8. Open Tu-Sa 10am-9pm. AmEx/D/MC/V.)

◤ APPROACHING DECATUR: 39 MILES
From Cullman, take **I-65 N** for 32 mi. to **Exit 340,** then follow **Rte. 20/72 W** for 5 mi.

DECATUR

An industrial town on the Tennessee River's Wheeler Lake, Decatur is home to the Meow Mix cat food plant, among other lakeside mega-factories. Point Mallard Park, on Point Mallard Dr., has a 35-acre waterpark with a wave pool, multiple waterslides, and other attractions. Because it's run by the town, admission is a bargain. (☎256-341-4900; www.pointmallardpark.com. Open May-Sept. M-Th 10am-6pm, F-Su 10am-9pm. $15, ages 5-11 $10.) ◤**Big Bob Gibson BBQ ❷**, 1715 6th Ave. SE (Rte. 31), claims to be the world's best barbecue, and the imposing forest of trophies next to the front door testifies to the restaurant's impressive barbecue resume. The food lives up to the reputation, with succulent ribs and saucy pulled pork. (☎256-350-6969; www.bigbobgibson.com. Plates $7-10. Open daily 9:30am-8:30pm.) If you need a break from barbecue, **Tony's Country Cooking ❷**, 2324 6th Ave. SE (Rte. 31), has breakfast specials ($6), meat-and-vegetable plates ($6.50), and a standard diner menu. (☎256-306-0012. Open daily 5am-10pm. MC/V.) Point Mallard has a **campground ❶**, 2600 Point Mallard Dr. SE, that has shady sites with water, electricity, showers, and laundry facilities. (☎256-351-7772; www.pointmallardpark.com. Sites $16-18. MC/V.)

◤ APPROACHING ATHENS: 14 MILES
Continue on **I-65 N,** and take **Exit 354** to Athens.

ATHENS

Athens' downtown has been all but conquered by a Super Wal-Mart near Exit 354 off I-65. The **Alabama Veterans Museum**, 100 W. Pryor St., downtown, has a collection of military artifacts from the Revolutionary War to the present-day. Because most of the museum's uniforms, guns, maps, and other artifacts have been donated by Alabama veterans, most are presented along with a story of how they were used or found by a particular soldier or sailor. (☎256-771-7568; www.alabamaveteransmuseum.com. Open W and F-Sa 9am-3pm. Free.) Just south of downtown, **Dubs Burgers ❶**, in a mini-mall on S. Jefferson St., is an ancient burger-and-fries restaurant. The handmade hamburgers ($3) are phenomenal. (☎256-232-6135. Open M-Sa 11am-2pm. Cash only.) **La Fiesta Mexicana ❷**, 600 S. Jefferson St., has good Mexican food with plentiful veggie options. (☎256-232-2323. Lunch specials $4-6. Dinner entrees $5-10. Open daily 11am-10pm. AmEx/D/MC/V.) **The Bomar Inn ❷**, 1101 Hwy. 31 S, is an independently owned motel, about a mile south of downtown, with clean, spacious rooms. (☎256-232-6944. Rooms $32-36. AmEx/D/MC/V.)

◤ APPROACHING COLUMBIA: 42 MILES
From Athens, take **I-65 N** for 36 mi. across the Alabama/Tennessee border. Take **Exit 46,** then follow **Rte. 412 W** for 6 mi. to downtown Columbia.

The Volunteer State
TENNESSEE
Welcomes You!

COLUMBIA. Columbia's main attraction is the **James K. Polk Presidential Home Site**, 301-305 W. 7th St., the only surviving residence of the 11th President of the United States. Restored with the original furnishings from Polk's time in Tennessee, the house also has a small exhibit on Polk's presidency and an outdoor garden. Tours are given every 30min. and last approximately 20min. (☎931-388-2354;

www.jameskpolk.com. Open Mar.-Nov. M-Sa 9am-5pm, Su 1-5pm; Nov.-Mar. M-Sa 9am-5pm, Su 1-4pm. $7, seniors $6, children $4.) North of Columbia on Rte. 31 in Spring Hill, the **General Motors/Saturn Spring Hill Manufacturing Welcome Center**, Saturn Pkwy., has a welcome center that takes visitors on a guided tour of the immense Saturn automobile assembly plant. Children must be 42 in. tall and accompanied by a parent. (☎800-326-3321. Open M-F 7:30am-5pm. Tours M-Tu and Th-F 8:30, 10am, 1, 2:30pm; W 10am, 1, 2:30pm.)

 DID YOU KNOW? Tennessee produces the largest number of Bibles in the US.

⚐ APPROACHING FRANKLIN: 24 MILES
From Columbia, take **Rte. 31 N,** following **Bus. 31** into Franklin.

FRANKLIN

A southern suburb of Nashville, Franklin has a small downtown that is absurdly adorable. **Franklin on Foot** arranges themed walking tours of the historic downtown, and the 90min. **Ghosts and Gore Tour** every Saturday night exposes Franklin's darker past. It features the sites of hangings, lynchings, "activities of the night," and even some allegedly haunted buildings. (☎615-400-3808; www.franklinonfoot.com. $15.) The **Carter House**, 1140 Columbia Ave., provides an in-depth account of the 1864 Civil War battle in Franklin, including a small diorama of the battle and a guided tour of a house that was at the center of the fighting. (☎615-791-1861; www.carter-house.org. Open Apr.-Oct. M-Sa 9am-5pm, Su 1-5pm; Nov.-Mar. M-Sa 9am-4pm, Su 1-4pm. $8, seniors $7, ages 6-12 $4.) Franklin's neoclassical plantation house, **Carnton Plantation**, 1345 Carnton Ln., is a majestic mansion with period furnishings. The house also served as a battlefield hospital during the Civil War, and visitors can see the Confederate cemetery on the grounds for free. (☎615-794-0903; www.carnton.org. Open M-Sa 9am-5pm, Su 1-5pm. 1hr. tours $10, seniors $9, children $3.) In downtown Franklin, **Merridee's Breadbasket ❶**, 110 Fourth Ave. S, is a cozy bakery with delicious homemade breakfasts, as well as a full menu of sandwiches. (☎615-790-3755; www.mer-ridees.com. Lunch entrees $3-6. Open M-Sa 7am-5pm. MC/V.) **McCreary's Irish Pub and Eatery ❷**, 414 Main St., has burgers, pot pies, and fancy baked potatoes in an informal pub atmosphere. (☎615-591-3197. Entrees $6-8. Open M-Th 11am-10pm, F-Sa 11am-midnight. AmEx/D/MC/V.)

⚐ APPROACHING NASHVILLE: 21 MILES
Take **Hwy. 96 E** for 3 mi. to **I-65.** Follow I-65 N for 18 mi. to downtown Nashville.

NASHVILLE

Nashville is often called "nouveau dixie," with much of its wealth invested in gaudy, glitzy entertainment. Nashville also bears a number of other unusual nicknames. Known as "the Athens of the South," the city is home to an array of Greek, or rather, imitation Greek architecture. The area has also been called the "buckle of the Bible belt," a reference to its Southern Baptists. But Nashville's most popular moniker by far is "Music City, USA," and for good reason: this town has long been the banjo-pickin', foot-stompin' capital of country music. No matter which Nashville you visit, you're sure to have a rollicking good time, with music and beer flowing around the clock.

VITAL STATS

Population: 545,530

Visitor Info: Nashville Visitor Information Center, 501 Broadway (☎615-259-4747; www.nashvillecvb.com), in the Gaylord Entertainment Center, at Exit 209A off I-65 N/I-40. Open M-Sa 8:30am-5:30pm, Su 10am-5pm.

Internet Access: Nashville Public Library, 615 Church St. (☎615-862-5800), between 6th and 7th Ave. Open M-Th 9am-8pm, F 9am-6pm, Sa 9am-5pm, Su 2-5pm. Free. **J & J's Market,** 1912 Broadway (☎615-327-9055), has 2 Internet terminals. $1 per 10min. Open M-F 7am-midnight, Sa 9am-midnight, Su noon-9pm.

Parking: Library Garage, at 7th Ave. N between Commerce and Church St. $1 per 30min., max. $5 per day.

Post Office: 901 Broadway (☎615-256-3088), in the same building as the Frist Center for the Visual Arts. Open M-F 8:30am-5pm. **Postal Code:** 37203.

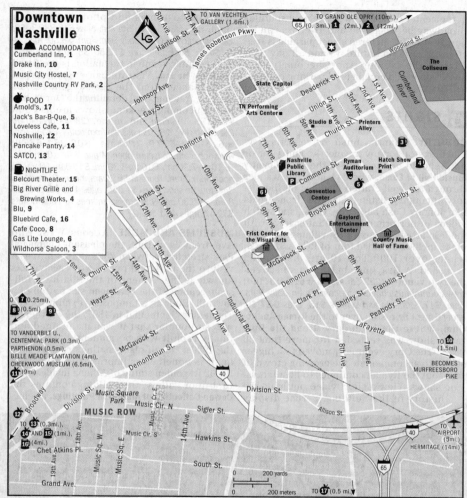

Downtown Nashville

▲▲▲ ACCOMMODATIONS
Cumberland Inn, 1
Drake Inn, 10
Music City Hostel, 7
Nashville Country RV Park, 2

● FOOD
Arnold's, 17
Jack's Bar-B-Que, 5
Loveless Cafe, 11
Noshville, 12
Pancake Pantry, 14
SATCO, 13

NIGHTLIFE
Belcourt Theater, 15
Big River Grille and
  Brewing Works, 4
Blu, 9
Bluebird Cafe, 16
Cafe Coco, 8
Gas Lite Lounge, 6
Wildhorse Saloon, 3

GETTING AROUND

Nashville's roads are fickle, often interrupted by curving parkways and one-way streets. Names change without warning. **Broadway,** the main east-west thoroughfare, runs through downtown, then veers left after passing over I-40; **West End Ave.** continues straight ahead. Broadway joins **21st Ave.** after a few blocks, passing through Vanderbilt University. In the downtown area, numbered avenues run north-south, parallel to the Cumberland River and divided by Broadway into north and south. The curve of **James Robertson Pkwy.** encloses the north end, becoming **Main St.** on the other side of the river (later Gallatin Pike) and turning into **8th Ave.**

in the center of downtown. The area south of Broadway between 2nd and 7th Ave. can be unsafe at night. Metered street parking is free after 12:30pm on Saturdays and all day Sundays; in the evening, spots become prized possessions and commercial parking costs up to $10.

👁 SIGHTS

COUNTRY. Country music drives this city. The first stop for any traveler—country fan or not—should be the state-of-the-art ◪**Country Music Hall of Fame,** where visitors can wander through the well-crafted displays on the history of country, listen to samples from greats like Johnny Cash and Patsy Cline, and watch videos of performances and interviews with modern artists. An extra $8 will upgrade tickets to include a guided tour of RCA's **Studio B,** where over 1000 Top 10 hits have been recorded. A Grayline shuttle runs between the two venues. *(222 5th Ave. S. ☎615-416-2001; www.countrymusichalloffame.com. Open daily 9am-5pm. $17, students and seniors $15, ages 6-17 $9, under 6 free.)* Two-step over to the **Ryman Auditorium,** where the legendary **Grand Ole Opry** radio show was recorded for more than 30 years. The Opry eventually moved to a bigger studio to accommodate the growing crowd of fans, but the Ryman continues to host fantastic shows. View a short video outlining the history of the building, peruse display cases of costumes and photos, and even climb on stage. *(116 5th Ave. N. ☎615-889-3060; www.ryman.com. Open daily 9am-4pm. $8.50, ages 4-11 $4.25. Backstage tour $12.50/$8.50.)* The premier country venue in the nation is the **Grand Ole Opry House.** Visitors can enjoy musical performances, tour the backstage areas, or visit the free museum detailing the Opry's history. Upcoming weekend shows are listed in *The Tennessean* and online. *(2804 Opryland Dr. Exit 11 off Hwy. 155, accessible from both I-40 and I-65. ☎615-871-6779, tickets 800-871-6779; www.opry.com. Museum open M and W-Th 10am-6pm, Tu 10am-7:30pm, F 10am-8:30pm, Sa 10am-10pm, Su noon-5pm. Free. Tours M-Sa 10am, noon, 2, 3pm; no 3pm tour on show days. $11.50, ages 4-11 $5. Shows F 8pm, Sa 6:30 and 9:30pm, sometimes Tu 7pm. Tickets $32-47, ages 4-11 $22-27.)*

MUSEUMS AND MORE. Across West End Ave. from Vanderbilt, the pleasant **Centennial Park** stretches between 25th and 28th Ave. A visit to the park will reveal why Nashville is known as the "Athens of the South": a full-scale replica of the **Parthenon** sits on top of a low hill. Built as a temporary exhibit for the Tennessee Centennial in 1897, the Parthenon was so popular that it was maintained and finally rebuilt with permanent materials in the 1920s. Out-of-place as the structure may be, it is nonetheless impressive—especially the 42 ft. golden statue of Athena inside. In its first-floor gallery, the building contains the **Cowan Collection of American Paintings,** a selec-

"YOU ARE SO NASHVILLE IF..."

Nashville's status as the glitzy capital of country music has resulted in some awkward cultural contradictions. For the past 18 years, Nashville's *Scene* magazine has lampooned the city's image-consciousness with its annual "You are so Nashville if . . ." contest. In the same vein as Jeff Foxworthy's "You might be a redneck if . . ." jokes, the contest has poked fun at Nashville's quirky fusion of New South money and Old South tradition. The inaugural winner of the contest referred to Nashville's status as the Athens of the South with "You are so Nashville if you think our Parthenon is better because the other one fell apart." The 1993 winner mocked Nashville's mega-churches with "You are so Nashville if your church congregation is referred to as 'the studio audience.'" The 2006 contest prompted such entries as "You'd rather keep your quarterback and trade your Senator" and "The wire holding your bumper to your car is a low E string." The 2006 winner reacted to the cultural impact of the film *Brokeback Mountain* with "You are so Nashville if you were a gay cowboy before being a gay cowboy was cool." Perhaps the best entry of the contest's history is the 1996 winner, which sums up the Music City's perplexing but enduring appeal with "You are so Nashville if you never meant to stay here this long."

tion of 19th- and early 20th-century American art. (☎615-862-8431; www.parthenon.org. Open in summer Tu-Sa 9am-4:30pm, Su 12:30-4:30pm; in winter Tu-Sa 9am-4:30pm. $5, 62+ and ages 4-17 $2.50.) Right in the heart of downtown, the **Frist Center for the Visual Arts** inspires both young and old with an interesting array of rotating exhibits. Some of the most popular exhibitions require additional entrance fees of $5-10. (919 Broadway. ☎615-244-3340; www.fristcenter.org. Open M-W and Sa 10am-5:30pm, Th 10am-8pm, F 10am-9pm, Su 1-5pm. $8.50, military and 65+ $7.50, college students with ID $6.50, under 19 free.) **Fisk University's Carl Van Vechten Gallery** consists of a portion of the private collection of Alfred Steiglitz, donated by his widow Georgia O'Keeffe. The gallery is small, but the fascinating Steiglitz photographs hanging among works by Picasso, Cézanne, and Renoir should not be missed. (At Jackson St. and D.B. Todd Blvd. ☎615-329-8720. Open Sept.-May Tu-F 10am-5pm, Sa-Su 1-5pm; June-Aug. Tu-F 10am-5pm, Sa 1-5pm. Donation suggested.) At the **Capitol**, a stately Greek Revival building on Charlotte Ave. north of downtown, visitors can tour the Governor's Reception Room, the legislative chambers, the former Tennessee Supreme Court, and the grounds, which include the tomb of President James K. Polk. (On Charlotte Ave., between 6th and 7th Ave. ☎615-741-0830. Photo ID required. Open M-F 8am-4pm. Tours every hr. M-F 9-11am and 1-3pm. Free.) A letter-press poster printing shop that first opened in 1879, **Hatch Show Print** has a collection of posters of Nashville country stars, vaudeville acts, and sporting events. Go wild and decorate your car Nashville style. (316 Broadway. ☎615-256-2805. Open M-F 9am-5pm, Sa 10am-5pm. Free.)

CHEEKWOOD MUSEUM AND BELLE MEADE MANSION. For a break from the bustle of downtown, head to the **Cheekwood Botanical Garden and Museum of Art.** The well-kept gardens, complete with a woodland sculpture trail, are a peaceful spot for a stroll. The museum features American and contemporary sculpture and paintings and a collection of English and American decorative arts. (1200 Forrest Park Dr., off Page Rd. ☎615-356-8000; www.cheekwood.org. Open June-Aug. Tu-W and F-Sa 9:30am-4:30pm, Th 9:30am-8pm, Su 11am-4:30pm; Sept.-May Tu-Sa 9:30am-4:30pm, Su 11am-4:30pm; .

$10, seniors $8, college students and ages 6-17 $5. Half-price after 3pm.) The nearby **Belle Meade Plantation** was once one of the nation's most famed thoroughbred nurseries. The lavish 1853 mansion has hosted seven US presidents, including the 380 lb. William Howard Taft, who allegedly spent some time lodged in the mansion's bathtub. Visitors can explore the house and grounds, including a collection of antique carriages. (5025 Harding Rd. ☎615-356-0501 or 800-270-3991; www.bellemeadeplantation.com. Open M-Sa 9am-5pm, Su 11am-5pm. $11, seniors $10, ages 6-12 $5.)

THE HERMITAGE. The graceful manor of US president Andrew Jackson, the Hermitage holds an impressive array of its original furnishings. Admission includes a 15min. film about Jackson's life, access to the house and grounds, and a visit to the nearby **Tulip Grove Mansion** and **Hermitage Church.** (4580 Rachel's Ln. Exit 221 off I-40 E, continue 4 mi. on Old Hickory Blvd.; entrance is on the right. ☎615-889-2941; www.thehermitage.com. Open daily 9am-5pm. Last tickets sold at 4:30pm. $12, 62+ and ages 13-18 $11, ages 6-12 $6.)

▓ FOOD

The famous Nashville candy **goo-goo clusters** (peanuts, pecans, chocolate, caramel, and marshmallow) are sold in specialty shops throughout the city. Nashville's other finger-lickin' traditions, barbecue and fried chicken, are no less sinful. Restaurants catering to collegiate tastes and budgets cram **21st Ave., West End Ave.,** and **Elliston Place,** near Vanderbilt.

▓ **Arnold's,** 605 8th Ave. S (☎615-256-4455). This cafeteria-style restaurant boasts the best meat-and-3-vegetable special ($7) for miles around. The roast beef au jus is delicious, and the pies are freshly made (slice $2). Open M-F 10:30am-3pm. MC/V. ❷

Loveless Cafe, 8400 Rte. 100 (☎615-646-9700; www.lovelesscafe.com), at the end of the Natchez Trace Pkwy. Follow West End Ave. to where it becomes Harding Pike/Rte. 100. A Nashville tradition since 1951. The fried chicken, country breakfasts, and delicious made-from-scratch biscuits are as good as ever. Breakfast ($9-12) served all day. Open daily 7am-9pm. AmEx/D/MC/V. ❸

Pancake Pantry, 1796 21st Ave. (☎615-383-9333), serves stacks of delicious, fluffy pancakes, from traditional buttermilk to orange-walnut or apricot-lemon ($7). Don't be scared off if there's a line out the door—it always goes fast. Open M-F 6am-3pm, Sa-Su 6am-4pm. MC/V. ❶

Jack's Bar-B-Que, 416A Broadway (☎615-254-5715; www.jacksbarbque.com), is a bit of a legend, both for the flashing neon-winged pigs above the door and for its succulent, tender pork. Sandwiches $3-5. Plates $8-12. Open in summer M-Th 10:30am-8pm, F-Sa 10:30am-10pm, Su noon-6pm; in winter Th 10:30am-8pm, F-Sa 10:30am-10pm. AmEx/D/MC/V. ❷

SATCO (San Antonio Taco Company), 416 21st Ave. S (☎615-327-4322), near Vanderbilt. Not gourmet, but crazy cheap. The outdoor patio is full of Vanderbilt students every evening. Fajitas $1.50-2. Enchilada plates $5-6. Open in summer M-W and Su 11am-midnight, Th-Sa 11am-1am; in winter M-W and Su 11am-11pm, Th-Sa 11am-midnight. AmEx/D/MC/V. ❶

Noshville, 1918 Broadway (☎615-329-6674; www.noshville.com), in Midtown. A New York-style deli with a menu that would please even the most die-hard Manhattanite, Noshville's selection ranges from matzoh ball soup ($4.50-5.50) to pastrami on rye ($10) and smoked whitefish on a bagel ($10). Open M 6:30am-2:30pm, Tu-Th 6:30am-9pm, F 6:30am-10:30pm, Sa 7:30am-10:30pm, Su 7:30am-9pm. AmEx/D/MC/V. ❸

ACCOMMODATIONS

Rooms in downtown Nashville can be expensive, especially in summer. The visitors center offers several deals on motel rooms, and budget motels are plentiful around **West Trinity Lane** and **Brick Church Pike,** off I-65 at Exit 87. There are cheap hotels around **Dickerson Rd.** and **Murfreesboro,** and near downtown, motels huddle on **Interstate Dr.** over the Woodland St. Bridge.

Music City Hostel, 1809 Patterson St. (☎615-692-1277; www.musiccityhostel.com), near Vanderbilt and Midtown. Friendly and reasonably clean, this hostel is a good, secure option close to Nashville's downtown attractions. Rooms are comfortable, though it can get crowded on weekends during the summer. Free Wi-Fi, full kitchen, and TV room. Dorms $25; private rooms $50-75. MC/V. ❶

Drake Inn, 420 Murfreesboro Rd. (☎615-256-7770). Close to downtown with small and clean rooms. Most rooms feature funky, country music-influenced wall paintings. Laundry and a pool. Singles $40; doubles $45. AmEx/D/MC/V. ❸

Nashville Country RV Park, 1200 Louisville Hwy. (☎615-859-0348), 12 mi. north of downtown at Exit 98 off I-65. Significantly cheaper than the campgrounds surrounding Opryland USA, with shaded sites, showers, laundry, a pool, an exercise room, and free Wi-Fi. Sites $16, with water and electricity $17.25. AmEx/D/MC/V. ❶

Cumberland Inn, 150 W. Trinity Ln. (☎615-226-1600 or 800-704-1028). From downtown on I-65 N, take Exit 87, and turn right at the bottom of the ramp even though it says "East Trinity Lane." The Inn is on the right. The rates are among Nashville's lowest and get you A/C, HBO, and laundry. Singles $35; doubles $41. AmEx/D/MC/V. ❷

♫ ENTERTAINMENT

The hordes of visitors that swoop upon Nashville have turned the **Grand Ole Opry** (p. 744) into a grand ole American institution. However, there are other great forms of entertainment in the capital city as well. The **Tennessee Performing Arts Center,** 505 Deaderick St., at 6th Ave. N, hosts the Nashville Symphony, opera, ballet, Broadway shows, and other theater productions. (☎615-255-2787; www.tpac.org. Tickets $15-75.) The **Dancin' in the District Music Festival** runs from mid-June to mid-September in Riverfront Park and features three live bands every Thursday evening. Past performers include Better Than Ezra, Cake, and Blondie. (☎800-594-8499. Gates open at 5:30pm. Tickets $5-8.) Listings for the area's music and events fill the free *Nashville Scene* and *Rage,* available at most establishments.

Two professional franchises dominate the Nashville sports scene. The NFL's **Tennessee Titans** play at **Adelphia Coliseum,** 460 Great Cir-

1941: Les Paul's first electric guitar, "The Log," is an un-sexy monstrosity.

cle Rd., across the river from downtown. (☎615-565-4200; www.titansonline.com. Tickets $12-52.) The NHL's **Nashville Predators** face off at the **Gaylord Entertainment Center**, 501 Broadway. (☎615-770-2040; www.nashvillepreadators.com. Open M-F 10am-5:30pm. Tickets $10-85.)

🎵 NIGHTLIFE

Nashville has a vivacious nightlife scene fueled by country music; if you are into line dancing, you're good to go. Other, smaller scenes, such as hip-hop spots and gay clubs, are a little more out of the way. Downtown, country nightlife centers on Broadway and 2nd Ave., where tourists flock to Broadway's country music-themed **Honky Tonks** and bars. Downtown parking can be difficult in summer, especially when something is going on at the Gaylord Entertainment Center. Near Vanderbilt, **Elliston Place** hops with college-oriented music venues, and **Hillsboro Village**, on 21st Ave. at Belcourt Ave., attracts a young crowd to its late-night bars and coffee shops. **Church St.** runs west out of downtown and has a variety of nightclubs and bars.

🦋 **Bluebird Cafe**, 4104 Hillsboro Pkwy. (☎615-383-1461; www.bluebirdcafe.com), near the mall at Green Hills. From 21st Ave., it's on the left after you cross Richard Jones Rd. This famous bird sings original country and acoustic every night. Country stars Kathy Mattea and Garth Brooks started their careers here. $7 food and drink min. if sitting at a table. Cover for shows $4-10; no cover Su. Open M-Sa 5:30pm-last customer, Su 6pm-last customer. Early show M-Th 6pm, F-Su 6:30pm. Late show M and F-Sa 9:30pm, Tu-Th 9pm, Su 8pm. AmEx/D/MC/V.

Wildhorse Saloon, 120 2nd Ave. N (☎615-902-8200; www.wildhorsesaloon.com). Bring your boots and two-step 'til dawn in this country dance hall. It's loud and brash, but ain't that country? M-F dance lessons 6pm, Sa noon, Su 2pm. Tu-Sa live music 7pm. Cover after 7pm M-Th and Su $4, F-Sa $6. Open M-Th and Su 11am-1am, F-Sa 11am-3am. AmEx/D/MC/V.

Cafe Coco, 210 Louise Ave. (☎615-321-2626; www.cafecoco.com), off Elliston Pl. A cozy coffeehouse, bar, and sandwich shop popular with the

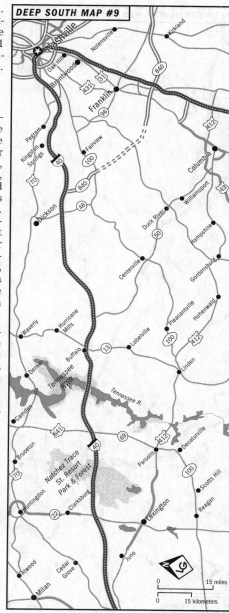

DEEP SOUTH MAP #9

DEEP SOUTH

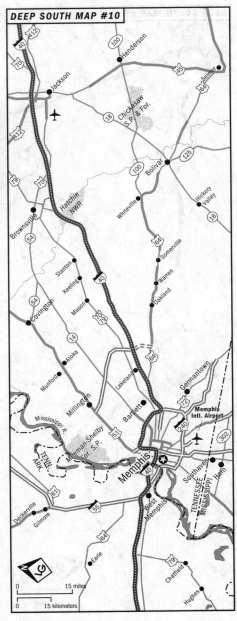

DEEP SOUTH MAP #10

0 — 15 miles
0 — 15 kilometers

college set. The patio and bar heat up with live music most nights starting around 7-8pm. Su jazz 4:30-7:30pm. Happy hour daily 7-11am and 3-6pm with $1 coffee and $2 domestic beers. Occasional cover F-Sa $3-5. Open 24hr. MC/V.

Belcourt Theater, 2102 Belcourt Ave. (☎615-383-9180; www.belcourt.org), at 21st St., in Hillsboro Village. Once a silent movie theater, the Belcourt now profits from the marketing miracle of blockbusters and booze. Films $7.75, students and seniors $6; matinees $6/$5.25. Call or check online for showtimes and events. AmEx/D/MC/V.

Big River Grille and Brewing Works, 111 Broadway (☎615-251-4677). A spacious microbrewery in the heart of downtown. The rotating choice of specialty beers ($3.75) and selection of salads will come as a relief to those in need of a fried-free night. Don't worry—you can still get ribs ($12). Open M-Th 11am-midnight, F-Sa 11am-1am. Kitchen closes M-Th 11pm, F-Sa midnight. AmEx/D/MC/V.

GLBT NIGHTLIFE

For info on GLBT nightlife in Nashville, check out the monthly *Out and About* or the weekly *Xenogeny*, available at venues downtown. Several gay nightclubs have opened on **Church St.**

Blu, 1713 Church St. (☎615-329-3838). A popular gay and lesbian nightclub, Blu has a downstairs dance floor. Th ladies night. F boys night. Su brunch noon. Open W-Sa 4pm-3am, Su noon-3pm and 6:30pm-midnight. MC/V.

Chute Nashville, 2535 Franklin Rd. (☎615-297-4571; www.chutenashville.com). Those in search of a theme party can stop at Chute Nashville, where the seven individual bars of this nightlife megaplex are given such raucous themes as The Sanctuary (dance club) and The Round-Up (country-themed). All this space allows for a variety of nightly events, from karaoke to talent shows to "high-energy" dance nights. Cover M and W $4, F-Sa $6. Tu, Th, Su no cover.

⚔ APPROACHING HURRICANE MILLS: 71 MILES
From Nashville, follow **I-40 W,** and take **Exit 143** to Hurricane Mills.

HURRICANE MILLS. Just off the I-40 exit ramp, the **Log Cabin Restaurant ❸,** on Rte. 13, has hunting-lodge style furnishings and delicious country cooking. Pork chops, catfish, or roast-beef plates are $10, but the adventurous can go for frog legs or liver and onions for $1 more. (☎931-296-5311. Open daily 6am-9pm. AmEx/D/MC/V.) Seven miles north of I-40, the **Coalminer's Daughter Museum,** within **Loretta Lynn's Ranch,** 44 Hurricane Mills Rd., celebrates the country music career of Loretta Lynn. The museum is packed with memorabilia, awards, dresses, cars, and videos charting Loretta Lynn's rise from rural childhood to Nashville mega-stardom. The ranch is home to an RV park, motocross course, horse stable, and fishing pond. (☎931-296-1840. Open Apr.-Oct. daily 9am-5pm. $10, children $5.)

◪ **APPROACHING JACKSON: 63 MILES**
Follow **I-40 W** to **Exit 80A** for Jackson.

JACKSON. The **Casey Jones Home and Railroad Museum,** 56 Casey Jones Lane, off Rte. 45, commemorates the heroic railroad conductor who "died on the throttle of Old 382" with a short video, a replica of his railroad engine, and a museum in his former home. (☎731-668-1223; www.caseyjones.com. $4, seniors $3.50, children $3.) Across the street from the museum, the **Old Country Store Restaurant and Buffet ❸,** is similar to country-style chain restaurants, but better, cheaper, and without the corporate aftertaste. (☎731-668-1223. Breakfast buffet $6-8. Soup and salad bar $7. Open daily 6:30am-9pm. MC/V.)

◪ **APPROACHING MEMPHIS: 80 MILES**
From Jackson, follow **I-40 W** to downtown Memphis.

MEMPHIS

Music is the pulse of Memphis and the reason why most visitors visit the city. Still, blues, funk, soul, country, and rock are deeply entwined with the history of civil rights and social change in the United States. White farmers brought country music, black workers brought the blues, and their synthesis resulted in a mixture of contemporary musical styles. Today, most visitors make the Memphis pilgrimage to see Graceland, the former home of Elvis Presley and one of the most deliciously tacky spots in the US. There's plenty to do after you've paid your respects to "The King"; unusual museums, fantastic ribs, and live music are just some of the reasons you might want to stay a few days.

▣ GETTING AROUND

Downtown, named avenues run east-west, and numbered streets run north-south. **Madison Ave.** divides north and south addresses. Two main thoroughfares, **Poplar** and **Union Ave.,** run east to west; **2nd** and **3rd St.** are the major north-south routes downtown. **I-240** and **I-55** encircle the city. **Riverside Dr.** takes you to **U.S. 61,** which becomes **Elvis Presley Blvd.** and leads south straight to Graceland. **Midtown,** east of downtown, is home to a funky music scene and gay venues and is a break from the tourist attractions (and tourist traps) of **Beale St.**

VITAL STATS
Population: 650,000
Visitor Info: Tennessee Welcome Center, 119 Riverside Dr. (☎901-543-6757; www.memphistravel.com), at Jefferson St. Open daily 7am-9pm.
Internet Access: Cossitt Branch Library, 33 S. Front St. (☎901-526-1712), downtown at Monroe. Open M-F 10am-5pm. Free.
Parking: Peabody Place, on Peabody Pl. Open M-W and Su 7am-2pm, Th-Sa 24hr. $1 per hr., max. $12 per day.
Post Office: 1 N. Front St. (☎901-576-2037). Open M-F 8:30am-5pm, Sa 9am-1pm. **Postal Code:** 38103.

◉ SIGHTS

▨ **GRACELAND.** The best strategy for visiting Elvis Presley's home is to know what you want to see before you go—it's easy to be overwhelmed by the crowds once you're there. Crowds are lightest in the mornings before 10am. The **Graceland Mansion** itself can be seen in about 1½-2hr.; it takes a whole morning or afternoon to visit the array of secondary shops, museums, and restaurants. The crush of tourists swarms in a delightful orgy of gaudiness around the tackiest mansion in the US. The faux-fur furnishings, mirrored ceilings, green shag-carpeted walls, ostrich-feather pillows, and yellow-and-orange decor of Elvis's 1974 renovations are not easily forgotten. A blinding sheen of hundreds of gold and platinum records illuminates the **Trophy Building**, where exhibits detail Elvis's stint in the army and his more than 30 movie roles. The King is buried in the adjacent **Meditation Gardens**. Be sure to check out the thousands of inscriptions carved on the stone wall next to the sidewalk in front of the mansion. *(3763 Elvis Presley Blvd. Take I-55 S to Exit 5B or bus #43 "Elvis Presley."* ☎901-332-3322 *or 800-238-2000; www.elvis.com. Ticket office open Mar.-Nov. M-Sa 9am-5pm, Su 10am-4pm; Dec.-Feb. M and W-Su 10am-4pm. Attractions open Mar.-Nov. M-Sa 9am-7pm, Su 10am-6pm; Dec.-Feb. M and W-Su 10am-6pm. Mansion closed Tu. Tour \$22; college students, ages 13-18, and 62+ \$20; ages 7-12 \$9.)*

MORE ELVIS. If you love him tender, love him true, visit the peripheral Elvis attractions across the street from the mansion. **Walk a Mile in My Shoes,** a free 20min. film screened every 30min., traces Elvis's career from the early (slim) years through the later (fat) ones. The **Elvis Presley Automobile Museum** houses a fleet of Elvis-mobiles, including pink and purple Cadillacs and motorized toys aplenty. *(*☎*901-332-3322 or 800-238-2000; www.elvis.com. \$8, students and seniors \$7.25, ages 7-12 \$4.)* Visitors to **Elvis' Custom Jets** can walk through the King's private plane, the *Lisa Marie*, complete with a blue suede bed and gold-plated seatbelts, and peek into the tiny *Hound Dog II* Jetstar. *(*☎*901-332-3322 or 800-238-2000; www.elvis.com. \$7, seniors \$6.50, children \$3.50.)* The **Sincerely Elvis** exhibit offers a glimpse into Elvis' private side, displaying his wedding announcements, a collection of Lisa Marie's toys, and items from his wild wardrobe, as well as memorabilia and heaps of fan letters. *(*☎*901-332-3322 or 800-238-2000; www.elvis.com. \$6, seniors \$5.50, children \$3.)* The **Platinum Tour Package** discounts admission to the mansion and other attractions. *(*☎*901-332-3322 or 800-238-2000; www.elvis.com. \$28, ages 13-18, college students and seniors \$27, ages 7-12 \$15.)* Graceland now offers an **Entourage Package** that lets you skip the lines to get in and includes a souvenir "backstage" pass. But at \$55 for all ages, it's a lot of money spent for

very little time saved: once inside, even VIPs have to wait behind hordes of visitors moving through The King's palace.

MUSICAL SIGHTS. Memphis's musical roots run deep into the fertile cultural soil of the Mississippi delta region. During the early- and mid-1900s, Memphis' musical scene blended jazz, soul, and folk traditions to create a new, unique blues sound. Downtown Memphis' historic **Beale St.** saw the invention of the blues and the soul hits of the Stax label. At the must-see ◨**Rock 'n' Soul Museum,** the numerous artifacts on display include celebrity stage costumes and B.B. King's famous guitar, Lucille. Best of all, the audio tour contains 100 complete songs. The museum also provides an account of rock 'n' roll's origins, from the cotton fields to the blending of black and white musical styles in Memphis recording studios. *(191 Beale St., across from the Gibson Guitar factory.* ☎*901-205-2533; www.memphisrocknsoul.org. Open daily 10am-7pm, last entry 6:15pm. \$9, ages 5-17 \$6.)* Long before Sam Phillips and Sun Studio produced Elvis and Jerry Lee Lewis, the **Gibson Guitar Factory** was lovingly constructing the quintessential rock instrument. The factory only produces about 35 instruments each day; tours detail the various stages of the guitar-making process. Visit during the week in the morning or early afternoon to see the craftsmen at work. Gibson's factory store is stocked with their entire lineup of guitars and will leave aspiring rock stars drooling. *(145 Lt. George W. Lee Ave.* ☎*901-543-0800, ext. 101; www.gibsonmemphis.com. 35-45min. tours M-Sa 11am-4pm on the hr., Su noon-4pm on the hr. \$10. Must be 5 or older.)* For rock 'n' roll fans, no visit to Memphis is complete without a visit to ◨**Sun Studio,** where rock 'n' roll was conceived. In this legendary one-room recording studio, Elvis rocked the jailhouse, Johnny Cash walked the line, and Jerry Lee Lewis was consumed by great balls of fire. Tours go through a small museum area and proceed to the studio itself, where visitors listen to the recording sessions that earned the studio its fame. *(706 Union Ave.* ☎*800-441-6249; www.sunstudio.com. Open daily 10am-6pm. 35min. tours every hr. on the half-hr. \$9.50, under 12 free.)*

1930: Edgar Leeteg pioneers black velvet painting, ensuring that Elvis will never die.

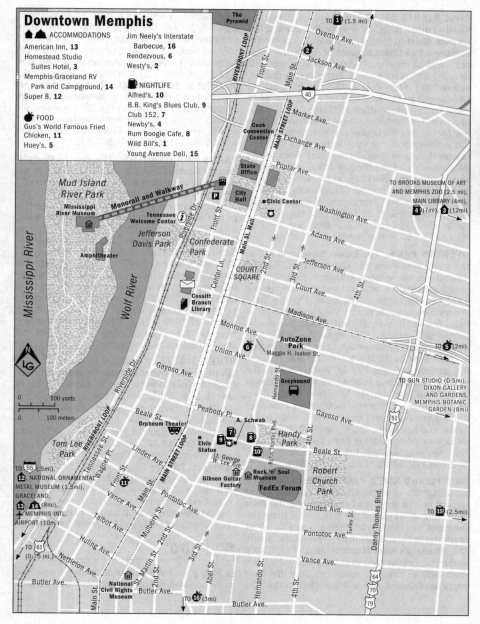

Downtown Memphis

▲▲ ACCOMMODATIONS

American Inn, **13**

Homestead Studio
  Suites Hotel, **3**

Memphis-Graceland RV
  Park and Campground, **14**

Super 8, **12**

Jim Neely's Interstate
  Barbecue, **16**

Rendezvous, **6**

Westy's, **2**

🍴 FOOD

Gus's World Famous Fried
Chicken, **11**

Huey's, **5**

🍸 NIGHTLIFE

Alfred's, **10**

B.B. King's Blues Club, **9**

Club 152, **7**

Newby's, **4**

Rum Boogie Cafe, **8**

Wild Bill's, **1**

Young Avenue Deli, **15**

CIVIL RIGHTS SIGHTS. On April 4, 1968, Dr. Martin Luther King, Jr. was assassinated at the **Lorraine Motel** in Memphis. Today, the powerful **☒National Civil Rights Museum** occupies the original building. Relive the courageous struggle of the Civil Rights movement through photographs, videos, and interviews in this moving exhibit, which ends in Dr. King's motel room. The main exhibition's presentation of the Civil Rights movement of the 1960s is comprehensive, engaging, and among the best of the South's many similar museums. Even so, the museum's annex across the street devotes an entire floor to the assassination of Dr. King and the investigation and trial of James Earl Ray, which some may find excessive and/or morbid. (450 Mulberry St. ☎ 901-521-9699; www.civilrightsmuseum.org. Open June-Aug. M and W-Sa 9am-6pm, Su 1-6pm; Sept.-May M and W-Sa 9am-5pm, Su 1-5pm. $12, students and 55+ $10, ages 4-17 $8.50. M after 3pm free.)

OVERTON PARK. The **Brooks Museum of Art,** in the southwest corner of Overton Park, east of downtown, showcases a diverse collection of paintings and decorative art and features visiting exhibits throughout the year. On the first Wednesday of each month, the museum hosts a celebration (6-9pm, $5) with food, films, live music, and drinks. (1934 Poplar Ave. ☎ 901-544-6200; www.brooksmuseum.org. Open Tu-F 10am-4pm, Sa 10am-5pm, Su 11:30am-5pm. $8, seniors $7, college students and ages 7-17 $4. W free.) Also in the park, the small but impressive **Memphis Zoo** is one of four places in the US where you can see giant pandas. The new "Northwest Passage" exhibit has polar and black bears, bald eagles, seals, and sea lions. (2000 Prentis Pl. ☎ 901-276-9453; www.memphiszoo.org. Open daily Mar.-Oct. 9am-6pm; Nov.-Feb. 9am-5pm. Last entry 1hr. before close. $13, 60+ $12, ages 2-11 $8. Tram tour $1.)

MUD ISLAND RIVER PARK. A quick walk or monorail ride over the Mississippi to **Mud Island** allows you to stroll and splash along the **River Walk,** a scale model of the Mississippi River the length of five city blocks. Free tours of the River Walk run several times daily. Also on the island, the **Mississippi River Museum** charts the history and culture of the river over the past 10,000 years with videos, musical recordings, and life-sized replicas of steamboats and iron-clad battleships.

(Monorail leaves from 125 N. Front St. every 10min. ☎ 901-576-7241 or 800-507-6507; www.mudisland.com. Park open June-Aug. daily 10am-6pm; Apr.-May and Sept.-Oct. Tu-Su 10am-5pm. Last entry 1hr. before close. 3-5 tours daily. Museum $8, 62+ $6, ages 5-12 $5. Monorail $2.) The newest feature is the **Sleep Out on the Mississippi,** scheduled for the 2nd Friday of each month during the summer. Though it may sound like a form of political protest, it's actually a camping excursion under the stars with dinner, music, kayaks, and breakfast. (Reservations ☎ 901-576-7241 or 800-507-6507. $40.)

PARKS AND GARDENS. The 96-acre **Memphis Botanic Garden,** with 22 distinct gardens, is the perfect place to take a long stroll. Relish the 57-variety rose garden, the sensory garden, or the Japanese garden. (750 Cherry Rd., in Audubon Park off Park Ave., 12 mi. east of downtown Memphis. ☎ 901-685-1566; www.memphisbotanicgarden.com. Open Apr.-Oct. M-Sa 9am-6pm, Su 11am-6pm; Nov.-Mar. M-Sa 9am-4:30pm, Su 11am-4:30pm. $5, 62+ $4, ages 3-12 $3, under 2 free.) Across Park Ave., the **Dixon Gallery and Gardens** flaunts an impeccable garden accented with an impressive range of sculptures and a collection of Impressionist art with works by Renoir, Degas, and Monet. (4339 Park Ave. ☎ 901-761-2409 or 901-761-5250; www.dixon.org. Open Tu-F 10am-4pm, Sa 10am-5pm, Su 1-5pm. $5, 60+ $4, students and children free.)

OTHER SIGHTS. South of downtown, the **☒National Ornamental Metal Museum,** the only institution of its kind in the US, displays fine metalwork from artists around the world. Get a better idea of the artistic process at the working blacksmith shop behind the museum, and check out the front gate as you walk in. (374 Metal Museum Dr. Exit 12C from I-55. ☎ 901-774-6380; www.metalmuseum.org. Open Tu-Sa 10am-5pm, Su noon-5pm. $5, 62+ $4, ages 5-18 $3.) A general store, antique museum, and clothing shop rolled into one, **A. Schwab** has stood on Beale St. since 1876. Used clothing, toys, gadgets, and miscellaneous treasures abound for the bargain-hunter. (163 Beale St. ☎ 901-523-9782. Open M-Sa 9am-5pm.)

◢ FOOD

In Memphis, barbecue is as common as rhinestone-studded jumpsuits; the city even hosts the

World Championship Barbecue Cooking Contest in May. Don't fret if gnawing on ribs isn't your thing—Memphis has plenty of other Southern restaurants with down-home favorites like fried chicken, catfish, chitlins, and grits.

Jim Neely's Interstate Barbecue, 2265 S. Third St. (☎901-775-2304; www.jimneelysinterstatebarbe-cue.com), off I-55 at Exit 7. Great barbecue, plain and simple. The chopped pork barbecue sandwich ($4.50-5.50) is tasty, as is the rib dinner (full rack of ribs; $8.50). Open M-Th 11am-11pm, F-Sa 11am-midnight. AmEx/MC/V. ❷

Rendezvous, 52 S. 2nd St. (☎901-523-2746). The entrance is around back on Maggie H. Isabel St., in the alley opposite the Peabody Hotel. A Memphis legend, serving charcoal-broiled ribs (half rack $14, full rack $17), cheese and sausages ($8), and sand-wiches ($6-7). Open Tu-Th 4:30-10:30pm, F 11am-11pm, Sa 11:30am-11pm. AmEx/D/MC/V. ❸

Huey's, 1927 Madison Ave. (☎901-726-4327 or 866-818-8094; www.hueyburger.com). The deli-cious Huey Burger ($5) comes with a toothpick holding the mouthwatering stack together. Look up and you'll see a forest of these colorful wooden spears stuck in the ceiling tiles. Open daily 11am-1am. AmEx/D/MC/V. ❷

Gus's World Famous Fried Chicken, 310 S. Front St. (☎901-527-4877). The sign out front says: "Today's Special: Chicken," and if their fried wings, thighs, and legs aren't the world's best, they come pretty close. Chicken plates with beans and cole slaw $4.50-5.50. Open daily 11am-9pm. AmEx/D/MC/V. ❶

Westy's, 346 N. Main St. (☎901-543-3278), at Jackson Ave., on the trolley line, downtown. Westy's serves deli-cious tamales, stuffed potatoes, and creole dishes (all $6-11) in a relaxed neighborhood pub atmosphere. Sandwiches on home-baked bread $5-9. Meat-and-three lunch specials $6.25. Happy hour daily 4-7pm. Open daily 10:45am-3am. AmEx/D/MC/V. ❷

ACCOMMODATIONS

A few downtown motels have prices in the bud-get range; more budget lodgings are available near Graceland at **Elvis Presley Blvd.** and **Brooks Rd.** Coupons from the visitors center are good for substantial discounts at many chain hotels, particularly midweek, but call ahead to confirm room availability. For the celebrations of Elvis's historic birth (Jan. 8) and death (Aug. 16), as well as for the month-long Memphis in May festival, book rooms six months to one year in advance.

Super 8, 340 W. Illinois St. (☎901-948-9005), Exit 12C off I-55. Close to downtown. Rooms are clean and include refrigerator, microwave, and access to a pool. Continental breakfast included. Shuttle to downtown $4. Rooms M-Th and Su $40-50, F-Sa $50-60. AmEx/D/MC/V. ❸

American Inn, 3265 Elvis Presley Blvd. (☎901-345-8444), Exit 5B off I-55, close to Graceland. Despite its shabby exterior, you can't help falling in love with the comfy rooms and the lobby's Elvis-themed mural. Cable TV, A/C, pool. Continental breakfast included. Singles $39; doubles $49. AmEx/D/MC/V. ❷

EAT LIKE ELVIS

Considering his booming voice and energetic personality, it's no surprise that Elvis Presley had an equally impressive appetite. Needless to say, Elvis lived in the era before weight-consciousness, the food pyra-mid, and low-carb dieting put a damper on good old-fashioned greasy deliciousness. As a southern boy raised in Tupelo, many of Elvis's favorite foods are Southern standards, including his all-time favorite meal: fried pork chops with brown gravy, mashed potatoes, apple pie and a Pepsi. Elvis's taste was not just traditional, however. Apparently, he also enjoyed his pork chops with sauerkraut and was known to fix himself ham salad for Thanksgiving dinner. Elvis devotees who wish to sample some of Elvis's more daring dishes can accompany their peanut butter and banana sandwich (fried in a skillet, with butter, of course) with some Swedish meatballs wrapped in bacon. Elvis's ample waistline during his sequined jumpsuit days later in his career are worth keeping in mind before you decide to go on an all-Elvis-food diet. But just like the decorations in Graceland, Elvis made his food uniquely his own. As he was fond of saying when ordering food: "I like it well done. I ain't ordering a pet."

Homestead Studio Suites Hotel, 6500 Poplar Ave. (☎901-767-5522). About 16 mi. from downtown. These impeccable rooms come with full kitchen, high-speed Internet, and access to laundry facilities. The surrounding area also offers plenty of dining options. Rooms $70-80. AmEx/D/MC/V. ❸

Memphis-Graceland RV Park and Campground, 3691 Elvis Presley Blvd. (☎901-396-7125 or 866-571-9236), beside the Heartbreak Hotel, a 2min. walk from Graceland. Very little privacy, but the location is great. Pool and laundry facilities. Reservations recommended. Sites $22, with water and electricity $32, with full hookup $35; cabins $36. D/MC/V. ❶

🎵 ENTERTAINMENT

The majestic **Orpheum Theatre,** 203 S. Main St., hosts Broadway shows and big-name performers. On Fridays during the summer, the grand old theater shows classic movies with an organ prelude and a cartoon. (☎901-525-3000; www.orpheum-memphis.com. Box office open M-F 9am-5pm and before shows. Movies $6, seniors and under 12 $5. Concerts and shows $15-55.) Just as things are really beginning to heat up in the South, the legendary **Memphis in May** celebration hits the city with concerts, art exhibits, food contests, and sporting events throughout the month. (☎901-525-4611; www.memphisinmay.org.) One such event is the **Beale Street Music Festival,** featuring some of the biggest names from a range of musical genres. There's also the **World Championship Barbecue Cooking Contest** and the **Sunset Symphony,** a concert near the river given by the Memphis Symphony Orchestra. In August, **Elvis Week** commemorates the King with events ranging from film festivals to impersonator contests. For more info, see www.elvis.com.

🎸 NIGHTLIFE

W.C. Handy's 1917 "Beale St. Blues" claims that "you'll find that business never closes 'til somebody gets killed." Today's visitors are more likely to encounter the Hard Rock Cafe and all the mega-commercialism that comes with it than the rough-and-tumble juke joints of old. Despite all the change, the strip between 2nd and 4th St. is still the place to go for live music. On Friday nights, a $12 wristband lets you into any club on the strip, except Alfred's. You must show ID to get into Beale St. at night; police officers card at entrances to the pedestrian area, which is 21+. The free *Memphis Flyer* and the "Playbook" section of the Friday *Memphis Commercial Appeal* can tell you what's goin' down in town. For a collegiate climate, try the **Highland St.** strip near **Memphis State University** or the intersection of **Young** and **Cooper Ave.** in Midtown. The city's gay bars are also in **Midtown.** For info on gay clubs and happenings, *Triangle Journal News* can be found in any gay venue. Memphis can be unsafe after dark outside the Beale St. area and downtown, so be careful and ask any bar to call you a cab.

Rum Boogie Cafe, 182 Beale St. (☎901-528-0150). One of the 1st clubs on Beale St., Rum Boogie still rocks with homegrown blues and a friendly ambience. Check out the celebrity guitars hanging from the ceiling. Nightly live music. Happy hour M-F 5-7pm. 21+ M-Th and Su after 9pm, F-Sa after 8pm. Cover $5-10. Open M-Th and Su 11am-12:30am, F-Sa 11am-2am. AmEx/D/MC/V.

B.B. King's Blues Club, 143 Beale St. (☎901-524-5464; www.bbkingsclub.com). Live blues makes this place popular with locals, visitors, and celebrities. Drinks are expensive, even for Beale St. B.B. himself occasionally plays a show, though tickets can reach $200 and typically sell out. Entrees $11-19. Music starts at 6pm, house band starts at 8:30pm. 21+ after 8pm. Cover $5-8. Open M-Th and Su noon-1:30am, F-Sa 11am-3am. AmEx/D/MC/V.

Club 152, 152 Beale St. (☎544-7011). One of the most popular clubs on Beale, offering 3 floors of dancing and drinks. Live music acts range from blues to techno. On weekends DJs spin upstairs. Check out the "mood elevator," a wildly painted elevator that takes you to hip-hop (F, 2nd fl.), techno (Sa, 3rd fl.), and beyond. Beer from $3.50. Cover $10-12. Open M-Th and Su 11am-2am, F-Sa 11am-5am. MC/V.

Alfred's, 197 Beale St. (☎901-525-3711; www.alfreds-on-beale.com). Known for its karaoke, live music, and DJs spinning into the wee hours. Upstairs patio overlooks Beale St.'s nightly debauchery. Nightly live music 6-10pm. 21+ after 10pm. Cover some Th and most F-Sa $5. Beale St. wristbands are not accepted. Open daily 11am-5am. AmEx/D/MC/V.

Newby's, 539 S. Highland St. (☎901-452-8408; www.newbysmemphis.com), is a lively college bar with pool tables, comfy red booths, and an outdoor patio.

Live bands play everything from rock to reggae almost every night beginning at 10pm. Happy hour daily 3-10pm. Cover usually $3-5. Open daily 3pm-3am.

Young Avenue Deli, 2119 Young Ave. (☎901-278-0034; www.youngavenuedeli.com), in Midtown. A cavernous bar with pool tables that attract a young crowd. 30 beers on tap, and hundreds of bottled beers to choose from, as well as a full deli menu and tasty french fries ($2.75). Cover usually $3-5. Happy hour M-F 4-7pm with $1.75 domestic beers. Open daily 11am-3am. Kitchen closes 2am. MC/V.

Wild Bill's, 1580 Vollintine Ave. (☎901-726-5473). A neighborhood restaurant and music joint way off the beaten track. Bill's is a far cry from Beale St.'s touristy joints. F-Sa live music 11pm, Su 10pm. Cover F-Su $5. Open M-Th 10am-11pm, F-Su 10am-3am. MC/V.

The Natural State

ARKANSAS

Welcomes You!

 BIG DETOUR. Explore the Southern soul in Mississippi on the **Barbecue, Blues, and Blue Suede Shoes Big Detour,** p. 756.

⚐ APPROACHING BRINKLEY: 79 MILES
From Memphis, take **I-40 W** to **Exit 216.** Follow **Rte. 49 S** for 2 mi. to downtown Brinkley.

BRINKLEY. The **Central Delta Cultural Center,** 100 W. Cypress St., in downtown Brinkley, has exhibits on the regional history of the Arkansas Delta including displays on the development of the railroads, the exploration of the Louisiana Purchase territory, and a feature on the 2004 discovery of the rare Ivory-Billed Woodpecker near Brinkley. (☎870-589-2124; www.eddm.org. Open M-Sa 9am-5pm, Su 1-4pm. $2, children $1.) **Gene's BBQ ❷,** 1107 N. Main St., between I-40 and downtown Brinkley, has pork barbecue, catfish, and burgers, (all $6-8). It may look like a big warehouse from the outside, but inside it's decorated like a cozy family dining room. (☎870-734-9965. Open daily 6am-10pm. AmEx/D/MC/V.)

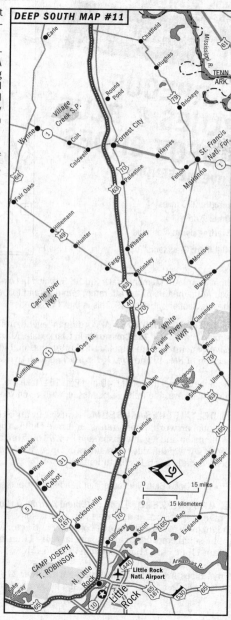

DEEP SOUTH MAP #11

BARBECUE, BLUES & BLUE SUEDE SHOES

LOVE ME FENDER

Length: 229 miles
Time: 2 days
Starting point: Memphis
Highlight: Graceland, Too

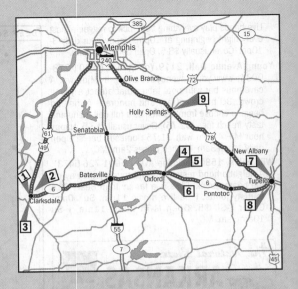

From downtown Memphis, take 3rd St. S, which becomes Rte. 61 S, for 70 mi. to the Clarksdale/Rte. 278/6 exit. At the bottom of the exit ramp, turn right and follow Rte. 278/6 W for ½ mi. Turn left onto Rte. 161 S to the intersection with Rte. 49. This is the "Crossroads."

1 THE CROSSROADS. According to legend, the pioneering blues guitarist Robert Johnson sold his soul to the devil at **The Crossroads** in Clarksdale, MS. Johnson's legendary guitar playing may or may not have benefitted from supernatural intervention, but the story lives on in Delta folklore, and the intersection of Rte. 49 and Rte. 161 is marked with two blue guitars to commemorate the alleged event.

From the intersection of Rte. 49 and Rte. 161, take Rte. 49 N (Decatur Ave.), and turn left onto 3rd St. Turn left onto Blues Ave. The Delta Blues Museum will be on your left.

2 DELTA BLUES MUSEUM. Housed in an old train depot, the Delta Blues Museum displays regional artwork, photographs, and rare Delta artifacts, including harmonicas owned by Sonny Boy Williamson and a guitar fashioned by ZZ Top from a log cabin Muddy Waters once lived in. (☎662-627-6820; www.deltabluesmuseum.org. Open Mar.-Oct. M-Sa 9am-5pm; Nov.-Feb. M-Sa 10am-5pm. $7, seniors and ages 6-12 $5, students $3.)

From the Delta Blues Museum, just head straight across the street for Ground Zero.

3 GROUND ZERO. Head to **Ground Zero ❶**, 0 Blues Alley, for a plate lunch ($7), complete with beverage, cornbread, and dessert. On Wednesday, Friday, and Saturday, stay late for local tunes. You might even catch a glimpse of co-owner and actor Morgan Freeman. (☎662-621-9009; www.groundzerobluesclub.com. Plate lunch special daily 11am-2pm. Open M-Tu 11am-2pm, W 11am-midnight, Th 11am-11pm, F-Sa 11am-midnight. AmEx/D/MC/V.)

From Blues Ave. in Clarksdale, backtrack to Rte. 278/6, and follow Rte. 6 E to the Lamar Ave./Downtown Oxford exit. Turn left on Lamar Ave., and follow it to Courthouse Sq. in downtown Oxford.

4 SQUARE BOOKS. Square Books is one of the best independent bookstores in the nation. The owner also happens to be the city's mayor. Expand your belly while opening your mind—coffee drinks and pastries are just $1-2 at the coffeeshop upstairs. (☎662-236-2262. Open M-Th 9am-9pm, F-Sa 9am-10pm, Su 10am-6pm.)

Take Lamar Ave. back toward Rte. 6, then turn right on University Ave. Follow University Ave. to Lyceum Circle. Park anywhere on the circle, and walk towards the Lyceum, the building with 6 white columns on the far side of the circle from University Ave. The Memorial and Blues archive are behind the Lyceum building.

5 CIVIL RIGHTS MEMORIAL AND BLUES ARCHIVE. Opened in 2006, the **Civil Rights Memorial** commemorates racial equality in higher education. A large stone doorway celebrates the successful struggle of James Meredith, the first African-American to enroll at the University of Mississippi. Next to the memorial in the main library, the **Ole Miss Blues Archive** will delight blues fans with one of the largest collections of Blues memorabilia in the world. (☎662-915-7753. Open M-F 8am-5pm. Free.)

From Lyceum Circle, follow University Ave. towards Lamar Ave. Turn right on Lamar Ave., and follow it until Old Taylor Rd. Turn right on Old Taylor Rd., and follow it to the parking area for Rowan Oak.

6 ROWAN OAK. Entranced by the house's history (it once belonged to a Confederate general), William Faulkner bought the place in 1930 and named the property after the Rowan tree, a symbol of peace and security. The plot outline of his 1954 novel *A Fable* is etched on the walls of the study. (☎662-234-3284. Mansion open for self-guided tours Tu-Sa 10am-4pm, Su 1-4pm. Grounds open sunrise to sunset. $5.)

Backtrack on Old Taylor Rd., turning right on Lamar Ave. and following it to Rte. 6. Take Rte. 6 E for 52 mi. Rte. 6 becomes Main St. near Tupelo. After passing through downtown Tupelo, turn right onto Franklin St. The Automobile Museum will be on your right.

7 TUPELO AUTOMOBILE MUSEUM. Antique car fanatics will be in heaven at the Tupelo Automobile Museum, 1 Otis Blvd., off E. Main St., which includes hot rides like a gull-wing DeLorean and a customized Corvette. (☎662-842-4242; www.tupeloauto.com. Open Tu-Su 10am-6pm. $10, seniors $8, children $5.)

Follow Rte. 6 E (Main St.) to the intersection with Veterans Blvd. Turn right on Veterans Blvd., and take the 1st right onto Reese St. The Elvis Birthplace Museum will be on the right.

8 ELVIS PRESLEY BIRTHPLACE. The Elvis Presley Birthplace, 306 Elvis Presley Blvd., is definitely worth a visit. There's also a museum, a memorial chapel, a fountain, and a statue of 13-year-old Elvis. (☎662-841-1245; www.elvispresleybirthplace.com. Open M-Sa 9am-5pm, Su 1-5pm. Birthplace $2.50, children $1.50.)

Head back on Reese St., turn right onto Veterans Blvd., and follow it to Rte. 78. Take Rte. 78 W to Rte. 4 E/7 N. Follow it to E. Gholson Ave., and turn right. Graceland Too is on your left. You really can't miss it.

9 GRACELAND TOO. Part museum and part Elvis shrine, **Graceland Too** is home to Paul MacLeod, the self-proclaimed "World's Number One Elvis Fan" and his son, Elvis Aaron MacLeod. The house's expansive collection of Elvis memorabilia is mind-boggling, but Paul's enthusiastic tours and encyclopedic knowledge of everything Elvis are equally stupifying. Tours can last anywhere from 1-4hr.; Paul's longest was 12hr. (☎662-252-2515. Open 24hr. If it's nighttime, just knock louder. $5.)

BACK TO THE ROUTE. From Graceland Too, backtrack to Rte. 78, and follow Rte. 78 W for 33 mi. to Memphis.

◤ APPROACHING LITTLE ROCK: 67 MILES
Take **Rte. 49 N** to I-40, and follow **I-40 W** for 63 mi. Take **Exit 153B** for **I-30 W** and take it to downtown Little Rock.

LITTLE ROCK

Located squarely in the middle of the state along the Arkansas River, Little Rock became a major trading city in the 19th century. A small rock served as an important landmark for boats pushing their way upstream. Though this "little rock" is still visible today, it doesn't loom as large as the historical landmark of Central High School, where, in 1957, Governor Orval Faubus and local white segregationists violently resisted nine black students who entered the school under the protection of the National Guard. Today, this and other historical events are remembered in the many museums in the downtown area. The newest attraction is the Clinton Presidential Library, which overlooks the Arkansas River..

VITAL STATS

Population: 184,500

Visitor Info: Little Rock Visitor Information Center, 615 E. Capitol Ave. (☎501-370-3290 or 877-220-2568; www.littlerock.com), in Curran Hall. Take the 6th or 9th St. exit off I-30, and follow the signs. Open M-Sa 8:30am-5pm, Su 1-5pm.

Internet Access: Main Library, 100 Rock St. (☎501-918-3000), near River Market. Open M-Th 9am-8pm, F-Sa 9am-6pm, Su 1-5pm. Free Wi-Fi.

Parking: Free parking beneath the overpass at 2nd Ave., between Commerce and Sherman St. Parking garage across 2nd Ave. ($1.50 per hr., $7.50 per 24hr.)

Post Office: 600 E. Capitol Ave. (☎501-375-5155). Open M-F 7am-5:30pm. **Postal Code:** 72701.

▣ GETTING AROUND

Little Rock is at the intersection of **I-40** and **I-30,** 140 mi. west of Memphis. Downtown, numbered streets run east-west, while named streets run north-south. The four major thoroughfares are **I-630, Cantrell Rd., University Ave.,** and **Rodney Parham Rd.** Near the river, Markham becomes 1st St. and Capitol becomes 5th St. The east side of Markham St. is now President Clinton Ave. and moves through the lively **River-**

walk district. North Little Rock is linked to downtown Little Rock by three bridges spanning the Arkansas River

◉ SIGHTS

▨ THE CLINTON PRESIDENTIAL CENTER. The Clinton Presidential Center was hailed by admirers as a metaphor for Clinton's "Bridge to the 21st Century" and lampooned by critics as a gigantic glass-walled mobile home. Highlights include Clinton's presidential limo, replicas of the Oval Office and Cabinet Room, and a compilation of humorous White House television moments. *(1200 E. President Clinton Ave. ☎501-374-4242; www.clintonpresidentialcenter.com. Open M-Sa 9am-5pm, Su 1-5pm. $7; students, military, and seniors $5; ages 6-17 $3.)*

CENTRAL HIGH SCHOOL. The aftermath of Little Rock's Civil Rights struggle is manifest at the corner of Daisy L. Gatson Bates Dr. (formerly 14th St.) and Park St., where **Central High School** remains a fully functional school. It is therefore closed to visitors, but a ▨**visitors center** in a restored gas station across the street contains an excellent exhibit on the "Little Rock Nine." *(2125 Daisy L. Gatson Bates Dr. ☎501-374-1957; www.nps.gov/chsc. Open M-Sa 9am-4:30pm, Su 1-4:30pm. Free.)*

MUSEUMS. In the middle of downtown, the **Historic Arkansas Museum** showcases rotating exhibits of art and artifacts from Arkansas. The museum also contains a small outdoor village that recreates life in 19th-century Little Rock using period actors who show off old-time frontier living. *(200 E. 3rd St. ☎501-324-9351; www.historicarkansas.org. Open M-Sa 9am-5pm, Su 1-5pm. 1hr. tour of historic homes $2.50, seniors $1.50, under 18 $1. Free.)* At the **Arkansas Inland Maritime Museum,** visitors can tour the *U.S.S. Razorback,* a World War II-era submarine. Quarters in the submarine are not for the claustrophobic, but this is a rare and undeniably cool chance to see the inside of a submarine. *(Off Riverfront Dr. in North Little Rock, accessible from I-30 at the Broadway exit. ☎501-371-8320. Open May-Sept. Th-Sa 10am-6pm, Su 1-6pm; Oct.-Apr. Sa 10am-sunset, Su 1pm-sunset. $6; seniors, military, and children $4.)* The **Arkansas Art Center** has an excellent permanent collection focusing on contemporary painting and sculpture. *(501 E. 9th St. ☎501-372-4000; www.arkarts.com. Open Tu-Sa*

10am-5pm, Su 11am-5pm. Permanent collection free, rotating exhibits $8-12.)

OTHER SIGHTS. When the legislature is not in session, visitors can explore the **State Capitol,** at the west end of Capitol St., which is modeled after the Capitol building in Washington, D.C. (☎501-682-5080. Open M-F 7am-5pm, Sa-Su 10am-3pm. Free.) Tourists can visit **"Le Petite Roche,"** the actual "little rock" of Little Rock, at Riverfront Park. From underneath the railroad bridge at the north end of Louisiana St., look straight down. Look carefully; the rock is part of the embankment (it's that small), and it's been covered in graffiti since its plaque was stolen. (At Riverfront Park, at the north end of Rock St.)

OUTDOORS. Just a 15min. drive to the west of the city is **Pinnacle Mountain State Park,** home to the **Arkansas Arboretum.** The 71-acre Arboretum highlights the different natural regions and flora in Arkansas with interpretive exhibits and a ½ mi. paved loop trail. Visitors can also walk down to the Little Maumelle River on the **Kingfisher Trail** (½ mi.) and see birds and giant cypress trees. For a more strenuous hike, visitors can climb to the top of the Pinnacle Mountain via the **West Summit Trail.** (11901 Pinnacle Valley Rd., in Roland. From Little Rock, take I-430 to Exit 9, and follow Rte. 10 W for 7 mi. Take Rte. 300 N for 2 mi., and follow the signs to the park. ☎501-868-5806; www.arkansasstateparks.com. Open M-F 8am-5pm, Sa-Su 8am-6pm. Free.)

🍴 FOOD

The city has revamped the downtown area starting with **River Market,** 400 President Clinton Ave. The downtown lunch crowd heads here for a wide selection of food shops, coffee stands, delis, and an outdoor **farmers market.** (☎501-375-2552; www.rivermarket.info. Market Hall open M-Sa 7am-6pm; many shops open only for lunch. Farmers market open May-Oct. Tu and Sa 7am-3pm.)

🐟 **The Flying Fish,** 511 President Clinton Ave. (☎501-375-3474), near Market Hall. Has quickly become downtown's most popular hangout for its unpretentious atmosphere and walls covered with photos of fish caught by patrons. Hungry diners clamor for platters of fried catfish, shrimp, and oysters ($5-9). Open daily 11am-10pm. MC/V. ❷

Cotham's in the City, 1401 W. 3rd St. (☎501-370-9177). Popularized by then-Governor Bill Clinton and

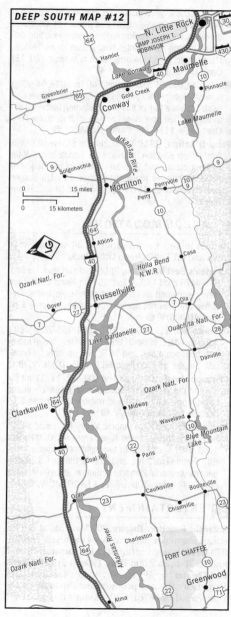

DEEP SOUTH MAP #12

other political types during the 1980s and 90s, which explains the campaign signs and posters that decorate the walls. Cotham's onion rings are enormous and delicious, but the restaurant is best known for its "Hubcap Hamburgers," grilled underneath a hubcap ($9.25). Open M-F 11am-2pm. MC/V. ❸

Whole Hog Cafe, 2516 Cantrell Rd. (☎501-664-5025; www.wholehogcafe.com), in the Riverdale Center strip mall. Eat like a hog at this award-winning barbecue restaurant. Pulled pork plates come with 2 sides for $6-7. Open M-Sa 11am-8pm. AmEx/D/MC/V. ❶

Pizza D'Action, 2919 W. Markham St. (☎501-666-5403), just past the Hillcrest area. Boasts some of the tastiest pizzas and liveliest crowds in the neighborhood. Nightly live music. Large pies $11-15. Burgers and sandwiches $5-7. Open daily 11am-1:30am. AmEx/D/MC/V. ❶

🏨 ACCOMMODATIONS

Budget motels crowd around I-30 southwest of town and off I-40 in **North Little Rock.**

America's Best Value Inn, 2508 Jackson Hwy. (☎501-945-4167), off I-40 at Exit 157, in North Little Rock. Newly renovated and spacious motel-style rooms. Free coffee and Internet access in the lobby. Rooms $39. AmEx/D/MC/V. ❷

Galloway Inn, 3124 Hwy. 391 (☎501-955-0700), off I-40 at Exit 161, in North Little Rock. New, clean rooms with free local calls, free Wi-Fi, and continental breakfast. Singles $57; doubles $62. AmEx/D/MC/V. ❸

Cimarron Motel, 10200 I-30 (☎501-565-1171), off Exit 130 on the westbound access road. Offers clean and basic rooms with fridge and microwave. Singles $35; doubles $40. AmEx/MC/V. ❷

Maumell Park, 9009 Pinnacle Valley Rd. (☎501-868-9477), on the Arkansas River. From I-430, take Rte. 10 (Exit 9) west 2½ mi., turn right on Pinnacle Valley Rd., continue for 2 mi., and look for the sign. 129 sites near the beautiful Pinnacle Mountain State Park. Office open daily 10am-10pm. Sites $18-20. MC/V. ❶

🎵 ENTERTAINMENT

Arkansas Repertory Theatre, 601 Main St., at 6th St., stages six major performances each year. (☎501-378-0445; www.therep.org. Performances W-F and Su 7pm, Sa 2 and 7pm. Tickets $18-35.) **Weekend Theater,** on W. 7th St., stages fantastic Off-Broadway theater productions throughout the year. (☎501-374-3761. Call for show times.)

NIGHTLIFE

Little Rock's growing nightlife scene centers around the **River Market District** on President Clinton Ave., downtown. West of downtown, a number of bars can be found in the **Hillcrest** neighborhood along Kavanaugh Blvd. For listings of shows, bands, and events, pick up a free copy of *Nightflying* or *Free Press*, available at most restaurants and bars around Little Rock.

The Flying Saucer, 322 President Clinton Ave. (☎501-372-7468; www.beerknurd.com). A beer-lover's paradise, with 75 beers on tap and hundreds of bottled beers. Settle into a cozy sofa, or relax at a table in their main tap room, which is decorated with—of course—flying saucers. Most beers $2.50-4. M $2.50 pints. F-Sa live music. Open M-Th and Sa 11am-1am, F 11am-2am. AmEx/D/MC/V.

Vino's, 923 W. 7th St. (☎501-375-8466; www.vinos-brewpub.com), at Chester St. Little Rock's original microbrewery-nightclub, with a clientele ranging from lunchtime's corporate businessmen to midnight's younger set. Live rock music most Th-Sa nights. Pizza slices $1.15. 18+ at night. Cover $5-10. Open M-W 11am-10pm, Th 11am-11pm, F 11am-1am, Sa 11:30am-1am, Su 1-9pm. MC/V.

Sticky Fingerz, 107 S. Commerce St. (☎501-372-7707; www.stickyfingerz.com), across President Clinton Ave. from the River Market. Sticky Fingerz serves its signature chicken fingers ($5.50) with a side of alt-rock. 21+ after 7pm. Open M-F 11am-1:30pm and 4pm-last customer, Sa 11am-1am. MC/V.

The Underground Pub, 500 President Clinton Ave. (☎501-707-2537). Offers British fare like fish and chips ($7) to go along with your Guinness. Enjoy music, darts, pool, foosball, and British football on big-screen TVs, or head to the outdoor patio overlooking the Arkansas River. Happy hour daily 4-7pm. Open M-W 11am-midnight, Th-F 11am-2am, Sa 11am-1am.

🚗 APPROACHING MORRILTON: 60 MILES

Take **I-40 W** for 45 mi. to **Exit 108.** Follow **Rte. 9 S** for 7½ mi., then turn right onto **Rte. 154 W** to head into Morrilton.

MORRILTON. The **Museum of Automobiles,** 8 Jones Ln., off Rte. 154, is Morrilton's main attraction, with over 50 restored classic cars. Highlights include Bill Clinton's '67 Mustang convertible, Elvis' Ranchero pickup, and antique vehicles dating back to the Model-T era. (☎501-727-5427; www.museumofautos.com. Open daily 10am-

5pm. $6, seniors $5.50, ages 6-17 $3.) Just down Rte. 154, **Petit Jean State Park,** 1285 Petit Jean Mountain Rd., is one of the largest state parks in Arkansas. Visitors can enjoy 20 mi. of hiking trails, drive to an overlook at the summit of Petit Jean Mountain, explore the 95 ft. ■**Cedar Falls,** fish or pedal-boat on Lake Bailey. The park also has a **campground ❶** with 125 campsites with water, electricity, and showers. (☎501-727-5441; www.petitjeanstatepark.com. Open sunrise-sunset. Sites $13-17; cabins $70-165. MC/V.)

◪ APPROACHING RUSSELLVILLE: 22 MILES
From Morrilton, continue on **Rte. 154 W** for 14 mi., then turn right onto **Rte. 7 N** to downtown Russellville.

RUSSELLVILLE. There are very few gas stations between Russellville and Fort Smith, so fill up here before you head out. The **Big Red Drive-In ❶**, 1520 S. Arkansas Ave. (Rte. 7), has been a Russellville mainstay for over 40 years, with tasty fried-chicken dinners ($4-6), catfish plates ($5-7), and burgers ($1-3). There's a small dine-in area, or you can just drive through. (☎479-968-1960. Open M-Th 9am-8pm, F-Sa 9am-9pm. MC/V.)

◪ APPROACHING FORT SMITH: 88 MILES
From downtown Russellville, take **Rte. 7 N** to I-40. Follow **I-40 W** for 74 mi. to **Exit 7 (I-540 S).** Take I-540 S to **Exit 7,** then take **Rogers Ave. (Hwy. 22 W)** to downtown Fort Smith.

FORT SMITH

An old frontier town, Fort Smith's biggest draw is the **Fort Smith National Historic Site,** 3rd St., comprised of two preserved military posts built on America's western frontier during the 1830s. The visitors center has a short video on the settlement of Oklahoma and the importance of the fort in enforcing the Indian Removal Act. Visitors can walk through the fort's basement jail and the chambers of Judge Parker, known as the "Hanging Judge," who sentenced over 160 men to death during his 21 years in office. (☎479-783-3961. Open daily 9am-5pm. $4, under 17 free.) The **Fort Smith Museum of History,** 320 Rogers Ave., chronicles the growth of the city around the fort from its beginnings as a small outpost during the Trail of Tears to its boomtown days as a gateway to America's western territories. The museum also has a working 1920s-era soda fountain with fountain sodas and ice-cream floats. (☎479-783-7841; www.fortsmithmuseum.org. Open June-Aug. Tu-Sa 10am-5pm, Su noon-5pm. $5, ages 6-11 $2.)

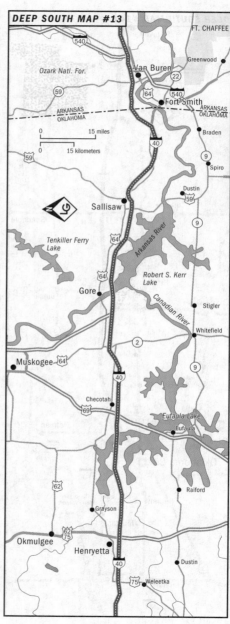

DEEP SOUTH MAP #13

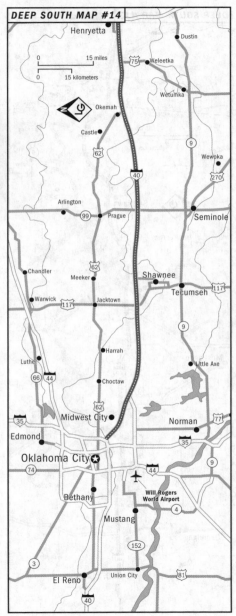

DEEP SOUTH MAP #14

In downtown Fort Smith, **R. Landry's New Orleans Cafe ❸**, 115 N. 10th St., at the corner of 10th and B St., in Brunwick Place, is a lively pub and restaurant that serves Cajun dishes like creole chicken and gumbo. (☎479-783-2505. Lunch entrees $5-10. Dinner entrees $9-14. Th night all-you-can-eat $11. W-Sa live music 7-9pm. Open W-Sa 11am-9pm. AmEx/D/MC/V.) Next door to Landry's, **Tammy's Tamales ❶**, 115 N. 10th St., has cheap, delicious tamales. A plate of two tamales with a side will set you back just $5. (☎479-783-8045. Open M-F 11am-2pm. MC/V.) A few blocks north of downtown, the **Inn Towne Lodge ❷**, 301 N. 11th St., has clean rooms with refrigerators, microwaves, coffeemakers, and free local calls. (☎479-783-0271; www.stay3rdnightfree.com. Rooms $35, 3rd night free. AmEx/D/MC/V.)

� APPROACHING SALLISAW: 40 MILES
Take **I-540 N** to **I-40 W**. Continue on I-40 W into Oklahoma, and take **Exit 311** to Sallisaw.

The Sooner State
OKLAHOMA
Welcomes You!

SALLISAW. For a cheap night's stay, the **Sallisaw Inn ❷**, 2503 E. Cherokee St., just off I-40, is a good deal with simple but spacious, impeccably clean rooms. (☎918-775-7981. Free Wi-Fi. Continental breakfast included. Singles $30-40; doubles $35-45. AmEx/D/MC/V.)

▢ APPROACHING GORE: 22 MILES
From Sallisaw, follow **I-40 W** to **Exit 291**. Take **Rte. 10 N** for 2 mi. to the intersection with **Rte. 64**.

GORE. At Rte. 64 and Rte. 10, the **Cherokee Courthouse Museum** commemorates Tahlonteeshee, which served as the capital of the Cherokee Nation from 1829-39 after the Cherokee were forcibly resettled in present-day Oklahoma. The museum has a reconstructed Cherokee log home as well as a courthouse that was the seat of the Cherokee government until they were again forced to move their capital north to Tehequa. The museum also has small exhibits on the Cherokee language, daily life on the frontier, and government in the territories. (☎918-489-5663. Open M-Sa 9am-5pm, Su noon-5pm. Free.)

🚏 APPROACHING HENRYETTA: 52 MILES
Take **Rte. 10 S** for 2 mi. to I-40, then **I-40 W** to **Exit 240.** Head north on **Rte. 62/75**, then turn left onto **E. Main St.**, which runs through downtown Henryetta.

HENRYETTA. Henryetta used to be a major oil-drilling and mining town, but since the oil and coal ran out, things have quieted down. Housed in an old one-room schoolhouse, the **Henryetta Territorial Museum,** 410 W. Moore St., tells the story of Henryetta's days as a frontier oil town and has memorabilia from famous Henryettans, including quarterback Troy Aikman and bull-rider Jim Shoulders. (From E. Main St., turn left onto 4th St., then right onto Moore St. ☎918-652-7112; www.territorialmuseum.org. Open W-Sa 10am-3pm. Free.) The **Colonial Pancake House and Restaurant ❶,** 608 E. Main St., serves fluffy pancakes and hearty diner food. (☎918-652-3562. Breakfast plates $3-4. Open daily 6am-8pm. AmEx/D/MC/V.)

🚏 APPROACHING SHAWNEE: 57 MILES
From Henryetta, take **I-40 W** for 55 mi. to **Exit 185.** Head south on **Kickapoo St.** to **MacArthur St.**

SHAWNEE. Shawnee is home to two universi-ties as well as the 🏛Mabee-Gerrer Museum of Art, 1900 W. MacArthur St. This gem of a museum contains artistic treasures collected by the Benedictine monk, Father Gregory Gerrer, dur-ing a lifetime of world travel. In addition to good collection of European and American art, from the Renaissance to the 20th century, the museum has ancient Greek and Roman objects, an Egyptian mummy, and a pair of shrunken heads from South America. (From Kickapoo St., follow MacArthur St. W to the entrance of St. Gregory University, on the right. ☎405-878-5300; www.mgmoa.org. Open Tu-Sa 10am-5pm, Su 1-4pm. $5, seniors $4, ages 6-17 $3.) At the intersection of Kickapoo and MacArthur St., **Abuelita Rosa's ❷,** 2313 N. Kickapoo St., serves authentic and delicious Mexican food. (☎405-214-5500. Lunch entrees $5-6. Dinner entrees $7-10. Open M 11am-8pm, W-Sa 11am-9pm, Su 11am-3pm. AmEx/D/MC/V.)

🚏 APPROACHING OKLAHOMA CITY: 39 MILES
From Shawnee, follow **I-40 W** for 35 mi. Take **Exit 150C** to reach downtown Oklahoma City.

OKLAHOMA CITY

For years, Oklahoma City was just a dusty stop for cattle drives and railroad trains. That all changed in the land run of 1889 when the city's population exploded from a few dozen people to 15,000 virtually overnight. The city remained relatively quiet until the tragic bombing of the Federal Building in 1995 suddenly thrust this self-proclaimed "cowtown" into the spotlight. As the site of the infamous terrorist attack, Oklahoma City became a symbol of American patriotism and solidarity around the world.

VITAL STATS

Population: 506,000

Visitor Info: Oklahoma City Convention and Visitors Bureau, 189 W. Sheridan Ave. (☎405-297-8912 or 800-225-5652; www.okccvb.org), at Robinson St. Open M-F 8:30am-5pm.

Internet Access: Oklahoma City Public Library, 131 Dean McGee Ave. (☎405-231-8650). Open M and W-F 9am-6pm, Tu 9am-9pm, Sa 9am-5pm. Free.

Post Office: 305 NW 5th St. (☎800-232-2198). Open M-F 7am-9pm, Sa 8am-5pm. **Postal Code:** 73102.

🖰 GETTING AROUND. Oklahoma City is constructed as a nearly perfect grid. **Santa Fe Ave.** divides the city east-west, and **Reno Ave.** slices it north-south. Cheap and plentiful park-ing makes driving by far the best way to get around. Some areas of the city are unsafe at night; be careful around Sheridan Ave. and Walker St.

 DID YOU KNOW? In 1935, the world's first parking meter was installed in Oklahoma City.

🖰 SIGHTS. The 🏛Oklahoma City National Memo-rial, at 5th and Harvey St., downtown, is a haunt-ing tribute to the victims of the bombing of the Murrah Federal Building. Outside lies the Field of Empty Chairs (one for each of the 168 victims), a stone gate, and a reflecting pool. Indoors, a museum tells the story of the bombing and the world's response through photographs, videos, and testimonials. (☎405-235-3313. Open M-Sa 9am-6pm, Su 1-6pm. $8, seniors $7, students $6, under 6 free.) The **National Cowboy and Western Her-itage Museum,** 1700 NE 63rd St., a popular tourist attraction, features an extensive collection of Western art and exhibits on rodeo, Native Ameri-cans, and frontier towns. (☎405-478-2250;

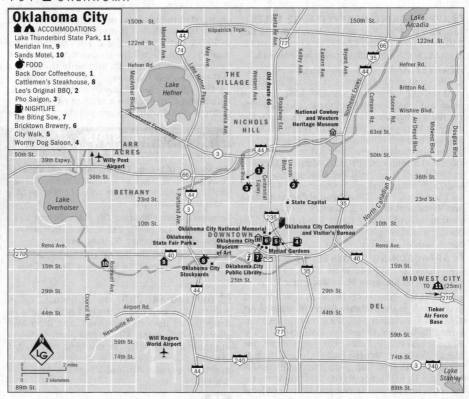

Oklahoma City

♠ ⌂ ACCOMMODATIONS
Lake Thunderbird State Park, **11**
Meridian Inn, **9**
Sands Motel, **10**
🍴 FOOD
Back Door Coffeehouse, **1**
Cattlemen's Steakhouse, **8**
Leo's Original BBQ, **2**
Pho Saigon, **3**
🍸 NIGHTLIFE
The Biting Sow, **7**
Bricktown Brewery, **6**
City Walk, **5**
Wormy Dog Saloon, **4**

www.nationalcowboymuseum.org. Open daily 9am-5pm. $8.50, seniors $7, ages 6-12 $4, under 5 free.) Monday is the time to visit the **Oklahoma City Stockyards,** 2500 Exchange Ave. (☎405-235-8675), the busiest in the world. Visitors enter via a catwalk over cow pens and cattle herds from the parking lot northeast of the auction house. The auction is as Old West as it gets. (☎405-235-8675. Auctions M-Tu 8am-last cow. Free.) The **Oklahoma City Museum of Art,** 415 Couch Dr., has a standard collection of modern and classical art, but the dazzling and wildly inventive 🔲**Dale Chihuly glass** pieces are alone worth the price of admission. (☎405-236-3100; www.okcmoa.com. Open Tu-Sa 10am-5pm, Th 10am-9pm, Su noon-5pm. $9; seniors, students, children $7; under 5 free.) Plant lovers should make a bee-line for **Myriad Gardens,** 301 W. Reno Ave., with 17 acres of vegetation from deserts and rainforests, or cross the **Crystal Bridge,** a 70 ft. diameter glass cylinder perched over a tropical ravine. (☎405-297-3995. Gardens open daily 7am-11pm. Free. Crystal Bridge open M-Sa 9am-6pm, Su noon-6pm. $6, students and seniors $5, ages 4-12 $3.)

Oklahoma City hosts the **Red Earth Festival** (☎405-427-5228), the country's largest celebration of Native American culture. Early summer finds the annual **Charlie Christian Jazz Festival** entertaining music lovers. Call the Black Liberated Arts Center, Inc. (☎405-424-2552) for more info. The **Cox Business Convention Center** (☎405-236-8666) hosts art fairs and dance competitions. Fall visitors catch the **World Championship Quarter Horse Show** (☎405-948-6800) in mid-November.

📑 **FOOD.** Oklahoma City contains the largest cattle market in the US, and beef tops most menus. Restaurants with longer hours lie east of town on **Sheridan Ave.,** in the Bricktown district, and north of downtown along **Classen Blvd.** and **Western Ave.** Asian restaurants congregate around the intersection of **Classen** and **NW 23rd St.** One of OKC's oldest restaurants and arguably its best steakhouse is **Cattlemen's Steakhouse ❹**, 1309 S. Agnew, in the heart of Stockyards City. Established in 1910, this famous restaurant was the prize in a craps game played in 1945. (☎405-236-0416; www.cattlemensrestaurant.com. Steaks $10-23. Open M-Th and Su 6am-10pm, F-Sa 6am-midnight. AmEx/D/MC/V.) **Pho Saigon ❷**, 2800 N. Classen Blvd., #108, has Vietnamese and Chinese food in a classy setting. (☎405-524-2233. Most entrees $6.75. Open Tu-F 11am-9pm, Sa 9am-9pm, Su 9am-8pm. MC/V.) Everyone's fighting for the rights to the late Leo's recipes at **Leo's Original BBQ ❸**, 3631 N. Kelley St., a classic hickory-smoking outfit in the northwest reaches of town. (☎405-424-5367. Beef sandwich and baked potato $5. Open M-Sa 11am-9pm. AmEx/D/MC/V.) The **Back Door Coffeehouse ❶**, 3214 N. Classen Blvd., is a great breakfast option with $5 waffles and coffee options from $2.50. (☎405-602-3354; www.backdoorcoffeeokc.com. Free Wi-Fi. Open M-Sa 7am-8pm, Su 9am-3pm. AmEx/D/MC/V.)

⌂ ACCOMMODATIONS. The Meridian Inn ❷, 1224 S. Meridian Ave., has large, clean rooms in a convenient location (Off Exit 145, on I-40. ☎405-948-7294. Singles $45; doubles $50. AmEx/D/MC/V.) For the cheapest of the cheap in rooms and RV parking, head to the **Sands Motel ❶**, 721 S. Rockwell Ave. (Off Exit 143 on I-40. ☎405-787-7353. RV sites $16; private rooms $20. AmEx/D/MC/V.) A more scenic option, **Lake Thunderbird State Park ❶** offers campsites near a beautiful lake fit for swimming and fishing. Rent canoes at the marina or a horse at the riding stables. (Take I-40 E to Exit 166, and go south 10 mi. until the road ends. Make a left, and drive 1 mi. ☎405-360-3572. Office open M-F 8am-5pm; call for late or weekend arrivals. Showers available. Sites $10, with water and electricity $16-23; huts $45. AmEx/D/DC/MC/V.)

⚑ NIGHTLIFE. Oklahoma City nightlife is growing by leaps and bounds—head to Bricktown to get into the thick of it all. To find Bricktown's best beer specials ($10 buckets) and experience Oklahoma's "red dirt" country music first hand, head to the **Wormy Dog Saloon,** 311 E. Sheridan Ave. (☎405-601-6276. Cover $3. Open W-Sa 6pm-2am. AmEx/D/MC/V.) The **Bricktown Brewery,** 1 N. Oklahoma St., at Sheridan Ave., brews five beers daily. (☎405-232-2739. Tu and F-Sa live music 9pm. Upstairs 21+. Cover $5-15 during live music. Open M and Su 11am-10pm, Tu-Th 11am-midnight, F-Sa 11am-1:30am. AmEx/D/MC/V.) **The Biting Sow,** 1 E. California Ave., is the place for live blues and jazz. (☎405-232-2639. Cover $5. AmEx/D/MC/V.) **City Walk,** 70 N. Oklahoma St., houses eight clubs. Enjoy the tropical Tequila Park, line dance inside the City Limits, or sing along at Stooge's piano bar. (☎405-232-9255. No athletic wear or excessive tattoos or piercings. Cover $8. No cover for women before 10pm. Open Th-Sa 8pm-2am. AmEx/D/MC/V.)

THE END OF THE ROAD

You've eaten your way through mounds of barbecue, hit every blues and country joint in the South, gained a new appreciation for Elvis's pelvis, and, dare we say it, developed a bit of a twang. Congratulations on your journey through the Deep South, but don't let the comfort food slow you down—you've seen one part of America, and it's time to see the rest. Stay in Oklahoma City to try out the Mother Road or drive up north to explore the National Road.

SPEED LIMIT 65

EXIT TO

Tulsa, OK   106 mi.
on route 66, p. 528

St. Louis, MO   499 mi.
on the national road route, p. 397

the southern border

TOP 5

1. Get cozy with snakes, gators, and American crocodiles in **Everglades National Park.**
2. *Parlez français* and sample **Cajun cuisine** in the bayou city of Lafayette, Louisiana.
3. Tour Mission Control and view moon rocks at Houston's **Johnson Space Center.**
4. Journey to the **Center of the World** (well, sort of) near Yuma, New Mexico.
5. Feed giraffes at the world-famous **San Diego Wild Animal Park** in Escondido, California.

Only the strong survived in the Old West, but you won't need spurs and a rifle to make it through this route—just a lot of water and a working air-conditioner. You'll experience both a wet heat and a dry heat as you gallop across eight states on your way from the semi-tropics of the South to the arid deserts of the Wild West. On the way, you'll visit all the gator-filled swamps, historic antebellum mansions, starkly beautiful monuments, and national parks that the borderlands have to offer.

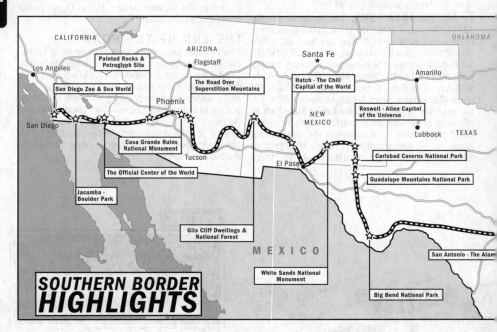

SOUTHERN BORDER HIGHLIGHTS

ROUTE STATS

Miles: c. 2700

Route: The Everglades, FL, to San Diego, CA

States: 8; Florida, Alabama, Mississippi, Louisiana, Texas, New Mexico, Arizona, and California

Driving Time: Two weeks will get you there, but you'll want four to catch all the best sights.

When to Go: Prices will be higher in winter, but the weather will be much, much hotter in summer.

Crossroads: The Pacific Coast in San Diego, CA (p. 888), **The East Coast** in the Everglades, FL (p. 57).

Your journey begins in the mangrove swamps of the **Everglades** (p. 768), where you'll meet alligators, dolphins, and sea turtles. Tracing Florida's coastline, you'll visit the mermaids of **Weeki Wachee** (p. 776) and the "Redneck Riviera" of **Panama City Beach** (p. 779). Continuing west across Florida's (not-so) "Forgotten Coast," you'll soon brush across coastal Alabama and Mississippi on your way to the French Quarter of resilient **New Orleans** (p. 789).

Louisiana has more good things in store, from bayous and crawfish to **Avery Island** (p. 799), home of the McIlhenny Company's spicy Tabasco empire.

You can have your steak and eat it, too, as the road leads deep into the heart of Texas. Learn about the Buffalo Soldiers in **Houston** (p. 808). Head straight into the heart of small-town Texas on the **Rocks, Ribs, and Revolvers Big Detour** (p. 820), before looping back to **Austin** (p. 815). Remember **The Alamo** (p. 822) in **San Antonio** and continue west through the Lone Star State, where the oil derricks are big and the steakhouses are bigger. In western Texas, see roadrunners, wily coyotes, and the mighty Río Grande at **Big Bend National Park** (p. 830), then chill out at **Guadalupe Mountains National Park** (p. 833).

Head north into New Mexico and the cool limestone grottoes of **Carlsbad Caverns** (p. 835), where at dusk 16 species of bat swarm out of the caves at a rate of 6000 bats per minute (BPM). That's a lot of bats. Don't get carried away at the **UFO Festival** in **Roswell** (p. 837)—you

SOUTHERN BORDER

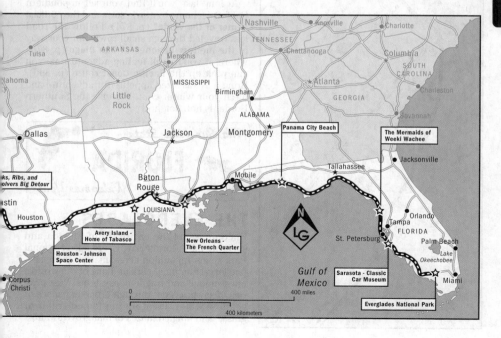

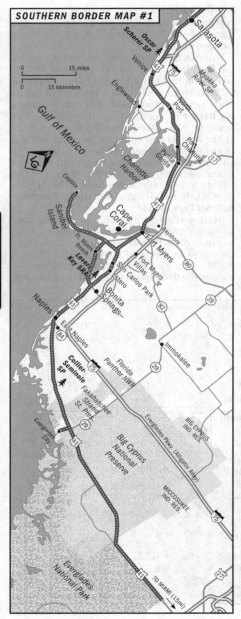

SOUTHERN BORDER MAP #1

still have miles to go. Ascend the 12,000 ft. peak of **Sierra Blanca** outside of **Ruidoso** (p. 839) for some of the most beautiful vistas of the trip, then duck test missiles and surf down the snowy dunes of **White Sands National Monument** (p. 841). Fall in love with the west Texas town of **El Paso** (p. 842), then bid it goodbye as you recross the border into New Mexico.

Back in the "land of enchantment," stop for a fiery bite in **Hatch** (p. 848), the "Chile Capital of the World." Head north to marvel at the 700-year-old **Gila Cliff Dwellings** (p. 849), then chase Billy the Kid through **Silver City** (p. 850) before slipping across the border into Arizona. Don't miss the otherworldly rock spires of **Chiricahua National Monument** (p. 852) as you make your way across the Arizona desert to the Wild West town of **Tombstone** (p. 856). Next up is laid-back **Tucson** (p. 857), then it's on to the mysterious **Casa Grande Ruins** (p. 866) and hip **Phoenix** (p. 866). Ponder ancient spirals and pictographs at **Painted Rocks Petroglyph Site** (p. 872), then stop for some lettuce head bowling in **Yuma** (p. 873), the mother of all truck stops.

At long last, you'll find yourself in southern California, home to movie stars and the **"Official Center of the World"** (p. 874). Follow the road less traveled through small towns on your way to the mellow beaches of **San Diego** (p. 878) where, if you're still feeling adventurous, you can pick up the **Pacific Coast** route (p. 896). Bring a Texas-sized appetite for adventure and ditch your winter coat, because the Southern Border is hot, hot, hot!

The Sunshine State
FLORIDA
Welcomes You!

THE EVERGLADES

Encompassing the entire tip of Florida and spearing into Florida Bay, Everglades National Park spans 1.6 million acres, making it the second largest national park and one of the world's most unique and fragile ecosystems. Vast prairies of sawgrass cut through broad expanses of shallow water, creating the famed "river of grass," and tangled mazes of mangrove swamps wind up and down the western coast. To the south, delicate coral reefs lie below the shimmering blue waters of the bay. Keep your eyes open for American alligators, dolphins, sea turtles, and various birds and fish, as well as the endangered Florida panther, Florida manatee, and American crocodile.

GETTING AROUND

The Everglades National Park stretches across the entire southern end of Florida. **Everglades City** lies on the very western edge of the park, some distance from other towns, though visitors centers are scattered throughout the park. **U.S. 41,** also known as the **Tamiami Trail,** is the only way to get from east to west. To reach the sights, food, and accommodations in **Florida City** and **Homestead,** take **U.S. 41 W** to **Rte. 997.** Homestead lies about 20 mi. south along Rte. 997. Florida City is just southwest of Homestead; go south on Rte. 997 and then take **Rte. 9336 W** to reach it. The main entrance to the park, Ernest Coe Visitors Center, is just inside the eastern edge of the Everglades, near Florida City. From here, Rte. 9366 cuts 40 mi. through the park past campgrounds, trailheads, and waterways to the Flamingo Visitors Center and the Flamingo Outpost Resort.

SIGHTS

For a truly bizarre experience, head up U.S. 1 to the **Coral Castle,** 28655 S. Dixie Hwy., in Homestead. After his fiancée changed her mind the day before the wedding, Latvian immigrant Ed Leedskalnin spent the next 20 years construct-ing a monument to lost love, turning hundreds of tons of coral rock into a sculpture garden. The site has since been studied by anthropologists, who think it might explain how humans built the Egyptian pyramids. (☎305-248-6345; www.coralcastle.com. Open M-Th 9am-8pm, F-Su 9am-9pm. Tours every hr. $9.75, seniors $6.50, ages 7-12 $5.) Gawk at gators, crocs, and snakes at the **Everglades Alligator Farm,** 40351 SW 192 Ave., 4 mi. south of Palm Dr., in Florida City. Though touristy, this is the place to see thousands of gators, from little hatchlings clambering for a bit of sunlight to 18-footers clambering for a bit of you. (☎305-247-2628; www.everglades.com. Open daily 9am-6pm. Alligator feeding 3 and 5pm. $11.50, ages 4-11 $6.50.)

Travelers seeking to commune more intimately with fauna can take the **Loop Road Detour,** a deserted dirt road that once led to Al Capone's headquarters and is now a great way to see alligators, birds, and the occasional turtle or deer. The 18 mi. detour takes about two hours and is well worth the trip. If you want a really close look at wildlife, head down one of the rough trails off the road, but as always, exercise caution. **Coopertown Airboat Tours,** 22700 Tamiami Tr., are also a good way to see alligators if you are pressed for time. In addition to the 8 mi. tours, Coopertown shelters a 14 ft. gator and serves up gator tail dinners for $23. (☎305-226-6048. Open daily 8am-6pm. Tours $18.) About 5 mi. after the sign for Bear Lake Campsite, **Clyde Butcher's Gallery and Studio,** 52388 Tamiami Tr., exhibits and sells photographs of the Everglades, Western US, and Cuba. (☎239-695-2428. Open M and Th-Su 10am-5pm. Free.)

OUTDOORS

The park is swamped with fishing, hiking, canoeing, biking, and wildlife-watching opportunities. Just don't think about swimming; alligators, sharks, and barracuda patrol the waters. From November through April, the park sponsors amphitheater programs, canoe trips, and ranger-guided Slough Slogs (swamp tours). Summer visitors can expect mosquitoes aplenty; stay away from swampy areas around sunrise and sunset. The best time to visit is winter or spring when heat, humidity, storms, and bugs are at a minimum, and wildlife congregate

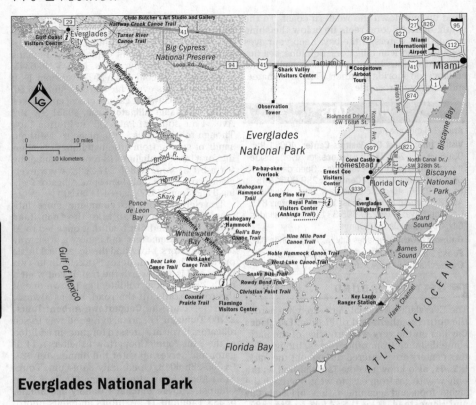

Everglades National Park

in shrinking pools of evaporating water. Wear long sleeves and bring insect repellent.

HIKING

The Everglades are accessible via a series of well-developed short trails. A good option is the **Pa-hay-okee Overlook,** 13 mi. from the main entrance off Rte. 9336, which rewards visitors with a stunning view of the park after only a quarter of a mile. One of the best hiking trails is the famous **Anhinga Trail,** which begins at the Royal Palm Visitors Center, 4 mi. from the main entrance, inside the park. Moderately difficult, this trail grants explorers up-close encounters with alligators, anhinga birds, and turtles. For a more strenuous trail through 10 mi. of slash pine forest, try the **Long Pine Key Trail,** 16 mi. from the main entrance. Another worthwhile

hike is the **Mahogany Hammock Trail,** 20 mi. from the main entrance. This ½ mi. boardwalk offers incredible routes through freshwater prairie and pineland. The trail is best in the winter, as the mosquitoes are vicious in summer months.

BOATING

If you really want to experience the Everglades, start paddling. The 99 mi. **Wilderness Waterway** winds its way from the northwest entrance to the Flamingo Visitors Center in the far south. **Everglades National Park Boat Tours,** at the Gulf Coast Visitors Center, rents canoes ($24 per day) and is the best option for guided boat tours. The **Ten Thousand Island Cruise** is a 1½hr. tour through the Everglades's myriad tiny islands; patrons often see bald eagles, dolphins, and manatees. (☎239-695-2591. $27.) The **Man-**

grove **Wilderness Cruise** is a 2hr. cruise through the inland swamps that brings its six passengers face-to-face with alligators. (☎239-695-2591. Tours 9, 11am, 1, 3pm. $30.) For those who would rather be on their own, **Hell's Bay Canoe Trail,** about 29 mi. from the entrance, is the best place to start. For more information on navigating the park's waterways, consult the rangers at the Flamingo Visitors Center.

BIKING

While the Everglades mostly caters to those with walking sticks and canoe paddles, it does offer some excellent biking trails. The best route is the 15 mi. loop at the **Shark Valley Visitors Center.** The trail peaks at an observation tower that offers incredible views of the park's rivers of grass, alligators, and even deer. (☎305-221-8776. Tram tours May-Nov. daily 9:30, 11am, 1, 3pm; Dec.-Apr. every hr. 9am-4pm. $14. Reservations recommended. Bike rental available daily 8:30am-3pm. $6 per hr., including helmets.)

🍴 FOOD

In 1959, six-year-old Robert sold his first bunch of cucumbers and **Robert Is Here ❶,** 19200 SW 344th St., off Palm Dr., in Florida City, was born. Today Robert sells tropical fruit, vegetables, local honey, and out-of-this-world key lime milkshakes ($3). While you're waiting for your shake, check out the emus out back. (☎305-246-1592; www.robertishere.com. Open Nov.-Aug. daily 8am-7pm. AmEx/D/MC/V.) **Rosita's ❷,** 199 Palm Dr., across the street from the hostel in Florida City, has the best Mexican food in the area. Cool your jets with a plate of hot tamales for $6.50. (☎305-246-3114. Open daily 8:30am-9pm. AmEx/MC/V.) Behind the aspirin in the Royal Palm drug store is its cure for what ails you, the **Royal Palm Grill and Deli ❶,** 806 N. Krome Ave., at Campbell Dr. Try the homemade biscuits and gravy ($4.50) or a good ol' Southern ham sandwich for $5. (☎305-246-5701. Open M-F 7am-4pm, Sa 7am-3pm, Su 7am-2pm. AmEx/D/MC/V.) At the southern end of Homestead, **Farmer's Market Restaurant ❷,** 300 N. Krome Ave., delivers "good home cooking." Enjoy the delicious two eggs, ham, and grits ($6.25) and other all-American breakfasts. (☎305-246-6334. Fried fish fingers $8.75. Open daily 5:30am-9pm. MC/V.)

🏠 ACCOMMODATIONS

The **Everglades International Hostel (HI-AYH) ❶,** 20 SW 2nd Ave., off Rte. 9336 (Palm Dr.), is a backpacker's delight with modern rooms and a friendly staff. After venturing into the Everglades, hang out with fellow travelers in the gazebo, gardens, or kitchen. The house has a big-screen TV, a piano, and an extensive video collection. (☎305-248-1122 or 800-372-3874; www.evergladeshostel.com. Bicycles $15 per day. Canoes $25 per day. Free Wi-Fi. Breakfast included. Linen $2. Dorms $20, members $17; private rooms $42-45. MC/V.) Outside the eastern entrance to the park, Florida City offers cheap motels along U.S. 1. One pleasant option is the **Inn of Homestead ❸,** 1020 N. Homestead Blvd. (U.S. 1), which has large, clean rooms and pool access. (☎305-248-2121. Rooms $60-80. AmEx/D/MC/V.) A few **campgrounds ❶** line Rte. 9336. All sites have drinking water, grills, dump sites, and restrooms, but none have hookups. (☎800-365-2267; www.reserveusa.com. Reservations required Nov.-Apr. Sites $16. AmEx/D/MC/V.) **Backcountry camping ❶** inside the park is accessible primarily by boat. Required permits are available on a first come, first served basis at the Flamingo and Gulf Coast Visitors Centers. Camping reservations must be made in person at the visitors centers within 24hr. of heading out. (☎239-695-3311. Permit $10. Sites may be unavailable due to hurricane damage. AmEx/D/MC/V.)

🚗 APPROACHING EVERGLADES CITY: 15 MILES

Take **U.S. 41 W (Tamiami Tr.)** across the northern border of Everglades National Park and through the **Big Cypress National Preserve.** Take the exit for Everglades City after passing the town of Ochopee.

EVERGLADES CITY. Everglades City is a bit of a waterlogged fishing town, but contains the Gulf Coast Visitors Center, the main eastern visitors center for the Everglades. For a bite to eat, **Burger Express ❶,** 203 Collier Ave., has burgers ($3) and fish sandwiches. (☎239-695-4210. Open M-F 9am-6pm, Sa-Su 10am-6pm. Cash only.) The **Seafood Depot ❶,** 102 Collier Ave., cooks up tasty seafood dishes. (☎239-695-0075. Dinners $11-20. Open daily 10am-9pm. AmEx/D/DC/MC/V.) The **Everglades City Motel ❷,** 310 Collier Ave. (Rte. 29), has clean and spacious rooms. (☎800-695-

8353. Reservations recommended. Rooms $70-95. AmEx/D/MC/V.)

■ APPROACHING NAPLES: 36 MILES

Continue north on **U.S. 41 (S. Tamiami Tr.)** until you reach Naples.

NAPLES. Quiet and affluent, Naples is mostly a retirement community for Midwesterners. Although the city is starting to diversify, a stroll down the ritzy main drag (5th Ave. S) is just what you would expect: beautifully kept buildings, expensive restaurants, and lots of elderly couples. For the budget traveler, Naples offers beautiful white-sand beaches lined with palm trees. Head down to the **Naples Pier** (at the westernmost end of 12th Ave. S) to see pelicans and the occasional dolphin family. The pier can get crowded; try to visit in the evening, when the crowds head home. **Lindburger's ❶**, 330 S. Tamiami Tr., a small diner with airplane-themed decor, grills 50 varieties of burgers. (☎239-262-1127. Burgers around $6. Open daily 11am-9pm. AmEx/MC/V.) The quiet **Lemon Tree Inn ❷**, 250 9th St. S (U.S. 41), has lovely rooms and a pool, garden, and gazebo. Some rooms even have screened-in porches to save you from the ravages of local mosquitoes. (☎239-262-1414. Breakfast included. Rooms Apr.-Dec. $89; Jan.-Mar. $149-179. AmEx/D/DC/MC/V.) Another option is the **Tamiami Motel ❷**, 2164 Tamiami Tr. E, which offers sparse but clean rooms. (About 2 mi. before downtown Naples and the beach. ☎239-774-4626. Rooms $55-90. AmEx/D/DC/MC/V.)

■ APPROACHING LOVERS KEY STATE PARK: 22 MILES

Head north on **U.S. 41 (S. Tamiami Tr.)** and turn left at **Bonita Beach Blvd.**, which becomes **Estero Blvd.** Follow the road 7 mi. until you see signs for Lovers Key. Turn left into the park.

LOVERS KEY STATE PARK. An exploration of Lovers Key State Park, 8700 Estero Blvd., is one of Florida's most romantic adventures. You can take short hikes in the park, or rent a kayak at the concession stand in Parking Lot A and paddle through the brackish streams between the narrow keys. The beaches are the highlight of the park but are often filled with families and young children. For real seclusion, walk about 30-45min. north or south along the beach. (☎941-463-4588. Kayaks $30

per day. Canoes $50 per day. Open daily sunrise-sunset. $5 per vehicle.)

■ APPROACHING FORT MYERS BEACH: 6 MILES

Turn left out of Lovers Key State Park and continue on **Estero Blvd. (U.S. 41).** After a few miles, you will cross a bridge and enter Fort Myers Beach. From U.S. 41, turn right on **Rte. 865 W**, then turn left on **Rte. 869 W** and left again onto **Rte. 865 S**, following signs for Fort Myers Beach. Rte. 865 S crosses the bridge over the San Carlos Bay as Estero Blvd.

FORT MYERS BEACH. Fort Myers is famous for its lively beach scene, attracting everyone from senior citizens and families with children to spring break partiers. Just over the bridge is the town square, where most of the action takes place. **Dusseldorf's ❷**, 1113 Estero Blvd., has over 140 imported beers and serves excellent German food. (☎239-463-5251. Sandwiches $7. Sausage sampler $12. F-Su accordion music 3-7pm. Open M-Th 11am-midnight, F-Sa 11am-2am. AmEx/D/MC/V.) The newly renovated **Beacon Motel ❹**, 1240 Estero Blvd., is the best deal you'll find along the beach. (☎239-463-5264; www.thebeaconmotel.com. Reservations recommended. Rooms from $89. AmEx/D/MC/V.)

◼ DETOUR
SANIBEL ISLAND

Take Estero Blvd. over the bridge out of Fort Myers and take a left on Summerlin Rd. Continue 8 mi., crossing over a toll bridge ($6) to Sanibel.

A quiet, affluent community of retirees and vacationers, Sanibel Island is famous for its seashells and for the **J.N. "Ding" Darling Wildlife Refuge**, 1 Wildlife Dr. The refuge has short hikes, tram rides, and canoe and kayak rentals. (☎239-472-1100, rentals 239-472-8900. Kayaks $20 per 2hr., $80 per day. Open M-Th and Sa-Su sunrise-sunset. $5 per vehicle.) Head to **Billy's Rentals**, 1509 Periwinkle Way, if you want to explore the island's 25 mi. of bike paths. (☎239-472-5248; www.billysrentals.com. Bikes $15 per day. Open daily 8:30am-5pm.) A 15 mi. drive to the end of the island will take you to **Captiva Beach**, where fabulous sunsets light up the sky.

■ APPROACHING OSCAR SCHERER STATE PARK: 6 MILES

Head south on **U.S. 41** until you reach the park entrance.

OSCAR SCHERER STATE PARK. Oscar Scherer State Park ❶, 1843 S. Tamiami Tr., has beautiful creekside camping, fishing, swimming, and canoeing (rentals $5 per hr., $25 per day) amid trees draped with Spanish moss. (☎941-483-5956. Open daily sunrise-sunset. $4 per vehicle. Sites with water and hookup $25. AmEx/D/DC/MC/V.) For cheaper camping, head 8 mi. east to **Myakka River State Park** ❶, State Rd. 72, Exit 205, which has a few sites about 2 mi. from the parking lot. (☎941-361-6511. Sites $4. AmEx/D/MC/V.)

APPROACHING SARASOTA: 6 MILES
Continue on **U.S. 41** to run straight into Sarasota.

SARASOTA

The self-proclaimed "cultural capital" of Florida, Sarasota doesn't disappoint. The city has a beautiful harbor and the stunning white-sand beaches that make the Florida Gulf Coast famous.

VITAL STATS

Population: 53,000

Visitor Info: Sarasota Convention and Visitors Bureau, 655 N. Tamiami Tr. (☎941-957-1877; www.sarasotafl.org). Open M-Sa 10am-4pm, Su noon-4pm.

Internet Access: Fruitville Library, 100 Coburn Rd. (☎941-861-2500). Open M-F 9am-9pm, Sa 9am-5pm. Free.

Post Office: 1661 Ringling Blvd. (☎941-331-4221). Open M-F 8am-5:30pm, Sa 9am-noon. **Postal Code:** 34240.

GETTING AROUND. U.S. 41 runs right into the center of town, where it changes to **Bayfront Dr.** and passes through Sarasota's lush harborfront area. Turn right on major streets like **Ringling Blvd., Main St.,** or **Fruitville Rd.** to reach downtown.

SIGHTS. The real reason to stop in Sarasota is the fabulous ▧**John and Mable Ringling Museum of Art,** 5401 Bayshore Rd., off U.S. 41. Built by circus baron John Ringling in an attempt to promote Sarasota (most of which he owned), the museum consists of three parts. The **Art Museum** houses an impressive collection of Rubens. The **Circus Museum** features all sorts of colorful circus relics and a model circus painstakingly assembled over 50 years by circus enthusiast Howard Tibbals. But the star of the show is the **Ca d'Zan Mansion,** the one-time Ringling winter quarters. Evoking Ringling's fondness for Venetian-Gothic palaces, the mansion has marble pillars, cathedral ceilings, and other opulent touches—all with an unbeatable view of the Gulf. (☎941-359-5700; www.ringling.org. Open daily 10am-5:30pm. $15, students and teachers $5.) Across the street from Ringling is the ▧**Sarasota Classic Car Museum,** 5500 N. Tamiami Tr. This world-class collection is comprised of nearly 100 classic cars that span automotive history. From Model-T Fords to a 1974 Bentley Formula Racer and everything in between, these cars deserve a look from both avid enthusiasts and curious roadtrippers. The collection is as amusing as it is astounding—the original caped crusader's Batmobile, Paul McCartney's humble Mini, John Lennon's funky "psychedelic roadster," and the 1982 Delorean of *Back to the Future* fame are all featured. (☎941-355-6228; www.sarasotacarmuseum.org. Open daily 9am-6pm. $8.50.)

FOOD AND ACCOMMODATIONS. Sarasota has a number of good restaurants. ▧**Yoder's Restaurant** ❸, 3434 Bahia Vista St., is an Amish restaurant in the heart of the Amish 'hood. Meals come with homemade bread and butter, and Mrs. Yoder's pies are divine. (☎941-955-7771; www.yodersrestaurant.com. Pie $4 per slice. Open M-Sa 6am-8pm. AmEx/MC/V.) If you've ever been curious about soft-shell crabs, head to **Phillipp Creek Village Oyster Bar** ❹, 5353 S. Tamiami Tr., for a soft-shell-crab sandwich and open-air dockside seating. (☎941-925-4444; www.creekseafood.com. Sandwiches $6.75. Entrees $13-15. Open M-Th 11am-10pm, F-Sa 11am-10:30pm. AmEx/D/MC/V.) **Sierra Station Cafe** ❸, 400 N. Lemon Ave., offers an intimate atmosphere in a restored 19th-century train station. It's a little pricey, but a good place to grab breakfast or lunch if you're downtown. The Cajun tuna sandwich ($8.50) and the eggs benedict ($7.50) come highly recommended. (☎941-906-1400; www.sierrastation.com. Open daily 8am-3pm. AmEx/MC/V.) The **Cadillac Motel** ❷, 4021 N. Tamiami Tr., has clean rooms and a pool. (☎941-355-7108. Rooms June-Sept. $38-48; Oct.-May $58. AmEx/D/MC/V.)

APPROACHING BRANDENTON: 13 MILES
From Sarasota, head north on **U.S. 41** to reach downtown Bradenton.

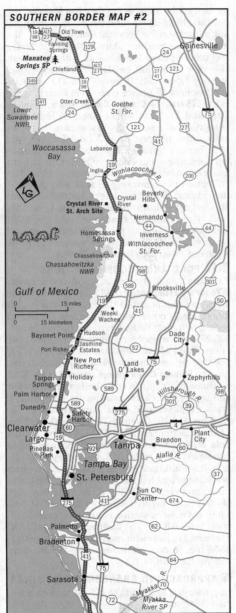

SOUTHERN BORDER MAP #2

SOUTHERN BORDER

BRADENTON. Take a left on Manatee Ave. and an immediate right at 10th St. to visit the **South Florida Museum,** 201 10th St., which chronicles southwestern Florida's history from the Pleistocene to the present. The **Parker Manatee Aquarium** houses Manatee County's official mascot, 58-year-old Snooty. Mornings at the museum are often devoted to programs for delightful but screaming children. (☎941-746-4131; www.southfloridamuseum.org. Open Jan.-Apr. and July M-Sa 10am-5pm, Su noon-5pm; May-June and Aug.-Dec. Tu-Sa 10am-5pm, Su noon-5pm. $13.75, 60+ $11.75, ages 4-12 $8.75.)

⚑ APPROACHING CLEARWATER AND ST. PETERSBURG: 46 MILES
Continue on **U.S. 41 N** and hang a left at **U.S. 19.** The toll ($1) to cross the **Sunshine Skyway Bridge** into Clearwater and St. Petersburg is well worth the view.

ST. PETERSBURG AND CLEARWATER

Just across the bay from Tampa, St. Petersburg is home to a relaxed beach community of retirees and young singles. The town basks in soft, white beaches, emerald water, and about 361 days of perfect sunshine every year. The St. Petersburg-to-Clearwater stretch caters to beach bums and city strollers alike. While the outdoor scenery draws crowds, indoor activities are equally captivating—the museums and restaurants rival even the sunset.

VITAL STATS

Population: 248,000/108,000

Visitor Info: St. Petersburg Visitors Center, 100 2nd Ave. N (☎727-821-4069; www.stpete.com). Open M-F 8am-5pm, Sa 10am-5pm, Su noon-5pm. **Suncoast Welcome Center,** 2001 Ulmerton Rd. (☎727-573-1449), in Clearwater. Open daily 9am-5pm.

Internet Access: St. Petersburg Main Library, 3745 9th Ave. N (☎727-893-7724). Open M-Th 9am-9pm, F-Sa 9am-6pm, Su 10am-6pm.

Parking: Parking garage at the corner of 2nd Ave. N and 2nd St. N ($1 per hr., $6 per day max.). There is ample free parking in downtown St. Pete's and all street parking is free after 6pm.

Post Office: 3135 1st Ave. N (☎727-322-6699), at 31st St. Open M-F 8am-6pm, Sa 8am-12:30pm. **Postal Code:** 33730.

GETTING AROUND

St. Petersburg and Clearwater are two separate cities along a peninsula connected by a number of smaller towns. In St. Petersburg, **Central Ave.** parallels numbered avenues, running east-west in the downtown area. **34th St. (U.S. 19), I-275,** and **4th St.** are major north-south thoroughfares. The beaches line a strip of barrier islands on the far west side of town facing the Gulf. Several causeways, including the **Clearwater Memorial Causeway (Rte. 60),** access the beaches from St. Petersburg. Clearwater sits at the far north of the peninsula. **Gulf Blvd.** runs down the coastline, connecting St. Petersburg, Clearwater, and all the towns in between.

SIGHTS

Grab a copy of *TBT* or *The Weekly Planet* at many restaurants in downtown St. Petersburg for the lowdown on area events. The *St. Petersburg Official Visitor's Guide* also has information about tourist attractions, coupons, and maps.

SALVADOR DALÍ MUSEUM. St. Petersburg got lucky: avid Dalí collectors Mr. and Mrs. A. Reynolds Morse were looking for a tourist-oriented town to give their collection public exposure, and St. Petersburg fit the bill. Since it opened in 1982, the Salvador Dalí Museum has housed the largest private collection of Dalí's work in the world. Be sure to check out his first Surrealist painting, the spectacular *Hallucinogenic Toreador*. The informative free tours offered throughout the day are worth the time. *(1000 3rd St. S. ☎800-442-3254; www.salvadordalimuseum.org. Open M-W and Sa 9:30am-5:30pm, Th-F 9:30am-8pm, Su noon-5:30pm. Tours every hr. $14, seniors $12, students $9, under 10 $3.50. Th after 5pm $5.)*

FLORIDA INTERNATIONAL MUSEUM. The Florida International Museum has no permanent exhibits but often hosts excellent traveling shows. Topics touch on history, anthropology, archaeology, and a little bit of everything in between. Tickets can be expensive (up to $25), so make sure to call ahead before purchasing. *(244 2nd Ave. N. ☎727-341-7900. Call ahead for hours and prices.)*

MUSEUM OF FINE ARTS. Though it is sometimes overshadowed by the Dalí Museum, the Museum of Fine Arts is fantastic and gives the discerning visitor a little taste of everything, from Impressionist to medieval painting to sculpture to glass. The contemporary art halls, which feature Georgia O'Keefe's *Poppy,* are especially worthwhile. The museum also has a small photo gallery with rotating exhibits of works by the likes of Ansel Adams. *(255 Beach Dr. NE. ☎727-896-2667; www.fine-arts.org. Open Tu-Sa 10am-5pm, Su 1-5pm. Free 45min. tours daily 11am, 1:30, 2:30pm. $8, seniors $7, students $4, under 7 free.)*

HASLAM'S BOOK STORE. A local landmark in St. Petersburg since 1933, Haslam's is the biggest bookstore in Florida, with a loyal contingent of shoppers and over 300,000 new and used books. It even has roadtripper credibility—Jack Kerouac used to hang here. Pick up a 10-cent romance novel for the road. *(2025 Central Ave. ☎727-822-8616; www.haslams.com. Open M-Sa 10am-6pm.)*

SUNKEN GARDENS. The Sunken Gardens have some of the oldest tropical plants in the region. The gardens were originally dug out of a large sink hole by plumber George Turner. The city later took over, adding 6000 plants and constructing a butterfly garden. *(1824 4th St. N. ☎727-551-3100. Open M-Sa 10am-4:30pm, Su noon-4:30pm. $8, seniors $6, children $4.)*

BEACHES. Beaches are the most worthwhile attraction along the coastline. Although its parking meters eat quarters by the bucket ($0.25 per 15min.), **Pass-a-Grille Beach** is the most beautiful beach in the area. For cheaper options, drive down to **Fort De Soto Park,** where parking is free, or check out **Clearwater Beach,** located at the northern end of Gulf Blvd. The touristy but fun **Sunsets at Pier 60 Festival** brings arts and entertainment to Clearwater Beach in the form of souvenir booths and buskers. *(☎727-449-1036; www.sunsetsatpier60.com. Festival daily from 2hr. before sundown to 2hr. after.)*

FOOD

St. Petersburg has a wide variety of restaurants, but you'll do best if you have a penchant for seafood. Night owls are out of luck—few dining options stay open after 9pm.

Frenchy's Cafe, 41 Baymont St. (☎727-446-3607). Though neither a cafe nor French, this place attracts tons of tourists from Clearwater Beach. The tasty fish sandwiches are made from fish caught by Frenchy's own fleet. Open M-Th 11am-11pm, F-Sa 11am-midnight, Su noon-11pm. AmEx/MC/V. ❸

Dockside Dave's, 119 Boardwalk Pl. W (☎727-392-9399), off Gulf Blvd., in Madeira Beach. A fun, down-to-earth restaurant where the fish is fresh and the grouper sandwich ($10) is simply sublime. Open M-Sa 11am-10pm, Su noon-10pm. MC/V. ❸

Tangelo's Bar and Grille, 226 1st Ave. N (☎727-894-1695). A Cuban restaurant with fabulous sangria ($3 per glass). Sandwiches $5-6. Open M 11am-4pm, Tu-Th 11am-8pm, F-Sa 11am-9pm. MC/V. ❸

Fourth Street Shrimp Store, 1006 4th St. N (☎727-822-0325). Purveyor of all things shrimp, the Shrimp Store is full of seafarer memorabilia and license plates. Chipotle shrimp salad $8. Open M-Th and Su 11am-9pm, F-Sa 11am-9:30pm. MC/V. ❸

The Chattaway Drive-In, 358 22nd Ave. S (☎727-823-1544). No longer a drive-in, this old school establishment has glowing galaxy tables and a large patio covered with twinkling lights. Fish 'n' chips $9.75. Slices of homemade pie $3.75. Fri-Sa night live blues. Open daily 11am-9:30pm. Cash only. ❷

Chiang Mai Thailand Restaurant, 1100 Central Ave. (☎727-895-4851). Famous among locals, Chiang Mai offers amazing Thai cuisine at reasonable prices. For a change from grouper, try some tofu red curry or a great Panang curry ($9). Sa night Thai dancing. Open M-Sa 11am-10pm. AmEx/MC/V. ❸

ACCOMMODATIONS

Cheap motels line **4th St. N** and **U.S. 19** in St. Petersburg. To avoid the worst neighborhoods, stay on the north end of 4th St. and the south end of U.S. 19. Several inexpensive motels are located on the beaches along **Gulf Blvd.** in the towns of **Madeira Beach** and **Indian Rocks Beach.**

Clearwater Beach International Hostel, 606 Bay Esplanade (☎727-443-1211), off Mandalay Ave., at the Sands Motel. This hostel feels more like a country club than a budget lodging, with a pool, canoes, a full kitchen, and a shaded patio. Internet $1 per 15min. Key deposit $5. Reception 9am-noon and 5-9pm. Dorms $15; private rooms $37-59. MC/V. ❶

Fort De Soto County Park, 3500 Pinellas Bayway S (☎727-464-3347 or 727-582-2267; www.pinellascounty.org/park). Fort De Soto, which is composed of 5 islands jutting into the Gulf of Mexico, was rated the top beach in the US by *Dr. Beach's*

2005. North Beach can get a little crowded, but there are plenty of deserted beach areas along the Gulf side. Park office open daily 8am-9pm. Curfew 10pm. Sites $28. MC/V. ❶

Suncoast Motel, 10264 Gulf Blvd. (☎727-360-9256), a hop, skip, and a jump from the beach. This quaint motel has basic rooms with small kitchens and free Wi-Fi. Singles $38-58. MC/V. ❷

◪ APPROACHING TARPON SPRINGS: 18 MILES
Leave St. Petersburg by heading north on **34th St. (U.S. 19).** Follow U.S. 19 until **U.S. 19A,** and then hang a left toward the Gulf. Turn onto **Dodecanese Blvd.** to reach Tarpon Springs.

TARPON SPRINGS. Sponge harvesters used hooks to retrieve the sponges off the coast of Tarpon Springs until Greek immigrant John Corcoris introduced Greek sponge-diving technology in 1905. Tarpon Springs subsequently emerged as a little piece of Greece in Florida, with a close-knit, Greek-speaking community and a thriving Greek Orthodox Church. Around Christmas, the bayou just south of the docks on Tarpon Ave. hosts a traditional festival in which young Greek Orthodox children dive into the chilly waters to retrieve a ceremonial cross. Having capitalized on the local culture, the waterfront "sponge district" is now a bit touristy, but still worth a stop. Buy a souvenir sponge and sample great Greek food at **Mama's Greek Cuisine ❸,** 735 Dodecanese Blvd. (☎727-944-2888. Gyros $6. Broiled octopus $12. Open daily 7am-10pm. MC/V.)

◪ APPROACHING WEEKI WACHEE: 28 MILES
Continue on **U.S. 19 N.**

WEEKI WACHEE. Since 1947, Weeki Wachee has been famous for the **Weeki Wachee Springs Park,** 6131 Commercial Way, where professional mermaids hold underwater spectacles and then pose for pictures with landlubbers. Nowadays the park's bread and butter are wilderness river cruises and a water park, which is generally filled with kids. The mermaids, though, remain the real attraction. The 1:30pm show is fantastic; mermaids demonstrate underwater eating, drinking, and dancing. Once a month, retired mermaids from decades past come back to relive their underwater glory days. (☎352-596-2062. Open daily 10am-4pm.

Shows 11am, 1:30, 3pm. In summer $22, ages 3-10 $16; in winter $16/$11.)

☛ APPROACHING CRYSTAL RIVER: 26 MILES
Follow **U.S. 19 N** to Crystal River.

CRYSTAL RIVER. Take a break from driving to wander around the **Yulee Sugar Mill Ruins Historic State Park,** 3400 N. Museum Point, the ruins of a sugar cane plantation owned by Florida's first senator, David Levy Yulee. (☎ 352-795-3817. Open daily 8am-sunset. Free.) The **Crystal River Archaeological State Park,** also on N. Museum Point, preserves the remains of a ceremonial mound complex and village that stood on the riverbank 1600 years ago. The small **visitors center** displays artifacts found at the site. (☎ 352-795-3817. Park open daily 8am-sunset. Visitors center open daily 9am-5pm. $2 per vehicle, $1 per pedestrian.) The park is surrounded by the **Crystal River Preserve State Park,** which offers a number of short hiking trails. In the winter, over 350 types of migratory birds frequent the area. (☎ 352-795-3817. Open daily 8am-sunset. Free.)

☛ APPROACHING MANATEE SPRINGS STATE PARK: 50 MILES
Continue on **U.S. 19** to the town of Chiefland, turn left on **Rte. 320,** and drive 7 mi.

MANATEE SPRINGS STATE PARK. This giant spring gushes forth water at a rate of 50 to 150 million gallons per day, providing excellent, if crowded, swimming on hot summer afternoons. The park is absolutely beautiful for canoeing and kayaking—paddle through the serene Suwannee River and look out for manatee, the gentle creatures for which the park is named. **Camping ❶** is also available. (☎ 352-493-6072; www.florid-astateparks.org. Open daily sunrise-sunset. $4 per vehicle. Sites $17. AmEx/D/MC/V.)

☛ APPROACHING OLD TOWN: 13 MILES
Continue on **U.S. 19 N** to reach Old Town.

OLD TOWN. The village of Old Town sits way down along the Suwannee River, where the lazy flow of the dark waterway creates an aura of tranquility along its banks. Enjoy long afternoons and warm, peaceful evenings at the **Suwannee Gables Motel ❸**, 27659 SE U.S. 19. Each room in this tiny motel has a great river view, pool access, and a gorgeous wooded backyard above the Suwannee's banks. Feel free to loll around the

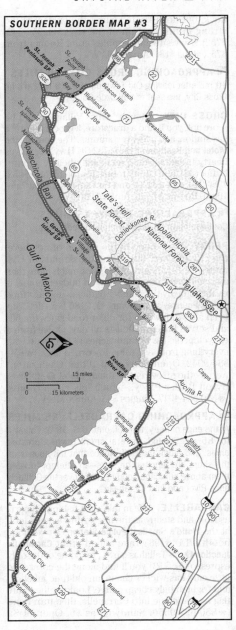

SOUTHERN BORDER MAP #3

dock, but don't try to swim—the current is too strong in this section of the river. (☎352-542-7752; www.suwanneegables.com. Rooms from $75; cabins $180. AmEx/MC/V.)

◪ APPROACHING CROSS CITY: 10 MILES
10 mi. after leaving Old Town on **U.S. 19 N,** you'll hit Cross City, the seat of tiny Dixie County.

CROSS CITY. Though "Cross Village" might be more apt, you'll find a drugstore, a grocery store, a gas station, and a few restaurants. The **Carriage Inn Motel and Restaurant ❷,** 16782 SE Hwy. 18, serves hearty breakfast fare, an equally hearty country buffet ($8), and comfy rooms for the night. (☎352-498-3910. Open M-Th and Su 7am-9pm, F-Sa 7am-10pm. Rooms $42-50. AmEx/D/MC/V.)

◪ APPROACHING PERRY: 45 MILES
Continue north on **U.S. 19** until you enter Perry.

PERRY. Very much in the middle of nowhere, the city of Perry sits at the crossroads of U.S. routes 98, 19, 27, and 221. It's not much more than a traveler's pit stop; the slew of budget motels is rivaled only by the number of diners and fast food joints. **Pouncey's Restaurant ❷,** 2186 U.S. 19 S, has been a town favorite for diner food since the 50s and serves huge breakfasts all day. Order from an encyclopedic list of sandwiches ($2-6) made with everything from egg salad to corned beef. (☎850-584-9942. Open daily 6am-10pm. Cash only.) Across the street is the **Gandy Motel ❷,** 2239 S. Byron Butler Pkwy., which has clean rooms. (☎850-584-4947. Singles $35. AmEx/MC/V.)

◪ APPROACHING CARRABELLE: 85 MILES
At the edge of Perry, turn left onto **U.S. 98 W.** Follow it for 85 mi. through several small towns, forested areas, and along the Gulf. Notice that the houses on the shore are perched on stilts—an attempt to keep them above hurricane flooding. Pass over the Ochlockonee River and into Carrabelle.

CARRABELLE. Life in this quiet fishing village is as slow and steady as the tides. After a quick look at the **World's Smallest Police Station** (a telephone booth off U.S. 98), take a load off at **Carrabelle Junction ❶,** 88 Tallahassee St., for some of the only espresso ($1.50-2) you'll find along the coast. The little cafe has wicker chairs, an old-time jukebox, and frighteningly cheap coffee. Look for the pirate flag as you come into Carrabelle, then turn right. (☎850-697-9550. Sandwiches $6. Open M-Sa

8am-4pm, Su 9am-3pm. Cash only.) For more robust fare, try **Miss Brenda's ❸,** on U.S. 98 just before you enter town. People travel for hours just to scarf down Miss Brenda's fried seafood, plucked straight from the Gulf. (☎850-697-5494. Grouper burger $8. Seafood plates $9-18. Open Tu-Su 11am-9pm. MC/V.)

◪ DETOUR
ST. GEORGE ISLAND STATE PARK
Continue 20 mi. down U.S. 98 through the ominous Tate's Hell Forest to Eastpoint and go left over the Gorrie Bridge. The state park is 4 mi. down, at the east end of the island.

The nine miles of undeveloped beaches and sand dunes that make up ◪**St. George Island State Park** are right at the end of St. George Island. Amid the sandy coves, salt marshes, shady pines, and oak forests of the pristine island sanctuary, you may hear the call of an American bald eagle or the rustle of a loggerhead turtle, raccoon, or ghost crab. (☎850-927-2111. Open daily sunrise-sunset. $4 per vehicle.)

◪ APPROACHING APALACHICOLA: 22 MILES
Head east on **Hwy. 98.**

APALACHICOLA. Apalachicola is a romantic fishing port on the shores of a peaceful bay, distinguished by the red-brick buildings of its historic downtown. Apalachicola is part of the Forgotten Coast that is not too forgotten—as indicated by the **Forgotten Coast Outfitters and Gift Shop,** 94 Market St. Head to the 100-year-old **Apalachicola Seafood Grill ❹,** 100 Market St., to enjoy the best oysters in town. (☎850-653-9510. Open M-Sa 11am-4pm. AmEx/D/DC/MC/V.) The **Rancho Inn ❸,** 240 U.S. 98 W, has large, well-equipped rooms with access to a pool and barbecue grill. (☎850-653-9435. Reception 8am-11pm. Rooms M-F $85, Sa-Su $95. AmEx/D/DC/MC/V.)

◪ DETOUR
ST. JOSEPH PENINSULA STATE PARK
Follow U.S. 98 out of Apalachicola for about 5 mi. until you reach the fork in the road at S.R. 30A (there is a small sign indicating the park on the right). Bear left, and follow 30A for 12 mi. to Cape San Blas Rd. Turn left, and continue another 10 mi.

Here on the edge of the world sits the astoundingly beautiful St. Joseph Peninsula State Park. Miles of white-sand beaches, sea-oat-covered dunes, and a heavily forested interior provide an incredible backdrop for campers, snorkelers, and fishermen. Nearly two-thirds of the park is a protected wilderness, serving as a sanctuary for brown pelicans, horseshoe crabs, sea turtles, peregrine falcons, and monarch butterflies. Camping is available at primitive sites in the wilderness area. (☎850-227-1327 or 800-326-3521. Open sunrise-sunset. $4 per vehicle. Primitive sites $4; regular sites $22; cabins $70. AmEx/D/MC/V.) For rentals, check out **Scallop Cove B.P.**, 4310 Cape San Blas Rd., just outside of the park entrance. (☎850-227-1573. Bikes $6 per 4hr. Canoes and kayaks $25 per 4hr. Open daily 8am-sunset.)

APPROACHING MEXICO BEACH: 35 MILES
From Apalachicola, head northwest on **U.S. 98/Rte. 30** to Mexico Beach.

MEXICO BEACH. This town prides itself on its lack of fast food, but it is still erecting condos to attract Panama City Beach tourists looking for quiet beaches. If you're feeling peckish, head to **Sharon's Cafe ❶**, 1100 U.S. 98, for pancakes, eggs, sandwiches, and a huge helping of happy faces. (☎850-648-8634. Breakfast $3-6. Open daily 6am-2pm. Cash only.) If you insist on stopping for the night, try the **Buena Vista Motel ❺**, 903 Hwy. 98, which has huge rooms right on the beach. (☎850-648-5323. Doubles $125. AmEx/D/MC/V.)

APPROACHING PANAMA CITY BEACH: 40 MILES
Continue on **U.S. 98,** passing through Panama City, to Panama City Beach.

A few miles before Panama City Beach, U.S. 98 enters the Central Time Zone, where it is 1hr. earlier.

PANAMA CITY BEACH

Whether you're in college or not, the Panama City Beach experience is the pinnacle of a spring break rampage. As the heart of the "Redneck Riviera," there is no pretension or high culture here—just 27 mi. of sand obscured by thousands of tourists, miles of parties, and loud, thumping bass. Warm-as-a-bath turquoise water, roller coasters, surf shops, and water parks round out the entertainment possibilities.

VITAL STATS

Population: 8000

Visitor Info: Panama City Visitors Center, 17001 Panama City Beach Pkwy. (☎800-722-3224; www.thebeachloversbeach.com), at the corner of U.S. 98 and Rte. 79. Open daily 8am-5pm.

Internet Access: Bay County Public Library, 25 W. Government St. (☎850-747-5748), in Panama City. Open M-W 9am-8pm, Th-Sa 9am-5pm, Su 1-5pm. Free.

Post Office: 1336 Sherman Ave. (☎850-747-4890). Open M-F 8:30am-6pm, Sa 9:30am-12:30pm. **Postal Code:** 32401.

GETTING AROUND. Panama City Beach (PCB) is essentially two roads: **U.S. 98 (Panama City Beach Pkwy.)** runs parallel to **Alt. U.S. 98 (Front Beach Rd.),** which runs along the beach. Front Beach Rd. becomes the glorious, tourist-crammed beachfront known as the **"Miracle Strip,"** PCB's main drag. As you enter PCB from the east, turn south (left) onto **Thomas Dr.** This will take you down to the beach, where it joins up with Front Beach Rd.

SIGHTS. Nearly a dozen submarines of various sizes are parked outside the **Museum of Man in the Sea,** 17314 Back Beach Rd. (U.S. 98), making this roadside attraction hard to miss. Inside the tiny museum, colorful displays are dedicated to the mysteries of the ocean and those who explore its depths. The museum also features exhibits on shipwrecks and allows visitors to crawl inside a small scientific submarine. (On the left side of U.S. 98 E. ☎850-235-4101. Open daily 10am-4pm. $5, ages 6-16 $2.50.) The **Treasure Island Marina,** 3605 Thomas Dr., has the "world's largest speed boat," the *Sea Screamer,* which cruises the Grand Lagoon. (☎850-233-9107. 4 cruises per day; call for times in spring and fall. $16, ages 4-12 $8.) If your penchant for cruising is still going strong, **Island Time Sailing Cruises,** 3605 Thomas Dr., offers 3½hr. snorkel-and-swim-with-dolphins ($25) tours or a 2hr. sunset sail and dolphin watch for $15. (☎850-234-7377. Cruises Mar.-Oct. daily 8am, noon, 4pm. Call ahead to confirm.)

FOOD. Along Thomas Dr. and the Miracle Mile you can have your fill at numerous buffets— most of which offer "early bird" half-price specials from 4-6pm. For something different, stop by the new **Liza's Kitchen ❷**, 7008 Thomas

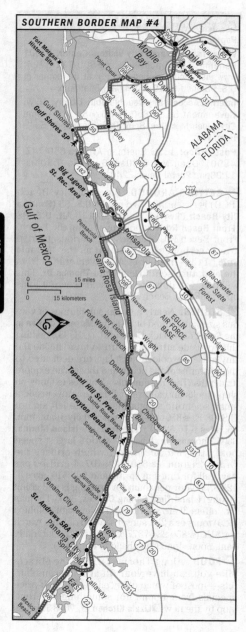

SOUTHERN BORDER MAP #4

SOUTHERN BORDER

Dr. All the breads and sauces are made from scratch, and the roasted chicken with red pepper, goat cheese, and spinach on homemade focaccia ($7) is delicious. (☎850-233-9000. Breakfast $4-6.50. Sandwiches $5-8. Open M-Sa 7am-4pm. D/MC/V.) **Scampy's ❹**, 4933 Thomas Dr., serves seafood in a less harried atmosphere than the mega-troughs. (☎850-235-4209. Lunch specials $4-8. Entrees $11-23. Open M-Th and Su 11am-10pm, F-Sa 11am-11pm. AmEx/D/MC/V.) A couple of doors down, the **Schooners Bar and Grill ❹**, 5121 Gulf Dr., calls itself "the last local beach club" and it's no surprise why—it's perched right on the beach. In the evenings, R&B bands croon tunes to a crowd of locals and tourists of all ages. (☎850-235-3555. Entrees $11-20. 21+ after 9pm. Open M-Th 11am-11pm, F-Su 11am-1am. Shows M-Th 9-11pm, F-Sa 9pm-1am. AmEx/D/MC/V.) Cool off with a Hurricane or a Sharkbite ($6.50) at **Sharky's ❸**, 15201 Front Beach Rd. Adventurous souls can savor "shark bites" (fried shark cubes; $7), Sharky's signature appetizer. (☎850-235-2420. Happy hour M-F 4-6pm with half-price drinks. Th-Su live music; in summer also W. Open daily 11am-2am. AmEx/D/MC/V.)

ACCOMMODATIONS. Finding an affordable hotel on the beach in PCB is no picnic. Call well in advance for summer reservations. Cheap motels can be found in Panama City on U.S. 98, just over the bridge from PCB. Though these rooms are rarely worth the $45 they average, they are the best bargain in town. The **Seafoam Motel ❸**, 6010 Thomas Dr., has 14 bright rooms and two cheery hosts. (☎850-234-3830. Singles from $50; doubles from $95. AmEx/D/MC/V.) The **Monterey Motel ❸**, 5501 Thomas Dr., has gargantuan singles with living rooms. (☎850-234-5062. Singles $60; doubles $70. AmEx/D/MC/V.) Closer to PCB proper is **Treasure Cove Motel ❷**, 2603 Thomas Dr. The rooms are a bit shabby (they were hit hard in the last hurricane), but it's cheap and sweet. (☎850-230-0712. Key deposit $5. Doubles $55. AmEx/D/MC/V.) At the **St. Andrews State Recreation Area**, 4607 State Park Ln., you can camp on 1000 acres of parkland near nature trails and beaches. You can also camp on beautiful Shell Island with special permission from a ranger. (At the east end of Thomas Dr. ☎850-233-5140, reservations 800-326-3521. Kayak rentals $20 per 4hr., $35 per day. Open daily 8am-sunset. Entrance fee $5. Reservations recommended. Sites $24. AmEx/D/MC/V.)

NIGHTLIFE. The largest club in the US (capacity 8000) and an MTV favorite is the behemoth **Club La Vela**, 8813 Thomas Dr. La Vela has eight sub-clubs and 48 bar stations under one jammin' roof. Live bands work the Rock Pavilion every night, and the "Kryogenics Room" freezes suddenly when the DJ presses a magic button. Wet t-shirt, bikini, and hardbody contests fill the weekends and every night during spring break. (☎850-234-3866. 18+. Dress code "sexy chic" in VIP rooms. Cover $5-35. Open daily 10am-5pm and 7pm-4am. AmEx/D/MC/V.) Next door, the **Spinnaker,** 8795 Thomas Dr., is a slightly more laid-back PCB icon. Ten bars, DJs, and live bands entertain partygoers. (☎850-234-7882, ext. 10. 21+ after 9pm. Cover varies. Open daily 11am-4am. AmEx/D/MC/V.)

APPROACHING FORT WALTON BEACH: 52 MILES

Take **Rte. 30A** out of Panama City Beach. Continue past the hidden entrance to Topsail Hill State Preserve, just outside of Destin. At this secluded beach area, roadtrippers can take a short drive down a dirt road through scrub pines to isolated white-sand dunes. Continue along Rte. 30A to rejoin **U.S. 98/Rte. 30** heading toward Fort Walton Beach.

FORT WALTON BEACH

The Fort Walton area was first settled around 12,000 BC by prehistoric peoples, who left their mark in the form of large mounds and middens. The area's bays and bayous were also home to pirate schooners that needed to recover from raiding and plundering. Tales of the notorious Billy Bowlegs are among the area's most famous pirate legends and are celebrated in the city's annual Billy Bowlegs Festival in June.

VITAL STATS

Population: 20,000

Visitor Info: Emerald Coast Convention and Visitors Bureau, 1540 Miracle Strip Pkwy. (☎800-322-3319; www.destin-fwb.com). Open M-F 8am-5pm, Sa-Su 9am-4pm.

Internet Access: Fort Walton Beach Library, 185 Miracle Strip Pkwy. SE (☎850-833-9590). Open M-Th 9am-9pm, F-Sa 9am-5pm. Free.

Post Office: 21 Walter Martin Rd. NE (☎850-244-2625). Open M-F 8:30am-4:45pm, Sa 10am-1pm. Postal Code: 32548.

GETTING AROUND. Fort Walton Beach is small and easily to navigate. **U.S. 98/Rte. 30** runs east-west along the coast as the **Miracle Strip Pkwy.** The town's other east-west thoroughfare is **Hollywood Blvd.**, which divides **Memorial Pkwy.** and **Wright Pkwy.** into northern and southern halves.

SIGHTS. Dolphin stars Princess, Delilah, and Lily perform comedic soccer games and 18 ft. skyward leaps daily at the **Gulfarium,** 1010 Miracle Strip Pkwy. In their shadow, sea lions, scuba divers, and multi-species acts also perform daily. The grounds feature many aquariums, a shark moat, and a stingray pool, in addition to gators and penguins. (On the right side of U.S. 98 E, just before the bridge. ☎850-243-9046; www.gulfarium.com. Dolphin shows 10am, noon, 2, 4pm. Open in summer 9am-6pm. Last entry 4pm. $17.50, ages 4-11 $10.50.) Explore the **Indian Temple Mound Museum,** 139 Miracle Strip Pkwy. (U.S. 98), to see a reconstruction of the Chief's Temple, the ancient political and ceremonial center of the area. The museum holds one of the finest collections of southeastern Native American ceramics and artifacts in the country. (On the right side of U.S. 98 E, after Rte. 85. ☎850-833-9595. Open June-Aug. M-Sa 10am-4:30pm, Su noon-4:30pm; Sept.-May M-F 10am-4pm, Sa 10am-4:30pm. $5, ages 6-17 $3.)

FOOD AND ACCOMMODATIONS. The **Brooks Bridge BBQ and Cafe ❷,** 240 Miracle Strip Pkwy., is a homey little place with daily specials on a blackboard and delectable barbecue dinners. (☎850-244-3003. Barbecue $6-12. Open M-Sa 11am-8pm. Cash only.) To enjoy a respite from American-style cooking, stop by **Kim's II ❸,** 234 W. Miracle Strip Pkwy. The Chicken Bok Um (pan-fried chicken in a spicy sauce with veggies; $9) is scrumptious. (☎850-244-2872. Noodle and rice entrees $9-12. Open M-Sa 11am-10pm. MC/V.)

If you're looking for a place to crash late, the **Classic Inn ❸,** 3 Miracle Strip Pkwy., does not accept reservations and may have vacancies when others do not. (☎850-243-3592. Singles $77, doubles $88. D/MC/V.) Don't be too shocked by the bright teal exterior of the **Dolphin Inn ❸,** 207 Miracle Strip Pkwy.; the rooms are spotless, very comfortable, and *not* teal. (☎850-244-2443. Reservations recommended. Rooms from $55. AmEx/D/DC/MC/V.)

SOUTHERN BORDER

⚲ APPROACHING PENSACOLA: 38 MILES

From Fort Walton Beach, head west on **U.S. 98/Rte. 30** to reach Pensacola.

PENSACOLA

Pensacola's military population and reputation for conservatism have been a part of the city's composition since the antebellum period, when three forts on the shores of Pensacola formed a triangular defense to guard its deepwater ports. For roadtrippers, Pensacola has a lovely downtown, noteworthy diners and barbecue joints, and the wacky T.T. Wentworth Museum. It's also the last major stop in Florida along the route, so take a moment to bid farewell to the Sunshine State.

VITAL STATS

Population: 56,000

Visitor Info: Pensacola Visitors Center, 1401 E. Gregory St. (☎800-874-1234; www.visitpensacola.com). Open daily 8am-5pm.

Internet Access: Pensacola Public Library, 200 W. Gregory St. (☎850-436-5060). Open Tu-Th 9am-8pm, F-Sa 9am-5pm, Su 2-7pm. Free.

Post Office: 101 S. Palafox St. (☎850-439-0171). Open M-F 8am-5pm. **Postal Code:** 32502.

⛢ GETTING AROUND.

Follow the Pensacola Bay Bridge 3 mi. into town, where it becomes **Bayfront Pkwy.** to the left and **Gregory St.** to the right. Both streets will lead you into Pensacola's historic downtown district. **Palafox St.** runs north-south, dividing the city into east and west sections. **Cervantes St.** is the main east-west artery, while **Palafox St., Davis Hwy.,** and **9th St.** are major north-south routes. Traveling east, Cervantes St. becomes **Scenic Hwy. (U.S. 90),** which hugs the coast of Pensacola Bay. The 11 mi. drive, high on some of the Gulf Coast's only bluffs, provides unforgettable views of the quiet bay below.

DID YOU KNOW? This section of the Gulf Coast is famous for its "sugar-white sand and emerald water." In fact, that fine, white sand is neither sugar nor sand: it's mostly quartz run-off from the Appalachian mountains. The sun reflecting off the quartz gives the water its emerald tint.

⚲ SIGHTS.

In the 1980s, millionaire junk collector T.T. Wentworth donated his eccentric collection to the city of Pensacola. The resulting **T.T. Wentworth Museum,** 830 S. Jefferson St., has one exhibit hall dedicated to Wentworth's collection, which includes oddities like a petrified cat, a shrunken head, and a gigantic shoe that belonged to the world's tallest man (who stood 8 ft. 8½ in. tall). The rest of the museum includes exhibits on Spanish explorers, model trains, sports, African-American history, and the area's shipwrecks. (☎850-595-5990. Open M-Sa 10am-4pm. Free.) At the **National Museum of Naval Aviation,** 1750 Radford Blvd., more than 130 planes will have pilot wannabes soaring on natural highs. The museum covers American aviation from WWI to the Vietnam War, and it even allows visitors to climb into a flight simulator. (Inside the Naval Air Station, at Exit 2 off I-10. ☎850-452-3604. Open daily 9am-5pm. Tours daily 10am, noon, 2pm. Must show picture ID to enter. Free.) For more grounded fun, escape to the relaxing paths that meander through the **Naval Live Oaks Area,** 1801 Gulf Breeze Pkwy. John Quincy Adams established this as the first and only naval tree reservation in the US, and set apart its oaks to make warships. (Head across the Pensacola Bay Bridge. ☎850-934-2600. Open daily 8am-5:30pm. Free.)

PHOTO OP. The 3 mi. **World's Longest Fishing Pier** shadows the Pensacola Bay Bridge.

⚎ FOOD AND ACCOMMODATIONS.

The owner of **King's BBQ ❷,** 2120 N. Palafox St., built this drive-up stand with his own hands 27 years ago and is often around to tell you about it. (½ mi. north of Cervantes St., at Maxwell Rd. ☎850-433-4479. Rib sandwiches $6.50. Open M-F 11am-6:30pm. MC/V.) A roadside grill, **Jerry's Drive-In ❷,** 2815 E. Cervantes St., dishes out standard diner fare with frosty milkshakes. (☎850-433-9910. Sandwiches and burgers $2-4. Dinner plates $5-6. Open daily 7am-10pm. Cash only.) A 10min. drive north on Davis Hwy. will lead you to **Tu-Do Restaurant ❷,** 7130 N. Davis Hwy., which serves incredible Vietnamese food. (☎850-473-8877. Entrees $4-8. Open daily 10:30am-9:30pm. AmEx/D/MC/V.)

Hotels along the beach cost at least $65 and get significantly more expensive during the summer. Cheaper options lie inland, north of downtown. One good choice is the **Harbor Inn ❷**, 200 N. Palafox St., which has clean and well-furnished rooms near downtown. (☎850-432-3441. Key deposit $5. Singles M-Th and Su $50, F-Sa $54; doubles $61/$65. AmEx/D/MC/V.) The **Red Roof Inn ❷**, 7340 Plantation Rd., is close to the airport and offers tidy rooms with Internet access. (☎850-476-7960. Reservations recommended. Singles from $40; doubles from $60. AmEx/D/DC/MC/V.)

◎ DETOUR
BIG LAGOON RECREATION AREA
Located on Rte. 292A (Gulf Beach Hwy.), 30min. west of Pensacola. Take Garden St., and hang a left when it splits. Follow Rte. 292 (Barrancas Ave.) to 292A, then turn left. The recreation area is on the right.

Sandpine scrub grows on dunes while gnarled underbrush testifies to the harsh coastal environment of this state recreation area. The park's rails and **campsites ❶** are situated alongside the lake, off Pensacola Bay. Quiet visitors may get a glimpse of the many foxes, raccoons, and blue herons that roam the area. (☎850-492-1595. Park open daily 8am-sunset. $4 per vehicle. Sites $17. AmEx/D/MC/V.)

⚑ APPROACHING FAIRHOPE: 35 MILES
From Pensacola, head west on **Garden St.**, which becomes **U.S. 98**. Continue west through strip malls for 30 mi. to Foley, crossing the Florida-Alabama divide. When U.S. 98 splits, take scenic **Alt. U.S. 98** to enter the oh-so-cute town of Fairhope.

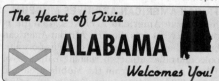

The Heart of Dixie
ALABAMA
Welcomes You!

FAIRHOPE. Founded by a group of Midwesterners seeking utopia, Fairhope still maintains its status as the largest "single-tax colony" in the country. Downtown's second stoplight is Fairhope Ave., and a right here leads to a panoramic view of Mobile Bay from the Fairhope pier. The **Down By the Bay Cafe ❸**, 4 Beach Rd., offers salads and sandwiches on a patio overlooking the pier. Peek

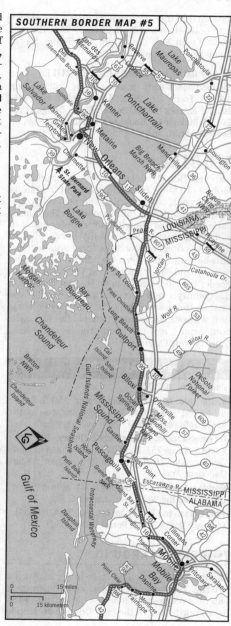

SOUTHERN BORDER MAP #5

SOUTHERN BORDER

through the large bay windows to look for whales with polka-dotted tails. (☎251-928-4363. Entrees $8-13. Open M-F 11am-3pm and 5-8pm, Sa-Su 11am-3pm. Cash only.)

⛟ APPROACHING MOBILE: 33 MILES
The road heads north for about 20 mi. before hitting **U.S. 98.** Follow U.S. 98 for 10 mi. until it joins **U.S. 90** and crosses the **Battleship Pkwy. Bridge.** Take **Exit 27** through the **Bankhead Tunnel** to emerge on **Government St.,** in the heart of downtown Mobile.

MOBILE

Although Bob Dylan lamented being stuck here, Mobile (MO-beel) has had plenty of fans in its time. French, Spanish, English, Sovereign Alabama, Confederate, and American flags have each flown over the city since its founding in 1702. This historical diversity is revealed in both the population and the local architecture; antebellum mansions, Italianate dwellings, Spanish and French forts, and Victorian homes border the city's azalea-lined streets. The site of the country's very first Mardi Gras, Mobile still hosts a three-week-long Fat Tuesday celebration without the hordes that plague its Cajun counterpart, giving the city the feel of a less-touristy New Orleans.

VITAL STATS

Population: 200,000

Visitor Info: Mobile Visitors Center, 150 S. Royal St. (☎251-208-7304), in a reconstructed French fort near Government St. Open daily 8am-5pm.

Internet Access: Mobile Public Library, 704 Government St. (☎251-208-7076). Call ahead for new location after 2007. Open M-Th 9am-9pm, Sa-Sa 9am-6pm. Free.

Parking: Free daytime parking is available in the lot across from the Welcome Center on S. Royal St.

Post Office: 168 Bay Shore Ave. (☎251-478-5639). Open M-F 9am-4:30pm. **Postal Code:** 36607.

⬚ GETTING AROUND

Mobile is surrounded by three major highways: **I-10** runs north-south to the south of downtown; **I-65** runs north-south near the airport; and **I-165** heads north, east of the city. Downtown Mobile

is a grid, surrounded by **Broad St.** to the west, **Canal St.** to the south, **Water St.** to the east, and **Beauregard St.** to the north. **Dauphin St.,** which is one-way downtown, and **Government Blvd. (U.S. 90),** which becomes **Government St.** downtown, are the major east-west routes. **Airport Blvd., Springhill Ave.,** and **Old Shell Rd.** are secondary east-west roads. **Royal St.** and **Broad St.** are major north-south byways.

⛏ SIGHTS

▦ USS ALABAMA BATTLEFIELD MEMORIAL PARK. The USS Alabama earned nine stars in WWII. Open passageways let civilians explore the ship's depths, and the park around the ship houses airplanes and the *USS Drum* submarine. (In Battleship Park, 2½ mi. east of town, accessible from I-10. ☎251-433-2703. Open daily Apr.-Sept. 8am-6pm; Oct.-Mar. 8am-4pm. $10, ages 6-11 $5, under 6 free.)

BIENVILLE SQUARE. With its oaks, white gazebo, and cast-iron fountain, Bienville Square is a picture of Southern charm. Eight historical districts, marked by signs downtown, showcase the city's architectural and cultural influences. (On Dauphin St., between Conception and St. Joseph St.)

THE MUSEUM OF MOBILE. This museum celebrates and documents 300 hundred years of Mobilian history in all its glory. Exhibits cover the founding of Mobile, the fate of the slave ship *Clotilda*, and the private collections of prominent Mobile families. (111 S. Royal St. ☎251-208-7569. Open M-Sa 9am-5pm, Su 1-5pm. $5, seniors $4, students $3. First Su of each month free.)

AFRICAN-AMERICAN ARCHIVES MUSEUM. The African-American Archives Museum is housed in what was the first African-American library in the US. The museum contains portraits, books, and other artifacts pertaining to the lives of African Americans from the Mobile area and beyond. (564 Dr. Martin Luther King, Jr. Ave. ☎251-433-8511. Open M-F 8am-4pm, Sa 10am-2pm. Free.)

OAKLEIGH HISTORICAL COMPLEX. This complex contains the grandiose **Oakleigh House Museum,** the working-class **Cox-Deasy House Museum,** and the **Mardi Gras Cottage Museum.** The complex features 19th- and 20th-century art collections, and each house portrays the lives of a different class of Mobilians in the 1800s. All visits are

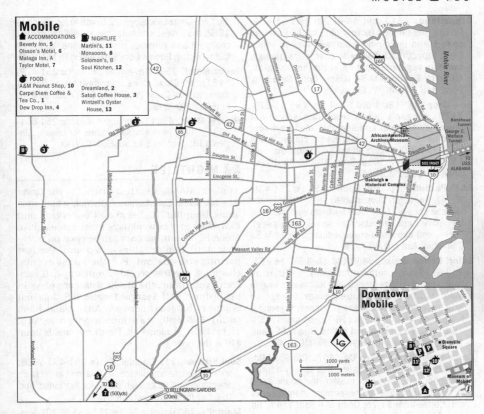

Mobile

▲ ACCOMMODATIONS
Beverly Inn, **5**
Olsson's Motel, **6**
Malaga Inn, **A**
Taylor Motel, **7**

♦ FOOD
A&M Peanut Shop, **10**
Carpe Diem Coffee &
Tea Co., **1**
Dew Drop Inn, **4**

◼ NIGHTLIFE
Martini's, **11**
Monsoons, **8**
Solomon's, **B**
Soul Kitchen, **12**

Dreamland, **2**
Satori Coffee House, **3**
Wintzell's Oyster
House, **13**

Downtown Mobile

SOUTHERN BORDER

chaperoned by costumed guides. *(350 Oakleigh Pl., 2½ blocks south of Government St., at George St. ☎251-432-1281. Open Tu-Sa 9am-3pm. Tours every 30min. 9am-2pm. $7, seniors $6.50, ages 6-11 $5.)*

BELLINGRATH GARDENS. The gardens on Mr. Bellingrath's estate-turned-museum were voted one of America's top five formal gardens for the 900 acres of lush roses, oriental displays, and bayou boardwalk. Visitors can also tour the **Bellingrath Museum Home** or take a narrated 45min. cruise on the **Southern Belle** riverboat. While the long drive and steep admission price may deter some, rose lovers should make the gardens a top priority. *(12401 Bellingrath Gardens Rd. Take Exit 15A off I-10 in Theodore. ☎800-247-8420. Open daily 8am-sunset. Gardens $10; gardens and home $18; gardens, home, and cruise $26.)*

🍴 FOOD

Mobile's Gulf location means fresh seafood, tasty barbecue, and good, old-fashioned Southern cookin'. But, unwilling to be pigeonholed, Mobile hosts restaurants serving a variety of cuisines.

◪ **Wintzell's Oyster House,** 605 Dauphin St. (☎251-432-4605; www.wintzellsoysterhouse.com). Wintzell's is a long-time local favorite; oysters are served "fried, stewed, or nude" amid wall decorations that range from the highly profound to the nearly profane. Beat the 1hr. oyster-eating record of 31 dozen (held by "Big Joe" Evans) to gain fame and $25. Happy hour M-F 4-7pm with $0.25 raw oysters and $1 draft beer. Open M-Th 11am-10pm, F-Sa 11am-11pm, Su 11am-10pm. AmEx/MC/V. ❸

Dreamland, 3314 Old Shell Rd. (☎251-479-9898). The famous Hickory ribs, cooked over an open fire in the dining room, will stick to yours. Don't expect much flora with your fauna, though; the only vegetarian option is the house salad. Half-rack $9. Open M-Sa 10am-10pm, Su 11am-9pm. AmEx/D/MC/V. ❷

Dew Drop Inn, 1808 Old Shell Rd. (☎251-273-7872). Mobile's oldest restaurant serves hot dogs, hamburgers, and seafood. Mull over your options as you sip a Coke from a classic green bottle ($1.30). Veggie plates $6. Dinner specials $5-7. Open Tu-F 10am-8pm, M and Sa 10am-3pm. AmEx/D/MC/V. ❷

A&M Peanut Shop, 209 Dauphin St. (☎251-438-9374). This candy shop is solely responsible for the extreme obesity of the local squirrels who snack on the leftover hot peanuts. Also serves other sweet, sticky, and chocolate-covered things. Open M-Sa 9am-6pm. AmEx/D/MC/V. ❶

Satori Coffee House, 5460 Old Shell Rd. (☎251-343-6677; www.satoricoffee.com). Satisfies all your hippie cravings for acoustic folk music, veggie food, and handmade pottery mugs. Lounge as long as you'd like on the snug couches, enjoying a full complement of wraps ($6-7) and salads ($3-7). Live music on weekend nights. Open M-F 7am-10pm, Sa-Su 7am-midnight. AmEx/MC/V. ❷

Carpe Diem Coffee & Tea Co., 4072 Old Shell Rd. (☎251-304-0448). Because this locally-adored coffeehouse has its own roaster, the beans used to make your coffee are never more than 2 weeks old. Coffee from $1.75. Open M-F 6am-11pm, Sa 7am-11pm, Su 8am-10pm. MC/V. ❷

ACCOMMODATIONS

There are few budget options in the historical part of downtown Mobile, but a 15-20min. drive from downtown will take you to the cheaper motels lining I-65. Pick up the *Alabama Travel Coupons* at the visitors center for discounts on a variety of chain motels.

⬛ Olsson's Motel, 4137 Government Blvd. (☎251-661-5331). Take Exit 1B off I-65. Though it's far from downtown, Olsson's makes up for it with quirky perks like cushy recliners and 4-poster beds. Singles $45; doubles $59. AmEx/D/MC/V. ❷

Malaga Inn, 359 Church St. (☎251-438-4701; www.malagainn.com), at Claiborne St., in front of the Civic Center. Occupying 2 townhouses dating to 1862, the pink-stucco hotel has a delightful central courtyard and gorgeous rooms. Continental breakfast included. Rooms from $79. AmEx/D/MC/V. ❹

Taylor Motel, 2598 Government Blvd. (☎251-479-5481), a 10min. drive from downtown. Decent rooms with A/C and TV. Singles $45; doubles $58. AmEx/D/MC/V. ❷

Beverly Motel, 4384 Government Blvd. (☎251-661-0331). Nice, fresh-smelling rooms for cheap. Singles $39; doubles $49. AmEx/MC/V. ❷

NIGHTLIFE

At night, Mobile's hottest district is the **Lower Dauphin Street Entertainment District,** which runs along Dauphin St., between Conception and Lawrence St. On weekdays most places close around 2 or 3am, but bars can be open on weekends until 4am or later—often until the last patrons straggle out. For the latest events, check out the free weekly *Lagniappe*. If bars aren't your thing, the **Mobile Symphony** plays in the historic 1927 **Seanger Theatre,** 6 S. Joachim St., every Saturday between August and June. (☎251-432-7080; www.mobilesymphony.org. Tickets $16, students $8. Dress rehearsals 2pm; $10 at the door.)

Soul Kitchen, 219 Dauphin St. (☎251-433-5958; www.soulkitchenmobile.com). This joint attracts an energetic and hip college crowd for live music and DJs. Call for showtimes. AmEx/D/MC/V.

Martini's, 250 Dauphin St. (☎251-433-9920). Martini's draws a slightly older crowd of young professionals to its chic, dimly-lit atmosphere. Sample one of 40 different martinis ($8-11). Live piano Th-Sa 7:30pm. Half-price martinis Tu-F 4-7pm. No cover. Open Tu-Sa 3pm-last customer. AmEx/D/MC/V.

Monsoon's, 9 N. Jackson St. (☎251-438-5500). A bit more laid-back than other live music venues, Monsoon's has folk and bluegrass performances throughout the week. Th nights acoustic only. Cover varies.

Solomon's, 5753 Old Shell Rd. (☎251-344-0380), at University Rd. A warehouse-sized space with 18 pool tables, darts, and video games. Happy hour 11am-7pm. Open 24hr. AmEx/MC/V.

APPROACHING PASCAGOULA: 42 MILES

Take **Government Blvd. (U.S. 90 W)** out of Mobile. After 20 mi., you will cross from "sweet home" Alabama into Mississippi, which, according to the road sign, is like "coming home."

The Magnolia State

MISSISSIPPI

Welcomes You

PASCAGOULA. The city of Pascagoula is a mess of oil rigs and shipping ports, though it does have a few places to sleep if you need a break. The **King's Inn Motel ❸,** 2303 Denny Ave., offers clean, basic rooms. (☎228-762-8110. Singles $65; doubles from $75. AmEx/MC/V.)

☈ APPROACHING GULF ISLANDS NATIONAL SEASHORE: 18 MILES

13 mi. past Pascagoula on **U.S. 90** is Ocean Springs—although it's hard to tell where one town ends and the other begins. The turnoff for the Gulf Islands National Seashore is in eastern Ocean Springs. Turn left (south) at the signs, and head down about 4 mi. to the park visitors center.

GULF ISLANDS NATIONAL SEASHORE.

Sheltered woods, palmetto groves, and grassy bayous make up the Davis Bayou segment of the Gulf Islands National Seashore, Mississippi District. Although Hurricane Katrina damaged many of the trees, visitors can still enjoy a few miles of nature trails, fishing, and picnicking. The small visitors center provides park info on the wildlife and geographic features of the area. (☎228-875-9057; www.nps.gov/guis). Unfortunately for roadtrippers, at press time the campground is currently housing Mississippians displaced by Katrina and is closed indefinitely. You can still hike and make use of free primitive camping sites on Horn, Petit Bois, Cat, and East Ship Islands, all designated wilderness areas, though visitors must arrange their own transportation to the islands. Contact the visitors center for information about local charter boats.

☈ APPROACHING OCEAN SPRINGS: 4 MILES

Exit the Gulf Islands National Seashore, and head left (west) on **U.S. 90.** Continue 3 mi., and take a right on **Washington Ave.** to reach downtown Ocean Springs.

OCEAN SPRINGS. The heart of Ocean Springs is on oak-lined Washington Ave. Life may move at a slower pace, but price tags still run high. Visitors can experience the bohemian flavor of the town at the **Walter Anderson Museum of Art,** 510 Washington Ave. The masterpieces of the museum are the murals that line the walls of the attached community center, which Anderson created in 1951 and gave to the community for $1. (☎228-872-3164; www.walterandersonmuseum.org. Open May-Sept. M-Sa 9:30am-5pm, Su 12:30-5pm; Oct.-Apr. M-Sa 9:30am-4:30pm, Su 12:30-4:30pm. $7, ages 16-24 $6, under 16 $3.) **Bayview Gourmet ❸,** 1010 Robinson St., serves upscale dishes like smoked-salmon omelettes and portobello mushroom sandwiches. (☎228-875-4252. Breakfast $5-12. Sandwiches $5-10. Open W-F 8am-3pm, Sa 7am-7pm, Su 7am-1pm. AmEx/D/MC/V.)

☈ APPROACHING BILOXI AND GULFPORT: 20 MILES

The bridge formerly connecting Ocean Springs and Biloxi has been washed away—with no rebuilding date scheduled. To get to Biloxi, head north on **Washington Ave.,** cross U.S. 90, and head west on **I-10** for 8 mi. Take **Exit 46,** heading south on **I-110** for 7 mi., until the highway ends in downtown Biloxi.

BILOXI AND GULFPORT

Once known for towering resort casinos, Biloxi and its neighbor Gulfport have been flattened by Hurricane Katrina. Fast-food chains and restaurants are mostly rubble, and stately old homes have been replaced with trailers. A number of oak trees remain, but even those are a lot worse for the wear. The beaches are closed, but the streets aren't empty; they're filled with construction crews, American flags, and posters proclaiming "Together we rebuild." Biloxi and the surrounding area is well-worth visiting if only to come face-to-face with the resilience of its citizens.

VITAL STATS

Vital Stats information is currently unavailable in Biloxi and Gulfport due to Hurricane Katrina. Please contact the **Mississippi Gulf Coast Convention and Visitors Bureau** for more information. (☎228-575-4297; www.gulfcoast.org.)

⬛ GETTING AROUND. U.S. 90 runs right along the shoreline as **Beach Blvd.** Some residential services line **Pass Rd.**, which parallels Beach Blvd. one block inland and is most easily accessible by turning on **Beauvoir Rd.**, next to the Coliseum in central Biloxi.

◙ **SIGHTS. Ship Island**, located 12 mi. off the coast of Biloxi, can be reached from Gulfport via a ferry run by the National Park Service. The marvelous white-sand beaches of this large island are as pure as they were when the Spanish discovered them in the 1500s. The Civil War-era **Fort Massachusetts** is also located on Ship Island. Free tours are offered every time a boatload of tourists docks. (Departs from Gulfport Yacht Harbor, adjacent to the intersection of U.S. 90 and Rte. 49. ☎ 866-466-7386; www.msshipisland.com. Ferries depart June-July daily 9am and noon; mid-Apr. to May and Aug. W-F 9am, Sa 9am and noon, Su noon; Sept. to late Oct. W-Sa 9am, Su noon. $20, under 10 $10.) The **Maritime and Seafood Industry Museum** is no longer open and does not yet have plans to rebuild. They are, however, still offering 2hr. tours in the Gulf Bay on full-scale replicas of 19th-century oyster schooners. (☎ 228-435-6320; www.maritimemuseum.org. Call ahead for times. $25.) The **Sailfish** takes guests on 70min. tours during which they loose their shrimping nets and discuss their catch. Don't worry—they throw all the sea critters back. (Departs from the Main St. Harbor. ☎ 800-289-7908; www.gcww.com/sailfish. Tours Feb.-Nov. Call for times. $12, ages 4-12 $8.) One of Biloxi's most upscale casinos, the **Beau Rivage**, is planning to reopen soon, but call ahead. (875 Beach Blvd. ☎ 888-595-2534; www.beaurivage.com. Open 24hr.) If you're looking to work the slots, head to the **Isle of Capri**, 151 Beach Blvd. (☎ 228-435-5400; www.isleofcapricasino.com. Open 24hr.) The **Palace Casino Resort**, 158 Howard Ave., also has gambling at slot machines. (☎ 800-725-2239; www.palacecasinoresort.com. Open 24hr.)

🍴🛏 FOOD AND ACCOMMODATIONS.
Most restaurants in Biloxi were obliterated by the hurricane, but more reopen every day. **Mary Mahoney's Old French House Restaurant ④**, 116 Rue Magnolia, is one of the only restaurants open on Beach Blvd. The beautiful courtyard and cozy interior seem worlds away from the rubble outside. Prices are high ($15-20), but they have lunch specials for $13. (☎ 228-436-6000; www.marymahoneys.com. Open daily 11am-9pm. Reservations recommended. AmEx/

D/MC/V.) For a less expensive lunch, head to **Port City Cafe ②**, 2418 14th St., right off Hwy. 49. The cafe has big windows, exposed brick, and a friendly owner who is extremely generous with pickles. (☎ 228-868-0037. Sandwiches $5-6. Salads $4-7.50. Open M-F 7am-3pm. AmEx/MC/V.) **Ben's Deli ①**, 1412 Pass Rd., is a tiny place with a takeout window and plenty of picnic tables. The deli serves burgers, po' boys, chicken dinners ($3-6), and a mean lo mein—it turns out Ben is Chinese-American. (☎ 228-214-4099. Chinese dishes $3.50-5.50. Open M-Sa 10am-7pm. Cash only.) Options for motels, hotels, and B&Bs are very limited in the Biloxi area. Those that are open have lowered capacity and often reserve all their rooms for out-of-town construction workers and clean-up volunteers. If you're thinking of staying the night, contact **Gulf Coast Hotel Reservations** (☎ 228-388-6117) to find out what is available. Hotels that offer tourist lodgings often charge inflated prices, generally $150 per night. One of the cheapest options is the **Southern Hotel ③**, 1870 Beach Blvd., just off Hwy. 90, which has new rooms with A/C and cable TV. (☎ 228-388-4331. Singles M-Th $85, F-Su $115. AmEx/D/DC/MC/V.)

🚩 APPROACHING PASS CHRISTIAN: 23 MILES
From Biloxi, take **I-10 W** to **Exit 24** at **Menge Ave.**, and bear left to reach Pass Christian.

PASS CHRISTIAN. Before Katrina, fabulous antebellum mansions lined the seashore and were visible from the aptly named **Scenic Dr.** Although it has seen better days, the street is still worth cruising, since some mansions remain and others are being reconstructed.

🚩 APPROACHING BAY ST. LOUIS: 21 MILES
From Pass Christian, take **Menge Ave.** 8 mi. to **I-10**, and then head west for 10 mi. Take **Exit 13,** and follow the signs for a few miles south to Bay St. Louis.

BAY ST. LOUIS. Bay St. Louis sustained a lot of damage in the hurricane, but the town still retains a quaint charm. Locals are working diligently to rebuild the charming shops and cafes that once lined the shopping district. The posh **Sycamore House ④**, 210 Main St., offers candlelit dining and fabulous desserts, like chocolate torte. (☎ 228-469-0107; www.thesycamorehouse.com. Entrees $15-25. Desserts $6-8. Open W-Sa 11am-2:30pm and 6-10pm, Su 11am-3pm.

AmEx/D/MC/V.) Near the railroad tracks, **The Bay City Grill ❸**, 136 Blaize Ave., serves Cajun and American-style food ($7-11). The late-night menu, served 10pm-1am, has similar dishes for slightly less. (☎228-466-0590. Lasagna $10. Open Tu-Th 11am-2pm and 5pm-midnight, F-Sa 11am-2pm and 5pm-2am. AmEx/MC/V.) If you want to stay the night, a good bet is the **Economy Inn ❷**, 810 U.S. 90. (☎228-467-8441. Singles $30; doubles $35. Cash only.)

⚑ APPROACHING NEW ORLEANS: 55 MILES
From Bay St. Louis, follow **U.S. 90 W** for 18 mi. to the junction with I-10. Get on **I-10 W,** and continue 37 mi. to New Orleans. Take the **Canal St./Superdome exit** to head directly into the French Quarter.

NEW ORLEANS

First explored by the French, La Nouvelle Orléans was secretly ceded to the Spanish in 1762, but its citizens didn't find out until 1766. Spain returned the city to France just in time for the US to grab it in 1803. Centuries of cultural cross-pollination have resulted in a vast melange of Spanish courtyards, Victorian verandas, Cajun jambalaya, Creole gumbo, and French *beignets*, to name but a few unique hallmarks of New Orleans. Life hasn't been easy since the city was devastated by Hurricane Katrina, but there is a perceptible air of pride in the residents as they return, rebuild, and try to keep the Big Easy's party going.

VITAL STATS

Vital Stats information is currently unavailable in New Orleans due to Hurricane Katrina. Contact the **New Orleans Convention and Visitors Bureau** for tourist information. (☎800-672-6124; www.neworleanscvb.com.)

▣ GETTING AROUND

Most sights in New Orleans are located within a central area. The city's main streets follow the curve of the **Mississippi River,** hence its nickname, "the Crescent City." Directions from locals are usually relative to bodies of water—lakeside means north, referring to Lake Pontchartrain, and "riverside" means south. Uptown lies west, upriver; downtown is downriver. "The East" refers only to the easternmost part of the city.

Tourists flock to the small **French Quarter,** bounded by the Mississippi River, **Canal St., Rampart St.,** and **Esplanade Ave.** Streets in the Quarter follow a grid pattern, making navigation easy. Just northeast of the Quarter, across Esplanade Ave., **Faubourg Marigny** is a residential neighborhood that has trendy nightclubs, bars, and cafes. Northwest of the Quarter, across from Rampart St., the African-American neighborhood of **Tremé** has a storied history. Its appearance has been marred by the encroaching highway overpass and the housing projects lining its Canal St. border. Be careful in Tremé and in **Central City** (the area southwest of the Superdome) at night. Uptown, the residential **Garden District,** bordered by **St. Charles Ave.** to the north and **Magazine St.** to the south, is distinguished by its elegant homes.

Parking in New Orleans is relatively easy (parking info ☎337-299-3700). Throughout the French Quarter (and in most other residential neighborhoods), signs along the streets designate 2hr. parking. Many streets throughout the city have meters (M-F after 6pm, weekends, and holidays free). Parking lots along Rampart St. sell day-long spaces ($5-12), but many lots within the French Quarter charge upwards of $15 for anything over 3hr. Another viable option is to park for free in the Garden District; just take the **St. Charles Streetcar** along St. Charles Ave. into downtown and the French Quarter. As a general rule, avoid parking on deserted streets at night. After sunset, it's often best to take a cab or the St. Charles Streetcar.

◉ SIGHTS

The St. Charles Streetcar route, which picks up at Canal St. and Carondelet St., passes through parts of the **Central Business District** ("CBD" or "downtown"), the Garden District, and the **Uptown** and **Carrollton** neighborhoods along **S. Carrollton Ave.** and passes Tulane and Loyola University.

The **Jean Lafitte National Historical Park and Preserve Visitors Center,** 419 Decatur St., conducts free 1½hr. walking tours through the French Quarter. (☎504-589-2636. Office open daily 9am-5pm. Tours daily 9:30am.) On the **Gay Heritage Tour,** Robert Batson, "history laureate" of New Orleans, gives a politically insightful and lively tour of the city's queer history and culture. (Leaves from 909 Bourbon St. ☎504-945-6789. 2½hr. tours W 4pm and Sa 1pm. Reservations required. $20.) For all things jazz, head to the **New Orleans Jazz National Historical Park Visitors Center.** Currently housed at 916 N. Peters St. in the French Quarter, the Center will eventually be re-located slightly north to Armstrong Park. Check www.nps.gov/jazz for updates. (☎504-589-4841. Visitors center open Tu-Sa 9am-5pm. Short film on jazz Tu-Sa 11am. Lectures Tu and Th 3-4pm. Call ahead for afternoon concert schedule. Free)

FRENCH QUARTER

Allow a full day in the Quarter. The oldest section of the city is famous for its ornate wrought-iron balconies—French, Spanish, and uniquely New Orleans architecture—and raucous atmosphere. Known as the **Vieux Carré** (vyuh ca-RAY), or Old Square, the historic district of New Orleans encompasses dusty used bookstores, voodoo shops, museums, art galleries, bars, and tourist traps. **Bourbon St.** is packed with touristy bars, strip clubs, and panhandlers disguised as clowns; **Decatur St.** has a more mellow version of the same. If you're searching for some bona fide New Orleans tunes, head northeast of the Quarter to **Frenchmen St.,** a block of bars that locals claim is what Bourbon St. was like 20 years ago.

ROYAL STREET. A streetcar named "Desire" once rolled down **Royal St.,** one of the French Quarter's most aesthetically pleasing avenues. Pick up the free *French Quarter Self-Guided Walking Tour* from the visitors center on St. Ann St.; they may be hiding it behind the counter.

JACKSON SQUARE. During the day, much of the activity in the French Quarter centers around Jackson Sq., a park dedicated to General Andrew Jackson, victor of the Battle of New Orleans. The square swarms with artists, mimes, musicians, psychics, magicians, and con artists. If you've got cash to burn, you can take a 30min. horse-drawn tour of the Quarter here for $60. The oldest Catholic cathedral in the US, **St. Louis Cathedral,** possesses a simple beauty and

has been fully operational since 1718. *(615 Père Antoine Alley. ☎504-525-9585. Open daily 7am-5pm.)* Behind the cathedral lies **Cathedral Garden,** also known as **St. Anthony's Garden,** bordered by Pirate Alley and Père Antoine Alley. Legend has it that Pirate Alley was the site of covert meetings between pirate Jean Lafitte and Andrew Jackson as they drafted their plans for the Battle of New Orleans. In reality, the alley wasn't even built until 16 years later. Pirate Alley is also home to **Faulkner House Books,** where the late American author wrote his first novel, *Soldier's Pay.* The bookshop is a treasure trove of Faulkner's books, alongside an extensive catalogue of other Southern writers. *(624 Pirate Alley. ☎504-524-2940. Open daily 10am-6pm.)*

FRENCH MARKET. The historic French Market takes up several city blocks east of Jackson Sq., toward the water along N. Peters and Decatur St. *(☎504-522-2621. Shops open daily 9am-8pm.)* The market begins at the famous **Café du Monde** (p. 795) and for the first few blocks is a strip mall of touristy shops in a historical building. By Gov. Nicholls St., it becomes the outdoor **Farmers' Market,** which never closes and has been selling "most anything that grows" since 1791. Beyond the Farmers Market is the **Flea Market,** where vendors offer everything from feather boas to woodcarvings. Since Hurricane Katrina these markets have specialized exclusively in tourist trinkets—perfect if you want to buy your mother a "N'awlins" salt-and-pepper shaker set.

OUTSIDE THE QUARTER

WATERFRONT. For an up-close view of the Mississippi River and a unique district of New Orleans, take the free **Canal Street Ferry** to **Algiers Point.** Once called "The Brooklyn of the South," Algiers was home to much of New Orleans's African-American population as well as the city's most famous jazz musicians. Nowadays there's not much to do there, but if you're hankering for a pretty neighborhood and a glimpse of a few brightly painted bungalows, it might be worth visiting. At night, the ferry's outdoor observation deck affords a panoramic view of the city's sights. *(Ferry departs from the end of Canal St. daily every 30min. 5:45am-midnight. $1 per vehicle.)*

WAREHOUSE ARTS DISTRICT. The Warehouse Arts District, at the intersection of Julia

New Orleans

🏠 ACCOMMODATIONS
India House, **2**
Jude Travel Park, **1**
Marquette House (HI-AYH) **4**
St. Charles Guest House, **5**

🍴 FOOD
Franky & Johnny's, **9**
Juan's Flying Burrito, **6**
Tee Eva's, **8**

🍺 NIGHTLIFE
Maple Leaf Bar, **3**
Tipitina's, **7**

and Camp St., contains several contemporary art galleries in revitalized warehouse buildings. Many galleries have exhibition openings on the first Saturday of every month. On **White Linen Night,** the first Saturday in August, thousands take to the streets in their fanciest white finery. In an old brick building with a modern, glass-and-chrome facade, the **Contemporary Arts Center** mounts exhibits of local artists' works, ranging from puzzling to positively cryptic. It also hosts music and performance art. (*900 Camp St. ☎504-528-3805; www.cacno.org. Open Tu-Su 11am-5pm. $5, students and seniors $3, under 12 free. Th free.*) Across the street, the **Ogden Museum of Southern Art** contains a huge collection of modern art and sculpture created in the Southern US. (*925 Camp St. ☎504-539-9600; www.ogdenmuseum.org. Open Tu-W and F-Su 9:30am-5:30pm, Th 9:30am-8:30pm. Th*

jazz show free after 6pm. $10, students and seniors $8, under 17 $5.) In the rear studio of the **New Orleans School of Glassworks and Printmaking,** you can watch students and instructors transform molten glass into vases and sculptures. (*727 Magazine St. ☎504-529-7277. Open in summer M-F 10am-5:30pm; in winter M-Sa 10am-6pm. Free.*) The **Jonathan Ferrara Gallery** hosts all sorts of local and regional artists. (*841 Carondelet St. ☎504-522-5471. Open Tu-Sa noon-6pm. Free.*) Just west of the Warehouse District, the **Zeitgeist Multi-Disciplinary Arts Center** has films, art exhibits, and theatrical and musical performances. (*1724 Oretha Castle Haley Blvd., 4 blocks north of St. Charles Ave. ☎504-525-2767. $6, students and seniors $5.*) A few blocks farther west on St. Charles St., in **Lee Circle,** stands a bronze **Confederate Gen. Robert E. Lee,** who stares down the Yankees to this day.

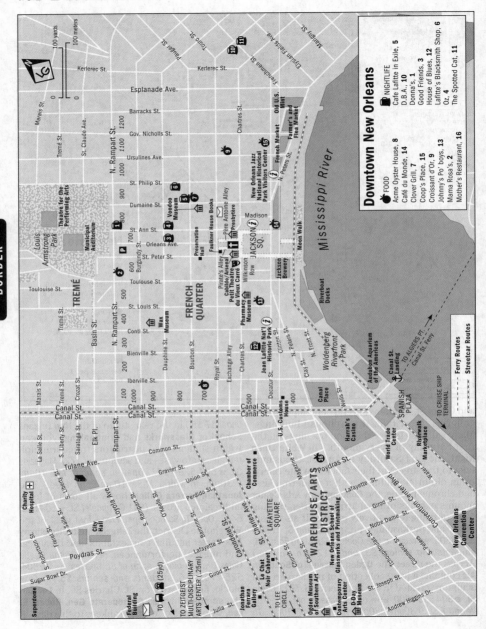

Downtown New Orleans

● FOOD
Acme Oyster House, **8**
Café du Monde, **14**
Clover Grill, **7**
Coop's Place, **15**
Croissant d'Or, **9**
Johnny's Po' boys, **13**
Mama Rosa's, **2**
Mother's Restaurant, **16**

● NIGHTLIFE
Cafe Lafitte in Exile, **5**
D.B.A., **10**
Donna's, **1**
Good Friends, **3**
House of Blues, **12**
Lafitte's Blacksmith Shop, **6**
Oz, **4**
The Spotted Cat, **11**

Ferry Routes
Streetcar Routes

PLANTATION RIVER ROAD. Across from downtown New Orleans, River Rd. curves along the Mississippi River. If you follow it 40 mi. west (or take I-10 W to Exit 194), you can access several plantations preserved from the 19th century. *Great River Road Plantation Parade: A River of Riches*, available at the New Orleans Visitors Center, contains a good map and descriptions of the houses. Choose wisely, since tours of the privately owned plantations are quite expensive. ▓**Laura Plantation** was owned and operated by slave-owning Creoles whose lives were very different from those of white antebellum planters. Br'er Rabbit hopped into his first briar patch here, the site of the first recorded "Compair Lapin" West African stories. The tours are fantastic and provide a unique view of plantation life. *(2247 Rte. 18/River Rd. ☎ 225-265-7690. Tours daily 9:30am-4pm. $10, students and seniors $5.)* The **San Francisco Plantation** is an example of Creole style, with its bright blue, peach, and green exterior; it also points to the aesthetic tastes of its Bavarian mistress. The inside features lavish furnishings and beautiful painted ceilings, all of which are original. *(2646 Hwy. 44. ☎ 985-535-2341; www.sanfranciscoplantation.org. Open daily Apr.-Oct. 9:30am-5pm; Nov.-Mar. 9am-5pm. $10, students and seniors $5.)* The name **Oak Alley** refers to the magnificent lawn-alley bordered by 28 evenly spaced oaks that correspond to the 28 columns surrounding the Greek Revival house. The Greeks wouldn't have approved, though—the mansion is bright pink. *(3645 Rte. 18, between St. James and Vacherie St. ☎ 225-265-2151; www.oakalleyplantation.com. Open daily 9am-5pm. $10, students and seniors $5.)*

🏛 MUSEUMS

▓**NATIONAL D-DAY MUSEUM.** This museum lives up to its hype as an engaging, exhaustive, and moving study of World War II. Through photos, recorded footage, and personal testimony, the museum explains how the US entered WWII and how D-Day was planned and executed. The museum also deals in great depth with the U.S.-Japanese Pacific war and confronts the ugly issues of race and propaganda that fueled hate against Japanese and Japanese-Americans. *(945 Magazine St., at the corner of Andrew Higgins Dr. ☎ 504-*527-6012; www.ddaymuseum.org. Open Tu-W and F-Sa 9am-5pm, Th 9am-7pm. $14, students and seniors $6, ages 5-17 $6. Th 5-7pm $10.)*

▓**NEW ORLEANS PHARMACY MUSEUM.** This enthralling look into medical history is housed in an apothecary shop built by America's first licensed pharmacist in 1923. Among the exhibits are 19th-century "miracle drugs" like cocaine and opium, voodoo powders, a collection of old spectacles, a rare 1855 soda fountain, and live leeches. *(514 Chartres St., between St. Louis and Toulouse St. ☎ 504-565-8027. Open Tu-Sa 9am-noon. $5, students and seniors $4, under 12 free.)*

LOUISIANA STATE MUSEUM. Eight separate museums are overseen by the "State Museum," three of which are open following Katrina. The **Cabildo** presents the history of Louisiana and houses Napoleon's death mask. *(701 Chartres St. ☎ 504-488-2631. $6, students and seniors $5, under 12 $3.)* The **Arsenal** recounts the history of the Mississippi River and New Orleans as a port city. *(615 St. Peter St. Enter through the Cabildo. ☎ 504-488-2631. $6, students and seniors $5, under 12 $3.)* The **Presbytère** features a gigantic exhibit on Mardi Gras, which allows visitors to try on costumes and clamber onto floats. *(751 Chartres St. ☎ 800-568-6968. $6, students and seniors $5, under 12 $3.)*

NEW ORLEANS MUSEUM OF ART (NOMA). This magnificent museum houses art from North and South America, a phenomenal glass collections, opulent works by the jeweler Fabergé, a strong exhibit of French paintings, and some of the best African and Japanese work in the country. The inspiring new sculpture garden sprawls over acres of walkways. *(In City Park, at the City Park/Metairie exit off I-10. ☎ 504-488-2631; www.noma.org. Open F-Su 10am-4:30pm. $8, students and seniors $7, ages 3-17 $4. Sculpture gardens free.)*

THE VOODOO MUSEUM. Learn why all those dusty shops in the Quarter sell gris-gris and alligator teeth at this quirky haunt. The owner, John Martin, doubles as a voodoo and druid priest and happily performs readings or rituals for a fee (readings on palms and cards from $30, rituals from $150). Ask John about his five pet pythons, all of which live in his apartment above the Museum—he'll proudly show you pictures. *(724 Dumaine St. ☎ 504-581-3824. Open M-Th 10:30am-5:30pm, F-Su 10am-6pm. $7, students and seniors $5.50, under 12 $3.50.)*

AUDUBON AQUARIUM OF THE AMERICAS. If you like aquariums, you'll love this one. The 110,000 sq. ft. facility has state-of-the-art exhibits, including sharks from the Gulf Coast, penguins, and a Coral Reef. Look for the 10 ft. albino alligator. *(1 Canal St. ☎800-774-7394; www.auduboninstitute.org/aoa. Open Tu-Sa and Su 10am-5pm. $16, seniors $13, children $9.50.)*

FOOD

If the eats in the Quarter prove too trendy, touristy, or tough on the wallet, there are plenty of options on **Magazine St.** and in the Tulane area. Be warned that many restaurants and bars, especially in the Quarter, have shortened their hours because of the drop in tourism.

Coop's Place, 1109 Decatur St. (☎504-525-9053). Some of the Quarter's best Southern cooking. The gumbo ($6.50) is thick and spicy, the beer-battered alligator bits ($8) have won awards, and the jambalaya ($6.50) has a flavor found nowhere else. A cozy neighborhood bar to boot. Open M-F 11am-1am, Sa-Su 11am-2am. D/MC/V. ❸

Tee Eva's, 4430 Magazine St. (☎504-899-8350). Eva used to sell her scrumptious pies from a picnic basket around town. Now she has a more permanent home—a brightly painted food counter. Soul food lunches ($3-6) change daily. Creole pralines $2. Crawfish pie $3. Sweet potato or pecan pie $2. Open daily 11am-7pm. Cash only. ❶

Juan's Flying Burrito, 2018 Magazine St. (☎504-569-0000). These crunchy burritos may be the best on the planet. Get the "gutter punk" burrito ($6.50), a meal the size of your head, and wash it down with some Mexican beer. Open M-Sa 11am-11pm, Su noon-10pm. AmEx/D/MC/V. ❷

Clover Grill, 900 Bourbon St. (☎504-598-1010). Open since 1950, serving greasy and delicious burgers (from $5) grilled under an American-made hubcap. Breakfast ($3-4) served all day. Open M-Th 7am-midnight, F-Sa 24hr. AmEx/MC/V. ❶

Franky and Johnny's, 321 Arabella St. (☎504-899-9146), southwest of downtown at the corner of Tchoupitoulas St. A noisy, dark, and very popular bar where you can sample alligator soup ($4.50) or fried crawfish ($11). The stuffed artichokes ($8) are fantastic. Open M-Th 11am-8pm, F 11am-9pm, Sa 11am-8pm. AmEx/D/MC/V. ❸

Johnny's Po' Boys, 511 St. Louis St. (☎504-524-8129), near the Decatur St. corner. This French Quarter institution has 40 varieties of the classic po' boy ($4-7.50). Open M and W-Su 9am-3pm. AmEx/MC/V. ❷

Acme Oyster House, 724 Iberville St. (☎504-522-5973). A touristy spot with excellent oysters (6 for $5, 12 for $8). Get your oysters shucked before your eyes by Hollywood, the senior shucker. Open M-Th and Su 11am-9pm, F-Sa 11am-10pm. AmEx/D/MC/V. ❸

Croissant d'Or, 617 Ursulines Ave. (☎504-524-4663). French pastries, sandwiches, and quiches are served to a crowd that comes to read

NOSHING IN N'AWLINS

Dining in New Orleans can be more than a little confusing without a guide to the most popular local cuisine.

Beignet: A "French-style" donut, the beignet is a deep-fried blob of dough that is typically smothered in powdered sugar.
Gumbo: Louisiana's signature soup, New Orleans's seafood gumbo starts with a *roux* broth with regional spices, is usually thickened with okra, and can include crab, shrimp, or crawfish.
Muffuletta: Invented in 1906 by Salvatore Lupo, the owner of the Central Grocery on Decatur St., the muffuletta sandwiches ham, salami, provolone cheese, and olive relish between slices of round muffuletta bread. These can get messy to eat, but are worth the extra napkins.
Po' boy: A New Orleanian pronunciation of "poor boy," this is basically New Orleans's version of the grinder, hoagie, submarine or hero sandwich. The name originates from the Great Depression of the 1930's, when oyster po' boys were the cheapest meal you could buy in the city. Served on french bread, today's po' boy may feature oysters, catfish, shrimp, or more traditional lunchmeats.

the morning paper. Fresh croissants $1.75. Chocolate mousse $3. Open M and W-Su 7am-5pm. AmEx/MC/V. ❷

Mama Rosa's, 616 N. Rampart St. (☎504-523-5546). Locals adore this Italian *ristorante*, and with good reason. Served in a cozy neighborhood setting, Mama Rosa's pizza is some of the best you'll ever eat. "Outrageous muffuletta" $8. Pizza $17. Open M-Th and Su 11am-10pm, F-Sa 11am-11pm. AmEx/D/MC/V. ❸

Café du Monde, 800 Decatur St. (☎504-587-0833). Picture old school tables, a sprawling patio, and a bustling waitstaff, and you have it. This people-watching paradise, open since 1862, only does two things—hot café au lait and scrumptious *beignets* ($1.75)—and it does them well. Open 24hr. Cash only. ❶

Mother's Restaurant, 401 Poydras St. (☎504-523-9656), at the corner of Tchoupitoulas St. A deli-style restaurant packed with locals and tourists. While you munch the "world's best baked ham po' boy" ($8), take a minute to appreciate the decor. The walls are covered with framed newspaper clippings and awards that attest to Mother's greatness. Open M-Sa 7:30am-8pm. AmEx/MC/V. ❷

ACCOMMODATIONS

Finding inexpensive, decent rooms in the **French Quarter** can be as difficult as staying sober during Mardi Gras. Luckily, other parts of the city compensate for the absence of cheap lodging downtown. Several hostels cater to the young and almost penniless, as do guesthouses near the **Garden District.** Accommodations for Mardi Gras and the Jazz Festival are booked solid up to a year in advance. During peak times, proprietors will rent out any extra space, so be sure you know what you're paying for.

St. Charles Guest House, 1748 Prytania St. (☎504-523-6556; www.stcharlesguesthouse.com), off Jackson St. Located in the heart of the beautiful Garden District, this large 19th-century home is luxury without the hefty price tag. Caring and quirky owner Dennis Hilton is the traveler's personal encyclopedia of all things New Orleans, Louisiana, and the South. Large courtyard and beautiful pool, in addition to A/C and private bath. No phones or TVs. Continental breakfast

included. Rooms with shared bath $45-65, with private bath $65-105. Cash only. ❸

India House, 124 S. Lopez St. (☎504-821-1904; www.indiahousehostel.com), at Canal St. This bohemian haunt has all the character you'd expect from a former brothel. Communal eating, comfy couches, and a backyard patio, as well as kitchen, pool, and turtle pond. Linen deposit $5. Internet $4 per hr. Dorms $17; 3- to 4-bed dorms $22.50; private rooms $45. AmEx/MC/V. ❶

Marquette House New Orleans International Hostel, 2249 Carondelet St. (☎504-523-3014), in the Garden District. This hostel has a sobriety policy, ensuring a quiet stay. 150 beds, A/C, kitchen (without stove), reading rooms, and lovely outdoor courtyards. Linen included. Key deposit $10. Storage $0.50. Dorms $22; private rooms $66. MC/V. ❷

Jude Travel Park and Guest House, 7400 Chef Menteur Hwy./U.S. 90 (☎504-241-0632), at Exit 240B, 5 mi. from the French Quarter. The guest house is expensive, so it's best to stay at the campground. 46 sites. Electricity, pool, showers, and 24hr. security. Laundry $2. Sites $25. AmEx/D/MC/V. ❷

ENTERTAINMENT

Uptown houses authentic Cajun dance halls and university hangouts, while the **Marigny** is home to New Orleans's alternative and local music scenes. There are good bars along **Frenchman St.** that often have live music and are less touristy than the French Quarter equivalents. Check out *Off Beat*, free in many restaurants, *Where Y'At*, another free weekly, or the Friday *Times-Picayune* to find out who's playing where.

Le Petit Théâtre du Vieux Carré, 616 St. Peter St. (☎504-522-2081). One of the city's most beloved historic theaters and the oldest continuously operating community theater in the US, the building replicates the early 18th-century abode of Louisiana's last Spanish governor. About 5 musicals and plays go up each year. Call for box office hours. Tickets $20-26.

Preservation Hall, 726 St. Peter St. (daytime ☎504-522-2841, after 8pm 504-523-8939). Traditional New Orleans jazz was born at the turn of the century, and it's alive and well here. With only 2 small ceiling fans to cool the place, most people only stay for 1 set, so you can usually find a spot. Cover $8, except special events. Shows F and Sa 8pm and 10 pm.

Le Chat Noir, 715 St. Charles Ave. (☎504-581-5812; www.cabaretlechatnoir.com). In a turn-of-the-century house on St. Charles, Le Chat Noir prides itself on being a "European-style cabaret" (dark interior and little white-clothed tables with candles). The venue seats 125 and hosts all sorts of shows. Ticket prices vary. Open most weeknights and every weekend from 7pm.

◈ NIGHTLIFE

Life in New Orleans is and always will be a party. On any night of the week, at any time of the year, the masses converge on Bourbon St. to drift in and out of bars and strip joints. Ask any local what to do on a weekend, and he'll probably tell you to avoid Bourbon at all costs; the street has become increasingly touristy as of late. **Decatur St.,** near the French market, is a quieter, though still touristy nightlife area. To experience what the Quarter was like before the tourist traps took over, head southeast to **Frenchmen St.,** which offers eclectic bars and clubs. Another good place to find nightlife is around Tulane University on **Oak St.**

BARS

Bars in New Orleans stay open late, and few keep a strict schedule; in general, they open around 11am and close around 3am, but many go all night when there's a crowd or a party.

Most blocks, especially in the Quarter, feature at least one establishment with cheap draft beer and "Hurricanes" (sweet juice-and-rum drinks).

☒ **Donna's,** 800 N. Rampart St. (☎504-596-6914), on the edge of the French Quarter. As one fan says, this is "the place where you can sit and watch New Orleans roll by." Brass and jazz bands play inside, the smell of ribs and chicken wafts out, and customers sit on the sidewalk and take it all in. Cover $10. Open M and Th-Su 6:30pm-last customer. AmEx/MC/V.

☒ **The Spotted Cat,** 623 Frenchmen St. (☎504-943-3887). This is what you might have imagined most New Orleans bars would be like: a small, dim place with passionate trumpet and piano solos that pour out onto the sidewalk. Caters to the local music community; call ahead if you want to know who's playing the following week. Plays blues, jazz, ragtime and swing. "Early" band 6:30pm, "late" band 10pm. Sa-Su live bands 2pm-2am. No cover; 1-drink min. Open daily 1pm-2am. Cash only.

D.B.A., 618 Frenchmen St. (☎504-942-3731; www.drinkgoodstuff.com). Modeled after the original in New York City, D.B.A. has a yuppie urban vibe with a great selection of beer, Wi-Fi, and a delightfully dark interior. Bands play jazz, rock, or blues every night. Cover $5-10. Open M-Th 5pm-4am, F-Sa 5pm-5am, Su 5pm-3am. AmEx/D/MC/V.

DANCE CLUBS

☒ **Tipitina's,** 501 Napoleon Ave. (☎504-895-8477; www.tipitina.com). The best local bands and some big national names play so close you can almost

---

THE BIG MOLDY

Whether you study it, admire it, or fear it, there's no denying the stupendous amount of mold in New Orleans. Persistent flooding and water stagnation following Hurricane Katrina has created an ideal and even unprecedented environment for mold spores. Christine Rogers, at the Department of Environmental Health, actually compared the city of New Orleans in September 2005 to "biological warfare." Wall-to-wall mold colonies of every conceivable hue greeted scientists and returning residents after the waters began to subside. Only a few colonies of Stachybotrys (a.k.a. "black toxic mold") were found, and scientists are still undecided as to how the mold will affect residents' health. To be safe, Rogers and her colleagues, with the help of the Red Cross, have distributed 30,000 respirators for New Orleans residents to wear while they scrub, bleach, and handle moldy material. On the bright side, scientists have been rubbing their hands with glee. The estimated 1.5 million species of mold currently in the Big Easy include 70,000 previously uncharacterized types. Entomologists have been equally delighted. They have named 65 new species of slime mold beetles in Katrina's wake. Not exactly the type of tourists the government was trying to attract!

touch them. Su 5-9pm Cajun *fais-do-dos.* 18+. Cover $7-25. Music usually W-Su 9pm-3am; call ahead for times and prices. AmEx/MC/V.

■ **Maple Leaf Bar,** 8316 Oak St. (☎504-866-9359; www.themapleleafbar.com), off Carrollton Ave. A staple of the New Orleans jazz, blues, zydeco, and brass-band scene. Chandeliers, a wooden dance floor, and a massive piano. Nightly live music. Cover from $5-10. Open daily 3pm-last customer. AmEx/D/MC/V.

House of Blues, 225 Decatur St. (☎504-310-4999). A sprawling complex with a large dance hall and a balcony and bar overlooking the action. Concerts nightly. Cover from $12. Open in summer Tu-Su 4-10pm; hours vary in winter. AmEx/D/DC/MC/V.

GLBT NIGHTLIFE

The New Orleans gay scene is more inclusive than that of other urban centers, and many straight people visit gay venues because the drinks are cheaper and stronger. The majority of gay establishments are located toward the northeast end of **Bourbon St.** ("downriver"), and along **St. Ann St.,** known to some as the **"Lavender Line."** A good point of reference is the intersection of St. Ann and Bourbon St. To get the lowdown on gay nightlife, pick up a copy of *Ambush Magazine.*

Cafe LaFitte in Exile, 901 Bourbon St. (☎504-522-8397). Banished from LaFitte's Blacksmith Shop in 1953 when the shop came under new management, the ousted gay patrons trooped up the street to found the oldest gay bar in America. On the opening night, surrounded by patrons dressed as their favorite exiles, Cafe Lafitte in Exile lit an "eternal flame" (it still burns today) that represents the soul of the gay community in New Orleans. Video screens, pool tables, and a rockin' dance scene. Happy hour M-F 4-9pm. Open M-Th and Su noon-2am, F-Sa noon-5am. MC/V.

Good Friends, 740 Dauphine St. (☎504-566-7191). Entering this bar is like stepping into a gay *Cheers* episode. A cozy, friendly neighborhood bar full of locals happy to welcome refugees from Bourbon St. Don't miss sing-a-long Su 3-11pm. Happy hour daily 4-9pm. Domestic beers $2.50. Open 24hr. MC/V.

Oz, 800 Bourbon St. (☎504-593-9491; www.ozneworleans.com). So you wanted a N'awlins party? Well, here it is. Oz, with 2 floors and a balcony,

has something crazy every night of the week. Strippers dance on the bar Th-Su night starting at 10pm. M and W drag shows. Th strip contest. F drag bingo. "Shirtless Sundays" (no shirt earns you $1 beers). Happy hour M-F 4-10pm, Sa-Su 4-8pm with half-price domestic beers. Open M-F 1pm to 3 or 4am, Sa-Su 24hr. Cash only.

⚑ APPROACHING HOUMA: 54 MILES
To leave the Big Easy, head west on **Claiborne St. (U.S. 90)** for 48 mi. Take **Exit 210 (Rte. 182 W),** and continue 8 mi. to Houma.

HOUMA

Fishing boats line the waterways here, at the confluence of seven bayous. Don't be surprised if one of them glides alongside as you meander down one of the swamp-hugging streets. Alligators, wandering from their bayou homes, have been known to approach humans on the sidewalks. One of the nicest ways to get a feel for Houma is to wander the historic downtown. You can pick up a self-guided tour at the **Houma Area Convention and Visitors Bureau,** 114 Tourist Dr. (☎985-868-2732. Open M-F 9am-5pm, Sa-Su 9:30am-3:30pm.) Houma also has numerous swamp tours run by locals. Bill Munson of **Munson's Swamp Tours,** 979 Bull Run Rd., is an expert in all things swamp-related and offers marvelous 2hr. excursions to see alligators, otters, and nutria. (☎985-851-3569. Call for times. $20, under 12 $15.)

The residents of Houma two-step to the rhythms of Cajun music, zydeco, and swamp pop at the ◪**Jolly Inn Dance Hall,** 1507 Barrow St. The hall boasts live bands, spry elderly locals, a wooden dance floor, and a cafe with sizzling Cajun dishes. (☎985-872-6114. Cafe open M-F 10:30am-2pm, Sa 6-10:30pm, Su 4-7pm. Dance hall open F 8-10pm, Su 4-8pm. $3, under 12 free.) On the right side of Rte. 182, ½ mi. east of downtown, **A-Bear's Motel ❷,** 342 New Orleans Blvd., has small rooms with cable TV. (☎985-872-4528. No non-smoking rooms. Singles $40; doubles $45. AmEx/D/MC/V.)

⚑ APPROACHING MORGAN CITY: 22 MILES
From Houma, take **U.S. 90 W** to Morgan City.

MORGAN CITY. Following the Civil War, Charles Morgan, a steamship and railroad tycoon, dredged the Atchafalaya Bay Channel to make Morgan City a bustling trade center.

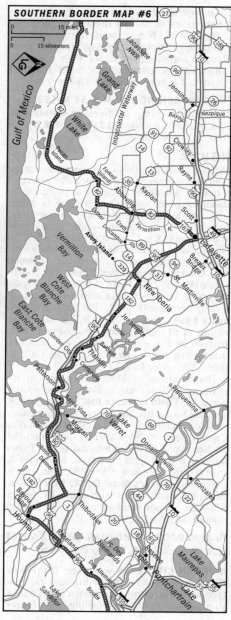

SOUTHERN BORDER MAP #6

The halfway point between New Orleans and Lafayette, the city remains an important crossroads of land and water routes at the edge of the swamp. Unfortunately, there isn't much to see or do here. Some may be interested in making the trek to the **International Petroleum Museum and Exposition,** also known as the "Rig Museum" because it's located on an abandoned oil rig known fondly as "Mr. Charlie." (☎985-384-3744; www.rigmuseum.com. Open M-Sa 8am-5pm. Tours 10am and 2pm. $5, seniors $4, under 12 $3.50.) For a food stop, check out **Manny's Restaurant ❷,** 725 Rte. 90, a diner with plastic furniture and video gambling. Hearty American breakfasts like pork chops and eggs ($7.25), roast-beef dinners ($8), and an all-you-can-eat lunch buffet ($9-11) mean no one goes home hungry. (On U.S. 90 E, on the left just before the underpass. ☎985-384-2359. Open M-Sa 6am-8:30pm, Su 7am-2pm. Buffet daily 11am-2pm. AmEx/D/MC/V.) The **Morgan City Motel ❷,** 505 Brashear Ave., has surprisingly large and comfy rooms. (☎985-384-6640. Key deposit $2. Singles $33; doubles $55. Cash only.)

⚑ APPROACHING FRANKLIN: 26 MILES
From Morgan City, take **U.S. 90 W** for 10 mi. to the junction with **Rte. 182.** Take Rte. 182 W for 16 mi.

FRANKLIN. Franklin's gas lamps, oak canopies, and antebellum mansions suggest the elegance of years gone by, even while its preserved slave quarters stand as constant reminders of the price of such opulence. The rooms at the **Billmar Motel ❷,** 1520 Main St., are clean and comfortable. (☎337-828-5130. Singles $40; doubles $55. AmEx/D/MC/V.)

⚑ APPROACHING JEANERETTE: 17 MILES
Rte. 182 follows the 125 mi. Bayou Teche, one of the longest of Louisiana's swampy waterways. It is easy to imagine the frustration of the steamboat captains who often navigated these sinuous waters. After 17 mi., you will reach Jeanerette.

JEANERETTE
Ivy climbs the lofty heights of the lonely brick spire in Jeanerette. The town was once home to a large cypress-logging operation; the solitary tower is all that remains of the industry. Otherwise, life in Jeanerette remains much the same as it was a century ago, and decaying brick buildings still line Main St. (Rte. 182). Jeaner-

ette's other name is **Sugar City,** and its sugarcane industry survives to this day. In the fall, the cane is harvested and brought to mills while the stalks burn in the fields, filling the air with sweet smoke. The **Jeanerette Bicentennial Museum,** 500 E. Main St., shows a 13min. video on sugarcane history that also indoctrinates viewers on the importance of sugar as part of a "balanced diet." The museum's real treasures are the knowledgeable guides who can tell you all about the sugar biz. (☎337-276-4408. Open Tu-F 10am-5pm, Sa 10am-2pm. Last tour 1hr. before close. $3, students $1.)

Just before you reach Jeanerette, look for the **Yellow Bowl Restaurant ❸,** 19478 Rte. 182 W, which derives its name from the use of "bowl" as a code word for speakeasy during prohibition. But alcohol is not its major claim to fame. A Cajun family acquired it in the 1950s and began serving crawfish; soon the crustacean was on every menu in the state. Try a crawfish *etouffée* ($13) or a cup of crawfish bisque ($4) for an authentic Cajun delight. (☎337-276-5512. Po' boys $6-8. Open W-Th 11am-9pm, F 11am-9:30pm, Sa 5-9:30pm, Su 11am-2:30pm. AmEx/D/MC/V.) The folks at **LeJeune's Bakery ❶,** 1510 W. Main St., bake French bread in an old-fashioned brick oven. They don't have a storefront, but they'll gladly sell the bread straight from the kitchen. Enter through the door on the left side of the building to get a hot loaf for $2.50. (☎337-276-5690. Open daily 7am-5pm or whenever they run out of bread. Cash only.)

DID YOU KNOW? Cajun legend holds that when the French Acadians left Nova Scotia for Louisiana, the local lobsters grew lonely and swam after them. The long journey left them so exhausted that they shrank to the size of shrimp, becoming the "mud bugs" (crawfish) that inhabit the waters of Louisiana today.

APPROACHING NEW IBERIA: 10 MILES
Continue west on **Rte. 182** to New Iberia.

NEW IBERIA

The "Queen City" of the Bayou Teche, New Iberia was the only Spanish settlement in Acadiana.

Later, it was the home to many wealthy sugar plantation owners during the Antebellum period. No trace of Spanish culture remains, but New Iberia is still the major city in these parts—at least compared to the other towns in New Iberia Parish—and it has many boutiques and restaurants, as well as a beautiful, oak-lined Main Street.

VITAL STATS

Population: 33,000
Visitor Info: Iberia Parish Visitors Bureau, 2704 Rte. 14 (☎337-365-1540). Open daily 9am-5pm.
Internet Access: Iberia Parish Library, 445 E. Main St. (☎337-373-0077). Open M-Th 8:30am-8pm, F-Sa 8:30am-5:30pm, Su 1:30-5:30pm. Free.
Post Office: 817 E. Dale St. (☎337-364-6972). Open M-F 8am-5pm, Sa 8:30am-noon. **Postal Code:** 70560.

GETTING AROUND. Main St. runs westward through town, while **St. Peter St.** handles the eastbound traffic one block south. **Center St.,** which runs perpendicular to Main St., is lined with fast-food restaurants and chain motels.

SIGHTS. New Iberia's sights are primarily historic. Surrounded by dazzling flower gardens and shaded by massive oaks draped in Spanish moss, **Shadows-on-the-Teche,** 317 E. Main St., is a lovely Classical Revival plantation built by sugar cane planter David Weeks in 1834. (☎337-364-6446. Open daily 9am-4:30pm. $7, children $4.) The **Konriko Rice Mill,** 301 Ann St., is the oldest functioning rice mill in the US. Tours highlight old equipment and explain Cajun culture. (☎337-367-6163; www.conradricemill.com. Open M-Sa 9am-5pm. $3.) Perhaps the most visited sight in New Iberia is **Avery Island,** home of Tabasco hot sauce. Over 130 years ago, E.A. McIlhenny planted a crop of capsicum peppers and combined their fiery juices with the island's natural salt to create the now-famous pepper sauce known as Tabasco. Today there is a toll ($1) for the island, but the charge is quickly made up in free samples, if you can handle the heat. On the **Tabasco Factory Tour,** visitors are exposed to 15min. of hardcore pro-Tabasco propaganda before viewing the assembly lines and bottlers. The next stop is the **Tabasco Country Store,** which sells Tabasco items ranging

SOUTHERN BORDER

from kitchenware to neckties. (Take Rte. 14 to Rte. 329, and follow it for 5 mi. to the toll booth. ☎337-365-8173; www.tabasco.com. Tours every 20min. daily 9am-4pm. Free.) Avery Island's natural beauty also rewards explorers. Drivers can take a 4 mi. tour of the beautifully landscaped **Jungle Gardens.** There is also a bird sanctuary that attracts some 20,000 snowy egrets to platforms in a pond nicknamed **"Bird City."** Just don't picnic too close to the ponds—impolite alligators lurking in the waters are known to take without asking. (☎337-369-6243. Open daily 8am-5pm. $6.50, ages 6-12 $4.25.) The visitors bureau has information on New Iberia's annual festivals, including the **Cajun Hot Sauce Festival** of early April, the **World Championship Gumbo Cookoff Contest** in mid-October, and **Hi Sugar!**, a sugar cane festival in late-September.

📇 FOOD AND ACCOMMODATIONS. New

Iberia has cheap eats and a few classy establishments. **Steve's Drive Inn ❷**, 1218 W. Main St., is a drive-in (not an inn) that has quick burgers, seafood, and po' boys. Hang out in the parking lot with locals, who sit in and on cars while chowing down. (☎337-365-0566. Sandwiches $4-7. Open M-W and Sa 10am-9pm, Th-F 10am-10pm, Su 10am-2pm. MC/V.) Named for the late folk artist Clementine Hunter, **Clementine ❸**, 113 E. Main St., is a gourmet eatery with a Cajun slant. Lunches include seafood gumbo ($5.50), po' boys ($7), and entrees like blackened redfish ($10). Dinners are quite a bit more expensive, but if you're willing to splurge, try the crabmeat *au gratin* for $19. (☎337-560-1007. Open M 11am-2pm, Tu-Th 6-9pm, F-Sa 6-10pm. AmEx/D/MC/V.) Each olive-green room of the 🏠**Teche Motel ❷**, 1830 E. Main St., makes up half of a cabin that sits underneath an oak canopy on the sleepy bayou's edge. Guests have access to the beautiful Bayou Garden, which includes a dock, a gazebo, a rope swing, and even a trampoline. The exceedingly friendly hosts aim to please; they will even lend you their barbecue grill for bayou-side grilling. (☎337-369-3756. Singles $40; doubles $45. Cash only.) For a little less, the **Kajun Inn ❷**, 1505 Center St., has standard rooms. (☎337-367-3608. Key deposit $2. Singles $37; doubles $47. AmEx/D/MC/V.)

🚩 APPROACHING LAFAYETTE: 20 MILES
Follow **Main St. (Rte. 182)** heading west.

LAFAYETTE

At the center of bayou land, Lafayette is the two-stepping, crawfish-eating heart of Acadiana. Although Lafayette advertises itself as a French-speaking oasis, very few people under the age of 65 actually speak French. Cajuns remain extremely proud of their Acadian heritage, however, and have started importing French teachers from Quebec, France, Belgium—even Martinique—to experiment with French immersion programs in Lafayette elementary schools. The jury's out on a French revival in the area, but Cajun culture reigns supreme in the music and food.

📇 GETTING AROUND

Lafayette is a crossroads at the center of the swamp. **I-10** leads east to New Orleans and west to Lake Charles; **U.S. 90** heads south to New Iberia and the Atchafalaya Basin and north to Alexandria and Shreveport; **U.S. 167/I-49** runs north into central Louisiana. Most of the city is west of the **Evangeline Throughway** (I-49 in the north, **U.S. 90** in the south), where most of the budget motels are located. **Johnston St.** marks the eastern border of downtown and has many fast-food restaurants.

VITAL STATS

Population: 110,000

Visitor Info: Lafayette Convention and Visitors Commission, 1400 NW Evangeline Throughway (☎800-346-1958; www.lafayettetravel.com). Open M-F 8:30am-5pm, Sa-Su 9am-5pm.

Internet Access: Lafayette Public Library, 301 W. Congress St. (☎337-261-5787). Open M-Th 9am-9pm, F 9am-6pm, Sa 9am-5pm, Su 1-5pm.

Post Office: 1105 Moss St. (☎337-269-7111). Open M-F 8am-5:30pm, Sa 8:30am-noon. **Postal Code:** 70501.

👁 SIGHTS

The **Acadian Cultural Center,** 501 Fisher Rd., is a unit of the **Jean Lafitte National Historic Park and Preserve,** which runs throughout the delta region of Louisiana. The Acadian Center has a dramatic 35min. documentary chronicling the arrival of the Acadians in Louisiana, as well as a film on conservation efforts in the Atchafalaya swamp. Check out the terrific bilingual exhibits on Cajun history and culture. (Take Johnston St. to Surrey, then follow the signs. ☎337-232-0789, ext. 11. Open daily 8am-5pm. Shows every hr. 9am-4pm. Free.) Next door, a "living museum" re-creates the Acadian settlement of **Vermilionville,** 300 Fisher Rd., with music, crafts, food, and dancing on the Bayou Vermilion banks. The buildings mostly date from 1790 to 1890, though a few, like the church, are reproductions. (☎337-233-4077. Su live bands 1-4pm. Cajun cooking demos daily 10:30, 11:30am, 12:30pm. Open Tu-Su 10am-4pm; last entry 3pm. $8, seniors $6.50, ages 6-18 $5.) **Acadian Village,** 200 Greenleaf Rd., features 19th-century Cajun homes with a fascinating array of artifacts and displays. Highlights include the **Thibodeaux House,** a collection of 19th-century medical paraphernalia at the **Doctor's House,** and the small replica 1850 chapel. (Take Johnston St. to Ridge Rd., turn left on Broussard, and follow the signs. ☎337-981-2489 or 800-962-9133. Open daily 10am-pm. $7, seniors $6, ages 6-14 $4.) Follow signs to **McGee's Landing,** 1337 Henderson Rd., which sends three 1½hr. boat tours into the Basin each day. (☎337-228-2384. Tours daily 10am, 1, 3pm. Sunset tours by reservation. $15, seniors $12, under 12 $8.)

Closer to downtown, the University of Louisiana's **University Art Museum,** 710 E. St. Mary Blvd., houses both temporary and permanent exhibits of sculpture, photography, and paintings in a gorgeous building. (☎337-482-2278; www.louisiana.edu/UAM. Open Tu-Sa 10am-5pm. $5, 50+ $4, ages 3-17 $3.) The **Cathedral of Saint John the Evangelist,** 515 Cathedral St., is worth a peek for its stunning 19th-century ecclesiastical architecture. (☎337-232-1322. Open daily 6am-6pm. Free.)

 PHOTO OP. Skip the church museum and check out the nearby **Saint John's Cathedral Oak,** 914 St. John St., which has a trunk 19 ft. in circumference. No matter where you're standing on the lawn, you're sure to get some shade.

The **Festival International de Louisiane** is the largest free outdoor francophone festival in the US. It transforms Lafayette into a gigantic French-speaking fairground for one wild weekend in April. (☎337-232-8086; www.festivalinternational.com.) The **Breaux Bridge Crawfish Festival,** in nearby Breaux Bridge, 10 mi. east, on I-10 at Exit 109, features crawfish races, live music, dance contests, cook-offs, and a crawfish eating contest. (☎337-332-6655; www.bbcrawfest.com.)

▓ FOOD

It's not hard to find reasonably-priced Cajun and Creole cuisine in Lafayette, a city that prides itself on its food. Of course, it also prides itself on music, which can be found

THE LOUISIANA EATIN' MACHINES

As you drive through the Louisiana bayou, keep your eyes peeled (and a trigger cocked) for Nutria, or **myocastor coypus.** Indigenous to Argentina, these small rat-like beavers were imported to Louisiana in the 1930s by Tabasco tycoon E.A. McIlhenny. He kept them as pets, but other enterprising souls used the creatures for fur farming. A few were released, either accidentally or intentionally, and they soon began to reproduce at alarming rates. Nutria begin breeding at 6 months and have 3 litters per year, with up to 13 offspring each time. Moreover, one 12 lb. nutria can eat 25% of its own body weight each day. The 20 million nutria currently frolicking in the Louisiana wetlands are particularly fond of the plants that keep the soil from eroding, causing a serious environmental problem. In a desperate attempt to thin out the population, the Department of Wildlife and Fisheries began a $2 million "eat nutria" campaign in 1997, paying premier Louisiana chefs to peddle nutria as haute cuisine. When the scheme failed, the government tried a new tack: paying trappers $4 for each nutria they shoot down. Hopefully the money will be incentive enough for nutria hunters because, word has it, the nearsighted rodents don't provide much sport.

live in many restaurants at night. Make sure to get to restaurants relatively early, since it is hard to find anything other than chains that stays open after 10pm.

Dwyer's Cafe, 323 Jefferson St. (☎337-235-9364). Since 1927, this diner has been the best place in town to get breakfast or lunch. They serve a bang-up breakfast special (grits, eggs, ham, biscuits, juice, and coffee; $4). At lunch and dinnertime, locals saunter in for plates of gigantic proportions ($6-8). Open M and Su 6am-2pm, Tu-Sa 6am-2pm and 5-10pm. AmEx/D/MC/V. ❷

The Judice Inn, 3134 Johnston St. (☎337-984-5614; www.judiceinn.com). A roadside time warp with booths and a wooden bar, almost always presided over by a member of the Judice family. Burgers $2.50. Open M-Sa 10am-10pm. AmEx/D/MC/V. ❶

Old Tyme Grocery, 218 W. St. Mary St. (☎337-235-8165; www.oldtymegrocery.com). Serves the best po' boys in town. A convenience store, a take-out counter, and a charming dining area with wood paneling and checkered tablecloths. Don't expect variety—all they serve is po' boys ($6-7) and the occasional salad ($5-6). Open M-F 8am-10pm, Sa 9am-7pm. Cash only. ❷

The Riverside Inn, 240 Tubing Rd. (☎866-837-6650; www.poorboysriversideinn.com). A standby since 1932, without the touristy schlock that plagues some other Cajun restaurants in Lafayette. Lunch specials M-F 11am-2pm $7.25. Veggie options $8-13. Entrees $12-25. Open M-Th 11am-10pm, F 11am-11pm, Sa 5-11pm. AmEx/D/MC/V. ❸

Guamas, 302 Jefferson St. (☎337-267-4242; www.guamas.com). The friendly Reuben and Julieta cook meals that combine a variety of Caribbean and Latin American dishes in this bright restaurant with a bar and outdoor tables. The coconut shrimp ($16) are mouthwatering. Entrees $10-16. Happy hour Tu-F 4-7pm. Sa salsa dancing 11pm-2am. Open Tu-Th 11am-10pm, F 11am-11pm, Sa 5pm-2am. Kitchen closes 10pm. AmEx/D/MC/V. ❸

Borden's, 1103 Jefferson St. (☎337-235-9291). Serving yummy sundaes ($2.50-3.50) and massive banana splits ($4) since 1940. Everyone, from grandparents to teen couples, indulges. Open Tu-Th 1-8pm, F-Sa noon-9pm, Su noon-8pm. Cash only. ❶

ACCOMMODATIONS

◪ **Blue Moon Guest House & Saloon,** 215 E. Convent St. (☎337-234-2422; www.bluemoonhostel.com). Driving south on Evangeline Throughway (U.S. 90), take a left on Johnston St. and a left on Convent St. One of the best lodgings in the South. A large dorm and comfy private rooms are accompanied by an inviting common area, a deck, and a "saloon" where bands whoop it up W-Sa. Guests get free concert access and a complimentary drink at the bar. Linen $2. Free Wi-Fi. Check-in 5-10pm. Dorms $18; private rooms $40-60. AmEx/MC/V. ❶

Travel Host Inn South, 1314 N. Evangeline Throughway (☎337-233-2090). Sweet-smelling rooms and pictures on the wall make it feel a bit more like home than your average motel. Continental breakfast included. Singles $30; doubles $50. AmEx/D/MC/V. ❷

Plantation Motor Inn, 2810 N.E. Evangeline Throughway (☎337-232-7285). Bright, spacious rooms with big windows. Rooms $45. AmEx/D/MC/V. ❷

Acadiana Park Campground, 1201 E. Alexander St. (☎337-291-8388), off Louisiana Ave. On the site of a former plantation, this campground is just a stone's throw from the center of Lafayette. 75 shaded sites near a stream. Access to tennis courts and a soccer field. Reception M-Th and Sa-Su 8am-5pm, F 8am-8pm. Sites $13. Cash only. ❶

KOA Lafayette, 537 Apollo Rd. (☎337-235-2739), in Scott, 5 mi. west of town, on I-10 at Exit 97. This lakeside campground has over 200 sites, a store, a mini-golf course, and 2 pools. Reception M-Th and Su 7:30am-8pm, F-Sa 7:30am-9pm. Water, electricity, and bathrooms. Reservations recommended. Sites $24-34. MC/V. ❷

NIGHTLIFE

To find the best zydeco in town, pick up a copy of *The Times*, free at restaurants and gas stations. There is also a variety of local music festivals throughout the year. The best of these is **Downtown Alive!,** a 12-week annual concert series held on the 700 block of Jefferson St., showcasing everything from New Wave to Cajun and zydeco. (☎337-291-5566. Apr.-June and Sept.-Nov. F 6-8:30pm.)

◪ **Angelle's Whiskey River Landing,** 1365 Henderson Levee Rd. (☎337-228-8567), in Breaux Bridge. On Su afternoons, this is the place to be. Live Cajun music has people dancing on the very lip of the levee

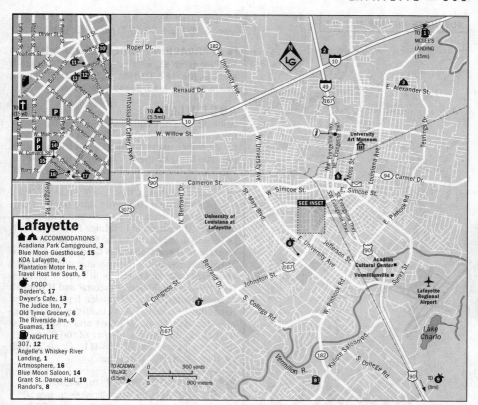

Lafayette

ACCOMMODATIONS
Acadiana Park Campground, 3
Blue Moon Guesthouse, 15
KOA Lafayette, 4
Plantation Motor Inn, 2
Travel Host Inn South, 5

FOOD
Borden's, 17
Dwyer's Cafe, 13
The Judice Inn, 7
Old Tyme Grocery, 6
The Riverside Inn, 9
Guamas, 11

NIGHTLIFE
307, 12
Angelle's Whiskey River
Landing, 1
Artmosphere, 16
Blue Moon Saloon, 14
Grant St. Dance Hall, 10
Randol's, 8

SOUTHERN BORDER

overlooking the swamp. Boatmen pull ashore right outside and come in to join the party—it sometimes feels like the whole floor could collapse into the swamp with all the stamping. Su live music 4-8pm.

Artmosphere, 902 Johnston St. (☎337-233-3331). Artmosphere (we *do* mean "art") has just about everything: live music nightly, hookahs ($5), free Internet access, and food seasoned with herbs from the backyard garden. Sa 2-for-1 daiquiris. Cover $3-5 after 8:30pm. Open daily 11am-2am. AmEx/D/MC/V.

Grant St. Dance Hall, 113 Grant St. (☎337-237-8513). This former United Fruit warehouse is now a venue for live music, playing everything from zydeco to metal, from local acts to big-name groups. 18+. Cover usually $5-10, up to $50 depending on the act. Open only on show days; call ahead. D/MC/V.

Blue Moon Saloon, 215 E. Convent St. (☎337-234-2422). Area bands play in the backyard bar. W cajun jam with lots of locals and often dancing. Cover $5. Open W-Sa 5pm-midnight. AmEx/MC/V.

307, 307 Jefferson St. (☎337-262-0307). A hip spot for locals to get dressed up and listen to live bands. Exposed brick, high tables with stools, dim lighting. Music ranges from DJs spinning Latin and reggae to "modern jazz" to "alternative country" to retro 80s—anything goes. W talent night. Cover up to $7. Open daily 7pm-2am. AmEx/D/MC/V.

Randol's, 2320 Kaliste Saloom Rd. (☎337-981-7080). One of many large, barn-like establishments in Lafayette. Cajun bands, a crowd of adorable elders dancing the two-step, and checkered table-cloths. You can hang out and listen to the bands if you order drinks, but you can only sit at the tables if

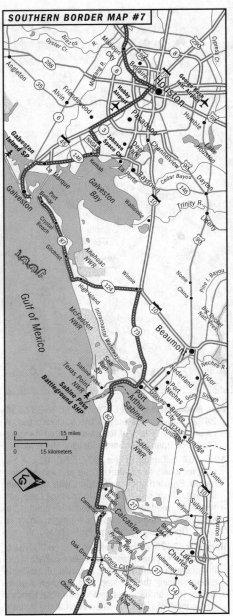

SOUTHERN BORDER MAP #7

you get food. Nightly live music 6-9pm. Open M-Th and Su 5-10pm, F-Sa 5-11pm. AmEx/D/MC/V.

APPROACHING ABBEVILLE: 17 MILES

Take **Johnston St.** west out of Lafayette. The road becomes **Rte. 167.** Take Rte. 167 S, and turn right on **Concorde St.** to reach downtown Abbeville.

ABBEVILLE

Abbeville is a rice mill town with a pretty downtown center, friendly locals, and a different festival almost every week. The quirkiest (and perhaps best) of these festivals is the **Omelette Festival,** on the first Sunday in November, when the town makes a 5000-egg omelette. Many of the historic buildings that line S. State St. (Rte. 82) in downtown Abbeville date back to the mid-19th century, when French immigrants settled here. Picturesque buildings form the heart of the city and lead up to the Greek Revival columns of the **Vermillion Parish Courthouse.** Next to Magdalen Square is the romanesque **St. Mary Magdalen Catholic Church,** built in 1911. Across the street is the **Abbeville Cultural and Historical Alliance Center,** 208 N. Magdalen Sq. Despite its formidable name, it's actually a charming museum with displays of art and antiques, as well as exhibits on the history of the town and the Cajun people. (☎337-898-4114. Open Tu and Sa 10am-3pm, W-F 10am-5pm.)

> **DID YOU KNOW?** In addition to 5,000 eggs, the Abbeville omelette uses 50 lb. onion, 75 chopped green peppers, 52 lb. butter, 6¼ gal. of milk, and some crawfish tails for good measure. The eggs are made in a 12 ft. skillet, stirred by 20 egg chefs, and cooked over an enormous log fire. In the end, the omelette is more scrambled than flipped, but it tastes good anyway!

Dupuy's Oyster Shop ❸, 108 S. Main St., has served oysters since 1869 and prepares other scrumptious seafood dishes as well. (☎337-893-2336. Entrees $11-15. Open Tu-Sa 11am-2pm and 5-9pm, F-Sa until 10pm. AmEx/D/MC/V.) The nearby **Riverfront Grill ❸,** 503 W. Port St., has a lovely riverside patio and specializes in seafood. The crab and corn bisque ($4.50) is famous in Abbeville. (☎337-898-9218. Open Tu-Th and Su 11am-9pm, F 11am-10pm, Sa 6pm-10pm. AmEx/

D/MC/V.) For a quick lunch with a side of town gossip, Abbevillians head to the **Comeaux Cafe ❷**, 106 S. State St. A laid-back diner, CC's serves po' boys ($3-5), sandwiches ($2.25-3), and burgers ($2.50-4.50). Don't be afraid to join the senior-citizen set for the $9 all-you-can-eat seafood lunch buffet. (☎337-898-9218. Buffet daily 11am-2pm. Open M-F 5:30am-2pm, Sa 5:30am-11am. MC/V.) On the main drag of Abbeville, the **Sunbelt Lodge ❷**, 1903 Veterans Dr., has large, bright rooms. (☎866-299-1480; www.sunbelt-lodge.com. Continental breakfast included. Singles $45; doubles $55. AmEx/D/MC/V.)

◪ APPROACHING CAMERON: 92 MILES
From Abbeville, continue straight on **Rte. 167,** which becomes **Rte. 82.** The rice paddies outside Abbeville quickly give way to miles of marsh and swamp. Keep your eyes peeled for the elusive American alligators that lurk in these waters. There are few gas stations along these roads, so be sure to fill up in Abbeville.

CAMERON. The tiny town of Cameron is the first real sign of life in this swampy area. Look for the sign for the **Hurricane Cafe ❶**, a small trailer that sells hot dogs ($1.25), boudin (rice-and-pork sausage; $1.85), and burgers ($2). They sometimes have fresh shrimp, if you ask for it. (☎337-775-2801. Open daily 6:30am-3pm. Cash only.) There's also a gas station in Cameron if you need to fill up; otherwise, just head right back on the road.

◪ APPROACHING PORT ARTHUR: 50 MILES
After Cameron, it's a short 3 mi. to the **Calcasieu Ferry,** which shuttles cars across a small channel to the continuation of **Rte. 82.** Service is free and continual, and while the jump across the canal is only a few hundred yards, the ferry is as slow as it is small—waits can exceed 30min. Continue on Rte. 82 until you cross the towering **Martin Luther King, Jr. Bridge.** As you emerge on the other side of the bridge, you are greeted by a sign welcoming you to Texas, "the proud home of President George W. Bush," and the sight of looming oil refineries belching smoke into the air.

PORT ARTHUR

The Port Arthur area is a confusing mess of intersecting highways. Perhaps the only thing more confusing than the geography are the miles of pipelines that wind around the endless natural gas and oil refineries that surround the city. This is the heart of the Texas petroleum industry, and natural gas fires burn high into the night. Other than the jaw-dropping enormity of the refineries, there is not much to see in Port Arthur. If you do end up here for the night, be sure to check out the great Vietnamese food, courtesy of Port Arthur's large population of Vietnamese immigrants.

VITAL STATS

Population: 58,000

Visitor Info: Port Arthur Convention and Visitors Bureau, 3401 Cultural Center Dr. (☎800-235-7822; www.portarthurtexas.com). Open M-F 9am-5pm.

Internet Access: Port Arthur Public Library, 4615 9th Ave. (☎409-985-8838). Open Sept.-May M-Th 10am-9pm, F 10am-6pm, Sa 10am-5pm, Su 2-5pm; June-Aug. M-Th 10am-9pm, F 10am-6pm, Sa 10am-5pm. Free.

Post Office: 345 Lakeshore Dr. (☎409-983-3423). Open M-F 8am-5pm. **Postal Code:** 77640.

▣ GETTING AROUND. Rte. 73 enters the Port Arthur area from the southwest. **Rte. 82** defines the southern border of the area, running perpendicular to Rte. 73; a few miles down Rte. 73 is **Memorial Blvd. (U.S. 69),** which runs through much of downtown Port Arthur. Farther down U.S. 73, **Twin City Hwy. (Rte. 347),** runs parallel to Memorial Blvd. between Port Arthur and Groves; this road is home to many of the area's attractions.

◪ SIGHTS. At the **Museum of the Gulf Coast,** 700 Procter St., Port Arthur displays its pride in some of its famous residents, including Jimmy Johnson and Janis Joplin. Aside from large exhibits dedicated to football and music, the two-story museum also features excellent displays on the petroleum industry, mariners, and prehistoric animals. (Take Memorial Blvd. all the way to its southeastern end at the intercostal canal. Head right onto Lakeshore Dr., which becomes 4th St. The museum is hidden on the right, across the street from the police station.

☎409-982-7000. Open M-Sa 9am-5pm, Su 1-5pm. $3.50, children $1.50.) The rest of Port Arthur's old downtown core is a ghost town—everyone has moved into the suburbs that are closer to the refineries. Built in 1900 as a winter home for the barbed-wire King, Isaac Ellwood, the pink **Pompeiian Villa,** 1953 Lakeshore Dr., is modeled after a house uncovered in Pompeii, Italy in 79 AD. (☎409-983-5977. Call ahead. Open M-F 10am-2pm. $2.) The **Queen of Peace Shrine & Gardens,** 801 9th Ave., is a picturesque Asian garden with a huge statue of the Virgin Mary. Built in the 1980s by Catholic Vietnamese who relocated to Port Arthur after the Vietnam War, the shrine is a tranquil place for contemplation. (☎409-983-7676. Open 24hr. Free.)

⌖ FOOD AND ACCOMMODATIONS. The unassuming **⌖Pho Vien Dong ❶,** 2523 Twin City Hwy., serves the best Vietnamese food in town. The Bun Bo Xao (vermicelli cooked with beef; $5) is big enough to satisfy any appetite. Try a Vietnamese iced coffee with condensed milk ($2.50) or an avocado smoothie ($2) for dessert. (☎409-962-8000. Open M-Sa 9am-9pm, Su 9:30am-3:30pm. MC/V.) There are numerous fast-food chains lining Twin City Hwy. One of the better (and smaller) of these chains is **Tony's BBQ ❷,** 4700 Twin City Hwy. Staffed by Vietnamese servers, Tony's serves tantalizing meats slow-cooked with hickory. (☎409-963-1005. Sandwiches $3.50-4. Dinner entrees $7.50-9.50. Open M-Sa 11am-9pm. AmEx/D/MC/V.) The best deal for accommodations in Port Arthur are the large rooms at the **Southwinds Inn ❷,** 5101 E. Parkway St. All rooms have TV, microwave, fridge, and pool access. (☎409-962-3000. Rooms $48. AmEx/D/MC/V.)

⌖ APPROACHING CRYSTAL BEACH: 78 MILES
From Port Arthur, head west on **Rte. 72** for 25 mi. Take **Rte. 124 S** for 53 mi. Rte. 124 will become **Rte. 87** through the Bolivar Peninsula.

CRYSTAL BEACH. If Bolivar's beaches strike your fancy or you just can't make it to Galveston Island before nightfall, Crystal Beach is a good place to stop. The **Outrigger Grill ❷,** 1035 Rte. 87, offers all-American meals. Eggs, pancakes, omelettes, and biscuits and gravy run about $4-6. Lunch options ($3-8) include burgers, sandwiches, po'boys, steaks, and chicken. (☎409-684-6212. Open M-Tu and Th-Su 7am-8:30pm, W 7am-

2pm, F-Sa 7am-10pm. AmEx/MC/V.) Lodgings are available at the **Joy Sands Motel ❸,** 1020 Rte. 87. The pastel-colored rooms at this coastal dwelling have A/C, TV, fridge, and microwave. (☎409-684-6152. Singles M-F $50, Sa-Su $65; doubles $65/$85. AmEx/D/MC/V.)

⌖ APPROACHING GALVESTON ISLAND: 8 MILES
Follow **Rte. 87** until it ends. Take the free **ferry** across the water. The ride is about 15min. but waits can exceed an hour on weekends.

GALVESTON ISLAND

This island is infamous as the base for swashbuckler Jean Lafitte's pirate fleet. In the 19th century, Galveston was the "Queen of the Gulf," the wealthiest city in Texas, a claim to which over 6000 historic buildings stand testament. Things changed in 1900, when a devastating hurricane ripped through the city and claimed 6000 lives. Today, the 32 mi. island is powered mainly by tourism, its cool sea breezes offering a much-needed respite from Houston's heat.

VITAL STATS

Population: 57,000

Visitor Info: Galveston Island Visitors Information Center, 2428 Seawall Blvd. (☎888-425-4753; www.galveston.com). Open daily 8:30am-5pm.

Internet Access: Rosenberg Library, 2310 Sealy Ave. (☎409-763-8854). Open M-Th 9am-9pm, F-Sa 9am-6pm. Free.

Parking: There is a municipal lot at 25th St. and Mechanics Row ($5 per day) and free parking along Seawall Blvd.

Post Office: 601 25th St. (☎409-763-6834). Open M-F 8:30am-5pm. **Postal Code:** 77550.

⌖ GETTING AROUND. The Bolivar Peninsula ferry deposits you on the eastern end of the island. From there, you can head west (right) on **Broadway St.,** which runs east-west in the center of the island, or on **Seawall Blvd.,** the main beachfront drag, which also runs east-west. On the far eastern edge of the island sits **Apffel Park,** the only beach in Galveston that permits alcoholic beverages. Downtown, most establishments and some beaches are located east along Seawall Blvd., while the western side of the island is more sparsely populated. Nine miles to the west lies **Galveston Island State Park.** Away from the waterfront, Galveston sports a revitalized downtown, known as the **Strand**, where five blocks of gas lamps evoke the 19th-century "Queen of the Gulf" era. **Strand St.** runs east-west along the north side of the island, and is most easily accessible from **Rosenberg St.**, which crosses north-south from Seawall Blvd. to Strand St. Another major north-south street is **61st St.**, which connects Seawall Blvd. to Broadway. Galveston is a grid, with streets running north-south and labeled by number (numbers rise as you head west) and avenues running east-west, labeled by letters.

◪ SIGHTS. Galveston Island's main attraction is **Seawall Blvd.**, brimming with hotels, mini golf, and chain restaurants. Driving down this strip can be difficult with all the SUVs circling to score a parking spot. On the Strand, in the Historic Downtown, you can find boutiques and outdoor vendors selling local art and kitschy souvenirs. The **Galveston Railroad Museum,** 123 Rosenberg St., at the west end of the Strand, pays homage to Texas railroad history with displays, model trains, and dozens of actual trains spanning an entire century. With no off-limits areas, visitors are free to explore every corner of the trains, from the luxurious Pullman car parlors to the kitchen galleys to the locomotive cabs. (☎409-765-5700; www.galvestonrrmuseum.com. Open Mar.-Dec. daily 10am-4pm; Jan.-Feb. W-Su 10am-4pm. $6, seniors $5, ages 4-12 $3.) The one-of-a-kind **Ocean Star Offshore Energy Center,** Pier 19, on Harborside Dr. at 20th St., demystifies the oil drilling rigs that dot the Gulf of Mexico horizon. The museum is located on a retired oil rig anchored just offshore and accessible by a causeway. (☎409-766-7827; www.oceanstaroec.com. Open daily June-Aug. 10am-6pm; Sept.-May 10am-5pm. $6, seniors $5, ages 7-18 $4.) Most of the historic Victorian buildings in the city are private homes, but a few are open to public tours. The elegant **Moody Mansion,** 2618 Broadway, is the former home of Galveston's leading family and contains original furnishings and stunning stained glass. (☎409-762-7668; www.moodymansion.org. Open M-Sa 10am-3pm, Su noon-3pm. $6, seniors $5, ages 4-18 $3.) Three glass pyramids house a tropical rainforest, aquarium, science museum, and IMAX theater at **Moody Gardens,** 1 Hope Blvd., a tourist-oriented theme

park. The well-manicured grounds themselves are beautiful and free. (Take the West Beach exit onto 61st St., and follow the signs south. ☎800-582-4673. Open in summer daily 10am-9pm; in winter M-Th and Su 10am-6pm, F-Sa 10am-9pm. Aquarium $13, seniors $10, ages 4-12 $7; rainforest $9/$7/$6; IMAX $9/$7/$6. Day pass to all attractions $30; after 6pm everything half-price.)

◪ FOOD AND ACCOMMODATIONS.
Benno's ❸, 1200 Seawall Blvd., can be crowded with tourists, but the food makes up for it. Try the Cajun platter (shrimp, oysters, and snapper; $14) with a cup of jambalaya ($3.75). The key lime pie ($2) is the perfect dessert. (☎409-762-4621. Po' boys $7. Open M-Th and Su 11am-10pm, F-Sa 11am-11pm. AmEx/D/MC/V.) Off the beachfront, **The Original Mexican Cafe ❷,** 1401 Market St., cooks up Tex-Mex meals with homemade flour tortillas. (Go east from Rosenberg St.; it's on the right. ☎409-762-6001. Lunch specials $6-8. Open M-Th 11am-9:30pm, F 11am-10pm, Sa-Su 8am-10pm. AmEx/D/MC/V.) Locals head to **The Diner ❷,** 1017 61st St., for cheap breakfasts. Expect to be called "baby doll" and "sugar" repeatedly. (☎409-744-3223. Breakfast $2.50-5.50. Open daily 6am-2pm. MC/V.) For a jolt of joe, head to **Java's 213 ❶,** 213 Tremont St., the island's hippie-student cafe par excellence. Lounge on the couches, surf the Internet, or just revel in the stained-glass windows. (☎409-762-5282. Open daily 7:30am-midnight. AmEx/D/MC/V.)

On summer weekends, even the shabbiest accommodations can get away with charging upwards of $100, but cheaper deals can be found during the week and in the winter. Although it looks a little shady from the outside, the **Rosenberg Inn ❷,** 2027 Rosenberg, has huge rooms with full kitchens only a few blocks from the beach. Try to get rooms on the second floor for better light. (☎409-765-7632. Key deposit $2. Rooms $45. AmEx/D/MC/V.) The **Driftwood Motel ❸,** 3128 Seawall Blvd., has bright, newly renovated rooms with balconies and views of the beach. (☎409-763-6431. Singles M-F $40, Sa-Su $50-70; doubles $50/$80-120. AmEx/D/MC/V.)

◪ APPROACHING HOUSTON: 55 MILES
Take **61st St.,** stopping along the way as you cross Offatts Bayou (the only bit of water you'll see) to look for pelicans, herons, and other water birds. Hang a left at **Broadway** and follow it as it turns into **I-45.** Follow the interstate for 50 mi. north to Houston.

SOUTHERN BORDER

HOUSTON

With the fourth-largest population of any US city, Houston can't hide its miles of strip malls and gridlocked traffic. Though known for sprawl and lack of planning, Houston has a revitalized downtown with a light rail line, glorious modern architecture, stadiums, and top-notch performing-arts centers. Houston's prosperity, built on the wealth of its oil and maritime industries, shows in its immaculate streetscapes, parks, and public buildings. Yet beyond the skyscrapers, culture abounds in an impressive array of world-class restaurants, museums, and cultural organizations.

VITAL STATS

Population: 5.3 million

Visitor Info: Houston City Hall (☎ 713-437-5200 or 800-446-8786; www.cityofhouston.gov), at the corner of Walker and Bagby St. Open daily 9am-4pm.

Internet Access: Houston Public Library, 500 McKinney St. (☎ 713-236-1313), at Bagby St. Open M-Th 9am-9pm, F-Sa 9am-6pm, Su 2-6pm. Free.

Parking: Free parking in the Museum District and on side streets around Westheimer. Downtown street parking is free after 5pm.

Post Office: 701 San Jacinto St. (☎ 713-223-4402). Open M-F 8am-5pm. **Postal Code:** 77052.

GETTING AROUND

Houston's freeway system is a traffic nightmare; the more you avoid it, the happier you'll be. Major interstates **I-45** and **I-10** intersect at the city's downtown and are constantly clogged with angry Texans. The **Sam Houston Tollway (Beltway 8),** an effort to alleviate traffic congestion, wraps around the outer edge of the city. **I-610** forms a tighter belt around the city closer to downtown. **U.S. 59** and **290,** as well as **Rte. 225** and **288,** also turn into large freeways as they approach the city.

Though the flat Texan terrain has sprouted several mini-downtowns, true downtown Houston borders the **Buffalo Bayou** at the intersection of I-10 and I-45. A grid of interlocking one-way streets, downtown centers on **Main St.** The Museum District sits just southwest of Midtown, centered at **Bissonnet St.** and Main St. To get to the **Rice Village** area, which has lots of shopping and restaurants, continue west on Bissonnet and go south (left) down **Kirby Dr.** The **Montrose** area (along **Westheimer St.** around Montrose St.) is filled with antique shops, piercing studios, vintage clothing stores, and cafes. It's one of the only places in Houston where people stroll around. A **transit rail** runs along Main St. and San Jacinto through downtown, Midtown, and the Museum District. Buses run on all major streets, although service on weekends is very slow. For $2 you can get a day-long pass for all modes of public transport.

👁 SIGHTS

JOHNSON SPACE CENTER. The city's most popular attraction, the Johnson Space Center is technically not even in Houston but 20 mi. away in Clear Lake. The Mission Control Center is fully operational; when today's astronauts say, "Houston, we have a problem," these people answer. Admission includes tours of the Mission Control Center and astronaut training facilities. Among the attractions are exhibits of astronaut suits from the past 30 years, simulator rides, lunar rocks, and out-of-this-world harnesses; strap in and bounce around like a real space explorer. The complex also houses models of the Gemini and Apollo crafts. (*1601 NASA Rd. 1. Take I-45 S to the NASA Rd. exit, and head east for 3 mi. ☎ 281-244-2100 or 800-972-0369; www.spacecenter.org. Open June-Aug. daily 9am-7pm; Sept.-May M-F 10am-5pm, Sa-Su 10am-7pm. $18, seniors $15, ages 4-11 $12.*)

BUFFALO SOLDIERS NATIONAL MUSEUM. Between the end of the Civil War in 1866 and the integration of the armed forces in 1944, the US Army had several all-black units. During the Indian Wars of the late 1800s, the Cheyenne warriors nicknamed these troops "Buffalo Soldiers," both because of their naturally curly hair and as a sign of respect for their fighting spirit. Learn the history of the Buffalo Soldiers and African-Americans in the military and NASA from the Revolutionary War to the present. (*1834 Southmore Blvd. ☎ 713-942-8920. Open M-F 10am-5pm, Sa 10am-3pm. Suggested donation $2.*)

SAN JACINTO STATE PARK. The **San Jacinto Battleground State Historical Park** is the most

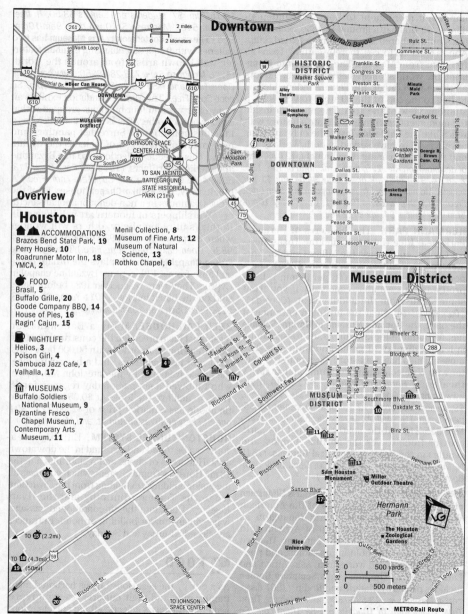

Overview

Houston

Downtown

Museum District

METRORail Route

important monument to Lone Star independence. On this battleground in 1836, Sam Houston's outnumbered Texan Army defeated Santa Anna's Mexican forces, thereby earning Texas its freedom from Mexico. The **San Jacinto Monument,** the world's tallest memorial tower, honors all those who fought for Texas's independence. Riding to the top of the 50-story tower yields a stunning view of the area. The museum inside the monument celebrates the state's history with relics like the **Battleship Texas,** the only surviving naval vessel to have served in both World Wars, and the last remaining dreadnought. *(21 mi. east of downtown on Rte. 225, then 3 mi. north on Rte. 134. ☎ 281-479-2421. Park open daily 9am-6pm. $1 per vehicle. Monument and museum open daily 9am-6pm. Free. Battleship ☎ 281-479-2431. Open daily 10am-5pm. $9, seniors $4, under 12 free.)*

HERMANN PARK. The 388 acres of Hermann Park, near Rice University and the Texas Medical Center, encompass the Miller Outdoor Theater, sports facilities, a mini-train ($2.25), and a pond with paddle boats ($8 per 30min.). It's a pretty area to wander, especially if you want some shade from the midday heat. *(Open daily 10am-6pm. Free.)* Near the northern entrance of the park, the **Houston Museum of Natural Science** has formidable-looking dinosaur fossils and a splendid display of gems and minerals. The museum also has a six-story glass butterfly center with 50 species, a planetarium, and an IMAX theater. *(1 Hermann Circle Dr. ☎ 713-639-4629; www.hmns.org. Open M-Sa 9am-6pm, Su 11am-6pm. $9, seniors and under 12 $6. Butterfly center $8/$5; planetarium $6/$4; IMAX $8/$5; day pass to all attractions $25/$15.)* At the southern end of the park, crowds flock to see the gorillas, hippos, and reptiles in the **Houston Zoological Gardens.** *(1513 N. MacGregor St. ☎ 713-533-6500. Open daily 9am-6pm. $8, seniors $6, ages 3-12 $4.)*

ART ATTRACTIONS. The world-class 🖾**Museum of Fine Arts** features paintings of the American West by artists such as Frederic Remington, as well as the largest collection of African gold pieces outside of the African continent. The two large buildings also hold Impressionist and post-Impressionist art and works from Asia, Africa, and Latin America. The museum's **Sculpture Garden** includes pieces by Matisse and Rodin. *(1001 Bissonet St. Museum: ☎ 713-639-7300; www.mfah.org. Open Tu-W 10am-5pm, Th 10am-9pm, F-Sa 10am-7pm, Su 12:15-7pm. $7, students and seniors $3.50. Th free. Garden: 5101 Montrose St. Open daily 9am-10pm. Free.)* The small **Contemporary Arts Museum** has two galleries with frequently changing exhibits featuring well-known artists from around the world. *(5216 Montrose St. ☎ 713-284-8250; www.camh.org. Open Tu-W and F-Sa 10am-5pm, Th 10am-9pm, Su noon-5pm. Free.)* The Menil Foundation exhibits an array of artwork in four buildings grouped within a block of each other. The 🖾**Menil Collection** has a fabulous collection of Surrealist paintings and modern art, one highlight of which is the Warhol room. This eclectic collection also has Byzantine and medieval artifacts. *(1515 Sul Ross St. ☎ 713-525-9400. Open W-Sa and Su 11am-7pm. Free.)* A block away, the **Rothko Chapel** houses 14 of the artist's paintings in a non-denominational sanctuary. Worshippers of modern art will delight in Rothko's ultra-simplicity; others will wonder where the paintings are. *(3900 Yupon St. ☎ 713-524-9839. Open daily 10am-6pm. Free.)* The **Byzantine Fresco Chapel Museum** displays the ornate dome and apse from a 13th-century Byzantine chapel in Cyprus. They were rescued in 1983 before being sold on the black market. *(4011 Yupon St. ☎ 713-521-3990. Open F-Su 10am-6pm. Free.)*

BEER CAN HOUSE. Many a Bacchanalian feast must have preceded the construction of the Beer Can House. Adorned with 50,000 beer cans, strings of beer-can tops, and a beer-can fence, the house was built by the late John Mikovisch, who followed a six pack-a-day regimen for 18 years to achieve the look. At $0.05 per can, the tin abode has a market price of $2500. *(222 Malone St., between Washington St. and Memorial Dr.)*

HOUSTON TUNNEL SYSTEM. Earthly pleasures can be found underground in the downtown area. Hundreds of shops and restaurants line the 18 mi. Houston Tunnel System, which connects all the major buildings, extending from the Civic Center to the Tenneco Building and the Hyatt Regency. Duck into the air-conditioned passageways via any major building or hotel. Entrances are closed Saturday and Sunday.

🍴 FOOD

As a city by the sea, Houston has harbored many immigrants, and their cultures are well represented in the city's eclectic ethnic cuisine. Along with the more indigenous barbecue and Southern soul food, you'll find Mexican, Cajun, and Asian fare. Search for reasonably priced restaurants along the chain-laden streets of **Westheimer** and **Richmond Ave.**, especially where they intersect with **Fountainview Ave.** Houston has two **China-town/Little Vietnam** areas. The older one is the district south of the George R. Brown Convention Center along Main St.; the newer one, called DiHo, is on **Bellaire Blvd.**, west of downtown. For authentic Mexican fare, try Houston's **East End.**

Brasil, 2604 Dunlavy St. (☎713-528-1993), at Westheimer. This hip coffee shop houses a bar, restaurant, and bakery. Munch on California-style salads and pizzas with toppings like goat cheese, spinach, eggplant, and basil. Sit inside, where the walls are adorned with local art, or head to the foliage-enclosed patio. Breakfast $3-6. Sandwiches $6-8. Open M-Sa 7:30am-2am, Su 7:30am-midnight. AmEx/MC/V. ❷

House of Pies, 3112 Kirby Dr. (☎713-528-3816). Little has changed in this classic 60s diner, where 44 kinds of pies and cakes grace formica countertops. Try the Bayoo Goo pie (or just "goo") with pecans, cream cheese, vanilla custard, and whipped cream ($3.25). Slice of pie $2.50-4. Breakfast $3-5. Sandwiches $5.50-7. Open 24hr. AmEx/D/MC/V. ❶

Goode Company BBQ, 5109 Kirby Dr. (☎713-522-2530), near Bissonnet St. Decorated with memorabilia, license plates, and a huge bison head, this little restaurant serves mouthwatering mesquite-smoked brisket, ribs, and sausage links all smothered in homemade sauce. Sandwiches from $5. Dinners $8-10. Open daily 11am-10pm. AmEx/D/MC/V. ❷

Buffalo Grille, 3116 Bissonnet St. (☎713-661-3663). Second location at 1201 S. Voss Rd. (☎713-784-3663). Hands down the best breakfast in town. Try the pancakes with fruit ($4-5), bigger than the plates on which they're served. The *huevos rancheros* ($6.75) satisfy even the most ferocious appetite. Open M 7am-2pm, Tu-F 7am-9pm, Sa 8am-9pm, Su 8am-2pm. AmEx/D/MC/V. ❷

Ragin' Cajun, 4302 Richmond Ave. (☎713-623-6321). Scarf down buckets of crawfish amid walls chock-full of postcards, while zydeco plays cheerfully in the background. Po'boys $6-9. Gumbo $4. Entrees $5-11. Open M-Th 11am-10pm, F-Sa 11am-11pm, Su 11am-9pm. AmEx/D/MC/V. ❷

ACCOMMODATIONS

Near downtown, **U.S. 59** is rife with budget motels. If you forgo the freeways and approach Houston via Alt. U.S. 90 on **Main St.**, you'll find the south Main St. area is also full of options, although some stretches may be unsafe at night.

Perry House Houston International Hostel, 5302 Crawford St. (☎713-523-1009). From Main St., turn east on Binz St., and north on Crawford St. Just past Hermann Park and near downtown, this beautiful 1920s home is tucked away in a quiet neighborhood. Minor chores. No alcohol. Internet access $5 per hr. Reception 8-10am and 5-11pm. Dorms $15; private rooms $23. Cash only. ❶

YMCA, 1600 Louisiana St. (☎713-758-9250; www.ymcahouston.org), between Pease and Leeland St., downtown. Small, spartan rooms—all singles—with daily maid service. Some have private baths. Towel deposit $2.50. Key deposit $10. Reception 24hr. Singles $28-35. AmEx/D/MC/V. ❶

Roadrunner Motor Inn, 6855 Southwest Fwy. (☎713-771-0641). Exit at Hillcroft Ave./West Park Dr., and take the access road on the east side of the freeway. Slightly cheaper than the Great Western Inn next door, this hotel offers rooms adjacent to a lovely courtyard. All rooms have TV, A/C, and pool access. Singles $40; doubles $45. AmEx/MC/V. ❷

Brazos Bend State Park, 21901 FM 762 (☎512-389-8900). From Houston, take Rte. 288 to Rosharon. Head west on FM 1462, then north on FM 762. This nature-lover's paradise is less than 1hr. from downtown. Along with a diversity of flora and fauna, visitors are sure to see American alligators, some over 12 ft. long. Sites have water and electricity, and the park offers fishing, picnicking, wildlife observation towers, and 22 mi. of trails. $4 per vehicle. Primitive sites $12, with electricity and water $16. D/MC/V. ❶

ENTERTAINMENT

From March to October, symphonies, dance companies, and theater companies stage free performances at the **Miller Outdoor Theatre**, in Hermann Park (☎713-284-8350; www.milleroutdoortheatre.com). The **Alley Theatre**, 615 Texas Ave., puts on excellent productions at moderate prices. (☎713-228-8421; www.alleytheatre.org.

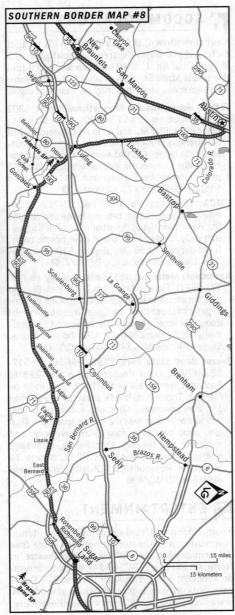

SOUTHERN BORDER MAP #8

15 miles

15 kilometers

Tickets $40-75; student rush tickets 1hr. before show M-Th and Su $12, F-Sa $20.) The **Houston Symphony,** 614 Louisiana St., performs from September to May. (☎713-227-2787. Tickets $20-95.) Various festivals are held throughout the year. Check out the **Texas Music Festival** in June. (☎713-743-3313; www.uh.edu.tmf. Locations vary. $10, students and seniors $5.)

🎷 NIGHTLIFE

There are a number of bars in the **Rice Village,** near Rice University. The once (in)famous Richmond Strip, along **Richmond St.,** has quieted down, though some bars remain. In the last few years, the downtown core's nightlife has been revitalized; there are numerous bar options along **Main St.,** accessible by transit rail. For indie-kid hangouts, head to the area around **Westheimer** and **Montrose St.** To find out what's going on where, grab a copy of the free weekly, *Houston Press*, or the free magazines *Envy* and *002houston*, all of which can be found at cafes and restaurants.

Helios, 411 Westheimer Ave. (☎713-526-4648; www.heliosrising.org). An eclectic bar in a rambling Victorian house. The "it" place for hip young people of all types, Helios has got an outdoor stage in the back, DJs spinning in the front yard, and random activities on the top floor like tango performances or an open figure drawing class (Tu; $5; models and food provided). M bluegrass M. F hip-hop. Sa reggae. Su funk and jazz. Cover for live music $5, under 21 $15. Open daily 8pm-2am. D/MC/V.

Poison Girl, 1641B Westheimer Ave. (☎713-527-9929). A trendy place whose walls are covered with beautiful "poison girls," vixens with sultry stares. The indie-cool clientele hang out on old furniture on the patio, while the inside features a number of old school pinball machines drawn from the owner's personal collection. Happy hour daily 6-8pm with $2.50 draft beer. First Su of the month all profits go to charity. No cover. Open daily 5pm-2am. AmEx/D/MC/V.

Sambuca Jazz Cafe, 909 Texas Ave. (☎713-224-5299). This bar and restaurant hosts nightly live music from 7pm. Business casual attire. No cover. Happy hour M-F 4-7pm with $2 appetizers and $4 martinis. Open M-Th and Su 11am-midnight, F 11am-1am, Sa 5pm-1am. AmEx/D/MC/V.

Valhalla, 6100 Main St. (☎713-348-3258). For "gods, heroes, mythical beings, and cheap beer," students, locals, and travelers descend to the depths of Keck

Hall in the center of the Rice campus. Beer $0.95. Happy hour F 4-8pm. Open M-F 11:30am-1pm and 4pm-2am, Su 7pm-2am. Cash only.

APPROACHING HALLETTSVILLE: 112 MILES
Houston has miles of sprawling suburbs, which becomes painfully apparent as you head out through stop-and-go traffic along **Alt. U.S. 90**, the continuation of **Wayside St.** Once you pass through the twin towns of Richmond and Rosenberg, the suburbs give way to rolling hills. Continue 30 mi. to Hallettsville.

HALLETTSVILLE. Hallettsville is the first stop in Lavaca County, a section of Texas settled by German and Czech immigrants in the 1880s. Nowadays, the people of Lavaca County have only smatterings of their grandparents' native tongues, but the influence remains—especially in the cooking. Hallettsville is famous for its yearly **Kolache Festival** (last weekend in Sept.), which features beer gardens, raucous dancing and kolache-eating contests. In town, the impressive clock tower of the **Lavaca County Courthouse** looms over the square. The **Hallettsville Chamber of Commerce**, 1614 N. Texana Rd., is located a half-mile north and provides more info on area attractions. (☎361-798-2662. Open M-Sa 8am-5pm.) **The Smokehouse Restaurant ❷**, 101 Rte. 77 S, cooks homestyle food like the "German-style" ham-and-cheese sandwich ($4) and chicken-fried steak ($7). Upgrade your steak to Texas size for an additional $3. (☎361-798-9504. Open M-Th and Su 7am-8:30pm, F-Sa 7am-9pm. AmEx/D/MC/V.) The **Hallettsville Inn ❷**, 608 W. Fairwinds Rd., offers the best combination of good rooms and good prices in town. (☎361-798-3257. Singles $40; doubles $45. AmEx/D/MC/V.)

APPROACHING SHINER: 14 MILES
Continue on **U.S. 90A** until you reach Shiner.

SHINER

Shiner is known as the "cleanest little city in Texas," though the "littlest clean city in Texas" would have been equally accurate; Shiner's population of 2100 warrants the title of "hamlet" rather than "city." The stunning **Sts. Cyril and Methodius Church**, 424 S. Ludmila St., is named after the saints who brought Catholicism to Bohemia. The church was built in 1921 and features a majestic altar, murals, beautiful statues, and stained glass windows—all imported from Bavaria.

Be sure to check out the **Spoetzl Brewery,** 603 E. Brewery St., founded in 1909 by a Bavarian immigrant and the oldest independent brewery in the state. (☎800-SHINER; www.shiner.com. Tours M-F 11am and 1:30pm. Free.) **Werner's Restaurant ❷**, 317 N Ave. E., has excellent steaks, barbecue, burgers, and sandwiches. There is also an 18ft. salad bar. (☎361-594-2928. Entrees $9-14. Open daily 6-10pm. MC/V.) The **Shiner Country Inn ❷**, 1016 N Ave. East, greets visitors with quaint rooms with a ranch-house feel. (☎361-594-3335; www.shinertx.com. Singles $42; doubles $50. AmEx/D/MC/V.)

APPROACHING GONZALES: 33 MILES
Head west on **Alt. U.S. 90.** Turn left onto **I-183 S,** and left again on **St. Joseph St.**

GONZALES

On October 2, 1835, the first shot of the Texas revolution was fired at Mexican troops who were marching into Gonzales demanding that the citizens hand over their cannon. The townsfolk rebelled and defeated the Mexicans, and the famous cannon still sits in the **Gonzales Memorial Museum,** 414 Smith St. The museum complex resembles a miniature version of the Washington Monument's mall and reflecting pool, honoring those who took part in the revolution. It also houses an eclectic collection of objects, from dolls to wedding dresses to muskets, that tell the story of the white settlers in the area. (☎830-672-6532. Open Tu-Sa 10am-noon and 1-5pm, Su 1-5pm. Donations suggested.) The **Gonzales County Jail Museum,** 414 St. Lawrence St., is a great little museum that gives a sense of the town's Wild West roots. You can wander the old cell blocks and gallows of the jail, constructed in 1887. The last hanging took place in 1921, before the electric chair came into fashion. Small exhibits show the tools of prisons, such as balls and chains, weapons, and wanted posters. Don't miss the cell for "women and lunatics" and the solitary confinement cell. (In the town square off St. Joseph St. ☎888-672-1095. Open M-Sa 8am-5pm, Su noon-4pm. Donation suggested.) A great place to stop in town is the **Sandy Fork Trading Post ❶**, 2100 Water St. (U.S. 183 N.), a family-run cafe that has perky flower arrangements on every table. (☎888-672-5900. Sandwiches $4.50-5.50. Open daily 9am-6pm. MC/V.)

SOUTHERN BORDER

⚐ APPROACHING PALMETTO STATE PARK: 12 MILES

To leave Gonzales, get on **U.S. 183** and head north past Alt. U.S. 90, toward Luling. 10 mi. down U.S. 183, look for signs for **Palmetto State Park.** Turn left and continue for 2 mi. to the park headquarters.

PALMETTO STATE PARK. This lush tropical oasis in the middle of the Texas grassland feels like the jungle of southern Florida. The dwarf palms of the park's namesake grow abundantly in the underbrush, where armadillos, deer, and other wildlife make their homes. Summer evenings flicker with the light of fireflies, who create a symphony of chirps, calls, and croaks. The San Marcos River and small Oxbow Lake run through the park, perfect for swimming and fishing. The park also features nature trails, picnic areas, a playground, and campsites. (☎512-389-8900; www.tpwd.state.tx.us. $2 per vehicle. Primitive sites with water $10, with electricity $16.)

⚐ APPROACHING LULING: 6 MILES

Take **U.S. 183 N** to reach Luling.

LULING. Luling is the name, and watermelons are the game. During the last weekend of June, the town hosts the **Luling Watermelon Thump.** Watermelon lovers from all over the state come for country music, street dancing, car rallies, seed-spitting competitions, and the crowning of the Watermelon Queen. See below for an interview with the 2006 Watermelon Queen. (☎830-875-3214 ext. 2; www.watermelonthump.com. Last full weekend of June.) Even if you're not

around for the Thump, you can still see watermelons everywhere you look. The water tower is painted like one and the oil drills feature amusing watermelon-y scenes (the most famous is a boy eating a watermelon in the parking lot of the Dollar General Store. Ask anyone to point out the way.) You can also buy delicious watermelons at outdoor stalls all over town (2 for $5). Ironically, no one in the town actually grows watermelons anymore—they are imported from nearby towns.

⚐ APPROACHING LOCKHART: 14 MILES

From Luling, be careful to stay on **U.S. 183 N** until you reach Lockhart; there is a sharp turn in the road that can be confusing.

LOCKHART. Lockhart is known by some as the "Barbecue capital of Texas." The title is contested by many other Texan towns, including Luling, but Lockhart is still worth a stop. The red-brick buildings have a real "Old West" feel, and the **county courthouse** in the center of town is sure to bemuse and amaze. **Black's BBQ ❶,** 708 N. Main St., is the self-proclaimed oldest family barbecue joint in Texas. That declaration may be as truthful as Black's claim to be open eight days a week, but either way, the food is yummy and dirt cheap. Try the beef brisket or the pork ribs, both $2.25. (2 blocks west of U.S. 183, on the north side of town. ☎512-398-2712; www.blacksbbq.com. Lunch special $5. Open daily 10am-8pm. AmEx/D/MC/V.)

⚐ APPROACHING AUSTIN: 30 MILES

Take **U.S. 183 N** to **Bastrop Hwy.** Take the **Airport Blvd. exit** and bear left on the **1st-5th St.** ramp into Austin.

WATERMELON THUMP-PICK

Let's Go *sat down with Megan Cox, a Luling high school student and the 2006 Luling Watermelon Thump Queen, and her mother, Shelly, to discuss the ins and outs of being crowned Queen of Watermelons.*

LG: First off, why "thump"?

MC: It's because you thump a watermelon to see if it's ripe.

LG: You drop it?

MC: No. "Thumping" it means you flick it or hit it a little—don't drop it. Definitely don't drop it.

LG: Oh. Yes, that makes more sense. So, how did you become Queen?

MC: It's by popular vote of the whole town...We started a year beforehand, cutting out (paper) watermelons and putting together posters. How long did cutting the watermelons take, Mom?

SC: Oh, about 4 months. At least.

LG: So what are your duties once you win the vote to be Queen?

MC: You find out on the Thursday of the Thump and then all through the the festival you're completely busy. You have to weigh watermelons, and you start the seed spitting contest.

AUSTIN

If the "Lone Star State" still inspires images of rough-and-tumble cattle ranchers riding horses across the plains, then Austin puts this stereotype to rest. In recent years, 17,000 new dot-com millionaires have made their fortunes in Austin. Nowadays, Fortune 500 companies and Internet startups play second fiddle to Austin's reputation for musical innovation as the "Live Music Capital of the World." For roadtrippers, Austin's live music scene won't disappoint; no matter what day you arrive, there are bound to be plenty of venues with great bands and DJs. With funky vintage stores, great restaurants, and a cool cafe scene, Austin is a vibrant, liberal, alternative oasis in an otherwise quite traditional state.

VITAL STATS

Population: 660,000

Visitor Info: Austin Visitors Center, 209 E. 6th St. (☎866-GO-AUSTIN). Open M-F 8:30am-5pm, Sa-Su 9am-5pm. **Capitol Visitors Center,** 112 E. 11th St. (☎512-305-8400). Open daily 9am-5pm.

Internet Access: Austin Public Library, 800 Guadalupe St. (☎512-974-7400). Open M-Th 10am-9pm, F-Sa 10am-6pm, Su noon-6pm. Free.

Parking: Free **Park 'n' Ride** lots on Toomey Rd. at Lamar, or on MoPac Expwy. at César Chavez (☎512-474-1200).

Post Office: 510 Guadalupe St. (☎512-494-2210), at 6th St. Open M-F 8:30am-6:30pm. **Postal Code:** 78701.

GETTING AROUND

Austin's roads feature steep climbs and tight curves, so be careful while you drive. Most of the city lies between **Mopac Expwy. (Rte. 1)** and **I-35,** which both run north-south. Students at the University of Texas inhabit central **Guadalupe St. ("The Drag"),** where music stores and cheap restaurants thrive. The state capitol governs the area a few blocks to the southeast. South of the capitol dome, **Congress Ave.** has upscale eateries and shops. The many bars and clubs of **6th St.** hop at night. Away from the urban sprawl, **Town Lake** is a haven for joggers, rowers, and cyclists.

Parking is easy to find outside the center of downtown for $4-5 per day. If parking is hard to find, drive either east or west on **4th St.** (away from Congress St.) until you find a spot—there are generally plenty available.

SIGHTS

Forming the backbone of the city's cultural life, the **University of Texas at Austin (UT)** is both the wealthiest public university in the country, with an annual budget of over a billion dollars, and one of the largest, with over 50,000 students. A number of the city's attractions, like the LBJ Library and Museum, are connected to the school. Austin is also Texas's capital city and the "Bat Capital" of the world, so be sure to check out both the government and the Congress Ave. Bridge bats.

LG: You, as Queen, start it?

MC: Yes. You spit the first seed. They have to draw names by lottery to see who can spit because so many people want to do it. The winner gets $500. But the Queen always spits the first seed.

LG: So are you famous now that you're Queen?

MC: Um...not that famous. Everybody here knows me now, but everybody pretty much knew me before. But I've been in lots of newspapers and on TV so locally...yeah. I'm a little famous.

SC: She comes from a line of Queens. There are six Queens on her Dad's side. So we're not playing around when a girl's born into the family! (laughs)

LG: So what are you planning now that you've graduated high school and are giving up your Thump crown in a couple weeks?

MC: Well, I get to keep the actual crown but, yes, I won't be Queen. I'm going to college. I want to be a teacher for little kids . . . so I can mold them.

LG: Into little Thump Queens?

MC: (Laughing) Exactly!

■ MEXICAN FREE-TAIL BATS. Just before dusk, head to the **Congress Ave. Bridge** near the Austin American Statesman parking lot and join thousands of others to watch the massive swarm of Mexican free-tail bats. When the bridge was reconstructed in 1980, the engineers unintentionally created crevices that formed ideal homes for the migratory bat colony. The city exterminated the night-flying creatures until **Bat Conservation International** moved to Austin to educate people about the bats' harmless behavior and the benefits of their presence—the bats eat up to 3000 lb. of insects each night. Stand on the bridge itself to see the bats fly out from underneath, or on the southern riverbank under the bridge for a more panoramic view. *(For flight times, call the bat hotline at ☎512-416-5700, ext. 3636. Bats fly Mar.-Nov.)*

GOVERNMENT BUILDINGS. Proving that everything *is* bigger in Texas, Texans built their state capitol 7 ft. taller than its federal counterpart. Its pink hue comes from Texas red granite, which was used instead of more traditional limestone. The capitol, its dome, the legislature chambers, and the underground extension are all open to the public. *(At Congress Ave. and 11th St. ☎512-463-0063. Open M-F 7am-10pm, Sa-Su 9am-8pm. 1hr. tours every 15min. Tours depart from the capitol steps. Free.)* The **Capitol Visitors Center** has exhibits on the capitol's history and construction. *(112 E. 11th St. ☎512-305-8400. Open daily 9am-5pm. 2hr. parking on 12th and San Jacinto St.)* Since the White House is closed to visitors, get an up-close look at Dubya's old stomping grounds by taking a tour of the **Texas Governor's Mansion.** *(1010 Colorado St. ☎512-463-5516. Free tours every 20min. M-Th 10-11:40am.)*

MUSEUMS. The first floor of the **Lyndon B. Johnson Library and Museum** sets the public and personal life of the Texas native against the backdrop of a broader history of the American presidency. A life-sized animatronic LBJ tells jokes and anecdotes on the second floor, while the 10th floor features a model of the Oval Office and an exhibit on Lady Bird Johnson, a great leader in her own right. *(2313 Red River St. ☎512-721-0200; www.lbjlib.utexas.edu. Open daily 9am-5pm. Free.)* If you've ever wondered about "the story of Texas," the **Bob Bullock Texas State History Museum** traces nearly 500 years of Western settlement, with the usual hero-worship of Travis, Houston, and Austin tempered by exhibits on the lives of minorities and the economy and culture of Texas over the years. *(1800 N. Congress Ave. ☎512-936-8746; www.thestoryoftexas.com. Open M-Sa 9am-6pm, Su noon-6pm. $5.50, seniors $4.50, ages 5-18 $3.)* The downtown **Austin Museum of Art** displays traveling exhibits of contemporary art, from photography to painting to installation. A second branch, housed in a Mediterranean-style villa, has exhibits that focus on nature. *(823 Congress Ave. ☎512-495-9224; www.amoa.org. Branch at 3809 W. 35th St. ☎512-458-8191. Open Tu-W and F-Sa 10am-6pm, Th 10am-8pm, Su noon-5pm. $5, students and seniors $4, under 12 free. Tu $1.)* The small **Mexic-Arte Museum** features traveling exhibits by Mexican, Mexican-American, and Latino artists. *(419 Congress Ave. ☎512-480-9373. Open M-Th 10am-6pm, F-Sa 10am-5pm, Su noon-5pm. $5, students and seniors $4, under 12 $1.)* The brand-new **Blanton Museum of Art** is the art giant in Austin, with over 17,000 works and an eclectic focus on European, American, and Latin American art. *(MLK Blvd. at Congress St., across from the Bob Bullock Museum. ☎512-471-7324; www.blantonmuseum.org. Open Tu-W and F-Sa 10am-5pm, Th 10am-8pm, Su 1-5pm. $5, seniors $4, ages 13-25 $3, under 13 free. Th free.)*

PARKS. Covert Park at Mt. Bonnell offers a sweeping view of Lake Austin and Westlake Hills from the highest point in the city. *(3800 Mt. Bonnell Rd., off W. 35th St.)* On hot afternoons, Austinites come in droves to riverside **Zilker Park,** just south of the Colorado River. *(2201 Barton Springs Rd. ☎512-974-6700. Open daily 5am-10pm. Free.)* Flanked by walnut and pecan trees in Zilker Park, the 1000 ft. long **■ Barton Springs Pool** is a spring-fed swimming hole that hovers around 68°F. Families crowd the shores by day, while many young people swim at night. *(☎512-499-6700. Pool open M-W and F-Su 5am-10pm. $3, ages 12-17 $2, under 12 $1. Free daily 5-8am and 9-10pm.)* The **Barton Springs Greenbelt** offers challenging hiking and biking trails.

◤ FOOD

Downtown, patrons often get free or cheap appetizers with drinks during happy hour and, as night falls, vendors appear on the streets, selling pizza, barbecue and burgers. Near UT, along

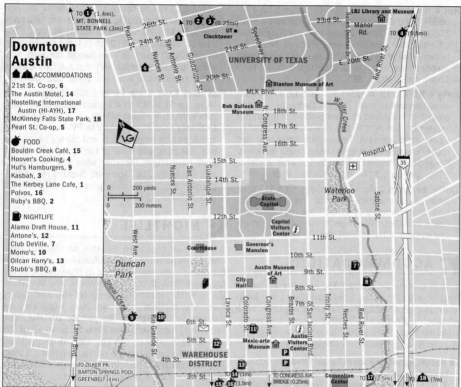

Downtown Austin

⌂⌂ ACCOMMODATIONS

21st St. Co-op, **6**
The Austin Motel, **14**
Hostelling International
  Austin (HI-AYH), **17**
McKinney Falls State Park, **18**
Pearl St. Co-op, **5**

🍎 FOOD

Bouldin Creek Café, **15**
Hoover's Cooking, **4**
Hut's Hamburgers, **9**
Kasbah, **3**
The Kerbey Lane Cafe, **1**
Polvos, **16**
Ruby's BBQ, **2**

🌙 NIGHTLIFE

Alamo Draft House, **11**
Antone's, **12**
Club DeVille, **7**
Momo's, **10**
Oilcan Harry's, **13**
Stubb's BBQ, **8**

SOUTHERN BORDER

Guadalupe St., there are a number of inexpensive restaurants. Though a bit removed from downtown, **Barton Springs Rd.** offers a diverse selection of eateries, including Mexican restaurants and Texas-style barbecue joints. If you want to cook or snack on free samples, head to **Whole Foods Market's** flagship store, 525 N. Lamar Blvd. The organic food chain started in Austin. (☎512-476-1206. Open daily 8am-10pm.)

☒ Polvos, 2004 S. 1st St. (☎512-441-5446). Scrumptious Mexican food and an extensive salsa bar. The *ceviche* (fresh, cold whitefish with tomato, cilantro, lemon and spice; $6.50) is a must. The chili *relleno al nogal* (poblano pepper stuffed with pastor and topped with pecan cream sauce; $9) is a terrific change from the usual tacos and burritos. Open M-F and Su 7am-10pm, Sa 7am-11pm. AmEx/D/MC/V. ❸

☒ Bouldin Creek, 1501 S. 1st St. (☎512-416-1601), at Elizabeth St. A hip cafe with murals, funky couches, and delicious vegan and vegetarian food. Try the heavenly portobello tacos ($6.25) or the vegan blueberry cornbread ($2). Free Wi-Fi. Open M-F 7am-midnight, Sa-Su 9am-midnight. MC/V. ❷

Kasbah, 2714 Guadalupe St. (☎512-542-9870). Sit on cushions beneath draped Moroccan cloths and sip mint tea ($2) from glasses brought to you on a silver tray, or sit on the outside patio amid candles and pottery. Try a *lait d'amandes* (almond milk) for $3. Entrees $8. Open daily 10am-3am. Cash only. ❷

Hoover's Cooking, 2002 Manor Rd. (☎512-479-5006), ½ mi. east of I-35. Also known as "the good taste place" or "the smoke, fire, and ice house," Hoover's has cooking that is just plain good. Chipotle chicken salad sandwich $7.50. Open M-F 11am-10pm, Sa-Su 9am-10pm. MC/V. ❸

Hut's Hamburgers, 807 W. 6th St. (☎512-472-0693). "God Bless Hut's" has been the motto since 1981, when a flood destroyed everything in the area but inexplicably spared Hut's. A haven for heavenly burgers ($5-6), Hut's has over 20 different varieties from which to choose. Open daily 11am-10pm. AmEx/MC/V. ❷

Ruby's BBQ, 512 W. 29th St. (☎512-477-1651; www.rubysbbq.com). Ruby's barbecue is good enough to be served on silver platters, but that just wouldn't seem right in this cow-skull-and-butcher-paper establishment. The owners order only hormone-free meat from farm-raised, grass-fed cows. Scrumptious brisket sandwich $5; brisket dinner $10. Open daily 11am-midnight. MC/V. ❸

The Kerbey Lane Cafe, 3704 Kerbey Ln. (☎512-451-1436; www.kerbeylanecafe.com). An Austin institution. The pancakes ($3.50-5) are renowned and come in buttermilk, gingerbread, or apple whole wheat. Open 24hr. AmEx/D/MC/V. ❷

🏠 ACCOMMODATIONS

Chain motels lie along **I-35,** which runs north and south of Austin. This funkified city, however, is a great place to find cheap options with character. **Co-ops** at UT offer rooms and meals to hostelers. Only a 10-20min. drive separates Austin from the nearest campgrounds.

🏕 Hostelling International Austin (HI-AYH), 2200 S. Lakeshore Blvd. (☎512-444-2294 or 800-725-2331), 3 mi. from downtown. From I-35, exit at Riverside, head east, and turn left at Lakeshore Blvd. Beautifully situated, quiet hostel with a 24hr. common room overlooking Town Lake. 42 dorm-style beds in mostly single-sex rooms. Rents bikes, kayaks, and canoes ($10 per day). Full kitchen and barbecue. Internet access $1 per day. No alcohol. Reception 8-11am and 5-10pm; arrivals after 10pm must call ahead to check in. Dorms $20, members $17. AmEx/MC/V. ❶

🏕 The Austin Motel, 1220 S. Congress (☎512-441-1157; www.austinmotel.com). Look for the oddly phallic sign. Bright, airy rooms are individually decorated with themes like "Zen" and "California Greenhouse." Reservations recommended. Singles M-Th and Su $65, F-Sa $75; doubles $85. AmEx/D/MC/V. ❸

UT Co-ops (☎512-476-5678), at various locations around the University of Texas campus, off Guada-lupe St. UT co-ops house students during the year and will usually accept summer hostelers for a nominal fee ($10-20 per night, including food). The 21st St. Co-op (707 W. 21st St.) and the Pearl St. Co-op (2000 Pearl St.) are two of the best. Call ahead to make arrangements and ask for the membership coordinator when you arrive. Cash only. ❶

McKinney Falls State Park, 5808 McKinney Falls Pkwy. (☎512-243-1643), southeast of the city. Turn right on Burleson off Rte. 71 E, then right on McKinney Falls Pkwy. Caters to RV and tent campers. Sites with ample shade and privacy near excellent swimming and 6 mi. of hiking trails. Reception daily 8am-10pm. Primitive sites $12, with water and electricity $16. Screened shelters for up to 8 people $35; no bedding provided. Day-use $2, under 13 free. D/MC/V. ❶

🎵 NIGHTLIFE

Austin has replaced Seattle as the nation's underground music hot spot, so keep an eye out for rising indie stars as well as blues, folk, country, and rock favorites. Downtown, **6th St.** is lined with warehouse nightclubs and fancy bars. The mellow, cigar-smoking, night-owl set gathers in the **4th St. Warehouse District.** The bars and clubs along **Red River St.** have all of the grit and glamour of 6th St., with more parking. The Austin coffeehouse scene provides a low-key alternative. The weekly *Austin Chronicle* and *XL-ent* have details on current music performances, shows, and movies. The *Gay Yellow Pages* is free at stands along Guadalupe St.

🎵 Antone's, 213 W. 5th St. (☎512-320-8424). Antone's namesake lives on: a blues paradise for all ages. Shows 8pm almost every night; call for details. Cover $5-25. Open daily 7pm-2am. AmEx/D/MC/V.

🎵 The Alamo Drafthouse Cinema, 409B Colorado St. (☎512-476-1320; www.originalalamo.com). Second runs, cult classics, and other offbeat films are shown at the Alamo. Revel in 1980s horror classics and sing-alongs while you chow down at the full-service restaurant and bar. Tickets up to $10. MC/V.

Club DeVille, 900 Red River (☎512-457-0900). Chandeliers cast a mellow glow over the funky furniture and black walls of this slick cocktail lounge. The patio is carved out of the side of a cliff. Occasional live music outdoors. Try their signature cucumber shot, made with plum ice wine ($6). Cover $2. Happy hour M 5pm-last customer, Tu-F 5-8pm with $1 off well drinks and drafts. Open daily 5pm-2am. AmEx/D/MC/V.

Momo's, 618 W. 6th St. (☎512-479-8848; www.momosclub.com), above Katz's. This laid-back 2nd fl. bar hosts local bands every night of the week and has a terrific wood patio overlooking the city. Music ranges from bluegrass to rock to acoustic. Music from 8pm. M-Th and Su $2 Lonestar beer. Cover $5-10. Open daily 7pm-2am. AmEx/D/MC/V.

Stubb's BBQ, 801 Red River St. (☎512-480-8341; www.stubbs.com). Stubb's inexpensive grub includes a fabulous all-you-can-eat buffet with live gospel for $17 (reservations recommended; seatings 11am and 1pm). Downstairs, an all-ages club hosts acts 3-4 nights per week, starting at 8pm. Cover $8-22. Restaurant open Tu-Th 11am-10pm, F-Sa 11am-11pm, Su 11am-9pm. Nightclub open Tu-Th 7pm-midnight, F-Sa 7pm-1am. AmEx/D/MC/V.

Oilcan Harry's, 211 W. 4th St. (☎512-320-8823). One of the best gay bars in Austin. 3 bars, pool table, and outdoor patio. Th and Su strip shows (21+). No cover. Open daily 2pm-2am. AmEx/MC/V.

 BIG DETOUR. Explore the wild back-country roads of Texas on the **Rocks, Ribs, and Revolvers Big Detour,** p. 820.

APPROACHING NEW BRAUNFELS: 48 MILES
Take **I-35 S** for 46 mi. to **Exit 189** and the town of New Braunfels.

NEW BRAUNFELS. If you like waterslides, you'll love the **Schlitterbahn Waterpark Resort** in the town of New Braunfels. Schlitterbahn is one of the largest waterparks in the US and has received accolades from the Travel Channel, which called it the best waterpark in America. It features 65 acres of slides, tube chutes, and wave pools; there are even three uphill "water coasters." (☎830-625-2351. $37, ages 3-11 $30. Open late May to late Aug. daily 10am-8pm; May and Sept. Sa-Su 10am-7pm.)

DETOUR
NATURAL BRIDGE CAVERNS
From I-35, take Exit 175 to Rte. 3009 and follow the signs for the caverns.

The Natural Bridge Caverns are Texas's largest underground cave system and always maintain a pleasant 70°F. Don't miss the famed Watchtower, an amazing 50 ft. rock formation that resembles a crystallized flower. (☎210-651-6101; www.natural-bridgecaverns.com. Open daily in summer 9am-7pm; in winter 9am-4pm. 1½hr. tours every 30min. $15, ages 3-11 $9. 1hr. tours of Jaremy Caves every hr. $17, ages 3-11 $9.50.)

APPROACHING SAN ANTONIO: 32 MILES
Continue south on **I-35**, which will take you into downtown San Antonio. Exit at **Alamo/Commercial Dr.**

SAN ANTONIO

Though best known as the home of the Alamo, San Antonio is better defined by its integration of Anglo and Hispanic cultures. The city proudly revels in its Mexican heritage, with missions, mariachis, and margaritas around every corner. Yet there are enough barbecue joints and ten-gallon hats to remind travelers that they're in the heart of Lone Star country.

VITAL STATS

Population: 1.1 million

Visitor Info: San Antonio Convention and Visitors Bureau, 317 Alamo Plaza (☎210-207-6748; www.sanantoniovisit.com), across from the Alamo. Open daily 9am-5pm.

Internet Access: San Antonio Public Library, 600 Soledad St. (☎210-207-2500). Open M-Th 9am-9pm, F-Sa 9am-5pm, Su 11am-5pm. Free.

Parking: Parking lots dot the downtown region and all cost about $6-8 for the day. If you're staying only a short time or moving about the city, meters are cheap ($0.10 per 30min.). Outside the small downtown core, free parking is easy to find.

Post Office: 615 E. Houston St. (☎210-212-8046), 1 block from the Alamo. Open M-F 8:30am-5:30pm. **Postal Code:** 78205.

GETTING AROUND

Commerce and **Market St.** are major east-west arteries—they pass most major attractions, like the Riverwalk, Market Square, and La Villita. **Durango Blvd.** runs east-west in the south end of

ROCKS, RIBS & REVOLVERS
SEND A TEX MESSAGE

Length: 314 miles
Days: 2 days
Starting point: Austin
Highlight: Stonehenge II (Return of the Killer Stonehenge)

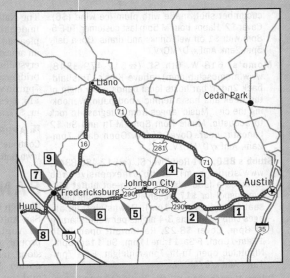

From Austin, get on Hwy. 290 W (Rte. 71), and go 40 mi. to F.M 1826 S. Turn left, and follow signs to Driftwood. After 13 mi., look for the small sign on the right that announces the Salt Lick.

1 THE SALT LICK. The **Salt Lick Barbecue Restaurant ❷** attracts tourists and Texans from miles around with its legendary smoked brisket. If any barbecue is worth a detour, this is it. Buy a bottle of Salt Lick brand barbecue sauce to take with you. (18001 F.M. 1826. ☎512-858-4959; www.saltlickbbq.com. Beef plate $9-10. Open daily 11am-10pm. Cash only.)

Continue 1 mi. west on F.M. 1826 to C.R. 150, and turn left (south). Go ½ mi. to C.R. 170 (also called Elder Hill Rd.), and turn left (west). Go 4 mi. and look for the sign for Driftwood Vineyard on your left.

2 DRIFTWOOD VINEYARDS. Driftwood offers you your first taste of Texas wine—a growing industry in the state. The Driftwood tasting house is situated on a beautiful hill that overlooks the vineyards. For $5 you can taste up to 9 wines. (4001 Elder Hill Rd. ☎512-692-6229; www.driftwoodvineyards.com. Tasting house open M-Th 10am-5pm, F-Sa 10am-6pm, Su noon-6pm.)

Head back to Hwy. 290, and go west (left) for about 25 mi. Pass through the town of Dripping Springs to the turn-off for Pedernales Falls State Park (Rte. 3232). Follow it 8 mi. into the park.

3 PEDERNALES FALLS STATE PARK. Pedernales is the gem of states parks in Texas Hill Country. The low-level waterfalls are strikingly beautiful as they cascade down limestone rock stacks. You can climb the limestone formations or hike along any of the 20 mi. of trails throughout the park if you have a bit more time to spare. (2585 Park Rd. ☎512-389-8900. Open daily 8am-10pm. $5 per vehicle.)

Leave Pedernales by following Rte. 2766 for 8 mi. until reaching the junction of Hwy. 281 and Hwy. 290. Go 4 mi. north (right) on Hwy 281 to reach the Exotic Resort Zoo.

4 EXOTIC RESORT ZOO. This rough 'n' tumble managerie is home to over 80 species. While you take a 90min. tram tour through the zoo's 137 acres, guides reveal the ins and outs of animal life. The zoo also sells exotic animals; the lemurs, which run about $1000, are their most popular sell. Consider snagging an African pygmy goat as an awfully cute souvenir. (235 Zoo Trail. ☎830-868-4357; www.zooexotics.com. Open daily 9am-6pm. $11, children under 12 $9.)

Head south on Hwy. 281 back to the junction of Hwy. 281 and Hwy. 290. Travel west on Hwy. 290 for 4 mi. to Stonewall, the Peach Capital of the World. Look for signs to the Lyndon B. Johnson Historic Site, and turn right.

5 LYNDON B. JOHNSON STATE PARK AND HISTORIC SITE. The State Park Visitors Center offers an interpretive bus tour that runs to a one-room school house, the President's reconstructed birthplace, the Johnson family cemetery, and the Johnson ranch. The site also contains the **Sauer-Beckmann Living History Farm** which highlights the history of German settlers in the area. (☎830-644-2252; www.tpwd.state.tx.com. Open 9am-sunset. Bus tours 10am-4pm. $6, 62+ and 7-17 $3.)

After getting your fill of Johnson (and Stonewall peaches), continue on Hwy. 290 toward Fredericksburg. After 11 mi., turn left (west) on R.R. 1376 toward Luckenbach. Go 4½ mi. to the Luckenbach loop, and turn right.

6 LUCKENBACH. Once a trading post established by German pioneers in 1849, Luckenbach was sold (beer joint, general store, dance hall, and all) to the Texan folk humorist, Hondo Crouch, in 1970. Crouch's purchase inspired his friends Willie Nelson and Waylon Jennings to pen the 1977 hit single, "Luckenbach Texas." Now tourists and locals come to the "town" to buy kitschy souvenies, listen to music, and two-step. (412 Luckenbach Town Loop. ☎830-997-3224; www.luckenbachtexas.com. Open daily 10am-9pm. Free.)

Retrace your path back to Hwy. 290, and head left (west) into the heart of Fredericksburg.

7 GISH'S OLD WEST MUSEUM. This small museum is tucked far away from Frederickburg's overpriced tourist scene and contains Joe Gish's personal collection of Old West artifacts. Exhibits include a fascinating display of "Wanted" posters, sheriffs' stars, and cowboy apparel. (502 N. Milam St. ☎830-997-2794. Hours vary according to when Joe is home, so call ahead. Free.)

From Main St. (Hwy. 290), go south on Hwy 16 (Adams Rd.) for 22 mi. until reaching Kerrville. Take Hwy. 27 west 6 mi. to the town of Ingram. Branch left onto Hwy. 39, and follow it 7 mi. until reaching the town of Hunt. Go right on F.M. 1340 for 2 mi. Stonehenge II will be on the left.

8 STONEHENGE II. Stonehenge II is a bizarre testament to its creators, Doug Hill and Al Shepperd, who built the structure in 1989. Two-thirds the size of the original, Stonehenge II is made of steel, plaster, and concrete and took 9 months to construct. One of the slabs is stone (a limestone chunk left over from Doug's new patio in 1989) but it can be tough to find. Doug and Al also added a few replica Easter Island heads for good measure. (F.M. 1340. Free.)

From Stonehenge II, loop back to Kerrville and then to Fredericksburg along Hwy. 16. Head north for 8 mi. to the Enchanted Rock Natural Area.

9 ENCHANTED ROCK STATE NATURAL AREA. "Enchanted Rock" isn't just a catchy title—Native Americans believed that this giant, pink granite dome formation was magical. Visitors can take the trek up the dome for stunning views. (16710 RR 965. ☎325-247-3903; www.tpwd.state.tx.us. Open daily 8am-10pm. $5 per person.)

BACK TO THE ROUTE. Head back to Hwy. 16, continuing north 13 mi. to Llano. At Llano, head southeast on Hwy. 71 about 80 mi. back to Austin.

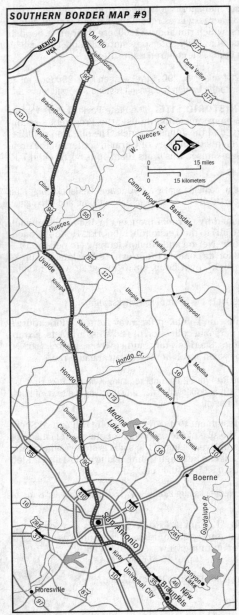

SOUTHERN BORDER MAP #9

0   15 miles

0   15 kilometers

the city. Major north-south streets are **Alamo,** which runs alongside the Alamo in the center of downtown, **Presa,** and **St. Mary's**—the latter runs down to the missions. **Flores St.** runs north-south in the east side. The two major north-south highways are **I-35** and **I-37.** I-37 (also called U.S 281) heads north toward of **Brackenridge Park,** the second-largest urban municipal park in the country. **Hwy. 410** rings the downtown area, connecting all highways that run into the city. Watch for traffic jams on I-37 and Hwy. 410, especially at rush hour.

👁 SIGHTS

THE ALAMO. Built as a Spanish mission during the colonization of the New World, the Alamo has come to serve as the symbol of Texas's break from Mexico and thus a touchstone of Lone Star pride. For 12 days in 1836, a motley crew of Americans (including ⬛**Davy Crockett**), Europeans, and Hispanic Tejanos defended the Alamo against the army of Mexican General Santa Anna, who was determined to reclaim the land for Mexico. The morning of the 13th day saw the end of their defiant stand, and all 189 men were killed. However, the massacre united Texans behind the independence movement, and "Remember the Alamo!" became the rallying cry for Sam Houston's ultimately victorious forces. After languishing for decades, the site is presently under the care of the Daughters of the Republic of Texas and is the focus of the city's downtown. (*At the center of Alamo Plaza.* ☎ *210-225-1391; www.thealamo.org. Open M-Sa 9am-5:30pm, Su 10am-5:30pm. Free.*)

OTHER MISSIONS. Four missions built in the 1720s and 30s supplied San Antonio with agricultural products and newly converted Catholics. Today they make up the **San Antonio Missions National Historical Park.** Stretching 23 mi. south of the city along the San Antonio River, they are connected by the brown-signed Mission Trail road, which begins at the Alamo. (*Visitors Center located at Mission San José.* ☎ *210-932-1001; www.nps.gov/saan. Open daily 9am-5pm.*) Stopping at each mission takes a good half-day; some may wish to see only the first two. The missions are connected by biking and hiking trails, and the first two are served by Bus #42. The first is **Mission Concepción,** the oldest unrestored stone church in North America.

(807 Mission Rd., 4 mi. south of the Alamo off E. Mitchell St. ☎ 210-534-1540.)

Mission San José, the "Queen of the Missions," contains remnants of its original irrigation system, a gorgeous sculpted rose window, and numerous restored buildings. *(6701 San José Dr., off Roosevelt Ave. ☎ 210-922-0543. Mass Su 7:45, 9, 10:30am; noon "Mariachi Mass.")* **Mission San Juan Capistrano** and **Mission San Francisco de la Espada** are smaller, but they surround the Espada Aqueduct, a remarkable engineering feat that provided irrigation to the river valley. Visitors can view the fully functional aqueduct as it carries water over the streams and valleys below. *(San Juan: 9101 Graf St. ☎ 210-534-0749. San Francisco: 10040 Espada Rd. ☎ 210-627-2021.)*

RIVERWALK. After the Alamo, the most famous symbol of San Antonio is its 2½ mi. long **Riverwalk (Paseo del Río),** built in the 1930s by the WPA as a combination flood control and real estate project. Following the original course of the San Antonio River, it is a 3 ft. deep river lined with shaded pathways, picturesque gardens, shops, and cafes, all of which are below street level. Along the southern arm of Riverwalk is **La Villita,** a preserved section of historic houses and streets that has been turned into a Spanish-style artisan village where the public can watch artists work and purchase their creations. *(418 Villita. ☎ 210-207-8612; www.lavillita.com. Open daily 10am-6pm. Free.)* **Market Sq.** is a part open-air, part-enclosed market where customers can haggle with vendors. Weekends feature the upbeat tunes of Tejano bands with a backbeat of buzzing frozen margarita machines. *(Between San Saba and Santa Rosa St. ☎ 210-207-8600. Outdoor vendors and indoor market area open daily May-Sept. 10am-8pm; Sept.-May 10am-6pm.)*

HEMISFAIR PARK. The site of the 1968 World's Fair, HemisFair Plaza still draws tourists with restaurants, museums, and historic houses. *(Plaza located between S. Alamo St., E. Market St., Bowie St., and Durango Blvd.)* The view is beautiful from the **Tower of the Americas,** which rises 750 ft. above the Texas hill country. *(600 HemisFair Park. ☎ 210-233-3101. Open M-Th and Su 9am-10pm, F-Sa 9am-11pm. $3, seniors $2, ages 4-11 $1.)* Inside the park, the **Institute of Texan Cultures** documents the histories and contributions of 27 different ethnic groups in Texas, from Czech to Chinese to Swedish. *(☎ 210-458-2300;*

www.texancultures.utsa.edu. Open Tu-Sa 9am-6pm, Su noon-5pm. $7, seniors and ages 3-12 $4.)

MUSEUMS. In continuous operation since 1881, the **Buckhorn Saloon & Museum** displays objects from the Old West as well as a huge collection of stuffed animals from around the world, an interactive wax museum of Texas history, and exhibits on ranching and gunfights. Stop in for a drink and a bite at the saloon. *(318 Houston St., 2 blocks west of the Alamo. ☎ 210-247-4000. Museum $11, children 3-11 $8. Open Memorial Day to Labor Day 10am-6pm; Labor Day to Memorial Day 10am-5pm.)* **The San Antonio Museum of Art,** housed in the former Lone Star Brewery, showcases a nice collection of Pre-Columbian, Egyptian, Oceanic, Asian, and Islamic folk art. In 1998, the museum established the Nelson A. Rockefeller Center for Latin American Art, the first of its kind in the U.S. Highlights include works by Diego Rivera. *(200 W. Jones Ave. ☎ 210-978-8100. Open Tu 10am-8pm, W-Sa 10am-5pm, Su noon-6pm. $8, seniors $7, students $5, ages 3-11 $3. Tu 4-8pm free.)* The **McNay Art Museum** displays the collection of Impressionist, Post-Impressionist, and Expressionist masterpieces accumulated by Mrs. McNay, who stirred up controversy in the early 20th century as the first promoter of modern art in otherwise conservative Texas. The museum and 23-acre grounds are free to the public. *(6000 N. New Braunfels Ave. ☎ 210-805-1756; www.mcnayart.org. Open Tu-W and F 10am-4pm, Th 10am-9pm, Sa 10am-5pm, Su noon-5pm. Grounds open daily 7am-7pm.)*

BRACKENRIDGE PARK. To escape San Antonio's urban congestion, amble down to Brackenridge Park. The 343-acre grounds include playgrounds, a miniature train, and a driving range. The main attraction of the park is a lush, perfumed **Japanese tea garden** with pathways weaving in and out of a pagoda and around a goldfish pond. *(3910 N. Saint Mary's St., 5 mi. north of the Alamo. ☎ 210-223-9534. Japanese gardens $3, children $2. Open daily 5am-11pm. Train daily 9am-6:30pm. $3, children $1.50.)* The park also houses the **San Antonio Zoo.** One of the country's largest zoos, it shelters over 3500 animals in re-creations of their natural settings. The extensive African mammal exhibit is particularly noteworthy. *(3903 N. Saint Mary's St. ☎ 210-734-7184. Open daily June-Aug. 9am-6pm; Sept.-May 9am-5pm. $8, seniors and ages 3-11 $6.)*

FOOD

Be prepared to pay dearly for dining along the **Riverwalk**. North of town, Asian restaurants line **Broadway** across from Brackenridge. On weekends, hundreds of carnival food booths crowd the walkways of **Market Sq.** If you come late in the day, prices drop and vendors are willing to haggle. (☎210-207-8600. Open daily May-Sept. 10am-8pm; Sept.-May 10am-6pm.)

Mi Tierra, 218 Produce Row (☎210-225-1262), in Market Sq. A huge restaurant filled with shining ceiling decorations, Mi Tierra gets packed full of tourists and locals come dinnertime. Mariachi musicians serenade diners while they munch delicious Mexican fare, like chicken enchiladas with *mole* sauce ($8.75). Daily lunch specials (M-F 11am-2pm) provide hearty meals at slightly lower prices. Lunch plates $7-8; Dinner plates $11-14. Open 24hr. AmEx/DC/MC/V. ❷

Rosario's, 910 S. Alamo St. (☎210-223-1806), at S. Saint Mary's St. Rosario's is known as the best Tex-Mex eatery in town. Scrumptious chicken quesadillas ($6) and *relleno de pascado* ($11) uphold the reputation. Live Latin-infused music F-Sa, starting around 8pm. Open M 11am-3pm, Tu-Th 11am-10pm, F-Sa 11am-12:30am. AmEx/D/MC/V. ❸

Liberty Bar, 328 E. Josephine St. (☎210-227-1187). Friendly service and a classy ambience. Napa Valley-inspired daily specials ($13-14) and sandwiches ($6-9). Try the *karkade,* an iced hibiscus and mint tea with fresh ginger and white grape juice ($2.50). Open M-Th 11am-10:30pm, F-Sa 11am-midnight, Su 10:30am-10:30pm. AmEx/D/MC/V. ❸

Ruta Maya, 107 E. Martin (☎210-223-6292; www.rutamayariverwalk.com), at Soledad. Serves organic Chiapas-grown coffee ($1.50) and homemade sandwiches and salads. Try the chicken on sourdough with olive *tapenade* ($6.75). Relaxed, lounging-friendly atmosphere. Free Wi-Fi. Th-Sa bands or DJs. Open M-Th 7am-11pm, F 7am-2am, Sa 8am-2am, Su 8am-10pm. AmEx/D/MC/V. ❷

Josephine St. Steaks/Whiskey, 400 Josephine St. (☎210-224-6169), at Ave. A. Josephine St.'s specialty is thick Texan steak, but they offer a wide array of other tasty dishes for less intense carnivores. Nice shaded patio. Entrees $7-15. Open M-Th 11am-10pm, F-Sa 11am-11pm. AmEx/D/MC/V. ❸

Twin Sisters, 124 Broadway and 6322 N. New Braunfels (☎210-354-1559). Some of the best vegetarian food in San Antonio. The tofu quesadillas ($6) are delicious. Open M-F 9am-3pm. AmEx/MC/V. ❷

ACCOMMODATIONS

For cheap motels, try **Roosevelt Ave.,** a southern extension of Saint Mary's St., and **Fredericksburg Rd.** Inexpensive motels also line **Broadway** between downtown and Brackenridge Park. Follow **I-35 N** or the **Austin Hwy.** to find cheaper and often safer lodging outside town.

San Antonio International Hostel, 621 Pierce St. (☎210-223-9426), off Grayson St. With friendly management, a pool, and a rec room, San Antonio's only hostel is a good one. 42 beds in a ranch-style building. Breakfast ($6) served in elegant dining room. Key deposit $10. Reception 8am-10pm. Dorms $25; private rooms $45. AmEx/D/MC/V. ❷

Alamo Lodge, 1126 E. Elmira St. (☎210-222-9463), off Grayson St. This budget motel provides clean rooms in a quiet neighborhood. Outdoor pool, A/C, and 5 free local calls. Key deposit $2. Rooms M-Th $40, F-Su $47. AmEx/D/MC/V. ❷

Roosevelt Inn, 2122 Roosevelt Ave. (☎210-533-2514), a few minutes from downtown. Clean, no-frills rooms with A/C and TV. You can borrow classic VHS movies from the office. Rooms M-F $35-40, Sa-Su $46. AmEx/D/MC/V. ❷

Alamo KOA, 602 Gembler Rd. (☎210-224-9296 or 800-833-7785), 6 mi. from downtown. From I-10 E, take Exit 580, drive 2 blocks north, then take a left onto Gembler Rd. Well-kept grounds with lots of shade. Each site has a grill and a patio. Showers, laundry, pool, and free movies. Reception 8am-8:30pm. Sites $26, with full hook-up $36. D/MC/V. ❷

NIGHTLIFE

In late April, the 10-day **Fiesta San Antonio** (☎210-227-5191) ushers in spring with concerts, carnivals, and hoopla in honor of Texas's many heroes and cultures. Clusters of funky, independent bars can be found in the residential areas of **King William, N. St. Mary's St.** (around Woodlawn Ave.) and **Josephine St.** The *Friday Express* and the weekly *Current* (available at the visitors center and in many bars and businesses) are guides to the city's nightlife.

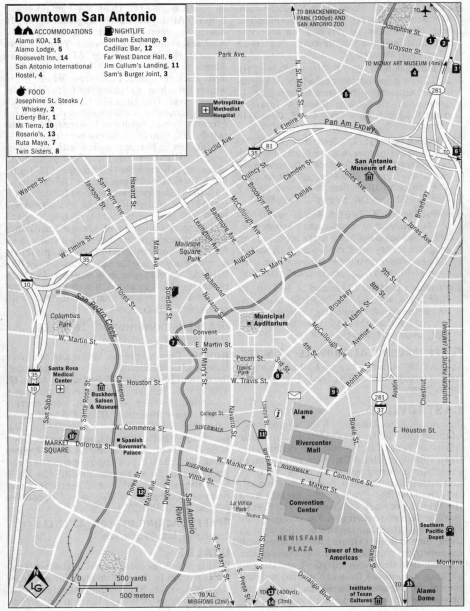

Downtown San Antonio

🏠🏠 ACCOMMODATIONS
Alamo KOA, **15**
Alamo Lodge, **5**
Roosevelt Inn, **14**
San Antonio International
Hostel, **4**

🍅 FOOD
Josephine St. Steaks /
    Whiskey, **2**
Liberty Bar, **1**
Mi Tierra, **10**
Rosario's, **13**
Ruta Maya, **7**
Twin Sisters, **8**

📺 NIGHTLIFE
Bonham Exchange, **9**
Cadillac Bar, **12**
Far West Dance Hall, **6**
Jim Cullum's Landing, **11**
Sam's Burger Joint, **3**

SOUTHERN BORDER

Cadillac Bar, 212 S. Flores St. (☎210-223-5533). This restaurant and bar fills to the brim after 9pm with locals dancing between the tables to authentic Tejano music. No cover. Open M-Sa 11am-2am. AmEx/MC/V.

Sam's Burger Joint, 330 E. Grayson St. (☎210-223-2830; www.samsburgerjoint.com). Brightly painted restaurant with outside bar and patio. Tu 10pm poetry slam. Swing dancing M 7pm. Live music W-Sa from 8pm. Cover $5-15. Open M-Th 11am-2am, F-Sa 11am-2am. AmEx/D/MC/V.

The Bonham Exchange, 411 Bonham St. (☎210-271-3811), around the corner from the Alamo. This 1200-person-capacity club is the place to be on weekend nights. Gay-friendly. W college night. Cover up to $20; free before 10pm. Open W-Th 4pm-2:30am, F 4pm-3am, Sa 8pm-3am, Su 8pm-2:30am. MC/V.

Far West Dance Hall, 3030 U.S. 410 NE (☎210-646-9378). Two types of music—country and western. With a mechanical bull and 2 dance floors, you best bring your cowboy hat. Can't two-step? No worries: Th-Sa evenings begin with free lessons at 7pm. 18+. Cover $3-20. Open W-Sa 8pm-3am. AmEx/D/MC/V.

Jim Cullum's Landing, 123 Losoya St. (☎210-223-7266; www.landing.com). Dixieland, bluegrass, jazz, and swing nightly, including the legendary Cullum and his band. Cover $6. Open M-F 4pm-midnight, Sa-Su noon-midnight. D/MC/V.

◼ **APPROACHING CASTROVILLE: 27 MILES**
To leave San Antonio, hop on **I-10** and follow it west—it turns into **U.S. 90.** Follow U.S. 90 W for 27 mi. to Castroville.

CASTROVILLE

Just outside San Antonio, on the sleepy banks of the Medina River, sits Castroville, "the little Alsace of Texas." In the mid-19th century, the town's founder, Henri Castro, a gentleman of French birth, Portuguese ancestry, Jewish faith, and American citizenship, began recruiting settlers from the Rhine Valley and especially from the French province of Alsace. As the French families flocked to their new Texas home, they constructed their houses in the same style as those they had left behind: little cottages with asymmetrical roof lines. Many of these quaint Alsatian-style structures still stand, and you can pick up a pamphlet for a self-guided walking tour at the **Chamber of Commerce,** 802 London St. (On the left when you enter town from U.S.

90 W. ☎830-538-3142. Open M-F 9am-noon and 1-3pm.) At the **Castroville Regional Park,** 816 Alsace St., camping, picnicking, and a public pool are available year-round. You can also swim in the Medina River. (Turn left onto Alsace St. and look for the signs. ☎830-931-4070. Park open daily in summer 5am-10pm; in winter 6am-9pm. Entrance fee $5 per vehicle. Picnic fee $5. Tent sites $10. Cash only.)

The denizens of a little Alsatian cottage serve excellent French cuisine at **La Normandie Restaurant ❹,** 1302 Fiorella St. Favorites include the beef medallions in bernaise sauce with artichoke hearts ($17) and roast duck. (☎830-538-3070. Champagne brunch Su 11:30am-3pm $15. Buffet lunch Tu-Sa 11am-2:30pm. Dinner Th-F 5-9pm, Sa-Su 5-10pm. Reservations required for dinner.) If you'd like to splurge on lodgings, try the **Landmark Inn ❸,** 402 Florence St., where you can stay in a 19th-century building with antique furnishings and few modern distractions. Bikes and canoes for guests. You can also tour the beautiful five-acre grounds or see the small museum. (☎830-931-2133. Museum open daily 8am-6pm; $2. Continental breakfast included. Reservations recommended. Rooms with shared bath $65, with private bath $80. D/MC/V.)

◼ **APPROACHING HONDO: 16 MILES**
Take **U.S. 90 W** toward Hondo.

HONDO. Picturesque gas lamps and old brick buildings line the railroad tracks running through the town of Hondo. Try ▨**El Restaurante Azteca ❷,** 1708 Ave. K. This family-owned restaurant has a no-tip policy—they believe that "good service comes at no extra charge." (From U.S. 90 E, take a left on Ave. K and cross the tracks. ☎830-426-4511. Lunch specials $5. Combination plates $8. Open M-Sa 11am-9pm. AmEx/D/MC/V.) At the **Regency Inn ❷,** 401 U.S. 90 E, you'll find comfortable country living in clean rooms. (☎830-426-3031; www.regencyinn-hondo.com. Reservations recommended. Singles M-F $39, Sa-Su $59; doubles $49/$89. AmEx/D/MC/V.)

◼ **APPROACHING UVALDE: 43 MILES**
Continue on **U.S. 90** to Uvalde.

UVALDE

Uvalde sits at the intersection of the two longest highways in the continental United States (U.S. 90 and U.S. 83). On the east side of town stands the home of lawless lawman Pat Garrett, who killed Billy the Kid. Wild West blood once flowed freely through the heart of the town, but at the turn of the century, Uvalde became as civilized as it once had been wild. The town is proud of its most famous resident, John Nance Garner, the two-term vice president who served under Franklin D. Roosevelt. **The Garner Museum,** 333 N. Park St., preserves his home and displays papers and memorabilia. (Turn right onto Park St. from U.S. 90. ☎ 830-278-5018. Open Tu-Sa 9am-5pm. Free.)

In a log cabin on the east side of town, **Jack's Steakhouse ❸,** 2500 E. Main St., serves good steaks and chicken. (☎ 830-278-9955. Entrees $13-15. Open M-Th and Su 4:30-9:30pm, F-Sa 4:30-11pm. AmEx/D/MC/V.) The large rooms of the **Amber Sky Motel ❸,** 2005 E. Main St., are the cheapest option in Uvalde. All rooms have A/C, TV, microwaves, and fridges. (☎ 830-278-5602. Singles $48; doubles $58. AmEx/D/MC/V.)

⚑ APPROACHING BRACKETVILLE AND FT. CLARK SPRINGS: 40 MILES

Once you leave Uvalde on **U.S. 90,** you enter Texas scrub brush country, and the scenery looks dramatically more like desert. 40 mi. along sit the old white brick buildings of Bracketville.

BRACKETVILLE AND FT. CLARK SPRINGS

Once the support town of Fort Clark, Bracketville had little left to offer after the army withdrew. An impressive **courthouse** stands in the center of town, accessible by turning north onto Rte. 674. The best attraction in Bracketville is **The Alamo Village Movie Location,** 7 mi. from Bracketville on Rte. 674. The Alamo Village was constructed for the 1960 John Wayne epic *Alamo,* and has since provided a backdrop for several other films and TV shows. See the Old West-style buildings and, in the summer, daily music and rodeo shows. Lots of employees have been extras in films—ask them about their experiences with stardom. (☎ 830-563-2580; www.alamovillage.com. Open daily in summer 9am-6pm; in winter 9am-5pm. Shows in summer 10:30am, 12:30, 2:30, 4:30pm. Tickets $10, under 11 $5.)

In contrast to Bracketville, the once-abandoned Ft. Clark base has been revitalized as a residential community, run collectively by an association of homeowners. Driving tours of the former barracks, parade grounds, guardhouses, and depots are available from the **visitors center** if you call them in advance. Otherwise, you can wander around the lovely grounds by yourself. There is also a small museum about the barracks. (☎ 830-563-9150. Visitors center open M-Th 8am-6pm, F 8am-7pm, Sa-Su 8am-1pm. Museum open Sa-Su 1-4pm. $2, children free.) The resort boasts a spacious 🏨**motel ❸** renovated from cavalry barracks. You get access to the spring-fed pool and the chance to sleep in a former barracks without emptying your wallet. All of the rooms have TV and A/C, but lack phones. (☎ 800-937-1590. Rooms in summer $30, in winter $57. AmEx/D/MC/V.)

THE GREAT BARBECUE DEBATE

There are many mysteries surrounding the Lone Star State. Why the big hats? What the heck is tumbleweed? Why exactly can't you mess with Texas? Yet the origin of Texas barbecue may be the most elusive. Here are some theories to gnaw on. Some argue that barbecue came from the Caribbean. Others maintain that the Taino indigenous nation began the barbecue craze with their "barabicoa," made by digging a hole in the ground, filling it up with meat (usually goat), and then covering it with leaves and smouldering coal for a few hours. Still others claim that "barbecue" originates from the French *barbe-et-queue* (head and tail), the places where a pig is skewered before being placed over an open fire. Despite the debate, everyone agrees that barbecue was originally pork—the Texas twist is the beef. In the mid-1800s, German immigrant butchers started substituting beef for pork, taking the idea from Mexican vaqueros. Taino? French? Mexican? German?. . . many Americans in the South don't buy the international connection. They say barbecue or, barbeque, is simply a corruption of BBQ, a term which comes from US roadhouses with pool tables that used to advertise, "Bar, Beer, and Cues" and serve up heaping plates of meat. Which theory is true? Who knows? But be sure to sample plenty of barbecue as you ponder.

[on the menu]

APPROACHING DEL RIO: 32 MILES

From Ft. Clark Springs, continue on **U.S. 90 W** for 32 mi. to Del Rio. Once in town, turn right onto **Veterans Blvd.** to reach motels and restaurants (many of them chains) or turn left to get to the historic downtown. Veterans Blvd. is also the continuation of U.S. 90, so to leave town, you'll head west until the chains fade away and you're back in the open country.

DEL RIO

Many colorful personalities have passed through Del Rio since it was founded in 1883. **The Whitehead Memorial Museum,** 1308 S. Main St., is the burial site of self-made lawman Judge Roy Bean, who held court in the saloon and infamously once fined a dead man for carrying a concealed weapon. Perry House is one of the oldest buildings in town; built as a general store, it later served as a court house, a masonic hall, a church, and a post office. Now a museum, it houses a collection of exhibits about Bean and the town's history. (Go straight when U.S. 90 turns at Gibbs St. ☎830-774-7568. Open Tu-Sa 9am-4:30pm, Su 1-5pm. $5, children $2.) The nearby **San Felipe Springs** was a watering hole for the US Army Camel Corps, a short-lived pre-Civil War cavalry experiment. The town was also home to Dr. John R. Brinkley, whose inventions included goat-gland implants (to improve the sex lives of men) and autographed pictures of Jesus Christ.

Don Marcelinos ❷, 3510 Veterans Blvd., offers Mexican food in a festive environment. Dinner options include combination plates ($6-8) and steaks ($12-15). A buffet ($6) is offered from 11am to 4pm. (☎830-774-2424. Open M-Sa 11am-10pm, Su 10am-8pm. AmEx/D/MC/V.) The **La Siesta Inn ❷,** 2000 Veterans Blvd., has clean, well-furnished rooms at affordable prices. The rooms have TVs with HBO, A/C, and pool access. (☎830-775-6323. Singles $35; doubles $47. AmEx/D/MC/V.)

⚲ DETOUR
AMISTAD NATIONAL RECREATION AREA
On U.S. 90, 8 mi. west of Del Rio, on the right-hand side. Look for the signs.

Amistad ("friendship") is an international recreation area on the US-Mexico border. The reservoir was created by the 6 mi. long dam on the Río Grande, and the water always appears strikingly blue by virtue of the area's limestone rock and exceptionally clear water. Run by the National Park Service, this area is renowned for its watersports, but it also protects prehistoric pictographs (accessible only by boat) and a diverse animal population. You can fish, snorkel, swim, kayak, or canoe in the river, but bring your own equipment. Great touristy photos await if you drive onto the reservoir dam (on your left off U.S. 90, just past the visitors center): between two bronze eagles, you can stand with one foot in Mexico and the other in the US. **Camping ❶** is available at Governor's Landing. (☎830-775-7491; www.nps.gov/amis. Visitors center open daily 8am-5pm. Primitive campsites $4, with water $8. Cash only.)

⚲ DETOUR
SEMINOLE CANYON STATE PARK
Off U.S. 90, 45 mi. past the Amistad Visitors Center.

Inspired by ancient peoples, the museum showcases small, well-executed exhibits about the Native Americans who left pictographs on the canyon walls thousands of years ago. The park features 10 mi. of trails, although a guided tour ($5) is required for the canyon trail, the only way to see the pictographs up close. Otherwise, you can walk a 6 mi. trail to catch a glimpse of some pictographs from across the canyon. (☎432-292-4464. Open daily 9am-5pm. Canyon tour in summer W-Su 10am; in winter 10am and 3pm. Entrance fee $3. Toilets and showers available. Sites $10, with hookup $14.)

⚲ DETOUR
PECOS RIVER CANYON
Off U.S. 90, 3 mi. past Seminole Canyon Park.

The awe-inspiring **Pecos Canyon** was formed by the eponymous river. Take the high road for beautiful views or the low road to get down to the boat launch area. A few feet along the high road is a lovely picnic spot with shelters. From there, you can look down to the old river roads that have now been washed out by floods.

APPROACHING LANGTRY: 62 MILES
From Pecos River Canyon, drive down **U.S. 90.**

LANGTRY. As the erstwhile home of Judge Roy Bean, who embodied "the law west of the Pecos," this town has one of the most colorful histories in the West. Judge Bean dispensed hard liquor and harsh justice—since Langtry had no jail, all offenses were punished by fines payable to Bean. To learn more about this classic Wild West character, stop by the impressive **Judge Roy Bean Visitor Center,** off U.S. 90 at W. Loop 25. The center houses a small museum dedicated to Bean, the original saloon/courtroom, and a labeled cactus garden. There are also state-of-the-art holographic history exhibits designed by Disney. (Turn right off U.S. 90 at the gas station. ☎ 432-291-3340. Free Wi-Fi. Open daily 8am-6pm. Free.)

> ⚠ There are no service stations at night for the next 120 mi., and even during the day you'll have to drive 66 mi. to find anything. Be sure to fill up your tank at the station just past the Amistad Visitors Center.

⛟ APPROACHING SANDERSON: 57 MILES

Head back on **U.S. 90** to reach Sanderson.

SANDERSON. Sanderson bills itself as the "Cactus Capital of Texas." Despite the slogan, there are surprisingly few cacti in the area. Similarly, despite the designation "town," there are surprisingly few people. Until recently, trains changed crews in Sanderson, and local businesses housed and fed resting workers. When crews began to switch at Alpine, businesses folded. Only a few diehards remain in this quasighost town. Get a meal with friendly service at **Mi Tierra Mexicana ❷,** at U.S. 90, on your left as you enter town. A little place run by Delores Rodriguez, Mi Tierra serves "authentic border Tex-Mex." Get a breakfast taco for $2 or a burger and fries for $6. (☎ 432-345-2266. Dinners $7-8. Steaks $11-12. Open daily 6:30am-7:30pm, but sometimes closed for siesta. MC/V.) The accommodations at the **Outback Oasis Motel ❷,** 800 U.S. 90, are spacious and have been remodeled in fine Southwestern style. The pool has been converted into a koi pond, and there's a reptile exhibit by the lobby. (☎ 888-466-8822; www.outbackoasismotel.com. Singles $29-33; doubles $49. AmEx/D/MC/V.)

⛟ APPROACHING MARATHON: 52 MILES

Continue 52 mi. on **U.S. 90** through mesa-topped mountain grasslands to Marathon.

MARATHON. Marathon is the tiny, touristy, expensive northern gateway town to Big Bend National Park. The cheapest place to stay is

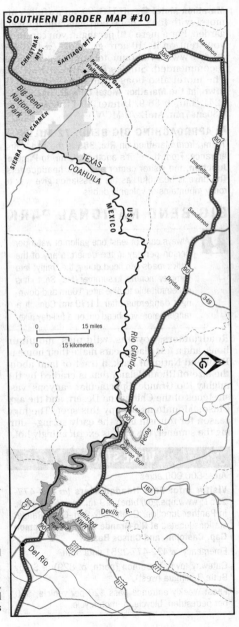

SOUTHERN BORDER MAP #10

0 — 15 miles
0 — 15 kilometers

SOUTHERN BORDER

Marathon Motel ❸, off U.S. 90, an awfully cute motel with faux-adobe cottages and a lovely garden. For a mere $10 per night, you can stake your tent on its 10-acre grounds. (☎432-386-4241; www.marathonmotel.com. Reservations recommended. Singles $60. AmEx/D/MC/V.) The motel also boasts the cheapest eats in town, at the **Marathon Motel Cafe ❷**. (☎432-386-4241. Lunch $6-9. Dinner $9-11. Open daily 6:30am-7pm. AmEx/D/MC/V.)

⚑ APPROACHING BIG BEND: 72 MILES

72 mi. from Marathon on **Rte. 385** is the park's first entrance. From there, it's another 30 mi. to **Panther Junction**, the visitor center and park headquarters. The drive is beautiful, as the grasslands give way to rocky mountains of volcanic debris.

BIG BEND NATIONAL PARK

> ❗ Always carry at least one gallon of water per person per day in the desert. Many of the park's roads can flood during the "rainy" late summer months. In summer (May-Sept.) it is uncomfortable to hike after 10am and downright dangerous after 11:30am. Consult a ranger before you head out on a full-day hike.

Roadrunners, coyotes, wild pigs, mountain lions, and a few black bears make their home in Big Bend National Park, a tract of land about the size of Rhode Island that is cradled by the mighty Río Grande. Spectacular canyons, vast stretches of the Chihuahua Desert, and the airy Chisos Mountains occupy this spot. The high season for tourism is in the early spring—during the summer, the park is excruciatingly hot.

VITAL STATS

Area: 800,000 acres

Visitor Info: Park Headquarters (☎432-477-2251; www.nps.gov/bibe), 29 mi. inside the park, in Panther Junction. Open daily 8am-6pm. Ranger stations located at **Río Grande Village, Persimmon Gap, Castolon, and Chisos Basin.**

Emergency: ☎432-477-2251 until 5pm.

Gateway town: Marathon (north; p. 829) or Study Butte/Terlingua (west).

Fees: Weekly entrance pass $20 per vehicle; $10 per pedestrian, bicycle, or motorcycle.

◧ GETTING AROUND. There are only five paved roads in the park. Of these, the best sightseeing is along the **Ross Maxwell Scenic Drive,** a 30 mi. paved route from the western edge of the Chisos Mountains that leads down to the Río Grande and Santa Elena Canyon. The 8 mi. drive that winds its way up into the Chisos Basin is also quite rewarding. However, the most spectacular drives in the park are unimproved, accessible only to 4WD jeeps and trucks: **River Road** (51 mi.) skirts along the Río Grande from Castolon to the Río Grande Village, and the 26 mi. **Old Ore Road** travels along the western edge of the Sierra del Caballo Muerto. Those interested in driving the backroads of Big Bend should purchase the guide to backcountry roads ($2) at the visitors center.

⚶ OUTDOORS. Big Bend encompasses several hundred miles of hiking trails, ranging from 30min. nature walks to backpacking trips of several days. Pick up the *Hiker's Guide to Big Bend* pamphlet ($2), available at Panther Junction. Free nature hikes are led by park rangers throughout the year. Inquire at any visitors center for schedules. In the middle of the park are the Chisos Mountains, which provide cooler hiking and camping. The Chisos are also home to a number of species that are found nowhere else in North America, such as the drooping juniper and the white-tailed deer. The Chisos offer several short hikes. The **Lost Mine Trail** (4¾ mi. round-trip) takes about 3hr. to complete and is the best in the park. It leads up somewhat steep switchbacks to an amazing view of the desert and the Sierra de Carmen in Mexico. Pick up a guide ($1) at the trail head. Also in the Chisos, **Emory Peak** (9 mi.) is an intense hike, and the easier **Santa Elena Canyon** trail (1¾ mi.) ambles along the Rio Grande.

Though upstream damming has decreased the river's pace, rafting is still big fun on the Río Grande. **Far-Flung Outdoor Center,** on Rte. 170, 2 mi. south of Rte. 118, in Terlingua, organizes one- to seven-day trips. (☎432-371-2633 or 800-839-7238; www.farflungoutdoorcenter.com. From $125 per person.) Across Hwy. 170, **Big Bend River Tours** rents canoes and inflatable kayaks and organizes rafting and paddling trips. (☎915-371-3033 or 800-545-4240; www.bigbendrivertours.com. Canoes $45 per day. Kayaks $35 per day.)

FOOD. The **Chisos Mountains Lodge ❸**, in the Chisos Basin, contains the only restaurant in the park, which serves three square meals per day. (☎432-477-2291. Lunch sandwiches $5-10. Dinner entrees $10-17. Open daily 7-10am, 11:30am-4pm, and 5:30-8pm. AmEx/D/MC/V.) At **Los Paisanos ❷**, on Rte. 170, get delicious, authentic Mexican food. (☎432-371-2101. Lunch $5-7. Dinner $7-10. Open M-Sa 11am-2pm and 5-9pm. Cash only.) **Starlight Theater Bar and Grill ❷**, off Rte. 170 in Terlingua, next to Ms. Tracy's, has healthy portions of Tex-Mex ($5-11), live music, and an indoor pool. (☎432-371-2326. Open M-F and Su 5pm-midnight, Sa 5pm-1am. Kitchen closes 10pm. AmEx/MC/V.)

ACCOMMODATIONS. The **Chisos Mining Co. Motel ❷**, on Rte. 170, west of the junction with Rte. 118, is the closest budget motel. (☎432-371-2254. Singles $47; doubles from $60; 6-person cabins $67-86. AmEx/D/MC/V.) There are three developed campsites within the park. The **Chisos Basin Campground ❶**, at 5400 ft., has sites with running water and flush toilets; it stays cooler than the other campgrounds in the summer. (☎877-444-6777; www.reserve-usa.com. Water and flush toilets. Sites $10.) The **Río Grande Village Campground ❶** has tent sites and an RV park with 25 full hookups near the only showers in the park. The RV park at Río Grande Village has 25 full hookups (☎877-444-6777; www.reserveusa.com. Tent sites $14; RV sites $14.50.) **Backcountry camping** is also available with a backcountry permit ($10) obtained at the Panther Junction Visitors Center.

APPROACHING ALPINE: 80 MILES

Rte. 118 runs west out of the park. Almost immediately you pass through the tiny, tourist-oriented town of Study Butte. If you're ready to press on to Alpine, stay on Rte. 118 as it curves northward for 80 mi. The desert mountains slowly give way to green shrublands, grassy foothills, and picturesque mountains. This part of Texas doesn't receive enough water to support tree growth, but occasional storms bring enough rain for grass to blanket the ground.

ALPINE. With a population of 5000, Alpine is the big metropolis in this area. High above town on the eastern hills, **Sul Ross State University** is Alpine's main attraction and has one of the nation's best rodeo teams. Sul Ross also houses the tiny **Museum of the Big Bend**, a collection of

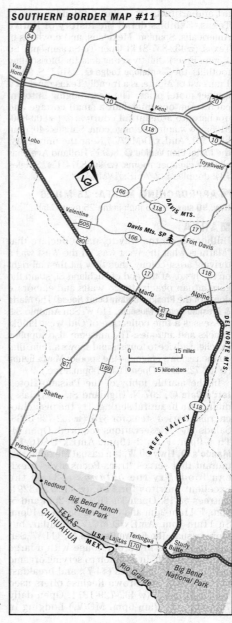

SOUTHERN BORDER MAP #11

art and artifacts from the Big Bend region of Texas. Exhibits detail the history of Native Americans, Spanish, Mexicans, and cowboys in Texas. (☎432-837-8143. Open Tu-Sa 9am-5pm, Su 1-5pm. Free.) Quietly set against the blossoming foothills, the ◪Antelope Lodge ❷, 2310 U.S. 90 W, 1 mi. east of Alpine, is a friendly Texas ranch at a budget motel price. The best lodging in town, each room occupies half a small cottage and opens onto a beautiful courtyard. (☎800-880-8106; www.antelopelodge.com. Singles $40; doubles $61. AmEx/D/MC/V.) Near the university, the **Motel Bien Venido** ❷, 809 E. Holland Ave., has slightly cheaper rooms. (☎432-837-3454. Singles $34; doubles $42. AmEx/D/MC/V.)

◪ APPROACHING MARFA: 25 MILES
Hwy. 90 slows to 55 mph in the 25 mi. to Marfa.

MARFA
Billboards on the way to Marfa declare that "Marfa is what the West was." If the West was a thriving artist colony, then they hit the nail right on the head. At the end of Highland St. stand the gargantuan peach stucco walls and elaborate dome of the **Presidio County Court House.** The **Marfa & Presidio County Museum,** 110 W. San Antonio St., possesses a fine collection of Old West knick-knacks and antiques. The museum also supplies excellent advice to tourists and shows a 7min. film on the region's enigma—the spooky Marfa lights. (☎432-729-4140. Open Tu-Sa 1-5pm. Free.)

In the marble lobby of the Paisano Hotel, **Jett's Cafe** ❸, 207 N. Highland St., has classy dining in a beautiful setting. Try the pistachio-encrusted fried steak for $16. (☎432-729-3838. Salads $6-7. Reservations required. Open M-Th 5-9pm, F-Su 2-10pm. AmEx/D/MC/V.) **Mando's** ❷, Hwy 90 W, is a casual Mexican restaurant that serves "trans-Pecos style" Mexican food. Try the *botanas* ($3) or the excellent burritos for $4-6. (☎432-729-3291. Entrees $5-18. Open Tu-Th 11am-2pm and 5-9pm, F 11am-2pm and 5-10pm, Sa noon-10pm, Su 11am-5pm. AmEx/D/MC/V.) Similar, but more casual, **The Brown Recluse** ❷, 111 W. San Antonio St., is in an old house with a large patio and porch. In addition to serving organic coffee, breakfast plates ($4-7), and breakfast burritos ($2), The Brown Recluse offers used books for sale. (☎432-729-1811. Open daily 7am-2pm, Sa 7am-6pm. MC/V.) Lodging in

Marfa will cost you dearly wherever you hang your hat, but try the **Riata Inn** ❸, Hwy 90 E, which has big, airy rooms. (☎432-729-2900. Pool. Free Wi-Fi. Rooms $54. AmEx/D/MC/V.)

◪ APPROACHING VAN HORN: 78 MILES
Continue west on **U.S. 90** for 34 mi. through tiny Valentine, where empty buildings line the highway. 5 mi. outside Valentine sits the avant-garde **Prada Marfa** (p. 833). Follow U.S. 90 through another bizarre project: **Lobo,** a ghost town/Internet venture (www.lobo-texas.com) that lures denizens of cyberspace into buying citizenship in a collection of ramshackle buildings with promises to turn the "town" into a rewarding vacation site. As of yet, recreational possibilities seem rather limited. 38 mi. from Valentine, the highway rolls into Van Horn, first real town in 72 mi. To get to motels, gas, and groceries, take a left on **Broadway,** the town's main drag.

VAN HORN. Van Horn was originally established as a support center for area ranchers. If you're looking for a bite to eat and the plentiful fast-food options aren't up your alley, try **Papa's Pantry** ❷, 515 Van Horn Dr. The little roadside grill, right on U.S. 90 as you leave town, serves up everything from burritos ($2-4) to steak and chicken dinners ($6-10). Chicken-fried steak ($8) is their specialty. (☎432-283-2302. Open M-Sa 7am-9pm. MC/V.) There are dozens of budget motels along Broadway Ave. that are inexplicably cheaper than the motels in any neighboring cities. The recently remodeled **Village Inn Motel** ❷, 403 W. Broadway Ave., offers good value, with microwaves, fridges, TV, A/C, and continental breakfast included. (☎432-283-7213. Singles $25; doubles $45. AmEx/D/MC/V.)

◪ APPROACHING GUADALUPE MOUNTAINS NATIONAL PARK: 69 MILES
To continue on to Guadalupe Mountains National Park, take a right on **Broadway** in Van Horn, and make an immediate left onto **Rte. 54.** Follow Rte. 54 for 53 mi. along a lonely stretch of asphalt until it merges with **Rte. 180/62.** Continue another 16 mi. on Rte. 180 to the well-marked entrance to Guadalupe Mountains National Park.

When Rte. 54 merges with Rte. 180/62, you re-enter the Central Time Zone, where it is 1hr. later.

GUADALUPE MOUNTAINS NATIONAL PARK

The Guadalupe Mountains are the highest and most remote of the major Texas ranges. The peaks are remnants of the ancient Capitan reef that formed 265 million years ago along the edge of a vast inland sea and covered much of what is now western Texas and southeastern New Mexico. After the sea receded, the reef was buried under layers of sediment until major block faulting and erosion excavated and exposed the petrified remains 26 million years ago. Drivers can glimpse the park's best sights from Rte. 180/62: El Capitan, a 2000 ft. high limestone cliff; and Guadalupe Peak, the highest point in Texas at 8749 ft.

VITAL STATS

Area: 86,500 acres.

Visitor Info: Headquarters Visitor Center (☎915-828-3251; www.nps.gov/gumo), in Pine Springs. Accessible by U.S. 62/180 between Carlsbad and El Paso. Open daily 8am-4:30pm.

Gateway town: Carlsbad (p. 836).

Fees: $3 per vehicle.

Ⅎ GETTING AROUND. Beautiful roadside vistas notwithstanding, the Guadalupe Mountains National Park isn't car-friendly. The road to McKittrick Canyon Visitors Center is the only paved road that strays far from Rte. 180. The **Williams Ranch Rd.** ventures deepest into the park, but this trail has soft sands and rocky sections that are only passable by 4x4, high-ground-clearance vehicles. The 7¼ mi. journey lies behind two locked gates, the keys to which may be checked out free of charge at the visitors center. The desert trail ends in Bone Canyon at the historic Williams Ranchhouse.

 DID YOU KNOW? Hikers in the high Guadalupe Mountains are treading on the same rock that forms the underground Carlsbad Caverns.

Ⅺ OUTDOORS. There are many rewarding day hikes that highlight the park's best features. A beautiful, moderate hike is **Devil's Hall** (4¼ mi.), which winds through the desert and then descends into Pine Springs Canyon amongst deer, velvet ash, and juniper. **Smith Spring Trail** (2¼ mi.) is a short, easy trail. **McKittrick Canyon Trail** (6¾ mi.) is the most popular hike in the park, meandering through McKittrick Stream. The **Bowl Loop** (9 mi.) gives hikers a chance to see the flora and fauna of the Guadalupe high country. **Guadalupe Peak** (8½ mi.), at 8749 ft., is the highest mountain in Texas and the trail that runs up it is strenuous (3,000 ft. of elevation gain) but marked by outstanding views. If you've got more time in the park, one lengthy hike (24 mi.) follows the **Tejas Trail** from Pine Springs all the way to the Dog Canyon Campground and then returns via the **Bush Mountain Trail.**

DESERT CHIC

Valentine, Texas (population 217) can now boast a Prada boutique that rivals any in Paris or New York. The grand opening, on October 1, 2005, was greeted by locals with, um, confusion. The boutique, Prada Marfa, is the new minimalist sculpture by Germany-based artists Michael Elmgreen and Ingar Dragset, constructed for a cool $100,000 and boasting hand-crafted Prada heels and bags from the 2005 Prada fall collection. Made of biodegradable materials, the adobe building will eventually melt back in to the earth, but not soon enough for Valentine residents. Locals were not impressed by the minimalist piece of art or the available products. Within 3 days of the opening, the store's glass windows were smashed, the merchandise was stolen, and the word "dumb" was spray-painted all over the walls. No arrests were made. Perhaps locals were protesting the boutique's name; the artists chose to name it Marfa, instead of Valentine, in honor of the famous artist's colony nearby. When asked why he built the sculpture on his land, the owner said, "There's no cattle or horses or anything, so I just thought 'why not.'" Whether you are an art connoisseur pondering the globalization of commerce or just looking for an American oddity, this bizarre boutique is a must-see.

🍴🛏 FOOD AND ACCOMMODATIONS. The **Nickel Creek Cafe ❷**, 5 mi. north of Pine Springs toward Carlsbad, is the only restaurant near the park. The friendly owner serves Mexican food ($4-7), burgers ($6), and beer. (☎432-828-3295. Open M-Sa 7am-2pm. Cash only.) The park's two beautiful campgrounds, **Pine Springs ❶**, just past park headquarters, and **Dog Canyon ❶**, at the north end of the park, have water and bathrooms but no hookups or showers. Wood and charcoal fires are not allowed. When making your choice, keep in mind that Dog Canyon is nearly 100 mi. from Pine Springs and is nowhere near the park's highlights. You'll need a hammer to peg down your tent in the hard-packed desert ground. (☎915-828-3251. Reservations for groups of 10-20 only. Tent sites $8. Cash only.) Free **backcountry camping** permits are available at the visitors center. None of the backcountry sites in the park have water or toilets.

 New Mexico is in the Mountain time zone, so turn your watch back 1hr.

🚗 APPROACHING WHITE'S CITY: 38 MILES The 38 mi. on **Rte. 180** between Guadalupe Mountains National Park and the Carlsbad Caverns is also known as the **Texas Mountain Trail.** As you leave, look westward to see the monolithic **El Capitan** peak thrusting out from the heart of the mountains, a 2000 ft. cliff formed by a Permian limestone reef deposit.
   16 mi. from the Guadalupe Mountains National Park Visitors Center, you will pass into New Mexico.

Land of Enchantment
NEW MEXICO
Welcomes You!

WHITE'S CITY. The sign at the state line promises that New Mexico is the land of enchantment, but the first "city" on this route is anything but. To reach Carlsbad Caverns, you must make a left through White's City, which should perhaps better be called "The Caverns Tourist Trap." White's City consists of two hotels, an RV park, a general store (filled with souvenirs), a museum, and no real populace aside from the tourists. The **Million Dollar Museum**, 17 Carlsbad Caverns Hwy., under the grocery store, is a collection of antiques from the 19th and 20th centuries. The highlights are four grotesque skulls and two 6000-year-old mummies believed to have been natives of the area. (☎505-785-2291. Open daily 7am-8pm. $4, ages 6-12 $2.50, ages 5 and under free.) If you're too hungry to make it to Carlsbad, grab a bite at **Velvet Garter/Jack's Restaurant ❸**, 17 Carlsbad Caverns Hwy., which serves burgers, ribs, steaks, and Tex-Mex (entrees $13-21) in the evening and breakfast staples ($5-7) in the mornings. (☎505-785-2291. Open daily 7am-2pm and 4-9:30pm. AmEx/D/MC/V.)

BORDER CROSSING

I was cruising north up Rte. 118 near Big Bend National Park, TX, when I was pulled up short by orange cones and police cars blocking the road. It was hot. Everyone looked annoyed. I pulled up and got out. "What's going on?" I asked one of the officers pacing back and forth. "This guy," he said, motioning to a man standing with his hands on the hood of his car, "tried to jump the border." I nodded and suddenly remembered that I was in the borderlands. I inched closer to the Border Patrol Officers and listened in. They berated the Mexican man, asking, "Why were you driving here? You have no green card!" "Yeah, I know," he responded, "But I'm not sneaking in. I've been here almost one year working. This is my car." "But you have no insurance or registration." "Yeah. I know." The whole thing was going nowhere, and the cops looked more agitated than the perpetrator. I went back to my car and joined the small group of spectators who had gathered waiting for the road to clear. One, it turned out, was a county judge from the area. He told me he had five men just like this one sitting in county jail right now, and he had no idea what to do with them. If it was up to him, he said, he'd just scare them and send them back. A 22-year old kid, who'd been through his courtroom a month ago, had been given a translator for the court proceedings and was told to plead guilty. They didn't tell him that they'd found traces of pot in his clothing, and he was charged with crossing with an

CARLSBAD CAVERNS NATIONAL PARK

Imagine the surprise of European explorers in the middle of the New Mexico desert when 250,000 bats appeared out of nowhere. Following the swarm led to the discovery of the Carlsbad Caverns. By 1926, the National Park Service had built trails and installed lights, and colonies of tourists were competing with the bats for space in the caves. Carlsbad Caverns National Park contains one of the world's largest and oldest known cave systems, and even the most experienced spelunker will be struck by its phenomenal geological formations.

VITAL STATS

Area: 47,000 acres

Visitor Info: Visitors Center (☎ 505-785-2232 or 800-967-2283; www.nps.gov/cave). Open daily June to mid-Aug. 8am-7pm; mid-Aug. to May 8am-5:30pm.

Gateway towns: White's City, Carlsbad (p. 836).

Fees: Entrance $6, ages 6-15 $3. Audio tour $3.

G GETTING AROUND. To check out the oft-forgotten aboveground areas of the park, the only way to go is the **Walnut Canyon Desert Drive,** a 9½ mi., one-way auto tour on dirt roads (passable to all vehicles). A road guide is available at the beginning of the road (½ mi. from the visitors center). The guide mostly points out plant features and the surface geology of the park, taking note of the fossilized coral reefs that cover the area. The road offers excellent views of the basin below the park, and follows a creek bed back to the main road.

⚠ OUTDOORS. The most accessible section of the caverns is the **Big Room,** which can be entered at any time either by the **Natural Entrance** (a 1 mi. steeply sloped entrance into the cave) or by elevator. Self-guided audio tours are available. The 1¼ mi. trail, which passes by beautiful naturally lit formations, generally takes 1-2hr. to complete. Those with severe asthma may have difficulty breathing the moist cave air. Guided tours in the Big Room include a lantern tour though the Left Hand Tunnel and a climbing tour of the Lower Cave. The guided **King's Palace Tour** passes through four of the cave's lowest rooms and some of the most awesome subterranean sights. (Natural entrance open daily June to mid-Aug. 8:30am-3:30pm; mid-Aug. to May 8:30am-2pm. Big Room open daily June to mid-Aug. 8:30am-5pm; mid-Aug. to May 8:30am-3:30pm. $6, ages 15 and under free. Audio guide $3. Left Hand Tunnel tour $7. Lower Cave Tour M-F, $20. King's Palace Tour $8, ages 6-15 $4; reservations required.) Plan your visit to the caverns for late afternoon and stick around for the **bat flight.** Watching the hungry bats storm out of the cavern at dusk is a major tourist draw but hasn't been quite as impressive in the last few years; the colony, which once numbered 300,000-500,000, has

illegal substance. They sentenced him to 2 years. "Poor kid," said the judge, "he thought he was going home. He cried and cried. I wouldn't scare them that bad or anything." Then he laughed: "When he gets out, I've gotta make a run for it! He thinks it's me who sold him down the river...but I didn't." A Chicana lady next to us joined in, nodding: "You just have to do what the law says. They're dangerous when they come in here...mostly because they get scared. Why doesn't their President stop them?" "Maybe he doesn't have much control?" I suggested. She nodded, "Well, anyway, they'll overrun us if we let them all in." The cops were getting increasingly frustrated. "*No comprendo?*" one of them asked, despite the fact that the culprit had been conversing fluently for the last 30 minutes. "You can't drive. You have to leave us the car." The Mexican man just stared into the desert. The cops began waving the rest of us through. When it was my turn, he barely looked at me, "American citizen?" "No," I replied, making him shudder. "I'm Canadian," I hastily remarked. "Oh! Great!" He was visibly relieved and said, "Go on through. Have a nice day!" I passed the checkpoint without so much as flashing my passport.

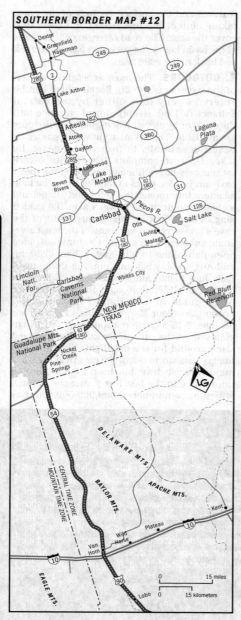

SOUTHERN BORDER MAP #12

(map labels:) Dexter, Greenfield, Hagerman, 249, 285, 2, Lake Arthur, 82, Artesia, Atoka, Dayton, 285, Lakewood, Lake McMillan, Seven Rivers, 360, Laguna Plata, 62/180, 31, Pecos R., 128, Salt Lake, 137, Carlsbad, Otis, Loving, Malaga, Lincoln Natl. For., Carlsbad Caverns National Park, Whites City, Red Bluff Reservoir, NEW MEXICO, TEXAS, Guadalupe Mts. National Park, 62/180, Nickel Creek, Pine Springs, DELAWARE MTS., 54, BAYLOR MTS., CENTRAL TIME ZONE, MOUNTAIN TIME ZONE, APACHE MTS., Kent, Plateau, 10, Wild Horse, Van Horn, 10, 90, EAGLE MTS., Lobo, 0 15 miles, 0 15 kilometers

SOUTHERN BORDER *(vertical side tab)*

dwindled to 24,000 because of pollution and drought. (May-Oct. daily just before sunset.)

Tours of the undeveloped **Slaughter Canyon Cave** offer a more rugged spelunking experience. The parking lot is 23 mi. down Rte. 418, an unpaved road several miles south of the park's main entrance on U.S. 62/180. The cave entrance is a steep, strenuous ½ mi. walk from the lot. Ranger-led tours traverse difficult terrain; there are no paved trails or handrails. (2hr. tours June-Aug. 2 per day; Sept.-May Sa-Su only. $15, ages 6-15 $7.50. Call the visitors center at least 2 days ahead to reserve. Bring a flashlight.) Tours of **Hall of the White Giant** and **Spider Cave** require crawling and climbing through tight passages. These tours are not for claustrophobes. (4hr. 1 per week. Call at least a month in advance to reserve. $20.) **Backcountry hiking** is permitted aboveground, but a free permit (available at the visitors center), a map, and massive quantities of water are required.

▛ **ACCOMMODATIONS.** There are no accommodations in Carlsbad Caverns National Park, but camping is close by in Guadalupe Mountains National Park (p. 833) and motels line the street in the town of Carlsbad.

▛ **APPROACHING CARLSBAD: 21 MILES**
Exit the park and head north along **U.S. 62/180** until you reach Carlsbad.

CARLSBAD

In 1899, townsfolk decided to name their riverside agricultural settlement after the Karlsbad Spa in the modern Czech Republic, hoping to attract tourists to the area's natural springs. In a weird twist of fate, their wish came true when the splendors of the Carlsbad Caverns became widely known in the 1920s. Courtesy of **Carlsbad Cruiselines,** you can rent paddleboats and kayaks or take a 45min. narrated tour aboard the George Washington Historic Paddleboat. (☎505-807-8313. Open Mar. to Labor Day M-F noon-8pm, Sa-Su 10am-8pm. All rentals $10 per hour. Paddleboat tour $4 per person.) If you're in town for the evening, don't miss a movie at the **Fiesta Drive-In ❶**, 401 W. Fiesta (look for signs on Canal St.). Do it 1950s-style by ordering dinner from their concession stand. (☎505-885-4126; www.fiestadrivein.com. 3 screens playing 3 movies nightly 8pm. $4, W $2.)

Rules and helpful hints pervade the **No Whiner Diner ❸**, 1801 S. Canal St., a classic roadside stop. The menu suggests you tell your waitress what kind of bread you want because "she can't read minds," while the sign out front gives civic advice: "bad officials are elected by good citizens who don't vote." Don't whine, and you'll enjoy huge dinner plates, pastas, and sandwiches. (☎505-239-2815. Entrees $8.50. Open Tu-Th 11am-2pm and 5-8pm, F-Sa 11am-2pm and 5-9pm. AmEx/D/MC/V.) **Mi Casita ❷**, 309 N. Main St., serves great New Mexican food and is often so packed with locals that you'll need to take your meal to the nearby beach. (☎505-628-1393. Huge burritos $2.50-2.75. Open Tu-F 10:30am-2pm and 4-8pm, Sa 7am-1pm. MC/V.) **Red Chimney Pit BBQ ❸**, 817 N. Canal St., does the best barbecue dinners in town ($6.50-9.50). They also serve amazing fruit cobblers ($3) for dessert. (☎505-885-8744. Open M-F 11am-2pm and 4:30-8:30pm. MC/V.) **Stage Coach Inn ❷**, 1819 S. Canal St., is the best of the budget motels and features an outdoor pool, laundry, and clean, comfortable rooms. (☎505-887-1148. Singles $36; doubles $53. AmEx/D/MC/V.) The **Driftwood Motel ❷**, 844 S. Canal St., has some of the cheapest, most respectable accommodations in town. (☎505-887-6522. Singles $35; doubles $45. AmEx/D/MC/V.) If you didn't get a spot at Guadalupe Mountains National Park, you can pay to pitch a tent in the **Carlsbad RV Park and Campground ❶**, 4301 National Parks Hwy., 4 mi. south of town. (☎505-885-6333; www.carlsbadrvpark.com. Tent sites $16.50; cabins $32. AmEx/D/MC/V.)

⚐ APPROACHING ARTESIA: 37 MILES
To leave Carlsbad, head north on **Canal St.** as it as it veers westward and becomes **Rte. 285.** Follow Rte. 285 for 35 mi. to Artesia.

ARTESIA

The city's slogan is "Artesia: Smells like Success." This might seem funny to a tourist who is struck by the stench of oil refineries but Artesians mean it literally: oil is the town's *raison d'être*. Even the name of the town comes from the nearby Artesian oil wells. On the left as you enter town, the **Visitors Center**, 107 N. 1st. St., has info and hosts the **Dairy Museum**, a room dedicated to Artesia's other main export. (☎505-746-2744. Open M-F 9am-5pm.)

The **Wellhead Restaurant ❸**, 332 W. Main St., has everything an oil tycoon could want, including tasty sandwiches, country-fried steak, catfish, salads, and handmade burgers ($6-7). Try the homemade beers by brewmaster Diane Riley at the on-site microbrewery; $3.50 buys you a sampler of

three of her favorites. (☎505-746-0640; www.thewellhead.com. Entrees $10-13. Open daily 11am-2pm and 5-9pm. Pub open M-Sa 11am-midnight, Su 11am-10pm. AmEx/D/MC/V.) For a place to relax, try **Jahva House ❷**, 105 N. 5th St., which has a modern decor, late hours, and great espresso. Try the Artesian sandwich ($6.50) with mesquite-smoked turkey, guacamole, and havarti. (☎505-746-9494; www.thejahvahouse.com. Open M-F 7am-10:30pm, Sa 8am-10:30pm. AmEx/D/MC/V.) On the way into town, the **Starlite Motel ❷**, 1018 S. 1st St., offers recently remodeled rooms. (☎505-746-9834. Continental breakfast included. Singles $40. AmEx/D/MC/V.)

⚐ APPROACHING ROSWELL: 40 MILES
Follow **1st St.** out of Artesia, where it turns back into **U.S. 285** and takes you to Roswell.

ROSWELL

Roswell was an otherwise small town known only for its dairy industry when life was unexpectedly shaken up by extraterrestrials. The fascination began in July 1947, when an alien spacecraft reportedly crashed on a ranch. The official press release reported that the military had recovered pieces of a "flying saucer," but a retraction followed the next day—the wreckage, the government claimed, was actually a weather balloon. The incident was the birth of Roswell's permanent craze and the beginning of multiple government-conspiracy theories. Today, traveling skeptics and alien enthusiasts have made tourism a far more lucrative industry than dairy cows. Contrary to expectations, however, aliens do not land on every corner, and there is a disappointing lack of spacecraft debris littering the highways into town.

VITAL STATS
Population: 45,000
Visitor Info: Roswell Visitors Center, 426 N. Main St. at 5th St. (☎505-624-7704; http://roswell-usa.com). Free Wi-Fi. Open M-F 8:30am-5:30pm, Sa-Su 10am-3pm.
Internet Access: Roswell Visitors Center (see above). Roswell Public Library, 301 N. Pennsylvania Ave. (☎505-622-7101). Open M-Tu 9am-9pm, W-Sa 9am-6pm, Su 2-6pm. Free.
Post Office: 5904 S. Main St. (☎505-347-2262). Open M-F 8:30am-1pm and 2-4:30pm. **Postal Code:** 88201.

GETTING AROUND. U.S. 70/U.S.380 runs through the middle of town, with intersections at **Sycamore Ave., Union Ave., Main St. (U.S. 285),** and **Atkinson Ave. (Rte. 93).** The main streets parallel to the highway are **Country Club Rd., College Blvd.,** and **8th St.** to the north, and **McGaffey St., Poe St.,** and **Brasher Rd.** to the south. Numbered streets begin a bit south of the highway and ascend heading north. Roswell has some close encounters of the natural kind, with a large park and trail system that runs parallel to **2nd St.**

SIGHTS. If you're convinced that the truth is out there, start looking at the **International UFO Museum,** 114 N. Main St., at the corner of 2nd St. This museum is the centerpiece of Roswell's UFO-oriented downtown. Surprisingly no-nonsense, it displays timelines, photographs, signed affidavits, and newspaper clippings from the historic incident. (☎505-625-9495. Open daily 9am-5pm. Suggested donation $2.) For something less alien, stroll through the **Historical Center of the Southeastern New Mexico,** 200 N. Lea Ave., which is housed in a beautiful 1910 home and tells the history of Roswell and the county. (☎505-622-8333. Open daily 1-4pm. Free.)

FOOD AND ACCOMMODATIONS. You've got to give the management props for the flashy outdoor decor at **Not of This World Coffee Bistro ❶,** 209 N. Main St.; they've got the alien theme down. Inside, the bistro is fairly normal and has good sandwiches ($5-6), baked goods ($1-3), and coffee. Try the heavenly turtle latte ($4), with chocolate, caramel, hazelnuts, and whipped cream. (☎505-627-0077. F live music 8-10pm. Open M-Th 7:30am-5:30pm, F 7-11pm. Sa 8:30am-5:30pm. D/MC/V.) **Cattle Baron ❹,** 1112 N. Main St., is famous across New Mexico for its steaks ($15-24), though the pasta, chicken, and fish are superb as well. (☎505-622-2465. Lunch $7-9. Entrees $13-24. Open M-Th 11am-9:30pm, F-Sa 11am-10pm, Su 11am-9pm. AmEx/D/MC/V.)

Definitely the best place to crash in Roswell, the recently remodeled rooms in the **Budget Inn ❶,** 2200 W. 2nd St., all come with refrigerators, microwaves, A/C, HBO, coffee, and pool access. (☎800-806-7030. Singles $28; doubles $45. AmEx/D/MC/V.) Nearby, the **Belmont Hotel ❷,** 2100 W. 2nd St., has smallish rooms that are clean and well-furnished. (☎505-623-4522. Singles $30. AmEx/D/MC/V.) On the same drag, **The Crane Motel ❷,** 1212 W. 2nd St., has an awesome illumi-nated sign and clean, comfy rooms with fridges, microwaves, A/C, TV, and pool access. (☎505-623-1293. Singles $34; doubles $45. AmEx/D/MC/V.) The **Bottomless Lakes State Park ❶,** Union Ave., has camping along the edges of seven pristine lakes formed when limestone caves collapsed and filled with water. (12 mi. east of Roswell on U.S. 70/U.S. 380; head south on Rte. 409. ☎505-624-6058. Park open daily 6am-9pm. Visitors center open daily June-Aug. 9am-6pm; Sept.-May 8am-5pm. Entrance fee $3 per vehicle. Tent sites $10; with full hookup $18. MC/V.)

APPROACHING LINCOLN: 68 MILES
From Roswell, take **2nd St.** westbound as it turns into **U.S. 380.** After 50 mi. you'll pass through the hamlet of Hondo, which has gas and minimal eats. When the road splits 1 mi. from Hondo, veer right, staying on U.S. 380, now called the **Billy the Kid Scenic Byway.** Follow the road 10 mi. down into the town of Lincoln.

LINCOLN. The town of Lincoln, first settled by Mexicans around the turn of the 19th century and then later by Americans in the 1850s, put the wild in Wild West. Its (in)famous inhabitants have included Kit Carson; Victorio, the last powerful Apache chief; cattle baron John Chisum; and Lew Wallace, author of *Ben Hur.* Perhaps the two most well-known residents of Lincoln, thanks to Hollywood and dime-store novels, are Sheriff Pat Garrett and his nemesis, William H. Bonney (a.k.a. Billy the Kid). These two lived at a time when Lincoln was so lawless that from 1876 to 1879 the area erupted in combat known as the "Lincoln County War." The town itself looks much as it did back at the time of the county war and its buildings have been maintained in close-to-original state. Five of the buildings are open to the public and feature museum-quality exhibits preserving the Lincoln of yore. The **Lincoln State Monument Visitors Center and Museum,** on your right as you enter town, tells the story of the county war and sells a combination ticket ($7) that includes the other buildings and museums. Make sure to see the **Tunstall Museum** and the **Courthouse,** featuring the bullet hole that, according to legend, Billy made when he escaped Garrett's jail. (☎505-653-4025. Open daily 8:30am-4:30pm. Single-site tickets $3.50, under 16 free. Cash only.)

APPROACHING SMOKEY THE BEAR STATE PARK: 7 MILES
Follow **U.S. 380** out of Lincoln as it winds its way to the junction with **Rte. 48.** The park is to the left.

SMOKEY THE BEAR STATE PARK. The gateway village to the park is the village of **Capitan,** where half the establishments are named for Smokey. The quaint log cabin at the **Smokey the Bear State Park** displays a large collection of Smokey memorabilia. The original Smokey is buried within view of the mountain where he was found in May of 1950, orphaned by a raging fire in the Lincoln National Forest. After the badly burnt black bear cub healed, he was sent to the National Zoo in Washington, D.C., where he became the spokesbear for preventing forest fires. (☎505-354-2748. Open daily 9am-5pm. $1, children $0.50.)

⚑ APPROACHING RUIDOSO: 18 MILES
From Capitan, take a left, heading southeast on **Rte. 48** for 18 mi. to Ruidoso. **Rte. 48** turns into **Mechem Dr.,** which takes you through the outskirts of town until it dead-ends at **Sudderth Dr.** Head left to see the full extent of Ruidoso's mountain tourist paradise.

RUIDOSO

During the summer months and ski season, the mountain hideaway of Ruidoso turns into a bustling tourist hub. Do not leave town without taking the scenic drive up 🏔**Sierra Blanca.** Towering at 12,000 ft., the peak of Sierra Blanca looms over Ruidoso's sprawl of expensive hotels and cabins, and the 11,000 ft. ascent offers views that only birds wouldn't envy. Switchbacks snake their way through pine forests and aspen groves up to the Windy Point Vista, where you can stare hundreds of miles eastward. Those fit enough to handle the demanding climb through thin air should take the **Lincoln National Forest Scenic Trail,** which departs from just outside the Ski Apache valley and connects with the crest trail; it heads above the tree line to wildflower meadows at the mountain's summit. After 3 mi., hikers are rewarded with a 360° panorama that encompasses everything from Mexico to White Sands to Texas. (Follow the signs for skiing and recreation that point you up a mountain road just outside Ruidoso on Rte. 48.)

Weber's Grill at Pub 48 ❸, 441 Mechem Dr., serves up Italian specialties and steaks in a mountain lodge atmosphere, complete with roaring hearth. They produce their own brews, like Alien Amber ($3.25), the best-selling microbrew in New Mexico. (☎505-257-9559. 10 in. pizza $8.50. Entrees $6-16. Open M and W-Su 11am-10pm. D/MC/V.) A lively twentysomething crowd enjoys pool, video games, a back patio, and 16 beers on tap at **Farley's ❸,** 1200 Mechem Dr., which doubles as a family restaurant serving burgers, hot dogs, chicken strips, and fajitas during the day. (☎505-258-5676. Entrees $8-12. Open M-Th 11:30am-midnight, F-Sa 11:30am-1am, Su 11am-11pm. AmEx/D/MC/V.) During the peak summer and winter seasons, it may be difficult to find an affordable room in town. A few budget motels can be found along U.S. 70, but most of the action is on Sudderth Dr. The **Alpine Lodge ❷,** 2805 Sudderth Dr., has small but clean rooms for decent prices. Jeanne, the owner, dispenses advice both in person and on her business cards. (☎505-257-4423.

ROSWELL RAKEOVER?

Something crashed onto Mac Brazel's ranch on July 4, 1947, but what it was is still up for debate. Most Roswell residents believe it was a flying saucer and have piles of evidence, even a museum, to prove it. Others, guffawing at the extraterrestrial hype, theorize that it was a weather balloon or a physics experiment gone awry. Either way, the series of events that took place after the crash are worthy of note. The perplexed Brazel took a sackful of the debris to Fort Worth and US Army Intelligence. Brazel was told to step out of the room, and claims that, when he returned, the original debris had been replaced with pieces of weather balloon wreckage. Later, Roswell undertaker Glenn Davis received a strange call from the Army airfield, asking how many child-sized caskets he had in stock and how to preserve bodies that had been exposed to the weather. A nurse was brought in to examine several bodies. She was transferred to England the next day, but before leaving, gave Davis hand-drawn pictures of the alien forms she had examined. The mysterious case has been closed for many years, and dozens of senators and even former presidents have been denied access to any information. So, do aliens exist? And did they crash at Roswell? No one really knows, but some peo-

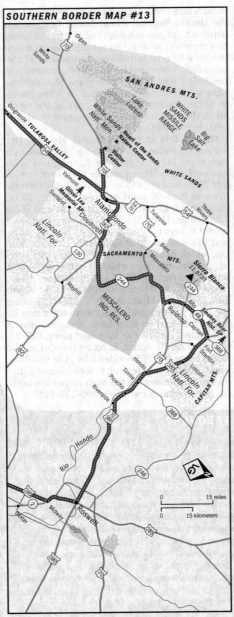

SOUTHERN BORDER MAP #13

0 — 15 miles
0 — 15 kilometers

Singles $40; doubles $45. Cash only.) **The Arrowhead Motel ❸**, 616 U.S. 70, west of town, has standard rooms and a friendly staff. (☎888-547-6652; www.ruidoso.net/arrowhead. Singles $54; doubles $64. D/MC/V.)

◪ APPROACHING CLOUDCROFT: 61 MILES

Leave town on **Rte. 70**, and a few miles down you'll pass a sign indicating that you're in the **Mescalero Indian Reservation**. During the 1st week of July, the Mescalero hold a traditional Apache coming-of-age ceremony; visitors are welcome to attend, but you must call the Mescalero Cultural Center (☎505-464-4494) beforehand for instructions regarding proper etiquette. Make a left turn and head southeast on **Rte. 244** for 30 mi. to the town of Cloudcroft.

CLOUDCROFT

Perched above 9000 ft., this mountaintop village is in a drastically different environment than the desert valley below. The "playland of the four seasons" lures visitors with a climate ranging from snowy flurries to breezy summer days. In the pricey **Lodge Hotel** (☎800-395-6343), **Rebecca's ❹** is named for the hotel ghost, who may well be sticking around for the gourmet food. The stately dining room serves affordable meals, with excellent fish and steak selections. (Take the last left as you exit Cloudcroft on U.S. 82, and look for the sign. ☎505-682-3131. Open daily 7-10:30am, 11:30am-2:30pm, and 5:30-9pm. AmEx/D/MC/V.) The premier budget accommodation in the area is the **◪Cloudcroft Mountain Park Hostel ❶**, 1049 U.S. 82, which opened in October 2005 and stands on 27 acres next to the Lincoln National Forest. It is quiet and clean, with a living room, kitchen, and large front porch. The private rooms are especially nice and should be reserved in advance. (5 mi. west of town; look for the oil drum with "hostel" painted across it. ☎505-682-0555; www.cloudcrofthostel.com; Dorms $17; private rooms $30. Cash only.) The **Aspen Motel ❷**, 1315 U.S. 82, features remodeled rooms nestled into the woodland hillside. (☎505-682-2526. Rooms $45. AmEx/D/MC/V.) Camping opportunities abound among the majestic pines of the Lincoln National Forest. The **Apache Campground ❶**, 3 mi. northeast of Cloudcroft along Rte. 244, has 24 wooded sites with hot showers and many cross-country ski trails. (☎505-682-2551. Showers $2. Sites $11. Cash only.)

APPROACHING ALAMOGORDO: 20 MILES

Head west on **Rte. 82.** As you depart, notice the old trestles in the gorges; these are remnants of the 19th-century tourist railroad that transported the summer's overheated Texans from El Paso to Cloudcroft. The road makes its way down 4312 ft. in these 16 mi., so exercise caution. Halfway down the mountain, the road passes through New Mexico's only tunnel. Stop just before this subterranean corridor at the tunnel vista turnout to enjoy an excellent view and discover a local secret: at the bottom of the steep hike down the canyon wall are rope swings and seasonal swimming holes. Rte. 82 intersects with **U.S. 70/Rte. 54;** take a left (south) on U.S. 70 to enter Alamogordo.

ALAMOGORDO

Alamogordo is Spanish for "fat poplar," though there are few trees in the town. Instead, there is a forest of motel, fast-food, and gas station signs along U.S. 70 (White Sands Blvd.). While sights in the town may be scarce, Alamogordo does provide plenty of eating and sleeping opportunities and is a good base for exploring the area. It serves as a convenient gateway to White Sands National Monument (p. 841). **The Lincoln National Forest Office,** 1101 New York Ave., provides info on hiking or camping trips in the Sacramento Mountains. (☎505-434-7200. Open M-F 7:30am-4:30pm.) **Outdoor Adventures,** 1516 10th St., rents bikes and provides advice on trails in the area. (☎505-434-1920 Bikes $20-25 per day. Open M-F 10am-6pm, Sa 10am-5pm.)

Memories ❸, 1223 New York Ave., is a beautiful restaurant in a restored historic home with reasonable prices and good seafood—a precious commodity in the desert. (☎505-437-0077. Burgers $4.50. Seafood dishes $11-15. Steaks $14-17. Open M-Sa 11am-9pm. MC/V.) **Maximinos ❷,** 2300 N. White Sands Blvd., has breakfast burritos for $3.75; their chicken *mole* runs $7. (☎505-443-6102. Tu and Th-Su all-you-can-eat lunch buffet 11am-2pm; $6.50. Open Tu-F 8am-2pm and 5-9pm, Sa 8am-9pm, Su 8am-3pm. AmEx/D/MC/V.) For dessert, don't miss **Caliche's Frozen Custard ❶,** 2251 N. White Sands Blvd., which serves sundaes, flurries, and malts at a walk-up window. The "Big Hawaiian" (custard, banana, pineapple, coconut, and pecans; $4) is amazing. (☎505-439-1000. Open daily May-Sept. 11am-10pm; Oct.-Apr. 11am-9pm. MC/V.) Head to the **Satellite Inn ❷,** 2224 N. White Sands Blvd., for clean rooms with Internet access. (☎800-221-7690; www.satelliteinn.com. Continental breakfast included. Singles $36; doubles $45. AmEx/D/MC/V.) **Budget Motel 7 ❷,** 2404 N. White Sands Blvd., provides few frills but has clean rooms. (☎505-437-9350. Singles $30; doubles $34. AmEx/D/MC/V.)

APPROACHING WHITE SANDS NATIONAL MONUMENT: 13 MILES

To get to White Sands National Monument, take **White Sands Blvd. (U.S. 70/Rte. 54)** out of town. 13 mi. down, on your right, is the National Monument Visitors Center.

WHITE SANDS NATIONAL MONUMENT

Perhaps the world's greatest beach (minus the water), the white gypsum dunes of the White Sands National Monument inspire awe both for their purity and for their bleakness. The Tularosa Basin, bordered by the Sacramento and San Andres Mountains, lacks any outlet to the sea, so rainwater collects at the low point, known as Lake Lucero. As the desert heat evaporates the lake, gypsum crystals collect on the dry bed and are swept away by the wind, transforming them into blindingly white sand that collects as dunes. In these forbidding and treacherous conditions only a few highly adaptive species can survive. The white lizards and fast-growing plants are nearly as astounding as the dunes themselves.

VITAL STATS

Area: 144,000 acres

Visitor Info: White Sands Visitor Center (☎505-479-6124; www.nps.gov/whsa), on U.S. 70. Open daily June-Aug. 8am-7pm; Sept.-May 8am-5pm. Park open daily June-Aug. 7am-9pm; Sept.-May 7am-sunset.

Gateway town: Alamogordo (p. 841).

Fees: $3, under 16 free.

GETTING AROUND. The **Dunes Drive** is the best way to enjoy the park. Beginning at the visitors center, the scenic road (16 mi. round-trip) winds from the edge of the dunes to the **Heart of the Sands** drive. Exhibits along the way provide information about geology and natural history. The park is occasionally closed for missile testing at the nearby **White Sands Missile Range,** so call ahead or check the website for closure times.

DID YOU KNOW? Why is a sand dune, like White Sands, a "monument?" Since the days of Teddy Roosevelt, presidents have been able to declare a site a "monument" in order to preserve it in a jiffy. A more lengthy process is required for Congress to declare a site a "national park."

OUTDOORS. The most popular activity at White Sands is **sand surfing** (though careening down the incredibly steep sides of 25 ft. dunes via sled is more akin to tobogganing than surfing). You can purchase a surfing disc (a saucer-shaped sled) from the gift shop for $9; they'll buy it back from you for $3.50, so keep your receipt. Roadies who are around for one of the monthly ranger-led **auto caravans** have the chance to travel across the open dunes to **Lake Lucero.** (Advance reservations required; contact the visitors center for information.) Informative ranger-led walks are held daily at sunset, a particularly beautiful time to be out on the dunes (walks begin 1hr. before sunset). At any time, you can walk along the **Interdune Boardwalk** (¼ mi.), which carves an easy route above the sands. Another easy but rewarding walkway is the **Dune Life Nature Trail** (1 mi.), which makes a loop through the edges of the dunes where plants and wildlife are more abundant. The strenuous **Alkali Flat Trail** (4½ mi.) loops from the **Heart of the Sands** drive to the edge of the salty lakebed of **Lake Otero.** Even if there isn't enough time or it's too hot for the whole Alkali trail, it's worth your while to hike just a short distance—you'll be struck by the sheer vastness of the seemingly interminable dunes. Off-trail hiking is permitted anywhere along the eastern edge of the park. On full moon nights in the summer, the park stays open until 11pm (last entrance 10pm). Ask the rangers about stargazing activities, including the yearly "star party" held in late September.

CAMPING. There are no established campgrounds available in the park, but 10 daily permits for the primitive backcountry campsites are available on a first come, first served basis. ($3 per person. Cash only.) The sites have no water or toilet facilities and are not accessible by any road, requiring a 1-2 mi. hike through the sand dunes. Campers must register in person at the visitors center and be in their sites before dark.

APPROACHING OLIVER LEE MEMORIAL STATE PARK: 14 MILES
Head east on **U.S. 70.** Pass through the outskirts of Alamogordo, and take **Rte. 54** 10 mi. to the entrance of Oliver Lee Memorial State Park. Turn left into the park gate and drive 4 mi. to the visitors center.

OLIVER LEE MEMORIAL STATE PARK.
Perched at the mouth of a vast canyon at the edge of the Sacramento Mountains, the Oliver Lee Memorial State Park provides a panoramic view of the canyon and the desert below. Those up for a challenge should think about trekking at least a half-mile up the mountain's face on the ludicrously steep **Dog Canyon Trail** (5½ mi. round-trip) to behold an astonishing vista of the Tularosa Basin. A less strenuous way to see some of the park is by walking the **Riparian Nature Trail** (½ mi.) through a stream-fed canyon. The park has excellent **camping ❶** with clean showers. (☎505-437-8284; www.emnrd.state.nm.us/nmparks. Visitors center open daily 9am-4pm. Sites $10, with hookup $14. Cash only.)

APPROACHING EL PASO: 75 MILES
Head back to **Rte. 54** and go westward. The only civilization that intrudes on the desert vistas is the busted mining town of Orogrande, which exists today only as a gas station strategically placed to save the lives of those who forgot to fill up in Alamogordo. Enter El Paso by following Rte. 54 until it branches into **I-10.** Follow I-10 to downtown, and take **Exit 19A (Mesa St.)** or **19B.**

The Lone Star State
TEXAS
Welcomes You!

EL PASO

Since it was first established in the 17th century, this Texas city has always been "the pass." It is a gateway to Mexico, the Río Grande, the western deserts, and the eastern Texas rangeland. As Americans have begun to worry increasingly about the Mexican border, El Paso's reputation has suffered. Residents are more than aware of the politics at stake and they aren't afraid to engage the issue while proudly promoting the city's reputation as "second-safest city in the US." The truth is that El Paso is a lively town with a world-class art museum, a lovely, historic downtown core, excellent Mexican restaurants, and fabulous desert scenery just minutes away.

VITAL STATS

Population: 560,000

Visitor Info: El Paso Convention and Visitors Bureau, 1 Civic Center Plaza (☎915-534-0600, 800-351-6024; www.visitelpaso.com), at Santa Fe and Mills Ave. Open M-F 8am-5pm.

Internet Access: El Paso Public Library, 501 N. Oregon St. (☎915-543-5433). Open M-Th 8:30am-8:30pm, F-Sa 8:30am-5:30pm, Su 1-5pm. Free.

Post Office: 219 E. Mills Ave. (☎915-532-8824), between Mesa and Stanton St. Open M-F 8:30am-5pm, Sa 8:30am-noon. **Postal Code:** 79901.

GETTING AROUND

While El Paso and Ciudad Juárez, its Mexican sister city, sprawl across the valley floor, the downtown districts of both cities are relatively small and easily navigable. **San Jacinto Plaza,** at the corner of Main and Oregon St., is the heart of El Paso. **I-10** runs east-west through the city and intersects with north-southbound **U.S. 54** in a mess of tangled concrete fondly dubbed "the spaghetti bowl." Rte. 85 becomes **Paisano St.** as it enters downtown. Paisano St. and **San Antonio Ave.** are two of the city's major east-west arteries. **Santa Fe Ave., Stanton St.,** and **El Paso St.** run north-south, with El Paso St. continuing to the border crossing. The main north-south artery is **Mesa St.,** which connects to the **Trans Mountain Rd.,** leading through Franklin State Park. Tourists should be wary of the streets between San Antonio and the border late at night.

 DID YOU KNOW? Some of the South's larger border crossings see hundreds of senior citizens making a run for the border every day. What do they come for? The drugs. Mexican border towns often have discount pharmacies, where regular prescription drugs are much cheaper than in the US. Let's Go does not recommend drug-running.

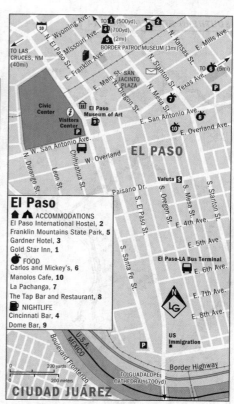

El Paso

♠ ▲ ACCOMMODATIONS
El Paso International Hostel, **2**
Franklin Mountains State Park, **5**
Gardner Hotel, **3**
Gold Star Inn, **1**

🍴 FOOD
Carlos and Mickey's, **6**
Manolos Cafe, **10**
La Pachanga, **7**
The Tap Bar and Restaurant, **8**

🍸 NIGHTLIFE
Cincinnati Bar, **4**
Dome Bar, **9**

SIGHTS

Self-guided walking tours of the historic downtown and its restored buildings are a great way to spend a couple of hours. The visitors center has pamphlets with the route laid out. The undisputed jewel of El Paso's museums is the **El Paso Museum of Art,** 1 Arts Festival Plaza, which features over 5000 works in a recently renovated building. Particularly impressive are the 19th- and 20th-century Southwestern and Mexican colonial collections. (☎915-532-1707. Open Tu-Sa 9am-5pm, Su noon-5pm. Free.) Regardless of your politics, the **National Border Patrol Museum,** 4315 Trans Mountain Rd., gives a sense of the very real issues at stake in El Paso. The exhibits, which span the Old West to the present and include vehicles, paint-

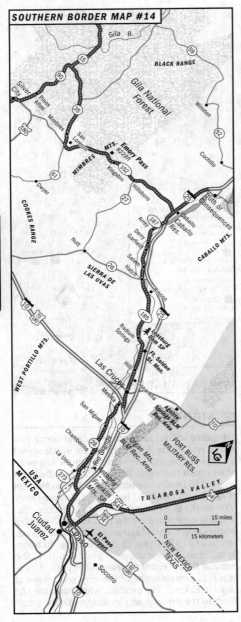

SOUTHERN BORDER MAP #14

SOUTHERN BORDER

ings, and photos, will leave you rolling your eyes or applauding the bravery of the border guards and vigilantes. (☎915-759-6060; www.borderpatrolmuseum.com. Open Tu-Su 9am-5pm. Free.)

◤ OUTDOORS

North of downtown, the **Franklin Mountains State Park** covers 24,000 acres, making it the largest urban wilderness park in the US. The park's visitors center is located in McKellington Canyon on the east side of the Franklin Mountains. (From downtown, take Scenic Dr. east, and turn left onto Alabama St., following it for a couple of miles. Turn left at McKellington Canyon Rd. Visitors center open daily 8am-4pm. Park open daily June-Sept. 8am-8pm; Oct.-May 8am-5pm. Park entrance $4.) There are many hiking routes throughout the park. The most popular hike is **West Cottonwood Spring** (1½ mi. one-way), which begins at Sneed's Cory and makes a loop leading to a spring with an amazing view of the valley. Also starting at Sneed's Cory, the **North Franklin Peak Trail** (9 mi. one-way) is a difficult hike to the top of 7200 ft. Mt. Franklin. The **Aztec Caves Trail** (1¼ mi. one-way) is a steep, 2hr. workout. (To reach the trailhead, take the 2nd. right after the fee station.) One of the easier hikes in the park is **Upper Sunset** (1¼ mi. one-way), which runs along the western edge of the mountain. The trail begins just after the fee station on the left side of the road. The Tom Mays section of the park is a perfect setting for hiking, mountain biking, and rock climbing, and is accessible only from the west side of the Franklin Mountains. Ask at the visitors center for trail maps. The **Wyler Aerial Tramway** takes visitors to the top of Ranger Peak (5632 ft.). The third tramway of its kind in the US, it was built in 1960 to service TV and radio antennas. On a clear day, you can see 7000 sq. mi. from the top—all the way to the Guadalupe Mountains and Ruidoso. (On the corner of Alabama St. and McKinley Ave. ☎915-562-9899. Open M and Th noon-6pm, F-Su noon-9pm. $7, children $4.)

◤ FOOD

There's no shortage of good Mexican food in downtown El Paso, and prices are generally cheap. El Paso's fast-food joints cluster around **Stanton St.** and **Texas St.** Be aware that many downtown restaurants close at 5pm and on the weekends. Don't be spooked by the dim lighting and mirrored walls at **The Tap Bar and Restaurant** ❷, 408 E. San Antonio Ave. The burritos ($1.75-4), enchiladas ($4.25), and chiles *relleno* ($6.75) are delicious. (☎915-532-1848. Open M-Sa 9am-2am, Su noon-2am. Kitchen closes 10pm. Cash only.) For cheap food in a spartan setting, try **Manolo's Cafe** ❶, 122 S. Mesa St., between Overland and San Antonio Ave. *Menudo* ($3-4), burritos ($2), and generous lunch specials ($5) are standard fare. (☎915-532-7661. Open M-Sa 7:30am-4:30pm, Su 7:30am-3pm. AmEx/D/MC/V.) **La Pachanga** ❶, 222 Texas Ave., between N. Mesa and N. Stanton St., sells sandwiches and excellent fruit smoothies for $3-4. (☎915-544-4454. Open M-Sa 8am-5pm. MC/V.) The best incarnation of fried ice cream, an El Paso specialty, can be found at **Carlos and Mickey's** ❶, 1310 Magruder St., off Montana St., where you can sit at the bar and get a bowl for $2.75. (☎915-778-3323. Open daily 11:30am-10:30pm. Bar open M-Th and Su 11:30am-11pm, F-Sa 11:30am-1:30am. AmEx/D/MC/V.)

ACCOMMODATIONS

The **Gardner Hotel** ❷, 311 E. Franklin, between Stanton and Kansas St., has housed weary travelers since 1922 and is El Paso's oldest operating hotel. John Dillinger, the famous bank robber, stayed here in 1934. Make calls from a wooden phone booth and take the cage elevator up from the ornate lobby. (☎915-532-3661; www.gardnerhotel.com. Singles $24, with private bath from $44. MC/V.) Located inside the hotel, the **El Paso International Hostel** ❶, 311 E. Franklin Ave., takes great pride in meeting the needs of backpackers, offering clean, four-bed, single-sex rooms with a full kitchen and a large lounge. (☎915-532-3661. Pool $5 per hr. HI, HA, ISIC, student, or teacher ID required. Laundry $1.50. Towels $0.50. Internet $1 per 15min. Check-out 10am. Dorms $20.50, members $18.50. MC/V.) Motels can be found along Dyer and Alameda St. Closer to downtown, the **Gold Star Inn** ❷, 1401 N. Mesa, has clean, spacious rooms for low prices. (☎915-533-2220. Singles $30; doubles $38. AmEx/D/MC/V.) Beautifully situated primitive camping is available in the **Franklin Mountains State Park** ❶. Four of the five sites have shelters and, while there are clean outhouses, there is no water or electricity. The sites are accessed from the park entrance along the Trans Mountain Rd., but if you're planning to arrive after the park closes, you must contact the rangers in advance to get the gate combination. (☎915-566-6441. Reservations recommended. Sites $8. Cash only.)

ENTERTAINMENT

Most nightlife seekers cross the border to take advantage of the younger drinking age in Ciudad Juárez. Still, there remain several options north of the Río Grande. For shows and events around town, leaf through the free weekly *What's Up.* If you're in town on a Sunday, don't miss **Music Under the Stars**, the hugely popular free summer concert series in Chamizal National Memorial Park. Shows range from Brazilian jazz to flamenco to symphonic, and there is always dancing and food. (☎915-541-4481; www.elpasotexas.gov/mcad. Shows June-Aug. Su 7:30pm.) Free concerts, dubbed **Alfresco Fridays**, are held every Friday in summer at Arts Festival Plaza, near the El Paso Museum of Art. Music is varied but is usually local bands. (☎915-541-4481; www.elpasotexas.gov/mcad. June-Aug. F 5:30pm.)

NIGHTLIFE

The aptly named **Cincinnati Bar**, 207 Cincinnati Ave., is one of the most happening places to be on a Friday night. (☎915-532-5592. "$2 Tuesdays"; all drinks $2. Th open mic. Cover Tu for men; $2 after 10pm. Open daily 2pm-2am. AmEx/D/MC/V.) Downtown, the classy **Dome Bar**, 101 S. El Paso St., in the Camino Real Hotel, serves martinis and mojitos in the lobby of a restored 1912 hotel. It's worth dropping by for the gorgeous decor, if not for the chocolate cake and raspberry sauce martini ($8). Live music (salsa, jazz, and instrumental) plays Th-Sa nights at 9:30pm. (☎915-534-3000, ext. 5012. Mixed drinks $8. Beers on tap $5. Open M-Th 3pm-midnight, F-Sa 3pm-2am. AmEx/D/MC/V.)

APPROACHING LAS CRUCES: 50 MILES
From El Paso, jump on **I-10 W** to get to Las Cruces.

Land of Enchantment
NEW MEXICO
Welcomes You!

LAS CRUCES

Las Cruces was named for the many crosses marking the graves of early pioneers. To make the most of your visit, bypass the car dealerships, strip malls, and chain motels that make up the city in favor of historic Mesilla, or go biking and hiking in the beautiful Organ Mountains.

VITAL STATS

Population: 74,000

Visitor Info: Las Cruces Convention and Visitors Bureau, 211 N. Water St. (☎505-541-2444; www.lascrucescvb.org). Open M-F 8am-5pm.

Internet Access: Thomas Branigan Memorial Library, 200 E. Picacho Ave. (☎505-528-4000). Open Aug.-May M-Th 10am-9pm, F-Sa 10am-6pm, Su 1-5pm; June-July M-Th 10am-9pm, F-Sa 10am-6pm. Free.

Post Office: 201 E. Las Cruces Ave. (☎505-524-2903). Open M-F 8am-6pm, Sa 8-11:30am. **Postal Code: 88001.**

GETTING AROUND

Las Cruces is framed by **I-25** to the east and **I-10** to the south. East to west, the major north-south streets are **Telshor Blvd. (I-25), Main St.,** and **Valley Dr. Lohman Ave.** runs east-west through the city, while **University Ave.** forms the southern boundary. This road leads east to the Organ Mountains and is the easiest route to the Mesilla plaza.

SIGHTS

Though Las Cruces is the demographic center of the area, **Mesilla,** 3 mi. away, is the cultural center. When the US acquired the land in 1854 with the Gadsden Purchase, Mesilla became an important stop for traders and travelers en route to San Francisco. By the 1880s, the town was as wild as any other in the West; it was in Mesilla that Billy the Kid was tried for murder and sentenced to hang in 1881. Mesilla looks much the same as it did in the 1880s, and most of the adobe buildings around the central plaza date back 150 years. While the shops are very touristy, selling arts and crafts, postcards and t-shirts, the adobe-ringed plaza is lovely. The majestic **San Albino Church,** 2250 Calle Principal,

originally built as an adobe structure in 1855, presides over the square. (☎505-526-9349. Open M-Sa 1-3pm. Su mass 8, 11am. Free.)

Mary Bird, the great-great-granddaughter of Billy the Kid's public defender, takes visitors on a tour of local history at the **Gadsden Museum,** on Boutz Rd., across from the plaza. Exhibits include a jail cell from which Billy the Kid once escaped, objects belonging to the mysterious "hermit of La Cueva," and Spanish-era artifacts. (☎505-526-6293. Open July-Aug. daily 10am-5pm; Sept.-June Sa-Su 10am-5pm. $3.)

Las Cruces has its own roadside oddity in the form of a ◙**giant roadrunner** made from recyclable trash, perched high on hillside rest stop. The roadrunner was made in the mid-1990s by a resident in protest of recyclable material being thrown into the city's dump. First displayed in the dump, the roadrunner was such a hit that the city moved him to his hilltop perch. From the 20 ft. roadrunner, you can see the entire Las Cruces/Río Grande Valley. (Take I-10 W out of Las Cruces to Exit 135. The bird can be seen from the westbound lanes, but the rest stop can only be visited from the eastbound lanes.)

OUTDOORS

Las Cruces provides decent mountain biking opportunities. The **"A" Mountain Trail** (3¼ mi. loop) is a moderately difficult ride around the base of the hill at the east end of New Mexico State University's campus. The trail takes its name from the "A" formed by the white stones that adorn the mountain's east face, visible from most of Las Cruces. The length of the **Sierra Vista Trail** (14½ mi. round-trip) makes it somewhat more difficult, though it is not particularly steep. The most technically challenging trail is the **SST Trail** (8 mi.). Check with the bike shop **Outdoor Adventures,** 1424 Missouri Ave., for more info on these and other trails. (☎505-521-1922. Bikes $20 per day. Open M-F 10am-7pm, Sa 10am-5pm.)

FOOD

Culinary options in Las Cruces revolve around chain restaurants, but there are a number of interesting places to dine in Mesilla. **La Posta ❸,** 2410 Calle de San Albino, off Avenida de Mesilla, is located in an adobe structure that once housed road-weary travelers from the

Butterfield Trail, including Billy the Kid, Kit Carson, and Pancho Villa. You might have a harder time finding lodging these days, but La Posta still serves excellent Mexican cuisine. Try a combination plate ($8.50) for a taste of everything. (☎505-524-3524; www.laposta-de-mesilla.com. Entrees $7-12. Open M-Th and Su 11am-9pm, F-Sa 11am-9:30pm. AmEx/D/MC/V.) Nearby, **El Comedor ❷**, 2190 Avenida de Mesilla, is an understated restaurant that serves up heaping Mexican specialty plates. Try the "Doña Ana Fajitas" ($10) or the tacos *al pastor* for $7.50. (☎505-524-7002. Entrees $7-10. Open M-Th 9am-8pm, F-Sa 9am-9pm, Su 9am-3pm. AmEx/D/MC/V.)

If you can't make it to Mesilla to eat, **International Delights ❶**, 1245 El Paseo, in the corner of the Albertson's shopping center, has a relaxed atmosphere and a full selection of coffee drinks ($1-3) and sandwiches (falafel $4.50). It's a comfortable haven away from the city's suburban sprawl. (☎505-647-5956. Open M-Sa 7am-midnight, Su 8am-midnight. AmEx/D/MC/V.) A mixed crowd hangs out at the **High Desert Brewing Co. ❷**, 1201 W. Hadley Ave., off Valley Rd., the only local brewery in town. The sampler, which isn't on the menu, includes four 4oz. glasses for $4. You can also taste up to three shots of beer for free. (☎505-525-6752. Pints $3.25. Burgers $5. Burrito plate $6. Th and Sa live music 8-11pm. Open M-Sa 11am-midnight, Su noon-10pm. Kitchen closes M-Sa 10pm, Su 9pm. D/MC/V.)

ACCOMMODATIONS

Cheap motels line Picacho Ave. to the west of Valley Dr. This area is not very safe at night, so exercise caution when walking alone. Other motels cluster around the I-10 and I-25 exits. Located in a beautifully decorated, 100-year-old adobe mansion, the **Lundeen Inn of the Arts Bed and Breakfast ❸**, 618 S. Alameda Blvd., serves as both a guest house and a local art gallery, and is worth the premium price. The spacious rooms are named after area artists, and each has a private bath. (☎505-526-3327 or 888-526-3326; www.innoft-hearts.com. Reception 8am-10pm. Reservations required. Singles $58-64; doubles $77-85. AmEx/D/MC/V.) For a cheaper room, **Day's End Lodge ❷**, 755 N. Valley Dr., offers clean accommodations with free popcorn and morning coffee. (☎505-524-7753. Singles $31; doubles $36. AmEx/D/MC/V.)

◤ DETOUR
ORGAN MOUNTAINS
Drive east. on U.S. 70 for 15 mi. Turn left on Aguirre Spring Rd. for camping, or follow Dripping Springs Rd. 11 mi. east of the city to reach the visitors center.

East of Las Cruces, opportunities for hiking, mountain biking, and rock climbing are plentiful. On the western slope of the Organ Mountains, **Dripping Springs** and **La Cueva Trails,** both easy 1 mi. hikes, are accessible via Dripping Springs Rd. For more info, check at the **A.B. Cox Visitors Center.** (Follow the signs from University Blvd. ☎505-522-1219. Open daily 8am-5pm.) On the eastern slope of the Organ Mountains, Aguirre Springs is farther from Las Cruces with more challenging hiking. The **Aguirre Spring National Recreation Area ❶** is an idyllic place to pitch your tent, with isolated, quiet campsites against the background of gorgeous mountains and desert valleys. Each site has a grill and is near an outhouse. (☎505-644-9143. Open daily mid-Apr. to mid-Oct. 8am-7pm; mid-Oct. to mid-Apr. 8am-6pm. Vault toilets. Water available at campground host's site. $3 per vehicle. Cash only.) To reach **hiking trails,** follow Aguirre Spring Rd. through the campground and look for the trail markers leading off the road. You can park your car at the pull-offs.

◤ APPROACHING RADIUM SPRINGS: 15 MILES
From Las Cruces, head north on **Valley Rd.** until it turns into **Rte. 185.** Follow Rte. 185 for 15 mi., and turn at the sign for Fort Selden.

RADIUM SPRINGS. While you'll be hard-pressed to find any radium or springs here, you can find intriguing ruins at the old **Fort Selden State Monument,** 1280 Ft. Selden Rd. The fort marks the beginning of the *jornada del muerto* (journey of death), where the era's longest highway, El Camino Real, curved away from the Río Grande. The combination of desert and vulnerability to Apache raids made this 90 mi. stretch particularly deadly. The fort was commissioned to protect this area in 1865 and was in operation until just before the turn of the century. It features a small but excellent collection of historic military artifacts. (☎505-526-8911. Open daily 8:30am-5pm. Activities such as cooking demonstrations, military reenactments, and lectures occur in summer most Sa-Su 10am-3pm. $3, 16 and under free.)

APPROACHING HATCH: 27 MILES
From Radium Springs, head back out to **Rte. 185**, and follow it north 25 mi. to the village of Hatch.

HATCH. All kinds of produce are grown in the fertile Rio Grande Valley. As you approach Hatch, Rte. 185 meanders through orchards, green fields, and cropland devoted to the most famous of all New Mexico exports: the chile. During the right season, these farms offer freshly picked chiles to passersby and in the off-season, dried chiles hang for sale on most houses, trailers, and stores. In fact, Hatch lays claim to the title of Chile Capital of the World. Every Labor Day weekend, the town celebrates its status at the annual **Chile Festival**, when it crowns two queens: one for red chiles and one for green. **The Pepper Pot ❷**, 207 W. Hall St., is on the main (and only) road through town. They serve up chile classics like *relleno* ($6.50). To taste several dishes, try the combo plate for $7.50. (☎505-267-3822. Open daily 6am-3pm. Cash only.)

APPROACHING TRUTH OR CONSE- QUENCES: 38 MILES
Follow **Rte. 185** out of the village and head north (right) on **Rte. 187 Scenic Byway**. The road continues through more farmlands until it hits a dead end; turn right and you're on the main road leading into town.

TRUTH OR CONSEQUENCES

In 1950, Ralph Edwards's popular radio game show "Truth or Consequences" celebrated its 10th anniversary by naming this small town, formerly Hot Springs, in its honor. Every year on the first weekend of May, residents celebrate the rechristening with a fiesta. Events include parades, rodeos, country music, high-energy drum circles, and canoe races. Day-to-day life in T or C is as quirky as one would expect, and many artists have recently opened studios in the area.

VITAL STATS

Population: 7300

Visitor Info: T or C Visitors Information Center, 211 Main St. (☎505-894-1968). Open M-Sa 9am-4:30pm, Su 11am-4pm.

Internet Access: Truth or Consequences Public Library, 325 Library Ln. (☎505-894-3027). Follow the signs from Main or 2nd St. northbound onto Foch St., then take a right at 3rd Ave.; the library is on the left. Open M-F 9am-7pm. Free.

Post Office: 300 Main St. (☎505-894-0876). Open M-F 9am-3pm. **Postal Code:** 87901.

GETTING AROUND

Taking the first exit off I-25 N into T or C puts you on **Broadway**. The road runs one way, forming a circle around downtown. On the north side of the circle, it becomes **Main St.** On the east side of town, **Date St.** leads up to **Elephant Butte SP**, and to the numbered streets. **Foch St.** and **Austin St.** lead down southward to the Rio Grande.

SIGHTS

T or C is proud of its status as an artist colony in the making. Inquire at the visitors center for a studio map, or just wander down Broadway between Daniels and Pershing St. to visit many of the artists' studios. Every second Saturday of the month, all the studios open 6-9pm and serve refreshments. T or C's **mineral baths** are the town's other main attraction; locals claim that they heal virtually everything. ($10 per hr.; private pool on the water's edge $15 per hr. Open 10am-7pm.) The only outdoor tubs are located at the **Riverbend Hot Springs Hostel and Resort** (p. 849), where four tubs abut the Río Grande. The **Geronimo Springs Museum,** 211 Main St., showcases Native American history, military history, 1950s television history, and much more. The highlight of the museum is the Native American pottery collection, which has intricately designed pots in pristine condition. (☎505-894-6600. Open M-Sa 9am-5pm. $3, ages 6-18 $1.50, under 6 free.)

Five miles north of T or C, **Elephant Butte Lake State Park** features New Mexico's largest lake, created by the construction of a dam in 1916. The park offers sandy beaches for swimming and a marina for boating. There is a **visitors center** at the entrance of the park with a small museum on the natural history of the area. Although the park has little hiking, there is an easy **nature trail** (1½ mi.) that begins in the nearby parking lot. (Head north on Date St. to a sign for Elephant Butte; turn right onto Rte. 181, and follow the signs. ☎505-784-5421. Open M-F 7:30am-4pm, Sa-Su 7:30am-10pm. $5 per vehicle.)

FOOD

Nearly all of T or C's restaurants are easy on the wallet. A little deli with a few tables, brightly painted walls, and a laid-back artist clientele, **The Happy Belly Deli ❶**, 313 Broadway, serves up sandwiches ($4-6), salads ($5), and yummy fruit smoothies for $3. (☎505-894-5555. Breakfast served all day. Open Tu-F 7:05am-3pm, Sa 8:05am-3pm. MC/V.) **Hacienda Mexican Restaurant ❷**, 1615 S. Broadway, is cozy and unassuming. Dishes like *arroz con pollo* (rice with chicken; $7), and breakfast *chorizo con huevos* (sausage with eggs; $5) are excellent. (☎505-894-1024 Open Tu-Su 11am-9pm. MC/V.)

ACCOMMODATIONS

The mineral baths in T or C add a touch of luxury to accommodations. At the ☕**Riverbend Hot Springs Hostel and Resort ❶**, 100 Austin St., you can stay on the banks of Río Grande and spend your days soaking in an outdoor mineral bath that overflows into the river. Riverbend is an eclectic place with brightly tiled courtyards, lots of plants, and mineral baths, which are free for guests. All dorms have common rooms and kitchens. (☎505-894-7625; www.riverbend.com. Free Wi-Fi. Reception 8am-10pm. Single-sex dorms $25; pensions with full bed and bath $39; rooms with kitchenettes from $49. Tent sites and 1 teepee $20. AmEx/D/MC/V.) The **Charles Motel and Spa ❷**, 601 Broadway, has simple, clean accommodations with free mineral baths on the premises (in bathtubs, not pools). Massages, reflexology, mud baths, and a host of other splurge-worthy spa treatments ($45-64 per hr.) are available on-site. (☎505-894-7154 or 800-317-4518; www.charlesspa.com. Some rooms have kitchenettes. Singles $37; doubles $46-52. AmEx/D/MC/V.) Campsites at the **Elephant Butte Lake State Park ❶**, north of T or C, have access to restrooms and hot showers. (☎505-744-5421 or 877-664-7787. Sites $10, with water and electricity $14; primitive beach camping $8. D/MC/V.)

NIGHTLIFE

The **Pine Knot Saloon**, 700 E. 3rd Ave., just past the curve on 3rd St. toward Elephant Butte, is a vintage Western saloon festooned with photos of John Wayne. Locals in cowboy hats sit around and listen to live music on weekend nights. The musical genre, according to the bartender, is "whatever the crowd wants...but they always want country and Western." (☎505-894-2714. Th night karaoke. Open M-Sa 10am-2am, Su noon-midnight. AmEx/D/MC/V.) **The Dam Site**, just past the Elephant Butte Dam on Rte. 51, is a bar and restaurant with spectacular views of the lake and surrounding mountains. (☎505-894-2073. Entrees $7-19. Drafts $3. Open M-Th and Su 11am-7pm, F-Sa 11am-midnight. AmEx/D/MC/V.)

DETOUR
GILA CLIFF DWELLINGS

From T or C, follow I-25 S to Rte. 152 W. After 66 mi., turn right onto Rte. 35. Follow Rte. 35 until it meets Forest Rd. 15, then turn north (right).

The mysterious ☕**Gila Cliff Dwellings National Monument** is set amid the mountains and pines of the Gila National Forest. The monument preserves over 40 stone-and-timber rooms, which were constructed on top of the cliff's natural caves by the Mogollon tribe during the late 13th century. About a dozen families lived here for 20 years, farming on the mesa top and along the river. In the early 14th century, the Mogollon abandoned their homes for unknown reasons. Today, visitors have the opportunity to explore inside the ruins using traditional ladders. The half-mile hike to the dwellings begins with a steep ascent up the canyon walls, but the rest of the hike is easy. Mogollon ruins are scattered throughout the area, and rangers can direct you to more remote sites. (☎505-536-9461; www.nps.gov/gicl. Tours depart from the dwellings in summer 11am and 2pm; in winter noon. Visitors center open daily Memorial Day to Labor Day 8am-5pm; Labor Day to Memorial Day 8am-4:30pm. Dwellings open daily Memorial Day to Labor Day 8am-6pm; Labor Day to Memorial Day 8am-4pm. Entrance fee $3; under 16 free. Trail guide $0.50.)

SOUTHERN BORDER

At the intersection of Rte. 35 and 15, the **Grey Feathers Lodge, Cafe, and Bakery ❷** is a quiet retreat in the midst of the great Gila wilderness. The lodge has cozy rooms and the cafe serves home-cooked meals, but the real attraction is its location in the path of the annual 🐦**hummingbird migration.** From mid-July to mid-August, 3000-4000 hummingbirds visit the lodge's feeders each day. (☎505-536-3206; www.greyfeathers.com. Breakfast $3-5. Cafe: Sandwiches $5-7. Open M and W-Su 8am-4pm. Motel: Breakfast included. Singles $40; doubles $50.) From here, the road climbs to a peak above the Gila River, where red, pine-covered rocks extend into endless vistas. Soon you'll pass the infinitesimally small hamlet of Gila Hot Springs, where supplies are available at **Doc Campbell's Post Vacation Center.** Like many of the building in Gila Hot Springs, Doc Campbell's is geothermally heated. Four miles past Gila Hot Springs, Forest Rd. 15 enters the Gila National Forest. The area encompasses hundreds of miles of hiking trails through mountains, canyons, and forest interspersed with **hot springs** and is ideal for backpacking, mountain biking, and rock climbing.

🚩 APPROACHING SILVER CITY: 92 MILES
Take **I-25 S** for 11 mi. to **Exit 63 (Hillsboro).** Take **Rte. 152 W** for 17 mi. to the little town of Hillsboro. At one time, gold chunks as heavy as 240 lb. attracted prospectors from all over the West to Hillsboro. The road climbs up into the pristine, pine-covered mountains. It's a mere 35 mi. to reach the turn-off for **Rte. 35,** which will take you north into the Gila Wilderness Area, or, if you want to continue to Silver City directly, follow the forested road another 10 mi. to Santa Clara, where it meets **Rte. 180.** A short 9 mi. drive westward on Rte. 180 brings you to Silver City.

SILVER CITY

In its heyday, Silver City was a rough and wild place that spawned the infamous outlaw Billy the Kid. Brown historical markers strewn about town point out the sites of his home, his school, his first bank robbery, his first jailbreak, and other typical landmarks of a Wild West childhood. Today, Billy would be more likely to find a latte in Silver City than a brawl. The very quaint Bullard St., in the heart of Silver City's historic downtown, has one civilized cafe and gallery after another—the sign of yet another artists' community in the making.

VITAL STATS

Population: 10,500

Visitor Info: 201 N. Hudson St. (☎505-538-3785), near Broadway. Open M-Sa 9am-5pm.

Internet Access: Silver City Public Library, 515 W. College Ave. (☎505-538-3672). Open M and Th 9am-8pm, Tu-W 9am-6pm, F 9am-5pm, Sa 9am-1pm. Free.

Post Office: 500 N. Hudson St. Open M-F 8:30am-5pm, Sa 10am-noon. **Postal Code:** 88061.

🔳 GETTING AROUND. Hudson St. (U.S. 90) and **Silver Heights Blvd. (U.S. 180)** are the major routes through town, running north-south and east-west, respectively. Around the center of town, **College Ave.** bisects Hudson St. and leads to the **University of Western New Mexico.** Most of the action in Silver City is along **Bullard St.,** which runs parallel to Hudson St. and is accessible from **Broadway.**

🔳 OUTDOORS. Silver City contains the main **Forestry Station** of the Gila National Forest, 3005 E. Camino del Bosque. The station provides excellent maps of the forest and its wilderness areas, as well as info on various outdoor activities in the region. (On the 32nd Bypass Rd. off U.S. 180, east of town. ☎505-388-8201. Open M-F 8am-4:30pm.) Rent mountain bikes for exploring Gila and the surrounding foothills at the **Gila Hike and Bike Shop,** 103 E. College Ave. They also repair bikes, sell outdoor equipment, and provide maps of the area. (☎505-388-3222. Bikes 1st day $20, 2nd day $15, 3rd day $10, each additional day $5. Helmets included. Open Apr.-Dec. M-F 9am-5:30pm, Sa 9am-5pm, Su 10am-4pm.) For a "wilderness" experience just off Bullard St., walk along the town's famed **"Big Ditch,"** a lush, tree-filled ditch that was created when the original Main St. washed away in a 1902 flood. Art enthusiasts will find an impressive collection of local **galleries** on Bullard and Yankie St.

🔳 FOOD AND ACCOMMODATIONS. Put on your gold-lamé bikini and visit **Java the Hut ❶,** 611-A N. Bullard St. Far from the dusty deserts of Tatooine, this coffee shop is like sitting in your grandma's living room—assuming she serves great espresso. Lounge on the sofas, at one of the two Formica tables, or on the little patio. The owner, Marcia, serves sandwiches ($3-4), coffee ($1-4), and a ¼ lb., all-beef hot dog for $3. (☎505-

534-4103. Open M-F 8am-4pm, Sa 8am-3pm. Cash only.) Local artwork and hard-to-find magazines are for sale in **Rejuvenations ❶**, 201 N. Bullard St., a spacious cafe that manages to be both hip and homey. Try the excellent carrot cake or the Karma Latte (caramel, vanilla, espresso), each for $4. Free Wi-Fi and comfy chairs make it easy to while away a few hours here. (☎505-388-1350; http://danandjohns.com. Open daily 6am-10pm. MC/V.) At the **Jalisco Cafe ❷**, 100 S. Bullard St., the chefs put the New Mexican chile pepper to good use. The jalapeño guacamole ($5.50) is delicious (in a masochistic sort of way); the menu warns people to ask for samples of their specialty red and green chile sauce before ordering—many guests just can't take the heat. (☎505-388-2060. Entrees $7-9. Open M-Sa 11am-8:30pm. D/MC/V.)

A night at the **Palace Hotel ❷**, 106 W. Broadway, at Bullard St., is yet another way to experience the mining-town history of Silver City. Established in 1882, this charming hotel echoes the grandeur of years gone by. Most of the tiny rooms open into the spacious sky-lit common room. (☎505-288-1811; www.zianet.com/palace-hotel. Continental breakfast included. Reservations recommended. Singles $44; doubles $57. AmEx/D/MC/V.) **The Drifter Motel and Cocktail Lounge ❷**, 711 Silver Heights Blvd., is another solid budget option that has a diner upstairs and a lounge with live music (DJs, rock, and reggae) downstairs. (☎800-853-2916, lounge 505-538-2916. Th-Sa live music. Lounge open daily 5pm-1:30am. Singles $38; doubles $48. D/MC/V.)

⚑ APPROACHING LORDSBURG: 44 MILES
An uneventful 44 mi. drive northeast on **U.S. 90** connects Silver City with Lordsburg. The only excitement on this road is cresting the **Continental Divide** which, at 6300 ft., consists of the region's foothills.

LORDSBURG. There's little reason to stop in Lordsburg unless you need to fill up your gas tank, buy groceries, or stop for the night. The **Holiday Motel ❶**, 600 E. Motel Dr., has clean beds and bathrooms, and all rooms have A/C and HBO. (☎505-542-3535. Rooms $29-39. AmEx/D/MC/V.) Next door, **Vicky's Restaurant ❷**, 604 E. Motel Dr., is one of the only possibilities besides McDonald's and DQ. Vicky serves Mexican and American food to patrons seated in comfy red booths. (☎505-542-4517. Open daily 6:30am-9:30pm. Burritos $2. Dinner $6-9. Cash only.)

⚑ APPROACHING PORTAL: 47 MILES
Take **I-10 W** and pass through a true dust bowl, where high winds can reduce visibility to almost zero. Use extreme caution when driving through dust storms. Drive 14 mi., and exit at **Rte. 80.** Head south for 25 mi. along flat, desert roads, and turn right (west) on **Rte. 533.** Continue for 8 mi. to Portal.

The Grand Canyon State **ARIZONA** *Welcomes You!*

 When you pass into the village of Portal, you will enter the Pacific Time Zone, where it is 1hr. earlier Apr.-Oct. There is no time change Nov.-Mar., since most of Arizona does not observe Daylight Saving time.

PORTAL. The village of Portal consists almost entirely of the **Portal Peak Lodge,** cafe, and attached store. (☎520-558-2223; www.portalpeaklodge.com. Office and store open daily 9:30am-7:30pm. Cafe open daily 7:30am-3:30pm and 5-7pm. AmEx/MC/V.) Its diminutive size aside, Portal is nonetheless a welcome bit of civilization before the road begins to climb steeply into the Chiricahua Mountains.

⚑ APPROACHING CHIRICAHUA NATIONAL MONUMENT: 30 MILES
Drive 30 mi. west along **Pinery Canyon Rd.** to reach the entrance to Chiricahua National Monument. The road passes through the beautiful **Chiricahua Mountains** and is extremely bumpy—it's impossible to exceed 15 mph for most of the drive. On the right 3 mi. past Portal is the **Cave Creek Visitors Information Center,** which welcomes you to the mountains and has an excellent view of the boulder-topped canyon walls. (☎520-558-2221. Open Sa-Su 8am-noon and 12:30-4pm.) Monday through Friday, contact the Coronado Forest Douglas Ranger District (☎520-364-6800) for info on the Cave Creek area.

 The road through the Chiricahua Mountains is not maintained for winter travel, so check with the Coronado Forest Douglas Ranger District office (☎520-364-6800) for information on road conditions and safe driving.

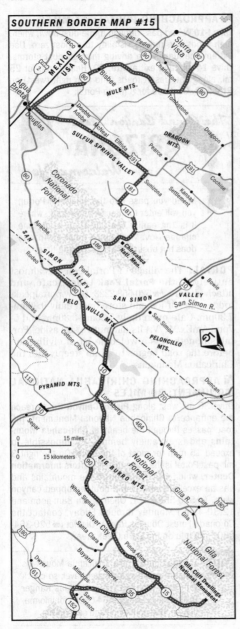

SOUTHERN BORDER MAP #15

CHIRICAHUA NATIONAL MONUMENT

Over 25 million years ago, the Turkey Creek Caldera spewed forth thick, white-hot ash that settled over the Chiricahua area. Since then, erosion has sculpted the fused-ash rock into peculiar formations that loom over the landscape and awe those who walk among them. The massive stone spires, weighing hundreds of tons and often perched precariously on small pedestals, inspired the Apaches to call the area "Land of the Standing-Up Rocks," and the pioneers to dub it "Wonderland of Rocks." Whatever you call it, it's nothing short of spectacular. The geological magnificence here could be the cousin of Zion or Bryce Canyons, yet it happily lacks their popularity.

VITAL STATS

Area: 12,000 acres

Visitor Info: Chiricahua Visitors Center, 13063 E. Bonita Rd., on your right 2 mi. beyond the entrance station (☎504-824-3560; www.nps.gov/chir). Open daily 8am-4:30pm.

Entrance Fees: $25 per vehicle, $5 per person; valid for 7 days.

GETTING AROUND. Extending from the park's entrance station to Massai Point at the back of the park is the **Bonita Canyon Drive,** a scenic 8 mi. road that is the only way to get through the monument. At the end of Bonita Canyon Dr., the road squeezes through the narrow gap between the towering granite walls of Bonita Canyon and then ascends to pine-studded **Massai Point** at the mountain's crest. A short interpretive nature trail encircles the peak and also serves as the starting point for the more demanding Echo Canyon Trail and other trails into the wilderness. All of the park, except for a strip around the main road, is federally designated wilderness; no biking or climbing is permitted.

HIKING. There is a terrific selection of day hikes in the monument. Many combinations are possible, since several loops and spurs provide flexibility, but all trails either lead to **Echo Canyon** or to the remote and more-spectacular **Heart of Rocks.** From the parking lot on Massai Point, the moderate **Echo Canyon Loop** (3½ mi., 2-

SOUTHERN BORDER

3hr.) is the best way to see many formations in a short period of time. The trail runs through an impressive cluster of formations, including rock grottoes, before descending into the wooded Echo Park area and then out through a more desert-like trail. For hikers with more time, an excellent route is the **Echo Canyon to Heart of Rocks Trail** (7½ mi.) that passes by the most spectacular formations in the park. The route follows the **Ed Riggs Trail** from the Echo Canyon trailhead through the forest and up to the top of the canyon, where you hike along the ridge on the **Big Balanced Rock Trail.** From there, follow the **Heart of Rocks Loop** to see the most unusual rock formations in the monument. The trail is strenuous, mostly because of length, and it requires about half of a day to complete. For info and trail maps, check the visitors center.

☀ CAMPING. No backcountry camping is allowed along the trails, but there is one established campground inside the park. The well-equipped **Bonita Canyon Campground ❶** has toilets, picnic grounds, water, and easy access to the park trails, but no showers. (☎504-824-3560. 24 sites. 14-day max. stay. No reservations. Sites $12. D/MC/V.) There are several campgrounds in the Cave Creek area along Pinery Rd. between Portal and the monument. The first of these, **Idle Wilde ❶,** has grills, outhouses, a water pump, and shaded sites. (Open 24hr. Sites $10. Cash only.) The road forks a few times, so keep a close eye on the well-marked signs for the National Monument. Pass many other well-developed camp-sites and short hiking or birding trails in the National Forest, as you begin the steep, switchback laden trip up into the mountains. The picturesque canyons and boulder formations are worth exploring before continuing to the National Monument. As the road makes its way up to the impressive ridgeline, it becomes to dirt. Reaching **Pinery Canyon Camp ❶** seems like a reward for those who've stuck it out: the campground has amenities like picnic tables and fire rings. (Open 24hr. Free.)

⚑ APPROACHING ELFRIDA: 39 MILES
From Chiricahua National Monument, drive 3 mi. to the junction of **Rte. 186/181,** and turn left on Rte. 181 toward Douglas. Follow the road for 22 mi. until the junction with **U.S. 191,** and take a left (south). 14 mi. down the road is the tiny village of Elfrida.

ELFRIDA. A smattering of houses and a gas station make up the tiny town of Elfrida. **The Longhorn ❷,** 10348 Hwy. 191, offers lunch, including a veggie burger ($5), steak dinners ($14-26), and $1 draft beer. (☎520-642-3496. Open daily 6am-midnight. MC/V.)

⚑ APPROACHING DOUGLAS: 24 MILES
Continue on **U.S. 191** for 24 mi. to the junction of **Rte. 80,** turning left into Douglas.

DOUGLAS
The quiet border town of Douglas sits at the intersection of Rte. 80 and Rte. 191. While Rte. 80 runs through the center of town, Rte. 191 makes a run for the border toward Mexican neighbor Agua

CACTUS CUISINE

During a road trip through the Southwest, there are the endless stretches between truck stops and drive-by shacks. But on this part of the trip, you're in luck! It turns out that cactus is edible. The cacti throughout Arizona and New Mexico can be divided into two culinary groups: cholla and prickly pears. Cholla have slender, rounded stems and are unpalatable, but prickly pears are delicious. When harvesting cactus, choose small specimens and use heavy gloves and a sharp knife. Cut off the pads, shave the spikes off with a knife, and trim the edges. To impress everyone at the hostel or campground, try this tasty recipe for Cactus Creole.

2 cups diced cactus
1 pound hamburger (cooked and drained)
6 oz tomato paste
1 cup water
1 diced jalapeño pepper
6-1/2 oz canned shrimp (drained)

Mix ingredients together in pan and cook over medium heat for 20min. or until the cactus turns a deep green. Eat it in a tortilla or serve it hot over noodles or rice. Yum!

Prieta. Stores swarm around Rte. 80 (rechristened **G Ave.** for municipal purposes), and most city services lie off this thoroughfare on **10th St.** The well-marked **Visitor Information Center,** 1125 Pan American Rte., is off Rte. 80 on your right as you enter town. (☎888-315-9999. Open M-F 8am-5pm, Sa 8am-1pm.) The city's main attraction is the **John Slaughter Ranch,** 6153 Geronimo Trail. The ranch's eponymous owner was a Confederate soldier, rancher, and lawman who was voted the Marshal of Tombstone. He proceeded to shoot or prosecute (in no particular order) Tombstone's worst. Slaughter's ranch buildings are now a museum where visitors can get a sense of the Wild West and get a great view of the town below. The ranch is located 15 mi. east of the city on an unpaved, bumpy road that takes about 45min. each way, so make sure you really like ranches before setting out. (Follow 15th St. east until it becomes the Geronimo Trail, which leads to the ranch. ☎520-558-2474. Open W-Su 10am-3pm. $4, children $1.)

The **Grand Cafe ❶,** 119 G Ave., has walls filled with pictures of Marilyn Monroe, an obsession of the first owner's wife. It also offers tasty Mexican food for under $7. (☎520-364-2344. Open M-Sa 10am-9pm. MC/V.) Across the street, the **Gadsden Hotel ❸,** 1046 G. Ave., is an extravagant yet inexpensive hotel. Established in 1907, this opulent palace hails itself as "the last of the grand hotels," and the white marble staircase, 14K gold-topped marble pillars, and ridiculously ornate lobby support the claim. While the rooms may not be as luxurious as the great hall, they are still nicely decorated, with big, bright windows. (☎520-364-4481; www.gadsdenhotel.com. Singles $50; doubles $60. AmEx/D/MC/V.)

◼ APPROACHING AGUA PRIETA: 100 FEET
Your best bet is to park your car in Douglas and walk across the border to Agua Prieta—Mexico requires foreign drivers to carry Mexican **liability insurance** (your existing American policy won't cover it), and those caught without it face stiff penalties. Within the 20km "free zone" south of the Arizona-Sonora border, you won't need a tourist card.

AGUA PRIETA

The 10-block area of Agua Prieta close to the border with Douglas is a far cry from the extreme poverty and sleaze of some Mexican border towns. A quick hop over the border is worth it for the cultural experience—it's much livelier than the American side—and the Mexican food. Street vendors sell *helado* (ice cream), *fruta* (fresh fruit), and *agua fresca* (juice and soda). Don't worry about exchanging money if you're only going to be in Mexico for a few hours; vendors will accept dollars or pesos, overcharging tourists either way. The city is laid out with *avenidas* running north-south and *calles* running east-west. The best Mexican food can be found on **Avenida 4.** Don't miss the **Plaza** at Calle 5 and Avenida 4, site of many a fiesta. The town also has beautiful churches, like the **Iglesia de Guadalupe,** at Avenida 4 and Calle 6. The border crossing is located on **Calle 3.** It is easiest to park your car on the American side of 3rd St., at Pan American, and walk across. If you decide to drive, be prepared to wait in lines returning through the crossing. If you're planning on roadtripping through Mexico, this is a great place to start; Agua Prieta marks the beginning of the **Janos Hwy.,** the shortest route to Mexico City from the US. For more coverage of Mexico, see ◪*Let's Go: Mexico.*

◼ APPROACHING BISBEE: 21 MILES
From Douglas, take **Rte. 80 W** for 21 mi. to Bisbee across more desert.

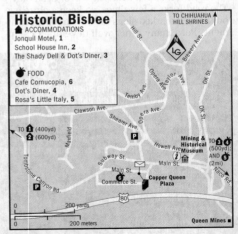

Historic Bisbee

▲ ACCOMMODATIONS
Jonquil Motel, **1**
School House Inn, **2**
The Shady Dell & Dot's Diner, **3**

🍎 FOOD
Cafe Cornucopia, **6**
Dot's Diner, **4**
Rosa's Little Italy, **5**

TO CHIHUAHUA HILL SHRINES

BISBEE

This rough-'n'-tumble mining-town-turned-artist-colony is famous for its eccentricity. Old miners give tours of prosperous shafts while bohemians hang out at cafes and galleries. The Victorian-style houses that line the narrow streets of the historic district could as easily be part of a European town as they are part of this Old West settlement. Some hail it as a land where time stands still, but Bisbee seems more like a community where time accumulates; the Western frontier, the Gold Rush, the 1950s, the summer of love, and the postmodern age are all alive and well here.

VITAL STATS

Population: 6100

Visitor Info: Bisbee Visitors Center, 2 Copper Queen Plaza (☎520-432-3554; www.discoverbisbee.com), on Main St. Open M-F 9am-5pm, Sa-Su 10am-4pm.

Internet Access: Copper Queen Library, 6 Main St. (☎520-432-4232). Open M noon-7pm, Tu and Th-F 10am-5pm, W 10am-7pm, Sa 10am-2pm. Free.

Post Office: Copper Queen, 6 Main St. (☎520-432-2052). Open M-F 8:30am-4:30pm. **Postal Code:** 85603.

⌐ **GETTING AROUND.** The streets of Bisbee are almost entirely unnavigable, but the downtown area is small and easy to walk. Get a map—you'll still be lost, but you'll feel better. The town's tiny alleys were designed for hooved travel, so the sooner you ditch your car and take to the street, the better off you'll be. Most restaurants and galleries lie along **Main St.,** which curves and turns into **Tombstone Canyon Rd.**

◗ **SIGHTS.** Copper mining built Bisbee, and although the mine became unprofitable and shut down in the mid-1970s, you can still learn about it on educational 1¼hr. tours at the **Queen Mines,** on the Rte. 80 interchange. Tours are led by former miners and require headlamps and safety gear. The miners also offer van tours of the town's historical sights. (☎866-432-2071. Mine tours daily 9, 10:30am, noon, 2, 3:30pm. $12, ages 4-15 $5. Van tours daily 10:30am, noon, 2, 3:30pm. $10.) After exploring the bowels of Bisbee's mines, you'll welcome the heavenly experience of the **Chihuahua Hill Shrines.** A

20min. hike over rocky ground leads to two shrines, the first Buddhist and the second Catholic. The Catholic shrine is exceptional in its complexity and was erected in the 1950s by a grieving family who lost their son at war. The more understated Buddhist shrine features several works of rock art in addition to innumerable prayer flags and pictures of the last two Dalai Lamas. (To reach the shrines, head up Brewery Ave.; there is a grocery store on the right. Behind the store are two staircases; take the left one. Next, turn left, and briefly follow a concrete driveway. Before the private property sign, turn right off the paved road. At the cross, follow the trail up.) For a retrospective view on the area, visit the **Mining and Historical Museum,** 5 Copper Queen. This Smithsonian-affiliated museum has excellent exhibits that highlight the discovery of Bisbee's copper surplus and the lives of the fortune-seekers who extracted it. The newest exhibit has been 7 years in the making and features a realistic faux mine. (☎520-432-7071. Open daily 10am-4pm. $5, seniors $4.50, under 3 free.)

 PHOTO OP. Head to the **Copper Queen Hotel,** 11 Howell Ave., to meet one of the four ghosts who haunt the hotel's long halls and winding staircases.

♖ **FOOD.** Eateries line the main drags of downtown. With fresh sandwiches and crisp salads, **Cafe Cornucopia ❷,** 14 Main St., was hollowed out of a turn-of-the-century structure. The chicken-salad sandwich ($7) will knock your socks off, and don't miss the tangy cilantro coleslaw. They also serve smoothies ($4) and soups ($5-6) in a bread bowl. (☎520-432-4820. Open W-Su 10am-5pm. Cash only.) At night, **Rosa's Little Italy ❸,** 7 Bisbee Rd., 1 mi. from the historic district, is so popular that you'll need reservations. Adorably romantic, it has small, candlelit tables inside and a beautiful vine-shaded courtyard with a fountain outside. The "Peasant's Pasta" ($14) is great, as is the extensive vegetarian menu ($11-13). Bring your own wine or beer at no charge. (☎520-432-1331. Open Th-Sa 5-9pm, Su 5-8pm. MC/V.)

▚ **ACCOMMODATIONS.** Lodging in Bisbee is expensive. Travel back in time to the 50s at ▨**The Shady Dell ❷,** 1 Douglas Rd., where you can stay in one of eight restored vintage trailers, complete with authentic period furnishings including propane stoves, refrigerators, and electric percolators. Each of the sleek aluminum trailers is unique, and some even have original black-and-white TVs. (Just before historic Bisbee, take a left after the rotary. ☎520-432-3567; www.theshadydell.com. No children under 10. Reservations recommended. Trailers $45-120. MC/V.) On the grounds you'll also find the unique **Dot's Diner ❶**, located in a 1957 trailer. A visit to Dot's means fighting the walls for elbow room, but the cozy family kitchen evokes the original atmosphere of diner eating. Classic breakfasts ($3) are served all day along with hamburgers, sandwiches, and Southwestern food. (☎520-432-1112. Lunch $4-5. Open Aug.-May W-Su 7:30am-2pm.) At the south end of town, the ☒**School House Inn ❸**, 818 Tombstone Canyon Rd., is located in a remodeled 1918 schoolhouse and has beautifully decorated rooms, a balcony, and a spacious oak-shaded patio for guest use. Check out the working 1950s soda machine by the balcony. All rooms have private baths. Ironically, no children under 14 are allowed. (☎520-432-2996 or 800-537-4333. Hot breakfast included. Singles $69; doubles $89. AmEx/D/MC/V.) The **Jonquil Motel ❸**, 317 Tombstone Canyon Rd., has clean, smoke-free rooms and a backyard perfect for barbecues or lounging. (☎520-432-7371 or 866-432-7371. Singles $60; doubles $70. D/MC/V.)

◤ **APPROACHING TOMBSTONE: 27 MILES**
From Bisbee, head northwest on **Rte. 80** out of town and continue 27 mi. to Tombstone.

TOMBSTONE

Long past its glory days as a silver-mining town that was also the largest city between the Mississippi River and the Pacific, Tombstone has abandoned its dangerous Old West history for a more-sanitized, Disney version of cowboy living. Despite the touristy feel, it's a fun place to spend a few hours; it gives you a real sense of how a Western town was built in the late-1800s, not to mention tons of cheesy but fabulous photo ops. The city offers a little bit of everything, and a lot of rot-gut and gunfight re-enactments.

VITAL STATS

Population: 1600

Visitor Info: City of Tombstone Visitor and Information Center, 317 Allen St. (☎520-457-3929; www.cityoftombstone.org), at 4th St. Open daily 9am-5pm.

Internet Access: Tombstone Public Library, 337 S. 4th St., at Toughnut St. (☎520-457-3612). Open M-F 8am-noon and 1-5pm. Free.

Post Office: 100 N. Haskell Ave. (☎520-457-3479). Open M-F 8:30am-4:30pm. **Postal Code:** 85638.

◩ **GETTING AROUND.** Historic Tombstone is basically two streets: **Rte. 80** rolls through town one block east of **Allen St.**, which is closed to traffic and is the main historic drag. Numbered streets run perpendicular to Allen St., and most attractions lie between 6th and 3rd St.

◧ **SIGHTS.** Tombstone has turned the shootout at the **O.K. Corral**, 308 E. Allen St., into a year-round tourist industry, inviting visitors to view the barnyard where Wyatt Earp and his posse showed outlaws who was boss. Besides a reenactment of the shootout daily at 2pm, the O.K. Corral has good exhibits on the history of the site, the town, and on legal prostitution in Tombstone in the 1880s. Attached to the Corral is the **Tombstone Historama**, where Vincent Price narrates the town's history as a plastic mountain revolves on stage and a dramatization of the gunfight is shown on a movie screen. (☎520-457-3456. Open daily 9:30am-4:30pm. Historama shows every 30min. Corral and Historama $5.50; with gunfight $7.50.) The site of the longest poker game in Western history (8 years, 5 months, and 3 days), the **Bird Cage Theater**, at 6th and Allen St., is named for the upper-level booths that once held "soiled doves" (prostitutes) with feathers in their hair. Men would pay $25 for 8hr. of "negotiable affection" with the lady of their choice. When the mines went bust in 1889, the Bird Cage was shut and left as it was—a time capsule preserving the history of Tombstone's men and the women who serviced them. It is unrestored today, with the original 1881 curtains, piano, tables, and chairs left essentially undisturbed. The museum also houses artifacts, including a

100-year-old "merman," original show posters, and the "crib" (bordello room) of Sadie Jo, Wyatt Earp's famous actress-lover. The Bird Cage is said to be haunted, with 26 violent deaths in its nine-year run. (☎505-457-3421. Open daily 8am-6pm. $8, seniors $7, ages 8-18 $6, under 8 free.) If hype and tall tales are not your style, visit the **Tombstone Courthouse State Historic Park,** at 3rd and Toughnut St. The impressive old building that tried to bring law to the lawless is now a museum offering the most accurate account of what really happened at high noon at the O.K. Corral. The most interesting part of the museum may be the historical gallows. (☎520-457-3311. Open daily 8am-5pm. In summer $3, in winter $4; under 13 free.) The actual tombstones of Tombstone—the results of all that gunplay—rest in the **Boothill Cemetery,** just outside of town on Rte. 80 N. Look for the graves of the O.K. Corral losers (the McLaury brothers and Billy Clanton) and other Tombstone notables like Dutch Annie, "Queen of the Red Light District." Pick up a map ($2) of the graveyard at the entrance. (☎800-457-3423. Open daily 7:30am-5:30pm. Free.)

 PHOTO OP. For something a little less high-noon and a little more horticulture, the **Rose Tree Museum,** at 4th and Toughnut St., shelters the **World's Largest Rose Tree,** which was planted in 1885 and is now over 8,000 sq. ft. Its annual flowering in April is a sight to behold. (☎520-457-3326. Open daily 9am-5pm. $3, under 14 free. Cash only.

FOOD AND ACCOMMODATIONS.
Food in Tombstone is a one-trick act consisting primarily of hamburgers. Once the "Bucket of Blood Saloon" where Virgil Earp was shot from the second-story window, **The Longhorn Restaurant ❷,** 501 E. Allen St., is now a boisterous family restaurant. Try the "too tough to die burger" ($11.25). Less-legendary burgers and sandwiches cost around $6, while dinner plates like roast beef or meatloaf are $11. (☎520-457-3405. Open daily 9am-9pm. AmEx/MC/V.) Named for "the girl who loved Doc Holiday and everyone else," **Big Nose Kate's Saloon ❸,** 417 Allen St., is done up like

an Old West saloon with live honky-tonk music daily. The ghost of "the swamper" is said to haunt these halls searching for his lost cache of silver, left here when the building was still the Grand Hotel. (☎520-457-3107. Lunch from $7. Open daily 10am-midnight. AmEx/MC/V.) Named after the "angel of the mining camps" who devoted her life to clean living and public service, **Nellie Cashman's Restaurant ❸,** 402 S. 5th St., off Allen St., is less Old West and a bit more down-home. (☎520-457-2212. Hamburgers from $6. Entrees $10-13. Open daily 7:30am-9pm. D/MC/V.)

Removed from the giddy-up ruckus of Allen St. but still only steps from the action, the **Larian Motel ❸,** at 5th St. and Rte. 80., offers spacious, clean rooms named for famous outlaws, vigilantes, and ruffians. All rooms have A/C, TV, and coffee; some have fridges and microwaves. (☎520-457-2272; www.tombstonemotels.com. Singles $55-65; doubles $65-75. Reservations recommended. MC/V.)

⚑ APPROACHING SONOITA: 22 MILES
Head north on **Rte. 80** for 3 mi. to **Rte. 82.** Head west 19 mi. to the town of Sonoita, located in Arizona's wine country, where a few scattered wineries offer wine tasting down back roads.

SONOITA. You might be surprised to learn that Sonoita is located in Arizona's wine country—the area is mostly open prairie. The town itself, situated at the crossroads of Rte. 82 and 83, has little to offer but an expensive hotel, gas, and a couple of restaurants. The aptly named **Sonoita Crossroads Cafe ❶,** 3172 Hwy. 83, fuels up passersby with gourmet coffees and classic American cuisine with the Madera Canyon and mountains as a backdrop. (☎520-455-5189. Breakfast $2-6. Lunch $4-6. Open daily 8am-2pm. MC/V.)

⚑ APPROACHING TUCSON: 48 MILES
Take **Rte. 82 W** to **Rte. 83.** Here, you'll see your first *saguaro,* the tall, standing cacti that make the Arizona landscape famous. Get on **I-10 W,** and take **Exit 265** to downtown Tucson.

TUCSON
A little bit country, a little bit south of the border, Tucson is a melting pot of culture, history, and contradictory influences. Mexi-

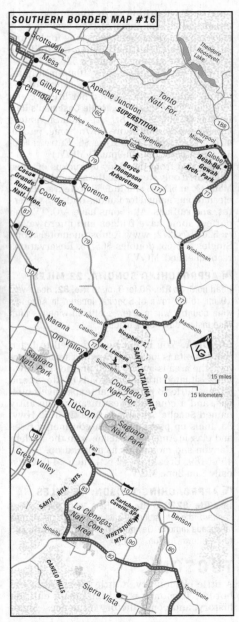

SOUTHERN BORDER MAP #16

can property until 1854, the city retains much of its Mexican influence while also championing the rugged individualism of the American West. Home to the students of the University of Arizona, the soldiers of the Davis-Monthan Air Force Base, ranching cowboys, downtown artists, and suburban retirees, Tucson is the colorful fusion of a seemingly disparate variety of folk. Somehow though, amid the war machines and creative photography, honky tonk and Latin techno, irony gradually fades away into desert sunsets and half-empty margarita glasses.

VITAL STATS

Population: 490,000

Visitor Info: Tucson Convention and Visitors Bureau, 100 S. Church Ave. (☎520-624-1817 or 800-638-8350; www.visittucson.org). Open M-F 8am-5pm, Sa-Su 9am-4pm.

Internet Access: Joel D. Valdez Main Public Library, 101 N. Stone Ave. (☎520-791-4393). Open M-W 9am-8pm, Th 9am-6pm, Sa 10am-5pm.

Post Office: 1501 S. Cherry Bell. (☎520-791-5043). Open M-F 8:30am-8pm, Sa 9am-1pm.
Postal Code: 85726.

GETTING AROUND

Just east of **I-10,** Tucson's downtown area surrounds the intersection of **Broadway Blvd.** and **Stone Ave.** The **University of Arizona** lies 1 mi. northeast of downtown at the intersection of **Park Ave.** and **Speedway Blvd.** Avenues run north-south, streets east-west; because some of each are numbered, intersections such as "6th and 6th" exist. Speedway, Broadway, and **Grant Rd.** are the quickest east-west routes through town. To go north-south, follow **Oracle Rd.** through the heart of the city or **Campbell Ave.** east of downtown. The hip, young crowd swings on **4th Ave.** and on **Congress St.,** both with small shops, quirky restaurants, and a slew of bars. Tucson is accustomed to bustle, and as in most of the Southwest, parking is not an issue. If you want to ditch your car downtown, ride the free TICET buses that circulate downtown between Tools Ave. and I-10 and 6th and 12th St. On weekends, a $1 electric trolley runs up and down 4th St.

SOUTHERN BORDER

SIGHTS

UNIVERSITY OF ARIZONA. Lined with cafes, restaurants, galleries, and vintage clothing shops, **4th Ave.** is an alternative magnet and a great place to take a stroll. Between Speedway and Broadway Blvd., the street becomes a shopping district with increasingly touristy shops. Lovely for its varied and elaborately irrigated vegetation, the University of Arizona's mall sits where E. 3rd St. should be. The **Center for Creative Photography** is home to the archives of over 50 great 20th-century photographers, including Ansel Adams, Edward Weston, and W. Eugene Smith. The museum also hosts temporary exhibits. *(1030 N. Olive Rd. ☎520-621-7968. Open M-F 9am-5pm, Sa-Su noon-5pm. Archives available to the public by appointment only. Free.)* The **Flandrau Science Center** dazzles visitors with a public observatory and a laser light show. *(1601 E. University Blvd. ☎520-621-7827. Open M-W 9am-5pm, Th-Sa 9am-5pm and 7-9pm, Su 1-5pm. $3, ages 3-14 $2, under 3 free. Planetarium shows $5.50, seniors $4.50, ages 3-13 $4.)* The **University of Arizona Museum of Art** displays modern American and 18th-century Latin American art, as well as the sculpture of Jacques Lipchitz. The museum also exhibits student art. *(☎520-621-7567. Open Tu-F 9am-5pm, Sa-Su noon-4pm. Free.)*

TUCSON MUSEUM OF ART. This major museum presents impressive traveling exhibits in all media to supplement its permanent collection of American, Mexican, and European art. Housed in the surrounding and affiliated Presidio Historic Block, it boasts an impressive collection of Pre-Columbian and Mexican folk art as well as art of the American West. *(140 N. Main Ave. ☎520-624-2333. Open Tu-Sa 10am-4pm, Su noon-4pm. $8, seniors $6, students $3, under 13 free. 1st Su of each month free.)*

DEGRAZIA GALLERY IN THE SUN. Stepping through the ornate iron doors of this old-fashioned pueblo home reveals the artistic world of Ettore "Ted" DeGrazia. The home itself, wonderfully spacious and colorful, breathes life into the paintings that adorn the walls. Wander the grounds before entering the gallery; wooden sculptures and sun-bleached metalwork are scattered throughout the cactus garden. Don't miss the chapel, dedicated to the Virgin Guadalupe. *(6300 N. Swan Rd., about ¼ mi. north of Sunrise Rd. ☎520-299-9191 or 800-545-2185; www.degrazia.org. Open daily 10am-3:45pm. Free.)*

SIGHTS ON WEST SPEEDWAY. As Speedway Blvd. winds its way west from Tucson's city center, it passes by a variety of sights. The left fork leads to **Old Tucson Studios**, an elaborate Old West-style town constructed for the 1938 movie *Arizona* and used as a backdrop for Westerns ever since, including many John Wayne films and the 1999 Will Smith blockbuster *Wild Wild West*. It's open year-round to tourists, who can walk around the Old West mock-up, watch comedy and musical shows, view gun fight reenactments, and, if fortunate, catch a filming. *(201 S. Kinney Rd. ☎520-883-0100. Open daily 10am-4pm. Occasionally closed for group functions; call ahead. $15, ages 4-11 $9.50, under 4 free.)* Those opting to take the right fork will eschew the Wild Wild West for the merely wild West; less than 2 mi. from the fork lies the **Arizona-Sonora Desert Museum**, a first-rate zoo and nature preserve. The living museum recreates a range of desert habitats and features over 300 kinds of animals. A visit requires at least 2hr., preferably in the morning before the animals take their afternoon siestas. *(2021 N. Kinney Rd. Follow Speedway Blvd. west of the city as it becomes Gates Pass Rd., then Kinney Rd. ☎520-883-1380; www.desertmuseum.org. Open daily June-Aug. 7:30am-10pm; Mar.-May and Sept. 7:30am-5pm; Oct.-Feb. 8:30am-5pm. June-Aug. $9, ages 6-12 $2; Sept.-May $12/$4.)*

CAVES. Kartchner Caverns State Park is enormously popular, filled with magnificent rock formations and home to over 1000 bats. This is a "living" cave, which contains water and is still experiencing the growth of its formations. The damp conditions cause the formations to shine and glisten in the light. Taking a tour is the only way to enter the cave. *(8 mi. off I-10 at Exit 302. ☎520-586-4100, reservations 520-586-2283. Open daily 7:30am-6pm. 1hr. tours every 30min. 8:30am-4:30pm. Entrance fee $5 per vehicle, free with reservation. Reservations strongly recommended. Tours $19-23, ages 7-13 $10-13.)* Near Saguaro National Park East, **Colossal Cave** is one of the only dor-

---

1973: 16 year old "Rolling Stone" writer Cameron Crowe hits the road with the Allman Brothers.

mant (no water or new formations) caves in the US. A variety of tours are offered; on Saturday evenings, a special ladder tour through otherwise sealed-off tunnels, crawl spaces, and corridors can be arranged. (☎520-647-7275. Open mid-Mar. to mid-Sept. M-Sa 8am-6pm, Su 8am-7pm; mid-Sept. to mid-Mar. M-Sa 9am-5pm, Su 9am-6pm. Entrance fee $5 per vehicle. Guided tours $8.50, ages 6-12 $5. Ladder tour $35, including dinner.)

PIMA AIR AND SPACE MUSEUM. This museum chronicles aviation history from the days of the Wright brothers to its modern military incarnations. While exhibits on female and African-American aviators are interesting, the main draw is a fleet of decommissioned warplanes. (6000 E. Valencia Rd. ☎520-574-0462. Open daily 9am-5pm; last entry 4pm. June-Oct. $9.75, seniors $8.75, ages 7-12 $6; Nov.-May $11.75/$9.75/$8.)

🏔 OUTDOORS

North of the desert museum, the western half of **Saguaro National Park** (Tucson Mountain District) has hiking trails and an auto loop. The **Bajada Loop Drive** runs less than 9 mi. but passes through some of the most striking desert scenery the park has to offer. The paved nature walk (¼ mi.) near the **Visitors Center**, 2700 N. Kinney Rd., has some of the best specimens of Saguaro cactus in the Tucson area. (☎520-733-5158. Open daily 9am-5pm. Entrance fee $10 per vehicle, good for 7 days.) There are a variety of hiking trails through Saguaro West; **Sendero Esperanza Trail** (3¼ mi.), beginning at the Ez-Kim-In-Zin picnic area, is the mildest approach to the summit of **Wasson Peak** (4687 ft.), the highest in the Tucson Mountain Range. The **Hugh Norris Trail** (5 mi.) is a slightly longer, more strenuous climb to the top but has great views of unique rock formations. The eastern half of Saguaro National Park, known as the **Rincon Mountain District,** has more hiking. Mountain biking is permitted only around the **Cactus Forest Loop Drive** (8 mi.) and **Cactus Forest Trail** (2 mi.), at the eastern end of the park near the visitors center. The trails in Saguaro East are much longer than those in the western segment of the park.

Northeast of downtown Tucson, the cliffs and desert pools of **Sabino Canyon** provide an ideal backdrop for picnics and day hikes. Locals beat Tucson heat by frolicking in the water holes. No cars are permitted, but a narrated 45min. shuttle bus ride makes trips through the canyon. A great day hike idea is to take the shuttle one-way from the visitors center to stop #9, then walk back along the **Phoneline Trail** (5¾ mi.), a picturesque route along the ridge of the canyon. The visitors center is at the park's entrance. (Take Speedway Blvd. to Swan Rd. to Sunrise Dr. The entrance is at the cross of Sunrise Dr. and Sabino Canyon Rd. ☎520-749-8700. Park open 24hr. $5 per vehicle. Visitor center open M-F 8am-4:30pm, Sa-Su 8:30am-4:30pm. Shuttle runs July-Nov. every hr. 9am-4pm; Dec.-June every 30min. sunrise-sunset. $7.50, ages 3-12 $3.)

🍴 FOOD

Like any good college town, Tucson brims with inexpensive, tasty eateries, and, as in any good Southwestern town, Mexican fare dominates the culinary scene.

Elle, 3048 E. Broadway Blvd. (☎520-327-0500). Cool jazz reverberates throughout this elegant eatery. Spoil yourself with a meal of butternut squash ravioli ($16) and a glass of Arizona wine (from $5). Open M-Th 11am-9pm, F-Sa 11am-10pm, Su 4-9pm. Entrees $13-16. AmEx/D/MC/V. ❸

El Charro, 311 N. Court Ave. (☎520-622-5465), at the corner of Franklin and Court St. Opened in 1922, El Charro is Tucson's oldest Mexican restaurant owned continuously by the same family. It is so popular that the USS Tucson submarine has named its galley "El Charro Down Under." Its most famous dish is the carne seca, beef dried for 48hr. on the restaurant's roof and then thinly sliced and grilled with tomatoes, onions, chiles, and spices ($13). Entrees $10-13. Open M-Th and Su 11am-9pm, F-Sa 11am-10pm. AmEx/D/MC/V. ❷

Gus Balon's Restaurant, 6027 E. 22nd St. (☎520-748-9731), just west of Wilmot. This classic diner serves up Tucson's best breakfast ($4-5) all day with heaping plates of eggs, potatoes, and toast. Lunch and dinner feature classics like roast sirloin ($6), grilled country ham ($6.75), and assorted sandwiches ($2-4). The pies lining one wall are an irresistibly sweet temptation ($2 per slice). Open M-Sa 7am-3pm. Cash only. ❶

La Indita, 622 N. 4th Ave. (☎520-792-0523). A small restaurant that delights customers with tra-

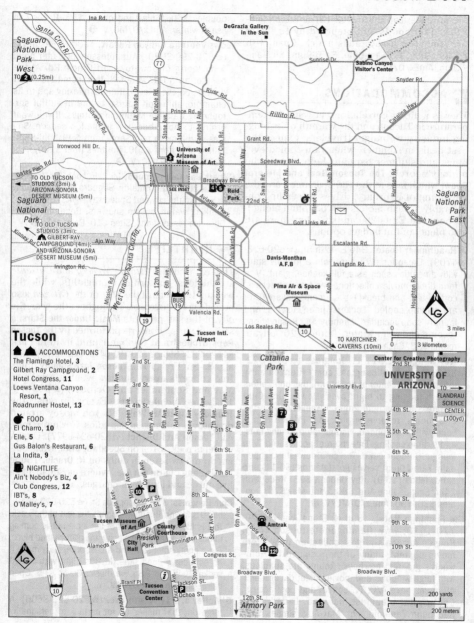

DeGrazia Gallery in the Sun

Ina Rd.

Skyline Dr.

Saguaro National Park West

TO 2 (0.25mi)

Sabino Canyon Visitor's Center

Sunrise Dr.

Snyder Rd.

Santa Cruz Rd.

River Rd.

Prince Rd.

Rillito R.

Catalina Hwy

Ironwood Hill Dr.

Grant Rd.

Speedway Blvd.

University of Arizona Museum of Art

SEE INSET

TO OLD TUCSON STUDIOS (3mi) & ARIZONA-SONORA DESERT MUSEUM (5mi)

Broadway Blvd.

Reid Park

22nd St.

Saguaro National Park East

Gates Pass Rd.

Saguaro National Park

TO OLD TUCSON STUDIOS (3mi); GILBERT-RAY CAMPGROUND (4mi); AND ARIZONA-SONORA DESERT MUSEUM (5mi)

Kinney Rd.

Ajo Way

Golf Links Rd.

Old Spanish Trail

Irvington Rd.

Escalante Rd.

Davis-Monthan A.F.B

Irvington Rd.

Pima Air & Space Museum

Valencia Rd.

Los Reales Rd.

Tucson Intl. Airport

TO KARTCHNER CAVERNS (10mi)

3 miles

3 kilometers

Tucson

ACCOMMODATIONS
The Flamingo Hotel, 3
Gilbert Ray Campground, 2
Hotel Congress, 11
Loews Ventana Canyon Resort, 1
Roadrunner Hostel, 13

FOOD
El Charro, 10
Elle, 5
Gus Balon's Restaurant, 6
La Indita, 9

NIGHTLIFE
Ain't Nobody's Biz, 4
Club Congress, 12
IBT's, 8
O'Malley's, 7

Catalina Park

Center for Creative Photography

UNIVERSITY OF ARIZONA

TO FLANDRAU SCIENCE CENTER (100yd)

University Blvd.

Amtrak

Tucson Museum of Art

El Presidio Park

County Courthouse

City Hall

Alameda St.

Congress St.

Broadway Blvd.

Tucson Convention Center

Armory Park

200 yards

200 meters

ditional Mexican cuisine ($3-12) served on tortillas. The food is still prepared by *La Indita* herself, who always adds a kick. Open M-Th 11am-9pm, F 11am-6pm, Sa 6-9pm, Su 9am-9pm. AmEx/D/MC/V. ❷

ACCOMMODATIONS

There's a direct correlation between the temperature in Tucson and the warmth of its lodging industry to budget travelers; expect the best deals in summer, when rain-cooled evenings and summer bargains help to ease the midday scorch. **The Tucson Gem and Mineral Show,** which falls at the end of January and the beginning of February, drives prices up considerably. Cheap motels can be found along **I-10** between Exits 260 and 262, but there are also plenty of fun budget options.

Roadrunner Hostel, 346 E. 12th St. (☎520-628-4709). Exceptionally clean, with a friendly staff, with amenities such as a full kitchen, giant TV, a formidable movie collection, free Internet access, coffee, tea, and breakfast. All rooms have A/C or are swamp cooled. Lockers, linen, towels, and laundry soap included. Laundry $1. Reservations recommended in winter. Dorms $20; private rooms $38. Cash only. ❶

Hotel Congress, 311 E. Congress (☎520-622-8848; www.hotelcongress.com). Conveniently located in the center of downtown, this hotel offers superb lodging to night owls. Downstairs, Club Congress booms until 2am on weekends; for quieter rooms, reserve in advance. Private rooms come with bath, phone, vintage radio, ceiling fans, and swamp cooling. Free Internet access and TV in lounge. Outdoor patio. The cafe downstairs (open daily 7am-10pm) serves great salads ($6-11) and sandwiches ($6-9). Key deposit $25. Reception 24hr. Singles June-Aug. $60; Sept.-May $70. Doubles $80/$90. AmEx/D/MC/V. ❸

The Flamingo Hotel, 1300 N. Stone Ave. (☎520-770-1910; www.flamingohoteltucson.com). Houses Arizona's largest collection of Western movie posters, many of them signed by Hollywood's greatest cowboys. Rooms are spacious, with large windows and movie poster decorations. All rooms have A/C, TV, coffee, and pool access. Continental breakfast included. Laundry $1. Reception 7am-midnight. May-Aug. singles $40;

doubles $50; triples and quads $55. Prices can rise in winter. AmEx/D/MC/V. ❷

Loews Ventana Canyon Resort, 7000 N. Resort Dr. (☎520-299-2020). A quintessential 5-star hotel 5 mi. north of downtown off Oracle Rd. At the base of an 80 ft. waterfall, this incredible resort delivers on every level, from its relaxing spa to its championship golf course to the beautiful surrounding Catalina Mountain foothills. If you want luxury, it's not a bad deal in the low season. Singles mid-May to mid-Sept. from $99; mid-Sept. to mid-May from $300. Doubles from $120/from $300. AmEx/D/MC/V. ❺

Gilbert Ray Campground, McCain Loop Rd. (☎520-883-4200), just outside Saguaro West. An easy drive from the city and Speedway sights. Toilets and drinking water, but no showers. Reception 9am-5pm. No reservations. Sites $10. Cash only. ❶

☯ NIGHTLIFE

The free weeklies *Tucson Weekly* and *Caliente* are the local authorities on nightlife, while the weekend sections of the *Star* or the *Citizen* also provide good coverage. Throughout the year, the city of the sun presents **Music Under the Stars,** a series of sunset concerts performed by the **Tucson Pops Orchestra** at the bandstand in Reid Park (☎520-722-5853 or 520-791-0479. Concerts generally Sa-Su. Free.) The **Tucson Jazz Society** holds free concerts every Sunday evening April and May and September and October. (☎520-903-1265. Free. Venue varies.) Every Thursday, the **Thursday Night Art Walk** lets you mosey around downtown galleries and studios. For more info, call **Tucson Arts District** (☎520-624-9977). U of A students rock 'n' roll on **Speedway Blvd.,** while others do the two-step in clubs on **N. Oracle.** Young locals hang out on **4th Ave.,** where most bars have live music and low cover charges.

Club Congress, 311 E. Congress St. (☎520-622-8848), has DJs M and Th and live bands the rest of the week. This is the venue for most of the indie music coming through town, including alt-country, alt-rock, and blues. The friendly hotel staff and a cast of regulars make it an especially good time. M 80s night with $0.80 vodka. Tu-W and F-Su live music. Cover $3-5. Open daily 9pm-2am. AmEx/D/MC/V.

O'Malley's, 247 N. 4th Ave. (☎520-623-8600). A large bar that makes up for its lack of personality with decent bar food, pool tables, and pinball. As its name implies, this is usually a better place to nurse your pint of Guinness than it is to get your groove on, although the dance floor gets packed on Th and Sa for 80s and 90s cover bands. No cover. Open daily 11am-2am. AmEx/D/MC/V.

IBT's, 616 N. 4th Ave. (☎520-882-3053). The single most popular gay venue in Tucson, IBT's pumps dance music in a classic club environment to a mixed weekend capacity crowd. Sa karaoke. F and Sa hip-hop DJs. W (8pm) and Sa (8:30pm) free drag shows. No cover. Open daily 9am-2am. Cash or debit only.

Ain't Nobody's Biz, 2900 E. Broadway Blvd. (☎520-318-4838). The little sister of its Phoenix namesake and the big mama of the Tucson lesbian scene. "Biz" is a cozy bar with cool mood lighting that attracts a diverse crowd for some of the best dancing in Tucson. Music ranges from hip-hop to Latin pop. Sa 80s and 90s. Happy hour M-Tu 2-10pm, W-F 2-8pm with 2-for-1 domestic beers and drafts. Open daily 11am-2am. AmEx/D/MC/V.

⛰ DETOUR
SKY ISLAND SCENIC BYWAY

Hop on Oracle Rd. heading north and follow it as it turns into Rte. 77. The road passes by the University of Arizona and the entrance to Coronado National Forest's Sky Island Scenic Byway (Gen. Hitchcock Hwy.). The entrance is on your right, before you've exited the city limits.

The Sky Island road isn't about islands—it's all about sky. The beautiful 30 mi. road leads up steep inclines and switchbacks through **Catalina State Park** (☎520-749-8700; $6 per vehicle) up to **Mt. Lemmon.** From there, you must backtrack on the same road to reach Rte. 77. The entire adventure, not including any hiking, takes several hours. In both temperature and terrain, the nearly mile-high climb can be compared to a transcontinental journey from Mexico to Canada. Every 1000 ft. change in elevation witnesses a metamorphosis that parallels a 300 mi. drive northward. As the road blasts through impressive granite formations and snakes along canyon walls, the temperature drops nearly 30° and the Sonoran desert gives way to forest.

Nearing the summit, the highway hugs the ridgeline, and the impressive vistas of the surrounding desert valleys are visible on both sides of the roadway. Stopping at one of the many turnouts or picnic areas for a picture is a must. At 8000 ft., **Inspiration Rock Picnic Ground** offers the brave a chance to take a few (cautious) steps out onto a giant granite precipice and gaze down at the miniature Tucson Valley below. At the top lies the teensy hamlet of **Summerhaven,** where a public restroom makes up half of the buildings in the town, and **Mt. Lemmon Ski Valley** (☎520-576-1321). The Forest Service offers campsites along the way, with **Rose Canyon Campground ❶,** on the shores of a lovely lake, being the most popular. **Spencer Canyon Campground ❶** is closer to the summit, so it stays cooler than many other sites. Both sites have toilets and potable water but no showers. (☎520-749-8700. $17 per vehicle.) Other campgrounds are primitive sites and cost $10-15. **Molino Basin ❶** and **General Hitchcock ❶** campsites have toilets but no potable water. (Closed June-Sept. Sites at both $7.) Call the Santa Catalina Ranger District (☎520-749-8700) for more info on camping.

⛰ APPROACHING BIOSPHERE 2: 18 MILES
Once you've seen or passed Catalina State Park, continue north on **Rte. 77** past the town of Oro Valley, essentially a suburb of Tucson, to Biosphere 2.

BIOSPHERE 2. The "earth-bound spaceship" ⛰**Biosphere 2,** 32540 S. Biosphere Rd., is a massive 3¼ acre laboratory that looks and feels like it is, indeed, independent of planet Earth, which scientists affectionately call Biosphere 1. Concrete, glass, and 500 tons of steel construct and close off this sealed ecosystem, which houses five biomes: a desert, a marsh, a savanna, a rainforest, and even an ocean. Ultra-high technology powers Biosphere 2, from the two dome-like "lungs" that manage air pressure to the wave machine that keeps 700,000 gallons of water moving through the reefs of the ocean biome. Perhaps best known for a 1991 experiment that examined whether humans could survive in a closed environment, the center now focuses on education and research. (☎520-838-6200; www.bio2.com. Open daily 9am-4pm. Last tour 3pm. $13, ages 13-17 $9, ages 6-12 $6, under 6 free. AmEx/D/MC/V.)

⛰ APPROACHING MAMMOTH: 17 MILES
Continue on **Rte. 77** for 17 mi. to reach Mammoth.

MAMMOTH. The prairies and foothills that surround the self-proclaimed wildflower capital

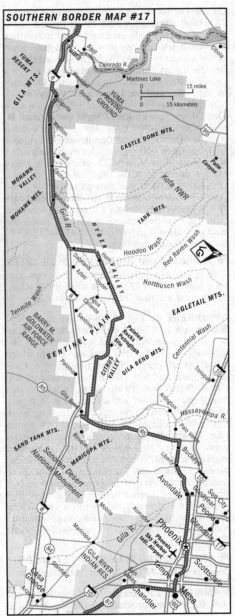

SOUTHERN BORDER MAP #17

of Arizona explode with color in springtime with adequate rainfall—which unfortunately hasn't happened in a few years. If you need a meal, **Alicia's Cafe ❷,** 337 Rte. 77, serves up Mexican and American food. Breakfast plates ($5) come with a tortilla or toast and hash browns or beans. For lunch Alicia's offers hamburgers ($2.75) and sandwiches ($4-5). Though it's not much to look at, the food hits the spot. (☎520-487-2380. Open Tu-Sa 7:30am-8pm, Su 7:30am-3pm. AmEx/D/MC/V.)

⛽ APPROACHING GLOBE-MIAMI: 59 MILES
From Mammoth, continue on **Rte. 77** to Globe. The road winds through foothills and cacti before passing the behemoth smokestacks of the mining operation in Winkelman, a town with little to offer besides gas. From there, the road gets steeper as it heads through the **Pinal Mountains** and a canyon known as **Carson's Pass,** named for Kit Carson's march through this region on his way to California in the late 1800s. Rte. 77 then runs into Globe, becoming **Willow St.** in town. Turn right at the signs for the "Historic District" to reach **Broad St.,** the town's main drag.

GLOBE-MIAMI
The history of these two small conjoined mountain towns is inextricably tied to the mineral deposits that lace the surrounding mountain walls. A quick stop at the **Gila County Historical Museum,** 1330 N. Broad St., reveals the impact mining has had on this community. (☎928-425-7385. Open M-F 10am-4pm, Sa 11am-3pm. Free.) Globe is also home to the **Besh-Ba-Gowah Archaeological Park,** a reconstructed 400-room pueblo. Few actual artifacts remain at the site, but if you don't mind the facsimile, you'll enjoy the intricate walls, multi-storied buildings, and recreated settings. The adjoining **Besh-Ba-Gowah Museum** houses actual artifacts and relates the natural history of the area. The name means "place of metal" and was given to the early mining towns of Globe and Miami by the Apache. (From U.S. 60, take Broad St. until it ends at the railroad tracks, then go left on Jess Hayes St. for ½ mi.; the park is up the hill on the left. ☎928-425-0320. Museum open daily 9am-5pm. Park open daily 9am-6pm. $3, seniors $2, under 11 free.)

Joe's Broad Street Grill ❷, 247 S. Broad St., sits in the heart of Globe's historic district, in the building that was once the Globe's first schoolhouse. This classic diner full of American flags serves tasty Italian food (pastas $7) and hand-made burgers ($5) hot off the grill. (☎928-425-6269. Open M-F 6am-2:30pm, Sa 6am-1pm. AmEx/D/MC/V.) Inexpensive rooms are located right off U.S. 60 at the **Willow Motel ❶**, 792 N. Willow St. Rooms are a bit scruffy but clean and decorated with a ragtag assortment of old-school furniture. (☎928-425-4573. Singles $25; doubles $33. AmEx/D/MC/V.)

▶ APPROACHING SUPERIOR: 22 MILES

Leave Globe on **Rte. 77**, and head 4 mi. to **U.S. 60 (Gila Pinal Scenic Road)**. Take a left toward Superior. The 18 mi. road to Superior takes you into the heart of the **Superstition Mountains**. The barren landscape gives way to oaks as the road winds up the rust-colored walls of the canyon. The aptly named **Oak Flat Campground ❶** offers a chance to explore the red boulder formations and oak groves of these heights. (Left turn 12 mi. after Globe. ☎928-402-6200. Picnic tables and grills. No water or toilets. Open 24hr. Free.) When the climb levels off, the road finds itself in a mountaintop valley speckled with oaks. The impressive scenery ends as you cruise into the mining town of Superior.

SUPERIOR

At the base of the Superstition Mountains sits the still-active mining community of Superior. The local copper smelter looms over the village, an imposing monument to the ore that runs this city. Superior has seen better days, but classic Old West facades maintain its mining-town character. The biggest attraction in Superior is, ironically, the ◪**World's Smallest Museum**, 1111 W. U.S. 60. This 15 ft. long museum displays everything from mining equipment to guns and a 1984 Compaq computer to a Barry M. Goldwater bobble-head. In an American society obsessed with the biggest and the best, it's nice to know that the smallest can still capture popular attention. Outside, the museum has an assortment of fountains made from old junk; one fountain is made from wheelbarrows and miscellaneous rusted farming equipment, while another is constructed entirely from old tires. (On the left as you leave Superior on U.S. 60 W, attached to the Buckboard City Cafe. ☎520-689-5857; www.smallestmuseum.com. Open M and W-Su 8am-1:30pm. Suggested donation $1.)

Next door, the **Buckboard City Cafe ❷**, 1111 W. U.S. 60, serves traditional breakfast fare, ham-burgers, sandwiches, salads, soups, and Mexican food. Try the "sweat-hog" (spicy wrap with sausage; $7) or the "Southwesty burger," a $6 heap of chili, bacon, and cheese. (☎520-689-5800. Open M and W-Su 6am-3pm. D/MC/V.) The **El Portal Motel ❷**, 70 W. Hwy. 60, has clean, well-decorated rooms with large windows against the backdrop of the Superstition Mountains. (☎520-689-2886. Singles $40; doubles $45. Cash only.)

▶ APPROACHING BOYCE THOMPSON ARBORETUM: 3 MILES

Continue on **U.S. 60** for 3 mi. after Superior.

BOYCE THOMPSON ARBORETUM. Nestled in the gorge created by Queen Creek lies the shady hollow of the ◪**Boyce Thompson Arboretum State Park**, 37615 U.S. 60. Founded in the mid-1920s, the botanical garden features plants from the world's deserts. Just a bunch of cacti? Think again. In addition to a large selection of domestic and exotic cacti, the gardens exhibit flora from the Australian Outback to the tropics to the native Sonoran desert. The tall trees assure enjoyable trails in almost any season, but avoid walking the 1½ mi. trail through the park at midday in summer. (☎520-689-2811; www.arboretum.ag.arizona.edu. Open daily May-Aug. 6am-3pm; Sept.-Apr. 8am-5pm. $7.50, ages 5-12 $3.)

▶ APPROACHING FLORENCE: 28 MILES

Continue on **U.S. 60** for 13 mi. to Florence Junction. From here, you can continue directly to Phoenix on U.S. 60, or dip south on **Rte. 79** to reach Florence.

FLORENCE

As Rte. 79 rolls into Florence it passes a sign that reads "State Prison: do not stop for hitchhikers." That, in a nutshell, is Florence. Home to Arizona's largest state prison, the town has a long penal history, having housed WWII internment camps for Japanese-Americans and German POWs. The **Pinal County Historical Museum**, 712 S. Main St., documents the town's penal history in grisly detail, displaying a collection of hangman's nooses, a two-seater from a gas chamber, and photos of criminals put to death. (☎520-868-4382. Open Sept. to mid-July Tu-Sa 11am-4pm, Su noon-4pm. Donation suggested.) Quietly meditate on all you've learned about the penal system at **St. Anthony's Greek Orthodox Monastery**, 4784 N. St. Joseph Way, a peaceful compound framed by the gold domes of the Eastern rite.

Built in 1995 by five Orthodox fathers from Greece, the monastery houses 40 fathers who encourage visitors to see the grounds on monk-led tours. (8 mi. south of Florence, off Rte. 79, at mi. 124. ☎520-868-3188. Appropriate dress required: men must wear long pants and long sleeves; women must wear skirts below the knee, long sleeves, and a head covering. Open daily 10:30am-4pm. Free.) For good eats any time of day or night, head to **Don Francisco's ❷**, 981 S. Main St., which offers decent Mexican food. (☎520-868-0200. Entrees $5-7.50. "Super Nachos" $6.25. Open 24hr. Cash only.) The out-rageously teal **Blue Mist Motel ❸**, 40 S. Pinal Pkwy., off Rte. 79, has clean and comfortable rooms. All rooms have HBO and pool access, but, surprisingly, are not painted teal. (☎520-868-5875. Singles $55; doubles $65. AmEx/D/MC/V.)

◖ DETOUR
CASA GRANDE RUINS NATIONAL MONUMENT
Go west on Rte. 287 for 9 mi. toward Coolidge. Follow Rte. 287 for 2 mi. as it curves southward, and look for the signs for Casa Grande. The ruins are on your right.

The nation's first archaeological preserve, the Casa Grande Ruins National Monument is also one of the most perplexing. Built around AD 1350 by the Hohokam people, the four-story structure is almost all that remains of one of North Amer-ica's most advanced civilizations. The structure, which mystified Spanish explorers called Casa Grande ("great house"), was part of a vast, innova-tive civilization. The walls of the house face the four cardinal points of the compass, and a circular hole in the upper west wall aligns with the setting sun during the summer solstice. The park has a visitors center with a small museum and offers self-guided tours through the ruins. (☎520-723-3172. Open daily 8am-5pm. $5, under 15 free.)

◖ APPROACHING PHOENIX: 63 MILES
From Casa Grande, go back out to **Rte. 287,** and retrace your route 2 mi. back toward Florence. When the road splits, take **Rte. 87 W** for 7 mi. to **I-10 W.** Although you're already technically in the greater Phoenix area, it takes another 30-45min. to drive into the center of town.

PHOENIX

Anglo settlers named their small farming com-munity Phoenix, believing that their oasis had risen from the ashes of ancient Native American

settlements. The 20th century has seen this unlikely metropolis live up to its name; the expansion of water resources, the proliferation of the railroad, and the introduction of air-condi-tioning have fueled Phoenix's ascent to the ranks of America's leading urban centers. Shiny high-rises now crowd the business district, while a vast web of six-lane highways and strip malls surround the downtown area. During the balmy winter, tourists, golfers, and businessmen flock to enjoy perfect temperatures, while in summer, the visitors flee, and the city crawls into its air-conditioned shell as temperatures exceed 100° F.

VITAL STATS

Population: 1.5 million

Visitor Info: Greater Phoenix Visitors and Conven-tion Bureau, 50 N. 2nd St. (☎602-254-6500 or 877-225-5749, recorded info 602-252-5588; www.visitphoenix.com), at Adams St. Open M-F 8am-5pm.

Internet Access: Burton Barr Central Library, 1221 N. Central Ave. (☎602-262-4636). Open M-Th 10am-9pm, F-Sa 9am-6pm, Su noon-6pm. Free.

Post Office: 522 N. Central Ave. (☎602-253-5045). Open M-F 9am-6pm. **Postal Code:** 85034.

▐ GETTING AROUND

The intersection of **Central Ave.** and **Washington St.** marks the center of downtown. Central Ave. runs north-south, Washington St. east-west. One of Phoenix's peculiarities is that numbered ave-nues and streets both run north-south; avenues are numbered sequentially west from Central Ave., while streets are numbered east. Think of Central Ave. as the heart of town; facing north, the first road to your right is **1st St.,** the first to your left is **1st Ave.** Large north-south thorough-fares include **7th St., 16th St., 7th Ave.,** and **19th Ave.,** while **McDowell Rd., Van Buren St., Indian School Rd.,** and **Camelback Rd.** are major east-west arteries. Greater Phoenix includes smaller independent municipalities that sometimes have different street-naming schemes. If you park and want to get around the downtown area (Adams, Washington, and Jefferson St.), look for the free "Dash" buses and jump aboard (6:30am-11pm).

Once a series of independent communities, the numerous townships of "the Valley of the

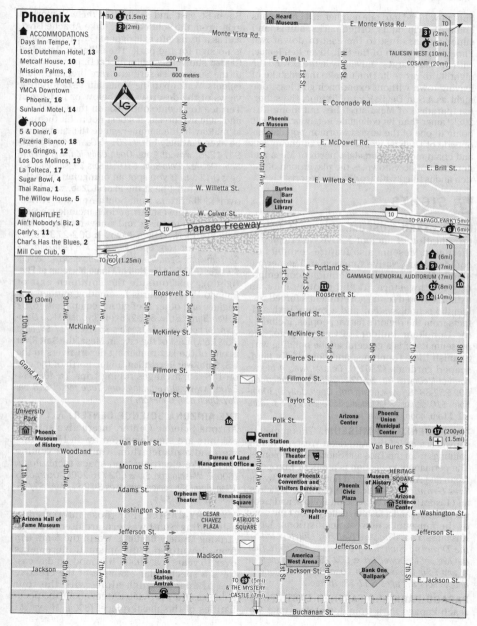

Phoenix

ACCOMMODATIONS
Days Inn Tempe, **7**
Lost Dutchman Hotel, **13**
Metcalf House, **10**
Mission Palms, **8**
Ranchouse Motel, **15**
YMCA Downtown
  Phoenix, **16**
Sunland Motel, **14**

FOOD
5 & Diner, **6**
Pizzeria Bianco, **18**
Dos Gringos, **12**
Los Dos Molinos, **19**
La Tolteca, **17**
Sugar Bowl, **4**
Thai Rama, **1**
The Willow House, **5**

NIGHTLIFE
Ain't Nobody's Biz, **3**
Carly's, **11**
Char's Has the Blues, **2**
Mill Cue Club, **9**

Sun" now bleed into one another in a continuous chain of strip malls, office parks, slums, and super-resorts. Just to the east of downtown Phoenix and south of the Salt River lies **Tempe**, with the third-largest university in the US and the nightlife to prove it. Don't make the mistake of leaving town without experiencing at least one night as a Sun Devil. East of Tempe, the suburban paradise of **Mesa** stretches out along Rte. 202. Tamer than its collegiate neighbor, Mesa is home to one of the largest Mormon populations outside of Utah as well as a bevy of cheap eats and chain motels. **Scottsdale,** north of Mesa and northeast of downtown, is the playground of the rich and is filled with world-class resorts.

👁 SIGHTS

■ THE HEARD MUSEUM. Renowned for its presentation of ancient Native American art, the Heard Museum also features exhibits on contemporary Native Americans. The permanent collection includes fabulous contemporary Southwestern art and photography, an exhibit devoted to the government's forced residential school system, and a gallery with artifacts from the region's native peoples, including the Hohokam, builders of Casa Grande. The museum itself is a graceful adobe building with Spanish tiles, fountains, and beautifully landscaped gardens. (2301 N. Central Ave., 4 blocks north of McDowell Rd. ☎602-252-8840, recorded info 602-252-8848; www.heard.org. Open daily 9:30am-5pm. $10, seniors $9, students $5, ages 6-12 $3. Tours 10, 11am, noon, 1:30pm; free.)

THE PHOENIX ART MUSEUM. This museum showcases art of the American West, including paintings from the Taos and Santa Fe art colonies. The permanent collection is a mix of European, Asian and American art and houses pieces by the *Tres Grandes* of Mexican art (Orozco, Siqueiros, and Rivera), works by Jackson Pollock and Georgia O'Keeffe, and a fashion gallery. Don't miss one of the museum's newest acquisitions, Yayoi Kusama's *You Who Are Getting Obliterated in the Dancing Swarm of Fireflies.* (1625 N. Central Ave., at McDowell Rd. ☎602-257-1880. Open Tu-W and F-Su 10am-5pm, Th 10am-9pm. $9, students and seniors $7, ages 6-17 $3. Th free.)

PAPAGO PARK AND FARTHER EAST. To reach Papago Park from downtown, take Van Buren St. east, and head left at the well-marked exit. From the south or east, take Apache Blvd. and as it turns left, exit right at Galvin Rd.; there is no sign for the park. The **■ Desert Botanical Garden** showcases colorful cacti, plants native to the Sonoran Desert, and rare breeds of succulents. Walk up to the Mountain Vista for great views of the desert valley below or to Ullman Terrace for scenic outlooks on the mountains and saguaro forests. It's best not to hit the park at midday in the summer, since the garden can be excruciatingly hot. (1201 N. Galvin Pkwy. ☎408-941-1225; www.dbg.org. Open daily May-Sept. 7am-8pm; Oct.-Apr. 8am-8pm. $10, seniors $9, students $5, ages 3-12 $4.) If you spot an orangutan amid the cacti, you must be at the **Phoenix Zoo,** which has over 1300 critters from South America, Africa, and the Southwest. Attractions include massive 100-year-old tortoises and a new monkey walkway. (455 N. Galvin Pkwy. ☎602-273-1341; www.phoenixzoo.org. Open June-Aug. M-F 7am-2pm, Sa-Su 7am-4pm; Sept.-May daily 9am-5pm. $14, seniors $9, ages 3-12 $6.) The **Hall of Flame Museum of Firefighting,** just outside the southern exit of Papago Park, features fascinating antique fire engines and other firefighting equipment. (6101 E. Van Buren St. ☎602-275-3473. Open M-Sa 9am-5pm, Su noon-4pm. $6, seniors $5, ages 6-17 $4, ages 3-5 $1.50.) East of the city, in Mesa, the **Salt River** is one of the last remaining desert rivers in the US. **Salt River Recreation,** 15 mi. north of the city on U.S. 60, arranges tubing trips. (☎408-984-3305; www.saltrivertubing.com. Tube rental $13 per day. Open daily 9am-7pm.)

THE ARIZONA SCIENCE CENTER. At the Arizona Science Center, interactive science exhibits are supplemented by an IMAX theater and a planetarium. Galleries examine topics like electricity and space technology. (600 E. Washington St. ☎602-716-2000. Open daily 10am-5pm. $9, seniors and ages 3-12 $7. IMAX $7/$6. Planetarium $5/$4.)

MYSTERY CASTLE. For those interested in astounding Southwestern architecture, the striking **Mystery Castle** is worth the 5 mi. trip from downtown. Built in small increments over 15 years (ca. 1930), this modern-day castle is a spectacular example of the creative use of space. Laugh along with the tour guides as they provide tidbits about the peculiarities of this masterpiece. (800 E. Mineral Rd.

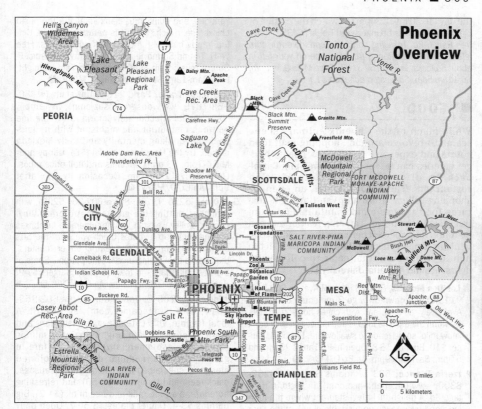

Phoenix Overview

Head south on Central Ave., and take a left on Mineral Rd. just before the South Mountain Park entrance. ☎ 602-268-1581. Open Oct.-May Th-Su 11am-4pm. $5, seniors $4, ages 5-15 $3.)

WRIGHT SIGHTS. Taliesin West was built as the winter camp of Frank Lloyd Wright's architectural collective; in his later years he lived there full-time. It is now a campus for an architectural college run by his foundation. The beautiful compound, entirely designed by the master, seems to blend naturally into the surrounding desert, and includes a studio, a Chinese cinema, and a performance hall. (12621 Frank Lloyd Wright Blvd. Head east off the Cactus St. exit from Rte. 101. ☎ 480-860-2700; www.franklloydwright.org. Open Sept.-June daily 9am-4pm. Guided tours required. 1½hr. tours $22.50, stu-

dents and seniors $18.50, ages 4-12 $10. 3hr. tours $35. 2hr. evening tours Th-F $25.) One of the last buildings Wright designed, the **Gammage Memorial Auditorium** is a stand-out with its unique rotunda shape and pink-and-beige earth tones in harmony with the surrounding environment. (At Mill Ave. and Apache Blvd., on the Arizona State University campus in Tempe. ☎ 408-965-0458. 1hr. tours Sept.-Apr. M 1-4pm. Free.) **Cosanti** is a working studio and bell foundry designed by the architect and sculptor Paolo Soleri, one of Wright's students and the mastermind behind the utopian community Arcosanti, located 70 mi. north of Phoenix. The buildings here fuse with the natural landscape even more strikingly than those at Taliesin West, and visitors are allowed to wander the grounds freely and observe artists working. Arrive early in the day (10:30am-12:30pm) to watch the casting of Cosanti's famous bronze wind bells. *(6433 Doubletree Ranch Rd. Traveling north on Scottsdale Rd., turn left on Doubletree Ranch Rd.; it will be on your left in about 5 blocks.* ☎800-752-3187. *Open M-Sa 9am-5pm, Su 11am-5pm. Suggested donation $1.)*

FOOD

While much of the Phoenix culinary scene seems to revolve around shopping mall food courts and expensive restaurants, quality budget eateries can be found. **McDowell** and **Camelback Rd.** offer a (small) variety of Asian restaurants. The **Arizona Center,** an open-air shopping gallery at 3rd and Van Buren St., features food venues amid fountains and palm trees. Downtown, cafes and hip restaurants can be found interspersed between the parking lots, while in **Tempe** you can fill up on bar food in the hybrid "resto-bars" that cater to college students, around **Mill** and **University St.**

Los Dos Molinos, 8646 S. Central Ave. (☎602-243-9113). From downtown, go 8 mi. south on Central Ave. Lively, colorful, and with chiles hotter than hell, it's worth the trip. The food is authentic, and they don't know mild, so be ready to swallow fire. Enchilada dinner $10. Burritos $6-8. Open Tu-F 11am-2:30pm and 5-9pm, Sa 11am-9pm. AmEx/D/MC/V. ❷

Pizzeria Bianco, 623 E. Adams St. (☎602-258-8300; www.pizzeriabianco.com), in Historic Heritage Sq. A delightful little restaurant where the roaring wood oven takes up a sizable chunk of the floor space. The freshly made pizzas are superb, particularly "The Rosa" (pistachios and rosemary; $10). Salads $6-9. Open Tu-Sa 5-10pm. Bar open 4-10pm. AmEx/MC/V. ❷

Thai Rama, 1221 W. Camelback Rd. (☎602-285-1123). Combines cool, modern decor with cozy booths and Thai decorations. Try a delicious coconut curry dish ($8-9), the cashew duck ($9), or one of the many vegetarian options. For dessert, sample homemade coconut ice cream with black sweet rice ($3.50). Open M-W 11am-2:30pm, Th 11am-2:30pm and 5-9:30pm, F 11am-2:30pm and 5-10:30pm, Sa noon-10:30pm, Su 5-9:30pm. AmEx/MC/V. ❷

The Willow House, 149 W. McDowell Rd. (☎602-252-0272; www.thewillowhouse.com). This self-proclaimed "artist's cove" in a rambling old house combines the best aspects of chic coffeehouse, New York deli, and quirky musicians' hangout. The pesto chicken sandwich ($6.25) is particularly good. Coffee happy hour M-F 4-6pm; half-price drinks. Free Wi-Fi. Tu and Su movie night. Th poetry open mic. F-Sa live music from 8pm. Open M-Th 7am-midnight, F-Sa 7am-1am, Su 7am-midnight. MC/V. ❶

Dos Gringos Trailer Park, 216 E. University (☎480-968-7879; www.dosgringosaz.com), in Tempe. "Dos," as its affectionately known, skirts the line between restaurant and nightspot with its laid-back day-drinking mentality and tasty Mexican dishes. Try the Hangover Special ($6). Happy hour M-F 4-7pm; $3 drink specials and half-price tacos. Open daily 11am-2am. Occasionally 21+ after 9pm. AmEx/D/MC/V. ❶

5 & Diner, 5220 N. 16th St. (☎602-264-5220), with branches dotting the greater metro area. Vinyl booths, smiley waitstaff, and innumerable jukeboxes playing sock-hop favorites teach you what the 50s could have been. Outdoor seating under "misters" that blow a cool, damp breeze onto patrons. Some of the best milkshakes in town ($4.50). Burgers $7-9. Sandwiches $6-9. Open 24hr. AmEx/MC/V. ❷

La Tolteca, 1205 E. Van Buren St. (☎602-253-1511; www.latoltecamex.com), at 12th St. A local favorite, this cafeteria-style restaurant and Mexican grocery, with brightly painted murals serves up uncommercialized Mexican fare in *grande* portions. Familiar dishes are offered alongside specialties like *cocido* soup (sausage, chickpeas, and tomatoes; $5.50) and refreshing *horchata,* a sweet, milk-and-rice drink ($1-2). Big burritos $3-4. Dinner plates $5.50-7. Open daily 6:30am-9pm. AmEx/MC/V. ❶

Sugar Bowl Ice Cream Parlor & Restaurant, 4005 N. Scottsdale Rd. (☎480-946-0051), in Scottsdale. Get out of the heat and into this fun ice-cream parlor, where everything is super cutesy and super pink. The sundaes are piled thick and high ($3-5) and the milkshakes ($4) are a meal in themselves. Sandwiches and salads ($7-8) are available if you're still hungry. Open M-Th 11am-11pm, F-Sa 11am-midnight, Su 11am-10pm. AmEx/D/MC/V. ❷

ACCOMMODATIONS

Budget travelers should consider visiting Phoenix during July and August, when motels slash their prices by as much as 70%. In the winter, when temperatures drop, the number of vacationers rises, vacancies are few, and prices go up; make reservations early. The reservationless should cruise the rows of motels on **Van Buren St.** east of downtown, toward the airport. Parts of this area can be unsafe; guests should examine a motel thoroughly before checking in. Although they are more distant, the areas around **Papago Fwy.** and **Black Canyon Hwy.** are loaded with motels and can present some safer options. Another alternative is to contact **Mi Casa Su Casa Advanced Reservations Arizona,** which arranges stays in B&Bs throughout Arizona, New Mexico, Utah, Nevada, and southern California. (☎800-456-0682; www.azres.com. Open daily 6am-9pm. From $50.)

Metcalf House (HI-AYH), 1026 N. 9th St. (☎602-254-9803), a few blocks northeast of downtown. The ebullient owner gives helpful advice about the area, and fosters a lively community in this decorative house. Evening gab sessions are common on the front porch. The neighborhood has seen better days, so the coin lockers available in the dorms are probably a good idea. Check-in 7-10am and 5-10pm. Lockout from kitchen 10am-5pm. Single-sex dorms $18, members $16; private rooms $30-35. Cash only. ❶

YMCA Downtown Phoenix, 350 N. 1st Ave. (☎602-257-5138). Another option in the downtown area with small, clean, single-occupancy rooms with shared bathrooms for both men and women. Temporary gym memberships $5. 18+. Reception daily 7am-10pm. No reservations. Rooms $25. AmEx/D/MC/V. ❶

The Ranchouse Motel, 1009 E. Monroe St. (☎623-386-420, ext. 13), 30 mi. west of downtown, in Buckeye. From Phoenix, follow I-10 to the Buckeye exit and go south. Turn right at the 1st stoplight; the motel is on your left. Each wrangler receives a plot of land with a ranchero-style, 2-room bungalow. Full kitchens or kitchenettes in rooms, TV, and A/C. Reception 24hr. Singles $40; doubles $50. Cash only. ❷

Lost Dutchman Motel, 560 S. Country Club Dr. (☎480-969-2200), in Mesa. A good location to many restaurants and clean rooms are the best reasons to stay at the Dutchman. Kitchenettes available for $3 extra. Check-in 3pm. Check-out noon. Singles in summer $49; doubles $69. Rates vary in winter; call ahead. AmEx/D/MC/V. ❸

Days Inn Tempe, 1221 E. Apache Blvd. (☎480-968-7793; www.daysinn.com), in Tempe. A chain with tidy rooms and reasonable prices. TV, pool,

jacuzzi, free Internet access. Breakfast included. Singles in summer $48; in winter $70. Doubles $55/$100. AmEx/D/MC/V. ❸

Sunland Motel, 2602 E. Main St. (☎480-833-1713), in Mesa. One of many motels along E. Main St., this is a solid option with clean standard rooms. Some rooms have kitchenettes. Singles from $45; doubles from $50. AmEx/V/MC. ❷

Mission Palms, 60 E. 5th St. (☎480-894-1400; www.missionpalms.com). At the base of the Tempe's Hayden Butte, this deluxe hotel is a steal in the summer, though prices more than double in the winter. Indulge in luxury (2 hot tubs, a pool, health club, tennis center, and standard laptop Internet hookups) with the knowledge that raucous Mill Ave. is just a minute's walk away. Singles in summer $99; in winter $190. Doubles $140/$230. AmEx/D/MC/V. ❺

🎵 ENTERTAINMENT

Phoenix is stacked with stadiums, and the large facilities make it easy to get last-minute tickets. NBA basketball action rises with the **Phoenix Suns** (☎602-379-7867) at the **America West Arena,** while the **Arizona Cardinals** (☎602-379-0101) provide American football excitement. The 2002 World Series Champions **Arizona Diamondbacks** play at the state-of-the-art **Bank One Ballpark,** complete with a retractable roof, an outfield swimming pool, and "beer gardens." (☎602-514-8400. Tickets from $10. $1 tickets available first come, first served 2hr. before games.) The **Phoenix Symphony,** 225 E. Adams St., plays regularly September to June and holds the occasional summer concert. (☎602-495-1999; www.www.phoenixsymphony.org. Tickets $20-60. Student discount 25%. Student rush tickets $10 1hr. before showtime.) For theater of all types, from musicals to Shakespearean tragedies, check out the historic **Orpheum Theatre,** 203 W. Adams St., which was built in 1929 as a movie house. (☎602-262-7272. Box Office open M-F 10am-4pm. Tickets $15-50.)

🔊 NIGHTLIFE

The free *New Times Weekly,* available on local magazine racks, lists club schedules for Phoenix's after-hours scene. The *Cultural Calendar of*

Events covers area entertainment in three-month intervals. *The Western Front,* found in bars and clubs, covers gay and lesbian nightlife. Happening bars are easy to find if you walk up **Mill St.** around ASU. Downtown, there are a few gems scattered about if you know where to look.

⚎ Char's Has the Blues, 4631 N. 7th Ave. (☎602-230-0205; www.charshastheblues.com). Intimate, laid-back bar with excellent live music that ranges from jazz to R&B to Motown. The thirtysomething crowd grooves on the small dance floor or sits with style at tables. Live music nightly from 9pm. Cover F-Sa $5-8. 2-drink min. Open daily 7:30pm-1am. AmEx/D/MC/V.

Carly's, 128 E. Roosevelt St. (☎602-262-2759). There's no doubt that Carly's is hip: cool modern decor, funky, well-dressed waitstaff, and indie kids playing music Tu-Sa nights. Often acoustic, always eclectic. Eat gourmet grilled paninis ($7-8) and salads ($6-7) or nurse a drink as you listen. Th 5-8pm wine happy hour with $3 per glass on selected wines. Open M 11am-10pm, Tu-Th 11am-midnight, F 11am-2am, Sa noon-2am, Su 4-10pm. MC/V.

Ain't Nobody's Biz, 3031 E. Indian School Rd. #7 (☎602-224-9977), in the east end of the mall. This lesbian bar is the big sister of the Tucson club (p. 863). Top 40 pumps over a packed dance floor where men and women, both gay and straight, get down. A more laid-back scene can be found around the pool tables. The abundance of drink specials (Tu $2 drinks for ladies; Sa $1 vodka until midnight) ensures an excellent time is had by all. Generally no cover. Open Th-Su 4pm-2am. Cash only.

Mill Cue Club, 607 S. Mill Ave. (☎480-858-9017). For those looking to mingle in a casual place that still exudes some class. The leather sofas in the corner complement the dark-paneled walls and the rows of pool tables in the back. The club gets packed for "reverse happy hour" W 8pm-midnight. Long Island iced tea $2.50-4. M and Su pool $3 per game. Happy hour 2-7pm. No cover. Some nights 21+. Open daily 2pm-2am. AmEx/D/MC/V.

⬔ APPROACHING GILA BEND: 68 MILES

Get on **I-10 W** and take **Exit 121.** When you get off the highway, head left (south) for 5 mi. to the traffic light and turn right onto **Buckeye Rd.** into Buckeye. Pass the Ranchhouse Motel, and continue to the junction with **Rte. 85.** Take a left (south), and follow Rte. 85 for 30 mi. to Gila Bend.

GILA BEND

Gila Bend has definitely seen better days. Once the proud crossroads joining Yuma, Phoenix, and Tucson, today the old town doesn't get a passing glance from motorists whizzing by on I-8. Gila Bend features a fine assortment of gas stations, a mechanic, and a laundromat, but otherwise it has little to offer. The one attraction that seems to have withstood the test of time is the **Space Age Outer Limits Hotel and Restaurant,** 401 E. Pima Ave., built in 1964-65 by Al Stovall, a rich industrialist with a thing for the NASA program—the building features a 28 ft. spaceship with a space-themed mural, and even the pool heater is shaped like a crash-lanmded satellite. The **Outer Limits Restaurant ❸** offers the best Mexican and American cuisine in town. (☎928-683-2273. Entrees $7.50-10. Open daily 5am-9pm. AmEx/D/MC/V.) After change of ownership, the motel is now the **Best Western Space Age Motel ❹** and has clean rooms. (☎928-683-2273. Continental breakfast included. Rooms $59-99. AmEx/D/MC/V.) For a less cosmic experience, it's best to check out one of the other motels along the East Pima strip. The **Yucca Motel ❷,** 836 E. Pima St., promises "service with a smile" and has clean rooms with pool access, microwave, fridge, and HBO. (☎928-683-2211. Singles $38; doubles $50. AmEx/D/MC/V.)

⬈ DETOUR
PAINTED ROCKS PETROGLYPH SITE
From Gila Bend, take I-8 W for 13 mi. to Exit 102 and turn right (north). Continue another 11 mi. down Painted Rocks Rd. to the site.

This national monument showcases one of the best collections of prehistoric Native American art in existence. Centuries ago, Native Americans in the area found a pile of boulders standing alone on the flat desert land and concluded that it must be of spiritual importance. They inscribed hundreds of spirals and unique figures, whose complex meanings can be loosely interpreted using guides available at the site. De Anza, the Mormon Battalion, Kit Carson, and many other pioneers passed by and left their own inscriptions. The site is run by the Phoenix Bureau of Land Management but has no visitors center. (☎602-580-5500. $2 per vehicle.) Next to the petroglyph site, the **Petroglyph Campground ❶** offers the chance to spend the night under the incredible desert stars at this sacred site, but has no running water and only one pit toilet. As with the petroglyphs, the campground is entirely self-serve. The area is dangerously hot in the summer and the campground should not be used. (☎602-580-5500. Free.)

APPROACHING DATELAND: 26 MILES
To get to Dateland, head back to **I-8,** and continue west for 26 mi. Get off at **Exit 67** for Dateland.

DATELAND. One might assume that Dateland is named after the numerous date trees scattered throughout the town. But here, as often happens on the backroads of America, logic fails. The name is derived from WWII-era General Datelan, who commanded a military base in the area. The dates came later, and with their arrival, the second "d" was added to the name. The gift shop tells about the wonders of the palm tree fruit, but visitors should actually experience it, in the form of the Dateland date milkshake. ■**Dateland Palms Village Restaurant ❷,** which basically constitutes the entire town of Dateland, serves up shakes ($3) and other date treats, in addition to a full diner menu. (☎928-454-2772; www.dateland.com. Entrees $6-8. Open daily 8am-10pm. MC/V.)

APPROACHING YUMA: 69 MILES
From Dateland, take **I-8 W** to Yuma.

YUMA

The mother of all truck stops, Yuma sits smack dab in the middle of nowhere, as far as modern-day travelers are concerned. For travelers of old, however, Yuma had the important distinction of being at the narrowest point on the Colorado River, which made it an ideal place to cross into California. The crossing at Yuma was first used by Native American traders and nomads, then by Spanish explorers, the US army, and gold miners. Nowadays, Yuma has a range of motels and restaurants to give respite to travelers before they cross the state line into California.

VITAL STATS

Population: 83,000

Visitor Info: Yuma Visitors Center, 377 S. Main St. (☎800-293-0071; www.visityuma.com), at the corner of Giss Pkwy. Open May-Oct. M-F 9am-5pm, Sa 9am-2pm; Nov.-Apr. M-F 9am-5pm, Sa 9am-4pm.

Internet Access: Yuma Public Library, 350 3rd Ave. (☎928-782-1871; www.yumalibrary.org), at the corner of 4th St. Open M-Th 9am-9pm, F-Sa 9am-5pm. Free.

Post Office: 2222 S. 4th Ave. (☎928-783-2124 or 928-783-2125). Open M-F 9am-5pm, Sa 9am-1pm. **Postal Code:** 85364.

GETTING AROUND. To hit **4th Ave.,** Yuma's main drag, exit I-8 at 4th Ave., and head south. Most hotels and fast-food chains are on 4th Ave., while the **Yuma Crossing State Historic Park** and other useful stops lie east on **Giss Pkwy.** A small downtown area with a restaurant and store-filled pedestrian walkway lies on **Main St.** between 2nd and 3rd St.

SIGHTS. Legend has it that the infamous prison in the **Yuma Territorial Prison State Historic Park,** 1 Prison Hill Rd., was home to some of the West's most ruthless bandits. In 1876, the inmates were forced to construct the walls that would confine them in the heart of the scorching desert. After the local high school burned down, the jail was used as a school from 1910-1914; Yuma High School's sports teams are still called "the Criminals" as a tribute. Tour what remains of the cell blocks and guard tower, and visit the museum, which perches on a hill overlooking the Colorado River. If you don't want to pay for jail time, visit the free park below the prison, where there are shaded picnic tables. (Take I-8 to Exit 1, head east on Giss Pkwy., and turn at Prison Hill Rd. ☎928-783-4771. Open daily 8am-5pm. $4.) Check out the **Saihati Camel Farm,** 15672 S. Ave. 1 E., which breeds camels. Twenty other species of animal also share the premises. (☎928-627-7511. Open Nov.-May M-Sa 10am-5pm. $3, seniors $2.50.)

 DID YOU KNOW? Yuma produces 93% of the world's winter lettuce (meaning lettuce consumed during the North American winter months). To celebrate this important part of Yuman culture, the town holds the annual **Lettuce Festival** the 3rd weekend in January. Activities include a street fair, a farmers' market and, to prove that Yuma has lettuce to spare, lettuce-head bowling. In 2005, Yuma tried to make the world's biggest salad, though the word is still out on whether Guinness will accept the claim.

FOOD AND ACCOMMODATIONS. Pool and dominoes are still played in **Lutes Casino ❶,** 221 S. Main St., as they have been since 1920 in the state's oldest pool hall. As you devour your burger or sandwich, you can

SOUTHERN BORDER

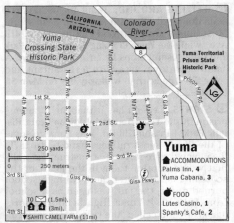

Yuma
California
Arizona
Colorado River
Yuma Crossing State Historic Park
Yuma Territorial Prison State Historic Park
N. Madison Ave.
N. 2nd Ave.
1st St.
4th Ave.
S. 2nd Ave.
S. 3rd Ave.
E. 2nd St.
W. 2nd St.
S. Main St.
S. Maiden Ln.
S. Gila St.
Prison Hill Rd.
S. Madison Ave.
S. 1st Ave.
3rd St.
Giss Pkwy.
Giss Pkwy.
3rd St.
4th St.
TO ✉ (1.5mi).
(3mi).
SAHITI CAMEL FARM (11mi)
0 250 yards
0 250 meters

Yuma

🏠 ACCOMMODATIONS
Palms Inn, 4
Yuma Cabana, 3

🔥 FOOD
Lutes Casino, 1
Spanky's Cafe, 2

ponder the truly wacky decor. (☎928-782-2192. Entrees $3.25-5.25. Pool $6 per hr. Open M-Th 9am-8pm, F-Sa 9am-9pm, Su 10am-6pm. Cash only.) For something healthier and less historical, check out brand spankin' new **Spanky's Cafe** ❷, 202 S. 1st Ave., a pretty little cafe serving sandwiches like grilled portobello ($7.25) and snazzy salads. (☎928-782-0818. Open M-F 7am-4pm, Sa 7am-1pm. AmEx/D/MC/V.)

The Palms Inn ❸, 2655 S. 4th Ave., has huge, nicely furnished rooms with all the standard amenities and pool access. (☎928-344-0082. Singles $33; doubles $39. AmEx/D/MC/V.) The tropically themed **Yuma Cabana** ❸, 2151 S. 4th Ave., is a resort by motel standards. Spacious and clean rooms come with free continental breakfast, fridge, microwave, Internet access, HBO, A/C, and a lovely pool. (☎520-783-8311. Singles $33; doubles $42. AmEx/D/MC/V.)

The Golden State
CALIFORNIA
Welcomes You!

 Nov.-Mar., you pass into the Mountain Time Zone, where it is 1hr. later. Apr.-Oct. there is no change here.

◣ DETOUR
THE CENTER OF THE WORLD
10 mi. west of Yuma on I-8. Exit at Sidewinder Rd., then go north and immediately west to find the spot.

Your first stop in California looks suspiciously like the Arizona desert. Well, cheer up: you've reached both the center of the world and one of kitschiest roadside attractions on the trip. The title ◩**The Official Center of the World** was originally made up by the writer of a children's book, but was officially set in stone in 1985, and tours are now given of the granite pyramid where this point resides. Admission comes with a photograph and a commemorative certificate. Outside, stare in wonder at a span of wall (in a pink that matches the pyramid) that commemorates great moments in French aviation, casualties of the Korean War, the entire 1949 class of Princeton University, and the genealogical history of the Taylor family. Michelangelo's Arm of God (from the Sistine Chapel) sets the local solar time at a giant sundial, while stairs from the Eiffel Tower sit nearby, awkwardly leading to nowhere but the desert sky. If it's not open, you can still wander the grounds—you just won't get a certificate. (☎760-572-0100. Open Thanksgiving to Easter daily. $2.)

◣ DETOUR
IMPERIAL SAND DUNES
Another 9 mi. west on I-8. Take Exit 156 (Grays Well Rd.), and enter the Imperial Sand Dunes Recreation Area. Continue down the road for about 2 mi. past the campground ($25 per week). Down the hill lies a section of the old planks.

If the shifting sands and rolling slopes of the Imperial Dunes remind you of another planet, they should. These sands appeared as the desert planet Tatooine in the classic movie *Star Wars: A New Hope*, and have been featured in many other films. Hundreds of buggies and motorcycles zip across the dunes each year, but before it served as a racing grounds, the area presented a formidable obstacle. Winds and migrating dunes quickly erased any trail, while soft sands slowed travelers to a crawl—if they didn't stop them entirely.

With the invention of the automobile, people became even more interested in finding a passage over the sands. The answer came in 1916, with a piece of desert ingenuity—the plank road. Thousands of wooden boards held together by metal bands traversed the dunes, effectively creating a boardwalk for Model Ts. This innovation lasted until 1926, when the paved road that became Rte. 80 was constructed, though a piece of the historic old plank road still remains in the desert. Permits ($25) are required to park your car for any significant period of time at the dunes. (For information and permits, contact the Bureau of Land Management, El Centro, 1661 4th St. ☎760-337-4400. You can also purchase permits at ☎800-278-0165 or at www.icso.org.)

⚐ APPROACHING HOLTVILLE: 33 MILES

Continue west on **I-8.** Take **Exit 131 (Holtville/Rte. 115),** turn right (north), and make another right (east) immediately onto **Evan Hewes Rd.** Follow the road 1 mi. over an aqueduct until you see the palm trees of a desert oasis on the right. Geothermal activity warms the water, and a fountain caps the source, shooting the hot water into a spa area. The oasis is a fun break from the road, and the palm-ringed pond next to it is perfect for an oasis-in-the-desert photo to send home to mom. Head north on Rte. 115 toward Holtville.

HOLTVILLE. The little farming town of Holtville doesn't see much action, nor will you while you're there. There is, however, a pretty central square and a few great Mexican food places, and it's a perfect place to grab a bite to eat after frolicking in the oasis. Stop at **Nueva Mexico Lindo ❶,** 411 E. 5th St., where the food is made with handmade tortillas in a friendly, family atmosphere. (☎760-356-2197. Entrees $4-6. Open daily 8am-9pm. Cash only.)

⚐ APPROACHING EL CENTRO: 8 MILES

Make your way through Holtville along the main street until you see a sign for El Centro. This is the continuation of **Rte. 115** and runs directly into El Centro.

EL CENTRO. El Centro's motto, "where the sun spends its winters" is a much better alternative to "where the sun bakes the hell out of everything in the summer." El Centro is the center of the Imperial Valley but there is little to do in town. The main reason to stop in El Centro is the abundance of inexpensive accommodations on Adams Ave. (which becomes Rte. 80). Many of these are rented out during the week by nomadic farmhands or county officials. Near the courthouse, **La Hacienda Family**

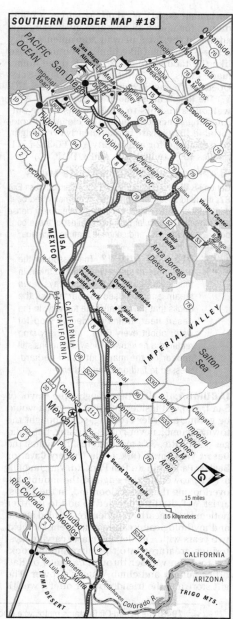

SOUTHERN BORDER MAP #18

Restaurant ❶, 841 W. Main St., serves a filling dinner for under $8 and also gives religious advice in the form of wall adornments ("Try Jesus—You might like him!"). You might also like the taco plate ($5.25) with three home-made tacos, rice, and beans. (☎ 760-353-8118. Open Tu-Th and Sa 8am-8pm, F 8am-9pm. MC/V.) **The Ranch House Motel ❷**, 808 Adams Ave., welcomes visitors to a lush oasis in the surrounding concrete jungle. The clean and comfortable 15 units are booked nearly every night, so call ahead for availability. (☎ 760-352-5571. Singles $30; doubles $35. AmEx/D/MC/V.)

APPROACHING JACUMBA: 46 MILES
Get on **I-8 W**, and continue for 41 mi. After you pass **Exit 87**, the road sheds all semblance of normalcy: red boulders appear on all sides, becoming increasingly dense and forming spectacular hills. In the midst of these boulders, exit on **Rte. 80**, and continue 5 mi. to Jacumba.

 DID YOU KNOW? The reason for the abundance of sparsely populated towns in this region goes back to the days when steam engines used to roar across the tracks that now parallel the freeway. In the desert heat, trains needed to stop for water about every 6 mi., and every stop required a new town. Today, the towns still appear on the map, but you'll be hard-pressed to find anything in them.

JACUMBA. In 1922 Bert Vaughn, the mayor of San Diego, got insider info that Jacumba would be getting a border crossing, so he bought the town. Jacumba never got its crossing, but it did get one of Rte. 80's most interesting sights: the **Desert View Tower** (a.k.a. the **Mystery Cave**, or **Boulder Park**), 1 In Ko Pah Park Rd. Vaughn built a 70 ft. tower on the edge of the mountains overlooking the desert floor and, in the 1930s, artist W.T. Ratliffe decided to add to it. After noticing how nearby boulders resembled actual and mythological creatures, he spent the next two years with a mallet and chisel carving mysterious creatures into the surrounding rock. Visitors can wander through carvings of Ratliffe's fantasy and climb Vaughn's tower. The gift store and the friendly owner offer a wealth of roadtrip info. (☎ 619-766-4612. Open daily 9am-5pm. $2.50, children $1.)

◼ DETOUR
THE SUNRISE HIGHWAY
From Jacumba, continue 7 mi. on Rte. 80 until it joins back up with I-8. Go west on I-8 for 15 mi. to Exit 47. Head north on S1 (Scenic Rte. 1) for 25 mi. through the Laguna Mountains.

This scenic drive carves through the oak canyons and pine peaks of the Cuyamaca and Laguna Mountains, which stand as a formidable barrier between the coast and the desert. Ten miles in you'll come to **Laguna Mountain Village**, which is the highest point on the drive at 6000 ft. and which contains a grocery store, an over-priced restaurant, and the **Cleveland Forest Visitor Center**, which is staffed by volunteers. (☎ 619-473-8824. Visitors center open F-Su 8am-4pm.) To park your car, picnic, hike, or camp, you must purchase an Adventure Pass ($5), which can be obtained at any of the three establishments in Laguna Mountain Village. Continue 200 ft. past the village to **Desert View Picnic Area**, which has a beautiful view of the desert valley below. Just 2 mi. farther down the road is an even better lookout with panoramic views and a wooden viewing platform. Continue on the winding highway through the ashen wasteland remaining from the 2002 pine fire, then into beautiful desert fields where agave and wildflowers grace the rolling hills.

APPROACHING JULIAN: 56 MILES
Head west on **I-8** for 33 mi. Take **Exit 40** onto **Rte. 79**, and continue for 23 mi. to Julian.

JULIAN
After the Civil War, Confederate soldiers wandered west looking for land and, in the process, stumbled across gold. Understandably, they decided to put roots down and established Julian, which became the biggest gold producing area in Southern California. In the late 1800s, the reserves dried up and Julian's residents discovered a new kind of gold: apples. Soon Julian's apples were famous across the US. Now the main industry in the picturesque little town is tourism and the townspeople have gone from mere apple sellers to apple bakers—

 1948: The Pissed Off Bastards motorcycle club changes its name to the Hells Angels.

making fresh apple pie that has tourists coming for miles. The little **Julian Pioneer Museum,** 2811 Washington St., off Main St., has Native American artifacts, pioneer and mining tools, and the best lace collection in the state. (☎760-765-0227. Open Apr.-Nov. Th-Su 10am-4pm; Dec.-Mar. Sa-Su 10am-4pm. $3.) Those looking for an educational adventure should take an interactive tour of the **Eagle and High Peak Mine,** at the end of C St., where visitors can take a 1hr. guided tour of the 1000 ft. of tunnels and pan for gold. (☎760-765-0036. Open daily 10am-2pm. Call ahead for tour times. $10, ages 5-15 $5, under 5 $1.) The **Town Hall,** 2129 Main St., distributes helpful information about the town and shows local art. (☎760-765-1857. Open daily 10am-4pm.)

For food in Julian, visit the **Miner's Diner & Soda Fountain ❷,** 2134 Main St. Housed in an 1886 building, this old-fashioned soda shop holds true to its roots with brickwork still visible behind the 1928 soda fountain. Don't miss their displays of license plates. (☎760-765-3753. Breakfast $4-7. Lunch $7-9. Open M-F 8am-5pm, Sa-Su 8am-6pm. MC/V.) For the bison-obsessed and the bison-curious, the bison-themed **Buffalo Bill's ❷,** at the corner of 3rd and B St., serves up bison burgers ($7.25). Bison meat has one-fourth the fat of beef, so chow down guilt-free. (☎760-765-1560. Sandwiches $4-7. Open M-F 7:30am-2pm, Sa-Su 7am-5 or 6pm. MC/V.) It would be a tragedy to leave town without a slice of Julian's apple pie, and many places on Main St. serve the all-American dessert by the slice for under $3. **Apple Alley Bakery ❷,** 2122 Main St., is one of the better-known pie purveyors ($2.75 per slice). For something different, try apple-boysenberry or apple-cherry mixes. (☎760-765-2532. Open M-Th 9am-5:30pm, F-Sa 9am-7pm. AmEx/D/MC/V.)

◤ APPROACHING SANTA YSABEL: 7 MILES
Continue west on **Rte. 78/79,** which becomes **Julian Rd.,** for 7 mi.

SANTA YSABEL. It may be a tiny pit-stop, but Santa Ysabel offers some of the world's best baked goods. Half of the town is ◩**Dudley's Bakery ❶,** 30218 Rte. 78, at Rte. 79, which is known across San Diego County for its fresh bread. Stop and buy a loaf ($2.75), or try the tasty fruit bars ($3) and other assorted

pastries. (☎800-225-3348. Open W-Su 8am-5pm. AmEx/D/MC/V.)

◤ APPROACHING RAMONA: 15 MILES
Continue along **Rte. 78/79 (Julian Rd.)** to Ramona.

RAMONA

This ranching community in the foothills of the Cuyamaca Mountains centers around horses. Don't miss the **Ramona Rodeo** in May and the **Country Fair** days in August. For more info, contact the **Ramona Chamber of Commerce/Information Center,** 960 Main St. (☎760-689-1311; www.ramona.com. Open M-F 8:30am-4:30pm, Sa 9am-2pm.) The **Woodward Museum,** 645 Main St., has displays on horses and horse-related gear, a memorial exhibit to a local championship rodeo rider, and a rose garden. (☎619-789-7644. Open Th-Su 1-4pm. $2.) Ramona is also known for its wine and antiques. You can taste the former at **Schwaesdall Winery,** 17677 Rancho de Oro Rd., at Hwy. 67, the only licensed taster in the Ramona Valley. (☎760-789-7547, tasting room 760-789-7542. Tastings Sa-Su 10am-6pm.) You can hunt for antiques at **Charlotte's,** 969 Main St., which has 6000 sq. ft. of antiques, including cool vintage clothing. (☎760-788-2784. Open M-Sa 9am-3pm or by appointment.) Other antique warehouses, which comprise "Antique Row," line a drab stretch of Main St. in the 700-1000 blocks.

Grab a home-cooked meal at the **Kountry Kitchen ❷,** 826 Main St., where they've been serving American favorites and misspelling "country" since 1939. (☎760-789-3200. Lunch $5.50-7. Dinner $7-9. Open M-Tu 5am-3pm, W-Su 5am-8:30pm. MC/V.) If you want to stay in Ramona, your best (and basically only) option is the clean, hospitable, and pricey **Ramona Valley Inn ❸,** 416 Main St. The bright rooms have pool access, free coffee, and TV. (☎760-789-6433 or 800-648-4618. 21+. Singles $68; doubles $74. Remodeled rooms $79/$88. AmEx/D/MC/V.)

◤ APPROACHING SAN DIEGO: 36 MILES
From Ramona you can head southwest on **Rte. 67** to the **Scripps Poway Pkwy.** Make a right on the Scripps Poway Pkwy., and take it west to **I-15 S,** which will lead you into downtown. If you want to visit Escondido's **Wild Animal Park** (p. 883) first, continue west on **Rte. 78** for 17 mi. through Escondido, and then go south on **I-15.** Follow the highway another 25 mi. into central San Diego.

SAN DIEGO

The natives call it "America's Finest City," and visitors pulling into this picturesque port will soon understand why. In a state where every other town has staked its claim as paradise, San Diego may be Southern California's best return on the promises of a golden state. Year-round sunny weather encourages abundant gardens, inviting beaches, friendly demeanors, and a vibrant city that is simultaneously cosmopolitan and chill.

VITAL STATS

Population: 1.4 million

Visitor Info: International Visitors Information Center, 1040 W. Broadway (☎619-236-1212; www.sandiego.org), at Harbor Dr. Open daily in summer 9am-5pm; in winter 9am-4pm.

Internet Access: San Diego Public Library, 820 E St. (☎619-236-5800). Open M and W noon-8pm, Tu and Th-Sa 9:30am-5:30pm, Su 1-5pm. Free.

Parking: There are free public parking lots in Old Town, off Congress St., and at Mission Beach, behind the roller coaster (Mission Beach Blvd.).

Post Office: 2535 Midway Dr. (☎619-758-7101). Open M 7am-5pm, Tu-F 8am-5pm, Sa 8am-4pm.

Postal Code: 92186.

GETTING AROUND

San Diego is beautiful but it's also a city of freeways and highways—there's no avoiding them. **I-5** runs north-south, skirting the eastern edge of downtown on its way to the Mexican border. **I-15** runs northeast through the desert to Las Vegas, and **I-8** runs east-west along downtown's northern boundary, connecting the desert with Ocean Beach. To get to downtown from I-5, take the **Civic Center** or **4th Ave. exit.** Downtown is just south of the freeway, and its grid layout is easy to navigate—one-way streets alternate every block.

The epicenter of San Diego tourism is **Balboa Park.** Northwest of the park is stylish **Hillcrest,** which centers on **5th Ave.** and **University Blvd.** It's the city's gay enclave and has great shopping and the most diverse restaurants in the city. The **Gaslamp Quarter** sits in the southern section of downtown between 4th and 6th St.

and contains signature theaters, restaurants, and nightclubs. Just north of downtown in the southeast corner of the I-5 and I-8 junction lies a little slice of old Mexico known as **Old Town.** Along the coast, **San Diego Bay** opens up south of downtown, bounded by classy **Coronado Island.** Northwest of town sits the collection of shiny beaches and man-made inlets known as **Mission Bay,** home to several laid-back, sun-soaked communities including **Ocean, Mission,** and **Pacific Beaches.** A jaunt up the coast leads to the swanky haven of **La Jolla.**

Parking lots are scattered throughout the downtown area and all charge around $5 per hr. If you plan to shop, parking at Horton Plaza (San Diego's gigantic outdoor mall at Broadway and 4th Ave.) is free with validation in one of the mall's stores (3hr. max.). **Balboa Park** has numerous parking lots, and from there you can take the free narrated park tram around to all the museums. Although most San Diegans seem content to battle traffic on the freeways, buses run throughout downtown and the suburbs and electric trolleys run in the downtown core. Buy a **Daytripper Pass** for unlimited rides in one day. (☎619-233-3004 or 800-COMMUTE; www.sdcommute.com. Passes available at the W. Broadway Visitors Info center or at the Transit Store at 1st St. and Broadway. $5.)

SIGHTS

San Diego's world-class attractions are extremely varied and enough to keep any traveler engaged. Pick up the free weekly *Reader* for local event listings. Special ticket deals, like the **San Diego 3 Days, 35 Attractions Pass** ($109) are available online (www.sandiego.org) or at the attraction ticket counters.

DOWNTOWN

San Diego's downtown attractions are concentrated in the corridor that includes its business, Gaslamp, and waterfront districts—all testaments to San Diego's continuing renaissance. Travelers should be careful outside of this area, the neighborhood to the southeast in particular is not safe.

GASLAMP QUARTER. The Gaslamp Quarter houses antique shops, Victorian buildings, trendy restaurants, and many nightclubs. The streets, especially 5th Ave., get packed on Friday and Saturday nights with well-dressed, well-tanned folks out to see and be seen. The **Gaslamp Quarter Foundation** offers guided walking tours as well as a small museum. *(410 Island Ave., at William Heath Davis House. ☎ 619-233-4692; www.gaslampquarter.org. Museum open Tu-Sa 10am-6pm, Su 9am-3pm. Suggested donation for museum $3. 2hr. walking tours Sa 11am. Tours $8, students and seniors $6, under 12 free. Self-guided tour maps $2.)* The jewel of San Diego's redevelopment is **Horton Plaza**, at Broadway and 4th Ave. This pastel-hued urban creation is an open-air shopping center covering seven blocks. The **Horton Grand Hotel,** is supposedly haunted. Believers may catch a glimpse of former guests Wyatt Earp or Babe Ruth. *(311 Island Ave. ☎ 619-544-1886.)*

SAN DIEGO MUSEUM OF CONTEMPORARY ART. The steel-and-glass San Diego Museum of Contemporary Art shows rotating exhibits of 20th-century works, generally post-1950. Exhibits are nicely curated and, best of all, free. *(1001 Kettner Blvd. ☎ 619-234-1001. Open M-Tu and Th-Su 11am-5pm. Free.)*

SAN DIEGO MARITIME MUSEUM. Displays at this museum showcase San Diego's rich maritime history. The museum also maintains the magnificently restored 1863 sailing vessel *Star of India*, along with nautical exhibits and old steamships. *(1492 N. Harbor Dr. ☎ 619-234-9153; www.sdmaritime.org. Open daily Memorial Day to Labor Day 9am-9pm; Labor Day to Memorial Day 9am-8pm. $12, seniors $9, ages 6-17 $8.)*

EMBARCADERO. Spanish for "dock," the Embarcadero has boardwalk shops and museums that face moored windjammers, cruise ships, and the occasional naval destroyer. To get out on the water, you can opt for a 1hr. **harbor cruise** that will take you around the bay for beautiful views of the cityscape and the Coronado Bridge. *(☎ 619-234-4111 or 800-442-7847; www.sdhe.com. Tours leave approximately every hr. in summer 10am-5:30pm; in winter 10am-4:15pm. $17, seniors $15, ages 4-12 $8.50.)* At the southern tip of the Embarcadero area lies **Seaport Village**, a cute Spanish village-like area filled with 57 touristy boutiques and restaurants. *(☎ 619-235-4014; www.seaportvillage.com. Shops open daily June-Aug. 10am-10pm; Sept.-May 10am-9pm.)*

BALBOA PARK

Balboa Park was created from the baked dirt of an abandoned pueblo tract when pioneering horticulturists planted its first redwood seedlings in 1889. Today, the park nurtures these spectacular trees, a profusion of flora, and many museums and cultural attractions. The **Balboa Park Visitors Center** sells maps and the **Passport to Balboa Park,** which allows admission into 13 of the parks. (1549 El Prado St. From I-5, merge onto Rte. 163 N and take the Balboa Park exit. ☎ 619-239-0512; www.balboapark.org. Open daily in summer 9am-4:30pm; in winter 9am-4pm. Passport $30.)

■■ **SAN DIEGO ZOO.** With over 100 acres of exquisite fenceless habitats, this zoo deserves its reputation as one of the finest in the world. Its unique "bioclimatic" exhibits group animals and plants by habitat. The panda exhibit is the most famous feature of the park, and the zoo invests over $1 million a year on panda habitat preservation in China. The most thorough way to tour the zoo is on foot, though visitors can board an educational 40min. double-decker bus tour that races across 75% of the zoo. Seats on the upper deck are popular, but trees can obstruct views, so the lower deck is often a better bet. *(2920 Zoo Dr., in Balboa Park. ☎ 619-234-3153; www.sandiegozoo.org. Open daily late June to early Sept. 9am-10pm, last entry 8pm; early Sept. to late June 9am-sunset. $22, with 35min. bus tour and 2 tickets for the aerial tramway $32; ages 3-11 $14.50/$20.)*

MUSEUM OF MAN. Creationists beware: the Museum of Man dedicates an entire floor to the 98.4% of DNA we share with chimpanzees. Downstairs has rotating exhibits and a section dedicated to Mexico. The real treat, however, is the museum's exterior, which features gleaming Spanish mosaic tiles on its much-photographed tower and dome. *(On the west end of the park. ☎ 619-239-2001; www.museumofman.org. Open daily 10am-4:30pm. $6, seniors $5, ages 6-17 $3. 3rd Tu of each month free.)*

SAN DIEGO AIR AND SPACE MUSEUM. The museum displays 24 full-scale replicas and 44 original planes, as well as information on aviation history and the International Space Station project. The museum also has a GPS satellite and flight simulators. *(2001 Pan American Plaza. ☎ 619-234-8291; www.aerospacemu-*

SOUTHERN BORDER

seum.org. Open daily in summer 10am-5:30pm; in winter 10am-4:30pm. $10, students and seniors $8, ages 6-17 $5. 4th Tu of each month free.)

REUBEN H. FLEET SPACE THEATER AND SCIENCE CENTER.
The Fleet houses the world's very first Omnimax theater, complete with 153 speakers and a hemispheric planetarium. The science center has interactive exhibits about the five senses, aging, and a host of other topics. Although it's filled with kids, it can be fun if you like science centers. Don't miss the aging machine, where you can see what you'll look like at age 70. (1875 El Prado Way. ☎619-238-1233; www.rhfleet.org. Open daily 9:30am-8pm. $6.75, with Omnimax show $11.50; seniors $6/ $8.50; ages 3-12 $5.50/$9.50. 1st Tu of each month free. F omnimax shows after 6pm $6.)

SAN DIEGO MUSEUM OF ART.
This museum has a collection ranging from ancient Asian to contemporary Californian works, in addition to rotating exhibits. (☎619-232-7931; www.sdmart.org. Open Tu-Su 10am-6pm, Th 10am-9pm. $10, seniors $8, students $7, ages 6-17 $4.)

MUSEUM OF PHOTOGRAPHIC ARTS (MOPA).
The small, ultra-modern Museum of Photographic Arts features excellent rotating exhibits. It occasionally shows films, which range from ultra-artsy to more traditional. (☎619-238-7559; www.mopa.org. Open M-W and F-Su 10am-5pm, Th 10am-9pm. $6, students $4. 2nd Tu of each month free. Films $5/$4.50.)

TIMKEN MUSEUM OF ART.
Right next to the Botanical Gardens is the small but impressive Timken Museum of Art. The collection, sustained by the wealthy Timken family, includes a few choice pieces by European masters and an excellent collection of Russian icons. (☎619-239-5548. Open Tu-Sa 10am-4:30pm, Su 1:30-4:30pm. Free.)

BALBOA PARK GARDENS.
The **Botanical Building** is a giant wooden structure filled with the scent of jasmine and the murmur of fountains; the orchid collection is particularly striking. The **Desert Garden** and the award-winning **Inez Grant Parker Memorial Rose Garden** offer a fascinating contrast of flora. The Desert Garden contains more than 1300 plants within its 2½ acres and is in full bloom from January to March. The Rose Gar-

den has approximately 2500 roses of nearly 200 varieties and is at its peak between April and May. (2200 Park Blvd. ☎619-235-1100, tour info 619-235-1121. Open M-W and F-Su 10am-4pm. Free.)

OLD GLOBE THEATER.
Constructed in 1937, the **Old Globe Theater** is the oldest professional theater in California and a Tony-award winning institution. (☎619-234-5623; www.theoldglobe.org. Tickets from $19. Students and seniors 50% discount for same-day tickets purchased at box office. Call ahead.)

OLD TOWN
In 1769, supported by a brigade of Spanish infantry, Father Serra established the first of 21 missions that would line the California coast in the area now known as Old Town. The remnants of this early settlement have become one of San Diego's tourist mainstays. Old Town is centered around State Park, where seven original buildings still stand, along with 21 reconstructed ones. (To reach Old Town, take the Old Town exit from I-5 N.)

STATE PARK.
The most popular of the area's attractions, the park's early 19th-century buildings contain museums, shops, and restaurants. On the square, **Seely Stable,** once the Yuma-San Diego stage coach stop, now houses a huge museum of 19th-century transportation, namely of the horse and carriage variety. (☎619-220-5427. Open daily 10am-5pm. Tours every hr. 11am-2pm.) The **Whaley House Museum** stands on the site of San Diego's first gallows, and the house itself was the site of several deaths. It is now one of two **official haunted houses** officially recognized by the State of California. Tours cover aspects of the Victorian era in San Diego, the Whaley family, and, of course, ghosts. (2482 San Diego Ave. ☎619-298-2482, tours 619-293-0117. Open daily in summer 10am-10pm. Reduced hours in winter; call ahead. Before 7pm $6, seniors $5, ages 3-12 $4; after 7pm $10, ages 3-12 $5.)

HERITAGE PARK.
Up the street from State Park is **Heritage Park,** a group of 150-year-old Victorian buildings that were transported to Old Town as part of preservation effort in the 1970s. Most of the buildings are now private offices, but you can tour tiny **Senlis Cottage,** an 1896 home, and **Temple Beth Israel,** the first

synagogue in San Diego. (☎619-291-9784. *Open daily 9am-5pm. Free.*)

COASTAL SAN DIEGO

CORONADO ISLAND

Lovely Coronado Island is now, in fact, a peninsula. A slender 7 mi. strip of hauled sand known as the "Silver Strand" tethers it to the mainland down near Imperial Beach. The island is perfect for strolling or browsing and outdoor enthusiasts can jog, roller-skate, and bike over 7 mi. of paved trails. Coronado has a huge military presence, and the entire northern chunk comprises the **North Island Naval Air Station,** the birthplace of naval aviation. This area was an island, until diligent navy men used wheelbarrows full of sand to connect it to the rest of Coronado. Also among the island's many military enterprises is the training area of the elite **Navy SEAL** (sea, air, and land) special forces teams. The graceful **Coronado Bridge** guides cars to Coronado from downtown San Diego along I-5. Bus #901 follows the same route. Those who would rather skim the ocean than the asphalt can take the **Bay Ferry.** (☎619-234-4111 or 800-442-7847; www.sdhe.com. Departs downtown every hr. M-Th and Su 9am-9pm, F-Sa 9am-10pm. Departs Coronado every hr. M-Th and Su 9:30am-9:30pm, F-Sa 9:30am-10:30pm. Round-trip $6.)

HOTEL DEL CORONADO. Coronado's most famed sight is the Victorian-style Hotel Del Coronado, 1500 Orange Ave., one of America's largest wooden buildings. The long, white verandas and the vermilion spires of the "Del" were built in 1888, and it has since become one of the world's great hotels (rooms from $270 per night), hosting 10 presidents and one blonde bombshell—Marilyn Monroe's 1959 *Some Like it Hot* was filmed here. You can scope it out for yourself or take one of the tours offered by the Coronado Visitors Center. (*1100 Orange Ave.* ☎619-437-8788; www.coronadovisitor-center.com. *Reservations recommended. Tours F-Su 2pm. $15, under 6 free.*)

BEACHES. San Diego's younger population flocks to these communities by the surf for the hopping nightlife. **Ocean Beach** ("OB") is the most hippie-flavored of the beaches, in large part because community groups have fought to keep out condo rental developers and chain restaurants. OB has a great **farmers market**

every Wednesday 4-7pm on the 4900 block of Newport Ave., the beach's main thoroughfare. Farther north, at the corner of W. Mission Bay Dr. and Mission Blvd., **Mission Beach** is a people-watcher's paradise. Belmont Park, a combination amusement park and shopping center, draws a youthful crowd. To find it, just look for the roller coaster ($4 per ride). **Pacific Beach** and its boisterous Garnet Ave. is home to the best nightlife. Ocean Front Walk is packed with joggers, cyclists, and the usual beachfront shops. Rent a bike from **Cheap Rentals Mission Beach** to cruise the strip and work on your tan. (*3685 and 3221 Mission Blvd.* ☎619-488-9070 or 800-941-7761; www.cheap-rent-als.com. *In-line skates and bikes $12 per day.*)

SEA WORLD. Since the 190-acre park opened in 1964, Sea World has welcomed more than 100 million guests. The A-list star here is the behemoth killer whale **Shamu,** whose signature move is a cannonball splash that soaks anyone in the first 20 rows. The original Shamu died long ago, but the name is still proudly carried as a stage name by all of Sea World's performing killer whales. In addition, there are animals from all walks of sea life in their natural habitats, including penguins, polar bears, and sharks. Try the ray petting pool and Shipwreck Rapids, Sea World's first adventure ride. (*From I-5, take the Sea World Dr. exit, and turn west toward the park.* ☎619-226-3901. *Open daily in summer M-Th 9am-10pm, F-Su 9am-11pm; call ahead for winter hours. $54, ages 3-9 $44.*)

LA JOLLA

The Spanish named this area *La Jolla* ("The Jewel") for its physical beauty. More recently, the craggy promontory developed as the exclusive hideaway for wealthy Easterners, and today it remains true to its tony roots. To reach La Jolla, take the Ardath exit west from I-5.

BEACHES. La Jolla claims some of the finest beaches in the city. **La Jolla Cove** is popular with scuba divers, snorkelers, and brilliantly colored Garibaldi goldfish. Wander south along the cliffs to a semi-circular inlet known as **The Children's Pool.** Established in 1931 by wealthy philanthropist Ellen Scripps, the inlet became the preferred sunbathing spot for a community of sea lions. Some of the best breaks in the county can be found at **Tourmaline Beach** and **Wind 'n' Sea Beach.** However, these are notoriously territorial spots, so outsiders might be advised to surf elsewhere. **La Jolla Shores** has gentle swells ideal for inexperienced surfers, boogie boarders, and swimmers. Learn to hang ten from **Surf Diva**. (*2160 Ave. de la Playa. ☎858-454-8273; www.surfdiva.com. Private lessons $65 per hr. 4hr. group lessons $135.*)

MUSEUMS AND DR. SEUSS. The ⚂**Birch Aquarium at the Scripps Institute of Oceanography** has great educational exhibits, including a tank of eerily lit jellyfish, a large collection of seahorses, and a 70,000 gal. kelp and shark tank. Just outside you'll find a tide pool exhibit and fabulous views of the ocean. (*2300 Expedition Way. ☎858-534-3474; http://aquarium.ucsd.edu. Open daily 9am-5pm. $11, seniors $9, students $8, ages 3-17 $7.*) The **San Diego Museum of Contemporary Art** shares its rotating collection of pop, minimalist, and conceptualist art with the downtown branch (p. 879). The museum is as visually stunning as the art it contains, with gorgeous ocean views and high-ceilinged, light-filled spaces. (*700 Prospect St. ☎858-454-3541. Open M-Tu and Th-F 10am-5pm, W and Sa-Su 11am-5pm. $6; students, seniors, and ages 12-18 $2. 1st Su and 3rd Tu of each month free.*) If you've got time, drop by to see the terraces and buttresses of **Geisel Library** at the University of California San Diego (UCSD), a space-age structure endowed by La Jolla resident Theodore Geisel, better known as the late and beloved children's books author, Dr. Seuss. Twice a year (usually in March and July or August), a collection of his original sketches and notes are on display. (*The library is in the center of campus. ☎858-534-3339. Open M-F 8am-6pm, Sa-Su 10am-6pm. Free.*)

ESCONDIDO

Escondido lies 30 mi. north of San Diego amid rolling, semi-arid hills that blossom with wildflowers in the spring.

SAN DIEGO WILD ANIMAL PARK. The real reason to head to Escondido is to see the free-roaming animals at the 1800-acre San Diego Wild Animal Park, a sister to the San Diego Zoo. Rhinos, giraffes, gazelles, and tigers roam the grounds. One of the park's highlights is the ⚂**giraffe-feeding station.** The open-air Wgasa Bush Line Railway, a 1hr. monorail safari, travels through four created habitat areas; sit on the right if possible. Another option is a **Photo Caravan**

Safari, which takes you close enough to the animals to touch them. (*From I-15, take the Via Rancho Pkwy. ☎619-747-8702; www.wildanimalpark.org. Open daily in summer 9am-10pm; in winter 9am-5pm. Last entry 2hr. before park closes. Rail tours June-Aug. 9:30am-9pm; Sept.-May 9:30am-4pm. $28.50, ages 3-11 $17.50. Safaris $90-130 per person. Parking $8.*)

▰ FOOD

With its large Hispanic population and proximity to Mexico, San Diego is renowned for its exemplary Mexican cuisine; **Old Town** serves some of the most authentic Mexican food in the state. San Diego also offers an assortment of ethnic and more traditional eateries. Good restaurants cluster downtown along **C St., Broadway Blvd.,** and in historic **Gaslamp Quarter.** The best food near Balboa Park and the zoo is in nearby **Hillcrest** and **University Heights.**

⚃ **Casa Guadalajara,** 4105 Taylor St. (☎619-295-5111; www.casaguadalajara.com), in Old Town. With its brightly painted tiles, heavy wooden furniture, and lush, shady patio, you'll feel like you're in a pristine version of Mexico. Colossal combo plates ($8-10) and soft taco fajitas ($12.25) are overshadowed only by the selection of margaritas ($5-12). Open M-Th and Su 7am-10pm, F-Sa 7am-midnight. AmEx/D/MC/V. ❷

⚃ **The Corvette Diner,** 3946 5th Ave. (☎619-542-1476; www.corvettediner.signonsandiego.com), in Hillcrest. This 50s-style diner has more chrome than Detroit and more neon than Las Vegas. Greasy-spoon classics and unique creations like the "Rory Burger" (with peanut butter and bacon; $8). A DJ spins oldies nightly 6-9pm while costumed waitstaff give as much lip as service. Open M-Th and Su 11am-10pm, F-Sa 11am-11pm. AmEx/D/MC/V. ❷

Pizza Port, 135 N. Rte. 101 (☎858-481-7332; www.pizzaport.com). If you're around Solana Beach, there's no better place for grub and grog than this surf-themed pizza parlor and microbrewery. After the sun sets, the bar fills up with laid-back, young locals discussing the finer points of the day's swell. Sit at long picnic tables, help yourself to plastic dinnerware, and create your own pizza ($6, plus $1 per topping) or try one of their favorites, like the San Clemente (black beans and cilantro; $7.25-17.75). Rotating selection of excellent homemade brews and ciders ($2-6). Open daily 7am-2am. AmEx/MC/V. ❷

Kono's Surf Club, 704 Garnet Ave. (☎858-483-1669), across from the Crystal Pier in Pacific Beach. Identifiable by the line stretching out the door, Kono's is a surfer's shrine that serves up legendary burritos. Mostly takeout, so you can eat on the beach. Try the huge "Egg Burrito #3," which includes bacon, cheese, potatoes, and sauce ($4.75). Open M-F 7am-3pm, Sa-Su 7am-4pm. D/MC/V. ❶

La Especial Norte, 664 N. Rte. 101 (☎760-942-1040), 25 mi. north of San Diego, in Leucadia. A great place to stop for well-made Mexican food. This family-run restaurant has huge portions, friendly service, and food so good that the San Diego Coast lifeguards rent the restaurant for their annual banquet. *Bistek ranchero* $12. Open daily 10am-10pm. AmEx/D/MC/V. ❷

Kansas City Barbecue, 610 W. Market St. (☎619-231-9680; www.kcbbq.net), near Seaport Village. The location of *Top Gun*'s "Great Balls of Fire" bar scene. While the wooden piano remains, all that's left of Goose and Maverick is an abundance of autographed posters and neon signs. Vegetarians will find themselves in the Danger Zone in this barbecue-slathered meatfest. Entrees $9-16. Open daily 11am-2am. Kitchen closes 1am. MC/V. ❷

🏠 ACCOMMODATIONS

Beyond the hostel and residential hotel scene, San Diego is littered with generic chain motels, which are generally clean and safe. There is a cluster of motels and hotels known as **Hotel Circle** (2-3 mi. east of I-5 along I-8), where summer prices begin at $60 for a single and $70 for a double during the week. Several beaches in North County, as well as one on Coronado, allow camping. For info call the San Diego and North County Coast Rangers Headquarters (☎619-688-3260), or for reservations contact ReserveAmerica (☎800-444-7275).

🍌 **Banana Bungalow,** 707 Reed Ave. (☎619-858-273-3060; www.bananabungalowsandiego.com), in the center of Pacific Beach. Smack dab on the beach, this hostel is like one big beach party with an open courtyard and gorgeous deck overlooking the water. Communal dinners cooked by friendly, travel-savvy hostel staff: Tu $1 cheeseburgers, W $5 dinner, Su free barbecue. Must have out-of-state ID, international passport, or proof of travel. Breakfast included. Lockers $0.25. Linen included. Laundry $1.50. Free Wi-Fi; Internet terminals $1 per 12min. Dorms in summer $25; in winter $18. Private rooms $95/$55. MC/V. ❷

🏠 **San Diego Downtown Hostel (HI-AYH),** 521 Market St. (☎619-525-1531; www.sandiegohostels.org), in the Gaslamp Quarter. Quiet, impeccably clean, and

close to popular attractions and clubs. Airy common rooms, big kitchen, and pretty courtyard. Bike rental $10. Pancake breakfast included. Dinner $5. No alcohol. Laundry $0.75. Free Wi-Fi. 4- to 6-bed dorms in summer $24-29, members $21-26; in winter $21-26/$18-23. Singles $58/$50. AmEx/D/MC/V. ❷

USA Hostels San Diego, 726 5th Ave. (☎619-232-3100 or 800-438-8622; www.usahostels.com), between F and G St. This colorful Euro-style fun house fits in with the happening atmosphere of the Gaslamp Quarter, hosting frequent parties, weekly W night pub crawls, and $12 Tijuana trips. Bottom-floor rooms can be very loud. Bike rental $10. International passport, out-of-state ID, or student ID required. Pancake breakfast included. Dinner $5. Lockers, linen, and laundry ($1.50). Free Wi-Fi; Internet terminals $2 per 20min. Dorms in summer $24; in winter $18-20. Private rooms $61. MC/V. ❷

Ocean Beach International (OBI), 4961 Newport Ave. (☎619-223-7873 or 800-339-7263). Clean rooms near the most laid-back beach in San Diego. Proof of international travel in the last 6 months required. Pancake breakfast included. Tu and F free barbecue. Internet $1 per 20min. 29-day max. stay. 4- to 6-bed dorms in summer $22, in winter $17; doubles $54/$44. MC/V. ❶

Roger's Dorms, 3204 Mission Blvd. (☎858-539-0043), across the street from Mission Beach roller coaster. Small, somewhat cramped hostel with over 2000 DVDs and videotapes lining the walls. Rooms painted according to theme—check out the cardboard palm trees. Small common room, coffee, microwave, and fridge. Free movies and popcorn nightly. Internet $1 per 10min. Deposit $20. Dorms $24; private singles $45; doubles $64. Cash only. ❷

San Elijo Beach State Park, off Rte. 101 (☎760-753-5091), south of Cardiff-by-the-Sea. Over 170 sites on seaside cliffs. Laundry and showers. Tent sites $16-25; with hookup $25-44. ❶

South Carlsbad Beach State Park, off Carlsbad Blvd. (☎760-438-3143), near Leucadia. Over 100 sites near beautiful beaches with good surfing. Laundry and showers. Sites $16-35. ❶

🎵 ENTERTAINMENT

The definitive source of entertainment info is the free *Reader*, found in shops, coffeehouses, and visitors centers. Listings can also be found in the *San Diego Union-Tribune*'s Thursday "Night and Day" section or the *What's Playing* pamphlet from the visitors center. If cruisin' and boozin' isn't your idea of fun, you can spend a more sedate evening at one of San Diego's excellent theaters, such as the **Balboa Theatre,** 225 Broadway Ave. (☎609-544-1000), and the **Horton Grand Theatre,** 444 4th Ave. (☎619-234-9583). The **La Jolla Playhouse,** 2910 La Jolla Village Dr., is an award-winning theater that presents shows on the UCSD campus. (☎858-550-1010; www.lajollaplayhouse.com. Tickets from $30.) The **San Diego Symphony** plays throughout the year. (☎619-235-0804; www.sandiegosymphony.com.)

🎤 NIGHTLIFE

Nightlife in San Diego is scattered across distinct pockets of action. Posh locals and party-seeking tourists flock to the **Gaslamp Quarter.** The **Hillcrest,** next to Balboa Park, draws a young, largely gay crowd to its clubs and eateries. Away from downtown, the beach areas (especially **Garnet Ave.** in Pacific Beach) are loaded with clubs, bars, and cheap eateries.

Pacific Beach Bar and Grill and **Club Tremors,** 860 Garnet Ave. (☎858-272-1242). One of the only dance clubs in Pacific Beach. Live DJ spins hip-hop, house, and retro for a packed 2-level dance floor filled with a young crowd. Respectable food, more than 20 beers on tap, and live music (generally rock) on Su from 6pm. 21+ at night. Cover Tu $5. Enter through the bar instead of Club Tremors Th-Sa to avoid the cover. Club open Tu-Su 9pm-1:30am. Bar open Tu-Su 11am-1:30am. Kitchen closes midnight. AmEx/D/MC/V.

Canes Bar and Grill, 3105 Ocean Front Walk (☎858-488-1780; www.canesbarandgrill.com), in Mission Beach. One of the best live music venues in the city, this beachside bar has unbeatable sunset views from the terrace. Music is usually rock, but check the website for schedule. Cover $5-25. Grill open M-F 11am to an hr. after sunset, Sa-Su 9am to an hr. after sunset. Club open 9pm-1 or 2am. AmEx/D/MC/V.

The Casbah, 2501 Kettner Blvd. (☎619-232-4355; www.casbahmusic.com). Intimate show venue with black walls, bar, and stage. Famous for attracting alt-rock greats before they became great: Pearl Jam, Nirvana, and The White Stripes have all played here. Music is generally alt-rock but can lean toward punk. Shows are sometimes sold out, so call ahead or purchase tickets online. Cover $10-18. Cash only.

Croce's Top Hat Bar and Grille and **Croce's Jazz Bar,** 802 5th Ave. (☎619-233-4355; www.croces.com), at F St. in the Gaslamp Quarter. Ingrid Croce, widow of singer Jim Croce, created this blues and jazz bar in memory of her late husband. Bypass the pricey restaurant and head to the wood-paneled piano bar with huge pictures of Jim adorning the walls. The live music is top-notch and the crowd is composed of jazz connoisseurs (most of whom are over 40). Don't wear your dirty backpacker gear. Music nightly from 8:30pm. 21+. Cover M-Th and Su $5, F-Sa $10. Top Hat open F-Sa 7pm-1:30am. Jazz bar open daily 5:30pm-12:30am. AmEx/D/MC/V.

Bourbon St., 4612 Park Blvd. (☎619-291-4043), in University Heights. Happening gay bar that's open nightly. There's a pub in the front area but most of the fun is in the back, where a covered patio is decorated to look like a street from the New Orleans French Quarter. Music is generally Top 40 and retro dance. Tu karaoke from 9pm. Th 4-7pm $3 martinis. Su $3 pitchers, $2 drafts. No cover. Open M-Sa 4pm-2am, Su 1pm-2am. MC/V.

THE END OF THE ROAD

Gawk at the beasties in the San Diego Zoo, build a massive sandcastle on the beach, and take a well-deserved surfing break. You survived the Southern Border, enduring desert heat, prickly cacti, lonely tumbleweed, and the occasional spicy chile, all while keeping your roadtripping spirit intact. Cool your fiery heels in the ocean, then head north along the Pacific Coast or meet up with Route 66 in L.A..

EXIT TO

Laguna Beach, CA 73 mi.
on the pacific coast route, p. 898

Los Angeles, CA 120 mi.
on route 66, p. 596

SPEED LIMIT 65

the pacific coast

TOP 5

1. Order from the secret menu at L.A.'s **In-N-Out Burger,** a mandatory lunch stop.
2. Sip cool apple cider in the shadow of Bishop's Peak in **San Luis Obispo, CA.**
3. Check out the colorful murals and excellent burritos of San Francisco's **Mission District.**
4. Marvel at the **Old Man of the Lake,** the famed vertically floating driftwood in Crater Lake, OR.
5. Head under the Aurora Bridge in Seattle, WA to meet the **Fremont Troll.**

Crashing waves, sheer coastal bluffs, monumental redwoods, expansive ocean sunsets—exhilaration doesn't begin to describe the way it feels to be poised on the western edge of the country. On the Pacific Coast, better times await in the cliff-hugging turns ahead, and the past recedes in your rearview mirror. The coast has a way of winning over even the stodgiest skeptic, usually with avocado sandwiches, vanilla-scented Jeffrey pines, and oceanside campsites. Our route takes you from San Diego, the southernmost of California's major cities, all the way to Seattle, on the foggy edge of Puget Sound.

From **San Diego** (p. 888), you'll cruise through California beach culture; unassuming beach communities begin near San Diego and dot the coast all the way to San Francisco. You'll pass by (or stop and surf) the mythical swells of **Huntington Beach** (p. 900) before reaching laid-back **Hermosa,** carnivalesque **Venice,** and **Santa Monica,** all of which bow year-round to the gods of sun and surf. Of course, you'll have to venture into **Los Angeles** (p. 902); visit the Getty Museum, see the silver-screen sights in Hollywood, and party on **Sunset Strip** before heading through **Zuma Beach** (p. 903), which has the best surfing and softest sand.

Continuing north, the 400 mi. stretch of coast between L.A. and San Francisco embodies all that is this route—rolling seas, an oceanside highway built for cruising, and dramatic bluffs topped by weathered pines. You'll pass through **Santa Barbara** (p. 919), home to stunning sunsets and Spanish architecture, before reaching **Big Sur** (p. 929), where the magnificence that inspired John Steinbeck's novels and Jack Kerouac's musings lives on, and clear skies, dense forests, and old seafaring towns beckon. The landmarks along the way—**Hearst Castle** (p. 928), the **Monterey Bay Aquarium** (p. 934), the historic

missions—are well worth visiting, but the highlight of this stretch is the road itself.

Give yourself ample time to explore **San Francisco** (p. 946)—wander the streets and cross the **Golden Gate Bridge** before continuing north. Windswept and larger than life, the coast then winds from the Bay Area to the Oregon border. Redwoods tower over undiscovered black sand beaches, and otters frolic next to jutting rock formations—the untouched wilderness is simply stunning. From the **Marin Headlands** (p. 946), the road snakes along craggy cliffs between pounding surf and monolithic redwoods. You'll drive along the **Avenue of the Giants,** home of the redwoods that make the region famous, and back to the coast where more redwoods tower, protected within the long strip of **Redwood National and State Park** (p. 958).

From there, it's on to **Oregon,** where a string of touristy resort towns and small, unspoiled fishing villages line the route. The road winds through the scenic **Oregon Dunes National Recreation Area** (p. 963), and, for those brave enough for the bone-chilling waves, some of the most pristine beaches along the entire coast. Don't leave Oregon before searching for adventure (and giant cinnamon rolls) on the **Cavemen, Craters, and Carnivores Big Detour** (p.

PACIFIC COAST

PACIFIC COAST

Calgary
ALBERTA

BRITISH
COLUMBIA

Vancouver

WASHINGTON

Olympic National Park

Seattle - Experience Music Project

★ Olympia

Missoula

MONTANA

Portland

Eugene

OREGON

IDAHO

★ Boise

Oregon Sand Dunes National Recreation Area

Cavemen, Craters, and Carnivores Big Detour

WYOMING

Redwoods National Park

Avenue of the Giants

Salt
Lake City

Reno

Napa

★ Sacramento

San Francisco - Golden Gate Bridge

UTAH

NEVADA

COLORADO

CALIFORNIA

Las Vegas

Big Sur

Hearst Castle

ARIZONA

Flagstaff

PACIFIC
OCEAN

Los Angeles - Sunset Strip & Zuma Beach

Albuquerque

San Diego - San Diego Zoo

★ Phoenix

Tucson

El Paso

Nogales

PACIFIC COAST
HIGHLIGHTS

Hermosillo

964). Finally, you'll cross into **Washington;** here, the road loops around the **Olympic Peninsula,** skirting the vast, lush, forests of **Olympic National Park** (p. 980), before reaching the end in **Seattle**—the Emerald City, where skyscrapers tower, the streets are nearly spotless, and every hilltop offers impressive views of the surrounding mountains and the glinting waters of Puget Sound. Try the **coffee.**

The Pacific Coast is no ordinary roadtrip; it's neither lonely nor especially kitschy. You'll probably end up eating more avocado sandwiches than burgers (although the **In-N-Out Burgers** of Southern California are hands-down the ultimate road food), but you'll return to wherever you came from relaxed, refreshed, and significantly tanner.

ROUTE STATS

Miles: c. 1500

Route: San Diego, CA to Seattle, WA.

States: 3; California, Oregon, and Washington.

Driving Time: At least 1 week; allow 2-3 weeks to take in the coast at a more leisurely pace.

When To Go: California is pleasant year-round; but a summer roadtrip will find warm days and decreased precipitation in the perpetually rainy Northwest.

Crossroads: The Southern Border, in San Diego, CA (p. 878); **Route 66,** in Santa Monica, CA (p. 598); **The National Road,** in San Francisco, CA (p. 479).

The Golden State
CALIFORNIA
Welcomes You!

SAN DIEGO

The natives call it "America's Finest City," and visitors pulling into this picturesque port will soon understand why. In a state where every other town has staked its claim as paradise, San Diego may be Southern California's best return on the promises of a golden state. Year-round sunny weather encourages abundant gardens, inviting beaches, friendly demeanors, and a vibrant city that is simultaneously cosmopolitan and chill.

VITAL STATS

Population: 1.4 million

Visitor Info: International Visitors Information Center, 1040 W. Broadway (☎619-236-1212; www.sandiego.org), at Harbor Dr. Open daily in summer 9am-5pm; in winter 9am-4pm.

Internet Access: San Diego Public Library, 820 E St. (☎619-236-5800). Open M and W noon-8pm, Tu and Th-Sa 9:30am-5:30pm, Su 1-5pm. Free.

Parking: There are free public parking lots in Old Town, off Congress St., and at Mission Beach, behind the roller coaster (Mission Beach Blvd.).

Post Office: 2535 Midway Dr. (☎619-758-7101). Open M 7am-5pm, Tu-F 8am-5pm, Sa 8am-4pm. **Postal Code:** 92186.

▐ GETTING AROUND

San Diego is beautiful but it's also a city of freeways and highways—there's no avoiding them. **I-5** runs north-south, skirting the eastern edge of downtown on its way to the Mexican border. **I-15** runs northeast through the desert to Las Vegas, and **I-8** runs east-west along downtown's northern boundary, connecting the desert with Ocean Beach. To get to downtown from I-5, take the **Civic Center** or **4th Ave. exit.** Downtown is just south of the freeway, and its grid layout is easy to navigate. One-way streets alternate every block.

The epicenter of San Diego tourism is **Balboa Park.** Northwest of the park is stylish **Hillcrest,** which centers on **5th Ave.** and **University Blvd.,** and is the city's gay enclave. The **Gaslamp Quarter** sits in the southern section of downtown, between 4th and 6th St., and contains signature theaters, restaurants, and nightclubs. Just north of downtown, in the southeast corner of the I-5 and I-8 junction, lies a little slice of old Mexico known as **Old Town.** Along the coast, **San Diego Bay** opens up south of downtown, bounded by classy **Coronado Island.** Northwest of town sits the collection of shiny beaches and man-made inlets known as **Mission Bay,** home to several laid-back, sun-soaked communities including **Ocean, Mission,** and **Pacific Beaches.**

Parking lots are scattered throughout the downtown area and all charge around $5 per hr. If you plan to shop, parking at Horton Plaza

TO MISSION BEACH (5mi),
6 7 8 9 10 11
PACIFIC BEACH (6mi),
LA JOLLA (8mi),
12 13
ESCONDIDO (30mi)
✈ San Diego
Intl. Airport

TO OLD TOWN,
AND **5** (2mi)

TO
HILLCREST (0.5mi) **1 2 3 4**

TO
SEA WORLD (2mi),
OCEAN BEACH (4mi)

SEE BALBOA PARK INSET

Maple St.
Laurel St.   El Prado
Kalmia St.
Juniper St.
Ivy St.
Hawthorn St.
Grape St.
Fir St.
Elm St.

Laurel St.

LITTLE ITALY

San Diego
Air and Space
Museum

Balboa Park

U.S. Naval
Medical
Center

Date St.
Cedar St.
Beech St.
Ash St.
A St.

Balboa
Stadium

Russ Blvd.
San Diego
City College

Medea
Berkeley   Maritime
Museum

Star of
India

EMBARCADERO

B Street
Pier

Broadway
Pier

Navy Pier

Santa Fe
Amtrak
Depot

Museum of
Contemporary
Art

City
Hall
Balboa
Theater

Copley
Symphony
Hall

Ferry to
Coronado

International Visitor
Information Center

Greyhound

Broadway

0   200 yards
0   200 meters

Tuna Harbor
Park

Pantaja
Park

15

Horton
Plaza
Center

E St.
F St.
G St.

**GASLAMP
QUARTER**

**SEE GASLAMP
QUARTER INSET**

Market St.
Island Ave.

Seaport
Village

Embarcadero
Marina Park

Horton
Grand
Theater

J St.
K St.
L St.

Imperial Ave.

San Diego

▲▲ **ACCOMMODATIONS**
Banana Bungalow, **7**
Ocean Beach International (OBI), **8**
Roger's Dorms, **9**
San Diego Downtown Hostel
(HI-AYH), **18**
San Elijo Beach State Park, **12**
South Carlsbad Beach State Park, **13**
USA Hostels San Diego, **17**

🍎 **FOOD**
The Corvette Diner, **1**
Casa Guadalajara, **5**
Kansas City Barbecue, **15**
Kono's Surf Club, **6**
La Especial Norte, **4**
Pizza Port, **3**

🎵 **NIGHTLIFE**
Bourbon St., **2**
Canes Bar and Grill, **11**
The Casbah, **14**
Croce's Top Hat Bar and Grill
& Croce's Jazz Bar, **16**
Pacific Beach Bar and Grill
and Club Tremors, **10**

Balboa Park

San Diego Zoo

Spanish
Village
Art
Center

The Old Globe
Theater

Botanical
Gardens

Balboa
Park
Gardens

Museum of Man   Museum
of Art

Timkin Museum
of Art

Visitor Info Center

Museum of
Photographic
Arts

Reuben H.
Fleet Space
Theater and
Science Center

Gaslamp Quarter   E St.

Horton
Plaza
Center

16

F St.

17

G St.

Market St.

**GASLAMP
QUARTER**

18

Horton
Grand
Hotel

Gaslamp
Quarter
Foundation

Island Ave.

**Coronado
Island**

**San Diego
Harbor**

TO CORONADO ISLAND (1mi)

(San Diego's gigantic outdoor mall at Broadway and 4th Ave.) is free with validation in one of the mall's stores (3hr. max.). **Balboa Park** has numerous parking lots, and from there you can take the free narrated park tram around to all the museums. Although most San Diegans seem content to battle traffic on the freeways, buses run throughout downtown and the suburbs and electric trolleys run in the downtown core. Buy a **Daytripper Pass** for unlimited rides in one day. (☎619-233-3004 or 800-COMMUTE; www.sdcommute.com. Passes can be bought at the W. Broadway Visitors Info center or at the Transit Store at 1st St. and Broadway. $5.)

 SIGHTS

San Diego's world-class attractions are extremely varied and enough to keep any traveler engaged. Pick up the free weekly *Reader* for local event listings. Special ticket deals, like the **San Diego 3 Days, 35 Attractions Pass** ($109) are available online (www.sandiego.org) or at attraction ticket counters.

DOWNTOWN

San Diego's downtown attractions are concentrated in the corridor that includes its business, Gaslamp, and waterfront districts—all testaments to San Diego's continuing renaissance. Travelers should be careful outside of this corridor, the area to the southeast in particular is not as safe.

GASLAMP QUARTER. The Gaslamp Quarter houses antique shops, Victorian buildings, trendy restaurants, and many nightclubs. The streets, especially 5th Ave., get packed on Friday and Saturday nights with well-dressed, well-tanned folks out to see and be seen. The **Gaslamp Quarter Foundation** offers guided walking tours as well as a small museum. *(410 Island Ave., at William Heath Davis House. ☎619-233-4692; www.gaslampquarter.org. Museum open Tu-Sa 10am-6pm, Su 9am-3pm. Suggested donation for museum $3. 2hr. walking tours Sa 11am. Tours $8, students and seniors $6, under 12 free.)* The jewel of San Diego's redevelopment is **Horton Plaza**, at Broadway and 4th Ave. This pastel-hued urban creation is an open-air, multi-level shopping center covering seven blocks. The **Horton Grand Hotel**, is supposedly haunted. Believers may catch a glimpse of

former guests Wyatt Earp or Babe Ruth. *(311 Island Ave. ☎619-544-1886.)*

SAN DIEGO MUSEUM OF CONTEMPORARY ART. The steel-and-glass San Diego Museum of Contemporary Art shows rotating exhibits of 20th-century works, generally post-1950. Exhibits are nicely curated and, best of all, free. *(1001 Kettner Blvd. ☎619-234-1001. Open M-Tu and Th-Su 11am-5pm. Free.)*

SAN DIEGO MARITIME MUSEUM. Displays at this museum showcase San Diego's rich maritime history. The museum also maintains the magnificently restored 1863 sailing vessel *Star of India*, along with nautical exhibits and old steamships. *(1492 N. Harbor Dr. ☎619-234-9153; www.sdmaritime.org. Open daily Memorial Day to Labor Day 9am-9pm; Labor Day to Memorial Day 9am-8pm. $12, seniors $9, ages 6-17 $8.)*

EMBARCADERO. Spanish for "dock," the Embarcadero has boardwalk shops and museums that face moored windjammers, cruise ships, and the occasional naval destroyer. To get out on the water, you can opt for a 1hr. **harbor cruise** that will take you around the bay for beautiful views of the cityscape and the Coronado Bridge. *(☎619-234-4111 or 800-442-7847; www.sdhe.com. Tours leave approximately every hr. in summer 10am-5:30pm; in winter 10am-4:15pm. $17, seniors $15, ages 4-12 $8.50.)* At the southern tip of the Embarcadero area lies **Seaport Village**, a cute Spanish village-like area filled with 57 touristy boutiques and restaurants. *(☎619-235-4014; www.seaportvillage.com. Open daily June-Aug. 10am-10pm; Sept.-May 10am-9pm.)*

BALBOA PARK

Balboa Park was created in an abandoned pueblo tract when pioneering horticulturists planted its first redwood seedlings in 1889. Today, the park nurtures these spectacular trees, a profusion of flora, and many museums and cultural attractions. The **Balboa Park Visitors Center** sells park maps and the **Passport to Balboa Park,** which allows admission into 13 of the park's attractions. (1549 El Prado St. From I-5, merge onto Rte. 163 N and take the Balboa Park exit. ☎619-239-0512; www.balboapark.org. Passport $30. Open daily in summer 9am-4:30pm; in winter 9am-4pm.)

🖼 **SAN DIEGO ZOO.** With over 100 acres of exquisite fenceless habitats, this zoo deserves its reputation as one of the finest in the world. Its unique "bioclimatic" exhibits group animals and plants by habitat. The panda exhibit is the most famous feature of the park, and the zoo invests over $1 million a year on panda habitat preservation in China. The most thorough way to tour the zoo is on foot, though visitors can board an educational 40min. double-decker bus tour that races across 75% of the zoo. Seats on the upper deck are popular, but trees can obstruct views, so the lower deck is often a better bet. *(2920 Zoo Dr., in Balboa Park. ☎619-234-3153; www.sandiegozoo.org. Open daily late June to early Sept. 9am-10pm, last entry 8pm; early Sept. to late June 9am-sunset. $22, with bus tour and 2 tickets for the aerial tramway $32; ages 3-11 $14.50/$20.)*

MUSEUM OF MAN. Creationists beware: the Museum of Man dedicates an entire floor to the 98.4% of DNA we share with chimpanzees. Downstairs has rotating exhibits and a section dedicated to Mexico. The real treat, however, is the museum's exterior, which features gleaming Spanish mosaic tiles on its much-photographed tower and dome. *(On the west end of the park. ☎619-239-2001; www.museumofman.org. Open daily 10am-4:30pm. $6, seniors $5, ages 6-17 $3. 3rd Tu of each month free.)*

SAN DIEGO AIR AND SPACE MUSEUM. The museum displays 24 full-scale replicas and 44 original planes, as well as information on aviation history and the International Space Station project. The museum also has a GPS satellite and flight simulators. *(2001 Pan American Plaza. ☎619-234-8291; www.aerospacemuseum.org. Open daily in summer 10am-5:30pm; in winter 10am-4:30pm. $10, students and seniors $8, ages 6-17 $5. 4th Tu of each month free.)*

REUBEN H. FLEET SPACE THEATER AND SCIENCE CENTER. The Fleet houses the world's very first Omnimax theater, complete with 153 speakers and a hemispheric planetarium. The science center has interactive exhibits about the five senses, aging, and a host of other topics. Although it's filled with kids, it can be fun if you like science centers. Don't miss the aging machine, where you can see what you'll look like at age 70. *(1875 El Prado Way. ☎619-238-1233; www.rhfleet.org. Open daily 9:30am-8pm. $6.75, with Omnimax show $11.50; seniors $6/$8.50; ages 3-12 $5.50/$9.50. 1st Tu of each month free.)*

SAN DIEGO MUSEUM OF ART. This museum has a collection ranging from ancient Asian to contemporary Californian works, in addition to rotating exhibits. *(☎619-232-7931; www.sdmart.org. Open Tu-W and F-Su 10am-6pm, Th 10am-9pm. $10, seniors $8, students $7, ages 6-17 $4.)*

MUSEUM OF PHOTOGRAPHIC ARTS (MOPA). The small, ultra-modern Museum of Photographic Arts features excellent rotating exhibits. It occasionally shows films, which range from ultra-artsy to more traditional. *(☎619-238-7559; www.mopa.org. Open M-W and F-Su 10am-5pm, Th 10am-9pm. $6, students $4. 2nd Tu of each month free. Films $5/$4.50.)*

TIMKEN MUSEUM OF ART. Right next to the Botanical Gardens is the small but impressive Timken Museum of Art. The collection, sustained by the wealthy Timken family, includes a few choice pieces by European masters and an excellent collection of Russian icons. *(☎619-239-5548. Open Tu-Sa 10am-4:30pm, Su 1:30-4:30pm. Free.)*

BALBOA PARK GARDENS. The **Botanical Building** is a giant wooden structure filled with the scent of jasmine and the murmur of fountains; the orchid collection is particularly striking. The **Desert Garden** and the award-winning **Inez Grant Parker Memorial Rose Garden** offer a fascinating contrast of flora. The Desert Garden contains more than 1300 plants within its 2½ acres and is in full bloom from January to March. The Rose Garden has 2500 roses of nearly 200 varieties and is at its peak in April and May. *(2200 Park Blvd. ☎619-235-1100. Open M-W and F-Su 10am-4pm. Free.)*

OLD GLOBE THEATER. Constructed in 1937, the **Old Globe Theater** is the oldest professional theater in California and a Tony-award winning institution. *(☎619-234-5623; www.theoldglobe.org. Tickets from $19. Students and seniors 50% discount for same-day tickets purchased at box office.)*

OLD TOWN

In 1769, supported by a brigade of Spanish infantry, Father Junípero Serra established the first of 21 missions that would line the California coast in the area now known as Old Town. The remnants of this early settlement have

PACIFIC COAST

become one of San Diego's tourist mainstays. Old Town is centered around State Park, where seven original buildings still stand, along with 21 reconstructed ones. (To reach Old Town, take the Old Town exit from I-5 N.)

STATE PARK. The most popular of the area's attractions, the park's early 19th-century buildings contain museums, shops, and restaurants. On the square, **Seely Stable,** once the Yuma-San Diego stage coach stop, now houses a huge museum of 19th-century transportation, namely of the horse and carriage variety. (*☎619-220-5427. Open daily 10am-5pm. Tours every hr. 11am-2pm.*) The **Whaley House Museum** stands on the site of San Diego's first gallows, and the house itself was the site of several deaths. It is now one of two **official haunted houses** officially recognized by the State of California. Tours cover aspects of the Victorian era in San Diego, the Whaley family, and, of course, ghosts. *(2482 San Diego Ave. ☎619-298-2482, tours 619-293-0117. Open daily in summer 10am-10pm; hours vary in winter. Before 7pm $6, seniors $5, ages 3-12 $4; after 7pm $10, ages 3-12 $5.)*

HERITAGE PARK. Up the street from State Park is **Heritage Park,** a group of 150-year-old Victorian buildings that were transported to Old Town as part of preservation effort in the 1970s. Most of the buildings are now private offices, but you can tour tiny **Senlis Cottage,** an 1896 home, and **Temple Beth Israel,** the first synagogue in San Diego. (*☎619-291-9784. Open daily 9am-5pm. Free.*)

COASTAL SAN DIEGO

CORONADO ISLAND

Lovely Coronado Island is now, in fact, a peninsula. A slender 7 mi. strip of hauled sand known as the "Silver Strand" tethers it to the mainland down near Imperial Beach. The island is perfect for strolling or browsing and outdoor enthusiasts can jog, roller-skate, and bike over 7 mi. of paved trails. Coronado has a huge military presence, and the entire northern chunk comprises the **North Island Naval Air Station,** the birthplace of naval aviation. This area was an island, until diligent navy men used wheelbarrows full of sand to connect it to the rest of Coronado. Also among the island's many military enterprises is the training area of the elite **Navy SEAL** (sea, air, and land) special forces teams. The graceful

Coronado Bridge guides cars to Coronado from downtown San Diego along I-5. Bus #901 follows the same route. Those who would rather skim the ocean than the asphalt can take the **Bay Ferry.** (*☎619-234-4111 or 800-442-7847; www.sdhe.com. Departs downtown every hr. M-Th and Su 9am-9pm, F-Sa 9am-10pm. Departs Coronado every hr. M-Th and Su 9:30am-9:30pm, F-Sa 9:30am-10:30pm. Round-trip $6.*)

HOTEL DEL CORONADO. Coronado's most famed sight is the Victorian-style Hotel Del Coronado, 1500 Orange Ave., one of America's largest wooden buildings. The long, white verandas and the vermilion spires of the "Del" were built in 1888, and it has since become one of the world's great hotels (rooms from $270 per night), hosting 10 presidents and one blonde bombshell—Marilyn Monroe's 1959 *Some Like it Hot* was filmed here. You can scope it out for yourself or take one of the tours offered by the Coronado Visitors Center. (*1100 Orange Ave. ☎619-437-8788; www.coronadovisitorcenter.com. Reservations recommended. Tours F-Su 2pm. $15, under 6 free.*)

BEACHES. San Diego's younger population flocks to these communities by the surf for the hopping nightlife. **Ocean Beach** ("OB") is the most hippie-flavored of the beaches, in large part because community groups have fought to keep out condo rental developers and chain restaurants. OB has a great **farmers market** every Wednesday 4-7pm on the 4900 block of Newport Ave., the beach's main thoroughfare. Farther north, at the corner of W. Mission Bay Dr. and Mission Blvd., **Mission Beach** is a people-watcher's paradise. Belmont Park, a combination amusement park and shopping center, draws a youthful crowd. To find it, just look for the roller coaster ($4 per ride). **Pacific Beach** and its boisterous Garnet Ave. is home to the best nightlife. Ocean Front Walk is packed with joggers, cyclists, and the usual beachfront shops. Rent a bike from **Cheap Rentals Mission Beach** to cruise the strip and work on your tan. (*3685 and 3221 Mission Blvd. ☎619-488-9070 or 800-941-7761; www.cheap-rentals.com. In-line skates and bikes $12 per day.*)

SEA WORLD. Since the 190-acre park opened in 1964, Sea World has welcomed more than 100 million guests. The A-list star here is the behemoth killer whale **Shamu,** whose signature move is a cannonball splash that soaks anyone in the first 20 rows. The original Shamu died long ago, but the name is still proudly carried as a stage name by all of Sea World's performing killer whales. In addition, there are animals from all walks of sea life in their natural habitats, including penguins, polar bears, and sharks. Try the ray petting pool and Shipwreck Rapids, Sea World's first adventure ride. (*From I-5, take the Sea World Dr. exit, and headwest toward the park.* ☎ *619-226-3901. Open daily in summer M-Th 9am-10pm, F-Su 9am-11pm; hours vary in winter. $54, ages 3-9 $44.*)

ESCONDIDO

Escondido lies 30 mi. north of San Diego amid rolling, semi-arid hills that blossom with wildflowers in the spring.

SAN DIEGO WILD ANIMAL PARK. The real reason to head to Escondido is to see the free-roaming animals at the 1800-acre San Diego Wild Animal Park, a sister to the San Diego Zoo. Rhinos, giraffes, gazelles, and tigers roam the grounds. One of the park's highlights is the ⚑**giraffe-feeding station.** The open-air Wgasa Bush Line Railway, a 1hr. monorail safari, travels through four created habitat areas; sit on the right if possible. Another option is a **Photo Caravan Safari,** which takes you close enough to the animals to touch them. (*From I-15, take the Via Rancho Pkwy.* ☎ *619-747-8702; www.wildanimalpark.org. Open daily in summer 9am-10pm; in winter 9am-5pm. Last entry 2hr. before park closes. Rail tours June-Aug. 9:30am-9pm; Sept.-May 9:30am-4pm. $28.50, ages 3-11 $17.50. Safaris $90-130.*)

⬥ FOOD

With its large Hispanic population and proximity to Mexico, San Diego is renowned for its exemplary Mexican cuisine; **Old Town** serves some of the most authentic Mexican food in the state. San Diego also offers an assortment of ethnic and more traditional eateries. Good restaurants cluster downtown along **C St., Broadway Blvd.,** and in historic **Gaslamp Quarter.** The best food near Balboa Park and the zoo is in nearby **Hillcrest** and **University Heights.**

■ **Casa Guadalajara,** 4105 Taylor St. (☎619-295-5111; www.casaguadalajara.com), in Old Town.

With its bright tiles, wooden furniture, and shady patio, you'll feel like you're in a pristine version of Mexico. Colossal combo plates ($8-10) and soft taco fajitas ($12.25) are overshadowed only by the intoxicating selection of margaritas ($5-12). Open M-Th and Su 7am-10pm, F-Sa 7am-midnight. AmEx/D/MC/V. ❷

■ **The Corvette Diner,** 3946 5th Ave. (☎619-542-1476; www.corvettediner.signonsandiego.com), in Hillcrest. This 50s-style diner has more chrome than Detroit and more neon than Las Vegas. Greasy-spoon classics and unique creations like the "Rory Burger" (with peanut butter and bacon; $8). A DJ spins oldies nightly 6-9pm while costumed waitstaff give as much lip as service. Open M-Th and Su 11am-10pm, F-Sa 11am-11pm. AmEx/D/MC/V. ❷

Pizza Port, 135 N. Rte. 101 (☎858-481-7332; www.pizzaport.com). If you're around Solana Beach, there's no better place for grub and grog than this surf-themed pizza parlor and microbrewery. After the sun sets, the bar fills up with laid-back, young locals discussing the finer points of the day's swell. Sit at long picnic tables, help yourself to plastic dinnerware, and create your own pizza ($6, plus $1 per topping) or try one of their favorites, like the San Clemente (black beans and cilantro; $7.25-17.75). Rotating selection of excellent homemade brews and ciders ($2-6). Open daily 7am-2am. AmEx/MC/V. ❷

Kono's Surf Club, 704 Garnet Ave. (☎858-483-1669), across from the Crystal Pier in Pacific Beach. Identifiable by the line stretching out the door, Kono's is a surfer's shrine that serves up legendary burritos. Mostly takeout, so you can eat on the beach. Try the huge "Egg Burrito #3," which includes bacon, cheese, potatoes, and sauce ($4.75). Open M-F 7am-3pm, Sa-Su 7am-4pm. D/MC/V. ❶

La Especial Norte, 664 N. Rte. 101 (☎760-942-1040), 25 mi. north of San Diego, in Leucadia. A great place to stop for well-made Mexican food. This family-run restaurant has huge portions, friendly service, and food so good that the San Diego Coast lifeguards rent the restaurant for their annual banquet. *Bistek ranchero* $12. Open daily 10am-10pm. AmEx/D/MC/V. ❷

Kansas City Barbecue, 610 W. Market St. (☎619-231-9680; www.kcbbq.net), near Seaport Village. The location of *Top Gun's* "Great Balls of Fire" bar scene. While the wooden piano remains, all that's left of Goose and Maverick is an abundance of

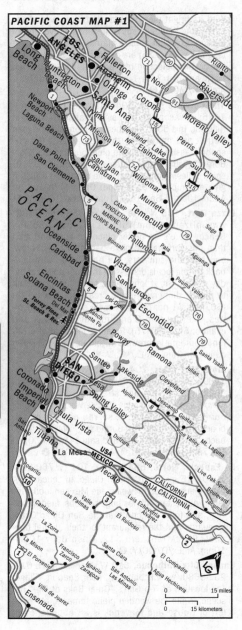

PACIFIC COAST MAP #1

PACIFIC COAST

autographed posters. Vegetarians will find themselves in the Danger Zone in this barbecue-slathered meatfest. Entrees $9-16. Open daily 11am-2am. Kitchen closes 1am. MC/V. ②

ACCOMMODATIONS

Beyond the hostel and residential hotel scene, San Diego is littered with generic chain motels, which are generally clean and safe. There is a cluster of hotels known as **Hotel Circle** (2-3 mi. east of I-5 along I-8), where summer prices begin at $60 for a single and $70 for a double during the week. Several beaches in North County, as well as one on Coronado, allow camping. For information call the San Diego and North County Coast Rangers Headquarters (☎619-688-3260), or for reservations contact ReserveAmerica (☎800-444-7275).

Banana Bungalow, 707 Reed Ave. (☎619-858-273-3060; www.bananabungalowsandiego.com), in the center of Pacific Beach. Smack dab on the beach, this hostel is like one big beach party with an open courtyard and gorgeous deck overlooking the water. Communal dinners cooked by friendly, travel-savvy hostel staff: Tu $1 cheeseburgers, W $5 dinner, Su free barbecue. Must have out-of-state ID, international passport, or proof of travel. Breakfast included. Lockers $0.25. Linen included. Laundry $1.50. Internet access $1 per 12min. Free parking. Dorms in summer $25, in winter $18; private rooms $95/$55. MC/V. ②

San Diego Downtown Hostel (HI-AYH), 521 Market St. (☎619-525-1531; www.sandiegohostels.org), in the Gaslamp Quarter. Quiet, impeccably clean, and close to popular attractions and clubs. Airy common rooms and a big kitchen. Free tours of the city. Bike rental $10. Pancake breakfast included. Dinner $5. No alcohol. Laundry $0.75. Free Wi-Fi. Dorms in summer $24-29, members $21-26; in winter $21-26/$18-23. Singles $58/$50. AmEx/D/MC/V. ②

USA Hostels San Diego, 726 5th Ave. (☎619-232-3100 or 800-438-8622; www.usahostels.com), between F and G St. This colorful Euro-style fun house fits in with the happening atmosphere of the Gaslamp Quarter, hosting frequent parties, weekly pub crawls, and $12 Tijuana trips. Bike rental $10. International passport, out-of-state ID, or student ID required. Pancake breakfast included. Dinner $5.

Lockers, linen, and coin-op laundry ($1.50). Internet terminals $2 per 20min. Dorms in summer $24, in winter $18-20; private rooms $61. MC/V. ❷

Ocean Beach International (OBI), 4961 Newport Ave. (☎619-223-7873 or 800-339-7263). Clean rooms near the most laid-back beach in San Diego. Proof of international travel in the last 6 months required. Pancake breakfast included. Tu and F barbecue. Internet access $1 per 20min. Dorms in summer $22, in winter $17; doubles $54/$44. MC/V. ❶

Roger's Dorms, 3204 Mission Blvd. (☎858-539-0043), across the street from Mission Beach roller coaster. Small, somewhat cramped hostel with over 2000 DVDs and videotapes lining the walls. Rooms painted according to theme—check out the cardboard palm trees. Small common room, coffee, microwave, and fridge. Free movies and popcorn nightly. Internet access $1 per 10min. Key deposit $20. Dorms $24; private singles $45; doubles $64. Cash only. ❷

🎵 ENTERTAINMENT

The definitive source of entertainment info is the free *Reader*, found in shops, coffeehouses, and visitors centers. Listings can also be found in the *San Diego Union-Tribune*'s Thursday "Night and Day" section or the *What's Playing* pamphlet from the visitors center. If cruisin' and boozin' isn't your idea of fun, you can spend a more sedate evening at one of San Diego's excellent theaters, such as the **Balboa Theatre,** 225 Broadway Ave. (☎609-544-1000), and the **Horton Grand Theatre,** 444 4th Ave. (☎619-234-9583). The **La Jolla Playhouse,** 2910 La Jolla Village Dr., is an award-winning theater that presents shows on the UCSD campus. (☎858-550-1010; www.lajollaplayhouse.com. Tickets from $30.) The **San Diego Symphony** plays throughout the year. (☎619-235-0804; www.sandiegosymphony.com.)

🔦 NIGHTLIFE

Nightlife in San Diego is scattered across distinct pockets of action. Posh locals and party-seeking tourists flock to the **Gaslamp Quarter.** The **Hillcrest,** next to Balboa Park, draws a young, largely gay crowd to its clubs and eateries. Away from downtown, the beach areas

(especially **Garnet Ave.** in Pacific Beach) are loaded with clubs, bars, and cheap eateries.

Pacific Beach Bar and Grill and **Club Tremors,** 860 Garnet Ave. (☎858-272-1242). One of the only dance clubs in Pacific Beach. Live DJ spins hip-hop, house, and retro for a packed 2-level dance floor filled with a young crowd. Respectable food, more than 20 beers on tap, and live music (generally rock) on Su from 6pm. 21+ at night. Cover Tu $5. Enter through the bar instead of Club Tremors Th-Sa to avoid the cover. Club open Tu-Su 9pm-1:30am. Bar open Tu-Su 11am-1:30am. Kitchen closes midnight. AmEx/D/MC/V.

Canes Bar and Grill, 3105 Ocean Front Walk (☎858-488-1780; www.canesbarandgrill.com), in Mission Beach. One of the best live music venues in the city, this beachside bar has unbeatable sunset views from the terrace. Music is usually rock, but check the website for schedule. Cover $5-25. Grill open M-F 11am to an hr. after sunset, Sa-Su 9am to an hr. after sunset. Club open 9pm-1 or 2am. AmEx/D/MC/V.

The Casbah, 2501 Kettner Blvd. (☎619-232-4355; www.casbahmusic.com). Intimate show venue with black walls, bar, and stage. Famous for attracting alt-rock greats before they became great: Pearl Jam, Nirvana, and The White Stripes have all played here. Music is generally alt-rock but can lean toward punk. Cover $10-18. Call ahead for schedule. Cash only.

Croce's Top Hat Bar and Grille and **Croce's Jazz Bar,** 802 5th Ave. (☎619-233-4355; www.croces.com), at F St., in the Gaslamp Quarter. Ingrid Croce, widow of singer Jim Croce, created this blues and jazz bar in memory of her late husband. Bypass the pricey restaurant and head to the wood-paneled piano bar with huge pictures of Jim adorning the walls. The live music is top-notch and the crowd is composed of jazz connoisseurs (most of whom are over 40). Don't wear your dirty backpacker gear. Music nightly from 8:30pm. 21+. Cover M-Th and Su $5, F-Sa $10. Top Hat open F-Sa 7pm-1:30am. Jazz bar open daily 5:30pm-12:30am. AmEx/D/MC/V.

Bourbon St., 4612 Park Blvd. (☎619-291-4043), in University Heights. Happening gay bar that's open nightly. There's a pub in the front area but most of the fun is in the back, where a covered patio is decorated to look like a street from the New Orleans French Quarter. Music is generally Top 40 and retro dance. Tu karaoke from 9pm. Th 4-7pm $3 martinis. Su $3 pitchers, $2 drafts. No cover. Open M-Sa 4pm-2am, Su 1pm-2am. MC/V.

APPROACHING LA JOLLA: 14 MILES
Head north on **9th Ave.**, turn right onto **Broadway,** then left onto **11th Ave.** Merge onto **I-5 N.** Take **Exit 26A** for the **La Jolla Pkwy.**, which becomes **Torrey Pines Rd.** Turn right onto **Prospect Pl.** and turn left onto **Herschel Ave.**

LA JOLLA

Pronounced *la-HOY-a*, this posh seaside locality has few budget accommodation options but offers some of the finest public beaches in the San Diego area. **La Jolla Cove,** the home of the brilliantly-colored Garibaldi goldfish, is popular with scuba divers and snorkelers. Wander south along the cliffs to a striking semi-circular inlet known as **The Children's Pool,** whose inhabitants are a famous thriving community of sea lions. Some of the best breaks in the county are at **Tourmaline Beach** and **Wind 'n Sea Beach.** However, these are notoriously territorial spots, so outsiders are advised to play nice. **La Jolla Shores** has gentle swells ideal for new surfers, boogie boarders, and swimmers. Up the road, the **◪Birch Aquarium at the Scripps Institute of Oceanography,** 2300 Expedition Way, has great educational exhibits including tanks of oozing jellyfish, well-camouflaged rockfish, and a 70,000 gal. shark tank. (☎858-534-3474; www.aquarium.ucsd.edu. Open daily 9am-5pm. $11, 60+ $9, college students $8, ages 3-17 $7.50.) The **San Diego Museum of Contemporary Art,** 700 Prospect St., shares its rotating collection of pop, minimalist, and conceptualist art with the downtown branch (p. 890). The museum is as visually stunning as the art it contains, with gorgeous ocean views and high-ceilinged, light-filled spaces. (☎858-454-3541. Open M-Tu and Th-F 10am-5pm, W and Sa-Su 11am-5pm. $6; students, seniors, and ages 12-18 $2. 1st Su and 3rd Tu of each month free.) The terraces and buttresses that support **Geisel Library** at the **University of California San Diego (UCSD)** are worth checking out. This space-age structure was endowed by the late Theodore Geisel, better known by his middle name as the beloved children's books author, Dr. Seuss. (☎858-534-3339. Open M-Th and Su 8am-midnight, F 8am-8pm, Sa 10am-6pm.)

APPROACHING TORREY PINES STATE PARK: 8 MILES
Go north on **Herschel Ave.** and turn right onto **Prospect St.** Turn left onto **Torrey Pines Rd.** to reach the state park.

TORREY PINES STATE PARK. The closest taste of nature near San Diego, **Torrey Pines State Park,** 12600 N. Torrey Pines Rd., is often crowded, but the hiking trails and beach are lovely. Be sure to watch for the frolicking dolphins along the coast. The park is also home to the scrub jay bird and the rarest kind of pine tree in the US. (About ½ mi. south of Del Mar Village. ☎858-755-2063; www.torreypine.org. Open 7am-sunset. $6 per vehicle.) The **Torrey Pines Lodge,** 11480 N. Torrey Pines Rd., provides info on hiking trails, as well as an exhibit on why the torrey pines are so unique. (☎858-453-4420. Open daily 9am-5:30pm.)

APPROACHING DEL MAR: 3 MILES
Torrey Pines Rd. becomes **Camino Del Mar** north of the park and leads into Del Mar.

DEL MAR

The affluent suburb of Del Mar is home to racehorses and famous fairgrounds, as well as small shops and some good eats along Camino Del Mar. During June and early July, Del Mar hosts the **San Diego County Fair,** one of the largest fairs in California. To the north, Solana Beach boasts the **Cedros Design District,** which is full of warehouses converted into specialty boutiques. Wander the streets for an eclectic array of boutiques from a salvage yard to upscale clothing stores. The celebrity-studded **Del Mar Thoroughbred Club,** at the corner of Via de la Valle and Jimmy Durante Blvd., fills with racing fans in late July and August. Founded in 1937 by Bing Crosby and Pat O'Brien, the racetrack is one of the most beautiful in the world. (☎858-755-1141; www.delmarracing.com. At least 8 races daily. Post time 2pm.)

Surf-weathered locals favor **Board and Brew ❷,** 1212 Camino Del Mar, for its cheap beer ($2-2.50) and delicious sandwiches. Try the California Delight ($4.50), with turkey, cream cheese, and sunflower seeds. (☎858-481-1021. Open daily 10am-7pm. Cash only.) Relax on the patio at the **Beach Grass Cafe ❷,** 159 S. Hwy 101., and enjoy tasty soups and fresh salads as you sample microbrews. (☎858-509-0632. Open M-Th and Su 7:30am-3:30pm and 5-9pm, F-Sa 5-10pm. AmEx/D/MC/V.) **Pizza Port ❷,** 135 N. U.S. 101, in Solana Beach, has awesome deep-dish pizza and "grog." Expect a wait at dinner time; the place is usually packed.

(☎858-481-7332; www.pizzaport.com. Pizzas from $6. Pints from $3. Open M-F 10:30am-11pm, Sa-Su 11am-11pm. AmEx/MC/V.)

⚑ APPROACHING CARLSBAD: 17 MILES
Camino Del Mar becomes **Old U.S. 101** and then **Carlsbad Blvd.** as it heads north along the coast. Turn right onto **Carlsbad Village Dr.**

CARLSBAD
Farther up the coast is the charming lagoon hideaway of Carlsbad, where U.S. 101, known here as Carlsbad Blvd., winds past silky sands and shingled homes adorned with wild rosebushes.

VITAL STATS

Population: 78,000

Visitor Info: Carlsbad Convention and Visitors Center, 400 Carlsbad Village Dr. (☎760-434-6093; www.carlsbadca.org). Open M-F 9am-5pm, Sa 10am-4pm, Su 10am-3pm.

Internet Access: Georgina Cole Library, 1250 Carlsbad Village Dr. (☎760-434-2870), downtown. Open M-Th 9am-9pm, F-Sa 9am-5pm. Free.

Post Office: 2772 Roosevelt St. (☎760-729-1244). Open 7:30am-5pm, Sa 9am-12:30pm. **Postal Code:** 92008.

⌸ GETTING AROUND. Carlsbad Blvd. (U.S. 101) is the major north-south route. Carlsbad Village Dr. runs inland toward I-5.

◪ SIGHTS. Legoland, 1 Legoland Dr., is a fun, goofball tribute to the interlocking kiddie blocks that have inspired countless junior architects. Visitors who pay the hefty admission price might be disappointed to find no gem-studded legos. (South of town, head east on Canyon Rd. ☎760-918-5346. Open in summer daily 10am-8pm; in fall M and Th-Su 10am-5pm; in spring daily 10am-5pm; hours vary in winter. $53, ages 3-12 $43.) Shake, rattle, and roll at the extensive **Museum of Making Music,** 5790 Armada Dr., where over 450 innovative musical instruments create a survey of 20th-century American music. (☎877-551-9976; www.museumofmakingmusic.org. Open Tu-Su 10am-5pm. $5; seniors, students, military, and ages 4-18 $3.) The California state park system maintains a number of breathtaking beaches. The long **Carlsbad State Beach** is

marred only slightly by the mammoth power plant which occupies the coast to the south. **Offshore Surf Shop,** 3179 Carlsbad Blvd., rents boogie boards and 6-8 ft. "soft" foam surfboards for beginners. (☎760-729-4934. Boogie boards $3 per hr., $10 per day. Surfboards $5/$25. Credit card or deposit of $40 for boogie board and $300 for surfboard is required. Open daily 9am-7pm.) On the first Sunday in May and November, the **Carlsbad Village Street Faire,** the largest one-day fair in California, attracts over 80,000 people.

◪⌂ FOOD AND ACCOMMODATIONS.
There are a variety of great beachfront restaurants along Pacific Coast Hwy. (Old U.S. 101). Locals and tourists cram the intimate dining area at ◪**Trattoria I Trulli ❸,** 830 S. Coast Hwy., for good reason: the food is delicious and the atmosphere is charmingly chic. (☎760-943-6800. Dinner entrees from $10. Open M-Th and Su 11:30am-2:30pm and 5-10pm, F-Sa 11:30am-2:30pm and 5-10:30pm. AmEx/D/MC/V.) Life is sweet at **Honey's Bistro and Bakery ❷,** 632 S. Coast Hwy., in Encinitas, where they serve large, fresh salads ($5-8), sandwiches ($4-7), and soups ($4-6), as well as mouth-watering baked goods. (☎760-942-5433. Open daily 5:30am-3:30pm and 5pm-last customer. AmEx/MC/V.) Karaoke your heart out at the **Coyote Bar and Grill ❸,** 300 Carlsbad Village Dr., or warm up next to the fire pits. Live music and Southern cuisine make this a popular local hangout. (☎760-729-4695. Open M-Th and Su 11am-12:30am, F-Sa 11am-2am. AmEx/MC/V.)

Though inexpensive lodging is nearly impossible to find in Carlsbad, the **Surf Motel ❹,** 3136 Carlsbad Blvd., is a decent value across the street from the beach. (☎760-729-7961. Rooms in summer $129-259; in winter $79-189. AmEx/D/MC/V.) A cheaper alternative is **Motel 6 ❸,** 1006 Carlsbad Village Dr., just east of Carlsbad Village. (☎760-434-7135. Singles $50-64; doubles $56-70. AmEx/D/MC/V.) **San Elijo Beach State Park ❶,** off Rte. 101, south of Cardiff-by-the-Sea, has over 170 sites on seaside cliffs. (☎760-753-5091. Laundry and showers. Sites $16-25, with hookup $25-44.) **South Carlsbad Beach State Park ❶,** off Carlsbad Blvd., has over 100 sites near beautiful beaches with good surfing. (☎760-438-3143. Laundry and showers. Reservations required in summer. Sites $16-35.)

PACIFIC COAST

◪ APPROACHING OCEANSIDE: 5 MILES
Carlsbad Blvd. becomes **Coast Hwy.** as it heads north toward Oceanside.

OCEANSIDE

Oceanside is the largest and least glamorous of San Diego's coastal resort towns. Neighbor to Camp Pendleton, a Marine Corps base, as well as one of the world's greatest surfing beaches at Oceanside Harbor, Oceanside is part military order, part surfer-chill. The pier gets crowded during the **World Body Surfing Championships** in mid-August. Call the Oceanside Special Events Office (☎760-435-5540) for info. Get a taste of surf culture at the ◪**California Surf Museum**, 223 N. Coast Hwy., where the exhibit changes yearly. (☎760-721-6876. Open M and Th-Su 10am-4pm. Free.) Catch your own dinner by renting gear at **Helgren's Sportfishing Trips,** 315 Harbor Dr. S. (☎760-722-2133. 1-day license $11.50. Rod rental $13; shark rod $15. Half-day trips on the fishing boat $39, full day $65. Non-fishing harbor cruise daily $14, ages 5-12 $7.) Find California's first pepper tree at **Mission San Luis Rey de Francia,** 4050 Mission Ave., founded by Father Lausen in 1798. The only original building still standing is the church and the five adjoining arches. (Follow Mission Ave. E from N. Coast Hwy. ☎760-757-3651. Open daily 10am-4pm. $5, ages 8-14 $3. Tours $7. Cemetery free.) Power up before hitting the waves at **The Longboarder ❷**, 228 N. Coast Hwy., which serves juicy burgers ($6-7) and heaping omelettes ($7-8) to hungry surfers. (☎760-721-6776. Open M-W 7am-2pm, Th-Sa 7am-9pm, Su 7am-3pm. MC/V.)

◪ APPROACHING SAN CLEMENTE AND DANA POINT: 24 MILES
Head east on **Mission Ave.** to **I-5 N.** Follow I-5 N through the Camp Pendleton Marine Base.

SAN CLEMENTE AND DANA POINT. San Clemente, a "small Spanish village by the sea," provides the waves of bigger beach towns without all the noise and antics. It is also the birthplace of former US President Richard Nixon. San Clemente's downtown is known as a mecca of antiques, with unrivaled shops and historic buildings lining the streets. Just south of town, **San Onofre State Beach** is a prime surfing zone for experienced thrill-seekers. Neighboring Dana Point's spectacular bluffs were popularized in namesake Richard Henry Dana's 1841 account of Southern California's sailing culture, *Two Years Before the Mast.* The harbor holds nearly 3000 yachts and serves as a point of departure for Catalina Island. If you're in the mood for a swim ask for Dana Point's **swimming beach,** which lies at Green Lantern Cove and Ensenada Place.

◪ DETOUR
SAN JUAN CAPISTRANO
From San Clemente or Dana Point, take I-5 N to Exit 82. Turn left on Ortega Hwy.

The **Mission San Juan Capistrano** was founded in 1776 by Father Serra and is the birthplace of Orange County. Full of romance and beauty, the mission stands as a monument to Native American, Mexican, and European cultures. Although most of the original structure collapsed in an earthquake in 1812, this is the oldest used building in California and the only standing site where Serra himself is known to have given mass. The crumbling walls of the beautiful **Serra Chapel** are warmed by a 17th-century Spanish altar and Native American designs. The courtyard garden is perhaps the most charming part of the mission. On March 19th each year, the city of San Juan Capistrano gathers here for the famous **"Return of the Swallows,"** a celebration of the flock of birds that always migrates back to the mission. (☎949-234-1300; www.missionsjc.com. Open daily 8:30am-5pm. $6, seniors $5, ages 3-12 $4.) **The Swallows Inn,** 31786 Camino Capistrano, has been the favorite local pub for over 50 years and is the best place to catch the **Swallows Day Parade** in March. It is also home to one of the country's largest chili cook-offs each May. (☎949-493-3188. Open daily 7am-2am. Cash only.)

◪ APPROACHING LAGUNA BEACH: 14 MILES
From the **Pacific Coast Hwy. (Rte. 1),** turn right onto **Forest Ave.,** and right again onto **Glenneyre St.** to reach Laguna Beach.

LAGUNA BEACH

A sign at the corner of Forest and Ocean Ave. sums up the industry-free pleasantness of Laguna with the message: "This Gate Hangs Well and Hinders None, Refresh and Rest, Then Travel On." Recent television fame has popularized this oceanside town, though its bustling beaches, rocky cliffs, coves, and lush hillside foliage don't need the extra publicity to appeal to visitors. Much of the town's charm is visible along the coastal highway, including dozens of displays of public art.

VITAL STATS

Population: 24,000

Visitor Info: 252 Broadway (☎800-877-1115; www.lagunabeachinfo.org). Open daily 9am-5pm.

Internet Access: Laguna Beach Library, 363 Geneyre St. (☎949-497-1733), 1 block south of Forest Ave. Open M-W 10am-8pm, Th 10am-6pm, F-Sa 10am-5pm. Free.

Parking: There's a large parking lot ($1.50 per hr.) between Park and Laguna on Glenneyre St.

Post Office: 24001 Calle de la Magdalena (☎949-837-1848). Open M-F 8:30am-5pm, Sa 9am-3pm.

Postal Code: 92654.

■ **GETTING AROUND. Ocean Ave.,** at the Pacific Coast Hwy., and **Main Beach** are the prime hangout spots in Laguna Beach. **Westry Beach,** which spreads south of Laguna just below Aliso Beach Park, and **Camel Point,** between Westry and Aliso, form the hub of the local gay community. You'll know you've reached the town center when you see the seaside Main Park; the main drags of **Forest Ave.** and **Ocean Ave.** run perpendicular to it. Parking downtown can be a problem; meters gobble quarters for 15min. of legality 8am-6pm. For beach access, park on residential streets to the east and look for "Public Access" signs between private properties.

◙ **SIGHTS.** The one-name native of Laguna Beach, painter **Wyland** has distinguished himself in the art world through public expression of the enchantment of whales and other underwater life. Wyland aims to paint 100 murals worldwide; 93 have been completed so far. Number 100 is scheduled for the Great Wall of China at the 2008 Olympics. You can see one, in tiles, next to the **Wyland Gallery,** 509 S. Coast Hwy. **Friends of Sea Lions Marine Mammal Center,** 20612 Laguna Canyon Rd., rescues sick sea lions and friends, whom you can visit. (☎949-494-3050; www.mammalmmc.org Open daily 10am-4pm.) The **Thousand Steps Beach** may be missing 800 of the steps it claims, but the beauty of the arched descent is enough to make you lean toward poetic exaggeration. The inconspicuous entrance is one block south of the medical center on 9th St.; park your car inland. Three miles north of Laguna Beach, **Crystal Cove State Park,** 8471 Rte. 1, is a beautiful nature preserve with a rocky shoreline. **El Moro Canyon** extends up the hills east of Rte. 1, offering hikes with coastal views. Choose one of the better hikes: a comfortable 3 mi. loop around No Dogs Rd., Poles Rd., and El Moro Canyon Rd. or the strenuous 10½ mi. ascent up Moro Ridge Rd. (☎949-494-3539. Open daily sunrise-sunset. $5 per vehicle.)

In the ◙**Pageant of the Masters,** the highlight of Laguna Beach's Festival of Arts, people

THE INS-N-OUTS OF IN-N-OUT

From its beginning in 1948 as a burger stand, **IN-N-OUT Burger** has come a long way. Its distinctive yellow-and-red sign is now ubiquitous across California, Nevada, and Arizona. Many first-time visitors are surprised to see a menu with just 5 choices (hamburger, cheeseburger, double-double, fries, and shake), but IN-N-OUT also has a "secret menu." These options aren't technically on the menu, but they're available at all locations.

Animal Style: Burger grilled in mustard with lettuce, tomato, pickles, grilled onions, and IN-N-OUT's special sandwich spread.
Protein Style: Burger of your choice wrapped in lettuce instead of a bun.
Double Meat: Two beef patties, no cheese.
Flying Dutchman: Two beef patties, two slices of cheese, nothing else.
Wish Burger: No meat.
3x3: 3 beef patties, 3 slices of cheese, lettuce, tomato, and spread on a bun. (Also available in 4x4)
Fries Animal Style: Fries with cheese, special spread, and onions.

faithfully recreate famous works of art as "living pictures." (☎949-494-1145; www.foapom.com. July-Aug. daily 8:30pm.) The **Sawdust Art Festival** showcases 200 local artists in a beautiful 3½ acre setting. (Open July-Aug. 10am-10pm. $7, seniors $6, ages 6-12 $3, under 6 free.)

▟ FOOD AND ACCOMMODATIONS. The **Orange Inn ❷**, 703 S. Coast Hwy, dates back to 1931, serving sandwiches ($4.50-7.25), smoothies ($4), and Mexicali dishes. Check out the pictures of old Laguna Beach in the back. (☎949-494-6085. Open daily 6am-5pm. D/MC/V.) **Ho Sum Bistro ❷**, 3112 Newport Blvd., at 32nd St., is a quintessentially Southern Californian mix of healthy Asian-influenced food and neon-lit white decor. The Ho Sum chicken salad ($5.25) will definitely fill you up. (☎949-675-0896. Open M-Th and Su 11am-10pm, F-Sa 11am-11pm. AmEx/MC/V.) Across the street from the park, **The White House ❸**, 340 S. Coast Hwy., has been serving upscale American food that won't break the bank since 1918. The "twilight dinner" (M-Th and Su 4-6:30pm) is a steal: only $12 for a two-course meal with choices like seafood pasta and peppered steak. (☎949-494-8088. Open M-Th and Su 11am-10pm, F-Sa 9am-11pm. AmEx/MC/V.) **Laguna Village Market and Cafe ❶**, 577 S. Coast Hwy., sits atop a cliff and houses an open-air gazebo market, though the oceanfront terrace is the real draw. (☎949-494-6344. Open daily 8am-sunset.)

Laguna Beach doesn't offer much in the way of budget accommodations. Your best bet is probably camping. In town, the **Seacliff Laguna Inn ❹**, 1661 S. Coast Hwy., is a cut above the average motel with some rooms overlooking the ocean (over other roofs) and a heated pool. (☎949-494-9717; www.seaclifflaguna.com. Rooms from $85. AmEx/D/DC/MC/V.)

▟ NIGHTLIFE. Locals and tourists head to the bars lining Ocean Ave. for a night out. The **Ocean Brewing Company**, 237 Ocean Ave., is a mellow bar that turns into a 21+ club after 10pm. Ask the bartender for a special brew ($5.50) or try one of their infamous martinis. (☎949-497-3381. Cover Tu and Th-Sa after 10pm $5. Open Tu-Su 11:30am-last customer. AmEx/MC/V.) The neighboring **Hennessey's Tavern**, 213 Ocean Ave., offers live music and dancing. Stop in for Two Timin' Tuesdays, when breakfast and burgers are 2-for-1.

(☎949-494-2743. Open M-F 10am-1:30am, Sa-Su 8:30am-1:30am. AmEx/MC/V.)

▟ APPROACHING NEWPORT BEACH: 12 MILES
Continue along **Rte. 1 N.**

NEWPORT BEACH

Multi-million-dollar homes, beach bums, and Balboa Peninsula are all packed closely enough on the Newport Beach oceanfront to make even New Yorkers feel claustrophobic. The young hedonists partying on the sand are a solid mix of locals and out-of-towners. Surfing and beach volleyball are popular, as is strolling the residential streets of Balboa Peninsula. Newport's **Harbor Nautical Museum**, 151 E. Pacific Coast Hwy., aboard the 189 ft. *Pride of Newport*, has exhibits on maritime history and model ships. (☎949-673-7863; www.nhnm.org. Open Tu-Sa and Su 10am-5pm. Free.) Get a dose of O.C. style at **Fashion Island**, just inland from the Pacific Coast Hwy., between MacArthur Blvd. and Jamboree Rd. Divided into seven courts, this outdoor mall is the Orange County version of a regular mall but lets you get a tan while you shop. **Joe's Crabshack ❸**, 2607 Pacific Coast Hwy., has brightly colored chairs, neon beer lights on the walls, and a fantastic view of the harbor. Happy hour (daily 5-7pm) has discounted eats and dirt-cheap drinks. (☎949-650-1818; www.joescrabshack.com. Entrees from $8. Open M-Th and Su 11am-10pm, F-Sa 11am-11pm. AmEx/D/DC/MC/V.) The **Balboa Inn ❺**, 105 Main St., is a renovated landmark that offers rooms with ocean views and access to a hot tub. (☎949-675-3412; www.balboainn.com. Continental breakfast included. Parking $8. Rooms from $119. AmEx/D/DC/MC/V.)

▟ APPROACHING HUNTINGTON BEACH: 6 MILES
Take **PCH/Rte. 1 N** for 6 mi.

HUNTINGTON BEACH

The prototypical Surf City of the US, Huntington Beach is a playground for beach bums. This town has surf lore galore, and proof is on the **Surfing Walk of Fame** (the sidewalk along PCH at Main St.) and in the **International Surfing Museum**, 411 Olive St. (☎714-960-3483. Open M-F noon-5pm, Sa-Su 11am-6pm. $2, students $1.) All you need to join the wave-riding is about $40 per hr., enough for an instructor, board, and wetsuit. Inquire at local surf shops or make an appointment with the lifeguard-staffed **Huntington Beach Surfing Instruction** (☎714-962-3515). The pier is the best place to watch the cavalcade of official surfing contests which occur periodically throughout the summer.

Turn off Rte. 1 onto Main St. for six blocks, and on your left you'll find **Jan's Health Bar ❷**, 510 Main St. This wholesome hold-over from the 60s sells scrumptious sandwiches ($4-7), salads, and smoothies. (☎714-536-4856. Open M-Sa 8am-7pm, Su 8am-6pm. Cash only.) **Ruby's ❸**, at the end of the Huntington Beach Pier, is a flashy white-and neon-red, 50s-style diner with great burgers ($8) and a fabulous ocean view. Try the shoestring fries ($3) for a shoestring budget price. (☎714-969-7829. Open daily 7am-9pm. AmEx/D/MC/V.) Cheap lodging is available at **Huntington Beach Colonial Inn Youth Hostel ❶**, 421 8th St., four blocks inland at Pecan Ave. This large, early 20th-century, yellow-and-blue house looks like it is from the set of a surfer movie. (From PCH, turn onto 8th St. ☎714-536-3315. Common bathroom, kitchen, reading room with TV, Internet access, deck, and shed with surfboards, boogie boards, and bikes. Linen and breakfast included. Key deposit $20. Check-in 8am-10pm. Reserve 3 months in advance for summer. Dorms $22; private doubles $50. MC/V.)

⬢ DETOUR
DISNEYLAND
From Huntington Beach, take Beach Blvd. (Rte. 39) N for 11 mi. Turn right on Ball Rd. and continue for 4 mi.

Disneyland calls itself the "Happiest Place on Earth," and a little bit of everyone agrees. But after a full day, your wallet might be in pain. Weekday and low-season visitors will be the happiest, but the clever budget travelers can wait for parades to distract families from the epic lines or utilize the line-busting FastPass program. New **California Adventure Park** lets you see recreated movie back lots, California sights, a beach boardwalk, an eight-acre mini-wilderness, a citrus grove, a winery, and a replica of San Francisco. (☎714-781-4565; www.disneyland.com. Open M-Th and Su 8am-11pm, F-Sa 8am-midnight; hours may vary. Disneyland passport $50, ages 3-9 $40, under 3 free. 2- and 3-day passes also available.

California Adventure $50, ages 3-9 $40, under 3 free. Park Hopper ticket $70, ages 3-9 $60.)

⬢ DETOUR
KNOTT'S BERRY FARM
Stay on Rte. 39 N 1 mi. after the turn-off for Disneyland on Ball Rd.

Knott's Berry Farm has long since given up on being the happiest place on Earth—it settles on being "America's 1st theme park." Highlights include roller coasters like Montezooma's Revenge, Boomerang, and Ghostrider. The latest addition is the Silver Bullet. (☎714-220-5200. Open M-F and Su 10am-8pm, Sa 10am-10pm; hours may vary. $40, ages 3-11 and 62+ $15, under 3 free.) Neighboring **Soak City USA** is Knott's 13-acre effort to make a splash in the drenched water park scene. (☎714-220-5200. Open daily 10am-7pm; hours may vary. $40, ages 3-11 and seniors $15, under 3 free.)

⬢ APPROACHING LONG BEACH: 19 MILES
Take **PCH/Rte. 1 N**. In Long Beach, turn left on **Alamitos Ave.** to head for the shore.

LONG BEACH

Long Beach is an industrial shipping center—massive, hulking, and impersonal. The fifth-largest city in California has less coastal charm than its neighbors. There are two main attractions on the coast, the Queen Mary luxury liner and the aquarium. Every April, Long Beach hosts a Grand Prix, and world-class racecar drivers and celebrities alike come to careen around the downtown track.

VITAL STATS
Population: 465,000
Visitor Information: Long Beach Visitors Bureau, 1 World Trade Ctr., Ste. 300 (☎800-452-7829), at Ocean Blvd. Open M-F 8am-5pm.
Internet Access: Long Beach Library, 101 Pacific Ave. (☎562-570-7500). Open Tu 10am-8pm, W-Sa 10am-5:30pm. Free.
Post Office: 300 N. Long Beach Blvd. (☎562-628-1303). Open M-F 8:30am-5pm, Sa 9am-2pm. **Postal Code:** 90802.

▣ GETTING AROUND. Long Beach's main tourist attractions lie by the bay. **Pine Ave.,** the backbone of downtown, runs north from the bay. **Ocean Blvd.** runs west to the boutiques of Belmont Shores. Be cautious in the inland areas of industrial Long Beach.

◎ SIGHTS. At the end of Queen's Way Dr., the legendary 1934 Cunard luxury liner **Queen Mary** has been transformed into a hotel with art exhibits, historical displays, and upscale bars. During WWII, the "Grey Ghost" (as she was known) carried 765,429 military personnel, sailing a total of 569,429 miles. The ship was so crucial to the Allied war effort that Hitler offered highest honors to anyone who sank her. Spookify the scene with the Haunted Encounters Passport. (☎ 562-435-3511; www.queenmary.com. Open daily 10am-6pm. $23, seniors and military $20, children $12.)

A $117 million, 156,735 sq. ft. celebration of the world's largest and most diverse body of water, the **Long Beach Aquarium of the Pacific,** 100 Aquarium Way, is situated atop one of the world's busiest and most polluted harbors. Meet the dazzling creatures of the deep that struggle to coexist with the harbor's flotsam, jetsam, and effluvium. The seals, sea lions, otters, sharks, and jellyfish are sure to please. (☎ 562-590-3100; www.aquariumofpacific.org. Open daily 9am-6pm. $20, seniors $17, ages 3-11 $12.) Just south of Ocean Blvd. and east of the Convention and Entertainment Center is an enormous **life-sized mural of whales,** cited by locals as the largest in the world. Ready your game face and head to **Gameworks,** 10 Aquarium Way, in The Pike at Rainbow Harbor. With bowling lanes and 2-for-Thursdays ($2 domestic drafts and specialty shots), you can play the night away. (☎ 562-308-7529. Open M-Th 11am-midnight, F 11am-2am, Sa 10am-2am, Su 10am-midnight. AmEx/MC/V.)

◢✸⸏ FOOD AND ACCOMMODATIONS. The comfy diner setting at **The Shorehouse Cafe ❸,** 5271 E. 2nd St., in Belmont Shores, assures that you can order anything at any time. (☎ 562-433-2266. Huge burgers $8-9. Open 24hr. AmEx/D/MC/V.) The health-conscious should head to **The Omelette Inn ❷,** 108 W. 3rd. St., for egg-white omelettes, brown rice, and veggie bacon strips. (☎ 562-437-5625. Open daily 7am-2:30pm. AmEx/MC/V.) Cheap accommodations are few, but the **Beach Inn Motel ❹,** 823 E. 3rd St., right off the water, is not wholly unreasonable and has all

the standard amenities. (☎ 562-437-3464. Doubles $90. AmEx/D/MC/V.) If money is not on your mind, try the newly renovated **Beach Plaza Hotel ❹,** 2010 E. Ocean Blvd., at Cherry Ave., with spacious rooms and a turquoise exterior that matches the ocean. (☎ 562-437-0771. Pool and beach access. Reservations recommended. Doubles $80-150, with ocean view and kitchenette $200. AmEx/MC/V.)

⁊ APPROACHING LOS ANGELES: 25 MILES Take **Atlantic Ave. N** to **I-405 N.**

LOS ANGELES

In a city where nothing seems to be more than 30 years old, the latest trends command more respect than does tradition. People flock to this historical vacuum in an effort to live like the stars. And what better place? Bring your sense of style and an attitude; both are mandatory in this city of celebrities. Cruise through the city and watch the sun set over the Pacific in Santa Monica, or stay to see the sights and the stars; either way, it's one hell of a show.

VITAL STATS

Population: 10 million

Visitor Info: L.A. Convention and Visitor Bureau, 685 S. Figueroa St. (☎ 213-689-8822; www.visitlanow.com), between Wilshire Blvd. and 7th St., in the Financial District. Open M-F 8:30am-5pm.

Internet Access: Los Angeles Public Library, Central Library, 630 W. 5th St. (☎ 213-228-7000). Open M-Th 10am-8pm, F-Sa 10am-6pm, Su 1-5pm. Free.

Post Office: 7101 S. Central Ave. (☎ 323-586-4414). Open M-F 7am-7pm, Sa 7am-3pm. **Postal Code:** 90001.

▛ GETTING AROUND

Five major freeways connect California's vainest city to the rest of the state. **I-5 (Golden State Fwy.), U.S. 101 (Hollywood Fwy.),** the **Pacific Coast Hwy. (PCH or Rte. 1), I-405 (San Diego Fwy.),** and **I-10 (Santa Monica Fwy.).** I-5, I-405, I-110 (Harbor Fwy.), U.S. 101, and Pacific Coast Hwy. all run north-south. I-10 runs east-west. I-5 intersects I-10 just east of downtown and is one of the two major north-south thoroughfares. I-405, which goes from **Orange County** in the south all the way through L.A., parallels I-5 closer to the coast, and separates **Santa Monica** and **Malibu** from the **L.A. Westside.**

A legitimate downtown L.A. exists, but few go there except to work. The heart of downtown is relatively safe on weekdays, but avoid walking there after dark and on weekends. **Monterey Park** is one of the few cities in the US with a predominantly Asian-American population. The **University of Southern California (USC), Exposition Park,** and the districts of **Inglewood, Watts,** and **Compton** stretch south of downtown. **South Central,** as this area is called, suffered the brunt of the 1992 riots, is known for rampant crime, and holds few attractions for tourists. The predominantly Latino section of the city is found east of downtown and is comprised of **Boyle Heights, East L.A.,** and **Montebello.**

Sunset Blvd. has virtually everything L.A. has to offer the food- and fashion-conscious. **Sunset Strip,** the hot seat of L.A.'s best nightlife, is the West Hollywood section of Sunset Blvd. closest to Beverly Hills. The region known as **The Westside** encompasses prestigious **West Hollywood, Westwood, Bel Air, Brentwood, Beverly Hills, Pacific Palisades, Santa Monica,** and **Venice.** A good portion of the city's gay community resides in West Hollywood, while Beverly Hills and Bel Air are home to the rich and famous. **West L.A.** is a municipal distinction that refers to Westwood and the no-man's land that includes Century City. The area west of downtown and south of West Hollywood is known as the **Wilshire District.**

Eighty miles of beaches line L.A.'s coastal region. **Long Beach** is the southernmost. North across the Palos Verdes Peninsula is **Venice,** followed by **Santa Monica, Malibu,** and **Zuma Beach.** The **San Fernando Valley** sprawls north of the Hollywood Hills and the Santa Monica Mountains. The basin is bounded to the north and west by the Santa Susana Mountains and Rte. 118 (Ronald Reagan Fwy.), to the south by Rte. 134 (Ventura Blvd.), and to the east by I-5 (Golden State Fwy.). The **San Bernardino Valley,** home to about two million people, stretches eastward from L.A., south of the San Gabriel Mountains. In between these two valleys lie the affluent foothills of **Pasadena** and its famed **Rose Parade.**

 SIGHTS

HOLLYWOOD

Exploring the Hollywood area requires a pair of sunglasses, a camera, some cash, and a whole lot of patience. Running east-west at the foot of the Hollywood Hills, **Hollywood Blvd.** is the center of L.A.'s tourist madness. Thousands come daily to the home of the Walk of Fame, famous theaters, souvenir shops, and museums.

HOLLYWOOD SIGN. Those 50 ft. high, 30 ft. wide, slightly erratic letters perched on Mt. Lee in Griffith Park stand as a universally recognized symbol of the city. The original 1923 sign read HOLLYWOODLAND and was an advertisement for a new subdivision in the Hollywood Hills. The sign has been a target of many college pranks, which have made it read everything from "Hollyweird" to "Ollywood" (after the infamous Lt. Col. Oliver North) to "Hollyweed," when California adopted a new marijuana law in 1976. A fence keeps you at a distance of 40 ft. *(To get as close to the sign as possible requires a strenuous 2½ mi. hike. Take the Bronson Canyon entrance to Griffith Park and follow Canyon Dr. to its end, where parking is free. The Brush Canyon Trail starts where Canyon Dr. becomes unpaved. At the top of the hill, follow the road to your left. For those satisfied with driving, go north on Vine St., take a right on Franklin Ave. and a left on Beachwood, and drive up until you are forced to drive down.)*

GRAUMAN'S CHINESE THEATRE. Loosely modeled on a Chinese temple, this monumental, eye-catching theater is a Hollywood icon that frequently rolls out the red carpet for movie premieres. The sculptures on the exterior columns—"Heaven Dogs"—were imported from China, where they once supported a Ming Dynasty temple. The theater houses a collection of celebrity foot- and handprints pressed into cement as well as other star trademarks, including Whoopi Goldberg's dreadlocks and R2-D2's wheels. *(6925 Hollywood Blvd., between Highland and Orange St. ☎ 323-461-3331. 7-12 tours per day; call ahead. $12, children $8, under 2 free.)*

WALK OF FAME. Tourists along Hollywood Blvd. stop mid-stride to gawk at the sidewalk's over 2000 bronze-inlaid stars, which are inscribed with the names of the famous, the infamous, and

PACIFIC COAST

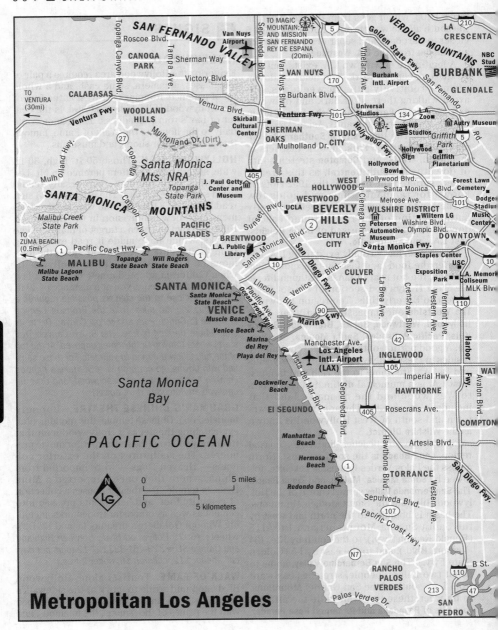

Metropolitan Los Angeles

Glendale Fwy.

Mt. Wilson 5,710ft

Mt. Wilson Observatory

Monrovia Peak 5,412ft

Pine Mountain 454ft

San Gabriel Res.

LA CAÑADA

NASA Jet Propulsion Laboratory

FLINTRIDGE

Descanso Gardens

Mt. Harvard 5,440ft

Angeles National Forest

Silver Mountain 3,391ft

San Gabriel Cyn. Rd.

Mt. Bliss 3,725ft

Morris Res.

San Dimas Experimental Forest

Glendora Mtn. Rd.

210

Washington Blvd.

Rose Bowl

PASADENA

Norton Simon Museum of Art

Sierra Madre Blvd.

Colorado Blvd.

Foothill Blvd.

GLENDORA

134

Ventura Fwy.

Pasadena Playhouse

Caltech

Huntington Gallery and Gardens

ARCADIA

210

Foothill Fwy.

39

Pasadena Fwy.

Huntington Dr.

Santa Anita Ave.

Live Oak Ave.

BALDWIN PARK

39

Arrow Hwy.

210

SAN DIMAS

110

SAN MARINO

SAN GABRIEL

Rosemead Blvd.

Peck Rd.

605

COVINA

Grand Ave.

Raging Waters

ALHAMBRA

El Pueblo Historic Park

Valley Blvd.

ROSEMEAD

Ramona Blvd.

San Bernardino Fwy.

10

CHINATOWN

10

City Hall

El Pueblo de Los Angeles Historical Monument

MONTEREY PARK

19

60

Valley Blvd.

Glandora Ave.

N8

Azusa Ave.

CITY OF INDUSTRY

POMONA

71

Convention and Visitors Bureau

5

EAST L.A.

Santa Ana Fwy.

605

19

60

Pomona Fwy.

60

HUNTINGTON PARK

710

DOWNEY

WHITTIER

72

Colima Rd.

Hacienda Blvd.

Fullerton Rd.

57

Orange Fwy.

142

Chino Hills State Park

Slauson Ave.

Firestone Blvd.

42

Century Fwy.

105

Lakewood Blvd.

N8

Whittier Blvd.

La Habra Blvd.

Long Beach Blvd.

Rosecrans Ave.

PARAMOUNT

Artesia Fwy.

NORWALK

Alondra Blvd.

La Mirada Rd.

Imperial Hwy.

Beach Blvd.

Harbor Blvd.

ORANGE COUNTY

90

Nixon Library

Alameda St.

Pasadena Fwy.

91

19

CERRITOS

605

Bellflower Blvd.

91

5

FULLERTON

Riverside Fwy.

91

55

Atlantic Ave.

LAKEWOOD

Carson St.

Knotts Berry Farm

Lincoln Ave.

ANAHEIM

57

Arrowhead Pond

Costa Mesa (Newport) Fwy.

Long Beach Municipal Airport

Valley View St.

Disneyland

Edison Intl. Field of Anaheim

710

1

LONG BEACH

Pacific Coast Hwy.

Willow St.

Beach Blvd.

Katella Ave.

GARDEN GROVE

Longbeach Aquarium

Ocean Blvd.

405

San Diego Fwy.

Bolsa Chica

Garden Grove Fwy.

22

5

SANTA ANA

Belmont Shores

Queen Mary

U.S. Naval Weapons Station

TO SUNSET BEACH (0.5mi)

Brookhurst St.

Euclid St.

39

1st St.

TO COSTA MESA (2mi) & NEWPORT BEACH (8mi).

TO IRVINE (2mi) & SAN DIEGO (70mi)

the downright obscure. Stars are awarded for achievements in one of five categories: movies, radio, TV, recording, and live performance. Only Gene Autry has all five stars. To catch today's stars in person, call the Chamber of Commerce for info on star-unveiling ceremonies. (☎323-469-8311; www.hollywoodchamber.net. Free.)

OTHER SIGHTS. The hillside **Hollywood Bowl** is synonymous with picnic dining and classy summer entertainment. All are welcome to listen to the L.A. Philharmonic's free rehearsals; call the box office for info. (2301 N. Highland Ave. ☎323-850-2058, concert line 323-850-2000; www.hollywoodbowl.org. Open July-Sept. Tu-Sa 10am-8pm; Nov.-June Tu-Sa 10am-4:30pm. Free.) The sprawling **Hollywood and Highland Mall** centers on two monstrous elephant sculptures and contains ritzy shops, high-profile restaurants, and the impressive **Kodak Theater,** built specifically to host the Academy Awards. (6801 Hollywood Blvd. Mall ☎323-467-6412, box office 323-308-6363. Open daily 10am-6pm, show days 10am-9pm. Tours daily every 30min. 10:30am-2:30pm. $15, under 12 $10.)

VENICE AND SOUTH BAY

Ocean Front Walk, Venice's main beachfront drag, is a seaside circus of fringe culture. In-line skaters, skateboarders, and almost anything else that moves can be seen along this strip of beach. Find the city's biggest bodybuilders at **Muscle Beach,** 1800 Ocean Front Walk, closest to 18th St. and Pacific Ave. Vendors sell everything from beach blankets to fake tattoos and define the colorful culture of this playground population.

About 20 mi. southwest of downtown L.A., the PCH passes through the heart of the beach scene at **Redondo Beach, Hermosa Beach,** and **Manhattan Beach.** Most visit Redondo Beach for its harbor, pier, and seafood-rich boardwalk. Hermosa Beach, the most popular urban beach in L.A. County, has a reputation for cleanliness. Manhattan Beach is favored for surfing. Both Manhattan and Hermosa beaches host elite beach volleyball and surf competitions (☎310-426-8000; www.avp.com or www.surffestival.org.) **The Strand** is a concrete bike path crowded with bikers and in-line skaters that runs along the beach from Santa Monica to Hermosa Beach.

BEVERLY HILLS

Conspicuous displays of wealth border on the vulgar in this center of extravagance. Residential ritz reaches its peak along **Beverly Dr.,** where the mansions are bigger than most city libraries. If stories of the rich and famous intrigue you, hop in a cab and ask for an informal tour of this street.

RODEO DRIVE. The greedy heart of the city, Rodeo Drive is known for its clothing boutiques and jewelry shops and is in the **Golden Triangle,** a wedge formed by Beverly Dr., Wilshire Blvd., and Santa Monica Blvd. Built to look like an old Italian church, **GP Deva** stands out on this ultramodern street. (413 N. Rodeo Dr. ☎310-858-6545). The triple-whammy of **Cartier** (370 N. Rodeo Dr.), **Gucci** (347 N. Rodeo Dr.), and **Chanel** (400 N. Rodeo Dr.) sits on prime real estate, with rents approaching $40,000 per month. At the south end of Rodeo Dr. (closest to Wilshire Blvd.), **2 Rodeo Drive,** a.k.a. **Via Rodeo,** is an all-pedestrian shopping complex that features Versace, Tiffany, and salons of the stars. Across the way is the **Beverly Wilshire Hotel,** featured in *Pretty Woman.* (9500 Wilshire Blvd.)

WEST HOLLYWOOD

Bring your walking shoes and spend a day on the 3 mi. strip of **Melrose Ave.** from Highland Ave. west to the intersection of Doheny Dr. and Santa Monica Blvd. This strip began to develop its funky flair in the late 1980s when art galleries, designer stores, lounge-like coffee shops, used clothing and music stores, and restaurants began to take over. Now it is home to the hip, with the choicest stretch lying between La Brea and Fairfax Ave. While much sold here is used ("vintage"), none of it is cheap. North of the Beverly Center is the **Pacific Design Center,** a royal-blue complex nicknamed the Blue Whale and constructed in the shape of a rippin' wave. (8687 Melrose Ave. ☎310-657-0800; www.pacificdesigncenter.com.)

DOWNTOWN

EL PUEBLO HISTORIC PARK. The historic birthplace of L.A. is now known as **El Pueblo de Los Angeles Historical Monument** and is bordered by César Chavez Ave., Alameda St., Hollywood Fwy., and Spring St. In 1781, 44 settlers started a pueblo and farming community here; today, 27 buildings from the eras of Spanish and then Mexican rule are preserved. Established in 1825, the **Plaza** is the center of El Pueblo and hosts festivals like the Mexican Independence

Los Angeles Westside

▲ ACCOMMODATIONS
The Beverly Hills Reeves Hotel, **16**
Claremont Hotel, **19**
Orbit Hotel and Hostel, **10**
USA Hostels Hollywood, **2**

● FOOD
Al Gelato, **17**
Belwood Bakery Café, **14**
Duke's Coffee Shop, **5**
Griddle Cafe, **4**
Mulberry Street Pizza, **18**
Nate 'n Al Delicatessen, **15**
Pink's Hot Dog Stand, **9**
Roscoe's House of Chicken and Waffles, **1**

■ NIGHTLIFE
Abbey Cafe, **11**
Jerry's Famous Deli, **13**
Largo, **12**
Miyagi's, **3**
3 of Clubs, **8**
Rainbow Bar & Grill, **7**
The Roxy, **6**

UCLA & Westwood

WESTWOOD VILLAGE
Murphy Sculpture Garden
Medical School
UCLA Hammer Museum
Los Angeles National Cemetery
BEL AIR

PACIFIC COAST

TO HOLLYWOOD SIGN (400m); GRIFFITH PARK (4mi)

Hollywood Bowl
Van Ness Ave.
Franklin Ave.
Hollywood Blvd.
Sunset Blvd.
Arclight Cinerama Dome
Paramount Studios
Hollywood Cemetery
Vine St.
Cahuenga Blvd.
Grauman's Chinese Theater
Hollywood and Highland Mall/Kodak Theater
Amoeba Music
El Capitan Movie Theater
Highland Ave.
Melrose Ave.
Wilshire Country Club
HOLLYWOOD
Fountain Ave.
La Brea Blvd.
Santa Monica Blvd.
Samuel French Bookshop
Fairfax Ave.
Sierra Bonita Ave.
Curson Ave.
Spaulding Ave.
Genesee Ave.
Gardner St
Crescent Heights Blvd.
WEST HOLLYWOOD
Sweetzer Ave.
Kings Rd.
Book Soup
Sunset Strip
Beverly Blvd.
CBS Television Studios
Farmer's Market
L.A. County Hancock Museum Park La Brea of Art
Tar Pits
Miracle Mile
San Vicente Blvd.
La Cienega Blvd.
Beverly Center
Robertson Blvd.
Wilshire Blvd.
Pacific Design Center
Doheny Dr.
Hillcrest Rd.
Doheny Rd.
Hillcrest Rd.
Palm Dr.
Elm Dr.
3rd St.
Burton Way
Reeves Dr.
Castle Heights Ave.
Beverwil Dr.
BEVERLY HILLS
Crescent Dr.
Canon Dr.
Rodeo Dr.
Beverly Dr.
Camden Dr.
Roxbury Dr.
Rexford Dr.
Golden Triangle
Pico Blvd.
Olympic Blvd.
Beverly Wilshire Hotel
Beverly Hills Hotel
Beverly Hills Country Club
Playboy Mansion
Bel Air Rd.
BEL AIR
Bel Air Country Club
Sunset Blvd.
UCLA
SEE INSET
Hilgard Ave.
Le Conte Dr.
Gayley Ave.
Landfair Ave.
WESTWOOD
Century City
CENTURY CITY
Ave. of the Stars
Century Park W.
Century City Shopping Center
Beverly Hills High
Beverly Glen Blvd.
Motor Ave.
Rancho Park
Patricia Ave.
Prosser Ave.
Overland Ave.
Westwood Blvd.
Veteran Ave.
Westside Pavilion
Manning Ave.
AAA Blvd.
Sepulveda Blvd.
San Diego Fwy.
WEST LOS ANGELES
Wilshire Blvd.
Santa Monica Blvd.
Bundy Dr.
San Vicente Blvd.
Federal Ave.
Barrington Ave.
Veterans Administration Center
BRENTWOOD
J. Paul Getty Museum and Getty Center
TO SKIRBALL CULTURAL CENTER (6mi)
TO PACIFIC PALISADES (2mi); MALIBU (10mi)
TO SANTA MONICA (2mi); VENICE (10mi)
TO LAX (8mi)
Santa Monica Fwy.
National Pl.
Washington Blvd.
Venice Blvd.
Airdrome St.
Robertson Blvd.
Crescent Hts. Blvd.

800 yards
800 meters

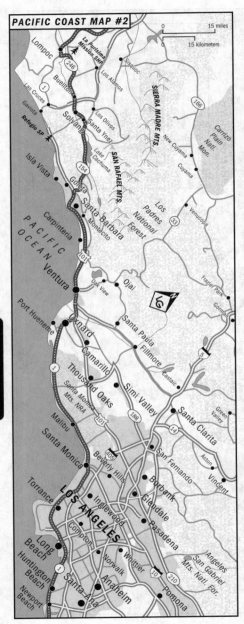

PACIFIC COAST MAP #2

PACIFIC COAST

celebration (Sept. 16), Dia de los Muertos celebrations (Nov. 1-2), and Cinco de Mayo (May 5). Treat yourself to the cheapest churros around (2 for $1) as you walk down historic **Olvera St.,** or bargain with *puestos* (vendors) selling everything from Mexican crafts to food and personalized t-shirts. The **Avila Adobe** (circa 1818) is the "oldest" house in the city. *(10 E. Olvera St. ☎213-680-2525. Open daily 9am-4pm. Free.)*

MUSIC CENTER. The beautiful Music Center is easily identified by the sweeping silver curves of the Frank Gehry-designed **Walt Disney Concert Hall.** This gleaming 2265-seat structure is the new home of the L.A. Philharmonic and the L.A. Master Chorale. *(151 S. Grand Ave. ☎213-972-7211; www.disneyhall.org.)* **The Dorothy Chandler Pavilion** houses the L.A. Opera and is the former site of the Academy Awards. *(☎213-972-8001; www.laopera.org.)* Also part of the Music Center are the **Mark Taper Forum** and the **Ahmanson Theatre,** both known for world-class shows. *(☎213-628-2772; www.taperahmanson.com. Open daily 10am-2pm as performance schedules permit. Self-guided tours $12, students and seniors $10.)*

OTHER SIGHTS. One of the best-known buildings in southern California, **City Hall** "has starred in more movies than most actors." *(200 N. Spring St.)* Bargain hounds can haggle to their hearts' delight in the **Fashion District,** between 6th and 9th St., along Los Angeles St. At 1018 ft., the **Library Tower** has a distinctive glass crown and is the tallest building between Chicago and Hong Kong. *(633 W. 5th St.)* The **Museum of Contemporary Art (MOCA)** features an extensive and varied collection of American and European art dating from 1940 to the present, including abstract expressionism and photography. *(250 S. Grand Ave. ☎213-626-6222; www.moca.org. Open M and F 11am-5pm, Th 11am-8pm, Sa 11am-midnight, Su 11am-6pm. $8, students and seniors $5, under 12 free.)*

NEAR DOWNTOWN

UNIVERSITY OF SOUTHERN CALIFORNIA
(USC). North of Exposition Park, USC's 30,000 students bring a youthful character to downtown. The alma mater of celebrities such as astronaut Neil Armstrong, the school has had a gold-medal-winning athlete in every summer Olympics since 1912. L.A. sports fans salivate when the burnished USC Trojans clash with the

blue-and-gold UCLA Bruins in annual football and basketball classics. *(From downtown, head south on Figueroa St., and turn right on 35th St. ☎ 213-740-2311; www.usc.edu. Campus tours M-F every hr. 10am-3pm. Free.)*

GRIFFITH PARK AND GLENDALE. For fresh air and a respite from city life, take to the slopes of Griffith Park, the nation's largest municipal park, nestled between U.S. 101, I-5, and Rte. 134. A stark contrast to the concrete of downtown and the star-studded streets of Hollywood, the park is a refuge from the city and the site of outdoor diversions. Fifty-two miles of hiking and horseback-riding trails, three golf courses, several museums, and a 6000-person Greek theater are contained within its 4107 rolling acres. *(4730 Crystal Spring Dr. ☎ 323-913-4688, emergency 323-913-7390. Park open daily 5am-10pm.)* The park has numerous equestrian trails and places to saddle up, such as **J.P. Stables.** No riding experience is necessary; guides are provided. *(1914 Mariposa St., in Burbank. ☎ 818-843-9890. Open daily 8am-6pm. No reservations. 1hr. $25, $15 per additional hr.)* The world-famous white stucco and copper domes of the **Planetarium and Observatory** would be visible from nearly any point in L.A. were it not for the smog. The observatory parking lot lends a terrific view of the Hollywood sign. You may remember the planetarium from the James Dean film *Rebel Without A Cause. (2800 E. Observatory Rd. ☎ 323-664-1181 or 323-664-1191; www.griffithobs.org. Open Tu-F 1-10pm, Sa-Su 10am-10pm.)* Rare animals from around the world are still on display throughout the **L.A. Zoo's** 113 well-kept acres. The zoo's five sea lions are a big hit, as are the red apes and chimps. *(5333 Zoo Dr. ☎ 323-644-4200; lazoo.org. Open daily July-Aug. 10am-6pm; Sept.-June 10am-5pm. Animals are tucked into bed starting 1hr. before closing. $10, seniors $7, ages 2-12 $5.)* A rather twisted sense of celebrity sightseeing may lead some to Glendale's **Forest Lawn Cemetery,** where you can gaze upon stars who can't run away. Among the illustrious dead are Clark Gable, George Burns, and Jimmy Stewart. The cemetery has a 30 ft. by 15 ft. stained-glass reproduction of Leonardo da Vinci's *The Last Supper*, presented every 20min. 9:30am-4pm. *(1712 S. Glendale Ave. ☎ 800-204-3131. Open daily 8am-6pm.)*

SAN FERNANDO VALLEY

TV and movie studios redeem the Valley (somewhat) from its bland warehouses, blonde "Valley Girls," and strip malls. Passing Burbank on Rte. 134, you might catch glimpses of the Valley's most lucrative trademark studios: **Universal, Warner Bros., NBC,** and **Disney.** To best experience the industry, attend a **free TV show taping** or take one of the tours offered by most studios.

■ **UNIVERSAL STUDIOS.** A movie and television studio with the world's first and largest movie-themed amusement park, Universal Studios Hollywood is the most popular tourist spot in Tinseltown. The park is located in its very own municipality, Universal City, which has its own police and fire stations. *(Take U.S. 101 to the Universal Studios Blvd. exits. ☎ 800-864-8377; www.universalstudios.com. Open July-Aug. M-F 9am-8pm, Sa-Su 9am-9pm; Sept.-June M-F 10am-6pm, Sa-Su 10am-7pm. $59, children $49, under 2 free.)*

MISSION SAN FERNANDO REY DE ESPAÑA. Founded in 1797, the **San Fernando Mission** is largest adobe structure in California. The grounds are beautifully kept and definitely worth a visit. *(15101 San Fernando Mission Blvd. ☎ 818-361-0186. Open daily 9am-4:30pm. Mass M-Tu and Th-Sa 7:25am, Su 9 and 10:30am. $4, seniors and ages 7-15 $3, under 7 free.)*

PASADENA

The excellent **Convention and Visitors Bureau,** 171 S. Los Robles Ave., is a useful first stop in Pasadena, with numerous promotional materials and guides to regional events. *(☎ 626-795-9311; www.pasadena-cal.com. Open M-F 8am-5pm, Sa 10am-4pm.)*

ROSE BOWL. In the gorge that forms the city's western boundary, this sand-colored, 90,000-seat stadium is home to "the grand-daddy of them all." The annual Rose Bowl game is a college football clash on January 1st between the champions of the Big Ten and Pac 10 conferences. College football's Bowl Championship Series comes every four years, and the UCLA Bruins play regular-season home games here as well. *(1001 Rose Bowl Dr. ☎ 626-577-3100; www.rosebowlstadium.com. Bruins info: ☎ 310-825-2946; www.cto.ucla.edu.)* The bowl also hosts a monthly **flea market** that attracts 2000 vendors selling nearly one million items. *(☎ 323-560-7469. 2nd Su of each month 5am-4:30pm. Admission after 9am $7.)*

PACIFIC COAST

SCIENCES. Some of the world's greatest scientific minds do their work at the **California Institute of Technology (Caltech).** Founded in 1891, Caltech has amassed a faculty that includes several Nobel laureates and a student body that prides itself on both its staggering collective intellect and its loony practical jokes. *(1200 E. California Blvd., about 2½ mi. southeast of Old Town. Take I-110 N until it becomes the Arroyo Pkwy. Turn right on California Blvd. and go 1¼ mi. Turn left on Hill Ave., left on San Pasqual St., and right on Holliston Ave. Register your car at 370 S. Holliston Ave.; $1 per hr., $5 per day. ☎626-395-6327. Tours M-F 2pm. Free.)* The **NASA Jet Propulsion Laboratory,** 5 mi. north of Old Town, sent the Mars Pathfinder on its way. Ask to see pictures of the face of Mars. *(4800 Oak Grove Dr. ☎818-354-9314. Free tours by appointment.)*

🏛 MUSEUMS

🖾 **J. Paul Getty Center and Museum,** 1200 Getty Center Dr. (☎310-440-7300; www.getty.edu), Exit I-405 (San Diego Fwy.), at Getty Center Dr. Above Bel Air and Brentwood, in the Santa Monica Mountains, shines a modern Coliseum, "the Getty." Wedding classical materials to modern designs, renowned architect Richard Meier designed the stunning $1 billion complex, which consists of 5 pavilions overlooking the Central Garden. The pavilions contain the world-class Getty collection of Impressionist paintings. Open Tu-Th and Su 10am-6pm, F-Sa 10am-9pm. $7 per vehicle.

🖾 **Los Angeles County Museum of Art (LACMA),** 5905 Wilshire Blvd. (☎323-857-6000; www.lacma.org). Opened in 1965, the LACMA is the largest museum on the West Coast and holds several of Steve Martin's Dada and Surrealist works. (This explains why Steve was able to rollerskate LACMA's halls in *L.A. Story*.) F 5:30-8:30pm free jazz. Su 6-7pm chamber music. Open M-Tu and Th noon-8pm, F noon-9pm, Sa-Su 11am-8pm. $9, students and seniors $5, under 18 free; 2nd Tu of each month free. Film tickets $9, students and seniors $6.

🖾 **Norton Simon Museum of Art,** 411 W. Colorado Blvd. (☎626-449-6840; www.nortonsimon.org). Rivaling the Getty in quality, this private collection chronicles Western art from Italian Gothic to 20th-century abstract. The Impressionist and Post-Impressionist hall, the Southeast Asian sculptures, and the 79,000 sq. ft. sculpture garden by Nancy Goslee Power are particularly impressive. Open M, W-Th, Sa-Su noon-6pm; F noon-9pm. $8, seniors $4, students and under 18 free.

UCLA Hammer Museum of Art, 10899 Wilshire Blvd. (☎310-443-7000; www.hammer.ucla.edu). This museum houses the world's largest collection of works by 19th-century French satirist and painter Honoré Daumier. The gem of the collection is Van Gogh's *Hospital at Saint Rémy*. Open Tu-W and F-Sa 11am-7pm, Th 11am-9pm, Su 11am-5pm. Free tours of traveling exhibits Tu 1pm; Th 1 and 6pm. Jazz concerts in summer Th 8pm. $5, seniors $3, under 17 free. Th free.

Autry Museum of Western Heritage, 4700 Western Heritage Way (☎323-667-2000; www.autrynationalcenter.org), in Griffith Park. City slickers and lone rangers may discover that the West is not what they thought—the museum insists that the real should not be confused with the reel, drawing the line between Old West fact and fiction. Open Tu-W and F-Su 10am-5pm, Th 10am-8pm. $7.50, students and seniors $5, ages 2-12 $3. Th after 4pm free.

Petersen Automotive Museum (PAM), 6060 Wilshire Blvd. (☎323-930-2277; www.petersen.org), at Fairfax Ave. The world's largest car museum, showcasing over 150 classic cars, hot rods, motorcycles, and celebrity cars, not to mention a 1920s service station, 50s body shop, and 60s suburban garage. Open Tu-Su 10am-6pm. Tours by appointment. $10, students and seniors $5, ages 5-12 $3, under 5 free.

🍴 FOOD

Los Angeles elevates chain restaurants to heights unknown. For the supreme burger-and-fries experience, try the beloved 🖾**In-N-Out Burger** (Many locations. ☎800-786-1000.) If you're looking to cook, **Trader Joe's** specializes in budget gourmet food. (☎800-746-7857. Most open daily 9am-9pm.) The **Farmer's Market,** 6333 W. 3rd St., at Fairfax Ave., attracts 3 million people every year and has over 160 produce stalls, as well as international food booths, handicraft shops, and a juice bar. (☎323-933-9211; www.farmersmarketla.com. Open M-F 9am-9pm, Sa 9am-8pm, Su 10am-7pm.)

HOLLYWOOD

🖾 **The Griddle Cafe,** 7916 Sunset Blvd. (☎323-874-0377), in West Hollywood. A popular brunch spot, the Griddle prides itself on breakfast creativity. The "Apple Cobbler French Toast" ($7) and "Black Magic" (Oreo-crumb-filled flapjacks; $7) are especially popular. A 45min. wait is not uncommon on weekends. Open M-Tu and Th-F 9am-4pm, W 10am-4pm, Sa-Su 8am-4pm. AmEx/D/DC/MC/V. ❷

▨ **Duke's Coffee Shop,** 8909 Sunset Blvd. (☎310-652-3100), in West Hollywood. Legendary Duke's is the best place to see hungry, hungover rockers slumped over tables. The walls are plastered with autographed album covers and movie memorabilia. Try the Howdy Doody (orange juice, hot cakes, fried eggs, and bacon or sausage; $6). Entrees $5-11. Open M-F 7:30am-8pm, Sa-Su 8am-3:30pm. MC/V. ❷

Roscoe's House of Chicken and Waffles, 1514 Gower St. (☎323-466-7453), at the corner of Sunset Blvd. A down-home feel makes this a popular spot; we even spotted Flavor Flav (wearing his clock) of Public Enemy. Try "1 succulent chicken breast and 1 delicious waffle" ($7.50). Open M-Th and Su 8:30am-midnight, F-Sa 8:30am-4am. AmEx/MC/V. ❸

Pink's Hot Dog Stand, 709 N. La Brea Ave. (☎323-931-4223; www.pinkshollywood.com), at Melrose Ave. An institution since 1939, Pink's serves up chili-slathered goodness in a bun. The aroma of chili and freshly cooked dogs draws crowds far into the night. Try the special "Martha Stewart Dog (It's a good thing)" for $5. Chili dogs $3.15. Chili fries $2.70. Open M-Th and Su 9:30am-2am, F-Sa 9:30am-3am. Cash only. ❶

VENICE AND THE SOUTH BAY

▨ **Rose Cafe and Market,** 220 Rose Ave. (☎310-399-0711), at Main St. Gigantic walls painted with roses, industrial architecture, local art, and a gift shop might make you think this is a museum, but the colorful cuisine is the main display. Healthy deli specials and indulgent bakery sweets. Vegetarian-friendly (roasted root veggie salad $4.50 per pint). Open M-F 7am-5:30pm, Sa 8am-6pm, Su 8am-5pm. AmEx/MC/V. ❷

Aunt Kizzy's Back Porch, 4325 Glencoe Ave. (☎310-578-1005), in a strip mall at Mindanao Way, in Marina del Rey. A little slice of Southern heaven, offering smothered pork chops with cornbread and veggies. Save room for sweet potato pie ($3). Lunch specials M-Sa 11am-4pm ($8). Dinner $12-15. Open M-Th and Su 11am-9pm, F-Sa 11am-11pm. AmEx/MC/V. ❹

Wahoo's Fish Tacos, 1129 Manhattan Ave. (☎310-796-1044), in Manhattan Beach. A small but quality chain, each Wahoo's pays homage to surfing and serves cheap and flavorful Mexican grub. Many swear by the teriyaki steak "Maui Bowl" ($7.50). Open M-Sa 11am-10pm, Su 11am-9pm. AmEx/MC/V. ❸

BEVERLY HILLS

▨ **Al Gelato,** 806 S. Robertson Blvd. (☎310-659-8069), between Wilshire and Olympic St. Popular among the theater crowd, this authentic gelateria also does pasta with a delicious basil tomato sauce ($9). If gelato isn't your thing, try the made-to-order cannoli ($5.25). Gelato $4.50-6.50. Open Tu-Su 10am-midnight. Cash only. ❶

Nate 'n' Al Delicatessen, 414 N. Beverly Dr. (☎310-274-0101; www.natenal.com), near Little Santa Monica Blvd. This deli has been serving up hand-pressed latkes ($9), blintzes ($9.50), and reubens ($12.75) for 55 years. Open daily 7am-9pm. AmEx/MC/V. ❸

Belwood Bakery Cafe, 246 N. Beverly Dr. (☎310-274-7500). Baked delights and paninis to refuel weary shoppers. Try the daily lunch special (soda, sandwich and cookie; $7). Yellow-and-green mosaic tables and chairs create a warm, kitchen-like atmosphere. Open M-F 7:30am-6pm, Sa 9am-6pm. MC/V. ❷

Mulberry Street Pizzeria, 240 S. Beverly Dr. (☎310-247-8100). Additional location at 347 N. Canon Dr., in Beverly Hills. The wide, flat pizza served at Mulberry Street is some of the best in the city. Slices $2.75-4, whole pies $17-26. Open M-Th 11am-11pm, F-Su 11am-midnight. MC/V. ❶

WESTWOOD AND THE WILSHIRE DISTRICT

▨ **Sandbag's Gourmet Sandwiches,** 1134 Westwood Blvd. (☎310-208-1133), in Westwood. A cheap, healthy lunch comes with a chocolate cookie. Try the "Sundowner" (turkey, herb stuffing, lettuce, and cranberries: $6). Open daily 10am-6pm. AmEx/MC/V. ❷

Gypsy Cafe, 940 Broxton Ave. (☎310-824-2119), next to Diddie Riese. Modeled after a sister spot in Paris, this cafe's fare is more Italian than French (penne cacciatore; $11), and its mood is more Turkish than Italian (hookahs $12). The tomato soup ($7) is famous throughout Westwood. Open M-W 9am-3am, Th-Sa 9am-5am. AmEx/D/MC/V. ❸

DOWNTOWN

■ **The Pantry,** 877 S. Figueroa St. (☎213-972-9279). Since 1924, it hasn't closed once—not for the earthquakes, not for the 1992 riots (when it served as a National Guard outpost), and not even when a taxicab punched through the front wall. There aren't even locks on the doors. Owned by former L.A. mayor Richard Riordan, this spot is known for its large portions and carnivore-friendly menu. Giant steak and egg breakfast specials $9. Open 24hr. Cash only. ❷

Philippe, The Original, 1001 N. Alameda St. (☎213-628-3781; www.philippes.com), 2 blocks north of Union Station. Sawdust covers the floor of this 98-year-old lunch eatery. Chow down on a pork, beef, ham, or turkey dip ($5). Top it off with pie ($2.75) and coffee (■ **$0.09**—no, that's not a typo). Open daily 6am-10pm. Cash only. ❶

PASADENA

Eateries line **Colorado Blvd.** from Los Robles Ave. to Orange Grove Blvd. in Old Town. The concentration of restaurants and sights around Colorado Blvd. make it Pasadena's answer to Santa Monica's Third St. Promenade.

■ **Fair Oaks Pharmacy and Soda Fountain,** 1516 Mission St. (☎626-799-1414), at Fair Oaks Ave., in South Pasadena. From Colorado Blvd., go south 1 mi. on Fair Oaks Ave. to Mission St. This old-fashioned drug store with a soda fountain and a lunch counter has been serving travelers on Rte. 66 since 1915; now, a bit of Pasa-dena's upscale flavor has crept in. Hand-dipped shakes and malts $4.25. Sandwiches $5-8. Soda fountain open M-F 9am-9pm, Sa 9am-10pm, Su 11am-8pm. Lunch counter open M-F 11am-9pm, Sa 11am-10pm, Su 11am-8pm. AmEx/D/MC/V. ❸

Pita! Pita!, 927 E. Colorado Blvd. (☎626-356-0106), 1 block east of Lake Ave. Never has pita deserved so many exclamation points. Try a breakfast pita ($5) or the spicy chicken pita ($6). Open M-Th and Su 7am-9pm, F-Sa 8am-10pm. AmEx/D/DC/MC/V. ❷

▶ ACCOMMODATIONS

When choosing where to stay, location should be the first consideration. Those looking for a tan should choose lodgings in Venice, Santa Monica, or the South Bay. Sightseers will be better off in Hollywood or the more expensive (but nicer) Westside. Chain motels can be found along Hollywood Blvd. south of Fairfax Ave. Listed prices do not include L.A.'s **14% hotel tax.**

■ **USA Hostels Hollywood,** 1624 Schrader Blvd. (☎323-462-3777 or 800-524-6783; www.usahostels.com), south of Hollywood Blvd. Crawling with young travelers, this green-and-yellow chain hostel is filled with energy. Special events nightly. Passport or proof of travel required. Breakfast included. Dinner $5. Lockers $3. Linen included. Parking $4.50 per day. 6- to 8-bed dorms with private bath $24-27; private rooms $58-64. MC/V. ❷

DOLLAR DIDDIE

A dollar doesn't buy much these days, especially around L.A., but anyone passing through Westwood Village can use a single greenback to get a piece of handheld goodness from **Diddie Reese Cookies.** A line of patrons stretching down the block from the storefront ensures that cookies, ranging from chocolate chip to white chocolate macadamia nut, are baked fresh throughout the day to meet demand. Each customer steps up to the counter, picks out two cookies and an ice cream flavor, and the clerks quickly put together a generous, neatly wrapped ice cream sandwich. You're free to mix-and-match, leading to mouthwatering combos like white chocolate cookie with espresso ice cream or double chocolate cookie with mint ice cream. Then hand the clerk your dollar and dig in. If you want to try Diddie Reese's baked goods but aren't ready for a full-on sugar coma, you can pick out three cookies for $1. A buck also gets you two cookies and milk or juice. Talk about your dollar going a long way.

Diddie Reese Cookies, 926 Broxton Ave. (☎310-208-0448). Open M-Th 10am-midnight, F 10am-1am, Sa

Orbit Hotel and Hostel, 7950 Melrose Ave. (☎323-655-1510 or 877-672-4887; www.orbithotel.com), 1 block west of Fairfax Ave. in West Hollywood. Opened by 2 young locals several years ago, Orbit sets new standards for swank budget living. Fashion-conscious furniture, spacious retro kitchen, big-screen TV lounge, small courtyard, and late-night party room. Dorms only accept international students with passport. Breakfast and lockers included. Free TV show tickets. 6-bed dorms $20; private quads from $89. MC/V. ❷

Los Angeles Surf City Hostel, 26 Pier Ave. (☎310-798-2323), in Hermosa Beach's Pier Plaza. A young international clientele enjoys the beach by day and the downstairs club by night. Showers, Internet access, kitchen, TV lounge. Boogie boards, breakfast, and linen included. Passport or driver's license required for all guests. Key deposit $10. No parking. 3-day max. stay for U.S. citizens. Reservations recommended. 4-bed dorms $23; private rooms $56. AmEx/MC/V. ❶

Hotel Claremont, 1044 Tiverton Ave. (☎310-208-5957 or 800-266-5957), in Westwood Village near UCLA. Still owned by the same family that built it 60 years ago, this hotel is pleasant and inexpensive. Clean rooms, ceiling fans, private baths, and a well-kept Victorian-style TV lounge. Reservations recommended, especially in June. Singles $60; doubles $70. AmEx/MC/V. ❸

The Beverly Hills Reeves Hotel, 120 S. Reeves Dr. (☎310-271-3006; www.bhreeves.com). If you want to save your money for shopping, stay at this reasonably priced hotel, only 2 blocks from L.A.'s shopping mecca. Rooms have A/C, TV, microwave, and fridge. Continental breakfast included. Rooms from $89. AmEx/MC/V. ❹

Venice Beach Hostel, 1515 Pacific Ave. (☎310-452-3052; www.caprica.com/venice-beach-hostel), just north of Windward Ave., in Venice. Central location with friendly staff and a lively atmosphere. A full kitchen, 2 enormous lounges, and 10 super-comfy couches encourage mingling. Lockers, storage rooms, and linen included. Laundry $2. Internet access $1 per 10min. Security deposit $25-100. 4- to 10-bed dorms $19-22; private rooms $55. AmEx/MC/V. ❶

🎵 ENTERTAINMENT

There are many ways to sample the silver screen glitz created and peddled by the entertainment capital of the world. Shopping is, like, a major pastime in the L.A. area. For after-hours fun, L.A. features some of the trendiest, most celeb-frenzied nightlife imaginable. For amusement parks, check out nearby giants **Disneyland** (p. 901), **Knott's Berry Farm** (p. 901), and **Universal Studios** (p. 909).

TELEVISION STUDIOS

A visit to L.A. isn't complete without exposure to the actual business of making a movie or TV show. Fortunately, most production companies oblige. **Paramount** (☎323-956-5000), **NBC** (☎818-840-3537), and **Warner Bros.** (☎818-972-8687) offer 70min., 2hr., and 2¼hr. (respectively) guided tours that take you onto sets and through back lots. Tickets to a taping are free, but studios tend to overbook, so holding a ticket doesn't guarantee you'll get in; show up early. **NBC,** 3000 W. Alameda Ave., at W. Olive Ave., in Burbank, is your best bet for getting in. Show up at the ticket office on a weekday at 8am for passes to Jay Leno's **Tonight Show,** filmed at 4:30pm the same evening. (Limit 2 tickets per person. 16+). Studio tours run on the hour. (☎818-840-3537. M-F 9am-3pm. Tickets $7.50, ages 5-12 $4.) Many of NBC's other shows are taped at **Warner Bros.,** 4000 Warner Blvd. (☎818-954-6000), in Burbank. A **CBS box office,** 7800 Beverly Blvd., next to the Farmer's Market in West Hollywood, hands out free tickets to *The Price is Right* (taped M-Th) up to one week in advance. (☎323-575-2458. Box office opens at 7:30am on days with show tapings. 18+. Open M-F 9am-5pm.) You can request up to ten tickets by sending a self-addressed, stamped envelope to *The Price is Right* Tickets, 7800 Beverly Blvd., Los Angeles, CA 90036, a few weeks in advance.

MOVIES

It would be a cinematic crime not to partake of L.A.'s moviegoing experiences. The city's movie palaces show films the way they were meant to be seen: on a big screen, in plush seats, and with gut-rumbling sound and top-quality air conditioning. The gargantuan theaters at **Universal City,** as well as those in **Westwood Village** near UCLA, are incredibly popular. In **Santa Monica,** there are 22 screens within the three blocks of the Third St. Promenade. Devotees of second-run, foreign-language, and experimental films can get their fix at the eight **Laemmle Theaters** in Beverly Hills, West Hollywood, Santa Monica, and Pasadena. (☎310-478-1041. $10; students $8.50; children, seniors, and matinee $7.) For info on what's playing around town, call ☎323-777-3456, or read the daily *Calendar* section of the *L.A. Times*.

■ **Arclight Cinerama Dome,** 6360 Sunset Blvd. (☎323-466-3401), in Hollywood, near Vine St. The ultimate cineplex for the serious moviegoer. 14 movie screens surround a gigantic dome that seats 850 people. The screen is 32 by 86 ft. Recent releases only. Don't be late—doors close 7min. after movies begin. Tickets $7.75-14.

■ **Grauman's Chinese Theatre,** 6925 Hollywood Blvd. (☎323-464-8111), between Highland and La Brea Ave., in Hollywood. Hype to the hilt. See **Hollywood Sights** (p. 903). Tickets M-Th $12, F-Su $12.50; matinee $9; seniors, children, and military $8.

El Capitan, 6838 Hollywood Blvd. (☎800-347-6396). The cineplex your inner child has always dreamed of. Shows Disney films and nothing else. Tickets $14, children and seniors $11, matinee $12.

Mann Village Theater, 961 Broxton Ave. (☎310-208-5576). Built to resemble a Spanish mission in 1931, this theater hosts some of Hollywood's biggest premieres. Tickets $10.75, seniors $8, children $7.50.

 DID YOU KNOW? The first movie theater opened in Los Angeles on April 2, 1902.

LIVE THEATER AND MUSIC

L.A.'s live-theater scene does not have the reputation of New York's Broadway, but its 115 "equity-waiver theaters" (under 100 seats) offer dizzying, eclectic choices for theatergoers, who can also view small productions in art galleries, universities, parks, and even garages. Browse listings in the *L.A. Weekly* to find out what's hot. L.A.'s music venues range from small clubs to massive amphitheaters. The **Hollywood Palladium** (☎323-962-7600) seats 3500. Mid-sized acts head for the **Gibson Ampitheatre** (☎818-777-3931). Huge indoor sports arenas like the **Staples Center** (☎213-742-7100), double as concert halls for big acts. Few dare to play at the 100,000-seat **Los Angeles Memorial Coliseum**

and Sports Arena; only U2, Depeche Mode, Guns 'n' Roses, and the Warped Tour have filled the stands in recent years. Call Ticketmaster (☎213-480-3232) to purchase tickets for any of these venues.

■ **Hollywood Bowl,** 2301 N. Highland Ave. (☎323-850-2000), in Hollywood. The premier outdoor music venue in L.A. Free open-house rehearsals by the Philharmonic and visiting performers usually Tu and Th; call the box office for info. Parking is limited and pricey ($12-14). It's better to park at one of the lots away from the Bowl and take a shuttle (every 20min. starting 3hr. before showtime; one-way $2.50).

Wiltern LG, 3790 Wilshire Blvd. (☎213-380-5005). Seating 2200, this mid-sized music venue has hosted acts like Belle & Sebastian, Sufjan Stevens, and The Pixies. Shows 3 nights per week. Tickets $25-85.

Pasadena Playhouse, 39 S. El Molino Ave. (☎626-356-7529; www.pasadenaplayhouse.org.), in Pasadena. California's premier theater and historical landmark. Come here to see soon-to-be Broadway stars and productions. Shows Tu-F 8pm, Sa 5 and 9pm, Su 2 and 7pm. Tickets $47-71.

Geffen Playhouse, 10886 LeConte Ave. (☎310-208-5454), in Westwood. Off-Broadway and Tony award-winning shows. Tickets $35-110. Student rush tickets 10min. before shows $15.

SPORTS

Exposition Park and the often dangerous city of **Inglewood,** southwest of the park, are home to many sports teams. The **USC Trojans** play football at the **L.A. Memorial Coliseum,** 3911 S. Figueroa St. (☎213-740-4672), which seats over 100,000 spectators. It is the only stadium in the world to have hosted the Olympic Games twice. Basketball's doormat, the **L.A. Clippers** (☎213-742-7500), and the dazzling 2000-02 NBA Champion **L.A. Lakers** (☎310-426-6000) play at the new **Staples Center,** 1111 S. Figueroa St. (☎213-742-7100, box office 213-742-7340), along with the **L.A. Kings** hockey team (☎888-546-4752) and the city's WNBA team, the **L.A. Sparks** (☎310-330-3939). Call Ticketmaster (☎213-480-3232) for tickets. **Elysian Park,** about 3 mi. northeast of downtown, curves around the northern portion of Chavez Ravine, home of **Dodger Stadium** and the popular **L.A. Dodgers** baseball team. Single-game tickets ($6-200) are a hot commodity during the April-October season, especially if the Dodgers are playing well. Call ☎866-DODGERS for more ticketing info.

SHOPPING

In L.A., shopping isn't just a practical necessity; it's a way of life. **Rodeo Dr.** may be too much for the average budget traveler's wallet, but you can't brag that you've shopped L.A. without taking a trip down the ritzy strip. Also be sure to stop by the downtown **Fashion District.** This nexus of all things trendy is home to designers, wholesalers, retail stores, and guys hawking "Gucci" bags from suitcases. The hub of the shop-'til-you-drop spots is the Westside. ◙**Book Soup,** 8818 Sunset Blvd., in West Hollywood, has a maze of new books, with especially strong film, architecture, poetry, and travel sections. The **addendum** next door is a gem for bargain-shopping book lovers, featuring discounts of up to 50%. (☎310-659-3110; www.booksoup.com. Main store open M-Sa 9am-10pm, Su 9am-7pm. Addendum open M-Sa noon-8pm, Su 11am-4pm.) The **Samuel French Bookshop,** 7623 Sunset Blvd., in Hollywood, can prep you for your audition. This wealth of entertainment-industry wisdom is filled with acting directories, TV and film reference books, trade papers, a vast selection of plays and screenplays. (☎323-876-0570. Open M-F 10am-6pm, Sa 10am-5pm.) Independent record store ◙**Amoeba Music,** 6400 Sunset Blvd. in Hollywood, carries all genres and titles, including a lot of underground music. Take advantage of daily $1 clearance sales. (☎323-245-6400; www.amoebamusic.com. Open M-Sa 10:30am-11pm, Su 11am-9pm.)

◙ NIGHTLIFE

LATE-NIGHT RESTAURANTS

Given the extremely short shelf-life and unpredictability of the L.A. club scene, late-night restaurants have become reliable hangouts.

◙ **Canter's,** 419 N. Fairfax Ave. (☎323-651-2030), in Fairfax, north of Beverly Blvd. The soul of historically Jewish Fairfax since 1931. Visit the Kibitz Room for nightly free rock, blues, jazz, and a chance to spot L.A.'s finest in the audience. Grapefruit-sized matzoh balls in chicken broth $4.50. Sandwiches $8-9. Beer from $1.50. Open 24hr. D/MC/V.

Fred 62, 1850 N. Vermont Ave. (☎323-667-0062), in Los Feliz. "Eat now, dine later," and look for a booth with headrests. Hip, edgy East L.A. crowd's jukebox selections rock the house. Try the "Mr. Frenchy" French toast ($6.25). Open 24hr. AmEx/D/DC/MC/V.

The Rainbow Bar and Grill, 9015 Sunset Blvd. (☎310-278-4232; www.rainbowbarandgrill.com), in West Hollywood. Dark red, vinyl booths, dim lighting, loud music, and colorful characters set the scene. Marilyn Monroe met Joe DiMaggio on a blind (and apparently, rather silent) date here. Calamari $6.50. Brooklyn-quality pizza $14. Open M-F 11am-2am, Sa-Su 5pm-2am. AmEx/D/MC/V.

Jerry's Famous Deli, 8701 Beverly Blvd. (☎310-289-1811), at the corner of San Vicente Ave., in West Hollywood. An L.A. deli with red leather and sky-high prices. There are more than 600 items on the menu—Jerry reportedly wanted "the longest menu possible while still maintaining structural integrity." Something here is bound to satisfy your 4am craving. Entrees $13-15. Open 24hr. AmEx/MC/V.

BARS

The 1996 film *Swingers* has had a homogenizing effect on L.A.'s hipsters. Grab your retro '70s polyester shirts, sunglasses, and throwback Cadillac convertibles, 'cause if you can't beat them, you have to swing with them, daddy-o.

◙ **Miyagi's,** 8225 Sunset Blvd. (☎323-650-3524), on Sunset Strip. With 3 levels, 5 sushi bars ($6-10), 6 liquor bars, waterfalls, and streams, this Japanese restaurant/bar/lounge/hip-hop dance club is a Strip hot spot. "Sake bomb, sake bomb, sake bomb" $10. No cover. Happy hour daily 5:30-7pm with 2-for-1 drinks. Open daily 5:30pm-2am. AmEx/D/MC/V.

◙ **3 of Clubs,** 1123 N. Vine St. (☎323-462-6441), in Hollywood. In a small strip mall beneath a Cocktails sign, this bar made a famous appearance in *Swingers.* Th live bands. F-Sa DJ. Happy hour daily 6-9pm. No cover. Open daily 6pm-2am. Knock before 8pm. AmEx/MC/V.

Beauty Bar, 1638 Cahuenga Blvd. (☎323-464-7676), in Hollywood. Where else can you get a manicure and henna tattoo while sipping a cocktail and schmoozing? It's like getting ready for the prom again, except that the drinking starts earlier. Drinks around $8. DJ nightly 10pm. Open M-W and Su 9pm-2am, Th-Sa 6pm-2am. AmEx/MC/V.

CLUBS

With the highest number of bands per capita in the world and more streaming in every day, L.A. is famous for its (often expensive) club scene. Coupons in *L.A. Weekly* and those handed out by the clubs can save you a bundle. To enter the club scene, it's best to be at least 21 (and/or beautiful) to avoid a cover charge for a less desirable venue.

The Derby, 4500 Los Feliz Blvd. (☎323-663-8979; www.the-derby.com), at the corner of Hillhurst Ave., in Los Feliz. Still jumpin' and jivin' with the kings of swing. Ladies, grab your snoods; many dress the 40s part. Italian fare from Louise's Trattoria next door. Full bar. Su 6:30 and 7:30pm free swing lessons with cover. Cover $7-15. Open daily 6pm-2am. AmEx/MC/V.

Largo, 432 N. Fairfax Ave. (☎323-852-1073), between Melrose Ave. and Beverly Blvd., in West Hollywood. Intimate sit-down (or, if you get there late, lean-back) club. Rock, pop, folk, and comedy acts. Cover $2-12. Open M-Sa 8:30pm-2am.

Roxy, 9009 Sunset Blvd. (☎310-278-9457), on Sunset Strip. One of the best-known Sunset Strip clubs, this is great option for the under-21 crowd. Bruce Springsteen got his start here. Live rock, blues, and occasional hip-hop. Many big touring acts. All ages. Cover $10-40. Open 8pm-last customer. AmEx/D/MC/V.

GLBT NIGHTLIFE

While the Sunset Strip features all the nightlife any Jack and Jill could desire, gay men and lesbians may find life more interesting a short tumble down the hill on **Santa Monica Blvd.** Still, many ostensibly straight clubs have gay nights; check *L.A. Weekly.* The free weekly magazine *fab!* lists happenings in the gay and lesbian community.

Abbey Cafe, 692 N. Robertson Blvd. (☎310-289-8410), at Santa Monica Blvd., in West Hollywood. 6 candlelit rooms, 2 huge bars, a large outdoor patio, and a hall of private booths make this beautiful lounge and dance club the best place around. On hot days they turn the mister on. Open daily 8am-2am. AmEx/D/DC/MC/V.

Motherlode, 8944 Santa Monica Blvd. (☎310-659-9700). A friendly and popular bar that steers clear of the surrounding West Hollywood trendiness. Pool, pinball machines, and cheap drinks are sure to delight. Open M-F 3pm-2am, Sa-Su noon-2am. Cash only.

Micky's, 8857 Santa Monica Blvd. (☎310-657-1176), in West Hollywood. Huge dance floor of delectable men. When other bars close, head to Micky's for another 2hr. of grooving. Music is mostly electronic dance. Drag shows M night. Cover $6-10. Happy hour M-F 5-9pm. Open M-W 4pm-2am, Th-F 4pm-4am, Sa noon-4am, Su noon-2am. Cash only.

APPROACHING SANTA MONICA: 16 MILES

Hop on **I-10 W** which drops off in Santa Monica at **Rte. 1.**

SANTA MONICA

The most striking characteristic of Santa Monica is its efficiency. It is safe, clean, and unpretentious—and you can usually find a parking spot. Its residential areas, once populated by

THANK YOU FOR NOT SMOKING

Just outside the city of Los Angeles lies an affluent community of 250,000 people known for their innovative smoking laws. The city of Calabasas recently adopted a smoke ordinance that prohibits smoking in all public areas or places where people could be exposed to second-hand smoke, sidewalks included. The Calabasas City Council unanimously passed the ordinance in February, and the measure took effect on March 15, 2006. The smoking ban is the follow-up to a recent declaration by the California Air Resources Board, which asserts that second-hand smoke is a toxic air pollutant. Not everyone is thrilled about the new ordinances. Robert Best, a coordinator for an international smoker's rights coalition, says he has gathered nearly 100 signatures in a petition to overturn the laws. These smokers have vowed to cease all shopping activities in Calabasas until their rights are protected. So when in Calabasas, just where can you light up? Smoking is allowed on private residential property, in up to 20 percent of the rooms in any hotel or motel, and in designated smoking outposts. Although the city asserts that first-time offenders will be given a warning, they also claim they will not hesitate to enforce harsher punishments for repeat offenders.

screen superstars, are just blocks away from its main districts. The area on and around the carnival pier is filled with hawkers, and street performers and a farmers market add a bit of spice to the pedestrian-only Third St. Promenade. Farther inland, along Main St. and beyond, a smattering of galleries, design shops, and museums testify to the city's love of art and culture.

 PAGE TURN. See p. 598 in **Route 66** for complete coverage of Santa Monica.

⚲ APPROACHING MALIBU: 21 MILES
From **Rte. 1** turn right onto **Malibu Canyon Rd.**

MALIBU

North of Santa Monica along the Pacific Coast Highway, the cityscape gives way to appealing stretches of sandy, sewage-free shoreline. Stop along the coast and you may see dolphin pods swimming close to shore, or at least pods of surfers trying to catch a wave. Malibu's beaches are clean and relatively uncrowded—easily the best in L.A. County for surfers and sunbathers.

VITAL STATS

Population: 13,300

Visitor Info: Malibu Chamber of Commerce, 23805 Stuart Ranch Rd., Ste. 100 (☎310-456-9025; www.ci.malibu.ca.us). Follow signs to City Hall; it's in the same building complex. Open M-F 9am-5pm.

Internet Access: 23519 W. Civic Center Way (☎310-456-6438). Open M-Tu 10am-8pm, W-Th 10am-6pm, F-Sa 10am-5pm. Free.

Post Office: 23648 Pacific Coast Hwy. (☎310-317-0328). Open M-F 9am-5pm, Sa 9:30am-1:30pm.

Postal Code: 90265

◪ SIGHTS. The prime beach spot in Malibu is ◪Zuma, L.A. County's largest beach. For a more intimate Malibu experience, check out **Escondido Beach**—look for the small brown coastal access sign 2½ mi. north of Pepperdine. **Will Rogers State Beach** hosts an annual volleyball tournament. You can jet through the wave tubes at **Surfrider Beach,** 23000 Pacific Coast Hwy., a section of **Malibu Lagoon State Beach** north of the pier. Walk there via the **Zonker Harris Access Way** (named after the

Doonesbury character), 22700 Pacific Coast Hwy. **Malibu Surf Shack,** 22935½ Pacific Coast Hwy., across from the pier, rents surfboards, kayaks, boogie boards, and wetsuits. The store offers surfing lessons and tours. (☎310-456-8508. Surfboards $10 per hr., $25 per day. Kayaks $15-20/$35-50. Boogie boards $12 per day. Wetsuits $10 per day. 1½hr. lesson and full-day gear rental $100. Open M-Tu 10am-6pm, W-Su 9am-6pm.)

Hike at **Leo Carrillo State Park,** 35000 W. Pacific Coast Hwy., which has beautiful trails on hills above the ocean. (☎818-880-0350. $10.) **Pepperdine University,** 24255 Pacific Coast Hwy., rising above the coast in sunny conservative glory, offers free tours of the campus as well as the **Weisman Museum of Art.** (Pepperdine: ☎310-506-4000; www.pepperdine.edu. Museum: ☎310-506-4851. Open Tu-Su 11am-5pm. Free.) The red-roofed **Malibu Lagoon Museum and Adamson House,** 23200 Pacific Coast Hwy., overlooks the Pacific in classic Californian style. The home, now owned by the state, serves as a museum and is open for tours. (☎310-456-8432. Open W-Sa 11am-3pm; last tour 2pm. $5, ages 7-16 $2, under 6 free.)

◪◪ FOOD AND ACCOMMODATIONS.
Cheap eats are hard to come by at Malibu's waterfront restaurants, which charge as much for their view as for their food. **Malibu Beach Grill ❷,** 22935 Pacific Coast Hwy., downstairs from Malibu Surf Shack, has a mix of Mexican and surfer food like tacos ($3) and wraps ($8). Try the "Surfrider" burger for $8. (☎310-456-9411. Open M-Th 11am-10pm, F 11am-2:30am, Su 11am-10pm. AmEx/DC/MC/V.) A roadside shack popular with barefoot surfers, **Neptune's Net Seafood ❸,** 42505 Pacific Coast Hwy., offers baskets of fried seafood ($8.75). Cross the street and eat overlooking the sea, dude. (☎310-457-3095. Open M-Th 10:30am-8pm, F 10:30am-9pm, Sa-Su 10am-8:30pm MC/V.) Motels in Malibu pay the same prices for real estate as the multi-million-dollar stars, so the best budget option is to head to L.A. or to camp. A good option is **Sycamore Canyon,** on the beach 19 mi. northwest of Malibu in Point Mugu State Park. (☎805-488-5223. Sites $25. Cash or check only.) Alternatively, **Leo Carrillo** has 139 sites in a lot across the highway from the beach. (☎805-488-1827. Cash or check only.)

1980: The Rubik's Cube becomes the hottest toy on the market.

PACIFIC COAST

⚲ APPROACHING OXNARD: 28 MILES
Once again, leaving town is as simple as getting on **Rte. 1 N.**

OXNARD. A sanctuary of sand awaits at **Oxnard State Beach Park,** about 5 mi. south of Ventura, which is quiet and peaceful except on weekends. Oxnard celebrates its farming roots and 8500 berry acres each May with a delightful **Strawberry Festival** (☎888-288-9242; www.strawberry-fest.org). A great pit stop is 24hr. **USA Gasoline,** 2251 N. Oxnard Blvd., which has ultracheap fuel, an ATM, and clean restrooms. (☎805-988-3933. Open 24hr.)

⚲ APPROACHING VENTURA: 11 MILES
Rte. 1 and **U.S. 101** merge heading into Ventura. Exit and turn right onto **S. California St.,** following it 3 blocks to **Main St.**

VENTURA

The Central Coast's southernmost city, Ventura is Southern in image and mentality, blessed with great weather and easygoing charm. Visitors to "California's Rising Star" flock to the revitalized downtown, home to numerous restaurants, shops, museums, galleries, and thrift stores. The locals come out at night and fill nearly every bar in town. Ventura Harbor is a bustling center of activity with over 30 restaurants and shops, concerts, and festivals.

VITAL STATS

Population: 106,000

Visitors Info: Ventura Visitors Bureau, 89 S. California St. (☎805-648-2075 or 800-333-2989; www.ventura-usa.com). Open M-F 8:30am-5pm, Sa 9am-5pm, Su 10am-4pm.

Internet Access: E.P. Foster Library, 651 E. Main St. (☎805-648-2716). Open M-Th 10am-8pm, F-Sa 10am-5pm. Free.

Post Office: 675 E. Santa Clara St. (☎805-643-3057). M-F 8:30am-5:30pm, Sa 9am-5pm. **Postal Code:** 93001

⬛ GETTING AROUND. Ventura lies 30 mi. south of Santa Barbara and 70 mi. north of L.A., off U.S. 101. **Main St.** runs east-west in the historic downtown area on the east side of town, intersecting with **California St.,** which runs to the pier. **Ventura Harbor** lies south of downtown

along the coast; from downtown, take Harbor Blvd. to **Spinnaker Dr.** To locate all that Ventura has to offer, pick up the historic walking tour map from the visitors bureau.

⬛ SIGHTS. Billed as California's "Gold Coast," the clean beaches near Ventura roar with surf. **Emma Wood State Beach,** on Main St. (take State Beaches exit off U.S. 101), and **Oxnard State Beach Park,** about 5 mi. south of Ventura, are quiet except on weekends. **San Buenaventura State Park,** at the end of San Pedro St., entertains families and casual beachgoers with its volleyball courts and nearby restaurants. **Surfer's Point,** at the end of Figueroa St., has the best waves around, but novices should start at **McGrath State Beach,** about 1 mi. south of Ventura down Harbor Blvd. Be forewarned that surfers can be territorial. Pick up insider surfing tips and Patagonia outlet gear at **Real Cheap Sports,** 36 W. Santa Clara St. (From Main St., go 1 block south on Ventura Ave., and turn right onto Santa Clara St. ☎805-648-3803. Open M-Sa 10am-6pm, Su 11am-5pm.)

Inland from Ventura Harbor on Olivas Park Dr. is the **Olivas Adobe.** The restored 1847 home sits on 5000 acres of land that the Mexican army gave to Raymundo Olivas for services rendered. The house is decorated in period furnishings and is a tribute to the early rancho period of Ventura's history. Olivas was not only one of the richest ranchers in California, but also an early friend of the budget traveler; next to visitors' beds, Raymundo placed bowls of coins from which guests could draw some pocket change. (From U.S. 101, take the Telephone Ave. exit south to Olivas Park Ave. and turn right. ☎805-658-4728. Open Tu-Su noon-4pm. Free.) **Mission San Buenaventura,** 211 E. Main St., still functions as a parish church. It also houses a tiny museum of treasures from Father Junípero Serra's order. A small and colorful courtyard lies between the church and gift shop. (☎805-643-4318. Open M-F 10am-5pm, Sa 9am-5pm, Su 10am-4pm. Suggested donation $1.) Across the street is the **Museum of History and Art,** 100 E. Main St., which has one permanent and two rotating exhibits. Among the stellar works are over 200 George Stuart Historical Figures, an acclaimed collection of small-scale sculptures of people from world history that George Stuart, a historian, created to accompany his lectures. (☎805-653-0323;

www.vcmha.org. Open Tu-Su 10am-5pm. $4, seniors $3, ages 6-17 $1, under 5 free.)

FOOD. Affordable restaurants cluster along **Main St.,** in the heart of historic downtown. **Franky's ❸,** 456 E. Main St., between California and Oak St., is a Ventura institution, showcasing local art on the walls and offering healthy, delectable breakfast. Sit in the mystery table and get two free meals. (☎805-648-6282; www.myfrankysplace.com. Spanish Flirt $8.50. Open daily 7am-3pm. D/MC/V.) **Top Hat ❶,** 299 E. Main St., at Palm St., is a roadside shack serving chili cheeseburgers ($2.50), hot dogs ($1.50), and fries ($1) to a local crowd. (☎805-643-9696. Open Tu-Sa 10am-6pm. Cash or debit only.) **Jonathan's at Peirano's ❹,** 204 E. Main St., is a popular Mediterranean spot. The beautiful patio is adjacent to a well-manicured park and large fountain. (☎805-648-4853; www.jonathansatpeiranos.com. Lunch entrees $9-15. Dinner entrees $12-25. Open M-Sa 11:30am-2:30pm and 5:30pm-last customer, Su 5:30pm-last customer. AmEx/D/MC/V.) **Capriccio Restaurant ❹,** 298 Main St., at the corner of Palm St., serves delicious pasta and other fine Italian dishes. (☎805-643-7115. Lunch entrees $7-10. Dinner entrees $8-15. Open M-Th 11:30am-8:45pm, F-Sa 11:30am-10pm, Su noon-8:45pm. AmEx/D/MC/V.)

ACCOMMODATIONS. Prior to its rejuvenation, Ventura was exclusively a stopover point along the coastal routes. As a result, the city has a number of budget motels, particularly along **E. Thompson Ave.,** though many are decades old and in need of renovation. Beach camping is not in short supply, but conditions lean towards the primitive, so make reservations through ReserveAmerica (☎805-654-4744) months in advance. Located in the heart of the city and formerly a firehouse, **Clocktower Inn ❺,** 181 E. Santa Clara St., offers an outdoor jacuzzi. (From Main St., go south 1 block on California St. and turn right on Santa Clara. ☎805-652-0141. Some rooms have balconies and fireplaces. Rooms M-F $105-115; Sa-Su $119-129. AmEx/D/MC/V.) **Mission Bell Motel ❸,** 3237 E. Main St., is your best bet for basic lodging. (Near Pacific View Mall. ☎805-642-6831. Rooms M-F from $60, Sa-Su from $109. AmEx/D/MC/V.) In addition to its 173 campsites, **McGrath State Beach Campground ❶,** 2211 Harbor Blvd., boasts bird-watching, swimming, nature trails and fishing. (South of town, in Oxnard. ☎805-654-4744. Sites $25. Cash only.)

NIGHTLIFE. Most of the bars that line Main St. are packed full of locals. **Wine Lovers Wine Bar,** 1067 E. Thompson Ave., serves up gourmet pizza and has live music nightly. On Reggae Wine Splash nights (Th 7pm-1am), you can enjoy the music in the wine garden. (☎805-652-1810; www.wineloversbar.com. Open daily W-Sa 5pm-1am. AmEx/MC/V.) **Winchester's Grill,** 632 E. Main St., is a western bar and grill where the locals go for beer variety. With 37 beers, 3 ciders, and 1 root beer on tap, this is a bar for some serious drinkers. (☎805-653-7446. Happy hour daily 4-6pm. Open M-F 4pm-last customer, Sa-Su 11am-last customer. AmEx/D/MC/V.)

APPROACHING SANTA BARBARA: 28 MILES
From Ventura, take **U.S. 101 N (Ventura Fwy.)** for about 27 mi.; exit at **Garden St.** to access downtown Santa Barbara.

SANTA BARBARA

If L.A. and Santa Cruz had a baby, her name would be Santa Barbara. The town is an enclave of wealth and privilege, true to its soap-opera image, but in a less aggressive and flashy way than its SoCal counterparts. Santa Barbara's golden beaches, museums, missions, and scenic drives make it a weekend escape for the rich and famous and an attractive destination for surfers, artists, shoppers and backpackers.

PACIFIC COAST

VITAL STATS

Population: 92,500

Visitor Info: Santa Barbara Visitor Information Center, 1 Garden St. (☎805-965-3021; www.santabarbaraca.com), at Cabrillo Blvd. across from the beach. Open M-Sa 9am-5pm, Su 10am-5pm.

Internet Access: Santa Barbara Public Library, 40 E. Anapamu St. (☎805-962-7653). Open M-Th 10am-9pm, F-Sa 10am-5:30pm, Su 1-5pm. Free.

Parking: Free street parking (except on State St.). Parking lots on State St. are free for the first 1¼hr., then $1.50 per hr. Su free.

Post Office: 836 Anacapa St. (☎805-564-2202), 1 block east of State St. Open M-F 8am-6pm, Sa 9am-5pm. **Postal Code:** 93102.

⊡ GETTING AROUND

Santa Barbara is 92 mi. northwest of L.A. and 27 mi. from Ventura on **Ventura Fwy. (U.S. 101).** Since the town is built along an east-west expanse of shoreline, its street grid is skewed. The beach lies at the south end of the city, and **State St.**, the main drag, runs northwest from the waterfront. All streets are designated east and west from State St. The major east-west arteries are U.S. 101 and **Cabrillo Blvd.**; U.S. 101, normally north-south, runs east-west between **Castillo St.** and **Hot Springs Rd.**

⊙ SIGHTS

Santa Barbara is best explored in three sections—the coast, swingin' State St., and the mountains. Essential to discovering local events and goings-on is the *Independent*, published every Thursday and available at city newsstands.

COASTAL SANTA BARBARA

Recently revamped, Santa Barbara's supreme coastal drive is **Cabrillo Blvd.**, the first leg of the city's scenic drive. Follow the green signs as they lead you on a loop into the mountains and around the city, winding through the hillside bordering the town along Alameda Padre Serra. This part of town is known as the "American Riviera" for its high concentration of wealthy residents.

SANTA BARBARA ZOO. This delightfully leafy habitat has such an open feel that the animals seem kept in captivity only by sheer lethargy. A miniature train provides park tours. There's also a miniaturized African plain where giraffes stroll lazily, silhouetted against the Pacific. Ask the admissions window for special biscuits ($3) to hand-feed the giraffes. (*500 Niños Dr., off Cabrillo Blvd. from U.S. 101. ☎805-962-5339. Open daily 10am-5pm. $10, seniors and children $8, under 2 free. Train $2, children $1.50.*)

SEA CENTER. Stearns Wharf, at the foot of State St., is the oldest working pier on the West Coast, housing the newly renovated Sea Center, restaurants, and shops. The center is now a working lab with hands-on exhibits for visitors. Crawl through a 1500 gal., tide-pool-tank tunnel to observe wildlife in their natural state. (*At State St. and Cabrillo Blvd. ☎805-962-2526. Open daily 10am-5pm. $7, seniors and ages 13-17 $6, children $4.*)

BEACHES AND OTHER SIGHTS. Santa Barbara's beaches are breathtaking, with sailboats bobbing around the local harbor and breeze-rustled palm trees lining the shore. **West Beach** and **Leadbetter Beach** flank the wharf. **Skater's Point Park**, along the waterfront on Cabrillo Blvd., south of Stearns Wharf, is a free park for skateboarders. Helmets and gear are required. **Wheel Rentals** rents out retro surreys, covered, Flintstone-esque bicycles with bench seats that looks a bit like a buggy. You and up to eight friends can cruise in style. (*23 E. Cabrillo St. ☎805-966-2282. Surreys $24-44 per 2hr., depending on number of riders. Open daily 8am-8pm.*) **Beach House** rents surfboards and body boards plus all the necessary equipment. (*10 State St. ☎805-963-1281. Surfboards $7-35. Body boards $4-16. Wetsuits $4-16. Credit card required.*) **Paddle Sports** offers kayak rentals and lessons. (*1176 Harbor Way. ☎805-899-4925. Rentals $20-40 per 2hr., $40-60 per day. Open in summer M-F 10am-6pm, Sa-Su 9am-6pm.*) Across the street from the visitors center is idyllic **Chase Palm Park**, complete with a vintage 1916 Spillman carousel. (*Open daily in summer 9am-9pm; in winter 11am-6pm. $2.*) For the best sunset around, have a drink ($8-18) at the bar at the **Four Seasons Biltmore Hotel.** This five-star lodging is off-limits to most budget travelers, but the view of the Pacific is priceless (and free) and there's often free evening music. (*1260 Channel Dr., in Montecito. Take U.S. 101 towards Montecito, and exit at Olive Mill. ☎805-969-2261. Take advantage of the complimentary valet parking.*)

STATE STREET

State St., Santa Barbara's monument to city planning, runs a straight, tree-lined 2 mi. through the center of the city. Among the countless shops and restaurants are some cultural and historical landmarks that should not be missed. Everything that doesn't move—malls, mailboxes, telephones, even the restrooms at the public library—is slathered in Spanish tile.

SANTA BARBARA MUSEUM OF ART. This art museum has an impressive collection of classical Greek, Asian, American, and European works that spans 3000 years. The 20th-century and Hindu collections are particularly good. Over 90% of the permanent collection consists of gifts from Santa Barbara's wealthy residents. (*1130 State St. ☎805-963-4364. Open*

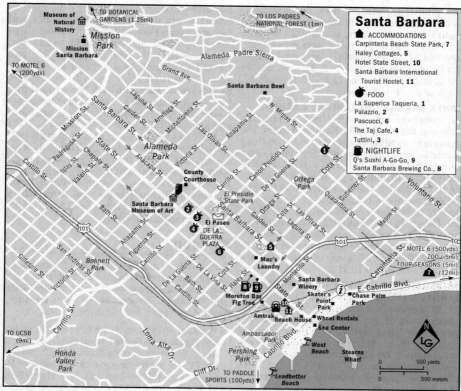

Santa Barbara

▲ ACCOMMODATIONS
Carpinteria Beach State Park, **7**
Haley Cottages, **5**
Hotel State Street, **10**
Santa Barbara International
  Tourist Hostel, **11**

● FOOD
La Superica Taqueria, **1**
Palazzio, **2**
Pascucci, **6**
The Taj Cafe, **4**
Tuttini, **3**

■ NIGHTLIFE
Q's Sushi A-Go-Go, **9**
Santa Barbara Brewing Co., **8**

Tu-Su 11am-5pm. Tours Tu-Su noon and 1pm. $9, seniors $7, students and ages 6-17 $6, under 6 free. Tu and Th 1-5pm and Su free.)

OTHER SIGHTS. At the corner of Montecito Ave. and Chapala St. stands the notable **Moreton Bay Fig Tree.** Brought from Australia by a sailor in 1877, the tree's gnarled branches now span 167 ft.; it can provide shade for more than 1000 people at once. If you'd rather drink than stand in the shade with 999 other people, sample award-winning wine at the **Santa Barbara Winery.** *(202 Anacapa St. ☎805-963-3633. Open daily 10am-5pm. Tastings $5 for 6 wines.)*

MISSION SANTA BARBARA. Praised as the "Queen of Missions" in 1786, the mission was restored after the 1812 earthquake. Towers containing splayed Moorish windows stand around

a Greco-Roman temple and facade while a Moorish fountain bubbles outside. The museum contains items from the mission archives, and visitors may attend mass in the colorful but solemn main chapel. The mission is also an infirmary and Franciscan friary. *(At the end of Las Olivas St. ☎805-682-4149. Open daily 9am-5pm. $4, ages 6-11 $1, under 6 free. Mass M-F 7:30am, Sa 4pm, Su 7:30, 9, 10:30am, noon.)*

SANTA BARBARA MUSEUM OF NATURAL HISTORY. Unlike your typical museum, the only way to get from one exhibit to the next here is to go outside. The founder's wish to establish a museum of ▓comparative oology (no, not zoology) were overturned by a Board of Trustees who thought devoting the space to the study of eggs was silly. So they hatched the current exhibitions, which include the largest collection of Chumash artifacts in the West, a natural-history gallery, and a planetarium. *(2559 Puesta del Sol Rd. Follow signs to parking lot. ☎805-682-4711. Open daily 10am-5pm. Planetarium shows in summer daily 1, 2, 3pm. $8, seniors and ages 13-17 $7, under 12 $5. Planetarium $2. 3rd Su of each month free.)*

SANTA BARBARA BOTANICAL GARDEN.

Far from town but close to Mission Santa Barbara and the Museum of Natural History, the botanical garden boasts non-native flora planted along easy, meandering paths. Five miles of hiking trails wind through 78 acres of native Californian trees, wildflowers, and cacti. The garden's water system was built by the Chumash and is now one of the last vestiges of the region's native heritage. *(1212 Mission Canyon Rd. ☎805-682-4726. Open daily Mar.-Oct. 9am-5pm; Nov.-Feb. 9am-4pm. Tours daily 2pm, Sa-Su also 11am. Special demonstrations F and Su 2pm, Sa 10:30am. $7, seniors $5, students and ages 13-17 $4, ages 5-12 $1.)*

UNIVERSITY OF CALIFORNIA AT SANTA BARBARA (UCSB).

This beautiful outpost of the UC system is stuck in Goleta, a shapeless mass of suburbs, gas stations, and coffee shops, but the beachside dorms and gorgeous student body more than make up for the town. The excellent **University Art Museum** is worth visiting. It houses the Sedgwick Collection of 15th- to 17th-century European paintings. *(Museum off U.S. 101. ☎805-893-2951. Open W-Su noon-5pm. Free.)*

![] OUTDOORS

The popular **Inspiration Point** is a 4 mi. round-trip hike that climbs 3000 ft. Half of the hike is an easy walk on a paved road. The other half is a series of mountain switchbacks. The reward on a clear day is an extensive view of the city, the ocean, and the Channel Islands. Following the creek upstream will lead to **Seven Falls.** (From Mission Santa Barbara, drive toward the mountains and turn right onto Foothill Rd. Turn left onto Mission Canyon Rd., and continue 1 mi. Bear left onto Tunnel Rd., and drive 1 mi. to its end.) **Rattlesnake Canyon Trail** is a moderate 3½ mi. round-trip hike to the Tunnel Trail junction with a 1000 ft. elevation. It passes waterfalls, pools, and secluded spots, but it is highly

popular—expect company. (From Mission Santa Barbara, drive toward the mountains, and turn right onto Foothill Rd. Turn left onto Mission Canyon Rd., and continue for ½ mi.; then make a sharp right onto Las Conas Rd., and travel 1¼ mi. Look for a large sign on the left side of the road.) The treks from the **Cold Springs Trail** to **Montecito Peak** (7 mi. round-trip, 2462 ft. elevation gain) or to **Camino Cielo** (9 mi. round-trip, 2675 ft. elevation gain) are more strenuous but offer great views. (From U.S. 101 S, take Hot Springs Rd. exit, and turn left. Travel 2½ mi. to Mountain Dr. Turn left, drive 1¼ mi., and stop by the creek crossing.) For a more extensive listing of trails, try the botanical garden gift shop or the visitors center in town. Another option is to join the local **Sierra Club** on one of their group hikes. (☎415-977-5500; www.sierraclub.org. Free.)

![] FOOD

Santa Barbara may well have more restaurants per capita than anywhere else in America, so finding a place to eat won't be a problem. **State** and **Milpas St.** are especially diner-friendly; State St. is hipper, but Milpas St. is cheaper.

⊠ Palazzio, 1026 State St. (☎805-564-1985). The reproduction of the Sistine Chapel ceiling is as impressive as the enormous pasta dishes ($19-22, half-portion $12-15) and the serve-yourself wine bar. Open M-Th and Su 11:30am-3pm and 5:30-10pm, F-Sa 11:30am-3pm and 5:30-11pm. AmEx/MC/V. ❺

Pascucci, 729 State St. (☎805-963-8123), in Paseo Nuevo. A neighborhood Italian spot that uses local ingredients in true California style. Panini comes on garlic cheese bread with a salad ($7.50-8.25). The Macadamia-crusted halibut salad is also a good bet ($8.25). Open M-Th and Su 11:30am-9pm, F-Sa 11:30am-10pm. AmEx/MC/V. ❸

La Superica Taqueria, 622 Milpas St. (☎805-963-4940). Rumored to have been Julia Child's favorite for Mexican. Maybe the culinary icon came for the freshest tortillas around (made while you watch), tamales, and excellent *pozole* on Su. Entrees under $10. Be prepared to wait. Open M-Tu, Th, Su 11am-9pm, F-Sa 11am-9:30pm. Cash only. ❸

Tuttini, 10 E. Carillo St. (☎805-963-8404), off State St. Great for breakfast, lunch, or Sunday brunch. Try the PBCB (Peanut-butter-chocolate-banana panini; $6.50) or indulge in polenta and poached eggs ($8.25). Open M-Sa 7am-2:30pm, Su 8am-2pm. MC/V. ❸

The Taj Cafe, 905 State St. (☎805-564-8280). Enjoy low-fat, village-style, Indian cooking with natural ingredients. Tandoori chicken in a sweet, tangy mango sauce ($10). Lunch specials $6.50-9. Many vegetarian entrees $6.50-8.50. Open M-Th and Su 11:30am-10pm, F-Sa 11:30am-11pm. AmEx/D/MC/V. ❸

🏠 ACCOMMODATIONS

A 10min. drive north or south on U.S. 101 will reward you with cheaper lodging than that in Santa Barbara proper. Trusty **Motel 6** is always an option. All Santa Barbara accommodations are more expensive on the weekends (peaking July-Aug. and on holidays).

> **DID YOU KNOW?** Santa Barbara is where Motel 6 first originated.

🏨 **Hotel State Street,** 121 State St. (☎805-966-6586; www.statestreethotel.com), 1 block from the beach. Welcoming, comfortable, and meticulously clean, this European-style inn offers a good (and relatively cheap) night's sleep. Common bathrooms are pristine. Rooms have sinks and cable TV; a few have private bathrooms, and others have skylights with origami cranes dangling from them. Reservations recommended. Rooms $89-109. MC/V. ❹

Haley Cottages, 227 E. Haley St. (☎805-963-0154; www.haleycottages.com), at Garden St. Run by the same folks as the International Hostel, the spirit of budget funk pervades these 14 private cottages. Each cottage has its own kitchen and bathroom and is a 5min. walk from the beach. In a formerly dodgy area that's starting to undergo gentrification. Rooms in summer $54-75; in winter $49-65. MC/V. ❸

Santa Barbara International Tourist Hostel, 134 Chapala St. (☎805-963-0154; www.sbhostel.com). Great location near the beach and State St. Bike ($6-15) and boogie board rentals ($5-8). Pool table and laundry. Internet access $1 per 10min. Dorms $21-24; private rooms $79. MC/V. ❶

Carpinteria Beach State Park, at the end of Palm Ave. (☎805-684-2811). 12 mi. south of Santa Bar-

bara; follow signs from U.S. 101. 261 developed sites with hot showers, fire rings, and picnic tables. Sites $25, with hookup $34-44. Day-use $8. ❶

🍸 NIGHTLIFE

Every night of the week, the clubs on **State St.,** mostly between Haley St. and Canon Perdido St., are packed. This town is full of people who love to eat and drink. Consult the *Independent* to see who's playing on any given night.

Q's Sushi A-Go-Go, 409 State St. (☎805-966-9177). Patrons enjoy a 3-level bar, 8 pool tables, and dancing. Sample the sushi ($3.50-13.50), and wash it all down with sake ($3.50). Happy hour M-Sa 4-7pm with 20% off sushi plates and half-price drinks and appetizers. M free pool. Cover Sa after 10pm $5. Open M-Sa 4pm-2am. AmEx/D/DC/MC/V.

Santa Barbard Brewing Company, 501 State St. (☎805-730-1040). Caters to those looking for drinks that hail from the U-S-of-A. Try the Rincon Red or the Santa Barbara Blonde. Happy hour M-F 3-6pm and 10pm-last customer with $2.75 pints and $3 Kamikazee shots. Open M-F 11:30am-last customer, Sa-Su 11am-last customer. AmEx/D/DC/MC/V.

🔍 DETOUR
LAKE CACHUMA COUNTRY PARK
From U.S. 101, take Rte. 154 toward Cachuma Lake.

If **Lake Cachuma's** clean, deep-blue waters placidly filling the crooks of the Santa Ynez Mountains are so stunning they seem almost unreal, that's because they are—they come from a man-made dam. The lake is nevertheless an unbelievably beautiful spot for hiking, boating (rentals from $15 per hr., $35-310 per day), fishing, wildlife observation, and camping. No swimming is allowed. Campers enjoy more than 400 sites—first come, first served—with a general store, gas station, nature center, outdoor theater, pool and marina. (☎805-686-5055; www.cachuma.com. Day use $6. Sites $18; yurts $45-65. D/MC/V.)

🚗 APPROACHING SOLVANG: 14 MILES
Take **Rte. 154** to **Rte. 246 W** to Solvang. Along Rte. 154 is the lovely **Santa Ynez Valley,** home to acres of vineyards, hundreds of ostriches, and Michael Jackson's Wonderland Ranch.

SOLVANG

Clydesdale horses pull tourist-packed trolleys down the street in Solvang ("sunny field" in Danish). Established in 1911, this former Danish colony will remind you of Disneyland's "Small World" ride. The town trumpets its Danish heritage—every shop and motel has a watered-down pitch related to Copenhagen or Hans Christian Anderson. Ironically, the Danish population has dwindled to a minority, even as the town's Danish thrust has become more concerted. In a formerly Mexican territory, this enclave is interesting simply for its novelty value.

VITAL STATS

Population: 5300

Visitor Info: Solvang Conference and Visitors Bureau, 639 Copenhagen Dr. (☎800-468-6765). Open daily 10am-4pm.

Internet Access: Solvang Branch Library, 1745 Mission Dr. (☎805-688-4214). Open M 2-7pm, Tu-Th 10am-7:30pm, F-Sa 10am-5:30pm. Free.

Post Office: 430 Alisal Rd. (☎805-688-9309). Open M-F 9am-5:30pm, Sa 9am-5pm. **Postal Code:** 93463.

GETTING AROUND. Activity centers on Mission Dr., the town's main drag in town, neighboring **Copenhagen Dr.,** and the intersecting **Alisal Rd.,** which features a turning windmill.

SIGHTS. Stroll around the themed streets and admire the elements of Scandanavian design—a thatched roof is at 1st St. and Copenhagen Dr.—and enjoy the cutesy storefronts, wine-tasting shops, and bakeries. **Elverhoj Museum,** 1624 Elverhoy Way, off 2nd St., has displays and artifacts from Danish-American pioneer life. (☎805-686-1211; www.elverhoj.org. Open W-Su; hours vary. Suggested donation $3.) **The Hans Christian Anderson Museum,** 1680 Mission Dr., in the Book Loft, pays homage to Hans Christian Anderson, the children's author of such tales as *The Ugly Duckling, The Emperor's New Clothes,* and *The Little Mermaid,* with a modest display of his valuable books as well as his paper cutouts. (☎805-688-6010. Open M and Su 9am-6pm, Tu-Th 9am-8pm, F-Sa 9am-9pm. Free.) Bike buffs

will enjoy the **Vintage Motorcycle Museum,** 320 Alisal Rd. (☎805-686-9522; www.motosolvang.com. Open Sa-Su 11am-5pm. $5.)

FOOD AND ACCOMMODATIONS. At **Olsen's Village Bakery and Coffee Shop ❶,** 1529 Mission Dr., the most authentic Danish bakery in town, the goods are delivered fresh every day by a third-generation Dane. The *Kringle* is particularly good. The Danish breakfast is a terrific value, with bread, cheese, pastry, coffee, and orange juice for $6. (☎805-688-6314; www.olsendanishbakery.com. Open in summer daily 7am-7pm; in winter M-F 7am-6pm, Sa-Su 7am-8pm. AmEx/MC/V.) The **Viking Motel ❸,** 1506 Mission Dr., has the lowest prices in town, depending on the time of year. Bear in mind, the cost can skyrocket up to $150 on summer weekends. (☎805-688-1337. Rooms from $49. AmEx/D/MC/V.)

APPROACHING BUELLTON: 4 MILES
Go west on **Mission Dr. (Rte. 246).**

BUELLTON. At the intersection of Rte. 246 and U.S. 101 is the town of Buellton, home of **Pea Soup Andersen's ❷,** where split pea soup has been sold thick, hot, and fresh since 1924. (☎805-688-5581. Soup $4.50. All-you-can-eat soup plus a milkshake $8.50. Open daily 7am-10pm. AmEx/D/MC/V.)

APPROACHING LOMPOC: 18 MILES
Continue on **Rte. 246 W.**

LOMPOC. The nation's largest producer of flower seed, Lompoc consists of every chain convenience you could imagine, alongside flower fields and a mission. The acres upon acres of blooms, which peak near the end of June, are both a visual and olfactory explosion. Lompoc holds a **Flower Festival** (☎805-735-8511; www.flowerfestival.org) at the season's peak, usually the last weekend in June. Stretch out at **La Purisima Mission State Park,** 2295 Purisima Rd. This mission, with Mexican blankets on display and horses grazing in pastures, is the most fully restored of Father Serra's missions. Ten buildings stand alongside 12 mi. of beautifully maintained trails. (☎805-733-3713; www.lapurisimamission.org. Open daily 9am-5pm. Free guided tours daily 1pm. $4, seniors $3.)

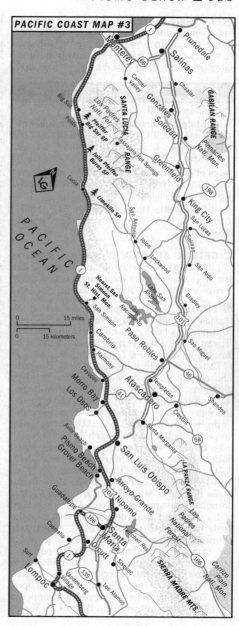

PACIFIC COAST MAP #3

APPROACHING PISMO BEACH: 49 MILES

Take **Rte. 246 W** to **Rte. 1 N**; follow Rte. 1 N to Pismo Beach.

PISMO BEACH

Pismo Beach is a honky-tonk town situated around one of California's longest and widest beaches. At the **Pismo Dunes,** the loveliness of the broad, white sand is enjoyed by the all-terrain vehicles (ATV) that cruise around like insects on a picnic spread. (Open 6am-11pm. $4.) Rent ATV equipment from **Steve's ATV,** 1206 W. Grand Ave., in Grover Beach. (☎805-474-6431; www.stevesatv.com. 2hr. ATV rental including helmet $48-140. Hummer beach tours $35, under 12 $15. Open daily 8am-6pm.) Those surpassing the speed limit of 15 mph risk a hefty fine and their lives, as careless driving on the dunes can be deadly. For more information, head to the **Pismo Beach Chamber of Commerce,** 581 Dolliver St. (☎805-773-4382; www.classicalifornia.com.) **Pismo SB North Beach Campground ❶,** on Dolliver St., on Rte. 1, has the nicest campsites in Pismo, though even these are in a parking lot. (☎800-444-7275. No hookups. Sites $15-20.) Another option is **Pismo Beach State Park ❶,** on Rte. 1, just south of scenic Pismo Beach. The huge campground is split into two areas; North Beach has 103 tent sites with showers and restrooms, while Oceano has 40 tent sites and 84 RV hookups with water, flush toilets, and showers. North Beach sites are larger and closer to the beach. (☎805-489-1869. Reservations recommended. Tent sites $25; RV sites $34. Cash only.)

APPROACHING SAN LUIS OBISPO: 13 MILES

Follow **Rte. 1 N** to San Luis Obispo.

SAN LUIS OBISPO

Amid sprawling green hills close to the rocky coast, San Luis Obispo (frequently condensed to SLO, pronounced "slow") is a town that lives up to its nickname. The mission, which has reigned as the center of local life since 1772, saw SLO become a full-fledged town after the Southern Pacific Railroad laid tracks here in 1894. Ranchers and oil-refinery employees comprise a large percentage of today's population, and California Poly-

PACIFIC COAST

technic State University (Cal Poly) students add a young, energetic component to the mix. Along the main downtown roads, hip students mingle with laid-back locals in outdoor eateries, trendy shops, and music-filled bars.

VITAL STATS

Population: 44,360

Visitor Info: Visitors Center for the Chamber of Commerce, 1039 Chorro St. (☎805-781-2777). Watch for signs on U.S. 101. Open M-W and Su 10am-5pm, Th-Sa 10am-7pm.

Internet Access: San Luis Obispo Branch Library, 995 Palm St. (☎805-781-5989). Open Tu 10am-8pm, W-Sa 10am-5pm. Free.

Post Office: 893 Marsh St. (☎805-541-9138). Open M-F 8:30am-5:30pm, Sa 9am-5pm. **Postal Code:** 93401.

GETTING AROUND. Downtown, **Monterey** and **Higuera St.** (north-south) and **Broad** and **Garden St.** (east-west) are the main drags. Walking here is easy and there is plenty of cheap parking.

SIGHTS. San Luis Obispo grew around the **Mission San Luis Obispo de Tolosa,** and the city continues to hold celebrations and socialize around its front steps and at the creek that runs through its courtyard. The mission was built in 1772 to resemble a steepled New England Church, but its appearance has changed over the years. In the late 1800s, the town began reviving the mission's Spanish origins; by the 1930s it was fully restored. It still serves as the Catholic parish church for SLO. The mission houses a small museum, which displays objects from the early days of the mission and a small collection of Chumash artifacts. (☎805-543-6850. Open daily Apr.-Oct. 9am-5pm; Nov.-Mar. 9am-4pm. Suggested donation $2.) The mission faces beautiful **Mission Plaza,** where Father Serra held the area's first mass. A gurgling 14 ft. waterwheel and shady deck await visitors at the **Apple Farm Mill,** 2015 Monterey St. Alternately churning ice cream and flour, the mill provides free samples of handmade ice cream, popcorn, and cider from a local farm. The mill is also home to a restaurant, bakery, gift shop, and inn. (☎805-544-2040. Open M-Th and Su 7am-9pm, F-Sa 7am-10pm.) The city recently dropped a cool $1 million to transform the public library

into the **SLO Historical Society Museum,** 696 Monterey St. The exhibits tell the story of SLO's past and change several times a year. (☎805-543-0638. Open W-Sa and Su 10am-4pm.) Every Thursday night, rain or shine, downtown SLO is transformed into a block party of sorts. Locals flock to the **Farmers' Market,** on Higuera St. for fresh fruit and produce or to pick up a hot meal from one of the food stands.

FOOD AND NIGHTLIFE. Higuera St. and its cross streets are lined with restaurants and cafes. Voted "Best Restaurant in SLO" and winner of many awards, **Big Sky Cafe ❸,** 1121 Broad St., delivers vegetarian-friendly food under the stars. (☎805-545-5401. Sandwiches $7-12. Open daily 7:30am-10pm. AmEx/D/MC/V.) Lavish surroundings and belly dancers enhance the Mediterranean and Moroccan cuisine at **Oasis ❹,** 675 Higuera St. The Oasis feast (appetizer, soup or salad, entree, baklava or cup of mint tea; $24) satisfies even the most weary desert traveler. (☎805-543-1155. Lunch $7-15. Open daily 11am-10pm. D/MC/V.) **Woodstock's Pizza Parlour ❶,** 1000 Higuera St., is a local hangout that invariably sweeps annual "best pizza" awards. Young crowds keep it lively all night. Lunch specials include all-you-can-eat pizza and bottomless soda for $7. (☎805-541-4420. Single slices $2.25. Open M-W 11am-midnight, Th-Sa 11am-1am, Su 11am-midnight. AmEx/D/MC/V.)

Mother's Tavern, 725 Higuera St., is a Yukon-inspired bar and restaurant that attracts mostly Cal Poly students. Try a Chumash chipotle steak wrap ($7.75) and top the evening off with karaoke, live music, and DJs. (☎805-541-8733. Cover $1-5. Open M-F 11:30am-1:30am, Sa-Su 8am-1:30am. Kitchen closes 9pm. AmEx/D/MC/V.)

ACCOMMODATIONS. The **Hotel Obispo (HI-AYH) ❶,** 1617 Santa Rosa St., is conveniently located three blocks from downtown. Free homemade sourdough pancakes are served daily from 8am-9:30am. (☎805-544-4678; www.hostelobispo.com. Linen included; towels $0.50. Laundry $3. Reception 7:30-10am and 4:30-10pm. Lockout 10am-4:30pm. Dorms $23, members $20; private rooms $50-85. Cash only.) Pitch a tent at **Montaña de Oro State Park ❶,** Pecho Rd., 15 mi. from SLO via Los Osos Valley Rd., which features 50 primitive sites in a gorgeous, secluded park. Gray whales, seals, otters, dolphins, and the occasional orca frequent Montaña de Oro State Park, whose 8000 acres and 7 mi. of shoreline remain relatively secluded. **Spooner's Cove,** across from the campground, ¾ mi. south of Coralina Cove, is a great day hangout. Up the coast, Coralina Cove has tide pools and whale-watching spots at Bluff's Trailhead. (☎805-528-0513. Outhouses and running water. Bring your own drinking water. Reservations recommended, especially in summer. Sites mid-May to mid-Sept. $15; mid-Sept. to mid-May $11. Cash only.)

⚠ **APPROACHING MORRO BAY: 14 MILES**
Follow **Rte. 1 N** to Morro Bay.

MORRO BAY

The Nine Sisters, a chain of small ex-volcanoes, are remnants of a time when SLO County was highly volcanically active. The lava that once flowed here formed the dramatic shorelines along Rte. 1 from Morro Rock to SLO. The northernmost sister, Morro Rock, and three large smokestacks from an electric company shadow the tiny burg of Morro Bay, just north of its eponymous park. **Morro Bay State Park** is home to coastal cypresses that are visited by Monarch butterflies from November to March. (☎800-444-7275.) The park's modern, hands-on **Museum of Natural History** flexes its curatorial muscle on the aquatic environment and wildlife of the coastal headlands. A bulletin board near the entrance lists free nature walks led by park docents. (☎805-772-2694. Reserve campsites year-round. Open daily 10am-5pm. $2, under 17 free.) South Bay Blvd., which links the town and the park, winds through the new **Morro Bay National Estuary,** a sanctuary for great blue herons, egrets, and sea otters. Take the trail or rent a kayak or canoe to explore. Pack a basket and paddle out to the sand dunes for a picnic lunch. Check tide schedules at Kayak Horizons, or ask at the marina to avoid (or take advantage of) numerous sandbars. **Kayak Horizons,** 551 Embarcadero, rents kayaks and offers instruction. (☎805-772-6444; www.kayakhorizons.com. Rentals $9-16 per hr. Open daily 9am-5pm. MC/V.)

Along the beach, the **Embarcadero** is the locus of Morro Bay activity and fish-'n'-chips bargains. The modest **Morro Bay Aquarium,** 595 Embarcadero, is a rehabilitation center for distressed marine animals and has over 100 ocean critters.

The seal-feeding station is a rare opportunity to see these animals from only feet away. (☎805-772-7647. Open daily in summer 9am-6:30pm; in winter 9:30am-5:30pm. $2, ages 5-11 $1, under 5 free. Cash only.) Morro Bay's pride and joy is the **Giant Chessboard,** 800 Embarcadero, in Centennial Park across from Southern Port Traders. The board is 256 sq. ft., with 18-30 lb. carved redwood pieces. (Call the Morro Bay Recreation office at ☎805-772-6278 to set up a game or watch for free M-F 8am-5pm. $38 per game.)

⚠ **APPROACHING CAMBRIA AND SAN SIMEON: 21 MILES**
Follow **Rte. 1 N** to Cambria.

CAMBRIA AND SAN SIMEON

The original Anglo-Saxon settlers of the southern end of the Big Sur coast were awestruck by the stunning pastoral views and rugged shoreline, reminiscent of the eastern coast of England. In homage to the natural beauty of their homeland, they named this equally impressive New World area Cambria, the ancient Roman name for Wales. Ten miles north of Cambria, neighboring New San Simeon, is a strip town along Rte. 1 with few roads and many motels near spectacular beaches. Old San Simeon is north of New San Simeon and consists only of a 150-year-old store, **Sebastian Store,** and the homes of Hearst Corporation ranchers.

VITAL STATS

Population: 6232

Visitor Information: Cambria Chamber of Commerce, 767 Main St. (☎805-927-3624). Open daily 9am-5pm. **San Simeon Chamber of Commerce,** 250 San Simeon Dr. (☎805-927-3500), on the west side of Rte. 1. Look for signs. Open daily 10am-4pm.

Internet Access: Cambria Branch Library, 900 Main St. (☎805-927-4336), in Cambria. Open Tu-F 11am-5pm, Sa noon-4pm. Free.

Post Offices: Cambria, 4100 Bridge St. (☎805-927-8610). Open M-F 9am-5pm. **Postal Code:** 93428. **San Simeon** (☎805-927-4156), on Rte. 1, in the back of Sebastian's General Store; take the road opposite the entrance to Hearst Castle. Open M-F 8:30am-noon and 1-5pm. **Postal Code:** 93452.

◄ GETTING AROUND. For a quick stop, turn off Rte. 1 at the Burton Dr. exit, which takes you straight to **Main St.** Drive north up Main St. through the town center to the West Village, where most of the action is. There (after passing the wonderful Robin's restaurant), in a one-block radius you'll find an **ATM**, a gas station, and old-timey **Soto's Market & Deli** (☎805-927-4411. Open M-Th 7am-7pm, F-Sa 7am-8pm, Su 8am-6pm.)

◙ SIGHTS. San Simeon marks the beginning of Big Sur's dramatic coastline. Sea otters, once near extinction, live in the kelp beds of **Moonstone Beach**, on Moonstone Dr., off Rte. 1, toward San Simeon. Along this stretch of coast, surfers are occasionally nudged off their boards by playful seals (and, far more rarely, by not-so-playful great white sharks). Scenic **Leffingwell's Landing** is the best spot for **whale-watching.** (Open Apr.-Dec. daily 8am-sunset.) Call **Virg's Landing** for info. (☎805-772-1222.) In addition to providing the best swimming for miles, **San Simeon** and **Hearst State Beaches,** just across from Hearst Castle (p. 928), are ideal for cliff climbing and beachcombing.

◙◭ FOOD AND ACCOMMODATIONS. Food is more plentiful in Cambria than in San Simeon. Many San Luis Obispo residents consider ◙**Robin's ❺**, 4095 Burton Dr., to be the only reason to drive the 30 mi. to Cambria. International cuisine and daily deli salads are served in a craftsman-style bungalow with outdoor gardens. (☎805-927-5007. Dinner entrees $13-22. Open daily 11am-9pm or later. Reservations recommended. MC/V.) Locals frequent **Creekside Gardens Cafe ❸**, 2114 Main St., at the Redwood Shopping Center, for a burger ($7-9.25) or hearty breakfast scramble for $8.75. (☎805-927-8646. Su brunch 10am-2:30pm. Open M-Sa 7am-2pm and 5-9pm, Su 7am-1pm. Cash only.)

Cambria has lovely but pricey B&Bs. Budget travelers will have better luck in San Simeon. The arrival of Motel 6 set off a pricing war that has led to wildly fluctuating rates, so it is always a good idea to call ahead. Beware of sky-high prices in summer. **San Simeon State Beach Campground ❶** is just north of Cambria on Rte. 1. **San Simeon Creek** has 134 developed sites near the beach. (Reservations ☎800-444-7275. Sites $25. Cash only.) Neighboring **Wash-burn** sits on a breezy hill overlooking the ocean and has primitive camping, pit toilets, and cold running water. (Reservations ☎800-444-7275. Sites $15. Cash only.) Originally built in the 1890s for the preacher at the church next door, **Bridge Street Inn ❶**, 4314 Bridge St., in Cambria, includes sunny and sparklingly clean rooms with sturdy bunks and a volleyball net in the yard. (☎805-927-7653. Continental breakfast included. Linen included. Reception 5-9pm. Dorms $20; private rooms $40-70. MC/V.)

◙ DETOUR
HEARST CASTLE
On Rte. 1, 3 mi. north of San Simeon and 9 mi. north of Cambria.

Newspaper magnate and multi-millionaire owner William Randolph Hearst casually referred to it as "the ranch," or in his more romantic moments, "La Cuesta Encantada" (the enchanted hill). The hilltop estate is an indescribably decadent dreamland castle of limestone, shaded cottages, pools almost too exquisite to swim in, fragrant gardens, and Mediterranean *esprit*. Hearst spent most of his life gathering Renaissance sculpture, tapestries, and ceilings, and telling his architect to incorporate them into his castle's design. Scores of celebrities and luminaries such as Charlie Chaplin, Charles Lindbergh, and Winston Churchill visited the castle (by invitation only) to bask in Hearst's legendary hospitality. Take the garden tour (#4) to stroll along the azalea walk that Cary Grant nicknamed "Lovers' Lane." The castle is impressive, and the colorful stories told by the tour guides are not to be missed.

The State Parks Department runs five different tours, all of them strictly hands-off experiences. Tour 1 is recommended for first-time visitors, and includes a viewing of a National Geographic documentary on the architectural wonder. The banisters and staircases are the only things you may touch in the castle, but there's plenty to occupy your eyes. Tour 5 is only available on most weekend evenings during the spring and fall and features costumed docents acting out the castle's legendary Hollywood history. (☎805-927-2020; www.hearstcastle.com. Call in advance, as tours often sell out. 4 different daytime tours leave frequently 8:20am-3:20pm. 1¾hr.

tours mid-May to mid-Sept. $24-30, ages 6-17 $12-15; mid-Sept. to mid-May $20-30/$10-15. Theater: ☎805-927-6811. Films show daily every 45min. 8:15am-5:15pm. $8, under 12 $6; included in Tour 1 pass.)

⚑ APPROACHING BIG SUR: 74 MILES

Follow **Rte. 1 N** to Big Sur. Big Sur is the stretch of highway that was left as wilderness, and you need to make preparations in advance. That means getting food, camping equipment, and gas before you hit the *Sur Grande*. There are few services in Big Sur and the ones that do exist are exorbitantly priced. Pick up a free copy of the newspaper leaflet *El Sur Grande*, which includes a good map of the stretch (www.big-surcalifornia.org).

BIG SUR

Monterey's Spanish settlers called the entire region below their town *El Sur Grande*—the Big South. Today, Big Sur is a more explicitly defined 90 mi. coastal stretch, bordered on the south by San Simeon and on the north by Carmel. Cutting the road into the cliff, whose wending ways and tremendous views make a spectacular driving experience, was quite a lot of work: the entire highway, completed in 1937, took 18 years to build and cost $10 million to finish. More of a region than a precise destination, the area draws a curious mix of hippies, rich folk, and outdoor enthusiasts who come for its enchanting wilderness. Outdoorsy travelers will find too much to do in Big Sur. River and creek water is swimmable in the summer months, and there are more hiking trails than year round inhabitants.

VITAL STATS

Visitor Info: Big Sur Station (☎831-667-2315), ½ mi. north of Pfeiffer Big Sur entrance on Rte. 1. Multi-agency station includes the State Park Office, the US Forest Service (USFS) Office, and the Cal-Trans Office. Provides permits, maps, and info on hikes and campfires. Open daily June-Sept. 8am-6pm; Oct.-May 8am-4:30pm.

Road Conditions: ☎800-427-7623.

Highway Patrol: ☎805-549-3261.

Post Office: 47500 Rte. 1 (☎831-667-2305), next to the Center Deli in Big Sur Center. Open M-F 8:30am-4pm. **Postal Code:** 93920.

▮ GETTING AROUND

Rte. 1 in Big Sur wraps itself around the curves of the mountain at heights up to 1,000 ft. above sea level. Don't feel pressured to drive faster because it's a one-lane road, and someone is tailing you; just pull over into one of the many turnouts to let them pass.

◉ SIGHTS

Before you hit the great outdoors, spend some time learning about one of the area's most celebrated former residents. Henry Miller, author of the *Rosy Crucifiction* trilogy: *Sexus*, *Plexus*, and *Nexus*. The **Henry Miller Memorial Library,** just south of Nepenthe and Cafe Kevah, displays books and artwork by the famous author. Miller's casual reminiscences and prophetic ecstasies introduced his readers to Big Sur. Many readers of his more explicit works came to Big Sur seeking a nonexistent sex cult that he purportedly led. While the sex cult is no longer a tourism draw, the cult of history suffices nicely.The library sells books and hosts concerts and readings such as the **West Coast Championship Poetry Slam.** There is also an interesting sculpture garden featuring a computer-and-wire crucifix. (☎831-667-2574; www.henrymiller.org. Open W-Sa and Su 11am-6pm and by appointment.)

🌲 OUTDOORS

Big Sur's state parks and **Los Padres National Forest** beckon to outdoor enthusiasts of all types. Their hiking trails penetrate redwood forests and cross low chaparral, offering even grander views of Big Sur than those available from Rte. 1. If you're driving through in one day, the best hikes to hit are the three waterfalls; they give you a taste of the area in various breathtaking incarnations. Swimmers will find that though the water is too cold for much of the year, brave souls can bear it best in the summer months.

The northern end of Los Padres National Forest, accessible from Pfeiffer Big Sur, has been designated the **Ventana Wilderness** and contains the popular **Pine Ridge Trail,** which runs 12 mi. through primitive sites and the **Sykes Hot Springs.** The Forest Service ranger station supplies maps and permits for the wilderness area. At **Limekiln State Park,** 56 mi. south of Carmel and 2 mi. south of Lucia (☎831-667-2403), a 30min. round-trip to a waterfall will take you through redwoods and the giant metal namesakes on this less trodden southern stretch of the coast. **Ewoldsen Trail** (round-trip 4½ mi.) starts in redwoods at McWay Creek, follows McWay Canyon, and climbs upwards, sometimes steeply. **Tan Bark Trail** starts east of Rte. 1 at Partington Cove. The 5½ mi. round-trip hike traverses oak and redwood forests to the Tin House and has excellent views. To shorten the trip, take the road at the end of the trail. It leads back to Rte. 1, a mile south of the trailhead.

HIKING

Terrific hiking can be found within **Pfeiffer Big Sur State Park** ($1 map available at park entrance). **Pfeiffer Falls Trail,** in Julia Pfeiffer Falls State Park, an easy 1½ mi. round-trip along Pfeiffer Big Sur Creek, winds through redwoods and ends in a 60-foot waterfall. (Day-use $4.) The **Valley View Trail** (2 mi. round-trip), from Pfeiffer Falls, offers views of Pt. Sur and Big Sur Valley. The more challenging **Oak Grove Trail** is a 3 mi. round-trip from the Big Sur Lodge that intersects with the Pfeiffer Falls trail. It features redwood groves, oak woodlands, dry chaparral, small-leaved evergreen trees, and shrubs. The strenuous **Mt. Manuel Trail** (round-trip 8 mi.) begins at the Oak Grove Trail and is a steep, dry climb to the 3379 ft. Manuel Peak. **Buzzard's Roost Trail** is a rugged 2hr. hike up torturous switchbacks, but from its peak you can see the Santa Lucia Mountains, Big Sur Valley, and the Pacific Ocean. The **McWay Waterfall Trail,** in Julia Pfeiffer Burns State Park, holds the only waterfall that spills directly into the great Pacific, an elegant, 80 ft. plume feeding a limitless ocean just south of Carmel; look for the sign.

BEACHES

Roughly 10½ mi. north of Julia Pfeiffer Burns State Park lies Big Sur's most jealously guarded treasure: the USFS-operated **Pfeiffer Beach.** Turn off Rte. 1 at the stop sign just past the bridge by Loma Vista. Follow the road 2 mi. to the parking area, where a path leads to the beach. An offshore rock formation protects sea caves and seagulls from the pounding ocean waves. (Day-use $5.) Other beaches can be found at **Andrew Molera**

State Park (5 mi. north of Big Sur station; day-use $8), **Sand Dollar Beach** (33 mi. south of the Big Sur station near Kirk and Plasket Creek campsites; day-use $5), and **Jade Cove** (36 mi. south of Big Sur station; free). The inhospitality of dark, rocky **Jade Cove** is perhaps what makes it so enthralling. Although it's illegal and inconsiderate, people reportedly go jade hunting on the beach, and over the years $50 million of jade have been removed. The stone is distinguished by its soapy texture, dark green color, and hardness. Roughly at the midpoint of the Big Sur coast lies the **Julia Pfeiffer Burns State Park,** where picnickers find McWay Cove's sea otters and the shelter of the redwood forest. (Backcountry camping permits at Big Sur Station. No dogs. Day-use $8.)

▧ FOOD

Grocery stores are located at Big Sur Lodge (in Pfeiffer Big Sur State Park), and in Pacific Valley and Gorda. Some packaged food is sold in Lucia and at Ragged Point, but it's better to arrive prepared—prices in Big Sur are generally high. Listings are ordered from south to north along Rte. 1.

- ▧ **Big Sur Restaurant and Bakery** (☎831-667-0520, bakery 831-667-0524), just south of the post office, by the Shell gas station and the Garden Gallery. Serves 12 in. wood-fired pizzas ($13-18.50) and entrees prepared with free range meats and fresh local vegetables ($27-36) in a garden setting. The bakery specializes in organic breads and pastries. Beer and wine available. Open daily 8am-8pm, until 9pm if busy. MC/V. ❺

- **Center Deli and General Store** (☎831-667-2225), 1 mi. south of Big Sur Station, next to the post office. This is where you'll find the most reasonably priced goods in the area. Sandwiches ($4-6.25) include veggie options like avocado and egg salad. Pasta salads $6.50 per lb. Open daily 7:30am-8:30pm. Cash or debit only. ❶

- **Fernwood Bar and Grill** (☎831-667-2422), on Rte. 1. Highly popular outdoor patio under redwood canopy. Chicken, veggie burritos, hot dogs, and hamburgers from $9. Barbecue specials ($8-10). Frequent live music. Open daily 11am-9pm. Bar open M-Th and Su 11am-midnight, F-Sa 11am-1:30am. Grocery store open daily 8am-10pm. MC/V. ❸

- **The Roadhouse** (☎831-667-2264), off Rte. 1, about 19 mi. south of Carmel, just south of Riverside Camp. A lively, intimate atmosphere and flavorful food, like pan-seared salmon with a green-cabbage-mango salad ($23). Soups and salads $7-15. Entrees $12-24. Open M and W-Su 5:30-last customer. MC/V. ❹

ACCOMMODATIONS

Camping in Big Sur is heavenly; in choosing your site, decide whether you'd prefer to be close to the beach (Andrew Molera, Kirk Creek, Limekiln) or in the redwood forest, which is darker and more protected from coastal winds (Ventana, Pfeiffer Big Sur, Fernwood). Reserve well in advance by calling ReserveAmerica (☎800-444-7275). Camping is free in the **Ventana Wilderness,** a backpack-only site at the northern end of Los Padres National Forest (permits at Big Sur Station).

Ventana Big Sur (☎831-667-2712; www.ventanawildernesscampground.com), on Rte. 1, about 24 mi. south of Carmel. 80 shady sites in a gorgeous redwood canyon with picnic tables, fire rings, flush toilets, and water faucets. Hot showers. Sites $29-40. AmEx/D/MC/V. ❶

Pfeiffer Big Sur State Park, (☎831-667-2315), on Rte. 1, about 22 mi. south of Carmel, just south of Fernwood Resort and Campground. The diverse wildlife and terrain, the beautiful Big Sur River, and several hiking trails ensure that all 218 bustling campsites are usually filled. Fire pits, picnic tables, softball field, flush toilets, and hot showers. As one ranger put it, "Your grandma can camp here." Trail maps $1. Sites mid-May to mid-Sept. $25, on the river $35; mid-Sept. to mid-May $20/$30. Cash only. ❶

Fernwood Resort and Campground (☎831-667-2422), on Rte. 1, about 19 mi. south of Carmel. 60 small but well-situated campsites and 2 swimming holes in a redwood forest on the Big Sur River. Several state park trails start from the campground. Reservations recommended. Sites $30, with hookup $35. MC/V. ❶

Big Sur Campground and Cabins, (☎831-667-2322), on Rte. 1, 18 mi. south of Carmel on the Big Sur River. Hot showers and laundry. Reservations recommended. Hookup $4. Tent sites in summer $30-40, in winter $25-35; 2-person tent cabins $62/$55; cabins $120-265/$95-230. Day-use $10. MC/V. ❶

Riverside Camp, (☎831-667-2414), next to the Big Sur Campground. 28 tent sites, each with a picnic table and fire pit. Showers ($0.25 per 3min.) Sites $28, with hookup $33; cabins $130. D/MC/V. ❶

DETOUR
POINT LOBOS RESERVE
On Rte. 1, 3 mi. south of Carmel. Park on Rte. 1 before the tollbooth, and walk or bike in for free.

This extraordinary 550-acre, state-run wildlife sanctuary is popular with skin divers and day hikers. Bring binoculars to view otters, sea lions, seals, brown pelicans, gulls, or migrating whales from the paths along the cliffs. At the water, Point Lobos offers tide pools and scuba access. (☎831-624-4909, reservations 831-624-8413. Open daily Apr.-Oct. 9am-7pm; Nov.-Mar. 9am-5pm. Free daily nature tours; call for times. Map $1. Reservations required. Dive fee $10. $8 per vehicle.)

APPROACHING CARMEL: 28 MILES
Go northwest on **Rte. 1** toward Carmel.

CARMEL
Moneyed Californians migrate to Carmel (officially Carmel-by-the-Sea) to live out their fantasies of small-town life. Carmel has beautiful beaches, a multitude of boutiques and art galleries, and a carefully manufactured aura of quaintness. Local ordinances forbid address numbers, parking meters, high heels, billboards, chain stores and, at one time, eating ice-cream cones outside—all considered undesirable symbols of urbanization.

VITAL STATS

Visitor Information: Carmel-by-the-Sea Chamber of Commerce and Visitor Information Center (☎831-624-2522 or 800-550-4333; www.carmel-california.org), next to the Eastwood Bldg., on San Carlos St., between 5th and 6th Ave. Open daily 10am-5pm.

Internet Access: Mail Mart (☎831-624-4900), at Dolores St. and 5th Ave. Open M-F 8:30am-5:30pm, Sa 9am-3pm. $3 per 15min.

Parking: Free parking can be found on the corner of Junípero Ave. and 3rd Ave.

Post Office: (☎831-624-3630), on 5th Ave., between San Carlos and Dolores St. Open M-F 9am-4:30pm. **Postal Code:** 93921.

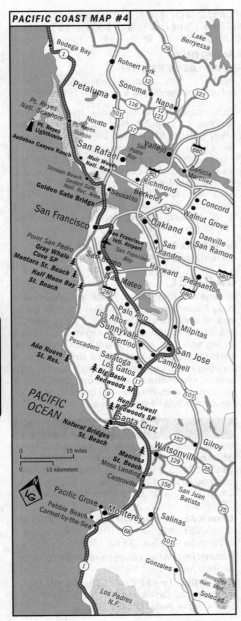

PACIFIC COAST MAP #4

GETTING AROUND. Carmel lies at the southern end of the Monterey Peninsula off **Rte. 1**, 126 mi. south of San Francisco. The town's main street, **Ocean Ave.,** cuts west from the freeway to (surprise) the ocean. All other east-west avenues are numbered; numbers ascend as you head south. **Junípero Ave.** crosses Ocean Ave. downtown and leads south to the mission at **Rio Rd.** Free town maps are available at most hotels and at the visitors center.

SIGHTS. Established at its present site in 1771 by Father Serra, "the great conquistador of the cross," the **Mission Basilica San Carlos Borromeo del Río Carmelo (Carmel Mission),** 3080 Rio Rd., at Lasuen Dr., off Rte. 1, welcomed 4000 converted Native Americans before it was abandoned in 1836. Fastidiously restored in 1931, the mission's marvels are still astounding. With a stone courtyard, a bell tower, lavish gardens, and a daily mass, the mission is one of the most elaborate in California. Father Serra and many Native Americans are buried here. The three museums display the original silver altar furnishings, handsome vestments, and the first library in California. (☎831-624-1271. Open M-Sa 9:30am-5pm, Su 10:30am-5pm. $5, seniors $4, children $1.) The Sunset Cultural Center, which once housed Ansel Adams and Edward Weston's Friends Photography, is now home to the **Center for Photographic Art,** on San Carlos St. between 8th and 9th Ave. The center exhibits top-notch work by local and international artists. Recent shows include Oliver Gagliani and German Herrera. (☎831-625-5181; www.photography.org. Open Tu-Su 1-5pm. Free.)

The northern Big Sur coast begins at the end of Ocean Ave., at **Carmel City Beach,** a white, sandy crescent framing a cove of chilly waters. The beach ends abruptly at the base of red cliffs, which make a fine grandstand for sunsets. **Carmel River State Beach,** just south of City Beach, is windier and colder than Carmel City Beach, but it is blessed with better surf, parking, and smaller crowds. Bring a jacket or sweater, even in summer. (To get to Carmel River State Beach, walk about 1 mi. along Scenic Rd., or drive to the end of Carmelo St., off Santa Lucía.)

FOOD AND ACCOMMODATIONS. Food, like everything else in Carmel, is overpriced. It is, however, occasionally good enough to justify the expense. **Em Le's ❸,** on

PACIFIC COAST

Dolores St., between 5th and 6th Ave., is known for its fabulous breakfasts, including omelettes with cottage cheese and toast ($8.50-13), and unique French toast ($9.45). For dinner, early birds (4:30-6:30pm) can get an entree with soup or salad for $10. (☎831-625-6780. Open daily 7am-3pm and 4:30-10pm. D/MC/V.) **The Forge in the Forest ❹**, at the southwest corner of 5th Ave. and Junípero St., has been voted best outdoor dining in Monterey County for the last 14 years. The popular restaurant serves pasta, seafood, grill items ($15-28), and gourmet pizza (roasted duck and caramelized onion; $13) on a gorgeous garden patio complete with open-fire forge. (☎831-624-2233. Open M-Th and Su 11:30am-9pm, F-Sa 11:30am-10pm. AmEx/MC/V.) Housed in a historic building dating from 1927, **The Tuck Box English Tea Room ❸**, on Dolores Ave., between Ocean and 7th Ave., is famous for scones ($4.75), preserves, and a fairy tale-esque facade. (☎831-624-6365. Omelettes $8-10. Open daily 7:30am-2:50pm. Cash only.)

The expensive inns and lodges in Carmel usually offer only double-occupancy rooms (which fall below $90 only midweek or in winter) and usually include full breakfasts. A 15min. drive to Monterey will yield lower rates at places with less charm. The upscale **Carmel Sands Lodge ❹**, on San Carlos St., between 4th and 5th Ave., is one of the least expensive options downtown. All rooms have cable TV, phone, and private bath. Some have fireplaces, wet bar, or balcony. (☎831-624-1255 or 800-252-1255. Free parking and pool. Rooms $85-199. AmEx/D/DC/MC/V.)

⚲ DETOUR
17-MILE DRIVE
The 17-Mile Drive meanders along the coast from Pacific Grove through Pebble Beach and the forests around Carmel. For the Carmel entrance, take Ocean Ave. down toward the beach, and turn right down San Antonio. From Rte. 1 N, take the Pebble Beach/Pacific Grove Hwy. 68 W exit, and turn left at the 1st stoplight. Follow signs for Pebble Beach.

Once owned by Del Monte Properties, Pebble Beach has become the playground of the fabulously well-to-do. Its enormous, manicured golf courses creep up almost to the shore's edge in bizarre contrast to the dramatically jagged cliffs and turbulent surf. The drive is rolling, looping, and often spectacular, though plagued by slow-driving tourists and a hefty entrance fee ($8.50). To drive in and out as you please over the course of a day, present your receipt to the guard, and have him record your license plate number. Save money by biking it (bicyclists and pedestrians are allowed in for free) or drive along Sunset Dr. instead (p. 934). Along 17-Mile Drive, make sure to stop at **Fanshell Overlook,** where massive harbor seals and their pups rest up on the shore, and at the **Lone Cypress,** an old, gnarled tree growing on a rock promontory. An image of this tree is now the official logo of the Pebble Beach community.

◪ **APPROACHING MONTEREY: 8 MILES**
Follow **Rte. 1 N** to Monterey.

MONTEREY

Monterey makes good on its public claim to have preserved more of its heritage than any other Californian city. Although luxury hotels and tourist shops abound, and the Cannery Row of Steinbeck fame has all but vanished, a number of important sites testify to the city's colorful past. The "Path of History," marked by yellow medallions embedded in the sidewalks, passes such landmarks as Colton Hall, the site of the California Constitutional Convention in 1849, and the Robert Louis Stevenson House, where the author lived in 1879. Most of these sites owe their preservation to Monterey's other distinguishing feature: abundant wealth. Multi-million-dollar homes and golf courses line the rocky shoreline, and luxury cars cruise the city streets.

VITAL STATS
Population: 33,000
Visitor Information: Monterey Peninsula Visitor and Convention Bureau, 150 Olivier St. (☎831-657-6400 or 888-221-1010; www.montereyinfo.org). Open in summer M-Sa 9am-6pm, Su 9am-5pm.
Internet Access: Monterey Public Library, 625 Pacific St. (☎831-646-3930), across from City Hall. Open M 1-9pm, Tu-W 10am-9pm, Th-F 10am-6pm, Sa-Su 1-5pm. Free.
Post Office: 565 Hartnell St. (☎831-372-4003). Open M-F 8:30am-5pm, Sa 10am-2pm. **Postal Code:** 93940.

PACIFIC COAST

▐ GETTING AROUND

The Monterey Peninsula, 116 mi. south of San Francisco, consists of **Monterey,** residential **Pacific Grove,** and **Pebble Beach,** a nest of mansions and golf courses. **Alvarado St.** runs north-south through Old Monterey and hosts most nightlife. Parallel to it is **Pacific St.** At Alvarado St.'s northern end stand luxury hotels and the giant DoubleTree Conference Center; beyond the plaza lies a parking lot, the marina, and Fisherman's Wharf. Perpendicular to Alvarado St., **Del Monte Ave.** runs northeast to the coast; on the other side, **Lighthouse Ave.** leads northwest through Pacific Grove, where it becomes **Central Ave.** and veers back to Lighthouse Ave., ending at Point Piños Lighthouse.

◉ SIGHTS

▨ MONTEREY BAY AQUARIUM. The largest of Monterey's attractions, this extraordinary aquarium benefits from the area's superb marine ecology. Gaze through the **world's 3rd-largest window** at an enormous marine habitat containing green sea turtles, giant ocean sunfish, large sharks, and yellowfin and bluefin tuna in one million gallons of water. Don't miss the provocative exhibit connecting the shape, movement, and beauty of jellyfish to various art forms, or the new exhibit exploring the myth and mystery of sharks. Kids and adults love watching the sea otters during feeding time, walking through the shorebird aviary, perusing the living kelp forest housed in a two-story glass aquarium, and checking out the touch pool of bay creatures (bat rays included). Be patient; the lines can be unbelievably long. Save 20-40min. by picking up tickets the day before. (*886 Cannery Row. ☎831-648-4888 or 800-756-3737; www.monterey-bayaquarium.org. Open daily June-Aug. 9:30am-6pm; Sept.-May 10am-6pm. $22; seniors, students, and ages 13-17 $20; ages 3-12 $13.*)

CANNERY ROW. Lying along the waterfront east of the aquarium, Cannery Row was once a dilapidated street crammed with languishing sardine-packing plants. The ¾ row has since been converted into tourist-packed mini-malls, bars, and a pint-sized carnival complex. All that remains of the earthiness and gruff camaraderie celebrated by John Steinbeck in *Cannery Row* and *Sweet Thursday* are a few building facades: 835 Cannery Row was the Wing Chong Market, the bright yellow building next door is where *Sweet Thursday* took place, and Doc Rickett's lab, 800 Cannery Row, is now closed to the public. Take a peek at the **Great Cannery Row Mural;** local artists have covered a construction-site barrier on the 700 block with depictions of 1930s Monterey and what "The Row" was like in its heyday. The "Taste of Monterey" **Wine Visitors Center,** on the second floor of the 700 building, offers a sampling of the county's wine industry with well-priced bottles and winery maps. (*700 Cannery Row. ☎888-646-5446. Open daily M-Th 10am-5pm, F-Sa 11am-6pm, Su 11am-4pm. $5 for 6 tastings.*)

SUNSET DRIVE. West of Monterey in Pacific Grove, Sunset Dr. provides a free, 6 mi. scenic alternative to 17-Mile Drive. Appropriately, Sunset Dr. is the best place in the area to watch the sun go down. People arrive a full 2hr. before sunset in order to secure front-row seats along the road, also known as Ocean Blvd. At the western tip of the peninsula stands **Point Piños Lighthouse,** the oldest continuously running Pacific Coast lighthouse, which has exhibits on Coast Guard history. (*☎831-648-5716. Open M and Th-Su 1-4pm. Free.*)

PACIFIC GROVE. Pacific Grove took root as a Methodist enclave over 100 years ago, and many of the Victorian houses are still in excellent condition. This unpretentious town (which falls eerily quiet at night) has a beautiful coastline, numerous lunch counters, and lots of antique and artsy home-furnishing stores. Browse secondhand clothing, book, and music stores along Lighthouse Ave., or outlet-shop 'til you drop at the **American Tin Cannery,** on Ocean View Blvd., near New Monterey. Thousands of **monarch butterflies** winter in Pacific Grove from October to March. Look, but don't touch; bothering the butterflies is a $1000 offense. The **Pacific Grove Museum of Natural History,** at Forest and Central Ave., one block west of Lighthouse Ave., has exhibits on monarchs and local wildlife. The stuffed birds are top-notch. (*☎831-648-5716. Open Tu-Sa 10am-5pm. Free.*)

MARITIME MUSEUM OF MONTEREY. This haven for sea buffs illustrates the maritime history of Monterey with ship models, photos, navigation tools, logs, and a free 14min. film. The museum's centerpiece is the original Fresnel lens of Point Sur Lighthouse. The lens is a two-story structure of gear-works and cut glass later replaced by the electric lighthouse. (*5 Custom House Plaza, across from Fisherman's Wharf. ☎831-372-2608. Open M-Tu and Th-Su 10am-5pm. $8; seniors, ages 13-17, and military $5; under 12 free.*)

PATH OF HISTORY WALKING TOUR. The early days of Monterey spawned a unique architectural trend that combined flourishes from the South, like wraparound porches, with Mexican adobe features like 3 ft. thick walls and exterior staircases. The Path of History, marked by yellow sidewalk medallions, snakes through Monterey State Historic Park in downtown, passing numerous historic buildings including the Royal Presidio Chapel, built in 1794, and the Larkin House, home to the US consul to Mexico during the 1840s. Use the visitors center brochure to walk the path unguided, or join a free tour led by state park guides. (*☎831-649-7118. Tour times and starting locations vary; call for details.*)

⚑ OUTDOORS

Companies on Fisherman's Wharf offer critter-spotting boat trips around Monterey Bay. The best time to go is during gray whale migration season (Nov.-Mar.), but the trips are hit-or-miss year-round. **Chris's Fishing Trips,** 48 Fisherman's Wharf, offers daily whale-watching tours and fishing boat charters. (☎831-375-5951. Open daily 4am-5pm. 2-3hr. whale-watching tours May-Nov. 11am, 2pm. $25, children $20. 2hr. gray whale migration tours Dec.-Apr. $22. Boat charters for tuna, salmon, rock cod, halibut, and sea bass also available.) Sea kayaking above kelp forests and among otters can be a heady experience. **Monterey Bay Kayaks,** 693 Del Monte Ave., provides rentals and tours. (☎831-373-5357 or 800-649-5357. Call for lesson info. Rentals $30 per person; includes gear, wetsuit, and instruction. 3hr. natural history guided tour $60. Open in summer M-Th and Su 9am-8pm; in winter daily 9am-6pm.) There are several bike paths in the area. The best is the **Monterey Penin-** sula Recreation Trail, which follows the coast for approximately 20 mi. from Castroville to Asilomar St. in Pacific Grove. Bikers can then continue through Pacific Grove to Pebble Beach along famous 17-Mile Drive.

▓ FOOD

Once a hot spot for the sardine industry, Monterey Bay now yields crab, red snapper, and salmon. Seafood is often expensive; look for free chowder samples or early-bird specials (usually 4-6pm). Stroll along the wharf, where most restaurants give out free samples of chowder. **Old Fisherman's Grotto,** Fisherman's Wharf (☎831-375-4606), has some of the best. Nibble on free samples at the **Old Monterey Market Place,** on Alvarado St. between Pearl St. and Del Monte Ave. (☎831-655-2607. Open in summer Tu 4-8pm; in winter Tu 4-8pm.)

▓ **Thai Bistro II,** 159 Central Ave. (☎831-372-8700), in Pacific Grove. Graced with a flower-encircled patio, this bistro offers top-quality Thai cuisine in a comfy atmosphere. Lunch combos ($7-9) come with soup, salad, egg roll, and rice. Extensive vegetarian menu. "Tuk-Tuk Delight" $9. Open daily 11:30am-2:30pm and 5-9:30pm. AmEx/D/MC/V. ❸

▓ **Tillie Gort's,** 111 Central Ave. (☎831-373-0335), in Pacific Grove. This vegetarian restaurant has been in business for over 30 years. Large portions of dishes like Mexican fiesta salad ($10.50), eggplant *francese* ($10.75), or spinach ravioli ($11.25), and sweet treats like berry cheesecake or chocolate vegan cake ($4.50) please even carnivores. Open June-Oct. M-F 10am-10pm, Sa-Su 8am-10pm; Nov.-May M-F 11am-10pm. MC/V. ❸

Bagel Bakery, 452 Alvarado St. (☎831-372-5242). Making delicious bagel sandwiches since 1976, this local chain has several additional locations in the area: Carmel (26539 Carmel Rancho Blvd.), Sand City (2160 California Ste. D), and Pacific Grove (1132 Forest Ave). Known for the "Kuperman's Delight" (triple-jack cheese, sprouts, and tomato; $2.75) and their omelettes-on-a-Bagel, like the Mexican Fiesta (Egg, jalapeno, cheddar, and avocado; $3.50). Open M-Sa 6am-6pm, Su 7am-4pm. AmEx/MC/V. ❶

Kalisa's, 851 Cannery Row, across from the Monterey Bay Aquarium. This simple yellow structure was the inspiration for La Ida Cafe in Steinbeck's *Cannery*

Row. Hearty, healthy, inexpensive sandwiches from $6. Lappert's ice cream from Hawaii ($2.50-6) and fresh coconuts drilled for drinking ($3) add a tropical flair. F 9pm belly dancing show; cover $5. Open daily 10am-7pm. AmEx/D/MC/V. ❷

🏠 ACCOMMODATIONS

Inexpensive hotels line the 2000 block of **Fremont St.** in Monterey. Others cluster along **Munras Ave.** between downtown Monterey and Rte. 1. The cheapest hotels in the area are in the less appealing towns of Seaside and Marina, just north of Monterey. Prices fluctuate depending on the season, day of the week, and events. In Monterey, camping is an excellent option for the budget traveler. Call **Monterey Parks** (☎831-755-4895) for camping info and ReserveAmerica (☎800-444-7275) for reservations.

Monterey Carpenter's Hall Hostel (HI-AYH), 778 Hawthorne St. (☎831-649-0375), 1 block west of Lighthouse Ave. This 45-bed hostel is fairly new and perfectly located. Modern facilities and a large, comfy living room with a piano, library, and games. Make-your-own pancake breakfast with tea, hot chocolate, and coffee. Limited shower time: visitors get 2 tokens per day, each good for 3½min. of hot water. Towels $0.50. Linen and parking included. Lockout 10:30am-5pm. Curfew 1am. Reservations essential June-Sept. Dorms $25, members $22, ages 7-17 with adult $17; private rooms $60-74. MC/V. ❶

Del Monte Beach Inn, 1110 Del Monte Blvd. (☎831-649-4410), near downtown, across from the beach. Cute, Victorian inn with pleasant rooms. Near a fairly loud road. One room has kitchenette. Continental breakfast included. Check-in 2-8pm. Reservations recommended. Rooms from $50. MC/V. ❸

Sea Breeze Lodge, (☎800-575-1805) 1101 Lighthouse Ave., minutes from Monterey and the ocean. 30 clean and comfortable rooms are set in the residential area of Pacific Grove. Outdoor pool. Continental breakfast included. Rooms $49-129. AmEx/D/MC/V. ❹

Veterans Memorial Park Campground, (☎831-646-3865), 1½ mi. from downtown. From Rte. 68, turn left onto Skyline Dr. From downtown, go south on Pacific St., turn right on Jefferson St., and follow the signs. Located on a hill with a view of the bay. Play-ground, barbecue pits, and hot showers. 40 sites. 3-night max. stay. No reservations; in summer and Sa-Su arrive before 3pm. Sites $20. Cash only. ❶

🎵 NIGHTLIFE

Monterey knows how to cut loose at night, but some areas of the peninsula quiet down early. The main action is downtown along **Alvarado St.;** there are also a few Lighthouse Ave. bars. Those under 21 have few options.

Mucky Duck British Pub, 479 Alvarado St. (☎831-655-3031). Empty front window booths might fool you--many patrons are in the back beer garden, listening to music or staying warm around a coal-burning fire. Monterey locals have voted the pub's beer the city's best for 7 years in a row. Come early to avoid waits. Live music, karaoke, or DJ from around 9pm; some live music during the day. Salads, sandwiches, and appetizers $5.25-13. Open daily noon-2am. AmEx/MC/V.

Club Octane, 321D Alvarado St. (☎831-646-9244; www.cluboctane.com), on the 2nd fl., at Del Monte Ave. Strobe lights and smoke machines throb like teenage hormones. 4 bars and 3 dance floors with different DJs. Pool tables and a smoking deck. Nightly drink specials. Male and female burlesque M 9:45pm. Th-Sa live music. F-Sa no hats, tennis shoes, or beach flip-flops. Cover M $7, F-Sa $5. Open M and Th-Su 9pm-1:45am. AmEx/D/MC/V.

🔀 DETOUR
SAN JUAN BAUTISTA
Take Rte. 1 N to Rte. 156 E.

A historic mission town founded in 1797, San Juan Bautista has retained the tranquility of a bygone era by pursuing policies of slow growth and forbidding development by chain commerce. **San Juan Bautista Mission** was the largest of the missions built in the 18th century to bring Catholicism to the "savage natives." The area around the town square—the mission, cemetery, garden, hotel, town hall, and stable—has been preserved in a historical park, and the buildings function like museums, although the mission still holds daily mass. At the end of the green lies a portion of **El Camino Real** ("the royal road"), the path that connected the 21 missions from San Diego to San Francisco, each a day's journey on horseback from the next. On the

PACIFIC COAST

first Saturday of every month, San Juan Bautista hosts a "living-history celebration" with displays of spinning, weaving, candle-making, and dancing. Pick up an events calendar at the mission or around town for other festivals. (☎831-623-2127. Mass in Spanish M-F 8am; Sa 5pm; Su 8:30, 10am, and noon. Open daily 9:30am-4:30pm. $3, ages 4-12 $1, under 3 free.)

⚑ APPROACHING CASTROVILLE: 18 MILES
Take **Rte. 1 N** toward Castroville.

CASTROVILLE. Though it's not worth more than a quick stop, **Castroville** distinguishes itself as "the artichoke center of the world" and hosts the Castroville Artichoke Festival in May. For a taste, head to the **Giant Artichoke Restaurant**, 11261 Merritt St., which is easy to spot with its enormous statue of an artichoke outside. A small order of deep-fried artichoke hearts runs $4.50. (☎831-633-3501. Open daily 6am-9pm. AmEx/MC/V.)

⚑ APPROACHING SANTA CRUZ: 28 MILES
Continue on **Rte. 1 N** toward Santa Cruz. Cruise past Watsonville, a chain-store center where the only site of interest is the **Sunset State Beach**, 201 Sunset Beach Rd. Wind through eucalyptus-lined roads and end up by a stunning beach. (Take the San Andreas Rd. exit, and turn right onto Sunset Beach Rd. ☎831-763-7063. Food lockers, picnic tables, and coin-operated showers. 90 sites with fire rings. Reserve three months in advance for the summer. Sites $25. Day-use $6. Cash only.)

SANTA CRUZ

One of the few places where the 1960s catchphrase "do your own thing" still applies, Santa Cruz embraces sculpted surfers, aging hippies, free-thinking students, and same-sex couples. The atmosphere here is fun-loving but far from hedonistic, intellectual but nowhere near stuffy. Friendly and unpretentious, Santa Cruz offers a mix of Southern California's surf culture and Northern California's laid-back vibe. Pacific Ave. teems with independent bookstores, cool bars, trendy cafes, and pricey boutiques. Be careful about visiting on Saturday or Sunday, since the town's population virtually doubles on summer weekends, clogging area highways as daytrippers make their way to and from the Bay Area.

VITAL STATS

Population: 55,717

Visitor Info: Santa Cruz County Conference and Visitor Council, 1211 Ocean St. (☎831-425-1234 or 800-833-3494; www.santacruz.org). Publishes the free *Santa Cruz County Traveler's Guide*. Open M-Sa 9am-5pm, Su 10am-4pm. **Downtown Info Center,** 1126 Pacific Ave. (☎831-459-9486). Open daily; hours vary.

Internet Access: Central Library, 224 Church St. (☎831-420-5730). Open M-Th 10am-8pm, F 10am-5pm, Sa 10am-5pm, Su 1-5pm. $3 per hr.

Parking: Free 2hr. public lots off Pacific Ave.

Post Office: 850 Front St. (☎831-426-8184). Open M-F 9am-5pm. **Postal Code:** 95060.

▣ GETTING AROUND

Santa Cruz is on the northern tip of Monterey Bay, 65 mi. south of San Francisco. Through west Santa Cruz, Rte. 1 becomes **Mission St.** The **University of California at Santa Cruz (UCSC)** stretches inland from Mission St. Southeast of Mission St. lie the waterfront and the downtown. Down by the ocean, **Beach St.** runs roughly east-west. The narrow **San Lorenzo River** runs north-south, dividing the Boardwalk scene from the quiet residences of the affluent. **Pacific Ave.** is the main street downtown. Along with **Cedar St.,** Pacific Ave. carves out a nightlife niche accessible from the beach motels. Resident-traffic-only zones, one-way streets, and dead-ends can make Santa Cruz frustrating to navigate by car.

◉ SIGHTS

BEACHES. For information on Santa Cruz's many beach facilities, head to the **California Parks and Recreation Department,** 600 Ocean St. (☎831-429-2850. Open M-F 8-am-5pm.) The **Santa Cruz Beach** (officially named Cowell Beach) is broad, reasonably clean, and packed with volleyball players. If you're seeking solitude, you'll have to venture farther afield. Away from the main drag, beach access points line Rte. 1. Railroad tracks, farmlands, and dune vegetation make several of these access points difficult to reach, but the beaches are correspondingly less crowded. Folks who want to bare everything head north on Rte. 1 to the **Red, White, and Blue Beach,** down Scaroni Rd. Look for a piece of wood painted in patriotic colors that marks the elusive turn-off to the beach. Sunbathers must be 18+ or accompanied by a parent. *(Beach open Mar.-Oct. daily 10am-6pm. Day-use $15, ages 6-17 $5, under 6 free.)* Around the point at the end of W. Cliff Dr. is **Natural Bridges State Beach.** Only one natural bridge remains, but the park offers a pristine beach and awe-inspiring tidepools. In November and December, thousands of stunning monarch butterflies swarm along the beach and blanket the nearby groves with their orange hues. *(☎831-423-4609. Open daily 8am-sunset. Free.)*

SANTA CRUZ BEACH BOARDWALK AND WHARF.

The beach is great at Santa Cruz, but the water is frigid. Casual beachgoers catch their thrills on the Boardwalk, a three-block strip of over 25 amusement park rides, shooting galleries, and corn-dog vendors. It's a gloriously tacky throwback to 50s beach culture. Don't miss the **Giant Dipper,** a 1924 wooden roller coaster where Dirty Harry met his enemy in 1983's *Sudden Impact. (Mini-golf $5. Boardwalk open daily June to Labor Day. Tickets $0.65, 60 tickets $33; all-day pass $27.)* Jutting off Beach St. is the longest car-accessible pier on the West Coast. Seafood restaurants and souvenir shops will try to distract you from the expansive views of the ocean. *(At the convergence of Beach St. and W. Cliff Dr. ☎831-423-7258.)* Munch on a caramel apple ($3.75) or gummy treats ($2.25 per lb.) from local favorite **Marini's at the Wharf,** Municipal Wharf #55A, while watching sea lions hang out on rafters beneath the end of the pier. *(☎831-425-7341. Open M-Th and Su 10am-9:30pm, F-Sa 10am-11pm.)*

UNIVERSITY OF CALIFORNIA AT SANTA CRUZ.

This sprawling, 2000-acre campus lies within a mile of downtown. Governor Ronald Reagan's plan to make UCSC a "riot-proof campus" (free of a central point where radicals could inflame a crowd) resulted in the university's decentralized and beautiful forested layout. Although the campus appears to be tranquil, amidst rolling hills and redwood groves, UCSC is famous (or infamous) for its leftist politics and conspicuous drug culture. If driving, make sure you have a parking permit ($5) on weekdays, available at the kiosk inside the main campus entrance, the police station, or the parking office. *(Parking office on the right, past the entrance*

kiosk. ☎831-459-3799; www.ucsc.edu.)* Be sure to visit the university's gorgeous **Arboretum,** which contains over 45 colorful kinds of flowers. *(1156 High St. ☎831-427-2998. Open daily 9am-5pm. Free.)* UCSC is also home to the **Seymour Marine Discovery Center,** which overlooks the Monterey Bay National Marine Sanctuary. Take a tour that includes an on-site laboratory. *(100 Shaffer Rd. ☎831-459-3800. Open Tu-Sa 10am-5pm, Su noon-5pm. $6; students, seniors, and ages 4-16 $4. 1st Tu of each month free.)*

OTHER SIGHTS. The **Mission Santa Cruz,** with a peaceful adobe church and fragrant garden, offers a quiet place to relax for an afternoon. *(130 Emmett. St., off Mission St. ☎831-426-5686. Open Tu-Sa 10am-4pm, Su 10am-2pm. Donation suggested.)* Two miles into the Santa Cruz Mountains lies a warped cabin where the trees grow twisted: the **Mystery Spot.** Don't bring your compass, as it's likely to stop working after your visit. Head up the hill to the center of the Mystery Spot, and try to discover its secrets. *(Head north on Branciforte Dr., then make a left on to Mystery Spot Rd. ☎831-423-8897. Open daily Memorial Day to Labor Day 9am-7pm; Labor Day to Memorial Day 9am-5pm. $5.)*

⚑ OUTDOORS

KAYAKING

Outdoor sports enthusiasts will find ample activities in Santa Cruz. Parasailing and other pricey pastimes are popular on the wharf. You must provide ACA certification for a closed-deck kayak unless you go to Elkhorn Slough, a beautiful estuary which is safe for inexperienced kayakers. **Kayak Connection,** 413 Lake Ave., offers tours of Elkhorn Slough (9:30am and 1:30pm; $40) and the Santa Cruz Harbor ($30-45), and rents ocean kayaks at decent rates. *(☎831-479-1121. Open M-F 10am-5pm, Sa-Su 9am-6pm. Open-deck singles $30 per day; closed-deck singles $33. Paddle, life jacket, brief instruction, and wetsuit included.)* Beware of rental agencies that don't include instruction sessions; closed-deck ocean kayaking can be dangerous.

SURFING

The best vantage points for watching surfers are along W. Cliff Dr. To learn more about the activity, stop in at **Steamer's Lane,** the deep water off the point where surfers have flocked

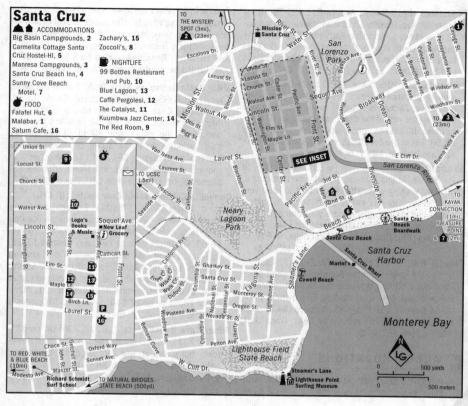

Santa Cruz

⛺ 🏠 ACCOMMODATIONS
Big Basin Campgrounds, **2**
Carmelita Cottage Santa
Cruz Hostel-HI, **5**
Manresa Campgrounds, **3**
Santa Cruz Beach Inn, **4**
Sunny Cove Beach
Motel, **7**

Zachary's, **15**
Zoccoli's, **8**

🍴 NIGHTLIFE
99 Bottles Restaurant
and Pub, **10**
Blue Lagoon, **13**
Caffe Pergolesi, **12**
The Catalyst, **11**
Kuumbwa Jazz Center, **14**
The Red Room, **9**

🍴 FOOD
Falafel Hut, **6**
Malabar, **1**
Saturn Cafe, **16**

since Hawaiian "Duke" Kahanamoku kick-started California's surf culture here 100 years ago. Surfers also gather at the more remote "Hook" along **Pleasure Point,** north of Santa Cruz in Live Oak. **Lighthouse Field State Beach**, on W. Cliff Dr., a surfing haven, is home to **Lighthouse Point** and the **Santa Cruz Surfing Museum,** housed in the Mark Abbott Memorial Lighthouse, which displays surfing artifacts from 100 years of Santa Cruz wave riding. (☎831-420-6289. Open M and W-Su noon-4pm. Free.) For surfing lessons, contact **Richard Schmidt Surf School,** 236 San Jose Ave., or ask for him at the beach. Locals boast that Schmidt can get anyone up and riding. (☎831-423-0928; www.richard-schmidt.com. 1hr. private lesson $80-100; 2hr. group lesson $80. Lessons include equipment.)

🍴 FOOD

Santa Cruz offers an astounding number of budget eateries. The restaurant community goes out of its way to embrace vegans—tofu can be substituted for just about anything. **New Leaf Grocery,** 1134 Pacific Ave., offers healthful snacks and fresh produce in Santa Cruz's first ozone-friendly store—the store has a refrigeration system that is free of all ozone-depleting gases. (☎831-425-1793. Open daily 9am-9pm.)

🍴 **Zoccoli's,** 1534 Pacific Ave. (☎831-423-1711). This phenomenal deli uses only fresh ingredients in its sandwiches. Daily pasta specials ($4.50-7.25) come with salad and bread. Sandwiches $4.75-6. Open M-Sa 10am-6pm, Su 11am-6pm. MC/V. ❶

PACIFIC COAST

Malabar, 1116 Soquel Ave. (☎831-423-7906), at Seabright Ave. Healthy Sri Lankan cuisine in a romantic atmosphere. Incredible flatbread ($3) served by candlelight with ghee and garlic. Entrees $5-9. Open M-Th 11am-2:30pm and 5:30-9pm, F 11am-2:30pm and 5:30-10pm, Sa 5:30-10pm. MC/V. ❷

Zachary's, 819 Pacific Ave. (☎831-427-0646). With savory potatoes, fresh bread, and enormous omelettes, Zachary's will give you a reason to laze about for the rest of the day. Basic breakfast (2 eggs, oatmeal-molasses toast, and hash browns) for $5.50. Eat at the counter to avoid the wait. Open Tu-Su 7am-2:30pm. MC/V. ❶

Saturn Cafe, 145 Laurel St. (☎831-429-8505), at Pacific Ave. At this planetary-punk-themed restaurant, the hard-working waitstaff does its best to keep your table clean and your coffee fresh. Veggie breakfast plates include a tofu scramble with homefries and sourdough toast ($6.50). The Spartacus Salad is also delicious ($8). Open M-W noon-midnight, Th-F noon-3am, Sa 10am-3am, Su 10am-midnight. MC/V. ❷

Falafel Hut, 309 Beach St. (☎831-423-0567), across the street from the Boardwalk. A good place for a quick late-night snack, the Hut serves Middle Eastern and American dishes. The owners pride themselves on their falafel sandwiches ($4.25), but the chicken ($5.25) is hard to beat. Open daily 11am-11pm. MC/V. ❶

ACCOMMODATIONS

Santa Cruz gets jam-packed during the summer, especially on weekends. Room rates skyrocket; reservations are always recommended. Surprisingly, the nicer motels tend to have more reasonable summer weekend rates. Reservations for state campgrounds are available through **ReserveAmerica** (☎800-444-7275) and should be made three months in advance.

Big Basin Redwoods State Park, 21600 Big Basin Way (☎831-338-8860), in Boulder Creek, 23 mi. from Santa Cruz. Go north on Rte. 9 to Rte. 236 through Boulder Creek. Big Basin offers the best camping in the region, with 80 mi. of cool, breezy trails, including the 2-day, 30 mi. Skyline to the Sea Trail (trailhead parking $6), and 145 campsites with showers. Reservations required. Reservation fee $5. Sites $25; backcountry sites $10. Day-use $6. ❶

Carmelita Cottage Santa Cruz Hostel (HI-AYH), 321 Main St. (☎831-423-8304), 2 blocks from the beach. A 40-bed Victorian house, centrally located in a quiet neighborhood. Linen included. Towels $0.50. Overnight parking free; day permits $1.25. July-Aug. 3-night max. stay. Reception 8-11am and 5-10pm. Lockout 11am-5pm. Strict curfew 11pm. Reservations recommended, but no refunds after 48hr. prior to reservation date. Dorms $21, members $18, ages 12-17 $14, ages 4-11 $10, ages 3 and under free. MC/V. ❶

Sunny Cove Beach Motel, 1610 E. Cliff Dr. (☎831-475-1741), near Schwan Lagoon. Far from downtown, but pleasant, well-kept suites have kitchens, cable TV, and access to an outdoor pool. Pets allowed. Rooms M-Th and Su $60-100, F-Sa $80-150. AmEx/MC/V. ❹

THE MYSTERY OF THE MYSTERY SPOT

Let's Go got the inside story about the Santa Cruz Mystery Spot from local UCSC alum, Lindsay Busby. As a biology and community studies major, Lindsay has compelling insight into the magnetic force behind the local attraction.

LG: How long have you lived in Santa Cruz?

LB: Five mystery-filled years, and it's a mystery why I'm still here.

LG: When did you first hear about the Mystery Spot?

LB: Well, I'd seen bumper stickers all over the Bay Area and had no idea what it was. Then I moved to Santa Cruz and realized it was an actual place as opposed to some sort of hippie joke.

LG: What do UCSC students say about the Mystery Spot?

LB: To tell you the truth, they think it's pretty lame because people build it up a lot and some people get dizzy and throw up.

LG: Does anybody really know what it is?

LB: Um, yeah, the people that have been there. Most people want to tell you about what they've seen, but

[in the passenger seat]

Santa Cruz Beach Inn, 600 Riverside Ave. (☎831-458-9660), off Laurel St. Close to the Boardwalk. Rooms are upscale but surprisingly budget-friendly. Outdoor pool and whirlpools. Continental breakfast included. Rooms from $99. AmEx/D/DC/MC/V. ❺

Manresa Uplands State Beach Park, 205 Manresa Rd. (☎831-761-1795), in La Selva Beach, 13 mi. south of Santa Cruz. Take Rte. 1, and exit at San Andreas Rd. Veer right, and follow San Andreas Rd. for 4 mi., then turn right on Sand Dollar Rd. Located in farm country, away from the hustle and bustle of Santa Cruz. Walk-in tent sites $25. Day-use $6. Cash only. ❶

▧ NIGHTLIFE

There are comprehensive weekly events listings in the free *Good Times* and *Metro Santa Cruz*, and also in the *Spotlight* section of Friday's *Sentinel* (all available at cafes and bookstores). The Boardwalk bandstand offers free summer concerts, usually by oldies bands on Friday evenings. The Santa Cruz Parks and Recreation Department publishes info in the free *Summer Activity Guide*. **Pacific Ave.** is home to a host of bustling coffee shops and laid-back bars.

▧ 99 Bottles of Beer on the Wall Restaurant and Pub, 110 Walnut Ave. (☎831-459-9999). This modest but lively bar in the heart of downtown offers standard bar meals and 99 different types of beer. Check the wall to see who has tried them all. W quiz night. Happy hour Th 11:30am-10pm with $1 off pints. Open M-Th 11:30am-1:30am, F-Sa 11:30am-2am, Su 11:30am-midnight. Kitchen closes midnight. AmEx/D/MC/V.

▧ Caffe Pergolesi, 418A Cedar St. (☎831-426-1775). A chill coffeehouse and bar with small rooms and a patio for reading or socializing. 4 types of hot chocolate. Open M-Th 7am-11pm, F-Sa 7am-midnight, Su 7:30am-11:30pm. Cash only.

The Red Room, 1003 Cedar St. (☎831-425-1913). You'll be seeing red everywhere you look as you mingle on plush couches. Downstairs, The Red Room is its smokier, rock 'n' roll counterpart. Su jazz band. Open daily 4pm-2am. AmEx/MC/V.

Blue Lagoon, 923 Pacific Ave. (☎831-423-7117). This mega-popular club has won all kinds of awards and is known as the city's best dance club. Bar in front, 2 pool tables in back, and dancing everywhere. Stronger-than-the-bouncer drinks $3-4. Cover $3-5. Open daily 4pm-2am. Cash only.

The Catalyst, 1011 Pacific Ave. (☎831-423-1338). The town's primary music and dance venue draws national, college, and local bands. Pool and arcade games upstairs, pizza and bar downstairs. Cover and age restrictions vary with show. Upstairs bar area is strictly 21+. Shows daily $5-30. Open daily 11am-1:30am. MC/V.

Kuumbwa Jazz Center, 320 Cedar St. (☎831-427-2227; www.kuumbwajazz.org, tickets www.ticketweb.com). Known throughout the region for great jazz and innovative off-night programs. M big-name bands. Th local acts. All ages welcome. Tickets $10-35. Shows M 7 and 9pm, Th 7pm. MC/V.

---

it's best not to give too much away. All I ever gleaned from student rumors was that it had something to do with physics.

LG: When did you finally go to the Mystery Spot?

LB: Just after I graduated. It took me four years to find it, though I drove by it once when I got lost in the woods trying to find a frat party.

LG: And what are your speculations about what causes the Mystery Spot to be so mysterious?

LB: Personally, I buy the UFO story. I think that a spacecraft landed and it had some sort of giant chunk of magnetic rock (from another planet) that disrupts the gravitational and magnetic forces of the earth surrounding the rock.

LG: Would you recommend that people visit the Mystery Spot?

LB: Yeah, I thought it was worth the trip; it did make me kind of dizzy, though.

The Mystery Spot, 465 Mystery Spot Rd. (☎831-423-8897; www.mysteryspot.com.) Open daily Memorial Day to Labor Day 9am-7pm; Labor Day to Memorial Day 9am-5pm. $5; children free.

⚄ DETOUR
AÑO NUEVO STATE RESERVE
20 mi. north of Santa Cruz on Rte. 1.

This wildlife reserve has several hiking trails that offer views of **Año Nuevo Island,** the site of an abandoned lighthouse now taken over by birds, seals, and sea lions. Free hiking permits are available at the ranger station by the entrance and at the visitors center (though seal-viewing permits are only issued until 3:30pm). From mid-December to late March, the reserve is the mating place of 15 ft., 4500 lb. elephant seals. Thousands of fat seals crowd the shore where, like frat boys looking to score, the males fight each other for dominance over a herd of females. Before mid-August, you can still see the last of the "molters" and the young who have yet to find their sea legs. Don't get too close—if the seals don't get you, the cops might; the law requires that visitors stay 25 ft. away. (☎831-879-0227. No pets. Open daily 8am-sunset. Visitors center open daily 10am-3:30pm.)

⚐ APPROACHING PESCADERO: 14 MILES
Follow **Rte. 1 N** toward Pescadero.

PESCADERO. Pescadero may be a one-horse town, but **Duarte's ❷,** is the place to go for awesome artichoke-and-green-chile soup ($6.50) or homemade pie. The simple wooden restaurant and tavern has been run by the Duarte family since 1894. Sound like a local by asking for a cup of "half and half." (☎831-879-0406. Open daily 7am-8:30pm. MC/V.)

⚐ APPROACHING SAN JOSE: 57 MILES
Take **Rte 1. N** to **Rte. 92 E.** Follow Rte. 92 E to **I-280 S,** toward San Jose. Take the **Rte. 87/Guadalupe Pkwy. exit** on the left.

SAN JOSE
Founded in 1777 in a bucolic valley of fruit and walnut orchards, San Jose was California's first civilian settlement. In 1939, the first computer company, Hewlett-Packard, had its modest beginnings here in Dave Packard's garage. By the early 1970s, many of San Jose's orchards had been replaced by offices, and the moniker "Silicon Valley" began to take hold. In recent years, San Jose residents have broadened their one-track focus on the high-tech to include

other industries. Museums, restaurants, hotels, and vineyards have all sprouted up as part of an effort to expand San Jose beyond the world of microchips and barefoot office techies.

VITAL STATS

Population: 945,000

Visitor Information: Visitor Information and Business Center, 150 W. San Carlos St. (☎408-792-4173; www.sanjose.org), in the San Jose McEnerny Convention Center. Open M-F 9am-5pm, Sa 11am-5pm.

Internet Access: Martin Luther King, Jr. Public Library (☎408-808-2000; www.sjlibrary.org), at the intersection of E. San Fernando and 4th St. Open M-W 8am-8pm, Th-Sa 9am-6pm, Su 1-5pm. Free.

Post Office: 105 N. 1st St. (☎408-292-0487). Open M-F 8:30am-5pm, Sa 7am-noon. **Postal Code:** 95110.

⬛ GETTING AROUND

San Jose is centered on the convention-hosting malls and plazas near the intersection of east-west **San Carlos St.** and north-south **Market St.** Numbered streets run north-south and alternate one-way directions. The **Transit Mall,** the center of San Jose's bus and trolley system, runs along 1st and 2nd St. in the downtown area. The Alameda lies at the east end of Santa Clara St. and leads to Santa Clara University and Santa Clara Mission.

⚅ SIGHTS

TECH MUSEUM OF INNOVATION. Curious kids and their parents love the hands-on, cutting-edge science exhibits and IMAX theater at this tourist-savvy attraction. Grow your own jellyfish DNA and watch it glow. The museum is underwritten by high-tech firms and housed in a sleek geometric building. (201 S. Market St. ☎408-795-6224; www.thetech.org. Open daily Apr.-Sept. 10am-5pm; Oct.-Mar. Tu-Su 10am-5pm. $10, seniors $8, ages 3-12 $7. Exhibits and IMAX $16/$11/$10.)

WINCHESTER MYSTERY HOUSE. This odd Victorian house is little more than, well, an odd Victorian house, but it will amuse those with a penchant for the unusual. Sarah Winchester was the eccentric heiress to the Winchester rifle fortune. After the death of her daughter and husband, she was convinced by an occultist that the spirits of all the men killed by her family's guns would seek revenge if construction on her home ever ceased. Work on the mansion continued 24hr. a day for over 38 years. A 160-room maze of doors, windows, and stairs elaborately designed to "confuse the spirits" is the end result. (525 S. Winchester Blvd., near the intersection of I-880 and I-280. ☎408-247-2101. Open daily June-Aug. 9am-7pm; Sept. to mid-Oct. M-Th and Su 9am-5pm, F-Sa 9am-7pm; mid-Oct. to May daily 9am-5pm. $22, ages 6-12 $16, under 6 free.)

ROSICRUCIAN EGYPTIAN MUSEUM AND PLANETARIUM. Rising out of the suburbs, this grand structure houses the largest exhibit of Egyptian artifacts in the western US, with a collection of over 4000 ancient pieces that includes a walk-in tomb and spooky animal mummies. This collection belongs to the ancient and mystical Rosicrucian Order, whose past members include Amenhotep IV, Pythagoras, Sir Francis Bacon, René Descartes, Benjamin Franklin, and Sir Isaac Newton. (1660 Park Ave., at Naglee Ave. ☎408-947-3635; www.egyptianmuseum.org. Open Tu-F 10am-5pm, Sa-Su 11am-6pm. $9, students and seniors $7, ages 5-10 $5, under 5 free.)

THE SAN JOSE MUSEUM OF ART. Neighbor to the Tech Museum, this modern museum features contemporary art and is itself progressive in design and mission. Admission is free to encourage public awareness of 20th- and 21st-century art, and the museum offers a wide range of exhibits, lectures, programs, and hands-on events for adults and children. (110 S. Market St. ☎408-271-8840; www.sjma.com. Open Tu-Su 11am-5pm. Free.)

MISSION SANTA CLARA DE ASIS AND SANTA CLARA UNIVERSITY. The first California mission to honor a woman as its patron saint, Mission Santa Clara de Asis was established on the Guadalupe River in 1777 and moved to its present site in 1828. (Mass M-F noon, Su 10am.) **Santa Clara University,** built around the mission, was established in 1851, making it California's oldest university. Subsequent restorations have refitted the structures to match the beauty of the surrounding rose gardens and 180-year-old olive trees. (500 El Camino Real, 5 mi. northwest of downtown San Jose off The Alameda. ☎408-554-4000; www.scu.edu.)

AMUSEMENT PARKS. Paramount's Great America theme park is a jungle of roller coasters, log rides, and fiendish contraptions designed to spin you, flip you, drop you, and generally separate you from your stomach. (☎408-988-1776; www.pgathrills.com. Off U.S. 101 at Great America Pkwy. in Santa Clara, 8 mi. northwest of downtown San Jose. Open June-Aug. M-F and Su 10am-8pm, Sa 10am-9pm; Sept.-Oct. and Mar.-May Sa-Su 10am-6pm. $52, seniors and ages 3-6 $35, under 3 free. Parking $10.) The area's best collection of waterslides is at Paramount's **Raging Waters.** Just don't expect to be the only one seeking a soaking. (Off U.S. 101 at the Tully Rd. exit, about 5 mi. east of downtown San Jose. ☎408-238-9900; www.rwsplash.com. Open June-Aug. M-F 10am-6pm, Sa-Su 10am-7pm; Sept. Sa-Su 10am-5pm. $26, under 48 in. $20, seniors $16. After 3pm $19/$14.)

⬛ FOOD

Familiar fast-food franchises and pizzerias surround SJSU. More international cheap eats lie along **S. 1st St.** or near **San Pedro Sq.,** at St. John and San Pedro St.

Bill's, 1115 Willow St. (☎408-294-1125), at Lincoln Ave. Lots of food for little cash. Hearty omelets ($6-9.45), and burgers ($8-9), but the real draw is the lightly fried calamari ($10.50). Open daily 7am-3pm. AmEx/D/MC/V. ❸

The Mini Gourmet, 599 S. Bascom Ave. (☎408-275-8973). Voted "best after-hours coffee shop." Build your own breakfast for $6.50. ½ sandwich and soup $5.50. Dinner entrees $9-15. Open 24hr. MC/V. ❷

Sonoma Chicken Coop, 31 North Main St. (☎408-287-4083), at San Pedro Sq. Quality food at inexpensive prices. Standard Italian-American fare with a few quirks like butterscotch bread pudding ($6.50) and surf-and-turf pizza ($10). Appetizers $3-9, Entrees $7-13. Open daily 11am. AmEx/MC/V. ❸

White Lotus, 80 N. Market St. (☎408-977-0540), between Santa Clara and St. John St. Strictly vegetarian, though some food is meat-flavored. Fried fish with ginger sauce $10. Banana-blossom, sweet-and-sour soup $7. Open M and W-Th 11am-9pm, F-Sa 11am-10pm. MC/V. ❷

■ ACCOMMODATIONS

County parks with campgrounds surround the city, as do chain motels.

Sanborn Park Hostel (HI-AYH), 15808 Sanborn Rd. (☎408-741-0166), in Sanborn County Park. This hostel features clean rooms and 39 beds for travelers in search of peace and quiet. Volleyball, badminton, and croquet. Linen included; towels $0.25. Reception 5-10:30pm. Check-out 9am. Curfew 11pm. Dorms $17, members $14, under 18 $6. Cash only. ❶

Santa Clara Inn, 2188 The Alameda (☎408-244-8860), just before Santa Clara University. Rooms with cable TV, kitchens, and complimentary breakfast. Rooms from $50. AmEx/D/DC/MC/V. ❸

Mount Madonna County Park, on Pole Line Rd. (☎408-842-2341, reservations 408-355-2201), off Hecker Pass Hwy. 117 sites in a beautiful setting, available by reservation or on a first come, first served basis. Tent sites $15; RV sites $25. ❶

Sanborn County Park, 16055 Sanborn Rd. (☎408-867-9959, reservations 408-355-2201). From Rte. 17 S, take Rte. 9 to Big Basin Wy., and turn left onto Sanborn Rd. This densely forested park features miles of horse and hiking trails. Open late Mar. to mid-Oct. for walk-in camping. Day use 8am-sunset. Tent sites $10; RV sites $25. D/MC/V. ❶

⬛ NIGHTLIFE

Downtown San Jose is a nightlife destination for many Bay Area locals. Known for dance clubs and all-night parties, the city has enough nightlife to keep even the wildest partiers busy. Most of the action is in or around **San Pedro Sq.** Most of SJ's hot spots enforce strict dress codes.

Fahrenheit Ultra Lounge, 99 E. San Fernando St. (☎408-998-9998). This plush lounge is the destination of choice for young professionals looking to unwind. The college crowd takes over Th night. Tu karaoke. W jazz. Th-Sa DJs and dancing. Open Tu-F 11:30am-2:30pm and 5pm-2am, Sa 5pm-2am. AmEx/MC/V.

Voodoo Lounge, 14 S. 2nd St. (☎408-286-8636). A popular local spot with drinks like the Voodoo Child (Jack Daniel's Lynchburg lemonade; $6) and Black Magic Margarita ($6). Open M, W, F-Sa 10pm-2am; Th 9:30pm-10am.

Club Havana Nights, 117 W. Santa Clara St. (☎408-279-3670), at the corner of N. San Pedro St., downtown. This is San Jose's premier salsa club. Th-F 7-9pm free salsa lessons. Semi-formal dress code strictly enforced. Open W 8pm-2am, Th-Sa 7:30pm-2am, Su 3-8pm. D/MC/V.

◤ APPROACHING PALO ALTO: 17 MILES
Take **Rte. 87 N** to **U.S. 101 N.**

PALO ALTO

Dominated by the beautiful 8000-acre Stanford University campus, Palo Alto is an upscale university town populated by affluent home owners and elite college students. Stanford's perfectly groomed grounds, sparkling lake, and Spanish mission-style buildings have a manufactured quality that suits the university's speedy rise to international acclaim. The city that Stanford calls home is equally manicured, with a tidy downtown strip of restaurants, bookstores, and boutiques. Its nightlife caters to students and suburbanites, while weekday happy hours help singles wind down.

VITAL STATS

Population: 60,000

Visitor Information: Palo Alto Chamber of Commerce, 122 Hamilton Ave. (☎650-324-3121), between Hude and Alta St. Open M-F 9am-5pm. **Stanford University Information Booth** (☎650-723-2560), across from Hoover Tower in Memorial Auditorium. Open M-F 8am-5pm, Sa-Su 9am-5pm.

Internet Access: Palo Alto Main Library, 1213 Newell Rd. (☎650-329-2436). Open M-W 10am-9pm, Th noon-9pm, F-Sa 10am-6pm, Su 1-5pm. Free.

Post Office: Main Office, 2085 E. Bayshore Rd. (☎650-321-1423). Open M-F 8:30am-5pm, Sa 9am-noon. **Postal Code:** 94303.

◰ GETTING AROUND. Residential Palo Alto is not easily distinguished from the Stanford campus. **Stanford University** spreads out from the west end of **University Ave.,** the main thoroughfare off U.S. 101. Despite its name, University Ave. belongs much more to the town than to the college. Cars coming off U.S. 101 onto University Ave. pass very briefly through **East Palo Alto** and into the university's side of town. **El Camino**

Real (Rte. 82) abuts University Ave. and runs northwest-southeast through town. From there, University Ave. turns into Palm Dr., which accesses the heart of Stanford's campus.

◙ **SIGHTS.** Palo Alto's main tourist attraction, **Stanford University,** was founded in 1885 by Jane and Leland Stanford to honor their son, who died of typhoid fever. The Stanfords loved Spanish colonial mission architecture and collaborated with Frederick Law Olmsted, designer of New York City's Central Park, to create a red-tiled campus of uncompromising beauty. The school has produced such eminent conservatives as Chief Justice William Rehnquist, and the campus has been called "a hotbed of social rest." The oldest part of campus is the **Main Quadrangle,** on Serra St., the location of most undergraduate classes. The walkways are dotted with diamond-shaped, gold-numbered stone tiles that mark the locations of time capsules put together by each year's graduating class. (☎ 650-723-2560. Tours depart from the Information booth in Memorial Auditorium daily 11am and 3:15pm. Free.) Just south of the Main Quad, at Escondido Mall and Duena, **Memorial Church** is a non-denominational gold shrine with stained-glass windows and glittering mosaic walls like those of an Eastern Orthodox church. (☎ 650-723-3469. Open M-F 8am-5pm. Tours F 2pm. Free.) The **Hoover Tower's** observation deck has views of campus, the East Bay, and San Francisco. (☎ 650-723-2053. Open daily 10am-4:30pm; closed during finals and academic breaks. $2, seniors and under 13 $1.) The **Visual Arts Center,** 328 Lomita Dr., at Museum Way off Palm Dr., displays an eclectic collection of painting and sculpture. (☎ 650-723-4177. Open W and F-Su 11am-5pm, Th 11am-8pm. Free.) The extensive **Rodin Sculpture Garden,** at Museum Way and Lomita Dr., contains a stunning bronze cast of *Gates of Hell,* among other larger figures. Enjoy a picnic lunch here while contemplating the next life. (☎ 650-723-4177. Tours Sa-Su 2pm. Free.)

🍴🍷 **FOOD AND NIGHTLIFE.** Dining in Palo Alto is centered around posh restaurants downtown. Those who are watching their wallets should stay on University Ave. 🍴**Café Borrone ❷,** 1010 El Camino Real, is a bustling, brasserie-style cafe that spills onto a large patio and serves freshly baked bread, sinful *gâteaux* ($2-4), coffee drinks, Italian soda, wine ($5-6), and beer (pints $3.75). Check the chalkboard for specials, or choose from a wide range of salads, sandwiches, and quiches for $4-10. (☎ 650-327-0830. Open M-Th 8am-11pm, F-Sa 8am-midnight, Su 8am-5pm. MC/V.) One block east of University Ave., **Mango Caribbean Restaurant and Bar ❷,** 435 Hamilton Ave., offers reggae music and Caribbean cuisine, like seriously spicy Jamaican "jerked joints" ($6.50) and tropical smoothies ($4.50). Veggie options are available. (☎ 650-324-9443. Delicious bread pudding $6. Open M-Th and Su 11am-10pm, F-Sa 11am-midnight. AmEx/D/MC/V.) Locals and students loosen

THE PLAY

The Bay Area is known for its intense sports rivalries, but none inspire the fiery devotion of the California-Stanford football game, known simply as "The Big Game." The most famous Big Game occurred on November 20, 1982 at University of California. Down by 1 at the last minute, the Stanford Cardinal managed to kick a desperate field goal to make the score 20-19. It looked as though the game was over. With only 3 seconds left on the clock, Bears fans were a deflated bunch. Stanford kicked off, certain they had an easy tackle and a historic win ahead. The Cal Bears caught the ball and started to run, taking advantage of the fact that until the ball was dead, the game couldn't be over. The Bears started passing the football back and forth like a hot potato, and out of a tangle of bodies a Cal player emerged with the ball. The Stanford football team was confused, but not as confused as the Stanford marching band. Not realizing that the game wasn't over, the band marched on to the field, blaring the Stanford fight song with celebratory enthusiasm. With only a marching band between them and the victory, the Cal team charged through the horde of trumpets and trombones, flattening a drum major in the end-zone for good measure and winning the game 20-25. It

up at **Oasis Burgers and Pizza** ❷, 241 El Camino Real, known as "The O." Burgers ($5.25-8) and pizza ($12-23) are served amidst tables and walls crudely carved by past patrons. (☎650-326-8896; www.theoasisbeergarden.com. Open daily 11am-2am. AmEx/D/MC/V.)

Though Palo Alto can't compete with San Francisco's wild nightlife, it still has a couple of hot spots and bars perfect for sitting back and having a few beers. There's a fiesta every day in the vibrant, super-popular **Nola,** 535 Ramona St. Colorful strings of lights and patio windows open onto a cool courtyard dining area. The late-night New Orleans-themed menu offers Cajun quesadillas ($8-10), Creole prawns ($9), and gumbo ($7) to accompany cocktails. (☎650-328-2722. Happy hour daily 4-6pm. Open M-F 11:30am-2am, Sa-Su 5:30pm-2am. Kitchen closes M-Th 10pm, F-Sa 11pm, Su 9pm. AmEx/MC/V.)

⚑ ACCOMMODATIONS. Motels are plentiful along **El Camino Real,** but rates can be steep. In general, rooms are cheaper farther away from Stanford and to the north. Many Palo Alto motels cater to business travelers and are actually busier on weekdays than on weekends. One budget option is **Hidden Villa Ranch Hostel (HI-AYH)** ❶, 26870 Moody Rd., about 10 mi. southwest of Palo Alto in the Los Altos Hills. The first hostel on the Pacific Coast (opened in 1937), it functions as a working ranch and farm in a wilderness preserve. Recent renovations have completely rebuilt the dorms and extended the living room, kitchen, and dining room. (☎650-949-8648. Reception 8am-noon and 4-9:30pm. Reservations required for weekends and groups. Open Sept.-May. Dorms $22, children $11; private cabins $40-56.) For something a little ritzier, try the **Stanford Inn** ❸, 115 El Camino Real, in Menlo Park. Full of character and charm, this yellow building dates back to 1937, when it was built as an apartment complex. (☎650-325-1428. Singles from $60; doubles from $65. AmEx/D/DC/MC/V.)

◪ APPROACHING SAN FRANCISCO: 34 MILES
Follow **U.S. 101 N** to downtown San Francisco.

SAN FRANCISCO

If California is a state of mind, then San Francisco is euphoria. Welcome to the city that will take you to new highs, leaving your mind spinning, your tastebuds tingling, and your calves aching. The dazzling views, daunting hills, one-of-a-kind neighborhoods, and laid-back, friendly people fascinate visitors. Though smaller than most "big" cities, the city manages to pack an incredible amount of vitality into its 47 sq. mi., from its thriving art communities and bustling shops to the pulsing beats in some of the country's hippest nightclubs and bars. For more coverage of the City by the Bay, see ▨*Let's Go: San Francisco.*

PAGE TURN. See p. 479 in **National Road** for complete coverage of San Francisco.

◪ APPROACHING MARIN HEADLANDS: 10 MILES
From San Francisco, follow **U.S. 101 N** across the Golden Gate Bridge. Take the first exit **(Alexander Ave.)** off 101, veer right off the ramp onto Alexander Ave. and then left on **Bunker Rd.** through a tunnel. For the most scenic drive and best view of the city, take your first left onto **McCullough Rd.** and turn right along Conzelman. For the visitors center, from Bunker Rd., take a left onto **Field Rd.**

MARIN HEADLANDS

The fog-shrouded hills just west of the Golden Gate Bridge constitute the Marin Headlands. Formerly a military installation charged with defending the San Francisco harbor, the Headlands are dotted with machine gun nests, missile sites, and soldiers' quarters dating from the Spanish-American War to the 1950s. These windswept ridges, precipitous cliffs, and hidden sandy beaches offer superb hiking and biking minutes from downtown. For more info, contact the **Marin Headlands Visitors Center,** Bldg. 948, Fort Barry. The center is also a museum and a store with artifacts. (At Bunker and Field Rd. ☎415-331-1540. Open daily 9:30am-4:30pm.) For instant gratification, drive up to any of the look-out spots and pose for your own postcard-perfect shot of the Golden Gate Bridge and the city skyline. One of the best short hikes is to the lighthouse at **Point Bonita,** a prime spot for seeing sunbathing California sea lions in summer and migrating gray whales in the cooler months. The lighthouse at the end of the point doesn't seem up to guarding the whole San Francisco Bay, but it has stood vigilant since 1855; in fact, its original glass lens is still in operation. At the end of a narrow, knife-like ridge lined with purple wildflowers, the lighthouse is reachable by a short tunnel through the rock and a miniature suspension bridge that will quicken your heart rate. Even when the lighthouse is closed, the short walk provides gorgeous views on sunny days. (No dogs or bikes through tunnel. Open M and Sa-Su 12:30-3:30pm. Guided walks M and Sa-Su 12:30pm. Free.) **Battery Spencer,** on Conzelman Rd. immediately west of U.S. 101, offers one of the best views of the city skyline and the Golden Gate Bridge, especially around sunset on the (rare) clear day. Tourists are known to wait for hours to catch a fogless shot of the Golden Gate Bridge.

To get to the **Marin Headlands Hostel (HI) ❶,** follow the signs from the visitors center. This charmingly austere hostel offers a kitchen, large common room with multiple couches, piano, fireplace and picnic tables, as well as a basement game room with pool, foosball and ping-pong tables. (☎415-331-2777; www.norcalhostels.org. Soap $0.50. Dorms $20, children $10; private rooms $60. AmEx/D/MC/V.) Accessible by car, **Kirby Cove ❶,** off Conzelman Rd. west of the Golden Gate Bridge, consists of four campsites in a grove of cypress and eucalyptus trees on the shore, with fire rings, food lockers, and pit toilets. (☎800-365-2267. Bring your own water. No pets. 3-day max. stay. Open Apr.-Nov. Sites $25. D/MC/V.)

⊼ APPROACHING SAUSALITO: 7 MILES
Sausalito is a few miles north of the Golden Gate Bridge on **U.S. 101.**

SAUSALITO

Originally a fishing center full of bars and bordellos, the city at Marin's extreme southeastern tip has long since traded its sea-dog days for retail boutiques and overpriced seafood restaurants. The palm trees and 14 ft. elephant statues of Plaza de Vina del Mar Park look out over a wonderful view of San Francisco Bay, making for a sunny, seaside tourist distraction. The sheer number and variety of quality art galleries in the small town make it worth checking out, regardless of the touristy feel. Half a mile north

of the town center is the **Bay Model and Marinship Museum,** 2100 Bridgeway, a massive working model of San Francisco Bay. Built in the 1950s to test proposals to dam the bay, the water-filled model recreates tides and currents in great detail. (☎415-332-3871. Open Tu-Sa 9am-4pm. Free.) Those tired of Rice-A-Roni should venture to the **Venice Gourmet Delicatessen ❶,** 625 Bridgeway, which serves massive sandwiches ($5-7) and side dishes ($2-5) in a Mediterranean-style marketplace; cross the street and eat by the water. (☎415-332-3544; www.venicegourmet.com. Open daily in summer 9am-7pm; in winter 9am-6pm. MC/V.)

 DID YOU KNOW? While staying on a houseboat in Sausalito, Otis Redding wrote his greatest hit, "The Dock on the Bay."

⧅ DETOUR
MUIR WOODS
5 mi. west of U.S. 101 on Rte. 1.

At the center of Mt. Tamalpais State Park is **Muir Woods National Monument,** a 560-acre stand of old coastal redwoods. Spared from logging by the steep sides of Redwood Canyon, these massive, centuries-old trees are shrouded in silence. The level, paved trails along the canyon floor are lined with wooden fences, but a hike up the canyon's sides will soon put you far from the tourists, face-to-face with nature. (☎415-388-7368. Open in summer 8am-5pm; in winter 9am-6pm. $3; under 15 free.) Avoid the fee by hiking 2 mi. from the Pantoll Ranger Station. It's also worth a detour to check out the Muir Beach Overlook.

⊼ APPROACHING STINSON BEACH: 10 MILES
Take **U.S. 101 N,** switching to **Rte. 1 N.** 3¼ mi. after the turn-off onto Rte. 1, you can choose to go to Muir Woods or Mt. Tamalpais.

STINSON BEACH. A younger, rowdier, and better-looking surfer crowd is attracted to Stinson Beach, although cold and windy conditions often leave them languishing on dry land. The Bard visits Stinson Beach from July to October during **Shakespeare at Stinson.** (☎415-868-1115; www.shakespeareatstinson.org. Tickets $25, 16 and under $18.) Bring a jacket, the town chills down after the sun sets. Turn west at the only stop sign in town to reach the **Parkside Cafe ❸**, 43 Arenal Ave., where a light interior and garden patio complement an American menu that edges towards the gourmet. Pick your favorite from the wine list to accompany your Parkside burger and applewood-smoked chicken salad. (☎415-868-1272; www.parkside-cafe.com. M Mexican night. Tu spaghetti night $7.50. W 2 soups and 2 salads $7.50. Sa live jazz. Open M-F 7:30am-4pm and 5-9:30pm, Sa-Su 8am-4pm and 5-9:30pm. MC/V.)

⚐ APPROACHING BOLINAS: 7 MILES
Continue along **Rte. 1 N** until you reach the exit for **Olema Bolinas Rd.** Travel south for a few miles to reach the city.

BOLINAS

Bolinas, a tiny colony of hippies, artists, and writers, is perhaps the most mellow place on earth—it is certainly the hardest to find. For years, locals have hoped to discourage tourist traffic by tearing down any and all signs marking the Bolinas-Olema road. Press coverage of the "sign war" won the people of Bolinas exactly the publicity they wanted to avoid, but for now, at least, the town remains unspoiled in ways that Sausalito is not—and they intend to keep it that way. But who needs signs anyway? Generations of locals walk and bike through town, mostly ignoring the tourist presence that creeps in on weekends. Restaurants and shops open and close at whim, which only exemplifies the town's laid-back attitude.

To graze while you gaze at the locals, try Northern California cuisine at **Coast Cafe ❷**, 46 Wharf Rd., open for breakfast, lunch, and dinner, but don't tell them we sent you. Try "The Unusual" (2 eggs, potatoes, biscuits and gravy; $8) if you're feeling feisty, or stick to "The Usual" (2 eggs, potatoes and meat; $8.50) if you fear change. (☎415-868-2298. Open Tu-F 11:30am-3pm and 5:30-9pm; Sa 7:30am-3pm and 5-9:30pm; Su 7:30-11:30am and 5-9pm. AmEx/D/MC/V.) At the end of Olema-Bolinas Rd. is the **Bolinas Gallery**, 52 Wharf Rd. Colorful paintings hang from the ceiling and perch on the floor. (☎415-868-0782. Open Sa-Su 1-5pm. Suggested donation.) Turn right and you can see the convergence of the lagoon and the ocean. Take the next-to-last right off Olema-Bolinas Rd. to reach **The Grand Hotel ❷**, 15 Brighton Ave., which has

two cozy rooms that share a bathroom and kitchen above a second-hand shop run by an old-timer. (☎415-868-1757. Rooms $50. MC/V.)

⚐ APPROACHING POINT REYES: 12 MILES
Follow **Rte. 1 N** for about 11 mi. Turn left onto **Bear Valley Rd.**, which leads to the Point Reyes Visitor Center. To reach Point Reyes Station, continue north on Rte. 1.

POINT REYES

A near-island surrounded by nearly 100 mi. of isolated coastline, the Point Reyes National Seashore is a wilderness of pine forests, chaparral ridges, and grassy flatlands. Five million years ago, this outcropping was a suburb of L.A., but it hitched a ride on the submerged Pacific Plate and has been creeping northward along the San Andreas Fault ever since. In summer, colorful wildflowers attract crowds of gawking tourists, but with hundreds of miles of amazing trails, it's quite possible to gawk alone.

VITAL STATS

Population: 350

Visitor Info: Point Reyes National Seashore Headquarters (also referred to as Bear Valley Visitor Center; ☎415-464-5100; www.nps.gov/pore), on Bear Valley Rd., ½ mi. west of Olema. Open M-F 9am-5pm, Sa-Su and holidays 8am-5pm.

Internet Access: Point Reyes Station Library, 11431 Rte. 1 (☎415-663-8375). Open M 10am-6pm, Tu and Th 2-9pm, F-Sa 10am-2pm. Free.

Post Office: 10155 Rte. 1 (☎415-663-1761), in Olema. Open M-F 8:15am-1pm and 1:30-4:15pm. **Postal Code:** 94950.

◗ SIGHTS. Before you do anything, make sure you've picked up a map from the visitors center. The **Earthquake Trail** is a paved half-mile walk along the infamous San Andreas Fault Line that starts right at Bear Valley. Lovely **Limantour Beach** sits at the end of Limantour Rd., 8 mi. west of the park headquarters. Both Limantour and Point Reyes Beaches have high, grassy dunes and long stretches of sand, but strong ocean currents along the point make swimming very dangerous. Swimming is safest at **Hearts Desire Beach**, north of the visitors center on sheltered **Tomales Bay** at **Tomales Bay State Park.** (Open daily 8am-8pm. No dogs. Day use $6 per vehicle.) To reach the dramatic **Point Reyes Lighthouse** at the very tip of the point, follow Sir Francis Drake Blvd. to its end (20 mi. from the visitors center) and head right along the stairway to Sea Lion Overlook. From December until February, migrating gray whales can be spotted from the overlook. (☎415-669-1534. Open M and Th-Su 10am-4:30pm.) To hike from the Coast Trail to **Bass Lake Swimming Hole,** take the unmarked Olema-Bolinas Rd. 2½ mi. north of Stinson. Take a left at the fork and then a right onto Mesa Rd., which will curve around for several miles past the bird observatory to the Palomarin trailhead. The hike will take you along the Pacific into the rocky cliffs, through trees, and finally to a secret swimming spot. Bring a picnic and take a dip, with or without a suit. To reach **Goat Rock Beach,** 2 mi. south of the Russian River, turn west for Goat Rock Beach where late May to early September you can see newborn baby seals; harbor seals and elephant seals are currently in a silent war over the territory.

🍴 FOOD AND ACCOMMODATIONS.
Across the street from an ATM in the town of Point Reyes, **Bovine Bakery ❶**, 11315 Rte. 1, proffers caffeinated drinks and vegan-friendly gooey treats like the morning bun ($2.50). Sandwiches are $6 when fresh (Tu and F) and $4.25 other days. (☎415-663-9420. Open M-F 6:30am-5pm, Sa-Su 7am-5pm. Cash only.) A popular area favorite, **The Station House Café ❹**, 11180 State Rte. 1, serves classic American food. The heavenly bread pudding costs $7. (☎415-663-1515. Open M-Tu, Th, and Su 8am-9pm, F-Sa 8am-10pm. AmEx/MC/V.)

The 📷**Point Reyes Hostel (HI-AYH) ❶** is just off Limatour Rd., 2 mi. from Limatour Beach. Miles from civilization, this excellent hostel provides shelter in the wilderness. The surrounding landscape is still scarred by a major forest fire that torched the region in 1995. (☎415-663-8811; www.norcalhostels.org. Linen $1; sleeping bags encouraged. Towels $1. Check-in 4:30-9:30pm. Check-out 10am. Lockout 10am-4:30pm. Dorms $18, under 17 $10. MC/V.) Camping sites are scattered throughout the park and are by permit only. **Sky Camp ❶**, has 12 sites with views of Drakes Bay, is on the western side of M. Wittenberg. 1.5mi. walk from Sky Trailhead, Limantour Rd. **Wildcat Camp ❶** has 7 sites with ocean views, 6 mi. from the Coast Trail. (☎415-663-8054. Picnic tables, charcoal grills, pit toilets, and food lockers. Bring water. Sites $15-30. AmEx/D/MC/V.)

🚗 APPROACHING VALLEY FORD: 23 MILES
Follow **Rte. 1/Shoreline Hwy.** for about 32 mi.

VALLEY FORD. The only reason to stop in Valley Ford is to go to 📷**Dinucci's Italian Dinners ❹**, 14485 Valley Ford Rd., an old-school, family-oriented and totally unpretentious restaurant with brown-checkered cloths on the table. Don't expect any delicate olive oil on the table here. Hearty five-course meals of spaghetti, lasagna, or ravioli come with anti-

WINE TASTING 101

While European wines are often known by their region of origin, California wines are generally known by the type of grape from which they are made. California white wines include Chardonnay, Riesling, and Sauvignon Blanc; reds include Pinot Noir, Merlot, Cabernet Sauvignon, and Zinfandel, which is indigenous to California. Blush or rosé wines come from red grapes that have their skins removed during fermentation, leaving just a kiss of pink. Dessert wines, such as Muscat, are made with grapes that have acquired the "noble rot" (botrytis) at the end of picking season, giving them an extra sweet flavor. When tasting, be sure to follow the proper procedure. Always start with a white, moving from dry to sweet. Proceed through the reds, which range from lighter to more full-bodied, depending on tannin content. Ideally, you should cleanse your palate between wines with a biscuit, some *fromage*, or fruit.

Tasting proceeds thus: stare, sniff, swirl, swallow. You will probably encounter tasters who slurp their wine and make concerned faces. These are serious tasters who are aerating the wine into their mouths to better bring out the flavor. Key words to help you seem more astute during tasting sessions are: dry, sweet, buttery, light, crisp, fruity, balanced, rounded, subtle, rich, woody, and complex.

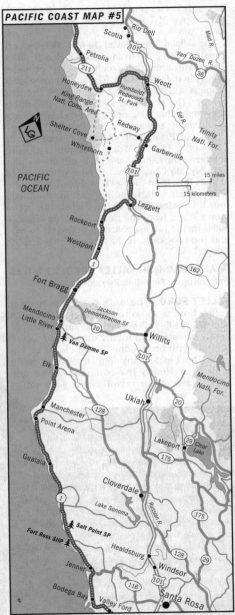

PACIFIC COAST MAP #5

pasto, fabulous minestrone, a starch (baked potato, rice pilaf, or french fries) side, and salad all from $14.75. Top it off with apple pie for $3.75. (☎707-876-3260. Open M and Th-Sa from 4pm, Su from noon. AmEx/D/MC/V.)

⚑ APPROACHING BODEGA BAY: 9 MILES
Continue on **Rte. 1/Shoreline Hwy.** to Bodega Bay.

BODEGA BAY

The small town of Bodega Bay displays its seafaring roots in the incredibly fresh salmon and crab at oceanside restaurants. Both the towns of Bodega Bay and Bodega, 1½ mi. away, were featured in Alfred Hitchcock's 1963 film *The Birds*. The **Bodega Bay Visitors Center**, 850 Rte. 1, has info on the North Coast. (☎707-875-3866; www.bodegabay.com. Open M-Th and Sa 9am-5pm, F 9am-6pm, Su 10am-5pm.) On the Sonoma coast, west of Bodega Bay, the **Bodega Head Loop** is a short coastal hike with pristine beach and ocean views. To reach the 1½ mi. trail from the town, turn left on E. Shore Rd., turn west on Bay Flat Rd., and continue around the bay past Spud Point Marina to Bodega Head parking for the trailhead. **Sonoma Coast State Beach** begins just north of Bodega Bay off Rte. 1. Unfortunately, unpredictable currents make the water unsafe (see Sleeper Waves; p. 955) for swimming. The 5000 acres of land offer 16 mi. of beautiful beach, spectacular views, and places to picnic, hike, and camp. One popular coastal campground is **Bodega Dunes ❶**. (☎707-875-3483. Hot showers. Sites $25. Cash only.) Another very popular site is **Wright's Beach ❶**. (☎707-875-3483. Sites $25. Cash only.) Call ReserveAmerica for reservations at ☎800-444-7275. If the campsites are full, the clean rooms at **Bodega Harbor Inn ❸**, 1345 Bodega Ave., off Rte. 1 in Bodega Bay, are your cheapest bet. (☎707-875-3594; www.bodegaharborinn.com. Rooms $65-95. MC/V.)

⚑ APPROACHING JENNER: 11 MILES
From Bodega, follow **Rte. 1 N** for 53 mi. and then turn right onto **Old State Hwy.**

JENNER. Heading north from Bodega Bay, Rte. 1 hits **Jenner** at the mouth of the Russian River. **Goat Rock Beach,** with its astounding waves and coast, is the site of a famous harbor seal rookery. **Reef Campground ❶**, 10 mi. north of Jenner, is part of **Fort Ross State Historic Park**

and provides 20 sites in a wooded gulch, a 5min. walk from a rocky secluded beach. (☎707-847-3286. No showers. Sites $15. Cash only.) **Salt Point State Park**, 20 mi. north of Jenner, is a 6000-acre park for the hiker or horseback rider with an inland campsite surrounded by woods, **Woodside Creek ❶**, and a coastal campground, **Gerstle Cove ❶**, on a bluff among scattered pines overlooking the sea. The Cove is a good spot for mushroom gathering (5 lb. per day) and abalone diving. (☎707-847-3221, reservations 800-444-7275. No showers. Drinking water and toilets. Open for day use sunrise-sunset. Sites $15-25. Day-use $6. Cash only.)

☒ APPROACHING GUALALA: 38 MILES
From Jenner, follow **Rte. 1** for 37 mi. and then turn right onto **Old State Hwy.**

GUALALA. Pass by Gualala if you can, but if you must stay, try **Gualala Hotel ❸**. The hotel has served as the central establishment in town for over 100 years, and recent, if incomplete, renovations have improved the once outdated rooms. Rooms lack TVs and phones, but some joint bathrooms have old-fashioned tubs. Downstairs is a good restaurant and **saloon** with pool tables and darts, pretty much the only nightlife around. (☎707-884-3441; www.thegualalahotel.com. Rooms M-F $50-70; Sa-Su $70-100. AmEx/MC/V.) Stop in at **Bones Roadhouse ❸**, 38920 S. Hwy 1, where you can dine on barbecue oysters amid roadtripping memorabilia. The food has a southwestern flair, but the Big Johnson (kielbasa sausage with mustard and relish; $9) will satisfy those looking for something simple. (☎707-884-1188. Open daily 11am-9pm. MC/V.)

☒ APPROACHING POINT ARENA: 14 MILES
Turn right onto **Rte. 1/Shoreline Hwy.** and continue for 14 mi.

POINT ARENA
Point Arena's center attraction is the **Point Arena Lighthouse**, 2 mi. north of town. The 115 ft. lighthouse, the tallest one accessible to the public in America, is vintage, built after the San Francisco earthquake demolished the 1870 original. Although no longer in commission, it contains a Fresnel lens, an intricate array of prisms and magnifying glass worth $3.5 million—an optician's paradise. The downstairs exhibit

includes a whale-watching information room. (☎707-882-2777; www.pointarenalighthouse.com. Open daily in summer 10am-4:30pm; in winter 10am-3pm. $5, under 12 $1.) **CityArt**, 284 Main St., is a nonprofit community arts gallery in the former home of a teacher who murdered her lover. It shows changing exhibits of local artists and hosts a poetry reading the third Thursday of every month. (☎707-882-3616; www.cityart.ws. Open Th-Su noon-4pm.) Surfers like swells at **the cove** (take the coastal access sign from Rte. 1) although there's not much to speak of in terms of beauty.

■**The Record ❷**, a cafe and natural gourmet market, is the best place to meet the town locals—mostly artists whose work decorates the walls. The chicken pesto sandwich ($8.50) is particularly good. (☎707-882-3663. Sandwiches $3.50-9. Open in summer M-Sa 7am-8pm, Su 9am-5pm; in winter M-Sa 7am-7pm, Su 8am-6pm. MC/V.) All organic, high-quality Mexican fare awaits at **El Burrito ❷**, 165 Main St. Their commitment to organic ingredients make them a true NorCal establishment and a borderline nonprofit. (☎707-882-2910. Burritos $5.75-7.50. Quesadillas $4.50-5.50. Open daily 11:30am-7pm. AmEx/MC/V.)

☒ APPROACHING ELK: 19 MILES
Take **Rte. 1** toward Elk.

ELK. Fans of Jack London should stop in Elk, where the famed author often stayed to write in a hotel room overlooking the ocean. The town is little more than a charming rest stop with a quaint inn and a few walking trails. Poor drainage, thin soil, and ocean winds have created an unusual bonsai garden 3 mi. south of Mendocino at the **Pygmy Forest** in **Van Damme State Park ❶**. The forest, off Rte. 1 past the park, is free to hikers. Take the 3½ mi. Fern Canyon Trail to see the Bonsai trees. (Sites $25. Day-use $6. Cash only.)

☒ APPROACHING MENDOCINO: 17 MILES
To enter Mendocino from **Rte. 1**, turn left onto **Little Lake Rd.**

MENDOCINO
Teetering on bluffs over the ocean, isolated Mendocino is a charming coastal community of art galleries, craft shops, bakeries, and B&Bs. The town's weathered shingles, white picket

fences, and clustered homes seem out of place on the West Coast; maybe that's why Mendocino was able to masquerade for years as the fictional Maine village of Cabot Cove in the TV series *Murder, She Wrote.*

VITAL STATS

Population: 1107

Visitor Info: Mendocino Headlands State Park Visitor Center, 735 Main St., at the Ford House. Open daily 11am-4pm.

Internet Access: Regional Branch Library of Mendocino, 499 Laurel St. (☎707-964-2020), in Fort Bragg. Open Tu-W 11am-7:45pm, Th-F 11am-5:45pm, Sa 10am-4:45pm. Free.

Post Office: 10500 Ford St. (☎707-937-5282). Open M-F 7:30am-4:30pm. **Postal Code:** 95460.

◪ GETTING AROUND. Mendocino sits on **Rte. 1,** right on the Pacific Coast, 30 mi. west of U.S. 101 and 12 mi. south of Fort Bragg. Once in Mendocino, exploring is best done on foot.

◪ SIGHTS. Mendocino's greatest natural feature lies 900 ft. to its west, where the earth comes to a halt and falls off into the Pacific, forming the impressive coastline of the ◪**Mendocino Headlands.** The windy quarter-mile stretch of land that separates the town from the rocky shore remains an undeveloped meadow of tall grass and wildflowers, despite its obvious value as a site for multi-million dollar vacation homes. The ecological staircase at **Jug Handle State Park,** 5 mi. north of town, is a terrace of five different ecosystems formed by a combination of erosion and tectonic uplift, with each ecosystem roughly 100,000 years older than the one below it. An abundance of hot springs in the Mendocino area proves once again that the region is a natural paradise. **Orr Hot Springs,** 13201 Orr Springs Rd., is an hour's drive east of Mendocino, in Ukiah, off U.S. 101. Sauna, steam room, and gardens make the world disappear at this clothing-optional resort. (☎707-462-6277. 18+ or accompanied by an adult. Open daily 10am-10pm. $25.) In July, enjoy the **Mendocino Music Festival,** a two-week melee of classical music, opera, and cultural dance. Tickets for some events go quickly. (☎707-937-4041; www.mendocinomusic.com. Tickets $15-40.)

◪◪ FOOD AND ACCOMMODATIONS. All of Mendocino's breads are freshly baked, all vegetables locally grown, all wheat unmilled, and almost all prices inflated. A trip to **Harvest at Mendosa's Market,** 10501 Lansing St., the closest thing in Mendocino, is a must before any picnic on the Mendocino Headlands. (☎707-937-5879. Open daily 7:30am-10pm.) **Moody's Cafe ❶,** 10450 Lansing, has a modern vibe. With free Wi-Fi, an adjoining Internet cafe ($6 per hr.), and tasty treats like Spiced apple cider and cookies. (☎707-37-4843. Open daily 5am-9:30pm. D/MC/V.) **Tote Fête ❶,** 10450 Lansing St., has delicious tote-out food. An asiago cheese, pesto, and artichoke heart sandwich ($4.75) hits the spot. (☎707-937-3383. Open M-F 8am-7pm, Sa 8am-8pm, Su 8am-6pm. MC/V.) **Lu's Kitchen ❷,** 45013 Ukiah St., west of Lansing St., is a local favorite. With leafy vegetarian cuisine, students get a break here; ask for the Mendo student burrito for $5. (☎707-937-4939. Entrees $6-10. Open W-Su 11:30am-5pm; closed Jan.-Mar. and on very rainy days. Cash or check only.)

If you're arriving after 10pm you can crash in the "late night" room at the ◪**Sweetwater Spa & Inn ❹,** 44840 Main St. where you'll get free exclusive use of the hot tub and sauna all night. The owner is unopposed to haggling. (☎707-937-4076 or 800-300-4140. Rooms from $60. MC/V.) **Medocino Hotel ❹,** 45080 Main St., is luxurious to say the least. Relax by the fireside in their sitting room, where newspapers and Wi-Fi are available. (☎707-937-0511. Rooms from $85. AmEx/MC/V.) The **Jug Handle Creek Farm ❷,** 5 mi. north of Mendocino off Rte. 1, across the street from the Jug Handle State Reserve, is a beautiful 133-year-old house on 40 acres of gardens. One hour of chores or $5 is required per night. (☎707-964-4630. Reservations recommended in summer. Sites $12, students $10, children $5; private rooms $30/$23/$10; cabins $38/$30/$13.)

◪ APPROACHING FORT BRAGG: 10 MILES Continue on **Rte. 1 N/Shoreline Hwy.** for 10 mi. Turn right onto **E. Laurel St.** to reach the town center.

FORT BRAGG

Fort Bragg is a little rougher around the edges than its genteel sibling Mendocino. The town's major industry, the lumber mill, was shut down in August 2002 and the town now relies on tourism, as well as smaller fishing and logging operations.

VITAL STATS

Population: 6963

Visitor Info: Fort-Bragg-Mendocino Coast Chamber of Commerce, 332 N. Main St. (☎707-961-6300). Open M-F 9am-5pm.

Internet Access: Regional Branch Library of Mendocino, 499 Laurel St. (☎707-964-2020). Open Tu and Th 10am-6pm, W noon-8pm, F-Sa 10am-5pm. Free.

Post Office: 203 N. Franklin St. (☎717-964-2302). Open M-F 8:30am-5pm. **Postal Code:** 95437.

◨ **SIGHTS.** There are only 6 tattoo museums in the world, and Fort Bragg has one of them. **Triangle Tattoo and Museum,** 356 B North Main St., in downtown, functions as a tattoo parlor and museum. Founded by the infamous Madame Chinchilla and Mr. G, the museum displays multicultural tattoo art from around the world. If you have an old tattoo, let them know; they document tattoos inked between 1920-1960. (☎707-964-8814. Open daily noon-6pm.) The much-lauded **North Coast Brewing Company,** 44 N. Main St., makes 11 of their own brews on the block. The excellent ▧**Old Rasputin** (8.6% alcohol) or Old Stock (a whopping 13% alcohol) will get you tipsy faster than you can destabilize czarist Russia—at the bar they'll only serve you two. The food is good too, with salad and burger lunch options ($9-11) and New American pasta, seafood and the like for dinner ($11-18). Across the street you can peek in at the enormous brewing vats behind the store or take a free tour. (☎707-964-3400; www.northcoastbrewing.com. Open daily noon-4pm and 5-9:30pm; F-Sa until 10:30pm. Tours Sa 12:30pm.) The California Western Railroad, also called the **Skunk Train,** at Rte. 1 and Laurel St., has offered a jolly, child-friendly diversion through its Redwood Route since 1885. A steam engine, diesel locomotive, and vintage motorcar take turns running between Fort Bragg and Northspur. (☎707-964-6371 or 800-45-SKUNK; www.skunktrain.com. 3hr. round-trip. Reservations recommended. Departs Fort Bragg daily 10am and 3:30pm. 10am train $45, child $20; 3:30pm train $65/$35.)

▚▟ **FOOD AND ACCOMMODATIONS. Eggheads** ❸, 326 Main St., offers omelettes ($6.50-12.75) stuffed with ingredients like cheese, bacon, and Dungeness crab, along with other cheery diner favorites. (☎707-964-5005. Open M-

Tu and Th-Su 7am-2pm. AmEx/MC/V.) The most budget-friendly option for lodgings is **Colombi Motel** ❷, 647 Oak St., five blocks east of Main St. It has clean single and double units with cable TV, phone, and private bath; some units also have a full kitchen. (☎707-964-5773. (☎707-964-2020)Check-out 11am. Singles $45; doubles $55. MC/V.) **MacKerricher State Park campground** ❶, 2½ mi. north of Fort Bragg, has excellent views of tidepool life, passing seals, sea lions, and migratory whales, as well as 9 mi. of beaches and a murky lake for trout fishing. Around this lake is Lake Cleone Trail, an easy, 1 mi. hike that features thick cypress trees and a pretty marsh. Access the trail from Cleone Camp or Surfwood Camp. (☎707-937-5804. Showers, bathrooms, and potable water. Reservations necessary in summer. Sites $25. Cash only.)

▦ **APPROACHING WESTPORT: 16 MILES**
Continue on **Rte. 1/Shoreline Hwy.** for about 16 mi.

WESTPORT. Blink and you'll miss Westport, a town with only a general store (gas available) and a couple of inns. Despite its size, however, it still manages to display a lot of tie-dye. If this kind of seclusion appeals to you, try the lovely **De Haven Valley Farm** ❺, housed in an 1875 Victorian ranch house, 1¾ mi. north of town on Rte. 1. The owners plan on turning the old barn into an artists' co-operative. (☎707-961-1660; www.dehaven-valley-farm.com. Rooms $100-150.)

▦ **APPROACHING GARBERVILLE: 51 MILES**
The **PCH** north of Westport becomes exceedingly curvy and therefore slow. North of **Rockport** it turns inland to **Leggett;** there is no possible way to continue along the coast here. Road-builders decided to circumvent the formidable King Range, abandoning this portion of land, the mysterious **Lost Coast** to, as it turns out, the wiles of marijuana farmers. Where Rte. 1 turns inland and snakes around the Lost Coast, stay on smoothly paved, speedy **U.S. 101** toward Garberville and the Avenue of the Giants for some of the most beautiful redwoods in the world.

GARBERVILLE. Garberville is a good jumping-off point for Humboldt State Park. The **Garberville-Redway Chamber of Commerce,** 728 Main St. in the Redwood Drive Center, offers information on local events and attractions. (☎707-923-2613. Open M-F 10am-5pm.) **Sentry**

PACIFIC COAST MAP #6

Market, on Redwood Dr., is the largest supermarket for miles. (☎707-923-2279. Open daily 7am-10pm.) Locals highly recommend **Calico's Cafe ❷,** on Redwood Dr. next to Sherwood Forest Motel, for its homemade pastas, salads, and burgers as well. Try the garlicky fettuccine gorgonzola ($10) made from scratch. (☎707-923-2253. Open M-Th 8am-9pm, F-Sa 8am-10pm, Su 11am-9pm. Cash only.) **Organic Bagelry ❶,** on Redwood Dr. after Sprowl Creek Rd. is an healthful smoothie and sandwich shop. A liquid rainbow smoothie (kiwi, blueberry, strawberry, banana, apple juice, and spirulina $4.25) or the S Hum Builder, a make your own bagel sandwich (starting from $5.50; depends on ingredients), makes for terrific roadside eats. (☎707-923-2939. Open in summer daily 7am-5pm; in winter M-Sa 7am-5pm. Cash only.)

⚐ APPROACHING HUMBOLDT REDWOODS STATE PARK: 35 MILES

Take **U.S. 101 N** for 24 mi. Take the ramp to **South Fork/Honeydew,** then quickly make a left onto **Rte. 254/Redwood Hwy./Avenue of the Giants.** Turn left onto **Mattole Rd.** and continue on Mattole Rd. to reach the park.

HUMBOLDT REDWOODS STATE PARK

About 24 mi. north of Garberville on U.S. 101 in the **Humboldt Redwoods State Park**, the Avenue of the Giants (the actual name of the road) splits off the highway and winds its way through 31 mi. of redwoods, the world's largest living organisms above ground level. Hiking, swimming, fishing, biking, and rafting opportunities abound in this rugged area. Garberville is the main town along the Avenue and is connected to its smaller neighbor, Redway, by Redwood Dr., the main street in both towns. Moving north up the Avenue, drivers encounter the tiny towns of Phillipsville, Miranda, Myers Flat, Weott, Redcrest, and Pepperwood.

The **Humboldt Redwoods State Park Visitors Center,** just south of Weott on the Avenue of the Giants, has a very knowledgeable staff that can direct you to the Avenue's groves, facilities and trails, while providing safety tips on camping. (☎707-946-2263. Open Apr.-Oct. daily 9am-5pm; Oct.-Apr. Th-Su 10am-4pm.) Each developed campsite offers coin-op showers, flush toilets, and fire rings. (☎707-946-2409. Sites $15.) The wildlife-filled **Albee Creek ❶**, on Mattole Rd. 5 mi. west of U.S. 101, near Rockefeller Forest, has access to biking and hiking trails and is open year-round. (☎707-946-2409. Sites $20. Cash only.) **Hidden Springs ❶**, near Myers Flat, is situated on a hillside in a mixed forest and has 154 semi-secluded sites with hot showers. Few hiking trails start directly at the campsite, but the South Fork of Eel River is a 10min. hike away. (707-943-3177. Open mid-May to mid-Oct. Sites $20. Cash only.)

 APPROACHING PETROLIA: 35 MILES
Continue on **Mattole Rd.** toward Petrolia.

PETROLIA. Named for being the site of the first oil drilling in California, Petrolia is now one of the few town outposts for the farm-dwellers of the region. Stop for a bite at the cosy, authentic Petrolia General Store. After Petrolia, the road passes by a stretch of the coast which is made all the sweeter by its remoteness. Chances are you'll be one of the few cars on this beautiful outpost, with only the wildflowers, dark sea rocks, and grazing cows for company.

> **❗ SLEEPER WAVES.**
> Sleeper waves are overpowering waves that crash ashore and then forcefully pull back whatever or whomever they happen upon. Many beaches have posted warnings about such dangerous currents, and it is safest to simply stay out of treacherous waters. However, if a sleeper wave yanks you into the surf, do not swim toward shore. Doing so will only tire you out in a futile battle against the current. Instead, swim parallel to the beach until you're out of the wave's clutches.

 APPROACHING FERNDALE: 30 MILES
From Petrolia, follow **Mattole Rd. (Rte. 211)** to reach Ferndale.

FERNDALE

The northernmost Lost Coast town of Ferndale exemplifies small-town perfection. The amphitheater-like cemeteries near **Russ Park** on Ocean Ave. give a sense of the town's history and provide a breathtaking view of the Victorian town with its grazing dairy cattle. The entire village is

a designated State Historical Landmark and as a result, there's not a franchise in sight, and the atmosphere is honest enough to allow for an unattended jam shop, **Jackie Jett Jam,** with a box for payments. The jams ($6) are delicious, too!

One of the area's oddest features, the annual Arcata Kinetic Sculpture Race (p. 957), ends at the studio of the event's founder, **Hobart Galleries**, 393 Main St., at Brown St. (☎707-786-9259. Call for hours. Donation suggested $1). See kooky contraptions from past races in the form of a raccoon, dragon, bumblebee, flying saucer, and purple crayon at the **Ferndale Kinetic Sculpture Museum,** inside the **Arts and Cultural Center,** 580 Main St., at Shaw Ave. (☎707-786-9634. Open daily 10am-5pm.) The **Ferndale Museum,** on Shaw Ave., around the corner from Main St., is worth a stop for its exhibits on local history. (☎707-786-4466. Open W-Sa 11am-4pm, Su 1-4pm. $1.) **Ferndale Repertory Theatre,** on Main St., hosts live productions and an art gallery showcasing local work. (☎707-786-5483. Performances F-Sa 2 and 8pm. Tickets $15.)

The Wild Blackberry Cafe ❶, 468 Main St., is worth a stop off the highway. Try the grilled goat cheese and caramelized onions ($5.75) and top it off with a sticky cinnamon roll for $3. (☎707-786-9440. Open M and W-Su 11am-4pm. MC/V.) The accommodations in Ferndale are mostly exorbitantly priced B&Bs, but if you have been saving for a splurge, this is the time. One option is California's oldest B&B, the **Shaw House ❺**, 703 Main St. Founded in 1860, the Carpenter Gothic Revival-style home has seven opulent rooms, a sit-down hot breakfast, and afternoon tea. (☎707-786-9958; www.shawhouse.com. Check-in 4-6pm. Check-out 11am. Rooms in summer $115-275; in winter $95-255. MC/V.) For a slightly cheaper rest, the **Francis Creek Inn ❹**, 577 Main St., offers simple rooms at the edge of downtown. (☎707-786-9611. Rooms $73-83. MC/V.)

> **DID YOU KNOW?** The films *The Majestic* and *Outbreak* were filmed in Ferndale.

 APPROACHING EUREKA: 20 MILES
Follow **Rte. 211** out of Ferndale, then merge onto **U.S. 101 N,** and continue to Eureka.

EUREKA

Eureka was born out of the demands of mid-19th-century gold prospectors who wanted a more convenient alternative to the tedious overland route from Sacramento. Humboldt Bay provided a landing spot, and Eureka was founded as its port. Its rugged beginnings formed a town less appealing than its neighbors to the north, but Old Town Eureka is regaining some of its historic attraction. Next to the harbor are quaint shops, restaurants, and art galleries in old Victorian-style buildings. Don't judge Eureka only by driving through; the city's perimeter may reek of fish matter, but the city center has a pleasant, old-time charm.

VITAL STATS

Population: 28,606

Visitor Info: Eureka/Humboldt Visitors Bureau, 1034 2nd St. (☎707-443-5097 or 800-346-3482). Open M-F 9am-5pm.

Internet Access: Eureka Public Library, 202 S. Main St. (☎309-467-2922). Open M-Tu and Th 10am-8pm, W and F 10am-6pm. Free.

Post Office: 337 W. Clark St. (☎707-442-1768), near Broadway St. Open M-F 8:30am-5pm, Sa noon-3pm. **Postal Code:** 95501.

▛ GETTING AROUND. Eureka straddles **U.S. 101,** 7 mi. south of Arcata and 280 mi. north of San Francisco. To the south, U.S. 101 is referred to as **Broadway.** In town, U.S. 101 is called **4th St.** (heading south) and **5th St.** (heading north).

▣ SIGHTS. Eureka is very proud of its bevy of restored Victorian homes, a few of which are worth driving past. Some of the more handsome houses are now expensive B&Bs. If you drive by, don't miss the much-photographed, dramatically stark **Carson Mansion,** 143 M St., which belonged to a prominent logger in the 1850s. Art galleries, Eureka's main claim to fame, cluster downtown. Ask at the visitors center for information on specific exhibits around town. Check out **First Street Gallery,** 422 1st St., which features cultural and educational exhibits. Rotating shows go up every four to six weeks, so it's best to call ahead. (☎707-443-6363. Open Tu-Su noon-5pm. Free.) The **Morris Graves Museum of Art,** 636 F St., has musical performances and a sculpture garden. (☎707-442-0278. Open Th-Su noon-5pm. Donations accepted.) **The Ink People Gallery,** 411 12th St., is also worth a visit. (☎707-442-8413. Open Tu-Sa 11am-4pm.)

▛▟ FOOD AND ACCOMMODATIONS. **Ramone's Bakery and Cafe ❶,** 209 E St., between 2nd and 3rd St., specializes in homemade truffles, fresh-baked pies, and the ever-popular "Chocolate Sin"—a chocolate and liqueur torte. Sandwiches ($5.25), soups ($2.50), and salads ($3.50) are also available. (☎707-445-2923. Open M-W and Sa 7am-6pm, Th 7am-7pm, Su 8am-4pm. AmEx/D/DC/MC/V.) **Half Empty ❷,** 525 2nd St., is located in the historic Vance Hotel. Munch on a roasted zucchini panini ($7) or sip on caramel apple cider ($2.25) or hot chocolate ($2) next to an old-fashioned brass elevator. (☎707-445-5887. Open M-Th 7am-6pm, F-Sa 7am-9pm. MC/V.) Another notable choice is **Los Bagels ❶,** 403 2nd St., a vibrant spot that combines Mexican and Jewish baking traditions with tasty results. (☎707-442-8525. Open M-F 6:30am-5pm, Sa 7am-5pm, Su 7am-4pm. MC/V.) **Cafe Marina ❸,** 601 Startare Dr., is off U.S. 101 at the Samoa Bridge Exit (Rte. 255). From there, take the Woodley Island exit north of town. Outdoor dining is the perfect way to enjoy their fresh seafood, like the spicy blackened snapper ($13). The polished bar is a popular night spot for local fishermen. (☎707-443-2233. Sandwiches $6-13. Entrees $10-16. Open daily in summer 7am-10pm; in winter 7am-9pm. AmEx/D/MC/V.)

Travelers will find many budget motels off U.S. 101, but most are unappealing, so be selective. Walking around alone at night, especially along Broadway, is not recommended. **Motel 6 ❸,** 1934 Broadway, lies south of town off U.S. 101 and offers satellite TV with standard amenities. (☎707-445-9631. Singles $47; doubles $53. Rates vary July-Aug. AmEx/D/DC/MC/V.) **Big Lagoon County Park ❶,** 20 mi. north of Eureka on U.S. 101, is a favorite. The park has 25 sites with flush toilets, drinking water, and a big lagoon for swimming, canoeing, and kayaking. Arrive early to beat the rush. (☎707-445-7652. No hookups. Sites $14. Day-use $2. Cash only.)

◪ DETOUR
SAMOA

From U.S. 101, take Rte. 255 over the Samoa Bridge, turn left on Samoa Blvd., then take the 1st left on Cookhouse Rd.

Built in 1893 to feed the lumberjacks of the mill company that owned the town, the **Samoa Cookhouse** ❸ opened to the public in the 60s. It remains a great place to roll up your sleeves and pack down some solid food. One set meal (no menu) is served for breakfast (7-11am; $10), lunch (11am-3:30pm; $11), and dinner (5-9pm; $14). At oil cloths on picnic-style tables, people enjoy the likes of pot roast and baked ham. Seconds are served for free. The building also houses a logging exhibit. (☎707-442-1659; www.humboldtdining.com/cookhouse. AmEx/D/MC/V.) The **dunes recreation area,** in Samoa off Rte. 255 (past the cookhouse and left at the Samoa Bridge, on the north end by the jetty), was once a thriving dune ecosystem. Now, this peninsula offers beach access and dune hiking.

⛟ APPROACHING ARCATA: 8 MILES
Follow **U.S. 101 N,** and take the **Rte. 255/Samora Blvd. exit** toward Arcata.

ARCATA

Arcata (ar-KAY-ta) is like a transplanted slice of Berkeley in a remote northern corner of California. At the intersection of U.S. 101 and Rte. 299, Arcata typifies the laid-back existence that characterizes the state's northern coast. Check out the town's many murals, Victorian homes, and characters living "alternative" lifestyles. Arcata's neighbor, Humboldt State University, focuses on forestry and marine biology (Earth First! was founded here). All over Humboldt County, students get baked in the sun—and on the county's number-one cash crop.

VITAL STATS

Population: 15,700
Visitor Info: Arcata Chamber of Commerce, 1635 Heindon Rd. (☎707-822-3619). Open daily 9am-5pm.
Internet Access: Humboldt County Library, Arcata Branch, 500 7th St. (☎707-822-5954). Open Tu and F noon-5pm, W and Sa 10am-5pm, Th noon-8pm. Free.
Post Office: 799 H St. (☎707-822-3370). Open M-F 8:30am-5pm. **Postal Code:** 95521.

◪ SIGHTS. Experience Arcata by taking a short stroll around the **Arcata Plaza,** in the center of town near the intersection of 8th and H St. The plaza hosts folk music on the weekends and is a great place for people watching. The **Natural History Museum,** at 13th and G St., a brief walk from the plaza, is home to a modest collection of prehistoric fossils and whale skulls. (☎707-826-4479. Open Tu-Sa 10am-5pm. Suggested donation $3.) Nearby **Redwood Park,** at 14th and Union St., contains lots of nooks for picnicking among giant trees. Behind the park lies **Arcata Community Forest,** which has picnic spaces, meadows, redwoods, and hiking trails. A former "sanitary" landfill, the 307 acre **Arcata Marsh and Wildlife Sanctuary** lies at the foot of I St., across from Samoa Blvd. Visitors can wander around the lake or take a tour to see how this saltwater marsh/converted sewer system treats waste. The **Sanctuary Trail** (2 mi., 1hr.), along Humboldt Bay, offers great bird-watching opportunities. (☎707-826-2359. Tours Sa 8:30am, 2pm. Open daily 9am-5pm.) The 36-year-old **◪Kinetic Sculpture Race,** held annually over Memorial Day weekend, is Humboldt County's oddest festival. A few dozen insane and artsy adventurers attempt to pilot homemade vehicles (like the squash-shaped "Gourd of the Rings") on a grueling three-day, 42 mi. trek from Arcata to Ferndale over road, sand, and water. Vehicles from previous competitions are on display in Ferndale (p. 955).

◪⛟ FOOD AND ACCOMMODATIONS. A **farmers market,** offering tie-dyed dresses, candles, and the usual fresh produce, livens up the Arcata Plaza (Apr.-Nov. Sa 9am-2pm). **◪Live From New York Pizza ❶,** 670 9th St., has pies to die for. Cheese is a well-spent $2, but try something more exciting, like the Godfather, with ricotta, fresh tomatoes, sun-dried tomatoes, pesto, and mozzarella. (☎707-822-6199. Open M-Th and Su 11am-9pm, F-Sa 11:30am-10pm. MC/V.) **Tomo's ❸,** 708 9th St., offers fresh and affordable sushi, with the occasional jazz accompaniment. Seek out the specials or any of the mango rolls. (☎707-822-1414. Open M-Sa 11:30am-2pm, Su 5pm-last customer. MC/V.) A popular breakfast venue, **Golden Harvest Cafe ❷,** 1062 G St., has menu options for vegetarians and vegans, like the California Cristo sandwich ($10), a grilled French toast sandwich. (☎707-822-8962. Entrees $4-10. Open M-F 6:30am-3pm, Sa-Su 7:30am-3pm. MC/V.) **Crosswinds ❷,** 860

10th St., offers a number of hearty breakfast and lunch options in a beautifully restored Victorian home. (☎707-826-2133. Lunch from $5. Open Tu-Sa and Su 7:30am-2pm. D/MC/V.)

Arcata has many budget motels off U.S. 101 at the Giuntoli exit. **Motel 6 ❸**, 4755 Valley W. Blvd., is clean and quiet and has cable TV, a pool, and A/C. (☎707-822-7061. Singles $55, under 17 free. AmEx/D/DC/MC/V.) Popular **Clam Beach County Park ❶**, on U.S. 101, 7½ mi. north of Arcata, has dunes and a huge beach with seasonal clam digging. (☎707-445-7651. $3 per vehicle. Sites with water and pit toilets $10. Cash only.) **Patrick's Point State Park ❶**, 15 mi. north of Arcata on U.S. 101, is an excellent spot for whale-watching and seals. The 124 sites feature terrific ocean views, lush vegetation, and treasure-hunting in the beach's tidepools. (☎707-677-3570, reservations 800-444-7275. Showers and flush toilets. Reservations recommended. No hookups. Sites $20. Day-use $6. Cash only.)

▛ APPROACHING TRINIDAD: 13 MILES
Continue on **U.S. 101 N**, and take the exit toward Trinidad. Turn left onto **Westhaven Dr./Main St.**, and continue to follow Main St.

TRINIDAD. Originally founded as a port during the gold-rush era, Trinidad's main attraction is the unofficially named **College Cove**. The beach provides sandy shores for the clothed to the north and the nudists to the south. (From the Trinidad exit, follow signs for the Trinidad Beach on Stagecoach Rd., then take the second left onto a gravel road at the Elk Head Park sign.) **Patrick's Point State Park**, 5 mi. north of Trinidad, is worth a stop for the 2 mi. walk along the Rim Trail, which sweeps by Agate Beach, Mussel Rocks, Patrick's Point and **▧Wedding Rock**, a tremendous boulder that juts out into the ocean. On the beach, you can hunt for the semi-precious agate stones. Sharing the 640-acre park is also a model **Yurok village** for visitors and a nice **campground ❶** with water and coin-operated showers. (☎707-677-3570. Sites $20. Day use $4. Cash only.)

▛ APPROACHING REDWOOD NATIONAL AND STATE PARKS: 23 MILES
Continue on **U.S. 101 N/Redwood Hwy.** The park's south entrance is a few miles up the road.

REDWOOD NATIONAL AND STATE PARKS

With ferns that grow to the height of humans and redwood trees the size of skyscrapers, Redwood National and State Parks will leave an impression. The redwoods are the last remaining stretch of the old-growth forest that used to blanket two million acres of Northern California and Oregon. Wildlife runs free here, with black bears and mountain lions roaming the backwoods and Roosevelt elk grazing in the meadows. While a short tour of the big sights and the drive-through trees certainly give visitors ample photo opportunities, a more memorable experience of the redwoods may require heading down a trail into the quiet of the forest, where you can see the trees as they have stood for thousands of years.

VITAL STATS

Area: 112,613 acres

Visitor Info: Redwood National Park Headquarters and Information Center, 1111 2nd St. (☎707-464-6101), in Crescent City. Open in summer daily 9am-5pm; in winter M-Sa 9am-5pm.

Gateway Towns: Orick, Klamath, Crescent City

Fees: Fees vary by park and are different for parking, camping, and hiking. There is usually no entrance fee. Day-use fees ($4 per car) for parking and picnic areas are typical.

▛ GETTING AROUND

Redwood National and State Parks is an umbrella term for four contiguous redwood parks. The parks span 40 mi. of coast and two counties, with information centers and unique attractions throughout. **Redwood National Park** is the southernmost of the four; the others, from south to north, are **Prairie Creek Redwoods State Park, Del Norte Coast Redwoods State Park,** and **Jedediah Smith Redwoods State Park.**

Orick and Klamath border the national forest to the south and north, respectively. **U.S. 101** traverses most of the parks. The slower but more scenic **Newton Drury Pkwy.** runs parallel to U.S. 101 for 31 mi. from Klamath to Prairie Creek (watch for bikers).

DID YOU KNOW? Native American's called the redwoods "the eternal spirit" because of their 2000-year life span, ability to adapt to climatic changes, and resistance to insects, fire, and even lightning.

⚠ OUTDOORS

All plants and animals in the part are protected—even feathers dropped by birds of prey are off-limits. California **fishing licenses** (1 day $10) are required for fresh and saltwater fishing off any natural formation, but fishing is free from any man-made structure (check out Battery Point in Crescent City). There are minimum-weight and maximum-catch requirements specific to both. Call the Fish and Game Department (☎707-445-6493; www.dfg.ca.gov) for more information.

The redwoods are best experienced on foot. Hikers should take particular care to wear protective clothing—ticks and poison oak thrive in these dark places. Roosevelt elk roam the woods and are interesting to watch but dangerous to approach, as encroachers on their territory are promptly circled and trampled. Also look out for the black bears and mountain lions that inhabit the park. Before setting out, get advice and trail maps at the visitors center.

ORICK AREA. The Orick Area covers the southernmost section of Redwood National and State Parks. The **visitors center** lies on U.S. 101, 1 mi. south of Orick and a half-mile south of the Greyhound bus stop. A popular sight is the **Tall Trees Grove,** accessible by car to those with permits (free from the visitors center) when the road is open. Allow at least 3-4hr. for the trip. From the trailhead at the end of Tall Trees Access Rd., off Bald Hills Rd. from U.S. 101 north of Orick, it's a 1¼ mi. hike down (about 30min.) to some of the tallest trees in the world. The return hike up is steep—allow 1hr. If the road is closed, hardy souls can see these giants by hiking the 16 mi. round-trip from **Dolason Prairie Trail** to **Emerald Ridge Trail,** which connects with **Tall Trees Trail.**

Orick is a somewhat desolate town overrun by cows (which outnumber the people) and souvenir stores selling burl sculptures (over-crafted and expensive wood carvings). However, those needing to stock up on the essentials will find a post office and a market for groceries.

PRAIRIE CREEK AREA. The Prairie Creek Area, equipped with a ranger station, visitors center, and state park campground, is perfect for hikers, who can explore 70 mi. of trails in the 14,000-acre park. Be sure to pick up a trail map ($1) at the ranger station before heading out; the loops of criss-crossing trails can confuse. Starting at the Prairie Creek Visitors Center, the **James Irvine Trail** (4½ mi. one-way) snakes through a prehistoric garden of towering old-growth redwoods. Winding past small waterfalls that trickle down 50 ft. fern-covered walls, the trail ends at ⊠**Fern Canyon** on **Gold Bluffs Beach. Rhododendron** (7¾ mi. one-way) is another choice pick because of its beautiful blossoms and many possibilities; if you get tired, you can take the convenient switchback, **South Fork Trail.** The less ambitious can elk-watch on the meadow in front of the ranger station or cruise part of the **Foothill Trail** (¾ mi. one-way) to the 1500-year-old 306 ft. high **Big Tree.** This behemoth is a satisfying alternative for those who don't want to trek to **Tall Trees Grove** (see above).

KLAMATH AREA. The Klamath area to the north consists of a thin stretch of parkland connecting Prairie Creek with Del Norte State Park. The town itself consists of a few stores stretched over 4 mi., so the main attraction here is the spectacular coastline. The **Klamath Overlook,** where Requa Rd. meets the steep **Coastal Trail** (8 mi.), is an excellent whale-watching site with a fantastic view (provided the fog doesn't obscure it).

The mouth of the **Klamath River** is a popular commercial fishing spot in fall and spring, when salmon spawn, and in winter, when steelhead trout do the same. (Permit required, contact the Redwood Visitors Info Center, ☎541-464-6101.) In spring and summer, sea lions and harbor seals congregate along Coastal Dr., which passes by the remains of the **Douglas Memorial Bridge** and continues along the ocean for 8 mi. of incredible views. Kitsch meets high-tech at **Trees of Mystery,** 15500 U.S. 101 N, just north of Klamath. It is a three-quarter-mile walk through a maze of curiously shaped trees and elaborate chainsaw sculptures that talk and play music. There is also a small, free Native American museum that displays ornate costumes, baskets, and tapestries. The tourist trap's latest addition, the **Sky Trail,** is a multi-million-dollar gondola snaking up the hill to offer an exclusive bird's eye view of the towering trees. A 49 ft. tall Paul Bunyan and his blue ox Babe mark the entrance to the sight. (☎541-482-2251 or 800-638-3389. Trail open daily 8am-6:30pm. Museum 8am-6:30pm. $13.50, seniors $10, children $6.50.)

CRESCENT CITY AREA. An outstanding location from which to explore the parks, Crescent City calls itself the city "where the redwoods meet the sea." The **Battery Point Lighthouse** is on a causeway jutting out from Front St.; turn left onto A St. at the top of Front St. The lighthouse contains a museum open only during low tide. (☎707-464-3089. Open Apr.-Sept. W-Su 10am-4pm, tide permitting. $3, students $1.) From June through August, the national park offers **tidepool walks,** which leave from the Enderts Beach parking lot. The trailhead is at the **Crescent Beach Overlook** on Enderts Beach Rd., just off U.S. 101. (Turn-off 4 mi. south of Crescent City. Schedules ☎707-464-6101.) A scenic drive from Crescent City along **Pebble Beach Dr.** to **Point Saint George** snakes past coastline that looks transplanted from New England; craggy cliffs, lush prairies, and an old lighthouse add to the atmosphere. The **World Championship Crab Races,** on the third Sunday in February, features races and crab feasts. The **Sea Cruise,** a parade of over 500 classic cars, occurs over three days on the first or second weekend in October. (☎800-343-8300 for information regarding any of these events.)

North of Crescent City, the **Smith River,** the state's last major un-dammed river, rushes through the rocky gorges on its way from the mountains to the coast. This area offers the best salmon, trout, and steelhead fishing around, and excellent camping awaits on the riverbanks. There are also numerous hiking trails throughout the forest.

HIOUCHI AREA. This inland region, known for its rugged beauty, sits in the northern part of the park region along U.S. 199 and contains some excellent hiking trails, most of which are in **Jedediah Smith Redwoods State Park.** Several trails lie off Howland Hill Rd., a dirt road accessible from both U.S. 101 and U.S. 199. From U.S. 199, turn onto South Fork Rd. in Hiouchi and right onto Douglas Park Rd., which then turns into Howland Hill Rd. From Crescent City, go south on U.S. 101, turn left onto Elk Valley Rd., and right onto Howland Hill Rd. Drive through **Stout Grove,** which some say surpasses even the Avenue of the Giants. From here, you can take the **Stout Grove Trail** (½ mi.) and admire the ancient redwoods up close. The trailhead is near the eastern end of Howland Hill Rd. The **Mill Creek Trail** (4mi.; moderate) provides excellent swimming, accessible from the Mill Creek Bridge on Howland Hill Rd., and from the footbridge in the Jedediah Smith campground during summer. The more strenuous **Boy Scout Trail** off Howland Hill Rd. splits after 3 mi.; the right-hand path goes to the monstrous Boy Scout Tree, and the left ends at Fern Falls.

FOOD

There are more picnic tables than restaurants in the area, so the best option for food is probably the supermarket. In Crescent City, head to the 24hr. **Safeway,** 475 M St. (☎707-465-3353).

Palm Cafe, 21130 Hwy. 101 (☎707-488-3381). Famous for its for Paul Bunyan rolls ($8) and enormous cinnamon rolls that can feed 5. Entrees $7. AmEx/D/MC/V. ❷

Glen's Bakery and Restaurant, at 3rd and G St. (☎707-464-2914), in Crescent City. A family affair since it opened in 1947. Dedicated regulars love the plate-sized pancakes. Breakfast served all day. Pancakes $4. Open Tu-F 5am-6:30pm, Sa 5am-2pm. MC/V. ❶

ACCOMMODATIONS

Redwood Hostel (HI), 14480 U.S. 101 (☎707-482-8265 or 800-295-1905; www.redwoodhostel.com), at Wilson Creek Rd., 7 mi. north of Klamath. A prime beach location and great sunset views. Check-in 8-10am and 5-9pm. Check-out 8-10am. Reservations recommended in summer. Dorms $20, under 17 $10; doubles $49. MC/V. ❶

Hiouchi Motel, 2097 Rte. 199 (☎707-458-3041), 8 mi. east of Crescent City. Offers basic amenities near the park. Singles $42; doubles $60. D/MC/V. ❷

Gold Bluffs Beach Campground (☎707-464-6101). Turn west on Davison Rd., 3 mi north of Orick, pass Elk Meadows to the pocked dirt ground (read: huge holes in the ground). The campsites sit among tall, yellow grass on a sandy shore that is surprisingly sheltered from the wind. This former port for gold miners is now one of the best spots for beach camping along the coast. Sites $12. Day-use $6. Cash only. ●

Jedediah Smith Redwoods State Park Campground (☎707-464-6101). Nestle in among old-growth redwoods at this campground. Flush toilets and water. No hookups. Sites $20. MC/V. ●

⛏ APPROACHING BROOKINGS: 26 MILES
Continue on **U.S. 101,** and cross into Oregon.

The Beaver State
OREGON
Welcomes You!

BROOKINGS

In Brookings, one of the few coastal towns that remains relatively tourist-free, hardware stores are easier to find than trinket shops, and the beaches are among Oregon's least spoiled. The city also sits in Oregon's "banana belt"; warm weather is not rare in January, and some Brookings backyards even boast scraggly palm trees. Brookings is known statewide for its flowers. In downtown's **Azalea Park,** azaleas encircle pristine lawns and bloom at intervals year round; call ahead to make sure the flowers are out. The pride of Brookings is its **Azalea Festival** (☎541-469-3181), held in Azalea Park over Memorial Day weekend. South Beach is just north of town and offers soft sand as well as haunting vistas of angular volcanic rocks strewn about the sea. **Harris Beach,** a bit farther north, has an equally excellent view of the rock formations, and has less obstructed views.

A number of seafood spots can be found near the harbor. The local favorite is **Oceanside Diner** ❷, 16403 Lower Harbor Rd. Regular customers and their orders are featured on the menu; ask for a ⬛**Berta** ("make me something") and see what you get. (☎541-469-7971. Open daily 4am-1:30pm. Cash only.) **The Bonn Motel** ❸, 1216 U.S. 101, has a heated indoor pool and cable TV. (☎541-469-2161. Singles $59-69; doubles $69-89. AmEx/D/MC/V.) **Harris Beach State Park Campground** ❶, at the north edge of Brookings, has 63 tent sites set back in the trees. (☎541-469-2021 or 800-452-5687. Free showers. Sites $21; RV sites $22; yurts $29. MC/V.)

⛏ APPROACHING GOLD BEACH: 29 MILES
Continue on **U.S. 101/Oregon Coast Hwy.** Explore 15 mi. of countless trails, some leading to beaches covered in volcanic rocks, at **Samuel Boardman State Park.** Don't be surprised if an exploratory hike unexpectedly ends at an intimate seaside cove.

GOLD BEACH. Thirty miles north of Brookings, in Gold Beach, you can ride a jet boat up the Rogue River. **Mail Boat Hydro-Jets,** 94294 Rogue River Rd., offers 6-7hr. whitewater daytrips. Longer trips get more whitewater, but all trips offer many wildlife viewing opportunities. (☎541-247-7033 or 800-458-3511. Trips May-Oct. $42-84. D/MC/V.)

⛏ APPROACHING BANDON-BY-THE-SEA: 56 MILES
Continue on **U.S. 101/Oregon Coast Hwy.** Bandon is 27 mi. north of Port Orford. **Humbug Mountain State Park,** 6 mi. south of Port Orford along U.S. 101, surrounds the heavily forested mountain. A 3 mi., moderate trail ascends the 1700 ft. peak, with lush ferns on the trail and amazing views on top. The trail is accessible from a campground at the foot of the mountain, which has 95 tightly packed sites with toilets. (☎541-332-6774. Sites $14, with hookup $16. MC/V.) **Cape Blanco State Park,** just north of Port Orford, offers a long stretch of empty beach; it is the farthest point west on the Oregon Coast, and its **lighthouse** is the coast's oldest, with views that stretch for miles. Take a tour of the lighthouse and its mesmerizing lens, located at the end of the road leading into the park. (Open Apr.-Oct. Tu-Su 10am-3:30pm. $2, under 16 free.) Few stop at the **Cape Blanco State Park campground** ❶ a few miles back from the lighthouse; it offers exceptional seclusion between hedges, plus a ¼ mi. walk to a beautiful isolated beach. (☎541-332-2973. Toilets and showers. RV sites $16; cabins $35. MC/V.)

BANDON-BY-THE-SEA

Despite a steady flow of summer tourists, the fishing town of Bandon-by-the-Sea has refrained from breaking out the pastels and making itself up like an amusement park. A few outdoor activities make Bandon worth a stop on a coastal tour.

PACIFIC COAST

VITAL STATS

Population: 2800

Visitor Info: Bandon-by-the-Sea Visitors Center, 300 SE 2nd St. (☎541-347-9616), in Old Town. Open daily in summer 10am-5pm; in winter 10am-4pm.

Internet Access: Bandon Public Library, Hwy. 101 (☎541-347-3221). Open Tu-Th 10:30am-8pm, F-Sa 10:30am-5pm. Free.

Post Office: 105 12th St. SE (☎541-347-1160). Open M-F 8:30am-4:30pm. **Postal Code:** 97411.

GETTING AROUND. Ocean Dr. runs along the pacific before heading inland through downtown Bandon. After it intersects with U.S. 101, Ocean Dr. becomes 2nd St.

SIGHTS. In September, the town holds an annual **Cranberry Festival** (☎541-347-9616; www.bandon.com). The **Old Town** actually just dates from 1936, when a giant fire swept through and destroyed all the living quarters, but not the industry, in Bandon. People were living in tents and hurried to put up "temporary" buildings, many of which are still standing today. At the traffic light turn onto Hwy. 42S for 1½ mi. and then right on Morrison Rd. for 1 mi., to reach the **cranberry bog** at **Faber Farms,** 54982 Morrison Rd. In October see the floating berries bob on the water as they're harvested. (☎866-347-1166; www.faber-farms.com. Open M-Sa 10am-4pm.) A visit to **Bandon's Historical Society Museum,** 270 Fillmore Ave., at U.S. 101, is like leafing through a grandmother's scrapbook filled with the area's Native American, industrial, maritime, and pioneer heritage. (☎541-347-2164; www.bandonhistoricalmuseum.org. Open M-Sa 10am-4pm. $2, under 12 free.)

FOOD AND ACCOMMODATIONS. Bandon Baking Co. and Deli ❶, 160 2nd St., offers soups and breads like pumpkin, hazelnut, and the regionally ubiquitous cranberry-nut. (☎541-347-9440; www.bandonbakingco.com. Open M-Sa 7am-4pm. Cash only.) **Alloro Wine Bar & Restaurant ❹,** 375 2nd St., has an extensive collection of wines that focuses on Oregon and Italy. The pricey Italian fare is worth a splurge. Try the *Caesar con Gancho* (Caesar salad with crab) for $11. (☎541-347-1850. Open Tu-Su 3-10pm. AmEx/D/MC/V.) The small **Sea Star Guest House ❶,** 375 2nd St., contains the remains of a once-thriving hostel as well as several elegant guesthouse rooms overlooking the marina. (☎541-347-9632; www.seastarbandon.com. Dorms $19; private rooms $39-75; guesthouse rooms with living room and kitchen $75-150. AmEx/D/MC/V.) Two miles north of town and across the bridge, **Bullard's Beach State Park ❶** houses the Coquille River Lighthouse, built in 1896. The park has 185 sites. (☎541-347-2209. Showers $2. Sites $20; yurts $27. MC/V.)

APPROACHING CHARLESTON: 22 MILES
Go north on **U.S. 101/Oregon Coast Hwy.,** turn left onto **Seven Devils Rd.,** and continue toward the coast.

CHARLESTON. Tiny Charleston sits peacefully on the coast. This is one of the few places on the Pacific where life slows down as you near the shore, with a string of state parks along the coastline and a pristine estuary near its bay. Four miles south of Charleston up Seven Devils Rd., the **South Slough National Estuarine Research Reserve** ("slough" is pronounced "slew") is one of the most fascinating and under-appreciated venues on the central coast. Spreading out from a small interpretive center, almost 4779 acres of salt and freshwater estuaries nurture all kinds of wildlife, from sand shrimp to blue herons.

Head to the interpretive center first to check if there are any guided hikes (free) or paddles going out ($10 per boat), or to begin one of the short trails starting at the center. A great way to observe wildlife by canoe or kayak is to start from the Charleston Marina (near the Charleston Bridge) at low tide. Paddle into the estuary with the tide and out as it subsides; the estuary turns into a wasteland of mud flats at low tide. (☎541-888-5558; www.southsloughestuary.com. Open June-Aug. daily 10am-4:30pm; Sept.-May M-Sa 10am-4:30pm. Trails open daily sunrise-sunset.)

APPROACHING COOS BAY: 9 MILES
From Charleston, head on to the **Cape Arago Hwy.,** then follow **Empire Coos Bay Hwy.** into town.

COOS BAY

The largest city on the Oregon Coast, Coos Bay still has the feel of a down-to-earth working town. For two weeks in mid-July, Coos Bay plays host to the **Oregon Coast Music Festival,** the most popular summer music event on the coast. A week of jazz, blues, and folk is followed by a week of performances by the renowned festival orchestra. Art exhibits and a free classical concert in Mingus Park make the festival an attraction for the ticketless. (☎541-267-0938. Tickets $5-20.) At the **Blue Heron Bistro ❸**, 100 Commercial Ave., at Broadway, German cuisine complements the WWII memorabilia on the walls. (☎541-267-3933. Sandwiches $8. Dinner $8-14. Open M-F 11am-9:30pm, Sa 5-9:30pm. MC/V.) **Cranberry Sweets ❷**, 1005 Newmark St., near the corner of Ocean Blvd., is a far-from-average candy factory with numerous original offerings such as beer pâtés and cheddar cheese fudge. Cheapskates can load up on free samples. (☎541-888-9824. Open M-Sa 9am-5:30pm, Su 11am-4pm. AmEx/D/MC/V.) **Euros International Grill ❷**, 274 S. Broadway, offers burgers but specializes in sandwiches ($7-9.50). Wednesdays have the best bargain; order a "Burger and Brew" for $6. (☎541-266-7708. AmEx/MC/V.)

Akin to camping in a well-landscaped parking lot, **Sunset Bay State Park ❶**, 89814 Cape Arago Hwy., 12 mi. south of Coos Bay and 3½ mi. west of Charleston, has 138 sites. The loop B sites have a bit more seclusion. (☎541-888-4902, reservations 800-452-5687. Sites $16; RV sites $20; yurts $27. MC/V.) Three miles north of North Bend, off U.S. 101, lies the **Bluebill Campground ❶**, which offers 18 sites among sandy scrub a half-mile from the ocean. (Follow the signs to the Horsfall Beach area, then continue down the road. ☎541-271-3611. Open Apr.-Oct. Sites $20. Cash only.)

BIG DETOUR. Explore the backcountry roads and stunning natural sights of Oregon on the **Cavemen, Craters, and Carnivores Big Detour**, p. 964.

⚑ APPROACHING WINCHESTER BAY: 23 MILES

Continue on **U.S. 101 N/Oregon Coast Hwy.** Along the way, nature's ever-changing sculpture, the **Oregon Dunes National Recreation Area**, presents sand in shapes and sizes unequaled in the Northwest. Perhaps the only hotbed of "reverse conservation," the dunes are actually greening rapidly as European beachgrass, planted in the 1920s, spreads its tenacious roots and sparks concerns

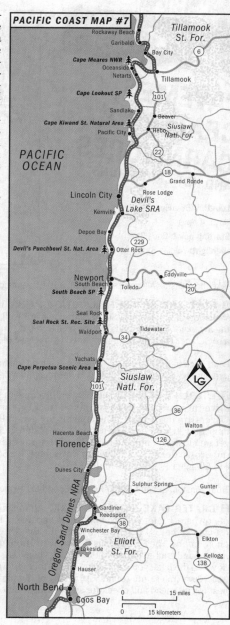

PACIFIC COAST MAP #7

Tillamook St. For.

Rockaway Beach
Garibaldi
Cape Meares NWR
Bay City
Oceanside
Netarts
Tillamook
Cape Lookout SP

PACIFIC OCEAN

Sandlake
Cape Kiwand St. Natural Area
Beaver
Siuslaw Nath. For.
Hebo
Pacific City

Grand Ronde
Rose Lodge
Lincoln City
Devil's Lake SRA
Kernville

Depoe Bay
Devil's Punchbowl St. Nat. Area
Otter Rock
Eddyville

Newport
South Beach
Toledo
South Beach SP

Seal Rock
Seal Rock St. Rec. Site
Tidewater
Waldport

Yachats
Cape Perpetua Scenic Area
Siuslaw Natl. For.

Walton

Hacenta Beach
Florence

Dunes City
Sulphur Springs
Gunter

Gardiner
Reedsport
Winchester Bay
Elliott St. For.
Elkton

Lakeside
Kellogg

Hauser
North Bend
Coos Bay

0   15 miles
0   15 kilometers

Oregon Sand Dunes NRA

PACIFIC COAST

CAVEMEN, CRATERS & CARNIVORES

AND HOT CROSS BUNS

Length: 456 miles
Days: 4 days
Starting point: Coos Bay
Highlight: Wildlife Safari

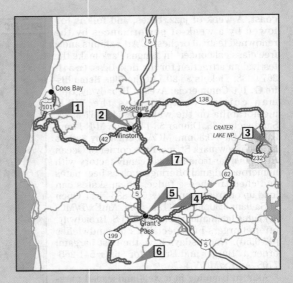

Take the Eastside-Allegany exit from U.S. 101 S, and continue east along a narrow, gravel road.

■ **GOLD AND SILVER FALLS STATE PARK.** It may be a little hard to find, but the beauty and seclusion of Golden and Silver State Falls are well worth your navigatory efforts. Three trails lead to the awesome Golden Falls, which plunge 100 ft., and Silver Falls, thin sheets of water cascading down a rock face. The falls are surrounded by massive old-growth firs and cedars. (Open 24hr.)

Head back to U.S. 101 S to Hwy 42 S. The road will turn into Hwy. 42., and after you pass through Winston, turn onto I-5 N. Get off at Exit 120 to Roseburg. Turn right onto Oak Ave., and make a left on Jackson St.

■ **WILDLIFE SAFARI.** Let the wildlife come to you at Wildlife Safari, in Winston, Oregon. At this drive-thru zoo, big signs warn you to "Keep moving if lion approaches" and remind you that "Tigers are dangerous." The animals are generally car friendly and remain at a distance, but you must stay in your car. The park also provides shelter to several endangered species. If you want to get up close and personal, call ahead for a "Get Inside" event, which ranges from "Breakfast with the Brown Bears" to a "Cheetah Encounter." (☎541-679-6761. Open daily 9am-5pm. $17.50, seniors $14.50, ages 4-12 $11.50, under 3 free.)

From Winston, get on **I-5 N** to **Hwy. 138,** and follow the signs to Crater Lake.

■ **CRATER LAKE NATIONAL PARK.** Although you have to drive through what seems to be middle of nowhere, Crater Lake National Park should not be missed. The impossibly steep banks of the deepest lake in the U.S. can be seen along the Rim Drive, where turnoffs offer the best vantage points for photographs. The **Steel Visitors Center,** 17 mi. from the Hwy. 138 park entrance, offers a wealth of information and trail maps. (☎541-594-3100. Open daily May-Oct. 9am-5pm; Nov.-Apr. 10am-4pm.) To get down to the lake, you can hop on a boat tour (☎541-594-3100; $24.50, ages 11-15 $15) or take the **Cleetwood Cove Trail** (2 mi. round-trip). Many of the park's features are inaccessible in winter months; it's best to call ahead and check for snow, which sometimes lingers through the summer months.

From Crater Lake, take Hwy. 62 W. Head towards Gold Hill, and turn left at Dardanelles St. Make a right at 2nd St., and follow the signs 5 mi. to the House of Mystery.

4 THE HOUSE OF MYSTERY. Travel into the Gold Hills to find the Oregon Vortex, at the House of Mystery. Originally built as a gold mining office, it was quickly abandoned when miners realized that their gold weighed less inside the cabin. The spherical field, referred to as the vortex, apparently creates a negative force that appears to push people forward; most people stand at a 7½ degree angle when inside. Take a tour to see the wonderous effects of the vortex, a three-quarter acre parcel of land that defies gravity. (☎541-855-1543. Open June-Sept. daily 9am-5:15pm; Mar.-May and Oct. Tu-Su 9am-4:15pm. $8.50, senior $7.50, ages 6-11 $6.50, under 6 free.)

From I-5 N take Exit 58 to downtown Grants Pass.

5 THE CAVEMAN. Just off I-5, a giant 18ft. caveman welcomes visitors to the city of Grants Pass. The town's unofficial mascot originates from the proximity of the town to the Oregon Caves National Monument which lies just outside of town. Realm of the Caveman, a local organization founded to promote the tourism industry in Gold Hills, puts on parades, and the members make appearances at special events throughout the Pacific Northwest.

From Grants Pass, head south on Redwoods Hwy. for 27 mi. In the town of Cave Junction, turn left onto Caves Hwy. After 14 mi., bear right on OR-46. The caves are 5 mi. down the road.

6 OREGON CAVES NATIONAL MONUMENT. This 488-acre monument may be small, but it packs a concentrated punch. Above ground, four hiking trails range throughout a spectacular, old-growth stand of Douglas Firs. The **Cliff Nature Trail** (1 mi.), with its gorgeous panoramas, is the most popular, but the more adventurous may want to consider the **Big Tree Trail** (3½ mi.), which passes the largest Douglas Fir in Oregon. Of course, the must-see attractions are below ground. Rangers give tours of the still-developing marble **caves** mid-March to November. The caves aren't warmer than your refrigerator, so dress accordingly. Also be sure to ask the ranger before you take any photographs; you don't want to disturb the hordes of sleeping bats. (Call Oregon Caves Headquarters, 1900 Caves Hwy., for info. ☎541-592-2100. Open daily in summer 9am-7pm; in spring and fall 10am-4pm. Tours mid-Mar. to Nov. Hours vary; call ahead. Cave tour $8.50, under 16 $6. Park entrance free.)

Head back the way you came, and then take I-5 N to Exit 86 for Azalea.

7 HEAVEN ON EARTH. Heaven on Earth ❷, 703 Quines Creek Rd., is no ordinary roadside cafe. The building used to house a thriving saloon and brothel, but there's a new sheriff in town, and his name is Jesus. You can pick up a copy of Gospel Guitars (#9, 10, 12, or 15) or any number of evangelical gifts if you like, but your money would be better spent on a cinnamon roll as big as your head ($10). If you're not up to the challenge, try the mini roll ($4). The typical diner fare is seriously livened up by the dessert table near the entrance, where cobblers, pie, and more delight any appetite. (☎541-837-3700. Open daily 6am-10pm. AmEx/D/DC/MC/V.)

BACK TO THE ROUTE. Head up I-5 until you reach Exit 119. Take the exit onto OR-42 W, which will take you back to Coos Bay.

that the dunes may disappear in as few as 100 years. Get them while they're hot: everyone, from the hard-partying buggy or ATV rider to the hiker seeking solitude enjoys the endless expanses of windblown sand. For an unmuffled and undeniably thrilling dune experience, venture out on wheels. Plenty of shops on U.S. 101 between Coos Bay and Florence rent and offer tours, and most either transport ATVs to the dunes or are located on them. The visitors center in Reedsport (p. 966) also offers a list of places that rent ATVs.

WINCHESTER BAY

The vast stretches of sand south of Winchester Bay and around Eel Creek represent Oregon Dunes at their most primal. The experience of any day hike is heightened by solitude, so go early or late to avoid other tourists. With little to guide you besides an occasional marking pole, the **John Dellenback Dunes Trail** (1 mi.), located off U.S. 101, wanders through unparalleled beauty in the sand slopes, wind cornices, and rippled surfaces of the dunes. Access the trailhead off U.S. 101. The area is ATV-free, and you'll probably find yourself wandering along the ridges of the dunes while exploring an occasional patch of vegetation. The views are best when the sun is low in the sky and the shadows highlight the precise transitions between slopes and other wind-sculptured features. The trail goes 6 mi. to the ocean over soft sand, requiring several hours of hiking.

Winchester Bay is also home to an excellent surf spot on the coast. Rent crab traps to try and capture the elusive creatures; even if you can't get one, cheap meal options abound here. The **Anchor Grill ❸**, 208 Bayfront Loop, is a classy but casual choice on the waterfront. Try the Halibut fish and chips for $16. (☎541-271-2104. Lunch $7-11. Dinner $15-23. Open daily 11am-9pm. AmEx/D/MC/V.) The **Harbor View Motel ❷**, 540 Beach Blvd., is so close to the marina that there are boats in the parking lot. A robotic frog welcomes guests to the office. Rooms are comfortable and clean, with striking color schemes. (☎541-271-3352. Rooms $42-45. D/MC/V.) For less private, but still well-sheltered campsites, **William M. Tugman State Park ❶**, 8 mi. south of Reedsport on U.S. 101, is close to gorgeous Eel Lake. (☎541-759-3604, reservations 800-452-5687. Water and electricity. Sites in summer $16, in winter $12; yurts $27. MC/V.)

⚐ APPROACHING REEDSPORT: 5 MILES

Follow **U.S. 101/Oregon Coast Hwy.,** then turn right to follow **Rte. 38** into Reedsport.

REEDSPORT

A popular stopover by the dunes, Reedsport has excellent camping and is a great place to rest between runs on the sand. Birdwatching is popular around town; lists of species and their seasons are available at the **Oregon Dunes National Recreation Area Visitors Center,** 855 U.S. 101, at Rte. 38, just south of the Umpqua River Bridge. The center also has a 10min. video on dune ecology and essential info on fees, regulations, hiking, and camping. (☎541-271-3611. Open June-Oct. daily 8am-4:30pm; Nov.-May M-F 8am-4:30pm.) Most tourists enjoy stopping at the **Oregon Dunes Overlook,** between Reedsport and Florence. Several 1½-3hr. walks depart from the overlook and explore a wide variety of dunes amidst the constant barrage of bird calls from nearby shrubs.

Harbor Lights Family Restaurant ❸, at U.S. 101 and Rte. 38, offers American food in a diner with no pretension. (☎541-271-3848. Salmon burger $9. Open daily 7am-9pm. AmEx/D/MC/V.) **Carter Lake Campground ❶,** 12 mi. north of Reedsport on U.S. 101, has boat access to the lake, and some sites are lakeside. The well-screened spots are about as quiet as it gets out here. (☎541-271-3611. 23 sites. No ATVs. Open May-Sept. Sites $17.)

⚐ APPROACHING FLORENCE: 23 MILES

Continue on **U.S. 101/Oregon Coast Hwy.**

FLORENCE. Florence is home to the most photographed lighthouse in the US as well as a cormorant rookery. The **Siuslaw Pioneer Museum** is worth a gander. (☎541-997-7884. Open Tu-Su noon-4pm. $2, children free.) Up the road, the picturesque, red-topped **Heceta Lighthouse,** built in 1894, is another worthy photo-op. (☎541-547-3416. Tours Memorial Day to Labor Day daily 11am-5pm; Mar., Apr., and Oct. M and F-Su 11am-3pm. $3.)

1969: The first Kinetic Sculpture Race is started by Hobart Brown, who rides a pentacycle.

⊠ DETOUR
ALPHA FARM

Drive 14 mi. east of Florence to the tiny community of Mapleton. Press on 30min. farther along Rte. 36 and then 7 mi. up Deadwood Creek Rd.

Alpha Farm offers a 280 acre communal alternative to the coast's bourgeois tourism. Members farm and produce gift shop-type items to support the communal purse. Anyone willing to lend a hand with the chores is welcome to camp out or stay in the beautiful, simple bedrooms. Visitors can stay up to three days; afterward, a long-term commitment to the farm is required. (☎541-964-5102.) The **Alpha Bit Cafe ❶**, in Mapleton on Rte. 126, is owned and staffed by the very chill members of Alpha Farm. (☎541-268-4311. Open M-Th and Sa-Su 10am-6pm, F 10am-9pm. Cash only.)

⚲ APPROACHING CAPE PERPETUA: 22 MILES

Continue on **U.S. 101/Oregon Coast Hwy.** until you reach the **Cape Perpetua Scenic Area.** In the fall and winter hundreds of boisterous sea lions make their home here in the **world's largest sea cave**, 91560 U.S. 101 (which accounts for the smell). In spring and summer months they prefer to sun themselves just outside on the rookery. (☎541-547-3111; www.sealioncaves.com. Open daily 8am-6pm. $8, ages 6-15 $4.50.)

CAPE PERPETUA

Cape Perpetua is the highest point on the coast that you can drive to (803 ft.) and arguably its high point for scenic beauty. Even if you're only passing through, drive to the top of the **Cape Perpetua Viewpoint** (2 mi.), and walk the quarter-mile loop. Gaze out at the ocean, as well as the headlands to the north and south. Those looking for a more challenging hike can take the difficult 1¼ mi. **St. Perpetua Trail** up to the same viewpoint. The trail departs from **Cape Perpetua Visitors Center**, 2400 U.S. 101, just south of the viewpoint turn-off, which has informative exhibits about the surrounding area and hilarious rangers. (☎541-547-3289. Open May-Nov. daily 9am-5pm.) At high tide, witness an orgy of thundering spray in the **Devil's Churn** (¼ mi. north of the interpretive center down Restless Water Trail) and **Spouting Horn** (¼ mi. south down Captain Cook Trail). The two sites, as well as the tidal pools, are con-

nected; the tidal pools can also be reached from the interpretive center. The **Cape Perpetua campground ❶** is an excellent place to sleep, with 37 sites alongside a tiny, fernbanked creek. (At the turn-off for the viewpoint. ☎877-444-6777. Water, toilets. Firewood $5. Sites $20. Cash only.) **The Rock Creek Campground ❶**, 8 mi. farther south, has 15 sites under mossy spruces a half-mile from the sea. (☎877-444-6777. Drinking water, toilets. Sites $20. Cash only.)

⚲ APPROACHING YACHATS: 4 MILES

From Cape Perpetua, follow **U.S. 101/Oregon Coast Hwy.**

YACHATS

Billing itself as the "Gem of the Oregon Coast," Yachats (YAH-hots) comes from the Native American word meaning "dark water between timbered hills." There's not much to do in this small resort town but stroll around and enjoy. The **Yachats Visitors Center**, 241 U.S. 101, next to the supermarket, is extremely helpful for information on local attractions. (☎800-929-0477; www.yachats.org. Open daily 10am-4pm.) Stop in at the **Green Salmon Coffee and Tea House ❶**, off U.S. 101 at 3rd St., where the menu is written on coffee bags, the cash register uses solar power, and the tables are giant tree stumps. (☎541-547-3077. Raspberries on toast $4.50. Open Tu-Su 7:30am-4pm. Cash only.) The cozy **Grand Occasions Cafe ❸**, 84 Beach St., off U.S. 101, at 3rd St., offers a delightful Dungeness Crab Melt ($12), alongside fresh pies, cookies, cobblers, and scones. (☎541-547-4409. Open in summer M-Th 10am-6pm, F-Su 10am-8pm; in winter daily 10am-5pm. D/MC/V.) A local favorite for jazz, blues, rock, and folk, as well as tasty cuisine, the **Drift Inn ❹**, 124 U.S. 101, showcases live music every night around 6:30pm. Sit in the Victorian parlor or drink and dine near the bar. (☎541-547-4477; www.the-drift-inn.com. Open daily 8am-last customer. MC/V.) **Silver Surf Motel ❸**, 3767 U.S. 101, at the north end of town, features sliding glass doors overlooking a grassy hill that rolls 120 ft. to the sea. Rooms have kitchenettes and access to a pool and hot tub. (☎800-281-5723 or 541-547-3175; www.silver-surf-motel.com. Rooms in summer $89-99; in winter $69-89. AmEx/D/MC/V.)

◤ APPROACHING SEAL ROCK: 14 MILES
Head north on **U.S. 101/Oregon Coast Hwy.**

SEAL ROCK. Home to striking yellow stone cliffs, Seal Rock has some terrific sights. The **Triad Art Gallery,** at milepost 153, shows surprisingly above-average pieces. Look for the neon horse out front. (☎541-563-5442. Open daily 10am-5pm.) Nearby, **Yuzen ❸,** on U.S. 101, has fantastic sushi. (☎541-563-4766. Daily specials $12-15. Open Tu-Su 11am-2pm and 4:30-9pm. MC/V.) **South Beach,** 2 mi. south of town on U.S. 101, offers haunting views of angular volcanic rocks strewn about the sea, plus sand that's soft on bare feet.

◤ APPROACHING NEWPORT: 10 MILES
Continue north on **U.S. 101/Oregon Coast Hwy.**

NEWPORT

After the miles of malls along U.S. 101, Newport's renovated waterfront area of pleasantly kitschy restaurants and shops is a delight. Newport's claim to fame, however, is the world-class Oregon Coast Aquarium. This, in addition to the Mark Hatfield Marine Science Center and loads of inexpensive seafood, make Newport a star attraction for marine lovers.

VITAL STATS

Population: 9500

Visitor Info: Chamber of Commerce, 555 SW Coast Hwy. (☎541-265-8801 or 800-262-7844; www.discovernewport.com). Open in summer M-F 8:30am-5pm, Sa 11am-3pm; in winter M-F 8:30am-5pm.

Internet Access: Newport Public Library, 35 Nye St. NW (☎541-265-2153), at Olive St. Open M-W 10am-9pm, Th-Sa 10am-6pm, Su noon-5pm. Free.

Post Office: 310 SW 2nd St. (☎541-867-3986). Open M-F 8:30am-5pm, Sa 10am-noon. **Postal Code:** 97365.

▣ GETTING AROUND. Newport is bordered on the west by the foggy Pacific Ocean and on the south by Yaquina Bay. U.S. 101, known in town as the **Coast Hwy.,** runs north-south through town. U.S. 20, known as **Olive St.,** bisects the north and south sides of town. Just north of the bridge, **Bay Blvd.** circles the bay and runs through the heart of the port. Historic **Nye Beach,** bustling with tiny shops, is on the northwest side of town, between 3rd and 6th St.

◉ SIGHTS. The ◼**Mark O. Jatfield Marine Science Center,** at the south end of the bridge on Marine Science Dr., is the hub of Oregon State University's coastal research. The 300 scientists working here maintain rigorous intellectual standards for the exhibits, which explore fascinating topics ranging from chaos—demonstrated by a paddle wheel/waterclock—to climatic change and a behavioral analysis of Wile E. Coyote's causality. While you can't play with the live octopus, a garden of sea anemones, slugs, and bottom-dwelling fish awaits you in the touch tanks. (☎541-867-0100. Open in summer daily 10am-5pm; in winter M and Th-Su 10am-4pm, Tu-W 10am-5pm. Donations accepted.) More famous, less serious, and much more expensive than the Science Center is the **Oregon Coast Aquarium,** 2820 Ferry Slip Rd. SE, at the south end of the bridge. This aquarium housed Keiko, the much-loved *Free Willy* Orca, during his rehabilitation before he returned to his childhood waters near Iceland. The Passages of the Deep exhibit features a 200 ft. undersea tunnel surrounded by sharks, rays, and fish. (☎541-867-3474; www.aquarium.org. Open daily late June to early Sept. 9am-6pm; late Sept. to early June 10am-5pm. $12, seniors $10, ages 3-12 $7.) The **Rogue Ale Brewery,** 2320 Oregon State University Dr. SE., has won more awards than you can shake a pint at. Cross the bay bridge, follow the signs to the aquarium, and you'll see it. Twenty brews, including Oregon Golden, Shakespeare Stout, and Dead Guy Ale, are available upstairs at **Brewers by the Bay,** where taster trays of four beers are $5.25. (Brewery: ☎541-867-3660. Brewers by the Bay: ☎541-867-3664. Pints $4.50. Open M-Th and Su 11am-10pm, F-Sa 11am-11pm. Tours daily noon, 4, 6pm, depending on demand. Free.)

◤▣ FOOD AND NIGHTLIFE. Food in Newport is surprisingly varied, but seafood is the dining option of choice. The granddaddy of all Newport establishments, **Mo's Restaurant ❷,** 622 Bay Blvd. SW, is famous for its clam chowder ($4.25) and is just about always filled to the gills. If "Old Mo's" is packed, head across the street to **Mo's Annex ❷,** at 657 Bay Blvd., which dishes up the same food in a less historical atmosphere. (Mo's Restaurant: ☎541-265-2979. Open daily 11am-10pm. Mo's Annex: ☎541-265-7512. Open M-W and F-Su 11am-9pm. AmEx/D/MC/V.) **April's ❺**, 749 3rd St. NW, by Nye Beach, is the pinnacle of local dining, and the serene ocean view and exceptional food are worth every penny. (☎541-265-6855. Entrees $16-21. Towering chocolate eclairs $4. Reservations recommended. Open W-Su 5pm-last customer. D/MC/V.)

Pubs and taverns line the Historic Harbor on SW Bay Blvd. **Apollo's**, 836 SW Bay Blvd., offers a pub and nightclub in one. Relax, take a Jell-O shot ($3), and play pool, darts, or pinball. (☎541-265-9307. M Latin night. Tu and Th karaoke. F-Sa night DJ. M, W, and F Texas Hold 'Em tournaments. Cover F-Sa after 10pm $3. Open M-Th and Su 11am-2am, F-Sa 11am-2:30am. MC/V.)

☐ ACCOMMODATIONS. Motel-studded U.S. 101 provides affordable but sometimes noisy rooms. The **▤Sylvia Beach Hotel ❹**, 267 NW Cliff St., is by far the best option around, with a variety of rooms devoted to literary themes. Stay in one of the luxurious Classics overlooking the ocean, a mid-ranged Bestseller, or a Novel, fun but without a view. (☎541-265-3707; www.sylviabeachhotel.com. Novels $68-94; bestsellers $94-131; classics from $183. AmEx/MC/V.) Opposite the visitors center stands **City Center Motel ❷**, 538 Coast Hwy. SW, which has spacious rooms. (☎541-265-7381 or 800-627-9099. Singles $40; doubles $60. AmEx/D/MC/V.) If you feel like camping near the beach, head to **Beverly Beach State Park ❶**, 198 123rd St. NE, 7 mi. north of Newport and just south of Devil's Punch Bowl. Beverly Beach is a year-round campground of gargantuan proportions. (☎541-265-9278, reservations 800-452-5687. Sites $4-22; yurts $29. MC/V.)

☐ APPROACHING DEPOE BAY: 13 MILES
Continue on **U.S. 101/Oregon Coast Hwy.** Detour on the renowned **Otter Crest Loop**, a twisting 4 mi. excursion high above the shore that affords spectacular views at every bend, including vistas of **Otter Rock** and the **Marine Gardens.** A lookout over the aptly named **Cape Foulweather** has telescopes ($0.50) for spotting sea lions lazing on the rocks. **The Devil's Punch Bowl,** formed when the roof of a seaside cave collapsed, is also accessible off the loop. It becomes

a frothing cauldron during high tide when waves crash through an opening in the side of the bowl. **Otter Rocks Beach** is a great place to learn to surf; beginners can try out smaller breaks close to shore.

DEPOE BAY. Diminutive Depoe Bay has whale watching along the town's low seawall at the **Depoe Bay State Park Wayside** and the **Observatory Lookout,** 4½ mi. to the south. Go early in the morning on a cloudy day during the annual migration (Dec.-May) for your best chance of spotting the gray giants. **Tradewinds Charters,** off U.S. 101, downtown, has 6hr. fishing and crabbing trips and 1-2hr. whale-watching trips (☎541-765-2345 or 800-445-8730; www.tradewindscharters.com. Crabbing trips $75. Whale-watching trips $15, seniors and ages 13-19 $13, ages 5-12 $7.)

☐ APPROACHING LINCOLN CITY: 12 MILES
Take **U.S. 101/N. Oregon Coast Hwy.** to Lincoln City.

LINCOLN CITY

Lincoln City is actually five towns wrapped around a 7 mi. strip of ocean-front motels, gas stations, and souvenir shops along U.S. 101. Most budget travelers (and *Let's Go*) will tell you that the Three Capes area to the north is far superior as a destination. As one of the largest "cities" on the North Coast, Lincoln City can, however, be used as a gateway to better points north and south. Four miles north of Lincoln City, life-long Oregon resident and author Ken Kesey *(One Flew Over a Cuckoo's Nest; Sometimes a Great Notion)* is memorialized in the "Sometimes a Great Notion" house on the Siletz River.

Dory Cove ❸, 5819 Logan Rd., at the far north of town, is the locals' unanimous choice for affordable seafood. (☎541-994-5180. Dinner from $10. Open in summer M-Sa 11:30am-9pm, Su noon-8pm; in winter M-Th 11:30am-8pm, F-Sa 11:30am-9pm, Su noon-8pm. AmEx/D/MC/V.) Pets are welcome in the beautiful, small rooms at the **Captain Cook Inn ❷**, 2626 U.S. 101 NE. A quaint New England-style exterior hides clean and charmingly adorned rooms. (☎541-994-2522 or 800-994-2522. Singles $48; doubles $52. AmEx/D/DC/MC/V.)

☐ APPROACHING PACIFIC CITY: 23 MILES
Follow **U.S. 101/S. Oregon Coast Hwy.,** and turn left onto **Brooten** (BRAW-ten) **Rd.**

PACIFIC CITY. The nearest town to Cape Kiwanda, Pacific City is a hidden gem that most travelers on U.S. 101 never even see. The town contains some surprisingly good restaurants. At the **Grateful Bread Bakery ❸**, 34805 Brooten Rd., enjoy vegetarian stuffed focaccia ($8.50) or sample one of the many excellent omelettes for $8. (☎503-965-7337. Open in summer M and Su 3:30-6pm, Tu and Th 8am-3:30pm, F-Sa 3:30-7:30pm; in winter M and Th-Su 8am-6pm. MC/V.) The **Anchorage Motel ❸**, 6585 Pacific Ave., offers homey rooms. (☎541-965-6773 or 800-941-6250. Rooms in summer from $49, in winter from $37. D/MC/V.) Camping on Oregon beaches is illegal, but local youth have been known to camp near the beach, or on more secluded beaches north of Cape Kiwanda. If the Anchorage is booked up, try **The Inn at Pacific City ❹**, 32515 Brooten Rd. Rustic, well furnished rooms are worth the cost. (☎503-965-6366. Rooms in summer from $80; in winter from $55. D/DC/MC/V.)

◪ DETOUR
CAPE KIWANDA STATE PARK
Along the Three Capes Loop, north of Lincoln City.

Cape Kiwanda State Park (☎800-551-6949. Open 24hr.), 1 mi. north of Pacific City, is the jewel of the Three Capes Loop's triple crown. This sheltered cape draws beachcombers, kite-flyers, volleyball players, surfers, and windsurfers, not to mention the odd snowboarder out to ride a giant sand hill. A walk up the sculptured sandstone on the north side reveals a hypnotic view of swells rising over the rocks, forming crests, and smashing into the cliffs. If the surf is up, head to **Seven Surfboards**, 33310 Cape Kiwanda Dr., a little ways of the beach, where the walls are lined with hand crafted surf boards and local artwork. Buy a pair of "Locals" (flip-flops) for $5. (☎503-965-7873. Surfboard rental $20 until 5pm. Boogieboards $10. Wetsuits $20. Package deal $45. Lessons $35 per hour. Open in summer daily 9am-6pm; hours vary in winter.)

◪ DETOUR
CAPE LOOKOUT STATE PARK
12 mi. southwest of Cape Meares.

Cape Lookout State Park offers a small, rocky beach with incredible views of the surrounding sights. From here, the **Cape Trail** (2½ mi.) heads past the 1943 crash site of a military plane to the end of the lookout, where a spectacular 360-degree view featuring **Haystack Rock** awaits. The **Cape Lookout Campground ❶** offers lovely camping near the dunes and the forests behind them, although sites with better privacy tend to go far in advance. (☎503-842-4981 or 800-551-6949. 216 sites. Sites May-Sept. $16, with hookup $20; Oct.-Apr. $12/$16. Yurts $27. Day-use $3. MC/V.)

◪ DETOUR
CAPE MEARES STATE PARK
At the tip of the promontory jutting out from Tillamook; 6 mi. south of Tillamook.

Cape Meares State Park protects one of the few remaining old-growth forests on the Oregon Coast. The mind-blowing **Octopus Tree,** a gnarled Sitka Spruce with six candelabra trunks, looks like the imaginative scribbles of an eight-year-old. The **Cape Meares Lighthouse** operates an illuminating on-site interpretive center. (☎503-842-2244. Open Apr.-Nov. daily 11am-4pm. Free.) If you walk down to the lighthouse, bring binoculars or use the $0.25 viewer to look at the amazing seabird colony on the giant volcanic rock. As you drive south of Cape Meares, a break in the trees reveals a beach between two cliffs; this is a beautiful place to pull off the road to explore.

The towns of Oceanside and Netarts lie a couple miles south of Cape Meares, and offer overpriced gas, a market, and a few places to stay. **The Terimore ❸**, 5103 Crab Ave., in Netarts, has the decent, clean rooms, some with ocean views. (☎541-842-4623 or 800-635-1821. Rooms in summer $50-65, with views $65-75; in winter $43-53/$56-66. AmEx/D/MC/V.) The **Whiskey Creek Cafe ❸**, 6060 Whiskey Creek Rd., in Netarts, is popular for its chile lime oysters ($11.50), fresh from the bay. (☎541-842-5117. Halibut and chips $12. Open daily 11am-9pm. Cash only.)

◪ APPROACHING TILLAMOOK: 35 MILES
Between Lincoln City and Tillamook, **U.S. 101** wanders east into wooded land, leaving the coast. The **Three Capes Loop** is a 35 mi. circle that connects a trio of spectacular promontories—**Cape Kiwanda, Cape Lookout, and Cape Meares State Parks,** that will almost certainly

PACIFIC COAST

make you linger longer than you expect; plan accordingly. The loop leaves U.S. 101 10 mi. north of Lincoln City and rejoins at Tillamook. Unless time is of the utmost importance, the loop is a far better choice than driving straight up U.S. 101.

TILLAMOOK

Although the word Tillamook (TILL-uh-muk) translates to "land of many waters," to the Northwest it is synonymous with "cheese." Tourists come by the hundreds to gaze at blocks of cheese being cut into smaller blocks on a conveyor belt at the **Tillamook Cheese Factory.** The dairy cows themselves give the town a rather bad odor; still, two good museums, hiking and biking in the nearby coastal mountains, and the Three Capes Loop redeem Tillamook for the adventurous traveler.

VITAL STATS

Population: 4400

Visitor Info: Tillamook Chamber of Commerce, 3705 U.S. 101 N (☎503-842-7525), in the big red barn near the Tillamook Cheese Factory, 1½ mi. north of town. Open daily M-F 9am-5pm, Sa 10am-3pm.

Internet Access: Tillamook County Library, 210 Ivy Ave. (☎503-842-4792). Open M-Th 9am-9pm, F-Sa 9am-5:30pm. Free.

Post Office: 2200 1st St. (☎503-842-2517). Open M-F 9am-5pm. **Postal Code:** 97141.

 GETTING AROUND. Tillamook's main drag, **U.S. 101,** splits into two one-way streets downtown; **Pacific Ave.** runs north and **Main Ave.** runs south. The cross streets are labeled numerically, increasing as you head south.

 SIGHTS. The **Tillamook Cheese Factory,** 4175 U.S. 101 N, gives out cheese samples and lets visitors take a free guided tour. (☎800-542-7290; www.tillamookcheese.com. Open daily in summer 8am-8pm; in winter 8am-6pm. Free.) Plane buffs and all who celebrate mechanical marvels will appreciate the impressive **Tillamook Naval Air Station Museum,** 2 mi. south of town. This hulking seven-acre

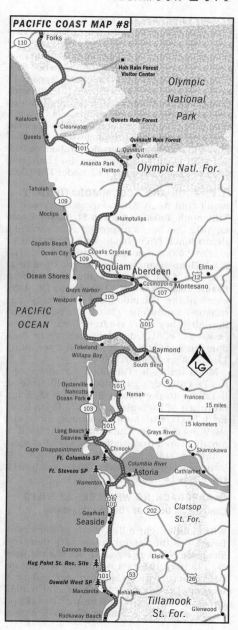

PACIFIC COAST MAP #8

former blimp hangar is the largest wooden clear-span structure in the world. The airy cavern is home to over 38 fully functional war planes, including WWII beauties like the P-38 Lightning and a PBY-5A Catalina. (☎503-842-1130. Open daily 9am-5pm. $11, ages 6-17 $6.50, under 6 $2.) Downtown, the **Tillamook County Pioneer Museum**, 2106 2nd St., features exceptionally thorough collections of WWII medals, rifles, and collectibles. The museum also displays the head-turning work of taxidermist and big game hunter Alex Walker. (☎503-842-4553. Open Tu-Sa 9am-5pm, Su 11am-5pm. $3, seniors and ages 12-17 $2, under 12 $0.50.)

▓▐ FOOD AND ACCOMMODATIONS. You won't find many alternatives to cheese in Tillamook. **Dekunsam's 2nd St. Coffee House ❶**, 1912 2nd St., is a colorful cafe serving a Bento lunch (rice, beans and vegetables or chicken; $5) and delicious drinks. (☎503-842-2299. Th open jam sessions 6-9pm. Open daily 9am-5pm. Cash only.) The **Blue Heron French Cheese Company ❶**, 2001 Blue Heron Dr., 1 mi. south of the Tillamook Cheese factory, has tasty deli sandwiches ($5). If you're still craving dairy, they also have free cheese samples. (☎503-842-8281. Open daily in summer 8am-8pm; in winter 8am-6pm. Deli open daily 11am-3:30pm. AmEx/D/MC/V.)

Motel prices in Tillamook are steep, and the 7% city lodging tax doesn't help. Instead, head out to the **Kilchis River Park ❶**, 6 mi. northeast of town at the end of Kilchis River Rd. It has 36 sites between a mossy forest and the Kilchis River. The campground itself is mostly geared towards families, with a baseball field, volleyball court, horseshoes, and swimming. (☎503-842-6694. Water and toilets. Open May-Oct. Sites $10. MC/V.)

▐ APPROACHING WHEELER: 23 MILES
Continue on **U.S. 101/Oregon Coast Hwy.**

WHEELER. Eight miles north of Rockaway Beach lies this quaint community that runs alongside Nehalem Bay. The **Old Wheeler Hotel ❹**, 495 Hwy 101, is a warm and welcoming B&B of sorts with antique furniture and a collection of the "greatest movies ever made." (☎503-368-6000. Continental breakfast included. Rooms in summer from $75; in win-

ter from $65. AmEx/D/MC/V.) The **Sea Shack ❸**, 380 Marine Dr., serves delightfully fresh seafood right on the waterfront. (☎503-368-7897. Halibut sandwich $7.50. Shrimp melt $7.50. Open daily 11am-11pm. AmEx/D/MC/V.)

▐ APPROACHING NEHALEM: 2 MILES
Head north on **U.S. 101/Oregon Coast Hwy.**

NEHALEM. Just north of Wheeler, a cluster of shops along U.S. 101 make up Nehalem. The **Nehalem Bay Winery**, 34965 Rte. 53, 2 mi. south of town, has free tastings of local cranberry and blackberry vintages. The winery sponsors performances in a small theater and an annual reggae and bluegrass festival, providing a forum for general bacchanalian revelry. (☎503-368-9463; www.nehalembaywinery.com. Open daily 9am-6pm.) Outside of town, **Nehalem Bay State Park ❶** has several camping options. (☎503-368-5154, reservations 800-452-5687. Sites May-Sept. $8-20; Oct.-Apr. $5-16. Day-use $3.)

◀ DETOUR
OSWALD WEST STATE PARK
Located off U.S. 101, 3 mi. south of Arch Cape.

Oswald West State Park is a tiny headland rainforest of hefty spruce and cedars. With a first-rate break and camping close by, **Short Sands Beach**, or Shorty's, is a premier surf destination. The beach and woodsy campsites are only accessible by a trail off U.S. 101, but the park provides wheelbarrows for transporting gear from the parking lot to the 30 sites. The campground fills quickly; call ahead. (Open Mar.-Nov. Sites $14. Cash only.) From the south side of the park, a segment of the Oregon Coast Trail leads over the headland to 1661 ft. **Neahkahnie Mountain.**

▐ APPROACHING CANNON BEACH: 8 MILES
Go north on **U.S. 101/Oregon Coast Hwy.** Along the way, you'll pass **Hug Point**, famous for tidal caves that are accessible only at low tide.

CANNON BEACH

Many moons ago, a rusty cannon from a shipwrecked schooner washed ashore at Arch Cape, giving this town its name. Today, home to a veritable army of boutiques, bakeries, and galleries, Cannon Beach is a more refined alternative to nearby Seaside's crass commercialism. Arguably the most desirable location on the entire Oregon Coast because of its amazing ocean views and interesting shops, Cannon Beach is always crowded with Portlanders and other tourists. Still, it's well worth the stop to take in the view.

VITAL STATS

Population: 1588

Visitor Info: Cannon Beach Chamber of Commerce and Visitor Info, 207 N. Spruce St. (☎503-436-2623), at 2nd St. Open M-Sa 10am-5pm, Su 11am-4pm.

Internet Access: Cannon Beach Library, 131 N. Hemlock St. (☎503-436-1391). Open M-Sa 1-5pm. $6 per hr.

Post Office: 163 N. Hemlock St. (☎503-436-2822). Open M-F 9am-5pm. **Postal Code:** 97110.

⬛ GETTING AROUND. Cannon Beach lies 8 mi. south of Seaside and 42 mi. north of Tillamook on U.S. 101. Lovely **Ecola** and **Oswald State Parks** lie just to the north and a few miles south of the town, respectively. The four exits into town from U.S. 101 all lead to **Hemlock St.,** which is lined with restaurants and galleries.

◙ SIGHTS. Cannon Beach has expensive, sporadically elegant galleries and gift shops. A stroll along the 7 mi. stretch of flat, bluff-framed beach suits many better. The best place to enjoy the dramatic volcanic coastline of Cannon Beach is at **Ecola State Park,** which attracts picnickers, hikers, and surfers alike. Have a look at Ecola Point's views of hulking **Haystack Rock,** which is spotted with seagulls, puffins, barnacles, anemones, and the occasional sea lion. Follow signs from U.S. 101. **Indian Beach** is a gorgeous surfing destination where you can catch waves between volcanic rock walls, before rinsing off in the freshwater stream that runs down the beach. Rent boards from **Cleanline Surf,** 171 Sunset Blvd. (☎503-436-9726. Surfboards and boogie-boards $15 per day. Wetsuits $20 per day. Open in summer daily 8am-8pm; in winter M-F 10am-6pm, Sa-Su 9am-6pm.)

There is also good hiking in the area. **Indian Beach Trail** (2 mi.) leads to the Indian Beach tide pools, which teem with colorful sea life. Follow signs to "Ecola" to reach the trailhead. **Tillamook**

Head Trail (12 mi. round-trip) leaves from Indian Beach, and hugs the coast to the mini-cape that separates Seaside Beach from Cannon Beach. The trail passes the top of Tillamook head (2 mi. up the trail), where five campsites await those willing to make the trek for free camping. Fourteen miles east of Cannon Beach, **Saddle Mountain Trail** (5 mi. round-trip) climbs the highest peak in the Coast Range. The trail leads to the mountain's 3283 ft. summit and ends with astounding views of the Pacific Ocean, Nehalem Bay, and the Cascades.

Coaster Theater, 108 N. Hemlock St., is a small playhouse that stages theater productions, concerts, dance performances, comedy, and musical revues throughout the year. (☎503-436-1242; www.coastertheater.com. Box office open W-Sa 1-5pm. Tickets $14-16.)

◼🍴 FOOD AND NIGHTLIFE. The deals are down **Hemlock St.,** in mid-town. If you're looking to stock up, **Mariner Market,** 139 N. Hemlock St., holds 8439 grocery items on its expansive shelves. (☎503-436-2442. Open July-Sept. M-Th and Su 8am-10pm, F-Sa 8am-11pm; Oct.-June M-Th and Su 8am-9pm, F-Sa 8am-10pm.) **Lazy Susan's Cafe ❷,** 126 N. Hemlock St., in Coaster Sq., is a Cannon Beach favorite with an intimate, woodsy interior. Excellent homemade scones are $2.25. (☎503-436-2816. Omelettes $7-8. Open in summer M and W-Th 8am-2:30pm, F-Sa 8am-8pm, Su 8am-4pm; in winter M and W-Th 8am-2:30pm, F-Sa 8am-7pm, Su 8am-4pm. Cash only.) **Bill's Tavern ❷,** 188 N. Hemlock St., brews beer upstairs that flows on tap downstairs. (☎503-436-2202. Basic pub grub $3-8.25. Pints $3. Open M-Tu and Th-Su 11:30am-last customer, W 4:30pm-last customer. Kitchen closes around 9:30pm. D/MC/V.)

🏠 ACCOMMODATIONS. During the winter months, inquire about specials; many motels offer two-for-one deals. In the summer, however, it's a seller's market, so most motels have two-night minimum stays if you want a reservation. Real budget deals are a short drive away: the **Seaside International Hostel** is 7 mi. north (see p. 975), and the stunning **Oswald West State Park** is 10 mi. south (see p. 972). **McBee Cottages ❸,** 888 S. Hemlock St., has bright and cheerful rooms a few blocks from

PACIFIC COAST

the beach. (☎800-238-4107. Some kitchen units and cottages available. Rooms in summer from $60; in winter from $45. AmEx/D/MC/V.) Nineteen tree-shaded sites make **Wright's for Camping ❶**, 334 Reservoir Rd., off U.S. 101, a relaxing retreat from RV mini-cities. (☎503-436-2347. Showers, toilets. Reservations recommended in summer. Sites $21-30. MC/V.)

APPROACHING SEASIDE: 8 MILES
Continue to follow **U.S. 101/Oregon Coast Hwy.**

SEASIDE

In the winter of 1805-1806, explorers Lewis and Clark made their westernmost camp near Seaside. While the amenities were few and far between at the time, the development of a resort in 1870 brought in hordes of tourists. The town center, replete with indoor mini-golf and barrels of saltwater taffy, has transformed Seaside from a remote coastal outpost to a bustling beachfront. For those uninterested in video arcades, Seaside still has merit as a base for exploring the beautiful Oregon Coast. Seaside is also less expensive than its nearby neighbors, and its hostel is one of the best in the Northwest.

VITAL STATS

Population: 5900

Visitor Info: Chamber of Commerce, 7 N. Roosevelt Dr. (☎503-738-6391 or 800-444-6740), on U.S. 101 and Broadway. **Seaside Visitor Bureau** (☎503-738-3097 or 888-306-2326; www.seasideor.com), in the same building. Open June-Aug. daily 8am-5pm; Oct.-May M-F 9am-5pm, Sa-Su 10am-4pm.

Internet Access: Seaside Library: 60 N. Roosevelt Dr. (☎503-738-6742). Open Tu-Th 9am-8pm, F-Sa 9am-5pm, Su 1-5pm. Free.

Post Office: 300 Ave. A (☎503-738-5190), off Columbia Ave. Open M-F 8:30am-5pm, Sa 8:30-10:30am. **Postal Code:** 97138.

GETTING AROUND. Seaside lies 17 mi. south of Astoria and 8 mi. north of Cannon Beach along **U.S. 101.** The Necanicum River runs north-south through Seaside, two blocks from the coastline. In town, U.S. 101 becomes **Roosevelt Dr.,** and another major road, **Holla-**day **Dr.,** splits off from it. **Broadway** runs perpendicular to the two, and is the town's main street and a tourist-dollar black hole. Streets north of Broadway are numbered, and those south of Broadway are lettered. The **Promenade** (or "Prom") is a paved foot-path that hugs the beach for the length of town.

SIGHTS. Seaside's tourist population (which often outnumbers that of locals) swarms around **Broadway,** a carnival-esque strip of arcades and shops running the half-mile from Roosevelt Dr. (U.S. 101) to the beach. "The Arcade," as it is called, is the focal point of downtown and attracts a youthful crowd. Bumper cars, basketball games, and other tourist trappings abound. The turnaround at the end of Broadway signals the end of the **Lewis and Clark Trail. The Seaside Aquarium,** 200 N. Promenade, is smaller than its companion in Newport, but it makes up for its small size by giving visitors the chance to feed playful harbor seals. (☎503-738-6211. Open Mar.-June daily 9am-7pm; hours vary in winter. $7, seniors $5, ages 6-13 $3.50, under 6 free. Seal feeding $1.) If it's a bright day, you might want to take a stroll down the beach, or bike or skate along the wooden walkway, **The Prom.** Get into the spirit by renting a beach bike, tossing back your hair, and eating an ice-cream cone by the sea. The **Salt Cairns** (8 blocks south of Broadway) are also worth a gander. Pots in a pile of stones are traditionally none too exciting but then, those other pots weren't on the spot where members of Lewis and Clark's party boiled sea water for two months, supplying the explorers with the essential salt to preserve their food. Seaside's beachfront is sometimes crowded despite bone-chilling water and strong undertows that more or less preclude swimming. For a slightly quieter beach, head to **Gearhart,** 2 mi. north of downtown off U.S. 101, where long stretches of dunes await exploration. Perhaps the premier recreational road race in the US, the **Hood to Coast Relay** is the ultimate team running event. Held annually at the end of August, runners tear up the trails between Mt. Hood and Seaside (195 mi.) to the cheers of 50,000 spectators. About 750 12-person teams run three 5 mi. shifts in this one- to two-day relay race. (For more info, call ☎503-292-4626.)

🔊🍴 FOOD AND ACCOMMODATIONS.

Prices on Broadway, especially toward the beach, are outrageous. At **Morning Star Cafe ❷**, 280 S. Roosevelt Dr., comfy couches and aging board games will remind you of your old basement recreation room. Enjoy a sandwich ($3.25-7.25) or quiche ($4.25) with a mocha. Get the grilled cheese royale ($6.50) for a dairy fix. (☎503-717-8188. Open in summer M-F 7am-7pm, Sa-Su 7am-2 or 4pm; in winter M-F 7am-6pm and Sa-Su 7am-2 or 4pm. D/MC/V.) **The Stand ❶**, 101 N. Holladay Dr., serves the cheapest Mexican meals around to a local crowd. (☎503-738-6592. Burritos $3-5. Open M-F 11am-6pm. Cash only.)

Seaside's expensive motels are hardly an issue for the budget traveler, thanks to the large hostel on the south side of town. Motel prices are directly proportional to their proximity to the beach and start at $50 (less during the low season). The lively **◪Seaside International Hostel (HI) ❶**, 930 N. Holladay Dr., offers free nightly movies, a well-equipped kitchen, an espresso bar, and a grassy yard along the river. (☎503-738-7911. Kayak and canoe rental. Reception 8am-11pm. Reservations recommended. Dorms $25, members $22; private rooms with bath $39-65/$36-42. D/MC/V.) **Saddle Mountain ❶**, 10 mi. east, off U.S. 26, offers sites with drinking water. Drive 8 mi. northeast of Necanicum Junction, then another 7 mi. up to the base camp. (☎800-551-6949. Sites Oct.-Apr. $5; May-Sept. $9. Cash only.)

🡆APPROACHING FORT CLATSTOP NATIONAL MEMORIAL: 10 MILES

Continue north on **U.S. 101.** Turn right at **SE Marlin Ave.,** and follow the signs to the memorial.

FORT CLATSTOP NATIONAL MEMORIAL.

This memorial reconstructs Lewis and Clark's winter headquarters from journal descriptions. The fort has been restored and contains exhibits about the explorers' quest for the Pacific Ocean. In summer, rangers in feathers and buckskin demonstrate quill writing, moccasin sewing, and musket firing. (☎503-861-2471. Open daily June to Labor Day 9am-6pm; Labor Day to May 9am-5pm. $5, ages 4-15 $2, under 4 free.)

🡆APPROACHING FORT STEVENS STATE PARK: 1 MILE

Head north on **Fort Stevens Hwy.** to the park.

FORT STEVENS STATE PARK.

Fort Stevens was constructed in 1863 to prevent attack by Confederate naval raiders. The fort was significantly upgraded in 1897 with the addition of eight concrete artillery batteries. Several of these remaining batteries are the focus of a 2hr. self-guided walking tour that begins up the road from the campground area. Great places to surf or kayak await at the South Jetty, near the northern tip of the peninsula in the park. Waves get big when the wave refraction off the jetty kicks in. Everyone loves catching a wave in front of the **Wreck of the Peter Iredale** that sticks out of the sand, even though the breaks are nothing special. (☎503-861-2000. Get a map and pass from the camp registration. Entrance fee $3.) Rugged, empty beaches and hiking and bike trails surround the **campground ❶**, though the 287 cramped sites don't offer much in the way of privacy. (☎503-861-1671, reservations 800-452-5687. Toilets, water. Reservations recommended; $6 fee. Sites $18; RV sites $22; hiker/biker sites $4 per person; yurts $30. MC/V.)

🡆APPROACHING ASTORIA: 9 MILES

Follow **Fort Stevens Hwy. (Alt. U.S. 101)** out of Fort Stevens Park, and turn left to follow **U.S. 101.**

ASTORIA

Established in 1811 by John Jacob Astor's trading party, Astoria is the oldest US city west of the Rocky Mountains. Originally built as a fort to guard the mouth of the Columbia River, it quickly became a port city for ships heading to Portland and Longview, WA. A much more pleasant and less expensive destination than the overrun resort cities to the south, Astoria offers the same beautiful views of the Pacific Ocean. Its Victorian homes, energetic waterfront, rolling hills, and persistent fog suggest a smaller-scale San Francisco. Differentiating it from that metropolis

PACIFIC COAST

1956: Art Ingels builds the first go-kart out of scrap metal and a surplus cycle engine.

is a microclimate with wicked winter storms; hurricane-force winds aren't uncommon, and many travelers come to watch storms roll into the Columbia River outlet.

VITAL STATS

Population: 9800

Visitor Info: Astoria-Warrenton Area Chamber of Commerce, 111 W. Marine Dr. (☎503-325-6311), just east of Astoria Bridge. Open June-Sept. M-Sa 9am-6pm, Su 9am-5pm; Oct.-May M-F 9am-5pm, Sa-Su 11am-4pm.

Internet Access: Astoria Library, 450 10th St. (☎503-325-7323). Open Tu-Th 10am-7pm, F-Sa 10am-5pm. Free.

Post Office: 750 Commercial St., Ste. 104 (☎503-338-0316). Open M-F 8:30am-5pm. **Postal Code:** 97103.

GETTING AROUND. Astoria is a peninsula that extends into the Columbia River, approximately 7 mi. from the ocean beaches in Fort Stevens and Washington. Two bridges run from the city: the **Youngs Bay Bridge** leads southwest when **Marine Dr.** becomes **U.S. 101,** and the **Astoria Bridge** spans the Columbia River into Washington. All streets parallel to the water are named in alphabetical order, except for the first one.

SIGHTS. On the rare clear day, **Astoria Column,** cradled between **Saddle Mountain** to the south and the **Columbia River Estuary** to the north, grants climbers a stupendous view of Astoria. Completed in 1926, the column on Coxcomb Hill Rd. encloses a dizzying 164 steps past newly repainted friezes depicting local history; picture something like an exceptionally well-decorated barber's pole jutting into the sky, albeit one that (luckily) doesn't spin. (Follow signs from 16th Ave. and Commercial St. Open sunrise-10pm.) The cavernous, wave-shaped **Columbia River Maritime Museum,** 1792 Marine Dr., on the waterfront, is packed with marine lore, including displays on the salmon fisheries that once dominated Astoria. Among the model boats is the 1792 vessel that Robert Grey first steered into the mouth of the Columbia River. (☎503-325-2323. Open daily 9:30am-5pm. $8, seniors $7, ages 6-17 $4, under 6 free.) The annual **Astoria-Warrenton Crab and Seafood Festival** is a misnomer for a large assembly of Oregon winemakers, brewers, and restaurants. (☎503-325-6311. $5.)

FOOD. A small but growing **farmers market** convenes each summer Sunday downtown at 12th St. from 10am-3pm. **Columbian Cafe ❸,** 1114 Marine Dr., offers local banter, wines by the glass, and fantastic pasta and seafood. Try "Seafood" or "Vegetarian Mercy"—name the heat your mouth can stand and the chef will design a meal for you. (☎503-325-2233. Lunch entrees $5-10. Dinner entrees $15-20. Open M-Tu 8am-2pm, W-Sa 8am-9pm, Su 9am-2pm. Cash only.) Check out the Meat Lover weekends (F-Sa) at **T. Paul's Urban Cafe ❸,** 1119 Commercial St., where they rotate pork loin, prime rib, and lamb. The veggie Baja Boca Burger ($7.50) is exceptional. (☎503-338-5133. Open in summer M-Th 11am-9pm, F-Sa 11am-10pm, Su 11am-4pm; in winter M-Th 11am-9pm, F-Sa 11am-10pm. MC/V.) Across the street, the **Danish Maid Bakery ❶** offers delicious sweets for pocket change. Crazy Coolies ($0.25) and Chocolate Chews ($0.75) are particularly popular. (☎503-325-3657. Open M-Sa 4am-5:30pm. AmEx/MC/V.)

ACCOMMODATIONS. Motel rooms can be expensive and elusive during summer. U.S. 101, both north and south of Astoria, is littered with clean and scenic campgrounds. **Grandview B&B ❸,** 1574 Grand Ave., has intimate, cheery, and luxurious rooms. (☎503-325-0000 or 325-5555. Breakfast included. Rooms $49; with bath from $79. D/MC/V.) **Lamplighter Motel ❸,** 131 W. Marine Dr., near the visitors center, has spotless, well-lit rooms with cable TV and large bathrooms. (☎503-325-4051 or 800-845-8847. Rooms in summer $67-85; in winter $40. AmEx/D/MC/V.)

NIGHTLIFE. The nightlife in Astoria has recently begun to come into its own. The **Voodoo Room,** adjacent to Columbian Cafe, is the new hot venue for live music, known by many as the artists' hang. Egyptian sarcophagi complete the scene. (☎503-325-2233. F-Sa funk, jazz, and every other kind of music. Th bluegrass. Cover F-Sa $3-5. Open daily 5-10pm or later. Cash only.) Youthful crowds flock to

Wet Dog Cafe & Pacific Rim Brewing Co., 144 11th St., for hip-hop and Top 40 on weekends. (☎503-325-6975. Burgers $8. Seafood burgers $10. Th-F DJs. 21+ after 10pm. Open M-Th 11am-10pm, F 11am-1:30am, Sa 8am-1:30am, Su 8am-10pm. AmEx/D/MC/V.)

⚑ APPROACHING CHINOOK: 10 MILES
Follow the **U.S. 101/Oregon Coast Hwy.** across the border into Washington.

The Evergreen State
WASHINGTON
Welcomes You!

CHINOOK. As you stop in the **Country Store,** 775 U.S. 101, for some candy or a bottle of juice, check out the photographs of how Chinook looked in days of yore with dirt streets and horses pulling in the fishing catch. (☎360-777-2248. Open M-Sa 5am-8pm, Su 5am-7:30pm.) One of the few intact coastal defense sites in the US, **Fort Columbia State Park** offers 5 mi. of hiking trails, an interpretive center, and wildlife viewing. (Center open daily 10am-5pm. Park open daily in summer 6:30am-9:30pm; in winter 8am-5pm. Donations accepted.)

⚑ APPROACHING ILWACO: 7 MILES
Head north on **U.S. 101** to Ilwaco.

ILWACO. The best thing to do once you've set foot in the beautiful, wet state of Washington is to traipse around its southernmost tip in Ilwaco, ◪**Cape Disappointment State Park.** The confluence of the Columbia and Pacific is breathtaking, and along the way you'll stumble over some unexpected beaches tucked into the jetty. The cape was named for that "aw, shucks" feeling felt by the British explorer Captain John Meares in 1788 when he missed the passage over the bar. Follow the signs to the **Lewis and Clark Interpretive Center,** park your car, and wander; you can't go too far without coming to the water's edge. If the weather turns on you (which is a frequent occurrence in Washington), you can pop into the center, which has excellent dis-

plays about the famous duo's journey, as well as maritime and Native American history. (☎360-642-3078. Hours vary; call ahead. $3, ages 7-17 $1, under 6 free.) A ¾ mi. trail leads to the **Cape Disappointment Lighthouse,** the oldest operating lighthouse on the West Coast.

Like most other towns along the bay, **Ilwaco** was nearly devastated when depleted salmon stocks required a shutdown of the fishery for several years. Salmon steaks are plentiful along the waterfront, where the industry is beginning to recover. **Pacific Salmon Charters** leads 8hr. fishing tours. (☎360-642-3466 or 800-831-2695. From $83.50. Open daily at 4:30am.)

⚑ APPROACHING LONG BEACH PENINSULA: 5 MILES
Continue north on **U.S. 101.**

PHOTO OP. The **world's largest frying pan** is in Long Beach Peninsula.

LONG BEACH PENINSULA

The 28 mi. of unbroken sand that is Long Beach Peninsula is a frenzy of kitsch and souvenir shops sporadically broken up by calm forests and beautiful ocean views. Just don't give into temptation and take a dip—the water is very cold and carries lethal riptide currents. Accessible by U.S. 101 and Rte. 103, every town has a clearly marked beach access road (unmarked roads end in private property). Fishing, boating, and kite-flying are how residents recuperate from pounding winter storms. Clamming season lasts from October to mid-March. **Short Stop,** in the Shell Station across from the visitors center, sells non-resident licenses (2-day license $7) along with tips and tide tables. For some entertainment, head to **Marsh's Free Museum,** 409 S. Pacific Way, home to a mechanical fortune teller, Jake the petrified alligator-man, and honky-tonk souvenirs. (☎360-642-2188. Open whenever tourists bring money.) During the 3rd full week of August, flyers from Thailand, China, Japan, and Australia compete in the spectacular **International Kite Festival.** Head to the **visitors bureau,** 5min. south of Long Beach on U.S. 101, for more info. (☎360-642-3466 or 800-831-2695. Open daily M-Sa 9am-5pm, Su 10am-4pm.)

For the best meal around, head up Rte. 103 in Ocean Park to historic **Oysterville.** The star draw of this tiny, whitewashed town is **Oysterville Sea Farms** ❸, at 1st St. and Oysterville Rd., which raises and dishes out its namesake mollusk. (☎360-665-6585. Open daily 10am-5pm. MC/V.) **Doogers** ❸, is a small regional family chain that offers seafood at its best. Salmon fish and chips ($10) and cheap beer. (☎360-642-4224. Open daily at 11am. AmEx/D/MC/V.) Hit the hay at the **Mermaid Inn** ❸, 1910 N. Pacific Hwy. (☎360-642-2600. Rooms $50-100. AmEx/MC/V.)

📍 **APPROACHING WILLAPA BAY: 8 MILES**
Follow **U.S. 101** as it heads off the peninsula and north toward Willapa Bay.

WILLAPA BAY. Willapa Bay stretches between the Long Beach Peninsula and the Washington mainland. Home to the last unpolluted estuary in the nation, this is an excellent place to watch birds, especially in late spring and early fall. From the north, stop at the headquarters of the **Willapa National Wildlife Refuge,** 12 mi. north of the junction between U.S. 101 and Rte. 13, just off U.S. 101, by Chinook. The headquarters has info on Canada geese, loons, grebes, cormorants, and trumpeter swans. (☎360-484-3482. Open M-F 7:30am-4pm.)

📍 **APPROACHING SOUTH BEND: 37 MILES**
Continue on **U.S. 101** to the tiny town of South Bend.

SOUTH BEND. South Bend grew into a township as the location of the Northern Pacific railroad terminus. As you drive through, pull over into the harbor for a closer view of the wooden statues dedicated to fishermen and women. Don't miss the beautiful 1910 **Courthouse,** 300 Memorial Dr., one block east of U.S. 101, set into stunning landscaped gardens. Take a look up at the kaleidoscopic-colored glass dome. (☎360-875-9320. Open M-F 8:30am-5pm.)

📍 **APPROACHING TOKELAND: 26 MILES**
Continue on **U.S. 101** to Raymond, and follow **Rte. 105** out of Raymond along the coast; it's worth it to take the little extra time to loop around the coastal route of Rte. 105, instead of staying inland on U.S.

101. Be careful of the low speed limits here, especially the 25 mph of the **Shoalwater Reservation,** which are enforced with particular diligence.

TOKELAND. A stop in Tokeland is worth it for the **Tokeland Hotel** ❸. Isolated on the Willapa Bay, the gracious 1889 hotel has pretty whitewashed rooms with quilts and shared bathrooms. The downstairs living room and restaurant are open from 8am to 8pm. (From Rte. 105 take the Tokeland exit. The hotel is 2 mi. down, on the left. ☎360-267-7006. Reservations required. Doubles $65. D/MC/V.)

📍 **APPROACHING WESTPORT: 14 MILES**
Continue on **Rte. 105** to Westport.

WESTPORT. Westport is a pleasant town, but aside from the fishing there's not much going on. The highlight is the beautiful **Westhaven State Park** (donations accepted.) where there is a 1½ mi. trail along the coast to the lighthouse. (Just northeast of town on Rte. 105. ☎360-268-9717. Donations accepted.) Charter a fishing boat or surf the cove; you can rent equipment from **Steepwater Surf,** 1200 N. Montesano St. (☎360-268-5527; www.steepwatersurfshop.com. Board and wetsuit $26 per 4hr. Open in summer daily 9am-5pm; in winter M and Th-Su 10am-4pm.)

📍 **APPROACHING ABERDEEN AND HOQUIAM: 22 MILES**
Continue on **Rte. 105** for about 18 mi., then turn left to approach Aberdeen and Hoquiam on **U.S. 101 N.**

ABERDEEN AND HOQUIAM

From Olympic National Park to the north, U.S. 101 passes Grays Harbor and the industrial cities of Aberdeen and Hoquiam at the mouth of the Chehalis River. The two towns, once deeply embedded in the now largely defunct fishing and timber industries, are now focusing on tourism. Aberdeen is best known as the childhood home of late Nirvana frontman Kurt Cobain.

📧 **GETTING AROUND.** Aberdeen is at the eastern side of Grays Harbor, on the banks of the Wishkah and Chehalis Rivers. **U.S. 101** runs through Aberdeen as two one-way streets a block apart. Hoquiam is west of Aberdeen, on the banks of the Hoquiam River. Both cities can be extremely confusing to navigate, so be sure to pick up a map from the Grays Harbor Chamber of Commerce.

VITAL STATS

Population: 16,600/9200

Visitor Info: Grays Harbor Chamber of Commerce and Visitors Center, 506 Duffy St. (☎360-532-1924). Open M-F 8-5, Sa-Su 9-4.

Internet Access: Timberland Regional Library, 121 E. Market St. (☎360-533-2360). Open M-Th 10:30am-8:30pm, F 10am-6pm, Sa 10am-5pm, Su 1-5pm. Free.

Post Office: in Aberdeen, 115 N. K St. (☎360-537-7205). Open M-F 8:30am-5pm, Sa 10am-2pm. **Postal Code:** 98520. In Hoquiam, 620 8th St. (☎360-537-7204). Open M-F 8:30am-5pm. Postal Code: 98550.

◙ SIGHTS. Head across the street from the visitors center to **Hubb's Muffler,** not to fix your car but to see a small statue and homemade shrine to Kurt Cobain. The statue is hidden in the corner. Aberdeen has a fraught relationship with its most famous resident, and controversy has raged over whether the statue should be displayed publicly; many residents have reservations about honoring a heroin addict who committed suicide. The sculptor, Randy, is married to the mechanic who runs the shop. (☎360-533-1957. Open M-F 8am-5pm, Sa-Su 10am-noon. Free.) The **Grays Harbor Historic Seaport,** now slightly obscured by a gigantic Wal-Mart, occasionally harbors the *Lady Washington.* Launched in 1750, the vessel was the first American ship to round Cape Horn and dock in the Northwest. The boat that exists today is a 1989 replica of the historic brig, and it is most recently famous for its appearance in Disney's *Pirates of the Caribbean.* The boat also offers a selection of 3hr. tours: a sunset sail, a "sailing adventure" where you can pull the ropes and navigate yourself, or the most exciting—a 18th-century sea battle. (☎800-200-5239 or 360-532-8611; www.ladywashington.org. Open daily 10am-1pm. $3, students and seniors $2, children $1.

Trips $35-50.) In Hoquiam, the **Polson Museum,** 1611 Riverside Ave., has an extensive collection of local artifacts, photographs, and period clothing. (☎360-533-5862. Open in summer W-Sa 11am-4pm; in winter Sa-Su noon-4pm or by appointment. $4, students $2, under 12 $1.)

▃◪ FOOD AND ACCOMMODATIONS. **Billy's Bar & Grill ❸,** 322 E. Heron St., at G St., crosses a rugged Old West saloon with Howard Johnson's. It's named for a sailor who used to keep his seafaring pals' money in his safe and then, when they came back after a few drinks to take it out, would pull a trap door on them and send them plummeting into the ocean. (☎360-533-7144. Entrees $8-11. Open M-Th 7am-11pm, F-Sa 8am-midnight, Su 7am-10pm. AmEx/D/DC/MC/V.) The **Olympic Inn Motel ❸,** 616 W. Heron St., on U.S. 101 N., has a flashing neon torch on the sign out front. (☎360-533-4200, or 800-562-8681. Rooms in summer $56-80; in winter $46-54. AmEx/D/MC/V.) More tourist attraction than lodging, **Hoquiam's Castle ❺,** 515 Chenault Ave., is not a castle at all, but a cloyingly cute 1897 Victorian inn with five rooms built by the lumber baron who started the town. Dolls crowd the windowsill in the Princess room, and some bathrooms have vanity tables and claw-footed tubs. (☎360-533-2005; www.hoquiamcastle.com. Rooms $145-195. MC/V.)

◪ APPROACHING OCEAN SHORES: 22 MILES
Follow **U.S. 101** out of Aberdeen, then turn left onto **Rte. 109.** About 16 mi. later, turn left on **Rte. 115.**

OCEAN SPRINGS. Declared "the richest little city in America" in 1969 because of its lucrative real estate, Ocean Shores remains an enviable destination for its antiquing, boating, and gambling. Grab your shillelagh and head to **Galway Bay Irish Pub ❸,** 880 Point Brown Ave. NE, for live music every Friday and Saturday nights. (☎360-289-2300. Open M-Th 11am-10pm, F-Sa 11am-midnight, Su 11am-10pm. AmEx/D/DC/MC/V.)

◪ APPROACHING OLYMPIC NATIONAL PARK: 109 MILES
Continue north on **U.S. 101** through Amanda Park and Queets toward Olympic National Park.

PACIFIC COAST

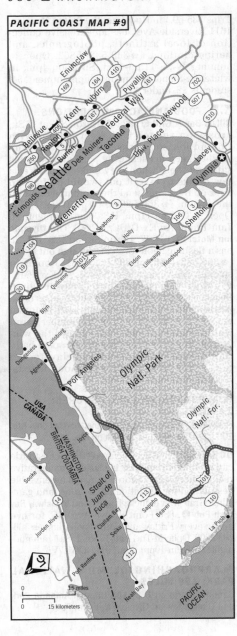

PACIFIC COAST MAP #9

OLYMPIC NATIONAL PARK

North of Aberdeen, U.S. 101 loops around the Olympic Peninsula, a remote backpacking paradise, before heading back south toward Seattle. To the west, the Pacific Ocean stretches to a distant horizon; to the north, the Strait of Juan de Fuca separates the Olympic Peninsula from Vancouver Island; and to the east, Hood Canal and the Kitsap Peninsula isolate this sparsely inhabited wilderness from Seattle's urban sprawl. The Olympic National Park, sheltering one of the most diverse landscapes of any region in the world, is certainly the centerpiece of the Olympic Peninsula. Roads lead to many corners of Olympic National Park, but they only hint at the depths of its wilderness. A dive into the backcountry leaves summer tourists behind and reveals the park's richness and diversity.

VITAL STATS

Area: 922,610 acres

Visitor Info: Olympic National Park Visitors Center, 3002 Mt. Angeles Rd. (☎360-565-3130), off Race St. in Port Angeles. Open daily in summer 9am-4:30pm; in winter 9am-4pm.

Gateway Towns: Forks and **Port Angeles.**

Fees: $15 per vehicle.

GETTING AROUND

U.S. 101 encircles the park in the shape of an upside-down U. Farthest south is **Forks,** a gateway to the park's rainforested **western rim.** Separate from the rest of the park, much of the Pacific coastline comprises a gorgeous **coastal zone.** The much-visited **northern rim** extends eastward to **Port Angeles,** the major gateway to the park and home to many food and lodging options. The park is huge, and U.S. 101 passes through far more than you could experience in one roadtrip; don't be in any hurry to get to Seattle.

SIGHTS

Port Angeles is the "gateway" to the Olympic National Park and has the most attractions to show for it. Near town, a trail (5 mi., 2hr.) leads out on the **Dungeness Spit**, the world's longest natural sand spit, which extends 6 mi. into the Strait of Juan de Fuca. The trail winds all the way to **New Dungeness Lighthouse**, once at the tip of the spit, now a half-mile from the end. (☎603-683-9166; www.newdungenesslighthouse.com. Open daily 9am until 2hr. before sunset. Free.) Over 200 species of birds inhabit this area, part of the **Dungeness National Wildlife Refuge.** Offshore, indigenous crabs, clams, seals, and sea lions populate the waters. When passing through Forks, take time to visit the **Forks Timber Museum.** (☎360-374-9663. Open June-Sept. Tu-Sa 10am-4pm. Logging and mill tours M, W, F 9am. Free.) East on U.S. 101 in the Northern Rim, 13 mi. of paved road penetrates the park's interior to the popular **Sol Duc Hot Springs Resort,** where retirees de-wrinkle in the springs and eat in the lodge. (☎360-327-3583; www.visitsolduc.com. Open late May-Aug. daily 9am-9pm; Mar.-Apr. and Sept.-Oct. 9am-7pm. Suit and towel rental available. $10.75, ages 4-12 $8.)

◤ OUTDOORS

EASTERN RIM

The eastern rim stuns visitors with its canals and grandiose views of the peninsula and Puget Sound. Steep trails lead up **Mt. Ellinor,** 5 mi. past Staircase Campground on Rte. 119. Hikers can choose the 3 mi. path or an equally steep but shorter journey to the summit; look for signs to the Upper Trailhead along Forest Rd. #2419-04. Adventurers who hit the mountain before late July should bring snow clothes to "mach" (as in Mach 1) down a ¼ mi. snow chute. In the nearby National Forest, a 3¼ mi. hike goes to **Lena Lake,** 14 mi. north of Hoodsport off U.S. 101; follow Forest Service Rd. 25 off U.S. 101 for 8 mi. to the trailhead. The Forest Service charges $3 per trailhead pass. The **West Forks Dosewallip Trail** (10½ mi.) to **Mount Anderson Glacier** is the shortest route to any glacier in the park. The road to **Mount Walker Viewpoint,** 5 mi. south of Quilcene on U.S. 101, has sheer drop-offs and shouldn't be attempted in bad weather or

with an unreliable car. A view of Hood Canal, Puget Sound, Mt. Rainier, and Seattle awaits travelers at the top.

NORTHERN RIM

The most developed section of Olympic National Park lies along its northern rim, near Port Angeles, where glaciers, rainforests, and sunsets over the Pacific are only a short drive away. Farthest east off U.S. 101 lies **Deer Park,** where trails tend to be uncrowded. Past Deer Park, the **Royal Basin Trail** meanders 6¼ mi. to the **Royal Basin Waterfall.** The road up **Hurricane Ridge** is a curvy drive, so be cautious. Before July, walking on the ridge usually involves some snow-stepping. Clear days provide splendid views of Mt. Olympus and Vancouver Island set against a foreground of snow and indigo lupine. From here, the uphill **High Ridge Trail** is a short walk from Sunset Point. On weekends from late December to late March, the Park Service organizes snowshoe walks on the ridge. The **Sol Duc trailhead** is a starting point for those heading up, but crowds thin dramatically above **Sol Duc Falls.** The **Eagle Ranger Station** has info. (☎360-327-3534. Open in summer daily 8am-4:30pm.) A massive body of water located in the north-central region of the peninsula, just off U.S. 101, **Lake Crescent** is often ignored by travelers. The lake offers brisk swimming, blissful picnicking, and frequent sunshine. **Storm King Ranger Station** is on a small peninsula in the center of the lake and offers the regular services. (☎360-928-3380. Open in summer daily 10am-5pm.) The **Lake Crescent Lodge,** next to the Storm King Station, rents rowboats to help summertime romantics. (☎360-928-3211. Rentals 7am-8pm. $9 per hr., $25 per half-day.)

NEAH BAY AND CAPE FLATTERY

At the westernmost point on the Juan de Fuca Strait and north of the park's western rim is **Neah Bay,** known as the "Pompeii of the Pacific." The only town in the **Makah Reservation,** Neah Bay is a 500-year-old village that was buried in a landslide at Cape Alava. The Makah Nation, whose recorded history goes back 2000 years, still lives here. Just inside the reservation, the **Makah Cultural and Research Center,** on Rte. 112, in Neah Bay, has artifacts from the archaeological site. (☎360-645-2711;

www.makah.com/mcrchome.htm. Open June to mid-Sept. daily 10am-5pm; mid-Sept. to May W-Su 10am-5pm. Free tours W-Su noon-4pm. $5, students and seniors $4.) For over 80 years, Native Americans from around the region have come for canoe races, dances, and bone games during **Makah Days,** a festival held the last weekend of August. (☎360-645-2711; www.makah.com/makahdays.htm. $10 per vehicle.) ■**Cape Flattery,** the northwesternmost point in the contiguous US, lies just outside Neah Bay. Head out of town on Neah Bay Rd., then take the right fork onto Arrow Head Rd. This will turn into Cape Loop Rd., which will lead you to the traihead. A ½ mi. trail leads to the breathtaking cape.

COASTAL ZONE

Pristine coastline traces the park's far western region for 57 mi., separated from the rest of Olympic National Park by U.S. 101 and non-park forest. Eerie fields of driftwood, sculptured arches, and dripping caves frame flaming sunsets, while the waves are punctuated by rugged sea stacks. Between the Quinalt and Hoh Reservations, U.S. 101 hugs the coast for 15 mi. with parking lots a short walk from the sand. North of where the highway meets the coast, **Beach #4** has abundant tide pools plastered with sea stars. **Beach #6,** 3 mi. north at Mi. 160, is a favorite whale-watching spot. Near Mi. 165, sea otters and eagles hang amid tide pools and sea stacks at **Ruby Beach,** a magical spot where lovers and photographers tend to congregate. Day hikers and backpackers adore the 9 mi. loop that begins at **Ozette Lake.** The trail leads along boardwalks through the rain forest. One heads toward sea stacks at **Cape Alava,** and the other goes to a beach at **Sand Point.**

FOOD

Pacific Pizza, 870 South Forks Ave. (☎360-374-2626), in Forks. The Italian dinner menu features classic spaghetti and meatballs ($6), as well as delicious slices of pizza ($3) and sandwiches ($6.50). Open daily 11am-10pm. AmEx/D/DC/MC/V. ❶

Crazy Fish, 229 W. 1st St. (☎360-457-1944), in Port Angeles. The hit restaurant in town. The fish

tacos (2 for $7) and the oddball mac-and-cheese wedges ($5) are guaranteed to brighten your day. Open M-Sa 11am-2am. DC/MC/V. ❷

Thai Peppers, 222 N. Lincoln St. (☎360-452-4995). Thai Peppers keeps patrons happy with an extensive menu and excellent seafood. Lunch specials $8. Dinner $9-12. Open M-Sa 11am-2:30pm and 4:30-9pm. D/MC/V. ❸

ACCOMMODATIONS

Rainforest Hostel, 169312 U.S. 101 (☎360-374-2270; www.rainforesthostel.com), 20 mi. south of Forks on U.S. 101, between Hoh Rain Forest and Kalaloch. To get there, follow hostel signs off U.S. 101, 4 mi. north of Ruby Beach. A large coed dorm, 2 rooms for couples, and a family room. Morning chore required. Campsites $4.50. Dorms $8.50; private doubles $18. Cash only. ❶

Thor Town Hostel, 316 N. Race St. (☎360-452-0931; www.thortown.com), in Port Angeles. A friendly refuge located in a big red house. Helpful staff and backpacker friendly. Laundry $2. Bike rental $8 per day. Dorms $15; private rooms $30. Cash only. ❶

Town Motel, 1080 S. Forks Ave. (☎360-374-6231), in Forks. Offers a beautiful garden, comfortable rooms, and an activities room with a tanning bed and exercise equipment. Singles from $43; doubles from $53. AmEx/D/DC/MC/V. ❷

South Beach Campground, 3 mi. south of the ranger station. Everywhere has a view of the ocean even though it can get quite windy. 50 sites first come, first served. No potable water. Sites $10. Cash only. ❶

◪ APPROACHING SEATTLE: 84 MILES

Leave Port Angeles on **U.S. 101;** continue east and then south. 35 mi. beyond Port Angeles, bear right onto **Rte. 104 S.** 25 mi. later, take the **ferry** to Edmonds, leaving the Olympic Peninsula, and take **I-5 S** into Seattle.

SEATTLE

Seattle's serendipitous mix of mountain views, clean streets, espresso stands, and rainy weather was the magic formula of the 90s, attracting transplants from across the US. The droves of newcomers provide an interesting contrast to the older residents who remember Seattle as a town, not a thriving metropolis bubbling over with millionaires. Software and coffee money have helped drive rents sky-high in some areas, but the grungy street culture prevails. In the end, there is a nook or cranny for almost anyone in Seattle. The city is shrouded in cloud 200 days a year, but when the skies clear, Seattleites rejoice that "the mountain is out" and head for the country.

VITAL STATS

Population: 573,911

Visitor Info: Seattle Convention and Visitors Bureau (☎206-461-5840; www.seeseattle.org), at 8th and Pike St. Open in summer daily 9am-5pm; in winter M-F 9am-5pm.

Internet Access: Seattle Public Library, 1000 4th Ave. (☎206-386-4636), at Madison St. Photo ID required. Open M-W 10am-8pm, Th-Sa 10am-6pm, Su 1-5pm. Hours vary; call ahead. Free.

Parking: Pacific Place Parking, between 6th and 7th Ave. and Olive and Pine St., with hourly rates comparable to the meters. There's also parking at **Seattle Center,** near the Space Needle. (☎206-652-0416. $2 per hr.; $24 per day.)

Post Office: 301 Union St. (☎206-748-5417), at 3rd Ave., downtown. Open M-F 7:30am-5:30pm. **Postal Code:** 98101.

GETTING AROUND

Seattle stretches from north to south on an isthmus between **Puget Sound** to the west and **Lake Washington** to the east. Get to **downtown** (including **Pioneer Square, Pike Place Market,** and the **waterfront**) from I-5 by taking any of the exits from James St. to Stewart St. Take the Mercer St. exit to the **Seattle Center.** The Denny Way exit leads to **Capitol Hill,** and, farther north, the 45th St. exit heads toward the **University District.** The city is easily accessible via **I-5,** which runs north-south through the city, and **I-90** from the east, which ends at I-5 southeast of downtown. The less crowded **Rte. 99** (also called **Aurora Ave.** and **Aurora Hwy.**) runs parallel to I-5 and skirts the western side

of downtown, with great views from the Alaskan Way Viaduct. Rte. 99 is often the better choice driving downtown or to **Queen Anne, Fremont, Green Lake,** and the northwestern part of the city. Even the most road-weary drivers can learn their way around the Emerald City. Street parking creates many blind pull-outs in Seattle, so be extra careful when turning onto crossroads. Downtown, **avenues** run northwest to southeast and **streets** run southwest to northeast. Outside downtown, everything is simplified: with few exceptions, avenues run north-south and streets east-west. The city is divided into quadrants: 1000 1st Ave. NW is a far walk from 1000 1st Ave. SE.

When driving in Seattle, yield to pedestrians. Locals drive slowly, calmly, and politely, and the police ticket mercilessly. Downtown driving can be a nightmare: parking is expensive, hills are steep, and one-way streets are ubiquitous. Read the street signs carefully, as many areas have time restrictions, and ticketers know them by heart. Prepare yourself for heavy traffic, especially on I-5, at almost any hour of the day.

SIGHTS

Most of the city's major sights are within walking distance. Seattle taxpayers spend more per capita on the arts than any other Americans, and the investment pays off in unparalleled public art installations throughout the city and plentiful galleries. The investments of Seattle-based millionaires have brought startlingly new and bold architecture in the Experience Music Project and International Fountain. Outside cosmopolitan downtown, Seattle boasts over 300 areas of well-watered greenery.

DOWNTOWN AND THE WATERFRONT

THE SEATTLE AQUARIUM. The star attraction of the Seattle Aquarium is a huge underwater dome, and the harbor seals, fur seals, otters, and endless supply of fish won't disappoint. Touch tanks and costumes delight kids, while a million-dollar salmon exhibit teaches about the state's favorite fish. Feedings occur throughout the day. (*Pier 59, near Pike St. ☎206-386-4320. Open daily in summer 9:30am-7pm; in fall and winter 10am-5pm; in spring*

9:30am-6pm. Last entry 1hr. before closing. $12.50, ages 6-12 $8.50, ages 3-5 $5.50.

■ **PIKE PLACE MARKET.** In 1907, angry citizens demanded the elimination of the middleman, and local farmers began selling produce by the waterfront, creating the Pike Place Market. Business thrived until an enormous fire burned the building in 1941. The early 1980s heralded a Pike Place renaissance, and today thousands of tourists mob the market daily. In the **Main Arcade,** on the west side of Pike St., fishmongers compete for audiences as they hurl fish from shelves to scales. (1531 Western Ave. ☎206-682-7453; www.pikeplacemarket.com. Open M-Sa 10am-6pm, Su 11am-5pm.) The **Pike Place Hillclimb** descends from the south end of Pike Place Market past chic shops and ethnic restaurants to the Alaskan Way and waterfront.

THE SEATTLE CENTER

The 1962 World's Fair demanded a Seattle Center to herald the city of the future. Now the Center houses everything from carnival rides to ballet. The center is bordered by Denny Way, W. Mercer St., 1st Ave., and 5th Ave. and has six gates, each with a model of the center and a map of its facilities. The anchor point is the **Center House,** which holds a food court, stage, and **Info Desk.** (☎206-684-8582. Info desk open daily 7am-9pm.)

EXPERIENCE MUSIC PROJECT. Undoubtedly the biggest and best attraction at the Seattle Center is the futuristic, abstract, and technologically brilliant Experience Music Project (EMP). The museum is the brainchild of Seattle billionaire and Microsoft co-founder Paul Allen, who originally wanted to build a shrine to his music idol, Jimi Hendrix. The project eventually ballooned to include dozens of ethnomusicologists and multimedia specialists, a collection of over 80,000 musical artifacts, the world-renowned architect Frank Gehry, and enough money to make the national debt appear small (fine, it was only $350 million). The result? The rock 'n' roll museum of the future. Even if you don't go inside, the building alone— sheet metal molded into abstract curves and then acid-dyed gold, silver, purple, light-blue, and red—is spectacular. Inside, check out the guitar Hendrix smashed on a London stage and On Stage, a karaoke stage gone haywire. (325 5th St., at Seattle Center. From

I-5, take Exit 167, and follow signs to Seattle Center. ☎206-367-5483 or 877-367-5483. Open daily 10am-8pm. $20, seniors and military $16, ages 7-17 $15, under 7 free.

SPACE NEEDLE. Built in 1962 for the World's Fair, this 607 ft. rotating building was hailed as avant-garde and daring. Today, the EMP has stolen part of the Needle's glory, but the Space Needle is still internationally recognized as the symbol of Seattle. On a clear day, the Needle provides a great view and an invaluable landmark for the disoriented. The elevator ride itself is a show—operators are hired for their unique talents. The Needle houses an observation tower and a high-end 360-degree rotating restaurant. (At Seattle Center. ☎206-905-2100. $14, seniors $12, ages 4-13 $7.)

PIONEER SQUARE

ELLIOT BAY BOOKS. Taking up an entire block in Pioneer Square, the Elliot Bay Books houses more books than you could ever read (a whopping 150,000 titles) and, of course, the omni-present Seattle coffee shop. With expansive children's and fiction sections, you can find almost any title imaginable. The bookstore employees detail their personal favorites on sticky notes throughout the store. (101 S. Main St. ☎206-624-6600. Open M-Sa 9:30am-10pm, Su 11am-7pm.)

SEATTLE UNDERGROUND. Originally, downtown Seattle stood 12 ft. lower than it does today. The Seattle Underground Tour guides visitors through the subterranean city of old. Be prepared for lots of company, comedy, and toilet jokes. The tour begins in **Doc Maynard's Public House,** 610 1st Ave., where a guide gives a brief and oh-so-witty overview of the history of Seattle and its famous resident, Crapper, before leading you into the dark depths of the underground. (☎206-682-4646; www.undergroundtour.com. 1½hr. tours daily, roughly every hr. 10am-6pm. No reservations–arrive early on weekends. $11, students and seniors ages 3-17 $9, ages $7-12 $5. Cash only.)

INTERNATIONAL DISTRICT AND CHINATOWN

■ **SEATTLE ASIAN ART MUSEUM.** What do you do when you have too much good art to

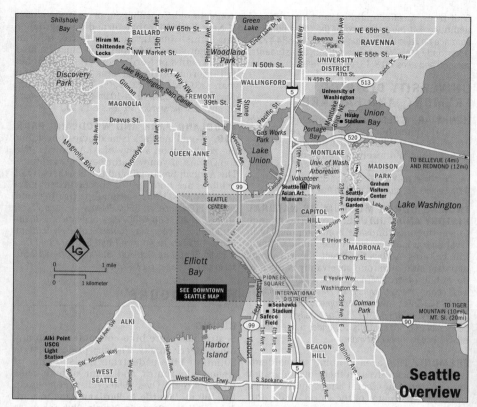

Seattle Overview

exhibit all at once? Open a second museum. This is just what the Seattle Museum of Art did, creating a wonderful stand-on-its-own attraction. The museum displays a particularly strong collection of Chinese art, but the majority of East Asia is admirably represented. (*In Volunteer Park, just beyond the water tower.* ☎ *206-654-3100. Open Tu-W and F-Su 10am-5pm, Th 10am-9pm. Suggested donation $5, students and seniors $3, under 12 free.*)

■ **WING LUKE ASIAN MUSEUM.** This museum gives a thorough description of life in an Asian-American community, investigates different Asian nationalities in Seattle, and shows work by local Asian artists. One permanent exhibit is **Camp Harmony**, a replica of barracks from a Japanese internment camp

during WWII. (*407 7th Ave. S.* ☎ *206-623-5124; www.wingluke.org. Open Tu-F 11am-4:30pm, Sa-Su noon-4pm. $4, students and seniors $3, ages 5-12 $2. 1st Th of the month free.*)

UNIVERSITY OF WASHINGTON ARBORETUM. The University of Washington Arboretum nurtures over 4000 species of trees, shrubs, and flowers, and maintains superb trails. Tours depart the **Graham Visitors Center**, at the southern end of the arboretum. (*8 blocks east of Volunteer Park. Visitors center on Arboretum Dr. E, off Lake Washington Blvd.* ☎ *206-543-8800. Open daily sunrise-sunset. Visitors center open daily 10am-4pm. Tours 1st and 3rd Su of the month. Free.*)

SEATTLE JAPANESE GARDEN. The tranquil 3½ acre park is a retreat of sculpted gardens, fruit trees, a reflecting pool, and a traditional teahouse. *(At the south end of the UW Arboretum, entrance on Lake Washington Blvd.* ☎ *206-684-4725. Open daily Mar.-Nov. 10am-sunset. $5; students, seniors, and ages 6-18 $3; under 6 free.)*

UNIVERSITY DISTRICT, FREMONT, AND BALLARD

HENRY ART GALLERY. Specializing in modern and contemporary, the Henry reflects its curators' enthusiasm with unconventional installations and rarely-exhibited artists. *(41st NE and 15th NE Ave.* ☎ *206-543-2280; www.henryart.org. Open Tu-W and F-Su 11am-5pm, Th 11am-8pm. $10, seniors $6, students free. Th free.)*

THOMAS BURKE MUSEUM OF NATURAL HISTORY AND CULTURE. Savor the chance to see the only dinosaur bones on display in Washington and a superb collection on Pacific Rim cultures. Across the street, the astronomy department's old stone **observatory** is open to the public. *(45th St. NE and 17th Ave. NE, in the northwest corner of the University of Washington campus.* ☎ *206-543-5590; www.washington.edu/burkemuseum. Observatory:* ☎ *206-542-0126. Open daily 10am-5pm. $8, seniors $6.50, students $5, under 5 free. Special exhibits occasionally cost more.)*

FREMONT. This area is home to residents who pride themselves on their love of art and antiques, and the liberal atmosphere of their self-declared "center of the world" under Rte. 99. Twice in the past 15 years Fremont has applied to secede from the United States. The immense **Fremont Troll**, beneath the Aurora Bridge on 35th St., grasps a Volkswagen Bug with a confounded expression. Some say kicking the bug's tire brings good luck; others say it hurts. A flamin' **Vladimir Lenin** resides at the corner of N. 36th and N. Fremont Pl.; this work from the former Soviet Union will be around until it is bought by a permanent collection.

NORDIC HERITAGE MUSEUM. Just east of the U District, the primarily Scandinavian neighborhood of **Ballard** offers a wide variety of Scandinavian eateries and shops along Market St. The museum presents realistic exhibits on the history of Nordic immigration and influence in the US. Stumble over cobble-stones in old Copenhagen, or visit the slums of New York City that turned photographer and Danish immigrant Jacob Riis into an important social reformer. The museum also hosts a series of Nordic concerts by national and international musicians throughout the year. *(3014 NW 67th St.* ☎ *206-789-5707; www.nordicmuseum.org. Open Tu-Sa 10am-4pm, Su noon-4pm. $6, students and seniors $5, ages 6-18 $4.)*

WOODLAND PARK AND WOODLAND PARK ZOO. Woodland Park is mediocre at best, but the zoo has won a bevy of AZA awards (the zoo Oscars, if you will) for best new exhibits. The African Savannah and the Northern Trail exhibits are both full of zoo favorites: grizzlies, wolves, lions, sasquatch, giraffes, and zebras. *(Entrances at 5500 Phinney Ave. and 750 N 50th St.* ☎ *206-684-4800. Park open daily 4:30am-11:30pm. Zoo open May to mid-Sept. daily 9:30am-6pm; mid-Mar. to Apr. and mid-Sept. to mid-Oct. 9:30am-5pm; late Oct.-Feb. 9:30am-4pm. $10.50, seniors $8.50, ages 6-17 $7.50.)*

▲ OUTDOORS

BIKING
Seattle has more bike-commuters than any other American city. The city prides itself on 30 mi. of bike-pedestrian trails, 90 mi. of signed bike routes, and 16 mi. of bike lanes on city streets. Over 1000 cyclists compete in the 190 mi. **Seattle to Portland Race** in mid-July. Call the **Cascade Bicycle Club** for more info. (☎206-522-3222; www.cascade.org.) On **Bicycle Saturdays/Sundays** from May to September, Lake Washington Blvd. is open only to cyclists from 10am-6pm. (usually on the 2nd Saturday and the 3rd Sunday of each month.) Contact the **Seattle Parks and Recreation Activities Office** for more info. (☎206-684-4075; www.cityofseattle.net/parks.)

HIKING
4167 ft. **Mt. Si** is the most climbed mountain in the state of Washington, and with good reason. Just an hour from downtown Seattle, hikers can reach a lookout that showcases Mt. Rainier, the Olympic Mountains, and Seattle in just a few hours (1 mi. one-way). A 4hr. hike (4 mi. one-way, 4hr.) brings you to **Hay-**

stack Basin, the false summit. Don't try climbing higher unless you have rock-climbing gear, though. To get to Mt. Si, take I-90 E to SE Mt. Si Rd. Cross the Snoqualmie River Bridge to the trailhead parking lot. **Tiger Mountain** (2522 ft.) is another great day-hike near Seattle. A 4hr. hike (5½ mi. round-trip) leads to the summit. Take I-90 to Tiger Mountain State Forest. From the Tradition Plateau trailhead, walk to Bus. Road Trail and then to West Tiger Trail.

WHITEWATER RAFTING
Although the rapids are hours away by car, over 50 whitewater rafting outfitters are based in Seattle and are often willing to undercut one another with merciless abandon. **Washington State Outfitter and Guides Association** provides advice and sends out info. (☎509-997-1080.) The **Northwest Outdoor Center,** 2100 Westlake Ave., on Lake Union, gives $50-70 instructional programs in whitewater and sea-kayaking. (☎206-281-9694; www.nwoc.com. Kayak rentals $12-17 per hr. Reservations recommended. Hours vary; call ahead.)

🍴 FOOD

Although Seattleites appear to subsist solely on espresso and steamed milk, they do occasionally eat. When they do, they seek out healthy cuisine, especially seafood. **Puget Sound Consumer Coops (PCCs)** are local health-food markets at 7504 Aurora Ave. North (☎206-525-3586), in Green Lake, and 600 34th St. North (☎206-632-6811), in Fremont. Capitol Hill, the U District, and Fremont close main thoroughfares on summer Saturdays for **Farmers Markets.**

PIKE PLACE MARKET AND DOWNTOWN
Restaurants south of Pike Place cater mostly to tourists and suits on lunch breaks, but there are many sandwich shops covering downtown.

Piroshky, Piroshky, 1908 Pike Pl. (☎206-441-6068). The Russian *piroshki* is a croissant-like dough baked around sausages, mushrooms, cheeses, salmon, or apples doused in cinnamon ($3.25-4.25). Watch the *piroshki* process in

progress. Open M-F and Su 8am-6:30pm, Sa 8am-7pm. MC/V. ❶

Soundview Cafe (☎206-623-5700), on the mezzanine in the Pike Place Main Arcade. The sandwich-and-salad bar is a good place to brown-bag a moment of solace. Breakfast and lunch from $4. Open in summer M-Th 8am-7:30pm, F-Su 8am-last customer; in winter M-Th 8am-6pm, F-Su 8am-8pm. AmEx/D/MC/V. ❸

Emmett Watson's Oyster Bar, 1916 Pike Place (☎206-448-7721). The Oyster Bar Special (2 oysters, 3 shrimp, bread and chowder; $8) will delight. Beer bottles line the shelves to showcase their selection. Open M-Th 11:30am-7pm, F-Sa 11:30am-8pm, Su 11:30am-6pm. MC/V. ❸

THE WATERFRONT
Budget eaters should steer clear of Pioneer Sq. Instead, take a picnic to **Waterfall Garden Park,** on the corner of S. Main St. and 2nd Ave. S. The garden sports tables and a manmade waterfall that masks traffic outside. (Open daily sunrise-sunset.)

Mae Phim Thai Restaurant, 94 Columbia St. (☎206-624-2979), a few blocks north of Pioneer Sq., between 1st Ave. and Alaskan Way. Slews of pad thai junkies crowd in for cheap, delicious Thai cuisine. All dishes $6. Open M-F 11am-7pm, Sa noon-7pm. Cash only. ❷

Ivar's Fish Bar, Pier 54 (☎206-467-8063), north of Pioneer Sq. A fast-food window serves the definitive Seattle clam chowder ($3). Clam and chips $5.75. Open daily 10am-midnight. MC/V. For a more upscale meal, try **Ivar's Restaurant** next door. Open M-Th and Su 11am-10pm, F-Sa 11am-11pm. MC/V. ❶/❸

INTERNATIONAL DISTRICT
Along King and Jackson St., between 5th and 8th Ave., Seattle's International District is packed with great eateries.

Uwajimaya, 600 5th Ave. S (☎206-624-6248). The Uwajimaya Center—the largest Japanese department store in the Northwest—is a full city block of groceries, gifts, videos, and CDs. There is even a food court, plying Korean barbecue and Taiwanese-style baked goods. Grilled saba fish $7. Pork dumpling $0.60. Open M-Sa 9am-10pm, Su 9am-9pm. ❷

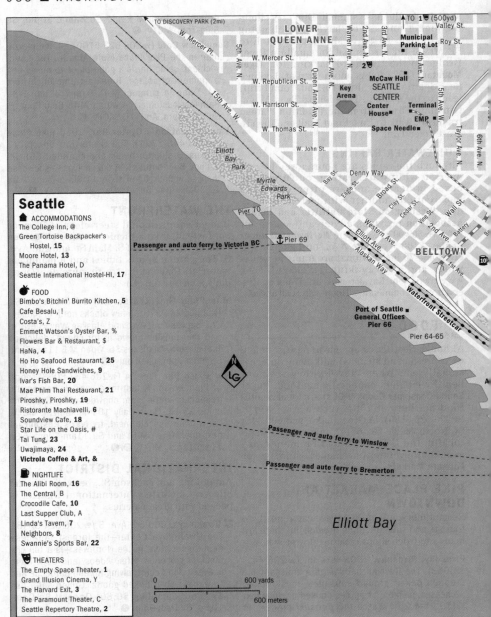

Seattle

🏠 ACCOMMODATIONS
The College Inn, @
Green Tortoise Backpacker's
   Hostel, **15**
Moore Hotel, **13**
The Panama Hotel, D
Seattle International Hostel-HI, **17**

🍽 FOOD
Bimbo's Bitchin' Burrito Kitchen, **5**
Cafe Besalu, !
Costa's, Z
Emmett Watson's Oyster Bar, %
Flowers Bar & Restaurant, $
HaNa, **4**
Ho Ho Seafood Restaurant, **25**
Honey Hole Sandwiches, **9**
Ivar's Fish Bar, **20**
Mae Phim Thai Restaurant, **21**
Piroshky, Piroshky, **19**
Ristorante Machiavelli, **6**
Soundview Cafe, **18**
Star Life on the Oasis, #
Tai Tung, **23**
Uwajimaya, **24**
Victrola Coffee & Art, &

🎭 NIGHTLIFE
The Alibi Room, **16**
The Central, B
Crocodile Cafe, **10**
Last Supper Club, A
Linda's Tavern, **7**
Neighbors, **8**
Swannie's Sports Bar, **22**

🎭 THEATERS
The Empty Space Theater, **1**
Grand Illusion Cinema, Y
The Harvard Exit, **3**
The Paramount Theater, C
Seattle Repertory Theatre, **2**

PACIFIC COAST

TO PUGET CONSUMER
CORPS (3.5mi)

TO @ (1mi),
(2mi)

TO 🏛 SEATTLE ASIAN ART MUSEUM (.25mi)
VOLUNTEER PARK (.5mi), LAKE
UNION, UNIVERSITY DISTRICT (3mi)

E Roy St.

Mercer St.

Republican St.

Harrison St.

John St.

Denny
Park

Denny Wy.

Dexter Ave. N.
8th Ave. N.
9th Ave. N.
Westlake Ave. N.
Terry Ave. N.
Boren Ave. N.
Fairview Ave. N.
Minor Ave. N.
Pontius Ave. N.
Yale Ave. N.
Eastlake Ave. E.
Melrose Ave. E.
Bellevue Ave. E.
Summit Ave. E.
Belmont Ave. E.
Boylston Ave. E.
Harvard Ave. E.
Broadway East
10th Ave. E.
11th Ave. E.
12th Ave. E.
13th Ave. E.
14th Ave. E.
Malden Ave. E.

3

E. Harrison St.

E. Thomas St.

CAPITOL HILL

E. John St.

4

13th Ave. E.
14th Ave. E.
15th Ave. E.
16th Ave. E.
17th Ave. E.
18th Ave. E.

9th Ave.

ℹ️ REI/National
Park Information

E. Olive Way

E. Denny Wy.

E. Howell St.

Broadway
Playfield

E. Olive St.

E. Pine St.

E. Pine St.

E. Howell St.

E. Olive St.

E. Pine St.

Blanchard St.
7th Ave.
Virginia St.
Stewart St.
Howell St.
Yale St.
Bellevue Ave.

Monorail

5th Ave.

4th Ave.

Greyhound 🚌

Olive Way

Pine St.

6

5

7

8

E. Pike St

9

E. Union St.

E. Union St.

Terminal ■

Pike St.

ℹ️

Boren Ave.

Minor Ave.

Terry Ave.

Seneca St.

Madison St.

E. Spring St.

13

Pike
Place
Market

Freeway
Park

FIRST
HILL

SEATTLE
UNIVERSITY

E. Marion St.

12th Ave.

E. Columbia St.

16
18
🌺
15
17 Benaroya
Hall

Union St.

University St.

🏛Seattle
Art Museum

✉️

8th Ave.
9th Ave.
7th Ave.
6th Ave.
Madison St.

✚ Virginia Mason
Medical Center

Swedish Medical
Center ✚

E. Cherry St.

Spring St.

Seattle
Public Library

Marion St.

Columbia St.

Broadway

E. Jefferson St.

🌺

E. Terrace St.

ront
Park

99

ter-

Post Ave.
Western Ave.
1st Ave.
2nd Ave.
3rd Ave.
Marion St.
Columbia Tower

Cherry St.

James St.

5th Ave.
4th Ave.
Jefferson St.

Columbia Tower

Alder St.

t 56

t 54

20

Pier 52

⚓

21

Underground
■ Tours

PIONEER
SQUARE

Harborview
Medical
Center ✚

Terry Ave.

Alder St.

E. Spruce St.

E. Fir St.

Boren Ave.

Washington
State Ferry
Terminal

Smith
Tower

Yesler Way

E. Yesler Way

Pier 48

B

S. Washington St.

A 22

S. Main St.

Union
Station

Maynard St.

6th Ave. S.

5

TO 🏛
MERCER
ISLAND

46

Eliott Bay
Books

King Street
Station

D

Wing Luke
🏛Asian American Museum

S. Jackson St.

23

S. King St.

S. King St.

24

25

S. Weller St.

S. Weller St.

INTERNATIONAL
DISTRICT

S. Dearborn St.

S. Lane St.

1st Ave. S.
Occidental Ave.
4th Ave. S.
E. Marginal Way S.
Alaskan Fwy.
Alaskan Way S.
8th Ave. S.
12th Ave. S.

Charles St.

S. Dearborn St.

90

Tai Tung, 655 S. King St. (☎206-622-7372). Select authentic Mandarin cuisine from a comprehensive menu. Entrees $5-12. Open M-Th and Su 10am-11pm, F-Sa 10am-1:30am. AmEx/MC/V. ❸

Ho Ho Seafood Restaurant, 653 S. Weller St. (☎206-382-9671). Eat generous portions of tank-fresh seafood inside Bruce Lee's old Kung Fu studio. Lunch $5-7. Dinner $6-12. Open M-Th and Su 11am-1am, F-Sa 11am-3am. MC/V. ❸

CAPITOL HILL

With bronze dance-steps emblazoned on the sidewalks and neon storefronts, **Broadway Ave.** is a land of espresso houses, imaginative shops, elegant clubs, and good eats.

Bimbo's Bitchin' Burrito Kitchen, 506 E. Pine St. (☎206-329-9978). The name explains it, and the decorations (fake palm trees and lots of plastic) prove it. Walk right on through the door to the Cha Cha for $3.50 tequila shots. Spicy Bimbo's burrito $4.25. Open M-Th noon-11pm, F-Sa noon-2am, Su 2-10pm. MC/V. ❶

Ristorante Machiavelli, 1215 Pine St. (☎206-621-7941), across the street from Bauhaus. This small, bustling Italian place. The gnocchi is widely considered to be the best in town. Pasta $8-10. Open M-Sa 5-11pm. MC/V. ❸

HaNa, 219 Broadway Ave. E (☎206-328-1187). Packed quarters testify to the popularity of the sushi here. Lunch sushi combo platter with rice and soup $7.50. Dinner $4-10. Open M-Sa 11am-10pm, Su 4-10pm. MC/V. ❸

Honey Hole Sandwiches, 703 E. Pike St. (☎206-709-1399). The primary colors and veggie-filled sandwiches make you feel healthy and happy. Try the pork- and pineapple-filled Buford T. Justice ($7.75). Open daily 10am-2am. MC/V. ❷

UNIVERSITY DISTRICT

The neighborhood around the immense **University of Washington** ("U-Dub"), north of downtown between Union and Portage Bay, supports funky shops, international restaurants, and coffeehouses. The best of each lies within a few blocks of **University Way,** known as "the Ave."

Flowers Bar & Restaurant, 4247 University Way NE (☎206-633-1903). This 1920s landmark was once a flower shop; now, the mirrored ceiling tastefully reflects an all-you-can-eat vegetarian buffet ($8). Great daily drink specials. Th Sour night $3. Sa Margarita night $3. Open M-Sa 11am-2am, Su 11am-midnight. AmEx/MC/V. ❷

Star Life on the Oasis, 1405 50th St. NE (☎206-729-3542). A secret gem, tucked in next to the Grand Illusions Cinema. Mostly sandwiches and other treats to snack on. Get the vegan open faced ($6.50). Open M-W and F-Sa 8am-11pm, Su 10am-10pm. MC/V. ❷

Costa's Restaurant, 4559 University Way NE (☎206-633-2751). Everything from *spanakopita* ($7.50) to burgers ($7.50-9.50). Try the "Garden skillet" for veggies or go for the "Farmer" if you need a meat fix ($8.50). Open daily 7am-10-pm. MC/V. ❸

📷 CAFES

The coffee bean is Seattle's first love; you can't walk a single block without passing an institution of caffeination. The city's obsession with Italian-style espresso drinks even has gas stations pumping out the dark, soupy java.

Victrola Coffee & Art, 411 15th Ave. (☎206-326-6520; www.victrolacoffee.com). This cafe posseses atmosphere in abundance, balancing private sitting space with inviting sofas. They also roast their own coffee beans. Open daily 5:30am-11pm. Cash only.

Cafe Besalu, 5909 24th Ave. NW (☎206-789-1463). The coffee is good, but the real draw is Cafe Besalu's delectable pastries—from artisan bread to croissants and brioches—baked fresh in the open kitchen. Open Tu-Su 7am-3pm. MC/V.

🏠 ACCOMMODATIONS

Seattle's hostel scene is not amazing, but there are plenty of choices and establishments to fit all types of personalities. **Pacific Reservation Service** (☎800-684-2932) arranges B&B singles for $50-65. For inexpensive motels farther from downtown, drive north on **Aurora Ave.**

Seattle International Hostel (HI), 84 Union St. (☎206-622-5443 or 888-622-5443), at Western Ave., by the waterfront. Take Union St. from downtown; follow signs down the stairs under the "Pike Pub & Brewery." Great location, laundry, and Internet access. Reception 24hr. Reservations recommended. Dorms $32, members $29; private doubles $79-92. AmEx/MC/V. ❷

Green Tortoise Backpacker's Hostel, 105 Pike St. (☎206-340-1222), at 1st Ave. A young party hostel downtown. Laundry, kitchen, Internet access. Key deposit $20. Towel $1. Breakfast (7-9:30am) and dinner (M, W, F) included. Reception 24hr. Dorms $23-27; private rooms $48-50. MC/V. ❶

Moore Hotel, 1926 2nd Ave. (☎206-448-4851 or 800-421-5508), at Virginia St. 1 block from Pike Place Market. Built in 1907, the Moore Hotel has a swanky lobby, cavernous hallways, and attentive service. Singles $50, with bath $65; doubles $60/$77. MC/V. ❸

Panama Hotel, 605½ S. Main St. (☎206-223-9242), in the International District. Opened in 1910, the rooms reflect its history. All rooms have shared bath and come with a *Yukata* (Japanese robe). Breakfast pastry and coffee included. Singles from $60; doubles from $70. MC/V. ❸

The College Inn, 4000 University Way NE (☎206-633-4441). Filled with youthful travelers, the friendly staff offers clean budget rooms adorned with brass fixtures. All rooms share bathrooms. Continental breakfast included. Singles in summer from $50, in winter $45; doubles $55-75. D/MC/V. ❸

🎵 ENTERTAINMENT

Seattle has world-renowned underground music scenes and a bustling theater community. In summer, the free **Out to Lunch** series (☎206-623-0340; www.downtownsummer.com) brings everything from reggae to folkdancing into parks, squares, and office buildings. Check cheeky free weekly *The Stranger* for event listings.

MUSIC

The **Seattle Opera** performs from August to May in **McCaw Hall**, 321 Mercer St. The culmination of a 10-year renovation, the Opera House reopened in 2003, with a glass facade, decked-out lobbies, and a modernized auditorium. Opera buffs should reserve well in advance, although rush tickets are sometimes available. (☎206-389-7676; www.seattleopera.com. Box office open M-Tu and Th-F 9am-5pm, W 9:30am-5pm. Tickets from $35. Students and seniors can get half-price tickets 2hr. before the performance.) The **Seattle Symphony** performs in the new **Benaroya Hall**, 200 University St., at 3rd Ave., from September to June. (☎206-215-4747; www.seattlesymphony.org. Box office open M-F 10am-6pm, Sa 1-6pm. Tickets from $15-39, seniors half-price. Same-day student tickets $10.)

THEATER

The city hosts an exciting array of first-run plays and alternative works, particularly by many talented amateur groups. Rush tickets are often available at nearly half-price on the day of the show from **Ticket/Ticket.** (☎206-324-2744. Cash only.) 🎟**The Empty Space Theatre,** 901 12th Ave., in the Lee Center for the Arts, presents comedies and bold dramatic works from April to December. (☎206-547-7500. Tickets $10-30.) **Seattle Repertory Theater,** 155 Mercer St., at the wonderful Bagley Wright Theater in the Seattle Center, presents contemporary and classic winter productions. (☎206-443-2222; www.seattlerep.org. Tickets $15-48, seniors $34, under 25 $10. Rush tickets 30min. before curtain $20.)

CINEMA

Seattle is a cinephile's paradise. Most of the theaters that screen non-Hollywood films are on Capitol Hill and in the University District. On summer Saturdays, outdoor cinema in Fremont begins at dusk at N. 35th St., at Phinney Ave., in the U-Park lot by the bridge, behind the Red Hook Brewery. (☎206-781-4230. Entrance 7:30pm. Suggested donation $5.) **TCI Outdoor Cinema** shows everything from classics to cartoons at the Gasworks Park. (Live music 7pm-sunset. Free.) **The Paramount Theatre,** 911 E. Pine St., is best known for hosting the **Seattle International Film Festival** in the last week of May and first two weeks of June. (☎206-467-5510. Box office open M-F 10am-6pm. Tickets $10.) **The Harvard Exit,** 807 E. Roy St., on Capitol Hill, near the north end of the Broadway business district, has its own ghost, an enormous antique projector, and offers quality classic and foreign films. (☎206-323-8986. $9.25, seniors and under 12 $6.25.) **Grand Illusion Cinema,** 1403 50th St. NE, in the U District at University Way, is one of the last independent theaters in Seattle and often shows old classics and hard-to-find films. (☎206-523-3935. $7, seniors and children $5.50.)

PACIFIC COAST

SPORTS

The **Mariners,** or "M's" play baseball in the $500 million, hangar-like **Safeco Field,** at 1st Ave. South and Royal Brougham Wy. S., under an enormous retractable roof. (☎206-622-4487. Tickets from $7.) Seattle's football team, the **Seahawks,** are stuck playing in UW's **Husky Stadium** until construction on their new stadium is finished. (☎206-628-0888. Tickets from $39.) On the other side of town, the sleek **Key Arena,** in the Seattle Center, hosts the NBA **Supersonics.** (☎206-628-0888. Tickets from $10.) The **University of Washington Huskies** football team has contended in the PAC-10 for years. Call the Athletic Ticket Office (☎206-543-2200) for schedules and prices.

FESTIVALS

Pick up the visitors center's *Calendar of Events* (www.seeseattle.org/events) for coupons and listings. The first Thursday of each month, the art community sponsors **First Thursday,** a free gallery walk where galleries and art cafes open to the city. The **Fremont Fair** (☎206-694-6706; www.fremontfair.com), honors of the summer solstice in in mid-June with the **Fremont Solstice Parade,** led by dozens of bicyclists wearing only body paint. **Bumbershoot** is a massive four-day festival that caps off Labor Day weekend with major rock bands, street musicians, and a young, exuberant crowd. (☎206-281-7788; www.bumbershoot.org. 1-day pass $18-30; 3-day pass $50-80. Some events require additional tickets.) Puget Sound's yachting season starts in May. **Maritime Week,** in the third week of May, and the **Shilshole Boats Afloat Show** (☎206-748-0012; www.boatsafloatshow.com), in mid-September, let boaters show off their craft. Over the 4th of July weekend, the Center for Wooden Boats sponsors the free **Wooden Boat Festival and Classic Speedboat Show** (☎206-382-2628; www.cwb.org) on Lake Union, which includes a demonstration of boat-building skills. The finale is the **Quick and Daring Boat-building Contest,** in which competitors sail wooden boats that they build in the previous 24hr. using limited tools and materials.

⬢ NIGHTLIFE

Seattle has moved beyond beer to a new nightlife frontier: the cafe-bar. The popularity of espresso bars in Seattle might lead one to conclude that caffeine is more intoxicating than alcohol, but often an establishment that poses as a diner by day brings on a band, breaks out the disco ball, and pumps out the microbrews by night. The best spot to go for guaranteed good beer, live music, and big crowds is **Pioneer Square,** where UW students from frat row dominate the bar stools. You may prefer to go to **Capitol Hill,** or up Rte. 99 to **Fremont,** where the atmosphere is usually more laid-back than in the Square.

DOWNTOWN

▨ **The Alibi Room,** 85 Pike St. (☎206-623-3180), across from the Market Cinema in the Post Alley in Pike Place. A remarkably friendly, local indie filmmaker hangout. Bar with music. Downstairs dance floor F-Sa. Brunch Sa-Su. No cover. Open M-F 4pm-2am, Sa-Su 11am-2am. AmEx/D/MC/V.

Crocodile Cafe, 2200 2nd Ave. (☎206-448-2114), at Blanchard St. in Belltown. Cooks veggie friendly from scratch by day, and features live music by night (Tu-Sa). Try the Swamp Water (iced tea with mango, lemonade, and hibiscus $1.50). Shows usually start 9pm; some require advance ticket purchase. 21+ after 9pm. Cover $6-22. Open Tu-F 11am-11pm, Sa 8am-11pm, Su 9am-3pm. MC/V.

PIONEER SQUARE

Most bars participate in a joint cover (M-Th and Su $5, F-Sa $10) that will let you wander from bar to bar to sample the bands. The larger venues are listed below. Two smaller venues, **Larry's,** 209 1st Ave. S. (☎206-624-7665), and **New Orleans,** 114 1st Ave. S. (☎206-622-2563), feature great blues and jazz nightly. Most clubs close at 2am weekends and midnight weekdays.

The Central, 207 1st Ave. S. (☎206-622-0209). One of the early venues for grunge has now become a favorite for bikers. Live rock nightly. Tu punk music. Joint cover. Open daily 11:30am-2am. Kitchen closes 9pm. AmEx/MC/V.

Last Supper Club, 124 S. Washington St. (☎206-748-9975), at Occidental. 2 dance floors, DJed with everything from 70s disco to funky house, drum 'n' bass, and trance. Open W-Su 6pm-2am. AmEx/MC/V.

Swannie's Sports Bar, 222 S. Main St. (☎206-622-9353). Share drink specials with pro ball-players who stop by post-game. Any Seattle sports junkie will swear this is the place to be. Drink specials change daily. Open daily 11:30am-2am. AmEx/MC/V.

CAPITOL HILL

East of Broadway, travelers can sit back in a cool lounge on **Pine St.** West of Broadway, **Pike St.** has the clubs that push the limits (punk, industrial, fetish, dance) and break the sound barrier.

■ **Linda's Tavern,** 707 Pine St. E (☎206-325-1220). A very chill post-gig scene for Seattle rockers. Tu night DJ plays jazz and classic rock. Expanded menu, liquor, and breakfast on week-ends. W movie night. No cover. Open M-F 11:30am-2am, Sa-Su 10am-2am. MC/V.

Neighbors, 1509 Broadway Ave. (☎206-324-5358). Enter from the alley on Pike St. A gay dance club for 24 years, Neighbors prides itself on techno slick-ness. Th-Sa drag nights. Tu Mark "Mom" Finley. Open Tu-Su at 6:30pm-last customer. MC/V.

THE END OF THE ROAD

Head over to the Pike Place Market for some hardcore fish-throwing, wander among the vintage shops on Capitol Hill, or spend a quiet afternoon at Elliot Bay Books. You've made it all the way up the sunny coast, the road of a thousand beaches and avocados. Do you think you've quenched your thirst for the road? You ain't seen nothing yet. Grab a cup of coffee (there's no better place than Seat-tle), and continue your adventures on the Great North or the Oregon Trail.

EXIT TO

Portland, OR   174 mi.
on the oregon trail route, p. 673

Victoria, BC   108 mi.
on the great north route, p. 344

SPEED LIMIT 65

MEASUREMENT CONVERSIONS

1 inch (in.) = 25.4mm	1 millimeter (mm) = 0.039 in.
1 foot (ft.) = 0.30m	1 meter (m) = 3.28 ft.
1 yard (yd.) = 0.914m	1 meter (m) = 1.09 yd.
1 mile = 1.61km	1 kilometer (km) = 0.62 mi.
1 ounce (oz.) = 28.35g	1 gram (g) = 0.035 oz.
1 pound (lb.) = 0.454kg	1 kilogram (kg) = 2.202 lb.
1 fluid ounce (fl. oz.) = 29.57mL	1 milliliter (ml) = 0.034 fl. oz.
1 gallon (gal.) = 3.785L	1 liter (L) = 0.264 gal.
1 acre (ac.) = 0.405ha	1 hectare (ha) = 2.47 ac.
1 square mile (sq. mi.) = 2.59 sq. km	1 square kilometer (sq. km) = 0.386 sq. mi.

DISTANCE CONVERSION SCALE

Miles	1	2	3	4	5	10	20	30	40	50	60	70	80	90	100	250	500	1000
Kilometers	1.6	3.2	4.8	6.4	8	16	32	48	64	81	97	113	115	145	161	402	805	1609
Kilometers	1	2	3	4	5	10	20	30	40	50	60	70	80	90	100	250	500	1000
Miles	.62	1.3	1.9	2.5	3.1	6.2	12.4	18.6	25	31	37	43	50	56	62	155	310	620

TEMPERATURE CONVERSION SCALE

Degrees Celsius	-20	-15	-10	-5	0	5	10	15	20	25	30	35	40	45
Degrees Fahrenheit	-4	5	14	23	32	41	50	59	68	77	86	95	104	113

LANGUAGE BASICS

FRENCH QUICK REFERENCE

Both English and French are official languages in Canada. Roadtrippers should have no trouble getting around in English, but a basic familiarity with French is helpful, especially in Quebec, where attempts to use French words will be much appreciated.

ENGLISH	FRENCH	PRONOUNCIATION
Hello/Good day	Bonjour	bohn-ZJHOOR
Good evening	Bonsoir	bohn-SWAH
Hi!	Salut!	SAH-LU
Goodbye	Au revoir	oh ruh-VWAHR
Good night	Bonne nuit	bon NWEE
Yes/No/Maybe	oui/non/peut-être	wee/nohn/puh-TET-ruh
Please	S'il vous plaît	see voo PLAY
Thank you	Merci	mehr-SEE

APPENDIX

You're welcome	De rien	duh rhee-EHN
Excuse me!	Excusez-moi!	ex-SKU-zay-MWAH
Go away!	Allez-vous en!	ah-lay vooz ON
Where is...?	Où se trouve?	oo s'TRHOOV
Closed/Open	fermé/ouvrir	ferh-MAY/ooVRAY
Help!	Au secours!	oh-skOOR
I'm lost	Je suis perdu(e)	zh'SWEE pehr-DU
I'm sorry	Je suis désolé(e)	zh'SWEE day-zoh-LAY
Do you speak English?	Parlez-vous anglais?	PAR-lay-vooz ahn-GLAY

SPANISH QUICK REFERENCE

Though Spanish is not an official language in the US, it is widely spoken, especially in California and along the states bordering Mexico and the Gulf of Mexico.

ENGLISH	SPANISH	PRONOUNCIATION
Hello	Hola	OH-la
Goodbye	Adios	ah-dee-OHS
Good day/night	Buenas días/noches	BWEH-nos DEE-ahs/NO-ches
Yes/No/Maybe	Si/No/Tal vez	SEE/no/tal VEHS
Please	Por favor	POHR fa-VOHR
Thank you	Gracias	GRA-see-ahs
You're welcome	De nada	DEH-NAH-da
Excuse me!	Perdón/Disculpe	pehr-DOHN/dees-SKOOL-pay
Go away!	¡Váyase!	VAH-yah-say
Where is...?	¿Dónde está?	DOAN-day eh-STAH
Closed/Open	Cerrado(a)/Abierto(a)	sehr-RAH-doh/ah-BYEHR-toh
Help!	¡Auxilio!	Ow-SEE-lee-yoh
I'm lost	Soy perdido	soy payr-DEE-doh
I'm sorry	Lo siento	low SYEN-toh
Do you speak English?	¿Habla inglés?	AH-blah een-GLAYS

index

INDEX

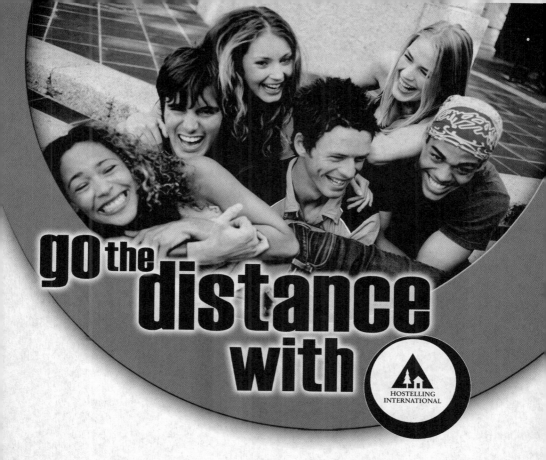

go the distance with

HOSTELLING INTERNATIONAL

Get into the groove with HI-USA, the largest network of quality hostels in America.

Stay with us and be close to all the sites, clubs, attractions and more. So you can really experience fantastic cities like New York, Boston, Chicago, Washington, San Francisco and Los Angeles, or explore the open road.

Enjoy great rates and a warm HI welcome!

For information or reservations: www.hiusa.org
or toll free (within USA and Canada): 1 (888) 464-4872

ORBITZ

AND GO!™

Visit www.orbitz.com today.

ABOUT LET'S GO

NOT YOUR PARENTS' TRAVEL GUIDE

At Let's Go, we see every trip as the chance of a lifetime. If your dream is to grab a machete and forge through the jungles of Brazil, we can take you there. If you'd rather bask in the Riviera sun at a beachside cafe, we'll set you a table. We write for readers who know that there's more to travel than sharing double deckers with tourists and who believe that travel can change both themselves and the world—whether they plan to spend six days in London or six months in Latin America. We'll show you just how far your money can go, and prove that the greatest limitation on your adventures is not your wallet, but your imagination.

BEYOND THE TOURIST EXPERIENCE

To help you gain a deeper connection with the places you travel, our fearless researchers scour the globe to give you the heads-up on both world-renowned and off-the-beaten-track attractions, sights, and destinations. They engage with the local culture, only to emerge with the freshest insights on everything from local festivals to regional cuisine. We've also opened our pages to respected writers and scholars to hear their takes on the countries and regions we cover, and asked travelers who have worked, studied, or volunteered abroad to contribute first-person accounts of their experiences. In addition, we increased our coverage of responsible travel and expanded each travel guide's Beyond Tourism chapter to share more ideas about how to give back while on the road.

FORTY-SEVEN YEARS OF WISDOM

Let's Go got its start in 1960, when a group of creative and well-traveled students compiled their experience and advice into a 20-page mimeographed pamphlet, which they gave to travelers on charter flights to Europe. Four and a half decades later, we've expanded to cover six continents and all kinds of travel—while retaining our founders' adventurous attitude toward the world. Laced with witty prose and total candor, our guides are still researched and written entirely by students on shoestring budgets, experienced travelers who know that train strikes, stolen luggage, food poisoning, and marriage proposals are all part of a day's work.

THE LET'S GO COMMUNITY

More than just a travel guide company, Let's Go is a community. Our small staff comes together because of our shared passion for travel and our desire to help other travelers see the world the way it was meant to be seen. We love it when our readers become part of the Let's Go community as well—when you travel, drop us a postcard (67 Mt. Auburn St., Cambridge, MA 02138, USA), send us an e-mail (feedback@letsgo.com), or post on our forum (http://www.letsgo.com/connect/forum) to tell us about your adventures and discoveries.

For more information, visit us online: www.letsgo.com.

map index

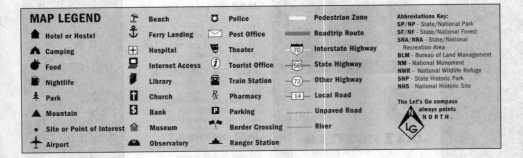

MAP LEGEND

🏠 Hotel or Hostel
🏕 Camping
🍎 Food
🍸 Nightlife
🌲 Park
⛰ Mountain
▪ Site or Point of Interest
✈ Airport

⚓ Beach
⚓ Ferry Landing
✛ Hospital
🖥 Internet Access
📖 Library
✝ Church
💲 Bank
🏛 Museum
⛑ Observatory

🚓 Police
✉ Post Office
🎭 Theater
ⓘ Tourist Office
🚉 Train Station
℞ Pharmacy
🅿 Parking
🏁 Border Crossing
⛴ Ranger Station

⬚ Pedestrian Zone
⬛ Roadtrip Route
70 Interstate Highway
56 State Highway
73 Other Highway
14 Local Road
------ Unpaved Road
—— River

Abbreviations Key:
SP/NP - State/National Park
SF/NF - State/National Forest
SRA/NRA - State/National
   Recreation Area
BLM - Bureau of Land Management
NM - National Monument
NWR - National Wildlife Refuge
SHP - State Historic Park
NHS - National Historic Site

The Let's Go compass
always points
NORTH.
LG